THE
WIND ENSEMBLE
CATALOG

THE
WIND ENSEMBLE
CATALOG

Jon A. Gillaspie,
Marshall Stoneham,
and David Lindsey Clark

Music Reference Collection, Number 63

GREENWOOD PRESS
Westport, Connecticut • London

Library of Congress Cataloging-in-Publication Data

Gillaspie, Jon A.
    The wind ensemble catalog / by Jon A. Gillaspie, Marshall
Stoneham, and David Lindsey Clark.
        p.   cm.—(Music reference collection, ISSN 0736–7740 ; no.
63)
    Companion to the authors' Wind ensemble sourcebook and
biographical guide.
    Includes bibliographical references and index.
    ISBN 0–313–25394–3 (alk. paper)
    1. Wind ensembles—Bibliography.   I. Stoneham, Marshall.
II. Clark, David Lindsey.   III. Stoneham, Marshall. Wind ensemble
sourcebook and biographical guide.   IV. Title.   V. Series.
ML128.W5G52   1998
016.7848′026—dc21   97–42759
                           MN

British Library Cataloguing in Publication Data is available.

Library of Congress Catalog Card Number: 97–42759
ISBN: 0–313–25394–3
ISSN: 0736–7740

First published in 1998

Greenwood Press, 88 Post Road West, Westport, CT 06881
An imprint of Greenwood Publishing Group, Inc.

Printed in the United States of America

The paper used in this book complies with the
Permanent Paper Standard issued by the National
Information Standards Organization (Z39.48–1984).

10 9 8 7 6 5 4 3 2

CONTENTS

PREFACE

This catalog represents the work of three researchers over the past twenty years. What began as a short list of works has grown into an attempt to document an entire musical genre. We cite, generally, works for five or more instruments up to about eighteen instruments - the wind section of a modern symphony orchestra - which include *at least one pair of wind instruments*. We omit music for the separate genres of large concert and military bands and of wind quintets or smaller groups of solo winds. For works in the first phase of wind harmony we exercise a certain amount of license based on titles and function: if a work for two horns and a bassoon is titled "Harmonie" it is included; similarly, many works of wind harmony include "honorary winds" such as the viola and violone. Where a composer's work stretches over the divide between wind harmony and larger military bands we tend to include a complete list of his works, especially when a smaller core group is given as an alternative to the full scoring. We are aware that many later bands employed more than one instrument per part, but our experience has shown that many of these works *can* be played as Harmoniemusik, especially with a bit of restraint on the part of the brass instruments. Even with the exclusion criteria, the catalog includes over 13,000 works by more than 2,400 composers and arrangers.

In the course of our researches we have slept everywhere from palaces to park benches. We have worked with librarians and archivists ranging from near-saints to, on at least on one occasion, a psychopath of the first water. After our mileage reached the equivalent of three times round the world, we gave up counting.

This catalog differs from other surveys of musical genres in a number of ways. First we have not relied on secondary sources for our information but have actually examined as many of the works as proved possible. In far too many cases we found that what was actually written on the manuscripts and early prints did not agree with information provided by some earlier researchers; in some cases we actually began to wonder whether there was a "Harmoniemusik Twilight Zone" into which they had inadvertently strayed.

Secondly, from the beginning we have been aware of the frustrations that result - both to researchers and to music librarians and archivists - through inadequate documentation of works. Wherever possible, we have included shelfmarks for works so that valuable time will not be wasted in trying to locate them. Librarians will thank you for quoting shelfmarks in your dealings with them.

Thirdly, we generally do not include works that remain lost or are "ghosts" (Geisterwerke). That said, we *do* note lost copies when doing so will save time and frustration for researchers and librarians. A list of untraced works is included as an appendix to our companion volume, *The Wind Ensemble Thematic Catalog 1700-1900*.

Fourthly, we have endeavored to document modern editions of early works. All too frequently works are published without provenance and we have found that a "Parthia in E♭" may actually be one of dozens of similar works. Wherever possible we have linked publications to the original source(s).

Finally, we have put considerable time and effort into matching up versions of the same work. This is especially critical for the large number of arrangements of operas and ballets, many of which were issued by more than one publisher, often without the arranger's attribution. Pirated copies, often omitting movements and ad lib instruments, have also muddied the waters. In Vienna, the earlier view of a market wholly dominated by Went, Triebensee and Sedlak has now given way to one of many such arrangers, from important figures such as Starke to shadowy and often anonymous house arrangers. Where it has been impossible to identify an arranger, *we have not made guesses*. Such works are listed in the supplementary Arrangements List as ANON.

We are prepared to admit that this catalog is far from comprehensive. There is still a great deal of work to be done in locating and cataloging collections in the Russian Federation, the Ukraine and other countries of the former USSR, the Baltic States and the Balkans. There are also many private collections across Europe where access is not possible. A number of collections lost during World War II are still missing, notably the Liechtenstein collection from Valtice (Feldsberg) - a collection which must have been truly magnificent considering that Triebensee and Sedlak were successive *Kapellmeistern*. The majority of works from the Imperial Harmonie transferred from the Austrian Nationalbibliothek to the Conservatorium in 1884 must now be presumed lost; with the assistance of Dr Otto Biba of the Gesellschaft der Musikfreunde in Wien we have ascertained that at least some of these works were presented by Dr Pohl to the town band of Weingirl but there the trail grows cold. Another major archive has been closed for the past 32 years. Nevertheless, we believe that this catalog includes over 90% of the *international* early repertoire. We do not expect that future research will turn up many surprises; rather, we predict that most of the works yet to be discovered will be of a local nature.

Modern works can also present problems. We have often been surprised by the number of works composed during the last half-century which cannot be located. In many cases, we have returned to a situation analogous to that in the late 18th century with publishers holding only a single manuscript from which copies are made. Amalgamation of publishers and the reduction of archives have often contributed to the problem of locating such works. Moreover, new works are continually being composed and it is often difficult to obtain any information on them. This is not a new problem by any means and we can only echo the plea of Johann Breitkopf in the introduction to his mid-18th century catalog: *If you know of works we have missed, please let us know.*

We are well aware that our work will probably generate numerous research projects and dissertations. We shall be delighted to enter into correspondence with other researchers. However, we must point out that, in most cases, we will not be able to respond to questions of an editorial nature, e.g. variants in the thirty-second bar of the third movement (or to requests to "send all our information"). *Our brief is to tell the researcher and musician where works can be found - and to make as much sense as is possible of erroneous attributions and information regarding these works.* Should you wish to contact us, we list below the principal areas of research undertaken by each of us; of course we also "swapped hats" on many occasions.

> Jon Gillaspie: principal fieldwork in Austria, Benelux, Czech Republic, France, Germany, Hungary, Italy, Poland, Scandinavia, Slovak Republic, Spain, Switzerland, United Kingdom, United States; also dealt in the later stages with modern works; database management
> Marshall Stoneham: Australia, Czech Republic, Hungary, Japan, New Zealand, Portugal, Switzerland, United Kingdom, United States; also text coordination for *The Wind Ensemble Sourcebook*
> David Clark: chiefly responsible for modern works & editions, also visits in Germany and Switzerland

For a project of this size our acknowledgments are, of necessity, wide-ranging. If we have inadvertently omitted names (or official titles) we apologise profusely.

We would like to thank the ERMULI Trust, now The Music Libraries Trust for grants partly funding Jon Gillaspie's first trip to Łańcut and Prague and his third trip (of 13) to the Czech Republic.

From our experiences, we realize that most archives and libraries are simply not geared to sweeping bibliographic searches - especially when we can examine eight to twelve works each hour. On the whole, the directors and staffs of the various places we visited coped admirably, giving unstintingly of their time and expertise. Quite simply, we could not have produced this work without their cooperation - and, in more than one instance, with recent government cut-backs and restricted service, it would now be nearly impossible to duplicate our research within the same time scale. We list below, in alphabetical order by location, the many archives and libraries to whom we owe so much:

Amberg (Staatliche Bibliothek Amberg) Dr Walter Lippe; *Amsterdam* (Stichting Toonkunst-Bibliotheek) Dr W.M.J. Dekker, Librarian; *Bergamo* (Civico Museo Bibliographico-Musicale) the Director & staff; (Biblioteca del Conservatorio di Musica "Giuseppe Donizetti") the Director & staff; *Berlin* (Hochschule der Künste, Bibliothek) Department Head, Dr Wolfgang Rathert; *Bethlehem, PA* (Northern Archives of the Moravian Church), Vernon H. Nelson, Archivist, & the staff; *Bologna* (Biblioteca del Conservatorio di Musica "G.B. Martini") the Director & staff; (Convento di San Francesco) Padre Stanislao Maria Rossi; *Boston* (Boston Public Library) the Director & staff; *Braga* (University of the Minho) Dr Marta Ramos; *Brno* (Moravské Muzeum) successive Directors Dr Jiží Sehnal & Dr František Malý & the staff; *Budapest* (Országos Széchényi Könyvtár) successive Directors of the Music Division, Dr Robert Murányi, Dr Veronika Vavrinecz, Mde. Katalin Szerző Abt. leiter & the staff; *Cambridge* (King's College, Rowe Music Library), Mrs Cramner; (Library of the Fitzwilliam Museum), the Director & staff; *Český Krumlov* (Schwarzenberg-Oettingen archives) Dr Jiří Záloha & the staff; *Darmstadt* (Hessische Landes- und Hochschulebibliothek) Dr Bill & the staff; *Detmold* (Lippische Landesbibliothek), Frau Melchert & the staff; *Donaueschingen* (Fürstlich Fürstenbergische Hofbibliothek) H.H. Joachim Fürst zu Fürstenberg for permission to examine, Frau Gisela Holzhüter for assistance; *Edinburgh* (Reid Library of the University of Edinburgh, Music Division) the Director and staff; *Einsiedeln* (Kloster Einsiedeln, Musikbibliothek), Pater Lukas Helg; *Eisenstadt* (Esterházy Archives) H.H. Princess Melinda Esterházy for permission, Dr Holzschuch & the staff of the Esterház'sche Guter-Direktion & Archives, *also* Dr Winkler, Haydn Muzeum and Dr Walter Reicher, Intendent, Haydn Festival; *Evanston, IL* (Northwestern Univertiy, Music Library), Don L. Roberts & the staff; *Florence* (Biblioteca del Conservatorio Statale di Musica 'Luigi Cherubini'): Prof. Gai & the staff; *Frankfurt am Main* (Répertoire International des Sources Musicales - Zentralredaktion): Dr Klaus Keil & the staff; (Stadt- und Universitätsbibliothek, Musiksammlung) Dr Ann Barabara Kersting, Boris Haken & the staff; *Genoa* (Biblioteca del Conservatorio di Musica "N. Paganini") Dr Andrea Sommariva, Librarian; *Geneva* (Bibliothèque Publique et Université de Genéve) the Director & staff; *Glasgow* (Euing Music Library) the Director and staff; *Kroměříž* (Státní zámek) successive Directors: Dr Antonín Lukáš (now Director of the Archives) & his successor, Ing. Jiří Čermák, Mme Obrtelová, Archivist, & Mme A. Bartošová, Deupty Archivist; *Łańcut* (Muzeum-Zamek) Director Dr Wit Karol Wojtowicz & the staff of the archives; *Leipzig* (Leipziger Städtische Bibliotheken, Musikbibliothek), Dr Krause, Fachinformator; *London* (British Broadcasting Corporation Music Library) Joan Redding & the staff; (British Library, Music, Reference, Manuscript & National Sound Archives Divisions) the Directors & staffs; (Royal College of Music) Pamela Thompson & the staff; *Mainz* (Schott Archives) Monika Motzko-Dollmann, archivist; *Madrid* (Bibiloteca Municiapal, Sección de musica), Dr Aurora Rodriguez & Carmen Hervas; *Meiningen* (Staatliche Museen) Frau Herta Müller, Leiterin der Abt. Musikgeschichte / Max-Reger-Archiv; *Melk,* (Benedictinerstiff), Pater Bruno Brandstetter, Abbot of Melk; *Milan* (Biblioteca del Conservatorio "Giuseppe Verdi") Prof. Agostina Zecca Laterza & the staff; (Ufficio Riverca Fondi Musicali) Il Direttore della Ricerca Dott. Mariangela Donà & her successor Dott. Massimo Gentili-Tedeschi; *Modena* (Biblioteca Estense) the Director & staff; (Instituto Musicale Pareggiato "Orazio Vecchi", Biblioteca) the Director & Librarian; *Münster* (Universitätsbibliothek, Musiksammlung) Dr Ernst; *Munich* (Bayerische Staatsbibliothek, Musikabteilung) the Director & staff; *Munich* (Répertoire International des Sources Musicales, Arbeitsgruppe Deutscheland e V. - Arbeitsstelle München): Dr Gertraut Haberkamp; *Neuchatel* (Bibliothèque publique de la ville de Neuchatel) the Director & staff; *New York* (New York Public Library) Susan T. Sommer; *Ostiglia* (Fondazione Greggiati) Dott. Claudio Sani; *Oxford* (Bodleian Library, Music Libary) Peter Ward Jones & the staff; *Paris* (Bibliothèque nationale, Départment de la musique) Madame Catherine Massip & the staff; (Bibliothèque nationale, RISM) Cécile Grand & the staff;

Prague (Státní knihovna ČR, hudební archiv) Head Dr Julius Hůlek; Deputy Head, Mme Zuzanna Petrášková & the staff; (Národní múzeum, hudební oddělení) Dr Jana Fojtíková, Head of the Historical Music Department, Dr Markéta Kabelková, Deputy Head, & the staff; (Český rozhlas / Czech Radio, Central Music Archive) Mgr. Václav Rysl & the staff; *Regensburg* (Thurn und Taxis Hausarchiv) H.S.H Gloria, Fürstin von Thurn & Taxis for permission to view, Herr Hugo Angerer (also for information on the regimental band) & the staff; *Rudolstadt* (Thüringisches Staatarchiv), Dr Langhof, Director; *Salzburg* (Salzburger Mezeum Carolino Augusteum, Bibliothek) Frau Ebeling-Winkler & the staff; *Schwerin* (Mecklenburgische Landesbibliothek) Herr Raimund Jedeck; *Stockholm* (Musikaliska Akademiens Bibliotek) Ms Anna Lena Holm; *Stuttgart* (Württembergische Landesbibliiothek) the Directors & staffs of the Music & MSS Depts; *Tübingen* (Musikwissenschaftliches Institut der Eberhard-Karls-Universitäts) Prof. Dr Hermann Manfred Schmid (Director) & Dr Schick (Assistant Director); (Swabische Landesbibliothek) Dr Georg Günther; *Uppsala* (Universitetsbiblioteket, Music & Manuscript Departments) Dr Anders Edeling, Inga Johansson & the staff; *Vaduz* (Fürstemtum Liechtenstein Landesarchiv) Dr Alois Ospelt; *Venice* (Biblioteca del Conservatorio "Benedetto Marcello") the Director & staff; (Santa Maria Consolazione detta 'al Fava') the Archivist; *Vienna* (Österreichische Nationalbibliothek) Hofrat Dr Günter Brosche & the staff; (Gesellschaft der Musikfreunde in Wien) Dr Otto Biba & the staff; (Stadtbibliothek): the Director & staff; (Stiftung Fürst Liechtenstein Hausarchiv) Dr Evelin Oberhammer; *Washington, DC* (Library of Congress, Music Dept.) the Director & staff; *Winston-Salem, NC* (The Moravian Music Foundation) Dr Nola Canouse, Director; *Zurich* (Zentralbibliothek, Music Department) the Director & staff.

We would also like to thank the directors and staffs of the many national Music Information Centers, notably: Amsterdam: Donemus; Brussels: Centre Belge de Documentation Musicale (CeBeDeM); Cardiff: Welsh Music Information Centre; Copenhagen: Dansk Musik Informations Center; Glasgow: Scottish Music Information Centre; London: British Music Information Centre; New York: American Music Center; Oslo: Norsk Musikkinformasion; Prague: Český hudební fond; Stockholm: Svensk Musik; Sydney: Australian Music Centre Ltd; Toronto: Canadian Music Centre; Vienna: Österreichische Gesellschaft für Musik; Wellington: New Zealand Music Center (SOUNZ); Zurich: Fondation SUISA pour la musique.

Our searches for modern works were often assisted by copyright collection agencies and we are especially grateful to the Performing Right Society (PRS, UK), the Mechanical Copyright Protection Society Ltd (including the National Discography; MCPS, UK), and the American Society of Composers, Authors and Publishers (ASCAP). Music publishers, too, have been enthusiastic in their support of our project and we would especially like to thank the following: The American Composers Alliance, Ariel Music, Bärenreiter-Verlag, Bote & Bock (also for information on Margun Music), Breitkopf & Härtel, Bruyere Music Publications, Camden Music, Castle Music, Chester Music (part of the Music Sales Group), CMA, Doblinger, Editions Robert Martin, Edition Musicus New York, Edition Wilhlem Hansen, Copenhagen, Emerson Edition (with special thanks to June Emerson and her staff), EMI Music Ltd (and EMI Records Ltd), Karthause-Schmülling Internationale Musikverlage, The Music Sales Group, Novello (part of the Music Sales Group), G. Schirmer, Inc., Musikverlag B. Schott's Söhne, Shawnee Press, UMI, Universal Music, WOODWINDplus, and Worldwide Music

Many individuals offered enthusiastic assistance and encouragement, including: Prof Igor and Dr Ira Abarenkov; Eric Baude-Delhommais & the Ensemble Philidor, Clifford Bartlett, Dr Steven Barnett, Dr Bastiaan Blomhert (for sharing so much research with us, notably our exchanges of Krommer information), Jack Brymer OBE, Dr Maureen Buja, Prof James A. Cairns, David Campbell, Carlos Chanfón, Katja Chermusheva, Dr Ulrich Drüner, Madame Arlette Durey, Robert Eccles, David Farneth (The Kurt Weill Foundation for Music Inc.), Dr Piero Gargiulo, Nessa Glen, Martin Harlow (for sharing information from the Biblioteca del Conservatorio, Florence), Herbert Huber (for information on works purchased from the Löwenstein collection), John Humphries, Dr Markéta Kabelková (for information on the Pachta Harmonie & for exceptional assistance in Prague), Prof Dieter Klöcker & the Consortium Classicum, Vera Kulikova, Christopher Larkin & the London Gabrieli Brass Ensemble; Ian Lowe & the Bournemouth Wind Quire, Dr William Mackrodt, Charles Neidich & Mozzafiato, Christopher & Frances Nex, Michael O'Donovan & the Pacific Wind Ensemble, Frau Pechotsch-Feichtinger (for exceptional assistance at the Österreichische Nationalbibliothek), Dr Andrew Pfister, Dr Howard Picton, Dr David J. Rhodes, Paul Rodriguez, Prof H. C. Robbins Landon, Gabrielle Rossi (RILM, Milan), John Smit & the Josef Triebensee Ensemble, Sotheby's (London & Frankfurt am Main), Peter Schreiber & the Collegium Vienense, Pamela & David Thompson, Ernest Warburton (for advance information on the J. C. Bach Thematic Catalog), Martha Kingdon Ward & Sweet Harmony, Jane Woolfenden. We must also acknowledge our debt to Dr Roger Hellyer and Dr David Whitwell, whose pioneering works provided us with a starting point to explore the many collections around the world.

We would also like to thank the many modern composers & arrangers who provided us with information, the numerous people who provided accommodations in many locations and, of course, our families and friends, who *remained* family and friends throughout the many years of our obsession.

Last but far from least, we owe a great debt to Greenwood Press, not only for their encouragement but also for their patience. We were nearing completion when political changes in Eastern Europe opened up undreamed of opportunities for further research. Marilyn Brownstein, Mary Blair, Alicia S. Merritt, Pamela St. Clair and Jane Lerner offered continuing insights and coped admirably as, over the six years that followed, the "book" grew to three volumes as research trips became more and more frequent. Telephone calls to discuss various points were invariably greeted with the question, "Where are you *now*?" We are proud to be their "Wayward Winds".

Now the question becomes, "Where do we go from here?" This is certainly *not* the end of our involvement in this rich area of music. We are committed to maintaining an up-to-date database and hope, at some point in the future, to prepare a hypertext version; an Internet web site is a distinct possibility. If you know of works that we have missed (or have just composed a new work, published a new edition, or made a recording) please let us know. Above all, we hope you enjoy playing - and hearing - works you have found in this catalog.

ABBREVIATIONS

a-	alto	nr	near
A	alto voice	ob	oboe
Abth.	Abtheil/Abteil	obdam	oboe d'amore
ad lib	ad libitum	obl	obbligato/obligé/required
amp-	amplified	oph	ophicleide
arr(s)	arrangement(s)	org	organ
Auto	autograph	p-	petit/small/klein
b	basso/unspecified bass instrument)	Pc	publication, contemporary*
b-	bass	perc	percussion
B	bass voice	pf	piano
bar-	baritone; (without hyphen: baryton)	pic(-)	piccolo
BAR	baritone voice	Pm	publication, modern**
bc	basso continuo	pn	plate number/edition number
Bd.	Band/volume	prin	principale
bomb	bombard/bombardone	prov	provenance
bn	bassoon	pt(s)	part(s)
bthn	basset horn, corno di bassetto	pub	published
c.	circa	red	reduction
C	canto (generally boy soprano)	repr	reprint/reprinted
cap	cornet á pistons	rip	ripieno/ripieni
cb(-)	contrabass; contrabasso	quart-	quarto (at the 4th above/below)
cbn	contrabassoon	quint-	quinto (at the 5th above)
cel	celeste	s-	soprano
cl	clarinet (in B♭ unless otherwise noted)	S	soprano voice
clar	clarino	sax	saxophone
con	concertante/concertanto	sd	sine dato/without date
crt	cornet	s-dr	snare/side/small drum, caisse claire
cym	cymbal(s)	Ser.	series
db	double bass	serp	serpent
dr	drum	sl	sine loco/without place
e-	electric	Sm.	Sammelband
ed	edited by/editor	sn	sine nomine/without name
euph	euphonium	Supp	supplement
f./ff.	folio(s), sheet	synth	synthesizer
	(f.1) = verso; (f.1b) = recto	t-	tenor
fig	figured/figurato	T	tenor voice
fl	flute	tamb	tambourine
fldam	flauto d'amore	tb	trombone
flug	flügelhorn	t-dr	caisse roulante/Wirbeltrommel
glock	glockenspiel	terz-	terzio (at the 3rd below)
gtr	guitar	Th.	Theil/Teil
harm	harmonium	timp	timpani
heck	heckelphone	tp	trumpet
hn	French horn, corno di caccia	tri	triangle
-hn	horn (brass instrument)	tu	tuba
hpcd	harpsichord	var	variation(s)
kl-	klappen-/keyed	vc	cello
liv	Livraison, installment, part	vib	vibraphone
M	mezzo-soprano	vl	violin
min	miniature	vla	viola
MS(S)	manuscript(s)	vladam	viola d'amore
mvt(s)	movement(s)	vlne	violone
No(s)	number(s)	wm	watermark
Nr(o)/Nr(s)	number(s)	xly	xylophone

J9/J6   *Journal für neunstimmige/sechsstimmige Harmonie.* (Chemische Druckerei: Wien).
KGS   *Oettingen-Wallerstein'sche Musiksammlung. Microfiche Edition.* K. G. Saur: Munich, etc., 1986.
Mag de mus fêtes nat   Magasin de Musique des Fêtes Nationales. (Publishing house of the Conservatoire de Musique, Paris, 1794 - 1799).
Rec des époques   *Recueil des Époques.* Unpublished, 1799; the only proof copy is in F-Pn.
RISM   *Répertoire International des Sources Musicales.* Series a/I. Printed music (generally) pre-1800. Bärenreiter: Kassel, 1971 *et seq.*
Steinquest   Steinquest, Eugene Waldo. *Royal Prussian Wind Band Music 1740 - 1797.* D.Ed. dissertation, George Peabody College for Teachers, (University of West Virginia), 1971.
Swanzy   Swansy, David Paul. *The Wind Ensemble and its Music During the French Revolution (1789 - 1795).* Ph.D. dissertation, Michigan State University, 1966.

*   **Pc** refers in *most cases* to printed publications. However, we also include here early commercially anailable manuscripts by publishers such as Breitkopf (Leipzig); Cappi, Hoftheater-Musik-Verlag, Laube, Traeg, T. Weigl (Vienna).

**   **Pm** refers to modern publications, generally post-1945, (which may also be only on hire in manuscript).

GUIDE TO THE CATALOG

The **Main Composer Sequence**, listed by composer for original works, or by arranger for arranged works, gives locations and shelfmarks wherever possible; modern editions are given without locations and shelfmarks. Concordances to standard thematic catalogs are given, e.g. of Mozart's works (WAM-) to Köchel (K).

Composers and arrangers are assigned a three-letter **Work Code**, with the initial of their surname as the last letter; this code is used systematically for cross-referencing. *The Work Code and number assigned to a work will never be altered; if, in future, a work should be re-attributed, the work will bear both the old and new Work Code and number.* A suffix indicates the type of work:

a	arrangements and transcriptions
c	conjectured; without contemporary attribution, but with supporting data
d	dubious and/or spurious works
e	excerpts from larger works, e.g. operas
f	fragments
m	military (marches and pieces for military bands)
s	supplemental and minor works
t	funeral music (Trauermusik), instrumental
v	vocal music

Works are listed in the order: original instrumental, original instrumental (marches), original vocal, arrangements. Note that it is possible to use more than one suffix for a single work, e.g. **tva** (arranged vocal music for funerals). It is also possible to qualify an excerpt from a collection, e.g. **1.1m(a)** (arranged work within a military work or collection).

Entries are given in the following format divided into 'sentences' by periods:

1. *Work Code, Title, Key, Number of movements.* Wherever possible an accurate short title has been provided; in these cases the title is separated from any additional information by a semi-colon (;).

2. *Instrumentation.* This generally follows modern usage with the following exceptions: horn parts *precede* bassoon parts, and contrabassoon parts *immediately follow* the bassoon parts. *Alternatives* are indicated by the use of an oblique: *ob/cl.* *Doublings* are indicated by a set of parentheses: **ob(ca).** *Keys* of instruments are also indicated by a set of parentheses: **cl(Eb).**

3. *Bibliographical Information: format, imprint* (for published works), *location(s), shelfmark(s) and additional comments.* Format takes the following order: Autograph manuscripts, manuscript scores, manuscript parts, early published versions, modern published versions.

Cross-referencing to the *Wind Ensemble Sourcebook* and *The Wind Ensemble Thematic Catalog 1700 - 1900* are indicated by the use of asterisks (*) and stars (★). An asterisk preceding the composer's name indicates that a biographical entry appears in the *Wind Ensemble Sourcebook;* an asterisk preceding an individual work indicates that it is discussed under the biographical entry. A star at the end of an entry indicates that the incipit and full information on movements can be found in *The Wind Ensemble Thematic Catalog 1700 -1900.*

Following the Main Composer Sequence are two additional sections:

Anonymous Works. This section is organized alphabetically by geographical region. Shelfmarks are given for both single works and those in collections from specific archives. Each item is given a specific **A-** identification number, e.g. **A-1**. Qualifying suffixes (a, c, d, f, m, t, v) are also applied as above; thus, vocal music with winds (excluding music solely for use at funerals) will have a separate numbered sequence with the code: **A-(number)v**.

Arrangements. Following sections of Anonymous Collections and Anonymous (Unidentified) Single Works, the principal list is ordered alphabetically by the *composer arranged* (not by the *arranger*). Works by each composer are listed in chronological order. Where the arranger has been identified, entries are in short form comprising the arranger's name, the Work Code, number of movements and scoring. Anonymous arrangements bear a specific **A-** identification number; in this case, with the qualifying suffix **a**, e.g. **A-1a**; these entries include full bibliographical information. Some arrangements are found among the preceding Anonymous Works section and their short form entries are recognizable by their *parenthetical* qualifier, e.g. **A-85.1m(a).**

The **Appendix** which follows the Arrangements section lists the most common alternative opera and ballet titles encountered during our researches. In many cases, archives and libraries have cataloged works under the alternative title without any further identification; the Appendix should eliminate any confusion which may arise.

LIBRARY and ARCHIVE SIGLA

The order of entries is alphabetical by siglum: first by country, then by town (capital letters), then by archive (lower case letters), then by individual collection (lower case letters in parentheses; note that this is solely for identification and does not form part of the official siglum). We have adopted 1997 national boundaries.

Country Sigla

Austria (Österreich)	A-	
Australia	AUS-	
Belgium (België/Belgique)	B-	
Bulgaria (Bulgarija)	BU-	
Canada	C-	
Croatia (Hrvatska)	HR-	
Czech Republic (Česká Republika)	CZ-	
Denmark (Danmark)	DK-	
Finland (Suomi)	FIN-	(formerly SF-)
France	F-	
Germany (Deutschland)	D-	
Hungary (Magyarország)	H-	
Iceland (Ísland)	IS-	
Ireland (Éire)	EIRE-	
Italy (Italia)	I-	
Japan (Nippon)	J-	
Netherlands (Nederland)	NL-	
New Zealand	NZ-	
Norway (Norge)	N-	
Poland (Polska)	PL-	
Russia (Rossiya)	RF-	
Slovakia (Slovensko)	SK-	(formerly SQ)
Slovenia (Slovenija)	SI-	
South Africa (Suid-Afrika)	SA-	
Spain (España)	E-	
Sweden (Sverige)	S-	
Switzerland (Schweiz/Suisse/Svizza)	CH-	
Ukraine (Ukraina)	UKR-	
United Kingdom (Great Britain)	GB-	
United States of America	US-	
Yugoslavia, Federal Republic of	YU-	(comprising Serbia & Montenegro)

Austria (Österreich)

A-Ed	Eisenstadt, Domarchiv
A-Ee	- Esterházy-Archiv
A-Eh	- Haydn-Museum
A-FK	Feldkirch, Domarchiv
A-Gk	Graz, Akademie für Musik und Darstellende Kunst und Landesmusikschule
A-GE	Geras, Niederösterreich, Stift Geras, Musikarchiv
A-GÖ	Fürst bei Göttweg, Benediktinerstift Göttweig, Musikarchiv
A-GT	Götz, Prämonstratenser-Stift, Musikarchiv
A-H	Herzogenburg, Chorherrenstift Herzogenburg, Bibliothek und Musikarchiv
A-HE	Heiligenkreuz, Zizterzienerstift
A-KN	Klosterneuburg: Augustiner-Chorherrenstift
A-KR	Kremsmünster, Benediktiner-Stift Kremsmünster, Regenterei oder Musikarchiv
A-L	Lilienfeld, Zisterzienster-Stift, Musikarchiv und Bibliothek
A-LA	Lambach, Benediktiner-Stift Lambach
A-LIm	Linz, Oberüsterreichisches-Landesmuseum
A-M	Melk, Benediktiner-Stift Melk
A-RB	Reichersberg, Stift Reichersberg
A-Sca	Salzburg: Salzburger Museum Carolino Augusteum, Bibliothek
A-Sm	- Mozarteum, Internationale Stiftung Mozarteum, Bibliotheca Mozartiana
A-Ssp	- St Peter (Erzstift oder Benetiktiner-Erzabtei Musikarchiv)
A-Sst	- Bundesstaatliche Studienbibliothek
A-SCH	Schlägl, Prämonstratenser-Stift
A-SEl	Seitenstetten, Benediktiner-Stift Musikarchiv
A-SF	St Florian, Augustiner-Chorherrenstift
A-TU	Tulln, Katholisches Pfarramt (Pfarrkirche St Stephan)
A-Wdo	Vienna (Wien), Zentralarchiv des Deutschen Ordens
A-Wgm	- Gesellschaft der Musikfreunde in Wien. *See also:* A-Wgm(c), A-Wgm(w).
A-Wgm(c)	- Gesellschaft der Musikfreunde in Wien, Gesellschaft Conservatorium collection

> *Note: Works with this siglum were originally part of the Imperial Harmonie collection and were not part of the music tranferred back to A-Wn in January, 1884. These works may have already been lost in 1884; despite the cooperation of the Gesellschaft der Musikfreunde we have not been able to trace these works. See also: A-Wgm(w).*

A-Wgm(w)   Vienna (Wien), Gesellschaft der Musikfreunde in Wien, Gesellschaft Conservatorium collection
        Note: Works with this siglum were originally part of the Imperial Harmonie collection but were not among music tranferred back to A-Wn in January 1884. Instead these works were given by the Conversatorium to the Weingirl town band in February 1886 (Bibliothek der Gesellschaft der Musikfreunde in Wien, Document 10981/139). These works remain lost.

A-Wkann	- Sammlung Prof. Hans Kann, private collection
A-Wmi	- Musikwissenschaftliches Institut der Universität
A-Wn	- Österreichische Nationalbibliothek, Musiksammling
A-Wn(h)	- Österreichische Nationalbibliothek, Sammlung von Anthony von Hoboken
A-Wögm	- Österreichische Gesellschaft für Musik (mic)
A-Wort	- Österreichische Radio, Musiksammlung
A-Ws	.- Schottenstift, (Benediktiner-Abtei Unserer Lieben Frau zu den Schotten), Bibliothek
A-Wst	- Stadtbibliothek, Musiksammlung
A-Wue	- Universal Edition archives
A-Wweinmann	- Prof. Dr. Alexander Weinmann, private collection
A-Z	Zettl, Zisterzienser-Stift, Bibliothek und Musikarchiv

Australia
AUS-Smc   Sydney, Australian Music Centre

Belgium (België/Belgique)

B-Ac	Antwerp (Antwerpen, Anvers), Koninklijk Vlaams Musiekconservatorium
B-Bc	Brussels (Bruxelles, Brussel), Conservatoire Royal de Musique, Bibliothèque
B-Bcdm	- Centre Belge de Documentation Musicale (CeBeDeM)
B-Br	- Bibliothèque Royale Albert 1er
B-Gc	Ghent (Gent, Gand), Koninklijk Muziekconservatorium, Bibliotheek
B-Lc	Liège (Luik), Conservatoire Royal de Musique, Bibliothèque

Bulgaria (Bulgarija)
BU-Sp   Sofia (Sofija), State Philharmonic Orchestra, Archives

Canada
C-Tcm   Toronto (Ontario), Canadian Music Council (mic)

Switzerland (Schweiz/Suisse/Svizza)

CH-Bchristen	Basle, Werner Christen, private collection
CH-Bmi	- Bibliothek des Musikwissenschaftlichen Instituts der Universitat Basle
CH-Bsacher	- Paul Sacher, private collection
CH-Bu	- Öffentliche Bibliothek der Universität Basle, Musiksammlung
CH-E	Einsiedeln, Benediktinerkloster. *NB. Only male visitors admitted, by appointment.*
CH-EN	Engleberg, Stift Engelberg, Musikbibliothek
CH-Fcu	Fribourg (Freiburg), Bibliotheque Cantonale et Universitaire
CH-Gc	Geneva (Genève, Genf) Bibliothèque du Conservatoire de Musique
CH-Gpu	- Bibliotheque Publique et Universitaire de Genève
CH-Lz	Lucerne (Luzern), Zentralbibliothek
CH-N	Neuchâtel (Neuenburg), Bibliothèque Publique
CH-Wr	Winterthur, Stiftung Rychenberg
CH-Zjacobi	Zürich, Dr Erwin Jacobi, private collection (in CH-Zz)
CH-Zma	- Schweizerisches Musik-Archiv (mic)
CH-Zwalter	- Walter private collection
CH-Zz	- Zentralbibliothek, Kantons-, Stadt- und Universitätsbibliothek. *Shelfmarks beginning "AMG" denote music from the collection of the Allgemeine Musik Gesellschaft.*

Czech Republic (Česká Republika)
CZ-Bm   Brno, Moravské Múzeum, Ústav dějin hudby. *Note: application for an appointment a month in advance is now recommended.*

(au)	Brno, Augustinian Monastery archive
(bh)	Bystřice pod Hostýnem, church arcives
(br)	Břeclav, church archives
(ck)	Českě Křídlovice, chruch archives
(cp)	Čehovice (Čehowitz) u Prostějova [near Prostějov], church archives
(dr)	Drnholec, church archives
(hr)	Hranice, church archives
(jb)	Júr u Bratislavy [near Bratislava], church of Svatý [Saint] Júr
(kj)	Kamenice u Jihlavy [near Jihlava], church archives
(kb)	Karlovice u Bruntálu [near Bruntál], Sbírka Aloise Englische
(ko)	Kojehín, church archives
(kv)	Kvasice (Kvasicich), Kůr Straka, church archive (cf. CZ-KV)
(lr)	Lomnice u Rýmařova [near Rýmařov], church archives
(lb)	Lukov - Horní Břečkov, combined church archives
(nm)	Nové Město na Moravo, church archives
(no)	Naměšť nad Oslavou, castle archives
(os)	Ostrava, church archives
(pe)	Brno, St Petrov
(re)	Rešov, church archives
(rj)	Rajhrad, Klášter [monastery] archives
(ro)	Rozstání, church archives
(sz)	Stražnice, castle archives

(CZ-Bm)	(te)	Tělc
	(tr)	Třebíč, church archive
CZ-Bparsch	Brno, Arnošt Parsch unpublished (apply to the composer *via* CZ-Pis)	
CZ-Brezniček	- Petr Rezniček, unpublished (apply to the composer *via* CZ-Pis)	
CZ-Bsa	- Státní archiv, (works from the Augustinian Monastery, Staré [Old] Brno)	
CZ-Bu	- Státní vědecká knihovna Universitní knihovna	
CZ-BA	Bakov nad Jizerou, pobočka Okresního archívu v Mladé Boleslavi	
CZ-BR	Březnice, Sv Ignace, church archives - all works may now be in CZ-PLa	
CZ-CH	Cheb, Okresný archív	
CZ-CI	Cítoliby, Státní múzeum, archives of Count Ernst Pachta of Rayhofen.	
CZ-K	Český Krumlov, Státní Archív Třeboň	
CZ-KRa	Kroměříž, Zámecký hudební archív	
CZ-KRk	- Kostela p Marie (Church of St Mary; now in CZ-KRa)	
CZ-KRsm	- Archive of the Collegiate Church of St Maurice (Chrám sv. Mořice; now in CZ-KRa)	
CZ-KV	Kvasice (Kvasicich), Kůr Straka, church archive (see also: CZ-Bm(kv).)	
CZ-Lla	Česká Lípa, Okresný archív	
	(je)	Jestřbí, castle/church archives
	(st)	Stráž pod Ralskem, castle/church archives
	(no)	Nový Bor (formerly Haida), church archives
	(ve)	Vejprnice, town archives
	(vl)	Velenice. church archives
	(za)	Zákupy, church archives
CZ-MH	Mnichovo Hradiště, Městské múzeum	
CZ-NR	Nova Říši, klášter premonstrátů, knihovna a hudební sbírka, (formerly in CZ-Bm)	
CZ-NYc	Nymburk, Chrám sv. Jiljí, church archive	
CZ-OLu	Olomouc, Státní vědecká knihovna Universitní knihovna	
CZ-OP	Opava, Slezské múzeum	
CZ-OSr	Ostrava, Český rozhlas (Czech Radio), hudební archív	
CZ-OSTpololáník	Ostrovačice, Zdeněk Pololáník, unpublished (apply to the composer *via* CZ-Pis)	
CZ-Ph	Prague (Praha), Církev Holěsovice, district archives - now in CZ-Pu(dm)	
CZ-Pis	- Hudební Informačni stredisko Českého hudebního fondu (mic)	
CZ-Pjiráčková	- Marta Jiráčková, unpublished (apply to the composer *via* CZ-Pis)	
CZ-Pk	- Archív Státní konzervatore v Praze, hudební archív	
CZ-Pkalach	- Jiří Kalach, unpublished (apply to the composer *via* CZ-Pis)	
CZ-Pmatousek	- Lukáš Matousek, unpublished (apply to the composer *via* CZ-Pis)	
CZ-Pnm	- Múzeum České Hudbi, Národní múzeum. *Note: Officially closed as of 15 April 1996 in preparation for relocation; microfilm copies remain possible. Letters should be directed c/o Novotného lávka 1, CZ 110 01 Praha, Czech Republic.*	

          Lobkovic. Archive of Prince Lobkowicz, Roudnice nad Labem
          XX. Archive of the Counts Kinsky, zámek Budenický
          XXII. Archive of the Counts Pachta
          XXXII (-XXXIV). Osek, Cistercian Monastery archive
          XXVII.D. Břevnov (Prague), monastery archives
          XXXVIII.A (-E). Broumov, monastery archives
          XXXVIII.F. Úterý, church archives
          XL.A (- D) Bertramka, Mozart Society collection (provenances generally unknown)
          XL.E. Klášterec nad Ohří
          XLI. Archive of the Counts Chotek, zámek Veltrusy & zámek Káčina
          XLII.A (- E). Archive of the Counts Clam-Gallas, Frýdlant & Prague
          XLII.F.1 (- 201). Svojšín, castle archives
          XLIII.A (- F). Rychnov nad Kněžnou, castle & church archives
          XLVI, XLVII. Prague, Strahov Praemonstratensian monastery
          XLIX.D.386 *bis*, XLIX.F.1 (-293) Kucs, church archives

CZ-Pp	- Archiv pražského hradu
CZ-Pr	- Český rozhlas, hudební archív (Czech Radio, Central Music Archive)
CZ-Pu	- Státní knihovna ČR, Universitní knihovna - hudební oddělění archív Mozartova.
	(dm) Langenbruck, now Dlouhý Most, Musikantengesellschaft. *Note: some earlier reference works use the now superceded "CZ-Ph" siglum & "DM" shelfmarks.*
CZ-Pvent	- Ventova komorni harmonie (Vent's Wind Harmonie), private collection
CZ-PLa	Plzeň, Městský archív
	(ba) Břetislava, town/church band
	(bl) Blovice, church archive
	(br) Březnice, castle/church archives, copies by František Vaněčka
	(ka) Kasejovice, church archives, copies by Ladislav Vaněčka
	(ne) Nepomuk, church archive
	(ve) Vejprnice, town/church archives (Jan Lašek, učitel)
	(vm) Václav Mentberg collection
CZ-PLr	- Česky rozhlas, hudební archív, (Czech Radio, Music Archive)
CZ-POL	Poličk, Múzeum: Pomátnik Bohuslav Martinů
CZ-RAJ	Rajhrad, Klášter (archives now mostly in CZ-Bm)
CZ-RO	Rokycany, Okresný múzeum, (sometimes cited using the old siglum: CZ-MR)
CZ-TRB	Česká Třebová, Městské múzeum
CZ-U	Ústí nad Orlicí, Okresný [church] archív

Germany (Deutschland)

D-As	Augsburg, Staats- und Stadtbibliothek
D-AB	Amorbach, Fürstlich Leiningische Bibliothek. *Collection currently inaccessible.*
D-AG	Augustusberg, Erzgebirge (Sachsen), Pfarrarchiv
D-ASh	Aschaffenburg, Hofbibliothek
D-B	Berlin, Staatsbibliothek Preussischer Kulturbesitz, now including the Deutsche Staatsbibliothek (Dddr-Bds). *Note: D-Bds shelfmarks are gradually being altered to conform to D-B usage; we have retained the D-Bds sigla for any works where we know only the old shelfmark.*
D-Bds	- Deutsche Staatsbibliothek (formerly East Berlin; see comments for D-B)
D-Bdso	- Deutsche Staatsoper
D-Bhm	- Hochschule der Künste Berlin (Staatliche Hochschule für Musik und Darstellende Kunst)
D-Bim	- Staatliches Institut für Musikforschung (formerly, 1917-1939, Fürstliches Institut fur Musikwissenschaftliche Forschung at Bückeburg)
D-Blandshoff	- Ludwig Landshoff, private collection
D-Bu	- Universitatsbibliothek der Freien Universität
D-BABhuber	Babenhausen, Herbert Huber, private collection (MSS formerly in D-WEMl; cf. GB-Ljag)
D-BAUd	Bautzen, Domstift und Bischöfliches Ordinariat, Bibliothek
D-BAUm	- Stadtmuseum
D-BAR	Bartenstein, Fürst zu Hohenlohe-Bartensteinsches Archiv
D-BB	Benediktbeuern, Pfarrkirche, Bibliothek
D-BE	Berleburg, Fürstlich Sayn-Wittenstein-Berleburgsche Bibliothek
D-BFa	Burgsteinfurt, Gymnasium Arnoldinum
D-BFb	- Fürstlich Bentheimsche Bibliothek (now in D-MÜu as a loan collection)
D-BNba	Bonn, Wissenschaftliches Beethovenarchiv
D-BÜ	Büdingen (Hessen), Fürstlich Ysenburg- und Büdingisches Archiv und Schlossbibliothek
D-Cl	Coburg, Landesbibliothek
D-Dla	Dresden (Sachsen), Staatsarchiv (formerly Sächsisches Landshauptarchiv)
D-Dl	- Sächsische Landesbibliothek (formerly used the siglum: D-Dlb)
D-Dmb	- Stadt und Bezirksbibliothek (formerly Städtische Musikbücherei; now in D-Dl)
D-DO	Donaueschingen, Fürstlich Fürstenbergische Hofbibliothek, private collection
	Note: the collection is now held in Switzerland but works must be examined at D-DO. This can only be done by placing an advance order. Please include the required shelfmark(s).
D-DS	Darmstadt, Hessische Landes- und Hochschulbibliothek, Musikabteilung
D-DSim	- Internationales Musikinstitut, Informationszentrum für Zeitgenössisches Musik (sim)
D-DT	Detmold, Lippische Landesbibliothek
D-DTF	Dietfurt, Franzizkanerkloster
D-DÜl	Düsseldorf, Landes- und Staatsbibliothek
D-ESpriv	Essen, private collection, owner unknown to us, cited by Whitwell
D-F	Frankfurt, Frankfurt am Main, Stadt- und Universitätsbibliothek
D-FÜS	Füssen, Pfarrkiche St Mang
D-GBR	Grossbreitenbach bei Arnstadt, Pfarrbibliothek
D-GOL	Goldbach bei Gotha, Thüringen Pfarrarchiv
D-GSA	Garmisch, Sammlung Strauss
D-Hch	Hamburg, Gymnasium Christianeum
D-Hs	- Staats- und Universitätsbibliothek, Musikabteilung
D-HEms	Heidelberg, Musikwissenschaftliches Seminar der Universität
D-HER	Herrnhut, Archiv der Bruder-Unität
D-HL	Haltenbergstetten, Schloss über Niederstetten (Baden-Württemberg), Fürst zu Hohenlohe-Jagstberg'sche Bibliothek, private collection
D-HR	Harburg über Donauwörth, Fürstlich Oettingen-Wallerstein'sche Bibliothek, private collection (now in D-Au, Augsburg, Universitätsbibliothek)
D-HRD	Herdringen, Schloss Herdringen Biblioteca Fürstenburgiana (administered by D-Kdma Kassel, Deutsches Musikgesichictliches Archiv)
D-Kl	Kassel, Murhard'sche Bibliothek der Stadt Kasssel und Landesbibliothek
D-KA	Karlsruhe, Badische Landesbibliothek, Musikabteilung
D-KIZklöcker	Kirchzarten, private collection of Dieter Klöcker (Director of the Consortium Classicum)
D-KNh	Cologne (Köln), Staatliche Hochschule für Musik
D-KPk	Kempten (Allgäu), Kirchenbibliothek, Evangelisch-Lutherisches Pfarramt St. Mang
D-LB	Langenburg (Württemberg), Fürstlich Hohenlohe-Langenburg'sche Schlossbibliothek
D-LEm	Leipzig, Musikbibliothek der Stadt Leipzig
D-LEt	- Thomasschule (Alumnat), Bibliothek
D-LIT	Lichtenstein (Sachsen), Stadtkirche St Laurentius Kantoreiarchiv
D-LÜh	Lübeck, Bibliothek der Hansestadt Lübeck, Musikabteilung
D-Mk	Munich (München), St Kajetan
D-Mbs	- Bayerische Staatsbibliothek
D-Mmb	- Städische Musikbibliothek, *includes:*
	D-Mf: Frauenkirche archives
D-Mv	- Verband Deutsche Musikerzieher und Konzertierender Künster e.V. Manuscriptarchiv
D-MEIr	Meiningen (Thüringen), Staatliche Museen mit Reger Archiv
D-MERz	Merseburg, Deutsches Zentral-Archiv, Historische Abteilung
D-MGmi	Marburg an der Lahn, Musikwissenschaftliches Institut der Philipps-Universität, Musikarchiv
D-MÜms	Münster, Musikwissenschaftliches Seminar des Bischöfliche Diözesanarchiv (Generalvikariat)
D-MÜu	- Universitätsbibliothek. (D-BFb & D-RH on loan). *Appointment strongly recommended.*

D-MZsch   Mainz, Musikverlag B. Schotts Söhne, Archiv
D-NEhz   Neuenstein, Hohenlohe-Zentral-Archiv
D-OB   Ottobeuren (Allgäu), Bibliothek der Benediktiner-Abtei
D-OF   Offenbach am Main, Verlagsarchiv André
D-PA   Paderborn, Erzbischöfliche Akademische Bibliothek
D-Rk   Regensburg, Der Künstlergilde
D-Rp   - Bischöfliche Zentralbibliothek (Proske - Musikbibliothek)
D-Rs   - Staatliche Bibliothek
D-Rtt   - Fürstlich Thurn und Taxis'sche Hofbibliothek
D-RH   Rheda, Fürst zu Bentheim-Tecklenburgische Bibliothek (on loan in D-MH and D-MÜu)
D-ROu   Rostock, Universitätsbibliothek
D-RUh   Rudolstadt, Hofkapelarchiv
D-RUl   - Staatsarchiv
D-SCHN   Schnaitsee, Pfarrkirche
D-SWl   Schwerin, Wissenschaftliche Allgemeinbibliothek (formerly Mecklenburgische Landesbibliothek)
D-SPlb   Speyer, Pfälzische Landesbibliothek, Musikabteilung
D-Tl   Tübingen, Swabische Landesbibliothek, (now part of the Musikwissenschaftliches Institut der
               Universität (D-Tmi), (formerly used siglum: D-Tsch)
               Signatur: B & Bb   Ochsenhausen, Benediktinerkloster und Pfarrkirche St George
                             G & Gg   Gutenzell, Pfarrkirche
                             R   Tübingen, Stiftkirche
                             Z   Bad Buchau
D-Tu   - Universitätsbibliothek der Eberhard-Karls Universität
D-W   Wolfenbüttel (Niedersachsen), Herzog August Bibliothek, Musikabteilung
D-WD   Wiesentheid (Bayern), Musiksammlung des Grafen von Schönborn-Wiesentheid
D-WEMl   Wertheim am Main, Fürstlich Löwenstein'sche Bibliothek, private collection
               *Note: the music collection was sold at Sotheby's, London, on 1 Dec 1995 and 15 May
               1996; virtually all of the Harmoniemusik is now at GB-Ljag; a few works are at
               D-BABhuber. The D-WEMl siglum has been retained only for works whose present
               locations are unknown.*
D-WRgs   Weimar, Goethe-Schiller Archiv
D-WRl   - Landeshauptarchiv, Bibliothek
D-WRtl   - Thüringische Landesbibliothek, Musiksammlung
D-WS   Wasserburg am Inn, Chorarchiv St. Jakob, Pfarramt Bibliothek
D-WSm   - Stadtmuseum (Heimathaus)
D-WÜd   Würzburg, Diözesanarchiv
D-Z   Zwickau (Sachsen), Ratsschulbibliothek
D-ZI   Zittau (Sachsen), Stadt- und Kreisbibliothek (now in D-Dl)
D-ZL   Zeil (Bayern), Fürstlich Waldburg-Zeil'sches Archiv, private collection

Denmark (Danmark)
DK-A   Åarhus (Aarhus), Staatsbiblioteket i Åarhus
DK-Kd   Copenhagen (København), Dansk Musik Informtion Center
DK-Kk   - Det kongelige Bibliotek
DK-Sa   Sørø, Sørø Akademis Bibliotek

Spain (España)
E-Bca   Barcelona, Biblioteca de Catalunya, Departament de Música de la Biblioteca
E-E   El Escorial, Real Monasterio de El Escorial
E-Mam   Madrid: Biblitoteca musical circulante, (part of the Biblioteca municipal)

Ireland (Éire)
EIRE-Da   Dublin: Royal Irish Academy
EIRE-Dn   - National Library and Museum of Ireland

France
F-AG   Agen, Archives départmentales
F-AIXmc   Aix-en-Provence, Bibliothèque de la maîtrise de la cathédrale
F-C   Carpentras, Bibliothèque Inguimbertine et Musée de Carpentras
F-Ep   Épernay, Bibliothèque municipale
F-G   Grenoble, Bibliothèque municipale
F-Nm   Nantes, Bibliothèque municipale
F-NEmic   Neuilly-sur-Seine, Centre de Documentation de la Musique Contemporaine Société des Auteurs,
               Compositeurs et Editeurs de Musique (SACEM), 225 Ave Charles de Gaulle, F-92521
F-Pa   Paris, Bibliothèque de l'Arsenal
F-Pd   - Centre de Documentation de la Musique Contemporaine, (Cité de la Musique, 16 Place de
               la Fontaine aux Lions, BP 11593, F-75920 PARIS CEDEX 19)
F-Pi   - Bibliothèque de l'Institut de France
F-Pn   - Bibliotheque nationale (includes F-Pc, Conservatoire National de Musique)
F-Po   - Bibliothèque - Musée de l'Opéra
F-Sim   Strasbourg, Institut de musicologie de l'Université
F-TO   Tours, Bibliothèque municipale
F-TOep   Tours, Ensemble Philidor, private collection (2 ter rue des Ursulines, 37000 Tours)
F-TOm   - Médiathèque de Musique Tchèque
F-V   Versailles, Bibliothèque municipale

Finland (Suomi)
FIN-A   Åbo (Turku), Sibeliusmuseum Musikvetenskapliga Institutionen (Akademi, Bibliotek & Arkiv)
FIN-Hmt   Helsinki, Finnish Music Information Center

United Kingdom (Great Britain)
GB-AB   Aberystwyth, National Library of Wales
GB-Bu   Birmingham, University Music Library, Barber Institute of Fine Arts
GB-BA   Bath, Municipal Library
GB-BFlowes   Blandford Forum, Ian Lowes, private collection
GB-Cfm   Cambridge, Fitzwilliam Museum
GB-Ckc   - Rowe Music Library, King's College
GB-Cpl   - Pendlebury Library of Music
GB-Cu   - University Library
GB-CDw   Cardiff, Welsh Music Information Centre. *Closed in 1997; GB-Lmic may be able to advice*
                on the current status.
GB-CDp   - Public Libraries, Central Library
GB-DEro   Derby, Derbyshire Record Office
GB-DIDbushell   Didcot (Oxon); Geoffrey Bushell, private collection
GB-DOTams   Dorchester-on-Thames (Oxon), Prof. Marshall Stoneham, private collection
GB-DRc   Durham, Cathedral Library
GB-DU   Dundee, Public Library
GB-En   Edinburgh, National Library of Scotland
GB-Ep   - Public Library, Central Public Library
GB-Er   - Reid Music Library of the University of Edinburgh
GB-Gm   Glasgow, Mitchell Library
GB-Gsma   - Scottish Music Archive (mic)
GB-Gu   - Glasgow University Library
GB-Lam   London, Royal Academy of Music
GB-Lbbc   - British Broadcasting Corporation
GB-Lbennett   - William Bennett, private collection
GB-Lbl   - British Library, Reference Division, Music Library, (formerly used siglum: GB-Lbm)
GB-Lcm   - Royal College of Music
GB-Lgbe   - Gabrieli Brass Ensemble, private collection
GB-Ljag   - Jon A. Gillaspie, private collection. GB-jag(w) indicates Harmoniemusik from D-WEMl.
                Consultation by appointment only, from 2000 onwards. Copies cannot be provided.
GB-Lhoffnung   - Annetta Hoffnung, private collection
GB-Lhumphries   - John Humphries, private collection
GB-Lkc   - King's College Library
GB-Lmic   - British Music Information Centre
GB-Lsm   - Royal Society of Musicians of Great Britain
GB-Lu   - University of London, Music Library
GB-Lwcm   - Central Music Library, Westminster
GB-LEbc   Leeds, Brotherton Collection
GB-LEc   - Leeds Public Library, Music Department, Central Library
GB-LVu   Liverpool, Liverpool University, Music Department
GB-Mp   Manchester, Central Public Library, Henry Watson Music Library
GB-Ob   Oxford, Bodleian Library
GB-P   Perth, Sandeman Music Library
GB-PLd   Plymouth, Devon Library Service
GB-SA   Saint Andrews (Fife, Scotland), University Library
GB-T   Tenbury, St Michael's College, (now mostly in GB-Ob)
GB-WOKbaker   Woking, Lance Baker, private collection
GB-Yu   York, York University Library

Hungary (Magyarország)
H-Bberkes   Budapest, Kalman Berkes/Budapest Wind Ensemble, private collection
H-Bl   - Liszt Ferenc Zenemüvészeti Föiskola Könyvtára (Library of the Conservotoire "Franz Liszt")
H-Bmz   - Hungarian Music Information Center c/o Association of Hungarian Musicians (Magyar
                Zenemüvészak Szövetsége)
H-Bn   - Országos Széchényi Könyvtár (National Library)
H-Bu   - Egyetemi Könyvtár (University Library), includes: Kiadjda a Magyar Nemzeti Muzeum
H-KE   Keszthely, Helikon Kastélymúzeum
H-P   Pécs (Fünfkirchen), Pécsegyházmegyei Könyvtár-volt Pécsi Papnevelöintezeti Könyvtár
                (Diözesanbibliothek Bibliothek)

Croatia (Hrvatska)
HR-Zha   Zagreb, Hrvatski glazbeni zavod (Croatian Music Institute)

Italy (Italia)
I-Bc	Bologna, Civico Museo Bibliografico-Musicale (including I-Bl, Conservatorio di Musica "G. B. Martini")
I-Bsf	- Archivio del Convento di San Francesco
I-BGc	Bergamo, Biblioteca civica "Angelo Mai"
	(jm) Fondo J.S. Mayr
	(lc) Fondo Lina e Rosa Calvi
I-BGi	- Civico Istituto musicale "Gaetano Donizetti"
	(bi) Biblioteca dell'Instituto
	(cm) Fondo Capella Musicale Basilica S. Maria Maggiore
	(md) Museo Donizettiano
I-BRd	Brescia, Archivio capitolare del Duomo
I-BZtoggenburg	Bolzano, Anton Melchior von Menz collection (1757-1801), private archives, Count Toggenburg
I-CORc	Correggio, Biblioteca comunale
I-Fc	Florence (Firenze), Conservatorio di Musica "Luigi Cherubini". *Closed since 1966.*
I-FZc	Faenza, Biblioteca communale
I-Gc	Genoa (Genova), Conservatorio di Musica "N. Paganini". [formerly I-Gi(l) and I-Gl]
I-GAN	Gandini, Archivo Parrocchiale di Gandino
I-Ls	Lucca, Seminario arcivescovile pressö la Curia
I-LEFpezzoli	Leffe, Raccolta Privata (private collection) Gianni Pezzoli
I-Mc	Milan (Milano), Biblioteca del Conservatorio "Giuseppe Verdi"
I-MOe	Modena, Biblioteca Estense
I-MOl	- Instituto Musicale Pareggiato "Orazio Vecchi", Biblioteca
I-MZ	Monza, Insigne Basilica di S Giovanni Battista
I-Nc	Naples (Napoli), Conservatorio del Musica S. Pietro a Maiella. *Currently closed.*
I-OS	Ostiglia, Fondazione Greggiati
I-Pc	Padua (Padova), Biblioteca Palatina presso il Conservatorio "Arrigo Boito"
I-Ppriv	- untraced private collection [see Ratti in Main Composer Section]
I-PAc	Parma, Sezione Musicale della Biblioteca Palatina presso il Conservatorio del Musica "Arrigo Boito"
I-PIs	Pisa, Fondo Simoneschi
I-PLcon	Palermo, Biblioteca del Conservatorio di Musica "Vincenzo Bellini"
I-PS	Pistoia, Archivio capitolare della Cattedrale
I-Rar	Rome (Roma): Radiotelevisione Italiana, music archives
I-Rsc	- Biblioteca Musicale governativi del Conservatorio di Santa Cecilia
I-TRc	Trento, Biblioteca communale
I-UDricardi	Udine, Ricardi private collection
I-Vc	Venice (Venezia), Conservatorio di Musica "Benedetto Marcello" (includes I-Vmc, Museo Civica Correr)
I-Vcdr	- Pia Casa di Ricovero
I-Vmc	- Museo Civico Correr (now apparently entirely in I-Vc)
I-Vnm	- Biblioteca nazionale Marciana
I-Vsmc	- S. Maria della Consolazione detta "della Fava"
I-VERbelotti	Vertrova, Raccolta Privata (private collection) Giuseppe Belotti
I-VId	Vicenza, Archivo e Biblioteca capitolare del Duomo (Archivo della Cattedrale)

Iceland (Ísland)
IS-Rmic	Reykjavik, Islensk Tónverkamidstöd / Icelandic Music Information Center

Japan (Nippon)
J-Tma	Tokyo (Tokjo), Biblioteca Musashino Academia Musicae (Musashino College of Music Library)
J-Tfc	- Japanese Federation of Composers

Norway (Norge)
N-Oic	Oslo, Norwegian Music Information Center

Netherlands (Nederland)
NL-Ad	Amsterdam, Donemus Foundation
NL-At	- Toonkunst-Bibliotheek
NL-DHgm	The Hague (Den Haag), Gemeente Museum
NL-Lu	Leiden, Bibliotheek der Rijksuniversiteit
NL-MOverheijen	Morgestel, Cees Verheijen, private collection
NL-Uu	Utrecht, Universiteitsbibliotheek
NL-Z	Zeist, Archief van de Evangelische Brodergemeente, (now in NL-Uu)

New Zealand
NZ-Wmc	Wellington, New Zealand Music Centre (SOUNZ)
NZ-Wn	- New Zealand National Library.

Portugal
P-La	Lisbon (Lisboa), Biblioteca do Palácio nacional da Ajuda

Poland (Polska)
PL-CZ	Górze w Częstochowie, Augustinian Cloister, Bibliotece, OO. Paulinów na Jasnej
PL-GDj	Gdansk, St Johann, Lirchenbibliothek
PL-Kj	Kraków (Cracow), Biblioteka Jagiellónska
PL-LA	Łańcut, Bioblioteka muszczna Zamku (Lubomirski Palace archives)
PL-Wpcm	Warsaw (Warszawa), Polish Music Center
PL-Wtm	- Warrszawskiego Towarzystwz Muzycznego, Bibliotecka
PL-Wu	- Biblioteka Uniwersytecka
PL-WRu	Wrocław (Breslau), Biblioteka Uniwersytecka

Russia (Rossiya)
RF-KL   Klim, Tchaikovsky Museum
RF-Mcm   Moscow (Moskva), Gosudarstvennaja Tsentral'niy Muzey Muzikal'noy Kul'turi M.I. Glinka
RF-Ml   - Gosudarstvennaja Biblioteka (formerly: SSSR imeni V.I. Lenina)
RF-Shenselt   St Petersburg (formerly Leningrad), Henselt private collection
RF-Sk   - Biblioteka Gosudarstvennoj Konservatorii imeni N.A. Rimskogo-Korsakova
RF-Slit   - Naučnaja biblioteka Gosudarstvennogo instituta teatra, muzyki i kinomatografii
RF-Ssc   - Gosudarstvennaja Ordena Trudovovo Krasnovo Znameni Publičnaja Bibliotekaimeni
               M.E. Saltykova-Sčedrina. *The Imperial Harmonie collection is now here rather than RF-Sk.*
RF-Stob   - Central'naya muzylal'naya biblioteka Teatra operay: baleta im S.M. Kirova.

Sweden (Sverige)
S-J   Jönköping, Per Brahegymnasiet
S-L   Lund, Universitetsbiblioteket
S-Snydal   Stockholm, R. Nydhahl, private collection
S-Sic   - Svensk Musik (STIMS; Informations Central för Svensk Musik)
S-Skma   - Kungliga Musikaliska Akademiens Bibliotek
S-Sm   - Musikhistoriska museet, Biblioteket
S-Ssr   - Sveriges Radio, Musikbiblioteket
S-St   - Kungliga Teaterns Bibliotek
S-SK   Skara, Stifts- och Landsbiblioteket (includes Lävroverkets Musikbibliotek)

South Africa (Suid-Afrika)
SA-Jsamro   Johannisberg, South African Music Rights Organisation Ltd.

Slovenia (Slovenija)
SI-Las   Ljubljana, Jettel collection
SI-Lu   - Narodna in univerzitetna knjižnica

Slovakia (Slovensko)
SK-BRhis   Bratislava, Hudobné informačné stredisko Slovenské hudobného fondu (mic)
SK-BRnm   - Slovenské národné múzeum, hudobné oddělenie (including the archives of Kežmarok and
               Svedlár Monasteries)

Ukraine (Ukraina)
UKR-Ku   Kiev, University Library

United States of America
US-Bm   Boston (MA), Boston University, Mugar Memorial Libary
US-Bp   - Boston Public Library - Music Department
US-BE   Berkeley (CA), University of California, Music Library
US-BETm   Bethlehem (PA), Archives of the Moravian Church, Northern Province Archive
US-BLu   Bloomington (IN), Indiana University, School of Music Library
US-CA   Cambridge (MA), Harvard University, Music Libraries
US-CAe   - Harvard University, Eda Kuhn-Loeb Library
US-Cn   Chicago (IL), Newberry Library
US-CDhs   Concord, (NH), New Hampshire State Library
US-CLwr   Cleveland (OH), Western Reserve University, Freiberger Library and Music House Library
US-Eu   Evanston (IL), Northwestern University, Music Library
US-EL   Elmira (NY), Elmira College, The Garnett Tripp Learning Center
US-GRBidrs   Greensboro (NC), University of North Carolina, International Double Reed Society Library
US-I   Ithaca (NY), Cornell University Music Library
US-Lu   Lawrence (KS), University of Kansas Libraries
US-MSu   Minneapolis (MN), University of Minnesota, Music Library
US-NH   New Haven (CT), Yale University, The Library of the School of Music
US-NRwhitwell Northridge (CA), Dr David Whitwell, private collection
US-NYaca   New York, (NY), American Composers Alliance, 170 W. 74th St, New York NY 10023;
               E-mail: info@composers.com. *All works are either available for purchase or hire.*
US-NYamc   - American Music Center Library, (mic)
US-NYp   - New York Public Library at Lincoln Center, Library and Museum of the Performing Arts
US-NYweill   - The Kurt Weill Foundation for Music, Inc.
US-PHci   Philadelphia (PA), The Curtis Institute of Music Library
US-PHf   - Free Library of Philadelphia, Music Department
US-PHu   - University of Pennsylvania Music Library
US-PHschoenbach - Sol Schoenbach, private collection
US-PT   Potsdam (NY), State University of New York at Potsdam, Crane School of Music Library.
US-R   Rochester (NY), State University of New York at Rochester, Eastman School of Music, Sibley
               Music Library
US-STu   Stanford (CA), Stanford University, Music Library, Division of Humanities & Social Sciences
US-Wc   Washington (DC), Library of Congress, Music Division
US-Ws   - Folger Shakespeare Library
US-WOa   Worcester (MA), American Antiquarian Society Library
US-WS   Winston-Salem (NC), Moravian Music Foundation, Peter Memorial Library. *By the end of
               1998 US-WS will also hold microfilms of the complete music collection at US-BETm.*

Federal Republic of Yugoslavia
YU-Bmic   Belgrade (Beograd), Union of Yugoslav Composers' Organization, Documentation and
               Information Section

ALTERNATIVE NAMES AND PLACES

Note: Vowels with an umlaut and the Danish "o" with a streg *(ø) are treated in all cases as if they are followed by an "e"; thus Göpfert can be found at Goepfert, and Nørholm at Noerholm. All other names follow English alphabetization.*

ALTERNATIVE NAMES

ALESSIO → ALEXIUS

BOIS, Rob Du → DU BOIS
BROR, Lille → SÖDERLUNDH
BUREBL → PUREBL

CHAIKOVSKY → TCHAIKOVSKY

DA → *Ignored in alphabetization*
DAUBRAWSKY → DOUBRAVSKÝ
DE → *Ignored in alphabetization*
DES → *Ignored in alphabetization*
DISCHER → FISCHER
DITTERSDORF → DITTERS VON DITTERSDORF
DRUŽECKÝ → DRUSCHETZKY
DUSSEK → DUŠEK

ENESCU → ENESCO
ERNEST → ERNST

FOLGERT → VOLKERT
FRANTZL, Jacopo, *Pater* → TRAUTZL

GABRIEL-MARIE, ( ) → MARIE, Gabriel
GALLUS, Gerog Anton → MEDERITSCH, Johann
GAMBARO, Vincenzo (Vincent) → GAMBARO, Giovanni Battista
GODZHIBEKOV → GADZHIBEKOV
GÖPFERT → GOEPFERT

JÍROVEC → GYROWETZ

KALIVODA → KALLIWODA
KATHALIERÝ → CARTELLIERI
KELLERI → CHELLEREI
KOŽELUH → KOZELUCH
KRECHTER → KRECHLER
KRAMÁŘ → KROMMER

LATTENBURG → BEUTEL VON LATTENBURG

MASCHEK → MAŠEK
MAXWELL DAVIES → DAVIES
Mc → Treated as MAC
MICHEL, J. → YOST
MÜLLER, C.F. *of Berlin* → MÜLLER, (Carl) Friedrich

R., I. → REID, John, *General*
ROESSLER → ROSETTI
RÖSSLER → ROSETTI

SAPUTO → TRAUTZL
SCHÖRINGER → SCHIRINGER
SCHTSCHEDRIN → SHCHEDRIN
STEFFAN, Josef Anton → ŠTĚPÁN
STEPHANI, Joseph → ŠTĚPÁN

TRÜBENSEE → TRIEBENSEE

VAGENSEIL → WAGENSEIL
VAN → *Ignored in alphabetization*
VENT → WENT
VISCHERING → DRÖSTE-HÜLSHOFF
VON → *Ignored in alphabetization*
VRANICKÝ → WRANIZKY

WANHAL(L) → VANHAL
WENDT → WENT
WENTH → WENT
WERBA → VRBA
WILLIAMS → VAUGHAN WILLIAMS
WIND, BLASIUS → MENTNER
WITSCHKA → VITSKA
WITSKA → VITSKA
WOLLANEK → VOLÁNEK
WRANITZKY → WRANIZKY
WRATNI → VRATNÝ
WRBA → VRBA

ALTERNATIVE PLACE NAMES
Here we give English equivalents of place names as cited in publishers' imprints and manuscripts.

ANVERS → ANTWERP
BRÜNN → BRNO
FELDSBURG → VALTICE
FIRENZE → FLORENCE
LANGENBRUCK → DLOUHÝ MOST
LENINGRAD → ST PETERSBURG
MAYENCE → MAINZ
MILANO → MILAN
MÜNCHEN → MUNICH
PARIGI → PARIS
PRAG → PRAGUE
PRAHA → PRAGUE
PRESSBURG → BRATISLAVA
ROMA → ROME
STALINGRAD → VOLGAGRAD
VENEZIA → VENICE
VIENNE → VIENNA
WIEN → VIENNA

THE
WIND ENSEMBLE
CATALOG

MAIN COMPOSER SEQUENCE

ABATE, Rocco
RXA-1. Tatà Requiem . . . oscuro gioco del tempo per doppio quintetti di fiati.   2fl 2ob 2cl 2hn 2bn.
Pm (Edipan: Roma, pn EP 7159, 1986), facsimilie AutoMS score in "New Notation".

*ABEL, Carl (Karl) Friedrich *22 Dec 1723, Cöthen - 20 June 1787, London*
CFA-1m, 2m. Duè Marcia di Cavalleria de d'Infanteria Le Prince Wallis della Gran Bretagne d'un Regimento di Dragoni Cavalleggiore; in E♭.   2cl 2hn bn.
MS parts: D-Bds, KH MM 382, (as by J. C. Bach); GB-Lbl, R.M.24.k.15, (piano reduction, as by Abel).   ★
Pm (Henmar Press Inc. (*via* Peters): New York, pn 66672a, 1983), score & parts.

ABER, Johann (Giovanni) *(?1740), active in Genoa, 2nd half of the 18th century*
GZA-1(-6). 6 Sonate; in D, C, G, A, G, F; all 3 mvts.   2fl 2hn basso.   MS parts: I-Mc, Noseda 1.12a.   ★

*ABINGTON, William *(1765), Lieutenant in the 1st Regiment, Royal East India Volunteers*
WXA-1m. The Royal East India Slow March.   2cl 2hn 2bn tp serp.
Pc (Printed for Culliford, Rolfe & Barrow: London, c.1796), score: GB-Lbl, h.3213.k.(1).   ★
WXA-2m. The Royal East India Quick March.   2cl 2hn 2bn tp serp.
Pc (Printed for Culliford, Rolfe & Barrow: London, c.1796), RISM [A 177], score: GB-Lbl, g.133.(1); GB-Ob, Mus.Instr.I.1(13).   ★

ABLE, ( ) *(1740) We cannot rule out the possibility that this is Carl Freidrich Abel (1723-1787)*
XYA-1m. The Buckingham March.   2ob 2hn bn.
Pc (sn: sl [London], c.1775), RISM [AA 178, I,1], score: GB-Lbl, h.1568.u.(8); GB-Lhumphries; US-NYp. ★

*ACERBI, Domenico *(1830), active 1859 - 1870s, Venice*
I-Vsmc also has many fragmentary sets of parts by Acerbi; some may have been for winds alone.
DXA-1v. Gloria, 1859.   TTB(concertante+ripieno), (fl) 2cl 2hn basso tp (tb) timp (organ).
MS score & parts: I-Vsmc, (instruments in parentheses appear in parts only).   ★
DXA-2v. Kyrie, 1866.   Solo TB, 2cl 2hn timp.   MS parts: I-Vsmc, (missing hn II).   ★
DXA-3v. Laudate pueri, 1871.   Solo T, TTB chorus, 2cl 2hn tp tb timp organ.   MS score & parts: I-Vsmc.   ★
DXA-4v. Tantum ergo, 1872.   TTB, 2cl 2hn tp tb organ(with registration).   MS score: I-Vsmc.   ★

ACKER, Dieter *3 Nov 1940, Hermannstadt/Siebenbürgen, Germany (previously Romania)*
DZA-1. Octet No. 2.   fl cl 2bn 2tp 2tb.   MS score: The composer.
DZA-2. Attitüden; 1968/1971.   2cl 2hn 2bn.
Pm (Breitkopf & Härtel: Wiesbaden, pn BG 1244, 1971), score & parts.
Pm (Gerig: Köln, pn HG 821, 1976), score & parts.

*ADAM, Adolphe Charles *24 June 1803, Paris - 3 May 1856, Paris*
ACA-1t. Marche exécutée en 1841 (translation des Cendres de Napoleon).
2pic(D♭) 2ob cl(E♭) 2cl(B♭) 2hn 4bn 2tp 4cap 3tb oph b tamtam.   *Bn III & IV are the same as bn II.*
MS parts (25 Feb 1842): F-Pn, L 17.118, No. 1, (63 pts in total).   ★

*ADAMS, Thomas *(1775), Organist of St George's, Camberwell*
TZA-1m. A Grand March and Quick Step Composed expressly for the 3rd. Regiment of Loyal London Volunteers.   fl 2cl 2hn bn+serp tp *(trio for 2cl bn serp).*
Pc (Printed for the Author by Clementi & Co.: London, c.1808), score: GB-Lbl, h.100.(9).   ★

*ADDISON, John *16 March 1930, Chobham, Surrey, UK*
*JOA-1. Sextet for Woodwind; 1949.   2fl 2cl 2bn.   MS score: GB-Lmic.

ADLER, ( ) [? Giovanni AZLER]
YYA-1(-6). [6] Quintetti (E♭, 4 mvts; E♭, 4 mvts; E♭, 5 mvts; B♭, 4 mvts; B♭, 3 mvts; B♭, 4 mvts).
2cl 2hn bn.   MS parts: I-UDricardi, Ms.146.   ★

ADLER, Samuel Hans *4 March 1928, Mannheim; US citizen from 1942*
SHA-1. Music for eleven.   2fl ob 2cl bn 5perc.
Pm (Oxford University Press: London, NY, 1968).
SHA-2. 7 Epigrams for woodwind sextet.   pic fl ob cl b-cl bn.
Pm (Oxford University Press, London, NY; pn 97007, 1970), score and parts.

*ADOLPH I.K.H.P. *(the initials are probably a motto)*
IKA-1. Quadrille ex Es [E♭].   2ob 2cl 2hn bn.   MS parts: CZ-Pnm, XLII.E.229.   ★

ADOLPHE, Bruce *1955, USA*
BYA-1. Chiaroscuro.   2fl 2ob 2cl 2hn 2bn.
Pm (American Composers Alliance: New York, 1984), score.

AGNOLO, Giacomo
GXA-1v. Salve Regina.   Solo T, 2cl(C) 2hn vlne organ(obbligato & bc-fig).   MS score & parts: I-Vsmc.   ★
GXA-2v. Tantum ergo.   TTB(solo+ripieno), 2ob 2hn (b-tb) organ(bc-fig).
MS score & parts: I-Vsmc, (the parts are incomplete & the b-tb is a later addition).   ★
GXA-3v. Tota pulchra.   Solo TTB, 2ob 2hn organ(bc-fig).
MS score & parts: I-Vsmc, (the oboes, although an integral part of the work, are not in the score).   ★

*AGRELL (Agrelli), Johann Joachim (Giovanni) *2 Feb 1701, Löth, East Gotland - 19 Jan 1765, Nüremburg*
JJA-1. Sinfonia à 5 in F; 5 mvts.   2ob 2hn basso.
MS parts (by F.G. Sander, c.1724 - 1726): S-Uu, Mus.instr.hs.13:22.   Modern MS score: GB-Ljag.   ★

AGUILAR-AHUMADA, Miguel del *1931, Chile*
MAA-1. Septet; 1954.   cl hn 2bn 2tp db.   MS score: The Composer.

ÁGÚSTSSON, Herbert Hriberschek *8 Aug 1926, Mürzzuschlag, Austria (of Icelandic parentage)*
HHA-1. Kammermusik Nr. 1, 1963. fl 2ob 2cl 2hn 2bn.
Pm (Islenzk Tonverkamidstüd: Rekjavik; c.1963); score.

*AHL, C., le cadet *(1780), active c.1806 - 1810*
CXA-1a. Paer: Griselda, Recueils 1 & 2, each 6 mvts. 2cl 2hn bn.
Pc (André: Offenbach s/M, pn 2226, 2227, 1806), parts: A-KR; A-Wn; CH-Zz; CZ-KRa, A4018/IV.B.191, (Recueil 1, with an additional bn I part by Havel); D-Tl, Z 44 & 45; H-KE, 677/VIIIa & 677/VIIIb; US-Wc.
CXA-2a. J. Weigl: Die Schweizerfamilie, Recueils 3 & 4, each 7 mvts. 2cl 2hn bn.
Pc (André: Offenbach s/M, c.1810), parts: A-KR; A-Wn; D-Bhm; US-Wc; US-WS, (Recueil 4).

*AHLBERG, Gunnar *29 May 1942, Mora, Sweden*
GQA-1. Fluente; 1984. 2fl 2cl b-cl bn. MS score: S-Sic.

*AIBLINGER, Johann Caspar *23 Feb 1779, Wasserburg, Bavaria - 6 May 1867, Munich*
JCA-1.1m. Militar Hymne; in E♭, AWV IX:8. 2fl 2cl 2hn 2bn cb.
AutoMS score (19 Nov 1850): D-WSm., Nr. 39. ★
JCA-1.2m. Militar Hymne. pic fl cl(A♭) 2cl(E♭) 3cl(B♭) 4hn 2bn 4tp 2flug a-hn t-hn 3tb baryton bomb drums.
MS score: D-WSm., Nr. 39.
Pc *(Münchener Lieblings-Stücke der neuesten Zeit, No. 70):* (Joseph Aibl: Munich, pn 728, sd), piano reduction: D-Mbs, Mus. pr.343/70.
JCA-1v. Missa per la notte di Natale; AWV I:18. SSATTB chorus, 2fl 2ob 2cl 2hn 2bn 2tp (2)vc+b timp organ.
AutoMS score & MS parts (1830): D-Mk, 128, 129, (the titlepage calls for the following number of singers: 2S.2S.4A.2T.2T.4B.). MS score: A-Wn, Mus.Hs.16,698, ff.28 - 51b, ("No. 389"). MS parts: D-Mk, 1002. ★
JCA-2v. Missa; in F, AWV I:19. SATB solo, SATB ripieno, 2fl 2cl 2hn 2bn 2tp a-tb t-tb b-tb 2vc b timp organ.
AutoMS score (1829): D-Mk 130, (with titlepage calls for 3 of each ripieno vocal part). ★
MS score: D-Mk, D-Mbs, Mus.mss.5532/2; D-Rp, (1841, with MS parts).
JCA-3v. Feyerliche Messe zur Allerhöchsten Geburts Feyer Seiner Majestät des Königs in allerunterthänigster Ehrfurcht gewidmet; AWV I:50. SATB chorus, 2fl(E♭) 2cl(E♭) 2cl(B♭) 4hn 2bn 2tp(clar) 2tb timp.
AutoMS score: D-Mk, 52. ★
JCA-4v. Hymne zur Auferstehung; "Halleluja, er lebt um unserer Sünden wilien", in C, AWV II:106.
Two SATB choruses, 2fl 2ob 2cl 4hn 2bn 2tp a-tb t-tb b-tb 2vc+b harp.
AutoMS score (27 Feb 1831): D-WSm, Nr. 47. MS parts: D-Mk. ★
JCA-5v. Sey herzlich uns willkommen hier; in C, AWV V:97. SATB, 2fl 2cl 2hn 2bn b-tb.
AutoMS score: D-Mk, 1050, ff.16 - 17. ★
JCA-6v. Sieh Vater deine Kinder treten; in F, AWV V:103. SATB, 2fl 2cl 2hn 2bn b-tb.
AutoMS score: D-Mk, 1050, ff.18 - 20. ★
JCA-1va. Mozart: La Clemenza di Tito, Act II, No. 16, Recitative, "Eh wir des Festes Spiel beginnen", AWV VII:15. T, 2fl 2ob 2cl 2hn 2bn 2tp. AutoMS score (1821): D-Mbs, St.Th.112.
JCA-1e. Rodrigo und Zemene [Zimene]; AWV VI:1. Scoring varies. AutoMS Score: D-Mbs, St.Th.140. ★
    1.1e. Act I, No. 5. Intermezzo; in F, 8 bars. fl(I) 2ob 2cl 2hn 2bn b-tb.
    1.1ve. Act I Finale [Nos. 45 & reprise at 47]. Coro dentro la Scena: "Von Spaniens Himmel ist gefallen".
        TTB chorus, 2pic 2cl(E♭) 2cl(B♭) 4hn 2bn 3tb serp timp b-dr "Tamburi coperti".
    1.2e. Act II, No. 12. [Balletmusik] Auf der Buhne in der Sentiefung; in E, 44 bars. fl 2ob 2cl 2hn 2bn.
    1.1e(m). Act II, No. 19. Tempo di marcia; in C, 8 bars. pic(D) 2cl(D) 2cl(A) 4hn 2bn b-tb serp b-dr.
JCA-2.1e(v), 2.2e(v). Cantata [libretto titlepage printed by Franz Seraph Hübschmann: zum ehrfurchtsvollsten Empfange Ihrer Königlichen Majestäten auf einem Festa-Balle weichen zur Feyer Allerhöchst- Ihrer fünf und zwanzigjähriger Regierung die Gesellschaft des Museums zu München gab am 2tem Februar 1824]; in D, "Heil unserm König" im Jubelkranze", text by Joseph von Baader, AWV IV:I. AutoMS score: D-WSm. Nr. 9. ★
    1.1ve. No. 2 [reprised as No. 8]. Volkslied: "Heil unserm König"; in B♭.
        SATB chorus, fl 2ob 2cl 2hn 2bn vc cb harp.
    1.2ve. No. 5. Volkslied [another setting of 1.1ve]. SATB chorus, fl 2ob 2cl 2hn 2bn vc cb harp.

AIGMÜLLER, Andreas *1952, Germany*
AZA-1. Octet. 2ob 2cl 2hn 2bn.
Pm (Miami Music Edition, *via* Bassoon Heritage Edition: Fort Lauderdale, FL, pn 41, sd), score & parts.

*ALBINONI, Tomasso *8 June 1671, Venice - 17 Jan 1751, Venice*
Note: All Albinoni wind works are now regarded as of highly questionable authenticity.
TXA-1. Concerto à 6 in F, (Mi.16). 3ob taille 2bn. MS parts: D-HRD, Fü 3720a.
TXA-2. Concerto à 5 in C; 3 mvts, (Mi.3). 3ob bn/bc tp.
MS parts: D-HRDf, Fü 3715a; D-BFb. ★
Pm (Sikorski, Hanburg, pn ED. 580, 1966), ed. Wojiechowski & Müller, score & parts.
TXA-3. Concerto à 5 in B♭, (Mi.30). ob(obl) 2ob taille bc. MS parts: D-HRDf, Fü 3607a.
TXA-4. Concerto a cinque; in D. ob 2obdam 2hn bn.
MS parts: D-BFb. *Unverified.*
*TXA-5. Concerto à 5; in F. 2obdam 2hn bn.
MS parts: D-BFb. *Unverified.*
Pm (edition untraced, advertized in agency catalog, Musica Rara, 1960s).

ALBISI, Abelardo *1872 - 1939, Italy*
ABA-1. Solo di concerto; 1925. fl ob 2cl 2bn. MS score: US-Wc.

*ALBRECHTSBERGER, Johann Georg *3 Feb 1736, Klosterneuberg - 7 March 1809, Vienna*
*JGA-1. Serenata a 5; in E♭, 3 mvts. 2ob cl hn bn.
(?Auto)MS score ("comp: Mense Nov. [1]806"): H-Bn, Ms.Mus.2359. ★

ALCALAY, Luna *21 Oct 1928, Zagreb, (Austrian citizen)*
LZA-1. Beauté homogène; 1967. 2cl 2hn 2bn.
In MS: A-Wögm will assist in contacting the composer.

*ALCOCK, John, *Doctor of Music 11 April 1715, London - 23 Feb 1806, Lichfield*
*JYA-1v. A favourite hymn for Christmas Day 1779; "Let chearful [sic] smiles in ev'ry Face".
Solo TB, Chorus (Treble, Contra-tenor [sic], Tenor, Bass), 2ob bn/bc-fig.
Pc (S.A.[&]P.T[hompson], London 1779/1780), RISM Supp [AA 762a], score: GB-Lbl, G.517.gg.(8). ★

ALCOCK, John, *Doctor of Music,* **and ALCOCK, John,** *the Younger, Batchelor in Music baptized 28 Jan 1740, Plymouth - buried 27 March 1791, Walsall*
*JYA-2v. Six New Anthems [3 by each composer] 2, 3 and 4 voices.   [CATB], 2ob 1/2bn organ(bc-fig).
Pc (Bland & Weller: London, 1795?), score: GB-Lbl, H.1187.f.(2). ★
Pm (Phylloscopus Publications: Lancaster, UK, pn PP41, 1991), No. 6 (Psalm XXVIII only), playing score.
Note: Although the titlepage states 2ob bn, Nos. 1 - 3 are with organ accompaniment (although No. 3 also includes a section for B solo, 2bn(with bc-fig) and the organ part comprises 2 treble line & bc-fig.
    2.1v. Alcock the Younger: Psalm X, Verse 13, "Arise O Lord God", 1778.   pp. 1 - 7.
    2.2v. Alcock the Younger: Psalm XC, "Lord Thou has been our refuge", 1778. pp. 8 - 15.
    2.3v. Alcock the Younger: Psalm CXXVIII, "Blessed are all they who fear the Lord", 1778. pp. 16 - 25.
    2.4v. Alcock the Elder: Psalm CXXVII, "When the Lord turned again", 1778. pp. 26 - 32.
    2.5v. Alcock the Elder: Psalm XIX, "The Heav'ns declare the Glory of God", 1779. pp. 35 - 39.
    2.6v. Alcock the Elder: Psalm XXVIII, Verse 7, "Praised be the Lord", 1779. pp. 40 - 49.

ALESSANDRI, Felice *1742 - 1798*
FYA-1m. Marsch; in C.   2ob 2cl bn tp.   MS parts: D-Bds, Hausbibl. Nr. 78. ★

*ALEXIUS (Alessio), František (Francesco) *1717 - 1780*
Alessius' works for the Pachta Harmonie (in CZ-Pnm) include later alto clarinet parts to replace those for the tailles. The Pachta collection also contains a number of works for two clarinets and bassoon.
FXA-1. Cassatio in D, 1768; 5 mvts.   2ob 2cl 2hn 2bn 2vla.   MS pts: CZ-Pnm, XXII.A.77. ★
FXA-2. Parthia in C; c.1770, 4 mvts.   2ob/cl 2hn 2bn.   MS pts: CZ-Pnm, XXII.A.33, (with an additional bn pt transposed to B♭ for use with clarinets in B♭; CZ-Bm, A.18.364, (for 2ob 2hn bn).
FXA-3. Parthia in C, 1768; 4 mvts.   2ob/cl 2hn 2bn.   MS parts: CZ-Pnm, XXII.A.34. ★
FXA-4. Parthia in C, 1768; 4 mvts.   2ob/cl 2hn 2bn.   MS parts: CZ-Pnm, XXII.A.35. ★
FXA-5. Parthia in F, 1768; 4 mvts.   2ob/cl 2hn 2bn.   MS parts: CZ-Pnm, XXII.A.36. ★
FXA-6. Parthia in F, 1768; 5 mvts.   2ob/cl 2hn 2bn.   MS parts: CZ-Pnm, XXII.A.37. ★
FXA-7. Parthia in F, 1768; 5 mvts.   2ob/cl 2hn 2bn.   MS parts: CZ-Pnm, XXII.A.38. ★
FXA-8. Parthia in F, 1768; 5 mvts.   2ob/cl 2hn 2bn.   MS parts: CZ-Pnm, XXII.A.39. ★
FXA-9. Parthia in F, 1768; 4 mvts.   2ob/cl 2hn 2bn.   MS parts: CZ-Pnm, XXII.A.40. ★
FXA-10. Parthia in F; 4 mvts.   2ob/cl 2hn 2bn.   MS parts: CS-Pnm, XXII.A.41. ★
FXA-11. Parthia in F; 4 mvts.   2ob/cl 2hn 2bn.   MS parts: CZ-Pnm, XXII.A.42. ★
FXA-12. Parthia in F; 4 mvts.   2ob/cl 2hn 2bn.   MS parts: CZ-Pnm, XXII.A.43. ★
FXA-13. Parthia in B[♭]; 5 mvts.   2cl 2hn bn.   MS parts: CZ-Pnm, XXII.A.44, (with an additional bn pt transposed to C for use with clarinets in C or oboes); D-DO, Mus.Ms.1551, Nos. 62-66. ★
FXA-14. Parthia in B[♭]; 5 mvts.   2cl 2hn bn.   MS parts: CZ-Pnm, XXII.A.45, (with an additional bn pt transposed to C for use with clarinets in C or oboes); D-DO, Mus.Ms.1551, Nos. 52-56. ★
FXA-15. Parthia in B[♭]; 5 mvts.   2cl 2hn bn.   MS parts: CZ-Pnm, XXII.A.46, (with an additional bn pt transposed to C for use with clarinets in C or oboes); D-DO, Mus.Ms.1551, Nos. 57-61. ★
FXA-16. Parthia in Dis [E♭]; 5 mvts.   2cl 2hn bn.
MS parts: CZ-Pnm, XXII.A.47, (with an additional bn part transposed to F for use with clarinets in C or oboes);
D-DO, Mus.Ms.1551, Nos. 84-88. ★
FXA-17. Parthia in Dis [E♭]; 5 mvts.   2cl 2hn bn.
MS parts: CZ-Pnm, XXII.A.48, (with an additional bn part transposed to F for use with clarinets in C or oboes);
D-DO, Mus.Ms.1551, Nos. 89-93. ★
FXA-18. Parthia in Dis [E♭]; 5 mvts.   2cl 2hn bn.
MS parts: CZ-Pnm, XXII.A.49, (with an additional bn part transposed to F for use with clarinets in C or oboes);
D-DO, Mus.Ms.1551, Nos. 71-75. ★
FXA-19. Parthia in B[♭]; 5 mvts.   2cl 2hn bn.
MS pts: CZ-Pnm, XXII.A.50, (with an additional bn pt transposed to C for use with clarinets in C or oboes). ★
FXA-20. Parthia in Dis [E♭]; 5 mvts.   2cl 2hn bn.
MS pts: CZ-Pnm, XXII.A.51, (with an additional bn pt transposed to F for use with clarinets in C or oboes). ★
FXA-21. Parthia in B[♭]; 5 mvts.   2cl 2hn bn.
MS pts: CZ-Pnm, XXII.A.52, (with an additional bn pt transposed to C for use with clarinets in C or oboes). ★
FXA-22. Parthia in Dis [E♭]; 5 mvts.   2cl 2hn bn.
MS pts: CZ-Pnm, XXII.A.53, (with an additional bn pt transposed to F for use with clarinets in C or oboes). ★
FXA-23. Parthia in B[♭]; 5 mvts.   2cl 2hn bn.
MS pts: CZ-Pnm, XXII.A.54, (with an additional bn pt transposed to C for use with clarinets in C or oboes). ★
FXA-24. Parthia in B[♭]; 22 August 1774, 5 mvts.   2cl 2hn bn.
MS pts: CZ-Pnm, XXII.A.55, (with an additional bn pt transposed to C for use with clarinets in C or oboes). ★
FXA-25. Parthia in Dis [E♭]; 5 mvts.   2cl 2hn bn.
MS pts: CZ-Pnm, XXII.A.56, (with an additional bn pt transposed to F for use with clarinets in C or oboes). ★
FXA-26. Parthia in B[♭]; 5 mvts.   2cl 2hn bn.
MS pts: CZ-Pnm, XXII.A.57, (with an additional bn pt transposed to C for use with clarinets in C or oboes). ★
FXA-27. Parthia in C; 4 mvts.   2cl 2hn 2bn.   MS pts: CZ-Pnm, XXII.A.58. ★
FXA-28. Parthia in Dis [E♭]; 4 mvts.   2talie/a-cl(E♭) 2hn 2bn.
MS parts: CZ-Pnm, XXII.A.59, (with 2 additional later a-cl parts in C transposing). ★
FXA-29. Parthia; in B♭, 5 mvts.   2talie/a-cl(E♭) 2hn 2bn.
MS parts: CZ-Pnm, XXII.A.60, (with 2 additional later a-cl pats in C transposing; the 2 horns were originally tacet in the 2nd mvt Andante but minimal parts have been added at the bottom of the sheets). ★
FXA-30. Parthia in Dis [E♭]; 5 mvts.   2talie/a-cl(E♭) 2hn 2bn.
MS parts: CZ-Pnm, XXII.A.61, (with 2 additional later a-cl pts in C transposing). ★
FXA-31. Parthia in Dis [E♭]; 5 mvts.   2talie/a-cl(E♭) 2hn 2bn.
MS parts: CZ-Pnm, XXII.A.62, (with 2 additional later a-cl parts in C transposing). ★

FXA-32. Parthia in Dis [E♭]; 5 mvts. 2talie/a-cl(E♭) 2hn 2bn.
MS parts: CZ-Pnm, XXII.A.63, (with 2 additional a-cl parts in C transposing). ★
FXA-33. Cassatio in Dis [E♭]; 5 mvts. 2talie/a-cl(E♭) 2hn 2bn.
MS parts: CZ-Pnm, XXII.A.64, (with 2 additional later a-cl parts in C transposing). ★
FXA-34. Parthia in B[♭]; 4 mvts. 2ob 2hn 2bn. MS parts: CZ-Pnm, XXII.A.65. ★
FXA-35. Parthia in B[♭]; 4 mvts. 2ob 2hn 2bn. MS parts: CZ-Pnm, XXII.A.66. ★
FXA-36. Parthia in C; 4 mvts. 2ob 2hn 2bn. MS parts: CZ-Pnm, XXII.A.67. ★
FXA-37. Parthia in D; 4 mvts. 2ob 2hn 2bn. MS parts: CZ-Pnm, XXII.A.68, (missing bn II). ★
FXA-38. Parthia in D; 4 mvts. 2ob 2hn 2bn. MS parts: CZ-Pnm, XXII.A.69. ★
FXA-39. Parthia in Dis [E♭]; 4 mvts. 2ob 2hn 2bn. MS parts: CZ-Pnm, XXII.A.70. ★
FXA-40. Parthia in Dis [E♭]; 4 mvts. 2ob 2hn 2bn. MS parts: CZ-Pnm, XXII.A.71, (missing 2ob). ★
FXA-41. Parthia in F; 4 mvts. 2ob 2hn 2bn. MS parts: CZ-Pnm, XXII.A.72, (missing ob II). ★
FXA-42. Parthia in F; 4 mvts. 2ob 2hn 2bn. MS parts: CZ-Pnm, XXII.A.73, (missing bn II). ★
FXA-43. Parthia in G; 4 mvts. 2ob 2hn 2bn. MS parts: CZ-Pnm, XXII.A.74. ★
FXA-44. Parthia in G; 4 mvts. 2ob 2hn 2bn. MS parts: CZ-Pnm, XXII.A.75. ★
FXA-45. Parthia in B[♭]; 6 mvts. 2ob 2hn 2bn. MS parts: CZ-Pnm, XXII.A.76. ★
FXA-46. Barthia [sic] in F; 4 mvts. 2ob 2hn 2bn. MS parts: CZ-Pnm. XXXII.A.99. ★
FXA-47. Parthia; in E♭, 4 mvts. 2cl 2hn bn. MS parts: D-DO, Mus.Ms.1551, Nos. 67-70. ★
FXA-48. Parthia; in E♭, 4 mvts. 2cl 2hn bn. MS parts: D-DO, Mus.Ms.1551, Nos. 80-83. ★

*ALKAN, Charles Henri Valentin *(pseud. for C.H.V. Morhange)* *30 Nov 1813, Paris - 29 March 1888, Paris*
CHA-1m. Pas Redoublé. pic(E♭) terz-fl fl 2ob cl(E♭) 3cl(B♭) 4hn (2E♭, B♭ alto, B♭ basso) 2bn crt 2tp 2t-tb b-tb 2oph(B♭) b-dr+cym t-dr+tri. AutoMS score (1 Oct 1840): F-Pn, MS. 2944. ★
*CHA-1v. Marcia funèbre sulla morte d'un pappagello. SSTB, 3ob bn.
Pc (Pour l'Auteur: Paris, 1859), score: F-Pn. ★
Pm (G. Schirmer: New York, London, 1972), ed. Raymond Lewenthal, score & parts.

ALKEMA, Henk *1944, Netherlands*
HXA-1. Openen en sluiten. 2fl 2ob 2cl 2hn 2bn.
Pm (Donemus: Amsterdam, 1982), score.

ALLEN, Herbert Philip *1883 - 1952*
HPA-1. The Muses. fl ob 2cl hn bn tp tb.
Pm (Whitney Blake: New York).

ALLERS, Hans Günther *1935, Germany*
HGA-1. Elegie & Capriccio. 2cl 2hn 2bn.
Pm (Möseler Verlag: Wolfenbüttel, pn 42157, 1977), score & parts.

ALLGÉN, Claude Loyola *16 April 1920, Calcutta - 18 Sept 1990, Stockholm*
CZA-1. Adagio och Fugue. fl(pic) a-fl ob ca cl b-cl a-sax hn bn(cbn) bar. MS: S-Sic.

ALMILA, Atso *1953, Finland*
ASA-1. Nonet. fl 2ob 2cl 2hn 2bn. MS score: FIN-Hmt, (No. 8393).

*ALPAERTS, Flor *12 Sept 1876, Antwerp - 5 Oct 1954, Antwerp*
FLA-1, FLA-2. Avondmuziek. Musique de soir (2 Serenades). 2fl 2ob 2cl(A) 2bn
Pc/m (Metropolis: Antwerp; 1915-1916, reissued 1953), scores.

ALTAFULLA, Ubaldo Antonio
UAA-1v. Messa; in C. TTB, fl(C, F) 2cl(C) 2hn b. MS score: I-Bsf, M.A.VII-13. ★

ALTMANN, Eddo *(editor) 1900*
EXA-1. Kleine Tanzsuite nach Tänzen einem alten Tanzbuch, c.1800. fl ob 2cl 2hn 2bn db.
Pm (Hofmeister: Leipzig, sd), score & parts (hire).

*ALYABYEV, Alexander Alexandrovich *15 Aug 1787, Tobolsk, Siberia - 6 March 1851, Moscow*
*AAA-1. Quintet in E♭ minor, c.1815. 2tp 2hn tb *(or, better:* 2cl 2hn bn.)
Pm (Russian State: Moscow; pn 28228, 1953, reiss. 1960), score & pts: GB-DOTams. ★

*AMALIE, *Princess of Prussia* *1723 - 1787*
It is possible that her teacher, Benda, actually scored her marches.
PVA-1m. Marsch pour le Reg. der Gen. F. de Millendorf. 2ob bn 3tp. MS: D-Bds, Mus.Ms.Amalie, 1.
PVA-2m(-4m). 3 Marsche, (Pour le Regiment du Comte Lottum, mars 29, 1767; Pour le Reg. du Gen. Bülow, août 14, 1767; Pour le Reg. du Gen. Saldern, mai 16, 1769). 2ob bn tp. MS: D-Bds, Mus.Ms.Amalie, 2.
PVA-2.1m. Marsch; in C. ob 2cl(C) 2hn bn. MS pts: D-DS, Mus.ms.1223/19, (A-104.1m; a later rescoring). ★
PVA-2.2m. Marsch; E♭. 2cl(E♭) 2cl(B♭) 2hn (2)bn 2tp. MSpts: D-DS, 1223/21, No. 1. *A later rescoring.*
The bassoon part is labelled "Fagotto"; the titlepage states "Fagotti" although the preceding "2" has been rubbed out. The cl(E♭) double the cl(B♭) pts.

*AMANTINO, ( ) *(c.1730)*
XXA-1. Nro 1mo Divertimento in F; 4 mvts. 2ob/cl 2hn 2bn. MS parts: CZ-Pnm, XXII.A.91. ★
XXA-2. Nro 2 Divertimento in F; 3 mvts. 2ob/cl 2hn bn. MS parts: CZ-Pnm, XXII.A.92. ★
XXA-3. Nro 3 Divertimento, in F; 3 mvts. 2ob/cl 2hn bn. MS parts: CZ-Pnm, XXII.A.93. ★
XXA-4. Nro 4 Divertimento in C; 3 mvts. 2ob/cl 2hn 2bn. MS parts: CZ-Pnm, XXII.A.94. ★
XXA-5. Nro 5 Divertimento in Dis [E♭]; 3 mvts. 2ob/cl 2hn 2bn. MS parts: CZ-Pnm, XXII.A.95. ★
XXA-6. Nro 6 Divertimento in G; 3 mvts. 2ob 2hn 2bn. MS parts: CZ-Pnm, XXII.A.96. ★
XXA-7. Nro 7 Divertimento in A; 3 mvts. 2ob 2hn 2bn. MS parts: CZ-Pnm, XXII.A.97. ★
XXA-8. Nro 8 Divertimento in B[♭]; 4 mvts. 2ob 2hn 2bn. MS parts: CZ-Pnm, XXII.A.98, (missing ob II). ★
XXA-9. Nro 9 Divertimento in F; 4 mvts. 2ob 2hn 2bn. MS parts: CZ-Pnm, XXII.A.99, (missing bn). ★
XXA-10. Nro 10 Divertimento, in G; 4 mvts. 2ob 2hn bn. MS parts: CZ-Pnm, XXII.A.100. ★
XXA-11. Nro 11 Divertimento, in C; 3 mvts. 2ob 2hn bn. MS parts: CZ-Pnm, XXII.A.101. ★
XXA-12. Nro 12 Divertimento, in D; 3 mvts. 2ob 2hn bn. MS parts: CZ-Pnm, XXII.A.102. ★

*AMBROZ, Anton *Kapellmeister, kk Österreich 57. Linien-Infant. Reg, Grossherzog von Mecklenburg-Schwerin*
AXA-1m. Verlobungs=Fest=Marsch für die Militär=Musik. pic(Db) fl(Db) cl(Ab) cl(Eb) 3cl(Bb) 4hn 4tp 2flug b-flug euph 3tb 2basso b-dr tambour. MS score: D-SWl, Mus. 740. ★

AMELSVOORT (Amelsfoort), J. van *1910, Netherlands*
JVA-1. Two Elégies. 2fl ob ob(ca) 3cl 4hn 2bn db/cbn.
Pm (Compusic: Amsterdam, pn 201, 1988), score & parts.

*AMON, Johann Andreas (André) *1763, Bamberg - 29 March 1825, ?Wallerstein*
JAA-1. VI Pièces, pour Musique turque, Op 40; 6 mvts.
pic 2flautino 2cl(Eb) 2cl(Bb) 2hn 2bn 2tp b-tb b-dr+cym("E.ct. [sic]") s-dr.
Pc (André: Offenbach s/M, pn 2233, 1806) pts: D-BFb, A-Mo 58; H-KE, 679/VIII. ★
JAA-2. Musik für Harmonie; 2 mvts, c.1820. fl 2cl/ob+cl 2hn 2bn.
MS pts: D-HR, HR III 4 1/2 2° 422. *The oboe and "Clarinetto" (+ cl II) parts are later additions on larger folio paper; the first 12 bars of No 2, marked "Terz Floete" in the fl pt have been crossed out and the fl is tacet.* ★
Pm (KGS), (fiche 2425).
JAA-3. [7] Pièces pour musique turque, Op. 57. Instrumentation unknown.
Pc (André: Offenbach s/M, pn 3170, c.1813), pts: A-Wgm, (4 pieces only), unverifed; D-AB.

*AMOS, Keith *b.1939*
KXA-1. Theme & Variations. 2fl 2ob 2cl 2hn 2bn.
Pm (Keith Amos: Kingston, UK, 1985), score & parts.
Pm (CMA Publications: Kingston, 1989), score & parts.
KXA-2. Prelude & Postlude. 2ob 2cl 2hn 2bn.
Pm (Ramsden, sl, 1983), score & parts.
KXA-3. Concertino for Clarinet and Wind Ensemble. Solo clarinet, 2fl 2ob cl hn bn.
Pm (CMA Publications: Kingston, 1989), score & parts.
KXA-4. Philadelphus. 2ob cl sax 2hn 2bn.
Pm (CMA Publications: Kingston, 1989), score & parts.
KXA-5. Catland. 2fl 2cl.
Pm (CMA Publications: Kingston, 1989), score & parts.
KXA-6. Sir Robert Walpole in Richmond Park. 2fl 2cl.
Pm (CMA Publications: Kingston, 1989), score & parts.

ANDERSON, Leroy *29 June 1908, Cambridge, MA - 18 May 1975, Woodbury, CT*
LXA-1. Suite of carols. pic 2fl 2ob ca 3cl a-cl b-cl cb-cl 2bn cbn. Pm (Mills Music: NY).

ANDERSSON, B. Tommy *26 July 1964, Borås*
BTA-1. Intrada. 3fl(pic) 2ob 3cl 4hn 2bn 3tp 3tb tu timp 2perc. MS score: S-Sic.

*ANDRÉ, Johann Anton *6 Oct 1775, Offenbach am Main - 6 April 1842, Offenbach am Main*
JTA-1. Ouverture militaire, Op. 24. 2ob 2cl 2hn 2bn.
Pc (André: Offenbach am Main), parts: CH-Bu.

*ANDREOZZI, Gaetano *22 May 1775, Aversa - 21 Dec 1826, Paris.*
GYA-1m. The celebrated March, In the Opera of La Vergine del Sole. fl cl(F) 2cl(Bb) 2hn (2)bn tp tb serp s-dr.
Pc (Printed for J. Dale: London, c.1804), score: GB-Lbl, g.1780.q.(8). ★

*ANDRIESSEN, Jurraan *15 Nov 1925, Haarlem*
JZA-1. Rouw past Elektra [Morning becomes] Elektra: symphonic suite. fl 2ob cl hn 2bn 2tp 2tb timp perc.
Pm (Donemus: Amsterdam, 1954), score & parts.
JZA-2. Concertino. Solo bassoon, 2fl 2ob 2cl 2hn 2bn.
Pm (Donemus: Amsterdam, 1962), score & parts.
*JZA-3. Respiration Suite. 2fl 2ob 2cl 2hn 2bn.
Pm (Donemus: Amsterdam, 1962) score & parts.
JZA-4. Antifone e fusione. fl ob cl 2hn bn 2tp 2tb timp.
Pm (Donemus: Amsterdam, 1966), score & parts.
JZA-5. Octuor Divertissement. fl 2ob 2cl 2bn b-cl/db.
Pm (Donemus: Amsterdam, 1948), score & parts.
JZA-6. Sinfonia dell'Arte. 2fl 2ob 2cl.
Pm (Mollenaar [via Donemus]: Amsterdam, 1972), score & parts.

ANDRIESSEN, Louis *6 June 1939, Utrecht*
LYA-1. Spektakel (Uproar), 1970. 3fl 3ob 2cl 4hn 3bn 6perc, electronic instruments.
Pm (Donemus: Amsterdam, 1971).

*ANGERER, Paul *16 May, 1927, Vienna*
PXA-1. Musica articolata. 2fl(pic) 2cl(ca) 2cl b-cl 2hn 2bn(cbn) tp tb.
Pm (Doblinger: Wien, 1970), score (pn DE 06612) & parts (pn DE 06605).
PXA-2. Concerto; 1946. ob ca 2bn tp hpcd vla.
Pm (Universal Edition: Wien, c.1946).

ANSIAUX, Hubert (Joseph) *16 Dec 1781, Huy, Belgium - 4 Dec 1826, Huy, Belgium*
HJA-1. Boléro, 1825. 2ob 2cl 2hn 2bn. MS parts: B-Lc, Ms.291-2.L.V1.

ANTONIOU, Theodore *10 Feb 1935, Athens*
TYA-1. Threnos. 2fl ob 2cl b-cl 2hn 2bn cbn 2tp tb tu db perc piano.
Pm (G. Schirmer: New York, London, 1972), score & parts.
TYA-2. Concertino, Op. 21, 1962/63. Solo piano, fl ob 2cl 2hn 2bn tp perc.
Pm (Bärenreiter: Kassel, pn BA 4377, 1964, reissued 1973), score & parts.
TYA-3. Dexiotechniká Idiómela. fl ob 2cl 2hn 2bn tp.
Pm (Margun Music: Newton Center, MA, 1989), hire score & parts (MP 1064).

ANZAGHI, Davide *29 Nov 1936, Milan*
DQA-1. Alena.   2fl 2ob 2cl 2hn 2bn.
Pm (Suvini Zerboni: Milano, pn S.8238Z., 1978), facsimile AutoMS score ("New Notation").

*APEL, ( ) *?David Aaron Apell (Kassel 1754 - post 1806)*
XZA-1m. Kronprinz-Marsch, Op. 27.   Instrumentation unknown.
MS: D-Bds, Hausbibliothek, (?lost).

APERGHIS, GEORGES *1945, Greece*
GEA-1. Puzzles.   2fl 2cl hn bn 2tp tb tu perc.
Pm (Amphion: Paris, c.1971), score.

APIVOR, (Ap Ivor), Denis *14 April 1916, Collinstown, Ireland*
DYA-1v. She stoops to conquer, Op. 12 (opera buffa, 4 acts, libretto by the composer, based on Goldsmith).
7 soloists, chorus, 2fl 2ob 2cl 2hn 2bn 4tp 3tb tu piano harp 2perc.   MS score: GB-CDmic.
DYA-2v. Yerma, Op. 28 (opera, 3 acts, libretto by Montague States, based on Lorca).
7 soloists, chorus, 2fl 2ob 2cl 2hn 2bn 4tp 3tb tu piano harp 3perc.   MS score: GB-CDmic.

*ARENSKY, Anton *12 July 1861, Novgorod - 25 Feb 1906, Terijoki, Finland*
ATA-1. 6 Children's Pictures.   fl ob 3cl 2hn 2bn 2tp tb.
Pm (Polskie Wydawnictwo Muzyczne: Kraków).

ARGENSINGER, Charles
CZA-1. Divertissement sur l'homme arme.   fl ob cl 2hn bn 2tp tb tu.   MS score (1987): NY-amc.

*ARICI, Marco *1778, Foresto - 1827, Chiari*
MXA-1. Cum Sancto, a 4 voci, con organo e fiati; in D.   SATB, fl 2cl 2hn tp tb organ.
MS parts: I-BGi(cm), Faldone 24, n. 1035.

ARMER, Elinor Florence *6 Oct 1939, Oakland, California*
EFA-1. Three sonnets for woodwinds.   fl ob ca 2cl bn.
MS score: The Composer, *via* US-NYamc.

*ARNE, Thomas Augustine *12 March 1710, London - 5 March 1778, London*
TAA-1e. Thomas and Sally: "The Ecnoing Horn calls the sportmen abroad".   T solo, TB chorus, 2cl 2hn.
Pc (Printed for the Author by J. Phillips: London, 1761), RISM [A 1024], score: GB-Bu; GB-Ckc; GB-Gm;
GB-Lam; GB-Lcm; GB-Ob; US-BE; US-Lu; US-MSu; US-Wc,
Pc (Printed for I. Walsh: London, c.1765), RISM [A 1025], score: D-Dl; F-Pn; GB-Bu; GB-Cfm; GB-Lbl,
(3 copies, including:) Hirsch M.1363; GB-Lcm; GB-LEbc; GB-Mp; US-Bp; US-CA; US-I; US-NH; US-NYp;
US-PHu; US-STu; US-Wc; US-Ws.
Pm (Eulengburg: London, pn EE 649, 1977), miniature score (No. 926).

*ARNELL, Richard Anthony Sayer *15 Sep, 1917, London*
*RAA-1. Serenade, Op. 57.   2fl 2ob 2cl 2hn 2bn cbn/db.
Pm (Hinrichsen: London), score: GB-Lmic.

*ARNOLD, *Sir* Malcolm Henry *21 Oct 1921, Northampton*
*MHA-1. Trevelyan Suite, Op. 96; 1967.   3fl 2ob 2cl 2hn vc/2bn.
Pm (Faber: London, pn F 0210 (score) 1970), score & parts.
Pm (Emerson Edition: Ampleforth, pn E142, sd), score & parts.
MHA-2. Octet, Op. 137, 1990.   2fl 2ob 2cl 2hn 2bn.
Pm (Novello: London, 1990), score & parts (hire).   (MS score in GB-Lmic).

*ARRIEU, Claude *30 Nov 1903, Paris - 7 March 1990, Paris*
*CYA-1. Dixtuor, 1967.   2fl(pic) ob 2cl hn 2bn tp tb.
Pm (Billaudot: Paris, pn MR 1198B, 1967), score.
CYA-2. Prélude et Scherzo.   2fl 2ob 2cl hn 2bn tp vc.
Pm (Amphion: Paris, 1973).

ARTEMOV (Artymov), Vyacheslav *29 June 1940, Moscow*
VXA-1. Concerto for 13, 1967.   2fl ob 2cl bn 2tp tb piano 3perc.
Pm (VAAP [copyright agency for the former Soviet Union: Moscow), ?score.

ARUNDELL, Robert Monckton, *Vicount Gallway* *1726 - 1782*
RMA-1.1, 1.2. Two favorite minuets; (Lady Galway's Minuet, Miss Buckley Mathew's Minuet).   2cl 2hn bn.
Pc (Smart: London, c.1790), RISM [A 2502], score: GB-Lbl, b.55.b.(2); GB-Ljag, (modern MS copy).   ★
RMA-1md. General Monckton's March.   2ob cl 2bn.
Untraced. Grove V (under "Military Band", p. 768) quotes part of the score - copies must survive.   ★

*ASCHE, W *(1840), Kapellmeister, 1st Hanseatic Regiment, Hamburg*
WYA-1m. Deutschland Hoch! Marsch, 1870.   fl 2ob 4cl 2hn 2bn cbn 5tp 2t-hn 3tb euph 2tu perc.
MS: D-B, Mus.Ms.800.

ASCHERL, ( )
YXA-1m. Marsch nebst 4 Ecouse [sic].   terz-fl 2cl(C) 2hn bn tp(prin) "Tampour" [sic].
MS parts: CZ-Pnm, XLII.F.193.   ★

ASHEIM, Nils Henrik *1960, Oslo*
NHA-1. Octopus, 1974.   2fl ob 2cl hn bn.   MS: N-Oic, (now withdrawn by the composer).

*ASHLEY, Josiah *1780, Bath - 1830, Bath.*
JQA-1m. The Royal Dorsetshire March, as Repeatedly Perform'd before their Majesties at Weymouth. Composed
expressly for that occasion By His Majesty's Obedient Humble Servant, Josiah Ashley.   2fl 2cl 2hn 2tp bass.
Pc (Bland & Weller's: London, 1797), score and pf reduction: GB-Lbl, g.133.(2); GB-Ob, Mus.Instr.I.3 (3).   ★

*ASIOLI, Bonifacio *30 Aug 1769, Corregio - 18 May 1832, Corregio*
We have no locations for Asioli's 2 Sextets of 1817 (cl 2hn bn vla pf), published in Milan c.1820, or his 16
kleinen Quartetten (also 1817) for cl 2hn bn. Asioli's orchestral works in I-Vsmc have a bassoon part and we
believe that the bassoonist read off the organ bass for the works listed below. I-Vsmc also has many fragmentary
sets of parts, of which some may have been for winds alone.
FXA-1. Dixit; in F. 2cl/2vl/fl+vl(II) 2hn organ.   MS parts: I-Vsmc.   ★
BXA-1v. Gloria; in F.   Solo TTB, fl 2cl 2hn tp(prin) tb timp organ.
MS score & parts: I-Vsmc. (with a long instrumental introduction).   ★
BXA-2v. Kyrie; in C minor.   TTB(solo+rip(2)), fl 2cl 2hn tp tb organ.   MS score & parts: I-Vsmc.   ★
BXA-3v. Laudate pueri; in G.   fl 2cl 2hn bn.
MS parts: B-Br, Mus.Ms.693/4, Fonds S Gudule, (missing vocal parts).   ★
BXA-1vf. Magnificat; in Bb.   2cl(C) 2hn tp tb organ.   MS score: I-Vscm, (incomplete, 2 pages only).   ★

*ASPLMAYR (Aspelmayr, Asplmayr, Aspelmayer), Franz (Francesco) D.
baptized 4 April 1728, Linz - 29 July 1786, Vienna
BHA below refers to VI Serenade di F Aspelmayer a Fl 2C Viola e Fag (actually 2fl 2hn vladam bn) Op.1.
Pc (Guera: Lyon, pn 12, sd), RISM [A 2625], pts: DK-Kk. The MS publication advertized in the Breitkopf
catalog, Supplement XII, 1778 as "FLUTE - CONCERTI ingagliati" appears to be a later version of: "Sei
serenade per flauto traverso o vero violino, due corni di caccia, violoncello e basso o vero fagotti...opera Ia."
*FDA-1. Partitta à 2 chori; in D, 5 mvts.   4ob 4hn 2bn.   AutoMS parts (c.1770): CZ-Pnm, XXII.A.251.   ★
FDA-2(-4). 3 Partittas; (Eb, F, Bb - all 4 mvts).   2ob 2cl 2hn 2bn.   MS parts: A-Ee, Mus.1176 - 1178.   ★
*FDA-5. Concertino A 7 Stromenti; in C, 5 mvts.   2ob/fl 2talia 2hn bn.
MS parts: A-Wgm, VIII 8544 (Q 16364).   ★
FDA-6. Partitta in F; 5 mvts, 1768.   2ob/cl 2hn 2bn.
MS parts: CZ-Pnm, (2 copies), XXII.A.194, XLII.A.227 (in G, for 2ob 2hn (2)bn).   ★
FDA-7. Partitta in F di Camera; 4 mvts.   2ob/cl 2hn (2)bn.   MS parts (c.1780): CZ-Pnm, XXII.A.204.   ★
FDA-8. Partitta di Campagne [sic] in F; 5 mvts.   2ob/cl 2hn 2bn.   (?Auto)MS pts (1767): CZ-Pnm, XXII.A.213.   ★
FDA-9. Partitta di Campagnia [sic] in F; 4 mvts, (c.1770); BHA-6.   2ob/cl 2hn 2bn.
(?Auto)MS parts: CZ-Pnm, XXII.A.214.
MS parts: CZ-Pnm, XLII.A.216, (in G, for 2fl 2hn bn); D-DO, Mus.Ms.1551, Nos. 99-102 (for 2cl 2hn bn).   ★
FDA-10. Partitta di Campagnia [sic] in G; 4 mvts.   2ob 2hn 2bn.   AutoMS pts (c.1770): CZ-Pnm, XXII.A.225.   ★
*FDA-11. Partitta di Campagnia [sic] in A; 4 mvts.   2ob 2hn 2bn.   AutoMS pts (c.1770): CZ-Pnm, XXII.A.226.   ★
FDA-12. Parthia in G; 5 mvts.   2ob 2hn 2bn.   AutoMS parts (c.1770): CZ-Pnm, XXII.A.227.   ★
FDA-13. Parttitta [sic] in D; 5 mvts.   2ob 2hn 2bn.   MS parts (c.1770): CZ-Pnm, XXII.A.228.   ★
*FDA-14. Partitta di Campagnia; in D, 7 mvts.   2ob 2hn 2bn.   AutoMS parts (1768): CZ-Pnm, XXII.A.235.   ★
FDA-15. Partitta in G; 5 mvts.   2ob 2hn 2bn.   AutoMS parts (1768): CZ-Pnm, XXII.A.236.   ★
FDA-16. Partitta in G di Campagna; 5 mvts, (c.1770), BHA-4.   2ob 2hn (2)bn.
MS parts: CZ-Pnm, (2 copies), XXII.A.246, XLII.C.64 (as "Partitta in G", for 2fl 2hn bn); D-DO, Mus.Ms.1551,
Nos. 103 - 107 (as "Partita in F" for 2cl 2hn bn).   ★
FDA-17. Partita in F; 3 mvts, 1769, BHA-2.   2ob 2hn bn.
(?Auto)MS parts (1769): CZ-Pnm, XXII.A.195.   MS parts: CZ-Pnm, XLII.D.92 (in G, for 2fl 2hn bn).   ★
Pm (Leuckart: München, sd), ed. Oldřich Polkert, parts (Leukertiana No 114).
FDA-18. Partita in F di Campagna; 4 mvts.   2ob/cl 2hn bn.   MS parts (c.1770): CZ-Pnm, XXII.A.196.   ★
FDA-19. Partitta in F, 4 mvts.   2ob/cl 2hn bn.   MS parts (c.1770): CZ-Pnm, XXII.A.197.   ★
FDA-20. Partitta in C di Campagna; 4 mvts, (c.1770).   2ob/cl 2hn bn.
MS parts: CZ-Pnm, (2 copies), XXII.A.198, XLII.A.328, (as "Partitta in C", for 2fl 2hn (2)bn).   ★
FDA-21. Partitta in C: di Campagnia [sic]; 5 mvts.   2ob/cl 2hn bn.   MS pts (c.1770): CZ-Pnm, XXII.A.199.   ★
FDA-22. Partitta in C: di Campagnia [sic]; 4 mvts.   2ob/cl 2hn bn.   MS pts (c.1770): CZ-Pnm, XXII.A.200.   ★
FDA-23. Partitta in F; 4 mvts, (c.1780).   2ob/cl 2hn bn.   MS parts: CZ-Pnm, (2 copies), XXII.A.201,
XLII.C.293 (in G, for 2cl 2hn bn); D-DO, Mus.Ms.1551, Nos. 128 - 131, (in Eb, for 2cl 2hn bn).   ★
FDA-24. Partitta in C di Campagna; 5 mvts.   2ob/cl 2hn bn.   MS parts (c.1770): CZ-Pnm, XXII.A.202.   ★
FDA-25. Partitta in F: di Campagna; 3 mvts, (c.1770), BHA-3.   2ob/cl 2hn bn.
MS parts: CZ-Pnm, 2 copies, XXII.A.203, XLII.C.175 (c.1778, in G for 2fl 2hn bn).   ★
FDA-26. Partitta in C di Campagna; 4 mvts.   2ob/cl 2hn bn.   MS parts (c.1780): CZ-Pnm, XXII.A.205.   ★
FDA-27. Partitta in C di Campagno [sic]; 4 mvts, (c.1780).   2ob/cl 2hn bn.
MS parts: CZ-Pnm, 2 copies, XXII.A.206, XLII.C.105, (as "Partitta in C", for 2fl 2hn bn); D-DO, Mus.Ms.1551,
Nos. 112 - 115 (as "Parthia in A" for 2cl 2hn bn).   ★
FDA-28. Partitta in C; 4 mvts.   2ob/cl 2hn bn.   MS parts (c.1780): CZ-Pnm, XXII.A.207.   ★
FDA-29. Partitta in C di Campagna; 4 mvts, (c.1780).   2ob/cl 2hn bn.
MS parts: CZ-Pnm, XXII.A.208; D-DO, Mus.Ms.1551, Nos. 116 - 119 (as "Partita in C" for 2cl 2hn bn).   ★
*FDA-30. Partitta in C di Campagna; 4 mvts.   2ob/cl 2hn bn.   MS parts (c.1780): CZ-Pnm, XXII.A.209.   ★
FDA-31. Partitta in C di Campagna; 5 mvts.   2ob/cl 2hn bn.   MS parts (c.1780): CZ-Pnm, XXII.A.210.   ★
FDA-32. Parthia à 5 Instrom. ex F; 6 mvts.   2ob/cl 2hn bn.   MS parts (c.1770): CZ-Pnm, XXII.A.211.   ★
FDA-33. Partitta; in C, 14 mvts.   2ob/cl 2hn bn.   MS parts (c.1770?): CZ-Pnm, XXII.A.212.   ★
FDA-34. Partitta da Camera in F; 4 mvts.   2ob/cl 2hn bn.   MS parts (1767): CZ-Pnm, XXII.A.215.   ★
FDA-35. Partitta in D: # [D major] di Campagno [sic]; 4 mvts.   2ob/cl 2hn bn.
MS parts (c.1770): CZ-Pnm, XXII.A.216.   ★
*FDA-36. Partita in b [Bb] Nro 24; 5 mvts, 1769.   2ob/cl/(ca or bthn) 2hn bn.
MS parts: CZ-Pnm, XXII.A.217, (with bn parts in Bb & Eb, slight variations).   ★
FDA-37. Partitta in C Nro 25, 5 mvts, 1769.   2ob/cl/(ca or bthn) 2hn bn.
MS pts: CZ-Pnm, (2 copies), XXII.A.218, (with bn pts in C & F, slight variations), XLII.C.173, (for 2fl 2hn bn).   ★
*FDA-38. Partitta in C; 5 mvts, (c.1769).   2ob 2hn bn.
MS parts: CZ-Pnm, (2 copies), XXII.A.219, XLII.B.140, (for 2fl 2hn bn).   ★
*FDA-39. Parthia ex D à 5 Instromenti; 6 mvts.   2ob 2hn bn.
MS parts (c.1770): CZ-Pnm, XXII.A.224.   ★
Pm (Leuckart: München, sd), edited Odlřich Polkert, parts (Leuckartiana No 113).
FDA-40. Parthia à 5 Instrom: ex G; 6 mvts.   2ob 2hn bn.   MS parts (c.1770): CZ-Pnm, XXII.A.229.   ★

*FDA-41. Partitta; in D, 9 mvts, (c.1780). 2ob 2hn bn.
MS parts: CZ-Pnm, 2 copies, XXII.A.230, XLII.B.191, (as "Partitta in D", for 2fl 2hn bn). ★
*FDA-42. Partitta; in G, 7 mvts. 2ob 2hn bn. MS parts (c.1770): CZ-Pnm, XXII.A.231. ★
FDA-43. Partita in G; 5 mvts. 2ob 2hn bn. MS parts (c.1770): CZ-Pnm, XXII.A.232. ★
FDA-44. Partita in D; 4 mvts. 2ob 2hn bn. AutoMS parts (c.1770): CZ-Pnm, XXII.A.233. ★
MS parts: CZ-Pnm, XLII.C.203 (as "Partitta in D", for 2fl 2hn bn).
FDA-45. Partitta in G; 4 mvts. 2ob 2hn bn. AutoMS parts (c.1770): CZ-Pnm, XXII.A.234. ★
*FDA-46/(FDA-1a). Partitta in F; 4 mvts. 2ob 2hn bn. MS parts (c.1773): CZ-Pnm, XXII.A.237. ★
*FDA-47/(FDA-2a). Partitta in A [minor]; 4 mvts. 2ob 2hn bn. MS parts (c.1773): CZ-Pnm, XXII.A.238. ★
*FDA-48. Partita in D; 4 mvts. 2ob 2hn bn. AutoMS pts (1769): CZ-Pnm, XXII.A.239. ★
FDA-49. Partitta in F di Campagnia [sic]; 5 mvts. 2ob 2hn bn. MS parts (c.1770): CZ-Pnm, XXII.A.240. ★
FDA-50. Partitta in G di Campagnia [sic]; 4 mvts. 2ob 2hn bn. MS parts (c.1770): CZ-Pnm, XXII.A.241. ★
FDA-51. Partitta in G di Campagnia [sic]; 4 mvts. 2ob 2hn bn. MS parts (c.1770): CZ-Pnm, XXII.A.242. ★
*FDA-52/(FDA-3a). Partitta in D; 3 mvts. 2ob 2hn bn. MS parts (c.1773): CZ-Pnm, XXII.A.243. ★
*FDA-53/(FDA-4a). Partitta in G; 8/9 mvts. 2ob 2hn bn. MS parts (c.1774-77): CZ-Pnm, XXII.A.244. ★
*FDA-54/(FDA-5a). Partitta in G Di Campagna; 4 mvts, (c.1770), BHA-1. 2ob 2hn bn.
MS parts: CZ-Pnm, XXII.A.245; D-DO, Mus.Ms.1551, Nos. 108 - 111 (as "Partita in F" for 2cl 2hn bn). ★
*FDA-55/(FDA-6a). Partitta: in G; 3 mvts. 2ob 2hn bn. MS parts (c.1773): CZ-Pnm, XXII.A.247. ★
FDA-56. Partitta in G: di Campagna; 4 mvts, (c.1770), BHA-5. 2ob 2hn bn.
MS parts: CZ-Pnm, XXII.A.248; D-DO, Mus.Ms.1551, Nos. 95 - 98 (as "Partita in F" for 2cl 2hn bn). ★
FDA-57. Partitta in F; 3 mvts, (c.1770). 2ob 2hn bn. MS parts: CZ-Pnm, XXII.A.249. ★
*FDA-58/(FDA-7a). Partitta In C; 4 mvts. 2ob 2hn bn. MS parts (c.1770): CZ-Pnm, XXII.A.250. ★
FDA-59. Partitta; in E♭, 7 mvts. 2ca/a-cl 2hn bn. MS parts (c.1770): CZ-Pnm, XXII.A.220. ★
FDA-60. Partitta; in E♭, 6 mvts. 2ca/a-cl 2hn bn. MS parts (c.1770): CZ-Pnm, XXII.A.221. ★
FDA-61. Partitta; in B♭, 4 mvts. 2ca/a-cl 2hn bn. (?Auto)MS parts, (c.1770): CZ-Pnm, XXII.A.222. ★
FDA-62. Partia Ex A; 5 mvts, (c.1778). 2ob 2hn basso.
MS parts: CZ-Pnm, XXII.A.223; CZ-KRa, A4758, (as "Parthia Ex G"). ★
FDA-63. Partitta in C; (c.1770), BHA-6. 2fl 2hn bn. MS parts (c.1778): CZ-Pnm, XLII.A.82. ★
FDA-64. Partitta in A, 4 mvts, (c.1770). 2fl 2hn bn.
MS parts: CZ-Pnm, XLII.C.102; D-DO, Mus.Ms.1551, Nos. 124 - 127, (for 2cl 2hn bn). ★
FDA-65. Partita; in C, 4 mvts. 2cl 2hn bn. MS parts: D-DO, Mus.Ms.1551, Nos. 120 - 123. ★
FDA-66. Parthia. Instrumentation unknown. MS parts: A-LA.
*FDA-1a/(FDA-46). Partitta in F, comprising 4 arranged works: Allegro. Episodes (?Asplmayr: Gli Incidenti);
Adagio. Adèle (Starzer: Adelheid von Ponthieu, 1773); Allegro. Episodes; Couplet (unidentified).
*FDA-2a/(FDA-47). Partitta in A, including a final Allegro from Episodes (?Asplmayr: Gli Incidenti).
*FDA-3a/(FDA-52). Partitta in D, including the mvt: Vivace. Alexandre (Asplmayr: Alexandre et Campaspe de
Larisse, 1773).
*FDA-4a/(FDA-53). Partitta in G, including 5 arranged mvts: Allegro. Diana (Starzer: Diana ed Endimione,
1770); Menuet [& Trio]. Diana; Andante Cantabile. Agamemnon (Asplmayr: Agamemnon vengé, 1771, revised
1772); Allegro. Tamborino (alternative title: "Pièce de Chasse", possibly original); Couplet (unidentified); Menuet.
Opera fiera di Venezia (Salieri: La Fiera di Venezia, 1772).
*FDA-5a/(FDA-54). Partitta in G Di Campagna, including 1 arranged mvt: Vivace. Opera Paride (Gluck: Paride
ed Elena, 1770).
*FDA-6a/(FDA-55). Partitta in G, including the first mvt: Andante. Acis (Asplmayr: Acis et Galathée, 1773).
*FDA-7a/(FDA-58). Partitta in C, including 3 arranged mvts: Allegretto. Acis (Asplmayr: Acis et Galathée,
1773); Menuet. Episodes (?Asplmayr: Gli Incidenti); Andante. Alexandre (Asplmayr: Alexandre et Campaspe
de Larisse, 1773); Finale. Allegro (perhaps original).
*FDA-1ad/ANON A-26a. Asplmayr: Alexandre et Campaspe de Larisse, 8 mvts. 2ob 2hn bn.
MS parts: CZ-Pnm, XLII.B.139.
*FDA-2ad/ANON A-23a. Asplmayr: Die kleine Weinlese (as "Die Wein Löess") No 2, 10 mvts (D, D, D, D,
A, D, D, D, A, D). 2ob 2hn bn. MS parts: CZ-Pnm, XLII.D.13.

*ASSMAYER, Ignaz *11 Feb 1790, Salzburg - 3 Aug 1862, Vienna*
IXA-1. Octet; in E♭, 6 mvts. 2ob 2cl 2hn 2bn. MS pts: untraced. Modern MS score & pts: D-KIZklöcker. ★

ASTRIAB, Jan *14 Sept 1937, Garlice, Poland*
JNA-1. Octet, 1971. 2ob 2cl 2hn 2bn.
Pm (Polish State: Warsaw, sd).

*ATTERBERG, Kurt *12 Dec 1887, Gottenburg - 15 Feb 1974, Stockholm*
KYA-1. Romance. 2fl ob 2cl 2hn bn. MS: S-Sic

*ATTWOOD, Thomas *23 Nov 1765, London - 24 March 1838, London.*
THA-1.1m, 1.2m. Royal Exchange March, Composed and Inscribed to Lieut Colonel Birch and the Rest of the
Officers of the Royal Exchange, or First Regiment of Loyal London Volunteers. *The (two) marches are (i)
Maestoso; (ii) Allegretto (Quick March, with a second section and da capo).* 2fl 2cl 2hn (2)bn 2tp serp
Pc (J. Dale: London, c.1803), score: GB-Lbl, g.133.(3); GB-Ob, Mus.Instr.I.3(7); GB-DOTams, modern score. ★

*AUBER, Daniel François Esprit *29 Jan 1782, - 12 May 1871, Paris*
DFA-1. [1 mvt: Andantino/ Allo]; AWV 182. pic fl 2ob 2cl(C) 4hn 2bn cym. MS score: F-Pn, MS 2823. ★
DFA-1m. Marche miliatire. pic(D♭) 2cl(E♭) 2cl(B♭) 2hn 2bn 2cap bugle 3tb serp+oph b-dr tambours.
MS parts (1836): F-Pn, D. 500 (16).
DFA-1t. Marche [for the translation of the ashes of Napoleon, 1841]; AWV 191.
2pic(D♭) 2ob cl(E♭) 2cl(B♭) 2cap 3tb oph tamtam. *Bns III & IV are the same as bn II.*
MS score (29 Feb 1842): F-Pn, L 17.118, No. 2 ★
DFA-1v. O Dieu puissant, Dieu créator; AWV 107. SATB chorus, 2cl(C) 2bn.
AutoMS score: F-Pn, MS. 2793. ★
DFA-1md. [3] Pas pour défiler sur les motifs de Gustave et Lestocq; AWV 195. Scoring varies.
MS parts: F-Po, Rés 1. *Probably arrangements by someone other than the composer.* ★

1.1md. pic cl(E♭) 3cl(B♭) 2hn 2bn 2tp 2crt bugle 3tb serp/oph b-dr t-dr.
1.2md. pic cl(D) 3cl(A) 2hn 2hn 4tp bugle 3tb serp/oph b-dr t-dr.
1.3md. pic cl(E♭) 3cl(B♭) 2hn 2bn 2tp 2crt bugle 3tb serp/oph b-dr t-dr.

*AUBÉRY du BOULLEY, Prudent Louis *9 Dec 1796, Verneuil - 28 Jan 1870, Verneuil*
PLA-1v. Cantate pour les réunions de S⁞ Cécile, Op. 96; text by Mr. Darde de Longuy.
SSB, pic(E♭) fl(F) cl(E♭) 2cl(B♭) 2hn 2bn tp cap bugle 3tb a-oph(E♭) 2b-oph(B♭) b-dr.
Pc (chez Richault: Paris, 1836), vocal score & parts: F-Pn, Acm 1009. ★

*AUBIGNY, L. d' *(1830)*
LDA-1. Prière. Solo ob principal, 2cl 2hn 2bn 2vla.
Pc (Imp. Michele-Garré: Paris, pn L.D.37, 1868), score: F-Pn, K. 692, (K. 693 is a piano reduction by Maurice Decourcelle, issued by the same publisher, pn F.T. 29). ★

AUBIN, Tony Louis Alexandre *1907 - 1981*
TLA-1. Cressida Fanfare. 4hn 2bn 3tp 3tb tu timp perc.
Pm (Leduc: Paris, pn 22986, c.1962), score.

AVNI, Tzni (Jacob) *2 Sept 1927, Saarbrücken (moving to what was Palestine in 1935)*
TJA-1. Mashav: Concertino. Solo xylophone, 2fl, 2ob 2cl hn 2bn tp 2perc.
Pm (Peters: New York, 1988).

*AVONI, Petronio, *Bolognese* *(1790)*
PYA-1. Armonia [3] Variazioni prese da un mottivo [sic] di Paisiello; in B♭. 2fl 2ob 2cl 2hn 2bn.
MS parts: I-Bc, LL.59, Nos. 2, 4, 6, 8, 10, 11, 13, 15, 18, 20. ★
PYA-1a. Armonia composta d'alcuni motivi i più conosciuiti dell' Insigne Cimarosa.
2fl 2ob 2cl 2hn 2bn 2tp b-tb. MS parts (1826): I-Bc, LL.58. ★
PYA-2a. Paer: Griselda; Armonia sopra il duetto Vederlo Sol Bramo del Mͬᵒ Paer nella Griselda.
2fl 2ob 2cl 2hn 2bn 2tp(tacet in section 1) b-tb. MS parts: I-Bc, LL.59, Nos. 1, 3, 5, 7, 9, 12, 14, 16, 17. 19, 21, 22, 23, (with many later MS alterations). ★

*AVSHALOMOV, Jacob *28 March 1919, Tsingtao, China; (US citizen from 1944)*
*JXA-1v. Inscriptions at the City of Brass, 1956. Narrator, chorus, pic 3fl 2ob ca cl cl(E♭) 4hn bn cbn 3tp 3tb tu timp 3perc pf 2gtr 2banjos 2db.
Pm (American Composers' Alliance: New York, 1956).
JXA-2v. Salmo 100. Chorus, winds *(rescored for organ & percussion, 1957).*
Pm (American Composers' Alliance: New York, 1956), possibly score & parts for hire.

*BACH, Carl (Karl) Philip Emanuel *8 March 1714, Weimar - 15 Dec 1788, Hamburg*
*CPB-1(-6). 6 kleine Sonate; (Wq184, H 629-634; D, F, G, E♭, A, C; each 1 mvt). 2fl 2cl 2hn bn.
MS parts: A-Wn, Mus.Hs.5525; B-Bc, (2 copies), Wotquenne 6367, (as "VI Sonate", copy by J.J.H. Westphal for the Schwerin court). ★
Pc (Giovanni Lorenz: Milano, sd), parts, (incorrectly attributed to C.F. Bach): I-Mc, Da Camera A.59.29.16.
Pm (Ricordi: Milano, pn E.R.1946, 1939), ed. Giovanni Lorenz, score & parts.
Pm (Simrock: Berlin, 1935).
Pm (Litolff: Frankfurt am Main, 1937), ed. Leupold, (Nos. 2, 3 & 5 only).
Pm (E.B. Marks: New York, 1937).
Pm (International Music Corporation: New York, 1944), ed. Piccioli, score & parts.
Pm (Musica rara: London, pn M.R. 1118, 1958), ed. Kurt Janetzky, miniature score & parts.
*CPB-7, 8. 2 kleine Stücke, (Wq186, H.620; C, F). 2cl 2hn bn. MS: B-Bc, (?lost). ★
*CPB-1m(-6m). 6 kleine Märsche (Wq185; H. 614-619; D, C, F, G, E♭, D). 2ob 2cl 2hn bn (perc ad lib).
MS parts: B-Bc, Wotquenne 6369; US-PHf. ★
Pm (E.B. Marks: New York, 1948), ed. Simon, score & parts.
Pm (together with CPB-7m, 8m): (Arthur Parrhysius: Berlin-Charlottenberg, 1952), score & parts.
*CPB-7m, 8m. 2 kleine Märsche (Wq187; H. 637; F, d). 2ob 2hn bn.
MS: B-Bc, Wotquenne 6370, score. ★
Pm (together with CPB-1m - 6m): (Arthur Parrhysius: Berlin-Charlottenberg, 1952), score & parts.

*BACH, Johann (John) Christian *5 Sept 1735, Leipzig - 1 Jan 1782, London.*
Scores of the music for winds are published as Vol. 37 of J. C. Bach's Collected Works (Garland Publishing: New York, 1990), ed. Richard Maunder, (Series Editor: Ernest Warburton).
*JCB-1(-6). Sei Sinfonia; E♭, B♭, E♭, B♭, E♭, B♭, all 4 mvts. 2cl 2hn 2bn/bn.
Pc (Longman and Broderip: London, 1782), RISM [B 259], parts, GB-Lbl, (2 copies): RM.16.b.17.(2), RM.17.b.1.(15); D-Bim. ★
Pc (J.J. Hummel: Berlin & Amsterdam, c.1783), RISM Supp [BB 259a], parts: D-HER. *Printed from the Longman & Broderip plates with a new titlepage, as "Six Simphonies".*
MS (post-1782): GB-Lbbc; US-PHf
Pm (VEB Friedrich Hoffmeister: Leipzig, 1957, 1958, reissued c.1996), ed. Fritz Stein, 2 Heft, scores (pn: Nos. 1 - 3: 7213, Nos. 4 - 6: 7234) and parts (pn 7213a, 7234a).
Pm (Bärenreiter-Verlag: Kassel, 1977), ed. Johannes H.E. Koch, (No. 6 only, with mvts 3 & 2 of Sinfonia No. 4 substituted for mvt 3).
*JCB-7(-10). 4 Military Pieces [4 Quintets]; E♭, 3 mvts; E♭, 3 mvts; B♭, 3 mvts; E♭, 2 mvts). 2cl 2hn bn.
Pc (B. Cooke: Dublin, c.1794), RISM [B 412], parts: EIRE-Da. ★
Pm (Boosey & Hawkes: London, etc., 1957), ed. Stanley Sadie, miniature score: Hawkes Pocket Scores, Nos. 269, 270 (pn B.&.H. 18151, - 18154), score and parts (pn B.18151 - 18154).
*JCB-1m, 2m. 2 Marches [E♭] No. 1 for the 1st, No. 2 for the 2nd Bataillon, Garde-Regiment Hannover.
2ob 2cl 2hn 2bn.
MS parts: D-Bds, KH MM 386. ★
Pm (Breitkopf & Härtel: Leipzig, sd), "Armee- und Präsentirmärsche" Nos. 75, 76, score & parts.
Pm (Bärenreiter: Kassel, pn 4135, 1970), score & parts: (In: Pätzig (qv), Vol. 2 Nos. 14, 15 pp. 19-22, 23-25.

*JCB-3m, 4m. Due Marce di Cavalleria e d'Infanteria della Maestra Regina della Gran Bretagna d'un Regimento di Dragoni; No.1: Marsch zu Fuss; No. 2: Marsch zu Pferd.   2ob 2cl 2hn bn.
MS parts: D-Bds, KH MM 381.   ★
Pm (with JCB-5m, 6m): (C.F. Peters: London; Henmar Press Inc.: NY *(via* Peters), pn 66672a, 1983), ed. Douglas Townsend, score & parts.
*JCB-5m(-7m). [3] Marche Ex Es di Bach a London, c.1780. (No. 1) Marche du Régiment de Prince Ernst, (No. 2) Marche du [Infanterie] Régiment de Braun[schweig], (No. 3) Marche de [Husaren] Régiment de Wür[tte]mb[erg].   2ob/fl 2hn basso.
MS parts: D-SWl, Mus. 831.   ★
Pm (Sikorski: Hamburg, pn 346, 1956), ed. J. Wojciechowski, score & parts.
JCB-1a (JCB-2/iv). Boccherini: Ballet Espagnol, (G.526/i).   2cl 2hn 2bn.
JCB-2a (JCB-3/ii). Gluck: Armide, Act II ballet.   2cl 2hn (2)bn.
*JCB-1d. Sujto in Dis [E♭], No. 1 a [9 crossed out] 10 p.; 3 mvts.   2ob/fl 2cl 2hn 2bn.
MS parts: E-Mn, M Ca/4429-8. *Almost certainly by Mysliveček. (qv).*
JCB-2d. Parthia; in D, 5 mvts.   2fl 2bthn 2hn bn.   MS parts: D-WRtl, HMA 3508.   ★
*JCB-1md, 2md. Due Marce di Cavalleria e d'Infanteria le Prince Wallis de la Gran Bretagna d'un Regimento di Dragoni.   2cl 2hn 2bn. *In fact, by C.F. Abel, CFA-1m, 2m.*
MS parts: D-Bds, KH MM 382.
Pm (with JCB-3m, 4m): (Peters: London, etc., pn P. 66672, 1983), score & parts.

*BACH, Johann Christoph Friedrich *21 June 1732, Leipzig - 26 Jan 1795, Bückeburg*
JFB-1. Septet in E♭, (S.V/15), 1794.   Oboe concertante, 2cl 2hn 2bn.
MS: D-Bim (?lost, formerly 2 citations): MS 1754 [in *MGG]* and XIII 18.   ★
Pm (Breitkopf & Härtel: Leipzig, 1982), hire score & parts, ed. Günther Raphael (incorrectly attributed to J.C. Bach); hire catalogue: Musikalien Gesamtkatalog, 1982.

*BACH, Johann Sebastian *21 March 1685, Eisenach - 28 July 1750, Leipzig*
*JSB-1m. Marche pour la Première Garde du Roy; (BWV deest).   3ob 2cl bn timp.
MS: [untraced, recorded by the London Baroque Ensemble].

*BACH, Otto *9 Feb 1833, Vienna - 3 July 1893, Unterwaltersdorf*
OXB-1tm. Trauer Marsch in F moll (und Trio in Des [D♭]) für grosses militär - Orchester.
pic(D♭) 2cl(A♭) 2cl(E♭) 4cl(B♭) 4hn 2bn cbn+tu 3tp 2cap 2flug b-flug 2tb b-tb+bomb euph b-dr+cym s-dr(damped).
AutoMS score (11 March 1861): A-Wn, Mus.Hs.9293.   ★
OXB-1v. Nachwachter Lied (nach Beranger, Ged. v. Chamisso).   TTBB, 2fl 2ob 2cl 4hn 2bn.
MS parts: A-Wn, Mus.Hs.9371.   ★

*BACH, Wilhelm Friedrich Ernst *baptised 24 May 1759, Bückeburg - 25 Dec 1845, Berlin*
*WFB-1. Parthia in E♭, 6 mvts.   2ob/fl 2cl 2hn 2bn.
AutoMS parts: GB-Lbl, Add 32,040.   ★
Pm (WINDS: Northridge, CA, W-81, c.1980), photocopy of AutoMS pts (incorrectly attributed to W.F. Bach).
Pm (Compusic: Amsterdam, pn 230, 1988), score & parts.
*WFB-2. Parthia; in B♭, 4 mvts.   2ob 2cl 2hn 2bn.
MS score: GB-Lbl, Add 32,316, (in the hand of Carl Zöller, 1840 - 1889).   ★
*WFB-3. 5 Konzertstücke.   2cl 2hn 2bn.
AutoMS score: D-Bds.   ★
Pm (Peters Edition: London, etc., 1983), score & parts, ed. Douglas Townsend (as "Five Parade Pieces").
*WFB-1m, 2m. 2 Märsche.   2ob 2cl 2bn tp.   AutoMS score: D-Bds.   ★

*BACHMANN, (?G; ?Anton) *(One of the Berlin-based family of musicians, probably the father Anton, 1716, Berlin - 8 March 1800, Berlin)*
GAB-1. Allegro molto & Andante [& Balletto].   2ob 2cl 2bn tp.
(?Auto)MS parts: D-Bds, Hausbibl.M.M.333; GB-Ljag (modern score).   ★
Pm (Steinquest), pp. 274 - 281, score.
GAB-1m. Marsch, in E♭.   2ob 2cl 2hn (2)bn.
MS score & piano reduction: D-Bds, Hausbibl.M.M.84 (missing horn parts).   ★
Pm (Steinquest), pp. 118 - 121, score.
GAB-2m. Marsch, in B♭.   2ob 2cl 2bn tp.
MS: D-Bds, Hausbibl.M.M.83.   ★
Pm (Steinquest), pp. 112 - 117, score.
Pm (In: Pätzig (qv), Vol. 1, No. 4, as "Marsch No. 2"), score & parts.
GAB-3m. Marsch, in F.   ob 2cl 2bn tp.
MS: D-Bds, Hausbibl.M.M.85.   ★
Pm (Steiquest), pp. 122 - 124, score.
GAB-4m. Marsch, in B♭.   2cl 2bn tp.
MS: D-Bds, Hausbibl.M.M.82.   ★
Pm (Steiquest), pp. 109 - 111, score.
Pm (In: Pätzig (qv), Heft 3, No. 19, as "Marsch No. 1"), score & parts.
GAB-5m. Marsch, in E♭.   2cl 2bn tp.   MS: D-Bds, Hausbibl.M.M.86.   ★
GAB-6m. Marsch.   Instrumentation unknown.
MS: D-MERz, 49.F/10.
GAB-7m, 1mv. Janitscharenmarsch & Marsch (with text).   Instrumentation unknown.
MS: D-Bds, Hausbibl, No. 95, (?lost).

BADINGS, Henk Hermann *1907 - 1987, Netherlands*
HHB-1. Azioni musicali; 1980.   2fl 2ob 2cl 2hn 2bn vc db.
Pm (Donemus: Amsterdam, c.1985), score.

BADINSKY, Nicolai *19 Dec 1937, Sofia*
NXB-1. Die Ruinen unter Sofia. 2ob 2cl 2hn 2bn.
Pm (Deutscher Verlag für Musik: Leipzig, pn DV 8523a/b, 1972), score & parts.

BÄCK, Sven-Erik *16 Sept 1919, Stockholm - 10 Jan 1994, Stockhom*
SEB-1. Architektur-60. 2fl(pic) 2cl 2hn 2bn 2tp 2tb db timp perc piano.
Pm (Ab Nordiska Musikforlaget: Stockholm, 1960), hire score & parts.
SEB-2. Architektur-65. 2fl(pic) 2cl 2hn 2bn 2tp 2tb db timp perc piano.
Pm (Ab Nordiska Musikforlaget: Stockholm, 1965), hire score & parts.

BAEKERS, Stephen *1948, Netherlands*
SYB-1. Serenata, 1976. 2fl 2ob 2cl 4hn 2bn 2tb.
Pm (Donemus: Amsterdam, pn DV 8521a/b, 1976), score & parts.

*BÄRR, Anton
AWB-1. [7] Variatione, "Seglich durch dich". 2cl 2hn 2bn. MS parts: CZ-KRa, A3838/IV.B.2, No. 1. ★
AWB-2. [6] Variatione Nro 2, "Beglückt durch dich". 2cl 2hn 2bn. MS pts: CZ-KRa, A3838/IV.B.2, No. 2. ★

BAGGIANI, Guido *1932, Italy*
GDB-1. Double. fl 2ob 2cl 2hn bn 2db.
Pm (Salabert: Paris, c.1979).
GDB-2. Profili 2. fl fl(a-fl) ob ob(ca) 2cl bthn 2bn.
Pm (Edipan: Edizione Musicale: Roma, sd).

BAILEY, Judith Margaret *18 July 1941, Camborne, Cornwall, UK*
JMB-1. Festive Concert Piece; 1983/1984. 2fl 2ob 2cl 4hn 2bn 2tp 2tb tu timp perc. MS score: GB-Lmic.
JMB-2. Havas, A period of Summer, Op. 44; 1992, 3 mvts (Lanyon Quoit, The Merry Maidens, Gwavas Lake).
2fl 2ob 2cl 4hn 2bn 2tp 3tb (*or* 2tb, timp perc, strings). MS score: GB-Lmic.
JMB-3. Concerto for Ten Wind Instruments, Op. 20; 1979. 2fl 2ob 2cl 2hn 2bn. MS score: GB-Lmic.
JMB-4. Wind Octet, Op. 26; 1983. 2ob 2b-cl 2hn 2bn. MS score: GB-Lmic.

*BAILLIE, R., Miss, (of Mellerstane) *(1760)*
RYB-1m. A favorite march & quick step…for the Edinburgh Volunteers…performed…1794. 2cl 2hn bn tp.
Pc (Neil Stewart & Co.: Edinburgh, 1794), RISM [B 708], score: GB-En, Glen 347-19; GB-Gu; US-NYp. ★
Pm (Swanzy), pp. 44 - 46, score.

*BAINES, Anthony Cuthbert *6 Oct 1912, London - 2 Feb 1997, London*
ACB-1. 9 Easy Pieces. 2fl 2ob 4cl 2hn bn.
Pm (Oxford University Press: Oxford, 1961), score & parts.

*BAKER, Lance *24 May 1947, Birmingham, UK*
Tickeridge Press music can be obtained through Emerson Music, Ampleforth, Yorks, UK.
LQB-1. Double Wind Quintet: Blow the Wind Southerly. pic fl ob ca cl(b-cl) cl(a-sax) hn hn(tam-tam) bn cbn.
Pm (Tickeridge Press: Uckfield, E Sussex, 1992), score & parts.
LQB-1a. Berlioz: Nuits d'Été, Op. 7. fl fl(pic) ob(ca) ca cl cl(b-cl) 2hn 2bn. MS score & pts: GB-WOKbaker.
LQB-2a. Ravel: Pavane pour un infante défunte. 2fl ob ob(ca) 2cl 2hn 2bn.
Pm (Tickeridge Press: Uckfield, E Sussex, 1988), score & parts.
LQB-1va. Mozart: Così fan tutte, "E Amore un ladroncello". Soprano or clarinet solo, 2ob 2cl 2hn 2bn.
Pm (Tickeridge Press: Uckfield, E Sussex, 1991), score & parts.

BAKSA Robert Frank *7 Feb 1938, New York*
RZB-1. Octet, Eb. 2fl 2ob 2cl 2bn.
Pm (Alexander Broude: New York).

*BALADA, Leonardo *2 Sept 1933, Barcelona*
LAB-1. Concerto for piano, winds and percussion.
Solo piano, 2fl 3ob 3cl 2b-cl a-sax(t-sax, bar-sax) 4hn 3bn 2tp 3crt 2tb bar tu timp 3perc.
Pm (G. Schirmer: New York, 1974), score & (hire) parts.
LAB-2. Sonata for 10 Winds. fl(pic) ob cl(Eb) 2hn bn 2tp tb b-tb.
Pm (G. Schirmer: New York, pn 50336460, 1980), score & (hire) parts.

BALAKIREV, Mily Aleksyeevich *2 Jan 1837, Nizhny-Novgorod - 29 May 1910, St Petersburg*
MIB-1e. King Lear: English Song (based on "The Men of Davey's Delight"). fl ca 2cl 2bn harp.
Pm (Издтельство Музыка; State Publishers Music: Moscow, 1969), score.

BALDAN, Angelo *(1747 or 1753), Venice - 23 April 1803, Venice*
AXB-1v. Credo; 1789. TTB, 2ob 2hn bn 2tp organ. MS: I-Vmc, N. 42.
AXB-2v, 3v. [2] Credo. TTB, ob 2hn bn organ. MS: I-Vcdr, Busta III A.53, 54.

*BALL, S. *(1780)*
SXB-1m. The Ipswich Volunteers, Slow & Quick Marche [sic], with a Funeral March.
Nos 1, 2: 2fl 2cl 2hn 2bn tp; No 3: 2fl 3cl 2hn 2bn 2tp serp.
Pc (Broderip & Wilkinson: London, c.1808), score: GB-Lbl, H.1895.(18). ★

BALLOU, Esther Williamson *17 July 1915, Elmira, NY - 12 March 1973, Chichester, UK*
EWB-1. Suite, 1957. 2fl 2ob 2cl 2hn 2bn.
Pm (American Composers' Alliance: NY, c.1957).

BANK, Jacques *18 April 1943, Borne, Netherlands*
JIB-1. Lost. 2fl 2ob 3cl 4hn 2bn tb.
Pm (Donemus: Amsterdam, 1976), score.
JAB-2. Alexander's Concerto. Solo piano, pic 2fl 2ob 2cl 3hn 2bn 2tp tb 3perc.
Pm (Donemus: Amsterdam, 1978), score, solo part.

*BANNER, John *(1780)*
JKB-1m. The Loyal London Volunteers March (8th Regiment).   pic 2cl 2hn (2)bn tp serp long-drum (= b- dr?).
Pc (Printed for & Sold by the Author: London, c.1805), score: GB-Lbl, g.271.h.(1).   ★

BARBAUD, Pierre *1911, France*
PIB-1. Variations Carlsberg.   fl 2ob 3cl hn bn tu perc.
Pm (Billaudot: Paris, sd), score.

BARCLAY-WILSON, R.
RWB-1. Kindergarten.   2ob 2cl 2hn 2bn.
Pm (Editions Henry Lengnick: South Croydon, Surrey, sd), score & parts.

BARDWELL, William *1913, UK*
WAB-1. Antiphony; (1966 - 1968).   2fl 2ob 2cl 2hn 2bn.   MS score & parts: GB-Lbbc.

BARRELL, Joyce *26 Nov 1917, Salisbury, UK*
JXB-1. 3 Ukranian impressions, Op 37.   2fl ob 2cl bn.
Pm (Anglian New Music, London, pn ANMS 129, 1983), score.

*BARRÈRE, Georges *31 Oct 1876, Bordeaux - 14 June 1944, Kingston, NY*
*GOB-1a. Elgar: Salut d'amour, Op. 12.   fl, wind ensemble.   MS: (location unknown), recorded.

BARRY, Gerald *28 April 1952, County Clare, Ireland*
GXB-1. Sur les pointes; (1985 revision of 1981 work) for piano.   2cl 2sax 2hn 2bn 2tp 2tb piano.
Pm (Oxford University Press: London, etc., 1985), score & parts (hire).
GXB-2. Sweet Punishment; 1987.   2cl b-cl bn cbn.
Pm (Oxford University Press: London, etc., 1987), score & parts.

BÁRTA (Bartta), Josef (Jiří) *1744 - 1787, Bohemia*
FJB-1. Nro 1 Parthia Ex C; 3 mvts.   2ob 2hn 2bn.   MS parts: CZ-Pnm, XXII.B.2, (missing bn II).   ★

BARTH, ( )
QZB-1. Parthia in Dis [E♭]; 4 mvts.   2cl 2hn bn.
MS parts (by Augustin Erasmus Hübner, Langenbruck): CZ-Pu(dm), 59 R 3333.   ★

BARTH, Christian Friderik *24 Feb 1787, Copenhagen - 17 July 1861, Middelfart, Fünen*
CSB-1. Grand Sinfonie pour instruments à vent, Op. 10; 3 mvts.   2fl 2ob 2cl 4hn 2bn 2tp tb serp timp.
Pc (André: Offenbach am Main, sd), parts: D-DS, (?lost in World War II).   ★

BARTH, Friedrich Augustus Wilhelm *9 May 1813, Leipzig - 10 Dec 1884, Biel*
FAB-1v. Cantata "Sey gesegnet stille Morgensone" [sic] Op. 54, (1839).
B solo, 3-part mixed chorus, winds.   MS: *(MGG says "in private hands").*

*BARTH, Wilhelm (Guillaume) Leberecht *10 May 1774 - 22 Aug 1829, Leipzig*
WLB-1a. Marschner: Der Templar und die Jüdin, Beliebte Stücke, 10 mvts.
2fl(terz-fl, pic) 2ob 4cl 2hn 2bn 2tp 3tb; (ad lib: serp b-dr+cym s-dr).
Pc (F. Hofmeister: Leipzig, pn 1151, c.1829), pts: US-BETm, Philharmonic Society of Bethlehem PSB Add 2.
WLB-2a. Paer: Léonora. Pièces d'harmonie, Premier Recueil, introduzione & 7 mvts.   fl 2cl 2hn 2bn.
Pc: (Chez Fred. Hoffmeister: Leipzig, pn 56, c.1810), parts: CZ-Pnm, XXI.C.178.   *See WLB-4a for Recueil 2.*
WLB-3.1a. Spohr: Jessonda, overture.   fl(pic E♭) terz-fl(pic E♭) 2ob cl(E♭) 3cl(B♭) 4hn 2bn tp a-tb t-tb b-tb
serp timp.   *Sold together with WLB-3.2a or separately.*
Pc (C.F. Peters: Leipzig, pn 1842, c.1825), parts: D-DT, Mus-n 940, (with duplicate parts: fl terz-fl 2ob).
WLB-3.2a. Spohr: Jessonda, 8 mvts.   fl(pic E♭) terz-fl(pic E♭) 2ob cl(E♭) 3cl(B♭) 2hn 2bn (2)tp serp.
Pc (C.F. Peters: Leipzig, pn 1842, c.1825), parts: D-DT, Mus-n 940.
WLB-4a. J.Weigl: Die Schweizerfamilie. Pièces d'Harmonie, Second Recueil; overture & 3 mvts.   fl 2cl 2hn 2bn.
Pc: (Hofmeister: Leipzig, pn 186, c.1805), parts: D-Rtt, Weigl Druck 3; H-Bn, Z 43,900.

*BARTHÉLÉMON, François-Hippolyte *27 July 1741, Bordeaux - 20 July 1808, London*
FHB-1m. The Prince of Wirtemberg's [sic] March.   2ob/vl 2hn 2bn vla.
Pc (Longman & Broderip: London, 1797), RISM [B 1113], score: GB-Lbl, g.133.(5); GB-Ob.   ★

*BARTÓK, Béla *25 March 1881, Nagyszentmiklós, Hungary (Sînnicolau Mare, Romania) - 26 Sept 1945, New York*
BXB-1e. Concerto No. 2, 1st mvt.   Piano solo, pic 2fl 2ob 2cl 4hn 2bn cbn 2tp 3tb tu timp perc.
Pm (Universal: London, etc., pn Ph 306, 1932), score.

*BARTOŠ, Jan Zdeněk *4 June 1908, Dvůr Králové-nad-Labem - 1 June 1981, Prague*
*JZB-1. I Divertimento per stromenti a fiato, Op. 14; 1957, 6 mvts.   fl 2ob 2cl(C) 2hn 2bn.
Pm (Panton: Praha/Prague, pn P.184, 1960), miniature score.

*BASSI, Luigi *(1800)*
LYB-1a. Donizetti: La Sancia di Castiglia, cavatina ("Se talor più nol rammento").   2cl hn bn tp tb.
MS parts: I-Mc, Da Camera MS.7.2.

*BASSUS, Jean Marie, *Baron* *(1770)*
JMB-1. In uso di Offertorium, Sestetto; in E♭, 1 mvt.   fl 2cl 2hn vla.   MS parts: D-Mbs, Mus.Mss.5506.
The hn II pt is marked "Corno Secondo Ripieno in E♭".   ★
JMB-2. Adagio e Rondo in uso di Offertorio; in D.   fl 2cl(D) 2hn bn.   MS parts: D-Mbs, Mus.Mss.5505.   ★
JMB-3. Sestetto Caratteristico; in D, 4 mvts.   2cl(D) 2hn vla basso.   MS parts: D-Mbs, Mus.Mss.5507.   ★
JMB-4. Sestetto; in D, 5 mvts.   fl cl(D) 2hn vl basso.   MS parts: D-Mbs, Mus.Mss.5508.   ★
JMB-5. Andante [altered to "Andantino"] e Allegretto in uso di Offertoio...Composta per la Chiesa di Sollem;
in D.   fl cl(D) hn (I, in D) vla.   MS parts: D-Mbs, Mus.Mss.5509.   ★

*BATISTE, Antoine-Edouard *28 March 1820, Paris - 9 Nov 1876, Paris*
EXB-1. Symphonie militaire; in F, 3 mvts.   fl 2ob 2cl 2hn 2bn tp tb oph.
AutoMS score (1845): F-Pn, MS. 3343.   ★

BAUDE-DELHOMMAIS, Eric *21 May 1957, Boulogne*
EDB-1a. Biber: La Battalia.   3ob 2ca 2bn b.   AutoMS score & parts: F-TOep.

BAUER, Marion Eugenie *15 Aug 1887, Walla Walla, Washington, USA - 9 Aug 1955, South Hadley*
MRB-1. Aquarelle, Op. 39, No. 2; 1948.   chamber orchestra *or* 2fl 2ob 2cl 2hn 2bn.   MS: US-CA.
MRB-2. Patterns, Op. 41, No. 2; 1968.   chamber orchestra *or* 2fl 2ob 2cl 2hn 2bn.   MS: US-CA.

BAUR, Jürg *1 Nov 1918, Düsseldorf*
JBB-1. Pour rien (ostinato senza fine); 1980.   2cl 2hn 2bn.
Pm (Breitkopf & Härtel: Wiesbaden, 1984), score (pn PB 5087) & parts (pn EB 8344).

*BAYER, ( ) *(1780)*
XXB-1. 4 Ländler, Ecoses, Allemande.   2ob 2cl 2hn 2bn cbn.   *(2ob tacet in Ländler 3; 2hn tacet in Ländler 4)*
MS parts: CZ-Pnm, XX.F.23.   ★

BAYER, Francis *1938, France*
FCB-1. Propositions 2; 1980.   fl(pic) 2ob 2cl 2hn 2bn 2tp 2tb; bns & tbs reputedly double on ocarinas.
MS score: F-Pd will assist in contacting the composer.

BAŽAN, Valentin *(1780) active c1810 - post-1859, Moravia (Chor-Rector, Mahr: Ostrava)*
VYB-1v. Píseň Pohřební která sě při pohřebu mladence neb panny spivati může.   CATB, 2cl 2hn bn.
AutoMS parts (c.1810): CZ-Bm(os), A.48.494, (missing A, 2cl 2hn).   ★

*BAŽANT, Jaromír *8 Aug 1926, Krásný Dvůr*
YJB-1. Divertimento, Op. 14, 1960.   2fl 2ob 2cl 4hn 2bn 3tp 3tb tu timp perc.
MS score & parts: CZ-PLr, O 967.

*BAZIN, François-Emmanuel Joseph *4 Sept 1816, Marseilles - 2 July 1878, Paris*
EJB-1. Mélodie; in F.   2 solo horns, fl 2ob 2cl 2bn.   AutoMS score & parts (1840): F-Pn, MS. 3214.   ★

BEALE, James *20 Jan 1924, Wellesley Hills, Mass.*
ZJB-1. 5 Still Lifes, Op. 32.   fl fl(pic) 3cl bn harp celeste vibraphone.
Pm (American Composers Alliance: New York).

BEAUMONT, Adrian *1 June 1937, Huddersfield*
AQB-1. Concerto, 1967.   2fl 2ob 2cl 2hn 2bn.   MS score: GB-Lmic.

*BECHLER, Johann Christian *7 June 1784, Oesel - 15 April 1857, Herrnhut*
JOB-1. Parthia, in Eb, 4 mvts.   2cl 2hn bn tp.
MS parts: US-BETm, Lititz Collegium Musicum 175; (?also copy in: US-WS).   ★
JOB-1m, 2m. 2 Marches; both in Eb.   2cl 2hn bn tp.
MS parts (1817): US-BETm, Lititz Collegium Musicum 203, Nos. II & VII.   ★
Pm (in: Henry H. Hall, *The Moravian Wind Ensemble*, Ph.D dissertation, Vanderbilt University, 1967), score.

BECKER, Günther *1 April 1924, Forbach*
GUB-1. "Quasi una fantasmagoria". Szenen nach Robert Schumanns "Sphinxes", 1980-81.   2cl 2hn 2bn.
Pm (Breitkopf & Härtel: Wiesbaden, pn KM 2196, c.1981), score & parts.

BECKER, John Joseph *22 Jan 1886, Henderson, KY - 21 Jan 1961, Wilmette, Ill, USA*
OJB-1. Mockery: a scherzo for dance or chamber orchestra, 1933 (first concert performance 1974).
2fl ob 3cl 3sax 2tp tb db piano perc.
Pm (American Composers Alliance: New York).

BECKERATH, Alfred Wilhelm von *4 Jan 1901, Hahenau, Alsace - 1978, ?Munich*
AFB-1. Divertimento 10.   fl fl(pic) 2ob 2cl 2hn 2bn 2tp 2tb tu perc.
Pm (?self published: sl, sd), score: D-Mmb.
AFB-2. Tricoro.   3fl 2ob 2hn bn 3tp 3tb.
Pm (Berkerath, [self-published]: sl, sd), score: D-Mmb.
AFB-3. Music.   fl/ob 2cl bn.
Pm (Matthias Hohner: Trossingen, sd), parts.

*BECKFORD, William *1 Oct 1759, Fonthill Gifford, Wiltshire - 2 May 1844, Bath*
WYB-1m. Marche; in F.   2ob 2cl 2hn (2)bn.   MS score: GB-Cfm, Mus.Ms.154; GB-Ljag, (modern MS).   *Note: the GB-Cfm shelfmark "32.F.25" is the old shelfmark for this work rather than another march.*   ★

*BÉDARD, Jean Baptiste *c.1765, Rennes - c.1815, Paris*
Bédard's "Hymne à Voltaire" has been recorded, and may exist for winds.
XYB-1. Harmonie No. 2.   Instrumentation unknown.
Pc (Frère, Fils: Paris, sd), parts: US-Wc.
XJB-1m. Nº. 1 Marches militaires. Attachés aux musiques des demies brigades de la République Française.
Instrumentation unknown.
Pc (Viguerie: Paris, (gravé Michot), post-1795), RISM Supp [BB 1604a], parts: H-KE.
XYB-1a. Pot-pouri d'airs connus, arrangé en harmonie à 6 parties . . . 1ere suite.   2cl 2hn 2bn.
Pc (Decombe: Paris, pn 152, c.1810), RISM [B 1605], parts: US-Wc.

*BEDFORD, David *4 Aug 1937, London*
*DXB-1. Susato Variations, 1992.   3fl 2ob 2cl 4hn 3bn 2tp 2tb tu 2perc.
Pm: available from the composer, GB-Lmic will assist in contacting.
DXB-1v. When I Heard the Learn'd Astronomer.   T solo, 2fl 2ob 2cl 3hn 2bn tb b-tb tu.
Pm (Universal Edition: London, etc., pn 15508, 1972), score & parts.

BEDŘICH, Jan *1932, Czechoslovakia*
AJB-1. Miniatury.   2fl 3ob 3cl perc; (also arranged for piano).
Pm (Český hudební fond: Prague, 1980), hire score & parts.

*BEECKE, Ignaz Franz von *28 Oct 1733, Wimpfen in Tal - 3 Jan 1803, Wallerstein*
*IVB-1. Partita in Dis [E♭]; (c.1780), 5 mvts.   fl ob 2cl 2hn bn.
MS parts: D-HR, HR III 4 1/2 4° 98.   Pm (KGS), fiche: 466. ★
IVB-1ad. Parthia in C; in fact, overture & 6 mvts from Beecke's 1786 opera *Nina*. 2fl(pic) 2ob 2cl 2hn 2bn cb.
MS score: D-Rtt, Beecke 12. ★
*IVB-2ad. Parthia Das Waldmaedchen; (arr of P. Wranitzky's ballet, *Das Waldmädchen*).   2ob 2cl 2hn 2bn.
MS pts: D-HR, HR III 4 1/2 2° 350. Pm (KGS), fiche: 2301, 2302. *In fact, Went's arrangement, JNW-72.1a.*

*BEETHOVEN, Ludwig van *15/16 Dec 1770, Bonn - 26 March 1827, Vienna*
The wind works are in these collected editions: GA: Ludwig van Beethoven's Werke. (Breitkopf & Härtel: Leipzig, 1862-90) wind works: Bd. VII, dramatic music: Bd. XX, marches: Bd. XXV. WH: Supplemente zur Gesamtausgabe. Herausgegeben von Willy Hess. (Breitkopf & Härtel: Wiesbaden), wind works: Bd. 7, dramatic music: Bds. 11-13. NA: Werke: Neue Ausgabe Sämtlicher Werke...im Auftrag des Beethoven-Archiv, Bonn, unterr Leitung von Joseph Schmidt-Görg. (G. Henle Verlag: Munich, Duisberg, etc., 1961). LEA: Chamber Music for Winds (Lea Pocket Scores: New York, 1959), includes LVB-1, 2 & 4 and the smaller chamber works (but not the marches, etc.).
*LVB-1. Rondino [Rondo für achtstimmige Harmonie]; WoO 25, 1793.   2ob 2cl 2hn 2bn.
Auto MS score: D-BNba. ★
Pc (Diabelli: Wien, pn 3044, 1829), parts: A-Wgm, VIII 16861; D-DT, Mus-n 1074; GB-Lbl, h.3213.h.(2.).
Pc (Artaria: Wien, 1830), parts.
Pc (Breitkopf & Härtel: Leipzig, pn B 60.15, sd), parts: A-Wgm, VIII 30438; D-DT, Mus-n 1074.
Pm (GA VIII, No. 2), repr: (Kalmus: London, etc.), min score (pn 1007, No. 2; pp. 29 - 36), parts (pn 9695).
Pm (Payne: London, etc., 1887), Payne's Miniature Scores, No. 252.
Pm (Eulenburg: London, 1952), miniature score: Edition Eulenburg, No. 252.
Pm (International Music Corp: London, 1952), miniature score (pn 1173), parts (pn 1168).
Pm (Schott: London, etc., pn CON 22, 1952), score & parts
Pm (Ricordi: Milano, etc., pn PR 623, 1954), score (Partitur tascabili Ricordi No. 623).
Pm (University of Cardiff Press: Cardiff 1954), score (pn P69001) & parts (pn P69002).
Pm (Presser: London, etc., pn 692, 1954), parts (with alternative parts: fl for ob I; b-cl for bn II).
Pm (Lea: New York), miniature score.
*LVB-2. Parthia in Es [Octett in E♭], Op. 103; 4 mvts.   2ob 2cl 2hn 2bn.
AutoMS score: D-Bds, Artaria Sammlung. MS score: D-DT, Mus-n 1059. ★
Pc (Breitkopf & Härtel: Leipzig, 1803), parts: A-Wgm, VIII 2726..
Pc (Artaria: Wien, pn 3032, 1830), parts: A-Wgm, VIII 2726; GB-Lbl, Hirsch IV.362.a; I-Mc, Noseda C.10.10.
Pm (GA VIII, No.1 reprints), (Kalmus: London, etc), score (pn A 1291), (Breitkopf & Härtel: Leipzig): score (pn PB 1332) & parts (pn KM 1554).
Pm (Payne: London, etc.), 1887), Payne's Miniature Scores No. 135.
Pm (Eulenburg: London, 1952) miniature score, ed. Wilhelm Altmann, Edition Eulenburg No.135 (Payne, reprint)
Pm (Kneusslin: Bern, 1952), score.
Pm (Rongwen: New York, 1969).
Pm (Lea: New York), miniature score.
Pm (Musica rara: London, pn MR 1201, 1969), parts.
Pm (Breitkopf & Härtel: Wiesbaden, pn KM 1554, sd), score & parts.
*LVB-3. Die Ruinen von Athen, Op. 113; No. 5: Musik hinter der Scene: Assai allegro ma non troppo (74 bars including reprise).   2ob 2cl(C) 2hn(C) 2bn.
Auto MS score: GB-Lbl, Zweig MS.9. ★
Pc (Artaria und Comp.: Wien, 1846), score: GB-Lbl, RM.11.b.4, Hirsch IV.377.
Pm (reprints of GA, Bd 20, No. 2, pp. 59 - 61): (Kalmus: London etc., 1978), score (pn A 1272), parts (pn A 1272), miniature score (pn 4. No. 38).
*LVB-4. Sextet in E♭, Op. 71; 1796.   2cl 2hn 2bn.
AutoMS (Menuetto & Rondo sketches): GB-Lbl, Add 29801, ff. 103 - 105. MS parts: D-DT, Mus-n 1070. ★
Pc (Breitkopf & Härtel: Leipzig, pn 1370, 1810; reprinted 1864), pts: A-Wgm, (2 copies), VIII 30439, VIII 6196; GB-Lbl, h.383.dd.
Pm (Rieter-Biedermann: Wintherthur, 1873).
Pm (C.F. Peters: London, etc., pn H 738, 1873).
Pm (Payne: London, etc., 1877), Payne's Miniature Scores No. 139.
Pm (Lea: New York), miniature score.
Pm (International Music Corp.: New York, 1959), ed. Lyman, min score (pn 1209) & parts (pn 946).
Pm (GA reprint, Bd. VIII, No. 3): (Kalmus: London etc., 1956), score & pts, miniature score (pn 1007, No. 3).
Pm (Breitkopf & Härtel: Wiesbaden, 1956), parts (pn KM 1551).
Pm (Hinrichsen-Peters: London, pn 738, 1963), score & parts.
*LVB-5. Quintet in E♭; WoO 62, revised 1793, 3 mvts of which only No 2 is complete.   ob 3hn bn.
Pm (completed by F.A. Zellner, ed. Willy Hess): (B Schott's Söhne: Mainz; Schott & Co.: London, 1956), score (pn 4517) & parts (pn 4529).
*LVB-1m. Marsch in D; WoO 24, 3 June 1816.   pic fl 2ob cl(F) 4cl(C) 4hn(D) dr tri cym.
AutoMS score: D-Bds, Artaria Sammlung
Pm (reprints of GA, Bd. 2, No. 6): (Breitkopf & Härtel); (Kalmus: London, etc., pn 1003, No. 3), min score.
*LVB-2m. Zapfenstreich No. 1 in F, "Yorck'scher Marsch"; WoO 18, 1809.   pic 2fl 3cl 2hn 2bn cbn 2tp perc.
AutoMS: D-Bds, 2 copies, Artaria Sammlung 144 (without trio), 145 (complete). ★
MS: A-Wgm (Haslinger-Rudolph collection, Vol.19), XVI 11788 (Q 20691).
MS parts: A-Wn, Mus.Hs.19,594; CZ-Pnm, (2 versions, without Trios), Lobkovic X.H.a.76, (for 2ob 2cl(F) 2hn 2bn cbn tp), (2 copies, for pic 2ob 2cl 2hn 2bn cbn tp tri cym b-dr s-dr:) X.H.a.77, XX.F.53, (missing bn II); F-Pn
MS: (facsimile): Trio published in May 1973 issue of *Atlantis*.
Pc (Steiner: Wien, pn 1620, 1810/11), *(A-93.2)*, parts: CS-Pnm, XLII.F.722.
Pc (Schlesinger: Berlin, pn 384, c.1818); [a separate issue of Heft 8, No. 37 of the collection of marches, A-74m, scored for 2fl(F) 2ob cl(F) 2cl(C) 2bthn 2hn 2bn cbn 2tp 3tb b-hn b-dr s-dr "tamb di Soldat" tri cym], score: GB-Lbl, (2 copies), h.400.r.(3), h.400.mm.
Pm (GA reprint, Bd. 25, No. 24/I): (Kalmus: London), score & pts (pn A 3166 No. 1), min score (pn 1028 No. 2).
Pm (Doblinger: Wien, 1979), ed. Otto Biba, score & parts (DM 698, No. 1).
Pm (Beethoven-Jahrbuch. 1953/54, pps. 251 ff.), score.

*LVB-3m. Zapfenstreich No. 3 in F; WoO 19, c.1809.   pic 2fl 2cl 2hn 2bn cbn 2tp perc.
AutoMS: A-Wdo; A-Wgm; D-Bds, Artaria Sammlung 145.
MS: A-Wgm (Haslinger-Rudolph coll., vol. 19; 3 other mss); A-Wn, Mus.Hs.19,595.
Pc (Steiner: Wien, pn 1620, 1810/11), *(A-93) No, 12,* parts: CZ-Pnm, XLII.F.722, (for pic 2fl cl(F) 2cl(C) 2hn 2bn cbn tp(princ) tp(C) b-dr s-dr).
Pm (GA reprint, Bd. 25, No. 24/II: (Kalmus: London), score & pts (pn A 3166 No. 3), min score (pn 1028 No. 3).
Pm (Doblinger: Wien, 1979), ed. Otto Biba, score & parts (DM 698, No. 2).
Pm (Beethoven-Jahrbuch. Jahrg. 1953/54, pp. 251 ff.), score.
*LVB-4m. Zapfenstreich No. 2 in C, (WoO 20, c.1809).   pic 2ob 2cl 2hn 2bn cbn 2tp perc.
AutoMS score: in private hands.
Pm (GA reprint, Bd. 25, No. 25): (Kalmus: London), score & pts (pn A 3163), min score (pn 1028 No. 4).
Pm (reprint of GA, Bd 25, No. 25): (Kalmus: London), score & pts (pn A 3163); min score (pn 1028, No. 4).
Pm (Doblinger: Wien, 1979), ed. Otto Biba, score & parts (DM 698, No. 3).
*LVB-5m. Polonaise in D; WoO 21, 1810.   pic 2ob 2cl 2hn 2bn cbn 2tp perc.
AutoMS: F-Pn, Collection Malherbe.
Pm (reprint of GA, Bd 25, No. 26): (Kalmus: London), score & pts (pn A 3165); min score (pn 1028, No. 5).
Pm (Doblinger: Wien, 1979), ed. Otto Biba, score & parts (DM 698, No. 4).
LVB-6m. Ecossaise in D; WoO 22, c. 1810.   pic 2ob 2cl 2hn 2bn cbn tp b-dr cym s-dr tri.
AutoMS: A-Wgm, G. Sig XV 17234 (Q 20445), (parts from the Sammlung Erzherzog Rudolfs);
GB-Ob, AutoMS: c.21. fol.19 and 21 (MS. M. Deneke Mendelssohn; private collection of Maria Wach).   ★
Pm (reprint of GA, Bd 25, No. 27): (Kalmus: London), score & pts (pn A 3165); min score (pn 1028, No. 6).
Pm (Breitkopf & Härtel: Wiesbaden, sd), hire score & parts.
Pm (Doblinger: Wien, 1979), ed. Otto Biba, score & parts (DM 698, No. 5).
*LVB-7m. Ecossaise in G. Lost; the piano version is WoO 23.
*LVB-8m. Marsch, "Grenadiers' March"; WoO 29, 1807.   2cl 2hn 2bn.
AutoMS: D-Bds, Nachlass Grasnick.
Pc (In **A-82.1m** Acht Märsche für Türkischen Musick [sic], 1 Heft, No. 6, as "March in C":) (Johann André: Offenbach am Main, pn 1822, 1803), pts: H-KE, K 731/VIII. *Scored for 2fl 2cl(C) 2hn 2bn serp 2tp(clar) b-dr.*
MS score & parts (copy of the André edition): I-Fc, F.P. S.553.
Pm (Schirmer: New York, etc., sd), score & parts.
Pm (Billaudot: Paris, pn GB 1710, 1977), score & parts.
Pm (reprint of GA, Bd 25, No. 29) (Kalmus: London, etc), miniature score.
*LVB-1v. Bundeslied "In allen guten Stunden erhüht von Lieb und Wein", Op. 122; (1822-4).
SA soli, 3-part chorus, 2cl 2hn 2bn.
AutoMS: D-Mbs, Mus.Ms.2760.   ★
Pc (B. Schott Söhne: Mainz, pn 2280, 1825): GB-Lbl, (score, 2 copies), H.725.i, Hirsch IV.391, (parts) H.725.l.
Pm (GA reprint, Bd XXII, No.4): (Kalmus: London, pn 1019, No.4), miniature score.
Pm (Breitkopf & Härtel: Wiesbaden, sd), hire score & parts.
Pm (Doblinger: Wien, pn DM 478, 1979), score & parts.
Pm (WINDS: Northridge, CA, pn W-170, c.1981), photocopy of Schott score, vocal score, and WIND'S MS pts.
*LVB-1ad. Beethoven: Septet, arranged for winds, incomplete *(See* The Wind Ensemble Sourcebook).
*LVB-1md. Alexander Marsch (blöde Ritter), K.-H. Anh. 11.   *See: PERSUIS.*

BEHREND, Fritz *3 Nov 1889, Berlin - 29 Dec 1972, Berlin*
FQB-1. Suite, Op. 116; 1956.   fl ob 2cl b-cl hn bn tp.   MS: D-DSim.

*BEINET (Bienet), ( )   *(1750), Musicien au Régiment des Gardes Suisses*
Marie-Anne Castignery died 6 Oct 1782; Beinet's works were advertized in Boüin's catalogs as late as 1788.
*XJB-1a. Amusemens Militaire Contenant un choix d'Ouvertures, d'Ariettes et autres Airs.   2ob 2cl 2hn 2bn.
Pc (Bouin; Castignery: Paris; Blaisot: Versailles, pre-1783), pts: S-Uu, Utl.instr.mus.tr. 145, 149 - 151, Takt 9, (missing ob I, II, cl II, hn II; with a printed slip bearing the imprint of Imbault, c.1787 - 1794, pasted over the original imprint).
    I.1a. Paisiello: Il Re Teodoro in Venezia, overture & 3 mvts.   Nos. 1, 2, 4. 5.
    1.2a. Salieri: Axur, Re d'Ormus (as "Tarare"), 2 mvts.   Nos. 3, 6.
    1.3a. Grétry: Richard Cœur de Lion, 6 mvts.   Nos. 7 - 12.
*XJB-2a Receuil de pot poury [sic] d'airs connus.   2ob 2cl(C) 2hn 2bn, ("Fagotti" but a single unison part).
Pc (Boüin, Mlle. Castignery: Paris; Blaisot: Versailles, pre-1783), RISM Supp [BB 1695, I, 2], parts: F-Pn, Vm7 6955.
Pc (Imbault: Paris, pn 537, c.1794) RISM Supp [BB 1695, I, 1], parts: S-Uu, Utl.instr.mus.tr. 145, 149 - 151, Takt 19, (missing ob I & II, cl II, hn II). *Retitled "Pot Pouri d'Airs Arrangés Pour Harmonie".*   ★
XJB-3.1a(-3.3a). [MS: 1ere - 3e] Suitte d'Airs Arrangés Pour Harmonie.   2cl 2hn 2bn.
Pc (Imbault: Paris, pn 533 - 535, c.1794), RISM Supp [BB 1695, I, 3], parts: CH-E; S-Uu, Utl.instr.mus.tr. 145, 149 -151, Takt 10 - 12, (missing cl II, hn II).
    3.1/1a. Dalayrac: L'Amant Statue, overture & 6 mvts.   Nos. 1, 4 - 8, 10.
        3.1/2a. Haydn: Symphony in D, ("L'Impériale"), Andante, (Hob. I/53ii).   No. 2.
        3.1/3a. Grétry: Panurge dans l'île des lanternes, Marche.   No. 3.
        3.1/4a. Grétry: Richard Cœur de Lion, "Ô Richard, ô mon Roi".   No. 4.
        3.1/5a. Grétry: La Rosière de Salency, "Quand le Rossignol".   No. 9.
        3.1/6a. Monsigny: Félix, trio. No. 11.
        3.1/7a. Giornavici ["Giarnóvick"]: Allemande. No. 12.
    3.2/1a. Grétry: Panurge dans l'île des lanternes, overture & 3 mvts.   Nos. 1 - 3.
        3.2/2a. Champein: La Mélomanie, 9 mvts.   Nos. 4 - 12.
    3.3/1a. Paisiello: Le Due Contesse, overture. No. 1.
        3.3/2a. Salieri: Axur, Re d'Ormus (as "Tarare"), 5 mvts.   Nos. 2, 4, 5, 8 & 9.
        3.3/3a. Paisiello: Il Re Teodoro in Venezia, 2 mvts.   Nos. 3 & 7.
        3.3/4a. Vogel: La Toison d'or, Marche. No. 6.
        3.3/5a. Grétry: Richard Cœur de Lion, 3 mvts.   Nos. 10 - 12.

BELFIORE, Turi *1917, Italy*
TXB-1. Dimensione; 1959.   fl ob 2cl 2sax hn 2bn tp tb timp.
Pm (Suvini-Zerboni: Milano, pn 5808, 1962), score & parts.

*BELLI-SANDRE, P.M.M. *(active 1869)*
PMB-1v. Tantum ergo, Op. 22.   Solo T, TTB chorus, fl 2cl 2hn tp tb organ.   MS parts: I-Vsmc.   ★
PMB-2v. Inno "O deux celi *etc.*" per S. Lorenzo Giustimiani, 1869.   TTB, 2cl 2hn organ(bc-fig).
AutoMS score & MS parts: I-Vsmc.   ★

*BELLOLI, Agostino *1778 - 1839, Italy*
ASB-1. Quartetto.   2cl hn bn.   MS: I-Mc, (unverified).
ASB-1a. Donizetti: L'Elisir d'amore, quintetto.   2fl 2ob cl(E♭) cl(B♭ obl) 3cl(B♭) 4hn 2bn 6tp 2tb serp fagottone.
MS parts: D-Hch, C 117/42.

BELLUCCI, Giacomo
GIB-1. Notesdieci; 1979, 1 continuous mvt.   2ob 2cl 2hn 2bn.
Pm (Rugginenti Editore: Milano, 1983), facsimile AutoMS score.

*BELOTTI, Giuseppe *(1820), active in the Bergamasco region, 1856 - 1898*
GSB-1. Suonata con variazioni per fagotto con accompagnamento.   Solo bassoon, fl 2cl 2hn tp cb organ.
AutoMS score: I-VERbelotti.
GSB-1v. Versetto; in B♭.   B obl, STB chorus, pic fl 2cl 2hn tp(obl) tp(II) tb(obl) 2tb oph cb timp;
organ("guida").   MS parts: I-VERbelotti.
GSB-2v. Inno per processione (Ave Maris Stella); in E♭.   STTB, fl(pic) 2cl 2hn 2bn 2tp 3tb cb+oph.
AutoMS score (1866): I-VERbelotti.
GSB-3v. Cum Sancto; in B♭.   STTBB, pic fl 2cl 2hn 2tp 2tb oph cb timp; organ("guida").
MS parts: I-VERbelotti.
GSB-4v. Dixit; in E♭.   TTB di concerto, pic fl("di concerto") 2cl 2hn 2tp tb("di concerto") tb(II)
tb("d'accompagnamento") cb timp; organ("guida").   MS parts: I-VERbelotti.
GSB-5v. Versetto; in B♭.   T obl, fl(obl) cl(obl) cl(II) 2hn 2tp tb("di concerto") 2tb cb timp; organ("guida").
MS parts: I-VERbelotti.
GSB-6v. Dixit; in F.   S(obl), T(I obl), T(II) B("di concerto"), B("di ripieno"), pic fl 2cl 2hn 2tp tb bomb cb
timp; organ("Guida").   MS parts: I-VERbelotti.
GSB-7v. Versetto; in C.   B obl, TTB chorus, pic fl(obl) 2cl(C) 2hn tp(obl) tp(II) tb(obl) tb(I [sic]) oph timp;
organ("guida").   MS parts: I-VERbelotti, (the vocal parts include another set of lyrics).
GSB-8v. Laudamus; in G.   ST obl, TTB chorus, fl(obl) 2cl(C) 2hn 2tp 2tb oph cb timp; organ("guida").
MS parts: I-VERbelotti, (the vocal parts also include another set of lyrics).
GSB-9v. Confitebor; in C.   Solo T, STB chorus, fl 2cl(C) 2hn 2tp 2tb oph cb timp; organ("guida").
MS parts: I-VERbelotti.
GSB-10v. Credo; in F.   TB di concerto, TB [chorus], fl("di concerto") 2cl(C) 2hn bn 2tp tb cb timp;
organ("guida").   MS pts: I-VERbelotti, (possibly missing bn II & tb II: the existing parts are both marked "1ᵒ").
GSB-11v. Versetto; in B♭.   TTB di concerto, TB (chorus), fl 2cl 2hn bn("di concerto) tp(I) tb("di concerto") tb
cb timp; organ("guida").   MS parts: I-VERbelotti.
GSB-12v. Tantum ergo; in F.   T solo, TTB chorus, fl 2cl 2hn bn 2tp tb cb timp; organ("guida").
MS parts: I-VERbelotti, (the fl & bn parts are marked "di concerto").
GSB-13v. Versetto; in D.   T obl, STB chorus, fl 2cl 2hn bn 2tp tb timp organ.   MS parts: I-VERbelotti.
GSB-14v. Magnificat; in B♭.   STTB, fl 2cl 2hn 2tp 2tb cb organ.   MS parts: I-VERbelotti.
GXB-15v. Dixit; in F.   TB di concerto, AT, fl 2cl 2hn 2tp 2tb cb timp; organ("guida").
MS parts: I-VERbelotti, (the fl, cl I, hn I, tp I & tb I are all marked "di concerto").
GSB-16v. Magnificat; in F.   TTB di concerto, TTB ripieco, fl 2cl 2hn 2tp 2tb cb timp; organ("guida").
MS parts: I-VERbelotti, (the fl, cl I, hn I, tp I & tb I are all marked "di concerto").
GSB-17v. Dixit; in E♭.   TTB, fl 2cl 2hn 2tp 2tb cb timp; organ("guida").   MS parts: I-VERbelotti.
GSB-18v. Sanctus; in C.   TTB di concerto, fl 2cl(C) 2hn 2tp 2tb cb timp; organ("guida").
MS parts (1880): I-VERbelotti, (the fl & tb I parts are marked "di concerto").
GSB-19v. Credo, in F.   SATTB, fl 2cl(C) 2hn 2tp tb cb timp organ.
AutoMS score (1861): I-VERbelotti.
GSB-20.1v. Gloria in excelsis Deo; in E♭.   S, T(I), T(II di ripieno), B("di concerto"), pic 2cl 2hn 2tp tb oph
cb timp; organ("Guida").   MS parts: I-VERbelotti.
GSB-20.2v. Istrumentazione in piccolo di un Gloris in excelsis Deo; in E♭.   fl 2cl 2hn 2tp tb.
AutoMS score: I-VERbelotti, (associated with GSB-20.1v).
GSB-21v. Credo, per pochi istrumenti; in E♭.   (S)TTB, pic 2cl 2hn tp (tp II) tb (tb II) cb (timp).
AutoMS score & MS parts: I-VERbelotti, (the parts in parentheses do not appear in the score).
GSB-22v. Gloria; in E♭.   (S)TTB, pic 2cl 2hn tp (tp II) tb (tb II) cb (timp).
Auto MS score & MS parts (1856): I-VERbelotti, (the parts in parentheses do not appear in the score).
GSB-23v. Kyrie; in B♭.   TTBB, fl(pic) 2cl hn(I £di concerto") hn(II) tp(I) tb("di concerto") tb cb timp;
organ("guida").   MS parts: I-VERbelotti, (possibly missing tp II).
GSB-24v. Miserere; in A minor.   (S)TTB, fl 2cl(C) 2hn tp (tp II) tb (tb ripieno) organ.
AutoMS score & MS parts: I-VERbelotti, (the parts in parentheses do not appear in the score).
GSB-25v. Versetto; in B♭.   TB obl, pic 2cl 2hn tp(obl) tp(II) cb timp; organ("guida").   MS parts: I-VERbelotti.
GSB-26v. Kyrie; in C.   TTB, fl 2cl(C) 2hn tp(I) 2tb cb; organ("guida").   MS pts: I-VERbelotti, (?missing tp II).
GSB-27v. Versetto; in F.   S solo, fl 2cl hn(obl) hn(II) tp(obl) tb cb organ.   MS parts: I-VERbelotti.
GSB-28v. Qui tollis.   T obl, TB chorus, fl cl(I obl) cl(II) 2hn tp tb organ.
MS parts: I-VERbelotti, (the organ part is incomplete and two parts show considerable deterioration).
GSB-29v. Vespro; in C.   CTB, pic 2cl(C) 2hn tb basso.   MS parts: I-VERbelotti.
GSB-30v. Credo, a tre voci; in E♭.   TTB("di concerto")B("2°."), pic 2cl 2hn tp("di concerto"); organ("guida").
MS parts: I-VERbelotti.
GSB-31v, 32v. [2] Iste confessor; in E♭.   TTB, pic 2cl tp tb timp.
AutoMS score: I-VERbelotti, (the second *Iste confessor* is found on the back of the sheets).

*BÉM (Behm), Václav (Venceslao, Wenceslao, Wenceslas) *(1740)*
VXB-1. Nro 1 Parthia in Dis [E♭]; 4 mvts.   2ob 2hn 2bn.   MS pts: CZ-Pnm, XXII.B.15, (missing hn I).   ★

*BENDA, ?Franz (František) [not Georg Benda nor Jan Jiři Benda]
baptized 22 Nov 1709, Staré Benátky, Bohemia -7 March 1786, Nowawes, near Potsdam.
XQB-1m. Dragoner-Marsch, (1764).   2ob 2bn tp.   MS score: D-Bds, Hausbibl, No 232.

*BENDA, Georg *baptized 30 June 1722, Stáre Benátky - 6 Nov 1795, Köstritz, Thuringia*
GQB-1em. Medea: March.   2ob 2hn bn.
AutoMS score: D-B, Mus.ms.autogr.Benda G. 1.   ★
Pm (Editio Supraphon: Praha/Prague, 1976), score, (Musica antiqua bohemica, Ser. 2, No. 8).

BENKERT, Johann Karl *(1800), Hautboisten im Regiment König Otto von Griechenland. (cf KOLB, Anton)*
KJB-1a, 2a. Jugend Polka [&] Münchner Posthorn-Schottisch, arrangiert.
pic(D♭) cl(E♭) 3cl(B♭) 2hn 2bn tp tb cb.   (?Auto)MS scores: GB-Ljag(w), (for the Löwenstein Kapelle).

*BENNETT, William *7 Feb 1936, London*
*WXB-1a. Theobald Boehm: Grande Polonaise.   solo fl, 2ob cl cl(C) 2hn 2bn.
MS score & parts: GB-Lbennett (English Chamber Orchestra Wind Ensemble).

*BENTZON, Niels Viggo *24 Aug 1919, Copenhagen.*
NVB-1. Concertino, Op. 483.   Solo piano, pic 2fl 2ob ca 2cl b-cl 2bn cbn 4perc.
Pm (Wilhelm Hansen: Copenhagen, 1986), hire score & parts.
NVB-2. 2 Hula-hula Compositions, Op. 395; 1977.   2fl 2ob ca 3cl bn cbn perc.   MS score: DK-Kd.

*BENZ, Johann Baptist (D.)
DYB-1v. Offertorium in Natavit Dm[m]i; "Hodie nobis cœlorum Rex"; in C.   CATB, 2cl 2hn 2tp organ.
MS score (Directionstimme) & MS parts (c.1840): CZ-KRsm, UHM A.963/Br.C-9. *The Directionstimme names the composer as, "D. Benz"; all the parts give "J. Benz". This is definitely Johann Baptist Benz.*   ★

*BERERA, Francesco Antonio *24 Aug 1737, Trento - 8 April 1811, Trento*
*FNB-1v. Messa, in F, a tre voci, Con strumenti di fiato per la Banda della Guardia Civica, Trento 1801.
TTB, 2terz-fl 2ob 2cl 2hn bn.   AutoMS score: I-TRc.

*BERG, Alban *9 Feb 1885, Vienna - 12 Dec 1935, Vienna*
*AYB-1. Kammerkonzert.   Solo Violin, Solo Piano, pic fl ob ca cl(E♭) cl(A) b-cl 2hn bn cbn tp tb.
Pc (Universal Edition: Wien, New York, 1925), score.
Pm (Universal Edition: Wien, New York, 1953), miniature score, Philharmonia No. 423; reprinted, with an introduction by Pierre Boulez, Wien & London, 1970.

BERGER, Arthur (Victor) *15 May 1912, New York*
AVB-1. Canzon otavi modi.   4ob 2ca 2bn.   Pm (Christlieb Products: Sherman Oaks, CA).

BERGER, František (Franz) *(1790), active c.1820*
FTB-1v. Stationes IV pro Festivitate Theophoriae.   CATB, 2cl(C) 2hn bn(vel vlne) 2tp(clar) timp.
MS parts (by Aloys Englisch, c.1820): CZ-Bm(kb), A.36.281.   ★

*BERGER, Ludwig *18 April 1777, Berlin - 18 Feb 1839, Berlin*
LZB-1m. Marche pour les armées anglaises-espagnoles dans les Pyrénées, Op. 1.   Instrumentation unknown.
AutoMS score: D-Bds, Mus.ms.auto.L.Berger 23.   *One of the few marches identified with the Peninsular War.*
LXB-2m. Marcia in E♭.   Instrumentation unknown.   AutoMS score: D-Bds, Mus.ms.auto.L.Berger 25.
LXB-3m. Triumphal Marsch (of the Prussian Army, 1814).   Instrumentation unknown.
AutoMS score: D-Bds, Mus.ms.auto.L.Berger 47.

BERGT, (Christian Gottlob) August *1771 - 1837*
CGB-1. [Divertimento, 21 mvts].   2cl 2hn bn.   AutoMS score: D-BAUm, R 15833, (Nos. 20 & 21 are Chorales, "Morgenlied. Des Morgens wenn ich früh" and "Ich dank' die Herr").   ★
CGB-1v. Aus dineem Quell Allvater; ("Preis Gottes des Allseligen" von Cramer).   TTB solo & chorus, 3cl 2hn bn b-tb timp.   AutoMS score (17 June 1836) & parts: D-BAUm, R 18468, (parts missing b-tb timp).   ★
CGB-2.1v, 2.2v. Asperges [me] & Offertorium, "Tu noster hymnus es".   TTB or SAB chorus, 2cl 2hn cb.
MS score & parts: D-BAUd, Mu I:360a.   ★
CGB-3v. Veni Sancte Spiritus.   SATB chorus, 2cl 2hn bn 2tp b-tb timp.
MS score (by Carl Wolf, 1834) & parts: D-BAUd, Mu II:58.   ★
CGB-1tv. Trauer=Motette und 2 Choräle, "Am Grabe tagt des Lebensdämmerung".   SATB, 2cl 2hn bn.
MS score & vocal parts (6S, 6A, 4T, 4B): D-LST, Mus.ant. 111:8.   ★
CGB-2tv. Trauer=Motette; "Am Ziel ist er! es wehen um ihr die Palmen schon".
SATB solo & chorus, 2fl 2ob 2cl 2hn 2bn 2tp b-tb timp.   MS score & parts: D-LST, Mus.ant. 111:9.   ★
CGB-3tv. Trauer=Motette: II. "Am Ziel ist er es wehen".   SATB solo & chorus, 2cl 3bn s-tb a-tb t-tb b-tb.
MS parts: D-LST, Mus.ant. 111:10.   ★

*BERKES, Kálmán *1952, Hungary*
KYB-1a. F.P. Schubert: 16 Deutsche (German Dances), (D.783), Nos. 6 & 7.   2ob 2cl 2hn 2bn.   MS: H-Bberkes.
KYB-2a. F.P. Schubert: Waltzes, (D.146), Nos. 12 & 20.   2ob 2cl 2hn 2bn.   MS: H-Bberkes.
KYB-3a. Leo Weiner: Two Hungarian Dances, Op. 20.   2ob 2cl 2hn 2bn.   MS: H-Bberkes.

*BERLIOZ, Louis Hector *11 Dec 1803, La Côte-Saint-André - 8 March 1869, Paris*
Major editions are: BW: Berlioz Werke. (Breitkopf & Härtel: Leipzig, 1899 - 1907), scores. NBW: New Edition of the complete Works of L. H. Berlioz (Bärenreiter: Kassel; Breitkopf & Härtel: Wiesbaden, 1967, etc.), scores. Below we write 4hn(12) meaning 4 parts, 12 players total, etc.
*LHB-1m(v). Grande Symphonie Funèbre et Triomphale, Op. 15; 1840.
SSTTBB chorus, Trombone solo, pic(4) fl(5) ob(5) cl(E♭)(5) 2cl(26) b-cl(2) 4hn(12) 2bn(8) cbn 4tp(8) 2cap(4) 3tb(10) btb 2oph(6) timp 2tambours (Voilés ou sans timbre)(8), grosse caisse, cym, pavillon chinois, tam-tam, 2v1(20/20) 2vla(15) vc(15) db(10); cbn, b-tb, timp, chorus & strings ad lib.
MS score (partly Autograph, pp. 1 - 6): F-Pn, MS. 1.164.   ★

Pc (Maurice Schlesinger: Paris, pn M.S. 3708, 1843), score: B-Bc, 7239; B-Br, Fétis 3074; B-Lc, 324-KK-IX; D-Bds, Mus. 442; F-Pn, (3 copies), Ac e10 887, D. 17550, Vm7 2238; GB-Cpl, X.Ra.850.80B.G1; GB-En, H.B.2/19(1); GB-Lbbc, (2 copies), Misc. 83A, Misc.83B; GB-Lbl, (3 copies), Hirsch M.788, h.456.(2), h.3250.a; GB-Lcm, I.K.25; GB-Ob, Mus.1.c.309.(21); US-Bp, M.341.19; US-NYp, MTA; US-Wc, M1203.B52op.15.
Pc (Brandus et Cie.: Paris, sd, post-1851), pts: D-Mbs, 2° Mus.pr 4161; F-Pc, D 16490, (with corrections by the composer); GB-En, H.B.2/19(2-3), (missing cap I, II; corrections by the composer); US-Cn, VM 100 1.B5 15g.
Pc (BW, 1900): Bd. III, Abteilung I, pp. 151 - 226), score.
Pm (E F Kalmus: New York, etc., sd), reprint of BW, score & parts, (pn A 1314), miniature score (pn 499).
Pm (NBW, vol. 19), score.
Pm (Ernst Eulenburg: London, 1976), miniature score (Edition Eulenburg No 595)
Pm (WINDS: Northridge, CA, pn W-96, c.1981), arranged for modern band (with optional sax parts) by David Whitwell, score & parts.
*LHB-2m(e). Te Deum, Op. 22: Marche pour la Présentation des Drapeaux.
4fl(pic) 2ob(ca) 2cl(b-cl) 4hn 4bn saxhorn(B♭) 2tp 2cap 3tb oph tu timp 4tambours, b-dr, cym(4/5 pairs), 2harps(12); (with minimal string parts; organ doubles the winds).
AutoMS sketch (Marche): F-Pn, MS. 1.508, (included in AutoMs score of *Benvenuto Cellini*, I, 128); facsimile in Holoman: *Berlioz Research*, opposite p.40.
AutoMS score (fair copy): RF-Ssc, (presented by Berlioz, 11 Sept 1862). ★
MS parts (partly Autograph): F-Pn, D. 16.466 & MS. 17995 *bis* 17997.
Pc (G. Brandus, Dufour et Cie.: Paris, 1855), score: A-Wn, S.A.83.C7; D-Bds, Mb.240; F-Pn, (4 copies), Rés. F.1044, (proofs: mvts I - III, VII, corrected by the composer), D.900, D.939, Vm1 22; GB-En, (2 copies), H.B.1/84 (proofs, without titlepage, corrected by the composer), H.B.2/48; GB-Lbl, R.M.14.c.14; GB-Lcm, I.K.26.
Pc (sn: Paris, 1880), score: GB-Lbl, h.1509.g.(3).
Pm (NBW, Vol 19), score.
Pm (Ernst Eulenburg: London, 1976), miniature score (Edition Eulenburg, No 1095).
Pm (WINDS: Northridge, CA, pn W-265, c.1981), score & wind parts (movement 7 only).

*BERNARD, (Jean August) Émile *11 Nov 1843, Marseilles - 11 Sept 1902, Paris*
*EYB-1. Divertissement, Op. 36; in F, 3 mvts.   2fl 2ob 2cl 2hn 2bn.
Pc (A. Durand & Fils: Paris, 1890), score (pn 7358) & parts (pn 7362): D-Bhm; F-Pn, D. 985 (2). ★
Pm (McGinnis & Marx, New York), parts.
Pm (Compusic: Amsterdam, pn 232, 1991), score & parts.

*BERNER, Friedrich Wilhelm *16 May 1780, Breslau - 9 May 1827, Breslau*
FWB-1v. Der Herr ist Gott.   TTBB, winds.
Pc (G. Cranz: Breslau, sd), score: D-Tl, AA 6, (with the added imprint of G.A. Zumsteeg, Stuttgart).
Pc (Leuckart: Breslau, sd), score: D-Bds.

*BERNHARD, M. *(1810), Lehrer, Donauwörth*
MWB-1tv. [attributed] Leichenlied; "Gottes Ruh".   CATB, terz-fl 2cl 2hn bomb.
MS parts (Donauwörth, Musiksammlung des Cassianeums): D-Tl, DWc 34.

*BERR, Friedrich (Frédéric) *17 April 1794, Mannheim - 24 Sept 1838, Paris*
We have not traced surviving copies of arrangements by Berr of works by Berton. The Journal d'Harmonie et de Musique Militiare, *a joint venture by F. Louis, C. Münchs and F. Berr was later reissued from the original plates as separate works by Les Fils de B. Schott.*
FXB-1. Journal d'Harmonie et de Musique Militaire.   Scoring varies.
Pc (*Année 2, Liv. 1-3 [or 5-7]:* Au Dépôt du Journal, Chez Pacini…et Chez les Auteurs: Paris; *Année 2, Liv. 4 & Année 3, Liv. 1-4 [or 8-12]:* Au Dépôt du Journal, Chez Pacini…et Chez Munchs [sic], pn 5-9, c.1822-1823), pts: F-Pn, Vm27 2969 (1, 2) & Vm27 2630, (2 copies of Liv. 7-9), (missing Année 3, Liv. 2-4 [or 10-12]). ★
  1/5/. An 2, Liv. 1 [Liv 5].   pic(D) cl(E♭) 2cl(B♭) 2hn 2bn tp 2tb 2serp b-dr; (Nos. 1 & 2 add solo cl in B♭).
  1/5/1. Marche, ¢.   1.5/2. Pas Redoublé, 6/8.   1.5/3. Waltz, Poco Lento, 3/8.
  1/6/. An 2, Liv. 2 [Liv. 6].   pic(D) cl(E♭) 2cl(I, B♭), 2cl(II, B♭) 2hn 2bn tp 2tb b-dr+t-dr.
  1/6/4. Pas Redoublé, 2/4.   1/6/5. Pas Redoublé, 6/8.   1/6/6. Waltz, 3/8 [+ Trio].
  1/7/. An 2, Liv. 3 [or Liv. 7].   fl(C) 2ob/cl(C) 2cl(B♭) 2hn 2bn 2tp 2tb serp(divisi No. 7); ?missing ad lib cb.
  1/7/1. Simphonie, 1 mvt. No. 7.   1/7/2. Andante. No. 8.   1/7/3. Menuetto [+ Trio]. No. 9.
  1/8/. An 2, Liv. 4 [or Liv. 8].
    1. Marche, C.   fl(D♭) cl(E♭) 3cl(I, B♭) 2cl(II, Bb) 2hn 2bn tp 2tb serp b-dr+t-dr.   No. 1.
    2. Pas Redoublé [+ Trio], 2/4.   fl(D♭) cl(E♭) 2cl(B♭)* 2hn 2bn crt(A♭) tb serp b-dr.   No. 2.
    3. Walz [sic] de la Duchesse de Berry, 3/8 [+ Trio].   fl(D♭) cl(E♭) 2cl(B♭) 2hn 2bn tp serp b-dr. No. 3.
  1/9/. An 3, Liv. 1 [or Liv. 9].
    1. Pas Redoublé, 2/4 [+ Trio].   fl(E♭) cl(E♭) 2cl(B♭) 2hn 2bn crt(A♭) tb serp b-dr.   No. 4.
    2. Pas Redoublé, 2/4 [+ Trio].   fl(E♭) cl(I, B♭) 2cl(II, B♭) 2hn 2bn tp tb 2serp b-dr.   No. 5.
    3. Waltz, Allegretto non troppo, 3/8 [+ Trio].   fl(E♭) cl(E♭) 2cl(B♭) 2hn 2bn tp tb serp b-dr.   No. 6.
FXB-1.1. Grand Harmonie, Cahier [MS: 1, 2]; 3 mvts.   *Reissued from the plates of FXB-1.*
Pc (Chex les Fils de B. Schott: Paris, Mayence et Anvers, pn 3022, 3023, 1827/1828), parts: D-DT, 1567, (Cah. 2); D-MZsch, (complete).   *1.1/1: Cahier 1 = Liv. 7; 1.1/2: Cahier 2 = Liv. 11.* ★
  1.1/2/1. Ouverture.   fl 2ob 2cl(C) 2hn bn(I) bn(II)+cb tp 2tb serp.
  1.1/2/2. Andante; scoring as 1.1/2/1.   1.1/2/3. Minuetto Vivace [& Trio]; scoring as 1.1/2/1.
FXB-1.2. Musique Militaire, Cahier 1 - 6.   *Reissued from the plates of FXB-1.*
Pc (Chex les Fils de B. Schott: Paris, Mayence et Anvers, pn 3006 - 3010, 1827/1828), pts: D-DT, 1569, (missing Cah. 2; in Cah. 1 the MS No. "5", corresponding to the original Journal No., has been crossed out & "1" has been added; there are additional local MS tp pts: 2tp in No. 1, cor de signal à clefs en La♭ [A♭] in No. 2, 2tps in No. 3); D-MZsch, (complete).   *Cah. 1 = Liv. 5; Cah. 2 = Liv. 6; Cah. 3 = Liv. 8; Cah. 4 = Liv. 9.* ★
  Cah. 5 [Liv. 10]: 1. Marche, C.   p-fl(D♭) cl(E♭) 2cl(I, B♭) 2cl(II, B♭) 2hn 2bn 2tp tb (2)serp b-dr.
    2. Pas Redoublé, 2/4 [+Trio].   p-fl(D♭) cl(E♭) 2cl(I, B♭) 2cl(II, B♭) 2hn 2bn crt(A♭) tb serp b-dr.
    3. Waltz, 3/8 [+Trio].   p-fl(D♭) cl(E♭) 2cl(I, B♭) 2cl(II, B♭) 2hn 2bn 2tp tb serp b-dr.
  Cah. 6 [Liv.11]: 1. Pas Redoublé, 2/4 [+Trio].   p-fl(C#) cl(E♭) 2cl(I B♭) 2cl(II B♭) 2hn 2bn 2tp 2tb serp b-dr+cym
    2. Pas Redoublé, 2/4 [+Trio].   p-fl(D♭) cl(E♭) cl(I, B♭) 2cl(II, B♭) 2hn 2bn tp(bugle) tb 2serp b-dr+cym.
    3. Waltz, 3/8 [+ Trio].   p-fl(D♭) cl(E♭) 2cl(I, B♭) 2cl(II, B♭) 2hn 2bn 2tp tb serp b-dr+cym.

FXB-2. Journal de Musique Militiare Authorisé par S. E. le Ministre de la Guerre. Année 1, Liv. 1, 6 mvts.
fl(Eb) cl(Eb) cl(solo, Bb) 2cl(Bb) 2hn 2bn tp(crt) b-tb serp b-dr+cym t-dr.
Pc (Chez Gambaro: Paris, pn 1, 1 Jan 1826), parts: D-DT, 1568. ★
FXB-3.1. [3 pieces in Année 1, Liv. 3 of Conrad Münchs' *Nouveau Journal d'Harmonie et de Musique Militaire.*
   3.1/1(a). Harmonie N°. 25. Mercadante: Elisa e Claudio, overture.
      fl(Eb) cl(Eb) cl(solo Bb) cl(I, Bb) cl(II, Bb) 2cl(Bb rip) 2hn 2bn tp 3tb (2)serp cb.
   3.1/2. N°. 26. Andantino. fl(C) cl(Eb) cl(solo Bb) cl(I, Bb) cl(II, Bb) 2cl(Bb rip) 2hn 2bn tp 3tb (2)serp cb.
   3.1/3. N°. 27. Menuetto. fl(Eb) cl(Eb) cl(solo Bb) cl(I, Bb) cl(II, Bb) 2cl(Bb rip) 2hn 2bn tp 3tb (2)serp cb.
FXB-3.2. 3 Pièces pour Musique Militaire. Scoring as FXB-3.1.
Pc (Chez les Fils de B. Schott: Paris, Myence et Anvers, pn (3), c.1823), parts: D-DT, 1590, (with additional
MS parts for serp transposed to C, b-dr [Nos. 25 & 27]; the cb pt bears the local note, "ou Corno di Basso"). ★
FXB-1m - FXB-6m may also be drawn from the (missing) Livraisons of FXB-2.
FXB-4. 4°. Air varié. Solo cl, orchestra, (harmonie or piano alternatives).
Pc (Gambaro: Paris, pn 103, 1818), parts: GB-Lbl, h.2189.c.(3), (full orchestral version).
FXB-5. 5ᵐᵉ Air Varié. Solo cl, orchestra (fl 2cl 2hn 2bn 2vl vla vc+b), (harmonie or piano alternatives)
MS parts (1836 by Philipp Schmutzer, owned by F. Anton Schmutzer, then by Julius Günter, Wellnitz bei
Heienstat): GB-Ljag, (full orchestral version).
FXB-1m. Marche du Couronnement de Charles X.   pic(Db) cl(Eb) 3cl(Bb) 2hn 2bn+2tb tp serp.
MS score: D-Tl, Z 136, No. 2, ff. 6 - 11. *Possibly from the missing FXB-1, Liv. 11 & 12 of FXB-1.* ★
FXB-2m. Marche; Eb. pic(Db) cl(Eb) 3cl(Bb 2hn 2bn tp 2tb serp. MS score: D-Tl, Z 136, No. 3, ff. 11b-17. ★
FXB-3m(-6m). 4 Pas redoublés (Ab, C minor, Eb, Eb).   pic(Db) cl(Eb) 2cl(Bb) 2hn serp+2bn tp.
MS score: D-Tl, Z 136, Nos. 6 - 9, ff. 26 - 30, 30b - 32b, 33 - 35b, 36 - 40b. ★
FXB-1a. Adam: Le Postillon de Lonjumeau, Suite 1 (Nos. 1 - 5), Suite 2 (Nos. 6 - 10).
fl cl(Eb) cl(solo, Bb) 3cl(Bb) 4hn 2bn 2tp 2cap(Suite 2 only) 3tb serp/oph cb(obl. Suite 1, ad lib Suite 2).
Pc (chez les Fils de B. Schott: Mayence et Anvers, pn 1348.(1.), 1348.(2), c.1837), parts: GB-Ljag(w). *The plate*
number is outside the main Schott sequence and probably indicates an original Parisian publisher.
FXB-2a. Auber: La Muette de Portici, overture.   pic cl(Eb) 2cl(Bb) 2hn 2bn, (ad lib: fl cl(III) tp 2tb serp).
Pc (chez E. Troupenas: Paris, pn 265, c.1828), parts: D-DO, Mus.Drkw.3249; I-Mc, Noseda B.19.4, (printed parts
missing hn II; prov: "Musique du Pensionnat du Freibourg", with MS parts for: pic(Eb), cl I (3 copies: 1 is a
simplified part, another the overture to Carafa's *Masaniello),* cl II, cl III, hn II, bn II, cap I, cap II, tb I, tb II
(simplified), oph(C), b-dr, s-dr).
FXB-3a. Auber: La Fiancée, overture. pic cl(Eb) 2cl(Bb) 2hn bn(I) serp, (ad lib: cl III & IV, bn II, tp 3tb db).
Pc (Chez E. Troupenas: Paris, pn 324, c.1829), parts: I-Mc, Noseda B.18.1, (printed parts missing hn II, bn I
& II; prov: "Musique du Pensionnat de Freibourg", with MS parts for: Partie-Direction (piano reduction), cl I
(2 copies, one including Bouifl's arrangement of the overture to Boieldieu's *La dame blanche),* cl II, hn II,
tp(á piston, Eb) II, tb I, tuba-cleide, b-dr s-dr).
FXB-4a. Auber: Fra Diavolo, overture.
fl cl(Eb) (solo)cl(Bb) 2cl(Bb) 2hn bn(I) 2tp serp, (ad lib: cl III & IV, bn II, 2tb db b-dr tri).
Pc (Chez Troupenas: Paris, pn 428, c.1830), parts: I-Mc, Noseda B.19.2, (with a printed slip: "Chez Rousset:
Lyon". The printed parts are missing hn III, db & Tambour Solo; cl II is *divisi* in the final 12/8 section.
Prov: "Musique du Pensionnat de Freibourg", with MS parts for: Partie-Direction (pf red), cl I, cl II (2 versions),
cornet III, oph(C), tuba-cleide, & an unspecified basso part).
FXB-5a. Auber: Le Philtre, overture.
fl(Eb) cl(Eb) cl(Bb solo) 2cl(Bb) 2hn bn serp; (ad lib: 2cl(Bb) bn(II) tp 3tb cb b-dr tri).
Pc (les Fils de B. Schott: Mayence et Anvers, pn 561, c.1831/32), parts: D-DT, Mus-n 285. *The plates are from*
Troupenas (Paris), 1831/1832.
FXB-6a. Auber: Le Serment, overture.
pic cl(Eb) 2cl(Bb) 2hn bn serp, (ad lib: cl III & IV, bn II, bugle 2tp 3tb b-dr s-dr).
Pc (Chez E. Troupenas: Paris; chez D'Almaine: London; chez les fils de B. Schott: Mainz & Antwerp, pn 619,
c.1832), parts: I-Mc, Noseda B.19.1, (printed pts missing bugle, and with a duplicate serp pt marked "serp/oph";
prov: "Bibl. Mus: Conv. Fr[ei]b[urg]", with MS parts for: Partie-Direction (pf red), cl I, cl II, cl III, hn II,
cap(Eb) II, 3tb, oph(C), tuba-cleide).
FXB-7a. Auber: Lestocq, overture. pic cl(Eb) 4cl(Bb) 4hn(Eb, Bb) 2bn 2tp 2cap 3tb serp+oph db b-dr cym.
Pc (au Dépôt Central de la Musique de la Bourse: Paris; chez d'Almaine et Cie: London; chez les fils de B.
Schott: Mayence et Anvers, pn 870, c.1834), parts: I-Mc, Noseda B.19.3, (printed parts missing 2hn, 2cap, tb
II, b-dr, cym; prov: Bibl. Mus. Conv. Fr[e]ib[urg], with MS parts for: Partie-Direction (pf red), (2 sets of) cl I -
III, hn II (Bb) basso, cap II, tb II (untitled), oph(C), tuba-cleide, b-dr, s-dr).
FXB-8a. Auber: Le Cheval de bronze, overture.
fl(Eb) cl(Eb) cl(Bb solo) 2cl(Bb) 2hn bn serp; (ad lib: 3cl(Bb) 2hn 2tp 2tb b-tb cb).
Pc (Chez E. Troupenas: Paris, pn T.135, 1835), parts: I-Mc, Noseda B.18.3, (printed pts missing hn I & II; prov:
"Musique du Pensionnat de Freibourg", with MS pts for: Partie-Direction (piano reduction) cl I, cl II, cl III,
hn II, tp(á piston, Eb) II, tb(á piston), tuba-cleide, a-oph, b-dr(+cym & tri) s-dr, unspecified perc part).
FXB-9a. Auber: Le Domino rouge, overture.
fl(Eb) cl(Eb solo) 4cl(Bb) 2hn 2bn 2tp(á piston) 2tp 3tb (solo)oph oph b-dr.
Pc (Chez E. Troupenas: Paris, pn T.635, c.1838), parts: I-Mc, Noseda B.18.4, (printed parts missing hn II, tp(á
piston) I; prov: "Musique du Pensionnat de Freibourg", with MS parts for: Partie-Direction (pf red), solo cl,
cl II, cl III, hn II, tb(á piston), a-oph, (solo)oph(C), tuba-cleide, s-dr).
Beethoven: Waltz, Le Désir (K.-H.Anh.14, No. 1). *See infra: SCHUBERT, F.P. Original-Tänze, Op. 9, No. 2.*
FXB-10a. Boieldieu: Les Deux Nuits, overture. pic cl(Eb) 2cl(Bb) 2hn 2bn serp; (ad lib: 2cl(Bb) tp 2tb cb).
Pc (sn: sl, [= Janet et Cotelle: Paris], pn 2296.J.C., c.1829), pts: I-Mc, Noseda C.57.4, (printed pts missing hn II;
prov: "Musique du Pensionnat de Freibourg", with MS parts for: Partie-Direction, cl I, cl II (2 copies), hn II,
cap(Bb) II, tb I, (untitled) tb II, a-oph, tuba-cleide, b-dr+tri s-dr; the printed db part has been altered to oph).
FXB-11a. Carafa: Masaniello, overture. pic cl(Eb) 2cl(Bb) 2hn bn(I) serp, (ad lib: cl III & IV, tp 2/3tb serp).
Pc (sn: sl, [Troupenas: Paris], pn 609, c.1829), parts: I-Mc, Neseda D.31.8, (printed parts missing cl I - IV &
possibly other parts; prov: "Musique du Pensionnat de Freibourg", with MS parts for: cl I(Bb (2 copies), cl IV,
untitled bass part (? = bn II), cap I, cap II, 2tp(Eb), tb(á piston), tb II, buccin (altered in pencil to tb III), a-oph,
b-oph(C). Following on in the tb II part only is "No. 15. Valse de Strauss"). *A simplified cl I is at: FXB-2a.*

FXB-12a. Carafa: Le Solitaire, overture. fl cl(Eb) 2cl(C) 2hn 2bn; (ad lib: cl III in C, tp (2)tb, serp ripieno).
Pc (Chez Meysenberg: Paris, pn 332 M.G., c.1823), pts: F-Pn, Vm27 737, (the headtitles in the bn pts are both in the plural, "Bassons").
FXB-13a. Grisar: Sarah, overture. fl(Eb) cl(Eb) 4cl(Bb) 4hn 2bn 2cap 3tb (2)serp.
Pc (les Fils de B. Schott: Mayence et Antvers, pn B.L.1304, c.1837), parts: D-DT, Mus-n 448, (missing cl(Bb) II & III; with MS pts for 2serp b-dr s-dr). *The plates are from the Parisian publisher, Bernard Latte.*
FXB-14a. Halévy: Le Dilettante d'Avignon, overture.
fl cl(Bb solo) 2cl(Bb) 2hn bn tp serp; (ad lib: 2cl(Bb) 2hn bn(II) tb b-dr).
Pc (Maurice Schlesinger: Paris, pn M.S.957, 1829/1830), parts: I-Mc, Noseda T.22.9, (missing hn III, b-dr, tri; with an additional MS part for a-oph).
FXB-15a. Hérold: Marie [Almédon], overture. (Here only: pic cl(Eb) cl(Bb, IV) 2hn bn(I); (ad lib: tp (2)tb serp).
Pc (Chez J. Meissonnier: Paris, pn J.M.248, c.1826), parts: I-Mc, Noseda R.15.16, No 1, (missing titlepage & (at least) cl I - III, bn II).
FXB-16a. Hérold: Le Dernier Jour de Missolonghi, overture.
fl(Eb) cl(Bb solo) 2cl(Bb) 2hn bn (2)serp; (ad lib: 2cl(Bb) tp 2tb cb b-dr+cym tri).
Pc (les Fils de B. Schott: Mayence et Anvers, pn J.M.428, 1832), parts: D-DT, Mus-n 518, (with MS serp II pt); D-MZsch. *Printed from the J. Meissonnier (Paris) plates.*
FXB-17a. Hérold: Zampa, overture.
fl cl(Bb solo) 2cl(Bb) 2hn bn serp; (ad lib: 2cl(Bb) hn(III) bn(II) bugle tp 3tb cb).
Pc (Chez J. Meissonnier: Paris, pn J.M.570, c.1831), parts: I-Mc, Noseda R.15.16, No 2, (missing hn II (hn III part altered to "2e cor"); provenance: "Musique du Pensionnat de Freiburg", with MS parts: fl, cl III & III, tb I & II, oph in C).
FXB-18a. Hérold: Le Médicine sans Médecin, overture.
fl(Eb) cl(Eb) cl(Bb solo) 2cl(Bb) 2hn bn serp; (ad lib: 2cl(Bb) tp bugle 3tb cb).
Pc (les Fils de B. Schott: Mayence et Anvers, pn 685, 1833), pts: D-DT, Mus-n 517, (with MS pts: a-tb b-dr s-dr). *The plate number is outside the main Schott sequence and is probably printed from the Troupenas (Paris) plates.*
FXB-19a. Hérold: Le Pré aus Clercs, overture.
fl(Eb) cl(Eb) cl(Bb solo) 2cl(Bb) 2hn bn serp; (ad lib: 2cl(Bb) bn(II) tp bugle 3tb b-dr).
Pc (Chez les Fils de B. Schott: Mayence et Anvers, pn 684, 1833), pts: D-DT, Mus-n 520, (with MS pts: a-tb bomb b-dr t-dr). *The plate number is outside the main Schott series and is probably printed from the Troupenas (Paris) plates.*
Mercadante: Elisa e Claudio, overture. *See supra: FXB-3.1/1(a).*
FXB-20a. Meyerbeer: Margherita d'Anjou, overture.
fl(pic) cl(Eb) cl(Bb solo) 2cl(Bb) 2hn bn serp; (ad lib: cl(Eb) 2cl(Bb) bn(II) 2tb cb b-dr tri).
Pc (Chez les Fils de B. Schott: Mayence et Anvers, pn J.M.427, c.1820): D-DT, Mus-n 718, (with MS pts for 2ob & solo cl (transposed); the cb pt has been altered to b-hn); D-MZsch. *Printed from the J. Meissonnier (Paris) plates.*
FXB-21a. Reissiger: Danses brillantes, Op. 26, No. 5 (as "La dernière Pensée de C. M. von Weber"). Valse et Pas redoublé. Military band.
Pc (Schott: Mainz, post-1826): D-MZsch.
***FXB-22a.** Rossini: Tancredi, overture. Instrumentation unknown, (probably as FXB-25a).
Pc (untraced but known to survive - ?I-Gc).
***FXB-23a.** Rossini: Il Turco in Italia, overture. Instrumentation unknown, (probably as FXB-25a).
Pc (untraced but known to survive - ?I-Gc).
FXB-24a. Rossini: La Cenerentola, Airs. Instrumentation unknown, (probably as FXB-25a).
Pc (Schott: Mains, c.1825), parts: D-MZsch.
***FXB-25a.** Rossini: Mathilda di Shabran, overture. Instrumentation unknown (probably as FXB-25a).
Pc (untraced but known to survive - ?I-Gc).
***FXB-26a.** Rossini: La Siège de Corinthe, overture. fl(Eb) cl(Eb) 2cl(Bb) 2hn 2bn; (ad lib: 2cl(Bb) tp 3tb serp cb; (if only one trombone available, the lowest part is to be preferred).
Pc (chez E. Troupenas: Paris, pn 184, c.1826), parts: F-Pn, K. 12.191; I-Fc, F.P. S.700.
FXB-27a. Rossini: Guillaume Tell, overture. Instrumentation unknown (probably as FXB-25a).
Pc (Schott: Mainz, c.1830): D-MZsch.
FXB-28a. F.P. Schubert: Original Tänze, Op. 9, No. 2 (misattributed to Beethoven as "Waltz, Le Désir" (K.-H.Anh.14, No. 1). fl cl(Eb) 2cl(C) 2hn 2bn; (ad lib: cl III in C, tp, (2)tb, serp ripieno).
Pc (as "Oeuv: 37") (Chez les Fils de B. Schott: Paris; chez les mêmes: Mayence; chez A. Schott: Anvers, c.1826), parts: F-Pn, Vm27 159, (4 copies).
FXB-29a. La Réunion. Pas Redoublés, Marches, Walses…Arrangés…Livraison [MS: 1 - 3].
p-fl(Eb) cl(Eb) 3cl(Bb) 2hn 2bn tp 3tb serp b-dr t-dr; (ad lib: hn III, bugle).
Pc (Chez A. Aulanger: Paris, pn AA.164 - 169, 1831), parts: F-Pn, Vm27 161.
Liv. 1: 29.1a. Rossini: Marche. 29.2a. Paganini: [Violin Concerto No. 2], La Clochettte. Morceau de répos.
Liv. 2: 29.3a. Niedermeyer: Le Ronde du Sabbat, pas redoublé. 29.4a. [Panseron]: Petit blanc. Pas redoublé.
Liv. 3: 29.5a. [Panseron]: Le [petit] Porteau d'eau. Pas redoublé. 29.6a. [Anon]: La Favorite. Valse.
FXB-1ma. Sowinski: Marche héroique des Parisiens composée et dedié au Général Lafayette, commandant et Chef des Gardes Nationales de France. pic(Db) cl(Eb) cl(Bb solo) 4cl(Bb) 2hn 2bn tp tb serp b-dr t-dr.
Pc (Launer, Paris; pn 2693, c.1831), parts: CH-Gpu, Ib.4921a; GB-Ljag, (photocopy).
FXS-2ma. Donizetti: Parisina, Pas Redoublé, No 5. fl cl(Eb) 2cl(Bb) 2hn 2bn 2tp 2tb oph b-dr s-dr.
Pc (sn: sl, Paris, c.1836), parts (small format): I-Mc, Noseda E.63.2, (missing cl I, tb II).
FXB-3ma. Mercadante: I Briganti, Pas Redoublé (No 6). fl cl(Eb) 2cl(Bb) 2hn 2bn 2tp 2tb oph b-dr s-dr.
Pc (sn: sl, Paris, c.1836), parts (small format): I-Mc, Noseda E.63.4, (missing cl I, tb II).
FXB-4ma. Schubry: (unidentified work as:) Pas Redoublé, No 3. fl cl(Eb) 2cl(Bb) 2hn 2bn tp 3tb oph b-dr s-dr.
Pc (sn: sl, Paris, c.1836), parts (small format): I-Mc, Noseda E.63.3, (missing cl I).
FXB-1ac. R.N.C. Bochsa: Le Roi et la Ligue, overture. p-fl(A) (2)fl 2cl(F) 2cl(C) 2hn 2bn tp cb.
MS pts (c.1816 - 1820): D-Rtt, Sm. 13, No. 53, (as "v[on] Baehr"). *We believe this is Berr's (lost) arrangement.*

BERR, José *29 Dec 1874, Regensburg - 15 April 1947, Zurich*
VJB-1. Variations and Fugue on "Der Osterhase", Op. 91. fl ob 2cl 2hn bn. MS: CH-Zma.

*BERTIE, Willoughby, *4th Earl of Abingdon* *16 Jan 1740, Gainsborough - 26 Sept 1799, Rycote*
WZB-1v. [attributed]. Hallelujah.   2cl 2hn 2bn; ad lib chorus.
Pc (T. Monzani: London, c.1800), RISM [A 151], score: GB-Lbl, H.2824.(31); GB-DOTams, (modern MS score
& parts); GB-Ljag, (modern MS score); GB-OBharding.
*WZB-1t. Funeral March.   2ob 2cl 2hn 2bn timp.
Pc (In: A Selection of Twelve Psalms and Hymns, set to music according to the rules laid down for the Church.
pp. 2 - 3. Theobald Monzani, Thomas Skillern: London, 1793), RISM [A 148], score: D-Rp; GB-BA, BR 209.C;
GB-En; GB-Lbl, E.577; GB-Ljag, (modern MS copy); GB-DOTams (modern score & pts); GB-OBharding; H-Bn,
(presumably the copy owned by Haydn, and likely to have been a presentation copy from the composer).   ★

*BERTON, Henri Montan   *17 Sept 1767, Paris - 22 April 1844, Paris*
HMB-1m. Marche Militaire, P.2318.   2p-fl 2cl 2hn 2bn tp serp.
Pc (Mag de mus fêtes nat: Paris, ventôse an III, 1795), liv. 12, No. 3, parts: F-Pn, H2. 12,3.   ★
HMB-1v. Hymne pour la Fête de l'Agriculture; "Hommage à la pompe rustique", P.117.
Solo voice, SATB chorus, p-fl 2cl 2hn 2bn 2tp a-tb t-tb b-tb serp timp tri, tambour turc.
Pc (Mag de mus fêtes nat.: Paris, c.1796), RISM [B 2338], vocal score & instrumental pts: H2. 43.   ★
Pc (Imprimerie du Conservatoire: Paris, c.1796), vocal score & instrumental parts: D-AB; F-Pn, D. 16082.
Pc (Hymnes de la Révolution français: Paris, sd), score: F-Pn, H2. 35,11.   ★

*BERTONI, Ferdinando Gasparo   *15 Aug 1725, Salò, Venice - 1 Dec 1813, Dessenzano*
FGB-1v. Gloria.   TTB, 2ob 2hn bn 2tp organ(bc-fig); (Gratias agimus: TTB, 2ob 2hn bn organ(bc-fig);
Domine Deus: TT, 2ob bn organ(bc-fig); Qui tollis: TTB, 2ob 2hn bn 2tp organ(bc-fig); Qui sedes: Solo T, 2ob
bn organ(bc-fig); Cum Sancto Spiritu: TTB, 2ob 2hn bn 2tp organ(bc-fig)).
MS score & parts: I-Vsmc, (with an additional full organ part).   ★
FGB-2v. Credo a 3.   Solo TTB, 2cl 2hn bn timp organ(bc-fig).
MS score & parts: I-Vsmc, (with an additional full organ pt).   ★
FGB-3v. Credo in Csolfaut.   TTB(solo+rip), 2cl 2hn bn timp organ(bc-fig).   MS parts: I-Vsmc.   ★
FGB-4v. Pastorale e Gloria.   Pastorale: 2fl 2ob 2cl 2hn bn organ(bc); Gloria: SATB, 2fl 2bo 2cl 2hn vla
organ(bc-fig)+bn, (Laudamus te: SATB, 2fl 2ob vla organ(bc-fig)+bn; Gratias agimus tibi: SATB, 2ob vla
organ(bc-fig)+bn; Domine Deus, Qui tollis, Quoniam: SATB, 2fl 2ob vla organ(bc-fig)+bn; Cum Sancto Spiritus:
SATB, organ(bc-fig)+bn).   AutoMS score: I-Bc, DD.155.   ★
FGB-5v. Credo.   TTB, ob 2hn bn.   MS: I-Vcr, Busta IV N. 62.

BERTRAND, Ginette   *8 June 1949, Montreal*
GTB-1. Octet for Woodwinds; 1972.   2ob 2cl 2hn 2bn.   In MS: C-Tcm will assist in contacting the composer.

*BERTUZZI, A.M.   *(?1770)*
AMB-1v. Credo a 2.   Solo TB, 2cl 2hn tp tb organ.   MS score & parts: I-Vsmc.   ★
AMB-2v. Kyrie.   Solo TB, 2cl(C) 2hn tp tb organ.   MS score & parts: I-Vsmc.   ★

*BERWALD, Franz   *23 Aug 1798, Stockholm - 3 April 1868, Stockholm*
*Here **BwGAi** stands for:* Sämtliche Werke. Editionsleitung Berwald-Kommitten. *Bärenreiter: Kassel, 1966, etc.*
*FYB-1v. Kantata: Konung Carl XII:s seger vid Narva (König Carls XII. Sieg bei Narva) oder Schwedisches
Soldatenlied; 1845.   Solo voices, fl 2cl 2hn.
AutoMS piano reduction & parts: S-Skma.
Pm (BwGA, Bd. 21), score.
*FYB-2v. Nordiska fantasibilder, 1846.   Male chorus, fl 3cl 2tp crt tb organ.
AutoMS score: S-Skma.
Pm (BwGA, Bd. 21), score.
FYB-3v. Kantate: Musik till industrieerpositionens invigningsfest den 15 juni 1866; Marsch, Hymne, Jubelchor.
Male chorus, pic 2fl 4cl 4hn 4tp 6crt 3t-tb 4b-tb 2b-tu bomb timp drum.
AutoMS (photocopy): S-Skma.
Pm (BwGA, Bd. 22), score.

BESEL, F., *Dr.*   *(1870)*
FUB-1m. Regiments=Marsch der 55er [Regt]. fl 2ob cl(E♭) 3cl(B♭) 4hn bn 4tp 3crt(2B♭, E♭) 2t-hn 3tb bar 2tu
b-dr t-dr glock.   MS (by "E.L.", 25 Nov 1912): D-DT, Mus-h 3 B 1, (with new copy by Gustav Kühne, 1947).   ★

*BESOZZI, Carlo   *c.1738, Naples - 22 March 1791*
*Critical editions of CXB-1 - CXB-24 also appear in score in Part 2 of Daniel Niemitz's PhD disseration
(University of Rochester, 1967). The wrappers of the A-Wgm copies are of a slightly later date than the parts.*
CXB-1. No 1 Parthia o [sic] Sonata in D; 4 mvts.   2ob 2hn bn.
MS parts: A-Wgm, VIII 8535 (Q 16366).   ★
CXB-2. Nro II Sonata; in D, 4 mvts.   2ob 2hn bn.
MS parts: A-Wgm, VIII 8535 (Q 16366).   ★
CXB-3. No: 3 Sonata in C; 4 mvts.   2ob 2ca 2hn bn.
MS parts: A-Wgm, VIII 8535 (Q 16366).   ★
CXB-4. No: 4 Sonata in F; 4 mvts.   2ob 2ca 2hn bn.
MS parts: A-Wgm, VIII 8535 (Q 16366).   ★
CXB-5. No: 5 Sonata in E♭; 4 mvts.   2ob 2ca 2hn bn.
MS parts: A-Wgm, VIII 8535 (Q 16366).   ★
CXB-6. No VI Sonata in E♭; 4 mvts.   2ob 2ca 2hn bn.
MS parts: A-Wgm, VIII 8535 (Q 16366).   ★
CXB-7. No 7 Sonata; in C; 4 mvts.   2ob 2ca 2hn bn.
MS parts: A-Wgm, VIII 8535 (Q 16366).   ★
CXB-8. No 8 Sonata; in F 4 mvts.   2ob 2ca 2hn bn.
MS parts: A-Wgm, VIII 8535 (Q 16366).   ★
CXB-9. No: 9 Sonata in C; 4 mvts.   2ob 2ca 2hn bn.
MS parts: A-Wgm, VIII 8535 (Q 16366).   ★

CXB-10. No: X Sonata; in F, 4 mvts.   2ob 2hn bn.   MS parts: A-Wgm, VIII 8535 (Q 16366);
CZ-Pnm. XLII.C.174, (as "Sonata in F"; leaf 2 of the bn pt is damaged). ★
CXB-11. No XI Sonata; in D, 4 mvts.   2ob 2hn bn.
MS parts: A-Wgm, VIII 8535 (Q 16366). *The head title on all parts is "Parthia".* ★
Pm (Leuckart: Basel, pn 122, 1973), ed. Daniel Nimetz, score & parts (as "Parthia in D"; with suggested
alternatives of flutes for oboes & clarinets for horns).
CXB-12. No: XII Sonata; in B♭, 4 mvts.   2ob 2hn bn.
MS parts: A-Wgm, VIII 8535 (Q 16366). ★
CXB-13. No: XIII Sonata; in C 4 mvts.   2ob 2hn bn.
MS parts: A-Wgm, VIII 8535 (Q 16366). ★
Pm (Leuckart: Basel, pn 122, 1973), ed. Daniel Nimetz, score & parts (as "Sonata in C"; for 2ob/fl 2hn/cl bn).
CXB-14. No: XIV Sonata; in C, 4 mvts.   2ob 2hn bn.
MS parts: A-Wgm, VIII 8535 (Q 16366). ★
CXB-15. No: XV Sonata; in G, 4 mvts.   2ob 2hn bn.
MS parts: A-Wgm, VIII 8535 (Q 16366). ★
CXB-16. No: XVI Sonata; in F, 4 mvts.   2ob 2hn bn.
MS parts: A-Wgm, VIII 8535 (Q 16366). ★
CXB-17. No: XVII Sonata; in C, 4 mvts.   2ob 2hn bn.
MS parts: A-Wgm, VIII 8535 (Q 16366). ★
CXB-18. No: XVIII Sonata; in D, 4 mvts.   2ob 2hn bn.
MS parts: A-Wgm, VIII 8535 (Q 16366). ★
CXB-19. No: XIX Sonata; in C, 4 mvts.   2ob 2hn bn.
MS parts: A-Wgm, VIII 8535 (Q 16366). ★
CXB-20. No: XX Sonata; in C, 4 mvts.   2ob 2hn bn.
MS parts: A-Wgm, VIII 8535 (Q 16366). ★
Pm (Leuckart: Basel, pn 124, 1973), ed. Daniel Nimetz, score & parts (as "Sonata in C", for 2ob/fl 2hn/cl bn).
CXB-21. Sonata Ia [altered, pencil, to "21"]; in F, 4 mvts.   2ob 2hn bn.
MS parts: A-Wgm, VIII 8535 (Q 16366). ★
CXB-22. Sonata VIIIa [altered, pencil, to "21"]; in F, 4 mvts.   2ob 2hn bn.
MS parts: A-Wgm, VIII 8535 (Q 16366). ★
CXB-23. No: VIIII [altered, pencil to "XXIII"] Sonata; in C, 4 mvts.   2ob 2hn bn.
MS parts: A-Wgm, VIII 8535 (Q 16366). ★
CXB-24. Sonata VI: [altered, pencil, to "24"]; in F, 4 mvts.   2ob 2hn bn.
MS parts: A-Wgm, VIII 8535 (Q 16366). ★
CXB-25. N: 3 Partita In F; 4 mvts.   2ob 2hn bn.
MS parts: CZ-Pnm, XLII.A.208. ★
CXB-26. N: 5 Partita in F; 4 mvts.   2ob 2hn bn.
MS parts: CZ-Pnm, XLII.A.213. ★
CXB-27. In D# [D major]. № 2. Marche [sic: in fact, a 5-mvt Parthia or Cassation in D major].   2ob 2hn bn.
MS parts: CZ-Pnm, XLII.A.235, (as by "Sig⁻ Matheo Besozzi"). ★

*BETTINELLI, Bruno *4 July 1913, Milan*
BYB-1. Ottetto, 1975.   2fl ob 2cl hn 2bn.
Pm (Carisch: Milano, pn 21966, 1976), score & parts

*BEUTEL VON LATTENBURG, Felix Valerian *(1780)*
FEL-1m. Marsch in C N.1.   2ob 2cl 2hn 2bn.   (?Auto)MS score (1815): CZ-Pu, 59 R 749. ★

BEVAN, Clifford James *1934, UK*
CJB-1. Suite.   fl ob 2cl bn.
Pm (MGP; now Piccolo Press: Winchester, Hampshire, UK, sd), score & parts.

*BIALAS, Günter *19 Sept 1907, Bielschowitz, Upper Silesia.*
GYB-1. Partita, 1963.   fl 2ob 2cl 2hn 2bn db.
Pm (Bärenreiter: Kassel, pn BA 3958, 1969), score.
GYB-2. Romanza e danza für Bläser-Oktett nach J. Meyerbeer [i.e. Meyerbeer's opera, *L'Africaine*], 1971.
2ob 2cl 2hn 2bn.
Pm (Bärenreiter: Kassel, pn BA 6179, 1977), score.

BIANCAMANO, Angelo *1964*
AGB-1. Il pioppo [The poplar].   2fl 2ob 2cl 2hn 2bn.
Pm (Berben: Ancona, Italy, pn 2978, c.1988), score & parts.

*BIBER, Heinrich Ignaz Franz von *12 Aug 1644, Wartenberg, Bohemia - 3 May 1704, Salzburg*
*HIB-1v. In Festo Regnum Mottetum Natale à 6.   CC, 2fl 2ob vlne org.
MS pts (provenance: parish church of Sv. Jakub, Brno): CZ-Bm, A.1547. ★

*BIBL, Rudolf *6 Jan 1832, Vienna - 2 Aug 1902, Vienna*
*RXB-1v. Zum 50 Jahrigen Regierungs-Jubiläum Sr Majestät Kaiser Franz Josef I. 1848 - 1898. Graduale.
Gloria et honore, coronasti eum, Du hast ihn gekrönt mit Ruhm und Ruhm.
SATB chorus, 2ob 2hn 2tp a-tb t-tb b-tb timp.
(?Auto)MS score ("comp im Jänner [sic] 1898"): A-Wn, Mus.Hs.3109. ★

*BIGGS, Edward Smith *(c.1765 - c.1820)*
ESB-1m. Lady Ann Townsend's March.   2ob(+ 2cl, doubling) 2hn 2bn.
Pc (Rt. Birchall: London, c. 1810), score: GB-Lbl, h.721.x.(7). ★

BILLEMA, Carl (Charles) *(?1830)*
CBB-1a. Verdi: Les Vêpres siciliennes, "Polka-Mazurka".   pic fl 2ob 2cl 4hn 2bn 2tp 3tb bomb timp b-dr+tri.
MS parts: D-DT, Mus-n 2047.

*BINDER, ( ) *(1770), active 1802*
QXB-1. Casacion [sic] in Dis [E♭]; 4 mvts.   2cl 2hn bn.
MS parts (by Augustin Erasmus Hübner, Langenbruck, 1802): CZ-Pu(dm), 59 R 3356.   ★
QXB-2. Parthia in Dis [E♭]; 4 mvts.   2cl 2hn bn.
MS parts (by Augustin Erasmus Hübner, Langenbruck): CZ-Pu(dm), 59 R 3348.   *"Author Mozart" appears (almost certainly incorrectly) on the cl I and bn parts; Binder's name appears on all parts.*   ★

*BIRD, Arthur H. *23 Sept 1856, Belmont, Mass. - 22 Dec 1923, Berlin*
*AHB-1. Serenade, Op. 40; 5 mvts, (1898).   2fl 2ob 2cl 2hn 2bn.
MS: US-Wc, ML96.B55 case.
Pm (Margun Music: Newton Center, MA, pn MM 069, c.1985) score & parts.   ★
*AHB-2. Suite in D, 4 mvts (WoO, 1889).   2fl 2ob 2cl(A) 2hn 2bn.
MS: US-Wc, ML96.B55 case.
Pm (Margun Music: Newton Center, MA, pn MP 1012, c.1986), score & parts.   ★
Pm (Compusic: Amsterdam, pn 233, 1988), score & parts.
AHB-3. Nonet for Woodwinds (Marche miniature); 1886 - 1887.   pic 2fl 2ob 2cl 2bn.
Pm (Margun Music: Newton Centre, MA, pn MM 057, 1985), score and parts.   ★

*BIRTWISTLE, *Sir* Harrison *15 July 1934, Accrington, UK*
*HXB-1. The World is Discovered, 1960.   2fl ob ca cl cl/bhn/(b-cl) 2hn 2bn harp guitar.
Pm (Universal Edition: London, pn UE 12937, 1963), score.
*HXB-2. Verses for Ensembles, 1969.   pic(a-fl) ob(ca) cl(E♭, cl B♭) cl(B♭)+b-cl hn bn(cbn) 3perc.
Pm (Universal Edition: London, pn UE 15331, 1972), score.
HXB-1v. The Fields of Sorrow, 1971-72.   SS chorus, 3fl 2ca 3b-cl hn 2bn vibraphone 2pianos.
Pm (Universal Edition: London pn 15462, 1973), score.

*BISCH (Bische), Johann *(1760)*
WJB-1m. Recueil de marches et pas redoublés.   pic 2cl 2hn 2bn serp b-dr cym.
MS parts: D-Bds, Hausbibl, No. 399.
WJB-1a. Pieces [sic] d'Harmonie à six parties, tirées des oeuvres de Mr Pleyel; 8 mvts.   2cl 2hn 2bn.
Pc (chez J. André: Offenbach s/M; pn 470, 1792), B.2038, RISM [P 3006]: pts: CZ-Pnm, XLII.A.211, (complete); D-HER, (cl I only); H-Bn, ZR 701/1-6 (missing hn II); S-Skma (cl I only); GB-Ljag, (modern MS score & pts).
Pc (Imbault: Paris, pn 262, 1792), B.2040, RISM [P 3007], parts: S-Uu, Utl.instr.mus.tr. 145, 149 - 151, (missing cl II, hn II).   *Details of movements are given in the Arrangements List at PLEYEL, Composite Works, p. 415.*

*BISCHOFF, Ernst Ferdinand *(?1800)*
EIB-1. Introduction und Thema mit Variationen nach C.M. v. Weber.
fl 2ob cl(E♭) 3cl(B♭) 2hn 2bn 2tp 3tb b-hn b-dr t-dr tri.   AutoMS score: D-DT, Mus-n 360.   ★

BISHOP, *Sir* Henry Rowley *18 Nov 1786, London - 30 April 1855, London.*
HRB-1m. Grand March composed Expressly for, and presented to The Royal Society of Musicians, London, by Henry R. Bishop[,] May 26th 1827.   fl 2ob 4cl 2hn 2bn 2tp b-tb serp.
AutoMS score: GB-Lbl, Add. 34,725, ff. 1 - 7.   *The Trio is occasionally mistaken for a second march.*   ★
HRB-1t. Funeral March for the Duke of Wellington, (October, 1852).
2fl 2ob 4cl b-sax 4hn 2bn 2tp 3tb oph serp perc.   AutoMS score: GB-Lbl, R.M. 21.d.14, f.83 bis.
HRB-1e. Fortunatus & his Sons.   scoring varies.   MS score: GB-Lbl, Add. 33,570.
  1.1e. Nos. 17 & 18. All° Spiritoso Alla Marcia.   2hn 2to b-tb timp.   ff. 43 - 44.   ★
  1.2e. No. 20. Behind Scenes. Andantino, 6/8, 16 bars.   2fl 2hn 2bn(unison) harp.   ff. 47 - 47b.   ★
  1.1ve. No. 6. Chorus: Fortunatus why delay?   SATB, 2fl 2cl 2hn 2bn 2tp b-tb.   ff. 14 - 17.   ★
HRB-2e. The Coronation of Charles X, overture & march, (1825).   Orchestra, with 2 military bands (one behind the curtains).   AutoMS score: GB-Lbl, Add. 33570, f.139 bis & f.172 bis, respectively.

BISSEL, Keith *12 Feb 1912, Medford, Ontario, Canada*
KXB-1. A Folk-song Suite; 1960.   2fl 2cl b-cl/bn.
Pm (Boosey & Hawkes: New York, pn 1322, 1963), score & parts.
KXB-2. Serenade; 1972.   2fl/ob 2hn bn.   MS score: C-Tcm.

*BITSCH, Marcel *29 Dec 1921, Paris*
MXB-1. Concerto.   Piano solo, 2fl ob 2cl 2hn 2bn 2tp 2tb.
Pm (Alphonse Leduc: Paris), score.

*BITTERMAN, Carl Friedrich (Charles Frédéric)
CDB-1m. Marche pour le Corps de Janitscharen.   fl 2ob 2cl(C) 2hn 2bn 2tp serp+b-tb b-dr+cym s-dr+tri.
MS score: D-Mbs, Mus.Mss.3052.   ★

BJÖRKMAN, Rune *12 April 1923 - 29 Aug 1976*
RUB-1. Melodes; 1976.   2fl 2ob 2cl 3hn 2bn 3tp 3tb tu db timp(glock) perc.   MS score: S-Sic.

*BLACHER, Boris *19 Jan 1903, Niu-chang, China - 30 Jan 1975, Berlin*
*BZB-1. Virtuose Musik, 1966.   Solo vl, 2fl ob 2cl 2hn bn tp tb timp perc harp.
Pm (Bote & Bock: Berlin, 1967), score.
*BZB-2. Sonata für 2 Violoncelli und 11 Instrumente ad libitum.   2 solo cellos, 2fl ob 2cl 2hn bn tp harp perc.
Pm (Bote & Bock: Berlin, 1972), score (2 cellos only), hire ad lib wind parts.
BZB-3. Estnische Tänze, Op. 9, 1936.   10 winds (?2fl 2ob 2cl 2hn 2bn).
Pm (Bote & Bock: Berlin, 1935). *Not published; MS presumed destroyed during World War II.*

BLACKBURN, Maurice *22 May 1922, Quebec - 29 March 1988, Montreal*
MYB-1. Concertino, C major.   Solo piano, 2fl 2ob 2cl 2hn 2bn 2tp 2tb.
Pm (Canadian Music Centre: Toronto 1948), score.

BLACKWELL, I[saac]. G. *(1780)*
IGB-1m. A Grand Divertimento[:] Military March [with minor section & trio].   2fl ob 2cl 2hn 2tp 2basso.
Pc (Printed for the Author: London, 1809), score: GB-Lbl, h.102.(8). *March only; not a full-scale divertimento.* ★

BLACKWOOD, Easley *21 April 1933, Indianapolis*
EZB-1. Chamber Symphony, Op. 2.   2fl ob 2cl hn bn tp tb db.
Pm (Elkan-Vogel: New York, pn 50339640 [Archive edition], 1955), score.
EZA-1v. Un Voyage à Cythère, Op. 20, 1966.
S, fl(pic) ob(ca) 2cl hn bn tp tb db; *(NB: Chester Hire Catalog lists 2fl ob).*
Pm (G. Schirmer: New York, 1967), aitograph facsimile (Schirmer's Study Scores No. 110) & hire parts.

***BLAKE, David Leonard** *2 Sept 1936, London*
***DZB-1.** Nonet, 1971/78.   fl(pic) ob ob(ca) cl cl(b-cl) 2hn 2bn.
Pm (Novello: Borough Green, pn 89 0098 01, 1979), facsimile study. (A set of parts is deposited in GB-Lmic.)
***DZB-2.** Cassation, 1979.   ob ob(ca) cl(sax) cl(cl in E♭, b-cl) hn hn(maracas) bn bn(cbn).
Pm (Novello: Borough Green, pn 89 0116 04), score.   (A set of parts is deposited in GB-Lmic.)

***BLAKE, Howard** *1938, London*
HZB-1. Serenade for wind octet.   2ob 2cl 2hn 2bn.
Pm (Faber Music, London, 1990), score & parts.

BLANK, Allan *27 Feb 1925, Bronx, NY*
AZB-1. Polymorphics; 1988.   2fl 2ob 2cl 2hn 2bn.   MS score: US-NYamc.
AZB-1a. Paganini: Caprice in A minor, Op.1, No. 24.   2fl 2ob 2cl 2hn 2bn.
Pm (Associated Music Publishers: New York, London, 1978), score & parts.

***BLASIUS, Matthieu (Matthäus) Frédéric** *23 April 1758, Lauterbach, Alsace - 1829, Versailles*
***MFB-1.1.** Ouverture; P.2308.   2fl 2ob 2cl 2hn 2bn 2tp 3tb serp.
Pc (Mag de mus fêtes nat: Paris, brumaire an III, 1794), liv 8, No. 1, RISM [B 2859], parts: D-WRtl;
F-Pn, (2 copies), H2. 8,1, H2. 125 a-n; F-Nm, vol 22207. ★
***MFB-1.2.** Ouverture [?rescored Leroy].   2p-fl(F) 2ob 2cl(III & IV, C) 2hn 2bn tp serp timp.
Pc (In: Leroy. PQL-1.12, No. 68/61, Journal d'Harmonie, 12me Livraison), CH-Zz, AMG XII 3075, No. 68/61.
MFB-2. Harmonie; 8 mvts.   2cl 2hn 2bn.
Pc (Chez Chanel: Lyon; sn: Paris, pn 31, sd), RISM Supp [BB 2859a], parts: I-Mc, Da Camera A.18.12. ★
   2.1. Blasius: Allegro Mod[era]to, C.   2.2(a). Haydn: String Quartet, Hob. III/61ii, Adagio [ma non troppo].
   2.3. Blasius: Minuetto (& Trio). 2.4. Blasius: Allegretto Louré, 6/8. 2.5(a). Leroy: Rondo, All^tto non troppo, 2/4.
   2.6. [?Blasius]: Andantino, 2/4.   2.7. Blasius, Waltz, 3/8.   2.8. Blasius: Pot Pourri.
MFB-1m. Harmonie Militaire Contenant Marches, Pas Redoublés, Roudeaux et Walse [sic]; 4 Liv., 4 mvts each.
fl(D) cl(F) 2cl(C) 2hn 2bn tp b-tb serp b-dr; (Liv. III, Nos. 2 & 3 add tri, also No. 3: Clarinette Solo in C).
Pc (Gaveaux ainé: Paris, sd, c.1816 - 1826), Livres 1 - 4, parts: F-Pn, Vm27 214, (1 - 4). ★
MFB-1a. Dalayrac: Ouverture et [5] Airs de Maison à vendre, (1800).   pic 2cl 2hn 2bn tp b-tb.
Pc (Imbault: Paris, pn 735, O.H.H.178 *and* 735, c.1800), RISM [D 392], parts: D-AB, (missing cl I, tp tb);
F-Pn, Vm27 1049. *The "O.H.H." plate number indicates that the Ouverture was sold as a separate work.*
MFB-2a(-4a). Suites d'Harmonie tirés des Opéras nouvelles, No. [1], [MS: 2e, 3e].   2cl 2hn 2bn.
Pc (Imbault: Paris, pn 22, 285, 286, 1799-1802), pts: F-Pn, (2 copies), Vm7 6960(-6962), Vm7 10,530(-10,532). ★
   2a. Suite 1: 6 mvts without titles. *Some mvts may be original works by Blasius.*
   3a. Suite 2: [possibly from Blasius' *Africo et Menzola*, 1798].
      3.1a. Nargue de la tendresse.   3.2a. Écoutez [sic] cet Oiseau. 3.3a. Ô toi pour l'amour m'enflame.
      3.4a. Chansonette. 3.5a. Allegro, 6/8.   3.6a. Andante, 2. 7. Allegro, 2/4.
   4a. Suite 3: 6 mvts without titles. *Some mvts may be original works by Blasius.*

BLATNÝ, Pavel *14 Sept 1931, Brno*
PXB-1. Suite; 1958.   Piano solo, 2cl 2hn 2bn tp tb tu.
Pm (Editio Supraphon: Praha/Prague, 1968), score & parts.

***BLATTNER, Orrin**
ORB-1. 2 American Sketches.   2fl 2ob 2cl 2hn 2bn.
Pm (Music Publishers' Holdings, *via* M. Witmark: New York, 1942), score & parts.

***BLAYNEY, James** *(1770), Master of the Band, 1st Regiment of Foot Guards.*
JPB-1m. Three Grand Military Pieces, [March, Pas Doublé, Quick March],…Dedicated to the Officers of the
Brigade of Foot Guards. *The GB-Ob copy bears an inscription from the 49th Demi Brigade in the French
Service (cf. JPB-2m).*   2fl 2cl(E♭) 2cl(B♭) 2hn 2bn tp serp b-dr, muffled drum, loud drum.
Pc (Goulding, Phipps & D'Almaine: London, c.1803), score: GB-Lbl, g.270.v.(4); GB-Ob, Mus.61c.56(19). ★
JPB-2m. A Second Grand March from the 49th Demi-Brigade, arranged for a Full Band…Humbly Dedicated…to
the Officers of the Brigade of Foot Guards.   2fifes pic cl(E♭) 2cl(B♭) 2hn 2bn tp serp, muffled drum, loud drum.
Pc (Goulding, Phipps & D'Almaine: London, c.1801), score: GB-Ob, Mus.1c.303. ★

***BLECHA, Oldřich** *(1910)*
See also: KARLOVSKÝ, K. KUK-1a. Malá dechová harmonie, (harmonized Blecha, scored Karlovský).
OZB-1. Pro jugoslav. No. 1: cl(E♭) cl(B♭) 2hn 3tp 2flug b; Nos. 2 - 4: cl(E♭) 3cl(B♭) 2hn 3tp 2b-flug b.
AutoMS score: CZ-PLa, Hu 4082.
   1.1. Oj, Kozaro, [8 bars].   1.2. Nabrosimo kose.   1.3. Mladá partyzánka.
   1.4. Slovanů stráž, [missing the text by Stanislav Petrbok].
   1.5. Jarní písnička, [text: Josef Sládek]; without instrument parts.
OZB-1m. Marchè [sic] Salut aux freres [sic] d'armes soldats Francias [sic]. Pozdrav francouzským bratřím.
Pochod koncertní. Marché dédiée s[ci] aux défenseurs héroïques de la Liberté-nobles fils de la grande France
par l'auteur.   pic 2ob cl(E♭) 3cl(B♭) 4hn 2bn 2crt 4tp b-tp t-hn bar-hn 2tb b-tb bassi b-dr+cym s-dr.
AutoMS score ("Siberia - Irkutsk: 27./6. 1919. Vydána partitura co rukopis Ministerstvem Voj, na Rusi"):
CZ-PLa, Hu 3913. AutoMS parts (as "Opus 66"): CZ-PLa, Hu 3914.

OZB-2m. Pochod - Branného sboru čs. motoristů [B.S.Č.M.], 1938.
pic fl 2ob cl(E♭) 3cl(B♭) 4hn 2bn 2crt 4tp b-tp t-hn bar-hn 2tb b-tb bassi b-dr+cym s-dr.
AutoMS score: CZ-PLa, Hu 4027. *Hu 4026 is the same work scored for orchestra.*
OZB-1ma. J. Nesnídal: [songs], Pochod plzeňské posádky, Op. 112, 1935.
pic 2ob cl(E♭) 3cl(B♭) 4hn 2bn 2crt 4tp b-tp t-hn bar-hn 2tb b-tb 2bassi b-dr s-dr.
AutoMS score: CZ-PLa, Hu 3997. *Hu 3998 is the same work scored for orchestra.*
OZB-1a. Lidové tance z Plzeňska. 2cl 2hn tp tb. AutoMS score (20 - 26 ledna [Jan] 1948): CZ-PLa, Hu 4083.
    1.1a. Trio pochodu mokřinské kapely.   1.2a. Měj se dobře staré košatino (Sousedská).
    1.3a. Andulko z Koterova (Sousedská).   1.4a. Co sedláci, co děláte? (Sousedská).   1.5a. Plzenačka (Polka).
    1.6a. Za tou, za tou, za tou . . . (Sousedská).
OZB-2.1a. "Plzeňka" (Polka) [= OZB-1.5a]. 2cl 2hn tp tb tu. AutoMS score: CZ-PLa, Hu 4084.
OZB-2.2. Masopustní polka [without Trio]. 2cl 2hn tp tb tu. AutoMS score (1948): CZ-PLa, Hu 4086.
OZB-3a. [Suite/Potpourri]. cl(E♭) cl(B♭) 2tp flug b-flug tu drums. AutoMS score: CZ-PLa, Hu 4085.
    1.1a. Co sedláci [= OZB-1.4a].   1.2a. Za tou [= OZB-1.6a].   1.3a. Co sedláci [= OZB-1.4a].
    1.4a. Měj se dobře [= OZB-1.2a].   1.5a. Za tou [= OZB-1.6a].   1.6a. Pochod v Es dur [March in E♭].
    1.7a. Emilka Polka [Anon, arr Blecha].   1.8a. [untitled piece in 3/4].   1.9a. "Plzeňka" Polka [= OZB-1.5a].
OZB-4a. [5 pieces from Plzeň]. cl(E♭) cl(B♭) 2tp b-tp 2flug b-flug b. AutoMS score: CZ-PLa, Hu 4157.
    4.1a. Přiletěla vrána. Skoro pochodem.   4.2a. V tom křimickém zámku.   4.3a. Ještě já se ohlídám.
    4.4a. U potůčka zarmoucený sedím.   4.5a. Když jsem k vám chodíval.
OZB-5a. [7 pieces]. cl(E♭) cl(B♭) 2tp b-tp 2flug b-flug b. MS score: CZ-PLa, Hu 4159.
    5.1a. Hubička [hezká je] (A já obrázek mám).   5.2a. Na Sv. Ducha.   5.3a. Já hezká, ty hezkej.
    5.4a. Hej duli.   5.5a. Hej šup.   5.6a. Na rozloučení.   5.7a. Ta Plneňská brána.
OZB-6a. [2 picese]. cl(E♭) cl(B♭) 2tp b-tp 2flug b-flug b. AutoMS score: CZ-PLa, Hu 4158.
    6.1a. Já mám jabloňku.   6.2a. Maděra.
OZB-7a. [Suite/Potporri], 28 mvts. cl(E♭) cl(B♭) 2tp b-tp 2flug t-hn bar-hn b. MS parts: CZ-PLa, Hu 4160.
    7.1a. U potůčka zarmoucený sedím [= OZB-4.4a].   7.2a. Když jsem k vám chodíval [= OZB-4.5a].
    7.3a. Na rozloučení [= OZB-5.6a].   7.4. V tom křimickém zámku [= OZB-4.2a].
    7.5a. Hubička hezká je [= OZB-5.1a].   7.6a. Šla Nanynka do zelí.   7.7a. Měj se dobře [= OZB-1.2a].
    7.8a. [reprise of 6.5a].   7.9a. Přiletěla vrána. Skoro pochodem [= OZB-4.1a].   7.10a. [reprise of mvt 5].
    7.11a. [reprise of mvt 6].   7.12a. Já hexká, ty hezkej [= OZB-5.3a].   7.13a. [reprise of mvt 5].
    7.14a. [reprise of mvt 12].   7.15a. Hrály dudy.   7.16a. Ta Plneňská brány [sic, = OZB-5.7a].
    7.17a. [reprise of mvt 12].   7.18a. Hej duli - duli.   7.19a. Pojdte chlapci (Půj dome se podívati).
    7.20a. [reprise of mvt 5].   7.21a. [reprise of mvt 15].   7.22a. [reprise of mvt 12].   7.23a. [reprise of mvt 5].
    7.24a. Ja mám jabloňku. [= OZB-6.1a].   7.25a. Na Sv. Ducha [=OZB-5.2a].   7.26a. [reprise of mvt 25].
    7.27a. [reprise of mvt 4].   7.28a. Maděra [= OZB-6.2a].

BLOCK, Hans Volker *1940, Austria*
HOB-1. Bläseroktett; 1971. 2fl ob cl hn bn tp tb.
Pm (Doblinger: Wien, 1978), miniature score (pn Stp 412), parts (pn 0 6613).

*BLOCKX, Jan *25 Jan 1851, Antwerp - 26 March 1912, Kapellenbos*
JWB-1. Het looze visschertje (The artful fisherman), folk song arrangement. 2ob 2bn. MS score: B-Ac.

*BLOMBERG, Erik *6 May 1922, Järnskog*
EKB-1. Blåsklang; 1981. 3fl 3ob 3cl 3hn 2bn cbn 3tp 3tb 2tu. MS score: S-Sic.
EKB-2. Blåsklang II; 1982. 3fl 3ob 3cl 3hn 2bn cbn 3tp 3tb 2tu. MS score: S-Sic.
EKB-3. Blåsklang III; 1982. 3fl 3ob 3cl 3hn 2bn cbn 3tp 3tb 2tu. MS score: S-Sic.

BLOMDAHL, Karl Bigger *1916 - 1968*
KBB-1. Kammerkonzert. Solo piano, pic 2fl 2ob ca 2cl b-cl 2bn cbn b-dr s-dr cym tri bongos tam-tam xly.
Pm (B. Schott's Söhne: Mainz, London, 1957), hire facsimile of AutoMS score: GB-Ob, Mus.131.b.16.(2).

*BLOMHERT, Bastiaan *3 May 1944, Groningen*
BQB-1a. Françaix: Concerto pour Contrebasse. Solo db, fl fl(pic) ob ob(ca) cl cl(b-cl) 2hn 2bn.
Pm (B. Schott's Söhne: Mainz, London, 1988), hire score & parts.
BQB-2a. Mozart: Die Zauberflöte, full opera arrangement (overture & 31 mvts).
fl(pic) ob ob(ca) 2cl 2hn 2bn db glock. MS score & parts: NL-DHblomhert.
*BQB-3a. Mozart: Orgalwalzemusik, K.594, (1994). 2ob 2c 2hn 2bn.
Pm (Doblinger: Wien, 1995), score & parts.
*BQB-4a. Mozart: Orgelwalzemusik, K.608, (1995). 2ob 2cl 2hn 2bn.
Pm (Doblinger: Wien, 1995), score & parts.
*BQB-5a. Mozart: Orgelwalzemusik, K.616, (1988). 2ob 2cl 2hn 2bn.
Pm (Doblinger: Wien, 1995), score & parts.
*BQB-6a. Poulenc: L'histoire de Babar. Speaker, fl fl(pic) ob ob(ca) cl cl(b-cl) 2hn bn bn(cbn) tp tu.
Pm (Chester Music: London, 1983), hire score & parts.
BQB-7a. Strauss the Younger: Die Fledermaus, overture. fl fl(pic) 2ob 2cl 2hn 2bn db/cbn.
Pm (Compusic: Amsterdam, 1994), score & parts.

*BLUMENTHAL, Casimir von *d. Lausanne 1849*
CYB-1. Harmonie in C, 4 mvts. 2ob 2cl 2hn 2bn 2tp - [& probably cbn with bn II].
MS parts (c.1819): CZ-Bm(au), A.35.153, (missing bn II, tp II).

BLUMENTHAL, Josef (Jacques) von *1 Nov 1782, Brussels - 9 May 1850, Vienna*
JVB-1a. Grosser Marsch aus dem Trauerspiel König Lear. 2ob 2cl(C) 2hn 2bn tp.
Pc (Im Verlage der k:k: priv: Chemischen Druckerey: Wien, pn 1474, 1810/1811), parts: E-Mm, K.846.(7). ★
MS parts (rescored by Anton Schneider, 1823, for fl(D) 2ob 4cl(C) 2hn 2bn tp b-tb cb): D-Rtt, Sm. 23, No. 13.

*BLUMENTHAL, Leopold von *(?1780)*
LDB-1m. II Märsche…für die erste Division der bürgl Grenadiers. 2ob cl(F) 2cl(C) 2hn 2bn cbn 2tp.
Pc (In Verlage der k: k: pr: chemische Druckerey: Wien, pn 2116, 1813/1814), parts: E-Mam, K.846.(8). ★

*BN. (B., Bnn.), E.S.T.M, *Mons.* *(the initials may be a motto) (1720)*
ETB-1. Ouverture ex D# [D major]; 5 mvts.   3ob 2hn 2bassi.   MS parts: D-SWl, Mus. 271.   ★
ETB-2. Ouverture ex D# [D major]; 5 mvts.   3ob 2hn 2bassi.   MS parts: D-SWl, Mus. 279.   ★
ETB-3. Ouverture ex D# [D major]; 5 mvts.   3ob 3hn 2bassi.   MS parts: D-SWl, Mus. 281.   ★
ETB-4. Ouverture ex F; 5 mvts.   3ob 2hn 2bassi.   MS parts: D-SWl, Mus. 283.   ★
ETB-5. Ouverture ex F; 5 mvts.   2ob 2hn 2bn.   MS parts: D-SWl, Mus. 272.   ★
ETB-6. Ouverture ex F; 5 mvts.   2ob 2hn 2bassi.   MS parts: D-SWl, Mus. 278.   ★
ETB-7. Ouverture ex D# [D major]; 6 mvts.   2ob 2hn 2bassi.   MS parts: D-SWl, Mus. 280.   ★
ETB-8. Ouverture ex F; 5 mvts.   2ob 2hn 2bassi.   MS parts: D-SWl, Mus. 282.   ★
ETB-9. Ouverture ex F; 5 mvts.   2ob 2hn 2bassi.   MS parts: D-SWl, Mus. 284.   ★
ETB-10. Ouverture alarmij ex D# [D major]; 2ob 2hn 2bassi.   MS pts: D-SWl, Mus. 285.   ★
ETB-11. Partia; in F, 2 mvts.   2cl(C) 2hn bn(I) bn(II)/basso tp.   MS parts: D-SWl, Mus. 556.   ★

BOARA, Giovanni, *"del fu Gio Veneziano"* *(active 1833 - 1860)*
Boara's works in I-Vsmc also include many fragmentary sets of parts, some of which may have been scored for
winds.   Boara's works in I-Vsmc are divided into 2 packets.
GZB-1. Marcia.   2cl 2hn tp tb timp organ.
MS parts: I-Vsmc, packet I.   ★
GZB-2. Marcia No. 2, 1857.   2cl 2hn tp tb timp organ.   MS score & pts: I-Vsmc, packet I.   ★
GZB-1v. No. 18 Credo, L.D.B.M.V, 1836.   Credo: TTB, 2cl 2hn bn 2tp timp organ(bc-fig); Et incarnatus est:
TTB, 2cl(C) 2hn bn organ(bc-fig); Crucifixus: Solo T, TTB chorus,2cl(C) bn 2tp organ(bc-fig); Et resurrexit:
TTB, 2cl(C) 2hn bn 2tp timp organ(bc-fig)).   MS score & parts: I-Vsmc, packet I.   ★
GZB-2v. No. 16 L.D.B.M.V. Gloria.   Solo TTB, 2cl 2hn bn 2tp timp organ(bc-fig).
MS score & parts: I-Vsmc, packet I.   ★
GZB-3v. Inno del Presioni Sangue, Festivis resonent compita vocibus.   TTB, 2cl 2hn bn 2tp vlne organ(bc-fig).
MS score & (incomplete) parts: I-Vsmc, packet II.   ★
GZB-4v. Kyrie N: 15, L.D.B.M.V., 1835.   TTB, 2cl 2hn bn 2tp timp organ(bc-fig).
MS score & parts: I-Vsmc, packet II.   ★
GZB-5v. Credo.   TB chorus, 2cl 2hn tp tb timp organ.   MS score & parts: I-Vsmc, packet I.   ★
GZB-7v. Haec tua Virgo: Inno di S. Catterina da Siena, "per la Chiesa di SS. Gio: e Paolo.
Solo TTB, 2cl 2hn tp tb timp organ(bc-fig).
MS score & pts: I-Vsmc, packet II.   ★
GZB-8v. Gloria.   Solo TB, 2cl 2hn tp tb timp organ.   MS score & parts: I-Vsmc.   ★
GZB-9v. Requiem.   TTB(solo+rip), 2cl 2hn tp tb vlne timp.
MS parts: I-Vsmc, packet III, (missing T(I) concertante & ripieno, B concertante, ?organ).   ★
GZB-10v. Kyrie a 2 [sic] voci & Credo.   TTB, 2cl 2hn tp tb vlne timp organ.
MS score & parts: I-Vsmc, packet II.   ★
GZB-11v. Domine Deus.   Solo Baritone, 2cl 2hn tp organ.   MS score & parts: I-Vsmc, packet I.   ★
GZB-12v. Inno di S. Spiridione, Anno 1860, ("Si questis miracula").   TTB, 2cl 2hn organ.
MS score & parts: I-Vsmc, packet II.   ★

BOCCADORO, Carlo *1963, Italy*
CCB-1. Octet.   2ob 2cl 2hn 2bn.
Pm (Casa Musicale Sonzongo di Piero Ostali: Milano, 1992), score & parts.

*BOCHMANN, ( ) *(?1800)*
XUB-1. Introd[uction] & Var[iationen] in A♭.   pic 2ob cl(E♭) cl(B♭ prin) 3cl(B♭) 2hn 2bn 2tp 3tb serp b-dr s-dr.
MS parts: D-DT, Mus-n 1579.   ★
XUB-2. 15 pièces.   fl(E♭, F) 2ob cl(E♭) cl(B♭ solo) 3cl(B♭) 2hn bn bn+serp 2tp a-tb t-tb b-tb b-dr s-dr.
MS parts: D-DT, Mus-n 1580.   ★

*BOCHSA, Carl (Karl, Charles), *Père* *c.1760, Bohemia - 1821, Paris*
Victor Dufaut purchased the stock of Bochsa's publishing firm in 1819 and some of the "self-published" works
were reissued c.1824 by Dufaut & Dubois (who became a partner in March 1821).
CZB-1. Ouverture Militaire, Op. 29.   2fl 2ob/cl(C) 2cl(C) 2hn 2bn tp b-tb serp b-dr.
Pc (Chez CH^LES Bochsa Père, Auteur: Paris, pn 88, c.1811/12), pts: F-Pn, (2 copies), Vm27 341, Vm7 10538.   ★
MS parts: D-Rtt, Sm.14, No. 25.
*CZB-2. Trois Pot-pourris, Op. 25.   2cl 2hn 2bn.
Pc (Chez Ch^les Bochsa Père, Auteur: Paris, 1811/12), parts: F-Pn, (2 copies), Vm7 10539, Vm27 342.   ★
Hoboken incorrectly assigns a date of 1809 and parts for b-dr tri in CZB-1a(-3a); he also incorrectly states that
the slow movement in CZB-3a is that of Haydn's Symphony No. 102.   We cannot rule out the possiblity that these
Haydn arrangements are, in fact, by R.N.C. Bochsa (qv).
CZB-1a. Haydn: Symphony No. 85 ("La Reine").   2fl 2cl 2hn 2bn tp b-tb serp.
Pc (Duhan, repr: Dufaut & Dubois: Paris, pn 1, 1802), parts: F-Pn, (2 copies), Vm 7 10542, Vm27 2073 (1).
CZB-2a. Haydn: Symphony No. 91.   2fl 2cl 2hn 2bn tp b-tb serp.
Pc (Duhan: Paris, pn 488, 1816) as "Symphony No. 3", parts: CH-Gpu, Ib.4726; F-Pn, (2 copies), Vm 7 10544,
Vm25 33.
CZB-3a. Haydn: Symphony No. 102, mvts 1, 3, 4, with mvt 2 of Symphony 104.   2fl 2cl 2hn 2bn tp b-tb serp.
Pc (Duhan: Paris, pn 487, 1816), as "Symphony No. 2", parts: CH-Gpu. Ib. 4727, F-Pn, (2 copies) Vm7 10543,
Vm27 2073, (2).

*BOCHSA, Robert Nicolas Charles, *Fils* *9 Aug 1789, Montmédy - 6 Jan 1856, Sydney, Australia*
RNB-1v. Messe de Requiem de Louis XVI; 1815/1816.
ATB chorus, 2terz-fl ob ob(ca) 2cl 4hn 2bn 4tp b-tb serp cb timp(muffled) tam-tam.
Pc (Pleyel & Bochsa: Paris, c.1816), parts: F-Pn, D. 7418; I-Fc, A.21.   ★
Pm (WINDS: Northridge, CA, pn W-36, c.1981), (photocopy) score & parts.
RNB-1ac. Boieldieu: La Dame blanche, cavatine.   cl(E♭) cl(B♭, premier) 2cl(Bb) 2hn 2bn 2tp b-tb.
MS parts: I-Mc, Noseda C.55.2, ("arrangé par Charles B.").

*BODE, ( ) *(? Johann Joachim Christoph Bode, 1730 - 1793)*
ZYB-1m. Marsch No 1 Mit Flautraver [sic] ex E# (E major).   2fl 2hn bn.
MS score: D-SWl, Mus. 3284, No 1.   ★
ZYB-2m. Marsch No 2 Mit Flautraver [sic] ex D# (D major).   2fl 2hn basso(= bn).
MS score: D-SWl, Mus. 3284, No 2.   ★
ZYB-3m. Marsch No 3 Mit Hobo [sic] de Amor ex D# (D major).   2obdam 2hn bn.
MS score: D-SWl, Mus. 3284, No 3.   ★

BODENSOHN, Ernst Freidrich Wilhelm *(1900)*
ENB-1. Kleine Bläserserenade "Im alten Stil".   2fl/2ob/ob+vl 2cl 2hn 2bn.
Pm (Edition Bodensohn: Baden-Baden, pn EA 55, 1935), score & parts.

*BODINUS (Bodini), Sebastian   *c.1700 - 1756, Dulach (Konzertmeister at Baden-Durlach)*
SQB-1. Symphony in D; 3 mvts (Siciliane, Aria, Tempo di Menuet).   2fl/ob 2hn b-c.
MS parts: D-KA, Mus.Hs.58.   ★
Pm (Mannheimer Musik-Verlag: Bonn, sd), ed. Kurt Janetzky, score & parts.

BOEDIJN, Gerd (Gerardus Hendrik; used the pseudonym: "Jack Harvay")
19 April 1893, Hoorn - 23 Sept 1972, Hoorn
GGB-1. 5 Concertante Epigram-Schetsen, Op. 159.   2fl 2ob 3cl 2hn 2bn 2tp timp perc piano.
Pm (Molenaar: Wormeveer, via Donemus: Amsterdam, 1959), score.

BÖGLE, ( ) [Georg, *OSB*, 1734 - 1796 *or* Anton, *OSA*, 1768 - 1825]
XWB-1v. Offertorium; in F.   CTB, fl cl 2hn organ.   MS parts: D-FÜS, 3, (missing vocal & organ pts).   ★

BOEHM, Yohanan *1936 - 1986, Israel*
YQB-1. Little Suite, Op. 27; 1957.   2fl 2ob 2cl 2bn.   MS score: US-BLu.
YQB-2. Divertimento, Op. 20.   2fl 2ob 2cl 2bn.
Pm (Israel Music Publications Ltd: Jerusalem, post-1958).

*BÖHNER, Johann Ludwig (Louis) *7 Jan 1787, Töttelstadt, nr. Gotha - 28 March 1860, Gotha.*
We have not located his 3 grosse Märsche und Trios *for* 3cl 2hn bn cbn 2tp *(Gombart: Augsburg, 1817).*
JLB-1v. Motetta "Preise Jerusalem den Herrn".   SATB, ob 2cl 2hn 2tp 3tb timp.   MS: D-Bds, Mus.Ms.2100.

BÖRJESSON, Lars-Ove *1953, Sweden*
LOB-1. Sextet, Op. 31; 1981.   2cl 2hn 2bn.   MS score: S-Sic.

*BOIELDIEU, (François) Adrien   *16 Dec 1775, Rouen - 8 Oct 1834, Jarcy*
FDB-1m. Six Marches Militaires.   2fl(D) 2cl(F) 2cl(C) 2hn bn 2tp tb serp b-dr cym.
Pc (Jean George Naigueli [Naegeli]: Zürich, post-1803 - 1814), pts: H-KE, K 2202, (No. 1, G, only).   ★
FDB-1v. Hymnes et Cantiques No. 1, "Amitié sainté et fraternelle" (text by Pouschkin [sic, i.e. Vasily Lvovich
Pushkin, uncle of Aleksander, the poet).   Nos. 2 - 4 are probably by Cavos (qv).   ATTB, ob ca 2cl(C) 2hn 2bn.
Pc (sn, "pour la R. des Amis Réunis": St Petersburg, c.1810 [the imprint is misleading, stating "à Jerusalem" with
the Masonic date 5810]), score: GB-Lbl, E.497.ii.   ★

BOLARDT, Thomas *(1820)*
TYB-1. Trauermarsch.   2cl 2hn 2tp tb flug.   AutoMS (1846): CZ-Pnm, XX.F.294.   ★

BON, Willem Frederik *1940 - 1983, Netherlands*
WIB-1. Passacaglia in blue.   2fl 2ob 2cl 2hn 2bn tp tb db.
Pm (Donemus: Amsterdam, 1972), score.
WIB-2. Sketches, Op. 21.   2fl 2ob 2cl hn 2bn tp 2vc db.
Pc (Donemus: Amsterdam, 1968), score.

*BONASEGLA, Carl Philipp *1779 - post-1810; horn I in the Kapelle of Gräfin Charlotte zu Bentheim-Steinfurt*
CHB-1a. Walzer et Eccoss [sic], c.1810.   2fl 2cl 2hn 2bn tp(clar).
MS parts (1810): D-BFb, B-on 40.   *An arrangement of his own Walzer, (D-BFb, B-on 46).*
CHB-2a. Gluck: Armide, Gesang, "Reçois de notre amour".   terz-fl ob 2cl 2hn bn tp(clar) cb.
MS parts: D-BFb, G-1u 6 hoch 2.

*BONDON, Jacques *6 Dec 1927, Boulbon, France*
QJB-1. Symphonie Concertante, 1978.   Solo piano, 2fl 2ob 2cl 2hn 2bn.
Pm (Eschig: Paris, 1979).

BONDT, Cornelius de *1953, Netherlands*
COB-1. Bassoon Concerto.   Solo bassoon, 2ob 2cl 2hn bn tp tb db.
Pm (Donemus: Amsterdam, 1977), score & solo part.

*BONNO (Bono), Joseph (Guiseppe) *29 Jan 1711, Vienna - 15 April 1788, Vienna*
See also: Anonymous Works - Austro-Bohemia: Český Krumlov, Schwarzenberg Harmonie.
JGB-1. No. 9, Parthia in Dis [E♭]; 5 mvts.   2ca 2hn bn 2vla.   MS parts: CZ-Pnm, XLII.C.274.   ★
JGB-2. Parthia in C; 12 mvts.   2ob 2hn bn.   MS parts: CZ-Pnm, XLII.B.164.   ★
JGB-3. Parthia in F; 4 mvts.   2ob 2hn bn.   MS parts: CZ-Pnm, XLII.C.26.   ★
JGB-4. Parthia in C; 6 mvts.   2ob 2hn bn.   MS parts: CZ-Pnm, XLII.C.176.   ★
JGB-5. No. 7 Parthia In C; 6 mvts.   2ob 2hn bn.   MS parts: CZ-Pnm, XLII.C.317.   ★
JGB-6. Parthia in Dis [E♭] alla Camare [sic]; 4 mvts.   2ca 2hn bn.   MS pts: CZ-K, symfonie Nr. 243.K.II.   ★
JGB-7. Parthia in Dis [overwritten correctly: C] alla Camare [sic]; 4 mvts.   2ca 2hn bn.
MS parts: CZ-K, symfonie Nr. 244.K.II.   ★
JGB-8. No: 4 Parthia In C; 5 mvts.   2ca 2hn bn.   MS parts: CZ-Pnm, XLII.A.300.   ★
JGB-9. Nro IIItio Parthia In C; 5 mvts.   2ca 2hn bn.   MS parts: CZ-Pnm, XLII.C.25.   ★
JGB-10. N: 1 Barthia [sic] in "E♭"; 5 mvts.   2ca 2hn bn.   MS parts: CZ-Pnm, XLII.C.50; CZ-K, symfonie
Nr. 223.K.II, (here as an anononymous "Parthia in Es" , with 2 sets of ca I & bn parts).   ★
JGB-11. Parthia in F; 4 mvts.   2ca 2hn bn.   MS parts: CZ-Pnm, XLII.C.191.   ★

BONSEL, Adriaan *4 Aug 1918, Hilversum*
ADB-1. Folkloristische Suite, 1958.   fl fl(pic) 2ob 3cl 2hn 2bn 2tp timp perc.
Pm (Donemus: Amsterdam, sd), score.
ADB-2. Octet.   fl(pic) 2ob 2cl hn 2bn.
Pm (Donemus: Amsterdam, 1975), score & parts.

BONVIN, Ludwig *17 Feb 1850, Siders, Switzerland - 18 Feb 1939, Buffalo, USA*
LXB-1. Mélodie, Op. 56b.   fl 2ob 2cl 2hn 2bn.
Pc (Breitkopf & Härtel: Leipzig).
LXB-2. Romanza, Op. 19a.   fl ob 2cl 2hn 2bn.
Pc (Breitkopf & Härtel: Leipzig).

*BOOREN, Jo van den *14 March 1935, Maastricht*
DJB-1. Rofena, Op. 79.   2fl 2ob 2cl 3hn 2bn 2tp tb tu timp.
Pm (Donemus: Amsterdam, 1990), score.
DJB-2. Sextet, Op. 60.   2cl 2hn 2bn.
Pm (Donemus: Amsterdam, 1987), score & parts.

*BORDES, Charles *12 May 1863, La Rochelcorbon - 8 Nov 1909, Toulon*
CAB-1. Divertissement (Fantaisie) pour trompette et orchestre [in fact, for winds and percussion: 3fl 2ob 2cl 2bn 4hn 2tp 3tb tu 4perc timp celeste 2pianos 2harps].
Pc (Salabert: Paris).

BORDORF (Bordoux), Jean Erneste *(1770)*
JNB-1m. Nouveau Marsch, in E♭, c.1800.   2ob 2cl 2hn 2bn tp.
MS score: D-B, Mus.Ms.2337 (with the MS imprint: "Marchand de Musique à Lewin").   ★

*BOROVÝ, Antonín *12 June 1755, Sedlak - 29 March 1832, Zlatá Koruna*
AOB-1v. Offertorium pastorale.   SATB, 2fl 2hn organ.
MS parts (24 Dec 1789): CZ-Pnm, VI.C.107, (provenance: parish church, Zlatá Koruna).   ★

BORREMANS, Joseph *25 Nov 1775, Brussels - 15 Dec 1858, Ukkel*
JQB-1. Sérénade nouvelle à huit parties.   2cl 2hn 2bn 2vla.
Pc (Gravée par Madame Neyts, se vend à Bruxelles chez Weissenbruch, sd), parts: B-Bc

BORRIS, Siegfried *4 Nov 1906, Berlin - 23 Aug 1987, Berlin*
SZB-1. Oktett, Op. 25, No. 3.   fl ob cl b-cl 2hn bn tp.
Pm (Sirius Verlag, now Heinrichshofen: Wilhelmshaven, 1952), score (pn 8816) & parts (pn 8817).
SZB-2. Oktett, Op. 55; 1951.   fl ob cl b-cl 2hn bn tp.
Pm (Sirius Verlag, now Heinrichshofen: Wilhelmshaven, 1978), score (pn 8828) & parts (pn 8829).

BORTOLOTTI, Mauro *1926, Italy*
MOB-1. Homage to India.   2ob 2cl 2hn 2bn.
Pm (Edipan Edizioni Musicale: Roma, sd).

*BOSER, ( ) *(1730) Possibly Carlo di Bose, composer of instrumental music at Dresden (cited by Sainsbury)*
YYB-1(-7). [8] Partia Nr. 1 [-3, 5 - 8]; (C, G, C, F, G, C, F).   2fl 2talia 2hn bn.
MS parts (1768): D-Z, Mus.VI, 1/1-7, missing No. 4.   ★

BOSSI, Renzo Rinaldo *1883 - 1965, Italy*
RRB-1. La Fata Morgana e l'orca.   2fl 2ob 2cl 2hn 2bn 2tp 2tb piano.
Pm (Francesco Bongiovanni: Bologna, sd).

BOSSLER, Kurt *10 July 1911, Duisburg - 1976*
KZB-1. Divertimento, 1974.   2cl 2hn 2bn.
Pm (privately printed: Heidelberg-Gaiberg, c.1974).

*BOST (Rost), ( )
YZB-1. Harmonien No. 1 [&] No. 2; 7 mvts (3 + 4, consecutively numbered), in B♭.   3cl 2hn 2bn tp.
MS parts: D-Tl, Gg 130.   ★

BOTTENBURG, Wolfgang Heinz *1930, now resident in Canada*
WHB-1. Octet; 1972.   fl(pic) ob cl 2hn bn tp tb.   MS score: C-Tmc.

*BOUFFIL (Boufil), Jacques-Jules *14 May 1783, Muret - 1868, ?Paris*
JJB-1. Six Airs Variés Précédé d'une Ouverture et suivis d'un Pot-pourri d'Airs nationaux, Oeuvre 6, [MS: 1ᵐᵉ] Livraison [Ouverture, Airs variées 1 - 4], [MS: 2ᵐ] Livraison [Airs variées, 5, 6, Potpourri] .   fl 2cl 2hn 2bn.
Pc (Chez Gambaro: Paris, pn 54, 1814), parts: GB-Ljag(w), (Liv. 1 only).   ★
JJB-1a. Boieldieu: La Dame blanche, overture & 4 Suites (mvts: 1 - 4, 5 - 8, 9 - [10.5], 11 - 13).
fl(pic) 2cl 2hn 2bn obbligato, (ad lib: 2cl tp b-tb serp).
Pc (Janet et Cotelle: Paris, pn 2051J.C.-2054J.C., 2126J.C., post-1825), parts: CH-Gpu, Ib.4810a (3ᵉ Suite), Ib.4810b (2ᵉ Suite), Ib.4810c (4ᵉ Suite); D-DO, Mus.Drkw.3250; I-Mc, Noseda C.57.5, (incomplete: missing hn II overture & cl I - III suites 1 - 4; provenance: "Musique du Pensionnat de Freibourg"; with MS parts (overture only) for: Partie-Direction, cl(Eb), cl(B♭) I & II, hn II, tp(II á piston Eb), tb I & II, a-oph, oph(C), tuba-cleide, b-dr+cym s-dr).
MS parts: I-Mc, Noseda C.55.2, (Cavatine only; parts for cl(E♭), premier cl(B♭) 2cl(Bb) 2hn 2bn 2tp b-tb).

BOULIANE, Denys *1955, Canada*
DEB-1. "A propos . . . et le Baron perché"; 1985.   2b-cl 2hn 2cbn tp 2tb db.   MS score: C-Tmc.

BOWEN, Edwin York *1884 - 1961, UK*
EOB-1. Miniature Suite.   fl ob 2cl bn.
Pm (De Wolfe: London, sd), score & parts.

BOWMAN, Kim *1957, Netherlands*
KXB-1. Ermita.   2fl 2ob 2cl 4hn 2bn 2tp tb tu.
Pm (Donemus: Amsterdam, 1992), score.

*BOYLE, Rory *11 March 1951*
RQB-1. Sorceries, Charms and Spells (1991, for the Bournemouth Wind Quire).   2cl 2hn 2bn.
MS parts: GB-BFlowes.   Pm (?Chester Music: London), hire score & parts.

*BOZZA, Eugène *4 April 1905, Nice - 28 Sept 1991*
*EUB-1. Octanphonie.   2ob 2cl 2hn 2bn.
Pm (Leduc: Paris, pn A.L.24.494, 1972) score & parts.
EUB-2. Symphonie da camera.   2ob 2cl 2hn 2bn.
Pm (Leduc: Paris, 1960), score & parts.

BRACCINI, Luigi (Roberto) *1756, Florence - 1791, Florence*
LRB-1v. Miserere.   SATB, 2cl 2hn 2bn.   MS score & parts: I-Fc, F.P. Ch.9, (with 2 sets of vocal parts).

*BRÄUTIGAM, Helmut *16 Feb 1914, Crimmitschau - 17 Jan 1942, Ilmensee*
HYB-1. Kleine Jagdmusik, Op. 11 (Veränderungenen über "Auf, auf zum fröhlichen Jagen").   fl 2ob 2cl 2hn 2bn.
Pm (Breitkopf & Härtel: Wiesbaden, 1939, repr 1956), score (pn PB 4970) and pts (pn OB 4070).

*BRAHMS, Johannes *7 May 1833, Hamburg - 3 April 1897, Vienna*
Brahms' wind works can also be found in the following collected edition: **(GA)** *Johannes Brahms. Sämtlicher Werke. Ausgabe der Gesellschaft der Musikfreunde in Wien (Breitkopf & Härtel: Leipzig; 1926-28; vol. 19). A complete Urtext edition is in preparation by G. Henle Verlag, Munich, but publication dates are not yet known.*
*JHB-1v. Begräbnissgesang, Op. 13, 1858.   SATBB chorus, 2ob 2cl 2hn 2bn 2tb tu timp.
Pc (J. Rieter-Biedermann: Winterthur, pn 167, 1861, repr. c.1865), score & parts.   ★
Pm (GA 19, No. 6, pp. 124 - 134) reprinted (Breitkopf & Härtel: Leipzig, 1906) score, (Kalmus: New York, pn 1161, No. 2, sd), miniature score.
Pm ([unidentified]: Evanston, Ill, 1970), score.
*JHB-1va. F.P. Schubert: Sieben Gesänge, Op. 52 No. 2.   Ellens zweiter Gesang aus [Sir] Walter Scott's "Fraulein vom See"; (M.Ahn.Ia/17, 2nd version 1873).   Soprano solo, SSA chorus, 2hn(E♭) 2hn(B♭ basso) 2bn.
Pm (Deutcher Brahms Gesellschaft: Berlin 1906), score.
Pm (Kalmus: New York, pn 1161 No. 4, sd), miniature score.
Pm (Phylloscopus Publications: Lancaster, UK, pn PP 157, 1994), score & parts, (with additional parts for 2ob 2cl to augment the vocal parts).

*BRAKKEE, Stefaan *(1960)*
STB-1.1a. Debussy: Petite Suite.   2ob 2cl 2hn 2bn.
Pm (Compusic: Amsterdam, pn 268, c.1994), score & parts.
STB-1.2a. Debussy: Petite Suite.   2ob 2ca 2hn 2bn.
Pm (Compusic: Amsterdam, pn 250, c.1994), score & parts.

BRAMBILLA, Paolo *(1786 or 9 July 1787), Milan - 1838, Milan*
PYB-1v. Tantum ergo.   Solo B, TTB chorus, 2cl(C) 2hn tp tb vlne timp organ.
MS score & parts: I-Vsmc.   ★

*BRAUER, Max *1855, Mannheim - 2 Jan 1918, Karlsruhe   A pupil of Franz Lachner.*
MZB-1. Pan suite.   2fl 2ob 2cl 2hn 2bn db.
Pm (Breitkopf & Härtel: Leipzig, 1934).

*BRAUN, C.A.P. *(1790)*
CRB-1. Quatuor, Oe. 1; in D, 3 mvts.   2fl 2hn
Pc (Au Bureau de Musique de A. Kühnel: Leipzig, pn 959, 1812), parts: GB-Ljag(w), L.270.   ★

*BRDIČKA, František (Franz) *(1770), active 1805*
FIB-1. Parthia 1 in B[♭]; 4 mvts.   2cl 2hn bn.
MS parts (by Augustin Erasmus Hübner, Langenbruck, 1805): CZ-Pu(dm), 59 R 3334, No. 1.   ★
FIB-2. Parthia 2 in B[♭]; 4 mvts.   2cl 2hn bn.
MS parts (by Augustin Erasmus Hübner, Langenbruck, 1805): CZ-Pu(dm), 59 R 3334, No. 2.   ★

*BREITENBACH, Joseph Heinrich *1809 - 1866, Switzerland*
HKB-1t. Marcia funèbre.   fl cl(E♭) 2cl 2hn 2bn.
MS: CH-E.

*BRENDLER, ( )
ZZB-1m. [?6] Maerche; (C, C, F, C, C, E♭).   2ob 2cl 2hn 2bn, ("flautino" given as option for ob I in No. 2; pic replaces ob I in No. 5).   MS pts: CZ-Pnm, XLII.C.205. *Only the first march is credited to Brendler.* ★

*BRESCIANI, Bartolomeo Antonio *(1790), Maestro di Capella Cattedral, 1827*
BAB-1v. Miserere.   TTB, 2fl 2ob 2cl 2hn 2bn 3tb timp.
AutoMS score & MS parts: I-BRd, palch. 5-39/I.

*BRESCIANI, Giovanni Battista *(1770), Maestro Concertatore al Teatro Grande, Brescia, 1810*
BNB-1v. [Messa breve in D minor] Chirie [sic], Gloria e Credo.   TTB solo & chorus, 2cl(A) 2hn cb organ.
MS parts: I-BRd, palch. 5-41/I, (with duplicate vocal & cb pts and a pt for "clar e cor").
BNB-2v. Pange Lingua Oblig^{to} [sic] con Istromenti di fiatto Per la Precessione del Corpus Domini a Quingano.
CATB, 2ob 2hn bn.   AutoMS score: I-BRd, palch. 5-35/I, (with a duplicate set of vocal parts).

*BRESGEN, Cesar *16 Oct 1913, Florence - 7 April 1988, Salzburg*
CEB-1. Jagdkonzert.   Solo horn, fl ob 2cl hn 2bn db.
Pm (B. Schott's Söhne: Mainz, 1939).

BRESNICK, Martin *13 Nov 1946, New York*
MTB-1. Introit; 1969.   2fl 2ob 2cl 4hn 2bn 2tp 2tb.
MTB-2. Bread and Salt; 1984.   2fl 2ob 2cl 2sax 2hn 2bn vc db.

*BRIDGEMAN, Charles *20 Aug 1778, Hertford, UK - 3 Aug 1873, Hertford, UK.*
CLB-1m. 18 Marches for the Use of the Hertfordshire Volunteers. (Nos 1, 2:) 2cl 2hn (2)bn tp; (Nos 3 - 8:)
2"B.Fifes" 2cl 2hn (2)bn tp; (Nos 9 - 18:) fife & piano.
Pc (Broderip & Wilkinson: London, c.1800), score: GB-Lbl, g.137.(28); GB-Ob. Mus. Instr. I.29(8).   ★
  1.1m, 1.2m. The Hertford Volunteers Slow March / Quick March.
  1.3m, 1.4m. The St Albans Volunteers Slow March / Quick March.
  1.5m, 1.6m. The Royston and Barkway Volunteers Slow March / Quick March.
  1.7m, 1.8m. The Bishop Hatfield Volunteers Slow March / Quick March.
  1.9m, 1.10m. The Ware Volunteers Slow March / Quick March.
  1.11m, 1.12m. The Hitchin Volunteers Slow March / Quick March.
  1.13m, 1.14m. The Bishop Stortford Volunteers Slow March / Quick March.
  1.15m, 1.16m. The Wormley Volunteers Slow March / Quick March.
  1.17m, 1.18m. The Hunsden Volunteers Slow March / Quick March.

*BRINER, Beat *(1960)*
BEB-1a. Arvo Pärt: Fratres; 1977.   2ob 2cl 2hn 2bn perc(claves tomtom).
Pm (Universal Edition: Wien, etc, 1990), score (pn UE 19 814) & parts (UE 19 815).
BEB-2a. Stravinsky: Four Norwegian Moods.   2ob 2cl 2hn 2bn.
Pm (? Universal Edition: Wien, 1996), hire score & parts.

*BRISCOLI, Domenico *(1770), flourished 1800-1815, Dublin.*
DOB-1.1(-1.3). Three Grand Overtures entitled The Conversation of the five Nations. 2fl 2cl 2hn tp b-hn.
Pc (S. Holden: Dublin, c.1810), parts: GB-Lbl, h.1560.e.   ★
Pm (WINDS: Northridge, CA, pn W-107, W-108, W-109, c.1981), photocopy of modern MS score & parts.
  1.1. The Italian. 1.2. The German and French. 1.3. Grand Medley of the Five Nations.

BRIXEL, Eugen *27 March 1939, Mährisch Schönberg (now Šumperk)*
EGB-1. Panharmonicon.   fl 2cl 2tp tb.
Pm (Halter: Karlsruhe, 1976), score & parts.

*BRIXI, František *2 Jan 1732 Prague - 14 Oct 1771 Prague*
FZB-1. Nro 4 Parthia; in D; 5 mvts.   2ob 2hn 2bn.
· MS parts: CZ-Pnm, (2 copies), XXII.B.82, XXII.E.61/35, (as an anonymous "Partita").   ★
FZB-2. Parthia in Dis [E♭] Nro 1; 5 mvts.   2talis/ca/a-cl(C) 2hn bn.
MS parts: CZ-Pnm, XXII.B.79. *The cover calls for "Talia 2bus" but the parts are marked "Corno Ingl[ese]:";*
the a-cl(C) pts are later replacements.   ★
FZB-3. Intermezzo Nro 2; in B♭; 4 mvts.   2talis/a-cl 2hn bn.
MS parts: CZ-Pnm, XXII.B.80.   ★
Pm (Česky hudební fond: Prague, 1988), hire MS score No. 2328, (for 2ca 2hn 2bn).
FZB-4. Nro 3 Parthia in Dis [E♭]; 4 mvts.   2talis/a-cl(C) 2hn bn.
MS parts: CZ-Pnm, XXII.B.81.   ★
FZB-5(+). Unverified works for octet and 2ob 2hn 2bn in CZ-Pk, (?MS parts).

BROEGE, Timothy David *1947*
TDB-1. Sonatas & Fantasies.   2ob 2cl 2hn 2bn.   MS score: US-NYamc.

BRÖSEL, ( ) *(1720)*
ZYB-1m. Parade à 7 ex Des dur [sic: E♭]; 3 mvts.   2ob 2bn bn(ripieno) tp.
MS pts (?c.1750): D-DS, Mus.ms.1223/2, (with a duplicate Oboe Primo part).   ★
ZYB-2m. Parade à 5 ex des dur [sic: E♭]; 3 mvts.   2ob 2bn tp.
MS pts (?c.1750): D-DS, Mus.ms.1223/1.   ★
ZYB-3m. Parade. Stücke à 5 ex dis [E♭]; 3 mvts.   2ob 2bn tp.
MS pts (?c.1750): D-DS, Mus.ms.1223/24.   ★

*BROOKS, James *(1760) - (pre-1813, Bath)*
*JRB-1m. Thirty Six Select Pieces for a Military Band Consisting of Marches, Quick-Steps, Minuets & Rondos.
2cl 2hn bn (tp - No. 15 in the hn II part & No. 16 in the hn I part only).
Pc (Culliford, Rolfe & Barrow: London, c.1796), RISM [B 4589], (Benton B.8676), parts: GB-Lbl, b.82;
GB-Ob, Mus.61.d.2(6). *These pieces are single movement divertimentos, rather than parade pieces: 1. Dibdin*
(not one of his original band pieces); 2 - 8. Brooks; 9 - 13. Pleyel (IJP-12.6; also falsely attributed to Mozart as
K.C.17.10); 14 - 36 are presumably all by Brooks, although Nos. 19, 25 - 29 do not identify the composer(s).   ★

BROWN, Christopher (Roland) *17 June 1943, Tunbridge Wells*
CTB-1v. Tres Cantus Sacri, Op. 60.   SATB, timp, perc, (ad lib: fl(pic) fl 2ob 2cl 4hn 2bn 3tp 3tb tu organ).
Pm (Chester Music: London, 1984), hire score & parts.

BROWN, J.W.
WOB-1a. Lyadov: 8 Russian Folk Songs, Op. 58.   fl fl(pic) ob ob(ca) 2cl 2hn 2bn (b-cl ad lib).
Pm WOODWINDplus: Leeds, 1991), score & parts.

BROŽÁK, Daniel *1947, Netherlands*
DAB-1. Pastorale; 1976.   2fl ob cl bn 2tp tb piano b-gtr 2perc.
Pm (Donemus: Amsterdam, 1978), score.

*BRUCHSCHLÖGL (Bruchschloegl), ( ) *(1825)*
QQB-1. [6] National Stey'er.   fl(D♭) cl(E♭) 2cl(B♭) 2hn 2bn tp flug.   MS parts (c.1844): A-Sca, Hs.266.   ★

*BRUCKNER, Anton *4 Sept 1824, Ansfelden, Austria - 11 Oct 1896, Vienna*
Bruckner's wind works can be found in: **(GO)** *Göllerich, August. Anton Bruckner: ein Lebens- und Schäffens-Bild (edited Max Auer). (1922-1927) (Deutsche Musikbücherei. Bd. 36, Bd. 37, Tl.2, Bd. 38 Tl.2); repr (Bosse: Regensburg 1974).* **(RH)** *Sämtliche Werke. Kritische Gesamtausgabe...) (edited Robert Haas; Brucknerverlag: Wiesbaden, 1949, 1952).* **(LN)** *Sämtliche Werke. Kritische Gesamtausgabe (2 revidierte Ausgabe). Herausgeben von der Generaldirektion der Österreichisches Nationalbibliothek und der Internationalen Bruckner-Gesellschaft. Unter Leitung von Leopold Novak (Musikwissenschaftlicher Verlag der Int. Bruckner-Gesellschaft: Wien, 1951).*
*ANB-1v. Dom-Kantate (Festkantate) "Preiset den Herrn", (1862).
Baritone solo, TTBBchorus, 2fl 2ob 2cl 4hn 2bn 3tp 3tb timp
Pm (facsimile): (GO), A III/2, No. 2, pp. 197 - 216, score.
*ANB-2.1v. Mass in E minor, (1866, revised 1869 and 1876; 2nd version: 1882, revised 1885 and 1896).
SSAATTBB chorus, 2ob 2cl 4hn 2bn 2tp 3tb.
Pm (LN), Bd. 17, No.1, miniature score.
*ANB-2.2v. Mass in E minor, (2nd version 1886; revised 1885 and 1896).
SSAATTBB chorus, 2ob 2cl 4hn 2bn 2tp 3tb.
Pm (L. Doblinger: Wien, 1896), score (pn D 2087) and parts (pn 2346).
Pm (Universal-Edition: Wien, Leipzig; c.1917), score.
Pm (Wiener Philharmonischer Verlag: Wien, 1924), ed. by Josef V. Wöss, Philharmonia Partituren 204.
Pm (RH), Bd. 13, miniature score.   Pm (LN), Bd. 17, No. 2.
*ANB-3v Kantate "Auf, Brüder! auf, und die Saiten zur Hand!", 1855.
TBB soli, TTBB chorus, solo horn, 2ob 2hn 2bn 2tp 3tb.
Pm (GO), 1928, A II/2, No. 35, pp. 229-239, (cued vocal score).
ANB-4v Kyrie from the (incomplete) Eb Mass.   SATB 2ob 3tb organ.
Pm (GO) A II/2, No. 17, pp. 86-93, (facsimile score, 58 bars).

BRÜGGEMANN, Kurt *1908, Germany*
KQB-1. Suite; 1954.   2ob ca 2bn.
Pm (Hieber Musikverlag: München, 1987), parts.

BRUGK, Hans Melchior *1909, Germany*
HAB-1. Divertimento, Op. 29; 1962.   fl ob cl 2hn bn tp.
Pm (Simrock: Berlin, now A.J. Benjamin Musikverlage: Hamburg, pn EE 3282, 1965), score & parts.

BRUMBY, Colin James *1933, Australia*
CNB-1. Doubles; 1965.   2fl 2ob 2cl 2hn 2bn.   MS score: GB-Lmic.

*BRUN, Georges *1878 - (?1918), France*
GRB-1. Passacaille, Op. 25.   2fl ob 2cl 2hn bn (db ad lib).
Pm (Lemoine: Paris, 1908).

BRUŠEK (Bruschek, Brusschek, Bruzzek), Joseph *(1770)*
JEB-1. Parthia in F [originally Eb]; 4 mvts.   2ob 2cl 2hn 2bn.
MS parts (by Johann Anton Handl): A-Wn, Mus.Hs.562. *The scoring of the parts differs from that listed on the titlepage: 3cl(C) 2hn 2bn. The clarinet parts are in the key of F (and may be for either C or Bb clarinets); the horn parts are marked "Corno Primo [Secundo] ex Dis [Eb]". There are 3 bassoon parts present: "Fagotto Primo" & "Fagotto Secundo", both in Eb, and a "Fagotto" part on different paper with the headtitle, "Parthia in F", with full divisi in mvts 2 - 4; at 3 points the Secundo part lies between the divisi of the Fagotto part. All parts except the Fagotto were hastily copied and the latter was probably added at a later date.* ★
JEB-2. Parthia in Dis [Eb], 4 mvts.   2cl 2hn 2bn.   MS parts (by Wydra): CZ-Pnm, XXIX.D.207.   ★
JEB-3. [7 Variations & a Coda].   2cl 2hn 2bn.   MS parts: CZ-KRa, A3841/IV.B.5.   ★
JEB-4. Parthia in Dis [Eb]; 4 mvts.   2cl 2hn bn.
MS parts (by Augustin Erasmus Hübner, Langenbruck): CZ-Pu(dm), 59 R 3352.   ★
JEB-5. Parthia in Dis [Eb]; 3 mvts.   2cl 2hn bn.
MS parts (by Augustin Erasmus Hübner, Schulgehilf aus Langenbruck, 1801): CZ-Pu(dm), 59 R 3353.   ★
JEB-6. Partia [headtitle: "Parthia"] in Dis [Eb]; 4 mvts.   2cl 2hn bn.
MS parts (by Augustin Erasmus Hübner, Schulgehilf aus Langenbruck): CZ-Pu(dm), 59 R 3354.   ★
JEB-1v. Salve Regina.   CAB, 2ob 2cl 2hn 2bn.   MS parts: I-MOe, Mus.D.38.   ★
JEB-2v. Salve Regina.   8 voices, winds.   MS: I-Fc, F.P. Ch.1033.

*BUCHAL (Bouchal, ?Buchnal), Johann Anton *(1770)*
JAB-1a. J.S. Mayr: Ginevra di Scozia & Méhul: Une Folie. Stücke aus Ginevra und Une Folie . . . N° 4 z cyklu Harmony Stücke, Łańcut den 16 July '804 [sic].   2cl 2hn bn.   MS parts: PL-LA, RM 38.
JAB-2a. Paer: [Achille], Achilles. N° 5 z cyklu Harmony Stücke, Łańcut den 10 Jully '804.   2cl 2hn bn.
MS parts: PL-LA, RM 39.
JAB-3a. J. Weigl: [Alcina, Stücke aus Allcina . . . z cyklu Harmony Stücke, Łańcut den 23 Jully . . . [1]804.
2cl 2hn bn.   MS parts: PL-LA, RM 36.
Buchal signed another version (PL-LA, RM 45, dated "Wien 22-25 April [1]803") as copyist, arranged for 2cl 2hn 2bn; he probably based his arrangement on that copy.
JAB-4a. J. Weigl: Richard Löwenherz & Die Spanier auf der Insel Christina. Stücke aus Richard Lövenherz [sic] und Insel Christina . . . N° 6 z cyklu Harmony Stücke, Łańcut den 24 July [1]804.   2cl 2hn bn.
MS parts: PL-LA, RM 40.
JAB-5a. P. von Winter: [Das unterbrochene Opferfest], Stücke . . . N°3 z cyklu Harmony Stücke, Łańcut den 2 July [1]804.   2cl 2hn bn.   MS parts: PL-LA, RM 37.
JAB-1c. Harmoniemusik; in Bb, 4 mvts.   2cl 2hn 2bn.
MS parts: PL-LA, RM 131, (anonymous; bn II part signed by Buchal).   ★
JAB-1tc. Todten-Marsch (by "J. Buchnal").   2cl 2hn 2bn.   MS parts: CZ-KRa, III.B.233.   ★

BUCHANAN, Dorothy *28 Sept 1945, Christchurch, New Zealand*
DQB-1. Five Sketches, 1981.   2ob 2cl 2hn 2bn.   MS score: NZ-Wn.

BUCHOLTZ, Johann Gottfried *1725, Aschersleben - c.1800*
JTB-1(-3). 3 Parthias; (D, 2 mvts; D, 4 mvts; D, 2 mvts), 1766. 2ob 2hn 2bn.
MS parts: CZ-KRa, A4024, A4025/IV.B.198, Part 2, Parthias 1 - 3. ★

BUCK, Ole *1 Feb 1945, Copenhagen*
OYB-1. White Flower Music. 2fl 2cl tp.
Pm (Wilhelm Hansen: Copenhagen, 1965), hire score & parts.

BÜCHLER, ( ) *(See: PICHLER, Placidus 1722 - 96)*

BÜCHLER, Ferdinand *1817 - 1891*
FEB-1t. Marcia funebre. Componirt zum Begräbniss meines Freundes und Schulers Hermann Cumerl, die 15<u>ten</u>
Sept. 1846. fl ob 2cl hn(F) hn(C) 2bn b-tb. MS score & parts: D-DS, Mus.ms.156. ★
FEB-1v. Choral: Jesus mein. 2ob+2cl(C) 2hn 2bn. MS parts: D-DS, Mus.ms.156. ★
FEB-1ad. Graun: Auferstehen, ja Auferstehen. 2ob+2cl(C) 2hn 2bn. MS parts: D-DS, Mus.ms.156.

BÜCHTGER, Fritz *14 Feb 1903, Munich - 26 Dec 1978, Munich*
FRB-1. Nyktodia, Oktet. 2ob 2cl 2hn 2bn. Pm (Orlando Musikverlag: Munich, sd), score.

*BÜHLER (Bihler), Franz (Francesco) Gregor, *Abbate* *12 April 1760, Nördlingen - 4 Feb 1824, Augsburg*
FOB-1. Nacht Musique [sic] zu den 27<u>te</u> August 1797 in Oberbolzen; in C, 4 mvts. ob 2hn 2vla b.
MS parts: I-BZtoggenburg.
FOB-1c. [Anon divertimento, in F, 8 mvts]. Oboe solo, 2hn bn/vc 2vla. MS pts: I-BZtoggenburg, A/IV,23. ★
FOB-1v. Messe; in E♭. SATB chorus, fl 2cl 2hn 2bn 2tp 2vla vlne, organ. MS parts: D-Tl, B 010. ★
FOB-2v. Ecce panis, [II. In figuris praesignatur; III. Jesu nostri miserere], Musica in Solenitate Corporis Christi.
CATB, 2fl 2ob 2cl 2hn(F, C) 2bn tp(prin)+tp(clar ad lib) [b-tb] timp. MS pts (c.1790; b-tb c.1830): D-FÜS, 9. ★
FOB-3v. Tantum ergo. CATB, solo ca, 2fl 2cl 2hn 2bn 2tp(clar) timp vlne organ.
MS parts (1796): I-BZtoggenburg, (possibly missing a trumpet part).
FOB-4v. IV. Hymni: [4] Pange lingua ad Processionem in Festo SS. Corporis Christi.
SATB, 2fl 2cl 2hn 2bn 2tp(clar) timp.
Pc (Joannis Jacobi Lotter Filii: Augustae [Augsburg], c.1826), parts: D-Tl, Gg 138, (with the slip of the Augsburg
publisher Gombart e Comp.; the bn pts are pasted into Gg 454, as Nos. 76 - 79). ★
FOB-5v. Pange Lingua pro Solenni Processione in festo Corporis Christi; in C.
CATB, 2fl/(solo fl + 2fl) 2ob 2cl(C) 2hn 2bn 2tp(clar) timp.
MS parts: I-BZtoggenburg, A/V,4 (with 3 sets of duplicate vocal parts).
FOB-6v. Pange lingua et Musica pro Solenni Processione SSmi Corporis Christi.
CATB, fl 2cl 2hn 2bn 2tp tb timp. MS parts: I-BZtoggenburg, A/V,5.
FOB-7v. Tantum ergo. CATB, fl 2ob 2hn 2bn 2tp vlne organ. MS parts (1800): I-BZtoggenburg, A/V,49
(includes a *Genitori* with strings & tps; the hn pts are on the reverse of the tp pts).
FOB-8v. Chorus; "Anbetung, Preis und Ehre". CCTB, 2terz-fl 2cl 2hn 2tp b-tb vlne organ. MS pts: D-Tl, ZZe 18.★
FOB-9v. Heil und dank dem Sieger; [cantata in C]. CATB, 2fl 2ob 2cl 2hn bn tp(clar).
MS parts: I-BZtoggenburg, A/V,52.
FOB-10v. Ein Lied; "Gold lacht der Lag" [?sic]. CCTB, 2fl 2ob 2cl 2hn bn tp(prin). MS pts: I-BZtoggenburg.
FOB-11v. Veni Creator Spiritus et ave O gloriosa Domina. CATB, fl 2cl(C) 2hn bn/organ.
AutoMS score: D-Mbs, Mus.Mss.3205. ★
FOB 12v. Deutscher Gesang. SATB, 2vl/cl(A & C) 2fl 2hn vlne organ(bc-fig).
MS parts: CZ-Pnm, XXXVIII.F.205, (with 2 additional flute pts "ohne A Clarinetto"). *This is a full Deutsche
Messe; the phrase "oder B u. C Clarinett [sic]" following "2 Violon" on the wrapper is a later addition.* ★

BUERIS, John de *(1910), USA*
HJB-1. Petite pastorale; in E♭. fl ob 2cl bn.
Pm (George F. Briegel: New York, 1937), score & parts: US-Wc.

*BUHL, Joseph David *1781, Amboise - (?) post-1829*
JDB-1m(-4m). Quatre Marches / 1803. 1804[,] an 13 [1805/06] et 1829). Instrumentation unknown.
MS parts (post-1829): F-Pn, L. 9.644, (trumpet part only). ★
   1m. Marche composée en 1803 par David Buhl pour toutes les troupes légères.
   2m. Marche composée en 1804 pour la Garde Impériale. (arrangée par la trompette major de la Garde).
   3m. Marche adaptée par le Ministre en l'antreiz pour toutes les troupes à cheval.
   4m. Marche adaptée par le Ministre en 1829. Composée par David Buhl.

BUHR, Glenn
GLB-1. Montage. fl(pic) ob(ca) cl(b-cl) 2hn 2bn 2tp tu 2perc.
Pm (Dorn Publications: Medfield, MA, USA, c.1981), score & parts.

BULL, Eduard-Hagerup *1922, Norway*
EHB-1. Posthumes: in memoria J. Østhus et E.F. Bræn, Op. 47. 2fl 2ob cl hn bn cbn db. MS score: N-Oic.

BURCKART, J.V. *(?1680), active in Uppsala*
UJB-1. Ouverture à 4; in F, 6 mvts. 2vl/ob vla/talia bc/bn.
MS parts: S-Uu, Mus.instr.hs.13:21. Modern MS: GB-Ljag. *The wind options are written on the parts.* ★
UJB-2. Sonata à 4; in F, 3 mvts. 2vl/ob vla/talia bc/bn.
MS parts: S-Uu, Mus.instr.hs.13:22. Modern MS: GB-Ljag. *The wind options are written on the parts.* ★

BURDICK, Richard Oscar *1961, USA*
ROB-1. The Seasons Suite. 2ob 2cl 2hn 2bn. In MS: US-NYamc will assist in contacting the composer.

BURGON, Geoffrey *15 July 1941, Hambleside, Hants, UK*
GEB-1. Gendling. fl fl(pic) 2ob cl(b♭) 2cl 4hn 2bn cbn 2tp 3tb tu amp-vc(or pf) timp perc.
Pm (Chester Music: London, 1968), hire score & parts.

BURKE, John *1951, Canada*
BJB-1. Far calls, coming, far!; 1988. fl(pic) ob cl 2hn bn tp b-tb 3perc piano. MS score: C-Tcm.

*BURRELL, Diana *25 Oct 1948, Norwich, UK*
*DIB-1 Archangel, 1987.   2ob ca 3tp concertante, 3fl/pic 3cl 4hn 2bn cbn 2tb tu.
Pm (United Music Publishers: London, 1987), hire score & parts.

BURTCH, Mervyn *7 Nov 1929, Ystrad Myrnach, Glamorgan*
MEB-1v. Et in terra pax.   S solo, SSA chorus, 2ob 2cl 3hn 2bn 2tp timp perc, (or piano accompaniment).
MS score: GB-CDmic.

*BUSBY, Thomas *Dec 1755, Westminster - 28 May 1838, London*
*TZB-1e. Mrs. Wybrow's Pas Seul in the *Tale of Mystery*.   2fl 2cl 2hn 2bn 2tp tb serp.
Pc (E. Riley: London, 1802), score: GB-Lbl, h.1568.b.(1).   *From Thomas Holcroft's "Melo-drame" (Act II,
Scene 1, first performed 13 Nov 1802, London.* ★
TZB-1.1m(-1.10m). 10 Marches in the *British Military Journal*.
Pc (Richard Phillips: London, 1798 - 1801), scores: GB-Lbl, P.P.4050.ga. ★
    1.1m. The Field of Honour.   2fl 2cl 2hn bn tp serp.   (With the additional imprint, "Published as the act
       directs Octr. 1st 1798. By Hookham & Carpenter[,] Bond Street"), Vol. I, No. 1, October 1798.
    1.2m. British Valour.   2pic 2cl 2hn (2)bn 2tp serp.   Vol. I, No. 2, November 1798.
    1.3m. The Soldiers [sic] Joy, a Quick Step.   2cl bn; piano.   Vol. I, No. 3, December 1798.
    1.4m. The Triumph.   2pic 2cl 2hn bn tp serp.   Vol. I, No. 4, January 1799.
    1.5m. Flying Colours, a Quick Step, 2cl (2)bn; piano.   Vol. I, No. 5, February 1799.
    1.6m. The General.   2cl 2hn (2)bn 2tp serp.   Vol. I, No. 7, April 1799.
    1.7m. The Expedition.   A Quick Step. 2cl bn; piano.   Vol. I, No. 8, May 1799.
    1.8m. The Field of Mars.   2cl 2hn (2)bn.   Vol. I, No. 9, June 1799.
    1.9m. The Flying Camp.   2cl 2hn (2)bn.   Vol. I, No. 11, August 1799.
    1.10m. The Encampment.   2cl bn 2tp timp.   Vol. II, No. 30, March 1801.

BUSCH, Carl Reinhold *29 March 1862 Bjerre - 19 Dec 1943, Kansas City*
CQB-1. Septet: An Ozark Reverie.   fl ob 2cl 2hn bn.
Pm (Albert J. Andraud: Cincinnati, now Southern Music Co.: San Antonio, Texas, sd).
Pm (Fitzsimmons: Chicago, sd).

BUSCH, Dennis
DNB-1. Serenades, Op. 328.   fl ob 2hn bn.   MS score: US-NYamc.

*BUSCHMANN, ( ) *(1730)*
NYB-1. Parthia; in E♭, 3 mvts.   2cl 2hn 2bn.   MS parts (c.1760): D-Rtt, Buschmann 1. ★
NYB-2. Partitta; in E♭, 5 mvts.   2cl 2hn 2bn.   MS parts (c.1760): D-Rtt, Buschmann 2. ★

*BUSHELL, Geoffrey Clifford *7 Feb 1958, Croydon*
GCB-1. Strawberries and Cream, Op 20, 1986.   fl 2ob 2cl 2hn 2bn db/hn(III).
MS score & parts: GB-DIDbushell; GB-DOTstoneham.
GCB-1a. Golliwog's Cakewalk (Debussy), Op 16.   2fl 2ob 2cl b-cl/vc 2hn 2bn cbn/db.
MS score & parts: GB-DIDbushell; GB-DOTstoneham.

BUSSOTTI, Sylvano *1931, Italy*
SLB-1. Solo; 1978.   2fl ob obdam cl(B♭, cl in E♭) 2hn 2bn perc vc piano celeste harp.
Pm (Ricordi: Milano, pn 132760, c.1979), score.

*BUTLER, Martin (Claines) *1 March 1960, Romsey, UK*
MAB-1. From an Antique Land, 1982.   2fl 2ob 2cl a-sax 2hn 2bn 2tp 2tb tuba 2perc piano.
Pm (Oxford University Press: London, 1982), facsimile score (& hire parts).
MAB-2. Craig's Progress Suite [from the opera, MAB-1v].   2fl 2ob 2cl 2hn 2bn piano(4 hands).
Pm (Oxford University Press: London, 1997), hire score & parts.
MAB-1v. Craig's Progress; opera.   Voices, 2fl 2ob 2cl 2hn 2bn piano(4 hands) perc.
Pm (Oxford University Press: London, 1994), hire score & parts.

BUZZOLLA, Antonio *2 March 1815, Adria - 20 March 1871, Venice.*
ATB-1. Marcia.   2cl 2hn tp tb timp organ.   MS score & parts: I-Vsmc. ★

*C., I.H. *(possibly the "G.H.C." who copied Reid's (qv) Parthia, for the Kinský Harmonie)*
IHC-1ad. Righini: Armonia in F (VYR-1.4, 1797), 4 mvts.   2cl 2hn 2bn.   MS parts: CZ-Pnm, XX.F.110.
I.H.C.is almost certainly the copyist rather than the arranger.

*C., J. *(1790)*
XJC-1a. Rossini: Elisabetta Regina d'Inghilterra, Chor·(Marziale).   pic fl 2ob 2cl(A) 2hn 2bn tp b-dr s-dr.
MS parts: CZ-Pnm, Lobkovic X.G.f.b.72, *(the wrapper bears performance dates 23 Oct 1824 and 28 Oct 1825).*
XJC-2a. C.M. von Weber: Euryanthe, Jägerchor.   2cl 4hn 2bn.   MS pts: CZ-Pnm, Lobkovic X.H.a.6. *The horn
parts are "Corno Soprano in Es [E♭], Corno Alto in Es, Corno Tenore in B[♭] alto, and Corno Basso in Es.*

*CADOW, Paul *19 June 1908, Lübeck*
PXC-1. Pastorale in alten Stil.   2ob ca hn 2bn.
Pm (Ultraton: Osthofen; 1953), score & parts.
Pm (Grosch: München, 1992), score & parts.

*CAGLIERO, Giovanni, *"di Torino"* *1838 - 1926*
GXC-1v. Credo.   TTB, fl 2cl 2hn tp tb organ.   MS score & parts: I-Vsmc. ★
GXC-2v. Domine ad adjuvandum.   TTB(solo+rip), 2cl 2hn tp tb timp organ.   MS score & parts: I-Vsmc. ★
GXC-3v. Gloria.   TTB, fl 2cl 2hn tp tb timp organ.   MS score & parts: I-Vsmc. ★
GXC-4v. Kyrie.   TTB, 2cl 2hn tp tb organ.   MS score & parts: I-Vsmc. ★
GXC-5v. Dixit.   TTB(solo+rip), 2cl 2hn tp tb timp organ.   MS score & parts: I-Vsmc. ★

CALEGARI, G.F. *(1780), active c.1815 onward, Naples*
GFC-1. [untitled piece in C, 2/4].   cl(D) 4cl(C) 2hn 4crt(G, C) tp(prin) 2tocatti(ripieno, C) 2tb basso.
MS score: I-Mc, Noseda D.5.7. *A transitional work to the genre of "Armonia di Metallo" (brass band).* ★
GFC-1a. Rossini: La Gazza ladra, sinfonia.   "Grande Armonia".   MS score: D-BFb, R-os 117 hoch 2.

CALIFANO, Archangelo *(?1730)*
ARC-1. Sonata a 4 voci; in Bb, 4 mvts. 2ob 2bn. MS parts: D-HRD, Fü 2649a. ★

*CALIFF, Pietro
XXC-1. Sanctus & Agnus Dei. TTB(solo+rip), fl 2cl 2hn vlne/bn tp timp organ. MS score & pts: I-Vsmc, (the fl pt is not in the score; the "Violon o Fagotto" part bears the later pencil note, "Trombone"). ★

CALLHOFF, Herbert *13 Aug 1933, Viersen, Rhineland*
HXC-1. Movimenti. fl 2ob 2cl hn 2bn.
Pm (Gerig: Köln, pn HG 1089, 1973; reissued Breitkopf & Härtel: Wiesbaden), score & parts.
HXC-2. Transfigurationen, 1980. 2cl 2hn 2bn.
Pm (Gravis: Bad Schwalbach, pn 1427, c.1980), score & parts.

*CALVI, Girolamo *?, Piazza Brembara - 1848*
GIC-1. Serenade. pic fl cl(G) cl(D) 4cl(C) 4hn 3bn cbn+serpentone 2tp(naturale, in D) 2tp (G) 4tp(D) 2flug(C, obl)+flug(G) posthorn. MS parts: I-BGc(lc), Faldone 7, n. 140.
GIC-2. Sinfonia. 2fl 3cl(C) 2hn 2bn 2tp tb (organ).
(?Auto)MS score: I-BGc(lc), Faldone 2, n. 39. *The score bears the note, "Per la parte dell'organo si trascriva quella del fagotto 2°."*
GIC-3. Finale. pic fl 3cl 2hn 2bn 2tp tb (organ).
(?Auto)MS score: I-BGc(lc), Faldone 2, n. 42. *The score bears the note, "Per la parte dell'organo si trascriva quella del fagotto 2°."*
GIC-4. Introduzione e pastorale. pic fl 3cl 2hn 2bn 2tp tb.
(?Auto)MS score & parts: I-BGc(lc), Faldone 2, n. 44, (with additional pts for ob, 2vl vla vc).
GIC-5(-7). Tre divertimenti. pic fl 2cl 2hn bn tb cym.
MS parts: I-BGc(lc), Faldone 11, n. 178.
GIC-8, 9. Due divertimenti. pic fl 2cl 2hn bn tb.
MS parts: I-BGc(lc), Faldone 2, n. 40.
GIC-10. [Untitled piece]. 2fl 2cl 2hn 2bn. (?Auto)MS score: I-BGc(lc), Faldone 2, n. 38.
GIC-11. [Untitled piece]. pic fl 2cl 2hn bn.
(?Auto)MS score: I-BGc(lc), Faldone 2, n. 41, (incomplete).
GIC-12. [Untitled piece]. fl 2cl 2hn bn cym.
(?Auto)MS score: I-BGc(lc), Faldone 6, n. 124, (incomplete).
GIC-13. Divertimento per due flauti e fagotto. 2fl bn.
(?Auto)MS score & parts: I-BGc(lc), Faldone 2, n. 45.
GIC-1m. Marcia per banda. pic terz-fl(F) 3cl 2hn 2bn 2tp tb b-dr [& 1 unidentified part].
(?Auto)MS score: I-BGc(lc), Faldone 2, n. 43.
GIC-1v. Godiam godiam la vita. SSTB, pic(Ab) pic(Eb) fl 2cl 2hn 2bn 2tp tb tb+bassi.
(?Auto)MS score: I-BGc(lc), Faldone 5, n. 97.
GIC-2v. Vexilla. TTB, pic fl 2ob 2cl 2hn bn 2tp tb timp. (?Auto)MS score & pts: I-BGc(lc), Faldone 3, n. 51.
GIC-3v. Si queris miracula. Inno per processione. TTB, pic 2cl 2hn bn tb.
(?Auto)MS score & pic part: I-BGc(lc), Faldone 4, n. 67, (incomplete score).
GIC-4v. Brindisi per Sig. Carlo Arioli. TTB, pic 2cl 2hn tp tb.
(?Auto)MS score (1841): I-BGc(lc), Faldone 5, n. 104.
GIC-5v. Sanctorum meritis. TTB, fl 2cl 2hn tb. (?Auto)MS score: I-BGc(lc), Faldone 4, n. 65.
GIC-6v. Beatus vir. TTB, 2cl tp tb. (?Auto)MS score: I-BGc(lc), Faldone 5, n. 107.
GIC-7v. Inno per processione (Mysterium ecclesiae). TTB, fl 2cl tb.
(?Auto)MS score: I-BGc(lc), Faldone 2, n. 36, (incomplete).

*CAMBINI, Giuseppe Maria Gioacchino (Giovanni) *13 Feb 1746, Legnano, Italy - 29 Dec 1825, nr Paris*
There are discrepancies in reported instrumentations; we have usually followed Constant Pierre.
GGC-1m. Marches militaires. Instrumentation unknown. MS score: D-DS, (?lost in World War II).
GGC-1mv. Le pas de charge républicain; (P.44). SSATB chorus, 2cl 2hn 2bn 2tb serp tambour.
Pc (Boyer: Paris, 1794), RISM [C 317], parts: F-Pn, (2 copies), Vm7 7081, Vm7 16761. ★
GGC-2mv. Hymne à l'Être suprême; (P.64). Solo voice, 2ob 2cl 2hn 2bn tb serp organ.
Pc (Imbault: Paris, pn A.HH.3, 1793), RISM [C 309], score: D-B; F-Pn, (4 copies, including:) Vm7 7056. ★
GGC-3mv. Hymne à l'Égalité; (P.77). Solo voice, 2ob/cl 2hn (2)bn tb serp organ.
Pc (Imbault: Paris, pn A.HH.4, 1793), RISM [C 307], score: F-Pn, (4 copies, including:) Vm7 7059. ★
GGC-4mv. Les rois, les grands, les prêtres; (P.81). Solo voice, 2cl 2hn 2bn (2)serp basse.
Pc (Imbault: Paris, pn A.HH.5, 1793), RISM [C 306], score: D-B; F-Pn, (2 copies), Vm7 7062, Vm7 16755. ★
GGC-5mv. Ode sur les deux jeunes héros Barra et Viala, à l'époque de leur translation au Panthéon français; (P.74). Solo voice, 2cl 2hn bn 2tb basse.
Pc (Imbault: Paris, pn A.HH.6, 1793), RISM [C 313], score: D-B; F-Pn, (3 copies, including:) Vm7 7063. ★
GGC-6mv. Ode sur nos Victoires; (P.85). Solo voice, 2ob/cl 2hn (2)bn tb serp.
Pc (Imbault: Paris, pn A.HH.1, 1793), RISM [C 315], score: D-B; F-Pn, (2 copies, including:) Vm7 7060. ★
GGC-7mv Ode sur la Victoire remportée dans les plaines de Fleurus; (P.67). Solo voice, 2ob/cl 2hn bn 2tb.
Pc (Boyer: Paris, 1794), RISM [C 314], pts: F-Pn, (2 copies, including:) Vm7 7064. *The battle was in 1794.* ★
GGC-8mv. Hymne à la Liberté; (P.760. Solo voice, 2ob/cl hn bn tb serp organ.
Pc (Imbault: Paris, pn A.HH.8, 1793), RISM [C 308], score: D-B; F-Pn, (9 copies, including:) Vm7 7058. ★
GGC-9mv. Hymne à la Vertu; (P.75). Solo voice, 2ob/cl hn bn tb serp organ.
Pc (Imbault: Paris, pn A.HH.7, 1793), RISM [C 311], score: D-B; F-Pn, (2 copies, including:) Vm7 7057. ★
GGC-10mv. Hymne à l'Être suprême pour l'usage des fêtes décadaires; (P.54). Solo voice, 2ob/cl 2hn bn tb.
Pc (Boyer: Paris, 1794), RISM [C 310], parts: F-Pn, (2 copies, including:) Vm7 7064. ★
GGC-11mv. Hymne à la victoire; (P.69). Solo voice, 2ob/cl bn tb serp.
Pc (Imbault: Paris, pn A.HH.2, 1793), RISM [C 312], score: D-B; F-Pn, (4 copies, including:) Vm7 7061. ★

CAMILLERI, Carlo Mario *1941, Malta, resident in UK*
CMC-1. Zeitgeist. 2fl 2ob 2cl 2hn 2bn 2tp timp perc xyl piano.
Pm (Novello: Borough Green).

*CAMPBELL, Arthur *? - April 1996*
Many of Campbell's excellent arrangements remain in MS; in time, GB-Lmic may be able to clarify the situation.
AWC-1a. Albéniz: España, Six album leaves, Op. 165, No. 2, Tango.   fl 2ob 2cl 2hn 2bn.
Pm (Phylloscopus: Lancaster, pn PP142, 1996), score & parts.
AQC-2a. Fauré: Dolly (Suite), Op. 56, Four Pieces.   fl 2ob 2cl 2hn 2bn.
Pm (Phylloscopus: Lancaster, pn PP144, 1996), score & parts.
AQC-3a. Handel: Sinfonia, from *Solomon*, ("Arrival of the Queen of Sheba").   2ob 2cl 2hn 2bn.
Pm (Emerson Edition: Ampleforth, pn E103, 1978), score & parts.
AQC-4a. Handel: Music for the Royal Fireworks.   2ob 2cl 2hn 2bn.
Pm (Phylloscopus: Lancaster, pn PP149, 1996), score & parts.
AQC-5a. Quilter: 4 Child Songs (as "Children's Suite").   2ob 2cl 2hn 2bn.   In MS.
AQC-6a. Warlock: Capriol Suite.   2ob 2cl 2hn 2bn.   In MS.
AQC-7a. C.M. von Weber: 5 Weber Movements.   2ob 2cl 2hn 2bn.
Pm (Emerson Edition: Ampleforth, pn E126, 1979), score & parts.

CAMPBELL-WATSON, Frank *22 Jan 1898, New York - 27 Feb 1980, New York*
FXC-1. Divertimento.   fl ob 2cl b-cl 2hn bn.
Pm (Witmark: New York, 1948), score & parts: US-PT; US-Wc.

*CAPLET, André *23 Nov 1878, Le Havre - 22 April 1925, Neuilly-sur-Seine*
*AXC-1. Suite Persane; c.1900, 3 mvts.   fl(pic) fl 2ob 2cl(A & B♭) 2hn 2bn.
?MS: US-PHci.   ★
Pm (Compusic: Amsterdam, pn 204, 1991), score & parts.

*CARAFA DI COLOBRANO, *Prince* Michele Enrico (Francesco Vincenzo Aloisio Paolo)
17 Nov 1787, Naples - 26 July 1872, Paris.   For F-Pn, MS. 3945 (3), See: DAUPRAT.
MCC-1. Les Souvenirs de Naples.   pic terz-fl fl 2ob cl(G) cl(E♭) cl(B♭ solo) 2cl(B♭) 2hn 2bn 3cap(2B♭, F) 2tp(B♭) a-tb 2b-tb 2oph b-dr s-dr.   MS score: F-Pn, MS. 3945 (1).   ★
MCC-2. Allegretto.   fl(F) 2ob 3cl 2hn 2bn cap.   AutoMS score (Paris, 19 Sept 1845): F-Pn, MS. 3929.   ★
MCC-3. Andante, Solo de Cor.   Solo horn, 2cl bn oph.   AutoMS score: F-Pn, MS. 3945 (2).   ★
MCC-4. Andantino Cantabile.   Cornet a piston in B♭, 2cl bn oph.   AutoMS score: MS. 3945 (4).
MCC-5. Allegro.   Solo clarinet, 2cl bn oph.   AutoMS score: F-Pn, MS. 3945 (5).   ★
MCC-1m. Collection of pieces for military band (including "Marche funèbre pour la translation des cendres de Napoleon", and works for 5 winds).   AutoMS: I-Nc.

CARCANI, Giuseppe (Gioseffo) *1703, Cremona - end of Jan 1779, Piacenza*
GYC-1. Quintetto ex G.   2fl 2hn bn.   MS: D-KA.

*CARPENTER, Gary *13 Jan 1951, Hackney, UK.*
*GQC-1. Pantomime; 5 mvts.   2ob 2cl 2bthn 4hn 2bn cbn/db.
Pm (Camden Music: London, 1996), score (& hire parts - possibly available for sale).
*GQC-2. Ein Musikalisches Snookerspiel, 1991, *(based on Mozart's Composing Game)*.   2ob 2cl 2hn 2bn.
Pm (Camden Music: London, pn CM050, 1992), score & parts.

CARR, Arthur *29 Feb 1908, Pontiac, Michigan, USA*
AYC-1v. As on the Night.   Voices, 2fl 2ob 2cl 2hn 2bn harp.
Pm (G. Schirmer: NY, sd), hire score & parts.

*CARRARA, Vittorio *(1890)*
VYC-1v. Pange Lingua processionale Facilissimo e melodico per coro di populo all' unisono con accompagnam[en]to di Banda.   Unison choir, pic 2cl(C) s-sax a-sax t-sax bar-sax 2hn 2crt s-flug a-flug t-flug bar-flug b-tb b-dr s-dr cym, (or organ).
Pc (V. Carrara: Bergamo, pn V.321C., *Terza Edizione*, c.1920), score & parts: CZ-Pnm, XLIII.C.264.   ★

*CARTELLIERI (Cartellier) Casimiro Antonio *27 Sept 1772, Danzig - 2 Sept 1807, Liebeshausen, Bohemia*
CAC-1. 6 Türkisches Stücke.   pic(F) 2fl 2cl(C) 2hn 2bn 2tp tri cym b-dr s-dr.
MS parts: CZ-Pnm, Lobkovic X.H.a.69.   ★
CAC-2. Nro 1 Divertimento; in F, 5 mvts.   2ob 2cl 2hn 2bn cbn.
MS parts: A-Wgm VIII 8868, (as "Divertimento [another hand:] II"); A-Wn, Mus.Hs.3615; CZ-Bm(no), A.16.629.   ★
CAC-3. Nro 2 Divertimento; in F, 4 mvts.   2ob 2cl 2hn 2bn cbn.
MS parts: A-Wn, Mus.Hs.3615; CZ-Bm(no), A.16.630.   ★
CAC-4. Nro 3 Divertimento; in F, 4 mvts.   2ob 2cl 2hn 2bn cbn.
MS parts: A-Wgm, VIII 8869; A-Wn, Mus.Hs.3615; CZ-Bm(no), A.16.631.   ★
The following works are attributed to Cartellieri; the MSS give "Kathalierý" or "Kataliery" as the composer.
CAC-1c. Parthia in E♭, 5 mvts.   2cl 2hn 2bn.
MS parts: CZ-KRa, A3895/IV.B.58; SK-BRnm, Mus.XII.99, No. 1, (from Ilava, church collection).   ★
CAK-2c. Parthia in E♭, 5 mvts.   2cl 2hn 2bn.   MS parts: CZ-KRa, A3896/IV.B.59.   ★

CARTER, Anthony *1936, UK*
AWC-1. 6 pieces for woodwind groups.   2fl 2ob 4cl bn.
Pm (Oxford University Press: Oxford, 1980), score.

*CARULLI, Benedetto *3 April 1797, Olginate - 8 April 1877, Milan*
*BYC-1. Divertimento; in F, 3 mvts.   Solo trombone, cl(F) 2cl(B♭) 2hn bn 4tp(B♭, F) serpentone.
(?Auto)MS score: I-Bsf, M.C. VII-15.   ★
BYC-1a. Bellini: Biancia e Fernando, "All'udir del padre afflitto".   2fl cl(F) 3cl(B♭ 2hn 2bn tb+b.
MS parts: I-Bsf, M.B. IV-10.
BYC-2a. Mercadante: Andronico, duetto ("Vanne se alberghi in petto").   fl 2cl hn bn.
MS parts: I-Mc, Noseda B.30.3.11 (Fasc. I°).

*CASADESUS, François (Francis) Louis *2 Dec 1870, Paris - 27 June 1954, Paris*
*FLC-1. London sketches, Petite suite humoristique; 3 mvts, 1916.   2fl 2ob 2cl 2hn 2bn.
Pm (Deiss & Crépin: Paris, 1916), score & parts: F-Pn, (3 copies).
Pm (Salabert: Paris, 1924).
Pm (R. Deiss: Paris, 1925), score & pts: F-Pn, (2 copies), K. 12.417 (score only), K. 12.484 (complete); US-Wc.

CASADESUS, Robert Marcel *7 April 1899, Paris - 19 Sept 1972, Paris*
RMC-1. Dixtuor.   2fl 2ob 2cl 2hn 2bn.
Pm: (A.J. Andraud: Cincinatti, now Southern Music Publishing: San Antonio, Texas).

CASAMORATA, ( )
YYC-1a. Raccolta di Armonie estrata da composizioni di gli diversi autori.   fl ob 2cl 2hn 2bn.
(?Auto)MS score & (16) parts (= Parti 1 & 2): I-Fc, F.P. S.168.

*CASKEN, John *15 Aug 1949, Barnsley, UK*
*JXC-1. Kagura; 1972-73.   Concertante a-sax, 2fl 2ob 2cl 2hn 2bn 2tp.
Pm (Schott & Co.: London, c.1982), hire score & parts, (study score in GB-Lmic).

CASTALDO, Joseph F. *1927, USA*
JFC-1. Theoria.   fl fl(pic) 2ob 2cl 2bn 2tb tu perc piano.
Pm (Southern Music Publishing Conpany: New York; Peer Musikverlage: Hamburg, sd), score.

CASTIGLIONI, Niccolò *1932, Italy*
NZC-1. Doppio coro; 1977.   2fl 2ob cl(B♭, cl in E♭) cl(B♭, b-cl) 2hn 2bn.
Pm (Riccordi: Milano, pn 132746, c.1979), score.
NZC-2. Motetto.   fl fl(pic) 2ob 2cl 2hn 2bn.
Pm (Ricordi: Milano, pn 132746, c.1979), score.

*CASTIL-BLAZE (Blaze), François Henri Joseph *1 Dec 1784, Cavaillon - 11 Dec 1857, Paris*
*FHC-1. Sextet No. 1 in E♭, Op. 18; 4 mvts.   2cl 2hn 2bn.
Pc (Aulanger: Paris, c.1832), parts.   ★
Pm (Musica Rara: London, pn 1280, 1971); ed. Roger Hellyer, score & parts
FHC-2. Marche en échos, Boléro et Pas Redoublé à Grand Orchestre Militaire [note that the title is given somewhat differently in several secondary sources].   2fl(F) cl(F) 2cl(C) 2hn 2bn 2tp tb cym+tambours.
Pc (Pleyel: Paris, pn 1193, 1817), parts: CH-Gpu, Ib.4812, (with the printed slip of: Marcillac dit Le Jeune: Geneva; au dépôt de musique: Lausanne); GB-Ljag, (photocopy).   ★

*CATEL, Charles Simon *10 June 1773, L'Aigle, Orne, France - 9 Nov 1830, Paris*
CSC-1. Ouverture: Bataille de Fleurus; in F, (P.2313).   2pic 2fl 2cl 2hn 2bn 2tp 3tb serp timp.
MS parts: F-Pn, H2. 87 e-k.   MS score (modern copy): GB-Ljag.   ★
Pc (Mag de mus fêtes nat: Paris, nivôse an III, 1794), liv. 10/1, pts: F-Pn, H2. 10,1, H2. 126; F-Nm, vol. 22207.
Pm (for modern band:) (Mercury Music Corp.: New York, 1958), ed. Richard Franko Goldman & Roger Smith, score & (35) parts.
Pm (WINDS: Northridge, CA, pn W-25, c. 1981), score & parts.
CSC-2. Symphonie; in F, P.2321.
2p-fl 2cl 2hn 2bn 2tp 3tb serp timp, b-dr, (buccin, tuba corva, cb, cym, tambour turc).
MS pts: (instruments in parentheses above only): F-Pn, musique d'harmonie, paquet 3, (old shelfmark, untraced).
Pc (Mag de mus fêtes nat: Paris, 1795), liv. 14, parts: F-Pn, H2.127 a-q & aa-pp.   ★
CSC-3. Symphonie militaire; in F, P.2298.   2p-fl 2cl 2hn 2bn 2tp tb serp db b-dr cym.
MS parts: F-Pn, H2.128 a-l.
Pc: Mag de mus fêtes nat: Paris, thermidor an II, 1794), liv. 5/1, pts: F-Pn, (2 copies), H2. 5,1; Vm7 7043.   ★
Pm (?for modern band:) (Atlantic Music Supply: New York), score & parts.
*CSC-4. Ouverture [in C minor/major; 1793], de la musique de l'Armée parisienne, executée dans le Temple de la Raison le 20 frimaire an 2e de la République; (P.2285).   2p-fl 2cl 2hn 2bn 2tp b-tb serp timp (tuba corva).
MS parts (2 copies of tuba corva part only): F-Pn, H.2 147 a-b.
Pc: Mag de mus fêtes nat: Paris, germinal an II, 1793), liv. 1/3 parts: F-Pn, (2 copies), H2.1, 3, Vm7 7019.   ★
Pm (Swanzy), pp. 190 - 212, score.
CSC-1m. Marche militaire, le 16 juillet 1791; (P. 2273).   p-fl 2cl 2hn 2bn 2tp serp b-dr cym.
AutoMS score: F-Pn, H2. 30A, B.   MS score: F-Pn, MS. 743.   ★
AutoMS parts (2cl 2hn 2bn 2tp serp 2vl vc db b-dr cym): F-Pn, H2. 1,3.
Pc (Mag de mus fêtes nat.: Paris, germinal an II, 1793), liv. 3, parts: F-Pn, (2 copies), H2. 1,3, Vm7 7021.   ★
Pm (Swanzy), score, pp. 213 - 229.
CSC-2m. Pas de manoeuvre; (P.2287).   2pic 2cl 2hn 2bn tp serp.
Pc (Mag de mus fêtes nat: Paris, germinal an II, 1793), liv. 1/4, parts: F-Pn, (4 copies) H2. 1,4, H2. 10,1, H2. 140.a-j, Vm7 7022.   ★
CSC-3m(-6m). [4] Marche militaire; (P.2291, 2294, 2300, 2309).   2p-fl 2cl 2hn 2bn tp serp.
Pc (Mag de mus fêtes nat: Paris, prairial, messidor, thermidor an II, brumaire an III, 1794), liv. 3, No. 3; liv. 4, No. 4; liv. 5, No. 3; liv. 8, No. 3, parts: F-Pn, (2 sets), H2. 3,3, H2. 4,4, H2. 5,3, H2. 8,3 and Vm7 7022, Vm7 7033, Vm7 7040, Vm7 7045, respectively.   ★
CSC-1.1a, 1.2a. Catel: Sémiramis, "Arrangée par l'Auteur"; 2 Suites, each of 5 mvts.
2cl(C) 2hn 2bn, (ad lib: pic 2ob 2tp tb serp b-dr cym timp).
Pc (A l'Imprimerie du Conservatoire: Paris, pn 28, 29, c.1802) 2 liv., parts: CH-Gpu, Ib.4814, 4815.
CSC-1.3a. Catel: Semiramis, Air des Africains.   2cl 2hn 2bn; (ad lib: pic 2ob 2tp tb timp b-dr cym).
Pc (Au Magasin de Musique [du Conservatoire]: Paris, pn 24, c.1802), parts: CH-Gpu, Ib.4813.
CSC-1mv. Hymne du 10 août (Anniversaire du Dix Août, 23 Thermidor); P.103.
SATB chorus, 2pic 2cl 2hn 2bn serp 2tp 3tb serp, buccin, tuba corva, timp, cym, tambour turc, b-dr.
MS score (by Pierre): F-Pn.
Pc (Mag de mus fêtes nat: Paris, 1795), liv. 16, parts: F-Pn, H2. 35,9.   ★
Pc (for: Voice, 2cl 2hn 2bn:) (Rec des époques: Paris, post-1797), liv. 2, No. 10, score: F-Pn, H2. 16,10.

CSC-2mv. Chant du banquet républicain pour la fête de la Victoire; P.116.
Solo voice, SATB chorus, 2fl/ob 2cl 2hn 2bn 2tp 3tb serp timp.
MS parts: F-Pn, H2. 61, (vocal parts). MS score (by Pierre): F-Pn. ★
Pc (for: Voice, 2cl 2hn (2)bn:) (Rec des époques: Paris, c.1799), liv. 1, No. 36, score: F-Pn, H2. 15,36.
CSC-3mv. Ode patriotique; P.31. ATB chorus, 2p-fl 2cl 2hn 2bn 2tp 3tb serp, tuba corva, timp.
MS parts: F-Pn, H2. 123 a-r, (? missing b-tb). MS score (by Pierre): F-Pn. ★
CSC-4mv. La bataille de Fleurus; P.66. ATB chorus, 2cl 2hn 2bn 2tp 3tb serp timp.
MS score (by Pierre): F-Pn. MS parts: F-Pn, H2. 88A a-tt.
Pc (Mag de mus fêtes nat: Paris, vendémiaire, brumaire an III, 1794), liv. 7/2 & liv. 8/2, parts: F-Pn, H2. 7,2, (1er strophe), H2. 8,2, (2e strophe).; F-Nm, vol. 22207, 22208. ★
CSC-5mv. Hymne à la victoire, sur la bataille de Fleurus; P.65. Solo voice, 2p-fl 2cl 2hn 2bn 2tp tb serp.
Pc (Mag de mus fêtes nat: Paris, thermidor an II, 1794), liv. 5/5, pts: F-Pn, (3 copies), H2.5, Vm7 7047, Vm7 16773; F-Nm, vol 22207. MS score (by Constant Pierre): F-Pn. ★
Pc (for: Voice, 2cl 2hn (2)bn:) (Rec des époques: Paris, c.1799), liv. 1, No. 27, score: F-Pn, H2. 15,27.
CSC-6mv. Ode sur le vaisseau "le Vengeur"; P.46. B solo, 2cl 2hn 2bn.
Pc (Rec des époques: Paris, c.1799), liv. 1, No. 27, pp. 73 - 75, score: F-Pn, H2. 15,27. ★
CSC-7mv. Hymne à l'Être suprème; P.51. Voice, 2cl 2hn 2bn.
Pc (Rec des époques: Paris, c.1799), liv. 1, No. 23, pp. 60 - 61, score: F-Pn, H2. 15,23. ★
CSC-8mv. Fête [Hymne] de la Souveraineté du Peuple; P.149b. Voice, 2cl 2hn 2bn.
Pc (Rec des époques: Paris, c.1799), liv 2, No. 2, pp. 134 - 136, score: F-Pn, H2. 16,3. ★
CSC-9mv. Ode sur la situation de la République pendant la Tyrannie décemvirale; P.88. Voice, 2cl 2hn (2)bn.
Pc (Rec des époques: Paris, c.1799), liv. 1, No. 29, pp. 79 - 81, score: F-Pn, H2. 15,29. ★
CSC-10v. Hymne à l'Égalité. Voice, 2cl(C) 2hn (2)bn.
Pc (Rec des époques: Paris, c.1799), liv. 1, No. 2, pp. 4 - 5, score: F-Pn, H2. 15,2. ★
CSC-1ad. Catel, Sémiramis, Air des Africains. 2cl 2hn 2bn; (ad lib: p-fl(C) 2ob 2tp tb timp b-dr cym).
Pc (Au Magasin de Musique [à l'usage du Conservatoire]: Paris, pn 24, c.1802), parts: CH-Gpu, Ib.4813.

*CAVOS, Catterino *30 Oct 1775 - 10 May 1840, St Petersburg*
See also: ANON, A-74m. Of the Masonic works below, No. 4 is scored for winds, and Nos. 2, 3 hint at similar scoring. No composer is identified for No. 3, and it may be by Boieldieu.
CZC-1v(-3v). Hymnes et Cantiques Nos. 2 - 4: "O toi que l'univers encense" (text: Dalmas); "Pour la Sante du V." (text by Pouschkin [sic, i.e. Vasily Lvovich Pushkin, uncle of Aleksander]); "Servir, adorer sa Patrie" (text Pouschkin [sic]). No 1 is by Boieldieu (qv). ATTB, ob ca 2cl(C) 2hn 2bn.
Pc (sn, "pour la R des Amis Réunis": St Petersburg, c.1810 [the imprint is misleading, stating "à Jerusalem" with a Masonic date 5810]), score: GB-Lbl, E.497.ii. ★

CAWKWELL, Roger *1950*
RXC-1a. Scott Joplin: Two Rags (The Entertainer; Ragtime Dance). 2ob 2cl 2hn 2bn
Pm (Chester Music: London, 1980), score & parts (Mixed Bag: No 5).

CAZDEN, Norman *23 Sept 1914, New York - 18 Aug 1980, Bangor, Maine*
NYC-1. Concerto, Op. 10. Solo piano, viola & Cello, fl ob cl 2hn bn tp.
Pm (Music Corporation of America, via Belwin Mills: New York, c.1938), score.
Pm (Composers Facsimile Edition, *via* American Composers Alliance: New York, 1958), score.
NYC-2. 6 Discussions, Op. 40, No. 5, Insistence. 2ob 2bn.
Pm (E.F. Kalmus: Fort Lauderdale, Florida, 1951), score & parts.
Pm (Jack Spratt: Old Greenwich, CN, 1961), score & parts.

CECCARELLI, Luigi
LXC-1. La naturale condizione del moto. fl 2ob 2cl 2hn 2bn.
Pm (Edipan Edizione Musicale: Roma, sd), parts.

CECCONI-BETELLA, Monic (Monique Gabrielle) *30 Sept 1936, Courbevoi*
MBC-1. Aura. 2fl 2ob(ca) 3cl(b-cl) 2hn bn 2tp 2tb.
Pm (Technisonar, *via* Billaudot: Paris, 1974), score.

*ČEJKA (Czeyka), Valentin, *Conte* *active c.1769, Prague*
See also: FUCHS, Johann Nepomuk, JAF-1c.
VXC-1. Nro 2 Partita, o sia Divertimento a sei Stromenti; in D, 5 mvts. 2ob 2hn 2bn.
MS parts: CZ-Pnm, XXII.B.185. ★
VXC-2. Nro 3 Divertimento; in G, 3 mvts. 2ob 2hn 2bn. MS parts: CZ-Pnm, XXII.B.186. ★
VXC-3. Nro 1 Divertimento; in A, 3 mvts. 2ob 2hn(non obligsti) bn. MS parts: CZ-Pnm, XXII.B.184. ★
VYC-4. Parthia in Dis [E♭]; 4 mvts. 2ob 2hn bn. MS parts: CZ-KRa, A3847/IV.B.11. ★
VXC-5. 3 Ländler & ein Walzer. Instrumentation unknown. MS parts: I-Mc, (unverified).

*CELESTINO, Eligio *20 March 1739, Pisa - 24 June 1812, Ludwigslust*
EXC-1. Andante con moto. 2ob 2hn bn tp.
MS parts: D-SWl, Mus. 1461. ★

CELIS, Fritz Lode *1929, Belgium*
FIC-1. Introduzione & Scherzo, Op. 36; 1990. 2fl 2ob 2cl 2hn 2bn. MS score: B-Bcdm.
FIC-2. Octet, Op. 40; 1992. 2ob 2cl 2hn 2bn. MS score: B-Bcdm.

*CERHA, Friedrich *17 Feb 1926, Vienna.*
*FYC-1. Divertimento: Hommage à Stravinsky.
2ob 2cl 2bn 2tp timp 6perc(b-dr 2s-dr t-dr tri tamtam woodblock cym castanets).
Pm (Universal Edition: Wien, 1948), score.
*FYC-2. Curriculum, 1972-73. ob obdam cl b-cl 2hn 2bn 2tp 2tb/bar tu.
Pm (Universal Edition: Wien, pn 14489, 1980), score.

CHAGRIN, Francis (*pseud*, i.e. Alexander Paucker) *15 Nov 1905, Bucharest - 19 July 1972, London*
FZC-1. 7 Petites Pièces pour 8 Instruments; 1966.   pic fl ob 2cl hn 2bn.
Pm (Novello: London, pn 09.0022.02, 1969), score & parts.
FZC-2. French Patrol 1 & 2; 1948.   2ob 2cl 2hn 2bn.   MS score: GB-Lmic.

CHAITKIN, David *16 May 1938, New York*
DZC-1. Summersong for 23 wind instruments.   pic fl a-fl 3ob 3cl 3hn 2bn cbn 3tp 3tb tu.
PM (Margun Music: Newton Center, MA, pn MM 1050, 1981), study score.

*CHANDLER, Mary *16 May 1911, London*
*MXC-1. Badinages (1975).   2fl 2ob 2cl 2hn 2bn.
Pm (Phylloscopus: Lancaster, pn PP67, 1996), score & parts.
MXC-2. Octet, 1957.   2ob 2cl 2hn 2bn.   MS score: GB-Lmic.
MXC-3. Cassation; 5 mvts.   2ob 2cl 2hn 2bn.   In MS: (untraced).

CHARPENTIER, Jacques *18 Oct 1933, Paris*
JYC-1. Vitrail pour un temps de guerre pour harmonie de chambre.   2fl ob ca cl b-cl 2hn 2bn 2tp 2tb tu.
Pm (Leduc: Paris, 1984), score.

CHAUN, František *26 Jan 1921, Kaplice - 31 Dec 1981, Prague*
PAC-1. Divertimento.   fl 2ob 2b-cl 2hn 2bn.
Pm (Panton; Praha/Prague, 1961), score.

*CHÉLARD, Hippolyte André Jean Baptiste *2 Jan 1789, Paris - 12 Feb 1861, Weimar*
HAC-1. Hymne à Orphée; in A♭.   2fl 2cl 4hn 2bn oph.   MS score: D-B, Mus.ms.3442/5.   ★
Die Hermannschlacht (opera, 1835, Munich).
HAC-1.1e. Entfernter Marsch der Römer.   pic 5cl 4hn 2bn 4tp a-tb t-tb b-tb oph b-dr.
MS parts: D-B, Mus.ms.3435/8.   ★
HAC-1.2e. Act III: Gebt acht genau durch ihre Kunst lernt unsern Sieg, Marsche.
pic 5cl 4hn 2bn serp 3tp b-tb b-dr s-dr.   MS parts: D-B, Mus.ms.3435/11.   ★

CHELLEREI (Kelleri), Fortunato *1690 - 1757*
FOC-1. Parttia [sic]; in E.   2obdam 2hn b.   MS parts: S-Uu, Instr.mus.i.hs.20:11.   ★

*CHERUBINI, Maria Luigi Carlo Zenobio Salvatore *14 Sept 1760, Florence - 15 March 1842, Paris*
GMC-1m. Marche du Department de Préfet d'Eure-et-Loir.   p-fl(C) 2cl(C) 2hn bn 2tp serp(s) b-dr, tambour turc+cym.   MS score: D-Bds, Bottée de Toulmon, No. 125 bis.   ★
*GMC-2m. Marcia in Fa [F; for Baron Peter von Braun, Vienna, 1805].   2ob 2cl(C) 2hn 2bn cbn.
AutoMS score: D-Bds.   ★
Pm (Suvini Zerboni: Milano, 1983), ed. G. C. Ballola, score (pn ESZ 7931) & pts (ESZ 7932), here with 2cl(B♭)
GMC-3m. Pas redoublé pour le Retour du Préfect de Department d'Eure-et-Loir.   p-fl(C) 2cl(C) 2hn (2)bn 2tp tb serp tri b-dr+cym.   MS score (Paris, 8 Oct 1808): D-Bds, Bottée de Toulmon, No. 145.   ★
*GMC-4m. March, in F, [for the Princesse de Chimay].   p-fl(C) 2ob 2cl(C) 2hn 2bn 2tp tb serp tri b-dr+cym.
MS score (Chimay, 12 July 1809): D-Bds, Bottée de Toulmon, No. 146.   ★
*GMC-5m. March, [for the Princesse de Chimay].   p-fl(C) 2cl 2hn 2bn 2tp tb serp tri b-dr+cym.
MS score (Chimay, 22 Sept 1810): D-Bds, Bottée de Toulmon, No. 152.   ★
GMC-6.1m(-6.3m). Marche [pour la Garde Nationale & 2 Pas redoublés].   Scoring varies.
MS score (Marche: 8 Feb 1814, Pas redoublés: 13 Feb 1814): D-Bds.   ★
   6.1m. Marche.   p-fl(C) 2cl(C) 2hn 2bn 2tp tb b-dr cym.
   6.2m, 6.3m. Pas redoublé 1 & 2.   p-fl(E♭) 2cl 2hn 2bn 2tp tb tri b-dr+cym.
*GMC-7m. Pas redoublés, May 1814 [there are 6 pas redoublés and two marches for Col. Witzleben].   tp 3hn tb.
AutoMS score: D-Bds.
Pm: (London: Mills Music 1962).
*GMC-1mt. Marche funèbre pour la pompe funèbre du général Hoche, P.131.
2p-fl 2ob 2cl 2hn 2bn 2tp 3tb, caisse roulante ou tambour, tam-tam.
MS score: D-Bds, Bottée du Toulmon, No. 116/5b.   ★
Pm (Boccaccini & Spada: Roma, pn BS 112, sd), score.
GMC-1v. Graduale in B[♭]; "Ave Maria".   SATB, 2cl 2hn 2bn db organ.
MS parts: CZ-KRsm, UHM A.1145/Br.C-258, (the gift of Archbishop Maximilian Josef in 1845).   ★
GMC-1ve. Lodoïska, Act II, Scene 13, Finale: "Amis que ce divin breuvage".   TBBB, 2fl 2ob 2cl 2hn 2bn.
Pc (H. Nadermann: Paris, c.1791), score.
Pm (Garland Press: New York, 1978), facsimile of the Naderman (Paris) score, (Early Romantic Opera, No. 33).
*GMC-1mv. Hymne funèbre sur la mort du général Hoche; P.131. *Later adapted as* Hymne funèbre sur la mort du général Joubert, 16 Sept 1799. Solo SATB, ATB chorus, 2p-fl 2cl 2hn 2bn 2tp 3tb serp timp.
MS score: D-Bds, Bottée de Toulmon, No. 116/5a; F-Pn, H2. 34.   ★
Pc (for: Voice, 2cl 2hn 2bn:) (Rec des époques: Paris, c.1799), RISM Supp [CC 2028 I,467], liv. 1, No. 38, pp. 109 - 111, score: F-Pn, H2. 15,38.
*GMC-2mv. Chant Républicain pour la Fête du 10 août (1795); P.104.
SATB chorus, 2p-fl 2cl 2hn 2bn 2tp 3tb serp buccin, tuba corva, b-dr t-dr cym.
Auto MS score: F-Pn, MS. 10948. (incomplete facsimile in Pierre: P.111).   ★
MS score: D-Bds, Bottée de Toulmon, No. 116/3.
MS parts: F-Pn, (2 copies) H2. 31, L. 17497, (19th century); F-Po.
Pc (for: Voice, 2cl 2hn 2bn) (Rec des époques: Paris, c.1799), liv. 1, No. 15, score: F-Pn, H2. 15,15.
*GMC-3mv. L'Hymne du Panthéon; P.790.   ATB chorus, 2p-fl 2cl 2hn 2bn 2tp 3tb serp timp tam-tam b-dr.
Pc (Mag de mus fêtes nat: Paris, ventôse an III, 1795), liv. 12/2, score: F-Pn, H2. 12,2.   ★
*GMC-4mv. Hymne à la Fraternité; P.810.   SATB chorus, 2p-fl 2cl 4hn 2bn 2tp serp b-dr cym, tambour turc.
MS score: D-Bds, Bottée de Toulmon, No. 116/2.   ★
MS parts: F-Pn, H2. 97 a-t, (contemporary), L. 17.487 *and* L. 17.501, (later copy).
Pc (for: Voice, 2cl 2hn 2bn:) (Rec des époques: Paris, c.1799), liv. 1, No. 31, score: F-Pn, H2. 15,31.   ★

GMC-5mv. Ode sur le 18 Fructidor, P.144.   ATB chorus, 2p-fl 2cl 2hn 2bn 2tp 3tb serp db timp.
AutoMS score: F-Pn, MS. 10.948.   MS score: D-Bds, Bottée de Toulmon, No. 116/6.   ★
MS parts: F-Pn, (2 copies), H2. 98 a-q, H2. 32.
Pc (for: Voice, 2cl 2hn 2bn:) (Rec des époques: Paris, c.1799), liv. 1, No. 37, score: F-Pn, H2. 15,37.
*GMC-6mv. Hymne à la Victoire; P.115.
Solo voice, SATB chorus, 2p-fl 2cl 2hn (2)bn 2tp 3tb serp buccin, tuba curva, timp b-dr.
MS score: D-Bds, Bottée de Toulmon, No 116/4; F-Pn, (by Pierre), Vm7 7956.   MS parts: F-Pn, H2. 99 a-u.   ★
*GMC-7mv. Le Salpêtre républicaine, 1794; P.140.   Solo voice, 2cl 2hn (2)bn.
MS score: D-Bds, Bottée de Toulmon, No. 116/7.
Pc (Rec des époques: Paris, c.1799), liv. 1, No. 21, pp. 56 - 58, score: F-Pn, H2. 15,21.   ★
GMC-8mv. Hymne pour la Fête de la Jeunesse, 10 germinal [30 March 1799]; P.150.   Solo voice, 2cl 2hn 2bn.
MS score: D-Bds, Bottée de Toulmon, No. 116/8.
Pc (Rec des époques: Paris, c.1799), liv. 2, No. 4, score: F-Pn, H2. 16, 4.   ★
GMC-9mv. Fête de la Reconnaissance, 10 prairial [29 May 1799]; P.154.   Solo voice, 2cl 2hn (2)bn.
MS score: D-Bds, Bottée de Toulmon, No. 116/9.
Pc (Rec des époques: Paris, c.1799), liv. 2, No. 6, pp. 160 - 162, score: F-Pn, H2. 16,6.   ★

CHILDS, Barney Sandford *13 Feb 1926, Spokane, Wash, USA*
BSC-1. Music for Winds.   2fl 2ob 2cl t-sax hn 2bn tp tb tu.
Pm (American Composers Alliance, New York. c.1964), score.

CHITI, Gian Paolo *1939, Italy*
GPC-1. Replay.   2ob 2cl 2hn 2bn.
Pm (Edipan Edizione Musicale: Roma, sd), score & parts.

CHRISTIAN, *Prince of Hesse-Darmstadt*   *(?1720)*
PHC-1m. March in E♭.   2cl(E♭) 2cl(B♭) 2hn (2)bn tp.   MS parts: D-DS, Mus.ms.1223/21, No 2. *The composer may not have done the instrumental scoring. The bassoon part is labelled "Fagotto"; the titlepage states "Fagotti" although the preceding "2" has been rubbed out. The cl(E♭) double the cl(B♭) parts.*   ★

*CHRISTIANSEN, Asger Lund *23 May 1927, Copenhagen*
*ASC-1. Octet for Winds.   2ob 2cl 2hn 2bn.
Pm (Self-published: Frederiksværk).   DK-Kd will assist in contacting the composer.

*CHRISTIANSEN, Carl *1890 - 7 Dec 1947, Sweden*
CXC-1. Leksaksasken Svit: Spielkasten [Toybox].   2fl ob 2cl 2hn 2bn tp tb; (scoring varies for each mvt:
1. Humoresque: 2fl ob 2cl 2bn, 2. Menuet & 3. Pacific: full group, 4. Pastoral: fl ob 2cl bn, 5. Tennsoldaternas
Marsch: fl ob cl 2hn bn tp tb).
Pm: (Gehrmans: Stockholm, pn 3017, 1938), score.

CHRISTIANSEN, Svend *1954, Denmark*
SXC-1. Fluktuation; 1975 - 1976.   2fl 2ob 2cl 2hn 2bn 2tp 2tb.   MS score: DK-Kd.

CHUNG YANG YÜEH T'NAN
YTC-1. K'uai le ti nü chan shih.   fl ob 2cl bn.
Pm (People's Publishing Corporation: sl [?Beijing], 1977), parts.

*CIANCHI, Emilio *1833 - 1890, Italy*
EZC-1. Nonetto; 4 mvts.   2ob 2cl 2hn 2bn cbn.
Pc (E. Paoletti,: Firenze, 1868), min score & pts: I-Bc, MM.148, (score); I-Mc, Da Camera A.28.13, (score).   ★
Pm (Compusic: Amsterdam, pn 205, 1988), score & parts.

CIBULKA (Cybulka, Zibulka), Masouš Alojs *22 Feb 1768, Prague - 1845, Pest*
MAC-1a. Wenzel Müller: Der lustige Beilager, 2 mvts.   2cl 2hn 2bn.
MS parts (by J. Pražáka, c.1800): CZ-Pnm, XLI.B.111.

*CIGLER, ( )
XYC-1. Barthia in F; 5 short mvts.   2ob 2hn bn.   MS parts: CZ-Pnm, XXXII.A.101.   ★

*CIMAROSA, Domenico *17 Dec 1749, Aversa, near Naples - 11 Jan 1801, Venice*
*DZC-1m. Marcia da suonarsi sotto L'Albero della Libertà nel bruciamento della immagini dei Tiranni.
2ob 2cl 2hn 2bn.
MS: I-Npriv, (in Torre del Greco).
Pm (Boccaccini & Spada: Roma, pn B.S. 1145, 1984), score & parts.   ★

*CIMOSO, Domenico *1780 - 1850*
DXC-1v. Tantum ergo, "Composto 1833 . . . Per la Festa di S. Giuseppe Calasanzio in S. Pantaleone".
Solo TB, 2cl 2hn vlne organ.   MS parts: I-Vsmc.   ★
DXC-2v. Tantum ergo.   Solo B, 2cl 2hn vlne organ.
MS parts: I-Vsmc, (the vlne part bears a later alternative of tb).   ★
DXC-1vf. Stabat Mater a Strumenti a Fiato.   MS parts: I-Vsmc, (incomplete, the trombone part only).

CIRY, Michael *1919, France*
MZC-1. La Crucifixion.   cl 2hn 2bn 2tp 3tb 2perc timp 2pianos.
Pm (Billaudot: Paris), score.

CISLER, ( )
YXC-1. Parttia [sic]; in C; 5 mvts .   2ob 2hn bn timp.   MS parts: A-Wn, Mus.Hs.3096.   ★

CIUFFOLOTTI, Vincenzo *(1760)*
VIC-1v. Motetto, 1796.   SATB, winds, basso.   MS: I-Nc.

*CLEMENTI, Aldo *25 May 1925, Catania*
ALC-1. Intermezzo per 14 fiati e pianoforte preparato, 1982.   2fl 2ob 2cl 2hn 2bn 2tp 2tb, prepared piano.
Pm (Suvini-Zerboni: Milano, S8782Z, 1982), score.
ALC-2. Ideogramini No. 1, 1959.   2fl 3cl 3hn bn db 2tp tb db piano xyl 2perc.
Pm (Suvini-Zerboni: Milano, pn S5595Z, 1960), score.
ALC-3. Elegia; 1981.   fl 4hn 4bn 4tb.
Pm (Suvini-Zerboni: Milano, pn S8863Z, 1983), score.

CLEMENTS, Patrick
PYC-1a. Brahms: Hungarian Dances Nos. 3 & 7.   2ob 2cl 2hn 2bn cbn/db
Pm (Boosey & Hawkes: London, 1981), score (pn B&H 20507) & parts (pn B&H 1366).
PYC-2a. Dvořák: Slavonic Dances Nos. 8, 9 and 15 (Op. 46, No. 8, Op. 72, No. 1 and No. 7).
2ob 2cl 2hn 2bn cbn/db.
Pm (Boosey & Hawkes: London, c.1978), score & pts (Exploring Music Series).

*COCCON (Cocconi), Nicole (Nicolò) *1826, Venice - 1903, Venice*
Many of Coccon's works include parts, possibly later additions, not found in the scores; we list these in parentheses.
NXC-1. Pastorale.   2cl 2hn organ.   AutoMS score & parts (1865): I-Vsmc. ★
NXC-1v. Credo; 1860.   TB(solo+rip), 2cl(C) 2hn (bn/basso) tp tb timp organ.
AutoMS score & MS pts: I-Vsmc. *With 2 sets of pts, the earlier in oblong folio for: 2cl(C) 2hn bn/basso tp timp (with an additional pt: hn II tranposed for tp in C); the later for: TB(solo[1]+rip[3]), 2cl(C) 2hn tp timp organ.* ★
NXC-2v. Kyrie; 1848.   TB(solo+rip), (fl) 2cl 2hn bn tp (vlne) timp organ.
AutoMS score & MS parts: I-Vsmc, (with an additional part, "organo senza Stromenti"). ★
NXC-3v. Kyrie; 1850.   TB(solo+rip), (fl) 2cl 2hn (tp tb vlne) organ.
AutoMS score & MS parts: I-Vsmc, (with additional pts: hn II transposed for tp II & hn I tranposed for tb). ★
NXC-4v. Gloria; 1847.   TB(solo+rip), 2cl 2hn (tp tb vlne) timp organ.   AutoMS score & MS parts: I-Vsmc. ★
NXC-5v. Gloria, 1850.   Solo TB, (fl) 2cl 2hn (2bassi tp tb) organ.
AutoMS score & MS parts: I-Vsmc, (with an additional cl II parts). ★
NXC-6v. Laudate letatus podes nostri.   TB(solo+rip), fl 2cl 2hn bn bn/vlne to tb timp organ.
MS parts: I-Vsmc. ★
NXC-7v. Letatus sum.   TTB(solo+rip), 2cl 2hn tp (tb) vlne (bomb) timp organ.
AutoMS score (1845) & MS parts: I-Vsmc, (missing cl II). ★
NXC-8v. Gloria.   Solo TB, TTB(solo+rip), fl 2cl 2hn vlne/bn organ.
AutoMS score: I-Vsmc, (missing all before the Quoniam; the complete mvts (all with the same instrumental scoring, except the last mvt) are: Quoniam, solo B; Cum Sancto Spiritu, TTB chorus; Domine Deus, solo TTB; Qui tollis, TTB chorus; Qui sedes, T solo with solo organ). ★
NXC-9v. Domine ad adjuvandum.   Solo TB, 2cl 2hn organ.   MS parts: I-Vsmc, (missing a clarinet part). ★
NXC-10v. Dixit Dominus, 1852.   Solo TB, 2cl 2hn timp organ(bc-fig).   MS pts: I-Vsmc, (missing the cl pts). ★

CODAVILLA, Filippo *1841 - 1923*
FQC-1. Ottetto in E♭.   fl ob cl 2hn bn crt tb.
Pc (Umberto Pizzi: Milano, 1919), score & parts.
Pm (Bongiovanni: Firenze, pn 1109, sd), score & parts (reprint of Pizzi edition).
Pm (M. Witmark: New York, sd), score & parts.

COENEN, Paul *8 Dec 1908, Saarlouis*
PQC-1. Bläsersextett in D minor, Op. 160.   2cl 2hn 2bn.
Pm (Astoria: Berlin).

COHEN, Karl Hubert *1851 - 1938*
KHC-1v. Te Deum.   5-part chorus, winds, organ.
Pc: (Pustet: Regensburg, sd).
KHC-2v. Requiem, Op. 2.   4-part chorus, winds.
Pc (Pustet: Regensburg, sd).

COJANIZ, Claudio
CLC-1. Apeiron.   pic 2fl b-fl 2ob cl bn 2tp 2tb perc xly piano.
Pm (Edipan Edizione Musicale: Roma, sd).

*COLE, Hugo *6 Aug 1917 London*
*HYC-1. Serenade for nine wind instruments; 8 mvts.   fl ob ob/fl(II) 2cl hn/cl(IV)/a-sax hn bn/cl(III) bn.
Pm: (Novello & Co: Borough Green, Sevenoaks, Kent, pn 12.0243.10, 1966, reprinted 1984), score & parts, (Music For Today, Series Two - Wind Ensemble, No. 5).

COLEMAN, Dan *USA*
DAC-1. The Animated Room; 1990.   pic ob(ca) cl cl(b-cl) bn 2tp 2tb db vib harp.   MS score: US-NYamc.

*COLEMAN, James *(1760)*
JMC-1m. Twelve slow & Twelve quick marches, in eight books, as now in use in the garrison of Gibraltar.
2fifes 2fl 2cl 2hn 2bn tp.
Pc (Longman & Broderip, for the Author: London, c.1790), RISM [C 3295], parts: EIRE-Dn, (incomplete; the additional harpsichord book only).

*COLLAUF (Collauff), ( ) *(?1770)*
XZC-1. No. I Parthia; in E♭, 4 mvts.   2cl 2hn bn.   MS parts: US-BETm, Lititz Collegium Musicum 178. ★
XZC-2. No. 2 Parthia; in E♭, 4 mvts.   2cl 2hn bn.   MS parts: US-BETm, Lititz Collegium Musicum 177. ★
XZC-3. No. 3 Parthia; in E♭, 4 mvts.   2cl 2hn bn.   MS parts: US-BETm, Lititz Collegium Musicum 176. ★
XZC-4. No. 4 Parthia; in E♭, 4 mvts.   2cl 2hn bn.   MS parts: US-BETm, Lititz Collegium Musicum 185. ★
XZC-5, 6. Parthias I & II; (both in E♭, 4 mvts).   2cl 2hn bn.
MS parts: US-BETm, Lititz Collegium Musicum 179.1, 179.2. ★
XZC-7. Parthia; in E♭, 8 mvts.   2cl 2hn bn.   MS parts: US-WS, SCM 260, (missing cl I). ★

COMER, Franz *1813 - 1897*
FRC-1v, 2v. "Abendlied" und "Die drei Sterne". TTBB, 2cl 2hn 2bn.
AutoMS score: D-Bds, Mus.Ms.Auto.F.Comer 55.

CONN, John Peebles *15 Sept 1883, Penicaik - 5 Feb 1960, Glasgow*
JPC-1a. Giovanni Bolzoni (1841 - 1919): Menuetto. fl ob 2cl a-cl b-cl.
Pm (C. Fischer: New York, sd).

*CONNOLLY, Justin *11 Aug 1933, London*
*JUC-1a. Brahms: Variationen über ein Thema von R Schumann für Pianoforte zu vier Händen, Op. 23 (1861).
fl 2ob 2cl 2hn 2bn.
Pm (Novello & Co.: London, pn 09 0577, c.1985), score & parts.

CONSOLI, Marc Antonio *1946, Italy, now resident in USA*
MRC-1. Odefonia; 1978. pic fl ob ca cl b-cl 2hn 2bn 2tp tb 4vc 2db perc.
Pm (untraced - ?T. Presser: Bryn Mawr, 1978).

*CONSTANT, Marius *7 Feb 1925, Bucharest*
MYC-1. Symphonie pour instruments à vent. 3fl 2ob 2cl b-cl 4hn 2bn/cbn 2flug 2tb tu.
Pm (Salabert: Paris, 1978), score.
MYC-2. Winds. 2fl ob 2cl 2hn bn db 2tp 2tb (ad lib: shofars, Swannee whistles, vacuum cleaners & bird calls).
Pm (Salabert: Paris, 1988), score.

CONSTANTINI, Francesco *1789 - 1854*
FNC-1v. O lingua benedicta. TTBB, 2ob 2hn 2tp tb/bn. MS: I-Bsf, Mss.N.253/3.

*COOKE, Thomas Simpson *1782, Dublin - 26 Feb 1847, London.*
TSC-1m, 2m. His Grace the Duke of Leinster's March and Quick Step; [and] The Kildare Quick Step.
2fl 2cl 2hn basso.
Pc (B. Cooke: Dublin, c.1795), score: GB-Lbl, g.271.qq.(7). ★

CORGHI, Azio *9 March 1937, Turin*
AZC-1. Intavolature; 1967. 2fl 2ob 2cl 2hn 2bn 2tp timp perc.
Pm (Ricordi: Milano, pn 131344, 1966), score & parts.
AZC-2. Actus I; 1975. 2fl 2ob 2cl 2hn 2bn.
Pm (Suvini-Zerboni: Milano, pn S7924Z, c.1976), score & parts.

*CORNECK, Mrs F. (Unclear, possibly: Mrs I./J. Corneck, or Mrs Horneck) *(1770)*
MFC-1m. Her Royal Highness the Duchess of York's March. 2cl 2hn bn 2tp timp *or* piano.
Pc (Printed by W.M. Cahusac: [London] & J. & W. Lintern: Bath, c.1800), score: GB-SA, Fin M1746,G7N5,
No. 73; GB-DOTams, (photocopy); GB-Ljag, (photocopy). ★

CORNELL (name originally: MEIER), Klaus *1932, Switzerland*
KXC-1. Versuch über Döblin; 1983. 2cl 2hn 2bn. MS: CH-Zma.

*CORRI, Montague P. *1784, Edinburgh - 19 Sept 1849, London.*
MPC-1m. A Complete Course of Instructions on the most efficient system of Arranging Music in Score for
Voices, Orchestras, Military Bands, Brass Bands &c. with a Description of the Power and Compass of All the
Wind Instruments in General Use. [Includes short original pieces for various configurations].
Pc (Published for the Proprietors, by Metzler & Co: London, c.1835), score: GB-Lbl, R.M.13.e.3.; GB-Ljag,
(modern MS copy).

CORTÉS, Ramiro, Jr *25 Nov 1933, Dallas - 2 July 1984, Salt Lake City*
RYC-1. Chamber Concerto No. 1, 1958. Cello solo, 12 winds.
Pm (?T. Presser & Co.: Bryn Mawr, PA, c.1959), autograph facsimile score.
RYC-1v. Missa breve. Women's voices, 3fl 2ob 3cl 3bn.
Pm (T. Presser & Co.: Bryn Mawr, PA).

*COSSART, Leland A. *1877, Funchal, Madeira - 1965, Lausanne*
*LAC-1. Suite in F, Op. 19; 4 mvts. 2fl 2ob 2cl 2hn 2bn harp.
Pm (Heinrichshofen: Wilhelmshaven, 1919). *Score & parts for hire* via *C.F. Peters.*

COULTER, John *South Africa*
JOC-1. "Fancy That . . ."; 1982. 4fl 2ob 4cl hn 2bn. MS score: SA-Jsamro.

*COURTIN, (M.) Henri *(1770)*
HZC-1a. Airs De differents Maîtres Etrangers...4ᵐᵉ Suitte. (2ob/fl ad lib) 2cl 2hn 2bn.
Pc (Aux deux Lyres, chez Mᵐᵉ Duhan et Cⁱᵉ: à Paris, pn 360, 1811/1812), parts: CH-Gpu, Ib.4818, (with
additional printed bassoon parts for clarinets in C).
    1.1a. Andreozzi: "Nò [sic: Ah] quest' anima non speri"; [included in the Sarti & Mazzinghi pasticcio, *Armide*].
    1.2a. Anon: La Biondina [in Gondoletta]. Barcarole.
    1.3a. Zingarelli: Giulietta e Romeo, "Ombra adorata aspetto". 1.4a. Mozart: La Clemenza di Tito, "Ah Perdo".
    1.5a. Martín y Soler: L'Arbore di Diana, "Oc[c]hietto furbetto".
    1.6a. Nicolini: Rondo, "Gia un dolce raggio", [?J.S. Mayr: polacca for Andreozzi's *La Principessa Filosofa*].
HZC-2.1a. Berton: Aline, Reine de Golconde, overture. 4cl(C) 2hn 2bn serp/cb.
Pc (Chez Sieber fils: Paris, pn 284, 1804), RISM Supp [BB 2178a], parts: CH-Gpu, Ib.4816.
HZC-2.2a. Berton: Aline, Reine de Golconde, [11] Airs. 2cl(C)+2cl(C ripieno) 2hn 2bn serp/cb, *or* 2cl 2hn 2bn.
Pc (Chez Sieber [fils]; Gravé par Bouret: Paris, pn 285, 1804), RISM Supp [BB 2173], parts: CH-Gpu, Ib.4817.
HZC-1ma. Lesueur: Marche du Sacre de Sa Majesté L'Empereur. Exécutée Le jour de la bataille d'Austerlitz
Par les Musiciens des chasseurs à Pieds de la Garde Impériale Recueillie d'après les Orders de Mr. Le Lieutenant
Général Baron Pelet, Directeur Général du Depôt de la Guerre.
pic(Db) cl(Eb) 2cl(Bb) 2hn 2bn 2cap 2tp 3tb oph b-dr s-dr.
MS score (late copy, probably rescored): F-Pn, Vma ms. 512. ★

COWIE, Edward *17 Aug 1943, Birmingham (now living in Australia)*
EYC-1. Cathedral Music. 4fl 3ob 3cl 2bn.
Pm (Schott & Co.: London).
EYC-1v. Leighton Moss: December Notebook.
Solo ST, SSAATTBB chorus, 2fl(pic) 2ob 2cl 4hn 2bn 4tp 3tb tu timp perc piano(celeste).
Pm (Chester Music: London, 1973), hire score & parts.

CRAMER, Wilhelm *2 June 1746, Mannheim - 5 Oct 1799, London*
WXC-1. Rondo, in B♭. 2ob 2cl 2hn 2bn. MS parts (c.1790): D-Rtt, Cramer 1. ★

CRESTON, Paul *10 Oct 1906, New York - 24 Aug 1985, San Diego*
PZC-1. Pavane variations, Op. 89; (version for:) 2fl 2ob 2cl 2hn 2bn 2tp.
Pm (G. Schirmer: New York, 1966).

CREUZBURG, Heinrich *1907, Germany*
HEC-1. Serenade; 1966. 2cl 2hn 2bn. MS score: D-Rk.
HEC-2. Divertimento; 1964. 2cl hn bn. MS score: D-Rk.

*CROES, Henri-Joseph de *16 Aug 1758, Brussels - 6 Jan 1842, Brussels*
HDC-1. Andante. fl 2ob 2cl 2hn 2bn 2vla vc vlne. MS parts (c.1802): D-Rtt, Sm. 32, No. 2. ★
HDC-2. [Parthia in E♭], [crossed out: Nro. 5] N♀ 2; 10 mvts. 2ob 2cl 4hn 2bn 2vla vlne.
MS parts: D-Rtt, H.de Croes 37. ★
HDC-3. Divertiment [sic], in E♭, 7 mvts. 2cl 4hn 2bn 2tp 2vla vlne.
AutoMS parts ("Le 2 de novembre 1796"): D-Rtt, H.de Croes 18. ★
HDC-4. [Parthia in E♭], d[en][3t[e]n Nov: 1793", 12 mvts. 2cl 4hn 2bn 2tp 2vla vlne.
MS parts: D-Rtt, H.de Croes 12. *Movements 9 - 12 are in a different hand and the 2tp pts (in the same hand) are on different paper and may be later additions. The title "13 Stim[m]ig is also a later addition.* ★
HDC-5. [Parthia in E♭], 10 mvts. 2cl 4hn 2bn 2tp 2vla vlne. MS pts (c.1793): D-Rtt, H.de Croes 13. ★
HDC-6. Andantino Variazioni; in B♭. fl 2ob 2cl 2hn 2bn 2vla vlne. MS pts (1823): D-Rtt, Sm. 18, No. 39. ★
HDC-7. Lento cantabile; in Eb. fl 2ob 2cl 2hn 2bn 2vla vlne. MS pts (1823): D-Rtt, Sm. 18, No. 40. ★
HDC-8. Andantino Variazione. fl 2ob 2cl 2hn 2bn 2vla vlne. MS pts (1823): D-Rtt, Sm. 18, Nos. 37. ★
HDC-9. Andante Romance; in F. fl 2ob 2cl 2hn 2bn 2vla vlne. MS pts (1823): D-Rtt, Sm 18, No. 38. ★
HDC-10. Andantino & Allegro; in F. fl 2ob 2cl 2hn 2bn 2vla vlne. MS pts (1823): D-Rtt, Sm 18, No. 39. ★
HDC-11. Andante; in B♭. fl 2ob 2cl 2hn 2bn 2vla vlne. MS parts (c.1790): D-Rtt, Sm. 32, No. 2. ★
HDC-12. [Parthia in E♭]; 6 connected sections. fl(pic) 2ob 2cl 2hn 2bn b-tb cb.
MS parts (1823): D-Rtt, Sm. 18, No. 19. ★
HDC-13. Divertissement, in B♭, 8 mvts. 2ob 2cl 2hn 2bn vlne.
AutoMS parts ("le 12. d'octobre 1792"): D-Rtt, H.de Croes 11. ★
HDC-14. Divertimento, in E♭, 12 mvts. 2cl 2hn 2bn 2vla vlne. MS parts (1794): D-Rtt, H.de Croes 14. ★
HDC-15. 9 Stim[m]ig / 12. Partien [sic: 12 mvts] v. Croes; in B♭, 12 mvts. 2cl 2hn 2bn 2vla vlne.
MS parts: D-Rtt, H.de Croes 10. ★
HDC-16. [Parthia in E♭]; 9 mvts. 2cl 2hn 2bn 2vla vlne. MS pts (5 April 1794): D-Rtt, H.de Croes 15. ★
HDC-17. [Parthia in E♭], 9 mvts. 2cl 2hn 2bn 2vla basso. AutoMS pts (c.1790): D-Rtt, H.de Croes 17. ★
HDC-18. [Parthia in B♭]; N: 1. 9.Stim[m]ige, 12 mvts. 2cl 2hn 2bn 2vla vlne.
MS parts (c.1790): D-Rtt, H de Croes 36. ★
HDC-19. [Parthia in B♭]; N: 2, 9 Stim[m]ig, N♀ 8; 12 mvts. 2cl 2hn 2bn 2vla vlne.
MS parts (c.1790): D-Rtt, H.de Croes 34. ★
HDC-20. [Parthia in B♭]; 9. Stim[m]ig, N♀ 3; 12 mvts. 2cl 2hn 2bn 2vla vlne.
MS parts (c.1790): D-Rtt, H de Croes 33. ★
HDC-21. [Parthia in B♭]; 9 Stim[m]ig, N♀ 7; 11 mvts. 2cl 2hn 2bn 2vla vlne.
MS parts (c.1790): D-Rtt, H.de Croes 35. ★
HDC-22. Le Galopade Varié…d. 12 Feb 1796. 2cl 2hn 2bn 2vla vlne. (?Auto)MS pts: D-Rtt, H.de Croes 21. ★
HDC-23. Douze morceaux. 2cl 2hn 2bn 2vla vlne. AutoMS pts (6 July 1790): D-Rtt, H.de Croes 9. ★
HDC-24. [Parthia in B♭], 6 mvts. 2cl 2hn 2bn 2tp(clar) timp. AutoMS score (c.1800): D-Rtt, H.de Croes 23. ★
HDC-25.1(-25.103). [Collection of 103 mvts]. 2hn 2tp 2vla vlne.
AutoMS parts (c.1800): D-Rtt, H.de Croes 22. ★
HDC-26(-31). [6] Partitas; all in E♭; Nos 1-5: 12 mvts; No 6: 14 mvts. 2cl 2hn 2tp.
MS parts (c.1786; No 5: "23 decembre 1786"): D-Rtt, H.de Croes 1 (-6). ★
HDC-32. N♀ 2 Divertimento, in Eb, 12 mvts. 2cl 2hn 2tp. MS pts (c.1780): D-Rtt, Inc.IVa.26/I. ★
HDC-33. [Divertimento in D], N♀ 3; 20 mvts (+ 5 mvts). 2cl(A) 2hn 2tp(clar).
MS parts (c.1780): D-Rtt, Inc.IVa.26/II. *The additional 5 mvts are separately numbered.* ★
HDC-34. Douze morceaux, "Partita Con Due Clarinetti in G Due Viole A Violone Del Henrico Croes anno 1788". 2cl 2hn 2tp.
AutoMS parts ("Compose a Tischingen par Henri Croes 1788 [sic]"): D-Rtt, H.de Croes 7. ★
Pm (Karthause-Schmülling Musikverlage: Kamen, 1993), ed. Uwe Müller, score & parts.
HDC-35. Partia in G; 13 mvts. 2a-cl(G) 2vla vlne. AutoMS pts ("anno 1788"): D-Rtt, H.de Croes 8. ★
HDC-36. Partia in G; 14 mvts. 2a-cl(G) 2vla vlne. AutoMS pts (23 Nov 1794): D-Rtt, H.de Croes 16. ★
HDC-37. [Partia in G]; N♀ 1. 5 Stim[m]ig; 12 mvts. 2a-cl(G) 2vla vlne.
MS parts (c.1788): D-Rtt, H.de Croes 32. ★
HDC-38. [Partia in G]; N♀ 5. 5 Stim[m]ig; 12 mvts. 2a-cl(G) 2vla vlne.
MS parts (c.1788): D-Rtt, H.de Croes 30. ★
HDC-39. [Partia in G]; N♀ 6. 5 Stim[m]ig; 12 mvts. 2a-cl(G) 2vla vlne.
MS parts (c.1788): D-Rtt, H.de Croes 31. ★
HDC-40. [Partia in G]; N♀ 8. 5 Stim[m]ig; 12 mvts. 2a-cl(G) 2vla vlne.
MS parts (c.1788): D-Rtt, H.de Croes 29. ★
HDC-41. [Partia in G]; N: 11. 5 Stim[m]ig; 12 mvts. 2a-cl(G) 2vla vlne.
MS parts (c.1788): D-Rtt, H.de Croes 28. ★
HDC-42. 32 Pieces für Harmonie-musik. Instrumentation unknown. (?MS): D-Rp, unverified.

*CROSS, William *d. 1826, Oxford.*
WYC-1m. The Oxford Loyal Volunteers, Slow & Quick March.   2cl 2hn (2)bn.
Pc (Henry Hardy: Oxford, c.1797); score: GB-Lbl, g.1780.q.(9). ★

*CROSSE Gordon *1 Dec 1937, Bury, Lancashire, UK*
GZC-1. Concerto da camera, Op. 6; 1962.   Solo violin, fl ob 2cl 2hn bn 2tp tb perc.
Pm (Oxford University Press: London, pn J 2451, 1966), score.

CRUFT, Adrian *10 Feb 1921, Mitcham, UK - 20 Feb 1987*
AHC-1. Stilestone Suite, Op. 62a.   pic 2fl ob 2cl 2hn 2bn 2tp 2tb (perc ad lib).
Pm (Joad Press: London, 1976).

*CRUSELL, Bernhard (Henrik) *15 Oct 1775, Nystad, Sweden - 28 July 1838 Stockholm*
BXC-1a. Beethoven: Septet, Op. 20.   terz-fl cl(Eb) 2cl(Bb) 2hn 2bn tp b-tb serp.
Pc (Peters: Leipzig; pn 1856, 1856II, 1825), 2 Parties, score & pts: D-Bhm, Mus.6983, 6984; GB-Ljag(w), (parts).
BXC-2a. Krommer: Concerto for 2 clarinets, Op. 35.   2 Solo cl, 2fl 2cl(Eb) 3cl(Bb) 4hn 2bn 2tp 3tb serp perc.
MS: S-Skma.

CUGLEY, Ian Robert Sebastian *1945, Australia*
IRC-1. Chamber Symphony.   2fl 2ob 2cl 2hn 2bn tp.
Pm (Albert & Sons Ltd.: Sydney, c.1972).

*CURSCHMANN, Karl Friedrich *21 June 1805, Berlin - 24 Aug 1841, Langfuhr, nr Danzig (now Gdansk)*
KFC-1v. Movement included in Grell's "Gemeine- und Chor-Gesänge zur Säkeular-Feier der Stiftung des Schindlerschen Waisenhauses, "Barmherzig und grädig ist der Herr".
SATB (solo & chorus), 2ob 2cl 2bthn 2hn 2bn cbn serp vc+db organ.   MS score: D-B, Mus.ms.8470/35, Nr. 2
MS score, Bläserdirektions-stimme & parts: D-B, Mus.ms.8470/50, Nr. 2. ★

*CUTLER, William Henry *14 Jan 1792, London - post 1824*
WHC-1m. March for the Full Band of the 6th Regt. Loyal London Volunteers.   2fl 2cl 2hn 2bn 2tp serp timp.
Pc (For the Author by Clementi & Co; London 1805): GB-Lbl, h.105.(26). ★

*CZERNY, Carl *20 Feb 1791, Vienna - 15 July 1857, Vienna*
CYC-1a. Beethoven: Septet, Op. 20.   2cl 2hn 2bn.   MS (1805): D-Bds, Artaria Sammlung.
CYC-2a. Winter: Das unterbrochene Opferfest, overture & 10 mvts.   (2fl) 2cl 2hn 2bn.
AutoMS pts ("den 28 April [1]804. Czernÿ [sic]"): CZ-KRa, A4005/IV.B.177, (with 2 additional fl pts by Havel).
MS parts: CZ-Pnm, (2 copies), XLI.B.128, XLI.B.131. *Possibly a reduction of Went's octet version.*

*CZŮBEK, ( ) *(1770), active in Langenbruck 1802*
YZC-1. Parthis in Dis [Eb]; 3 mvts.   2cl 2hn bn tp(prin).
MS parts (by Augustin Erasmus Hübner, Langenbruck, now Dlouhý Most, 1802): CZ-Pu(dm), 59 R 3330. ★

DAHLHOFF, Walter
WXD-1. Waldgeheimnisse (Forest Secrets).   fl ob 2cl bn.
Pm (C.F. Schmidt: Heilbronn, 1925), score & parts.

DALAYRAC (D'Alayrac, Talirak), Nicolas Marie *8 June 1753, Muret, Haute Garonne - 28 Nov 1809, Paris*
NMD-1v. Hymne à la Liberté ("Veillons au salut de l'empire").   Voice, 2cl 2hn (2)bn.
Pc (Rec des époques: Paris, c.1799), liv. 1, No. 5, pp. 11 - 13, score: F-Pn, H2. 15,5.   *Adapted (?by the composer) from his opera,* Renaud d'Ast. ★

DALBY, Martin *25 April 1942, Aberdeen*
MXD-1. Cancionero para una mariposa, 1971.   2fl bn 2tp(C) 2tb 2vc.
Pm (Novello: Borough Green, 1975), score & (hire parts): GB-Gsma; GB-Lbl, f.641.aa.(6.)
MXD-2. Fair Women Like Fair Jewels Are: Variations for Wind Octet on the Theme by Robert Jones, 1963.
fl fl(pic) ob cl hn 2bn tp.
Pm (The composer). Facsimile score available from GB-Gsma.
MXD-3. Songs my mother taught me: Caprice for Wind Sextet; (Waltz; Slow; Bird cries).   fl ob cl b-cl hn bn.
Pm (Novello: Borough Green, 1986), score.
Pm (The composer). Facsimile score available from GB-Gsma.

DALE, Gordon Alan *13 July 1935, Wrexham, UK*
GQD-1. Songs of the Forest.   fl fl(pic) ob 2cl 2hn 2bn 2tp timp 2perc.
Pm (Piper Music, Girvan, pn S046, sd), score & parts.

*DALE, Joseph *1750 - 21 Aug 1821, Edinburgh.*
JZD-1m. The Loyal March . . . for The Gentlemen Volunteers of England.   2cl 2hn 2bn.
Pc (Printed for the Author: London, c.1796), RISM [D 765], score: GB-Lbl, g.133.(12);
GB-Ob, Mus.Instr.I.79 (38). ★

DALLEY, Orien E. *1903, USA*
OED-1. Rêverie.   2fl ob 2cl hn 2bn.   Pm (M. Witmark: New York, 1933).
OED-2. Serenade.   2fl ob 2cl 2bn.   Pm (Music Publisher's Holding Association: New York).

DAL VASCO, Agostino
AXD-1v. Tantum ergo a due voci e Genitori a tre.   Solo TB, TTB chorus, 2cl 2hn bn tp timp organ.
MS score (1855) & parts: I-Vsmc. ★

*DANZI, Franz *15 May 1763, Mannheim - 13 April 1826, Karlsruhe*
FAD-1. Pot-pourri, Op. 45.   fl 2ob 2hn 2bn.   MS parts: D-HEms.
*FAD-2. Sestetto; in Eb, 4 mvts.   2cl 2hn 2bn.
MS parts: D-Rtt, Danzi 66. *A version for ob/vl 2vla 2hn vc as "Op. 10" was published by Falter in Munich (D-Rtt, Danzi 7) and by Macario Falter: Monaco, pn 95 (GB-Lbljag).* ★
Pm (Hans Sikorski: Hamburg, pn 656, 1965), ed. Johannes Wojciechowski, score & parts.

FAD-3. [Quintet in G minor, Op. 56, No. 2], Trois [sic] Quintetti. fl ob/cl(C) cl(Bb) hn bn.
MS parts: D-Rtt, Danzi 5. *Dedicated to Anton Reicha.* ★
FAD-1v. Graduale et Offertorium in Coena Domini, "Christus factus est", in F. SATB, 2ob 2hn (2)bn vc organ.
MS parts (by E. Vogel, c.1810): D-Mbm, Mf 194. ★
FAD-2v. Herr Gott, Dich loben wir; in Eb. SATB, 2cl 2hn 2bn vc+contrabasso(bc-fig).
AutoMS score & MS parts: D-Sl, H.B.XVII. 127 a.b., (with duplicate vocal pts: 3S, 2A, 2T, 2B) ★

*DASSEL, Johann Anton *(1800)*
JBD-1.1a, 1.2a. Strauss the Elder: Venetianer-Galop[p], Op. 74 & Reise-Galop[p], Op. 85.
fl 2ob cl(Eb) 3cl(Bb) 2hn 2bn 2tp 3tb serp b-dr t-dr. MS parts (c.1835): D-DT, Mus-h 1 D 1.

*DAUNEY, ( ) Dr *[Not the composer Dr William Dauney (1800-1843), also of Aberdeen.]*
DWD-1m. A Slow March Composed for the Aberdeen Fencibles. 2cl 2hn 2bn serp timp; *or* piano.
Pc (Longman & Broderip: London, c.1795), score: GB-Lbl, g.133.(52); GB-Ob, Mus.Instr.I.212.(3). ★

*DAUPRAT, Louis François *24 May 1781, Paris - 16 July 1868, Paris*
LFD-1. Solo de Cor. Solo horn, 2cl bn oph. AutoMS score: F-Pn, MS. 3945.3. ★

DAVID, Thomas Christian *1923, Wels, Austria*
TCD-1. Serenade. 2ob 2cl 2hn 2bn.
Pm (Doblinger: Wien, 1986), miniature score (pn Stp 634) & parts (pn 06 594).

*DAVIDE DA BERGAMO, Felice Moretti, *Pater (Minore Riformato)* 1791 - 1863
FMD-1. [Untitled work]. cl(F) 3cl(C) 2hn 2bn 2tp serpentone+tb drum("cassa").
AutoMS score: I-BGc, Faldone D,7,5 (36).

*DAVIES, *Sir* Peter Maxwell *8 Sept 1934, Salford, UK*
*PMD-1. St Michael: Sonata for 17 Winds, 1957. 2fl 2ob 2cl 2bn 3hn 2tp 3tb tu.
Pm (Schott & Co.: London, 1963), miniature score (pn 10792; S & Co. 6210).
PMD-2. Alma Redemptoris Mater, 1957. fl ob 2cl hn bn.
Pm (Schott & Co.: London, pn 10802, 1965), miniature score (pn 10802).
PMD-1v. Ecce manus tradentis, 1965.
SATB soli, chorus, fl ob hn 2bn cbn 2tb harp, hand-bells, crotales.
Pm (Boosey & Hawkes: London, etc., 1981), score.
PMD-2v. Te lucis ante terminum, 1961. SATB chorus, 2fl ob 2cl 2tp vc glock gtr.
Pm (Schott & Co.: London, pn 10871b, 1967), playing score.

*DAVIS, Carl *1936, New York*
*CAD-1. Pickwick Papers, 1984. 2fl 2ob 2cl 4hn 2bn cbn.
Pm (Studio Music: London, 1985), score & parts.
*CAD-2. The Searle Suite, 1974, 4 mvts. 2ob cl cl(b-cl, mvt 1 only) 2hn bn(cbn).
Pm (Eaton Music: Sundergrade).

*DAVY, John *23 Dec 1763, Crediton - 22 Feb 1824, London.*
*JHD-1mv. To Arms: To Arms! - or - John Bull's Charge to his Country. Solo voice, 2fl 2cl 2hn (2)bn 2tp.
Pc (Thomas Clio Rickman: London, c.1802), score: GB-Lbl, R.M.14.b.1.(23). *Text by James Fisher.* ★

DEÁK, Csaba *16 April 1932, Budapest (resident in Sweden since 1957)*
CYD-1. I 21. [sic]; 1969. fl ob 2cl 2hn 2bn 2tp timp piano perc.
Pm (Carl Gehrmans Musikförlag: Stockholm, pn CG 6326, c.1970), score.

DEGEN, Helmut *14 Jan 1911, Aglasterhausen, Baden*
HXD-1. Kleine Suite. Instrumentation unknown. Pm (Bärenreiter: Kassel, 1960).

DELDEN, Lex van *10 Sept 1919, Amsterdam - 7 Jan 1988, Amsterdam*
LVD-1. Violin Concerto, Op. 104. Solo Violin, 2fl 3ob 3cl 4hn 2bn cbn perc.
Pm (Donemus: Amsterdam, 1978), score, piano reduction & solo part.
LVD-2. Piccolo concerto, Op. 67; 1960. 2fl 2ob 2cl 2hn 2bn 2tp timp perc pianof.
Pm (Donemus: Amsterdam; 1960), score.
LVD-3. Sinfonia (concertante) No. 7, Op. 83; 1964. 2fl 2ob 2cl b-cl 2hn 2bn.
Pm (Donemus: Amsterdam; 1971), miniature score & parts.
LVD-4. Fantasia, Op. 87. Solo harp, 2ob 2cl 2hn 2bn.
Pm (Donemus: Amsterdam, 1965), score & parts

DELLA MARIA, Pierre Antoine Dominique *14 June 1769, Marseilles - 9 March 1800, Paris*
PAD-1. Pièces d'harmonie. 2cl 2hn 2bn.
Pc (B. Schott: Mainz, pn 231, c.1799), parts: D-MZsch.

*DELLO JOIO, Norman *24 Jan 1913, New York*
NJD-1. Satiric Dances for a comedy by Aristophanes. 2fl 2ob 4cl sax hn bn tp tb 2tu 2timp.
Pm (Associated Music Publishers: New York, 1975), score (pn 50244630) & parts (pn 502433620).

DENISOV (Denissow), Edison Vassilievich *1929, Tomsk*
EVD-1. Bläseroktett; 1991. 2ob 2cl 2hn 2bn.
Pm (Anglo-Soviet Music Press, Boosey & Hawkes: London, pn 9464, 1991 *also via Döblinger)*, score.
Pm (Hans Sikorski: Hamburg, (pn ex nova 155), sd), score.

*DEOLA, Paolo *(1800), active 1845 - 1856*
Many of Deola's works include additional pts not found in the autograph scores; we indicate these pts in parentheses. I-Vsmc also holds many fragmentary sets of pts by Deola, some of which may be for voices & winds; there are also several choral works with 2 horns & organ. Works in I-Vsmc are divided into 3 packets.
PXD-1. Marcia. 2ob 2hn bn 2tp timp organ(obbligato). MS parts: I-Vsmc, packet I. ★
PXD-1v. Sanctus & Agnus Dei; 1851. Solo TB, , (fl) 2cl 2hn (vlne/bn tp timp) organ.
AutoMS score & MS parts: I-Vsmc, packet II. ★

PXD-2v. Beatus vir; 1845.   TTB(solo+ripieno), 2cl 2hn bn tp (vlne) timp organ.
AutoMS score & MS parts: I-Vsmc, packet I.   ★
PXD-3v. Confitebor; 1851.   Solo TB, fl 2cl 2hn bn (vlne) organ.
AutoMS score & MS parts: I-Vsmc, packet I.   ★
PXD-4v. Credo. Solo TB, (2cl) 2hn (vlne/bn timp) organ. Auto MS score & MS pts (1850): I-Vsmc, packet I. ★
PXD-5v. Dixit Dominus; 1847.   TTB(solo+rip), 2cl 2hn bn tp (vlne) timp organ.
AutoMS score & MS parts: I-Vsmc, packet I.   ★
PXD-6v. Dixit Dominus; 1845.   Solo TB, 2cl 2hn (vlne) organ(bc-fig).
AutoMS score & MS parts: I-Vsmc, packet I, (missing cl II, with additional full organ pt).   ★
PXD-7v. Gloria; 1847.   TB(solo+rip), 2cl 2hn bn tp (vlne) timp organ(bc-fig).
AutoMS score & MS parts: I-Vsmc, packet I, (with an additional full organ part).   ★
PXD-8v. Kyrie; 1847.   TTB(solo+rip), 2cl 2hn bn tp (vlne) timp organ(bc-fig).
AutoMS score & MS parts: I-Vsmc, packet II, (with an additional full organ part).   ★
PXD-9v. Kyrie e Gloria; 1850. TB(Solo+rip), (2cl) 2hn (vlne+bn timp) organ.
AutoMS score & MS parts: I-Vsmc, packet II.   ★
PXD-10v. Laudate Dominum omnes gentes; 1845.   TTB(solo+rip), 2cl(C) 2hn bn (bn/vlne) tp timp organ.
AutoMS score & MS parts: I-Vsmc, packet II.   ★
PXD-11v. Laudate pueri.   TTB(solo+rip), fl(ad lib) 2cl 2hn bn tp(2) (vlne) timp organ.
AutoMS score & MS parts: I-Vsmc, packet II, (the bn marked "Col Basso dell'Organo").   ★
PXD-12v. Regina coeli; 1852.   TTB, 2cl(C) 2hn bn (tp tb) organ(bc-fig).
AutoMS score & MS parts: I-Vsmc, packet II, (with an additional full organ part).   ★
PXD-13v. Regina coeli; 1855.   TTB chorus, fl 2cl 2hn tp timp organ.
AutoMS score & MS parts: I-Vscm, packet II. *The parts include 2vl vla; however, a note on the last verso page states that if the work is to be performed with "Soli Stromenti da fiato" the clarinets replace the violins. There follows scoring list: vl I(2) vl II(2) vla(1) fl(1) cl(2) hn(2) tp(1) bn(1) vlne(1) timp(1) organ(1), T I(2) T II(2) B(3) for a total of 23 musicians. The bassoon & violone would have played off the organ bass.* ★
PXD-14v. Salve Regina.   TTB, 2cl 2hn bn (tp) organ(bc-fig).
AutoMS score & MS parts: I-Vsmc, packet II, (with an additional full organ part; the bassoon part bears the pencil addition, "o Violon").   ★
PXD-15v. Salve Regina.   TTB, 2cl 2hn (bn/vlne vlne tp tb) organ.
AutoMS score & MS parts (1845): I-Vsmc, packet II.   ★

*DERENZIS (De Renzis), Raffaelo *17 Feb 1879, Casacalenda, Campobasso - 3 Nov 1970, Rome*
RZD-1va. F.P. Schubert: Mass in G.   Soli, SATB chorus, 2fl 2cl a-cl b-cl.
Pc (Shawnee Press: Delaware Water Gap), hire score & parts.

DERUNGS, Gion Antoni *1935, Switzerland*
GAD-1. Oktett, Op. 79; 1978.   2ob 2cl 2hn 2bn.   MS: CH-Zma.

*DESHAYES, Prosper Didier *1751 - 1815, Paris*
PDD-1. Première Suite d'Harmonie; 6 substantial mvts.   2cl 2hn 2bn.
Pc (A l'Imprimerie du Conservatoire de Musique: Paris c.1798), RISM [D 1765], parts: F-Pn, Vm7 6960.   ★
MS parts: CZ-Pnm,(MS parts), XLI.B.108.
Pc (Schlesinger: Paris, c.1820), parts: F-Pn.

*DESIRO, ( )
XXD-1v. Gloria.   TTB(solo+rip), 2cl 2hn bn/vlne tp timp organ.   MS score & parts: I-Vsmc.   ★
XXD-2v. Kyrie.   TTB(solo+rip), 2cl 2hn bn/vlne tp timp organ.   MS score & parts: I-Vsmc.   ★

DESPORTES, Yvonne Berythe Melitta *18 July 1907, Coburg, Saxony*
YBD-1. Sérénade exotique; 1973.   2ob 2cl 2hn 2bn.   MS score: F-Pd.

*DESVIGNES, Pierre (Louis Augustin) *27 Sept 1764, Vélars - 21 Jan 1827, Paris*
*PLD-1v. Deprofundis [sic].   CATB, 2ob 2cl 2hn 2bn 3tb timp bassi.
AutoMS score (1806): F-Pn, (2 copies), MS. 9347 (1), MS. 7209.   ★
PLD-2v. 4e Messe.   CATB, 2cl hn bn vc bc.   AutoMS score: F-Pn, MS. 9330.   ★
PLD-3v. 2e Messe.   CATB, cl bn vc b.   AutoMS score: F-Pn, MS. 9330 (1), (missing sheet 1).   ★
PLD-1vf. Resurrexit.   C, 2cl hn b.   AutoMS score: F-Pn, MS. 9330, following PLD-2.   ★

*DEVASINI, Giuseppe *20 Marvh 1822, Milan - 21 June 1878, Cairo*
*GXD-1. Sestetto; in F, 4 mvts.   fl ob 2cl(C) hn bn.
Pc (Ricordi: Milano, pn L13625L, 1850s), parts: I-Mc, (2 copies), Da Camera A.30.12, Da Camera A.30.13.   ★

DEVČIČ, Natko *1914*
NXD-1. Prolog.   pic 2fl 2ob 3cl 4hn 2bn 4tp 4tb tu 2perc.
Pm (H. Gerig: Köln, 1965), full score *(via Breitkopf & Härtel: Wiesbaden, pn BG 634)*.

*DEVIENNE, François *31 Jan 1759, Joinville - 5 Sept 1803, Charenton.*
FZD-1. Ouverture, in F, P.2305.   2p-fl 2ob 2cl 2hn 2bn 2tp tb serp timp.
Pc (Mag de mus fêtes nat: Paris, vendemiaire an III, 1795), liv. 7, No. 1, RISM [D 1920], parts: D-WRtl; F-Pn, H2. 7,1; F-Nm, Vol 22207.   ★
Pm (Hofmeister: Leipzig, pn 1434, 1954), ed. Franz von Glasenapp, (suggests bn III/cbn for serp), score & parts.
FZD-1a. Beffroy de Reigny & P. Gaveaux: Le Club de bonnes [sic] gens, overture & 6 morceaux.
2p-fl/ob(ad lib) 2cl 2hn 2bn serp 2tp b-dr cym tri, *or* 2p-fl/ob 2cl 2hn 2bn.
Pc (les frères Gaveaux: Paris, pn 38, c.1792), RISM [B 1661], parts: D-AB.
FZD-2a. P. Gaveaux: L'Amour filial, overture & 6 morceaux. 2p-fl/ob(ad lib) 2cl 2hn 2bn 2tp serp b-dr cym tri, *or* 2p-fl/ob 2cl 2hn 2bn; *(surviving copies are missing: 2tp serp perc).*
Pc (les frères Gaveaux: Paris, pn 36, c.1792), RISM [G 624], parts: D-AB; US-BETm.
Pc (as "2nd Suite d'harmonie": (sn [?les frères Gaveaux]: Paris, sd), parts: D-DS, (?lost in World War II).
FZD-3a. P. Gaveaux: Le petit matelot, 6 mvts.   2pic/ob 2cl 2hn 2bn, (ad lib: tp[s] serp b-dr cym tri).
Pc (les frères Gaveaux: Paris, pn 37, c.1796), RISM Supp [DD 1920a = GG 670a], parts: US-BETm.

FZD-1mv. Le Chant du rétour; (P.127).   Solo voice, 2pic 2cl 2hn 2bn timp.
MS: F-Pn, Archives national, F17 1295.   ★
FZD-2mv. Hymne à l'Éternel; (P.570.   Solo voice, 2cl 2hn 2bn.
Pc (Rec des époques: Paris, c.1799), liv. 1, No. 25, pp. 66 - 70, score: F-Pc, H2. 15,25.   ★
FZD-1ac. P. Gaveaux: Sophie et Moncars, ouverture.   2pic/ob(ad lib) 2cl 2hn 2bn serp 2tp b-dr cym tri, *or*
2pic/ob 2cl 2hn 2bn.
Pc (sn: sl [= les frères Gaveaux: Paris], pn 45, c.1797), RISM [G 692], parts: D-AB, (incomplete: only pic/ob(I)
cl(II) 2hn 2bn serp).

*DIBDIN, Charles *baptized 15 March 1745, Southampton - 25 July 1814, London*
Modern MS scores and parts of all these works are at GB-DOTams and GB-Ljag. In all the titled works, the
wind band version (apparently by Dibdin himself) omits vocal parts.
*CXD-1. The Lancashire Witches: Allegro.   2cl 2hn bassi.   AutoMS score: GB-Lbl, Add. 39052, f.127.   ★
*CXD-1m. Ode in honour of his Majesty's birthday. 2cl 2hn 2bn bassi.
Pc (Printed & Sold by the Author: London, 1792), RISM [D 2945], score: GB-Gu; GB-Lbl, G.363.(4);
GB-Ob, Mus.Voc.I.19(31).   ★
*CXD-2m. Ode to Gratitude on the preservation of his Majesty.   2cl 2hn bn.
Pc (Printed & Sold by the Author: London, 1800), RISM [D 2947], score: GB-Lcm; GB-Lbl, G.368.(8);
GB-Ob, Mus.Voc.I.19(19); GB-SA; I-Rsc.   ★
CXD-3m. March; in Eb.   2cl bn (unfilled staves for: 2hn tp timp).
AutoMS score: GB-Lbl, Add. 30950, f.132b.   ★
*CXD-4m. British War-Songs (Nos. 1 - 6, 8, 9 from the numbered series for chorus and orchestra).
  *4.1m. Fall or Conquer, A Parody on Robert Burns's Poem called "Bruce's Address to his Army."
  2cl 2hn 2bn bassi 2tp.
  AutoMS score: GB-Lbl, Add. 30950, f.134.   ★
  Pc (Printed & Sold by the Author, June 4 1803), score: GB-Lbl, G.376.(2); GB-Ob, Mus.Voc.I.19(20).   ★
  *4.2m. The British Heroines.   2cl 2hn 2bn bassi.
  AutoMS score: GB-Lbl, Add. 30953, f.180.   ★
  Pc (Printed & Sold by the Author: London, July 4 1803), score: GB-Lbl, G.376.(2); GB-Ob, Mus.Voc.I.19(21).
  4.3m. The Song of Death.   2cl 2hn 2bn bassi.
  Pc (Printed & Publish'd by the Composer: London, Augt 4 1803), score: GB-Lbl, G.376.(2);
  GB-Ob, Mus.Voc.I.19(22).   ★
  4.4m. The Soldier's Oath of Allegiance.   2cl 2hn 2bn bassi.
  Pc (Printed & Sold by the Author: London, Sepr. 5th, 1803), score: GB-Lbl, (2 copies), G.376.(2),
  R.M.13.e.8.(88); GB-Ob, Mus.Voc.I.19(23).   ★
  *4.5m. The Song of Acre.   2cl 2hn bassi.
  Pc (Printed & Publish'd by the Composer: London, Octr. 4th 1803), score: GB-Lbl, G.376.(2);
  GB-Ob, Mus.Voc.I.19(24).   ★
  4.6m. The Volunteer (text: The Reverend W. Butler).   2ob/cl 2hn 2bn bassi.
  AutoMS score: GB-Lbl, Add.30952, f.25.   ★
  Pc (Printed for the Composer: London, [Nov 4] 1803), score: GB-Lbl, G.376.(2); GB-Ob, Mus.Voc.I.19(25).
  4.7m. Love and Glory.   2cl 2hn 2bn bassi.
  Pc (Printed & Sold by the Author: London, Jany. 4th 1804), score: GB-Lbl, (2 copies), G.376.(2),
  R.M.13.e.8.(89); GB-Ob, Mus.Voc.I.19(27).   ★
  4.8m. The Duty of a Soldier, a Brother, a Father and a Briton.   2cl 2hn bassi.
  Pc (Printed & Sold by the Author: London, [Feb 4] 1804), score: GB-Lbl, R.M.13.e.8.(90).   ★
*CXD-5m. [3 Songs from] Britons Strike Home!, (separate issues).
  5.1m. The Auld Pibrough.   2cl 2hn bassi.
  Pc (Printed & Sold by the Author: London, 1803), score: GB-Lbl, G.380.(1); GB-Ob, Mus.Voc.I.17(43).   ★
  *5.2m. The Subscription at Lloyds.   2cl 2hn (2)bn(col bassi) bassi.
  Pc (Printed & Sold by the Author: London, 1803), score: GB-Lbl, G.380.(4).   ★
  *5.3m. Victory and George the Third.   2cl 2hn 2bn bassi.
  Pc (Printed & Sold by the Author: London, 1803), score: GB-Lbl, G.380.(11).   ★

DICKSON, Stanley
SXD-1. Thanks be to God, in Db.   Solo cornet, fl ob 3cl cl(Eb) a-sax 4hn 2bn 2ct 2b-tb euph drum.
Pm (Edwin Ashdown: London), hire score & parts.

DIEHL, Paula Jespersen
PJD-1. Portage.   3cl b-cl 2bn.   MS score: US-NYamc.

DIESELBACH, ( )
XYD-1. N: 1. Parthia Toni B[b] a 8 Stromt:; 6 mvts.   2ob 2cl 2hn 2bn.
MS parts (provenance: Franz Culmberger): D-F, Mus.Hs.1565.   ★

*DIETHE, Johann Friedrich *(oboist) 1810 - 1891*
FYD-1. Romance.   Solo clarinet, 2ob 2cl 2hn 2bn.
Pm (Merseburger: Berlin, 1928; later reissue, sd), score.
FYD-2. Romance.   2ob cl b-cl hn bn.
Pm (Leduc, Paris, sd).
Pc (A.J. Andraud: Cincinatti, sd).

DIETRICHSTEIN (Dittrichstein), Moritz, *Graf* von   *19 Feb 1775, Vienna - 27 Aug 1864, Vienna*
MVD-1. Minuetto [& Trio]; in G.   2ob 2ca 2hn (2)bn.   MS parts: A-Wgm, VIII 8548 (Q 16372).   ★
Although the titlepage lists "Fagotto" there is a single divisi bar, suggesting 1 or 2 bassoons.

DIJK, Jan H. van   *4 June 1918, Oostzaan, Netherlands*
JVD-1. Sérénade, 1959.   2fl 2ob 3cl 2hn 2bn 2tp timp perc piano.
Pm (Donemus: Amsterdam, sd), score.

*DIJKSTRA, Lowell *1952, Netherlands*
LXD-1. Fantasia.   2fl 2ob 2cl 4hn 3bn 3tp 3tb tu.
Pm (Donemus: Amsterdam, 1988), score.
LXD-2. Peccadillos.   fl 2ob 2cl 2hn 2bn.
Pm (Donemus: Amsterdam, 1991), score.

DILLON, James *1950, Glasgow*
JMD-1. La Femme Invisible.   fl(pic) a-fl(b-fl) ob ob(ca) cl b-cl s-sax s-sax(a-sax) piano 3perc.
Pm (Peters Edition: London, 1989), score & (hire parts).

*DIMITRAKOPOULOS, Apostolos *4 Jan 1955, Greece*
APD-1. Void; 1985.   3fl(pic) 2ob(ca) 2cl(b-cl) 4hn 2bn 4tp 2tb 2tu 2db timp 2perc.   MS score: S-Sic.
APD-2. Impexus; 1987.   2fl 2ob 2cl 4hn 2bn 2tp 2tb 2tu timp 2 perc.   MS score: S-Sic.
APD-3. 5.1.8. [sic].   2fl 2ob 2cl 2hn 2bn db tape.   MS score: S-Sic.
APD-4. Lux prima; 1993.   fl cl 2bn 2tp 2tb xylophone piano.   MS score: S-Sic.

DIRRIWACHTER, Wim *1937, Netherlands*
WZD-1v. Missa brevis, 1975.   SATB chorus, 2ob ca 3bn.
Pm (Donemus: Amsterdam, 1981), score.

DISCHER, J.D. *See under* **Fischer, J.**

*DITTERS VON DITTERSDORF, Carl *2 Nov 1739, Vienna - 24 Oct 1799, zámek Červená Lhota, Bohemia*
We have been unable to verify or identify this modern edition but believe it to be from the set CDD-40(-46):
Partita in D minor.   2ob 2hn bn.   Pm (A.J. Benjamin: Hamburg).
*CDD-1. Partita No. 1 in C; 7 mvts.   fl 2ob 2hn bn.
MS parts: D-Bds, Hausbibl. Nr 336 (?lost); CZ-Pnm, XXII.B.256 (as "Parthia in C, No. 17").   ★
CDD-2. Partita No. 2.   4ob 2hn 2bn 2tp.   MS parts: D-Bds, Hausbibl. Nr.336, (?lost).
CDD-3. Partita No. 3.   2fl 2ob 2hn 2bn 2tp timp.   MS parts: D-Bds, Hausbibl. Nr. 336, (?lost).
CDD-4, 5. 2 Parthien.   2fl 2ob 2cl 2hn bn.   MS: D-Bds, (unverified).
CDD-6. Parthia in C; 7 mvts.   2vl/(?ob) 2ca 2hn bn.
MS parts: A-KR, H39/74.   ★
Pm (Mannheimer Musik-Verlag: Bonn, pn E6-61, sd), ed. Helmut Wirth, hire score & pts, (for 2ob 2ca 2hn 2bn).
CDD-7. Partita ex F; 9 mvts.   2vl 2ca 2hn bn.
MS parts: A-KR, H 39/74.   ★
Pm (Mannheimer Musik-Verlag: Bonn, pn E6-61, sd), ed. Helmut Wirth, hire score & parts.
CDD-8. Parthia ex C, Nro. 1; 4 mvts.   2ob 2hn bn.   MS parts: CZ-Pnm, XXII.B.240.   ★
*CDD-9. Partita Nro. 2; in F, 6 mvts.   2ob 2hn bn.
MS parts: CZ-Pnm, (2 copies), XXII.B.241, XXXII.B.139, (as "N: 1 Partitta in F"; omits mvts 4 & 5).   ★
Pm (Breitkopf & Hartel: Wiesbaden, c.1948), ed. Günter Rhau (from CZ-Pnm XXII.B.241), electrostatic copy
of Rhau's MS score, (Kammerbibliothek 2101): GB-Lbl, f.244.gg.(1).
CDD-10. Partita Nro. 3; in B♭, 5 mvts.   2ca/cl 2hn bn.   MS parts: CZ-Pnm, XXII.B.242.   ★
*CDD-11. Partitta Nro 4; in D, 4 mvts.   2ob 2hn bn.
MS parts: CZ-Pnm (2 copies), XXII.B.243, XLII.B.183, (as "Parthia in D").   ★
Pm (Breitkopf & Hartel: Wiesbaden, c.1948), ed. Günter Rhau (from CZ-Pnm XXII.B.243), electrostatic copy
of Rhau's MS score, (Kammerbibliothek 2101): GB-Lbl, f.244.gg.(1).
CDD-12. Partitta, Nro. 5; in B♭, 4 mvts.   2ob 2hn bn.   MS parts: CZ-Pnm, XXII.B.244.   ★
CDD-13. Partita In D, Nro. 6; 4 mvts.   2ob 2hn bn.   MS parts: CZ-Pnm, XXII.B.245.   ★
CDD-14. Partita In F, Nro. 7; 5 mvts.   2ob 2hn bn.   MS parts: CZ-Pnm, XXII.B.246.   ★
CDD-15. Partitta No. 8; in D, 5 mvts.   2ob 2hn bn.
MS parts: CZ-Pnm, XXII.B.247; GB-Lbl (c.1765), RM.21.a.13.(2).   ★
Pm (Musica rara: London, 1958), ed. Karl Haas, score & parts.
CDD-16. Partita in B[♭], Nro 9; 6 mvts.   2ob 2hn bn.
MS parts: CZ-Pnm, (2 copies), XXII.B.248, XXXII.B.145. ★
CDD-17. Parthia In G, Nro 10; 4 mvts.   2ob 2hn 2bn.   MS parts: CZ-Pnm, XXII.B.249.   ★
CDD-18. Parthia In D, Nro. 11; 4 mvts.   2ob 2hn 2bn.   MS parts: CZ-Pnm, XXII.B.250.   ★
CDD-19. Parthia In C, Nro. 12; 4 mvts.   2ob 2hn 2bn.   MS parts: CZ-Pnm, XXII.B.251.   ★
CDD-20. Parthia in C, Nro. 13; 4 mvts.   2ob 2hn 2bn.   MS parts: CZ-Pnm, XXII.B.252;
CDD-21. In Dis [E♭] Parthia, Nro. 14, 4 mvts.   2ob 2hn 2bn.   MS parts: CZ-Pnm, XXII.B.253.   ★
CDD-22. Parthia In D, Nro. 15; 4 mvts.   2ob 2hn bn.   MS parts: CZ-Pnm, XXII.B.254.   ★
CDD-23. Parthia in Dis [E♭], Nro. 16; 5 mvts.   2ob 2hn bn.   MS parts: CZ-Pnm, XXII.B.255.   ★
CDD-24. Parthia in D, Nro 18; 5 mvts.   2ob 2hn bn.   MS parts: CZ-Pnm, XXII.B.257.   ★
CDD-25. Parthia Ex A, Nro. 19; 5 mvts.   2ob 2hn 2bn.   MS parts: CZ-Pnm, XXII.B.258.   ★
*CDD-26. Parthia Ex A, Nro. 20; 5 mvts.   2ob 2hn bn.   MS parts: CZ-Pnm, XXII.B.259.   ★
Pm (Breitkopf & Hartel: Wiesbaden, c.1948), ed. Günter Rhau (from CZ-Pnm XXII.B.241), electrostatic copy
of Rhau's MS score (Kammerbihliothek 2101): GB-Lbl, f.244.gg.(1).
CDD-27 . Parthia ex G, Nro. 21; 5 mvts.   2ob 2hn bn.   MS parts: CZ-Pnm, XXII.B.260.   ★
*CDD-28. Parthia Ex Dis [E♭], Nro. 22; 4 mvts.   2ob 2hn bn.   MS parts: CZ-Pnm (2 copies), XXII.B.261,
XXXII.B.146, (as "Partitta in Dis / N: 3").   ★
CDD-29. Parthia Nro. 23; in D, 5 mvts.   2ob 2hn bn.   MS parts: CZ-Pnm, XXII.B.262.   ★
CDD-30. Partia in G, Nro. 24; 5 mvts.   2ob 2hn bn.   MS parts: CZ-Pnm, XXII.B.263.   ★
CDD-31. Partitta in F; 5 mvts.   2ob 2hn 2bn.   MS parts: CZ-Pnm, XXII.B.264.   ★
*CDD-32. N: 1 Parthia in G; 5 mvts.   2ob 2hn bn.   MS parts: CZ-Pnm, XXXII.B.140.   ★
CDD-33. N: 4. Partitta in G; 5 mvts.   2ob 2hn bn.   MS parts: CZ-Pnm, XXXII.B.142.   ★
CDD-34. N: 5 Partitta in C; 5 mvts.   2ob 2hn bn.   MS parts: CZ-Pnm, XXXII.B.147; D-HER, Mus.C.13=1,
(as "Partia in C", for 2ob/(fl vl) 2hn bn).   ★
*CDD-35. N: 8. Partitta in G; 6 mvts.   2ob 2hn bn.   MS pts: CZ-Pnm, XXXII.B.141.   ★
CDD-36. Parthia in D# [i.e. D major]; 4 mvts.   2ob 2hn bn.   MS pts: CZ-NR, A.18.235/B.250.   ★
CDD-37. Parthia in D; 5 mvts.   2ob 2hn bn.   MS parts: CZ-NR, A.18.264/B/280.   ★

CDD-38.1. [Parthia in E♭], 5 mvts.   2cl 2hn bn.
MS pts: D-Rtt, Sammelband 8, Nos. 53-57; D-DO, Mus.Ms.332, (as "Parthie in Dis" [E♭]; with score, c.1920).   ★
CDD-38.8. [Parthia], in E♭; 12 mvts.   MS parts: D-Rtt, Dittersdorf 39. *Probably a local arrangement: the first 2 mvts are the same as those of CDD-22.2; mvts 3 - 12 are completely different.*
CDD-39. Divertimento in B[♭]; 5 mvts, (Krebs 136).   2ob 2cl (2)bn.
AutoMS score: A-Wgm VIII 8871.   ★
MS parts (both as "Parthia in B[♭]"): CZ-Pnm, XXXII.C.103, (post-1773); D-Dl, Mus.3411-P-5.
Pm (Sikorski: Hamburg, pn 294, 1954), ed. J Wojciechowski, score & parts.
CDD-40(-46). 7 Partite.   2ob 2hn 2bn.   MS parts: D-Bds, Hausbibl., Nr. 335.
CDD-1m. 2 Märsche.   2ob 2cl 2hn 2bn.   MS parts: D-Bds, Hausbibl. M.M.98.
CDD-1e(m). Das Gespenst mit der Trommel (Geisterbanner; opera, 16 Aug 1794), Act II, No 7 (Sestetto): march & presentation of arms.   2ob 2hn (2)bn + unison voices.
AutoMS score: D-Dl.   MS score: A-Wgm, IV 7737 (Q 1318); D-B, Mus.ms.5021 (not D-Bds, *pace* MGG).   ★
★CDD-1d. Parthia in E♭ (actually Rosetti, FAR-9.1).   2ob 2cl 2hn 2bn.   MS score: D-Mbs, Mus.Mss.1723, (fair copy by Druschetzky, as "Parthia. Del: Sig: Carlo Dittersdorff [sic]").

★DITTRICH, Francis *(1770)*
★FQD-1m. A Collection of Military Music For a whole band. Chiefly for the bugle, Consisting of Marches[,] Quicksteps, Troops and Waltzes.   2fl 2cl 2hn 2bn tp bugle(tacet in No. 10) serp.
Pc (sn, ?The Author: sl [Edinburgh], 1801), parts: GB-Lbl, h.107.(24).   ★
  1.1m. Lord Dalkeith's Troop. 1.2m. Duke of Buccleugh's March. 1.3m. Lord Montague['s] Fancy. Quickstep.
  1.4m. Dutchess [sic] of Bucleugh['s] Menuet. 1.5m. Lord Dalkeith['s] Bugle Poloness [sic].
  1.6m. Lord Elebank['s] Delight. 1.7m. 4th N[orth] B[erwick]. Militia Troop. 1.8m. Lt. General Vyse's March.
  1.9m. Capt. Campbell['s] Quick Step. 1.10m. A Scotch Ayr [sic]. 1.11m. Lord Elbank['s] Fancy. Jigg [sic].
  1.12m. Capt. Burnett['s] Quick Step. 1.13m. Capt. Crichton['s] Bugle Waltz.
  1.14m. Sir Chas. Douglas['s] Bugle Waltz. 1.15m. Major Riddell['s] Fancy. Quickstep.
  1.16m. Lady Dalkeith's Waltz. 1.17m. Lady Caroline Montague['s] Delight.
  1.18m. Schultz: Grand Waltz Lt. Don's Favourate [sic]. Not to [sic] Quick.

DIXON, Hugh *1927, New Zealand*
HYD-1. Mosaic[1989, (11 minutes).   ob (ob(ca) cl cl(b-cl) 2hn 2bn.   MS score: NZ-Wmc.
HYD-2. Folksong Frolic; 1990, (3 minutes).   2ob 2cl 2hn 2bn.   MS score: NZ-Wmc.

★DIXON, William *(c.1760)*
WYD-1v. Four services in score with Accompaniment for flutes & oboes, a bassoon or violoncello, Designed for the use of Country Choirs.
Pc (Engraved, Printed, & Sold by the Author: London, 1792), RISM [D 3295], score: GB-Cu; GB-Lbl, G.502.(1).

DMITRIEV, Sergej *15 Jan 1964*
SYD-1. Conversions; 1992.   fl(pic) cl(b-cl) 2bn 2tp 2tb perc piano/conductor.   MS: S-Sic.

★DOBIHAL, Josef (Joseph) *1779 - 1824*
★JUD-1m. Romani (composer/compiler): Die Fee und der Ritter, Marsch.   2ob 2cl 2hn 2bn cbn 2tp.
MS parts: A-Wn, Mus.Hs.3880.   ★
JUD-2m. 9 Märsche vom 1ten k.k. Landess=Pataillon [sic] der Nord Wien.   2ob cl(F) 2cl(C) 2hn 2bn cbn 2tp.
MS parts: CZ-Pnm, Lobkovic X.H.b.13.   ★
JUD-1a. [composer unknown - ?Dobihal]:·Larighetto, overture & 11 mvts.   2ob 2cl 2hn 2bn cbn.
MS parts: CZ-KRa, A3853/IV.B.17.

DODD, Peter *(1930?)*
PYD-1. Octet.   2ob 2cl 2hn 2bn.
Pm (New Wind Music: Wembley Park, Middlesex, UK, sd).

DÖHL, Friedhelm *7 July 1936, Göttingen.*
FHD-1. Ballet mécanique, 1984.   2fl 2cl vc piano perc.
Pm (Breitkopf & Härtel: Wiesbaden, pn 2209, 1985), score.

DOLETSCHEK, Joseph Johann
JPD-1m. Marsch; (with Trio), in D.   cl(G) cl(D) 2bn klappen-tp(D) tp(G hoch) tp(A ti[e]f).
AutoMS parts: CZ-Pnm, XIII.B.53, (inserted loose with funeral marches by Josef Mrvkvička). *Note: Doletschek was the copyist for Mrkvička's marches; however, we believe that this is an original work by Doletschek.*   ★

DOMANSKY, Alfred *1883 - ?*
AYD-1. Octet.   fl ob 2cl 2hn 2bn.
Pc (E. Müller, Süddeutscher Musikverlag: Heidelberg, c.1923).
AYD-2. Quintet No. 2.   2ob 2cl bn
Pc (C.F. Schmidt: Heilbronn, 1936).
AYD-3. Divertimento.   2cl 2bn. *Some sources give: 2cl hn bn.*
Pc (C.F. Schmidt: Heilbronn, 1936).

★DOMAŽLICKÝ, František *13 May 1913, Prague*
FKD-1. Concerto for Wind Octet, Op. 45.   2ob 2cl 2hn 2bn.
Pm (Český Hudební fond: Prague, 1973), (hire) score & parts.

★DONATONI, Franco *9 June 1927, Verona*
FCD-1. Movimento; 1959.   Solo piano, harpsichord, 3fl 2cl 2hn bn tp.
Pm (Suvini Zerboni: Milano, 1960). *There is also a 1962 version for full orchestra.*
FCD-2. Cadeau;1984.   2ob 2hn 2bn tu marimba vib glock harp.
Pm (Ricordi: Milano, pn 133840, c.1984), score.
FCD-3. Terzo estratto; 1975.   2ob 2bn 2tp 2tb piano.
Pm (Suvini-Zerboni: Milano, pn S8133, c.1976), score.

DONE, Joshua *(1790?) London*
JYD-1v. A Selection ... of Psalm & Hymn Tunes, Chants, &c. harmonized in four parts, for voices, Piano Forte, Organ or Band. 2vl/2fl/2ob vla basso
Pc (George & Manby: London, "Second Edition, augmented", 1835?), score: GB-Lbl, H.3047.

DONELLI, Benedetto *(1790)*
BXD-1 Armonia in F per soli strumenti di fiati; 3 mvts. 2fl 2ob 2ca 2cl(C) 2hn 2bn.
AutoMS score (1821): I-Bc, MM.232. ★

*DONIZETTI, (Domenico) Gaetano (Maria) *29 Nov 1797, Bergamo - 8 April 1848, Bergamo*
*DGD-1. Sinfonia; in G minor, 1 mvt. fl 2ob 2cl 2hn 2bn.
AutoMS score ("Bologna, lì 19 Aprile 1817"): I-BGi(md), Collocazione: I, 2ª, Ca, 5. ★
Pm (Tetra Music *via* Alexander Broude: New York, pn A.B.137-16, 1967), ed. Douglas Townsend, score & parts.
Pm (Edition Eulenberg: Zürich, c.1975), ed. Bernhard Päuler, score (pn 10015) & parts (pn 10015a).
DGD-2. Larghetto in Fa Magg [F major]. 2fl 2bthn 2hn bn.
(Auto?)MS: US-Eu.
Pm (Boccaccini & Spada: Roma, pn BS 1163, 1989), ed. Don L. Roberts, score & parts.
DGD-3. Moderato. fl 2cl 2hn tp tb organ.
(?Auto)MS: I-BGi(md), Collocazione: I, 1a, Ca, 2.
Pm (Boccaccini & Spada: Roma, pn BS 1164, 1989), edited Pietro Spada, parts.
*DGD-1m. Marcia in F Magg. pic cl(D) 2cl(C) 2hn tp tb drum.
MS: (untraced - ? I-BGi).
Pm (Boccaccini & Spada: Roma, pn BS 1165, 1989), ed. Pietro Spada, ?score & parts.
DGD-1tv. Luga qui Legis. Marcia funebre composta...nell'anno 1842 in Milano per il rinomato scultore Pompeo Marchesi. Unison voices, fl(Eb) ob cl(Ab) 3cl(Bb) 4hn 2bn 2tp(F) 2tp(Ab basso) Trombe a Macchina (Eb) 2flicorno(Bb) 3tb 2basso b-dr dr(muffled).
Pm (G. Ricordi: Milano, pn 30309, c.1910), score: GB-Lbl, H.375.b.(4).
DGD-1v. Qui tollis per Tenore, Clarinetto obbligato e piccola orcheatra; in F.
T solo, 2fl 2ob 2hn 2bn organ, cb(ad lib). MS parts: I-BGi(md), Collocazione: I, 2a, E, 51.
DGD-2v. Salve Regina; in F. CTB, 2ob 2cl 2hn tb vc vlne.
AutoMS Score: F-Pn. MS parts: I-BGi(md), Collocazione: I, 2a, E, 57.
DGD-3v. Tantum ergo; Eb major. T solo, fl 2cl 2hn 2bn cb.
MS parts: I-BGi(md), Collocazione: I, 2a, E, 60.
DGD-4v. Domine [ad adjuvandum]; in C. CTB, 2ob 2hn organ (tp tb cb).
MS parts: I-BGi(md), Collocazione: I, 2a, E, 16, (the instruments in parentheses appear only in the parts).
DGD-5v. Tantum ergo; Eb major. T solo, fl 2cl 2hn 2bn cb.
MS parts: I-BGi(md), Collocazione: I, 2a, E, 60.
DGD-6v. Kyrie, C minor. CTB, 2ob 2hn organ (cb).
AutoMS score & MS parts: I-BGi(md), Collocazione: I, 1a, E. 26, (the appears in the parts only).
DGD-7v. Kyrie; in C minor. CTB, 2ob 2hn basso.
AutoMS score & MS parts: I-BGi(md), Collocazione: I, 1a, E. 27.
*DGD-1va. Mayr: Miserere. Solo CCATTB, ATB chorus, pic 3fl 2ob 2cl 3hn 2bn 4tp 2tb.
MS parts: I-BGc, Mayr fald. 214/17, (with duplicate parts: ob I, hn I, hn III, tp IV).

DONNINGER, Ferdinand *1716 - 1781*
*FND-1. Parthia a 8 instr.; in Bb, 10 mvts. 2cl 2hn 2bn 2vla.
(?Auto)MS pts: D-Rtt, Donninger 18. *The viola parts, written in the bass clef, appear to be a later addition.* ★

DORDA, Gerhard *1922, Germany*
JFD-1. Images de la vie; 1981 - 1982. ob ca hn 2bn.
Pm (Deutscher Tonkünstlerverbend e.V.: München, pn 604, c.1983), score & parts.

DOTAS, Chuck
CZD-1a. Richard C. Peaslea: Nightsongs. Solo flug/tp, 2fl ob ca 3cl 2hn 2bn piano db 2perc.
Pm (Margun Music: Newton Center, MA, pn MM 061B, 1994), score & parts.

*DOUBRAVSKÝ (Dobrawský, Däubrawsky), František *7 Feb 1790, Lomnice - 28 April 1867, Lomnice*
FRD-1v. [4] Stationes in F. CATB, fl 2cl 2hn 2tp flüg b-tb timp. MS parts (1860): CZ-Pnm, VIII.D.133. ★
FRD-2v. Stabat Mater, C mol: [minor]. CATB, 2cl hn 2tp(muted) timp.
AutoMS parts (16 March 1834): CZ-Pnm, VIII.D.137. ★
FRD-1tv. Pišeň pohřební pro manźela [funeral song for a husband].
CATB, fl cl(Eb) cl(Bb) 2hn bn 3tp b-tb. MS parts (by Josef Erlebach, 19 Sept 1874): CZ-Pnm, XII.E.318. ★

DOUGLAS, Clive Martin
CMD-1. Divertimento No. 1, Op. 83. fl ob 2cl bn. MS score: AUS-Smc.

*DOUW, André *1951, Netherlands*
AQD-1. Octet. 2fl 2ob 2cl hn bn.
Pm (Donemus: Amsterdam, 1990), score.

*DOVE, Jonathan *1959, UK*
*JQD-1. Figures in the Garden, 7 mvts. 2ob 2cl 2hn 2bn; (for 18th century instruments).
MS: GB-Lmic will assist in contacting the composer.

*DOWNEY, John Wilham *5 Oct 1927, Chicago*
JWD-1. Octet; 1954, revised 1976). fl ob cl b-cl hn 2bn tp.
Pm (T. Presser: Bryn Mawr, PA, 1958), score & parts. *(Revised version: MS score: US-NYamc)*

*DRAHLOVSKÝ, Josef C.
JED-1v. [4 Stationes] Zum heiligen Frohnleichnamsfeste, Op. 92. CATB, 2cl 2hn bn organ.
MS parts: CZ-Bm(br), A.6278. ★

*DRANREL, ( ) *(1790)*
ZZD-1. VI Variations; in E♭.   2cl 2hn bn.
MS parts (by Augustin Erasmus Hübner, Langenbruck, 1810): CZ-Pu(dm), 59 R 3316.   ★

*DREHER, Josef Anton
JAD-1. Harmonie; in F, 4 mvts.   fl 2cl 2hn bn b-tb.   MS parts: D-Tl, Gg 158.   ★

DREYFUS, George *22 July 1928, Wuppertal; (resident in Australia)*
GZD-1. Rush.   2cl 2hn 2bn.
Pm (Allens Music: Melbourne, Australia, 1974).

DRIESSLER, Johannes *26 Jan 1921, Friedrichsthal, Saar*
JOD-1. Aphorismen, Op. 78, 1948.   fl ob ca cl b-cl bn.
Pm (Bärenreiter: Kassel, pn BA 3698, c.1948).

*DROBISCH, Carl (Karl) Ludwig (Carlo Luigi) *1803 - 1854   See also: ARRANGEMENTS LIST.*
KLD-1v. Offertorium, Ave verum corpus, in E♭.   SATB, 2fl 2ob 2cl 2hn 2bn vc+db.
AutoMS parts (c.1830): D-Mbm, Mf 257, (with a duplicate set of parts by Anton Schröfl).   ★
KLD-2v. Te deum laudamus, in C.   SATB, 2ob 2hn 2bn serp 2tp(clar) vc db timp.
MS score (by Anton Schörfl, 5 Feb 1833): D-Mbm, Mf 326, Ex. 1.   *Ex. 1 bears the note, "Dr[obisch] comp 9 Dec. 1832"; Ex. 2 is an AutoMS re-scoring for SATB, 2vl vla db 2ob 2tp(clar) 3tb timp, dating from 1833; the later version was published by Lotter in Augsburg, 1844.*

*DROBISCH, Johann Gottfried Trautgott *d. 1807, St Petersburg*
ZXD-1. 6 Angloises neuves.   2cl/ob 2cl 2hn 2bn 2tp.   MS: D-SWl, Mus. 1704, (keyboard reduction only).   ★

*DRÖSLER, ( )
YXD-1. 12 Ländler Tänz.   2cl 2hn 2bn.   MS parts: CZ-KRa, A3855/IV.B.19.   ★
This is possibly an arrangement of a work by Josef Dreschler.

*DROSTE-HÜLSHOFF, Maximilian Friedrich, *Freiherr von Vischering*
22 Oct 1764, Hülshoff, Münster - 8 March 1840, Alte Hülshoff bei Münster
*MDV-1v. Das Hallelujah von Pfeffel . . . Zur Verherrlichung des Gottesdienstes.
Solo SATB, SATB chorus, 2cl 2hn 2bn b-tb.
Pc (W.A.W. Logier: Berlin, sd), RISM [D 3583], score & piano reduction: D-Mbs, 2 Mus.pr. 1213; NL-At.   ★

*DRUOT, ( )
YYD-1. [Parthia in B♭], 4 mvts.   2cl 2hn 2bn 2vl vlne.   MS pts (c.1800): D-Rtt, Drout 1.   *A 5th mvt (Andantino, 6/8) appears in the cl I, hn I & II pts only.*   ★

*DRUSCHETZKY (Družecký, Druscheczky, Druschetzchi), Georg (Jiří, Giorgio) *7 April 1745, Jemníky (nr Kladko), Bohemia - 6 Sept 1819, Buda (now Budapest), Hungary*
Note: All MSS by Druschetzky in H-KE were a bequest in 1802 from Johann Gallyus, Advocat (lawyer) in Zagreb, to Graf Georg Festetics I. The modern editions of GYD-11a & 12a (Haydn: Die Schöpfung & Die Jahreszeiten, respectively), announced by Cardiff University Press, edited by Dr Roger Hellyer, were never issued.   The **Concerto for 6 Timpani** *in H-Bn is scored for* orchestra *rather than Harmonie as is often erroneously stated; the* **Messlied und Heilig** *(GYD-1) and the* **Motetto** *(GYD-19), both in H-Bn, do* not *have vocal parts.*
*GYD-1. Messlied und Heilig /: Wir werfen uns darmieder :/ acomodel del Sig: Druschetzkÿ [sic].
2ob 2cl(C) 2hn 2bn cbn, (cl in F, 2tp b-tb ad lib).   MS parts: H-Bn, Ms.Mus.1536, (with 2 earlier horn parts, tacet except for the Heilig; the cl(F) only plays in the Heilig).   ★
*GYD-2. [Nº 3] Adagio con un Imatazione [sic; organ pt: "Offertorium de Sᶜᵗᵒ Stephan"]; in E♭.
2ob 2cl 2hn 2bn 2tp(clar) timp organ(bc-fig).
MS parts: H-Bn, Ms.Mus.1582.   *The 2tp & timp are not listed on the title page and may be later additions; "Organo" has been added to the titlepage at a slightly later - but still contemporary - date.*   ★
Pm (WINDS: Northridge, CA, pn W-48, c.1981), score (photostat) & parts.
*GYD-3. Partitta Berdlersgarn; in C, 3 mvts.   2ob 2cl(C) 2hn 2bn, "Violino Pigola" ["Picilino" on part], "Dambornino" [tambourine].
MS parts: A-Wn, Mus.Hs.11377.   *The winds also play toy instruments: ob I (Wachtel-Weibl = female quail call, Trompetta, Schelerl [bells]), ob II (Schelerl), cl I (Schelerl), cl II (C-gugu [cuckoo], D-gugu, Scherel), hns I & II (Trompetta), bn I (Ratschen), bn II (Rohlerl, C Schelerl, Wachtl-Manntl = male quail call).*   ★
*GYD-4. Nº 7 Rondo Fresco ungaria; in F.   2ob 2 bthn 2hn 2bn cbn.
MS parts: H-Bn, Ms.Mus.1523.   *Follows the arrangement of Bohr's work of the same title & scoring.*   ★
GYD-5. [No.] 9. Rondo; in C minor/E♭ major.   2ob 2cl 2hn 2bn cbn.   MS pts: H-Bn, Ms.Mus.1523, (last item).   ★
*GYD-6. Parthia; in B♭, 6 mvts.   2ob 2cl 2hn 2bn (players alternating on folk instruments); later cimbalon part.
MS parts: H-Bn, Ms.Mus.1569.   *The cimbalon part is a later addition in autograph expanding the work to 13 mvts by inserting 7 new solo mvts between the original mvts 1 & 2 (1 & 9).*   ★
*GYD-7(-12). 6 Parthien; in B[♭], B[♭], Dis [E♭], Dis, Dis, Dis, all 4 mvts.   2ob 2cl 2hn 2bn.
Pc (Christoph Torricella: Wien, pn 3, 1784), RISM [D 3588], parts: A-M, V 1488.   ★
MS parts: CZ-Pnm, XXII.C.38 - 43, (Torricella Nos. 2, 4, 5, 3, 6, 1, respectively).
Pm (Doblinger: Wien, 1969), ed. A. Weinmann, min score (pn Stp 240 - 245) & pts (Diletto musicale 264 269.
*GYD-13. Parthia in B[♭]; 3 mvts.   ob cl hn bn + Echo ob cl hn bn.   MS pts: A-Wgm, VIII 38670.   ★
GYD-14. Parthia Ex Dis [E♭]; 4 mvts.   2ob 2cl 2hn 2bn.   MS pts: D-WRgs, Noten-Sgl. Goethe Nr. 518.   ★
GYD-15. Partitta in F; 4 mvts.   2ob 2cl 2hn 2bn.
MS parts: CZ-Pnm, XX.F.106; CZ-KRa, A38856/IV.B.20, (as "Parthia in F" for 2cl 2hn 2bn).   ★
GYD-16. Partia; in C; 3 mvts.   2ob 2cl 2hn 2bn.   MS pts: CZ-Pnm, XXVII.B.84.   ★
GYD-17. Partia; in C, 4 mvts .   2ob 2cl(C) 2hn 2bn.   MS score: CZ-Pnm, XII.E.343.   ★
*GYD-18. Mottetto [sic], Adagio et Allegro; in E♭.   2ob 2cl 2hn 2bn.   MS pts: H-Bn, Ms.Mus.1529, No. 2.   ★
*GYD-19. Des Herrn V. Zmeskal Takt Messer Wiener Zoll. Des Herrn Mälzel's bestimmung des Tempo durch das Metronome...Sind die Thema aus sein Sonate Von Herrn Anton Halm gerste Lieutenant in der K.K. Armee. acomodato Di Druschetzki[sic]; 5 short movements.   2ob 2cl(C) 2hn 2bn.   MS parts: H-Bn, Ms.Mus.1519.   ★

GYD-20. Marche No. 1 . . . Composèes [sic] par le Comte Louis de Szechenij [Széchény] et arrangèes par Druschetzki [sic]; (march with 2 variations, the variations probably by Druschetzky). 2ob 2cl 2hn 2bn. MS parts ("Vor das Monats Jullÿ [1]805"): H-Bn, Ms.Mus.1530. ★
Pm (WINDS: Northridge, CA, pn W-84, c.1980), parts (photocopy of H-Bn MSS).
*GYD-21. Variazioni; in B♭. 2ob 2cl 2hn 2bn.
Pc (sn: sl, sd, =Torricella: Vienna, pn 8, 1784), RISM [D 3589], parts: A-M; H-Bn, Mus.pr.13123. ★
*GYD-22. N⁰ 55: Zrini Ungaria: Entre Act [sic]. adagiosissima [sic] dopoi And͟ᵉ [incipit] acomodato in Harmoni di Druschetzki [sic]. 2ob 2cl(C) 2hn 2bn. MS pts: H-Bn, Ms.Mus.1534, (the ob I pt is a 5-bar fragment only, on the verso of the bn I pt). ★
*GYD-23(-39). 17 Partia / Parthia. 2ob 2ca 2hn bn. MS parts (post-1776): A-Wgm, VIII 8536. *All of these works have late 18th century added wrappers giving the titles as "Parthia"; in some cases the original titlepage is present and in all these cases the titles are given as "Partia". As these works are from the Schwarzenberg Harmonie, we cannot rule out the possibility that they are transcriptions by Johann Nepomuk Went.*
  GYD-23. No. 1 Partia in F; 4 mvts. ★
  GYD-24. Parthia in C; 4 mvts. ★
  GYD-25. N: 3tio in F Partia; 4 mvts. *In the original title the composer's name has been omitted ("Del Sig [left blank]"; the name "Wagenseil" can be made out in faint pencil). We believe that this is a later addition; stylistically the work is unquestionably from this set of Druschetzky's Parthien.* ★
  GYD-26. [In pencil: "N 4"] Parthia in F; 4 mvts. ★
  GYD-27. No. 5to Ex F Partia; 3 mvts. ★
  GYD-28. N: 6 Parthia in F; 4 mvts. ★
  GYD-29. Ex C. VIIta Partia; 4 mvts. ★
  GYD-30. No 8, 7. S[tr]⁰[menti] Parthia in B[♭]; 5 mvts. ★
  GYD-31. IXma Partia; in C, 4 mvts. ★
  GYD-32. Xmo Partia in F; 4 mvts. ★
  GYD-33. XIma Partia in G; 4 mvts. ★
  GYD-34. XIIma Parthia in F; 5 mvts. 2ob 2ca 2hn basso. The final mvt is an arrangement of an aria from Dittersdorf's opera, *La Contadina Fedele* ★
  GYD-35. No. 13 Parthia in E♭; 5 mvts. (A pencil note above the Menuet I on hn I reads, "Nihil valet".)
  GYD-36. No. 14 Parthia in E♭; 5 mvts. ★
  GYD-37. No. 15 Parthia in F; 5 mvts. ★
  GYD-38. N. 16 Parthia in B[♭]; 4 mvts.
  GYD-39. No. 17 Parthia in E♭; 5 mvts. ★
*GYD-40. Partitta a La Camera [sic], in G, No. 23; 4 mvts. ob 3bthn 2hn bn. MS pts: CZ-Pnm, XLII.E.35. ★
*GYD-41. Partitta in G, No. 24; 4 mvts. ob 3bthn 2hn 2bn. MS pts: CZ-Pnm, XLII.E.221. ★
*GYD-42. No. 25 Partitta la Camera in G; 4 mvts. 3bthn 2hn 2bn. MS pts: CZ-Pnm, XLII.E.222. ★
*GYD-43. Partitta in G, No. 26; 4 mvts. ob 3bthn 2hn bn. MS pts: CZ-Pnm, XLII.E.41. ★
*GYD-44. Partitta; in G, 4 mvts. ob 3bthn 2hn 2bn. MS pts: CZ-Pnm, XLII.E.223. ★
*GYD-45. Partitta in G, No. 28; 4 mvts. ob 3bthn 2hn 2bn. MS pts: CZ-Pnm, XLII.E.227. ★
GYD-46. Concerto; in E♭, 3 mvts. Fortepiano, 2cl 2hn 2bn.
MS parts: H-KE, K 0/139; H-Bn, (microfilm) FM 4/2021. ★
*GYD-47. Parthia in F; 4 mvts. fl 2ob 2hn bn. MS pts: CZ-Pnm, XLII.E.226. ★
*GYD-48. Parthia in A Minore; 4 mvts. fl 2ob 2hn bn.
MS parts: CZ-Pnm, XLII.E.230. Modern MS score & parts: GB-Ljag, (modern MS score & parts). ★
*GYD-49. Partitta in G; 4 mvts. fl 2ob 2hn bn. MS parts: CZ-Pnm, XLII.E.237. ★
*GYD-50. Parthia in C Concertino; 4 mvts. fl 2ob 2hn bn. MS parts: CZ-Pnm, XLII.E.284. ★
*GYD-51. Parthia in C; 4 mvts. fl 2ob 2hn bn. MS parts: CZ-Pnm, XLII.E.285. ★
*GYD-52. Partitta in G; 4 mvts. fl 2ob 2hn bn. MS pts: CZ-Pnm, XLII.E.287, (missing hn I & II). ★
*GYD-53. Partitta in C; 4 mvts. fl 2ob 2hn bn. MS parts: CZ-Pnm, XLII.E.288. ★
GYD-54. Parthia in Dis [E♭]; 4 mvts. 2cl 2hn 2bn. MS parts (c.1780): CH-Zz, AMG XII.103, a-e. ★
*GYD-55.1. Parthia in Dis [E♭] Concertand; 4 mvts. 2cl 2hn 2bn.
MS parts: CH-Zz, AMG XII.700, a-e; PL-LA; RM 43, (as "Parthia Es-dur"). ★
Pm (Kneuslin: Basle, 1967), score & parts, (für Kenner und Liebhaber No. 35).
GYD-55.2. Partita; in F, 4 mvts. 2ob 2hn 2bn. MS parts: I-Gc, SS.A.2.12. ★
GYD-56. Parthia: Concertand, in E♭. 2cl 2hn 2bn. MS pts: CH-Zz, AMG XII.701, a-e. ★
Here **MD** *stands for the modern edition edited by Dorottya Somorjay, published by Musicalia Danubiana: Budapest, 1985, score & parts, (Musicalia Danubiana 4); page numbers refer to the volume of scores.*
*GYD-57. Concerto; in E♭, 3 mvts. Solo clarinet, cl 2hn 2bn.
MS parts: H-KE, K 0/134; H-Bn, (microfilm), FM 4/2016. Pm (MD), pp. 385 - 460. ★
*GYD-58. Concerto in E♭; 3 mvts. Solo clarinet, cl 2hn 2bn.
MS parts: H-KE, K 0/147; H-Bn, (microfilm), FM 4/2029. ★
*GYD-59. Partie en E♭; 7 mvts. 2cl 2hn 2bn.
MS parts: H-KE, K 0/126; H-Bn, (microfilm), FM 4/2008. Pm (MD), pp. 59 - 124, (omits mvts 4 & 6). ★
GYD-60. Partitta in F; 4 mvts. 2cl 2hn 2bn.
MS parts: H-KE, K 0/127; H-Bn, (microfilm), FM 4/2009. Pm (MD), pp. 125 - 150. ★
GYD-61. Partitta in F; 3 mvts. 2cl 2hn 2bn.
MS parts: H-KE, K 0/129; H-Bn, (microfilm), FM 4/2011. Pm (MD), ppp 151 - 190. ★
GYD-62. Partitta in B[♭]; 4 mvts. 2cl 2hn 2bn.
MS parts: H-KE, K 0/130; H-Bn, (microfilm) FM 4/2012. Pm (MD), pp. 191 - 234. ★
*GYD-63. Partitta Concertante in E♭; 4 mvts. 2cl 2hn 2bn.
MS parts: H-KE, K 0/131; H-Bn, (microfilm), FM 4/2013. Pm (MD), pp. 235 - 298. ★
GYD-64. Parhia In Dis [E♭]; 4 mvts. 2cl 2hn 2bn.
MS parts: H-KE, K 0/132; H-Bn, (microfilm), FM 4/2014. Pm (MD), pp. 299 - 338. ★
GYD-65. Partitta; in F, 4 mvts. 2cl 2hn 2bn.
MS parts: H-KE, K 0/133; H-Bn, (microfilm), FM 4/2015. Pm (MD), pp. 339 - 384. ★

GYD-66. Parthie en B[♭]; 6 mvts.   2cl 2hn 2bn.
MS parts: H-KE, K 0/135; H-Bn, (microfilm), FM 4/2017.   Pm (MD), pp. 461 - 504.   ★
*GYD-67. Partitta Concertante en E♭; 4 mvts.   2cl 2hn 2bn.
MS parts: H-KE, K 0/136; H-Bn, (microfilm), FM 4/2018.   Pm (MD), pp. 505 - 550.   ★
*GYD-68. Partitta in G [Echo Partitta]; 4 mvts.   2cl(C) 2hn 2bn.
MS parts: H-KE, K 0/137; H-Bn, (microfilm) FM 4/2019.   ★
GYD-69. Partitta; in E♭, 5 mvts.   2cl 2hn 2bn.   MS parts: H-KE, K 0/138; H-Bn, (microfilm), FM 4/2020.   ★
GYD-70. [Partie en C], 6 mvts.   2cl(C) 2hn 2bn.   MS pts: H-KE, K 0/140; H-Bn, (microfilm), FM 4/2022.   ★
GYD-71. Partitta in E♭; 4 mvts.   2cl 2hn 2bn.   MS parts: H-KE, K 0/141; H-Bn, (microfilm), FM 4/2023.   ★
GYD-72. Partitta in C; 4 mvts.   2cl(C) 2hn 2bn.   MS pts: H-KE, K 0/142; H-Bn, (microfilm), FM 4/2024.   ★
*GYD-73. Partitta in D [Echo Partie]; 4 mvts.   2cl(D) 2hn 2bn.
MS parts: H-KE, K 0/143; H-Bn, (microfilm), FM 4/2025.   ★
GYD-74. Partitta in D; 4 mvts.   2cl(C) 2hn 2bn.   MS parts: H-KE, K 0/144; H-Bn, (microfilm), FM 4/2026.   ★
GYD-75. [Partie en C], 5 mvts.   2cl(C) 2hn 2bn.   MS pts: H-KE, K 0/145; H-Bn, (microfilm), FM 4/2027.   ★
GYD-76. Partitta [in] B[♭]; 4 mvts.   2cl 2hn 2bn.   MS parts: H-KE, K 0/146; H-Bn, (microfilm), FM 4/2028.   ★
GYD-77. Partitta in E♭; 4 mvts.   2cl 2hn 2bn.   MS parts: H-KE, K 0/148; H-Bn, (microfilm), FM 4/2030.   ★
GYD-78. Parthia In B[♭]; 4 mvts.   2cl 2hn 2bn.   MS pts: H-KE, K 0/149; H-Bn, (microfilm), FM 4/2031.   ★
GYD-79. Partitta in E♭; 4 mvts.   2cl 2hn 2bn.   MS parts: H-KE, K 0/150, Koll.1; H-Bn, (microfilm),
FM 4/2032; SK-BRnm, (Ilava, church archive) Mus.XII.99, No. 3.   ★
GYD-80. Partie in E♭; 4 mvts.   2cl 2hn 2bn.   MS parts: H-KE, K 0/151; H-Bn, (microfilm), FM 4/2033.   ★
GYD-81. Partitta; in E♭, 4 mvts.   2cl 2hn 2bn.   MS parts: H-KE, K 0/152; H-Bn, (microfilm), FM 4/2034.   ★
GYD-82. Partitta; in B♭, 4 mvts.   2cl 2hn 2bn.   MS parts: H-KE, K 0/153; H-Bn, (microfilm), FM 4/2035.   ★
GYD-83. Partitta in C; 3 mvts.   2cl(C) 2hn 2bn.   MS pts: H-KE, K 0/154; H-Bn, (microfilm), FM 4/2036.   ★
GYD-84. Partitta in E♭; 4 mvts.   2cl 2hn 2bn.
MS pts: H-KE, K 0/155; H-Bn, (microfilm), FM 4/2037; SK-BRnm, (Ilava, church archive), Mus.XII.99, No. 2. ★
GYD-85.1. Partitta in B[♭]; 4 mvts.   2cl 2hn 2bn.   MS pts: H-KE, K 0/156; H-Bn, (microfilm), FM 4/2038.   ★
GYD-85.2. Parthia à 6 in B[♭]; 4 mvts.   2cl 2hn 2bn.   MS pts: CZ-Pnm, XLI.B.112.   *Mvts 1, 2 & 4 are
identical with GYD-87.1; mvt 3 (Andante Sustenuto [sic], C) is completely different and does not match any other
mvt in the H-KE set.* ★
GYD-86. Partitta; in B♭, 4 mvts.   2cl 2hn 2bn.   MS parts: H-KE, K 0/157; H-Bn, (microfilm), FM 4/2039.   ★
GYD-87. Parthia; in E♭, 3 mvts.   2cl 2hn 2bn.   MS parts: H-KE, K 0/158; H-Bn, (microfilm), FM 4/2040.   ★
GYD-88. Partitta in B[♭]; 4 mvts.   2cl 2hn 2bn.   MS parts: H-KE, K 0/159; H-Bn, (microfilm), FM 4/2041.   ★
GYD-89. Partitta in E♭; 4 mvts.   2cl 2hn 2bn.   MS parts: H-KE, K 0/160; H-Bn, (microfilm), FM 4/2042.   ★
GYD-90. Partitta in E♭; 4 mvts.   2cl 2hn 2bn.   MS parts: H-KE, K 0/161; H-Bn, (microfilm), FM 4/2043.   ★
GYD-91. Parthia; in F, 4 mvts.   2cl 2hn 2bn.   MS parts: H-KE, K 0/162; H-Bn, (microfilm), FM 4/2044.   ★
GYD-92. Partitta in F; 4 mvts.   2cl 2hn 2bn.   MS parts: H-KE, K 0/163; H-Bn, (microfilm), FM 4/2045.   ★
GYD-93. Partitta in F; 4 mvts.   2cl 2hn 2bn.   MS parts: H-KE, K 0/164; H-Bn, (microfilm), FM 4/2046.   ★
GYD-94. Partitta In B[♭]; 4 mvts.   2cl 2hn 2bn.   MS parts: H-KE, K 0/165; H-Bn, (microfilm), FM 4/2047.   ★
GYD-95. Serenata In E♭; 5 mvts.   2cl 2hn 2bn.   MS parts: H-KE, K 0/166; H-Bn, (microfilm), FM 4/2048.   ★
GYD-96. Partitta; in E♭, 4 mvts.   2cl 2hn 2bn.   MS parts: H-KE, K 0/167; H-Bn, (microfilm), FM 4/2049.   ★
GYD-97. Partitta; in E♭, 4 mvts.   2cl 2hn 2bn.   MS parts: H-KE, K 0/168; H-Bn, (microfilm), FM 4/2050;
A-Wn, Mus.Hs.567, (MS by Johann Handl, as "Parthia in Dis").   ★
GYD-98. Partitta in F; 4 mvts.   2cl 2hn 2bn.   MS parts: H-KE, K 0/169; H-Bn, (microfilm), FM 4/2051.   ★
GYD-99. Parthia In E♭; 4 mvts.   2cl 2hn 2bn.   MS parts: H-KE, K 0/170; H-Bn, (microfilm), FM 4/2052.   ★
GYD-100. Partitta in E♭; 4 mvts.   2cl 2hn 2bn.   MS parts: H-KE, K 0/171; H-Bn, (microfilm), FM 4/2053.   ★
GYD-101. Partitta in E♭; 4 mvts.   2cl 2hn 2bn.   MS parts: H-KE, K 0/172; H-Bn, (microfilm), FM 4/2054.   ★
GYD-102. Partitta; in E♭, 4 mvts.   2cl 2hn 2bn.   MS parts: H-KE, K 0/173; H-Bn, (microfilm), FM 4/2055.   ★
GYD-103. Partitta; in E♭, 4 mvts.   2cl 2hn 2bn.   MS parts: H-KE, K 0/174; H-Bn, (microfilm), FM 4/2056.   ★
GYD-104. Partitta; in E♭, 4 mvts.   2cl 2hn 2bn.   MS parts: H-KE, K 0/175; H-Bn, (microfilm), FM 4/2057.   ★
GYD-105. [Partitta in E♭], 6 mvts.   2cl 2hn 2bn.   MS pts: H-KE, K 0/176; H-Bn, (microfilm), FM 4/2058.   ★
GYD-106. Partitta; in E♭, 4 mvts.   2cl 2hn 2bn.   MS parts: H-KE, K 0/177; H-Bn, (microfilm), FM 4/2059.   ★
GYD-107. Partitta In E♭; 4 mvts.   2cl 2hn 2bn.   MS parts: H-KE, K 0/178; H-Bn, (microfilm), FM 4/2060.   ★
GYD-108. Parthia in B[♭]; 4 mvts.   2cl 2hn 2bn.   MS parts: H-KE, K 0/179; H-Bn, (microfilm), FM 4/2061.   ★
GYD-109. Partitta in G; 4 mvts.   2cl(C) 2hn 2bn.   MS parts: H-KE, K 0/180; H-Bn, (microfilm), FM 4/2062.   ★
GYD-110. Partitta in E♭; 4 mvts.   2cl 2hn 2bn.   MS parts: H-KE, K 0/181; H-Bn, (microfilm), FM 4/2063.   ★
GYD-111. Partitta in C; 4 mvts.   2cl(C) 2hn 2bn.   MS parts: H-KE, K 0/182; H-Bn, (microfilm), FM 4/2064.   ★
GYD-112. Partitta in D; 4 mvts.   2cl(C) 2hn 2bn.   MS pts: H-KE, K 0/183; H-Bn, (microfilm), FM 4/2065.   ★
GYD-113. Parthia in F; 4 mvts.   2cl 2hn 2bn.   MS parts: H-KE, K 0/184; H-Bn, (microfilm), FM 4/2066.   ★
GYD-114. Parthia in F; 4 mvts.   2cl 2hn 2bn.   MS parts: H-KE, K 0/185; H-Bn, (microfilm), FM 4/2067.   ★
GYD-115. Serenata in E♭; 6 mvts.   2cl(C) 2hn 2bn.   MS parts: H-KE, K 0/186; H-Bn, (microfilm), FM 4/2068;
RF-Ssc, Ф 891 собрюосуповыiх N44, pp. 19 - 54, (mvts 1 2, 5 & 6 only).   ★
GYD-116. Parthia; in E♭, 4 mvts.   2cl 2hn 2bn.
MS parts: H-KE, K 0/187; H-Bn, (microfilm), FM 4/2069, (there may also be a contemporary MS copy).   ★
Pm (B. Schott's Söhne: Mainz, 1965), ed. L. Kalmar, score (pn 5502) & parts (pn 5466), (as "Sestetto").
GYD-117. Partitta; in E♭, 4 mvts.   2cl 2hn 2bn.   MS parts: H-KE, K 0/188; H-Bn, (microfilm), FM 4/2070.   ★
GYD-118. Partitta in E♭; 4 mvts.   2cl 2hn 2bn.   MS parts: H-KE, K 0/189; H-Bn, (microfilm), FM 4/2071.   ★
GYD-119. Partitta in C; 4 mvts.   2cl(C) 2hn 2bn.   MS parts: H-KE, K 0/190; H-Bn, (microfilm), FM 4/2072.   ★
GYD-120. Partitta in G; 4 mvts.   2cl(C) 2hn 2bn.   MS parts: H-KE, K 0/191; H-Bn, (microfilm), FM 4/2073.   ★
GYD-121. Partitta in D; 4 mvts.   2cl(C) 2hn 2bn.   MS parts: H-KE, K 0/192; H-Bn, (microfilm), FM 4/2074.   ★
GYD-122. Partitta; in F, 4 mvts.   2cl(C)/2ob 2hn 2bn.   MS pts: H-KE, K 0/193; H-Bn, (microfilm), FM 4/2075. ★
*GYD-123. Partitta La Fantasia; in E♭, 6 mvts.   2cl 2hn 2bn.
MS parts: H-KE, K 0/194; H-Bn, (microfilm), FM 4/2076. ★
GYD-124. Partitta In A; 4 mvts.   2cl(A) 2hn 2bn.   MS pts: H-KE, K 0/195; H-Bn, (microfilm), FM 4/2077.   ★
*GYD-125. Les Danses Paysannes; 88 dances.   2cl 2hn 2bn.
MS parts: H-KE, K 0/118, (missing cl I); H-Bn, (microfilm), FM 4/2000.
GYD-126. Partita in F; 4 mvts   2ob 2hn bn.   MS parts: CZ-Bm(au), A.18.231.   ★
Pm (Státní Hudební vydavatelství: Praha, 1973), ed. Vrátislav Bělský, score, (Musica antiqua bohemica No. 35).

GYD-127. Partitta a la Camera; in E♭, 4 mvts. 2ob 2hn bn. MS parts: CZ-NR, A.18.322/B.247. ★
*GYD-128. N: 1mo Partitta In C; 4 mvts. 2ob 2hn bn. MS parts: A-Wgm, VIII 8537. ★
*GYD-129. N⁰ 2⁰ Partitta In C; 4 mvts. 2ob 2hn bn. MS parts: A-Wgm, VIII 8537. ★
*GYD-130. N⁰ 3to Partitta In C; 4 mvts. 2ob 2hn bn. MS parts: A-Wgm, VIII 8537. ★
*GYD-131. N⁰ 4mo Partitta In C; 4 mvts. 2ob 2hn bn.
MS parts: A-Wgm, VIII 8537, (the title is preceded by the note "Favorito" in another hand). ★
*GYD-132. Nro 5to Partitta In C; 4 mvts. Solo ob, ob 2hn bn. MS parts: A-Wgm, VIII 8537. ★
*GYD-133. N⁰ 6to Partitta In C; 4 mvts. Solo bn, 2ob 2hn. MS parts: A-Wgm, VIII 8537. ★
*GYD-134. N⁰ 7mo Partitta In C; 4 mvts. 2ob 2hn bn. MS parts: A-Wgm, VIII 8537. ★
*GYD-135. N⁰ 8 Partitta In F; 4 mvts. 2ob 2hn bn.
MS parts: A-Wgm, VIII 8537, (the title is preceded by the note "Favorito" in another hand). ★
*GYD-136. N⁰ 9⁰ Partitta In F; 4 mvts. Solo ob, ob 2hn bn.
MS parts: A-Wgm, VIII 8537. ★
Pm (Breitkopf & Härtel: Wiesbaden, 1969), ed. Alexander Weinmann, (Kammermusik Bibliothek/Collegium musicum Nr. 2113), score & parts.
*GYD-137. N⁰ 10⁰ Partitta In F; 4 mvts. 2 oboes "Solli" [sic], 2hn bn.
MS parts: A-Wgm, VIII 8537. ★
Pm (Breitkopf & Härtel: Wiesbaden, 1969), ed. Alexander Weinmann, (Kammermusik Bibliothek/Collegium musicum Nr. 2114), score & parts.
*GYD-138. N⁰ 11mo Partitta In-F; 4 mvts. Solo bn, 2ob 2hn. MS parts: A-Wgm, VIII 8537. ★
*GYD-139. N: 12⁰ Partitta In B[♭]; 4 mvts. 2ob 2hn bn. MS parts: A-Wgm, VIII 8537. ★
*GYD-140. N⁰ 13⁰ Partitta In B[♭]; 4 mvts. 2ob 2hn bn.
MS parts: A-Wgm, VIII 8537. ★
Pm (Breitkopf & Härtel: Wiesbaden, 1969), ed. Alexander Weinmann, (Kammermusik Bibliothek/Collegium musicum Nr. 2115), score & parts.
*GYD-141. N⁰ 14⁰ Partitta In B[♭]; 4 mvts. 2ob 2hn bn. MS parts: A-Wgm, VIII 8537. ★
*GYD-142. Nro 15⁰ Partitta In E♭; 4 mvts. 2ob 2hn bn. MS parts: A-Wgm, VIII 8537. ★
*GYD-143. N⁰ 16to Partitta In Dis [E♭]; 4 mvts. 2ob 2hn bn. MS parts: A-Wgm, VIII 8537. ★
*GYD-144. N⁰ 17⁰ Partitta In Dis [E♭]; 4 mvts. Solo hn II, 2ob hn(I) bn. MS parts: A-Wgm, VIII 8537. ★
*GYD-145. N: 18⁰ Partitta In G; 4 mvts. 2ob 2hn bn. MS parts: A-Wgm, VIII 8537. ★
*GYD-146. N⁰ 19⁰ Partitta In G; 4 mvts. 2ob 2hn bn. MS parts: A-Wgm, VIII 8537. ★
*GYD-147. N⁰ 20⁰ Partitta In G; 4 mvts. 2ob 2hn bn. MS parts: A-Wgm, VIII 8537. ★
*GYD-148. N⁰ 21 Partitta In G: al Valet; 4 mvts. 2ob 2hn bn.
MS parts: A-Wgm, VIII 8537. ★
Pm (Breitkopf & Härtel: Wiesbaden, 1969), ed. Alexander Weinmann, (Kammermusik Bibliothek/Collegium musicum Nr. 2116), score & parts.
*GYD-149. N= 22⁰ Partitta In D; 4 mvts. 2ob 2hn bn. MS parts: A-Wgm, VIII 8537. ★
*GYD-150. N⁰ 23= Partitta In D; 4 mvts. 2ob 2hn bn. MS parts: A-Wgm, VIII 8537. ★
*GYD-151. N⁰ 24⁰ Partitta In D; 4 mvts. 2ob 2hn bn. MS parts: A-Wgm, VIII 8537. ★
GYD-152. In C, Partitta; 4 mvts. 2ob 2hn bn. MS parts: CZ-Pnm, XLII.E.286. ★
GYD-153. Partitta in C; 4 mvts. 2ob 2hn bn. MS parts: A-Wn, Mus.Hs.2919, (MS by Johann Michael Winkler); D-Rtt, Sammelband 8, Nr. 9 - 12, (untitled, in A, for 2cl 2hn bn).
GYD-154. [Partita in A], 4 mvts. 2cl 2hn bn. MS parts: D-Rtt, Sammelband 8, No. 58 - 61. ★
GYD-155. [Partita in A], 4 mvts. 2cl 2hn bn. MS parts: D-Rtt, Sammelband 8, No. 66 - 69. ★
GYD-156. [Partita in E♭], 4 mvts. 2cl 2hn bn. MS parts: D-Rtt, Sammelband 8, No. 78 - 81. ★
GYD-157. [Partita in E♭], 4 mvts. 2cl 2hn bn. MS parts: D-Rtt, Sammelband 8, No. 87 - 90. ★
GYD-158. [Partita in E♭], 4 mvts. 2cl 2hn bn. MS parts: D-Rtt, Sammelband 8, No. 91 - 94. ★
*GYD-159. Miserere . . . Accomodato di Giorgio Druschetzkÿ [sic]; (14 connceted Miserere).
2bthn(2cl in Nos. 6 - 10 & 13) 2hn 2bn.
AutoMS score (Nos. 1 & 4 only, score for 2cl 2bn). MS parts: H-Bn, Ms.Mus.1598. ★
GYD-160. Partia in F. Instrumentation unknown. MS: CZ-K, (?lost).
GYD-161. Theme & Variations. Instrumentation unknown. MS: CZ-K, (?lost).
GYD-162, 163. 2 Parthias, both 4 mvts. Turkish music. MS parts: I-Fc, F.P. S.463.
GYD-164. Divertissement; in F, 32 mvts (Nos. 1 - 33, but No. 14 is not written out). 3bthn.
MS parts: H-KE, K 0/120; H-Bn, (microfilm), FM 4/2002. ★
Pm (OTMS: Dolní Sytová, 1989), ed. Jiří Kratochvil, score & pts, (Nos 2, 5-10, 12, 13, 20, 22-25, 27, 29-32).
Pm (Kliment: Wien, 1993), ed. Bernard Habla, score & parts.
GYD-165. [62 mvts] Composés et Arrangés par Druschezky [sic]. 2cl 2hn 2bn.
MS parts: H-KE, K 0/116; H-Bn, (microfilm), FM 4/1998.
    165.1(m) - 165.6(m). [6] Marche; E♭, E♭, E♭, E♭, B♭, B♭. Nos. 1 - 6. ★
    165.7, 165.8. [2] Englese. Nos. 7, 8.★   165.9. Polonesse. No. 9. ★ 165.10. A la Strassbourg. No. 10. ★
    165.11. Allegro. No. 11. ★   165.12. Presto. No. 12. ★   165.13. La Chasse; Allegro. No. 13. ★
    165.14. La Chasse; Allegro. No. 14. ★   165.15. Andante con [6] Variazioni. No. 15. ★
    165.16(a). Grétry: Zemire und Azor, Spiegel Arie [as by "Sallieri"]. No. 16.
    165.17(a). W. Müller: Das Sonnenfest in Braminen, 2 mvts ("Schwermuth und Grillen", "Noch ist sie nicht
       verplüht"). Nos. 17 & 18. (=GYD-7.1a, Nos 6 & 11).
    165.18(a). Righini: L'incontro inaspettato, "Sposa Sonia". No. 19. (= GYD-7.5a, No. 19).
    165.19. Allegro. No. 20. ★   165.20. Romance. No. 21. ★
    165.21(a). Süssmayr: Der Spiegel in Arkadien, 2 mvts. Nos. 22 & 23.
    165.22(a). W Müller: Kaspar der Fagottist, 1 mvt. No. 24. (= GYD-7.6a, No. 39).
    165.23. Grand Polonesse con [6] Variationi. ★   165.24. Adagio; in E♭, 3/4. No. 26. ★
    165.25. La Russia; Allegro moderato. No. 27. ★   165.26. Vivace con [5] Variazioni. No. 28. ★
    165.27. Adagio. No. 29. ★   165.28. Allegretto. No. 30. ★   165.29, 165.30. [2] Englese. Nos. 31, 32. ★
    165.31. Polonesse. No. 33. ★   165.32. Wirbel Tanz der Fourlaner; Moderato. No. 34. ★
    165.33. Andantino. No. 35. ★   165.34. Allegretto. No. 36. ★   165.35. Andante. No. 37. ★
    165.36. Ala [sic] Malbrug; Allegretto, 6/8. No. 38. ★

165.37. Haydn: Andante con [2] Variazionen. No. 39. (=GYD-3a).
165.38. Andante. No. 40. ★   165.39. Adagio. No. 41. ★   165.40. Polonesse. No. 42. ★
165.41. Ballarina; Adagio. No. 43. ★   165.42. Moderato. No. 44. ★   165.43. Harlekino; Allegro. No. 45. ★
165.44. Der Jäger; Andantino. No. 46. ★   165.45. Das Schwerdt schmieden; Allegro. No. 47. ★
165.46. Adagio. No. 48. ★   165.47. Andante. No. 49. ★   165.48(m). Marche. No. 50. ★
165.49. Allegretto. No. 51. ★   165.50. Adagio, Moderato con [5] Variazioni. No. 52. ★
165.51. Alla Majen [sic], Presto. No. 53. ★   165.52. Allegretto. No. 54. ★   165.53. Presto. No. 55. ★
165.54. Allegro. No. 56. ★   165.55. Andante. No. 57. ★   165.56. Larghetto. No. 58. ★
165.57. Ariette sur le Tombeau, Largo. No. 59. ★
165.58. [5] Variation sur le Menuet danse par Mademeiselle Venturini a Vienne [sic]. No. 60 (= GYD-1a).
  165.59(m). La Marche pour la Serenade. No. 61. ★   165.60(t). Der Todten, March, adagio [sic]. No. 62. ★
*GYD-1.1m(a), 1.2m(a). Franzosischen [sic] Zapfenstreich et March der französischen Division des Generl [sic]
Gudon [sic: Gudin]; both in B♭. Accomodato di Giorgio Druschetzkÿ [sic]. 2ob 2cl 2hn 2bn.
AutoMS ("15 Vor das Monats April [1]806): H-Bn, Ms.Mus.1527. ★
Pm (WINDS: Northridge, CA, pn W-82, c.1981), parts (photocopy).
*GYD-2m. Marche: du Couronnement de L'Empereur Napoleon a Paris [sic]; in B♭. 2ob 2cl 2hn 2bn cbn.
MS parts: H-Bn, Ms.Mus.1528, (with performance dates: 21 June, 10 July, 13 July, 14 Aug 1805). ★
Pm (WINDS: Northridge, CA, pn W-45, c.1981), parts (photocopy).
*GYD-3m. Regimentsoboisten Marsch. 2ob+2cl 2hn 2bn.
MS pts: D-Mbs, Mus.Mss.3672; H-Bn, Z 46.694 Koll. 1 (as "Regiments Marsch von Palatines Husarn", 1818). ★
GYD-4m. Märsche für Blasinstrumente. Instrumentation: unknown. MS: A-Wgm, (untraced, cited by Eitner).
*GYD-1v. Der Frühling, N° 1; text Schiller. SATB, 2ob 2cl(C) 2hn 2bn.
MS parts (only the wind parts are AutoMS): H-Bn, Ms.Mus.1538. ★
*GYD-2v. Der Frühling, N° II; text Schiller. SATB, 2ob 2cl 2hn 2bn.
MS parts (only the ob I part is autograph): H-Bn, Ms.Mus.1539. ★
*GYD-3v. Punschlied; text Schller. SATB, 2ob 2cl 2hn 2bn.
MS parts: H-Bn, Ms.Mus.1541. ★
Pm (WINDS: Northridge, CA, pn W-112, c.1981), parts (photostat).
*GYD-4v. Sehnsucht; text Schiller. SATB, 2ob 2cl 2hn(con sordini) 2bn. MS parts: H-Bn, Ms.Mus.1537. ★
*GYD-5v. Einladung zum Ball; text Schiller. SATB, 2ob 2cl 2hn 2bn. MS parts: H-Bn, Ms.Mus.1540. ★
*GYD-1a(-6a). 6 Thema Con Variazioni . . . Diversi Authori Acomodato. 2cl 2hn 2bn.
MS parts: CZ-KRa, A3857/IV.B.21; H-KE, K 0/116, (GYD-167.) Nos (1a) 60, (3a) 39; H-Bn, (microfilm of
H-KE), FM 4/1998.
Pm (No. 5 only:) (Kneusslin: Basel, 1967, 1973), ed. A. Myslík, score & parts, *(für Kenner und Liebhaber 50).*
  1a. Anon: [5] Variazione Sur le Menuetto Danse [sic] par Mademoiselle Venturini. (= GYD-165.58)
  2a. Mozart: [6 Variations on "Ah, vous dirai-je, Maman", K.265/K6.300e].
  3a. Haydn: [2 Variations on the Andante from the Symphony in G, Hob. I/81]. (= GYD-165.37)
  4a. Haydn: [6 Variations on *Die Schöpfung:* No. 13, "Die Himmel erzählen"].
  5a. Mozart: [6 Variations on Gluck's "Unser dummer Pöbel meint", K.455].
  6a. Mozart: [6 Variations on *La Clemenza di Tito:* 6 "Tanto affanno soffre un core", (Sesto's aria, No. 13,
      beginning bar 53, Allegro)].
*GYD-7a. 42 Arien aus verschiedenen Opern. 2cl 2hn 2bn.
MS pts (associated with the Harmonie of *Graf* Josef Batthyány): H-KE, K 0/117; H-Bn, (microfilm), FM 4/1999.
  7.1a. W. Müller: Das Sonnenfest der Braminen, sinfonia & 10 mvts. Nos. 1 - 11. *See also:* GYD-165.17a,
        (= Nos. 6 & 11).
  7.2a. W. Müller: Die zwei Schwestern von Prag, sinfonia & 2 mvts (as "Gruss dem . . ."). Nos. 12 - 14.
  7.3a. W. Müller: Das neu Sonntagskind, sinfonia & 2 mvts (as "Gruss dem . . ."). Nos. 15 - 17.
  7.4a. Righini: L'Incontro in aspettato, sinfonia & "Sposa Sonia". Nos. 18 & 19. [No. 18 = GYD-165.18(a)]
  7.5a. Naumann: Cora och Alonzo, 8 mvts. Nos. 20 - 27.
  7.6a. W. Müller: Kaspar der Fagottist, sinfonia & 14 mvts. Nos. 28 - 42. [No. 39 = GYD-165.22(a)]
*GYD-8a. Beethoven: Grand Septetto, Op. 20. 2ob 2cl 2hn 2bn cbn/vlne.
MS parts: CZ-Bm, A.35.149, (as an anonymous work; hn I part missing central sheet, mvt 4).
Pc (Au magasin de l'imprimerie chimique: Vienna, pn 1886, 1812), parts: A-M, V 1346; A-Wgm.
Pc (Haslinger: Vienna, post-1826), parts, (reprint of Chemische Druckeri/Steiner edition).
Pm (Artia [now Supraphon]: Praha/Prague, 1984), score (Musica viva historica 49a/H 6711).
Pm (Astoria: Berlin), edited Werner Schulze, parts.
*GYD-9a. Jos. Bohr: Rondo. Fresco Hungaria. 2ob cl bthn 2hn 2bn cbn..
MS parts ("ofen, 31 März 1803"): H-Bn, Ms.Mus.1523. *Bohr's name is crossed out in red pencil; cf. GYD-4.*
*GYD-10a. Dreschler: Nelsons Leichenfeier, Op. 5, ein Trauermarsch. 2ob 2cl 2hn 2bn.
MS parts: H-Bn, Ms.Mus.1529, No. 1, (as "Marcia [added] Mor. di Nelson").
GYD-11a. Hänsel: Rondo Allegretto a la ungaria [B♭]. 2ob talia cl bthn 2hn 2bn.
(?Auto)MS parts: H-Bb, 51,477, (missing 2ob)
*GYD-12a. Hassler: [single mvt in F minor/major; Andte poco Largo / Andtino]. 2ob cl bthn 2hn 2bn cbn.
MS parts: H-Bn, Ms.Mus.1523, (item 3).
*GYD-13a. Haydn: Die Schöpfung [The Creation], Einleitung & 15 mvts. 2ob 2cl 2hn 2bn (cbn ad lib).
MS parts: A-Wgm, VIII 40509; D-DO, Mus.Ms.727; I-Fc, F.P. S.352.
*GYD-14a. Haydn: Die Jahreszeiten [The Seasons], 14 mvts. 2ob 2cl 2hn 2bn.
MS pts: A-KR, H 42/109; A-Wgm, VIII 47734; I-Fc, F.P. S.352. *The contemporary piccolo pt found with the
A-Wgm copy is* not *part of this arrangement, being in a different hand on different paper, with different bar counts.*
GYD-15.1a. Mozart: Die Zauberflöte, 18 mvts. 2cl 2hn 2bn.
MS parts: H-KE, K 0/124; H-Bn, (microfilm), FM 4/2006.
GYD-15.2a. Mozart: Die Zauberflöte, Priester Marsch, in E♭. 2cl 2hn 2bn. MS parts: H-KE, K 0/150 Koll.2,
(as Anon; the 2hn parts are also present transposed to B♭); H-Bn, (microfilm), FM 4/2032.
GYD-16a. Paer: La Passione di Gesù Cristu. 2ob 2cl 2hn 2bn cbn. MS parts: I-Fc, F.P. S.351.
GYD-17a. Paer: Cantata per la festività del S. Natale. 2ob 2cl 2hn 2bn.
MS parts: I-Fc, F.P. S.351, (as "Cantata per il Natale di N. S. G[esù]. C[risto]").

GYD-18a. Gottfried Rieger: Allegretto, in F, 6/8, *(Note:* there are original Harmonie works & arrangements by Rieger in CZ-Bm). 2ob 2cl 2hn 2bn. MS parts: H-Bn, Z 46,694, Koll. 2.
GYD-19a. Süssmayr: Ländlerlische aus dem Spiegel von Arkadien. 2cl 2hn 2bn.
MS parts: H-KE, K 0/118, unnumbered item before No. 1; H-Bn, (microfilm), FM 4/2000.
GYD-1.1va. F.J. Haydn: "Gott erhalte den Kaiser" [sic]. SATB, 2ob 2cl 2hn 2bn.
MS parts: H-Bn, Ms.Mus.1579, (with duplicate vocal parts).
GYD-1.2va. F.J. Haydn: "Gott erhalte den Kaiser" [sic]. TTBB, ob cl hn bn. MS parts: H-Bn, Ms.Mus.1578.
GYD-2av. Kirnberger: Miserere, (Introduzione, 14 mvts & Canon). SATB, 2cl 2hn 2bn org.
MS parts: H-KE, K 0/125; H-Bn, (microfilm), FM 4/2007.
GYD-1ad. [Collection of arrangements = A-6a]. 2ob 2cl 2hn 2bn. MS pts: A-Wn, Mus.Hs.3792. *Attributed to Druschetzky by Alexander Weinmann, also earlier attributed to Triebensee. Many of the mvts are, in fact, arrangements by Went; the sets of variations may be by Triebensee. The Druschetzky attribution is most unlikely.*
*GYD-2ad. Beethoven: Sonata ("Pathetique"), Op. 13. 2ob 2cl 2hn 2bn cbn.
Pc (as Anon:) (Chemische Druckerei: Wien, pn 1488, 1810), parts: NL-DHgm, hk 19 C 4.
MS parts (as Anon): CZ-Bm(au), A.37.330, (missing cbn; ob II marked "ad lib").
Pm (performing edition prepared by Alexander Weinmann, broadcast ORF, Vienna, pre-1986, attributed without source to Druschetzky), MS score & parts: A-Worf.
Pm (Compusic: Amsterdam, pn 202, 1991, attrib. "probably Druschetzky"), score & parts.

DSPILER, ( )
XZD-1. Parthia in C, 4 mvts. 2cl 2hn 2bn. MS pts: CZ-NR, A.18.240/B.255. ★

*DUBOIS, Pierre-Max *1 March 1930, Graulhet, France - 1995*
PID-1. Huit plus un, Op. 90; 5 mvts. fl(pic) 2ob cl cl(sax) 2hn 2bn.
Pm (Billaudot: Paris, pn GB 1711, 1977), score & parts.
PID-2. Les nouvealles saisons. 2fl 2ob 2cl 2hn 2bn piano.
Pm (Billaudot: Paris, sd), score & parts.
PID-3. Les trois mousequetaires: Divertimento. ob 2cl bn; (a-sax alternative for cl II).
Pm (Leduc: Paris).

*DU BOIS, Rob *28 May 1934, Amsterdam*
RXD-1. Sinfonia da camera. 2fl 2ob 2cl 4hn 2bn cbn.
Pm (Donemus: Amsterdam, 1980), score.
RXD-2. Cercle. fl ob 2cl 2hn 2bn tp pf perc.
Pm (Donemus: Amsterdam, 1963), score & parts
RXD-3. Chansons pour appâter les cheiroptères *(to lure bats)*, 1975. ob 2obdam 2ca.
Pm (Donemus: Amsterdam, 1977), score & parts.
RXD-4. Vertiges. 2fl 2ob 2cl 4hn 2bn cbn.
Pm (Donemus: Amsterdam, 1987), score.

*DUBOIS, (Clement François) Théodore *24 Aug 1837, Rosnay - 11 June 1924, Paris*
*CFD-1. Première Suite; 3 mvts. 2fl ob 2cl hn 2bn.
Pc (Au Ménestrel, Heugel & Cⁱᵉ: Paris, pn H & Cⁱᵉ 192541898, c.1877), score & parts: F-Pn, D. 3605; GB-Lbbc, Orch. 10291, (score only). ★
Pm (E.F. Kalmus: New York, pn A 3953, sd), score & parts (reprint of Heugel edition).
*CFD-2. Deuxième Suite; 3 mvts, (c.1877). 2fl ob 2cl hn 2bn.
Pc (Alphonse Leduc: Paris, pn A.L. 9928, 1898), score (pn 11567) & parts (pn 11568), Bibliothèque Leduc No. 334: D-Bhm; F-Pn, D. 3606; I-Fc, F.P. S. 13250; US-PT. ★
Pm (E.F. Kalmus: New York, pn A 3275, sd), score & parts (reprint of Leduc edition).
*CFD-3. Au Jardin: Petite Suite; 3 mvts. fl fl/pic ob 2cl(A) hn bn.
Pc (Au Ménestrel, Heugel & Cⁱᵉ: Paris, pn H. & Cⁱᵉ 23,466, 1908), score & parts: F-Pn, D. 3607; GB-Lbbc, Orch. 5309. ★
Pm (E.F. Kalmus: New York, pn A 41 54, sd), score & parts (reprint of Heugel edition).
Pm (Compusic: Amsterdam, pn 206, 1988), score & parts.

DÜRING, J.C. [?Johann Chrisitian] *(1770)*
JCD-1a. Himmel: Fanchon, das Leiermädchen, overture & 12 mvts. 2fl 2ob 2cl 2hn 2bn tp cb.
MS pts: D-F, Mus.Ms.1788; NL-DHgm, hk 19 C 1, (as anon). *Essentially for 2cl 2hn 2bn cb with ripieno parts.*

DUK, August *(active 1834, Český Krumlov)*
AZD-1v. Religiöser Chor . . . Op. Eccl. I. 16.Sept.[1]834; in C, "Allmächtiger! im Staube knien wir".
SATB, 2fl 2cl(C) 2hn 2bn 2tp 2tb timp. MS parts: CZ-K, rodina Šimečkova Sign.1333. *A note offers the option of organ accompaniment when the winds are not available* ★

DURAND, Paul Jules *(c.1900)*
PZD-1. Let us take a walk in the woods. 2fl 2ob 2cl b-cl bn.
Pm (Mills Music: New York, 1961).

*DUREY, Louis-Edmond *27 May 1888, Paris - 3 July 1979, St Tropez*
LED-1. Concertino, Op. 83; 1957. Piano solo, pic 2fl 2ob 2cl 2hn 2bn cbn 2tp tb tu db timp.
Photocopy of the autograph score available from Madame Durey; apply *via* SACEM: Paris.
*LED-1v. Le Bestiaire du Cortège d'Orphée, Poèmes de Guillaume Apollinaire, Op 17. Voice, 13 winds (1958 version of 1921 piano original).
Pc (J. & W. Chester: London, Geneva, 1921), piano: GB-Lbl, G.1270.b.(16).
*LED-2v. Le Printemps au fond de la mer, Cantate sur une poésie de Jean Cocteau, Op. 24, (1920, revised 1954). S, 2fl ob ca 2cl(A) hn 2bn tp.
Pm (Editions du Chant du Monde *via* United Music Publishers: Paris, London, sd), score & parts.

*DURKÓ, Zsolt *10 April 1934, Szeged, Hungary*
ZYD-1. Octet; 1988. 2ob 2cl 2hn 2bn cbn(ad lib).
Pm (Editio Musica: Budapest, pn 13837, sd), score. MS score: H-Bmzs.

*DUŠEK (Dussek, Duschek), František (Franz) Xaver *8 Dec 1731, Chotěborky - 12 Feb 1799, Prague*
FXD-1. Parthia in C; 4 mvts, (S.55).   2ob 2hn 2bn.   MS parts: CZ-Pnm, XXII.C.136. ★
FXD-2. Parthia in B[♭]; 4 mvts, (S.56).   2ob 2hn 2bn.
MS parts: CZ-Pnm, (2 copies), XXII.C.137 (dated 1762), XXXII.B.8. ★
FXD-3. Parthia in F; 4 mvts, (S.57).   2ob 2hn 2bn.   MS parts (1762): CZ-Pnm, XXII.C.138. *The original date,*
"1764" has been corrected in the same hand to the earlier date ★
FXD-4. Parthia in G; 4 mvts, (S.58).   2ob 2hn 2bn.   MS parts: CZ-Pnm, XXII.C.139. ★
FXD-5. Parthia in D; 4 mvts, (S.59).   2ob 2hn 2bn.   MS parts: CZ-Pnm, XXII.C.140. ★
FXD-6. Parthia in F; 4 mvts, (S.60).   2ob 2hn 2bn.   MS parts (1762): CZ-Pnm, XXII.C.141. *The original date,*
"1764" has been corrected in the same hand (but with a different ink) to the earlier date. ★
FXD-7. Parthia in F; 4 mvts, (S.61).   2ob 2hn 2bn.   MS parts (1762): CZ-Pnm, XXII.C.142. ★
FXD-8. Partia in F; 4 mvts, (S.62).   2ob 2hn 2bn.   MS parts: CZ-Pnm, XXII.C.147. ★
FXD-9. Parthia in C; 4 mvts, (S.63).   2ob 2hn 2bn.   MS parts: CZ-Pnm, XXII.C.148. ★
FXD-10. Parthia in F; 4 mvts, (S.64).   2ob 2hn 2bn.   MS parts (1763): CZ-Pnm, XXII.C.149. ★
FXD-11. Parthia in D; 4 mvts, (S.65).   2ob 2hn 2bn.   MS parts (1764): CZ-Pnm, XXII.C.150. ★
FXD-12. Parthia Ex F; 4 mvts, (S.66).   2ob 2hn 2bn.   MS parts (1764): CZ-Pnm, XXII.C.151. ★
FXD-13. Parthia in D; 4 mvts, (S.67).   2ob 2hn 2bn.   MS parts: CZ-Pnm, XXII.C.152. ★
*FXD-14. Partia in A; 4 mvts (S.68).   2ob 2hn 2bn.
MS parts: CZ-Pnm, (2 copies), XXII.C.153, XLII.E.143 (as "Parthia Ex A"). ★
*FXD-15. Partia in D; 4 mvts, (S.69).   2ob 2hn 2bn.
MS parts: CZ-Pnm, (2 copies), XXII.C.154, XXXII.A.104, (as "Parthia ex D"). ★
FXD-16. Partia in F; 4 mvts, (S.70).   2ob 2hn 2bn.   MS parts: CZ-Pnm, XXII.C.155. ★
FXD-17.1. Parthia Ex D; 4 mvts, (S.71).   2ob 2hn 2bn.   MS parts: CZ-Pnm, XXII.C.156. ★
FXD-17.2. Parthia in D, №̲ 15; 4 mvts, (S.deest).   2ob 2hn bn.   MS parts: H-Bn, Ms.Mus.IV 747.
FXD-18. Partitta; in D, 4 mvts, (S.73).   2ob 2hn 2bn.
MS parts: CZ-Pnm, XXII.C.120a.   Modern MS score: CZ-Pnm, XXVI.C.2. ★
FXD-19. Partitta; in B♭, 4 mvts, (S.74).   2ob 2hn 2bn.   MS parts: CZ-Pnm, XXII.C.120b. ★
FXD-20. Partitta; in B♭, 4 mvts, (S.75).   2ob 2hn 2bn.   MS parts: CZ-Pnm, XXII.C.121. ★
FXD-21. Partitta; in F, 3 mvts, (S.76).   2ob 2hn 2bn.   MS parts: CZ-Pnm, XXII.C.122. ★
FXD-22. Partitta In D; 4 mvts, (S.77).   2ob 2hn 2bn.   MS parts: CZ-Pnm, XXII.C.123. ★
FXD-23. Partitta In A; 4 mvts, (S.78).   2ob 2hn 2bn.   MS parts: CZ-Pnm, XXII.C.124. ★
FXD-24. Partitta In F; 4 mvts, (S.79).   2ob 2hn 2bn.   MS parts: CZ-Pnm, XXII.C.125. ★
FXD-25. Partitta In B[♭]; 4 mvts, (S.80).   2ob 2hn 2bn.   MS parts: CZ-Pnm, XXII.C.126. ★
FXD-26. Parttit[a] in F; 4 mvts, (S.81).   2ob 2hn 2bn.
MS parts: CZ-Pnm, (2 copies)., XXII.C.127, XL.D.438.   Modern MS score: CZ-Pk, Sign. 942/30. ★
FXD-27. Parthia in A; 4 mvts, (S.82).   2ob 2hn 2bn.
MS parts: CZ-Pnm, (2 copies) XXII.C.128; XL.D.436, (modern MS score). ★
FXD-28. Parthia in C; 4 mvts, (S.83).   2ob 2hn 2bn.   MS parts: CZ-Pnm, XXII.C.129. ★
FXD-29. Parthia in F; 4 mvts, (S.84).   2ob 2hn 2bn.   MS parts: CZ-Pnm, XXII.C.130. ★
FXD-30. Parthia in B[♭]; 4 mvts, (S.85).   2ob 2hn 2bn.
MS parts: CZ-Pnm, (2 copies), XXII.C.132, XL.D.437, (modern MS score); CZ-Pk, Sign. 949/30. ★
FXD-31. Partitta in A; 4 mvts, (S.86).   2ob 2hn 2bn.   MS parts: CZ-Pnm, XXII.C.133. ★
FXD-32.1. Parthia in C; 4 mvts, (S. 87).   2ob 2hn 2bn.   MS parts: CZ-Pnm, XLII.E.149. ★
*FXD-32.2. Partihia [sic] in B[♭], 4 mvts.   2cl 2hn 2bn.   MS parts: D-F, Mus.Hs.1558, (missing 2 hn - the
horn parts present are not for this work; there is also a duplicate bn I part in C). ★
FXD-33. Parthia in F; 4 mvts, (S. 88).   2ob 2hn 2bn.   MS parts: CZ-Pnm, XLII.E.135. ★
FXD-34. Parthia in b [B♭]; 4 mvts, (S.89).   2ob 2hn 2bn.   MS parts: CZ-Pnm, XLII.E.134. ★
FXD-35. Parthia in F; 4 mvts, (S deest).   2ob 2hn 2bn.   MS parts: CZ-Pnm, XLII.E.151. ★
FXD-36. Parthia Ex F; 4 mvts, (S.48).   2ob 2hn bn.   MS parts: CZ-Pnm, XXII.C.135. ★
FXD-37. Parthia in F; 4 mvts, (S.49).   2ob 2hn bn.
MS parts (1762): CZ-Pnm, XXII.C.143. ★
Pm (Artia: Prague), score (Musica antiqua bohemica 35, No. 3).
FXD-38. Parthia in A; 4 mvts, (S.50).   2ob 2hn bn.   MS parts: CZ-Pnm, XXII.C.144. ★
FXD-39. Parthia in F; 4 mvts, (S.51).   2ob 2hn 2bn.   MS parts: CZ-Pnm, XXII.C.145. ★
FXD-40. Parthia in G; 3 mvts, (S.52).   2ob 2hn 2bn.   MS parts: CZ-Pnm, XXII.C.146. ★
FXD-41. Parthia in F; 3 mvts, (S. 53).   2ob 2hn bn.   MS parts: CZ-Pnm, XXII.C.131. ★
FXD-42. Partitta; in G; 4 mvts, (S.54).   2ob 2hn bn.   MS parts: CZ-Pnm, XXII.C.134. ★
FXD-43.1. Parthia; in F, 4 mvts, (S.72).   2ob/cl 2hn bn.
MS parts (1762): CZ-Pnm, XXII.C.119, (with an additional bn. part transposed to E♭ for use with B♭ clarinets;
the oboe parts have been marked "clarineto [sic] Imo" and "Clarino [sic] IIdo" at a later date).
FXD-43.2 Parthia in G №̲ 14; 5 mvts, (S.deest).   2ob 2hn bn.   MS parts: H-Bn, Ms.Mus.IV 748. ★
FXD-44. Parthia in F, №̲ 10; 3 mvts, (S. deest).   2ob 2hn bn.   MS parts: H-Bn, Ms.Mus.IV 746. ★
FXD-45 (-48). 4 Parthien ("Tuschek").   Instrumentation unknown.   MS parts: D-DO, (?lost).
Here MVH indicates: Edition Supraphon: Prague, 1979), ed. Miloslav Klement, score & parts (Musica viva
historica. 39). The set has also been issued by A. J. Benjamin: Hamburg, sd, ed. Degen; and by E.C. Kerby Ltd:
Toronto, ed. Komorous (2 vol. pn ECK 15947 & 16047).
FXD-49. Parthia in G; 3 mvts, (S. 43).   2ob bn.   MS parts: CZ-Pnm, XXII.C.68.   Pm (MHV: No 6). ★
FXD-50. Parthia in F; 4 mvts, (S. 44).   2ob bn.   MS parts(1763): CZ-Pnm, XXII.C.69.   Pm (MHV: No 1). ★
FXD-51. Parthia in G; 4 mvts, (S. 45).   2ob bn.
MS parts: CZ-Pnm, XXII.C.70, (dated 1763); CZ-Pu(am), Sigl.O 1085.   Pm (MHV: No 5). ★
FXD-52. Parthia in C; 4 mvts, (S. 46).   2ob bn.
MS parts: CZ-Pnm, XXII.C.71; CZ-Pu(am), Sigl.O 1083.   Pm (MHV: No 4). ★
FXD-53. Parthia in C; 4 mvts, (S. 47).   2ob bn.
MS parts (1763): CZ-Pnm, XXII.C.72; CZ-Pu(am), Sigl.O 1087.   Pm (MHV: No 3). ★
FXD-54. Parthia in F, 4 mvts, (S deest).   2ob bn.
MS parts: CZ-Pu(am), Sigl.O 1086.   Pm (MHV: No 2). ★

FXD-1m. Marsch in D; (S. 180). 2cl(A) 2hn bn 2tp(clar) tp(prin) timp.
AutoMS (from Kunvald): CZ-Pnm, VIII.F.40, (an additional part labelled "Cornuo [crossed out: Clarinetto] primo in C" comprising 2 Stücke is, in fact, from some other work). ★
FXD-1v. Ex D Pangelingua [sic]; (S.193). 2fl 2cl 2hn bn.
MS parts (by Johann Mategna, from Choceň: CZ-Pnm, VIII.F.25, (missing 2fl 2hn & vocal parts). ★
FXD-2v. Cantilena funeralis; in E♭, ("Zhasnnl život diery milé [sic]"), (S.187). CATB, 2cl 2hn bn.
MS parts (from Kunvald): CZ-Pnm, VIII.F.42. ★

*DUVERNOY, Frédéric Nicolas *16 Oct 1765, Montbéliard - 19 Sept 1838, Paris*
FED-1mv. Pas de manoeuvre; (P.2295). 2p-fl 2cl 2hn 2bn tp serp.
Pc (Mag de mus fêtes nat: Paris, messidor an II, 1794), liv. 4, No. 5, pts: F-Pn, (2 copies), H2. 4,5, Vm7 7041. ★

*DUYN, Wilhelm *1922, Netherlands*
WQD-1. Rhapsody. 2fl 2ob 2cl 2hn 2bn.
Pm (Donemus: Amsterdam, 1990), score.

*DVOŘÁK, Antonín Leopold *8 Sept 1841, Nelahozeves, nr Prague - 1 May 1904, Prague*
*ALD-1. Serenade in D minor, Op. 44; 1878, 4 mvts. 2ob 2cl 3hn 2bn vc db.
Pc (N. Simrock: Berlin, 1879), score: CZ-Pu, Vp 13052; GB-Lbl, h.1573.b.(2.); I-Mc, Da Camera A.36.13. ★
Pm (SNKLHU: Prague, 1956), score & parts, miniature score.
Pm (Ernst Eulenburg: London, Edition Eulenburg No. 1314, c.1960), score.
Pm (Musica rara: London, pn 1039, 1961), parts.
Pm (Supraphon: Prague, pn 1928, c.1984), score & parts, miniature score (No. 86).
Pm (Artia: Prague, pn H 1952, sd), score.
Pm (E.F. Kalmus: New York, pn A 3423, sd), score & parts.
Pm (International Music Corp.: New York, sd), min score (pn 1399) & parts (pn 1397).
Pm (Anton J. Benjamin: Hamburg & London, sd). Pm (A. Noël: Paris, sd).

*EASTLAND, Edwin *(1760)*
EYE-1m. Twelve Marches for 2 Hautboys, German flutes or Clarinets and a Bassoon. As an Introduction to Play in Different Keys; *(in fact, only 7 keys are used; the marches are respectively in G, G, F, C, F, A, D, F, G, B♭, D, E♭).* Nos. 1 - 11: 2ob/fl/cl bn; No. 12: 2vl 2cl basso.
Pc (Longman and Broderip: London, 1787), RISM [E 23], score: GB-Lbl, b.60.(2); GB-Ob, Mus.86d.2. ★

EATON, John Charles *1935, USA*
JCE-1. Concert Piece. fl 2ob 2cl.
Pm (Malcolm Music, *via* Shawnee Press: Delaware Water Gap, Pa, 1956), hire score & parts.
JCE-2. Variations for Wind Quintet. fl 2ob 2cl.
Pm (Associated Music Publishers: New York), score & (hire) parts.

*EBDON, Thomas *1738, Durham - 23 Sept 1811, Durham*
*TXE-1(m). A Favorite March, Performed at the Installation of Wm: Hen: Lambton Esqr., Grand Provincial Master of Free and Accepted Masons for the County of Durham. 2ob 2hn bn timp.
Pc (J. Dale: London, c.1795), RISM [E 40], score: GB-Gu; GB-Lbl, g.133.(14); GB-Ob, Mus.Instr.I.91(3). ★

EBELL, Heinrich Carl *30 Dec 1775, Neuruppin - 12 March 1824, Opole, Poland*
HCE-1. Partita. 2ob 2cl 2hn bn. MS parts: PL-Wu, Ka. 4, 5, 6.

*EBERWEIN, Trautgott Maximilian *27 Oct 1775, Weimar - 2 Dec 1831, Rudolstadt*
TME-1. Parthia in C. 2ob 2cl(C) 2hn 2bn tp. (original provenance unknown)
Pm (Worldwide Music Services: New York, now Jacksonville, Florida, 1982), ed. Kurt Janetzky, score & pts. ★
Pm (Hofmeister: Hofheim/Taunus, 1992), ed. Kurt Janetzky, score & parts.
TME-2(-5). 4 Partien. 2fl ob cl 2hn 2bn. MS parts: D-DS, (?lost during World War II).

*EDELING, Johann *(?1770)*
*JXE-1. [Concerto(?) in E♭], 4 mvts. 2cl(2)bn 2vla vc/vlne. MS pts: GB-Lbl, R.M.21.d.4.(8), (?missing 2hn). ★
*JXE-2. Parthia; in B♭, 4 mvts. 2cl 2hn bn 2vla vc/vlne. MS pts: GB-Lbl, RM.21.d.4.(9). ★

*EDENHOFER, F.H. *(1780)*
PFE-1a. Türkische Musique Militair [sic]. pic 2cl(E♭) 2cl(B♭) 2hn 2bn 2tp b-tb serp b-dr t-dr.
MS parts: A-Sca, Hs.77, (the cl I in B♭ pt is incomplete, missing the sheet for the end of No. 4 and the beginning of No. 5, the last sheet of No. 9 and all of No. 10; cataloged at "A. Fendt").
1.1a. Simphonia; 4 mvts. Nos. 1 - 4.
1.2a. Simphonia; 4 mvts. Nos. 5 - 8.
1.3a. Simphonia, "orango [sic] F.H.E."; 4 mvts. Nos. 9 - 12.

*EDER, Helmut *26 Dec 1916, Linz*
*HYE-1. Suite mit Intermezzi, Op. 71. 2ob 2cl 4hn 2bn cbn.
Pm (Doblinger: Wien, 1981), score (pn DE 06597) & parts (pn DE 06598).
HYE-2. Septet for Winds, Op. 55: Homage to Johannes Kepler; 1970. fl ob cl 2hn bn tp.
Pm (Doblinger: Wien, 1972), miniature score (pn STP 291), parts (pn DE 6606).
HYE-3. Litzlberg-Serenade, Op. 67. 2cl hn bn tp.
Pm (Doblinger: Wien, 1980), score & parts.

EDER, Philipp
PXE-1tv. Leichengesang in Es [E♭]; "Lebet wohl geliebte Kinder". CATB, 2cl 2hn bn.
MS parts: A-Wn, Mus.Hs.21,727. ★

EDLUND, Lars *1922, Sweden*
LXE-1v. Triad, (text: Dag Hammarskjöld). SATB chorus, fl ob 3cl a-sax 3hn 2bn 2tp 3tb tu 4perc 3vc 2db.
Pm (Ab Nordiska Musikforlaget: Stockholm, 1973), hire score & parts.

EDLUND, Mikael *19 Jan 1950, Tranås, Sweden*
MXE-1. Music for Double Wind Quintet; 1983 - 1984.   2fl 2ob 2cl 2hn 2bn.
Pm (Ab Nordiska Musikforlaget: Stockholm, 1984), hire score & parts (also *via* Wilhelm Hansen: Copenhagen).

EGGAR (Egger), Franz *(1790)*
FXE-1a. Donizetti: L'Esula di Roma.   fl(E♭) cl(E♭) cl(B♭) 2hn bn, keyed-bugle(ad lib).
MS parts: A-Wn, Mus.Hs.23968.

*EGK, Werner (*pseudonym for Werner Mayer*) *17 May 1901, Auchsesheim - 10 July 1983, Inning*
*WXE-1. Divertissement; 1973.   fl(pic) 2ob cl cl(b-cl) 2hn bn bn(cbn, ad lib) tp.
Pm (B. Schott's Söhne: Mainz, 1975), score (pn 6465) & parts (pn 6465-10).
*WXE-1a. Egk: Die Zaubergeige: Overture; (1935, arranged 1980).   fl fl(pic) ob ob(ca) 2cl 2hn 2bn tp db.
Pm (B. Schott's Söhne: Mainz, London, 1980), hire score & parts.
*WXE-2a. Mozart: Sinfonia Concertante, K297b, 1982/83.   2ob 2cl 2hn 2bn db.
Pm (B. Schott's Söhne: Mainz, London, 1986), score (pn 7525) & parts (pn 7526).

EHMANN, ( ) *(1770)*
XZE-1m. Marsch.   2pic 2cl(A) 2cl(D) 2hn 2bn tp serp.   MS: D-Bds, Hausbibl.M.M.98a.
XZE-2m. Marsch, in E♭, c.1800.   2cl 2hn 2bn tp.
Pm (In: Pätzig (qv), Heft 2, No. 16), score & parts.

*EHRENFRIED, Franz Heinrich *(c.1750)*
*FHE-1a. Dalayrac: Nina (as "Parthia", No. 1, 6 mvts; No. 2, 5 mvts), 1788.   2ob 2cl 2hn (2)basso.
MS parts: D-HR, HR III 4 1/2 2° 351/352.   Pm (KGS), fiche 2303.
D-DO, Mus.Ms.2017 (A-100a) may also be Ehrenfried's arrangement, slightly adapted by Rosinack.
*FHE-2a. Grétry: Raoul Barbe-Bleue. Parthia No. 1, 6 mvts; No 2, 6 mvts; No. 3, 5 mvts.
Nos. 1, 3.   2ob 2cl 2hn (2)basso; No. 2: 2ob 2cl 2hn bn (2)basso.
MS parts: D-HR; HR III 4 1/2 2° 353 - 355.   Pm (KGS), fiche 2304.
FHE-3a. Monsigny: Le Déserteur, (as "Parthia"), 6 mvts.   2ob 2cl 2hn bn vlne.
MS parts: D-F, Mus.Hs.1556, (with the added note, "per la Capella Principale [Bern, Switzerland]").
FHE-4a. Mozart: Don Giovanni.   2ob 2cl 2hn 2bn vlne/cb.   MS parts: I-Fc, F.P. S.477.
FHE-5a. Righini: Armida, overture & 17 mvts.   2ob 2cl 2hn 2bn vlne/cb.
MS parts: D-HR, HR III 4 1/2 2° 357.   Pm (KGS), fiche 2306 - 2308.

*EICHHORN, Johann (Paul) *born 22 Feb 1787, Coburg - ?*
JYE-1. Variations pour la Basson.   Solo bn, 2cl 2hn.   MS parts: CH-Lz, Mus.311.

*EICHNER, Ernst (Ernesto) Dietrich Adolf *9 Feb 1740, Arolsen, nr Mannheim - pre-10 Oct 1777, Potsdam*
*EXE-1. Divertissement [sic]; in E♭; 7 mvts.   2ob 2cl 2hn 2bn.
MS pts: GB-Lbl, RM.21.d.4, No. 10; GB-DOTams, (microfilm).   ★
EXE-2. Divertissement [parts: "I. Suite"] in C; 6 mvts.   2ob 2cl 2hn 2bn.
Pc (Mme Berault: Paris, 1780), RISM [E 531], parts: D-BFb, E-ich 70.
Pm (Compusic: Amsterdam, pn 234, 1988), score & parts.

*EILHARDT, Friedrich Christian Carl *(1830)*
FCE-1m. Sieges Triumph Festmarsch, 1866.   2 military bands: "Infanterie": pic(E♭) fl 2ob 2cl(E♭) 4cl(B♭) 4hn
2bn cbn 4tp 3tb 2t-hn 2tu b-dr s-dr; "Cavalerie": pic(E♭) 2crt(E♭) 2crt(B♭) 4tp flug 2t-hn bar-hn 2tu.
MS score: D-B, Mus.Ms.5560. *This large work is listed because of the way it contrasts two different bands.*

*EINEM, Gottfried von *24 Jan 1918, Berne (now Austria) - 14 July 1996, Oberdürchbach*
GVE-1. Rindlberger March, Op. 54.   2cl 2hn 2bn 2tp tb tu timp b-dr s-dr.
Pm (Bote & Bock, Berlin, 1979), hire score & parts.
GVE-2. Glück, Tod und Traum, Alpbacher Tanzserenade, Ballet, Op. 17, 1953.   ob 2cl 2hn 2bn tp.
Pm: (B Schott's Söhne: Mainz; Universal Edition: Wien, c.1957), hire score & parts.

EISMA, Will *13 May 1929, Sungaailat, Indonesia*
WYE-1. 5 Roses for Diana, 1969.   3fl 3ob 3cl 4hn 3bn electronics.
Pm (Donemus: Amsterdam, 1971). score.
WYE-2. Gadget.   2fl 2ob 3cl a-sax 2hn bn db.
Pm (Donemus: Amsterdam, 1979), score.

EK, Gunnar *26 June 1900, Asarum - 21 June 1981, Lund*
GXE-1. Octet; 1970.   2fl 2ob 2cl 2bn.   MS score: S-Sic.

*EK, Hans *31 Jan 1964, Sweden*
HQE-1. CNN [sic]; 1991.   fl cl 2bn 2tp 2tb.   MS score: S-Sic.

EKLUND, Hans *1927, Sweden*
HAE-1. Zodinal; 1986.   fl 2cl bn piano.   MS score: S-Sic.

*EKSTRÖM, Lars *1956, Sweden*
LYE-1. Teroni (Bondläppens erogena zon); 1986.   2cl 2bn.   MS score: S-Sic.

*ÉLER, André Fréderic *1764, Alsace - 21 April 1821, Paris*
AFE-1. Ouverture N° 16; P.2322.   2p-fl 2ob 2cl 2hn 2bn 2tp 3tb serp timp, (buccin, tuba corva, vla, cb ad lib).
Pc (Mag de mus fêtes nat: Paris, c.1795), liv. 16, RISM [E 602], pts: F-Pn, (2 copies), H2. 44,7, H2. 130B a-q. ★
MS parts (probably including instruments in parentheses above): F-Pn, H2. 130A.
AFE-2. Six walzes & un anglaise.   2cl 2hn 2bn.
Pc (Mlles. Erard: Paris; Garnier, Lyon, (Gravé par Mlle. Garbet), pn 639, 1806), RISM Supp [EE 615a], parts:
B-Gc, (missing hn II); F-Pn, Vm12g 15586, (3 copies). *Also issued for solo piano (F-Pn, Vm12g 4169).* ★
AFE-3. Trois Quatours, Oeuv. Xᵉ; (E♭, E♭, B♭).   2cl hn bn.
Pc (chez Pleyel: Paris, pn 698, 1806), parts: F-Pn, A. 33895.
*AFE-1mv. Ode sur la situation de la République en prairial an VII; (1799), P.155.   Solo voice, 2cl 2hn (2)bn.
Pc (Rec des époques: Paris, post-1797), liv. 1, No. 41, score: F-Pn, H2. 15,41. ★

*ELEY, Charles Frederick (Francis) *July 1756, Hanover - 1832, (?) London*
It is likely that Eley was involved in the preparation of the works in A-202 - A-204; CFE-1.8m & 1.11m can be found in A-204 (Nos. 5 & 7). Elrington's New Short Troop, CRE-1.2m(a), was probably scored by Eley .
CFE-1m. Twelve Select Military Pieces . . . Performed by the Band of the Coldstream Regiment of Guards. 2cl 2hn (2)bn tp(ad lib).
Pc (Printed for C.F. Eley at Mr Fike[']s: London, 1789), RISM [E 618], pts: GB-Lbl, b.80.(1); GB-Ob, 61.d.3. ★
MS parts (No. 1 only): D-Bds, Hausbibl.M.M.376, (with CFE-5m, as Anon).
  1.1m. The Duke of York's March [and Trio], [arranged Eley].   1.2m(a). W. Elrington: New Short Troop.
  1.3m. Baltioram Quick March.   1.4m. The Prince of Wales [sic] Favorite Quick March.
  1.5m. The Duke of Clarence [sic] Favorite Menuet.   1.6m. [C.] F. Eley: Quick March.
  1.7m. [C.] F. Eley: Troop.   1.8m(t). March Fonebre [sic].   1.9m. C.F. Eley: Menuet.
  1.10m. The Austrian Grenadiers Quick March [with Trio].   1.11m. C.F. Eley: Menuetto.
  1.12m. Quick March.
CFE-2m. A [MS: 2d] Set of Select Military Pieces. 2ob/cl 2cl 2hn 2bn tp; (2terz-fl replace 2ob in No. 4).
Pc (Longman & Broderip: London, 1791/1792), RISM [E 618], parts: GB-Lbl, b.80.(2); GB-Ob, Mus. 61.d.3. ★
  2.1m. [C.] F. Eley: Slow March.
  2.2m(a). W. Reeve: Oscar & Malvina, Adagio [or rather, Rondo Allegro / Andante; the two 1st cl parts are marked "Solo" & "ad Libm.", the latter with an Alberti accompaniment].
  2.3m(a). J.W. Callcott: Glee, in [S. Arnold's opera, the] Battle of Hexham.
  2.4m. [C.] F. Eley: Cotillion [with Trio].
  2.5m(a). Pleyel: Adagio (B.331/ii) [& Allegro (B.350/ii].   2.6m. [C.] F. Eley: Walzer [& Trio].
  2.7m(a). W. Reeve: In Oscar & Malvina. Adagio and Allegretto.
  2.8m(a). S. Arnold: [The Surrender of Calais], Andante ("From Night till Morn I take my glass").
CFE-3m. A Third Set of Military Pieces. 2ob/cl 2cl 2hn 2bn tp.
Pc (Longman & Broderip: London, c.1792), RISM [E 618], parts: GB-Lbl, b.80.(3); GB-Ob, Mus.61.d.3. ★
  3.1m. [C.] F. Eley: March.   3.2m(a). W Shield: Finale to the Woodman.
  3.3m(a). Pleyel: Adagio & Presto (B.302/iii+iv; IJP-12.5).   3.4m. [C.] F. Eley: Sherzando [sic].
  3.5m(a). Pleyel: Minuetto (B.322/iii, iiia).   3.6m(a). S. Storace: Andante.
  3.7m(a). Paisiello: Catch. [Clarinets in C].
  3.8m(a). Duetto. Sung by Mr. [Michael] Kelly and Mrs. Crouch. Andante Sostenuto.
CFE-4m. Ten Military Divertimentos, with Fifes & Drums (ad libitum) also proper directions for beating the side Drum by Notes. Book [1]. *Missing band parts, here only:* 2fifes timps muffled-drums loud-drums b-dr cym.
Pc (Clementi, Banger, Hyde, Collard & Davis, Successors to Longman & Broderip: London, c. 1801 - 1805), score: GB-Lbl, R.M.17.f.9.(1). *Only 5 of the 10 pieces are included in the score.* ★
  4.1m. Adagio / Short Troop [with Trio].   4.2m. Quick March / Light Infantry.
  4.3m. Slow March / Light Infantry [cymbals added to b-drum part].   4.5m. Allegretto.   4.10m. March.
CFE-5m. The favorite Short Troop as Performed by His Royal Highness the Duke of York's new Band in the Coldstream Regt. of Guards. 2cl 2hn 2bn tp.
Pc (Longman & Broderip: London, c.1789), RISM [E 624], score: GB-Gu; GB-Lbl, g.133.(15); GB-Ob, Mus.Instr.I.91(8); US-Bu; US-Wc. ★
MS parts: D-Bds, Hausbibl.M.M.376, (with CFE-1.1m, as Anon).
CFE-1me. The Grand March as Performed in the Pantomime of Hercules & Omphale. 2ob/cl(ripieno) 2cl 2hn 2bn tp serp(ad lib).
Pc (G. Smart: London, 1795), RISM [E 621], score: GB-Gu; GB-Lbl, g.133.(19); GB-Ob. ★
CFE-1ma. M. Arne: Cymon, "The favourite Quick March in Cymon". 2cl 2hn 2bn tp.
Pc (Longman & Broderip: London, c.1785), RISM [E 620], score: GB-Gu, GB-Lbl, g.133.(16); GB-Ob, Mus.Instr.I.91(17). ★
MS parts: D-Bds, Hausbibl.M.M.380.
CFE-2ma. [Mozart: Le Nozze di Figaro, "Non più andrai"]. The Duke of York's New March as Performed by His Royal Highness's new Band in the Coldstream Regt. of Guards Composed, and Arranged . . . by C.F. Eley. 2cl 2hn 2bn tp.
Pc (Longman & Broderip: London, 1792), RISM [M 4495], score: GB-Ckc; GB-En, Glen 347-15; GB-Lbl, g.271.t.(10); GB-Ljag (photocopy), GB-Lhumphries.

*ELGAR, Sir Edward William, Bart *2 June 1857, Broadheath, nr Worcester - 23 Feb 1934, Worcester*
Elgar's wind works present a number of problems. The original MS pts are found at: GB-Lbl, Add. 60,316 A-E. Only the bassoon part is in Elgar's hand and the order of works is different for each part. The bassoon part is labelled by Elgar on the wrapper: "[pencil] Bassoon / [original, ink] 'Cello / E. W. Elgar / (only)."; many of the works are clearly intended for a cello, with multiple stops & pizzicato and arco markings. In most cases, the works are in single movements. A second set including "Sheds" 6 and 7 have a part for violin. The works were rediscovered by John Parr, of Sheffield, who edited and grouped the works for local performance in 1935 & 1936; Parr's MS versions (in several hands) are held at GB-Lbl, Add. 58,051 and Add. 58,052. The Belwin Mills publications represent yet a further grouping of works. We list here first the Belwin Mills publications as EWE-1 - EWE-6; annotations in italics follow the entries. Omitted works - primarily arrangements - follow.
*EWE-1.1(1.6). Six Promenades; 1878. 2fl ob cl bn.
Pm (Belwin Mills: London, pn Ap 394-399, 1976), score & parts.
No.1 is titled "Nancy", with vc rather than bn. No. 2 is titled in pencil, "Waxworks!", with vc rather than bn. No. 4 has the original title, "Sleep" altered to "Somniferous". No. 5 is marked (?titled) in pencil, "Skip". No. 6 is titled, "Hell & Tommy", with vc rather than bn.
*EWE-2.1(-2.5). Harmony Music [Sheds] 1 - 5.
Pm (Belwin Mills: London, pn Ap 395, 1976), score & parts.
No. 2 is titled, "Nelly Shed". No. 3 is incomplete. No. 4 ("Shed No. 4") is titled "Farmyard" & dated 7 Sept 1878; No. 5 ("Shed No. 5") is in 2 mvts, the first titled in pencil, "The Mission", the second, a Menuetto & Trio (the latter with vc rather than bn) plus "Noah's Ark", (Andante, 6/8) and Finale Allegretto, C.
*EWE-3. Five Intermezzi. 2fl ob cl bn.
Pm (Belwin Mills: London, pn Ap 395, 1976), score & pts, (with EWE-13/iv & 16 as "Five Intermezzi").
Nos. 2 & 5 are for vc rather than bn; No. 3 is dated 27 April 1879.

*EWE-4. Four Dances [Menuetto; Gavotte, "The Alphonsa"; Sarabande; Gigue].   2fl ob cl bn.
Pm (Belwin Mills: London, pn Ap 395, 1976), score & pts, (with EWE-14/i, ii, & EWE-14, as "Four Dances").
Originally separate works.   The Menuetto in titled in pencil, "Glee Club"; the Gavotte is titled in pencil,
"Alphonsa Gavotte"; Nos. 3 & 4 are titled "Sarabanda & Giga", respectively.
*EWE-5. Adagio cantabile, "Mrs. Winslow's Soothing Syrup"; 22 Aug 1878.   2fl ob cl bn.
Pm (Belwin Mills: London, pn Ap 395, 1976), score & parts.
*EWE-6. Andante con Variazione (Evesham Andante).   2fl ob cl bn.
Pm (Belwin Mills: London, pn Ap 395, 1976), score & parts.
With vc rather than bn, (pizzicato & arco markings).
EWE-1m. Peckham March[,] EWE Xmas 1877.   2fl ob cl bn.
EWE-1a. Anon: Where is now the Merry Party? (Musical Bouquet: London, 1876, Nos. 561, Song; 5567, Duet.
EWE-2a. Anon: In the Hour of Softened Spendour.   **EWE-3a.** Anon: Raise Again the Bowl.
EWE-4a. Angot, *Fille de M.*: Hence now Away.   **EWE-5a.** Angot, *Madame*: Song of the Brotherhood
EWE-6a. Barnby: Sweet and Low.   **EWE-7a.** Beethoven: Violin Sonata, Op. 23, Allegro molto.
EWE-8a. J.W. Callcott: Forgive, Blest Shade (Epitaph).   **EWE-9a.** Dowland: Awake, Sweet Rose [sic: Love].
EWE-10a. Garrett, George Mursell: May Carol.
EWE-11a, 12a. Hallah: Solfeggio No. 196 & 225. (? John Pyne HULLAH)
EWE-13a. Morley, Thomas: Now is the Month of Maying.   **EWE-14a.** Pinsuti: Tell me, Flora
EWE-15a. Seybach: March (?Teybach).   **EWE-16a.** Spofforth: Hail, Smiling Morn.

*ELIASSON, Anders *1947, Sweden*
ANE-1. Hymn; Latin text, 1970.   6+ unison male voices, 2ob 2ca 3tp 3tb 3perc.   MS score: S-Sic.

ELISCU, Robert *1944*
RXE-1. Kalenda Maya; 1976.   ob 2ca heck 2bn tabla.
Pm (Edition Modern (Hans Wewerka): München, pn 2127, c.1980).
RXE-2. Hommage a Susato; 1979.   ob 2ca bn tabla.
Pm (Edition Modern (Hans Wewerka): München, pn 2130, c.1980).

*ELLIOT, Willard Somers *18 July 1926, Fort Worth, Texas, USA*
Bruyere Music Publications can be contacted at: 6731 Trail Cliff Way, Fort Worth, TX 76132, USA.
*WSE-1. 5 Impressions, 1982.   2ob 2cl 2hn 2bn.
Pm (Novello: London, pn 120643, 1989), score & parts.
WSE-1a. Granados: Goyescos, Lament of [sic] the Mainden and the Nightingale.   2ob 2cl 2hn 2bn.
Pm (Bruyere Music: Evanston, IL, now Fort Worth, Texas, sd), score & parts.
WSE-2a. Grieg: Four Lyric Pieces.   2ob 2cl 2hn 2bn.
Pm (Bruyere Music: Evanston, IL, now Fort Worth, Texas, sd), score & parts.
WSE-3a. C.M. Weber: Peter Schmoll, overture.   2ob 2cl 2hn 2bn.
Pm (Bruyere Music: Evanston, IL, now Fort Worth, Texas, sd), score & parts.
WSE-4a. C.M. Weber: Musik zu Turandot, March.   2ob 2cl 2hn 2bn.
Pm (Bruyere Music: Evanston, IL, now Fort Worth, Texas, sd), score & parts.

ELMSLY, John *1952, New Zealand*
JOE-1. As Time Goes By; 1978.   fl 2cl 2bn.   MS score: NZ-Wmc.

ELSNER, Józef Ksawery *1 June 1769, Grotków, nr Śląsku - 18 April 1854, Elsnerówka pod Warszawa*
We have no locations for the following work: Requiem, Op. 2, *(CATB, 2cl 2bthn 2hn 2bn; L'vov, 1793).*
JKE-1m. Dwa Marsze dla Gwardji Narodowej.   pic 2fl cl(Eb) 4cl(Bb) 4hn bn 2tp b-tb serp timp b-dr tri.
MS: PL-Wtm, Ms. 939.

*EMERSON, Geoffrey *30 Jan 1938, Ramsgate*
GZE-1a. Christmas pieces.   2fl ob 3cl hn bn.
Pm (Emerson Edition: Ampleforth, pn E172, 1988), score & parts.
    1.1a. Mendelssohn: [6 Kinderstücke] Six Childrens's/Christmas Pieces, Op. 72, No. 1.
    1.2a. Humperdinck: [Der Wunder] The Miracle, Prelude.
    1.3a. Domenico Scarlatti: [Sonatas, K.446], Siciliano, in F
    1.4a. Tchaikovsky: Sixteen Children's Songs, Op. 54, No. 5, Legend, Christ in His Garden
    1.5a. Cornelius: [6 Weihnachtslieder] Six Christmas Songs, Op. 8, No. 1, Der Tannenbaum [Der Christbaum].
GZE-2a. J.S. Bach: 3 Sarabandes.   2fl ob 3cl bn.
Pm (Emerson Edition: Ampleforth, pn E47, 1997), score & parts.
GZE-3a. Dvořák: Slavonic Dance, Op. 46, No. 2.   fl 2ob 2cl 2hn 2bn (cbn ad lib).
Pm (Emerson Edition: Ampleforth, pn E197, c.1990), score & parts.
GZE-4a. Percy Whitlock: Five Short Pieces for Organ, No. 2: Folk Song.   2fl ob 3cl hn bn.
Pm (Emerson Edition: Ampleforth, pn E24, 1974), score & parts

EMILSSON, Anders *17 Feb 1963, Sweden*
ADE-1. Pajso: Kammermusikalisk dikt; 1985.   2fl 2ob 2cl 2hn 2bn 2tp tb.   MS score: S-Sic.

EMMERICH (Emmerig), Joseph *1772, Kemnath, Bavaria - 13 June 1834, Regensburg*
JZE-1v. Theodolindens Traumgeschicht [for the birthday of the Queen of Bavaria, 1827].
TTBB, fl 2cl 2hn bn 2tp.   MS: A-Sca, Hs.734. ★

*EMMERT, Adam Joseph *24 December 1765, Würzburg - 16 Sept 1812, Vienna*
Duyle published the texts of AJE-1v(-4v) as: Vier Kirchenlieder für die Hauskapelle des Franz Xaver Duyle. Zum
Besten Armen. [Salzburg] 1802; *this pre-dates the publication of AJE-4v. A copy is held in A-Sca, Hs.14665.*
*AJE-1. Harmonieen, Erste Sammlung, 7 mvts.   2cl(C) 2hn 2bn tp.
Pc (Franz Xaver Duyle: Salzburg, 1807), RISM [E 675], parts: A-Sca, Hs.20219; CZ-Pnm, XLI.B.109.   ★
Both copies are dated 1807; there is no 1805 (RISM [E 674]) version.
Pm (WINDS: Northridge, CA, pn W-86, c.1980), parts (photostat of modern MS).
AJE-2. Harmonieen, Erste Sammlung, 11 mvts.   2cl 2hn 2bn.
Pc (Franz Xaver Duyle: Salzburg, 1804), RISM [E 672], parts: A-Sca; CH-E; CZ-Pnm; D-Rtt, Emmert 1.   ★

AJE-3. Harmonieen, Erste Sammlung. 2fl 2hn bn.
Pc (Franz Xaver Duyle: Salzburg, 1804), RISM [E 673], parts: A-Sca, Hs.20709; A-Sm; D-Rtt.
*AJE-4, 5. Harmonieen, Sammlung 1 [8 mvts]; Sammlung 2. 2hn bn.
Pc (Franz Xaver Duyle: Salzburg, 1799, 1805), RISM [E 671], pts: A-Sca. (?lost); D-Rtt, Emmert 2, (Sm. 1). ★
Pm (Simrock: Hamburg, London, 1966), ed. Walter Höckner, (Elite Ed. 3297).
AJE-1m. Janitscharenmusik. pic flauticco [sic] 2fl 2ob+2cl(C) 2hn 2bn 3tp(clar) "tambourin" cym tri.
MS parts: A-KR, H 41/97, (with duplicate hn pts). ★
*AJE-1a. Emmert: Don Sylvio von Rosario, overture & 20 mvts. 2ob 2cl 2hn 2bn (ad lib tp & turkish perc in Nos. 1 & 21). MS parts (9): I-Fc, F.P. S.375, (incorrectly attributed to Cherubini).
AJE-1v(-5v) all bear the same RISM number: [E 668]; the A-Sca set is not noted; HR-Zha holds some of the set.
*AJE-1v. Kirchenlied auf das Fest des Heiligen Kreuzes, Nro. I. TTBB, (ad lib: 2cl 2hn 2bn).
Pc (Franz Xaver Duyle: Salzburg, 1800), vocal pts, instrumental score: A-Gd; A-Sca, 20694; D-Mbs, 8 Mus.pr. 2637. *The instrumental score is printed in AJE-2v rather than here.* ★
*AJE-2v. Kirchenlied auf das Fest Maria Himmelfahrt, Nro. II. TTBB, (ad lib: 2cl 2hn 2bn).
Pc (Franz Xaver Duyle: Salzburg, 1800), vocal pts, instrumental score: A-Sca, 20694; D-Mbs, 8 Mus.pr.2637. ★
*AJE-3v. Kirchenlied auf den Frieden, Nro. III. TTBB, (ad lib: 2cl(C) 2hn 2bn).
Pc (Franz Xaver Duyle: Salzburg, 1801), vocal parts, instrumental score: A-Sca, 20694. ★
*AJE-4v. Kirchenlied auf das Kirchweihfest, Nro. IV. TTBB, (ad lib: 2cl(C) 2hn 2bn).
Pc (Franz Xaver Duyle: Salzburg, 1803), vocal parts, instrumental score: A-L; A-Sca, 20694. ★
*AJE-5v. Kirchenlied als Gebeth fuer den Durchlauchtigsten Landesherrn, Nro. V. TTBB, (ad lib: 2cl 2hn 2bn).
Pc (Franz Xaver Duyle: Salzburg, 1803), vocal parts, instrumental score: A-Sca, 20694. ★

EMMERT, František *19 May 1940, Mstišov, nr Teplice, North Bohemia*
FYE-1. Double Quintet. 2fl 2ob 2cl 2hn 2bn.
Pm (Český hudební fond: Prague, 1981), (hire) score & parts.
FYE-2. Sextet. 2ob 2hn 2bn.
Pm (Český hudební fond: Prague, 1983), (hire) score & parts.
FYE-3. Concerto for harpsichord and winds. Instumentation unknown.
Pm (Český hudební fond: Prague, 1986), (hire) score & parts.

ENCKHAUSEN, Heinrich *(?1800)*
HXE-1. Militair Musik, 1° Werk; 6 mvts. Incomplete: here only: fl(Eb) cl(Eb) cl(I Bb).
Pc (C. Bachmann: Hannover, pn 59, c.1835), parts: D-DT, Mus-n 1601. ★

ENDRES, Franz Andreas *(1780)*
FAE-1. Serenata; in C, 7 mvts. 2fl 2hn tp db timp.
MS parts (c.1805): D-Mbs, Mus.Mss.10467, (formerly in D-HL). ★
FAE-2. II. Märshe und I. Waltzer; all in C, (c.1810). 2cl(C) 2hn bn cb. MS parts: D-BAR. ★

*ENESCO (Enescu), Georges *19 Aug 1881, Leveni-Vîrav (Dorohoiu), Romania - 4 May 1955, Paris*
*GYE-1. Dixtuor, "No. 1", Op. 14; in D major, 3 mvts, 1906. 2fl ob ca 2cl 2hn 2bn.
Pc (Enoch: London), score.
Pm (Salabert: Paris, 1956), score.
Pm (McGinnis & Marx: New York, sd), parts.
Pm (Editura muzicală a Uniunii compozitorilor din Republica socialistă România: Bucharest, 1965), score.
Pm (Edwin Ashdown: London), hire score & parts.

*ENGLEMANN, C. *(1790)*
CZE-1a. Boieldieu: La Dame blanche, 3 mvts. fl(Eb) cl(Eb) cl(Bb solo) 3cl(Bb) 2hn 2bn 2tp 3tb serp b-dr s-dr.
MS parts: D-DT, Mus-h 4 E 1.

ENGLER, Augustin Joseph *1853 - 1929*
AOE-1v. Dem Männergesangbereine "Sängerbund Bautzen" zum 20. Stiftungsfeste zugeeignet. "Glück auf!", Op. 4. Text by Novalis. TTBB double quartet & chorus, fl 2cl(A) 2hn bn tb tu. MS pts: D-BAUd, Mu 183. ★

*ENGSTRÖM, Torbjörn *11 Oct 1963*
TZE-1. Musik för bläsirkester; 1984 - 1985. 4fl(pic) 2ob 4cl 2hn 2bn 2tp 2tb. MS score: S-Sic.

ENNIS, Barry *(1950), USA*
HRE-1. Western Suite. fl ob 2cl hn bn.
Pm (1975), parts: US-Wc.

ERBSE, Heimo *27 Feb 1924, Rudolstadt*
HZE-1. Divertimento für Mozart, No. 3. für Bläser. 2fl 2ob 2cl 2bthn 2hn 2bn cbn tp timp.
Pm: (B. Schott's Söhne: Mainz, London, etc.), hire score & parts.
HZE-2. Allegro - Lento - Allegro. 2fl 2ob 2cl 2bthn 2hn 2bn cbn 2tp timp.
Pm (Universal Edition: Wien, sd).

*ERCOLANI, Giuseppe *(active in Naples, c.1800 - 1820)* *See also:* FETTER & ERCOLANI.
GQE-1a. Mayr: Ginevra di Scozia, Due Marcie. Instrumentation unknown.
Pc (Venanzio Salvoni: Napoli, post-1801), score: I-Fc, F.P. S.682.

ERDMANN, Veit *1944, Germany*
VXE-1. Drei Variations; 1968. fl 2cl sax 2bn tp tb perc.
Pm (Döring Musikverlag: Herrenberg, c.1969), score & parts.

ERIKSON, Robert *1917, USA*
RYE-1. Variants. 2fl 2ob 2cl 2bn.
Pm (G. Schirmer: New York, sd).

ERMITASCH (?Cremitasch), ( ) *(1760)*
XXE-1. Parthia ex Dis [Eb], 4 mvts. 2cl 2hn bn.
MS parts ("Ex Rebus Joh[ann Anton] Handl, [1]814": A-Wn, Mus.Hs.571, (with an additional bn pt transposed to F for use with clarinets in C). ★

*ERNST (ERNEST), Franz (François) Anton *21 Feb 1745, Georgenthal - 13 Jan 1805, Gotha*
*FRE-1a. Haydn: Symphony in C, "L'Ours", (Hob.I/82). 2cl 2hn 2bn. MS parts: CZ-Bm(no), A.16.635.
FRE-2a. Sacchini: Oedipe à Colonne; Suite 1: 8 mvts, Suite 2: 8 mvts. 2cl 2hn 2bn.
Pc (Imbault: Paris, pn 124, 1787/1788), RISM [S 239], parts: D-AB; S-Uu, Utl.instr.mus.tr.145, 149 - 151,
Takt 25, 26, (missing cl II, hn II; the hn I pt is defective).
FRE-3a. Salieri: Tarare, Suite 1: 13 mvts, Suite 2: 12 mvts. 2cl 2hn 2bn.
Pc (Imbault: Paris, pn 93, 125, 1787/1788), parts: S-Uu, Utl.instr.mus.tr.145, 149 - 151, Takt 15, 16, (missing
cl II, hn II).
Pc (J.J. Hummel: Berlin; Au grand magazin de musique: Amsterdam, pn 805, c.1791), RISM [E 768 = S 603],
parts: D-Dl, Mus.3796/F/24a; FIN-A.
MS parts: D-Tl, Gg 176, (as "Harmonien de Opera Tarrare", Suite 1 only, divided after No. 7 into 2 Suites).
FRE-4a. Vogel: Démophon, Suite No. 87, 10 mvts. 2cl 2hn 2bn (2tp serp b-dr cym ad lib).
Pc (Sieber: Paris, pn 1108, c.1790), RISM [V 2304], parts: D-F, Mus.pr. 1937/182.

ERÖD, Ivan *2 Jan 1936, Budapest (now living in Austria)*
IXE-1. Capriccio, Op. 23; 1977. 2fl 2ob 2cl 2hn 2bn.
Pm (Doblinger: Wien, 1980), score (pn STP 410) & parts (pn 06611).
IXE-2. Schnappschüsse: 5 Portraits [Snapshots], Op. 52; 1986. fl 2ob 2cl 2hn 2bn.
Pm (Doblinger: Wien, pn 06592, sd), score & parts.

*ESCH, Louis von *(?1760)   See also under JOUVE.*
*LVE-1. Airs Champêtres, Oeuvre IV; 7 mvts. Solo harp, cl 2hn bn db/b.
Pc (Sieber; Mme Broullard; Cousineau: Paris, pre-1789), RISM [E 789], pts: F-Pn, Vm7 6137. ★

*ESCHLER, J. *(1810), active with the Löwenstein Kapelle, Wertheim*
JQE-1. Larghetto; in E♭. terz-fl cl(E♭) 2cl(B♭) 2hn 2bn tp b timp. (?Auto)MS score: GB-Ljag(w), 356. ★

ESMEISTER, ( )
XYE-1. Partitta In C; 6 mvts. 2ob 2hn 2bn timp. MS parts: CZ-Pnm, XLII.C.202. ★
XYE-2. N° 2 Partitta In C; 6 mvts. 2ob 2hn bn timp. MS parts: CZ-Pnm, XLII.A.214. ★
XYE-3. Nʳᵉ 3 Partitta ex F; 5 mvts. 2ob 2hn 2bn.
MS parts: CZ-Pnm, XLII.A.215. *The 2bn are divisi only in the Trios of the 2 Menuetts.* ★

*ESSEX, Timothy *1764, Coventry - 27 Sept 1847, London*
TYE-1m. The Royal Westminster Volunteers March, as it is Performed by theirs, and ... the Duke of York's Band.
fl 2cl 2hn 2bn tp serp timp.
Pc (Printed & Sold for the Composer, by Mess. Longman & Broderip: London, c.1797), RISM [E 873], score:
GB-Lbl, g.133.(23); GB-Ob, Mus.Instr.I.93(11); US-Bp, Brown Collection, M.441.100. ★
TYE-2m. The Quick Step of The Royal Westminster Volunteers. fl 2cl 2hn 2bn tp serp timp.
Pc (Printed for the Composer by Messrs. Longman & Broderip, etc.: London, c.1797), RISM [E 874], score:
GB-Lbl, g.133.(21); GB-Ob, Mus.Instr.I.93(10); US-Bp, (as "[from op. 1]"; RISM [E 875], without titlepage). ★
TYE-3m. The Angus Fencibles March and Quick Step. 2cl 2hn 2bn tp timp; with 2fifes in the Quick Step only.
Pc (Printed for the Composer: London, c.1795), RISM [E 872], score: GB-Lbl, g.133.(22);
GB-Ob, Mus.Instr.I.93(12); US-Bp, Brown Collection, M.441.100. ★
TYE-4m. The Grand March of the Hampstead Loyal Association as it is performed by ... the Duke of York's Band.
fl 2cl 2hn 2bn tp serp timp.
Pc (Printed for the Composer & Sold by Mesrs. Longman, Broderip, etc.: London, 1799), RISM [E 877], score:
GB-Lbl, g.133.(20); GB-Ob, Mus.Instr.I.93(9); US-Bp, Brown Collection, M.441.100. ★
TYE-5m. A Grand March Composed for, and Dedicated to Sir John de la Pole. 2ob 2cl 2hn 2bn timp.
Pc (Printed for the Author: London, c.1795), RISM [E 878], score: GB-Gu; GB-Lbl, g.133.(24);
GB-Ob, Mus.Voc.I.20(44); US-Bp, Brown Collection, M.441.100. ★
TYE-6m. The Hampstead Volunteers Quick March; [plate title: "Essex. Marches Op. 1"].
fl 2cl 2hn bn tp serp timp; with piano reduction.
Pc (sn: sl [London], sd), RISM [E 876], score: US-Bp, Brown Collection, M.441.100, (without titlepage). ★

EST, ( )
YXE-1v. Kurze Advent=Messe; in C. CATB, 2fl 2hn organ.
MS pts (by Ant. Kutzbauer): CZ-Pnm, XXXVIII.F.216. *The Credo only appears at the end of the fl I pt.* ★

*ETT, Caspar *5 Jan 1788, Eresing - 16 May 1847, Munich*
CXE-1v. Hochzeitgesang, "Hymn windet Rosenketter". SATB, fl ob 2cl 2hn 2bn.
AutoMS score (1822): D-Mbs, Mus.Mss.3695, pp. 23 - 35. ★
*CXE-2v. Grablied; "Auferstehn, ja Auferstehn". SATB, 2cl 2hn tb.
AutoMS score (1819): D-Mbs, Mus.Mss.4321/1. ★

*EVANS, Charles *(1780)*
CYE-1m. March, for a Military Band . . . [for] the Loyal Ludlow Volunteer Infantry, Op. 7. [Followed by
variations for fl & pf]. 2cl 2hn 2bn tp.
Pc (Goulding, Phipps & D'Almaine: London, pn 112, 1807 [wm 1803]), score: GB-Lbl, h.109.(33). ★

*EYBLER, Johann Leopold, *Edler von* *8 Feb 1765, Schwehat, nr Vienna - 24 July 1846, Vienna*
Eybler's 5 Menuetti mit Trios (AutoMS, A-Wgm) often cited as for winds is, in fact, for full orchestra.
JLE-1.1v. Libera me Domine; (EWV deest). CATB Coro 1mo, CATB Coro 2do, 2ob/cl 2cl 2bn cbn.
AutoMS score: A-Wn, Mus.Hs.16,591.
MS parts: A-M, (missing C); CZ-Pnm, III.B.131, (the cl(B♭) II pt is not written out after bar 2; bars 1 & 2 are
the same as cl I. The bn II pt is not written out and a note calls for it to double the bn I). ★
JLE-1.2v. Libera me, Domine. CATB, 2bthn 2hn 2bn 2tp 3tb timp organ.
MS parts: D-BB, MS 173, No. 2, (a local rescoring).
JLE-2v. Offertorium in C minor ("Si consistant adversum"); (EWV V/86). SATB/TTBB, 2ob 2hn 2bn.
MS score: CZ-Bm(au), A.20.748. *The AutoMS copy in A-Ws - as well as the published edition (Haslinger:
Vienna, pn 5013, 1827) - is scored for full orchestra; the CZ-Bm(au) copy is probably a local arrangement.* ★

JLE-3v. Unam Petri; in C, (EWV III/43). TTBB, 2ob 2hn 2bn.
AutoMS score: A-Ws, Cod. 569/3. MS score: A-Wn, Fonds St Peters Kirche, (unverified). ★
JLE-4v. Te Deum in C; (EWV VI/114). CCAATTBB, 2ob 2cl 3tb vc. MS parts: A-KN, 364. *The AutoMS
score in A-Ws is scored for full orchestra; the A-KN copy is undoubtedly a local arrangement.* ★
JLE-5v. Ecce quomodo; (EWV VI/125). SATB, 2ob.
MS score (1830): A-Wn, Mus.Hs.13,040, No. 3, ff. 5 - 5b. ★

EYSER, Eberhard *1 Aug 1932, Kwidzym*
EZE-1. Cirkus-Uvertyr: Clownernas upptåg, Entfesslte Possenreisser [Circus Overture], 1976.
fl(pic) ob cl(Eb) 2cl(Bb) a-sax hn 2bn 2tp tu perc db. MS score & pts: S-Sic, (score) T-2653, (pts) T-2654.
EZE-2. [Drömmen om mannen] Liten Svit, 1978. 2cl a-cl/hn bthn/hn s-sax a-sax bn cbn/cb-cl. MS score: S-Sic.
EZE-3. Folkviseparafraser piccolo, 1979. cl(Eb) 2cl(Bb) b-cl/bn cbn/cbn a-sax t-sax bar-sax. MS score: S-Sic.
EZE-4. Stochasta; 1974. fl ob 3sax hn bn 2tp 3tb tu 3perc. MS score: S-Sic.
EZE-5. Tempestes du printemps; 1974. fl ob 3cl hn bn cbn 2tp 3tb tu db. MS score: S-Sic.
EZE-6. Variationem über ein Thema von Bartók, 1956/1974. fl ob 3cl hn bn 2tp tu. MS score: S-Sic.
EZE-7. Serenata; 1976. 2cl hn bn. MS score: S-Sic.
EZE-8. El fuego de oro; 1978. 2cl 2bn. MS score: S-Sic.
EZE-9. Seremata 2; 1976. 2cl 2bn. MS score: S-Sic.

F., L.
FÜL-1v. Pange Lingua Per la processione introduzione; in F. SATB, 2ob 2hn bn organ(bc-fig).
MS score (by J.S. Mayr) & MS parts (ATB only): I-BGc, fald. 309/10, (with a duplicate ob II pt). ★

FABIO, (Angelo) *or* **(Ermarcora)** *These works are more likely to be by Ermacora FABIO.*
XXF-1v. Beati omnes. TTB, 2cl 2hn bn tp(2) (vlne) timp organ. MS score & pts: I-Vsmc, (vlne in pts only). ★
AZF-2v. Si queris maricola. Responsorio di S. Antonio di Padova.
TTB(solo+rip), (fl) 2cl 2hn bn (tp tb) organ(bc-fig).
MS score & parts: I-Vsmc, (the fl tp & tb parts are not included in the score). ★

FABIO, Ermarcora
AZF-1v. Domine ad adjuvandum. TTB, fl 2cl 2hn tp basso timp organ. MS score (1856) & pts: I-Vsmc. ★
EZF-2v. Salve Regina. Solo TB, 2cl 2hn bn organ. MS parts: I-Vsmc. ★

*FAHRBACH, Joseph (Giuseppe) *(1840)*
JBF-1a. Verdi: Aida, Due Fantasie, Op. 86. fl cl(Eb) cl(Bb) 2hn bombardino/bn tp flug bombardone.
Pc (Ricordi: Milano, etc., pn 45224, 45225, c.1872), parts: I-Mc, Da Camera A.37.10, (Prima Fantasia only).

FALTIS, (Jan) Josef *16 Nov 1744, Vičkovice - 10 Jan 1795, Prague*
JOF-1v. N: 7 Stationen für das hohe Frohenleichnams-Feste. CATB, 2fl 4cl(2D, 2C) 2hn 2bn 2tp(clar) tp(prin) timp.
MS parts (by Johann Stépan, from Chroustovice): CZ-Pnm, IX.A.52, (with later pts for 2cl(A) 2tp(D) b-tp). *With
a list of performance dates between 1831 and 1864.* ★
JOF-2v. Quatuor Stationes in Harmonia. CATB, 2cl(C) 2hn bn+basso 2tp(clar) timp.
MS parts (by Johann Michalička, from Kunvald): CZ-Pnm, IX.A.53. ★
JOF-3v. Pange lingua; in G. CATB, organ, (ad lib: 2fl 2hn bn).
MS parts (by Franz Kopp): CZ-Pnm, XXXVIII.B.130, (with a duplicate organ pt tranposed to F). ★

*FANE, John, 11th Earl of Westmorland (Lord Burghersh) *3 Feb 1784, London - 16 Oct 1859, Althorpe
House, Northamptonshire, UK*
JHF-1m. Untitled martial composition. pic(ottavino) 2fl ob 2cl 2hn 2bn 2tp 2tb timp; with an additional double
band placed on the left and right of the core band, each comprising: pic(ottavino) 2cl 2hn 2bn 2tp timp b-dr.
MS score (mostly Autograph): GB-Lbl, Add. 33313, f.19b. ★

FANTINI, I. *(1760)*
IYF-1m. A Grand March, Performed by the Austrian Band Commanded by the Arch Duke Charles.
2cl 2hn 2bn serp(col bn II) tp(col hn I).
Pc (Longman & Broderip: London, pre-1799),' score: GB-Lbl, g.847.d.(10). ★

FANUCCHI, Domenico *c.1795, Lucca - 24 June 1862, Lucca, Italy*
DXF-1v. Cantata, "Se dell'or la wete [sic?] avara", 1839. AATB, fl 2cl 2hn 2bn cbn 2tp tb. MS: I-Ls, B.41.
DXF-2v. Il figlio reconosciuto, 1822. Voices, 2fl ob 2cl 2hn bn cbn. MS: I-Ls, B.41.
DXF-3v. Aria con cori. SAB, ob cl 2hn. MS: I-Ls, B.41.

*FARKAS, Ferenc *15 Dec 1905, Nagykanizsza*
FXF-1. Contrafacta hungarica [after 16th century dances and melodies], 1977. 2ob 2cl 2hn 2bn.
Pm (Editio Musica: Budapest, pn Z 12827, c.1986), score & parts.

*FARQUHAR, David Andross *5 April 1928, Cambridge, NZ*
*DYF-1. Homage to Stravinsky. 2ob 2bn 2tp 2tb. MS score: NZ-Wn.

FASCH, Johann Firedrich *15 April 1688, Buttelstadt, (nr Weimar) - 5 Dec 1758, Zerbst*
Fasch's I. Concerto (2ob 2bn) & I. Concerto *(2ob 2obdam 2bn)*, *(Breitkopf Supplement I, 1766) are untraced.*
JIF-1. Concerto in G. 2ob 2taille/vla 2bn cembalo. MS parts: D-Dl, CX.212, Nr. 37 Sth.
JIF-2. Concerto grosso; on C, 4 mvts. 3 bands, each of: 3ob 1bn 3tp timp.
AutoMS score: D-Bds, Amalienbibl. Ms. No. 589. ★
Pm (WINDS, Northridge, CA, pn W-184, c.1985), score & parts, (arranged by David Whitwell for modern band).
JIF-3. Sonata in D minor. 2ob 2bn b. MS parts: D-Dl.
JIF-4. Sonata a 4; in F, 3 mvts. 2ob 2bn.
MS parts: D-HRD, Fü 3639a. ★
Pm (Deutsche Verlag für Musik, *via* Breitkopf & Härtel: Wiesbaden, 1981), ed. Angenhöfer, score & pts (pn 8441).

FEDELI, Pietro
PQF-1. Adagi per la Benedizione, Adagio Marcia. 2cl 2hn (2)bn (tp tb timp) organ.
MS score & parts: I-Vsmc, (the tp tb & timp parts do not appear in the score). ★

FELDERHOF, Jan Reinhert Adriaan *25 Sept 1907, Bussum*
JRF-1. Musik, 1930.   2fl 2ob 2cl a-sx 2hn 2bn 2tp tb tu timp perc.
Pm (Donemus: Amsterdam, sd), score.

*FELDMAYR (Feldmayer, Feldmair), Georg (Johann) *1757, Pfaffenhofen/Ilm - post-1831, (?Hamburg)*
*GJF-1.1. Parthia; in D, 1794, 4 mvts.   2fl 2ob 2cl(A) 2hn 2bn tp vlne timp.
MS parts (by F.X. Link, 3 Aug 1794): D-HR, HR III 4 1/2 2° 594.   ★
Pm (KGS), fiche (2701, 2702).
*GJF-1.2. Romance Adagio; in D, (following the Finale in the MS parts).
MS parts (by F.X. Link, 3 Aug 1794): D-HR, HR III 4 1/2 2° 594.   ★
Pm (KGS), fiche (2701, 2702).
GJF-2. Parthia in D dur . . . Compost. nell Mese d'April: 1790; 4 mvts.   2fl 2ob 2cl(A) 3hn 2bn vlne.
AutoMS score: D-HR, HR III 4 1/2 4° 479.   MS parts (by F.X. Link): D-HR, HR III 4 1/2 2° 589.   ★
Pm (KGS) fiche (score 962, 963; parts 2690, 2691).
GJF-3. Parthia in F; c.1787, 4 mvts *(not 5 as per the catalog)*.   2fl 2ob 2cl 3hn 2bn vlne.
AutoMS score (c.1787) & MS pts (by F.X. Link, 1787): D-HR, HR III 4 1/2 2° 585.   ★
Pm (KGS), fiche (2680 - 2682).
GJF-4. Parthia: in F dur; c.1788, 4 mvts.   2fl 2ob 2cl 3hn 2bn vlne.
AutoMS (& MS parts by F.X. Link): D-HR, HR III 4 1/2 2° 587.   ★
Pm (KGS), fiche (2684 - 2686).
*GJF-5.1. Parthia; in F, c.1788, 4 mvts.   2fl 2ob 2cl 3hn 2bn vlne.
AutoMS score: D-HR, HR III 4 1/2 4° 502.   MS pts (by F.X. Link, 1788): D-HR, HR III 4 1/2 2° 595.   ★
Pm (KGS), fiche (score: 997; parts: 2703, 2704).
*GJF-5.2. Minuett.   2fl 2ob 2cl 3hn 2bn vlne.
AutoMS score (3 loose sheets): D-HR, HR III 4 1/2 4° 502.   *This is the original Minuett for the Parthia in F. The fl I & II & ob I parts have this Minuett written in, with the Minuetto Fresco replacement added; the other parts were copied after the substitution and do not include the original Minuett.*   ★
*GJF-6. Partitta à 11. Inst:; in F, 1786, 4 mvts.   2fl ob 2cl 3hn 2bn vlne.
MS parts (by J.S.A. Link, 1786): D-HR, HR III 4 1/2 4° 473.
Pm (KGS), fiche (955, 956).   ★
*GJF-7. Parthia; in F, c.1790, 4 mvts.   2fl ob 2cl 3hn 2bn vlne.
AutoMS score: D-HR, HR III 4 1/2 4° 481.   Pm (KGS), fiche (965).   ★
GJF-8. Parthia in F dur; c.1788, 4 mvts.   2fl ob 2cl 3hn 2bn vlne.
AutoMS score & MS parts (by F.X. Link, 1788): D-HR, HR III 4 1/2 2° 593.
Pm (KGS), fiche (2698 - 2700).   ★
GJF-9. Parthia; in D, c.1795, 4/5 mvts.   fl 2ob cl(A) 3hn 2bn tp vlne.
AutoMS score & MS parts (by F.X. Link, as "Serenata": D-HR, HR III 4 1/2 2° 596.   ★
Pm (KGS), fiche (2705 - 2707).
GJF-10. Parthia; in D, c.1790, 4 mvts.   2fl 2ob 2cl(A) 2hn 2bn.
MS parts (by F.X. Link): D-HR, HR III 4 1/2 2° 591.
Pm (KGS), fiche (2695).   ★
GJF-11. Parthia; in G, c.1785, 4 mvts.   2fl 2ob cl 2hn 2bn vlne
MS parts (by F.X. Link): D-HR, HR III 4 1/2 4° 472.
Pm (KGS), fiche (953, 954).   ★
GJF-12. Parthia; in D# [i.e. D major]; c.1797, 5 mvts.   fl 2ob cl(A) 3hn 2bn tp vlne.
AutoMS score & MS pts (by F.X. Link, 1797): D-HR, HR III 4 1/2 2° 588.   Pm (KGS), fiche (2687 - 2689).   ★
GJF-13. Parthia; in G, c.1788, 4 mvts.   2fl 2ob 3hn 2bn vlne.
MS parts (by F.X. Link): D-HR, HR III 4 1/2 2° 590.   Pm (KGS), fiche (2692, 2693).   ★
GJF-14. Parthia in G dur; c.1786, 4 mvts.   2fl 2ob 3hn 2bn vlne.
AutoMS score & MS parts (?by J. Nagel, 1786): D-HR, HR III 4 1/2 2° 592.   ★
Pm (KGS), fiche (2696, 2697).   ★
GJF-15. Parthia; in F, 1798, 8 mvts.   2ob 2hn 2bn 2vla vlne.
MS parts (by F.X. Link, 1798): D-HR, HR III 4 1/2 2° 584.   ★
Pm (KGS), fiche (2678, 2679).
GJF-16. Parthia in E♭; 11 mvts (of which the 11th is from Mozart's *Die Zauberflöte*).   2ob 2hn bn vla.
MS parts: D-DO, Mus.Ms.418.   ★
GJF-17. Parthia; in F, 4 mvts & coda.   2ob 2hn bn vla.
MS parts (by F.X. Link, Oettingen-Wallerstein): D-DO, Mus.Ms.419.   ★
GJF-18. Parthia: in F; 6 mvts.   2ob 2hn bn vla.
AutoMS score: D-HR, HR III 4 1/2 4° 475 & HR III 4 1/2 4° 478, (mvt 5).   ★
MS parts (by F.X. Link, Oettingen-Wallerstein): D-DO, Mus.Ms.420, (8 mvts).
Pm (KGS), fiche (958, D-HR score).
GJF-19. Parthia; in F, c.1785, 1 continuous mvt.   2ob 2hn bn vla.
MS parts: D-HR, HR III 4 1/2 2° 586.   Pm (KGS), fiche 2683. *Although the parts list the viola in the singular, the titlepage has been altered to read "Viole"; "Violone" has also been added after "e Fagotto".*   ★
GJF-20. Una Parthia Concertante; in F, c.1795, 6 mvts.   2ob 2hn bn vla.
AutoMS score: D-HR, HR III 4 1/2 4° 476.   MS parts: D-DO, Mus.Ms.421.   ★
Pm (KGS), fiche (959, score).
*GJF-21. Parthia in E♭; c.1795, 18 mvts.   2cl 2hn 2bn.
AutoMS score: D-HR, HR III 4 1/2 4° 480.   ★
Pm (KGS), fiche (964, score).
GJF-1v. Cantate [Willkommen Fürsten, unser Lust und Freund].   2 solo voices, SATB chorus, 2ob 2hn 2bn.
AutoMS score: D-HR, HR III 4 1/2 4° 17.   ★
Pm (KGS), fiche (123, 124).
GJF-1a. Mozart: Die Zauberflöte, as "Parthia in F"; c.1795, 9 mvts.   2ob 2hn bn vla.
MS parts (by F.X. Link): D-HR, HR III 4 1/2 40 474.   Pm (KGS), fiche (957).   ★

*FELSHUT, C. *(1780), active in Tischingen, 1819*
*CFF-1. 12 Danses, Dédié A. V. Altesse rejale [sic] Madame L. Princesse A:J: de Thurn e Taxis reig. née Princesse r. de Meklenbourg Strelitz par C. Felshut. Dischingen [sic] a. 12 Octbr. 1819. Ov. 23. . . Zu dem Hohen Namersfeier Ihro Königl. Hoheit, sowie zu der Huldigungsfeier bestimmt. [5 Wals[er], 1 Ländler, 6 Eccossaise, all in F]. 2vl fl 2hn bn. MS pts: D-Rtt, Pr.D.1819. *Beneath the dedication is the note, "Felshut Vater und Sohn Franz".* ★

*FENDT, A. *(1780), Lieutenant und Musik-Inspektor, Salzburg*
Note: All five sets previously attributed to Fendt bear specially printed title slips for each part pasted onto the marbled paper of the covers and specially printed titlepages, all stating "der K. National=Garde III. Klasse zum Andenken gewidmet von A. Fendt, Lieutenant und Musik=Inspektor - Salzburg den 2ten Juny 1812." In several cases the volumes contain music from different dates, in different hands on different paper. In the case of AXF-5a, the marbled paper of the part covers has been pasted over the original titlepage which clearly identifies F.H. Edenhofer as the composer (and arranger). We believe that these collections were simply brought together, bound and presented to the band of the National-Garde by Fendt in 1812.
AXF-1d. Türkische Musik. Scoring varies. MS parts: A-Sca, Hs.76. *The first set of 4 pieces are by (von) Kriset; we list here the set that follows. Although consecutively numbered, both the paper and hand changes after No. 26 and again after No. 51. Our subdivisions are based on the an analysis of the contents.* ★
   1.1d. [26 Marches & Dances]. Nos. 1 - 26. pic 2cl(Eb) 2cl(Bb) 2hn(Eb) 2hn(Ab) (2)bn tp(prin) b-tb glock timp b-dr s-dr. *In No. 25 (Allemande) the first 8 bars of cl II are divisi.*
   1.2d. [Unidentified ?ballet]. sinfonia & 7 mvts. Nos. 27 - 34.
       pic 2cl(Eb) 2cl(Bb) 2hn(Eb) 2hn(Ab) (2)bn 2tp b-tb timp b-dr.
   1.3d. 10 Allemandes with Trios & Coda. Nos. 35 - 44.
       pic 2cl(Eb) 2cl(Bb) 2hn(Eb) 2hn(Ab) (2)bn 2tp b-tb timp b-dr.
   1.4d. 3 Allemandes. Nos. 45 - 47.   pic 2cl(Eb) 2cl(Bb) 2hn(Eb) 2hn(Ab) (2)bn 2tp b-tb timp b-dr s-dr.
   1.5d. [? Allemande] & Marche. No. 48.   pic 2cl(Eb) 2cl(Bb) 2hn(Eb) 2hn(Ab) (2)bn b-tb timp b-dr s-dr.
   1.6ad. [? Overture]. No. 49.   pic 2cl(Eb) 2cl(Bb) 2hn(Eb) 2hn(Ab) (2)bn tp(prin) b-tb timp b-dr s-dr.
   1.7d. [Theme & 8 Variations; in Ab]. No. 50   pic 2cl(Eb) 2cl(Bb) 2hn(Eb) 2hn(Ab) (2)bn b-tb timp b-dr.
   1.8ad. [? Opera mvt]. No. 51. pic 2cl(Eb) 2cl(Bb) 2hn(Eb) 2hn(Ab) (2)bn tp(prin) b-tb glock timp b-dr s-dr.
   1.9d. [19 Marches & Dances]. Nos. 52 - 70.
       pic 2cl(Eb) 2cl(Bb) 2hn(Eb) 2hn(Ab) (2)bn 2tp(prin) b-tb timp b-dr s-dr.
   1.10d. Allegro moderato. No. 71. pic 2cl(Eb) 2cl(Bb) 2hn(Eb) 2hn(Ab) (2)bn 2tp(prin) b-tb timp b-dr s-dr.
AXF-2d. Harmoniestuecke Nº I. 2fl 2cl(C & Bb) 2cl(C) 2hn 2bn cb/cbn. MS parts (1812): A-Sca, Hs.260.
   2.1ad. [Unidentified ballet, overture & 11 mvts]. Nos. 1 - 12.
   2.2ad. Mozart: Così fan tutte, 28 mvts & overture. Nos. 13 - 41.
   2.3ad - 2.5ad. [4 unidentifed mvts]. Nos. 42 - 44.   2.6da. Stumpf: [4 unidentified] mvts. Nos. 45 - 48.
AXF-3ad. Harmonie-Stücke. Scoring varies. MS parts: A-Sca, Hs.75.
   3.1ad. [Unidentified ballet]. overture & 15 mvts.   2cl(Eb) 2cl(C & Bb) 2hn 2bn 2tp(Nos. 1-5) b-tb(Nos. 1-6).
   3.2ad. [Untitled mvt with Trio in 2/4]. pic 2cl(Eb) 3cl(C & Bb) 2hn 2bn 2tp b-tb.
   3.2ad. Gyrowetz: Der Augenarzt, overture, Act 1: 8 mvts, Act 2: Entreact [sic] & 7 mvts.
       2cl(Eb) 3cl(C & Bb) 2hn 2bn 2tp b-tb. *Possibly adapted from Starke's arrangement, FRS-10a.*
   3.3ad. Méhul: Joseph [as "Jacob und seine Söhne"], 2 Romanzes. pic 2cl(Eb) 3cl(C & Bb) 2hn 2bn.
   3.4ad. J. Weigl: Die Schweizerfamilie, overture &12 mvts. pic 4cl(Bb & C) 2hn 2bn 2tp.
   3.5ad. Himmel: Fanchon, introduzione & 7 mvts. pic 2cl(Eb)/ob 2cl(Bb) 2hn 2bn b-tb.
AXF-4d. Verschiedene Stuecke in Partitur. Scoring varies. MS scores: A-Sca, Hs.78. ★
   4.1/1. Marcia; 6/8 [& Trio], Eb. fl(Db) 2cl(Eb) 3cl(Bb) 2hn 2bn 2tp(clar) serp+b-tb b-dr s-dr. *The cl(II,Bb) includes a number of divisi bars.*
   4.1/2. Duple [March]; 2/4 [& Trio], Bb. fl(Db) 2cl(Eb) 2cl(Bb) 2hn 2bn 2tp(clar) serp b-dr s-dr.
   4.1/3. Duple [March]; 2/4 [& Trio], Eb. fl(Db) 2cl(Eb) 3cl(Bb) 2hn 2bn 2tp(clar) serp timp pic[c]olo-timp.
   4.1/4. Marche; C [& Trio], Eb. fl(Db) 2cl(Eb) 3cl(Bb) 2hn 2bn 2tp(clar) serp b-dr s-dr.
   4.1/5. Duple; 2/4 [& Trio], Eb. fl(Db) cl(Eb) 3cl(Bb) 2hn 2bn 2tp(clar) serp timp piccolo-timp.
   4.2. 9 mvts. 2cl(Eb) 2cl(Bb) 2hn bn b-tb tp.
       1. Marche; ¢. 2. Allegro Moderatto [sic], 3/4. 3. Polonaise, 3/4 [& Trio]. 4. Allegro Modoratto [sic], 2/4.
       5. Andante con [4] Variasione [sic], ¢. 6. Allemando [sic] Tempo Allegretto, 3/4. 7. Andante,, ¢.
       8. Tempo Maeethe [sic], ¢. 9. Allegro, ¢.
   4.3/1. Allemande, 3/4 [& Trio]; Eb. pic(Db) 2cl(Eb) 2cl(Bb) 2hn 2bn 2tp serp b-dr s-dr.
   4.3/2. [Dance with Trio in 2/4]; Ab. fl(Db) 2cl(Eb) 2cl(Bb) 2hn 2bn 2tp serp timp pic[c]olo-timpani.
   4.3/3. [Dance with Trio in 2/4]; Eb. pic(Db) 2cl(Eb) 2cl(Bb) 2hn 2bn 2tp b-tb serp timp.
AXF-5d. Türkishche Musik. Scoring varies. MS pts: A-Sca, Hs.77. *In fact, by F.H. Edenhofer (qv).*

FENNELLY, Brian Leo *1937, USA*
BLF-1. Empirical Rag; 1979. 2ob 2cl 2hn 2bn. MS score: US-NYamc, (also wind quintet version).

*FERGUS, John *1767, Huntley, Aberdeenshire - 10 June 1825*
JNF-1m. A Grand March . . . [for] The Royal Glasgow Volunteers. 2cl 2hn 2bn.
Pc (Printed for the Author: Edinburgh, c.1795), RISM [F 248], score: GB-En, Glen 347-33; GB-Lbl, h.1568.b.(4). ★

FERRARI, Giorgio *1925, Italy*
GIF-1. Piccolo Concerto. Piano, fl ob 2cl 2hn 2bn 3perc.
Pm (Casa Musicale Sonzogno: Milano, pn 6081, sd).

FERRERO, Lorenzo *1951, Italy*
LOF-1. My Blues; 1982. 2fl 2ob 2cl 2hn 2bn.
Pm (Ricordi: Milano, pn 133492, c.1983), score & parts, (also version for mixed ensemble, pn 133651).

FERRI, Angelo *(1800)*
AYF-1v. Gloria. TTB(solo+rip), fl 2ob 2hn bn 2tp vlne organ(bc-fig) organ. MS score & parts: I-Vsmc. ★
AYF-2v. Tantum ergo, 1832. TTB(solo+rip), fl 2cl 2hn bn (timp) organ(bc-fig).
MS score & parts: I-Vsmc, (the timp part does not appear in the score). ★

*FESCA, Friedrich Ernst *15 Feb 1789, Magdeburg - 24 May 1826, Karlsruhe*
FEF-1v. Tenor-Arie: "Ja sterben o, es thut so wohl!" aus der Oper "Casemir" [altered to "Catemire"].
T, 2ob 2cl 2hn 2bn; *or piano.*
Pc (Beilage zur allgem. musik. Zeitung, Jahrgang 1820, No. 43), short score (piano accomapniment with 4-note chords marked "Fl. [sic; &] Clar", and cues for oboes & bassoons): D-SWl, Mus. 1822. ★

FETTER, (Giuseppe) & ERCOLANI (Giuseppe)
FFF-1a. Paisiello: La Serva padrona, Parte primo.   2ob 2cl 2hn 2bn.   MS parts: I-Fc, F.P. S.323.
FFF-2a. Paisiello: Nina, Parte 1 & 2.   2ob 2cl 2hn 2bn.   MS parts: I-Fc, F.P. S.323.

FEUCH, ( ) *(?1780)*
XYF-1. Menuetto [& Trio] in Es [E♭].   terz-fl 2cl 2hn 2bn tp b-tb.
MS parts (by Dominik Hübner, Langenbruck): CZ-Pu(dm), 59 R 3367. ★

FÉYER, ( ) *active 2nd half of the 18th century, ?St Petersburg*
QXF-1(-3). [3 sets of] Pièces d'Harmonie; (B♭, B♭, E♭; all 3 mvts).   2cl 2hn bn.
MS parts: RF-Ssc, Ф 891 собр юосуповыix N45, (NN 10 - 12), pp. 76 - 118. ★

*FIALA, Joseph (Josef) *3 Feb 1748, Lochovice, nr Příbram, Bohemia - 31 July 1816, Donaueschingen*
*JSF-1. Divertimento I; in E♭, c.1780, 4 mvts.   2ca 2cl 3hn 2bn.   MS parts: D-DO, Mus.Ms.427. ★
JSF-2. Parthia in F; 4 mvts.   2fl 2ob 2hn 2bn.   MS parts: D-DO, Mus.Ms.443. ★
Pm (Castle Music: Sheriff Hutton, York, pn F3/131, 1992), ed. J.S. Taylorson, score & parts *(with ad lib double bass part; also includes JSF-6).*
JSF-3. Parthia in G [No.] VI; 4 mvts.   2fl 2ob 2hn 2bn.   MS parts: D-DO, Mus.Ms.444. ★
Pm (Castle Music: Sheriff Hutton, York, pn F3/131, 1992), ed. J.S. Taylerson, score & parts *(with ad lib double bass part; also includes JSF-5).*
JSF-4. Parthia Ex Dis [E♭]; 4 mvts.   2ob 2cl 3hn bn(obl).   MS parts: D-DO, Mus.Ms.440. ★
JSF-5. Parthia in Dis [E♭] II; 6 mvts.   2talie 2cl 3hn bn.   MS parts: D-DO, Mus.Ms.451. ★
JSF-6. Divertimento IV; in D, 4 mvts.   2ob 2cl 2hn bn.   MS parts: D-DO, Mus.Ms.434. ★
JSF-7. Divertimento V; in A, 4 mvts.   2ob 2cl(A or B♭) 2hn bn.   MS pts: D-DO, Mus.Ms.451 (missing ob I). ★
JSF-8. Divertimento VI, in D, 4 mvts.   2ob 2cl 2hn bn.   MS parts: D-DO, Mus.Ms.437. ★
JSF-9. Divertimento I; in E♭, c.1780, 4 mvts.   2ca 2cl 2hn bn.   MS pts: D-DO, Mus.Ms.428. ★
JSF-10. Divertimento II; in B♭, 4 mvts.   2ca 2cl 2hn bn.   MS parts: D-DO, Mus.Ms.430. ★
*JSF-11. Divertimento No. III; in E♭; 4 mvts.   2ca 2cl 2hn (2)bn.
MS parts: D-DO, Mus.Ms.431. *The bn part is for a single instrument - altered in another (later) hand from "Fagotto" to "Due Fagottj [sic]".* ★
JSF-12. Divertimento IV, in B[♭]; 4 mvts.   2ca 2cl 2hn bn.   MS pts: D-DO, Mus.Ms.435. ★
*JSF-13. Divertimento VI Pastorale, in B[♭], 4 mvts.   2ob/ca 2cl 2hn bn.   MS parts: D-DO, Mus.Ms.439. *The titlepage lists 2 oboes; although the parts call for cor anglais, they are, in fact, untransposed oboe parts.* ★
JSF-14. Partita in Dis [E♭] IV; 4 mvts.   2ca 2cl 2hn bn.   MS parts: D-DO, Mus.Ms.442. ★
JSF-15. Divertimento III; in E♭, 3 mvts.   2ca 3hn 2bn.   MS parts (c.1780): D-DO, Mus.Ms.429. ★
Pm (Edition Kunzelmann: Zürich, pn GM 720, 1983), ed. Kurt Janetzky, score & parts.
JSF-16. Divertimento II; in E♭, 4 mvts.   2ca 3hn 2bn.   MS parts (c.1780): D-DO, Mus.Ms.432. ★
JSF-17. Divertimento IV; in F, 4 mvts.   2ob 2hn 2bn.   MS parts: D-DO, Mus.Ms.433. ★
JSF-18. Divertimento V; in G, 4 mvts.   2ob 2hn 2bn.   MS parts: D-DO, Mus.Ms.436. ★
JSF-19. Divertimento VI; in D, 4 mvts.   2ob 2hn 2bn.   MS pts: D-DO, Mus.Ms.438. ★
JSF-20. Barthia [sic] in G. Del Sig Viala [sic]; 5 mvts.   2ob 2hn 2bn.
MS parts: CZ-Pnm, XXXII.A.100; D-DO, (photocopy), Mus.Ms.445. ★
*JSF-21. Nº 4 di Fyala [sic; untitled Divertimento in F]; 5 mvts.   2ob 2hn 2bn.
MS parts: CZ-Pnm, XLII.E.249. ★
Pm (Edition Robert Martin: Charnay-Lès-Mâcon, 1996), ed. Eric Baude-Delhommais, score & parts.
JSF-22. Parthia in Dis [E♭]; 4 mvts.   2talia 2hn 2bn.
MS parts: CZ-Bm(au), A.18.764.   MS score (by Prof B. Štedroň, 1938): CZ-Bm(au), A.36.743. ★
JSF-23. Parthia in Dis [E♭]; 4 mvts.   2talia 2hn bn.
MS parts: CZ-Bm(au), A.18.765. ★
Pm (Anglo American Music Publishers: New York, 1981), ed. Kurt Janetzky, score (for 2ca 2hn bn).
JSF-24(-26). Quintettos I - III; (B♭, E♭, E♭; all 4 mvts).   2ca 2hn bn.
MS parts: D-DO, Mus.Ms.447, 448, 449. ★
Pm (Hofmeister: Leipzig, Frankfurt, pn 7442, 1969), ed. Kurt Janetzky, score & parts.
JSF-27. No. 1 Partthia [sic] Ex Dis [E♭]; 4 short mvts.   2talie 2hn bn(obl).
MS parts: A-Wgm, VIII 8581 (Q 16384), (as "Parthia ex Dis"); CZ-Pnm, XLII.E.48. ★
*JSF-28. No. 2 Partthia [sic] in Dies [sic: E♭]; 4 short mvts.   2talie 2hn bn(obl).   MS pts: CZ-Pnm, XLII.E.52. ★

FIALA, Petr *25 March 1943, Pelhřimov*
PZF-1. Rondo-concerto.   Solo piano, winds, perc.
Pm (Český hudební fond: Prague, 1986), (hire) score & parts.

FIBIGER, Jan (Johann) Augustin
JZF-1v. Salve Regina ex Dis [E♭].   CATB, 2cl 2hn bn organ(bc).   AutoMS parts: CZ-Pnm, XII.E.310. ★

FICK, Peter Johann *d. 1743, Altona*
PJF-1. Concerto a 7; in F, 4 mvts.   2fl(a bec) 2ob 2hn vlne cembalo(bc-fig).
AutoMS parts: D-SWl, Mus. 352a. ★
PJF-2. No. 27 Concerto a 7; in F, 4 mvts.   2fl(a bec) 2ob 2hn cembalo(bc-fig).
AutoMS parts: D-SWl, Mus. 352b. ★
PJF-3. No. 4. Ouverture a 5, ex D# [D major]; 7 mvts.   2ob 2hn bn.   (?Auto)MS parts: D-SWl, Mus. 287.
This is, in fact, a 7-movement suite; the Ouverture (mvt 1) is in three contrasting sections. ★

FIEDLER, ( )
XZF-1. Parthia in Dis [E♭]; 4 mvts.   2cl 2hn bn.
MS parts (by Dominik Hübner, Langenbruck): CZ-Pu(dm), 59 R 3340. ★

FIELDS, Frank Gasken *(c.1900)*
FGF-1. Chant Rituel No. 1.   pic 2fl 2ob 2cl b-cl 2bn cbn timp.
Pm (Peer International Corp.: New York, pn PS1648, 1954), score: GB-Lbl, g.727.hh.(3); US-Wc.

FILICH, ( ) *(active 1822, Langenbruck, now Dlouhý Most)*
YYF-1m. Marcia [and Trio]; in D.   2pic 2cl(C) 2hn 3bn 2tp(clar) posthorn timp.
MS parts (by Augustin Erasmus Hübner, Langenbruck, 1822): CZ-Pu(dm), 59 R 3384, No. II. ★

FINKE, Fidelio Friedrich *1891 - 1968, Germany*
FIF-1. Suite No. 5; 1955.   fl ob cl 2hn bn 2tp 2tb db/tu.
Pm (Breitkopf & Härtel: Wiesbaden, c.1956).

*FINNISSY, Michael (Peter) *17 March 1946, London*
*MYF-1. Obrecht Motet V, 1992.   fl/pic 3s-sax hn 3tp 2t-tb b-tb db pf.
Pm (Oxford University Press: London, 1992), hire score & parts.

*FISCHER, ( ), *1st of the name* *(possibly the same as the 2nd of the name)*
HXF-1t. Todten Marsch; C minor.   terz-fl 2cl 2hn 2bn.   MS pts: CZ-Pnm, II.F.125; GB-Ljag, (modern copy). ★

*FISCHER, ( ), *2nd of the name* *(possibly the same as the first of the name)*
YXF-1. [9] Landlerische.   2cl 2hn bn.
MS parts (by Augustin Erasmus Hübner, Langenbruck, 1808): CZ-Pu(dm), 59 R 3383. ★

FISCHER, ( ), *Third of the name* *(1800) We cannot rule out the possibility that this is Carl Fischer.*
ZZF-1a. Mozart: La Clemenza di Tito, "Parto, parto".
fl cl(B♭ obl) cl(B♭ solo) 3cl(B♭) 2hn 2bn cbn/serp 2tp b-tb.   MS parts: D-DT, Mus-n 1864.
ZZF-2a. Tausch: Rondo aus einer [?clarinet] Concerto.   fl cl(E♭) 3cl(B♭) 2hn 2bn 2tp 3tb serp b-dr s-dr.
MS parts: D-DT, Mus-n 2037.

FISCHER, Alois *(1870), "Oberlehrer und Regenschori", active 1901, Radonitz*
ALF-1tv. Vier Begräbnislieder.   BAR solo (No. 1), B solo (No. 2), T solo (No. 3), SATB, cl(I, B♭) cl(II, E♭)
2hn basso; (fl(E♭) 2tp flug b-flug b-tp euph b-tb ad lib).
Pc (Eigenthum & Verlageres Componisten: Radonitz, pn 2, 3, 1901), parts: CZ-LIa(za), No. 2664 hud, (missing
some parts). ★
   1.1tv. Guter Vater, schlaf in Frieden!.   1.2tv. O Herr und Gott, Du ew'ge Macht.
   1.3tv. O klaget laut ihr Trauerklänge.   1.4tv. Ach, es fliessen Trauerthränen.

*FISCHER, C[arl]. (Karl, Ch[arles].) *(1800)*
CYF-1m. 10 Märsche für die Infanterie, 14tes Werk.   pic(D) 2ob cl(F) 3cl(C) 4hn 2bn 2tp a-tb t-tb b-tb) (2)serp
b-dr s-dr.
Pc (bei F.J. Mompour: Bonn, pn 154, c.1834), parts: D-DT, Mus-n 1617. *With Subscribers List.* ★
*CYF-1a. Potpouri brillant, Oeuvre 5.   terz-fl cl(F) 4cl(C) 2hn 2bn 2tp a-tb t-tb b-tb serp b-dr t-dr.
Pc (André: Offenbach a/M, pn 4949, 1826), parts: D-DT, Mus-n 1618, (with MS pts: pic(E♭) 4cl(B♭) 2hn 2bn
2tp a-tb t-tb b-dr; the MS parts have been transposed down one whole step). ★
*CYF-2a. 2me Pot-pourri pour musique militaire d'après des thêmes favoris de divers Opéras, Oeuvre 6.
fl(E♭) cl(E♭) 4cl(B♭) 4hn 2bn 2tp tp(clar)/posthorn(A♭) a-tb t-tb b-tb (2)serp b-dr s-dr.
Pc (André: Offenbach a/M, pn 4973, 1827), pts: D-DT, Mus-n 1620. *Includes the Chor, "Schmüket mit Blumen"*
& a "Tema de Caraffa" with 2 variations.
*CYF-3a. Boieldieu: Potpourri tiré de l'Opéra La Dame blanche, Op: 7.
(TTBB ad lib), terz-fl(fl in F, pic in D) cl(F) 4cl(C) 2hn 2bn 2tp a-tb t-tb b-tb serp b-dr s-dr.
Pc (N. Simrock: Bonn, pn 2640, c.1827), parts: D-DT, Mus-n 1619, (missing the ad lib vocal pts, t-tb b-tb; with
MS pts transposed down one whole step: pic(E♭), bn I & II, a-tb t-tb b-tb).
*CYF-4a. Introduction et Polonaise d'après des Thèmes [sic] de Kalkbrenner & Kalliwoda. Opus 13.
fl(F) 2ob cl(E♭) 3cl(B♭) 4hn 2/3bn(divisi in bn I) 2tp a-tb t-tb b-tb serp b-dr t-dr; (ad lib: fl in C).
Pc (chez les Fils de B. Schott: Mayence, Paris et Anvers, pn 3674, 1832), parts: D-DT, Mus-n 1616.

FISCHER, Ernst *1900 - 1975, Germany*
ERF-1. Legnania.   3fl ob ca 2cl hn 2bn db harp.
Pm (Hans Gerig: Köln, *via* Breitkopf & Härtel: Wiesbaden, 1965).

*FISCHER, Heinrich Wilhelm *(1790)*
HWF-1t. Die Trauer-Musick: an [sic] Grabe! Unsers Vielgeliebten Herzogs Friedrich Wilhelms, Braunschweig,
den 14. December 1815.   2ob 2cl 2hn 2bn.   MS parts: D-SWl, Mus. 1870. ★

*FISCHER, I.G.C. *(1810)*
IGF-1. Militair Musik; 6 mvts.   fl(E♭) 2ob cl(F) 3cl(B♭) 2hn bn(I) bn(II)+serp 2tp b-tb b-dr s-dr.
Pc (in der Hofmusikhandlung von C. Bachmann: Hanover, pn 134, c.1835), parts: D-DT, Mus-n 1615. ★

*FISCHER (Tischer, Tisher, Ficher; in CZ-KRa as "J Discher"), J. *(1750)*
JYF-1. [Parthia in E♭], 4 mvts.   2cl 2hn bn.   MS parts: D-Rtt, Sm. 8, Nos. 13 - 16;
CZ-KRa, A3849/IV.B.13, (as "Partie Nro 9 ala [sic] Camera"). ★
JYF-2. [Parthia in E♭], 5 mvts.   2cl 2hn bn.   MS parts (c.1770): D-Rtt, Sm. 8, Nos. 43 - 47. ★
JYF-3. Parthia; in E♭, 8 mvts.   2cl 2hn bn.   MS parts: D-Rtt, Sm. 8, Nos. 70 - 77. ★
JYF-4. [Parthia in E♭], 5 mvts.   2cl 2hn bn.   MS parts: D-Rtt, Sm. 8, Nos. 82 - 86. ★
JYF-5. [Parthia in E♭], 5 mvts.   2cl 2hn bn.   MS parts: D-Rtt, Sm. 8, Nos. 95 - 99. ★
JYF-6. Partie alla camera Nro 1, in E♭, 4 mvts.   2cl 2hn bn.   MS parts: CZ-KRa, A3848/IV.B.12. ★
JYF-7. Nro. 10 Pardia alla Camera, in E♭, 4 mvts.   2cl 2hn bn.   MS parts: CZ-KRa, A3850/IV.B.14. ★
JYF-8. Nro. 11 Partie alla camera, in E♭, 4 mvts.   2cl 2hn bn.   MS pts: CZ-KRa, A3851/IV.B.15. ★
JYF-9. N: 12 Quintetto, in E♭, 4 mvts.   2cl 2hn bn.   MS parts: CZ-KRa, A3852/IV.B.16. ★
JYF-10. [Parthia in E♭], 13 mvts.   2cl 2hn 2bn 2vla vlne.   MS pts (c.1780): D-Rtt, Fischer 9.
The basso pt is with the bn II; the hn pts for Nos. 5 - 7 are reversed. We believe this 2nd version to be a later,
local arrangement: mvt 1 = JYF-1, mvt 1; mvts 5 - 7 & 11 = mvts 1 - 3, 7, respectively, of JYF-3; mvts 2 - 4,
6, 8 - 10, 12 & 13 do not match any of the mvts in the other D-Rtt copies. ★

*FISCHER, Johann Christian *1733, Freiburg im Breisgau - 29 April 1800, London*
JCF-1. Triumphmarsche, E♭, 4 mvts (Marsch No 1; Marsch No 2; Amoroso (which omits the trumpets and percussion); Finale Allegro).   2ob 2cl 2hn 2bn 2tp tri cym dr(trommel).
MS parts: D-Bds, Hausbibl. M.M.99.   ★
Pm (Steinquest), pp. 129 - 155, score.

FISCHER, Matthäus (Matthias) Karl Konrad *baptized 28 Nov 1763, Ried, Swabia - 5 May 1840, Augsburg*
MKF-1v. Pange lingua vorzüglich bei feyerlichen Prozessionen anwendbar.   CATB, fl 2cl 2hn 2tp *or* organ.
Pc (Anton Böhm: Augsburg, pn 521, sd), RISM Supp [FF 1040a], parts: A-RB.

FISCHER, T.W. [also incorrectly cataloged as "Joseph"] *(1760), active 1797, Kremsmünster*
TWF-1v. Missa à la Camp; in E♭.   CATB, 2ob 2cl 2hn 2bn.
MS parts ("A: Z: 14 April 1797"): A-KR, C 17/807.   ★
TWF-2v. Eucharisticon seu 4 Stationes pro festo Corporis Christi a la Musica di Camp.
CATB, 2cl 2hn (2)bn tp(prin) timp.
MS parts: A-KR, F 20/5, (cl in A is suggested as an alternative if tp clarino in Dis [E♭] is unavailable).   ★

*FISCHER, Thoma, *Functionaire (1740)*
*TXF-1. Il Couraggio [sic]; in B♭, 5 mvts.   Solo ob & ca, 2cl 2hn 2bn.
MS parts: A-Wgm, VIII 2283.   ★
Pm (WINDS: Northridge, CA, pn W-46, c.1980) photostat of modern copies.

FISCHER-MÜNSTER, Gerhard *1952, Germany*
GMF-1. 3 Karikaturen über eine Querflöte; 1973.   2fl 2ob 2cl 2hn 2bn.   MS score: D-Mv, No. 89.

*FIŠER, Luboš *30 Sept 1935, Prague*
LXF-1. Chamber Concerto.   1964, orchestra; 1970, 12 winds.
MS score & parts: CZ-Pfiš; CZ-Pph; (?) CZ-Pchf.

*FLACHS, Karl *(1790)*
KXF-1a. Rossini: Tancredi, overture.   fl ob 2cl 2hn 2bn.
Pm (Compusic: Amsterdam, pn 220, 1988), score & parts, (original provenance unknown - ?D-BFb).
KXF-2a. Rossini: L'Italiana in Algeri, overture.   fl ob 2cl 2hn 2bn.
Pm (Compusic: Amsterdam, pn 221, 1988), score & parts, (original provenance unknown - ?D-BFb).
*KXF-3a. Weber: Der Freischütz.   fl 2ob 2cl 2hn 2bn db. *There are 2bn and not 2fl, contrary to Jähns's catalog.*
MS parts: D-BFb, W-eb 35.
Pc (Hoffmeister: Leipzig, 1823), parts.
Pm (Bärenreiter: Kassel, 1976), ed. Kurt Janetzky, *(advertized, possibly not issued).*

*FLACK, (John) Caspar *(?1750), Horn player with the 1st Regiment of Guards (Grenadiers), London*
CXF-1m. Thirty Six Military Divertimentos . . . as they are Perform'd by his Majesty's bands at St James's; [in fact making up 9 four-mvt divertimentos].   2cl/ob 2hn (2)bn.
Pc (To be had of the Author . . . and at Welcker's Music Shop: London, 1776), RISM [F 1102], score: GB-Ckc, 104.119 (1) RES; D-Bds, Hausbibl.No.395, (?lost). *The bn pt is divisi in Nos. 1, 5, 8, 10, 11, 14 & 22; the titlepage bears the note, "NB They may be play'd with Hautboys by transposing the Bass a Note higher".*   ★

FLAMENT, Edouard *27 Aug 1880, Douai - 27 Dec 1958, Bois-Colombes*
EXF-1. Fantasia con fuga (Fantasy and Fugue), Op. 28.   fl ob ca cl hn 2bn. *Some sources omit the ca & give 2cl.*
Pm (Evette & Schaeffer: Paris, sd).
Pm (McGinnis & Marx: New York, sd).

FLEISCHMANN, Friedrich *1766 - 1798*
FZF-1. Parthia in B[♭].   fl 2ob 2cl 2hn cb+quart-bn.   MS parts: D-RUl, RH-F 24, (with a cbn pt).

FLEMMING, Wilhelm *(1780), active 1806 - 1820*
WXF-1. Partie.   2cl 2hn bn tp.   MS parts: PL-WRu.

FLORSCHÜTZ, Eucharius *baptized 5 May 1756 - 20 March 1831, Rostock*
EYF-1v. Ave Maria, Componirt und der Feier des 10.Dec.1829 (Geburtstag des Grossherzogs Friedrich Franz I).
SATB, fl 2cl 2bn db.   MS parts: D-SWl, Mus. 1887.   ★

*FLOSMAN, Oldřich *5 April 1925, Plzeň*
OXF-1. Overture for Wind Instruments.   3fl 3ob 3cl 4hn 2bn 2tp 3tb tu timp xyl perc.
Pm (Český hudební fond: Prague, 1974), hire score & parts.

FLOWERS, Geoffrey Edward *6 June 1811, Boston, Lincolnshire, UK - 14 June 1872, Hammersmith, London*
GOF-1. Miniature Suite.   fl ob 2cl bn 2tp 2tb.
Pm (Novello: London, pn 19434, 1966), score & parts.

FODI, John *1944, Canada*
JDF-1. Sonata; 1983.   2fl 2ob 2cl 2hn 2bn.   MS score: C-Tcm.
JDF-2. Octet, Op. 63; 1981.   2ob 2cl 2hn 2bn.   MS score: C-Tcm.

*FOERSTER (Förster), Christoph Heinrich *30 Nov 1693, Bibra bei Laucha - 6 Dec 1745, Rudolstadt*
*CHF-1. Concerto à 6 in C; (c.1740).   2ob concertante, 3ob bn.   MS parts: D-HRDf, Fü 3663a.   ★
CHF-2. Concerto à 5 in C; 4 mvts.   3ob 2bn.
MS parts: D-HRDf, Fü 3666a.   ★
Pm (Compusic: Amsterdam, pn 597, c.1994), score & parts.

FÖRSTER, Josef *řídící učitel v Osenich [Moravia], active 1881*
Förster's funeral songs appear in Roman Nejedlý's (cf.) 12 Pohřebních Písní. Pc (Ant. Kindl: Brno, 1881), parts.
JFF-1tv (= RZN1.3tv). Spi, rozmilé nemluvňátko.   SAB, 2cl 2hn basso.
JFF-2tv (= RZN-1.10tv). Hlas tě Boha všemocného (Otci neb matce) [for funerals of fathers or mothers].
SAB, 2cl 2hn basso.

*FOJTÍK, Bohumil *1927, Czechoslovakia*
BYF-1. Impressioni, pět písní o kratochvilných hrách větru s oblaky.   fl 2ob 2cl 2hn 2bn.
Pm (Český hudební fold: Prague, 1983), hire score & parts.

FONTEBASSO, Pietro
PXF-1v. Tantum ergo.   TTB(solo+rip), 2cl 2hn bn tp (tb) timp organ.
MS score & parts: I-Vsmc, (the trombone part does not appear in the score). ★

*FORSTMAYER (Forstmeyer), Ehrenfried Andreas *1730 - 1787, Chamber musician at Karlsruhe, c.1780*
EAF-1, 2. 2 Quintetto Partien; (Eb, 4 mvts, Eb, 5 mvts).   2cl 2hn bn.   MS parts: D-DO, Mus.Ms.472. ★
EAF-3, 4. 2 Quintetti, (Eb, Eb, each of 7 mvts).   2cl 2hn bn.   MS parts: D-DO, Mus.Ms.473, 474. ★

*FORSYTH, Malcolm Dennis *8 Dec 1936, Pietermaritzberg, S. Africa, (Canadian citizen since 1974)*
MDF-1. Fanfare and 3 Masquerades.   Solo horn, 2ob 2cl 2hn 2bn cbn.
Pm (E.C. Kirby: Toronto, 1983).
MDF-2. Music for Haydn's Band; 1980.   2ob 2hn 2bn.   MS score: C-Tcm.

FORTNER, Wolfgang *12 Oct 1907, Leipzig - 5 Sept 1987, Heidelberg*
WYF-1. Bläsermusik zur 500 Jahr-Feier der Universität Freiburg; 1957.   2fl 2ob ca 2cl b-cl 3hn 2bn cbn tp tb.
Pm (B Schott's Söhne: Mainz, c.1957), hire score & parts.
WYF-2. Zyklus. Solo cello, fl 2ob 2cl hn 2bn tp tb tu harp perc.
Pm (B Schott's Söhne: Mainz; 1971), ?hire score & parts.
WYF-3. Preludium & Hymnus; 1957.   2fl 2ob ca 2cl b-cl 3hn 2bn cbn tp tb.
Pm (B. Schott's Söhne: Mainz, 1977).

FOUNTAIN, Primous, III [sic] *1 Aug 1949, St Petersburg, Florida, USA*
PYF-1. Poème; 1978.   2fl ob ca 2cl 2hn 2bn 2tp 2tb tu.
Pm (Margun Music: Newton Center, MA, pn MM 040, 1980), score & parts.

FOURNIER, A. Giuseppe *(1750)*
AGF-1. Nº 3. Quartetti Notturni; No 1: in Eb, 3 mvts, No 2: in Eb, 2 mvts, No 3: in Eb, 1 mvt.   cl 2hn bn.
MS parts: CH-Zz, AMG XII 320 &a-c; GB-Lgillaspie, (photocopy). ★

*FOWLER, Jennifer Joan *14 April 1939, Bunbury, W. Australia*
*JJF-1. Chimes, fractured; 1971.   2fl(pic) 2ob 2cl bn bn(cbn) organ 2bagpipes 6perc (including bells glock vibr).
Pm (Universal Edition: London, pn UE 29147, 1971), score.
JJF-1v. Hours of the day; 1968.   4M, 2ob 2cl.
Pm (Universal Edition: London, pn UE 29144, 1971), score.

FOWLER, Tommy *1948, Aberdeenshire*
TYF-1. Visions Before Midnight; 1994.   3fl 2cl b-sax.   MS score: GB-Gsma, (available for purchase).

*FOX, Christopher *10 March 1955, York*
*CZF-1. Some Creation Myths (Heliotrope 3); 1991.   fl/pic ob cl cl/b-cl hn bn.   MS score & tape: GB-Lbmic.

FOX, Frederick Alfred *1931, USA*
FAF-1. Essay.   2fl ob 3cl hn 2bn 2tp 2tb perc.
Pm (University Microfilm: Ann Arbor, Mich, 1967), score, (copy in US-Wc, M985.F).

*FRACKENPOHL, Arthur Roland *23 April 1924, Irvington, New Jersey, USA*
ARF-1. Aria with fughetta.   2fl ob sax 7cl 4sax 3bn.
Pm (Shawnee Press: Delaware Water Gap, PA, sd).

*FRÄNZEL, Ferdinand *24 May 1770, Schwetzingen - Nov 1833, Mannheim*
FYF-1, 2. Echo für die Harmonie, No 1 in Eb [1 mvt], No 2 in Ab [1 mvt].   2cl 2hn 2bn.
MS parts: CZ-KRa, A3861/IV.B.25. ★
Pm (Mannheimer Musik-Verlag: Bonn, pn E2-63, sd), hire score & parts.

*FRÄNZL, Ignaz *3 June 1736, Mannheim - 3 Sept 1811, Mannheim*
IXF-1. Partia a 8.   2ob 2cl 2hn 2bn.
MS parts: D-DS, unverified.
Pm (Breitkopf & Härtel: Wiesbaden, 1967).

*FRANÇAIX, Jean *23 May 1912, Le Mans*
JEF-1. Rhapsodie for viola and small orchestra.   Solo viola, 2fl 2ob 2cl 2hn 2bn cbn 2tp harp perc.
Pm (B. Schott's Söhne: Mainz; Schott & Co.: London, c.1977), score & hire parts.
JEF-2. Divertissement for violin and winds, 1953.
(?) In MS, (untraced - not published by Schott).
*JEF-3. 8 Danses exotiques, 1981.   2fl(pic) 2ob 2cl a-sax 2hn bn bn(cbn) perc.
Pm (B. Schott's Söhne: Mainz, 1981), hire score & parts
*JEF-4. Petite valse européenne, 1979.   Solo tuba, 2fl 2ob 2cl 2hn bn cbn.
Pm (B. Schott's Söhne: Mainz, pn 6934, 1980), score & hire parts.
JEF-5. Concerto pour trombone.   Solo trombone, 2fl 2ob 2cl 2hn bn cbn.
Pm (B. Schott's Söhne: Mainz, etc., 1984), hire score & parts.
*JEF-6. Quasi improvvisando [sic], 1975.   pic fl 2ob cl cl(b-cl) 2hn bn cbn tp.
Pm (B. Schott's Söhne: Mainz, 1978), score (pn ED 6762) & parts (pn ED 6763).
*JEF-7. Variations sur un thème plaisant.   Solo piano, 2fl 2ob 2cl 2hn bn bn(cbn).
Pm (B. Schott's Söhne: Mainz, etc., 1977), hire score & parts.
*JEF-8. Mozart-new-look: petite fantasie sur la sérénade de Don Giovanni.   2fl 2ob 2cl 2hn bn bn(cbn) db.
Pm (B. Schott's Söhne: Mainz, 1983), score (pn ED 7205) & parts (pn ED 7206).
*JEF-9. Hommage à l'ami Papageno, 1987.   fl fl(pic) ob ca cl cl(b-cl) 2hn bn bn(cbn) piano.
Pm (B. Schott's Söhne: Mainz), score (pn ED 7513) & parts (pn ED 7514).
*JEF-10. Les Malheurs de Sophie, Sept danses, 1970.   2fl 2ob 2cl 2hn 2bn.
Pm (B. Schott's Söhne: Mainz, 1972), score (pn 6459) & parts (pn 6460).

*JEF-11. 9 pièces charactéristiques. 1973.   fl(pic) fl 2ob 2cl 2hn bn bn+(cbn ad lib).
Pm (B. Schott's Söhne: Mainz, 1974), score (pn 6471) & parts (pn 6472).
*JEF-12. Le Gai Paris, 1974.   Solo trumpet, fl 2ob 2cl 2hn bn cbn.
Pm: (B. Schotts Söhne: Mainz, 1975), score (pn 6142), parts (pn 6143), min score (pn 6959).
*JEF-13. 11 Variations on a theme of Haydn.   2ob 2cl 2hn 2bn tp db.
Pm (B. Schott's Söhne: Mainz, 1982), hire score & parts.
JEF-14. Élégie, pour commémorer le Bicentenaire de la mort de W.A. Mozart. fl a-fl ob ca bthn b-cl 2hn bn cbn.
Pm (B. Schott's Söhne: Mainz, 1992), hire score & parts.
JEF-15. Sextuor, 1991.   fl ob cl b-cl hn bn.
Pm (B. Schott's Söhne: Mainz, 1991), hire score & parts.
JEF-1a. Chabrier: Huit Pièces Pittoresques.   2fl 2ob 2cl 2hn 2bn.
Pm (B. Schott's Söhne: Mainz, 1984), hire score & parts.
JEF-2a. Chabrier: Cortège Burlesque, (1989).   pic fl ob ca cl b-cl 2hn bn cbn.
Pm (B. Schott's Söhne: Mainz), hire score & parts.
JEF-3a. Chopin: Variations sur un Air Populaire Allemand et Trois Ecossaises.   fl fl(pic) 2ob 2cl 2hn 2bn.
Pm (B. Schott's Söhne: Mainz, 1989), hire score & parts.
*JEF-4a. Poulenc: Valse, Élégie, L'Embarquement pour Cythère, (as "Musique pour faire plaisir").
2fl ob ob(ca) cl cl(b-cl) 2hn bn bn/cbn.
Pm (Max Eschig: Paris (now B. Schott's Söhne: Mainz), 1984), hire score & parts.
JEF-5a. Schubert: Trois Marches Militaires.   fl fl(pic) 2ob 2cl 2hn bn bn(cbn).
Pm (B. Schott's Söhne Mainz, 1987), score (pn ED 7621) & parts (pn ED 7622).

*FRANKE-BLON, Lars-Åke *1941, Sweden*
LAF-1. Ekon från svunnen tid: Tre fantasistycken; 1978.   fl ob 2cl 2hn bn tp euph tu timp.   MS score: S-Sic.

*FRANZEN, Olov *22 Jan 1946, Umeå*
OZF-1. In memoriam 1791 sopra Requiem di W.A. Mozart; 1991.   2fl ob cl(ca) cl cl(b-cl) 2hn 2bn.
MS score: S-Sic.

FRANTZL, Jacopo, *Pater*   *SEE:* **TRAUTZL, Jan Jakub.**

*FREEMAN, Thomas Augustine *(1750)*
TAF-1m. The Earl of Carlisle's March [& Quick Step].   2cl 2hn hpcd.
Pc (Longman & Broderip: London, c.1780), RISM [F 1835], score: GB-Lbl, g.271.t.(11).   ★

FRELICH, Lorenz (Lorenzo) *(active 1886, Venice)*
LXF-1va. Pellegrini: Credo.   TTB, 2cl 2hn tp tb timp organ.   AutoMS score (1886) & 2 pts: I-Vsmc.   ★
LXF-2v. Pellagrini: Kyrie.   Score: 2cl 2hn tp tb organ; parts: B(rip), timp only.
AutoMS score (1886, Venezia) & 2 parts: I-Vsmc, (incomplete, missing the vocal parts).   ★

FREUER, Norbert, *R.C.* *(active c.1825, Kunvald, Bohemia*
NXF-1v. Stationes pro Festo Theophoria.   CATB, 2fl 2ob 2hn bn.
MS parts: (by Johann Simon, from Kunvald): CZ-Pnm, IX.B.46.   ★

*FREUNDTHALER, Cajatan *(1760), active in Austria, pre-1799*
We have no locations for his 2 Divertimentos (2cl bthn 2hn bn; 2cl 2hn bn) & his 2 sets of Harmoniestücke
(No. 1: 2bthn 2bn; No. 2: 2cl bthn bn), MS publications by Traeg (listed in his 1799 catalog).
CQF-1v. Aria pro Particulis de Functis [sic], in G minor, ("Ich bin noch ein Kind").   CATB, 2cl 2hn bn.
MS parts: A-GE, I 424.   ★

*FRICKE, Elias Christian *(editor)* *(1750)*
*ECF-1. Neue Sammlung englischer Tänze für das Jahr 1776. 2fl 2ob 2hn 2tp timp; (D-SWl copy also has 2vl b).
Pc (Bey Christian Iversen: Lübeck, c.1775), RISM [F 1927], pts: D-SWl, Mus. 563/b; GB-Lbl, Hirsch III.206.   ★

*FRICKER, Peter Racine *5 Sept 1920, London - 1 Feb 1990, Santa Barbara, California*
PRF-1. Sinfonia, In memoriam Benjamin Britten, Op. 76.   17 winds.
PRF-2. Five canons, (1966).   2fl 2ob/cl.
Pm (British & Continental Music Agencies: London, 1969), score & parts.

*FRID, Géza *25 Jan 1904, Máramarossziget - 13 Sept 1989, Bevernik*
GXF-1. 12 Metamorphosen, Op. 54a; 1963.   2fl 2ob 2cl hn 2bn piano harp.
Pm (Donemus: Amsterdam, 1966), score & parts.
GXF-2. Serenade, Op. 4; 1928.   fl 2cl hn bn.
Pm (Donemus: Amsterdam, sd).

FRIDOLFSON, Ruben *18 Feb 1933, Oderljunga*
RYF-1. Fantasia on a twelvetone system; 1991/1993.   3fl(pic) 2ob 2cl 2hn 2bn 2tp 3tb tu timp perc.
MS score: S-Sic.

FRIED, Gottl[ieb] *(1780)*
GLF-1m. IV Märsche für die Türkische Musik.   pic(F) cl(F) 2cl(C) 2hn 2bn cbn 2tp b-dr s-dr.
Pc (Im Verlag der K. K. priv. chemischen Druckerey: Wien, pn 1294, 1810), parts: E-Mam, K.846.(10).   ★

FRIED, Oskar *(1880)*
OYF-1. Adagio und Scherzo, Op. 2.   fl(pic) 2fl 2ob a-ob 2cl b-cl 3hn 2bn cbn 2harps timp.
Pc (Breitkopf & Härtel: Leipzig, pn Part.B.1846, 1904), facsimile AutoMS score.

*FRIEDRICH II, *(called "the Great") King of Prussia* *24 Jan 1712, - 17 Aug 1786*
TGF-1m. 4 Preussischer Armée-marsch.   Instrumentation unknown.   MS: D-Bds, Hausbibl, (?lost).
TGF-2m. Marsch, Der Hohenfriedberger (Ansbach-Bayreuth-Dragoner Regt.). Original instrumentation unknown.
Pc (Schlesinger: Berlin, c.1865), arr. for large military band, (in "Märschen für Türkische Musik", No. 1c), score:
GB-Lbl, R.M.11.h.6.
Pm (reconstruction for 2ob 2cl 2hn 2bn tp:) (In: Pätzig (qv), Heft 2, No. 17), score & parts.
TGF-3m. Mollen Marsch; 1741.   2ob bn tp.   MS parts: D-DS, Mus.ms.1224, S.231 - 237, No. 1.   ★

*FRIEND, John *(1780)*
JQF-1m. The Durham City Loyal Volunteers, March & Quick Step.   pic(doubling cl I) 2cl 2hn bn serp tp.
Pc (Preston: London, c.1810), score: GB-Lbl, G.295.t.(8).   ★

FRITSCHE, Volkmar *1936, Germany*
VXF-1. Rondino; 1984.   2ob 2cl 2hn 2bn.   In MS (1st perf 1986): D-DSim can assist in contacting the composer.
VXF-2. Prologo sereno; 1986.   2ob 2cl 2hn 2bn.   In MS: D-DSim can assist in contacting the composer.

FRITSCHEK (Fryček), Jan *1758 - 24 April 1820, Nová Říše*
JWF-1. Parthia ex B[♭]; 4 mvts.   2vl 2cl vc.   MS parts: CZ-NR, A.18.258/B.273.   ★
JXF-1v. Ecce! quo modo pestus moritur.   CATB, 2cl 2hn 2bn.
MS parts: CZ-NR, A.18.226/B.241, (?missing 2bn).   ★

FRÖHLICH, Friedrich Theodor *25 Feb 1803, Brugg - 16 Oct 1836, Aarau*
FTF-1. Walzer.   fl ob 2cl 2hn 2bn tb.   (original source untraced).
Pm (B. Schott's Söhne: Mainz, 1954), Ars viva (edited H. Scherchen).
Pm (Willy Müller: Heidelberg, sd), ed. H. Scherchen.
FTF-2. Gentil Housard varié.   fl 2cl(A) hn 2bn.   MS parts: D-DO, Mus.Ms.475/2.   ★

FROMMEL, Gerhard *7 Aug 1906, Heidelberg - 1984*
GYF-1. Bläser-Suite, Op. 18.   fl ob 2cl 2hn bn cbn(ad lib).
Pm (Müller: Heidelberg, 1944), parts.
GYF-2. Concertino, Op. 24.   Solo tenor horn or trombone, fl ob 2cl hn bn.
Pm (B. Schott's Söhne: Mainz, 1944).

FROSCHAUER, Helmut *22 Sept 1933, Wiener Neustadt*
HYF-1. Sextet.   fl ob 2cl hn bn.
Pm (Doblinger: Wien, 1962), miniature score (pn Stp 71) & parts (pn 06602).

*FUCHS, Georg Friedrich *3 Dec 1752, Mainz - 9 Oct 1821, Paris*
GFF-1. La Bataille de Marengo, Musique militaire.   fl(obl) 2cl(C) 2hn 2bn tp b-tb serp s-dr+cym timp/t-dr.
Pc (Chez l'Auteur et chez Winnen: Paris, pn 3, c.1800), pts: F-Pn Vm27 1594; GB-Ljag, (photocopy).   ★
*GFF-2. 3ème Harmonie, Le Siège de Thionville.   4cl 2hn 2bn tp serp perc.
Pc (Henri Naderman: Paris, 1793), pts: F-Pn, (unverified; Vm2 8353, sometimes cited for this work, is incorrect).
*GFF-3. 5ème Harmonie, ou Bataille de Genape, et prise de la ville de Mons.   4cl(C) 2hn 2bn tp b-tb.
Pc (Henri Naderman: Paris, 1793), RISM [F 2044], parts: D-Tu.
GFF-4.1, 4.2. [2] Walze [sic].   2fl(ad lib) 2cl(C) 2hn 2bn.
Pc (the 5th item in each liv. of Fuch's arrangement of Paer's *Una in bene ed una in male*, GFF-30.2a).   ★
GFF-5. 104me Suite militaire, marche, pas redoublé et fanfare.   2cl 2hn 2bn.
Pc (Sieber [père]: Paris, pn 1497, 1799), RISM [F 2045], parts: D-AB.
GFF-6. Trois Quatuors; 1: in E♭, 2 mvts; 2: in E♭, 3 mvts; 3: in F, 3 mvts.   cl 2hn bn.
Pc (chez Boyer et Naderman: Paris, 1797), RISM Supp [FF 2053a], pts: F-Pn, A. 34041, (clarinet pt only).   ★
GFF-7. Douze Nocturnes lettre A, (each 1 mvt).   2hn bn.
Pc (Henry [sic] Lemoine: Paris, pn 508, c.1805), pts: F-Pn, Vm17 340; GB-Ljag, (modern MS).   ★
GFF-1m. Six marches et six pas doublés, Ier Suite.   2fl 3cl 2hn (2)bn tp b-tb timp b-dr.
Pc (Jouve: Paris, pn 20, sd), RISM Supp [FF 2044a], parts: RF-Ml.
GFF-1ma. Marche en pas redoublé de la Landwehere de la Ville de Vienne. Arrangée.
pic cl(F) 2cl(C) 2hn 2bn tp tb serp b-dr.
Pc (Chez Imbault: Paris, c.1807 - 1811), parts: F-Pn, Vm27 1587.   ★
GFF-2ma. Marche de la Garde Nationale à Cheval de la Ville de Vienne. Arrangée.
pic cl(F) 2cl(C) 2hn 2b tp tb serp b-dr.
Pc (Chez Imbault: Paris, c.1807 - 1811), parts: F-Pn, Vm27 1586.   ★
*GFF-1a. Première Suite d'Airs d'Opéra Comiques.   2fl 2cl(C) 2hn 2bn.
Pc (Imbault: Paris, c.1799), RISM [F 2074], pts: D-AB, (fl II, cl II only); F-Pn, (3 copies), Vm7 6965,
(incomplete: a duplicate sheet, pages 3/4 replaces pages 5/6 in the cl I pt),Vm27 1591, Vm27 1603; US-Cn.
   1.1a. Tarchi: Le Trente et Quarante, 3 mvts.   1.2a. Tarchi: Le Cabriolet jaune, 1 mvt.
   1.3a. Dalayrac: Une journée [sic: matinée] de Catinat, 2 mvts.
   1.4a. Bruni: Le Rencontre en voyage, 1 mvt.   1.5a. (unidentified): Un Nuit d'éte, 1 mvt.
GFF-2a. Première Suite d'Airs d'Opéra Buffa.   2fl 2cl(C) 2hn 2bn.
Pc (Imbault: Paris, pn 535, c.1799), RISM [F2075], parts: F-Pn, Vm27 1591; US-Cn, VM 858.
   2.1a. Cimarosa: L'Impresario in augustie, duo "Che l'alma mia discacci" & air "Chi dice mal d'amore". Nos. 1, 4.
   2.2a. Cimarosa: Gianina e Bernadone, duo, "Gianina amabile", No. 2.
   2.3a. Palma: La Pietra simpatica, Polaca [sic], "Sento che son vicino", No. 3.
   2.4a. Bernardini: [Don Simoncino, ossia] Furberia e Puntiglio, Air, "Per amar Abbiamo il core", No. 5.
   2.5a. Bianchi: La Villanella rapita, duo, "Vanne in preda", No. 6.
GFF-3a. Deuxième Suite d'Airs d'Opéra Buffa.   2fl 2cl(C) 2hn 2bn.
Pc (Imbault: Paris, pn 794, c.1801), RISM [F 2076], parts: D-AB, (fl II, cl II only); F-Pn, (2 copies), Vm7 6966,
Vm27 1584.   MS parts: D-Rtt, Sm. 14, Nos. 60 - 63.
   3.1a. Martín y Soler: La Scuola dei maritati (as "La capricciosa correttà"), polacca, ("La Donna hà bello il
   core").   *Note: the same incipit appears in D-Rtt for arrangements in Sm. 17 (Cherubini) & Guglielmi 5/III.*
   3.2a. Paisiello: L'Inganno felice, quatuor ("Infedeli dov' è l'affetto") & duo ("Via dite cosa avete").
   3.3a. Sarti: Fra i due litiganti (as "Le Nozze di Dorina"), polacca.
GFF-4a. Pot-pourri.   4cl 2hn 2bn.
Pc (Henri Naderman: Paris, pn 177, c.1791), RISM [F 2082], parts: F-Pn (2 copies), Vm7 6967, Vm18 151.
Includes pieces from Grétry's Richard Coeur de Lion *and Dalayrac's* Les deux petites Savoyards.
GFF-5a. Le carillon national, Ah! ça ira, dictum populaire.   2cl 2hn 2bn.
Pc (Sieber: Paris, c.1790?), RISM [F 2084], parts: D-AB.
GFF-6a. No. 2 Pas redoublé, la Carmagnole.   4cl 2hn 2bn.
Pc (Naderman: Paris, c.1792), RISM Supp [FF 2043b], pts: CZ-Pnm, XLII.A.212, (the imprint overpasted with a
slip for Cousineau Père et Fils, Paris; *pace* RISM, the work is complete with headtitle rather than titlepage).

GFF-7a. Berton: Montano et Stephanie, [7] Airs Choisis.   2fl(ad lib) 2cl(C) 2hn 2bn.
Pc (Imbault: Paris, pn 796, c.1803), RISM [B 2276 = F 2080], pts: D-AB (fl II, cl II only); D-Bhm, Mus. 6932;
CH-Gpu, Ib.4825; F-Pn, Vm27 1592; US-Wc.
GFF-8a. Blasius: Nouvelle suitte d'harmonie, (as "Suite 110me").   Instrumentation unknown - ?2cl 2hn 2bn.
Pc (Sieber: Paris, pn 1563, c.1802), RISM Supplement [BB 2851a], parts: D-AB. *(Possibly an arrangement of
Blasius' melodrama of 1802,* Don Pèdre et Zulika).
GFF-9a. Bruni: Spinette et Marini, Ouverture italienne.   4cl 2hn 2bn tp.
Pc (Nadermann: Paris, pn 163, 1791), RISM [B 4722], parts: D-Tu; F-Pn (2 copies) Vm7 6972, Vm27 1601.
GFF-10a. Bruni: Le Rencontre en voyage, overture.   2fl 2cl(C) 2hn 2bn, (ad lib: tp tb serp).
Pc (Imbault: Paris, c.1799), parts: F-Pn, Vm27 1598.
GFF-11a. Cimarosa: L'Impressario in augustie.   2cl 2hn 2bn.
Pc (Imbault: Paris, pn 106, c.1786), RISM [C 2281], parts: D-BFb, C-im 30, (with the printed slip of J.C. Gayl,
Frankfurt am Main).   *We believe this anonymous copy is Fuchs's arrangement.*
GFF-12.1a. Cimarosa: Il Matrimonio segreto, overture.   2fl 2cl(C) 2hn 2bn.
Pc (Imbault: Paris, pn O.H.H.179, 1802), parts: F-Pn, Vm27 1599.
GFF-12.2a. Cimarosa: Il Matrimonio segreto, Morceaux choisis, 8 mvts.   2fl 2cl(C) 2hn 2bn.
Pc (Imbault: Paris, pn 750, 1802), RISM [C 2314], parts: F-Pn, (3 copies), H2. 177. (missing fl I & II, bn II),
Vm7 6980, (complete), Vm27 1589, (complete).
GFF-12.3a. Cimarosa: Il Matrimonio segreto, ouverture et airs.   2fl 2cl(C) 2hn 2bn.
Pc (Janet et Cie.: Paris, post-1814), parts: F-Pn, (a re-issue from the Imbault plates).
GFF-13a. Dalayrac: Azémia. As: "Suite No. (94 d'Azémia)".   4cl 2hn 2bn serp/db, *or* 2cl 2hn 2bn.
Pc (Sieber [père]: Paris, pn 1247, c.1792), RISM [D 106], pts: D-AB; D-BFb, D-al 15.
GFF-14a. Dalayrac [arr. attributed Fuchs]: Camille, ouverture [No. 62].   4cl 2hn 2bn tp serp, *or* 2cl 2hn 2bn.
Pc (Sieber [père]: Paris, pn 1333, 1794), RISM [D 144], pts: D-AB; S-Uu, Utl.instr.mus.tr. 145, 149 - 151,
Takt 21, (cl I, bn I & II, hn I only). *Fuch's name have been removed from the plate (a faint impression remains).*
GFF-15.1a. Dalayrac [arranged Anon, attributed Fuchs]: Gulnare, overture.   2pic(C) 2cl(C) 2hn 2bn tp.
Pc (Imbault: Paris, pn O.H.H.164, c.1798), RISM [D 296], parts: F-Pn (2 copies), Vm7 6984.
GFF-15.2a. Dalayrac: Gulnare, [6] Airs.   2fl 2cl(C) 2hn 2bn. *(The flutes are essentially ripieno.)*
Pc (Chez Imbault: Paris, pn 866, c.1807), parts: F-Pn, (2 copies), Vm27 1583.
Pc (Janet et Cie.: Paris, post-1814), parts: D-BFb.
GFF-16.1a. Devienne: Les Visitandines, ouverture [No. 61].   4cl 2hn 2bn tp serp, *or* 2cl 2hn 2bn.
Pc (Sieber [père]: Paris, pn 1328, 1793), RISM [D 1874], parts: D-AB; S-Uu, Utl.instr.mus.tr. 145, 149 - 151,
Takt 20, (cl I, bn I & II, hn I only).
GFF-16.2a. Devienne: Les Visitandines, airs, as: "Suite (No. 97)".   4cl 2hn 2bn *or* 2cl 2hn 2bn.
Pc (Sieber [père]: Paris, pn 1310, 1793), RISM [D 1871], parts: D-AB, (missing cl IV).
GFF-17a. Foignet: Le mont Alphéa, ouverture.   4cl(C) 2hn 2bn.
Pc (Naderman: Paris, pn 166, c.1792), RISM [F 1456], parts: D-Tu; F-Pn, (2 copies), Vm7 6971, Vm27 1600.
GFF-18.1a. Gossec: Le Triomphe de la République, ou Le Camp de Grand-Pré, ouverture.   4cl(C) 2hn 2bn tp.
Pc (Naderman: Paris, pn 152, 1793), RISM [G 3075], parts: F-Pn, (9 copies, 2 editions, including:) Vm7 6977,
Vm27 1876; GB-Lhumphies, (modern MS).
GFF-18.2a. Gossec: Le Triomphe de la République, ou Le Camp de Grand-Pré, airs, 7 mvts.   4cl(B♭) 2hn 2bn.
Pc (Naderman: Paris, pn 158, 1793), RISM [G 3078], parts: F-Pn, (at least 2 copies), Vm7 6978, Vm27 1875.
GFF-19a. R. Kreutzer: Paul et Virginie, overture, [No. 60].   4cl 2hn 2bn tp serp, *or* 2cl 2hn 2bn.
Pc (Sieber: Paris: pn 1329, 1793), RISM [K 2147], parts: S-Uu, Utl.instr.mus.tr. 145, 149 - 151, Takt 22, (cl I,
bn I & II, hn I only).
GFF-20a. La Borde (Delaborde): La Cinquantaine, ouverture.   2cl 2hn 2bn.
Pc (Naderman: Paris, [gravée par la Cne. Chaume], 1796/1797), RISM Supp [LL 71a], parts: F-Pn, (3 copies),
Vm7 1029, Vm7 6975, Vm27 1597; GB-Ljag, (photocopy of F-Pn, Vm27 1597).
GFF-21a. Lesueur: La Caverne, ouverture.   4cl 2hn 2bn tp.
Pc (H. Naderman: Paris, pn 160, 1794), RISM Supp [LL 2111a], pts: F-Pn, (2 copies), Vm7 6974, Vm27 2586.
GFF-22a. Lesueur: Paul et Virginie, ouverture.   4cl(C) 2hn 2bn tp.
Pc (Naderman: Paris, pn 159, 1794), RISM [L 2144], parts: F-Pn, (2 copies), Vm7 6974, Vm27 2587; US-Cn.
*GFF-23.1a. Lesueur: Ossian, ou les Bardes, overture.   2cl 2hn 2bn.
Pc (Imbault: Paris, pn O.H.H.190, c.1804), RISM [L 2128], parts: D-AB, F-Pn, Vm27 2585; I-Mc, Noseda T.9.2.
Although the publication is anonymous, stylistically this arrangement is almost certainly by Fuchs.
GFF-23.2a. Lesueur: Ossian, ou les Bardes, Morceaux choisis; Suites 1 & 2, 6 mvts, 8 mvts.   2cl 2hn 2bn.
Pc (Imbault: Paris, pn 59 [Suite 1], 152 [Suite 2], c.1804), parts: F-Pn, Vm27 1588.
GFF-24a. Méhul: Euphrosine, [MS: 96] Suite; 7 mvts.   4cl(C) 2hn 2bn serp/cb, *or* 2cl(C) 2hn 2bn.
Pc (Sieber: Paris, pn 1291, 1793), RISM [M 1826], parts: S-Uu, Utl.instr.mus.tr. 145, 149 - 151, Takt 14, (cl I,
bn I & II, hn I only).
GFF-25a. Méhul: Ariodant. Morceaux choisis.   2fl 2cl(C) 2hn 2bn.
Pc (Imbault: Paris, pn 748, 1802), RISM [M 1762], parts: D-AB (missing fl 1); F-Pn (2 copies), Vm7 6981,
Vm27 2899; GB-Lhumphries (modern copy).
GFF-26a. Mozart: Don Giovanni, Airs, 7 mvts.   2fl(ad lib) 2cl 2hn 2bn.
Pc (Sieber: Paris, pn 367, c.1805), RISM [F 2079], parts: CH-Gpu, Ib.4824; GB-DOTams, (photocopy).
GFF-27.1a. Mozart: La Clemenza di Tito, Ouverture (I Suite).   2ob 2hn 2bn.
Pc (Decombe: Paris, 1801 - 1806), RISM [F 2077], parts: CH-Gpu, Ib.4822.
GFF-27.2a. Mozart: La Clemenza di Tito, Airs, (2 Suite), 6 mvts.   2fl 2cl 2hn 2bn.
Pc (Decombe: Paris, 1802 - 1805), RISM [M 5227], parts: CH-Zz, AMG XIII 1085 a-g.
GFF-27.3a. Mozart: La Clemenza di Tito, Airs, (3 Suite); 5 mvts.   2cl 2hn 2bn.
Pc (Decombe: Paris, 1802 - 1805), RISM [F 2077 = M 5228], parts: CH-Gpu, Ib.4823; I-Fc, B.2733.
GFF-28.1a. Paer [arranged Anon, attributed Fuchs]: Griselda, as "La Griselda", overture.   2cl 2hn 2bn.
Pc (Imbault: Paris, pn O.H.188, c.1798), parts: F-Pn, Vm27 3295.
GFF-28.2a. Paer: Griselda, Airs; 9 mvts.   2cl 2hn 2bn.
Pc (Imbault: Paris, pn 348, 1802 - 1805), parts: F-Pn, Vm27 3292; GB-Ljag(w), (missing cl II).
GFF-29a. Paer: Achille, overture.   2cl(C) 2hn 2bn; (ad lib: 2fl tp b-tb b-dr).
Pc (Imbault: Paris, pn O.H.198, 1802 - 1805); parts: F-Pn, (2 copies), Vm27 3297, Vm27 1596.

GFF-30.1a. Paer: Una in bene ed una in male, ouverture. 2fl(ad lib) 2cl(C) 2hn 2bn.
Pc (Imbault: Paris, pn O.H.201, c.1805), parts: F-Pn, Vm27 3298.
GFF-30.2a. Paer: Una in bene e una in male, [8] airs. 2fl(ad lib) 2cl(C) 2hn 2bn.
Pc (Imbault: Paris, c.1805), liv. 1 & 2, parts: F-Pn, Vm27 3293 (1, 2). *A 5th mvt in each liv. is a waltz by Fuchs, GFF-4.1, 4.2.*
GFF-31a. Paisiello: I Zingari in fiera, Morceaux choisis, 6 mvts; No. 6 is, in fact, "E vero che in casa" from Cimarosa's *Il Matrimonio segreto.* 2fl 2cl(C) 2hn 2bn.
Pc (Imbault: Paris, pn 418, 1793), RISM [C 2445, *incorrectly cited at Cimarosa],* pts: D-AB; F-Pn, Vm27 1590.
GFF-32.1a. Paisiello: Proserpine, ouverture. 2cl 2hn 2bn, (pic, serp ad lib).
Pc (Imbault: Paris, pn O.H.H.186, c.1803), parts: F-Pn, Vm27 3305.
GFF-32.2a. Paisiello: Proserpine, Airs, Suite 1: 7 mvts, Suite 2: 8 mvts. 2cl 2hn 2bn.
Pc (Imbault, Paris, pn 304, 399, c.1803), RISM [P 479, P 480 - citing the D-AB copies only], parts: D-AB (cl II only); F-Pn, (several copies, including:) Vm7 6953, Vm27 3304 (1, 2).
GFF-33a. Persuis: Estelle, ouverture. 4cl 2hn 2bn tp.
Pc (Naderman: Paris, c.1794), parts: F-Pn (2 copies), Vm7 6970, Vm27 3357.
GFF-34.1a. Rossini: Il Barbiere di Siviglia, ouverture. pic cl(F) 2cl(B♭) 2hn 2bn b-tb serp.
Pc (Carli: Paris, 1076, 1820), parts: F-Pn, Vm27 3691.
GFF-34.2a. Rossini: Il Barbiere di Siviglia, airs, 2 Suites: Nos 1 - 6, 7 - 13. 2fl cl(F) 2cl(B♭) 2hn 2bn tb serp.
Pc (Carli: Paris, pn 1145, 1820/1821), parts: F-Pn, Vm27 3665 (1, 2), (missing cl(F) tb serp parts).
GFF-35.1a. Solié: Jean et Geneviève, Airs . . . Mêlés de petits Airs Patriotiques, 7 mvts. 4cl(B♭, C) 2hn 2bn.
Pc (Naderman: Paris, pn 172, 1794), RISM [S 3878], parts: F-Pn, (2 copies), Vm7 6979, Vm27 3937.
   35.1a. Solié: Jean et Généviève, 3 mvts. *The 4cl are in B♭.*
   35.2a - 35.5a. Anon: Airs Patriotiques: Air de la Montagne, Air du Siege [sic] de Lille, Air du Cadet Rousselle, Air de la Carmagnolle [sic]. *The 4cl are in C.*
GFF-35.2a. Solié: Jean et Geneviève, airs. 2fl 2cl 2hn 2bn.
Pc (Naderman: Paris, sd), parts: F-Pn, Vm22 4.
GFF-36.1a. Solié: Le Chapitre second, ouverture. 2fl 2cl 2hn 2bn.
Pc (Imbault: Paris, pn O.H.H.171, c.1799), RISM [S 3862], parts: F-Pn, Vm 27 3936, (2 copies).
GFF-36.2a. Solié: Le Chapitre second, airs choisis; 7 mvts. 2fl 2cl(C) 2hn 2bn.
Pc (Imbault: Paris, pn 761, 1802), RISM [S 3864], parts: F-Pn, (2 copies), Vm22 4, Vm27 3934.
GFF-37a. Steibelt: Bataille d'Austerlitz. 2cl(C) 2hn 2bn, (ad lib: pic tp tb timp b-dr).
Pc (Imbault: Paris, pn 777, c.1806; *the battle was on 2 Dec 1805),* parts: F-Pn, Vm27 1593.
MS parts: D-Bds, Hausbibl., No 312.
GFF-38a. Steibelt: Cinquième Pot-pourry. 4cl 2hn 2bn. *Includes an Air from Paisiello's Nina, the Andante from Haydn's Symphony in G (Hob. I/63ii) & an Air from Sarti's Fra due Litiganti, (as "Les Noces de Dorine").*
Pc (Naderman: Paris, pn 200, sd), RISM [S 5522 = F 2081], parts: F-Pn, (3 copies), Vm7 6969, Vm27 1602, Vm27 3982. *Fuchs is styled, "G.F. Fuchs Ordinarie de la Garde Natle. Parisienne".*
Pc (Naderman: Paris, "Gravé par la Cne Chaume", pn 202, c.1792), RISM [F 2083], pts, as "Pot Pourri Pour huit Instruments": F-Pn, Vm7 6968. *Steibelt is not mentioned; Fuchs is styled, "GEORGE FERID [sic] FUCHS Ordinaire de l'Armée Parisienne".*
GFF-39a. Steibelt: La Journée d'Ulm. 2cl 2hn 2bn, (fl tp tb b-dr ad lib).
Pc (Imbault: Paris, pn 777, 1802), RISM [S 5326], parts: D-AB. *The plate number cited in RISM is questionable (= GFF-37a).*
GFF-40a. Vogel: Démophon. 4cl 2hn 2bn tp serp, *or* 2cl 2hn 2bn.
Pc (Sieber [fils]: Paris, pn 1093, 1790/1791), parts: F-Pn, D. 16265.
GFF-1d. Pot-pourri. 4cl 2hn 2bn.
Pc (Henri Naderman: Paris, pn 202, c.1792), RISM [F 2083], pts: F-Pn. *Not an original work; in fact, GFF-38a.*

*FUCHS, Johann (Giovanni) Nepomuk *1766 - 29 Oct 1839, Eisenstadt*
*JAF-1. Nro 8 Parthia ex Dis [E♭]; 4 mvts. 2ob 2cl 2hn 2bn.
MS parts: A-Ee, Mus.1175, *(as "Fuchs I" in Hummel's 1806 Esterházy catalog).* ★
*JAF-2. [9] Messlied in Es [E♭]; "Wir werfen uns darnieder". fl 2cl 2hn 2bn (2tp timp).
AutoMS score & MS parts: A-Ee, Mus.272, (with a simplified fl pt for Nos 3 & 4; parts in parentheses - for Nos. 1-6 only - do not appear in the score and are probably later additions). *This work comprises 9 instrumental settings, all with the same opening section but with progressively more complicated conclusions.* ★
JAF-1v. Deutsche Messe in D, 1822. SATB, fl 2cl 2hn 2bn 2tp(clar) vlne timp organ(full part).
AutoMS parts: A-Ee, Mus.260, (with duplicate vocal parts: 3S, 3A, 2T, 2B). ★
JAF-2v. Zum heiligen Segen "Unsern Heiland, unsern Lehrer." SATB, fl 2cl 2hn 2bn 2tp(clar) timp organ(full part & bc with a few fig). AutoMS parts: A-Ee, Mus.349, with duplicate vocal parts: 3S, 2A, 2T, 2B). ★
JAF-3v. Deutsche Messe in F. Solo & ripieno SATB, fl 2cl 2hn vl vlne organ. AutoMS scores (SATB & organ, full part and/or bc-fig with separate instrumental score) & MS parts: A-Ee, Mus.271. *The instrumental parts in the score do not agree with the listing on the titlepage: 2cl(C & A) 2hn bn 2tp(clar) timp organ. The MS instrumental parts are: SATB concto, (2)S,ATB ripieno, fl cl 2hn vc vlne organ(bc-fig).* ★
JAF-1c. Adagio, die Introduction von der Messe componirt von Gapellmeister Ceÿka [sic; ?Valentin Čejka]. 2ob cl(F) 2cl(C) 2hn 2bn cbn tp(clar, C) 2tp(prin) b-tb. MS score: A-Ee, Mus.1199. *Besides the Adagio, the work comprises 4 "Nachspiel zum Messlied", a Vorspiel vor Segenlied with 2 Nachspiels, "Adagio No. 5" (without tps) & "No. 6. Larghetto", 3/8. This appears to be a local addition to one of Čejka's Masses.* ★
JAF-1vc. Das Lied "Wir werfen uns darnieder, Introducione [sic], 12 verses & 4 Nachspiels. Voice, 2ob cl(F) 2cl(C) 2hn 2bn cbn tp(prin) tb. MS score: A-Ee, Mus.1200. ★
On f.2, a trumpet solo is marked, "Cavallerie Kirchen Hoffe" (to be played in the church courtyard).
JAF-2vc. Harmonie für Heiligen Messe. Voice, 2ob cl(F) 3cl(C) 2hn 2bn cbn 2tp(prin).
MS parts: A-Ee, Mus.1199. *The work comprises a 4-verse hymn, a 2-verse Segenlied, "die Erklärung macht für bekannt, wir ed vor Segung bid Ende", and "by Cominition".* ★

*FÜHRER, Robert (Johann Nepomuk) *2 June 1807, Prague - 28 Nov 1861, Vienna*
RXF-1v, 2v. [2] Veni Sancte Spiritus. SATB, fl 2cl 2hn 2tp timp organ. MS pts: CZ-Pnm, XLVII.E.263. ★
RXF-3v. Te Deum in C. TTBB, 2cl(C) 2hn 2tp b-tb timp. MS pts: CZ-Pnm, XLIII.C.29. ★
RXF-4v. Choral Requiem. SATB, fl 2cl hn bn organ. MS pts: CZ-Pnm, XLVII.E.263.

RXF-5.1v. Frohnleichnamsmusik enthaltent: Die vier Stationes sammt Da pacem Domine e Pange lingua, Op. 263.   SATB, 2cl(C) 2hn 2tp(chromatic) b-tb.   MS parts: CZ-Pnm, IX.D.122.   ★
Pc (Jos. Kränzl: Ried, sd), parts: CZ-Bm(bh), A.9121, (missing vocal parts, signed "J Šubert, 25.10.1875"), CZ-Pnm, XLIII.F.70, (with MS score: 2cl 2hn 2tp "Bassorka in B[♭]" tb timp).
RXF-5.2v. [4] Stationen, Fronleichnamsmusik, Op. 263.   SATB, cl hn 2tp tb.   MS pts: CZ-Pnm, IX.D.122.   ★
RXF-5.3v. Frohnaleichnamsmusik [sic].   CATB, 2cl hn 2tp b-tb.   MS parts: CZ-KV, B.179.
RXF-6v. [6] O Salutaris hostia.   SAB, 2vl/2cl(C) 2hn vlne+tb organ.
Pc (Anton Böhm: Augsburg, pn 2550, sd), parts: CZ-Pnm, XLIII.D.93.   ★
RXF-7v. Harmonie Messe in Es [E♭] nebst Graduale, Offertorium und Tantum ergo, Op. 188.
SATB, fl 2cl 2hn 2tp(E♭) flug(B♭) a-hn(B♭) bar-tu(B♭) bomb+b-tb organ.
Pc (Verlags=Eigenthum des Johann Gross: Innsbruck, c.1850), parts: CZ-PLa, Hu 2845; CZ-Pnm, XLIII.E.34.   ★
MS parts: CZ-Pnm, XXIX.D.305, (flug replaces a-hn(B♭), with an additional euph part).
RXW-8v. Schwert und Schild, Gedicht von Julius Rodenberg, Op. 187.
TTBB chorus, pic(E♭) fl 2ob 2cl 4hn 2bn 3tp 2tb tu/b-hn/bomb timp, *or* piano.
Pc (Reid: Oberösterreich; Fr. Whistling: Leipzig; Fr. Glöggl: Wien, , sd), score: A-Sca, 43006.   ★
RXW-9v. III Marien Lieder.   SATB, organ, 2cl(C) 2hn bomb(ad lib).
MS pts (by R. Fleck, Lehrer, copy of Jos. Kränal: Reid, Oberösterreich edition): A-Wn, Mus.Hs.23,272.   ★

FÜRST, Paul Walter *1926, Austria*
PWF-1. Oktibet II [sic].   2ob 2cl 2hn 2bn.
Pm (Doblinger: Wien, sd), miniature score (Stp 647) & parts (pn 6591).

FULKERSON, James Orville *1945, USA*
JMF-1. A Screaming Comes Across the Sky; 1985.   2ob 2cl 2hn 2bn.   MS score: US-NYamc.

FULTON, Robert Norman *1909 - 1980, UK*
RNF-1. Curtain Wells Sketches.   2fl 2cl bn harpsichord harp.
Pm (Chester Music: London, sd), score & parts.

FURBE, ( )
ZXF-1v. Tenebrae in G♮ [sic, = F major].   CATB, ob organ, (2ca ad lib).
MS parts (by František Černý): CZ-Pnm, XXXVIII.B.155.   ★

FURLANETTO, Bonaventura *27 May 1738, Venice - 6 April 1817, Venice*
BXF-1v. Gloria.   SSB, 4ob 2hn 2bn 2tp organ.   MS: I-Vcdr, Busta V N.98.
BXF-2v. Kyrie.   SSB, 4ob 2hn 2bn 2tp organ.   MS: I-Vcdr, Busta V N.99.
BXF-3v. Credo.   SSB, 2ob 2cl 2hn bn tp organ.   MS: I-Vcdr, Busta V N.88.
BXF-4v. Tantum ergo.   TTB, 2ob 2hn bn organ.   MS: I-Vcdr, Busta VI N.115.
BXF-5v. Alma Redemptoris.   Solo T, 2ob 2hn bn organ(bc).   MS score: I-Vsmc, packet I.   ★
BXF-6v. Beatus Vir, 1796.   TTB(solo+rip), fl 2cl 2hn bn (timp) organ(bc-fig).
MS score & parts: I-Vsmc, packet I, (the timp part is not in the score).   ★

*FUSCO, Michele *(?1780)*
MZF-1(a). Sinfonia a tutto Orchestra obbligato del Maestro Fusco Eseguita in circostanza della Cantata per l'apertura del Teatro Filodrammatico in onore del Reale Infante, il Principe Ferdinand, Carlo Vittorio, [sic] ridotta dal medesimo per gli Strumenti da fiato della Reale Armonia.   *Orchestra version only: fl 2ob 2cl 2hn 2bn 2tp 2vl vla vc b timp.*   AutoMS score: I-MOe, Mus.F.398.   ★

FUSSELL, Charles *14 Feb 1938, Winston-Salem, NC*
CAF-1. Three Processionals.   fl(pic) fl ob ca cl(E♭) a-cl b-cl 2hn bn cbn 2tp 2tb 4perc harp.
Pm (G. Schirmer: New York, 1973), score & (hire) parts.

*FUX (Fuchs), ( ) *(1770), active at Březnice, nr Plzeň, c.1800*
ZYF-1v. Ecco quomodo in Dis [E♭].   CATB, 2cl 2hn 2bn.   MS pts: CZ-BR, sign. 411, No. 1, (MS by Horetsky, with 3 sets of vocal parts); CZ-PLa(br), Hu 1711/1, (MS by František Vaněček; missing Canto pt).   ★
ZYF-1va. Luopiccini: Vexilla Regis; in F.   CATB, 2cl 2hn 2bn.
MS parts: CZ-BR, sign. 411, No 2, (MS by Horetsky, with 3 sets of vocal parts); CZ-PLa(br), Hu 1711/2, (MS by František Vaněček).   *The original composition, "Del Sig. Luopiccini / Chori SS. Ignatii Xaverii / Brzeznicii 1765" can be found at CZ-BR, Sign. 411.*

GAALMAN, A. *1914 - 1986, Netherlands*
AAG-1. Introduction et Burlesque.   fl ob ob/ca cl cl/b-cl 2hn 2bn bn/cbn.
Pm (Compusic: Amsterdam, pn 207, 1988), score & parts.

GAATHAUG, Morten *1955, Norway*
MXG-1. Orff'evs i blåsarlunden (Orff'ers in the wind grove).   2fl ob 2cl hn bn tp tb tu, "Orff instruments"(= school percussion).   MS score: N-Oic.
MXG-2. 3 Slovakian Bagatelle, Op. 22b; 1983.   2ob 2cl 2hn 2bn.   MS score: N-Oic.

*GABRIELI, Giovanni *c.1554 - 12 July 1612, Venice*
GZG-1dv. Jubilemus Singuli.   SSAATTBB chorus, ob ca 2cl 2hn 2bn 2tp.
Pm (G. Schirmer: New York), score & (hire) parts.   *Presumably a modern arrangement.*

GADZHIBEKOV (Godzhibekov), Sultan Ismail Oglui *9 May 1919, Shucha - 19 Sept 1974, Baku*
SSG-1. Sextet.   fl ob 2cl hn bn.   Pm (Azernemr: Baku, 1965), score & parts.

*GÄNSBACHER, Johann Baptist *8 May 1778, Bolzano - 13 July 1844, Vienna*
JBG-1m. II Märsche in C.   pic 2ob 2cl 2hn 2bn tp.   MS parts: CZ-Pnm, Lobkovic X.H.a.78.   ★
JBG-2m. Marsch in C.   2fl(G) 2cl(F) 2cl(C) 2hn 2bn cbn 2tp b-dr.
MS parts: CZ-Pnm, Lobkovic X.H.a.80, *(the final item: all others are by Krechler).*   ★
JBG-1v. Alpenlied.   SSAATTBB, 2fl 2cl 2hn 2bn cbn.
(?Auto)MS score (Innsbruck, Oct. 5, 1822): A-LIm, Autographensammlung I.   ★

GAGNEBIN, Henri *13 March 1886, Liège - 2 June 1977, Geneva*
HXG-1. Divertissement; 1959. pic 2fl 2ob 2cl 2bn 2tp perc.
Pm (self-published: ?Geneva, 1959), parts: CH-Zma.
HXG-2. Octet, Op. 150; 1970. 2ob 2cl 2hn 2bn. MS score: CH-Zma.
HXG-3. Sextet, Op. 160; 1970. 2ob 2cl 2bn. MS score: CH-Zma.

*GAILLARD, Marius François *13 Oct 1900, Paris - 23 July 1973, Evequemont, Yvelines*
*MFG-1. Guyanes. (Voice), fl fl(pic) ob 2cl 2hn bn 2tp b-dr boite-clour, tam-tam, whistle, tambour, cym, piano.
AutoMS score (1925): F-Pn, MS. 21714. Pm (Heugel: Paris, sd), piano reduction.

*GÁL, Hans *5 Aug 1890, Brunn, nr Vienna - 3 Oct 1987, Edinburgh*
Gál's A Pickwickian Overture, sometimes cited as for winds only, is actually for full orchestra.
HAG-1. Divertimento, Op. 22; 1924. fl ob 2cl 2hn bn tp.
Pm (Leduc: Paris, 1925). Pm (Leuckart: München, 1927), score: US-Wc.

GALANTE, Carlo *1959, Italy*
CLG-1. Rondela amoureux; 1982. 2fl ob 2cl 2hn 2bn.
Pm (Suvini-Zerboni: Milano, pn S9050Z, 1982), score & parts.
CLG-2. Rondela amoureux; 1985. 2ob 2cl 2hn 2bn.
Pm (Suvini-Zerboni: Milano, pn S9447Z, 1985), score & parts.

GALLIGNANI, Giuseppe *9 Jan 1851, Faenza - 14 Dec 1923, Milan*
GXG-1. Suonatina - Studio. fl ob cl hn 2bn. MS parts: I-Bc, NN.461. ⋆

GALLINI, ( ) *(1800), active Rajhrad, Moravia, 1828*
ZYG-1. Kassatio am Iter May, 4 mvts. 2cl(C) 2hn bn 4tp timp. MS parts (1828): CZ-Bm(rj), A.14.206. ⋆

*GALOTTI, All[esandr]o *(1790)*
ALG-1a. Rossini: Semiramide, sinfonia & 9 mvts. pic fl 3cl 2hn 2bn 2tp b-tb.
MS parts: I-OS, Mus.Musiche B 4153, (with the stamps of the Duke of Verona & the music seller, Picinelli).

*GAMBARO, Giovanni Battista *baptized 1785, Genoa - 1828, Paris*
It is almost certain that Giovanni Battista Gambaro & Vincent (Vincenzo) Gambaro are, in fact, the same person.
VXG-1. [MS: 2°] Ouverture de Tivoli. Composée pour le Fête extrordinaire du 10 Août 1815, Dédiée à leurs
Majestés Les Souverains Alliés. fl 2cl 2hn 2bn, (ad lib: tp tb serp db timp).
Pc (Gambaro: Paris, pn 75, 1816), parts: F-Pn, (2 copies), Vm27 1621, Vm27 1625. ⋆
VXG-2. Premiere [sic] Suite de musique militaire; 3 mvts. pic(D) cl(F) 2cl(C) 2hn 2bn tp tb serp b-dr.
Pc (Chez Gambaro: Paris, pn 24, 1814), parts: F-Pn, Vm27 1623 (1). ⋆
VXG-3. Musique militaire, [MS: 2°] Suite. Oeuvre 2; 6 mvts. pic(D♭) cl(E♭) 2cl(B♭) 2hn tp tb serp b-dr.
Pc (Gambaro: Paris, pn 46, 1814), parts: F-Pn, Vm27 1623 (2). ⋆
VXG-4. Musique militaire [MS: 3°] Suite; mvts 1-6. pic(D♭) cl(E♭) 2cl(B♭) 2hn (2)bn tp tb serp b-dr+cym.
Pc (Gambaro: Paris, pn 69, 1816), parts: F-Pn, Vm27 1623 (3). ⋆
  4.1(a). Haydn: Andante with variations / Menuetto All° & Trio; (Hob. I/53, ii, iii, iiia).
  4.2(a). Rummel: Valse.   4.3(a). [?Rummel or Gambaro]: Valse.   4.4(a). Schaffner: Rondo.
  4.5(a). Berbiguier: Marche des volontaires Royaux.   4.6(a). Piccini: Pas redoublé.
VXG-5. Musique militaire, [MS: 4°] Suite; mvts 7-12. pic(D♭) cl(E♭) 2cl(B♭) 2hn 2bn tp tb serp b-dr (s-dr).
Pc (Chez Gambaro: Paris, pn 44 [titlepage: 69], 1816), parts: F-Pn, Vm27 1623 (4). ⋆
  5.1(a). 7. Rummel: Andante with 4 variations.   5.2(a). 8. Rummel: Valse.   5.3(a). 9. Schaffner: Marche.
  5.4. 10. [?Gambaro]: Valse de la Garde Nationale.   5.5. 11. [?Gambaro]: Valse [& Trio].
  5.6. 12. [?Gambaro]: Pas Redoublé avec les Tambours. (b-dr part adds "Caisses à Tambour".)
VXG-1a. Gallenberg: Amleto, overture. fl 2cl 2hn bn bn+cb, (ad lib: cl(E♭ ripieno) tp tb serp timp b-dr+cym).
Pc (Chez Gambaro: Paris, pn 25, post-1817), parts: F-Pn, Vm27 1624.
VXG-2a. F.J. Haydn: Harmonie Tirée des Œuvres de Haydn; 4 mvts. 2fl 2cl 2hn 2bn, (ad lib: tp tb serp).
Pc (Gambaro: Paris, pn 45, 1814), parts: F-Pn, Vm27 1622. *The bn(II) part is titled "FAGOTTO 2° ou*
VIOLONCELLO", with numerous pizzicato & arco markings.
  2.1a. String Quartet No. 4, (1799, Hob. III/78i), Allegro [con spirito].
  2.2a. String Quartet No. 1, (1787, Hob. III/44ii), Adagio [non lento].   (tp tb serp tacet)
  2.3/1a. String Quartet No. 2 (c.1788, Hob. III/58/ii) Menuetto.
  2.3/2a. Symphony in E♭, (Hob. I/91iiia), Trio of Menuetto.   (tp tb serp tacet)
  2.4/1a. Trio for pf, vl & vc (Hob. XV/18ii), Andante, Majeur, (tp tb serp tacet) ⇒ 2.4/2a. [unidentified,
  ?Spurious] Polonaise in F.
*VXG-3a. Paer: Agnese di Fitz-Henry ("L'Agnese"), [MS: V] Suite, [parts: "1ère Suite"]; 4 mvts; Suite 2, 4 mvts.
fl 2cl 2hn 2bn; (ad lib: b-tb serp).
Pc (Chez Janet et Cotelle: Paris, [Suite 1] pn 1132, post-1810), parts: F-Pn, Vm27 1619.
MS parts (pre-1821): D-Rtt, Sm. 14, Nos. 2 - 5, (Suite 2).
VXG-4a. Persuis: Vive le Roi, Vive la France, Marche de M.M. Les Gardes du corps Musique.
fl(F) cl(F) 2cl(B♭) 2hn (2)bn tp tb serp(B♭) b-dr.
Pc (Chex Gambaro: Paris, pn 66, 1816), parts: F-Pn, Vm27 3359, (2 copies, each with 2 sets of B♭ cl pts).
*VXG-5a. Rossini: L'Italiana in Algeri, overture. fl 2cl(B♭) 2hn 2bn; (ad lib: cl(E♭) 2cl(B♭) 2tp b-tb serp b-dr).
Pc (Chez Gambaro: Paris, pn 110, 1818), parts: D-DT, Mus-n 862.
*VXG-6a. Rossini: Il Barbiere di Siviglia, ouverture & 4 suites, (4, 4, 5, 5 mvts).
fl cl(Eb, overture) 2cl(Bb) 2hn 2bn; (ad lib: cl[Bb] III & IV, tp[2tp in Suites 2 - 4] tb serp).
Pc (Chez Janet et Cotelle: Paris, pn (overture) 1410, (suites) 1381, 1382, 1383, 1383 [sic], post-1816), parts:
I-Fc, F.P. S.702; I-Mc, Noseda M.37.2, (missing many parts). MS pts (1823): D-Rtt, Rossini 2, (Suite 1 only).
*VXG-7a. Rossini: Otello, overture. fl(E♭) 2cl(B♭) 2hn 2bn; (ad lib: cl(E♭) 2cl(B♭ ripieno) tp 3tb timp b-dr.
Pc (Chez Gambaro: Paris, pn (190) [?sic, ?90], 1817), parts: D-DT, Mus-n 866.
VXG-8a. Rossini: La Gazza ladra, overture. fl(E♭) cl(E♭) 2cl(B♭) 2hn 2bn; (ad lib: tp tb serp timp).
Pc (Chez Gambaro: Paris, post-1817), parts: I-Fc, F.P. S.701.

VXG-9a. Rossini: Mosè in Egitto, overture.   12 parts [? fl cl(Eb) 2cl(Bb) 2hn 2bn tp tb serp b-dr].
Pc (Chez Gambaro: Paris, post-1818), parts: I-Fc, F.P. S.703.
*VXG-10a. Rossini: Ricciardo e Zoraide, overture.   fl 2cl 2hn 2bn; (ad lib: cl(Eb) tp tb serp timp).
Pc (Chez Gambaro: Paris, post-1818), parts: I-Fc, F.P. S.699.
VXG-11a. Rossini: Semiramide, overture.   Instrumentation unknown, 15 parts, probably similar to VXG-7a.
Pc (chez Gambaro: Paris, post-1823), parts: I-Fc, F.P. S.696. *The overture was inserted in the pastiche* Ivanhoé.
VXG-12a. N.A. Schaffner: Ouverture de Chasse [in F].   fl 2cl 2hn 2bn, (ad lib: 2cl 2tp tb serp).
Pc (Chez Gambaro: Paris, pn 6, 1814), parts: F-Pn, Vm27 1620.

GAMBARO, Vincenzo (Vincent)   *See GAMBARO, Giovanni Battista*

*GAMSTORP, Göran *17 May 1957, Stockholm*
GOG-1. Caccia per flauto e fiati da camera; 1984.   Solo flute, fl(pic) ob ob(ca) cl cl(b-cl) 2hn bn bn(cbn).
MS score: S-Sic.

*GAN, Nikolay Karlovich *28 April 1908, Tbilisi*
NKG-1. Dyerskiye Kartyinki [Children's pictures].   2fl ob 2cl hn bn.
Pm (Musgis/Soviet Music Center: Moscow, 1955), score & parts.

GANDA (Janda), ( )
YYG-1. Parthia in Dis (Eb), 4 mvts.   2cl 2hn bn.   MS parts: CZ-NR, A.18.234/B.249.   ★

GANDINI, Antonio *20 Aug 1786, Modena - 10 Sept 1842, Modena*
AXG-1v. Tantum ergo - Opure Qui tollis; in F.   T solo, pic(D) cl(Eb) 3cl(Bb) 2hn 2tp b-signal-hn 2tb bassi.
AutoMS score & MS parts: I-MOe, Mus.D.93, (the MS parts differ from the score: pic(Db) fl(Db) cl(Eb)
2cl(Bb) 3hn 2tp signal-hn b-signal-hn 2tb 2bombardone; with duplicate parts: 2cl(I) in Bb, cl(II) in Bb).   ★

GANGE, Kenneth Edward *13 June 1939, Burry Port, Carmarthenshire, Wales*
KEG-1. A Welsh March.   2fl 2ob 3cl 2hn bn 2tp tb tu.   MS score: GB-CDmic.

*GANZ, Rudolf *24 Feb 1877, Zurich - 2 Aug 1972, Chicago.*
RXG-1. Woody Scherzo, Op. 33, No. 3.   pic 2fl 2ob cl(Eb) 2cl(Bb) b-cl(Bb) 2bn cbn/db.
Pm (Mills Music: New York, 1946), score: GB-Lbl, g.727.p.(7); US-Wc.

GARANT, (Albert Antonio) Serge *1929 - 1986, Canada*
SAG-1. Jeu à quarte; 1968.   fl ob 2cl 2hn bn 2tp tb db 3perc piano+celeste harp.   MS score: C-Tcm.

GARCIA, Joaquin *? - 1799*
JQG-1v. Noble, magestuosa arquitectura; 1757.   TB, 2ob 2bn.
Pm (Musica Barroca Espanola: sl, 1973), score & parts.

GASPARINI, Giovanni Battista *(1800), active 1854, Venice*
GIG-1. Marcia & Allegro.   fl 2cl(Eb) 2cl(Bb) 2hn 2tp flug bomb "bombardino" db.   MS parts: I-Vsmc.   ★
GIG-1v. Tantum ergo et Genitori in Eb, 1850.   TTB(solo+ripieno), 2cl 2hn 2tp(tacet in Tantum ergo) tb timp.
MS score & parts: I-Vsmc, (with an additional vla part).   ★
GIG-1vf. Salve Regina, (1850).   Bass solo, winds, organ.
MS score & parts: I-Vsmc, (incomplete: the score is for voice & organ only; missing all parts except fl & bn).   ★

*GASSMANN (Gasman), Florian Leopold *3 May 1729. Most, Bohemia - 20 Jan 1774, Vienna*
*Note: Many of Gassmann's Parthias also exist in string quintet versions to which Hill assigns earlier thematic
catalog numbers; we cite Hill numbers in the order: winds, strings.*
FLG-1. Notturno; in Bb, 5 mvts, (H.621).   2clalumeau 2hn 2vla vc b.   MS parts: A-Wn, Mus.Hs.11,394.   ★
FLG-2. Parthia in C; 5 mvts, (H.601).   2ob 2hn 2bn.   MS parts: CZ-Pnm, XLII.E.200.   ★
FLG-3. Parthia in B[b]; 5 mvts, (Hill deest).   2ob/cl 2hn bn.   MS parts: CZ-Bsa, fond Staré Brno 1092/E4.   ★
FLG-4. Cassatio a 5; in Eb, 5 mvts, (H.532).   2ca 2hn bn.   MS parts: CZ-K, No.261.K.II.   ★
FLG-5. Parthia Imo; in Eb, 5 mvts, (H.524, 504).   2cl 2hn bn.
MS parts: D-Rtt, (2 copies), Inc.IVa/31/I, Nos. 1 - 5, (1773); Sm. 8, Nos. 38 - 42, (c.1780).   ★
FLG-6. Parthia IIdo; in Eb, 5 mvts, (H.525, 505).   2cl 2hn bn.
MS parts: D-Rtt, (2 copies), Inc.IVa/31/I, Nos. 6-10, (1773); Sm. 8, Nos. 21-24, (c.1780, missing mvt 2). ★
FLG-7. Parthia IV; in Eb, 4 mvts, (H.528, 518).   2cl 2hn bn.
MS parts: D-Rtt, (2 copies), Inc.IVa/31/I, Nos. 16 - 19, (1773); Sm. 8, Nos. 100 - 103, (c.1770).   ★
FLG-8. Parthia V; in Eb, 5 mvts, (H.527, 517).   2cl 2hn bn.
MS parts: D-Rtt, (2 copies), Inc.IVa/31/I, Nos. 20 - 24, (c1773); Sm. 8, Nos. 30 - 34, (c.1770).   ★
FLG-9.1. Parthia VI; in Eb, 5 mvts, (H.522, 502).   2ob 2hn bn.
MS parts: D-Rtt, (2 copies) Inc.IVa/31/I, (1773); Sammelband 8, Nos. 1 - 4, (c.1770).
FGL-9.2 [untitled - Parthia] in Bb, 13 mvts.   2cl 2hn 2bn 2vla.   MS parts (c.1780): D-Rtt, Gassmann 8.   ★
FLG-10. [Parthia in Eb], 4 mvts, (H.529).   2cl 2hn bn.   MS parts: D-Rtt, Sm. 8, Nos. 104 - 107.   ★
FLG-11. [Parthia in Eb], 5 mvts, (H.530).   2cl 2hn bn.   MS parts: D-Rtt, Sm. 8, Nos. 108 - 112.   ★
FLG-12. [Parthia in Eb], 5 mvts, (H.526, 506).   2cl 2hn bn.   MS parts (c.1770): D-Rtt, Sm. 8, Nos. 113 - 117.   ★
FLG-1d. [Untitled - Parthia], in Bb, (H.531).   2ob 2hn bn.   MS parts: CZ-Pnm, XXXII.C.246. *Gassmann
identified as composer only in the CZ-Pnm card catalog, possibly based on the contemporary catalog.*   ★

GASTYNE, Serge de *1930, France (resident in USA)*
SDG-1. Partita.   2fl 2cl bn.
Pm (Fereol Publications: Alexandria, VA, sd).

GAUBERT, Philippe *3 Aug 1879, Cahors - 8 Aug 1941, Paris*
PHG-1. Siciliano.   2fl ob 2cl 2hn 2bn harp.
Pm (Heugel: Paris).

*GAZZANIGA, Giuseppe *5 Oct 1743, Verona - 1 Feb 1818, Cremona*
GYC-1. Suonata.   2cl 2hn (timp) organ.   MS parts: I-Vsmc, (incomplete, the timp part only).
GYG-1v. Quoniam.   Solo B, 2cl 2hn bn 2tp organ(bc-fig).
MS score & parts: I-Vsmc, (with additional db & full organ parts).   ★

*GEBAUER, Étienne François *1777, Versailles - 1823, Paris*
EFG-1. Trois Quatours Concertants, Oe. 10; F, F, F minor/major; all 2 mvts).   2cl(C) hn(II) bn.
Pc (Mag de mus fêtes nat: Paris, sd), parts: F-Pn, A. 34.809, (as by "L.C.F. Gebauer", missing cl I).   ★
EFG-1a.[Attributed to E.F. Gebauer] Boieldieu: Le Calife de Bagdad, overture.   pic 2cl 2hn 2bn.
Pc (Mlles. Erard: Paris; Garnier: Lyon, pn 12, 1810), parts: CH-Gpu, Ib.4826; GB-DOTams, (photocopy).
MS parts (as Anon): CH-E, Th.54,4 (Ms.1922).
EFG-2a. Dalayrac: Léhemann, overture.   Instrumentation unknown, (probably similar to EFG-5a).
Pc (Mlles Erard: Paris, 1801), RISM [D 346], parts: D-AB.
EFG-3.1a. Dalayrac: La Boucle de cheveux, ouverture.   Instrumentation unknown, (probably similar to EFG-5a).
Pc (Mlles Erard: Paris, 1802), RISM [D 134], parts: D-AB.
EFG-3.2a. Dalayrac: La Boucle de cheveux, airs et duo.   Instrumentation unknown, (probably similar to EFG-5a).
Pc (Mlles Erard: Paris, 1802), RISM [D 131], parts: D-AB.
EFG-4a. Spontini: La Vestale, ouverture.   2fl 2ob 2cl(C) 2hn 2bn tp b-tb+serp.
Pc (Mlles. Erard: Paris, pn 711, 1808), parts: F-Pn, Vm27 3973.
EFG-5a. Spontini: Fernand Cortez, overture.   2pic 2fl 2ob 2cl(F) 2cl(C) 2hn 3bn 2tp timp b-dr tri tambour.
Pc (Mlles Erard: Paris, pn 890, 1819), parts: CH-Gpu, Ib.4829.
EFG-6a. Spontini: Les Dieux rivaux, airs.   Instrumentation unknown, (probably similar to EFG-5a).
Pc (Mlles Erard: Paris, 1816), parts: D-Bds.

*GEBAUER, François Réné *15 March 1773, Versailles - 28 July 1845, Paris*
FRG-1m. Pas de manoeuvre; P.2299.   2p-fl 2cl 2hn 2bn tp serp.
Pc (Mag de mus fêtes nat: Paris, thermidor an II, 1794), liv. 5, No. 4, pts: F-Pn, (2 copies), H2. 5,4, Vm7 7046;
F-Nm, Vol 22207.
FRG-2m. Pas de manoeuvre; P.2310.   2p-fl 2cl 2hn 2bn tp serp.
Pc (Mag de mus fêtes nat: Paris, brumaire an III, 1794), liv. 8, No. 4, pts: F-Pn, H2. 8; F-Nm, Vol 22207.   ★
FRG-3m. [6] Marches et [6] Pas Redoublés de différens Caractères.
fl cl(F) 2cl(C) 2hn 2bn tp tb serp b-dr+cym+tri
Pc (Chez Beaucé: Paris, pn G.M. 3ᵉ L., c.1805 - 1814), parts: F-Pn, Vm27 1742, (as by "F.N. Gebaver").   ★
FRG-4m. Six Marches et Pas-Redoublés Composés Pour la Garde Royale.
p-fl(F) cl(F) 2cl(C) 2hn 2bn tp tb serp b-dr+cym.
Pc (Chez J. Frey: Paris, c.1814), parts: F-Pn, Vm27 1740.   ★
FRG-5m. Marches à l'usage des Musiques Militaires.   2cl 2hn 2bn.
Pc (sn: Paris, sd), parts: D-DS, (?lost in World War II).
FRG-1a. Haydn: Symphony No. 73 "La Chasse", mvts 1, 4.   2fl 2cl(C) 2hn 2bn tp(ad lib), *or* 2cl 2hn bn.
Pc (P. Porro: Paris, sd), RISM [H 4111], parts: I-Bc, GG.43, (with MS pts for 2ob based on the clarinet pts; with
the printed slips of Pacquet: Marseille, and Naderman: Paris).
EFG-2a. Isouard: Cendrillon, Suite 1: 6 mvts, Suite 2: 6 mvts.   fl 2cl 2hn 2bn, (serp/cb ad lib).
Pc (Chez Nicolo, Auteur: Paris, pn A 20, A 21, c.1810 - 1812), parts: CH-Gpu, Ib.4827, 4828.

*GEBAUER, François Réné & FREY, Jacques Joseph Désiré *1782, Paris - 9 June 1838, Paris*
*FFG-1m. Trois Marches Composées pour l'entrée de Sa Majesté Louis XVIII dans la Ville de Paris Le ___ [sic]
1814.   pic(F) fl(F) cl(F) 2cl(C) 2hn 2bn(unison) 2tp tp serp b-dr cym, (No. 2 only: tamb tri, pavillon chinois).
Pc (Chez J. Frey: Paris, 1814), parts: F-Pn, Vm27 1741, (2 copies).   ★

*GEBAUER, Franz Xaver *1784, Eckersdorf, Prussian Silesia - 13 Dec 1822, Vienna*
FXG-1. Overture Pastorale; in F.   fl 2ob 2cl 2hn 2bn serp.   MS parts (post-1803): D-AB, S.32.   ★

*GEBAUER, Michel Joseph *1763, La Fère, Aisne - 1812, ?Russia*
MJG-1m. Marche militaire, P.2312.   2p-fl 2cl 2hn 2bn tp serp.
Pc (Mag de mus fêtes nat: Paris, frimaire an III, c.1795), liv. 9, No. 3, parts: F-Pn, H2. 9,3.   ★
MJG-2m. Pas de manoeuvre, P.2311.   2p-fl 2cl 2hn 2bn tp serp.
Pc (Mag de mus fêtes nat: Paris, frimaire an III, c.1795), liv. 9, No. 4, parts: F-Pn, H2. 9,4.   ★
MJG-3m. 5 Marches de la Garde Imp. françoise [sic].   Instrumentation unknown.
MS: D-Bds, Mus.Ms.7205.
MJG-1ms. 12 Marches nouvelles exécutées à l'occasion des grandes parades.   piano reduction only.
Pc (T. Weigl: Wien, pn 1100, c.1808), RISM [G 798]: A-Wgm, XVI 9461/2 (Q 20542).   ★
MJG-1a. Nouveau Journal d'Harmonie A l'Usage des Musiques Militaires.
fl(F) cl(F) 2cl(C) 2hn 2bn tp serp/b-tb b-dr cym tri; *or* fl(F) 2cl(C) 2hn 2bn serp.
Pc (P. et J.J. Le Duc: Paris, 1807 et seq.), pts: CH-Zz, AMG XIII. 3070-3073, (Livrason 1 - 4); I-Fc, F.P. S.477,
(33 pages - ? Liv. 1). *The numbering of the Livraisons (Suites) is continuous.*
    1.1/1a. Paisiello: Marche [& Mineur]; No. 1.   1.1/2. M.J. Gebauer: Marche; No. 2.   ★
    1.1/3a. Paisiello: Marche; No. 3.   1.1/4. M.J. Gebauer: Drapeau; No. 4.   ★
    1.1/5a. Paisiello: Pas redoublé [& Mineur]; No. 5.   1.1/6. M.J. Gebauer: Pas Redoublé; No. 6.   ★
    1.1/7a. Paisiello: Pas Redoublé [& Trio]; No. 7.
    1.1/8a. Haydn [in fact, Roman Hoffstetter]: Walzer [& Trio], (Hob. III/14), here in 3/8; No. 8.
    1.2/1a. Viotti: Simphonie (Maestoso, C / Allegro, ¢); No. 9.
    1.2/2a. Haydn: Andantino Gratioso, (Hob. III/13iii); No. 10.
    1.2/3a. Fioravanti: des comédiens ambulans, "Quelle fête l'on nous donne"; (tp tb tacet), No. 11.
    1.2/4a. Fioravanti: des comédiens ambulans, "Je me sens né pour la Guerre"; (tp tb tacet), No. 12.
    1.2/5a. Haydn: Walzer [& Trio], (Hob. deest); No. 13.
    1.3/1a(-1.3/6a). G.F. Fuchs: [6 unidentified mvts].   Nos. 14 - 19.
    1.4a. Solié: Mademoiselle de Guise, ouverture & 5 mvts; Nos. 20 - 26.
MJG-2a. Bianchi: La Villanella rapita. Nouvelle Suite d'Harmonie No. 3.   2ob 2cl 2hn 2bn serp/db(ad lib).
Pc (Boyer, Le Menu: Paris; Philippeaux: Bordeaux, c.1783), RISM [B 2561], parts: D-BFb, B-ia 59.
MJG-3a. Bruni: Toberne.   (fl, pic ad lib) 2cl 2hn 2bn.
Pc (les frères Gaveau: Paris, sd), parts: D-AB.
MJG-4a. Champein: La Mélomanie, Nouvelle Suite d'Harmonie No. 1.   2ob 2cl 2hn 2bn serp/db(ad lib)
Pc (Boyer, Le Menu: Paris; Philippeaux: Bordeaux, 1782), RISM Supp [CC 1816a], parts: D-BFb, C-ha 50.

MJG-5a. Dalayrac: Sargines, Suite [MS: 95], 8 mvts.   4cl 2hn 2bn.
Pc (Sieber: Paris, pn 1248, 1792/1793), RISM [D 586], parts: D-F, Mus.1939/184, (stamped "A FRANCFORT CHES [sic] JEAN J. GAYL."; the Gayl copy does not include mvt 1); D-BFb, D-al 25.
MJG-6a. Dalayrac: Les deux petits Savoyards, Nouvelle Suite d'Harmonie No. 11.   2ob 2cl 2hn 2bn serp/db(ad lib).
Pc (Boyer, Le Menu: Paris; Philippeaux: Bordeaux, c.1789), RISM [D 1171], parts: D-BFb.
MJG-7a. Della Maria: L'Opéra Comique, overture.   fl 2cl(C) 2hn 2bn tp tb serp.
Pc (Lemoine: Paris, c.1798), parts: F-Pn, Vm27 1743, (the tb pt is marked "Tromboni" but there is only 1 pt).
MJG-8.1a. Gaveaux: Le Diable couleur de rose, overture.   11 parts.
Pc (les frères Gaveaux: Paris, pn 216, 1805), RISM [G 633], parts: D-AB.
MJG-8.2a. Gaveaux: Le Diable couleur de rose, airs, duo, trio.   8 winds.
Pc (les frères Gaveaux: Paris, pn 217, 1805), RISM [G 634], parts: D-AB.
MJG-9a. Haydn: Symphony in B♭, (Hob. I/51; omits Menuetto & Trio, mvt 3).
pic cl(F) 2cl(C) 2hn 2bn tp b-tb serp b-dr
Pc (Sieber père: Paris, pn 1364, 1795), RISM [H 4110], pts: D-F, Mus.pr. 1939/184, (missing b-dr).
The titlepage for the following 4 works reads: "N° [108, 109, 115, 116] / à la demie Brigade d'infanterie / [MS: 1, 2, 8, 9] Livraison / DOUZE NOUVELLES / suites d'Harmonie / à [MS: 8] Parties / Par [MS: W.A. Mozart] / Suivies de Marches et pas Redoublés / Par J. GEBAUER Chef / de la Musique de la Gardes des Consuls. / Dediés [sic] aux Armées Françaises / — / Chaque Suite sevend [sic] Separément. 9 francs. — / — / A PARIS / chez SIEBER pere [sic] Editeur de Musique rue Honoré." The wording clearly indicates that the Marche & Pas Redoublé which follow the arrangments are original works by Gebauer; the scoring differs substantially from the arrangement and the parts are printed four-to-the-page. Surviving copies of the other numbers in this series have not been located.
MJG-10a. Mozart: Così fan tutte, Suite 108, liv. 1, sinfonia & Act I, Nos 1 - 4, 6, 7.   2fl/ob 2cl 2hn 2bn.
Pc (Sieber père: Paris, pn 1558, c.1802), RISM [M 4764], parts: D-F, Mus.pr. Q50/449.
   10.1 & 10.2. Gebauer: Marche [E♭] & Pas Redoublé [E♭].   2pic cl(F) 2cl(C) 2hn 2bn tp tb serp b-dr+cym. ★
MJG-11a. Mozart: Così fan tutte, Suite 115, liv. 8, Act I, Nos. 16 - 22.   2fl/ob 2cl 2hn 2bn.
Pc (Sieber père: Paris, c.1802), RISM [M 4769], parts: D-F, Mus.pr. Q50/449. *(RISM suggests this is only item 14 of the opera, based on Stumpf's arrangement; no marches are included in the D-F copy).*
MJG-12a. Mozart: Così fan tutte Suite 116, liv. 9, Act II, Nos. 23bis.   2fl/ob 2cl 2hn 2bn.
Pc (Sieber père: Paris, c.1802), RISM [M 4770], parts: D-F, Mus.pr Q50/449. *(RISM cites item 23 only).*
   12.1 & 12.2. Gebauer: Marche [E♭] & Pas Redoublé [E♭].   2pic cl(F) 2cl(C) 2hn 2bn tp tb serp b-dr+cym. ★
MJG-13a. Mozart: Gran Partita, K.361, mvts 1 - 3, 7; as Suite 109, liv. 2.   2fl/ob 2cl 2hn 2bn.
Pc (Sieber père: Paris, pn 1561, c.1802), RISM [M 5904], parts: D-F, Mus.pr. Q50/449. *RISM gives KV 361: Anh B zu 361 (K370a)).*
   13.1 - 13.3. Gebauer: Marche [E♭] & Pas Redoublé I & II [E♭].   2pic cl(F) 2cl(C) 2hn 2bn tp tb serp b-dr+cym. ★

GEBEL, A. Franz (François) *probably Franz Xaver (1787, Furstenau nr Breslau; buried 3 May 1843, Moscow)*
AFG-1, 2. Deux Harmonies, Op. 11; both in Eb, 3 mvts.   2cl 2hn 2bn.
Pc (Au Magazin de Imprimerie Chimique: Vienne, pn 882, c.1810), parts: H-Bn, ZR 691; H-KE, 717/VIII. ★

*GEBHARD, Johann Gottfried *(1780), Moravian Brethren composer*
JNG-1m. March in E♭.   2cl 2hn bn tp.   MS parts: US-BETm, Lititz Collegium Musicum 203, No. 11. ★

GEDDES, (John) Maxwell *26 May 1941, Glasgow*
JMG-1. 4 Gothic Pieces; 1963.   2fl 2ob 2cl 2bn.   MS score: GB-Lmic.

GEFORS, Hans *8 Dec 1952, Stockholm*
HNG-1. Snurra; 1994.   fl(pic) 2ob 4hn 3tp 3tb tu perc.   MS score: S-Sic.

GEHLHAAR, Rolf (Rainer) *30 Dec 1943, Breslau (from 1953 living in the USA)*
RRG-1. Pixels; 1981.   2fl 2cl 2hn 2vc.
Pm (Feedback Studios, Köln, *via* Bärenreiter: Kassel, 1981).

*GEHOT, (Jean) Joseph *8 April 1756, Brussels (?Liège) - c.1820, USA*
JOG-1m. Twenty four military pieces, consisting of marches, minuets, quick-movements, &c, Op. 4th. 2cl 2hn bn.
Pc (William Napier: London, c.1780), RISM [G 825], parts: D-SWl, Mus. 2011, (missing the cl parts).
Pm (Spratt Music Publishing: Fort Lauderdale, FL, sd). *No complete versions known - ?modern completion.*

*GELLERT, Josef *1787 - 17 Nov 1842, Chomutov*
JXG-1v. [4] Stations-Arien in D pro Festo Corpus Christi.   CATB, fl [2ob] cl(C) 2cl(A) 2hn bn [cbn] 4tp(2clar, prin, A basso) [b-tb] timp.   MS parts: CZ-LI(a), No. 2112 hud, (missing cl in C; with duplicate C & B pts. The instruments in square brackets are not listed on the titlepage]. ★
JXG-2v. Messe in D.   CATB, fl 2cl(C) 2hn bn organ.
MS parts (1835): CZ-Pnm, XXXII.D.116. (as "Deutsche Messe in D"; missing cl II; with 2 copies of voice & organ pts). *Although the printed edition includes violins, we believe that this work was performed at Osek with wind accompaniment; the clarinet pts closely follow the violins and the flute generally doubles an octave above.* Pc (s.n., "Steindruck von I. Zwettler": Prag[ue], s.d. [c.1835]), parts: CZ-Pu, 59-A-6293. *The printed edition is scored for CATB, 2vl vlne organ, (fl 2cl(C)+2ob 2hn 2tp timp ad lib).* ★
JXG-1.1tv. Drei neue Grabgesänge, 1te Sammlung.   (Nos 1 & 2:) SATB, fl 2cl 2hn bn+b-tb 2tp; (No 3:) SAB, 2cl 2hn bn.
Pc (s.n: s.l., s.d, c.1835), score: CZ-Pu, 59 E 2663; GB-Ljag, (photocopy). ★
MS pts (1837): CZ-LIa(je), No. 262 hud., (Nos. 2 & 3; both for CATB, terz-fl cl(I, B♭) cl(II, E♭) 2hn bn+b-tb 2tp); CZ-LIa(vl), No. 2451 hud., No. 2, (No. 2 only), No. 2494 hud., No. 1, (No. 3 only).
   1.1/1tv. Grabgesang bei der Leiche eines Kindes; "Gleich der juengen Morgen nahe".
   1.1/2tv. Gragbesang bei der Leiche einer erwachsenen Person; "Die du in jenen [sic] Höhem".
   1.1/3tv. Grabgesang mit 3 Singstimmen bei der Leiche einer erwachsenen Person; "Ruhe frei von aller Klage".
JXG-1.2tv. [= JXG-1.1/2]. 2 Grablieder bei Kindern und Erwachsenen; No. 2.   CATB, 2terz-fl 2cl 2hn bn(vel b-tb) 2tp(clar).   MS parts: CZ-LIa(vl), No. 2451 hud.
JXG-2tv. 2 Grablieder bei Kindern und Erwachsenen; No. 1: Nimm hier an meines Grabes Rande.
CATB, 2terz-fl 2cl 2hn bn(vel b-tb) 2tp(clar).   MS parts: CZ-LIa(vl), No. 2451 hud., (No. 2 is JXG-1.1/2). ★

JXG-3tv. Todten=Arie in Es [E♭]; "O Herr und Gott du ew'ge Macht".   CATB, terz-fl 2cl 2hn bn+b-tb 2tp.
MS parts (by Josef Jentsch): CZ-Lla(je), No, 273 hud, (the title lists tp "Prinzipal con Sardini [sic]" and
"Pomparton" rather than bn+b-tb).   ★
JXG-4tv. Grabgesang bey der Leiche einer erwachsenen Person mit Harmoniemusick [sic] Begleitung.
CAB, 3cl 2hn 2bn 2tp b-tb(ad lib).   MS parts (by Wolleschensky): CZ-Lla(je), No. 275 hud., (missing cl I &
II, hn II, tp I).   ★
JXG-5tv. Grab=Arie bein einer jungen Person.; "Freunde denkt an meine Bahre".   CATB, 2terz-fl 2cl 2hn tp b-tb.
MS parts (by Josef Jentsch): CZ-Lla(je), No. 276 hud.   ★
JXG-6.1tv. 2 Grabgesänge, No. 1; "Sey [sic] willig dem zurückgegeben.   CAB, fl(F) 2cl 2hn bn+b-tb 2tp(clar).
MS parts: CZ-LI(a), No. 2414 hud., No. 1.   *No. 2, for CATB was also arranged by A.J. Gruss (qv).*   ★
JXG-6.2tv. 2 Begräbnislieder für Kindern, No. 1; "Sei willig".   CATB, fl(ad lib) 2cl 2hn bn.
MS parts: CZ-Lla(vl), No. 2394 hud., (the T pt missing all notes).   *Possibly rescored by A.J. Gruss.*
JXG-7. 2 Grablieder, No. 1 bei Kinder ["Dass viele Kinder sterben"], No. 2 bei Erwachsenen ["Gottes Ruh,
Gottes Ruh"].   CATB, fl(F) 2cl 2hn b-tb.   MS parts: CZ-Lla(vl), No. 2421 hud.   ★
JXG-8tv. 2 Grablieder bei Erwachsenen.   Scoring varies.   MS parts: CZ-LI(vl), No. 2472 hud.   ★
   8.1tv. Schlaf geliebter Bruder ein.   CATB, 2cl 2hn bn+b-tb 2tp(clar).
   8.2tv. Er ruft nun in Frieden in Gottes Schoos.   CATB, terz-fl cl(E♭) 3cl(B♭) 2hn bn+b-tb 2tp.
JXG-9tv. 2 Grablieder beim Begräbnisse eines Vater oder Mutter.   CATB, 2cl 2hn bn.
MS parts: CZ-Lla(vl), No. 2458 hud, (the bn part is missing the notes for No. 1).   ★
   9.1tv. Ein Vater [Mutter] musste sterben.   9.2tv. Weinend, weinend, weinend, und in vollem Jammer.

*GEMROT, Jiří   *15 April 1957, Prague*
*JZG-1. Returns and Metamorphoses.   Piano, 9 winds.
Pm (Český hudební fond: Prague, 1981), (hire) score & parts.

GENARO, Ulisse
UXG-1v. Kyrie & Gloria.   TTB, 2cl 2hn tp tb organ.   MS score: I-Vsmc.   ★

*GENERALI, Pietro   *23 Oct 1773, Masserano, Vercelli - 3 Nov 1832, Novara*
PXG-1v. Litanie.   TTB(solo+rip), 2cl 2hn tp tb timp organ.   MS score: I-Vsmc.   ★
PXG-2v. Tantum ergo.   TTB(solo+rip), 2cl(A) 2hn tp tb timp organ.   MS score: I-Vsmc.   ★

GENTILUCCI, Armando   *8 Oct 1939, Lecce*
ARG-1. Trama; 1977, 1 continuous mvt.   2fl 2ob 2cl 2hn 2bn.
Pm (Ricordi: Milano, pn 132629, 1979), facsimile AutoMS score, (in "New Notation").
ARG-2. Un mutevole intreccio; 1984.   2fl 2ob 2cl 2hn 2bn.
Pm (Ricordi: Milano, pn 133631, c.1985), facsimile AutoMS score (in "New Notation").

*GENZMER, Harald   *2 Feb 1909, Blumenthal, nr Bremen*
*HQG-1. Divertimento für sinfonische Bläser.   pic 2fl 2ob ca 2cl b-cl bn 4hn 2tp 2tb tu harp timp perc.
Pm (Henry Litolff's Verlag; C.F. Peters: Frankfurt am Main, 1968), score: GB-Lbl, c.160.dd.(12).
*HQG-2. Sextett; 1966.   2cl 2hn 2bn.
Pm (Litolff/Peters: Frankfurt am Main, 1970), min. score (pn P8051a) and parts (pn P8051).
HQG-3. Chamber Concerto for viola and cello.   Solo viola & cello, 2ob 3cl 4hn 2bn.
Pc (Henry Litolff's Verlag: Frankfurt am Main, 1931), score: US-Wc.
Pm (Peters: Frankfurt am Main, 1950).

GERBER, René   *29 June 1908, Travers, Neuchâtel, Switzerland*
RYG-1. Concerto; 1949.   Piano, fl ob ca 2cl 2hn 2tp tb.   MS score: CH-Zma.
RYG-2. Concertino; 1935.   Piano, fl(pic) ob cl 2hn bn tp perc.   MS score: CH-Zma.
RYG-3. Suite, 1933.   2fl 2cl bn.   MS score: CH-Zma.

*GERHARD, Roberto   *25 Sept 1896, Valls, Catalonia - 5 Jan 1970, Cambridge*
RUG-1. Sardana I; 1928.   pic(fl) ob ca 2cl 2hn bn tp tb tu perc.   MS score & parts: GB-Lbbc.

*GERKE, August   *1790, Lüneburg - 1847, (?)*
AWG-1a. Six Pièces pour la musique turque, Oeuvre 12.   2fl 2ob 2cl(C) 2bthn 2hn 2bn cbn 2tp(clar) b-dr+cym
s-dr; (the 2bthn are *tacet* in No. 1).
Pc (Chez Breitkopf & Härtel: Leipsic [sic], pn 2064, 1804), parts: I-Fc, F.P. S.475.   ★
AWG-2. Deux Pièces pour la musique turque tiré da Requiem de Mr. le Comte V. Rzewunki, Oeuvre 2.
pic 2fl 2ob 2cl bthn 2hn 2bn cbn 2tp(clar) timp b-dr+cym s-dr.
Pc (Chez Breikopf & Härtel: Leipsic [sic], pn 2061, 1804), parts: I-Fc, F.P. S.475.   ★

GERKE, Otto   *1807 - 1878, Germany*
OXG-1. Notturno, Marcia, Adagio e Polonaise, Op. 24.   2hn 2bn.
Pm (Mompour: Bonn, sd), parts: D-B

*GEROLD, J.   *(?1820)*
JWG-1a. Beethoven: Sonate Pathètique, Op. 13, Adagio.   terz-fl ob cl(E♭) 2cl(B♭) 2hn bn 2tp crt a-crt tb euph
tambours.   MS score (by Karl Kaiser, 13 June 1877): D-DT, Mus-n 9083, (possibly a rescoring).

GERSCHEFSKI, Peter Edwin   *10 June 1909, Mendon, CN, USA*
EYG-1. Prelude Op. 6, No. 5.   2fl 2ob 2cl bn hp 3perc.
Pm (American Composers Alliance: New York, 1957).

*GERSHWIN, (Jacob) George   *25 Sept 1898, Brooklyn - 11 July 1937, Hollywood*
*GJG-1. Figured Chorale, for George White's *Scandals of 1921.*   cl 2hn 2bn vc db.   AutoMS score: US-Wc.

GHEDINI, Giorgio Federico
GFG-1a. Andrea Gabrielli: Aria della Battaglia "per sonar d'Instrumenti da Fiato - a 8".
fl fl(pic) 2ob ca 3cl b-cl 4hn 3bn 3tp 3tb b-tu.
Pm (G. Ricordi: Milano, pn P.R.673, 1954), miniature score.

GHERARDESCHI, Giuseppe *3 Nov 1759, Pistoia - 6 Aug 1815, Pistoia*
GQG-1(-3). 3 Quintetti; dedicated to "Cav. Luigi Cellesi", 1793. 2ob 2hn bn.   AutoMS: I-PS, B.124.8.
GQG-1v. Miserere. SATB, winds.   AutoMS (1786): I-PS, B.78.2.

*GIANELLA, Luigi *1778 (1788?) - 1817, Paris*
LXG-1.1/1(-1.1/3). Trois nocturnes, Oeuvre 12; C minor/major, F minor/major, G minor/major, each 1 mvt in
2 sections. fl 2bn/bn+b.
Pc (a la typographie de la syrène: Paris, sd), RISM Supp [GG 1836 I, 17], parts: GB-Lbl, g.409.gg. ★
LXG-1.2/1(-1.2/3). Trois nocturnes, Oeuvre 12; identical to KXG-1.1. 2fl/fl+vl bn.
Pc (a la typographie de la syrène: Paris, sd), RISM Supp [GG 1836 I, 18], parts: GB-Lbl, g.409.hh.
LXG-1a. Cimarosa: Il matrimonio segreto. fl 2ob 2hn 2bn.   MS parts: I-Fc, F.P. S.353.
LXG-2a. Paisiello: Nina, 12 mvts. fl 2ob 2hn 2bn.
MS score: I-Vmc, Fondo Correr, Busta B.14, No. 15 (No. 72).

GIEFFER, Willy *1930, Germany*
WYG-1. Diskontinuum; 1974. 2cl 2hn 2bn.
Pm: (W. Gerig: Cologne, *via* Breitkopf & Härtel: Wiesbaden, pn HG 1178, c.1975), score & parts.

*GIESLER, D. Victor *(1790)*
VYG-1tv. Ecce! quomodo moritur justus. CATB, fl 2cl 2hn 2bn 2tp(clar, con sordine).
MS parts (by František Czerný): CZ-Pnm, IX.D.200. ★

*GILLASPIE, Jon Alan *16 June 1950, Potsdam, New York*
*JAG-1. In Memoriam: Francis Poulenc, (1982). fl ob 2cl 2hn 2bn cbn. AutoMS score: GB-Ljag; GB-DOTams.
*JAG-2. Wolf Song, (1985).   fl ob(ca) cl cl(b-cl) 2hn 2bn cbn sampler/tape.   AutoMS score: GB-Ljag.
*JAG-3. Une Nuit dans le Palais de Tango; (1996). 2ob 2ca 2hn 2bn db/cbn.
AutoMS score: GB-Ljag.   MS score & parts: F-TOep.
*JAG-1a. Berlioz: Trois morceaux pour l'orgue Alexandre.   fl(pic) ob 2cl 2hn 2bn cbn(ad lib).
AutoMS score: GB-Ljag; score & parts: GB-DOTams.
JAG-2a. Bertie (4th Earl of Abingdon): Three Minuets. fl ob 2cl 2hn 2bn.
AutoMS score: GB-Ljag; score & parts: GB-DOTams.
JAG-3a. Donizetti: L'Elisir d'amore, overture. 2fl 2ob 2cl 2hn 2bn cbn/db.   AutoMS score: GB-Ljag.
JAG-4a. Donizetti: L'Elisir d'amore. Opera accompaniment. 2fl 2ob 2cl 2hn 2bn cbn/db.
AutoMS score: GB-Ljag.
JAG-5a. Gossec: Symphony in E♭, Op. 12, No. 5. fl 2ob 2cl 2hn 2bn cbn.
AutoMS score & parts: GB-Ljag; parts: GB-DOTams.
*JA6-6a. Joplin: Cleopha, March & Two-Step. fl ob 2cl 2hn 2bn cbn.
AutoMS score & parts: GB-Ljag; parts: GB-DOTams.
*JA6-7a. Joplin: The Entertainer. 2ob 2cl 2hn 2bn cbn.   AutoMS score & parts: GB-Ljag; parts: GB-DOTams.
*JAG-8a. Joplin: Bethena, Concert Waltz. fl ob 2cl 2hn 2bn cbn.
AutoMS score & parts: GB-Ljag; pts: GB-DOTams.
*JAG-9a. Joplin: Euphonic Sounds. 2ob 2cl 2hn 2bn cbn. AutoMS score & pts: GB-Ljag; parts: GB-DOTams.
*JAG-10a. Joplin: Stoptime Rag. fl ob 2cl 2hn 2bn cbn. AutoMS score & pts: GB-Ljag; parts: GB-DOTams.
*JAG-11a. Joplin: The Cascades. fl ob 2cl 2hn 2bn cbn. AutoMS score & pts: GB-Ljag; parts: GB-DOTams.
*JAG-12a. Joplin: Solace, a Mexican Serenade. fl ob 2cl 2hn 2bn cbn.
AutoMS score: GB-Ljag; parts: GB-DOTams.
*JAG-13a. Joplin: Great Crush Collision March. 2ob 2cl 2hn 2bn cbn.
AutoMS score & parts: GB-Ljag; parts: GB-DOTams.
*JAG-14a. Joplin: Maple Leaf Rag. 2ob 2cl 2hn 2bn cbn. AutoMS score & pts: GB-Ljag; parts: GB-DOTams.
*JAG-15a. Joplin: Eugenia. 2ob 2cl 2hn 2bn cbn. AutoMS score & parts: GB-Ljag; parts: GB-DOTams.
*JAG-16a. Joplin: Ragtime Dance. 2ob 2cl 2hn 2bn cbn. AutoMS score & pts: GB-Ljag; parts: GB-DOTams.
*JAG-17a. Joplin: Scott Joplin's New Rag. 2ob 2cl 2hn 2bn. AutoMS score & pts: GB-Ljag; pts: GB-DOTams.
*JAG-18a. Joplin: Pine Apple Rag. 2ob 2cl 2hn 2bn cbn. AutoMS score & pts: GB-Ljag; parts: GB-DOTams.
*JAG-19a. Joplin: Magnetic Rag. 2ob 2cl 2hn 2bn cbn. AutoMS score & pts: GB-Ljag; parts: GB-DOTams.
*JAG-20a. Joplin: A Breeze from Alabama - A Ragtime Two Step. 2ob 2ca 2hn 2bn db/cbn.
AutoMS score: GB-Ljag.   MS score & parts: F-TOep.
*JAG-21a. Joplin: Pleasant Moments - Rag-time Waltz. 2ob 2ca 2hn 2bn db/cbn.
AutoMS score: GB-Ljag.   MS score & parts: F-TOep.
*JAG-22a. Joplin: The Entertainer. 2ob 2ca 2hn 2bn db/cbn.
AutoMS score: GB-Ljag.   MS score & parts: F-TOep.
*JAG-23a. Mozart: Le Nozze di Figaro. Complete opera accompaniment. 2fl 2ob 2cl 2hn 2bn cbn/db.
AutoMS score & parts: GB-Ljag. Photocopy: F-TOep.
*JAG-24a. Mozart: Le Nozze di Figaro. Complete accompaniment. fl ob cl hn bn hpcd.
AutoMS score & parts: GB-Ljag.
JAG-25a. Mozart: Le Nozze di Figaro, "In quel'anni, in cui val poco". Solo hn, 2ob 2cl 2hn 2bn cbn.
AutoMS score: GB-Ljag; AutoMS parts: GB-DOTams.
JAG-26a. Rossini: La Scala di seta, overture. fl(pic) 2ob 2cl 2hn 2bn cbn.
AutoMS score: GB-Ljag; score & parts: GB-DOTams.
JAG-27a(v). Rossini: Otello, "Sommeil à ma prière". S, fl ob 2cl 2hn 2bn cbn.
AutoMS score: GB-Ljag; score & parts: GB-DOTams.
*JAG-28a. Strauss the Younger: Tales from the Vienna Woods, Op. 325. fl 2ob 2cl 2bthn 4hn 2bn db/cbn.
AutoMS score: GB-Ljag.
JAG-29a. Sullivan: Yeomen of the Guard, overture. 2fl ob 2cl 2hn 2bn cbn/vc/db. AutoMS score & pts: GB-Ljag.
JAG-30a. Sullivan: Yeomen of the Guard. Opera accompaniment. 2fl ob 2cl 2hn 2bn cbn/vc/db.
AutoMS score & parts: GB-Ljag.
JAG-31a. Suppé: Poet & Peasant, overture. fl fl(pic) 2ob 2cl 2hn 2bn cbn.   AutoMS score: GB-Ljag.
JAG-32a. A von Suppé Potpourri. 2ob 2cl 2hn 2bn cbn. AutoMS score: GB-Ljag.
JAG-33a. Verdi: Il Trovatore, Tango Paraphrase on the Miserere Scene. 2ob 2cl 2hn 2bn cbn.
AutoMS score: GB-Ljag.

GILLES, Jean *1669, Tarascon - 5 Feb 1705, Avignon*
JTG-1v. 14 Motets à grand choeur et symphonie. 4/5-part chorus; some with strings, some with 2fl 2ob 2bn.
MS: F-AIXmc; F-C; F-Pn; US-Wc.

GINZBURG, Dov *1906, Poland (resident in Israel)*
DXG-1. Cupid and Psyche. fl 2ob cl bn tp perc.
Pm (Israel Music Publications Ltd: Jerusalem, 1964), score.

*GIORGI, Andrea di *1836, Bergamo - 1900, Gandino*
AUG-1. Pezzo concertato originale con obbligazione di clarinetto.
Clarinetto obbligato, fl(Db) cl(Eb) 3cl(Bb) 2hn 5tp 2flug clavicorno+bombardino 3tb bassi timp.
MS score (by Giuseppe Mapelli of Bologna, 6 Jan 1887): I-GAN.
AUG-2. Armonia religiosa; in Ab.   cl(Eb) 2cl(Bb) 2hn clavicorno geni 2tb bombardone(F) pelitone.
AutoMS score & parts: I-GAN.
AUG-3. Sequenzia della B.V. Addolorata; in F.   fl 2cl(C) 2hn 2tp tromboni cb; organ("guida").
AutoMS score & MS parts: I-GAN.
AUG-1v. (Breve) Ave Maris Stella, a tre voci per processione; in Ab.
TTB, fl+pic 2ob 2cl 2hn 2bn 2tp 3tb bombardoni cb timp (rullante e catuba).
AutoMS score & MS parts: I-GAN, (the parts in parentheses are not in the score).
AUG-2v. (Solenne) Pange lingua, a canto unisono; in Ab.   T,T,BAR,B, fl+pic 2ob 2cl 2hn 4tp 2bombardini
3tp bombardoni, rollante e catuba.   AutoMS score & MS parts: I-GAN.
AUG-3v. Tantum ergo, a baritono solo con coro; in Eb.
BAR solo, chorus, 2fl 2ob 2cl 2hn 2bn 2tp 3tb cb timp organ.   AutoMS score & MS parts: I-GAN.
AUG-4v. (Inno) Iste confessor, a due voci per processione; in Db.
TB chorus, fl(pic) 2ob 2cl 2hn 2bn 2tp 3tb 2bomb cb timp.   AutoMS score & MA parts: I-GAN.
AUG-5v. (Piccolo) Pange lingua, a due voci per processione; in Eb.
TB chorus, fl+pic 2ob 2cl 2hn 2bn 2tp 2tb 2bomb timp, rollante e catuba.   AutoMS score & MS parts: I-GAN.
AUG-6v. Versetto (Tantum ergo, per soprano con coro a tre voci; in Bb.
TB chorus, 2fl 2ob 2cl 2hn 2tp tromboni cb timp organ.   AutoMS score & MS parts: I-GAN, (?complete).
AUG-7v. Inno (Pange lingua), a tre voci per processione; in Eb.
TTB, 2fl 2ob 2cl 2hn 2bn 2tp tromboni cb timp.   AutoMS score & MS parts: I-GAN.
AUG-8v. Inno per processione (Pange lingua); in Bb.
TTB, 2fl 2ob 2cl 2hn 2bn 2tp tromboni cb timp.   AutoMS score & MS parts: I-GAN.
AUG-9v. (Numero quatro) Litanie della B.V.M.   Solo TTB, 2fl 2ob 2cl 2hn 2bn 2tp tromboni cb timp.
AutoMS score & MS parts: I-GAN.
AUG-10v. (Solenne) Pange lingua unisono per processione; in Eb.
TB chorus, pic fl 2ob 2cl 2hn 2bn 2tp 2tb bassi.   AutoMS score & MS parts: I-GAN.
AUG-11v. Tantum ergo; in Eb.   T solo, pic fl 2ob 2cl 2hn 2bn 2tp tromboni timp organ.
AutoMS score & MS parts: I-GAN.
AUG-12v. Versetto a tenore e basso, indi duetto a tenore e baritono, con Introduzione, Intermezzi in forma di
variazione e Finale a flauto e corno in fa obbligati; in F.   Solo T, BAR, B, Solo flute & horn, fl(II) ob 2cl 2hn
2bn 2tp tromboni timp organo.   AutoMS score (31 Oct 1887) & MS parts: I-GAN.
AUG-13v. Verseto (I salutaris hostia), a tenore solo con coro ripieno; in Ab.
T solo, chorus, 2fl 2ob 2cl 2hn 2bn 2tp tromboni timp organ.   AutoMS score & MS parts: I-GAN.
AUG-14v. Kyrie, a tre voci con ripieno; in Bb.   TTB, fl 2ob 2cl 2hn 2bn 2tp 3tb organ.
AutoMS score & MS parts: I-GAN.
AUG-15v. Laudamus, Gratias e Domine Deus, per baritone con coro; in Bb.
Solo BAR, TTB chorus, fl+pic 2ob 2cl 2hn 2bn 2tp 3tb organ.   AutoMS score & MS parts: I-GAN. *A note
on p. 1 of the score states, "Servibile anche per Tantum Ergo per Baritono con Coro".*
AUG-16v. (Breve) Versetto (Tantum ergo); in Db.   T solo, TTB chorus, 2fl 2cl 2hn 2bn 2tp timp organ(obl).
AutoMS score & MS parts: I-GAN, (the score also includes a reduction for strings by the composer).
AUG-17v. Quoniam; in C.   Solo T, TTB chorus, fl+pic 2ob 2cl(C) 2hn 2tp 3tb timp; organ("guida").
AutoMS score & MS parts: I-GAN.
AUG-18v. Duetto; in Ab.   Solo BAR & B, chorus, pic fl ob 2cl 2hn 2bn 2tp tromboni cb organ.
AutoMS score & MS parts: I-GAN, (on the reverse of the score is a reduction for strings by the composer).
AUG-19v. Kyrie, a tre voci con ripieni; in D minor.   TTB, pic fl ob 2cl 2hn 2bn 2tp tromboni timp organ.
AutoMS score & MS parts: I-GAN.
AUG-20v. Ave Maris Stella, a due voci per processione; in D.   TB chorus, fi(pic) 2ob 2cl 2hn 2bn 2tp tromboni
timp cb. AutoMS score & MS parts: I-GAN. *A note on p. 1 of the score states, "Questo Inno serve anche per
l'Inno del Sacro Cuore di Gesù (Cor Arca legem continens)".*
AUG-21v. Credo; in Bb.   TTB solo & ripieno, fl(pic) 2cl 2hn 2bn 2tp 3tb timp organ.
AutoMS score (2 Jan 1886) & parts: I-GAN, (the last sheet of the score is missing).
AUG-22v. Qui sedes, meno il Quoniam a basso solo con trombone obbligato; in Ab.
B solo, trombone obbligato, fl+pic 2cl 2hn bn 2tp 2tb organ.   AutoMS score & MS parts: I-GAN.
AUG-23v. (Piccolo) Qui tollis; in G minor.   Solo T, TTB chorus, fl 2cl 2hn 2bn 2tp tromboni timp organ.
AutoMS score & MS parts: I-GAN.
AUG-24v. Domine ad adjuvandum; in C.   CATTB, fl 2cl(C) 2hn 2bn 2tp tromboni timp organ.
AutoMS score (16 April 1888) & MS parts: I-GAN.
AUG-25v. Inno lugubre, per processione; in C minor.   TTB, fl(pic) ob 2cl 2hn 2bn 2tp tromboni timp;
organ("guida").   AutoMS score & MS parts: I-GAN. *A note on p. 1 of the score states, "Servibile per Stabat
Mater, oppure anche per il Salmo Miserere".*
AUG-26v. Inno per processione; in Bb.   TTB, fl ob 2cl 2hn 2bn 2tp tromboni timp.
AutoMS score & MS parts: I-GAN.
AUG-27v. Laudamus, Gratias e Domine Deus, duetto a tenore e basso; in Db.
Solo TB, fl+pic 2cl 2hn 2bn 2tp tromboni timp organ.   AutoMS score & MS parts: I-GAN.
AUG-28v. Salve Regina; in Eb.   TTB, fl 2cl(C) 2hn 2tp tromboni cb timp organ.
AutoMS score & MS parts: I-GAN.

AUG-29v. Tantum ergo, duetto; in F.   Solo ST/TT, fl 2cl 2hn 2bn 2tp tromboni timp; organ("guida").
AutoMS score (16 Dec 1893) & MS parts: I-GAN.
AUG-30v. (Salmo) Confitebor tibi Domine; in C.   Solo T, coro di ripieno, pic fl 2cl(C) 2hn 2tp tb cb timp.
AutoMS score (1880, although possibly composed in 1864) & MS parts: I-GAN, (?complete).
AUG-31v. Inno per verpro ["Inno proprio di S. Giuseppe e di S. Antonio di Padova"]; in C.
TTB, fl 2cl(C) 2hn 2tp tromboni cb timp.   AutoMS score & MS parts: I-GAN.
AUG-32v. Pange lingua (oppure: Stabat Mater), Inno a quatro voci per processione; in B♭.
STB, fl cl(E♭) 2cl(B♭) 2hn 2tp tromboni timp.   AutoMS score & MS parts: I-GAN.
AUG-33v. Sanctus, Benedictus e Agnus Dei; in C.   TTB, fl 2cl(C) 2hn 2tp tromboni timp organ.
AutoMS score & MS parts: I-GAN.
AUG-34v. Versetto (Tantum ergo) a basso con coro; in D.   Solo B, chorus, fl 2cl(A) 2hn 2tp tromboni timp org.
AutoMS score & MS pts: I-GAN. *A p. 1 note states, "Servibile anche per il Salmo "Lauda Jerusalem Dominum".*
AUG-35v. Domine ad adjuvandum; in C.   TTB, fl 2cl(C) 2hn 2tp tromboni cb organ.
AutoMS score & MS parts: I-GAN.
AUG-36v. Pange lingua, a tre voci per processione; in B♭.   TTB, fl 2cl 2hn 2tp tb timp organ.
AutoMS score: I-GAN.
AUG-37v. Domine ad adjuvandum; in C.   TTB, fl 2cl(C) 2hn 2tp tromboni cb timp.
AutoMS score & MS parts: I-GAN.
AUG-38v. (Salmo) Laudate Dominum (oppure: Tantum ergo), versetto a baritono solo con coro nel finale; in E.
BAR solo, chorus, fl 2cl(A) 2hn 2tp tromboni timp.   AutoMS score & MS parts: I-GAN.
AUG-39v. Inno (Pange lingua), a quatro voci per processione; in E♭.   SATB, fl 2cl 2hn 2tp tb timp.
AutoMS score & MS parts: I-GAN.
AUG-40v. Litanie dell B.V.   TB chorus, fl 2cl(C) 2hn tb.   AutoMS score & MS parts: I-GAN.

*GIORGI, Andrea di & GIORGI, Federico di
FAG-1v. Lungo inno a quatro voci per processione; in E♭.   SATB, 2fl 2cl 2hn 2tp tb timp.
MS score & pts: I-GAN.

*GIPPS, Ruth *20 Feb, 1921, Bexhill, UK*
Tickerage Press music can be obtained via Emerson Music, Windmill Farm, Ampleforth, Yorks, YO6 4HF, UK.
RZG-1. Seascape, Op. 53; 1 continuous mvt.   2fl ob ca 2cl(A) 2hn 2bn
Pm (Keith Prowse: London; Sam Fox Publishing Co: New York, 1961), score & pts.
Pm (Tickerage Press: Uckfield, East Sussex, c.1982), score & parts.   (Copy in GB-Lmic)
*RZG-2. Wind Sinfonietta, Op. 73; 4 mvts.   2fl(2pic) ob ob/ca 2cl 2hn 2bn (tam-tam ad lib).
Pm (Tickerage Press: Uckfield, East Sussex, 1989), score & parts.
*RZG-3. Wind Octet, Op. 65; 3 mvts.   2ob 2cl(A) 2hn 2bn.
Pm (Tickerage Press: Uckfield, East Sussex, 1983), score & parts.

GIRARDI, ( )
ZZG-1f. Marcia (with Trio & Coda), 1847.   Instrumentation unknown, here only: fl bn tp(II) tb vc vlne timp.
MS parts: I-Vsmc.   ★

GIROUST (Giroult, Giroux), François *1738 - 1799*
FCG-1v. Chant de Versailles; ("Quel accents! quels transports"), P.980.   Voice, 2cl 2hn (2)bn.
Pc (Rec des époques: Paris, c.1799), liv. 1, No. 10, pp. 23 - 25, score: F-Pn, H.2 15,10.   ★

GIULIANO, Giuseppe *1948, Italy*
GLG-1. Cela sans plus.   2ob 2cl 2hn 2bn.
Pm (Suvini-Zerboni: Milano, pn S9112Z, 1982), score & parts.

GIURANNA, Barbara Elena *18 Nov 1902, Palermo*
BEG-1. Episodi; 1942.   2fl 2ob 2cl 2hn 2bn 2tp timp piano.   Pm (Ricordi: Milano, sd).

*GLASER, Werner Wolf *16 April 1910*
WWG-1. Konsert; 1966.   fl ob 3cl sax 4hn 2bn 4tp 3tb tu timp.   MS score: S-Sic.
WWG-2. Marsch i blåsväder: "Aufforderung zum Marsch"; 1974.   2fl 2ob 2cl 2hn 2bn perc.   MS score: S-Sic.
WWG-3. Capriccio e canzone; 1978.   2cl 2bn.   MS score: S-Sic.

*GLASS, Philip *31 Jan 1937, Baltimore*
PYG-1. Glassworks.   2fl s-sax t-sax 2hn pf vla vc.
Pm (Dunvagen Music Publishers, via Music Sales: 1981), hire score & parts.
PYG-2. Floe.   fl s-sax t-sax 2hn pf/DX7 *(DX7 = Yamaha DX7 synthesizer).*
Pm (Dunvagen Music Publishers, via Music Sales: 1983), hire score & parts.

*GLEISSNER, Franz Johann *6 April 1761, Neustadt an der Waldnab - 18 Sept 1818, Munich*
FOG-1. Journal de Musique militaire.   2cl(D) 2cl(A) 2hn 2bn.
Pc (Götz: München, Mannheim, Düsseldorf, sd), parts: D-BFb, G-le 31.
FOG-2. 6 Pièces d'harmonie.   fl 2cl 2hn bn.
Pc (chés [sic] J. André: Offenbach s/M, pn 1694, 1803), RISM Supp [GG 2601a], parts: H-Bn, Z 44,291;
GB-Ljag, (microfilm).   ★
Pc (Johann André: Offenbach s/M, pn 3890, 1819), RISM [G 2602], pts: D-OF.

*GLUCK, Christoph Willibald *2 July 1714, Erasbach - 15 Nov 1787, Vienna*
CWG-1v. De profundis, in D minor, Graduale vel Offertorium, (W. C Nr. 1, S.154).
S(I),A+S(II),T,B, ob hn bn a-tb t-tb b-tb vla vc(s) b.
MS vocal score & instrumental parts (by Johann Baptist Schröfl, c.1825): D-Mbm, Mf 549, (scored for:
SATB, ob hn 2bn 3tb vla vc(s) cb).   MS parts (with printed vocal parts): D-Dl, Mus.3030-D-4.
Pc (À l'imprimerie du conservatoire de musique: Paris, c.1805), score: GB-Lbl, (2 copies), E.601.g.(4),
Hirsch IV.746.   ★
Pc (Cianchettini & Sperati: London, c.1809), score: GB-Lbl, D.298.b, (copy owned by *Sir* Henry R. Bishop).
Pc (Chez P. Porro: Paris, c.1820), score & parts (Musique sacre. no. 6): GB-Lbl, (3 copies), R.M.14.f.4.(6),
H.1028.b.(2), Hirsch IV.747, (score only).
Pc (Chez N. Simrock: Bonn, c.1870), score: GB-Lbl, Hirsch IV.745.

*GNOCCHI, Pietro *(?1690) - 1775, Brescia*
PZG-1v. Miserere; in G minor. CATB, 2ob bn 2vla vlne.
AutoMS score & MS parts: I-BRd, palch. 3-50/VI.
PZG-2v. Benedictus. CCATB, 2ob bn 2vla vlne. AutoMS score & MS parts: I-BRd, palch. 3-44/III.

*GODDARD, Mark Timothy Robert *28 June 1960, Aylesbury, UK.*
*MAG-1. Fanfare, Romance and Jig, 1986. 2cl 2hn 2bn.
MS score & parts: GB-DOTams. Pm: (Spartan Press, Oxford, pn SP 116, 1988), score & parts.
*MAG-2. Marshall's Diversion; (published as *Freestyle*). 2cl 2hn 2bn. MS score & pts: GB-DOTams.
Pm: (Spartan Press, Monmouth, 1995), score & pts, (with alternative instrumentation).
MAG-1a. Verdi: La Forza del destino, overture. fl 2ob 2cl 2hn 2bn.
Pm (Spartan Press, Oxford, pn SP 162, 1989), score & parts.
*MAG-2a. Sousa: Washington Post. 2cl 2hn 2bn.
MS score & parts (1986): GB-DOTams. Pm (Spartan Press, Oxford, pn SP 164, 1989), score & parts.
*MAG-1va. Completion (with A.M. Stoneham & R. Eccles) of C.M. von Weber: Trauermusik, (CMW-3v).
BAR solo, SATB chorus, fl 2cl 2bn 2hn 2tp b-tb timp. MS score & parts: GB-DOTams.

*GODFREY, Charles, *the Elder 22 Nov 1790, Kingston, Surrey, UK - 12 Dec 1863, London*
CXG-1a. Auber: Gustave. Overture, Finale (Act I), Galop. pic(F/E♭) cl(E♭) 3cl(B♭) 2hn 2bn serp;
(ad lib: cl(B♭) 2tp a-tb t-tb b-tb drums cym tri).
Pc (D'Almaine & Co.: London, 1834), parts: GB-Lbl, h.129.(1), (2).

*GODFREY, William *(1780) We have not linked him to the famous family of bandmasters.*
WXG-1. The Thrush, A Favorite Rondo. pic(oblig) 2cl 2hn (2)bn serp.
Pc (H. Robinson: London, 1804), score: GB-Lbl, h.111.(12). ★

GOEB, Roger John *1914, USA*
RJG-1. Concertante IIIb; 1951. Viola, fl ob cl 2hn bn 2tp tb tu. MS score: US-NYamc.
RJG-2. Winds Playing; 1988. fl ob cl 2hn bn 2tp tb tu. MS score: US-NYamc.

GOEDECKE, Hermann *(?1800)*
HWG-1m. Marsch; in E♭. pic 2ob cl(E♭) cl(B♭ solo) 3cl(B♭) 4hn 2bn 2tp 3tb bomb/b-hn b-dr s-dr tri cym.
MS parts: D-DT, Mus-h 3 G 19.

*GOEHR, Alexander *10 Aug 1932, Berlin*
AYG-1. 3 Pieces from *Arden Must Die*, Op. 21a. 3fl 3ob 4cl 4hn 3bn 3tp 3tb tu harp timp 4perc.
Pm (B. Schott's Söhne: Mainz, pn 11003, sd), score.
AYG-2. Chaconne, Op. 35. 2fl 2ob ca cl(E♭) cl 2hn 2bn cbn 3tp 3tb.
Pm (B. Schott's Söhne: Mainz), hire score & parts (copy of score in GB-Lmic).
AYG-3. Lyric piece, Op. 36. fl ob cl 2hn bn 2tp tb tu db.
Pm (B. Schott's Söhne: Mainz, pn 11279, sd), score.
AYG-4. Variations on Bach's Sarabande from the English Suite in E; 1990. 2cl 2sax 2bn 2tp tb timp.
Pm (B. Schott's Söhne: Mainz, 1990).

*GÖLLER, ( )
XYG-1. [untitled (?) Parthia in E♭], 12 mvts. 2cl 2hn bn. MS parts: D-DO, Mus.Ms.542. ★
*The attribution "v[on]. Göller" has been added in another hand at the beginning of the cl I part; at the end of
this part is the note, in the copyist's hand, "Dell: S: Forstmeyero [sic]".*

*GOEPFERT, Carl (Karl, Charles) Andreas (André) *16 Jan 1768, Rampad - 11 April 1818, Meiningen*
*CAG-1. Harmonie. 2ob/cl 2cl(C) 2hn 2bn tp serp.
MS parts (post-6 June 1800 - c.1801): F-Pn, Vm7 4951. MS score (modern copy): GB-Ljag. ★
   1.1. 10 Marches; (No. 10 is a Todten Marsch). No. 3, 3rd section: pic replaces cl(I); No. 5: fl replaces cl(I).
   1.2. 15 Dances.
   VI Sinfonien [parts titled: Parthia I - VI].
   1.3. Parthia I; in F, 4 mvts.
   1.4. Parthia II; in C, 3 mvts.
   1.5. Parthia III; in C, 3 mvts.
   1.6. Parthia IV; in C, 4 mvts. 2tp(clar) rather than one in mvt 4 ("La Caccia").
   1.7. Parthia V; in C, 4 mvts.
   1.8. Parthia VI; in C minor/major, 4 mvts.
CAG-2. Dix-huit Pièces. ob/fl 2cl 2hn bn tp cb/serp. (fl replaces ob in No. 3, p-fl replaces ob in No. 4).
Pc (André: Offenbach s/M, pn 3198, 1814), RISM [G 2953], parts: D-OF; NL-DHgm, hk 19 C 4. ★
CAG-3, 4. Douze Pièces, Op. 26, Nos. 1, 2; 12 mvts each. 2cl 2hn bn.
Pc (André: Offenbach s/M, pn 3129, 3130, 1813/14), RISM [G 2943], pts: D-OF; DK-A; NL-DHgm, hk 19 C 4. ★
CAG-5. Cassation. ob 2cl 2hn 2bn 2db. MS parts: D-BE.
CAG-1a. Cherubini: Les deux Journées, 6 Pièces. fl 2cl 2hn bn tp serp.
Pc (André: Offenbach s/M, pn 3191, 1814), RISM Supp [CC 2028 I, 145], parts: D-AB.
CAG-2a. Mozart: Lieder (as "Six Pièces d'Harmonie"), N° 1. 2ob/fl 2cl 2hn bn serp/bn (tp ad lib).
Pc (N. Simrock: Bonn; H. Simrock: Paris, pn 456, 1806), RISM [M 5426], pts: D-B, DMS.86.548; CH-E.
   2.1a. Das Traumbild, K.530. 2.2a. Des kleinen Friedrichs Geburtstag, K.529.
   2.3a. Sehnsucht nach dem Frühlinge, K.596. 2.4a. Lorenz Schneider: Vergiss mein nicht!, K.C.08.06.
   2.5a. Die Verschweigung, K.518. 2.6a. Verdankt sei es dem Glanz, K.392.
CAG-3a. Mozart: Lieder (as "Six Pièces d'Harmonie"), N° II. 2ob/fl 2cl 2hn bn serp/bn (2tp ad lib).
Pc (N. Simrock: Bonn; H. Simrock: Paris, pn 457, 1806), RISM [M 5415 = M 5414 & M 5416], parts: CH-E;
D-B; D-LEm, Poel.mus. 106, (Note: D-LEm holds only N° II).
   3.1a. Gesellenreise, K.468. 3.2a. Die kleine Spinnerin, K.531. 3.3a. An die Einsamkeit, K.391 (340d).
   3.4a. Im Frühlingsanfange, K.597. 3.5a. Das Lied der Trennung, K.519.
   3.6a. Arietta for Bass: "Männer suchen stets", K.433 (416c).

CAG-4.1a. Mozart: Pièces d'Harmonie . . . arrangées d'après divers airs et chansons de W.A. Mozart; 6 mvts. ob 2cl(C) 2hn 2bn tp.
Pc (André: Offenbach s/M, pn 1798, 1803), RISM [M 5422], parts: A-Wgm, VIII 29300, (Köchel's copy; the last page of the bn I part is damaged, affecting 2 systems); D-OF; GB-Ljag(w), (missing cl I & titlepage).
    4.1/1a. Abendempfindung, K.523.   4.1/2a. Das Veilchen, K.476.   4.1/3a. An Chloe, K.524.
    4.1/4a. Variations on "Lison dormait" [from Dezéde's opera, *Julie*], K.264.
    4.1/5a. Oiseaux si tous les ans, K.307.
    4.1/6a. Ein deutsches Kriegslied, "Ich möchte wohl der Kaiser sein", K.539.
CAG-4.2a. Mozart: Pièces d'Harmonie . . . arrangées d'après divers airs et chansons de W.A. Mozart; 6 mvts. ob 2cl 2hn 2bn tp.
Pc (Vernay: Charenton, pn 179, sd, c.1804), parts: F-Pn, Vm 27 1872; GB-Ljag (photocopy).
    4.2/1a. Abendempfindung, K.523.   4.2/2a. Das Veilchen, K.476.   4.2/3a. An Chloe, K.524.
    4.2/4a. Trio, Leibes Mandel, wo is's Bandel, K.441.   4.2/5a. Oiseaux si tous les ans, K.307.
    4.2/6a. Ein deutsches Kriegslied, "Ich möchte wohl der Kaiser sein", K.539, (as "Meine Wünsche").
CAG-5a. Mozart: Sinfonie in D ("Paris", K.297), "Sinfonie en Harmonie". 2ob/fl 2cl(C) 2hn 2bn/(bn serp) tp.
MS parts: D-HER, Mus.N.1:6, (missing bassoons).
Pc (N. Simrock: Bonn, pn 415, 1805-06), RISM [M 5578], pts: CZ-Bm(au), A.18.828; D-HR, HR III 4 1/2 2° 387; D-Rtt, (incomplete: missing 2hn 2bn tp).
Pm (KGS), fiche (2368), D-HR copy.
Pm (Karthuse-Schmülling Verlag: Kamen, 1993), ed. Uwe Müller, score (pn 0103a) & parts (pn 0103b).
*****CAG-6a.** Mozart: Gran Partita, K.361 (with an extra, 3rd, Trio to the 2nd Menuet). 2ob 2cl 2hn 2bn cb/cbn.
Pc (N. Simrock, pn 994, 1813), pts: A-Wn(hob); B-Bc; D-HR, HR III 4 1/2 2° 610; GB-DOTams; NL-DHgm, hk 19 C 4; S-Skma.
MS parts: CZ-Pnm, XX.F.55, (missing ob II); D-Rtt, W.A.Mozart 19.
Pm (KGS), fiche (2733), D-HR copy.
*****CAG-7a.** Mozart: Piano Sonata in A, K.331/3, as "Marche à la turque". pic 2ob/fl 2cl(C) 2hn bn serp tp b-dr.
Pc (N. Simrock: Bonn, pn 421, 1804), RISM [M 6909], parts: A-Wweinmann.
MS parts (as "Allegrini alla Turca"): D-Rtt, Sammelband 14, No. 70.
Pm (Doblinger: Wien, 1995), ed. Bastiaan Blomhert, score & parts.
*****CAG-8a.** Mozart: 6 Marches. 2ob/fl 2cl(C) 2hn 2bn tp(clar) serp b-dr.
Pc (N. Simrock: Bonn; H. Simrock: Paris, pn 420, 1804), RISM [M 5719], parts: A-Wweinmann; D-LEm; F-Pn, Vm 26 9233, (2 copies). *Also possibly issued in single numbers from the same plates; D-LEm apparently holds a copy of No. 2 in this format, RISM [M 5664].*
    8.1a. K.408/1, (K7.383e).   8.2a. K.335/1, (K7.320a).   8.3a. K.408/3, (K7.383F).   8.4a. K.335/2, (K7.320a).
    8.5a. La Clemenza di Tito, Act I, No. 4 (K.621/4).   8.6a. Idomeneo, Act I, No. 8 (K366/8).
*****CAG-9a.** Steibelt: Combat Naval. 2ob 2cl 2hn 2bn, (ad lib: tp serp b-dr).
Pc (N. Simrock: Bonn; H. Simrock: Paris, pn 346, 1803), RISM [S 5304], parts: A-Wmi; CH-N, 50.1591; D-AB, (missing ob 1); D-HR, HR III 4 1/2 2° 387; D-Bds; D-Dl; F-Pn, K.1852; H-KE, 2048; S-J.
Pm (KGS), fiche (2367), D-HR copy.
CAG-1ad. Neukomm: Marcia, in C. 2pic 2ob 3cl(C) 2hn 2bn 2tp b-tb+serp+cbn b. MS parts (c.1820): D-Rtt, Sammelband 14, No. 71. *Goepfert's name appears in pencil in the cl(Eb) part; however, this is clearly a copyit's error and, in fact, refers to CAG-7a which precedes it in Sm. 14.*

GÖTTLING, ( )
XZG-1. 6 Harmoniestücke. ob 2cl 2hn 2bn.
MS parts: D-Bds.

GÖTZ, František (Franz, Francesco) *29 July 1755, Strasniče, Bohemia - 17 Dec 1815, (?Kroměříž)*
FYG-1. Musica â [sic] la Turca in C; 9 mvts. 2pic 2cl 2hn 2bn 2tp tp(prin) b-dr tondi["plates" = cym], tamburino. MS parts: CZ-KRa, A3869/IV.B.33. ★

*****GOŁĄBEK, Jakub** *1739, Silesia - 30 March 1789, Kraków*
JYG-1. Parthia in C; 3 mvts. 2cl 2hn bn.
MS parts: PL-S, A.VII.II.(251), (missing cl II). ★
Pm (In: *Źróda do historii muzyki polsiej*, Vol 4): (Polskie Wydawnictwo Muzyczne: Kraków, 1961), pp. 288 - 296, edited & cl II part composed by Karol Mrowiec, score.

GOLD, Morton *1933, USA*
MNG-1. A Song of Praise. 2ob 2cl 2hn 2bn.
Pm (Transcontinental Music Publishers: New York, pn 9702152, c.1972).

*****GOLLER, Martin,** *OSB 1764 - 1836, Innsbruck*
MOG-1v. Tantum ergo, Innsbruck 1829. CATB, 2ob 2cl 2bn tp timp organ.
MS parts (c.1840): D-FÜS 22, (included in a Tantum ergo by Fischer). ★

GOLLER, V.
VZG-1v. Zweite einstimmige Messe mit Orgel- oder Harmoniebegleitung, Op. 63. Instrumentation unknown.
Pc (Alfred Coppenrath's Verlag (H. Pawelek): Regensburg; J. Fischer & Bro.: New York, pn H.P. 1297, sd), vocal score: D-Tl, Gg 191.

GOLUB, Peter *1952, USA*
PTG-1. Liquid Shapes; 1979. 2fl 2ob 2cl 2hn 2bn. MS score: US-NYamc.

GOODMAN, Alfred Alexander Grant *1 March 1920, Berlin (now resident in the USA)*
AGG-1. 5 Aphorismes; 1977. 2ob 2cl 2hn 2bn.
MS score: D-Mv.

GOOSEN, Jacques G. *1952, Holland*
JCG-1. Bläsermusik in 2 Sätzen; 1980/81. 2fl cl 2hn bn tp 2tb.
Pm (Donemus: Amersterdam, 1981), score & parts.

*GOOSSENS, *Sir* (Aynsley) Eugène *26 May 1893, London - 13 June 1962, Hillingdon*
*AEG-1. Fantasy for nine winds, Op. 36 (40); 1924. fl ob 2cl 2hn 2bn tp.
Pc (J. Curwen & Sons: London, 1926), score: GB-Lbl, g.1211.(9).
Pm (New revised edition:) (Alphonse Leduc et Cie,: Paris, 1961), score (pn BL 855): F-Pn; GB-Lbl, e.668.ee.(3).

GORLI, Sandro *19 June, 1948, Como*
SXG-1. Serenata Secondo per doppio quintetto di fiati; 1976, 1 continuous mvt.
Quintet 1: fl(C) ob ob(ca) cl(Bb/Eb) bn; Quintet 2: fl(C/G) cl(b-cl) 2hn bn.
Pm (Suvini-Zerboni: Milano, pn S.8244Z., 1976), facsimile AutoMS score.

*GOSSEC, François Joseph *17 Jan 1734, Vergnies, Hainault, Belgium - 16 Feb 1829, Passy, nr Paris*
*FJG-1, 2. Piéces pour . . . S.A.S. Mgr. Le Prince De Condé. 2cl 2hn 2bn.
  FJG-1. Andante.   AutoMS score: F-Pn, MS. 1436.   MS (modern score): GB-Ljag. ★
  FJG-2. La grande Chassę de Chantilly.   MS pts: F-Pn, MS. 1490 a-f.   MS (modern copy): L-jag. ★
Pm (In: Georges Cucuel: *Étude sur un orchestre au XVIIIme siècle*. Librairie Fischbacher: Paris 1913), score:
F-Pn; GB-Lbl (main library), 7896.g.47.
FJG-3. Simphonie à 6, Eb. 2cl 2hn 2bn. AutoMS score: F-Pn, MS. 1436(2).   MS pts: F-Pn, MS. 1490 a-f. ★
*FJG-4. Chasse d'Hÿlas et Silvie. 2cl 2hn 2bn.
AutoMS score: F-Pn, MS.1436(3).   MS (modern score): GB-Ljag. ★
Pm (Heugel: Paris, 1970), score & parts: F-Pn, H. 32060.
*FJG-5. La Bataille. 2cl 2hn 2bn.   AutoMS pts: F-Pn, MS. 1491 a-f.   MS (modern score): GB-Ljag. ★
*FJG-6. Cosac (Turkana). 2cl 2hn 2bn.
AutoMS score: F-Pn, MS. 1436, (f.15b).   MS (modern score): GB-Ljag. ★

Revolutionary Works
*FJG-7. Symphonie en ut; [C major; performance 10 Aug 1794], P.2301.
2p-fl 2ob 2cl 2hn (2)bn 2tp a-tb t-tb b-tb serp, buccin, tuba corva, timp.
MS score: F-Pn, MS. 1772. ★
MS parts (for: 2p-fl(6) 4cl(24) 2hn(4) bn(6) 3tb serp(4), buccin/tuba corva cb(6)): F-Pn, H2. 154.
Pm (Swanzy), pp. 168 - 176, score.
Pm (Mercury Music Corp.: New York, s.d), score & parts.
*FJG-8. Sinfonie Concertante; P.2279. 2 solo ob, 2cl 2hn 2bn 2tp a-tb t-tb b-tb serp timp.
MS parts: F-Pn, L. 18133. ★
FJG-9. Symphonie militaire; (perf 30 May 1794), P.2288. 2p-fl 2fl 2ob 2cl 2hn 2bn 2tp serp/cb timp b-dr.
Pc (Mag de mus fêtes nat: Paris, floreal an II, 1794), liv. 2, No. 1, pts: F-Pn, (2 copies), H2. 2,1, Vm7 7025. ★
Pm (Mercury Music Corp.: New York), score & parts.
Pm (University of Southern California Press: Berkeley), ed. William Schaefer.
*FJG-1m. Marche lugubre; P.2270.
2p-fl 2cl 2hn 2bn 2tp a-tb t-tb b-tb serp, tuba corva, cloche(tam-tam), b-dr t-dr.
MS score: F-Pn, H2. 143 a-q. ★
Pc (Mag de mus fêtes nat: Paris, ventôse an III, 1795), liv. 12, No. 1, pts (omits cloche, tuba corva): F-Pn, H2. 12.
Pm (In: Constant Pierre. *Musique exécutée dans les fêtes nationales.* 1893, p. 45), score.
Pm (Swanzy), pp. 262 - 265, score.
Pm (Franco Colombo: New York, sd), score & parts, (No. 4 of "Gossec Suite").
*FJG-2m. Marche funèbre; P.2280. 2p-fl 2cl 2hn 2bn 2tp a-tb t-tb b-tb serp, tuba corva, tam-tam, (b-)dr/timp.
MS parts (first performed 20 Nov 1793): F-Pn, H2.14. ★
Pc (Ozi, Paris, 1817), parts: (?lost).
FJG-3m. Marche religieuse; P.2272.   2fl 2cl(C) 2hn 2bn tp serp; (Lefèvre: bn(III)+serp same as bn(1+II) pt).
Pc (In: J.X. Lefèvre. JXL-1m(-12)m, between the marches & pas redoublés. c.1792), pts: F-Pn, Vm7 7100.
Pc (Mag de mus fêtes nat: Paris, fructidor an II, 1794), liv. 6, No. 3, pts: F-Pn, (2 copies), H2.6, Vm7 7050. ★
FJG-4m. Marche victorieuse; P.2304. 2p-fl 2cl 2hn 2bn serp tp.
Pc (Mag de mus fêtes nat: Paris, fructidor an II, 1794), liv. 6, No. 4, pts: F-Pn, (2 copies), H2.6, Vm7 7051. ★
FJG-5m. Marche; in C, P.2314. 2p-fl 2cl 2hn 2bn tp serp.
Pc (Mag de mus fêtes nat: Paris, nivôse an III, 1795), liv. 10, No. 3, parts: F-Pn, H2.10; F-Nm, Vol 22207. ★
FJG-6m. March; in F, P.2317. 2p-fl 2cl 2hn 2bn tp serp.
Pc (Mag de mus fêtes nat: Paris, pluviôse an III, 1795), liv. 11, No. 3, parts: F-Pn, H2.11. ★
*FJG-1.1mv. Hymne à l'Être suprême; ("Source de véreté"), P.47.
SATB chorus, p-fl fl 2ob 2cl 2hn 2bn 2tp a-tb t-tb b-tb serp buccin, tuba corva, b-dr cym, tambour turc.
AutoMS score (stanzas 1 & 5): F-Pn, MS. 1461. ★
MS parts: F-Pn, H2. 83 a-n, (incomplete; TB, 2cl 2hn 2bn tp).
MS score (reconstructed by Pierre, stanzas 2 & 4; stanza 4 remains incomplete): F-Pn.
*FJG-1.2mv. Hymne à l'Être suprême; (Père de l'univers"), P.48.
SATB chorus, (2)p-fl (2)fl 2ob 2cl 2hn 2bn 2tp a-tb t-tb b-tb serp, b-dr, cym, tambour turc.
AutoMS score: F-Pn, MS. 1461. ★
Pc (Mag de mus fêtes nat: Paris, messidor an II, 1794), liv. 4, No. 2, RISM [G 3123], score (chorus) &
instrumental parts: D-AB; F-Pn, (4 or 5 copies including:) H2. 4,2, Vm7 7039.
FJG-2mv. Aux mânes de la Gironde; P.108.
Solo voice, ATB trio, SATB chorus, 2p-fl 2fl 2ob 3cl 4hn 2bn 2tp a-tb t-tb b-tb serp cb timp.
AutoMS score: F-Pn, MS. 1460.   MS parts (missing 2ob cb timp): F-Pn, H2. 104 a-w.
*FJG-3mv. Te Deum; P.3. ATB chorus, 2p-fl 2ob 2cl 2hn 2bn 2tp a-tb t-tb b-tb serp 2vla timp cym b-dr, "gros
tambour", tonnerre("thunder"). AutoMS score: F-Pn, MS. 1430. ★
FJG-4mv. Domine salvum fac. ATB chorus, 2p-fl 2ob 2cl 2hn 2bn serp 2tp a-tb t-tb b-tb 2vla timp cym, gros
tambour, b-dr, tonnerre("thunder"). AutoMS score: F-Pn, MS 1430 appendix. ★
FJG-5mv. Choeur patriotique, Le triomphe de la loi; P.16.
ATB chorus, 2p-fl 2ob 2cl 2hn 2bn 2tp a-tb t-tb b-tb serp buccin, tuba corva, b-dr cym.
AutoMS score: F-Pc, MS 1463. ★
Pc (Mag de mus fêtes nationales: Paris, floréal an II, 1794), liv. 2, No. 2, RISM [G 3128], score & parts (omits
a-tb t-tb buccin, tuba corva): D-AB; F-Pc, H2.2; F-Pn, Vm7 7026; F-Nm, Vol 22207; US-Wc, (score).

FJG-6mv. Choeur patriotique exécuté à la translation de Voltaire au Panthéon français en 1791; P.8.
ATB chorus, 2ob 2cl 2hn 2bn 2tp a-tb t-tb b-tb serp timp, "petites et grandes trompes antiques".
AutoMS score: F-Pn, MS. 1463. _"Petites et grandes trompes antiques" = buccin & tuba corva._ ★
Pc (Mag de mus fêtes nat: Paris, 1794), RISM [G 3127], score & parts: D-AB, (score & 11 parts);
F-Pn, (2 copies) H2. 80 a-q, Vm7 16901 (score & 13 parts).
FJG-7mv. Hymne à l'Être suprême; P.49. Solo voice, chorus, 2p-fl 2fl 2ob 2cl 2hn 2bn serp 2tp 2tp a-tb t-tb b-tb.
Pc (Mag de mus fêtes nat: Paris, messidor an II, 1794), liv. 4, No. 2, score (chorus) & instrumental parts: D-AB;
F-Pn, (2 copies), H2. 4.3, Vm7 7038. ★
Pc (for: Voice, 2cl 2hn 2bn:) (Rec des époques: Paris, c.1799), liv. 1, No. 22, score: F-Pn, H2. 15,22.
FJG-8mv. Chant funèbre sur la mort de Ferraud; 1795, P.3119.
Solo voice, male chorus, 2fl 2ob 2cl 4hn 2bn 2tp a-tb t-tb b-tb serp.
MS parts (missing chorus, ob I & II, hn II): F-Pn, H2.100 a-p. MS score (reconstructed by Pierre): F-Pn. ★
FJG-9mv. Hymne à la Victoire; 1796, P.113.
SATB chorus, 2p-fl 2ob 2cl 2hn (2)bn 2tp a-tb t-tb b-tb serp buccin, tuba corva, timp.
AutoMS score: F-Pn, MS. 1463. MS parts: F-Pn, H2. 121 a-v. ★
FJG-10mv. Chant martial pour la Fête de la Victoire.
Solo voice with SATB chorus (refrain only), 2fl 2ob 2cl 2hn 2bn 2tp a-tb t-tb b-tb serp, tuba corva, timp.
AutoMS score: F-Pn, MS. 1463. MS parts: F-Pn, H2. 105 a-s. ★
FJG-11.1mv. Chant [Choeur] à la Liberté; 1792, P.12. SSATB chorus, p-fl fl cl 4hn 2bn a-tb t-tb b-tb serp timp.
MS pts: F-Pn, H2.103 a-r [and] H2.68. _Adapted by Gossec from his opera,_ Le Triomphe de la République. ★
FJG-11.2mv. Chant pour la Fête de Chateau vieux; P.13. Voice, 2cl(C) 2hn 2bn(divisi 3 bars only).
Pc (Rec des époques: Paris, c.1799), liv. 1, No. 4, pp. 9 - 10, score: F-Pn, H2. 15.4. ★
FJG-12mv. Rondo [sic: Ronde] nationale; 1792, P.13. SATB chorus, p-fl fl 2cl 4hn 2bn a-tb t-tb b-tb serp timp.
MS parts: F-Pn, H2.103 a-r, (No. II). _Adapted by Gossec from his opera,_ Le Triomphe de la République. ★
Pc (for: Voice, 2cl 2hn 2bn:) (Rec des époques: Paris, c.1799), liv. 1, No. 8, score: F-Pn, H2. 15,8.
FJG-13mv. Hymne à la Liberté; ?1793, P.18. SSATB chorus, 2p-fl 2cl 2hn 2bn 2tp a-tb t-tb b-tb serp timp.
MS score (by Pierre): F-Pn.
Pc (Mag de mus fêtes nat: Paris, 1795), liv. 15, RISM [G 3133], score (chorus) & instrumental parts: D-AB;
F-Pn, (5 - 8 copies including:) H2. 35,8. ★
FJG-14mv. Hymne à l'Humanité, P.102. SATB chorus, 2fl 2cl 2hn 2bn 2tp a-tb t-tb b-tb serp cb.
MS parts: F-Pn, H2. 106 a-s. ★
FJG-15mv. Choeur ("Quel peuple immense"); 1793, P.24.
SATB chorus, 2p-fl 2cl 2hn 2bn 2tp a-tb t-tb b-tb serp timp. MS score: F-Po, No. 350. ★
FJG-16mv. Le Chant de 14 juillet; 1790, P.6. ATB chorus, 2fl 2cl 2hn 2bn 2tp a-tb t-tb b-tb serp.
MS score (by Pierre): F-Pn.
Pc (Mag de mus fêtes nat: Paris, c.1796), liv 17, parts: F-Pn, H2. 37,17; F-Nm, Vol 22208. ★
FJG-17mv. Hymne à la Nature exécuté à la fête de la Réunion du 10 août an Ier, _[original title: Hymne à la Liberté]_; P.22. SATB chorus, p-fl 2cl 2bn tp a-tb t-tb b-tb serp.
MS score: F-Po, No. 350. ★
Pc (with 2p-fl/fl, 2hn ad lib, omits a-tb & t-tb:) (Mag de mus fêtes nat: Paris, thermidor an II, 1794), liv. 5, No. 2,
RISM [G 3131], score (chorus) & instrumental pts: D-AB; F-Pn, (3 copies), H2. 5, H2. 101 a-n, Vm7 7044.
Pm (In: Pierre, Constant, _Les Hymnes et Chansons de la Révolution._ Imprimerie Nationale: Paris, 1904), p. 126.
FJG-18mv. Hymne à l'Égalité, _[original title: Hymne à la Nature];_ P.23.
SATB chorus, p-fl 2cl 2bn 2tp 3tb timp serp.
MS score: F-Po, No. 350. ★
Pc (chorus in score, 2cl 2hn 2bn:) (Mag de mus fêtes nat: Paris, nivôse an III, 1794), liv. 10, No. 2, RISM
[G 3115], score (chorus) & instrumental pts: F-Pn, (7 scores, 5 sets of parts including:) H2. 10, H2. 35,5; S-Sm.
FJG-19mv. Hymne à la Liberté, _[original title: Hymne à la statue de la Liberté];_ P.25.
ATB chorus, 2p-fl 2hn 2bn 2tp.
MS parts (instruments only): F-Pn, H2. 87 e-k. ★
Pc (Mag de mus fêtes nat: Paris, sd), RISM [G 3105], score (chorus) & 11 parts: D-AB.
FJG-20mv. Hymne sur la translation du corps de Voltaire au Panthéon; P.7. Solo voice, 2cl 2hn 2bn.
MS parts (instruments only): F-Pn, H2. 52. ★
Pc (Voice only:) (Mag de mus fêtes nat: Paris, sd), parts: F-Pn, (sn: sl; RISM [3106]; US-Wc, (with publisher's
imprint; RISM [G 3107]).
FJG-21mv. Hymne à Jean-Jacques Rousseau; P.86. Solo unison voices, 2cl(C) 2hn (2)bn.
Pc (Rec des époques: Paris, c.1799), liv. 1, No. 32, pp. 89 - 92, score: F-Pn, H2. 15,32. ★
FJG-22mv. Chant en Honneur des Martyrs de la Liberté; P.979. Voice, 2cl(C) 2hn (2)bn
Pc (Rec des époques: Paris, c.1799), liv. 1, No. 13, pp. 30 - 32, score: F-Pn, H2. 15,13. ★
FJG-23mv. Choeur pour la fête de M. Bernard Sarrette. Coriphée (solo & chorus), ATB chorus, 2cl 2hn 2bn
bn(III)+serp 2tp. MS pts (2 copies): F-Pn, D. 6696, (with duplicate vocal pts) , L. 18136, (with duplicate pts). ★
FJG-1amv. Rouget de Lisle: La Marseillaise; P.26. ATB chorus, 2p-fl 2cl 2hn 2bn 2tp serp timp.
MS score: F-Po, No. 350. MS pts: F-Pn, (3 copies), H2. 49,4, H2. 151,8a/8b, H2. 55.

*GOULD, Morton _10 Dec 1913, Richmond Hill, NY_
MYG-1. Concertette for Viola & Band. Solo viola, fl(pic) fl ob ob(ca) 2cl b-cl 4hn 2bn 3tp 3tb tu vc db timp
perc harp.   Pm (G. Schirmer: New York, 1943), hire score & parts.
MYG-2. Inventions. 4 solo pianos, 3fl 3ob 3cl 4hn 3bn 3tp 3tb tu timp 3perc.
Pm (G. Schirmer: New York, 1953), hire score & parts.
MYG-3. Fanfare for Freedom. 3fl 3ob 3cl 4hn 2bn 3tp 2tb tu timp 4perc.
Pm (G. Schirmer: New York, 1971), score & hire parts.
MYG-4. Bird Movements (from Audubon). 3fl ob ca 3cl 2bn cbn tu db perc.
Pm (G. Schirmer: New York, 1971), score & hire parts.
MYG-1v. Salutations. Narrator, 2fl(pic) 3cl 4hn 2bn 3tp 3tb tu timp 2/3perc celesta harp.
Pm (G. Schirmer: New York, 1966), hire score & parts.
MYG-2v. Quotations. SSAATTBB chorus, 2fl 2ob 2cl 4hn 2bn 3tp 3tb tu 2db timp 2/3perc harp piano.
Pm (G. Schirmer: New York, 1983), hire score & parts.
MYG-3v. Something To Do. Solo voice & narrator, Chorus, fl(pic) ob(ca) 3cl b-cl 2hn bn 2tp 2tb tu 2perc
e-gtr 2e-kbd e-db.   Pm (G. Schirmer: New York, 1976), hire score & parts.

*GOUNOD, Charles François *18 June 1818, Paris - 18 Oct 1893, St Cloud*
*CFG-1. Hymne à Sainte Cécile. Solo violin, 2fl ob 2cl 4hn(E) 2bn 2tp(D) db timp 2 harps.
Pc (Le Duc: Paris, pn NL 438, 1866), score: F-Pn, D. 4801 (1); GB-Lbl, h.80.a.(9.); GB-Ob, Mus.183.c.81;
I-Bc, NN.122, (with MS wind parts). ★
*CFG-2. Petite Symphonie; in B♭, 4 mvts, 1885. fl (2)ob 2cl 2hn 2bn.
Pc (Costallat &. Cie.: Paris, 1904), score: F-Pn; GB-Lbl, f.244.f.(1.); I-Mc, Part. 73.6. ★
Pc (Costallat &. Cie.: Paris, 1957), parts: GB-Lwcm.
Pm (Billaudot: Paris, sd), score (pn GB 1714) & parts (pn GB 1715).
Pm (International Music Co.: New York, sd), min score (pn 3092) & parts (pn 3027),
Pm (E.F. Kalmus: New York, pn A 1514, sd), score & parts.
Pm (Edition Peters: Leipzig, pn E.P.13429, c.1987), ed. Klaus Burmeister.

*GOUVY, Louis Théodore *2 July 1819, Goffontaine, Saarbrücken - 21 April 1898, Leipzig*
*LTG-1. Petite Suite Gauloise, Op. 90. fl 2ob 2cl 2hn 2bn.
Pc (Jos. Aibl: München, c.1900), score & parts: A-Wgm, VIII 30079; I-Mc, Da Camera A.46.13, (score);
US-Wc, M 957 G 75. ★
Pc/m (Universal Edition: Wien, 1898, repr 1985), score (pn UE 3480) & parts (pn UE 3481).
*LTG-2. Ottetto, Op. 71. fl ob 2cl 2hn 2bn.
Pc (F. Kistner: Leipzig, pn 5891, 1882), score & pts: A-Wgm, VIII 28213 (H 25485), (score), VIII 28213 (H 25486),
(parts); D-Bhm, 4809; GB-Lbl, e.705; I-Mc, Da Camera A.46.5; US-Wc, M 857 G 18. ★
Pm (A.J. Andraud, now Southern Music: San Antonio, Texas, sd), score & parts.
Pm (Compusic: Amsterdam, pn 235, 1988), score & parts.
Pm (Doblinger: Wien, 1991), score & parts.

*GOW, Nathaniel *28 May 1763, Inver, nr Dunkeld - 19 Jan 1831, Edinburgh*
NXG-1m. The Hon. Mr Ramsay Maule of Panmure's March & Quick Step. 2cl 2hn bn tp.
Pc (Neil Stewart & Co.: Edinburgh, c.1794), RISM [G 3235], score: GB-En, Glen 347-28; GB-Ep;
GB-Lbl, h.830.j.(2). ★

GRÄFE, Johann Friedrich *1711 - 1787, Prussia*
JRG-1m. March. 2ob bn tp. MS parts (1770): D-B.

*GRAESCHL, ( ) *(? = Franz Joseph Graetzl, 1770 - 1824)*
XWB-1v. Komm heiliger Geist mit deiner Gnad; in C. CATB, 2cl 2hn(solo)+2hn(tutti) 2tp(clar) timp.
MS parts (c.1820, by Joseph Spät): D-SCHN, 28. ★

*GRAF, Christian Ernst *30 June 1723, Rudolstadt - 17 July 1804, The Hague*
CEG-1d. Die Schlacht bei Austerlitz. Türkische Musik. MS: D-Bds, Hausbibl., No. 312.
*(Since the Battle of Austerlitz did not take place until 2 December 1805, when Graf had been dead for 18
months, there is an inconsistency here which may simply indicate an imaginative re-titling by his successors).*

GRAF, Johann *(1720)*
JVG-1. Parthia ex F. 2vl 2hn bn. MS parts: D-RH.

GRANT, Julian *3 Oct 1960, London*
JUG-1. Octet. 2ob 2cl 2hn 2bn. MS score & parts: with the composer, GB-Lmic will assist in contacting.

*GRAUGAARD, Lars *1957, Denmark*
*LZG-1. Seven Summerscapes. 2ob 2cl 2hn 2bn. MS score: DK-Kd.

GRAUN ( ) *(Probably Carl Heinrich, qv, 1702 - 1771)*
ZZG-1. Auferstehen [ja Auferstehen]. 2ob+2cl(C) 2hn 2bn.
MS parts: D-DS, Mus.ms.156. *Without vocal parts. Possibly arranged by Ferdinand Bühler (qv).* ★

*GRAUN, Carl Heinrich *7 May 1703, Wahrenbrück, nr Dresden - 8 Aug 1759, Berlin*
CHG-1m, 2m. 2 Marches. No. 1: 2ob 2hn bn; No. 2: 2ob bn cbn tp. MS score: GB-Lbl, Add., 31,641. ★
CHG-3m. March ex E♭. 2ob tp basso. MS parts (?c.1750): D-DS, Mus.ms.1223/17. ★

GRAUN, Johann Gottlieb *28 Oct 1702, Wahrenbrück, nr Dresden - 27 Oct 1771, Berlin*
JGG-1. Intrada. 2fl 3ob 2hn 2bn. MS: D-Bds, Mus.ms.8239/2, (?lost).
JGG-2(-4). 3 Overtures: D, F E♭. 2ob 2hn bc. MS: D-Bds, Mus.ms.8239/27-29, (?lost).

GRAZIOLI, Giambattista Ignazio (Giovanni Battista) *6 July 1746, Bogliaro, Brescia, - c.1820, Venice*
GAG-1v. Credo. TTB, 2cl 2hn (vlne timp) organ.
MS score & parts: I-Vsmc, (vlne & timp do not appear in the score). ★

GREAVES, Terence (Gervase) *16 Nov 1933, Hodthorpe, Derbyshire, UK*
TGG-1. 4 Bagatelles. 2fl 2cl.
Pm (Emerson Edition: Ampleforth, UK, pn E48, 1989), two scores.

*GRECO, José-Luis *1953*
JIG-1. Swallows. 2ob 2cl 2hn 2bn piano.
Pm (Donemus: Amsterdam, 1992), score.

GREEN, Anthony Robert *1946*
ATG-1. Concertino. 2fl 2ob 2cl 2hn 2bn. In MS.

GREGOR, František (Franz) *(1840), Ředitel (Chorregent) at Sv Barbora, Písek*
FZG-1tv. [24] Pohřební písně a sbory s jednoduchou hudbou. Nos 10, 18, 19: SATB, 2cl b-flug+euph bomb;
No. 20: unison voices, 2cl b-flug+euph bomb.
Pc (Nakladetel Fr. A. Urbánek: Praha [Prague], 1873), score: CZ-PL(br), Hu 1200. *Nos. 1, 3 - 7, 9, 11 - 15
include ad lib parts for 2hn; No. 6 "Obligátní" pts for 2hn; Nos 2, 8, 16 & 21 are for TTBB only; No. 17 is for
three unspecified voices with b-flug+euph bomb; No. 22, without vocal parts, is for b-flug+euph bomb;
Nos. 23 & 24 for SATB & organ.* ★

FZG-1.1tv. 10. Ku pohřbu manžela [for a husband]. "Konám poslední svou cestu do váčnosti". Kancionál svatojánský II č.800, 1864. TTBB, 2cl b-flug+euph bomb.
FXG-1.2tv. 18. Ku pohřbu představeného. "Bůh vyměřil dráhu tobě, za úkol". Z Pohana č. za 1850. TTBB, 2cl b-flug+euph bomb. p. 39.
FXG-1.3tv. 19. Ku pohřbu školního učitěle [for a teacher]. "Tmavá rakev jast tvé lůžko, pod hrudami obyt tvůj". Z Pohana č 3 1850. TTBB, 2cl b-flug+euph bomb. p. 44.
FZG-1.20tv(a). Ku pohřbu duchovního pastýře [for a singing pastor]; text "Z Pohana čis. 1", 1850, "Truchlitemné zvonů znění stádo rmoutí Kristovo". SATB, cl(Eb) cl(Bb) 2hn tp(Eb) b-flug tb. MS parts (by Josef Florián, Kasejovice): CZ-PL(ka), Hu 1702, (missing cl in Eb; with duplicate vocal parts: S(2)A(2)T(3)B(4)). *An arrangement of No. 20 of FZG-1tv; probably not arranged by Gregor.* ★

*GRELL, (August) Eduard *6 Nov 1800, Berlin - 10 Aug 1886, Berlin*
EXG-1v. Waisen Musik, 1830.   Solo SATBB, SSATTB chorus, 2fl 2ob 2cl 2a-cl 2bthn 4hn 4bn cbn 3tp a-tb t-tb 3b-tb b-hn serp vc+db organ timp.
AutoMS score: D-B, Mus.ms.8470/35 (formerly D-Bds, Mus.ms.auto.E.Grell 322). *On f.2 is pasted a printed program with the title, "Gemeine= und Chor=Gesänge beim Gottesdeinst in der St. Nikolai=Kirche am Sonntage Rogate den 16.Mai, 1830. Sur Säkular=Feier der Stiftung des Schindlerschen Waisenhauses."*
MS score, Bläserdirektions-stimme & parts: D-B, Mus.ms.8470/35, with duplicate parts: Solo A for No 1 only; Chorus: S1(12) S2(12) A(16) T1(8) T2(8) B(24) 2cl(2) serp(2) vc+db(2).
    1.1v. "Lobet ihr Völker unserm Gott", in Eb. ★
    1.2v. K.F. Curschmann: "Barmherzig und gnädig ist der Herr", Tenor solo, in Bb.
        Solo SATB, SATB chorus, 2ob 2cl 2bthn 2hn 2bn cbn serp vc+db organ. *A note has been added in another hand, "Von / Fr. Curschmann / und dem Freunde Grell / an / Fr. Curschmann / am 21sten Juni 1830." We believe this to be an original work by K.F. Curschmann rather than an arrangement.*
    1.3v. "Wie soll ich dem Herrrn vergelten", Soprano solo, in Eb.
    1.4v. "Dienst dem Herrn mit Freuden", [quartet] Soli, in Eb.
    1.5v. Choral, "Halleluja, Lob, Preis uns Ehr sey unserm Gott", in Eb
EXG-2v, 3v. 2 Chöre: "Herr Gott, dich loben wir" & "Komm heiliger Geist".   SATB, winds.
AutoMS score: D-Bds, Mus.ms.auto.E.Grell 237.
EXG-4v. Chöre, "Non sic excubiae non circumstantia" (1831).   TTBB, winds.
AutoMS score: D-Bds, Mus.ms.auto.E.Grell 468.
EXG-5v. Chöre, "Hic dies vere mihi festus", (1831).   TTBB, winds.
AutoMS score: D-Bds, Mus.ms.auto.E.Grell 469.
EXG-6v. Chöre, "Saepins ventis agitatur" (1832).   TTBB, winds.
AutoMS score: D-Bds, Mus.ms.auto.E.Grell 471.
EXG-7v. Lateinische Festgesänge, (1830).   TTBB, winds.
AutoMS score: D-Bds: Mus.ms.auto.E.Grell 470.

*GRENSER, (Grenzer), Johann Friedrich *1758, Dresden - 17 March 1794, Stockholm*
JFG-1. Parthia, (c.1800).   2ob 2cl 2hn 2bn.   MS parts: D-Z, Mus.Ms.500.
JFG-2(-7). 6 Partitas.   2cl 2hn bn.   MS (score): DK-Kk, (2 copies), mu. 7410.0831 - 7410.0836; Mu. 6506.1833, (in the hand of F. Heyper, "Contra Bassista Amico suo"). ★
    JFG-2. Partita N.1, in Eb, 4 mvts.   JFG-3. Parthia N.2da, in Eb, 4 mvts.
    JFG-4. Partita 3tia, in Bb, 4 mvts.   JFG-5. Partita 4ta, in Bb, 4 mvts.
    JFG-6. Partita N.5, in Eb, 4 mvts.   JFG-7. Parthia N.6, in Eb, 4 mvts.
JFG-1a. Kraus: Intermedes pour Amphitryon.   2ob 3cl 2hn 2bn.   MS parts: S-Skma.

GRÉTRY, André Ernest Modeste *10/11 Feb 1741, Liège - 24 Sept 1813, nr Montmorency*
AMG-1mv. Plantation des arbres de la liberté; P.148b.   Voice, 2cl(C) 2hn (2)bn.
Pc (Rec des époques: Paris, c.1799), liv. 2, No. 3, pp. 130 - 133, score: F-Pn, H2. 16,2. ★

*GRETSCH, Johann Konrad *1710 - 1784, Regensberg*
JKG-1. Parthia VII, in Eb, 7 mvts.   2cl 2hn bn.   MS pts: D-Rtt, Inc. IVa/3l/I, Nos. 29 - 35. ★
JKG-2. Parthia XV, in Eb, 7 mvts.   2cl 2hn bn.   MS parts: D-Rtt, Inc. IVa/3l/I, Nos. 83 - 89. ★
Following mvt 6 is the note, "Fine del Sig. Gretsch"; the 7th mvt is, in fact, by "Rudolff" [i.e. Anton Rudolph]. "Madame la Princesse Regnat" has been added in pencil above the start of mvt 2 in the hn I part; this may indicate that the mvt is an arrangement.

*GRIESBACH, Charles *(1770) We have not linked him to the other (Austrian) musicians of this name.*
CYG-1m. Twelve Military Divertimentos.   fl/terz-fl(Nos. 8, 9) fl cl(Eb ad lib) 2cl 2hn 2bn serp tp; *or* 2cl 2hn 2bn.
Pc (Smart: London, 1800), RISM [G 4590], parts: GB-Lbl, h.129.(3); GB-Ob, Mus.Instr.I.102(19). ★
    1.1m. March.   1.2m. Quick March.   1.3m. Walzer [with Trio in the minor].   1.4m. March.
    1.5m. Quick March.   1.6m. Walzer [with Trio in the minor].
    1.7m. Troop [Introduction, sections in 4/4 & 6/8, then the March & Trio].   1.8m. Andante.
    1.9m. German Cottillion [sic; with Trio].
    1.10m. Grave [in 3/4, followed by an Andante section, and 4/4 Tempo Primo section; *Volte Subito* to:]
    1.11m. Rondo (Scherzanto [sic]), in 3/8.   1.12m. Walzer.

*GRIESBACH (Griesbacher), Reimund (Raymund) *1752, Vienna - 1818, Vienna*
REG-1. Allegro und Romanza [sic]; in Eb, 6 mvts.   2cl 2hn 2bn.   MS parts: D-SWl, Mus. 2212. ★

*GRIFFES, Charles Tomlinson *17 Sept 1884, Elmira, NY - 8 April 1920, New York City*
*CTG-1. The Kairn of Koridwen: a dance drama in 2 Scenes; 1916 - 1917.   fl 2cl 2hn celeste harp piano.
AutoMS score (Scene 1 complete, Scene 2 incomplete), AutoMS sketches (Scene 2) & MS parts: US-NYp, Performing Arts Research Center, Music Division.
Pm (Kallisti Music Press: Philadelphia, 1993), score.
*CTG-2. Three Tone Pictures, Op. 5; (piano).   Rescored by the composer for: fl 2ob 2cl 2hn 2bn harp.
AutoMS score: US-EL, (No. 1 only); US-NYp, Performing Arts Research Center, Music Division, (Nos. 2 & 3).
    2.1. The Lake at Evening.   2.2. The Vale of Dreams.   2.3. The Night Winds.
*CGT-3(f). Salut au Monde. 1919.   fl(pic) cl 2hn tp 2tb timp perc 2harps piano.
AutoMS sketches (Act I only) & MS score (completed by Edmond Rickett, who also composed the music for Act III): US-NYp, Performing Arts Research Center, Music Division.

*GROH, Josef *(1830), active in Velenice, 1864*
JSG-1tv. 2 Grab-Arien.   CATB, fl cl(E♭) 2cl(B♭) 2hn 2tp 2flug b-tb.
MS parts (by Konrad Zimmer, 2 June 1864): CZ-LIa(vl), No. 2454. ★
   1.1tv. Hier Mensch, hier lerne was du bist.   1.2tv. Schlummernd gingst du sanft in jene Welt hinüber.
JSG-2tv. 2 Gräbnisslieder bei Kindern und Erwachsenen.   CATB, 2terz-fl 2cl 2hn bn(vel b-tb) 2tp(clar).
MS parts: CZ-LIa(vl), No. 2950 hud.   ★
   2.1tv. Wenn an des Vaters Aschengrube.   2.2tv. Unvermuthet, eh wir es vermeinen.
JSG-3tv. Grab-Candate [sic] in Ass [sic, A♭]; "Hier an meines Grabes Scheidewege.   SATB, terz-fl (cl in E♭)
2cl(B♭) 2hn 2tp b-tb.   MS parts: CZ-LIa(vl), No. 2497 hud, (the cl in E♭ is not listed on the titlepage).   ★
JSG-4tv. 2 Grablieder in Es [E♭] et As [A♭].   CATB, fl(D) 2cl 2hn (bn) 2tp b-tb.
MS parts: CZ-LIa(vl), No. 2476 hud, (the bn pt is not listed on the titlepage).   ★
   4.1tv. Alle Müssen wir verwesen.   4.2tv. Begrabt den Leib in seine Grust.
JSG-5tv. 2 Grablieder.   CATB, fl(D) 2cl 2hn 2bn (b-tb).
MS parts: CZ-LIa(vl), No. 2470 hud, (the b-tb is not listed on the titlepage.   ★
   5.1tv. Wie die Blume einst zu Staube.   5.2tv. Da, wo ein ewiger Morgen.
JSG-6tv. 2 Gradlieder.   CATB, 2cl 2hn bomb.   MS parts: CZ-LIa(vl), No. 2498 hud.   ★
   6.1tv. Ihr Trauernden, stillet die Thränen.   6.2tv. Die Stund ist uns verborgen.

GROSS, Eric *1926, Austria (now resident in Australia)*
EYG-1. Suite, Op. 115.   3ob 2ca 3bn.
Pm (Leeds Music: London, New York, c.1980).

*GROSS, Johann Gottlieb *c.1748 - 8 June 1820, (?Berlin)*
YXG-1. Echo à 6 ex Tief B[♭]; 5 mvts.   ob(echo) 2ob 2bn tp.   MS pts (?c.1750): D-DS, Mus.ms.1223/23.
The "Hautb[ois]. Echo" is used in mvts 1 and 5 only.   ★

GROT (?Grotz), ( )
YZG-1. Parthia in C; 4 mvts.   2cl(C) 2hn 2bn.   MS parts (by Johann Anton Handl): A-Wn, Mus.Hs.347.   ★

GROTTO, Antonio, vicentino *18 Sept 1753, Vicenza - 20 Jan 1831, Vicenza*
ANG-1v. Mazzo [sic] I, N.1. Kyrie – Gloria.   CATB, organo di concerto, organo obbligato, ob 2hn bn tb vlne.
MS score & parts: I-VId, Mazzo I, N.1.

*GROVLEZ, Gabriel (Marie) *4 April 1879, Lille - 20 Oct 1944, Paris*
*GMG-1a. Fauré: Première Nocturne pour piano, Op. 35, No. 1.   fl 2ob 2cl 2hn bn.
Pm (Hamelle: Paris, 1925).
Pm (A.J. Andraud: Cincinatti; now Southern Music: San Antonio, Texas, sd), score & parts.

*GRUBER, Johann Georg *Not the Gruber who composed "Stille Nacht" ("Silent Night").*
JEG-1m. Marsch in F.   2fl 2cl 2hn bn tp(prin) b-dr.
MS parts: A-Wn, Mus.Hs.5645, (the flutes are not listed on the titlepage).   ★

GRUBER, Leopold *(?1760)*
LYG-1. Parthia in B[♭]; 6 mvts.   2ob 2hn bn.   MS pts: CZ-Bm(no), A.18.851.   ★

GRÜBER (Gruber), Josef *18 April 1855, Wöserdorf, Lower Austria - 2 Dec 1933, Linz*
QJG-1v. Te Deum laudamus, Op. 296.   SATB, 3cl 2hn 2tp b-tb timp *or* organ.
MS parts: CZ-Pnm, XLIII.A.165, (here cl(B♭) I & II only, ?missing cl in E♭).   ★
QJG-2v. Neun Fronleichnamsgesänge, Op. 178.   SATB, (2cl/flug 2hn t-hn/b-flug t-tb b-tb/bomb/helikon; *or*
organ ad lib).
Pc (Anton Böhm u. Sohn: Augsburg & Wien, pn 5279, 1908), parts: CZ-Pnm, XLIII.A.166, (with duplicate voice
parts, 4S, 4A, 2T, 2B).   ★

GRUND, Friedrich Wilhelm *10 Aug 1791, Hamburg - 24 Nov 1874, Hamburg*
FWG-1. Octet.   7 winds & piano.
Pc (Aug. Cranz: Hamburg, c.1830), parts.

GRUNDMANN, Clare Ewing *1913, USA*
CEG-1. March of the Gnervous Gnomes.   2fl cl bn 3tp 3tb tu perc.
Pm (Boosey & Hawkes: London, etc., sd).

*GRUSS, Anton Josef *(?1840), Lehrer zu Holtschitz (nr Česká Lípa)*
AJG-1a. Gellert: Begräbnisslied für Kinder; "Nimm dies Kind des Lebensende.   CATB fl(F ad lib) 2cl 2hn bn.
MS parts: CZ-LIa(vl), No. 2394 hud., No. 2. *(No. 1, "Sei willig" may also hav been rescored by Gruss).*   ★

GUBICH, ( ) *(?1760) (? only the copyist; the following may be Went's arrangement.)*
WZG-1ad. Cimaroso: Il Matrimonio segretto.   2ob 2cl 2hn 2bn.   MS parts: A-KR, G 9/24.

GUDMUNDSEN-HOLMGREN, Pelle *1932, Denmark*
PLG-1. October; 1977.   pic 2fl 2ob ca 2cl b-cl bn cbn.   MS score: DK-Kd.

*GÜNTHER, Carl Friedrich *Possibly the bass Friedrich Günther who sang at the Weimar and Gotha theaters
between 1770 and 1780.*
CRG-1m. 12 Märsche.   10-part military band.   MS: D-Bds, Hausbibl.M.M.460.

*GUERINGE (Guering), ( ) *(1750 - post-1818), "Directeur de Musique de ... la Princesse de Bade Bade"*
ZXG-1. Serenade; 3 mvts.   fl ob 2cl 2hn 2bn.   MS parts (1818): CZ-Bm(au), A.18.854.   ★
ZXG-1a. Paisiello: Il Re Teodoro in Venezia, overture & 21 mvts.   2cl 2hn 2bn.
Pc (Author: Baden Baden, sd), RISM [P 485], parts: CZ-KRa, A3942/IV.B.105; D-BFb, P-ai 39; D-F.
MS parts (purchased from Johann Gallyus, Advocat in Zagreb, 1802): H-KE, 0/119, (No. 10 in the print is
divided into 3 mvts); H-Bm (microfilm) FM 4/2001.

GUERRANT, Mary Thorington *7 May 1925, Taft, Tennessee, USA*
MHG-1. Pecos ruins.   2ob 2cl 2hn 2bn.   MS: NY-amc will assist in contacting the composer.

GUERRERO, Francisco *1951, Spain*
FNG-1. Anemos C.   2fl(pic) 2ob 2cl 2hn 2bn tp tb 2perc.
(Editorial Alpuerto: Madrid, pn 1449, 1976).

GÜRSHING, Albrecht *9 Sept 1934, Nuremburg*
AZG-1. Pas encore.   2fl 2ob 2cl 2hn 2bn.
Pm (H. Peer: Hamburg, 1972), score & parts.
AZG-2. Oktett.   2ob 2cl 2hn 2bn.
Pm (H. Peer: Hamburg, 1974), score & parts.
AZG-3. Stops.   2cl 2hn 2bn.
Pm (H. Peer: Hamburg, sd), score & parts.

*GUEST, George *1 May 1771, Bury St Edmunds - (?10) Sept 1831, Wisbech*
GEG-1m. A New Troop, Composed for the Wisbech Volunteer Band.   2fl 2cl 2bn tp/bugle serp b-dr s-dr.
Pc (Printed & Sold for the Author by Preston: London, 1805), score: GB-Lbl, h.129.(4).   ★
GEG-2m. A Second Troop, Composed for the Wisbech Volunteer Band. 2fl 2cl 2hn 2bn serp b-dr. s-dr tamb
cym tri. *("N.B. The Side Drum, Tambourine, Cymbals & Triangle to come in only on the repeat of the first
strain").   (GEG-1m & 2m refer to the Wisbech United Batallion of Volunteer Infantry)*
Pc (Printed & Sold for the Author by Preston: London, 1805), score: GB-Lbl, h.129.(6).   ★
GEG-3m. A Third or Grand Bugle Horn Troop,... Inscribed to... the first Regiment of Norfolk Volunteer Infantry.
2fl 2cl 2hn 2bn bugle serp b-dr side-drum,*("Drums &c to come in only on the repeat of the 1st and 2nd strains").*
Pc (Printed & Sold by Preston: London, 1806), score: GB-Lbl, h.129.(7).   ★
GEG-4m. A Fourth Troop...Inscribed to...the Third Regiment of Cambridgeshire Volunteer Infantry.
2fl 2cl 2hn 2bn serp b-dr s-dr.   [Adagio / Andante / Clarinet cadenza / Troop (3/8)].
Pc (Printed & Sold for the Author by Preston: London, 1807), score: GB-Lbl, h.129.(8).   ★
GEG-5m. A Fifth Troop March...Inscribed to...The Isle of Ely Regt. of Local Militia.
2fl 2cl 2hn 2bn tp serp b-dr s-dr.
Pc (Printed & Sold for the Author, by Preston: London, 1809), score: GB-Lbl, h.129.(9).   ★
GEG-6m. A Second Grand Bugle Horn Piece or Sixth Troop,...Inscribed to...The Isle of Ely Regiment of Local
Militia.   2fl 2cl 2hn 2bn bugle tp serp b-dr side-dr (tamb, cym, tri). *("N.B. The side-Drum, Tamborim [sic],
Cymbals and Triangle to come in only on the repeat of the 1st strain.")*
Pc (Printed & Sold for the Author, by Preston: London, 1810), score: GB-Lbl, h.129.(5).   ★

*GÜTTLER, Josef *(1840), active 1870 - 1890*
XJG-1. Offertorium, Op. 21.   2cl(C) 2hn 2tp tp(chromatic) t-hn(C).
MS parts (c.1870): GB-Ljag, (purchased in Český Krumlov, 1993); CZ-Pu, (photocopy).   ★
XJG-1v. Miserere, in E♭, "Arrangirt von J. Güttler".   SATB, 2cl 2hn 2tp t-hn(B♭) b-tb.
Pc (A. Pietsch: in Ziegenhals in Schlesien, pn A.P.823, c.1880), parts: CZ-Pnm, XLIII.A.38.   ★
XJG-1tv. Neun Begräbnislieder, Op. 110.   SATB, 2cl 2hn 2tp t-hn b-tb.
Pc (A. Pietsch: in Ziegenhals in Schlesien, pn A.P.1148, c.1900), vocal score & parts:
CZ-LIa(za), No. 2663 hud. ★
    1.1tv. O gönn' den Himmel deinem Kinde.   1.2tv. Das liebe, treue Mutterherz.
    1.3tv. Bei einem Vater oder einer Mutter, "Gutter Vater [Mutter], schlaf in Frieden".
    1.4tv. Klage un die Mutter, "Meine Liebe ruht im Grabe!".
    1.5tv. Am Grabe eines Kindes, "O weinet nicht".
    1.6tv. Bein einem Vater oder einer Mutter, "Schlaf, Vater/Mutter, nun in stillem Frieden".
    1.7tv. Für alle Fälle, "Weine nicht".   1.8tv. Am Brage einer Veteranen, "Leb' wohl, Kam'rad!".
    1.9tv. Für alle Fälle, "Wenn aus dem stillen Vaterhaus".
XJG-2tv. "O weinet nicht" Lied am Grab eines Kind, Op. 34.   B solo, 2cl 2hn t-hn(ad lib) b-tb.
Pc (A. Pietsch: Zeigenhals in Schlesien, pn A.P.822, c.1890), parts: CZ-LIa(za), No. 2660 hud.   *An earlier setting
than XJG-1.5tv.*   ★
XJG-3tv. Am Grabe eines Kindes. Lied, Op. 16, "Lebet wohl, ihr meine Lieben".   B solo, 2cl 2hn t-hn tb.
Pc (s.n.: s.l., pn 72, s.d.), parts: CZ-LIa(za), No. 2665 hud.   MS parts: CZ-Bm(ro), A.23.274.   ★
XJG-4tv. Am Grabe. Lied, "Wenn aus dein stillen Vaterhaus".   B solo, 2cl 2hn t-hn tb, (2tp ad lib).
Pc (A. Pietsch: Ziegenhals in Schlesisien, sd) parts: CZ-Bm(ro), A.23.275; CZ-LIa(za), No. 2661 hud., (missing
the ad lib tp pts).   *An earlier setting than XJG-1.9tv.*   ★

GUÉZEC, Jean-Pierre *29 Aug 1934, Dijon - 9 March 1971, Paris*
JPG-1. Assemblages.   pic 3fl 2ob ca cl(E♭) 2cl b-cl 4hn 2bn tp(D) 2tp(C) 2t-tb b-tb tu 3perc.
Pm (Editions Salabert: Paris, 1967), score: F-Pn.
JPG-2. Textures enchaînées.   2fl ob cl(E♭) cl b-cl 2hn 2tp(C) t-tb b-tb 3perc harp
Pm (Editions Salabert: Paris, 1967), score: F-Pn.
JPG-3. Forme coleurs.   2fl ob 2cl hn tp 2perc.
Pm (Salabert: Paris, 1969).

GUIDE, Richard Jules Joseph de *1909 - 1962, Belgium*
RDG-1. Concert à onze, Op. 12; 1940.   fl ob cl 2hn 2bn tp tb timp cym.
MS score: B-Bcdm.

*GWILT, David William *3 Nov 1932, Edinburgh*
*DWG-1. Suite for Woodwind and Brass Instruments.   2fl ob 2cl 2hn bn/cl(III) 2tp 2tb perc(ad ib).
Pm (Novello: London, 1966), score (09 0512 0700) & pts (09 0512 0701), (Music for Today, Series 2, No. 6).
DWG-2. Retrograde Steps.   2fl 2ob 2cl 2hn 2bn.
Pm (facsimile score): GB-Gsma, (available for purchase).
Pm (Horn Realm: Far Hills, NJ, sd), score.

GWINNER, Volker *18 Aug 1912*
VZG-1. 6 Low-German folk dances.   2cl 2hn bn.
Pm (Möseler: Wolfenbüttel, Series "Aulos" No. 104, sd), score & parts.

*GYROWETZ (Jírovec), Adalbert Mathias (Vojtĕch Matyáš) *19 Feb 1763, Budweis (now České Budějovice) - 19 March 1850, Vienna*
*ADG-1. Parthia in Dis [E♭]; 3 mvts. 2ob 2cl 2hn 2bn cbn.
MS parts: CZ-Pnm, XX.F.11. ★
Pm (Compusic: Amsterdam, pn 208, 1988), score & parts.
Pm (Doblinger: Wien, 1991), score & parts.
*ADG-2. Parthia in B[♭]; 3 mvts. 2ob 2cl 2hn 2bn cbn.
MS parts: CZ-Pnm, XX.F.12; D-SWl, (attributed to C. Stamitz; unverified). ★
ADG-3. Nocturno in Dis [E♭]; 3 mvts. 2cl 2hn 2bn.
MS parts (11 Dec 1812): CZ-KRa, A3866/IV.B.30. ★
ADG-4. Parthia V [Parthia / Not[t]urno]; in E♭, 5 mvts. 2cl 2hn 2bn. MS parts: CZ-KRa, IV.B.28. ★
*ADG-5, 6. 2 Serenades, Op. 3 (E♭, 5 mvts; B♭, 4 mvts). 2cl 2hn bn.
MS pts: CH-E, (copy by Joannes Tschudi, 1806 - see also CZ-Pnm); CH-Zz, AMG XIII.7090. a-d, (Nos. 1 & 2; as "Harmonia"); CZ-Pnm, V.B.179, (No. 1 only: MS score & parts by Dr J. Pohl, advocat in Zbirov, dated 18 April 1914 - based on the copy in CH-E); NL-Z, Z1184/M.Á.Zcm.20, (Nos. 1 & 2 - both missing cl II; as "oeuvre 5"); US-BETm, Philharmonic Society of Bethlehem PSB 1350.1a, 1350.1b, (cataloged as "Op. 2").
Pc (as "Deux Sérénates" [sic]) (J. André: Offenbach s/Main, pn 315, c.1790), RISM [G 5337], parts: D-B (Nos. 1 & 2); D-Dl (Nos. 1 & 2); DK-A (Nos. 1 & 2); RF-Ssc, (Nos. 1 & 2). ★
Pc (as "Deux Sérénates Op. 5" [sic]) (Johann Julius Hummel: Berlin; Grand Magasin de musique: Amsterdam, pn 819, 1802), RISM [G 5338], parts: D-Mmb.
Pm (No. 1 only:) (Nova Music: London, pn NM 235, 1983), score & parts.
ADG-7(-11). [5] Quintetti; (B♭, 3 mvts; E♭, 3 mvts; E♭, 5 mvts; E♭, 3 mvts; E♭, 2 mvts). 2cl 2hn bn.
MS parts: I-UDricardi, Ms.146. ★
ADG-12. Parthia in Dis [E♭] Concertando [sic]; 4 mvts. 2cl 2hn bn.
MS parts (by Augustin Erasmus Hübner, Langenbruck): CZ-Pu(dm), 59 R 3332. ★
ADG-13. Parthia in B[♭]. 2cl 2hn bn.
MS parts (by František Vanĕček): CZ-Pla(br), Hu 959, (the hn I part is missing the beginning of the work). ★
*ADG-1e. Incidental music for Grillparzer's play, *Der Traum ein Leben.*
MS score (?late 19th century): A-Wst, MH 13817/c.
   1.1e. Act I (end) & Verwandlung (end): fl 2cl harp. ★
   1.2e. Act IV, Janitscharenmusik, 7 bars. pic 2cl(C) 2hn 2bn 2tp(C, a2) b-tb cym tri. ★
*ADG-1v. "Lasst Fenisens Lob". Solo voice, fl 2cl 2bn tp guitar 2timp. MS: D-DS.
ADG-2v. Zu einem Prozessions-Tantum ergo in C, Andante. fl 2cl(C) 2hn 2tp bomb.
MS parts: CZ-Pnm, XXXIV.A.174, (missing hn I). *Possibly an arrangement. The blank verso of each part has been used for a geography lesson for 10-year-olds at the Osek Monastery, March 1850.* ★
ADG-1d. Divertimento, in D, 1826. Instrumentation unknown.
MS: A-M. *Whitwell citation: this work is not known at the Benedictine monastery at Melk, nor does it appear in the contemporary inventories.*

H., ( ), *Signore (Possibly, H., C. G.)*
ZXH-1. 6 Poloneso e 2 Masur. 2ob 2cl 2hn 2bn cbn.
MS parts: CZ-Pnm, XX.F.107. ★

H., F. *(1720) - active in Kromĕříž*
FUH-1. Parthia Ex G; 5 mvts. 2ob 2hn 2bn.
MS parts: CZ-KRa, A4030/IV.B.203. ★

*HAAN, Stefan de *25 Jan 1921, Darmstadt*
SDH-1. Octet. 2ob 2cl 2hn 2bn.
Pm (Schott & Co.: London, 1972), score & parts.
Pm (Highgate Music: London, c.1990), score & parts.
SDH-2. Studies and Pieces. 2fl ob 3cl hn bn tp vc.
Pm (Highgate Music: London, c.1990), score & parts.

*HABERHAUER, Maurus (Mauro, Mauritius) *1749 - 1799*
MRH-1v. Missa Adventalis. SATB, 2cl 2tb 2vla organ.
MS parts (1849): CZ-Bm(rj), A.14.215, (missing 2vla; probably a local rescoring). ★

*HABERT, ( ) *M[ons]: Musicien de M: le Duc de Deuxponts*
MQH-1a. Grétry: Richard Coeur-de-Lion, 8 mvts. 2ob/fl+ob 2cl 2hn 2bn.
AutoMS score: D-DS, Mus.ms.486, (as by "M: Habert").

HABERT, Johannes Evangelista *18 Oct 1833, Oberplan, (now Horní Planá) - 1 Sept 1896, Gmunden*
ZJH-1a. Scherzo [Vivace], Op. 107, No. 1, arr by the composer as Op. 107, No. 1b (Allegretto). fl ob cl 2hn 2bn.
Pc (in: *Johannes Ev. Habert's Werke.* Breitkopf & Härtel: Leipzig, c.1915; Ser. XII, No. 4, pp. 51-54), score: GB-Lbl, H.602 (specify "ser. 12 no. 2" on application slip). ★
Pm (Albert J. Andraud: Cincinnati, now Southern Music Co.: San Antonio, Texas, sd).
Pm (Associated Music Publishers: New York, sd).

HACKER, Benedikt *30 May 1769, Deggendorf, Metten, Bavaria - 2 May 1829, Salzburg*
BYH-1v. Juvaviens Gruss bey der höchsterfreulichten Ankunft Sr Hochfürstl: Gauden des Hochwürdigsten Fürst-Erzbischofs Augustin Gruber von Rudolph Hinterhuber...abgesungen 22 Marz 1824. TTBB, 2cl 2hn 2bn.
MS parts: A-Sca, Hs.1858, (the vocal pts only); A-Wn, Mus.Hs.9773. ★

HÄBERLING, Albert *5 Sept 1919, Affolten, Zurich*
AZH-1. Musik für 5 Bläser. 2cl bn 2tp.
Pm (Möseler: Wolfenbüttel, pn 42160, 1978), score & parts.

HAEFELIN, Max *1898 - 1952, Switzerland*
MYH-1. Divertimento. fl ob 2cl hn 2bn. MS score: CH-Zma.

*HAEFFNER (HÄFFNER), Johann Christian Friedrich *1759 - 1833*; *Kapellmeister, Uppsala*
CJH-1. Den 20 Psalm [added:] af Tingstadius. 2ob 2cl(C) 2hn 2bn vc cb. MS score: S-Uu, Vok.mus.hs.93:4,
No. 1. *Related to the Musikalist Tidsfördrif (Stockholm, 1807), a setting for SATB to Tingstadius' text.* ★
CJH-2. Partie; in E♭, 3 mvts. 2ob 2cl 2hn 2bn. AutoMS score: S-Uu, Instr.mus.hs.72:17. ★
CJH-3. Sinfonia; in C, 2 mvts. 2ob 2cl(C) 2hn 2bn.
AutoMS score: S-Uu, Instr.mus.hs.72:16. *Mvt 2 bears the note, "Contredance af Konungen [?Gustav IV]
arrangirad af H.r Kapellmäst Haeffner".* ★
CJH-4. Allegro non tanto & Tempo Allemande; in E♭. 2ob 2cl 2hn 2bn.
AutoMS score: S-Uu, Instr.mus.hs.72:13. ★
CJH-5. Maestoso / Allegro, in B♭. 2ob 2cl 2hn 2bn. AutoMS score: S-Uu, Instr.mus.hs.72:12b. ★
CJH-6. Allegro non molto; in F. 2ob 2cl(C) 2hn 2bn. AutoMS score: S-Uu, Instr.mus.hs.72:12a. ★
CJH-7. Allegretto; in C. 2ob 2cl(C) 2hn 2bn. AutoMS score: S-Uu, Instr.mus.hs.72:1f. ★
CKJ-1m. March, Allegro maestoso. 2ob 2cl(C) 2hn 2bn. AutoMS score: S-Uu, Instr.mus.hs.72:2a. ★
CJH-2m. [Marche, in C]. 2ob 2cl(C) 2hn 2bn. AutoMS score: S-Uu, Instr.mus.hs.72:1e. ★
CJH-3m. [Untitled march]. 2ob 2cl(C) 2hn 2bn. AutoMS score: S-Uu, Instr.mus.hs.73:19. ★
CJH-1a. [?Gustav IV, King of Sweden]: Contredance. 2ob 2cl 2hn 2bn. Mvt 2 of **CJH-2.**
CJH-2a. Mozart: Harmonie Musik Aus das Operett [sic] Die Hochzeit das Figaro [Le Nozze di Figaro], Nos. 3,
20, 2 & 9. 2ob 2cl 2hn 2bn. AutoMS score: S-Uu, Instr.mus.hs.72:1a.

*HAERING, Joseph *(1780)*
JQH-1. Pièces d'Harmonie . . . dediés aux Élèves du louable colége [sic] de Notre Dame des Hermites; (40 short
pieces). 2p-fl 2cl(E♭) 2cl(B♭) 2hn 2bn tp serp timp. MS parts: CH-E, Th.185,3 (Ms.2578). ★
JQH-2. XVIII Pièces Pour la Musique Militaire dediés a l'usage de l'École de Notre Dames des Hermites
arrangé [sic] Par Jos: Haering; all in E♭. 2p-fl 2cl 2hn 2bn tp timp.
MS parts: CH-E, Th.185,2 (Ms.2577), (with 2 copies of the clarinet parts).
　2.1. Marche de parade, ₵. ★   2.2. Marche, ₵.   2.3. Pas redoublé, 6/8.   2.4. Marche de parade, C.
　2.5. Marche, C. 2.6. Pas redoublé. 2.7. Marche Moderato, 2/4.   2.8. Pas redoublé. 2.9. Marche Par Haering.
　2.10. Marche Par Haering. 2.11. Pas redoublé. 2.12. Tempo di minuetto. Moderato, 3/4.
　2.13. Pas redoublé.   2.14. Allemande anglaise, 2/4.   2.15(a). Allemande, arrangé par Jos. Haering, 2/4.
　2.16. Walze par Jos. Haering, 3/8.   2.17. Allemande. Allegro, 2/4.
　2.18(a). Mozart: Die Zauberflöte, "Bei Männern".
JQH-3. Deux Simphonies et un Rondau a Plusieurs Instruments en vents [crossed out: dediées aus Eleves du
louable Colége de Notre Dame des Hermites Par Jos: Haering de Schwytz] [sic]. 2fl 4cl 2hn 2bn tp serp timp.
MS parts: CH-E, Th.185,11 (Ms.2579).
　3.1. Grand Ouverture, E♭. ★   3.2. Rondo allegretto, 2/4.   3.3. Grand Simphonie.

HÄSER, Wilhelm *(1810)*
WIH-1v. Grablied, Lieblich tönt. Here only: cl(I) 2hn bn. MS parts: D-Tl, B 144, Nr. 5,5 M, (missing voice
part(s), (?fl) & cl II; written on the reverse of the cl I, hn 1 & 2, bn pts of Nr. 5,5, another Grablied).

*HAGMANN, L. *(1790)* *"Chef de Musique des Pionniers"*
LQH-1m. Harmonie militaire . . . dédié à la Garde Nationale de France, Œuv. Ier.
Solo Trompette à clefs, cl(D) 2cl(A) 2hn bn(I) bn(II)+cbn tb("Troma" [sic] in A basso).
Pc (Richault: Paris, pn 2769:R., 1830/1831), parts: CH-Gpu, Ib.4830; GB-Ljag, (photocopy). ★
LQH-1ac. Podpouri [sic] v[on] Hagman [sic] aus [C.M. Weber's] *[Der] Freischütz.* 2cl 2hn bn tp.
MS score: GB-Ljag(w). *The chromatic trumpet part was clearly intended for a keyed instrument; this is possibly
a local rescoring for the forces at Wertheim.* ★

HAGNER, M.E. *(1770)*
ZZH-1a. Mozart: Die Zauberflöte, overture. 2cl 2hn 2bn. MS pts: D-Rtt, W.A. Mozart 27/VI.

HAHN, Bernhard *1780 - 1852*
BQH-1v. Offertorium: "Jesu, dulcis memoria". CATB, vlne basso, (ad lib: 2cl 2hn).
MS score & parts: D-Tl, Gg 198, No. II, (copy of the edition published by F.E.C. Leuckart: Breslau). ★

HAHN, Joseph
YJH-1v. Deutsche Fest=Messe für Land Chöre. SSTB, organ, (ad lib: fl(D) 2cl(C) 2hn 2tp t-tb basso timp.
Pc (sn: sl, sd), parts: D-Tl, Gg 199. ★

*HAHN, Reynaldo *8 Sept 1875, Caracas - 28 Jan 1947, Paris*
*RXH-1. La Bal de Béatrice d'Este; ballet suite. 2fl ob 2cl 2hn 2bn tp piano 2harps perc(timp cym tri).
Pc (Heugel & Cie.: Paris, 1909), score: F-Pn; GB-Lbl, h.1507.ee.(4).

*HÁJEK, Aleš *1937, Czechoslovakia*
ALH-1. Octet. 2ob 2cl 2hn 2bn.
Pm (Český hudební fond: Prague, 1982), hire score & parts.

*HÁJEK, Jan (Johann) *Rector chori zu Teschen (now Český Těšín)*
DJH-1v. Solemnes Requiem aus dem Lateinischen in Deutsch; 7 mvts. SATB, 2ob 2cl 2hn(B♭, E♭) bn.
MS pts: CZ-Bm(au), A.20.782, (missing 2hn); CZ-Bm(kv), A.24.304. ★

*HALE, Samuel *(1770)*
SYH-1m. A Select Collection of Martial Music, Consisting of Marches, Quick Steps, Waltzes, Rondeaux, and
Favorite Divertisements. Comprised in 2 Books. 2fl 2cl 2hn bn serp.
Pc (C. Wheatstone: London, c.1804?), score: GB-Lbl, h.1570.h., (Book 1 only).
　1.1m. The Grenadiers Slow March.   1.2m. Hale: Waltz.   1.3m. Lord Cathcart's March.
　1.4m(a). Mozart: Quick Step.   1.5m(a). Jouve: The Austrian Retreat; [1 flute rather than 2].
　1.6m(a). Mozart: [Le Nozze di Figaro, Non più andrai]. The Duke of York's New March.
　1.7m. Hale: Quick Step.   1.8m. The Duke of York's New March.
　1.9m. The Royal Westminster Slow March & Waltz.   1.10m(a). R. Kreutzer: Lodoïska, march.
　1.11m(a). Jouve: The Downfall of Paris.   1.12m. The Prince of Wales's Volunteers March.
　1.13m(a). Mozart: Quick Step; [loosely based on the Finale to K.388].

*HALLAGER, A.
AWH-1. Reminiscenzen aus den letzten Tagen [last days] auf St Helena. Grosses Tongemälde [tone painting] in 3 Abtheilungen für grosse Militär-Musik. Instrumentation unknown.
MS score: D-Bds, Hausbibl. M.M.371.

HALLAM, Norman *(1960)*
NXH-1. Seven Variations for Six; (1991, for the Bournemouth Wind Quire).2cl 2hn 2bn. MS pts: GB-BFlowes.

*HALLBERG, Bengt *13 Sept 1932, Göteborg*
BQH-1. Hällristningar. Tondikt; 1974. 6 jazz soloists, 2fl 2ob 2cl 2hn 2bn 2tp tb timp perc.
Pc (Gehrmans musikförlag: Stockholm, c.1974).

HALLER, Michael (Georg) *13 Jan 1840, Neusaat, Oberpfalz - 4 Jan 1915 Regensburg*
MGH-1v. Das Deutsche Amt. CATB, vlne organ(+bc-fig), (2ob 2hn 2bn ad lib).
MS parts (by Jos. Pfreimer): A-Wn, Mus.Hs.22,986, (missing 2bn; with later parts in the same hand for 2fl; with a duplicate Canto parts; the organ part comprises a top line and bc-fig). ★

*HAMBRAEUS, Bengt *19 Jan 1928, Stockholm*
BEH-1. Strata; 1979 - 1980. 2ob 2cl 2bthn/a-cl 4hn 2bn b.
Pm (Edition Suecia, c/o S-Sic: Stockholm, c.1980), score & parts.

*HAMILTON, Iain (Ellis) *6 June 1922, Glasgow*
*IEH-1. Antigone, 1992. fl cl 2bn 2tp 2tb.
Pm (Alfred A. Kalmus: London, 1992), hire score & parts.
IEH-2. Sonatas and Variants. fl ob cl 2hn bn 2tp tb tu.
Pm (Schott: Mainz, London, 1963), score, (copies in GB-Lmic & GB-Gsma).

*HAMMER, August *"Prémière [sic] Hautbois chez le 7tiem Reg: d'Hollande"*
AXH-1. Fantasie; in F, 3 continuous sections. Solo oboe, fl 4cl 4hn 2bn 2tp a-tb t-tb b-tb serp perc.
MS pts: D-SWl, Mus. 2286. *Although the work is for "Orchestre Militaire", the Solo Oboe pt includes vl cues.* ★

*HAMMERL, Carl Anton *(1770)*
CAH-1. Partita; Eb (c.1800). ob 2cl 2hn bn. MS parts: D-ZL, (the 2nd mvt bears a note, "da Haydn").

*HAMMERL, Paul Cornelius *13 Dec (some sources give: Oct) 1769, Munich - 27 April 1839, Ludwigslust*
*PCH-1(-3). 3 Parties; (partly composed, partly arrangements. 2ob 2cl 2hn 3bn tp serp.
MS parts: D-SWl, Mus. 2288. *The numbering of movements is continuous.* ★
    1.1(a). Mussini: Ouverture. 1.2(a). Haydn: Symphony in G ("Surprise"; Hob. I/94), Andante.
    1.3(a). Winter: Das unterbrochene Opferfest: Allegretto. 1.4. Hammerl: Menuetto [& Trio].
    1.5. Hammerl: Rondo. 1.6. Hammerl: Menuetto [& Trio]. 1.7(a). Winter : Andante, Thema di Winter.
PCH-4. Pollonaisse [sic]; in C. 2ob 2cl 2hn 2bn tp serp. MS parts: D-SWl, Mus. 2288/2. ★
PCH-5. Suite; in C, 4 mvts. 2ob 2cl 2hn 2bn tp serp.
MS parts ("Decembre 25, 1802"): D-SWl, Mus. 2288/1, (missing ob II). ★
PCH-1a. Mozart: Le Nozze di Figaro, overture. 2fl 2cl(C) 2hn 2bn cbn/serp tp.
Pc (J.A. Böhme: Hamburg, pn M.1., sd), RISM [M 4451], parts: CH-Lz.
PCH-2a. Mozart: La Clemenza di Tito, overture. 2fl 2cl 2hn 2bn tp serp.
Pc (J.A. Böhme: Hamburg, sd), RISM [M 5215], parts: CH-Lz.
PCH-3a. Andante [by Pleyel, B.580ii; in F] et: Pollaca [by F. Witt; in C]. 2ob 2cl 2hn 2bn tp serp.
MS parts: D-SWl, Mus. 2288/3.

*HANDEL (Händel, Haendel), George Frideric (Georg Friedrich) *23 Feb 1685, Halle - 14 April 1759, London.*
CHR: *Georg Friedrich Händel's Werke. Ausgabe der Deutschen Händelgesellschaft, (Breitkopf & Härtel: Leipzig, 1859-1903).* **HH-A**: *Hallische Handel-Ausgabe. Im Auftrag der Georg-Friedrich-Händel-Gesellschaft (ed. Max Schneider & Rudolf Steglich). (Barenreiter: Kassel, 1955), scores.*
*GFH-1. Musick for the Royal Fireworks (HWV. 351). 3ob 3hn 2bn 3tp timp.
AutoMS score: GB-Lbl, RM.20.g.7, ff.16r - 29v. ★
Pc (Printed for I. Walsh: London, 1749), with strings, pts: GB-Lbl, h.435.k.(1); GB-Ob, Mus.221c.282.(3/1-5), missing 6 parts.
Pm (CHR. Bd. XLVII, p.100 ff.), score.
Pm (HH-A. Bd. IV/3, pp. 61-96), score, miniature score, parts.
Pm (Boosey & Hawkes: London, etc., 1943), ed. Charles Cudworth, score (Hawkes Pocket Scores, No.255), (version with strings).
Pm (C.F. Peters: New York, etc., 1959), ed. Robert Austin Boudreau, score & parts (wind version with 2fl 2cl 2hn 3tb ad lib).
Pm (Oxford University Press: London, 1960), ed. Anthony Baines & Charles Mackerras, score (both versions, with alternative scorings).
Pm (Bärenreiter: Kassel, Basel, 1964), score (winds), ed. Hans Ferdinand Redlich, (Taschenpartitur 173).
*GFH-2.1, 2.2. 2 Arias in F; (HWV. 410, HWV. 411; c.1725). 2ob 2hn bn.
MS: GB-Lbl, RM.18.b.8, ff.25-32, (GFF-2.2, fragment); GB-Cfm, Ms. 260, f.22. ★
Pm (Musica rara: London, pn 1215, 1958), ed. Karl Haas, parts.
*GFH-3. Minuet in G; (HWV. 422; 1746/7). 2ob 2hn bn. MS: GB-Cfm, Ms. 260, f.25. ★
GPH-4. Minuet in G; (HWV. 423; 1746/7). 2ob 2hn bn. MS: GB-Cfm, Ms. 263, f.77. ★
GFH-5. March in F; (HWV. 346, c.1740). 2ob 2hn bn.
MS score: GB-Lbl, Add.31641. ★
Pc (horn parts only), at the end of *Ptolemy* [sic]: GB-Lbl, g.74.11.(4).
*GFH-6. March in G; *(Judas Maccabeus).* 2ob 2hn bn. MS: GB-Cfm, Ms. 263, f.26. ★
*GFH-7. March in D; (HWV. 417b). 2ob 1/2hn bn.
MS (fragment): GB-Cfm, Ms. 252, f.34 ("a 3"); MS (horn 2 only): GB-Cfm, Ms, 263, f.78. ★
*GFH-8. March in D; (HWV. 345). 2ob bn tp.
MS: GB-Cfm, Barrett-Lennard Collection v.10 Miscellanys Mus.Ms.798, Sinfonie diverse No.7, p.243, Marche. ★
GFH-9. March in D; (HWV. 416; Dragoons' March, c.1740). 2ob bn tp. MS: GB-Cfm, Ms. 263, f.55. ★

*GFH-10. Overture [Suite] in D, (HWV. 424).   2cl hn.
MS: GB-Cfm, Ms. 264, ff.17 - 23.   ★
Pm (Mercury Music Corporation: New York, 1950), ed. J.M. Coopersmith & Jan La Rue, score & pts (for 2cl hn or 3cl).
Pm (McGinnis & Marx: New York, 1950).
Pm (Schott & Co.: London, 1952), ed. Karl Haas, score & parts.
*GFH-11. Rigaudon [D minor] & Bouree [G minor].   2ob bn (sd-dr ad lib).
MS: GB-Lbl, R.M.18.b, ff.65-66b.   ★
Pm (Musica rara: London, pn 1134 No. 1, 1958), ed. Karl Haas, score & parts.
*GFH-12. March in G.   2ob bn.
MS: GB-Cfm, Ms. 263, f.57.   ★
Pm (Musica rara: London, pn 1134 No. 2, 1958), ed. Karl Haas, score & parts.

*HANDL, Johann *(1770). Known mainly as a copyist: all attributions are suspect.*
JXH-1a. Salieri: Palmira, Harmonie Stück in Dis [E♭].   2cl 2hn bn tp(prin).
AutoMS parts: A-Wn, Mus.Hs.352, (with additional later parts: Fagotto tranposed to F for use with clarinets in C, Clarinetto 1mo with cues for "Horn", "Fagotto" & "Tromba").
JXH-1d. 13 Polonaisen.   2ob 2cl 2hn 2bn.   MS: A-Wn, (?lost).
JXH-1mad. Alpenhorn [Marsch] und Zwicker Marsch für 6st: [sic] Harmonie.   No. 1: cl(D) cl(A) 2hn 3tp b-tb b-dr; No. 2: cl(G) cl(D) 3tp tb b-dr.   MS parts: A-Wn, Mus.Hs.355, (with later pts for cl I in D to replace the cl I in G in No. 2, with the b-flug and 3tp parts transposed to C).   ★
JXH-1vd (= **A-5v**). Pange lingua a 4 Vocibus.   CATB, 2cl 2hn bn organ.
MS parts (by Handl): A-Wn, Mus.Hs.657, (with duplicate CAB, & 2 Organo pts - one in C and the other in D for use with clarinets in C; "Fagotto" is listed on the titlepage and probably read off the organ pt).   ★

HANDSCHUCH, ( ) *(1750)*
YZH-1. Parthia in Dis [E♭]; .   2ob 2cl 2hn 2bn.   MS pts: CZ-Pnm, Lobkovic X.H.a.11.   ★

HANFF, Wilhelm, See: HAUFF, Wilhelm Gottlieb *(1740 - d ?1777)*

*HANMER, Ronald (Charles Douglas) *1917, Reigate, UK*
RCH-1. Serenade for 7 winds.   2fl ob 3cl hn.
Pm (Emerson Edition: Ampleforth, pn E52, 1973), score & parts.
RCH-2. Suite for 7.   2fl ob 3cl bn.
Pm (Emerson: Ampleforth, pn E7, 1973), score & parts.
RCH-3. Five for Five.   fl fl/ob 2cl bn/b-cl.
Pm (Studio Music: London, c.1987), score & parts.
      3.1(a). Beethoven: Für Elise.   3.2(a). Traditional: The Fairy Reel.   3.3. Hanmer: Gracious Gavotte.   3.4(a). Traditional: Amazing Grace.   3.5. Hanmer: Finale for Five. Allegro molto, 3/8.
RCH-4. Cuckoo Quartet.   2fl 2cl.
Pm (Emerson: Ampleforth, pn E30, c.1974), score & parts.
RCH-1a. Woodwind Quintets. 1. All Through the Night; 2. Hanmer: Merry Minuet; 3. Over the Hills and Far Away; 4. Swing Low, Sweet Chariot; 5. Hanmer: Quintet Finale.   fl fl/ob 3cl.
Pm (Studio Music: London 1987), score & parts.

*HANSCHKE (Handscke, Hanisch), Anton *(1770) - active c.1801, Vienna*
AYH-1. Partia; in E♭, 2 mvts.   2cl 2hn 2bn.   MS parts: CZ-Pnm, XLI.B.105.   ★
AYH-1v. Chora [sic] a 4 Vocibus.   SATB, 2cl 2hn [bn].   MS pts: CZ-Pnm, XLI.B.202, (with 4 sets of S & A parts; although no bn part is present, we believe that the bassoonist read off the Bass voice part).   ★

HANSEN, Johannes *1915, Denmark*
HJH-1. Dedikation, Op. 100; 1974.   fl ob 2cl hn bn tb flüg 2perc.   MS: DK-Kd.

HANSEN, Peter *3 March 1958, Örebro*
PQR-1. Kolofon, Op. 10; 1993.   2fl 2cl b-cl 3hn bn 2tp 3tb tu timp.   MS score: S-Sic.

HANTKE (Handke), Mořic (Mauritius, Moritz) *c.1723 - 1804, Kroměříž*
MOH-1(-4). 4 Parthias, (ex C, 3 mvts; C, 4 mvts; C, 5 mvts; E♭, 6 mvts).   2ca 2hn bn.
MS parts: CZ-KRa, A4026/IV.B.199 a-e, Nos. 7 - 10.   ★
MOH-1v. Hymnus pro festo Theophoricae [Pange lingua].   CA, 2fl 2vla organ.
MS parts (1776, Schol Piarum ad S. Jeom Baptam.): CZ-KRa, A2071.   ★

HARBISON, John *20 Dec 1938, Orange, NJ, USA*
QJH-1. Music for 18 winds.   fl fl/pic 2ob 2cl a-sax 4hn bn bn/cbn 2crt 2tb tu.
Pm (Associated Music Publishers: New York, 1986), score (pn 50488840) & hire parts.

HARBORDT, Gottfried *1768 - 1837*
GXH-1t. Trauer Marsch; in B♭ minor.   2cl 2hn bn timp("con sordini").   MS parts: D-DS, Mus.ms.518.   ★

*HARKE, Friedrich *(1770)*
FZH-1m. 6 Märschen (C, F, A minor, A minor, D minor, C) . . . für eine zehnstimmige Harmonie Nach dem neuen für die k.k. Oester. Armée [sic] eingefürten geschwindern Tempo Siener der Generalissimus E.H. Carl Königl Hoheit in aller Unterhänigkeit gewidmet von Friedrich Harke Kappelmeister [sic] in 2-ten Inf Reg E.H. Ferdinand, c.1800.   2ob 2cl 2hn 2bn cbn tp.   MS parts: PL-LA, RM 66.   ★

*HARPER, Edward *17 March 1941, Taunton, Devon, UK*
EZH-1. Double Variations; 1989.   Solo oboe & bassoon, pic 2fl 2ob 2cl 4hn 2bn cbn 3tp 3tb tu timp 2perc (perc I: b-dr s-dr cym tamtam 3bongos glock xyl; perc II: cym, 3temple blocks, vibraphone xyl).
Pm: (Oxford University Press: London, pn 363084, c.1991), hire score & pts; pf reduction (pn J 3910).

*HARREX, Patrick *26 Sept 1946, London*
PXH-1. Antiphonies for 2 wind quartets; 1967.   fl a-fl ob ca cl b-cl 2hn 2bn.   MS score: GB-Lmic.

*HARRINGTON (Harrington), Thomas *(1760)*
TQM-1m. Lord Broom's March.   2cl 2hn 2bn, *or* piano, *or* flute, *or* guitar.
Pc (Printed & Sold by the Author: Bury St Edmunds, and at the Engravers (E. Riley): London, c.1800), score:
GB-SA, Fin M1746.G7N5, No. 140; GB-DOTams, (photocopy); GB-Ljag, (photocopy).   ★
TQH-1md. [attributed] Grand March in Honor of Admiral Nelson's Victory.   2cl 2hn bn tp , *or* piano.
Pc (Printed for Thoˢ Cahusac: London, c.1805), RISM Supp [HH 2111a], score: GB-SA, Fin M1746.G7N5,
No. 162; GB-DOTams, (photocopy); GB-Ljag, (photocopy).   ★

*HARTMANN, (Wilhelm) Emil *21 Feb 1836, Copenhagen - 8 Aug 1898, Copenhagen*
*JPH-1. Serenade, Op. 43; 1888, in B♭, 4 mvts.   fl ob 2cl 2hn 2bn vc/db.
Pc (Ries & Erler: Berlin, 1890).   ★
Pm (Compusic: Amsterdam, pn 209, 1991), score & parts.

*HARTMANN, Erich *1920, Germany*
*EQH-1. Nachtstück; 1992.   3ob ca 3bn cbn.
Pm (Compusic: Amsterdam, pn 513, c.1994), score & parts.

*HARVEY, Jonathan (Dean) *3 May 1939, Sutton Coldfield, UK*
*JIH-1. Serenade in Homage to Mozart; 2 mvts, (to precede Mozart's *Die Zauberflöte* at Glyndebourne).
fl fl(pic) 2ob cl(B♭, cl in E♭) cl(B♭, b-cl) 2hn 2bn.
Pm (Faber Music: London, 1991), hire score & parts.
JIH-2. Triptych.   fl ob 2cl bn piano.
Pm (Schott: London, 1961), score & parts.

HASENÖHRL, Franz *1 Oct 1885, Vienna - 13 Dec 1970, Vienna*
We do not know the current locations of FXH-4 & 5; A-Wögm may be able to assist.
FXH-1. Sinfonietta.   2fl 2ob 2cl 2hn 2bn.
Pm (Universal Edition/A.A. Kalmus: Wien, etc, 1951), MS score.
FXH-2. Serenade.   2fl 2ob 2cl 2hn 2bn.
Pm (Europäischer Verlag: Wien, 1953). *Materials now held in Universal Edition/A.A. Kalmus archives, Vienna.*
FXH-3. Divertimento; 1958.   4fl 4cl 2bn.
Pm (Schott: Mains, 1958), MS score held in archives, possibly available for hire.
FXH-4. Nocturne & Scherzo; 1958.   2fl 2cl bn.   MS: untraced, try A-Wögm.
FXH-5. Sextet; 1949.   fl ob cl b-cl hn bn.   MS: untraced, try A-Wögm.

*HASLINGER, Tobias *1 March 1787, Zell, Upper Austria - 18 June 1842, Zell*
*TZH-1. Europa's [sic] Sieges Feyer. Eine grosse musikalische Darstellung für die türkische Musik. Den
althöchs'ten verbunden siegreichen Kaisern und Königen den tapferen Heerfürrern und Helden der errungenen
Siege gewidmet.   pic 2fl 2ob cl(F) 3cl(B♭) 4hn(C, F) 2bn cbn 3tp(2C, F) b-dr s-dr cym.
Pc (Chemische Druckerei: Wien, pn 2465, pre-Oct 1816), pts: CZ-Pnm, XXXII.C.165, (MS pts by Jos. Hüller).   ★
1.1. Triumph Marsch der Terzen zur Siegesfeyer.   1.2. Dankhymne der Allmacht. Andante / Marsch & Trio.
1.3. Siegesjubel. Rondo militar [sic]. Allegro.
TZH-1v. Messe in C.   CATB, 2fl 2cl(C & B♭) 2hn bn 2vla organ.
MS parts: CZ-Pnm, XXXVIII.F.187, ("Herausgegeben [edited] v. Tobias Haslinger, Musikverleger in Wien").   ★

*HASSE, ( ) *(1800)*
YYH-1m. Geschwindmarsch des "Volhynischen Leib-Garde Regiments".   Instrumentation unknown.
MS score: D-Bds, Hausbibl.M.M.452.
YYH-1ma. Auber: La Muette de Portici: Geschwindmarsch de "Polnischen Leib-Garde-Grenadier-Regiments".
Instrumentation unknown.   MS score: D-Bds, Hausbibl.M.M.451.

HASSE, Johann Adolf (Giovanni Adolfo), *Il Sassone* *1699 - 1783*
DJH-1m. Marcia & Minuetto Marziale, in D.   2ob 2hn bn.   MS score & parts: I-Mc, Noseda Q.8.10.   ★

*HASSLOCH, Carl *1769 - 1829*
CYH-1. Zu Ubal; No. 1: Pastorale in G, fl ob cl(A) 2hn 2bn; No. 2: Chor: Komm lieblicher Engel, SATB, 2fl
2ob 2cl(A) 2hn 2bn db.   AutoMS score & MS parts: D-DS, Mus.ms.1214, (the vocal parts are missing).   ★
CYH-1.1m(-1.3m). III Märsche.   MS parts (c.1810): D-DS, Mus.ms.234.   ★
1.1m. Marche De Sauvages; in A minor.   2pic 2ob 2cl(C) 2hn 2bn 2tp b-dr cym tri.
1.2m. Trauer Marsch; in C minor.   2fl 2ob 2cl(C) 2hn 2bn.
1.3m. Quikmarch [sic]; in C.   2pic 2ob 2cl(C) 2hn 2bn 2tp b-dr.
*CYH-1v. Hexen Chöre zu Mekbet [sic, Macbeth].   MS pts: D-DS, Mus.ms.231, (with duplicate vla pts).   ★
1.1v. Acto 1; "Hui wir Schwestern Hand in Hand".   SSS, 2hn 2bn vla bassi.
1.2v. No. 2; "Lodre, bradte".   SSS, 2hn 2bn vla bassi.
1.3v. Hexentanz [pts: "hexentanz Walzer"]; "Geister schwarz und weiss".   (3)S, 2cl 2hn 2bn basso
1.4(v). Marsch; in C.   2ob 2hn bn.
*CYH-2v. Cantate bei Einweihung der neuen ▭ [i.e. Masonic Lodge] Johannes der Evangelist zur Eintracht im
O: zu Darmstadt Vom Br: Cer: Mˢᵗʳ Hassloch.   AutoMS score (c.1810): D-DS, Mus.ms.228.   ★
2.1v. Chorale, Bei dem Einzug; "Dankt dem Herrn".   TTB chorus, 2cl 2hn 2bn.
(Includes cues for the entrance of the Worshipful Grand Master, etc.)
2.2v. Cantata; 5 mvts, (begins "Aus Dunkel strahlt der Morgens uns").   TTB chorus, 2cl 2hn 2bn vc.

*HATAŠ (Hattasch, Hattisch), Ivan Wenzel (Jan Václav, Jean) *3 Dec 1727 - post-1752*
Not the same person as Hotiš; or T. Dismas Hataš. We have not been able to confirm two Parthias cited in
MGG: a Parthia in G (for fl 2ob 2hn bn; MS: D-SWl) and a Parthia in Dis (2ob 2hn 2bn, location not cited).
IWH-1. Parthia in D; 5 mvts.   2fl 2cl(A) 2hn bn.   MS parts: CZ-Pnm, XLII.E.292.   ★
IWH-2. Parthia per il Flant Stromenti in Dis [E♭]; 4 mvts.   2ob 2hn 2bn.   MS pts: CZ-Pnm, XLII.E.295.   ★
IWH-3. Parthia; in G, 5 mvts.   2fl 2cl 2hn.   MS parts: CZ-Pnm, XLII.E.294.   ★
IWH-4. N. 4 Parthia Pastoritia in C; (4 mvts).   2ob 2hn 2bn.   MS parts: CZ-Pnm, XLII.E.261.   ★
IWH-5. N: 1ᵐᵒ Parthia Pastoritia in D; 4 mvts.   2ob 2hn bn.   MS parts: CZ-Pnm, XLII.E.262.   ★
IWH-6. N: 3ᵗⁱᵒ Parthia Pastoritia in F; 4 mvts.   2ob 2hn bn.   MS parts: CZ-Pnm, XLII.E.263.   ★

IWH-7. Parthia Pastorita in G; 4 mvts.   2ob 2hn bn.   MS parts: CZ-Pnm, XLII.E.296.   ★
IWH-8. Parthia Pastoritia in G; 4 mvts.   2ob 2hn bn.   MS parts: CZ-Pnm, XLII.E.297.   ★
IWH-9. 4to Parthia in F per il Flant Stromenti; 4 mvts.   2ob 2hn bn.   MS parts: CZ-Pnm, XLII.E.293.   ★
IWH-10. N: 5° Parthia per il Flant Stromenti in G; 4 mvts.   2ob 2hn bn.   MS parts: CZ-Pnm, XLII.E.291.   ★
IWH-11. Cantata mit Türkischer Musik[,] Abgefalten bei ihr Warenrechnung Sr durchlaucht ihr Fürsten Carl [probably Carl Anselm] Thurn & Taxis [sic].   pic[I], flauto militar 2do, cl(F) 2cl(C) 2hn 2bn 2tp(clar).
MS parts (from Opočno, Bohemia): CZ-Pnm, XLII.F.725, *(apparently complete, but may lack vocal pts).*   ★

*HAUFF (HANFF), Wilhelm Gottlieb   *(1740 - ?c.1777)*
WXH-1(-6). 6 Sextets.   2cl 2hn 2bn.   *The bassoon parts are virtually unison.*
Pc (Mandhare: Paris; Godefroi: Brussels; et aux Addresses ordinaire, sd [c.1776/77]), RISM Supp [HH 2364a], parts: I-Rsc, (missing hn I & II, bn II).
MS parts: D-F, Mus.Hs.1567 (Sextuor II in E♭, 3 mvts), Mus.Hs.1563, (Sextuor III; in E♭, 3 mvts).   ★

HAUSCHILD, ( )
QZH-1. Fest-Schottisch, für Harmonie.   fl 2ob 2cl(E♭) 3cl(B♭) 2hn 2bn 2cap/tp(obl) 3tb.
MS parts: D-DT, Mus-n 1664

*HAUSLER (HÄUSLER, HAUSSLER, HAUSSER), (? Ernst)   *1760/1761 - 1837*
EXH-1. Parthia [C] National Marche & Aria François Saira [sic]; c.1792.   pic 2fl 2ob 2cl 2hn 2bn 2tp tamboro.
MS parts: D-HR, HR III 4 1/2 2° 360.   Pm (KGS), fiche (2312).   ★
EXH-2. 2 Kirchencantaten *(one for orchestra, the other for winds).*   MS score: D-As.
EXH-3. 6 Notturni, Op. 23; (all 2 mvts).   2hn 2bn.
(?Auto)MS parts (c.1800): D-Rtt, Häusler 1.   ★
Pc (Breitkopf & Hartel: Leipzig, pn 147, 1804), parts: D-SWl, Mus.Ms.2524.
Pc (Giov. André: Offenbach s/M, pn 2019), Nos. 1 - 3 as "Tre Notturni, Op. 23", parts: H-KE, 1037/IX.
No. 1 = Nos. 1i, 2ii, 3ii; No. 2 = Nos. 6ii, 3i; No. 3 = Nos. 4i, 5ii, 1ii.   ★
EXH-1v. Kirchen-Musik; "Lasset uns mit Andachts hören.   SATB concertante, ob 2hn bn vc cb.
AutoMS score: D-Mbs, Mus.Ms.1799.   ★

*HAUSSER, Joseph   *(1800, active 1837) Kapellmeister, 14ten Linien Infanterie Regt Richter von Bienenthal*
SJH-1a. Donizetti: Marino Faliero, aria.   (Solo) flug, fl(E♭) 2ob cl(A♭) cl(E♭) 2cl(B♭) 2hn 2bn cbn 2tp b-tb.
(?Auto)MS score: A-Wn, Mus.Hs.20,521.

HAVEL, Václav (Wenzel)   *c.1778, Prague - post-1826, [?Kroměříž]*
VXH-1. Allegro ut pastorela [sic], B♭, 21 Jan 1806.   2cl 2hn 2bn, tuba pastorela principale [alphorn].
AutoMS parts (21 Jan 1806): CZ-KRa, A4468/R.I.38.   ★
VXH-2. Echo; in B♭, (3 original movements attached to VXH-45a).   2cl 2hn bn.
AutoMS parts: CZ-KRa, IV.B.165, (5th mvt).   ★
VXH-3. Echo in Dis [E♭].   2cl 2hn 2bn.   AutoMS parts: CZ-KRa, A4465/R.I.35.   ★
VXH-4. Ländler, mvt 6 of Havel's arrangement of Winter's *Das unterbrochene Opferfest.*   2cl 2hn 2bn.
AutoMS parts: CZ-KRa, A4006/IV.B.178.   ★
VXH-5. Theme & 5 variations ("Partitur für die Harmonie").   2cl(C) 2hn 2bn.
(?Auto)MS score: CZ-KRa, A.4013/IV.B.169, (included with Havel's arrangement of works from J. Weigl's operas - for 2cl 2hn bn; the theme matches none of the works in this set).   ★
VXH-6. N^{ro} 27. Sei Variatione; in E♭.   2cl 2hn 2bn.
AutoMS parts (by Havel, 4 Sept 1809): CZ-KRa, A4459/R.I.29.   ★
VXH-7. N^{ro} 28. Variatione in E♭; (theme, 4 vars, coda).   2cl 2hn 2bn.
AutoMS parts (by Havel, 7 Sept 1811): CZ-KRa, A4460/R.I.30.   ★
VXH-8. N^{ro} 29. Sei Variatione ut Allegretto; in E♭.   2cl 2hn 2bn.
AutoMS parts (by Havel, 9 Sept 1809): CZ-KRa, A4461/R.I.31.   ★
VXH-9(a). N^{ro} 33. Variatione in F. Acomo. [sic] di Harmonia Hawell [sic]; (in fact, Theme, 5 vars, [Ländler] & Quadril [sic]).   2cl 2hn 2bn.   AutoMS parts (31 Jan [1]806): CZ-KRa, A4462/R.I.32.   *Probably an original set of variations for piano, later scored for Harmonie.*   ★
VXH-10. N^{ro} 36. [6] Variatione in B[♭].   2cl 2hn 2bn.   AutoMS parts: CZ-KRa, A4463/R.I.34.   ★
VXH-11. N^{ro} [crossed out: 121] 120. Variatione in G; (on "Wenn ich in der Früh aufsteh" Tost's *Der Lugner;* theme, 5 vars, coda).   2cl 2hn 2bn.   AutoMS pts: CZ-KRa, (2 copies) A4486/R.I.57, A4488/R.I.58, No. 1, (in C).   *Possibly based on Triebensee's Variations for pf vl & gtr (Artaria: Wien, pn 300, c.1796). See also VXH-40a.*   ★
VXH-12. Variatione in B[♭], No. 2 [Haydn: Symphony in G, "Surprise", Hob. I/94ii, Andante; theme, 9 vars, coda].   2cl 2hn 2bn.   MS parts: CZ-KRa, A4488/R.I.58, No. 2.   ★
VXH-13.1, 13.2. Variatione [Thema, 5 vars, coda] und Ländler.   2cl 2hn 2bn.
AutoMS parts: CZ-KRa, A4490/R.I.60.   ★
VXH-1s. Additional bn I part for Lickl's Quintetto, Op. 21.
AutoMS parts: CZ-KRa, A3917/IV.B.80; GB-Ljag, (photocopy); GB-DOTams, (edited modern copy).
VXH-2s. Additional tp II part for Nos. 6 & 10 of Triebensee's *Miscellannées de Musique,* Jg. I, Oe. 8.
AutoMS part: CZ-KRa, A3930/IV.B.93.
VXH-3s. Additional bn I part for Ahl's arrangement of Paer's opera *Griselda,* Recueil 1, (CXA-1a).
AutoMS part: CZ-KRa, A4018/IV.B.191.
VXH-4s. Additional 2ob & 2tp parts for Pechatschek's Variatione in B(♭), (FMP-1, 2cl 2hn 2bn).
AutoMS parts: CZ-KRa, A3949/IV.B.112.
VXH-5s. Additional 2fl parts for Czerny's arrangement (2cl 2hn 2bn, CYC-2a) of Winter's *Das unterbrochene Opferfest,* overture & 11 mvts.   AutoMS pts: CZ-KRa, A4005/IV.B.177.
VXH-1a. Cimarosa: Gli Orazi e Curiazi, Parthe [sic] I: overture & 8 mvts, Parthe [sic] IIdo: 9 mvts.   2cl 2hn 2bn.
MS parts: CZ-KRa, A4452/R.I.22, [Nos. 4 & 5].
VXH-2a. Eybler: 7 Variations on "A Schüsserl und a Reinell".   2cl 2hn 2bn.   MS pts: CZ-KRa, A3860/IV.B.24.
VXH-3a. Fräntzel: 1 mvt, as "N. 1mo Serenatta [sic]".   2cl 2hn 2bn.   MS pts: CZ-KRa, A4476/R.I.46, No. 1.
VXH-4a. Gyrowetz: Aria Russe.   2cl 2hn 2bn.   MS parts (4 Aug 1808): CZ-KRa, A3864/IV.B.28.
VXH-5a. Hradecký: 6 Variationen ut Coda.   2cl 2hn 2bn.   MS parts: CZ-KRa, A3893/IV.B.56.
VXH-6a. Kozeluch: Il ritrovata figlia di Ottone II, overture & 8 mvts.   2cl 2hn bn.
MS parts: CZ-KRa, A4482/R.I.52.

VXH-7a. Krommer: Partita in B♭, Op. 45, No. 1 (as "Parthia 3tia", 1808).   2cl 2hn 2bn tp(ad lib).
MS parts: CZ-KRa, A3905/IV.B.68.
VXH-8a. Krommer: Partita in E♭, Op. 45, No. 2 (as "Nro 3 [Parthia] Sig. Kromer [sic] acc. Havel").
2cl 2hn 2bn.   MS parts: A4455/R.I.25, No. 3.
VXH-9a. Krommer: Partita in B♭, Op. 45, No. 3 (as "Nro 2 Parthia in B", 1808).   2cl 2hn 2bn tp(ad lib).
MS parts: CZ-KRa, A3904/IV.B.67.
VXH-10a. Krommer: Harmonie in F, Op. 57 (as "Nro 1mo Parthia In F", 27 July 1808).   2cl 2hn 2bn tp(ad lib).
MS parts: CZ-KRa, A3903/IV.B.66; GB-Ljag, (photocopy).
VXH-11a. Krommer: Harmonie in B♭, Op. 67 (as "Parthia V in B").   2cl 2hn 2bn tp(ad lib).
MS parts: CZ-KRa, A3907/IV.B.70.
VXH-12a. Krommer: Harmonie in E♭, Op. 69 (as "Parthia IVta", 1808).   2cl 2hn 2bn tp(ad lib).
MS parts: CZ-KRa, A3906/IV.B.69.
VXH-13a. Krommer: Partita in E♭, (FVK-16), (as "Nro 6 Parthia in dis", 2 mvts: Allegro, Finale).   2cl 2hn 2bn.
MS parts: CZ-KRa, A3910/IV.B.73.
VXH-14a. Krommer: Parthia in.E♭, (FVK-17), (as "Nro 1mo Parthia in dis", 6 Aug 1808).   2cl 2hn 2bn.
MS parts: CZ-KRa, A3909/IV.B.72.
VXH-15a. Krommer: Partita in B♭, (FVK-21.1), (as "Nro 2do Parthia In B").   2cl 2hn 2bn.
MS parts (8 Aug 1808): CZ-KRa, A3911/IV.B.74.
VXH-16.1a. Martín y Soler: L'Arbore di Diana, overture, (Act 1) Nos. 1-14, (Act 2) Nos. 15-25.   2cl 2hn 2bn.
AutoMS parts: CZ-KRa, A4452/R.I.22, [No. 10].   *Possibly a reduction of Went's octet arrangement; the*
Overture [0] and the Finales (Nos. 14 & 25) are missing sections found in Went's version.
VXH-16.2a. Martín y Soler: L'Arbore di Diana, overture & 9 mvts.   2cl 2hn bn.
AutoMS parts (18 Aug 1813): CZ-KRa, A4481/R.I.51.
One of the three following works may be Mašek's lost "Parthia vel Variazione" cited by Jerkowitz.
VXH-17a. V.V. Mašek: [7] Variatione in G [or rather, in F].   2cl 2hn 2bn.
MS parts (1805): CZ-KRa, A3919/IV.B.82.
VXH-18a. V.V. Mašek: [7] Variatione in B[♭].   2cl 2hn 2bn.   MS parts: CZ-KRa, A3920/IV.B.83.
VXH-19a. V.V. Mašek: [5] Variatione in B[♭].   2cl 2hn 2bn.   MS parts: CZ-KRa, A3921/IV.B.84.
VXH-20a. Maurer: Niederländen Bauern, Pas de deux für die Pantomime Arlequin und Colombini auf der Alpen.
2cl 2hn(B♭ basso) 2bn, tuba pastoralis(C).   MS parts: CZ-KRa, A3367/R.I.38.   *Here Havel rescores a movement*
from Triebensee's Miscellanées de Musique, Jg. I, Oe. 1, No. 6.
VXH-21a. Mayr: La Lodoiska, overture & 13 mvts.   2cl 2hn 2bn.
AutoMS parts (13 Jan 1808): CZ-KRa, A3845/IV.B.9, (here incorrectly attributed to Cherubini).
VXH-22a. Mozart: Divertimento in E♭, (WAM-4d, K6.C.17.01, as "Partitta IIIta, E♭"), 5 mvts.   2cl 2hn 2bn.
MS parts: CZ-KRa, A4457/R.I.27 a-f, No. 3, ("Acod: [sic] Ha[vel]").
VXH-23a. W. Müller: Die Teufelsmühle, overture & 20 mvts.   2cl 2hn 2bn.
MS parts: CZ-KRa, A4452/R.I.22, No. 3.
VXH-24a. Paer: L'intrigo amoroso, overture & 11 mvts.   2cl 2hn 2bn.   MS parts: CZ-KRa, A4484/R.I.54.
VXH-25a. Paer: Camilla, overture & 3 mvts.   2cl 2hn bn.   MS parts (17 April 1806): CZ-KRa, A4479/R.I.49.
VXH-26a. Paer: Achille, arr. Sedlak (2cl 2hn 2bn), overture & 16 mvts.   Rescored by Havel for 2cl 2hn bn.
MS parts: CZ-KRa, A3945/IV.B.108.
VXH-27a. Pleyel: String Quartet, (B.308).   2cl 2hn 2bn.
MS parts: CZ-KRa, A4455/R.I.25, No. 24, (as "Parthia 24").
VXH-28a. Pleyel: String Quartet, (B.310), mvts 1 & 4 only.   2cl 2hn 2bn.
MS parts: CZ-KRa, A4455/R.I.25, No. 11, (as "Parthia 11").
VXH-29a. Pleyel: 6 String Quartets (1786), Moderato (B.319/i).   2cl 2hn 2bn.
MS parts (18 Jan 1805): CZ-KRa, A4476/R.I.46, No. 2, (as "Serenatta [sic] 2da").
VXH-30a. Pleyel: String Quartet, (B.321).   2cl 2hn 2bn.   MS pts: CZ-KRa, A4455/R.I.25, No. 7, (as "Parthie 7").
VXH-31a. Pleyel: String Quartet, (B.322).   2cl 2hn 2bn.   MS pts: CZ-KRa, A4455/R.I.25, No. 9, (as "Parthie 9").
VXH-32a. Pleyel: String Quartet, (B.323).   2cl 2hn 2bn.
MS parts: CZ-KRa, A4455/R.I.25, No. 15, (as "Parthie 15").
VXH-33a. Pleyel: String Quartet, (B.324).   2cl 2hn 2bn.
MS pts: CZ-KRa, A4455/R.I.25, No. 10, (as "Parthia 10").
VXH-34a. Pleyel: Sting Quartet, (B.325), (as "Nro. 15"); mvts 1 & 4 only.   2cl 2hn 2bn.
MS parts: CZ-KRa, A4471/R.I.43.
VXH-35a. Pleyel: String Quartet, (B.334).   2cl 2hn 2bn.
MS parts: CZ-KRa, A4455/R.I.25, No. 16, (as "Parthie 16").
VXH-36a. Pleyel: String Quartet, (B.343).   2cl 2hn 2bn.
MS parts: CZ-KRa, A4455/R.I.25, No. 12, (as "Parthae 12").
VXH-37a. Pleyel: String Quartet, (B.347).   2cl 2hn 2bn.
MS parts: CZ-KRa, A4455/R.I.25, No. 19, (as "Parthia 19").
VXH-38a. Pleyel: String Quartet, (B.358/i, ii).   2cl 2hn 2bn.
MS parts: CZ-KRa, A4455/R.I.25, No. 6, (as "Parthie 6").
VXH-39a. Pleyel: 6 Quartets for fl/vl vl vla vc, (B.381-386); 3 mvts: Allegro (B.384/i), Andante (B.386/ii),
Rondo Allegro non troppo (B.384/iii).   2cl 2hn 2bn.
MS parts (19 Sept 1806): CZ-KRa, A3950/IV.B.113, No. 1, (as "Nro VIta Parthia, in E♭").
VXH-40a. Tost: Der Lügner, Cadentz, 6 Ländler & Coda.   2cl 2hn 2bn.   MS parts (13 July 1810): CZ-KRa,
A4485/R.I.55.   *Ländler 1 is "Wenn ich in der Früh aufsteh", (cf. VXH-11 & 5.3a).*
VXH-41a. Triebensee (as arranger): Miscellanées de Musique, Jg. I, Oe. 1.   Rescored for: 2cl 2hn 2bn tp.
MS parts (7 Dec 1812): CZ-KRa, A3978/IV.B.144.
VXH-42a. M. Umlauf: Das eigensinnige Landmädchen, overture & 9 mvts.   2cl 2hn 2bn.
MS parts: CZ-KRa, A3979/IV.B.147.
VXH-43a. J. Weigl: Das Sinnbild des menschlichen Lebens, overture & 6 mvts.   2cl 2hn bn.
MS parts: CZ-KRa, A3945/IV.B.108.   *The mvts (overture, Nos. 4, 2, 9, 10, 14, 15, 6) are probably a reduction*
of Went's sextet arrangement.
VXH-44a. J. Weigl: Richard Löwenherz, overture & 16 mvts.   2cl 2hn 2bn.
MS parts: CZ-KRa, A4452/R.I.22, No. 8.

VXH-45a. J. Weigl: Clothilde, (overture & 3 mvts, with 3 original mvts, VXH-2).   2cl 2hn 2bn.
MS parts: CZ-KRa, A3995/IV.B.165.   *The order of movements corresponds to the first four movements of the anonymous arrangement in CZ-KRa, A3995/IV.B.165b.*
VXH-46a. T. Weigl: Bacchus et Ariadne, overture & 12 mvts.   2cl 2hn 2bn.   AutoMS parts: ("Chrást, 14/2 1807"): CZ-KRa, A4452/R.I.22, No. 8.   *Probably a reduction of Triebensee's nonet arrangement.*
VXH-47a. Wilde: Tänze des Brassilianischen Ballfeste, 8 Walzer & Coda, Quadrille, Polonaise & Trio. 2cl(C) 2hn 2bn.   MS parts: CZ-KRa, A4191/R.I.61.
VXH-48a. Winter: Das unterbrochene Opferfest, overture & 4 mvts.   2cl 2hn 2bn.
MS parts: CZ-KRa, A4006/IV.B.178.   *The four mvts match mvts 5, 8, 4 & 10, respectively, of Czerny's arrangement for 2cl 2hn 2bn (CYC-2a), possibly rescored.*
VXH-49. P. Wranizky: Oberon, overture & 13 mvts.   2cl 2hn 2bn.
MS parts: CZ-KRa, A4452/R.I.22, No. 6.   *Havel states "Aut[hore]: Stumpf". This may indicate that the arrangement is based on Stumpf's arrangement, Recueils 4 & 5; Stumpf does not usually include an overture so this may have been added by Havel.).*
VXH-50.1a. Zingarelli: Giulietta e Romeo, overture & 6 mvts.   2cl 2hn 2bn.
MS parts (2 copies): CZ-KRa, A4177/IV.B.181, (Chr[ást], 24 Oct 1808) & A4452/R.I.22, No. 2, ("Sig. Maestro Zincarely [sic] per il Clavi Cembalo. Acomo. de Harmo= Havel").
VXH-50.2a. Zingarelli: Giuletta e Romeo, overture.   2cl 2hn 2bn.   MS pts: CZ-KRa, A3919/IV.B.82, No. 2.
VXH-51a. Anon: Kaiser Alex, Favorit Tänze. N° 119. IV Poloness und Zwey Quadril [sic].   2cl 2hn 2bn. AutoMS parts: CZ-KRa, A4486/R.I.56.
VXH-52a. N° 23. 3: Arien.   2cl 2hn 2bn.   AutoMS parts: CZ-KRa, A4458/R.I.28.
    52.1a. Anon: das Nachtständchen.   52.2a. Anon: Wiegenleid ("Schlafe mein Prinzessin").
    52.3a. Tost: Der Lugner, "Wenn ich in der Früh aufsteh".
VXH-53a. N° 100. 10 Arien für die Fünf Stimige Harmonie [sic]. Weigl. Accomodata H[avel].   2cl 2hn bn.
MS parts: CZ-KRa, A4176/IV.B.163.
    53.1a. [Anon]: Kaiser Alex, duett, No. 1.   53.2a. Weigl: Alcina, No. 2.
    53.3a. Die Reue des Pygmalion, No. 3.   53.4a. [Méhul]: Une Folie], beiden Füchse, Nos. 4 & 5.
    53.5a. [W. Müller]: Die Teufelsmühle [auf der Danube], Nos. 6 - 10.
VXH-54a. Anon: Aria in F, "Wilkommen Schüster".   2cl 2hn 2bn.
MS parts (by Havel, 1810): CZ-KRa, A4464/R.I.34.
VXH-1.ma(-1.5ma). IV Märsche [with one added later].   2cl 2hn 2bn tp(prin).
MS parts (by Havel): CZ-KRa, A4467/R.I.37.
    1.1ma. Anon: Bey Eröffnungs des Monument des S[t] S: [word illegible] Joseph d: 2ten.
    1.2ma. [?Paer: Sargino] Kaysers Napoloen Lieblings March (Sarsano Marsch).
    1.3ma. Der Nachwächter.   1.4ma. [?Thern]: Aufzug bei der Wachtparade.   1.5ma. [Anon: untitled march].
VXH-1c. N° 61. Parthia . . . Aut. N: N: [i.e. Anon; added later in pencil: "Havel"]; in E♭, 3 mvts.   2cl 2hn 2bn.
MS parts (by Havel): CZ-KRa, A4477/R.I.47.   ★
VXH-2c. N° 62. Parthia in dis [E♭]; 3 mvts.   2cl 2hn 2bn.
MS parts ("1800 Chras [sic] Havel"): CZ-KRa, A4478/R.I.48.   ★
VXH-3c. Parthia in Dis Nro 3 . . . Author N: N: [i.e. Anon; added later in ink: "Hawel"]; in E♭, 3 mvts. 2cl 2hn 2bn.   MS parts (29 Oct [1]806): CZ-KRa, A4469/R.I.40.   ★
VXH-1ac - VXH-12ac, in the bound volumes titled, "XXIV Parthien del Sig Krommer et Pleyel / N:5", are almost certainly arrangements by Havel, possibly of string quartets by Krommer.
VXH-1ac. Anon: Parthie 4; in E♭, 3 mvts.   2cl 2hn 2bn.   MS parts: CZ-KRa, A4455/R.I.25, No. 4.   ★
VXH-2ac. Anon: Parthie N:5; in E♭, 4 mvts.   2cl 2hn 2bn.   MS parts: CZ-KRa, A4455/R.I.25, No. 5.   ★
VXH-3ac. Anon: Parthie 8; in E♭, 2 mvts.   2cl 2hn 2bn.   MS parts: CZ-KRa, A4455/R.I.25, No. 8.   ★
VXH-4ac. Anon: Parthie 13; in B♭, 3 mvts.   2cl 2hn 2bn.   MS parts: CZ-KRa, A4455/R.I.25, No. 13.   ★
VXH-5ac. Anon: Parthie 14; in F, 4 mvts.   2cl 2hn 2bn.
MS parts (12 Aug 1805): CZ-KRa, A4455/R.I.25, No. 14.   ★
VXH-6ac. Anon: Parthie 17; in E♭, 3 mvts.   2cl 2hn 2bn.   MS parts: CZ-KRa, A4455/R.I.25, No. 17.   ★
VXH-7ac. Anon: Parthie 18; in E♭, 3 mvts.   2cl 2hn 2bn.   MS parts: CZ-KRa, A4455/R.I.25, No. 18.   ★
VXH-8ac. Anon: Parthie 19; in E♭, 3 mvts.   2cl 2hn 2bn.   MS parts: CZ-KRa, A4455/R.I.25, No. 19.   ★
VXH-9ac. Anon: Parthie 20; in B♭, 4 mvts.   2cl 2hn 2bn.   MS parts: CZ-KRa, A4455/R.I.25, No. 20.   ★
VXH-10ac. Anon: Parthie 21; in E♭, 4 mvts.   2cl 2hn 2bn.   MS parts: CZ-KRa, A4455/R.I.25, No. 21.   ★
VXH-11ac. Anon: Parthie 22; in A♭, 2 mvts.   2cl 2hn 2bn.   MS parts: CZ-KRa, A4455/R.I.25, No. 22.   ★
VXH-12ac. Haibl: Der Tiroler Wastel, 7 mvts.   2cl 2hn 2bn.
MS parts (by Havel, 25 Jan 1805): CZ-KRa, A3938/IV.B.101.
VXS-13ac. Solié: Le Chapitre second, overture & 13 mvts.   2cl 2hn 2bn.
MS parts: CZ-KRa, A4453/R.I.23, No. 4, (here as "Das zweyte Capitel, von Winter").
VXH-14ac. P. Wranizky: Das Urtheil des Paris, overture & 12 mvts.   2cl 2hn 2bn.
MS parts: CZ-KRa, A4453/R.I.23, No. 6.
VXH-15ac. N° 39. Arien.   2cl 2hn 2bn.   MS pts: CZ-KRa, A4466/R.I.36, (16.7ac & 16.8ac are later additions).
    15.1ac. Krommer: [4] Variatione.   15.2ac. Krommer: Finalle [sic].
    15.3ac. Hoffmeister: Aria et Echo.   *Note VXH-16.2c which attributes the Echo to Pleyel (B. deest).*
    15.4ac. P. Wranizky [?arranged Stumpf]: Arie aus Oper Oberon /Sig. Stumpf/.
    15.5ac. Anon: Martzia.   15.6ac. Winter: Das unterbrochene Opferfest, Arie.
    15.7ac. Anon: Martzia; in C.   15.8ac. Anon: Martzia IIdo; in C.
VXH-16ac. Echo N°1 in F von Triebensee, N° 2 in Es [E♭] von Pleyel (B. deest).   2fl 2cl 2hn 2bn.
AutoMS parts: CZ-KRa, A4452/R.I.22, No. 7.   *The Echo by Pleyel is attributed is Hoffmeister at VXH-17.3ac.*
VXH-1ad. Kozeluch: Il ritrovato figlia d'Ottone II, overture & 16 mvts.
AutoMS pts: CZ-KRa, A4452/R.I.22, No. 7.   *Essentially Went's sextet arrangement with some key tranpositions.*
VXH-2ad. Paer: Camilla, overture & 10 mvts.   2cl 2hn 2bn.   MS parts: CZ-KRa, A4452/R.I.22, No. 1.   *This is essentially Went's sextet arrangement with the clarinet parts transposed so that all mvts use cl(B♭).*

HAWKES, Jack Richards *18 May 1916, Ipswich, UK*
JRH-1. Pieces of Eight.   2fl 2ob 2cl 2bn.
Pm (Emerson Edition: Ampleforth, pn E58, 1979), score & parts.

*HAYDN, Franz Joseph *31 March 1732, Rohrau, Lower Austria - 31 May 1809, Vienna*
JHW: Joseph Haydn Werke. Herausgegeben vom Joseph Haydn-Institut, Köln, unter der Leitung von Jens Peter Larsen. (G. Henle Verlag: München, Duisberg, 1958, etc.), scores; the wind divertimenti are to be found in Reihe VIII, Bd. 2, Bläserdivertimenti und "Scherzandi", ed. Sonja Gerlach & Horst Walter, in association with Makoto Ohmiya, 1991. The numbers "N27", etc., are those of the New Grove, and "Hellyer 8", etc, are from the Haydn Jahrbuch, XV 5. The "old Clam Gallas No." numbers (from Robbins Landon) are not current in CZ-Pnm. These numbers were added by Speer when he prepared the Clam Gallas catalog; Speer also supplied the numbering of the Parthien. Modern titles given as "Divertimento No. 1", etc. are equivalent to the "Stp" (Studentpartitur) numbers of the Doblinger miniature scores.
*FJH-1. Introduzione, Die Worte des Erlösers am Kreuze (The Seven Last Words of the Redeemer on the Cross), A minor, Introduction to Part II, 1795-96, (Hob. XX/1A). fl 2ob 2cl 2hn 2bn cbn 2tb.
Pc (Breitkopf & Härtel: Leipzig, 1801), score: GB-Lbl, (3 copies), E.409.a., Hirsch IV.810, RM.8.g.18. ★
Pm (JHW: Reihe XXVII, pp. 93 - 102).
Pm (WINDS: Northridge, CA, pn W-259 c.1981), score & parts (photocopies).
*FJH-2. Divertimento [Feld-Parthie]; in F, 1760, Hob II/16, N27, Hellyer 8. 2vl 2ca 2hn 2bn.
AutoMS score: H-Bn, Ms.Mus.I.47. ★
MS score (19th century): A-Wgm, XI 40913 (Q 17271), (MS by Pohl); D-B, Mus.ms.10023, (MS by Otto Jahn).
MS parts (c.1790): D-Rtt, J.Haydn 89, (as "Concertino"; bn I+II pt incomplete in Adagio).
Pm (pp. 10 - 32 of the music supplement to A Reissmann's *Joseph Haydn*. Berlin, 1879), score: GB-Lbl (main book catalog), 010708.h.67.
Pm (Friedrich Hofmeister: Leipzig, 1954), ed. Kurt Janetzky, score (pn 1542) & pts (pn 1543), based on D-B.
Pm (JHW: Reihe VIII, Bd. 2, 1991, pp. 43 - 60), score.
*FJH-3. Divertimento [Parthia]; in F, 1760, (Hob II/15, N29, Hellyer 1), 5 mvts. 2ob 2hn 2bn.
AutoMS score: A-Wn, (Harrach Archives), MS. 784., (incomplete after bar 18 of 5th mvt). ★
MS parts: A-Wgm; CZ-KRa, A4024-4025/IV.B.198 a-f, Part 1, No. 4, (dated 1766); CZ-Pnm, (2 copies), XLII.D.33 [old Clam Gallas No. 371, as "Parthia in G"], XLII.D.21 (as "Parthia in F" [old Clam Gallas No. 423/3]).
Pm (Doblinger: Wien, 1959), ed. H.C. Robbins Landon, score & pts (Diletto musicale 29), min score (pn Stp 180 No. 1).
Pm (Oxford University Press: London, 1960), ed. Fritz Spiegl, score & parts (for 2ob/fl hn/cl 2bn).
Pm (G. Schirmer: New York, 1965), score & parts (Musica da camera, pn 3/45788).
Pm (JHW: Reihe VIII, Bd. 2, 1991, pp. 18 - 23), score.
*FJH-4. Divertimento [Feldparthie, Parthia]; in F, pre-1765, (Hob II/23, N22, Hellyer 2), 5 mvts. 2ob 2hn 2bn.
AutoMS: D-B, Ms.auto. Haydn 8 (only 4th & 5th mvts in autograph). ★
MS parts: A-Wgm, VIII 40898; A-Wn; CZ-K, Piarislische Sig.; CZ-KRa (2 copies), A3876/IV.B.39, A4024 & A4025/IV.B.198 a-f, Part 1, No. 5, (as "Parthia, 1766"); CZ-Pnm, (2 copies), XLII.D.34 [old Clam Gallas No. 423/4, as "Parthia (No. 4) In F"], XLII.D.22 [old Clam Gallas No. 371], (as "Parthia in G", with an extra (spurious?) Allegro between the 4th and 5th movements].
Pm (Musica rara: London, 1959), ed. A.F. Lumsden, score & parts.
Pm (Doblinger: Wien, 1959), ed. H.C. Robbins Landon, score & parts (Diletto musicale 30), miniature score (pn Stp 180 No. 2), with the extra Allegro from CZ-Pnm.
Pm (Boosey & Hawkes: London, pn 20405, 1978), ed. Peter Wastall, score & parts (part of "Exploring Music Series: Ensemble Series").
Pm (JHW: Reihe VIII, Bd. 2, 1991, pp. 24 - 30), score.
*FJH-5. Divertimento [Feldpartie]; in C, 1760-62, (Hob II/7, N23, Hellyer 3), 5 mvts. 2ob 2hn 2bn.
MS parts: CZ-KRa, (2 copies), A3873/IV.B.36, A4024 & A4025/IV.B.198 a-f, Part 1, No. 1, dated 1766); CZ-Pnm, XLII.D.31 [old Clam Gallas No. 423/1, as "Divertimento: In: C. (No. 1)"]; D-Rtt, J Haydn 90, (as "Divertimento Ex C a 6 Vocibus"). ★
Pm (Münchener Haydn-Renaissance: München, 1935), Abt. 4, No. 2, score: GB-Lbl, Hirsch M.909.
Pm (Musica rara: London, 1958), ed. Karl Haas, score & parts.
Pm (Doblinger: Wien, 1959), ed. H.C. Robbins Landon, score and parts (Diletto musicale 31) miniature score (pn STP 180, No. 3).
Pm (Boosey & Hawkes: London, pn B.&H. 20384, 1978), ed. Peter Wastall, score & parts, (omits mvt 2).
Pm (JHW: Reihe VIII, Bd. 2, 1991, pp. 12 - 17), score.
*FJH-6. Parthia [Cassatio]; in D, pre-1765, (Hob II/D18, N25, Hellyer 4). 2ob 2hn 2bn.
MS parts: CZ-KRa, A4024 & A4025/IV.B.198 a-f, Part 1, No. 3, (dated 1766); CZ-U, (copy by Jos. Zábrodský, as "Divertimento"). ★
Pm (Doblinger: Wien, 1959), ed. H.C. Robbins Landon, score & parts (Diletto musicale 33), miniature score (pn STP 180, No. 5). This edition includes the extra movement (Allegro, in D, mvt 6 of the CZ-KRa copy), probably spurious.
Pm (JHW: Reihe VIII, Bd. 2, 1991, pp. 31 - 37), score.
*FJH-7. Divertimento; in G, pre-1766, (Hob II/3, N24, Hellyer 5), 5 mvts. 2ob 2hn 2bn.
MS parts: CZ-KRa, (2 copies), A3875/IV.B.38, A4024 & 4025/IV.B.198 a-f, Part 1, No. 6, (dated 1766); CZ-Pnm, XLII.D.35 [old Clam Gallas No. 423/5]. ★
Pm (Doblinger: Wien, 1960), ed. H.C. Robbins Landon; score & parts (Diletto musicale 84), miniature score (pn STP 180, No. 6).
Pm (JHW: Reihe VIII, Bd. 2, 1991, pp. 6 - 11), score.
*FJH-8. Parthia; in G, 1766, (Hob. II/G9=II/C12 Add., N26, Hellyer 6), 5 mvts. 2ob 2hn 2bn.
MS parts: CZ-KRa, A4024 & 4025/IV.B.198 a-f, Part 1, No. 2, (in C; dated "1766"); CZ-Pnm, XLII.D.36, (as "Parttia [sic] Ex: G") [old Clam Gallas No. 423/5]. ★
Pm (G major version:) (Doblinger, Wien, 1960), ed. H.C. Robbins Landon, score and parts (Diletto musicale 85), miniature score (pn STP 180, No. 7).
Pm (JHW: Reihe VIII, Bd. 2, 1991, pp. 38 - 42), score.
*FJH-9. Divertimento Ex D: [No. 2 Clam Gallas]; 4 mvts, (Hob. II/D23, N(App)26, Hellyer 7). 2ob 2hn 2bn.
MS parts (c.1760): CZ-Pnm XLII.D.32 [old Clam Gallas No. 423/2]. ★
Pm (Doblinger: Wien, 1960), ed. H.C. Robbins Landon, score & parts (Diletto musicale 86), miniature score (pn STP 180, No. 8).

*FJH-10. Divertimento; in D, (Hob. II/5, N32).   2cl 2hn bn.
Pm (University of Cardiff Press: Cardiff, pn P 65817, 1983), reconstructed by Roger Hellyer from the version
for baryton 2vl 2hn, score & parts. ★
*FJH-11. Divertimento; in C, 1761, (Hob. II/14, N30).   2cl 2hn.
AutoMS: RF-Sk, "Divertimento Giuseppe Haydn 761".
MS parts: A-Wgm, VIII 23669. ★
Pm (Wilhelm Hansen: Copenhagen; Georg Kallmeyer Verlag: Wolfenbüttel, Berlin, 1932), ed. Hermann
Reichenbach, parts (Das Hauskonzert No. 5): A-Wgm; GB-Lbl, g.455.y.(4.).
Pm (Muzika: Leningrad, 1957), score.
Pm (Doblinger: Wien, 1960), ed. H.C. Robbins Landon, score & parts (Diletto musicale 32), miniature score
(pn STP 180, No. 4).
Pm (JHW: Reihe VIII, Bd. 2, 1991, pp. 3 - 5), score.
*FJH-1v. Alfred, König der Angelsachsen: Aria des Schützgeistes (Guardian Spirit's Aria), 1796,
(Hob. XXXb/5).   Solo soprano, 2cl 2hn 2bn.
Pm (Haydn-Mozart Presse: Salzburg, pn HMP 110, 1961), score.
*FJH-1m(a) Symphony No. 100, 2nd mvt: March in C.   fl 2ob 2cl(C) 2hn 2bn 2tp(C) tb serp s-dr.
AutoMS score (c.1794 - 1795): S-Snydahl.
Pm (HW: I/17, pp. 227 - 233).
*FJH-2.1m, 2.2m. 2 Marches composed . . . for Sir Henry Harpur Bart. and presented by him to the Volunteer
Cavalry of Derbyshire . . . 1794; in E♭ & C.   2cl 2hn 2bn tp serp.
AutoMS scores: (No. 1): H-Bn, Mus.Ms. I.43/b; (No. 2): A-Eh, Inv. Nr. 2420; (Nos. 1, 2): GB-DEro, *(AutoMS
scores, plus original plates, correspondence and early prints are to be found in the Derbyshire Records Office,
refs D2375/287/1-30).*
Pc (Printed for Sir Henry Harpur Bart by Willm. Simpkins: London, c.1794), RISM [H 4025], score with piano
reduction: GB-Lbl, K.8.k.(15).; US-R. ★
Pc (Joseph Eder: Wien, pn 268, c.1796), score (omits serpent; the order of the marches is reversed), RISM
[H 4026]: H-Bn, Z 22.016.
Pc (A. Kühnel, Bureau de Musique: Leipzig, pn 489, 1806), RISM [H 4027], parts (follows Eder version):
CZ-Pnm, Lobkovic X.H.a.79; D-ZI; H-Bn; H-KE, 726/VIII. ★
Pm (Doblinger: Wien, München, 1960), ed. H.C. Robbins Landon, score, (Diletto musicale 34, Nos. 5 & 6,
pp. 8, 9).
Pm (Musica rara: London, 1960), ed. Karl Haas, score & parts (with FJH-4m).
*FJH-3m. Hungarian National March, E♭, (Hob. VIII/4).   2ob 2cl 2hn 2bn tp.
AutoMS score (before Nov 27, 1802): H-Bn, Mus Ms I.43[a]. ★
Pm (AutoMS facsimile): (In: Jeno Vecsey (editor) *Haydn Compositions in the National Széchényi Library.*
Hungarian Academy of Science: Budapest, 1960), figs. 22a-22d.
Pm (Doblinger: Wien, 1960), ed. H.C. Robbins Landon, score & pts (Diletto musicale 34, No. 4, p. 10).
*FJH-4m. March for the Prince of Wales, E♭, 1792, (Hob. VIII/3).   2cl 2hn 2bn tp serp.
AutoMS score: GB-Lrs. ★
Pm (In: *The Score* No. 2, p. 52, 1950), ed. Karl Haas, score.
Pm (Doblinger: Wien, 1960), ed. H.C. Robbins Landon, score & parts (Diletto musicale 34, No. 4, p. 6).
Pm (Musica rara: London, 1960), score & parts (with FJH-2m).
*FJH-5m. March (fragment, 8 bars), E♭. c.1792, (Hob. VIII/7).   2cl 2hn 2bn tp serp.
AutoMS score: GB-Lbl.   Ms score: A-Eh (incomplete). ★
Pm (Doblinger: Wien, 1960), completed H.C. Robbins Landon, score and pts (Diletto Musicale 34, No. 3, p. 5).
*FJH-6m. Marche Regimento de Marshall; in G, (Hob Vol. iii, p. 315).   2ob 2hn 2bn.
AutoMS score: F-Pn, MS.1192.   MS parts (dated 1772): CZ-Pnm, XLII.D.72. ★
Pm (Doblinger: Wien, 1960), ed. H.C. Robbins Landon, score & pts (Diletto musicale 34, No. 1, pps. 3 - 4).
Pm (Musica rara: London, 1959), ed. A.F. Lumsden, score & parts.
Pm (Editio Supraphon: Prague, 1976), ed. M. Rutova, score & pts, (Musica viva historica 37).
*FJH-7m. Marcia, E♭, (Hob. VIII/6).   2cl 2hn 2bn.
AutoMS score: CZ-Pnm.   Pm (HW: XXV/12, p. 316). ★
Pm (Doblinger: Wien, 1960), ed. H.C. Robbins Landon, score & parts (Diletto musicale 34, No. 2, p. 4).
*FJH-8m(e). Armida (Hob. XXVIII/12), 1783, Act I, scene iv: March, B♭.   2cl 2hn 2bn.
Pm (HW: Reihe XXV/12, p. 69, ed. Karl Geiringer).

Haydn: Doubtful & Spurious Works
*FJH-1d. Feldparthie in B♭, 4 mvts, (Hob. II/46).   2ob 2hn 3bn serp.
MS parts: D-Dl, Mus.3356-P-520,1 (formerly: D-ZI, Sigl Exner; as "Divertimento I"). ★
MS parts: A-Wgm, VIII 39900, ("mit St Anthony', cbn replaces serp).
MS score (by Pohl, after the Breitkopf edition of c.1782): A-Wgm, VIII 41541.
MS score (mvt 2, by Brahms): A-Wgm, Konvolut A 130, fol. 44v.
Pc: (6 Divertimenti, No. 1) (Breitkopf & Härtel: Leipzig, c.1782), parts.
Pm (F. Schuberth Jr.: Leipzig, 1932), ed. Karl Geiringer, score & parts.
Pm (C.F. Peters: New York, etc, 1960), ed. Robert Austin Boudreau, score & parts.
Pm (Edition Eulenburg: London, etc., 1969), ed. R.A. Boudreau, miniature score (Edition Eulenburg. No. 1324).
Pm (Phylloscopus: Lancaster, pn PP 10, 1989), score & parts (2cl replace bns 1, 2).
*FJH-2d. Feldparthie in B♭, 5 mvts, (Hob. II/42).   2ob 2cl 2hn 2bn.
MS score (by Pohl, after Breitkopf edition of c.1782): A-Wgm, VIII 41541.
MS parts: D-Dl, Mus. 3356-P-520,2 (formerly: D-ZI, Sigl Exner; as "Divertimento II"). ★
Pc: (6 Divertimenti, No. 2) (Breitkopf & Härtel: Leipzig, c.1782), parts.
*FJH-3d. Feldparthie in E♭, 4 mvts, (Hob. II/4l).   2ob 2cl 2hn 2bn.
MS score (by Pohl, after Breitkopf edition of c.1782): A-Wgm, VIII 41541.
MS parts: D-Dl, Mus. 3356-P-520,2 (formerly: D-ZI, Sigl Exner; as "Divertimento III"). ★
Pc: (6 Divertimenti, No. 3) (Breitkopf & Hartel: Leipzig, c.1782), parts.
Pm (Universal-Edition A.G.: Wien, Leipzig, 1931), edited Karl Geiringer, score.

*FJH-4d. Feldparthie in F, 4 mvts, (Hob. II/45).   2ob 2hn 3bn serp.
MS score (by Pohl, after Breitkopf edition of c. 1782): A-Wgm, VIII 41541.
MS parts (for 2ob 2hn 2bn(obl) bn(rip) serp/quart-bn): D-Dl, Mus. 3356-P-520,3 (formerly: D-ZI, Sigl Exner; as "Divertimento IV"). ★
Pc: (6 Divertimenti, No. 4) (Breitkopf & Härtel: Leipzig, c.1782), parts.
*FJH-5d. Feldparthie in B♭; 4 mvts, (Hob. II/43).   2ob 2cl 2hn 2bn.
MS score (by Pohl, after Breitkopf edition of c.1782): A-Wgm, VIII 41541.
MS parts: D-Dl, Mus. 3356-P-520,5 (formerly: D-ZI, Sigl Exner; as "Divertimento V"). ★
Pc: (6 Divertimenti, No. 5) (Breitkopf & Härtel: Leipzig, c.1782), parts.
Pm (B. Schott's Söhne: Mainz, 1970), ed. Helmut May, score & parts, (part ot the "Concertino" series).
*FJH-6d. Feldparthie in F, 4 mvts, (Hob. II/44).   2ob 2hn 3bn serp.
MS score (by Pohl, after Breitkopf edition of c. 1782): A-Wgm, VIII 41541.
MS parts (for 2ob 2hn 2bn(obl) bn+serp): D-Dl, Mus. 3356-P-520,5 (formerly: D-ZI, Sigl Exner; as "Divertimento VI"). ★
Pc: (6 Divertimenti, No. 6) (Breitkopf & Härtel: Leipzig, c.1782), parts.
FJH-7d. Divertimento in E♭; (Hob. II/Es12).   2ob 2cl 2hn 2bn.   MS parts: A-Wgm, VIII 41159. ★
FJH-8d. [Untitled Divertimento in E♭], 4 mvts, (Hob. II/Es13).   2ob 2cl 2hn 2bn.
(Probably by Hoffmeister - See: **FAH-10**). MS score (by Pohl): A-Wgm, VIII 40899 (Q 16389). ★
FJH-9d. N⁰ 4 Parthia in Dis [Divertimento in E♭], 4 mvts, (Hob. II/Esl4).   2ob 2cl 2hn 2bn.
MS parts: A-Wgm, VIII 39998, ("Del Sigᵉ Hayd [sic]"). ★
FJH-10d. Parthia; in E♭, 4 mvts, (Hob. II/Es16).   2ob 2cl 2hn 2bn.
MS: D-B, Mus.ms. 9847, (originally 2 parthien, only one survives). ★
FJH-11d. N⁰ 1 Parthia In F; 4 mvts, (Hob. II/F7), *probably by Paul Wranitzky; see: PAW-2*.   2ob 2cl 2hn 2bn.
MS: A-Wgm, VIII 40752. ★
MS pts: CZ-K, symfonie Nr 240.K.II, No. 1, (defective pts; as "Divertimento"); CZ-Pu, 59 R 16 (as "Harmonie", parts: "No. 1"; for 2ob/fl 2cl 2hn 2bn; post-1850 by Barnabus Weil, stamped "Kapuziner-Kloster / St. Josef / PRAG NEUSTADT"; the title slip on the folder has a fuller title beginning with the crossed out phrase, "Ochenmenuett und"); D-DO, Mus.Ms.2062, (as "Wranitzky"); D-HER, (2 copies), Mus. C.16=1, Mus.N.1=3.
Pc (as "Harmonie No. 1", 2ob/fl 2cl 2hn 2bn:) (N. Simrock: Bonn; H Simrock: Paris, pn 262, 1802-03), RISM [H 3342], parts: A-Wgm, VIII 40752; B-Bc; CZ-Pnm, V.E.85; S-J. *This is probably the Parthia advertized in Traeg's 1804 Nachtrag catalog as (octet) No. 208.*
Pm (C.F. Kahnt: Leipzig, 1902), ed. Friedrich Grützmacher, score: A-Wgm, VIII 41092 (H 25487).
Pm (International Music Co.: New York, pre-1965), miniature score (pn 999) & parts (pn 998).
FJH-12d. Adagio in E♭, (Hob. deest).   fl ob 2cl 2hn 2bn.   MS pts: I-Fc, unverified. *Possibly WENT, JNW-22a.*
FJH-13d. Suite in E♭, (Hob. II/Esl7).   2cl 2hn 2bn.   MS parts: D-B, Mus.Ms.10000. ★
FJH-14d. [untitled: Parthia in E♭], 5 mvts.   2cl 2hn 2bn.
MS parts: CZ-Pnm, XLI.B.149, (missing titlepage and/or wrapper). ★
*FJH-15d. Parthia in E♭, 4 mvts, (Hob. deest).   2cl 2hn 2bn.   MS parts: CZ-Pnm, XLI.F.36, No. 2. ★
FJH-16d. Parthia in Dis [E♭]; 4 mvts, (Hob. deest).   2cl 2hn 2bn.
MS parts: CZ-Pnm, XLI.B.153. *The MS is earlier than FJH-17d, XLI.B.152.* ★
*FJH-17d. Parthia in E♭ (Sextet), (Hob. II/B7), also attributed to Joseph Morris and to Mozart (K.C 17.09), 4 mvts.   2cl 2hn 2bn.
MS parts: CZ-Bm, (2 copies): CZ-Bm(au) A.19.095, (copy by Carl Honisch, as "Parthia ex B del Sig. Hayden [sic]", CZ-Bm(rj) A.14.282, ("Del Sig. Mozart"); CZ-KRa, A4457/R.I.27 a-f, (as "Parthia 5ta [B♭] Haÿden"); CZ-Pnm, XLI.B.152, ("Haydn", copy by Josef Pražák); US-BETm, Lititz Collegium Musicum 202 (copy by John Levering, "by Jos. Morris"); US-WS, Ms.24, (as "Parthie in B . . . del Sig. Haydn", missing hn I). ★
FJH-18d. Parthia 4ta, in B♭, 4 mvts, (uncited).   2cl 2hn 2bn.
MS pts: CZ-KRa, A4457/R.I.27 a-f, No. 4; CZ-Pnm, XLI.B.151, (as "Parthia in B[♭]", copy by Josef Pražák). ★
*FJH-19d. Parthia in G, 4 mvts, (Hellyer H15).   2ob 2hn 2bn.
MS parts (c.1800): CZ-Bm(au), A.19.005. ★
Pm (Doblinger: Wien, 1960), ed. H. C. Robbins Landon, score & parts (Diletto musicale 66).
FJH-20d. [Divertimento in G, 6 mvts, 1766, (Hob. II/G8, Hellyer H11).   2ob 2hn bn.
MS parts: CZ-KRa, A3874/IV.B.37, (end of bn pt: "Dell [sic] Sig Hayden / [1]766"). ★
FJH-21d. Partita in F; 5 mvts (Hob. II/F12; Hellyer H12).   2ob 2hn bn.
MS parts: CZ-K, Nr 240.K.II; CZ-Pnm, XLII.D.24, (as "Parthia. Ex F (No. 7 Clam Gallas)"). ★
FJH-22d. Divertimento in F, (Hellyer H13).   2cl 2hn bn.   MS parts: CZ-K, 240.K.II. ★
FJH-23d. [Parthia] "No. 9 Hayden"; in F, 7 mvts, (Hellyer H14).   2ob 2hn bn.
MS parts (without titlepage): CZ-Pnm, XLII.D.39, (old Clam Gallas No. 566). ★
FJH-24d. Parthia in Dis [E♭]; 4 mvts (of which the last is a 4-mvt "Pallo" [sic: Ballo]), Hob. deest, JHI Es20). 2cl 2hn bn.   MS parts ("für mich Augustin Hübner - Schulgehielf aus Langenbruck [now Dlouhý Most] 1801"): CZ-Pu(dm), 59 R 3325. ★
FJH-25d. Quartetto/Notturni; 12 mvts (Hob. II/D5).   2fl 2hn.
MS parts: Dresden, Staatskapelle, (lost since 1952, a copy is in private hands); D-LEm, PM 4494. ★
Pm (Edition pro Musica: Leipzig, pn 83, 1952), ed. Kurt Janetzky, score & parts.
Pm (Amadeus Verlag: Winterthur,pn BP 2399, sd), ed. Bernhard Päuler, parts.
FJH-26d. Divertimento (Cassation) in E♭, (Hob. II/Es7) - See: J.M. Haydn, JMH-2.
FJH-27d. 28d. 2 Cassations, E♭, (Hob. II/Es1-2) - See: J.M. Haydn, JMH-5, 6.
FJH-29d. Serenata; E♭, 3 mvts.   2ob 2cl 2hn 2bn.   MS pts: A-Ee. *Recorded by the Consortium Classicum.* ★
FJH-30d. Pièces d'harmonie; in B♭, 4 mvts.   2cl 2hn 2bn.
MS parts: RF-Ssc, Ф 891 собрюосуповых N44, pp. 119 - 130.
FJH-1vd. N≗ 2 Libera; in E♭, (Hob. XXIIb:Es3).   CATB, 2cl 2hn 2bn.
MS parts (from Potšejn [Potstýn, Pottenstein]): CZ-Pnm, X.A.69, (marked in pencil, "Heyden"; all dynamics have been added later, in another hand and the parts marked "Revisum"). ★
FJH-2vd. Terzetto in Dis; "Huc piae mentes venite" [an arrangement of "Zu Dir, o Herr, blickt alles auf", from *Die Schöpfung*, Teil 2, No. 14).   CTB 2cl 2hn 2bn.
MS parts ("N≗ 150 Ecclesias. Bartholomai. Inv. N≗ 170. Musicatium Fran: Krzepelka h.t. Chori regentes", in Plzeň; collectd 3 Sept 1901 by Ondřej Horník): CZ-Pnm, X.A.50. ★

*HAYDN, Johann Michael *14 Sept 1737, Rohrau, Austria - 10 Aug 1806, Salzburg*
JMH-1. Marcia Turchesa; in C, (P65, MH 601).   2fl 2ob 2cl 2hn 2bn 2tp cym, "tambour turc".
AutoMS score (Salzburg, 6 aug 1795): A-Ssp, Hay 1890.1. ★
Pm (*In:* Denkmäler der Tonkunst in Österreich: Jg. XIV/2, pp. 55-61), ed. Lothar H. Perger. ★
Pm (Bärenreiter: Kassel, pn BA 1080), parts.
JMH-2. Cassatio in Es [E♭]; 6 mvts, (formerly attributed to F.J. Haydn, Hob. II/Eb7), c.1758-1760, (MH 55).
2ca 2hn bn 2vla b.
MS parts: A-KR, H.39.55; A-Wgm. ★
Pm (Medici: St Cloud, Minnesota, 1983), score & parts.
*JMH-3. Divertimento in D; 5 mvts, (P95, MH 418), 5 mvts.   2ob 2hn 2bn.
MS parts (Salzburg, 9 March 1786): H-Bn, Ms.mus.2510. ★
Pm (Doblinger: Wien, 1969), ed. Werner Rainer, score & pts (Diletto musicale 312), min score (pn Stp 235).
Pm (Medici: St Cloud, Minnesota, 1983), score & parts.
*JMH-4. Divertimento à 6 ex G; 4 mvts, (P96).   ob 2hn bn vla b.
MS parts ("Salzburg, Sept 4, 1790"): H-Bn, Ms.mus.2511. ★
Pm (Doblinger: Wien, 1969), ed. Werner Rainer, score (Diletto musicale 275; miniature score pn Stp 189).
Pm (Medici: St Cloud, Minnesota, pn HS 16, 1983), score & parts.
JMH-5, 6. 2 Cassations, E♭, (once attributed to F.J. Haydn, Hob. II/Es1, 2).   2ca hn tp(clar) b.
MS parts: A-KR, H.40.82. ★
Pm (Medici: St Cloud, Minnesota, pn EHO 1, 1982), score & parts.
*JMH-7. Divertimento in D; 6 mvts, (P100, MH 464).   fl ob hn bn.
MS parts: A-Wn, Mus.Hs.11,944, (dated 1796); A-Wgm; VIII 8886. ★
MS score (by Dr Paul, 1958, photocopy, "nach Spartieruns des Rundfunks"): A-Wgm, VIII 8886.
Pm (Hofmeister: Frankfurt a/M, 1951), score & parts (Hofmeister Studienwerk).
Pm (Medici: St Cloud, Minnesota, pn QQ01, 1983), score & parts.
Although the earliest version of JMH-1v (not autograph) is scored for SSA rip, 2vl organ, many versions exist
with wind accompaniment, often scored for local forces.
*JMH-1.1v. Deutsches Hochamt (Deutsche Messe), (K VI/6c; MH 560).   (Scoring varies)
MS parts: A-Wn, Mus.Hs.22,260, (for SATB, 2fl 2ob 2cl 2hn 2bn 2tp timp organ), Mus.Hs.22,261 (for CATB,
2ob 2hn/vla, organ vlne); CH-E, Th.123,31 (for SATB, 2fl 2ob 2hn organ); CZ-Bm(br), A.9921, (as "Píseň ke
Mssi swaté Zde w shraussenosti padáme etc.", for SATB, 2cl 2hn organ; copy by Dominic Kinisky - a donation
by Tomáše Zlška, Brno; missing all parts except TB, 2hn); CZ-Bm(hr), A.5929, (as Píseň ke mse", for SAB,
2ob+2fl 2hn organ); CZ-KRa, A4157/VI.A.17, (9 mvts, for CA, 2fl 2cl 2hn organ); CZ-Pnm, XLIX.F.232, (as
an anonymous "Deutsche Messe", for CATB 2cl 2hn 2bn organ, with 2 later flute parts which are, in fact, the
2 clarinet parts transposed up an octave; MS by Franz Kücker, 1820); CZ-Pnm, XXXVIII.F.200, (for SATB, ad
lib: 2fl 2cl 2hn vlne organ, 1820); I-MOe, Mus.D.169, (for CATB, 2fl 2ob 2cl(C) 2hn 2bn 2tp timp organ). ★
JMH-1.2v. No. I. Michael Haydn's Deutsche Hochamt "Hier liegt vor Deiner Majestät" für Stadt- und
Landkirchen. Ausgabe 3".   SATB, 2cl(C) 2hn 2bn vlne/cbn 2tp timp
Pc (Carl Haslinger qᵐ Tobias K.K. Hof- und priv. Kunst- und Musikalien-Handlung: Vienna, pn 4595, c.1900),
(reissue from the 1824 plates), parts: CZ-Pnm, XLIII.A.124, (at this shelfmark can also be found a MS score
(as "Mše No. 1") with Czech text, for SATB, organ, 2cl(C)/vl 2hn 2bn cbn+db/vlne 2tp timp, with MS parts:
S(4)A(4)T(2)B(2), 2hn bn - the other instruments presumably read off the printed pts).
JMH-1.3v. Mose česka v čas postní; Czech text.   CATB, 2cl(C) 2hn 2bn organ(= C+bc).
MS parts (by František Michalička, from Kunvald, 1818): CXZ-Pnm, XII.F.78, (previously attributed to
Michalička; with 2 later duplicate Canto parts and a later "Basso e Fagotto" part).
JMH-1.4v. Gesang bey dem Heiligen Mess Opfer in der K:K: Landesfürstl: Stadtpfarrkirche zu Enns.
CATB, 2cl 2hn bn organ.   MS parts: A-Wn, Mus.Hs.20,001, (missing 2cl; the concluding instrumental *Lied nach*
der Wandlung only appears in the 2hn pts).
JMH-1.5v. Heiligen Messe.   CATB, terz-fl fl(C) 2cl(B♭) cl(III in C) 2hn bn; with later pts for flug & b-flug.
MS parts: A-Wn, Mus.Hs.20,002, (missing hn I; with duplicate A pt and a later C pt.
JMH-1.6v. Messe No. 3.   SATB, fl 2cl 2hn bn b-tb timp organ.   MS pts: D-BAUd, Mu 54, (missing instruments).
*JMH-2v. Missa Sancti Hieronymi, ("Salzburg, Sept 14 1777"), (KI/11).   *(See also under: Neukomm.)*
SATB soli, SATB chorus, 2ob soli, 2ob ripieni, 2bn 3tb db organ. *(Note 3tb, not the 2tb sometimes suggested).*
AutoMS score: F-Pc, Ms.2046; A-Ssp, (copy by Maximilian Raab with corrections by J.M. Haydn). ★
MS score: A-Wgm, I 7698.   MS parts: A-KR, A.3.13; A-L, Ms. 1423; A-SEI, D.XV.1b (1796):
A-Ssp, Hay 390.2; D-Mbs, Mus.Ms.1289, (missing some wind parts).
Pm (Universal Edition: Mainz, 1961, reprinted 1970), ed. Marius Flothius & Charles H. Sherman, score
(Accademia musicale 7) & parts (pn UE25 C007).
JMH-4v. Tantum ergo; in C, (Klafsky V, 12e; MH 371)   SATB, 2fl 2ob 2cl 2hn 2bn 2tp timp.
MS pts: D-Mbm, Mf 844.   *D-Mbm, Mf 845 is the same work transposed to Bb, arranged for full orchestra).* ★
*JMH-5v. Offertorium; Timete Dominum, (MH 256).   CATB concertante & ripieno, 2ob 2bn 3tb organ.
AutoMS score (29 Oct 1777): H-Bn, Ms.mus.2502. MS score: I-Fc, F.P. Ch.367/1. ★
MS parts: A-Ee; A-GT, MS.1283; A-M, MS.262; A-LA, M.1375; A-Ssp, Hay 1540.1, (copy by Maximilian
Raab); A-Wn, F.4.BADEN 168, (missing trombones); A-Ws, Nr. 92; D-LAm; H-Bn, Ms.Mus.IV.330.
Pm (G. Schirmer: New York, pn 2589, 1964), ed. Reinhard G. Pauly, score.

*HEDWALL, Lennart *16 Sept 1932, Göteborg, Sweden*
LXH-1. Partita; 1961.   2fl 2ob 2cl 2hn 2bn 2tp tb.   MS score: S-Sic.
LXH-2. Danssvit och sorgmarch; 1975.   2fl 2ob 2cl 2hn 2bn timp(ad lib).   MS score: S-Sic.

*HEIDENREICH (Haydenreich, Haydnreich), Josef (Georg) *(1760) - post 1821*
JYH-1v. Tantum ergo.   SATB, 2cl 2hn 2bn cbn.   MS pts: CZ-Bm(au), A.20.671, (missing cbn). ★
JYH-1a. Gerl & Schack: Der dumme Gärtner, 16 mvts.   2ob 2cl 2hn 2bn.
Pc (Traeg: Vienna, pre-1799), MS parts: I-Fc, F.P. S.333, (as "Die beyden Anton").
JYH-2a. Mayr: Adelasia ed Aleramo, overture & 14 mvts.   2ob 2cl 2hn 2bn [cbn].
MS pts: A-Ee, Mus.1140, (Hummel 1806 catalog: "Mayer 4"); I-Fc, F.P. S.346; CZ-KRa, A3923/IV.B.86, (with
an added cbn in the bn(II) pt, with only a few divisi. The MS is in the same scribal hand as Sedlak's arr. of
Mayr's *Alonso e Cora*, WXS-29a; the titlepage bears the pencil note, "54 bg [Bögen] [crossed out]: N᷂ᵒ 5").

JYH-3a. Mozart: Die Zauberflöte, sinfonia & 17 mvts. 2ob 2cl 2hn 2bn.
MS parts: D-DO, Mus.Ms.1396/2, (previously attributed to Rosinack); I-Fc, F.P. S.334.
Pm (Musica rara: London, pn MR 1888, 1889, 1977), 2 books, score & parts.
JYH-4a. Mozart: Horn Quintet, (K.407).   2ob 2cl 2hn 2bn.
MS parts: A-Ee, Mus.1134, (Hummel catalog of 1806: "Mozart 5").
JYH-5a. Mozart: String Quintet in Eb, (K.614).   2ob 2cl 2hn 2bn.
MS parts: A-Ee, Mus.1113; D-DO (minuet & trio, previously attributed to Rosiniack). *The arrangement was first advertized in the* Wiener Zeitung, *30 April 1794.*
JYH-6a. W. Müller: Das Sonnenfest in Braminen.   2ob 2cl 2hn 2bn.   MS parts: I-Fc, F.P. S.334.
JYH-7.1a. W. Müller: Die neu Sonntagskind, sinfonia & 12 mvts.   2ob 2cl 2hn 2bn.
MS parts: D-Rtt, W.Müller 2, (as Anon); I-Fc, F.P. S.322. *No. 13 is, in fact, by Joseph Schuster.*
JYH-7.2a. W. Müller: Die neu Sonntagskind, sinfonia & 12 mvts.   2cl 2hn 2bn.
MS parts (purchased from Johann Gallyus, Advocat in Zagreb, 1802): H-KE, K 0/121.
JYH-8a. W. Müller: Die Schwestern von Prag, sinfonia & 13 mvts.   2ob 2cl 2hn 2bn.
MS parts: A-Ee, Mus.1147, (Hummel catalog of 1806: "Müller 4"); I-Fc, F.P. S.332.
JYH-9a. W. Müller: Der Alte überall und nirgends, sinfonia & 10 mvts.   2ob 2cl 2hn 2bn.
MS parts: A-Ee, Mus.1157; I-Fc, F.P. S.341.
JYH-10a. W. Müller: Die zwölf schlafenden Jungfrau, sinfonia & 11 mvts. 2ob 2cl 2hn 2bn.
MS parts: A-Ee, Mus.1146; I-Fc, F.P. S.341.
JYH-11a. Nasolini: Il Sesostri.   2ob 2cl 2hn 2bn.   MS parts: I-Fc, F.P. S.374.
JYH-12a. Satzenhoven: Der Körbenflechter, introduzione & 15 mvts.   2ob 2cl 2hn 2bn.
MS parts: A-Ee, A.M.4105 *is Heidenreich's bill which includes this work, Prince Esterházy's authorization of payment (6 April 1811) & Heidenreich's receipt of the same date; although the bill describes the work as "Eine Neue Harmonie Musick, 9 stim[m]ige aus der Oppera [sic] der Körbel flachter [sic] ...... 80fl", the wrapper does not mention the contrabassoon and no part for it is present or extant.*
JYH-1ad. Mozart: Gran Partita, (K.361).   2ob 2cl 2hn 2bn.
MS parts: A-Ee, Mus.1133, (Hummel catalog of 1806: "Mozart 5"). *The MS gives no indication that the arrangement is by Heidenreich; the attribution was first suggested in* Köchel 6, *p. 779.*
JYH-2ad. Mozart: Don Giovanni, 7 mvts.   2ob 2cl 2hn 2bn.
MS parts: D-DO, Mus.Ms.1388/1.
Pm (B. Schott's Söhne: Mainz, 1975), score (pn 6621) & parts (6622).

HEILMANN, Harald Arthur *9 April 1924, Alle, Saxony*
HAH-1. Serenade.   fl ob cl 2hn bn tu.
Pm (Astoria: Berlin, 1951), score & parts.
HAH-2. Sextet.   2cl 2hn 2bn.
Pm (Astoria: Berlin. 1967), score & parts.

*HEINE, Gotthelf Sigismund *(1780), Kapellmeister, Sebnitz in Sachen.*
GSH-1v. Te Deum.   SATB, 2cl 2hn 2bn 2tp 3tb timp.
Pc (Klinkicht: Meissen, 1805), parts: A-Wn; A-Wgm; D-Bu.

*HEINE, Samuel Friedrich *(1770), Member of the Ludwigslust Hofkapelle.*
SFH-1tv. Auferstehn, ja Auferstehn, 1803 [for the death of *Erbprinzess* Helene Paulowna].
SSATB, 2cl 4hn 2bn serp 2vla b(vc).   MS parts (performed 2 Dec 1803): D-SWl, Mus. 2653. ★

*HEINRICH, ( ) *(1810)*
ZYH-1. Harmonie Piece; in G, 1 mvt.   fl(D) 2cl(C) 2hn 2bn tp flug.   MS parts: A-Sca, Hs.266, No. 41. ★

HEINZE, ( ) *(1760)*
QXH-1. Parthia in Dis [Eb]; 3/5 mvts.   2cl 2hn bn.
MS pts (by Ignaz Hübner, Langenbruck, pre-1800): CZ-Pu(dm), 59 R 3331, (mvts 4 & 5 are later additions). ★

HEITZ, Theobald *(1770)*
TXH-1. 3 Quatuors concertans.   2cl hn bn.
Pc (Gaveaux frères: Paris, c.1800), RISM [H 4964], parts: D-AB; US-Wc.

HEJTMÁNEK, J. *20 Jan 1816, Hoštice, near Tabor - 16 Nov 1875, Prague*
JZH-1v. Salve [Regina] in Es [Eb].   CATB, 2cl 2hn bn.
MS parts (by Anton F. Kraus, from Švabín, 1839): CZ-Pnm, X.D.11. ★

HEKSTER, Walter *29 March 1937, Amsterdam*
WYH-1. Early one morning; 1971.   2fl ob 3cl 4hn 2tp 2tb tu.
Pm (Donemus: Amsterdam, 1973), score.
WYH-2. Relief No. 3, for 9 winds in 3 groups; 1968.   fl 2ob 2cl 2hn 2bn.
Pm (Donemus: Amsterdam, pn E1973, 1970), score, parts (with 1973 edition).

HEMEL, Oscar van *3 Aug 1892, Antwerp - 9 July 1981, Hilversum*
OVH-1. Divertimento II.   2fl 2ob 2cl 2hn 2bn 2tp pf.
Pm (Donemus: Amsterdam, 1959), score & parts.
OVH-1v. Hart von Nederland (Ballade of Hollands Water Vaarvel Land).
Male chorus, fl 2ob cl hn bn 2tp timp perc pf(ad lib).
Pm (Donemus: Amsterdam, c.1960), score.

*HEMMERLEIN, Ignaz Carl *(1770), Konzertmeister in Fulda, 1798 - 1802*
ICH-1. IV Stücke für türkische Musick; (C, F, C, F).   pic 2cl 2hn tp basso.   MS pts: D-F, Mus.Hs.1175. ★
ICH-2. 4 Stücke für türkische Musick [sic], (C, F, C, C).   pic 2cl 2hn bn tp basso.
MS parts: D-F, Mus.Hs.1176. *Another movement, "Cosaca" numbered "4", has been added to all the parts - possibly to replace the original "a la Polacca".* ★

HÉMON, Sedje *(1940)*
SXH-1. Oboe Concerto. Solo oboe, fl ca 2cl 2hn bn cbn.
Pm (Donemus: Amsterdam, 1970), score & parts.

*HENNEBERG, Johann Baptist *6 Dec 1768, Vienna - 26 Nov 1822, Vienna*
BJH-1v. Pangelingua [sic].   SATB, 2cl 2hn (2)bn.   MS score: A-Wn, Mus.Hs.13,040, No. 4, ff.5 - 5b.   ★
BJH-2v. Vexilla regis.   SATB, 2ob/fl bn 2t-tb.   MS score: A-Wn, Mus.Hs.13,040, No. 2, f.2b.   ★

HENNEBERG, (Carl Albert Wilhelm) Robert *5 Aug 1853, Berlin - 19 Oct 1925, Malmö*
RZH-1. Serenad: Oktett; 1916.   fl ob 2cl 2hn 2bn.
Pc (Musikaliska kunstföreningen. Föreningen Svenska Tonsättare Ärg: Stockholm, 1918), pf score:
GB-Lbl, H.700./85.

*HENNIG, T. *9 Dec 1813, Glückstadt/Holstein - 23 June 1887, Güstrow (Civic Music Director in Güstrow)*
TYH-1m. 3 Märsche für das Gardehautboistencorps des 89sten Regiments (1. Geschwind Marsch, 2. Armee=
Marsch, 3. Defilir=Marsch).   fl(E♭) fl(C) 2ob 2cl(E♭) 3cl(B♭) 4hn(F, E♭) 2bn 4tp(F, E♭) 2flug(B♭) 2a-hn(E♭)
2t-hn(B♭) bar 3tb 2tu b-dr+cym s-dr.   MS score: D-SWl, Mus. 2674.   ★

*HENSHER, Raymond *12 Nov 1934, Rotherhithe, London*
*Except for RYH-1, Hensher's works remain in MS. Many of his scores are deposited (along with cassettes) at
GB-Lmic, who can also arrange acquisition of other scores and/or contact with the composer.*
RYH-1. English Countryside Suite; 3 mvts, 1974.   2fl 2ob 4cl 2hn 2bn cbn 2tp.
Pm (Emerson Edition: Ampleforth, pn E67, 1988), score & parts.
RYH-2. Latin Horns; 1980.   4 solo horns, 2fl 2ob 3cl 2bn cbn 2tp (perc); (b-cl ad lib).
RYH-3. Fantasy for Horn & Wind; 1975.   Solo horn, 2fl 2ob 4cl b-cl 2hn 2bn cbn 2tp (perc ad lib). *Also
available with piano accompaniment.*
RYH-4. North Country Suite; 3 mvts, 1977.   2fl 2ob 4cl 2hn/(+2hn ad lib) 2bn cbn 2tp perc; (b-cl ad lib).
RYH-5. Overture "Broomhill"; 1976.   2fl 2ob 4cl 2hn/(+2hn ad lib) 2bn cbn; (2tp perc ad lib).
RYH-6. Hungarian Impressions; 1977.   2fl 2ob 4cl 2hn 2bn 2tp perc.
RYH-7. Clarinet Polka; 1979.   2 solo clarinets, 2fl 2ob 2cl 2hn 2bn cbn; (b-cl 2hn tp perc ad lib). *Also
available with piano accompaniment.*
RYH-8. English Folk Song Suite; 3 mvts, 1977.   2fl 2ob 3cl 2hn/(+2hn ad lib) 2bn cbn 2tp (perc).
RYH-9. A Dale Morning; 1980.   2fl 2ob 3cl b-cl 2hn 2bn cbn; (perc ad lib).
RYH-11. Sinfoniette for Wind Ensemble; 4 mvts, 1981.   2fl 2ob 3cl b-cl 3hn 2bn cbn 2tp (perc).
RYH-12. Folk Songs of Provence; 3 mvts, 1982.   2fl 2ob 3cl b-cl 2hn 2bn cbn 2tp (perc).
RYH-13. Samba for Wind; 1983.   2fl 2ob 3cl b-cl 2hn 2bn cbn 2tp (perc).
RYH-14. Mexican Village Scenes; 3 mvts, 1977.   2fl 2ob 3cl 3hn 2bn cbn 2tp (perc); (b-cl ad lib).
RYH-15. Fantasia for Clarinet and Wind; 1974.   Solo clarinet, 2fl 2ob 2cl 2hn 2bn cbn.
RYH-16. Lakeland Suite; 4 mvts, 1975.   2fl 2ob 3cl 2hn 2bn cbn 2tp (perc).
RYH-17. St. Mary's Suite; 1984.   2fl 2ob 3cl b-cl 2hn 2bn cbn 2tp.
RYH-18. Holiday in Provence Suite; 1986.   2fl 2ob 3cl 2hn 2bn cbn 2tp.
RYH-19. Serenade for Wind; 1987.   2fl 2ob 2cl 2hn 2bn cbn 2tp.
RYH-20. South American Dance No. 1; 1988.   2fl 2ob 2cl 2hn 2bn cbn 2tp.
RYH-21. South American Dance No. 3; 1989.   2fl 2ob 2cl 2hn 2bn cbn 2tp.
RYH-22. Suite: Mr. Joplin in St. Louis; 3 mvts, 1989.   2fl 2ob 2cl 2hn 2bn cbn 2tp.
RYH-23. 1930 Palais Dance - Fox Trot - Tango; 1980.   2fl 2ob 2cl sax(E♭) b-cl 2hn 2bn cbn 2tp (perc).
RYH-24. Mister Joplin's Holiday; 2 mvts, 1978.   2fl 2ob 2cl 2hn/(+2hn ad lib) 2bn cbn 2tp (perc); (b-cl ad lib).
RYH-25. Three Surrey Landscapes; 1974.   2fl 2ob 2cl 2hn 2bn cbn (perc).
RYH-26. In Lathkill Dale; 1978.   Solo oboe, 2fl 2cl b-cl 3hn 2bn cbn.
RYH-27. Second XI Polka; 1981.   2fl 2cl b-cl hn bn cbn 2tp (perc).
RYH-1v. "Mother Make My Bed".   SATB chorus *or* S solo, 2fl 2ob 4cl b-cl 3hn 2bn cbn (perc ad lib).
RYH-2v. The Garden, descriptive piece with pre-narration; 1992.   Narrator, 2fl 2ob 2cl 2hn 2bn cbn 2tp.

*HENZE, Hans Werner *1 July 1926, Gütersloh, Westphalia*
HWH-1. Concertino, 1947.   Solo piano, 2fl 2ob 2cl 2hn 2bn 2tp 2tb tu 3perc.
Pm (B. Schott's Söhne: Mainz), hire score & parts; solo piano with piano reduction (pn 6988).

HERBAIN, ( ) *Chevalier d'* *1734, Paris - 28 May 1768, Paris*
CDH-1. Overture: Célime (ballet en un acte, réspresenté par l'Accademie [sic] royale de musique le 28e jour de
Sept 1756).   2ob 2cl 2hn.
AutoMS score: F-Po, with clarinets in F.
MS score (RISM [H 5085]): F-Po (Vendôme), with clarinets in F.

HERMANS, Nico (Niko) *1919, Netherlands*
NYH-1. Ballett des petits pieds, 1972.   2fl 2ob 2cl 2hn 2bn 2tp.
Pm (Donemus, Amsterdam, c.1973), score.
NYH-2. Bagatellen.   fl 2ob 2cl bn tp.
Pm (Donemus: Amsterdam, 1964), score & parts.

*HERMSTEDT, Johann Simon *29 Dec 1778, Langensalza, Thüringia - 10 Aug 1846. Sondershausen*
EJH-1.1a(-1.3a). Musique d'Harmonie contennant Trois Quatuors de Mozart; Cahier 1: K.428, (Cah. 2 & 3
untraced).   terz-fl 2ob 2cl 2hn 2bn 2tp(prin) b-tb b-hn.
Pc (au Bureau de Musique de C.F. Peters: Leipzig, pn 1678, sd), parts: GB-Ljag(w), (Cah. 1 only).
EJH-2a. Mozart: Allegro (1st mvt) from King of Prussia Set of String Quartets, No. 1, (K.575).
fl 2ob 3cl 2hn 2bn 2tp b-tb(C, G) b-hn timp.
AutoMS score: F-Pn, MS. 11830, (includes a 3-page biography of Hermstedt dated 11 Oct 1860).

*HERTEL, Johann Wilhelm *9 Oct 1727, Eisenach - 14 June 1789, Schwerin*
*JWH-1. Concerto à 5; in D.   2ob 2bn tp.
AutoMS score: B-Bc, No. 7682.
Pm (Heinrichshofen: Wilhelmshaven, pn 3146, 1941), score & parts; reprinted Noetzel, 1959.

JWH-2. Sonata à Quatro; in E♭, 3 mvts.   2hn 2bn.
AutoMS score (for the Schwerin court): B-Bc, No. 6695.   ★
Pm (Otto Heinrich Noetzel Verlag: Wilhelmshaven, pn 3147, 1959), ed. Johann Hermann Sallagar, score & parts.
JWH-1m. 6 Märsche.   2ob 2hn bn tp.
AutoMS score & MS parts: D-SWl, Mus. 2777.   MS: B-Bc, No. 7688   ★

HESS, Willy *12 Oct 1906, Winterthur*
WZH-1. Suite für 12 Bläsinstrumente, Op. 53; 1945-49.   2fl 2ob 2cl 2bn 2hn tp tb.
Pm: (Breitkopf & Härtel: Wiesbaden, 1951).
WZH-1a. Beethoven: 5 Stücke für die Flötenuhr, No. 1, Adagio, (WoO 33).   fl 2ob 2cl 2hn 2bn.
Pm (Breitkopf & Härtel: Wiesbaden, 1957, reissued 1986), score & parts, (Kammermusik-Bibliothek 2216).

HÉTU, Jacques (Joseph Robert) *8 Aug 1938, Quebec*
JJH-1. Cycle, Op. 16; 1969.   Solo piano, fl 2cl hn bn 2tp 2tb.   MS score: C-Tcm.

*HEUSCHKEL, Johann Peter *4 Jan 1773, Harras - 5 Dec 1853, Biebrich*
JEH-1a. Premier Recueil d'harmonie tiré de l'Opera Semiramis de Rossini [sic]; 6 mvts.   fl 2cl 2hn 2bn.
Pc (chez B. Schott Fils: Mayence, pn 2181, c.1823), parts: D-MZsch. *Nos. IV & V are different versions of the Introduzione, "Belo si celebri": No. IV uses a clarinet in A; No. V uses a clarinet in B♭, omitting the flute part and with bassoons marked "en Fa", scored a 6th above the part in No. IV.*
JEH-2a. Deuxieme Recueil d'harmonie tiré de l'opera Semiramis de Rossini et de l'opera Euryanthe de C.M. de Weber [sic]; 3 & 4 mvts, respectively.   fl 2cl 2hn 2bn.
Pc (chez B. Schott Fils: Mayence, pn 2182, c.1823), parts: D-MZsch; GB-Ljag(w).
JEH-3a. Troisieme Recueil d'harmonie tiré de . . . Euryanthe de C.M. de Weber [sic]; 6 mvts.   fl 2cl 2hn 2bn.
Pc (chez B. Schott Fils: Mayemce, pn 2206, 1824), parts: D-MZsch.

*HEWITT, J. (?James) *(1770 - 1827)*
JHH-1m. Four Quick Marches . . . [for] the Lichfield Loyal Association.   2cl/(and, or)2fl 2hn (2)bn tp.
Pc (Printed for the Author by Preston: London, 1800), RISM [H 5224], score: GB-Lbl, g.137.(29); GB-Ob, Mus.Instr.I.121(2).   ★

*HEYSE, Anton Gottlieb *(1770) - flautist, active c.1800 Halle*
AGH-1. Serenade, Op. 2 [Jansen] or Op. 6 [Vester citation].   2fl 2hn bn harp.
Pc (J.A. Boehm: Hamburg, c.1800), parts: DK-A.

HIDAS, Frigyes *1928, Hungary*
FIH-1. Divertimento.   2ob 2cl 2hn 2bn.
Pm (Editio Musica Budapest: Budapest, 1985), score & parts.
FIH-2. 5 Miniatures.   2cl 2hn 2bn.
Pm (Editio Musica Budapest: Budapest, pn 136531, 1991), score & parts.

*HIEBESCH, Johann Nepomuk *18 May 1766, Birkhausen nr Wallerstein - 1820, Wallerstein*
JKH-1. Parthia in F; c.1790, 4 mvts.   2fl 2ob 2cl 3hn 2bn vlne.
MS parts: D-HR, HR III 4 1/2 2° 607.   ★
Pm (KGS), fiche (2727, 2728).
JKH-2. Parthia in F; c. 1800, 4 mvts.   2fl 2ob 2cl 3hn 2bn vlne.
MS parts: D-HR, HR III 4 1/2 2° 609.   ★
Pm (KGS), fiche (2731, 2732).
JKH-3. [Parthia in D]; c.1800, 4 mvts.   2fl 2ob 2cl 2hn 2bn vlne.
AutoMS score: D-HR, HR III 4 1/2 2° 99.   ★
Pm (KGS), fiche (467).
*JKH-4. Partita in D, "Richtig mit Leipsig im 18t. Octbr: 1813"; 5 mvts.   fl 2ob 2cl 2hn 2bn tp db.
MS parts: D-HR, HR III 4 1/2 2° 606.   ★
Pm (KGS), fiche (2725, 2726).
*JKH-5. Parthia in F; 1791, 13 mvts.   fl 2ob 2cl 3hn 2bn vlne.
MS parts: D-HR, HR III 4 1/2 2° 608.   ★
Pm (KGS), fiche (2729, 2730).
JKH-1a. Mozart: Die Zauberflöte. See supra: JKH-5, (mvts 2, 4, 6, 7 & 8).

HIJMAN, Julius *25 Jan 1901, Almelo - 6 Jan 1969, New York*
JUH-1. Piece for 10 winds.   2fl 2ob 2cl 2hn 2bn. *No known locations; try US-Wc.*

*HILL, Frederick *1760, Louth, Lincolnshire - ? York*
FYH-1m. A Favourite Quick Step, . . . With a Relief For the Fife and Drum . . . [for] the Yeomanry, Cavalry, & Infantry, In the County of Leicester.   2cl/fl 2hn 2bn, (with a Relief (trio) for 2fifes & drums).
Pc (Printed for the Author by Cahusac & Sons: London, 1795), RISM [H 5245], score: GB-Gu; GB-Lbl, g.133.(26); GB-Ob, Mus.Instr.I.121(5), GB-Lhumphries.   ★

HILL, Peter *14 June 1948, Lyndhurst, Hampshire, UK*
PYH-1a. Gounod: Marche funèbre d'une Marionette.   2fl 2ob 2cl 2hn 2bn.
Pm (Westerleigh Publications: Lustleigh, Devon, UK, c.1988), score & parts.

*HIMMEL, Friedrich Heinrich *20 Nov 1765, Traubriezen - 8 June 1814, Berlin*
FHH-1tv. Trauer-Cantate, [for the funeral of Friedrich Wilhelm II, who died in 1797]. Quartetto, "Neuer Lebenshauch umwelt".   SSTB, 2cl(A) 2bn 2tp(muted) 3timp(muted), pp. 46 - 49; Chorale, Wahrend der Einsenkung des Sarges in ide Gruft.   2fl 2ob 2hn 2bn 2tp a-tb t-tb 2b-tb timp.
Pc (sn [The Author]: Potsdam, 1798), score: D-SWl, (3 copies), Mus. 2823.   ★
Pc (Meyn: Hamburg, c.1798), score: D-Rtt, Himmel (Druck) 4.
FHH-1m. [2] Marches, Op. 34.   2sept-flutes, 2cl 2bn serp 2tp tambour.
Pc (A Kühnel, Bureau de Musique: Leipzig, pn 792, 1810), RISM [H 5547], parts: A-Wgm; D-AB; I-Fc, F.P. S.475.   ★
FHH-2m. Marsch vom 2. Bataillon Garde.   2ob 2cl bn tp.   MS: D-Bds, Hausbibl, No. 56, (?lost).

*HINDEMITH, Paul *16 Nov 1895, Hanau, Frankfurt - 28 Dec 1963, Frankfurt am Main*
*PAH-1. Symphonia serena; 2nd movement, paraphrase on Beethoven's March LVB-2m.
pic 2fl 2ob ca 2cl(Eb) 4hn 2bn cbn 2tp 2tb tu glock celeste.
Pm (B. Schott's Söhne: Mainz, pn AMP 162, 1947, reissued 1954), score & pts, min score (full work, pn 4422).
*PAH-2. Der Schwanendreher; 3 mvts. Solo viola, fl(pic) fl ob 2cl 3hn 2bn tp tb hp 4vc 3db.
Pm (B. Schott's Söhne, Mainz, pn 3306, 1936, 1964).
PAH-3. Kammermusik No. 5 (Viola Concerto), Op. 36, No. 4; 1927.
Solo viola, pic ob 3cl hn 3bn 2tp 2tb tu 4vc 4db.
Pm (B. Schott's Söhne, Mainz, pn 3343, 1928), score.
PAH-4. Kammermusik No. 6 (Viola d'amore Concerto), Op. 46, No. 1; 1927.
Solo viola d'amore, fl ob 2cl hn bn tp tb 3vc 2db.
Pm (B. Schott's Söhne, Mainz, pn 6315, 1930).
PAH-5. Konzertmusik, Op. 48, 1930. Solo viola, pic fl ca cl b-cl 3hn 2bn cbn 2tp tb tu 4vc 4db.
Pm (B. Schott's Söhne, Mainz, pn 3491, 1930).
PAH-6. Concerto for orchestra, Op. 38: March. pic fl 2ob cl(Eb) cl b-cl 2bn cbn.
Pm (B. Schott's Söhne: Mainz, pn 3444, 1925), miniature score (complete work).
*PAH-7. Septet; 1948, 4 mvts. fl ob cl b-cl hn bn tp.
Pm (B. Schott's Söhne: Mainz, 1949), miniature score (pn ED 3540) & pts (pn ED 919).
PAH-1f. Sonata for 10 wind; 1917, (Op. 10a, fragments only)
Pm (to appear in: *Sämtliche Werke*. B. Schott's Söhne: Mainz), score.

*HINDMARCH (Hindmarsh), John *c.1755 - 1796*
JGH-1m. The favourite Grand March as Performed by The Staffordshire Band. 2fl 2cl 2hn tp basso.
Pc (Longman and Broderip: London, c.1795), RISM [H 5612], score: GB-Gu; GB-Lbl, g.133.(26); GB-Ob; US-Wc. ★

*HINTZE, W. *(?1820)*
WQH-1m. Die 55ger (Geschwindmarsch); in Ab. pic 2ob cl(Eb) 3cl(Bb) 4hn 2bn 4tp crt 2t-hn 3tb euph tu b-dr s-dr. AutoMS score: D-DT, Mus-h 5 H 2.
WQH-2m. Geschwindmarsch; in C. pic terz-fl 2ob 2cl(Eb) 3cl(C) 4hn 2bn 4tp 2t-hn 3tb "bastrophon" t-tu b-tu b-dr s-dr. MS score: D-DT, Mus-h 5 H 2.

*HLADKÝ, ( ) *(1810)*
XXH-1a. J. Strauss the Elder: Erinnerung an Pest, Op. 66, ("Emlek Pestre a nenus Nemzetnek ajubilon. Strauss Janostol. Erinnerung an Pesth"). 3cl 2hn bn 2tp b-tb. MS parts (c.1844): CZ-Bm, A.37.349, (missing cl I).

HLAVÁČ, Miroslav *23 Oct 1923, Protivín*
MLH-1. Elegikon, Symfonieta (1964). Piano, pic 2fl 2ob ca 2cl b-cl 4hn 2bn cbn 4tp 3tb tu timp vib xly s-dr+tri cym+tam-tam.
Pm (Panton: Prague, 1979), score (Studijní partitury, 106). *Recorded by Panton Records, Prague.*

*HLOBIL, Emil *11 Oct 1901, Veselí nad Lužnicí, near Tábor*
EYH-1. Octet, Op. 52. 2ob 2cl 2hn 2bn.
Pm (Panton: Prague, 1956), score & parts.
EYH-2. Komorníhudba, Op. 67. 2cl bthn b-cl.
Pm (Český hudební fond: Prague, 1965), hire score & parts.

*HNOJIL (Hnogill), Jan *5 July 1795, Sloupno, near Hradec Králové - 20 Nov 1852, Brno*
JAH-1. 6 Deutsche, c.1820. pic cl(F) 2cl(C) 2hn 2bn cbn 4tp b-dr s-dr. MS parts: CZ-Bm(au), A.18.911. ★
JAH-2, 3. 2 sets of 2 Deutsche. cl(D, Eb) 2cl 2hn 2bn cbn timp. MS parts: CZ-Bm(au), A.35.927. ★
JAH-4. Proba Marsch für die Türkische Musik. Componirt und gewidmet [sic] die k.k. H. Hauptmann des Herzog Nassan 29ten Linien Infanterie Regiments von (?)Kurz Wohlegeborn.
pic cl(F) 3cl(C) 2hn (D, G) 2bn serp 4tp(A, G, D, D) b-dr cym s-dr. MS pts (1820): CZ-Bm(au), A.18.910. ★
JAH-1v. Regina coeli. CATB, 2ob 2cl 2hn 2bn cbn 2tp timp.
MS parts ("die 7ma Marhi 1819"): CZ-Bm(au), A.18.909. ★
JAH-2.1v. Regina coeli, c.1822. CATB, 2ob 2cl 2hn 2bn 2tp (b-tb) timp.
MS parts: CZ-Bm(au), A.20.675, (b-tb in parts only). ★
JAH-2.2v. Regina coeli, 1824. CATB, 2ob 2cl(C, G) 4hn(C, G) 2bn cbn, "Basson Basso", 4tp(C, C, F, G) timp.
AutoMS score: CZ-Bm(au), A.20.675.
JAH-2.3v. Regina coeli. CATB, 2ob 2cl(C) 4hn(C, G) 2bn cbn, "Basson Basso", 4tp(C, C, F, G) timp.
MS score: CZ-Bm(au), A.35.300. *The Basson Basso part in not the same as the cbn pt.*
JAH-1.1a. Rossini: Il Barbiere di Siviglia, 9 mvts. 2ob 2cl 2hn 2bn cbn 2tp.
(?Auto)MS score: CZ-Bm(au), A.35.210, (possibly with stitching errors). MS pts: CZ-Bm(au), A.36.888, (without Op. omits No. 4). *The wrapper of the Beethoven Septetto (A.35.149) states,* "N^{ro} 25 / Barbier von Se= / villa / Oper / für / 2= Oboen / 2= Clarinetten, / 2= Horn / 2= Fagotten, / und Grand Fagott / Rossini / Eingerichtet für Harmonie / v- / J. Hnojil für H.H. C.J. Napp." *and probably should be with JAH-1.1a.*
JAH-1.2a. Rossini: Il Barbieri di Siviglia, Alla marcia. 2ob 2cl 2hn 2bn cbn.
MS pts: CZ-BM(au), A.35.149, (following the arrangement of Beethoven's *Septetto, Op 20*).

HOCH, Francesco *14 Feb 1943, Lugano, Switzerland*
FQH-1. Spurlos; 1978. 2fl 2ob 2cl 2hn 2bn.
Pm (Suvini-Zerboni: Milan, pn S8476Z, c.1979), score & parts.
FQH-2. Metafigure; 1978 - 1979. cl sax 2hn bn 2tp tu 2perc.
Pm (Suvini-Zerboni: Milan, pn S8589Z, c.1982), score & parts.

HODKINSON, Sydney Phillip *1934, USA*
SPH-1. Taula. fl ob cl 2hn bn 2tp tb tu.
Pm (Merion, *via* T. Presser: Bryn Mawr, PA, 1974).

HOEBERECHTS (Hoberechts), John Lewis *(1760), Holland - (1820), London*
JLH-1m. A Grand Military Piece; 4 mvts. 2cl+2cl(ad lib) 2hn 2bn tp serp.
Pc (Goulding, Phipps & D'Almaine: London, 1799), RISM [H 5708], parts: GB-Lbl, h.3213.k.(7). ★

*HOEDL (Hödl), Al[?bert] *(1825) active at the Collegium Mariano Rupertinum, Salzburg, c.1845*
Note: other anonymous works in A-Sca, Hs.266 may be composed or arranged by Hoedl; for a full list of these works see the Anonymous Works List under: Austria - Collegium Mariano Rupertinum, Salzburg.
ADH-1m. Friedrichslust [March with Trio]. fl(Eb) cl(Eb) 2cl(Bb) 2hn 2bn 2tp.
MS parts: A-Sca, Hs.266, No. 40. ★
ADH-2m. Marsch v[on]. Marian Eleven. 2cl(Eb) 2cl(Bb) 2hn 2bn 2tp. MS parts: A-Sca, Hs.266, No. 43. ★
ADH-3m. Marsch; [& Trio], in . 3cl(Eb) cl(Bb) 2hn 2bn 2tp. MS parts: A-Sca, Hs.266, No. 44. ★
ADH-4m. Der Abschied! Marsch [& Trio]. cl(Eb) 2cl(Bb) 2hn 2bn 2tp. MS parts: A-Sca, Hs.266, No. 51.
ADH-1t. Trauermarsch und Grabgesang. 2cl(Eb) 2cl(Bb) 2hn 2bn 2tp.
MS parts: A-Sca, Hs.266, No. 46, (the Grabgesang is without text). ★
ADH-1a. Quodlibet. 2cl(Eb) 2cl(Bb) 2hn 2bn 2tp. MS pts: A-Sca, Hs.266, No. 48. ★

HÖLLER, Karl Heinz *25 July 1907, Bamberg*
KXH-1. Scherzo, Op. 24a. 2ob 2cl 2hn 2bn.
Pm (Leuckart: München, pn 10675, 1972), score & parts.

*HÖNIG, ( ) *(1790), "Herrn Capellmeister Hönig"*
XZH-1a. Livorka: [7] Walzer, with Coda. 2ob cl(F) 2cl 2hn 2bn cbn 2tp.
MS parts (c.1818): CZ-Bm(au), A.37.338.

*HÖPPLER, ( ) *Possibly Simon Höpler, whose religious compositions are in CZ-Bm.*
YXH-1v. IV Stationes pro Festo SSmi Corporis Christi. CATB, 2fl 2cl 2hn 2bn 2tp(clar) tp(prin) vlne timp.
MS parts: CZ-Pnm, (2 copies), XXXVIII.B.137, XL.F.85, (Statio 1 only,"Ecce panis Angelorum", missing bn II;
the clarino parts have been incorrectly cataloged as clarinetts rather than trumpets). ★

*HÖRGER, G. *(?1810)*
GZH-1. No. 1 Ouverture; in Eb. Incomplete, here only: cl(Eb) bn(II) serp/cbn b-dr.
MS parts: D-DT, Mus-n 1046.

HOFER, Achim (editor)
AQH-1m(-10m). Die Infanteriemarsche der vormeligen Churfürstlich-Sachsischen Armee 1729. 2ob 2hn bn.
(Original) MS score: D-Dla, H27.8 (Old shelfmark: Loc.10945).
Pm (facsimile of first page of score, No. 8 only) in G. Joppig, 1988, *The Oboe*, from MS score at D-Dla, H27.8.
Pm (Fritz Schultz: Freiburg, 1981), edited Achim Hofer, score & parts.
    1.1m Garde [Marsch des Regiments "Erste Garde"].
    1.2m. March [sic] Regiment 2te Garde.
    1.3m. [Marsch des Regiments] Königl[licher] Prinz.
    1.4m. March [sic] von Gotha Regiment.
    1.5m. Alte Rgt-March [sic] [des] Obristen v. Böhnen.
    1.6m. [Marsch des Regiments du] Caila.
    1.7m. [Marsch des Regiments] von Löwendahl.
    1.8m. [Marsch des Regiments] Herzog von Weissenfels.
    1.9m. Marsch ex G [for the] Regiment de Descky.
    1.10m. Grafen Rutowsky March [sic].

*HOFER, Frédéric *"Chef de Musique au 5e Régiment d'Infanterie Légère".*
FRH-1m. Pas redoublé favori de Sa Majesté Louis Philippe 1er Roi des Française…Dédié à la Garde Nationale
et à l'Armée Française. pic(D) cl(Eb) 3cl(Bb) 2hn bn tp tb serp/oph b-dr tambour.
Pc (Richault: Paris, pn 2754.R, 1830), parts: CH-Gpu, Ib.4921e; GB-Ljag, (photocopy). ★

HOFFMANN, Adolf *(1850)*
ADH-1v. Fronleichnams-Stationen, Op. 2, Ausgabe A. SATB, 2fl 2ob 2cl 2hn 2bn 2tp t-hn, Directionstimme.
Pc (A. Pietsch: in Ziegenhals in Schlesien, pn 30, c.1880), pts: CZ-Pnm, (2 copies), XLIII.A.122, XLIII.A.123. ★

*HOFFMANN, Carl Heinrich, Oberaufseher *(1810)*
CHH-1(-3). [2] Feldschritt [in F & Exb; & 1 Walzer, in F].
pic(F) 2cl(Eb) 2cl(Bb) 4hn 2bn tp(clar) 2tp(chromatic) 2tb oph b-dr s-dr. MS parts (1840): D-SCHN, 42. ★

*HOFFMANN, Ernst Theodor Amadeus *24 Jan 1776, Königsberg-25 June 1822, Berlin*
ETH-1e *Das Kreuz an der Ostsee*, Trauerspiel, 1805
AutoMS score: D-Bds, Mus.ms.autogr.Hoffmann, E.T. 3, Akz. Nr. M 1174.
    1.1e. [without No.], Marsch der Ordersritter, in D, 28 bars. 2fl 2ob 2cl 2hn 2bn cbn 2tp. "Der Marsch wird
        bis zu Veränderung des Theatres wiederholt." ★
    1.2e. [without Number], Bey dem Schlusse des Epilogs, Bb, 17 bars. Harp, 2fl 2cl bthn 2bn 2tp 3tb timp. ★
    1ve. No. 3, Schlachtgesang der Preussen, 41 bars. TB chorus, 2fl 2ob 2cl 4hn 2bn cbn b-dr. ★
ETH-2e. *Wiedersehl!* Prolog in einem Akte, Nov 1808: Marcia guerriera sopra il Theatre, Molto Andante, in C,
24 bars. pic 2cl 2hn 2tp tb(ossia cbn) b-dr s-dr+cym.
AutoMS score & parts: D-DS. MS score: D-B, Mus.ms.10710. ★
This work also includes: No. 1, Chor, "Welch Leiden"), STB, 2fl 2ob, strings with an on-stage band (2cl 2hn 2bn).
ETH-3e. Aurora, grosse heroische Oper, 1811/12, Act 3 Finale, No. 14/1, Marsch der Priester.
2cl 2hn 2bn 2tp 3tb 2vla 2vc db.
AutoMS score & MS parts (with Auto corrections): D-WÜs. AutoMS score: D-BAa, Msc.Var.1t. ★
Pm (Denkmäler des Tonkünst in Bayern. Breitkopf & Härtel: Wiesbaden, 1984), Neue Folge Bd. 5.

*HOFFMANN, Leopold *c.1730, Vienna - 17 March 1793, Vienna*
LEH-1. Divertimento; in D, 6 mvts. 2ob 2hn bn.
MS parts: CZ-Pnm, (2 copies), XLII.B.243; XL.E.342, (MS score c.1850 as "Feld-Partitta in D"). ★

*HOFFMEISTER, Franz Anton   *12 May 1754, Rottenburg - 9 Feb 1812, Vienna*
The anonymous works sometimes attributed to Krommer in the bound volumes, CZ-KRa, A4451/R.I.21, Nos.
9 - 14 may also be by Hoffmeister; details are given in the ANONYMOUS WORKS LIST.
*FAH-1.1. Parthie in B♭, 3 mvts.   2ob 2cl 2hn 2bn.
MS parts: CZ-KRa,A3382/IV.B.45; NL-Z, Z1215/M.A.Zcm.26, No. 1; D-DO, Mus.Ms.767, (possibly attributed
to Kurzweil); D-RUl, RH. R.93, (attributed to Rosetti). ★
*FAH-1.2. No: 6: Parthia in F; 3 mvts.   3bthn 2hn bn.   MS parts: PL-LA, RM 60. ★
FAH-2.1. Serenade No. 1; in E♭, 5 mvts (as "No. 1 [- 5]").   2ob/fl 2cl 2hn 2bn cbn/db(ad lib).
Pc (N. Simrock: Bonn, pn 975, 1812/1813), RISM [H 6221], parts: CZ-K; D-HR, HR III 4 1/2 2° 382. ★
Pm (KGS), fiche (2263), D-HR Simrock edition.
Pm (Kneusslin: Basel, 1962), ed. with transitions & cadences by Ernst Hess, score & parts (Für Kenner und
Liebhaber, No. 24).
Pm (Ricordi: Milano, sd), score & parts.
FAH-2.2. Parthia No. 5; in E♭, 2/3 mvts (= Nos. 1 & 2 of FAH-2.1).   2ob 2cl 2hn 2bn.
MS pts: A-Ee, Mus.1128, (as "N: 5 in E♭ Partia", No. 2 split into 2 mvts); CZ-KRa, A3879/IV.B.42. (as "Nro V
Parthia in Dis", No. 1 split into 2 mvts); NL-Z, Z1215/M.A.Zcm 26, No. 5 (as "Parthie V", No. 1 split
into 2 mvts). *This is likely to be an earlier version of FAH-2.1.*
FAH-3. Harmonie in F; 4 mvts.   2ob 2cl 2hn 2bn.
Pc (Broderip & Wilkinson: London, c.1800), RISM [H 6229], parts: GB-Lbl, h.114.(8); GB-Ob,
Mus.Instr. I.122(16). ★
Pc (sn: Paris, sd), parts: D-DS, (Eitner citation - lost during World War II).
*FAH-4. Parthia, No. 2; in B♭, 4 mvts. 2ob 2cl 2hn 2bn.
MS parts: CZ-KRa, A3883/IV.B.46.; D-DO, Mus.Ms.1679, (as "No. 7" after "6 Partitas par Rosetti");
NL-Z, Z1215/M.A.Zcm 26, No. 2. ★
FAH-5.1. Parthia in B[♭]; 4 mvts.   2ob 2cl 2hn 2bn.   MS parts: A-Wgm, VIII 39983. ★
*FAH-5.2. No: 5: Parthia; in F, 3mvts.   3bthn 2hn.   MS pts: PL-LA, RM 59. *Without mvt 2, Menuetto & Trio.*
FAH-6. Nro 8 Pardia alla Camera; in A, 4 mvts.   2ob 2cl 2hn 2bn.   MS parts: CZ-KRa, A3885/IV.B.48. ★
FAH-7. Nro 10 Pardia; in A, 5 mvts.   2ob 2cl 2hn 2bn.   MS parts: CZ-KRa, A3885/IV.B.49. ★
FAH-8. No. 14 Pardia alie [sic] Camera; in E♭, 4 mvts.   2ob 2cl 2hn 2bn.   MS pts: CZ-KRa, A3884/IV.B.47. ★
*FAH-9.1. Parthia in D; 3 mvts (with Da Capo to mvt 1).   2ob 2cl(A) 2hn 2bn.
MS parts: CZ-KRa, A3881/IV.B.44.
*FAH-9.2. Parthia Nº VI in D; one continuous mvt, in 4 sections.   2ob 2cl(A) 2hn 2bn.
MS parts: A-Wgm, VIII 39982, (omits mvt 2, Romance, and the Da Capo to movement/section 1).
*FAH-9.3. Parthie in D; 2 mvts.   2ob 2cl 2hn 2bn.
MS parts: NL-Z, M.A.Zcm 26, No. 3, (omits mvt 2, Romance, and the Da Capo to movement/section 1).
*FAH-10. Parthie in D; 3 mvts.   2ob 2cl 2hn 2bn.   MS parts: NL-Z, Z1215/M.A.Zcm 26, No. 4, (as by
Hoffmeister); A-Wgm, VIII 40899, *(attributed to F.J. Haydn, as Hob.II/Es12, FJH-8d).* ★
FAH-11. Parthie, in E♭; 3 mvts.   2ob 2cl 2hn 2bn.
MS parts: NL-Z, Z1215/M.A.Zcm 26, No. 6; CZ-KRa, A3880/IV.B.43. (as "Nro VI Parthia in Dis"). ★
FAH-12. Parthia No. 15; in F.   2ob 2cl 2hn 2bn.   MS parts: D-RUl, RH-H.143.
FAH-13. Parthia in E♭.   2ob 2cl 2hn 2bn.   MS parts: PL-WRü.
FAH-14. Divertimento; in E♭, 3 mvts.   2ob 2cl 2hn 2bn.
MS pts: US-BETm, Philharmonic Society of Bethlehem PSB 1340.2, *(oboe pts are loose sheets in bn I book).* ★
FAH-15. [Untitled Parthia].   2fl 2cl 2hn 2bn.
MS parts: D-HER, Mus.N.1=15, (incomplete: fl II, cl I, hn I only).
*FAH-16.1. Notturno; in E♭, 4 mvts.   fl fldam 2hn 2vla vc/bn.
Pc (presso Hofmeister: Wien, pn 52, 1786), parts: F-Pn, A. 34.423. ★
*FAH-16.2. Notturno; in E♭, 4 mvts.   Solo fl, solo cl/ob, 2hn 2vla vc(vel bn).
MS parts: CZ-Pnm, XLI.B.264. *The alternative Solo oboe part is a slightly later addition.* ★
*FAH-17. Parthia Nro.1; in E♭; 4 mvts.   cl hn hn, with echo cl hn bn.
Pc (Traeg: [Vienna], pre-1799), No. 163, MS pts: CZ-Pnm, XLI.B.119; GB-Lcm, microfilm of CZ-Pnm MS. ★
*FAH-18. Parthia Nro. 2; in E♭; 3 mvts.   cl hn bn, with echo cl hn bn.
Pc (Traeg: [Vienna], pre-1799), No. 164, MS pts: CZ-Pnm, XLI.B.118; GB-Lcm, microfilm of CZ-Pnm MS. ★
*FAH-19. Parthia Nro.3; in B♭; 4 mvts.   2cl 2hn 2bn.
Pc (Traeg: [Vienna], pre-1799), No. 165, MS parts: CZ-Pnm, XLI.B.117.; D-DO, Mus.Ms.767, No. 2;
GB-Lcm, microfilm of CZ-Pnm MS. ★
FAH-20. Nro 54 Parthia in Es [E♭] Concertans; 4 mvts.   2cl 2hn 2bn.
MS parts: CZ-Bm(no), 16.641, (as "Parthia in Dis"); CZ-KRa, A3887/IV.B.50. ★
FAH-21. Nro 57 Parthia in Dis [E♭]; 3 mvts.   2cl 2hn 2bn.   MS parts: CZ-KRa, A3888/IV.B.51. ★
FAH-22. Nro 58 Parthia in Dis [E♭]; 4 mvts.   2cl 2hn 2bn.   MS parts: CZ-KRa, A3889/IV.B.52. ★
FAH-23.1. Nro 60 Parthia in dis [E♭]; 4 mvts.   2cl 2hn 2bn.   MS parts: CZ-KRa, A3890/IV.B.53. ★
FAH-23.2. Rondo; in F, (the first 82 bars, i.e. to the fermata, of the 4th mvt of FAH-23.1).   cl 2bthn bn.
MS score: CZ-KRa, A3888/IV.B.51 wrapper, ff. 1b-2b.
FAH-24. Parthia in B♭, 2 mvts.   2cl 2hn 2bn.   MS parts: CZ-Pnm, XLII.F.36, No. 12. ★
*FAH-25. Partita in B♭.   2cl 2hn 2bn.   MS parts: D-DO, Mus.Ms.767, No. 1.
*FAH-26. Partita in E♭, 4 mvts.   2cl 2hn 2bn.
MS parts: D-DO, Mus.Ms.767, No. 3; CZ-Bn(no), (as "Serenata V. in B[♭]", for 2cl 2hn bn). ★
*FAH-27. Partita in E♭, 3mvts.   2cl 2hn 2bn.   MS pts: D-DO, Mus.Ms.767, No. 4; CZ-Bm(no), (as "Serenata
VI. in E♭", for 2cl 2hn bn); CZ-NR, A.18.249/B.265. ★
FAH-28. Parthia in E♭; 4 mvts .   2cl 2hn 2bn.   MS parts: PL-LA, RM 57. ★
FAH-29. Parthia in E♭.   2cl 2hn 2bn.   MS parts: US-Wc.
FAH-30. Parthia in E♭, 5 mvts.   2cl 2hn 2bn.   MS parts: CZ-NR, A.18.243/B.259. ★
FAH-31. Parthia in E♭; 4 mvts.   2cl 2hn 2bn.   MS parts: CZ-NR, A.18.252/B.267. ★
*FAH-32. Parthia; in E♭, 4 mvts.   2cl 2hn 2bn.
MS parts: CZ-Bm(no), A.16.640b; CZ-KRa, A4451/R.I.21, No. 5, (hn I: "Bagio [sic] in Dis"). ★
FAH-33. Parthia in E[♭] la fa; 4 mvts.   2cl 2hn 2bn.   MS parts: CZ-Bm(no), A.16.639. ★

FAH-34. Sextetto; in E♭, 2 mvts, ("und Ein Aria auf [F Kauer's] Donau Weibchen"). 2cl 2hn 2bn.
MS parts: CZ-KRa, A3878/IV.B.41. ★
FAH-35. Parthia; in E♭, 4 mvts. 2cl 2hn 2bn.
MS parts: US-BETm, Philharmonic Society of Bethlehem PSB 1351.3. ★
*FAH-36. Parthia in E♭ ("Ankunfts- und Abschiedsparthia"), 3 mvts. 2cl 2hn 2bn.
MS parts: (provenance unknown). Modern MS score & parts: D-KIZklöcker. ★
FAH-37. Variazioni No. I. 2cl 2hn 2bn.
Pc (Hoffmeister & Kühnel: Leipzig; Hoffmeister & Co.: Wien, pn 151, 1803), RISM [H 6198], parts:
A-Wgm, VIII 9268; D-WEMl, (present location unknown); H-KE. MS parts: CZ-Pnm, XLII.F.36, No. 12. ★
FAH-38. Parthia in D moli [minor]; 4 mvts. 2ob 2hn bn. MS parts: CZ-KRa, A3891/IV.B.53. ★
FAH-39. Douze Ariettes, Op. 17. 2cl 2hn bn.
Pc (J.J. Hummel: Berlin; Amsterdam: Au grand magasin de musique, pn 826, c.1800), RISM [H 6222], parts:
CZ-Pnm, XLII.C.120. ★
Pc: (as "XII Pièces favoris":) (Hoffmeister & Kühnel: Leipzig, pn 347, 1804), RISM Supp [HH 6222a], parts:
H-Bn, ZR 684; GB-DOTams, (microfilm).
*FAH-40. No: 4: Parthia; in F, 3 mvts. 3bthn 2hn. MS parts: PL-LA, Mus. RM 58. ★
Note the similar scoring of FAH-1.2, FAH-5.2.
FAH-41. Quintetto; in F, 5 mvts. ob hn bn 2vla. MS parts (by Clement Stros): CZ-PLa(ne), Hu 91. ★
FAH-42. Quintetto; in E♭, 5 mvts. ob hn bn 2vla. MS parts (by Clement Stros): CZ-PLa(ne), Hu 92. ★
FAH-43. Quintetto; in D, 5 mvts. ob hn bn 2vla.
MS parts: A-Sca, Hs.1698, (with vlne doubling the bn); CZ-PLa(ne), Hu 202, (MS pts by Clement Stros). ★
FAH-44. Quintetto; in E♭, 5 mvts. ob hn bn 2vla. MS parts (by Clement Stros): CZ-PLa(ne), Hu 203. ★

HOFMANN, Wolfgang *1922, Germany*
WLH-1. Sinfonietta. 2fl 2ob 2cl 2hn 2bn 2tp tb perc.
Pm (Noetzel, *via* Heinrichhofen Verlag: Wilhelmshaven, 1984).
WLH-2. Concertino Palatino. 2ob ca 2bn tp hpcd.
Pm (Musikverlag Egbert Lewark: Frankenthal, c.1990).

HOHMANN, Edmond *1858, Germany*
EDH-1. Octet. 2ob 2cl 2hn 2bn.
Pm (Verlag Max Brockhaus: Bonn, sd).

HOLLER, (Georg) Augustin *baptized 14 June 1745, Sperlhammer - 13 Feb 1814, Munich*
GAH-1. Avertis[se]mentes in C; 12 allemandes. 2pic 2cl(C) 2hn bn tp(clar prin) tp(dugetto) "tampuro".
MS parts ("Ad me Petrum Hüber"): D-Mbs, Mus.Ms.7356. ★
GAH-2. Parthie in F; 12 mvts. 2fl 2cl(C) 2hn vla vlne.
MS parts ("Ad me Petrum Hüber): D-Mbs, Mus.Ms.7437. ★

*HOLLOWAY, Robin (Greville) *21 Oct 1943, Leamington Spa*
RGH-1. Concerto for solo organ, Op. 6, 1965-66. Solo organ, 2pic ob ca b-cl sax 2hn bn cbn tp tb tu.
Pm (Oxford University Press: London, 1966).
RGH-2. Divertimento No. 2, Op. 18, 1972. fl(pic) ob ob(ca) 2cl 2hn 2bn.
Pm (Boosey & Hawkes: London, 1966), hire score & parts.

*HOLMBOE, Vagn *20 Dec 1909, Horsens, Denmark - 1 Sept 1996, Ramlose*
Rights to Holmboe's works are owned by Edition Wilhelm Hansen, Copenhagen, (part of the Music Sales Group),
who should be contacted in the first instance regarding performance materials.
VYH-1. Music for fugle og grøer, Op. 106b; 1971. 2fl 16bn. AutoMS score: DK-Kk.
VYH-2. Divertimento No. 3; 1933. 2ob 2tp 2tb. AutoMS score: the Holmboe estate.

*HOLST, Gustav (Theodore) *21 Sept 1874, Cheltenham, UK - 25 May 1934, London*
GTH-1. Septet, Allegro (5pp, incomplete) 1896. fl ob 2cl(A) 2hn bn. AutoMS score: GB-Lholst.
GTH-1s. First Suite in E♭, Op. 28, No. 1 (Op. 28a); (H 105; M248), 3 mvts.
pic fl 2ob 2cl(E♭) 3cl(B♭) a-sax t-sax bar-sar 4hn 2bn 2crt tp 3tb euph 2b timp perc.
AutoMS score: GB-Lbl, Add. 47,824.
Pc (Boosey & Hawkes: London, 1921), parts and Piano-Conductor score.
Pm (Boosey & Hawkes: London, 1948), score, (with a-cl(B♭) b-cl b-sax cb-cl 2flug not in the original score).
GTH-2s. Second Suite in F, Op. 28, No. 2 (Op. 28b); (H 105; M249), 4 mvts.
pic fl ob cl(E♭) 3cl(B♭) a-sax t-sax bar-sar 4hn 2bn 3crt 2tp 3tb euph 2b timp perc.
(Partly) AutoMS score: GB-Lbl, Add. 47,825, (with the omitted opening, "Young Riley").
Pc (Boosey & Hawkes: London, 1922), parts and Piano-Conductor score.
Pm (Boosey & Hawkes: London, 1948), score, (with a-cl(B♭) b-cl b-sax cb-cl 2flug not in the original score).
GTH-3s. Hammersmith - A Prelude and Scherzo, Op. 52, (1st version); (H 178; M91).
pic 2fl 2ob 2cl(E♭) 3cl(B♭) a-sax t-sax 4hn 2bn 2crt 2tp 3tb bass(E♭) bass(B♭) b-dr s-dr cym tri gong glock xly.
AutoMS score (incomplete: part of the Prelude only): GB-Lbl, Add. 57, 904.
MS parts (mostly autograph): GB-Lbbc.
Pm (Boosey & Hawkes: London, 1956), score.

HOLSTEIN, Jean-Pierre *1939, France*
PJH-1. Variations concertantes; 1967. 2fl 2ob 2cl 2hn 2bn 2tp 3tb. MS score: B-Bcdm.

*HOLYOKE, Samuel Adams *15 Oct 1762, Boxford, Mass - 7 Feb 1820, Concord, New Hampshire*
*SAH-1. Quintet in B♭. 2cl 2hn bn. [Untraced; possibly in: *The Instrumental Instructor.* Pc (Henry Ranlet:
Exeter, NH, 1807): RISM [H 6364]: US-Clwr; US-CDhs; US-Wc; US-WS.]
*SAH-1ma. Kotzwara: The Battle of Prague, Turkish Quick Step. 2cl(C) 2hn basso.
Pc (In: *The Instrumental Assistant:*) (Samuel Holyoke: Exeter, NH, 1807), Vol. 2, score.
Pm (In: F.J. Cipolla & D. Hunsberger. *The Wind Ensemble and its Repertoire:*) (University of Rochester Press:
Rochester, NY, 1994), R.F. Camus (also editor): "The Early American Wind Band", p. 71, score.

*HOLZBAUER, Ignaz *17 Sept 1711, Vienna - 7 April 1783, Mannheim*
IXH-1. Divertimento pro Cassatione in C; 6 mvts. 2hn 2bn.
MS parts: CZ-KRa, A3892/IV.B.55, (bn II pt: "Fagotto 2o vel Viola di Alto"). ★
Pm (Hofmeister: Leipzig, pn 7433, 1969), ed. Kurt Janetzky, score & parts.
Pm (Mannheimer Musik-Verlag: Bonn, pn E3-63, sd), hire score & parts.

*HOLZINGER, Peter Benedictus *(1720) Aibach, Bavaria; flourished 1747-1805*
PBH-1. Die Belagerung und Eroberung Mantoua [sic] auf Türkische Musik; 9 mvts.
pic 2fl 2ob 2cl(C) 2hn bn tp b-dr s-dr cym.   MS parts: H-KE, 1157/IX. ★
PBH-2. Die Belagerung end Eroberung Allessandria auf Türkische Musik; 6 mvts.
2fl 2ob 2cl(C) 2hn bn tp b-dr s-dr cym.   MS parts: H-KE, 1156/IX. ★
PBH-1v. Missa in B♭.   STB, 2fl 2ob 2cl 2hn 2bn vlne, (organ *sine* vlne).   MS parts: D-DO, Mus.Ms.777.

HOMS (OLLER), Joaquín *21 Aug 1906, Barcelona*
JOH-1. Octet.   fl ob 2cl 2hn 2bn.
Pm (Seesaw Music Corp: New York, 1967), score & parts.

*HONAUER, Lorenz (Leontzi, Leonz) *1728, Paris - c.1790*
LYH-1. Suite de Pièces No. 1 in B♭, 7 mvts.   2cl 2hn 2bn pianoforte.
MS parts: D-B, Mus.ms.10840, Nr. 1; D-SWl, Mus. 2917. ★
LYH-2. Suite de Pièces No. 2, in Es (E♭), 4 mvts.   2cl 2hn 2bn pianoforte.
MS parts: D-B, Mus.ms.10840, Nr. 2; D-SWl, Mus. 2918. ★

*HONEGGER, Arthur *10 March 1892, Le Havre - 28 Nov 1955, Paris*
ARH-1. Musique pour Pasiphae.   2ob 2cl a-sax 2bn.
Pm (Salabert: Paris, c.1943).
*ARH-1v. Le Roi David; (original version, 1921).   SAT solo, SATB, pic(fl) fl ob(ca) cl cl(b-cl) hn bn 2tp tb,
(vc ad lib) db, perc (b-dr s-dr cymsgong tamb) cel harm piano.   (Version 2, the oratorio, 1923, adds narrator.)
Pm (Foetisch: Lausanne, *via* A.A. Kalmus: Tonbridge, Kent, UK), hire score & parts.

HONEY, Albert Edward *1919, South Africa*
AEH-1. Rondo for Reeds; 1966.   fl ob 2cl 2sax hn bn, (db ad lib).   MS score: SA-Jsamro.
AEH-2. Music to "Dr. Faustus"; 1968.   fl ob 2cl sax 2hn bn 2tp tb euph perc vc.   MS score: SA-Jsamro.
AEH-3. Fantasia on Tallis; 1966.   fl ob 2cl hn bn.   MS score: SA-Jsamro.
AEH-4. Passacaglia; 1966.   fl ob 2cl hn bn.   MS score: SA-Jsamro.

HORÁK, Jan Hyppolit *(1850)*
XJH-1tv. Pohřební zpěvy sborové s průvodem hudby. Složil Jan Ippo [sic] Horák. Zalmy při průvodech o
pohřbech dospělých osob i dětí. (scoring varies).
Pc (Fr. A. Urbánek, kněhkupec: Praha [Prague], 1875 - wrapper date: 1877), score: CZ-PLa, Hu 1068. ★
   XJH-1.1tv(a). 1. Při pohřbu dítěte [for a child]. ([text by] Bradáč, kancionál č.790) "Sotra jsem v svě
      nevinnosti". CATB, cl(E♭) cl(B♭) 2hn b-flug(B♭) bomb. pp. 2 - 6.
   XJH-1.2tv(a). 2. Při pohřbu nemluvněte [for a baby] (Z kancionalu) "Nechte dítek ke mně".
      SAB, 2cl(B♭) 2hn basso. pp. 7 - 9.
   XJH-1.3tv(a). 3. Jiná ku pohřbu nemluvněte. (Slova z kancionalu..) "Spi, rozmilé nemluvňátko!".
      SAB, 2cl(C) 2hn bomb. pp. 10 - 12.
   XJH.1.4tv. 4. Pohřební píseň dítěti. (Slova od Jos. Wünsche.) "Máti, máti, tvoje dítě".
      CAB, cl(E♭) cl(B♭) 2hn b-flug bomb. pp. 13 - 15.
   XJH.1.5tv. 5. Při pohřbu dítek. (Slova od [left blank].) "Plyň o duše do věčnosti mezi kůry andělské".
      CAB, 2cl(C) 2hn bomb. pp. 16 - 18.
   XJH.1.6tv. 6. Při pohřbu děcka [child]. (Slova od [left blank]). "Útlý plod jest v rakvi chladné".
      CA, cl(E♭) cl(B♭) 2hn basso. pp. 19 - 22.
   XJH.1.7tv(a). 7. Při pohřbu dítek (u hrobu) [for a child, at the grave] (Kancional.) "Již tu tebe více není".
      SATB, cl(E♭) cl(B♭) 2hn bomb. pp. 23 - 24.
   XJH.1.8tv(a). 8. Při pohřbu školního žaka neb žákyně [sic; for a male or female child of shool age].
      (Kancional.) "Sbohem, vy rodiče drazí". SAB, cl(E♭) cl(B♭) 2hn basso. pp. 25 - 27.
   XJH.1.9tv(a). 9. Při pohřbu pacholete neb děvčete [for a boy or girl]. (Kancional.) "Ubírám se do věčnosti".
      CAB, 2cl(C) 2hn bomb. pp. 28 - 29.
   [10. "Čís." [sic] vynecháno též u dalších skladeb. Žci pái pořřubu svého spolužáka. (Slova od Jos.
      Wünsche.)   "Již ti svadly růže v tváři". S+A, žáci [begin], B - učitel [teacher, kantor]. p. 30.]
   [11. Píseň žákyň při pohřbu jich spolužačky. (Slova od Jos. Wünsche.) "Aj, co že jsi". SSAA. p. 31.]
   XJH-1.10tv(a). 12. Při pohřbu mládence [for a youth]. (Kancional.) "Rychke mizí světa sláva".
      CAB, cl(E♭) cl(B♭) 2hn 2tp basso. pp. 32 - 34.
   XJH-1.11tv. 13. Jiná píseň při pohřbu mládence [Another funeral hymn for a youth]. Slova z Kanc., hudba
      od J. Ip. Horáka. "Pozoru jte moudré rady". SAB, cl(E♭) cl(B♭)/flug 2hn bomb. pp. 35 - 37.
   XJH-1.12tv. 14. Pohřební píseň jinochu neb panně. Slova J. Wünsche, hudba J. Ip. Horáka. "Uvadla růže
      krutě skosena". SAB, cl(D) cl(A) 2tp bomb. pp. 38 - 39.
   XJH-1.13tv(a). 15. Při pohřbu panny [for a vigin]. Dle Kancionalu upravil J. Ip. Horák. "Hle, tu opadala rů".
      CAB, cl(E♭) 2hn flug(B♭) bass. pp. 40 - 41.
   XJH-1.14tv(a). 16. Při pohřbu panny [for a maiden, virgin]. Z kancionalu. "Zhasnul život dcery milé".
      CAB, 2cl 2hn basso. pp. 42 - 44.
   XJH-1.15tv. 17. Při pohřbu osoby dospělé, muže neb ženy, i úda spolku neb bratrstva [for an adult, husband
      or wife, sister or brother.] Slova z kancionálu, hudba od J. Ip. Horáka. "Hle tu příklad změnli vosti."
      CAB, cl(E♭) cl(B♭/flug) 2hn bomb. pp. 45 - 47.
   XJH-1.16tv(a). 18. Při pohřbu osoby dospělé, též i úda některého bratrstva neb spolku [for an adult who had
      brothers or sisters]. Slova z kancionálu, hudba od J. Ip. Horáka. "Musí simě musí shníti".
      SAB, 2cl(C) 2hn basso. pp. 48 - 51.

XJH-1.17tv. 19. Při pohřbu dospělých osob [for an adult]. Slova i hudba od Jana Ippo Horáka. "Sečteny jsou dny života mého". SAB, cl(E♭) cl(B♭)/flug 2hn bomb. pp. 52 - 54.
XJH-1.18tv. 20. Pohřební píseň otci [for a father]. Slova F. Wünsche, nápěv i hudba J. Ip. Horáka. "Tatiča nám pochovají". CAB, 2cl(C) 2hn bass. pp. 55 - 56.
XJH-1.19tv. 21. Jiná píseň při pohřbu otce [another hymn for a father]. Slova pod. Jos. Wünsch [sic] v hudbu uvedl Jan Ippo. Horák. "Otče náš!". CAB, cl(E♭) cl(B♭) 2hn bass. pp. 57 - 59.
XJH-1.20tv. 22. Pohřební píseň Matce [for a mother]. Slova od F. [sic] Wünsche, hudba od J. Ip. Horáka. "Ach, matko matičko." CAB, 2cl 2hn bomb. pp. 60 - 62.
XJH-1.21tv. 23. Jiná píseň při pohřbu matky [another hymn for a mother]. Slova od F. Wünsche.
The music and scoring is the same as XJH-1.14tv.
XJH-1.22tv(a). 24. Při pohřbu ženy šestinedělky [for a mother six weeks after childbirth]. Dle kancionálu sv. J. "Matko! ty v svém povokíní". CAB, cl(C) cl(B♭) 2tp bomb. pp. 64 - 65.
XJH-1.23tv. 25. Při pohřbu manžela a otce [for a husband and father]. (Kancionál sv. J.) J. Ip. Horák. "Konám poslední svou cestu do věčnosti z ciziny". SAB, cl(C) cl(B♭)/flug 2hn bass. pp. 66 - 67.
XJH-1.24tv(a). 26. Při pohřbu manželů zdětilých [for a husband with children]. Dle kancionálu pro hudby upravil J. Ipp. Horák. "Já jsem život a rzkříšení". CAB, 2cl(C) flug(C) euph bomb. pp. 68 - 70.
XJH-1.25tv. 27. Při slavných pohřbech dospělých osob vůbec [for any famous adult]. Slova i hudba od J. Ip. Horáka. "A mdloby vytrhla tě ruka Páně." CAB, Cl(C) 2hn b-flug euph bomb. pp. 71 - 75.
XJH-1.26tv. 28. Pohřební píseň nad manželem [for a married couple]. Hudba J. Ip. H. Slova od [left blank]. "Posledně mě již vidíte". CA, cl(E♭) cl(B♭) euph bomb. pp. 76 - 79.
XJH-1.27tv(a). 29. Při pohřbu ovdovělých osob, spolu rodičů [for a widowed person, also a parent]. Dle kancionálu. "Dítky drahé, přišla chvíle". CAB, 2cl(C) 2hn bomb. pp. 80 - 82.
XJH-1.28tv. 30. Pohřední píseň dle potřeby bud mladým neb starým [for the young or old]. Slova od Jos. Wünsche, hudba od J. Ip. Horáka. CAB, cl(C) cl(B♭) 2tp bomb. pp. 83 - 84.
XJH-1.29tv. 31. Při pohřbu vůbec [for anyone]. "Hodina již udeřila". CAB, 2cl(B) 2tp bomb. pp. 85 - 86.
XJH-1.30tv. 32. Při pohřbu starých osob [for an old person]. Slova i hudba od J. Ippo. Horáka. "Hle popatřte". CAB, cl(E♭) 2tp(E♭) flug(B♭) bass. pp. 87 - 89.
XJH-1.31tv. 33. Při pohřbu výše postaveného muže [for a man of high position]. Slova z kanc[ional], hudbu od Jana Ippo. Horáka. "Četných přátel sbor u rakve stojí". CAB, 2cl(C) 2tp bomb. pp. 90 - 91.
XJH-1.32tv, 1.33tv. 34. a 35. Dvé písní o pohřbu kněze [2 funeral hymns for a priest]. Slova od Jana Krause, fáráře Blánského, hudba od J. Ip. Horáka. I. U domu [at the church] "Nastal odchodu čas mého". II. U hrobu [at the grave]. "Již v svém domku kosti skládám". CAB, cl(E♭) cl(B♭)/flug 2hn basso. pp. 92 - 96.
XJH-1.34tv(a). 36. Jiná píseň při pohřbu kněze vůbec [another hymn for any sort of priest]. Dle kancionálu. " Není sluhy. Páně více". CATB, 2cl(C) 2tp bomb. pp. 97 - 99.
[37. Pohřební zpěv duchovnímu. Slova od Jos. Wünsche, nápěv od J. Ip. Horáka. (Pro mužský sbor). "Ty povolal jsi". TTBB. p. 100.]
XJH-1.35tv(a). 38. Při pohřbu pastýře duchovního [for a singing priest]. Z kancionálu, pro hudba upravil Jan Ippo Horák. "Plačme v Pánu zesnulého Krista Pána". CAB, 2cl(C) 2tp(C) bomb. pp. 101 - 103.
[39. Pohřební píseň učiteli [for a teacher]. Slova od J. Wünsche, nápěv od J. Ip. Horáka. "Oněměla ústa drahá". SATB. p. 104.]
XJH-1.36tv. 40. Při pohřbu učitele [for a teacher]. Slova z kancionálu, nápěv od J. Ip. Horáka. "Dělník kráčí po své práci umdlen domu". CAB, 2cl(C) 2tp(C) bomb. pp. 105 - 106.
XJH-1.37v. 41. Příteli mládeže o pohřbu [for a young friend]. Slova od Josefa Wünsche, hudba od J. Ipp. Horáka. "Nech maličkých přijiti ke mně". SAB, cl(E♭) cl(B♭)/flug 2tp tb. pp. 107 - 108.
XJH-1.38tv. 42. Jiná píseň při pohřbu přítele mládeže [another funeral hymn for a young friend]. Slova od Jos. Wünsche, hudba od J. Ip. Horáka. "Ani ucho neslýchalo". CAB, cl(E♭) cl(B♭) 2hn basso. pp. 109 - 110.
XJH-1.39tv. 43. Pohřební píseň vojínovi [military funeral hymn]. Slova i hudba od Jana Ippo Horáka. "V žití kráčels v šiku bratrů chrobrých". TTB, cl(E♭) 2hn(E♭) 2tp(E♭) flug(B♭) bomb. pp. 111 - 114.
XJH-1.40tv. 44. Při slavném pohřbu [for a famous person]. Slova od Jos. Wünsche, hudba od J. Ip. Horáka. "Padá hvězada, zrak se trhá". CAB, 2cl(C) 2tp flug basso. pp. 115 - 118.
[45. Při pohřbu studujícího [for a student]. Slova v Jos. Wünsche, zpěv od J. Ip. Horáka. "Kniha psaná rozevř se". CAB. p. 119.]
[46. Ku pohřbu vůbec [for any sort of person]. Slova od Jos. Wünsche, nápěv od J. Ip. Horáka. "Zajisté přijde jednou den". TTBB. p. 120.]
XJH-1.41tv. 47. Ku pohřbu žebráka [for a beggar]. Slova z kancionálu, zpěv od J. Ip. Horáka. "Za všeliké dobrodiní". SAB, 2hn. p.121.
[48. Též ku pohřbu žebráka [for a beggar]. Slóva z kancionálu, zpěv od J. Ip. Horáka. "Lazare! již konac boje". CAB. p. 122.]
XJH-1.42tv(a). 49. Píseň obecná při pohřech slavných, na něž se předešlé nadpisy nehodí. (Libera me, Domine) Dle kancionálu. "Zbav nás věčné smrti Pane". CAB, 2cl 2hn flug bomb. pp. 123 - 125.
[50. Píseň na hřbitově, když se tělo ukládá. Z kancionálu. "Rozžehnejme se stím tělem". SATB. pp. 126 - 130. With the additional note, "Žalmy při průvodech o pohřbech dospělých osob i dětí. (Z Manuale pro sacris funtionibus) Mezihrami a dohrami opatřil Jan Hypolit Horák."]
XJH-1.43tv(a). 51. Žalm [Psalm] 50., jejž zpívá sbor při průvodu o pohřbech osob dospělých [hymn that one sings for an adult's funeral procession or burial]. "Miserere mei Deus". SATB, 2cl(C) 2hn/tb bomb. pp. 131 - 132.
XJH-1.44tv(a). 52. Žalm [Psalm] 148., jenž se zpívá při průvodech o pohřbech dětí [hymn that one sings for a child's funeral procession or burial]. "Laudate Dominum". SATB, 2cl(C) 2hn/tp basso. p. 133.
[53. Píseň na hřbitově, když tělo již pochováno. (Jak se zpívá na některých místech v diecési pražské). "Milosrdný Bože prosím za to". Bass solo. p. 134.]

*HORÁK, Josef *23 Dec 1883, Rožďalovice - 10 June 1968, Nymburk*
RJH-1am. Suda (qv): "Michálek" pochod [march]. pic fl cl(E♭) 3cl(B♭) 4hn 2flug t-hn bar-hn 2basso b-dr s-dr.
AutoMS score: CZ-PLa, Hu 2389.

*HOROVITZ, Joseph *26 May 1926, Vienna*
JVH-1. Fantasia on a theme of Couperin.   fl ob ca 2cl 2hn 2bn.
Pm (Mills Music: London, 1959; reprinted Novello, London 1988), score (pn 090591) & parts (pn 09059101).
JPH-2. Jazz Suite. 2fl 2cl.
Pm (Boosey & Hawkes: London, pn 3336, 1980), score & pts.

HORVÁTH, Josef Maria *20 Dec 1931, Pécs, Hungary*
JFH-1. Redundanz 1; 1966 - 1967.   ob ob(ca) cl(Bb, cl in Eb) cl(b-cl) 2hn bn bn(cbn).
Pm (Doblinger: Wien, 1970), miniature score (pn Stp 256) & parts (pn 6601).

HORWOOD, Michael Stephen *1947, USA*
MSH-1. Double Quintet; 1978.   2fl 2ob 2cl 2hn 2bn.   MS score: C-Tcm.

HOSCHNA, Jacob Phil. Gregor
PJH-1. Parthia in F; 4 mvts.   2cl 2hn bn.   MS parts: CZ-Pu, 59 R 165. ★

HOTIŠ (Hottisch), Jan Křitl F. Engelbert
KJH-1v. Salve [Regina] Es [Eb].   CATB, 2cl 2hn bn organ.
MS parts (by Jos: Uhlír, from Rychov nad Kněžnou): CZ-Pnm, X.E.105. ★

*HOTTETERRE, Martin *(d c.1712, Paris)*
MZH-1m. Marche des fusilliers in C.   4-parts "des hautbois" (with drum part by Lully).
MS (c.1705): F-Pn, Rés.F.671, No. 12. *This, the "Philidor MS", contains other early marches, often for 3ob bn.*
Related collections are in F-Pn, Rés.F.494 and Rés.F.533, and in F-V. ★

HOVHANNES (CHAKMAKJIAN), Alan (Vaness Scott) *8 Feb 1911, Somerville, Mass,USA*
HCH-1. Tower Music, Op. 129.   fl ob cl 2hn bn tp tb tu.
Pm (Rongwen, *via* Broude Brothers: Williamstown, Mass, 1954).

HOYLAND, Vic *11 Dec 1945, Wombwell, Yorkshire, UK*
VZH-1. Reel; 1980.   3ob 3ca 2bn cbn.
Pm (Universal Edition: London, pn UE 17328 K, 1990), score (photocopy) for sale, parts for hire.

HR., B.
BZH-1v. Offertorium, Puer natus in Bethlehem, pro Die Natali D: n. J. Christi.   Solo SS, fl 2cl 2hn bn serp vla.
MS parts: CZ-Bm(rj), A.14.223, (with later parts for: Solo B, 2vl, basso, Fagotto vel Organo). ★

HUBER, Jacob (Jakub) *(1740) - c.1788, Břevnov*
JCH-1v. Missa choralis in C.   SATB, bn+vlne+organ concertante, (2ob 2hn ad lib).
MS pts (by W. Janský): CZ-Pnm, XXXVII.D.23. *The title lists "2 Clarini" but the pts are undoubtedly for horns.* ★
JCH-2v. Missa choralis in G.   SATB, organ concertante, (ad lib: 2ob 2hn ad lib).
MS parts: CZ-Pnm, XXXVII.D.22. ★

HÜBSCHMANN (Huebschmann), C. *(1780)*
CXH-1. Harmonie No. 1; in Bb, 3 mvts.   2ob/fl 2cl 2hn 2bn.
MS parts: CH-E; D-AB, S.41.
Pc (N. Simrock: Bonn, pn 897, 1812), parts: CH-E; D-HR, HR III 4 1/2 2° 383. ★
Pm (KGS), fiche (2364).

HUGGLER, John *30 Aug 1928, Rochester, NY*
OJH-1. Music for 13 Instruments, Op. 75.   2fl ob 3cl 2hn 2bn tp tb vc.
Pm (Peters: New York, c.1974), parts.

**HUGO, *Prinz zu Hohenlohe-Öhringen*, *(Fürst from 1849)* *1816 - 1897*
Hugo used the pseudonym "Siebeneicher" (Seven oaks). Other works are treated as arrangements of his original
compositions; a full list can be found in the Arangements List.
HOH-1. Mazurek, in D.   fl 2ob 2cl 2hn 2bn tp tb db.   (?Auto)MS score (C.1840): D-NEhz, 115. ★

HULT, John *29 Nov 1899 - 16 Feb 1987, Västerås*
OHN-1. Rondo capricco [sic]; 1976.   2fl 2ob 4cl 2hn 2bn 3tp 3tb tu 2perc.   MS score: S-Sic.

HULTMARK, Torbjörn *31 Dec 1957, Sweden*
TOH-1. Konsertmusik.   fl fl(pic) ob 3cl 3hn 2bn 2tp 3tb tu timp perc piano.
MS score: The composer c/o S-Sic.

*HUMMEL, Berthold *27 Nov 1925, Hüfingen, Baden*
BXH-1. Octet, Op. 47.   fl cl 2bn 2tp 2tb.
Pm (Arthur J. Benjamin: Hamburg, 1972), score & parts.

HUMMEL, Johann Bernard *1760, Berlin - pre 1806, Berlin. Pianist son of the famous publisher, J.J. Hummel.*
JBH-1m. 2 Militarmärsche.   2ob 2cl 2hn 2bn 2tp.   MS score: D-Bds, Hausbibl.M.M.108.

*HUMMEL, Johann Nepomuk *14 Nov 1778, Pressburg (now Bratislava) - 17 Oct 1837, Weimar*
*JNH-1. N° 1 Parthia in Eb à 8 parti; 3 mvts.   2ob 2cl 2hn 2bn (serp ad lib, not in the score).
AutoMS score (27 Oct 1803): GB-Lbl, Add. 32217.   MS parts: GB-Lbl, Add. 71204, ff. 145 - 178. ★
Pm (Musica rara: London, pn MR 1250, 1970), ed. Roger Hellyer, score & parts.
Pm (WINDS: Northridge, CA, c.1981), score (photocopy of AutoMS) & parts (photocopy of modern MS).
*JNH-2. Statt Graduale Harmonie Stücke; uncited in any thematic catalog.
Solo Klappentrompett(D), 2cl 2hn 2bn.   MS parts: CZ-KV, B.301.
JNH-1.1m(-1.3m). Trois grandes Marches militaires composées pour Son Altesse Imperial Monseigneur le Grand
Duc Nicolas de Russie & &.   scoring varies.   AutoMS score: GB-Lbl, Add. 32,217, ff. 1 - 25b. ★
    1.1m. Marcia maestoso; in C.   fl(F) 2fl(C) 2ob cl(F) 2cl(C, Bb) 2bthn 2hn 2bn 2tp 3t-tb 2b-hn(octaves)
        Tambour des Soldat; Tambourin, tri cym & b-dr.   ff. 1 - 6b, Anfang (for percussion), ff.7 - 8.
    1.2m. Marcia; in Eb.   fl(F) 2fl(C) 2ob cl(F) 2cl(Bb) 2bthn 2hn 2bn cbn 2tp 3t-tb 2b-hn; Trio adds Klappen-
        Signalhorn and replaces the 2tp with 2hn.   ff. 9 - 13, Trio ff. 13b - 15.

1.3m. Marcia 16 Juilÿ [sic], Allò [sic] con energia e con fuoco; in C minor. fl(F) 2fl(C) 2ob cl(F) 2cl(C) 2bthn 2hn 2bn cbn 2tp 3t-tb 2b-hn perc (as 1.1m). ff. 16 - 18; cancelled Trio: ff. 18b - 19b; Trio: ff.20 - 22; Coda: ff. 22b -23; Anfang: ff. 24 - 25b. *The Anfang comprises the 2bthn & perc parts. The cancelled Trio adds 2hn but the parts have not been written out; after bar 8 only the parts for 2cl 3t-tb 2b-hn have been written out, although f.19b has been written out in full. The revised Trio shifts the 2ob from the melody to a counter line; the 2tp and 3t-tb are now tacet and the 2hn(C) play for 2 bars only.*
JNH-2m(e). [3 mvt work; titled in pencil, "Marcia di Hummel"]. 2vl vla vc+b, 2fl 2ob 2cl 2hn 2bn timp tri. MS score: GB-Lbl, Add. 32,217, ff. 26 - 41. *A harp is listed on the titlepage but no part appears. The triangle part has been misbound at GB-Lbl, Add. 32,216, f.29.*
   No. 1. Marcia; in D, [common time]. 2cl(A) 2hn 2bn timp; Trio: 2vl vla vc+b, fl(I) ob(I).
   No. 2. Andante; in Eb, 3/4. 2fl 2cl 2hn 2bn.
   No. 3. Grave, 2/4 (3 bars) / Allo, 2/4. 2vl vla vc+b, 2ob 2hn 2bn tri.
*JNH-1tv. Leichen-Gesang, in As [Ab] für vier Männerstimmen; text by Henneberg ("Rosen auf den Weg gestreut"); 5 stanzas; uncited in all thematic catalogs. TTBB, 2cl 2hn 2bn.
MS parts (by Johann Winkler): A-Wn, Mus.Hs.2734, (Canto is given as an option for Tenore Imo; there are additional parts for C & A; parts at this shelfmark for 2tp(clar) timp are from an entirely different work, in another key and in a different hand). ★
JNH-1e. Freuden=Ouverture für Orchester; mit [crosssed out: Anwendung] Benutzung der Volkslieder: 1. God save the King. 2. Gott erhalte [ranz den Kaiser] Jos. Haydn. 3. Volkslied aller Deutschen. Hummel. Zur Anwendung [crossed out: beim] am Geburtstag der Landesfürsten von J.N. Hummel. № 4.
AutoMS score: GB-Lbl, Add. 32,226, ff.1-25b.
   1.1e. № [2 crossed out] 1. God save the King. Englisches Volkslied. 8+8+8+8 bars. Phrases 1 & 3: 2cl(A) 2hn 2bn; phrases 2 & 4 (= repeat): 2vl vla basso, 2fl 2ob 2tp timp. ff.14 - 15, (on different paper).
   1.2e. № [3 overwritten:] 2. Gott erhalte - östreichisches [sic] Volkslied von J. Haydn. 4+4+4+4 bars. Phrases 1 & 3: fl(phrase 3 only) 2cl 2hn 2bn; phrases 2 & 4 (= repeat): orchestra as 1.1e. ff.16 - 19.
   1.3e. № 3. Volkslied aller Deutschen, von Hummel. 8+8+8+8 bars. Phrases 1 & 3: 2cl(A) 2hn 2bn; phrases 2 & 4: 2vl vla basso, 2fl 2ob 2tp a-tb t-tb b-tb b-dr+cym, Milit[är]Tambour.
JNH-2e. Johann von Finland, overture & incidental music. Orchestra, with fl/pic 2ob 2cl(A) 2hn 2bn "auf dem Theater" and "im Theater". AutoMS score: GB-Lbl, Add. 32,216, ff.1 - 100.
*JNH-1.1d. Concertino; in C, 2 mvts. Solo oboe, fl 2cl(C) cl(I, Bb)(bthn) cl(II, Bb, C) 2hn 2bn tp b-tb cb. MS parts: GB-Ljag(w), 100/4. ★
JNH-1.2d. Concertino; in F, 10 sections. Solo oboe, fl 2cl 2hn 2bn cb. *A modern, spurious arrangement.*
JNH-2d. Serenade [Octet No. 2] für Bläseroktett Es-Dur [b]; 4 mvts. 2ob 2cl 2hn 2bn cb. *Triebensee JYT-6.1.*
JNH-3d [= WITT, FZW-1c]. Sextett für Bläser F-Dur; 4 mvts. 2cl 2hn bn bn/b-tb.
MS parts: D-BABhuber, (formerly D-WEMl, No. 417). ★
Modern MS score & pts: D-FIZklöcker, (recorded with db). *"Witt Sextett" has been added in pencil; the scoring is unusual for either composer but stylistically it is more likely to be by Friedrich Witt.*
JNH-1ad. Mozart: Symphony in , K.425 ("Linz"). 2terz-fl 2cl 2hn 2bn. MS parts: D-Rtt, Mozart 17/II, (missing fl). *Hummel's name appears on the MS; this is, in fact, an arrangement of Mozart's symphony based on Hummel's arrangement for piano flute violin & cello.*

HUNTH, ( )
XYH-1. Pangelingua [sic] in C. CATB, fl 2cl 2hn bn.
MS parts (c.1853): CZ-Bm(ko), A.11.745, (missing 2cl 2hn; with performance dates between 1853 & 1858). ★

HURÉ, Jean *17 Sept 1877, Gien, Loiret - 27 Jan 1930, Paris*
JSH-1. Pastoral. Piano, 3fl ob cl(Eb) 2cl hn 2bn.
Pc (?A. Zunz Mathot: Paris).

HURNÍK, Ilja *25 Nov 1922, Poruba, Ostrava, Moravia*
IYH-1. Konzert. Winds, pf, timp.
Pm (Český hudební fond: Prague, 1956), hire score & parts.
IYH-2. Moments musicaux; 1962. fl 2ob 2cl 2hn 2bn tp tb.
Pm (Supraphon: Prague, pn H. 3856, 1964), score; *recorded Supraphon, Panton.*

HUSA, Karel *7 Aug 1921, Prague*
KYH-1. Concerto for Trumpet and Wind Orchestra.
Solo trumpet, pic 2fl ob ca 2cl a-sax 4hn 2bn cbn 3tp 3tb tu timp 3+perc 3+db.
Pm (Associated Music Publishers: New York, 1973), score.

HUTSCHENRUYTER (Hutschenreiyter), Wouter, *the Elder*
28 Dec 1796, Rotterdam - 18 Nov 1878, Rotterdam
WOH-1a. Beethoven: Symphony No. 1. 2fl 2ob 2cl 2hn 2bn tp.
MS (c.1830): NL-MOverheijen, (photocopy).
Pm (Compusic: Amsterdam, pn 266, c.1994), score & parts.

IBERT, Jacques (François Antoine) *15 Aug 1890, Paris - 5 Dec 1962, Paris*
*JFI-1. Cello Concerto, 1925. Solo cello, fl fl/pic 2ob cl cl(b-cl) hn 2bn tp.
Pc (Au Ménestral; Heugel: Paris 1926), score & parts.
Pm (Mercury Music Corp, now T. Presser: New York), score & parts.
JFI-2. Deux Mouvements. 2fl cl bn. Pm (A Leduc: Paris, 1923), score & parts.

IGNOTO, ( ) *Sig[no]ᵘˢ ?(pseudonym or anonymous)*
XXI-1. Quartetto; in F, 5 mvts. ob 2hn bn.
MS parts ("1802/Grdg."): D-Rtt, Inc.IIb/9. *"Stamitz" has been added in pencil on the titlepage.* ★

ILIEV, Iliya Kristov *1912, Bulgaria*
IKI-1. Theme & Variations, Op. 2; 1946. 2fl 2ob 2cl 2hn 2bn piano. MS score & parts: BU-Sp.

ILLÍN, Evžen *2 Nov 1924, Biskupice pri Dunaji, nr Podunajské, Biskupice - 1985*
EXI-1. Embarassing episodes. Solo trumpet, 2fl 2ob 2cl 2hn 2bn tb. Pm (Panton: Prague, 1966), score & pts.

*d'INDY, (Paul Marie Theodore) Vincent *27 March 1851, Paris - 1 Dec 1931, Paris*
*PVI-1. Chanson et Danses, Divertissement, Op. 50, 1898.   fl ob 2cl hn 2bn.
Pc (A. Durand & Fils: Paris, 1899 and reprints), score (pn 3592): F-Pn; GB-Lbl, f.656.a.(1); parts (pn 5593).   ★
Pm (Editions Durand & Cie: Paris; United Music Publishers: London; T. Presser: Bryn Mayr, sd), score & parts reprinted from the original plates.
*PVI-1v. La Vengeance du Mari, Op. 105.   Solo STT, SATB chorus, ca cl hn bn.
AutoMS score (14 July 1931): F-Pn, MS. 9232.

INGALLS, Albert M.
AMI-1. Woodwind Octet, Largo Movement.   fl ob 2cl b-cl 2hn bn.
Pm (in MS:) (The Author: Seattle, Washington, sd), score & pts. *This MS existed as late as 1962, available from the composer, then residing at 6551 24 Ave., NE Seattle 5, WA, USA; we have not been able to trace the MS.*

INGHELBRECHT, Desiré-Émile *17 Sept 1880, Paris - 14 Feb 1965, Paris*
DEI-1. 6 Danses suédoises.   2fl 2ob 2cl 2hn 2bn 2tp 3tb timp perc.
Pm (Editions Salabert: Paris, New York, 1929), score.

*ISAKSSON, Madeleine *3 Dec 1956, Stockholm*
MXI-1. Modell Maddes Modul Tvärskur; 1985.   fl fl(pic) 2ob cl cl(b-cl) 2hn 2bn.   MS score: S-Sic.

ITOH, Hiroyuki *1963, Japan*
HXI-1. Time Perspective; 1985.   2ob ca 3bn.   MS score: J-Tfc.

*IVES, Charles Edward *20 Oct 1874, Danbury, Conn. - 19 May 1954, New York*
CEI-1. Overture & March "1776", for theater orchestra, 1903 (K/V/13).   pic/2fl ob cl 2cornets tb piano 2perc.
Pm (Merion Music: Bryn Mawr, PA., 1973), edited James B. Sinclair, score.

*JACOB, Gordon (Percival Septimus) *5 July 1895, London - 8 June 1984, Saffron Walden, Essex, UK*
Jacob's Orchestral Technique *(Oxford University Press, 1931) includes four short sections arranged for winds, namely: p. 39, Grieg: Piano Sonata, for 2fl 2ob 2cl 2hn 2bn; p. 41, Schumann: Faschungsschwank aus Wien, for 2 fl 2ob 2cl 2hn 2bn; p. 42, Tchaikovsky, Scherzo Op. 21, No. 6, for 2fl ob cl hn 2bn; p. 44, from Mussorgsky, Pictures at an Exhibition, for 2fl 2ob 2cl 2hn.*
*GPJ-1. Old Wine in New Bottles; 4 mvts.   2fl 2ob 2cl 2bn 2hn (cbn 2tp ad lib).
MS score (facsimile): GB-Lmic.
Pm (Oxford University Press: London, 1960, r1980), score (pn J4992) & parts (pn J5006).
*GPJ-2. More Old Wine in New Bottles; 4 mvts.   2fl 2ob 2cl 2hn 2bn cbn/db 2tp.
Pm (Emerson Edition: Ampleforth, pn E93, 1981), score & parts.
*GPJ-3. Variations on Annie Laurie.   2pic heckelphone 2cb-cl 2cbn 3tu/serp+cb-serp+sub-cb-tu), hurdy-gurdy, harmonium.   MS score & parts: GB-Lhoffnung.
GPJ-4. Serenade for woodwind. in B♭, 1950.   2fl(pic) 2ob(ca) 2cl 2bn.
Pm (Hawkes & Son: London, 1953), score.
GPJ-5. 3 Elizabethan Fancies.   2ob 2cl 2hn 2bn.
Pm (Emerson Edition, Ampleforth, pn E134, c.1984), score & parts.
*GPJ-6. Divertimento in E♭; 3 mvts.   2ob 2cl 2hn 2bn.
Pm (Musica rara: London, pn 1171, 1969), score & parts.
GPJ-7. Two Pieces (Adagio doloroso, Allegro giocoso).   2ob ca
Pm (Joseph Williams: London, 1954), score (pn W.5973) & parts (pn W.5973a), Woodwind and Brass Series, No. 2.

*JADASSOHN, Salomon *13 Aug 1831, Breslau - 1 Feb 1902, Leipzig*
*SXJ-1. Serenade, Op. 104c, 4 mvts.   2fl 2ob 2cl 2hn 2bn.
Pc (Arthur P. Schmidt: Boston, Leipzig, pn S.100, printed in Leipzig, 1890), score & pts: GB-Lbl, f.244.ww.(2).   ★
Pm (Compusic: Amsterdam, pn 237, 1991), parts.

*JADIN, Hyacinthe *1769, Versailles - Oct 1802, Paris*
*HYJ-1. Ouverture; in F, P.2320.   2fl 2cl 2hn 2bn 2tp tb serp db timp.
Pc (Mag de mus fêtes nat: Paris, 1795), liv. 13, RISM [J 247], parts: F-Pn, (2 copies), H2. 47, H2. 132 a-m.   ★
HXJ-1mv. Chant pour la Fête d'Agriculture; P.118.   Solo voice, chorus, p-fl 2ob 2cl 2hn 2bn 2tp 3tb serp.
MS score: F-Pn, H2. 107 a-p. MS parts: F-Pn, H2. 20, (missing hn II, tp I & II parts).   ★
HXJ-2mv. Hymne du vignt-un janvier; P.39.   Solo voice, 2cl(C) 2hn 2bn.
Pc (Rec des époques: Paris, post-1797), liv. 1, No. 20, pp. 52 - 55, score: F-Pn, H2. 15,20.   ★
*HXJ-1a. Méhul: Le Jeune Henri, ouverture.   2fl 2cl(C) 4hn(2C, 2G) 2bn b-tb serp.
Pc (Mag de mus fêtes nat: Paris, pn 17, 1802), RISM [J 246 = M 1905], parts: D-AB; CH-Gpu, Ib.4832, (with a pasted printed slip, "Se trouve chez Lejeune au Bourg-de-Four, maison *Turetini* Nº. 219.").   -

*JADIN, Louis Emmanuel *21 Sept 1768 Versailles - 11 April 1853 Paris*
LEJ-1(-3). Trois Sextuors concertantes; E♭, F, A minor, all 3 mvts.   2cl 2hn 2bn.
Pc (Dufaut & Dubois: Paris, pn 546, c.1823 - 1826), RISM [J 338], parts: A-Wgm, VIII 9198.   ★
Revolutionary Works
*LEJ-4. Ouverture; in C minor/major, P.2303.   2p-fl 2fl 2ob 2cl 2hn 2bn 2tp tb serp timp.
AutoMS score: F-Pn, MS. 6470.   ★
Pc (Mag de mus fêtes nat: Paris, fructidor an II, 1794), liv. 6, No. 1, RISM [J 335], parts: D-WRtl; F-Pn, (2 copies), H2.6, Vm7 7048.
Pm (Swanzy), pp. 230 - 238, score.
*LEJ-5. Simphonie; P.2293.   2p-fl 2cl 2hn 2bn 2tp b-tb serp.
MS parts: F-Pn, (3 copies) H2. 46, H2. 133A a-l, H2.133B a-l.   ★
Pc (Mag de mus fêtes nat: Paris, messidor an II, 1794), liv. 4, No. 1, RISM [J 333], parts: F-Pn, (2 copies), H2. 4, Vm7 7037.
Pc (Ozi: Paris, pn 4. 1804), RISM [J 334], parts: A-Wkann. *Possibly a reissue; Ozi was director of the Magasin de Musique and Ozi et Cie was the successor company.*
Pc (Maurice Schlesinger: Paris, sd), parts (2fl replace 2pic): D-Bds.

Pm (Shawnee Press: Delaware Water Gap, PA; F. Hofmeister-Verlag: Leipzig & Frankfurt am Main, pn 1419, 1953), ed. Franz von Glasenapp & Herbert Schulze, score & parts, (Studien-Werke Nr. 1419).
Pm (Swanzy), pp. 230 - 238, score.
LEJ-1m. Marche; P.2306.   2p-fl 2cl 2hn 2bn tp serp.
Pc (Mag de mus fêtes nat: Paris, vendemiaire an III, 1794), liv. 7, No. 3, parts: F-Pn, H2. 7,3.   ★
Modern MS score: GB-Ljag.
LEJ-2m. Pas de manoeuvre; P.2307.   2p-fl 2cl 2hn 2bn tp serp.
Pc (Mag de mus fêtes nat: Paris, vendémiaire an III, 1794), liv. 7, No. 4, parts: F-Pn, H2. 7,4.   ★
Modern MS score: GB-Ljag.
LEJ-1mv. Hymne [Ode] à J.-J. Rousseau; P.87.   Chorus, 2fl 2cl 2hn 2bn 2tp serp.
AutoMS score: H2. 18.   ★
MS parts: F-Pn, (3 copies), H.2. 18, H2. 108 a-m, L.18361.
LEJ-2mv. Chant d'une esclave affranchie par le décret de la Convention Nationale sur le berceau de son fils; P 1435.   Solo voice, 2cl 2hn 2bn.
Pc (Mag de mus fêtes nat: Paris, prairial an II, 1794), liv. 3, No. 6, RISM [J 296], parts: F-Pn, H2. 3,6.   ★

JAEGER, David *1947, Canada*
DXJ-1. Double-quintette à vent, 1977.   2fl 2ob 2cl 2hn 2bn.   MS score: C-Tcm.

JAHN, A.W.F. *(1770) ?Musician at Ludwigslust (Mecklenburg-Schwerin)*
XZJ-1m. Reveille Nos. 1 & 2, Vergatterung Nos. 1 & 2, Zappenstreich Nos. 1 - 5.   2fife 2cl perc(3 parts: ?b-dr s-dr cym).   MS pts: D-SWl, Mus. 2950, (the unspecified perc pts are for the 2 Vergatterungen & Zapfenstreich Nos. 1 - 3; Zapfenstreich Nos. 4 & 5 do not bear Jahn's name, but stylistically fit with the other works).   ★

JAMES, Christopher *1952, South Africa, (?now resident in the USA)*
CXJ-1. Octet; (c.1983).   2ob 2cl 2hn 2bn.   MS score: US-NYamc.

*JANÁČEK, Leoš *3 July 1854, Hukvaldy - 12 Aug 1928, Ostrava*
*LXJ-1. Mládí; (Youth), 1924, 4 mvts.   fl(pic) ob cl b-cl hn bn.
Pm (Hudební matice Umělecké besedy: Praha [Prague], 1925), score & parts.
Pm (revised edition): (Hudební matice Umělecké besedy: Prague, 1947), score (Sbírka kapesnich partitur, sv. 32).
Pm (Státní nakladatelství krásné literatury, hudby a umění (now Supraphon): Prague, 1958), (miniature score: pn HM 341; parts: pn H2609, 1949).
Pm (C.F. Peters; London, etc.); miniature score (pn 9864a) & parts (pn 9864).
Pm (International Music Corp; New York, 1970), ed. Affelder, miniature score (pn 3111) & parts (pn 3104).
Pm (Bärenreiter: Kassel, pn BA 6854, post-1991), score & parts (= Supraphon edition).
*LXJ-1v Říkadla: 18 Nursery Rhymes; 1926.
SSAATTBB, fl fl(pic) 2cl(Eb) bn bn(cbn) db pf, child's drum, ocarina.
Pm (Universal Edition: Wien, pn UE 9688, 1929), score: GB-Lbl.

*JANSSEN, Guus *1951, Netherlands*
*GUJ-1 Dans van de malic matrijzen (Dance of the Malic Moulds).
Solo piano, fl(pic) fl 2ob sax(Bb sop) cl(Eb/Bb) cl(Bb) b-cl(Bb)/cl(Bb) bn bn/cbn 3tp 2tb.
Pm (Donemus: Amsterdam, pn Don 0092, 1978), score & piano reduction.
GUJ-2. Music for 6 woodwind instruments; 1972.   fl ob 3cl bn.
Pm (Donemus: Amsterdam, 1976).

JANSSON, Johannes *1950, Sweden*
JHJ-1. Guld i natten; 1980 - 1983.   ob 3cl hn bn db.   MS score: S-Sic.
JHJ-2. Etude; 1983.   ob 3cl hn bn db.   MS score: S-Sic.

*JAROCH, Jiří *23 Sept 1920, Smilkov (nr Votice), Czechoslovakia - 30 Dec 1986, Prague*
*JXJ-1. Metamorfózy; 1967 - 1968.   2fl 2ob 2cl 2hn 2bn tp tb.
Pm (Panton: Prague, 1970 - 1972), score & parts.

*JAVAULT, Alexandre *(1780)*
AYJ-1m. Harmonie militarie, IIᵉ Suite; 5 mvts (C, G minor, Eb, F, C).   fl ob 3cl 2hn 2bn tp tb serp/cb.
Pc (Gaveaux aîné: Paris, pn G.G.419, 1799 - 1802), RISM Supp [JJ 500 I, 1], parts: CH-Gpu, Ib.4833, (the tp & tb parts are not listed on the titlepage).   ★
AYJ-1.1a. Cherubini: Les deux Journées, overture.   fl ob 3cl 2hn(F, C) 2bn tp tb serp(Bb).
Pc (Chez G. Gaveaux, Aîné: Paris, pn G.G.116, c.1815), parts: F-Pn, (2 copies), Vm25 12, Vm25 12A.
AYJ-1.2a. Cherubini: Les deux Journées; Airs (as "Simphonie Militaire").   fl ob 3cl 2hn 2bn tp tb serp.
Pc (Chez G. Gaveaux, Aîné: Paris, pn G.G.117, c.1815), parts: F-Pn, (1ère Suite, 5 mvts; 2 copies), Vm25 13, Vm25 13A.

JEFFRIES, Kenneth
KYJ-1a. F.P. Schubert: Marche Militaire, Op. 51, No. 1.   2fl ob 4cl 2hn bn 2tp tb/tu.
Pm (Piper Publications: Girvan, Scotland, sd), score & parts.

JELEN, J.
JQJ-1v. Pohřební píseň; in Eb, "Dokonav život svůj".   SATB, 2cl(Eb) 2cl(Bb) 2hn 2tp b-flug tb.
MS parts (?by Joseph Florián): CZ-PLa(ka), Hu 1694, (missing cl II in Eb; with duplicate vocal parts).   ★

JELÍNEK, Stanislav *1945, Czechoslovakia*
SZJ-1. Unter dem Fenster von J. Haydn.   2ob 2cl 2hn 2bn.
Pm(Český hudební fond: Prague, 1989), hire score & parts.

*JELL, Josef (Jean) *(1770)*
JYJ-1. [4] Variationen.   2cl 2hn 2bn.   AutoMS parts: A-Wgm, Autograph Jell 1.   ★

JEPSEN, Henning *26 Feb 1954, Copenhagen*
HEJ-1. Sus; 1978.   2fl 2ob 2cl 2hn 2bn tb 5perc.   MS score: DK-Kd.

*JETSCHMANN, ( )
XYJ-1m. Parade- und Geschwind-Marsch für das I Bataillon Kgl. Leib-Garde.   ob 2cl(C) 2hn 2bn tp.
MS parts: D-Bds, Hausbibl.M.M.53.

JETTEL, Rudolf *1903 - 1981, Austria*
RXJ-1. Ouvertüre für Bläsorchester.   Instrumentation unknown.
Pm (Kunzelmann: Zurich), score (pn GM15) & parts (GM15/01).
RXJ-2. Sextet.   fl ob 2cl hn bn.
MS: SLV-Lsa.
Pm (Rubato: Wien, 1949), miniature score.   Pm (Doblinger: Vienna).

JEŽEK, Jaroslav *25 Sept 1906 - 1 Jan 1942, New York*
*JAJ-1. Konzert [for violin and wind orchestra, 1930]; 3 mvts.   Solo Violin, pic 2fl 2ob cl(Eb) 2cl(Bb) 4hn
2bn 3tp 2tb tu timp b-dr+cym s-dr.   MS score (autograph facsimile): CZ-Pr, 0-7319.

*JIRÁČKOVÁ, Marta *22 March 1932, Kladno*
MYJ-1. Centre of Gravity of Humanity, Op. 49; one continuous mvt.   8 double-reed winds.
MS score (1993): CZ-Pjiráčková.

*JIRÁSEK, Ivo *16 July 1920, Prague*
IYJ-1. Partita for winds.   2fl 2ob 2cl 2hn 2bn 2tp 2tb.
Pm (Český hudební fond/Panton: Prague, 1972), hire score & parts.

*JIRKO, Ivan *7 Oct 1926, Prague - 20 Aug 1978, Prague*
IXJ-1. Sonata for 14 Winds; 1967 - 1968.   2fl 2ob 2cl 2hn 2tp 2tb timp.
Pm (Panton: Prague, pn 32072-P1320, 1972), score; (parts for hire).

JOCHUM, Otto *18 March 1898, Bobenhausen, Swabia - 24 Oct 1969, Bad Reichenhall*
OTJ-1. Liederspiegel, Op. 38.   2fl 2cl 2bn.
Pm (Anton Böhm & Sohn: Augsburg, sd), (?parts): D-Bhm, 27,200.

JOERG (Jörg), Nikolas *(1770)*
NXJ-1a. (Collections): 12 Piecen für Harmoniemusik.   Winds.
Pc (Schott: Mainz, c.1800), parts: D-MZsch.
NXJ-2a. Della Maria: L'Opéra Comique.   2cl 2hn bn cbn.
Pc (B. Schott: Mainz, pn 231, c.1799), RISM [D 1424], pts: D-RH, Rheda 320, (missing horn pts); D-MZsch.

*JÖRNS, Helge *1943, Germany*
*HYJ-1 Dectet [sic].   fl 2ob 2cl 2hn 2bn db.
MS score & parts: D-KIZklöcker; written for the Consortium Classicum; reviewed in *The Times*, c.1981)

*JOHANSON, Sven-Eric Emanuel *10 Dec 1919, Västerrik*
SEJ-1. Hornpipe; 1985.   2lf ob 2cl 2hn bn 2tp tb tu 3perc.
Pm (Gehrmans musikförlag: Stockholm, 1985).
SEJ-2. Fanfar för Expo Norr; 1967.   fl ob ob(ca) 2hn 2tp 2tb euph 2batteria.   MS score: S-Sic.

*JOHANSSON, Gunnar *23 March 1906*
GXJ-1a. Yngve Sköld: Festpolonäs.   2fl 2ob 2cl 2hn 2bn perc.   MS score (1938): S-Sic.

*JOLAS, Betsy *5 Aug 1926, Paris*
BXJ-1. Points d'Aube.   Solo viola, fl fl(pic) 2cl b-cl cb-cl 2hn 3tp 3tb.
Pm (Heugel & Cie.: Paris, 1969), score (AutoMS facsimile).

*JOLIVET, André *8 Aug 1905, Paris - 20 Dec 1974, Paris*
AXJ-1. Ile concerto pour trompette, 1954.   Solo tp, 2fl ca cl 2sax cbn tb pf harp 2perc.
Pm (Heugel & Cie.: Paris, pn PH 210, 1955), score.

*JOMMELLI, Niccolò *10 Sept 1714, Averso, nr Naples - 25 Aug 1774, Naples*
NYJ-1v. Messa di Requiem solenne.   Voices & winds.   MS: I-Fc, Chiesa di S. Gaetano, E.1019.
NYJ-1m. Marche, in C.   2pic 2cl 2hn (2)bn tr cym timp.
MS parts (c.1780): D-HR, HR III 4 1/2 2° 380.   Pm (KGS), fiche (2361).   ★
NYJ-2m. Marcia; in C.   2ob 2tp bn.   MS parts: D-DS, Mus.Ms.1224, S.398 a-1.   ★
NYJ-3m. March de la Garde à pied (Marsch der Garde zu Fuss).   2ob tp basso.
MS: D-SWl, Mus. 3009; D-ROu, (with 2 anonymous marches under the title "3 Militärmärsche"; the other two
marches - probably not by Jommelli - are "March de Gen. Röther" et "March de General Werneck").   ★

*JONES, Daniel Jenkyn *7 Dec 1912, Pembroke - 29 April 1993, Swansea*
DJJ-1v. Epicedium, (words: Prudentius).   SATB soli, SATB chorus, 2ob ca cl(Eb) 2cl b-cl 3hn 2bn cbn 2tp tb 2hp.
MS score: GB-CDmic.

*JONES, John *1728, ?London - 17 Feb 1796, London*
*JZJ-1m. Sixteen select military pieces.   2fl 2cl 2hn bn tp, *or* harpsichord.
Pc (E. Riley for the Author: London, c.1795), RISM Supp [JJ 637a], parts: D-Kl, (hpcd only).

JONES, Lewis Ernest Beddoe *3 May 1933, UK*
LWJ-1. Music for wind.   2fl 2ob 2cl 2hn 2bn.   MS score: GB-Lmic.

JONES, Robert William *16 Dec 1932, Oak Park, Illinois*
RWJ-1. Declamation and Dance.   Solo tb, pic 3fl 2ob 3cl cl(Eb) a-cl b-cl cb-cl(Bb) 4hn 2bn 3tp 3tb tu perc.
Pm (Shawnee Press: Delaware Water Gap, Pa), hire score & parts.

*JONSSON, Josef Petrus *21 Jan 1887, Enköping - 9 May 1969 Norköping*
JPJ-1. Svit [Suite], Op. 53.   2fl 2ob 2cl 2hn 2bn 2tp 2tb 2perc.   MS score (1950): S-Sic.

*JORDAN, ( ) *Mr.* *(1760)*
XXJ-1m. March of the 3rd and 17th Regiment.   2 treble instruments, 2hn basso.
Pc (I. F-m [Jonathan Fentum: London, c.1790]), RISM Supp [JJ 653 I, 1], score: GB-Lbl, h.1568.q.(2).   ★

*JOSEPHS, Wilfred *24 July 1927, Newcastle*
WXJ-1. Concerto a dodici, Op. 21; 1959.   fl fl(pic) ob ob(ca) cl cl(b-cl) hn bn bn(cbn) tp tb tu.
Pm (Weinberger: London, 1977), score & hire parts.
*WXJ-2. Papageno Variations, Op. 153; 1989.   fl(pic) ob cl b-cl hn bn.
Pm (Mornington Music, *via* Novello: London, 1992), score & parts.

JOUARD, Paul *28 May 1928, Mt Vernon, NY*
PXJ-1a. Byrd: The Earl of Oxford's March.   2fl 2ob 2cl 2hn 2bn 3tp tb tu.
Pm (Shawnee Press: Delaware Water Gap, PA; Chester: London, [hire]), score & parts.
PXJ-2a. Alec Andrew Templeton: Merry Christmas.   2fl 2ob 2cl 2hn 2bn.
Pm (Shawnee Press: Delaware Water Gap, PA; Chester: London [hire]), score & parts.

*JOUVE, Joseph *1766, Aix - 1832, Paris.   See also supra: Hale, S.*
JOJ-1m. The Austrian Retreat, . . . for the Band of the First Regt. of Life Guards.
2pic 2cl 2hn bn tp serp b-dr "common-drums" cym.
Pc (Goulding & Co: London, c.1800), RISM [J 683], score: GB-Lbl, h.1480.x.(15).   ★
JOJ-1ma. L. von Esch: A select collection of [8] military divertimentos, arranged for a military band. Dedicated
to His Royal Highness the Duke of Cumberland by L. von Esch And arranged for a Military Band by J. Jouve;
8 single mvts.   2fl 2cl(F) 2cl(B♭) 2hn 2bn tp serp "big drum Cimb &c [sic]".
Pc (Broderip & Wilkinson: London, c.1798 - 1808), RISM Supp [EE 819a], parts: US-BETm, Lititz 210.   ★

JUNGK, Klaus *1 May 1916, Stettin*
KXJ-1. Serenade, Op. 71; 1979.   2ob 2cl 2bthn 4hn 2bn cbn.
Pm (privately printed; *via* Deutscher Komponisten-Verband: Berlin).

JURACOPA, Matteo *(?1770)*
MXJ-1. Primo Quatro.   2cl 2hn.   MS parts: D-Rtt.
MXJ-2. Secondo Quatro.   2cl 2hn.   MS parts: D-Rtt.

*K, E., *a Lady* *(1770)*
ELK-1m. A New March Composed for a Regiment of Bengal Sepoys.   2pic 3cl 2hn basso tp (drums).
Pc (Printed for the Author, & to be had at Bland & Weller's: London, wm1800), score: GB-Lbl, h.116.(1).   ★

*KAA, (Franz) Ignaz *baptized 27 Oct 1739, Offenburg, Baden - 8 May 1818, Cologne*
FIK-1v. Motetto per la Processione della Madonna del Rosario.   CATB, 2fl 2ob 2hn 2tp basso organ(bc-fig).
MS parts: CH-E, Th. 506,4.   ★

KABALIN, Fedor
FDK-1. Divertimento, Op. 7.   fl ob cl 2hn bn tp.
Pm (Tritone, *via* T. Presser: Bryn Mawr, PA, 1963).

*KABELÁČ, Miroslav *1 Aug 1908, Prague - 17 Sept 1979, Prague*
MXK-1. Sextet, Op. 8; 1940, 4 mvts.   fl ca 2cl(or sax, b-cl) hn bn.
Pm (Artia: Praha/Prague, 1956), score.

KAFFKA, Wilhelm *1751, Regensburg - 1806, Regensburg*
WXK-1. Divertimento, in E♭, 4 mvts.   2cl 2hn 2bn 2vla vlne.   (?Auto)MS pts (1790): D-Rtt, W.Kaffka 1.   ★

*KAGEL, Mauricio Raûl *24 Dec 1931, Buenos Aires*
*MRK-1. 10 Märsche um den Sieg zu verfehlen [10 marches to miss the victory].
pic fl 2ob ca cl sax bn cbn tp tu perc(sd-dr, t-dr, b-dr 2cym tam tri hi-hat, sleigh bells).
Pm (C.F. Peters: London, etc., pn 8458, 1983), score.

*KAISER, Karl *(1850) - post-1924, Detmold*
KAK-1a. Auber: La Muette de Portici, Schlummer-Arie.   cl(E♭) cl(solo, B♭) 2cl(B♭) 4hn 2bn 2t-hn b.
MS parts: D-DT, Mus-h 2 K 2, (in "Arrangements für Militair=Musik von Jahre 1882, 6 Jahrgang").
KAK-2a. Beethoven: Sechs Lieder, Op. 48, No. 4, Hymnus, "Die Ehre Gottes".
terz-fl ob cl(E♭) 2cl(B♭) 2hn bn 2tp (2)crt a-crt tb euph tambours.   MS parts: D-DT, Mus-h 2 K 100.
KAK-3a. Kloss: Militair=Musik, "Da untern ist Friede".   cl(E♭) 2cl(B♭) 2hn 2tp t-hn bar tu.
(?Auto)MS score (27 May 1879): D-DT, Mus-h 2 K 218.
KAK-4a. Méhul: Joseph en Egypte, overture.   fl cl(E♭) 2cl(B♭) 2hn 2tp 2t-hn tb tu b-dr s-dr.
MS parts: D-DT, Mus-h 2 K 10 1.
KAK-5a. Mendelssohn: 6 Lieder, Op. 47, No. 4, Volkslied.   cl(E♭) 2cl(B♭) 2hn 2tp t-hn bar tu.
MS pts (17 July 1878): D-DT, Mus-h 2 K 2, (in "Arrangements für Militair=Musik von Jahre 1878, 2 Jahrgang").
KAK-6a. Neefe: Der Friedhof.   cl(E♭) 2cl(B♭) 2hn 2tp t-hn bar tu.
MS pts (16 July 1878): D-DT, Mus-h 2 K 2, (in "Arrangements für Militair=Musik von Jahre 1882, 2 Jahrgang").

*KALABIS, Viktor *27 Feb 1923, Červený Kostelek*
VXK-1. Incantations, Op. 69.   2fl ob ca 2cl 4hn 2bn cbn.
Pm (Compusic: Amsterdam, pn 261, 1993), parts.
*VXK-2. Jarni Pístalky (Spring Whistles), Op. 50, 1974.   2ob 2cl 2hn 2bn.
Pm (Panton: Praha/Prague, c.1981), score & parts.
VXK-3. Strange Pipers (Der wundersame Pfeiffer), Op. 72.   2ob 2ca 2bn cbn.
Pm (Compusic: Amsterdam, pn 509, 1992), score & parts.

*KALACH, Jiří *9 March 1934, Prague*
JUK-1. Octet for Wind Instruments.   2ob 2cl 2hn 2bn.   MS score (1982): CZ-Pkalach.

*KALICK, R.D. *(?1770) German composer based in Vienna.*
RDK-1. Sinfonia; in C; 3 mvts.   2ob 2cl(C) 2hn 2bn 2tp(clar) timp.
AutoMS score (?c.1800): A-Wgm, XIII 7873 Autograph Kallick 1.   ★

*KALINSKY, Jan
JGK-1. Andante.   2ob 2ca bn.
Pm (Karthause Schmüling Verlag: Kamen, c.1993), ed. Birgit Welpmann, score & parts.

*KALLIWODA (Kalivoda), Johann Baptist Wenzel (Johan Wenzeslaus; Jan Křtitel Václav)
21 Feb 1801, Prague - 3 Dec 1866, Karlsruhe
*JWK-1. 6 Pièces d'Harmonie pour Musique militaire.   Vocal chorus (2 parts, Nos. 3 & 6), pic(A♭) 2ob cl(E♭) 3cl(B♭) 4hn 2bn 2crt 2tp t-hn 3tb bomb oph b-dr s-dr cym tri.
Pc (C.F. Peters: Leipzig, pn 3698, 3699, c.1845), 2 liv, parts: GB-Lbl, h.1570.(1) & h.1570.(2).   ★
JWK-2. Festmarsch.   2fl 2ob 2cl 3hn 2bn 3tp 3tb timp.   MS parts: D-DO, Mus.Ms.940.
*JWK-3. Harmonie.   fl 2cl 2hn 2bn.   MS parts: D-DO, Mus.Ms.939.
JWK-4. Galopp in E♭.   fl 2cl 2hn 2bn.   MS parts: D-DO, Mus.Ms.897.
*JWK-5. Harmoniemusik für heil[igen] Comunion.   2cl 2hn 2bn (ca ad lib).   MS parts: D-DO, Mus.Ms.941.
JWK-1v. Volkslied, "Hört ertönen uns're Lieder".   SATB, 2fl 2ob 2cl 2hn 2bn 2tp 3tb.
MS parts: D-DO, Mus.Ms.927.
JWK-2v. Lied während der Firmung.   SATB, 2fl 2ob 2cl 3hn 2bn 3tp tb.   MS parts: D-DO, Mus.Ms.881.
JWK-3v. Lied: "Stimmt an, Ihr Freunde".   TTBB, 2fl 2ob 2cl 2hn 2bn 2tp timp.   MS pts: D-DO, Mus.Ms.928.
JWK-4v. Abschiedslied, "Hier, wo sonst die Freude laut erklinget".   TTBB, fl ob 3cl 2hn 2bn tp tb.
MS parts: D-DO, Mus.Ms.923.
JWK-5v. Musik zur Trauung, "Jehova, Deinem Namem sei Ehre".   SATB, fl 2cl 2hn 2bn 2tp timp.
MS parts: D-DO, Mus.Ms.987.
JWK-6v. Festgesang, "Wie war die Zeit so voll von Schmerzen [sic]".   Solo SSTTBB, 2ob 2cl 2hn 2bn.
MS parts: D-DO, Mus.Ms.944.
JWK-7v. Der Gesang der Meuzzi in der Wüste, No. 2 ("Heil Dir, Euch das Heil").   SATB, 2hn 2bn 2tp tb db.
MS parts: D-DO, Mus.Ms.864.
JWK-8v. Duetto, "Sey, Geliebter, uns wilkommen".   TB, 2fl 2hn guitar.
MS parts: D-DO, Mus.Ms.900.
JWK-9v(-11v). [3 Duets], "Singst heit in frohen Chören", "Sonntagsfeuer", "Steht an des Himmels gold'nem Tor".
SS, 2ob bn.   MS parts: D-DO, Mus.MS.887.
JWK-12v. Additional aria (Titus) for Mozart's opera, *La Clemenza di Tito*.   Solo voice, chorus & winds.
MS parts: D-DO, Mus.Ms.1564, No. 2.
JWK-13v. Mass.   SATB, winds.   MS parts: D-DO, Mus.Ms.974.
JWK-14v. Deutsche Messe.   SATB, winds.   MS parts: D-DO, Mus.Ms.956.

KALLSTENIUS, Edvin *29 Aug 1881, Filipstad, Wärmland - 22 Nov 1967, Stockholm*
EXK-1. Svit [Suite], Op. 23; 1938.   2fl 2ob 2cl 2hn 2bn 2tp 2tb timp.   MS score: S-Sic.

KALMÁR, László *1931, Hungary*
LSK-1. Chamber Concerto; 1986.   fl cl cl(b-cl) 2hn bn tp tb tu harp.   MS score: H-Bmz.

*KAMMEL (Kamel[l], Kamml, Khaml, Cammell), Antonín *baptized 21 April 1730, Běleč - early 1788, London*
*ANK-1. Serenata in G; 3 mvts.   ob 2hn bn.
MS parts: CZ-Bm(sz), A.123.   ★
Pm (Artia: Praha/Prague, pn H 2304, 1973), ed. V. Belski, score (Musica antiqua bohemica 35).
Pm (McGinnis & Marx: New York, sd), score & parts.

KANITZ, Ernest *1896, Austria - 1978, USA*
ENK-1. Serenade; 1968.   2fl ob 2cl sax hn 2bn 2tp 2perc piano.   (?Auto)MS score: US-Wc.

*KANNE, Friedrich August *1778 - 1833*
FAK-1m. Marsch für die k.k. Oester Armee.   pic ob 2cl(C) 2hn 2bn serp tp(D).
Pc (Chemische Druckerei: Wien, pn 732, 1809), parts: CZ-Pnm, Lobkovic X.H.b.2.   ★

*KANTCHELI, Gia *1935, Tblisi*
UZK-1. Magnum ignotium.   fl 2ob 2cl 2hn 2bn db tape.
Pm (Sikorki: Hamburg, 1994), hire score & parts.

*KARG-ELERT, Sigfrid *21 Nov 1877, Oberndorf am Neckar - 4 Sept 1933, Leipzig*
*SXK-1. Quintet in C minor, Op. 30; 1904.   ob 2cl hn bn.
Pc (C.F. Kahnt Nachfolger: Leipzig, 1913), score (pn 6961) & parts: GB-Lbl, f.390.d.(12).   ★

KARKOFF, Ingvar *14 Sept 1958, Stockholm*
INK-1. Process; 1979 - 1980.   4fl ob ob(ca) 3cl 3hn 2bn 4tp 3tb tu 4db 4perc piano.   MS score: S-Sic.
INK-2. Parad; 1993.   fl cl 2bn 2tp 2tb perc.   MS score: S-Sic.

*KARKOFF, Maurice *17 March 1927, Stockholm*
MIK-1. Concerto da camera, Op. 56; (1961, revised 1965).   2fl 2ob 2cl 2hn 2bn 2tp tb tu db timp 2perc.
MS score: S-Sic.
*MIK-2. Kammerkonsert nr 2 "från 803" [sic], Op. 120.   fl(pic) ob(ca) 5cl 2hn 2bn 2tp 2tb euph tu 2perc.
MS score: S-Sic.
MIK-3. Quasi una marcia, Op. 123; 1974.   fl fl(pic) 2ob 2cl 2hn 2bn perc.   MS score: S-Sic.
MIK-4. Djurens karneval; 1974.   pic fl 2cl t-sax bn perc.   MS score: S-Sic.
MIK-5. Divertimento, Op. 141; 1978.   2cl 2bn.   MS score: S-Sic.

KARLOVSKÝ, K.
KUK-1a. Blecha: Malá dechová harmonie.   cl(E♭) cl(B♭) 2tp 2flug b-flug tb b bící.
MS (Plzeň, 25/9 1948): CZ-PLa, Hu 4088. *Traditional, harmonized Blecha; scored Karlovský.*
   1.1a. Čsá-stía hymna I. díl [Part 1].   1.2a. 2 díl [Part 2].   1.3a. Kdož jste boží bojovníci.

KARLSEN, Kjell Mørk *1947, Norway*
KMK-1. Musica decima, Op. 85; 1987.   fl 2ob 2cl 2hn 2bn db.
Pm (Norsk Musikfirlag A/S: Oslo, pn 103001, 1992).

KARLY, Gyula Antal *(1925)*
GAK-1. Serenata, Op 17, 1951-52, 1 mvt. fl ob cl 2hn 2bn. AutoMS score: H-Bn, Ms.Mus.3726/a.

KARNEVAL, Djurens
DXK-1. Stads musikanterna, 1974. pic fl 2cl sax bn perc. MS: S-Sic.

KAT, Jack *1955, Holland*
JZK-1. 3 Pieces. fl 2cl 2hn bn 2tp 2tb tu b-gtr piano.
Pm (Donemus: Amsterdam, 1978), score.

KATHALIERÝ (Kataliery), ( ) *See: CARTELLIERI.*

*KATZER, Ignaz *30 Sept 1785, Gross Auerschin, Bohemia - post-1820*
IXK-1. Zwölf Veränderungen über der beliebten Franzbrunner Deutschen [for Fürst Eugen zu Bentheim-Bentheim].
terz-fl 2cl 2hn 2bn cbn tp. MS parts (c.1820): D-BFb, K-at-90b, (with duplicate bn pts). ★

*KAUER, Ferdinand *18 Jan 1751, Klein Thaya (Tayax) nr Znaim; now Dyjákovičky, nr Znojmo, Moravia -*
13 April 1831, Vienna
FXK-1. Partia Ex C; 5 mvts. 2ob 2hn bn. MS parts (by Johann Prezt): A-Wn, Mus.Hs.2493. ★
FXK-2. Partia Ex D; 4 mvts. 2ob 2hn bn. MS parts (by Johann Prezt): A-Wn, Mus.Hs.2944. ★
FXK-1tv, 2tv. 2 Grab-Arien in'C moll [minor] bein erwachsenen Personen; "Der Freunde is uns gestorben" &
"Das Grab ist tief und stille". CATB, fl 2cl 2hn 2bn 2tp(clar) b-tb. MS parts: CZ-Lla(vl), No. 2441 hud. ★

*KEIL, Johann *(? = Joseph Kail, early 19th century horn virtuoso from Prague)*
JXK-1. Parthia, No. 12, in F. 2ob 2cl 2hn 2bn quart-bn. MS parts: D-RUl, RH-K 37. ★

*KÉLER, Béla, [pseud. Adalbert Paul von Kéler] *13 Feb 1820, Bártfa, Hungary - 20 Nov 1880, Wiesbaden*
*BXK-1a. Lortzing: Undine, scena. pic fl ob cl(A♭) cl(E♭) 3cl(B♭) 4hn 2bn 5tp tp(B basso)♭ cap 2flug flug(B♭
basso) 3tb euph b tambour. MS parts: D-DT, Mus-L 69 h 11.

*KELLER, Georg Friedrich *1806 - 1849*
GFK-1(-6). VI Versette in G. fl 2ob 2hn 2bn.
AutoMS score (Würzburg, 10 - 17 April 1848): D-WÜd, K.1.A.II.7. ★

*KELLER, Max *7 Oct 1783, Trostberg, Bavaria - 16 Sept 1855, Altötting*
MQK-1. Menuett. 2cl 2hn bn/db.
MS parts: D- (Stadt Burghausen).
Pm (Bezirk Oberbayern: München, 1989), ed. Robert Münster, (Musik in Oberbayern, Mappe 3), score & parts.

KELTERBORN, Rudolf *3 Sept 1931, Basle*
RXK-1. Meditationen, 1962-63. 2cl 2hn 2bn.
Pm (Heinrichshofen: Wilhelmshaven, 1964), miniature score (pn 6070) & parts (pn 6071).
RXK-2. Music; 1970. fl ob 2cl hn bn tp tb piano. MS score: CH-Zma.

*KEMPTER, Karl *17 Jan 1819, Limpach, Bavaria - 11 March 1871, Augsburg*
KEK-1v. Tantum ergo. SATB, fl 2cl 2hn 5tp tb bomb timp. MS (c.1860): D-Bds, MS.207.
KEK-2v. Responsorien zu den vier Evangelien am heiligen Frohnleichnamsfeste auch brauchter als Gradualien
oder Offertorium, 37tes Werk. CATB, ("mit oder ohne Begleitung": 2cl(C) 2hn 2tp b-tb/vlne timp org).
Pc (Anton Böhm u. Sohn: Augsburg, sd), parts: CZ-Pnm, XLIII.B.237. ★
*KEK-3v. Veni Sancte Spiritus zum Gebrauche bei Primizen am h[ei]l[igen]. Pfingstfest und bei anderen
Gelegenheiten. Für kleinere Musikchöre componirt", Op 53. SATB, organ *or* 2cl(C) 2hn 2tp(clar) vlne timp.
Pc (Anton Böhn: Augsburg, pn 3112, sd), parts: CZ-Pnm, XLIII.E.129; D-Tl, Gg 232. ★
KEK-4v. "Pange lingua" Hymnus zur Fronleichnams-Prozession, [arranged] zum Schluss-Segenlied bei
Hochämter, am grünen Donnerstag und so oft eine feierliche Funktion mit dem Hochwürdigsten Gute verkömmt,
Op. 75. SATB, organ, *or* 2hn 2tp obligat, timp ad lib; *or* 2cl(C) 2hn obligat, (2tp timp ad lib).
Pc (Verlag von Anton Böhn: Augsburg, pn 3417, sd), parts: CZ-Pnm, XLIII.D.181. ★

KENNAWAY, Lamont *1899 - Dec 1971, UK*
LXK-1a. J.S. Bach: Englische Suitten, No. 2, Sarabande. 2fl ob 3cl bn.
Pm (Emerson Edition: Ampleforth, pn E2, 1972), score.

KESZTLER, Lorínc & KOVACS, Imre (editors)
KZK-1a. Baroque music for woodwind. 3/2fl ob 2cl hn bn.
Pm (Editio musica: Budapest, c.1971), score & parts.

*KETTING, Otto *3 Sept 1935, The Hague*
*OYK-1. 2 Canzoni; 1957. fl ob 2cl 2hn bn tp tb cel harp 3perc.
Pm (Donemus: Amsterdam, c.1958), score.
OYK-2. Variazioni per orchestra; 1960. 2fl 2ob 3cl 2hn 2bn 2tp harp perc.
Pm (Donemus: Amsterdam, c.1960), score.
OYK-3. Time machine. 3cl 4hn 3bn 3tp 3tb 3perc.
Pm (Donemus: Amsterdam, pn Don 0032, 1972), score.

*KEULEN, Geert Synco van *1943, Holland*
*GVK-1. Chords for 15 winds; 1960. 3ob 3cl 3hn 2bn 2tp 2tb
Pm (Donemus: Amsterdam, pn Don 0031, 1974), pts. *Recorded Composer's Voice CV 7804.*
GVK-2. Interchromie. 3ob 3cl 3hn 2bn 2tp 2tb.
Pm (Donemus: Amsterdam, 1973), score.

*KEURIS, Tristan *3 Oct 1946, Amersfoort, Holland - 14 Dec 1996*
*TRK-1. Capriccio. 2ob cl(E♭) 2cl(B♭) b-cl 4hn 2bn db.
Pm (Donemus: Amsterdam, pn Don 0083, 1978), score.
TRK-2. Intermezzi. 2fl 2ob 2cl 2hn 2bn.
Pm (Novello: Borough Green, 1989), hire score & parts.

KEY, Thomas *? - pre-1805, Nuneaton*
TYK-1v. Eleven Anthems on General and Particular Occasions Interspersed With Symphonies and Thorough Basses, . . . Being particularly design'd for the Use of Parochial Choirs.   CATB, 2ob bn, organ.
Pc (Printed & Sold by the Author: Nuneaton; Messrs Thompson: London, c.1798 - 1804), RISM [K 495], score: GB-Lbl, G.521.a; US-NYp.   *Only Anthems I, III, VI - VIII & XI include wind parts.* ★
TYK-2v. Eight Anthems on Various Occasions. vix. For Easter-day, Ascension-day, Christmas Day; Thankgiving, Funerals, &c. Also Te deum. To which is now added Jubilate. Book I. The second Edition. CATB, ob vl/[ob] basso.   *Anthems I, II & VIII only scored for CATB, ob vl basso; Anthems III & IV scored for CATB, ob basso.*
Pc (Printed by Purday & Button Successors to Mr. Thompson: London, 1805 - 1807), scores: GB-L, G.521. ★

KEYSER, M.
MWK-1. Ouverture [or rather, Suite] a 4; in D, 6 mvts.   3ob bn.   MS parts: S-L, Saml. Wenster L:3. ★

KHUN, Ignaz *(?1790)*
IZK-1tv. Grablied; "Schlummere sanft".   CATB, fl 2cl 2hn bn.
MS parts (by Leeder): A-Wn, Mus.Hs.34,759. ★

*KIEL, August *1813 - 1871*
AYK-1. Walzer; in E♭.   fl 2ob cl(E♭) 3cl(B♭) 4hn 2bn tp ventil-tp klappen-hn a-tb t-tb b-tb serp b-dr s-dr.
MS parts: D-DT, Mus-h 3 K 30.
AYK-1m. Fest-Marsch; in E♭.   terz-fl fl 2ob 2cl(E♭) 3cl(B♭) 5hn 2bn 3tp kenthorn a-tb t-tb b-tb bomb/cbn b-dr+cym+tri s-dr.   MS parts: D-DT, Mus-h 3 K 13.
AYK-1a. Auber: Le Sirène, overture.   2fl 2ob cl(E♭) 4cl(B♭) 4hn 2tp a-hn 3tb b b-dr s-dr tri cym.
MS parts: D-DT, Mus-h 3 K 16.

KIEVMAN, Carron *27 Dec 1949, Los Angeles*
CAK-1. Piano Concert [sic].   Solo piano, 2fl 2ob 3cl 2hn bn 2tp b-tu perc(=choir bells).
Pm (Associated Music Publishers: New York, sd).   *"Amplification" is said to be needed.*

KIMPTON, Geoffrey *1927*
GXK-1. Sinfonietta, 1967.   2fl 2ob 2cl 2hn 2bn.   MS score: GB-Lmic.

*KING, Matthew Peter *1733, London - Jan 1823, London.*
MPK-1m. The British March as Performed by . . . the Duke of York's Band, Composed for the Brave Defenders of their King and Country.   2fife fl 2ob 2cl 2hn 2bn serp tp timp long-drum s-dr; *or* 2cl 2hn 2bn.
Pc (Printed by Longman and Broderip; also sold by the Author: London, 1798), RISM [K 597], score: GB-Lbl, g.133.(33); GB-Ob, Mus.Instr.I.142(5); GB-Lhumphries (modern MS score & parts). ★
MPK-2m. The Mary-le-Bone [sic] March.   2cl 2hn 2bn bn.
Pc (John Booth: London, c.1798), RISM [K 600], score: GB-Lbl, g.133.(32). ★
MPK-3m. The Siege of Valenciennes.   2cl 2hn 2bn bn.
Pc (Longman and Broderip: London, 1794), RISM [K 601], score: GB-Gu; GB-Lbl, g.133.(31); GB-Ob, Mus.Instr.I.142(2). ★

KINSKY (Kinky, Kinzi), Josef *2 March 1789, Sternberg - 2 Feb 1853, Olomouc*
HXK-1a. Piéces d'harmonie choisise des Opera les plus agréable [sic]; 8 mvts.   fl(F) 4cl 2hn 2bn.
MS parts: H-KE, 2755. ★
HXK-2a. Mozart: Die Zauberflöte, overture.   2pic 2cl(E♭) 2cl(B♭) 4hn 2bn cbn serp 3tp b-tb b-dr s-dr timp.
MS score (Augsburg den 12ten July 1818): D-HR, HR III 4 1/2 2° 925.   Pm (KGS), fiche (3223). ★

*KIRCHHOFF, Wilhelm *(1800)*
WZK-1. Divertimento, in D minor.   fl 2ob 2cl 2hn 2bn tp tb db timp.
AutoMS score (c.1836 - 1840) & MS parts: D-NEhz, 19, No. 3. ★
WZK-2. Ouverture, in E♭.   fl 2ob 2cl 2hn 2bn tp tb db timp.
AutoMS score (c.1836 - 1840) & MS parts: D-NEhz, 19, No. 1. ★
WZK-3. 2te Ouverture, in C.   fl 2ob 2cl 3hn 2bn tp tb db timp.
AutoMS score (c.1836 - 1840) & MS parts: D-NEhz, 19, No. 4. ★
WZK-4. Ouverture [No. 3], in F.   fl 2ob 2cl 2hn 2bn tb db.
AutoMS score (c.1836 - 1840) & MS parts: D-NEhz, 19, No. 5. ★
WZK-5. Ouverture No. 4, in A minor.   fl 2ob 2cl 2hn 2bn tp tb db.
AutoMS score (c.1836 - 1840) & MS parts: D-NEhz, 19, No. 6. ★
WZK-6.1(-6.5). [?Divertimento], 5 mvts.   fl 2ob 2cl 2hn 2bn tp tb db timp.
AutoMS score & MS parts: D-NEhz, 75. *At the beginning of the score is the note, "Sr. Hochfürstlichen Durchlaucht zum Geburtsfeste in tiefster Ehrfurcht gewidmet." There is some doubt that mvts 2 - 5 were composed by Kirchhoff since only the 2 Ouverturen are definitely identify him as the composer. However, we are inclined to believe that this birthday offering is entirely by Kirchhoff; D-NEhz, 35 - a work for Princess Louise's birthday clearly identifies the mvts in the parts are numbered consecutively.* ★
    6.1.   Ouverture, in F, pp 1 - 4.   6.2d.   Larghetto et Polacca, in B♭, pp 5 - 28.
    6.3d.   Marsch, in E♭, pp 29 - 39.   6.4d.   Walzer, in A♭, pp 40 - 46.   6.5.   Ouverture, in C, pp 47ff.
WZK-7.1. Schäfer Ballet.   fl 2ob 2cl 2hn 2bn tb db.
AutoMS score & MS parts: D-NEhz, 61, No. 13, (parts missing tb). ★
WZK-7.2. [Schäfer Ballet] Bauern Marsch und Tanz mit dem Lied (: vom hohen Olimp herab :).
fl 2ob 2cl 2hn 2bn tb db.   AutoMS score & MS parts: D-NEhz, 61, No. 14, (parts missing tb). ★
WZK-7.3. [Schäfer Ballet] Pas de deux.   fl 2ob 2cl 2hn 2bn tb db.
AutoMS score & MS parts: D-NEhz, 61, No. 15, (parts missing tb). ★
WZK-1m. Marcia, in E♭.   fl 2ob 2cl 2hn 2bn tb db.
AutoMS score (c.1836 - 1840) & MS parts: D-NEhz, 19, No. 7. ★
WZK-1a. Anon: Galopade, in D.   fl 2ob 2cl 2hn 2bn tp tb db.
AutoMS score: D-NEhz, 141, No. 13.   MS parts: D-NEhz, 137, No. 22.
WZK-2a. Anon: Galopp, in F.   fl 2ob 2cl 2hn 2bn tp tb db.
AutoMS score: D-NEhz, 141, No. 9.   MS parts: D-NEhz, 137, No. 23.

WZK-3a. Anon: Galopp, in F.   fl 2ob 2cl 2hn 2bn tp tb db.
AutoMS score: D-NEhz, 141, No. 11.   MS parts: D-NEhz, 137, No. 20.
WZK-4a. Anon: Galopp, in D.   fl 2ob 2cl 2hn 2bn tp tb db.
AutoMS score: D-NEhz, 141, No. 14.   MS parts: D-NEhz, 137, No. 18.
WZK-5a. Anon: Gräfenberger Polka.   fl 2ob 2cl 2hn 2bn tb db.   MS parts: D-NEhz, 137, No. 25.
WZK-6a. Anon: Lied "Es kann ja nicht immer so beliben".   fl 2ob 2cl 2hn 2bn tb db.
AutoMS score & MS parts: D-NEhz, 61, No. 18, (parts missing tb).
WZK-7a. Anon: Masur.   fl 2ob 2cl 2hn 2bn tb db.   MS parts: D-NEhz, 137, No. 27.
WZK-8a. Anon: Prisnitz Polka.   fl 2ob 2cl 2hn 2bn tb db.   MS parts: D-NEhz, 137, No. 24.
WZK-9a. Anon: Schnellsegler Ländler, in G.   fl 2ob 2cl 2hn 2bn tp tb db.   AutoMS score: D-NEhz, 141, No. 5.
WZK-10.1a(-10.14a). Anon: 14 [unidentified] Tänze.   fl 2ob 2cl 2hn 2bn tp tb db.
AutoMS score: D-NEhz, 141, No. 1.   *No. 1/2 is [Hérold] Zampa-Galopp.*
WZK-11.1a(-11.6a). Anon: 6 Tänze (Walzer, Galopps, Carlsbader Tänze).   fl 2ob 2cl 2hn 2bn tp tb db.
AutoMS score: D-NEhz, 141, No. 2.
WZK-12.1a(-12.7a). Anon: 7 Tänze.   fl 2ob 2cl 2hn 2bn tp tb db.   AutoMS score: D-NEhz, 141, No. 4.
MS parts (by either G. Schmitt or W.E. Scholz): D-NEhz, 134, Nos. 25 - 31, (for fl 2ob 3cl 2hn 2hn 2bn tb b).
WZK-13.1a(-13.4a). Anon: 18 Tänze (including otherwise untitled Walzer, Marsch, Hopswalzer, Galopp).
fl 2ob 2cl 2hn 2bn tb db.
AutoMS score (Nos. 10 - 13 only): D-NEhz, 137.
MS parts: D-NEhz, 137, Nos. 2 - 5, 8 - 10, 12 - 14, 16, 17, 21, 26.
WZK-14a. Anon: Walzer.   fl 2ob 2cl 2hn 2bn tp tb db.
AutoMS score: D-NEhz, 141, No. 3.   MS parts: D-NEhz, 137, No. 1.
WZK-15.1a(-15.3a). Anon: 3 Walzer.   fl 2ob 2cl 2hn 2bn tp tb db.
AutoMS score: D-NEhz, 141, No. 7.   MS parts: D-NEhz, 137, Nos. 7, 15, 19.
WZK-16a. Anon: Walzer.   fl 2ob 2cl 2hn 2bn tp tb db.   AutoMS score: D-NEhz, 141, No. 8.
WZK-17a. Anon: Walzer.   fl 2ob 2cl 2hn 2bn tp tb db.   AutoMS score: D-NEhz, 141, No. 10.
WZK-18a. Anon: Walzer, in B♭.   fl 2ob 2cl 2hn 2bn tp tb db.   AutoMS score: D-NEhz, 141, No. 12.
WZK-19.1a. Anon: Der Desauer Marsch, overture.   fl 2ob 2cl 2hn 2bn tp tb db.   MS score: D-NEhz, 44.
WZK-19.2a. Anon: Der Desauer Marsch, overture.   fl ob 2cl 3hn 2bn tp tb db timp.
MS parts: D-NEhz, 44, (old number 28).
WZK-20a. Anon: Der kleine Hans, "Nein ich will nicht länger leiden.   fl 2ob 2cl 2hn 2bn tp tb db.
MS score & parts: D-NEhz, 35, Bd 2, No. 16.
*WZK-21a. Adam: Le postillon de Lonjumeau, 3 Arien (Madelaine: "Glaube Männchen mir", Rondo: "Freunde
vernehmet die Geschichte", Grand Air: "Ich werde dem Adel").   fl 2ob 2cl 2hn 2bn tp tb db.
AutoMS score & MS parts: D-NEhz, 35, Bd 2, Nos. 9 - 11.
WZK-22a. Auber: Léocadie, 2 mvts.   fl 2ob 2cl 2hn bn 2tb basso.
AutoMS score ("Stuttgart 9. Aprill [sic] 1826") & MS parts: D-NEhz, 4, Nos. 1 & 2.
WZK-23a. Auber: Lestocq, 2 mvts (Entre Act [sic] et Air, "Schon naht die Mitternicht", Cavatine, "Wonniger
Augenblick").   fl 2ob 2cl 2hn 2bn tp tb db.   AutoMS score & MS parts: D-NEhz, 35, Bd 2, Nos. 13 & 14.
WZK-24a. Auber: Le Cheval de bronze, 2 mvts ("Ach für ein liebend Herz", Cavatine: "Wie kann die Freude
walten").   fl 2ob 2cl 2hn 2bn tp tb db.
AutoMS score & MS parts: D-NEhz, 35, Bd. 2, Nos. 12 & 15, (here attributed to Adam).
WZK-25a. Beethoven: Fidelio, overture & 1 Bd.   fl 2ob 2cl 2hn 2bn 2tp tb db timp.
AutoMS score ("den 8. 9rbr [Nov] 1834) & MS parts: D-NEhz, 7b.
WZK-26a. Beethoven: Adelaide, Op. 46.   fl 2ob 2cl 2hn tb db.
AutoMS score & MS parts: D-NEhz, 61, No. 11, (parts missing tb).
WZK-27a. Beethoven: Egmont, Op. 84, overture.   fl 2ob 3cl 2hn 2bn tp tb db.
AutoMS score (1834): D-NEhz, 28, Bd. 4, following the arr. of Marschner's opera, *Der Templer und die Jüdin.*
*WZK-28a. Bellini: I Capuleti ed i Montecchi, overture & 2 Bds.   fl 2ob 2cl 2hn 2bn tb db.
AutoMS score (c.1830): D-NEhz, 56.
WZK-29a. Bellini: La Sonnambula, Introduzion [sic], Arie & Duetto.   fl 2ob 2cl 2hn 2bn tb db.
AutoMS score & MS parts: D-NEhz, 84, Nos. 1 - 3.
WZK-30.1a. Bellini: I Puritani, "Diess war mein Lied, o Himmel".   fl 2ob 2cl 2hn 2bn tp tb db.
AutoMS score & MS parts: D-NEhz, 61, No. 1, (parts missing tb).
WZK-30.2a. Bellini: I Puritani, duetto ("Den Rival").   fl 2ob 2cl 3hn 2bn tp tb db.
AutoMS score & MS parts: D-NEhz, 61, No. 2, (hn III appears only in the score; parts missing tb).
WZK-31a. Donizetti: Anna Bolena, 2 Bds.   fl 2ob 2cl 3hn 2bn (2)tp(clar) tb db timp.
AutoMS score & MS parts: D-NEhz, 13, (hn III in Nos. 1 & 5 only); the score only includes one trumpet).
WZK-32a. Friedrich, Prinz von Hohenlohe-Oehringen: Walzer, in C.   fl 2ob 2cl 2hn 2bn tb db.
MS parts: D-NEhz, 137, No. 6.
WZK-33.1a. Hérold: Zampa, 3 mvts: Act III (1 mvt), Act II Introzudion, Act I finale.
fl 2ob 2cl 2hn 2bn tp tb db.   AutoMS score & MS parts: D-NEhz, 84, Nos. 7 - 9.
WZK-33.2a. Hérold: Zampa-Galopp.   fl 2ob 2cl 2hn 2bn tp tb db.   AutoMS score: D-NEhz, 141, No. 1/2.
WZK-34a. Himmel: Alexis und Ida, Op. 43, No. 40, Die Sendung (as "An Alexis").
fl 2ob 2cl 2hn 2bn tp tb db (?timp).   AutoMS score & MS parts: D-NEhz, 61, No. 17, (parts missing tb).
*WZK-35a. C. Kreutzer: Das Nachtlager in Granada, "Da mir alles".   fl 2ob 2cl 2hn 2bn tp tb db.
MS score & parts: D-NEhz, 35, Bd 2, No. 17.
WZK-36a. Lanner (arr for pf by A. Hollenstein): Vermählungs Walzer, Op. 15.   fl 2ob 2cl 2hn 2bn tp tb db.
AutoMS score: D-NEhz, 141, No. 6.
WZK-37a. Lindpaintener: [unidentified] Romance et Ballet.   fl 2ob 2cl 2hn 2bn tb db.
AutoMS score & MS parts: D-NEhz, 61, No. 16, (parts missing tb).
WZK-38a. Lindpaintner: [unidentified] Arie Einlage v[on]. Lindpaintner, in G.   fl 2ob 2cl 2hn 2bn 2tb db.
AutoMS score ("Stuttgart 9 April [sic] 1826") & MS parts: D-NEhz, 4, No. 3.
WZK-39a. Marschner: Der Templer und die Jüdin, 3 Bds.   fl 2ob 3cl 2hn 2bn tp tb db.
AutoMS score ("im Mai 1834") & MS parts: D-NEhz, 28, Bd. 2 - 4. *A completion of the arrangement by Georg
Schmitt, beginning with "Nr. 4, 1.Akt".*

WZK-40a. Marschner: Hans Heiling, Arie und Finale des 1ten Acts ("Wehe mir wohin").
fl 2ob 2cl 2hn 2bn tp tb db.   AutoMS score & MS parts: D-NEhz, 84, No. 4.
WZK-41a. Mathilde, Fürstin von Schwarzburg-Sondershausen: Lied von Prutz ("Um Mitternacht").
fl ob(I) 2cl 2hn 2bn tp tb db.   AutoMS score ("den 19ten Sept. 1841"): D-NEhz, 173.
WZK-42a. Meyerbeer: Robert le Diable, overture & 5 Acts.   fl 2ob 2cl 2hn 2bn (2)tp tb db timp.
AutoMS score (c.1845) & MS parts: D-NEhz, 26, (the score comprises Acts 4 & 5 only; the parts are complete).
*WZK-43a. Mozart: Die Entführung aus dem Serail, overture & Act I (5 mvts).   fl(pic) 2ob 2cl 2hn 2bn tb db.
AutoMS score (c.1830) & MS pts: D-NEhz, 56, Bd. 2. *Ouverture - Arie des Osmin ("Wer ein Liebchen") -
"Solche hergelaufen Laffen" - "Erste geköpft" - "Constanze, O wie ängstlich" - "Singt dem grossen Bassa".*
WZK-44.1a. Mozart: Don Giovanni, overture.   fl 2ob 2cl 2h 2bn tp tb db timp.
AutoMS score (c.1836) & MS parts: D-NEhz, 66, No. 6.
WZK-44.2a. Mozart: Don Giovanni, introduzione.   fl 2ob 2cl 2hn 2bn tp tb db.
AutoMS score & MS parts: D-NEhz, 66, No. 7.
WZK-44.3a. Mozart: Don Giovanni, Act I finale.   fl 2ob 2cl 2hn 2bn tp tb db timp.
AutoMS score (end of score: "S[ch]lawentitz d. 8. März [18]36") & MS parts: D-NEhz, 66, No. 2.
WZK-44.4a. Mozart: Don Giovanni, sextett ("Sola, sola in bujo loco").   fl 2ob 2cl 2hn 2bn tb db timp.
AutoMS score & MS parts: D-NEhz, 66, No. 8.
WZK-44.5a. Mozart: Don Giovanni: Act II finale.   fl 2ob 2cl 2hn 2bn tp tb db timp.
AutoMS score & MS parts: D-NEhz, 66, No. 9.
WZK-45.1a. Mozart: Die Zauberflöte, introduzione.   fl 2ob 2cl 2hn 2bn tb db.
AutoMS score & MS parts: D-NEhz, 66, No. 2.
WZK-45.2a. Mozart: Die Zauberflöte, "Dies Bildnis ist bezaubernd schön".   fl 2ob 2cl 2hn 2bn tb db.
AutoMS score & MS parts: D-NEhz, 66, No. 3.
WZK-45.3a. Mozart: Die Zauberföte, Act I finale.   fl 2ob 2cl 2hn 2bn tp tb db timp.
AutoMS score & MS parts: D-NEhz, 61, No. 4, (parts missing tb).
WZK-45.4a. Mozart: Die Zauberföte, Act II [Priester] Marsch.   fl 2ob 2cl 2hn 2bn tp tb db timp.
AutoMS score & MS parts: D-NEhz, 61, No. 9, (parts missing tb).
WZK-45.5a. Mozart: Die Zauberföte, Act II, Arie-Chor-Terzett ("Seid uns zum zweitenmal willkommen" - "Ach
ist fühls" [sic: "Alles fühlt"] - "O Isis").   fl 2ob 2cl 2hn 2bn tp tb db timp.
AutoMS score & MS parts: D-NEhz, 61, No. 10, (parts missing tb).
WZK-45.6a. Mozart: Die Zauberföte, Act II finale.   fl 2ob 2cl 2hn 2bn tp tb db timp.
AutoMS score & MS parts: D-NEhz, 61, No. 8, (parts missing tb).
WZK-46a. Reissiger: Yelva, die Waise aus Russland., overture.   fl 2ob 3cl 2hn 2bn tp tb db.
AutoMS score (1834) & MS pts: D-NEhz, 28, Bd. 4, following Kirchhoff's arr of Beethoven's *Egmont Overture.*
*WZK-47a. Reissiger: Die Felsenmühle von Etalières, 8 mvts.   fl 2ob 2cl 2hn 2bn tp tb db.
MS score & parts: D-NEhz, 35, Bd. 1, Nos. 1 - 8.
WZK-48a. Rossini: Otello, Arie.   fl 2ob 2cl 2hn 2bn tb db.   AutoMS score & MS pts: D-NEhz, 66, No. 3.
WZK-49a. Rossini: Semiramide, overture & 1 Bd.   fl ob 2cl 2hn bn(I)/tb bn(II).
AutoMS score ("d[en]. 24, Jänner 1834"): D-NEhz, 85.
WZK-50a. Spohr: Faust, Arie ("Der Hölle selbst").   fl 2ob 2cl 3hn 2bn tb db.
AutoMS score & MS parts: D-NEhz, 66, No. 4.
WZK-51a. Spohr: Zemire und Azor, Romance ("An die Rose" ["Rose wie bist du"]).   fl 2ob 2cl 2hn 2bn tb db.
AutoMS score & MS parts: D-NEhz, 61, No. 12, (parts missing tb).
WZK-52a. Spohr: Der Alchymist, 2 mvts: Arie mit Chor et Finale des 2ten Acts & Arie ("Das Wort, das seiner
Lipp entschwebt").   fl 2ob 2cl 2hn 2bn tp tb db.   AutoMS score & MS parts: D-NEhz, 84, Nos. 5 & 6.
WZK-53a. Strauss the Elder: Venetianer-Galopp, Op. 74.   fl 2ob 2cl 2hn 2bn tb db.
MS parts: D-NEhz, 137, No. 11.
WZK-54a. Weber: Der Freischütz, Scene und Arie.   fl 2ob 2cl 2hn 2bn tb db.
AutoMS score & MS parts: D-NEhz, 61, No. 6, (parts missing tb). *The Index bears the note, "Hier is die
Partitur bloss Correction der frühern Partitur des Freischütz un in derselben enthalten".*
WZK-55.1a. Weber: Euryanthe: overture.   fl 2ob 2cl 3hn 2bn tp tb db timp.
AutoMS score & MS parts: D-NEhz, 66, No. 1.
WZK-55.2a. Weber: Euryanthe, Romance ("Unter blühenden Mandelbäumen").   fl 2ob 2cl 2hn 2bn tb db.
AutoMS score: NEha, 73, between sheets 147 & 148. AutoMS score & MS parts: D-NEhz, 61, No. 3, (parts
missing tb).
WZK-55.3a. Weber: Euryanthe, Jägerchor.   fl 2ob 2cl 2hn 2bn tb db.
AutoMS score & MS parts: D-NEhz, 61, No. 5, (parts missing tb).
WZK-56a. Weber: Oberon, Ariette ("A lonely Arab maid").   fl 2ob 2cl 2hn 2bn tb db.
AutoMS score & MS parts: D-NEhz, 61, No. 7, (parts missing tb).
WZK-57a. Weber: Jubel Ouverture.   fl 2ob 2cl 2hn 2bn 2tp tb db timp.
AutoMS score (c.1836 - 1840) & MS parts: D-NEhz, 19, No. 2.

KIRCHNER, Volker David *25 June 1942, Mainz*
VDK-1. Der blaue Harlekin (Hommage à Picasso): Eine Groteske.   fl cl 2bn 2tp 2tb.
Pm (B. Schott's Söhne: Mainz, 1981), score & parts

KIRSCHNER, Johann Heinrich *1765 - 1831*
JDK-1v. Sittenfest [17]95 u[nd] 96. 1806. 1811. Wird jedesmal zum Sittenfest auf hohen gnädigsten Befehl den
Montag nach Quasimodogen gesungen. An die Weissheit. ("O du durch die wir auf der Bahn"); in Eb.
CATB, 2fl 2cl 2hn 2bn.   MS vocal short score & MS parts: D-RUl, RH-K 48, (missing the vocal parts).
JDK-2v. Sittenfest. [17]97. [added: 98]. "Wir sind nur einer Kette Glieder".   CATB, 2fl 2cl 2hn 2bn cb.
MS short score & parts: D-RUl, RH-K 48, (missing the vocal parts & possibly some instrumental parts).
JDK-3v. Sittenfest [17]99. "Ihr Gott und Vater".   CATB, 2fl 2ob 2cl 2hn cbn 2tp timp.
MS short score & parts: D-RUl, RH-K 48, (missing the S part).

*KIRSTEN (Kirstin), (Friedrich?) *(1750), flourished 1770 - 1797; organist in Dresden.*
FYK-1. Partita, in C, 5 mvts.   2fl 2taille 2hn bn.   MS parts: CZ-Pnm, XLII.C.201. ★
FYK-2. Partita, in Eb, 5 mvts.   2fl 2taille 2hn bn.   MS parts: CZ-Pnm, XLII.C.204. ★

*KLAUS (Klauss), Josef *(?1800)*
JSK-1tv(-3tv). [3 funeral cantatas:] I. Aufsterstehn, ja Aufsternstehn wirst du; II. Des Todes Graun, des Grabes Nacht; III. Alles schläft den Todesschlummer. CATB, 2cl 2hn 2bn 2tp.
MS score (by F.S. Knosel): A-Wn, Mus.Hs.5727. ★
JSK-4tv, 5.1tv. 2 Grablieder. C solo (No. 1), CATB chorus, fl(D) 2cl 2hn 2bn 2tp s-flug b-flug b-tb.
MS parts: CZ-LIa(vl), No. 2502 hud, (with a duplicate C part for No. 2). ★
  4tv. Wir gehn ans Grabe, und glauben doch. No. 1.
  5.1tv. Wohl auf, wohl auf, zum letzten Gang! No. 2.
JSK-5.2tv. Wohlauf [sic] zum letzten Gang! CATB, 2cl 2hn bn bn(vel b-tb) 2tp.
MS parts: CZ-LIa(vl), No. 2446 hud., No. 1.
JSK-6tv. Grablied für Erwachsene; "Ausgelitten hast du gute Seele". CATB, cl(Eb) 2cl(Bb) 2hn bn 2tp flug b-tb.
MS parts: CZ-LIa(vl), No. 2439 hud. ★
JSK-7tv. 2 Begräbnisslieder für Erwachsene; No. 2, "Stiller Kirchhof". CATB, 2cl 2hn bn 2tp b-tb.
MS parts: CZ-LIa(vl), No. 2446 hud. ★

KLEBE, Giselher Wolfgang *28 June 1925, Mannheim*
GWK-1. Missa Miserere nobis, Op. 45. 2fl 2ob 3cl 3hn 2bn 2tp 3tb tu.
Pm (Bote & Bock: Berlin, 1965).

*KLECZINSKY (Kletzinsky), Jan (Johann Baptist) *14 June 1756 - 6 Aug 1828, Berlin*
JBK-1. Partie. 7 winds.
MS parts: D-DO, (?lost).

*KLEIN, Bernhard *6 March 1793, Cologne - 9 Sept 1832, Berlin*
BYK-1, 2. 2 Divertimenti. Solo cl, 2ob 2cl 2hn 2bn.
MS: A-Wn(c), (lost).

*KLEIN, Gideon *6 Dec 1919, Přerov - ? Jan 1945, Fürstengrube concentration camp, Silesia*
*GIK-1. Divertimento; 1939 - 1940. 2ob 2cl 2hn 2bn.
Pm (Bote & Bock: Berlin; in association with the Český hudební fond: Prague, 1994), study score, score & parts.

KLEIN, Lothar *27 Feb 1932, Hannover*
LYK-1. Janitscharmusik für symphonisches Blasorchester. pic 2fl ob ca 2cl 2hn 2bn 2tp 2tb 4vc 3db timp perc.
Pm (Bote & Bock: Berlin, 1969), hire score & parts.
LYK-2. Variations; 1981. 2ob 2cl 2hn 2bn cbn. MS score: C-Tcm.

*KLEINPETER (Kleinpetter), Joseph *(1770)*
JFK-1. Parthia in Dis [Eb]; 4 mvts. 2cl 2hn bn(vel basso - but no divisi).
MS parts (by Augustin Erasmus Hübner, Langenbruck, 1799): CZ-Pu(dm), 59 R 3343. ★
JFK-2. Parthia in Dis [Eb]; 4 mvts. 2cl 2hn bn.
MS parts (by Augustin Erasmus Hübner, Langenbruck): CZ-Pu(dm), 59 R 3322. *The Finale is a rare fugue.* ★
JFK-3. Parthia in Dis [Eb]; 4 mvts. 2cl 2hn bn.
MS parts (by Augustin Erasmus Hübner, Langenbruck, 1806): CZ-Pu(dm), 59 R 3346, No. 1. ★
JFK-4. Parthia in Dis [Eb]; 4 mvts. 2cl 2hn bn.
MS parts (by Augustin Erasmus Hübner, Langenbruck, 1806): CZ-Pu(dm), 59 R 3346, No. 2. ★
JFK-5. Parthia in F; 4 mvts. 2cl 2hn bn.
MS parts (by Augustin Erasmus Hübner, Langenbruck, 1809): CZ-Pu(dm), 59 R 3347. ★

KLEINSINGER, George *1914 - 1982, USA*
GEK-1. Designs for Woodwinds. fl ob 2cl hn bn.
Pm (Broadcast Music: New York, 1946).

KLEITZ, F. *(1770)*
XFK-1a. Dalayrac: Adolphe et Clara, "Airs et morceaux d'ensemble...terminées par les walsses [sic]".
2ob/flautini(ad lib), 2cl 2hn 2bn.
Pc (P. Porro: Paris, c.1800), parts: CH-N, 5R 1593, (possibly suite 2 only.)

*KLEITZ, F. & FALTZANN, ( )
*XFK-2.1a, 2.2a. Six Harmonies Extraites des Compositions de Mozart. Arrangés; 1ère Livre/Harmonie *[Gran Partita*, K.361, mvts 1 - 3, & 7]; 2ème Harmonie: K.C.17.01, 5 mvts. *Note: Both works appear to have been pirated from earlier (spurious) sources.*
2ob 2cl 2hn 2bn; (Liv. 1ère: ob I & II marked "o flautino").
Pm (P. Porro: Paris, pn 1.H.M. 2.H.M., c.1807 - 1814), 2 liv., parts: CH-Gpu, Ib.4834, 4835, (liv. 1 missing cl II & bn II); GB-Ljag, (photocopy).

KLERK, Albert de *4 Oct 1917, Haarlem*
ADK-1v. 5 Noëls français. Alto, 2fl 2ob 2cl 2hn 2bn.
Pm (Donemus: Amsterdam, 1963), score & parts.

KLICKMANN, ( )
QZK-1a. Hoagy Carmichael: Stardust. fl ob 2cl hn bn.
Pm (Mills Music: New York, sd), score & parts.

*KLIEBENSCHÄDL (Kliebenschaedl), Johann Joseph *(1800)*
JJK-1v. Zwei Marienlieder von Guido Görres, 1. Die Nachtigalten, II. Schön wie der Mond.
No. 1: SATB, fl(F) cl(C) 2hn flug bomb/tb organ; No. 2: SATB, fl(C) cl(C) 2hn flug bomb/tb organ.
Pc (Verlag von Josef Anton Möst: Innsbruck, sd, pre-1850), parts: A-Sca, 20605. ★

KLING, Henri Adrien Louis *14 Feb 1842, Paris - 2 May 1918, Geneva*
HEK-1 Spring Poetry: Idyl. Solo horn, fl 2ob 2cl hn 2bn.
Pc (J. Oertel: Hannover), parts.
Pm (A.J. Andraud: Cincinnati, now Southern Music Co.: San Antonio, Texas).

*KLOB, Stephan *(1750), active 1770s - 1790s, Regensburg*
STK-1. Divertimento in Eb; 13 mvts.   2cl 4hn(Eb, Bb) 2bn 2tp(clar) 2vla vlne.
MS parts (c.1790): D-Rtt, Klob 14. ★
STK-2. Vaudeville; in Eb.   2cl 4hn(Eb, Bb) 2bn 2tp(clar) 2vla vlne.   MS parts (c.1790): D-Rtt, Klob 18. ★
STK-3. Divertimento in B[b]; 14 mvts.   2cl 2hn 2bn 2vla basso.   MS parts (c.1790): D-Rtt, Klob 13. ★
STK-4.1. [Parthia in Eb], 4 mvts.   2c 2hn 2bn.
MS parts (c.1770): D-Rtt, Sm. 8, Nos. 17 - 20.   *Mvt 3 does not appear in STK-4.2.* ★
STK-4.2. [Parthia in Eb]; 12 mvts.   2cl 2hn 2bn 2vla.   MS parts (c.1780): D-Rtt, Klob 16.
STK-5. Contradantz [sic] in b [Bb];   (Allegro molto / Allemande).   2cl 2hn 2bn 2vla db.
MS parts (c.1780): D-Rtt, Klob 17. ★
STK-6. [Parthia in Eb], 4 mvts.   2cl 2hn bn.   MS parts (c.1770): D-Rtt, Sm. 8, Nos. 62 - 65. ★
STK-7. Parthia Prima; in G, 5 mvts.   2cl(G) 2vla basso.   MS parts (c.1780): D-Rtt, Klob 15/I. ★
STK-8. Parthia IIda; in G; 5 mvts.   2cl(G) 2vla basso.   MS parts (c.1780): D-Rtt, Klob 15/II. ★
STK-9. Divertimento in G; 10 mvts.   2cl(G) 2vla basso.   MS parts (c.1790): D-Rtt, Klob 11. ★
STK-10. in G. Divertimento; 14 mvts.   2cl(G) 2vla basso.   MS parts (c.1790): D-Rtt, Klob 12/I. ★
STK-11. Divertimento in G; 8 mvts.   2cl(G) 2vla basso.   MS parts (c.1790): D-Rtt, Klob 12/II. ★
STK-1a. Haydn: [Symphonies, Hob I/85ii, 63ii, 79ii, 97ii, 97iii, 94ii, 90iii, 81ii, 94iii, 91ii, 91iii, 79ii], 12 mvts.
2cl 2hn bn 2vla vlne.   MS score & parts (c.1795): D-Rtt, Kolb 19.   *A 13th mvt which appears in the score only
is, in fact, von Schacht's arrangement (TVS-1a, No. 13) of "Il core vi dono" from Mozart's* Così fan tutte.

*KLOS, ( )
XXK-1. Parthia in Dis (Eb), 4 mvts; *(apparently early, ?c.1780, with a final contradanz).*   2ob 2cl 2hn 2bn.
MS parts: CZ-Pnm, Lobkovic X.H.a.28. ★

KLUPÁK, Jaroslav *26 May 1920, Prague - 2 June 1983, Plzeň*
JRK-1. Reinkarnace, Introdukce a quasi fugato.   2 solo accordions, 2fl ob cl 2hn bn tp tu timp piano xyl perc.
Pm (Český hudební fond: Prague, c.1970s). hire score & parts.

*KLUSÁK, Jan Filip *18 April 1934, Prague*
*JAK-1. Obrazy (Images), 4 mvts, 1960.   2fl 2ob 2cl hn 2bn 2tp tb.
Pm (SVH (Panton): Praha, 1967), score: CZ-Pnm, XXI.D.126; CZ-Pis.
JAK-2. Sonata, 1964-65.   Violin solo, fl 2ob 2cl 2hn 2bn tp tb.
Pm (Panton: Praha; Modern Edition: München, pn 1335, 1966), score & parts.
JAK-1v. 4 kleine Studien nach Kafka.   Soprano, fl 2ob 2cl 2hn 2bn tp tb.
Pm (Privately printed for the composer: Prague, 1960), score.
JAK-2v. Dämmerklarheit (six Rückert songs) for low voice with 2fl 2ob 2cl 2hn 2bn.
Pm (Compusic: Amsterdam, pn 262, 1991), parts.   *Original Czech title: Přísloví.*

KNAB, Armin *1891 - 1951, Germany*
ARK-1. Serenade; 1949 - 1950.   fl ob 2cl bn.
Pm (Litolff, now C.F. Peters: Frankfurt am Main, London, New York, pn 12240, 1964), score & parts.

KNAPE, Walter *14 Jan 1906, Bernburg*
WQK-1. Regensburger Festmusik, Op 72; 1974.   2ob 2hn 2bn 2tp.
Pm (Corona, Rolf Budde: Berlin, 1978).

*KNECHT (Kneht), (?Justin Heinrich) *(1810)*
ZZK-1va [= FCN-1v]. Neubauer: Vier Stationen=Gesänge.   CATB, (ad lib: organ *and/or* 3cl(C) 2hn b-tb vlne).
MS parts ("Scripsimus 1841 ad chorum Bonacellensem" [Gutenzell, Swabia]): D-Tl, Gg 284, (with additional
parts for tb/vlne & organ/vlne and duplicate S, A, & cl(III) pts; the titlepage bears the note, "Nota: Kne[c]ht von
Biberach soll die Begleitung der Instrumente gemacht haben").
ZZK-2va [= FCN-3.2v]. Neubauer: Quatuor Stationes.   CATB, 3cl 2hn basso.
MS parts: D-Tl, B 327, (with FCN-3.1; one of the two cl(III) pts bears the note, "Begleitung v. Knecht").

*KNĚŽEK (Knieschek, Knischek), Václav *1745, Prague - 1806, Regensburg*
VZK-1. [Parthia in Bb], Nº 4; 12 mvts.   2cl 2hn 2bn 2vla vlne.   MS parts: D-Rtt, Kněžek 13. ★
VZK-2. [Parthia in Bb], 9 Stim[m]ig Nº 2; 12 mvts.   2cl 2hn 2bn 2vla vlne.   MS parts: D-Rtt, Kněžek 14. ★
*VZK-3. [Parthia in G], Nº 9; 12 mvts.   2cl(G) 2vla vlne.   MS parts: D-Rtt, Kněžek 11. ★
VZK-4. [Parthia in G], N: 1. 5 stim[m]ig; 12 mvts.   2cl(G) 2vla vlne.   MS parts: D-Rtt, Kněžek 12. ★

KNORR, Bernhard, *Baron/Freiherr von* *18th century (Vienna)*
BVK-1. Quintetto; in C, 3 mvts.   fl ca 2hn bn.   MS parts: A-Wgm, VIII 1495. ★

KNUSSEN, (Stuart) Oliver *12 June 1952, Glasgow*
OSK-1. Choral, Op. 8; 1970 - 1972, revised 1981.   4fl 4ob 5cl 4sax 4hn 4bn 3tp 4tb 2tu 4db perc.
Pm (Faber Music: London, 1970, 1981), hire score & parts.

KOCH, Heinrich Christoph *10 Oct 1749, Rudolstadt - 12 March 1816, Rudolstadt.*
HCK-1m. 3 Pas redoublés pour Musique Militaire, Op. 48.   Military band.
Pc (Schott: Mainz, sd), parts: D-MZsch.

*KOECHLIN, Charles *27 Nov 1867, Paris - 30 Dec 1950, Le Canadel, France*
*CHK-1. Septet, Op. 165; 6 mvts.   fl ob ca cl sax hn bn.
Pm (Editions de l'Oiseau Lyre: Paris, 1948).

*KOEHLER, Benjamin Frédéric *1 Oct 1773, Leignitz, Silesia - post-1818, Guhrau*
*BFK-1. Jeu de déz [sic] d'écossaises à composer.   2cl 2hn bn tp.
Pc (Leuckart: Breslau, 1803), score.   *No locations known.*

*KÖHLER, Ernst *28 May 1799, Langenbielau, Silesia - 26 June 1847, Breslau*
We have no locations for his 1835 Septet for fl ob cl 2bn 2hn.
EYK-1v. Chor, (1831).   Solo, TTBB, 2 TTBB choirs, (4hn 2bn ad lib).   AutoMS score: F-Pn, MS.7311. ★

KÖHLER, Gottlieb Heinrich *6 July 1765, Dresden - 29 Jan 1833, Leipzig*
GHK-1(-3). 3 Parties, (E♭, B♭, E♭,). 2cl 2hn 2bn.
Pc (F. Becker: Leipzig, 1798), parts: D-Dl.

*KÖHLER, Nicolaus *(1800)*
NXK-1v. Lateinische Messe für die Advent- und Fastenzeit. SATB, organ/vlne obligat, 2cl 2hn nicht obligat.
Pc (Verlag von Anton Böhn: Augsburg, pn 1050, c.1825), parts: CZ-Pnm, XLIII.D.294. ★

KÖLB, ( ) von
XVK-1m. Marsch in D. fl/pic cl(G) 2cl(C) 2hn 2tp(D) tp(A) a-tp(G) b-tp(D) contrabasso.
MS parts (by Augustin Fibiger): CZ-BA, 186 (38-592), (missing fl/pic & cl I in C). ★

*KÖNIG, M.
MZK-1m. Marsch, in B♭. 2ob 2cl 2bn tp.
MS parts: D-Bds, Hausbibl.M.M.109.
Pm (In: Pätzig (qv), Heft 1, No. 5), score & parts.
MZK-2m. 6 Halberstädtische Märsche. ob 2cl 2bn tp(clarino).
MS parts: D-Bds, Hausbibl.M.M.110.
Pm (In: Pätzig (qv), Heft 3, Nos. 20 - 25), score & parts.

KÖPER, Karl Heinz *13 May 1927, Hanover*
KHK-1. Sextet. 2cl 2hn 2bn.
Pm (Privately printed: sl [West Germany], 1973), score.

KÖRNLEIN, Justus *? - 1866*
JVK-1. Introduction, Waltz & Galop. fl cl 2hn bn tp tb. MS parts (1841): D-DO, Mus.Ms.1083.

*KOETSIER, Jan *14 Aug 1911, Amsterdam*
JNK-1. Intrada classica, Op. 62. 2fl 2ob 2cl 2hn 2bn 2tp 4tb harp 3perc(ad lib).
Pm (Donemus: Amsterdam, 1971), score.
JNK-2. Baroque suite, E major, Op. 10, No. 2. Solo cello, 3fl 3ob 3cl 3bn.
Pm (Sirius Verlag: Berlin, sd).
JNK-3. Octet. 2ob 2cl 2hn 2bn.
Pm (Donemus: Amsterdam, 1969), score & parts.

KOFROŇ, Petr *15 Aug 1955, Prague*
PYK-1. 3 Pieces for Orchesra, 1981-82.
3fl 2ob ca 2cl s-sax t-sax bar-sax b-cl 2hn 2bn cbn 2tb tu organino/e-organ e-grt 4perc.
Pm (Český hudební fond: Prague, 1982), hire score.

*KOHN, Karl Georg *Aug 1, 1926, Vienna*
*KGK-1. Concert music; 1956, 8 mvts. pic 2fl 2ob ca 2cl b-cl 2hn 2bn.
Pm (Carl Fischer: New York, 1957), score & parts.
KGK-2. Impromptus; 1969. fl cl 2bn 2tp 2tb.
Pm (McGinnis & Marx, New York), parts.
Pm (Carl Fischer: New York, 1972), score & parts.

KOLB, Anton *Hautboist, im 12t Regmt. "König Otto v[on]. Greich[en]l[an]d". (cf. BENKERT, J.K.)*
AXK-1a. Hérold: Zampa, overture. pic(E♭) cl(E♭) 2cl(B♭) 2hn bn serp 2tp b-tb+cb b-dr s-dr.
Pc (s.n.: s.l., s.d., c.1841), MS parts: GB-Ljag, L.151, (with local duplicate parts: pic cl(E♭) hn I, hn II, b-tb).

KOLB, Barbara Anne *10 Feb 1939, Hartford, Connecticut, USA*
BAK-1. Double Wind Quintet. 2fl 2ob 2cl 2hn 2bn.
Pm (Boosey & Hawkes: New York, etc.), hire score & parts.

*KOLB, Johann Baptist *31 August 1743, Fürth, nr Nuremburg - c.1801 - 1810, Neudetreithau, Franconia*
JCK-1. [Parthia in B♭], 12 mvts. 2cl 2hn 2bn 2vla vlne. MS parts (c.1780): D-Rtt, Kolb 3. ★
JCK-2. [Parthia in E♭], 12 mvts. 2cl 2hn 2bn 2vla vlne. MS parts (c.1790): D-Rtt, Kolb 4. ★
JCK-3. [Parthia in B♭], 10 mvts. 2cl 2hn 2bn 2vla vlne. MS parts (c.1790): D-Rtt, Kolb 5. ★
JCK-4.1. [Parthia in G], 36 mvts. 2cl(G) 2vla. MS parts (pre-1776): D-Rtt, Kolb 1, No. 1. *2 Notes appear in the pts: (cl1, No. 12), "Pallet [sic] De comedia Abschi Von Kindth."; (cl II, No. 16), "Monssenie" (?Monsigny).* ★
JCK-4.2. [Parthia in G] No: 1; 24 mvts. 2cl(G) 2vla basso.
MS parts (c.1790): D-Rtt, Kolb 2, No. 2. *Except for some different mvts, identical with 4.1.*
JCK-5(-7). [3 Parthias in G], No. 2 (55 mvts), No. 3 (12 mvts), No. 4 (10 mvts). 2cl(G) 2vla.
MS parts (pre-1776): D-Rtt, Kolb 1, Nos. 2 - 4, (with later continuous numbering). ★
JCK-8. [Parthia in G], 24 mvts. 2cl(G) 2vla basso. MS parts (c.1790): D-Rtt, Kolb 2, No. 2. ★
JCK-9. [65 mvts]. 2cl 2hn. MS parts (c.1780): D-Rtt, Kolb 7. ★
JCK-10. [65 mvts]. 2bthn 2hn. MS parts (c.1780): D-Rtt, Kolb 8. *A note on the rear endpaper of the bthn I part states, "Dass ich Endes gesezter Meine Monatlich zu Laage A:3 f[ür]. den Monatt Augusti empfangen habe. Ein solche bescheine. [sic]".* ★
JCK-11. [115 mvts]. 2cl 2vla. MS parts (c.1790): D-Rtt, Kolb 6. *Except for some deviations identical with JCK-4.1 & JCK-5(-7). The mvts are divided into 4 sets of 36, 55, 12 & 12 mvts, with an additional continuous numbering added; it is likely that this set pre-dates JCK-9 & 10.* ★

*KOLBE, Oscar *10 Aug 1838, Berlin - 2 Jan 1878, Berlin*
OXK-1a. Leidersdorf: Fest Overture bei Gelegenheit der Feierlichen Krönung Ihrer Majestät Carolina Kaiserin von Oesterreich zur Königen von Ungarn. 2ob 2cl 2hn 2bn.
MS (1867): H-BuNM, Ms.Mus.1498.

KOLBINGER, Karl *1921, Germany*
KXK-1. Octet, 1981. fl(pic) ob 2cl 2hn 2bn. MS score: D-Mv, Nr. 847.
KXK-2. Divertimento. 3cl 2bn. MS score: D-Mv, Nr. 875.

*KOLLESCHOWSKY, Zigmund Michael *2 May 1817, Prague - 22 July 1868, Prague*
*ZMK-1. Adagio Religioso.   2cl 2bn.
Pc (Joh. Hoffmann: Prag, c.1846), parts: GB-Lbl, g.1067.a.(2.), (includes a MS score in the hand of John Parr, Leeds, dated 1949). ★

*KOLLMANN, August Friedrich Christoph *c.1756 - 1829*
AFK-1m. A New March Composed for the Corps of the Light Horse Volunteers of the Cities of London and Westminster.   2cl 2hn 2bn tp serp timp.
Pc (J. Dale: London, c.1794), RISM [K 1321], score: GB-Lbl, g.133.(34).

*KOLOVRÁTEK (Kollovratek), Tomáš (?Johann/Jan) *(1770); active 1797 - 1831*
All of Kolovrátek's works are originally from Choceň, Bohemia.
TXK-1. Parthia pastoralis ex F; 1 mvt.   Solo flute, 2cl 2hn 2bn.   MS parts: CZ-Pnm, XI.D.93. ★
TXK-2. Cassatae in Dis [E♭].   Solo vl, Solo cl, 2hn bn 2vla.   (?Auto) MS parts: CZ-Pnm, XI.D.62. ★
TXK-1v. Stationes Theophorices.   CATB, 2cl 2hn 2bn.   AutoMS parts (1812): CZ-Pnm, XI.D.92. ★
TXK-2v. Cantus de Venerabile Sacramento.   CC, 2cl 2hn bn.   AutoMS parts: CZ-Pnm, XI.D.72. ★
TXK-1tv. Cantus Funebris productus Sub funere A 2 ai Eximý Domini Domini Joanis Kollovratek Decani Chorerensium Zelozissimi.   CATB, 2cl 2hn 2bn 2tp(clar con sordin) timp.
AutoMS parts: CZ-Pnm, XI.D.75, (missing timp). ★
TXK-2tv. Píseň pohřebni při pohřbu panny [for the funeral of a young girl].   CATB, 2cl 2hn 2bn 2tp(clar) timp.
AutoMS parts (1823): CZ-Pnm, XI.D.90. ★
TXK-3tv. Pjseň pohřebnj při pohřbu manželky, a hospodině [for the funeral of a wife and housekeeper].
CATB, 2cl 2hn 2bn.   AutoMS parts: CZ-Pnm, XI.D.89. ★
TXK-4tv. Aria Funebris.   CATB, 2cl 2hn bn.   AutoMS parts: CZ-Pnm, IX.C.64. ★

KONECZNÝ, ( ) *18th century*
QXR-1. Parthia Ex Dis [E♭], 4 mvts.   2cl 2hn bn.
MS parts: CZ-NR, A.18.241/B.256. ★

KONÍČEK, František *1937, Czechoslovakia*
FNK-1. Divertimento per 8 stromenti a fiato; 1978.   2ob 2cl 2hn 2bn.
Pm (Panton: Praha/Prague, pn 05287-P2436, 1987), score; (parts for hire).

*KONTZVINDT (Ganswind), ( ) *1775, Čechách - ?*
QYK-1. Notturno ex F; 5 mvts.   2vadam 2a-cl bn+basso.
MS parts: CZ-Pnm, XLII.E.37b. ★
QYK-2. Parthia ex F; 3 mvts.   2vadam 2a-cl basso.
MS parts: CZ-Pnm, XLII.E.37a. ★
QYK-3. Parthia ex F; 3 mvts.   2vadam 2a-cl basso.
MS parts: CZ-Pnm, XLII.E.37c. ★

KOPPEL, Hermann David *1908, Denmark*
HDK-1. Octet, Op. 123.   2ob 2cl 2hn 2bn.   MS score: DK-Kd.

*KOPPRASCH, Wenzel *c.1750 - post-1844*
WYK-1. Serenata No. 11, in C.   2ob 2cl 2hn 2bn quart-fagott 2tp timp.   MS parts: D-RUl, RH-K 72.

*KORN, Peter Jona *30 March 1922, Berlin*
PJK-1. Octet, Op. 58.   2ob 2cl 2hn 2bn.
Pm (Nymphenburg: München, 1976), parts.
PJK-2. Variations and Fugue on a theme of Carrie Jacobs-Bond ("I love you truly"), Op. 5.   2fl ob cl b-cl 2hn bn.
Pm (Nymphemburg: München, 1947).

*KORTE, Oldřich František *26 April 1926, Šala*
OFK-1. Retrospektivy.   pic fl 2cl 4hn 3tp 3flug bart/euph 3tb tu db harp b-dr+tri+cym s-dr tamb suspended-cym.
MS score & parts: CZ-Pr, O-7534.

KOSCHINSKY, Fritz *1903 - 1965, Germany*
FQK-1. Variations über das Mantellied.   2ob 2cl 2hn 2bn.
Pm (Heinrichshofen: Willhelmshafen), parts.

*KOSPOTH, Otto Carl Erdmann, Baron von *1753, Mültroff, Saxony - 23 June 1817, Berlin*
OCK-1. Parthie in E♭; 3 mvts.   2cl 2hn 2bn.   MS parts: CZ-Pnm, XLII.F.36, No. 1. ★
OCK-2. Serenata, Op. 19.   Hpcd/pf ob/fl 2bthn/vla 2bn/vc.
MS parts: D-LB.
Pc (Johann André: Offenbach am Main, pn 728, 1794), RISM [K 1364], parts: A-SF; B-Bc.

*KOTTERZ, ( )
XZK-1. Barthia [sic] Ex F; 4 short mvts.   2ob 2hn 2bn.
MS parts: CZ-Pnm, XXXII.A.103. ★

KOŬBEK, ( )
YXK-1v. 4 Zastaveni k Bož Zělu [Statio 1 - 4].   CATB, fl 2cl(A) 2hn 2basso[ons] 2tp timp.
MS parts: CZ-Pnm, XI.D.155. *The wrapper, with the "Zastaveni" title, was added by O. Horník on 20 July 1901; the parts identify the works as "Statio 1 [- 4]" i.e. for the Frohnleichnamsfest.* ★

*KOWANDO, ( ) *(1770)*
UYK-1. Parthia in B[♭]; 4 mvts.   2cl 2hn bn.
MS parts (by Augustin Erasmus Hübner, Langenbruck, 1801): CZ-Pu(dm), 59 R 3328. ★

KOX, Hans *19 May 1930, Arnheim, Netherlands*
HAK-1. Concertino for alto sax(E♭) and 10 winds, for Ed Bogaard.   Solo a-sax, pic fl a-fl bcl 2hn 2tp tb tu.
Pm (Donemus: Amsterdam, 1982), score (revised 1991).

*KOZELUCH (Koželuh, CZ-KRa: "Gosheloch"), Jan (Johann Evangelista) Antonín Tomás
14 Dec 1738, Velvary - 3 Feb 1814, Prague. It is often hard to determine whether Jan Kozeluch or Leopold Kozeluch wrote a particular work. Here we usually agree with Poštolka's thematic catalog. Work details are given in full under Leopold Kozeluch, with doubtful cases (probably by Jan Kozeluch) only listed in this entry.
*JTK-1d. Nro. 1: Pardia ala Camera, C minor, (P.VI:c1).   2ob 2cl 2hn 2bn.
JTK-2d. Nro. 2 Parthia, D minor, (P.VI:d1).   2ob 2cl 2hn 2bn.
JTK-3d. Parthia in B♭, (P.VI:B3).   2ob 2cl 2hn bn.
JTK-4d. Parthia No. 4, D minor, (P.VI:d2).   2ob 2cl 2hn 2bn.
JTK-5d. Nro. 6 Partie ala Camera in B♭, (P.VI:B1).   Solo oboe, 2ob 2cl 2hn bn.
JTK-6d. Partie ala Camera No. 6, B♭, (P.VI:B2).   2ob 2cl 2hn 2bn.
JTK-7d. Parthia in F, (P.VI:F1).   2cl 2hn 2bn.
JTK-8d. Cassation in Es (E♭), 5 mvts, (P.VI:Es1).   2cl 2hn bn.

*KOZELUCH (Koželuh), Leopold Anton (Jan Antonín)   *9 Dec 1747, Velvary - 7 May 1818, Vienna*
LAK-1.1. Harmonie, No. 2; in F, 4 mvts, (P.VI:8, citing LAK-1.2 only).   2ob/fl 2cl 2hn 2bn cbn/db.
MS parts: D-Mbs, Mus.Ms.6854.
Pc (Chez N. Simrock: Bonn, H. Simrock: Paris, pn 270, 1802/1803), RISM [K 1458], parts: CZ-Pu, 59 A 10439; D-Bds; GB-Ljag(w), (ob I & II only) & (modern photocopy of CZ-Pu); US-Wc, ML30.4c no. 2593 Miller. ★
Pc (Breitkopf & Härtel: Leipzig, c.1807), parts. *Possibly only as agent for Simrock rather than a new edition.*
Pm (Hornseth Music Co: Washington, DC, c.1990), score & parts.
LAK-1.2. No. 22 Parthia; in F, 4 mvts, (P.VI:8).   2fl 2cl 2hn 2bn.
MS parts: RF-Ssc, (?2 copies), Ф 891 собр юосуповых N43, pp. 95 - 120, & N209b.
Pm (Český hudební fond: Prague, 1992), ed. František Laštůka, hire score & parts, No 08857.
LAK-2.1. Parthia in F; 4 mvts, (P. deest; LAK- 2.3 only = P.VI:3).   2ob 2cl 2hn 2bn cbn.
MS parts: D-HR, HR III 4 1/2 2° 356, (c.1790). *Possibly the untraced companion, "No. 1" to LAK-1.* ★
Pm (KGS), fiche (2305).
LAK-2.2. No. 23 Parthia; in F, 4 mvts, (P. deest; LAK-2.3 only = P.VI:3).   2fl 2cl 2hn 2bn.
MS parts: RF-Ssc, (?2 copies), Ф 891 собр юосуповых N43, pp. 95 - 120, & N209e.
Pm (Český hudební fond: Prague, 1992), ed. František Laštůka, hire score & parts, No 03074.
LAK-2.3. Parthia in F, arranged Kajetan Vogel, (P.VI:3).   fl 2cl 2hn 2bn 2vla/2bthn.
MS parts: D-W, Ms.Vogel 141. ★
LAK-3. Parthia in B♭, (P. deest).   2ob 2cl 2hn 2bn.   MS parts: D-HER, Mus.C.19=1. ★
For LAK-4 & 5 the titlepages give a scoring of Clavicembalo with 2cl 2hn 2bn, but the surviving parts are for Clavicembalo, 2vl 2ob 2bn; the violin parts are, generally, transcriptions of the right hand of the Clavicembalo part. The Roman numerals on the titlepages may be slightly later additions.
LAK-4. Divertimento I; in E♭, 4 mvts, (P.VI:9).   Clavicembalo, 2cl 2hn 2bn, (*or* 2vl 2ob 2bn).
MS parts: A-Wn, Mus.Hs.11,390. ★
LAK-5. Divertimento in E♭ II; 4 mvts, (P.VI:10).   Clavicembalo, 2cl 2hn 2bn, (*or* 2vl 2ob 2bn).
MS parts: A-Wn, Mus.Hs.11,391. ★
LAK-6. Divertimento 1mo in D; 3 mvts, (P.VI:5).   2cl(A) 2hn bn.
MS parts: CZ-Pnm, XXXII.A.87, (missing cl II). ★
LAK-7. Divertimento in D# [D major]; 5 mvts, (P.VI:5).   2cl 2hn bn.
MS parts: CZ-Pnm XXXII.A.88, (missing cl II). ★
LAK-8. Divertimento 3tio [in] E♭; 4 mvts, (P.VI:7).   2cl 2hn bn.
MS parts: CZ-Pnm XXXII.A.89, (missing cl II). ★
LAK-9. Quintetto in Dis [E♭] . . . Leopoldo Koželuch; (P.VI:Es2).   2cl 2hn bn.
MS parts: CZ-Pk, i.č.4769. ★
LAK-1m. March in C; (P.VI: without number).   2fl 2cl(C) 2hn 2bn serp 2tp(clar) b-dr.
Pc (In **A-82.1m** Acht Märsche für Türkische Musick [sic], 1 Heft, No. 1; as by "Kozeliuch":) (Johann André: Offenbach am Main, pn 1822, 1803), parts: H-KE, K 731/VIII. ★
MS score & parts (copy of the André edition): I-Fc, F.P. S.553.
LAK-2m. Marsch für das Corps der Freywilligen des Handelstandes von Wien, (P.XIV:10).   Winds.
We have not located the Traeg (pre-1799, MS. No. 135) wind parts.
Pc (Gombartische Musik Handlung: Augsburg, pn 160, c.1799), RISM [K 1815], piano only: CH-Bchristen; CZ-Pnm, XLI.D.279; H-KE. ★
Pc (Kozeluchische Musikalien Handlung: Wien, c.1799), RISM [K 1814], piano: CZ-K, CZ-KRa.
LAK-3m. Prag [collection of works for military band including marches & a theme and variations].   Winds.
AutoMS piano score: A-Wn, Mus.Hs.2091. *We have not traced wind versions of these works.*
The following works we believe to be by Jan Antonín Kozeluch (qv).
*LAK-1d. Nro. 1: Pardia ala [sic] Camera; in C minor, 3 mvts, (P.VI:c1).   2ob 2cl 2hn bn.
MS parts: CZ-Kra, A3897/IV.B.60. ★
LAK-2d. Nro. 2: Parthia ala [sic] Camera; in D minor, 4 mvts, (P.VI:d1).   2ob 2cl 2hn bn.
MS parts: CZ-KRa, A3898IV.B.61, (with an extra copy of the ob I part). ★
LAK-3d. 3 Pardie alla Camera; in B♭, 3 mvts, (P.VI:B3).   2ob 2cl 2hn bn.
MS parts: CZ-Kra, A3899/IV.B.62. ★
LAK-4d. Nro: 4 Pardia all [sic] Camera; in D minor, 4 mvts, (P.VI:d2).   2ob 2cl 2hn bn.
MS parts: CZ-KRa, A3900/IV.B.63. ★
LAK-5d. Nro: 6 Partie ala [sic] Camera; in B♭, 4 mvts, (P.VI:B1).   Solo oboe, 2ob 2cl 2hn bn.
MS parts: CZ-KRa, A3901/IV.B.64. ★
Pm (as "Parthia à la Camara" [sic] for solo ob, solo bn, 2ob 2cl 2hn bn:) (Compusic: Amsterdam, pn 238, 1991), score & parts.
LAK-6d. N: 5 Partie alla Camera; in B♭, 4 mvts, (P.VI:B2).   2ob 2cl 2hn 2bn.
MS parts: CZ-KRa, A3902/IV.B.65. ★
LAK-7d. Parthia in F; 4 mvts, (P.VI:F1).   2cl 2hn 2bn.   MS parts: CZ-NR, A.31.764/B.274. ★
LAK-8d. Cassation in Es [E♭]; 5 mvts, (P.VI:Es1).   2cl 2hn bn.   MS parts: CZ-Pnm, XXX.B.14. ★

*KOZLOWSKI (Koslowsky, Koslovsky), Josef Anton (Józef Ossip Antonowitsch)
1757, Warsaw - 27 Feb 1831, St Petersburg
*JOK-1. Adagio & Largo, C minor.   2fl 2cl 2hn 2bn.
MS parts: PL-LA, RM 81/1-5/, 1 (missing fl I, hn I, bn II).   ★
*JOK-2. Polonoises, B♭.   2fl 2cl 2hn 2bn.   MS parts: PL-LA, RM 81/1-5/, 74 (missing fl I, hn I, bn II).   ★
*JOK-3. Terzetto.   2fl 2cl 2hn 2bn.   MS parts: PL-LA, RM 81/1-5/, 31 (missing fl I, hn I, bn II).   ★
JOK-1t. Marche pour la Procession Funèbre; in E♭.   2cl 2hn bn+hn(III)+b-tb (2)bn/hn(IV)+b-tb.
MS parts: D-Tl, Gg 435, No. 2.   ★
JOK-2t. Marche [pour la Procession Funèbre]; in E♭.   2cl 2hn bn+hn(III)+b-tb (2)bn/hn(IV)+b-tb.
MS parts: D-Tl, Gg 435, No. 3.   ★
JOK-1ma. Trois Polonaises composées pour le Grand Orchestre Exécutées à l'occasion du Jour des fiançailles et du mariage de Son Altesse Impériale Monseigneur le Grand Duc Nicolai Pawlowitch avec Son Altesse Impériale Madame la Grande Duchesse Alexandra Feodorowna…arrangées pour la musique militaire et dédiées à S.A.J. Monseigneur le Grand Duc Nicolai Pawlowitch par L'Auteur.
pic 2fl 2ob cl(F) 2cl(C) 2bthn 2hn 2bn cbn+b-hn 2tp 2a-tb b-tb timp b-dr+cym t-dr tri.
Pc (chez Paez: gravé à S⸱ Petersbourg, post-1817), RISM [K 1829], score: CH-Gpu, Ib.2918.   ★
*JOK-1ve. Fingal, Tragédie en trois actes.
Pc (sn: St Petersburg, 1808), RISM Supp [KK 1824a], score, pp. 98-100, 121-125: GB-Lbl, H.1875.
Pc (sn: St Petersburg, pn 40, 1808), RISM Supp [KK 1824b], another edition, score: D-Cl; RF-Ml.
 1.1ev. Act I, No. 5: "Maître des cieux et de la terre".   TTBB chorus, 2cl(C) 2hn(C) 2bn cbn 3tb.
 1.2ev. "Ne planne plus dans le sejour", (Adagio).   TTBB chorus, 2cl(C) 2hn(C) 2bn cbn 3tb.
JOK-1a. Boieldieu: Ma tante Aurore, 1803, Ouverture.   2fl 2cl 2hn 2bn.
MS parts: PL-LA, RM 81/1-5/, 172 (missing fl I, cl I, bn II).   ★

KRACHER, Er[nst] *(1825)*
ERK-1m. Marsch.   2cl(E♭) 2cl(B♭) 2hn 2bn 2tp.   MS parts: A-Sca, Hs.266, No. 45.

*KRÁL, Johann Nepomuk
Mus.Hs.20,822 bears the stamp: K.K. INFTR.-RE[gi]M[en]T. FR[ei]H[err] v. HESS Nº 49 / Musikverwaltung.
JEK-1m. Hoch=Habsburg Marsch.   cl(E♭) 2cl(B♭) 2hn 3tp 2flug b-flug b-tb basso "Banda"(= b-dr s-dr).
MS parts: A-Wn, Mus.Hs.20,822, No. 1.   ★
JEK-2m. Donaugruss Marsch.   fl+pic(D♭) cl(A♭) cl(E♭) 2cl(B♭) 4hn 5tp cap b-tp 2flug 2t-hn b-flug 3tb euph helikon b-dr s-dr.   MS parts: A-Wn, Mus.Hs.20,822, No. 2.   ★

*KRÁSA, ( ) *(Not Joseph Martin Krása. Probably a member of the Chotek Harmonie)*
JMK-1. Parthia in B[♭]; 4 mvts.   2cl 2hn 2bn.   MS parts: CZ-Pnm, XLI.B.159.   ★
JMK-2. Parthia in E♭; 4 mvts.   2cl 2hn 2bn.   MS parts: CZ-Pnm, XLI.B.160.   ★
JMK-1v. Missa in B♭.   CATB, 2ob 2cl 2hn 2bn 3tp(2clar, 1prin) timp.
MS parts: CZ-Pu, 59 R 1624. *A substantial work, probably dating from the 1790s.*   ★

KRAUS, Freidrich
FEK-1. Partia A 4; in C, 5 mvts.   2obdam vladam bc.   MS parts: S-L. Saml. Kraus 40.   ★

KRAUS, Johann Martin
JMK-1a. Mozart: Idomeneo, Marche, (K. 366, No. 8).   2ob 2cl 2hn 2bn.   MS: S-St, (without shelfmark).

KRAUTMACHER, Erich *1927, Germany*
EQK-1. Divertimento in D; 1960.   fl 2ob 2cl hn bn.
Pm (Privately printed for the Author: Leichlingen, Rheinland, c.1961), score, (obtainable via Deutscher Komponist-Verband: Berlin).

*KRECHLER (Kechtler, Krechter), F., Faknrich (Officer-cadet) *(1780)*
Krechler presents unusal problems, both through his re-use of material and in his role as a compiler. The Auszug compilations include movements drawn from the works of other arrangers such as Triebensee.
*FFK-1m(-5m). Vergatterung & 4 Marches *(a fifth march in this set is by Gänsbacher).*
pic 2fl(G) 2cl(C) 2hn 2bn cbn 2tp b-dr.   MS parts: CZ-Pnm, Lobkovic X.H.a.80
FFK-1a. Stücke für die türkische Musik.   pic 2fl(G) 2ob cl(F) 2cl(C) 2hn 2bn cbn 2tp b-dr s-dr(as "Tamburo Picolo" [sic]).   MS parts: CZ-Pnm, Lobkovic X.H.a.70.
*FFK-2a. Harmonie, Oeuvre I.   2ob 2cl 2hn 2bn (cbn tp ad lib).
MS parts: CZ-Pnm, Lobkovic X.H.a.13; CZ-Bm(no), A.16.791, (mvts 1 - 4, 9, 5, 7, 10).
 2.1a, 2.2a. Paer: La Testa riscaldata, overture & aria ("La donna con amore").   (cf. FFK-4.1a)
 2.3a. Mayr: Adelasia ed Aleramo, quartetto ("Madre tu sei se l'amo").
 2.4a. Paer: La Testa riscaldata, aria ("Calmo mio bene").
 2.5a. Paer: Ginevra degli Almieri, overture.   (cf. FFK-9.1a)
 2.6a. Mayr: Adelasia ed Aleramo, duetto ("Che al mio bene al mio tesoro").
 2.7a. Paer: Polonaise, in B♭.   (cf. FFK-16.2a).
 2.8a. Paer: Poche ma buone ("La donna cambiata"), overture.   (cf. FFK-9.5a)
 2.9a. Haydn: Symphony in B♭, Hob. I/102, 3rd mvt, Menuetto.   (cf. FFK-9.6a)
 2.10a. Haydn: Drumroll Symphony, Hob. I/103, finale.   (cf. FFK-9.7a)
FFK-3a. Harmonie, Oe. II⁼.   2ob 2cl 2hn 2bn (cbn tp ad lib).   MS pts: CZ-Pnm, Lobkovic X.H.a.14.
 3.1a - 3.5a. [Unidentified opera/ballet], overture (?and 4 mvts).   3.6a. Méhul: Hélèna, overture.
 3.7a. [unidentified, possibly from Méhul's opera, *Hélèna*], 1 mvt.
FFK-4a. Harmonie, Lib: II (catalog: "Oe. 3").   2ob 2cl 2hn 2bn cbn.   MS parts: CZ-Pnm, Lobkovic X.H.a.15.
 4.1a. Paer: La Testa riscaldata, overture.   (cf. FFK-2.1a).
 4.2a. Beethoven: Zapfenstreich No. 1 (LVB-2m; Marche des Fürst Joseph von Lobkowitzischen Bataillons).
 4.3a. Zinek: [Kriegslied], Romance für Oestreichs [sic] Landswehr.
 4.4a. Zinek: Marche [originally part of 4.3a, cf. ZINEK, CZ-Pnm, XX.F.104).
 4.5a. Spontini: Fernand Čortez: Marché [sic] espagnol.
 4.6a. Gyrowetz: Emerike, arie & duetto, (2ob tacet in aria).   (cf. FFK-7.3a).
 4.7a. Anon: Marche [& Trio]. Allegro ¢.   4.8a. Anon: Marche [without Trio]. Allegro, C

FFK-5a. Harmonie, Oeuvre 4tre. 2ob 2cl 2hn 2bn (cbn tp ad lib). MS pts: CZ-Pnm, Lobkovic X.H.a.16.
    5.1a. J. Weigl: Richard Löwenherz, marche.
    5.2a. Mozart: Le Nozze di Figaro, Aria, "Non più andrai".
    5.3a. Paer: Numa Pompilio, 1 mvt.
    5.4a. Haydn: Die Jahreszeiten, Der Frühling, Arie, "Schon eilet froh der Ackermann".
    5.5a. Paer: Numa Pompilio, overture.
    5.6a. Haydn: Die Jahreszeiten, Der Winzer, Lied mit Chor, "Ein Mädchen".
    5.7a. Haydn, Die Jahreszeiten, Der Herbst, Einleitung.
    5.8a. Krechler: 8 Walzer. (cf. FFK-7.7a).
    5.9a. Paer: Numo Pompilio, ballo. Andantino, 2/4
    5.10a. ?Paer: Numo Pompilio, Coro Ecco.
FFK-6a. Miscellanées de Musique. 2ob 2cl 2hn 2bn cbn 2tp. MS parts: CZ-Pnm, Lobkovic X.H.a.48.
    6.1a. Mayr: L'intrigo della lettra, overture. 6.2a. Anon: Marche de Moura [sic], in F, 6/8.
    6.3a. Haydn: Ochsen Menuet (Hob. IX/27, spurious). 6.4a. Anon: Marsch [& Trio], ¢.
    6.5a. J. Weigl: Kaiser Hadrian, duetto. (cf. FFK-7.6a). 6.6a. Cherubini: Les deux Journées, Marche in C.
    6.7a. Kanne: Miranda, Marsch. (cf. FFK-7.5a). 6.8a. Paer: Griselda, duetto.
    6.9a. Mozart: Die Zauberflöte, arie (Act II, No. 14, "Der Hölle Rache"). (cf. FFK-12.3a)
    6.10a. Kanne: Orpheus, Marsche, in C. (cf.FFK-12.4a).
FFK-7a. Miscellanées. 2ob 2cl 2hn 2bn cbn tp. MS parts: CZ-Pnm, Lobkovic X.H.a.55.
    7.1a. Spontini: Fernand Cortez, choeur (Tempo di marcia con poco di moto).
    7.2a. Mayr: Ginevra di Scozia, cavatina. 7.3a. Gyrowetz: Emerike, arie et duo. (cf. FFK-4.6a).
    7.4a. Cherubini: Les deux Journées: marche, choeur et marche.
    7.5a. Kanne: Miranda, marche. (cf. FFK-6.7a). 7.6a. J Weigl: Kaiser Hadrian, duetto. (cf. FFK-6.5a).
    7.7(a). Krechler: 8 Walzer. (cf. FFK-5.8a). 7.8a. Paisiello: Il Re Teodoro in Venezia, Marche.
FFK-8a. Auszug aus verschiedene Opern & Ballets; 7 mvts. 2ob 2cl 2hn 2bn cbn tp.
MS score (as "Miscellanees [sic] pour le Harmonia", allegedly in the hand of J.S. Mayr): I-BGc, Mayr 607.
MS parts (post-1811): CZ-Pnm, Lobkovic X.H.a.65.
    8.1a. (unidentified opera/ballet): overture.
    8.2a. Mosel: Das Feuerprobe: 1 mvt. (cf. FFK-9.3a). 8.3a. Spontini: Milton, [Schluss Chor]. (cf. FFK-9.5a).
    8.4a. M. Umlauf: Aneas in Karthago, 4 mvts. (cf. FFK-15.2a).
FFK-9a. Auszug aus: [Paer] Ginevra [degli Almieri], [Cherubini] Medea, [Paer] Feuerprobe.
2ob 2cl 2hn 2bn cbn. MS parts: CZ-Pnm, Lobkovic X.H.a.12. *Included with the* Auszug, *on smaller sheets, are Nos. 3 - 8 of FFK-18a.*
    9.1a. Paer: Ginevra degli Almieri, overture. (cf. FFK-2.5a).
    9.2a. Cherubini: Medée, introduzione & marcia. Nos. 2 & 3. (cf. FFK-18a, Nos. 1 & 2).
    9.3a. Mosel: Die Feuerprobe, 1 mvt. (cf. FFK-8.2a). 9.4a. Spontini: Milton, Schluss Chor (cf. FFK-8.3a).
    9.5a. Paer: Poche ma buone, overture. (cf. FFK-2.8a).
    9.6a. Haydn: Symphony (Hob. I/102iii) Menuetto + Trio. (cf. FFK-2.9a).
    9.7a. Haydn: Symphony (Hob. I/103),Finale. Allo con Spirito, C. (cf. FFK-2.10a).
FFK-10a. Auszuge. Der besten Stücke aus verschesdene Opern für 9 Stimmige Harmonie. Aus: Grétry: Raoul der Blaubarth, Mozart: La Clemenza di Tito, Mayr: Ercole in Lidien. 2ob 2cl 2hn 2bn cbn.
MS parts: CZ-Pnm, Lobkovic X.H.a.60.
    10.1a. Grétrty: Raoul der Blaubarth, overture.
    10.2a. Mozart: La Clemenza di Tito, overture & 4 mvts (I/2, I/9, II/15, II/23). (cf. FFK-12.1a).
    10.3a. Mayr: Ercole in Lidien, overture & 1 mvt.
FFK-11a. Auszug der besten Stücke. aus verschiedene Opern; Cherubini: Giulio et Sabino, Cherubini: [Élisa] Bernhardsberg, Méhul: [Le Trésor supposé] Schatzgräber, T. Weigl: Bachus et Ariadne, (No. 71).
2ob 2cl 2hn 2bn cbn. MS parts: CZ-Pnm (2 copies), Lobkovic X.H.a.61/1, 61/2.
    11.1a. Cherubini: Gjulio Sabino (as "Giulio et Sabino"), overture
    11.2a. Cherubini: [Élisa] Mont St Bernard, 3 mvts
    11.3a. Méhul: Le Trésor supposé (as "Die Schatzgräber"), 1 mvt.
    11.4a. T. Weigl: Bacchus et Ariadne, 3 mvts.
FFK-12a. Auszug der besten Stücke aus [Mozart: La] Clemenza di Titto [sic], [Mayr: La] Lodoiska, [Mozart: Die] Zauberflöte etc: für Harmonie. 2ob 2cl 2hn 2bn cbn tp. MS parts: CZ-Pnm, Lobkovic X.H.a.62.
    12.1a. Mozart: La Clemenza di Tito, overture & 2 mvts (I/2, II/15). (cf. FFK-10.2a & FFK-21a)
    12.2a. Mayr: La Lodoiska, overture & Nos. 3, 6. (cf. FFK-13.2, Nos. 1 - 3)
    12.3a. Mozart: Die Zauberflöte, 5 mvts (I/2, I/3, I/8 "Zum Ziele", I/15). Nos. 7 - 11. (cf. FFK-6.9a)
    12.4a. Kanne: Orpheus, Marche. No. 12. (cf. FFK-6.10a).
FFK-13a. Auszug aus: Selico [Gyrowetz] & Lodoiska [Mayr]. 2ob 2cl 2hn 2bn.
MS parts: CZ-Pnm, Lobkovic X.H.a.63.
    13.1a. Gyrowetz: Selico, overture, duetto & 1 mvt.
    13.2a. Mayr: La Lodoiska, overture & 3 mvts. (cf. FFK-12.2a)
FFK-14a. Auszuk [sic]: Winter: Vologesus & J. Weigl: Die isthmischen Spiel. 2ob 2cl 2hn 2bn.
MS parts: CZ-Pnm, Lobkovic X.H.a.64.
    14.1a. Winter: Vologesus, overture & 9 mvts. (cf. FFK-24).
    14.2a(d). J. Weigl: Die isthmischen Spiele, 6 mvts. (= TRIEBENSEE JZT-64a)
FFK-15a. Harmonie; 11 mvts. 2ob 2cl 2hn 2bn cbn [tp]. MS pts with autograph amendments and corrections:
CZ-Pnm, Lobkovic (2 copies), X.H.a.9, (Nos. 1 - 6), X.H.a.67, (Nos. 1 - 6, 6½ only; with an additional tp part).
    15.1a. J. Weigl: Cantate [in fact, *Das Waisenhaus*], overture & 5/6 mvts.
    15.2a. M. Umlauf: Aeneas in Karthago, 4 mvts. (cf. FFK-8.4a).
*FFK-16a. Miscellanées pour Harmonie. 2ob 2cl 2hn 2bn. MS parts: CZ-Pnm, Lobkovic X.H.a.56.
    16.1a. (unidentified) Marcia, ¢ (Sotto voce). 16.2a. Paer: Polonaise, 3/4 [crayon: "7"]. (cf. FFK-2.7a)
    16.3a, 16.4a. [2 unidentified mvts], Allegro Modto, C; Andante 6/8.
FFK-17.1a. Boieldieu: Jean de Paris, overture & 9 mvts. 2ob 2cl 2hn 2bn cbn.
MS parts: CZ-Pnm, Lobkovic X.G.f.58. *Although this work is certainly claimed by Krechler, it may be an adaptation of Poessinger's arrangement (FAP-1a).*

FFK-17.2a. Boieldieu: Jean de Paris, overture & 10 mvts.   2ob 2cl 2hn 2bn cbn 2tp.
MS parts: D-Tl, Z 52, (as by "Kechtler").   *Another copy, now lost, is listed in the Hoftheater Invertory for 1834, Stuttgart; this uses the same variant spelling as the D-Tl copy.*
FFK-18a. Cherubini: Médée (Medea), introduzione & 7 mvts.   2ob 2cl 2hn 2bn cbn.
MS parts: CZ-Pnm, (2 copies), Lobkovic X.G.f.59, Lobkovic X.H.a.12, Nos. 2 & 3 (with Nos. 3 - 8 of the arrangement, on smaller sheets added at the end of the work).
FFK 19.1a, 19.2a. Isouard: Dix Pièces de Michel-Ange (overture & 4 mvts) et Le Billet de Loterie (5 mvts).
2ob 2cl 2hn 2bn (cbn tp ad lib).   MS parts: CZ-Pnm, Lobkovic X.G.f.63.
FFK-20a. Mayr: Allonso [sic: Alonzo] e Cora, overture & 7 mvts.   2ob 2cl 2hn 2bn cbn.
MS parts: CZ-Pnm, Lobkovic X.G.f.74; CZ-Bm(au), A.36.869, (Anon, "für 11 stimmige [sic] Harmonie", incorrectly cites Méhul as composer); I-Fc, F.P. S.342.
FFK-21a. Mozart: La Clemenza di Tito, overture & 12 mvts.   2ob 2cl 2hn 2bn (cbn listed with bn II, no divisi).
MS score (as Anon, in the hand of J.S. Mayr): I-Bc, Mayr 564, (for 2ob 2cl 2hn 2bn).
MS parts: CZ-Bm(au), A.35.192, (omits No. 8; the ob I pt states, "Copie Bouraiche / en Hautbois au / premier régiment d'Infantérie [sic] de Ligne de sa majesté l'empereur", dated by copyists 1817); I-MOe, Mus.D.262, (as by "Krechtler"; with additional local pts for ob II in the key of C & cl II in C for the overture; copy by Stohl).
FFK-22a. Spontini: La Vestale, overture & 7 mvts.   2ob 2cl 2hn 2bn cbn.   MS pts: CZ-Pnm, Lobkovic X.H.a.2.
*FFK-23a. Spontini: Fernand Cortez, overture & 14 mvts.   2ob 2cl 2hn 2bn cbn (tp).
AutoMS score & parts: CZ-Pnm, Lobkovic X.H.a.1. *The score, in 7 sewn blocks, is a working copy with many changes & corrections. No. 8 ("Choeur des Espagnols") has added parts in the score only for tri, cym(s), b-dr, tamburo militaire & 2 sections where pic doubles ob I. Scores like this are extremely rare. Both sets of parts are in the same hand. Set 1, on thick brown paper, includes a trumpet part not found in the score; Set 2, on Italian paper (wm 3 half-moons) lacks the trumpet part. The scoring is often thin, using only 2cl 2bn.*
MS score (as Anon, in the hand of J.S. Mayr): I-BGc, Mayr 608, (with the tp pt, tacet in Nos. 3 & 13).
*FFK-24a. Vogler: Samori, overture & 23 mvts.   2ob 2cl 2hn 2bn (cbn tp ad lib).
MS score & parts: CZ-Pnm, Lobkovic X.H.a.5. *Scores like this are extremely rare; unlike FFK-26a, this is in fair-copy. The cbn appears in the Finale (No. 23) only; the trumpet is used in the overture & mvts 5, 8, 10, 15 (a few bars only), 16, 18, 22, 23. As with FFK-26 the scoring often uses only 2cl 2bn.*
FFK-25a. Winter: Vologesus (as "Der Triumph der Treue"), overture & 9 mvts.   2ob 2cl 2hn 2bn cbn.
MS parts: CZ-Pnm, Lobkovic X.H.a.10/1; H-KE, 1179/IX, (as Anon, without cbn).   (cf. FFK-14.1a) *The cbn is with bn II with minimal divisi. The wrapper is a spoiled wrapper for FFK-17a.*
FFK-1ac. Miscellanées.   2ob 2cl 2hn 2bn cbn tp.   MS parts: CZ-Pnm, Lobkovic X.H.a.58.   *Some mvts, notably 1.2ac & 1.4ac may be drawn from arrangements by Triebensee.*
   1.1ac. Paer: I Fuorusciti, overture. No. 1.   1.2ac. Mozart: Le Nozze di Figaro, duetto "Sull' aria". No. 2.
   1.3ac. Mayr: Ginevra di Scozia, marcia, duetto. Nos. 3 & 5.
   1.4ac. Nicolini: Trajano in Dacia, duetto. No. 4.
   1.5ac. Cimarosa: Il Matrimonio segreto, aria, Tempo Pollacco sic]. No. 6.
   1.6ac. Haydn: Concerto for 2 Lire organizette in F, (Hob. VIIh/5ii), Andante con molto [sic].
   1.7ac. Haydn: Symphony in F, (Hob. I/89iii), Menuetto.
   1.8ac. Anon: Marcia.   1.9ac. Anon: Marcia.
FFK-1ad. Miselln [sic; pencil on bn I part].   2ob 2cl 2hn 2bn.   MS parts: CZ-Pnm, Lobkovic X.H.a.57.
These selections are almost certainly drawn from Went's arrangements.
   1.1/1-4ad. Gluck: La Rencontre imprévue [Der Pilgrim aus Mekka], 4 mvts ("A ma maîtresse j'avais promis", "Mahomet, notre grand prophète", "Un ruisselet bien clair" [variant]. Nos. 1 - 3.
   1.2ad. Gluck: Iphigénie aus Tauride, "Unis des la plus tendre enfance". No. 4.
   1.3/1-3ad. Gluck: Orfeo, 3 mvts. No. 5.
   1.4ad. Gluck: Alceste, "Non vi turbate". No. 6.
   1.5/1-2ad. I. Umlauf: Das Irrlicht, 2 mvts. No. 7 (Andante) & 10 (Andante moderato).
   1.6/1-2ad. Salieri: Der Rauchfangkehrer, 2 mvts. Nos. 8 & 9.   1.7ad. [unidentified] Andante, 2/4. No. 11.

*KREITH (Greith), Carl (Carlo, Karl) *1748 - 1807 (some sources give 1809)*
*CXK-1. Parthia in B[♭]; 4 mvts.   2ob 2cl 2hn 2bn.   MS parts: D-DO, Mus.Ms.1108.   ★
CXK-2. Parthia in Dis [E♭]; 5 mvts.   2ob 2cl 2hn 2bn.   MS parts: D-DO, Mus.Ms.1109.   ★
CXK-3. Parthia in Dis [E♭]; 5 mvts.   2ob 2cl 2hn 2bn.   MS parts: D-DO, Mus.Ms.1110, (with an additional bn(obl) pt in another hand, probably a compression of the 2bn pts).   ★
CXK-4. Partita; in C; 4 mvts.   2ob 2cl 2hn 2bn.
MS parts: I-Gc, SS.B.1.10.   ★
Pm (WINDS: Northridge, CA, c.1981), parts (modern MS photocopies).
CXK-5. Partitta in D mol [minor]; 4 mvts.   2ob 2cl 2hn 2bn.   MS parts: CZ-Pnm, XXII.D.185.   ★
*CKC-6. Serenata in B[♭]; 3 mvts.   2ob 2cl 2hn 2bn.   MS parts: CZ-Pnm, XXVII.B.78, (as by "Greith").   ★
CXK-7. Musique harmonique.   2ob 2cl 2hn 2bn.   MS parts: D-Bds, Hausbibl. Mus.Ms.432.
CXK-8. Partitta in B[♭], Op. 57; 4 mvts.   2ob 2cl 2hn 2bn.
Pc (apresso Giuseppe Eder: Vienna, pn 199, 1802), RISM [K 1955], pts: H-KE, K 663/VIII.   ★
CXK-9.1. Partitta in B[♭], Op. 58; 4 mvts.   2cl 2hn 2bn.
Pc (apresso Giuseppe Eder: Wien, pn 202, 1802), RISM [K 1957], parts: H-Bn, Z.43,656; H-KE, K 663a. ★
CKC-9.2. Partitta Tono B [B♭]; 4 mvts.   2ob 2cl 2hn 2bn.
Pc (apresso Giuseppe Eder: Wien, pn 425, c.1806), parts: H-KE, K 656-657.   ★
CXK-10. Partitta in D, Op. 59; 5 mvts.   2cl 2hn 2bn.
Pc (apresso Giuseppe Eder: Wien, pn 203, 1802), RISM [K 1958], parts: GB-Ljag(w); H-KE, K 665/VIII.   ★
CXK-11. Partita in E♭, Op. 60; 3 mvts.   2cl 2hn 2bn.
Pc (apreso Giuseppe Eder: Wien, pn 200, 1802), RISM Supp [KK 1955a], parts: GB-Ljag(w), (overpasted with the printed imprint slip of Gayl & Hedler: Frankfurt a/M).   ★
MS parts (arranged by Canon Giuseppe Greggiati, 14 Jan 1815, as "Divertimento Per Organo e [2] Corni"): I-OS, Mus.Musiche B 1184.
*CXK-12. Partitta in Es [E♭], Op. 63; 4 mvts.   2cl 2hn 2bn.
Pc (Giuseppe Eder: Wien, pn 201, 1802), RISM [K 1956], pts: D-WEMl; H-Bn, Z.43,657; H-KE, K 664/VIII.   ★
CXK-13. Parthia in Dis [E♭], Nro 12; 4 mvts.   2cl 2hn 2bn.   MS parts: CZ-Pnm, XXII.D.183.   ★

CXK-14. Parthia in Dis [Eb], Nro 13; 3 mvts. 2cl 2hn bn. MS pts: CZ-Pnm, XXII.D.184. ★
CXK-15. Parthia in Dis [Eb]; 4 mvts. 2cl 2hn bn. MS parts (from Bohdaneč): CZ-Pnm, XI.E.158. ★
CKC-16. Parthia in Dis [Eb]; 4 mvts. 2cl 2hn bn. MS parts: CZ-Pu(dm), (2 copies), 59 R 3345, (by Augustin Erasmus Hübner, Langenbruck, 1805), 59 R 3344, (later copy by Dominik Hübner). ★
CKC-17. Parthia in Dis [Eb]; 4 mvts. 2cl 2hn bn.
MS parts (by Dominik Hübner, Langenbruck): CZ-Pu(dm), 59 R 3357, No. 2. ★
CXK-18(-20). Tre Terzetti. 2cl bn/vc.
Pc (Joseph Eder: Wien, pn 148, 1800), RISM Supp [KK 1952a], parts: HR-Zha.
CXK-1t. Marcia per i Morti, Op. 52. 2ob 2cl 2hn 2bn basso.
Pc (Joseph Eder: Wien, pn 177, 1801), parts: CZ-Bm(au), A.19.283; H-KE, K 660/VIII. ★
***CXK-1m.** Marsch für das neu errichtete Wiener Scharfschützen Korps. pic 2ob 2cl 2hn 2bn 2tp(clar) tp(prin, obbligato), b-dr s-dr Teller(samt Czinellen). *Note: there are 2 bars of divisi in the ob II part.*
Pc (Joseph Eder: Wien, pn 122, 1799), RISM [K 1959], parts: A-Wn, M.S.9960, (?missing Teller pt: the perc pts are "Timpano Grande [sic]" & "Tambore"; with another set of ob pts in MS - the oboe II pt takes the top line in the divisi in the printed ob II part); H-KE, 659, (?complete). ★
CXK-2m. Deux Marches in B[b], Op. 95. 2ob 2cl 2hn 2bn.
Pc (Joseph Eder: Wien, pn 452, 1807), RISM [K 1961], parts: H-KE, K 666/VIII, (RISM A/1 states missing the 2bn parts; H-KE 1993 catalog has no mention of missing parts). ★
CXK-3m. VI Märsche. 2cl 2hn bn tp.
Pc (Joseph Eder: Vienna, pn 126, 1799), RISM [K 1960], parts: H-Bn, Z.22,015; H-KE, K 667/VIII. ★
CXK-1a. [Paisiello:] Quintetto del Opera Il Re Theodoro [sic]; 8 mvts. 2fldam 2hn bn.
Pc (apresso Giuseppe Eder: Vienna; München apresso Hahn. Francoforto apresso Gaille Hedler. Hamborgo apresso Böhm. Zürch apresso Negeli [sic], pn 267, wm 1803), RISM Supp [KK 1962c], parts: A-Wgm, VIII 30603.

***KREJČÍ, Iša** *10 July 1904, Prague - 6 March 1968, Prague*
IYK-1. Concertino for Piano & Winds, 1935. Solo piano, 2fl 2ob 2cl a-sax 2hn 2bn 2tp tb perc.
MS score & parts: CZ-Pr, O 1281.
IYK-2. Concertino for Violin & Winds, 1936. Solo violin, 2fl 2ob 2cl 2hn 2bn cbn 2tp 3tb perc celeste.
MS score & parts: CZ-Pr, O 1819.

***KREJČÍ, Miroslav** *4 Nov 1891, Rychnov nad Kněžnou - 29 Dec 1964, Prague*
MJK-1. Dectet, Op. 94. 2fl 2ob 2cl 2hn 2bn.
Pm (Český hudební fond: Prague, 1952), hire score & parts.
MJK-1. Octet, Op. 108. 2ob 2cl 2hn 2bn.
Pm (Český hudební fond: Prague, 1956), hire score & parts.
MYK-2. Sextet, Op. 79. 2cl bthn 2hn bn.
Pm (Český hudební fond: Prague, 1949), hire score & parts.

***KRENEK (Křenek), Ernst** *23 Aug 1900, Vienna - 23 Dec 1991, Palm Springs, CA*
EZK-1. Sinfonie für Blasinstrumente und Schlagwerke, Op. 34 (1926, Leipzig). 4fl 4ob 4cl 4bn 4hn 4tp 3tb tu.
Pm (Universal Edition: Wien, c.1927), score (pn UE 17153) & hire parts.
EZK-2. 3 lustige Märsche, Op. 44. fl ob 4cl 2hn 2tp tb tu timp perc.
Pm (Universal Edition: Wien, pn UE 9640, 1929), score & hire parts.
EZK-3. Kleine Blasmusik, Op. 70a (1932). fl ob 4cl 2hn 2tp tb tu timp perc.
Pm (Universal Edition: Wien, c.1932), hire parts.
***EZK-1v.** O Lacrimosa, Op. 48a. MS solo, 2fl 2cl 2bn harp.
Pm (Universal Edition: Wien, pn UE 8729, 1926/27), vocal score & hire parts.
***EZK-2v.** 4 Gesänge nach alten Gedichten, Op. 53a. MS solo, fl 3cl hn tp.
Pm (Universal Edition: Wien, 1927), vocal score & hire parts.

KRENN, Franz *(1810)*
FRK-1m. Marsch; in Eb. fl(Eb) 3cl(Eb) 2cl(Bb) 2hn 2tp basso.
MS parts (1 July 1844): A-Wn, Mus.Hs.24,410. ★

KRETSCHMARIK, Matthias *(1780) active in Oberbotzen c.1803 - post-1814*
MAK-1. Quodl Aufruff [...] Quodlibet [...] Fräule Nannette v: Menz gewidmet von Matt: Kretschmarik den 23 [Oc]t[o]ber [1]814. S(A)TB, 2ob 2cl 2hn 2bn tp.
MS score & parts: I-BZtoggenburg, C/V 89, (alto voice in parts only; 2 copies of S & B parts).

***KREUTZER, Conradin (Konradin)** *22 Nov 1780, Messkirch, Badenia - 14 Dec 1849, Riga*
CYK-1. VI Walzer und VI Trios; (KWV 5207). 2cl 2hn 2bn.
Pc (Chemische Druckerei [Steiner]: Wien, pn 1093, c.1810), parts: A-Wgm, XV 4307. ★
Pm (Ernst Eulenburg (Amadeus): London, pn BP2029, 1980), ed. Otto Biba, score & parts.
CYK-1m. March in D. (MS c.1820). fl 2ob 2cl 2hn 2tp tb serp db.
MS parts (c.1820): D-Rtt, Sm. 15, No. 27, (possibly an arrangement). ★
CYK-1v. Offertorium in Es [Eb]; "Venite exultemus". SATB, fl 2ob 2cl(C) 2hn 2bn 2tp flug b-flug b-tb vc cb.
MS parts (by Alois Jirsák): CZ-OScr,2099, (missing bn II, tp II). ★
CYK-2v. Chor der Bergleute in Brautschmuk, "Glück auf, weit wiehr als Silber". TTB, fl 2cl 2hn bn.
MS parts: D-DO, Mus.Ms.1119, (with 2 sets of voice parts).
CYK-1vf. Tantum Ergo, in As [Ab]. SATB, 2ob 2bn 2tp 3tb vc cb timp.
MS vocal score & vocal parts only: A-Wn, Fonds 24 ST PETER-WIEN B 148 (I).

***KREUTZER, Rudolphe** *16 Nov 1766, Versailles - 6 Jan 1831, Geneva*
RZK-1ma. Ouverture de la Journée de Marathon; (opera, 1793). 2p-fl 2cl(C) 2hn 2bn tp b-tb serp timp.
Pc (Mag de mus fêtes nat: Paris, frimaire an III, 1794), liv. 9, No. 1, parts: F-Pn, H2. 9,1.

***KRICKEL, ( )**
YZK-1v. No. 2 Missa Bohemica in B[b]. CATB, 2cl 2bthn 2hn 2bn b-tb organ.
MS pts (from Kratochvilka, Moravia): CZ-Pnm, XI.E.210, (with a unfigured basso pt but no other organ pt). ★

*KRIEGER, Johann Philipp *26 Feb 1649, Nuremberg - 6 Feb 1725, Weissenfels*
JIK-1. Lustigen Feldmusik; (6 overtures). 2ob taille bn; (the preface recommends: 6ob 3taille 3bn).
Pc (Nuremberg, 1704), score: D-Bds, (lost in World War II). *No other surviving copies known.*
Pm (Monatschefte für Musikgeschichte, 1897/8), *2 Partie für Oboes*, (F, C), No. 1, pp. 98-114; No. 2, pp. 114-128.
Pm (Schering: Leipzig, 1912), "Suite aus Lustigen Feldmusik", in *Perlen alter Kam*, score.
Pm (Kistner & Siegel: Leipzig, 1951), ed. Seiffert, *Partie aus "Feldmusik"*.

*KRISET, ( ) (?von Kriset) *(1780)*
VQK-1. Harmonie Stück [sic]; 4 mvts.
pic(Nos. 2 & 4; No. 3: flautino in Eb) 2cl(Eb) 2cl(Bb) 2hn(Eb) 2bn 2tp b-tb+serp(Nos. 1 & 3) timp b-dr s-dr.
MS parts: A-Sca, Hs.76, Nos. 1 - 4, (1st set, cataloged as by A. Fendt). ★

*KRISTINUS, Carl Raimund *(1870)*
CRK-1v. Sequenz am Frohnleichnamsfeste, Op. 66. 2cl(C) 2hn 2tp b-tb timp.
Pc (sn: sl, c.1900-1910), parts: CZ-Pnm, XLIII.A.307, (missing vocal parts & organ). ★

KROEGER, Karl *4 April 1932, Louisville, Kentucky*
KRK-1. Suite. 2fl 2ob cl(Eb) 3cl(Bb) 2b-cl bn.
Pm (American Composers' Alliance: New York), facsimile edition.

*KROL, Bernhard *24 June 1920, Berlin*
BZK-1. Concertina sereno, Op. 50; 1970.
Solo violin & doublebass, pic fl ob ca cl b-cl 4hn bn cbn 2tp 3tb b-tu cembalo piano, harp mandolin guitar.
Pm (N. Simrock: Hamburg & London, 1980).
BZK-2. Konzertante Musik, Op. 6; 1950. Solo viola, 2ob 2cl 2hn 2bn.
Pm (Breitkopf & Härtel: Leipzig, Wiesbaden, pn EB 5795, 1953), parts.
BZK-3. Linzer Harmoniemusik, Op. 67; 1977. 2ob 2cl 2hn 2bn.
Pm (Bote & Bock: Berlin, Wiesbaden, pn 22780, 1980), score.
BZK-4. 8 Spielstücke, Op. 5; 1950. fl ob 2hn 2bn (cbn ad lib).
Pm (Pro Musica Edition: Leipzig, pn PM 54, 1951), score & parts.
BZK-5. Feiertagsmusik, Op. 107. 2ob ca heck bn. In MS: D-DSim will assist in contacting the composer.
BZK-6. Pezzo Lirico, Op. 95a; 1985. 2ob 2ca.
Pm (Bote & Bock: Berlin & Wiesbaden, 1986).
BZK-1v. "Willst du dein Herz mir schenken" Liebeslieder-Kantate, Op. 52. SATB choir, fl ca cl b-cl 2hn bn cbn.
In MS: D-DSim will assist in contacting the composer.
BZK-2v. "In dulci jubilo" Kantate nach alten Weihnachtsliedern, Op. 25; 1956. S, Bar, 2ca 2bthn b-cl bn.
Pm (Marbot: Hamburg, 1950).
Pm (N. Simrock: Hamburg & London, 1963).
BZK-3v. Ein volles Gals - ein leeres Glas, Gesellig-klassiches Quodlibet, Op. 106; 1987.
Solo BAR, TTBB chorus, fl ob cl 2hn bn, (combalo or piano ad lib).
Pm (Anton Böhm & Sohn: Augsburg, 1988).

*KROMMER (KRAMÁŘ, Cromer, Kromer), Franz Vincent (František Vincenc) *1759 - 1831*
For arrangements, reductions and transcriptions of Krommer's wind works, see also: HAVEL, and ROSINACK.
   Scoring discrepancies between the titlepages and parts in the Bureau des Arts et d'Industrie and Chemische Druckerei (Vienna) editions result from the production of a common titlepage for consecutive opus numbers.
   Apparent Chemische Druckerei reissues by Siegmund Anton Steiner (a partner from 1809 and sole proprietor from 1812) with a new titlepage in German rather than the original French, but using the original music plates, almost certainly reflect changing relations with France (after the occupations of Vienna in 1805 and 1809).
   The Paris publications present considerable problems. It is likely that Krommer brought copies of the Viennese published parts with him in 1814/1815 and made an agreement with Charles Bochsa (père); Bochsa's publishing plans appear to have been disrupted by the severe reduction of the army and the subsequent collapse of the military wind music market, c.1816. Victor Dufaut (the firm did not become "Dufaut et Dubois" until March 1821) purchased the stock of Bochsa in Dec. 1819 (some sources suggest 1821, i.e. on Bochsa's death) and the Krommer works were almost certainly included. Dufaut & Dubois prepared editions c.1822 - 1825. These remarkably corrupt editions are discussed on p. 215 of The Wind Ensemble Sourcebook.
   Unless noted otherwise all Italian MS scores of FVK-4 - FVK-13 were issued (or derived from) the set issued as: "ARMONIA I [- X] / Al' Celebre Maestro / CAVALIERE / G. ROSSINI / COLLEZIONE / delle dieci Armonie in partitura / Composte / DA / F. KROMMER / per 2. Oboe, 2. Clarinetti, 2. Corni, 2. Fagotti, / e un Contrafagotto / Pubblicata per la prima volta in Italia / L' EDITORE / FERDINANDO LORENZI / Umilmente Dedica / N.° 3691. al 3700. Prezza di Ciascuna Armonia F.2.5 / l'Opera Completa F. [blank] / FIRENZE / Dalla Stabibmento Musicale i FERDINANDO LORENZI presso la I." S Trunta in faccia al Casse Doray". The complete set of scores & parts at held at I-Fc, F.P. S.179, (the 2-vol set of 10 "Armonie" scores at I-Fc, F.P. S.727 and the parts at I-Fc, F.P. S.1168 are almost certainly from this issue) & I-Mc, Partitura G.F.XI.33. This set is ultimately based on the Chemische Druckerei/Steiner, Vienna set.
*FVK-1. Partita, Op. 45, No. 1; in Bb, 4 mvts. 2ob 2cl 2hn 2bn cbn.
MS score: F-Pn, L. 3123 (2) (tb replaces cbn, MS copy associated with the Dufaut & Dubois edition, prepared for the Gymnase Musical Militaire, ?1830s).
MS parts: CZ-Bm(no), A.16.647; D-NEhz, 205b; D-Rtt, Krommer 7/I, (as "Parthie. 12 in B[b]", purchased from Scheffauer in Stuttgart, June, 1820); CZ-KRa, A3905/IV.B.68., as "Parthia 3tia" for 2cl 2hn 2bn tp(ad lib) arranged by Havel, 1808).
Pc (Nel Negozio di Ignazio Sauer: Vienna, c.1803), MS parts: H-KE, 700, (as "Nr. 3 Partitta").
Pc (Bureau des Arts et d'Industrie: Vienne, pn 99, 1803), RISM [K 2532/i], parts: A-Ee, Mus.1116; A-Wgm, VIII 1291; A-Wn, MS.9242; CZ-Bm(no), A.16.794; CZ-Bsa, fond Staré Brno, 1092/E4; CZ-Pnm, Lobkovic X.H.a.23; D-RU1. ★
Pc (Breitkopf & Härtel: Leipzig, c.1804), parts. *Untraced: probably only advertized as Bureau des Arts agent.*
Pc (Dufaut & Dubois: Paris, pn V.D. et D. 192, c.1826), pts, as "2e Suite. Op. 45 N° 2 [sic]": GB-Lcm, LIX.D.1; I-Bc. *With alternate fl(Db) arranged Modrux for ob I; b/tb/serp replaces cbn; the ad lib tp pt was not printed.*
Pm (WINDS: Northridge, CA, pn W-50, c.1981), parts, (photocopy of Bureau des Arts et d'Industrie edition).

*FVK-2. Partita, Op. 45, No. 2; in E♭, 4 mvts.   2ob 2cl 2hn 2bn cbn tp(ad lib).
MS score: F-Pn, L. 3123 (1), (tb/oph replaces cbn, MS copy associated with the Dufaut & Dubois edition, prepared by A. Loulmont for the Gymnase Musical Militaire, 1830-40s).
MS parts: D-NEhz, 205a; GB-Ljag, (as "N♀ 5 Parthia" without the ad lib tp); NL-DHgm, hk 19 B 20; US-NRwhitwell, (4 copies), 168 (pts), 363(early MS pts), 316 (score by Middelhoven), 366 (score by Schwebel); CZ-KRA, A4455/R.OI.25, No. 3, (arranged Havel for 2cl 2hn 2bn). *The GB-Ljag(w) copy listed above may also be a MS from Ignaz Sauer.*
Pc (nel Negozio di Ignazio Sauer: Wien, c.1803), MS parts: CZ-Pnm, XX.F.5, (as "Parthia in Dis", "Vienna nel Negozio di Ignazio Sauer"; the cbn is give as "ad lib" & there is no mention of a tp pt).
Pc (Bureau des Arts et d'Industrie: Vienne, pn 135, 1803), RISM [K 2532/ii], parts: A-Ee, Mus.1117; A-Wn, MS.9242; CZ-Bm(no), A.16.795; CZ-Bsa, fond Staré Brno, 1092/E4; CZ-Pnm, Lobkovic X.H.a.24; D-DT, Mus-n 587; D-Rtt, Krommer (Druck) 2; D-RUl; H-KE, 2012; NL-DHgm. ★
Pc (Breitkopf & Härtel: Leipzig, c.1804), parts. *Untraced: probably only advertized as Bureau des Arts agent.*
Pc (Dufaut & Dubois: Paris, pn V. D. et D 144, c.1823), pts, as "1ᵉ Suite. Op 45 N♀ 1 [sic]": GB-Lcm, LIX.D.1; I-Bc. *With fl(C) arranged by Modrux as alternative for ob I; b/tb/serp replaces cbn.*
Pm (Dufaut & Dubois: Paris, pn W-168, c. 1981), parts (photocopy of Bureau des Arts et d'Industrie edition).
*FVK-3. Partita, Op. 45, No. 3; in Bb, 4 mvts.   2ob 2cl 2hn 2bn cbn tp(ad lib).
MS score: F-Pn, L. 3123 (3), (tb replaces cbn, MS copy associated with the Dufaut & Dubois edition, prepared by A. Loulmont for the Gymnase Musical Militaire, 1830-40s; a tp pt is marked in the score but has not been written out).
MS parts: CZ-Bm(no), A.16.646, (as "Parthia in B", missing tp); CZ-Pnm, (3 copies), XI.E.244, XX.F.4, (as "Partitta", "Vienna nel Negozio di Ignazio Sauer"; the cbn pt is given as "ad lib" & there is no mentin of a tp pt), Lobkovic X.H.a.26; D-Rtt, Krommer 7/II, (as "Parthia", purchased from Scheffauer in Stuttgart, June, 1820); GB-Ljag, (modern score ed. John Smit, Josef Triebensee Ensemble); CZ-KRa, A3904/IV.B.67, (as "Nro 2 Parthia in B", for 2cl 2hn 2bn tp(ad lib), arranged by Havel, 1808).
Pc (nel Negozio di Ignazio Sauer: Wien, c.1803), MS parts: XX.F.4, (as "Partitta", the cbn pt is given as "ad lib" and there is no mention of a tp pt). *Other copies listed above may also be MSS from Ignaz Sauer.*
Pc (Bureau des Arts et d'Industrie: Vienne, pn 142, 1803) RISM [K 2532/iii], parts: A-Ee, Mus.1118; A-Wn, MS.9242; CZ-Bsa, fond Staré Brno, 1092/E4, CZ-Pnm, Lobkovic X.H.a.25, D-Bds; D-DT, Mus-n 588; NL-DHgm, hk 19 C 5. ★
Pc (Breitkopf & Härtel: Leipzig, 1804), parts. *Untraced: probably only advertized as Bureau des Arts agent.*
Pc (Dufaut & Dubois: Paris, pn V. D. et D. 1352, c.1826), parts, as "3ᵉ Suite": GB-Lcm, LIX.D.1; I-Bc. *With fl(C) arranged by Modrux as alternative for ob I; b/tb/serp replaces cbn.*
Pm (WINDS: Northridge, CA, pn W-167, c.1981), parts (photocopy of Bureau des Arts et d'Industrie edition).
*FVK-4. Harmonie in F, Op. 57; 4 mvts.   2ob 2cl 2hn 2bn cbn.
MS score: F-Pn, L. 3123 (4), (tb replaces cbn, MS copy associated with the Dufaut & Dubois edition, prepared by A. Loulmont for the Gymnase Musical Militaire, 1830-40s); I-Mc, Noseda 45.27; I-PAc, F-V-7, No. 1.
MS parts: D-Rtt, Krommer 8, (purchased from Scheffauer in Stuttgart, June 1820); D-RUl, RH-K. 110; CZ-KRa, A3903/IV.B.66, (as "Nro 1mo Parthia in F", for 2cl 2hn 2bn tp(ad lib), arranged by Havel, 27 July 1808).
Pc (Chemische Druckerei: Wien, pn 600, 1807), RISM [K 2533], parts: A-Wgm, VIII 17357; A-Wn, MS.9243; D-AB; D-B, DMS.197.107; D-MGmi; H-Bn, ZR 673; H-KE; I-Bl. ★
Pc (Dufaut & Dubois: Paris, pn V. D. et D. 1346, c.1826), RISM [K 2534], pts, as "4ᵉ Suite": GB-Lcm, LIX.D.1; I-Bc. *With fl(C) arranged by Modrux as alternative for ob I; b/tb/serp replaces cbn.*
Pm (Musica rara: London, pn 1264, 1971), ed. Roger Hellyer, score & parts.
Pm (WINDS: Northridge, CA, pn W-11, c.1981), parts (photocopy of the Chemische Druckerei edition).
*FVK-5. Harmonie in B[♭], Op. 67; 4 mvts.   2ob 2cl 2hn 2bn cbn.
MS score: I-Mc, (2 copies), Noseda M.45.24, No. 3, Da Camera MS. 12.1, No. 2; F-Pn, L. 3123 (5), (tb replaces cbn, MS copy associated with the Dufaut & Dubois edition, prepared by A. Loulmont for the Gymnase Musical Militaire, 1830-40s); I-PAc, F-V-7, No. 2.
MS parts: CZ-Bm(no), A.16.645, (as "No. 2 Partia in B"); D-Rtt, Sm. 13, Nos. 47 - 50 (as Anon "Sinfonie"); CZ-KRa, A3907/IV.B.70., (as "Parthia V in B", for 2cl 2hn 2bn tp(ad lib), arranged by Havel, c.1808).
Pc (as "Op. 67"): (Au Magasin de l'imprimerie chimique J. Reprio: Vienne, pn 775, 1807/1808), RISM [K 2537], parts: A-Wgm, VIII 17358; A-Wn, MS. 9243; CZ-Bm(au), A.35.173; D-AB; D-DT, Mus-n 1699, (missing 2cl); H-Bn, Z 43,623; H-KE, 2010; I-Mc; S-Skma; D-MGmi, RISM [K 2536], as "op 61"; we believe this to be a modern typographical error). ★
Pc (Dufaut & Dubois: Paris, pn V. D. et D. 1347, c.1826), parts, as "5ᵉ Suite": GB-Lcm, LIX.D.1; I-Fc. *With fl(C) arranged by Modrux as alternative for ob I; b/tb/serp replaces cbn.*
Pm (Musica rara: London, pn 1266, 1971), edited Roger Hellyer, score & parts.
Pm (WINDS: Northridge, CA, pn W-12, c.1981), parts (photocopy of the Chemische Druckerei edition).
*FVK-6. Harmonie in E♭, Op. 69; 4 mvts.   2ob 2cl 2hn 2bn cbn.
MS score: F-Pn, L. 3123 (6), (for fl in E♭, 2ob 2cl 2hn 2bn tb/b, MS copy associated with the Dufaut & Dubois edition, prepared in 1850 for the Gymnase Musical Militaire); I-Mc, Da Noseda M.45.26, (MS by Peter Lichtenthal); I-PAc, F-V-7, No. 3; I-Rsc, Governativo G.Mss.32 - 33, No. 3.
MS parts: CZ-Bm(no), A.16.649, (as "No. 3 Partia in Dis"); D-Rtt, Krommer 9, (purchased from Scheffauer in Stuttgart, June 1820); CZ-KRa, A3906/IV.B.69, (as "Parthia IVta", for 2cl 2hn 2bn tp(ad lib), arranged by Havel, 1808); I-Mc, Da Camera MS.10.6.
Pc (Au Magasin de l'imprimerie chimique I.R. priv.: Vienne, pn 877, 1808), RISM [K 2538], parts: A-Wgm; A-Wn, MS.9243; D-AB; D-B, DMS.197.108.; D-DT, Mus-n 1700, (missing 2cl); D-MGmi; H-Bn, ZR 671; H-KE, 2021, (possibly missing 2 horns); S-Skma. ★
Pc (Chemische Druckerei/Steiner: Wien, pn 877, c.1812), RISM [K 2539], parts: A-Wgm, VIII 17352 (H 26803); CZ-Bm(au), A.35.179; I-Nc; US-Wc, M957.K76 op. 69.
Pc Dufaut & Dubois: Paris, pn V. D. et D. 1348, c.1828), parts, as "6ᵉ Suite": GB-Lcm, LIX.D.1. *With fl(D♭) arranged by Modrux as alternative for ob I, b/tb/serp replaces cbn.*
Pm (Musica rara: London, pn 1256, 1970), edited Roger Hellyer, score & parts.
Pm (WINDS: Northridge, CA, pn W-13, c.1981), parts (Steiner edition photocopy, pn 877).

*FVK-7. Harmonie in E♭, Op. 71 ("La Chasse"); 4 mvts.   2ob 2cl 2hn 2bn cbn.
AutoMS score: I-Mc, Noseda Q.31.5, (owned by Peter Lichtenthal).   ★
MS score: F-Pn, L. 3123 (7), (for fl in E♭ 2ob 2cl 2hn 2bn tb/b, MS associated with the Dufaut & Dubois ed.,
made in 1850 for the Gymnase Musical Militaire); I-PAc, F-V-7, No. 4; I-Rsc, Governativo G.Mss.32 - 33, No. 4.
MS parts: A-Wn, Mus.Hs.3711, No. 3, (as "Partia", dated "[1]819"); CZ-Bm(no), A.16.645, (as "No. 2 Partia
in B"); CZ-KRa, A3914/IV.B.77, (copy by Havel, 21 March 1813); D-RUl, RH K.108.
Pc (Au Magasin de l'imprimerie chimique: Vienne, pn 999, 1808), RISM [K 2541], parts: A-M; CZ-Bm(au), (2
copies), A.35.180, A.35.253, No. 15, (mvt 1 only); D-AB; D-B, DMS.197.109; D-DT, Mus-n 1701, (missing 2cl);
D-MGmi; D-Rtt; Krommer (Druck) 5; H-Bn, ZR 633; I-Vc; S-Skma.
Pc (Dufaut & Dubois: Paris, pn V. D. et D. 1367, c.1826), parts, as "7ᵉ Suite": GB-Lcm, LIX.D.1. *With fl(D♭)
arranged by Modrux as alternative for ob I; b/tb/serp replaces cbn.*
Pm (Robert Lienau: Berlin).
Pm (WINDS: Northridge, CA, pn W-59, c.1981), pts, (photocopy of AutoMS score, & Chemische Druckerei pts).
Pm (WOODWINDplus: Leeds, UK, 1992), ed. J.W. Brown, score & parts.
*FVK-8. Harmonie in F, Op. 73; 4 mvts.   2ob 2cl 2hn 2bn cbn.
AutoMS score: F-Pn, MS. 6579. ★
MS score: I-BGc, Mayr 601, (? by J.S. Mayr); I-PAc, F-V-7, No. 5; I-Rsc, Governativo G.Mss.32 - 33, No. 5.
MS parts: A-Wn, Mus.Hs.3711, No. 1, (as "Partia in F", dated "[1]819"); CZ-Bm(au), A.35.202, (acquired 1814);
NL-DHgm, hk 19 C 2.
Pc (Au Magasin de l'imprimerie chimique: Vienne, pn 1092, 1810), RISM [K 2542], parts: D-AB; D-DT, Mus-n
1702, (missing 2cl); H-Bn, ZR 672; I-Vc; S-Skma.
Pc (Chemische Druckerei/Steiner: Wien, pn 1092, c.1812), RISM [K 2543], pts: A-Wgm, VIII 17355 (H 26804).
Pc (Bochsa père: Paris, pn 92, c.1816), parts.
Pc (Dufaut & Dubois: Paris, pn V. D. et D. 92, c.1826), parts, as "8ᵉ Suite": GB-Lcm, LIX.D.1. *With fl(C)
arranged by Modrux as alternative for ob I; b/tb/serp replaces cbn.*
Pm (WINDS: Northridge, CA, pn W-61, c.1981), parts (photocopy of the Chemische Druckerei edition).
*FVK-8.1. Parthie...opus 73 [sic] in B♭, 3 mvts.   2ob 2cl 2hn 2bn.
MS pts (by the same copyist as the D-DO and D-Rtt copies of FVK-20.1; purchased from Scheffauer in Stuttgart,
June 1820): D-Rtt, Krommer 10. *Mvts 3 & 4 of Op. 73, followed by an otherwise unknown Andante, 2/4, in C.* ★
*FVK-9. Harmonie in C, Op. 76; 4 mvts.   2ob 2cl(C) 2hn 2bn bn.
MS score: I-PAc, F-V-7, No. 6; I-Rsc, Governativo G.Mss.32 - 33, No. 6.
MS pts: A-Wn, Mus.Hs.3711, No. 2, (as "Partia in C", dated "[1]819"); CZ-KRa, A3915/IV.B.78, (by Havel, 1813).
Pc (Au Magasin de l'imprimerie chimique: Vienne, pn 1187, 1810), RISM [K 2544], parts: CZ-Pnm, XX.F.3,
(missing clarinet parts); H-Bn, Z 43,314; I-Vc; S-Skma. ★
Pc (Chemische Druckerei/Steiner: Wien, pn 1187, c.1812), RISM [K 2545], parts: A-Wgm, VIII 17354 (26805);
CZ-Bm(au), A.35.175, (missing hn I); I-Nc.
Pc (Bochsa père: Paris, pn 141, c.1816), as "2ᵉ Suite", parts: D-Rtt, Krommer (Druck) 3.
Pc (Dufaut & Dubois: Paris, pn V. D. et D. 141, c.1826), parts, as "9ᵉ Suite": GB-Lcm, LIX.D.1. *With fl(C)
arranged by Modrux as an alternative for ob I; b/tb/serp replaces bn.*
Pm (WINDS: Northridge, CA, pn W-63, c.1981), pts (photocopy of Steiner reissue).
Pm (WOODWINDplus: Louth, Lincolnshire, UK, 1994), score & pts (with alternate cl(B♭) pts; the cbn/db pt
is marked "ad lib").
*FVK-10. Harmonie in F, Op. 77; 4 mvts.   2ob 2cl 2hn 2bn cbn.
MS score: I-Mc, (2 copies), Noseda M.45.25, No. 1, Da Camera MS.12.1, No. 1; I-PAc, F-V-7, No. 7;
I-Rsc, Governativo G.Mss.32 - 33, No. 7.
Pc (Au Magasin de l'imprimerie chimique: Vienne, pn 1380, 1810), as "Oeuvre. 7[MS: 7]", RISM [K 2546], parts:
A-Wn, MS.8237; CZ-Bm(au), A.35.177; D-Rtt, Krommer (Druck) 4; H-Bn, Z 43,666; S-Skma. ★
Pc (Chemische Druckerei/Steiner: Wien, pn 1380, c.1812), RISM [K 2547], pts: A-Wgm, VIII 17351 (H 26806);
A-Wn, MS.8237; I-Nc; I-Vc.
Pc (Dufaut & Dubois: Paris, pn V. D. et D 1353, c.1826), parts, as "10ᵉ Suite": GB-Lcm, LXI.D.1. *With fl(C)
arranged by Modrux as alternative for ob I; b/tb/serp replaces cbn.*
Pm (WINDS: Northridge, CA, pn W-85, c.1981), parts (photocopy of Steiner reissue).
*FVK-11. Harmonie in B♭, Op. 78; 4 mvts.   2ob 2cl 2hn 2bn cbn.
MS score: I-Mc, Noseda M.45.25, No. 2; I-PAc, F-V-7, No. 8; I-Rsc, Governativo G.Mss.32 - 33, No. 8.
MS parts: CZ-Bm(au), A.35.174, (octet, dated 1831); CZ-KRA, A3916/IV.B.79, (copy by Havel, 24 May 1813);
I-Mc, Da Camera MS 10.6, (as "Opera 69. [added] recte 78").
Pc (Au Magasin de l'imprimerie chimique: Vienne, pn 1381, 1810/1811), as "Oeuvre. 7[MS: 8]", RISM [K 2549],
pts: A-Wn, MS.8237; CZ-Pnm, Lobkovic X.H.a.22; D-Rtt, Krommer (Druck) 6; D-RUl; H-Bn; I-Vc; S-Skma. ★
Pc (Chemische Druckerei/Steiner: Wien, pn 1381, c.1812), RISM [K 2550], parts: A-Wgm, VIII 1598 (26807);
I-Nc; I-Vc; I-Mc, Da Camera Nonetto Fiati B.9.h.75, (misattributed in RISM [K 2548]: the Op. 69 (FVK-6) plate
number is given instead).
Pc (Steiner: Wien, pn 1381, c.1812), RISM [K 2550], pts: D-RUl; I-Mc, Da Camera Nonetto Fiati B.9.h.74; I-Nc.
Pc (Dufaut & Dubois: Paris, pn V. D. et D. 1353, c.1826), parts, as "11ᵉ Suite": GB-Lcm, LXI.D.1. *With fl(C)
arranged by Modrux as an alternative for ob I; b/tb/serp replaces cbn.*
Pm (WINDS: Northridge, CA, pn W-68, c.1981), parts, (photocopy of the Chemische Druckerei/Steiner reissue).
*FVK-12. Harmonie in E♭, Op. 79; 4 mvts.   2ob 2cl 2hn 2bn cbn.
MS score: I-Mc, (2 copies), Noseda M.45.24, No. 1, Da Camera MS.12/1, No. 3; I-PAc, F-V-7, No. 9;
I-Rsc, Governativo G.Mss.32 - 33, No. 9.
MS parts: D-Rtt, Krommer 11, (purchased from Scheffauer in Stuttgart, June 1820); D-HER, Mus. C.21=2.
Pc (Au Magasin de l'imprimerie chimique: Vienne, pn 1382, 1810/1811), as "Oeuvr. 7[MS: 9]", RISM [K 2551],
parts: A-Wn, MS. 8237; CZ-Bm(au), A.35.176; CZ-Pnm, (2 copies), XX.F.2, Lobkovic X.H.a.21;
H-Bn, Z 43,640; I-Vc; S-Skma. ★
Pc (S.A. Steiner/Chemische Druckerei: Wien, pn 1382, c.1812), RISM [K 2552], parts: I-Nc.
Pc (Dufaut & Dubois: Paris, pn V. D. et D. 1350, c.1826), parts, as "12ᵉ Suite": GB-Lcm, LIX.D.1. *With fl(C)
arranged by Modrux as an alternative for ob I; b/tb/serp replaces cbn.*
Pm (Friedrich Hofmeister: Leipzig, 1962), ed. Kurt Janetzky, score (pn 7341) & parts (pn 7341a).
Pm (Musica rara: London, pn 1278, 1971), ed. Roger Hellyer, score & parts.
Pm (WINDS: Northridge, CA, pn W-70, c.1981), parts (photocopy of the Chemische Druckerei parts).

*FVK-13. Harmonie in F, Op. 83; 3 mvts.   2ob 2cl 2hn 2bn (cbn) tp. *Note: the Chemische Druckerei titlepage lists tp & omits cbn; the Steiner titlepage (reissue) lists cbn & omits tp.*
MS score: I-Mc, Noseda M.45.24, No. 2; I-PAc, F-V-7, No. 10; I-Rsc, Governativo G.Mss.32 - 33, No. 10.
MS pts: CZ-Bm(au), A.35.189; D-Rtt, Krommer 12, (purchased from Scheffauer, Stuttgart, June, 1820; cbn & tp).
Pc (Au Magasin de l'imprimerie chimique: Vienne: Wien, pn 1509, c.1811), RISM [K 2553], parts: CZ-Bm(au), A.35.181; H-Bn, Z 43,639; S-Skma. ★
Pc (Steiner: Wien, pn 1509, c.1812), RISM [K 2554], pts: A-Wgm, VIII 17356 (H 26808), (missing cbn); I-Mc.
Pc (Dufaut & Dubois: Paris, pn V. D. et D. 1395, c.1826), parts, as "13ᵉ Suite": GB-Lcm, LIX.D.1. *With fl(Db) arranged by Modrux as an alternative for ob I; b-tb/serp (divisi part) replaces cbn; includes tp pt.*
Pm (WINDS: Northridge, CA, pn W-72, c.1981), parts (photocopy of the Chemische Druckerei edition).
*FVK-14.1. Parthia in Eb; 5 mvts.   2ob 2cl 2hn 2bn.
MS parts: A-Ee, Mus.1127, (with 1st mvt pickup, as "Parthia in Eb", No. 6 of 6, "7ten May scripsit"; hn I, end: "Finis um 1794"); A-M, VI 2165; D-Rtt, Krommer 14/I, (as "Parthia"; purchased from Graf von Klenau, 1820); CZ-Bm(no), A.16.649, (as "Partia in Dis No. 3", 4 mvts); D-DO, (for 2ob cl bn, arranged by Rosinack). ★
FVK-14.2. Parthia; in Eb, 5 mvts.   2cl 2hn 2bn.   MS parts: CZ-KRa, A4451/R.I.21.
*FVK-15. Partita in Eb, 4 mvts.   2ob 2cl 2hn 2bn.
MS parts: CZ-Pnm; D-DO, Mus.Ms.1529; D-Rtt, Krommer 13/IV, (as "Nro: 11. Parthia in Dis [Eb]", scored for ob cl(III)/ob(II) 2cl 2hn 2bn; MS by Rosinack at D-DO; purchased from Scheffauer in Stuttgart, June 1820). ★
*FVK-16. Partita in Eb; 4 mvts.   2ob 2cl 2hn 2bn.
MS parts: D-DO, Mus.Ms.1160; CZ-KRa, A3910/IV.B.73, (for 2cl 2hn 2bn, as "Nro 6 Parthia in dis", arranged by Havel, c.1808). ★
*FVK-17. Partita in Eb, 4 mvts.   2ob 2cl 2hn 2bn.
MS parts: CZ-Pnm, XX.F.6.; D-DO, Mus.Ms.1159, (hn II part incomplete); D-Rtt, Krommer 13/II, (as "Nro. 8. Parthia in Dis [Eb]", scored for ob cl(III)/ob(II) 2cl 2hn 2bn; MS by Rosinack at D-DO; purchased from Scheffauer in Stuttgart, June 1820); GB-Lcm, (microfilm of CZ-Pnm copy); CZ-KRa, A3909/IV.B.72, (for 2cl 2hn 2bn, as "Partita No. 1mo in dis", arranged by Havel, 6 Aug 1808). ★
*FVK-18.1. Parthia in Eb, 4 mvts.   2ob 2cl 2hn 2bn (cbn).
MS score: I-Mc, Noseda 45.23. *A note at the bottom of f.1 states, "Manca la parte del Fagotto grande"; this has been altered to "Fagottone". A cbn part runs throughout but comprises merely rests or the instruction, "col Fag 2°". No other copy possesses a cbn part and we believe that this is a local addition.*
MS pts: CZ-Bm(no), A.16.651, (as "Partita in Dis concertans"); D-DO, Mus.Ms.1161; D-DO, (for 2ob cl bn, arranged by Rosinack). ★
*FVK-18.2. Partita in Eb, 4 mvts.   2cl 2hn 2bn.   MS parts: CZ-KRa, A4451/R.I.21, No. I. ★
This is the "lost" version cited by Jerkowitz.
*FVK-19.1. Harmonie in Es [Eb]; 3 mvts.   2ob 2cl 2hn 2bn cbn.
MS parts: CZ-Bm(au), A.35.178, (as "Harmonie in E [sic]", copy by "George Bouraiche [?Burčs], ex Hautbois an premier Régement de Ligne. Abbaye à St. Thomas ce 5 Octobre 1817"); D-DO, Mus.Ms.1162; D-DO, for 2ob cl bn, arranged by Rosinack). ★
*FVK-19.2. Parthia in Eb, 4 mvts.   2cl 2hn 2bn, (probably original in this form).
MS parts: CZ-Pnm, (2 copies), XX.F.8, (missing bn II), XLI.B.143, (missing hn II, bn I; as "N VI: Parthia in Eb"); CZ-KRa, A4451/R.I.21, No. 3, (3 mvts only: Allegro, Menuetto & Trio, Adagio); GB-Ljag, (modern MS score & parts, based on CZ-Pnm copies). ★
*FVK-20.1. Partita in Bb; 4 mvts.   2ob 2cl 2hn 2bn.
MS parts: D-DO, Mus.Ms.1530; D-DO, (for 2ob cl bn, arranged by Rosinack); D-Rtt, Krommer 14/III, (as "Barthia [sic] in b [Bb]", with an additional cl(III) vel ob(II) part; with annotations by Rosinack and another copyist at D-DO). *D-DO Mus.Ms.1530 & D-Rtt Krommer 14/III were prepared by the same copyist - who also prepared FVK-26.*
*FVK-20.2. Parthia in B[b]; 4 mvts.   2cl 2hn 2bn, (probably original in this form).
MS pts: CZ-Bm, (unverified); CZ-KRa, A4451/R.I.21, No. IV; CZ-Pnm, (2 copies), XX.F.10, XLI.B.145, (as "Nº IV. Parthia in B"). ★
*FVK-21.1. Parthia in Bb; 4 mvts.   2ob 2cl 2hn 2bn.
MS parts: GB-Ljag, (as "Nº 6 Parthia in B"); CZ-KRa, A3911/IV.B.74, (for 2cl 2hn 2bn, as "Nro 2do Parthia in B[b]", arranged by Havel, 8 Aug 1808, mvts 1, 3 & 4). *Here the 2nd mvt is an Adagio* ★
*FVK-21.2. Nro 7. Parthia in B[b]; variant of FVK-21.1, 4 mvts.   ob cl(III)/ob(II) 2cl 2hn 2bn.
MS parts: D-DO, Mus.Ms.1163; D-Rtt, Krommer 13/I, (MS pts by Rosinack at D-DO, purchased from Scheffauer in Stuttgart, 1820). *Here the 2nd mvt is an Andante con Variazione, possibly spurious.* ★
FVK-22. Partita in Bb; 4 mvts.   2ob 2cl 2hn 2bn.   MS pts: D-DO, Mus.Ms.1164; D-Rtt, Krommer 14/II, (as "Parthia. in B[b]"; purchased from Graf von Klenau, 1820). ★
*FVK-23. Partita in Eb, "La Chasse"; 5 mvts.   *(Only the 1st mvt bears this title; note FVK-7, Op. 71 is known by the same title).*   2ob 2cl 2hn 2bn.   MS parts: CZ-Bm(no), A.16.650; CZ-Bm(au), A.35.253, (with cbn, mvt 1 only, arranged by F. Starke, FRS-18a [= 1.3a]); CZ-Pnm, XX.F.9, (as "Parthia", missing the 4th mvt "Polonesse" & Trio); D-DO, Mus.Ms.1165; D-Rtt, Krommer 13/III, (as "Parthia in Dis. La Chasse", scored for ob cl(III)/ob(II) 2cl 2hn 2bn; MS by Rosinack at D-DO; purchased from Scheffauer in Stuttgart, June, 1820); D-DO, Mus.Ms.479, No. 6, (for 2ob cl bn, arranged by Rosinack). ★
Pm (WINDS: Northridge, CA, pn W-88, c.1981), parts.
Pm (Doblinger: Wien, 1989), ed. Antonín Myslík, score (hire only) & parts (Diletto musicale 982).
*FVK-24. Partita in Bb; 3 mvts.   2cl 2hn 2bn.
MS parts: CZ-Bm(no), A.16.648. *A string quintet version dated 1799 is in A-Wn.* ★
FVK-25. Parthia; in Eb, 3 mvts.   2ob 2cl 2hn 2bn, (cbn tp ad lib). MS pts: CZ-Pnm, XX.F.7, (missing bn II). ★
Modern MS score (completed by John Smit, for the Josef Triebensee Ensemble): GB-Ljag.
*FVK-26. Harmonie in E[b]; 3 mvts.   2ob 2cl 2hn 2bn.   MS parts (5 Oct 1817): CZ-Bm(au), A.35.178. ★
FVK-27. No. 4 Parthia in B[b]; 4 mvts.   2ob 2cl 2hn 2bn.
MS parts (Viennese scribal hand, probably from the firm of Ignaz Sauer): GB-Ljag.
*FVK-28. Partita in C minor; (1800), 3 mvts.   2cl 2hn 2bn.
MS parts: CZ-KRa, A4451/R.I.21, No. II; CZ-Pnm, (2 copies), XLI.B.144, (as "Parthia in C Mol No. IIIto"), XLII.F.36, No. 3, (as " Parthie"). ★
Pm (Supraphon: Prague, pn 5226, 1972), ed. Antonín Myslík, score & parts, (Musica viva historica No. 29).

*FVK-29. Parthia; in E♭, 4 mvts. 2cl 2hn 2bn.   MS parts: CZ-Pnm, XLII.F.36, No. 7, (as Anon); CZ-KRa, A3908/IV.B.71, (mvts 1 & 4 only; MS parts by Havel c.1808, as "Nro 6 Parthia in dis"; the titlepage lists the cl 1 as "Clarinet Primo Concertanto"; 2 mvts only: 1, Allegro & 4, Finale). *This is another "Lost" work incorrectly cited by Jerkowitz as "Partitta in C minor".* ★
FVK-30. Parthia; in B♭, 3 mvts.   2cl 2hn 2bn.   MS parts: CZ-Pnm, XLII.F.36, No. 10. ★
*FVK-31. Parthia in A♭.   "Clarinet concertanto", cl 2hn 2bn.
MS parts: CZ-KRa, IV.B.75. ★
Pm (Compusic: Amsterdam, pn 239, 1988), score & parts.
*FVK-32. Parthia, in E♭, 3 mvts.   2cl 2hn 2bn.   MS parts (by J.A. Buchal): PL-LA, RM 34. ★
FVK-33. Variationes.   2ob 2hn bn.   MS parts: CZ-Pnm, XLII.F.36, No. 9. ★
FVK-34. Nro IVto. Trio in F, 4 mvts.   2ob ca.   MS parts: CZ-K, No.34.K.23. ★
FVK-1s. Harmonie; in E♭, 4 mvts.   2ob 2cl 2hn 2bn.   MS parts (1836): A-M, VI 1768. *Mvt 3 of FVK-14.1, mvt 1 of FVK-14.1, unknown Romance, mvt 1 of Op. 83; this work was probably used for the Frohnleichnams-Umgang in 1836.* ★
FVK-2s. Harmonie Stücke für den Frohnleichnams-Umgang von Franz Krommer 1829. 2ob 2cl 2hn 2bn cbn tp.
MS parts: A-M, V 1189. *1. Romance of FVK-1s, mvt 3 of FVK-14.1 without upbeat, mvt 2 of Op. 45, FVK-2, mvt 2 of Op. 45, FVK-3.*
*FVK-1c. Harmonie Stücke fur des Frohnleichnams Umgänge.   2ob 2cl(C & B♭) 2hn 2bn cbn tp.
MS parts (1830): A-M, V.1189. *Adaptations, possibly by the composer.* ★
Unidentified: Partita in E♭.   2cl 2hn 2bn.   MS parts: D-Dl.

FVK-1.1a. Pleyel: 12 string quartets, dedicated to the King of Prussia, No. 8, (B.338/ii). Variazioni in F: Thema di Pleyel, [& Polonesse - possibly by Krommer].   2ob ca.
MS parts: CZ-K, No.35.K.23, No. 3.
Pm (Edition Kneusslin: Basle, 1978), ed. Antonín Myslík, parts, (Für Kenner und Liebhaber, No. 65).
Pm (Supraphon: Prague, 1979), ed. Miloslav Klement, score & parts, (Musica viva Historica 43).
FVK-1.2a. Pleyel: 12 string quartets, dedicated to the King of Prussia, No. 8, (B.338/ii). Variazioni in F: Thema di Pleyel, [& Polonesse - possibly by Krommer]].   2fl ca.   MS parts: A-Wgm, VIII 1228, No. 3.

*FVK-1ma. Haydn: Gott erhalte Franz den Kaiser, Volkslied, als Marsch für türkische Musik eingerichtet. pic(E♭) cl(Ab) 4cl(E♭) 5hn(F, 2E♭, 2F) 5tp(2E♭, D, Bb, F) 2klappen-tp 2tb b-tb basse b-dr s-dr.
Pc (Tobias Haslinger: Wien, pn 4951, 1827), RISM [K 2560], parts: A-Wgm, XVI 1331.
MS parts: (based on the Haslinger edition): A-Wgm, XVI 1331a.
*FVK-2ma. 12 Marsche.   2ob 2cl 2hn 2bn cbn.
MS parts (possibly by Ignaz Sauer, Vienna, c.1805): CZ-KRa, A3912/IV.B.76. *Krommer's name has been added to the titlepage at a later date; on internal evidence this attribution is probably correct.*
    2.1a Marcia & Trio (title illegible).   2.2a Marcia & Trio, (?Krommer), Segue No. 3.
    2.3a Anton Fischer: Svetard's Zaubergürtel (Zaubertal), (no Trio).
    2.4a Grétry (adapted Anton Fischer): Raoul Barbe-Bleu [as "Blaubart"], (no Trio).
    2.5a Mozart: La Clemenza di Tito, (no Trio).   2.6a Lasser: Der Kapellmeister, (no Trio).
    2.7a Seyfried: Cirus [in Persia], (no Trio, Minore section).
    2.8a Berton: Aline, Reine de Golconda, (no Trio, Minore section).
    2.9a. T. Weigl: Bacchus et Ariadne, (no Trio, Segue No. 10).   2.10a Winter: Maria von Montalban, (no Trio).
    2.11a. J. Weigl: Die isthmischen Spiele, (no Trio).   2.12a. Winter: Vologesus, (with Trio).
FVK-1m. Six Märsche, Op. 31; in F, E♭, C, E♭, F, E♭.   2ob 2cl 2hn 2bn cbn tp.
Pc (Bureau des Arts et d'Industrie: Vienne, pn 175, 1803), RISM [K 2531], parts: A-Wgm, XVI 1292; D-B, DMS.197.106; H-Bn, ZR 689; H-KE, K 2009. ★
Pc (Bureau des Arts et d'Industrie: Vienne, pn 161, 1803), piano reduction: A-Wgm VIII 11111 (Q 13596).
Pc ("2de edition"): (Johann André: Offenbach am Main, pn 3135, 1812), RISM [K 2530], parts: D-OF.
Note: the Bureau des Arts et d'Industrie editions do not bear an opus number.
    1.1m. Marche du Regiment Archiduc [sic] Charles [E.H. Carl]; in F.
    1.2m. Marche du Regiment Deutschmeister; in E♭.   1.3m. Marche: in C.
    1.4m. Marche du Regiment Arciduc [sic] Charles; in E♭.
    1.5m. Marche du Regiment Prince Auersperg; in F.   1.6m. Marche; in E♭.
MS parts: CZ-Pu, 59 R 3383, III, Nos. 5 & 6, (Nos. 1 & 5 only, rescored locally in E♭, for 2cl 2hn bn; No. 5 consistently replaces the original eighth note figures with dotted eighth and sixteenth notes; MS by Augustin Erasmus Hübner, Langenbruck (Dlouhý Most), 1808); PL-LA, RM 117, 118, 120, (Nos. 2, 5 & 4, rescored by J.A. Buchal, for 2cl 2hn 2bn tp); D-Rtt, Krommer 16, Nos. 1, 3 & 4, (= Nos. 6, 5 & 3; without cbn).
*FVK-2m. 3 Märsche, Op. 60; in F, E♭, E♭.   2ob 2cl 2hn 2bn cbn tp.
Pc (Chemische Druckerei: Vienna, pn 1262, 1810), RISM [K 2535], parts: E-Mam, K.846.(3); GB-Ljag, (microfilm); H-Bn, ZR 704; I-MOl; I-Nc. ★
FVK-3m. Marsch, Op. 82, in F.   2ob 2cl 2hn 2bn tp(F, with a simplified pt for tp in C if no other tp available).
Pc (chemischer Druckerey: Wien, pn 1508, c.1811), RISM Supp KK 2552a], pts: D-RUl; E-Mam, K.846.(1). ★
MS parts: CZ-Pnm, Lobkovic X.H.a.82. *See also FVK-1mc.*
The following three sets of marches, dedicated to Archduke Constantine of Russia, use the same titlepage with MS alterations. The marches, numbered 1 - 6 in pairs, were clearly a single original set.
FVK-4.1m. [2] Marsche für türkische Musik, 9[MS: 7]ᵗᵉ Werk.   2ob cl(F) cl(C) 4hn 2bn 5tp serp b-dr s-dr.
Pc (chemie Druckerey/Steiner: Wien, pn 2807, 1818), RISM Supp [KK 2555a], pts: E-Mam, K.846.(4); I-MOl; GB-Ljag, (photocopy). *"Op. 97" was also used for a fl vl vla vc quartet (Gombart: Augsburg, pn 798, c.1818).* ★
FVK-4.2m. [2] Märsche für türkische Musik, 9[MS: 8]ᵗᵉ Werk.   2ob cl(F) cl(B♭/C) 4hn 2bn 5tp serp b-dr s-dr.
Pc (chemie Druckerey/Steiner: Wien, pn 2808, 1818), parts: E-Mam, K.846.(6). ★
MS parts (copy by P.A. Osswald): CZ-Bm(au), A.19.289.
FVK-4.3m. [2] Märsche für türkische Musik, 9[MS: 9]ᵗᵉ Werk.   2ob cl(F) cl(B♭/C) 4hn 2bn 5tp serp b-dr s-dr.
Pc (chemie Druckerey/Steiner: Wien, pn 2809, 1818), parts: E-Mam, K.846.(5). ★
FVK-5m. Marsch für türkische Musik, Op. 100.   2ob cl(E♭) 2cl(B♭) 4hn 2bn cbn 4tp b-dr s-dr.
Pc (Chemische Druckerei (Haslinger): Wien, pn 2810, 1818), RISM [K 2555]), pts: A-Wgm; E-Mam, K.846.(2).
Note: "Op. 100" was also used for a set of 3 string quintets (Ricordi: Milan, c.1815; Mme Sieber: Paris, post-1822), a common type of inconsistency. ★

*FVK-6m. VI neue Regiments Harmonie-Märsche nach dem geschwinderen Tempo. 2ob 2cl(C) 2hn 2bn cbn tp.
Pc (Im Verlage der k.k. priv. chemisch: Druckerey: Wien, pn 286, c.1807), RISM [K 2559], parts:
A-Wgm, VIII 9472; CZ-Pnm, Lobkovic X.H.a.81 (missing bn II, cbn). *Note: the RISM plate number, "2860"
is a typographical error. This published work does not bear an opus number.* ★
FVK-7.1m(7.3m). VI Märsche; Nos. 2, 5 & 6, (Nos. 1, 3 & 4 are Nos. 6, 5 & 3, respectively of FVK-1m).
2ob 2cl 2hn 2bn tp. MS parts: D-Rtt, Krommer 16, (purchased from the estate of Graf von Klenau, 1820). ★
FVK-8m. March in C. 2fl 2cl(C) 2hn 2bn 2tp(clar) serp b-dr.
Pc (In **A-82.1m**: Acht Märsche für Türkische Musick [sic], 1 Heft, No. 7:) (Johann André: Offenbach, pn 1822,
1803), parts: H-KE, K 731/VIII. MS score & parts (copy of the André edition): I-Fc, F.P. S.553. ★
*FVK-1mc. Marcia; in E♭. 2ob 2cl 2hn 2bn cbn tp. MS pts: CZ-Pnm, Lobkovic X.H.a.82, verso of sheets. ★

*FVK-1d. Partita in Es (E♭), 4 mvts. 2cl 2hn 2bn.
Krommer denied authorship of this work in a notice in the Allgemeine musikaische Zeitung *in 1817.*
MS score: I-Mc, (2 copies), Noseda M.45.22, Da Camera MS.12.2, (with 2 sets of cl parts).
MS parts: D-HER, Mus. C.21=1.
Pc (C.F. Peters: Leipzig, pn 1341, 1817), RISM [K 2558], pts: CZ-Pu, (2 copies), 59 A 10438 (imprint
overpasted with printed slip, "à Bonn chez N Simrock / [MS: 3frs: 34ᶜ.]"), 59 B 7903; D-Dl;
D-Rtt, Krommer (Druck) 1; D-WEMl, (sold at Sotheby's, London, 1 Dec 1995, in Lot 192); I-Mc; S-Skma. ★
Pm (Friedrich Hofmeister: Leipzig, pn 7133, 1955), ed. Karl-Heinz Gutte, score & parts.
*FVK-2d [= Schoen, SZS-1c]. Parthia in Dis [E♭]; 3 mvts. 2 horns "Concertantto [sic]", 2ob 2cl 2bn cb/cbn.
MS parts: D-Rtt, Krommer 15, (the titlepage states, "Del Sig. Schoen"; "Kromer [sic]" has been added in pencil.
In the Gardemusik Katalog, this is item No. 34, attributed to Krommer). ★
Pm (WINDS: Northridge, CA, pn W-99, c.1981), score & parts (photocopies of modern MS score & parts).
Pm (Compusic: Amsterdam, pn 211, 1988), score & parts.
*FVK-3d. Sestetto Pastorale, 4 mvts. 2cl 2hn 2bn. MS: D-KIZklöcker, provenance unknown. *Recorded as
"Krommer" by Consortium Classicum on Claves CD 50-9004; the work is, in fact, Lickl's* Quintetto, Op. 21, *with
minor changes and an additional bassoon part; Havel also produced a version with a new bn I part.*

*The following 8 works are cataloged as "Krommer" in D-Rtt based on a note in the Regensburg Gardemusik
Katalog. The style, scoring and movement titles are unlike any other of his works. The paper (wm: IAV
WOLFEG; = Joseph Anton Vnold, Württemberg) appears to date from before 1785. The headtitle in the pts to
FVK-11d, "De Lucile" suggests that movements may be arrangements of numbers from Grétry's opera of 1779;
the parts version of this work includes three movements not found in the score. The order of the Parthien is not
the same in the MS score and parts, and "Parthia 7", FVK-11d, is not found in the score. The basset horn II
part is found separately on sheets 99 - 113 of the score.*
*FVK-4d. Partitta No. 1; in B♭, 5 mvts. 2cl 2bthn 2hn 2bn 2vla.
MS score: D-Rtt, Krommer 17/I, No. 1. MS pts (pre-1785): D-Rtt, Krommer 17/II, No. 1, (as "Parthia:No:I"). ★
*FVK-5d. Partitta No: 2; in B♭, 5 mvts. 2cl 2bthn 2hn 2bn 2vla.
MS score: D-Rtt, Krommer 17/I, No. 2. MS pts (pre-1785): D-Rtt, Krommer 17/II, No. 3, (as "Parthia:No:3"). ★
*FVK-6d. Partita:Ex b [B♭]:No:3:, 6 mvts. 2cl 2bthn 2hn 2bn 2vla.
MS score: D-Rtt, Krommer 17/I, No. 3. MS pts (pre-1785): D-Rtt, Krommer 17/II, No. 4, (as "Parthia:No:4"). ★
*FVK-7d. Partita:No:4 in B[♭]; 6 mvts. 2cl 2bthn 2hn 2bn 2vla.
MS score: D-Rtt, Krommer 17/I, No. 4. MS parts (c.1800): D-Rtt, Krommer 17/II, No. 5, (as "Parthia:No:5"). ★
*FVK-8d. Partitta No:5; in E♭, 7 mvts. 2cl 2bthn 2hn 2bn 2vla.
MS score: D-Rtt, Krommer 17/I, No. 5. MS pts (pre-1785): D-Rtt, Krommer 17/II, No. 2, (as "Parthia:No:2"). ★
*FVK-9d. Partita N:6; in B♭, 4 mvts. 2cl 2bthn 2hn 2bn 2vla.
MS score: D-Rtt, Krommer 17/I, No. 6. MS pts (pre-1785): D-Rtt, Krommer 17/II, No. 6, (as "Parthia:No:6"). ★
*FVK-10d. Partita:No:7 in B[♭]; 3 mvts. 2cl 2bthn 2hn 2bn 2vla.
MS parts: D-Rtt, Krommer 17/II, No. 8, (as "Parthia:No:8"; the cl II pt is incomplete). ★
*FVK-11d. Parthia 7, "De Lucile"; in B♭, 3 mvts (score), 6 mvts (parts). 2cl 2bthn 2hn 2bn 2vla.
MS score: D-Rtt, Krommer 17/I, No. 7. MS parts: D-Rtt, Krommer 17/II, No. 7. ★
FVK-12.1d. [Theme & 4] Variationen von Krammer [sic]; (= HAVEL, VXH-15.1ac). 2cl 2hn 2bn.
MS parts (by Václav Havel): CZ-KRa, A4466/R.I.36, "N° 39 / Arien", No. 1. *Probably arranged by Havel.* ★
FVK-12.2d. Finalle detto [sic]; (= HAVEL, VXH-15.2ac). 2cl 2hn 2bn.
MS parts (by Václav Havel): CZ-KRa, A4466/R.I.36, "N° 39 / Arien", No. 2. *Probably arranged by Havel.* ★
*Note: Works in CZ-KRa in the bound volumes in the Rudolfs Archiv (although dating from Trauttmanndorf's
tenure as Archbishop of Olomouc) must be regarded with great caution. Václav Havel, arranger and copyist,
was in the habit of giving a title to the volumes at the time the first works were copied in; subsequent works
could come from any source. The anonymous works sometimes attributed to Krommer found in CZ-KRa,
A4451/R.I.21, "Serenade / del Sig Kromer [sic] / Variazioni de Sig. Mozart", (Nos. 6, 9 - 14) are undoubtedly
spurious and may be by F.A. Hoffmeister (who composed No. 5); details are given in the ANONYMOUS WORKS
LIST: Austro-Moravia, Kroměříž. We list No. 8 below with reservations; the style suggests Krommer but no
other copies are known; it may turn out to be an arrangement by Havel of a chamber work by Krommer. All
of the works in the bound volumes, CZ-KRA, A4455/R.I.25, "XXIV Parthien del Sig. Krommer et Pleyel / N: 5"
are undoubtedly arrangements by Havel; Nos. 1, 4 & 5 may be arrangements of string (or flute & string)
quartets by Krommer; Nos. 8, 13, 14, 18 - 22 remain unidentified but do not appear stylistically to be by
Krommer. We list these works as arrangements at: HAVEL, Václav, as VXH-1ac - VXH-12ac.*
FVK-13d. [Anon: Parthia] N° 8; in B♭, 5 mvts. 2cl 2hn 2bn.
MS parts (by Havel): CZ-KRa, A4451/R.I.21, No. 8. ★
FVK-14d. Parthia 1ᵐᵒ; in E♭, 4 mvts. 2cl 2hn 2bn.
MS parts (by Havel, c.1805): CZ-KRa, A4455/R.I.25, No. 1. *Probably an arrangement by Havel.* ★

KRÜGER, Ulrich *27 Nov 1896, Graudenz*
UXK-1. Kammermusik für 7 Bläser. fl ob 2cl hn 2bn.
Pm (Hans Busch Musikförlag: Lidingö, 1981), score & parts.

KRZISH, ( ) *(1750)*
YYK-1. Parthia in C, 5 mvts. 2ob 2cl 2hn 2bn. MS parts: CZ-Pnm, Lobkovic X.H.a.29. ★

*KUBÁT, Norbert *7 July 1891, Kolín - 20 March 1966, Prague*
NYK-1. [1] "Fanfára" ku svěvení zvonů a vorhan v Doubravce, dne 19.VII.1931. [2] "Tisíckrát pozdravujeme Tebe." [3] "Ježíši, králi nebe a země." [4] "Ejhle oltář Hospodinův září."   2cl 2tp 2flug 2tb.
AutoMS score: CZ-PLa, Hu 3393.
NYK-1v. "Kantáta" k svěvení zvonů "Bartoloměje", "Marie", "Anny" v arciděkanském chrámu Páně v Plzni, 25.X.1931.   (Text by Jitty Zdeňka Honzíková.   CATB, fl 2cl 2hn 3tp 3tb timp.
AutoMS score, 2 piano reductions & CATB parts: CZ-PLa, Hu 3502.

*KUBÍČEK (Kubitschek), Adalbert *1776, Hodětín, nr Tábor - 26 Jan 1838, Brno*
These works may be drawn from the composer's dance collections - possibly arranged by the composer. Other arranged sets can be found in the Arrangements List.
VYK-1. [Intro & 7] Ländler.   pic 2fl cl(F) 3cl(C) 4hn(F, C) 2bn cbn 3tp(G, C, C) tb b-dr tri s-dr.
MS parts ("Comp. und übersetzt auf die Türkische Musik von Ad. Kubitschek 1821"): CZ-Bm(au), A.19.294.   ★
VYK-2. [7] Deutsche [with Coda] für Türkische Musik.   Incomplete, here only: 2pic(C, G) fl cl(II, A) cl(III, C) 2tp(G, G) 2tp(A basso) tb b-tb s-dr.   MS parts (1823): CZ-Bm(au), A.35.182.   ★
VYK-3. Partitta, in B♭, 2 mvts.   2cl(B♭) 2hn 2bn cbn tp(prin).   MS parts: CZ-Bm(au), A.20.825.   ★
VYK-4, 5. [Intro & 3] Redout Deutsche, [and 3] Milioner Valzer [?based on Carafa's work].
Incomplete, here only: cl(E♭) 2tp(No. 4: E♭, No. 5: B♭).   MS parts (c.1825): CZ-Bm(au), A.35.273.   ★

*KUČERA (Kuchera), ( ) *(?1820)*
YYK-1. Polonese für Türkische Mussik [sic].   2pic(C, G) cl(F) 3cl(C) 2cl(B♭) 3hn(C, F, F) 2bn 3tp(C, C, F) b-tb b-dr s-dr.   MS parts: CZ-Bm(au), A.19.296.   ★
YYK-2. No. 5 Ländler für Musica Turca.   pic 2cl 2hn cimbasso+bn(II) 4tp(2 keyed, 2 without keys) 2tb.
MS parts: I-OS, Mss.Musiche B 2243, (with duplicate cl II pt; possibly missing bn I).   *With a printed decorated sheet used for the titlepage, "Si vende in Verona presso Vincenzo Priori".*   ★

KUCHARZ, Lawrence W.
LWK-1. "1977 #3".   2fl 2ob 2cl 2hn 2bn.   Pm (American Composers Alliance: New York, 1977).
LWK-2. "1977 #11".   2ob 2cl 2hn 2bn.   Pm (American Composers Alliance: New York, 1977).

*KÜFFNER, Joseph (Josef) *31 March 1776, Würzburg - 9 Sept 1856, Würzburg*
MGG cites "20 volumes" of works for 6, 8, 9 and 12 winds [fantasias, marches, overtures and variations in manuscript] in D-Bds; D-Dl; D-Mbs; D-SWl. We have not been able to confirm these items - except to state that there are no manuscript wind works in D-Mbs or D-SWl.
JYK-1. Musique Militaire, Pantomime, Walses et Danses bavaroises, Op. 170; 9 mvts.
pic 2cl(E♭) 3cl(B♭) 4hn 2bn 2tp 2sig-hn(keyed) 2tb serp b-dr t-dr.
Pc (Chez les fils de B Schott: Mayence, pn 2445, 1826), parts: D-B, DMS.85.394; D-DT, Mus-n 1718; D-MZsch; GB-Ljag(w), L/265.8, (missing perc parts).   ★
Pc (Johann André: Offenbach am Main, sd), parts, (as "Potpourri pour Musique Militaire").
JYK-2. Trois Polonaises, Musique Militaire, Op. 235.   pic(E♭) 2cl(E♭) 3cl(B♭) 4hn 2bn 2tp 2tb serp b-dr t-dr.
Pc (Schott: Mainz, Paris, pn 3467, 1830), parts: D-B; D-MZsch.   ★
JYK-3. Musique Militaire Contenant La Polonaise du Général Uminsky, une Walse et cinq Galoppades, Op. 237.
fl(F, E♭) 2cl(E♭) 3cl(B♭) 4hn 2bn 3tp 2tb serp b-dr t-dr.
Pc (Les Fils de B. Schott: Mayence, Paris et Anvers, pn 3562, 1831), pts: D-B; D-DT, Mus-n 1709; D-MZsch.   ★
JYK-4. Sept Pièces d'Harmonie.   fl 2ob 2cl(C) 2hn 2bn cbn.   MS score & parts: I-Fc, F.P. S.473.   ★
*JYK-5. 6 Pièces [sic] d'harmonie, Oeuvre 205.   fl(F) 2cl 2hn 2bn.
Pc (chez les fils de B. Schott: Mayence; A. Schott: Anvers, pn 2980, 1828), parts: A-Wgm, VIII 9148; D-MZsch; F-Pn, Vm27 2288.   ★
   5.1(a). F.P. Schubert: Original-Tänze, Op. 9, No. 2 (here misattributed as "Beethoven: Le Désir Walse").
   5.2a. Küffner: Walse [& Trio].
   5.3(a). C.M. von Weber: Aufforderung zum Tanze, Op. 65, [L'Invitation á la Danse], Walse [& 2 Trios].
   5.4. Küffner: Walse [& Trio].   5.5. Küffner: Galoppe.   5.6. Küffner: Galoppe.
JYK-6.1, 6.2, 6.3. Pièces d'harmonie, Op. 40.   Liv. 1, 2: fl 2cl hn bn; Liv. 3 (1 long mvt): fl cl bthn hn bn.
MS parts (CZ-Pnm, V.C.427, (No. 3 only as "Quintet").   ★
Pc (Schott frères: Mayence et Paris, pn 848, 849, 1815), parts: CH-Zz, Mus. 114 & a-d, (Liv. 3 only); D-B; D-DT, Mus-n 1168, (Liv. 3 only); D-MZsch; GB-Ljag(w), L.69, (Liv. 1, missing bn); S-Skma.   ★
   6.1/1(a). J. Weigl: Die Schweizerfamilie, "Setz dich liebe Emeline".
   6.1/2(a). J. Weigl: Die Schweizerfamilie, "Wenn sie mich nur von weitem sieht".
   6.1/3. Küffner: Andante [B♭].   6.1/4(a). Méhel: Joseph, Romance "Ich war Jüngling noch an Jahren".
   6.1/5. Küffner: Adagio/Andante [E♭] & Allegro with 5 Variations [B♭].   6.1/6. Küffner: Allemande [C minor].
JYK-7. Pièces d'harmonie, Op. 92, (4me Cahier d'harmonie); 4 mvts.   fl 2cl hn bn.
Pc (Schott frères: Mayence et Paris, pn 1537, c.1822), parts: D-B; D-HR, HR III 4 1/2 2° 390, (missing fl).   ★
Pm (KGS), fiche (2371).
JYK-8. Pièces d'harmonie, 108tes Werk; in F.   fl(F) 2cl(E♭) 3/5cl(B♭; I & II divisi) 4hn 2bn 2tp b-tb serp b-dr s-dr.
Pc (bey Johann André: Offenbach a/m, pn 4460, 1822/1823), parts: D-DT, Mus-n 597.   *An arr. by the composer of his Overture, Op. 74.*   ★
JYK-9. Musique Militiare, Ouverture [in F], Op. 160 [altered in ink to 164].
fl(F) 2cl(E♭) 3cl(B♭) 4hn 2bn 2tp signal-hn(ad lib) 3tb serp b-dr t-dr.
Pc (chez B. Schott Fils: Mayence, pn 2257, 1825), pts: D-DT, Mus-n 598.   *An arr. by the composer of his Overture, Op. 74.*   ★
JYK-10. Musique Militaire, Ouverture [in F], Op. 161.   pic(E♭) 2cl(Eb) 3cl(Bb) 4hn 2bn 2tb serp b-dr t-dr.
Pc (Schott frères: Mayence et Paris, pn 2304, 1825), parts: B-Bc, (MS pts); D-B; D-DT, Mus-n 1712; D-MZsch; GB-Ljag(w), 265.7, (missing perc pts).   *An arr. by the composer of his Overture, Op. 130.*   ★
*JYK-11. Musique Militaire, Sinfonie, Op. 163; 4 mvts.   pic 2cl(Eb) 3cl(Bb) 4hn 2bn 2tp 2tb serp b-dr t-dr.
Pc (chez les fils de B. Schott: Mayence, pn 2315, 1825/26), pts: A-Wgm, XVI 17368; D-B; D-DT, Mus-n 599; D-MZsch; GB-Ljag(w), 265.6, (missing perc pts).   *An arr. by the composer of his Symphony No. 4, Op. 141.*   ★

JYK-12(-26). Musique turque, 15 Requeils.
MS parts: D-Bds, Mus.Ms.22065, (Pas redoublé; ?incomplete, scored for pic 2cl bn tp serp). *We have not been able to verify or match this particular mvt.*
JYK-12. Musique Turque, Recueil 1.　pic 2cl(E♭) 2cl(B♭) 2hn 2bn 2tp b-tb serp b-dr t-dr.
Pc (André: Offenbach, pn 3251, 1812/13), parts: D-OF.
JYK-13. Musique Turque, Recueil 2; 11 mvts.　pic 2cl(E♭) 2cl(B♭) 2hn 2bn 2tp b-tb serp b-dr t-dr.
Pc (Jean André: Offenbach, pn 3509, 1815/16), parts: D-OF; GB-Ljag(w), 265.4.　MS parts: D-Tl, Z 85. ★
JYK-14. Musique Turque, Recueil 3; 7 mvts.　pic 2cl(E♭) 2cl(B♭) 2hn 2bn 2tp b-tb serp b-dr t-dr carillon(ad lib).
Pc (André: Offenbach, pn 3510, 1815/16), pts: D-OF; GB-jag(w), 265.3, (missing perc & ad lib carillon pts). ★
JYK-15. Musique Turque, Recueil 4.　pic 2cl(E♭) 2cl(B♭) 2hn 2bn 2tp b-tb serp b-dr t-dr.
Pc (André: Offenbach, pn 3481, 1815), parts: D-OF.
JYK-16. Musique Turque, Recueil 5.　pic 2cl(E♭) 2cl(B♭) 2hn 2bn 2tp b-tb serp b-dr t-dr.
Pc (André: Offenbach, pn 3541, 1816), parts: D-OF.
JYK-17. Musique Turque, Recueil 6.　pic 2cl(E♭) 2cl(B♭) 2hn 2bn 2tp b-tb serp b-dr t-dr.
Pc (André: Offenbach, pn 3542, 1816), parts: D-OF.
JYK-18. Musique Turque, Recueil 7, 5 mvts.　2pic 2cl(E♭) 2cl(B♭) 2hn 2bn 2tp 2b-tb serp b-dr t-dr.
Pc (chez Jean André: Offenbach s/m, pn 3543, 1816), parts: D-OF; D-Rtt, Küffner (Druck) 1, (with modern MS parts for flute in C = transposed pic I, & b-tb). *The bass trombones are only divisi in No. 4.* ★
JYK-19. Musique Turque, Recueil 8.　pic 2cl(E♭) 2cl(B♭) 2hn 2bn 2tp b-tb serp b-dr t-dr.
Pc (André: Offenbach, pn 3544,·1816), parts: D-OF
JYK-20. Musique Turque, Recueil 9; 7 mvts.　pic 2cl(E♭) 2cl(B♭) 2hn 2bn 2tp b-tb serp b-dr s-dr.
Pc (André: Offenbach, pn 3508, 1816), parts: D-OF.
Pc (Schott: Mainz, pn 835, 1816), parts, (as "Recueil 1" or "Cah: 9"): D-DT, Mus-n 594, (missing titlepage). ★
MS score: I-Ria, Ms.313.
JYK-21. Musique Turque, Recueil 10.　pic 2cl(E♭) 2cl(B♭) 2hn 2bn 2tp b-tb serp b-dr t-dr.
Pc (André: Offenbach, pn 3509, 1816), parts: D-OF.
Pc (Schott: Mainz, pn 836, 1816), parts, (as "Recueil 2"): D-MZsch.
MS score: I-Ria, Ms.350.
JYK-22. Musique Turque, Recueil 11.　pic 2cl(E♭) 2cl(B♭) 2hn 2bn 2tp b-tb serp b-dr t-dr.
Pc (André: Offenbach, pn 3547, 1816), parts: D-OF.　MS score: I-Ria, Ms.350.
JYK-23. Musique Turque, Recueil 12.　pic 2cl(E♭) 2cl(B♭) 2hn 2bn 2tp b-tb serp b-dr t-dr.
Pc (André: Offenbach, pn 3550, 1816), parts: D-OF.　MS score: I-Ria, Ms.350
JYK-24. Musique Turque, Recueil 13; 9 mvts.　fl(E♭) 2cl(E♭) 2cl(B♭) 2hn 2bn 2tp b-tb serp b-dr t-dr.
Pc (André: Offenbach, pn 3510, 1816), parts: D-OF.　MS score: I-Ria, Ms.350.
Pc (Schott: Mainz, pn 940, 1817), parts: D-DT, Mus-n 1711.　MS score: I-Ria, Ms.350. ★
JYK-25. Musique Turque, Recueil 14.　pic 2cl(E♭) 2cl(B♭) 2hn 2bn 2tp b-tb serp b-dr t-dr.
Pc (André: Offenbach, pn 3746, 1818), parts: D-OF.
JYK-26. Musique Turque, Recueil 15, 6 mvts.
pic 2cl(Eb) 2cl(B♭) 2hn 2bn tp(E♭), 2cor de postillon/tp(A♭), tb serp b-dr t-dr.
Pc (chez Jean André: Offenbach s/M, pn 3773, 1818), parts: US-BETm, Philharmonic Society of Bethlehem PSB L-20. ★
JYK-27. Musique militaire contenant trois pièces favorites[:] ein Geschwind=Marsch und zwey Jubel=Ländler, Op. 146.　pic 2cl(B♭) 3cl(B♭) 4hn 2bn 3tp 2sg-hn 2tb serp b-dr t-dr.
MS score: I-Ria, Ms.274.
Pc (Schott: Mainz, pn 2077, 1824), parts: D-B; D-MZsch.
JYK-28. Pot-Pourri No.1 [&] No. 2, Op. 109.　fl(E♭) 2cl(E♭) 2cl(B♭) 2hn 2bn 2tp(clar, 2E♭, A♭/B♭ alto) serp.
Pc (André: Offenbach a/M, pn 4461, 1822/1823), parts: D-DT, Mus-n 1714. ★
JYK-29. Quatrième Potpourry [sic], Op. 102.　pic 2cl(E♭) 2cl(B♭) 2hn 2bn 2tp posthorn 2tb serp b-dr t-dr.
Pc (chez B. Schott Fils: Mayence, pn 1582, 1821), parts: D-B; D-DT, Mus-n 1716. ★
JYK-30. [5] Variationen aus der Thema: Beste Mutter, mein Herz ist offen.
pic(Eb) 2cl(E♭) 3cl(B♭) 2hn 2bn 2tp b-tb serp b-hn b-dr s-dr.　MS parts: D-DT, Mus-n 1723, No. 1. ★
JYK-31. [5] Schweizer Walzer mit Introduction und Coda zur Feyer des Rigi Festes, Op. 268.　fl(F) 2cl hn bn.
Pc (les fils de B. Schott: Mayence , Paris et Anvers, pn 4583, 1835), parts: D-Mbs, 4 Mus.pr. 23401. ★
JYK-32. Harm[onie] v[on] Küffner; 6 mvts, (WoO).　fl 2ob clf(?) 2cl(C) 2hn 2bn b-tb basso.
MS pts: GB-Ljag(w), 121A, (missing ob I; with a fl(D) pt to replace fl in C & a cl in B♭ II to replace cl in C). ★
JYK-1m. Trois Marches et quatre Pas-redoublés, Oeuv. 188.
fl(E♭) 2cl(E♭) 3cl(B♭) 4hn 2bn 2/3tp signal-horn(keyed) 2tb serp b-dr t-dr.
Pc (le Fils de B. Schott: Mayence, pn 2485, 1826), parts: D-Bds, DMS.85.397; D-DT, Mus-n 1707; D-MZsch. ★
JYK-2m. Drey Duplir Märsche [= Pas Redoublés], Op. 51.
pic(E♭) 2cl(E♭) 2cl(B♭) 3hn 2bn 2tp 2posthorn b-tb serp b-dr.
Pc (Mainz: Schott, pn 965, c.1817), parts: D-B. ★
*JYK-3m. Sechs Duplir Märsche, Op. 61.　pic(E♭) 2cl(E♭) 2cl(B♭) 4hn 2bn 2tp 2posthorn b-tb serp b-dr.
Pc (Schott: Mainz, pn 1086, 1818), parts: D-B; D-Mmb. ★
JYK-4m. Trois Grandes Marches, Oe. 207. fl(E♭) 2cl(E♭) 3cl(B♭) 2hn 2bn 2tp 2tb serp b-dr t-dr (2hn tp ad lib).
Pc (le Fils de B. Schott: Mayence, pn 3039, 1828), parts: D-DT, Mus-n 1708; D-MZsch. ★
JYK-5m. Tuerkische Musik. Drey grosse Parade=Maersche. pic 2cl(Eb) 2cl(B♭) 2hn 2bn 2tp b-tb serp b-dr s-dr.
Pc (bei Joh. André: Offenbach a/m, pn 3490, 1815/1816), parts: D-DT, Mus-n 1713. ★
JYK-1a. Pottpourri [sic; based on music by Auber & "Bethofen", K.-H.Anh.14].
pic(E♭, terz-fl) cl(E♭) 3cl(B♭) 4hn(Eb, A♭) 2bn 2tp a-tb t-tb b-tb serp b-dr s-dr.　MS parts: D-Tl, Z 24. ★
JYK-2a. Grand Valse, Op. 232, (quotes Auber's "La Parisienne" and Rouget de Lisle's "La Marseillaise").
Military band.　Pc (Schott: Mainz, sd, c.1831), parts: D-MZsch.
*JYK-3a. Pièces d'Harmonie, Op. 138, Liv. 1: 4 mvts, Liv. 2: 3 mvts (includes pieces from Rossini's *Otello* and Weber's *Preciosa*).　fl 2cl 2hn 2bn.
Pc (Schott frères: Mainz, Paris, pn 1985, 1823), parts: A-Wgm, VIII 4, (Liv. 1); D-B; D-RUl, (Liv. 1); D-MZsch; D-SPlb.

JYK-4a. Auber: Le Concert à la Cour, as "Potpourri sir des Thêmes favoris de l'opéra Le Concert de la Cour",
Op. 182". fl(F) 2cl 2hn 2bn.
Pc (Schott: Mainz, pn 2431, 1826), parts: D-B, DMS.85.368); D-MZsch; D-RUl.
JYK-5a. Auber: Fiorella, (overture & airs), Op. 208.   fl 2cl 2hn 2bn.
Pc (Schott: Mainz, c.1826), parts: D-B, DMS.85.363; D-MZsch.
JYK-6a. [Potpourri, including Theme & 5 variations on an Allegretto from Auber's opera, *La Muette de Portici]*.
fl(F) cl(Eb) 2cl(Bb) 2hn bn 2tp b-tb serp.   MS score: GB-Ljag(w), 337.
JYK-7a. Auber: La Muette de Portici, La Guarache, Air de Ballet, Oeuv. 218.
p-fl(Eb) 2cl(Eb) 3cl(Bb) 4hn 2bn 3tp(2Eb, 1Bb alto) 2tb serp b-dr t-dr.
Pc (Chez les Fils de B. Schott: Mayence, pn 3168, 1829), parts: D-DT, Mus-n 595; D-MZsch.
JYK-8a. Auber: La Muette di Portici, "Bolero", as Op. 29. Military band. (Scoring probably similar to JYK-7a.)
Pc (Chez les Fils de B. Schott: Mayence, c.1828), parts: D-B, DMS.85.399; D-MZsch.
JYK-9a. Auber: Fra Diavolo, overture. pic(Eb) fl(F) cl(Eb) 3cl(Bb) 4hn 3tp(2Eb, 1Bb), (ad lib: 2bn a-tb *and/or*
2tb b-hn("Russe") serp timp tri b-dr t-dr.
Pc (Chez les fils de B. Schott: Mayence et Anvers; E. Troupenas: Paris, pn 3314, 1831), parts: GB-Ljag(w), 155.
JYK-10a. Benedict: The Gipsy's Warning; WoO 8.   Musique militaire.
Pc (Schott: Mainz, pn 5462, 1839), parts: D-MZsch.
JYK-11a. Ries: Grande Ouverture et Marche triomphale pour la Fête Musicale de Cologne, Op. 172.
Military band.   Pc (Schott: Mainz, post-1820), parts: D-MZsch.
JYK-12a. Roser: Johann von Wieselburg, as "Potpourri musical"; WoO 7.
2fl 2cl(Eb) 3cl(Bb) 4hn 2bn 2tp 2sig-hn 2tb serp b-dr t-dr.
Pc (Schott: Mainz, pn 1711, 1822), parts: D-MZsch.
JYK-13a. Rossini: Corradino [Matilda di Shabran] & Mosé [in Egitto] as "Potpourri, Op. 183". fl 2cl 2hn 2bn.
Pc (Schott: Mainz, c.1818), parts: D-B, DMS.85.368; D-MZsch.
JYK-14.1a. [Rossini: Otello], Fünftes Pot-Pourri, Opus 110; (headtitle: V Potpourry di Ottello [sic]).
1/2pic(Eb, F)(fl F) 2cl(Eb) 3cl(Bb) 2hn 2bn 3tp(2Eb, 1Bb alto) 2tb serp b-dr t-dr.
Pc (in der Grossh: Hess Hofmusikhandlung v. B. Schott Söhne: Mainz, pn 1689, c.1823), pts: D-DT, Mus-n 1717.
JYK-14.2a. Pot pourri Militaire en Harmonie Complette Tiré de l'Opéra d'Otello de Rossini...Œuv. no [blank].
pic(Eb) 2cl(Eb) 3cl(Bb) 2hn 2bn 2tp(clar, Eb) tp(Bb alto) 2tb serp b-dr t-dr.
Pc (Chez Richault: Paris, pn 674 R, c.1824), pts: CH-Gpu, Ib 4836.
JYK-15a. Rossini: Tancredi, as "Troisième Potpourry [sic]", Op. 101; 5 mvts.
pic 2cl(Eb) 2cl(Bb) 2hn 2bn 2tp posthorn 2tb serp b-dr t-dr.
Pc (Schott fils: Mayence, pn 1581, 1821), pts: D-B; D-DT, Mus-n 1715; GB-Ljag(w), 265.5, (missing perc pts). ★
Pc (Richault: Paris, post-1821), parts: B-Bc.
JYK-16a. VIIᵗᵉˢ Potpourri, Op. 126; (d'opéras de Rossini), 6 mvts.
2pic 2cl(Eb) 3cl(Bb) 4hn 2bn 2tp 2sig-hn b-tb serp b-dr t-dr.
Pc (chez B. Schott Fils: Mayence, pn 1928, 1823), parts: D-B; D-DT, Mus-n 1718; D-MZsch.
JYK-17a. VIIIᵐᵉ Pot-pourri tiré de l'Opéra der Freischütz, Op. 132; 5 mvts.
p-fl(Eb) fl(F) 2cl(Eb) 3cl(Bb) 4hn 2bn 3tp(2F, Bb basso) 2signal-hn(à clefs, Eb) 2tb serp b-dr t-dr.
Pc (chez B. Schott Fils: Mayence, pn 1954, 1823), parts: D-B, D-DT, Mus-n 1719.
JYK-18.1a. Weber: IX Pot Pourri [Der Freischütz].
2fl(F, Eb) 2cl(Eb) 3cl(Bb) 2hn 2bn 2tp 2signal-hn(à clefs) 2tb b-dr t-dr.
Pc (Schott: Mainz, pn 1978, 1824), parts: D-DT, Mus-n 1720, (missing titlepage, bn I, 2tp signal-hn I, b-dr t-dr).
JYK-18.2a. Harmonie Complette ou Pot Pourri Militaire de l'Opéra de Robin des Bois, Œuv. [MS: 134. 3ᵉ Suite].
2fl(F) 2cl(Eb) 3cl(Bb) 4hn(2Bb,2Eb) 2bn 3tp(Eb, F, Bb basso/"corno à signal à clefs en Sib") 2tb serp b-dr t-dr.
Pc: (Richault: Paris, pn 1139, 1825), parts: CH-Gpu, Ib.4837., (headtitle: "9.ᵉ pot-pourri de J. Kuffner. Oe. 134").
JYK-19a. Weber: Der Freischütz, 5 Stücke.   fl cl bthn 2hn bn.
Pc (B. Schott Fils: Mayence: c.1821), parts: D-MZsch; US-BETm, Philh. Soc of Bethlehem 1365.6.
JYK-20a. Dixieme [sic] Pot=Pourri tiré de l'opéra Euryanthe de C.M. de Weber, Oeuv. 153.
fl(F, pic Eb) 2cl(Eb) 3cl(Bb - all divisi) 4hn 2bn 4tp 2tb serp b-dr t-dr.
Pc (chez B. Schott Fils: Mayence, pn 2242, 1824), parts: D-DT, Mus-n 1721.
JYK-21a. Potpourri (de thèmes favoris) No. 11, Op. 169.
2cl(Eb) 3cl(Bb) 4hn 2bn 2tp(F) tp(Ab)/posthorn 2signal-horn 2tb serp b-dr t-dr.
Pc (Schott, Mainz, pn 2422, 1826), parts: D-B, DMS.85.393; D-DT, Mus-n 1722, (missing titlepage); D-MZsch.
JYK-1ad. Weber: Euryanthe.   fl 2cl 2hn 2bn.   Pc (Schott: Mainz), pts: D-MZsch.

KÜHN, ( )   *(most unlikely that this is Joseph Karl Kühn, born 1803)*
QQK-1. [Carousel Rondo] Harmonie, nebst einem Carousel Ruf für die Trompete.   2ob 2cl 2hn bn(I) cbn.
MS parts: H-KE, 760/VIII. ★

KUIPER, Klaus *1956, Holland*
KQK-1. Tentakel.   2fl 2ob 2cl 2hn 2bn.   Pm (Donemus: Amsterdam, 1982), score.

*KULAK, J. *(1770), copyist & member of the are Harmonie at Łańcut, Poland*
JQK-1ad. J Weigl: Die Athenienische Tänzerin, overture & 9 mvts.   2cl 2hn 2bn.
MS parts: PL-LA, RM 47, (wrongly cataloged as Sedlak; the MS bears the inscription "Acomodato [sic] J. Kulak.
Wien den Mai...[sic] [1]804". However, the arrangement closely resembles anonymous versions in CZ-KRa and
CZ-Pnm, so Kulak's claim must be taken with great caution. It may be a reduction of P. Mašek's nonet arr.).

KULESHA, Gary *1954, Canada*
GRK-1. Chamber Concerto No. 3; 1981.   fl 2ob 2cl 2hn 2bn.   MS score: C-Tcm.

*KULKA, Ignác (Ignaz) *(?1800)*
*Other anonymous works at CZ-TRB are signed by Kulka; we have not been able to determine whether he was
the composer, arranger or copyist and list these in the Anonymous Works List: Austro-Bohemia: Ceská Třebová.*
IQK-1. Verschiedene Stücke für eine 6stimmige Harmonie; 6 mvts.   fl(G) 2cl(C) 2hn bn.
AutoMS parts: CZ-TRB, H 496. ★

*KUNERTH, Johann (Jan) Leopold *27 Dec 1784, Hucová - 8 Aug 1865, Kroměříž.*
JLK-1v. [3 Mass mvts], Gloria [in F]; Graduale [in B♭, "Sicut in holocaustis arietum"]; Offertorium [in B♭, "Domine in auxilium"]. T solo, SATB chorus, 2cl 2hn 2bn tp a-tb t-tb b-tb vc(2) db organ.
MS parts: CZ-KRsm, UHM A.1175/Br.C-269. ★
JLK-2v. Gloria in excelsis. Tenor solo, SATB chorus, 2cl 2hn 2flug 2tb vc organ.
MS parts: CZ-KRsm, UHM Br.C-701.
JLK-3v. Die 4 Evangelien zur Fronleichnamsfeier, 1854. SATB, 2fl 2cl 2tp 2flug bomb. MS parts: CZ-KRa.
JLK-4v. 4 Stationen. SATB, 2cl 2hn bn 2tp. MS parts: CZ-KRa.
JLK-5v. Die 4 Evangelien zur Fronleichnamsfeier. SATB, 2cl 3tp flug bomb. MS parts: CZ-KRa.

KUNTZE, Carl *17 May 1817, Trier - 7 Sept 1883, Delitzsch*
CZK-1v. Voms Fels zum Meer. T solo, SATB chorus, military band. MS: D-Bds, Hausbibliothek (?lost).
CZK-2v. Herr, bleib' bei uns, Op. 300. Male chorus, fl cl 2hn 2tp tp tu 2t-hn, piano.
MS: D-DS, Mus.1627, (?lost in World War II).

*KUNTZEN, Adolph Karl *22 Sept 1720, Wittemberg - 11 Nov 1781, Ludwigslust*
ACK-1.1m. Marsch No. 4 Mit Hobo [sic] ex Dis [E♭]. 2ob 2hn bn 2tp(clar).
MS score: D-SWl, Mus. 3284, No. 4. ★
ACK-1.2m. Marsch No. 5 Mit Hobo [sic] ex D# [D major]. 2ob 2hn bn.
MS score: D-SWl, Mus. 3284, No. 5. ★
ACK-1.3m. Marsch No. 6 Mit Hobo [sic] ex Dis [E♭]. 2ob 2hn bn 2tp(clar).
MS score: D-SWl, Mus. 3284, No. 6. ★
ACK-2m. Marsch. 2ob 2hn bn tp. MS score: D-SWl, Mus. 3283. ★

KUNZ, Konrad *30 Dec 1812, Schwanndorf - 3 Aug 1875, Munich*
KYK-1v. Reiterlied (zu Wallersteins Lager), [an extra mvt composed for Destouches' opera, *Wallersteins Lager]*.
TTB, pic 2cl 2hn 2bn tp (2)tb s-dr. MS score (1868): D-Mbs, St.th.643. ★

KUNZEN, Friedrich Ludwig Aemilius *24 Sept 1761, Lübeck - 28 Jan 1817, Copenhagen*
FLK-1v. Chorale, "O Jesu Christ, Guda Salvede". Solo voice, 2ob 2cl 2hn 2bn 2tp 3tb.
AutoMS score (c.1790 - 1800): DK-Kk, Mu. 6506.1138. ★

KUNZER, ( )
ZXK-1. 6 Deutsche Tänze. Winds. MS parts: D-DO, (?lost).

KUPKOVIČ, Ladislav Karol *1936, (now Slovakia; currently resident in Germany)*
LKK-1. Tower Music. fl ob cl 2hn bn 2tp tb tu.
Pm (Alexander Broude Brothers Ltd: Williamstown, MA, USA).
LKK-2. Serenade; 1981. 2fl 2ob 2cl 2hn 2bn 2tp. In MS: D-DSim can assist in contacting the composer.
LKK-3. Octet in D Major; 1986. 2ob 2cl 2hn 2bn. In MS: D-DSim can assist in contacting the composer.

*KURKA, Robert *22 Dec 1921, Cicero, Illinois - 12 Dec 1957, New York*
RYK-1. The Good Soldier Schweik: (**RYK-1.1** Suite (after the opera), Op 22. **RYK-1.2.** Polka and Waltz).
pic fl ob ca cl b-cl 3hn bn cbn/db 2tp tb timp s-dr.
Pm (Eugene Weintraub: New York, 1958), score (RYK-1.2: pn WB11006) & hire parts.

KURTZ, ( ) & SCHILHA, ( )
XSK-1v. IV Statio in F Pro Corporis Christi. CATB, 2cl 2hn basso (flug vla organ).
MS parts: CZ-Bm(kj), A.40.102, (with additional, later parts for flug vla organ). *From the titlepage attribution, "Authore Kurtz et Schilha", it is impossible to assign particular pieces to either composer.* ★

KURTZ, Arthur Digby *1929, USA*
ATK-1. Small Suite. 2fl 2ob cl 2hn bn. MS score: US-Wc.

KURZ, Siegfried *18 July 1930, Dresden*
SYK-1. Sonatina for orchestra, Op. 35. 2fl 2ob 2cl 2hn 2bn 2tp timp perc.
Pm (Tetra Music: Fort Lauderdale, Florida, 1969), score.

*KURZWEIL (Kurtzweil), Franz *(1770) - 1806 (?Vienna)*
FZK-1d (formerly FZK-7) was attributed to Kurzweil by earlier researchers; the style and structure do not agree with FZK-1(-6) and this work is undoubtedly by Hoffmeister.
FZK-1(-6). Partita No. 1 [-6]; (E♭; B♭; B♭; E♭; B♭; E♭, each of 4 mvts). 2ob 2cl 2hn 2bn.
MS parts: D-DO, Mus.Ms.767; A-Wgm, VIII 39991, (No. 1, attributed to Rosetti, as "in E♭ Partia"). ★
FZK-1d. [= Hoffmeister. FAH-1.1]. Parthia; in E♭, 3 mvts. 2ob 2cl 2hn 2bn.
MS parts: D-DO, Mus.Ms.767, No. 7; CZ-KRa, A3283/IV.B.45, (as Hoffmeister); NL-Z, 1215, No. 1, (as Hoffmeister); D-RUl, RH. R.93, (as Rosetti). ★

*KUTTICH, Franz *(1800)*
FWK-1a. Pergler: Polka. fl 2ob 2cl 2hn 2bn cbn 2tp tb. MS pts: CZ-Bm(au), A.36.928.
FWK-1ad. Wolfram: Schloss Candra, overture. 2ob 2cl 2hn 2bn cbn 2tp.
MS parts (copy by Kuttich, c.1835): CZ-Bm(au), A.40.169, (missing cl I, hn II). (= A-623a)

*KVANDAL, Johann *8 Sept 1919, Oslo*
JHK-1. Octet, in G (Dorian mode), Op. 54; 1946 (revised as "Nonet No. 1", 1980). 2ob 2cl 2hn 2bn db.
Pm (Norsk Musikforlag: Oslo, c.1980). *The db was originally ad lib in the 1946 version.*
*JHK-2. Night Music, Op. 57, 1981 ("Nonet No. 2"). 2ob 2cl 2hn 2bn db.
Pm (Norsk Musikforlag: Oslo, c.1981).

*KYPTA, Jan *30 Nov 1813, Borotín, nr Tábor - 5 April 1868, Telč*
There are a number of fragmentary sets (in parts) from Telč, CZ-Bm(te); some may be for winds alone.
JPK-1v. Pangelingua [sic]. SATB, 2fl 2cl 2hn bn organ. MS pts: CZ-Bm(te), A.1468. ★

*L., Sig[no]re
YYB-1. [6] Variazioni in B(♭). Solo cl, 3bthn. MS parts: CZ-Pnm, XLII.E.228. ★

*LABLER, František Xaver Martin *11 Nov 1805, Unhošť - 15 Nov 1851, Prague*
*FML-1v. IV Stationen in Solennitatem Corporis Christi.
CATB, 2fl 2cl 2hn bn(I ad lib) bn(II oblig: vel organo, with bc-fig) 2tp(clar) tp(prin) timp.
Pc (Auth: Franc: Labler: sl, sd), parts: CZ-BR, sign. 379; CZ-Lla, No. 2593 hud., (from Cvikov, with a pencil
note, "Zwickau"); CZ-Pnm, XI.F.183, (4 copies: (1) from Příbram; (2) "pro choro Horzicensÿ", Hořice, near
Hradec Králové; (3) from Plzeň, "Ecclesia S. Bartholomai, Inv. Nro 7, missing CATB, bn II/organo pts, with
additional MS pts for fl ("finis 30/5 [1]872") & flug(C) ("4/6 [1]860"); (4) provenance unknown, with MS
alterations of the texts of the Responses & MS pts: cl(C) I, hn I & II, 2 sets of tp I & II); CZ-PLa, (2 copies),
Hu 4627, (Václav Mentberg collection, Březnice), Hu 3840, (from Břetislav, with MS vocal pts by P.V. Picka,
1871). ★
MS parts: CZ-Pnm, (2 copies), XL.E.268; XLIII.F.13.
FML-2.1v, 2.2v. Asperges me et Vidi aquam in B[♭].   CATB, 2cl 2hn bn organ(bc).
MS parts (by J.J. Wagner, post-1830): CZ-NYc, DU 197. ★

*LABURA, Jiří *3 April 1931, Sobělav*
JRL-1. Ottetto per stromenti a fiato.   2ob 2cl 2hn 2bn.
Pm (Český hudební fond: Prague, 1987), hire score & parts.

*LACHNER, Franz *2 April 1803, Rain am Lech - 29 Jan 1890, Munich*
*FXL-1. Octet [B♭], Op. 156; 1850, 4 mvts.   fl ob 2cl 2hn 2bn.
Pc (Kistner: Leipzig, 1872), score (pn 3843) & parts (pn 3844): D-Bhm, Ms. 5692; GB-Lbl, e.66.b;
I-Mc, Da Camera A.63.19. ★
Pm (Musica rara: London, Ms.M.R.1263, 1970), score & parts.
FXL-1v. Hornesklange, 1876.   Male chorus, 4hn bn tp.   MS score: D-Mbs, Mus.Mss.6073.

*LACHNER, Ignaz *11 Sept 1807, Rain am Lech - 24 Feb 1895, Hanover*
*IQL-1v. Messe; in F.   SATB solo & chorus & organ, (2fl 2cl 2hn ad lib).
Pc (Verlagshundlung Zum Haydn: Stuttgart, 1844), parts: D-Tl, (4 copies), B 275, (Ochenhausen; with MS
Canto-ripieno & vlne pts), C 061, (Weingarten), G 104, (Gutenzell), N 67, (Obermarchtal), C-C 29, (Bad
Waldsee).   MS parts (by Mittermayr): A-KR, C 29/869. ★

LADERMAN, Ezra *29 June 1924, Brooklyn, NY*
EXL-1. Octet for Winds, 1957.   2ob 2cl 2hn 2bn.
Pm (Oxford University Press: London, 1971), score.

*LAHOTKA, Gábor *(1960)*
GYL-1. Suite Hongoise; 5 mvts.   2ob ca 2bn.   MS score & parts: F-TOep.

LÁLO, Aleksander *1948*
ALL-1. Albanian Folk Dances.   2fl 2ob 2cl 2bn.
Pm (Emerson Edition: Ampleforth, pn E248, 1995), score & parts.

*LAMAN, Wim (Willem Fredrik) *1946, Netherlands*
*WIL-1 Musica Subitilor.   Solo viola (amplified), 2ob 3cl bthn 2a-sax 2hn 2bn 2tp 2tb perc.
Pm (Donemus: Amsterdam, 1976).

*LAMPE, Walther *28 April 1872, Leipzig - 23 Jan 1964, Munich*
*WXL-1. Serenade, Op. 7; 4 mvts.   2fl 2ob ca 2cl b-cl 4hn 2bn cbn.
Pc: (Simrock: Berlin; for the British Empire, Alfred Lengnick: London, pn 11964, c.1895), score:
A-Wgm, VIII 30768 (H 25489); D-Mbs. ★

LAMPERINI, ( )
XXL-1. Kyrie.   TTB(solo+rip), 2cl 2hn tp (vlne) timp organ.
MS score & parts: I-Vsmc, (with full organ pt; the vlne does not appear in the score). ★

LANCEN, Serge Jean Mathieu *1922, France*
SJL-1. Talaut!   2fl ob ca 2cl 2hn 2bn 2tp perc vl db hpcd.
Pm (Editions Française de Musique, now Billaudot: Paris: 1969).

LANG, ( )
XZL-1. Partita de la Musica di Turca degli Tutti Stromenti utili; 5 mvts (including Contradanse and Eccoisse
[sic]).   2pic fl cl(F) 2cl(C) 2hn bn tp timp("Grand Timpano").   MS pts: CZ-Pnm, Lobkovic X.H.a.71. ★

*LANGE, Gustav Friedrich *22 Feb 1861, Fredrikshald - 1889*
GFL-1. Nonett in F; 4 mvts.   fl 2ob 2cl 2hn 2bn.
Pc (Seeling [now Erdmann]: Dresden, pn 6606 (score), 7305 (parts), 1879), score & parts:
A-Wgm, VIII 28210 (Q 16338), (score); D-Bhm, 6606, (score & parts); GB-Lbbc, Cm 363, (score). ★
Pm (Compusic: Amsterdam, pn 212, 1988), score & parts.
GFL-2. Pastoral-Quartett.   2ob ca/cl bn.
Pc (Seeling (now Erdmann): Dresden, 1880), score & parts.
Pm (Compusic: Amsterdam, pn 510, c.1994), score & parts (with the clarinet option).
GFL-1a. Auber: Fra Diavolo, overture.   2cl bn.   MS parts: A-Wgm, VIII 35509.

LANGER, Hans-Klaus *1903 - 1987, Germany*
HKL-1. Ouverture für 11 Holzbläser.   2pic fl ob ca cl(E♭) cl(B♭) b-cl 2bn cbn.
Pm (Astoria Verlag: Berlin).

*LANGLÉ (L'Anglé), Honoré François Marie *1741, Monaco - 20 Sept 1807, Villiers le bel, nr Paris*
HFL-1v. Hymne à l'Éternel; P.56.   Solo voice, 2cl 2hn 2bn.
Pc (Rec des époques: Paris, c.1799), liv. 1, No. 24, pp. 62 - 65, parts: F-Pn, H2. 15,24. ★

LANGLEY, James *1927, UK*
JCL-1. Sinfonia; 1967.   2fl 2ob 2cl 2hn 2bn.   MS score: GB-Lmic.

LANNER, Alois Václav (Wenzel) *(1810)*
AVL-1tm. Trauer Marsch [& Trio]; in C minor.   cl(E♭) 2cl(B♭) bn 2tp bomb("Basspombardo").
MS parts: CZ-TRB, H 70.   ★

LANNOY, Heinrich Edouard Josef, *Freiherr* von   *3 Dec 1787, Brussels - 28 March 1853, Vienna*
HEL-1. 6 Morceaux, Op. 7.   2cl 2hn 2bn.   MS parts: A-Gk(h).

LANTIER, Paul *1944, France*
PL-1. Fugue Jazz; 1944.   2cl 2sax bn tp tb perc.
Pm (self-published: Paris, post-1944).

LANZ, Engelbert *(1830)*
EYL-1v. Er naht im leichten Tanz der Horen.   TTBB, 2cl 2hn 2bn.   AutoMS score: A-Sca, Hs.693.   ★
EYL-2v. Franz-Josef Lied . . . 1887 das Alterhochsten Namensfestes Seiner Majestät des Kaisers Franz Josef.
SATB, 2fl 2cl 4hn 2tp a-tb t-tb b-tb oph tu.   MS score: A-Wn, Mus.Hs.21832, (incomplete, bars 1 - 5 only;
with a printed program of the event).   ★

LARSEN, Libby (Elizabeth) Brown *24 Dec 1950, Wilmington, Delaware, USA*
LBL-1. Love & Hisses.   2fl 2ob 2cl 2hn 2bn.   In MS.

*****LARSSON, Håkan** *7 Nov 1959, Sweden*
HZL-1. Oktett; 1993.   fl cl 2bn 2tp 2tb.   MS score: S-Sic.

LASALLE, E.
EQL-1m. Marsch; in C.   terz-fl 2cl(C) 2bthn 2hn 2bn cbn.   MS parts: D-F, Mus.Ms.1174.   ★

*****LAUBE, Antonín** *13 Nov 17ì8, Most - 24 Feb 1784, Hradčany, Prague*
AXL-1. Nro 1. Parthia in Dis [E♭]; 4 mvts.   2ob 2hn 2bn.   MS parts: CZ-Pnm, XXII.D.190.   ★
AXL-2. Nro 2. Parthia Ex D## [D major]; 5 mvts.   2ob 2hn 2bn.
MS parts: CZ-Pnm, (2 copies), XXII.D.191, XLII.E.58 (as "Nº 4 in D. Barthia [sic]").   ★
AXL-3. Nro 3. Parthia in D## [D major]; 5 mvts.   2ob 2hn 2bn.   MS parts: CZ-Pnm, XXII.D.192.   ★
AXL-4. Nro 4. Parthia in A### [A major]; 5 mvts.   2ob 2hn 2bn.
MS parts: CZ-Pnm, XXII.D.193, (missing hn I).   ★
AXL-5. Nro 5. Parthia Ex F; 5 mvts.   2ob 2hn 2bn.   MS parts: CZ-Pnm, XXII.D.194.   ★
AXL-6. Nro 6. Parthia in F; 5 mvts.   2ob 2hn 2bn.   MS parts: CZ-Pnm, XXII.D.195.   ★
AXL-7. Nro 7. Parthia Ex G# [i.e. G major]; 5 mvts.   2ob 2hn 2bn.   MS parts: CZ-Pnm, XXII.D.196.   ★
AXL-8. Nro 8. Parthia Ex D##; 5 mvts.   2ob 2hn 2bn.
MS parts: CZ-Pnm, (2 copies), XXII.D.197, XXII.E.61/50, (as an anonymous "Parthia in D").   ★
AXL-9. Nro 9. Parthia in C; 5 mvts.   2ob 2hn 2bn.   MS parts: CZ-Pnm, XXII.D.198.   ★
AXL-10. No. 2 in C. Barthia [sic]; 5 mvts.   2ob 2hn 2bn.   MZ parts: CZ-Pnm, XLII.E.59.   ★
AXL-11. No. 3 in D. Barthia [sic]; 5 mvts.   2ob 2hn 2bn.   MS parts: CZ-Pnm, XLII.E.89.   ★

LAURISCHKUS, Max *18 Feb 1876, Insterburg, Prussian Lithuania - 11 Nov 1929, Berlin*
MXL-1. Suite.   fl ob ca cl 2hn 2bn.
Pc (Simrock: Berlin, sd), score & parts.

*****LAWTON, D.** *(1760)*
DXL-1m. The Leeds Volunteers' March.   2cl 2hn bn.
Pc (Printed and Sold for the Author by Longman and Broderip: London, 1794), RISM [L 1176], score: GB-Gu;
GB-Lbl, g.133.(35); GB-Ob, Mus.Instr.156(2).   ★

*****LAZZARI, Joseph Sylvio** *30 Dec 1857, Bozen - 18 June 1944, Paris*
JSL-1. Octuor, Op. 20; 3 mvts, (dedicated to Taffanel).   fl ob ca cl 2hn 2bn.
AutoMS score (1889): F-Pn, MS. 9412.   ★
Pc (Evette & Schaeffer: Paris, pn E.S.867, 1920), score & parts: F-Pn, K. 650; US-Wc.
Pm (Compusic: Amsterdam, pn 269, c.1994), score & parts.

*****LEACH, Thomas** *(1770), Organist of Cheshunt, Herts.*
TXL-1m. The Hatfield Royal Review, A Full Military Piece.   2cl 2hn bn tp.
Pc (Printed for the Author by Thos. Jones & D. Corri: London, 1801), score: GB-Lbl, h.61.h.(10).   *(For other
music for this Review, see: Bridgeman).*   ★

LEEUW, Reinbert de
RDL-1. Hymns and chorals, with a commentary on the music of Eric Satie.
Group 1: 2cl 2sax 2hn 2tp 2tb, Group 2: 2e-gtr e-org tape, Group 3: 2ob cl 2b-cl.
Pm (Donemus: Amsterdam, 1970), score.

LEEUWEN, Are van *25 May 1873, Arnhem, Netherlands - 1953*
AVL-1. 4 Miniatures.   2cl 2bn.
Pm (Albert J. Andraud: Cincinnati (now Southern Music Co.: San Antonio, Texas), score & parts.

LEFÈBVRE, Charles Édouard *19 June 1843, Paris - 8 Sept 1917 Aix-les-Bains*
CEL-1. Intermezzo scherzando, after the String Quartet Op. 80.   fl ob 2cl hn bn.
Pc (A. Noël: Paris, 1898), score & parts: F-Pn, Vm20 50; US-Wc.   ★
CEL-2. Suite No. 2, Op. 122.   fl ob 2cl hn bn.
Pc (Evette et Schaeffer: Paris, 1910), score & parts: F-Pn, Vm15 152.   ★
Pm (Albert J. Andraud: Cincinnati (now Southern Music Co.: San Antonio, Texas), score & parts.

*****LEFÈVRE, Jean Xavier** *6 March 1763, Lausanne - 9 Nov 1829, Paris*
JXL-1. Ouverture; P.2323.   ob/p-fl 2cl 2hn 2bn serp buccin, tuba corva, cb.
MS pts: F-Pn, [old shelfmark: musique d'harmonie paquet 22; missing some parts; ?lost].   ★
JXL-1m(-12m). Recueil de [6] Marches & [6] Pas redoublés; P.2258-2269; (also includes Gossec, FJG-3mv).
2fl(D) 2cl(C) 2hn (2)bn bn(III)+serp tp b-dr+cym; (2bn unison except 2 bars in JXL-9m; the bn(III)+serp is
exactly the same as the parts for 2bn).
Pc (Imbault: Paris, pn 388, c.1792), parts: F-Pn, Vm7 7100.   ★

JXL-13m. Marche militaire; in F, P.2289.   2p-fl 2cl 2hn 2bn tp tb serp timp.
Pc (Mag de mus fêtes nat: Paris, floréal an II, 1794), liv. 2, No. 3, pts: F-Pn, H2. 2, Vm7 7027.   ★
Pm (Swanzy), pp. 270 - 272, score.
JXL-14m. Pas de manoeuvre; P.2290.   2p-fl 2cl 2hn 2bn tp tb serp.
AutoMS score: MS. 1465.   ★
Pc (Mag de mus fêtes nat: Paris, floréal an II, 1794), liv 2, No. 4, parts: F-Pn, (2 copies), H2.2, Vm7 7028.   ★
Pm (Swanzy), pp. 273 - 277, score.
JXL-1mv. Hymne à l'Agriculture; P.119.   Solo voice, SATB chorus, 2fl 2cl 2hn 2bn 2tp 3tb serp.
AutoMS score: F-Pn, H2. 19.   MS score & parts: F-Pn, H2. 109 a-o.   ★

*LE FLEMING, Christopher *26 Feb 1908, Wimborne (UK) - 19 June 1985, Woodbury (UK)*
*CLF-1. Homage to Beatrix Potter; [piano version: Op 6], 6 mvts.   fl ob 2cl bn.
Pm (J. & W. Chester: London, pn CH00383, 1971), score (pn JWC 467) & parts (pn JWC 467a).

LEGRAND, Robert
RXL-1. Symphonie maritime.   2fl 2ob 2cl 4hn 2bn 2tp 3tb cbn timp perc harp.
Pc (Editions Salabert: Paris, sd), parts.

*LEGRAND (Le Grand), Wilhelm (Guillaume) *5 March 1770, Zweibrücken - 1845, (?Munich)*
*WYL-1.1 (1.549). [549] Pièces d'Harmonie Arrangée [sic] par Guillaume Legrand; (part books in bound volumes). Nos. 1 - 70/71, 144, 147, 148, 245 - 249: 2ob 2cl 2hn 2bn; Nos. 71 *bis*: fl ob/fl 2cl 2hn 2bn; (fl III, ob III, bn III ad lib).   MS parts: D-Mbs, Mus.Mss.2316.   *Because of numbering irregularities, we retain the original numbers: Vol. 1 ends with No. 400 and Vol. 2 incorrectly begins with No. 400 (to avoid confusion we refer to these mvts below as "400/1" & "400/2"); Nos. 533 & 534 in the 2nd Vol. have not been used. Virtually all of the works in Vol. 1 are unidentified; many of the dances may, in fact, be original compositions by Legrand. A separate volume of ad lib parts comprises flute III (Nos. 1, 2, 4, 6, 8, 10, 12 - 14, 16, 20, 21, 23 - 25, 27, 29, 37, 38, 40, 61 - 63, 68, 70, 82, 84 - 102, 104 - 110, 123, 137, 129, 130, 139, 141 - 143, 150, 151, 153, 164, 167, 174, 180, 187, 204, 212, 235, 237, 239 - 243 (No. 242 is only lined out; no music is present), 247, 260; Nos. 103 & 262 are marked "Flauti" but only one part is present; No. 261 is marked "Echo Flauti / Oboe / Clarin[etti] / Corni F / Fagat [sic]" - all are, however, single parts; Nos. 535 - 550 comprise parts for Fagotto III. To minimise confusion we list first all unidentified Nos., then identified arrangements in alphabetical order by composer; where more than one No. is from a single work, they are listed together.*

Band 1.   1. Largo, 3/4, B♭ / non troppo Allegro, C, E♭.   2. Menuett alleg[re]tto, (& Trio), 3/4, both E♭.
   3. Poco adagio, 3/4, F.   4. Allemande (& Trio), 3/8, both B♭.   5. Allegro, ¢, F, (a long mvt).
6. Allemande, 3/4, E♭.   7. Larghetto, 2/4, E♭.   8. Allemande (& Trio), 3/4, both B♭.
9. Andante, C, F / Allo, C, F.   10. Allemande, 3/4, B♭.   11. Andantino, 6/8, E♭.
12. Allemande (& Trio), 3/4, both B♭.   13. Larghetto, 2/4, E♭.   14. Allemande (& Trio), 3/4, both B♭.
15. Allegretto, 6/8, F.   16. Allemande (& Trio), 3/8, both B♭.   17. Andante, ¢, E♭ / Allo, 3/4, E♭.
18. Allemande, 3/4, B♭.   19. Allegro, 6/8, F.   20. Chasse Allegro, 6/8, D.
21. Alleg[re]tto mod[era]to gratioso, 2/4, D.   22. Andantino, 3/4, F.
23. Allemande (& Trio), 3/4, both F. (In the Trio, bars 13 & 24 are marked "Flauti", bars 16 & 29, "Oboe").
24. Allegretto, ¢, B♭ (& Trio, E♭).   25. Allemande, 3/8, B♭ (& Trio, E♭).   26. Rondo Moderato, 2/4, B♭.
27. Allemande, 3/8, B♭ (& Trio, F).   28. Rondo Moderato, 2/4, F (& Coda).
29. Anglaise, 2/4, B♭ (& Trio, F).   30. Allegro, 2/4, B♭ / Adagio, 3/4, B♭ / Allegro, 2/4, B♭ [reprise].
31. Allegretto Allemande, 3/4, E♭ / Andantino, 6/8, E♭.   32. Allemande (& Trio), 3/8, both B♭.
33. Allemande (& Trio), 3/8, both E♭.   34. Allemande (& Trio), 3/4, both E♭.
38. Allemande, 3/8, F (& Trio, C).   39. [no tempo - ?Allemande], 3/4, B♭ (& Trio, E♭).
40. [no tempo - ?Allemande], 3/8, B♭ (& Trio, E♭).   41. Alleg[re]tto, 2/4, B♭.   42. Allem[an]de, 3/8, B♭.
43. Allegretto, 6/8, B♭.   44. And[an]te, ¢, F / Tempo di March [sic], ¢, F.
45. Larghetto ["Andante" crossed out], 6/8, E♭.   46. Allo, 3/8, B♭.   47. Andante, 6/8, E♭.   48. Allo, 3/8, E♭.
49. Larghetto, 3/4, E♭.   50. Allemande, 3/8, B♭.   51. And[an]te, 3/8, E♭.   52. Allem[an]de Mod[era]to, 3/8, E♭.
53. And[an]te, 3/4, F.   54. Andantino, 2/4, B♭.
55. And[an]te, ¢, F, (bars 3 - 5 & 7 - 9 of ob II marked "Clar[inett]").   56. And[an]te, 2/4, E♭.
57. Gratioso, 3/8, E♭.   58. All[e]g[re]tto, ¢, B♭.   59. All[e]g[re]tto, 3/4, E♭.
60. All[e]g[re]tto, 6/8, B♭, (ob II part marked "Flauto").   61. Andante Romance, C, B♭.
62. Allegro con Molto, 2/4, F.   63. Andantino, 6/8, F.   64. Allegretto, 2/4, E♭.
65. Andante, 6/8, G minor, (ob II: sections 1 & 3 marked "Flauti"; section 2, "Oboe").
66. Allegro, 2/4, E♭.   67. Andantino, 6/8, F.   68. Allegretto, 6/8, F.
69. Allegro Moderato Concertant, 2/4, F, (ob pt: "Solo"; a long bravura piece, 258 bars).
70. Allem[an]de, 3/8, E♭, (ob II, second section: "Flauti").
71. Alleg[re]tto Variationi, 6/8, G. (Theme & 5 variations; ob II, Variation 4 marked "Flauti [sic] Secondo").
72. Andante Variatione, 2/4, F.   73. Allem[an]de Mod[era]to, 3/4, B♭ (& Trio, F).
74. Andante [Theme & Variations] / Adagio / Allegro / Tempo Primo [with Minore & Majore]; all 2/4, G.
75. Andantino, 2/4, C, (with a bravura ob part).   76. Allo Concertante, ¢, F, (with Cadenza Andante).
77. Romance, 3/4m C.   78. Grazioso, 2/4, F.   79. Allemande, 3/8, F.   80. Allem[an]de, 3/8, C.
81. Adagio, 3/4, E♭ / Allo, ¢, E♭.   82. Allem[an]de, 3/8, B♭.   83. Allegro, 6/8, E♭.   84. All[e]g[re]tto, 3/4, E♭.
85. March, ¢, E♭.   86. Alleg[re]tto, ¢, E♭.   87. Allo Mod[era]to, C, F / Allo, C, F.   88. Allegro, 2/4, F.
90. Allegro, ¢ / Andante, 3/4 / Allo, ¢; all E♭.   91. Allegretto, 6/8, D.   92. Allem[ande], 3/8, G (& Trio, D).
93. Allegretto, 2/4, D, (& Trio, G).   94. Allem[ande]:, 3/8, G, (& Trio, D).
95. Maestoso, C / Allo, C / Tempo 1mo; all E♭.   96. Allegro Mod[era]to, C, E♭.   97. Alleg[re]tto, 2/4, E♭.
98. Allo Maestoso, C, F / March, 2/4, F.   99. Allo Mod[era]to, C, F / Andante, 3/4 / Tempo 1 mo; all B♭.
100. And[an]tino, C, G.   102. Allo, ¢, C.   103. Allo molto, ¢, C.   104. Allem[an]de (& Trio), 3/8, both F.
105. Andante, 2/4, B♭.   106. And[an]tino, 6/8, E♭, (& [Trio], A♭).
107. Romance Andante, 6/8, C / Polonaise, 3/4, C.   109. Alleg[re]tto, 2/4, D.
110. And[an]tino, C, D / Allegro, 6/8.   111. Alleg[re]tto Mod[era]to, 3/4, E♭.   112. March, C, E♭.
113. Allem[an]de, 3/8, F.   114. Allem[an]de, 3/8, B♭, (& Trio, E♭).   115. Allem[an]de, 3/8, F, (& Trio, B♭).
116. Allem[an]de (& Trio), 3/8, both F.   117. Allem[an]de, 3/8, F.   118. Allem[an]de, 3/8, B♭.

119. Allo Assai, 2/4, B♭. 120. Polonaise, 3/4, C. 121. Polonaise, 3/4, C. 122. March, C, D.
123. Allo, ¢, E♭. 124. Andante, 2/4, B♭ / Allo, 6/8, B♭. 125. Presto, 2/4, B♭.
126. All[e]g[re]tto, 6/8, D. 128. And[an]te, 6/8, B♭. 129. March, C, E♭. 130. Alleg[re]tto, 2/4, G.
131. All[e]g[re]tto, C, G / Allo, 3/8, G. 132. Allem[an]de, 3/4, D. 133. Polonaise, 3/4, C.
134. Allegro, C, C. 135. Larghetto, 2/4, G. 136. Allegro Molto, 2/4, C.
137. Allegro non tropo [sic], C, G. 138. Allegretto, 2/4, C.
139. [unidentified] Sinfonia, Allegro, C, E♭. *It is possible that Nos. 140 -149 are also from the same (?)opera.*
140. Larghetto, 3/4, E♭ / Alleg[re]tto, 2/4, E♭. 141. Polonaise, 3/4, E♭. 142. March, ¢, E♭.
143. March, ¢, E♭. 144. [unidentified] Cavatina, Alleg[re]tto, 3/4, E♭. 145. Allegro, 2/4, E♭.
146. And[an]te, 2/4, E♭. 147. Allegro Molto, ¢, C; (lead part marked, "Oboe Primo et Flauti").
148. La chasse Royale, 6/8, F / Menuetto grazioso, 3/4, F; (lead part marked, "Oboe").
149. Allegretto, C, F. 150. Allem[an]de, 3/4, C. 151. Allem[an]de, 3/8, C. 152. Chasse, 6/8, E♭.
153. Allem[an]de, 3/8, E♭. 154. Cont[re]d[a]n[c]e, 6/8, D, (& Coda). 155. Polonaise (& Trio), 3/4, D.
156. Allem[an]de, 3/8, D. 157. [no tempo - ?Allemande], 3/8, D. 158. Allem[an]de, 3/8, G.
159. Alleg[re]tto, 2/4, D, (& Coda). 160. Alleg[re]tto, 6/8, G. 161. Allo, C, D. 162. March, ¢, D.
163. March, ¢, G. 164. Allegro Meastoso, C, G / Allo, C, F. 165. And[an]tino, 3/4, F, (& Trio, B♭).
166. Allo, 2/4, F. 167. March, C, D; (lead pt marked, "Flauti[,] Oboe"). 168. March, C, D.
169. Alleg[re]tto, 6/8, F. 170. Allegro Assai, 2/4, C. 171. Polonaise, 3/4, C / Alleg[re]tto, 3/4, C.
172. Polonaise, 3/4, D. 173. Allo, 2/4, D. 174. Polonaise, 3/4, C. 175. Andantino, 3/4, B♭.
176. March, ¢, C. 177. Allegro, ¢, C. 178. Allegro, C, C. 179. Allegro, 6/8, F. 180. Maestoso, 2/4, F.
181. Allegro, 6/8, G. 182. Allegro, C, G. 183. Allo Assai, 3/4, G. 184. Alleg[re]tto, 3/4, F.
185. March, C, D. 186. March, C, D. 187. March, ¢, D. 188. Allo Mod[era]to, 2/4, D. 189. March, ¢, G.
190. Allem[an]de, 3/8, D. 191. Allegro, ¢, D. 192. Allegro, ¢, D. 193. Allegro, 6/8, D.
194. Alleg[re]tto, 6/8, E♭. 196. Allem[an]de, 3/8, F. 197. Allem[ande]., 3/4, F, (& Trio, C).
198. Allem[ande]., 3/4, F, (& Trio, C). 199. Allem[ande]., 3/4, D, (& Trio, G).
200. Contreda[n]z (& Trio), 2/4, both D. 201. March, ¢, D. 202. Tempo March [sic], C, D.
203. Allegro, ¢, D. 204. March, ¢, D. 205. Allem[an]de, 3/4, D, (& Trio, G). 206. Allegro, C, E♭.
207. Allegro, ¢, D. 208. ["Modto", crossed out] Allegro, 3/4, G. 209. Allegro (& Coda), 2/4, D.
210. Men[uetto]:, 3/4, G, (& Trio, D). 211. March, C, D. 212. Allem[an]de, 3/8, G.
213. Alleg[re]tto, 2/4, D. 214. Andantino, 6/8, C. 216. Allem[ande: mod[erato], 3/8, B♭.
217. Andante, 2/4, C. 218. And[an]tino, 2/4, C. 219. Allo, ¢, G / And[an]te, 2/4, D, (& Da Capo).
220. March, 2/4, G, (& Trio, D). 221. All[egre]tto, 2/4, C. 222. Allo mod[erato], C, C.
223. Romance, 2/4, G. 224. And[an]tino, 2/4, G. 225. Allem[ande]:, 3/8, C. 227. Allem[ande], 3/8, F.
228. [no tempo - ?Allemande], 3/8, G. 229. [no tempo - ?Allemande], 3/8, F.
230. [no tempo - ?Allemande], 3/8, G. 231. [no tempo - ?Allemande], 3/8, C.
232. [no tempo -?Allemande], 3/4, G. 233. Alleg[re]tto, G / Ländler, G. 236. And[an]tino, 3/4, F.
237. Alleg[re]tto non troppo, 2/4, C. 238. Maestoso, ¢, F / And[an]te, ¢, F / Allo, ¢, F.
239. And[an]tino, 6/8, F, (& Trio, B♭). 240. Rondo Alleg[re]tto, F, (& Trio, C) & Coda.
242. And[an]te, 6/8, B♭ / più moto / Allegro, 6/8, B♭. 243. And[an]te, ¢, C.
244. Concertant. Oboe Solo, Allegro Mod[er]ato, C, F. 245. Adagio, 3/4, F. 246. Rondo, 6/8, F.
   It is possible that the Nos. 244 - 246 comprise a single work.
250. Allemand[e], 3/8, F, (& Trio, B♭). 251. Allem[an]de, 3/8, G, (& Trio, C).
252. Allem[an]de (& Trio), 3/8, both C. 253. Allem[an]de (& Trio), 3/8, both C.
254. Allem[an]de (& Trio), 3/8, both C. 255. Allem[an]de (& Trio), 3/8, both C.
256. Allem[an]de, 3/8, F, (& Trio, C). 257. Allem[an]de, 3/8, B♭, (& Trio, F).
258. Allem[an]de, 3/8, F. 259. Allem[an]de, 3/8, C. 260. Ecossais [sic], 2/4, C.
261. Allem[an]te [Echo], 2/4, F. fl ob cl hn bn, (fl ob cl hn bn echo).
262. Largo, 3/8 / Allo, 3/8 / Largo, 3/8 / Allo, 3/8 / Largo, 3/8 / Allem[an]d[e], 3/8; all mvts in C.
263. And[an]te, 6/8, E♭. 264. And[an]te Sostenuto, 6/8 / Tempo Polonaise, 3/4; both in F.
265. Allegretto, ¢, E♭. 266. Tempo Marche, C, C. 267. And[an]te, 2/4, G / Allo risoluto, C, G.
268. Marche, ¢, D. 269. Allegro agitato, C, B♭. 270. Alleg[re]tto, 2/4, F. 271. Larghetto, 2/4, C.
272. Polonaiss [sic], 3/4, B♭. 273. And[an]te, ¢, D / Alleg[re]tto, ¢, D / Allo, 6/8, D.
274. Polonaiss [sic], 3/4, D. 275. Allo molto, ¢, D. 276. Allem[an]de, 3/4, F.
277. Allo, C, C. 278. Polonaiss [sic], 3/4, F / Allo, ¢, C / Allo assai, ¢, C.
279. Allegro, C / Allo, 6/8 / Andante, C / Allo, C; all in E♭. 280. Alleg[re]tto, 3/4, C / Alleg[re]tto, 6/8, C.
281. Contred[an]ce (& 2 Trio), 6/8, all in B♭. 282. Allem[ande]., 3/8, F.
283. Allem[ande (& Trio), 3/4, both F. 284. Allegro vivace, ¢, F. 285. Allegretto, 6/8, B♭.
286. Allegro, 2/4, B♭. 287. Allegro, ¢ / And[an]tino, ¢ / Allo, ¢ / And[an]tino, ¢ / Allo, ¢; all in B♭.
288. Allegro, C, B♭ / Allegretto, 6/8, B♭. 289. Allegretto Mo[era]to, 2/4, F. 290. March, ¢, F.
291. Allemande (& Trio), 3/4, both F. 292. Allemande (& Trio), 3/4, both C.
293. Allem[ande]; (& Trio), 3/4, both F. 294. Alleg[re]tto mod[er]ato, 6/8, B♭. 295. March, 2/4, F.
296. Allegro, C, G. 297. Alleg[re]tto, 6/8, G. 298. Allegretto, ¢, G. 299. Allegretto, 2/4, C.
300. And[an]tino, ¢, C. 301. Allo, ¢, C / And[an]te, ¢, C / Allo, ¢, C. 302. Allo, 6/8, C.
303. Cont[re]d[an]se, 2/4, G, (& 3 Trios, G, A, G). 304. Allegro, 2/4, C. 305. March, ¢, C.
306. Allem[an]de (& Trio), 3/4, B♭. 307. [no tempo - ?Allemande] (& Trio), 3/4, both C.
308. [no tempo - ?Allemande] (& Trio), 3/4, both F. 309. [no tempo - ?Allemande] (& Trio), 3/4, both B♭.
310. [no tempo - ?Allemande] (& Trio), 3/4, both G. 311. [no tempo - ?Allemande] (& Trio), 3/4, both C.
312. Tempo March, C, F. 313. And[an]te Romance, 2/4, C. 314. Allo Mod[era]to, C minor, (& major).
315. Romance Allo Mod[era]to, 3/8, B♭. 316. Allegro, 6/8, G. 317. March (& Trio), ¢, both F.
318. March, ¢, C. 319. Allemande (& Trio), 3/4, both F. 320. [no tempo - ?Allemande] (& Trio), 3/4, C.
322. Allo, C, E♭. 323. March Alleg[re]tto, 2/4, E♭. 324. [no tempo - ?Allemande] (& Trio), 3/4, both E♭.
325. [no tempo - ?Allemande] (& Trio), 3/4, both E♭. 326. [no tempo -?Allemande] (& Trio), 3/4, both G.
327. [no tempo - ?Allemande] (& Trio), 3/4, both C. 328. [no tempo - ?Allemande] (& Trio), 3/4, both C.
329. [no tempo - ?Allemande] (& Trio), 3.4, both C. 330. Allegro Mod[era]to, C, C.
331. [unidentified] Sinfonia, Allo non troppo, C, D; (lead part marked, "Flauto[,] Oboe").
   It is possible that some of the following Nos. are also part of this (?)opera.

332. Allegro, 6/8, C, (& Coda).   333. Allegro, ¢, E♭.   334. Allegro, C, E♭.
335. Andantino, 6/8, G / Allemande, 3/4, C.   336. Allegretto, ¢, F / [no tempo], 2/4, F / Coda.
337. March, ¢, F.   338. [no tempo - ?March], ¢, E♭.   339. Larghetto, 3/4. E♭ / Allegro, 3/4, E♭.
340. Allo mod[era]to, C, G.   341. March, ¢, F.   342. Allo, 3/4, E♭ / Andante, ¢, E♭ / Allo, 3/4, E♭.
343. March, ¢, F.   344. Alleg[re]tto, 2/4, C.   345. And[an]te, 3/4, E♭.   346. Chasse, 6/8, E♭.
347. Allegro, 6/8, F.   348. Allegro, 6/8, F.   349. Allo Mod[era]to, ¢, G / And[an]tino, 6/8, G.
350. March, ¢, D.   351. March, ¢, G.   352. Chasse, 6/8, E♭.   353. Chasse, 6/8, E♭.
354. Intrada Allegro, 6/8, F / And[an]te, C, F / da Capo Allegro.   355. March, ¢, F.
356. Allem[an]de, 3/4, F.   357. Allem[an]de, 3/4, G.   358. Allem[an]de, 3/4, F.   359. Allem[an]de, 3/4, G.
360. Allem[an]de, 3/4, F.   361. Allem[an]de, 3/4, B♭.   362. [no tempo - ?Allemande], 3/4, C.
363. Rondo And[an]te 3/4, E♭ / Allegretto, 2/4, E♭ / [2 more cycles] / al segno Alleg[re]tto.
364. Allem[an]de (& Trio), 3/4, both in F.   365. Allem[an]de (& Trio), 3/4, both F.
366. [no tempo - ?Allemande] (& Trio), 3/4, both F.   367. Andante, 2/4, G.   368. Andante, 2/4, E♭.
369. Alleg[re]tto, 2/4, C.   370. Marcia, ¢, E♭.   371. March, 2/4, D.   372. March, ¢, D.
373. Allegretto Gratioso, 6/8, D.   374. Allegro, 6/8, D.   375. Allegro, 2/4, G.
376. Allem[an]de, 3/4, D, (& Trio, G).   377. Allo, 2/4, G.   378. Andantino con [6] Variat[ioni], 3/4, B♭.
379. [unidentified] Ouverture, Allo viv[ace], ¢, C. *The following 4 Nos. may also be part of this (?)opera.*
380. Lento, C, C minor.   381. Romance Andante sost[enuto], 2/4, F.   383. Moderato, C, C.
385. Allegretto, 2/4, D.   386. Russischer Zapfenst[reich] Allegro, 2/4, D.
387. Chasse Allegro, 6/8, C / Andante, 3/4, C / Tempo primo.   388. Andante con [6] Var[ia]t[ioni], 3/4, C.
389. Allem[an]de, 3/4, B♭, (& Trio, F).   390. March, ¢, D.   391. Polonaise, 3/4, C, (& Trio, F).
392. Polonaise, 3/4, C.   393. Polonaise, 3/4, C.   394. Maestoso, C, B♭ / Mod[era]to, C, B♭.
395. Allegretto, 6/8, E♭.   396. Allo Mod[era]to, ¢, E♭.   397. March, ¢, E♭.   398. Andante, 3/4, G.
399. Andantino, 3/4, C / Allegro, C, C.   400/1. Allem[an]de (& Trio), 3/4, both C.
Band 2.   404. Andante, C, E♭ / Allegro, C, E♭.
408. Allegretto con [6] Variatione, 3/4, D, (a *tutti* follows each variation).
409. Allem[an]de (& Trio & Coda), 3/4, all in C.   410. [no tempo - ?Allemande] (& Trio), 3/4, both C.
411. [no tempo - ?Allemande] (& Trio), 3/4, both C.   412. Allo: Mod[era]to: Allemande (& Trio), 3/4, both F.
413. Allegro, C, F / Presto, C, F / Tempo 1 mo.   422. March, ¢, A.   423. Andante, C, B♭ / Allegro, 3/4, B♭.
424. Moderato, C, B♭ / Larghetto, C, B♭ /Allegro, C, B♭.   431. Alleg[re]tto, 3/4, D.
437. Allo, ¢, F / Andante, ¢ / Allo, ¢ / And[an]te, ¢ / Allo, ¢ / And[an]te, ¢ / Tempo 1mo.
441. Allo Mod[era]to, C, F.   442. And[an]te Vivace, 2/4, C / Allo, 2/4, C / più Allo, 2/4, C.   443. Marsch, ¢, C.
444. Marsch, ¢, C.   445. Allemando [sic] (& Trio), 3/4, both C.   447. Allemando [sic] (& Trio), 3/4, both C.
457. Andantino, 2/4, C / Polonaisse [sic], 3/4, C.   458. Moderato, ¢, B♭ / più Mosso.
461. Andante, 6/8, B♭ / And[an]tino, 6/8, F.   494. March, ¢, F.   495. March, ¢, F.
496. All[e]g[re]tto [= Allemande & Trio], 3/4, F.   498. March, 6/8, F.   499. Chasse, 6/8, F.
500. Allemande (& Trio), 3/4, both C.   501. All[e]m[an]do [sic] (& Trio), 3/4, both F.
502. Allemando [sic]. 3/4, B♭.   507. March, ¢, F.   508. March Vivace, 2/4, C.   509. Allegero [sic], 2/4, F.
512. Allo Vivace, 6/8, F, (& Coda).   513. Larghetto, 6/8.   514. Allegro, C.
518. Andante con moto, 6/8 / Allegro, ¢ / [no tempo], 3/8 / Allegro, ¢.   528. Allo Maest[o]so, C.
529. Marsch Maest[o]so, C.   530. Marsch Maest[o]so (& Trio), C.   540. Allegro, 6/8.
542. Andante, 9/8, C.   544. Andante sostenuto, C, F.   545. Andante, 3/4, B♭.   546. Più Adagio, 6/8, E.
549. Andante, 3/4, G.   [551]. Intrada, And[an]te, ¢.

WYL-1a. Aiblinger: Demetrio, 1 mvt. No. 490 (Marsch Maestoso). *(Possibly Rossini's* Demetrio e Polibio).
WYL-2a. Auber: La Neige, 2 mvts. Nos. 517 & 518.
WYL-3a. Auber: La Muette di Portici, 3 mvts. Nos. 526, 527, 531.
WYL-4a. Auber: Gustave III, 1 mvt. No. 536.
WYL-5a. Bellini: La Sonnambula, 3 mvts. Nos. 537 - 539.
WYL-6a. Bellini: Norma,1 mvt. No. 521.
WYL-7a. Bellini: (unidentified) Cavatine. No. 543.
WYL-8a. Carl Cannabich: Palmer und Amalia, 3 mvts. Nos. 215, 234, 235.
    Nos. 236 - 241 may also be from this opera.
WYL-9a. Chélard: Macbeth, 1 mvt. No. 521.
WYL-10a. Chélard: Mitternacht, 1 mvt (Ländler). No. 522.
WYL-11a. Cherubini: Les deux Journées (as "Graf Armand"), 1 mvt. No. 195.
WYL-12a. Coccia: Clothilde, 1 mvt. No. 448.
WYL-13a. Coccia: Evvelina, overture. No. 468, (here incorrectly attributed to Rossini).
WYL-14a. Coccia: La Poeta fortunato, 1 mvt. No. 470.
WYL-15a. Dalayrac: Léhéman, 3 mvts. Nos. 247, 248 (marked "Macdonalt"), 249.
WYL-16a. Danzi: (unidentified mvt), Allegretto, 3/8, G. No. 108.
WYL-17a. Duport: (unidentified ballet), 1 mvt. No. 470.
WYL-18a. Generali: Adelina, overture & 1 mvt. No. 402 (overture) & No. 416.
WYL-19a. Generali: La Contessa di colle erbe, 1 mvt. No. 418.
WYL-20a. Generali: La Locandiera, 1 mvt. No. 429. *Probably Farinelli's opera.*
WYL-21a. C. Kreutzer: Der Nachlager in Granada, 2 mvts. Nos. 547 (Jagd Chor); 548 (Bolero).
WYL-22a. Marschner: Der Templer und die Jüdin, 1 mvt. No. 550 (Tempo March, ¢).
WYL-23a. Méhul: Joseph, 1 mvt. No. 311. *Nos. 312 - 318 may also be from this opera.*
WYL-24a. Meyerbeer: Emma de Resburgo, 2 mvts. Nos. 478 & 479. *cf. WYL-52.4a, 52.5a.*
WYL-25a. Mozart: Le Nozze di Figaro, 3 mvts, ("Non più andrai", "Se vuol ballare, Signor Contino?", "Che soave zefiretto"). Nos. 35 - 37.
WYL-26a. Mozart: Così fan tutte, overture. No. 101.
WYL-27a. Mozart: La Clemenza di Tito, overture. No. 127.
WYL-28a. A. Müller: Zu ebner Erde und ersten Stock, 1 mvt. No. 535.
WYL-29a. Nicolini: Balduiro, 2 mvts. Nos. 465 & 466. *For No. 465, cf. WYL-52.3a.*
WYL-30a. Nicolini: Quinto Fabio, 2 mvts. Nos. 459 & 471, (Marsch, ¢). *For No. 459, cf. WYL-52.1a.*

WYL-31a. Orlando: La Dama soldato, 1 mvt. No. 403.
WYL-32a. Paer: Camilla, 2 mvts. Nos. 89 & 241.
WYL-33a. Pavesi: Celanira, 2 mvts. No. 463, (incorrectly attributed to Nicolini; also No. 464, untitled).
WYL-34a. Pavesi: Ser Marcantonio, 2 mvts. Nos. 414 & 491. *No. 414 is incorrectly attributed to Orlandi.*
WYL-35a. Rossini: Demetrio e Polibio, 1 mvt. No. 475. *cf. WYL-1a.*
WYL-36a. Rossini: La Pietra di Paragone, 5 mvts. Nos. 435, 436, 438 - 440.
WYL-37a. Rossini: L'Inganno felice, 1 mvt. No. 406.
WYL-38a. Rossini: Tancredi, overture & 6 mvts. Nos. 401 (overture), 405, 407, 426, 427, 428, 472.
WYL-39a. Rossini: L'Italiana in Algeri, overture & 6 mvts. Nos. 400/2 (overture), 417, 419 - 421, 425, 469.
WYL-40a. Rossini: Elisabetta, Regina d'Inghilterra, 1 mvt. No. 467.
WYL-41a. Rossini: Il Barbiere di Siviglia, 11 mvts. Nos. 449, 452 - 454, 480 - 486.
WYL-42a. Rossini: Otello, overture & 1 mvt. Nos. 460 (overture), 489.
WYL-43a. Rossini: La Gazza ladra, overture (No. 432), & 8 mvts (430, 433, 434, 475, 476, 487, 488, 492).
WYL-44a. Rossini: La Cenerentola, 5 mvts. Nos. 446, 451, 455, 473, 474.
WYL-45a. Rossini: Mosè in Egitto, 2 mvts. Nos. 456 & 493.
WYL-46a. Rossini: Ricciardo e Zoraide, 4 mvts. Nos. 503 - 506.
WYL-47a. Strauss the Elder: (unidentified) Walzer. No. 532.
WYL-48a. C.M. von Weber: Leyer und Schwert, Op. 42, No. 2, "Lützow's wilde Jagd". No. 471.
WYL-49a. J. Weigl: Der Waisenhaus, 1 mvt. No. 384. *No. 385 may also be from this opera.*
WYL-50a. J. Weigl: Die Schweizerfamilie, 2 mvts. Nos. 321 & 382. *No. 383 may also be from this opera.*
WYL-51a. Winter: Der Bettelstudent, 1 mvt. No. 226 (no tempo), 3/8, F.

WYL-52a. 6 Pièces d'Harmonie tirées des Opéras de Meyerbeer et Nicolini. fl 2cl 2hn 2bn.
Pc (Chez Breitkopf & Härtel: à Leipsic [sic], pn 3516, c.1820), parts: CH-Gpu, Ib.4838.
The (untitled) mvts, without the ob/fl part are: WYL-30.1a, 33.1a, 29.1a, 24.1a, 24.2a, 33.2.
WYL-53a. 6 Pièces d'Harmonie tirées des Opéras de Rossini, Nicolini et Pacini…N°. 2. fl ob 2cl 2hn 2bn.
Pc (Chez Breitkopf & Härtel: à Leipsic [sic], pn 3524, c.1820), parts: CH-Gpu, Ib.4839, (missing the fl pt).
　53.1a. Rossini [or rather, Coccia]: Evvelina, overture. (= WYL-13a)
　53.2a. Nicolini: Carlo Magno, 2 mvts.
　53.3a. Pacini: Barbieri [sic, Rossini].
　53.4a. Rossini: Mosé in Egitto, 1 mvt.
　53.5a. Anon [?Legrand]: Allemande.
WYL-54a. Mozart: Così fan tutte, as "Parthia Nro 8"), 8 mvts. fl ob 2cl 2hn 2bn.
MS parts: D-Rtt, Mozart 25/III.
WYL-55a. Rossini: Ouverture et [2] Airs des Opéras L'inganne [sic] felice et [2] La gazza ladra. fl 2cl 2hn 2bn.
Pc (Breitkopf & Härtel: Leipzig, pn 3302, 1821), parts: D-Tl, Gg 307.
MS parts: D-Rtt, Sm. 13, Nos. 54 - 58.
WYL-56a. Rossini: Tancredi, overture & 5 mvts. fl ob 2cl 2hn 2bn. (WYL-38a: 401, 472, 405, 407, 426, 427)
Pc (P. Petit: Paris, c.1814), parts: D-HR, HR III 4 1/2 2° 927.
MS parts: D-Rtt, Sm.13, Nos. 28 - 33, (followed by 4 mvts with the same scoring, possibly Legrand's arrs.).
Pm (KGS), fiche (3226), (of D-HR, Petit edition).
WYL-57a. Rossini: L'Italiana in Algeri, overture & 5 mvts. fl ob 2cl 2hn 2bn. (WYL-39a, omits No. 425)
Pc (Breitkopf & Härtel: Leipzig; P. Petit: Paris, pn 2856, 1818/19), pts: D-HR, HR III 4 1/2 2° 928, (Breitkopf).
Pm (KGS), fiche (3227).
WYL-58a. J. Weigl: L'amor marinaro, 1 mvt. fl ob 2cl 2hn 2bn.
MS parts: D-Rtt, Mozart 25/III, (the 9th mvt of WYL-54a).

*LEHMANN, Friedrich Adolphe von *(1770)*
FAL-1m. Six Marches qui peuvent s'exécuter aussi bien en Entre-actes à plein Orchestre qu'en Harmonie par les Instruments à vent; in E♭, C, D, E♭ D, C. 2fl 2ob 2cl 2hn 2bn 2b-tb timp, 2vl vla vc+basso.
Pc (Hoffmeister & Kühnel: Leipzig, pn 328, 1804), RISM [L 1645], parts: A-Wgm, XVI 4484, (uncut). ★

LEHMANN, Hans Ulrich *1937, Germany*
HUL-1. zu Blasen, 1975-6. pic fl a-fl 2ob 2cl b-cl 4hn 2bn cbn 3tp 3tb tu.
Pm (Breitkopf & Härtel: Wiesbaden, 1976), hire score & parts.

*LEIBL, Carl *3 Sept 1784, Fussgonheim, Pfalz - 4 Oct 1870, Cologne*
*CXL-1v. Fest Cantate aufgeführt bei der Feier der Grundsteinlegung für den Fortbau des Kölner Domes, [for the laying of the foundation of the Cologne Cathedral, 1842]. TTBB, 4hn 3bn tp 3tb db timp.
MS: CZ-Pnm, XXXI.E.235. ★
Pm (Musikverlag Schwann: Düsseldorf, 1955), score, (Denkmäler rheinischer Musik. Bd. 5): GB-Lbl, G.1391, (specify: DRM. Bd. 5).

LEICHTLING, Alan Robert *1947, USA*
ARL-1. Item 72-D. fl ob 3cl 2hn 2bn 2tp db.
Pm (Seesaw Music Corp: New York, c.1966).

*LEITERMEYER, Fritz *4 April 1925, Vienna*
FQL-1. Concerto for Violin and 21 winds, Op. 21. Solo Violin, pic fl fl(pic) 2ob ca cl(E♭) cl(B♭) cl(A) 3hn 2bn cbn 3tp 3tb. AutoMS score: A-Wn, Mus.Hs.34,378.
FQL-2. Divertimento, Op. 53. pic fl ob ca cl b-cl 2hn bn cbn tp tb.
Pm (Doblinger: Wien, 1976), miniature score (pn Stp 384) & parts (pn 06607).

LELEU, Jeanne *29 Dec 1889, St Mihiel, France - 11 March 1979, Paris*
JEL-1. Suite Symphonique; 5 mvts. 2fl 2ob cl hn bn 2tp tb piano perc.
Pm (Alphonse Leduc: Paris, 1926), score: GB-Lbl, h.1508.bb.(7.).

*LENOT, Jacques *29 Aug 1945, St.-Jean d'Angely, France*
*JQL-1. Comme un loin; 1976. fl(C) fl(G) ob ca cl b-cl 2hn 2bn.
(Gruppo 1: fl(C) ob bn, Gruppo 2: ca cl hn bn; Gruppo 3: fl(G) b-cl hn).
Pm (Suvini-Zerboni: Milano, pn S.8297Z., 1977), facsimile AutoMS score.

*LENZI, Carlo *1735, Azzone - 1805, Bergamo*
CYL-1v. Pange lingua, a 4 voci; in C.   CATB, 2ob 2cl 2hn 2bn (timp).
AutoMS score (11 June 1794) & parts: Faldone 28, n. 298, (the timpani are not in the score).
CYL-2v. Ave maris stella, a 4 voci, per processione; in C.   CATB, 2ob 2hn bn basso/organ timp.
AutoMS parts (11 Oct 1795): I-BGi(cm), Faldone 6, n. 58.
CYL-3v. Ave maris stella, a 3 e 4 voci, per processione; in D.   CATB, 2ob 2hn bn (timp).
AutoMS score (16 Aug 1780) & parts: I-BGi(cm), Faldone 6, n. 56, (timpani are not in the score).
CYL-4v. Laudate pueri, 1 3 voci; in F.   CATB, 2ob 2hn bn.   AutoMS score: I-GBi(cm), Faldone 23, n. 256.
CYL-5v. Pange lingua.   CATB, 2ob 2hn bn.   AutoMS score & parts: I-BGc, Mayr fald. 352/8.   ★
CYL-6v. Pange linga a 4 per processione.   CATB, 2ob 2hn bn.
AutoMS score & parts: I-BGc, Mayr fald. 332/9, (missing the bn pt).   ★
CYL-7v. Vexilla Regis, Inno.   CATB chorus, 2ob 2hn b/bn.
AutoMS score & pts: I-BGc, Mayr fald. 296/34.   AutoMS pts (CATB, bn only): I-BGc, Mayr fald. 298/10.   ★
CYL-8v. Ave maris stella, per processione; in F.   CATB, 2ob bn organ/basso.
AutoMS parts (1791): I-BGi(cm), Faldone 6, n. 60.

*LERCH, Vendelín *(attributed)* *(1810)*
VXL-1v. Graduale Pastoralis in F, "Jesu Redemptor omnium".   B solo, 2cl 2flug 2tp(keyed) b-tb 2bomb organ.
MS parts (23 Dec 1844): CZ-Bm(bh), A.33,139, (missing flug II, tp II, b-tb, bomb II).   ★

*LEROY, Pierre *(1770), active 1806*
PQL-1.1(-1.6). Journal de Musique Militaire Arrangé . . . Redigé par une Société d'Artistes. (Scoring varies).
Pc (Chez P. Leroy: Lyon; Chez Pleyel: Paris, Gravé par Richomme, 1806 - 1807), Liv. 1 - 6, parts: CH-Zz, AMG XIII 3074. *Continues as:*
PQL-1.7(-1.12). Journal d'Harmonie . . . Composé par une Société d'Artistes. (Scoring varies).
Pc (Chez Chanel: Lyon; au magasin de Musique, dirigé par les C^{ens} Cherubini, Méhul, Kreutzer, Rode, Nicolo Isouard et Boieldieu, Gravé par Leroy, 1807), Liv. 7 - 12, parts: CH-Zz, AMG XIII 3075. *After Liv. 1, the printed numbering of items returns to No. 1 and all items are consecutively numbered from there; the CH-Zz copy also bears contemporary MS numbers continuing from Liv. 1, No. 7. Below we list first the MS and then the printed number of each item. Nos. 1.2/1, 1.2/4 & 1.2/5 also appear in the 2nd Moitié of von Sydow & Werckmeister's* Journal de Musique Militaire *(1804), A-78.2a; for a discussion, See* The Wind Ensemble Sourcebook, *pp. 22- 23 & 25 - 26. When oboes replace the F clarinets; the C clarinets are labelled "III & IV". For want of further information to the contrary we treat all works as compositions or arrangements by Leroy.*
  1.1/1(a). Charles, Fils: Marche. No. 1.   2p-fl(F) 2cl(F) 2cl(C) 2hn 2bn tp serp b-dr.
    1.1/2. Leroy: Waltze. No. 2.   2p-fl(F) 2cl(F) 2cl(C) 2hn (2)bn tp serp b-dr.
    1.1/3. Leroy: Pas Redoublé. No. 3.   2p-fl(F) 2cl(F) 2cl(C) 2hn (2)bn tp serp b-dr.
    1.1/4. Leroy: Pas Redoublé. No. 4.   2p-fl(F) 2cl(F) 2cl(C) 2hn 2bn tp serp b-dr.
    1.1/5. Leroy: Marche.   No. 5.   2p-fl(F) 2cl(F) 2cl(C) 2hn (2)bn tp serp b-dr.
    1.1/6. Leroy: Waltze. No. 6.   2p-fl(F) 2cl(F) 2cl(C) 2hn 2bn tp serp b-dr.
    1.1/7. Leroy: Pas Redoublé. No. 7.   2p-fl(F) 2cl(F) 2cl(C) 2hn 2bn tp serp b-dr.
  1.2/1(a). Fleury: Ouverture. No. 8/1.   2p-fl(F) 2ob 2cl(III & IV, C) 2hn 2bn tp serp b-dr.
    1.2/2(a). D., H.: Rondo Finale. No. 9/2.   2p-fl(F) 2cl(F) 2cl(C) 2hn 2bn tp serp b-dr.
    1.2/3. Leroy: Marche. No. 10/3.   2p-fl(F) 2cl(F) 2cl(C) 2hn 2bn tp serp b-dr tambour.
    1.2/4. Leroy: Pas Redoublé. No. 11/4.   2p-fl(F) 2cl(F) 2cl(C) 2hn 2bn tp serp b-dr.
    1.2/5. Leroy: Walze [sic: Haydn, Hob. I/101iii]. No. 12/5.   2p-fl(F) 2cl(F) 2cl(C) 2hn 2bn tp serp b-dr.
    1.2/6. Leroy: Rondo en Pas Redoublé. No. 13/6.   2p-fl(F) 2cl(F) 2cl(C) 2hn 2bn tp serp b-dr.
  1.3/1(a). L. Jadin: Ouverture. No. 14/7.   2p-fl(F) 2cl(F) 2cl(C) 2hn 2bn tp serp b-dr.
    1.3/2. Leroy: Rondeau. No. 15/8.   2p-fl(F) 2cl(F) 2cl(C) 2hn 2bn tp serp b-dr.
    1.3/3. Leroy: Marche. No. 16/9.   2p-fl(F) 2cl(F) 2cl(C) 2hn 2bn tp serp b-dr.
    1.3/4. Leroy: Allemande. No. 17/10.   2p-fl(F) 2cl(F) 2cl(C) 2hn 2bn tp serp b-dr.
    1.3/5. Leroy: Walze. No. 18/11.   2p-fl(F) 2cl(F) 2cl(C) 2hn 2bn tp serp b-dr.
    1.3/6. Leroy: Rondeau en Pas Redoublé. No. 19/12.   2p-fl(F) 2cl(F) 2cl(C) 2hn 2bn tp serp b-dr.
  1.4/1(a). R.N.C. Bochsa, Fils: Ouverture. No. 20/13.   2fl(F) 2ob 2cl(III & IV, C) 2hn 2bn tp serp b-dr.
    1.4/2(a). R.N.C. Bochsa, Fils: Rondeau. No. 21/14.   2fl(F) 2ob 2cl(III & IV, C) 2hn 2bn tp serp b-dr.
    1.4/3(a). C. Bochsa, Père: Marche Funèbre. No. 22/15.   2fl(F) 2cl(F) 2cl(C) 2hn 2bn tp serp b-dr.
    1.4/4. Leroy: Allemande. No. 23/16.   2fl(F) 2cl(F) 2cl(C) 2hn (2)bn tp serp b-dr.
    1.4/5. Leroy: Fandango. No. 24/17.   2fl(F) 2cl(F) 2cl(C) 2hn (2)bn tp serp b-dr.
    1.4/6. Leroy: Allemande. No. 25/18.   2fl(F) 2cl(F) 2cl(C) 2hn 2bn tp serp b-dr.
  1.5/1(a). Fleury: Ouverture. No. 26/19.   2fl(F) 2ob 2cl(III & IV, C) 2hn 2bn tp serp b-dr.
    1.5/2(a). L. Jadin: Rondeau. No. 27/20.   2fl(F) 2cl(F) 2cl(C) 2hn 2bn tp serp b-dr.
    1.5/3. Leroy: Marche. No. 28/21.   2fl(F) 2cl(F) 2cl(C) 2hn 2bn tp serp b-dr.
    1.5/4. Leroy: Rondeau. No. 29/22.   2fl(F) 2cl(F) 2cl(C) 2hn 2bn tp serp b-dr.
    1.5/5. Leroy: Walze. No. 30/23.   2fl(F) 2cl(F) 2cl(C) 2hn 2bn tp serp b-dr.
    1.5/6. Leroy: Chasse. No. 31/24.   2fl(F) 2cl(F) 2cl(C) 2hn 2bn tp serp b-dr.
  1.6/1a. Haydn: Ouverture [Hob. XVI/38ii]. No. 32/25.   2fl(F) 2cl(F) 2cl(C) 2hn 2bn tp serp b-dr.
    1.6/2a. Haydn: Andantino [Hob. I/101ii]. No. 33/26.   2fl(F) 2ob 2cl(III & IV, C) 2hn 2bn tp serp b-dr.
    1.6/3(a). Alday: Rondeau. No. 34/27.   2fl(F) 2cl(F) 2cl(C) 2hn 2bn tp serp b-dr.
    1.6/4(a). Desormes: Marche. No. 35/28.   2fl(F) 2cl(F) 2cl(C) 2hn 2bn tp serp b-dr.
    1.6/5. Leroy: Walze. No. 36/29.   2fl(F) 2cl(F) 2cl(C) 2hn 2bn tp serp b-dr.
    1.6/6. Leroy: Ras Redoublé. No. 37/30.   2fl(F) 2cl(F) 2cl(C) 2hn (2)bn tp serp b-dr.
  1.7/1(a). L. Jadin: Ouverture. No. 38/31.   2fl(F) 2ob 2cl(III & IV, C) 2hn 2bn tp serp timp.
    1.7/2a. Haydn: Andantino [Hob. I/73ii]. No. 39/32.   2p-fl(F) 2cl(F) 2cl(C) 2hn 2bn tp serp.
    1.7/3(a). L. Jadin: Chasse. No. 40/33.   2fl(F) 2ob 2cl(III & IV, C) 2hn (2)bn tp serp timp.
    1.7/4(a). Lxxx.: Marche. No. 41/34.   2fl(F) 2cl(F) 2cl(C) 2hn 2bn 2tp serp timp b-dr.
    1.7/5. Leroy: Walze. No. 42/35.   2fl(F) 2cl(F) 2cl(C) 2hn 2bn 2tp serp timp b-dr.
    1.7/6. Leroy: Allemande. No. 43/36.   2fl(F) 2cl(F) 2cl(C) 2hn 2bn 2tp serp timp b-dr.

1.8/1(a). [G.] Walter: Ouverture. No. 44/37.   2p-fl(F) 2ob 2cl(III & IV, C) 2hn 2bn tp serp.
  1.8/2a. Haydn: Andante [Hob. I/94ii]. No. 45/38.   fl(C) 2ob 2cl(III & IV, C) 2hn 2bn serp.
  1.8/3(a). Walter: Polonoise. No. 46/39.   2p-fl(F) 2ob 2cl(III & IV, C) 2hn 2bn tp serp.
  1.8/4. Leroy: Marche. No. 47/40.   2p-fl(F) 2cl(F) 2cl(C) 2hn 2bn 2tp serp.
  1.8/5. Leroy: Walze. No. 48/41.   2p-fl(F) 2cl(F) 2cl(C) 2hn 2bn 2tp serp.
  1.8/6. Leroy: Rondeau en Pas Redoublé. No. 49/42.   2p-fl(F) 2cl(F) 2cl(C) 2hn 2bn tp serp.
1.9/1(a), Alday: Ouverture. No. 50/43.   2p-fl(F) 2ob 2cl(III & IV, C) 2hn 2bn tp serp.
  1.9/2a. Haydn: Andantino [Hob. I/104ii]. No. 51/44.   2fl(F) 2ob 2cl(III & IV, C) 2hn 2bn serp.
  1.9/3(a). Alday: All⁰ Finale. No. 52/45.   2p-fl(F) 2ob 2cl(III & IV, C) 2hn 2bn tp serp.
  1.9/4(a). Saramia: Marche. No. 53/46.   2p-fl(F) 2cl(F) 2cl(C) 2hn 2bn tp serp.
  1.9/5(a). Ch[arles] Bochsa [?père]: Valzer. No. 54/47.   2p-fl(F) 2cl(F) 2cl(C) 2hn 2bn tp serp.
  1.9/6(a). Fournier: Rondeau. No. 55/48.   2p-fl(F) 2cl(F) 2cl(C) 2hn 2bn tp serp.
1.10/1(a). Fleury: Ouverture. No. 56/49.   2p-fl(F) 2ob 2cl(III & IV, C) 2hn 2bn tp serp timp.
  1.10/2a. Haydn: Andantino, [Hob. I/92ii]. No. 57/50.   fl(F) 2ob 2cl(III & IV, C) 2hn 2bn serp.
  1.10/3a. Haydn: Minuetto & Trio, [Hob. 92/iii]. No. 58/51.   2p-fl(F) 2ob 2cl(III & IV, C) 2hn 2bn serp.
  1.10/4(a). Fleury: Polonaise. No. 59/52.   2p-fl(F) 2ob 2cl(III & IV, C) 2hn 2bn serp timp.
  1.10/5a. Cimarosa: Marche. No. 60/53.   2p-fl(F) 2cl(F) 2cl(C) 2hn (2)bn tp serp timp.
  1.10/6(a). Fleury: Pas Redoublé. No. 61/54.   2p-fl(F) 2cl(F) 2cl(C) 2hn (2)bn tp serp timp.
1.11/1(a). G. Walter: Ouverture; F minor/major. No. 62/55.   2fl(F) 2ob 2cl(III & IV, C) 2hn 2bn 2tp serp timp.
  1.11/2a. Haydn: Andante un poco Adagio [Hob. I/92ii]. No. 63/56.   2fl 2ob 2cl(III & IV, C) 2hn 2bn serp.
  1.11/3a. Haydn: Minuetto & Trio, [Hob. I/92/iii] No. 64/57.   2p-fl(F) 2ob 2cl(III & IV, C) 2hn 2bn serp.
  1.11/4(a). [G.] Walter: Rondeau. No. 65/58.   2p-fl(F) 2ob 2cl(III & IV, C) 2hn 2bn 2tp serp timp.
  1.11/5(a). [G.] Walter: Marche. No. 66/59.   2p-fl(F) 2cl(F) 2cl(C) 2hn (2)bn 2tp serp timp.
  1.11/6. Leroy: Pas Redoublé. No. 67/60.   2p-fl(F) 2cl(F) 2cl(C) 2hn 2bn 2tp serp timp.
1.12/1a. Blasius: Ouverture (= MFB-1.2). No. 68/61.   2p-fl(F) 2ob 2cl(III & IV, C) 2hn 2bn tp serp timp.
  1.12/2a. Haydn: Andantino [Hob. I/100iii]. No. 69/62.   2fl(C) 2ob 2cl(III & IV, C) 2hn 2bn tp serp.
  1.12/3a. Haydn: Minuetto & Trio [Hob. 100/iii]. No. 70/63.   2p-fl(F) 2ob 2cl(III & IV, C) 2hn 2bn tp serp.
  1.12/4(a). Fleury: Chasse. No. 71/64.   2p-fl(F) 2ob 2cl(III & IV, C) 2hn 2bn tp serp timp.
  1.12/5. Leroy: Marche. No. 72/65.   2p-fl(F) 2cl(F) 2cl(C) 2hn (2)bn 2tp serp timp.
  1.12/6. Leroy: Fandango. No. 73/66.   2p-fl(F) 2cl(F) 2cl(C) 2hn (2)bn 2tp serp.
  1.12/7. Leroy: Allemande. No. 74/67.   2p-fl(F) 2cl(F) 2cl(C) 2hn (2)bn 2tp serp timp.

LERSTAD, Torje Bjørn *1955, Norway*
TBL-1. The Last Serenade in D Sharp Major.   ob ca 2cl 2hn bn cbn.   MS score: N-Oic.
TBL-2. Septet, Op. 91; 1976.   pic fl 2ob cl b-cl cbn.   MS score: N-Oic.

*LESSARD, John Ayres *3 July 1920, San Francisco*
JOL-1. Concerto; 1949.   2fl ob 2cl 2hn 2bn 2tp tb.
Pm (Merrymount: sl, c.1951), score.
JOL-2. Octet; 1952.   fl cl 2hn bn 2tp b-tb.
Pm (General Music Publishers: New York, 1965), score. *Originally published by the Joshua Corporation, 1953.*

*LESSEL, Franciszek (Franz) *(1780), Puławy, Warsaw - 26 Dec 1838, Piotrków*
FYL-1 was recorded (with db) by the Consortium Classicum as "Parthia concertante Es-dur [E♭]" on EMI
Electrola, using the A-Wgm copy. The Parthia in E♭ (Billaudot: Paris) is also probably of the same work.
FYL-1. Nro 1mo Parthia in Dis [E♭]; 5 mvts.   2cl 2hn 2bn.
MS parts: A-Wgm, VIII 5226, (as "N⁰ 1 Partitta in E♭"); CZ-Pnm, XLI.B.162, (omits the 3rd mvt Pollonesse [sic] & Trio). ★
FYL-2. Nro 2 [altered to 4] Parthia; in E♭, 5 mvts.   2cl 2hn 2bn.   MS parts: CZ-Pnm, XLI.B.163. ★
FYL-3. Nro 3 Parthia, in E♭; 4 mvts.   2cl 2hn 2bn.   MS parts: CZ-Pnm, XLI.B.164. ★
FYL-1v. Kantata do świętej Cecylii [Sainte Cécile]; Warsaw, 21 Nov 1812. CATB, 2cl 2hn vc b/organ(bc) timp.
MS: PL-CZ. ★
Pm (PWM: Kraków, 1987), ed. Bohdun Muchenberg, score. *(copy in F-Pn, Vmg. 26556).*

*LESUEUR (Le Sueur), Jean François *15 Feb 1760, nr Abbeville - 6 Oct 1837, Paris*
JFL-1. Le Chant des Triomphes de la République française; P.2323.   2ob 2cl 2hn 2bn b-dr cym.
Constant Pierre cited this as a separate work from JFL-1mv (qv) based on the incomplete set of parts originally
at Musique pour inst. à vent, paquet 39 (now at H2. 89).
JFL-1mv. Le Chant des Triomphes de la République française; P.91.
4-part chorus, 2fl 2ob 2cl 2hn 2bn 2tp a-tb t-tb b-tb serp timp.   MS score (by Pierre): F-Pn.
MS parts: F-Pn, H2. 89 a-o, (vocal parts of KFL-1mv & incomplete instrumental parts). ★
Pc (Mag de mus fêtes nat: Paris, frimaire an III, 1794), liv. 9, No. 2, parts: F-Pn, H2. 9,2.
JFL-2mv. Scène Patriotique; P.93.   ATB chorus, 2p-fl 2fl 2ob 2cl 4hn 4bn(=2 de choeur + 2 d'accompagnment) 2tp a-tb t-tb b-tb serp, tuba corva, cb timp.
MS parts: F-Pn, H2. 113 a-h-i, (missing some chorus parts and all wind parts except cl I). ★
JFL-3mv. Hymne pour l'inauguration d'un Temple à la liberté; P.140.   Solo voice, 2cl(C) 2hn (2)bn.
Pc (Rec des époques: Paris, c.1799), liv. 1, No. 17, score: F-Pn, H2. 15,17. ★
JFL-4mv. Hymne [Le Chant] du neuf Thermidor; P.100.   Solo voice, 2cl(C) 2hn (2)bn.
Pc (Rec des époques: Paris, c.1799), liv. 1, No. 30, pp. 82 - 85, score: F-Pn, H2. 15,30. ★
JFL-5mv. Chant dithyrambique pour l'entrée triomphale des monuments conquis; P.143 *(P.138 is for full orchestra; P.143 is distinct).*   Solo voice, 2cl(C) 2hn (2)bn.
Pc (Rec des époques: Paris, c.1799), liv. 1, No. 39, pp. 112 - 116, score: F-Pn, H2. 15,39. ★
JFL-6mv. Hymne pour la fête de l'Agriculture; (10 messidor, c.1798), P.157.   Solo voice, 2cl 2hn 2bn.
Pc (Rec des époques: Paris, c.1799), liv. 2, No. 7, pp. 153 - 155, score: F-Pn, H2. 16,7. ★
JFL-7mv. Hymne pour la fête de la Vieillesse; (10 fructidor, c.1798), P.159.   Solo voice, 2cl 2hn 2bn.
AutoMS score: F-Pn, MS. 4713. ★
Pc (Rec des époques: Paris, c.1799), liv. 2, No. 10, pp. 162 - 165, score: F-Pn, H2. 16,10.

LEVINSON, Gerald *1951, USA*
GEL-1. Chant des rochers.   2fl ob 2cl hn bn 2tp tb tu 3perc piano harp.
Pm (T. Presser: Bryn Mawr, PA).

LEVY, Morton *1939, Denmark*
MOL-1. Christianias sejr; 1976.   fl ob 2cl hn bn.   MS score: DK-Kd.

LEWIS, Art
ATL-1. Pieces of Eight.   fl 2ob 3cl 2sax hn bn 2tp tb perc.
Pm (Composers Autograph Press: New York, 1969), facsimile autograph score, (copy in US-Wc).

LEWIS, James *1938, USA*
JML-1. You must remember this, for jazz quartet and wind ensemble.
Solo a-sax vib e-bass drums, pic fl ob ca cl(Eb) cl(Bb) b-cl 4hn 2bn 3tp 2tb tu timp 4perc.
Pm (Margun Music: Newton Center, MA, pn MP 4025, 1983), hire score & parts.

LEWIS, Jeffrey *28 Nov 1942, Neath, Glamorganshire, UK*
JYL-1. Strata.   2fl(pic) ob 2cl b-cl 3hn bn 3tb perc.   MS score: GB-CDmic; GB-LEc (score & parts).

LEWIS, Paul
PUL-1. Groucho.   2fl ob 2cl 2hn bn 2tp tb db perc piano(celeste) harp.
Pm (Boosey & Hawkes: London, Sydney, New York).
PUL-2. March for a Microbe.   2fl ob 2cl 2hn bn 2tp tb db perc piano(celeste) harp.
Pm (Boosey & Hawkes: London, Sydney, New York).

LEWIS, Peter Todd *6 Nov 1932, Charlottesville, VA, USA*
PTL-1. Sestina.   2fl 2ob 2cl b-cl 2hn 2bn.
Pm (American Composers' Alliance: New York), facsimile edition.

LEWKOWITCH, Bernhard *28 May 1927, Copenhagen*
BYL-1v. Mass, Op. 15.   SATB, fl 2ob ca 2bn 2tp 2tb harp.
Pm (Wilhelm Hansen: Copenhagen, 1954), hire score & parts.

LEYE, Ludwig *1796 - 1853*
LXL-1. Sextet, Op. 3.   fl bthn/cl 2hn bn, with piano accompaniment.
Pc (Sinner: Coburg, 1844), parts: GB-Lbl, R.M.17.f.15.(1). ★

LEZGUS (LETZGUS), D.H. *(1780)*
DHL-1. [3] Harmonien; (Theil I: F, 12 mvts; Theil II: F, 6 mvts; Theil III: F, 9 mvts).   2cl(C) 2hn bn.
MS parts: D-Tl, Gg 263, (bn part missing Theil 1). *Theil III, mvt 7 is an Andante Thema mit Variations; mvt 8 is a Marsch from Spontini's La Vestale; mvt 9 is C.M. von Weber's "Leyer und Schwert", Op. 42, No. 2, as "Lutzo [sic: Lützow's] wilde Jag[d]".* ★

LIBER, Joseph Anton *1732, Sulzbach, nr Regensberg - 1809, Regensberg*
JAL-1. Divertimento in Bb, 19 mvts.   2cl 2hn 2bn 2vla db.   MS parts: D-Rtt, Liber 2. ★
JAL-2. [attributed: Divertimento in Eb], 12 mvts.   2cl 4hn(Eb, Bb) 2bn 2tp.   MS parts: D-Rtt, Liber 4. ★

LICHTENTHAL, Peter *10 May 1780, Pressburg - 18 Aug 1853, Milan*
PZL-1. Primi due Tempi del Ballabile nella Regia di Nettuno nel Ballo mitologico <u>Dedalo</u> [sic], composta nel Carnevale del 1818 da Salvatore Viganò [choreographer] con musica di Peitro Lichtenthal. N.B. La presente continuazione de' predetti due Tempi, incominciando dal fu da quest' ultimo fatta in aprile 1842 per divertimento [incipit] privato in casa, e il tutto adattato.   Piano, 2cl 2hn vc.   MS parts: I-Mc, Noseda L.50.29. ★

LICKL (Likl, Lickel), Johann Georg, the Elder *11 April 1769, Korneuburg - 12 May 1843, Fünfkirchen*
JGL-1, 2. Deux Harmonies; No. I: in Eb, 5 mvts; No. II, in Eb, 4 mvts.   2cl 2hn 2bn.
Pc (Au Magasin de l'imprimerie chimique I:R:pr:: Vienne, pn 1878, 1879, c.1812), RISM Supp [LL 2349f], parts: H-Bn, Z 43,626; GB-Ljag, (microfilm of H-Bn copy). ★
JGL-3.1. Quintetto, Op. 21; 4 mvts.   2cl 2hn bn.
Pc (Nel Magasino della Caes. Real priv. Stamperia chimica: Vienna, pn 22, sd), RISM Supp [LL 2349a], parts: CZ-KRa, A3917/IV.B.80, (with an additional bn I part composed by Havel); GB-Ljag, (photocopy of CZ-KRa copy); H-KE, K 757/VIII; HR-Zh; PL-LA, DM 73, (missing titlepage). ★
JGL-3.2. attributed to Krommer as "Sestetto Pastorale" [FVK-3d (qv)].   2cl 2hn 2bn.
MS parts (post-1808): provenance unknown.   Modern MS score & parts: D-KIZklöcker.
JGL-4. Quintetto; Op. 22.   2cl 2hn bn.
Pc (Chemische Druckerei: Wien, pn 575, 1808), RISM Supp [LL 2348a], parts: CR-Zh; H-Bn, Z 43,939; H-KE, K 700. ★
JGL-5. Quintetto concertante in F; 5 mvts.   fl ob cl hn bn.
MS parts: CZ-Bm(rj), A.12.724, (1830); D-Rtt. ★
Pc (au Magasin de l'imprimerie chimique: Vienna, pn 490, 1806), RISM Supp [LL 2349g], parts: A-M; A-Wgm, VIII 8076; A-Wst, M 24255/a; I-CORc; I-Mc, Noseda S.17.3. ★
Pm (F. Kneusslin: Basel, pn 31, 1966), score & parts.
JGL-6. Cassatio; Eb, 5 mvts (incorrectly attributed to Mozart as K. C.17.11, WAM-20d).   ob cl hn bn.
MS parts: CZ-Pnm, XLII.F.36, No. 14, (for ob/cl(C) cl hn bn).
Pc (au Magasin de Musique chez Joseph Eder: Wienne [sic], pn 55, 1799), RISM Supp [LL 2349h], parts: A-LIm, (missing bn); A-Sca, 70303; H-KE, K 756/VIII. ★
Pm (Albert J. Andraud Wind Instrument Library: Cincinatti; (now Southern Music Co.: San Antonio, 1936), parts, (as by Mozart): GB-Lbl, g.382.(5); US-Wc.
JGL-1v. Mass in Eb.   SAB, 2cl 2hn bn organ.   AutoMS score (Sept 1814): H-P, L 127. ★

LIEBERMANN, Rolf *14 Sept 1910, Zurich*
ROL-1. Capriccio; 1958.
S solo, violin solo, 3fl 2ob ca 2cl b-cl 4hn 2bn cbn db 3tp 3tb tu timp vib xly perc hp cel 2pf.
Pc (Universal Edition: Vienna, pn UE 13 153, 1960), miniature score.

*LIEBERSON, Peter *25 Oct 1946, New York*
PXL-1. Wind Messengers.   3fl 2ob 2cl 2b-cl 2hn 2bn.
Pm (Associated Music Publishers: New York, 1990), hire score & parts.

LIGETI, György Sandor *28 May 1923, Dicsöszentmárton, Transylvania*
GSL-1. 6 Miniatures; 1953, revised 1975.   2fl 2ob 2cl 2hn 2bn.
Pm (B. Schott's Söhne: Mainz, etc., 1976), score.

*LILIEN, Ignacy (Ignace) *29 May 1897, L'vov - 10 May 1964, The Hague*
IXL-1. Sonatine apollinique; in C.   2fl 2ob 2cl 2hn 2bn.
Pm (Donemus: Amsterdam, 1939), score & parts.
IXL-1v. Nyuk-Tsin (The Perfect Jade).   Solo S, BAR, B; Chorus of T,T,BAR,BAR,B,B; 2fl 2ob 2cl 4hn 2bn
2tp 3tb tu db piano celeste 5perc xly vibraphone.
Pm (Donemus: Amsterdam, 1961), score & parts.

*LILJEFORS, Ruben *30 Sept 1871, Uppsala - 4 March 1936, Gävle*
RUL-1. Marionett-Ouverture.   2fl 2ob 2cl 2bn glock.   MS score: S-Sic.

LINDE, Bo *1 Jan 1933, Gävle - 2 Oct 1970, Gävle*
BOL-1. Fanfar för Gävle musikkolas blåsorkester; 1970.   3fl(pic) 2cl hn 2tp tb tu 2perc.   MS score: S-Sic.

LINDEN, Robert van der *1936, Netherlands*
RVL-1. In an old-fashioned way.   2fl 2ob 2cl a-sax 2hn bn tb tu 2perc.
Pm (Donemus: Amsterdam, 1972), score.

LINDNER, H[einrich]. *(1790) - post-1837*
HYL-1m. Musique militaire; 6 mvts.   2fl 2ob 2cl 2hn 2bn 2tp tb serp perc.
MS parts: D-Rtt, Sm.14, Nos. 64 - 69, *(copy of the (lost) edition published by Breitkopf & Härtel in Leipzig).* ★

*LINDPAINTNER, Peter Joseph von *9 Dec 1791, Koblenz - 21 Aug 1856, Constance*
PJL-1. Quadrille zum Königlichen Caroussel, 1839.   Abth. 1: von Lindpaintner neu komponirt; Abth. 2: nach
Themer aus der Hugenotten [Meyerbeer] und dem Zewikampf [Hérold]; Abth. 3: nach Themen von Auber,
Bellini, Strauss [the Elder] arrangirt und mit Zusäatzen verschen.
pic cl(Eb) 4cl(Bb) 2hn 2bn 5tp klappenhorn 2tb timp b-dr+cym t-dr tri glock.   MS pts: D-Sl, H.B.XVII. 813. ★
PJL-1v(-9v). 9 Chörale aus dem Württembergischen Choralbuch [Des Christmann-Knechtchen Choralbuchs
von Jahre 1799].   SATB, 2fl 2ob 2cl(C) 2hn 2bn 2tp(tacet in Nos. 3 & 4) 2a-tb b-tb cb timp.
AutoMS score (No. 9 is in another hand): D-Sl, H.B.XVII 880. ★
  1v. Anbetung Jubel und Gesang und Lob.   2v. Nimm denen falter Volk das Gasse.
  3v. Schauigns heilige Gedanke.   4v. Ach, taih ihe diel den bluten sterben!
  5v. Noch und Missle dem ferd wir.   6v. Glaubet, glaubt er ist das Leben!   7v. Finis dem Todes ubenmir dir!
  8v. Mein Glaub ist meines Lebend.   9v. Herr ihr sind dem nemlass eur Schluss.
*PJL-10v. Psalm zur Confirmations-feyer der beiden Königlichen Prinzessen Marie u[nd]. Sophie [von
Württemberg]; "Einst ist im Himmel unser Teil".   SATB, 2fl 2ob 2cl 2hn 2bn a-tb t-tb b-tb bassi.
AutoMS score (1832): D-Sl, H.B.XVII. 881. ★
PFL-11v. Frühlingslied, "Regst du, o Lenz die jungen Glieder" Am Todestage Schillers; text by Ritter.
SATB, 2fl 2ob 2cl 2hn 2bn.   AutoMS parts: D-Sl, H.B.XVII. 390 Kaps, (with duplicate set of vocal pts).   ★
PJL-12v. Schlumerlied; ("Schweigend über'm Thale schwebt"); text by Grünersen.
SSTB, fl cl 6hn(3F, 2C, Bb basso).
AutoMS score (Stutgart, 17 Sept 1841): D-Sl, H.B.XVII. 867.
Pc (s.n: s.l., s.d.), score: CZ-Pnm, II.C.5. ★
PJL-13v. Württemberger Lied, "Von dir o Vaterland zu singen", Am Begräbnisstage meines Freundes Fr. Ritter".
S solo, SSTB chorus, 2fl 2ob 2cl 4hn 2bn 2tp a-tb t-tb oph cb.   AutoMS score ("Stuttgart am 10. Mai 1843"):
D-Sl, H.B.XVII. 397 & 398.   *An orchestration by the composer from his setting for voice & piano of 1842.*   ★
PJL-1ve. Börsenglück (Schauspiel von Giesecke): Chor für Knabenstimmen, "Singet laut in froher Weise"; 38
bars.   CCA [= boys choir], 2cl 2hn 2bn.   AutoMS score (27 Nov 1855): D-Sl, H.B.XVII. 349.

LINDROTH, Peter *1950, Sweden*
PEL-1. Six ninety six = 6-96 [sic]; 1992.   fl cl 2bn 2tp 2tb piano marimba; (all amplified).   MS score: S-Sic.

LINEK, Jiří Ignác *21 Jan 1725, Bakov nad Jizerov, Bohemia - 30 Dec 1791, Bakov*
JIL-1v. Ex D: Vidi aquam.   CATB, 2fl 2cl(A) 2tp(clar) tp(prin) timp organ(bc-fig).
MS parts (by Joh. Aug. Fibiger): CZ-Pnm, XIX.F.267. ★

LINN, Robert *11 Aug 1925, San Francisco*
RZL-1. Concertino for violin and wind octet; 1965.   Solo violin, 2ob 2cl 2hn 2bn.
Pm (Pillin Music, *via* Western International Music, Inc.: Greeley, Colorado, pn WIM 052, 1976), score & parts.

LINSTEAD, George Frederick *1925*
GFL-1. Recitative & in Nomine.   fl ob 2cl hn bn.   MS score: GB-Lmic.

LIPAVSKÝ (Lipawsky), Josef (Giuseppe) *22 Feb 1772, Vysóke Mýto, Bohemia - 7 Jan 1810, Vienna*
JZL-1. Cantata, "La liberazione d'Italia".   Instrumentation unknown.
MS score & (11) parts: I-Fc, F.P. T.189.
JZL-1m. Marsch; in C.   2fl 2cl(C) 2hn 2bn tp(clar) serp b-dr.
Pc (In A-82.1m Acht Märsche für Türkische Musick [sic], 1 Heft, No. 8:) (Johann André: Offenbach am Main,
pn 1822, 1803), parts: H-KE, K 731/VIII. ★
MS score & parts (copy of the André edition): I-Fc, F.P. S.553.

*LIQUORISH, William *(1770)*
WZL-1m. The Loyal Hampstead Association March & Quick Step. 2fl 2cl 2hn bn serp tp.
Pc (W. Hodsoll, Successor to Mr. Bland: London, c.1799), RISM [L 2583], score: GB-Lbl, g.133.(37);
GB-Ob, Mus.Instr.I.159(3). ★
Pm (arranged A.C. Baines, **ACB-1a**) (Oxford University Press: Oxford), score & parts.
WZL-2m. The first Regiment of Royal Tower Hamlets Militia March & Quick Step as Performed by the
Regimental Band. 2cl 2hn bn serp tp.
Pc (W. Hodsoll: London, c.1800), RISM [L 2583], score: GB-Lbl, g.133.(36); GB-Ob, Mus.Instr.I.159(4). ★

*LISZT, Franz (Ferenc) *22 Oct 1811, Raiding, Hungary - 31 July 1886, Bayreuth. See also: RAFF.*
FZL-1v. Der 18te Psalm ("Coeli enarrant gloriam Dei", "Die Himmel erzählen die Ehre Gottes"), (S14; R490),
3rd version. TTBB chorus, 2fl 2ob 2cl 4hn 2bn 2tp 3tb tu (s-drum, timp, ad lib).
MS: D-Mbs, Mus Pr 5291. ★
Pc (J. Schuberth & Co.: Leipzig, 1870), score.
Pc (In: Franz Liszt's musikalische Werke. (Kirchliche und geistliche Gesangswerke. Bd. 5: Hymnen, etc.,
pp. 40 - 57): (Breitkopf & Härtel: Leipzig, 1918 - 1936), score.
Pm (Reprint): (Music Press, Aug 1960, pn 5291, pp. 40 - 57).
Pm (Reprint): (Gregg Press: Farnborough, Hampshire, 1972).
FZL-2v. Weimars Volkslied, zur Carl-August-Feier, (S87), (September 1857).   Male chorus, winds.
MS score: D-Blandshoff; D-WRgs.

LIVERATI, Giovanni *27 March 1772, Bologna - 18 Feb 1846, Florence*
GXL-1v. Giaculatore per la tre ore dell'Agonia di N S G[iesù]. C[risto]. nel Venerdi Santo; [Seven Last Words,
for Good Friday, c.1790].   3 voices, winds.   MS score & parts: I-Fc, F.P. Ch.566.

LOEPER, Hans *1922, Germany*
HXL-1. 6 Etüden.   2ob 2cl 2hn 2bn.   Pm (Privately printed, 1972), score.

LOEWE, Johann Heinrich *1766, Berlin - 1815, Bremen*
JHL-1. Notturno in D, Op. 5.   2fl 2hn bn 2vla cb.
Pc (Johann André: Offenbach am Main, pn 1930, 1804), RISM [L 2745], parts: D-DO; D-DT, Mus-n 1181,
(missing 1 part).

LÖWENSTEIN (Loewenstein)-WERTHEIM-FREUDENBERG, Carl Friedrich, *Erbprinz* von *1783 - 1849*
See also the dubious and spurious works by HUMMEL, JNW-1d, 2d, and C.M. von WEBER, CMW-1d(-5d); some
of these works were probably composed - and/or transcribed - by Carl Friedrich von Löwenstein. The peculiar
spelling of "Pièces" appears to have been derived from publications by Schott, Mainz; (cf. Küffner, Witt).
CAL-1. [17 Variations on the Menuetto in Mozart's *Don Giovanni,* Act I finale].
fl(F) ob cl(F) 2cl(C) bthn 2hn 2bn tp b-tb cb.   AutoMS score, AutoMS sketches & MS parts: GB-Ljag(w). ★
CAL-2. Harmonie No. 1; in E♭, 7 mvts.   2cl 2hn 2bn cb; with later pts for: fl(D - mvts 1 - 3, 7), 2terz-fl: (fl I
marked "Obligato [sic]"), czackan (mvt 7 only).   MS parts: (3 copies), GB-Ljag(w). ★
CAL-3. Harmonie No. 4; in E♭, 6 mvts.   2cl 2hn bn.   MS parts: GB-Ljag(w). ★
CAL-4. H[armonie]. No. 13; in E♭, 10 mvts.   2cl 2hn bn.   MS parts: GB-Ljag(w). ★
CAL-5. [Harmonie in F, one continuous mvt in 2 sections].   2cl 2hn bn.   MS parts: GB-Ljag(w). ★
CAL-6. [Collection of 77 dance mvts composed ? & arranged].   fl(F, terz-fl, D, pic F, E♭) 2cl(E♭) 2cl(B♭) 2hn
2bn tp b-tb cb.   AutoMS scores (incomplete, in separate numbers) & MS parts: GB-Ljag(w), 8/264.
    6.1(-6.12). 12 Walzer.   6.13(-6.15). Introdutione, 3 Walzer & Coda.   6.16(-6.26). 11 Walzer.
    6.27. Ecossaise Walzer.   6.28. Frankfurter Kampfschiff Walzer.   6.29.(-6.34). 6 Walzer.
    6.35. Allemande.   6.36. Galopp.   6.37. Linger Loch [sic] Walzer.   6.39. Française.
    6.40. Polonaise.   6.41, 6.42. 2 Walzer.   6.43. Polonaise.   6.44 Ländler.
    6.45. Bassethorn Walzer [& Trio].   Solo bthn, terz-pic(terz-fl) 2cl(E♭) cl(II in B♭) 2hn 2bn tp b-tb cb.
    6.46(a). C.M. Weber: Walzer aus Oberon.
    6.47(a). Ragotzi [sic] Marsch.   6.48, 6.49. 2 Walzer.   6.50. Dreher.   6.51. Polonoise.
    6.52. Schlacht bei Watterloo [sic], Walzer [with Trio & Coda].
    6.53(a). C.M. Weber: Walzer aus Oberon.   6.54(-6.66). 13. Walzer.   6.67. Marsch.   6.68. Polacca.
    [69. F. Witt: [5] Variazioni Concertante [sic]; in F.   2 solo horns, fl(F) 2cl(E♭) 2cl(B♭) 2bn tp b-tb cb.]
    6.70. Walzer.   6.71. Anon: [opera mvt].   6.72. Anon: Duetto.
    6.73(-6.76). 4 Walzer.   6.77. Dreher.   6.78. Walzer.
CAL-7. [Collection of 55 works, generally dances].   fl(F, terz; pic E♭, F) 2cl(E♭) 2cl(B♭) 2hn 2bn tp b-tb cb.
AutoMS scores & MS parts: GB-Ljag(w), 4/266, No. 3.
    7.1(-7.3). 3 Walzer with Trios.   7.4. Geschwind Walzer.   7.5, 7.6. 2 Schottischer.
    7.7(-7.9). 3 Walzer with Trios.   7.10. Pas double [sic] & Trio.   7.11(-7.13). 3 Walzer with Trios.
    7.14(-7.16). 3 Ländler with Trios & a Coda.   7.17. Ländler.   7.18. Presto, 2/4 with Trio.
    7.19. Walzer.   7.20. Ländler.   7.21. Ecosaise [sic] & Trio.
    7.22. Andantino with 7 Variations / 3/8 / Var. alla Polacca. ★
    7.23. Ecosaise [sic] & Trio.   8.24. 8.25. 2 Walzer with Trios.
    7.26. Andantino, 6/8 / Allo Vivace, 2/4 / Allo Riso[luto], 3/4 / 2ter Walzer, 3/4 / Andante, 3/4. ★
    7.27. [?Ecossaise & Trio], 2/4.   7.28. Polon[aise] with Trio.   7.29. [?Ecossaise & Trio], 2/4.
    7.30. Walzer & Trio.   7.31, 7.32. 2 Ecosaise [sic] with Trios.   7.33. Walzer & Trio.   7.34. Eccose [sic] & Trio.
    7.35. La Cavottino [sic], 2/4.   7.36(-7.38). 3 Française.   7.39. Ecossaise.   7.40. Geschwind Walzer.
    7.41. Ecossaise.   7.42. Ecossaise.   7.43. Geschwind Walzer.   7.44. Quadrille, 3/8 & Trio.
    7.45. Walzer & Trio.   7.46, 7.47. 2 Geschwind Walzer with Trios.   7.48. Walzer & Trio.
    7.49. Tema con [6] Variazione [& Coda], Andantino, 2/4. ★
    7.50. Ecossaise.   7.51. Walzer & Trio.   7.52. Ecose [sic] & Trio.   7.53. Polonaise & Trio.
    7.54(a). Küffner: Walzer & Trio.   7.55. Allegretto con [15] Variazione, 2/4 / Adagio (3 bars) / Walzer, 3/8. ★
CAL-8. [Collection of 26 Walzer; No. 13 titled "Darkelions Walzer", No. 21 "Schnelle Segler", No. 25 "Schnell
Walzer"].   fl ob 2cl(E♭, C) 2cl(B♭, C) 2hn 2bn tp(signal-horn in Nos. 3 - 7, 11) 2bn b-tb cb.
AutoMS scores & MS parts: GB-Ljag(w), 10/258, No. 1. *No. 13 is dedicated to Freidrich Witt (qv).* ★

CAL-1m. Marche Espagnole; in C. fl 2czackan 3cl(C) bn cb. MS pts: GB-Ljag(w), (missing czackan II, cl II).
The czackan was an unusual instrument combining a traverse flute with a walking stick. Among the Wertheim MSS is a fingering chart and exercises prepared for Erbprinz *Carl Friedrich by Joseph Freidlowsky.* ★
CAL-1a. Harmonie 14. Pieçes [sic] d'harmonie arrangées; in B♭, 3 mvts. 2cl(C) 2hn bn b-tb/bn.
MS pts: GB-Ljag(w). *Although called "Tromba" the part is clearly for bass trombone; a separate Fagotto 2ᵈᵒ part is also present, occasionally lying an octave below the b-tb part* ★
  1.2a. Menuet de Boeuf. [Dubious Haydn. Hob. XI/27]. (No other mvts are identified.)
CAL-2a. Taenze . . . zusammlungetragen und arrangiert. 2cl 2hn 2bn. MS pts: GB-Ljag(w), (missing 2hn). ★
  2.1a. Sammlung 1: 12 Laendler with Coda.
  2.2a. Sammlung 2: Deutsch, Ecossaise, Laendler, Tempete, Polonaise, Laendler.
  2.3a. Sammlung 3: Laendler, Ecossaise, Polonaise, Ecossaise, Française, Laendler.
CAL-3a. [Collection of opera mvts]. fl 2cl 2hn 2bn.
  3.1a. Gyrowetz: Wilhelm Tell, Hirtenlied.   3.2a. Haibl: Rochus Pumpernickel, overture & duetto.
  3.3a. Anon: [?also from 3.2a], Polonoise [& Trio]. 3.4a. J. Weigl: Das Waisenhaus, overture.
  3.5a. Anon: [? also from J. Weigl's *Die Waisenhaus*]: Andante / Allegro.
CAL-4a. Pieçes [sic] d'harmonie arrangées [parts: "Harmonie No. 6"]; in B♭, 6 mvts. 2cl 2hn 2bn.
MS parts: GB-Ljag(w). ★
CAL-5a. Harmonie [parts: "Partia"] No. 5 arrangiert; in E♭, 6 mvts. 2cl 2hn bn. MS parts: GB-Ljag(w). ★
CAL-6a. Pieçes [sic] d'harmonie [parts: "Partia"] No. 7 arrangées; in C, 5 mvts. 2cl 2hn bn.
MS parts: GB-Ljag(w). ★
CAL-7a. Pieçes [sic] d'harmonie No. 8 arrangées; in B♭, 4 mvts. 2cl 2hn bn. MS pts: GB-Ljag(w). ★
CAL-8a. Pieçes [sic] d'harmonie No. 9 arrangées; in E♭, 4 mvts. 2cl 2hn bn.
MS parts: GB-Ljag(w), (with later parts for b-tb [Marcia section of mvt 1, mvt 4] and 2hn for mvt 4 only, "wenn das Fagott mit des Posaune geblassen wird"). ★
CAL-9a. Pieçes [sic] d'harmonie [No. 10] arrangées; in E♭, 6 mvts. 2cl 2hn bn. MS pts: GB-Ljag(w). ★
CAL-10a. Pieçes [sic] d'harmonie [No. 11] arrangées; in B♭, 6 mvts. 2cl 2hn bn. MS pts: GB-Ljag(w). ★
CAL-11a. H[armonie] No. 13; in E♭, 10 mvts. 2cl 2hn bn. MS parts: GB-Ljag(w). ★
CAL-12a. Harmonie No. 14 Quatuor . . . arrangé; in E♭, 6 mvts. 2cl 2hn, *or* 2cl hn bn.
MS parts: GB-Ljag(w), (with a separate hn part to be used when hn I plays with the bn, and with 2 bn parts replacing hn I & II, respectively). ★
CAL-13a. [Harmonie; in C minor.major, 3 mvts]. 2cl(C) 2hn bn tb(mvt 1 only). MS parts: GB-Ljag(w).
  13.1a. Mozart: Die Entführung aus dem Serail, "Hier soll ich dich dem sehen" / overture.
  13.2. Polonaise; in C minor, 3/4 & Trio in C major. 13.3. Andante con moto; in C, ¢.
CAL-14a. Auber: La Muette de Portici, overture & 5 mvts. fl(pic D) 2cl(E♭) 2cl(B♭) 2hn 2bn tp b-tb cb.
AutoMS score & MS pts: GB-Ljag(w), (with later additional parts for: hn III ad lib, timp b-dr t-dr cym tri) bell.
CAL-15a. Boieldieu: Jean de Paris, overture. 2cl 2hn bn tp. MS parts: GB-Ljag(w).
CAL-16a. Crusell: Concertante for solo clarinet, horn & bassoon, with orchestra, Op. 3.
Solo clarinet, horn, bassoon; terz-fl 2cl(E♭) 2cl(B♭) 2hn (2)bn 2tp(clar) b-tb+cb.
AutoMS score & MS parts: GB-Ljag(w), (with the printed solo parts; a note on the accompanying bn(I) part states that it is only to used if 3bn are available).
CAL-17a. Himmel: Fanchon das Leyermädchen, overutre & 48 mvts. fl(F, D, pic F, D) 2cl(C) 2cl(B♭) 2hn 2bn tp b-tb cb. AutoMS score & MS parts: GB-Ljag(w), (2cl in E♭ replace 2cl in C in the parts).
CAL-18a. C. Kreutzer: Die Alpenhütte, overture & 13 mvts. fl(D♭) 2cl(C, E♭) 2cl(B♭) 2hn 2bn tp b-tb cb.
AutoMS score & MS parts: GB-Ljag(w).
CAL-19a. C. Kreutzer: Der deutsche Rhein. pic(F) 2cl(E♭) 2cl(B♭) 3hn 2bn tp b-tb+cb, (ad lib: tp II).
AutoMS score & MS parts: GB-Ljag(w), 362, No. 5.
CAL-20a. R. Kreutzer: Lodoiska, overture. 2cl(C) 2hn 2bn b-tb. MS parts: GB-Ljag(w).
CAL-21a. Kunzen: Das Fest der Winzer, overture. 2cl 2hn bn b-tb.
MS parts: GB-Ljag, (the b-tb may be a later addition).
CAL-22a. Lindpaintner: Concertino for 2 horns & orchestra, Op. 60. 2 horns, fl(pic) 2cl(A) 2bn tp b-tb cb.
AutoMS score, MS parts & original printed parts (Schott: Mainz, pn 2018, c.1825: 2fl 2cl b-tb): GB-Ljag(w).
CAL-23a. Méhul: Une Folie, overture & 9 mvts. 2cl 2hn 2bn. MS parts: GB-Ljag(w).
CAL-24a. Mozart: Idomeneo, overture & 14 mvts. fl(F) 2cl(E♭) 2cl(B♭) 2hn 2bn tp b-tb cb.
AutoMS score & MS parts: GB-Ljag(w).
CAL-25a. Mozart: Don Giovanni, overture. 2cl(C) 2hn bn b-tb. MS parts: GB-Ljag(w).
CAL-26.1a. Mozart: La Clemenza di Tito, overture. 2fl 2cl(C) 2cl(B♭) 2hn 2bn tp(clar) b-tb cb timp.
AutoMS score & MS parts: GB-Ljag(w), (with an additional basso part; cl I in C pt missing last 16 bars).
CAL-26.2. Mozart: La Clemenza di Tito, 26 mvts. fl(F, E♭, C) 1/2cl(E♭, C, B♭) 2cl(C, B♭) 2hn 2bn tp b-tb timp.
AutoMS score: GB-Ljag(w).
CAL-26.3a. Mozart: La Clemenza di Tito, overture & 26 mvts. fl(C, D, F) 2cl(E♭, C) 2cl(B♭, C) 2hn 2bn tp b-tb cb timp. AutoMS score & MS pts: GB-Ljag(w), (score missing the overture; with additional pts for cl in F: overture, cl in C III ripieno ad lib: overture, Nos. 10, 12). *f.1b of the hn II pt bears the note, "Suivez Göpfert".*
CAL-27a. Mozart: Die Zauberflöte, overture. 2cl 2hn bn tp(clar) b-tb/bn(II). MS parts: GB-Ljag(w).
CAL-28a. Weber: Silvana, overture & 19 mvts. terz-fl(fl in F, pic in F) 2cl(E♭) 2cl(B♭) 2hn 2bn tp b-tb cb.
AutoMS score & MS parts: GB-Ljag(w), 1/263, No. 2.
CAL-29a. C.M. Weber: Preciosa, overture & 10 mvts. fl(F, terz-fl, pic in F & E♭) 2cl(E♭) 2cl(B♭) 2hn tp b-tb+cb. AutoMS score & MS parts: GB-Ljag(w), 4/266, No. 4, (with additional bn I & timp parts).
CAL-30.1a, 30.2a. Anon: God Save the King, 2 settings. 1: fl(F) cl(E♭) 2cl(B♭) 3hn 2bn b-tb; 2: 2cl(E♭) 2cl(B♭) 2hn 2bn tp b-tb cb timp, (ad lib: tp II). AutoMS score & MS parts: GB-Ljag(w), 362, Nos. 2 & 3.
CAL-31a. [unidentified work, 5 mvts]. fl(F) cl(E♭) 2cl(B♭) 2hn 2bn tp b-tb. MS pts: GB-Ljag(w), 9/258, No. 3.
CAL-32a. [unidentified work, ?opera], 6 mvts. 2cl(E♭) 2cl(B♭) 2hn 2bn tp b-tb cb.
MS parts: GB-Ljag(w), 9/258, No. 5.
CAL-1va. Cherubini: Offertorium [Ave Maria]; in F. S solo, cl(C) solo/fl, 2cl(II, III, C) 2hn bn(I = vla pt) vla.
MS pts: GB-Ljag(w), (with printed S, cl/fl & vla pts: pn D. et C. No. 3700 = Diabelli und Cappi: Wien).
CAL-1c. Anon [?Carl Friedrich]: Con [7] Variazione. Solo bassoon, cl(E♭) cl(C) 2cl(B♭) 2hn bn tp b-tb cb.
MS parts: GB-Ljag(w), 9/258, No. 6. ★

CAL-2c. [3 mvts: Larghetto non tanto; Walser, Polonoise]. 2cl(E♭) 2cl(B♭) 2hn 2bn. MS pts: GB-Ljag(w). ★
CAL-3c. [Set of 7 dances with Trios: 1. Walzer, 2. Française, 3. Française, 4. Walser, 5. (?Française), 6. Polacca, 7. Française]. cl(E♭) 2cl(B♭) 2hn 2bn tp b-tb timp. MS parts: GB-Ljag(w). ★
CAL-4c. [Set of 7 dances, ?or Cassation: 1. Marcia, 2. Walzer [sic], 3. Contratanz, 4. Allegro, 6/8, 5. Walzer, 6. Polonaise, 7. Allegro con fuoco a furore + Minore section.] pic(E♭, No. 7) 2cl(E♭) 2cl(B♭) 2hn 2bn tp b-tb. MS parts: GB-Ljag(w). ★
CAL-5c. [Menuetto & 5 Walzer]. 2pic(F) 2cl(E♭) 2cl(B♭)+2cl(B♭ rip) 2hn 2bn tp b-tb cb timp. MS parts: GB-Ljag(w), 413. ★
CAL-6c. [6 mvts: 1. Menuetto & Trio; 2. Andantino, C / All° Moderato, C; 3. Geschwind Walzer & Trio; 4. Andante amoroso, 2/4; 5. [untitled] 3/8 / 2/4; 6. Quadrille, 2/4.] 2cl(E♭) 2cl(B♭) 2hn 2bn tp b-tb cb timp. MS parts: GB-Ljag(w), 389. ★
CAL-7c. [Set of 5 mvts]. fl(F, No. 5: pic in E♭) 2cl(E♭) 2cl(B♭) 2hn 2bn b-tb.
AutoMS scores (Nos. 2 & 5) & MS parts: GB-Ljag(w), 365. ★
   7.1c. Marcia. 7.2c(a). C.M. Weber: Volkslied, "Mein Schatzerl is hübsch", (J.234). 7.3c. Menuetto & Trio. 7.4c. Presto. 7.5c(a). Anon: Feldschritt, Der Jäger aus der Pfalz.
CAL-1vc. [Duet, "Denn mit der Freude Feier-klange"]. ST, fl(intro only, 2 bars) 2cl(C) 2cl(B♭) 2hn 2bn (2)cb.
AutoMS vocal score with piano accompaniment & instrumental introduction (16 bars) & MS pts: GB-Ljag(w). ★
CAL-1ac. Paer: Sargino, overture. 2cl(B♭) 2hn 2bn tp.
MS parts: GB-Ljag(w), (with a later tp part in the hand of Friedrich Witt (qv)).
CAL-2ac. Rossini: L'Italiana in Algeri, overture. cl(F) 3cl(C) 2hn 2bn tp b-tb timp.
MS parts: GB-Ljag(w), (with a later variant b-tb part).
CAL-3ac. [Set of 8 mvts, possibly all arrangments]. Scoring varies. MS parts: GB-Ljag(w), 429.
   3.1ac. Anon: Aria, Allegretto, 3/4. fl(D) bthn 3cl(C, II - IV) 2hn cb+bn bn(II). 3.2ac. Anon: Larghetto, 2/4. fl (D) 4cl(C) 2hn 2bn. 3.3ac. Kunzen: Der Fest der Winzer, Aria. fl(D) 4cl(C) 2hn 2bn.
   3.4ac. C.M. Weber: Der Freischütz, Allo feroco ma non troppo Presto. 2cl(C) 2cl(A) 2hn 2bn cb+bn.
   3.5ac. Anon: Allegro non tanto. fl(D) 2cl(E♭) 2cl(B♭) 2hn 2bn. 4.6ac. Anon: Allegro. fl(D) 4cl(C) 2hn 2bn.
   3.7ac. Mozart: Don Giovanni, Madamina. fl(D) 2cl(C) 2cl(A) 2hn 2bn.
   3.8ac. Mozart: Don Giovanni, Finch' han dal vino. 2cl(E♭) 2cl(B♭) 2hn 2bn.

LOIBL, Anselm Benedikt, *OSB [Order of St Benedict] 1766 - 1822*
BAL-1. Parthia in E♭; 5 mvts. 2cl 2hn 2bn. MS parts ("Ad me Petrum Hüber"): D-Mbs, Mus.Ms.7511. ★

***LOLLI, Antonio** c.1730, Bergamo - 10 Aug 1802, Palermo*
AQL-1. Sonata in F; 3 mvts. Solo violin, 2talie 2hn basso. MS parts: CZ-Pnm, XXXII.A.139. ★

LOQUAY (possibly Loguay or Lognay), ( )
YXK-1. Divertimento ex B[♭]; 4 mvts. 2cl 2hn bn. MS parts: CZ-Pnm, XXXII.A.301, (missing cl II). ★

***LORENTZ, ( )** active 1772*
XYL-1. Nro 1mo Parthia Ex C; 5 mvts. 2ob 2hn 2bn. MS parts: CZ-Pnm, XXII.D.215. ★
XYL-2. Nro 2do Parthia Ex F; 4 mvts. 2ob 2hn 2bn. MS parts: CZ-Pnm, XXII.D.216. ★
XYL-3. Nro 3tio Parthia Ex B[♭]; 5 mvts. 2ob 2hn 2bn. MS parts: CZ-Pnm, XXII.D.217. ★
XYL-4. Nro [4] Parthia Ex G# [G major]; 4 mvts. 2ob 2hn 2bn. MS parts: CZ-Pnm, XXII.D.218. ★
XYL-5. Nro 5 Parthia Ex D# [D major]; 5 mvts. 2ob 2hn 2bn. MS parts: CZ-Pnm, XXII.D.219. ★
XYL-6. Nro 6 Parthia Ex C; 5 mvts. 2ob 2hn 2bn.
MS parts: CZ-Pnm, (2 copies), XXII.D.220, XXXII.B.150. ★
XYL-7. Nro 7 Parthia Ex F; 4 mvts. 2ob 2hn 2bn. MS pts: CZ-Pnm, (2 copies), XXII.D.221, XXXII.B.149.★
XYL-8. Nro 8 Parthia Ex B♭]; 4 mvts. 2ob 2hn 2bn. MS parts: CZ-Pnm, XXII.D.222. ★
XYL-9. Nro 9 Parthia Ex G# [G major]; 5 mvts. 2ob 2hn 2bn. MS parts: CZ-Pnm, XXII.D.223. ★
XYL-10. Nro 10 Parthia Ex D## [D major]; 4 mvts. 2ob 2hn 2bn. MS parts: CZ-Pnm, XXII.D.224. ★
XYL-11. Nro 11 Parthia Ex C; 5 mvts. 2ob 2hn 2bn. MS pts: CZ-Pnm, XXII.D.225. ★
XYL-12. Nro 12 Parthia Ex F; 4 mvts. 2ob 2hn 2bn.
MS parts ("Finis 4. 8bi [Oct] 1772): CZ-Pnm, XXII.D.226. ★

***LORENTZEN, Bent** 11 Feb 1935, Stenvad - 1987*
BZL-1. Concerto for Alto Saxophone.
Solo a-sax, fl(pic) fl 2ob cl(cl E♭) cl(b-cl) 2hn 2bn 2tp tu timp 3perc pf.
Pm (Edition Wilhelm Hansen: Copenhagen, 1986), hire score & parts.
BZL-1v. Min Brud er en Lukket have (My Bride is like a Garden). Solo S, 2fl 2hn 3perc keyboard pf/celeste.
Pm (Edition Wilhelm Hansen: Copenhagen, 1972), hire score & parts.

***LORENZINI, Danilo** 1952, Italy*
DYL-1. Serenata in Forma di Variazioni su un Tema di Scriabin. 2ob 2cl 2hn 2bn.
Pm (Carish S.p.A.: Milano, pn 22131, 1984), miniature score.

LORENZINI, Raimondo *c.1730, Rome - May 1806, Rome*
RYL-1(-6). 6 Nocturnes. 2cl 2hn bn serp. MS parts: D-Bds.

***LORENZITI, Bernardo** (Parisian violinist, active 1764, Kirchheim - 1813, Paris*
BXL-1. Canon ou divertissement; in B♭, 2 mvts. 2cl 2bn.
Pc (Chez David (gravé par Michot): Paris, sd), RISM [L 2841], parts: F-Pn, Vm27 2587; H-KE; S-Skma. ★

***LORTZING, Gustav Albert** 23 Oct 1801, Berlin - 21 Jan 1851, Berlin*
***GAL-1v.** Lied zu Friedrich Schiller, "Wallersteins Lager": "Frisch auf, Kameraden aufs Pferd; March 1828, (LoWV 14). 2Kürassier, Chor der Soldaten (TTB), 2cl 4hn 2bn 2tp b-tb timp.
AutoMS score: D-DT, Mus-L 18 a 1. ★
GAL-2v. Chor zu M. Tenelly *Die Mönche oder Die Carabiniers im Kloster der Carmeliterinnen*, Lustspiel in 3 Acts (6 Aug 1850), (LoWV 98), "Sanctus Dominus". SSST, 2cl 2hn bn 2tp b-tb.
AutoMS score: D-DT, Mus-L 101 a 1. MS score: D-DT, Mus-L 101 a 2. MS parts: D-DT. ★
***GAL-1e.** Schauspielmusik zu Christian Dietrich Grabbe's *Don Juan und Faust*; 1829, (LoWV 16): Act I, Tafelmusik [after Mozart's "Finch'han dal vino"], 46 bars. 2cl 2hn 2bn. AutoMS score: D-DT, Mus-L 19 a 1. ★

*GAL-2e. *Uranias Festmorgen,* Festspiel zum 50 jährigen bestehen der Privat-Theater-Gesellschafts "Urania" in Berlin, 1842, (LoWV 55): No. 4, 37 bars. 2fl 2cl 2hn 2bn. MS score: D-DT. *An expanded version of GAL-3, incorporating the "Marseilaise".*
*GAL-1ve. *Die Weihnachtsabend, Launigte Szenen aus dem Familienlebe;* 1832, (LoWV 26): No. 6, Quintetto, "Es freuen sich die Kleinen", 48 bars. SATTB, fl 2cl 2hn bn..
AutoMS score: D-DT, Mus-L 35 a 1. MS parts: D-DT. ★
*GAL-2ve. *Andreas Hofer,* Singspiel in 1 Act; 1833, (LoWV 27). MS score & parts: D-DT.
  2.1ve. No. 2, "Ich fliehe nicht", 36 bars. S, 2cl 2hn 2bn 3vc db. ★
  2.2ve. No. 6, "Selig sind die Toten", 18 bars. Solo STBB, 2cl 2hn 2bn timp. ★
*GAL-3ve, 2.1e. *Szenen auf Mozarts Leben,* Singspiel in 1 Act; May/June 1833, (LoWV 28).
AutoMS score: CZ-Pnm, XX.C.103. MS score: D-DT.
  3ve. No. 5, Quartet, "Es gibt kein süsser Glück", 32 bars. Solo SATB, 2cl 2hn 2bn. ★
  3e. No. 8, Musik auf dem Theater, 25 bars. 2cl 2hn 2bn. *See also supra:* GAL-2e.
*GAL-4ve. *Undine,* Romantische Zauberoper in 4 Acts, 1844, (LoWV 64): No. 6: Finale, "Friede mit euch!".
Solo S, A, T, BAR, B, Chor des Fischer und Fischerinnen (SATB), 2fl(pic) 2ob 2cl 4hn 2bn 2tp 3tb timp.
AutoMS score: D-DT. MS score & parts: D-Cl; D-Dl; D-DT; D-RUl; US-Wc. ★
*GAL-5ve. Schauspielmusik zu Rudolph Gottscholl *Ferdinand von Schiller,* Vaterlandisches Drama in 5 Aufzügen, Nov 1850, (LoWV 101): No. 1, Lied, "Bei [zu] Kolberg, an der Ostsee Strand".
Solo voice, Männerchor, fl 2cl 2bn. AutoMS score & MS parts: D-DT, Mus-L 103 a 1. ★

*LOUDOVÁ, Ivana *8 March 1941, Chlumec nad Cidlinou*
*IZL-1. Don Giovanni's Dream; 1989. ob ca 2cl 2hn 2bn cbn.
Pm (Compusic: Amsterdam, pn 263, 1991), score & parts, (copy in CZ-Pis).
IZL-2. Zařivý hlas [Luminous Voice] Concerto for cor anglais, winds & percussion.
Pm (C.F. Peters: New York, 1986), hire score & parts, (copy in CZ-Pis).
IZL-3. Hymnos. 2fl fl(pic) 3ob 3cl 6hn 2bn bn(cbn) 3tp 3tb tu 3s-dr.
Pm (C.F. Peters: New York, 1973), hire score & parts, (copy in CZ-Pr, O 8082).

*LOUEL (Louël), Jean Hippolyte Oscar *3 Jan 1914, Ostend, Belgium*
JNL-1. Toccata et fugue; 1973. 2fl 2ob 2cl 2hn 2bn 2tp 3tb. MS score: B-Bcdm.

*LOUIS, F., *Chevalier active c.1794 (Paris) - post-1841 (Paris)*
Année 2 & 3 of the Journal d'Harmonie et de Musique Militiare, *a joint venture by F. Louis, C. Münchs and F. Berr was later reissued from the original plates as separate works by Les Fils de B. Schott, Mayence (Mainz). Each composer's contributions are listed at their separate entries.*
FCL-1. Journal d'Harmonie et de Musique Militaire. Scoring varies.
Pc (*Année 1:* Au Dépôt du Journal, Chez Mr Baumann: Paris; *Année 2, Liv. 1 - 3 [5 - 7]:* Au Dépôt du Journal, Chez Pacini . . . et Chez les Auteurs: Paris; *Année 2, Liv 4 [8] & Année 3, Liv. 1 - 4 [9 - 12]:* Au Dépôt du Journal, Chez Pacini . . . et Chez Munchs [sic], pn 5 - 9, c.1822 - 1823), parts: F-Pn, Vm 27 2630 (1 - 4), Vm27 2969 (1, 2) & Vm27 2630, (2 copies of Liv. 7 - 9), (missing Année 3, Liv. 10-12, FCL-1/10-1/12). ★
  1/1/1. Marche, C. No. 1. fl(E♭) cl(E♭) 2cl(B♭) 2hn tp tb serp b-dr.
  1/1/2. Pas Redoublé, 2/4 [+Trio]. No. 3. fl(E♭) cl(E♭) 2cl(B♭) 2hn 2bn tp tb serp b-dr.
  1/1/3. Polonaise, 3/4+Trio]. No. 8. fl(E♭) cl(E♭) 2cl(B♭) 2hn 2bn tp tb serp b-dr.
  1/2/1. Pas Redoublé, 2/4. No. 4. fl(E♭) cl(E♭) 2cl(I, B♭) 2cl(II, B♭) 2hn 2bn tp tb serp b-dr.
  1/2/2. Air varié, Andantino, 2/4 (Theme + 3Var +Tutti). No. 8.
      fl(E♭) cl(E♭) 2cl(I, B♭) 2cl(II, B♭) 2hn 2bn tp tb serp.
  1/2/3. Menuetto, 3/4 [+Trio]. No. 8. fl(E♭) cl(E♭) 2cl(B♭) 2hn 2bn tp tb serp b-dr
      There are only a few divisi in cl II in No. 4; in No. 8, cl II is only divisi in Variation 2. A few octave divisi occur in Var. 1 of No. 8 in the bn II pt; a few octave divisi occur in No. 4 of the serp. (The divisi in the lower instruments may be, in fact, simply alternative parts.)
  1/3/1. Marche, C. No. 1. fl(E♭) cl(E♭) cl(I, B♭) 2cl(II, B♭) 2hn 2bn tp tb serp b-dr.
  1/3/2. Pas Redoublé, 6/8. No. 3. fl(E♭) cl(E♭) 2cl(B♭) 2hn 2bn tp tb serp b-dr.
  1/3/3. Harmonie. Polonaise 3/4 [& Trio]. No. 7. fl(E♭) cl(E♭) 2cl(I, B♭) cl(II, B♭) 2hn 2bn tp tb serp.
  1/4/1. Marche Composée pour la Convoi funèbre de feu Monseigner Le Duc de Berri [sic]. No. 1.
      fl(E♭) cl(E♭) 2cl(B♭) + 2cl(B♭ ripieno) 2hn 2bn tp tb serp b-dr(muffled).
  1/4/2. Pas Redoublé, 6/8 [+Trio & Coda]. No. 3. fl(E♭) cl(E♭) 2cl(B♭) 2hn bn(I) 2bn(II) 2tp tb serp b-dr.
  1/4/3. Waltz, 3/8 [+ Trio]. No. 5. fl(E♭) cl(E♭) 2cl(B♭) 2hn 2bn tp tb serp b-dr.
  1/5/1. Louis: Ouverture. No. 7. fl(C) 2cl(B♭)+2/3cl(B♭ rip) 2hn 2bn tp 2tb 2serp cb.
  1/5/2. And^{te} non troppo. No. 8. fl(C) 2cl(B♭) 2hn 2bn serp cb.
  1/5/3. Menuetto, Allegro vivace [& Trio], 3/4. fl(C) 2cl(B♭) 2hn 2bn tp serp cb.
      The 2bn are on a single (divisi) pt for Nos. 1 - 6, and on separate pts for Nos. 7 - 9. The 2serp pt is marked "Serpents" with divisi in 1 - 7, Nos. 8 & 9 are either unison or for a single instrument. The Contre Basse (Nos. 7 - 9 only) is definitely for a string instrument with "arco" and "pizz" markings; in the next issue it is marked "ad libitum".
  1/6/1. Marche, C. No. 1. pic(D) cl(E♭) cl(I, B♭) 2cl(II, B♭) 2hn 2bn tp tb b-dr.
  1/6/2. Pas Redoublé, 2/4. pic(D) cl(E♭) 2cl(I, B♭) cl(II, B♭) 2hn 2bn tp tb b-dr.
  1/6/3. Valz [sic] [& Trio, Coda], 3/8. pic(D) cl(E♭) 2cl(I, B♭) 2cl(II, B♭) 2hn 2bn tp 2tb b-dr+t-dr.
  1/7/1. Pas Redoublé [& Trio], 2/4. No. 4. fl(E♭) cl(E♭) 2cl(B♭) 2hn 2bn tp tb 2serp b-dr.
  1/7/2. Pas Redoublé, 2/4. No. 5. fl(E♭) cl(E♭) cl(I, B♭) cl(II, B♭)* 2hn 2bn tp tb 2serp b-dr.
  1/7/3. Valz [sic] [& Trio], 3/8. No. 6. fl(E♭) cl(E♭) 2cl(I, B♭)* cl(II, B♭) 2hn 2bn tp 2tb 2serp b-dr.
  1/8/1. Ouverture. No. 7. fl(C) 2ob/cl(C) 2cl(C) 2hn 2bn tp tb 2serp cb.
  1/8/2. Adagio,Thema con [3] Variations. No. 8. fl(C) 2ob-cl/cl(I, C) 2cl(II, C) 2hn 2bn tp tb 2serp cb.
  1/8/3. Polonaise, Allegro, 3/4 [+ Trio]. No. 9. fl(C) 2ob/cl(C) 2cl(C) 2hn 2bn tp tb 2serp cb.
  1/9/1. Marche, C. No. 1. fl(E♭) cl(E♭) 2cl(B♭) 2hn 2bn tp tb 2serp b-dr. cl(I, II in B♭) divisi.
  1/9/2. Pas Redoublé.2/4 [+ Trio]. No. 2.
      fl(E♭) cl(E♭) cl(I, B♭) 2cl(II, B♭) 2hn 2bn tp 2tb 2serp b-dr tambours.
  1/9/3. Waltz, 3/8 [+ Trio]. No. 3. fl(E♭) cl(E♭) 2cl(I, B♭) 2cl(II, B♭) 2hn 2bn tp 2serp b-dr.

FCL-1.1/1(-1.1/3). Grand Harmonie, Cahier [MS: 1 - 3]; in F, each in 3 mvts.   fl 2ob 2cl 2hn 2bn tp serp/cb.
Pc (Chez les Fils de B. Schott: Paris, Mayence et Anvers, pn 3024 - 3026, 1828), parts: D-MZsch, (complete);
GB-Ljag(w), (Cah. 3 only). *Cah. 1 = Liv. 5; Cah. 2 = Liv. 8; Cah. 3 =Liv. 11).* ★
FCL-1.2/1(-1.2/5). Musique Militaire, Cahier 1 - 5.
Pc (Chex les Fils de B. Schott: Paris, Mayence et Anvers, pn 3012 - 3016, 1828), parts: D-MZsch, (complete).
Cah. 1 = Liv. 6; Cah. 2 = Liv. 7; Cah. 3 = Liv. 9; Cah. 4 = Liv. 10; Cah. 5 = Liv. 12.
FCL-1m. Pas Redoublé; in B♭. *(Journal de Musique Militaire, Liv. 1, No. 1.)* (=LAM-1.1m)
fl(E♭/F) cl(E♭/F) cl(solo B♭/C) 2cl(B♭/C) 2hn(E♭/F) 2bn(B♭/C) tp(E♭/F) 2tb serp/oph(C) b-dr t-dr+s-dr.
Pc (au Maison de Musique et d'Instrumens: Paris, c.1832 - 1835), parts: F-Pn, Vm27 2628, (the 2tb pt bears the
note, "Nª. Losqu'il un Trombone seul il faut jouer les notes en bas"; the single drum pt is marked "Caisse
roulante et Caisse clair"). *Although the composers (Louis & Mürchs are not named specifically, from the scoring
we believe this to be the contribution of F. Louis.* ★
FCL-1a. Adam: Le Brasseur de Preston, overture.   fl cl(E♭) cl(solo B♭) 4cl(B♭) 4hn(E♭, B♭) 2bn 2cap 2tp 3tb
oph/serp cb(ad lib) b-dr+cym s-dr.
Pc (chez les Fils de B. Schott: Mayence et Anvers, pn 1490, 1821), parts: GB-Ljag(w), 152.
FCL-2a(m). Lesueur: Marche séraphique (Taceat terra) du couronnement (of Napoleon) executée à Rheims dans
la cérémonie du sacre.   fl(E♭) cl(E♭) 2cl(B♭) 2hn 2bn tp b-tb serp b-dr.
Pc (Henry: Paris, pn 219, c.1803), RISM [L 2157], parts: S-Skma, Oh; GB-Ljag, photocopy.

LOUIS, F., *Chevalier*, MARCHAL, François, & MÜNCHS, Conrad
*Individual contributions can be found listed under the individual composers; the separate contributions from
Année 2 onwards were reissued in 1828 by Les Fils de B. Schott. For further information on this complicated
journal, See:* The Wind Ensemble Source Book and Biographical Guide, *Part 1, Appendix 1.*
LMM-1.1(-1.4). Journal d'Harmonie et de Musique Militaire; Année 1, Liv. 1 - 4.   Scoring varies.
Pc (Au Dépôt du Journal, Chez Mᵉ Baumann: Paris, pn 1 - 4, c.1820), parts: F-Pn, Vm27 2630 (1 - 4). *Liv. 1
& 2 are marked "Gravé par Mᵉᶦᵉ. S. VAIDY"; from Liv. 3 onward Michot was the engraver.*
Continued as: **LOUIS, F., *Chevalier*, BERR, Frédéric, & MÜNCHS, Conrad**
LMM-1.5(-1.12). Journal d'Harmonie et de Musique Militaire; Année 2, Liv. 1 - 4 [5 - 9], Année 3, Liv. 1 -
4 [9 - 12].   Scoring varies.
Pc (Au Dépôt du Journal, Chez Pacini . . . et Chez les Auteurs: Paris; Liv. 8 & 9: Au Dépôt du Journal, Chez
Pacini . . . et Chez Munchs [sic], pn 5 - 9, c.1822 - 1823), parts: F-Pn, Vm27 2969 (1, 2) & Vm27 2630,
(2 copies of Liv. 7 - 9), (missing Année 3, Liv. 2 - 4 [10 - 12]).

LOUIS, F., *Chevalier* & MÜNCHS, Conrad
The only surviving issue comprises 2 works without attribution; we believe No. 1 is by Louis & No. 2 by Münchs.
LAM-1. Journal de Musique Militiare; Année 1, Liv. 1 (no other issues traced).   Scoring varies.
Pc (au Maison de Musique et d'Instrumens: Paris, c.1832 - 1835), parts: F-Pn, Vm27 2628. ★
   1.1m. Pas redoublé, in B♭. p-fl(E♭/F) cl(E♭/F) cl(B♭/C) 2cl(B♭/C) 2hn 2bn tp 2tb serp/oph b-dr t-dr+s-dr.
     (with 2 sets of bn tb serp/oph pts in the keys of B♭ & C; the tb pt calls for b-tb if only one available).
   1.2m. Pas redoublé, in E♭. p-fl(E♭) cl(E♭) cl(B♭ solo) 2cl(B♭) 2hn 2bn tp 3tb serp/oph b-dr t-dr.

LOWE, Thomas, *(pseudonym)* *1911*
THL-1. Suite of Dances, 1975.   2fl ob 3cl hn bn.
Pm (Emerson Edition: Ampleforth, pn 22, 1977), score & parts.

*LOWES, Ian *1947, Bishop Auckland, County Durham, UK*
IYL-1. Octet, 1985, 3 mvts.   2ob 2cl 2hn 2bn.   MS parts: GB-BFlowes.
Pm (Camden Music: London), score & parts.
IYL-1a. Dave Brubeck: Three to get ready; Blue shadows in the street; Blue Rondo à la Turk.   2cl 2hn 2bn.
Pm (Camden Music: London, 1992), score & parts.

*LUCAS, Charles *28 July 1808, Salisbury - 30 March 1869, London*
*CHL-1. Septet; single mvt in E♭ minor & major.   fl ob 2cl 2hn 2bn.
MS parts: GB-Lbl, RM.21.d.6, ff.76 - 96b; GB-Lra, Ms. 1102. ★
Pm (Phylloscopus: Lancaster, 1989), score & parts.

LUCCHINI, P.
PYL-1v. Kyrie & Gloria.   Solo TB. 2cl 2hn tp tb timp organ.   MS score: I-Vsmc. ★

*LUCKÝ, Štěpán *20 Jan 1919, Žilina*
SXL-1. Musica collegialis.   2ob 2cl 2hn 2bn tp db.
Pm (Český hudební fond: Prague, 1980), hire score & parts.
SXL-2. Children's Suite.   fl ob 2cl hn bn.
Pm (Český hudební fond: Prague, 1951), hire score & parts.

LUDEWIG (Ludwig) IX, *Fürst zu Hesse-Darmstadt* *1719 - 1790, Darmstadt*
The titles have been added to the MS in a later hand; the composer may not have scored these works.
FHL-1m. Bataillonsmarsch, v. Ludewig IX, comp[onirt]. 1.I.1764.   ob 2cl(C) 2hn bn 2tp.
MS parts: D-DS, Mus.ms.1223/19, No. 3. ★
FHL-2m. Marsch, comp[onirt] v. Ludewig IX fü sein französ[ische]. Regiment Royal Hesse Darmstadt.
ob 2cl(C) 2hn bn 2tp.   MS parts: D-DS, Mus.Ms.1223/19, No. 6. ★

LUENING, Otto (Clarence) *15 June 1900, Milwaukee*
OCL-1. Mexican Serenades, 1974.   pic fl ob ca cl b-cl hn bn db 2perc.
Pm (Highgate Press: Boston; via Galaxy).
OCL-1v. Theater piece no 2.   Narrator, soprano(recorded on tape), 2fl 2cl 2hn bn 2tp 2tbn tu.
AutoMS: (unpublished).

LÜTGEN, W.A. *(1790)*
WAL-1. Notturno.   2fl 2hn.
Pc (B. Schott fils: Mainz, c.1819), parts: US-Wc.

LUIGINI, Alexandre *9 March 1850, Lyons - 29 July 1906, Paris*
AZL-1. Aubade, Op. 13. 3fl ob 2cl hn bn harp/piano; *(also cited as for: 2ob 2cl 2hn 2bn piano).*
Pm (Albert J. Andraud Wind Instrument Library: Cincinatti; (now Southern Music Co.: San Antonio, c.1935), score & parts.

*LUKÁŠ, Zdeněk *21 Aug 1928, Prague*
ZEL-1. Musica Boema, 2 Symphonic Movements, Op. 137. 3fl 3ob 3cl 4sax 4hn 2bn 3tp 3tb tu harp perc xyl campanile.
Pm (Český hudební fond: Prague, 1978), hire score & parts.
ZEL-2. Sonata concertata, Op. 49. Piano, 2fl 2ob 2cl 2hn 2bn 2tp tb perc.
Pm (Český hudební fond: Prague, 1966), hire score & parts.
ZEL-3. Musica ritmica, Concerto for percussion instruments, Op. 51. Percussion solo, 8 winds.
Pm (Český hudební fond: Prague, c.1966), hire score & parts.

*LULLY (Lulli), Jean Baptiste (Giovanni Battista) *28 Nov 1632, Florence - 22 March 1687, Paris*
JBL-1. Airs . . . pour le Carousel de Monseigneur Lan; 1686. ob 2taille(oboe da caccia) 3tp 2b timp.
MS: F-V, Ms.Mus.1163. ★
Pm (Heugel: Paris 1969), 2 vols, score, (Plein Jeu, Nos. 68, 69).
Pm (Musica rara: Monteux, pn 2112, repr 1984), ed. R.L. Minter & C.W. Smith, score & parts, (rescored for 2ob ca/ob bn 3tp tb timp).
Pm (Nova: London, pn NM 174, sd) as "Marches & Airs for the Court Band of Louis XIV, compiled by André Philidor".
JBL-2. Les Folies d'Espagne; in C, 1702. 3ob bn. MS: F-Pn, Rés.F.671, No. 10/2.
JBL-1m(-3m). Air de la Marche française, No. 1 [G], 2 [C], 4 [C]. 3ob bn.
MS: F-Pn, Rés.F.671, Nos. 4/2, 4/3, 4/5. ★
JBL-4m(-9m). Air de la Marche des Mousquetaires, Nos. 1 - 6 [all in C]. 3ob bn.
MS: F-Pn, Rés.F.671, Nos. 6/1 - 6/6, (the interior parts of Nos. 4 - 6 are completed by Philidor). ★
JBL-10m. Air de l'Retraite [sic]; in C. 3ob bn. MS: F-Pn, Rés.F.671, No. 6/2. ★
JBL-11m. Marche de la Garde Marine; in C. 3ob bn. MS: F-Pn, Rés.F.671, No. 9. ★
JBL-12m. Marche du Régiment du Roy; in F, 1670. 3ob bn. MS: F-Pn Rés.F.671, No. 10/1. ★
JBL-13m. Marche des Dragons de Monterey; in C. 3ob bn. MS: F-Pn, Rés.F.671, No. 22. ★
JBL-14m, 15m. Marche de Savoye, Nos. 1 & 2; both in C. 3ob bn. MS: F-Pn, Rés.F.671, Nos. 24/1, 24/2. ★
JBL-16m, 17m. Air de l'Assemblée, Nos. 1 & "; both in C. 3ob bn. MS: F-Pn, Rés.F.671, Nos. 24/3, 24/4. ★

LUNDÉN, Lennart *11 Sept 1914, Ytterlännäs - 18 Nov 1966, Stockholm*
LYL-1. 4 Pieces [Quadrilles]. 2fl 2cl b-cl/sax bn.
Pm (Nordiska Musikförlaget: Stockholm, sd), score & parts.
LYL-2. Queen Christina's Song. 2fl 2cl b-cl/sax bn.
Pm (Nordiska Musikförlaget: Stockholm, sd), score & parts.
LYL-3. 3 Swedish Tunes. fl ob 2cl bn.
Pm (Hansen: Copenhagen).
Pm (Nordiska Musikförlaget: Stockholm, sd), score & parts.
LYL-1a. Bellman: Blåsen nu alla: Bellmansvit. 2fl ob 2cl b-cl 2hn bn b. MS score (1960): S-Sic.

LUNDEN-WELDEN, Gunnar *1914 - 1988, Sweden*
GWL-1. 4 småbitar för 6 träblåsare; 4 mvts, 1976. fl(pic) fl(II) fl(III)/ob 2cl bn.
Pm (Edition suecia, c/o S-Sic: Stockholm, 1976), score & parts.

*LUNDQUIST, Torbjörn Iwan *1920, Sweden*
TIL-1. Vindkraft (Wind power): Symphonic sketch. fl ob 4cl 2sax 2hn bn 4tp euph 2tb 2tu db timp perc.
MS score: S-Sic.

LUTOSLAWSKI (Lutosławsli), Witold *25 Jan 1913, Warsaw - 7 Feb 1994, Warsaw*
WQL-1. Fanfare for Louisville. 3fl 2ob 2cl 4hn 3bn 4tp 3tb tu timp perc.
Pm (Chester Music: London, etc, 1986), hire score & parts.
WQK-1v. Trois Poèmes d'Henri Michaux. 20-pt mixed chorus, 16 winds, harp 2pianos perc.

LUTTER, ( )
ZXL-1. Parthia in Dis [E♭]; 3 mvts. 2a-cl(E♭) 2hn bn. MS pts (by Johann Anton Handl): A-Wn, Mus.Hs.600, (with additional clarinet parts transposed for clarinets in B♭). ★

*LUTYENS, (Agnes) Elisabeth *9 July 1906, London - 14 April 1983, London*
*EAL-1. Symphonies, Op. 46. Solo piano, pic 2fl 2ob ca cl(E♭) 2cl 4hn 2bn cbn 3tp 3tb tu timp 6perc 2harps.
Pm (Schott & Co.: London, pn 6616, 1969), score (hire) & hire parts. *Composed 1961.*
EAL-2. Nox, for piano and 2 chamber orchestras, Op. 118.
Solo piano plus (orch 1): 2fl 2cl 2tp 2tu perc harp; (orch 2): 2ob 2bn 2bn 2tb perc harp.
Pm (Olivan Press/Universal Edition (London) Ltd.: London, 1977), hire score & parts.
*EAL-3. Music for Wind, Op. 60; 1964. 2fl 2ob 2cl 2hn 2bn.
Pm (Schott & Co.: London, 1965), hire score & parts.
*EAL-4. Rape of the Moone, Op. 90. 2ob 2cl 2hn 2bn.
Pc (Olivan Press/Universal Edition (London) Ltd.: London, 1973), score & parts.
*EAL-5. Suite Gauloise (later version). 2ob 2cl 2hn 2bn.
Pm (de Wolfe: London, 1944), score & parts; not readily available. (AutoMS score: GB-Yu.)
EAL-1v. Isis & Osiris, Op. 74. 8 solo voices, fl 3cl bn 3tp 2b-tp tb harp cimbalom piano/celeste 3perc.
Pm (Olivan Press/Universal Editions (London) Ltd.: London, 1970), score; (parts for hire).

*LYADOV (Liadow, Lyadow), Anatoly Konstantinovich *11 May 1855, St Petersburg - 28 Aug 1914, Novgorod*
AKL-1a. Une Tabatière à Musique [Musical snuff box]: Valse Badinage pour Piano, Op. 32, (version arranged by the composer). pic 2fl 3cl(A) harp campanella[bells].
Pc (M.P. Balaïeff: Leipzig, pn 1556, 1893), score & parts: GB-Lbl, e.668.bb.(5.). ★

*LYON, (Samuel) Thomas *1776 - post-1824*
TYL-1a. Anon: Madame del Caro's Celebrated Hornpipe...as performed at Ranelagh. 2cl 2hn bn timp; *or* piano.
Pc (Printed for Longman & Broderip: London, sd), RISM Supp [LL 3140a]: US-NYp, Mus.Res.*MTK. ★

M., C. *(1750)*
CCM-1. Parthia in D, 1776; 5 mvts.   2cl(A) 2hn bn.
MS parts: CZ-KRa, A4028/IV.B.201. ★
CCM-2. Parthia in D, 1776; 5 mvts.   2cl(A) 2hn 2bn.
MS parts: CZ-KRa, A4029/IV.B.202. ★

*MABELLINI, Teodulo *2 April 1817, Pistoia - 10 March 1897, Florence*
*TEM-1. Sinfonia, in B♭, 4 mvts.   fl 2ob 2cl 2hn 2bn cbn.
Pc (E. Paoletti: Firenze, pn 141, 1868), miniature score: I-Bc; I-Fc, (2 copies), D.IX.2423, D.XIII.1180;
I-Mc, Da Camera A.65.29, (with MS parts including an additional cl part to replace ob II). ★

*McCABE, John *21 April 1939, Huyton, Lancs, UK*
JBM-1. Rainforest III.   2ob 2cl 2bthn 4hn 2bn cbn.
Pm (Novello: London, 1997).
JBM-2. Symphony for 10 winds, Op. 33; 1964.   pic(fl) fl ob ob(ca) cl cl(b-cl) 2hn 2bn.
Pm (Novello: London, 1990), score & parts.
JBM-3. Canzona; 1970.   fl ob 2cl bn hn 2tp tb perc timp.
Pm (Novello, London), facsimile score.

McCAULEY, William Alexander *1917, Canada*
WLM-1. 5 Miniatures.   fl ob cl 2hn bn 2tp 2tb tu.
MS score: C-Tcm.

*McGUIRE, Edward *15 Feb 1948, Glasgow*
*EXM-1. Wind Octet; 1980.   2ob 2cl 2hn 2bn.
MS score (& cassette): GB-Lmic; GB-Sma, (available for purchase).

MÂCHE, François Bernhard *4 April 1935, Clermont-Ferrand*
FCM-1. Rituel d'oubli.   2fl 2ob 3cl cb-cl 2bn 3tp 3tb b-tb, tape.
Pm (Salabert: Paris, 1969).
FCM-2. Kassandra.   ob ob(ca) cl b-cl bn cbn 2tp 2tb 3perc 2pianos tape.
Pm (Durand: Paris, 1977).
FCM-3. Safous mélè.   9 voices, 2fl 2ob harp perc.
Pm (Salabert: Paris, 1971).

*MACKINTOSH (Macintosh), Robert *1745 - 1807*
RXM-1m. A New March for the Edinburgh Volunteers.   2cl 2hn 2bn tp.
Pc (Printed for the Author: Edinburgh, c.1794), RISM [M 70], score: GB-En, Glen 347-12. ★

MacKINNONS, Robert
RZM-1. Suite.   2fl 2ob 2cl b-cl bn.
Pm (McGinnis & Marx: New York, sd), score & parts.

*McLEAN (MacLean), J.M. *"of the 29th Regiment", (1760)*
*JMM-1m. The Brighton Camp March.   2ob 2cl 2hn bn tp serp.
Pc (Longman and Broderip: London, c.1795), RISM [M 83], score: GB-Gu; GB-Lbl, g.133.(42);
GB-Ob, Mus.Instr.I.161(14). ★
*JMM-2m. The Brighton Camp Quick March.   2cl 2hn bn tp serp.
Pc (Longman & Broderip: London, c.1795), RISM [M 84], score: GB-Lbl, g.133.(43);
GB-Ob, Mus.Instr.I.161(13). ★
*JMM-3m. The Bagshot Slow March.   2fife 2cl 2hn 2bn tp.
Pc (Longman & Broderip: London, c.1795), RISM [M 81], score: GB-Gu; GB-Lbl (2 copies), g.133.(41),
h.1568.b.(10); GB-Ob, Mus.Instr.I.161(11). ★
*JMM-4m. The Bagshot Quick March.   2fife 2cl 2hn 2bn tp.
Pc (Longman and Broderip: London, c.1795), RISM [M 82], score: GB-Gu; GB-Lbl (2 copies), g.133.(40),
h.3213.k.(9); GB-Ob, Mus.Instr.I.161(12); US-Wc. ★

MACONCHY, *Dame* Elisabeth *19 March 1907, Broxbourne, Hants, UK*
EUM-1. Music for Woodwind and Brass, 1966.   fl fl(pic) ob ob(ca) 2cl 4hn 2bn 3tp 3tb tu timp.
Pm: (Chester Music: London &c, pn CH55692, 1986), score & hire parts.
EUM-2. Tribute.   Solo violin, 2fl 2ob 2cl 2bn.
Pm (Chester Music: London, 1983), hire score & parts.

*McPHEE, Colin Carhart *15 March 1901, Montreal - 7 Jan 1964, Los Angeles*
*COM-1. Concerto for Piano, 1928.   Piano solo, fl 2ob cl hn bn tp tb 2timp.
Pc (The New Music Society of California: San Francisco, 1931), score (In: *New Music*. Vol. 4, No. 2. Jan 1931):
GB-Lbl, 1.493.a.
Pm (Associated Music Publishers: London), hire score & parts.

McQUEEN, Ian *1954, London*
IYM-1. The Glen is Mine; 1980.   2ob 2cl 2hn 2bn.
MS score: GB-Gsma, (available for purchase).

MAGANINI, Quinto E. *1897 - 1974, USA*
QEM-1a. Mussorgsky: Pictures at an Exhibition, Ballet of the Chicks in their Shells.   fl ob 2cl bn 2tp.
Pm (Edition Musicus New York: New York, pn M 628, 1940), score & parts.

*MAGNELLI, Giuseppe *active 1787 - 1845, Florence*
We believe that all the works at I-Fc, F.P. S.834 and F.P. S.835 are compositions by Magnelli.
GPM-1. Concertone, 1799.   2fl 2ob cl 2hn 2bn tp serp timp.   MS score: I-Fc, F.P. S.835.
GPM-2. Notturno.   2ob 2cl 2hn 2bn.   MS score: I-Fc, F.P. S.835.
GPM-3. Sonata.   2ob 2cl 2hn 2bn.   MS score: I-Fc, F.P. S.835.
GPM-4. Notturni, 1799.   2fl 2bn.   MS score: I-Fc, F.P. S.835.
GPM-5. Larghetto.   Instrumentation unknown.   MS score: I-Fc, F.P. S.834.
GPM-1m. Marciale.   Instrumentation unknown.   MS score: I-Fc, F.P. S.835.
GPM-1v. Lauda al Signore.   SSS, winds.   AutoMS score & MS parts: I-Fc, F.P. T.1019.
GPM-2v. Miserere, 1792.   SATB, winds, vc.   MS score: I-Fc, F.P. Ch.1356.
GPM-3v. Miserere, 1792.   SATB, winds.   MS score: I-Fc, F.P. Ch.1444.
GPM-4v. Offertorium Per il Lunedi Santo, 1839.   S solo, winds.
MS score & parts, I-FC, F.P. Ch.1172, (33 voice parts, 32 instrument parts).
GPM-1c. Larghetto maestoso.   Instrumentation unknown.   MS score: I-Fc, F.P. S.834.
GPM-2c. Andante Maestoso.   Instrumentation unknown.   MS score: O-Fc, F.P. S.834.
GPM-3c. Allegro.   Instrumentation unknown.   MS score: I-Fc, F.P. S.835.
GPM-4c. Allegro ma non tanto.   Instrumentation unknown.   MS score: I-Fc, F.P. S.835.
GPM-5c. Larghetto.   Instrumentation unknown.   MS score: I-Fc, F.P. S.835.
GPM-6c. Minuetto.   Instrumentation unknown.   MS score: I-Fc, F.P. S.835.
GPM-7c. Pastorale.   Instrumentation unknown.   MS score: I-Fc, F.P. S.835.
GPM-8c. Pastorale.   Instrumentation unknown.   MS score: I-Fc, F.P. S.835.
GPM-9c. Rondo.   Instrumentation unknown.   MS score: I-Fc, F.P. S.835.

*MAHLER, Gustav *7 July 1860, Kalist, Bohemia - 18 May 1911, Vienna*
GUM-1v. Um Mitternacht (No. 5 of *Rückertlieder* and also No. 6 of *Lieder aus letzter Zeit;* note: *Ich atmet' einen Linden Duft*, also from the *Rückert Lieder*, is largely for winds and voice).
Soloist, 2fl 2ob 2cl 4hn 2bn cbn 2tp 3tb tu timp harp.
Pm: (Kalmus: New York, pn A2890), score & parts.

*MAHON, John *1746, (? Oxford) - 1834, Dublin*
JDM-1m. The Oxford Association, Slow & Quick-March...As approved by the Committee. 2fl 2cl 2hn bn tp serp
Pc (L. Lavenu: London, c.1797), RISM [M 168], score: GB-Lbl, g.271.ww.(1).   ★

*MAIER, L. *(1750), flautist, active 1782*
LXM-1. Parthia in C.   2ob 2cl 2hn 2bn quart-fagotto 2tp timp.
MS parts: D-RUl, RH-M.81.   ★
*LXM-2. Partia a 8 stromenti; in C.   2ob 2cl 2hn 2bn.
MS parts: D-Dl, Mus.3309-P-1.

MAJO, Gian Francesco de (known as "Ciccio") *24 March 1732, Naples - 17 Nov 1770, Naples*
GFM-1v. Salve Regina, antifono in Eb.   S, 2ob 2hn 2bn 2vla db.
MS score: I-BGi, 288.37/3 & 288.37/3.1 (modified copy, both owned by J.S. Mayr); I-Nc, Mus.22.4.1.

*MÁLEK, Jan *18 May 1938, Prague*
JQM-1. Sinfonia Il Fenice.   3ob 3bn clavier(hpcd).
Pm (Český hudební fond: Prague, 1976), hire score & parts.
JQM-2. 7 Studii for wind and percussion; 1964.
MS score & parts: CZ-PLr.

*MALIPIERO, Gian Francesco *18 March 1882, Venice - 1 Aug 1973, Treviso*
*GGM-1. Serenata mattutina.   fl ob cl 2hn 2bn 2vla celeste.
Pm (Universal Edition: Wien, London, 1960), score & miniature score (Philharmonia Partituren 388).

MALOTTE, Albert Hay *19 May 1895, Philadelphia - 16 Nov 1964, Hollywood*
AHM-1. 23rd Psalm.   Chorus, fl ob 3cl 3hn 2tp tb perc harp piano.
Pm (G. Schirmer: New York), hire score & parts.

MALZAT, Ignaz *4 March 1757, Vienna - 20 March 1804, Passau*
IXM-1. N° 1 in Eb Parthia; 6 mvts.   pic 2cl 2hn bn tp.
AutoMS score (1799): A-Sca, Hs. 242, (the end of a mvt & 4 other mvts have been added in another hand at the end of the cl II pt). *Probably the "Türkische Parthia, No. 134" advertized in Traeg's 1804 Nachtrag.*   ★
Pm (WINDS: Northridge, CA, pn W-7, c.1981), parts (modern photocopy).
IXM-2. Parthia in Eb.   2ob 2hn 2bn.   MS parts: A-KR, H 37/6.   ★
IXM-3. Parthia in Eb Nro 5.   2cl 2hn bn.
Pc (Traeg: [Vienna], pre-1799), No. 196, MS pts: A-KR, H 37/22, (MS by J. Fineberger; cl 1 part incomplete).   ★

MALZAT, Josef *(1790)*
JIM-1. Parthia ex Es [Eb]; 5 mvts.   2cl 2hn 2bn.
MS parts: CZ-Bm(rj), A.12.738, (with performance dates: 1824, (2 perf:) 1830).   ★

MANDANICI, Placido *1798, Barcellona di Sicilia - 6 June 1852, Genoa*
PXM-1v. Gloria.   TTB, 2cl 2hn bn basso/vlne (tp timp) organ.
MS score & parts: I-Vsmc, (the tp & timp pts do not appear in the score).   ★
PXM-2v. Credo.   TTB, (fl) 2cl 2hn bn timp organ.
MS score & parts: I-Vsmc, (the flute part does not appear in the score).   ★

MANERI, Joseph Gabriel *9 Feb 1927, New York*
YJM-1. Maranatha.   2fl 2ob 2cl hn 2bn 2tp 2tb tu 3perc.
Pm (Margun Music: Newton Center, MA, pn MP 5017SC, 1968), score.

MANFRIN, Giuseppe *(1800)*
GXM-1v. Tantum ergo. TTB(solo+rip), 2cl 2hn tp tb timp organ.
MS score & parts: I-Vsmc. ★

*MANGOLD, Johann Wilhelm *19 Nov 1796, Darmstadt - 23 May 1875, Darmstadt*
We have not located a Quintet (?No. 1, 1833) for 2fl 2hn bn cited by Jansen.
JWM-1. Zu Seigeisnug die am 12ᵗᵉⁿ July 1830. cl(Eb) 3cl 4hn 4bn cbn 4tp a-tb t-tb b-tb timp b-dr+cym tri.
AutoMS score (8 July 1830): D-DS, Mus.ms.734.
JWM-2. Harmonie für das am 5ᵗᵉⁿ July 1835 gefeierte Johannisfest der ⊏⊐ [i.e. Masonic Lodge].
fl ob 2cl 2hn 2bn cbn tp (timp ad lib). AutoMS score (29 June 1835): D-DS, Mus.ms.730. ★
JWM-3. No.1. In den 13ᵗᵉⁿ Mai in d[er]. ⊏⊐ [i.e. Masonic Lodge] geschrieben. fl ob 2cl 2hn 2bn cbn tp.
AutoMS score & parts: D-DS, Mus.Ms.733/1. ★
JWM-4. Nr. 2 Maestoso in Bb, "für den [?wie] das ein [?fest] das Ex Dr [?Hueh] geschrieben. fl 3cl 2hn 2bn
cbn tp (db). AutoMS score & pts: D-DS, Mus.ms.733/2, (with an additional cb pt not found in the score). ★
JWM-5. [untitled mvt]. 2cl 2hn 2bn 2tp timp. AutoMS score (1 Feb 1827): D-DS, Mus.ms.704/1. ★
JWM-6. Für die Schusten ⊏⊐ [i.e. Lodge]; Andantino. fl ob cl(C) 2hn bn(I) bn(II)/vc+cb.
AutoMS score & pts: D-DS, Mus.ms.704/2, (the autograph pts are for: fl ob cl(II, Bb) 2hn bn(I) bn(II)+cb). ★
JWM-7. [untitled mvt: Andante Semplice]. 2cl 4hn 2bn b-tb. AutoMS score: D-DS, Mus.ms.704. ★
JWM-8. Zum Schauspiel Hermann & Dorothea. am Schluss des IIIᵗᵉⁿ Acts. fl 2ob 2cl(C) 2hn 2bn.
AutoMS score & parts: D-DS, Mus.ms.754.
JWM-9. 4 movements, 1844-61. 4hn bn. AutoMS: D-DS, Mus.ms.874, (unverified).
JWM-10. 4 movements, 1845. 2hn bn. AutoMS: D-DS, Mus.ms.873, (unverified).
JWM-1m. Heimats-Klänge für Militärmusik. pic(Eb) terz-fl ob cl(Eb) 3cl(Bb) 4hn 2bn tp 2cap a-hn a-tb t-tb
b-tb euph oph bomb b-dr s-dr. AutoMS score (Feb 1854): D-DS, Mus.ms.753. ★
JWM-1t. Trauermarsch; in C minor. fl ob cl hn 2bn b-tb 2vla (2)vc cb.
AutoMS score (19 may 1843) & MS parts: D-DS, Mus.ms.735. ★
JWM-1v. für das Konzert am 17ᵗᵉⁿ Mai, "O sing heras Gestalten findben".
SATB, harp, 2fl 2ob+2cl(C) 2hn 2bn 2tp timp. AutoMS score (12 May 1832): D-DS, Mus.ms.710. ★
JWM-2.1v. Tempo di Marcia Funebre [chorus in Hamlet]. Solo SSA, 2cl 2hn 2bn; *then* Solo SSA with TTBB
chorus, 2cl 2hn 2bn a-tb t-tb b-tb. AutoMS score: D-DS, Mus.ms.708. ★
JWM-2.2v. № 2 Chor zu Hamlet, Tempo di Marcia Funebre. SSATTB chorus, 2cl 2hn 2bn a-tb t-tb b-tb.
AutoMS score & MS vocal pts: D-DS, Mus.ms.751, No. 1, (with duplicate pts: 3S(I)/3S(II)/4A/3B; missing T(I)). ★
JWM-3v. [title illegible]. SATB, 2fl 2hn 2bn. AutoMS score: D-DS, Mus.ms.758.
JWM-1tv. Trauerkantate; in C minor. TTBB, ob 3cl 3hn 2bn cbn.
AutoMS score (17 May 1830): D-DS, Mus.ms.739. ★

MANICKE, Dietrich *29 Oct 1923, Wurzen*
DXM-1. Sextett. 2cl 2hn 2bn.
Pm (N. Simrock: Hamburg, London, 1964), score (pn 3254) & parts (pn 3296).

MANINA (Monina), Fortunato, *di Genova* *(1800)*
FXM-1v. Tantum ergo. TTB, 2cl 2hn tp tb timp organ.
MS score & parts: I-Vsmc. ★

*MANKELL (Manckol[l], Mankol; ? formerly MANGOLD), Johann (Giovanni) Hermann M.
19 Nov 1763, Assia - 4 Nov 1835, Karlskronn (now Karlskrona), Sweden
HMM-1(-3). 3 suittes [sic], Divertimento I, in Eb, 4 mvts; Divertimento II, in C, 4 mvts; Divertimento III, in
Eb, 4 mvts. 2fl 2cl 2hn 2bn cb, (cl in Eb ad lib).
MS parts: NL-Z, Z1132, Nos. 1 - 3, (the cl in Eb may be a later addition; there are also incomplete parts for
2fl(C) transposed up a semi-tone from the originals). ★
HMM-4(-6). Parthias I - III, 1794, (all in Eb, 4 mvts). 2fl 2cl 2hn 2bn (cb ad lib).
MS parts: NL-Z, Z1231/M.A.Zcm.30, Nos. 1 - 3.
HMM-7. Suite de pièces d'harmonie, in Eb, 20 mvts. 2fl 2cl 2hn 2bn, (cl in Eb, cb ad lib).
MS parts: NL-Z, Z1232/M.A.Zcm.29.
HMM-8. Divertissement; [cl I pt, p. 1: "Partia I Di H. Mankell"], (4 mvts). 2cl 2hn 2bn.
Pc (chés [sic] Günther & Böhme: Hamburg, sd), RISM [M 363], pts: GB-Ckc, 104 5/10 RES; US-BETm,
Philharmonic Society of Bethlehem PSB 1351.1 (Partie 1ᵉʳᵉ only, 3 mvts, *"Imported & sold G Willig, No. 185
Market St. Philadelphia").*
HMM-9. Divertissement, in Eb, 12/13 mvts. 2cl 2hn 2bn, (2fl/ob cb ad lib).
MS parts: NL-Z, Z1229/M.A.Zcm.4, Nos. 1 - 3, (missing hn I & II, bn II; the final unnumbered mvt, Allegro
molto, ¢, has been added at a later date on separate sheets). *Although the title is in the singular, this work may
have been intended to be performed as 3 separate divertimentos (mvts 1 - 3, 4 - 6, 7 - 12).* ★
HMM-10. Divertissement, 10/11 mvts. 2cl 2hn bn, (cl in Eb, cb ad lib).
MS parts: NL-Z, Z1230/M.A.Zcm.28, (the 11th mvt, Allemande (6/8) / Allegro moderato (3/8) has been added
later in the same hand; it does not appear in the cl(Eb) & the bn is marked "Fagotto Primo" although there is
no other bassoon part present). ★
*HMM-1.1m. March, in Eb. 2fl ob 2cl(Bb) 2hn 2bn 2tp, (cl in Eb ad lib).
MS parts: NL-Z, Z1133, No. 6, (missing hn II - where No. 5 has been copied out again by mistake; the cl(Eb)
is another hand but in similar wrappers). ★
HMM-1.2m. March No. 1, in Eb. 2fl cl(Eb) 2cl(Bb) 2hn 2bn tp cb.
MS parts: NL-Z, (2 copies), Z1137/1, (missing hn II).
*HMM-2m. March maestoso, in Eb. 2fl ob 2cl(Bb) 2hn 2bn 2tp, (cl in Eb ad lib).
MS parts: NL-Z, Z1133, No. 8. ★

MANN, Tor
TXM-1a. Nielsen: Humoresque-Bagatelles, Op. 11. fl 2cl bn.
Pm (Wilhelm Hansen: Copenhagen, 1974), score (pn 29237) & parts (pn 29237A).

MANZONI, Giacomo *26 Sept 1932, Milan*
GQM-1. Percorso à otto; 1975. *Recommended:* Quartet 1: fl(fl in G, pic) heck cl bn, Quartet 2: b-fl(fl) ca
cb-cl(Bb) cbn; *or* Quartet 1: fl(fl in G, pic) ob cl bn, Quartet 2: fl ca b-cl bn.
Pm (Ricordi: Milano, 1976), facsimile AutoMS score, (in "New Notation").

*MARCHAL, François *(1790) active c.1821 in Paris*
FOM-1. Journal d'Harmonie et de Musique Militaire [with F. Louis & C. Münchs]. Scoring varies.
Pc (Au Dépôt du Journal, Chez Mʳ Baumann: Paris, pn 1 - 4, c.1821), parts: F-Pn, Vm27 2630 (Liv. 1 - 4).
  1/1/1. Marche, C. No. 2. fl(Eb) cl(Eb) 2cl(Bb) 2hn 2bn tp tb serp b-dr.
    1/1/2. Waltz [&Trio], 3/8. No. 5.   fl(Eb) cl(Eb) 2cl(Bb)+2cl(Bb rip) 2hn 2bn tp tb serp b-dr.
    1/1/3. Harmonie, Andᵗᵉ, C / Allᵒ assai, 6/8. No. 7. fl(Eb) cl(Eb) 2cl(Bb)+2cl(Bb rip) 2hn 2bn tp tb serp b-dr.
  1/2/1. Marche, ¢. No. 2.   fl(Eb) cl(Eb) 2cl(I, Bb) cl(II, Bb) 2hn 2bn("avec le Serpent") tp tb serp b-dr.
    1/2/2. Waltz, 3/8. No. 6. fl(Eb) cl(Eb) 2cl(Bb) 2hn 2bn("avec le Serpent") tp tb serp b-dr.
  1/2/3. Harmonie, Andante, 3/4 / Allegretto, 2/4. No. 7. fl(Eb) cl(Eb) 4cl(Bb) 2hn 2bn tp tb serp.
  1/3/1. Pas Redoublé, 2/4. No. 4. fl(Eb) cl(Eb) 2cl(Bb) 2hn 2bn("avec le Serpent") tp tb serp b-dr.
    1/3/2. Waltz, 3/8. No. 6. fl(Eb) cl(Eb) 2cl(Bb) 2hn 2bn("avec le Serpent") tp tb serp b-dr.
    1/3/3. Menuetto. Vivace, 3/4. No. 9. fl(Eb) cl(Eb) 4cl(Bb) 2hn 2bn tp tb serp.
  1/4/1. Waltz, Moderato, 3/8. No. 6. fl(Eb) cl(Eb) 2cl(I, Bb, "solo" + cl I) cl(II, Bb) 2hn tp tb serp b-dr.
    1/4/2. Harmonie. Allᵒ Brillante, ¢. No. 7. fl(C) cl(Eb) 4cl(Bb) 2hn 2bn tp tb serp.
    1/4/3. Andante, Grazioso, 3/4. No. 8. fl(C) cl(Eb) 4cl(Bb) 2hn 2bn tp tb serp.

MAROCCHINI, Enrico
ERM-1. Octet No. 2, Op. 23. 2ob 2cl 2hn 2bn.
Pm (Edipan Edizione Musicale: Roma, sd).

*MAROS, Miklós *14 Nov 1943, (?Hungary - now resident in Sweden)*
MQM-1. Symphonie Nr. 2; (1979). 3fl(pic) 3ob(ca) 4cl 4hn 2bn cbn 4tp 4tb tu timp perc. MS score: S-Sic.
MQM-2. Mutazioni; 1971. 3fl(pic) 3ob(ca) 3cl 4hn 2bn cbn 4tp 3tb 2tu. MS score & parts: S-Ssr.

*MARPURG, Wilhelm *(1790), active in Detmold, 1826 - d. 6 Aug 1836, Detmold*
WYM-1. [6 pieces]. pic 2ob cl(Eb) 3cl(Bb) 2hn 2bn 2tp a-tb t-tb b-tb serp b-dr t-dr.
MS parts: D-DT, Mus-h 3 M 3.
  1.1(a). Küffner: Der Kornett, 1 mvt.   1.2(a). Spohr: Jessonda, 1 mvt.
  1.3(m)(-1.6m). [Anon - ? Marpurg]: 4 Geschwindmärsche, F, F, Bb, Bb.
WYM-1a. 5 Pièces. pic 2ob cl(Eb) 3cl(Bb) 2hn 2bn 2tp a-tb t-tb b-tb serp b-dr s-dr.
MS parts: D-DT, Mus-h 3 M 5.
  1.1a. Wolfram: Der Bergmönch, overture.   1.2a, 1.3a. Bellini: La Straniera, Balletto [Ballet-Musik].
  1.4a. Bellini: La Straniera, introduction.   1.5a. Bellini: Norma, overture.
WYM-2a. [3 Pieces]. pic 2ob 2cl(Eb) 4cl(Bb) 5hn 2bn 2tp a-tb t-tb b-tb b-hn b-dr s-dr.
MS parts: D-DT, Mus-h 3 M 6.
  2.1a. Fränzl: Carlo Fioras, overture.   2.2a. C.M. von Weber: Jubel-Ouverture.
  2.3a. Auber: Fra Diavolo, Lied.
WYM-3a. [3 Pieces]. pic 2ob 2cl(Eb) 4cl(Bb) 2hn 2bn 2tp a-tb t-tb b-tb b-hn b-dr t-dr.
  3.1a. Auber: Fra Diavolo, overture.   3.2a. Labitzky: Polonaise in Ab.   3.3a. Labitzky: Walzer in F minor.
WYM-4a. Auber: La Muette de Portici, overture.   cl(Eb) 3cl(Bb) 2hn 2bn tp 3tb b-hn b-dr.
MS parts: D-DT, Mus-n 291.

MARSANO (MARSAND), Luigi, *"Ex Monaco"* *1769 - 1841*
LYM-1v. Inno per la Festivale della Reliquie. TTB, 2ob 2hn bn organ(bc-fig + full).
MS score & parts: I-Vsmc. ★

*MARSH, Roger Michael *10 Dec 1949, Bournemouth*
RMM-1. Point-to-Point, 1979 *(first performed Sheffield, 19 May 1979).* 2ob 2cl 2hn 2bn.
Pm (Novello: London, 1979), hire score & parts.
RQM-2. Jesters (for Sicks [sic]), 1972 *(first performed York, June 1972).* 2ob 2cl 2bn.
Pm (Novello, London, 1972), hire score & parts.

*MARTEAU, Henri *31 March 1874, Rheims - 3 Oct 1934, Lichtenberg*
HXM-1. Serenade in D, Op. 20; 4 mvts. 2fl 2ob 2cl b-cl 2bn.
Pm (Steingräber: Leipzig, 1922), score & parts: D-Mbs, 8 Mus.pr. 5525; US-Wc, M957.M4 op. 20..

*MARTIN, Frank *15 Sept 1890, Geneva - 21 Nov 1974, Naarden*
*FYM-1. Ballade fur Viola. Solo viola, pic ob ca cl b-cl 2hn bn cbn 2tp tb hpcd harp timp.
Pm (Universal Edition: Zürich, 1973), score.

*MARTINI, Giovanni (Jean), *il Tedesco (pseud., i.e. Johann Paul Aegidius Schwartzendorf)*
31 Aug 1741, Freystadt, Bavaria - 10 Feb 1816, Paris
GSM-1mv. Hymne à la République; (Chant du 1ᵉʳ vendémiaire; Anniversaire de la fond[ation]...; 1798), P.146.
SATB chorus, 2p-fl 2fl 2cl 2hn 2bn 2tp b-tb serp db b-dr cym.
Pc (Mag de mus fêtes nat: Paris, c.1798), liv. 22, RISM [M 1131], score (chorus) & instrumental parts: D-AB,
(missing tp II, cym, b-dr); F-Pn, H2. 114 a - t. ★
Pc (for Voice, 2cl 2hn (2)bn:) (Rec des époques: Paris, c.1799), liv. 2, No. 1, pp. 127-129, score: F-Pn, H2. 16,1.
GSM-2mv. Cœur [Chant triomphale] pour la fête du 1er vendémiaire an VII; (1798), P.147.
SATB chorus, p-fl fl 2ob 2cl 2hn 2bn tb serp db b-dr cym.
MS parts: F-Pn, H2. 120 a-p. MS score (by Pierre): F-Pn. ★

MARTINIDES, Carlo *c.1731 - 1794*
CXM-1. [Partita in Eb], 5 mvts. 2cl 2hn bn. MS parts (c.1770): D-Rtt, Sm. 8, Nrs 25 - 29. ★

MARTINO, Cesare Giovanni
CEM-1. La Vittoria. 3ob 3bn.
Pm (Hieber: München, 1985).

*MARTINŮ, Bohuslav *8 Dec 1890, Polička, eastern Bohemia - 28 Aug 1959, Liestal, nr Basle*
*BXM-1. Concertino in C minor; (H 143).   Solo cello, fl 2ob 2cl hn bn tp tb piano timp side-drum cym.
AutoMS: CZ-Pnm.
Pm (Český hudební fond: Prague, 1964), score & parts.
Pm (Panton: Prague, pn P. 535, 1973), score & parts.
*BXM-2. Sextet in E♭; 1929 (H174).   Piano, fl ob cl 2bn.
AutoMS: CZ-POpbm.
Pm (Český hudební fond: Prague, pn 466, 1960), score & parts.
Pm (Panton: Prague, pn P403, 1966, reprinted 1986), score & parts.
*BXM-2. Polní mse (Field Mass; La Messe aux Champs d'honneur), (H279).   Baritone solo, male chorus, 2fl
2cl 3tp 2tb pf harm perc(timp b-drum t-drum snare-drum s-drum cym tri fingercym, sanctuary bells).
AutoMS: CZ-POpbm.
Pm (Melantrich: Prague, pn M277, 1947), score & parts.
Pm (Státní hudební vydavatel': Prague), score & parts.
*BXM-2v. Legend of the Smoke from Potato Fires (Legenda z dýmu bramborové nati).
SA,BAR solo, SATB, fl cl hn accordion piano.
AutoMS: CZ-POpbm.
Pm (Státní nakladatelství: Prague, pn H2996, 1960), score: GB-Ob Mus 21.c.200(2).

MARTÍN Y SOLER, Vicente *2 May 1754, Valencia - 11 Feb 1806, St Petersburg*
VXM-1ev. Andromaca: Revitativo & Duet, 'Lascia bel Idol mio'.   ST, 2ob 2hn 2bn basso.
MS: DK-Sa, R 128.   *Possibly not arranged by the composer.* ★
*The following 4 works, previously attributed to the composer as original works are, in fact, principally arranged
mvts from his opera,* Una cosa rara; *the last mvts of VXM-1, 2 & 4 are short "Cottillions" almost certainly
composed by Charles Francis Eley. There is a strong possibility that Went's Schwarzenburg arrangement served
as the source from which these works were compiled for performances at Vauxhall Gardens, 1789.*
VXM-1(-4)da. N° 2, 3, 4 & 6 Divertimento; (all in B♭, 4 mvts).   2ob 2bthn 2hn 2bn serp.
MS parts: GB-Lbl, R.M.21.d.3, (the ob I pt of "Nro 2" was originally numbered "Nro 5"); GB-Lbbc, (No. 6 only,
in a modern score edited by Karl Hass, with photocopies of the GB-Lbl parts). ★
Pm (? Universal Edition: London, etc., sd), ed. Erik Smith, score & parts. *Unverified; probably No. 6 only.*
Pm (No. 6) (DINSIC Publicacions Musicals: Barcelona, 1995), ed. Colin Lawson & Carles Riera, score & parts.

*MARTLAND, Steve *1958, Liverpool*
*SEM-1a. Wolf-gang; Six Mozart Opera Arias.   ob ob(ca) cl(s-sax) cl(b-cl) 2hn 2bn.
Pm (Schott: London, 1991), hire score & parts.

MARULLI, Angelo *(1800)*
AXM-1v. Stabat Mater.   TTB(solo+rip), 2cl(C) 2hn bn organ(bc-fig).
MS score & parts: I-Vsmc, (with additional parts for 2vl - if cls are not available - tb (2 parts: one if bn is not
available; the other is simplified), vlne, timp, full organ). ★

*MARX, Karl Julius *12 Nov 1897, Munich - 8 May 1985, Stuttgart*
KYM-1. Divertimento, Op. 21; 1934.   2fl 2ob 3cl 2hn bn 2tp 2tb tu.
Pm (privately printed; *via* Deutscher Komponist-Verband: Berlin).

*MAŠEK (Mashek, Maschek, Masheck), Pavel (Paul) Lambert *14 Sept 1761, Zvíkovec - 22 Nov 1826, Vienna*
*PLM-1. Die Schlacht bey Leipzig den 18 Oct. A° [1]813; 8 mvts.
pic 2fl 2ob cl(F) 2cl(C) 2hn 2bn cbn tp(prin) b-tb serp tri Wirbl(= t-dr) b-dr+Teller(= cym).
MS parts: A-Wn, Mus.Hs.11,384. ★
Pm (as "The Battle of Leipzig") (WINDS: Northridge, CA, pn W-58, c.1981), modern score & MS parts in
photocopies.
*PLM-2.1. Die Besitznahme von Paris durch die Hohen Verbündeten siegreichen Truppen den 30 April
A°[1]814; 12 mvts.   pic 2fl 2ob cl(F) 2cl(C) 2hn 2bn cbn tp(prin) b-tb serp tri b-dr+Teller(cym)+Tamburino
Wirbl(= t-dr).
MS parts: A-Wn, Mus.Hs.11,387. ★
Pm (as "The Occupation of Paris") (WINDS: Northridge, CA, pn W-89, c. 1981), modern score & MS parts in
photocopies.
*PLM-2.2. Heil dir Europa!!! oder die Besitznahme von Paris durch die Verbündeten siegreichen [Truppen].
Mächte den 31 Marz A°[1]814; 15 mvts.   2ob 2cl 2hn 2bn cbn tp.
MS parts: A-Wn, Mus.Hs.11,386. ★
Pc (Joseph Eder: Vienna, 1814), piano reduction: A-Wst, M.14013.
*PLM-3. Oesterreichs Triumpf. oder die Rückkunft S⁰ Maj. Franz den 1ᵗᵉⁿ in seine Residenz Stadt Wiene [sic]
den 16 Juny A° [1]814; 9 mvts.   pic 2fl 2ob cl(F) 2cl(C) 2hn 2bn cbn tp(prin) b-tb+serp tri
b-dr+Teller(cym)+Tambur[in]o Wirbl(= t-dr).
MS parts: A-Wn, Mus.Hs.11,385, (missing horn parts). ★
Pm (as "The Return of the Allies":) (WINDS: Northridge, CA, pn W-92, c.1981), modern score & photocopy
of the MS parts.
*PLM-4(-9). Sei Partitte, (E♭, 4 mvts; B♭, 4 mvts; E♭, 2 mvts; D, 3 mvts, B♭, 4 mvts; E♭, 4 mvts).
2ob 2cl 2hn 2bn.   MS parts: A-Ee, Mus.1126. ★
PLM-1.1a. Cherubini: Les deux Journées, overture & 9 mvts.   2ob 2cl 2hn 2bn cbn.
MS parts: CZ-Bm(no), A.16.943, (as Anon); I-Fc, F.P. S.337; A-Wn, Sm.3795, (2 mvts: as Anon, A-8.2a).
PLM-1.2a. Cheubini: Les deux Journées, overture & 9 mvts.   2ob 2cl 2hn 2bn.
Pc (Sauers Kunsthandlung: Vienna., c.1801); MS pts: H-KE, (2 copies), K 1189/IX, K 1181/IX (? local copy).
*PLM-2a. J. Weigl: Die Atheneinische Tänzerin, 10 mvts.   2ob 2cl 2hn 2bn cbn.
MS parts: CZ-KRa, A3993/IV.B.163.

*MAŠEK (Maschek, Machek), Václav Vincenc (Vincent, Winzenz)
5 April 1755, Zvíkovic - 15 Nov 1831, Prague
*VVM-1. Concerto in D, 3 mvts.   3 clavicembalis, 2ob 2cl 2hn bn.
MS parts (c.1796): D-Bds, Mus.ms.13795. ★
VVM-2. Concertino [Parita] in E♭ per due Piano-Forti; in E♭, 3 mvts.   2 fortepianos, 2cl 2hn 2bn.
MS parts: CZ-Pnm, XXXVIII.C.281; D-Bds, Mus.ms.13795/3, ("Prag / Zu haben auf der Kleinseite in der Pfaargasse No. 155, in 1ten Stock").
VVM-3. Concertino; in F, 3 mvts.   Fortepiano duet (4 hands), 2fl 2cl 2hn 2bn.
Pc (Breitkopf & Härtel: Leipzig, pn 111, 1801), parts: CZ-Pnm, (2 copies), II.C.19, XIII.F.375; D-Bu. ★
Pm (Compusic: Amsterdam, 1991), score (pn 240A) & parts (pn 240B).
*VVM-4(-6). 3 Partitas; in A, E♭, D.   harpsichord or fortepiano, 2cl 2hn 2bn.
MS parts: CZ-CI.   Pm (untraced).
*VVM-7. Serenata in Dis [E♭] a due chori; 3 mvts.   (2cl 2hn bn) + (2ob 2hn bn).
MS parts: CZ-Pnm, XXII.D.251. ★
Pm (Doblinger: Wien, 1977), ed. Antonín Myslík, score (for hire only) & parts (pn Diletto musicale 889).
VVM-8. Partitta in F; 3 mvts.   fl ob cl bthn 2hn 2bn (cbn tp ad lib).   MS parts: CZ-Pnm, XX.F.13. ★
*VVM-9.1. Partitta in E♭; 3 mvts.   fl ob 2cl hn(tp clarino) hn(II) bn cbn.
MS parts: CZ-Pnm, XX.F.14.   Modern MS score (ed. John Smit, Josef Triebensee Ensemble): GB-Ljag. ★
VVM-9.2. Parthia in Dis [E♭]; 3 mvts.   fl cl(F, well [sic: vel] ob) 2cl(B♭) 2hn 2bn tp(prin).
MS parts: CZ-Pu(dm), 59 R 3319.   *Rescored by Anton Zasche, (AZZ-1a).*
*VVM-10, 11. 2 Serenaden; (E♭, 4 mvts; E♭, 4 mvts).   2ob 2cl 2hn 2bn.
MS parts: CZ-Pnm, XX.F.15, (both); D-Rtt, Masek 4, (No. 2, as "Parthia in E♭ . . . del Sig: Mascheck", with the last 3 mvts of No. 1, replacing the last mvt of No. 2 in the CZ-Pnm set); H-KE, 767/VIII. ★
AutoMS piano arrangement: CZ-PLa, H 30.77.
Pm (No. 2, in the CZ-Pnm version:) (Supraphon: Praha/Prague, 1984), ed. Antonín Myslík, score & piano reduction, (Musica antiqua bohemica Series 1, No. 81, pn H6707).
Pm (Parthia in E♭, probably one of this set:) (Compusic, Amsterdam, pn 241, 1991), score & parts.
Pm (Döblinger: Wien, pn DM 890, sd), score & parts, (No. 2).
VVM-12. Parthia; in B[♭], 3mvts.   2ob 2cl 2hn 2bn.
MS parts: D-DO, Mus.Ms.1597, No. 4.   *D-DO, Mus.Ms.1290 is a piano reduction.* ★
VVM-13. Serenata in E♭; 1 mvt.   2ob 2cl 2hn 2bn.   MS parts: H-KE, K 767. ★
VVM-14. Partitta in F.   fl ob cl bthn 2bn.   MS parts: CZ-OSr.
*VVM-15. Allegretto con [3] Variationi; in B♭.   Solo cl, fl/ob cl 2hn bn.
MS parts: A-Wn, Mus.Hs.5855. ★
Pm (WINDS: Northridge, CA, pn W-33, c. 1981), parts (photocopies of A-Wn manuscript).
*VVM-16. Notturno in F; 4 mvts.   2ob 2hn (2)bn.
MS parts: CZ-Bm(sz), A.66; CZ-Pnm, Pachta archives (XXII, untraced: possbily a ghost reference). ★
Pm (In: "Serenate boeme", No. 4:) (Statní nakladatelství krasné literatury, hudby a umeni: Praha/Prague, 1958), ed. Vratislav Belskí, score, (Musica antiqua bohemica, Series 1, No. 35).
VVM-17. Nro 1mo Partitta; in B♭, 4 mvts.   2cl 2hn 2bn.   MS parts: CZ-Pnm, XXII.D.228. ★
VVM-18. Nro 2 Partitta; in B♭, 4 mvts.   2cl 2hn 2bn.   MS parts: CZ-Pnm, XXII.D.229. ★
VVM-19. Nro 3 Partitta; in B♭, 4 mvts.   2cl 2hn 2bn.   MS parts: CZ-Pnm, XXII.D.230. ★
VVM-20. Nro 4 Partia in F; 4 mvts.   2ob/cl 2hn 2bn.   MS parts: CZ-Pnm, XXII.D.231. ★
VVM-21. Nro 5 Parthia in F; 4 mvts.   2ob/cl 2hn 2bn.   MS parts: CZ-Pnm, XXII.D.232. ★
VVM-22. N: 6 Parthia in F; 3 mvts.   2ob/cl 2hn 2bn.   MS parts: CZ-Pnm, XXII.D.233. ★
VVM-23. N: 7 Parthia in C; 4 mvts.   2ob/cl 2hn 2bn.   MS parts: CZ-Pnm, XXII.D.234. ★
VVM-24. N: 8 Parthia in B[♭]; 4 mvts.   2ob/cl 2hn 2bn.   MS parts: CZ-Pnm, XXII.D.235. ★
VVM-25. N: 9 Parthia in B[♭]; 2 mvts.   2ob 2hn 2bn.   MS parts: CZ-Pnm, XXII.D.236. ★
VVM-26. N: 10 Parthia in C; 3 mvts.   2cl 2hn 2bn.   MS parts: CZ-Pnm, XXII.D.237, (missing ob I). ★
VVM-27. N: 11 Parhtia in B[♭]; 4 mvts.   2cl 2hn 2bn.   MS parts: CZ-Pnm, XXII.D.238. ★
VVM-28. N: 12 Parthia in F; 4 mvts.   2ob/cl 2hn 2bn.   MS pts: CZ-Pnm, XXII.D.239, (missing ob II). ★
VVM-29. N: 13 Parthia in A; 2 mvts.   2ob 2hn 2bn.   MS parts: CZ-Pnm, XXII.D.240. ★
VVM-30. N: 14 Parthia in D; 4 mvts.   2cl 2hn 2bn.   MS parts: CZ-Pnm, XXII.D.241. ★
*VVM-31. N: 15 Parthia in D; 4 mvts.   2cl 2hn 2bn.
MS parts: CZ-Pnm, XXII.D.242. ★
Pm (as "Partita pastoralis") (Panton, Praha/Prague, P 2625, 1988), ed. Antonín Myslík, score & parts.
VVM-32. Nro 16 Parthia in D; 4 mvts.   2ob 2hn 2bn.   MS parts: CZ-Pnm, XXII.D.243. ★
VVM-34. N: 17 Parthia in G; 4 mvts.   2ob 2hn 2bn.   MS parts: CZ-Pnm, XXII.D.244. ★
VVM-35. N: 18 Parthia in Dis [E♭]; 4 mvts.   2ob 2hn 2bn.   MS pts: CZ-Pnm, XXII.D.245, (missing hn I). ★
VVM-36. N: 19 Parthia in F; 4 mvts.   2ob 2hn 2bn.   MS parts: CZ-Pnm, XXII.D.246. ★
VVM-37. No. 20 Parthia in C; 4 mvts.   2ob 2hn 2bn.   MS parts: CZ-Pnm, XXII.D.247, (missing ob II). ★
VVM-38. Nro 21 Parthia in C; 4 mvts.   2cl 2hn 2bn.   MS parts: CZ-Pnm, XXII.D.248. ★
VVM-39. Nro 22 Parthia in Dis [E♭]; 4 mvts.   2ob 2hn 2bn.   MS parts: CZ-Pnm, XXII.D.249. ★
VVM-40. Nro 23 Parthia in F; 4 mvts.   2ob 2hn 2bn.   MS parts: CZ-Pnm, XXII.D.250. ★
VVM-41. Nro 25 Parthia in B[♭]; 3 mvts.   2cl 2hn 2bn.   MS parts: CZ-Pnm, XXII.D.252. ★
VVM-42. N° 1 Parthia in B[♭]; 4 mvts.   2cl 2hn 2bn.   MS pts (by Josef Doletschek): CZ-Pnm, XXX.C.112. ★
VVM-43. Ballo, 4 mvts.   2fl 2hn bn.   MS parts: CZ-Bm(sz), A.108.   *Possibly an arrangement.* ★
VVM-44. Nro 3 Partitta in F, 4mvts.   2ob 2hn bn.
MS parts: CZ-Pnm, (2 copies), XXXII.B.27, (oboes & bn marked "a 2"), XXXII.C.46, (as "Partita in F"; "Procuravit / Fr[ater]. Ioachim [sic] Cron / Osseca prof:"; all parts marked "a 1"). ★
VVM-45. Partitta in G.   2ob 2hn bn, (oboes & bassoon parts marked "a.2").
MS parts: CZ-Pnm, XXXII.B.28. ★
VVM-46. Nro 2 Partitta in D; 4 mvts.   2ob 2hn bn.
MS parts ("Procuravit Fr Joachim Čron Ossecca prof. ao 1781"): CZ-Pnm, XXXII.B.29. ★

VVM-47. Partitta in C.   2ob 2hn bn, (oboes & bassoon parts marked "a 2").
MS parts: CZ-Pnm, XXXII.B.31.   ★
VVM-48. Partitta in C.   2ob 2hn bn, (oboe I & bassoon parts marked "a 2").
MS parts: CZ-Pnm, XXXII.B.32.   ★
VVM-49. Partitta in D.   2ob 2hn bn, (bassoon part marked "a.2").
MS parts: CZ-Pnm, XXXII.B.33.   ★
VVM-50(-52). 3 Parthias, (F, 4 mvts; F, 3 mvts; F, 3 mvts).   3bthn 2hn 2bn.
MS parts: PL-LA, RM 51/1, 51/2, 51/3 *(Note: RM 51 is not by Mašek)*.   ★
VVM-1t. Todten Marsch; in C.   2cl 2hn(C) 2bn 2tp(C).
MS parts (by Kantsky, from Žleb): CZ-Pnm, XII.E.119, (the scoring as given follows the parts; the titlepage incorrectly lists "2 Tromboni" instead of trumpets).   ★
VVM-2t. Todten Marsch.   2cl 2hn 2bn tp.   MS parts: CZ-Pnm, XII.F.318.
***VVM-1.1v.** 4 Stationis [sic].   CATB, 2fl 2cl 2hn bn 2tp(clar) tp(prin).
MS parts (c.1830): CZ-NYc, DÚ 201.   ★
***VVM-1.2v.** [4] Stationes.   SATB, 2fl 2cl 2hn 2bn tp timp.   MS parts: CZ-Pnm, XL.A.72.
***VVM-2.1v.** Pangelingua; in C.   CATB, 2fl 2cl 2hn bn 2tp(clar) tp(prin).
MS parts (c.1830): CZ-NYc, DÚ 206, (missing B pt; with Czech text; all 4 Stationes use the same music).   ★
***VVM-2.2v.** Pange Lingua; in D.   CATB, 2fl 2cl(A) 2hn bn timp.
MS parts (by Herle, from Mladá Boloslav): CZ-Pnm, XII.E.109, (the inside wrapper includes a simplified & incomplete timpani part, written with notes at pitch rather than the key of C conventional at this time).   ★
***VVM-3.1v.** Salve Regina; in B♭.   CA, 2cl 2hn 2bn.   MS parts: CZ-Pnm, XXII.F.282, (MS by Thom. W. Bolardt); CZ-PLa, Hu 576, (as "Salve in B[♭]", MS by J. Háj).   ★
***VVM-3.2v.** Duet, "Adorare".   CA, 2cl 2hn 2bn.   MS parts: CZ-Pnm, XXII.E.90.   ★
***VVM-3.3v.** Salve Regina in B[♭].   CA, 2cl 4hn(B♭, E♭) 2bn.   MS parts: CZ-BR, sign. 323.
***VVM-1tv.** Leichenlied; in F, "Begrabt den Lieb in seine Gruft".   SATB, fl 2cl(A) 2hn (2)bn.
MS parts: CZ-Pnm, XXXVIII.F.300, (the bn pt is marked "Fagotto Octavo" - here meaning *in octaves*, rather than calling for a cbn).   ★

MASSANA (Bertrán), Antonio (P. Antoni)   *24 Feb 1890, Barcelona - 9 Sept 1966, Raimat*
APM-1. Ouvertura.   2fl 2ob ca 2cl b-cl 2bn cbn 4tp(F) 3tp(C) 3tb tu b-dr timp.
MS parts: E-Bca, Fons Antonio Massana, BC M. 2982.

***MASSIAS, Gérard**   *25 May 1933, Paris*
GEM-1. Concert bref.   Piano solo, fl ob 2cl 2hn 2bn 2tp perc.
Pm (Jobert: Paris, 1966).

***MASSIS, Amable**   *2 June 1893, Cambrai - 10 June 1980, Troyes*
AYM-1. Ballade.   Solo vl, fl ob ca 2cl 2hn 2bn harp, piano.
Pm (Billaudot: Paris; sd), (reprint), score & parts.

***MAŠTALÍŘ, Jaroslav**   *1 May 1906, Karviná - 22 May 1988, Prague*
JNM-1. Sonatina.   fl 2ob 2cl 2hn 2bn.
Pm (Český hudební fond: Prague, 1975), hire score & parts.

***MAŤÁTKO (Matatko), Jan (Johann)**   *(1780)*
JHM-1ma. Reisskreutz: Marsch in C [& Trio].   cl(F) 2cl 2hn bn tp(prin).
MS parts (Langenbruck, c.1810): CZ-Pu(dm), 59 R 3394.   ★

MATĚJ, Jožka   *19 Feb 1922, Brušperk*
VJM-1. Ophelia: 3 vocal frescoes.   S solo, narrator, female choir, 2ob ca 2cl b-cl db piano.
Pm (Panton: Prague, pn 01900, sd), score.

***MATIEGKA, Wenzel Thomas (Václav Tomáš** *baptized 6 July 1773, Choceň - 29 Jan 1830, Vienna*
WTM-1v. Píseň pohřebni.   CATB, 2cl 2hn bn 2tp.   MS parts: CZ-Bm(rj), A.14.453.   ★

***MATOUŠ (Mattausch), ( )**   *(1760)*
XXM-1. Parthia ex Dis [E♭]; 4 mvts.   2cl 2hn bn.   MS parts (by Joh. Aug. Fibiger): CZ-Pnm, IX.C.12.   ★

***MATOUŠEK, Lukáš**   *29 May 1943, Prague*
LKM-1. Garden Music, 1962.   12 winds.   MS score: CZ-Pmatoušek.
LKM-2. Hudba pro Bayerreuth - II invense (Music for Bayreuth, 2nd Invention).   10 winds.
MS score: CZ-Pmatoušek.

***MATTHEWS, Colin**   *13 Feb 1946, London*
***CYM-1.** To compose without the least knowledge of music . . .   fl ob 2cl hn bn.
Pm (Faber Music: London, 1991), hire score & parts.

***MATYÁŠ (Matias, Matiaš), Mikoláš (Nikolaus)**   *(1820)*
MIM-1a. Donizetti: La Fille du régiment, marziale, arie & Rataplan.   fl 2cl(C & A) 2hn cbn 2tp flug b-flug tb "Tambure".   AutoMS parts (1851): CZ-TRB, H 64, (missing tb & tambure).
MIM-2a. Verdi: Nabuccodonosor, "Sperate, o figli".   cl(G) 2cl(C oblig) 2hn bn 3tp flug(C) 2bomb.
AutoMS parts: CZ-TRB, H 45.
MIM-3a. Verdi: Alzira, cavatina.   cl(C) obbligato, fl cl(D) cl(II C) 2hn bn 3tp 2flug bomb.
AutoMS parts (post-1845): CZ-TRB, H 494.

***MAW, (John) Nicholas**   *5 Nov 1935, Grantham, UK*
***NYM-1.** Minuet, 1991.   fl cl 2bn 2tp 2tb.   MS parts: GB-Lmic will assist in contacting the composer.

MAXWELL DAVIES, *Sir* **Peter**   *See under: DAVIES*

MAYER (Maier), Ambros
AZM-1v. [4] Stationes Pro Festo Corporis Christi.   SATB, 2cl 2hn bn.   MS: CH-Fcu, Ebaz II-80.

MAYER, Bert *(c.1950)*
BYM-1a. Mozart: Sonata in A, K.331/iii, Rondo à la turque.   2ob 2cl 2hn 2bn.
Pm (Universal Edition: Wien, c.1989), score & parts.

*MAYER (Mayer), Franz, *of Kroměříž (1750), Clarinettist active 1775 - 1779, Kroměříž, Moravia*
FNM-1. Parthia in G; 3 mvts.   2ob ob(princ) 2hn 2bn.
MS parts: CZ-KRa, A3927/IV.B.90. *The oboe principale part is* not *a solo part as sometimes suggested, rather a low part analogous to a trumpet principale part.* ★
FNM-2. Parthia in A; 3 mvts.   2ob 2hn 2bn.   MS parts: CZ-KRa, A3924/IV.B.87. ★
FNM-3. Parthia in F; 5 mvts.   2ob 2hn 2bn.   MS parts: CZ-KRa, A3925/IV.B.88. ★
FNM-4. Parthia in hoch C; 7 mvts.   2ob 2hn 2bn.   MS parts: CZ-KRa, A3926/IV.B.89. ★
FNM-5. Parthia in G; 5 mvts.   2ob 2hn 2bn.   MS parts: CZ-KRa, A2938/IV.B.91. ★

MAYER, Franz, *of Vienna (1800)*
FZM-1. Three Serenades; E♭, 5 mvts; E♭, 5 mvts; E♭, 7 mvts.   2fl t-fl(B) bn/vc.
Pc (Monzani & Hill: London, c.1825), parts: GB-Lbl, h.250.e.(3), (missing bn/vc). ★

*MAYR (Mayer, Mair), Johann Simon (Giovanni Simone) *14 June 1763, Mendorf - 2 Dec 1845, Bergamo*
JSM-1. [1 mvt in C].   fl 2ob 2cl 2hn bn 2tp tb timp.
(?Auto)MS score: I-BGc, Mayr fald. 297/2.   ★
JSM-2. [1 mvt in E♭].   fl 2ob 2cl 2hn 2bn tp tb timp.
AutoMS score: I-BGc, Mayr fald. 297/3.   ★
JSM-3. Intermezzo; in E♭.   fl 2ob 2cl 2hn 2bn.   (?Auto)MS score: I-BGc, Mayr fald. 311/34.   ★
*JSM-4. [1 mvt in F].   pic pic-cl 2cbn serp 3tb b-dr.
(?Auto)MS score: I-BGc, Mayr fald. 297/5.   ★
JSM-5. 4 Nocturnes; (A-544 as "nonets").   fl 2cl 2hn 2bn tp tb.
MS: I-BGi, XXIV.1.576.9751.
Pm (Cattaneo: Bergamo, sd), score & parts.
JSM-6. [1 mvt in D minor]; (octets, A-541).   fl 2cl 2hn bn 2db/vc. AutoMS score: I-BGc, Mayr fald. 314/25. ★
JSM-7. [1 mvt in C minor].   2ob 2cl 2hn bn tb.   AutoMS score: I-BGc, Mayr fald. 317/3.   ★
*JSM-8. [Divertimento (Suite di 8 Pezzi), in E♭], (A-534).   ob 2cl hn 2bn.
(?Auto)MS score: I-BGc, Mayr fald. 252/16; GB-DOTams, (modern photocopy).   ★
Pm: (Boccaccini & Spada: Roma, pn BS1282, sd), score & parts.
JSM-9. [1 mvt in E♭].   2cl bthn 2hn 2bn.   AutoMS score: I-BGc, Mayr fald. 303/33/2.   ★
JSM-10. [2 mvts in F]; (A-539).   2fl 2cl bthn 2hn.   AutoMS score: I-BGc, Mayr fald. 319/5.   ★
JSM-11. [Allegretto vivace, E♭, 6/8 - Larghetto, ¢, E♭].   2cl 3hn 2bn.
(?Auto)MS score: I-BGc, Mayr fald. 302/16.   ★
JSM-12. [1 mvt in C minor].   fl ob cl 2hn tp.   AutoMS score: I-BGc, Mayr fald. 297/4.   ★
*JSM-13.1. Suonate a N 6 Istrumenti; in E♭; 5 mvts, (A-533).   2cl bthn 2hn bn.
AutoMS score: I-BGc, Mayr fald. 306/2; GB-DOTams, (photocopy).   ★
Pm (Cattaneo: Bergamo, sd).
Pm (C.F. Peters: Leipzig, etc., sd), score & parts, (as "Serenata Bergamasca").
JSM-13.2. [Settimino in E♭], 4 mvts (omits mvt 5).   2cl bthn 2hn bn vla.
AutoMS score: I-BGc, Mayr fald. 306/3.
*JSM-14, 15. Sextuor, Op. 9, Nos. 1, 2; (E♭, 4 mvts; E♭, 5 mvts), (?A-543).   2cl 2hn 2bn.
Pc (Gombart: Augsburg, pn 423, 465, 1805), composer given as "MAIR", pts: D-Tu, (Nos. 1 & 2);
D-SWl, Ms.3505a, (No. 2 only, at "Mair"); H-Bn, ZR 42,909, (No. 2 only); GB-DOTams, (No. 2, photocopy). ★
MS parts: D-HR, HR III 4 1/2 4° 96, HR III 4 1/2 4° 97, (order reversed, for 2ob 2hn 2bn, as by "D.S. Mair",
both here in F).
Pm (KGS), fiche (465, 464), D-HR MS version.
*JSM-16. Sestetto in Si Bemoll [B♭]; (A-536).   2cl 2hn 2bn.
AutoMS score ("Dono sella S.a.M. Chiesa Cernovich"): I-Mc, MS.Autogr.26.6. *This is, in fact, a large-scale work: Tema (Andante, ¢) with 12 variations & a concluding 6/8 section (Allegro).* ★
JSM-17. [1 complete mvt in E♭ - ?A-532 "Sextet in E♭ (incomplete)"].   2cl 2hn 2bn.
AutoMS score: I-BGc, (2 copies), Mayr fald. 302/8, Mayr fald. 319/6. ★
JSM-18. [1 mvt in E♭].   2cl 2hn 2bn.   AutoMS score: I-BGc, Mayr fald. 303/17.   ★
JSM-19. [Marcia & Minuetto allegro in E♭].   2ob cl hn 2bn.   AutoMS score: I-BGc, Mayr fald. 252/16.   ★
JSM-20. [Sestetto in C]; 6 mvts.   ob/cl 2hn b/bn 2vla.   AutoMS score: I-BGc, Mayr fald. 335/4.   ★
JSM-21. [Sestetto in]; 3 mvts.   cl 2hn bn 2vla.   AutoMS score: I-BGc, Mayr fald. 335/5.   ★
*JSM-1m(t). Marcia lugubre; in C minor, (A-532).   2fl 2ob 2cl 2bthn 4hn(E♭, C) 2bn cbn/db 3tp b-tb timp b-dr.
(?Auto)MS score: I-BGc, Mayr fald. 47/37; GB-DOTams, (photocopy).   ★
MS parts: I-BGc, (with additional parts for pic, vla I & II, vc I & II; the horns are marked "con sordini" & the
timpani "Coperti", muffled).
Pm (Boccaccini & Spada, Roma, pn BS 1147, sd), score.
JSM-2m. March in D; (not in Allitt?).   pic 2fl 2ob 2cl(A) 2hn bn 2tp db timp "tamburlano".
MS score & parts: I-BGc, Mayr fald. 252/14, ("tamburlano" in the pts only); GB-DOTams, (photocopy).   ★
JSM-3m. [March] N:7 alla francese; in G minor.   2ob 2cl 3hn.
AutoMS score: I-BGc, Mayr fald. 299/6.   ★
JSM-4m. Marcia in E♭; (A-531).   2ob cl hn 2bn.   (?Auto)MS score: I-BGc, Mayr fald. 256/16.   ★
*JSM-1v. Laudate Dominum; in E♭.   CATB, 2fl ob 2cl 2hn 2bn tp tb("Tromboni") timp basso+organ.
AutoMS Score & MS parts: I-BGc(jm), Mayr fald. 8.
JSM-2v. Messa da Requiem; in E♭.   CATB, fl 2cl 2hn bn tp tb timp vlne organ.
AutoMS score & MS parts: I-BGc(jm), Mayr fald. 36

JSM-3v. Graduale per S. Luigi; in F. CCC, fl 2cl 2hn bn tp tb vlne timp.
AutoMS score & MS parts: I-BGc(jm), Mayr fald. 72.
JSM-4v. O salutaris hostia; in B♭. TTTB, fl ob cl 2hn bn tp tb vlne organ.
AutoMS score: I-BGc(jm), Mayr fald. 15.
JSM-5v. Alma redemptoris; in B♭. T solo, 2ob 2cl 2hn 2bn tb organ.
AutoMS score & MS parts: I-BGc(jm), Mayr fald. 15, (the score is incomplete).
*JSM-6v. Domine ad adjuvandum, e Magnificat; in C. TTB, fl 2cl/ob 2hn tp tb vlne organ.
AutoMS score & MS parts: I-BGc(jm), Mayr fald. 139, (the oboe alternative is only noted on the parts).
JSM-7v. Miserere in F. CCC, 2ob 2cl 2hn bn. AutoMS score & MS pts (2ob only): I-BGc, Mayr fald. 216.11.
JSM-8v. Viderunt te aqua, per benedizione di campane; in D. CTB, 2cl 2hn tb cb organ.
(?Auto)MS score & MS parts: I-BGc(jm), Mayr fald. 11.
*JSM-9v. Miserere; in C minor. CATB, 2cl 2hn tp(con sordini) tb timp(coperti), [cb].
MS score & pts: I-BGc(jm), Mayr fald. 214/17; I-BGi(cm), Faldone 1, n. 1022, (the cb is in this set of pts only).
The parts are, in fact, the later rescoring by Donizetti, (DGD-1va).
JSM-10v. Eja mater, a 4 voci; in F. CATB, 2ob 2cl 2hn vc. MS score: I-BGi(cm), Mayr fald. 112, n. 998.
JSM-11v. Salve Regina; in C. C/B solo, 2ob 2hn bn vlne organ.
AutoMS score & MS parts: I-BGc(jm), Mayr fald. 307.
JSM-12v. O salutaris hostia; in B♭. TTTB, ob cl 2hn bn tb vlne. (?Auto)MS score: I-BGc, Mayr fald. 15.5. ★
JSM-13v. Qui tollis; in E♭. CTTB, ob ca 2cl 2hn bn. AutoMS score: I-BGc, Mayr fald. 305.55. ★
JSM-14v. Stabat Mater, in F. SS, 2cl 2hn bn basso. (?Auto)MS score: I-BGc, Mayr fald. 16.38. ★
JSM-15v. Gratias agimus; in B♭. B solo, 2ob cl 2hn bn. (?Auto)MS score: I-BGc, Mayr fald. 323.28. ★
JSM-16v. Averte faciem; in F. CCC, 2cl 2hn bn. AutoMS score: I-BGc(jm), Mayr fald. 216.
JSM-17v. Pange lingua; in C. CATB, 2ob cl 2hn bn. AutoMS score & MS pts: I-BGc, Mayr fald. 16.37. ★
JSM-18v. Sicut erat; in B♭. CTB, 2ob 2hn basso. MS score: I-BGi(cm), Faldone 48, n. 1045.
JSM-19v. Te Joseph celebrent; in C. CTB, ob 2hn. (?Auto)MS score & MS pts: I-BGc(jm), Mayr fald. 11.
JSM-1vf. Stabat Mater; in G. CATB, 2ob 2hn bn. (?Auto)MS score: I-BGc, Mayr fald. 16.40, (incomplete). ★
JSM-2vf. Stabat Mater; in F. 3 voices, 2cl 2hn bn.
(?Auto)MS score: I-BGc(jm), Mayr fald. 16, (the score in incomplete and disorganized).
JSM-1va. Haydn: Credo in B♭. SATTTB, 2cl 2hn tp tb timp vc vlne organ.
MS score (partly autograph): I-BGc, Mayr fald. 315. ★
Pm (sn: London, 1991), ed. Ian Caddy, (arrangement attributed as Mayr *and* Donizetti), score & parts.
JSM-2va. Seyfried: Libera me. STBB, 2fl 2ob 2cl 2hn bn 2tp 2tb timp.
AutoMS score & MS parts: I-BGc, Mayr fald. 47.29, with duplicate parts: S(4) T(5) B(7), 2hn(3) tb(3)).
JSM-1vs. Passio nostri Jesu Christi. TB solo, SATB chorus, fl ob ob(ca) 2hn bn 2vla vc db organ.
Pm (in MS), reconstructed & revised by Pierangelo Pelucchi from numerous fragments in I-BGc. *Recorded in 1995 on Agorà Musica (Italy) CD: AG 005.2.*

*MAYR, Placidus, *O.S.B. (Order of St Benedict) (1770; active in Switzerland)*
PYM-1. [2] Kleine und leichte Walzer. 3cl(C) 3hn bn. MS parts: CH-EN, Ms. A 469 (Ms.5841). ★
PYM-2. Sextetto; in B♭, 6 mvts. 2cl 2hn 2bn. MS parts: CH-EN, Ms. A 461 (Ms.5833). ★
PYM-3. Sinphonie; in F, 1 mvt. 2cl(C) 2hn bn. MS parts: CH-EN, Ms. A 468 (Ms.5840). ★

MAYR, Sebastian *1845, Munich - 1899, La Chaux de Fonds*
SZM-1. Am Morgen (In the morning), Idyll. Solo trumpet or horn, fl ob 2cl 2bn.
Pm (Albert J. Andraud: Cincinnati, now Southern Music Co.: San Antonio, Texas, sd).

*MAZELLIER, Jules *1879 - 1959*
JXM-1. Prelude and dance. Solo bassoon, winds. *(The original version has not been traced.)*
Pc (Costallat: Paris, 1931), solo part & piano reduction: F-Pn, Vm10 c.20.
Pm (Leduc: Paris, 1931), solo part & piano reduction.

*MAZZORIN (MANZORIN), Michele *(1810) - active 1848, Venice*
MXM-1v. Credo, 1848. TTB, fl 2cl 2hn bn 2tp (vlne) timp organ(bc-fig).
MS score & parts: I-Vsmc, (with full organ pt; the vlne does not appear in the score). ★
MXM-2v. Gloria, 1848. TTB, fl 2cl 2hn bn 2tp (vlne) timp organ(bc-fig).
MS score & parts: I-Vsmc, (with full organ part; the vlne does not appear in the score). ★
MXM-3v. Kyrie, 1848. TTB, fl 2cl(C) 2hn bn 2tp (vlne) timp organ(bc-fig).
MS score & parts: I-Vsmc, (with additional vlne part). ★
MXM-4v. Lauda Jerusalem. TTB(solo+rip), 2cl(C) 2hn bn (vlne timp) organ.
MS score (missing last sheet) & parts(complete): I-Vsmc, (the vlne & timp do not appear in the score). ★
MXM-5v. Tantum ergo. Bass solo, TTB chorus, 2ob 2hn 2bn tp organ. MS parts: I-Vcr, Busta X.N.140.
MXM-6v. Salve Regina. TTB, 2ob 2hn bn (vlne) organ(bc-fig).
MS score & parts: I-Vsmc, (with full organ pt; the vlne does not appear in the score). ★
MXM-7v. Iste Confessor. TTB, 2cl 2hn 2tp organ(bc-fig). MS score & voice pts: I-Vsmc. ★
MXM-8v. Tantum ergo. Solo T, TB(solo+rip) chorus, 2cl(C) 2hn (bn) organ.
MS score (complete) & parts (fragments): I-Vsmc, (bassoon cues in the organ part in the score). ★
MXM-9v. Stabat Mater. 2cl 2hn bn tb(I) timp. MS parts: I-Vsmc, (missing voices & all other parts). ★

Mc is listed as Mac. Thus names like McPHEE, etc, are listed as if MacPHEE, etc.

*MEDER, Johann Gabriel *(1770)*
JGM-1m. 6 Märsche. 2cl 2hn bn.
Pc (Johann Julius Hummel: Berlin, pn 914, c.1795), RISM [M 1701], parts: CZ-Pnm; FIN-A.

*MEDERITSCH, Johann (known as: Georg Anton Gallus)
26 Dec 1752, Vienna - 18 Dec 1835, Lemburg (now L'vov).
*JYM-1ve. Der Tempelherrn (Schauspiel, 1794): Chor der Tempelherrn. SATB, 2fl 2cl bn tb organ.
AutoMS score: A-Sm, M.s. 1881; copy A-Sm, M.s.105/35.

*MÉHUL, Étienne Nicolas *22 June 1763, Givet, nr Mézières - 18 Oct 1817, Paris*
*ENM-1. Ouverture; in F, P.2286, (10 Dec 1793). 2p-fl 2cl 2hn 2bn 2tp b-tb serp timp.
MS score: F-Pn, D.7.855.   MS parts: F-Pn, H2. 135 a-q. ★
Pc (Mag de mus fêtes nat: Paris, prairial an II, 1794), liv. 3, No. 1, RISM [M 2135], parts: F-Pn, (2 copies),
H2 3,1, Vm7 7031; D-WRtl.
Pm (Swanzy), pp. 239 - 261, score.
Pm (Southern Music Corp.: San Antonio, Texas; H. Peer: Hamburg, pn PS 1983, 1952), ed. Goldman & Smith,
for modern band, 55 parts.
*ENM-1mv. Le Chant de Retour; P.136.   Solo voice, SATB chorus, 2pic 2cl 2hn 2bn 2tp 3tb serp.
Pc (Mag de mus.fêtes nat: Paris, c.1797), RISM [M 2141], vocal score & instrumental parts: D-AB.
Pc (for: Voice, 2cl 2hn (2)bn:) (Rec des époques: Paris, c.1799), liv. 1, No. 40, score: F-Pn, H2. 15,40. ★
Pm (Swanzy, 1966), p. 239, score.
*ENM-2mv. L'Hymne des Vingt-deux [Girondins]; P.109.
Solo voice, SATB chorus, 2p-fl 2cl 2hn 2bn 2tp 3tb serp buccin db timp cym b-dr.
MS parts: F-Pn, H2. 116 a-y.   MS score (by Pierre): F-Pn. ★
Pc (for: Voice, 2cl 2hn (2)bn:) (Rec des époques: Paris, c.1799), liv. 2, No. 35, score: F-Pn, H2. 15,35.
ENM-3mv. Le Chant des Victoires; P.70.   SATB chorus, 2ob 2cl 2hn 2bn 2tp 3tb serp buccin db cym b-dr.
Pc (for Solo voice, 2cl 2hn 2bn:) (Rec des époques: Paris, c.1799), liv. 2, No. 28, score: F-Pn, H2. 15,28. ★
ENM-4mv. Chant funèbre à la mémoire du réprésentant du peuple Féraud, assassiné à son poste le 1er prairial
an 3e; P.97.   Solo voice, 2p-fl 2cl 2hn 2bn 2tp 3tb serp.
AutoMS score: F-Pn, MS. 2295. ★
MS parts: F-Pn, H2. 117 a-m.   MS parts (by Constant Pierre): F-Pn, Fol² Y 688, (missing hn II).
Pc (for: Voice, 2cl 2hn 2bn; omits recitative:) (Rec des époques: Paris, c.1799), liv. 1, No. 33, score:
F-Pn, H2. 15,33.
*ENM-5mv. Le Chant du départ; P.68.   Solo voice, SATB chorus, 2cl(C) 2hn (2)bn 2tp serp timp.
Pc (Mag de mus fêtes nat: Paris, fructidor an II, 1794), liv. 6, No. 2, RISM [M 2135], vocal score & instrumental
parts: D-AB; F-Pn, (3 copies), H2. 6,2, H2. 84 a-n, Vm7 7049; F-Nm, Vol 22208. ★
Pc (for: Voice, 2cl 2hn (2)bn:) (Rec des époques: Paris, c.1799), liv. 1, No. 16, score: F-Pn, H2. 15,16.
Pm (Swanzy), pp. 273 - 276, score.
ENM-6mv. Anniversaire du neuf Thermidor. Hymne; P.101b.   Solo voice, 2cl 2hn 2bn.
Pc (Rec des époques: Paris, c.1799), liv. 2, No. 9, pp. 157 - 159, score: F-Pn, H2. 16,9. ★
ENM-7mv. Hymne pour la Fête des Époux, 10 floréal; (1799), P.152.   Solo voice, 2cl 2hn (2)bn.
Pc (Rec des époques: Paris, c.1799), liv. 2, No. 5, pp. 142 - 146, score: F-Pn, H2. 16,5. ★

MEIER, Daniel *1934, France*
DNM-1. Vitrail 2; 1981.   2fl 2ob 2cl 2hn 2bn 2tp 2tb tu.   MS score: F-Pd.

*MEIER, G. *(?1800)*
GWM-1a. Blauvels: Ouverture [E♭].   fl cl(E♭) cl(B♭ obl) 3cl(B♭) 2hn 2bn tp 3tb serp b-dr.
MS parts: D-DT, Mus-n 1578, (with a duplicate cl II pt).

MEIJERING, Chiel *1954, Netherlands*
CHM-1. Electric blue, 1977 (revised 1980)   2ob 2cl a-sax 2hn 2bn 2tp 2tb tu 2perc.
Pm (Donemus: Amsterdam, 1980), score.
CHM-2. Het pijporgel, (1981, revised 1982).   2fl 2ob 2cl 3hn 2bn db.
Pm (Donemus: Amsterdam, 1982), score.

MEILINK, Stef *14 Dec 1950, Groesbeck*
SQM-1. 5 Bagatelles.   2fl 2ob 2cl 2bn.
Pm (Teeseling: Nijmegen).

*MEISSNER, F.W. *(1790)*
*FWM-1. Pièces d'Harmonie, Liv. 1; in E♭, 4 mvts.   2ob/fl 2cl 2hn 2bn.
Pc (Breitkopf & Härtel: Leipzig, pn 3368, 1821), parts: A-Wgm, VIII 17359. ★
*FWM-2. Pièces d'Harmonie, Liv. 2; in E♭, 4 mvts.   2ob/fl 2cl 2hn 2bn.
Pc (Breitkopf & Härtel: Leipzig, pn 3371, 1821), parts: A-Wgm, VIII 17360. ★
MS parts (1822): D-Rtt, Sm. 15, No. 63.

*MEJO (Majo), Guillaume (Wilhelm) August *1793, Nossen, Silesia - post-1846*
We have not traced his Sextet for 2hn 2bn 2serp/cbn (Verlag Faber: Leinzau, 1821), *or the* "Var. p[our]. Fl.
2Htb. 2 Clarin. 2 Cors, 2 Bassons, Serpent (et Trombonne ad lib) No. 3 in C" *published by C.F. Peters in
Leipzig, cited in Whistling's Supplement 10, 1827.*
*GAM-1. Variations sur la Chanson: Gaudeamus igitur; (?= Op. 3).
fl(E♭) cl(E♭) 2cl(B♭) 3hn 2bn b-tb, (ad lib: cl III in B♭, a-tb t-tb serp).
Pc (Breitkopf & Härtel: Leipzig, pn 3908, 1824), pts: CH-Gpu, Ib.4841; GB-Lbl, g.474.r; GB-Ljag, (photocopy). ★
GAM-2. Variations, Op. 5; in F.   fl 2ob 2cl 2hn 2bn, (serp b-tb ad lib).
Pc (Breitkopf & Härtel: Leipzig, pn 4414, 1824/25), parts: A-Wgm, VIII 5240. ★

MELBY, John B. *1941, USA*
ZJM-1. Epitaph (in memoriam Carl Ruggles).   pic fl 2ob ca 2cl b-cl 2hn 2bn cbn 2tp 2tb tu 4perc.
Pm (Margun Music: Newton Center, MA, 1975).

*MELIN, ( ), (? G. Mellin)
XZM-1. Menuet Badin.   2fl 2ob 2cl 2hn 2bn.
Pm (Albert J. Andraud: Cincinnati, now Southern Music: San Antonio, sd), score & parts.

*MELIN, Sten *1957, Sweden*
SNM-1. Vågform 114 [sic]; 1980.   fl ob cl s-sax 2bn 2tp 2tb timp perc piano.   MS score: S-Sic.

*MELLERS, Wilfred Howard *26 April 1914, Leamington Spa*
WHM-1. Noctambule and Sun Dance; 1962.   2fl 2ob 2cl 2hn 2bn 2tp 2tb tu perc piano.
Pm (Novello & Co.: London, 1967), score (pn 090513 0500) & pts (pn 909513 0501), (Music for Today,
Ser. 2, No. 10).

*MENDELSSOHN, (Ludwig) Arnold *26 Dec 1855, Ratibor, Silesia (now Poland) - 19 Feb 1933, Darmstadt*
ARM-1. Suite, Op. 62. 2fl(pic) 2ob 2cl 2hn 2bn 2tp 3tb timp perc.
Pm (Leuckart: München, 1916), score & parts: D-Mbs, 2 Mus.pr. 7467.

*MENDELSSOHN BARTHOLDY, Jacob Ludwig Felix *3 Feb 1809, Hamburg - 4 Nov 1847, Leipzig*
FMBW: Felix Mendelssohn Bartholdy's Werke. (Breitkopf & Härtel: Leipzig, 1874-80), scores. (Reprinted:) (Gregg Press: Farnborough, Hampshire, UK, 1967-70). LAW: Leipziger Ausgabe der Werke Felix Mendelssohn Bartholdys. (Deutscher Verlag für Musik: Leipzig, 1960, etc.), scores.
*FJM-1.1. Ouverture fur Harmoniemusik, in C, Op. 24, (1838 version).
fl 2ob 2cl(F) 2cl(C) 2bthn 2hn 2bn cbn 2tp 3tb tu timp.
Pc (N. Simrock: Bonn, pts, pn 3586, 1839; score, pn Musikbibliothek PM 830, 1852): GB-Lbl, Hirsch M.280, score only.
Pc (FMBW: Series 7, No. 29, pp. 1-32), score (pn MB 29, as "Doberaber lasmusik").
Pm (E.F. Kalmus: New York), parts (pn A 1718), min score (pn 1186, No. 1, pp. 1-32).
*FJM-1.2. Notturno in C, Op. 24, (1824 version). fl 2ob 2cl 2hn 2bn tp b-hn(corno basso).
MS score: D-DÜl.
Pm (LAW: from 1972. Series III; to be issued), score.
Pm (Breitkopf & Härtel: Wiesbaden, sd), hire score & parts.
Pm (WINDS: Northridge, CA, pn W-192, c.1981), score & parts (photocopies of modern manuscript).
Pm (Compusic: Amsterdam, pn 242, 1988), score & parts (cbn replaces bass horn).
FJM-1.3. Ouverture für Harmoniemusik, Op. 24; in C, local rescoring. pic fl 2ob 2cl(F) 2cl(C) 2bthn 4hn 2bn cbn 2tp 3tb oph "Janitscharen" (= perc). MS parts: D-DT, Mus-n 697.
*FJM-2. Trauermarsch, in A minor, Op. 103; 1836. fl 2ob 2cl 2a-cl(Eb) 4hn 2bn 2tp 3tb b-dr s-dr cym tri.
Pc (J. Rieter-Biedermann: Leipzig, Winterthur, pn 552; PM 1071, 1868, 1869), score & parts.
Pm (FMBW: Series 7, No. 29a, pp. 33 - 38), score.
Pm (E.F. Kalmus: New York), parts (pn A 1719), min score (pn 1186, No. 2, pp. 33 - 38).
*FJM-1v. Begrüssung; componirt für die Naturforscher-Versammlung, in Berlin, September 1828; 7 mvts.
TTBB, 2cl 2hn 2bn timp celli db.
Pm (Breitkopf & Härtel: Leipzig, 1930), score: A-Wgm, III 42334 (H 28395).
*FJM-2v. Ave Maria, (Kirchen-Musik, Op. 23, No. 2). SSAATTBB, organ *or* 2cl 2bn basse.
Pc (N. Simrock: Bonn, pn 3479, 1838), score: CZ-Bm(rj), A.22.453; GB-Lbl, F.370.p.(1, 2). ★
Pc (Novello: London, sd), score: I-Bc.
Pc (FMBW: Series 17, pp. 118-120), score.
Pm (LAW: Series VI), score.

MENGELBERG, Mischa (Misja) *5 June 1935, Kiev*
MYM-1. Hello windyboys [sic]. 2fl 2ob 2cl 2hn 2bn electronics.
Pm (Donemus: Amsterdam, 1968), score.

*MENTNER, Karl *(pseudonym: Blasius Wind) c.1800 - 1860, Germany*
*KZM-1. Sérénade amusante, Op. 1399 [sic; or 139]. fl ob 2cl 2hn bn.
Pm (Louis Oertel: Hannover).
Pm (Albert J. Andraud: Cincinnati, now Southern Music Co.: San Antonio, Texas, sd), score & parts.

MENUCCI, Giuseppe *(?1780)*
GIM-1v. Messe. TTB, fl 2cl 2bn vc db. MS: CH-E, Th.548,1.

*MERCADANTE, (Guiseppe) Saverio (Raffaele) *17 Sept 1795, Altamura - 12 Dec 1870, Naples*
SXM-1v. Gloria. TTB(solo+rip), (fl) 2cl 2hn tp tb vlne timp organ.
MS score & parts: I-Vsmc, (the flute part does not appear in the score). ★
SXM-2v. Tantum ergo. TTB, 2cl 2hn tp tb timp organ. MS score & parts: I-Vsmc. ★

MERCURE, Pierre *21 Feb 1927, Montreal - 29 Jan 1966, Avallon, France*
PZM-1. Pantomime. (3rd version 1949). 2fl 2ob 2cl 4hn 2bn 2tp 2tb 3perc.
MS score: C-Tcm.
Pm (Ricordi: New York, pn RCI.171, 1971), score.
Pm (Sikorski; Hamburg, sd), score.

MERIKANTO, Aarre *1893 - 1958, Finland*
AIM-1. Partita, for harp and winds. Harp, 2fl ob 2cl bn. MS score: FIN-Hmt.

MERING, ( ) *(?1740)*
XYM-1. Parthia "in C"; 4 mvts. 2ca 2hn bn. MS parts: CZ-Pnm, XLII.B.55. ★

*MERKLEIN, ( ) *(?1760), probably a member of the Chotek Harmonie, zámek Kačina*
ZXM-1a. Mozart: Don Giovanni, overture & 19 mvts. 2cl 2hn 2bn.
MS pts: CZ-Pnm, XLI.B.154. *This is, in fact, the same as the arr at XLI.B.150 with the exception of cuts.*

*MESSIAEN, Olivier *10 Dec 1908, Avignon - 27 April 1992, Paris*
OXM-1. Et exspecto resurrectionem mortuorum, 1964. 5fl 4ob 5cl 6hn 4bn 4tp 4tb 2tu 3perc.
Pm (Alphonse Leduc: Paris, 1966), score.
OXM-2. Oiseaux exotiques, 1956. Solo piano, pic fl ob 3cl b-cl 2hn bn tp 7perc glock.
Pm (Universal Edition: London, 1960), score.
OXM-3. L'Ascension (orchestral version), 1st mvt: Majesté du Christ demandant sa Gloire à son Père.
3fl 2cl 3bn 4hn 3tp 3tb tu.
Pm (Leduc: Paris, 1948), score & hire parts.
OXM-4. Un vitrail et des oiseaux, 1986. Piano solo, 16 winds, tp xly xylorimba marimbaphon perc.
Pm (Leduc: Paris, 1992), score.

METZLER, Friedrich *18 Feb 1910, Kanth, Silesia*
FDM-1. Octet, 1953. 2ob 2cl 2hn 2bn.
Pm: (untraced; earlier citations to Sikorski: Hamburg appear to be in error).

*MEYER, Karl Heinrich (Charles Henri) *1784, Buchholz bei Annaberg - 1837, Leipzig*
KHM-1. Partita No. 1; in E♭, c.1821, 4 mvts. 2ob 2cl 2hn 2bn tp(ad lib).
MS parts: D-DO; D-Rtt, Meyer 1, (dated 1821). ★
Pc (A. Kühnel, Leipzig, 1807), parts: H-Bn.
*KHM-2. Journal de Harmonie, Contenant XII Pièces. Collection XV. Livraison II; mvts Nos. 13 - 24.
terz-fl cl(E♭) 2cl(B♭) 2hn tp b-tb; ad lib: 2bn serp timp b-dr+cym s-dr.
Pc (Chez Frederic [sic] Hofmeister: Leipzig, pn 670, 1808), parts: GB-Ljag(w), L.368, (with a MS b-tb part
transposed to concert pitch - the printed part is written a semitone below concert pitch). ★
KHM-1a. Lindpaintner: Joko, overture. fl+pic cl(E♭) 3cl(B♭, C) 2hn 2bn 2tp a-tb t-tb b-tb serp timp/b-dr.
Pc (au Bureau de Musique de C.F. Peters: Leipzig, pn 2073, 1828/29), parts: GB-Ljag(w), L.142.

MEYER, Rene
REN-1. Winkle Bar; 1978. 4fl 4cl 4bn. MS score: US-ṄYamc.

*MEYERBEER, Giacomo *5 Sept 1791, Berlin - 2 May 1864, Paris*
GZM-1v. Königslied, Dec 28, 1813. fl 2ob 2cl 2bn.
AutoMS score: D-Bds, Mus.Ms.Auto.Meyerbeer.1008.
GZM-2v. Der Bayerische Schützenmarsch, (January 1814). TTBB, 5hn 4bn cbn serp 4tp 4tb perc.
MS: D-Mbs, St.Th.405.

MEYLAN, Raymond *22 Sept 1924, Onex*
RYM-1. Swiss Renaissance dances, after a 16th century lute book. 2pic ob ob/ca 2hn 2bn tp tb 2perc(timp s-dr
tamb, "Basle drum").
Pm (Amadeus Verlag: Winterthur, pn BP 2069, 1981), score & parts.

*MICHAEL, David Moritz *21 Oct 1751, Erfurt - 26 Feb 1827, Neuwied*
Here **PhilSoc** *stands for the Philharmonic Society of Bethlehem collection and* **Lititz** *for the Lititz Collegium
Musicum collection, both at US-BETm.*
DMM-1. Parthia I; in E♭, 3 mvts. 2cl hn bn tp.
MS parts: US-BETm, Lititz 197; US-WS, (incomplete). ★
DMM-2. Parthia II; in E♭, 5 mvts. fl 2cl 2hn bn.
MS parts: US-BETm, Lititz 198A; US-WS. ★
Pm (Boosey & Hawkes: New York, pn B. Ens, 170, 1970), ed. Henry H. Hall, score & parts, (part of "Moramus
Edition of the Moravian Foundation Inc.").
DMM-3. Parthia III; in B♭, 3 mvts. 2cl 2hn 2bn.
MS parts: US-BETm, Lititiz 188. ★
DMM-4. Parthia IV; in E♭, 3 mvts. 2cl 2hn 2bn.
MS parts: US-BETm, Lititz 193; US-WS. ★
Pm (Boosey & Hawkes: New York, pn B.Ens.171, 1970), ed. Henry H. Hall, score & parts, (part of "Moramus
Edition of the Moravian Foundation, Inc.").
DMM-5. Parthia V; in E♭, 4 mvts. 2cl 2hn 2bn.
MS parts: US-BETm, Lititz 194. ★
DMM-6. Parthia VI; in F, 4 mvts. 2cl 2hn 2bn.
MS parts: US-BETm, Lititz 186. ★
Pm (Boosey & Hawkes: New York, pn B. Ens. 152, 1966), ed. Donald M. McCorkle, score & parts (part of the
"Moramus Edition" of the Moravian Foundation, Inc).
DMM-7. Parthia VII; in C minor, 4 mvts. 2cl 2hn bn.
MS parts: US-BETm, (two copies), PhilSoc PSB 1350.3, Lititz 195. ★
DMM-8. Parthia VIII; in C minor, 4 mvts. 2cl 2hn bn.
MS parts: US-BETm, (two copies), PhilSoc PSB 1350.4, Lititz 196. ★
Pm (MS score in:) Roger P. Phelps *The History and Practice of Chamber Music in the United States from
Earliest Times up to 1875.* Ph.D dissertation, University of Iowa, 1951, p. 826.
DMM-9. Parthia X; in E♭, 3 mvts. 2cl 2hn 2bn.
MS parts: US-BETm, (2 copies), PhilSoc PSB 1350.5, Lititz 187. ★
DMM-10. Parthia XI; in E♭, 4 mvts. 2cl 2hn 2bn tp.
MS parts: US-BETm, (two copies), PhilSoc PSB 1350.6, Lititz 189, (missing tp). ★
DMM-11. Parthia XII; in F, 4 mvts. 2cl 2hn 2bn.
MS parts: US-BETm, (two copies), PhilSoc PSB 1350.7, Lititz 190. ★
DMM-12. Parthia XIII; in E♭, 3 mvts. 2cl 2hn bn.
MS parts: US-BETm, (two copies), PhilSoc PSB 1350.8, Lititz 191. ★
DMM-13. Parthia XIV; in E♭, 4 mvts. 2cl hn bn.
MS parts: US-BETm, (two copies), PhilSoc PSB 1350.9, Lititz 192. ★
*DMM-14. Parthia "bestimmt zu einer Wasserfahrt auf der Lecha"; 15 mvts. 2cl 2hn 2bn.
MS parts: US-BETm, Bethlehem Misc Collection 58A, 58B (two copies); US-WS. ★
*DMM-15. Suiten, "bey einer Quelle zu blasen", Introductio, Pars [sic] 1 (4 mvts), 2 (4 mvts), 3 (5 mvts).
2cl 2hn bn. MS parts: US-BETm, PhilSoc PSB 1351.4; US-WS. ★
*DMM-1d. Parthia IX; 3 mvts. 2cl 2hn bn.
MS parts: US-BETm *(possibly lost or unidentified, if ever present. See* The Wind Ensemble Sourcebook).

*MICHALIČKA, František *(1780), active Kunvald, Bohemia, 1818*
FQM-1vd. Mose česka v čas postní. CATB, 2cl 2hn 2bn.
MS parts (1818, from Kunvald): CZ-Pnm, XII.F.78. *In fact, by Michael Haydn, JMH-1.2v.*

*MICHALIČKA, Ján (Johann) *(1780), active as učitel,* Kunvald, Bohemia, 1817 - 1859
JVM-1v. №̠ 8, Píseň před kazánjm. CATB, 2cl(C) 2hn 2bn 2tp(clar) timp organ(bc-fig).
AutoMS parts (from Kunvald): CZ-Pnm, XII.F.100. ★
JVM-2v. №̠ 2, Píseň při slawném wzkřjssenj Krysta Pána. CATB, 2fl 2cl 2hn bn 2tp(clar) tp(prin) timp.
AutoMS parts, (from Kunvald): CZ-Pnm, XII.F.101, (missing the instrumental parts & with later, duplicate parts
in the key of C: 2C, A, T, B; and in the key of D: CAB. A later titlepage on one of the Basso parts gives the
title as "Pjseň radoštá" with b-tb replacing the trumpet principale part). ★
JVM-3v. №̠ 1, Homo quidem pro Corporis Xsti [sic: Christi]. CAB, 2fl 2cl(C) 2hn bn.
AutoMS parts: CZ-Pnm, XII.F.82. ★
*JVM-4v. Libra český; in Es [E♭]. CATB, 2cl 2hn bn basso.
AutoMS parts (from Kunvald, 7 Nov 1851): CZ-Pnm, XII.F.97. ★
JVM-1tv. Cantus Funebris. Zhotowená k pohřbu Pana faráře Josefa Magwalda dne 4ᵗᵒ Aprile 1823.
CATB, 2cl 2hn 2bn. AutoMS parts (from Kunvald): CZ-Pnm, XII.F.102. ★
JVM-2tv. Cantus funebris na Mladence a na Pannu [for children or men]. CATB, 2cl 2hn bn.
AutoMS parts (Kunvald, 2 April 1830): CZ-Pnm, (with the same text reflecting case changes, using the same
setting: "Na Mladence", 11 verses, "Na Pannu", 7 verses). ★

MICHALSKY, Donal Rau *13 July 1928, Pasadena - 13 Dec 1975, Newport Beach, CA*
DRM-1a. Fanfare after 17th century dances. fl fl(pic) ob ca cl cl(B-cl) 2hn 2bn tp(C *or* B♭) tb.
Pm (Shawnee Press: Delaware Water Gap, PA, 1973), score & parts (LD129), score (LC571), parts (LC572).
   1.1a. Paul Peurl: Newe Rodouan, Intrada, Dantz und Galliarda. 1.2a. Johann H. Schein: Banchetto Musicale.
   1.3a. Isaak Posch: Musicalische ehm-Freudt.

*MICHEL, Franz Ludwig *(1770) Active 1790s, in the Harmonie of Sophie Potocka, Tulchin, Ukraine. Many
anonymous works & arrangements in PL-LA (RM 81/1-5), & RF-Ssc (Yosupov Collection), may be by Michel.*
FLM-1a. Haydn: Symphony in D (here E♭, Hob I/55). 2fl 2cl 2hn 2bn.
MS parts: PL-LA, RM 81/1-5/161, (missing fl I, hn I, bn II).
FLM-2a. Haydn: Symphony in G (here E♭; Hob I/70). 2fl 2cl 2hn 2bn.
MS parts: PL-LA, RM 81/1-5/166, (missing fl I, hn I, bn II).
FLM-3a. Haydn: Symphony in D (here E♭; Hob I/73, La Chasse). 2fl 2cl 2hn 2bn.
MS parts: PL-LA, RM 81/1-5/139, (missing fl I, hn I, bn II).
FLM-4a. Haydn: Symphony in D (here E♭; Hob I/75). 2fl 2cl 2hn 2bn.
MS parts: PL-LA, RM 81/1-5/138, (missing fl I, hn I, bn II).
Pm (Compusic: Amsterdam, pn 236, 1988), completed by Jan Nieuwenhuis, score & parts.
FLM-5a. Haydn: Symphony in E♭, Hob I/76. 2fl 2cl 2hn 2bn.
MS parts: PL-LA, RM 81/1-5/160, (missing fl I, hn I, bn II).
FLM-6.1a. Mozart: Sinfonia in G (K.318, here used as the overture to Bianchi's opera, *La Villanella rapita).*
2fl 2cl 2hn 2bn. MS parts: PL-LA, RM 81/1-5/149, (missing fl I, hn I, bn II).
FLM-6.2a. Mozart: "Mandina amabile", (K.480, additional number for Bianchi's opera, *La Villanella rapita).*
2fl 2cl 2hn 2bn. MS parts: PL-LA, RM 81/1-5/107, (missing fl I, hn I, bn II).
FLM-7a. Pleyel: Quartetto "Op. 6 No. 3", (B.321i; B.134iii; B.134iv, iva; B.321ii). 2fl 2cl 2hn 2bn.
MS parts: PL-LA, 81/1-5/68, (missing fl I, hn I, bn II).
FLM-8a. Pleyel: Quartetto, E♭, (B.111v; ?B.433i; B.111ii, all slight variants; B.332iii). 2fl 2cl 2hn 2bn.
MS parts: PL-LA, 81/1-5/69, (missing fl I, hn I, bn II).
FLM-9a. Pleyel: Quartetto, E♭, (B.312ii; B.331ii; B.349ii; B.349iii; the latter two mvts are based on similar
themes). 2fl 2cl 2hn 2bn. MS parts: PL-LA, 81/1-5/70, (missing fl I, hn I, bn II).
FLM-10a. Pleyel: Quartetto, E♭, (B.331ii (variant?); B.303ii; B.303iii; B.304iii). 2fl 2cl 2hn 2bn.
MS parts: PL-LA, 81/1-5/71, (missing fl I, hn I, bn II).
FLM-11a. Pleyel: Quartetto, B♭, (B.386i; B.338ii; B.386ii; B.334iii). 2fl 2cl 2hn 2bn.
MS parts: PL-LA, 81/1-5/72, (missing fl I, hn I, bn II).
FLM-12a. Pleyel: Quartetto Es-dur, (B.111i; B.382ii; B.382iii; ?variant of B.381iii). 2fl 2cl 2hn 2bn.
MS parts: PL-LA, 81/1-5/73, (missing fl I, hn I, bn II).
FLM-13a. Pleyel: Quartetto "Op 1 No. 4", (B.304i; B.355ii; B.354ii variant; B.353iii). 2fl 2cl 2hn 2bn.
MS parts: PL-LA, 81/1-5/140, (missing fl I, hn I, bn II).
FLM-14a. Pleyel: Quartetto "Op 6 No. 4", (B.322i; B.322iii, iiia; B.319/ii; B.323iii). 2fl 2cl 2hn 2bn.
MS parts: PL-LA, 81/1-5/141, (missing fl I, hn I, bn II).
FLM-15a. Pleyel: Quintetto, E♭, (No. 3 of the Trois Harmonies IJP-16; B.384i-iva). 2fl 2cl 2hn 2bn.
MS pts: PL-LA, 81/1-5/159, (missing fl I, hn I, bn II); RF-Ssc, Ф 891 собр юосуповыіх N44, pp. 1 - 18.
FLM-16a. Pleyel: Quartetto, E♭; (B.346i, B.346ii, B.382ii, B.382iii, B.284iv). 2fl 2cl 2hn 2bn.
MS parts: RF-Ssc, Ф 891 собр юосуповыіх N46, pp. 41 - 58.
FLM-17a. Pleyel: Sérenata [sic], E♭; (B.216i, B.359iii, B.358iii, iiia, B.216v). 2fl 2cl 2hn 2bn.
MS parts: RF-Ssc, Ф 891 собр юосуповыіх N46, pp. 59 - 75.

MICHL (Michel), Joseph Christian Willibald *9 Sept 1745, Neumarkt - 1 Aug 1816, Neumarkt*
JCM-1. Polonaise concertante. fl 2cl 2hn 2bn. MS parts: B-Lc, 26 1-2. L-VI.

MIHELČIČ, Pavel *8 Nov 1937, Nové Město*
PAM-1. Moderato cantabile, 1962. Solo viola, 2fl 2ob 2cl 4hn 2bn harp.
Pm (Društvo slovenskih skladateljev: Ljubljana). Pm (H. Gerig: Köln, 1968), score.

*MILHAUD, Darius *4 Sept 1892, Aix-en-Provence - 22 June 1974, Geneva*
DYM-1. Grands feux: film music, Op. 182; (1st performance: Paris, 30 Nov 1937).
2fl cl sax 2hn 2bn 2tp 2tb tu perc timp piano. *MS score untraced.*
*DYM-2. Cinquième Petite Symphonie (Dixtuor), Op. 75; 1922, 3 mvts. fl(pic) fl ob ca cl b-cl 2hn 2bn.
Pm (Universal Edition: London, 1922, reprinted 1950), score (pn UE 7192eN) & parts (pn UE 7192eNJ).
DYM-3. Concertino (Suite) d'Automne. 2 pianos (solo), fl ob 3hn 2vla vc.
Pm (Heugel: Paris, pn H.31604, 1952), score.
DYM-1v. 5 Chansons de Charles Vildrac, Op. 167, (1st version, 1936-37).
Solo voice, fl ob 2cl bn 2tp tb perc harp piano. Pm (Salabert: Paris, c.1938), score.

MILLER, Edward Jay *1930, USA*
EZM-1. Fantasy Concerto for Alto Saxophone; 1971.   Solo a-sax, 2fl 2ob 2cl 2hn 2bn 2tp 2tb tu bar.
Pm (American Composers Alliance: New York).
EZM-2. Serenade; 1982.   2fl 2ob 2cl hn 2bn tp tb.
Pm (American Composers Alliance, New York).

*MILLER (Millard), M. *(1760)*
MZM-1m. Twelve Military Marches . . . Dedicated to the Royal Family.   2cl 2hn 2bn serp.
Pc (Longman and Broderip: London, 1794), RISM [M 2795], parts: GB-Lbl, b.81; GB-Ob, Mus.61d(5).   ★
  1.1m, 1.2m. The King['s] [slow & quick] March.
  1.3m, 1.4m. The Queen['ls [slow & quick] March.
  1.5m, 1.6m. The Prince of Wales's [slow & quick] March.
  1.7m, 1.8m. The Duke of Clarence's [slow & quick] March.
  1.9m, 1.10m. Prince Edward's [slow & quick] March.
  1.11m, 1.12m. Prince Augustus's [slow & quick] March.

MILLER, Philip *29 April 1961, USA (now resident in Sweden)*
PHM-1. Celebration music; 1987.   2fl 2ob 4cl 4hn 2bn 2tp 2crt 3tb tu timp 2perc.
MS score: S-Sic.
PHM-2. Uvertyr (Overture); 1986.   3fl(pic) 3ob(ca) 3cl 4hn 3bn 3tp 3tb tu.   MS score: S-Sic.

*MILLING, Anton *(1740)*
ANM-1. Parthia, in A, 1776; 13 mvts.   2ob 2hn 2bn.
MS parts: CZ-KRa, A4024, 4025/IV.B.198, Part 1, No. 11.   ★
ANM-2. Parthia ex C et B[b]; 8 mvts (4 in each key).   2ob 2hn bn.
MS parts: CZ-KRa, A4032/IV.B.205.   ★
ANM-3. Parthia ex C cum March; 9 mvts.   2ob 2hn basso.   MS parts: CZ-KRa, A4756.   ★
*ANM-4. Symphionia [sic] ex g: b [Bb]: A, 12 mvts (4 in each key).   2ob 2hn basso.
MS parts: CZ-KRa, A4757.   ★
*ANM-5. Sonata 9e la parata ex c. f. et g [sic]; 13 mvts (5 in C, 4 each in F & G).   2ob 2hn basso.
MS parts: CZ-KRa, A4759.   ★
ANM-6. Parthia ex C et b [Bb]; 12 mvts (1-4 in C, 5-8 in Bb, 9-12 in C).   2ob 2hn basso.
MS parts: CZ-KRa, A4760.   ★
ANM-7. Parthias ex b [Bb] et A; 8 mvts (4 in each key).   2ob 2hn basso.
MS parts: CZ-KRa, A4761.   ★

MILLS, Charles Borromeo *8 Jan 1914, Asheville, NC - 7 March 1982, New York*
CZM-1. Concerto sereno, Op. 77; 1948.   2ob 2cl 2hn 2bn.
Pm (American Composers Alliance: New York).

*MINAŘIK, ( ) *(1800) - active c.1824, Brno*
YXM-1a. Spohr: Jessonda, aria & duett.   2ob 2cl 2hn 2bn cbn 2tp.
AutoMS score & MS parts: CZ-Bm(au), 35.230.

MISIASZEK, Stephen
STM-1. Fanfare.   2fl 2ob 2cl 2hn 2bn.
Pm (International Double Reed Society: North Howard, Indiana), score & parts.

*MIŠÍK (Mischik, Mischick, Mischk), František Vojtěch (Franz Adalbert) *(?1730)*
FAM-1. Partia Cassatio A 8 Stromenti; in F, 4 mvts.   2ob 2tallie [sic] 2hn 2bn.
MS parts: CZ-Pnm, XXVII.E.53.   ★
FAM-2. Nro 12 Partitta A 8 Stromenti; in F, 6 mvts.   2ob 2talie 2hn 2bn.   MS parts: CZ-Pnm, XXII.D.270.   ★
FAM-3. Nro 15 Partia A 8 Stromenti; in C, 4 mvts.   2ob 2talie 2hn bn, (tp(prin) ad lib).
MS parts: CZ-Pnm, XXII.D.273, (missing hn II).   ★
FAM-4. Partitta à 7 Stromento [sic]; in F.   2ob 2talia 2hn bn.   MS parts: CZ-Pnm, XVII.B.300.   ★
FAM-5. Nro 9 Partitta A 7 Stromenti; in F, 5 mvts.   2ob 2ca 2hn bn.   MS parts: CZ-Pnm,XXII.D.269.   ★
FAM-6. Nro 5 Partia A 7: Stromenti; in F, 5 mvts.   2ob 2talie 2hn bn.   MS parts: CZ-Pnm, XXII.D.265.   ★
FAM-7. Nro 6 Partitta A 7 Stromenti; in F, 4 mvts.   2ob 2talie 2hn bn.   MS pts: CZ-Pnm, XXII.D.266.   ★
FAM-8. Nro 7 Parthia A 7 Stromenti; in C, 6 mvts.   2ob Concertandi [sic], 2tallie Concertandi, 2hn bn.
MS parts: CZ-Pnm, XXII.D.267.   ★
FAM-9. Nro 8 Partitta A 7 Stromenti; in Bb, 4 mvts.   2ob Concerti [sic]. 2tallie Concertati, 2hn bn.
MS parts: CZ-Pnm, XXII.D.268.   ★
FAM-10. Nro 13 Parthia Ex F a 7 Stromenti; 5 mvts.   2ob 2talia 2hn bn.   MS parts: CZ-Pnm, XXII.D.271.   ★
FAM-11. Nro 14 Partia A 7 stromenti; in C, 6 mvts.   2ob 2talie 2hn bn.
MS pts: CZ-Pnm, (2 copies), XXII.D.272., XXII.E.61/49 (as Anon, "Divertimento ex C", for 2ob 2hn bn).   ★
FAM-12. Nro 16 Parhia Ex F: a 7 Stromenti; 6 mvts.   2ob 2talie 2hn bn.   MS pts: CZ-Pnm, XXII.D.274.   ★
FAM-13. Nro 17 Parhia A 6: Strom[enti]; in D, 4 mvts.   2ob 2hn 2bn.
MS parts: CZ-Pnm, XXII.D.275, ("Fagotto" on title page, but divisi in Trio of Menuetto).   ★
FAM-14. Parthia a 6 Stromenti; in A; 4 mvts.   2ob 2hn bn.   MS parts: CZ-Pnm, XXII.D.278.   ★
FAM-15. Nro 18 Partitta A. 5 Strom[enti]; in C, 4 mvts.   2ob 2hn bn.   MS parts: CZ-Pnm, XXII.D.276.   ★
FAM-16. Nro 19 Parthia Ex D# [i.e. D major]; 3 mvts.   2ob 2hn bn.   MS parts: CZ-Pnm, XXII.D.277.   ★
FAM-17. Nro 1 Parthia Ex [Bb]; 5 mvts.   2talia/a-cl 2hn bn.
MS parts: CZ-Pnm, XXII.D.261, (the a-cl pts are later additions).   ★
FAM-18. Parthia Ex B[b]; 4 mvts.   2talia 2hn bn.   MS parts: CZ-Pnm, XXII.D.262.   ★
FAM-19. Nro 3. Parttita [sic] A. 5 Strom[enti]; in Bb, 4 mvts.   2talia/a-cl 2hn bn.
MS parts: CZ-Pnm, XXII.D.263, (the a-cl pts are later additions).   ★
FAM-20. Nro 4 Parhia in A; 5 mvts.   2tallie/a-cl 2hn bn.
MS parts: CZ-Pnm, XXII.D.264, (the a-cl pts are later additions).   ★

MITREA-CELDRIDNU, Mihai *20 Jan 1935, Bucharest*
MCM-1. Janvier; 1985.   fl cl 2sax 2bn tb 2db vib.   Pm (Salabert: Paris, 1985).

*MOHR, J. *(1810)*
JPM-1a. Auber: Actéon, overture.   pic(fl) cl(D) cl(solo) 4cl(A) 2hn bn(I) cbn 2tp a-tb t-tb b-tb quint-oph
oph+serp b-dr+cym.
Pc (V. Gambaro: Paris; Aug. Gambaro: Brussels, pn 460, c.1836), parts: I-Mc, Noseda B.18.2, (provenance:
"Musique du Pensionnat de Freibourg"; with additional MS parts: Partie-Direction, cl I & II, hn II, tp(á piston) II,
a-tb, t-tb, quint-oph, oph(C) tuba-cleide, b-dr).
JPM-2.1a. Auber: Zanetta, overture.   pic cl(E♭) cl(B♭, solo) 4cl(B♭) 4hn(2B♭ basso obligés, 2F[ripieno]) bn(I)
bn(II)+cb 2tp 2cap bugle 2a-tb b-tb a-oph oph(C) oph(B♭) serp b-dr tri.
Pc (chez les fils de B. Schott: Mayence et Anvers, pn T. 971, c.1841), pas: GB-Ljag(w), (with additional MS
parts, largely transpositions, & a local timp pt). *The titlepage lists the scoring as: fl cl(E♭) 2cl(B♭) 2hn bn serp
tp cap obligés, 2cl(B♭) bn(II) 2cap tb b-dr tri ad lib. The plate number, outside the main Schott series, indicates
that the plates came from the Parisian publisher, E. Troupenas.*
JPM-2.2a. Auber: Zanetta, airs, 5 mvts. fl cl(E♭) cl(B♭, solo) 4cl(B♭) 4hn bn(I) bn(II)+cb 2tp 2cap bugle 3tb oph.
Pc (chez les fils de B. Schott: Mayence et Anvers, pn T. 975, c.1841), parts: GB-Ljag(w). *The comments for
JPM-2a apply here as well.*

*MOLTER, Johann Melchior (Giovanni Melchiore) *10 Feb 1696, Tiefenort, Werra - 12 Jan 1765, Durlach*
JOM-1. Concerto in D.   2ob 2hn bn tp.
MS: D-KA, Mus.Ms.597.   Pm (Medici: Bellingham, WA; pn MNO 3, 1983), score & parts.
JOM-2. Concerto in D.   2ob 2hn bn tp.
MS: D-KA.   Pm (Medici: Bellingham, WA; pn MNO 4, 1983), score & parts.
JOM-3. Sinfonia (concertante), (MWV VIII/1), in D.   Solo tp, 2ob 2hn bn.
MS: D-KA.
Pm (Musica rara: London, pn 1674, 1974), edited Robert Minter, score & parts, (17th and 18th Century Sonatas,
Concerti and Overtures for Trumpets & Orchestra. No. 60).
JOM-4. Sinfonia (concertante), (MWV VIII/2).   Solo tp, 2ob 2hn bn.
MS: D-KA.
Pm (Musica rara: London, pn 1675, 1974), edited Robert Minter, score & parts, (17th and 18th Century Sonatas,
Concerti and Overtures for Trumpets & Orchestra. No. 61).
*JOM-5. Sonata in F.   2chalumeaux 2hn bn.   MS: D-KA, Mus.Ms.508.
JOM-6. Sonata in D.   2ob 2hn bn.
MS: D-KA.   Pm (Medici: Bellingham, WA; pn MNO 2, 1983), score & parts.
JOM-7. Sinfonia in D, (MWV VIII/15).   2fl 2hn bn.
MS: D-KA.   Pm (Medici: Bellingham, WA; pn OF 18, 1983), ed. Sherman, score & parts (as "Concertino")
JOM-8. Sinfonia in D.   2fl 2hn bn.
MS: D-KA, Mus.Ms.596.   Pm (Medici: Bellingham, WA; pn OF 19, 1983), ed. Sherman, score & parts.
JOM-9. Harmoniemusik.   2cl 2hn bn.   MS: D-KA, Mus.Ms.675.
JOM-10. Symphonia in C.   2chalumeaux 2hn bn.
MS: D-KA.   Pm (Musica rara: London, c.1973), score & parts.
JOM-11, 12. 2 Concertos.   2chalumeaux 2hn bn.   MS: D-KA, (1 incomplete).
JOM-13. Concertino in D, (MWV VIII/5), after 1742.   Solo tp, 2ob 2hn bn.
MS: D-KA, Mus.Ms.546.
Pm (Musica Rara: London, pn 1596, 1973), ed. Georg Meerwein, score & parts, (17th and 18th Century Sonatas,
Concerti and Overtures for Trumpets & Orchestra. No. 62).
JOM-14. Concertino in D, (MWV VIII/6).   Solo tp, 2ob 2hn bn.
MS: D-KA, Mus.Ms.547.
Pm (Musica rara: London, pn 1596, 1973), ed. Georg Meerwein, score & parts, (17th and 18th Century Sonatas,
Concerti and Overtures for Trumpets & Orchestra. No. 63.
JOM-15. Concertino in D, (MWV VIII/7).   Solo tp, 2ob 2hn bn.
MS: D-KA, Mus.Ms.673.
Pm (Musica rara: London, pn 1597, 1973), ed. Georg Meerwein, score & parts, (17th and 18th Century Sonatas,
Concerti and Overtures for Trumpets & Orchestra. No. 64).
JOM-1m. 7 Marches.   2ob 2hn bn.
MS: D-KA.   Pm (Medici: Bellingham, WA; pn MNO 7, 1985), score & parts.

*MONNIKENDAM, Marius *28 May 1896, Haarlem - 22 May 1977, Haarlem*
MAM-1v. De Kinderkruistocht. SA chorus, pic fl ob 2cl b-cl bn timp perc.
Pm (Donemus: Amersterdam, 1967), score.
MAM-2v. Madrigalesca. SA choruus, 2fl ob 2cl b-cl bn tp tb timp perc.
Pm (Donemus: Amsterdam, 1967), score.

MONTIS, Vittorio
VIM-1. Masque en jeu. fl 2ob 2cl 2hn 2bn.
Pm (Edipan Edizione Musicale: Roma, sd).

MONTORLO, Antonio
ATM-1v. Che Fernando. SS, 2cl 2hn bn.   MS: I-Mc.

*MONTSALVATGE, (Bassols) Xavier *11 March 1912, Gerona, Catalonia*
XAM-1. Cinco Invocaciones al Crucificado. fl 2ob 2cl 2hn bn tp perc celeste harp piano db.
Pm (Union Musical Ediciones: Madrid, 1969), hire score & parts (*via* Music Sales).
*XAM-2. Peqeña suite burlesca.   Violin, woodwinds.
Pm (?UME: Madrid), score.

*MORBERG, Gösta *29 June 1923, Sweden*
GOM-1a. Erland von Koch: En sommarlåt (A summer tune). 2fl 2ob 2cl 2hn 2bn.
Pm (Gehrmans musikförlag: Stockholm, 1978), score & parts.

*MORETTI, Niccolò *(1800) - active 1823 - 1833, Venice*
I-Vsmc also possesses fragments of a Credo and Gloria which probably used winds alone.
NXM-1v. Gloria. TTB, fl 2ob/(2cl in C) 2hn bn 2tp (vlne) timp organ(bc-fig).
MS score & parts: I-Vsmc, (the alternative cls & vlne appear in parts only). ★
NXM-2v. Credo, 1823. TTB, 2cl 2hn (bn tp vlne) timp organ(bc-fig).
MS score & parts: I-Vsmc, (with full organ part; the bn tp & vlne appear in the parts only). ★
NXM-3v. Kyrie, 1833. TTB, 2cl(C) 2hn (bn tp vlne) timp organ(bc-fig).
MS score & parts: I-Vsmc, (with full organ part; the bn tp & vlne appear in the parts only). ★
NXM-4v. Quoniam. BB, 2fl 2ob 2hn bn organ. MS: I-Vcr, Busta X.N.143.

*MORGAN, David Stanley *18 May 1932, Ewell, Surrey, UK*
DSM-1. Concerto. Solo violin, winds, db perc. MS: AUS-Samc?
DSM-2. Trine, Op. 47; 1966. pic fl ob ca cl b-cl 2hn 2bn. MS score: GB-Lmic.
DSM-3. Serenade in F, Op. 34; 1964. 2ob 2cl 2hn 2bn. MS score: GB-Lmic.
DSM-4. Elegy and scherzo. 2cl 2hn 2bn.
Pm (Horn Realm: Far Hills, NJ, sd).

*MORRIS, Joseph *(1750?)*
JZM-1. Seven Pieces. fl 2cl 2hn 2bn tp.
MS pts: US-BETm (two copies), Philharmonic Society of Bethlehem PSB 1299, Lititz Collegium Musicum 201.
*JZM-2. Parthia, in B♭, 4 mvts. 2cl 2hn 2bn . *Also attributed to Haydn (FJH-17d) & to Mozart (WAM-15d).*
MS parts: (by John Liverins): US-BETm, Lititz Collegium Musicum 202. ★

*MORSE, Samuel *(1780)*
SYM-1. [Collection of works (c.1811) for five or more winds, including: The Pandean Waltz, as arranged for King George's (III) Band]. 2cl 2hn bn. MS: US-Wc, M177., M88 case., Mic. no. Music-1993.

*MORTELMANS, Lodewijk *5 Feb 1868, Antwerp - 24 June 1952, Antwerp*
LZM-1. Oud-Vlaamsche Kerstliederen (Old Flemish Carols). 2fl ob 2cl 2hn 2bn (varies), (strings ad lib).
AutoMS orchestra score: B-Bcdm.
Pc (Edition Het Muziekfons: Antwerp, pn H.M.F. 95, sd; available *via* Susato: Antwerp), vocal score only.
 1.1. Herders brengt melk en soetigheid. fl ob 2cl 2hn 2bn.
 1.2. In 't stalleken van Bethlehem. fl ob 2cl 2hn 2bn, (string orchestra ad lib).
 1.3. Er is een kinneken geboren op strooi. fl ob 2cl 2hn 2bn tri, (string orchestra ad lib).
 1.4. Het was een maghet uytvercoren. 2fl ob 2cl 2hn bn, (string orchestra ad lib).
 1.5. Er is een jonge maagd gelegen. 2fl ob 2cl 2hn bn, (string orchestra ad lib).
 1.6. Ons is gheboren een kindekijn. fl ob 2cl 2hn, (string orchestra ad lib).
 1.7, 1.8. Het viel een hemelsch dauwe & Een kindekijn is ons gheboren. string orchestra only.
 1.9. O herderkens, al soetjes. ob 2cl 2hn bn, (string orchestra ad lib).
 1.10. Maria die soude naar Bethlehem gaan. fl ob 2cl 2hn bn, (string orchestra ad lib).
 1.11. Herders, Hij is geboren. 2fl ob 2cl 2hn 2bn harp, (string orchestra ad lib).
LZM-2. Le Berger solitaire. fl ob 2cl 2hn bn.
Pc (Edition Het Muziekfon: Antwerp; 1920; *via* Susato: Antwerp), score & parts.

MORTHENSON, Jan Wilhelm *7 April 1940, Örnsküldsvik*
JKM-1. Antiphonia I. fl fl(pic) obdam ca cl cl(b-cl) a-sax 2hn 2bn 2tu 4perc cel el-gtr(or harp) e-gtr org pf 4vc.
Pm (Ab Nordiske Musikforlaget: Stockholm, 1963), hire score & parts.
JKM-2. Attacca; 1977 - 1978. 2fl 2ob 4cl 6hn 2bn 4tp 3tb 4tu 3perc.
Pm (Edition Reimers: Bromma, Sweden, c.1979), score.

MOSELL, Egisto *(1800) - active c.1831, (?)Florence*
EGM-1. Tema con Variazioni per Fagotto; in B♭. Solo bassoon, pic fl 3cl 2hn bn(II) 2tp b-tb.
MS parts: I-OS, Mss.Musiche B.3841, (missing the Fagotto principale part; the wrapper bears the stamp of Picinelli, negoziante). ★
EGM-1m. Scelta di Musica. Marcie, Passi raddoppiati ecc. Instrumentation unknown.
Pc (Presso G. Lorenzi: Firenze, sd), parts (10): I-Fc, F.P. S.477.
EGM-1a. Bellini: Norma. Instrumentation unknown. MS score & 15 parts: I-Fc, F.P. S.668.
EGM-2a. VII Quartetti . . . cavati da diversi pezzi favoriti del celebre Maestro Rossini; also includes a Duetto e Terzetto di Jwan [sic] Müller. fl 2cl bn.
Pc (Presso G. Lorenzi: Firenze, sd), parts: I-Fc, F.P. S.16719, (missing the fl pt).

MOSER, Franz Joseph *20 March 1880, Vienna - 27 March 1939, Vienna*
FRM-1. Serenade No. 2 (Suite), Op. 37. 17 winds.
Pc (Universal Edition: Wien, 1925), score & parts.
FRM-2. Serenade No. 1, Op. 35, 1921. 2fl 2ob ca 2cl b-cl 4hn 2bn cbn.
Pc (Universal Edition: Wien, 1922), score & parts.

*MOUQUET, Jules *10 July 1867, Paris - 25 Oct 1946, Paris*
JUM-1. Symphonietta in C, Op. 12. 2fl 2ob 2cl 2hn 2bn.
Pc (Henri Lemoine: Paris, 1900), score & parts: F-Pn.
*JUM-2. Suite; 3 mvts (Adagio - Aubade - Scherzo). fl ob 2cl hn 2bn.
Pc (Henri Lemoine: Paris, 1910), score & parts: F-Pn, (score) Vm14 17, (parts) Vm14 62; US-Wc.
Pm (Compusic: Amsterdam, pn 271, c.1994), score & parts.

*MOYSE, Louis *14 July 1912, Scheveningen, (lived in Paris, now resident in USA)*
LQM-1. Divertimento; 1961. 2fl 2ob 2cl 2hn 2bn 2vc db.
Pm (McGinnis & Marx: New York), hire score & parts (ed. No. 1199).

174 The Wind Ensemble Catalog

*MOZART, (Johannes Chrysostomus) [Wolfgangus] Wolfgang [Theophilus] Amadeus
27 Jan 1756, Salsburg - 5 Dec 1791, Vienna
MW: Wolfgang Amadeus Mozart's Werke (Breitkopf & Härtel: Leipzig, 1877-1905), scores. (Reprinted as:) 17 Divertimenti for various Instruments. From the the Breitkopf & Härtel Complete Works edition. Edited by M.G. Nottebohm, (Dover Publications: New York, pn 23862-8 Pa., 1979), scores. NMA: Neue Ausgabe samtlicher Werke (Bärenreiter-Verlag: Kassel, Basel, 1955, etc.), scores. (Reprinted in paperback), 1991. The Mozart autographs, previously in D-B, are now partly in Grüssau, Poland, having been in PL-Kj; some have now been returned, and are listed under D-B.

*WAM-1. Serenade (Gran Partita) in B♭; 7 mvts, (K.361/370a).   2ob 2cl 2bthn 4hn 2bn db.
See the ARRANGEMENTS LIST *for descriptions of reductions and arrangements.*
AutoMS score: US-Wc, (Whittall Foundation Collection). ★
MS score: A-Wgm, VIII 17361, (Köchel Nachlass MS score); D-B, (5 copies), Mus.ms. 15338, 15351/1 (2 copies), 15424, 15424/1.
MS parts: CZ-Pu, M.I/29; I-Mc, Da Camera MS. 18.2, (mid-19th century).
Pc (Bureau des Arts et d'Industrie: Vienne, pn 62, c.1803) RISM [M 5887], (as "Grand Sérénade"), parts: A-Wgm, VIII 17361; A-Wn-h; CH-Zz; CZ-Bm(au), A.19.495; CZ-K, symfonie Nr 77.K.II; D-Mbs; I-Fc; I-Mc, Noseda L.45.11; NL-DHgm, hk 19 C 6; S-Skma.
Pc (J. Reidl: Wien, pn 62, c.1820), RISM [M 5888], reprint from the Bureau des Arts et d'Industrie plates, parts: A-Wgm.
Pm (as "Serenade No. 10"), MW: Ser. IX, Bd. 1, No. 12, pp. 399 - 454.
Pm (A.H. Payne: London, 1877, etc.), miniature score, (Payne's Miniature Scores No. 100).
Pm (Breitkopf & Härtel: Leipzig, Wiesbaden, sd), score (pn PB 4393) & parts (Leipzig: pn OB 590, Wiesbaden: OB 4393).
Pm (E.F. Kalmus: New York, sd), score & pts (pn A 1836), miniature score (pn EK 958, No. 1; F 628, No. 4).
Pm (Musica rara: London, pn 1047, 1961), parts.
Pm (Ernst Eulenburg, London, 1965), miniature score, (Edition Eulenburg No. 100).
Pm (The Library of Congress: Washington, Stock No. 030-007-00005-11976), AutoMS facsimile.
Pm (NMA: Ser. VII, Bd. 17/ii, pp. 141 - 222), score.
Pm (Emerson Edition: Ampleforth, UK, pn E 200, 1992, Urtext edition edited Roger Hellyer), score & parts.
*WAM-2. Divertimento in B♭; 5 mvts, (K.186/159b).   2ob 2ca 2cl 2hn 2bn.
AutoMS score: D-B, Mus.ms.Auto.W.A.Mozart 186.
MS score: D-B, Mus.Ms.15313.
MS parts (post-1850): I-Mc, Da Camera MS.17.8, No. 2.
Pm (as "Divertimento No. 4"), MW: Ser. IX, Bd. 2, No. 18, pp. 57 - 62.
Pm (E.F. Kalmus: New York, sd), miniature score (pn EK 959, No. 4).
Pm (Breitkopf & Härtel: Leipzig, sd), hire score & parts.
Pm (NMA: Ser. VII, Bd. 17/i, pp. 3 - 16), score.
Pm (Phylloscopus, Lancaster, UK, pn PP11, 1989), parts.
Pm (Harmonia: Amsterdam, sd), arr. Hans P. Keuning (for: 2fl 2ob 2cl 2bn 2tp), score (pn 3404) & pts (3404A).
Pm (Castle Music: Sherriff Hutton, Yorks, UK, pn H24/122, 1992), ed. J.S. Taylorson, score & parts.
*WAM-3. Divertimento in E♭, 5 mvts, (K.166/159d).   2ob 2ca 2cl 2hn 2bn.
AutoMS score: PL-Kj. ★
MS score: A-Wgm VIII 29305 (H 25500), (by Köchel); D-B, Mus.ms.15312, (?lost).
MS parts (post-1850): I-Mc, Da Camera MS.17/8, No. 1.
Pm (as "Divertimento No. 3"), MW: Ser. IX, Bd. II, No. 17, pp. 47 - 56), score.
Pm (Breitkopf & Härtel: Leipzig), score (pn PB 394) & parts (pn OB 2414).
Pm (E.F. Kalmus: New York, sd), miniature score (pn EK 959, No.3).
Pm (Musica rara: London, pn 2090, 1981), parts.
Pm (NMA: Ser. VII, Bd. 17/i, pp. 17 - 38), score.
*WAM-4. Serenade in C minor; 4 mvts, (K.388/384a) (Serenade No. 12).   2ob 2cl 2hn 2bn.
Note: the version for 2ob 2ca 2hn 2bn in A-Wgm, VIII 8570b is almost certainly a transcription by Went and is listed under Went at JNW-1ac.
AutoMS score: D-B, Mus.ms.auto.W.A.Mozart 388 (one page is in another hand, namely bars 230 - 252 of the 4th movement). ★
MS score & parts (alleged autograph; ?parts in the hand of J.S. Mayr): I-BGi, Faldone 243.
MS score: CZ-Pu, M.I/30/2, (as "Parthia in C minore", c.1837); GB-Lbl, Loan 4.1874, (Royal Philharmonic Society, mvts 2 - 4 only, with the note, "The original and only (MS.) copy in score for Wind Instruments of Mozart's celebrated Notturno as performed at the Philharmonic Concerts").
MS parts: CZ-Bm(no), A.16.818; CZ-Pnm, Lobkovic X.H.a.30 (as "Parthia in C moll"); CZ-Pu, 59 R 10, (Kapuchiner Kloster St Josef, Prag-Neustadt, mid-19th century); I-Mc, Da Camera MS.18.1, ("Serie g-No. 14 / Serenade No. 12", c.1840-1850; hn II replaced by tb).
Pc (Traeg: [Vienna], from c.1792), MS parts, (part of the set numbered "77 / 25"): ; D-F, Mus.Hs.220.
Pc (J. André: Offenbach am Main, pn 2883, c.1809), ("Sérénade No. 2" of André's "Zwei Serenaden für 2 Oboen, 2 Clarinetten, 2 Hörner und 2 Fagotte..."; wrapper title "Verschiedene Werke...in Partitur"), RISM [M 5895], score: A-Wgm, VIII 8570(a); A-Wn-h.
Pc (as "Sérénade No. 2") (J. André: Offenbach am Main, pn 2883, c.1809), RISM [M 5894], parts: A-Wgm, VIII 29289; A-Wst; CZ-Pnm, XL.B.124.; D-AB; D-F; D-OF; I-Mc, Noseda S.17.2; US-Wc.
Pc (as "Ottetto":) (A. Kühnel: Leipzig, pn 900, c.1811), RISM [M 5893], pts: A-Wn-h; D-HR, HR III 4 1/2 2° 494; D-Dl; D-NEhz; D-RUl; I-Fc, F.P. S.475, (with MS score); I-Fc, F.P. S.475; S-Skma.
Pc (Breitkopf & Härtel: Leipzig, pn 10103, 1861), score: A-Wgm, VIII 36142, (presentation copy from Clara Schumann to Brahms, 1861).
Pc (as "Divertimento No. 12") MW: Ser. IX.
Pc (A.H. Payne: London, 1887, etc.), miniature score, (Payne's Miniature Scores, No. 309).
Pm (Breitkopf & Härtel: Leipzig, Wiesbaden, sd), score (Leipzig: pn PB 406; Wiesbaden: PB 4395) & parts (Leipzig: pn 406; Wiesbaden: OB 4395).
Pm (Ernst Eulenburg: London, pn 8821, 1949), miniature score, (Edition Eulenburg. No. 309).

Pm (E.F. Kalmus: New York, sd), score & pts (pn A 1838), min score (pn EK 958, No. 3; (reprint) F 628, No. 6).
Pm (Broude Brothers: New York), score & parts.
Pm (Peters: London), miniature score (pn 1216a) & parts (pn 1216).
Pm (Musica rara: London, pn 1045, 1961), parts.
Pm (KGS), fiche (2500), (of Kühnel edition).
Pm (NMA: Ser. VII, Bd. 17/ii, pp. 97 - 100), score.
Pm (Camden Music: London, pn CM001, 1992), Urtext Edition, ed. Andrew Skirrow, score & parts.
Pm (Boosey & Hawkes: London, etc., pn 3856, sd), Adagio only, for 2cl 2hn 2bn or 6cl.
*WAM-5.1. Serenade in E♭; 2nd version, 5 mvts, (K.375/375b) (Serenade No. 11).   2ob 2cl 2hn 2bn.
AutoMS score: D-B, Mus.ms.auto.W.A.Mozart 375 (pages 1 - 38, autograph movements 1, 3, 5; movements 2 & 4 in another hand); D-KNh, (first movement fragment, previously at Catalog No. 184, now lost).   ★
MS score: D-B, Mus.ms.15310, No. 7.
Pc (J. André: Offenbach am Main, pn 2833, c.1809), ("Sérénade No. 1" of André's "Zwei Serenaden für 2 Oboen, 2 Clarinetten, 2 Hörner, und 2 Fagotte . . ."; wrapper title: "Verschiedene Werke . . .in Partitur"), RISM [M 5895], score: A-Wgm, VIII 29311, A-Wn-h.
Pc (as "Sérénade No. 2":) (J. André: Offenbach am Main, pn 2883, c.1809), RISM [M 5891], parts: A-Wgm, VIII 29311 (H 25495); A-Wn-h; A-Wst; D-KNh; D-NEhz; D-OF; S-Skma; US-Wc.
Pc (J. André: Offenbach am Main, pn 7261, 1853), score: A-Wgm, VIII 29289 (H 25498), (presentation copy from Th. Avé Lallemant to Brahms, 5 June 1858).
Pc ("Divertimento No. 11":) MW: Ser. IX, Bd. 1, No. 13, pps 455 - 480), score.
Pc (A.H. Payne: London, 1887, etc.), miniature score (Payne's Miniature Scores. No. 308).
Pm (Ernst Eulenburg: London, pn 3320, 1949), miniature score (Edition Eulenburg. No. 308).
Pm (Breitkopf & Härtel: Leipzig, Wiesbaden), score (pn PB 405, Leipzig; PB 4394, Wiesbaden) & parts (pn 405, Leipzig; OB 4394, Wiesbaden).
Pm (Broude Brothers: New York, pn BB. 37, sd), parts.
Pm (Musica rara: London, pn MR 1044, 1961), score & parts.
Pm (Peters: London), miniature score (pn 1215a) & parts (pn 1215).
Pm (E.F. Kalmus: New York, sd), score & pts (pn A 1837), min. score (EK 958, No. 2; reprinted: F 628, No. 5).
Pm (NMA: Ser. VII, Bd. 17/ii, pp. 41 - 96), score.
Pm (Camden Music: London, pn CM024, 1992), Urtext edition, ed. Andrew Skirrow , score & parts.
*WAM-5.2. Serenade in E♭; 1st version, 5 mvts, (K.375/375a).   2cl 2hn 2bn.
AutoMS: D-B, Mus.ms.auto.W.A.Mozart 375, (pp. 39 - 73).   ★
MS score: D-B, Mus.ms.15310/7, (Aloys Fuchs MS, c.1836); CZ-Pu, M.I/30/1, (as "Parthia in E la fa"; with the stamp of "Mozarts Denkmal in seinen Werken 1837").
MS parts: CZ-Kra, A4457/R.I. a-f, (as "Parthia Ima"); CZ-Pnm, XLI.B.155, (as "Parthia in Dis [E♭]"); D-LEm, Becker III.12.12; I-Gc, C.2.3.7.Sc.35; PL-LA, RM 17.
Pc (as "Sérénade, Oeuvre 27me":) (J André: Offenbach am Main, pn 530, 1792), RISM [M 5890], parts: A-M; CH-E, Th.86,14; F-Pn; GB-Lbl, h.405.y.
Pc (Liv. 3, No. 6 of "Pièces d'harmonie":) (Breitkopf & Härtel: Leipzig, pn 202,1804), RISM [M 5892], parts: A-Sm; A-Wgm, (2 copies) VIII 17365, VIII 29301; A-Wn; CZ-Bm; D-LÜh; D-Mbs; D-ZI; GB-Lbl, (unverified).
Pm (Musica rara: London, pn 1044, 1955, reprinted 1969), ed. Karl Haas, score & parts.
Pm (Schott & Co.: London; B. Schott's Söhne: Mainz, pn 5923, 1958), ed. Fritz Spiegl, pts.
Pm (Oxford University Press: London, 1979), score (pn N 7939) & pts (pn N 7940), (Musica da camera No. 75).
Pm (NMA: Ser. VII, Bd. 17/ii, No. 1, pp. 3 - 40), score.
*Here **AND**: refers to the specific editions of K.213, 240, 252/240a, 253, 270, namely Cinq Divertissemens [sic] Oeuvre 90. Édition après l'original auteur. RISM [M 5885]. (J. André: Offenbach am Main, pn 1504, 1800), parts: A-Sm; A-Wgm, VIII 29296; A-Wn-h; A-Wst, M 9203/c; D-MGmi; D-OF; GB-Lbl, Hirsch IV.13; I-Mc, (2 copies), Da Camera A.83.6.*
(Mme Duhan: Paris, pn 1504), RISM [M 5886], parts: F-Pn.
MS score (early 19th century): I-Mc, Noseda L.20.21.
*WAM-6. Divertimento in F, 5 mvts, (K.213).   2ob 2hn 2bn.
AutoMS score: PL-Kj.   ★
MS score: A-Wgm, VIII 29292 (Q 16355), (by Köchel, after Aloys Fuchs); D-B, Mus.ms 15310, No. 1, (Aloys Fuchs MS, c.1836); CZ-Pu, M.I/28/3, Sigl.A.Fuchs, (c.1836).
MS parts: D-B, Mus.ms.15317; D-Mbs, Mus.Ms.1704; I-Mc, Da Camera MS.17.9, (with WAM-8).
Pc (AND: as "Divertissement No. 1").
Pm (as "Divertimento No. 8":) (MW: Ser IX, Bd. 2, No. 22, pp. 83 - 85), score.
Pm (Breitkopf & Härtel: Leipzig & Wiesbaden), score (pn 398, Leipzig) & parts (Leipzig: pn OB 2422; Wiesbaden: OB 4972).
Pm (E.F. Kalmus: New York, sd), miniature score (pn EK 959) & parts (pn 3729).
Pm (Ernst Eulenburg: London, pn 394, 1967), ed. Jürgen Braun, miniature score.
Pm (NMA: Ser. VII, Bd. 17/i, pp. 49 - 58), score.
*WAM-7. Divertimento in B♭, 4 mvts, (K.240).   2ob 2hn 2bn.
AutoMS score: PL-Kj.   ★
MS score: A-Wgm, VIII 29293 (Q 16355), (by Köchel, after Aloys Fuchs); D-B, Mus.ms.15310, No. 2, (Aloys Fuchs MS, c.1836); CZ-Pu, M.I/28/3, Sigl.A.Fuchs, (c.1836).
MS parts: D-B, Mus.Ms.15318; D-Mbs, Mus.Ms.1705; I-Mc, Da Camera MS.17.9, (with WAM-7).
Pc (AND: as "Divertissement No. 2").
Pm (as "Divertimento No. 9":) (MW: Ser. IX, Bd. 2, No. 23, pp. 89 - 97), score.
Pm (Breitkopf & Härtel: Leipzig & Wiesbaden), score & parts (pn OB 2424/25, Leipzig; OB 4973, Wiesbaden).
Pm (E.F. Kalmus: New York), miniature score (pn EK 959) & parts (pn 3730).
Pm (Ernst Eulenburg: London, 1967), ed. Jürgen Braun, miniature score, (Edition Eulenburg No. 395).
Pm (NMA: Ser. VII, Bd. 17/i, pp. 73 - 81), score.

*WAM-8. Divertimento in E♭, 4 mvts, (K.252/240a).   2ob 2hn 2bn.
AutoMS score: PL-Kj. ★
MS score: A-Wgm, VIII 29294 (Q 16355), (by Köchel, after Aloys Fuchs); D-B, Mus.ms.15310, No. 3, (Aloys Fuchs MS, c.1836); CZ-Pu, M.I/28/4, Sigl.A.Fuchs, (c.1836).
MS parts: D-Mbs, Mus.Ms.1706; I-Mc, Da Camera MS.17.11.
Pc (AND: as "Divertissement No. 3").
Pm (as "Divertimento No. 12":) (MW: Ser. IX, Bd. 2, pp. 147 - 151), score.
Pm (Breitkopf & Härtel: Leipzig, Wiesbaden), score and parts (pn OB 2431, Leipzig; OB 4974, Wiesbaden).
Pm (E.F. Kalmus, New York, sd) score (pn EK 960, No. 3) & parts (pn 3731).
Pm (Ernst Eulenburg: London, 1967), ed. Jürgen Braun, miniature score.
Pm (NMA: Ser. VII, Bd. 17/i, pp. 73 - 81), score.
*WAM-9. Divertimento in F; 3 mvts, (K.253).   2ob 2hn 2bn.
AutoMS score: PL-Kj. ★
MS score: A-Wgm, (2 copies), VIII 17701, (by Aloys Fuchs, 1 June 1836), VIII 17701 (Q 16341), (by Köchel, after Aloys Fuchs); D-B, Mus.ms.15310, No. 4, (Fuchs MS); CZ-Pu, M.I/28/6, Sigl.A.Fuchs, (c.1836).
MS parts: D-B, Mus.Ms.15321; D-Mbs, Mus.MS.1707.
Pc (AND: as "Divertissement No. 4").
Pm (as "Divertimento No. 13":) (MW: Ser. IX, Bd. 2, pp. 152 - 158), score.
Pm (Ernst Eulenburg: Leipzig, Wien, pn 3339, 1928; reprinted London, 1951), miniature score, (Eulenburgs kleine Partitur-Ausgabe. No. 351).
Pm (Breitkopf & Härtel: Leipzig & Wiesbaden), score & parts.
Pm (E.F. Kalmus: New York, sd), miniature score (pn EK 960, No. 3) & parts (pn 3732) *(we have also been quoted pn 2175, but our copy has 3732)*.
Pm (NMA: Ser. VII, Bd. 17/i, pp. 82 - 92), score.
*WAM-10. Divertimento in B♭; 4 mvts, (K.270).   2ob 2hn 2bn.
AutoMS score: PL-Kj. ★
MS score: A-Wgm, (2 copies), VIII 17701 (Q 16354), (by Aloys Fuchs, c.1836), VIII 29295 (Q 16355), (by Köchel, after Aloys Fuchs); D-B, Mus.ms.15310, No. 5, (Aloys Fuchs MS, c.1836); CZ-Pu, M.I/28/5, Sigl.A.Fuchs, (c.1836).
MS parts: D-B, Mus.Ms.15322, (for 2cl 2hn 2bn); D-Mbs, Mus.Ms.1708.
Pc (AND: as "Divertissement No. 5").
Pm (as "Divertimento No. 14":) (MW: Ser. IX, Bd. 2, pp. 159 - 167), score.
Pm (Ernst Eulenburg: Leipzig, Wien, pn 3340, 1928, reprinted London 1951), miniature score, (Eulenburgs kleine Partitur-Ausgabe No. 352).
Pm (Breitkopf & Härtel: Leipzig, Wiesbaden, pn OB 2433), score & parts *(some sources quote pn OB 4976 from Wiesbaden; our copy has 2433)*.
Pm (G. Ricordi & Co.: Milano, pn PR 622, 1954), miniature score.
Pm (E.F. Kalmus: New York, sd), miniature score (pn EK 960, No. 4) & parts (pn 3733).
Pm (NMA: Ser. VII, Bd. 17/i, pp. 93 - 109), score.
Mozart: Supplementary List of Wind Works
*WAM-1s. March of the Janissaries, (Köchel deest; appended to *Die Entführung aus dem Serail)*, C major. 2fl 2cl 2hn 2bn tp 2side-drums.
Pm (Bärenreiter: Kassel, pn BA 4792), ed. G. Croll, score & parts.
*WAM-2s. Additional Trio in Sextet versions of K.375.   *See supra:* WAM-6. 2cl 2bn (2hn)
*WAM-3s. Adagio in B♭, (K.411, K3. 440a, K6. 484a).   2cl 3bthn.
AutoMS score: ? PL-Kj.
Pm (Joh. André: Offenbach am Main; Novello & Ewer: London; G. André: Philadelphia, pn 7263, 1853), score: CZ-Pnm, V.B.103; GB-Lbl, E.1050.g.(3); I-Mc.   ★
Pm (MW: Ser. X, Bd. 17, pp. 80 - 83), score.
Pm (Breitkopf & Härtel: Leipzig, pn PB 1342, sd), score.
Pm (E.F. Kalmus: New York), miniature score, (EK 961, No. 17, pp. 80 - 83).
Pm (Oxford Universary Press: London, 1961), arranged by C.J. Haskins, (for 4cl b-cl/bn, *or* 2ob 2cl bn).
Pm (Rubank: Chicago, 1962), arranged by Hymie Voxman, (for 3cl cl(E♭) b-cl).
Pm (Musica rara: London, pn 2106, 1984) completed J. Newhill, (with alternative for 4cl b-cl/bn), score & pts.
Pm (NMA: Ser. III, Bd. 17/ii, pp. 223 - 232), score.
*WAM-4s(-8s). 5 Divertimenti (B♭), Nos. 1 - 5, (K.Anh.229, K6. 439b) *(No. 6 in the Simrock set comprises anonymous arrangements from* Le Nozze di Figaro & Don Giovanni). 3bthn (or 2bthn/2cl bn).
AutoMS score: ? PL-Kj.
Pc (as "Trois sérénades":) (Chez N. Simrock: Bonn, pn 926, c.1812), 2 liv., (Liv. I) RISM [M 6265]; (Liv. II), RISM [M 6247 & M 6265], parts: A-Wn-h, (Liv.I); B-Bc,(Liv.I, II); F-Pn,(Liv.I); GB-Lbl,(Liv.II), h.405.w.(2); S-Skma,(Liv.I,II).   ★
Pc (as "Trois sérénades", with added spurious horn parts:) (N. Simrock: Bonn, pn 926, c.1812), RISM [M 6264], 2 liv., parts: B-Bc,(Liv. I & II); GB-Lbl, (Liv. I), h.405.w.(1.).
*WAM-4s. Divertimento in B♭, No. 1.   3bthn, or 2cl bn.
Pm (Boosey & Hawkes: London, etc., 1941), ed. by F.J. Thurston (for 2cl bn), min score with analysis (Hawkes Pocket Scores, No. 206), score & parts (pn 8601, 3873, part of "Chamber Music for Wind Instruments").
Pm (Oxford University Press: London, 1967), edited & arranged (for 3cl) by Michael Whewell, score (pn N7903) & parts (pn N7304-6).
*WAM-5s. Divertimento in B♭, No. 2.   3bthn, or 2cl bn.
Pc (as "Petites pièces pour deux cors de bassette et basson:) (Breitkopf & Härtel: Leipzig, pn 162, 1803/1804), Liv.1 (?Liv.2 not issued), RISM (misprinted as [M 6273], in fact, [M 6263]), (the first Minuet & Trio, the Larghetto, the second Minuet and Trio, with a Finale of dubious authenticity), parts: A-Sm; A-Wgm, VIII 29297; A-Wn-h; D-Mbs; D-Dl; GB-Lbl, Hirsch IV.71.a.
Pm (Boosey & Hawkes: London, etc., 1941), ed. F.J. Thurston (for No. 207), score & parts (pn 8660, 3874, part of "Chamber Music for Wind Instruments").
Pm (Oxford University Press: London, pn N7908, 1967), ed. & arr. (for 3cl) by Michael Whewell, score & parts.

*WAM-6s. Divertimento in B♭, No. 3.   3bthn, or 2cl bn.
Pm (Musica rara: London, pn 1042, 1961), parts.
Pm (Oxford University Press: London, pn N7913, 1967), ed. & arr. (for 3cl) by Michael Whewell, score & parts.
*WAM-7s. Divertimento in B♭, No. 4.   3bthn, or 2cl bn.
Pm (Musica rara: London, pn 1043 No. 1, 1961), parts.
Pm (Oxford University Press: London, pn N7918, 1967), ed. & arr. (for 3cl) by Michael Whewell, score and pts.
*WAM-8s. Divertimento in B♭, No. 5.   3bthn, or 2cl bn
Pm (Musica rara: London, pn 1043 No. 2, 1961), parts.
*WAM-9s. Canonic adagio in F, (K.410 / K3. 440d / K6. 484d).   2bthn bn.
This incomplete work is placed here in the supplement, rather than with fragments, since it exists in several acceptable completions.
AutoMS score: D-B, Mus.ms.15349. ★
Pc (Breitkopf & Härtel: Leipzig, 1804), score.
Pm (MW: Ser. X, Bd. 15, p. 79), score. (reprinted: Breitkopf & Härtel: Leipzig, pn PB 1341), score. (reprinted: E.F. Kalmus: New York, pn EK 961. Nos. 16 & 19), miniature score.
Pm (NMA: Ser. VIII, Bd. 21, p. 120), score.
Pm (G.K. Kallmeyer: Wolfenbüttel), completed by Hans Fischer, (Lose Blätter der Musikantengilde No. 245).
Pm (Musica rara: London, pn 2105, 1984), completed by J.P. Newhill, score & parts.
Pm (Sikorski: Hamburg, pn 757 No. 1), completed J. Wojciechowski, (with WAM-6f), parts.
Mozart: Fragments for winds alone
*WAM-1f. March in B♭, (K3; considered part of *Die Entführung* / K6. 384b).   4 bars.
2ob 2cl 2hn 2bn.   AutoMS score: CH-Zwalter. ★
Pm (Schweizerisches Jahrbuch für Musikwissenschaft II (Agran), 1927), p. 68, score.
Pm (NMA: Ser. VII, Bd. 17, No. 2, p. 234), score.
*WAM-2f. (?Andante) in E♭, (K3. suggests it is the start of slow movement of K.388 / K6. 384B).   18 bars.
2ob 2cl 2hn 2bn.   AutoMS score: A-Wgm. ★
Pm (NMA: Ser. VII, Bd. 17, No. 2, pp. 233 - 234), score.
*WAM-3f. (Allegro) in B♭, (K Anh.96 / K3. 196g / K6. 384c).   16 bars.   2ob 2cl 2hn 2bn.
MS (?Auto) score: A-Sm, No. 54; D-Bds, Mus.Ms.15589. ★
Pm (NMA: Ser. VII, Bd. 17, No. 2, p. 235), score.
*WAM-4f. Allegro assai in B♭, (K Anh.95 / K3. 440b / K6. 484b).   22 bars.   2cl 3bthn.
AutoMS score: A-Sm, No. 53.   MS: D-B Mus.ms.15573I(f.15v), 15589. ★
Pm (NMA: Ser. VII, Bd. 17, No. 2, pp. 236 - 237), score.
*WAM-5f. Adagio in F, (K Anh.93 / K3. 440c / K6. 484c).   6 bars.   cl 3bthn.
AutoMS score: A-Sm, No. 52.   MS: D-B, Mus.ms.15573I (f.15r), 15589. ★
Pm (NMA: Ser VII, Bd 17, No. 2, p. 237), score.
*WAM-6f. Adagio in F, (K.Anh.94 / K3. 580a).   ca 2hn bn.
AutoMS: A-Sm, No. 49. ★
Pm (F. Kneusslin: Basel, pn FKuL 17, 1959), completed & arr. by E. Hess (for 2hn(C)/2cl/2hn(F)/2bthn & bn).
Pm (Edition Peters; Hinrichsen Edition: London, etc., 1959), completed & arr. (for fl ob 2cl hn bn) by D.H.R. Brearley, score & parts.
Pm (Sikorski: Hamburg, pn 757 No. 1, sd), completed by J. Wojciechowski, (with WAM-9s), parts.
Pm (Editio Supraphon: Prague, 1975), completed by Milan Munclinger, (with optional violin parts to replace horns), score & parts, (Musica viva historica No. 33).
Pm (Eulenburg: Zürich, pn GM 779, 1976), completed by F. Beyer (with optional violin parts to replace horns), score & parts with facsimiles.
Pm (NMA: Ser. VII, Bd. 17, No. 2, pp. 238 - 240), score.
Pm (WOODWINDplus: Leeds, UK, 1992), completed by Philip Wilby, score & parts, (also version for 3cl b-cl).
*WAM-7f. Menuetto & Trio in B♭, (K6. 594b).   ca 2hn bn.
Pm (Edition Peters; Hinrichsen Edition: London, etc, 1960), completed and arranged by D.H.R. Brearley (for fl ob 2cl hn bn), score & parts.
WAM-8f. (Beginning of a ?1st mvt in C minor), K6. deest.   2 bars.   2ob 2cl 2hn 2bn.
AutoMS score: (on f.8 of the autograph of K.388, WAM-4).
Pm (NMA: Ser. VII, Bd. 17, No. 2, pp. 241), score.
Mozart: Voice plus Winds
Here GL refers to the specific edition of scores ed. by Dr Bernhard Paumgartner (Drei Masken Verlag: Munich, 1920; one of the "Musikalische Studiebücher", reprinted: Bärenreiter: Kassel, pn BA 1767).
WAM-1.1ve. *Così fan tutte* (K.588): Secondare aurette amiche (No. 21).
TB solo, SATB chorus, 2fl 2cl 2hn 2bn.   MS: I-Fc.
WAM-1.2ve. *Così fan tutte* (K.588): Secondare aurette amiche (No. 21), as "Graduale in Es [E♭]", with 2 texts: Denom: Jesu ("Ave Jesu Summe bonus") & De Beatà ("Omne Die dio Mariae").   CATB, 2fl 2cl 2hn 2bn.
MS parts ("Ex Rebus Augustini Wünsch[,] Cantore Gablonzensis"): CZ-Pnm, XII.A.259.
WAM-2ve. Ascanio in Alba, Coro di Pastori, "Venga de' sommi eroi".   Male voices, 2fl 2ob 2hn 2bn vc db.
Pm (MW: Ser. VI, Bd. 1, No. 6), score.
WAM-1v. Ecco quel fiero istante, (K.436).   SSB, 3bthn.   AutoMS score: ? PL-Kj.
Pm (MW: Ser. VI, Bd. 30, pp. 65-66), score (reprinted: Breitkopf & Härtel: Leipzig, pn P 801), score (reprinted: E.F. Kalmus: New York, pn EK 945 No. 7, sd), score. ★
Pm (GL: No. 3), score.   Pm (NMA: Ser. III, Bd. 9, pp. 31 - 34, (sketch: p. 60), score.
WAM-2v. Mi lagnerò tacendo, (K.437).   SSB, 2cl bthn.
AutoMS score: ? PL-Kj. ★
Pc (N. Simrock: Bonn, pn 127, 1800), parts.
Pm (MW: Ser. VI, Bd. 31, pp. 67 - 69), score (reprinted: Breitkopf & Härtel: Leipzig, pn PB 810), score; (reprinted: E.F. Kalmus: New York, pn EK 945 No. 8, sd), score.
Pm (GL: No. 4), score.   Pm (NMA: Ser. VI, Bd. 31, pp. 35 - 41), score.
WAM-3v. Luci care, Luci belle, (K.346 / K6.439a).   SSB, 2cl bthn.
AutoMS: ? PL-Kj.   Pm (GL: No. 2), score.   Pm (NMA: Ser. III, Bd. 9, pp. 42 - 43), score. ★

WAM-4v. Più non si trovano, (K.549).   SSB, 2cl bthn.
AutoMS score: Not known; possibly in the Jul. André collection in 1869.
Pm (NWM: Ser. VI, Bd. 2, No. 41, pp. 185 - 186), score (reprinted: Breitkopf & Härtel: Leipzig, pn PB 825), score; (reprinted: E.F. Kalmus: New York, pn EK 946 No. 7), score. ★
Pm (GL: No. 3), score.   Pm (NWM: Ser. III, Bd. 9, pp. 44 - 47), score.
WAM-1vf. Canzonetta: La Libertà a Nice (Grazie agl'inganni tuoi), K.532, sketch (incomplete).
STB, fl 2cl 2hn 2bn db.
AutoMS score: A-Wn, Mus.Hs.16,474.   MS score: D-Bds, Mus.ms.15573(II), (Jähns copy). ★
Pm (MW: Ser. VII, Abt. 1, No. 35), score.
Pm (GL: No. 4), score.
Pm (NMA: Ser. III, Bd. 9, pp. 62 - 63), score.
WAM-2vf. Due pupile amabili, (K.439), 24 bars (incomplete).   SSB, 3bhn.
AutoMS score: ? PL-Kj. ★
Pm (GL: No. 6), score.   Pm (NMA: Ser. III, Bd. 9, pp. 26 - 28), score.
WAM-3vf. Se lontan, ben mio, tu sei, (K.438), fragment (7 bars vocal, 21 bars instrumental).   SSB 2cl bthn.
AutoMS score: ? PL-Kj.
Pm (MW: Ser. XXIV, Bd. 46, p. 67), score (reprinted: Breitkopf & Härtel: Leipzig, pn PB 831) (reprinted: E. F. Kalmus: New York, pn EK 945 No. 7, sd), score.
Pm (GL: No. 5), score.   Pm (NMA: Ser. III, Bd. 9, pp. 29 - 30, (sketch: p. 60), score.

Arrangements and possible arrangements by Mozart
*WAM-1a. Paisiello: Sinfonia in tre tempi, 3rd mvt.   2ob 2ca 2cl 2hn 2bn.
See the *Wind Ensembke Sourcebook* , under Mozart, WAM-2.
*WAM-2a. Don Giovanni: Act II Finale.   2ob 2cl 2hn 2bn (vlne/db).
  2.1a: Martin y Soler: *Una cosa rara,* finale to Act I. 2.2a: Sarti: *Fra í due litiganti,* "Come un angello".
  2.3a: Mozart: *Le Nozze di Figaro,* "Non più andrai".
Pm (Bruyere Music: Evanston, IL, now Fort Worth, TX sd), ed. Willard Elliot, parts.
*WAM-3a. *Die Entführung aus dem Serail,* sinfonia & 16 mvts.   2ob 2cl 2hn 2bn.
Increasingly accepted as authentic.   (See *The Wind Ensemble Sourcebook*).
MS parts: D-DO, Mus.Ms.1392.
Pm (In: Bastiaan Blomhert: *The Harmoniemusik of Die Entführung as dem Serail by Wolfgang Amadeus Mozart: study about its authenticity and ciritical edition.* Ph.D dissertation, published s.n: s.l, ISBM: 90-9001770-4, 1987), ed. B. Blomhert, score.
Pm (Bärenreiter Verlag: Kassel-Wilhelmshöhe, c.1988), ed. Bastiaan Blomhert, score & parts (hire only).

Mozart: Dubious & Spurious Works
*WAM-1d. Divertimento in C, (K.188 / K3. 240b; probably by Starzer).   2fl 5tp timp.
AutoMS score: F-Pi.   MS score: D-B, Mus.ms.15315. ★
Pm (MW: Ser. IX, Bd. 2, No. 6, pp. 69 - 72), score; (reprinted: Breitkopf & Härtel: Leipzig), score & parts; (reprinted: E.F. Kalmus: New York, etc., pn EK 959, sd), score.
Pm (Musica rara: London, pn 20900), parts.
Pm (Brightstar Music, *via* Western Inernational Music, Inc.: Greelely, Colorado, pn BMP 17, sd), score & parts.
*WAM-2d. 10 Stücke (Divertimento) in C, (K.187 / K3. 159c / K6. C.17.12); (Nos. 1 - 6 from works by Starzer, *La Gelosie del Seraglio,* Nos. 7 - 10 by Gluck, *Paride ed Elena).*   2fl 5tp timp.
AutoMS score (No. 8 in the hand of W.A. Mozart, all other movements in the hand of Leopold Mozart): PL-Kj.
MS score (by Köchel): A-Wgm, VIII 29308 (H 25500). ★
Pm (MW: Ser. IX, Bd. 2, No. 5, pp. 63 - 68) (repr: E.F. Kalmus: New York, pn EK 959, sd), miniature score.
Here **BH** *refers to the specific early edition published under Mozart's name, viz. Trois (Deux) pièces d'harmonie . . .: Liv. I, RISM [M 5905, M 5918], Liv. II, RISM [M 5919].* 2ob 2cl 2hn 2bn. *(Breitkopf & Härtel: Leipzig, pn 61, 65, 1801), parts: A-Sm (liv. I, II); A-Wgm (Liv. I, 2 copies; liv. II, 4 copies); A-Wn-h, (Liv. I, II); CZ-Bm(au), (Liv. I, II), A.19.490; D-Dl, (Liv. I, II); D-Zl (Liv. I, cl l & 2 only); GB-DOTams (Liv. I, II); H-KE, 1019/IX, (Liv. II); I-Fc, (Liv. I).   Liv III (Nos. 6 & 7) can be found in the ARRANGEMENTS LIST infra at MOZART.*
*WAM-3d. Divertimento in E♭, (K.Anh.226/K3. 196e/K.C.17.01). (Possibly by G. Puschmann); 5 mvts.
2ob 2cl 2hn 2bn, *or* 2cl/ob 2hn 2bn.
MS score: D-B, 2 copies; Mus.ms.15351, No. 1 (MS by Aloys Fuchs, for 2ob 4cl 2hn 2bn) and Mus.Ms.15351, No. 2, (MS by Otto Jahn). ★
MS parts: A-KR, H.38.46 (under "Puschmann, Giu."); CH-E, Th.91,18 (Ms.2365), No. 2 (the 2cl pts are at Th.928.18); CZ-Bm(rj), A.12.793 (for 2cl 2hn 2bn, as "Parthia ex E♭", 1804); CZ-KRa, A4457/R.I.27 (as "Parthia IIIta [E♭] Sig: Mozart, Acod [arranged]: Ha[vel]", for 2cl 2hn 2bn); I-Fc, No. 477.B.II, (for 2cl 2hn 2bn). ★
Pc (Traeg: [Vienna], c.1799), MS parts (part of the set numbered "77 / 25"): D-F, Mus.Hs.223.
Pc (BH: Liv. I, No. 2), parts.
Pc (Kleitz & Faltzann: Six Harmonie Extraits des Compositions de Mozart Arrangées; Liv. 2 = XFK-2.2a:) (P. Porro: Paris, pn 2.H.M., c.1807 - 1814), pts: CH-Gpu, Ib.4835; GB-Ljag, (photocopy). *Octet version, 5 mvts.*
Pm (Schott: London, etc., pn 10746, 1956), parts.
Pm (McGinnis & Marx: New York), parts.
Pm (Musica rara: London, pn MR 2062, 1967), ed. William Waterhouse, score & parts.
Pm (C.F. Peters Corp.: New York, etc., pn 6307, 6307a, 1971), ed. Alfred Einstein, miniature score & parts.
*WAM-4d. Divertimento (Serenade) in B♭, (K.Anh.227 / K3. 196f / K6. C.17.02).
2ob(doubling clarinets) 2cl 2hn 2bn.
MS score: A-Wgm, VIII 17701 (Q 16354), (by Aloys Fuchs, c.1836); D-B, (2 copies), Mus.ms.15310, No. 6, (MS by Fuchs, for 2cl 2hn 2bn), Mus.Ms.15310, No. 4, (MS by Otto Jahn). ★
MS parts: CH-E, Th.91,18 (Ms.2365) No. 4, (the cl parts are at Th.928.18); F-Pn, Vma.ms. 262, (for 2cl 2hn 2bn).
Pc (BH: Liv. II, No. 4), parts.
Pm (Schott & Co.: London, pn 10476, 1956), ed. Fritz Spiegl, parts.
Pm (C.F. Peters Corp.: New York, 1971), ed. Alfred Einstein, miniature score (pn P6308) & parts (pn P6308a).
Pm (WINDS: Northridge, CA, pn W-44, c.1981), parts (photostat of BH).

*WAM-5d. Divertimento in E♭, (K.Anh.228 / K. C.17.03, actually by Pleyel, IJP-6). 2ob 2cl 2hn 2bn.
MS score: D-B, Mus.ms.15351, No. 5, (MS by Otto Jahn); D-Bhm, Ms.11521. ★
MS parts: CH-E, Th.91,18 (Ms.2365) No. 5 (with an additional cl I part for the first movement only; the complete cl pts are at Th.982.18); D-Bhm, Ms.11248; D-DO, Mus.1592, (under "Pleyel").
Pc (BH: Liv. II, No. 5), parts.
Pm (C.F. Peters Corp: New York, c.1971), miniature score (pn P6306) & parts (pn P6306a).
Pm (WINDS: Northridge, CA, pn W-38, c. 1981), photocopies of an early anonymous 19th century score & modern MS parts.
*WAM-6d. Partita III, in E♭, (K.Anh.224 / K. C.17.04). 2ob 2cl 2hn 2bn. (Adagio; Menuetto & Trio; Adagio, Tema e Variazioni; Menuetto & Trio.)
MS score (by Aloys Fuchs, c.1836): D-B, Mus.ms.15310/1, No. 3. ★
*WAM-7d. Divertimento in F, (K.Anh.225 / K6. C.17.05). 2ob 2cl 2hn 2bn. (Adagio/Allegro; Andante).
MS score: D-B, Mus.ms.15310/1, No. 2, (MS by A. Fuchs, c.1836); D-Bhm, (2 copies), Ms.11620, Ms.11260. ★
*WAM-8d. Divertimenti, in E♭, 32 mvts, (Köchel deest). 2fl 2ob 2hn 2bn.
MS parts (?c.1775 - 1780, with a pencil note, "Mozart"): D-HR, HR III 4 1/2 4° 499. ★
Pm (KGS), fiche (987, 988).
*WAM-9d. Partitta in Es (E♭), 8 mvts, (Köchel deest). 2ob 2cl 2hn 2bn. MS pts: CZ-Bm(au), A.19.489. ★
*WAM-10d. Tema e Variazioni; in F, (Köchel deest). 2cl 2hn 2bn cbn. MS pts: CZ-Pnm, XLII.F.770. ★
The so-called "Prague Divertimentos"
*WAM-11d. Parthia I, in F, (Whitwell "Prague Divertimento", K. C.17.05 plus Menuetto & Trio, Rondo, K7.Anh.B zu 370a). 2ob 2cl 2hn 2bn.
Pm (WINDS: Northridge, CA, pn W-41, c.1981), photocopy of Traeg score & modern MS parts.
*WAM-12d. Parthia III, in E♭, (Whitwell & Klöcker "Prague Divertimento", K6. C.17.01 plus Rondo, K7.Anh.B zu 370a). 2ob 2cl 2hn 2bn.
MS score (?by Aloys Fuchs, c.1836): CZ-Pu, M.I/31, (Rondo only).
Pm (WINDS: Northridge, CA, pn W-43, c.1981), photocopy of Traeg score & modern MS parts.
*WAM-13d. Adagio & Allegro in F, (K. C.17.07). 2ob 2cl 2hn 2bn.
Pc (Traeg, [Vienna], 1792), MS parts: CZ-Pu, M.I/31, (MS score by Aloys Fuchs, c.1836). ★
*WAM-14d. Parthia I, in F, (Klöcker "Prague Divertimento", K. C.17.07 plus K. C.17.05), 2ob 2cl 2hn 2bn.
Pc (Traeg, [Vienna], 1792), MS parts: CZ-Pu, M.I/31, (MS score by Aloys Fuchs, c.1836). ★
Smaller ensembles
*WAM-15d. Divertimento in E♭, (K.289 /K3. 271g). 2ob 2hn 2bn.
Autograph (unverified MS score): GB-in private hands, (untraced).
MS score: A-Wgm, VIII 29309 (H 25492), (by Köchel, after Aloys Fuchs); CZ-Pu, M.I/28/1, Sigl.A.Fuchs, (c.1836); D-B, (2 copies) Mus.ms.15325 (MS by ?Jähns), Mus.ms.15310, No. 1, (MS by Aloys Fuchs, c.1836).
MS parts: A-Wgm, Mus.Hs.25,492; D-Mbs, Mus.Mss.1709; I-Mc, Da Camera MS.18.1, (late 19th century, as "Divertimento No. 16", after the MW edition). ★
Pm (MW: Ser. IX, Bd. 2, No. 30, pp. 198 - 207), score.
Pm (Breitkopf & Härtel: Leipzig (pn OB 2435), Wiesbaden (pn OB 4977), parts, (as "Divertimento Nr. 16" - ?based on I-Mc copy).
Pm (Belwin Mills: Melville, NY, pn 3734), parts.
*WAM-16d. Variations on a theme by Umlauf, (K.Anh.288, K. C.17.06, ? by Eberl). 2cl 2hn 2bn.
MS parts: CZ-KRa, R.21.g. ★
WAM-17d. Parthia in F, 4 mvts, (K. C.17.08). 2cl 2hn 2bn. MS parts: CZ-Bm(no), A.16.817. ★
*WAM-18d. Sextet in B♭, 3 mvts, (K. C.17.09; see also: Haydn, FJH-17d, Morris JZM-2). 2cl 2hn 2bn.
MS parts: CZ-Bm(rj), A.14.282, (as by "Haydn"); CZ-Pu (under "Haydn"): US-WS, (as by "Haydn"); US-BETm, Lititz Collegium Musicum 202, (as by "Jos. Morris"). ★
*WAM-19d. Parthia No. 2; in E♭, 3 mvts, (K. C.17.10, by Pleyel, IJP-12.3). 2cl 2hn bn.
MS pts: A-Wn, Mus.Hs.622, No. 2, ("IV Parthien in Dis / a / 2 Clarinetten / 2 Cornu / con / Fagotto / Auth. 3. Ritter / 1. Mozart"). *All other copies cite Pleyel, (qv; IJP-12 gives a full list of copies).* ★
*WAM-20d. Cassazione, (K. C.17.11; actually by Lickl, JGL-6, cf). ob cl hn bn. ★
*WAM-21d. Parthia Nro. 7mo; 4 mvts, (Köchel deest; by Went, JNW-35). 2cl 2hn 2bn.
MS parts: CZ-KRA, A4457 /R.I.27. No. 7, (formerly in: CZ-OLu, Sammlung Erzherzog Rudolph). ★
*WAM-22d. [untitled Parthia in E♭], 4 mvts, (Köchel deest). 2cl 2hn bn. MS parts: CZ-Bm(rj), A.14.283. ★
WAM-23d. Parthia in Dis [E♭]; 4 mvts (not in Köchel; actually by Binder). 2cl 2hn bn.
MS parts (by Augustin Erasmus Höbner, Langenbruck, 1809): CZ-Pu(dm), 59 R 3356. *"Author Mozart" appears, incorrectly on the cl I & bn parts; Binder's name appears on all parts.* ★
*WAM-24d. Trio in B♭, (Köchel deest). 3bthn, or 2cl bn.
MS parts: CZ-Pk; D-KIZklöcker, (modern MS score & parts). ★
WAM-25d. [5] Variatione [& Coda], in F. 2cl 2hn 2bn. MS parts: CZ-KRa, A4454/R.I.24, No. 9. ★

*MRKVIČKA, Josef *(?1800)*
JEM-1t. Trauer Marsche; (with Trio), in F. 2cl 2hn 2bn 2tp timp.
MS parts (by Joseph Johann Doletschek, Kunvald): CZ-Pnm, XIII.B.53. ★
JEM-2t. [Trauer Marsch in D minor, without Trio]. 2cl 2hn 2bn 2tp timp.
MS parts (by Joseph Johann Doletschek, Kunvald): CZ-Pnm, XIII.B.53, (on the verso of JEM-1t; with a later part for flügelhorn in B♭). ★

*MÜCK (Müch, Muck), Beda *(1800)*
BEM-1v. Halleluja. CATB. 2fl 2cl(C) 2hn/tp bn timp. MS pts: CZ-Pnm, (2 copies), XLIX.D.518 (by Kücker, 18 Oct 1833, with duplicate 2C, T pts), XLIX.F.40 (by Cech, 27 June 1836, with duplicate CAB pts). ★

*MÜLLER, Adolf *(1820)*
ADM-1e. Stadt und Land (Posse mit Gesang): Auf der Theater Allegro Vivace N° 1 Marsch /: in der Scene :/. pic fl 2ob 2cl(C) 2hn 2bn 2tp a-tb t-tb b-tb. MS score (1854): D-Sl, H.B.XVII. 466, ff. 33 - 34b. ★

MÜLLER, August Eberhard *13 Dec 1767, Hanover - 3 Dec 1817, Weimar*
AEM-1v. Cantatine zu Familienfesten.   4 solo voices, chorus, 2ob 2cl 2hn 2bn.
Pc (Hoffmeister: Leipzig, pn 917, 1811/12), parts: A-Wgm; D-Bhm; CH-E, 17.45 (score).

MÜLLER, Christian Gottlieb *6 Feb 1800, Nieder-Odernitz - 29 June 1863, Berlin*
CGM-1. Morgengruss.   terz-fl 2ob cl(E♭) 3cl(B♭) 3hn 2bn 2tp(clar) a-tb t-tb b-tb timp.
MS score: D-B, Mus.ms.15679/35. ★
CGM-2. Allegretto in E♭.   ob cl(E♭) 3cl(B♭) 2hn 2bn 2tp b-tb tu.   MS pts: D-B, Mus.ms.15679/31, Nr. 1. ★
CGM-3. Andante in B♭.   ob cl(E♭) 3cl(B♭) 2hn 2bn 2tp b-tb tu.   MS parts: D-B, Mus.ms.15679/31, Nr. 2. ★
CGM-4. Potpourri über Deutsche Volkslieder.   Military band.   AutoMS: D-Bds, Mus.ms.auto.C.G.Müller.99.
CGM-1v. Singt dem Herrn.   SATB, 2cl 2hn bn.   AutoMS (c.1830): D-Bds, Mus.ms.auto.C.G.Müller.60.

*MÜLLER, Christian Paul *(1790)*
CPM-1v. [attributed]. Danksagungslied; "Unsre vollgefüllten Scheunen"; in C.   CAB, 2cl 2hn.
MS parts: (by Joseph Spät, 1815 - 1820): D-SCHN, 56, (with the additional text, "Für unsern König bethen wir";
the MS attributes the work, "v[on]. Pfarrer zu Obersirebach [sic]"). ★

MÜLLER, Donat *(?) 1806 - 1879*
DQM-1. [Movement in C].   fl 2hn.   MS parts: D-FÜS, 211, (included in *4 Stationes*). ★

*MÜLLER, Franz Carl (Francesco Carlo) *(?1750)*
FEM-1v. Offertorium; "In laeto choro Angelorum", in E♭.   CTBB, 2cl 2hn 2bn organ.
MS parts: CZ-KRsm, UHM A.1249/Br.C-345. ★

*MÜLLER, (Carl) Friedrich (Frédéric) *10 Dec 1786, Orlamünde, nr Rudolstadt - 12 Dec 1871, Rudolstadt*
FIM-1. Pièces d'Harmonie, Op. 28.   fl 2ob 2cl 2hn 2bn serp 2tp.
Pc (Breitkopf & Härtel: Leipzig, 1827), 2 liv., parts: A-Wgm, VIII 5326, (complete). ★
FIM-1m. Douze Grandes Marches Originales, Oeuv. 55, Cahier I.
2fl(E♭) 2ob 2cl(E♭) 2cl(B♭) 2bthn 4hn 2bn 2tp a-tb t-tb b-tb serp+cbn+b-hn b-dr s-dr.
Pc (Hoffmeister & Kühnel: Leipzig, sd), parts: A-Ee, (with engraved portrait of Müller). ★
FIM-2m. Grand Musique militaire.   Large wind band.   MS: A-Gk, (?uncataloged).
FIM-1v. Cantatina…Dem Hohen Geburtsfeste Sr: Excellenz des wirklichen Königl. Preuß. Staats=Ministers
Herrn Freiherrn von Altenstein gewidmet; "Willkommen Tag der reinsten Lust".   SATBB, piano, 2cl 2bn.
AutoMS score (provenance: Freiherr von Stein-Hochberg, "Berlin 21t. Octobr 1829"): D-WRtl, Mus. 1a:74. ★

MÜLLER, J.M. *(?1800)*
MJM-1v. Ecce panis [Cum Isac, Jesu usatri].   CATB, 2fl 2ob 2cl 2hn 2bn 2a-tb b-tb timp organ(b).
MS score: D-Sl, Mss.Mus.220. ★

*MÜLLER, Johann Michael (Jeam-Marie) *1683, Schmalkalden - 1754, Paris*
XMM-1. XII Sonates, premier ouvrage.   Oboe "de concert", 2ob/vl taille bn/bc(clavecin ou basse de violon).
Pc (Roger: Amsterdam, c.1730), parts: D-WD; S-L.
Pm (2 sets of 3:) (Compusic: Amsterdam, pn 512A, 512B, c.1994), score & parts.

*MÜLLER, Joseph *(?1760)*
JRM-1m. Marcia in B[♭].   2ob 2cl 2hn 2bn cbn tamburo.   MS parts: XLII.C.33. ★

MÜLLER, Uwe
UXM-1a. J.S. Bach: Die Kunst der Fugue, Contrapuncti 1, 9, 10, 18 [sic, in fact, 19].   ob ca 2bn.
Pm (Karthause-Schmülling Internationale Musikverlag: Kamen, pn K 91, 1993), score & parts.

*MÜLLER, Wilhelm August *(1790) - active at Herrenberg*
Müller's works are performance parts to accompany works in the printed volume, Sammlung verschiedener
Kirchenmusiken, *a copy of which can be found at D-Tl, H 59 - 64.*
WIM-1(v). Weihnachts-Cantate; ("Ein Kind ist uns geboren"); Hh 64, Bd. III, Heft IV of H 64).
(CATB), terz-fl 2ob 2cl 2hn 2bn 2tp a-tb t-tb b-tb vla/bn cb.   MS parts: D-Tl, Hh 63.
WIM-2(v). Weihnachts-Cantate, a) Gloria sey dir gesungen, b) Jauchzet all ihr From[m]en, [Op. 40; Bd. I, Heft
III of H 60].   (CATB), terz-fl 2ob 2cl 2hn 2bn 2tp a-tb t-tb b-tb vla/bn cb.
MS parts: D-Tl, Hh 64, (missing tp II, a-tb). ★
WIM-3(v). Oster-Cantate, "Wachet auf!"; [Op. 33.1; Bd. I of H 59].
(CATB), terz-fl 2ob 2cl 2hn 2bn 2tp a-tb t-tb b-tb vla/bn cb timp organ.   MS parts: D-Tl, Hh 66. ★
WIM-4(v). Pfingst-Cantate, "Triumph, Triumph, [Gott und die Tugend siegen"; Op. 33.2; Bd. I of H 59].
(CATB), terz-fl 2ob 2cl 2hn 2bn 2tp a-tb t-tb b-tb vla/bn cb timp organ.   MS pts: D-Tl, Hh 67, (missing tp II). ★
WIM-5(v)-8(v). IV Cantate.   CAT, fl 2ob 2cl 2hn 2bn 2tp b-tb vla/bn timp organ; (vl vla ad lib).
MS parts: D-Tl, Hh 71, (?missing a-tb t-tb).
  5(v). Die Himmel rühmen des Ewigen Ehre; [Op. 48.2; Bd. II, Heft II].
  6(v). Es lebt ein Gott; [Op. 40.1; Bd. I, Heft IV].
  7(v). Cantate auf das Erndtefest; "Ewiger, Weiser, Unerforschlicher, [Op. 48.1; Bd. 1, Heft IV].
  8(v). Nicht um ein flüchtig Gut; [Op. 48.2; Bd. II, Heft I].

MÜLLER-HORNBACH, Gerhard *1951, Germany*
GHM-1. Moments.   2ob 2hn 2bn.
Pm (Breitkopf & Härtel: Wiesbaden, c.1983).

*MÜLLER von KULM, Walter *31 Aug 1899 Basel - 3 Oct 1967 Arlesheim*
WXM-1v. Der 10 Psalm, Op. 43.   Male chorus, fl 2ob 2cl 4hn 2bn cbn 3tp 3tb tu timp perc.
Pm (Hug & Co.: Zürich, sd), score.

MÜLLING *( ) (Possibly Anton Milling?, qv)*
YZM-1. Parthia ex b [B♭]; 5 mvts.   2ob 2hn bn.   MS parts: CZ-Pnm, XXII.E.1. ★

*MÜNCHS, Conrad *22 Feb 1788, Heertz, Prussia - 11 Sept 1835, Paris*
Année 2 & 3 of the Journal d'Harmonie et de Musique Militiare, *a joint venture by F. Louis, C. Münchs, & F. Berr was later reissued from the original plates in 1828 as separate works by Les Fils de B. Schott.*
CNM-1. Journal d'Harmonie et de Musique Militaire. Scoring varies.
Pc (*Année 1:* Au Dépôt du Journal, Chez Mr Baumann: Paris; *Année 2, Liv. 1 - 3 [5 - 7]:* Au Dépôt du Journal, Chez Pacini . . . et Chez les Auteurs: Paris; *Année 2, Liv 4 [8] & Année 3, Liv. 1 - 4 [9 - 12]:* Au Dépôt du Journal, Chez Pacini . . . et Chez Munchs [sic], pn 5 - 9, c.1822 - 1823), parts: F-Pn, (Année 1:) Vm 27 2630 (1 - 4), (Année 2, Liv 1 & 2:) Vm27 2969 (1, 2) & Vm27 2630, (2 copies of Année 2, Liv. 3 & 4 [7 & 8] & Année 3, Liv 1 [9]). (missing Année 3, Liv. 2 - 4 [10 - 12]). ★
   Liv. 1: fl(E♭) cl(E♭) 2cl(B♭) 2hn 2bn tp tb serp b-dr.
      1/1/1. Pas redouble [sic], 2/4 [+Trio]. No. 4.   1/1/2. Waltz, 3/4 [+Trio]. No. 6.
      1/1/3. Menuetto [+ Trio], All° 3/8 [sic = 3/4]. No. 9.
   Liv. 2: fl(E♭) cl(E♭) 2cl(B♭) 2hn 2bn tp tb serp b-dr. *The B♭ cl I is divisi in No. 9. The tb & serp pts are divisi in Nos. 4 & 6.*
      1/2/1. Marche, ¢. No. 1.   1/2/2. Pas Redouble, 2/4. No. 3.   1/2/3. Waltz, Gratioso, 3/4 [+Trio]. No. 5.
   Liv. 3: fl(E♭) cl(E♭) cl(I, B♭) 2cl(II, B♭) 2hn 2bn tp tb serp b-dr. *The B♭ cl I pt is divisi in No. 8; the B♭ cl II pt is divisi in Nos. 2 & 5.*
      1/3/1. Marche, C. No. 2.   1/3/2. Waltz, poco lento 3/8. No. 5.   1/3/3. Adagio non troppo. No. 8.
   1/4/1. Marche, C. No. 2.   fl(E♭) cl(E♭) 2cl(I, B♭) cl(II, B♭) 2hn 2bn tp tb serp b-dr.
      1/4/2. Pas Redoublé, 2/4 [+ Trio]. No. 4.   fl(E♭) cl(E♭) cl(I, B♭) 2cl(II, B♭) 2hn 2bn tp tb serp b-dr.
      1/4/3. Menuetto [& Trio], Allegro, 3/4. No. 9.   fl(E♭) cl(E♭) 4cl(B♭) 2hn 2bn tp tb serp.
   1/5/1. Pas Redoublé [& Trio], 2/4. No. 4.   pic(D) cl(E♭) 2cl(solo B♭) 2hn 2bn tp 2tb 2serp b-dr.
      1/5/2. Pas Redoublé [& Trio], 2/4. No. 5.   pic(D) cl(E♭) 2cl(B♭) 2hn 2bn tp 2tb 2serp b-dr t-dr.
         The b-dr pt has an additional "Partie pour les TAMBOURS" [t-dr]. A note on the cl I pt states, "Ce P[as]. R[edoublé]. peut être joué avec les tambours, leurs parties se trouve sur la Grosse Caisse".
      1/5/3. Waltz [& Trio], 3/4. No. 6.   pic(D) 2cl(B♭) 2hn 2bn tp 2tb 2serp b-dr.
   Liv. 6: fl(C) 2ob/cl(C) 2cl(C) 2hn 2bn tp tb cb(ad lib).
      1/6/1. Ouverture. No. 7.   1/6/2. Romance Varié. No. 8.   1/6/3. Menuetto Allegro [+ Trio], 3/4. No. 9.
   1/7/1. Allegro Militaire, C. No. 1.   fl(D♭) cl(E♭) 2cl(I, B♭) 2cl(II, B♭) 2hn 2bn 2tp 2serp b-dr.
      1/7/2. Pas-Redoublé [& Trio], 2/4. No. 2.   fl(D♭) cl(E♭) cl(I, B♭) 2cl(II, B♭) 2hn 2bn tp tb serp b-dr.
         The cl(E♭) bears the note, "N^{ta}. ce PAS REDOUBLÉ peut être joué par la Flûte en cas que la petite Clarinette manque. Les Solos se trouvent dans la partie de Flute [sic] en petites notes."
      1/7/3. Waltz [& Trio], 3/4. No. 3.   fl(D♭) cl(E♭) 2cl(I, B♭) 2cl(II, B♭) 2hn 2bn tp tb serp b-dr.
   1/8/1. Pas Redoublé, 2/4 [+ Trio]. No. 4.   pic(D♭) cl(E♭) 2cl(I, B♭) 2cl(II, B♭) 2hn 2bn tp 2tb (2)serp b-dr+t-dr.
      1/8/2. Pas Redoublé avec les Tambours, 2/4 [+Trio]. No. 5.   pic(D♭) cl(E♭) 2cl(B♭) 2hn 2bn tp (2)tb 2serp b-dr tambours.
      1/8/3. Waltz, 3/4 [+ Trio]. No. 6.   pic(D♭) cl(E♭) cl(I, B♭) 2cl(II, B♭) 2hn 2bn tp (2)tb 2serp b-dr.
   1/9/1. Simphonie, 1 mvt. No. 7.   fl(C) 2ob/cl(C) 2cl(C) 2hn 2bn tp tb (2)serp cb.
      1/9/2. Adagio. No. 8.   fl(C) 2ob/cl(C) 2cl(C) 2hn 2bn tp tb serp cb.
      1/9/3. Menuetto, Vivace, 3/4 [+ Trio]. No. 9.   fl(C) 2ob/cl(C) 2cl(C) 2hn 2bn tp tb serp cb.
CNM-1.1. Grande Harmonie, [MS: 1 - 3]. Scoring varies.
Pc (Chez les Fils de B. Schott: Paris, Mayence et Anvers, pn 3027 - 3029, 1828), parts: D-MZsch.
CNM-1.2. Musique Militaire, Cahier [MS: 1 - 6].
Pc (Chez les Fils de B. Schott: Paris, Mayence et Anvers, pn 3017 - 3021, 1828), parts: D-MZsch.
CNM-1.3. [untitled collection = 1/11/1 - 1/11/3; 1/5/1; 1/8/1].
fl(D♭) cl(E♭) 2cl(B♭) 2hn 2bn tp(crt in Trio of No. 1) 2tb serp b-dr s-dr.
MS parts: D-DT, 1867. *Nos. 1 - 3: 2 Pas Redoublés & Waltz.* ★
CNM-2. Nouveau Journal d'Harmonie et de Musique Militaire Publié sous l'Autorisation de S.E. Le Ministre de la Guerre. Scoring varies.
Pc (Propriété de l'Auteur: [Paris], pn 1 - 4, 1823/1824), parts: F-Pn, Vm27 3243, (missing Liv. 1 & 4, with a duplicate copy of Liv. 3; p. 1 of the serp pt in Liv. 2 is missing). ★
   Liv. 2: p-fl(D♭) cl(E♭) cl(B♭ solo) 2cl(B♭) 2hn 2bn tp(crt) 2tp(hn B♭ alto) 2tb serp+oph b-dr+cym t-dr. *In Nos. 14 & 15 the solo B♭ cl pt is marked "à deux". The B♭ cl I pt is labelled "1ere CLARINETTES"; the B♭ cl II is divisi in Nos. 10 - 13. In the Trio of No. 11 & Trio 1 of No. 14, the tp is replaced by cornet in A♭.*
      2.2/1. Marche; B♭ minor/major. No. 10.
      2.2/2(a). Pas redoublé de la Sémiramide de Rossini [& Trio]. No. 11.
      2.2/3(a). Pas redoublé Sur des motifs de Rossini. No. 12.   2.2/4. Pas redoublé [& Trio]. No. 13.
      2.2/5. Waltz à deux [& 2 Trios]. No. 14.   2.2/6. Waltz [& Trio]. No. 15.
   Nos. 16 - 18: p-fl(D♭) cl(E♭) cl(B♭ solo) 3cl(B♭) 2hn 2tp(hn B♭ alto) 2tb serp cb(ad lib).
      2.2/7(a). Cimarosa: Gli Orazi e Curiazi, overture. No. 16.
      2.2/8. Andante Sostenuto. No. 17.   2.2/9. Polonaise [& Trio]. No. 18.
   Liv. 3: p-fl(D♭) cl(E♭) cl(B♭ solo) 2cl(B♭) 2hn 2bn tp(crt in A♭, No. 20) 2/3tb serp b-dr+cym t-dr. *The solo B♭ cl is divisi in No. 19; B♭ cl I is divisi in Nos. 22, 22 & 24; B♭ cl II is divisi in Nos. 19 - 23. Horn I is divisi in Nos. 20 & 24, hn II in Nos. 20 & 22. Nos. 21 & 22 call for 2tb, the other Nos. for 3tb. The b-dr part of No. 19 also includes a separate "Partie pour les Tambours"; Nos. 20 - 24 include a part for t-dr (Caisse Roulante). For Nos. 25 - 27, see BERR, FXB-3.1.*
      2.3/1. Marche pour défiler. No. 19.   2.3/2. Pas redoublé [& Trio]. No. 20.   2.3/3. Pas redoublé . No. 21.
      2.3/4. Pas redoublé [& Trio]. No. 22.   2.3/5. Walz [sic], 3/8, [& Trio]. No. 23.
      2.3/6. Walz [sic], 3/4, [& Trio]. No. 24.
   Nos. 25 - 27 are arranged or composed by F. Berr (FXB-3.1).
CNM-1m, 2m. Marsch [C minor] & Pas redoublé, [A♭]. pic(D♭) cl(E♭) 2cl(B♭) 2hn 2bn tp(crt No. 5) b-tb serp.
MS score: D-Tl, Z 136, Nos. 4 & 5, ff. 17b - 22, 22b - 25b. *Possibly from the missing Nos. of CNM-1.* ★

MÜNCHS, Conrad, & LOUIS, F., *Chevalier*
The only surviving issue comprises 2 pas redoublés without attribution; we list both at LOUIS & MÜNCHS.
LAM-1. Journal de Musique Militiare; Année 1, Liv. 1 (no other issues traced). Scoring varies.
Pc (au Maison de Musique et d'Instrumens: Paris, c.1832 - 1835), parts: F-Pn, Vm27 2628. ★

*MÜNST, Matth[ias] *(?1780)*
MTM-1v. Feyerliche Messe zur Primiz-Feyer des Hochwürdigen Herrn Matth: Münst von Huggenlaubach; E♭.
CATB, cl(E♭) 2cl(B♭) 2hn 2tp b-tb.   MS score: D-Tl, Gg 208.   *The attribution may be questionable.*   ★

*MÜNSTER, Johann Baptist *(?1730)*
JLM-1. Concertatio; in F.   2ob 2hn basso.
MS parts: (provenance unknown - ?H-Bn).
Pm (Editio Musica Budapest: Budapest, pn 12648, c.1993), ed. Balla, score & parts (Alte Kammermusik).

*MUGNONE, Leopoldo *29 Sept 1858, Naples - 22 Dec 1941, Naples*
LEM-1a. J. Burgmein [pseudonym of Guido (di Tito) Ricordi]: Sette Pezzi Caratteristici, No. 5, Il Racconto della
Nonna, Preghiera, "O mamma cara".   2fl ob ca 2cl hn bn harp.
Pc (Ricordi: Milano, 1917), score (pn 116861) & parts (pn 116862): I-Mc, Da Camera A.8.2.I.
LEM-2a. J. Burgmein: Impressions de route, No. 2, "Dans la montagne".   2ob 2cl 2hn 2bn cbn.
Pc (Ricordi: Milano, 1916), score (pn 116828) & parts (pn 116829): I-Mc, Da Camera A.24.15.
LEM-3a. J. Burgmein: Mon carnot de jeunesse, "Dors, dors, mon enfant".   fl ca 2cl hn bn harp.
Pc (Ricordi: Milano, 1917), score & parts: US-Wc, M.779.R.

*MULDOWNEY, Dominic *19 July 1952, Southampton, UK*
DZM-1. Macbeth; ballet 1979.   2fl 2ob 2cl 2a-sax 4hn 2bn 3tp 3tb tu   3perc.
Pm (Universal Edition: London, pn UE 16441K, 1979), facsimile of the autograph score.
DZM-2. Garland of Chansons; 1978.   6ob 3bn.
Pm (Universal Edition: London, 1978), hire score & parts.   (MS parts: GB-Lmic.)
DZM-3. 3 Hymns to Agape; 1978.   ob obdam ca.   MS parts: GB-Lmic?
DZM-1v. 5 Psalms; 1979.   ST soli, SATB chorus, 2ob ca 2bn 2tp 3tb & optional tape.
Pm (Universal Edition London) Ltd: London, 1979), vocal score (pn UE 16378K), score & parts for hire.

MYSLÍK, Antonín *3 Feb 1933, Humpolec - 19 Feb 1983, Prague*
AOM-1a. Pichl: VXP-3.4d. as "Partita Pastoralis (in F)", 4 mvts.   2ob 2cl 2hn 2bn db tambourine.
AutoMS score (4th mvt only, 7 Aug 1948): CZ-Pu, 59 R 4147.

*MYSLIVEČEK, Josef *9 March 1737, Prague - 4 Feb 1781, Rome*
Below **MAB** *refers to the specific edition:* Tre Ottetti *(Státní hudební vydavatelství: Prague, pn H3406, 1962),*
edited by C. Schoenbaum, score & parts, (Musica antiqua bohemica, No. 55). The copy in CZ-OLu, II.322459,
sometimes cited as a contemporary MS is, in fact, the MAB modern edition.
*JFM-1.1. Partita in E♭, 3 mvts.   2ob 2cl 2hn 2bn.
MS parts: D-DO, Mus.Ms.1597, No. 5.   Pm (MAB: No. 2), score & parts.   ★
*JFM-2.1. Partita in E♭, 3 mvts.   2ob 2cl 2hn 2bn.
MS parts: D-DO, Mus.Ms.1597, No. 6.   Pm (MAB: No. 1), score & parts.   ★
*JFM-3. Partita in B♭, 3 mvts.   2ob 2cl 2hn 2bn.
MS parts: D-DO, Mus.Ms.1597, No. 7.   Pm (MAB: No. 3), score & parts.   ★
JFM-1.2, 2.2. [2 Sets of] Pièces d'Harmonie.   2fl 2cl 2hn 2bn.
MS parts: RF-Ssc, Ф 891 собр юосуповъ ı х N43, pp. 18 - 35, 56 - 71.
*JFM-4. Cassation ex B[♭], 5 mvts.   2cl 2hn bn.
MS parts: CZ-Bm(au), A.19.416; GB-BFlowes, (modern copy as "Lovecka parthia").   ★
*JFM-1c. Suito in Dis [E♭] No. 1. a [8 overwritten 9, then crossed out] 10 p[artes]; 3 mvts.   2ob/fl 2cl 2hn 2bn.
MS parts: E-Mn, M Ca/4429-8; GB-Ljag, (modern score ed. Ernest Warburton).   *Incorrectly attributed "del: Sig*
[added later: J.C.] Bach.". Following "Due Oboi." is the added phrase, "et ["2" added later] Flauto Traverse.";
however there are no separate flute parts.   ★

*N., K. *active in Elbeteinitz, Bohemia, c.1800 - 1850*
KYN-1m. 6 Märsche nebst 1 Pollaca und 1 Monfrin [sic].   cl(F) 2cl(B♭) 2hn 2tp serp.
MS parts: CZ-TRB, H 88, (missing hn I; the hn II & tp II pts are incomplete).   ★

NADELMANN, Leo *16 Jan 1912, Germany*
LXN-1. Passacaglia für 8 Holzinstrumente; 1960.   2fl ob ca cl b-cl bn cbn.
Pm (Astoria Verlag: Berlin, c.1980).

*NÄTHER, Gilbert *1948, Germany*
GZN-1. Two South-American Songs; (Angelitos Negres; Los Oprimidos); 1993.   S solo, ob 2bn cbn.
Pm (Compusic: Amsterdam, pn 524, c.1994), score & parts.

NAGILLER, Matthäus *24 Oct 1815, Münster, Tyrol - 8 July 1874, Innsbruck*
MXN-1v. Missa in F, N⁰ 3.   SATB, fl 2cl(C) 2hn 2tp(clar) tb timp organ.
MS parts (by J. Constantin): A-Wn, Mus.Hs.20,290.   ★

NAGNZAUN, Michael, *O.S. Bened. ad St. Petrum* *(1790)*
MZN-1v. Libera me Domine; in B♭.   SATB, 2cl 2hn bn.   MS pts (1816); A-KR, E 3/89, (with 3 later tb pts).   ★

*NANKE, Alois, *the Elder* *d. 1834, active around Brno*
AEN-1v. Offertorium in B♭.   TT, 2cl 2hn bn.   MS parts: CZ-KRa.

*NANKE, Carl (Karel) *1768, Nový Jičín, 30 Dec 1831, Brno*
CXN-1v. Osterlied, "Alles Lob und Preis".   SATB, 2fl 2cl 2hn 2bn 2tp timp, *or* organ.
MS parts: CZ-Bm(rj), A.12.823, (acquired 1829, performed [Easter] 11 April 1830).   ★

NARCISSE, ( )
XYN-1m. Pas redoublé; in E♭.   pic(D♭) cl(E♭) 2cl(B♭) 2hn tp bassi.
MS score: D-Tl, Z 136, No. 10, ff. 41 - 43. ★
XYN-2m. Pas redoublé; C minor.   pic(D♭) cl(E♭) 2cl(B♭) 2hn tp tb serp.
MS score: D-Tl, Z 136, No. 11, ff. 43b - 46b.   ★

*NAUMANN, Johann Gottlieb *17 April 1741, Blasewitz - 23 Oct 1801, Dresden*
JGN-1m. 6 Märsche (E♭, B♭, B♭, E♭, B♭, E♭) (No. 5 is a march from Naumann's 1791 opera, *La Dame Soldato;* see also JGN-1mad). Scoring varies: Nos. 1.1m - 1.4m: 2ob 2cl 2hn 2bn 2tp basso(?serp); No. 1.5m: 2ob 2cl 2bn basso(?serp); No. 1.6m: 2ob 2cl 2hn 2bn basso(?serp).
MS parts: D-Bds, Hausbibl.M.M.172.   Pm (Steinquest), pp. 225 - 260, score.   ★
JGN-2m. Erster Marsch des Regiments von Kalckstein, B♭.   2cl 2hn 2bn tp.
MS parts: D-Bds, Hausbibl.M.M.62, (the tp doubles hn I).   ★
Pm (Steinquest), pp. 95 - 99, score, (Steinquest suggests 2hn *or* 2tp).
Pm: (In: Pätzig (qv). Vol. 2, No. 12), score & parts.
JGN-3m. Zweiter Marsch von Kalckstein, E♭.   ob 2cl 2hn bn.
MS parts: D-Bds, Hausbibl.M.M.63.   ★
Pm: (Steinquest, pp. 100 - 104).   Pm: (In: Pätzig (qv), Vol. 2, No. 13), score & parts.
JGN-4m. 6 Märsche.   Instrumentation unknown.   AutoMS score: D-Bds, Mus.Ms.Auto.J.G.Naumann 13.
JGN-1.1v. Quartetto 29 ["Deh ti piaccia il tuo potere", B♭, from the oratorio "Davide in Terebinto", Dresden 1794].   SSTT, 2fl 2cl 2hn 3bn.   MS: D-B, (2 copies), Mus.ms.15938, Mus.ms.15944/5.   ★
JGN-1.2v. Quartetto [B♭, with the text, "Terulich, Herr, auf deinen Wegen lass mich wandeln immerdar!"].
SSTT *or* SSTB, 2cl 3hn 3bn.   MS parts: D-B, Mus.ms.15956.
JGN-2v. Terzetto in F, "Was Gott ordnet das ist löblich und herrlich".
SAT, (2ob) 2cl 2hn 2bn fondamento(bc-fig).   MS pts: CZ-Pnm, XXXVIII.F.525, (possibly missing bn II, which may have played off the fondamento part; the two unlisted ob pts appear on the back of the cl pts).   ★
JGN-1ve. Duetto nell' Opera Protesilao, "Caro Ben", in G.   SS, solo ob & bn, 2fl 2hn bn.
MS parts: D-B, Mus.ms.15967/14.
JGN-1mad. Retiret, in C (Allegretto, arranged from his 1791 opera *La Dama Soldata).*
2ob 2cl(C) 2hn 2bn 2tp serp *(of which the 2ob 2tp serp play only for the opening fanfare and the D.S al segno).*
MS parts: D-Bds, Hausbibl.M.M.343.   Pm (Steinquest), pp. 398 - 410, score.   ★

NAUMANN, Siegfried *27 Nov 1919, Malmö*
SXN-1. Music for 10 instruments, contrabassoon & timpani.   2fl 2ob 2cl 2hn 2bn cbn timp.   MS score: S-Sic.

*NAVA, Gaetano *16 May 1802, Milan - 31 March 1875, Milan*
GXN-1v. Tantum ergo.   B solo, TTB chorus, fl 2cl(C) 2hn bn tp (vlne) timp organ(bc-fig).
MS score & parts: I-Vsmc. (with full organ pt; the cl pts are marked "senza Violini" and the vlne pt does not appear in the score).   ★

NAVRÁTIL, František *c.1732 - 28 June 1802, Valašské Meziříčí (Wallachisch Meseritsch)*
FXN-1. Parthia in A; 5 mvts.   2cl(A) 2hn bn.   MS parts: CZ-KRa, A3839/IV.B.102.   ★

*NECCHI, Francesco Antonio *(?1770)*
FAN-1v. Gloria a 3ᵉ Voci [sic], con Stromenti; in F.   CATB, 2ob 2hn basso.
MS parts: CH-E, Th. 566,2 (Ms.4212).   ★
FAN-2v. Credo; in F.   CCC, ob 2hn bn.   MS parts: CH-E, Th. 285,2 hoch 3 (Ms.3243).   ★

NEIKRUG, Marc *24 Sept 1946, New York*
MYN-1. Rosacae.   3ob 3cl 4hn 2bn cbn 3tp 3tb 2perc.
Pm (Chester Music: London, etc., 1986), hire score & parts.

*NEITHARDT, August Heinrich *10 Aug 1793, Schleiz - 18 April 1861, Berlin*
For other marches by Neithardt (possibly not in their original scorings) see: ANONYMOUS WORKS, A-74m.
AHN-1m(-4m). Acht Märsche für die Infanterie, Nos. 5 - 8, (Nos. 1 - 4 are by F. Weller, qv).
Nos. 5 (B♭), 6 (F), 7 (B♭): pic 2ob 2cl(F) 3cl(C) 2bthn 4hn 3bn cbn+serp(doubles bn III) 4tp 3tb b-dr+cym tamb+tri; No. 8.   (B♭, without a trio): pic 2ob 2cl(F) 2cl(C) 2bthn 4hn 3bn cbn+serp 5tp 3tb tamb.
Pc (Eigenthum des Componisten: Berlin, c.1835, pp. 59 - 90), scores: D-Bds, Hausbibl, (?lost); GB-Lbl, e.43.   ★
AHN-5m. Drei Märsche.   pic 2ob 2cl(F) 2cl(C) 2bthn 4hn 2bn cbn+serp 4tp a-tb t-tb b-tb b-dr+cym s-dr+tri.
MS score (Nov 1825): A-Wn, Mus.Hs.11,358, (with the stamp of the Musikverein in Graz; later published by Laue: Berlin; Schlesinger: Berlin, and Hofmeister: Leipzig, as "Op. 25").   ★
AHN-1mv. [Chorgesang, "Jubellieder hört man schallen"].   Zum vierzigjährigen Regierungs=Jubiläum Seiner Majestät des Kaisers von Oesterreich; ein Chorgesang ausgeführt, am 1ᵗᵉⁿ März 1832, von der Musik= und Sänger=Chor des Kaiser Franz Grenadier Regiments in Berlin.
TTB chorus, flautino terz-fl 2ob 2cl(E♭) 2cl(B♭) 2bthn 4hn 2bn serp+cbn 2tp 3tb b-dr s-dr.
MS score: A-Wn, Mus.Hs.10,198, (with the stamp of the Musikverein in Graz).   ★
AHN-1a. Spontini: Alcidor, march.   pic quart-fl 2ob cl(F) 2cl(C) 4hn 2bn cbn+serp/2b-hn 2tp 3tb b-dr t-dr tamb cym.   *See ANONYMOUS WORKS, A-74.11/10m(a).*

*NEJEDLÝ, Roman *9 April 1844, Dětenice u Libáně - 25 Feb 1920, Manichovo Hradiště*
RZN-1tv. 12 Pohřebních Písní [funeral songs].   SAB (Nos. 1, 4 - 6 & 11: S/T,A/T,B), 2cl 2hn basso.
Pc (Ant. Kindl: Brno, 1881), pts: CZ-Pnm, XL.F.191, (missing cl I & the vocal parts for Nos. 1 - 3, 11, 12); CZ-PLa(ka), Hu 1709.   ★
   RZN-1.1tv. Nejedlý: Zapěj ardce u bolesti.
   RZN-1.2tv. Nejedlý: Bohem naše děťátko; text by Boleslav Jablonský.
   RZN-1.3tv = JFF-1tv. Josef Förster: Spi, rozmilé nemluvňátko.
   RZN-1.4tv = FNV-1tv. Franz Vogner: Uložme k spánku.
   RZN-1.5tv. Nejedlý: Nevíme, v kterou chvílní. *This uses the same music as RZN-1.1v.*
   RZN-1.6tv = FNV-2tv. Franz Vogner: Kynul Pán (Mládenci neb panně) [for the funerals of youths or virgins].
   RZN-1.7tv = FNV-3tv. Franz Vogner: Slze bolné (U hrobu) [for performance at the grave].
   RZN-1.8tv. Nejedlý: Zde na márách (Starci) [for the funerals of elderly men].
   RNZ-1.9tv. Nejedlý: Pouť má došla (Stařeně) [for the funerals of elderly women].
   RZN-1.10tv = JFF-2tv. Josef Förster: Hlas tě Boha všemocného (Otci neb matce) [for fathers or mothers].
   RZN-1.11tv. Nejedlý: Ach již nemůže jinak býti; text by Boleslav Jablonský.
   RZN-1.12tva. Nejedlý (arranger): Stara píseň [old song] Stala se vůle Tvá.

NELHÝBEL, Václav *24 Sept 1919, Polanka*
VYN-1. Toccata.   3fl ob 3cl hn bn 2tp 2tb 2perc hpcd.
Pm (E.C. Kerby Ltd: Toronto, 1973).
VYN-2. Auriel Variations.   fl ob ca 3cl bn perc.
Pm (Barta: sl, 1979).
VYN-3. Impromptus; 1963.   2fl(pic) ob 2cl bn.
Pm (General Music: New York, c.1963), *now published by:* (Colgems EMI Music Inc.: New York, sd).

*NELSON, Oliver Edward *6 April 1932, St. Louis, Missouri - 27 Oct 1975, Los Angeles*
OEN-1. Divertimento.   2fl 2ob 2cl 2hn 2bn cbn.
Pm (Modern Edition, now Hans Wewerka: München, 1962), score & parts.

NESVADBA (Noswadba), Josef *14 Jan 1822, Vyskeř - 20 May 1876, Darmstadt*
JXN-1a. Mendelssohn: Hochzeitsmarsch aus dem Sommernachtstraum [Midsummer's Night Dream, Wedding March].   2fl(Eb) 2ob 2cl(Eb) 4cl(Bb) 4hn(G, F) 2bn 2tp 2cap flug a-hn 3t-hn 3tb euph 2tu b-dr s-dr.
AutoMS score: D-DS, Mus.ms.810.

*NEUBAUER (Neubaur, Naibauer), Franz Christoph (Giovanni)
21 March 1750, Mělník, nr Prague - 11 Oct 1795, Bückeburg
FCN-1. Parthia; in Eb, 6 mvts.   2fl 2cl 2hn 2bn db.   MS parts: NL-Z, Z1132/M.A.Zcm.4, No. 4.   ★
FCN-2. Parthia No. 5; in Bb.   fl 2ob 2cl 2hn 2bn cbn. MS parts: D-RUl, RH. No.16.   ★
FCN-3. Parthia No. 3; in Eb.   fl ob 2cl 2hn 2bn quart-fagott. MS parts: D-RUl, RH. No. 13.   ★
FCN-4. Parthia in G; 4 mvts.   2ob 2cl(A) 2hn 2bn.
MS parts: D-DO, Mus.Ms.1423, (2 sets of parts, the second missing hn I).   ★
FCN-5. Barthia [sic] in B[b]; 4 mvts.   2ob 2cl 2hn 2bn.   MS parts: D-DO, Mus.Ms.1424, (missing cl II).   ★
FCN-6. Barthia [sic] in Dis [Eb]; 4 mvts   2ob 2cl 2hn 2bn.   MS parts: D-DO, Mus.Ms.1425.   ★
FCN-7. Parthia in B[b]; 4 mvts.   2ob 2cl 2hn 2bn.   MS parts: D-DO, Mus.Ms.1426.   ★
FCN-8. Barthia [sic] in Dis [Eb]; 4 mvts.   2ob 2cl 2hn 2bn.   MS parts: D-DO, Mus.Ms.1427.   ★
FCN-9. Harmonia, No. 1 [subtitled "Parthie 4 und 5"]; 10 mvts.   2ob 2cl 2hn 2bn.
MS parts: D-RUl, RH. No. 15.   ★
FCN-10. Parthia No. 2; in Eb.   2ob 2cl 2hn 2bn.   MS parts: D-RUl, RH. No.14.   ★
FCN-11. Parthia in F; 4 mvts.   2ob 2cl 2hn 2bn.   MS parts: D-Rtt, Neubauer 6.   ★
FCN-12. Partita in G; 4 mvts.   2ob 2cl 2hn 2bn.
MS parts: I-Gc, SS.B.1.14.(H.8.).   ★
Pm (WINDS: Northridge, CA, pn W-80, c.1981), photocopy, modern MS parts.
FCN-13. Cassatio in F.   fl fldam 2hn 2vla vc.   MS parts: I-Fc, F.P. S.168.
FCN-14. Parthia; in Eb, 4 mvts.   2cl 2hn 2bn.   MS parts: CZ-Bm(no), A.16.653.   ★
FCN-15. Parthia; in Eb, 3 mvts.   2cl 2hn 2bn.   MS parts: CZ-Bm(no), A.16.654.   ★
FCN-16. Parthia in Dis [Eb]; 4 mvts.   2cl 2hn bn.   MS parts: A-KR, H 37/7.   ★
FCN-17. Parthia; in Eb.   2cl 2hn bn.   MS parts (by Langthaller): A-KR, H 37/9.   ★
FCN-18. Parthis in Dis [Eb].   2cl 2hn 2bn.   MS parts: A-KR, H 37/10.   ★
FCN-19. Parthia; in Eb.   2cl 2hn bn.   MS parts (by Langthaller): A-KR, H 37/11.   ★
FCN-20. Parthia; in Eb.   2cl 2hn bn.   MS parts (by Langthaller): A-KR, H 37/13.   ★
FCN-21. Parthia in Dis [Eb].   2cl 2hn bn.   MS parts: A-KR, H 37/17.   ★
FCN-22. Parthia in Eb.   2cl 2hn bn.   MS parts: A-KR, H 37/23.   ★
FCN-23. Parthia in dis [Eb].   2cl 2hn bn.   MS parts: A-KR, H 37/24.   ★
FCN-24. Parthia in dis [Eb].   2cl 2hn bn.   MS parts: A-KR, H 37/29.   ★
FCN-25(-30) 6 Parthien; 1791.   fl(oblig) ob(oblig) 2cl 2hn 2bn vlne(ad lib).
AutoMS score & parts: D-DS, (?lost in World War II).   *FCN-2 & 3 probably match this set.*
FCN-1v [= ZZK-1va]. Vier Stationen=Gesäange.   SATB, (organ ad lib) *and/or* (3cl(C) 2hn tb vlne ad lib).
MS parts ("Scripsimus 1841 ad chorum Bonacellensem"; probably a late copy): D-Tl, Gg 284, (with additional parts for tb/vlne and organ/vlne).   *A note on the titlepage states, "Nota: Kne[c]ht von Biberach soll die Begleitung der Instrumente gemacht haben."; we have not been able to verify this supposed attribution.*   ★
FCN-2v. Pro Festo EPIPHANIE D[e].N[ostra].I[esu].C[hristus]., MISSA, 1783.
SATB, fl 2cl 2hn vlne organ(ad pulpitum) organ(2).   MS parts: D-OB, MO 67c, (a Graduale, Offertorium & Postcommunio by "A.R.P. Corrado Bagg, Prof: Ottob:" is listed on the titlepage but is not present).   ★
FCN-3.1v. Quatuor Stationes pro Festo SS. Corporis Christi.   CATB, 2(C) 2hn(C, F) bn+b-tb organ.
MS parts (by Loritz): D-Tl, B 327, (here with duplicate vocal parts for: S, A, B).   ★
FCN-3.2v [= ZZK-2va]. Quatuor Stationes.   CATB, 3cl 2hn basso.
MS parts: D-Tl, B 327, (with FCN-3.1; one of the two cl(III) pts bears the note, "Begleitung v. [? Justin Heinrich] Knecht", cf. FCN-1.2v *supra*).
FCN-4v. O Salutaris Hostia; in A.   SATB, 2ob 2hn basso organ.
MS parts: D-Rtt, Neubauer 9, (with 2 duplicate Soprano parts).   ★
FCN-5v. Pro Festo Purificationis, Graduale ("Suscepimus Deus"), Offertorium ("Diffusa est gratia", Bb) & Postcommunio ("Responsum accepit", Eb), 1783.   SATB, 2cl 2hn vlne organ.
MS parts: D-OB, Mo 665, (with 2 sets of vocal, vlne & organ parts; the wind parts are in a different hand).   ★
FCN-6v. Stabat Mater; in F minor.   SSS, cl bn 2vla(obl) organ.
MS parts: D-DTF, 176, (possibly missing a 4th vocal part).   ★

*NEUKOMM, Sigismond von *10 July 1778, Salzburg - 3 April 1858, Paris*
The New Grove *lists 10 marches for wind band (1 published), 2 phantasies for winds, 6 marches for winds, and several works "mostly" for winds (1 nonet, 1 octet (presumably SVN-8), 2 septets (one being NV 517, for fl 2cl hn bn tp db) and 1 sextet (NV 469, for 2hn tp 3tb). We cannot relate the others to our lists, although we note many marches for large wind bands (NV 122, 142, 143, 153, 158, 166, 416, 445, 496, 568, 600, 623). No. and Vol. references follow Neukomm's own chronological thematic list (most of the surviving works are now in F-Pn).*
SVN-1.1, 1.2. 9 Marches & Dances [sic: Although usually attributed to Neukomm, only the marches, Nos. 71 & 72 are by him; "Goepfert" appears in pencil in the Eb cl vol. (here used for cl III in C) for No. 71 but is clearly an error and refers to No. 70, CAG-7a]; Marsch, Eb].   2pic 2ob 3cl(C/Bb) 2hn 2bn 2tp b-tb+serp+cbn b(?serp).
MS parts: D-Rtt, Sm. 14, Nos. 71 - 2.   ★

SVN-2. Waltz, "La Blosseville". fl 3cl hn bn tp b-drum. MS: F-Pn, MS. 6653.
SVN-3. Fantasie: L'Adoration du St Sépulchre, E♭, (NV 170, 17 March 1819). Winds. MS: Vol. 4.
***SVN-4.** Serenade in B♭, 1796. 2ob 2cl 2hn 2bn. MS: D-F.
SVN-1e. Trauermärsche in the tragedy of Hanno, (NV 11, St Petersburg, 19 Oct 1804). Winds. MS: Vol. 70.
***SVN-1m.** 13 Märsch à grand orchestre militaire, (NV 166, Rio de Janeiro, Feb 1819). Winds.
Pc (as: Helden-Denkmal für Preussen. Zwölfe Märsche nebst Einleitung, für kriegerische Instrumente, seiner Majestät dem Könige Friedrich Wilhelm III ... gewidmet) (N. Simrock: Bonn & Cologne, pn 1697, 1819); parts: NL-Z, Z1245/M.A.Zcm.116, (No. [MS: 1]; only the "Gebet. Preghiera" & 2 marches, "Der Kronprinz" & "Der König"; incomplete: only the 2pic (2ob ad lib) 3cl b-dr s-dr cym parts).
SVN-2m, 3m. 2 Marches (C, C; titled "Prinz Carl von Mecklenburg" and "Prinz Friedrich"; c.1820).
2pic 2ob 3cl 2hn 2bn serp 2tp b-drum b(?serp). MS parts: D-Rtt, Sm. 14, Nos. 92 - 3. ★
SVN-4m, 5m. Marcia Prinz Albert, E♭; Marcia Prinz Heinrich, E♭, 1823. fl 2ob 4cl 2hn 2bn tp tb serp 2vla.
MS parts: D-Rtt, Sammelband 18, Nos. 42, 43, (possibly rescored by Anton Schneider). ★
SVN-6.1m. Marche triomphale, (NV 142 bis, 27 Sept 1816). Winds.
It is possible, but unconfirmed, that SVN-6.1m(-6.4m) are all the same march.
MS: Vol. 53. Pc (Mechetti: Vienna, c.1820), parts.
SVN-6.2m. Marche triomphale, (6 Dec 1816). Winds.
AutoMS score: D-Bds, Mus.Ms.Auto.S.Neukomm 12.
SVN-6.3m. Triumphmarsch, Op. 20, (1816). Winds.
Pc (Breitkopf & Härtel: Leipzig), parts: (in private hands).
SVN-6.4m. Marche triomphale. Military band. MS: B-Bc.
SVN-7m. Marche pour la fête de S.A.R., (NV 158, 19 Jan 1818). Winds. MS: Vol. 4; Vol. 36.
SVN-1t. Marche funèbre sur la morte du Comte da Barca, D minor, (NV 153, Rio de Janeiro, 22 June 1817).
Winds. MS: Vol. 4; Vol. 36 - 72.
SVN-2t. Marche pour les funerailles du Géneral Walter, D minor, (NV 122). Winds. MS: Vol. 55 - 67.
SVN-1v. Messe solonnelle ... St. Philippe avec un Dominus salvum fac Regem et un Tantum ergo; (NV 582).
Unison (& octave) voices (or SATB), 3fl 2ob cl(E♭) 2cl(B♭) 2hn 2bn 2tp a-tb t-tb b-tp oph timp tri b-dr+cym
s-dr organ, (2vl vla vc+db ad lib).
Pc (les fils de B. Schott: Mayence, pn 5850, 5851, 1840), score: CZ-Bm(au), A.20.689. ★
***SVN-2v.** 33rd Messe solonnelle. TTBB, 2fl 2cl 2hn 2tp 3tb vc db timp.
Pc (sn: Paris, 1858), score & parts: F-Pn, Vm1 2159, (missing tb pts).
SVN-3v. Messe des morts pour un grand service funèbre; (NV 791). Unison voices or SATB, fl(E♭) 2fl 2ob
cl(E♭) 2cl(B♭) 2hn 2bn 2tp a-tb t-tb b-tb 2oph 2vc cb timp; *also versions for:* organ (with registration), and 2vl
vla 2vc cb organ, (2ob 2hn timp ad lib).
MS score (presentation fair copy to Kaiser Franz Josef I): A-Wn, Mus.Hs.3220. ★
***SVN-1va.** J.M. Haydn: Missa St Hieronymi, (NV 55, 24 April 1809, Montbéliard). Voices & winds.
MS score: Vol. 55.

***NEUMANN, Anton (Franz)** *baptized 28 Feb 1740, Brno - Nov 1776 (?Kroměříž)*
AFN-1(-6). [6] Parthia a 5 Strom; each 6 mvts in C. 2ca 2hn bn.
MS parts: CZ-KRa, A4026/IV.B.199 a-e, Nos. 1 - 6. ★

***NEUMANN, Heinrich** *1792, Heiligenstadt - 4 April 1861, Heiligenstadt*
HYN-1. Polonaise. cl(E♭) cl(B♭ solo) 3cl(B♭) 2hn+2hn(ad lib) 2bn 2tp t-hn a-tb t-tb b-tb serp vc/b b-dr s-dr.
MS parts: D-DT, Mus-h 1 N 7, No. 2.
HYN-2. Walzer; in E♭. terz-fl ob cl(E♭) 3cl(B♭) 2hn 2bn 2tp a-tb t-tb b-tb serp b-dr t-dr tri.
MS parts: D-DT, Mus-h 1 N 6, No. 3.
HYN-3. Variations über den Sehnsuchts=Walzer. terz-fl cl(E♭) 3cl(B♭) 2hn 2bn 2tp a-tb t-tb b-tb serp b-dr s-dr.
MS parts: D-DT, Mus-h 1 N 3.
HYN-4. Ouverture No. 1. fl(E♭) ob cl(E♭) 3cl(B♭) 2hn 2bn 2tp b-tb b-hn. MS parts: D-DT, Mus-h 1 N 2.
HYN-5. Harmonie, Op. 20. 2ob 2cl 2hn 2bn cbn/db(ad lib).
Pc (Mompour: Bonn, sd), parts: US-NC, M952.N3.
HYN-1a. Carafa: Violette, aria. terz-fl ob cl(E♭) 3cl(B♭) 2hn 2bn 2tp a-tb t-tb b-tb serp .
MS parts: D-DT, Mus-h 1 N 5.
HYN-2a. Carafa: Violette, 2 arias. Oboe solo, terz-fl cl(E♭) 3cl(B♭) 2hn 2bn 2tp a-tb t-tb b-tb serp b-dr t-dr.
MS parts: D-DT, Mus-h 1 N 6, Nos. 1 & 2.
HYN-3a. Cherubini: Lodoïska, overture. cl(E♭) cl(B♭ solo) 3cl(B♭) 2hn 2bn 2tp t-hn a-tb t-tb b-tb serp b-dr s-dr.
MS parts: D-DT, Mus-h 1 N 7.

NEUNER, Carl Borrimäus *1778 - 1830*
CBN-1v. Psa[lm]: 122, Offertorium, 5 vocum, Ad te Domine levavi coulos meos; in A♭.
SATBB, (2cl 2bn 3tb ad lib). AutoMS score & AutoMS parts ("Vorstadt Au am 17t. Oktober 1827"):
D-Mbm, Mf 1039, (Chorus) Bl.1r-3r, (winds) Bl.3v-6v, (duplicate vocal parts). ★

NEWBURY, Kent Alan *25 Nov 1925, Chicago*
KXN-1. The Sepulchre of Famous Men. SATB, 2fl ob 3cl b-cl 4hn 2bn 3tp 3tb tu timp perc.
Pm (G. Schirmer: New York, sd), vocal score (pn GS 1972, out-of-print), full score & parts *not available*.

NEWSON, George John *1932, UK*
GJN-1. Octet; 1951. fl ob cl hn 2bn tp tb. MS score: GB-Lmic.

***NEX, Christopher** *10 June 1945, Capetown, South Africa*
***NEX (née TURNER),** Frances Hillary *11 May 1945, Bideford, UK*
CYN-1a. F.P. Schubert, arranged Brahms: Ellens zweiter Gesang. 2ob 2cl 4hn 2bn.
Pm (Phylloscopus Publications: Lancaster, UK, pn PP 157B, 1995), score & parts.

NEZWAL, Joseph
JYN-1tv. Todtenlieder, "Der Mensch vom Weib gebohren". CATB, 2cl 2hn b-tb.
MS parts: CZ-Bm(pe), A.21.374. ★

*NICHOLS, 'Red' (Ernest Loring) *8 May 1905, Ogden, Utah - 28 June 1965, Las Vegas*
RYN-1. Holiday for woodwinds [jazz)]. pic 2fl ob 4cl b-cl 4sax bn.
Pm (Lawson-Gould Music Publishers: New York, pn AMC 2792, 1957), score & parts.
Pm (G. Schirmer: New York).

NICHOLSON, G. Gordon *1942, Canada*
GGN-1. Contrapunctus; 1969. 2fl 2cl hn bn. MS score: C-Tcm.

NICULESCU, Stefan *31 July 1927, Moreni*
SYN-1. 2 Scènes; 1962 - 1965. 2fl(pic) ob(ca) 2cl(b-cl) bn tp tb 2db 2perc(cel vibr xyl) piano.
Pm (Salabert: Paris, c.1965).

NIEDERSTE-SCHEE, Wolfgang *1910*
WXN-1. Chamber Concerto. Solo violin, 10 winds, perc.
Pm (Wilhelm Hansen: Frankfurt; Chester Music: London), hire score & parts.

*NIELSEN, Carl August *9 June 1865, Nørre Lyndelse, nr Odense - 3 Oct 1931, Copenhagen*
We assume all these works are to be found in DK-Kk (and in the archives of Danmarks Radio); we believe the scorings "winds" correspond to a normal symphonic wind section.
*CAN-1. Paraphrase on "Naermere Gud til dig" ("Nearer, my God, to Thee"); (FS-63), 1912. Winds.
*CAN-2. Wind Quintet, Op. 43, 1923. fl ob cl hn bn.
Pm: (Wilhelm Hansen: Copenhagen, 1949), miniature score and parts.
CAN-1v. Hymne til Kunsten (FS-141), 1929. Solo ST, SSATB, 2fl ob cl(Eb) 2cl(Bb) 4hn bn 2crt 2tb tu timp. MS score: DK-Kk.
*CAN-2v. Incidental Music to "Ebbe Skammelsen" (FS-117), 1925.
Vocal soloists, unison male & female choirs, fl/ob ob 2cl 4hn 2bn tu gong.
*CAN-3v. Svømmehals-Kantate (FS-153a), 1930. Male voices, winds.

NIELSEN, Ludolf *1876 - 1939*
LYN-1. Bagpipe, Op. 30. 2fl/pic+fl 2ob 2cl 2bn triangles cym.
Pm (A.J. Andraud: Cincinnati, now Southern Music Co.: San Antonio, Texas, sd), score & parts.
LYN-2. Aus dem Skizzenbuch, Op. 50. pic fl 2ob 2cl 2bn perc.
Pc (Simon: s.l., s.d.), score & parts: US-Wc.

NILSSON, Torsten *1920, Sweden*
TXN-1. Chamber Concerto Op. 3; 1953, revised 1982. 2fl 2ob 2bn organ. MS score: S-Sic.

*NINI, Alessandro *1805, Fano - 1880, Bergamo*
AYN-1v. Stabat Mater, per processione; in Eb. CATTBB, 2fl (?2)ob 2cl 2hn 2tp 3tb timp.
(?Auto)MS score & MS parts: I-BGi(cm), Faldone 228, n. 784.

*NIPEL, Francesco *Maestro della Accademia filarmonica in Lecco*
FYN-1m. La Rocca di Bellagio, Marcia (& trio). pic cl(G) cl(D) cl(I, A) cl(II & II, C) 4hn(D, A basso) 2bn 4tp(D) 3tb b-tb 2basso b-dr s-dr. MS score: I-Mc, Noseda L.17.18. ★
FYN-1a. Donizetti: La Gitana, marcia (& trio). pic cl(G) cl(D) cl(A) 2cl(C) 4hn(D, A basso) 2bn 4tp flug(A) 2tb b-tp b-tb 2bassi b-dr. (?Auto)MS score: I-Mc, Noseda L.17.12.

*NOACK, ( ) *(active c.1800)*
XXN-1 Parthia III; in Eb, 5 mvts. 2cl 2hn bn.
MS parts: US-BETm, Lititz Collegium Musicum 180.3, (Parthias I & II are by Collauf). ★

NOBLE, Harold *3 June 1903, Blackpool, UK*
HXN-1. Hertfordshire Suite. 2fl 2ob 2cl 2bn.
Pm (Studio Music: London, 1984), score & parts.

*NOCENTINO (Nocentini), Domenico *18 March 1848, Laterino, Arezzo - 29 Dec 1924, Florence*
*DXN-1. Sinfonia in Bb, "Labor Omnia Vincit"; 3 mvts. fl 2ob 2cl 2hn 2bn db(ad lib).
MS score ("Con courso accademico a 1886"): I-Fc, D.IX.2804. ★
Pm (Compusic: Amsterdam, pn 245, 1990), score & parts, (cbn replaces db).
DXN-1m. Santa Maria, Marcia religiosa. Military band. MS score: I-LEFpezzoli.

NØRGÅRD, Per *13 July 1932, Gentofe, nr Copenhagen*
PXN-1. Modlys (Backlight); 1970. 2fl/pic 2ob cl cl/b-cl 2s-sax(or 2cl) 2bn 2tp 4tb 2tu 2perc 2pf.
Pm (Edition Wilhelm Hansen: Copenhagen, 1970), hire score & parts.
PXN-1v. Libra; (text: Rudolph Steiner). T solo, 2 SATB choruses, winds (ad lib), 2vib gtr.
Pm (Edition Wilhelm Hansen: Copenhagen, 1973), hire score & parts.
PXN-2v. Triptychon, Op. 18; 1957 - 1960. SATB, pic fl ob cl 2hn bn tp tb timp vc db.
Pm (Edition Wilhelm Hansen: Copenhagen, 1970), hire score & parts.

*NØRHOLM, Ib *2 Jan 1931, Copenhagen*
IXN-1. Idylles d'Apocalypse. Solo organ, 2fl 2ob 2cl 2hn 2bn 2tp 2tb tu, 2vl va vc db.
Pm (Wilhelm Hansen: Copenhagen, 1980), score (pn WH 29748) & hire parts.

NORDHAGEN, Stig *1966, Norway*
STN-1. Concertino; 1987. 3fl 3ob 3cl 2bn cbn. MS score: N-Oic.

*NOVÁČEK, Rudolf *7 April 1860, Weisskirchen, Hungary (now Bela Crkva, Serbia) - 12 Aug 1929, Prague*
RXN-1. Sinfonietta, Op. 4; 4 mvts. fl ob 2cl 2hn 2bn.
Pc (Breitkopf & Härtel: Leipzig, 1905); score (Breitkopf & Härtel's Partitur-Bibliotek No. 1917) & parts: D-Bhm, 17988; GB-Lbl, h.2785.1.(3); I-Mc, Da Camera A.87.13; US-PHf, 2387. ★
Pm (McGinnis & Marx: New York), score & parts.
Pm (Emerson Edition: Ampleforth, pn E141), score & parts.
Pm (Compusic: Amsterdam, pn 214, 1988), score & parts.
Pm (Western Music International, Inc.: Greeley, Colorado, pn WIM 320, 1984), ed. R. Dishinger, score & parts.

*NOVOTNÝ (Novotni), A. *(Probably not Ferenc Novotny, c.1749 - 1806)*
AYN-1a. Mozart: Le Nozze di Figaro, overture.   2ob 2cl(C) 2hn 2bn cbn(basso) 2tp.
MS parts (1846): CZ-Bm(au), A.37.343.
AYN-2a. Mozart: Don Giovanni, aria.   2ob 2cl 3hn 2bn cbn tp.
MS parts: CZ-Bm(au), A.37.342, (missing cl II).

*NOVOTNÝ (Nowotný), Johann *Lehrer zu Rychnov nad Kněžnou*
AYN-1v. 4 Stationen zum Frohen-Leichnamsfeste.   CATB, 2cl 2hn 3tp(2clar, 1prin) 2flug timp basso.
MS parts: CZ-Pnm, XLIII.D.207, (missing 3tp 2flug timp). ★

*NUDERA, Adalbert (Vojtěch Jovanne) *(active in 1796; violinist at Prague Cathedral)*
Note: Keys for VXN-5 to VXN-9 are as written (untransposed) for bassethorn; the actual key follows in brackets.
VXN-1. Parthia la Campagna in C; 4 mvts.   2ob 2hn bn.   MS parts: CZ-NR, A.18.263/B.279. ★
*VXN-2. Parthia La Campagna in C No. 3tio; 4 mvts.   2ob 2hn bn.   MS parts: CZ-NR, A.18.266/B.282. ★
VXN-3. Parthia in Dis [E♭]; 4 mvts.   2cl 2hn bn.   MS parts: CZ-Pnm, XXVII.C.60. ★
*VXN-4. Parthia in B[♭]; 3 mvts.   2cl 2hn bn.   MS parts (by Aug. Fibiger): CZ-Pnm, X.C.91. ★
VXN-5. Divertimento A Tre in F [in fact, in B♭]; 4 mvts.   3bthn.   MS parts: CZ-Pnm, XXVII.C.54. ★
VXN-6. Divertimento in G [in fact, in C]; 5 mvts.   3bthn.   MS parts: CZ-Pnm, XXVII.C.55. ★
VXN-7. Divertimento in G [in fact in C]; 4 mvts.   3bthn.   MS parts: CZ-Pnm, XXVII.C.56. ★
*VXN-8. Divertimento in C [in fact in F]; 4 mvts.   3bthn.   MS parts: CZ-Pnm, XXVII.C.57. ★
VXN-9. Divertimento in F [in fact, in B♭]; 4 mvts.   3bthn.   MS parts: CZ-Pnm, XXVII.C.58. ★
VXN-10. IV Ponolesse con Trio.   3bthn.   MS parts: CZ-Pnm, XXVII.C.59. ★

NUNES, Emmanuel *31 Aug 1941, Lisbon*
EXN-1. Dawn Wo; 1971.   fl(pic) a-fl(pic) ob ca cl(E♭) cl b-cl 2hn bn cbn tp tb.
Pm (Jean Jobert: Paris, 1974), score.

NYSTROEM, Gösta *13 Oct 1890, Silverg - 9 Aug 1966, Göteberg*
GYN-1v. Sommarmusik (Summer music); 1964.   S solo, fl ob cl 2hn bn tp perc celeste harp.
Pm (Ab Nordiske Musikforlaget: Stockholm, 1964), hire score & parts.

*OBERSTEINER, Johann
JXO-1v. Harmonie Feste Messe, Op. 237.   SATB, fl 2cl 2hn 4tp 2tb euph 2bomb timp organ.
MS: A-Wn, Mus.Hs.23,272.

*ODSTRČIL, Karel *1930, Valašském Meziříčí*
KYO-1. Stříbrná kniha [The Silver Book], Concerto for trombone.
Solo trombone *(or horn, bass clarinet, bassoon)*, fl ob 2cl 2hn bn 2tp tb tu timp xly vib perc.
Pm (Český hudební fond: Prague, 1975), hire score & parts.

ÖSTERLING, Ulf *4 Dec 1948, Sweden*
UXO-1. et parmi les piliers d'arabes [sic]; 1992.   2fl 2ob 2cl 2hn 2bn 2tp tb tu db.
MS score: The composer c/o S-Sic.

*OESTREICH (Östreich, Ostreich), Carl *(1800)*
CXO-1. Sinfonie; in E♭, 4 mvts.   fl(E♭)+terz-fl cl(E♭) 4cl(B♭) 2hn 2bn 2tp klappen-hn(B♭) b-tb serp b-dr s-dr, (2ob 2hn a-tb b-tb ad lib).   AutoMS score (26 Oct - 29 Nov 1831) & separate AutoMS score for the ad lib instruments: D-F, Mus.Hs.686. ★
Pm (WINDS: Northridge, CA, pn W-157, c.1981), photocopy of original score & (?modern) parts.
*CXO-2. Fantasie.   terz-fl 2ob cl(E♭) 4cl(B♭) 4hn 2tp a-tb t-tb b-tb serp b-dr s-dr.
AutoMS score & fair-copy score: D-F, Mus.Hs.708.   *A piano sketch for the opening bars can be found at Mus.Hs.713, p. 21.* ★
CXO-3. Polonoise.   2fl(E♭) 2ob 2cl(E♭) 4cl(B♭) 2hn 2bn 2tp a-tb t-tb b-tb serp b-dr s-dr.
AutoMS score: D-F, Mus.Hs.712. ★
CXO-4. Moderato, in A♭ & Ecos[saise].   fl(E♭) cl(E♭) 4cl(B♭) 2hn 2bn tp a-tb t-tb b-tb serp b-dr s-dr.
AutoMS score: D-F, Mus.Hs.712. ★
CXO-5. Walzer; in E♭.   fl(E♭) cl(E♭) 4cl(B♭) 2hn 2bn tp a-tb t-tb b-tb serp b-dr s-dr.
AutoMS score: D-F, Mus.Hs.712. ★
CXO-6. Octet, (1831).   fl 2cl 2hn 2bn tp.   MS parts: D-F, Mus.Hs.716.
CXO-7. Adagio; in E♭.   fl 2cl 2hn bn.   MS parts: D-F, Mus.Hs.750/5. ★
*CXO-8. [untitled Sextet]; in B♭, 3 mvts.   2cl 2hn 2bn.   MS parts: D-F, Mus.Hs.674, (2 sets of pts). ★
CXO-9.1. [untitled Sextet]; in B♭, 8 mvts.   fl bthn 3hn b-tb.
AutoMS score (Nos. 5 - 8) & MS parts: D-F, Mus.Hs.749, (the flute pt. for Nos. 5 - 8 only, is in a different hand & on different paper and may be a later addition).   ★
CXO-9.2. Allegretto [additional 9th mvt added to the pts of CXO-9.1].   fl bthn 3hn b-tb.
MS parts: D-F, Mus.Hs.749, No. [9]. ★
CXO-10.1. [untitled sextet]; in C, 4 mvts.   bthn 3hn b-tb.   AutoMS score (mvt 4 only) & MS parts: D-F, Mus.Hs.750/2. *The 4th mvt, Adagio (CXO-10.2), has been added to the parts at a later date.* ★
CXO-10.2. Adagio; in C.   fl bthn 3hn b-tb.   AutoMS score & MS parts (CXO-10.1): D-F, Mus.Hs.750/2. ★
CXO-11. [untitled sextet]; in C, 2 mvts.   fl bthn 3hn b-tb.   MS parts: D-F, Mus.Hs.750/9. ★
CXO-12. Horn-musik [headtitle: "Quintetto"]; in C minor, 3 mvts.   (titlepage lists:) fl 3hn posthorn b-tb; (parts present: bthn, hn I, hn III, hn IV.   MS parts: D-F, Mus.Hs.750/4, (?incomplete). ★
CXO-13. [untitled quintet]; in C, 3 - 4 mvts.   fl bthn 3hn.   MS parts: D-F, Mus.Hs.750/3. *The 4th mvt, (Common time without tempo marking), has been added at a later date to the flute part only.* ★
CXO-14. [untitled quintet]; in C, 5 mvts.   bthn 3hn b-tb.   MS pts: D-F, Mus.Hs.750/1. *See also: CXO-17.* ★
CXO-15. untitled quintet]; in C, 3 mvts.   bthn hn(I)/posthorn hn(II) hn(III) b-tb.   MS pts: D-F, Mus.Hs.750/8. ★
CXO-16. [untitled quartet]; in F, 3 mvts.   bthn 3hn.   MS parts: D-F, Mus.Hs.750/6, (?complete). *Mvts 2 & 3 appear to have been added at a later date.* ★
CXO-17. [untitled quartet]; in C, 6 mvts.   bthn 3hn.   MS parts: D-F, Mus.Hs.750/7. *Mvt 6 is the same as the mvt 2 of CXO-10.* ★

CXO-1m. [collection of 6 works, Nos. 1 - 4, 6 for Harmonie, No. 5 for orchestra].
fl ob cl(E♭) 4cl(B♭) 2hn 2bn tp a-tb t-tb b-tb serp b-dr s-dr. AutoMS score: D-F, Mus.Hs.712. ★
    1.1m. Marsch (& Trio). 1.2m. Marsch & Walzer. 1.3m. Allegro risoluto (& Trio).
    1.4m. Marsch (& Trio). 1.4m. Marsch (& Trio). 1.5m. Marsch *(for orchestra).* 1.6m. Marsch.
CXO-2m. [2] Marsch; both in C. fl 2ob 2hn bn. AutoMS score: D-F, Mus.Hs.712. ★
CXO-1t. Trauermarsch; in A♭.   cl 4hn(A♭, F) 2klappenhorn a-tb t-tb b-tb.
Contemporary MS parts & modern MS score: D-F, Mus.Hs.713. ★

*OHNEWALD, Joseph *(1781 - 1856)*
JYD-1v. Deutsche Messe, auch für die Frohnleichnams Prozession. CATB, 2cl 2hn bass.
MS parts ("Scripsimus ad chorum Bonac[ellensem] 1847"): D-Tl, Gg 285. ★

*OLBRICH, Fl. [?Florian] *(1810)*
FXO-1. Erinnerung an Schlawentzitz, Walzer; in E♭.   fl 2ob 2cl 4hn(E♭, F) 2bn tp tb db.
AutoMS score: D-NEhz, 140. MS parts: D-NEhz, 133, No. 31. ★
FXO-2. Die Gemüthlichen Walzer; in E♭.   fl 2ob 2cl 2hn 2bn "cor chromatica" b-tb db.
MS parts: D-NEhz, 109, No. 1.
FXO-3. Andeken an Fürstenstein, Walzer; in F. fl 2ob 2cl 2hn 2bn "cor chromatica" b-tb db.
MS parts: D-NEhz, 109, No. 2.
FXO-4. Pollonaise; in E♭.   fl 2ob 2cl 2hn 2bn "cor chromatica" b-tb db. MS parts: D-NEhz, 109, No. 3.
FXO-5. Heimath-Galopp; in B♭.   fl 2ob 2cl 2hn 2bn "cor chromatica" b-tb db. MS pts: D-NEhz, 109, No. 4. ★
FXO-6. Galopp; in E♭.   fl 2ob 2cl 2hn 2bn "cor chromatica" b-tb db. MS parts: D-NEhz, 109, No. 5.
FXO-7. Cavalerie=Galopp; in E♭.   fl 2ob 2cl 2hn 2bn tb db.   MS parts: D-NEhz, 133, No. 13.
FXO-8. Ländler; in Bb.   fl 2ob 2cl 2hn 2bn b-tb db.   MS parts: D-NEhz, 133, No. 15.
FXO-1a. Lanner: Die Kosenden, Op. 128. fl 2ob 2cl 2hn 2bn b-tb db.   MS parts: D-NEhz, 133, No. 11.

*OLIVER, Stephen *3 March 1950, Chester - 30 April 1992, London*
SXO-1. Ricercare 2, 1981. 2ob 2cl 2hn 2bn cbn.
Pm (Novello: London, c.1985), score (pn 12 0607 09) & parts (pn 12 0607 01).
*SXO-2. Character Pieces for wind octet derived from Metastasio's *La Clemenza di Tito,* 7 mvts.
2ob 2cl 2hn 2bn.
Pm (Novello & Co: London, 1991), hire score & parts.

*OLSSON, Sture *3 Sept 1919 - 6 Jan 1987, Sweden*
SYO-1. Divertimento; 1974. 3fl 2ob 3cl 2hn 2bn 2tp 3tb timp 2perc. MS score: S-Sic.
SYO-2. Billstroem Blues; 1983. 2fl 2ob 2cl t-sax 3hn 2bn 3tp db drums. MS score: The composer c/o S-Sic.

OLTHIUS, Kees *1940 (Member of the Netherlands Wind Ensemble)*
KXO-1. Marionetten; 1972. 2fl 2ob 2cl 3hn 2bn 2tp.
Pm (Donemus: Amsterdam, 1973), score.

OOSTEN, Roel van *1958, Netherlands*
RVO-1. Gioco; 1979. fl(pic) 3cl b-cl hn bn harp 2perc.
Pm (Donemus: Amsterdam, c.1979), score & parts.

OPPO, Franco *1935, Italy*
FYO-1. Musica.   2ob 2cl 2hn 2bn.
Pm (Edipan Edizione Musicale: Roma, sd).

*ORDOÑEZ (Ordonitz), Carlo d' *19 April 1734, Vienna - 6 Sept 1786, Vienna*
CDO-1. Notturno; in F, 5 mvts, (Brown IIIa:F1). 2ob 2ca 2hn 2bn.
MS parts: CZ-K, No.260.K.II, (missing ca I). *Possibly transcribed by Went.* ★

ORGAN, Robert J. *1895 - 1967, USA*
RJO-1. Divertimento. 3ob ca 3bn.   Pm (Rebo Music Publications: Denver, 1956).
RJO-2. Maulawiyah: Dancing Dervish. 3ob ca 3bn.   Pm (Rebo Music Publications: Denver, 1956).
RJO-3. Suite petite. 3ob ca 3bn.   Pm (Rebo Music Publications: Denver, 1956).
RJO-4. Air & Variations. 2ob 2bn.   Pm (Rebo Music Publications: Denver, 1956).
RJO-5. Serenade to a Young Lady. 2ob 2bn.   Pm (Rebo Music Publications: Denver, 1956).
RJO-6. In a Garden. 2ob 2bn.   Pm (Rebo Music Publications: Denver, 1959).

ORR, Buxton Daeblitz *18 April 1924, Glasgow*
BXO-1. Sonata per dieci; 1967. pic fl ob ca cl b-cl 2hn 2bn. MS score: GB-Gsma.

*OSBORNE, Nigel *23 June 1948, Manchester*
*NXO-1. Albanian Nights. 2fl 2ob 2cl 2hn 2bn *(for period instruments).*
Pm (Universal Edition: London, 1991), hire score & parts.

*OSCHMANN, ( ) *(?1800)*
XXO-1. Variations über Die Flasche.   fl cl(E♭) 3cl(B♭) 2hn 2bn 2tp b-tb serp b b-dr.
MS parts: D-DT, Mus-n 1876.

*OSSWALD, Paul Anton *(1790), (active 1815-1830s, St Thomas Monastery, Brno)*
*PAO-1v. Cantate zur namensfeyer des Hochwürden und Hochgelehten Herrn Friedrich Franz verdienstvollen
Professor der Physik aus Philosophischen Institute zu Brünn. SATB, 2cl 2hn 2bn cbn 2tp.
MS parts: CZ-NŘ, A.17.819/A.169. *This piece was probably borrowed for the Nová Říše Harmonie but never
returned to the Augustinian monastery at Brno.* ★
PAO-1a. [Anon]: 5 Allegmannes [sic] (with trios), c.1827. 2ob 2cl 2hn 2bn cbn 2tp.
MS parts: CZ-Bm(au), A.35.198. *"Arrangées", possibly also composed by Osswald.*
PAO-2a. [Anon]: Deutsche Nro. 3, (Intro & 3 Deutsche). 2ob 2cl 2hn 2bn cbn 2tp.
MS parts: CZ-Bm(au), A.35.197, ("übersetzt v. A. Osswald"). *Possibly by Schiedermayr, See below: PAO-8a.*
PAO-3a. Boieldieu: La Dame blanche, overture & 11 mvts. 2ob 2cl 2hn 2bn cbn 2tp.
MS parts (1828): CZ-Bm(au), (1 Partie) A.40.152, (2 Partie) A.40.153, (7 mvts). *Partie 1, No. 1 (Marsch &
Trio) has been added to all parts at a later date.*

PAO-4a. Mozart: Don Giovanni, overture. 2ob 2cl(C) 2hn 2bn cbn 2tp. MS pts (1828): CZ-Bm(au), A.40.158.
PAO-5a. Mozart: Die Zauberflöte, (Theil 1) overture & 6 mvts, (Theil 2) 6 mvts. 2ob 2cl 2hn 2bn cbn 2tp.
MS parts (1828): CZ-Bm(au), (Theil 1) A.35.193, (Theil 2) A.40.160.
PAO-6a. Osswald: L'uomo Négro (Der schwarz Mann), (Theil 1) overture & 9 mvts, (Theil 2) overture & 5
mvts, (Theil 3) 5 mvts. 2ob 2cl(C) 2hn 2bn cbn 2tp.
MS parts: CZ-Bm(au),(Theil 1) A.35.199, (Theil 2) A.18.380, (Theil 3), A.35.200.
PAO-7a. Rossini: Il Barbiere di Siviglia, overture. 2ob 2cl(C) 2cl(A) 2hn 2bn cbn 2tp b-tb.
MS parts: CZ-Bm(au), A.37.346.
PAO-8a. Schiedermayr: Deutsche Nro 2. Scoring incomplete, here only: ob I & II, cl(C).
MS parts: CZ-Bm(au), A.35.229.

OSTERMAYR, Johann Baptist, *a S. Emeran*
JBO-1v. Domine ad adjuvandum. CATB, 2ob 2cl 2hn 2bn 2tp(clar) organ(bc-fig).
MS parts: D-B, Mus.ms.16385. ★

OTTEN, Ludwig *24 Feb 1914, Zandvoort*
LXO-1. Divertimento No. 3. fl 2ob 2cl 2hn 2bn.
Pm (Donemus: Amsterdam, 1964), score & parts.
LXO-2. Suite. 2ob 2hn 2bn.
Pm (Donemus: Amsterdam, c.1953), score & parts.

*OTTERLOO, Willem van *27 Dec 1907, Winterswilk - 27 July 1978, Melbourne*
*WVO-1. Symphonietta, 1943. pic 2fl 2ob ca 2cl b-cl 4hn 2bn cbn.
Pm (Donemus: Amsterdam, 1948), score.

*OZI, Étienne *9 Dec 1754, Nîmes - 5 Aug 1813, Paris*
EXO-1m. Pas de manoeuvre ou Rondeau; P.2292. 2pic 2cl 2hn 2bn tp serp.
Pc (Mag de mus fêtes nat: Paris, prairial an II, 1794), liv 3, No. 4, pts: F-Pn, (2 copies), H2. 3,4, Vm7 7034. ★
EXO-2m. Pas de manoeuvre ou Rondeau; P.2319. 2pic 2cl 2hn 2bn tp serp.
Pc (Mag de mus fêtes nat: Paris, ventôse an III, 1795), liv 12: No. 4, parts: F-Pn, H2. 12. ★
*EXO-1mv. Hymne à l'Hymen pour la célébration des mariages. Solo voice, 2cl 2hn 2bn.
Pc (Rec des époques: Paris, post-1797), liv. 2, No. 11, score: F-Pn, H2. 15,11. ★
EXO-1a. Nouvelle Suite de pieces d'harmonie Contenant des Ouvertures, Airs et Ariettes d'Opera et Opera
comiques [sic]. 2cl(C) 2hn 2bn.
Pc (Boyer, Le Menu: Paris, c.1784 - 1791), RISM [O 321], Nos. 1 - 32, parts: D-DS, (probably lost in World
War II); F-Pn, D. 16.233. (Nos. 6), Vm7 6956, (Nos. 19 & 20); S-Uu, Utl.inst.mus.tr. 138 - 141, Nos. 1 - 11,
(Nos. 17, 18, 20 - 22, 24, 26 - 30, 32; missing cl II, hn II, with the overpasted printed imprint slip of Imbault,
dating from c.1794 - 1799).
    1.6/1a. Champein: La Mélomanie, overture, No. 1. **1.6**/2a. Sacchini: Renaud, 2 airs, Nos. 2 & 5.
        1.6/3a. Grétry: Colinette à la cour, air, duo, air, duo, Nos. 3, 4, 6 - 8.
    I.17/1a. Piccinni: Pénélope, overture & air de danse, Nos. 1, 8.
        1.17/2a. Dalayrac: L'Amant Statue, 6 mvts, Nos. 2 - 7.
    1.18/1a. Grétry: Richard Cœur de Lion, overture & 5 mvts, Nos. 1 - 6. 2cl(C) 2hn 2bn.
        1.18/2a. Dalayrac: La Dot, romance ("Vous que je viens de cueiller pour elle", No. 7.
        1.18/3a. Pleyel: (B.308iii), Finale de Quatours de Pleyel, No. 8.
    1.19/1a. Dalayrac: Nina, overture & 4 mvts. **1.19**/2a. F.A.D. Philidor: Thémistocle, 1 mvt.
        1.19/3a. Chardiny: Le Pouvoir de la Nature, "O moment délicieux".
        1.19/4a. Chapelle: L'Herueux Dépit, "Toujours de tes rigueurs".
    1.20/1a. Deshayes: Le Faux Serment, overture & 8 mvts (= RISM [D 1748]). 2cl(C) 2hn 2bn.
    1.21/1a. Paisiello: Il Re Teodoro in Venezia, overture & 4 mvts, Nos. 1 - 4, 6.
        1.21/2a. Anon: L'Amour Turc, 3 mvts, Nos. 5, 7, 8.
    1.22/1a. Vogel: Le Toison d'or, overture & 4 mvts, Nos. 1, 2, 4 - 6.
        1.22/2a. Gardel: Gavotte d'un des ballets de Gardel, No. 3.
        1.22/3a. Anon: L'Amour Turc, duo & air, Nos. 7, 8.
    1.24/1a. Haydn: Symphony in D (Hob. I/86i) [here in C], mvt 1 only, No. 1. 2cl(C) 2hn 2bn.
        1.24/2a. Salieri: Tarare (Axur, Rè d'Ormus), 3 mvts, Nos. 2, 3, 8.
        1.24/3a. Sacchini: Œdipus à Colonne, duo, gavotte & air, Nos. 4 - 6.
        1.24/4a. Dalayrac: Renaud d'Ast, air, No. 7.
    1.26/1a. F.A.D. Philidor: La belle Esclave, overture (2 parts) & 1 mvt, Nos. 1+2, 4. 2cl(C) 2hn 2bn.
        1.26/2a. Dalayrac: Renaud d'Ast, 4 mvts, Nos. 3, 5 - 7.
    1.27/1. Ozi: Marche. 1/27/2. Ozi: Air de Danse Cosaque. 1.27/3. Ozi: Gavotte. 1.27/4. Ozi: Marche.
        1.27/5. Ozi: Air de Danse Pas de Deux. 1.27/6. Ozi: Allemande. 1.27/7. Ozi: Marche.
        1.27/8. Ozi: Air de Danse Pas Russe. 1.27/9. Ozi: Allemande. 1.27/10. Ozi: Marche.
        1.27/11. Ozi: Air de Danse Provançal [sic]. 1.27/12. Ozi: Air de Danse tambourin. ★
    1.28/1. Ozi: Grande Marche. 1.28/2. Ozi: Air de Danse. 1.28/3. Ozi: Air de Danse. 1.28/4. Ozi: Marche.
        1.28/5. Ozi: Air de Danse Rondo. 1.28/6. Ozi: Pas de Maneuvre [sic]. 1.28/7. Ozi: Grande Marche.
        1.28/8. Ozi: Pastoral. 1.28/9. Ozi: Pas de Maneuvre [sic]. 1.29/10. Ozi: Marche.
        1.28/11. Ozi: Pas Redouble [sic]. 1.28/12. Ozi: Pas de Maneuvre [sic]. ★
    1.29/1a. Vogel: Démophon, overture & 4 mvts, Nos. 1 - 4, 7.
        1.29/2a. Méhul: Euphrosine, quatuor & duo, Nos. 5, 6.
    1.30/1a. Dalayrac: La Soirée orageuse, overture & 2 mvts, Nos. 1, 4, 7.
        1.30/2a. Giroult [= F. Giroust]: Petit chœur, No. 2. 1.30/3a. Méhul: Euphrosine, 3 mvts, Nos. 3, 5, 6.
    1.32/1a. Grétry: Pierre le Grand, overture. 1.32/2a. Trietto [?Tritto]: [?La Virgine del Sol], duetto, No. 2.
        1.32/3a. R. Kreutzer: Paul et Virgine, 3 mvts, Nos. 3, 5, 6. 1.32/4a. Paisiello: Nina, duetto, No. 4.
        1.32/5a. Viotti: Polaca [sic] di la Cosa Rara [inserted in Paris version of Martin y Soler's opera], No. 7.
        1.32/6a. Martín y Soler: Una cosa rara, aria, No. 8.
        1.32/7a. Rouget de Lisle: Marche des Marseillois [sic]. No. 9.
EXO-2a. Méhul: L'Irato, N°. 1. Ouverture & [6] Airs. 2cl(C & B♭) 2hn 2bn.
Pc (Chez Pleyel: Paris, pn 154, 1803), RISM [O 322], parts: CH-Gpu, Ib.4843, (2 copies).

PABLO COSTALES, Luis Alfonso de *28 Jan 1930, Bilbao*
LDP-1. Credo, 1976.   2fl 2ob 2cl 2hn 2bn.
Pm (Suvini Zerboni: Milano, pn S8243Z, 1977), score & parts.

***PACAK (Patzek), František** *(?1800)*
FXP-1v. Statio[nes] IVor [sic: quatuor] de Corporis Christi.   CATB, fl 2cl(C) 2hn bn 2tp timp.
MS parts (by Josef Leden, from Nový Brdžov): CZ-Pnm, XIII.E.163, (with later pts for 2vl, in fact doubling the 2cl; an even later set of different parts for 2vl vla & basso are also present).   ★

PACKER, George (Leonard) *28 Oct 1948, Philadelphia*
GLP-1. Octet in 4 Acts.   2fl 2ob 2cl 2bn.
Pm (International Double Reed Society: Indianola, Iowa), copy of MS parts.

***PAER, Ferdinando** *1 June 1771, Parma - 3 May 1839, Paris*
FYP-1. La douce Victoire; (sometimes cited as "Fantaisie").   Piano, 2fl 2hn bn.
Pc (Schlesinger: Paris), parts: *untraced.*
FYP-1m. [4] Grand Marches Exécutées dans les Galeries du Museum au moment du passage de Leurs MM. JJ. et RR. Le Jour de la Bénédiction Nuptiale de leur Mariage.   pic 2ob cl(F) 2cl(C) 2hn 2bn 2tp b-tb serp b-dr.
(No. 3: pic 2ob 2cl(B♭: "Petite Clarinette en Si ♭" [sic]) 2cl(C) 2hn 2bn 2tp b-tb serp b-dr).
Pc (Chez Imbault: Paris, 1810), parts: F-Pn, Vm27 3294 (1 - 4); GB-Lbl, (2 copies), h.721.v.(17), i.171.(3).   ★
Pm (Galaxy Music Corp.: New York; Galliard: London, 1965), Nos. 2 & 3, ed. Douglas Townsend, for modern (large) concert band, score, condensed score.
FYP-1v. Offertorium in G, "Quod requiro".   TTBB, 2fl 2ob 2cl 2hn 2bn; (or: 2vl db).
MS parts: CZ-Bm(au), A.19.617.   ★
FYP-1ad. Pièces favoris tiré de l'Opéra Numa Pompilio, sinfonia & 3 mvts.
2ob 2cl 2hn 2bn cbn tp.   MS parts: CZ-Bm(au), A.40.163, (missing cbn; arrargement attributed to Paer). *This is, in fact, Nos. 1, 2, 6 & 10 of Triebensee's arrangement, JZT-48.1a.*

PÄTZIG, Gerhard, (editor)
GDP-1m. Historische Bläsermusik - 25 Militärmärsche des 18. Jahrhunderts.
Performing version based on manuscripts in D-Bds.
Pm: (Bärenreiter: Kassel, etc., 1971), 3 volumes with facsimiles, score & parts.
Nos. 1 - 9 are in Vol. 1, Nos. 10 - 17 in Vol. 2, and Nos. 18 - 25 in Vol. 3.
   1.1m. Herzögin Philippa Charlotte von Braunschweig: Marsch 2, E♭, 1751.   2ob bn tp.   (= CBP-2m)
   1.2m. Anon: Prinz Ferdinand Regt. Marsch, c.1790.   2ob 2cl bn tp.
   1.3m. Anon: Prinz Heinrich Regt., c.1790.   2ob 2cl bn tp.
   1.4m. G. Bachmann: Marsch No. 2, in B♭.   2ob 2cl 2bn tp.   (= GAB-2m)
   1.5m. H. König: Marsch in B♭.   2ob 2cl 2bn tp.   (= MZK-1m)
   1.6m. Mozart, arranged Anon: Figaro Marsch, post-1786.   2ob 2cl bn tp.
   1.7m. Roetsche, senior: Marsch, 1799.   2ob 2cl 2bn tp.   (= ZYR-3m)
   1.8m. Anon: Dessauer Marsch, c.1705, reconstructed by Pätzig for 2ob bn.
   1.9m. Anon: Marsch (from the period of Friedrich II), reconstructed Pätzig for 2ob bn tp.
   1.10m,1.11m. Anon: Coburger Josias-Marsches; Jung Bornstedt Regt, 1792. (No. 1: 2cl 2hn 2bn tp;
      No. 2: 2cl 2hn bn tp).
   1.12m. J.G. Naumann: Marsch No. 1 von Kalckstein Regt.   2cl 2hn 2bn tp (doubling hn I).   (= JGN-2m)
   1.13m. J.G. Naumann: Marsch No. 2 von Kalckstein Regt.   ob 2cl 2hn 2bn.   (= JGN-3m)
   1.14m. J.C. Bach: 1st Bataillon [sic] des Gardes-Regt, Hannover.   2ob 2cl 2hn 2bn.   (= JCB-1m)
   1.15m. J.C. Bach: 2nd Bataillon [sic] des Gardes-Regt, Hannover.   2ob 2cl 2hn 2bn.   (=JCB-2m)
   1.16m. Ehmann: Marsch in E♭, (c.1800).   2cl 2hn 2bn tp.   (XZE-2m)
   1.17m. Attributed to Friedrich II: Der Hohenfriedberger Ansbach-Bayreuth-Dragoner Regt. (Reconstructed by
      Pätzig for 2ob 2cl 2hn 2bn tp.)   (= TGF-2m)
   1.18m. Schoenfeld: March for the Army of the Rhine, 1792.   ob 2cl bn tp.   (= ZFS-1m)
   1.19m. G. Bachmann: Marsch No. 1, in B♭.   2cl bn tp.   (= GAB-4m)
   1.20m(-1.25m). M. König: 6 Halberstädtische Märsche.   ob 2cl 2bn tp.   (= MZK-2m)

PAHOR, Karol *6 Aug 1896, Vrdela Kraj Trsta - 25 Nov 1974, Ljubljana*
KXP-1. Istrijanka (The lady from Istria), 15 dance miniatures.   fl fl(pic) 2ob 2cl 2hn 2bn 3tp 3tb timp 5perc.
Pm (Savez Kompozitora: Ljubljana, 1956; reprinted by Društvo slovenskih skladateljev: Ljubljana, 1964), score.

***PAISIELLO, Giovanni** *9 May 1740, Roccaforzata - 5 June 1816, Naples*
***GXP-1.** Serenata in C; 2 mvts.   2ob cl 2hn (2)bn guitar. *This, in fact, follows the Preludio opening Paisiello's opera, Elvira, (Naples, 12 Jan 1794). For other excerpts & contemporary scores, see infra: GXP-1e.*
Pm (Suvini Zerboni: Milano, 1985), ed. Giovanni Carli Ballola, score (pn S.8000Z) & parts (pn S.8001Z).   ★
***GXP-2(-5).** 4 Divertimentos; all in E♭, all 1 mvt.   2fl 2cl 2hn 2bn.
MS score (mid-19th century): RF-Ssc, Ф N674 САНТИНИ Ф N142.   ★
MS piano reduction (GXP-2): RF-Ssc, Арх Н ф ИНДЕЙЗЕНА Ф 816ОП N858, (incomplete & inaccurate).
   GXP-2. La Diana.   **GXP-3.** Il Mezzo Giorno.   **GXP-4.** Il Tramontar del Sole.   **GXP-5.** L'Andare a Letto.
***GXP-6(-17).** Docici Divertimenti, (E♭, E♭, E♭, B♭, B♭, E♭, E♭, C, A, D, D, D; all 1 mvt).
Nos. 1 - 3, 5 - 7, 9 - 12: 2fl 2cl 2hn bn; No. 4: 2cl bn; No. 8: 2fl bn.
MS score (mid-19th century): RF-Ssc, Ф N674 САНТИНИ фN143.   ★
Pm (Nos. 1, 2, 4, 6, 8, 10, 12:) (Muzika: Leningrad, pn 1455, 1973), ed. A.G. Aslatozov, score & pts.
Pm (Muzika: Leningrad, pn 2109, 1977), ed. A.G. Aslatozov, score & parts.
***GXP-1m(-3m).** Marche [in F]; Marche [in C]; Pas redoublé [in C].   fl 2cl(C) 2hn 2bn tp b-tb serp.
Pc (in M.J. Gebauer: Nouveau Journal de Musique Militaire, Nos. 1 - 3:) (Le Duc, Paris, 1808 - 1810), parts: CH-Zz, AMG XIII 3070 a-i. *Possibly arranged by M.J. Gebauer.*   ★
GXP-1e. Nitteti, (St Petersburg, c.28 [17 old style] Jan 1777), Act I, No. 6.1: March in D.
2fl 2ob 2cl 2hn 2bn 2tp timp cym(s) tri.
AutoMS score: I-Nc, Rari 2.8.21/22.   ★
MS score: D-B, Mus.Ms.16614; F-Pn, D. 10195 (1, 2); G-OB, Tenbury Wells 453 - 455.

*GXP-2e. Achille in Sciro, (St Petersburg, 6 Feb [26 Jan old style] 1778), Act I, No. 4: March. 2fl 2cl 2hn 2bn. AutoMS score: I-Nc, Rari 3.4.1/2. ★
MS scores: D-B, Mus.Ms.16616; F-Pn, (Version 2), D 10128 (1 - 2); GB-Lbl, Add. 32066; GB-Ob, Tenbury Wells 450 (= Act I); RF-Mcm, Φ187 11a-б, (Acts I & III); RF-Stob; US-Wc, M1500 P23 A2.
*GXP-3.1e(-3.3e). Alcide al Bivio, (St Petersburg, 6 Dec [25 Nov old style] 1780).
AutoMS score: I-Nc, Rari 3.3.22/23. MS score: B-Bc, 2259 K; GB-Lcm, MS 436; GB-Ob, Tenbury Wells 459; RF-Sit, Φ2опед 744. MS parts: RF-Stob, I 1 P126.5 O Alc 23375.
   3.1e. Scene 2.3: Accompanied Recitative ("Grazie, o numi del ciel") & March in C.
     strings + 2fl 2ob 2bn ("sopra il teatro"). ★
   3.2e. Scene 4.2: March in D. 2pic("ottavini") 2fl 2ob 2hn 2bn 2timp s-dr cym tri. *Reused, for GXP-6e.* ★
   3.3e. Scene 4.4: March in D [= reprise, probably without 2pic s-dr tri].
*GXP-4.1e(-4.5e). Il Mondo della Luna, (St Petersburg, 5 Oct [24 Sept old style] 1783).
AutoMS score: I-Nc, 2.8.19/20. MS score: A-Wn, Mus.Hs.17,806; RF-Ltob, I 1 P126.5 п M.d.L. 3024; US-Wc, M 1500 P23 M8 case, (copy made in 1923 from the A-Wn source).
   4.1e. Scene 9.2: Orchestral ritornello. 2cl 2hn bn + 2cl 2hn bn. ★
   4.2e. Scene 11.2: Accompanied Recitative ("Io resto stupefatto"): Ecclittico with echoes (B voices).
     B solo, cl solo, vl solo, orchestra: 2fl 2ob + strings, with 4cl 4hn 2bn "sopra il teatro".
   4.3e. Scene 11.2: Aria ("Che mondo amabile"). orchestra: 2fl 2ob + strings, with 4cl 4hn 2bn "sopra il teatro".
   4.4e. Scene 12: Marcia sopra il teatro; in E♭. 4cl 2hn 2bn.
   4.5e. Scene 15: Aria (Quà la mano"). 2cl 2hn 2bn + 2cl 2hn 2bn (in orchestra) + strings. ★
GXP-5.1e. Il Re Teodoro in Venezia, (Vienna, 23 Aug 1784), Act II, No. 8: Chorus ("Chi brama viver lieto"). Lisetta & Teodoro, Belisa & Acmet, Bafforio & Taddeo, Chorus of gondoliers, 2fl 2ob 2hn 2bn.
MS scores: A-Wgm, (Q 1808); A-Wn, Mus.Hs.17,804; B-Bc, 2262 K; D-HR, HR III 4 1/2 4° 76; D-Mbs, Mus.Mss.3057; DK-Kk, MU 7502.0636 CI 295; F-Pn, (3 copies), D 10205 (1, 2), (shortened version as 5.2e). D. 10206 (1, 2), D. 10208 (1, 2); F-Po, 4008 (1, 2); GB-Lbl, Add. 16076/16077/16078; I-Gc, A.7.3-6; I-PAc, (2 copies) SL 99-102(18433-18436), SL 103-106(10379-10382); I-Pc, ATVa 33/I-II; I-OS, Mus.Musiche.B.6531-6532; I-Vnm, (2 copies), It.cl.IV.cod.814/815/816, It.cl.IV.cod.1764/1765(11361/11362); US-CAe, Mus 779.8.651; US-Wc, M1550 P23 R4, (shortened version as 5.2e). ★
GXP-5.2e. Il Re Teodoro in Venezia, Act II, No. 8: Chorus (as GXP-5.1e but shortened version). Same scoring.
AutoMS score: I-Nc, Rari 3.2.1/2, (also replaces No. 26). MS score: A-Wn, (2 copies), Mus.Hs.25,282, K.T.440; B-Bc, S.G.H. Coll I 35; D-B, (2 copies), Mus.Ms.16617/1, Mus.Ms.16617, (without text for 5.2e); F-Po, A 322 (I-II); I-Mc, Part.Tr.M.301; RF-Stob, I 1 P126.5 п R.T. 3103.
GXP-6e. Pirro, (Naples, 12 Jan 1787). March in D. 2pic 2fl 2ob 2hn 2bn 2timp s-dr cym(s) tri.
MS score: B-Bc, 2268 K; F-Pn, (4 copies), Vm4 67, Vm468, D. 10199 (1, 2), D. 10200 (1, 2); I-Vnm, It.cl.IV.cod.831/832(10237/10238). *Note: this is, in fact, GXP-3.2e; many scores of Pirro omit this march.* ★
GXP-7.1e, 7.2e. Fedra, (Naples, 1 Jan 1788). AutoMS score: I-Nc, Rari 2.10.14/15.
MS score: A-Wn, Mus.Hs.9986; D-B, Mus.MS.16619; F-Pn, D 10167 (1,2); P-La, 45-III-35/36, (omits 7.1e).
   7.1e. Act II, No. 2.2. Marcia di sopra il teatro; in E♭. 4cl 2hn 2bn. ★
   7.2e. Act II, No. 6.1. March in D. 2cl 2hn 2bn drums. ★
GXP-8.1e, 8.2e. Catone in Utica, (Naples, 5 Feb 1789). MS score: F-Pn, D. 10145 (1, 2).
   8.1e. Act III, No. 2.1. March in D. 2ob 2cl 2hn 2bn s-dr. ★
   8.2e. Act II, No. 2.2. March (= 2.1e) & Chorus in, "Non più affenni". 4cl 2hn 2bn s-dr, SATB chorus.
GXP-9e. La Locanda, (London, 16 June 1791), Act II, No. 12.March & accompanied recitative, "Ma zitto parmi budir dell' istrumenti". STB, 2ob 2cl 2hn 2bn s-dr(s). AutoMS score: I-Nc, Rari 2.8.5/6. ★
GXP-10.1e(-10.3e). Elfrida, (Naples, 4 Nov 1792). *See also supra: GXP-1.*
AutoMS score: I-Nc, Rari 2.10.8/9.
MS score: B-Bc, 2273 K, (omits No. 11); F-Pn, D. 10159 (1, 2), (omits Nos. 10, 19, 20); GB-Lbl, Add. 32068, (No. 11 only with the note, "Si replica la marcia"); GB-OB, Tenbury Wells 472.473; I-Nc, Rari cornicione 38, (includes only Nos. 19 & 20); I-PAc, SL 109 - 110 (18135 - 18136); I-Rmass, Mus.MS. 284; I-Rsc, A.MSS 3701/3702; I-Vnm, It.cl.IV.cod.783/784 (10189/10190); S-St, Ital.partitur E3, (omits No. 11); US-Bp, XX M340.1.
   10.1e. Act I, No. 3: March; in C. 2ob 2cl 2hn 2bn. (Reprised as No. 10 in D, & No. 11 in C).
   10.2e. Act II, No. 1 (No. 19): Military March; in D. 2fl 2ob 2cl 2hn 2bn 2tp 2timp. ★
   10.3me. Act II, No. 2 (No. 20): Suono la battagila; in D. 2fl 2ob 2cl 2hn 2bn 2tp 2timp. ★
GXP-11e. Elvirda, (Naples, 12 Jan 1794): Act I, No. 10, March in C. 2ob 2cl 2hn 2bn b-dr tri, tamburo Albanese, small cyms. AutoMS score (Version 2): I-Nc, Rari 2.10.10/11. MS score (Version 1): B-Bc, 16665 K; F-Pn, D.10160; I-PAc, SL 107-108 (18274-18275); I-Vcm, It.cl.IV.cod.773/774(10179/10180); US-Bp, XX M402b.9. ★
GXP-12e. Didone Abbondonata, (Naples, 4 Nov 1794), Act I, No. 5, March; in C. 2ob 2cl 2hn 2bn b-dr s-dr rattles triangles cymbal. AutoMS score: I-Nc, Rari 3.3.20/21. MS score: A-Wgm, (Q 1818); D-B, Mus.MS.16608/50; F-Pn, D. 10151 (1, 2); GB-Lbl, Add. 32069; I-Rsc, A.MSS.377/378; I-Vnm, It.cl.IV.cod.777/778(10183/10184); US-Bp, XX M51.4. ★
GXP-13e. Andromaca: Act II, No. 9: March, in E♭. 2ob 2cl 2hn 2bn b-dr s-dr. MS score: A-Wn, Mus.Hs.9985; F-Pn, D. 10133 (1, 2), RF-Ssc, Φсобр юсупоВб ix N172/173; RF-Stob, I 1 P126.5 п A 4212.
GXP-1v, 2v. 2 Notturni; No. 1, "Selva romita e oscura", No. 2, "Ah, voi dite erbose sponde".
No. 1: SS, 2fl/cl 2hn [2bn] basso; No. 2: SS, 2cl/vl 2hn [2bn] basso.
MS score: D-B, Mus.ms.16644, No. 4, (No. 2 includes strings); D-Rtt, Paisiello 14, (No. 1 only); GB-Lbl, (3 copies, all in reverse order), R.M.22.k.3, (vls replace cls in GXP-2v), Add. 31731, R.M.22.l.13.(2) (No. 2 only); GB-Lcm, MS 701, Nos. 11 & 14; GB-OB, (4 copies): Tenbury Wells 431 Nos. 1 & 2, Tenbury Wells 449 Nos. 1 & 2, Tenbury Wells 491 No. 5, Tenbury Wells 496 No. 1 (No. 1 only); HR-Zha, XXXVII.32, ("Falli per S.M. Siciliana Nell' Estate 1780"); I-Bc, II-57, (No. 1 only, in D); I-Li, C V 71, (No. 1 only), I-OS, MUS.B.2608; I-Vnm, It.cl.IV.cod.835 (10241), "Composti l'anno 1775"); RF-Ssc, (2 copies),Φ 891 собр юсуповвı x N188, *and* Φ 891 собр юсуповвı x N24; S-Skma, (2 copies), 250-R SN vol.14, T-SE-R Oxenst. vol.15; S-Sk, 831:6; US-SFsc; US-Wc, M1505 A1 Vol 169, (No. 1), M1505 A1 Vol 186 (No. 2). ★
MS vocal score (voice & basso only): F-Pn, D 14680, "Composti per Divertimento Delle Dame Dilettanti di Musica, nell'anno 1778").

MS parts: D-MÜu, P-ai 30, (No. 1 with additional wind parts); D-Rtt, Paisiello 14, (instrument parts only); I-Gl, M.3.18, (No. 2 only); I-Mc, Noseda P.48.37, (with additional parts for 2ob); GB-Lbl, Add. 32149, (arranged for 2fl basso).

*GXP-1ve. Mass in B♭ for Napoleon's coronation, 2 Feb 1804: No. 14, Prayer, Domine salvum fac.
B solo, SSTB chorus, 2 orchestras of: 2fl 2ob 2cl 2hn 2bn 2tp timp b-dr s-dr.
MS score: F-Pn, (2 copies), Rés Vma MS 867, L. 19391 A-B. ★
MS parts: F-Pn, L. 19391 B-Q. *Note: This mvt is* not *in the AutoMS score in I-Nc.*
GXP-2ve. Proserpine, Act I, Scene IV: Chorus of Nymphs, "Les beaux jours et la paix sont revenus ensemble".
SS chorus, 2fl 2cl 2hn (2)bn.
MS score: F-Po, (2 copies) Rés A 386/I-II-III, Rés 386b/I-II-III; F-Pn, Vm2 930.
Pc (Imbault: Paris, pn 182, c.1803), score: A-Wn, M.S. 9121 4°; B-Bc, 1891; D-Hs, M B/2118; E-Mc, Roda 751; F-Pn, D. 10213; F-TLm; GB-Ckc, 107.80 Res; GB-Lbl, (2 copies), G.274.e, Hirsch IV.1575; GB-Lcm, XXIV.D.4; I-Bc, II 51; I-Bsf, Paisiello I-II-III; I-BGc, Sala 32 c.7.22; I-Mc, Part.Tr.298; I-Nc, (Version 1, Rari cornicione 120/121/122 (presentation copy from Imbault to the composer, later presented to King Ferdinand IV of Naples), (Version 6),123/124/125; I-PAc, R-III-2 (6941-6942); I-Rvat; US-Bp, XX M.293.24; US-Cn, Thomas 110, (Version 5 in Italian). ★
*GXP-1mv, 2mv. La Voluntaria. Ode per Marica [&] Marcia per Attacco.
No. 1: SSB chorus, 2ob 2cl 2hn 2bn b-dr s-dr; No. 2: SSTB chorus, 2pic 2ob 2cl 2hn 2bn b-dr s-dr.
MS score: I-Vlevi, CF.B.72, ("In Napoli 1798"); I-Vnm, It.cl.IV.cod.835 (10241). ★
Pc (as "La Voluntaria Marcia Militaire con Attacco, e Coro":) (Presso Luigi Marescalchi: Naples, c.1797), score: US-BE, M1531 P22 V6 caseX.
GXP-1md. Marcia di Paisiello; in B♭.   2cl 2hn 2bn 2tp.   MS parts: I-Rvat, Vat.Mus.148.

*PALKOVSKÝ, Pavel *18 Dec 1939, Zlín*
PQP-1. 3 Studie.   Solo baritone accordion, fl ob 2lc hn bn tp 2tb.
Pm (Český hudební fond: Prague, 1967), hire score & parts.
PQP-2. Sextet, Op. 81.   fl ob 2cl hn bn.
Pm (Český hudební fond: Prague, 1981), hire score & parts.

PÁLSSON, Páll Pampichler *1928, Iceland*
PPP-1. Nonet; 1984.   ob 2cl 2hn 2bn tp.   MS score: IS-Rmic.

*PANIZZA, Giacomo (Jacques) *27 March 1803, Castellazo Bormida - 1 May 1860, Milan*
GYP-1. Sestetto; in E♭, 3 mvts.   fl 2cl 2hn bn.
Pc (Artaria: Vienna, pn 2672, 1822), parts: A-Wgm, VIII 5193; D-Bds; GB-Lbl, h.1507.oo.(1). ★

*PANUFNIK, Sir Andrzej *24 Sept 1914, Warsaw - 27 Oct 1991, London*
AXP-1. Lyric Piece No. 1; 1963.   2cl hn b-cl/bn tp tb.
Pm (Boosey & Hawkes: London, etc., 1966), score & parts.
AXP-2. 5 pieśni ludowych (Five Polish peasant songs, (1940, reconstructed 1945, revised 1959).
Unison sopranos, 2fl cl b-cl.
Pm (Polskie wydawnictwo muzyczne: Kraków, 1946), score (text in Polish, English, French & Russian).
Pm (Boosey & Co.: London, etc., 1961), score (text in Polish & English).

PANWITSCHKA (occasionally given as 'PANOITSCHKA'), ( )
XXP-1. Parthia in Dis [E♭]; 4 mvts.   2cl 2hn 2bn.
MS parts: D-F, Mus.Hs.1559. ★

PARFREY, Raymond *6 May 1928, Harrow, UK*
RXP-1. Melodies for 7.   fl ob 3cl hn bn.
Pm (Cinque Port Music: Deal, UK, 1986).
RXP-2. Four Sketches.   fl 2cl bn/b-cl.
Pm (WOODWINDplus: Louth, Lincolnshire, UK, 1994), score & parts.

*PARISOT, Octave *(?1790)*
OXP-1m. Pas Redoublé Favori de S.A.R. le Duc d'Orléans . . . Dédié a l'Armée Française en Belgique, No. 2.
fl(E♭) cl(E♭) 3cl(B♭) 2hn 2bn tp bugle tb oph/serp b-dr.
Pc (Richault: Paris, pn 2875.R, 1831), parts: CH-Gpu, Ib.4921d; GB-Ljag, (photocopy). ★
OXP-2m. Pas de charge Favori de S.A.R. le Duc de Nemours . . . Dédié au Roi, No. 4.
fl(Eb) cl(E♭) 3cl(B♭) 2hn 2bn tp bugle tb oph/serp b-dr.
Pc (Richault: Paris, pn 2876.R. [2877.R. on parts], 1831), parts: CH-Gpu, Ib.4921c; GB-Ljag, (photocopy). *The titlepage calls for ophicleide but the part is marked "Serpent".* ★

*PAŘÍZEK, Alexis (Alexius) Vincent *1748 - post 1808*
AVP-1. Nocturno in C; 6 mvts.   2ob 2cl 2hn 2bn.   MS parts: CZ-Pnm, XL.C.379. ★
AVP-1m. Marcia militaire in B[♭].   2ob 2cl 2hn 2bn bn(pedale).   MS pts (1808): CZ-Pnm, XL.C.378. ★
*AVP-1v. [4] Messliedern.   CATB, 2fl 2cl 2hn 2bn organ(bc).   MS parts: CZ-PLa(cd), Hu 410. ★
    1.1v. Vor der Wandlung; "Herr deiner Kirche Glieder erfüllen ihr Gebot".
    1.2v. Nach der Wandlung; "O Jesu höchstes Gut wir denken an dein Leiden".
    1.3v. Zun Segen; "Kommet, lobet ohne end."   1.4v. Unter der Wandlung; "Du Segen volles Englebrod".
AVP-2v. Pater noster; in B♭.   CATB, 2cl 2hn 2bn organ.
MS parts: CZ-Pla(ve), Hu 2263 (MS by Jan Lašek, 1867); CZ-Pnm, XLVII.E.14, No. 1, (missing organ). ★

*PARRY, Sir Charles Hubert Hastings, Bart *27 Feb 1848, Bournemouth - 7 Oct 1918, Rustington*
CHP-1. Nonet in B♭, Op. 70; 1870, 4 mvts.   fl ob ob(ca) 2cl 2hn 2bn.
AutoMS score: GB-Lcm, MS 4216.   MS parts: GB-Lcm, MS 4217. ★
Pm (Emerson Edition: Ampleforth, sd), parts.
Pm (Compusic: Amsterdam, pn 215, 1991), score & parts.

*PARRY, John, *Bardd Alaw* *18 Feb 1776, Denbigh - 8 April 1851, London*
We have no locations for the two sets of Welsh airs from 1804 known as "The Ancient Briton's Martial Music" and the "Aeolian Harmonies", apparently arrangements.
JBP-1m. The Barouche Quick Step, Performed by H.R.H. the Duke of York's Band.
(pic) 2fl 2cl 2hn 2bn 2bugle-horns, *or* pic 2fife 2bugle-horns.
Pc (J. Power: London, c. 1815), score: GB-Lbl, g.270.y.(5). ★
*JBP-2m Royal Denbigh Militia March. *One of a series, each bearing the name of an officer of the regiment.*
2fl 2cl 2hn 2bn 2tp serp.
Pm: *Grove V*: "Military Band", p. 769 quotes without source part of the score of one march in F. ★
JBP-1ma. Twelve of Mr J[ames] Hook's most Popular Songs Adapted for a Military Band. 2fl 2cl 2hn 2bn serp.
Pc (Bland & Weller: London, c.1803), parts: GB-Lbl, b.229.a.
　1.1ma. Listen to the Voice of Love.　1.2ma. Lucy Gray [of Allendale].
　1.3ma. Tarry awhile [with me, my Love].　1.4ma. Sweet Kathlane [sic] McCree.　1.5ma. The Match Boy.
　1.6ma. The Celdonian [sic] Laddy.　1.7ma. The Linnet. (Moderato).　1.8ma. She lives in the Valley below.
　1.9ma. The Cottager's Daughter.　1.10ma. The Turtle Dove [Coos round my Cot].
　1.11ma. I never lov'd any, Dear Mary, but you.　1.12ma. A Soldier for Me.

*PARRY-JONES, Gwyn *23 Oct 1946, Cardiff*
GWP-1. Three Course Meal.　2fl 2ob 3cl b-cl 4sax 2hn bn tp tb perc.
Pm (Phylloscopus Publications: Lancaster, UK, pn PP 182, 1996), score & parts.
GWP-1a. Mozart: Fantasia in F, K.594.　2ob 2cl 2hn 2bn cbn.
Pm (Phylloscopus Publications: Lancaster, UK, pn PP 110, 1994), score & parts.
GWP-2a. Mozart: Fantasia in F minor, K.608.　fl 2ob 2cl 2hn 2bn cbn.
Pm (Phylloscopus Publications: Lancaster, UK, pn PP 46, 1991), score & parts.

*PARSCH, Arnošt *12 Feb 1936, Bučovice*
ARP-1. Concerto for Winds, Percussion Instruments and Piano, 1964.
MS score: CZ-Bparsch.

*PASCAL, Claude *19 Feb 1921, Paris*
CXP-1. Octuor, 1944; in A, 4 mvts.　fl fl(pic) ob cl hn 2bn tp.
Pm (Durand: Paris, pn D.&F. 13,254, 1947), score & pts: D-Mbs, 4 Mus.pr. 24668, GB-Lcml; US-PT, M857.P302.

*PASSER, Alois Wolfgang *(1790)*
AWP-1v. 2 Prozessions-Lieder, 1 mit deutsch. und 1 mit latein. Texte [sic: both with German text: "Dir soll mein Herz", "Wie kann ich dir vergelten"], auf das Fest Corporis Christi, auch als Offertorium ["Pange Lingua"], Zweite Lieferung, Für kleine Landchöre.　S, organ, (AB, 2vl/cl(C) 2hn/tp ad lib).
Pc (Verlag von Anton Böhm: Augsburg; in commission bei Fr. X. Duyle: Salzburg, 580, sd), parts:
A-Sca, 70151. ★

*PAUER, Jiří *22 Feb 1919, Libušin*
JIP-1. Koncertní hudba (Musica da concerto); 1971.　2fl 2ob 2cl 2hn 2bn 2tp tb.
Pm (Artia: Prague, 1971), score.
Pm (Bärenreiter Editio Supraphon: Kassel & Prague, pn H 5544/AP 1861, post-1991), score.

*PAUKERT, Stephan (J.) *(1800)*
JUP-1tv. Cantus funebris in Es [E♭]; German ["Hann, ach hinn ist meine Freude"] & Czech ["Mogi mylj Rodičowé"] texts.　CATB, 2cl 2hn 2tp.　AutoMS parts (3 June 1831): CZ-TRB, H 275. ★
JUP-2tv. Todtenlied beim Grabe; "Menschen weihet nicht zu rücke".　B solo, 2cl 2hn bn.
AutoMS parts (11 June 1840): CZ-TRB, H 463. ★

PAUL, Ernst Julius *18 Nov 1907, Vienna - 1979*
EJP-1. Serenade für Bläser, Harfe u. Schlagzeug, Op. 127, (1961, in A).　3fl 3ob 3cl 6hn 3bn 3tp hp perc.
MS score (location unknown).
EJP-2. 3 Pieces, Op. 122.　fl ob 2cl 2hn bn vc db perc.
Pm (sn: sl, 1958), score.

*PAYER, Hieronymous (Jérome) *15 Feb 1787, Meidling, nr Vienna - 17 Aug 1845, Wiedburg*
JYP-1. Eichenkränze, Rondo Andnate; in B♭.　pic(F) 3cl(D) cl(G) 2hn(D, G) 3bn cbn+serp 6tp(clar: A, G, F, E, 2B♭) quart-tb tb b-dr+cyn s-dr.
Pc (Pietro Mechetti: Wien, pn 702, 703, c.1821), parts: A-Wgm, X 1293; H-KE, K 1191a. ★
JYP-2. 7 Walzer.　cl(D) 2cl(A) 2hn 2bn cbn 2tp.　MS pts (c.1810): D-DO, Mus.Ms.1533/1. ★
JYP-3(-6). 8 Walzer samt Coda, 2 grosse Märsche, Ein Adagio und Rondo.　Scoring varies.
AutoMS score ("Wien, am 8-August 1821"): A-Wn, Mus.Hs.28,849.
　JYP-3. 8 Walzer. Nos. 1 - 6 & 8: cl(G) 2cl(D) 2hn bn cbn tp(clar, D); No. 7: cl(G) 2cl(D) bn cbn klappen-tp 2tp(clar, D). ★
　JYP-4. Triumph Marsch [& Trio].　cl(F) 2cl(E♭) bn cbn tp(clar, E♭) tp(clar, tief B[♭]). ★
　JYP-5. Marsch [& Trio]; in G.　cl(G) 2cl(C) bn cbn klappen-tp tp(clar, hoch G) tp(clar, hoch C). ★
　JYP-6. Adagio & Rondo; in D.　2cl(D) cl(A) 2hn(D) bn cbn klappen-tp. ★
JYP-1m. Marsch; in C.　pic(F) 3cl(D) cl(G) 4hn(2E, A, G) 3bn cbn+serp 4tp(2E, hoch A, tief A) klappen-tp(ad lib) quart-tb b-dr+cym s-dr.
Pc (Pietro Mechetti: Wien, pn 704, c.1821), parts: H-KE, K 1191b. ★
JYP-1ma. Gallenberg: Alfred der Grosse, Triumph-Marsch.
pic(D) 4cl(D) cl(G) 4hn(D, C, 2G) 2bn cbn 7tp(G Hoch, 2A, F, G teif, B, C) tb b-tb b-dr s-dr.
Pc (Maketti [sic: Mechetti: Vienna], c.1822), MS parts: H-KE, K 2044.

PAYNE, Anthony Edward *2 Aug 1936, London*
ANP-1. Alleluias and Hockets.　SATB, 2ob ca 2bn 2tp 3tb.
Pm (Chester Music: London, etc., 1987), hire score & parts.

*PAZ, Juan Carlos *5 Aug 1901, Buenos Aires - 25 Aug 1972, Buenos Aires*
JCP-1. Tema y transformaciones; 1928 -1929.   fl ob 2cl b-cl 2hn 2bn 2tp.
Pm (? Instituto interamericano de musicologica: Montevideo), score, (possibly in series: Editorial Cooperativa interamericano de compositores).
JCP-2. Octet, Op. 16; 1930.   fl ob 2hn 2bn 2tp.
Pm (? Instituto interamericano de musicologica: Montevideo), score, (possibly in series: Editorial Cooperativa interamericana de compositores).
JCP-2. Concerto No. 2, Op. 24; 1934.   ob 2hn bn tp piano.
Pc (Albert J. Andraud: Cincinnati, Now Southern Music Corp: Can Antonio, 1935), score & parts.

*PEARSALL, Robert Lucas *14 March 1795, Bristol - 5 Aug 1856, Wartensee, Lake Constance. We have not been able to verify the following works for voices and winds, all said to be in CH-E: Introitus in D; Adeste Fidelis (1847); Ecce quam bonum (1846); Lamentatio III in Sabbato Sancto Oratio Jeremiae (1852); Pange Lingua (1847); Requiem (1853-56); Te Deum (1847); Tenebrae (1849); Veni Creator, (sd).*
RLP-1. March in E♭ (No. 2).   pic 2fl 2ob 2cl 6hn 2bn cbn 2tp 3tb serp b-dr s-dr.   MS: (?CH-E).
RLP-2. March in C.   Winds & organ.   MS: CH-E.
RLP-3. Introitus in D.   Winds & organ.   MS: CH-E.

*PECHATSCHEK (Pechaczec, Pecháček, Petraczek), František (Franz) Martin
10 Nov 1763, Ustí nad Orlicí - 26 Sept 1816, Vienna
FMP-1. (6) Variatione in B(♭) (with Coda).   2ob 2cl 2hn 2bn 2tp.   MS parts: CZ-KRa, A3949/IV.B.112.
This appears to have originally scored for 2cl 2hn 2bn; the oboe & trumpet parts are on different (oblong) paper and were probably added by Havel, who was also the copyist, 3 Sept 1805. Possibly an arrangement. ★
FMP-2. 12 Ländler.   2cl 2hn bn.
Pc (Jos. Sig. Reitmayer: Straubing, 1801), parts: D-Mbs, 2 Mus.pr 248. ★
FMP-1m. 3 Bürger-Märsche, welche bey Gelegenheit der am 8ten December gehaltenen Feyerlichkeit producit werden; in E♭, C & F.   2ob 2cl(B♭ & C) 2hn 2bn tp(E♭, C & F).
Pc (Im Verlag der K.K. priv. chemische Druckerey: Vienne [sic], pn 91, 1805), parts: H-KE, K 1051/IX. ★

PEHRSON, Joseph Ralph *1950, USA*
JRP-1. Patina.   2fl 2ob 2cl 2bn 3tp 2perc piano.
Pm (Seesaw Music Corp: New York, 1978).

PEJŘINOVSKY, Martin *(1810)*
MXP-1v. Cantate.   SATB, fl 3cl 2hn 2bn 2tp tb timp.   AutoMS score (1844): CZ-Pnm, XXXVIII.B.30.

*PELLARINI (Pellarin), Giuseppe *(active 1841 - 1850)*
Instruments in parentheses appear in the parts only.
GZP-1v. Beatus vir.   TTB, 2cl(A) 2hn (bn 2tp tb bn+vlne) timp organ(bc-fig).   MS score & parts: I-Vsmc. ★
GZP-2v. Dixit, 1841.   TTB(solo+rip), (fl) 2cl(A) 2hn bn (tp tb vlne) timp organ(bc-fig).
MS score & parts: I-Vsmc, (with full organ part). ★
GZP-3v. Laudate pueri, 1841.   TTB, 2cl 2hn bn (tp tb vlne) timp organ(bc-fig).   MS score & pts: I-Vsmc. ★
GZP-4v. Kyrie.   TTB, 2cl 2hn bn tp (bn+bassi) tp timp organ(bc-fig).   MS score & parts: I-Vsmc. ★
GZP-5v. Confitebor.   TTB, 2cl 2hn bn (vlne) organ(bc-fig).   MS score & parts: I-Vsmc. ★

PENBERTHY, James *5 May 1917, Melbourne*
JXP-1. Variations on a Russian theme, Op. 70.   3fl 3ob 3cl 4hn 3bn 2tp 3tb tu harp.
Pm (Australasian Performing Rights Association: Crow's Nest, Australia, sd), score.
JXP-2. Octet. 2fl 2ob 2cl 2bn.
Pm (Australasian Performing Rights Association: Crow's Nest, Australia, sd), score.

PENTLAND, Barbara Lally *2 Jan 1912, Winnipeg*
BLP-1. Octet; 1950.   fl ob cl 2hn bn tp tb.   MS score: C-Tcm.

*PERCIVAL, John *(1760)*
JVP-1m. The Bristol Volunteers Troop.   2cl 2hn bn serp tp.
Pc (Broderip & Wilkinson: London, c. 1799), RISM [P 1280], score: GB-Lbl, g.133.(47). ★

PERILHOU, Albert *2 April 1846, Doumazau, Arriège - 28 Aug 1936, Tain l'Hermitage, Drôme*
AZP-1. Divertissement.   2fl 2ob 2cl 4hn 2bn.
Pm (Heugel: Paris, 1905), score: F-Pn, D. 12.595 (3).

*PERSUIS, Louis Luc Loiseau de *4 July 1769, Metz - 20 Dec 1819, Paris*
LLP-1a. Lesueur: Ossian, notturno.   fl 2cl 2hn 2bn serp/db(ad lib).
Pc (Imbault: Paris, pn O.n.58, c.1805), RISM [L 2128], parts: CZ-Bm(au), A.40.164; D-AB, (?missing serp); F-Pn, Vm27 3358.

PETERSEN, Nils Holger *1946, Norway*
NHP-1. Prelude; 1985.   2fl ob 2cl b-cl bar-sax 2hn bn 2tp tb tu.   MS score: DK-Kd.

PETRALI, Giuliano *(?1800)*
GIP-1v. Quoniam.   B solo, fl 2ob 2hn bn tp timp organ.   MS score: I-Vsmc. ★

PETRI, Antonio *(?1780)*
AQP-1v. Adoramus te Christi.   SATB, 2ob bn 2tp.   MS score: A-Wn, Mus.Hs.13,040, No. 5, ff. 6 - 7. ★

*PETTER, Jan František (Johann Franz) *(1790), active Česká Třebová, Bohemia, 1818*
Other anonymous works at CZ-TRB may be by Petter. We list here only works on which his name appears.
JFP-1v. Hymnus de B: V: M: Ave maris Stella.   CATB, 2cl (B♭/C) 2hn(E♭/F) b-tb.
AutoMS parts (1818): CZ-TRB, H 423. ★
JFP-1tv. Pjseň při wskřjssenj; "Wstal z mrtwých wykupitel".   CATB, 2cl(A) 2cl(C) 2hn bn 2tp timp.
AutoMS parts: CZ-TRB, H 436. ★
JFP-2tv. Todtenlied Bei der Leich eine Mutter; "Lernt, Kinder früh bedenken".   CAB, 2cl 2hn bn 2tp.
AutoMS parts: CZ-TRB, H 424. ★

JFP-3tv. Pohřebnj Pjseň pro Djkky [child]; "Eyhle angel od wysosti".   CAB, 2cl(C/B♭) 2hn(C) bn 2tp(C).
AutoMS parts: CZ-TRB, H 433. ★
JFP-4tv. Pjseň Pohřebnj pro dospěly lide [adults]; "Wssecko spy a mrtwe ležj".   CATB, 2cl 2hn bn.
AutoMS pts: CZ-TRB, H 435. ★
JFP-5tv. Todtenlied; "Mein Leben ist schön aus".   CAB, 2cl 2hn bn.
AutoMS parts: CZ-TRB, H 434, (missing Alto voice part). ★
JFP-6tv. Todtenlied in G; "Zum Grabe geht die Reise".   CAB, 2cl(C vel B♭) 2hn 2bn.
AutoMS parts: CZ-TRB, H 461, (missing 2hn). ★

*PETYREK, Felix *14 May 1892, Brno - 1 Dec 1951, Vienna*
*FZP-1. Divertimento für 8 Bläser.   fl fl(pic) ob cl 2hn 2bn.
Pm (Universal Edition: Wien, 1922), score & parts (hire).
Pm (Albert J. Andraud: Cincinnati, now Southern Music Co.: San Antonio, sd), score & parts.

PETZ (Pez), Johann Christoph *9 Sept 1664, Munich - 25 Sept 1716, Stuttgart*
JHP-1. Ouverture.   2ob obdam[hautcontre] taille bn bc.   MS parts: D-ROu.

*PEZZOLI, Antonio *1842, Leffe - 1908, Leffe*
ATP-1v. Duettino [Qui tollis]; in F.   TB, fl 2cl 2hn bn 2tp tromboni cb.
AutoMS score (19 July 1898): I-LEFpezzoli.

*PEZZOLI, Giovanni *1870, Leffe - 1934, Leffe*
GOP-1v. Domine ad adjuvandum; in F.   (BAR, B), fl 2cl 2hn bn 2tp tb+bomb cb (timp).
AutoMS score (1895) & MS parts: I-LEFpezzoli, (the parts in parentheses are not found in the score).
GOP-2v. Kyrie; in F minor.   TB chorus, 2fl 2cl 2hn 2tp tromboni cb timp.
AutoMS score (1892): I-LEFpezzoli.

*PEZZOLI, Giuseppe *1831, Leffe - 1908, Leffe*
GUP-1v. Stabat Mater n. 1, Inno per Processione dedicato all'Addolorata di Leffe; in F minor.
T, T, BAR, B, pic fl ob 2cl 2hn 2tp 3tb bombardone(F).   AutoMS score (1894) & MS parts: I-LEFpezzoli.
GUP-2v. Stabat Mater n. 2, Inno per Processione dedicato all'Addolorata di Leffe; in F minor.
T, T, BAR, B, pic fl ob 2cl 2hn 2tp 3tb oph.   AutoMS score (1894) & MS parts: I-LEFpezzoli.
GUP-3v. Credo; in F.   TTB, 2fl 2cl 2hn 2tp 2tb bomb cb timp.   AutoMS score: I-LEFpezzoli.
GUP-4v. Laudamus, versetto; in D.   T solo, pic fl 2cl 2tp genis 3tb bombardone cb.
AutoMS score & MS parts: I-LEFpezzoli.
GUP-5v. Domine Deus; in B♭.   TTB, fl cl(I obl) 2cl 2hn 2tp 2tb bomb/oph/cb.
AutoMS score (1889) & MS parts: I-LEFpezzoli.
GUP-6v. Qui tollis; in E♭.   (BAR), chorus, fl 2cl (bn) tp(I obl) tp(II) genis tb bombardone cb.
AutoMS score & MS parts: I-LEFpezzoli, (?incomplete - the only vocal part is the Basso di coro; the bn part
does not appear in the score).
GUP-7v. Sanctus, Benedictus e Agnus Dei; in B♭.   Voices, fl 2cl bn 2tp genis tromboni oph cb (timp).
AutoMS score & MS parts: I-LEFpezzoli, (?complete - the only surviving vocal parts are the tenor 1° di rinforzo
and the basso del coro; the bn does not appear in the score).
GUP-8v. Kyrie; in C.   TTB, (fl) 2cl 2tp flug genis 3tb cb/bomb.
AutoMS score & MS parts: I-LEFpezzoli, (the flute does not appear in the score).
GUP-9v. Inno (Iste confessor o Ave Maris Stella); in E♭.   TB chorus, fl 2cl 2hn 2tp tromboni timp.
AutoMS score: I-LEFpezzoli.
GUP-10v. Laudate pieri Dominum; in B♭.   T,T,BAR,B, fl cl(I obl) cl(II) bn tp(I) genis tb(I) cb/bombardone
timp.   AutoMS vocal score & MS parts: I-LEFpezzoli.

PFEIFFNER, Ernst *1922, Switzerland*
EXP-1. Capricci ed Elegie; 1958.   2cl 2bn 2tp tb perc.   MS score: CH-Zma.

*PFEILSTICKER, Nicolas
NYP-1. 3 morceaux de musique mil[itai]re, (1. Marche, 2. Pas Redoublé, 3. Walzer).
2fl 2cl(F) 2cl(C) 2hn bn serp 2tp tb b-dr.   (?Auto)MS score: D-Mbs, Mus.Mss.3054. ★

*PFLÜGER, Hans Georg *26 Aug 1944, Swabisch Gmünd*
HGP-1. Metamorphosen.   Solo Violin & Piano, pic fl ob ca 2cl b-cl 2hn bn cbn tp tb timp.
Pm (Bote & Bock: Berlin, 1988).
HGP-2. Ama-Deus.   2ob 2cl 2hn 2bn db.
Pm (Bote & Bock: Berlin, 1990), score & parts.

PFOHL, Thadeas *(active 1808, Langenbruch, now Dlouhý Most)*
TXP-1. [17] Ländlerische [and Coda].   2cl 2hn bn.
MS parts: (by Augustin Erasmus Hübner, Langenbruck, 1808): CZ-Pu(dm), 59 R 3383, No. II. ★

PHILIDOR, André Danican [l'aîné] *c.1647, Versailles - 11 Aug 1730, Dreux*
ADP-1. [Music for the Grand Écurie].   Scoring varies [the (dr) parts are by Lully].
MS score: F-Pn, Rés.F.671. ★
1.1. Air des hautbois: Le Générale de la garde française. 2ob taille bn (dr).   No. 2.
1.2. Le Descente des armes, No. 1.   2ob taille bn (dr).   No. 4/7.
1.3 Le Retraite.   2ob taille bn.   No. 4/9.   1.4. Le Descente des armes [1674].   2ob taille bn.   No. 6/3.
1.5. L'Air des hautbois.   2ob taille bn (dr).   No. 8.   1.1m. Marche royale [1679].   2ob bn.   No. 4/6.
2.1m Marche du Régiment de Saluced.   2ob taille bn.   No. 16.   3.1m. Marche Liegeoise. 2ob taille bn.   No. 20.
4.1m Marche Hollandaise.   2ob taille bn.   No. 21.
1.1t. Marche des Pompes funèbre ("pour Mad^e La Dauphine").   2ob bn.   No. 41.

PHILIDOR, Jacques Danican [le cadet] *5 May 1657, Paris - 27 May 1708, Versailles*
JAP-1. [Music for the Grand Écurie].   2ob taille bn.   MS score: F-Pn, Rés.F.671. ★
1.1. Le Retraite.   No. 11/3.   1.2. Le Descente des armes.   No. 11/4.
1.3. La Générale des Dragons du Roy.   No.11/5.

*PHILLIPA (Philippine) CHARLOTTE, *Herzogin von Braunschweig-Wolfenbüttel* 1716 - 1801
CBP-1m. Regiments-Marsch, in B♭.   2ob 2cl 2bn tp.
AutoMS score & MS parts: D-Bds, Hausbibl.M.M.43.   ★
Pm (Steinquest), pp. 93 - 94, score.
CBP-2m. Marsch *("componiert von I. K. H. Herzogin Phillippine Charlotte von Braunschweig. Schwester Friedrichs des Grossen, für ihren Bruder, den Prinzen August Wilhelm v. Preussen, 1751"),* in B♭.   2ob 2bn tp.
AutoMS score & MS parts: D-Bds, Hausbibl.M.M.39.   ★
Pm (Steinquest), pp. 88 - 90, score.
Pm (In: Pätzig (qv), Heft 1, No. 1), score & parts.
CBP-1md. Marsch der Herzogin von Braunschweig, in D.   2ob "bassen" tp(D).
(?Auto)MS parts: D-Bds, Hausbibl.M.M.41, (missing trumpet).

*PHILLIPS (afterwards JAGGER), Bryony *10 March 1948, Salford, UK (now resident in New Zealand)*
BJP-1. "Magnifipuss", "arranged from the Magnificat, for the Kappa Wind Ensemble".   fl 2ob 2cl bn.
MS score: NZ-Wn.

PHILIPPS, Ivan C.
ICP-1. 3 Hunting Songs.   2ob 2cl 2bn.   Pm (Oxford University Press: London, 1963), parts.

PHILLIPS, Peter *1930, USA*
PZP-1. Gesualdo Variations.   Solo hn 2tp t-tb b-tb, pic 2fl 2ob ca 2cl b-cl 4hn 2bn 4tp 3tb tu 7perc; (optional substitutions 2ob/2s-sax ca/a-sax 2bn/t-sax, b-sax).
Pm (Associated Music Publishers: New York, sd), hire score & parts.

*PIAZZA, Felice *(18th century, Italy)*
FEP-1(-12). Quintetti XII; (F, F, F, Eb, C, F, F, F, Eb, Eb; all 2 mvts).   2ob 2hn bn/vc.
MS parts: I-Mc, Noseda O.7.11.   *The 1st mvts of Nos. 5 & 9 bear the note "Con Trauersiera", possibly suggesting the use of flutes.*

*PICCINNI, Niccolò Vincenzo *16 Jan 1728, Bari, nr Naples - 7 May 1800, Passy, nr Paris*
*NXP-1em. Marcia da *Allesandro nella India*; Act IV Scene 5 (second version, Naples 1774).   2ob 2cl 2hn 2bn.
MS score: I-Rri.   ★
Pm (Boccaccini & Spada: Roma, pn B.S.1146, 1984), edited G. C. Ballola, score & parts.
NXP-1mv. Hymne à l'Hymen pour la célébration des mariages; P.153.   Two voices, 2ob+2cl 2hn 2bn.
Pc (Rec des époques: Paris, c.1799), liv. 2, No. 12, score: F-Pn, H2. 15,12.   ★

*PICHL (Pichel), Václav (Wenzel, Wentzel) *25 Sept 1741, Tábor - 4 June 1804, Vienna*
VXP-1. Partitta Nro 1; in C, 4 mvts.   2ob/cl 2hn bn.
MS parts: CZ-Pnm, XXII.E.46; D-DO, Mus.Ms.1551, Nos. 36 - 39, (for: 2cl 2hn bn).   ★
VXP-2. Partitta Nro 2; in F, 4 mvts.   2ob/cl 2hn bn.   MS parts: CZ-Pnm, XXII.E.47; D-DO, Mus.Ms.1551, Nos. 44 - 47 (for: 2cl 2hn bn); I-Vcm, Fondo Correr Busta B9, N1-5, No. IV.   ★
*VXP-3.1. Concertino in F con Pastorello; 4 mvts.   2ob 2ca 2hn 2bn.   MS parts: CZ-Pnm, XLII.E.23.   ★
VXP-3.2. Partitta; in Eb, 4 mvts.   2ob 2hn bn 2vla.
MS parts: CZ-NR, A.18.245/B.261, (with strings given as an alternative on the wrapper).   ★
VXP-3.3. Partitta Nro 3; in Eb, 4 mvts.   2cl 2hn 2bn.
MS parts: CZ-Pnm, XXII.E.48; D-DO, Mus.Ms.1551, Nos. 1 - 4.
*VXP-3.4(d). Concertino in F con Pastorella, 4 mvts.   2ob 2cl 2hn 2bn db tambourine.   *Note: this version, recorded by the Collegium musicum Pragense, is actually arranged by Antonín Myslík (qv).*
VXP-4. Partitta Nro 4; in F, 5 mvts.   2cl 2hn 2bn.
MS parts: CZ-Pnm, XXII.E.49; D-DO, Mus.Ms.1551, Nos. 27 - 31.   ★
VXP-5. Partitta Nro 5; in F, 4 mvts.   2cl 2hn 2bn.
MS parts: CZ-Pnm, XXII.E.50; D-DO, Mus.Ms.1551, Nos. 5 - 8. ★
VXP-6. Partitta Nro 6; in F, 4 mvts.   2ob 2hn bn.
MS parts: CZ-Pnm, XXII.E.51; D-DO, Mus.Ms.1551, Nos. 32 - 35. ★
VXP-6.1. Additional final mvt "Tamborina/Finale", in 6/8 and with a Minore section added in another hand in the Pachta version.   2cl 2hn bn.   MS parts: CZ-Pnm, XXII.E.51 (last sheet of each part).   ★
VXP-7. Partitta Nro 7; in F, 4 mvts.   2ob/cl 2hn bn.
MS parts: CZ-Pnm, XXII.E.52; D-DO, Mus.Ms.1551, Nos. 9 - 12, (for 2cl 2hn bn).   ★
*VXP-8. Partitta Nro 8; in F, 4 mvts.   2cl 2hn 2bn.
MS parts: CZ-Pnm, XXII.E.53; D-DO, Mus.Ms.1551, Nos. 40 - 43; *possibly related to VXP-19.*   ★
*VXP-9. Partitta Nro 9; in Eb, 4 mvts.   2ob 2hn 2bn.   MS parts: CZ-Pnm, XXII.E.54.   ★
VXP-10. Partitta Nro 10; in C, 4 mvts.   2ob/cl 2hn 2bn. MS parts: CZ-Pnm, XXII.E.55.   ★
*VXP-11. Partitta Nro 11; in C, 4 mvts.   2ob 2hn 2bn.
MS parts: CZ-Pnm (2 copies), XXII.E.56 (4 mvts), XXXII.A.302 (as "Divertimento ex B[♭]", for 2cl 2hn bn; missing cl II; with a reprise of the 1st section of mvt 1 after mvt 4).   ★
VXP-12.1. Nro 16 Partitta In A; 6 mvts.   2ob 2hn bn.
MS parts: CZ-Pnm, XXII.E.57; D-DO, Mus.Ms.1551, Nos. 17-21; D-HER, Mus.C.23=3, No. 1.   ★
VXP-12.2. Parthia in A#; 5 mvts.   2ob 2cl(A) 2hn bn.   MS parts: D-SWl, Mus. 4243.
VXP-13. Nro 17 Partitta d'Stromenti à Fiato In D; 5 mvts.   2ob 2hn bn.   MS parts: CZ-Pnm, (2 copies), XXII.E.58, XLII.E.272, (as "Parthia Ex D", 4 mvts, dated [1]770; omits mvt 2, Menuetto & Trio).   ★
VXP-14. in D# [D major] Nro 18 Partitta; 4 mvts.   2ob 2hn bn.   MS parts: CZ-Pnm, XXII.E.59.   ★
VXP-15. Parthia in b [B♭]; 4 mvts.   2cl 2hn bn.   MS parts: CZ-Pnm, XXXIV.A.82, (missing cl II; the bn pt is marked "á 2"); I-Vcm, Fondo Correr, Busta B.9, N1-5, No. VII.   ★
VXP-16. Partitta; in Eb, 4 mvts.   2cl 2hn bn.   MS parts: D-DO, Mus.Ms.1551, Nos. 13 - 16.   ★
VXP-17. Partia; in Eb, 5 mvts.   2cl 2hn bn.   MS parts: D-DO, Mus.Ms.1551, Nos. 22 - 26.   ★
VXP-18. Partia; in B♭, 4 mvts.   2cl 2hn bn.
MS parts: D-DO, Mus.Ms.1551, Nos. 48 - 51; I-Vcm, Fondo Correr Busta B9, N1-5, No. II.   ★
VXP-19. Harmonie; in Eb, 4 mvts.   2cl 2hn bn.   MS parts: D-SWl, Mus. 4244.   ★

*VXP-20(-28). Parthias I, III, V, VI, VIII - XII; (1: in G, 4 mvts; 3: in F, 4 mvts; 5: in F, 5 mvts; 6: in B♭, 4 mvts; 8: in F, 4 mvts; 9: in C, 3 mvts; 10: in B♭, 4 mvts; 11: in F, 4 mvts; 12: in E♭: 4 mvts). 2ob 2hn 2bn. MS parts: I-Vcm, Fondo Correr Busta B9, N1-5. *Nos. II, IV & VII match known works by Pichl; we believe that the other works in this set are also his compositions.* ★
VXP-29. Parthie. 2chalumeaux taille bn. MS parts: A-GÖ, MS.2873.
VXP-30(-33). 5 Parthien, Nos. 3 - 6 [sic]. 2cl 2hn bn. MS parts: D-HER, Mus.C.23=3, Nos. 2 - 6.
As No. 1 is VXP-12, we suspect but cannot verify the rest match works in CZ-Pnm, D-DO.

PICHLER (Bichler, Bechler, Büchler), (?Placidus) *1722 - 1796*
XZB-1. Concerto a 4; in F. 2fl ob 2hn basso. MS parts: D-RH, Ms.632. ★
XZB-2. Ex G# [G major] Partia; 4 mvts. fl fl/vl vl b. MS pts: D-Rtt, Büchler 1, (with 2 copies of the b pt). ★

*PICK, Henry *(1770)*
HXP-1. [Untitled collection of 10 works]. 2fl 4cl(B♭/C) 2hn 2bn 2tp b-tb serp perc (bugle horn, timp in No. 10). AutoMS score (c.1800): GB-Lbl, R.M.21.b.16. ★
HXP-2. Harmonie as Performed before their Majesty's Selected from the Works of celebrated composers and Arranged; 20 mvts. 2fl(B♭, C, terz-fl) 4cl 2bn 2hn tp bugle-hn serp/b-tb b-dr; (scoring varies).
Pc (Printed by Geo. Astor & Cº: London, c.1801), pts: GB-Lbl, R.M.17.f.10.(1), (missing bugle horn and b-dr). ★
   2.1(m). March.   2.2(m). Janizaren Quick March.   2.3(m). Gen[era]ˡ Vukasovich's March.
   2.4(m). Janizaren Quick March.   2.5. Andante Moderato.
   2.6. Romance. Andante / Allº. *Possibly an arrangement.*   2.7(m). March.
   2.8(a). Salieri: [Tarare], Axur Re d'Ormus, Introduzione & 5 mvts. Nos. 8 - 13.   2.9(m). Pick: March in E♭.
   2.10(a). Dalayrac: Le Deux petits Savoyards, 5 mvts. Nos. 15 - 19.   2.10. Pick: Waltz [with Trio].
HXP-1a. J. C. Bach: Lucio Silla, overture. 2fl 2ob 3cl(C) 2hn 2bn 2tp a-tb t-tb serp.
AutoMS score: GB-Lbl, R.M.21.d.4, ff. 1 - 18b.   MS parts (modern): GB-Lhumphries.

*PIERNÉ, (Henri Constant) Gabriel *16 Aug 1863, Metz - 17 July 1937, Ploujean*
HCP-1. Preludio & Fughetta, Op. 40. 2fl ob cl hn 2bn.
Pm (Hamelle: Paris, 1906), score & parts: F-Pn.
Pm (International Music Corp.: New York, pn 1804, sd), score & parts: D-Bhm, DA.1002; US-Wc.
HCP-2. Pastoral variée dans le style ancien, Op. 30; in B♭. fl ob cl hn 2bn tp.
Pm (Durand: Paris, pn D.&F. 5435, 1961), score: F-Pn; GB-Lbl, h.3979.c.(2); US-PT.
Pm (Albert J. Andraud: Cincinnati, now Southern Music Co.: San Antonio, Texas, sd), score.

PILLIN, Boris William *31 May 1940, Chicago*
BWP-1. 3 pieces for double reed septet; 1971. 2ob 2ca 2bn cbn.
Pm (Pillin Music, *via* Western Music International: Greeley, CO, pn PIL 22, 1972), score (copy in US-NYamc).

PILLNEY, Karl Hermann *8 April 1896, Graz*
KHP-1a. Mozart: Fantasie für eine Orgelwalze, K.608. fl 2ob 2cl 2hn 2bn.
Pm (Breitkopf & Härtel: Leipzig, Wiesbaden, pn EB 6496, sd), parts.

PILSS, Karl *7 April 1902, Vienna*
KYP-1. Octet in A; 1946-47. fl 2ob 2cl 2hn bn.
Pm (Doblinger: Wien, c.1947), MS materials in the Doblinger archives, can be hired.

*PINKHAM, Daniel *5 June 1923, Lynn, Mass*
DYP-1v. Magnificat. S solo, female chorus, 2ob 2bn harp/piano.
Pm (Peters: New York), vocal score with pf red, (hire score & parts).

*PIÑOS, Alois Simandl *2 Oct 1925, Vyškov*
ASP-1. Double Concerto for cello (violin), piano, winds and percussion.
Pm (Český hudební fond: Prague, 1966), hire score & parts.

*PINSUTI, Ciro *9 May 1829, Sinalunga, Florence - 10 March 1888, Florence*
CYP-1. Scherzino. fl fl/ob 2cl bn. (original provenance untraced.)
Pm (Music Publishers' Holding Co: New York, sd), ed. M.A. Springer.

*PIRCH, G(eorg) von *(1760), "Lieutenant im Regiment 'von Graevenitz'"*
GVP-1(-3)m. Märsche Nos. 1(-3); (C, C, C). 2ob 2cl(C) 2hn 2bn tp.
MS: D-Bds, Hausbibl.M.M.123.   Pm (Steinquest), pp. 156 - 180, score. ★
GVP-4(-9)m. Märsche Nos. 1(-6); (C, F, C, F, C, F). 2ob 2cl 2hn 2bn.
MS: D-Bds, Hausbibl.M.M.123a.   Pm (Steinquest), pp. 181 - 204, score. ★

PIRNSLER, ( ) *(1810)*
XYP-1a. Körnlein: Kegeltanz. fl ob 2cl 2hn bn tp tb. MS parts (1847): D-DO, Mus.Ms.1084.

PIŠTĚK, František *(1800)*
FCP-1v. V noci při narozemí Páně. CATB, fl(obl) 2cl(C) 2hn vlne organ(bc).
MS parts (by Joseph John, Pilsenetz [now Plnnec] 14 Dec 1837): CZ-PLa, Hu 334. ★

*PISTON, Walter *20 Jan 1894, Rockland, Maine - 12 Nov 1976, Belmont, Mass*
WXP-1. Concerto for String Quartet; 1976. Solo 2vl vla vc, 3fl 3ob 3cl 2hn 2bn 2tp 2tb timp perc.
Pm (Associated Music Publishers: New York, 1976), score & hire parts.
WXP-2. Divertimento; 1946. 2fl 2ob 2cl hn 2bn.
Pm (Associated Music Publishers: New York), score & hire parts.

*PITICCHIO (Pittichio, Pitichio), Francesco *(1740/1750), Palermo - post-1798*
FQP-1(-6). Concerti No. 6 [sic]; (C, C, F, F, B♭, Bb; all 3 mvts). 2ob/cl 2hn bn. MS pts: CZ-Bm(sz), A.14. ★
FQP-7. Quintetto. 1779. 2ob 2hn bn. AutoMS: D-Bds. *Possibly one of FQP-1 - 6.*

PIZER, Elizabeth Faw Hayden *9 Jan 1954, Watertown, NY, USA*
EFP-1. Pieces of Eight, Op. 42; 1977. 2ob 2cl 2hn 2bn.
Pm (American Music Center: New York, c.1977), parts.

PLAETNER, Jørgen *1930, Denmark*
JGP-1. 15 Miniatures; 1985.   4cl 2bn.   MS score: DK-Kd.

*PLEYEL (PLAJELLO, PLEIEL), Ignaz (Ignace) Joseph *1 June 1757, Ruppertsthal - 14 Nov 1831, Paris*
We list here works either by Pleyel or attributed to him (many of which are unlisted in Benton's thematic catalog). Works by known arrangers (or those prepared post-1831) are listed in the ARRANGEMENTS LIST.
*IJP-1. Patita [sic] pour l'Harmonie arrangé...par Mr: Pleyel appartient à l'Harmonie du Couvent des Augustines 1818; in D, 5 mvts, (B. deest).   fl ob 2cl(A) 2hn 2bn cbn.
MS parts ("Decembre 1818"): CZ-Bm(au), A.35.206, (all parts titled "Serenade").   ★
*IJP-2. Partita in E♭; (based on B.285), 5 mvts.   2ob 2cl 2hn 2bn cbn.
MS parts (c.1800): D-HR, HR III 4 1/2 2° 361.   Pm (KGS), fiche (2313).   ★
*IJP-3. Serenade in F; (B.2041 = B.321/i, ii, 138/iii, 305/iii; RISM [P 3009]).   2ob/fl 2cl 2hn 2bn (cb ad lib).
Pc (N. Simrock: Bonn, pn 980, 1813), liv. I, parts: D-Bds.   ★
Pm (Bureau de Musique Mario Bois: Paris, sd).
*IJP-4. Serenade in F, (B.2041 = B.383/i, ii, B.313/iii, iiia, B.573/ii; RISM [P 3010]).   2ob/fl 2cl 2hn 2bn (cb ad lib).
Pc (N. Simrock: Bonn, pn 981, 1813), liv. II, parts: D-HR, HR III 4 1/2 2° 381; I-Fc, D.X.2000.   ★
MS parts: D-Rtt, Sm. 14, 56 - 59, (incomplete: here only ob/fl I & II, cl I [in cl II volume], bn I).
Pm (Edition Engel: Puchheim, post-1990), score & parts.
*IJP-5. Parthia in Dis [E♭]; 2 mvts, (Benton deest).   2ob 2cl 2hn 2bn cbn.
MS parts (by C.J.H.): CZ-Pnm, XX.F.57.   ★
*IJP-6. Pièces d'Harmonie; (also attributed to Mozart, *See:* WAM-5d, K.C17.03); 5 mvts.   2ob 2cl 2hn 2bn.
MS parts: CH-E, Th. 91,18/No. 5, (?missing 2cl; as "Mozart"); D-DO, Mus.Ms.1592 (as "Pleyel", with an additional, unidentified Adagio as No. 6).   ★
MS score: D-B, Mus.Ms.15351, No. 5, (MS by Otto Jahn, attributed to Mozart); D-Bhm, Mus.11521 (score), Mus.11248 (parts).
Pc (attributed to Mozart:) (Breitkopf & Härtel: Leipzig, pn 65, 1801), RISM [M 5919], "Deux Pièces d'Harmonie", liv. II, No. 5, parts: A-Sm; A-Wgm (4 copies); A-Wn-h; CZ-Bm; D-Dl; GB-DOTams; H-KE.
Pm (WINDS: Northridge, CA, pn W-38, c.1981), Jahn score photocopy & modern MS parts.
*IJP-7. Partita in F; 3 mvts, (B.3047 = B.302).   2ob 2cl 2hn 2bn.   MS parts: D-DO, Mus.Ms.1574.   ★
Pm (Edition Engel: Puchheim, post-1990), score & parts.
*IJP-8.1. Partita in B[♭]; 4 mvts, (B.3546 = B.353i, 355iii, 354ii & iia, 353iii).   2ob 2cl 2hn 2bn.
MS parts: D-DO, Mus.Ms.1572.   ★
*IJP-8.2. Sextet in B[♭]; 4 mvts, (B.3547 = B.353i, 353iii, 355ii, 354ii & iia).
Clavicembalo (harpsichord) ob cl 2hn bn.   MS parts: A-Wgm, XI 10984 (Q 17658).
*IJP-8.3. Quintet; in B♭, 4 mvts, (B.3548 = B.353i, 353iii, 355ii, 354ii & iia).   Piano, ob cl hn bn.
MS parts: A-Wgm.
Pm (Musica rara: London, c.1969), ed. Werner Genuit & Dieter Klöcker, score & parts.
*IJP-9. Parthia in Dis [E♭]; 2 mvts, (B.3324 = B.338i & ii).   2ob 2cl 2hn 2bn.   MS pts: D-DO, Mus.Ms.1575.   ★
*IJP-10. Parthia in B[♭]; 4 mvts, (B.2046 = B.311i, X23+X24, 311ii, 312iii).   2ob 2cl 2hn 2bn.
MS parts: D-DO, Mus.Ms.1570.   ★
*IJP-11.1. Parthia in B[♭]; 3 mvts, (B.2047 = B.334/i, 303iii, 303iii, 334iii).   2ob 2cl 2hn 2bn.
MS parts: D-DO, Mus.Ms.1573.   ★
*IJP-11.2. Sestetto VI; in E♭, 4 mvts, probably arr. by Havel.   2cl 2hn 2bn.   MS pts: CZ-KRa, A4470/R.I.42.   ★
*IJP-12.1. Parthia Ite; in E♭ (B.111; Allegro - Andante con [6] Variazio - Menuetto & Trio - Adagio / Presto; the Adagio is from B.302).   2ob 2cl 2hn 2bn.
MS parts: D-DO, Mus.Ms.1597.   ★
Pm (Edition Engel: Puchheim, post-1990), score & parts.
*IJP-12.2. Parthia in Dis [E♭]; 5 mvts, (B.111 = B.1212), (Allegro - Andante con [5] variatione - Menuetto & Trio - Adagio - Rondo. Allegro).   2ob 2cl 2hn 2bn.   MS parts: D-DO, Mus.Ms.1571.   ★
*IJP-12.3. Parthia in Dis [E♭]; (Adagio - Rondo [finale] - Minuet & 2 Trios (Not in Benton); attributed to Mozart as K.C17.10; WAM-19d).   2cl 2hn bn.   MS parts: A-Wn, Mus.Hs.622, No. 2.   ★
*IJP-12.4. Divertimento...Storace, Pleyel, Attwood; [B.311ii: Adagio / Allegretto].   2ob 2bthn 2hn 2bn.
MS parts (A-202.1/2(a)): GB-LBl, RM.21.d.2, ff. 1 - 11b, (mvt 2).
*IJP-12.5. [Rondo finale].   *In:* C.F. Eley. "Twelve Select Military Pieces...Perform'd by the Band of the Coldstream Guards".   2cl 2hn bn tp(ad lib).
Pc (Longman & Broderip: London, 1792), Book 3, No. 3, parts: GB-Lbl, b.80.   ★
*IJP-12.6. [Andante & 1 variation; Minuet & Trio; Adagio; Rondo with Minore section & Da Capo].   *In:* James Brooks *Thirty six select pieces for a military band*, (Nos. 11, 12, 9, 10, respectively), B.8676.   2cl 2hn bn.
Pc (Culliford, Rolfe & Barrow: London, 1796), parts: GB-Lbl, b.82; GB-Ob, Mus.61.d.2(6).   ★
IJP-12.7. Andante con [Variazioni (mvt 3).   2cl 2hn 2bn.   MS parts: CZ-Pnm, XLI.A.98, No. 2.
*IJP-13. Pieces from the Royal Music Collection; B.2043 = B.349ii, B.321ii, 322i, 319ii.   2ob 2bthn 2hn 2bn serp.
MS parts: GB-Lbl, RM.21.d.2, respectively ff.12b (in C) & f.14b (in F), f.18, f.18b, f.20.   ★
   13.1, 13.2.   (B.349ii, iii).   [untitled 4-mvt divertimento, mvt 3, Andante / Presto].   A-202.2/3(a), missing 2hn.
   13.3.   (B.321ii).   [Moderato. 2/4 = Theme, 2 Variations & Theme reprise].   No. 1.   A-202.3/1(a).
   13.4.   (B.322i)   Andante Grazioso, 3/8 / (B. deest) Swabisch, 3/8.   No. 2.   A-202.3/2(a).
   13.5.   (B.319ii).   Andante con [2] Vars. Comp. by Pleyel.   No. 9.   A-202.3/9(a).
IJP-13.6. Piece from the Royal Music Collection (missed by Benton), Adagio (B.112/iv) / Allegretto (B.404/iii).
2fl 2bthn 2hn 2bn serp.   MS parts: GB-Lbl, R.M.21.c.34-40, No. 6.   [= A-204.6(a)]
*IJP-14(-16). Trois harmonies, (E♭, 3 mvts; E♭, 4 mvts; E♭, 4 mvts), (No. 1: B.2050; No. 2: B.2608 = B.284, *the Menuetto of No. 2 is not that of the string quartet B.284, although the Trio does correspond to this version; the Menuetto is not found in Benton*; No. 3: B.2609 = B.2610 & B.384)   2cl 2hn 2bn.
AutoMS score: D-Bds, Mus.Ms.Auto.J.Pleyel 2, (No. 3 only, IJP-16, Benton as: B.2610, dated 1780).
MS pts: A-Sca, Hs.421, (No. 1, as anonymous); CZ-KRa, A4455/R.I.25, (No. 3, as "Parthia 2, E♭"; the Romanze, mvt 2 is a variant of B.384/ii); CZ-Pnm, (2 copies), XLI.B.113, (No. 3 only), XLII.F.36, No. 15, (No. 3 only).
Pc (Au Magasin de l'imprimerie chemique: Vienne, pn 1557-1559, 1810/11), RISM [P 3011 - 3013], parts: A-Z (Nos. 1 - 3); CH-E, 62.11, (No. 2), 62.12, (No. 3); GB-Ljag(w), L.89, (Nos. 2 & 3).   ★
Pm (No. 2 only) (Musica rara: London, pn 1810, 1975), ed. H Voxman, score & parts.

*IJP-17. Parthia in Eb; 4 mvts, (B.261i - iv). 2cl 2hn 2bn.
MS pts: CZ-KRa, A3950/IV.B.114; CZ-Pnm, XX.F.56, (copy by Podratski; cl pts reversed in mvt 4, Rondo). ★
Pm (Edition Engel: Puchheim, post-1990), score & parts.
*IJP-18. [Arranged by Havel] Parthia No. VI; in Eb, 3 mvts, (B.384i, B.386ii, B.384iii). 2cl 2hn 2bn.
MS parts: CZ-KRa, A3950/IV.B.113. ★
*IJP-19. [Probably arranged by Buchal] Parthia in Eb; 4 mvts, (B.384/i, B.136/iii, B.385/ii, B.380/ii).
2cl 2hn 2bn. MS parts ("Wien den 4 Juny [1]803 JAB"): PL-LA, RM 50. ★
*IJP-20(-22). Drey Parthia, (Eb, Eb, Bb; B 2049; *IJP-20* = B.575i, B.577i, B.577iii, B.576iii; *IJP-21* = B.579i,
B.X63, B.X52, B.138iii & iv(middle section); *IJP-22* = B.574, B.575iii, B.578iii). 2cl 2hn bn.
MS parts: US-BETm, Philharmonic Society of Bethlehem PSB 1351.2a, b, c. ★
IJP-23, 24. Due Quintetti; No. 1: in Eb, 5 mvts (1st mvt = B.338ii), No. 2: in Eb, 4 mvts (Benton deest).
2cl 2hn bn. MS parts: I-UDricardi, Ms.147. ★
*IJP-25. Parthia in Dis [Eb]; 2 mvts, (Benton deest). 2cl 2hn bn.
MS parts ("Ex Partibus Ignaz Hübner", Langenbruck, 1805): CZ-Pu(dm), 59 R 3351. ★
*IJP-26. Parthia in B[b]; 6 mvts, (Benton deest). 2cl 2hn bn.
MS parts ("Ex Partibus Aug[ustin] Eras[mus] Hübner", Langenbruck, 1805): CZ-Pu(dm), 59 R 3350. ★
*IJP-27. [4] Menuetto [& Trios], [8] Salti [tedeschi] et [15] Marchia [sic] ex Dis; (Benton deest). 2cl 2hn bn.
MS parts ("pro me Augustin Erasmus Hübner", Langenbruck, 1804): CZ-Pu(dm), 59 R 3369. ★
  27.1(-27.4). Minuetto [& Trio] Nro 1 [-4]; all in F.   27.5(-27.12). Salti Tedeschi 1 [-8]; all in F.
  27.13. Marchia [sic] Nro 1; [& Trio], in F.   27.14. Marchia [sic] Nro 2; in F.
  27.15. Französischer Marsch bey der Schlacht Genua Nro 3; in F.   27.16. Marsch Nro 4; in F.
  27.17. Marsch Nro 5; in F.   27.18. Marsch von Regiment Prinz Maximilian in Gemnitz Nro 6; [& Trio], in F.
  27.19. Marsch des Regiments Kuhrfürst in Zeits Nro 7; [& Trio], in F.
  27.20. Marsch von Regiments General Reitzenstein in Leipzig Nro 8; [& Trio], in F.
  27.21. Marsch des Regiments General von Lind in Zwikau Nro 9; [& Trio], in F.
  27.22. Marsch von Regiments der Leibgarde in Dresden Nro 10; [& Trio], in F.
  27.23. Marsch von Prinz Anton in Grosslager Nro 11; [& Trio], in F.   27.24. Marsch Nro 12; [& Trio], in F.
  27.25. Marsch Nro 13; in F.   27.26. Marsch Nro 14; in F.   27.27. Marsch Nro 15; in F.
IJP-28. Rondo in C; (arr. based on B.311/iii). 2ob 2cl 2hn 2bn tp serp. MS parts: D-SWl, Mus. 4280/8. ★
IJP-29. Pièces d'harmonie; in Eb, 4 mvts, (Benton deest). Scoring uncertain: (?2cl 2hn 2bn)
MS parts: RF-Ssc, Ф 891 собрюосуповых N44, pp. 131 - 144. ★
IJP-30. Quartet in Bb, (B.395). fl 2cl bn.
MS score: D-ASh.   Pm (Musica rara: London, pn 1240, 1970), ed. Georg Meerwein, score & parts. ★
IJP-31. Quartetti. Del Sigr Pleyel, 7 mvts (B.353/iii, 354/ii, 355/ii, 358/iii, 357/ii, iii, deest). cl 3bthn.
MS parts (post-1791): CZ-Pnm, XLII.A.68. *Mvts 1 - 6 from Pleyel's 6 Quatuors, dedicated to the King of
Naples, published in 1791.* ★
*IJP-1v. Hymne à la Liberté; (B.705 (7033); P.11e).   Solo voice, 2cl(C) 2hn (2)bn.
Pc (Rec des époques: Paris, c.1799), RISM [P 2621], liv. 1, No. 9, pp. 20 - 22, score: F-Pn, H2. 15,9. ★
IJP-1c. Oktett Es-dur [Eb major]; 4 mvts, (Benton deest). 2ob 2cl 2hn 2bn (cb).
MS: provenance unknown. Modern MS score & parts: D-KIZklöcker. *Recorded on MD+G L 3460 (CD).* ★
*IJP-1d. Divertimento; in C, 15 mvts, (Benton deest). 2fl 2hn bn.
MS parts: D-DO, Mus.Ms.351/1, (missing 2fl). *This work, not in Benton, is only identified as being by Pleyel
in the D-DO catalog of 1803/04 (p. 58, Nr 39); provenance is attributed to "L.v.L".*
*IJP-2d. Parthia in Dis [Eb] - Authore Vogel; 5 mvts, (Benton deest). 2cl 2hn bn.
MS parts (by Dominik Hübner, Langenbruck): CZ-Pu(dm), 59 R 3337; (with an additional violin II part, in fact
a transcribed clarinet II part). *The wind parts all bear the headtitle, "Parthia von Pleyel"; the vl II part bears
the headtitle, "Sonata von Vogel". We believe that this work is, in fact, by Kajetan Vogel (KXV-1).* ★

*PLIMPTON, Job *(?1760) USA*
*JZP-1m. Washington's March. 2ob 2hn bn.
Score (in *The Universal Repository of Music*, 1808): US-NYp. ★
Pm (In: F.J. Cipolla & D. Hunsberger. *The Wind Ensemble and its Repertoire:)* (University of Rochester Press:
Rochester, NY, 1994), R.F. Camus (also editor): "The Early American Wind Band", pp. 73 & 74, score.
Note: This march can also be found as No. 16 of A-64m, (1775).

*POESSINGER (PÖSSINGER), Franz Alexander *c.1767, Vienna - 19 Aug 1827*
FAP-1. Nro VIto. Trio in F; 4 mvts. 2ob ca.
MS parts: CZ-K. No.34.K.23. ★
Pc (for: 2cl bn:) (Chemische Druckerei: Vienna, pn 1392, 1810), parts.
Pm (Edition Kneusslin: Basle, 1979), ed. Antonín Myslík, (Für Kenner und Liebhaber No. 73).
*FAP-1ac. Boieldieu: Jean de Paris. 2ob 2cl 2hn 2bn cbn. MS parts: I-Fc, F.P. S.362.
*FAP-2ac. J. Weigl: Die Schweizerfamilie; Part I, II. 2ob 2cl 2hn 2bn cbn.
Pc (chez Thadé Weigl: Vienne, pn 1114, 1115, 1810) parts: A-Ee, Mus.1121, 1122, (complete; Doć.A.M.4089
comprises Weigl's bill of Sept 4, 1811, Prince Esterházy's payment authorization & Kapellmeister Johann Fuch's
receipt for 36 gulden); CZ-Pnm, Lobkovic X.H.a.7, (liv. I; overture & 12 mvts; with MS pts [?by Krechler] of
the overture, Nos. 5 & 4: The ob, hn & bn pts of the overture transposed from C to Bb, Nos. 5 & 4 from Bb
to C to accomodate Bb clarinets; the first 14 bars of the overture in cl II have been been altered to Alberti
("woodle") accompaniment, and No. 4 has been altered throughout to provide a more complex accompaniment).

*POISSL, Johann Nepomuk, *Baron (Freiherr)* von *15 Feb 1783, Haukenzell, Bavaria - 17 Aug 1865, Munich*
JNP-1a. 10 Harmoniestücke für die Harmonie der Königl. Tafelmusik [of Ludwig I]. fl ob 2cl 2hn 2bn.
MS score (post-1840): D-Mbs, Mus.Mss.2438.
  1.1a. Donizetti: Belisario, "Trema Bisanzio", ff.1 - 3.   1.2a. Anon: Kom [sic] du lila flicka, ff.3 - 4.
  1.3a. Donizetti: Belisario, "Dunque andiam", ff.4 - 6.
  1.4a. Auber: Gustave III, "Au près du vous Madame", f.7 - 7b.
  1.5a. I. Lachner: Drei Jahrl nach'en letzten Fenster'ln, [untitled], ff.8 - 9.
  1.6a. I. Lachner: Drei Jahrl nach'en letzten Fenster'ln, "Mit di Fahna und Trummin", ff.9 - 10.
  1.7a - 1.10a. Donizetti: La Fille du régiment, 4 mvts, ff.11 - 22.

*POKORNY, Franz (František) Xaver Thomas *20 Dec 1728, Městec-Králové - 2 July 1794, Regensburg*
FTP-1. [Parthia in E♭], 10 mvts.   2cl 4hn(E♭, Bb) 2bn 2tp 2vla vlne.
AutoMS score & MS parts (c.1770): D-Rtt, Pokorny 171.   ★
FTP-2. Presto assai, in D.   2ob 2bn 2tp(clar) timp.   AutoMS score (c.1770): D-Rtt, Pokorny 196.   ★
*FTP-3. [Parthia in E♭], 6 mvts.   2cl 3hn.   AutoMS score (c.1760): D-Rtt, Pokorny 182/7.   ★
FTP-4. [Quintett in E♭], 3 mvts.   Cembalo, ob/vl 2hn basso.   AutoMS score (c.1770): D-Rtt, Pokorny 150.   ★

*POKORNY, G.J. *(active 1840), Brno*
GJP-1a. Lanner: Hoffnungs-Strahlen Walzer, Op. 158.   ob cl(D) cl(G) 2hn 2bn cbn 2tp.
MS parts: CZ-Bm(au), A.40.154.   *Other Lanner arrs. in CZ-Bm(au) may also be by Pokorny.*

*POKORNÝ, Petr *16 Nov 1932, Prague*
PEP-1. Notturno; 1992.   2ob 2ca 4bn.
Pm (Compusic: Amsterdam, pn 523, c.1994), score & parts.
PEP-1v. Die Reise, 3 pieces on the words of Günter Eich, Op. 33.   M-S, fl 2ob 2cl 2hn 2bn cbn.
Pm (Český hudební fond: Prague, 1990), hire score & parts.
Pm (Compusic: Amsterdam, pn 274, c.1994), score & parts.

*POLDOWSKI, *Mme (pseudonym of:* Irène Regina Wieniawski, *Lady* Dean Paul)
16 May 1880, Brussels - 28 Jan 1932, London
*XZP-1. Suite miniature de chansons à danser, (c.1912).   2fl ob obdam ca cl bthn b-cl.   MS: untraced.

POLI, Giovanni Batta *(1830)*
GBP-1v. Kyrie, 1861.   TB(solo3+rip3), 2cl(C) 2hn basso tp (tb) timp organ.
MS score & parts: I-Vsmc, (the tb part does not appear in the score).   ★

*POLLAK, ( ) *(1770) Possibly a member of the Chotek Harmonie, zámek Veltrusy & zámek Káčina*
YXP-1. Parthia in Dis [E♭]; 4 mvts.   2ob 2cl 2hn 2bn.   MS parts: CZ-Pnm, XX.F.105.   ★

POLOLÁNÍK, Zdeněk *25 Oct 1935, Tišnov*
ZXP-1. Komorní Koncert No. 2.   Winds.   MS score & parts: CZ-OSTpololáník; CZ-Pph.

*POML, ( )
YYP-1. Divertimento.   2ob 2hn 3bn serp.   MS: US-PHschoenbach.

PONCE, Luctor *11 Oct 1914, Geneva*
LXP-1. Euterpe, Suite, Op. 37; 1964.   2fl 2ob 3cl 2hn 2bn.
Pm (Donemus: Amsterdam, 1974), score & parts.

*PONTVIK, Peter *24 April 1963, Copenhagen*
PTP-1. Candombe: Una danza afro-uruguaiana; 1990/1991.   3fl(pic) 3ob(ca) 4cl 2hn 2bn cbn 3tp 3tb tu timp 2perc.
MS score: S-Sic.

*POOT, Marcel *7 May 1901, Vilvoorde, nr Brussels - 12 June 1988, Brussels*
MYP-1. Suite, 1940.   2fl 2ob 2cl 2hn 2bn 2tp 2tb timp perc.
Pm (Universal Edition: Wien, pn 11199, sd), score.
*MYP-2. Mozaïek (Mosaique).   2fl 2ob 2cl 2bn.
Pm (Universal Edition: Wien, London, 1969), miniature score (Philharmonia No. 431) & parts (pn UE 13571).

*POPKIN, Mark *(1960)*
MZP-1a. Brahms: Sextet, Op. 18.   2fl 2ob 2cl 2hn 2bn.
Pm (Compusic: Amsterdam, pn 267, c.1994), score & parts.

PORCELIJN, David *7 Jan 1947, Acht Karspelen, Friesland*
DXP-1. Continuations, 1968.   2fl 2ob 2cl 2hn 2bn tp.
Pm (Donemus: Amsterdam, 1971), score & parts.

*PORPORA, Nicolò Antonio *19 Aug 1686, Naples - Feb 1766, Naples*
NAP-1. Overture Roiale.   2ob 2hn bn 2tp timp.
MS: Provenance unknown.
Pm (Boccaccini & Spada: Roma, pn BS 1146, sd), score & parts; (perhaps an arrangement).

*POSSELT (BOHSELT), František (Franz) *1729 - 27 Jan 1801, Prague*
FNP-1. No. 1 Partitta; in G, 5 mvts.   ob 2hn bn vla.   MS parts: CZ-Pnm, XLII.E.298.   ★

*POSSIO, Gianni *(1950)*
*GQP-1. Serenata (Les Couleurs du Son-ge); 1983, 4 sections.   2ob 2cl 2hn 2bn.
Pm (Rugginenti Editore: Milano, 1984), score (in "New Notation").

POST, Jos *1955, Netherlands*
JDP-1. The Next Call.   fl ob cl 2hn bn tp tb 2db.
Pm (Donemus: Amsterdam, 1979), score.

*POULENC, Francis *7 Jan 1899, Paris - 30 Jan 1963, Paris*
FRP-1. Aubade, Concerto choréographique.   Piano, 2fl 2ob 2cl 2hn 2bn tp timp 2vla 2vc db.
Pm (Roualt, Lerolle & Cie: Paris, 1931), score.
FRP-2. Fanfare.   2cl 2hn 2bn cbn 2tp 2tb timp perc.
Pm (Chester Music: London, sd), hire score & parts.
*FRP-3. Suite française d'après Claude Gervaise (16e siècle); (1935).   Harpsichord, 2ob 2bn 2tp 3tb perc.
Pm (Durand: Paris, pn 13315, 1948), score.

POWELL, Kit (Christopher Bolland) *2 Dec 1937, Wellington, New Zealand*
KCP-1. Stone Poem, 1976.   2 speakers, 2fl 2ob 2cl 2hn 2bn stones.   MS score: NZ-Wn.
KCP-2. Metamorphoses: Theme & variations for woodwind septet.   2fl/ob 2cl 2hn bn.   MS score: NZ-Wn.

*POWNING, Graham *1949, Sydney, Australia*
*GRP-1. Wind Octet; 1984, 5 mvts.   2ob 2cl 2hn 2bn.   In MS: AUS-Smc will assist in contacting the composer.
GRP-2. Bionic Music.   3ob 2bn cbn.   In MS: AUS-Smc will assist in contacting the composer.

PRAAG, Henri C. VAN *18 July 1894, Amsterdam - 11 Dec 1968, Amsterdam*
HVP-1. Music for wind instruments; 1965.   2fl 2ob 3cl 2hn 2bn.
Pm (Donemus: Amsterdam, 1971), score & parts.
HVP-2. Fantasy for bassoon and wind ensemble.   Solo bn, 2fl 2ob 2cl 2hn 2bn.
Pm (Donemus: Amsterdam, 1962), score & parts.
HVP-3. 3 Schetsen voor 7 houtblazers.   fl 2ob 2cl 2bn.
Pm (Donemus: Amsterdam, 1960), score & parts.

*PRACHEŃSKI (Prachenskÿ), Joaues (Jeau, Jounis) *(1760)*
JOP-1. Parthia Turcika, 1798; in C, 5 mvts.   2pic "fletine" 2ob 2cl 2hn 2bn 2tp timp.
Pc (Traeg: [Vienna], pre-1804), No. 236, MS parts: A-Wgm, VIII 39979. ★
JOP-2. Parthia Turcika [in] G, 4 mvts.   2fl "fletine" 2ob 2cl(C) 2hn 2bn tp(prin) pagal+cym.
Pc (Traeg: [Vienna], pre-1804), No. 236, MS parts: A-Wgm, VIII 39978. ★
JOP-3. A[nn]⁰ 1801 Parthia; in C, 4 mvts.   2fl "fletine" 2ob 2cl 2hn 2bn tp(prin) pagal+cym.
Pc (Traeg: [Vienna], pre-1804), No. 236, MS parts: A-Wgm, VIII 39985. ★
JOP-4. Nᵒ II Parthia Turzika; in C, 4 mvts.   2fl "fletin" 2ob 2cl 2hn 2bn tp(prin) pagal+cym.
MS parts: A-Wgm, VIII 38671. ★

*PRAEGER, Heinrich Aloys *1783 - 1854*
HZP-1. Quintetto, Oeuv. 12; in B♭, 4 mvts.   fl 2cl bn vla.
Pc (Breitkopf & Härtel: Leipzig, pn 2046, 1814/1815), parts: GB-Ljag(w), L.62, (with the printed slip of J.C.
Gayl, Frankfurt an Main). ★

*PREISSER, M.A. *(1800)*
MAP-1m. Journal de Musique Militaire contenant Les Journées des 27, 28 et 29 Juillet [1830]; 6 mvts.
fl(E♭) cl(B♭) 4hn tp(bugle+crt) 3clairons(bugles, No. 2 only) 3tb ophr serp b-dr+cym s-dr t-dr.
Pc (Chez Hᵗᵉ Collin: Paris, 18), parts: CH-Gpu, Ib. 4845, GB-Ljag, (photocopy). ★
MAP-1mt. Marche funèbre . . . pour l'Anniversaire des 27, 28 & 29 Juillet [1830] et Dédiée à la mémoire des
victims. fl(E♭) cl(E♭) 4cl(B♭ principale)+2cl(B♭ ripieno) 2hn(solo)+2hn(ripieno) tp 3tb oph serp b-dr s-dr+t-dr.
Pc (Richault: Paris, pn 2244.R., post-1830), parts: CH-Gpu, Ib.4921b; GB-Ljag, (photocopy). ★

PRENRL, Stanko *1880 - 1965*
STP-1. Octet.   2ob 2cl 2hn 2bn.   MS score & parts: SI-Lu.

PRINZ, Alfred *1930, Austria*
AYP-1. Danzas; 1982.   2ob 2cl 2hn 2bn.
Pm (Doblinger: Wien, 1986), miniature score (Stp 543) & parts (pn 06596).

*PROCH, Heinrich *22 July 1809, Česká Lipa (Böhmisch-Leipa) - 18 Dec 1878, Vienna*
HYP-1v. Motette.   SATB, 2cl 2hn 2bn organ.   AutoMS score & parts: A-Wgm, III 53298 (Q 987).
HYP-2v. Herr du riefst uns ins Leben.   SATB, 2hn 2bn organ.   MS parts: A-Ed, B 299. ★

PROCHÁSKA, Franz (František) *(1830)*
FIP-1. Kirchen aufzug (Kostelú pochod) [church march], in E♭.   2cl 2hn 2tp 2flug 2b.
MS parts (c.1870): CŽ-Bm(ro), A.27.185. ★

PRODIGO, Sergio *1949, Italy*
SXP-1. Kammerkonzert II, Op. 81.   Solo pf, 2fl 2ob 2cl 2hn 2bn.
Pm (Berben: Ancona, Italy, pn 2907, c.1988), score & parts.
SXP-2. Ottetto II, Op. 67.   fl ob cl b-cl hn bn tp tb.
Pm (Berben: Ancona, Italy, pn 2920, c.1988), score & parts.

*PROWO (Browos), Pierre *8 April 1697, Altona, nr Hamburg - 8 Nov 1757, Altona*
PYP-1(-6). 6 Concertos à 6; (G, F, C, F, A minor, C), c.1735.   2recorders 2ob 2bn.
MS parts: D-SWl, Mus. 4314 - 4319. ★
Pm (No. 3) (Das Erbe deutsches Musik, XIV, 1941), ed. Schultz, score, pp. 38 - 48.
Pm (No. 4, for 2fl 2ob 2bn) (Hofmeister: Hofheim/Taunus, pn 7303, 1960; reprinted E.F. Kalmus: New York,
pn 9797), ed. G. Hausswald, score & parts.
Pm (No. 6) (Moeck: Celle, pn 1075, 1963), ed. Ochs, score.
Pm (Belwin & Mills: New York, 1980).
PYP-7. Intrada a 6 [or rather, a suite]; in F, 4 mvts.   2ob 2hn 2bn.   MS parts: S-L, Saml. Engelhart 420. ★
PYP-8(-13). 6 Concertos à 5; (F, C, D minor, G, B♭, G minor).   3ob 2bn.
MS parts: D-SWl, Mus. 4313. ★
Pm (No. 1, for 3ob 2bn) (Möseler: Wolfenbüttel, pn 13001, 1959), ed. R.J. Koch, score & parts.
PYP-14. Concerto à 6, in C, No. 2.   2ob 2bn 2b-tp.
Pm (Nagel: Hanover).   *(Original provenance untraced - ? a modern adaptation/arrangement of PYP-14)*

*PUGNI, Cesare *31 May 1802, Genoa - 26 Jan 1870, St Petersburg*
CZP-1. Serenata in Eb, 4 mvts.   fl ca cl 2hn 2bn.   MS pts: I-Mc, Da Camera MS.21.7, (with later substitute
MS parts of cornetta(B♭) for cl, tp(F) for ca, 2tb for 2bn). ★

PUJOLAS, Joseph *(?1770)*
JQP-1m. Nᵒ [MS: 1] Nouvelles marches militaires à Plusieurs Instruments; Marche & Pas redoublé.
2ob 2cl(F) 2cl(C) 2hn 2bn 2tp serp s-dr+cym t-dr.
Pc (Richomme: Sieber: Paris, sd), RISM [P.5628], parts: F-Pn, (2 copies), Vm27 10.487 (1).
Pc (Imbault: Paris, sd), RISM (P 5629), parts: D-HER; F-Pn, Vm7 7096 (1). ★
JQP-2m. Nᵒ [MS: 2] Nouvelles marches militaires à plusieurs instruments; Marche & Pas redoublé.
2fl, 2cl(F) 2cl(C) 2hn 2bn 2tp serp s-dr+cym.
Pc (Richomme: Sieber: Paris, sd), parts, RISM [P 5630], parts: F-Pn, Vm27 10.487 (2).
Pc (Imbault: Paris, sd), RISM (P 5631), parts: D-HER; (bn I, serp, tp only); F-Pn, Vm7 7096 (2). ★

JQP-3m. Nº [MS: 3] Nouvelles marches militaires à Plusieurs Instruments; Marche.
2fifes 2ob 2cl(C) 2hn 2bn tp s-dr cym.
Pc (Richomme; Sieber: Paris, sd), RISM [P 5632], parts: F-Pn, Vm27 10.487 (3).
Pc (Imbault: Paris, s.d.), parts: F-Pn, Vm7 7096 (3). ★
JQP-4m. Nº [MS: 4] Nouvelles marches militaires à Plusieurs Instruments; Marche.
2fifes 2cl(F) 2cl(C) 4hn 2bn tp serp s-dr cym.
Pc (Imbault: Paris, sd), RISM [P 5633], parts: F-Pn, Vm7 7096 (4). ★
JQP-5m. Nº [MS: 5] Nouvelles marches militaires à Plusieurs Instruments; Marche.
2fifes 2cl(Eb) 2cl(Bb) 4hn(2Eb, 2Bb basso) 2bn tp serp s-dr cym; (2ob as option for 2cl(Eb), reading fife pts).
Pc (Imbault: Paris, sd), RISM [P 5634], parts: F-Pn, Vm7 7096 (5). ★
JQP-6m. Nº [MS: 6] Nouvelles marches militaires à Plusieurs Instruments; Marche.
2fifes 2cl(Eb) 2cl(Bb) 4hn(Eb, Bb) 2bn tp serp s-dr cym.
Pc (Richomme: Paris, sd), RISM [P 5635, as published by Imbault], parts: F-Pn, Vm7 7096 (6), (the Imbault printed imprint slip is pasted over the Richomme imprint). ★
JQP-7m.Nº [MS: 7] Nouvelles marches militaires à Plusieurs Instruments; Marche.   2fifes 4cl(C) 2hn 2bn tp.
Pc (Imbault: Paris, sd), RISM [P 5636], parts: CH-E; F-Pn, Vm7 7096 (7). ★
JQP-8m. Nº [MS: 8] Nouvelles marches militaires à Plusieurs Instruments; Marche.
2fifes 2cl(C) 2hn 2bn tp serp s-dr cym.
Pc (Imbault: Paris, sd), RISM [P 5637], parts: F-Pn, Vm7 7096 (8). ★

*PUREBL (Purebel, Burebl), Josef *1768, Vienna - 5 March 1833, Vienna*
Some confusion remains as to the relation between the manuscript sets of Türkische Stücke in CZ-Bm(au) and the sets printed in Vienna by the Chemische Druckerei, 1808 (one set in C, pn 1006, the other in F, pn 1018; we have not located copies of either). A similar problem appears for JSP-1a, where the Chemische Druckerei published "4 Stücke aus den Ballete Figaro" (pn 1485, 1810/1811) and the "Rundtanz" from the same work (not Mozart's opera); JSP-1a are probably drawn from these publications. See also: TRIEBENSEE, JZT-1a.
JSP-1. Nro 4 Türckische Stück [sic] samt Trios; 5 mvts. pic 2fl cl(F) 2cl(C) 2hn 2bn 2tp(prin) b-dr s-dr.
MS parts: CZ-Bm(au), A.19.716. *Not the same work as JSP-1.*
JSP-2.1. Nro 5 Türckische Stücke samt Trios; 5 mvts. pic 2fl cl(F) 2cl(C) 2hn 2bn cbn 2tp(prin) b-dr s-dr.
MS parts: CZ-Bm(au), A.19.717. ★
JSP-2.2. Türkische Stücke; 5 mvts.   Solo cl(Eb), fl cl(Eb) 2cl(Bb) a-cl(Eb) 2hn 2bn tp(prin).
MS parts (by Johann Handl - possibly partly rescored by him): A-Wn, Mus.Hs.608. ★
Pm (WINDS: Northridge, CA, pn W-8, c.1981), photocopy of original parts.
JSP-3. VI. Eccosaises [sic] mit VI. Trios oder militärische Reise Märsche für die Türkische Musik.
pic(F) 2fl cl(F) 2cl(C) 2hn 2bn cbn(with bn II) 2tp b-dr s-dr.
Pc (Im Verlag der K. K. priv. chemischen Druckery: Vienna, pn 1096, 1808/1809), parts: CZ-Pnm, Lobkovic X.H.b.28. ★
JSP-4. No. 3 Parthia auf Thürcische Music [sic]; 5 mvts.   2fl 2cl(F) 2hn 2bn serp 2tp(prin) glock b-dr s-dr.
MS parts: CZ-Bm(au), A.19.719, (the serp part, on different paper, is for mvts 1-4 only). ★
JSP-5. Miscellen in Türkische Musick gesstzt; 5 mvts.   2fl cl(F) 2cl(C) 2hn 2bn cbn 2tp(prin) b-dr s-dr.
MS parts: I-Fc, F.P. S.473. ★
JSP-6. Parthia in Türkische Musik gesetzt; 4 mvts.   2fl cl(F) 2cl(C) 2hn 2bn cbn 2tp(prin) b-dr s-dr.
MS parts: I-Fc, F.P. S.473. ★
JSP-7. 42 Türkische Stücke.   cl(F) 2cl 2hn 2bn tp b-dr.   MS parts: A-KR, H 38/52. ★
JSP-1m. VI [sic: 4] Märsche für die Türkische Musik.   2fl(F) pic+cl(F) 2cl(C) 2hn 2bn cbn 2tp(prin) s-dr.
Pc (Im Verlage der k: k: priv: chemischen Druckerey: Wien, pn 1896, 1812), parts: CZ-Pnm, XLII.F.155. ★
MS parts: A-Sca, Hs.266, No. 53, (No. 1, for: fl(F) 2cl(C) 2hn 2bn 2tp).
JSP-2m. Marcia turca; 2.   2fl(F) pic+cl(F) 2cl(C) 2hn bn 2tp(prin) b-tb b-dr.
MS parts: D-Tl, Z 113, (missing cl I in C). ★
*JSP-3m. VI Märsche mit Trios für Zehnstimmige Harmonie.   2ob cl(F) 2cl(C) 2hn 2/3bn cbn 1/2tp(prin).
Pc (Im Verlage der k: k: priv chemischen Druckerey: Vienna, pn 1496, 1811) parts: A-Wst, M 20675/c; GB-Ljag,, (photocopy). ★
JSP-4m. Marcia, [& Trio] in F.   2ob cl(F) 2cl(C) 2hn 2bn cbn tp(prin).
MS pts: A-Ee, Mus.1141. *Cataloged under "Bubel"; despite reports to the contrary, this work is complete.* ★
JSP-5m. "Der Nachtwächter", Türkischer Zapfenstreich.   Janitscharmusik.
MS parts: D-Bds, Hausbibliothek, Thouret, No. 334, (under "Burebl").
*JSP-1a. 3 Pièces de Ballet Figaro pour la Musique Militaire, du Sieur Jos: Purebl, Musicien de la Cour.
2fl cl(Eb) 2cl(Bb) 2hn 2bn 2tp(prin) b-dr s-dr.
MS parts: D-Tl, Z 114. *These pieces are not from Mozart's opera.*
JSP-2a. Rundtanz aus dem Ballette Figaro [possibly composed by Purebl].   2ob 2cl 2hn 2bn cbn.
Pc (chemischen Druckerey: Vienna, pn 960, 1808), pts: CZ-Pnm, XLI.B.123. Modern MS score & pts: GB-Ljag.
JSP-3a. VI Stücke aus dem Ballet Paul und Virginne für Türkische Musick.   2fl cl(F) 2cl(C) 2hn 2bn tp b-dr s-dr cym.   MS parts: A-KR, H 38/52.
JSP-4a. Nicolini: Quinto Fabio, Marsch.   pic 2fl cl(F) 2cl(C) 2hn 2bn cbn tp(prin) b-dr s-dr.
MS parts: I-Fc, F.P. S.473.

*PUSCHMANN, Josef (Giuseppe) *c.1740, Mladá, nr Bezděz, Boleslav district - 3 Feb 1794 (?Olomouc)*
*JEP-1. Partitta in Eb; *(also attributed to Mozart as K.C17.01, WAM-3d)*, 5 mvts.   2ob 2cl 2hn 2bn.
MS parts: A-KR, H.38/46, ("Giuseppe Puschmann"). *Editions pub. post-1800 are listed at MOZART.* ★
JEP-2. No. 6 Partitta in F; 4 mvts.   2cl(C) 2hn 2bn.
Pc (Traeg: [Vienna], pre-1799], No. 162, MS parts: CZ-KRa, A3950/IV.B.115, (with later parts for fl(D), ob II [sic], & bn I & II transposed to D). ★
JEP-3. No. 4 Partitta in F; 4 mvts.   2cl(C) 2hn 2bn.
Pc (Traeg: [Vienna], pre-1799), No. 162, MS parts: CZ-KRa, A3951/IV.B.116. ★
JEP-4. No. 5 Partitta in F; 4 mvts.   2cl 2hn 2bn.
Pc (Traeg: [Vienna], pre-1799), No. 162, MS parts: CZ-KRa, A3952/IV.B.117. ★
JEP-5. Partitta in Eb; 5 mvts.   2cl(C) 2hn bn.   MS parts: CZ-Bm(au). A.19.697. ★
JEP-1v. Regina Coeli in C.   CATB. 2ob 4hn 2bn 2tp(clar) timp.
MS parts: CZ-OP, (2 copies), minorité A,17,489, minorité A.171 (hn I & II only). ★

*QUEST, Theodor *(?1800)*
TXQ-1m. Marsch.   fl cl(Eb) 2cl(Bb) 2hn 3tp a-hn 3tb bar "bässe" b-dr s-dr.   MS pts: D-DT, Mus-n 1889.

QUILICI, Domenico *23 Oct 1757, Lucca - 9 Nov 1831*
DXQ-1v. Miserere.   TTB, fl ob cl 2hn bn.   MS: I-PAc.
DXQ-2v. Stabat Mater, 1805.   TTB, fl ob cl 2hn bn.   MS: I-PAc.

QUIRICI, Giovanni
GXQ-1v. Credo.   TTB(solo+rip), 2cl 2hn tp tb timp organ.   MS score & parts: I-Vsmc.   ★
GXQ-2v. Kyrie.   TTB(solo+rip), 2cl(C) 2hn tp tb timp organ.   MS score & parts: I-Vsmc.   ★

*RADAUER, Irmfried *1928,*
IRR-1. Hommage . . . Mozart [sic].   2ob 2cl 2bthn 4hn 2bn db.
Pm (Gravis Editions: Bad Schwalbach, pn 1564, 1984), score & parts.

RAE, Allan *3 July 1942, Blairemore, Alberta, Canada*
ALR-1. Fun and games; 1962.   2fl ob 2cl bn.   MS: C-Tcm.

*RAFF, Joseph Joachim *27 May 1822, Lachen, Lake of Zürich - 24/25 June 1882, Frankfurt am Main*
*JJR-1. Sinfonietta, Op. 188; 1878, 4 mvts.   2fl 2ob 2cl 2hn 2bn.
AutoMS score: GB-Lcm, MS. 4119.   ★
MS (1906): US-Wc, M957.R13.
Pc (C.F.W. Siegel's Musikalienhandlung: Leipzig, 1878), parts: US-Wc, M957.R13C.
Pm (Eulenburg: Zürich, 1976), 1st ed. facsimile score, ed. by Hans Steinbeck (pn 10127) & pts (pn 10127a).
*JJR-1a. Liszt: Domine salvum fac regem.   T solo, TTBB chorus, 2ob 2cl 2hn(C) 2hn(F) 2bn 2tp(D) 3tb tu db.
Pc (Breitkopf & Härtel: Leipzig, 1871; reprinted: Gregg Press: Farnborough, Hants, 1972), score, in: *Franz Liszt Musikalisches Werke,* herausgegeben Liszt Stiftung, Bd. V, No. 5 ("Hymnen sowie sonstige Chorgesänge mit Orchester").

*RAFFAEL, ( ) *(1770)*
UXR-1m, 2m. [2] March in C.   2fl 2cl(C) 2hn 2bn serp 2tp(clar) b-dr.
Pc (In **A-82.1m** Acht Märsche für Türkische Musick [sic], 1 Heft, Nos. 2 & 3:) (Johann André: Offenbach am Main, pn 1822, 1803), parts: H-KE, K 731/VIII.   ★
MS score & parts (copy of the André edition): I-Fc, F.P. S.553.

RAIGORODSKY, (Leda) Natalia (*Mrs Harter*) *(?1938), Tulsa, Oklahoma*
LNR-1. Fantasy; 1962.   Piano, fl ob cl 2hn bn.   MS score: US-Wc.

*RAIMONDI, Ignazio *c.1737, Naples - 14 Jan 1813, London*
IXR-1m. Six Grand Marches.   2ob/vl 2cl 2hn 2bn/bn tp timp.
Pc (Printed for the Author, & to be had of T. Skillern: London, 1798), RISM [R 96], with subscribers list, score:
GB-Cu; GB-Gu; GB-Lbl, e.108.(12); GB-Ob, Mus.Instr.I.240(16); US-NYp; US-R.   ★

RAJNA, Thomas *1926*
TXR-1. Serenade; 1959.   2fl ob cl 2hn bn 2tp tb timp perc piano cimbalon.   MS score: GB-Lmic.

*RALSTON, Alfred *c.1910 - c.1985*
AFR-1. Nocturne Sentimentale.   fl 2cl bn.
Pm (New Wind Music: London, 1960).
AFR-1a. Grieg: Seven Norwegian Miniatures.   fl ob 2cl bn/b-cl
Pm (New Wind Music Co.: London, pn A.504, 1960), parts.
   1.1a. Poestiske Tonebilleder, Op. 3, No. 5 (as "Norwegian Tone Picture").
   1.2a. Lyrische Stücke, Op. 12, No. 5, Norske Folkevise (as "Norwegian Folk Song").
   1.3a. Humoresker, Op. 6, No. 3, (as "Humoresque").
   1.4a. Lyrische Stücke, Op. 12, No. 7, Albumblad (as "Albumleaf").
   1.5a(-1.7a). Lyrische Stücke, Op. 12, No. 2, Valse; No. 1 Arietta; No. 4, Elversdans, (as "Dance of the Elves").

*RAMEAU, Jean Philippe *baptized 25 Sept 1683, Dijon - 12 Sept 1764, Paris*
*JPR-1e. Acante et Céphise, ou La sympathie, pastorale-heroique.   2cl 2hn, (continuo ad lib).
Pc (Chez l'auteur; Vve Boivin; Le Clerc: Paris, 1751/52), score: A-Wn; B-Bc (2 copies); CH-Zjacobi; D-Dl; F-AG; F-Pa (2 copies); F-Pn, (2 copies); F-Po, (2 copies, one of incomplete page proofs with autograph amendments); F-Sim; F-V; GB-Lbl, Hirsch II.761; NL-DHgm; US-BE; US-Cn.
Pm (EFM Technisonor: Paris, sd), Vol. 2, pp. 142-144, (continuous pagination, pp. 306-308).
Pm (In: Albert R. Rice, *The Baroque Concerto.* Oxford University Press: London, 1992), scores; Rigaudon, pp. 121 - 122; Entr'acte (pp.126 - 127); Aria, pp. 123 - 126 (bars 1- 8 brs only).
   JPR-1e. Rigaudon. Act II.   2cl 2hn, (continuo ad lib).
   JPR-2e. Entr'acte between Acts II & III.   2cl 2hn, (continuo ad lib).
   JPR-1ve. Aria, "L'amour est heureux"; Act II.   S, 2cl 2hn, (continuo ad lib).

RAMPINI, Domenico *d. 1816*
DXR-1v. Kyrie.   TTB(solo+rip), 2cl(C) 2hn bn timp (vlne) organ(bc-fig).
MS score & parts: I-Vsmc, (with full organ part; additional pts: 2cl "Con Violini", 2tb (to replace hns), vlne).   ★

RAN, Shulamit *1949, USA*
SHR-1. Double Vision.   fl ob 2cl hn bn 2tp 2tb piano.
Pm (T. Presser: Bryn Mawr, PA, 1976).

*RANDHARTINGER, Benedict *27 June 1802, Ruprechtshofen - 22 Dec 1893, Vienna*
BXR-1v. Missa Nro 14 in B[b] und . . . Asperges [me].   TTBB solo & chorus, fl 2ob 2cl 2hn 2bn 2tp a-tb t-tb b-tb bomb timp.   *The Asperges me, which precedes the Missa, is acapella.*
AutoMS score (1858): A-Wn, Mus.Hs.145, (missing the top & timp Anfang; with a reduction for Philharmonica).
MS parts: A-Wn, HK 1207, (with 5 sets of vocal pts & an organ pt - the opening chords of the mvts only).   ★
BXR-2v. Militärisches Te Deum.   SATB chorus (all divisi), fl 2ob 2cl 2hn 2bn 2tp a-tb t-tb b-tb+bomb timp.
MS parts: A-Wn, HK 1216, (with 6 sets of vocal parts).   ★

RANGSTRÖM, (Anders Johan) Ture *1884 - 1947, Sweden*
TUR-1. Dramatisches Intermezzo.   2fl ob 2cl 2hn bn.   MS score: S-Sic.
TUR-2. 3 Pastizen.   2fl 2ob 2cl 2bn.
Pm (Lundquist Abr. Musikförlag: Stockholm).

*RATHGEN, Adam *(1750)*
The Breitkopf catalog Supplement X 1775 lists: 7 Sonate, Op. 1, for 2cl 2hn bn; these have not been traced.
AQR-1m. Six military divertimentos . . . Composed by Rathgen and other Eminent Authors Residing in England;
(all in E♭, 3 mvts; *no other composers are named in this work).*   2cl 2hn bn.
Pc (Printed for & Sold by J. Betz: London, c.1780), parts: GB-Ckc, 104.119 (2) RES.   ★

*RATTI, Leo *(1770?)*
LXR-1a. Mayr: I Solitari, scena.   fl 2cl 2hn bn serp.
MS parts: I-Ppriv.

RAUSCH, Carlos *1924, USA*
CAR-1. Danza.   2ob 2cl 2hn 2bn.
Pm (American Composers Alliance: New York, 1964).

*RAUSCHER, J[ohann]
JWR-1m, 2m. March, E♭ & Pas redoublé, E♭.   2fl ob cl(E♭) 2cl(B♭) 2hn 2bn 2tp serp.
MS parts: NL-Z, Z1433, Nos. 9 & 10.   ★

*RAUTAVAARA, Einojuhani *9 Oct 1928, Helsinki*
EYR-1. Wind Octet, Op. 21; 1962.   fl ob cl 2hn bn tp tb.
Pm (Musikiin Tiedotuskeskus: Helsinki, 1964).
Pm (Josef Weinberger Ltd.: London, 1977).

*RAWLINGS, Thomas A. *1775, London - 1850, London*
TAR-1m. A Grand Military March.   2ob 2cl 2hn 2bn tp timp.
Pc (Printed for the Author: London, c.1798), RISM [R 475], score: GB-Gu; GB-Lbl, g.133.(48);
GB-Ob, Mus.Instr.I.198; GB-Lhumphries (modern MS score & parts).   ★

*RAYKI, György *3 Feb 1921, Budapest*
*GXR-1. Burleske für 11 Bläser (a mi querido amigo Juan Astorga anta), 1953.   fl(pic) ob 2cl 3hn 2bn tp tb.
Pm (Universal Edition: Wien, London, pn UE 14313, 1966), score.

RAZZI, Fausto *4 May 1932, Rome*
FXR-1. Improvisatione I; 1965.   Solo viola, 3fl 2ob 3cl 3hn bn 3tp 3tb timp perc.
Pm (Suvini-Zerboni: Milano, 1966), score.
FXR-2. Musica (Music for 10 winds).   2ob ob(ca) cl 2bn 2tp 2tb.
Pm (Suvini-Zerboni: Milano, pn S6846, 1968), score & parts.

*REBNER, Edward Wolfgang *20 Dec 1910, Frankfurt am Main*
WER-1. Suite, "1492".   2ob 2hn 2bn 2tp 2tb perc.
Pm (Hans Wewerke: München).

REETZ, Gernot
GRR-1. 3 Etudes.   2pic 4fl ob ca 2cl b-cl 3bn cbn.
Pm (BKJ Publications: Boston, Mass, 1984).

*REEVE, William *1757, London - 22 June 1815, London*
*WYR-1em. Tippoo Saib: "Minuet un Militare [sic]".   2ob 2hn 2bn.
Pc (Longman & Broderip: London, 1791), RISM [R 697], vocal score p. 4: GB-Gu; GB-Lbl, G.367.(40);
GB-Lcm.   ★

*REGER, (Johann Baptist Joseph) Max *19 March 1873, Brand, Bavaria - 11 May 1916, Leipzig*
*MXR-1. Serenade in B♭; unfinished, 1 mvt.   2fl 2ob 2cl 4hn 2bn.
Pm (Sämtliche Werke. Unter Mitarbeit des Max-Reger-Institutes (Elsa-Reyer-Stiftung), Bonn:) (Breitkopf &
Härtel: Wiesbaden 1986), Band 38, Supplement III, score.
Pm (Breitkopf & Härtel: Wiesbaden, 1985), hire score & parts.
Pm (Compusic: Amsterdam, pn 246, 1988), score & parts.
*MXR-1v. Weihegesang (dedication hymn for the 350th anniversary of the University of Jena, July 30/31, 1908),
(S. WoO II, 2, p 436).   M or A solo, SATB chorus, 2fl 2ob 2cl 4hn 2bn timp.
Pc (Ed. Bote & Bock: Berlin, 1909), score: GB-Lbl, H.1326.b.(1.).
Pm (Sämtliche Werke. 1966), Band 28, score.

REGT, Hendrik de *1950, Netherlands*
HDR-1. Musica, Op. 26.   2fl 2cl 2bn hpcd.
Pm (Donemus: Amsterdam, 1973), score.

REHFELD, Kurt *1920, Germany*
KRR-1. Heiteres Bläserspiel.   2ob 2cl 2hn 2bn.
Pm (Georg Bauer Musikverlag: Karlsruhe, sd).

*REICHA (Rejcha), Antonin (Antonín, Anton, Antoine) Joseph *26 Feb 1770, Prague - 28 May 1836, Paris*
AJR-1.1m, 1.2m. 1.1m: Musique pour célébrer la mémoire des grands hommes qui se sont illustrés au service
de la Nation française.   Solo ensemble: 3pic 2ob 2cl 2hn(6) 2bn 3db; Ripieno ensemble: 2ob(4) 2cl(4) 2bn(4).
1.2m: Marche funèbre. Solo ensemble: 2ob 2cl 2hn(6) 2bn 2cbn; Ripieno ensemble: 4ob 4cl 4bn 6s-dr 4cannon.
AutoMS score: F-Pn, MS. 2495 & 8425.   ★
Pm (WINDS: Northridge, CA, pn W-90, c.1981), score & parts.

*REICHA, Josef (Joseph, Giuseppe) *13 March 1752, Chudenice, nr Klatovy - 5 March 1795, Bonn*
*JXR-1. Parthia ex D; 4 mvts.   2fl 2ob 2cl(A) 3hn 2bn vlne.
AutoMS score (c.1783): D-HR, HR III 4 1/2 4° 651, (the headtitle of the last mvt - formerly cataloged at HR III
4 1/2 4° 483 falsely states, "Parthia in D von J.G. Feldmayer"; this is definitely the last mvt of this work, in
Reicha's hand).   MS parts (1783): D-HR, HR III 4 1/2 4° 651. ★
Pm (KGS), score (fiche 1299) & parts (fiche 1300).
*JXR-2. Parthia ex D, 4 mvts.   2fl 2ob 2cl(A) 2hn 2bn db(vlne).
AutoMS score (c.1784): D-HR, HR III 4 1/2 4° 496, (the Contro Basso reads off the bn II part). ★
MS parts: D-HR, HR III 4 1/2 4° 94.   Pm (KGS), score (fiche 984) & parts (fiche 461, 462).
*JXR-3. Parthia Ex D; 4 mvts.   2fl 2ob 2cl(A) 2hn bn bn+db(vlne).
AutoMS score (c.1782): D-HR, HR III 4 1/2 2° 497, (the Contro Basso reads off the bn II pt). ★
MS pts: D-HR, HR III 4 1/2 4° 477.   *The pts (by X. Ernst, as "Parthia in D") are falsely attributed to Feldmayr.*
Pm (KGS), score (fiche 985) & parts (fiche 960, 961).
*JXR-4. Parthia Ex D; 4 mvts.   2fl 2ob 2cl(A) 2hn 2bn.
AutoMS Score (c.1783): D-HR, HR III 4 1/2 4° 489.   MS parts: D-HR, HR III 4 1/2 4° 489. ★
Pm (KGS), score (fiche 972) & parts (fiche 973, 974).
JXR-5.1, 5.2 appear to be two versions of the same work with minor differences.
JXR-5.1. Parthia Ex F; 4 mvts.   fl(oblig) 2ob 2cl 2hn.
AutoMS parts (c.1780): D-HR, HR III 4 1/2 4° 498.   Pm (KGS), parts (fiche 986). ★
JXR-5.2. Parthia Ex F; 4 mvts, (a rescoring of JXR-5.2).   2fl 2ob 2cl 2hn 2bn.
AutoMS parts (c.1780): D-HR, HR III 4 1/2 4° 570, (there is no fl 1 pt; probably used the pt from JXR-5.1). ★
Pm (KGS), parts (fiche 1100).
Pm (Compusic: Amsterdam, pn 216, 1988), score & parts.
Pm (Doblinger: Wien, 1991), score & parts.
*JXR-6. Parthia Ex F; 4 mvts.   (2fl) 2ob 2cl 3hn bn bn+vlne.
AutoMS score (1783): D-HR, HR III 4 1/2 4° 490, (without flute parts).
MS parts: D-HR, HR III 4 1/2 4° 490, (with later autograph flute parts). ★
Pm (KGS), score (fiche 975) & parts (fiche 976).
JXR-7. Parthia Ex E♭; 4 mvts.   2ob 2cl 2hn 2bn vlne.
AutoMS score ("le 3 Aoust 1783"): D-HR, HR III 4 1/2 4° 494. ★
Pm (KGS), score (fiche 981).
Pm (Edition Engel: Puchheim, c.1992), score & parts.
JXR-8. Parthia; in D, 4 mvts.   fl(oblig) 2ob 2cl 2hn bn.
Partly AutoMS pts (c.1780): D-HR, HR III 4 1/2 4° 492.   *The title and hn II pt are in the hand of F.X. Link.* ★
Pm (KGS), parts (fiche 979).
Pm (as unidentified Parthia in D:) (Compusic: Amsterdam, pn 247, 1991), score & parts.
*JXR-9.1. Parthia Ex D; 4 mvts.   2ob 2cl(A) 2hn bn.   **JXR-9.2.** Scoring as 9.1 with 2fl ad lib.
AutoMS score ("An: 1782"): D-HR, HR III 4 1/2 4° 495, (JXR-9.1, without flute parts). ★
MS parts: D-HR, HR III 4 1/2 4° 495, (JXR-9.2, as "Parthia in D", with later ad lib flute parts). ★
Pm (KGS), score (fiche 983) & parts (fiche 984).   *The fl pts are missing in the score; the bn part is autograph.*
Pm (Edition Engel: Puchheim, 1992), score (pn 9107) & parts (pn 9007), (omits the ad lib flutes).
JXR-10. Parthia Ex B[♭]; 4 mvts.   2ob 2cl 2hn bn.
AutoMS score ("An. 1782"): D-HR, HR III 4 1/2 4° 493. ★
Pm (KGS), score (fiche 980).
Pm (Edition Engel: Puchheim, c.1992), score & parts.
JXR-11. Parthia Ex Dis [E♭]; 4 mvts.   ob(oblig) 2cl 2hn bn.
AutoMS score ("An: 1782"): D-HR, HR III 4 1/2 4° 491.   MS parts: D-HR, HR III 4 1/2 4° 491. ★
Pm (KGS), score (fiche 977) & parts (fiche 978).

REICHEL, Bernhard   *3 Aug 1901, Neuchâtel*
BYR-1. Divertissement, 1966.   2ob 2cl 2hn 2bn.   MS: CH-Zma.

*REICHMANN, Carl *(1800)*
CXR-1. Marcia für XI-stimmige Harmonie componirt u. instrumentirt . . . Zur heil[ge]n Auferstehung
[Resurrection = Easter Sunday] 1833.   fl cl(I, in F) cl(II & III, in C) 2hn bn 2tp.
MS parts: CZ-Bm(no), A.16.774a, (?missing bn II & cbn parts). ★

*REID, ( )
YYR-1. Parthia in Dis [E♭]; 2 mvts.   2ob 2cl 2hn 2bn cbn.   MS parts (by "C.G.H"): CZ-Pnm, XX.F.57. ★

*REID, John, *General*, (*pseudonym*: "I.R.") *13 Feb 1721, Straloch, Perthshire - 6 Feb 1807, London.*
GJR-1m. A Set of Marches.   2cl/2ob/2fl 2hn bn.
Pc (R. Bremner: London, 1778), RISM [R 1002], parts: GB-CDp; GB-P; GB-Lbl, b.79.(1). ★
   1.1m. 17th Regt. of Foot, Lord Amherst's.   1.2m. 22d Regt., General Gage's.
   1.3m. 51st Regt., Earl of Eglington's.   1.4m. 35th Regt., General Campbell's.
   1.5m. 32d Regt., General Amherst's.   1.6m. 44th Regt., General Abercrombie's.
   1.7m. 63rd Regt., General F. Grant's.   1.8m. 16th Regt., General Robertson's.
   1.9m. 1st Battalion, 60th Regt., General Haldimand's.   1.10m. 70th Regt., General Tryon's.
   1.11m. 2d Battalion, 60th Regt., Colonel Christie's.
   1.12m. 77th Regt. or Atholl Highlanders, Colonel Murray's Strathspey.
   1.13m. 76th Regt., Lord Macdonald's Highlanders.   1.14m. Chatam [sic] Division of Marines.
   1.15m. 12th Regt. of Dragoons.
GJR-2m. A Sett of Minuets and Marches.   (Most are scored for 2vl 2hn b, except where noted below.)
Pc (Printed and Sold by R. Bremner: London, c.1778), RISM [R 1003], score: GB-Lbl, b.79.(2). ★
Pm (Phylloscopus: Lancaster, pn PP147, c.1995), parts.
   2.1m. Minuet 16th; p. 20.   2ob 2hn (2)bn.
   2.2m. March of the 3d. Regt. of Guards; pp. 26 - 27.   2ob 2hn (2)bn.
   2.3m. March of the 42 or Old Highland Regt; pp. 28 - 29.   2ob 2hn basso.
   2.4m. March of the 95th Regiment; p. 30.   2ob 2hn basso.

*REILL, Josef *1793 - 1865*
JYR-1tv. 3 Grablieder, c.1840.   SATB, fl 2cl 2hn 2bn tp tb.   MS: D-WS, MS. 544.

REIMANN, Aribert *4 March 1936, Berlin*
AXR-1. Monumenta.   2fl ob ca 2cl 3hn 2bn 3tp 2tb timp.
Pm (Bote & Bock: Berlin, 1960), hire score & parts.

*REIMANN, Ignaz *27 Dec 1820, Albendorf, Silesia - 17 June 1885, Rengersdorf*
IYR-1v. Ausgabe Nr. 1. IV Stationem mit Pange lingua für das heilige Fronleichnamsfeste Leicht ausfürbar für
SATB, 2fl 2cl(A) 2hn 2tp t-hn b-tb timp.
MS score (2) & pts: CZ-Pnm, XLIII.D.205, (with duplicate pts: S(2),A(4),T,B, fl I & II, hn I & II, t-hn b-tb. ★
*IYR-1.1tv. 14 Begräbniss für Kinder.   CATB, 2cl 2hn 2tp t-hn basso.
Pc (sn: sl [A Pietsch: Neustadt ob. Schl., sd), parts: CZ-Bm(ro), A.23.340.
   1.1/1tv. Lebe wohl geliebtes Elterngaar.   1.1/2tv. Engel schweben jetzt hernieder dich.
   1.1/3tv. Kommt, o Eltern und erfüllet eure.   1.1/4tv. "Kaum zum Leben est geboren.
   1.1/5tv. Erhebt die Blicke von der Erde.   1.1/6tv. Das Blaume gleich vom Sturm geknickt.
   1.1/7tv. Wir im Blüthenmond die Sonne.   1.1/8tv. Unerbittlich ist des Todes Bote.
   1.1/9tv. Nimm dies Kind in deinen Hände, Jesus. 1.1/10tv. Klagend stehn an ihres Kindes Leiche.
   1.1/11tv. Sind Kinder ihrer Eltern Freude.   1.1/12tv. Goldes Kind! das schmerzlich wir beweinen.
   1.1/13tv. Ruh, sanft, schaft wohl.   1.1/14tv. Schonungstos und ohn' Erbarmen.
IYR-1.2tv. 2 Grablieder 1. u. 2 [3. .u. 4; 5. u. 6; 7. u. 8; 9. u. 10].   CATB, 2cl 2hn 2tp flug b-tb.
MS parts: CZ-LIa(vl), No. 2406 - 2410 hud., respectively.
IYR-1.3tv. [= IYR-1.1/4tv, 1.1/6tv].   2 Grablieder bei Kindern.   CATB, 2cl 2hn 2tp(clar) bomb.
MS parts: CZ-LIa(vl), No. 2398 hud., (b-flug & b-tb replace the bomb pt listed on the titlepage).
IYR-1.4tv. [= IYR-1.1/7tv, 1.1/8tv].   2 Grablieder in As [A♭].   CATB, fl 2cl 2hn 2tp b-flug bomb.
MS parts: CZ-LIa(vl), No. 2425 hud.
IYR-1.5tv. [= IYR-1.1/13].   Grablied in As [A♭].   CATB, fl cl(E♭) 2cl(B♭) 2hn 2tp b-flug bomb.
MS parts (by Anton Ullrich - ?also the arranger - 20 Feb 1879): CZ-LIa(vl), No. 2449 hud.
IYR-1.6tv. [= IYR-1.1/13, 1.1/14].   2 Grablieder. Bei erwachesenen Person.   CATB, 2cl 2hn 2tp flug b-tb.
MS parts: CZ-LIa(vl), No. 2444 hud., (as Anonymous).
*IYR-2.1tv. 16 Begräbnisslieder für Erwachsene.   CATB, (2cl 2hn 2tp(chrom) t-hn basso ad lib).
Pc (A. Pietsch: Neustadt ob. Schl., sd), parts: CZ-Bm(ro), A.23.339. ★
   2.1/1tv. Bei einen Jünglinge. "Uiber Moder, über Leichen".
   2.1/2tv. Bei einer Jünglinge oder einer Jungfrau. "In der schönsten Blüthe deines Lebens".
   2.1/3tv. Bei einer Mutter. "Leb' wohl, leb' wohl du treues Herze".
   2.1/4tv. Bei einer Mutter. "Trauernd stehn wir hier und weinen".
   2.1/5tv. Bei einem Vater oder Mutter. "Guter Vater [Mutter]! du hast nun vollendet".
   2.1/6tv. Bei einer Person welch lange und schwer gelitten hat. "Schlummre sanft in kühler Erde".
   2.1/7tv. Bei alten Personen. "Vollendet hinnieden ist nun mein Lauf".
   2.1/8tv. Bei alten Personen. "Endlich kamm ich doch zum Ziele".
   2.1/9tv. Bei einem Armen. "Ruhen lass nun deine Hände".
   1.10tv. "Mensch o Mensch mit deinem Plänen".   2.1/11tv. "Jetzt da ich augerungen habe des Lebens".
   1.12tv. "O weint und betet frömme Herzen".   2.1/13tv. "Ein Jammerthal ist uns're Erde".
   2.1/14tv. "Ruhig ist der Todesschlummer".   2.1/15tv. "Mussten wir solch Leid erleben?"
   2.1/16tv. Am Grabe eines Lehrens. [1] "Von Verklärungsbauch umflossen".
     [2] Salve Regina, [for CAT only, in MS].
IYR-2.2tv. 2 Grablieder [1, 2; 3, 4; 5, 6; 7, 8; 9, 10, 11, 12; 13, 14; 15, 16].   CATB, 2cl 2hn 2tp t-hn b-tb.
MS parts: CZ-LIa(vl), No. 2488, 2481 - 2487 hud., respectively, (IYR-2.1/16 is scored for CATB, 4hn t-hn b-tb).
IYR-2.3tv. [= IYR-2.1/10tv, 2.1/4tv].   2 Grablieder.   CATB, fl 2cl 2hn 2tp b-flug bomb.
MS parts: CZ-LIa(vl), No. 2499 hud.
IYR-3.1/1tv. [= IVR-2.1/4tv, IYR-1.1/13tv]   II Grablieder: Trauernd stehn wir hier und weinen, [&] Ruh sanft,
schlaf wohl![,] für vier Singstimmen und Harmoniebegleitung.   SATB, fl cl(E♭ 2cl(B♭) 2hn 3tp 2flug b-flug
b-tb 2tu.   MS parts (by N. Roesler, 21 Jan 1873): CZ-LIa(je), No. 219 hud., (with duplicate SA parts).

*REINAGLE, Joseph *1762, Portsmouth - 12 Nov 1825, Oxford*
JNR-1m. The Oxford University Volunteers [Slow & Quick] March.   2cl 2hn bn.
Pc (Printed for the Author, by Messrs. Goulding & Co: London, wm1798), RISM [R 1050], score: GB-AB;
GB-CDp; GB-Lbl, g.272.u.(20). ★

*REINECKE, Carl Heinrich Carsten *23 June 1824, Altona - 10 March 1910, Leipzig*
*CHR-1. Oktett, Op. 216; 3 mvts.   fl ob 2cl 2hn 2bn.
Pc (Kistner: Leipzig, 1892), score & pts: D-Bhm, 6602, 6003; I-Mc, Part. e Parti 56.4; US-Wc. ★
Pm (Musica rara: London, sd), score & parts.
Pm (Hänssler Verlag, *via* Carus-Verlag: Stuttgart, 1973), parts.
Pm (sn: sl, 1980), score & parts reproduced from the Kistner edition in US-Wc.
Pm (Compusic: Amsterdam, pn 217, 1988), score & parts.
Pm (International Music Co: New York, pn 2942, 1989), ed. Stewart, score & parts.
Pm (Doblinger: Wien, 1991), score & parts.
*CHR-2. Sextet in B♭, Op. 271; 1903, 3 mvts.   fl ob cl 2hn bn.
Pc (J.H. Zimmermann: Leipzig, pn Z.4079, 1904), score & pts: I-Mc, Da Camera 1.106.5, (missing ob); US-R. ★
Pm (Compusic: Amsterdam, pn 248, 1988), score & parts.

*REINER, Karel *27 June 1910, Žatec - 17 Oct 1979, Prague*
KXR-1. Koncertantní Suite; 1947.   Winds & percussion.
Pm (Český hudební fond: Prague), hire score & parts.
KKR-2. Malá suita [Little Suite].   fl 2ob 2cl 2hn bn.
Pm (Český hudební fond: Prague, 1960), hire score & parts.

REINHARDT, Bruno *1929, Israel*
BRR-1. Allegro moderato.   2hn 2bn.   Pm (International Music Co: NY, sd), score & parts.

REINHARTH, J.G. *(?1710)*
XJG-1. Parthie; in C, 7 mvts. 2ob 2bn 2tp(clar) 2vl. MS parts: D-WD, Sig. 724.

*REINISCH, Hermann *(1800)*
*HXR-1. N. 1 Walzer Erinnrung [sic] an die Egg'stersteine [sic: Externstein].
terz-fl ob cl(Eb) 3cl(Bb) 2hn 2bn 2tp a-tb t-tb b-tb serp b-dr s-dr. MS parts: D-DT, Mus-h 3 R 2.

*REISSIGER, Carl Gottlieb *31 Jan 1798, Wittenberg - 7 Nov 1859, Dresden*
CGR-1v. 2 Lieder ("Wiedersehn" & "Pilgrim und Wiederhall"). Voice & winds. MS: in private hands.

*REIZENSTEIN, Franz *7 June 1911, Nuremburg - 15 Oct 1968, London*
FYR-1. Serenade in F, Op. 29; in F, 1951. Concertante trumpet, fl 2ob 2cl 2hn 2bn cbn/db.
Pm (Boosey & Hawkes: London, etc., pn 2234, 1977), score & parts (with a foreword by Margaret Reizenstein).

REKOLA, Jukka *1948, Sweden*
UJR-1. Malinchorali: Musik; 1978. fl(pic) ob 2cl 2hn bn tp tb tu 2perc. MS score: S-Sic.

*RELLUZI, Paolo *(?1740)*
ZXR-1. Parthia Ex D; 4 mvts. 2ob 2hn bn. MS parts: CZ-KRa, A3955/IV.B.118. ★

RENOSTO, Paolo *10 Oct 1935, Florence*
PXR-1. Musica per dieci, 1977. 2fl 2ob 2cl 2hn 2bn.
Pm (Carisch: Milano, pn 22055, 1980), score.

RESPIGHI, Ottorino *9 July 1879, Bologna - 18 April 1936, Rome*
OXR-1. Suite della tabacchiera; 1930. 2fl(pic) 2ob 2bn, pf duet (4 hands).
Pm (Ricordi: Milano, pn 133689, 1984), score & parts.

REUSS, August *6 March 1871, Liliendorf bei Znaim, Moravia - 18 June 1935, Munich*
AYR-1. Octet in Bb, Op. 37; 1918. 2ob 2cl 2hn 2bn.
Pc (J. H. Zimmermann: Leipzig, 1920), score & parts.
Pm (Zierfuss: München, sd), score & parts: D-Bhm, 32242.

*REUTTER, Georg, *the Younger* *baptized 6 April 1708, Vienna - 11 March 1772, Vienna*
GZR-1. Quintett; in F. 2ob 2hn bn. AutoMS score: A-H, (2 Teils, incomplete: Teil 2 breaks off after bar 15).

REVERDY, Michele *12 Dec 1943, Alexandria, Egypt*
MYR-1. Scenic Railway, 1983. fl(pic) fl(b-fl) ob(ca) 2cl cl(cl Eb) b-cl 2hn bn(cbn) tp tb tu db 3perc.
Pm (Salabert: Paris, 1983), hire score & parts.

REVUELTAS, Silvestre *31 Dec 1899, Santiago Papasquiaro, Mexico - 5 Oct 1940, Mexico City*
SYR-1. 3 Sonetos. 2cl b-cl hn bn 2tp tb piano tam-tam.
Pm (Southern Music Publishing Co. c/o Peer-Southern Organization: New York, pn 61500-794, sd), score & pts.
SYR-2. Toccata without a fugue. Violin, pic 3cl hn tp timp.
Pm (Southern Music Publishing Co. c/o Peer-Southern Organization: New York, 1959), score (pn 61470-791)
& parts (pn 61470-792).

*ŘEZAČ, Ivan *9 Nov 1924, Řevnice, nr Prague - 26 Dec 1977, Prague*
IZR-1. Dechový [wind] octet. 2ob 2cl 2hn 2bn.
Pm (Český hudební fond: Prague, 1976), hire score & parts.

*REZNICEK (Reznicek), ( ) *(1790) Kapellmeister to the k.k. Ignatz Graf Gyulai 60th Infantry Regiment*
XZR-1a. Krommer: [unidentified] Parthia; 3 mvts.
pic(Eb) cl(Ab) 4cl(Eb) cl(Bb) 4hn 3bn 2klappen-tp 5tp(2Eb, Ab, Bb, G) contrabassi b-dr s-dr.
AutoMS score (Wien am 3/8 1825): A-Wn, Mus.Hs.2280; GB-Lhumphries (modern MS parts). ★

*ŘEZNÍČEK, Petr *18 Feb 1938, Hradec Králové*
*PZR-1. Prelude & Toccata for Winds and Percussion Instruments, 1965. MS score: CZ-Březníček.

*RHEINBERGER, Josef Gabriel *17 March 1839, Vaduz - 25 Nov 1901 Munich*
*JGR-1v. Messe in Bb, Op. 172, 1892. TTBB chorus, 2fl 2ob 2cl 2hn 2bn 2tp db timp.
Pc (F.E.C.Leuckart: Leipzig, pn 4544 - 4588, 1897), score & pts: CZ-Pnm, XLIII.E.140; GB-Lbl, F.274.rr.(8.). ★
Pm (Carus-Verlag: Stuttgart, sd), score (pn 50,172) & parts (pn 50172/09), db pt (pn 50172/11).

*RHENÉ-BATON, (*pseudonym of* René Bâton) *5 Sept 1879, Courseilles - 23 Sept 1940, Le Mans*
*YXR-1. Aubade, Op. 53; in G, 1 continuous mvt. fl ob 2cl hn 2bn.
Pm (Durand: Paris, 1940), score & parts: F-Pn; GB-Lcml.

RICHETTI, Antonio *(?1780)*
AIR-1v. Dixit Dominus; in Ab. TTB solo & chorus, fl ob 2cl 2hn 2tp tb cb timp organ.
MS vocal score & parts: I-BRd, palch. 6-6/XVII, (missing tp II).

*RICHTER, ( ) *1st of the name* *(1770)*
QZR-1. Parthia in B[b]; 4 mvts. 2cl 2hn basso/bn.
MS parts (by Dominik Hübner, Langenbruck): CZ-Pu(dm), 59 R 3338. ★

*RICHTER, ( ) *(1780), Kapellmeister of the Neugebaur Regiment, afterwards Kapellmeister in Stuttgart, c.1835*
QYR-1a. Beethoven: Sonata in Ab, Op. 26, 3rd mvt, as "Todten Marsch für die Begräbniss der H[errn] General
von Bennendorf. 2ob 2cl(Eb) 3cl(Bb) 2bthn 6hn(4 Eb, 2 Ab) 2bn 2tp("H" = Bᵇ) 2tp(Eb) a-tb t-tb b-tb/serp.
MS parts (1828): D-Tl, Z 49.
QYR-2a. Mayr: Il carretto del venditor d'aceto. 2ob 2cl 2hn 2bn cbn.
MS parts: D-DO, Mus.Ms.1294, (with duplicate bn parts).
*QYR-3.1a(-3.7a). Harmonie[:] 1tes Finale aus der Oper: Don Juan [Mozart: Don Giovanni]: in 3 Abtheilungen[,]
Ouverture[,] Hirten Chor[,] Cavatine und Romanze aus der Oper: Rothkaepchen [Le petit chaperon rouge] von
Boieldieu. fl(G, Nos. 4, 5 & 7)/2fl(F, No. 6) cl(F, Nos. 1 - 4, 7; Eb, No. 6; D), No. 5) 3cl(C - cl II & III in Bb
in No. 6) 2hn 2bn 2tp b-tb serp/cbn. MS parts: D-Rtt, Sm. 19, Nos. 1 -3, (Mozart), 4 - 7 (Boieldieu).
QYR-1ad. Meyer [sic: ?Farinelli]: Theresa et Claudio. 2ob 2cl 2hn 2bn. MS pts: D-DO, (?lost).

*RICHTER, Anton *? - 1853*
AZR-1. Overtura; in E♭. fl 2cl(C) 2hn 2bn. AutoMS score & parts: A-Wgm, VIII 38550. ★
AZR-2. Septetto; in E♭, 4 mvts. fl 2cl 2hn bn.
AutoMS score & parts (14 Jan 1829): A-Wgm, VIII 37678, (parts missing hn I). ★
AZR-3. Serenata; in F, 4 mvts. fl 2cl 2hn bn. AutoMS score & pts (4 Dec 1827): A-Wgm, VIII 37680. ★

*RICHTER, Pius *11 Dec 1818, Warnsdorf - 10 Dec 1893, Vienna. (k.k. Hof-Organist).*
PYR-1v. [4] Stationen zum Frohnleichnamsfeste. SATB, fl 2cl(A) 2hn 2bn 2tp cbn/b-bomb timp.
MS parts(?1840s): A-Wn, Mus.Hs.2192, (the cbn pt is original, and has been altered to "Bassbombardon";
addditional SATB & b-bomb parts dating from c.1880 are also present). ★

RIDOUT, Godfrey *1918 - 1984, Canada*
GDR-1. Tafelmusik; 1976. 2fl 2ob 2cl 2hn 2bn 2tp 3tb tu. MS score: C-Tcm.

*RIEDEL, Georg *8 Jan 1934, Czechoslovakia, now resident in Sweden*
GOR-1. Intrada för blåsork & jazzgrupp; 1972. 2sax guitar db drums, fl fl(pic) 2ob 2cl 4hn 2bn 3tp 3tb tu timp.
MS score: S-Sic.
GOR-2. Tre danser för jazzgrupp' & blåsork; 1966.
fl a-sax tp guitar piano db drums, 2fl 2ob 2cl 2hn 2bn 2tp tb timp. MS score: S-Sic.
GOR-3. Skriket; 1982. 2fl 2ob 2cl 2hn 2bn. MS score: S-Sic.

*RIEDELBAUCH, Václav *1 April 1947, Dyšina nr Plzeň*
VZR-1. Concerti e Trenodi. 2ob 2cl 2hn 2bn.
Pm (Český hudební fond: Prague, 1979), hire score & parts.
Pm (Artia: Prague).

*RIEGER, Gottfried *1764, Troplowitz, Silesia - 13 Oct 1855, Brno*
GYR-1. Harmonie; in B♭, 6 mvts. 2ob 2cl 2hn 2bn cbn 2tp.
MS parts: CZ-Bm(au), A.36.887, (missing horn II, bn I & II). ★
GYR-2. Casatione in B[♭]; 5 mvts. 2cl 2hn 2bn. MS parts: CZ-Bm(no), A.16.666. ★
GYR-3. Parthia in F, La chasse; 4 mvts. 2cl 2hn 2bn. MS parts: CZ-Bm(no), A,16.665. ★
GYR-4. Parthia in C; 4 mvts. 2cl(C) 2hn 2bn. MS parts: CZ-Bm(no), A.16.664. ★
GYR-5. Romance; in B♭, 1 long mvt. 2cl 2hn 2bn. Ms pts: CZ-Bm(no), A.16.667. ★
GYR-6 & GYR-y are based on pieces from Das Labyrinth, *Winter's sequel to Mozart's* Die Zauberflöte.
GYR-6. Variations aus dem zweyter Theil der Zauberflöte, [Act II, Finale, Glöckenspiel, "Höll und Teufel!"].
2cl 2hn 2bn. MS parts: CZ-Bm(no), A.16.662, (theme, 7 vars, finale). ★
GYR-7. Variations aus dem zweyter Theil der Zauberflöte; [Act I, No. 3, Duetto Papagena & Papageno, "Herbei
ihr Leute, um unser Gluck zu fehn"]. 2cl 2hn 2bn. MS pts: CZ-Bm(no), A.16.861, (theme, 6 vars, coda). ★
GYR-1m. Marche. 2cl 2hn 2bn. MS parts: CZ-Bm(no), A.16.667, (?lost). *The Haugwitz inventory lists this
work, linked with the* Romance *GYR-5; it now appears to be missing.*
GYR-1a. Opern Stücke . . . nebst einem Contradanse. 2cl 2hn 2bn.
    1.1a. Hoffmeister: Der Königssohn aus Ithaka, 1mvt. 1.2a. K. Liechtenstein: Der Steinerne Braut, Allegretto.
    1.3. Rieger: Contradanse. 1.4a. Schenck: Der Dorfbarbier, Alla Pollaca.
    1.5. [?Rieger]: Thema con Variations, [in fact, one variation only].
GYR-2a. Dalayrac: Azémia (as "Die Wilden), overture & 6 mvts. 2cl 2hn 2bn. MS pts: CZ-Bm(no), A.16.661.
GYR-3a. Mozart: La Clemenza di Tito, overture & 5 mvts. 2cl 2hn 2bn. MS parts: CZ-Bm(no), A.16.659.
GYR-4a. Winter: Die unterbrochene Opferfest, overture & 7 mvts. 2cl 2hn 2bn.
MS parts: CZ-Bm(no), A.16.663.

*RIEGGER, Wallingford *29 April 1885, Albany, Georgia, USA - 2 April 1961, New York*
WZR-1a. Introduction and Fugue, Op. 74; arranged by the composer from his Op. 69 version (1957) for 4vc or
cello orchestra, 1960. Solo cello, 3fl 2ob 3cl 4hn 2bn 3tp 3tb tu timp.
Pm (Associated Music Publishers: New York, 1960), hire score & parts.
WZR-1v. Eternity, Op. 32a; (text by Emily Dickinson), 1942. SSA, fl 2hn db.
Pm (Harold Flammar: New York, 1945), vocal score (pn 2460) only; hire possibilities unknown.

*RIEPEL, Josef (Giuseppe) *22 Jan 1709, Horschlag - 23 Oct 1782, Regensburg*
JFR-1. Divertimento; in E♭, 12 mvts, (RWV 33). 2cl 4hn(E♭, B♭) 2bn 2tp 2vla basso.
AutoMS parts (c.1780): D-Rtt, Riepel 19. ★
JFR-2. Divertimento; in E♭, 17 mvts, (RWV 34). 2cl 2hn 2bn 2vla vlne.
(?Auto)MS parts (c.1780): D-Rtt, Riepel 21. ★
JFR-3. Divertimento; in G, 15 mvts, RWV 35). 2a-cl(G) 2vla vlne. MS pts (Dec, 1780): D-Rtt, Riepel 20. ★

*RIES, Ferdinand *baptized 28 Nov 1784, Godesburg - 13 Jan 1838, Frankfurt*
FZR-1. Nocturne; in E♭; 6 mvts, WoO 50. fl 2cl hn 2bn.
AutoMS score (1834): D-Bds, Mus.Ms.Auto.F.Ries.76N. ★
Pm (Ries & Erler: Berlin, 1993), ed. Helge Bartholomäus, score & parts.
FZR-2. Nocturne; in E♭, 4 mvts, WoO 60. fl 2cl hn 2bn.
AutoMS score (1836, Frunkfurt): D-Bds, Mus.Ms.Auto.F.Ries.77N. ★
Pm (Ries & Erler: Berlin, 1994), ed. Helge Bartholomäus, score & parts.
FZR-1tv. Nun lasset uns den Leib begraben; lyrics by Klopstock. S solo, TTBB, 2hn 2bn 2vla vc db.
Pc (A. Kuhnel: Leipzig, pn 1027, 1812/13), *No. 6 der Gesangstücke*, parts: CZ-Bm(au), A.19.783. ★
FZR-1m. March, ("The Return of the Troops"), Op. 53, No. 2.
Military band (original for piano duet; no copies of band version traced).
AutoMS score: D-Bds, Mus.Ms.Auto.F.Ries.51N, (for small orchestra). ★
FZR-2m. Introduction and Grand March, as performed by the Band of his Royal Highness, the Prince Regent,
at Brighton, Op. 53, No. 3. Military band. AutoMS piano score (1817): D-Bds, Mus.Ms.Auto.F.Ries.52N. ★

RIESS, J.H. (?Johann Heinrich)
JKR-1m, 2m. 2 Marches, both E♭. 2fl ob cl(E♭) 2cl(B♭) 2hn 2bn 2tp. MS pts: NL-Z, Z1133, Nos. 5 & 7. ★

*RIETI, Vittorio *28 Jan 1898, Alexandria, Egypt - 19 Feb 1994, New York*
VXR-1. Cello Concerto; 1934. Solo cello, fl ob 2cl 2hn 2bn tp db timp perc.
Pm (Ricordi: Milano, etc., 1936), solo part & piano reduction only (pn 123690).
Pm (General Music Company, G. Schirmer: New York), score.
VXR-2. Recital for Young Chambrer Players: Valsette No. 4.   2fl 2cl bn.
Pm (General Music Co.: New York, 1967), score & parts.

RIGEL, ( ) (? = Henri Joseph, qv)
ZZR-1 (= **HJR-1c**). Parthia Ex C; 4 mvts.   2ob 2hn bn.   MS parts: CZ-Pnm, XLII.B.215.   ★
ZZR-1a (= **HJR-1ac**). W. Müller: Das Schlagenfest in Sangora, quartet "Was nüken Trepter".   2cl 2hn 2bn.
MS parts: CZ-Bm(au), A.36.663.

*RIGEL (Riegel), Henri Joseph, *père* *9 Feb 1741, Wertheim, Franconia - May 1799, Paris*
HJR-1mv. Hymne à la Liberté (Hymne pour la fête du 10 août); P.106.
CATB, p-fl 2cl 2hn 2bn 2tp serp cb timp.   AutoMS score: F-Pn, H2 21.   ★
MS parts: F-Pn, (2 copies), H2. 145 a-g, L.19711, (the latter with duplicate pts: C(19), A(11), T(12), B(16),
p-fl(2) cl I (4), cl II (5), hn I, (2), hn II, (2) bn I (3), bn II (3), cb (5); the serp & 2tp are single pts only).   ★
HJR-1c. Parthia Ex C; 4 mvts.   2ob 2hn bn.   MS parts: CZ-Pnm, XLII.B.215.   ★
HJR-1ac. W. Müller: Das Schlagenfest in Sangora, quartet "Was nüken Trepter".   2cl 2hn 2bn.
MS parts: CZ-Bm(au), A.36.663.

*RIGHINI, Vincenzo *22 Jan 1756, Bologna - 19 Aug 1812, Bologna*
*VYR-1.1. Armonia, in F, 1797, 6 mvts.   2ob 2cl 2hn 2bn vlne/cb.
MS parts: D-B, RKZ-B-1; I-Fc, F.P. S.411.   ★
Pm (Steinquest), pp. 282 - 397, score.
VYR-1.2. Parthia in Eb; 4 mvts (omits mvts 4 & 5 of VYR-1.1).   2ob 2cl 2hn 2bn.
MS parts (purchased from the estate of Graf von Klenau, c.1820): D-Rtt, Righini 12.
VYR-1.3. Serenata Concertante; in Eb, 6 mvts.   2cl 2hn 2bn.   MS parts: CZ-Bm(no), A.16.658.   ★
VYR-1.4. Serenata; in Eb, 4 mvts (divides mvt 1 into 2 mvts; omits mvts 2, 3 & 6).   2cl 2hn 2bn.
Pc (Schmidt & Rau: Leipsic [sic], pn 9, c.1796), RISM [R 1666], parts: H-KE, K 1024/IX; S-L; US-WS.   ★
Pc (Breitkopf & Härtel: Leipsic [sic], pn 9, post-1796), RISM [R 1667], parts, (from the same plates as the
Schmidt & Rau edition): S-Skma.
Pc (chez Gombart & Co: Augsbourg [sic], pn 374, c.1797), RISM [R 1668], as by "Rhighini [sic]", parts:
A-Wgm, VIII 5200; D-B; GB-Ljag(w).
MS parts (by "I.H.C", IHC-1ad): CZ-Pnm, XX.F.110, (as "Serenata in Es").
*VYR-2.1. Serenata in Eb; 4 mvts.   2ob 2cl 2hn 2bn.   MS parts: A-Wgm, VIII 39990; US-WS.   ★
*VYR-2.2. Sonata; in Eb, 3 mvts, (omits mvt 3).   2cl 2hn 2bn.
(?Auto)MS parts: A-Wgm, VIII 21579 (Q 16429).   ★
Pc (Traeg: [Vienna], pre-1799), No. 165, MS parts: (untraced).
*VYR-3. Armonia con Capricio [sic], in D; 2 mvts.   vl hn 2bn vc.   MS parts: D-B, Mus.ms.18571/60.   ★

RIISAGER, Knudåge *6 March 1897, Port Kunda, Estonia - 26 Dec 1974, Copenhagen*
KYR-1. Sinfonietta, Op. 7; 1924.   fl cl 2bn 2tp 2tb.
Pm (Samfundet til udgivelse af Dansk Musik: Copenhagen, sd), score.
Pm (Southern Music Co.: San Antonio, Texas, sd), score.

RIKL, Václav (Wenceslaus)
VKR-1v. Requiem.   CATB, 2cl 2hn 2bn.
AutoMS parts: CZ-Pnm, XIV.D.141, (with alternative parts for 2 violins replacing the clarinets).   ★

RIMMER, John Francis *1939, New Zealand*
JOR-1. Octet for winds; 1964-65.   2ob 2cl 2hn 2bn.   MS score: NZ-Wn.

*RINCK, Johann Christian Heinrich *18 Feb 1770, Elgersburg - 7 Aug 1846, Darmstadt*
None of these works are cited in Donat's thematic catalog. A microfilm of the Yale collection is in D-DS.
JCR-1. [Choral:] "Nun danket alle Gott".   2ob 2hn 2bn 2tp 3tb timp.
AutoMS score: US-NH, Ma21 Y11 R47 ms.56 LM 4458.
JCR-2. [Choral:] "Wie schön leuchtet der Morgenstern".   2cl 2hn 2bn 2tp 3tb timp.
AutoMS score: US-NH, Ma21 Y11 R47 ms.56 LM 4558.
JCR-1t. Zur Begräbnissfeuer des Capellmeisters [Carl] Wagners, 1822.   2fl ob 2cl 2hn 2bn cbn a-tb t-tb b-tb.
AutoMS score: US-NH, Ma21 Y11 R47 ms.29 LM 4402.   ★
JCR-1v. Choral: Herr Gott dich loben wir.   SATB, 2ob 2hn 2bn 2tp 4tb organ.
AutoMS score: US-NH, Ma21 Y11 R47 ms.53 LM 4454.   ★
JCR-2v. Hallelujah.   ATB, 2cl 2hn 2bn 2tp(clar) 2vlne db timp.
AutoMS score: US-NH, Ma21 Y11 R47 ms.38 LM 4435, (the vocal lines are without text).   ★
JCR-3v. [Cantata, "Anbetung Dir"], "Dieses Musikstücke weuden den 3 Octbr. 1832 . . . aufgeführt".
SATB, 2fl 2cl 2hn 2bn 2tp timp.   AutoMS score: US-NH, Ma21 Y11 R47 ms.34 LM 4432.   ★
JCR-4v. [Choral:] Dich von ewiger Preissen wir.   SSTB, 2fl 2cl(C) 2hn 2bn 2tp(clar) timp organ.
AutoMS score (9 Nov 1812): US-NH, Ma21 Y11 R47 ms.27 LM 4400.   ★
JCR-5v. [Osterlied:] Preis dem Ueberwinder.   SSTB, 2fl 2cl 2hn 2bn 2tp timp organ.
AutoMS score: US-NH, Ma21 Y11 R47 ms.41 LM 4439.   ★
JCR-6v. [Cantata, "Die Freundschaft ist des Himmelsbild"] Lied an der Treu.   SATB, fl 2cl 2hn 2bn 2tp db timp.
AutoMS score ("Dieses Musikstücke wirden beim Herbst-Examen 1833 aufgeführt"):
US-NH, Ma21 Y11 R47 ms.37 LM 4434. *Includes "Menschenlied", Solo TB, fl 2cl 2hn 2bn.*   ★
JCR-7v. [Choral: "Gross ist der Herr"].   SATB, fl 2cl 2hn 2bn 2tp timp.   (Includes "Auf und singtst"
(SA, fl 2cl 2hn 2bn).   AutoMS score (1831): US-NH, Ma21 Y11 R47 ms.42 LM 4440a.   ★
JCR-8v. Heilig, Heilig; "Siehe Schöpfung in der Stane".   SATB, fl 2cl 2hn 2bn 2tp.
AutoMS score: US-NH, Ma21 Y11 R47 ms.36 LM 4433b.   ★
*JCR-9v. Lob, Preis und Dank, 1830.   SATB, fl 2cl 2hn 2bn 2tp db timp.
AutoMS score: US-NH, Ma21 Y11 R47 ms.40 LM 4437, No. 5.   ★

*JCR-10v. Preis Gottes, 1830.   SATB, fl 2cl 2hn 2bn cbn 2tp timp.
AutoMS score: US-NH, MS 40 LM 4437, No. 2. ★
JCR-11v. Psalm, "Singst dem Herrn".   SATB, fl 2cl 2hn cbn 2tp timp.
AutoMS score: US-NH, Ma21 Y11 R47 ms.43 LM 4440b.   ★
*JCR-12v. Cantata, gedichtet von Baur; "Stimmt an in Chören".   SSTB, fl 2cl 2hn 2bn 2tp(clar) db timp.
AutoMS score (1832): US-NH, Ma21 Y11 R47 ms.32 LM 4405.   ★
*JCR-13v. [Choral: "Wie gross ist der Allmächtiger"].   SATB, fl 2cl 2hn 2bn cbn.
AutoMS score: US-NH, Ma21 Y11 R47 ms.44 LM 4441a.   ★
JCR-14v. Chor [or rather, Cantata]: Beym Herbst-Examen 1838 aufgeführt; "Unsre Lebenzeit verschwindet"l
text by Baur.   SSTB, 2cl 2hn 2bn 2tp.   AutoMS score: US-NH, Ma21 Y11 R47 ms.39 LM 4436.   ★
JCR-15v. Cantata wurde beim Oster-Examen 1834; "O Jubeltag, o wonne Tag".   SATB, fl 2cl 2hn 2bn timp.
AutoMS score: US-NH, Ma21 Y11 R47 ms.33 LM 4406.   ★
JCR-16v. Cantata zur Feier des Gymnasiums zu Darmstadt nach zweihundert Jahre dessen Stiftung;
"Allmächtiger".   SATB, 2fl 2cl 2hn 2bn cbn 2tp timp.
AutoMS score (1829): US-NH, Ma21 Y11 R47 ms.49 LM 4489.   ★
JCR-17v. Cantata, "Der Frühling".   Solo SATB, SATB chorus, fl 2cl 2hn 2bn cbn 2tp(clar) timp.
AutoMS score ("Aufgefuhrt den 30, Marz 1833"): US-NH, Ma21 Y11 R47 ms.31 LM 4404.   ★
JCR-18v. "An die Freundschaft".   Solo B, fl 2cl 2hn 2bn db.
AutoMS score (1832): US-NH, Ma21 Y11 R47 ms.32 LM 4405.   ★
JCR-19v. "Aufmunterung zum Gesang".   SA, fl 2cl 2hn 2bn db.
AutoMS score (1832): US-NH, Ma21 Y11 R47 ms.32 LM 4405. ★
JCR-20v. Mailied, von Hölty.   SATB, fl 2cl 2hn 2bn db.
AutoMS score: US-NH, Ma21 Y11 R47 ms.35 LM 4433a.   ★
*JCR-21v. Sammelt Euch, Freunde, 1830.   SATB, fl 2cl(A) 2hn 2bn db.
AutoMS score: US-NH, Ma21 Y11 R47 ms.40 LM 4437, No. 1.   ★
*JCR-22v. Das Vaterland (Rundgesang), 1830.   SATB, fl 2cl 2hn 2bn cbn.
AutoMS score: US-NH, Ma21 Y11 R47 ms.40 LM 4437, No. 4.   ★
*JCR-23v. Duettino: "Bünder", 1830.   SA, fl 2cl 2hn 2bn cbn.
AutoMS score: US-NH, MS 40 LM 4437, No. 3.   ★
JCR-24v. Cantata: Die Auferstehung.   SSTB, fl 2cl 2hn 2bn organ.
AutoMS score ("Angefanmen im Mon: Dec 1822"): US-NH, Ma21 Y11 R47 ms., LM 4442.   ★
JCR-1a. Anon: God Save the King (as "Vaterlandslied").   TTBB, fl 2cl 2hn 2bn 2tp db timp.
AutoMS score (1832): US-NH, Ma21 Y11 R47 ms.32 LM 4405.   ★
JCR-2va. Mozart: Arie aus der Zauberflöte.   Solo B, fl 2cl 2hn 2bn cbn.
AutoMS score: US-NH, Ma21 Y11 R47 ms.35 LM 4433a.
JCR-3va. Mozart: "Dem höchsten Regierer sich Jubelgesang".   SATB, fl 2cl 2hn 2bn cbn.
AutoMS score: US-NH, Ma21 Y11 R47 ms.44 LM 4441b.
JCR-4va. Weber: [Der Freischütz], "Leise, leise, fromme Weise".   STB, fl 2cl 2hn 2bn cbn.
AutoMS score: US-NH, MS Ma21 Y11 R47 ms.LM 4441c.

*RINDL, P *[?Pater]* Hermann *(1770), "Catecheten an der Saazer Stadtschule" [?Prague]*
*HXR-1v. Prüfungslied zur 42ten öffentlichen Prüfung im Jahre [1]799 den 23ten July.
CATB, 2fl 2cl 2bn 2tp timp.   MS parts: CZ-Pnm, XLVI.F.107, (missing Tenor voice part).   ★
*HXR-2v. Prüfungslied zur 44ten offentlichen Prüfung im Jahre [1]800 den 21ten July.
CATB, 2fl 2ob 2cl 2bn 2tp timp.   MS parts: CZ-Pnm, XLVI.F.106, (missing Canto voice part).   ★

*RINSLER, ( ) *(? Musician at Donaueschingen, c.1822 - 1848)*
YZR-1va. Kalliwoda: Messe.   SATB, winds.   MS parts: D-DO, Mus.Ms.871.

RISINGER, Karel *1920*
KAR-1. Divertimento.   2ob 2cl 2hn 2bn.
Pm (Český hudební fond: Prague, 1954), hird score & parts.
KAR-2. Octet.   2ob 2cl 2hn 2bn.
Pm (Český hudební fond: Prague, 1985), hird score & parts.

RITCHIE, John Anthony *1960, New Zealand*
OJR-1. Partita; 1970.   fl cl 2bn 2tp 2tb.   MS score: NZ-Wmc.

*RITTER, (?Georg Wenzel) *7 April 1748, Mannheim - 16 June 1808, Berlin*
GWR-1(-3). Parthia I, II & IV in Dis [E♭]; (4 mvts, 2 mvts, 3 mvts).   2cl 2hn bn.
MS pts: A-Wn, Mus.Hs.622.   *Parthia II is attributed to Pleyel (IJP-12.3) and to Mozart (WAM-16d).*   ★

RITTER, J. Peter *1763 - 1846*
EJR-1. 12 kleine Stücke.   fl ob 2cl 2hn 2bn.   MS parts: US-Wc, ML96.R5E22.

*RIVIER, Jean *1896 - 1987*
JER-1. Concerto.   Solo alto saxophone & trumpet, fl 6cl b-sax 2bn (2)db.
Pm (Universal Edition: London, etc., c.1985), hire score & parts.

ROBERTSSON, Stig *11 Sept 1940, Sweden*
SZR-1. Gloria in excelsis Deo; 1982.   fl ob ob(ca) 2cl 2hn 2bn 2tp 2tb tu timp perc.
MS score: The composer c/o S-Sic.

ROBINSON, Stanford *1904*
SFR-1. Waltz Serenade.   fl ob 2cl 2hn bn 2tp 3tb perc piano(harpsichord) celeste.
Pm (Boosey & Hawkes: London,

*ROCKEMAN (Roeckeman, Rakeman), ( ) & ALTERS, ( )
XXR-1m. Six Sonatas in 5 parts…as performed in the Militia; (I: E♭, 3 mvts; II: B♭, 3 mvts; III: E♭, 4 mvts;
IV: E♭, 4 mvts; V: E♭, 4 mvts; VI: E♭, 4 mvts).   2cl 2hn bn.
Pc (Printed for C. & S. Thompson: London, 1773), parts: GB-Ckc, 104.119 (3) RES; GB-Lbl, b.206.   ★

*RÖDER, Georg Vincent *1780, Rammungen - 30 Dec 1848, Altötting*
*GVR-1v. Deutsche Messe, "In der Fastenzeit...1835 im Palmsonntag den 12. Aprill".
SATB, 2fl cl(C) 2hn vlne organ(bc-fig).   MS parts: CZ-Pnm, XXXVIII.F.203, (the organ part bears the inscription, "18 12/4 35 / Soukup 61 Jahre alt"). ★
GVR-2v. Regina coeli.   SATB, 2cl 2hn 3tp timp organ.   MS parts: CZ-Pnm, XIV.F.36.

*ROENTGEN, Julius Englebert *9 May 1855, Leipzig - 13 Sept 1932, Utrecht*
*JUR-1. Serenade, Op. 14; in A, 4 mvts.   fl ob cl(A & B♭) 2hn 2bn.
Pm (Breitkopf & Härtel: Leipzig, pn 14744, 1878, rep. 1964), score: D-Bhm, 3898, 3899; GB-Lbl, e.606. ★
Pm (Compusic: Amsterdam, pn 218, 1991), score & parts.

*ROESER (Röser), Valentin *(?1735, ?Monaco or Germany - ?1782, ?Paris)*
Item 29 - 81 in the anonymous collection in D-Rtt, Inc. IVa/21/II may be drawn from Roeser's arrangements.
*VAR-1. *Essai d'instruction à l'Usage de ceux qui composent pour la clarinette et le cor. Avec des Remarques sur l'Harmonie et des Examples à deux Clarinettes, deux Cors et deux Bassons.*
MS: F-TO.
Pc (Chez Mercier: Paris, 1764): B-Br.
Pm (facsimile:) (Minkoff: Geneva, 1972).
*VAR-2. [56 sets] Divertissements militaires. 2cl 2hn 2bn.
Pc (Sieber: Paris, 1771 - 1782), parts: D-DS, Nos. 39, 42, 50, 55, 56, (lost in World War II).
MS parts: D-SWl, Mus. 593, Nr. 1, (1 mvt, Presto, in E♭, as "Dievertissement [sic]"). ★
VAR-3. Andante grazioso.   2ob 2bthn 2hn 2bn serp.
MS parts: GB-Lbl, RM.21.d.3. [= A-203.1/4(a)] *Undoubtedly an arrangement.* ★
*VAR-1a. N°. [MS: 1 - 46] Suite de pièces d'harmonie tirées des opéra et opéra comique...arrangées. 2cl 2hn 2bn.
Pc (Sieber: Paris, 1771 - 1782), RISM [R 1868], parts: D-DS, (?lost in World War II); D-Dl, (?lost in World
War II; VAR-2a & VAR-3a may be from these sets); F-Pn, "No. [MS: 45]", Vmg. 14853
Pm (sn: Paris, 1964), score & parts (of No. 45).
   1.45/1. Gossec: Midas, ariette, "Toi qui fait n'altre dans mon âme"
   1.45/2. Gossec: Midas, duo, "Non, non, ma mère"
   1.453/3 - 1.45/8, 1.45/12. [?Duni - attribution now in question]: Ninette à la cour, (1755), 6 mvts (Andante,
      Amoroso, Menuet, Marche, Larghetto, Allemande; Contredanse)
   1.45/9 - 1.45/11. Anon: Les Ruses d'amour, 3 mvts (untitled, Allegretto, Pastorale)
*VAR-2a. Grétry: Silvain (5 mvts) & Lucille (2 mvts).   2cl 2hn 2bn.   MS pts: D-Dl, Mus.3486-F-7 hoch a.
*VAR-3a. Philidor: Ernelinde, Princesse de Norvège, ariettes & airs de danse, 12 items.   2cl 2hn 2bn.
MS parts: D-Dl.

RÖSLER, ( ) M[ons]. *(?1730)*
UYR-1. March Ex: F [sic; in fact 10 mvts, of which the titled mvt is the first].   2ob/vl 2hn basso.
MS parts: D-DS, Mus.ms.1224, S.79 - 89. ★
UYR-2. March Ex G# [sic; in fact 12 mvts, of which the titled mvt, in G major, is the first].   2ob 2hn basso.
MS parts: D-DS, Mus.ms.1224, S.119 - 138. ★

*ROETH (RÖTH), Philipp Jakob *1779 - 1850*
PJR-1v. Lateinishce Vesper; in D.   SATB, 2cl 2hn 2bn 2tp(Clar) timp organ.
MS parts (by J.A. Steigenberger, c.1840): D-Mbm, Mf 1191, (comprises Domine, Dixit, Confitebor, Beatus vir,
Laudate pueri, Lauda Jerusalem, Coelestis urbs, Magnificat). ★
PRJ-2v, 3v. [2] Tantum ergo; in C & E♭.   SATB, 2cl 2hn 2bn 2tp(clar) timp.
MS parts (by J.A. Steigenberger, c.1840): D-Mbm, Mf 1183. *These 2 works can also be found in MS scores
c.1840 with full orchestral setting at MF 1184, No. 1 (autograph) & Mf 1186, respectively.* ★
PJR-4v. Tantum ergo No. III; in E♭.   SATB, 2cl 2hn 2bn 2tp(clar) timp.
AutoMS parts (c.1835): D-Mbm, Mf 1185. ★
PJR-5v. Salve Regina; in C.   SATB, organ *or* 2cl 2hn 2bn.
MS parts (by J.A. Steigenberger, c.1840): D-Mbm, Mf 1181. ★
PJR-6v. Veni sancte Spiritus, Antiphona; in D.   SATB, 2cl 2hn bn.
MS parts (c.1840): D-Mbm, Mf 1190. *Mf 1189 is a version (c.1850) for SATB organ db.* ★

*ROETSCHE (Roetscher), ( ), Senior *(1770) - post-1806*
ZYR-1m. Marsch, in C.   2ob 2cl(C) 2hn 2bn.   MS: D-Bds, Hausbibl.M.M.126.
ZYR-2m. Marsch, in C.   2ob 2cl(C) 2hn 2bn.   MS: D-Bds, Hausbibl.M.M.128.
ZYR-3m. Marsch, 1799.   2ob 2cl(C) 2bn tp.
Pm (In: Pätzig (qv), Vol 1, No. 7), score & parts.
*ZYR-4m. Marsch (& "Gesang", cf ZYR-1mv).   Winds.   MS: D-Bds, Hausbibl.M.M.54, (?lost).
*ZYR-1v. Lied am Geburtstage Friedrich Wilhelms II von den Waisenkindern gesungen (1806).
Voices & winds.   MS: D-Bds, Hausbibl.M.M.264, (?lost). *The melody is drawn from ZYR-4m.*

ROGER (Rogers), ( ) *(1760)*
XYR-1m. Vingt [or, XX] Divertissements en Harmonie.   2cl 2hn bn.
Pc (Pleyel: Paris, pn 156, c.1798; *also* Meyn Bros.: Hamburg, 1798; Smart: London, c.1800), parts: D-Dl.

*RÓHLÍK, Antonín *(active 1871 - 1877, Nové Město na Moravě)*
ANR-1v. Mše do b[♭] s česk. slov.; (with Graduale, Offertorium & Pange lingua).   Solo CAB/TTB, CC/TT
chorus (BB ad lib), fl 2cl tp(E♭) 2a-hn(B♭) b-tb timp organ, (flug(B hoch) & b-flug(B♭) ad lib).   MS parts
(9 April 1871): CZ-Bm(nm), A.790, (with a note of 3 performances: 1871, 1872, 1877). *An earlier version "od
roku 1842", (dated 24 Feb 1876), for SATB & organ, (tp 2a-hn b-tb timp ad lib) is held at CZ-Bm(nm), A.528.* ★
ANR-2v. V. Česka mše; (including Graduale, Offertorium & Pange lingua).
Solo SAB, SABB chorus, fl 2cl(A) tp(D) flug(C) 2a-hn(A) b-tb timp organ.
MS parts (29 June 1870), CZ-Bm(nm), A.707. ★
ANR-3v. Messe [Latin] in C, Op. IV; (with Graduale, Offertorium & Pange lingua).   Solo SAB, CABB/TTBB
chorus, fl 2cl tp 2a-hn b-tb vla 2organ.   MS parts (10 June 1870): CZ-Bm(nm), A.791, (performed 17 June 1871,
for the engagement celebration of P.T. Koutesky of Clam Gallas, and again on 15 Aug 1872). ★

*RÓHLÍK, Johann *(attributed; active 1821)*
JBR-1v. Echo Misa [sic]. SS, 2cl 2hn bn tp(prin) timp.
MS parts ("2ten August [1]821 / Kudrna / Revidens"): CZ-Bm(nm), A.551. ★

*ROLLER, (Samuel Andreas) *(1730, active 1758 - 1773)*
SAR-1. Partia a: 10 voci: in D; 5 mvts.   2ob 2cl 2hn 2bn 2vla.   MS parts: CZ-KRa, A3959/IV.B.122. ★
SAR-2. [Parthia in D], 3 mvts.   2cl(A) 2hn 2bn 2tp.   MS parts: CZ-KRa, A3956/IV.B.120. ★
SAR-3. No. 2 [Parthia] Ex: D:; 3 mvts.   2cl(A) 2hn 2bn 2tp.   MS parts: CZ-KRa, A3962/IV.B.123. ★
SAR-4. No. 3 [Parthia] Ex D; 3 mvts.   2cl(A) 2hn 2bn 2tp.   MS parts: CZ-KRa, A3957/IV.B.124. ★
SAR-5. No. 4 Parthia in D, 1773; 3 mvts.   2cl(A) 2hn 2bn 2tp.   MS parts: CZ-KRa, A3960/IV.B.119. ★
SAR-6. Ex D Parthia; 3 mvts.   2cl(A) 2hn 2bn 2tp.   MS parts: CZ-KRa, A3961/IV.B.124. ★
SAR-7(-12). 6 Parthias, 1766, (all in D; SAR-7 = 6 mvts, all others = 5 mvts).   2cl(A,A,C,A,A,A) 2hn 2bn.
MS parts: CZ-KRa, A4024, A4025/IV.B.198, Part 2, Nos. 4 - 9. ★
SAR-13. N: 2 Partia Campagne [sic] in D, 1772; 5 mvts.   2cl(A) 2hn 2bn.
MS parts: CZ-KRa, A3958/IV.B.121. ★

ROMBERG, Andreas *27 April 1767, Vechta, nr Münster - 10 Nov 1821, Gotha*
ANR-1. Psalmus in C.   2hn bn 2tp timp.   MS parts: A-Wn, Fonds 4 BADEN 361.
ANR-2. Psalmus in Es [E♭].   2hn 2bn.   MS parts: A-Wn, Fonds 4 BADEN 361.

*RONG, Wilhelm Ferdinand *5 Aug 1759, Niedertrübenwasser, Bohemia - 13 Nov 1842, Bützow.*
WFR-1m(-6m). 6 Märsche; (all in F).   2fl 2bthn 2hn (2)bn.
AutoMS score (1795): D-Bds, Hausbibl.M.M.131. ★
Pm (Steinquest), pp. 205 - 221, score.
WFR-7m. Marsch, 1789, in F.   2ob 2cl tp b-fig *(the basso part is marked (prime) "Tasto Solo", implying it is merely a bass, even though figured).*
AutoMS score & parts: D-Bds, Hausbibl.M.M.131a. ★
Pm (Steinquest), pp. 222 - 224, score.

*ROPARTZ, (Joseph) Guy (Marie) *15 June 1864, Guingamp, Côtes du Nord - 22 Nov 1955, Lanloup*
JMR-1. Lamento.   Solo oboe, 2fl ob 2cl hn 2bn.
Pc (Salabert: Paris, sd), score.

*ROREM, Ned *23 Oct 1923, Richmond, Indiana*
*NXR-1. Sinfonia; 4 mvts.   pic 2fl 2ob ca cl(E♭) 2cl(A & B♭) b-cl 2hn 2bn cbn perc(ad lib; timp(3) b-dr s-dr cym, large gong or tam-tam, tri) xly piano+celeste.
Pm (Henmar Press Inc: New York, *via* C.F. Peters Corp: New York, etc., *and* Hinrichsen Edition Ltd: London, 1957), miniature score: GB-Lbl, c.140.mm.(8); US-Wc.
NXR-1v. Lift Up Your Heads (The Ascension), 1963.   SATB chorus, 2fl 2ob 2cl 2hn 2bn 3tp 3tb tu timp.
Pm (Boosey & Hawkes: New York, etc., 1971), score.

ROSE, Johann Daniel *30 July 1784, Quedlinberg - 14 March 1852, Quedlinberg*
JDR-1a. Hummel: Notturno, Op. 99.   fl 4cl 2hn 2bn tp tb.
Pc (Hoffmeister: Leipzig, pn 1228, 1817), as Vol. 3 of Journal für Militärmusik, parts: US-BETm, Philharmonic Society of Bethlehem, Add 1.   *This may be a re-issue, as Hoffmeister was purchased by Peters c.1814.*

*ROSE, J.H. *A member of the 1st Battalion Breadalbane Fencibles.   Conceivably Johann Heinrich Rose, c.1750 Trassdorf - 3 Aug 1844, Quedlinberg; note, too, Johann Daniel Rose (1784-1852), also from Quedlinberg.*
JHR-1m. The 1st Ba[ta]ll[io]n Breadalbane Fencibles New March.   2cl 2hn 2bn tp.
Pc (Printed for the Author & Sold by J. Johnson: Edinburgh, c.1800), RISM [R 2522], score: GB-DU, Wighton Collection 10470. ★
JHR-2m. Tay Side Fencibles Slow and Quick March.   2cl 2hn bn tp.
Pc (Printed for the Author: Edinburgh, c.1795), RISM [R 2525], score: GB-DU; GB-Gu; GB-Lbl, g.133.(50); GB-Ob, Mus.Instr.I.203(25). ★
JHR-3m. The Glasgow Volunteers March.   2cl 2hn bn tp.
Pc (Printed for the Author and Sold by him at Glasgow: Edinburgh, c.1800), RISM [R 2524], score: GB-DU, Wighton Collection 10470; GB-Ep. ★

ROSELL, Lars-Erik *9 Aug 1944, Nybro*
LER-1. Five to five: Svit; 1982.   fl(pic) ob cl 2hn bn 2tp tb tu.   MS score: S-Sic.

*ROSENBERG, Hilding Constantin *21 June 1892, Bosjökloster, Ringsjön, Skåne - 19 May 1985, Stockholm*
HCR-1. Symphonie für Bläser und Schlagzeug; 1966, (based on the ballet *Babels Torn*).
fl fl(pic) ob ca cl b-cl bn cbn 3tp 3tb timp 3perc(campinelli, xyl, 3tri 3cym, suspended cym, tamburo piccolo, tamburo rullante, 2bongos, 4tom-toms, rattle [raganella], verga di ferro [anvil], 3marble slabs with different pitches & hammer, wood block, 3 temple blocks).
Pm (Ab Nordiska Musikförlaget; Edition Wilhelm Hansen: Stockholm, Ringsted; pn NMS 6401, 1973), min score: GB-Lbl, b.276.s.(3); S-Sic; also hire score & parts.

*ROSENGART (Rosengarth), Aemilian, R.P. *(1760)*
AER-1v. Ave Maria pro Adventu Dni; in A.   CATB, 2fl 2cl/vla 2hn vlne.
MS parts (1795): D-Tl, B 372. ★
AER-2v. Ave Maria pro Adventu; in E♭.   CATB, 2fl 2hn/cl.
MS parts (1795): D-Tl, B 371. ★

*ROSER von REITER, Franz de Paula *17 Aug 1779, Naarn, Austria - 12 Aug 1830 Budapest*
We have not traced his dances for military band.
FPR-1v. In C[,] Tantum ergo.   SATB, 2ob 2cl(C) 2hn 2bn organ.
MS parts: H-Bn, Ms.Mus.1187. ★
FPR-1a. Mosel: Salem.   2ob 2cl 2hn 2bn cbn.
Pc (Thade [sic] Weigl: Wien, c.1813), MS parts: I-Fc, F.P. S.366.

*ROSETTI (Roessler, Rössler), Franz Anton *c.1750, Litoměřice, Bohemia - 30 June 1792, Ludwigslust*
Here sources are abbreviated: DTB: Denkmäler der Tonkunst in Bayern. Denkmäler deutscher Tonkunst. Zweite
Folge. (Breitkopf & Härtel: Leipzig; (Dr Benno Filser Verlag: Augsburg), 1925), Jg. XXV, Bd. 33, (reprinted:
Breitkopf & Härtel: Wiesbaden, 1967). MUR: Five Wind Partitas. (A-R Editions Inc: Madison, Wisconsin, 1989,
ed. Sterling E. Murray, (Recent Researches in the Music of the Classical Era, Vols. XXX, XXXI), score and pts.
Rosetti may well have written more works: the bassoon part only of a Partitta for 2cl 2hn bn survives at
*US-WS, and Tafel-Musik for Solo ob, 2cl 2hn bn appears to be lost from D-Bds, Hausbibl., No. 338. **Note:** The*
versions of works for ob concertante, 2ca 2hn 2bn in A-Wgm are probably transcriptions by Went; the versions
for ob 2cl 2hn 2bn in D-DO are probably transcriptions by Rosinack (possibly based on Went's versions).
*FAR-1. pour la Chasse. Parthia in F; 1785; 4 mvts, (K.II, 13).   2fl 2ob 2cl 3hn bn(solo) vlne+bn.
AutoMS score ("Composta nel mese di Settembre 1785 a Wallerstein"): D-HR, HR III 4 1/2 4° 284.   ★
AutoMS parts (c.1788): D-HR, HR III 4 1/2 4° 571, (mvt 1 only).
Pm (Mannheimer Musik-Verlag: Mannheim, pn E-11-57, sd), ed. Eugen Bodart, hire score & pts (mvt 1 only).
Pm (Oxford University Press: London, pn 3586509, 1972), ed. Roger Hellyer, score & parts.
Pm (KGS), fiche, scores (710, 711 & 1101) & parts (2708, 2709).
FAR-2. Parthia; in F, 4 mvts, (K.II, 15).   2fl 2ob 2cl 3hn vc+bn vlne+bn.
MS score: D-HR, HR III 4 1/2 2° 598.   ★
Pm (Denkmäler der Tonkünst in Bayern, Bd. 34), ed. Kaul, score.
Pm (KGS), fiche (2708, 2709).   Pm (MUR, No. 5), score & parts.
FAR-3. Parthia; in F, 4 mvts, (K.II, 12).   2fl 2ob 2cl 2hn bn bn+vlne.
MS score: D-HR, HR III 4 1/2 2° 599.   ★
Pm (G. Schirmer: New York, 1964), ed. Douglas Townsend.
Pm (KGS), fiche (2712, 2713).
FAR-4. Parthia in D; 4 mvts, (K.II, 11).   2fl 2ob 2cl 2hn bn vlne.
MS score ("Composta nel mese di febraro 1784"): D-HR, HR III 4 1/2 2° 600.   ★
Pm (KGS), fiche (2714).
Pm (Compusic: Amsterdam, pn 219, 1988), score & parts.
Pm (MUR, No. 3), score & parts.
Pm (Doblinger: Vienna, 1991), score & parts.
FAR-5. Parthia in D; 3 mvts, (K.II, 14).   2fl 2ob cl(A) 2hn 2bn vlne.
MS score: D-HR, HR III 4 1/2 2° 601.   ★
Pm (KGS), fiche (2715).   Pm (MUR, No. 4), score & parts.
*FAR-6.1. Divertimento; in B♭, 3 mvts, (K.II, 23).   2ob 2bthn 2hn 2vla vlne.
MS parts: GB-Lbl, R.M.21.d.3, f.121 et seq. *Probably a transcription,* (A-203, last work in the volumes).   ★
FAR-6.2. Partia I; in E♭.   2cl 2hn bn.
MS pts: US-BETm, Philharmonic Society of Bethlehem PSB 1351.6, (mvt 1 only, on f.2b of the cl I & II pts).
FAR-7.1. Partita in E♭; 4 mvts, (also exists as Rosetti's *Sinfonia in E♭*; K.I, 35).   2ob 2cl 2hn bn.
MS parts: D-DO, Mus.Ms.1597, No. 3; D-DS, Mus.Ms.1679/2, (?lost in World War II; as "Partia in Dis").   ★
Pc (as "Pièces de [sic] Harmonie No. 3") (Pleyel: Paris, pn 102, sd), RISM [R 2588], parts: D-KNh, (with the
imprint of N. Simrock, Bonn, pn 102); D-HER, Mus.C.1.17, (cl I & II, and bn I in contemporary MS, N.1=8).
FAR-7.2. Pièces d'Harmonie; in E♭, 4 mvts, (also exists as Rosetti's *Sinfonia in E♭*, K.I, 35).   2fl 2cl 2hn 2bn.
MS parts: RF-Ssc, Ф 891 собр юосуповьіх N44, pp. 55 - 74.
*FAR-8.1. Partia; in F, 4 mvts, (K.II, 16).   3ob 2hn bn vlne.
MS parts: D-HR, HR III 4 1/2 4° 488.   ★
Pm (DTB), XXV, Bd. 33, pp 20 - 33, ed. Kaul, score.
Pm (Eulenburg: London, pn GM 12, 1970), ed. Päuler, score (pn 10010) & parts.
Pm (KGS), fiche (971).
*FAR-8.2. Partia in Dis [E♭]; 4 mvts.   ob concertante, 2ca 2hn 2bn.   MS pts: A-Wgm, VIII 8538, No. 2.
*FAR-8.3. Partia in Dis [E♭], 5 mvts.   ob 2cl 2hn 2bn.
MS parts: D-DO, Mus.Ms.1679/1.
Pm (Edition Kunzlemann: Adliswil/Zürich, 1970), score & parts, (General Music series Nr. 11).
FAR-9.1. Partia in Dis [E♭]; 4 mvts, (K.II, 6).   2 oboes concertante, 2cl 2hn 2bn.
MS score: D-Mbs, Mus.Mss.1723, (fair copy by Druschetzky, under Dittersdorf's name).   ★
MS parts: D-DO, Mus.Ms.1679/2.
*FAR-9.2. Partia in Dis [E♭]; 4 mvts.   ob concertante, 2ca 2hn 2bn.   MS parts: A-Wgm, VIII 8538, No. 7.
FAR-10.1. Partia in Dis [E♭]; 4 mvts, (K.II, 4).   2ob 2cl 2hn 2bn.   MS pts: D-DO, Mus.Ms.1679/3.   ★
*FAR-10.2. Partia in Dis [E♭]; 4 mvts.   ob concertante, 2ca 2hn 2bn.   MS parts: A-Wgm, VIII 8538, No. 6.
*FAR-10.3 (&12.3). [Parthia], 2 mvts.   ob 2cl 2hn bn.
MS score (by Theodor von Schacht, c.1790): D-Rtt, Schacht 79/I, (last mvt only; follows FAR-12.1, 1st mvt).
FAR-11.1. Parthia in Dis [E♭]; (K.II, 5, as "Sextetto").   2ob 2cl 2hn 2bn.   MS pts: D-DO, Mus.Ms.1679/4.   ★
*FAR-11.2. Partia in Dis [E♭]; 4 mvts.   ob concertante, 2ca 2hn 2bn.   MS parts: A-Wgm, VIII 8538, No. 1.
*FAR-11.3. Partia in Dis [E♭].   ob 2cl 2hn 2bn.   MS parts: D-DO, Mus.Ms.1675.   ★
FAR-12.1. Partia in Dis [E♭]; 4 mvts, (K.II, 7, as "Sextetto").   2ob 2cl 2hn 2bn.
MS parts: D-DO, Mus.Ms.1679/5.   ★
*FAR-12.2. Partia in Dis [E♭]; 4 mvts.   ob concertante, 2ca 2hn 2bn.   MS parts: A-Wgm, VIII 8538, No. 4.
*FAR-12.3. Partia in Dis [E♭].   ob 2cl 2hn bn.
MS parts: D-DO, Mus.1669.   ★
MS score (by Theodor von Schacht, c.1790): D-Rtt, Schacht 79/I, (mvt 1 only; precedes FAR-10.1, last mvt).
FAR-13.1. Partita in E♭; 5 mvts, (K.II, 3, as "Sextetto").   2ob 2cl 2hn 2bn.
MS parts: D-DO, Mus.Ms.1679/6, No. 6, (for: 2ob 2cl 2hn 2bn).   ★
*FAR-13.2. Partia in Dis [E♭]; 5 mvts.   ob concertante, 2ca 2hn 2bn.   MS parts: A-Wgm, VIII 8538, No. 3.
*FAR-13.3. Partia in Dis [E♭].   ob 2cl 2hn bn.   MS parts: D-DO, Mus.Ms.1676.
FAR-14. N. V: Parthia [added: I] in A [in fact in D]; 4 mvts, (K.II, 8).   2ob 2cl(A) 2hn bn.
MS parts (1781): D-HR, HR III 4 1/2 4° 484.   Pm (KGS), fiche (968).   ★
*FAR-15. N. VI: Parthia [added: IIª]; in D, 4 mvts, (K.II, 9).   2ob 2cl(A) 2hn bn.
MS parts (1781): D-HR, HR III 4 1/2 4° 485.   Pm (KGS), fiche (969).   ★

FAR-16. Parthia III^{za}; in D, 4 mvts, (K.II, 10).   2ob 2cl(A) 2hn bn.
MS parts: D-HR, HR III 4 1/2 4° 486.   ★
Pm (DTB), XXV, Bd. 33, pp. 20 - 33, ed. Kaul, score.
Pm (Kneusslin: Basel, 1954), ed. Fritz Kneusslin, score & parts, (für Kenner und Liebhaver No. 5).
Pm (KGS), fiche (970).   ★
FAR-17. Septetto; in Eb, 9 mvts, (K.II, 20).   fl ob 2cl 2hn bn.
MS parts: D-DO, Mus.Ms.1664; A-KR, H.38.45, (as "Parthia in Dis", in 4 mvts).   ★
***FAR-18.1.** Sextetto (Partita), in Bb; 6 mvts, (K.II, 2).   ob/fl 2cl 2hn bn.
Pc (Traeg: [Vienna], pre-1799), No.36, MS pts: D-Bds, Hausbibl. Nr. 126; D-DO, Mus.Ms1657, (as "Partia in Dis",
with MS score; a MS piano reduction is at Mus.Ms1657b); D-DS, Mus.Ms.3859, (?lost in World War II).   ★
Pm (D-DO version:) (DTB), Jg. XXV, Bd. 33, pp. 34 - 40), ed. Kaul, score.   *NB. This is the work listed in the
GB-Lbbc Chamber Music Catalog; some earlier secondary sources have taken this to be an original MS.*
Pm (Eulenburg: London, pn GMI 1, 1970), score & parts, (with 2cl/ca parts).
Pm (Henry Litolff's Verlag; C.F. Peters: Frankfurt, etc., pn P8210, 1976), ed. Kurt Janetzky, (with parts for
2ca/2cl), (Peters Edition No. 8210).
***FAR-18.2.** Parthia in B[b]; 6 mvts.   ob concertante, 2ca 2hn bn.   MS parts: A-Wgm, VIII 8538, No. 5.
FAR-19. Parthia No. 12.   2cl 2hn 2bn.   MS parts: PL-WRu.
***FAR-20.** Parthia; in Eb, (K. II, 22), 5 mvts.   2cl 2hn bn.
MS parts: CZ-Pnm, XIV.E.58.; D-DO, Mus.Ms.1830, (attributed to Sperger; the 4th mvt Menuetto is written out
twice in the clarinet parts with different Trios); US-BETm, Philharmonic Society of Bethlehem PSB 1351.5.   ★
FAR-21. Partia in Bb.   2cl 2hn bn.   MS parts: US-BETm, Lititz Collegium Musicum 103, (missing cl I).   ★
***FAR-22.** Quintetto; in Eb, 3 mvts, (K.II, 17).   fl ob taille cl bn.
MS parts: D-HR, HR III 4 1/2 4° 285; D-Mbs.   ★
Pm (KGS), fiche (712).
Pm (Kneusslin: Basel, pn FKuL22, 1961), parts, (with ca/hn part).
Pm (Theodore Presser: Bryn Mawr, PA, pn Pr 257, 1962), arranged and edited by the Phildelphia Woodwind
Quintet, score & parts, (with horn replacing the cor anglais).
FAR-1s. Serenade; in D, 4 mvts, (K.I, 56).   2fl2(pic) 2ob 2cl 2hn 2bn tp(clar), 2vl vla vc vlne.
MS parts (1788): D-HR, HR III 4 1/2 2° 658.   Pm (KGS), fiche (2809, 2810).   ★
***FAR-1d.** Parthia in Eb.   2ob 2cl 2hn 2bn.
MS parts: A-Wgm, VIII 39991, (Rosetti); D-DO, Mus.Ms.767, No. 6, (attributed to Kurzweil).
***FAR-2d.** [= Hoffmeister. FAH-1.1] Parthia in Bb; 3 mvts.   2ob 2cl 2hn 2bn.
MS parts (attributed to Rosetti): D-RUl, RH-R 93.
MS parts (attributed to Hoffmeister): CZ-KRa, IV.B.45., (as "Parthia, No. 1"); D-DO, Mus.Ms.767, No. 7;
NL-Ura/mZ, M.A.Zcm 26, No. 1 (of a set of 6).

***ROSINACK (ROSINIACK), Franz Joseph** *pre-1750/1763 - 1823, Donaueschingen*
BB Bastiaan Blomhert 1987 Ph.D disseration: The Harmoniemusik of Die Entführung aus dem Serail
(Rijksuniversiteit Utrecht, 1987) points out that in many cases Rosinack merely copied arrangements by others;
*misattributions were largely the fault of the court catalogers at D-DO after Rosinack's death. The Parthias by
Hoffmeister, Krommer, Kurzweil, Pleyel and Rosetti (qv) found in D-DO also show signs of Rosinack's tampering
and should be regarded with suspicion as original works.*
FJR-1a. Haydn: Orlando Paladino (as *Ritter Roland*).   2ob 2cl 2hn 2bn.   MS parts: D-DO, Mus.Ms.736/I.
FJR-2a. Mozart: Die Zauberflöte, March of the Priests (Act II, No. 9).   2ob 2cl 2hn 2bn.
MS parts: D-DO, Mus.Ms.1396.   Pm (BB: pp. 375 - 376), ed. Bastiaan Blomhert, score.
FJR-3a. J. Sixt: Six Allemands [sic].   2ob 2cl 2hn 2bn.
MS parts: D-DO, Mus.Ms.1809.   *Note, Rosinack's arrangement of Sixt's 12 Waltzes appears to be lost.*
Pm (BB: pp. 361 - 370), ed. Bastiaan Blomhert, score.
FJR-4a. J. Sixt: 12 Waltzes.   2ob 2cl 2hn 2bn.   MS parts: D-DO, (?lost).
FJR-5a. Winter: Der Liebe Heninrich IV, overture & 17 mvts.   2ob 2cl 2hn 2bn. MS pts: D-DO, Mus.Ms.2038.
FJR-1va. Gleissner: Missa brevis; C. SATB, 2ob 2cl 2hn 2bn org.   MS pts: D-DO, Mus.Ms.536, (missing org).
FJR-1as. Krommer: Parthia in Bb, (FVK-18.1).   2ob cl bn.   MS parts: D-DO, Mus.Ms.479/1.
FJR-2as. Krommer: Parthia in Bb, (FVK-20.1).   2ob cl bn.   MS parts: D-DO, Mus.Ms.479/2.
FJR-3as. Krommer: Partita in Eb, (FVK-14).   2ob cl bn.   MS parts: D-DO, Mus.Ms.479/3.
FJR-4as. Krommer: [unidentified, ?String Quartet], Quartetto in B[b].   2ob cl bn. MS pts: D-DO, Mus.Ms.479/4.
FJR-5as. Krommer: Harmonie in Eb, (FVK-19.1).   2ob cl bn.   MS parts: D-DO, Mus.Ms.479/5.
FJR-6as. Krommer: Partita in Eb, "La Chasse", (FVK-23).   2ob cl bn.   MS parts: D-DO, Mus.Ms.479/6.
FJR-7as. Schörtzel: Balli Tedeschi, 6 mvts.   2ob cl bn.   MS parts: D-DO, Mus.Ms.479.
FJR-8as. Schörtzel: Balli Tedeschi.   2ob cl bn.   MS parts: D-DO, Mus.Ms.479/12.
FJR-9as. Schörtzel: Balli Tedeschi.   2ob cl bn.   MS parts: D-DO, Mus.Ms.479/19.
FJR-1mas, 2mas. Anon: [1] Marsch; in F, C.   2ob cl bn.   MS parts: D-DO, Mus.Ms.479/22-23.
FJR-1ad. Dittersdorf: Der Doktor und Apotheker.   2ob 2cl 2hn 2bn.
MS parts: D-DO, Mus.Ms.349, (2 Teils, = Went JNW-13.1a).
FJR-2ad. Martín y Soler: Una cosa rara, 6 mvts.   2ob 2cl 2hn 2bn.
MS parts: NL-DHgm, hk 19 C 1 (= Went JNW-25.1a).
FJR-3ad. Mozart: Die Entführung aus dem Serail.   2ob 2cl 2hn 2bn.
MS parts: D-DO, Mus.Ms.1392, (see text under Mozart: WAM-3a).
FJR-4ad. Mozart: Le Nozze di Figaro.   2ob 2cl 2hn 2bn.   MS pts: D-DO, Mus.Ms.1394, (= Went JNW-28.1a).
FJR-5ad. Mozart: Die Zauberflöte.   2ob 2cl 2hn 2bn.   MS pts: D-DO, Mus.Ms.1396, (= Heidenreich JYH-3a).
FJR-6ad. Mozart: String Quintet in Eb, K.614, Minuet and Trio.   2ob 2cl 2hn 2bn.
MS parts: D-DO, Mus.Ms.1809, (= Heidenreich JYH-5a).   Pm (BB: pp. 371 - 374), score.
FJR-7ad. W. Müller: Das neu Sonntagskind.   2cl 2hn 2bn.   MS pts: D-DO, Mus.Ms.1411. *Long believed lost;
Rosinack also prepared an arr. for ob & string quartet. The sextet arrangement is probably by Heidenreich.*
FJR-8ad. Paisiello: La Frascatana, (as "G. Pizzini: Das Mädchen von Frascati").   2ob 2cl 2hn 2bn.
MS parts: D-DO, Mus.Ms.1544, (= Went, JNW-36.1a).
FJR-9ad. Paisiello: Il Re Teodoro.   2ob 2cl 2hn 2bn.   MS parts: D-DO, Mus.Ms.1525, (= Went JNW-41.1a).
FJR-10ad. P. Wranizky: Oberon.   2ob 2cl 2hn 2bn.   MS parts: D-DO, Mus.Ms.2067.

ROSS, Walter Beghtol *1936, USA*
WLR-1. Suite. 2fl 2ob 2cl 4hn 3bn. MS score: US-NYamc.

ROSSEM, Andries van *1957, Netherlands*
AVR-1. Pier & Ocean. 2fl 2ob 2cl 2hn 2bn.
Pm (Donemus: Amsterdam, 1988), score.

ROSSINI, Gioacchino (Antonio) *29 Feb 1792, Pesaro - 13 Nov 1868, Passy, nr Paris*
Note: the first 5 of the "Wind Quartets" are arrangements by Berr after Rossini's String Quartets.
GAR-1m. Marche du Sultan Abd-ul-Medjid. fl(F) pic(F)/fl(F) cl(E♭) 3cl(B♭) 4hn(A♭/B♭) 2bn, solo tp(A♭)
4tp(E♭) tp(B♭) 4tb bombardino bombardon oph(B♭) b-dr s-dr, solo tri.
Pc (Chez les fils de B Schott: Mayence, pn 13386, c.1858), score: GB-Lbl, h.625.d. ★
GAR-2m. Pas redoublé. Military band. MS (1836): S-Skma.
GAR-3m. Tre Marce per il Duca di Orléans. Military band.
Pc (?Breitkopf & Härtel: Leipzig, 1837), parts.
Pm (In: Vessella, Alessandro. *La banda dalle origini fino ai nostri giorni. Notizie storiche con documenti inediti e un'appendice musicale.* Instituto Editoriale Nazionale: Milano, 1935), pp. 331 - 344, score.
GAR-1e. Guillaume Tell: Act IV, Terzetto, "Sottrado a orribil nembo". SSA, 2fl 2ob 2cl 4hn 2bn tb.
Pm (Garland Publishing: New York, London, 1980), score, (Early romantic Opera. 17).
*****GAR-1d.** Parthia. 2cl 2hn bn.
Pm (Compusic: Amsterdam, pn 251, 1988), score & parts. (Provenance unknown)

ROSŮLEK, Antonín Pavel *12 Nov 1803, Ohništani u Nového Byolžova - 29 Sept 1862, Bohdenei*
APR-1v. Quatuor Stationes v. D, 31 Werk. CATB, fl 2cl(A or C) 2hn 2tp 2tb organ timp.
AutoMS score & MS pts (by F. Tichý, Bohdaneč, 1846): CZ-Pnm, XIV.E.139. *The wrapper bears dates of use:*
1846 - 1851, 10 June 1852, 15 June 1854, 22 May 1856, 4 June 1863, 26 May 1864, 1 June 1866. ★

*****ROTH (Rothe, Rode), Johann Traugott** *23 Feb 1768, Zwickau - 5 May 1847, Dresden*
JTR-1. Andante & Allegro scherzando. 2ob 2cl 2hn 2bn; ad lib: 2tp serp("serbano"). MS parts: D-Dl, (?lost).

*****ROTH, Sinforiano** *(1720)*
SXR-1m. Marcia della guardia Reale Svizera del Re di Napoli, (c.1750). 2cl 2hn bn. MS pts: D-Rtt, Roth 1. ★
SXR-2m. Marcia, in E♭, (c.1750). 2cl 2hn bn. MS parts: D-Rtt, Roth 2. ★

ROTTER, Ludwig *1810 - 1895*
LYR-1v. Pater noster in D. SATB, 2ob 2hn 2bn cbn 2tp(clar) timp.
(?Auto)MS score & MS parts (by G. Weininger, c.1850): A-KR, D 8/362, (with 3 duplicate sets of vocal pts). ★

ROUGET DE LISLE, Claude-Joseph *10 May 1760, Lons-le-Saunier - 26/27 June 1836, Choisy-le-Roi*
CLR-1v. Le Chant de Marseillais. Solo voice, 2cl(C) 2hn (2)bn. *See also: ARRANGEMENTS LIST*
Pc (Rec des époques: Paris, c.1799), liv. 1, No. 6, pp. 13 - 16, score: F-Pn, H2. 15,6. *Probably arranged.* ★
CLR-2v. Roland à Ronceveaux. Solo voice, 2cl(C) 2hn 2bn.
Pc (Rec des époques: Paris, c.1799), liv. 1, No. 11, pp. 26 - 28, score: F-Pn, H2. 15,11. *Probably arranged.* ★

*****ROVA, Giovanni Battista,** *"di Venezia"* *(active 1830 - 1846)*
GBR-1. Grave. 2cl 2hn bn 2tp organ(bc-fig). MS score & parts: I-Vsmc, (parts for 2cl & organ only). ★
GBR-1v. Tantum ergo, 1832. T solo, TTB chorus, 2ob (2cl) 2hn bn (2tp) organ(bc-fig).
MS score & parts: I-Vsmc, (the 2cl & 2tp parts are not in the score; the 2cl largely double the 2ob and may be either ripieni parts or later replacements). ★
GBR-2v. Credo, 1830. TTB(solo+rip), 2ob 2hn bn (tp) timp organ(bc-fig).
MS score & parts: I-Vsmc, (with full organ part; the tp does not appear in the score). ★
GBR-3v. Messa, 1832 TTB(solo+rip), (fl) 2ob 2hn (bn 2tp) organ(bc-fig) .
MS score & parts: I-Vsmc, (with full organ part; the fl bn & 2tp do not appear in the score). ★
GBR-4v. Kyrie, 1832. TTB, 2cl 2hn (vlne+basso timp) organ.
MS score & parts: I-Vsmc, (with full organ part; the vlne & timp do not appear in the score). ★
GBR-5v. Veni Creator. TTB(solo+rip), 2cl(C) 2hn bn (timp) organ(bc-fig).
MS score & parts: I-Vsmc, (with full organ part; the timps do not appear in the score). ★
GBR-6v. Motetto: O Jesu mi dulcissime. TTB, 2ob 2hn (b-tb) organ(bc-fig).
MS score & parts: I-Vsmc, (the b-tb does not appear in the score). ★

ROXBURGH, Edwin *6 Oct 1937, Liverpool*
EXR-1. Voyager. 3ob 3ca 3bn.
Pm (United Music Publishers: London, 1989), score & hire parts.
EXR-2. Hexham Tropes. ob/obdam obdam bn hpcd.
Pm (United Music Publishers: London, 1979), score & hire parts.

ROZIERS, ( ) *(1650) "Le Fifre de la Compagnie des Mousquestaires"*
UZR-1. Air de l'Assemblé. 2ob taille bn. MS score: F-Pn, Rés671, No. 6/1. ★

*****RUDOLPH, Anton** *1742 - post-1784, (?Regensburg)*
ATR-1. Parthia; in F, 6 mvts. 2bthn 2hn bn 2vla db. (?Auto)MS parts (c.1780): D-Rtt, Rudolph 1. ★
ATR-2. Parthia N° II^do . . . in Mense Xbris [October] 1779; in D, 12 mvts. 2cl(A) 2hn 2tp.
(?Auto)MS parts: D-Rtt, Rudolph 2.
ATR-3. Parthia; in E♭, 10 mvts. 2cl 2hn 2tp(clar).
(?Auto)MS parts (1784): D-Rtt, Rudolph 3, (missing all parts except tp II). ★
ATR-4. Parthia VIII; in E♭, 5 mvts. 2cl 2hn bn. MS parts (1773): D-Rtt, Inc. IVa/31/I, Nos. 36 - 40. ★
ATR-5. Parthia XVI in Echo; in E♭, 6 mvts. 2cl 2hn bn. MS pts (1773): D-Rtt, Inc.IVa/31/I, Nos. 90 - 95. ★
ATR-6. Single mvt, added to the end of J.K. Gretsch's Parthia XV, E♭. 2cl 2hn 2bn.
MS parts: D-Rtt, Inc.IVa/31/I, No. 89 (= mvt 7). ★
ATR-7. Partita. Janitscharmusik. Instrumentation unknown.
MS parts: D-Bds, Hausbibl., No. 339.

*RUDOLPH (Johann Joseph Rainer), *Archduke* *8 Jan 1788, Florence - 24 July 1831, Baden, Vienna*
*JRR-1a. Mozart: Sonata K.497 for 4 hands. 2ob 2cl 2hn 2bn.
MS parts: CZ-Pnm, Lobkovic X.G.f.70.
Pm (Compusic: Amsterdam, pn 213, 1988), score & parts.

RUITER, Wim de *11 Aug 1943, Heemstede, Holland*
WDR-1. To be or not to be; 1976. 2fl 2ob 4cl 2hn bn tb vibraphone.
Pm (Donemus: Amsterdam, c.1976), score.

*RULOFFS (Roeloffs), Bartolomeus (Bartholomäus) *Oct, 1741, Amsterdam - 13 May 1801, Amsterdam*
BZR-1. Musique militaire . . . Composées Pour les Compagnies Bourgeoises, des M[onsieu]rs. E:G: van Beaumont, & H: van Slingelandt; 5 mvts. 2cl 2hn bn.
Pc (chez Jean Julius Hummel: Amsterdam, c.1780-85), parts: CZ-Pnm, XLII.A.210. ★

RUMLER, Johann (Jean) *(c.1780), (Bohemia)*
JLR-1. Quintuor, Oeuver [sic] 6; in E♭, 4 mvts. 2cl 2hn bn.
Pc (chez Gombart et Comp: Augsbourg [sic], pn 428, c.1798), pts: A-Wgm, (2 copies), VIII 2551; D-Bds. ★

*RUMMEL, Christian (Chrétien) Franz Ludwig Friedrich Alexander
27 Nov 1787, Brichsenstadt, Bavaria - 13 Feb 1849, Wiesbaden
CFR-1. Variations sur le thème de l'opéra Joseph de Méhul, Op. 40. 2ob 2cl 2hn 2bn cbn/cb.
Pc (Schott: Mainz, 1823), parts: D-MZsch.
CFR-2. Fantasie sur "Il ultimo giorno di Pompoji" [sic; opera by Pacini]. 2ob 2cl hn 2bn cbn.
Pc (Les Fils de B. Schott: Mayence, c.1826), parts: D-MZsch.
CFR-1.2m. Musique militaire, Cahier 2; 6 mvts. pic(E♭) cl(E♭) 3cl(B♭) 2hn 2bn tp b-tb serp b-dr+cym.
Pc (Chez B. Schott: Mayence, pn 834, c.1815), parts: currently untraced, sold as part of Lot 183 at the Sotheby's, London, on 6 Dec 1996. ★
CFR-1.4m. Militär Musik, N° 4; 6 mvts. pic cl(E♭) 4cl(B♭) 2hn 2bn tp b-tb serp b-dr+cym.
Pc (in der Grosherzogl: Hessischen Hofmusikhandlung von B. Schott: Mainz, pn 1076, c.1819), parts: D-Rtt, Rummel 1, (with a MS pt duplicating the bn II pt). *Divisi appear in the clarinet I (Nos. 2, 3, 6), clarinet II (Nos. 1 - 4) & clarinet III (Nos. 1 - 4); the Clarinette terzo part is marked in pencil, "Oboe".* ★
CFR-1.6m. Militaer Musick [sic], VIᵗᵉ Heft; 7 mvts. fl(E♭) cl(E♭) cl(B♭ prin) 3cl(B♭) 2hn 2bn 2to(clar) b-tb, 2serp b-dr; (Klappenflügelhorn/Cor de Signal à Clefs; a-tb, t-tb ad lib).
Pc (in der Groshzl: Hessischen Hofmusikhandlung von B. Schott Söhne: Mainz, pn 1336, 1820), parts: currently untraced, sold as part of Lot 183 at the Sotheby's, London, on 6 Dec 1996. *Although one serpent is called for on the titlepage, the part, marked "Serpent 1° et 2°" is divisi in all but No. 4; p. 1 of the Klappenflügelhorn part is a fingering chart with a picture of the instrument.* ★
CFR-1a. Deux Grandes Pièces d'aprés des motifs de Kalkbrenner et de [J L] Dussec [sic] et l'Ouverture jubilaire de C.M. de [sic] Weber, arrangées . . . Oeuvre 52. 2ob/fl 2cl 2hn 2bn cbn.
Pc (chez B. Schott Fils: Mainz, pn 2263, 1825), parts: A-Wgm, VIII 5146; CZ-KRa, A3963/IV.B.126; D-MZsch. *Weber's overture may have also been issued as a separate publication by Schott.*
CFR-2a. Boieldieu: Jean de Paris, overture. fl(D) cl(I principale, C)/ob cl(II, C) 2cl(B♭) 2hn 2bn serp; (ad lib: fl(E♭) cl(III, B♭) 2tp 2b-tb serp b-dr).
Pc (B. Schott fils: Mayence, pn 1268, c.1819), parts: D-DT, Mus.n 365, (the 2serp pt has been marked at a later date, "Basshorn"; with additional MS parts for: ob I & II, hn III & IV, 2tp, alt-hn, a-tb, Wirbel Trommel(t-dr)).
CFR-3a. Rossini: Tancredi, overture. pic(D) cl(E♭) cl(B♭ principale) 3cl(B♭) 2hn 2bn 2tp 2tb 2serp b-dr.
Pc (Chez Richault: Paris, pn 676.R., 1824), parts: CH-Gpu, Ib.4848.

RUPPERT, Anton *1936, Germany*
AOR-1. Reprisen; 1970. 2fl 2ob 2cl 2bn.
Pm (Orlando Musikverlag: München, 1972), score & parts.

*RUSSELL, William *6 Oct 1777, London - 21 Nov 1813, London*
WXR-1m. A favorite March Composed for the Guildford Volunteers. 2ob 2hn basso.
Pc (Printed for the Author by Longman and Broderip: London, c.1795), RISM [R 3288], score: GB-Ckc; GB-Gu; GB-Lbl, g.133.(51); GB-Ob, Mus.Instr.I.211; GB-Lhumphries (modern MS). ★

RUT, Josef *21 Nov 1926, Kutná Hora*
JVR-1. Suite; 1984. 2ob ca 2bn.
Pm (Český hudební fond: Prague, 1984), hire score & parts.

*RUZITSKA, Georg (György) *1789, Vienna - 3 Dec 1869, Kolozsug (now Romania)*
GER-1v. Pater noster, mit einem Praeludium; in C. CATB. Physharmonica, *or* ca 2cl 2hn 2bn, *or* 2cl 2vla vc.
MS: H-Bn, Ms.Mus.221. *Comprsing: (1) Vocal parts (C, 3S, 2A with added alternative "Soprano 2do", 2T, 2B) & physharmonica (= vocal parts), missing the wind parts; (2) a later AutoMS score, "Pater noster - à 4 Voci et accompagnement d'un Physharmonica [added: oder Harmonium], avec une prélude, écrit pour Mme la Baronne de Bánty, née Comtesse Agnes Ezterházi [sic] par G: Rusitska. 1859; (3) a later AutoMS score & MS pts, "Begleitung des Pater noster ad Libitum 1863", for 2cl(C) 2vla vc; (4) an AutoMS score of an entirely different work, "Ecce quomodo moritur justus. 1: Am Chorfreitage nach dem Pater noster :/", dating from c.1863.* ★

RÚZNÍ (Ruzni, Rugni), ( ) *NOTE: Some earlier researchers have mistaken the Czech word for "various" ("Sammlung") for the name of a composer/arranger. NO SUCH PERSON EXISTS.*

*RYBA, Jakub Šimon Jan *26 Oct 1765, Přeštice - 8 April 1815, Rožmitál pod Třemšínem*
JSR-1. Aufzug in D. 2pic 2fl 2cl(A) 4hn(G, D) 2bn 2tp(clar, in D) 2tp(prin, in D) timp.
MS parts: CZ-Pnm, XL.F.245. ★
JSR-1t. (= **JSR-1.18tv**). [Funeral] Marche; in E♭. CATB, 2cl 2bn - possibly missing 2hn.
JSR-2t. (= **JSR-1.19tv**). Marche funebre; in C minor. CATB, 2cl 2bn - possibly missing 2hn.
JSR-1v. Stationes in C in Processione Festo Corporis Christi; (N.306/a-d).
CCAATTBB, 2fl 2cl(C, vel ob) 2cl(B♭) 2hn 2bn 2tp(clar) tp(prin) timp.
AutoMS score (1803) : CZ-Pnm, III.D.76. MS pts (by Antonín Horetsky, Regenschori): CZ-BR, sign. 443. ★

JSR-2v. Stationes in C; (N.307/a-d). CATB, 2fl 2cl(C) 2hn 2bn 2tp(clar) to(prin) serp "Marche Bass" timp. MS pts: CZ-BR, sign. 376, (copy by Horetsky); CZ-Pnm, XL.F.101; CZ-PLa, Hu 1660, (as Anon; for CATB, fl 2cl(C) 2hn 2bn tp, with duplicate C & A pts, and a later tp(E♭) pt); CZ-PLa(ka), Hu 761, (missing all but 2cl). ★
JSR-3v. Stationes; in D, (N.308a-d). CATB, 2fl 2cl 2bn 2tp. MS parts: CZ-Pnm, XIV.A.112. ★
JSR-4v. Nábožný chod se 4ma zastávky neb Stati; (N.310/1-d). CATB, 3cl 3hn bn 2tp(clar) tp(prin) timp. MS parts: CZ-Pnm, XV.A.126, (missing T, cl III). ★
JSV-5v. Offertorium in F; "Per signum crucis", (N.230). CATB, 2fl 2cl 2bn 2tp timp. MS parts: CZ-Pnm, V.A.54, (with later parts for tb and fl & ob replacing the clarinets). ★
JSR-6v. Missa; in C, (N.404). CATB, 2fl 2cl 2hn 2bn 2tp(prin) timp. MS parts: CZ-Pnm, XIV.F.105; CZ-BR, Hu 50, (with later parts for: 2ob cbn serp organ). ★
JSR-7v. Oktáw neb Osmidenj pobožnost K swatemu Gánu Nepomuckému pozustáwagicý w osmi Chwalozpě wjch ktere k wětssj cti a sláwě Božj, a tohoto welkeho swateho složil [sic]. [Octave of songs of praise for the feast of St Johann Nepomuk], (N.1 - 8, citing the CZ-Pnm copy only). CAB, 2cl 2hn 2bn organ. AutoMS score: CZ-Pnm, XIV.F.88; CZ-PLa, Hu 4335, (Nos. 2 - 8 without text; Rožmitále, 1803). ★
  7.1v. Na den prwnj w oktáwa [sic]. "Weleb ctiteli, Gána swateho [sic]", in F.
  7.2v. Na den slavnosti S: Jána Nepomuckeho; in C. 7.3v. Na den druhý w oktáwu [sic]; in E♭.
  7.4v. Na den třetj w oktáwu [sic]; in G. 7.5v. Na den čtwrtý w okátavu [sic]; in D.
  7.6v. Na den patý w oktávu [sic]; in F. 7.7v. Na den ssestý w oktávu; in C minor.
  7.8v. Na den Octávu [sic]; in C.
JSR-8v. Missa pro Dom[inica]. III in Quadragesima; in G minor, (N.396). CATB, 2cl 2hn 2vla cb organ. AutoMS score (1814): CZ-Pnm, XIV.F.93, No. 3. ★
JSR-9v. Missa pro Dom[inica]. IV. in [Quadregesima]; in A minor, (N.398). CATB, fl(solo, Benedictus only) 2cl 2hn 2vla cb organ. AutoMS score (1814): CZ-Pnm, XIV.F.93, No. 4. ★
JSR-10v. Missa pro Dominica de Passione; in F minor, (N.398). CATB, 2cl 2hn bn(solo, Benedictus only) 2vla cb organ. AutoMS score (1814): CZ-Pnm, XIV.F.93, No. 5. ★
JSR-11v. Missa pro Dominica in Palmis; in A♭, (N.399). CATB, 2cl 2hn 2vla cb organ. AutoMS score (1814): CZ-Pnm, XIV.F.93, No. 6. ★
JSR-12v. Libera [me] in Es [E♭]; (N.318). CATB, 2fl 2cl 2hn bn 2tp(clar). MS pts: CZ-RO, No. 1058. ★
JSR-13v. Salve [Regina] in Es [E♭]; (N.303). CATB, fl 2cl 2hn bn. MS pts: CZ-RO, No. 537, (missing T). ★
JSR-14v. Animas; in E♭, (N.319). CATB, 2cl 2hn 2bn. MS parts: CZ-RO, No. 537, (missing 2hn). ★
JSR-15v. Animas; in E♭, (N.320). CATB, 2cl 2hn 2bn. MS parts: CZ-RO, No. 1059. ★
JSR-16v. Cursus Sacro-Harmonicus Tom. II. continens XVI Offert. a Dom. prima Adventus usque ad Quadrages. oblatus et dedicatus Regiae Urbi Plsnae; Offertorium de Dom[iunica]. IV, Adventus; "Ave Maria", (N.159). CATB, ob(conc) bn(conc) 2hn 2vla cb organ. AutoMS score (1811): CZ-Pnm, XIV.F.91, No. 4. ★
JSR-17v. Nº 49. Msse Ceska; in C, (N. deest). CAB, 2cl 2hn bn organ. MS parts ("Hijan [Hyan] mp 1821" = Josef Hyan, Blovice): CZ-PLa(bl), Hu 4336, (with duplicate CAB pts). ★
JSR-18v, 19v. Libera [me] et Salve [Regina] in Dis [E♭]; (N. deest & N.293). CATB, 2cl 2hn 2bn. AutoMS parts ("fecit a 44 ae.s."; 1809): CZ-Pnm, XV.A.105, (Salve Regina in Dis only). ★
MS pts: CZ-Pnm, XLIII.A.169, (both works, by Mathias Al. Pruscha, c.1830); CZ-PLa(br), Hu 757, No. 26, ("Salve I" only, for CATB, 2cl 2bn, possibly missing 2hn; see our general comments concerning JSR-1tv). ★
JSR-20v. Salve [Regina] in B[♭]; (N.300). CA, 2cl 2hn 2bn. MS parts (by Horetsky): CZ-BR, sign. 328. ★
JSR-21v. Salve II; in B♭; (N deest). CATB, 2cl 2bn - possibly missing 2hn. MS parts: CZ-PLa(br), Hu 757, No. 27, (see our general comments on JSR-1tv). ★
JSR-22v. IV Stationes in Processione Theophorica; (N.305/a-d). CATB, 2cl 2hn bn. MS parts: CZ-PLa(ka), Hu 681, (copy by F. Kassparec, missing T); CZ-PLa, Hu 761, (C, cl(E♭) only). ★
JSR-23v. Graduale na sv. Ducha do F; (N.265). CATB, 2cl 2hn bn organ. MS parts: CZ-Pu, 59 r 224. ★
JSR-24v. Offertorium z Missa minus solemnis in B[♭]; (N.232). CATB, 2cl 2hn cb+organ. MS parts: CZ-Pnm, XIV.G.7. ★
JSR-25.1v. Duetto; "Jesu dukis memoria", in E♭, (N.40). CA, 2hn 2vla organ(bc). MS parts: CZ-BR, sign. 383; CZ-Pnm, XV.A.71; CZ-Pu, (3 copies), 59 R 1392, 59 R 1396, 59 R 1852. ★
JSR-25.2v. Duetto; "Jesu dulcis memoria", in E♭, (N.40). ÇA, 2cl 2vla organ(bc). MS parts (by Karel Mindl, from Zagjček, 1845): CZ-NYc, DÚ 118. ★
JSR-1va, 2va. [Possibly arranged by the composer]. Octo Ariae et Duetto [orchestra]: Aria I ("Offero tibi cor meum") & Aria II ("O Deus ego amo te"), (N.32, N.33). S solo, 2cl(No. I: B♭; No. II: A) 2hn vla organ+basso. MS parts (by Schreyer, 1817; Chrám sv. Mikuláše collection): CZ-CH, S-40-5-102. ★

The funeral works which follow present considerable difficulties for the researcher. The principal MS, titled "Funebria", is in the hand of František Vaněček, Chorrector in Březnice, Bohemia; this comprises 27 anonymous works, of which two are instrumental. Single MSS of Nos. 1, 2, 6, 8, 9, 16, 19, 20 - in the hand of Vaněček's brother, Ladislav, a teacher in Kasejovice, Bohemia, identify Ryba as the composer. Earlier Czech catalogers have suggested that the entire contents of the Funebria MSS are by Ryba. This tends to be borne out by our research, especially since No. 26, "Salve I" exists in the collection from Rychnov nad Kněžnou (now in CZ-Pnm) under Ryba's name; we assign this work the identification number: JSR-5v. Neither of these sets are cited in Jan Němeček's thematic catalog (Jakub Jan Ryba. Život a dílo. Praha: Státní Huberní Vydavatelství, 1963).

Neither of the South Bohemian sets comprise a complete set of parts. The Březnice set are for CATB, 2cl 2bn; in most cases the texts are not included in the vocal parts - beyond the provision of the first line as a title. The Kasejovice set generaly comprises vocal parts; in three cases parts exist for 2hn. The exception in the latter set is Funebria No. 6 (CZ-PLa, Hu 758c), where the scoring is given as CATB, 2cl 2hn & "Bassy 1.2". We believe that this is the full scoring for all of the works in this collection (although the possibility exists that some, at least, of the works may have used one bassoon - or two in unison).

Some duplication exists in the CZ-Pnm sets, (No. 10 = No. 3, N.19; No. 11 = No. 8, N.24; No. 14 = No. 2, N.18; No. 15 = No. 1, N.17; "No. 12" is not present). Although Nos. 10 - 12, 14 & 15 appear to be missing from the Březnice set we note that - apart from No. 22 - the numbering corresponds to the CZ-Pnm set, omitting duplications. None of the duplicate works appear in the Kasejovice set - although CZ-Pla(ka), Hu 758ch ["ch" comes between "h" & "i" in the Czech alphabet] bears the note "N.13 z Ryb [sic]"; this, however, does not correspond to No. 13 in the Březnice Funebria set and may, in fact, be a numbering error by the copyist for the missing No. 12. CZ-PLa(ka), Hu 758ch is the only work in this set which is dated: "4/10 [1]837". The unusual numbering suggests a common source for the Prague and Březnice manuscripts.

JSR-1.1 - 1.18tv. Pohřební pisně; (N.17 - 31, with 3 deest).   CATB, 2cl 2hn 2bn 2tp(clar) tp(prin).
MS parts (provenance: Strahov monastery): CZ-Pnm, (individual numbers at:), XV.A.123, XX.B.58, XXIX.D.138,
XXX.E.26; CZ-PLa(br), Hu 757, (as "Funebria"; all for: CATB, 2cl 2bn, except Nos. 23 & 24 which are for 2cl
2bn; missing texts for Nos. 1 - 3, 13, 16, 18 & 20; texts incomplete after the first phrase for Nos. 5 - 9, 17, 19
& 21; MS by František Vaněček); CZ-PLa(ka), Hu 758a-ch, (Nos. 1, 2, 6, 8, 9, 16, 19, 20; MS by Ladislav
Vaněček; incomplete parts, scoring varies).
 1.1tv. Nro 1. Plyň, ó duše, do věčnosti mezi kůry anjelské; in F, (N.17).
       CZ-PLA(br): CATB, 2cl(C) 2bn, without text; CZ-PLa(ka): Hu 758a (CATB, cl(II, B♭) 2hn(F); full text). ★
 1.2tv. Nro 2. [Na dítě dospělejší. For a mature child] Pospěšte sem, bratřičkové; in C, (N.18).
       CZ-PLa(br): CATB, 2cl(C) 2bn, without text; CZ-PLa(ka): CATB; full text. ★
 1.3tv. Nro 3. [Jiná na dítě. Another for a child] Krásný ráj již se otvírá; in F, (N.19).
       CZ-PLa(br): CATB, 2cl 2bn, (without text). ★
 1.4tv. Nro 4. [Jiná na dítě] Kvítečku, ó jak ty kveteš; in E♭, (N.20).   CZ-PLa(br): CATB, 2cl(B♭) 2bn. ★
 1.5tv. Nro 5. [Na žačku. For pupils] Tu se s tebou [CZ-PLa: milý žačku) spolužáčku; in E♭, (N.21).
       CZ-PLa(br): CATB, 2cl(B♭) 2bn. ★
 1.6tv. Nro 6. Na žačku [sic: Na školačku. For a schoolboy]. Překrásná dívčinka není již zde; in B♭, (N.22).
       CZ-PLa(br): CATB, 2cl(C) 2bn, without text; CZ-PLa(ka): Hu 758c (CATB, 2cl(B♭) 2hn(F) 2"bassy"; full
       text; (missing C & basso/bn II parts). ★
 1.7tv. Nro 7. [Na mladíka-mládence. For young woman-man] [Z] Strašlivého kosto hradu; in B♭, (N.23).
       CZ-PLa(br): CATB, 2cl(B♭) 2bn. ★
 1.8tv. Nro 8. [Na děvče - pannu. For a girl - virgin. "Kde tvá krása, kde trá čilost?"]; in A, (N.24).
       CZ-PLa(br): CATB, 2cl(A) 2bn, (incomplete text); CZ-PLa(ka): Hu 758d, (CATB only, full text). *Note:
       both use an alternative text, "Libě plynuly nám dnové".* ★
 1.9tv. Nro 9. [Na manžela. For a husband.] Svazek, který věrnost, láska, [srdce]; in E♭, (N.25).
       CZ-PLa(br): CATB, 2cl(C) 2bn, incomplete text; CZ-PLa(ka): Hu 758e, CATB, 2cl(B♭) 2hn(F), full text. ★
 1.10tv. Nro 13. [Na otce. For a man. "Bůh, jenž mne vám"]; in D, (N.26).
       CZ-PLa(br): CATB, 2cl(D) 2bn, (without text). ★
 1.11tv. Nro 16. [Jiná na matku. Another for a mother] Kam se vrhnem, co si počnem, matko! [matko! nyní];
       in E♭, (N.27).   CZ-PLa(br): CATB, 2cl(B♭) 2bn, (without text); CZ-PLa(ka): Hu 758f, (CT, 2hn(E♭) only;
       full text). ★
 1.12tv. Nro 17. [Na starce - stařenu. For an old man - old woman] Každý pohřeb můž čilost; in C, (N.28).
       CZ-PLa(br): CATB, 2cl(C) 2bn. ★
 1.13tv. Nro 18. Kde tvá krása tvá čilost; (N. deest).   CZ-PLa(br): CATB, 2cl(B♭) 2bn.
 1.14tv. Nro 19. Sousedové ejhle [sic: eihle] přítel [obecného dobrého]; in E♭, (N. deest).
       CZ-PLa(br): CATB, 2cl(B♭) 2bn, incomplete text; CZ-PLa(ka): Hu 758g, (as "Ryba. Na úředníka. [For
       officials] Č[islo] 19."; CATB only; full text). ★
 1.15tv. Nro 20. [Na učitele. For a teacher] Libý oddech, tiché lůžko budiž tobě muži ctný; in E♭, (N.30).
       CZ-PLa(br): CATB, 2cl(B♭) 2bn, without text; CZ-PLa(ka): Hu 758h, (C only; full text). ★
 1.16tv. Nro 21. [Na duchovnihu pastýře. For a spiritual shepherd, cleric] Usedavý po dědinách; in E♭, (N.31).
       CZ-PLa(br): CATB, 2cl(B♭) 2bn. ★
 1.17tv. Nro 22. [No. 18. Na vesnického rychtáře. For a village magistrate] Dokonal jsem Bohu díky že jsem
       štastně; in E♭, (N.29).   CZ-PLa(br): CATB, 2cl(B♭) 2bn. ★
 No. 23 (= JSR-1t). No. 23. [Funeral] Marche; in E♭ [with Minore section]. CZ-PLa(br): 2cl(B♭) 2bn. ★
 No. 24 (= JSR-2t). No. 24. Marche funebre; in C minor. CZ-PLa(br): 2cl(B♭) 2bn. ★
 1.18tv. No. 25. "In paradisum." [deducant te Angeli]; in E♭. CZ-PLa(br): CATB, 2cl(B♭); Latin text. ★
 No. 26. (= JSR-5v). Salve [Regina] I; in E♭, (N.293).   CZ-PLa(br): CATB, 2cl(B♭) 2bn; Latin text. ★
 No. 27. (= JSR-21v). Salve [Regina] II; in B♭, (N. deest).   CZ-PLa(br): CATB, 2cl(B♭) 2bn. ★
JSR-2tv. Na otce [For fathers]. N 13 [sic] z Ryb[a].; "Bůh jenž mě vám milé díky", in E♭, (N. deest).
Here only: CATB, hn(E♭).   MS parts (by Ladislav Vaněček, 4/10 [1]837): CZ-PLa(ka), Hu 758ch. *Although
the text matches "Nro 13" above (JSR-1.10tv), the setting is completely different.* ★

*RYBÁŘ, Jaroslav *1942*
JZR-1. Otetto, 1982, in 1 mvt (duration 10').   2ob 2cl 2hn 2bn.
Pm (Panton: Prague, pn P2698, 1990), score (ISBN 80-7039-095-6).
JZR-2. Sonata.   10 winds.
MS score & parts: CZ-Prybar. *Recorded by Panton.*

*RYCHLÍK, Jan *27 April 1916, Prague - 20 Jan 1964, Prague*
JAR-1. Serenáda (Vapominky) [Memoirs], 1957.   2ob 2cl 2hn 2bn.
Pm (Český hudební fond: Prague, 1964), score.
*JAR-2. Africký cyklus, 1961, 5 mvts.   Piano, fl ob cl 2hn bn 2tp.
Pm (SHV/Artia, now Supraphon: Prague, pn H.3574, 1962), score. *Recorded Supraphon (number not known).*

RYDBERG, Bo *28 Feb 1960, Göteborg*
SMR-1. Event: Action; 1986.   3fl(pic) ob 2cl hn 2bn 2tp.   MS score: The composer c/o S-Sic.

SACCHINI (Sachini), Antonio Maria Gaspare *14 June 1730, Florence - 6 Oct 1786, Paris*
AGS-1v. Terzetto ex Es [E♭]; "O Deus te animo te ardenter".   C(I), T(vel C II) B, fl 2cl 2hn 2bn.
MS parts (by F. Jos. Grimm): CZ-CH, S-40-7-185. *Possibly an arrangement.* ★

SACHER, Josef (Joseph) *(1740)*
JXS-1. Partiha [sic]; in E♭, 5 mvts, c.1770.   2cl 2hn 2bn.
(Auto)MS parts ("Spectant adussum Joseph Sacher"): D-F, Mus.Hs.1566. ★
Pm (Hans Gerig: Köln, sd), score & parts (as "Feldpartie").

SADLER, Helmut *23 June 1921, Streitford (Seibenbürgen)*
HMS-1. Sinfonie Concertante for 15 winds.   2fl 2ob 2cl 2hn bn cbn 2tp 2tb tu 2perc.
Pm (Breitkopf & Härtel: Wiesbaden).

*SADLO, Franz *pre-1778 - 1829, Regensburg*
FBS-1. Bantomin [sic] Zur Hamlets Geschichte; (performed Regensburg, 1778), 3 mvts.   2fl 2hn bn.
MS parts: D-Rtt, (2 copies), Sadlo 15, Inc. VIIb/13.   ★

SAGVIK, Stellan *25 July 1952, Orebro, Sweden*
SXS-1. Guenilles des jogleurs: ballet music, Op. 74.   fl(pic, a-fl) ob(ca) cl(Eb) 2cl a-sax/batteria bn crt.
MS score: S-Sic.

*SALIERI, Antonio *18 Aug 1750, Legnano, nr Verona - 7 May 1825, Vienna*
*AXS-1. Armonia per un tempio di notte.   2ob 2cl 2hn 2bn.
AutoMS score: A-Wn, Mus.Hs.3756.   ★
Pm (Suvini Zerboni: Milano, 1976), ed. Giovanni Carli Ballola, score (pn S.7074Z) & pts (pn S.7975Z).
Pm (WINDS: Northridge, CA, pn W-6, c.1981), photocopy of A-Wn score & modern MS parts.
Pm (Doblinger: Wien, pn D. 17346, 1989), ed. W. Rainer, score & parts.
*AXS-2.1. Serenata in Bb; 6 mvts.   2cl 2hn 2bn vlne.
AutoMS score: A-Wn, Mus.Hs.3759.   ★
Pm (Suvini Zerboni: Milano, 1980), ed. Giovanni Carli Ballola, score (pn S.7976.Z.) & parts (pn S.7977.Z.).
*AXS-2.2(-2.5). 4 Serenatas, (C, F, G, Bb; all 2 mvts).   Nos. 1 - 3: 2fl 2ob 2hn 2bn; No. 4: 2ob 2cl 2hn 2bn.
MS score: A-Wn, Mus.Hs.3759. *Serenata 3, 2 mvts, is new material.*   ★
Pm (Doblinger: Wien, München, c.1977), ed. W. Rainer, score & parts, (Diletto musicale 898), Nos. 1 & 2 only.
Pm (WINDS: Northridge, CA, pn W-24(-27), c.1981), photocopies of the autograph score & modern MS parts,
(Nos. 1 - 4 issued separately).
Pm (Suvini Zerboni: Milano, pn S.8805.Z., 1986), ed. Giovanni Carli Ballola, score & parts (Nos. 1 - 3 only,
as a unified single work with ad lib cello part doubling bassoon II).
*AXS-2.6, 2.7 [= 2.2, 2.3]. Serenatta [sic] In C & Serenatta in F; (each 2 mvts).   2fl 2ob 2hn (2)bn vlne.
MS parts: D-Rtt, Salieri 1/I & 1/II. *Purchased from the estate of Graf von Klenau, 1820.*
Pm (Bailey Music: Minneapolis, Minnesota, sd), ed. Höckner.
*AXS-2.8 [= 2.2 & 2.3]. Cassazione in C, 4 mvts.   2ob 2ca 2hn 2bn.   MS parts: A-Wgm, VIII 8542 (Q 16407).
Obviously intended for the Schwarzerberg Harmonie - probably transcribed by Went.
*AXS-3. Picciola Serenata; in Bb, 4 mvts.   2ob 2hn (2)bn.
AutoMS score (1778): A-Wn, Mus.Hs.3758; CZ-Pnm, (unverified); F-Pn.   ★
Pm (Doblinger: Wien, München, 1977), ed. Rudolph Angermüller, score. (Doblingers Studienpartituren. No. 313,
1977) & parts (Diletto musicale No. 589).
Pm (Universal Edition: London, Wien, sd), score & parts.
Pm (Suvini Zerboni: Milano, pn S8034Z, c.1985), ed. Piero Spada, parts.
AXS-4.1s(-4.3s). 3 Trios; (G, 3 mvts; Eb, 3 mvts; C, 2 mvts).   2ob bn.
AutoMS score: A-Wn, Mus.Hs.3768.   ★
Pm (Universal Edition: London, Wien, pn UE 17512, 1983), ed. Gunther Joppig, score & parts.
*AXS-1m. Marcia [altered to "March" + Alternativo]; in C.   2cl(C)+2ob 2hn 2bn 2tp cbn.
AutoMS score: A-Wn, Mus.Hs.4472, No. 1.   ★
*AXS-2m. Marsch [& Trio]; in C. 2ob+2cl(C) 2hn (2)bn 2tp.   AutoMS score: A-Wn, Mus.Hs.4471, [No. 2].   ★
*AXS-1mv. Parade Marsch; in C, with the text beginning, "Prägt tief in eure Herzen Brüder die Jahrzahl eins
acht null und neun" [Impress deep in your hearts, brothers, the year 1809; i.e. when France occupied Vienna].
Unison voices, 2ob+2cl(C) 2hn 2bn 2tp.   AutoMS score: A-Wn, Mus.Hs.4471, [No. 1].   ★

*SALNER, G.P. *(1770)*
GPS-1m. Slow March . . . Dedicated to Capt. Den. Taaffe, Island of St. Helena.
fl(oblig, F) 2fl(Bb) 2cl 2hn 2bn tp serp timp side-drum tamb.
Pc (E. Riley: London, c.1800), RISM [S 632], score: GB-Lbl, g.271.t.(16).   ★
GPS-2m. The German grand march.   2pic 2cl(Eb) 2cl 2hn 2bn tp serp timp side-drum tamb drum [sic].
Pc (E. Riley: London, c.1800), RISM [S 631], score: GB-Lbl, g.271.q.(9).   ★

SALTER, Timothy *15 Dec 1942, Mexborough, Yorks, UK*
TXS-1. Divertimento; 5 mvts.   2ob 2cl 2hn 2bn.
Pm (Usk Edition: London, 1968, *reprinted* 1986), score (facsimile of AutoMS): GB-Ob, 209.c.27.(5).

SALZEDO (Salzédo), (Léon) Carlo *6 April 1895, Arcachon, France - 17 Aug 1961, Waterville, Maine*
CAS-1. Concerto; 1935.   Harp, fl ob 2cl hn bn tp tb.   MS score: US-Wc.

SAMANA, Leo *1951, Netherlands*
LES-1. Caged Memories II, Op. 31.   2fl 2ob 2cl 2hn 2bn.
Pm (Donemus: Amsterdam, 1987), score.

*SAMMARTINI (San Marino, Martino), Giovanni Battista *1698, Milan - 15 Jan 1775, Milan*
GBS-1d. Concertino; in C, 2 mvts, (SWV 80).   Scoring 1: 2fl 2hn b; Scoring 2: 2fl 2ob 2hn 2tp b.
MS parts: D-KA, (Scoring 1), Mus.Hs.794, (Scoring 2), Mus.Hs.783, (1st mvt), Mus.Hs.782, (2nd mvt).   ★
GBS-2d. Concertino; in C, (SWV 79).   2ob/vl 2hn 2bn.
MS score: D-KA, Mus.Hs.792. MS parts: CH-E, 84/11, (for 2vl/ob 2hn basso); CZ-Pnm, XXXIV.C.332.   ★
GBS-3d. Sinfonia; in A, 3 mvts, (SWV 65).   2fl 2ob bn.
MS parts: D-Dl, Musica 2763 N/3. *Originally for 2vl vla b.* ★
GBS-4d. Symphony in G; 3 mvts, (SWV 44).   2fl 2ob 2hn bn cembalo. *Originally for 2vl vla b 2tp.*
MS parts: D-Dl, Musica 2763, N. 1. *The 2fl replace the 2vl; the independent ob pts are probably spurious.*   ★
GBS-5d. Symphony in C; 3 mvts, (SWV 1).   2ob 2hn bn. *Originally 2vl vla b 2hn.*
MS parts: DK-Kk, Sammlung C, Sinfonia 21.   ★

SANDI, Luis   *22 Feb 1905, Mexico City*
LYS-1v. Las Troyanas, 1936.   SATB chorus, 2ob ca bn harp perc.
Pm Ediciones Mexicanasae Musica: Mexico City, 1953), score (Series II/8)
Pm (Peer: New York).

***SANDRED, Örjan**   *15 June 1964, Sweden*
OYS-1. Sabda; 1991.   pic cl/pic-cl 2bn 2tp 2tb tabla.   MS score: S-Sic.

***SARO, Heinrich**   *1827 - 1891*
HNS-1m, 2m.   Difiler Marsch & Armee-Marsch No. 176.
pic 2ob cl(Eb) cl(Bb solo) 3cl(Bb) 4hn 2bn 3tp t-hn 3tb b-hn/bomb vc/b b-dr s-dr.
MS score & parts: D-DT, Mus-n 1903.   ★
HNS-3m.   Prinz-Friedrich-Wilhelm-Marsch.
fl 2ob cl(Eb) cl(Bb solo) 3cl(Bb) 4hn 2bn 3tp t-hn 3tb b-hn bomb b-dr s-dr.
MS parts: D-DT, Mus-n 1986, No. 2.
HNS-4m.   Armee-Marsch No. 172.   pic 2ob cl(Eb) 3cl(Bb) 4hn 2bn 3tp t-hn 3tb bomb/b-hn vc/b b-dr s-dr.
MS parts: D-DT, Mus-n 1906a.
HNS-1a.   Strauss the Younger: Kammerball-Polka, Op. 230.
fl 2ob cl(Eb) cl(Bb solo) 3cl(Bb) 4hn 2bn 3tp t-hn 3tb b-hn bomb b-dr s-dr.
MS parts: D-DT, Mus-n 1986, No. 1.

***SARTI, Giuseppe**   *baptized 1 Dec 1729, Faenza - 28 July 1802, Berlin*
GXS-1m. Marcia; in C.   2fl 2ob 2cl 2bn 2timp.
AutoMS score: I-FZc, RM cart.32.2.   ★

***SARTORIUS (Sartorus), Georg Caspar**   *? - (c.1813, Darmstadt)*
Sartorius' arrangement of J.K. Wagner's Liebe und Freundschaft was lost in D-DS during World War II.
GCS-1m. Marsch des Hochfürstliche Hessen-Darmstädischen Leibregiments.   Instrumentation unknown.
MS: D-Bds, Hausbibl., Thouret, No. 402.
GCS-1a. Danzi: Chöre aus dem Freudenfest.   2cl 2hn 2bn cbn.
MS score: D-DS, Mus.ms.215.
GCS-2a. Himmel: Fanchon, 7 mvts.   2cl 2hn 2bn cbn.
MS score: D-DS, Mus.ms.247.
GCS-3a. Hoffmeister: Der Königssohn aus Ithaka, 9 mvts.   2cl 2hn 2bn cbn.
MS score: D-DS, Mus.ms.248.
GCS-4a. Kauer: Das Donauweibchen; 7 mvts.   2cl 2hn 2bn cbn.
MS score: D-DS, Mus.ms.243.
GCS-5a. Kozeluch: La ritrovata Figlia d'Ottone II, Theil II: 9 mvts.   2cl 2hn 2bn cbn.
MS score: D-DS, Mus.ms.804.
GCS-6a. Martín y Soler: Una cosa rara, 9 mvts.   2cl 2hn 2bn cbn.
MS score: D-DS, Mus.ms.800.
GCS-7a. Martín y Soler: L'Arbore di Diana, introduzione & 9 mvts.   2ob 2cl 2hn 2bn 2tp.
MS score: D-DS, Mus.ms.797.
GCS-8a. Martín y Soler: La Scuola de' maritati, 6 mvts.   2cl 2hn 2bn cbn.
MS score: D-DS, Mus.ms.798.
***GCS-9a.** Mozart: Le Nozze di Figaro, overture & 5 mvts.   2cl 2hn 2bn cbn.
MS score: D-DS, Mus.ms.818.
GCS-10a. Mozart: Favorit-Gesänge aus Il D[on]. Giovanni, 6 mvts.   2cl 2hn 2bn cbn.
MS score: D-DS, Mus.ms.817.
GCS-11a. Mozart: Così fan tutte, overture & 11 mvts.   2cl 2hn 2bn cbn.
MS score: D-DS, Mus.ms.816.
GCS-12a. Mozart: La Clemenza di Tito, 6 mvts.   2cl 2hn 2bn cbn.
MS score: D-DS, Mus.ms.815.
GCS-13.1a. Mozart: Die Zauberflöte, 7 mvts.   pic-fife 2fife 2ob 2cl(C) 2hn 2bn 2tp serp b-dr s-dr cym+"Halber
Mond" [Jingling Johnny].   MS score: D-DS, Mus.ms.820.
GCS-13.2a. Mozart: Die Zauberflöte, 12 mvts.   2ob 2cl 2hn 2bn 2tp.
MS score: D-DS, Mus.ms.819/1.
GCS-13.3. Mozart: Die Zauberflöte, 13 mvts.   2cl 2hn bn cbn.
MS score: D-DS, Mus.ms.819/2.
GCS-14a. Müller: Kaspar der Fagottist, 8 mvts.   2cl 2hn 2bn.
MS score: D-DS, Mus.ms.830.
GCS-15a. Paisiello: La Frascatana, overture & 7 mvts.   2cl 2hn 2bn cbn.
MS score: D-DS, Mus.ms.849.
GCS-16a. Piccinni: Didon, 8 mvts.   2cl 2hn 2bn cbn.
MS score: D-DS, Mus.ms.863.
GCS-17a. Süssmayr: Der Spiegel in Arkadien, overture & 8 mvts.   2cl(C) 2hn 2bn cbn.
MS score: D-DS, Mus.ms.1173.
GCS-18a. Winter: Helena und Paris, 6 mvts.   2cl 2hn 2bn cbn.
MS score: D-DS, Mus.ms.1025.
GCS-19a. Winter: Belisa, 6 mvts.   2cl 2hn 2bn cbn.
MS score: D-DS, Mus.ms.1026.
GCS-20a. Winter: Das unterbrochene Opferfest, Bd. 1: 9 mvts; Bd. 2: 6 mvts.   2cl 2hn 2bn cbn.
MS score: D-DS, Mus.ms.1024/I.
GCS-21a. Gossec: Te Deum, Choere [sic], Allegro maestoso.   2cl 2hn 2bn cbn.
MS parts: D-DS, Mus.ms.350.

*SAUER (Saver), Ignaz *1 April 1759, Třebušin - 2 Dec 1833, Vienna*
IYS-1. Messe-Lied; in B♭. 2ob 2cl 2hn 2bn cbn. MS parts: CZ-Pu, 59 r 82. ★
*IYS-1t. Charakteristische Trauergefühle am Grabe eines geistlichen oder weltlichen Lehrers vorzutragen.
[Headtitle:] Characteristische Trauergefühle am Grabe des Herrn Johann Theodor Persche, gewesenen Lehrers
der vierten Classe und der Zeichnungskunst an der Hauptschule des k.k. Waiseninstitutes in Wien, vorgetragen
an seinem Begräbnisstage den 9 Juli 1825. 2fl 2ob 2cl(C) 2hn 2bn cbn t-tb b-tb(ad lib) timp, *or* piano
Pc (bei ihm [Ignaz] Sauer: Wien, pn S.S.185, 1825), pts: A-Wgm, I 8350, (with 2 sets of instrumental pts). ★
*IYS-1v. Vierstimmiger Fest-Gesang einer ganzen Pfarrgemeinde oder Schule, an jenem Tage, wo ein Seelsorger
oder Lehrer sein fünfzigjähriges Sæculum feyert, oder mit der goldenen Enrenmedaille gezeiret wird.
[Headtitle:] Gesang der Waisen in Wien am 5. Febr. a [1]824. als dem Herrn Johann Föls Lehrer und Senior
im k.k. Waiseninstitute der goldene Ehrenmedaille ertheilet wurde. Worte bon Vierthaler, Musik von Sauer.
Solo TB, SATB choir, Waisenchor(S), 2fl 2cl(C) 2hn 2bn cbn 2tp timp.
Pc (Ignaz Sauer: Wien, pn S.S.182/c, 1824), parts & vocal score with piano accompaniment: A-Wgm, I 3117,
(uncut, with a printed program of the event). *The vocal score calls for "36 Hohe und 8 niedere Frauenstimmen,
6 Hohe und 6 niedere Männerstimmen".* ★
IYS-2v. Vierstimmiger Fest-Gesang an jenem Tage, wo ein neugeweihter Priester sein erstes Messopfer darbringt.
[Headtitle:] Gesang der Waisen in Wien am 19. April 1824, als der Hochwürdige Herr Carl Berger aus dem
Orden der frommen Schulen und Präfect des Löwenburgischen Convictes in der Kirche des k.k. Waiseninstitutes,
dessen Zögling er einst war, seine erste Messe sang. Worte von Vierthaler, Musik von Sauer.
Basso Paridon Solo, SATB chorus, 24Waisenknaben (S), 12 Waisenmädchen, 2fl 2cl(C) 2hn 2bn cbn 2tp timp.
Pc (Ignaz Sauer: Wien, pn S.S.183/c, 1824), pts: A-Wgm, I 3118, (uncut, with a printed program of the event).
*IYS-3v. Wo ist das Land, wo Milch und Honig fliesst? Vierstimmiger Gesang des Waisen in Wien am höchsten
Vermählungsfeste Seiner Kai. Hohert Franz Carl Erzherzogs von Oestreich [sic], Kön Prinzen von Ungarn und
Böhmen &c, mit Ihrer Kön. Hoheit Sophia Friederica Dorothea Kön. Prinzessin von Bayern.
[Headtitle:] Gesang der Waisen in Wien mit zwölfstimmiger Harmoniebegleitung den 4. Nov. à [sic] 1824
gesungen im Speissaal des k.k. Waiseninstitutes am höchsten Vermählungsfeste Seiner Kai. Hoheit Franz Carl
Erzherzogs von Oestreich etc. etc mit Ihrer kön. Hoheit Sophia Friederica Dorothea kön. Prinzessinn von Bayern.
Werte von Vierthaler, Music [sic] von Sauer. Solo TB, SATB chorus, 36Waisen (including 12 Waisenmädchen),
2fl 2cl(C) 2hn 2bn cbn 2tp timp.
Pc (Ignaz Sauer: Wien, pn S.S. 184, 1825), parts & vocal score with piano accompaniment: A-Wgm, I 8434,
(uncut; with a printed program of the event). ★
IYS-5v. Libera me. Solo CATB, 2ob 2bn a-tb t-tb. MS parts: A-Wgm, I 2341, (with a duplicate vocal pts). ★
*IYS-6v. Kriegslied. TTBB, winds.
Pc (Author: Wien, c.1825), parts: CZ-Pnm, [Old shelfmark: Slg. Kačina, VI.1073], unverified.
IYS-7v. Dankgefühle der Niederösterreichische Ständischen Freiwilligen "Lasst uns unserm Kaiser danken" (bei
Vierfacher Harmonie mit 2 Wechselchören), gesungen am 5. September 1797 im Landhaussaale.
Pc (Joseph Eder: Wien, pn 47, 1797), piano vocal score only: A-Wgm, V 6628.

*SAUGUET, Henri-Pierre *(pseud.* **Jean-Pierre Poupart)** *18 May 1901, Bordeaux - 22 June 1989, Paris*
HPS-1. Alentours saxophonistiques; 1941. Solo [?alto] sax, 2fl 2ob 2cl 2hn 2bn.
MS: untraced [?with the publishers].
Pm (Choudens: Paris, 1979), solo part & piano reduction.
HPS-2. Bocages. fl 2ob 2cl 2hn 2bn harp/piano.
Pm (Choudens: Paris).

SAVERY, Finn *1933, Denmark*
FGS-1. Lufttrykket er hojt over Skandinavien; 1978. 2fl ob 3cl bn 3tb tu 3perc. MS score: DK-Kd.

*SAVI, Antonio *(1875), active 1901*
ATS-1. Andantino Patetico, in F. fl 2cl(C) hn bn tp. MS score & pts (1901): I-Mc, Da Camera U.122.12. ★

*SAXTON, Robert *8 Oct 1953, London*
*RZS-1. Paraphrase on Mozart's Idomeneo; 1991. ob ob(ca) 2cl 2hn 2bn.
Pm (Chester Music: London 1991), hire score & parts.

SCARLATO, A.
AUS-1. Colours [sic]. 2ob 2cl 2hn 2bn.
Pm (Edipan Edizione Musicale: Roma, sd).

SCAVARDA, Donald *1928, USA*
DOS-1. Sounds for 11; 1961. fl ob 2cl bn 2perc vib e-gtr piano, conductor.
Pm (Lingua Press: La Jolla, CA, 1980).

*SCHACHT, Theodor, Freiherr (Baron) von *1748, Strasbourg - 20 June 1823, Regensburg*
TVS-1. Partitta in D, 1794, 6 mvts. 2flautini 2ob 2cl(D) 2cl(A) 2hn 2bn tp tri cym,Tamburo Turco, Tamburo,
Tamburino. MS parts: D-Rtt, Schacht 77. ★
*Note: Schacht 86/I is an AutoMS score, Allemanda con [6] Variazioni [B♭], for an orchestra of 2vl 2vla b 2ob
cl 2hn 2bn. On the last sheet, Schacht notes, "Den grössten gefallen könnte H. Miny mir erweisen wenn alles
abgeschrieben wäre biss um 5 Uhr wo bey der Erbprintzess [sic] Concert ist." Miny was one of the second
hornists in the Kapelle & Harmonie from at least 1783 (cf. his name on one of the hn II parts for Schacht's,
"Prolog Von 4ten obre 1783 / Prologue pour L'anèe [sic] 1783".) Although the theme is the same, the variations
in the 7 sets for Harmonie listed below show considerable differences.*
TVS-2.1. No. I. Allemande varie. B♭. 2cl(B♭) 4hn(B♭, E♭) 2bn 2tp(clar) 2vla vlne.
MS parts: D-Rtt, Inc.IVa/21/I, (Theme & 11 vars - Allegretto (& Trio) - Andante - Lento [& 2 vars]). ★
TVS-2.2. No. II. Allemande variée. B♭. 2cl(B♭) 4hn(B♭, E♭) 2bn 2tp(clar) 2vla vlne.
MS parts: D-Rtt, Inc.IVa/21/I, (Theme & 12 vars; TVS-2.1 with an additional variation).

TVS-2.3. No. III. Allemande variée, G.   2cl(G) 2vla b.
MS parts: D-Rtt, Inc.IVa/21/I, (Theme & 6 vars; as Schacht 86/I).
TVS-2.4. Parthia ["II" crossed out] N° IV; in B♭.   2cl(B♭) 2hn 2bn 2vla b.
MS parts: D-Rtt, Inc.IVa/21/I, (Theme & 6 vars; as Schacht 86/I).
TVS-2.5. Parthia ["III" crossed out] N° V; in A.   2cl(A) 2vla b.
MS parts: D-Rtt, Inc.IVa/21/I, (Theme & 6 vars; as Schacht 86/I).
TVS-2.6. Parthia ["IV" crossed out] N° VI; in A.   2cl(A) 2hn 2bn 2vla b.
MS parts: D-Rtt, Inc.IVa/21/I, (Theme & 6 vars); as Schacht 86/I).
TVS-2.7. Allemande variée, B♭.   2cl(B♭) 4hn(B♭, E♭) 2bn 2tp vla vlne.
MS parts: D-Rtt, Schacht 86/II, (Theme & 11 vars, 3/8; as TVS-2.1).
TVS-3, 4. [2] Anglaises Favorites Variées [sic], Anno 1793.
No. 1, in B♭, 6 variations (on No. 1 of TVS-12): 2cl 4hn(E♭, B♭) 2bn 2tp(clar) 2vla vlne; No. 2, in B♭,
12 variations, 2cl 2hn 2bn 2vla vlne. AutoMS score (No. 2 only) & MS parts: D-Rtt, Schacht 87/II. ★
TVS-5. Parthia in F, 13 mvts.   2cl 4hn(F, C) 2bn 2tp 2vla db. AutoMS score: D-Rtt, Schacht 80/III. ★
TVS-6. [Parthia in C], 12 mvts. 2cl 4hn 2bn 2tp(clar) 2vla vlne. MS parts: D-Rtt, Schacht 162. ★
TVS-7. [Parthia in E♭] N: 1, 13 Stim[m]ige, 12 mvts. 2cl 4hn(Eb, B♭) 2bn 2tp 2vla vlne.
MS parts (c.1790): D-Rtt, Schacht 163. ★
TVS-8. Thema Tedesco con 48 Var[iations].   2cl 2hn 2bn 2tp 2vla vlne.
AutoMS score: D-Rtt, Schacht 84, (unfinished sketch; missing the Thema & all after Variation 12). ★
TVS-9. Turco.   fl 2cl(A) 2cl(D) 2hn bn tp tri cym tamburo. · MS score: D-Rtt, Schacht 78. ★
TVS-10.1. [Parthia in B♭], N° 9; 12 mvts. 2cl 2hn 2bn 2vla vlne. AutoMS pts (c.1790): D-Rtt, Schacht 160.
Mvt 1 is an arrangement of "Malbrough s'en va t'en guerre" ; mvt 8 bears the title, "Krautschneider". ★
TVS-10.2. Allemande [& Trio].   2cl 2hn 2bn 2vla vlne. AutoMS score: D-Rtt, Schacht 160, loose sheet. ★
TVS-11. Theme & [2] Variations. 2cl 2hn 2bn 2vla vlne. AutoMS score: D-Rtt, Schacht 79/II, (incomplete). ★
TVS-12. 6 Anglaises. 2cl 2hn 2bn 2vla b.   MS parts: D-Rtt, Inc.IVb/13. *See also: TVS-3.*
TVS-13. Partitta d'Armonia, in B♭, 12 mvts. 2ob 2cl 2hn 2bn. AutoMS score (c.1790): D-Rtt, Schacht 73/II. ★
TVS-14. [Partitta in G]; 12 mvts. 2ca 2cl 2hn (2)bn.
AutoMS score & 2 sets of MS parts, one incomplete, (1789): D-Rtt, Schacht 74. *Incomplete pts are in F.* ★
TVS-15. Partitta in G, 2 mvts. 2ca 2cl(G) 2hn 2bn.
MS parts, (c.1790): D-Rtt, Schacht 74, (originally at Inc.IVa/25). ★
TVS-16. [Parthia in E♭], 2 mvts. ob 2cl 2hn bn. AutoMS score: D-Rtt, Schacht 79/I. ★
TVS-17. [Parthia], in E♭, 18 mvts. ob 2cl 2hn (2)bn(unison). AutoMS score: D-Rtt, Schacht 72. ★
TVS-18. Harmonie e Sinfonia; in B♭, 1 mvt, inserted in Act II, Scene 3 of Anfossi's opera, *Isabella e Rodrigo.*
2cl 2hn bn. MS score (c.1780): D-Rtt, Anfossi 7. *The two other numbers are for orchestra: Andante cantabile
(2fl 2hn, 2vl vla b 2 cannon) and Marcia Andantino (2pic 2cl(C) 2hn, 2vl vla b)* ★
TVS-19. Partitta Armonica; in G, 16 mvts. 2cl(G) 2vla vlne. MS parts (c.1780): D-Rtt, Schacht 73/I. ★
TVS-20. Sonata 3za, in G, 2 mvts. cembalo, fl 2hn b.
AutoMS score (c.1790): D-Rtt, Schacht 64/III, (incomplete: mvt 2 in sketch only in the cembalo part). *Published
without the winds as No. 3 of:* XII Sonates de Clavecin…Gravées à Ratisbonne, (D-Rtt, Schacht 64). ★
TVS-21. Partia; in F, 12 mvts. 2ca 2vla(con sordini).
AutoMS score (missing No. 9) & MS parts: D-Rtt, Schacht 75, (pts missing ca II, vla I). ★
*Only partly original: in the score the following mvts are identified: Nos. 1 & 10, "De Mr:de Schacht; No. 6,
"de Mr:Vachon", No. 7, "de Mr:Haidn [sic: Haydn = Menuetto & Trio of Symphony Hob. I/75]"; Nos. 9 & 12,
"De Mr:Ballestrini [sic: Palestrina]".* ★
TVS-22. Rondeau Andantino B♭ (with 6 Trios, all in B♭). Rondeau: 2vl 2vla vc vlne; Trio 1: 2cl 2hn 2bn;
Trio 2: harp 2vc vlne; Trio 3: 2ca cl 2bn; Trio 4: 2vl 2vla vc vlne harp 2cl 2hn bn; Trio 5: 2bn 2vc vlne; Trio 6:
2vl 2vla 2vc vlne harp 2ca 2cl 2hn 2bn. AutoMS score (c.1780): D-Rtt, Schacht 158. ★
TVS-1m. Sei Marsche de Parada, Scritte per S.A.S. e Reale l'Arciduca Carlo, 1807. 2ob 2cl 2hn 2bn cbn.
MS parts: I-Fc, F.P. S.473. *No. 5, Vivace, is marked, "Suonata lentamente e Sempre piano puo Servir di Marcia
funebre e allora il tempo e Andante per altro sarà".* ★
TVS-1e. Rosamund, Ein Serioses Pantomimisches Ballet, Act III, No. 1. 2cl(A) 2hn 2tp timp.
AutoMS score (1st performance in Regensburg, 7 Nov 1778): D-Rtt, Schacht 153. ★
TVS-1a. [Untitled collection of ?original & arranged mvts], 9 mvts. 2cl 2hn 2bn 2vla cb.
AutoMS score: D-Rtt, W.A. Mozart 17/III.
   1.1a. [?Schacht]: Beginnt mit Nr. 2: Andantino, 3/4, Eb.
   1.2a. [?Schacht]: Nr. 3, [without tempo marking], 3/4, B♭.
   1.3a. Mozart [attrib.]: Nr 4, [without tempo marking], 3/4, B♭. 1mo Finale di Don Giovanni / in Armonia /
        porto da T: di Schacht [sic]. *Note: this mvt does not match any section of Mozart's opera.*
   1.4a. [?Schacht]: Nr. 12: Allegro assai, C, B♭.
   1.5a. Mozart: Don Giovanni, "Là ci darem la mano".
   1.6a. Mozart: Le Nozze di Figaro, duettino, "Cinque, dieci, venti".
   1.7a. Mozart: Le Nozze di Figaro, overture.
   1.8a. [?Schacht]: Nr. 13. Cantabile, ¢, Eb.   1.9a. [?Schacht]: Largo, 2/4, B♭.
TVS-2a. [Parthia in B♭], N° 7; 13 mvts largely based on Mozart themes. 2cl 2hn 2bn 2vla vlne.
MS parts: D-Rtt, Schacht 161. *The last mvt, an arrangement of "Il core vi dono" from Mozart's opera,* Così
fan tutte. *is also found as the last mvt in the score of Stephan Klob's set of Haydn arrangements (STK-1a).* ★
TVS-1v. [Chorus] Reception des Wallersteins im Englischen Wald ("Göttin! dir opfern wir"), den 2.7bris [i.e.
September] Anno 1795. ST, 2ob 2cl 2hn 2bn. AutoMS score & MS instrumental pts: D-Rtt, Schacht 119. ★
TVS-2v. VI Notturni, Op. I. SSTB, 2ob 2cl 2hn 2bn, *or piano.*
Pc (sn: sl, pn 1, sd), RISM [S 1223], vocal score & instrumental parts: A-Wn; D-WUu, ("2da ediz.", with the
notice, "Stampati in Vienna, J.T. Trattner"); D-Bds; D-Dl; H-Bn.
TVS-3v. Stroffe [sic] Epitalamiche . . . Anno 1789, ("Viva ormai la Principessa"). STB, 2ca 2cl 2hn 2bn.
AutoMS score & MS parts: D-Rtt, Schacht 115, (with 2 S pts). ★

TVS-4v. [Chorus: "Hò perduto il mio tesoro" from Metastasio's "Ruggiero", E♭]. SSTTB, 2cl 2hn 2vla vc.
MS score: D-Rtt, Schacht 124. ★
TVS-1d. [Parthia in E♭], 2 mvts; in fact, by F A Rosetti, (K.II, 7). ob 2cl 2hn bn.
MS score (in Schacht's hand, c.1790): D-Rtt, Schacht 79/I, (mvt 1 is the 1st mvt of FAR-12; mvt 2 is the last mvt of FAR-10).

SCHÄFFER, Boguslaw Julien *1929, Poland*
BJS-1. Azione a due. fl ob ca 2cl sax hn bn to tb tu piano.
Pm (Ahn & Simrock: München, 1963).

*SCHAFFNER, Nicolaus Albert *c.1790 - 1860*
*We have no locations for his [2] Divertissements militaires, polonaises, allemandes et walses [sic] for 12 winds
Pc (Dufaut et Dubois: Paris, 1824), parts.*
NAS-1. Polonaise, in F, c.1820. 2fl 2ob 2cl 2hn 2bn 2tp b-tb serp b-dr cym tri.
MS parts: D-Rtt, Sm 14, No. 91. ★

*SCHALL, Claus Nielsen *28 April 1757, Copenhagen - 9 Aug 1835, Copenhagen*
*CNS-1. Carasel Musique, 1791; 28 mvts. "Fuer Harmonie:": 2ob 3cl 2hn 2bn; "fuer Trompetten": 3tp timp; "fuer Janitschar": pic "picoletto" 2fl 2cl 2hn 2bn 2tp b-dr "tamburazo".
MS parts: DK-Sa, R.237. *Performed at the Royal Riding Academy, Copenhagen; Schall composed the Schild- und Tanztour music; other movements were composed by Skalle (qv).*

*SCHALLER, ( ) *(?1800)*
WQS-1a. Sacchini: Oedipe à Colonne, ballet. fl(F) 2ob cl(F) cl(B♭ solo) 4cl(C) 2hn 2bn tp 3tb serp timp b-dr.
MS parts: D-DT, Mus-n 880, (the cl III gives cl(F) as an option; cl IV gives bthn as an option).

SCHAT, Peter *5 June 1935, Utrecht*
PYS-1. Clockwise and Anti-clockwise; 1967. 3fl 3ob 3cl 4hn 3bn.
Pm (Donemus: Amsterdam, 1971), score.

SCHAUB, Hans Ferdinand *1880 - 1965, Germany*
HFS-1. Speilmusik für 12 Blasinstrumente. 3fl 2ob 2cl 2hn 2bn tp.
Pm (A.J. Benjamin: Hamburg, pn EE 3292, 1957), score & parts.

SCHELLE, George Michael *1950, USA*
GMS-1. Double Quartet; 1980. fl(pic) ob cl cl(b-cl) 2hn bn perc. MS score: US-NYaca.

*SCHENK (Schenck), Johann Baptist *30 Nov 1753, Wiener Neustadt - 29 Dec 1836, Vienna*
JBS-1. Quartetto; in F, 4 mvts. fl 2ca bn.
AutoMS score: A-Wgm.
Pm (Doblinger: Wien, 1968), ed. Hans Steinbeck, miniature score (pn Stp.218) & parts (pn D.12.860), (Diletto musicale Nr 142). ★
JBS-1v. [7] Nocturnen; [Italian texts]. SATB, fl cl 2hn bn. AutoMS score: A-Wgm, VI 17684 (Q 3910). ★
Pm (photocopy, 1980), ed. Wolfgang Wetter, score & piano reduction: A-Wgm.
  1.1v. Sureami che ah non pirate.   1.2v. Bei labri che amore.
  1.3v. Trova un sol mia bella èlore.   1.4v. Gia notte saviana; Andante Canone con Variazioni.
  1.5v. Placito Zephiretto.   1.6v. Bella fiama del mio core.
  1.7v. Marcia. Perdonate, il nostro ardire.
JBS-2. Das Veilchen. Voice, piano, 2cl 2hn bn.
MS short score (voice & basso, with instrumental cues) & parts (by Perschl): A-Wgm, VI 17625 (Q 9345). ★

*SCHERER, ( ) *(?1780)*
YQS-1. Adagio in Dis [♭] mit [Theme & 6] Variation in B[♭]. 2cl 2hn 2bn.
MS parts ("Ex Musicalibus Josepha Labler m.p."; cl II: "L[adislav] Vaněček""): CZ-PLa(ka), (missing cl I). ★
YQS-1v. Harmonie Messe in Es [E♭]. SATB, 2fl 2ob 2cl 4hn 2bn 2tp vlne timp.
MS parts: CZ-Bm(au), A.20.063. ★

SCHERZER, A.P. *(1780)*
APS-1m. 6 Märsche, 1805. 2ob 2cl 2hn 2bn tp. (?Auto)MS score: D-Bds, Hausbibl.M.M.136.

*SCHETKY, Johann Georg Christoph *19 Aug 1737, Darmstadt - 30 Nov 1824, Edinburgh*
*JGS-1. A Collection of Scottish music, consisting of twelve slow airs, and twelve reels and strathspeys.
2fl 2cl 2hn bn tp.
Pc (Preston: London, c.1800), RISM [S 1521], parts: GB-En.
MS: GB-DOTams (modern MS parts ed. by Marshall Stoneham & Robert Eccles).
  Slow Airs 1.1. Busk Ye (The Braes of Yarrow). 1.2. The Bush aboon Traquair. 1.3. Waly Waly.
    1.4. The Broom of Cowdenknows. 1.5. Peggy I must love thee. 1.6. Gilderoy.
    1.7. An thou were my ain thing. 1.8. The last time I came o'er the Muir. 1.9. Braes of Ballandyne.
    1.10. Thou are gone awa. 1.11. Donald. 1.12. Within a mile of Edinburgh.
  Reels & Strathspeys 1.13. Short Life to Stepmothers [Strathspey]. 1.14. Mrs Garden of Troup's Reel.
    1.15. Miss Heron's Reel. 1.16. Mrs McDonald Grant's Strathspey. 1.17. Mrs Morthland's Reel.
    1.18. Lady C: Keith's Reel. 1.19. Kempshot Hunt [Reel]. 1.20. Lady Mary Murray's Delight [Strathspey].
    1.21. Village Reel. 1.22. Jarnovik's [Giornovichi's] Reel. 1.23. Miss Graham of Finty's Reel.
    1.24. Miss A: McKenzie's Reel.

SCHICHT, ( ) *(1790)*
QXS-1v. Choro: Jubilate Deo, Psalm 99 alla Capella. SSAATTBB, 2ob 2hn 2bn.
MS parts: CZ-Bm(au), A.20.065, (with a note of performance, "[1]822 den 22 Sept in festo S. Martini"). ★

SCHICK, F.
FKS-1a. Auber: La Muette de Portici, march.
pic quart-fl 2ob cl(F) 2cl(C) 4hn 2bn cbn+serp 2b-hn 2tp 3tb b-dr t-dr tamb cym.   Pc [In: A-74.12/2m(a)].

*SCHICKELE, Peter, (composing as "P.D.Q. Bach")   *17 July 1935, Amos, Iowa*
PXS-1. Capriccio. "La Pucelle de New Orleans".   2fl 2ob cl 2bn tp tb.
Pm (Theodore Presser: Bryn Mawr, PA, pn 2482, 1983), score & parts.
*PXS-2. Octoot, ("S.8").   2fl 2ob 2cl 2bn.
Pm (Theodore Presser: Bryn Mawr, PA, pn 414-4115-7, 1983), score & parts.
PXS-3. No-No-Nonette.   2ob 2cl 2hn 2bn 3toys.
Pm (Theodore Presser: Bryn Mawr, PA), score & parts.
*PXS-4. Suite from "The Civilian Barber", ("S.4F").   2hn 2bn 2tp tb tu vc db.
Pm (Elkan Vogel Inc: Philadelphia).

*SCHIEDERMAYR, Johann Baptist   *23 June 1779, Pfaffenmünster nr Straubing, Bavaria - 6 Jan 1840, Linz*
JOS-1. Deux Harmonies; No. 1, in F, 3 mvts; No. 2, in F, 3 mvts.   2ob/cl(C) 2hn 2bn tp.
Pc (Au Magasin de l'imprimerie chemique: Vienna, pn 1892, 1893, 1812), parts: CZ-Bm(au), A.20.144, (No. 2 only); D-Rtt, Schiedermayr 1, (complete).   ★
JOS-2. VIII Neue Türkische Stücke, Op. 2; 8 mvts.
2fl/2pic(Regimentspfeiffen) cl(F) 2cl(C)/2ob 2hn 2bn cbn/serp 2tp b-dr+cym s-dr.
Pc (Verlag: Bürgl. Noten und Kupferdruckery: Linz, c.1805), parts: A-Wgm, XVI 5105; CZ-Pnm, Lobkovic X.H.a.72; I-Fc, F.P. S.475.   MS parts: CZ-Pnm, XLII.F.154.   ★
JOS-3. Parthia in F.   2fl cl(F) 2cl(C) 2hn 2bn 2tp(clar) b-dr s-dr.
MS pts: A-KR, H 37/29. *Virtually the some scoring as JOS-2; is this the "Old" Türkische Stücke [?Op. 1]?*   ★
JOS-1m. VI Märsche für neumstimmige Harmonie.   2ob 2cl(Nos. 1 - 3: 3, No. 4: B♭) 2hn 2bn cbn.
Pc (Im Verlage der k: k: pr: chemischen Druckerey: Vienna, pn 1294, 1810), parts: E-Mm, K.846.(10).   ★
JOS-2m. Marsch [für] der Landwehr im Erzherzogthum Österreich ob der Enns.   2cl(C) 2hn 2bn tp.
Pc (Im Verlage des Kunst und Industrie=Comtoirs: Linz, c.1805), parts: A-Wgm, XVI 5105 (Q 20630); I-Fc, F.P. S.475.   ★
JOS-1.1v. No. 4 Deutsche Messe; 9 mvts.   CATB, 2fl 2cl 2hn 2bn 2tp timp organ.
MS parts: D-BAUd, Mu 290a, (with duplicate cl pts in B♭ & C).   ★
JOS-1.2v. Deutscher Gesang.   CATB, 2fl(2) 2cl 2hn basso organ+bc.   MS pts: CZ-Pnm, XXXVIII.F.219, (missing mvt 9, the order of mvts is 1 - 3, 5, 7, 4, 6, 8; with 2 different sets of fl pts).
JOS-2v. Deutsche Messe, No. 53, 1815.   SATB, 2bthn 2hn 2bn organ.   MS parts: A-Llm, VI/3.
*JOS-3.1v. IV Evangelien zum Gebrauchte bei dem Frohleichnamsfeste, 71tes Werk.   SATB, 2cl 2hn 2bn.
Pc (bei Tobias Haslinger: Vienna, pn T.H.5032, 1827), pts: A-Wgm, I,5326, (H 24614); CZ-Pnm, XLIII.A.109; CZ-Pu, 59 B 7683; GB-Ljag, (photocopy of CZ-Pu; *?A reissue, post-1818: a new price in Conventionsmünze - "C.M." - has been added across the partly effaced original price on the titlepage).*   ★
MS parts: A-Wn, Mus.Hs.27151, (copy by Ignatius Schnellew, with additional S & A parts; the accompaniment is marked "ad lib"); D-Tl, Gg 329, (as "Gesänge zu den vier Evangelium am Frohnleichnamsfeste oder zum heiligen Segen"; "Scripsimus 1837 ad chorum Bonacellensem"; the wind parts are given as ad lib).
JOS-3.2v. 4 Evangelium.   CATB, 2cl 2hn 2bn organ.
MS parts (from the Catholic church at Spiśké Podhradie): SK-BRnm, Mus.XI.163, (as Anon).
JOS-3.3v. IV Evangelium.   CATB, fl 2cl/vl 2hn bn(I) bn(II)/vlne 2tp(clar) timp.
MS parts (by Hyan, 1836): CZ-PLa(bl), Hu 214, (with performance dates of 1839 & 1842).
JOS-3.4v. [4 Stationes].   CATB, fl 2cl(C) 2cl(B♭) 2hn 3flug vlne(+ organ).   MS parts: CZ-Bm(kj), A.40.050.
JOS-3.5v. Am Fronleichnams Festtag a Homo quidam…und Pangelingua [sic].
CATB, fl 2cl(E♭) 2hn tp(prin) 2flug(C) b-flug(C) bomb.   MS parts (possibly arranged Ignace Scheiwein): CZ-Bm(lb), A.46.846, (missing cl(E♭) I; with duplicate vocal parts & bomb; the *Homo quidam* calls for CATB).
JOS-3.6v. 4 Evangelium.   SATB, 2fl 2cl 2hn 2bn.   MS parts (c.1830): CZ-Bm(kb), A.36.574.
JOS-3.7v. 4 Stationes.   SATB, fl 2cl 2hn 2tp tb.   MS parts (1856): CZ-Pnm, XLVII.D.223.
JOS-3.8v. Stationes pro Festo Corporis Christi.   SATB, fl 2cl 2bn 2tp timp.
MS parts: CZ-Pnm, (2 copies), XVI.A.66, XXVI.F.255.
JOS-3.9v. [Stationes].   CATB, 2cl 2hn 2tp 2flug bomb timp.   MS parts: (c.1870): CZ-Bm(ro), A.27.237.
JOS-3.10v. [4 Stationes Theophoricae].   CATB, 2cl 2hn 2tp(clar) tb timp.   MS parts: CZ-Bm(dr), A.34.015.
JOS-3.11v. IV Stationes pro Festo Corporis Christi.   SATB, 2cl 2hn 2bn 2flug.
MS parts: CZ-Bm(bh), A.9427, (copy by Anton Litschmann, *Lehrer,* 18 Aug 1854, with performance dates: 1873, 4 June 1874, 27 May 1875).
JOS-3.12v. IV Stationes pro Festo Corporis Christi.   CATB, 2cl 2hn 2bn tb.
MS parts ("Joh. Adolf Krist a razítko: Sigillum eccl. Reschnoviensis. 1845"): CZ-Bm(re), A.42.727.
JOS-3.13v. IV. Evang[elium].   [CATB], 2cl 2bn 2tp(clar) tp(prin). Contra Bass, organ, timp.
MS parts: A-Wn, Fonds 4 Baden 571, (missing vocal parts & possibly 2hn; the work shows heavy use and the parts were copied at four times, as follows: (1, original parts) bn I & II, tp(prin); (2) cl I & II, Contra Bass, timp; (3) tp(clar) I & II; (4) organ; texts are given at the bottom of each piece in the organ part).
JOS-3.14v. Stationen.   CATB, 2fl 2cl(C) 2hn 2bn 2tp timp.
MS parts (by Ignác Kulka & V. Matyáš): CZ-TRB, H 133.
JOS-4v. Pange lingua, Zum Gebrauche bei dem Frohnleichnamsfeste, 70tes Werk.   SATB, 2cl 2hn 2bn.
Pc (Tobias Haslinger: Vienna, pn T.H.5031, c.1827), pts: A-Wgm, I 3156 (H24614); CZ-Pnm, XLIII.A.112.   ★
MS parts (copy of Haslinger edition): CZ-Pnm, XLVII.B.284; SK-BRnm, Mus. VII 305, (with duplicate C, A & cl I pts; also with later parts for 2tp b-flug).
JOS-1tv. O weinet eure etc. Todtenlied bey Erwachsenen und Jungen.   CATB, 2cl 2hn bn 2tp b-tb.
MS parts: CZ-TRB, H 432.   ★

SCHIFFMAN, Harold Anthony *1928, USA*
HAS-1. Chamber Concerto. Piano, 2fl 2ob 2cl 2hn 2bn. MS score: US-NYamc.

SCHILDKNECHT, Björn *1905 - 1946, Sweden*
BQS-1. Fugerat förspel [Prelude fugué]; 1946. 2fl 2ob 2cl 2hn bn.
MS score & parts: S-Smic, T-0948. T-0909.

SCHILHA, ( ) *See: KURTZ, ( ) & SCHILHA, ( ).*

SCHILLINGS, Max von *19 April 1868, Düren - 24 July 1933, Berlin*
MVS-1v. Weihchor zum Festspiel bei Einweihung des Künstlerhauses für Trauerstimmen.
Two SA choruses, 2harps, 2fl 2ob 2cl 2hn 2bn.
AutoMS score (1900) & MS parts: D-Mbs, Mus.Mss.10074, (parts missing voices, fl I & ob II). ★

SCHIMPKE, Christoph *(?1722/1725) - 1789*
CQS-1. Parthia in Dis [Eb]; 4 mvts. 2cl 2hn bn.
MS parts (Augustus Eramus Hübner, Langenbrück, 1806): CZ-Pu(dm), 59 R 3335. ★

*SCHINN, Georg Johann *14 Sept 1768, Sinzing, nr Regensberg - 18 Feb 1833, Munich*
*GJS-1. Pièces d'Harmonie; 6 mvts. 2fl 2ob 2cl 2hn 2bn 2vla vc+vlne.
MS parts: CZ-K, symfonie Nr 144.K.II. ★

*SCHIRINGER (SCHÖRINGER), Karl (Carl) *(1740), active 1767 - 1790*
CXS-1. Parthia in G, 5 mvts. 2ob 2hn bn.
MS parts (c.1770): CZ-Bm(au), A.20.893, (missing ob I). ★

SCHLIER, Johann (Giovanni) Evangelist *22 Oct 1792, Salzburg - 27 May 1873, Salzburg*
JHS-1v. Libera me Domine. CATB, 2cl 2hn 2bn cbn 2tp a-tb t-tb b-tb.
(?Auto)MS score (performed 2 April 1835): A-Sca, Hs.573. ★

*SCHMELLING, ( ) *(?1800)*
*QUS-1. Ouverture. fl cl(Eb) 3cl(Bb) 2hn 2bn 2tp b-tb.
MS parts: D-DT, Mus-n 1723, No. 2. ★

*SCHMETS, ( ) *(1780)*
QYS-1a. Seyfried & Haibel (compilers): Rochus Pumpernickel, Ouverture a Polonese (Maestoso/Tempo di Menuetto/Tedesco & 2 Trios/Tempo 1mo; Polonese & Trio). 2ob 2cl 2hn 2bn cbn.
MS parts: CZ-Pnm, XX.F.109.

*SCHMID, Josef *30 Aug 1868, Munich - post 1904*
JSS-1. Serenata, Op. 42; 4 mvts. 2fl 2ob 2cl 2hn 2bn cbn.
AutoMS score (Munich, 20 April - 25 May 1904): D-Mbs, Mus.Mss.7173. ★

SCHMIDEK, Kurt *18 March 1919, Vienna - 13 April 1986, Vienna*
KXS-1. Suite für acht Bläser, Op. 40a; c.1961. fl 2ob 2cl hn 2bn.
Pm (Doblinger: Wien, 1963, reprinted 1981), score, (MS materials in the Döblinger archives, possibly for hire).

SCHMIDT, Franz *22 Dec 1874, Bratislava - 12 Feb 1939, Perchtoldsdorf, nr Vienna*
FAS-1. Variations and fugue on an original theme: 3rd version, 1925. 14 winds, timp, organ.
Pm (Weinberger: Wien), (?)hire score & parts.
FAS-2. Tullnerbacher Blasmusik, (Lied, Ländler, Marsch), c.1904-09. 2ob 3hn 2tp bar-hn s-dr.
Pm (Verlag Doblinger: Wien, München, 1975), arranged Rudolf Scholz (db replaces bar-hn), score (pn DE 06608) & parts (pn DE 06609).

*SCHMIDT (Schmid), Jakob *(?1790)*
OJS-1tv. Gedicht v. H. Harnach gewordener Praffer in Langau, Trauerlied in E[b], Für erwachsene Personen, "Du Musstest o Schöpfer". CATB, 2cl 2hn bn.
MS parts: A-GE, I 242. ★
OJS-2tv. Grabe Lied ex Dis, "Nun des kindes Lebens ende". CATB, 2cl 2hn bn.
MS parts: A-GE, I 241. ★
OJS-3tv. [Funeral] Melodie und Gesang, Für einen Ehegatten oder Gattin, [for a husband or wife] "Wir ruhen zu dir o grosser Gott". CATB, 2cl 2hn bn.
MS parts: A-GE, I 230. ★
OJS-4tv. Todtenaria in Es [Eb] Bey einer erwachsenen Person zu singen, "Du der du lebest".
CAB. (2cl 2hn ad lib). AutoMS parts: A-GE, I 236. ★

*SCHMIDT, Ole *14 July 1928, Copenhagen*
OXS-1. Concerto for Tuba. Solo tuba, 2fl 2ob 2cl 4hn 2bn timp perc 8vc 6db.
Pm (Wilhelm Hansen: Copenhagen, 1976), hire score & parts.

SCHMIDT, William Joseph *6 March 1926, Chicago*
WJS-1a. Joplin: Chrysanthemum Rag. pic fl ob 2cl b-cl a-sax t-sax 2bn.
Pm (Western International Music, Inc.: Greeley, Colorado, pn WIM 469, sd), score & parts.

*SCHMITT, Florent *28 Sept 1870, Blamont Meurthe-et-Moselle - 17 Aug 1958, Neuilly-sur-Seine*
*FYS-1. Lied et Scherzo, Op. 54. Solo horn, fl(pic) fl 2ob/ca 2cl hn 2bn.
Pc (A. Durand & Fils: Paris, pn D&F8365, 1912), score & parts: GB-Lbl, g.1060.(3); US-Wc.
Pm (Roland père et fils: Paris, 1962), score & parts.

*SCHMITT (Schmidt), Georg *(active Amorbach c.1803 - 1816, Öhringen & Schlawentzitz, 1816 - c.1839.)*
*NOTE. D-NEhz, 134, a Collection of 61 dances (Hopwalzer, Walzer, Galopps, Marsch, Cottillon, Polonaisen)
is a set of parts in the hands of Schmitt & W.E. Scholz. Only No. 32 (Kühn: Der alte Feldherr, walzer) identifies
Schmitt as the arranger, and we list this work at GYS-37a; other arrangments in this volume are probably also
by Schmitt. The complete collection is listed in Anonymous Collections at A-10a.*
GYS-1. 7 Walzer fürs Orchester [sic].   fl 2ob 2cl 3hn 2bn tp tb db.
AutoMS score: D-NEhz, 111f, (missing the opening pages; complete from No. 2).
GYS-1a. Collection of 63 Dances (Walzer, Cottillon, Hopswalzer, Polonaisen).
2fl 2ob 2cl 2hn 2bn 1/2tp (?t-)tb db. MS parts ("Walzer Band N° 1"): D-NEhz, 132, (fl II incomplete; missing
bn I. A single tp part is included in the cl I part except for Nos. 40 - 45 where there is a separate part for 2tp).
Only 3 dances are titled:
  1.8a: [Boieldieu: Le Petite Chaperon rouge], "aus dem Rothkaepchen".
  1.32a: [C.M. von Weber],"Walzer aus dem Frieschütz".   1.40a: [C.M. von Weber]: "aus Preciosa".
GYS-2a. Anon: Moderato in F minor.   fl 2ob 2cl 2hn 2bn tp tb db.
AutoMS score ("Friedrichruhe d. [ ]ten Septbr. 1828") & MS parts: D-NEhz, 100, No. 6, (missing some pts).
GYS-3a(-5)a. 3 unidentified arrangements, one said to be by V. Fioravanti, another said to be by Mozart.
2pic 2ob cl(E♭) 2cl(Bb) 4hn 2bn 2tp serp timp.   MS parts: D-AB, N. I/1, I/5, I/6 .
GYS-6a. Auber: La Neige, 1 Bd.   fl 2ob 2cl 2hn 2bn tp 2tb db (timp).
AutoMS score ("Eigenthum Schmitt") & MS parts: D-NEhz, 5, (parts missing bn I; with 2 additional tp parts.
The timp part does not appear in the score, where a note at the beginning states that it is to be found in Bd 22 -
now D-NEhz, 49/1. Although a note at the end of the score states "Ende des 3 Acts.", both the score & parts
end with No. 7 of Act II.)
GYS-7.1a. Auber: Le Concert à la cour.   fl 2ob 2cl 2hn 2bn tb(solo) 2tb db!
MS score & parts: D-NEhz, 2, (the parts differ slightly from the score: fl 2ob 2cl 2bn tp tb(obl) b-tb db).
GYS-7.2a. Auber: La Concert à la cour, 1 mvt.   fl 2ob 2cl 2hn 2bn tp tb db.
AutoMS score ("Friedrichruhe d. [ ]ten Septbr. 1828") & MS parts: D-NEhz, 100, No. 3, (missing some parts).
GYS-8a. Auber: Le Maçon, 1 Bd.   fl 2ob 2cl 2hn 2bn 2tb db.
(?Auto)MS score & MS parts: D-NEhz, 6, (the parts call for: tp tb, instead of 2tb).
GYS-9a. Auber: La Muette de Portici, 4 Bds.   pic fl 2ob 2cl 2hn 2bn 2tp 2tb b-tb bd.
AutoMS score ("Oehringen 30t Julij [18]29"; completed 15 July 1830) & MS pts: D-NEhz, 1, (the parts differ
slightly from the score: fl 2ob cl(solo) 2cl 2hn 2bn tp(clar) tb db timp).
GYS-10a. Auber: La Fiancée, 2 Bds.   fl 2ob 2cl 2hn 2bn tp tb(solo) tb db.
(?Auto)MS score & MS parts: D-NEhz, 53, (?missing the solo tb part).
GYS-11a. Auber: Fra Diavolo, overture & 3 Teils.   fl 2ob 3cl 2hn 2bn tp tb(obl) 3tb db timp.
(?Auto)MS score ("Schlawentzitz d. 10 Mai 1837, 12 Junj 1837") & MS pts: D-NEhz, 3, (?missing the 3tb pts;
the tp & timp are only used in the overture).
GYS-12a. Beethoven: Fidelio.   2fl 2ob 2cl 2hn 2bn tp tb db.
AutoMS score ("Eigenthum G. Schmitt. den 25t Octob[er] 1820") & MS parts: D-NEhz, 7a.
GYS-13a. Beethoven: Septetto, Op. 20.   2fl 2ob 2cl 2hn 2bn tb db.
(?Auto)MS score (1817) & parts: D-NEhz, 86, No. 5 - 8, (without tb part).
GYS-14a. Beethoven: Symphony No. 1 in C, Op. 21.   2fl 2ob 2cl 2hn 2bn tb db.
(?Auto)MS score (8 Sept 1817) & MS parts: D-NEhz, 86, Nos. 1 - 4, (without tb part).
GYS-15.1a. Boieldieu: Jean de Paris, overture.   2fl 2ob 2cl 2hn 2bn tb db timp.
MS parts: D-NEhz, 86, No. 23.
GYS-15.2a. Boieldieu: Jean de Paris.   fl 2ob 2cl 2hn 2bn tp tb db.
(?Auto)MS score & pts (1829): D-NEhz, 33.
GYS-16a. Boieldieu: La Fête du village voisin, overture.   2fl 2ob 2cl 2hn 2bn tb db.
MS parts: D-NEhz, 86, No. 24.
GYS-17.1a, 17.2a. Boieldieu: Le Petit Chaperon rouge & Cherubini: Les deux Journées [as "Graf Armand"].
2fl 2ob 2cl 2hn 2bn tp(2) tb db timp.
(?Auto)MS score & MS parts: D-NEhz, 10/1, (with a duplicate tp part; timpani do not appear in the score).
GYS-18.1a. Boieldieu: La Dame blanche, 2 Bd.   fl 2ob 2cl 2hn 2bn tp tb db (timp).
(?Auto)MS score & parts: D-NEhz, 9, (with a timp part for Nos. 23 - 25).
GYS-18.2a. Boieldieu: La Dame blanche, 1 mvt.   fl 2ob 2cl 2hn 2bn tp tb db.
AutoMS score ("Friedrichruhe d. [ ]ten Septbr. 1828") & MS parts: D-NEhz, 100, No. 6, (missing some parts).
GYS-19a. Catel: Sémiramis, air.   2pic 2ob cl(E♭) 2cl(B♭) 4hn 2bn 2tp serp timp.
MS parts: D-AB, N. I/8.
GYS-20a. Cherubini: Lodoïska, overture.   2pic 2ob cl(E♭) 2cl(B♭) 4hn 2bn 2tp serp timp.
MS parts: D-AB, N. I/7.
GYS-21.1a. Cherubini: Les deux Journées, overture.   2pic 2ob cl(E♭) 2cl(B♭) 4hn 2bn 2tp serp timp.
MS parts: D-AB, N. I/9.
GYS-21.2a. Cherubini: Les deux Journées, overture.   2pic 2ob 2cl(E♭) 4cl(B♭) 3hn 2bn 2tp tb serp timp.
MS parts: D-AB, S.27.
GYS-21.3a. Cherubini: Les deux Journées, 3 Acts.   2fl 2ob 2cl 2hn 2bn tp tb db timp.
(?Auto)MS score & MS parts: D-NEhz, 10, (with a duplicate tp part; the timpani do not appear in the score).
GYS-21.4a. Cherubini: Les deux Journées, romance.   fl 2ob 2cl(C) 2hn 2bn tb db.
MS parts: D-NEhz, 233.
See also supra: GYS-17.2a. Cherubini: Les deux Journées. 2fl 2ob 2cl 2hn 2bn tp(2) tb db timp.
GYS-22a. Dalayrac: Adolphe et Clara, overture.   2fl 2ob 4cl 2hn 2bn 2tp serp.
MS parts: D-AB, S.26.
GYS-23a. Dalayrac: Maison à vendre, "O ciel! qu'ai-je lu?".   3fl 3ob 4cl 2hn 2bn tb serp. MS pts: D-AB, S.55.

GYS-24.1a. Dalayrac: Deux mots, overture.   2fl 2ob 2cl 2hn 2bn 2tp tb db.   MS parts: D-AB, T.13
GYS-24.2a. Dalayrac: Deux mots, polonaise & pas redoublé.
terz-fl 2pic 2ob cl(F) 2cl(B♭) 2bthn 4hn (F, hoch B♭) 2bn cbn 2tp b-dr s-dr (tambour Soldat).
MS parts: D-AB, S.31.
GYS-25a. Eugen, Herzog von Würtemberg: Ouverture in C minor.   2fl 2ob 3cl 2hn 2bn tp tb db.
MS parts: D-NEhz, 193.
GYS-26.1a. V. Fioravanti: La Cantatrice villane, overture.   fl 2ob 2cl 2hn 2bn tp tb db.
AutoMS score ("Friedrichruhe d. [ ]ten Septbr. 1828") & MS parts: D-NEhz, 100, No. 1, (missing some parts).
GYS-26.2a. V. Fioravanti: La Cantatrice villane, overture & Act I (9 mvts).   2pic 2ob 3cl 4hn 2bn 2tp timp serp.
MS parts (c.1803 - 1816): D-AB, N. I/12 (overture), 13 (chor), & then mvts Nos. "2 - 9".
GYS-26.3a. V. Fioravanti: La Cantatrice villane, Act II, 6 mvts.   2fl 2ob 2cl 2hn 2bn 2tp.
MS parts: D-AB, S.4. *Although the mvts are numbered 11 - 16, this arrangement follows on from the 10 numbers of GYS- 27.2a*
GYS-27a. Gaveaux: Monsieur des Chalumeaux, overture.   fl 2ob 2cl 2hn 2bn 2tp tb serp perc.
MS parts: D-AB, S.29.
GYS-28a. Gyrowetz: Der Augenarzt, 1 mvt followed by 4 Walzer.   2fl 2ob cl(F) 2cl(B♭) 2bthn 4hn 2bn 2tp tb+db b-dr.   (?Auto)MS parts ("nach einem Clavier Auszug"): D-AB, S.10.
GYS-29a. Hérold: Almédon [here under the later title "Marie"], 2 Bds.   fl 2ob 3cl 2hn 2bn tp tb db.
(?Auto)MS score & MS parts: D-NEhz, 17.
GYS-30a. Hérold: Zampa, overture & 1 Bd.   fl 2ob 3cl 3hn 2bn 2tp tb db timp.
Partly AutoMS score (Act II only) & MS parts: D-NEhz, 18, (hn III appears in the overture & No. 4 only; the timpani are not in the score).
GYS-31a. Isouard: Le Médicin turc, overture.   3fl 2ob 4cl 4hn 2bn 2tp serp.
MS parts: D-AB, T.8, ("Fürstliche Leiningische Musik, No. 6").
GYS-32a. Kauer: Das Donauweibchen, overture.   2fl 2ob 2cl 2hn 2bn 2tp serp.   MS parts: D-AB, S.9.
GYS-33.1a. C. Kreutzer: Feodora, overture & 6 mvts.   2fl 2ob 2cl 2bthn 2hn 2bn 2tp tb+db.
MS parts: D-AB, S.5.
GYS-33.2a. C. Kreutzer: Feodora, quartetto ("So sieget denn die gute Sache").   2fl 2ob 2cl 2hn 2bn tp tb db.
AutoMS parts: D-NEhz, 32, No. 1.
GYS-34a. C. Kreutzer: Die Alpenhütte, overture & 6 mvts.   2fl 2ob 2cl 2hn 2bn tp tb db.
(?Auto)MS score (1818) & MS parts: D-NEhz, 86, Nos. 9 - 15, (without tb part).
Cited without composer in RISM A/2; there are 4 possibilities of which Kreutzer is most likely.
GYS-35.1a. R. Kreutzer: Paul et Virginie, overture.   fl 2ob 4cl 4hn 2bn 2tp 2tb serp.
MS parts: D-AB, S.25.
GYS-35.2a. R. Kreutzer: Paul et Virginie, (untitled excerpt).   3fl 2ob 4cl 2hn 2bn cbn 2tp tb perc.
MS parts: D-AB, T.9.
GYS-35.3a. R. Kreutzer: Paul et Virginie, Chor des Negrès.   2fl 2ob 4cl 2hn 2bn cbn.
MS parts: D-AB, S.61.
GYS-35.4a. R. Kreutzer: Paul et Virginie, finale.   fl 2ob 4cl 4hn 2bn 2tp 2tb serp.   MS parts: D-AB, S.54.
GYS-36a. Krommer: Symphony, Op. 12.   2fl 2ob 2cl 2hn 2bn tb db.
MS parts (1818): D-NEhz, 86, Nos. 25 - 28.
GYS-37a. Kühn: Der alte Feldherr, Walzer.   fl 2ob 3cl 2hn 2bn tb db.
MS score & parts: D-NEhz, 134, No. 32.
GYS-38a. Lesueur: Ossian, duo.   2fl 2ob 2cl 2hn 2bn.   MS parts: D-AB, S.59.
GYS-39a. Lindpaintner: Moses' Errettung, overture.   fl 2ob 2cl 2hn 2bn tp tb db.
AutoMS score & MS parts: D-NEhz, 34, (the parts differ slightly from the score: fl 2ob 2cl 2hn 2bn tp tb b-tb db timp; the bn I & timp pts are in duplicate).
GYS-40a. Lindpaintner: Aglae, 1 Bd.   fl 2ob 2cl 2hn 2bn tp tb(solo) a-tb t-tb db.
AutoMS score ("Oehringen d. 5t Aprill [sic] 1828") & MS pts: D-NEhz, 22, (the tp does not appear in the score).
GYS-41.1a. Lindpaintner: Janina, overture.   fl 2ob 2cl 2hn 2bn tb(obl).   MS parts (c.1830): D-NEhz, 1/2.
GYS-41.2a. Lindpaintner: Janina, Act II Introduction & Act IV, No. 5.   fl 2ob 2cl 2hn 2bn 2tb b-tb db.
AutoMS score (1828) & (incomplete) MS parts: D-NEhz, 27.
GYS-41.3a. Lindpaintner: Janina, 1Bd.   fl 2ob 2cl 2hn bn 2tp 2tb db.
AutoMS score (?c.1840) & MS parts: D-NEhz, 23, (the parts, in another hand, call for: fl 2ob 2cl 2hn bn tp 2tp(only in the overture) 2a-tb 2(?t)-tb b-tb db.   A note at the beginning of the score states that the timp pt is to be found in (old number) "Bd. 23.24.25".)
GYS-42a. Lindpaintner: Zeila, 2 Bds.   fl 2ob 2cl 2hn 2bn tp 2a-tb b-tb db.
AutoMS score ("Oehringen d. 26t April 1828"; end of score: "beendigt d. 18t May Vormittags 11 Uhr.") & MS parts: D-NEhz, 21.
GYS-43a. Marschner: Der Vampyr, 2 Bds.   fl 2ob 2cl 2hn 2bn 2tp a-tb t-tb b-tb db.
AutoMS score ("Oehringen d. 26tn Septbr. 1829") & MS parts: D-NEhz, 20, (the parts, in another hand, call for: fl 2ob 2cl 3hn(hn III in overture only) 2bn tp tb db timp.)
GYS-44a. Marschner: Templer und Jüdin, overture & 3 Nos. in Act I.   fl 2ob 3cl 2hn 2bn tp tb db.
AutoMS score ("Friedrichsruhe den 22t Juni 1833") & MS parts: D-NEhz, 28, Bd. 1 - 2, (with an additional timp part). *Band 2 of the arrangement, beginning with Act I, No. 4, was completed by W. Kirchhoff in May 1834.*
GYS-45a. Méhul: La chasse de jeune Henri, overture.   fl 2ob 2cl 3hn 2bn tp tb db timp.
MS score in the hand of W. Kirchhoff, c.1840) & parts: D-NEhz, 65, No. 10, (hn III does not appear in the score).
GYS-46.1a. Méhul: Joseph, overture.   2fl 2ob 2cl 2hn 2bn tp tb db.
AutoMS score ("den 20t Jan 1820") & parts: D-NEhz, 46/1.
GYS-46.2a. Méhul: Joseph, 6 mvts.   2fl 2ob 2cl 2hn 2bn (tp) tb db.
AutoMS score ("im Decemb. 1815") & parts: D-NEhz, 46/2, (the tp part does not appear in the score).

GYS-47a. Meyerbeer: Il Crociato in Egitto, overture.   fl 2ob 2cl 2hn 2bn 2tb b-tb db.
AutoMS score ("Friedrichsruhe den 22tn October 1828") & MS parts: D-NEhz, 27, (here missing all pts except 2db; pts for the overture are at D-NEhz, 1/1: fl 2ob 2cl 2hn 2bn tb).
GYS-48.1a. Mozart: Idomeneo, overture.   4fl 2ob 4cl 2hn 2bn 2tp tb serp.   MS parts: D-AB, S.23.
GYS-48.2a. Mozart: Idomeneo, finale.   3fl 2ob 4cl 2hn 2bn 2tp tb serp.   MS parts: D-AB, S.43.
GYS-49.1a. Mozart: Le Nozze di Figaro, overture & Act II finale. 2fl 2ob 2cl 2hn 2bn tp(2) tb db timp. (?Auto)MS score & parts: D-NEhz, 38.
GYS-49.2a. Mozart: Le Nozze di Figaro, 1 mvt.   2fl 2ob 2cl 2hn 2bn tp tb db.
(?Auto)MS score & parts: D-NEhz, 32, No. 5.
GYS-50.1a. Mozart: Don Giovanni, 2 Bds.   fl 2ob 2cl 3hn bn 2tp 2tb db.
AutoMS score ("Fini d. 12t März 1826") & parts: D-Nehz, 30, (parts missing fl II).
GYS-50.2a. Mozart: Don Giovanni, 2 Bds.   2fl 2ob 3cl 2hn 2bn tp 2tb db.
AutoMS score (1826) & parts: D-NEhz, 31, (missing fl I & (?) a tb pt; with a duplicate tp pt).
GYS-51.1a. Mozart: La Clemenza di Tito, overture.   2pic 2ob cl(E♭) 2cl(B♭) 4hn 2bn 2tp serp timp. MS parts: D-AB, N. I/4.
GYS-51.2a. Mozart: La Clemenza di Tito, 1 Bd.   2fl 2ob 2cl 2hn 2bn tp tb db.
AutoMS score ("Eigenthum G. Schmitt") & parts: D-NEhz, 82.
GYS-52.1a. Mozart: Die Zauberflöte, overture.   2fl 2ob 4cl 2hn 2bn tp tb db.
MS score (in the hand of W. Kirchhoff, c.1840) & parts: D-NEhz, 65, No. 11.
GYS-52.2a. Mozart: Die Zauberflöte, overture & 4 mvts.   4cl 2hn 2bn.
MS: (original untraced: D-AB?); (modern copy): D-KIZklöcker.
GYS-53a. Müller: Kaspar der Fagottist, cavatina (Allegro, 3/8).   2fl 2ob 2cl 2hn 2bn tb serp. MS parts: D-AB, S.57.
GYS-54.1a. Müller: Das neu Sonntagskind, overture.   2pic 2ob cl(E♭) 2cl(B♭) 4hn 2bn 2tp serp timp. MS parts: D-AB, N. I/3.
GYS-54.2a. Müller: Das neu Sonntagskind, 3 mvts: Chor, Act I finale; Duetto, Act II, No. 12, "Lasst un diesen Zwug entfliehen"; Chor, Act II finale.   2fl 2ob 4cl 4hn 2bn 2tp serp timp.   MS parts: D-AB, S.48.
GYS-54.3a. Müller: Das neu Sonntagskind, Duett, Act II, No. 5, "Wenn lieserl nur wollt".
2fl 2ob 2cl 2hn 2bn serp.   MS parts: D-AB, S.45.
GYS-55a. Müller: Die Teufelsmühle am Wienerberge, overture & 9 mvts.
2fl 2ob 2cl 2bthn 2hn 2bn 2tp vlne/serp.   MS parts: D-AB, S.8.
GYS-56a. Naumann: Protesilao, overture.   2fl 2ob 2cl 2bthn 2hn 2bn 2tp db.   MS parts: D-AB, S.7a.
GYS-57a. Pacini: Il Ultimo giorno di Pompei, 2 Bds.   fl 2ob 2cl 3hn 2bn tp tb db.
AutoMS score ("Oehringen d. 13t Junj 1829 angeangen") & MS pts: D-NEhz, 34/1, (pts possibly missing hn III).
GYS-58.1a. Paer: Camilla, overture & 2 mvts.   2fl 2ob 4cl 2hn 2bn 2tp tb serp.   MS parts: D-AB, S.53a.
GYS-58.2.a. Paer: Camilla, Act I, Nos. 4 & 5.   2fl 2ob 4cl 2hn 2bn 2tp tb serp.   MS parts: D-AB, S.47.
GYS-58.3a. Paer: Camilla, Act I, No. 6, "Notre Meunier charge d'argent" & No. 7, "Amis ne nous effrayés pas".
2fl 2ob 2cl(C) 2cl(B♭) 2hn 2bn 2tp tb serp.   MS parts: D-AB, S.58.
GYS-58.4a. Paer: Camilla, Act II, No. 8, Duett, Loredan - Fabio & No. 9, Ariette d. Fabio.
2fl 2ob 2cl 2hn 2bn tb serp.   MS parts: D-AB, S.60.
GYS-58.5a. Paer: Camilla, Act II, No. 10, Duett, Camille - Alberti.   2fl 2ob 4cl 2hn 2bn tb serp.
MS parts: D-AB, S.50.
GYS-59a. Paer: Poche ma buone, overture.   2pic 2ob cl(E♭) 2cl(Bb) 2hn 2bn 2tp serp timp.
MS parts: D-AB, N.I/2.
GYS-60.1a. Paer: Achille, overture.   2fl 2ob 4cl 2hn 2bn 2tp tb serp.   MS parts: D-AB, S.30.
The Overture differs from the piano reduction made by Arnold (N. Simrock: Bonn, pn 276, 1802/1803): after the opening 28-bar Allegro, there follows in the piano reduction an Allegro maestoso section ("Allegro di Marche" in Schmitt's version); Schmitt's arrangement includes the following sections: Allegro / Allegro non troppo / Allegro di Marche / Allegro - all in common time.
GYS-60.2a. Paer: Achille, terzetto ("Dunque andiam più no si tardi").   2fl 2ob 2cl 2hn 2bn tp tb db.
MS parts: D-NEhz, 32, No. 1.
GYS-61.1a. Paer: Sargino, 1 Bd.   2fl 2ob 3cl 2hn 2bn tp tb db.
AutoMS score ("Eigenthum G. Schmitt") & MS parts: D-NEhz, 32, (?parts missing cl III).
GYS-61.2a. Paer: Sargino, Larghetto.   2fl 2ob 2cl 2hn 2bn tp tb db.   MS parts (1829): D-NEhz, 33.
GYS-62a. Paer: Numa Pompilio, overture.   2fl 2ob 2cl 2hn 2bn tp tb db.
AutoMS score ("den 16. Merz [sic] 1829") & MS parts: D-NEhz, 33.
GYS-63a. Righini: Enea nel Lazio, terzetto.   2fl 2ob 2cl 2bthn 2hn 2bn 2tp db.   MS parts: D-AB, S.7b.
GYS-64a. Righini: Gerusalemme liberata, quartetto ("Fallisce in ogni impressa").
2fl 2ob 2cl 2hn 2bn (tp) tb db. AutoMS score ("Den 29ten Feb. 1816"): D-NEhz, 103, (the tp does not apper in the earlier score).   MS parts: D-NEhz, 32, No. 2.
GYS-65a. Rossini: Tancredi, 1 Bd.   fl 2ob 2cl 2hn 2bn tp 2tb db.
AutoMS score & MS pts: D-NEhz, 49/1, (the parts differ from the score: fl 2ob 2cl 2hn 2bn tp 2tp 2tb db timp).
GYS-66a. Rossini: Il Turco in Italia, 1 Bd.   2fl 2ob 2cl 2hn 2bn tp tb db.   AutoMS score & pts: D-NEhz, 37.
Bound between Acts I & II of the score of Schmitt's arrangement of Otello; *the arr. follows* Otello *in the parts.*
GYS-67a. Rossini: Il Barbiere di Siviglia, 1Bd.   2fl 2ob 2cl 2hn 2bn tp tb db.
AutoMS score ("Eigenthum G. Schmitt") & parts: D-NEhz, 42, (with duplicate tp pt).
GYS-68a. Rossini: Otello, 1 Bd.   2fl 2ob 2cl 2hn 2bn tp tb db.   AutoMS score & MS parts: D-NEhz, 37.
GYS-69a. Rossini: La Cenerentola, overture & Act I.   2fl 2ob 2cl 2hn 2bn tp tb db timp.
AutoMS score ("Oehringen d. 12tn Junij 1823") & parts: D-NEhz, 41, (parts missing fl II; with a duplicate tp pt; the timpani do not appear in the score).   *Attached to the parts are an incomplete set of parts for 2 mvts of Act II (fl 2ob cl hn(II) bn db timp); the arrangement in score is possibly missing Band 2.*

GYS-79a. Rossini: La Gazza ladra, 2 Acts. pic 2fl 2ob 2cl 2hn 2bn tp tb db.
AutoMS score ("d. 22t Junij 182[?]") & MS parts: D-NEhz, 39, (pts missing pic & fl II).
GYS-71a. Rossini: Armida, 1 Bd. 2fl 2ob 2cl 2hn 2bn tp tb db (timp).
AutoMS score ("Oehringen d. 30t Maij 1823") & parts ("Eigenthum Schmitt"): D-NEhz, 38, (with a duplicate trumpet part; the timpani do not appear in the score).
GYS-72a. Rossini: Mosè in Egitto, 5 mvts. Here only: fl 2ob cl 2hn tp tb db timp.
MS parts: D-NEhz, 93, (incomplete parts).
GYS-73a. Rossini: Ricciardo e Zoraide, 1 Bd. 2fl 2ob 2cl 2hn 2bn tp tb db.
AutoMS score & MS parts: D-NEhz, 36, (with a duplicate bn I part).
GYS-74a. Rossini: La Siège de Corinth, 2 Bd. fl 2ob 2cl 2hn 2bn tp tb 2tb db.
AutoMS score ("Oehringen d. 22tn Junij 1828") & MS parts: D-NEhz, 43, (the parts differ from the score: fl 2ob 2cl 2hn 2bn tp tb(obl) 2a-tb b-tb db timp.
GYS-75a. Rossini: Guillaume Tell, overture & 3 mvts. fl 2ob 2cl 2hn 2bn tp tb db.
AutoMS score & MS parts: D-NEhz, 40a, (parts with hn III & timp).
GYS-76a. Salieri: Palmira, overture. 2pic 2ob cl(E♭) 2cl(B♭) 4hn 2bn 2tp serp timp. MS pts: D-AB, N. I/10.
GYS-77a. Spohr: Jessonda, introduzione & 4 mvts. fl 2ob 2cl 2hn 2bn tp 2tb db.
AutoMS score & MS parts: D-NEhz, 95, (missing bn II part).
GYS-78a. Spohr: 1 unidentified mvt. fl 2ob 2cl 2hn 2bn tp tb db.
AutoMS score ("Friedrichruhe d. [ ]ten Septbr. 1828") & MS parts: D-NEhz, 100, No. 7, (missing some parts).
GYS-79.1a. Spontini: La Vestale, overture & 7 mvts. 2fl 2ob cl(E♭ obl) 2cl(B♭) 2bthn 4hn(C, E♭) 2bn cbn 2tp tb b-dr s-dr tri. MS parts: D-AB, T.12. *Mvts 6 & 7 are the extensive finales of Acts I & II, respectively.*
GYS-79.2a. Spontini: La Vestale, overture & 1 Bd. fl 2ob 2cl 2hn 2bn tp 2tb db timp.
AutoMS score & MS parts: D-NEhz, 44.
GYS-80a. Spontini: Fernand Cortez, overture & 1 Bd. 2fl 2ob 2cl 2hn 2bn tp tb db.
AutoMS score & MS parts: D-NEhz, 45a, (with an additional hn III part).
GYS-81a. Sterkel: Farnace, overture. 2fl 2ob 2cl 2hn 2bn tb db.
(?Auto)MS score (30 Jan 1818) & MS parts: D-NEhz, 86, No. 3.
GYS-82a. Süssmayr: Der Spiegel von Arkadien, duetto. 2fl 2ob 2cl 2hn 2bn serp. MS parts: D-AB, S.46.
GYS-83a. W. [unidentified]: Ouverture in C minor. 2fl 2ob 3cl 2hn 2bn tp tb db.
AutoMS score: D-NEhz, 31, Bd. 2, (follows on from the arrangement of Mozart's *Don Giovanni*).
GYS-84a. B.A. Weber: Jolanta, Königin von Jerusalem, 3 mvts. 2cl 2hn bn. MS parts: D-AB, K.8a.
GYS-85.1a. C.M. von Weber: Preciosa, 1 mvt. fl 2ob 2cl 2hn 2bn tp tb db.
AutoMS score ("Friedrichruhe d. [ ]ten Septbr. 1828") & MS parts: D-NEhz, 100, No. 2, (missing some parts).
GYS-85.2a. C.M. von Weber: Preciosa, 1 Bd. 2fl 2ob 2cl 2hn 2bn tp 2tb db.
AutoMS score & MS parts: D-NEhz, 49, (the parts differ from the score: fl 2ob 2cl 2hn 2bn 3tp 2tb db timp, with a duplicate hn II part; the timp part is to be found with Auber's *La Neige*, at D-NEhz, 5).
GYS-85.3a. C.M. von Weber: Preciosa, Zigeuner Marsch. fl 2ob 2cl 2hn 2bn 2tb b-tb db.
AutoMS score: D-NEhz, 49.
GYS-86.1a. C.M. von Weber: Der Freischütz, 1 Bd. 2fl 2ob 2cl 3hn 2bn tp tb db (timp).
AutoMS score & MS parts: D-NEhz, 51, (with duplicate tp part; the timpani do not appear in the score).
GYS-86.2a. C.M. von Weber: Der Freischütz, Jägerchor ("Was gleicht wohl auf Erden").
2fl 2ob 2cl 4hn 2bn tb db. AutoMS score & MS parts: D-NEhz, 51, (parts missing fl II, cl II).
GYS-86.3a. C.M. von Weber: Der Freischütz, 2 mvts. fl 2ob 2cl 2hn 2bn tp tb db.
AutoMS score ("Friedrichruhe d. [ ]ten Septbr. 1828") & MS parts: D-NEhz, 100, No. 5, (missing some parts).
GYS-87a. Weber: Euryanthe, Jägerchor (No. 18, "Die Thale dempfen" & "In grün belaubter Heide").
fl 2ob 2cl 5hn(B♭, 4E♭) bn tb db. AutoMS parts: D-NEhz, 153.
GYS-88.1a. Weber: Oberon, 3 Bds. fl 2ob 2cl 2hn 2bn 2tp tp 3tb db timp.
AutoMS score & MS parts: D-NEhz, 50, (the parts differ from the score: fl 2ob 2cl 3hn 2bn tp(2) tb db timp).
GYS-88.2a. Weber: Oberon, overture. fl 2ob 2cl 2hn 2bn tp 2tb db. AutoMS score & MS pts: D-NEhz, 95.
GYS-89a. J. Weigl: Das Dorf in Gebirge, overture. 2fl 2ob 2cl 2hn 2bn db. MS parts: D-NEhz, 193.
GYS-90a. J. Weigl: Vestas Feuer, overture. 2fl 2ob 2cl 2hn 2bn tp tb db.
AutoMS score ("Eigenthum G. Schmitt") & parts: D-NEhz, 82, (as "Ouverture Vestalin [sic] par Weigl").
GYS-91.1a. J. Weigl: Die Schweizerfamilie, overture. 2pic 2ob cl(E♭) 2cl(B♭) 4hn 2bn 2tp serp timp.
MS parts (c.1810 - 1816): D-AB, N. I/11.
GYS-91.2a. J. Weigl: Die Schweizerfamilie, overture & 6 mvts. 2fl 2ob 2cl 2hn 2bn tb db.
(?Auto)MS score (1818) & MS parts: D-NEhz, 86, Nos. 16 - 22.
GYS-92a. J. Weigl: Nachtigall und Raabe, 1 Bd. 2fl 2ob 2cl 2hn 2bn tp db.
AutoMS score ("12 Feb. 1820. nach einem Clavier Auszug.") & MS parts: D-NEhz, 46.
GYS-93a. Winter: Das unterbrochene Opferfest, duetto. 2fl 2ob 2cl 2hn 2bn tp tb db.
MS parts: D-NEhz, 32, No. 4.

*SCHMITT, Georg Aloys (Alois) *2 Feb 1827, Hanover - 15 Oct 1902, Dresden*
GAS-1tv. Trauer-Cantate [for the Duke of Mecklenburg's mother, Alexandrine, 1892]; in E♭ minor.
SATB chorus, 2ob 2cl 2hn 2bn 2tp 3tb organ timp. MS score (27 April 1892) & parts: D-SWl, Mus. 4893/1. ★

*SCHMITT, Nicolaus *(1760) ?Bassoonist in Paris, active 1778, d. c.1802*
NXS-1. Divertimento. 2hn 2bn.
Pc (Pleyel: Paris, pn 644, 1806), parts: D-Bds, (?lost).
NXS-1a. Choix de 12 Airs, 2e suite, Nos. 1 - 6. 4cl 2hn 2bn.
Pc (Chez J. [sic] Pleyel: Paris, pn 592, 1806), parts: CH-Zz, AMG XII.125 a-g.
    1.1a, 1.2a. Paisiello: Dal Finto il vero: "Se constante, se fidele" & "Reste in pace".
    1.3a. F. Orlandi: Podestà di Chioggia, "Degl' angelletti al canto.
    1.4a. Anon: L'Amour est un bien suprême. 1.5a. V. Trento: Polacca, "Sento che son vicino".
    1.6a. F. Orlandi: Podestà di Chioggia, "Cheta cheta qui masscondo.

*SCHMITTBAUER (Schmidbauer, Bauerschmitt, Bauerschmidt), Joseph Aloys
8 Nov 1718, Bamberg - 24 Sept 1809, Karlsruhe
JAS-1 (-8). 8 Divertimenti [in F] per usirsi alla Tavola. 2pic 2fl 2ob 2hn 2bn.
MS parts: D-KA, MS.891.
JAS-9. Divertimento; in C, 5 mvts. 2ob 2cl 2hn 2bn tp.
MS parts: D-SWl, Mus. 4902. ★
JAS-10. Partitta ex D; 4 mvts. 2ob 2hn bn.
MS parts: CZ-Bm(au), A.20.096. ★
JAS-11. Partitta in G; 4 mvts. 2ob 2hn bn.
MS parts: CZ-Bm(au), A.20.097. ★
JAS-12. Parthia in F. 2cl 2hn bn. MS parts (c.1770): D-RH, Mus.Ms.701, (cl I incomplete).

SCHNABEL, Arthur *1882 - 1951, Austria*
AKS-1. Duodecimet, (Op. posth). fl ob 2cl hn bn perc harp. *Instrumentation by René Leobowitz.*
Pm (Boosey & Hawkes: New York, 1963), miniature score (Arthur Schnabel memorial Edition).

*SCHNABEL, Joseph Ignaz (August) *24 May 1767, Naumberg am Queiss, Silesia - 16 June 1831, Breslau*
JIS-1.1v. Stationes in usum Theoforicae Processionis [&] Pange lingua [in] C.
SATB, 2fl 2ob 2cl 2hn 2bn 4tp a-tb t-tb b-tb timp. MS score & pts: CZ-KRsm, UHM A.1369/Br.C-490. ★
JIS-1.2v. [4] Stationen. SATB, 2fl 2ob 2cl 2hn 2bn 2tp timp. MS: D-Bds, Mus.Ms.20010.
JIS-2.1v. Missa Quadragesimalis in F. SATB solo & chorus, organ, (2bthn 2hn 2bn a-tb t-tb b-tb ad lib).
Pc (Leuckart: Breslau, sd), parts: A-Wgm, I 5315 (Q 381).
JIS-2.2v. Missa in F; (omits the Gloria). CATB solo & chorus, 2cl 2hn 2bn tp a-tb t-tb b-tb vc+vlne organ.
MS parts: CZ-KRsm, UHM a.1360/Br.C-480, (with duplicate vocal & vc+vlne parts; possibly missing 2cl).
JIS-2.3v. Missa Quadregesimalis in F. CATB solo & chorus, 2cl 2hn 2bn a-tb t-tb b-tb vlne organ.
MS parts: CZ-Bm(au), A.20.102, (with extra parts: organ, 2S, 2A, 3B, 2vlne; a note records performances in 1831, 1847 & 1851); D-BAUd, Mu 327, (copy by Carl Wolf, 19 Aug 1854). ★

*SCHNAUBELT, Heinrich *(1810)*
HQS-1. Marsch für die Frohnleichsnams-Prozession, 1866. terz-fl 2fl 3cl 2hn 2bn 2tp a-tb t-tb b-tb timp.
AutoMS score: A-Sca, Hs.485, (with a piano reduction). *A MS piano reduction is also at Hs.486.* ★
HQS-2. Marsch für die Frohnleichnams-Prezession, 1868. terz-fl fl 3cl 2hn 2bn 2tp 3tb oph timp.
AutoMS score & parts: A-Sca, Hs.487, (with a piano reduction). ★
HQS-1v. 6tes Tantum ergo (: für die heilige Weihnachtszeit :). CATB, 4hn bn vl vc vlne organ.
AutoMS score (16 Dec 1838): A-Sca, Hs.481. ★

SCHNEIDER, ( ), *first of the name* *(1740)*
XXS-1. Partitta (in C) à 5 Stromenti, 4 mvts. 2ca 2hn bn.
MS parts (c.1770): D-HR, HR III 4 1/2 4° 723. ★
Pm (KGS), fiche (1384).

SCHNEIDER ( ), *second of the name*
XYS-1(-21). 21 Partiten, Op. 6. 2ob 2cl 2hn 2bn. MS parts: PL-Wu, Ka.16.

SCHNEIDER, (?L.)
XLS-1a. Leontiff: Polonaise. fl 2ob 2hn 2bn serp. MS parts: D-AB, S.40.

*SCHNEIDER, Anton *1773 - post-1827*
AYS-1. Divertissement; in F, 9 mvts, 1822. fl/bthn(mvts 3, 4, 6 - 9) 2ob 2cl hn bn.
MS parts (1822): D-Rtt, Schneider 1. *Mvt 2 bears the note, "v[on]. Him[m]el".* ★
AYS-2. Variationen für Waldhorner; in F minor/B♭ major. Solo horn, fl(D) 2ob 2cl(C) 2cl(B♭) 2hn 2bn b-tb cb.
MS parts (1823): D-Rtt, Sm. 23, No. 14, (hn III replaces tp). ★
AYS-3. Variationen für die Flöte; in G. Solo fl, 2ob 2cl(C) 2cl(A) 3hn 2bn b-tb cb.
MS parts (1823): D-Rtt, Sm. 23, No. 15. ★
AYS-4. Cantabile [in C] mit Polonoise [in G]. fl 2ob 2cl(C) 2cl(B♭) 3hn 2bn b-tb cb.
MS parts (1823): D-Rtt, Sm. 30, No. 24, (hn III replaces tp). ★
AYS-5. [6] Walzer, (E♭, C, C, E♭, Eb, Eb). fl(E♭, D, D, F, F, E♭) 2ob 2cl(B♭, C, C, B♭, E♭, E♭, E♭) 2cl(B♭)
2hn 2bn tp(posthorn in No. 21) b-tb cb. MS parts (1823): D-Rtt, Sm. 23, Nos. 17 - 22. ★
AYS-6. [6] Walzer [& Trios & Coda], (C minor, B, A, C, E, D minor). fl(E♭, D) 2ob 2cl+2cl(rip) 2hn 2bn
tp(posthorn No. 101) b-tb serp. MS parts (1823): D-Rtt, Sm. 16, Nos. 96 - 101. ★
AYS-7. [6] Walzer [with Trios & Coda]. fl 2ob 4cl 2hn 2bn tp b-tb serp.
MS parts (1823): D-Rtt, Sm. 17, Nos. 201 - 206. ★
AYS-8. Adagio; in C minor. fl 2ob 2cl+2cl(rip) 2hn 2bn tp tb serp.
MS parts (1823): D-Rtt, Sm. 16, No. 102. ★
AYS-9. Walzer; in D. fl 2ob 4cl 2hn 2bn tp b-tb serp.
MS parts (c.1823): D-Rtt, Sm. 16, No. 148. ★
AYS-10. Ouverture; in D minor/major. fl 2ob 2cl(A) 2hn 2bn tp b-tb 2vla cb.
MS parts (1826): D-Rtt, Sm. 12, No. 15. ★
AYS-11. Ouverture; in C minor/major. fl 2ob 2cl 2hn 2bn tp b-tb 2vla cb.
MS parts (1826): D-Rtt, Sm. 12, Nos. 16. *AYS-11 may be linked to AYS-12.* ★
AYS-12. [Adagio, ¢ / poco adagio, 3/4]; in F. fl 2ob 2cl 2hn 2bn tp b-tb 2vla cb.
MS parts (1826): D-Rtt, Sm. 12, No. 17. ★
AYS-13. Ouverture; in D. fl 2ob 2cl(A) 2hn 2bn tp b-tb 2vla cb.
MS parts (1826): D-Rtt, Sm. 12, No. 18. ★
AYS-14. Ouverture; in F. fl 2ob 2cl 2hn 2bn tp b-tb 2vla cb.
MS parts (1827): D-Rtt, Sm 28, No. 1. ★

Here we list, in D-Rtt catalog order, anonymous works which we believe are by Schneider. We continue our numbering from the above and do not treat them as doubtful or spurious works.

Sammelband 12, (1826):   fl 2ob 2cl 2hn 2bn tp b-tb 2vla cb.
AYS-15(-58). 44 Walzer. MS parts: D-Rtt, Sm. 12, Nos. 1 - 42, 45 (Dutelsack [sic] Walzer), 46. *The cl I part of AYS-14 is marked, "Segue Walzer". No. 44 is an arrangement of Amadée de Beauplan's Romance, "Belle et Sensible" and is listed in the arrangements section infra; No. 43, an anonymous Romance (in C) may also be an arrangement of a work by Beauplan. Some of the Walzer may also be arrangements.*
Sammelband 16, (1822):   fl 2ob 2cl+2cl(rip) 2hn 2bn tp b-tb serp.
Note: Nos. 77 - 79 are marked "Tacet" in all parts; the fl pt bears the note "Tacet. Stehen in die andern / Bücher, von Stumpf abgeschrieben".
AYS-59, 60. Walzer; in D.   MS parts: D-Rtt, Sm. 16, No. 17.
AYS-61. Cottillon; in D.   MS parts: D-Rtt, Sm. 16, No. 18.
AYS-62. [6] Eccossaisen [sic], (G, C, F, D minor, D, G).   MS parts: D-Rtt, Sm. 16, Nos. 19 - 24.
AYS-63. [8] Walzer [& Coda]; (1 in F, 2 - 8 & Coda in B♭).
MS parts: D-Rtt, Sm. 16, Nos. 25 - 32, (Solo posthorn replaces trumpet in the Coda).
AYS-64. Andantino; in A♭.   (tp tacet).   MS parts: D-Rtt, Sm. 16, No. 34.
AYS-65. Larghetto; in F.   MS parts: D-Rtt, Sm. 16, No. 82.
AYS-66. Adagio; in E♭.   (hn III replaces tp).   MS pts: D-Rtt, Sm. 16, No. 102.
AYS-67. 3 Polonaisen, (B♭, F, D).   fl(D) 2ob 4cl 2hn 2bn tp(posthorn in No. 117) b-tb serp.
MS parts: D-Rtt, Sm. 16, Nos. 117 - 119, (posthorn may also replace tp in No. 118).
AYS-68. Aus Marienbad, Walzer; in D.   MS parts: D-Rtt, Sm. 16, No. 147. *Possibly an arrangement.*
AYS-69. Allegro maestoso, C / And. Sost:, 3/4 / Allegro Mod: ¢; in B♭.
MS parts: D-Rtt, Sm. 16, No. 150.
Sammelband 17, (1823, "Harmonie Music/ v[on]. Schneider 1813" appears in the top right corner of the first page of music in most parts; this has been crossed out; the cl I key in the headtitle has also been altered from "Dis" to "C". It is possible that this Sammelband was brought in by Schneider from his previous employment.)
fl 2ob 4cl 2hn tp b-tb serp.
AYS-70. Potpourie e la Quottlibet [sic]; 13 sections.   MS parts: D-Rtt, Sm. 17, No. 155.
AYS-71. Andante Expressione; in .   MS parts: D-Rtt, Sm. 17, No. 157.
AYS-72. Larghetto & Adagio tenuto.   MS parts: D-Rtt, Sm. 17, No. 158.
AYS-73. Adagio.   MS parts: D-Rtt, Sm. 17, No. 159.
AYS-74. Adagio.   MS parts: D-Rtt, Sm. 17, No. 161.
AYS-75. Adagio / Rondo, 2/4 / Adagio, 3/4.   MS parts: D-Rtt, Sm. 17, No. 162.
AYS-76. Walzer [& Trio]; in F.   MS parts: D-Rtt, Sm. 17, No. 165.
AYS-77. Walzer [& Trio]; in B♭.   MS parts: D-Rtt, Sm. 17, No. 171.
AYS-78. Menuetto [& Trio]; in D.   MS parts: D-Rtt, Sm. 17, No. 172.
AYS-79. Polonoise [& Trio]; in B♭.   MS parts: D-Rtt, Sm. 17, No. 173.
AYS-80. Adagio [with cadenza], 3/4 / Allegro, ¢.   MS parts: D-Rtt, Sm. 17, No. 175.
AYS-81. Menuetto [& Trio].   MS pts: D-Rtt, Sm. 17, No. 176.
AYS-82. Andante, C / Allegretto, 2/4.   MS parts: D-Rtt, Sm. 17, No. 177.
AYS-83. Polonoise [& Trio].   MS parts: D-Rtt, Sm. 17, No. 178.
AYS-84. Adagio [with 9 variations].   MS parts: D-Rtt, Sm. 17, No. 179.
AYS-85. Polonoise.   terz-fl 2ob 4cl 2hn 2bn tp b-tb serp.   MS parts: D-Rtt, Sm. 17, No. 180.
AYS-86. [4] Walzer [& Trios].   terz-fl 2ob 2cl 2hn 2bn tp b-tb serp.
MS parts: D-Rtt, Sm. 17, No. 181 - 184.
AYS-87. Angloise [& Trio].   MS parts: D-Rtt, Sm. 17, No. 185.
AYS-88. Allegretto [?Contradanz & Coda].   MS parts: D-Rtt, Sm. 17, No. 186.
AYS-89. Polonoise [& Trio].   MS parts: D-Rtt, Sm. 17, No. 187.
AYS-90. [?Overture] Largo, ¢ / Allegro, ¢.   MS parts: D-Rtt, Sm. 17, No. 188.
AYS-91. Walzer.   MS parts: D-Rtt, Sm. 17, No. 192.
AYS-92, 93. [2] Schottischer Tanz..   MS parts: D-Rtt, Sm. 17, No. 194, 195.
AYS-94. Menuetto [& Trio].   MS parts: D-Rtt, Sm. 17, No. 197.
AYS-95. [5] Walzer, (G, D, D, G, A).   MS parts: D-Rtt, Sm. 17, Nos. 202 - 206.
AYS-96. Romance [with cadenza], ¢.   MS parts: D-Rtt, Sm. 17, No. 197.
AYS-97. [6] Ländler; in A.   MS parts: D-Rtt, Sm. 17, Nos. 211 - 216.
*AYS-98. Schlacht Simphonie, Unterhandlung [sic]; in G, 3 mvts.   fl 2ob 4cl 2hn 2bn tp b-tb serp timp.
MS pts (1823): D-Rtt, Sm. 17, Nos. 217 - 219, (the timp pt is a loose sheet in the back of the serp volume).   ★
AYS-99. Allegretto, 2/4; in G.   MS parts: D-Rtt, Sm. 17, No. 220.
AYS-100. [4] Walzer [& Trios]; in D.   MS parts: D-Rtt, Sm. 17, Nos. 221 - 224.
AYS-101. Polonaise [& Trio], in G.   MS parts: D-Rtt, Sm. 17, No. 226.
AYS-102. Schottischer Tanz, in B♭.   MS parts: D-Rtt, Sm. 17, No. 230.
AYS-103. Walzer; in D.   MS parts: D-Rtt, Sm. 17, No. 231.
AYS-104. Menuetto [& Trio]; in F.   MS parts: D-Rtt, Sm. 17, No. 232.
AYS-105. Rondo Allegretto, 2/4 / Adagio, C / Allegretto Moderato, 6/8 / più Allegro, 6/8.
MS pts: D-Rtt, Sm. 17, No. 233.
AYS-106. Hops Walzer [& Trio]; in B minor.   MS parts: D-Rtt, Sm. 17, No. 235.
AYS-107. Walzer; in D.   MS parts: D-Rtt, Sm. 17, No. 236.
Sammelband 18, (1823).
AYS-108. [Walzer, in E♭].   2hn 2bn 2vla.   MS parts: D-Rtt, Sm. 18, No. 40.
AYS-109. Walzer; in E♭.   fl(Trio only) 2hn 2bn 2vla.   MS parts: D-Rtt, Sm. 18, No. 41.
Sammelband 22 (1823): fl(C, D, E♭) 2ob 4cl 2hn 2bn tp(posthorn in Nos. 26 & 27) b-tb cb.
AYS-110. 8 Walzer [with Trios & a Coda].   MS parts: D-Rtt, Sm. 22, Nos. 23 - 31.
AYS-111. 11 Walzer [with Trios].   MS parts: D-Rtt, Sm. 22, Nos. 32 - 42.

Sammelband 25, (1824): fl 2ob 2cl 2hn 2bn tp tb 2vla cb.
AYS-112. Menuetto [& Trio]; in D.   MS parts: D-Rtt, Sm. 25, No. 19.
AYS-113. Walzer [& Trio]; in C minor.   fl 2ob 2cl 2hn 2bn tp b-tb 2vla cb.   MS pts: D-Rtt, Sm. 25, No. 26.
AYS-114(-121). Overture & 7 mvts - possibly a ballet arrangement.   MS pts: D-Rtt, Sm. 25, Nos. 27 - 34.
Sammelband 28, (1827): fl 2ob 2cl 2hn 2bn tp b-tb 2vla cb.
AYS-122. Andantino & Polonoise [with Trio], in D.   MS parts: D-Rtt, Sm. 28, No. 2.
AYS-123. Adagio / Andante, (= Theme & 6 Variations); in F.   MS pts: D-Rtt, Sm. 28, No. 3.   ★
AYS-124. Andante Maestoso / Thema con [6] Variationi; in F.   MS pts: D-Rtt, Sm. 28, No. 11.   ★
AYS-125. Adagio [D minor] / Allegretto [= Theme & 10 Variations, D major] / Adagio / Allegro.
MS parts: D-Rtt, Sm. 27, No. 12. ★
Sammelband 29, (1827): fl(C, terz-) 2ob 2cl 2hn 2bn tp b-tb 2vla cb.
AYS-126. [6] Walzer, (E♭, D, B♭, A, C, E♭).   MS parts: D-Rtt, Sm. 29, Nos. 22 - 27.
AYS-127, 128. 2 Polonaisen, (C, B♭).   MS parts: D-Rtt, Sm. 29, Nos. 38, 39.
AYS-129. [4] Mazurken, (Bb, E♭, E♭, D).   MS parts: D-Rtt, Sm. 29, Nos. 40 - 43.
Sammelband 30, (1823): fl 2ob 4cl 3hn 2bn tp(with hn III) b-tb cb.
AYS-130(a). Böhmischer Posthorn Walzer [in F].   fl(F) 2ob 4cl 2hn 2bn posthorn b-tb cb.
MS parts: D-Rtt, Sm. 30, No. 25.
AYS-131(a). Kalopp [sic: Galopp] Walzer [in F].   fl(F) 2ob 4cl 2hn 2bn posthorn b-tb cb.
MS parts: D-Rtt, Sm. 30, No. 26.
Sammelband 32, (c.1820): fl 2ob 2cl 2hn 2bn 2vla cb.
AYS-132. Andantino; in F.   MS parts: D-Rtt, Sm. 32, No. 4.

AYS-1m. Marsch; in C.   fl 2ob 2cl+2cl(rip) 2hn 2bn tp b-tb serp.   MS pts (1823): D-Rtt, Sm. 16, No. 103.   ★
AYS-2m(-11m). 10 Märsche & Geschwindmärsche.   fl 2ob 2cl+2cl(rip) 2hn 2bn tp(poshorn No. 113) b-tb serp.
MS pts (1822): D-Rtt, Sm. 16, Nos. 105 - 114.   ★
AYS-12m. Marche Vivace [& Trio].   fl 2ob 4cl 2hn 2bn tp b-tb serp.   MS pts: D-Rtt, Sm. 17, No. 160.   ★
AYS-13m. Marsch; in E♭.   fl 2ob 4cl 2hn 2bn tp b-tb serp.   MS parts (1823): D-Rtt, Sm. 17, No. 166.   ★
AYS-14m. Marsch [& Trio].   fl 2ob 4cl 2hn 2bn tp b-tb serp.   MS parts (1823): D-Rtt, Sm. 17, No. 189.   ★
AYS-15m. Geschwind Marsch [& Trio].   fl 2ob 4cl 2hn 2bn tp b-tb serp.
MS parts (1823): D-Rtt, Sm. 17, No. 190.   ★
AYS-16m. Marsch.   fl 2ob 4cl 2hn 2bn tp b-tb serp.   MS parts (1823): D-Rtt, Sm. 17, No. 191.   ★
AYS-17m. Marsch.   fl 2ob 4cl 2hn 2bn tp b-tb serp.   MS parts (1823): D-Rtt, Sm. 17, No. 193.   ★
AYS-18. Marsch Maestoso.   fl 2ob 4cl 2hn 2bn tp b-tb serp.   MS parts (1823): D-Rtt, Sm. 17, No. 196.   ★
AYS-19m(-21m). 3 Märsche; (D, D, D).   fl 2ob 4cl 2hn 2bn tp b-tb serp.
MS parts (1823): D-Rtt, Sm. 17, Nos. 208 - 210.   ★
AYS-22m. Marsch; in A.   fl 2ob 4cl 2hn 2bn tp b-tb serp.   MS parts (1823): D-Rtt, Sm. 17, No. 227.   ★
AYS-23m. Marsch; in G.   fl 2ob 4cl 2hn 2bn tp b-tb serp.   MS parts (1823): D-Rtt, Sm. 17, No. 237.   ★

*AYS-1v. Lied zur ankunft Ihro Durlaucht [sic] F[ürst]: v[on]. E[sterházy]: "Freudig rufen wir willkommen".
B solo (MS loose in bn I pt), fl 2ob 2cl+2cl(rip) 2hn 2bn tp b-tb serp.   MS parts: D-Rtt, Sm. 16, No. 104.   ★
*AYS-2v. Cantate von Cotischau, Wunsch und gebett für Seiner Höchfürstliche Durchlaucht: zum Geburts Fest
v[on]. Gottischau [sic];   2 Arias, Duetto & Chor.   fl(D) 2ob 2cl(C & B♭) 2hn 2bn tp b-tb 2vla cb.
MS pts: D-Rtt, Sm. 23, Nos. 23 - 26, (missing the text).   *?Instrumental arrangement?*   ★

Details now follow of arrangements by - and attributed to - Schneider. Because of the unique composition of
the Thurn und Taxis Regimentaal Harmonie we include all the arrangements in volumes associated with
Schneider in this list (unless identified otherwise). It should be noted, however, that in some cases these works
may be rescorings for the Regensburg forces of earlier arrangements
AYS-1a. Lebe wohl mein Lieb!   fl 2ob 2cl+2cl(rip) 2hn 2bn serp.   MS parts (1822): D-Rtt, Sm. 16, No. 35.
AYS-2a. Anon: Cavatina, Die schöne Schifferin.   fl 2ob 2cl+2cl(rip) 2hn 2bn b-tb serp.
MS parts (1822): D-Rtt, Sm. 16, No. 36.
AYS-3a. Anon [posssibly by Schneider]: Ouverture, in C minor/major.   fl 2ob 2cl 2hn 2bn 2vla cb.
MS parts (1822): D-Rtt, Sm. 16, No. 37.
AYS-4a. Anon: Him[m]en. an die Nacht.   fl 2ob 2cl+2cl(rip) 2hn 2bn tp b-tb serp.
MS parts (1822): D-Rtt, Sm. 16, No. 38, (possibly associated with AYS-6a).
AYS-5a. Anon [possibly by Schneider]: Ouverture, in Es [E♭].   fl 2ob 2cl+2cl(rip) 2hn 2bn tp b-tb serp.
MS parts (1822): D-Rtt, Sm. 16, No. 116.
AYS-6a. Anon: Romanze; in G.   fl 2ob 2cl+2cl(rip) 2hn 2bn b-tb serp.   MS pts (1822): D-Rtt, Sm. 16, No. 145.
AYS-7a. Anon: Romanze, "Partela [sic: Parte la] nave"; in F.   fl 2ob 2cl+2cl(rip) 3hn 2bn b-tb serp.
MS parts (1822): D-Rtt, Sm. 16, No. 146.
AYS-8.1a. Anon (?von Schacht): Der Corsar aus Liebe, overture & 21 mvts.   fl 2ob 2cl 2hn 2bn 2vla (2)cb.
MS pts: D-Rtt, Inv.VIIb/15. *This work is not J. Wiegl's opera, L'amor marinaro; nor does it appear in AYS-8.1a.*
AYS-8.2a. Anon (?von Schacht): Der Corsar aus Liebe, Allegretto, ¢, in D.   fl 2ob 4cl 2hn 2bn tp b-tb serp.
MS parts (1823): D-Rtt, Sm. 17, No. 199. *This mvt is not found in J. Wiegl's opera, L'amor marinaro.*
*AYS-9a. Anon: Der Kosak und sein Mädchen, (song, as "Liebe Minka, ich mus [sic] scheiden").
fl 2ob 4cl 2hn 2bn tp b-tb serp.   MS parts (1823): D-Rtt, Sm. 17, No. 174.
*AYS-10. Anon: Russisches Volkslied; in B minor.   fl 2ob 4cl 2hn 2bn tp b-tb serp.
MS parts (1823): D-Rtt, Sm. 17, Nos. 221.
AYS-11a. Anon: v[on]: Spring ins Feld, (5 Walzer with Coda).   fl 2ob 2cl 2hn 2bn tp b-tb 2vla cb.
MS pts (1827): D-Rtt, Sm. 27, Nos. 13 - 18. *We believe "Spring ins Feld" to be a title rather than a pseudonym.*
AYS-12a. Anon: v[on]: Schnips Schnaps: [6] Walzer [& Trios].   fl 2ob 2cl 2hn 2bn tp b-tb 2vla cb.
MS pts (1827): D-Rtt, Sm. 28, Nos. 25 - 30. *We believe "Schnips Schnaps" to be a title rather than a pseudonym.*
AYS-13a. Anon (?Rossini): Adagio & Chor, in G.   fl 2ob 2cl 2hn 2bn tp b-tb 2vla cb.
MS parts: D-Rtt, Sm. 29, No. 21.   ★

AYS-14a. T.A. Arne: Alfred, "Rule Britannia" (as "When Britain"; in A♭). fl 2ob 2cl 2hn 2bn tp b-tb 2vla cb.
MS parts: D-Rtt, Sm. 25, No. 36.
AYS-15a. Auber: La Neige (as "Der Schnee"), overture & 15 mvts. fl 2ob 2cl 2hn 2bn tp b-tb 2vla cb.
MS parts (1826): D-Rtt, Sm. 27, (2nd arrangement in Sm. 27).
AYS-16a. Augustin: 12 Walzer [& Trios]. fl 2ob 2cl 2hn 2bn tp b-tb 2vla cb. MS pts (1825): D-Rtt, Sm. 31.
AYS-17a. Beauplan: Romance, Belle et Sensible. fl 2ob 2cl 2hn 2bn tp b-tb 2vla cb.
MS parts (1826): D-Rtt, Sm. 12, No. 44 of 46 Walzer following No. 18 in the Sammelband.
AYS-18a. Beethoven: Egmont, overture. fl 2ob 2cl 2hn 2bn tp b-tb 2vla cb.
MS parts (1826): D-Rtt, Sm. 12, No. 14.
AYS-19a. Beethoven: Trois grandes marches, Op. 45, No. 1. fl 2ob 4cl 2hn 2bn tp b-tb serp.
MS parts (1823): D-Rtt, Sm. 17, No. 207.
AYS-20a. J. Blumenthal: Marsch aus König Lear. fl(D) 2ob 4cl(C) 2hn 2bn tp b-tb cb.
MS parts (1823): D-Rtt, Sm. 23, No. 13. *A rescoring of Blumenthal, JVB-1a.*
AYS-21a. Boieldieu: Jean de Paris, overture & 13 mvts. fl 2ob 2cl 2hn 2bn tp b-tb 2vla cb.
MS parts (1825): D-Rtt, Sm. 26, Nos. [0], 1 - 13.
AYS-22a. Boieldieu: Le petite Chaperon rouge, overture. fl 2ob 2cl 2hn 2bn tp b-tb 2vla cb.
MS parts (1824): D-Rtt, Sm. 25, No. 20. *Not Dittersdorf as cataloged.*
AYS-23a. Carl Cannabich: Grand Simphonie in C, Op. 8, (mvt 1). fl(E♭) 2ob 2cl+2cl(rip) 2hn 2bn tp b-tb serp.
MS parts (1822): D-Rtt, Sm. 16, No. 120.
AYS-24a. Catel: Semiramis, overture & 1 mvt. fl 2ob 2cl 2hn 2bn tp b-tb 2vla b.
MS parts (1824): D-Rtt, Sm. 25, No. 2.
AYS-25a. Cherubini: [unidentified] Polonoise; in D. fl 2ob 4cl 2hn 2bn tp b-tb serp.
MS parts (1823): D-Rtt, Sm. 17, No. 234.
AYS-26a. Dittersdorf: Das Rotkäppchen, "Hab ich in den jungen Jahren" (sometimes found with the text, "Lustig leben di Soldaten". fl 2ob 2cl 2hn 2bn tp b-tb 2vla vlne. MS parts (1824): D-Rtt, Sm. 25, No. 20.
AYS-27a. Endrers: 9 Walzer & 1 Allegretto. fl 2ob 4cl 2hn 2bn tp(hn III, Nos. 11, 13, 15 - 17) b-tb cb.
MS parts (1823): D-Rtt, Sm. 21, Nos. 10 - 19.
AYS-28a. Erhard: Der Geistlichen Rath, 6 Walzer. fl(D,terz-fl) 2ob 4cl 2hn 2bn tp b-tb serp.
MS parts (1822, "aus Böhmen erhalten"): D-Rtt, Sm. 18, Nos. 3 - 8. *MS orchestral parts for these Walzer can be found at D-Rtt, Erhard 1, Nos. 1 - 6.*
AYS-29a. Esterházy von Galantha, *Prinzessin* Rosa: Walzer; [& Trio] in G. fl 2ob cl 2hn 2bn tp b-tb 2vla cb.
MS parts (1826): D-Rtt, Sm. 27, (last item).
AYS-30a. Gallenberg: Alfred der Grosse, Grosse Marsch in B♭. fl 2ob 4cl 2hn 2bn tp b-tb cb.
MS parts (1823): D-Rtt, Sm. 23, No. 16.
AYS-31a. Garnie (?Garnier): Polonaise [& Trio]; in D minor. fl 2ob 4cl 2hn 2bn tp b-tb serp.
MS parts (1822): D-Rtt, Sm. 16, No. 156.
AYS-32a. Grétry: Les deux Avares, Marsch. fl 2ob 4cl 2hn 2bn tp b-tb serp. MS pts (1823): D-Rtt, Sm. 18, No2.
AYS-33a. Grétry: Zémire et Azor, overture & 23 mvts. fl 2ob 2cl+cl(rip) 2hn 2bn tp b-tb serp.
MS parts (1822): Sm. 16, Nos. 121 - 144, (incorrectly attributed to Dalayrac; based on Italian pf red. in D-Rtt).
AYS-34a. Grétry: Raoul Barbe-Bleu, overture & 11 mvts. fl(E♭) 2ob 2cl 2hn 2bn tp(hn III) b-tb vlne.
MS parts (1823): D-Rtt, Sm. 23, Nos. 1 - 11. *Mvts 1, 3, 5, 7, & 9 - 11 in the cl I pt are marked in pencil, "Kyrie", "Gloria", "Vene [sic] Sancte Spiritus", "Te Deum", "Ofertorium [sic]", "Agnus Dei" & "Gratuale [sic] Dona nobis", respectively.*
AYS-35a. Gunngerl: [6] Walzer [& Trios]. fl 2ob 2cl 2hn 2bn tp b-tb 2vla cb.
MS parts (1827): D-Rtt, Sm. 27, Nos. 48 - 53.
AYS-36a. Hanisch: Polonoise [& Trio]; in B♭. fl 2ob 4cl 2hn 2bn tp b-tb serp.
MS parts (1823): D-Rtt, Sm. 17, No. 163.
AYS-37a. Hanisch: Polacca [& Trio]; in B♭. fl 2ob 4cl 2hn 2bn tp b-tb serp.
MS parts (1823): D-Rtt, Sm. 17, No. 164.
AYS-38a. Haydn: Die Schöpfung [The Creation]. fl 2ob 2cl 2hn 2bn tp b-tb 2vla cb.
MS parts (1825): D-Rtt, J.Haydn 116/III.
AYS-39a. Haydn: Die Jahreszeiten, overture & 15 mvts. fl(pic) 2ob 2cl 2hn 2bn tp(No. 11: hn III) b-tb 2vla cb.
MS parts (c.1825): D-Rtt, J.Haydn 118/II, (mvts from all 4 sections of the oratorio).
*AYS-40a. Haydn: Symphony in C, ("La Roxelane" Hob. I/63, as "Lieblings Symphonie, No. 23").
fl 2ob 2cl(C & B♭) 2hn 2bn tp b-tb 2vla cb. MS parts (1826): D-Rtt, Sm. 12, Nos. 1 - 4.
AYS-41a. Haydn: Symphony in F (here in D), (Hob. I/67). fl 2ob 2cl(C & B♭) 2hn 2bn tp b-tb 2vla cb.
MS parts (1826): D-Rtt, Sm. 12, Nos. 5 - 8.
AYS-42a. Haydn: Symphony in D, (Hob. I/93). fl 2ob 4cl 2hn 2bn tp b-tb cb.
MS parts (1823): D-Rtt, Sm. 18, Nos. 79 - 82.
AYS-43a. Haydn: Symphony in G, ("Surprise", Hob. I/94). fl 2ob 4cl 2hn 2bn tb b-tb serp.
MS parts (1823): D-Rtt, Sm. 17, Nos. 151 - 154.
AYS-44a. Haydn: Symphony in E♭, (Hob. I/99). fl 2ob 4cl 2hn 2bn tp b-tb cb.
MS parts (1823): D-Rtt, Sm. 18, Nos. 71 - 74.
AYS-45a. Haydn: Symphony in D major/minor, ("The Clock", Hob. I/101). fl 2ob 4cl 2hn 2bn tp b-tb cb.
MS parts: D-Rtt, Sm. 18, Nos. 75 - 78.
AYS-46a. Haydn: Symphony in E♭, ("Drumroll", Hob. I/103). fl 2ob 4cl 2hn 2bn tp b-tb cb.
MS parts (1823): D-Rtt, Sm. 18, Nos. 83 - 86.
AYS-47a. Haydn: Symphony in D major/minor, ("London" Hob. I/104). fl 2ob 4cl 2hn 2bn tp b-tb cb.
MS parts (1823): D-Rtt, Sm. 18, Nos. 87 - 90.
AYS-48. Himmel: unidentifed 2nd mvt in Schneider's Divertissement, in F (AYS-1). fl 2ob cl hn bn.
AutoMS parts (1822): D-Rtt, Schneider 1.
AYS-49a. Hitzigmann: [6] Walzer [& Trios]. fl 2ob 2cl 2hn 2bn tp b-tb 2vla cb.
MS parts (1827): D-Rtt, Sm. 28, Nos. 60 - 65.

AYS-50a. Horzalka: [6] Bassionierte [sic] Walzer [& 5 Allemandes].
fl(D, terz-fl, pic) 2ob 2cl 2hn 2bn tp(hn III) b-tb 2vla cb.   MS pts (1825): D-Rtt, Sm. 26, (last work in Sm. 26).
AYS-51a. Hummel: Die Rückfahrt des Kaisers, Op. 69, overture.   fl 2ob 2cl 2hn 2bn tp b-tb 2vla cb.
MS parts (1827): D-Rtt, Sm. 29, No. 19.
AYS-52a. Isouard: Michel-Ange, overture & 7 mvts.   fl 2ob 2cl 2hn 2bn cb.
MS parts (1823): D-Rtt, Sm. 18, Nos. 11 - 18.
AYS-53a. Isouard: Cendrillon, overture & 16 mvts.   fl(pic No. 24) 2ob 2cl 2hn 2bn b-tb 2vla vlne.
MS parts (1823): D-Rtt, Sm. 18, Nos. 20 - 36, (b-tb tacet in Nos. 21, 23, 25, 28 - 31, 33 - 35, Andante of 36).
AYS-54a. Kauer: Der Donauweibchen, 2 Romanzen; Theil 2, "Ich thron auf Silberwellen"; Theil 1, "In meinen
Schloss ists gar fein".   fl 2ob 4cl 2hn 2bn tp b-tb serp.   MS parts (1823): D-Rtt, Sm. 17, Nos. 168, 169.
AYS-55a. (?C.) Kreutzer: [cl I: Rondo] A la chasse col Echo; E♭.   fl 2ob 2cl+cl(rip) 2hn 2bn b-tb.
MS parts (1822): D-Rtt, Sm. 16, No. 33.
AYS-56a. C. Kreutzer: Fünf Frühlings Lieder von Uhland, 33tes Werk.   fl 2ob 2cl+2cl(rip) 3hn 2bn b-tb serp.
MS parts (1822): D-Rtt, Sm. 16, Nos. 91 - 95, (hn III replaces tp).
AYS-57a. C. Kreutzer: Neun Wander Lieder von Uhland, 34tes Werk.   fl 2ob 2cl+2cl(rip) 3hn 2bn b-tb serp.
MS pts (1822): D-Rtt, Sm. 16, Nos. 35, 83 - 90, (tp & b-tb tacet in No. 35; hn III replaces tp in the other Nos.).
AYS-58a. [?W.] Krumpholz (as "Krämplpelz): [6] Walzer [& Trios].   fl 2ob 2cl 2hn 2bn tp b-tb 2vla cb.
MS parts (1827): D-Rtt, Sm. 28, Nos. 19 - 24.
AYS-59a. Kuhlau: Trylleharpen (Die Zauberharfe), overture.   fl 2ob 4cl(C) 2hn 2bn tp b-tb cb.
MS parts (1823): D-Rtt, Sm. 21, No. 4.
AYS-60a. Kuhlau: Elisa (Elise), overture.   fl 2ob 2cl(A)+2cl(rip, C) 2hn 2bn tp b-tb serp.
MS parts (1822): D-Rtt, Sm. 16, No. 15.
AYS-61a. Lafont: Polonoise Heroique, in C minor.   fl 2ob 4cl 2hn 2bn tp b-tb cb.
MS parts (1823): D-Rtt, Sm. 30, No. 23.
AYS-62a. Lindpaintner: Sinfonie Concertante in B♭, for fl ob cl hn bn & orchestra.
fl 2ob 2cl 3hn 2bn b-tb 2vla cb.   MS parts (1827): D-Rtt, Sm. 29, No. 46, (hn III replaces tp).
AYS-63a. Méhul: Les deux Aveugles de Tolède, overture.   fl 2ob 2cl 2hn 2bn tp b-tb 2vla cb.
MS parts (1827): D-Rtt, Sm. 29, No. 5.
AYS-64a. Méhul: Joseph [und seine Brüder], overture & 13 mvts.
fl(pic) 2ob 2cl 2hn 2bn tp(hn III) b-tb(tp II) 2vla cb.   MS pts (1827): D-Rtt, Sm. 27, (3rd arrangement).
AYS-65a. Mozart: Die Entführung aus den Serail, overture & 21 mvts.
fl(pic) 2ob 2cl 2hn 2bn tp(hn III, Nos. 10, 14, 15) b-tb 2vla cb.   MS pts (1825): D-Rtt, Sm. 26, (arrangement 2).
AYS-66. Mozart: Le Nozze di Figaro, overture & 23 mvts.   fl 2ob 2cl 2hn 2bn tp(hn III) b-tb 2vla cb.
MS pts (1825): D-Rtt, Sm. 31, Nos. [0], 1 - 11, 11½, 12 - 22, (hn III replaces tp, Nos. 1 - 4, 7 - 10, 14, 16, 17).
AYS-67a. Mozart: Don Giovanni, overture & 35 mvts.   fl 2ob 2cl+2cl(rip) 2hn 2bn tp b-tb serp.
MS parts (1822): D-Rtt, Sm. 16, Nos. 41 - 76, (missing Nos. 54 - 60). *The Ouverture is duplicated at No. 42,
leading directly to the (unnumbered) Introduzione.*
AYS-68a. Mozart: Così fan tutte, overture.   fl 2ob 2cl+2cl(rip) 2hn 2bn tp b-tb serp.
MS parts (1822): D-Rtt, Sm. 16, No. 149.
AYS-69a. Mozart: La Clemenza di Tito (as "Titus der gütige), overture & 26 mvts.
fl 2ob 2cl 2hn 2bn tp b-tb 2vla b.   MS parts (1826): D-Rtt, Sm. 27, (first arrangement in the Sm.).
AYS-70a. Mozart: Die Zauberflöte, overture & 21 mvts.   fl(pic) 2ob 4cl 2hn 2bn tp(hn III) b-tb cb.
MS parts (1822): D-Rtt, Sm. 30, Nos. 1 - 22.
AYS-71a Mozart: Zaide, overture in G, (Symphony 32, K.318).   fl 2ob 4cl 3hn 2bn b-tb cb.
MS parts (1823): D-Rtt, Sm. 21, No. 1, *(the headtitle attributes this work to Bianchi's opera,* La villanella rapita,
and indeed Köchel observes that Mozart's Sinfonie was frequently used as an overture for Bianchi's work).
AYS-72a. Mozart: 2 additional numbers for Bianchi's opera *La Villanella rapita,* Quartetto, "Dite almeno"
(K.479) & Terzetto, "Mandina amabile" (K.480).   fl 2ob 4cl 3hn 2bn b-tb cb.
MS parts (1823): D-Rtt, Sm. 21, Nos. 2, 3.
AYS-73a. Mozart: [unidentified] "Scene, aus Einer Italienische oper".   fl 2ob 2cl 2hn 2bn tp b-tb 2vla cb.
MS parts (1824): D-Rtt, Sm. 25, No. 18. *Köchel deest.*
AYS-74a. W. Müller: Die Schlangenfest in Sangora, overture & 5 mvts.
fl 2ob 2cl 2hn 2bn tp(hn III in No. 25) b-tb 2vla cb.   MS parts (1824): D-Rtt, Sm. 25, Nos. 21 - 26.
AYS-75a. W. Müller: Der österreichische [here: "Ungarische"] Grenadier, overture.
fl 2ob 4cl 2hn 2bn tp b-tb serp.   MS parts (1823): D-Rtt, Sm. 17, No. 229.
AYS-76a. W. Müller: Hamlet, overture & 13 mvts.   fl 2ob 2cl 2hn 2bn tp b-tb 2vla cb.
MS parts (1824): D-Rtt, Sm. 25, Nos. 4 - 17. *Many of these mvts may be drawn from the ballet in the opera.*
AYS-77a. Paer: Achille (as "Agiles"), Trauer Marsch, in C minor.   fl 2ob 2cl 2hn 2bn tp b-tb 2vla cb.
MS parts (1827): D-Rtt, Sm. 29, No. 6.
AYS-78a. Paer: Der Kapellmeister von Venedig (Der Scheinbetrügt), overture.
fl 2ob 2cl 2hn 2bn tp b-tb 2vla cb.   MS parts (1827): D-Rtt, Sm. 29, No. 18.
AYS-79a. Righini: Armida, overture.   fl 2ob 4cl 2hn 2bn tp b-tb serp.
MS parts (c.1823): D-Rtt, Sm. 17, No. 228.
AYS-80a. Rossini: L'Italiana in Algeri, overture & 6 mvts.   fl 2ob 2cl 2hn 2bn tp b-tb 2vla cb.
MS parts (1827): D-Rtt, Sm. 28, Nos. 4 - 10.
AYS-81a. Rossini: Il Turco in Italia, overture & 14 mvts.   fl 2ob 2cl 2hn 2bn tp tb 2vla cb.
MS parts (1824): D-Rtt, Sm. 25, Nos. 37 - 51.
AYS-82.1a. Rossini: Elisabetta, Regina d'Inghilterra, overture.   fl 2ob 2cl(A) 2cl(C) 2hn 2bn tp b-tb serp.
MS parts (1823): D-Rtt, Sm. 18, No. 1.
AYS-82.2a. Rossini: Elisabetta, Regina d'Inghilterra, overture & 11 mvts.
fl(pic) 2ob 2cl 2hn 2bn tp(hn III) b-tb 2vla cb.
MS parts (1824): D-Rtt, Sm 24, Nos. [0], 1 - 11, (horn III replaces tp in one section of No. 7 only).

AYS-83.1a. Rossini: Il Barbiere di Siviglia, overture.   fl 2ob 2cl 2hn 2bn tp b-tb 2vla cb.
MS parts (1826): D-Rtt, Sm. 12, No. 9.
AYS-83.2a. Rossini: Il Barbiere di Siviglia, 15 mvts (without overture).   fl 2ob 2cl 2hn 2bn tp b-tb 2vla cb.
MS parts (1827): D-Rtt, Sm. 28, [following No. 65, as "Nos. 1 - 16"].   *No. 16 [Act II Finale] is the same work as No. 15, transposed from G to F.*
AYS-84a. Rossini: Otello, 12 mvts.   fl 2ob 2cl 2hn 2bn 2vla cb.
MS parts (1824): D-Rtt, Paer 8, Nos. 17 - 28.
AYS-85a. Rossini: La Cenerentola, overture.   fl 2ob 4cl 2hn 2bn tp b-tb cb.
MS parts (1823): D-Rtt, Sm. 18, No. 10.
AYS-86a. Rossini: (unidentified Quartetto in B♭).   fl 2ob 2cl 2hn 2bn tp tb 2vla cb.
MS pts (1827): D-Rtt, Sm. 29, No. 20.   *Sm. 29, No. 21 (AYS-13a), Adagio, 6/8 / Chor, 6/8, may also be by Rossini.*
AYS-87a. Rummel: 5 Walzer [with Trios].   fl(E♭) 2ob 2cl(E♭, Nos. 28 - 31, B♭, No. 27) 2cl(B♭) 2hn 2bn tp(posthorn, Nos. 27, 28) b-tb cb.   MS parts (1823): D-Rtt, Sm. 30, Nos. 27 - 31.
AYS-88.1a. Schenk: Der Dorfbarbier, overture.   fl 2ob 2cl 2hn 2bn tp b-tb 2vla cb.
MS parts (1824): D-Rtt, Sm. 25, No. 35.
AYS-88.2a. Schenk: Der Dorfbarbier, Polonoise in B♭.   fl 2ob 4cl 2hn 2bn tp b-tb serp.
MS parts (1823): D-Rtt, Sm. 17, No. 167.
AYS-89a. J. Schmid: Polonoise [& Trio]; in D minor.   fl 2ob 4cl 2hn 2bn tp b-tb serp.
MS parts (1823): D-Rtt, Sm. 17, No. 170.
AYS-90a. Schmitt: Ouverture in B♭, Op. 36a (as "Ouverture di Lipsia").   fl 2ob 2cl 2hn 2bn tp b-tb 2vla cb.
MS parts (1826): D-Rtt, Sm. 12, No. 12.
AYS-91a. Seyfried: König Saul, overture & 9 mvts.   fl 2ob 4cl 2hn 2bn tp b-tb serp.
MS parts (1823): D-Rtt, Sm. 18, Nos. 44 - 53; (in No. 53 the cl III pt is marked "Corno in C" [sic]).
AYS-92a. Spohr: Faust, overture.   fl 2ob 2cl(C) 2hn 2bn tp b-tb 2vla cb.   MS pts (1826): D-Rtt, Sm. 12, No. 11.
AYS-93a. Spohr, Jessonda, overture.   fl(C, E♭, pic in E♭) 2ob 2cl(A & B♭) 2hn 2bn tp b-tb 2vla cb.
MS parts (1826): D-Rtt, Sm. 12, No. 13.
AYS-94a. Spontini: Olympia, overture.   fl 2ob 2cl(C) 2hn 2bn tp b-tb 2vla cb.
MS parts (1825): D-Rtt, Sm. 26, arrangement 3 (immediately following *Die Entführung aus dem Serail*).
AYS-95a. Steinacker: 4 Polonoise.   fl 2ob 4cl 2hn 2bn tp(hn III in Nos. 6 - 8) b-tb cb.
MS parts (1823): D-Rtt, Sm. 21, Nos. 6 - 9.
AYS-96a. Steinacker: Walzer, in D.   fl 2ob 2cl(A)+2cl(rip, C) 2hn 2bn tp b-tb serp.
MS parts (1822): D-Rtt, Sm. 16, No. 16.
AYS-97a. Stumpf: Harmonie v[on] Stumpf et Schneider; [overture & 13 mvts].   2ob 4cl 2hn 2bn tp b-tb serp.
MS parts: D-Rtt, Sm. 16, Nos. 1 - 14, (Nos. 1, 2, 5 & 13 match mvts in Stumpf, JUS-1.1).
AYS-98a. Vogler: Sinfonia in C (Bayernische National-Sinfonie).   fl 2ob 2cl 2hn 2bn tp b-tb 2vla cb.
MS parts (1827): D-Rtt, Sm. 29, Nos. 1 - 4.
AYS-99a. C.M. Weber: Abu Hassan, overture.   fl 2ob 2cl 2hn 2bn tp b-tb 2vla cb.
MS parts (1827): D-Rtt, Sm. 29, No. 37.
AYS-100a. C.M. Weber: Der Beherrscher der Geister, overture.   fl 2ob 2cl 2hn 2bn tp b-tb 2vla cb.
MS parts (1826): D-Rtt, Sm. 12, No. 10.   *A note at the end states, "Segue Finale aus Euryanthe" [AYS-100.1a].*
AYS-101a. C.M. Weber: Preciosa, overture & 8 mvts.   fl(drum) 2ob 2cl(B♭) 2hn 2bn tp(hn III, tri) b-tb 2vla cb.
MS pts (1823): D-Rtt, Sm. 23, Nos. 27 - 35.   *The fl & tp double on perc in the Marsch section of the Ouverture.*
AYS-102.1a. C.M. Weber: Der Freischütz, overture & 16 mvts.   fl 2ob 4cl(hn IV replaces cl II in overture) 2hn 2bn tp(hn III: Nos. 54, 56, 58: 2hn, 59 - 70) b-tb serp.   MS parts (1823): D-Rtt, Sm. 18, Nos. 54 - 70.
AYS-102.2a. C.M. Weber: Der Freischütz; overture & 16 mvts.   fl 2ob 4cl 2hn(2tp) 2bn b-tb cb.
MS parts (c.1825): D-Rtt, C.M.v.Weber 1/I, Nos. [0], 1 - 16, (both horns double on tps in the Molto Vivace section of the Overture; tp replaces hn I in No. 1 & the first section of No. 3).
AYS-102.3a. C.M. Weber: Der Freischütz, overture.   fl(pic) 2ob 2cl+2cl(rip) 2hn 2bn tp b-tb serp.
MS parts (1822): D-Rtt, Sm. 16, No. 40.
AYS-102.4a. C.M. Weber: Der Freischütz, Marsche; in C.   fl 2ob 2cl+2cl(rip) 2hn 2bn tp b-tb serp.
MS parts (1822): D-Rtt, Sm. 16, No. 39.
AYS-103.1a. C.M. Weber: Euryanthe, overture & 9 mvts.   fl 2ob 2cl 2hn 2bn tp(hn III No. 33) b-tb 2vla cb.
MS parts (1827): D-Rtt, Sm. 29, Nos. 28 - 36, 45 (Finale).
AYS-103.2a. C.M. Weber: Euryanthe, Jaegerchor ("Die thalle dampfen die Höhen glühen").
fl 2ob 2cl 5hn 2bn tp b-tb 2vla cb.   MS pts (1823): D-Rtt, Sm. 23, No. 36.   *The 5hn pts are found in various volumes & give the names of the musicians: hn I(E♭): Hrr v[on]. Widl; hn II(E♭) (in tp vol): Härtl; hn III(A♭) (in cl II in E♭ vol): Zeller; hn IV(B[♭]) (in hn II vol): Dambacher; hn V(E♭) (in cl I in E♭ vol).*
AYS-104a. C.M. Weber: Oberon, overture.   fl 2ob 2cl 2hn 2bn tp b-tb 2vla cb.
MS parts (1827): D-Rtt, Sm. 29, No. 44.
AYS-105a. C.M. Weber: Grosse Symphonie No. 1 in C.   fl 2ob 2cl(C) 2hn 2bn tp b-tb(tp II No. 38) 2vla cb.
MS parts (1823): D-Rtt, Sm. 23, Nos. 37 - 40.
AYS-106a. C.M. Weber: [Leyer und Schwert, Op. 42, No. 2; J.169] Lützow's wilde Jagd.
fl 2ob 3cl(I, II, IV) 4hn 2bn b-tb cb.   MS pts (1823): D-Rtt, Sm. 21, No. 5, (hn III replaces tp, hn IV replaces cl III).
AYS-107a. J.G. Weber: Triumph Marsch, Op. 20, in F.   pic/fl 2ob 2cl(F) 2cl(C) 2hn 2bn tp b-tb cb.
MS parts: D-Rtt, Sammelband 23, No. 12.
AYS-108a. J. Weigl: Die Schweizerfamilie, overture & 18 mvts.   fl 2ob 2cl 2hn 2bn tp(hn III) b-tb 2vla cb.
MS parts: D-Rtt, Sm. 24, Nos. 12 - 30.
AYS-109a. *Graf* Westerholt: 11 Walzer.   fl(C, D, E♭) 2ob 2cl 2hn 2bn tp b-tb 2vla cb.
MS parts (1827): D-Rtt, Sm. 29, Nos. 7 - 17.   *Nos. 1, 6, 8, 3 - 5, 10, 7, 11, 2, respectively of the MS orchestral version at D-Rtt, Westerholt 1; Sm. 29, Nos. 13, 15 & 16 are Hops Walzer.*
AYS-110a. Winter: Das unterbrochene Opferfest, overture & 22 mvts.   fl 2ob 4cl 2hn 2bn tp(hn III) b-tb cb.
MS parts: D-Rtt, Sm. 22, Nos. [0], 1 - 22, (the fl & ob I pts are reversed in No. 21; tp in Nos. 5 & 8 only).

AYS-111a. Winter: Das Labyrint, overture.   fl 2ob 2cl 2hn 2bn tp b-tb 2vla cb.
MS parts (1824): D-Rtt, Sm. 25, No. 1, (as "Der Kampf den Elemente").
AYS-112a. Wunderlich: [6] Walzer [& Trios].   fl(C, D, E♭) 2ob 2cl 2hn 2bn tp b-tb 2vla cb.
MS parts (1827): D-Rtt, Sm. 28, Nos. 37 - 42.
AYS-113a. Zergansy: [6] Walzer [& Tios].   fl 2ob 2cl 2hn 2bn tp b-tb 2vla cb.
MS parts (1827): D-Rtt, Sm. 28, Nos. 54 - 59.
AYS-114a. Zimmarotsky: [5] Walzer [& Trios].   fl 2ob 2cl 2hn 2bn tp b-tb 2vla cb.
MS parts (1827): D-Rtt, Sm. 28, Nos. 43 - 47.
AYS-115a. Zingarelli: [6] Walzer [& Trios].   fl 2ob 2l 2hn 2bn tp b-tb 2vla cb.
MS parts (1827): D-Rtt, Sm. 28, Nos. 31 - 36, (as by "Zinggarnelly").
AYS-116a. Zwerger: Walzer [& Trio].   fl 2ob 2cl 2hn 2bn tp b-tb 2vla cb.
MS parts (1826): D-Rtt, Sm. 27, (penultimate piece).
AYS-1ma. Anon: Highland Marsch [sic]; in C.   fl 2ob 4cl(C) 2hn 2bn tp b-tb serp.
MS parts (1823): D-Rtt, Sm. 18, No. 9.
AYS-2ma. Anon: Duple; in D.   fl(D) 2ob 2cl+2cl(rip) 2hn 2bn tp b-tb serp.
MS parts (1823): D-Rtt, Sm. 16, No. 81.
AYS-3ma. Cavos (arr. Dörffeld, rescored Schneider): Duple [in F], Bey der K[aiserlich]: Russischen Arme[e],
See A-74m, Heft 3, No. 13).   terz-fl 2ob 2cl+2cl(rip) 2hn 2bn tp b-tb serp.
MS parts (1823): D-Rtt, Sm. 16, No. 80, (as by "Derffeld").
AYS-4ma. Dedroi [?Dederoi]: Marsch, in G.   fl 2ob 2cl+2cl(rip) 2hn 2bn tp b-tb serp.
MS parts (1822): D-Rtt, Sm. 16, No. 115.
AYS-5ma, 6ma. Neukomm (?rescored Schneider): 2 Marcia in E♭: Prinz Albert & Prinz Heinrich.
2pic 2ob(non obligat) 3cl 2hn 2bn tp b-tb serp.   MS parts: D-Rtt, Sm. 18, Nos. 42, 43, (pic II replaces cl IV).
AYS-7ma. Walter: Marsch; in D.   fl 2ob 4cl 2hn 2bn tp b-tb serp.   MS pts (1823): D-Rtt, Sm. 17, No. 200.

*SCHNEIDER, Friedrich *(?1800)*
FHS-1. Ouverture; in E♭.   pic 2ob cl(E♭) 4cl(B♭) 2hn+2hn(ad lib) 2bn 3tp 3tb serp b-dr s-dr.
MS parts: D-DT, Mus-n 963.

*SCHNEIDER, Georg Abraham *19 April 1770, Darmstadt - 19 Jan 1839, Berlin.*
GES-1. Harmonie.   2fl 2ob 2cl 2hn 2bn tp serp.
AutoMS score: D-Bds, Mus.Ms.Auto.G.A.Schneider 46.
GES-2(-13). 12 Harmonien.   2fl 2cl 2hn 2bn.
AutoMS score: D-Bds, Mus.Ms.Auto.G.A.Schneider 47.
GES-14. Harmonie.   2fl 2cl 2hn 2bn.
AutoMS Score: D-Bds, Mus.Ms.Auto.G.A.Schneider 48.
GES-15. Harmonie.   2fl 2cl 2hn 2bn.
AutoMS score: D-Bds, Mus.Ms.Auto.G.A.Schneider 109.
*GES-16. Terpodium Concert.   2ob 2hn 2bn.
AutoMS score: D-Bds, Mus.Ms.Auto.G.A.Schneider 84.
*GES-17. VI Pièces d'Harmonie, Op. 8.   2cl 2hn (2)bn.
Pc (Gombart: Augsburg, c.1801), parts: A-Wgm; D-B.
*GES-18. Harmoniemusik, in F.   2fl 2cl 2hn 2bn.   MS: ?D-Bds.
Pm (Bote & Bock: Wiesbaden, sd), ed. Heinrich Wohlheim, hire score & parts.
GES-19(-24). 6 Sextettes für Blasinstrumente.   Instrumentation unknown.
AutoMS score: D-Bds, (Eitner citation, ?lost).
GES-25(-31). 7 Quintetten für Blasinstrumente.   Instrumentation unknown.
AutoMS score: D-Bds, (Eitner citation, ?lost).
GES-1m, 2m. 2 langsame Märsche.   pic quart-fl 2ob cl(F) 2cl(C) 4hn 2bn cbn+serp/2b-hn 2tp 3tb b-dr t-dr tamb cym.   *See: ANONYMOUS WORKS, A-74.2/11m, 12m, (possibly rescored).*

SCHNEIDER, René *1931*
RQS-1. Exorde.   fl ob 3cl 2bn 3hn 2tp 3tb 2tu.
Pm (Jobert: Paris, pn J.J.847, 1971), score.

SCHNEIDER, Urs Peter *14 Feb 1939, Bern*
UPS-1. Achtzehn Stationen, 1979-81: 2. Langer Marsch, einige Stationen.   Instrumentation unknown.
Pm (Edition Zwachen: Aarau, Switzerland, 1981), ?score.

*SCHÖN, ( ) *(1740) - post-1782 (20 April 1794, if Schön was the Chorregens at Marienkirche am Rhein)*
XQS-1. Serenata…A l'usage Fr: Jos: Kohler; in E♭, 8 mvts.   2cl 2hn 2bn.
MS: CH-E, Th. 91,28 (Ms.2364). ★
XQS-2. Parthia a 5que; in F, 5 mvts, (c.1778).   2ob 2hn bn.
MS parts: CH-E, Th. 61,32 (Ms.1978); D-Bds. ★

*SCHOEN, ( ), *Sig.* *(?1770)*
*SZS-1c. Parthia in Dis [E♭]; 3 mvts.   2 horns "concertantto", 2ob 2cl 2bn cbn.
MS parts (?late 1780s): D-Rtt, Krommer 15. *See KROMMER, FVK-2d. Schoen's name appears on the original titlepage; Krommer's name ("Kromer") has been added in pencil, and is also noted as composer in the Gardemusik Katalog c.1820 (Nr. 34). The MS may have been purchased as part of a set of Krommer wind works from Scheffauer, in Stuttgart, July 1820, with the Krommer attribution an assumption by the cataloger.* ★

*SCHOENFELD, ( ) *(1760)*
*ZFS-1m. March for the Army of the Rhine, 1792.   ob 2cl bn tp.
Pm (In: Pätzig (qv), Heft 3, No. 18), score & parts. ★

*SCHOENFELD, William C.
WCS-1.1a. Beethoven: Piano Sonata in F minor, Op. 10, No. 2, Finale (Presto).   fl ob 2cl 2bn.
Pm (Music Publishers Holding Co: New York, sd), score & parts.
WCS-1.2a. Beethoven: Piano Sonata in F minor, Op. 10, No. 2, Finale (Presto).   fl ob 2cl hn bn.
Pm (Albert J. Andraud: Cincinnati, now Southern Music Co.: San Antonio, Texas), score & parts.

SCHOEPS, ( )
XZS-1. Partiten (number unknown).   2ob 2hn bn.
MS parts: PL-Wu, Ka 17.

*SCHOLL, Nicolaus (Miklós) *(1790) - post-1827 (?post-1841)*
NYS-1m. Racouzy [sic, Rákóczy] Marsch.   2ob cl(D) 2cl(B♭) 2hn 2bn+cbn 2tp(clar) b-tb serp timp.
MS parts: D-Tl, Z 123, (later pts: pic replaces cl in D, 2cl in C replace 2cl in B♭).   ★
NYS-1a. Musikalischer Sammler [sic] N: 2, 58tes Werk.   2ob 2cl 2hn 2bn cbn 2tp.
MS parts: I-MOe, Mus.F.1410, (with a later flute part on different paper).
     1.1a. Bresciani: L'Arbore di Diana, Overture.
     1.2a (1.4a). Generali: I Baccanti [Baccanali] di Roma, Scena e Rondo, Cavatina, Scena ed Aria.
     1.5a. Pacini: Allesandro nell' Indie, Cavatina.
NYS-2a. Viviani: Le Morte di Virginia, (Act I) sinfonia & 5 mvts, (Act II) 4 mvts.   2ob 2cl 2hn 2bn cbn 2tp.
MS parts: A-Ee, Mus.1119 (Act I), Mus.1120 (Act II), (without cbn & 2tp pts); A.35.259, (as Anon; = Act I
only); I-MOe, Mus.D.667, (with a flute part in another hand on different paper; the ob I pt bears many notes
relating to its adaptation for the flute part. I-MOe, Mus.F.1344 is Scholl's piano reduction).

*We believe that the following works, long-attributed to Sedlak without any verification, are actually by Scholl.
In most of the A-Wn copies made by Perschl the bass trombone parts are in another hand (designated the "b-tb
Hand") and probably post-date Perschl's copies; we indicate these parts by the abbreviation: **[b-tb]**. See* The
Wind Ensemble Source Book, Part 2, *SEDLAK, for a discussion of Perschl's copies. Sedlak **WXS-ad** codes
appear at the end of each entry in parentheses.*
NYS-1ac. Auber: Le Maçon (as: Maurer and Schlosser), Marsch.   2ob 2cl 2hn 2bn cbn (2tp).
Mvt No. 2 of the arrangement of Pacini's Amazilla, WXS-19ad.   (WXS-4ad)
NYS-2ac. Auber: Le Duc d'Olonne, 3 mvts (Ballade, Aria, Pas redoublé).   2ob 2cl 2hn 2bn cbn 2tp.
MS parts (by Perschl): A-Wn, Mus.Hs.3796. (WXS-5ad)
NYS-3ac. Bellini: La Straniera, 11 mvts.   2ob 2cl 2hn 2bn cbn 2tp [b-tb, Nos. 10 & 11 only].
MS parts (by Perschl, A-37a): A-Wn, Mus.Hs.3801. (WXS-6ad)
NYS-4ac. Bellini: I Capuleti ed i Montecchi, (Theil 1) 2 mvts, (Theil 2) 4 mvts.   2ob 2cl 2hn 2bn cbn (2tp, Theil
2 only).   MS pts (1834): A-Wn, Mus.Hs.3798, (at the end of the bn II pt is the pencil date 1834;
simplified parts for Theil 1, No. 2, Allegro modto section are marked in many of the pts in red crayon; further
simplified pts in another hand for Theil 1, No. 2, section 1 are inserted as loose sheets in the ob I, ob II, cl II, bn I,
bn II & cbn pts; corrections and interpretive additions in another hand have been added to Theil 2). (WXS-7ad)
NYS-5ac. Bellini: La Sonnambula, 5 mvts.   2ob 2cl 2hn 2bn 2tp [b-tb].
MS parts (by Perschl, 1837, A-41a): A-Wn, Mus.Hs.3800. (WXS-8ad)
NYS-6ac. Bellini: Norma, 4 mvts.   2ob 2cl 2hn 2bn cbn 2tp [b-tb].
MS parts (by Perschl, A-42a): A-Wn, Mus.Hs.3799. (WXS-9ad)
NYS-7ac. Bellini: Beatrice di Tenda, terzetto.   2ob 2cl 2hn 2bn cbn 2tp [b-tb].
MS parts (by Perschl): A-Wn, Mus.Hs.3797. (WXS-10ad)
NYS-8ac. Bellini: I Puritani di Scozia, [2] duetti e aria.   2ob 2cl 2hn 2bn cbn 2tp [b-tb].
MS parts (b-tb Hand): A-Wn, Mus.Hs.4459. (WXS-11ad)
NYS-9ac. Donizetti: L'Elisir d'amore, 4 mvts.   2ob 2cl 2hn 2bn cbn 2tp [b-tb].
MS parts (by Perschl, 1837): A-Wn, Mus.Hs.3808, (cropping affects a few bars in the b-tb pt). (WXS-11ad)
NYS-10ac. Donizetti: Torquato Tasto, 6 mvts.   2ob 2cl 2hn 2bn 2tp [b-tb].
MS parts (mvts 1-5 by Perschl, 1837; mvt 6 in the b-tb Hand): A-Wn, Mus.Hs.3810. *Statements that mvt 6 is
in Sedlak's hand are completely unfounded.* (WXS-13ad)
NYS-11ac. Donizetti: Mario Faliero, 3 mvts.   2ob 2cl 2hn 2bn cbn 2tp b-tb.
MS parts (by Perschel): A-Wn, Mus.Hs.3967. (WXS-14d)
NYS-12ac. Donizetti: Lucia di Lammermoor, 3 mvts (duetto, aria, cavatina).   2ob 2cl 2hn 2bn cbn 2tp b-tb.
MS parts (in the b-tb Hand): A-Wn, Mus.Hs.3809. (WXS-15ad)
NYS-13ac. Hérold: Le Pré aus Clercs, 3 mvts.   2ob 2cl 2hn 2bn cbn 2tp.
MS parts (by Perschl): A-Wn, Mus.Hs.3812, (the 2tp tacet in No. 3). (WXS-16ad)
NYS-14ac. Mercadante: Andronico, duetto.   2ob 2cl 2hn 2bn cbn 2tp [b-tb].
MS parts (by Perschl): A-Wn, Mus.Hs.3819. (WXS-17ad)
NYS-15ac. Meyerbeer: Les Huguenots, 6 mvts (Trinklied, Coro, Finale, Balatta, Ziguenertanz, Duetto).
2ob 2cl 2hn 2bn cbn 2tp b-tb.
MS parts (by Perschl): A-Wn, Mus.Hs.3820, (each piece with a separate titlepage). (WXS-18ad)
NYS-16ac. Pacini: Amazilla, overture & 4 mvts.   2ob 2cl 2hn 2bn cbn 2tp.
MS pts: CZ-Bm(au), A.40.101. *No. 2 is a march from Auber's* Le Maçon *(Maurer und Schlosser)*. (WXS-19ad)
NYS-17ac. Ricci: Il nuovo Figaro, overture.   2ob 2cl 2hn 2bn 2tp b-tb.
MS parts (by Perschl): A-Wn, Mus.Hs.3834. (WXS-20ad)
NYS-18ac. Ricci: Il Desertore per amore, cavatina & scene e cavatina.   2ob 2cl 2hn 2bn cbn 2tp [b-tb].
MS parts (the first cavatina by Perschl; the scena e cavatina in another hand): A-Wn, Mus.Hs.3833. *Statements
that this work is partly by Sedlak & completed by Perschl are completely without foundation.* (WXS-21ad)

SCHOLZ, Bernhard E. *30 March 1835, Mainz - 26 Dec 1916, Munich*
BXS-1. Serenade.   fl ob cl 2hn bn.   MS score: D-Bds, Mus.Ms.20167/7.

SCHOLZ, Robert
RBS-1. Country Tunes: 9 Dances.   2ob 2cl 2hn 2bn.
Pm (Asian Composers' League: New York). *Copy in US-NYamc.*

*SCHOLZ, W.E. (?Wilhelm Ernst) *(1810)*
Scholz also arranged 23 works for brass ensemble (D-NEhz, 141). D-NEhz 134, comprises 61 dances in parts reputedly in the hands of Georg Schmitt & W.E. Scholz; it is impossible to separate out the arrangers of these pieces; also, at least one of the anonymous dance collections at Neuenstein may have been arranged by Scholz.
WES-1. Overtura No. 2, 1832.   fl 2ob 2cl 3hn 2bn tp tb db timp.   AutoMS score ("Schl[a]w[entzi]tz 3.5/[18]41"; end of score: "Schlwtz. 11/5.41") & MS parts: D-NEhz, 58, No. 6, (parts missing cl I). ★
WES-2. Ouverture, in C.   fl 2ob 2cl 2hn 2bn tp tb db timp.
MS score (1843/1844) & MS parts: D-NEhz, 87, Bd. 1, No. 1. ★
WES-3. Ouverture, C minor.   fl 2ob 2cl 3hn 2bn tb db timp.
MS parts: D-Nehz, 244, (bn I incomplete, 5 sheets only). ★
WES-4. [Overture, E♭].   fl 2ob 2cl 2hn 2bn tp tb vc db timp.   AutoMS parts: D-Nehz, 245, No. 1. ★
WES-5. Ouverture, in F.   fl 2ob 2cl(C) 2hn 2bn tp tb vc db timp.   AutoMS parts: D-Nehz, 245, No. 2. ★
WES-6. Scherzo, in G.   fl 2ob 3cl 2hn 2bn tp tb db.   AutoMS score & MS parts: D-NEhz, 60, No. 1. ★
WES-7. Second Scherzo, in G.   fl 2ob 2cl 2hn 2bn tb.   AutoMS score & MS parts: D-NEhz, 60, No. 3. ★
WES-8. Scherzo.   fl 2ob 2cl 3hn 2bn tb db timp.
AutoMS score (1840/1841) & MS parts: D-NEhz, 58, Nó. 3, (parts missing cl I). ★
WES-9. Scholz: Fest-Ouverture Op. 17, in C.   fl 2ob 2cl 3hn 2bn tp tb db timp.
AutoMS score ("6.ten Octobr. 1838", end of score: "d. 1ten Nvbr. 1838") & MS parts: D-NEhz, 8, No. [0]. ★
WES-10(a). Scholz: Der Komet, overture, 16tes Arrangement, Schl[a]w[entzi]tz. 2/3.[18]39.
fl 2ob 2cl 3hn 2bn tp tb db timp.   AutoMS score (end of score: "Schlwtz. 7/3.39") & MS parts: D-NEhz, 59, No. 4, (missing fl part).
WES-1m. Fest Marsch, in F.   fl 2ob 2cl 3hn 2bn tp tb db.   (?Auto)MS score & MS pts: D-NEhz, 60, No. 13. ★
WES-2m(a). Scholz: Marsch, 17tes Arrangement, d.12/3.[1839].   fl 2ob 2cl 3hn 2bn tp tb db timp.
AutoMS score (end of score: "Schlwtz. 14/3.39") & MS parts: D-NEhz, 59, No. 6, (parts missing fl). ★
WES-1v. Fest Polonaise, componirt...Breslau d. 12ten Januar 1834.   SABB, fl 2ob 2cl 2hn 2bn tp tb db timp.
AutoMS score (?c.1841) & MS parts: D-NEhz, 58, No. 5, (parts missing cl I). ★
WES-1a. Potpourri, 3tes Arrangement.   fl 2ob 2cl 3hn 2bn tp tb db timp.
AutoMS score ("Schlawentzitz d. 4 9br. [September] 1838") & MS parts: D-NEhz, 8, No. 1.
The only identified piece is the opening section based on the overture to Auber's opera, La Muette de Portici.
WES-2a. Potpourri.   fl 2ob 2cl 2hn 2bn tp tb db timp.   MS score (c.1840) & MS parts: D-NEhz, 8, No. 1.
The works named in the Potpourri are: [Halévy:] Robert [le diable]; [Anon:] Die Welt ist zur Freude; [Anon:] Masurek; [Anon:] Dessauer Marsch; Lanner: Ankunft im Olymp Walzer; [Anon:] So leb denn wohl"; [Auber:] Fra Diavolo; [Donizetti:] La Fille du régiment, Martea [sic, Marsch]; [Anon:] Der Schmerz; [Strauss the Elder:] Haut-Volée-Quadrille; [Anon:] Duett, "Alba Kara [sic]"; [Anon:] Kinder-Freuden Polka; Kücken: Gretelein; [Bellini:] Duett; [Flotow:] Alessandro Stradella, "Trinke Lindaus"; [Beethoven:] Adelaide; [Anon:] Polka; [Donizetti:] Belisario, aria; [Anon:] Komersch Lied [sic]; [Anon:] Soldaten Abschied; [Benedict:] Les Quatre fils d'Aymon, quadrille; Abt: [7 Lieder, Op. 39, No. 1, "Agathe"], "Wenn die Schwalben"; [Donizetti:] Lucrezia Borghia; [?Lortzing: Czaar und Zimmermann] Lied des Czaaren; Kücken: Korblied; [Anon:] Postillons Heimkehr; [Anon:] "O wie wohl ist mir etc. dass ich fertig bin.".
WES-3a. Anon: [unidentified] Recitative, Scene et Arie.   fl 2ob 2cl 3hn 2bn tp tb db timp.
MS parts: D-NEhz, 244, (following Scholz's Ouverture in C minor; bn I part incomplete).
WES-4a. Anon: Cäcilien-Polka, in D.   fl 2ob 2cl 2hn 2bn tp tb db.
MS parts (c.1845): D-NEhz, 135, No. 12, (missing fl).
WES-5a. Anon: Courier-Galop, in D.   fl 2ob 2cl 2hn 2bn tp tb db.
MS parts (c.1845): D-NEhz, 135, No. 11, (missing fl).
WES-6a. Anon: Erinnerungs-Polka.   fl 2ob 2cl 2hn 2bn 2tp tb db timp.
AutoMS score & MS parts: D-Nehz, 107, No. 34.
WES-7a. Anon: Faschings-Polka.   fl 2ob 2cl 2hn 2bn 2tp tb db timp.
AutoMS score (c.1843) & MS parts: D-Nehz, 107, No. 33.
WES-8a. Anon: Freundschafts-Polka.   fl 2ob 2cl 2hn 2bn 2tp tb db timp.
AutoMS score (c.1843) & MS parts: D-Nehz, 107, No. 32.
WES-9a. Anon: Infanterie-Signal-Galopp.   fl 2ob 2cl 3hn 2bn tb db.
AutoMS score (c.1843) & MS parts: D-Nehz, 107, No. 27.
WES-10a. Anon: Mathilde Polka.   fl 2ob 2cl 3hn 2bn tb db timp.
AutoMS score (c.1843) & MS parts: D-NEhz, 107, No. 5.
WES-11a. Anon (?Gung'l): Polka, in C.   fl 2ob 2cl 2hn 2bn tp tb db timp.
MS score (c.1840) & MS parts: D-NEhz, No. 7.
WES-12a. Anon: (?Gung'l): Polka, in F.   fl 2ob 2cl 2hn 2bn tp tb db timp.
MS score (c.1840) & MS parts: D-NEhz, No. 8.
WES-13a. Anon: Polka, in C.   fl 2ob 2cl cl(E♭) 2cl(B♭) 2hn 2bn tp tb db timp.
AutoMS score (c.1849) & MS parts: D-NEhz, 120, No. 5.
WES-14a. Anon: Polka, in A minor.   fl 2ob 2cl 2hn 2bn tp tb db timp.
AutoMS score (c.1849) & MS parts: D-NEhz, 120, No. 6.
WES-15a. Anon: Polka.   fl 2ob 2cl 2hn 2bn 2tp tb db timp.
AutoMS score (c.1843) & MS parts: D-NEhz, 107, No. 31.
WES-16a. Anon (?Hugo, Prinz von Hohenlohe-Öhringen): Polka, in D.   fl 2ob 2cl 2hn 2bn tp tb db.
MS parts (c.1845): D-NEhz, 135, No. 17, (missing fl).
WES-17a(-19a). Anon (?Hugo, Prinz von Hohenlohe-Öhringen): 3 Polkas.   fl 2ob 2cl 2hn 2bn tp tb db.
AutoMS score (c.1843) & MS parts: D-NEhz, 107, Nos. 17 - 19.
WES-20a. Anon (?Hugo, Prinz von Hohenlohe-Öhringen): Schnepfen Polka.   fl 2ob 2cl 2hn 2bn tp tb db.
AutoMS score (c.1843) & MS parts: D-NEhz, 107, No. 16.
WES-21a. Adam: Le Roi d'Yvetot, overture.   fl 2ob 2cl 2hn 2bn tp tb db timp.
AutoMS score (c.1845) & MS parts: D-NEhz, 63, 1st unnumbered item, ff. 1 - 32b.

WES-22a. Auber: Le Lac de fées, chor & duett. fl 2ob 2cl 3hn 2bn tp tb db timp.
AutoMS score (end of No. 6: "Schl[a]w[enti]tz 3/5.[18]41"; end of No. 8: "Schlwtz. 11/6.41") & MS parts:
D-NEhz, 58, Nos. 8 & 9, (parts missing cl I).
WES-23.1a. Auber: Les Diamants de la couronne, ensemble ("Seht nach jenen düstren").
fl 2ob 2cl 2hn 2bn tp tb db.   AutoMS score & MS parts: D-NEhz, 73, No. 1.
WES-23.2a. Auber: Les Diamants de la couronne, duo & finale ("Das ist recht schön").
fl 2ob 2cl 2hn 2bn tp tb db timp. AutoMS score & MS parts: D-Nehz, 73, No. 2.
WES-24.1a. Auber: Carlo Broschi, ou le Part du diable, overture, "Schl[a]w[entzi]tz] 20.3.[18]44.
fl 2ob 2cl 2hn 2bn tp tb db timp. MS score (end of score: "Schlwtz 13.4.44") & MS parts: D-NEhz, 87, Bd. 1,
No. 2, (as "Carlo Broschi").
WES-24.2a. Auber: Carlo Broschi, ou le Part du diable, aria ("Was hab ich da gehört", "Ohne Freund auf
diesen").   fl 2ob 2cl 2hn 2bn tb db.   MS score (c.1844) & MS pts: D-NEhz, 87, Bd. 1, No. 6. (as
"Carlo Broschi").
WES-25a. Auber: Le Sirène, overture, Schl[a]w[entzi]tz. 5.7.[18]45.   fl 2ob 2cl 3hn 2bn 2tp tb db timp.
AutoMS score & MS parts: D-Nehz, 64, 1st unnumbered item.
WES-26a. Balfe: The Bohemian Girl, duet ("Die Wunde auf deinem Arm").   fl 2ob 2cl 2hn 2bn tp tb db.
AutoMS score (c.1847) & MS parts: D-NEhz, 72, No. 1.
WES-27a. Balfe: Les Quatre Fils d'Aymon, aria ("Auf ihr Wachen, habet Achtung").
fl 2ob 2cl 2hn 2bn tp tb db.   AutoMS score (1845) & MS parts: D-NEhz, 69, No. 3.
WES-28a. Beethoven: Fidelio, 3 mvts.   fl 2ob 2cl 2hn (hn III in No. 5) 2bn tp tb(No. 6) db timp(No. 6).
AutoMS score (1842) & MS parts: D-NEhz, 87, Bd. 1, Nos. 5 - 7. *Aria ("Abscheulicher, wo eilst du hin"), duett ("O
namen, namenlose Freunde"), quartett ("Mir ist so wunderbar").*
WES-29a. Beethoven: Lenore, overture No. 1, "Schl[a]w[entzi]tz 3.11.[18]45". fl 2ob 2cl 2hn 2bn tp tb db timp.
AutoMS score & MS parts: D-NEhz, 87, Bd. 1, No. 3.
WES-30a. Beethoven: Lenore, overture No. 2.   fl 2ob 2cl 2hn 2bn tp tb db timp.
AutoMS score ("Schl[a]w[entzi]tz 14/2.[1843]"; end of score: "Schlwtz 21/2.[1843]") & MS parts: D-NEhz, 55,
unnumbered 1st arrangement.
WES-31a. Beethoven: Die Geschöpfe des Prometheus, overture.   fl 2ob 2cl 2hn 2bn tp tb db timp.
AutoMS score (1842) & MS parts: D-NEhz, 70, No. 8.
WES-32a. Beethoven: Violin Sonata in A, Op. 12, No. 2/iii, Allegro, 10/5.[18]42.   fl 2ob 2cl 2hn 2bn tb db.
AutoMS score (end of score: "S[chlawentzitz] 13/5.42") & MS parts: D-NEhz, 62, No. 5.
WES-33a. Beethoven: Piano Sonata, Op. 26/i, Andante con Variazioni.   fl 2ob 2cl 2hn 2bn tb db.
AutoMS score & MS parts: D-NEhz, 29, No. 2, (parts missing cl I).
WES-34a. Beethoven: Symphony No. 3 (Eroica), Op. 55, Scherzo, "Schl[a]w[entzi]tz. 23/4.[18]39", 27tes
Arr[an]g[e]m[en]t.   fl 2ob 2cl 3hn 2bn tb db.
AutoMS score (end of score: "Schlwtz. d.27/4.39") & MS parts: D-NEhz, 68, Bd. 1, No. 1.
WES-35a. Beethoven: Coriolan, overture, Op. 62.   fl 2ob 2cl 4hn 2bn tb db timp.
AutoMS score ("Schl[a]w[entzi]tz 24/7.[18]41") & MS pts: D-NEhz, 29, No. 4, (parts missing cl I).
WES-36a. Beethoven: Ah! perfido, scene und aria, Op. 65.   fl 2ob 2cl 2hn 2bn tp tb db timp.
AutoMS score (c.1842) & MS parts: D-NEhz, 70, No. 4.
WES-37a. Beethoven: Symphony No. 5 in C minor, Op. 67, mvts 1 & 2, "3tes Arrangement".
fl 2ob 2cl 2hn 2bn tp tb db timp.   AutoMS score (dated between 17 & 24 May 1839) & MS parts: D-NEhz,
68, Bd. 2, 1st (unnumbered) item.
WES-38a. Beethoven: Overture Namensfeier, Op. 115.   fl 2ob 2cl 2hn 2bn tp tb db timp.
AutoMS score ("Schl[a]w[entzi]tz 7.4.[18]43") & MS parts: D-NEhz, 65, No. 5.
WES-39a. Beethoven: König Stephan, Op. 117, overture, ensemble, duo u[nd]. finale.
fl 2ob 2cl 2hn 2bn tp tb db timp.   AutoMS score (c.1843) & MS parts: D-NEhz, 73, 1st (unnumbered) item,
& Nos. 1 & 2.
WES-40a. Beethoven: Andante favori in F, WoO 57.   fl 2ob 2cl 2hn 2bn tb db.
AutoMS score (end: "Schl[a]w[entzi]tz. d. 7/5.[18]42") & MS parts: D-NEhz, 62, No. 3.
WES-41a. Bellini: La Sonnambula, quintett und finale. fl 2ob 2cl 3hn 2bn tp tb db timp.
AutoMS score (1839) & MS parts: D-NEhz, 8, No. 13.
WES-42.1a. Bellini: Norma, overture & 10 mvts.   fl 2ob 2cl 3hn 2bn tp tb vlne timp.
AutoMS score (1838 - 1839) & MS parts: D-NEhz, 8, Nos. 2 - 12. *Scholz labels Nos. 9 - 11 as 12th, 11th, &
13 arrangements, respectively. The mvts were prepared separately and later bound together out of order; the
overture is No. 11.*
WES-42.2a. Bellini: Norma, finale Act II ("Er sehet zurück").   fl 2ob 2cl 2hn 2bn tp tb db timp.
AutoMS score ("Salzbrunn d. 17.7.[18]45"; end of score: "Schlwtz 18.8.45") & MS ptars: D-NEhz, 69, No. 1.
WES-43a. Bellini: I Puritani, 6 mvts, (19tes, 21tes - 25tes Arrangement), 19/3.[18]39 - 18/4.[18]39.
fl 2ob 2cl 3hn 2bn tp tb db timp. AutoMS score & MS pts: D-NEhz, 59, Bd. 2, Nos. 8 - 13, (parts missing fl).
WES-44.1a. Benedict: The Gipsy's Warning, Op. 3, overture.   fl 2ob 2cl 2hn 2bn tp tb/bn db timp.
AutoMS score ("Schl[a]w[entzi]tz 22/1.[18]42") & MS parts: D-NEhz, 62, 1st unnumbered item, (parts missing
cl II, and possibly hn III, bn I & II).
WES-44.2a. Benedict: The Gipsy's Warning, Op. 3., arietta, ("Meister! die teiten des Mondes Lauf").
fl 2ob 2cl 2hn 2bn tb db.   AutoMS score & MS parts: D-Nehz, 62, No. 1.
WES-45a. Boieldieu: La Dame blanche, finale Act I. fl 2ob 2cl 2hn 2bn tp tb db timp.
MS score (1849) & MS parts: D-NEhz, 88, Bd. 1, No. 5.
WES-46a. Catel: Sémiramis, overture.   fl 2ob 2cl 3hn 2bn tb db timp.
AutoMS score ("Schl[a]w[entzi]tz 14/8.[18]41") & MS parts: D-NEhz, 29, No. 8, (parts missing cl I).
WES-47a. Cherubini: Medée, overture.   fl 2ob 2cl 2hn 2bn tp tb db timp.
AutoMS score ("Schl[a]w[entzi]tz 30.5.[18]43"; end of score dated "13.6.[18]43") & MS parts: D-NEhz, 57, 1st
unnumbered item.

WES-48a. Chopin: Valze brillante, Op. 18.   fl 2ob 2cl 3hn 2bn tp tb db.
AutoMS score ("Schl[a]w[entzi]tz 2/11.[18]39"): D-Nehz, 118. MS pts: D-Nehz, 133, No. 12.
WES-49a. David: Le Désert, Zug.   fl 2ob 2cl 2hn 2bn tp tb vla db timp.
AutoMS score (c.1847) & MS parts: D-NEhz, 72, No. 2.
WES-50a. Donizetti: L'Elisir d'amore, overture & 8 mvts.   fl 2ob 2cl 3hn 2bn tp tb db timp.
AutoMS score (beginning: "Schl[a]w[entzi]tz 12/5.[18]40; end: "Mit Gottes Hilfe vollendet d. 6 Februar 1841")
& MS parts: D-Nehz, 15.
WES-51a. Donizetti: Lucrezia Borgia, overture & 1 mvt.   fl 2ob 2cl 2hn 2bn tp tb db timp.
AutoMS score (beginning: "Schl[a]w[entzi]tz d. 4/5.[18]40"; end: "Vollendet Schlawentzitz d. 27ten April 1841")
& MS parts: D-NEhz, 12.
WES-52.1a. Donizetti: Marino Faliero, aria.   fl 2ob 2cl 3hn 2bn tb db timp.
AutoMS score (1847) & MS parts: D-NEhz, 11, Bd. 2, No. 11.
WES-52.2a. Donizetti: Marino Faliero, aria.   fl 2ob 2cl 2hn 2bn tp tb db timp.
AutoMS score (1847) & MS parts: D-NEhz, 11, Bd. 2, No. 12.
WES-53.1a. Donizetti: Lucia di Lammermoor, 4 mvts.   fl 2ob 2cl 2hn 2bn tp tb db timp.
MS score (c.1844) & MS parts: D-NEhz, 87, Bd. 2, No. 9. *Praeludio e coro di intruduzione; scene e cavatina;
cavatine und aria; aria.*   ,
WES-53.2a. Donizetti: Lucia di Lammermoor, duet ("Bei der Asche des Verblichnen").
fl 2ob 2cl 2hn 2bn tp tb db timp.   AutoMS score (c.1843) & MS pts: D-Nehz, 65, No. 2.
WES-53.3a. Donizetti: Lucia di Lammermoor, 5 mvts.   fl 2ob 2cl 3hn 2bn 2tp tb db timp.
AutoMS score (ends of scores dated between 5 Dec 1844 & 6 Feb 1845) & MS parts: D-NEhz, 63, Nos. 3 -7.
Finale, Act II; Duett; Chor; Scene & Aria; Finale Act II.
WES-54a. Donizetti: Belisario, overture & 1 Band.   fl 2ob 2cl 3hn 2bn tp(clar) tb db timp.
AutoMS score (dated between 7 April & 3 Dec 1840) & MS parts: D-Nehz, 14.
WES-55.1a. Donizetti: La Fille du régiment, overture.   fl 2ob 2cl 2hn 2bn tp tb db timp.
AutoMS score (c.1845) & MS parts: D-NEhz, 69, 1st (unnumbered) item.
WES-55.2a. Donizetti: La Fille du régiment, introduzione ("Bruder auf").   fl 2ob 2cl 3hn 2bn tb db timp.
MS score (end of score: "19.9.44") & MS pts: D-NEhz, 87, Bd. 2, Nos. 7, (here incorrectly attributed to Halévy).
WES-55.3a. Donizetti: La Fille du régiment, duett.   fl 2ob 2cl 2hn 2bn tp tb db.
MS score (c.1844) & MS parts: D-NEhz, 87, Bd. 2, No. 8.
WES-55.4a. Donizetti: La Fille du régiment, 3 mvts.   fl 2ob 2cl 2hn 2bn tp tb db timp.
AutoMS score (end of score dated "Vollendet d. 5ten August 1843") & MS parts: D-NEhz, 57, Nos. 6 - 8.
Ensemble, ("Ferne mit fir, fort, fort"); Duett, ("Wie, di liebst mich"); Finale Act I, ("Hoch, lebe hoch").
WES-55.5a. Donizetti: La Fille du régiment, aria ("Ach umsonst denkt, ihr").   fl 2ob 2cl 2hn 2bn tp tb db timp.
AutoMS score (c.1845) & MS pts: D-NEhz, 63, No. 1.
WES-56a. Donizetti: Linda de Chamounix, 2 mvts & overture.   fl 2ob 2cl 2hn 2bn tp tb db timp.
AutoMS score (1846): D-NEhz, 67, Nos. 1, 2 & (unnumbered) item following No. 9. *Duett ("Wie beruhist mich
die Freude"); aria; overture.*
WES-57a. Donizetti: Don Pasquale, overture & 9 mvts.   fl 2ob 2cl 2hn 2bn tp tb db timp.
AutoMS score (beginning of overture: "Schl[a]w[enti]tz d. 20ten Febr. 1848") & MS parts: D-NEhz, 11, (parts
include vla & vc in No. 5; missing fl).
WES-58a. Eugen, Herzog von Württemberg: Der Geisterbraut, quartett ("O reich dem Freunde").
fl 2ob 2cl 2hn 2bn tb db timp. AutoMS score & MS pts: D-NEhz, 65, No. 1.
WES-59a. Eugen, Herzog von Württemberg: Scene aus Lenore, ("Bald wird die Rache siegen").
fl 2ob 2cl 2hn 2bn tp tb db. MS score (4 Dec 1843) & MS parts: D-NEhz, 87, Bd. 1, No. 4.
WES-60a. J. Fahrbach the Elder: Döblers Zauber Walzer.   fl 2ob 2cl 2hn 2bn tp tb db timp.
MS   parts (c.1845): D-NEhz, 135, No. 5, (missing fl).
WES-61a. J. Fahrbach the Elder: Dombrunoc Polka.   fl 2ob 2cl 2hn 2bn tp tb db timp.
MS parts (c.1845): D-NEhz, 135, No. 4, (missing fl).
WES-62.1a. Flotow: Alessandro Stradella, 4 mvts.   fl 2ob 2cl 2hn 2bn tp tb db timp.
AutoMS score (c.1845) & MS parts: D-NEhz, 63, Nos. 2 - 5. *Act II Introduction ("So wär es denn erreicht");
Wechselgesang, Act III ("Italia, mein Vaterland"); Finale, Act III ("Wie freundlich strahlt der Tag"); Pilger-Chor
hinter der Scene, Act III ("Rosig strahlt die Morgensonne").*
WES-62.2a. Flotow: Alessandro Stradella, finale Act II ("Glockenklänge, hurtig auf").
fl 2ob 2cl 2hn 2bn tp tb db timp. AutoMS score (1845) & MS parts: D-NEhz, 69, No. 2.
WES-63a. Flotow: Martha, overture & finale Act I ("Raum und Platz der Obrigkeit").
fl 2ob 2cl 3hn 2bn tp tb db. AutoMS score (c.1848): D-NEhz, 105.
WES-64a. Friedrich, Prince zu Hohenlohe-Öhringen: Polka in F.   fl 2ob 2cl 2hn 2bn tp tb db.
AutoMS score (c.1849) & MS parts: D-Nehz, 120, No. 4. MS score (1848): D-NEhz, 119.
WES-65a. Gläser: Des Adlers Horst, terzett, ("Die Flaschen zur Hand"), 18tes Arrangement, 15/3.[18]39.
fl 2ob 2cl 3hn 2bn tp tb db timp.   AutoMS score (end of score: "Schl[a]w[entzi]tz. 18/3.39") & MS parts:
D-NEhz, 59, No. 7, (parts missing fl).
Gung'l, Joszef. See also supra: Anon: 2 Polkas.
WES-66a. Gung'l: Venus-Reigen Walzer, Op. 63.   fl 2ob 2cl 2hn 2bn tp tb db timp.
AutoMS score (c.1850) & MS parts: D-Nehz, 74, No. 1.
WES-67a. Gung'l: Illustrirte-Polka, Op. 65.   fl 2ob 2cl 2hn 2bn tp tb db timp.
AutoMS score (c.1850) & MS parts: D-NEhz, 74, No. 12.
WES-68a. Gung'l: Ideal und Leben-Walzer, Op. 67.   fl 2ob 2cl 2hn 2bn tp tb db timp.
AutoMS score (c.1850) & MS parts: D-NEhz, 74, No. 17.
WES-69a. Gung'l: Träume auf dem Ocean Walzer, Op. 80.   fl 2ob 2cl 2hn 2bn tp tb db timp.
AutoMS score (c.1850) & MS parts: D-NEhz, 120, No. 14.
WES-70a. Gung'l: Klänge von Delaware Walzer, Op. 89.   fl 2ob 2cl 2hn 2bn tp tb db timp.
AutoMS score (c.1849) & MS parts: D-NEhz, 120, No. 13.

WES-71a. Gung'l: Columbinen-Galopp. fl 2ob 2cl 2hn 2bn tp tb db timp.
MS parts (c.1850): D-NEhz, 135, No. 3, (missing fl).
WES-72a. Gung'l: Gambrinus Polka. fl 2ob 2cl 2hn 2bn tp tb db timp.
MS parts (c.1850): D-NEhz, 135, No. 23, (missing fl).
WES-73a. Gung'l: Gazellen-Polka. fl 2ob 2cl 2hn 2bn tp tb db timp.
MS parts (c.1850): D-NEhz, 135, No. 21, (missing fl).
WES-74a. Gung'l: Grazien-Polka. fl 2ob 2cl 2hn 2bn tp tb db timp.
AutoMS score (c.1850) & MS parts: D-NEhz, 74, No. 11.
WES-75a. Gung'l: Schlesische Lieder Walzer. fl 2ob 2cl 2hn 2bn tp tb db timp.
AutoMS score (c.1850) & MS parts: D-NEhz, 74, No. 2.
WES-76a. Gung'l: Vagabonden Polka. fl 2ob 2cl 2hn 2bn tp tb db timp.
AutoMS score (c.1850) & MS parts: D-NEhz, 74, No. 9.
WES-77a. Gung'l: Vielliebchen Polka. fl 2ob 2cl 2hn 2bn tp tb db timp.
AutoMS score (c.1850) & MS parts: D-NEhz, 74, No. 13.
WES-78a. Gung'l: Wiederschen Walzer. fl 2ob 2cl 2hn 2bn tp tb db timp.
AutoMS score (c.1850) & MS parts: D-NEhz, 74, No. 14.
WES-79.1a. Halévy: La Juive, 4 mvts. fl 2ob 2cl 3hn 2bn tp tb timp.
AutoMS score (mvts dated between 10 March & 9 April 1840) & MS parts: D-NEhz, 60, Nos. 4 - 7, (hn III in
Nos. 4 - 6; tp in Nos. 4 - 6; timp in Nos. 4, 6 & 7). *Grand Trio ("Was wollt ihr thun"); Aria ("Das Toderurthel
sprich"); Duo, ("Blond und schön zum Entzücken"); romance ("Er kommt zurück").*
WES-79.2a. Halévy: La Juive, 4 mvts. fl 2ob 2cl 2hn 2bn tp tb timp.
AutoMS score (dated between 15 Sept 1841 & 6 Dec 1841) & MS parts: D-NEhz, 62, Nos. 6 - 9. *Recit & Aria,
Act III ("Nur allzu lang"); Trink-Chor Act I; Duett Act II ("Er ist's, ich fühle mich vernichtet"); Finale Act I.*
WES-80.1a. Halévy: Le guitarero, 3 mvts. fl 2ob 2cl 2hn 2bn tp tb db timp. AutoMS score (No. 3 dated
"Schl[a]w[entzi]tz. 6/1.[18]43") & MS parts: D-NEhz, 55, Nos. 1- 3, (tp in No. 2 only; timp in Nos. 1 & 2 only).
WES-80.2a. Halévy: Le guitarero, ensemble & chor ("Gnädiger Herr! Was sagen Sie!").
fl 2ob 2cl 2hn 2bn tp tb db timp. AutoMS score (c.1843) & MS pts: D-NEhz, 73, No. 5.
WES-81a. Halévy: Les Mousquetaires de la Reine, aria & ensemble. fl 2ob 2cl 2hn 2bn tp tb db timp.
AutoMS score (c.1847) & MS parts: D-NEhz, 67, Nos. 4 & 5.
WES-82a. Halévy: Le Val d'Andorre, overture & 3 mvts. fl 2ob 2cl 2hn 2bn tp tb db timp.
MS score & MS parts: D-NEhz, 88, Bd. 1, 1st (unnumbered) item & Nos. 1 - 3. *Nos. 1 -3: Chor & aria ("Seht
da die reizende Georgette", "Schl[a]w[enti]tz 19.4.[18]49"; Gesang der Ziegenhirten ("Ja der alte Zauberer");
Finale Act II ("Hallet ein, erfahrt wer diese ist").*
WES-83a. Haydn: Die Jahreszeiten, 2 Theils. fl 2ob 2cl 2hn 2bn 2tp(clar) tb db timp.
AutoMS score (11 Feb - 30 April 1842) & MS parts: D-Nehz, 16.
WES-84a. Hérold: unidentified overture. fl 2ob 2cl 2hn 2bn 2tp tb timp tri.
AutoMS score: D-NEhz, 201, No. 6. *Does not match any of Hérold's popular operas; possibly a misattribution.*
WES-85a. Hugo, Prinz von Hohenlohe-Öhringen: Bathy Massurka [sic].
fl 2ob 2cl 2hn 2bn tb db. AutoMS score (c.1840) & MS parts: D-NEhz, 107, No. 11.
WES-86a. Hugo, Prinz von Hohenlohe-Öhringen: Furuska Polka. fl 2ob 2cl 2hn 2bn 2tp tb db timp.
AutoMS score (c.1843) & MS parts: D-NEhz, 107, No. 20.
WES-87a. Hugo, Prinz von Hohenlohe-Öhringen: Masurek. fl 2ob 2cl 2hn 2bn tp tb db timp.
MS pts (c.1845): D-NEhz, 135, No. 15, (missing fl). *Attributed under Prince Hugo's pseudonym, "Siebeneicher".*
WES-88a. Hugo, Prinz von Hohenlohe-Öhringen: Melancolie-Polka, in C minor.
fl 2ob 2cl 2hn 2bn tp tb db. MS parts (c.1845): D-NEhz, 135, No. 1, (missing fl). *Attributed under Prince
Hugo's pseudonym, "Siebeneicher".*
WES-89a. Hugo, Prinz von Hohenlohe-Öhringen: Polka, in F. fl 2ob 2cl 2hn 2bn tp tb db timp.
MS parts (c.1845): D-NEhz, 135, No. 22, (missing fl).
WES-90a. Hugo, Prinz von Hohenlohe-Öhringen: Setimitäts Polka. fl 2ob 2cl 3hn 2bn 2tp tb db.
AutoMS score (c.1843) & MS parts: D-NEhz, 107, No. 7.
WES-91a. Hugo, Prinz von Hohenlohe-Öhringen: Sylvester Polka. fl 2ob 2cl 2hn 2bn tb db.
AutoMS score (c.1843) & MS parts: D-NEhz, 107, No. 12.
WES-92a. [attrib] Hugo, Prinz von Hohenlohe-Öhringen: Der Geisterbraut, 3 mvts. fl 2ob 2cl 2hn 2bn tp tb db.
AutoMS score (c.1842) & MS pts: D-Nehz, 107, Nos. 13 - 15. *Marsch; Walzer; Gallop. These mvts appear
to be interpolations in Eugen, Herzog von Württemberg's opera.*
WES-93a. [attrib] Hugo, Prinz von Hohenlohe-Öhringen: Anna Polka. fl 2ob 2cl 2hn 2bn 2tp tb db.
AutoMS score (c.1840) & MS parts: D-Nehz, 107, No. 8.
WES-94a. [attrib] Hugo, Prinz von Hohenlohe-Öhringen: Electricitäts-Polka. fl 2ob 2cl 2hn 2bn 2tp tb db timp.
AutoMS score (c.1843) & MS parts: D-Nehz, 107, No. 22.
WES-95a. [attrib] Hugo, Prinz von Hohenlohe-Öhringen: Mitternachts-Polka. fl 2ob 2cl 2hn 2bn 2tp tb db.
AutoMS score (c.1843) & MS parts: D-Nehz, 107, No. 9.
WES-96a. [attrib] Hugo, Prinz von Hohenlohe-Öhringen: Polka. fl 2ob 2cl 2hn 2bn 2tp tb db.
AutoMS score (c.1843) & MS parts: D-NEhz, 107, No. 23.
WES-97a. [attrib] Hugo, Prinz von Hohenlohe-Öhringen: Die Ungetauften, Mazurka.
fl 2ob 2cl 2hn 2bn tp tb db. AutoMS score (c.1843) & MS parts: D-NEhz, 107, No. 21.
WES-98a. Kalliwoda: Ouverture No. 1 in D minor, Op. 38. fl 2ob 2cl 2hn 2bn tb db.
MS score & parts: D-Nehz, 60, No. 8.
WES-99a. E. Köhler: Fest Ouverture, in E♭. fl 2ob 2cl 2hn 2bn tp tb db timp.
MS score (end of score: "Schl[a]w[entzi]tz 1.9.[18]44") & MS parts: D-NEhz, 87, Bd. 1, No. 5.
WES-100.1a. C. Kreutzer: Das Nachtlager in Granada, overture. fl 2ob 2cl 2hn 2bn tp tb db timp.
AutoMS score (c.1845) & MS parts: D-NEhz, 63, 2nd unnumbered item, ff. 33 - 62b.
WES-100.2a. C. Kreutzer: Das Nachtlager in Granada, romance. fl 2ob 2cl 2hn 2bn tb db.
MS score & parts: D-NEhz, 60, No. 9.

WES-100.3a. C. Kreutzer: Das Nachtlager in Granada, quintett. fl 2ob 2cl 3hn 2bn tb db timp.
AutoMS score (1841) & MS parts: D-NEhz, 58, No. 9, (parts missing cl I).
WES-101a. Kreuzenacher: Favorit-Polka, in F. fl 2ob 2cl 2hn 2bn tp tb db timp.
MS parts (c.1845): D-NEhz, 135, No. 2, (missing fl).
WES-102a. Kücken: Der Prätendent, overture & 3 Bands. fl 2ob 2cl 2hn 2bn tp tb db timp.
AutoMS score ("Im Jahre 1848 den 17ten Julij angefangen und Im Jahre 1849 den 14ten Januar mit Gottes Hilfe vollendet. Scholz.") & MS parts: D-NEhz, 52, (parts missing fl I & cl I; the timpani do not appear in the score).
WES-103a. Kühner: Erinnerungs-Galopp. fl 2ob 2cl 2hn 2bn tp tb db timp.
MS parts (c.1845): D-NEhz, 135, No. 1, (missing fl).
WES-104a. Kühner: Europa-Walzer. fl 2ob 2cl 3hn 2bn tb db timp.
AutoMS score (c.1843) & MS parts: D-NEhz, 107, No. 2.
WES-105a. Kühner: Hugo Galopp. fl 2ob 2cl 3hn 2bn tb db timp.
AutoMS score (c.1843) & MS parts: D-NEhz, 107, No. 4.
WES-106a. Laade: Künstler-Grüsse Walzer. fl 2ob 2cl 2hn 2bn tp tb db timp.
AutoMS score (c.1848) & MS parts: D-NEhz, 110, No. 2.
WES-107a. Labitzky: Charlotten Polka. fl 2ob 2cl 2hn 2bn tp tb db timp.
AutoMS score (c.1849) & MS parts: D-NEhz, 110, No. 9.
WES-108a. Labitzky: Druskeniky-Mazurka, Op. 101. fl 2ob 2cl 2hn 2bn tp tb db timp.
AutoMS score (c.1848) & MS parts: D-NEhz, 110, No. 9.
WES-109a. Labitzky: Kinder-Freuden Polka, Op. 115. fl 2ob 2cl 2hn 2bn tp tb db timp.
AutoMS score (c.1848) & MS parts: D-NEhz, 110, No. 8.
WES-110a. Labitzky: Seelen-Spiegel Walzer, Op. 126. fl 2ob 2cl 2hn 2bn tp tb db timp.
AutoMS score (c.1849) & MS parts: D-NEhz, 120, No. 7.
WES-111a. Labitzky: Esterhazy [sic] Walzer, Op. 129. fl 2ob 2cl 2hn 2bn tp tb db timp.
MS parts (c.1845): D-NEhz, 135, No. 8, (missing fl).
WES-112a. Labitzky: Carlsbader-Sprudel Galop, Op. 131. fl 2ob 2cl 2hn 2bn tp tb db timp.
AutoMS score (c.1840 & MS parts: D-NEhz, 74, No. 10.
WES-113a. Labitzky: Seraphinen Quadrille, Op. 135. fl 2ob 2cl 2hn 2bn tp tb db timp.
AutoMS score (c.1848) & MS parts: D-NEhz, 110, No. 6.
WES-114a. Labitzky: Sträusschen am Wege Walzer, Op. 143. fl 2ob 2cl 2hn 2bn tp tb db timp.
MS parts (c.1847): D-NEhz, 135, No. 9, (missing fl).
WES-115a. Labitzky: Liverpool-Walzer, (1846). fl 2ob 2cl 2hn 2bn tp tb db timp.
AutoMS score (c.1848) & MS parts: D-NEhz, 110, No. 4.
WES-116a. Labitzky: Liebes-Grüsse Walzer, (1847). fl 2ob 2cl 2hn 2bn tp tb db timp.
AutoMS score (c.1847 & MS parts: D-NEhz, 74, No. 15.
WES-117a. Labitzky: Mödlinger-Polka. fl 2ob 2cl 2hn 2bn tp tb db timp.
AutoMS score (c.1847) & MS parts: D-NEhz, 74, No. 1.
WES-118a. Labitzky: Polka, in G (unidentified). fl 2ob 2cl 2hn 2bn tp tb db timp.
AutoMS score (c.1849) & MS parts: D-NEhz, 120, No. 10.
WES-119a. Labitzky: Polka, in E♭ (unidentified). fl 2ob 2cl 2hn 2bn tp tb db timp.
AutoMS score (c.1849) & MS parts: D-NEhz, 120, No. 11.
WES-120.1a. Lachner: Katherina Cornaro, finale. fl 2ob 2cl 2hn 2bn tp tb db timp.
AutoMS score ("Schl[a]w[entzi]tz 29.11.[18]46") & MS parts: D-NEhz, 67, No. 3.
WES-120.2a. Lachner: Katherina Cornaro, aria ("Wie leben auf") & Act II finale ("Wie? Hab ich recht verstanden"). fl 2ob 2cl 2hn 2bn tp tb db timp. AutoMS score (c.1845) & MS pts: D-NEhz, 76, Nos. 1 & 2.
WES-121a. Lanner: Die Aelpler, Walzer, Op. 124. fl 2ob 2cl 2hn 2bn tp tb db.
AutoMS score (c.1843) & MS parts: D-NEhz, 107, No. 24.
WES-122a. Lanner: Die Abendsterne, Walzer, Op. 129. fl 2ob 2cl 2hn 2bn tp tb db timp.
AutoMS score (c.1843) & MS parts: D-NEhz, 107, No. 29.
WES-123a. K.G. Lickl: Bravour Galopp. fl 2ob 2cl 2hn 2bn tp tb db.
AutoMS score (c.1843) & MS parts: D-NEhz, 107, No. 26.
WES-124a. Lieder: Ruda-Klänge Masurka [sic]. fl 2ob 2cl 2hn 2bn tp tb db.
AutoMS score (c.1849) & MS parts: D-NEhz, 120, No. 12.
WES-125a. Lindpaintner: Faust, overture. fl 2ob 2cl 3hn 2bn tb db timp.
AutoMS score (c.1839) & MS parts: D-NEhz, 29, No. 9, (parts missing cl I).
WES-126a. Litolff: Die Braut von Kynast, overture. 2ob 2cl 2hn 2bn tp tb vla vc db timp.
AutoMS score (c.1848/49) & MS parts: D-NEhz, 24.
WES-127.1a. Lortzing: Der Waffenschmied, overture. fl 2ob 2cl 2hn 2bn tp tb vla db timp.
AutoMS score (c.1847) & MS parts: D-NEhz, 72, No. 3.
WES-127.2a. Lortzing: Der Waffenschmied, 3 mvts. fl 2ob 2cl 2hn 2bn tp tb db timp.
AutoMS score (c.1846) & MS parts: D-NEhz, 67, Nos. 7 - 9. *Introduction; Aria ("Man wird ja einmal nur geboren"); Finale Act I.*
WES-128a. Lumbye: Fest-Galopp. fl 2ob 2cl 2hn 2bn tp tb db timp.
AutoMS score (c.1848) & MS parts: D-NEhz, 110, No. 11.
WES-129a. Lumbye: Der Günstlings-Walzer. fl 2ob 2cl 2hn 2bn tp tb db timp.
AutoMS score (c.1848) & MS parts: D-NEhz, 110, No. 12.
WES-130a. Marschner: Der Vampyr, 5 mvts. fl 2ob 2cl 2hn 2bn tp tb db timp.
AutoMS score (May 1843) & MS parts: D-NEhz, 65, Nos. 9 - 13, (Nos. 9, 11 & 12 without timp; Nos. 11 & 12 without tp; No. 12 with hn III). *Duett ("Du bist's, es ist kein Traum"); Terzett ("Ihr wollt mich nur beschämen"); Aria ("Wie ein schöner Frühlingsmorgen"); Trinklied und Quintett mit Chor ("Im Herbst da muss man trinken"); Duett ("Halt ein").*
WES-131a. Marschner: Der Bäbu, 5 mvts. fl 2ob 2cl 2hn 2bn tp tb db timp. MS score (1849) & MS parts: D-NEhz, 88, Bd. 2, Nos. 6 - 10. *Introduzione; duett; romance & aria; finale (2 sections).*

WES-132a. Mendelssohn-Bartholdy: Ein Sommernachtstraume, marsch. fl 2ob 2cl 2hn 2bn tp tb db timp.
AutoMS score (1845) & MS parts: D-NEhz, 69, No. 4.
WES-133a. Mendelssohn-Bartholdy: Sechs Lieder ohne Worte, Op. 19, Nos. 1 (Andante con moto), 3 (Molto
Allegro vivace) & 6 (Venetianisches Goldellied, Andante sostenuto), "Schl[a]w[entzi]tz. 18/6.[18]39, 33tes
Argmt". fl 2ob 2cl 2hn 2bn tb db. AutoMS score (end of No. 5: "Schlwtz 19/6.39"; end of No. 7: "Schlwtz.
21/6.39") & MS parts: D-Nehz, 68, Nos. 5 - 7.
WES-134a. Mendelssohn-Bartholdy: Die Hebriden (as "Fingals Höhle"), Op. 26, Schl[a]w[entzi[tz 14/11.[18]39.
fl 2ob 2cl 3hn 2bn tp tb db timp. AutoMS score (end of score "Schlawentitz. d. 23 Nvbr. 1839") & MS parts:
D-NEhz, 60, 1st (unnumbered) item.
WES-135a. Mendelssohn-Bartholdy: Meeresstille und glückliche Fahrt, overture, Op. 27; Schl[a]w[entzi]tz. d
19ten 12/[18]39. fl 2ob 2cl 3hn 2bn tp tb db timp.
AutoMS score (end of score: "Vollendet d. 12/1.[18]40") & MS parts: D-NEhz, 60, 2nd (unnumbered) item.
WES-136a. Mendelssohn-Bartholdy: Der schönen Melusine, overture, Op. 32. fl 2ob 2cl 3hn 2bn tp tb db timp.
AutoMS score ("Schl[a]w[entzi]tz 23.6.[18]41") & MS parts: D-NEhz, 29, 1st (unnumbered) arrangement, (parts
missing cl I).
WES-137a. Mercadante: Il Bravo, terzett & finale. fl 2ob 2cl 3hn 2bn 2tp tb db timp.
AutoMS score (end dated "Vollendet Schl[a]w[entzi]tz. 10.6.[18]45") & MS parts: D-NEhz, 64, Nos. 8 & 9.
WES-138.1a. Meyerbeer: Les Huguenots, overture & 2 Bands. fl 2ob 2cl 3hn 2bn tp tb db timp.
AutoMS score (beginning: "Schl[a]w[entzi]tz d. 25/6.[18]39"; end: "Schlawentzitz d. 7ten October 1839
vollendet.") & MS parts: D-NEhz, 25, (parts missing fl; the tp & timp do not appear in the score).
WES-138.2a. Meyerbeer: Les Huguenots, romance & chor. fl 2ob 2cl 3hn 2bn tb db.
MS score & parts: D-Nehz, 60, No. 12.
WES-139a. Meyerbeer: Ein Feldlager in Schlesien, overture. fl 2ob 2cl 2hn 2bn tp tb db timp.
AutoMS score (c.1847) & MS parts: D-NEhz, 72, No. 6.
WES-140.1a. Meyerbeer: Struensee, overture. fl 2ob 2cl 2hn 2bn tp tb db timp.
AutoMS score (26.9.[18]47) & MS parts: D-NEhz, 11, Bd. 2, No. 10, (parts missing fl).
WES-140.2a. Meyerbeer: Struensee, 2 mvts. fl 2ob 2cl 2hn 2bn tp tb db timp. AutoMS score (c.1847) &
MS parts: D-NEhz, 72, Nos. 4 & 5. *2ter Zwischenakt, polonaise; 1ter Zwischenakt der Aufruhr.*
WES-141a. Meyerbeer: Le Prophète, overture & 2 Bds. fl 2ob 2cl 2hn 2bn tp tb db timp.
AutoMS score (beginning dated 29 Oct 1849) & MS parts: D-NEhz, 78.
WES-142a. Mozart: Idomeneo, quartett ("Andrò ramingo"). fl 2ob 2cl 2hn 2bn tb db.
AutoMS score (c.1839) & MS parts: D-NEhz, 29, No. 10, (parts missing cl I).
WES-143a. Mozart: La Nozze di Figaro, terzett ("Cosa sento, tosto andate"). fl 2ob 2cl 2hn 2bn tb db.
AutoMS score ("Schl[a]w[entzi]tz 17/7.[18]41") & MS parts: D-NEhz, 29, No. 3, (parts missing cl I).
WES-144a. Mozart: Don Giovanni, 2 arias, ("In quali eccessi, o Numi"; "Batti, Batti").
fl 2ob 2cl 3hn 2bn tp tb db timp. AutoMS score (No. 11: "Schl[a]w[entzi]tz19/5.[18]41"; end of score: "Schlztz.
21/5.41"; No. 12, end of score: "26/5.41") & MS parts: D-NEhz, Nos. 11 & 12, (parts missing cl I).
WES-145a. Mozart: Symphony in G minor, (K.550), "Schl[a]w[entzi]tz d. 27/5.[18]39, [unmarked]-tes
Arrangement. fl 2ob 2cl 3hn 2bn tb db. AutoMS score (dated between 27 May & 11 June 1839) & MS parts:
D-NEhz, 68, Bd. 2, 2nd (unnumbered) item.
WES-146a. Nicolai: Gildippe e Odoardo, cavatine ("Ach ewig füllt die Seele"). fl 2ob 2cl 2hn 2bn tp tb db.
AutoMS score (1847) & MS parts: D-NEhz, 11, Bd. 2, No. 14, (parts missing fl).
WES-147a. Nicolai: Il Proscritto, Introduzion. fl 2ob 2cl 2hn 2bn tp tb db timp.
AutoMS score (c.1846 - 1847) & MS parts: D-NEhz, 67, No. 6.
WES-148a. Offenbach: [unidentified] Polka. fl 2ob 2cl 3hn 2bn tb db.
AutoMS score (c.1843) & MS parts: D-NEhz, 107, No. 35.
WES-149a. Olbrich: Polon[e]se. fl 2ob 2cl 3hn 2bn tb db timp.
AutoMS score (c.1843) & MS parts: D-Nehz, 107, No. 6.
WES-150a. Paer: Camilla, introduzione, 15tes Arrangement. Schl[a]w[entzi]tz d. 25/2.[18]39.
fl 2ob 2cl 3hn 2bn tp tb db timp. AutoMS score (end of score: "Schlwtz. d. 1/3.39") & MS parts: D-NEhz, 59,
No. 2, (parts missing fl).
WES-151a. Prochaska: Theresien-Polka. fl 2ob 2cl 2hn 2bn tp tb db.
AutoMS score (c.1843) & MS parts: D-NEhz, 107, No. 10.
WES-152a. Raymond: Wintergarten-Polka. fl 2ob 2cl 2hn 2bn tp tb db timp.
MS parts (c.1845): D-NEhz, 135, No. 10, (missing fl).
WES-153a. Reissiger: Adele de Foix: terzett ("Was doch so ein Man thut") & aria ("Wie sehnt mein Herz zurück
sich"). fl 2ob 2cl 2hn 2bn tp tb db timp. AutoMS score & MS parts: D-NEhz, 65, Nos. 3 & 4.
WES-154a. Righini: Tigrane, Rè d'Armenia, overture. fl 2ob 2cl 3hn 2bn tp tb db timp.
AutoMS score ("Schl[a]w[enti]tz 6/9.[18]40"; end of score: "Schlwtz 8/9.40") & MS parts: D-NEhz, 58, No. 1,
(parts missing cl I).
WES-155.1a. Rossini: Otello, finale Act III, "13tes Arrangement, Schlawentzitz d. 6/2.[18]39."
fl 2ob 2cl 3hn 2bn tp tb db timp. AutoMS score (end of score: "Schlwntz. d. 13/2.39") & MS parts: D-NEhz,
59, No. 1, (parts missing fl).
WES-155.2a. Rossini: Otello, finale Act III, "Schl[a]w[entzi]tz. 12/6.39, 32tes Arrangement". fl 2ob 2cl 3hn
2bn tp tb db timp. AutoMS score (end of score: "Schlwtz. 17/6.39") & MS parts: D-NEhz, 68, Bd. 1, No. 4.
WES-156a. Rossini: La Cenerentola, 5 mvts. fl 2ob 2cl 2hn 2bn tp tb db timp.
Auto MS score (No. 8 dated 7 Sept 1842) & MS parts: D-NEhz, 55, Nos. 4 - 8.
WES-157.1a. Rossini: Mosè in Egitto, 4 mvts. fl 2ob 2cl 2hn 2bn tp tb db timp.
AutoMS score (1843) & MS parts: D-NEhz, 57, Nos. 1 - 4, (timp in Nos. 1, 2 & 4 only).
WES-157.2a. Rossini: Mosè in Egitto, invocazione ("O Ewger, Erhabner") & Duett ("Ach kannt du so von mir
scheiden"). fl 2ob 2cl 2hn 2bn tp tb db timp. AutoMS score (1843) & MS parts: D-NEhz, 65, Nos. 6 & 7.
WES-158a. Rossini: Le Comte Ory, Act II finale, 2 sections ("Nun enthüllt", & "Ach, Amor, sei von stiller
Nacht unfangen"). fl 2ob 2cl 2hn 2bn tp tb db timp.
AutoMS score (end of No. 4: "Schl[a]w[entzi]tz 5.9.[18]43") & MS parts: D-NEhz, 73, Nos. 3 & 4.

WES-159.1a. Rossini: Guillaume Tell, overture, introduzione & 1 aria.   fl 2ob 2cl 3hn 2bn tb db timp.
AutoMS score (1839) & MS parts: D-NEhz, 29, Nos. 11, 6 & 7, (parts missing cl I).
WES-159.2a. Rossini: Guillaume Tell, 2 Bds.   fl 2ob 2cl 2hn 2bn tp tb db timp.
AutoMS score (1842-43) & MS parts: D-NEhz, 40b, (styled "Fortsetzung", i.e. continuation).
WES-160a. Rossini: unidentifed duett.   fl 2ob 2cl 2hn 2bn tb db.
AutoMS score & MS parts: D-Nehz, 60, No. 11.
WES-161a. Schubert: Fierrabras, overture, Op. 76.   fl 2ob 2cl 2hn 2bn tp tb db timp.
AutoMS score (beginning: "Schl[a]w[entzi]tz. d. 26ten April 1843; end: "Schlwtz. 3.5.43") & MS parts:
D-NEhz, 65, No. 8.
WES-162a. Seyfried: Faust, overture, Schl[a]w[entzi]tz. 1.11.[18]44.   fl 2ob 2cl 3hn 2bn 2tp tb db timp.
AutoMS score (end dated 6.11.[18]44) & MS parts: D-NEhz, 64, No. 2.
WES-163a. Spohr: Alruna, overture.   fl 2ob 2cl 2hn 2bn tp tb db timp.
AutoMS score (c.1845) & MS parts: D-NEhz, 71, 2nd (unnumbered) item.
WES-164.1a. Spohr: Faust, overture.   fl 2ob 2cl 2hn 2bn tp tb db timp.
AutoMS score (c.1845) & MS parts: D-NEhz, 71, 1st (unnumbered) item.
WES-164.2a. Spohr: Faust, scene & chor ("Lang mögen die Theuren leben"), "14tes Arrangement.
Schl[a]w[entzi]tz d. 16/2.[18]39.   fl 2ob 2cl 3hn 2bn tp tb db timp.
AutoMS score (end of score: "Schlwtz. 25/2.39") & MS parts: D-NEhz, 59, No. 3.
WES-164.3a. Spohr: Faust, introduction ("Ja Sinnenlust"), "Schl[a]w[entzi]tz. d. 21/6.[18]39, 34tes
Arr[an]g[ement]".   fl 2ob 2cl 3hn 2bn tb db timp.   AutoMS score (end of score: "Schlwtz. d. 24/6.39") &
MS parts: D-NEhz, 68, Bd. 1, No. 3.
WES-164.4a. Spohr: Faust, aria with chorus ("Beflügle deinen Lauf").   fl 2ob 2cl 2hn 2bn tp tb db timp.
MS score (front of score: "19.6.[18]49") & MS pts: D-NEhz, 88, Bd. 1, No. 4.
WES-164.5a. Spohr: Faust, sextet & aria.   2ob 2cl 2hn 2bn tp tb db timp.
AutoMS score ("Finis 15.4.[18]49") & MS parts: D-NEhz, 24/2.
WES-165.1a. Spohr: Jessonda, overture, "Schl[a]w[entzi]tz 19.4.[18]39, 26tes Arr[an]g[e]m[en]t.
fl 2ob 2cl 3hn 2bn tp tb db timp.
AutoMS score (end of score: "Schlwtz. d. 23/4.39") & MS parts: D-NEhz, 68, Bd. 1, 1st (unnumbered) item.
WES-165.2a. Spohr: Jessonda, introductione.   fl 2ob 2cl 2hn 2bn tb db.   MS score & pts: D-NEhz, 60, No. 10.
WES-165.3a. Spohr: Jessonda, duet ("Schönes Mädchen, wirst mich hassen").   fl 2ob 2cl 2hn 2bn tb db.
AutoMS score & MS parts: D-NEhz, 29, No. 1, (parts missing cl I).
WES-166a. Spohr: Des Heilands letzte Stunden, WoO 62, aria ("Ewig fliesset meine Zähren").
fl 2ob 2cl 2hn 2bn tb db.   AutoMS score (1842) & MS parts: D-NEhz, 70, No. 9.
WES-167.1a. Spontini: La Vestale, 3 mvts.   fl 2ob 2cl 2hn 2bn tp tb db timp.
AutoMS score (dated between 7 June & 2 July 1842) & MS parts: D-NEhz, Nos. 1 - 3. *Finale Act II ("Ach,
wenn in deinem Herzen"); Act III, ("Bald übt Nemesis"); finale Act III ("Er ist neber ungeweihter Stelle").*
WES-167.2a. Spontini: La Vestale, ensemble & finale.   fl 2ob 2cl 2hn 2bn tp tb db timp.
Auto MS score (1843) & parts: D-NEhz, 57, No. 5.
WES-168a. Spontini: Fernand Cortez, overture & 1 Band.   fl 2ob 2cl 3hn 2bn tp tb db timp.
AutoMS score ("Schl[awenti]tz. d. 25/4.[18]40"; end: "Vollendet Schlwtz. 6/6.42") & MS pts: D-NEhz, 45b.
WES-169a. Spontini: Olympie, overture.   fl 2ob 2cl 2hn 2bn tp tb db timp.
AutoMS score (end of score: "Schl[a]w[entzi]tz 7.6.[18]47.") & MS parts: D-NEhz, 72, No. 7.
WES-170a. Spontini: Sieges- und Festmarsch, in C.   fl 2ob 2cl 2hn 2bn tp tb vc db timp.
AutoMS score (c.1847) & MS parts: D-NEhz, 72, 1st (unnumbered) item.
WES-171a. Strauss the Elder: Heimat-Klänge Walzer, Op. 84, ("Schlawentzitz d. 1t 1obr 1838, 7tes
Arrangement".   fl 2ob 2cl 3hn 2bn tb db.
AutoMS score (end: "Schlawentzitz d. 7ten 1obr 1838") & MS parts: D-NEhz, 151.
WES-172a. Strauss the Elder: Künstler-Ball-Tänze, Op. 94.   fl 2ob 2cl 2hn 2bn tp tb db timp.
AutoMS score (c.1840) & MS parts: D-NEhz, 74, No. 3.
WES-173a. Strauss the Elder: Brusseler Spitzen-Walzer, Op. 95.   fl 2ob 2cl 2hn 2bn tp tb db timp.
MS parts (c.1845): D-NEhz, 135, No. 6, (missing fl).
WES-174a. Strauss the Elder: Rosenblätter Walzer, Op. 115.   fl 2ob 2cl 3hn 2bn tb db.
AutoMS score (c.1843) & MS parts: D-NEhz, 107, No. 2.
WES-175a. Strauss the Elder: Beliebte Annen-Polka, Op. 137.   fl 2ob 2cl 2hn 2bn tp tb db.
AutoMS score (c.1843) & MS parts: D-NEhz, 107, No. 35.
WES-176a. Strauss the Elder: Haut-Volée-Quadrille, Op. 142.   fl 2ob 2cl 2hn 2bn tp tb db.
MS parts (c.1845): D-NEhz, 135, No. 7, (missing fl).
WES-177a. Strauss the Elder: Walhalla-Toaste-Walzer, Op. 147.   fl 2ob 2cl 2hn 2bn tp tb db timp.
AutoMS score (c.1843) & MS parts: D-NEhz, 107, No. 30.
WES-178a. Strauss the Elder: Wilkommen-Rufe Walzer, Op. 168.   fl 2ob 2cl 2hn 2bn tp tb db timp.
MS parts (c.1845): D-NEhz, 135, No. 14, (missing fl).
WES-179a. Strauss the Elder: Maskenlieder Walzer, Op. 170.   fl 2ob 2cl 2hn 2bn tp tb db timp.
MS parts (c.1845): D-NEhz, 135, No. 13, (missing fl).
WES-180a. Strauss the Elder: Eunomien-Tänze, Op. 171.   fl 2ob 2cl 2hn 2bn tp tb db timp.
MS parts (c.1845): D-NEhz, 135, No. 20, (missing fl).
WES-181a. Strauss the Elder: Flora-Quadrille, Op. 177.   fl 2ob 2cl 2hn 2bn tp tb db timp.
MS parts (c.1845): D-NEhz, 135, No. 18, (missing fl).
WES-182a. Strauss the Elder: Sommernachts-Träume Walzer, Op. 180.   fl 2ob 2cl 2hn 2bn tp tb db timp.
MS parts (c.1845): D-NEhz, 135, No. 19, (missing fl).
WES-183a. Strauss the Elder: Amoretten-Quadrille, Op. 183.   fl 2ob 2cl 2hn 2bn tp tb db timp.
AutoMS score (c.1849) & MS parts: D-NEhz, 120, No. 2.

WES-184a. Strauss the Elder: Bouquets Walzer, Op. 197. fl 2ob 2cl 2hn 2bn tp tb db timp.
AutoMS score (c.1847) & MS parts: D-NEhz, 74, No. 4.
WES-185a. Strauss the Elder: Themis-Klänge Walzer, Op. 201. fl 2ob 2cl 2hn 2bn tp tb db timp.
AutoMS score (c.1848) & MS parts: D-NEhz, 110, No. 5.
WES-186a. Strauss the Elder: Eisele- und Beisele-Sprünge Polka, Op. 202. fl 2ob 2cl 2hn 2bn tp tb db timp.
AutoMS score (c.1848) & MS parts: D-NEhz, 110, No. 7.
WES-187a. Strauss the Elder: Herz-Töne Walzer, Op. 203. fl 2ob 2cl 2hn 2bn tp tb db timp.
AutoMS score (c.1848) & MS parts: D-NEhz, 110, No. 1.
WES-188a. Strauss the Elder: Helenen-Walzer, Op. 204. fl 2ob 2cl 2hn 2bn tp tb db timp.
AutoMS score (c.1848) & MS parts: D-NEhz, 110, No. 10.
WES-189a. Strauss the Elder: Triumph-Quadrille, Op. 205. fl 2ob 2cl 2hn 2bn tp tb db timp.
AutoMS score (c.1848) & MS parts: D-NEhz, 110, No. 2.
WES-190a. Strauss the Elder: Najaden-Quadrille, Op. 206 (16 mvts). fl 2ob 2cl 2hn 2bn tp tb db timp.
AutoMS score (c.1848) & MS parts: D-NEhz, 74, No. 6
WES-191a. Strauss the Elder: Schwedische Lieder Walzer, Op. 207. fl 2ob 2cl 2hn 2bn tp tb db timp.
MS score (c.1848) & MS parts: D-NEhz, 74, No. 5.
WES-192a. Strauss the Elder: Marien-Walzer, Op. 212. fl 2ob 2cl 2hn 2bn tp tb db timp.
AutoMS score (c.1848) & MS parts: D-NEhz, 110, No. 13.
WES-193a. Strauss the Elder: Martha Quadrille, Op. 215. fl 2ob 2cl 2hn 2bn tp tb db timp.
AutoMS score (c.1849) & MS parts: D-NEhz, 120, No. 3.
WES-194a. Strauss the Elder: Sorgenbrecher Walzer, Op. 230. fl 2ob 2cl 2hn 2bn tp tb db timp.
AutoMS score (c.1849) & MS parts: D-NEhz, 120, No. 1.
WES-195a. Strauss the Elder: Louisen-Quadrille, Op. 234. fl 2ob 2cl 2hn 2bn tp tb db timp.
AutoMS score (c.1849) & MS parts: D-NEhz, 120, No. 8.
WES-196a. Thomas: Le Panier fleuri, overture, Schl[a]w[entzi]tz 21.10.[18]44.
fl 2ob 2cl 3hn 2bn 2tp tb db timp. AutoMs score (end: "Schlwtz. 1.11.44") & MS parts: D-NEhz, 63, No. 1.
WES-197a. Verdi: Oberto di San Bonifazio, cavatine & finale. fl 2ob 2cl 2hn 2bn tp tb db timp.
AutoMS score (c.1845) & MS parts: D-NEhz, 76, Nos. 3 & 4.
WES-198.1a. Verdi: I Lombardi alla prima crociata, 6 mvts. fl 2ob 2cl 2hn 2bn tp tb db timp.
AutoMS score (c.1845) & MS parts: D-NEhz, 71, Nos. 1 - 6, (timpani tacet in Nos. 1 & 4). *Scene & cavatina; grand scene (Andante); scene; coro della prozession; duett; terzett.*
WES-198.2a. Verdi: I Lombardi alla prima corciata, 4 mvts. fl 2ob 2cl 2hn 2bn tp tb db timp.
AutoMS score (c.1845) & MS parts: D-NEhz, 76, Nos. 5 - 8. *Praeludio e Coro, Chor e Aria, Preghiera, finale.*
WES-199.1a. Verdi: Ernani, overture & 2 Bds. fl 2ob 2cl 2hn 2bn tp tb db timp.
AutoMS score (20 Aug - 6 Dec 1845) & parts: D-NEhz, 48, (the timpani do not appear in the score).
WES-199.2a. Verdi: Ernani, overture & 2 Bds. fl 2ob 2cl 2hn 2bn tp tb db timp. AutoMS score (end Bd 2: "Schl[a]w[entzi]tz 24.11.[18]46") & parts (end: "d. 28ten Feb. [18]47"): D-NEhz, 47, (parts missing fl & cl I).
WES-200a. Verdi: Macbeth, overture & 2 Bds. 2ob 2cl 2hn 2bn tp tb db timp.
AutoMS score (beginning: "28.2.[18]48"; end: "Mit Gottes hilfe d. 22ten Maerz 1849") & parts: D-NEhz, 24.
WES-201a. B.A. Weber: Der Ganz nach dem Eisenhammer, 1 mvt. fl 2ob 2cl 2hn 2bn tp tb db timp.
AutoMS score ("Schl[a]w[entzi]tz d. 24/1.[18]41") & MS parts: D-NEhz, 58, No. 4, (parts missing cl I).
WES-202.1a. C.M. von Weber: Der Beherrischer der Geister, overture, Schl[a]w[entzi]tz. 7/3.[18]39, 17tes Arrangement. fl 2ob 2cl 3hn 2bn tp tb db timp.
AutoMS score (end of score: "Schlwtz. 11/3.39") & MS parts: D-NEhz, 59, No. 5, (pts missing fl).
WES-202.2a. C.M. von Weber: Der Beherrischer der Geister, overture. fl 2ob 2cl 2hn 2bn tp tb db timp.
AutoMS score (1847) & MS parts: D-NEhz, 11, Band 2, No. 13, (parts missing fl).
WES-203.1a. C.M. von Weber: Euryanthe, finale Act I, "Schl[a]w[entzi]tz. 1/5.39, 28tes Arrangement.
fl 2ob 2cl 3hn 2bn tp tb db timp.
AutoMS score (end of score: "Schlwtz. d. 6ten Maij 1839") & MS parts: D-NEhz, 68, Bd. 1, No. 2.
WES-203.2a. C.M. von Weber: Euryanthe, scene & aria ("Wo berg ich mich"), "Schl[a]w[entzi]tz. 1/5.[18]39, 29tes Arrangement. fl 2ob 2cl 3hn 2bn tp tb db timp.
AutoMS score (end of score: "Schlwtz. 1/5.39") & MS parts: D-NEhz, 68, Bd. 1, No. 3.
WES-203.3a. C.M. von Weber: Euryanthe, cavatina ("Glöcllein im Thale"). fl 2ob 2cl 2hn 2bn tb db.
AutoMS score (1839) & MS parts: D-NEhz, 29, No. 5, (parts missing cl I).
WES-203.4a. C.M. von Weber: Euryanthe, aria ("Wehen mir Lüfte"). fl 2ob 2cl 2hn 2bn tb db.
AutoMS score (end: "Schl[a]w[entzi]tz 3/3.40") & MS parts: D-NEhz, 60, No. 2.
WES-203.5a. von Weber: Euryanthe, scene & cavatine ("So bin ich nun verlassen" - "Hier dicht am Quelle") & Finale Act II, ("Leuchtend fällt die Königshalle"). fl 2ob 2cl 2hn 2bn tp tb db timp.
AutoMS score (No. 9: "Schl[a]w[entzi]tz. 13.1.[18]43"; No. 10: "d.29/1.[18]43") & MS parts: D-NEhz, 55, Nos. 9 & 10.
WES-203.6a. C.M. von Weber: Euryanthe, Act I introduzion ("Dem Frieden Heil"). fl 2ob 2cl 2hn 2bn tp tb db timp. AutoMS score (end of score: "Schl[a]w[entzi]tz. 30.9.[18]43") & MS parts: D-NEhz, 73, No. 6.
WES-204a. C.M. von Weber: Oberon, overture. fl 2ob 2cl 2hn 2bn tb db timp.
MS parts: D-NEhz, 50, (following Schmitt's arrangement of the opera).
WES-205a. C.M. von Weber: Piano Sonata No. 2 in A♭, Op. 39, Capriccioso. fl 2ob 2cl 2hn 2bn tb db.
AutoMS score & MS parts: D-NEhz, 62, No. 4.
WES-206a. C.M. von Weber: Rondo brillant, Aufforderung zum Tanze, Op. 65. Schl[a]w[entzi]tz. 3/4.[1842].
fl 2ob 2cl 2hn 2bn tp tb db timp. AutoMS score & MS parts: D-NEhz, 62, No. 2.
WES-207a. Winter: Tamerlan, overture. fl 2ob 2cl 3hn 2bn tp tb db timp.
AutoMS score ("Schl[a]w[entzi]tz 13/5.[18]41"; end of score: "Schlwtz. d. 18/5.41") & MS parts: D-NEhz, 58, No. 10, (parts missing cl I).

SCHOONENBEEK, Kees *1947, Netherlands*
KES-1. Rijp en groen. 2fl 2cl s-sax a-sax 2hn bn tp 2tb piano.
Pm (Donemus: Amsterdam, 1980), score.

*SCHRECK, Gustav E. *9 Sept 1849, Zeulenroda - 22 Jan 1918, Leipzig*
*GZS-1. Nonet Divertimento, in E, Op. 40; 4 mvts. 2fl ob 2cl(A) 2hn 2bn.
Pc (Breitkopf & Härtel: Leipzig, 1905), score (pn Part.B.1837) & parts (K.M.1576/77): D-Bhm, 9984/9985;
I-Mc, Da Camera A.123.4; US-Wc, M957.S37 op. 40. ★
Pm (Compusic: Amsterdam, pn 225, 1990), score & parts.

SCHRIER (SCHREJER), ( ) *(1780)*
QQS-1v. Messe in C, "Die 15 - 18 Juny 1807". ATTBB, 2fl 2cl 2hn 2tp(clar) basso.
MS parts (from the Trenčín church collection): SK-BRnm, Mus.XIII.172. ★

*SCHROEDER, H.B. *(1760)*
HBS-1m. A favorite Slow March...Dedicated (by W.W. Jones) To the Earl of Radnor. 2cl 2hn 2bn tp serp timp.
Pc (Printed and Sold for the Author by Longman and Broderip: London, c.1795), RISM [S 2144], score: GB-Gu;
GB-Lbl, g.133.(56); GB-Ob, Mus.Instr.I.213(11). ★
HBS-2m. A favorite Quick March...Dedicated (by W.W. Jones) To the Earl of Radnor. 2cl 2hn 2bn tp serp timp.
Pc (Printed and Sold for the Author by Longman and Broderip: London, c.1795), RISM [S 2141], score: GB-Gu;
GB-Lbl, g.133.(54); GB-Ob, Mus.Voc.51(34). ★
HBS-3m. The West London Militia Slow March. 2cl 2hn 2bn tp serp timp.
Pc (Culliford, Rolfe, & Barrow: London, c.1796), RISM [S 2147], score: GB-Lbl, g.133.(53);
GB-Ob, Mus.Instr.I.213(14). ★
HBS-4m. The West London Militia Quick March. 2cl 2hn 2bn tp serp timp.
Pc (Culliford, Rolfe, & Barrow: London, c.1796), RISM [S 2146], score: GB-Lbl, g.133.(58);
GB-Ob, Mus.Instr.I.213.(9). ★
HBS-5m. Troop March Composed for the Berkshire Militia . . . at the request of W.W. Jones, Late of the
Berkshire Band. 2cl 2hn 2bn tp.
Pc (Printed for the Author by Longman and Broderip: London, c.1795), RISM [S 2145], score:
GB-Lbl, g.133.(56); GB-Ob, Mus.Instr.I.213(8); GB-Ljag, (modern MS); GB-DOTams, (modern MS score & pts). ★
HBS-6m. Quick March Composed for the Berkshire Militia . . . at the request of W.W. Jones, Late of the
Berkshire Band. 2cl 2hn 2bn tp.
Pc (Printed for the Author by Longman and Broderip: London, c.1795), RISM [S 2143], score:
GB-Lbl, g.133.(57); GB-Ob, Mus.Instr.I.213(3); GB-Ljag, (modern MS score); GB-DOTams (modern MS score
& parts); GB-Lhumphries (MS score & parts). ★
HBS-7m. A favorite Quick March . . . Dedicated to . . . the Duke of York. 2cl 2hn 2bn tp serp timp.
Pc (Printed and Sold for the Author by Longman and Broderip: London, 1795), RISM [S 2140], score:
GB-Lbl, g.133.(55); GB-Ob, Mus.Instr.I.213(10). ★
HBS-8m. A Favorite Quick March . . . Dedicated to His Royal Highness The Duke of Clarence.
2cl 2hn 2bn tp serp timp.
Pc (sn: sl [London], c.1795 - 1800), RISM [S 2142], score: GB-Lbl, h.1567.yy.(3). ★
*HBS-1mv. The Sussex Yeomanry Cavalry. The Words by Arthur Lee: "Since Virgil wrote in Yeoman's
praise . . ."; seven verses, with opening and closing music for band. Voice, 2cl 2hn 2bn.
Pc (Longman & Broderip: London, c.1795) score: GB-Ob, Mus.2c.99(35). ★

*SCHRÖDER, Hermann *26 March 1904, Bernkastel - 7 Oct 1984, Bad Orb*
HRS-1. Musik zu "Das Wort der Bibel", (1962). fl ob ca cl b-cl bn cbn.
MS score & parts: (location unknown; recorded Ariola GG).
HRS-2. Sextet, Op. 49, 1973. 2cl 2hn 2bn.
Pm (H. Gerig: Köln, 1975; now Breitkopf & Härtel: Wiesbaden, pn HG 1209, 1976), score. & parts.

*SCHUBERT, Ferdinand Lukas *18 Oct 1794, Vienna - 26 Feb 1859, Vienna*
*FLS-1v. Salve Regina in B[♭], 12tes Werk. SATB, 2ob 2hn 2bn, (2tp a-tb t-tb b-tb timp organ ad lib).
Pc (bei Ant. Diabelli & Comp: Wien, pn D. et C. № 4523, c.1845), score: A-Wgm, I 3621, (missing the ad lib
2tp t-tb b-tb timp parts). *Previously attributed to Franz Schubert as D.386.* ★
FLS-2v. Lied am Tage der ersten heiligen Communion (Für bitte zu Gott), Op. 31. SATB, organ, *or* 2ob 2bn.
AutoMS score ("Wien, am 20. April 1844") & MS parts (voices & organ/piano pts only): A-Wgm, I 42257,
(with duplicate vocal parts 6S. 5A, 3T, 4B; one of the S pts bears the later date "20/4 [1]861" at the end). ★
FLS-3v. Laudate Dominum! TTB, 2ob 2tp(clar) timp organ.
AutoMS score ("Wien, am 9. Apr. 1852") & MS parts: A-Wgm, I 42197. ★
*FLS-4v. Veni sancte Spiritus, 40 Werk. SATB, 2ob 2cl(C) 2hn 2bn 2tp(clar) a-tb t-tb b-tb timp, *or* organ.
Pc (bei F. Glöggl: Vienna; bei F. Whistling: Leipzig, pn 236, 1849), score: A-Wgm, I 22030. ★
FLS-5v. Gebeth für unsern geliebte Kaiserin Elisabetha Eugenia. SATB, 2ob 2hn 2bn 2tp timp.
AutoMS score ("Wien, am 6. Apr. [1]854") & MS vocal parts: A-Wgm, V 31117, No. 1. ★
FLS-6v. Oesterreichs Jugend an die Kaiserin. SATB, 2ob 2hn 2bn (3tp b-tb timp).
AutoMS score (1854), AutoMS short score (3tp b-tb timp) & AutoMS piano reduction vocal score:
A-Wgm, V 31117, No. 2. (tp I & II double the 2ob pts; the b-tb doubles bn II). ★
FLS-7v. Pange lingua; in C. SATB, 2cl(C) 2hn 2bn. AutoMS score ("Wien, am 9. May 1837"):
A-Wgm, I 42188, (the first stanza is in Latin, stanzas 2 - 4 are in German).
FLS-8v. Filiae regum. SATB, fl 2ob bn. AutoMS score: A-Wgm, I 31115. ★
FLS-1av. Mozart: Alma Dei, K.277. SATB, fl 2ob 2hn bn tp timp. MS: D-KNh, MS.307, (?lost).
FLS-2av. Franz Schubert: Salve Regina; in F, (D.386).
SATB chorus, 2ob 2hn 2bn 2tp 3tb organ(ad lib). AutoMS parts: GB-Lbl, Add 50,253.

*SCHUBERT, Franz Peter *31 Jan 1797, Vienna - 19 Nov 1828, Vienna*
GA: F Schubert's Werke. Kritisch durchgesehene Gesamtausgabe. Pc (Breitkopf & Härtel: Leipzig, 1884 - 1897), scores. Pm (E.F. Kalmus: New York, etc., sd), miniature scores. Pm (facsimile:) (Dover Publications: New York; Breitkopf & Härtel: Wiesbaden, 1965-69), scores.
NSA: Neue Ausgabe sämtlicher Werke. Pm (Bärenreiter: Kassel, etc. 1967), scores; paperback edition, 1997.
*FPS-1 Franz Schuberts Begräbniss-Feyer; ("Eine kleine Trauermusik", D.79).   2cl 2hn 2bn cbn 2tb.
AutoMS score (19 Sept 1813): A-Wst, MH 133/c. ★
Pc (GA: Ser. III, No. 3, pp. 81 - 82; reprinted Kalmus: EK1034), score.
Pm (McGinnis & Marx: New York, 1983), ed. Christopher Weait, photocopy parts.
Pm (Emerson Edition: Ampleforth), parts.
Pm (NSA: Ser. VI, Bd. 1, No. 2, pp. 25 - 26), score.   (1997 paperback edition: Bd. 1).
*FPS-2. 6 Minuets, (D.2D / D995; only Nos. 1 - 3 scored).   2fl/ob 2cl 2hn 2bn tp.
AutoMS score & sketches (18 Aug 1813): A-Wmv, Schubert MS. D *(Nos. 4 - 6 are piano drafts only);* S-L. ★
Pm (NSA: Ser. VI, Bd. 9, p. 25), score.   (1997 paperback edition: Bd. 1).
Pm (Bärenreiter: Kassel, pn 19109-19110 (score) 19109a-19110a (parts), 1970), Nos. 4 - 6 completed by Alexander Weinmann, ed. by Christa Landon, score & parts.
*FPS-3. Octet, in F, D.72.   2ob 2cl 2hn 2bn.   AutoMS score: A-Wst, MH132/c.
Pc (GA: Ser. III, No. 2, pp. 69 - 80), score (mvts 3 & 4 only); Kalmus reprint: score (pn A 9134) & miniature score (pn EK 1034 No. 2). ★
Pm (E.B. Marks: New York, c.1948), ed. Kahn, score & parts, (Menuetto only), Marks Educational Music Library Wind Ensemble, No. 5.
Pm (Reinhard Van Hoorickx: Ghent, c.1965), mvts 1 & 2 reconstructed from sketches by *Fr.* Reinhard Van Hoorickx, score (Provisory edition, Pro manuscripto).
Pm (McGinnis & Marx: New York, pn 147b, 1983), completed by *Fr.* Reinhard Van Hoorickx, edited & revised by Christopher Weait, score (facsimile), & parts.
Pm (NSA: Ser. VI, Bd. 1, mvts 3 & 4, pp. 3 - 24), score.   (1997 paperback edition: Bd. 1).
Pm (Nova Music: London, pn NM 121, 1979), mvts 3 & 4 only, ed. by James Brown.
FPS-1f. Fragment of an Allegro (D.72a), 1813, possibly associated with FPS-3.   2ob 2cl 2hn 2bn.
Pm (NSA: Ser. VI, Bd. 1, pp. 151 - 154), score.   (1997 paperback edition: Bd. 1). ★
Schubert: Instrumental Excerpts
FPS-1e. Fierrabras, Op. 76, D.796: No. 21, part 2, Marcia funebre (Andante, 16 bars).   2ob 2cl 2hn 2bn 2tp 3tb.
Pc (GA: Ser. XV, Bd. 6, No. 10 pp. 477 - 479); Kalmus reprint: pn EK 462, pp. 477 - 479, miniature score. Pm (NSA: Ser. II, Bd. 8), score.
FPS-2e. Des Teufels Lustschloss, D.84: No. 10, Trauermusik.   2cl 2bn 3tb.
Pc (GA: Ser. XV, Bd. 1, No. 1, p. 100), score.
Pm (NSA: Ser. II, Bd. 1 Teil a (1st version) p. 126 (1989)), score.
FPS-3e. Rosamunde, Op. 26, D.797: No. 6, Hirtenmelodie.   2cl 2hn 2bn.
Pc (GA: Ser. XV, Bd. 4, No. 2, p. 98), score.
Pm (NSA: Ser. II, Bd. 9), score.
FPS-4e. Alfonso ed Estrella, D.732: Act I, No. 10, Tempo di marcia.   2fl 2ob 2hn 2bn.
Pc (GA: Ser. XV, Bd. 5, No. 9, pp. 138 - 139), score.
Pm (NSA: Ser. II, Bd. 6), score.
Schubert: Vocal Works with Winds
*FPS-1v. Gesänge zur Feier des heiligen Opfers der Messe [Deutsche Messe], D.872.
SATB chorus, 2ob 2cl 2hn(G) 2tp 3tb timp organ(ad lib).
AutoMS score: A-Wst, MH 14. ★
Pc (Ant. Diabelli und Comp.: Vienna, 1826), (incorrectly attributed to F.L. Schubert), score & parts: GB-Lbl, Hirsch IV.900.a.
Pc (J.P. Gotthard: Vienna, pn 117-119, 1870), score & parts: GB-Lbl, H.2150.t.(1).
Pc (GA: Ser. XIII, Bd. 2, No. 7, pp. 325 - 341), score.
Pm (NSA: Ser. I, Bd. 6), score.
*FPS-2v. Hymnus an den Heiligen Geist, "Herr, unser Gott!", 2nd version, Op. posth 154, D.948, 1828.
TTTTBBBB, 2ob 2cl 2hn 2bn 2tp 3tb timp.
AutoMS score: A-Wn, MHS 19488. ★
Pc (A. Diabelli et Comp.: Vienne, 1847), score: GB-Lbl, Hirsch IV.632.
Pc (GA: Ser. XVI, Bd. 2, pp. 11 - 23), score.   Pm (NSA: Ser. I, Bd. 8), score.
Pm (WINDS: Northridge, CA, pn W-93, c.1980), score (photocopy of the Diabelli edition) & modern MS (photocopy) parts.
*FPS-3v. Glaube, Hoffnung und Liebe, D.954.   SATTBB 2ob 2cl 2hn 2bn 2tb.
Pc (T. Mollo: Wien, 1828), score & vocal score.
Pc (Zu haben bey der Pfarre der P.P. Minoriten: Wien, c.1828), score (misattributed as "Op. 97"): GB-Lbl, G.450.h. ★
Pc (GA: Ser. XVII, Bd. 5, pp. 152 - 155), score.
Pm (NSA: Ser. III, Bds. 1 & 2), score.
Schubert: Vocal Excerpts with Winds
*FPS-1ve. Stabat Mater, D.383: No. 5, "Wer wird Zähren sanften Mitleids".   SSAATTBB, 2fl 2ob 2hn 2bn 3tb.
Pc (GA: Ser. XIV, No. 13, p. 15), score.   Pm (NSA: Ser. I, Bd. 7), score.
*FPS-2ve. Die Zauberharfe, (D.644): No. 7, Chor der Ritter.   TTBB 2ob 2cl 2hn 2bn 2tp 3tb timp.
Pc (GA: Ser. XV, Bd. 4, No. 7, pp. 228 - 232), score.
Pm (NSA: Ser. II, Bd. 4, pp. 219 - 224), score.

*FPS-3ve. Die Zauberharfe, D.644: No. 8, Melodrama.   Spoken voice, 2fl 2ob 2cl 2hn 2bn tp 3tb.
Pc (GA: Ser. XV, Bd. 4, No. 7, pp. 233 - 237), score.
Pm (NSA: Ser. II, Bd. 4, pp. 225 - 229), score.
*FPS-4ve. Die Zauberharfe, D.644: alternative to No. 9, Romance des Palmerin (in sketch).   2hn 2bn harp.
Pc (GA: Ser. XV, Bd. 4, Appendix, No. 7, pp. 345 - 348), score.
Pm (NSA: Ser. II, Bd. 4), score.
*FPS-5ve. Die Zauberharfe, D.644: No. 11, Melodrama.   Spoken voice, 2ob 2cl bthn 2hn 2bn.
Pc (GA: Ser. II, Bd. 4, No. 11, pp. 282 - 283), score.
*FPS-6ve. Der vierjährige Posten, D.190: No. 5, Katchen's Aria, Andante con moto, 30 bars.   S, 2cl 2hn 2bn.
Pc (GA: Ser. XV, Bd. 2, No. 2 pp. 58 - 59), score.
*FPS-7ve, 8ve. Der vierjährige Posten, D. 190: Nos. 6 & 7, Marsch, Soldatenchor, Aufritt.
TTB, 2ob 2cl 2hn 2bn tp.
Pc (GA: Bd. 2, No. 2, pp. 69 - 71), score.
*FPS-9ve. Die Verschworenen, (D.787): Chor der Ritter "Wenn Mutt und Schönheit sich vereinen".
TTBB chorus, 2fl ob 2cl 2hn 2bn.
Pc (GA: Ser. II, Bd. 3, pp. 230 - 231), score.

*SCHUBERT, Johann Christian *(1760)*
QCS-1. Parthia in E♭; 1 mvt.   2ob 2cl 2hn 2bn.   MS parts: CZ-Pnm, XX.F.108.   ★

*SCHUBERTH (Schubert), Joseph *(1790)*
EJS-1v. Salve Regina in Es [E♭].   CATB, 2cl 2hn 2bn.
MS parts (by Johann Josef Wagner, c.1825): CZ-NYc, DÚ 137.   ★

*SCHUESTER (Schuster, Schüster), ( ) *(1730)*
YXS-1(-4). 4 Parthias; (G, 5 mvts; G, 6 mvts; F, 4 mvts; C, 5 mvts).   2ob 2hn 2bn.
MS parts (1766): CZ-KRa, A4024, 4025/IV.B.198, Part 1, Parthias 7 - 10.   ★
YXS-5. Parthia ex D; 12 mvts.   2ob 2hn 2bn.   MS parts: CZ-Pnm, XLII.C.190.   ★
YXS-6. Parthia in: G; 5 mvts.   2cl 2hn 2bn.   MS parts: CZ-KRa, A3969/IV.B.133.   ★
YXS-6. Parthia in D; 5 mvts.   2ob 2hn bn.   MS parts (1766): CZ-KRa, A3965/IV.B.129.   ★
YXS-7. Parthia; in G, 6 mvts.   2ob 2hn bn.   MS parts (1766): CZ-KRa, A3966/IV.B.130.   ★
YXS-8. Parthia; in D, 6 mvts.   2ob 2hn bn.   MS parts (1766): CZ-KRa, A3967/IV.B.131.   ★
YXS-9. Parthia; in C, 6 mvts.   2ob 2hn bn.   MS parts (1766): CZ-KRa, A3968/IV.B.132.   ★

*SCHULLER, Gunther Alexander *22 Nov 1925, New York*
*GQS-1. Eine kleine Posaunemusik.   Solo trombone, fl fl(pic) ob ob(ca) 2cl b-cl/cb-cl 2hn bn 2tp 3tb tu db perc harp piano/celeste.
Pm (Associated Music Publishers: New York, 1980), hire score & parts.
GQS-2. 3 Invenzioni.   2fl ob ca cl(E♭) b-cl a-sax 2hn bn cbn 3tp flüg 3tb tu bar celeste harp harpsichord piano.
Pm (Associated Music Publishers: New York), hire score & parts.
GQS-3. Fanfare for St Louis.   3fl 3ob 3cl 4hn 3bn 4tp 3tb tu perc.
Pm (Margun Music: Newton Center, MA, pn MP 70305S, 1968), score.
GQS-4. Pavane (Hommage à Maurice Ravel), 1943.   Solo Cornet, 3fl 4cl 4hn 2euph 4tu.
Pm (Margun Music: Newton Center, MA, pn MP 7031, sd), score & parts.
GQS-5. Double Quintet, for Wind & Brass Quintets.   fl ob cl 2hn bn 2tp tb tu.
Pm (Associated Music Publishers: New York, 1961), hire score & parts.

SCHULTZ, Andrew *1960, Australia*
AES-1. Cloud burning; 1986.   2fl 2ob 2cl 2hn 2bn 2tp perc.   MS score: AUS-Smc.

SCHULTZ, Helmut (editor)
HLS-1 Deutsche Blasmusik vom Barock bis zur Klassik.
Pc: (Nagel: Kassel, 1941, *reprinted* 1961, as Kammermusik, Bd. II).
Contains works by Speer (No. 4 c-d), Stranensky (No. 7) and Schwegler (No. 8).

SCHULTZ (Schulz), (Johann Abraham) Peter *31 March 1747, Lüneburg - 10 June 1800, Schwedt an der Oder*
JPS-1. Sonata à 5; in D, 4 mvts.   2fl 2ob bn. (The ob parts are marked (?later) - "Con Violino")
MS parts: S-Uu, Mus.instr.hs.59:1. *The "con Violino" option does not appear on the titlepage.*   ★
Pm (Broekmans & van Poppel: Amsterdam, pn 1356, 1978), ed. Verhagen, score & parts.

*SCHULTZ, Svend Simon *30 Dec 1913, Denmark*
*SSS-1. Divertimento for blaseroktet; 1961/1963.   2ob 2cl 2hn 2bn.
In MS: DK-Kd will assist in contacting the composer.

SCHULZ, C. [= **Johann Philipp Christian**] *24 Sept 1773, Langensalza - 20 Jan 1827, Leipzig*
We believe that the pieces are all from Schulz's works, probably incidental music for plays produced in Leipzig.
It was Schulz's version of the "Harmonie zu dem Monolog der Jung frau von Orleans what was rescored by
Triebensee for his Miscellanées de Musique *(JZT-50a) rather than the version composed by B.A. Weber.*
JCS-1a. VIII pièces d'harmonies de diverses Comédies favorites dont 5 à 6 Parties et 5 à 7. composées par C.
Schulz [sic]; 8 mvts.   fl 2cl(A & B♭) 2hn bn.
Pc (Hoffmeister & Kühnel: Leipzig, pn 352, 1804), parts: H-Bn, Z 43,933; GB-Ljag, (microfilm).
   1.1a. Harmonie zu dem Monolog der Jungfrau von Orleans. No. 1
   1.2a. Menikov und Natalie, 1 mvt. No. 2.
   1.3a. Aus dem Soldaten, 2 mvts. Nos. 3 & 7.
   1.4a. Die Kreuzfahrer, 2 mvts. Nos. 4 & 5.
   1.5a. Aus dem Schreibepult, 1 mvt. No. 8.

SCHULZ, Stephan *1965, New Zealand*
STS-1. Throb; 1986.   ob 2cl hn bn.
MS score: NZ-Wmc.

SCHUMANN, Gerhard *29 July 1914, Görlitz - 1976*
GRS-1. Elegia.   Solo horn, 2ob bn 2tp 4tb.
Pm (untraced, possibly: Sirius Edition; Heinrichshofen: Wilhelmshaven).

*SCHUMANN, Robert Alexander *8 June 1810, Zwickau - 29 July 1856, Endenich, nr Bonn*
RSW: Robert Schumanns Werke. Herausgegeben von Clara Schumann. *Pc (Breitkopf & Härtel: Leipzig, 1880 - 1893); reprinted: E.F. Kalmus: New York, etc., pn EK 1125, No. 1, sd), miniature score; also reprinted: Gregg Press: Farnborough, Hants, ISBN 057628301 0, 1967).*
RAS-1v. Beim Abschied zu singen, Op. 84.   SATB solo & chorus, 2fl 2ob 2cl 2hn 2bn; *or* piano.
Pc (F. Whistling: Leipzig, pn 578, 1859), score: GB-Lbl, F.432.o. ★
Pm (RSW), Ser. IX, Bd. 3, No. 84, score.
Pm (WINDS: Northridge, CA, c.1981), score & parts.
Pm (Compusic: Amsterdam, pn 252, c.1988), score & parts.
RAS-1ve. Der Rose Pilgerfahrt, Märchen, Op. 112, No. 10, Gebet, 19 bars.   S solo, 2cl 2hn 2bn.
Pc (Bei Fr. Kistner: Leipzig, 1852), score: GB-Lbl, (2 copies), G.245.e, Hirsch IV.918. ★
Pm (RSW), Ser. IX, Bd. 3, No. 86, score.

*SCHUYT, Nico (Nicolaas) *2 Jan 1922, Alkmaar, Netherlands - 1992*
NZS-1. Discorsi capricciosi; 1965.   fl 2ob 2cl 2hn 2bn tp tb tu timp perc.
Pm (Donemus: Amsterdam, 1971), score.
NZS-2. Alla notturna.   2ob obdam ca.
Pm (Donemus: Amsterdam, 1971), score & parts.

*SCHWARZ, ( ) [?M] *(?1760)*
UXS-1m. Marcia [& Trio] in F.   2cl(C) cl(C) cl(Bb) 2hn 2bn tp posthorn(Solo in Trio only).
MS parts (from Langenbruck, now Dlouhý Most): CZ-Pu(dm), 59 R 3375. ★

*SCHWARZ, A. *Flautist at Mecklenburg-Schwerin (Kapellmeister, 4. Brandenburgischen Infanterie-Regiment. No. 24, Grossherzog von Mecklenburg-Schwerin)*
AQS-1m. Fest-Marsch; in Eb.   pic fl 2ob 2cl(Eb) 5cl(Bb) 4hn 2bn 4tp 2crt t-hn 2t-tb b-tb b-dr+cym s-dr.
MS score: D-SWl, Mus. 5021. ★

*SCHWARZ, M. *(1780)*
MYS-1m. 11 Märsche für die ganze Türkische Musick oder neun-stimmige Harmonie.
pic 2ob cl(D) 3cl(C) 2hn 2bn cbn 3tp posthorn/tp(G) posthorn(Bb) tb b-dr s-dr.
Pc (Im Verlage der k: k: pr: chemischen Druckerey: Vienna, pn 2254, 1814), RISM [S 2464], parts: D-Mmb.
MYS-2m. 6 Märsche.   pic(C, F) 2fl 2ob(No. 3 only) cl(F) 3cl(C) 2hn 2bn cbn 2tp b-dr s-dr.
Pc (Im Verlage der k: k: pr: chemischen Druckerey: Wien, pn 2273, 1814/1815), pts: E-Mam, K.846.(11). ★

*SCHWEGLER, Johann David *1759, Endersbach, Württemberg - 1817, Stuttgart*
Schwegler's 10 Harmonien (2fl 2ob 2cl 2hn 2bn 2tp timp) appear to have been lost in the Stuttgart Hoftheater fire in 1902. These works are listed in the Inventorium über die Musikalien der Kgl. Hoftheaters in Stuttgart nach dem Pfand von 1. July 1834 *(D-Sl, H.B.XVII. 904). We believe that these Harmonien were, in fact, the basis for Jähns suggestion that one might be the missing* Harmonie in B[b] *by C.M. von Weber (CMW-6d).*
JDS-1. Quatre quatuors, Oeuv. 3; (D, Eb, G, F; each 3 mvts).   2fl 2hn.
Pc (Breitkopf & Härtel: Leipzig, pn 347, 1806/07), RISM [S 2472], pts: D-Dl; DK-Kk; GB-Lbl, i.28; S-Skma. ★
Pm (No. 2 only, in:) *(Das Erbe deutscher Musik.* Reihe 1. Reichsdenkmale. Bd. 14. Deutsche Bläsermusik vom Barock bis zur Klassik. Edited by Helmut Schultz. Breitkopf & Härtel: Leipzig, 1941, reprinted 1961), score.
Pm (No. 2 only:) (Western International Music Inc.: Greeley, Colorado, pn WIM 052, sd), score & parts.
JDS-1.1e, 1.2e. Deux Marches. Zur Braut von Messina; No. 1 Marche Vivace; No. 2: Todten Marsch.
2fl 2ob 2cl 2hn(F, C) 2bn 2tp timp.   MS parts: D-Sl, H.B.XVII. 586. ★

SCHWEINITZ, Wolfgang von *7 Feb 1953, Hamburg*
WVS-1. Englische Serenade, 1984.   3 Variations on 27 x 12 Töne, Op. 24.   2cl 2hn 2bn.
Pm (Boosey & Hawkes: London, 1985), score.

SCHWENKE, Christian Friedrich Gottlieb *(?1770)*
CFS-1a. [6 Marches & Dances], par Differents Auteurs Mecueillées [sic].   2fl(Eb) 2cl 2hn 2bn tp(ad lib).
Pc (J.A. Böhme: Hambourg [sic], sd), parts: H-KE, K 2188. ★

*SCIARRINO, Salvatore *4 April 1947, Palermo*
SYS-1. Di Zefiro e Pan, Poemetta; 1976.   2fl 2ob cl(Bb) cl(A) 2hn 2bn.
Pm (Ricordi: Milano, pn 132484, 1976), facsimile AutoMS score, (in "New Notation").

SCONTRINO, Antonio *17 May 1850, Trapani - 7 Feb 1922, Florence*
ANS-1. Adagio.   Solo violin, winds.
MS score: I-Fc, D.XIII.1770; I-PLcon.

*SEDLAK (Sedlach, Sedlack, Sedlash, Sedlatch), Wenzel (Václav) *4 Aug 1776, ? Bohemia - 2 Nov 1851, ? Vienna After 1812 a number of Sedlak's arrangements carry the note "mit Begleitung 2 Trombe". Although these trumpet parts enhance the arrangements, they are not essential, and whether or not the parts have been discarded often explains discrepancies in scoring between different collections. These parts are indicated as: (2tp). MSS in what we refer to as the professional "Auswahl" hand are indicated by the abbreviation: (AH). MSS which describe the combined bn II & cbn part as "Fagotti Bassi" are indicated by the abbreviation: (FB). We believe that both the "Auswahl Hand" and the use of "Fagotti Bassi" indicate that these MSS were produced & sold by the Viennese publisher, Pietro Mechetti. Works attributed on stylistic features are preceded by: +.*

WXS-1a. Auswahl der beliebter Arien aus Joconde, Joseph & Der kleinen [sic] Diebin, No. 1.
2ob 2cl 2hn 2bn cbn.   MS parts (AH): A-Wn, Mus.Hs.3852.
   1.1a. Isouard: Joconde, overture & 9 mvts. Nos. 1 - 9, (omits Nos. 7 & 12 of WXS-27a).
   1.2a. Méhul: Joseph und seiner Brüder, overture & 5 mvts (= WXS-32a: 1 - 3, 6 - 8). Nos. 10 - 15.
   1.3a. Kinsky: Die kleine Diebin, overture & 7 mvts. Nos. 16 - 22.
WXS-2a. Auswahl. Aus der Ballet, Die Pagen, und der Nina, Nro 2. 2ob 2cl 2hn 2bn cbn 2tp(tacet in 2.2a).
MS parts: A-Wn, Mus.Hs.3851, (AH); CZ-Bm(au), A.35.171, (Nos. 1 - 3, 5, 8 & 12; missing the 2tp).
   2.1a. Gyrowetz: Die Pagen des Herzoge von Vendome, introduzione & 7 mvts. Nos. 1 - 8.
   2.2a. Persuis: Nina, oder die Wahnsinnige aus Liebe, 4 mvts, Nos. 9 - 12 (= WXS-39a: 2, 4+5, 9 & 12).
WXS-3a. Auswahl. Aus der Oper Agnes Sorel, und Balletten, der Wald bey Kis, Bér [sic], Don Quixotte, und Antonius und Cleopatra, Nro 3. 2ob 2cl 2hn 2bn cbn.   MS parts (AH): A-Wn, Mus.Hs.3791.
   3.1a. Gyrowetz: Agnes Sorel, overture, duetto & 1 mvt (Largo, 2/4) (= WXS-20.1a: 1, 5 & 8). Nos. 1 - 3.
   3.2a. Kinsky: Der Wald bei Kis-Bér [sic: Das ländlich Fest im Wäldhen bei Kis-Bér], 5 mvts. Nos. 4 - 8.
   3.3a. M. Umlauf: Die Hochzeit des Gamacho oder Don Quixote, 2 mvts. Nos. 9 & 10.
   3.4a. R. Kreutzer: Antonius und Cleopatra, 1 mvt & marcia. Nos. 11 & 12.
WXS-4a. Auber: La Muette de Portici, Theil 1: overture & 11 mvts; Theil 2: 12 mvts; Theil 3: 13 mvts.
2ob 2cl 2hn 2bn cbn 2tp. MS parts: A-Wn, Mus.Hs.3795, (complete; AH, except ob I Theils; FB); CZ-Bm(au), A.35.146, (local copy, Theil 1, mvts 2, 3, 5, 6, 7, 12), A.35.147, (Theil 2, mvts 1, 6, 7 & Theil 3 mvts 8 - 10; with an added ad lib b-tb part). Although the wrapper of CZ-Bm(au) A.35.146 asserts "Ouverture nebst den 1ten Theil" the overture is not present; A.36.856 (for 2ob cl(F) 2cl(C) 2hn 2bn cbn 3tp tb, (missing ob II), is probably a local rescoring of the missing overture.
*WXS-5a. Beethoven: Fidelio, overture & 10 mvts.   2ob 2cl 2hn 2bn cbn.
Pc (bey Artaria et Comp: Wien, 1814), parts: A-Wn, (2 copies), MS.10812, MS.40105; A-Wst, M. 12355/c; GB-Ljag(w), (sold by J. Velten, Kunsthändler in Karlsruhe); I-Fc, (2 copies), D.X.80-101, F.P. S.359, (MS pts); NL-DHgm, hk 19 B 18.
Pm (WINDS: Northridge, CA, pn W-10, c.1981), photocopy of Artaria parts.
Pm (Musica rara: London, pn 1631, 1637, 1973), 2 books, ed. R. Block & H. Voxman, score & parts.
WXS-6a. Bellini: I Pirata, (Theil 1) overture & 11 mvts, (Theil 2) 12 mvts.   2ob 2cl 2hn 2bn cbn (2tp).
MS parts (local copy by Minařík): CZ-Bm(au), (Theil 1) A.35.151, (Theil 2), A.35.152.
+WXS-7a. Berton: Aline, Reine de Golconde, overture & 9 mvts.   2cl 2hn 2bn.   MS parts: PL-LA, RM 49.
WXS-8a. Boieldieu: Jean de Paris, overture & 9 mvts.   2ob 2cl 2hn 2bn cbn.   MS parts: A-Wgm, VIII 41157.
WXS-9a. Carafa di Colobrano: Gabrielle di Vergy, overture & 10 mvts.   2fl 2ob 2cl 2hn 2bn cbn 2tp.
MS parts (local copy, but retains FB): CZ-Bm(au), A.35.155 (overture), A.35.156, (10 mvts).
WXS-10a. Cherubini: Lodoiska, overture & 10 mvts.   2cl 2hn 2bn.
MS parts: CZ-KRa, A3843IV.B.7, (as Anon, complete); CZ-Pnm, XLI.B.120, (overture only as No. 13 of Sedlak's arrangement of Rossini's *Il Barbiere di Siviglia*, here incorrectly attrirbuted to Paer); PL-LA, RM 73, (copy by J.A. Buchal, 1803). *This is probably a reduction by Sedlak of the octet/nonet version.*
WXS-11a. Cherubini: Medée, overture & 9 mvts.   2cl 2hn 2bn.
MS parts: PL-LA, RM 129. *This is probably a reduction by Sedlak from Triebensee's octet arrangement.*
*WXS-12a. Cherubini: Faniska, overture & 11 mvts.   2ob 2cl 2hn 2bn cbn.
AutoMS score: A-Wgm, VIII 43277.
MS parts: A-Ee, Mus.1139; A-Wgm, VIII 43277 (Q 16373), (?lost); CZ-Bm(no), A.16.937; I-Fc, F.P. S.347.
WXS-13.1a. Dalayrac: Les deux petits Savoyards, overture & 8 mvts.   2ob 2cl 2hn 2bn cbn.   MS pts: I-Fc, F.P.S.345.
WXS-13.2a. Dalayrac: Les deux petits Savoyards, overture & 8 mvts.   2cl 2hn 2bn.   MS pts: PL-LA, RM 42.
WXS-14a. Dalayrac: La Poète et le musicien, overture & 6 mvts.   2ob 2cl 2hn 2bn cbn (2tp).
MS parts: CZ-Bm(au), A.35.159, (FB; Nos. 8 - 12 are from Gyrowetz & Persuis' ballet, *Die Hochzeit der Thetis und des Peleus*); I-Fc, (2 copies), F.P. S.381, F.P. S.365, (incorrectly attributed to Peter von Winter).
*WXS-15.1a. Duport (compiler): Der blöde Ritter, overture & 9 mvts.   2ob 2cl 2hn 2bn cbn.
Pc (Im Verlage den K.K. priv: chemische Druckerey: Wien, pn 2242, 1812), parts: CZ-Bm(rj), A.13.309, (acquired 1819).   MS parts: D-Rtt, Sm. 15, Nos. 52 - 61, (serp/db replaces cbn).
*WXS-15.2a. Duport (compiler): Der blöde Ritter, overture & 9 mvts.   2cl 2hn 2bn (cbn).
Pc (Im Verlage den K.K. priv: chemischen Druckerey: Wien, pn 2241, 2242, 1812), parts: (no copies traced.
See The Wind Ensemble Sourcebook p. 31, for a discussion of the rogue cbn part).
MS parts: CZ-KRa, A3859/IV.B.23; CZ-Pnm, XLI.B.167, (as "Suita").
WXS-16.1a. V. Fioravanti: La Capricciosa pentita, overture & 11 mvts.   2ob 2cl 2hn 2bn cbn.
MS parts (probably commercially produced by Johann Cappi: Vienna): CZ-Pnm, Lobkovic X.G.f.62; I-Fc, F.P. S.343, (as Anon).
WXS-16.2a. V. Fioravanti: La Capricciosa pentita, overture & 11 mvts.   2cl 2hn 2bn.
MS parts (local copy, 27 July 1808): CZ-KRa, A3977/IV.B.143; CZ-Pnm, XLI.B.89.
*WXS-17.1a. Gallenberg: Alfred der Grosse, "24tes Werk", (Theil 1) overture & 12 mvts, (Theil 2) 12 mvts.
2ob 2cl 2hn 2bn cbn (2tp).   MS parts: A-Wn, Mus.Hs.3862.
+WXS-17.2a. Gallenberg: Alfred der Grosse, Marsch.   2ob 2cl 2hn 2bn cbn 2tp.
MS parts: A-Wn, Mus.Hs.3863, (MS by Perschl); CZ-Bm(au), A.35.257, (incomplete).
*WXS-18a. Gallenberg: Ottavio Pinelli, (Theil 1) overture & 11 mvts, (Theil 2) 13 mvts.
2ob 2cl 2hn 2bn cbn (2tp).   MS parts (FB): A-Wn, Mus.Hs.3864.

WXS-19a. Grétry (adapted by Anton Fischer): Raoul Barbe-Bleue, overture & 13 mvts.   2cl 2hn 2bn.
MS parts: CZ-KRa, A3871/IV.B.34(b), (as Anon); CZ-Pnm, XLI.A.88, (as Anon, missing cl I); PL-LA, RM 44.
WXS-20.1a. Gyrowetz: Agnes Sorel, overture & 12 mvts.   2ob 2cl 2hn 2bn cbn.
MS parts: CZ-Pnm, XXVII.B.231; GB-Ljag(w); H-KE, 1173/IX; I-Fc, D.V.503.
WXS-20.2a Gyrowetz: Agnes Sorel, overture & 12 mts.   2cl 2hn 2bn.
MS parts: CZ-KRa, A3868/IV.B.32, (local copy, overture & 10 mvts); CZ-Pnm, XLI.B.106.
See also: **WXS-3.1a.** Gyrowetz: Agnes Sorel, overture & 2 mvts (Nos. 5 & 8).   2ob 2cl 2hn 2bn cbn.
See also: **WXS-2.1a.** Gyrowetz: Die Pagen des Herzoge von Vendome.   2ob 2cl 2hn 2bn cbn 2tp.
WXS-21.1a. Gyrowetz & Persuis: Die Hochzeit der Thetis und des Peleus: overture & 11 mvts.
2ob 2cl 2hn 2bn cbn.   MS pts: A-Wn, Mus.Hs.3865, (AH, FB); CZ-Bm(rj), A.13.281, (local copy, 1819; the
ob(I) pt has been tranposed for cl(F); although the cl(I) pt also gives ob(I) as an option, some of the mvts remain
in keys for cl in Bb).
WXS-21.2a. Gyrowetz & Persuis: Die Hochzeit der Thetis und des Peleus, 5 mvts.   2ob 2cl 2hn 2bn cbn (2tp).
MS parts: CZ-Bm(au), A.35.159, Nos. 8 - 12, (5 mvts following Sedlak's arrangement of Dalayrac's opera, *Le
Poëte et la Musicien;* professional scribal copy, FB).
WXS-22a. Gyrowetz & Persuis: Der Zauberschlaf, overture & 13 mvts.   2ob 2cl 2hn 2bn cbn (2tp).
MS parts (AH, FB): A-Wn, Mus.Hs.3867.
+**WXS-23a.** Hérold: Zampa, Theil 1: overture & 8 mvts; Theil 2: 6 mvts.   2ob 2cl 2hn 2bn cbn 2tp.
MS parts (FB): A-Wn, Mus.Hs.3811.
WXS-24a. Hummel: Helena und Paris, overture & 13 mvts.   2ob 2cl 2hn 2bn cbn.   MS parts: A-Ee, Mus.1164.
WXS-25a. Hummel: Prinzessin Eselshaut, (as "Die Eselshaut"), overture & 6 mvts.   2ob 2cl 2hn 2bn cbn.
Pc (Im Verlage den k: k: pr: chemischen Druckerey: Wien, pn 2281, 1814/15), **J9**, No. VIII, parts:
US-Wc, M959.H; GB-Ljag (photocopy).
MS score (allegedly in the hand of J.S. Mayr): I-BGc, Mayr 601.   MS pts: I-Fc, F.P. S.401.
WXS-26a. Hummel: Sappho von Mytilene, (as "Die Rache du [sic] Venus"), overture.   2ob 2cl 2hn 2bn cbn 2tp.
MS parts: CZ-Bm, A.35.209(au), No. 1, (replaces Rossini's overture in *Il Barbiere di Siviglia*).
*****WXS-27a.** Isouard: Joconde, overture & 11 mvts.   2ob 2cl 2hn 2bn cbn (2tp).   MS pts: A-Wgm, VIII 41156,
(AH, FB); CZ-Bm; CZ-KRa, A4011/IV.B.184; I-Fc, F.P. S.387. *See also* WXS-1.1a.
For Kinsky: Die kleine Diebin, see **WXS-1.3a,** overture & 7 mvts.   2ob 2cl 2hn 2bn cbn.
WXS-28.1a. Liverati: David, oder Goliaths Tod, overture & 6 mvts.   2ob 2cl 2hn 2bn cbn.
Pc (Chemische Druckerei: Wien, pn 2141, 2142, 1813), parts: (no copies traced).
MS parts (copies of Chemische Druckerei edition): A-Wgm, VIII 38236; CZ-KRa, A3918/IV.B.81;
I-Fc, (2 copies), F.P. S.367, F.P. S.400.
WXS-28.2a. Liverati: David, oder Goliaths Tod, overture & 6 mvts.   2cl 2hn 2bn.
Pc (Chemische Druckerei: Vienna, pn 2141, 2142, 1813), parts: (no copies traced).
MS parts (copies of Chemische Druckerei edition): CZ-Bm(au), (2 copies), ; CZ-Pnm, XLI.B.107.
WXS-29a. Mayr: Alonso e Cora, sinfonia & 7 mvts.   2cl 2hn 2bn.   MS parts: CZ-KRa, A3922/IV.B.85.
+**WXS-30a.** Mayr: Ercole in Lidien, overture & 14 mvts.   2cl 2hn 2bn.   MS pts: CZ-KRa, A4453/R.I.23, No. 2.
WXS-31a. Méhul: Un Folie, overture & 7 mvts.   2cl 2hn 2bn.
MS parts: CZ-KRa, A4453/R.I.23, No. 3; PL-LA, RM 41.
WXS-32a. Méhul: Joseph, overture & 7 mvts.   2ob 2cl 2hn 2bn cbn.   MS parts: CZ-KRa, IV.B.185.
See also: **WXS-1.2a.** overture & 5 mvts, (omits Nos. 4 & 5).   2ob 2cl 2hn 2bn cbn.
WXS-33a. Mercadante: Elisa e Claudio, Theil 1: overture & 11 mvts; Theil 2: 6 mvts.
2ob 2cl 2hn 2bn cbn (2tp).   MS parts: CZ-Bm(au), (Theil 1) A.35.188, (Theil 2) A.35.187. *Some mvts (?6) of
Theil 2 may have been omitted by the local copyist.*
WXS-34a. Niccolini: Traiano in Dacia, Theil 1, overture & 9 mvts.   2ob 2cl 2hn 2bn cbn (2tp).
MS parts CZ-Bm(au), A.35.196.
WXS-35a. Pacini: L'Ultimo giorno di Pompei, Theil 1: preludio & 7 mvts; Theil 2: 6 mvts.
2ob 2cl 2hn 2bn cbn (2tp).   MS parts: CZ-Bm(au), (Theil 1) A.19.613a, (Theil) A.19.613b.
WXS-36.1a. Paer: Achille, overture & 14 mvts.   2ob 2cl 2hn 2bn cbn.
MS pts: A-Ee, Mus.1076, (as Anon); A-Wn, Mus.Hs.3823, (as Anon); CZ-Bm(no), A.16.657; CZ-Pnm, (2 copies),
XLI.B.148, (as Anon, with 2 sets of bn parts), XLII.C.158, (for ob 2cl 2hn 2bn).
Pc (Nel Magazina di Musica dei Teatri Impr: Real: Vienna [sic], c.1801), MS parts: I-Fc, F.P. S.410.
WXS-36.2a Paer: Achille, overture & 14 mvts.   2cl 2hn 2bn.
MS pts: CZ-KRa, (2 copies), A3945/IV.B.108, (for 2cl 2hn bn), A4456/R.I.26, (copy by Havel); PL-LA, RM 71.
WXS-37.1a. Paer: Sargino, overture & 12 mvts.   2ob 2cl 2hn 2bn.
MS parts: A-Wn, Mus.Hs.3828 (overture, dated 1819), Mus.Hs.3829, (6 mvts; = Nos. 2, 4, 7, 9, 11, 12;
MS probably commercially produced by Cappi: Vienna); CZ-Bm(au), A.35.202, (No. 7 only, for 2ob 2cl 2hn
2bn, as No. 7 of the arrangement by Went of Paer's *Camilla* which, in turn, follows Krommer's Op. 73);
CZ-Bm(no),A.16.657; CZ-Bm(rj), A.355, (overture & Nos. 3, 6, 7 & 12 in a local copy, 1819; with a slightly
later pt for cl(F) closely based on the ob(I) pt, & a local tp pt; there is also a cl(I) pt with No. 2 transposed from
cl in C to cl in Bb); CZ-Pnm, Lobkovic X.G.f.71; D-NEhz, 32.
WXS-37.2a. Paer: Sargino, overture & 8 mvts (Nos. 3, 6, 7.1, 7.2, 8.2, 9, 12).   2ob 2cl 2hn 2bn.
MS parts: H-KE, 866/VIII, (as Anon); I-Fc, F.P. S.345, (as Anon).
WXS-37.3a. Paer: Sargino, overture & 12 mvts.   2cl 2hn 2bn.   MS parts: CZ-Pnm, XLI.B.147, (as Anon).
WXS-38a. Pavesi: Ser Marcantonio, overture & 12 mvts.   2ob 2cl 2hn 2bn cbn (2tp).
MS parts: A-Wn, Mus.Hs.3831, (AH, FB); I-Fc, F.P. S.374, (missing the two ad lib tp parts).
WXS-39a. Persuis, after Dalayrac: Nina; introductione & 11 mvts.   2ob 2cl 2hn 2bn cbn.
Pc (im Verlag der k:k: priv: chemy: Druckery: Wien, pn 2305, 1815), parts: GB-Ljag(w).
MS parts: CZ-Bm(au), A.35.203, (with a lithographed titlepage, s.n.: s.l., pn 2305); CZ-KRa, A3947/IV.B.110.
The CZ-Bm plate number of 2305 identifies the arrangement as that published by Chemische Druckerei.
See also: **WXS-3.2a.** 4 mvts.   2ob 2cl 2hn 2bn cbn.
WXS-40a. Rode: Air varié in G. Op. 10.   2ob 2cl 2hn 2bn cbn (2tp).
MS parts (Theil 2, No. 11 of the arrangement of Rossini's *Il Barbiere di Siviglia*, WXS-59.1a).

WXS-41a. Romani (composer & compiler): Die Fee und der Ritter (ballet pastiche, including works by Aiblinger, Mercadante, Pacini, Paer, Pensel, Romani, Rossini), Theil 1: overture & 11 mvts; Theil 2: 12 mvts, *56th & 57th Werke.*   2ob 2cl 2hn 2bn cbn 2tp.
Pc (Mechetti: Wien, c.1817), MS parts: A-Wn, Mus.Hs.3881, (AH, FB); CZ-Bm(au), A.36.872, (Theil 1, local).
WXS-42a. Rossini: Ciro in Babilonia, (Theil 1) overture & 11 mvts, (Theil 2) 12 mvts.   2ob 2cl 2hn 2bn cbn (2tp).
MS parts: A-Wgm(w), (?lost);   CZ-Bm(au), A.35.212, (Theil 1); I-Fc, F.P. S.387, (complete);
I-OS, Mus.Musiche B 4061, (Theil 1 as Anon, with a later b-tb pt for Nos. 2, 3 & 7 in another hand).
WXS-43.1a. Rossini: Tancredi, overture & 11 mvts.   2ob 2cl 2hn 2bn cbn (2tp).
MS parts: A-Wn, Mus.Hs.3841, (complete. AH); CZ-Bm(au), A.35.224; D-Tl, Z 116; I-Fc, F.P. S.386.
Pm (Compusic: Amsterdam, pn 220, 1991), overture only, score & parts.
WXS-43.2a. Rossini: Tancredi, an additional 5 mvts not found in WXS-43.1a, inserted in Sedlak's arrangement of Rossini's *L'Italiana in Algeri,* WXS-44a.   2ob 2cl 2hn 2bn cbn (2tp).
***WXS-44a.** Rossini: L'Italiana in Algeri, overture & 11 mvts.   2ob 2cl 2hn 2bn cbn (2tp).
MS parts: A-Wn, Mus.Hs.3838, (?lost; ?missing 2tp; Nos. 6 - 11 are from *Tancredi;* FB; a microfilm copy is available at: A-Wn, M.S.1124b (Photo M 261/91)); CZ-Bm(au), A.35.217, (local copy, 1819); I-Fc, F.P. S.386.
Pm (Compusic: Amsterdam, 1991), overture only, score & parts.
***WXS-45a.** Rossini: Elisabetta, Regina d'Inghilterra, *26 & 27 Werke*; Theil 1: overture & 11 mvts; Theil 2: 12 mvts.   2ob 2cl 2hn 2bn cbn (2tp). ,
MS parts (AH, FB): A-Wn, Mus.Hs.3837.   *Note: The arrangement in CZ-Bm is by Starke.*
Pm (Compusic: Amsterdam, 1988), overture only, score & parts.
***WXS-46.1a.** Rossini: Il Barbiere di Siviglia, (Theil 1) *22tes Werk:* overture & 11 mvts, (Theil 2) *30tes Werk:* 12 mvts (No. 11 is Rode's *Variazione in G,* used by Madame Catalani as the singing lesson in Act II). 2ob 2cl 2hn 2bn cbn (2tp).
MS pts: A-Wn, Mus.Hs.3855, (complete; AH, FB); CZ-Bm(au), A.35.209, (Theil 2, local copy; the overture to Hummel's ballet, *Sappho von Myrtilene,* as "Die Rache von Venus" replaces the Marciale as No. 1; Nos. 7 - 10 have been omitted).   *See* The Wind Ensemble Sourcebook *for a discussion of the gap in Werke numbers.*
Pm (Nova Music: London, 1983), ed. Stanley E. De Rusha, overture only, score & parts.
Pm (Musica rara: Monteux, pn MR 2134, c.1988), overture only, score & parts.
Pm (Compusic: Amsterdam, pn 224, 1988), overture only, score & parts.
WXS-46.2a. Rossini: Il Barbiere di Siviglia, overture & 11 mvts.   2cl 2hn 2bn.
MS parts (AH): CZ-Pnm, XLI.B.120, (No. 13 is the overture to Paer's opera, *Lodoiska)*; PL-LA, RM 87.
WXS-47a. Rossini: Otello, Theil 1: overture & 11 mvts, Theil 2: overture & 9 mvts.   2ob 2cl 2hn 2bn cbn (2tp).
MS parts: A-Wgm(w), (?lost = A-274a); I-Fc, F.P. S.413; I-OS, Mss.Musiche B.4140, (Theil 1 only, FB, with a later b-tb pt for the Overture and Introduzione only, in another hand on different paper).
+WXS-48a. Rossini: La Cenerentola, Theil 1: overture & 7 mvts; Theil 2: 8 mvts; Theil 3: 8 mvts.
2ob 2cl 2hn 2bn cbn (2tp).   MS parts (FB): I-Fc, F.P. S.414.
WXS-49.1a. Rossini: Mosè in Egitto, Theil 1: introduzione & 11 mvts, Theil 2: 12 mvts. 2ob 2cl 2hn 2bn cbn (2tp).
MS parts: CZ-Bm(au), A.37.347, (Theil 2 only); I-Fc, F.P. S.416, (divided into 3 Abtheilungen, each of 8 mvts); A-Wgm(w), (?lost).
+WXS-49.2a. Rossini: Mosè in Egitto, duetto.   2ob 2cl 2hn 2bn cbn 2tp.   MS parts: CZ-Bm(au), A.40.165.
+WXS-49.3a. Rossini: Mosè in Egitto, Preghiera.   (? 2ob 2cl 2hn 2bn cbn 2tp).   MS parts: A-Wgm(w), (?lost).
WXS-50a. Rossini: Ricciardo e Zoraide.   2ob 2cl 2hn 2bn cbn (2tp).
MS parts: CZ-Bm(au), (Theil 1, overture & 10 mvts) A.35.220, (Theil 2, 14 mvts) A.36.876; A-Wgm(w), (?lost).
***WXS-51a.** Rossini: Matilda di Shabran (as "Il Corradino"), *46tes - 48tes Werk:* (Theil 1) overture & 11 mvts, (Theil 2) 12 mvts, (Theil 3) 12 mvts.   2ob 2cl 2hn 2bn cbn 2tp.
MS parts: A-Wn, Mus.Hs.3836, (complete; AH, FB).
Pm (Compusic: Amsterdam, pn 223, 1991), overture only, score & parts.
***WXS-52.1a.** Rossini: Zelmira, *39 & 40 Werk,* (Theil 1) overture & 11 mvts, (Theil 2) 13 mvts.
2ob 2cl 2hn 2bn cbn (2tp).   MS pts: A-Wn, Mus.Hs.3844, (complete; AH, FB); CZ-Bm(au), (Theil 1) A.37.348, (Theil 2), A.35.226, (local copy); I-Fc, F.P. S.388.
***WXS-52.2a.** Rossini: Zelmira, *39 & 40 Werk,* (Theil 1) overture & 13 mvts, (Theil 2) 1st finale & 9 mvts.
2cl 2hn 2bn.   MS parts: PL-LA, RM 88/1 and 2.
***WXS-53a.** Rossini: Semiramide, *52tes & 53tes Werk,* (Theil 1) overture & 11 mvts, (Theil 2) 13 mvts.
2ob 2cl 2hn 2bn cbn (2tp).   MS parts: A-Wgm, VIII 4572 (also at shelfmark: 362 S. Xerox; AH, FB); A-Wn; CZ-Bm(au), (Theil 2) A.40.166, (Theil 2, duetto only, missing cbn), A.40.165.
Pm (Compusic: Amsterdam, pn 222, 1991), overture only, score & parts.
***WXS-54a.** Rossini: Le Siège de Corinthe, Theil 1: overture & 13 mvts, Theil 2: 6 mvts.
2ob 2cl 2hn 2bn cbn (2tp).   MS parts (local copy, 1826): CZ-Bm(au), (Theil 1) A.35.222, (Theil 2) A.35.223.
+WXS-55a. Rossini: Le Comte Ory, [Theil 1]: 5 mvts, [Theil 2]: 7 mvts.   2ob 2cl 2hn 2bn cbn 2tp.
MS parts (local copy, 18 Jan 1832, but uses FB): CZ-Bm(au), (Theil 1) A.36.873, (Theil 2) 35.216. *The Theil division is probably a local alteration.*
***+WXS-56a.** Rossini: Guillaume Tell, Theil 1: overture & 7 mvts, Theil 2: 8 mvts.   2ob 2cl 2hn 2bn cbn 2tp (b-tb).
MS pts: A-Wn(w), (?lost); CZ-Bm(au), (Theil 1) A.36.664, (Theil 2) A.35.225, (with a much later flute pt for the overture, *not* by Sedlak. The b-tb part, not listed on the titlepage, is in the same hand as the rest of the MS; the pt ends after Theil 2, No. 6). *This copy, made by members of the Augustinian Harmonie at Brno is incomplete: a long "Duetto Agita [sic]", the original No. 4 of Theil 2, is found (crossed out) only in the Fagotti Bassi part.*
Pm (Compusic: Amsterdam, pn 250, 1991), overture only (without fl/pic), score & parts.
WXS-57a. Rossini: Blaubart (ballet pastiche), overture & 11 mvts.   2ob 2cl 2hn 2bn cbn (2tp).
MS parts: CZ-Bm(au), A.36.871.
+WXS-58a. Seyfried, after Grétry: Richard Löwenherz, overture & 12 mvts.   2ob 2cl 2hn 2bn cbn.
MS parts: I-Fc, F.P. S.355, (the MS is divided into 2 Abtheilungen, probably a local alteration).
+WXS-59a. M. Umlauff: Paul et Rosette, overture & 11 mvts.   2ob 2cl 2hn 2bn cbn.
Pc (bey Johann Cappi: Wien, c.1806), MS parts: A-Wn, Mus.Hs.3870; CZ-Bm(no), A.16.673; GB-Ljag(w).
WXS-60a. M. Umlauf: Die Spiele des Paris auf dem Berg Ida, overture & 9 mvts.   2ob 2cl 2hn 2bn cbn.
Pc [Johann Cappi: Vienna, 1806]. MS parts: CZ-Pnm, Lobkovic X.H.a.3.

+WXS-61a. M. Umlauff: Aeneas in Carthago, 2 mvts.   2ob 2cl 2hn 2bn cbn.   MS parts: A-Wn, Mus.Hs.3869.
For M. Umlauf: Die Hochzeit des Gamacho, *2 mvts.   2ob 2cl 2hn 2bn cbn 2tp, See:* **WXS-3.3a.**
*WXS-62a. Weber: Der Freischütz, Theil 1 ("35 Werk"), overture & 11 mvts; Theil 2 [36 Werk], 9 mvts.
2ob 2cl 2hn 2bn cbn (2tp).   MS parts: CZ-Bm(au), (Theil 1, 2 copies) A.35.242, A.40.166 (missing ob II, bn II,
cbn; 1822), (Theil 2) A.35.243; D-Rtt, Weber 1/II, (Theil 1; AH); I-Fc, F.P. S.384 (in 3 Theils: overture & 8
mvts, 7 mvts [Theil 1, No. 10 split into 2 sections], 6 mvts); A-Wgm(w), (?lost).
Pm (Compusic: Amsterdam, pn (Overture) 259A, (Theils 1, 2) 259B, 259C, 1988), score & parts.
+WXS-63a. Weber: Euryanthe, overture & 16 mvts.   2ob 2cl 2hn 2bn cbn 2tp.
MS parts (FB): CZ-Bm(au), A.40.167, (copy dated 1841); D-Tl, Z 128, (as Anon).
Pc (as Anon, FB:) (Chemische Druckerei/Steiner: Vienna, pn 4578, 1823), parts: NL-DHgm, hk 19 C 5.
Pc (as Anon, FB:) (Richault: Paris, pn 1294 R., 1825/1826), parts: CH-Gpu, Ib. 4685.
+WXS-64a. J. Weigl: Die Reue des Pigmalion, overture & 8 mvts.   2cl 2hn 2bn.
MS parts: CZ-KRa, A4453/R.I.23, No. 9.
+WXS-65a. J. Weigl: Die isthmischen Spiele, overture & 8 mvts.   2cl 2hn 2bn.
MS parts: CZ-KRa, A4453/R.I.23, No. 8, (as Anon).
WXS-66a J. Weigl: Die Uniform, overture & 11 mvts.   2ob 2cl 2hn 2bn cbn.
Pc (bey Johann Cappi: Wien, c.1805), MS parts: GB-Ljag(w); H-KE, 884/VIII; I-Fc, F.P. S.342.
*WXS-67a. Winter: Das Labyrinth, overture & 13 mvts.   2cl 2hn 2bn.
MS parts: CZ-KRa, A4003/IV.B.176; CZ-Pnm, XLI.B.132. *A reduction of Triebensee's octet arrangement.*
WXS-68a. Winter: Marie von Montalban, overture & 11 mvts.   2cl 2hn 2bn.   MS pts: A-KR, G 8/19, (as Anon);
CZ-KRa, A4453/R.I.23, No. 1, (with duplicate parts for some numbers); CZ-Pnm, XLI.B.130; PL-LA, RM 27.
WXS-69a. Zingarelli: Giulietta e Romeo, overture & 8 mvts.   2cl 2hn 2bn.   MS parts: PL-LA, RM 68.
WXS-1ad. Beethoven: Symphony No. 7 in A (here, G), Op. 92.   2ob 2cl 2hn 2bn cbn. *Probably by Druschetzky.*
Pc (Chemische Druckerei/Steiner: Vienna, pn 2563, 1816), **J9**, parts: D-BNbh; D-ESpriv.
MS score: D-NEhz, 54, (with parts for fl 2ob 2cl 2hn 2bn tp tb db timp, probably rescored by Georg Schmitt).
Pm (WINDS: Northridge, CA, pn W-185, c.1981), parts.
Pm (Compusic: Amsterdam, 1988), score (pn 231A) & parts (pn 231B).
*WXS-2ad/*JNW-10ac. Palma: La Pietra simpatica, sinfonia & 7 (+ 1) mvts.   2ob 2cl 2hn 2bn.
Pc (k.k. Hoftheater: Wien, 1796; Traeg: [Vienna], No. 196, 1799), MS pts: A-Wn, Mus.Hs.3830; I-Fc, F.P. S.326,
(misattributed to Nasolini). *Earlier suggestions that Nos. 1 - 8 of the A-Wn copy are in Sedlak's hand, with mvt
9 in Went's hand are completely unfounded: two hands are involved, one a professional copyist, the other
possibly Went (cf. - the most likely choice as arranger).*
WXS-3ad. Süssmayr: Der Retter in Gefahr, recitativo & aria.   2ob 2cl 2hn 2bn.
MS parts: A-Wn, Mus.Hs.3853. (= A-554a)
*The following works have long been attributed without proof to Sedlak; we now believe that Nicolaus Scholl was
more likely to have been the arranger:*
WXS-4ad. Auber: Le Maçon (as Maurer und Schlosser), Marsch.   2ob 2cl 2hn 2bn cbn (2tp). *Mvt No. 2 of
the arrangement of Pacini's Amazilla, WXS-19ad.*
WXS-5ad. Auber: Le Duc d'Olonne, 3 mvts (Ballade, Aria, Pas redoublé).   2ob 2cl 2hn 2bn cbn 2tp.
MS parts (by Perschl): A-Wn, Mus.Hs.3796.
WXS-6ad. Bellini: La Straniera, 11 mvts.   2ob 2cl 2hn 2bn cbn 2tp [b-tb, Nos. 10 & 11 only].
MS parts (by Perschl, A-37a): A-Wn, Mus.Hs.3801, (the b-tb pt is in another, later, hand).
WXS-7ad. Bellini: I Capuleti ed i Montecchi, (Theil 1) 2 mvts, (Theil 2) 4 mvts.   2ob 2cl 2hn 2bn cbn 2tp(Theil
2 only).   MS pts (1834): A-Wn, Mus.Hs.3798, (at the end of the bn II & cbn pt is the pencil date 1834;
simplified parts for Theil 1, No. 2, Allegro modto section are marked in many of the pts in red crayon; further
simplified parts in another hand for Theil 1, No. 2, section 1 are inserted as loose sheets in the ob I, ob II, cl II,
bn I, bn II & cbn pts; corrections and interpretive additions in another hand have been added to Theil 2).
WXS-8ad. Bellini: La Sonnambula, 5 mvts.   2ob 2cl 2hn 2bn 2tp [b-tb].
MS parts (by Perschl, 1837): A-Wn, Mus.Hs.3800.
WXS-9ad. Bellini: Norma, 4 mvts.   2ob 2cl 2hn 2bn cbn 2tp [b-tb].   MS parts: A-Wn, Mus.Hs.3799.
WXS-10ad. Bellini: Beatrice di Tenda, terzetto.   2ob 2cl 2hn 2bn cbn 2tp [b-tb].
MS parts (by Perschl): A-Wn, Mus.Hs.3797.
WXS-11ad. Bellini: I Puritani di Scozia, 3 mvts.   2ob 2cl 2hn 2bn cbn 2tp [b-tb].
MS parts (b-tb Hand): A-Wn, Mus.Hs.4459.
WXS-12ad. Donizetti: L'Elisir d'amore, 4 mvts.   2ob 2cl 2hn 2bn cbn 2tp [b-tb].
MS parts (by Perschl, 1837): A-Wn, Mus.Hs.3808, (cropping affects a few bars in the b-tb pt).
WXS-13ad. Donizetti: Torquato Tasto, 6 mvts.   2ob 2cl 2hn 2bn 2tp [b-tb].
MS parts (mvts 1-5 by Perschl, 1837; mvt 6 in the b-tb Hand): A-Wn, Mus.Hs.3810.
Statements that mvt 6 is in Sedlak's hand are completely unfounded.
WXS-14ad. Donizetti: Mario Faliero, 3 mvts.   2ob 2cl 2hn 2bn cbn 2tp b-tb.
MS parts (by Perschel): A-Wn, Mus.Hs.3967.
WXS-15ad. Donizetti: Lucia di Lammermoor, 3 mvts (duetto, aria, cavatina).   2ob 2cl 2hn 2bn cbn 2tp b-tb.
MS parts (in the b-tb Hand): A-Wn, Mus.Hs.3809.
WXS-16ad. Hérold: Le Pré aux Clercs, 3 mvts.   2ob 2cl 2hn 2bn cbn 2tp.
MS parts (by Perschl): A-Wn, Mus.Hs.3812, (the 2tp are tacet in No. 3).
WXS-17ad. Mercadante: Andronico, duetto.   2ob 2cl 2hn 2bn 2tp b-tb.   MS parts: A-Wn, Mus.Hs.3819.
WXS-18ad. Meyerbeer: Les Huguenots, 6 mvts (Trinklied, Coro, Finale, Balatta, Ziguenertanz, Duetto).
2ob 2cl 2hn 2bn cbn 2tp b-tb.   MS pts (by Perschl): A-Wn, Mus.Hs.3820, (each piece with a separate titlepage).
WXS-19ad. Pacini: Amazilla, overture & 4 mvts.   2ob 2cl 2hn 2bn cbn 2tp.
MS parts: CZ-Bm(au), A.40.101. *No. 2 is a march from Auber's Maurer und Schlosset (Le Maçon).*
WXS-20ad. Ricci: Il nuovo Figaro, overture.   2ob 2cl 2hn 2bn 2tp b-tb.
MS parts (by Perschl): A-Wn, Mus.Hs.3834.
WXS-21ad. Ricci: Il Desertore per amore, cavatina & scene e cavatina.   2ob 2cl 2hn 2bn cbn 2tp [b-tb].
MS parts (the first cavatina by Perschl; the scena e cavatina in another hand): A-Wn, Mus.Hs.3833.
Statements that this work is partly by Sedlak & completed by Perschl are completely without foundation.

SEDSTRÖM, Hugo *1862 - 1941, Sweden*
HXS-1. Aftonstimming (Eventide).   2fl 2ob 2cl 2hn 2bn 2tp.
Pm (Elkan & Schildknecht: Stockholm), score & parts.

*SEIBER, Mátyás György *4 May 1905, Budapest - 24 Sept 1960, Capetown, South Africa*
*MGS-1. Serenade, 1925.   2cl 2hn 2bn.
AutoMS scores: GB-Lbl, Add.Ms.62800, ("Szerenad"; three versions).
Pm (Wilhelm Hansen: Copenhagen, pn 27413,1957), score & parts.

*SEIDEL, ( )
YYS-1v. Salve Regina; in E♭.   B solo, 2cl 2hn bn.   MS parts (by Josef Holeček): CZ-Pnm, XLIII.A.315.   ★

SEIDEL, Friedrich Ludwig *14 July 1765, Truenbriezen - 7 May 1838 Berlin*
FUS-1. Sestetto; in C.   fl ob 2hn bn, harpsichord/piano.
Pc (J.J. Hummel: Berlin, Amsterdam, 1800), parts: B-Bc, No. 7050.
Pm (McGinnis & Marx: New York, sd), score & parts.
Pm (De Wolfe: London), score & parts.

*SEIFF (Sieff), Jacob [G.] *(1780)*
We have no locations for other Harmonie pieces for fl 2cl 2hn bn 2tp (Falter et fils: München).
JYS-1. Six Pièces d'Harmonie.   2cl 2hn bn.
Pc (Falter et fils: München, sd), parts.
MS parts ("Ad me Thomas Daune"): D-Mbs, 4 Mus.pr 10481, (Nos. 1 - 5 only).   ★
JYS-2. Six Pièces d'Harmonie, Livre 1.   2cl 2hn bn.
Pc (chez les Fils de B. Schott: Mayence et Paris; A. Schott: Anvers, pn 557, 1811), pts: D-MZsch, (as "G. Seiff").   ★
JYS-1m. Militaer Musik Bestimmt für die National-Garden dritter Klasse des Königreichs Baiern. [? 1]tes Heft;
6 mvts.   pic 2cl(E♭) 2cl(B♭) 2hn 2bn 2tp b-tb b-dr.
Pc (bey Falter und Sohn: München, sd), parts: GB-Ljag(w), (missing b-dr).   ★
MS parts: D-Tl, Gg 454, Nos. 58 - 63, (missing pic 2cl(B♭) 2hn).
JYS-1a. 6 Pièces d'Harmonie tirées des Opéras favoris: La Muette de Portici [Auber], Macbeth [Chélard], Comte
Ory [Rossini], et Les 2 [sic] Nuits [Boieldieu].   2cl 2hn 2bn.
Pc (Schott: Mainz, Paris, c.1830), liv. I, parts: D-MZsch; DK-Kk.
JYS-2a. 6 Pièces d'Harmonie tirées des Opéras favoris: Macbeth [Chelard], Le Siège de Corinth [Rossini], [Der]
Vampyr [Marschner or Lindpaintner], La Muette de Portici [Auber], Comte Ory [Rossini], et Guill[aume] Tell
[Rossini].   2cl 2hn 2bn.
Pc (Schott: Mainz, Paris, c.1830), liv. 2, parts: D-MZsch.

*SEIFFERT, ( ) *(1800)*
YZS-1. [Introduction & 6] Wälzer, c.1830.   2cl(E♭) cl(B♭) 2hn bn cbn 2tp.   MS pts: CZ-Bm(au), A.35.933.   ★

*SELLNER, Josef *13 March 1787, Landau - 17 May 1843, Vienna*
JZS-1. Divertimento per Corno principale in F; 1 continuous mvt.   Solo horn, 2ob 2cl 2hn 2bn cbn 2tp.
MS score: A-Wn, Mus.Hs.3771, (Sellner's name has been crossed out in the title and all parts).   ★
JZS-2. [red crayon:] I [untitled work: Allegro in B♭ = I Pièce].   2ob 2cl 2hn 2bn cbn 2tp.
AutoMS score (1834): A-Wn, Mus.Hs.3772.   ★
JZS-3. [red crayon: II] Piéce [sic] pour la Harmonie; in E♭.   2ob 2cl 2hn 2bn cbn 2tp.
MS parts (by Perschl): A-Wn, Mus.Hs.3373.   ★
*JZS-4. [untitled work in a single mvt including a Theme & variations; in A♭].
Solo clarinet, 2ob cl 2hn 2bn cbn 2tp.
AutoMS score ("Wien aus 30ten Jann 1835"): A-Wn, Mus.Hs.3769, (title given incorrectly in the A-Wn catalog
as "Variations No. 1").   ★
Pm (WINDS: Northridge, CA, pn W-75, c.1981), photocopy of autograph & modern parts.
*JZS-5. [untitled Theme, 4 Variations & Polero [sic] in A♭].   Solo clarinet, 2ob cl 2hn 2bn cbn.
AutoMS score ("Wien aus 14ten Jaunn [sic] 1834"): A-Wn, Mus.Hs.3770. (title given incorrectly in the A-Wn
catalog as "Variations No. 2").   ★
Pm (WINDS: Northridge, CA, pn W-74, c.1981), photocopy of autograph & modern parts.

SERAFINO, Nino
NQS-1a. Tchaikovsky: Serenata, Op. 48, Elegia.   fl ob 2cl 2hn bn tp.
Pm (Edizione Musicali "Ortipe": Roma, sd), score & parts: I-Mc.

*ŠESTÁK, Zdeněk *10 Dec 1925, Cítoliby*
ZXS-1. Sonata da camera; 1978.   2ob 2cl 2hn 2bn.
Pm (Panton: Prague, 1981), score & parts.
ZXS-2. Partita Profana.   2ob ca 2bn.
Pm (Panton: Prague, 1976), score & parts.
ZXS-3. Congratulations Cassation.   fl cl 2bn tp.
Pm (Panton: Prague, 1979), score & parts.

*SETACCIOLI, Giacomo *8 Dec 1868, Corneto, Tarquinia - 5 Dec 1925, Sienna*
GIS-1. Nonett.   Piano, 2fl 2ob 2cl 2bn.
Pc (?Ricordi: Milano), parts, (cited in *MGG*).
GIS-1a. D. Scarlatti: Allegro in Si♭ [B♭] della Suite VIIIa per clavicembalo.   fl 2ob 2cl 2hn 2bn.
Pc (Ricordi: Milano, 1921), score & parts: US-Wc, M.779.R.

*SEXTARIUS, ( ) *(1770)*
UYS-1. Parthia in Dis [E♭]; 3 mvts.   2cl 2hn 2bn,
MS parts (by Augustin Erasmus Hübner, Langenbruck, 1801): CZ-Pn(dm), 59 R 3327.   ★

***SEYFRIED, Ignaz Xaver, *Ritter von* ** *15 Aug 1776, Vienna - 27/26 Aug 1841, Vienna*
*IXS-1. Serenata con una Cantatina Per li 4. Ottobre 1805 in Hetzendorf. Per due Orchestre d'Armonia;
(SWV VIII/5). Orchestra "A": 2ob 2cl 2hn 2bn cbn; Orchestra "B": ob ob/ca 2cl/2bthn 2hn 2bn cbn.
Voices: Solo STTB & SATB choruses.
MS score (with Auto amendments): A-Wn, Mus.Hs.11,105. ★
Pm (IXS-1.2 only:) (WINDS: Northridge, CA, c.1981), score & parts.
   IXS-1.1(a). Serenata Nro. 1. Grétry: Raoul Barbe-Bleue (as "Raul der Blaubarb [sic]"). 2ob 2cl 2hn 2bn cbn.
   IXS-1.2. Serenata Nro. 2. Divertimento per l'armonia a due Orchestre con l'Eco.
Orch A: 2ob 2cl 2hn 2bn cbn; Orch B: 2ob 2cl 2hn 2bn cbn.
   IXS-1.3(v). Serenata Nr 3. Cantatina.
      1.3/1(v). Cantata. SATB chorus; Orch A: 2ob 2cl(C) 2hn 2bn cbn; Orch B: 2ob 2cl 2hn 2bn cbn.
      1.3/2(v). Canone. Solo STTB, SATB chorus; Orch A: 2ob 2cl 2hn 2bn cbn; Orch B: ca cl 2bthn bn cbn.
      1.3/3(v). Coro. SATB chorus; Orch A: 2ob 2cl 2hn 2bn cbn; Orch B: 2ob 2cl 2hn 2bn cbn.
   IXS-1.4(a). Serenata Nr 4. Quodlibet; 24 short mvts.
Orchestra 1: 2ob 2cl 2hn 2bn cbn; Orchestra 2: 2ob 2cl 2hn 2bn cbn.
      1.4/1(a). Mozart: La Clemenza di Tito, overture, 29 bars. 2ob 2cl 2hn 2bn cbn, (A).
      1.4/2(a). Andantino, 12 bars. 2ob 2cl 2hn 2bn cbn, (B).
      1.4/3(a). Gluck: La Rencontre imprévu, "Unser dummer Pöbel meint", 13 bars. 2ob 2cl 2hn 2bn cbn, (A).
      1.4/4(a). Allegro, 16 bars. 2ob 2cl 2hn 2bn cbn, (B).
      1.4/5(a). Mozart: Die Zauberflöte, "Dies Bildnis ist bezaubernd schön". 2ob 2cl 2hn 2bn cbn, (A).
      1.4/6(a). J. Weigl: L'Amor marinaro. 2ob 2cl 2hn 2bn cbn, (A).
      1.4/7(a). Paisiello: La Molinara. 2ob 2hn 2bn, (A).
      1.4/8(a). Scherzando, 8 bars. ob 2cl 2hn 2bn, (A).
      1.4/9(a). Sostenuto, 12 bars. 2ob 2cl 2hn 2bn, (B).
      1.4/10(a). Larghetto, 8 bars. ob 2cl 2hn 2bn, (A). *Segue subito*
      1.4/11(a). Moderato, 16 bars. 2ob 2cl 2hn 2bn, (B).
      1.4/12(a). And.^{te} Sostenuto, 23 bars. 2ob 2cl 2hn 2bn, (A).
      1.4/13(a). Allegro, 20 bars. 2ob 2cl 2hn 2bn cbn, (B).
      1.4/14(a). Mozart: Die Zauberflöte, "In diesen heilgen Hallen", 8 bars. 2cl hn(solo in Es) 2bn, (B).
      1.4/15(a). And^{lino} Scherzando, 16 bars. 2cl(A) 2bn, (A).
      1.4/16(a). Poco Allegretto, 8 bars, 2ob 2hn 2bn, (A) / 2/4, cbn solo, (A).
      1.4/17(a). Andante, 8 bars. 2ob 2cl 2hn 2bn (B).
      1.4/18(a). Allo vivace, 12 bars. ob 2hn 2bn (A).
      1.4/19(a). Salieri: Palmira. 2bn + 2bn (A + B).
      1.4/20(a). Anon: O du lieber Augustine, 28 bars. ob 2cl 2hn 2bn cbn (B)
      1.4/21(a). Mozart: Le Nozze di Figaro, "Non più andrai", 10 bars. 2ob 2cl 2hn 2bn (A).
      1.4/22(a). Andantino, 6/8, 8 bars. 2cl 2hn 2bn cbn, (B).
      1.4/23(a). Mozart: Die Zauberflöte, "Zum Ziele", 18 bars/ob(I), (A) cadenza/24 bars. 2cl 2hn 2bn cbn (A+B).
      1.4/24(a). Haydn: Gott erhalte Franz den Kaiser, 22 bars. 2ob 2cl 2hn 2bn cbn, (A & B)
   IXS-1.5(a). Serenata Nr 5. Cherubini: Les deux Journées (as "Die Tage der Gefahr"), Marsch.
2ob 2cl 2hn 2bn cbn.
IXS-1e. Julius Caesar, Trauerspiel in fünf Aufzügen; 1811.
AutoMS score: D-DS, Mus.ms.1016. MS score: A-Wn, Mus.Hs.3276; D-F, Mus.Hs. Opern 537.
   1.1e. Tempo di Marcia funebre; bars 1 - 24. ★
   1.2e. Act I, No. 2: Aufzug beÿden [sic] Lupernalien. 2flautino 2ob 2cl(C) 2hn 2bn tri "tamburin". ★
   1.3e. Act III, No. 5: Marsch und Chor beÿ dem Leichenzug. SA chorus [Klage-Frauen], 2fl 2ob 2cl 2hn 2bn
      2tp 2a-tb b-tb timp(con Sordini), tamburo milit: coperto. Act III, No. 5. ★
   1.4e. Act III, No. 6: Marsch der Brutus [with Alternativo]. 2cl 2tp cbn. ★
IXS-1v. Julius Caesar, Larghetto. Female chorus, 2fl 2ob 2cl 2hn 2bn 2tp 3tb timp perc.
AutoMS score: D-DS, Mus.ms.1016, No. 5. ★
*IXS-2v. [Requiem No. 1 in As [A♭] Con Libera; (SWV XII/1)] Libera. SATB, 2bthn 2bn 2tp 3tb organ timp.
AutoMS score (Libera me): A-Wn, Mus.Hs.37,635. ★
MS score & parts (by A. Rockinger, c.1840): D-BB, Ms.173, No. 2, (parts missing 2bn; 3tb = a-tb 2t-tb; with
2cl parts to replace 2bthn).
Pc (Bei Tobias Haslinger: Vienna, 1827), score & pts: A-Wn, MS. 39910; D-B; D-SWl; GB-Lbl, H.1187.g.(3).
IXS-3v. Libera zum Gebrauche bei Mozart's Requiem; 1827/1828, (SWV XV/5).
SATB, 2bthn(vel cl) 2hn 2bn 2tp 2tb vlne timp organ.
AutoMS score: A-Wn, Mus.Hs.5117. ★
MS parts: A-HE, III d 1; A-Wm, Sign. 191, (SATB, 2tp vlne); D-BB, 173, (missing 2bn).
Pc (Haslinger: Vienna, 1828), score (pn 5042) & parts (pn 5043): A-M; A-SEI; A-Wn, (2 copies); D-Mbs.
*IXS-4v. Motette. Psalm 23; "Der Herr ist mein Hirte". SATB solo & chorus, 2cl 2hn 2bn 2tp b-hn timp.
MS score: D-SWl, Mus. 5077. ★
IXS-5v. Tantum ergo, No. 3; (SWV XV/10, No. 3). S/T, fl 2ob 2cl 2hn 2bn 2tp(clar) timp *or* organ.
AutoMS score (May 1835): A-Wn, Mus.Hs.37,672. MS parts: A-Wn, Mus.Hs.37,676. ★
IXS-6v. Cantata, "Singst und Freut Euch"; (SWV VII/5), 4 mvts. SATB, 2fl 2ob 2cl 2tp(clar) vlne timp.
MS parts: A-M, IV 129.
IXS-1va. Mozart: La Clemenza di Tito, Coro, "Che del ciel", as Offertorium, "Justuts ut palma".
CATB, 2vl vla vc b, 2ob 2tp(clar) 3tb organ timp *or* 2cl 2hn 2bn.
MS score (1837): A-Wn, Fond Nr. 24 St. Peter - Wien, E. 236 (I).
IXS-1tv, 2tv. 2 Grablieder in Es [E♭] für Erwachsene: "Trocknet erues Jammers Thränen" & "Die so zärtlich
fü mich wachtet, liebe Kinder!". No. 1: CATB, fl(F) cl(E♭) 3cl(B♭) 2hn bn 2tp b-tb; No. 2: CATB, fl(F) 2cl
2hn bn 2tp b-tb. MS parts: CZ-LIa(vl), No. 2456 hud. ★
IXS-3tv, 4tv. 2 Grablieder in Es [E♭]; "Meiner Jahre Luaf hab ich vollstrecket" & "Wenn oft in feierlicher
Stille"; (SWV deest). CATB, fl(F) 2cl 2hn bn 2tp(clar) a-tb t-tb b-tb. MS pts: CZ-LIa(vl), No. 2438 hud. ★

*IXS-1ad (= A-500a). Seyfried: Saul, König in Israel, overture & 14 mvts.   2ob 2cl 2hn 2bn cbn.
Pc (Im Verlage der k:k: priv chemischen Druckerey: Wien, pn 1486, 1810), *Journal für neunstimmige Harmonie,*
No. II, parts: A-Wst, M.24772/c, (without cbn part); CZ-KRa, A3842/IV.B.6, (in MS, missing cbn; overture &
Nos. 3, 4, 9, 12, here attributed to "Cherubiny"); CZ-Pnm, Lobkovic X.G.f.73 (complete); GB-Ljag, (photocopy);
H-Bn, Z 22,012, (complete); I-Fc, F.P. S.355, (MS parts).

SHCHEDRIN (Schtschedrin), Rodion Konstantinovich *16 Dec 1932, Moscow*
RKS-1. Musikalisches Opfer (1983, zum Geburtstag von J.S. Bach); 1 long continuous mvt.   Organ, 3fl 3bn 3tb.
Pm (Universal Edition: Wien, pn UE 18100, 1984), facsimile AutoMS score.

*SHEEN, Graham *18 Feb 1952, Southampton*
All of the E.F. Kalmus editions are also available in extra large score format.
*GHS-1a. Bizet: Carmen suite, (1990), 6 mvts.   fl ob ob(ca) 2cl 2hn 2bn cbn.
Pm (E.F. Kalmus: New York, pn A2460, c.1992), score & parts.
*GHS-2a. Bizet: Jeux d'Enfants.   fl(pic) 2ob 2cl 2hn 2bn.
Pm (E.F. Kalmus: New York, pn A2745, c.1993), score & parts.
GHS-3a. Brahms: Hungarian Dances, Nos. 3, 5, 11, 16.   2fl fl(pic) 2ob 2cl b-cl 4hn 2bn cbn.
Pm (E.F. Kalmus: New York, pn A7215, 1989), score & parts.
GHS-4a. Brahms: Variations & Fugue on a theme of Handel, Op. 24.   fl fl(pic) 2ob 2cl b-cl 3hn 2bn.
Pm (E.F. Kalmus: New York, pn A7216, 1989), score & parts.
GHS-5a. Debussy: Marsche écossaise (Earl of Ross March).   fl fl(pic) ob ca 2cl b-cl 2hn 2bn cbn.
Pm (E.F. Kalmus: New York, pn A5439, c.1993), score & parts.
*GHS-6a. Debussy: Coin des Enfants, (as "Three Pieces from Children's Corner": "The Little Shepherd",
"Jimbo's Lullaby", "Golliwog's Cake-Walk").   fl(pic) ob ca cl b-cl 2hn bn cbn.
Pm (E.F. Kalmus: New York, pn A7209, 1989), score & parts.
GHS-7a. Debussy: Six Épigraphes antiques.   2fl fl(pic) ob ca 2cl b-cl 2hn 2bn cbn.
Pm (E.F. Kalmus: New York, pn A7999, c.1994), score & parts.
GHS-8a. Dvořák: Czech suite, Op. 39.   2fl ob ob(ca) 2cl 2hn 2bn.
Pm (E.F. Kalmus: New York, pn A7214, 1989), score & parts.
GHS-9a. Dvořák: Bagatelles, Op. 47.   2ob 2cl 2bthn/cl 2hn 2bn cbn.
Pm (E.F. Kalmus: New York, pn A2330, c.1993), score & parts.
GHS-10a. Janáček: [3] Lachian Dances.   2fl 2ob 2cl 2hn 2bn (cbn ad lib).
Pm (E.F. Kalmus: New York, pn A7494, c.1991), score & parts.
GHS-11a. Mendelssohn: Konzertstück in F minor, Op. 113.   Solo clarinet & basset horn, fl 2ob 2hn 2bn.
Pn (E.F. Kalmus: New York, pn A7284, c.1992), score & parts.
*GHS-12a. Mendelssohn: Konzertstück in D minor, Op. 114.   Solo clarinet & basset horn, fl 2ob 2hn 2bn.
Pm (E.F. Kalmus: New York, pn A7210, 1989), score & parts.
GHS-13a. Mozart: Idomeneo, overture.   2ob 2cl 2hn 2bn.
Pm (E.F. Kalmus: New York, pn A7211, 1989), score & parts.
GHS-14a. Mozart: Die Schauspieldirektor, overture.   2ob 2cl 2hn 2bn.
Pm (E.F. Kalmus: New York, pn A7213, 1989), score & parts.
GHS-15a. Mozart: La Clemenza di Tito, overture.   2ob 2cl 2hn 2bn.
Pm (E.F. Kalmus: New York, pn A7212, 1989), score & parts.
GHS-16a. Mozart: Die Zauberflöte, "Alles fühlt der Liebe Freuden".   pic ob 2cl 2hn 2bn.
Pm (Park Music: London, 1988), hire score & parts.
GHS-17a. Mozart: Eine kleine Nachtmusik (K.525).   2ob 2cl 2hn 2bn.
Pm (Park Music: London, 1988), hire score & parts, *(arranged for the film* Amadeus *but unused).*
*GHS-18a. Schubert: 16 German Dances, (Op. 33, D.783).   fl(pic) ob ca cl b-cl 2hn bn cbn.
Pm (E.F. Kalmus: New York, pn A7208, 1989), score & parts.

*SHERIFF, Noam *7 Jan 1935, Tel Aviv*
*NOS-1. Music for Woodwinds, Trombone, Piano and Bass, 3 mvts.   3fl(pic) 2ob ca 3cl 3bn db piano.
Pm (Israeli Music Institute: Tel Aviv; 1961), score.

SHEWAN, Douglas
DXS-1. Wind octet.   2fl 2ob 2cl hn bn.
Pm (Hansen House: London, etc., 1975), score & parts.

*SHIELD, William *5 March 1748, Whickham, Durham - 25 Jan 1829, London*
*WYS-1e. Robin Hood [comic opera, 17 April 1784]: Finale, music to accompany the banquet.   2cl 2hn 2bn.
Pc (In: *The Piano-Forte Magazine.* Vol. XII. No. 3. 1800. Printed for Harrison and Co.: London), score: GB-Bu:
GB-Cu; GB-Lbl, D.854; GB-Ljag, (modern score); GB-Lsl; GB-Lu; GB-LVu; GB-T.   ★
*WYS-2e. The Magic Cavern or Virtue's Triumphs: Horns and Clarinets under the Stage, 16 bars.   2cl 2hn bn.
Pc (Longman & Broderip: London, 1785), RISM [S3047], pp. 8 - 9, score: F-Pn; GB-BA; GB-Lbl, H.230.b.(5);
GB-Lcm; GB-Ljag, (photocopy); US-Bp; US-Wc.
*WYS-1m. March in the Siege of Gibralter [sic] Perform'd by the Military Band while the Fleet sail into the Bay.
2ob 2cl 2hn (2)bn 2tp "Kettle Drums".
Pc (Wm. Napier: London; c.1780), score: GB-Er; GB-DOTams, (photocopy); GB-Ljag, (photocopy).   ★

*SHORT, Michael *27 Feb 1937, Bermuda (now resident in the UK)*
*MZS-1. 3 Pieces for Wind Octet.   2ob 2cl 2hn 2bn.
Pm (Studio Music: London, 1988), score & parts.

*SHOSTAKOVICH, Dmitri Dmitrievich *25 Sept 1906, St Petersburg - 9 Aug 1975, Moscow*
*DDS-1a. Two Scarlatti Pieces (L413 Pastorale; L375 Capriccio), Op. 17; 1928.
pic 2fl 2ob 2cl 2hn 2bn 2tp tb timp.
AutoMS score facsimile: Muzyka No. 27, 1983 (as "Op. 16").
Pm (Boccaccini & Spada: Roma, pn B.S.1162, 1985), revised Franco Mannino, score, (without pic).
Pm (E.F. Kalmus: New York, pn GEN 1653, c.1988), score.

SHOUJOUNIAN, Petros *1957, Canada*
PES-1. Akhtamar; 1983. Solo bassoon, 4fl 4ob 4cl. MS score: C-Tcm.

*SIBELIUS, Jean *8 Dec 1865, Tavastehus - 20 Sept 1957, Järvenpää.*
For the works for Hornseptett, some sources give a scoring with clarinet instead of Eb cornet. This alternative is sensible but, so far as we can tell, not authentic.
*JES-1. King Christian Suite: Musette, Op. 27. 2cl 2bn.
Pm (Breitkopf & Härtel: Leipzig, etc., 1932), score.
*JES-2. Allegro, Eb minor, 1889. s-crt(Eb) 2crt(Bb) a-hn(Eb) t-hn(Bb) b-hn(Bb) euph tu(Eb) tri.
AutoMS: FIN-Hy, Wo.0499, draft of score.
Pm (ed. Christopher Larkin from AutoMS), MS score & parts: GB-Lgbe.
JES-3. Overture in F minor, 1889-1890. s-crt(Eb) 2crt(Bb) a-hn(Eb) t-hn(Bb) b-hn(Bb) euph tu(Eb) perc.
AutoMS: FIN-Hy, Wo.0502 (score), Wo.0501 (parts, lacks ctII, tu).
Pm (ed. Christopher Larkin from AutoMS), MS score & parts: GB-Lgbe.
Pm (Fazer musiiki Oy, Helsinki, pn FM 07851-9, 1988), arr. Holger Fransman), score & parts.
JES-4. Andantino & Minuetto in C minor; 1890-91. s-crt(Eb) 2crt(Bb) a-hn(Eb) t-hn(Bb) b-hn(Bb) euph tu(Eb) perc.
MS score, (prepared by Haupt): FIN-Hy, Wo.0500.
Pm (Fazer musiiki Oy, Helsinki, pn FM 07852-7, 1988), with JES-5, as "Petite Suite", score & pts, (?without perc).
JES-5. Praeludium; 1891. s-crt(Eb) 2crt(Bb) a-hn(Eb) t-hn(Bb) b-hn(Bb) euph tu(Eb) perc.
MS (prepared by Haupt), score: FIN-Hy, Wo.0419/22.
Pm (Fazer musiiki Oy, Helsinki, pn FM 07852-7, 1988), with JES-4, as "Petite Suite", score & pts, (?without perc).
JES-6. Tiera; tone poem, 1894. s-crt(Eb) 2crt(Bb) a-hn(Eb) t-hn(Bb) b-hn(Bb) euph tu(Eb) perc.
(?Auto)MS score: FIN-Hy, Wo.0503.
Pc (Fazer musiiki Oy: Helsinki, c.1899), score: FIN-Hy, Wo.1874, (with autograph markings).
Pm (K[ansan] V[alistus] S[eura], 1934), score.
Pm (Kunstannusosakeyhotiö Otava, Finland, 1898), score.
*JES-1v. Aténarnes sång; 1898.
Chorus for boys' and mens' voices, s-crt(Eb) 2crt(Bb) a-hn(Eb) t-hn(Bb) b-hn(Bb) euph tu(Eb) perc.
Pm (Breitkopf & Härtel: Leipzig, 1899), score.

SIEBERT, Friedrich *25 May 1906, Bad Orb*
FZS-1. Scherzetto. Solo horn, 2fl 2ob 2cl 2bn.
Pm (Ernst Eulenberg: London, etc., pn GM 16, 1970), score & parts.

*SIGL (SIGEL, SICHEL), Georg *(1750)*
GGS-1. Partia Nro. 1; in Eb, 5 mvts. 2cl 2hn 2bn.
(?Auto)MS parts (c.1780): D-Rtt, Sigl 1. MS parts: D-DO. *The last mvt is a 4-section Balletto.* ★
GGS-2. Partia Nro. 2; in Bb, 5 mvts. 2cl 2hn 2bn.
(?Auto)MS parts (c.1780): D-Rtt, Sigl 2. MS parts: D-DO. ★
GGS-3. Partia Nro. 3; in Eb, 5 mvts. 2cl 2hn 2bn.
(?Auto)MS parts (c.1780): D-Rtt, Sigl 4. MS parts: D-DO. ★
GGS-4. Partia Nro. 4; in Bb, 5 mvts. 2cl 2hn 2bn.
(?Auto)MS parts (c.1780): D-Rtt, Sigl 3. MS parts: D-DO. ★
GGS-5. Partia Nro. 6; in Bb, 5 mvts. 2cl 2hn 2bn.
(?Auto)MS parts (c.1780): D-Rtt, Sigl 5. ★
GGS-6.1. No. 1 Parthitta [sic]; in Eb, 5 mvts. 2cl 2hn 2bn.
MS parts: CZ-KRa, A3971/IV.B.135, (titled); D-Rtt, Sm 8, Nos. 48 - 52, (untitled). ★
GGS-6.2. [Parthia in Eb], Di Sichel [sic] No. 5; 15 mvts. 2cl 2hn 2bn 2vla.
MS parts (c.1780): D-Rtt, Sigl 6. ★
GGS-7. Partita; in Eb, 4 mvts. 2cl 2hn bn.
MS parts (c.1770): D-Rtt, Sm. 8, Nos. 5-8. ★
GGS-8. No. 2. Parthitta [sic]; in Bb, 4 mvts. 2cl 2hn bn.
MS parts: CZ-KRa, A3972/IV.B.136. ★
GGS-9. No. 1. Parthia ex D; 5 mvts. 2cl 2hn bn.
MS parts: CZ-KRa, A3970/IV B.134. ★
GGS-10. Parthia in Dis [Eb]; 4 mvts. 2ca 2hn bn.
MS parts: CZ-Pnm, XLII.C.192. ★
GGS-1v. Deutsche Messe in C. CAB, 2ob 2hn bn+vlne organ.
MS parts (1816): D-BB, Ms. 151. ★

SILCHER, Friedrich *(1800)*
FIS-1. Figuralgesang aufs Christfest: Ehre sei Gott in der Höhe. 2cl 2bn b.
(?Auto)MS parts: D-Tl, R 9/2, (?missing vocal part). *The scoring is taken from the title; the parts present comprise: 2cl 2hn 2bn 2tp vc b timp.*
FIS-1v. Figuralgesang am Todestage des Erlösers "Schau hin nach Golgotha. S, 2cl 2hn 2bn basso organ.
(?Auto)MS parts: D-Tl, R 9/3, (with 5 copies of the Soprano vocal part).
FIS-1va. Vogler: Hymnus (Pfingsten u[nd]. Reformationsfest). TTBB, 2cl 2hn 2bn basso.
(?Auto)MS parts ("am Confessionsfest 1830"): D-Tl, R 6/1.

SILLANI, Francesco
FCS-1v. Pange lingua, in F. SATB, 2ob 2tb/tp basso.
MS score & parts: I-BGc, Mayr fald. 302/2; (the score calls for 2ob 2tb basso; the parts call for 2 oboes, 2 Tromba (written in the G clef) & basso; with mounting holes on the oboe II parts for outdoor performance). ★

*SIMAKU, Thoma *1958, Kavajë, Albania*
TZS-1. Elephas Maximus.   fl(pic) fl(a-fl) ob ob(ca) cl cl(b-cl) 2hn 2bn cbn 2tp.
Pm (Emerson Edition: Ampleforth, pn E243, 1994), score & parts.

*ŠIMON (Simoni), ( ) *(?1740)*
ZYS-1. Partita in C; 4 mvts.   2fl 2taille 2hn bn.
MS parts: CZ-Pnm, XLII.C.228. ★
ZYS-2. Partita in E♭; 4 mvts.   2fl 2taille 2hn bn.
MS parts: CZ-Pnm, XLII.D.100. ★
ZXS-3. Partita in C; 4 mvts.   2fl 2taille 2hn bn.
MS parts: CZ-Pnm, XLII.D.102. ★
ZXS-4. Partita in E♭; 4 mvts.   2fl 2taille 2hn bn.
MS parts: CZ-Pnm, XLII.D.103. ★

*SIMON, Ladislav *3 April 1929, Klánovics, nr Prague*
LXS-1. Sinfonietta for 13 wind instruments, 1988.
Pm (Český hudební fond: Prague, 1988), hire score.
LXS-2. Episodi.   2cl 2bthn b-cl.
Pm (Česky hudební fond: Prague, 1989), hire score & parts.

*SIMONET (Simone), François M. *(1760) 1st horn at the Théâtre Français in 1793.*
FMS-1.1a. Solié: Le Jockei, overture.   2fl 2cl 2hn 2bn.
Pc (Imbault: Paris, pn 163, c.1796), RISM [S 3882], parts: F-Pn, (2 copies), Vm7 6982, Vm27 3925.
FMS-1.2a. Solié: Le Jockei, suite d'harmonie.   2fl 2cl 2hn 2bn.
Pc (Imbault: Paris, pn 222, c.1797), RISM [S 3890], parts: F-Pn, (2 copies), Vm7 6983, Vm27 3911.

*SIMONI (Simony), Pietro de *(1770)*
*PDS-1a. Kunzen: Das Fest der Winzer, 22 mvts.   2fl 2hn basso.
MS parts: CZ-K, opery Nr 7.K.I, (mvts 17 - 22 are from the opera ballet, separately numbered 1 - 6).

SIMS, Ezra *16 Jan 1928, Birmingham, Alabama, USA*
EAS-1. Night unto Night.   3fl 2ob 2cl 3hn 2bn 2tb.
In MS: US-NYamc may be able to assist in contacting the composer.

SIQUEIRA, José de Lima *1907, Brazil*
LJS-1. Divertimento.   2fl 2ob cl 2hn 2bn.
Pm (Soviet State (VAAP): Moscow, 1907), score & parts.

*SIRLETTI, Ludovica
LQS-1a. Rossini: Le Comte Ory, terzetto.   fl ob 2cl(A) 2hn bn.
Pc (G. Ricordi: Milano, pn 5060, sd), parts: I-Mc, Da Camera A.118.4.
LQS-2a. Rossini: Le Comte Ory, coro e preghiera.   fl ob 2cl 2hn bn.
Pc (G. Ricordi: Milano, pn 5476, sd), parts: I-Mc, Da Camera A.118.5.II.

SIXTA, Jozef *12 May 1940, Jičín, Czechoslovakia (now Slovakia)*
JNS-1. Octet; 1977, 5 mvts.   2fl 2ob 2cl 2bn.
Pm (Opus: Bratislava, pn 9110 0755-8, 1983), score & parts.

SJÖBERG, Johann-Magnus *7 June 1953, Sweden*
HKS-1. En liten Hipp serenad; 1993.   2fl 2ob 2cl 2hn 2bn.   MS score: The composer c/o S-Sic.

SJÖBLOM, Heimer *1910, Sweden*
HOS-1. Kleine Suite im Spielmanneton.   fl ob 3cl hn b tp db.   MS score: S-Sic.

*SKÁCEL (SKAZEL, SKAKEL), ( ) *(1790)*
ZZS-1a. Rossini: Bianca e Falliero, quartetto.   2ob 2cl 2hn 2bn cbn 2tp.
MS parts (1827): CZ-Bm(au), A.35.211.

*SKALLE, ( ) *(1760). Oboist of the Royal Danish Foot Life-Guards.*
*CNS-1. Carasel Musique, 1791; 28 mvts.   "Fuer Harmonie:": 2ob 3cl 2hn 2bn; "fuer Trompetten": 3tp timp;
"Fuer Janitschar": pic "picoletto" 2fl 2cl 2hn 2bn 2tp b-dr "tamburazo".
MS parts: DK-Sa, R.237.   *Skalle composed the Märschen, Ring- & Koptour music; other movements were composed by C.N. Schal (qv).*

SKINDER, Kazimiera
KAS-1. Romantic Miniatures.   fl ob 2cl bn.   MS score: US-Wc.

*SKIRROW, Andrew M *15 April 1961, Birkenhead, UK*
ARS-1a. Brahms: Intermezzo, Op. 117, No. 1.   fl 2ob 2cl 2hn 2bn.
Pm (Camden Music: London, pn CM026, 1991), score & parts.
*ARS-2a. Gershwin: Scenes from Porgy & Bess.   2ob 2cl 2hn 2bn.
Pm (Camden Music: London, pn CM019, 1991), score & parts.
ARS-3a. Schumann: Introduction, Allegro and Finale, Op. 92.   fl 2ob 2cl 2hn 2bn cbn(ad lib).
Pm (Camden Music: London, pn CM029, 1991), score & parts.
ARS-4a. Tchaikovsky: Humoreske (No. 2 of Deux Morceux pour Piano, Op. 10).   2ob 2cl 2hn 2bn.
Pm (Camden Music: London, pn CM025, 1991), score & parts.
ARS-5a. Walton: Facade, 7 mvts.   fl 2ob 2cl 2hn 2bn.
MS score & parts: GB-Lskirrow.

*SKLENIČKA, Karel *1933, Czechoslovakia*
LZS-1. Konzert pro dechové nástroje a kontrabass.   2fl 2ob 2cl 2hn 2bn 2tp 2tb db.
Pm (Český hudební fond: Prague, 1963), hire score & parts.
KZS-2. Legendy.   fl 2ob 2cl 2hn 2bn.
Pm (Český hudební fond: Prague, 1981), hire score & parts.

*SKÖLD, Yngve *29 April 1899, Vallby - 6 Dec 1992, Ingarö   See also: JOHANSSON, Gunnar.*
YNS-1. [Sinfonia de chiesa, Op. 38, 1939] Passacaglia.   fl fl(pic) ob ob(ca) 2cl 4hn 2bn cbn 2tp 3tb tu timp.
MS score: S-Sic.

*SLAVICKÝ, Milan *7 May 1947, Prague*
MQS-1. La voce soave, Omaggio a Mozart.   Harmonica or celeste, 2ob 2cl 2hn 2bn.
Pm (Český hudební fond: Prague, 1981), hire score & parts.

SLETTHOLM, Yngve *1955, Norway*
YGS-1. 13 Monomainias, Op. 5; 1979.   fl ob cl cl(b-cl) hn bn.
MS score: N-Oic.

*SLIMÁČEK, Jan (Joseph) *31 July 1939, Kelč, Moravia*
AJS-1. Etudy.   10 winds.
Pm (Český hudební fond: Prague), hire score & parts.   *A tape recording is held by CZ-Plcr.*

*SMART, Timothy (Thymothy) *(?1760), Musician with the 1st Regiment of Guards (Grenadiers), London*
TYS-1m. Twenty four select military peices [sic].   2cl 2hn 2bn.
Pc (John Fentum: London, sd), RISM [S 3613], parts: D-SWl, Mus. 5872/4, (cl II & hn II parts only).

SMET, Raoul C.R. de *1936, Belgium*
RCS-1. Housneden; 1990.   2fl 2ob 2cl 2hn 2bn.   MS score: B-Bcdm.

SMET, Robin John de *1935, UK*
RYD-1a. Mozart: Eine kleine Nachtmusik, romanze, minuet & trio.   2ob 2cl 2bn.
Pm (C.F. Peters: London, pn H 773, 1963), score & parts.

SMIT, P.
PQS-1. Sinfonia secca, Op. 7.   ob 2cl 2bn.   MS score: SA-Jsamro.

*SMITH, Clement, M.B. *1760, Richmond, Surrey - 16 Nov 1826, Richmond.*
CYS-1m. Favorite March as Performed by the Duke of York's Band.   2cl 2hn (2)bn.
Pc (Published by Permission of the Author by Longman and Broderip: London, c.1790), score:
GB-Lbl, g.934.x.(2). ★
CYS-2m. Lady Nelson's Fancy, a Favorite Quick Step.   2cl 2hn bn.
Pc (In: J. Tebay, The Bath Volunteers March, pp. 2 - 3. T. & M. W. Cahusac: London, c.1800), score:
GB-Lbl, h.1586.b.(22). ★

SMITH, Dwayne
DZS-1. Septet.   2ob ca 2bn cbn perc.   MS score: US-GRBidrs.

SMITH (Vielehr), Julia Frances *25 Jan 1911, Denton, Texas*
CJS-1. Octet for Woodwinds.   2ob 2cl 2hn 2bn.
Pm (Mowbray Music: sl [USA], c.1980).   *Copy in US-NYamc.*

SMITH, Robert *4 Dec 1922, Whitchurch, Glamorgan*
RXS-1. The Masque of the Red Death, (for ballet or mime group).   2fl 2cl 2hn piano harp perc.
MS score: GB-CDmic.
RXS-2. 5 Myxolydian Variations.   Violin, 2fl ob 2cl 2hn 2bar-hn.
MS score: GB-CDmic.

*SMITH, William *(1760), Master of the Band of Music, West Norfolk Regiment of Militia.*
WZS-1m. The Favorite West Norfolk Troop.   2cl 2hn 2bn tp bugle-horn serp.
Pc (H. Wright: London, wm1794), score: GB-Lbl, h.1255.e.(2). ★

SMOLIANSKY, Suska *19 July 1894 - 25 Nov 1972, Stockholm*
SUS-1e. [Pontius Pilatus: Svit] No. 4. Pilatus-Marsch.   2fl 2ob 2cl 4hn 2bn 2tp 3tb.
MS score: S-Sic.

*SÖDERLUNDH, Bror Axel (known as: Lille BROR) *21 May 1912, Kristinehamm - 23 Aug 1957, Leksand*
*LBS-1. Klockrikesvit: Lyriska vinjetter [Suite from *Vagen till Klockrike*; *The Road to the Land o' Bells*], 6 mvts.
Narrator, fl 2cl bn.   MS score & parts: S-Ssr.

SØNSTEVOLD, Gunnar Johannes *1912 - 1991, Norway*
GUS-1. Dobbelt ror; 1989.   2ob ca bn cbn.   MS score: N-Oic.

SOETEMAN, Iman *1936, Netherlands (formerly horn player with Netherlands Wind Ensemble)*
IZS-1. Sho jo ji: Overture.   ob ca 2cl 2hn 2bn cbn/db.
Pm (Donemus: Amsterdam, 1983), score.
IZS-1a. 4 Satie-ren; (arrangements of Satie).   ob ob(ca) cl(Eb) 2cl b-cl 4hn 2bn cbn/db.
Pm (A.B. Reimers Edition: Stockholm, 1980), ?score.

SOKOLOV, Elliot *1953, USA*
ELS-1. Aeolus; 1977.   2ob 2cl 2hn 2bn.   MS score: US-NYamc.

SOLER, José (Josep) *25 March 1935, Barcelona*
JJS-1. Diaphonia; 1968.   3fl 3ob 3cl 4hn 4bn.
Pm (Southern Music Co.: San Antonio, Texas; Peer International Corp.: New York, 1971), score.

*SOLÈRE (Soler), Étienne (Pedro) *4 April 1753, Mont-Louis - 1817, Paris*
EPS-1. Ouverture; P.2316.   2p-fl 2cl 2hn 2bn tp serp.
Pc (Mag de mus fêtes nat: Paris, pluvôse an III, 1795), liv 11, No. 1, parts: F-Pn, H2.11; F-Pars, D.LI.20.   ★
Pm (In: Dudley, Walter Sherwood, Jr. *Orchestration in the Musique d' harmonie of the French Revolution.* Ph.D.
dissertation. University of California, Berkeley. 1968. University Microfilms International: Ann Arbor, Michigan,
London, UK, 1978), score.
*EPS-1m. Chant de bataille d'Austerlitz. Grand Marche à l'usage des Musiques Militaires suivie d'un
Pas-Redoublé.   No. 4. Marche: 2p-fl 2cl(F) 2cl(C) 2hn 2bn tp tb serp b-dr t-dr; No. 7. Pas Redoublé: scoring
as the Marche except 2fl replace 2p-fl.
Pc (Chez Imbault: Paris, c.1806), parts: F-Pn, Vm27 3931, (2 copies).   *The numbering & small format (4-parts
per page printed on large folio sheets) suggest that the plates originally came from another publication.*   ★
EPS-2m. Pas redoublé à l'usage des Musiques Militaires.   p-fl cl(F) 2cl(C) 2hn 2bn tp tb serp b-dr.
Pc (Chez Imbault: Paris, s.d.), parts: F-Pn, Vm27 3933 (1), (2), (2 copies).   ★
EPS-3m(-5m). Marche à l'usage des Musiques Militaires Nº [MS: 1 - 3].
p-fl cl(F) 2cl(C) 2hn 2bn tp tb serp b-dr.
Pc (Chez Imbault: Paris, s.d.), parts: F-Pn, Vm27 3932 (1 - 3), (2 copies of each).   ★

*SOLGERT, ( ) *(1800)*
ZWS-1v. Salve Regina; in B♭.   S solo, 2cl 2hn bn.
MS parts (by J. Holeček, c.1830): CZ-Pnm, XLIII.A.111.   ★

*SOLIÉ (Solier, Soulier) Jean Pierre *1755, Nîmes - 6 Aug 1812, Paris*
XJS-1m. Pas de manoeuvre, P.2315.   2pic 2cl 2hn 2bn tp serp.
Pc (Mag de mus fêtes nat: Paris, nivôse an III, 1794), liv. 10, No. 4, pts: F-Pn, H2. 10,4; F-Nm, Vol 22207.   ★

*SOLIVA, Carlo Evasio *1792, Casale Monferrrato, Piedmont - 20 Dec 1851, Paris*
CES-1. Divertimento Pastorale; in Eb, 3 mvts.   Clavicembalo, flob 2hn vla vc.
MS parts: I-Mc, Noseda Q.16.10.   ★

*SOMMER, Johann Matthias (Giovanni Mattia) *(1740)*
*MJS-1. Pieze a 13 Stromenti; in F, 10 mvts.   2cl(C) 4hn(F, C) 2bn 2tp(clar) 2vla vlne.
MS parts (c.1770): D-Rtt, Sommer 26.   ★

*SONNENLEITER (SONNELEITER), Antonius *(1750)*
AZS-1. No. 8 Parthia ex A; 5 mvts.   2cl 2hn bn.
MS parts: CZ-KRA, A3973/IV.B.137.   ★

*SONNENLEITER (SONNENLEITHER), L. *(?1750)*
LUS-1va. Haydn: Die Beredsamkeit (Hob.XXVc, 4).   SATB, 2ob 2cl 2hn 2bn.
MS parts: A-Wgm. *Hoboken citation.*
LUS-2va. Haydn: Aus dem Danklied zu Gott (Hob.XXVc, 8).   SATB, 2ob 2cl 2hn 2bn.
MS parts: A-Wgm. *Hoboken citation.*

*SPÄT, Joseph *d. 1829, Schnaitsee*
ZJS-1v. [Hirten]Lied in der Christnacht.   CAB, 2cl 2hn organ.
AutoMS parts (1817): D-SCHN, 67, (the title calls for the vocal parts as "2 Engelstim[m]en, 2 Hirtenstim[m]en";
the work was also performed in 1819 & 1820).   ★

*SPÄTH (Spaeth), Andreas (André) *9 Oct 1792, Rosach, Coburg - 26 April 1876, Gotha*
*ADS-1. Six Fantaisies dont les motifs sont tirés des romances de . . . le Prince Albert.
3fl 2ob 4cl 4hn 2bn 3tp 3tb oph perc.
AutoMS score: GB-Lbl, RM.21.g.36.   ★
ADS-2. Die Heuerndte [sic: Huerente]: Ländliche Scene in Form eines Pot-Pourri für vollständige Harmonie,
52tes Werk; in F, in 1 continuous mvt of 8 sections.
terz-fl 2ob cl(Eb) 2cl(Bb)+2cl(B♭ ripieno) 2hn 2bn tp(clar) serp.
Pc (bei J. André: Offenbach ˢ/m, pn 4720, 1824), parts: A-Wgm, VIII 5144.   ★
MS score: CH-Zz, AMG XIV 391, (with additional pic(F) & b-tb parts).
*ADS-3. Sérénade en forme de Pot-Pourri [in Eb] . . . composé & dédiée à la Société de musique à Zuric [sic],
Oeuvre 54.   terz-fl cl(Eb) 3cl(Bb) 2hn 2bn tp(clar) b-tb tu serp guitar(ad lib).
Pc (chez J. André: Offenbach ˢ/m, pn 5111, 1827), parts: CH-Zz, AMG XIII 484 a-m; GB-Ljag(w), L.118.   ★
ADS-4. Scène pastorale suisse pour l'Harmonie complète, Oeuvre 93; 1 continuous mvt, 10 sections.
pic terz-fl cl(Eb) 2cl(Bb)+2cl(B♭ ripieno) 2hn 2bn tp(clar) b-tb serp.
Pc (chez Jean André: Offenbach ˢ/m, pn 4912, 1825), parts: A-Wgm, VIII 5143.   ★
ADS-1v. Deutsche Militarische Te Deum, Op. 210.   TTBB, "Janisarmusik".
MS score: D-Bds, Mus.ms.20930.
ADS-2v. Deutsche Militar Messe.   TTBB, pic terz-fl 3cl 4hn 2bn 2tp 2cap 2t-tb b-tb a-hn oph bomb.
AutoMS score ("componirt von 20 Juli bis auf 7t August 1854"): A-Wn, Mus.Hs.15,542.   ★

*SPENCER, Hon. Capt. John *(1760)*
*CJS-1m. The Favourite Troop. Performed by the Band of the Oxford Shire [sic] Militia.
2fl cl(F) 2cl 2hn (2)bn tp serp.
Pc (G. Smart: London, 1794), RISM [S 4084], score: GB-Lbl, h.1586.b.(21).   ★

*SPERGER, Johann Matthias *23 March, 1750, Feldsberg (Valtice) - 13 May 1812, Ludwigslust*
*JWS-1. Parthia in F; 4 mvts, (Maier deest). 2ob 2cl(C) 2hn 2bn 2tp.
(probably Auto)MS score (c.1780): D-DS, Mus.ms.1233. ★
*JWS-2. Cassatio; in D, 5 mvts, C IV/6). fl 2ob 2hn bn/db bn(rip).
AutoMS score (c.1786) & MS parts: D-SWl, Mus. 5188/4. ★
JWS-3. Parthia Ex B[♭]; 4 mvts, (D VI/1). 2ob 2cl 2hn 2bn. AutoMS score: D-SWl, Mus. 5189/1. ★
*JWS-4. Adagio in Es-dur [E♭] Con Sordini; (D VI/2). 2ob 2cl 2hn 2bn.
AutoMS score: D-SWl, Mus. 5189/15. ★
*JWS-5. Parthia Ex b [Bb]; 5 mvts, (D VII/1). 2ob cl 2hn bn.
AutoMS score (c.1777 - 1783): D-SWl, Mus. 5189/14. ★
JWS-6. Parthia in B[♭]; 3 mvts, (D IV/1). 2ob 2hn 2bn. MS parts: D-SWl, Mus. 5189/44. ★
JWS-7.1. in B[♭]. Parthie; 3 mvts, (D IV/2). 2ob 2hn 2bn. MS parts: D-SWl, Mus. 5189/45. ★
JWS-7.2. Parthie in B[♭]; 3 mvts, (D IV/2). 2cl bn. MS parts: D-SWl, Mus. 5189/45a.
JWS-8. in A: Parthia; 4 mvts, (D IV/3). 2ob 2hn 2bn. MS parts: D-SWl, Mus. 5189/48. ★
*JWS-9. in C. Parthia; 4 mvts, (D IV/4). 2ob 2hn 2bn. MS parts: D-SWl, Mus. 5189/49. ★
JWS-10. in F. Parthia; 4 mvts, (D IV/5). 2ob 2hn 2bn. MS parts: D-SWl, Mus. 5189/51; A-KR, H 39/72. ★
JWS-11. in G: Parthia; 3 mvts, (D IV/6). 2ob 2hn 2bn. MS parts: D-SWl, Mus. 5189/53, (missing hn I). ★
JWS-12. in D: Parthia; 1 mvt in 5 sections, (D IV/7). 2ob 2hn 2bn.
MS parts: D-SWl, Mus. 5189/54. *The tempo alternates between Adagio, 2/4 & Allegro, 2/4.* ★
JWS-13. Parthia; in G 3 mvts, (D IV/8). 2ob 2hn 2bn. MS parts: D-SWl, Mus. 5189/55. ★
*JWS-14. Parthia in Dis [E♭]; 3 mvts, (D IV/9). 2ob 2hn 2bn. MS pts (1786): D-SWl, Mus. 5189/47. ★
JWS-15. Parthia In C; 4 mvts, (D IV/10). 2ob 2hn 2bn. MS parts: D-SWl, Mus. 5189/50. ★
*JWS-16. Pathia [sic] IV, in E♭; 4 mvts, (D IV/11). 2ob 2hn 2bn.
AutoMS score & parts (2 ob only): D-SWl, Mus. 5189/2. ★
JWS-17. Parthia Nr [number missing]; in A, 3 mvts, (D IV/12). 2ob 2hn 2bn.
AutoMS score: D-SWl, Mus. 5189/30; H-Bn, IV 745, (as "Parthia in A: N: 86"). ★
*JWS-18. Parthia Nr [number missing]; in F, 3 mvts, (D IV/13). 2ob 2hn 2bn.
AutoMS score: D-SWl, Mus. 5189/43. ★
JWS-19. Parthia Ex f: [F major]; 3 mvts, (D IV/46). 2ob 2hn 2bn.
MS parts: D-SWl, Mus. 5189/46; A-KR, H 39/71, (as "Parthia in F"). ★
JWS-20.1. in C. Parthia; 4 mvts, (D IV/15). 2ob 2hn 2bn.
MS parts: D-SWl, Mus. 5189/21, (with a later viola part, JWS-20.3). ★
*JWS-20.2. Parthia in C; 4 mvts, (D IV/15). 2cl 2hn 2bn.
(?Auto)MS score: D-SWl, Mus. 5189/21a. *Although the entire piece is laid out, only the cl I part is completely written out; a new coda has been added to the last mvt.*
JWS-20.3. Parthia in C; 4 mvts, (D IV/15). New viola part.
MS parts: D-SWl, Mus. 5189/21. *This is a separate part in a different hand.*
JWS-21. Parthia Ex D# [D major]; 4 mvts, (D IV/16). 2ob 2hn 2bn.
AutoMS score (1796-1798): D-SWl, Mus. 5189/11. ★
*JWS-22. [Parthia in E♭]; 5 mvts, (D V/1). 2ob/2cl 2hn 2bn.
MS parts: CZ-KRa, A4457/R.I.27, No. 6, (for 2ob 2hn 2bn). ★
AutoMS score: D-SWl, Mus. 5189/3, (a later version, for 2cl 2hn 2bn).
JWS-23.1. Parthia in B[♭]; 3 mvts, (D V/2B). 2ob 2hn 2bn. MS parts: H-Bn, Ms.Mus.IV.299, Nr. 4. ★
*JWS-23.2. Parthia Ex C; 4 mvts, (D V/2A). 2cl 2hn 2bn.
AutoMS score: D-SWl, Mus. 5189/43, (the bn parts are in B♭). ★
MS parts (as "Divertimento in B[♭] . . . il Mese 23ten Maerz L'anno 1810"): D-SWl, Mus. 43a.
JWS-24. [Parthia in D], 4 mvts, (D I/1). 2ob 2hn bn. MS parts: D-SWl, Mus. 5189/22. ★
JWS-25. [Parthia in C], 3 mvts, (D I/2). 2ob 2hn bn. MS parts: D-SWl, Mus. 5189/25. ★
JWS-26. [Parthia in C], 3 mvts, (D I/3). 2ob 2hn bn. MS parts: D-SWl, Mus. 5189/27. ★
JWS-27. [Parthia in F], 3 mvts, (D I/4). 2ob 2hn bn. MS parts: D-SWl, Mus. 5189/24. ★
JWS-28. [Parthia in B♭], 3 mvts, (D I/5). 2ob 2hn bn. MS parts: D-SWl, Mus. 5189/23. ★
JWS-29. [Parthia in E♭], 3 mvts, (D I/6). 2ob 2hn bn. MS parts: D-SWl, Mus. 5189/26. ★
JWS-30. [Parthia in C], 4 mvts, (D I/7). 2ob 2hn bn. MS parts: D-SWl, Mus. 5189/9. ★
JWS-31. [Parthia in C], 3 mvts, (D I/8). 2ob 2hn bn. MS parts: D-SWl, Mus. 5189/31. ★
JWS-32. [Parthia in C], 3 mvts, (D I/9). 2ob 2hn bn.
MS parts: D-SWl, Mus. 5189/40; D-DO, Mus.Ms.1826, (as "Parthia Ex C"). ★
JWS-33. [Parthia in E♭], 3 mvts, (D I/10). 2ob 2hn bn. MS parts: D-SWl, Mus. 5189/41. ★
JWS-34. [Parthia in F], 4 mvts, (D I/11). 2ob 2hn bn. MS parts: D-SWl, Mus. 5189/42. ★
JWS-35. [Parthia in D], 4 mvts, (D I/12). 2ob 2hn bn.
MS parts: D-SWl, Mus. 5189/22; H-Bn, Ms.Mus.IV.299, Nr. 7, (as "Parthia in D#"). ★
*JSW-36. [Parthia in F], 3 mvts, (D I/13). 2ob 2hn bn. MS parts: D-SWl, Mus. 5189/12; H-Bn, Ms.Mus.IV.299, Nr. 1, (as "Parthia. in F"; "1780" has been added in another hand). ★
JWS-37. [Parthia in F], 4 mvts, (D I/14). 2ob 2hn bn.
MS parts: D-SWl, Mus 5189/13; H-Bn, Ms.Mus.IV.299, Nr. 6, (as "Parthia in F"). *The opening Allegro is in 3/4 in the D-SWl version; in the H-Bn version it is in 3/8.* ★
*JWS-38. Parthia in F; 4 mvts, (D I/15). 2ob 2hn bn. MS parts: D-SWl, Mus. 5189/19; D-DO, Mus.Ms.1827; H-Bn, Ms.Mus.IV.299, Nr. 2, ("1780" added in another hand). ★
JWS-39. [Parthia in Bb], 3 mvts, (D I/16). 2ob 2hn bn.
MS parts: D-SWl, Mus. 5189/28; H-Bn, Ms.Mus.IV.299, Nr. 3, (as "Parthia in B"). ★
JWS-40. [Parthia in D], 4 mvts, (D I/17). 2ob 2hn bn.
MS parts: D-SWl, Mus. 5189/38; H-Bn, Ms.Mus.IV.299, Nr. 5, (as "Parthia in D#"). ★
JWS-41. [Parthia in G], 4 mvts, (D I/18). 2ob 2hn bn. MS parts: D-SWl, Mus. 5189/17. ★

*JWS-42. Parthia Da Giovanni Sperger; in F, 4 mvts, (D I/19).   2ob 2hn bn.   MS parts ("Fine die 10t Juli 1781"): D-SWl, Mus. 5189/32; D-DO, Mus.1828, (as "Parthia Ex F:", for 2cl 2hn bn).   ★
JWS-43. [Parthia in C], 3 mvts, (D I/20).   2ob 2hn bn.   MS parts: D-SWl, Mus. 5189/37.   ★
JWS-44. Parthia in D; 3 mvts, (D I/21).   2ob 2hn bn.   MS parts: D-SWl, Mus. 5189/52.   ★
JWS-45. [Parthia in G], 3 mvts, (D I/22).   2ob 2hn bn.   MS parts (c.1782): D-SWl, Mus. 5189/10.   ★
JWS-46. Parthia E[x] G; 4 mvts, (D I/23).   2ob 2hn bn.
(?Auto)MS score & MS parts: D-SWl, Mus. 5189/33, (the parts are titled "Parthia Ex G").   ★
JWS-47. Parthia Ex D; 4 mvts, (D I/24).   2ob 2hn bn.
AutoMS score ("Anno 1785") & MS parts: D-SWl, Mus. 5189/34.   ★
MS parts (2cl & bn transposed to E): D-SWl, Mus. 5189/34a.
JWS-48. Parthia Nro 1mo; in D, 4 mvts, (D I/25).   2ob 2hn bn.   MS parts: D-SWl, Mus. 5189/35.   ★
*JWS-49. Parthia Ex b. [Bb] in dieser Parthia wird Menuett, und Trio gleich nach dem Andante geschrieben, hernach das Allegro Finale; 3 mvts, (D I/19).   2ob 2hn bn.   AutoMS score: D-SWl, Mus. 5189/18.   ★
JWS-50. [Parthia in C], 3/4 mvts, (D I/21).   2ob 2hn bn.
AutoMS score: D-SWl, Mus. 5189/20.   *On the last verso sheet a 4th mvt, "N4 [sic] Andante" has been crossed out; this is, in fact, a variant of the Andante in JWS-52.1.*   ★
JWS-51.1. Parthia Ex b [Bb]. in dieser Parthia wird Menuett, und Trio gleich nach dem Andante geschrieben, hernach des Allegro Finale; 2 mvts, (D I/26).   2ob 2hn bn.   AutoMS score: D-SWl, Mus. 5189/18.   *The movements are in the wrong order, with the Menuett & Trio following the Finale.*   ★
*JWS-51.2. [Divertimento in C], 5 mvts, (C IV/8).   2ob 2cl(C) 2hn 2bn tp(clar, C) serp.
AutoMS score ("Fine Mese 2do Maÿ l'anno 1801"): D-SWl, Mus. 5190/22.   *A later reworking.*   ★
JWS-52. Parthia Ex Eb; 4 mvts, (D II/1).   2cl 2hn bn.   AutoMS score: D-SWl, Mus. 5189/8.   ★
JWS-53. Parthia Nro 2do; in D, 3 mvts, (D II/2).   2cl 2hn bn.
AutoMS score (1777 - 1782): D-SWl, Mus. 5189/5a.   MS pts: D-DO, Mus.Ms.1829, (as "Partitta in D").   ★
JWS-54. Parthia Ex F; 4 mvts, (D II/3).   2cl 2hn bn.   AutoMS score (1777 - 1782): D-SWl, Mus. 5189/5.   ★
JWS-55. Parthia Ex Dis [Eb]; 4 mvts, (D II/4).   2cl 2hn bn.
AutoMS score (1777 - 1783): D-SWl, Mus.5189/6.   ★
JWS-56. Parthia Ex Eb; 5 mvts, (D II/5).   2cl 2hn bn.   AutoMS score (1786/87): D-SWl, Mus. 5189/7.   ★
JWS-57. Parthia Ex A# [A major]; 4 mvts, (D III/1).   2ob bn 2tp.   AutoMS score: D-SWl, Mus. 5189/16.   ★
JWS-58. Parthia Ex b [Bb]; 4 mvts, (D III/2).   2ob bn 2tp.   AutoMS score: D-SWl, Mus. 5189/36.   ★
JWS-59. Parthia Ex C; 3 mvts, (D III/3).   2ob bn 2tp.   AutoMS score (1777 - 1783): D-SWl, Mus. 5189/8.   ★
JWS-60. Notturno. di Sperger Mense Junio 1796; in Eb, 6 mvts.   2vla 2hn bn.
AutoMS score: D-SWl, Mus. 5198.   ★
JWS-1v. Choral, "O, komm zu uns, verheisser Geist, du Lehrer, du zu Jesu weist", nach der Melodie "Wie schön leuchtet der Morgenstern", (J II/3).   Solo S, 2ob 2cl 2hn 2bn 2tp(clar) timp organ(bc).
AutoMS score ("Nro 136. Vor der Preedigt. Am Hln. Pfingst Tage. Anno 1797"): D-SWl, Mus. 34/2.   ★
JWS-2v. Choral, "Nicht un ein flüchtig Gut der Zeit", (J II/4).   Solo S, 2ob 2cl 2hn 2bn 2tp(clar) timp organ(bc).   AutoMS score ("Nro 139. nach der Predigt. am Heil. Pfingst=Feeste 1797"): D-SWl, Mus. 34/3.   ★
*JWS-3v. Chor, "Auf, Brüder, ergreifet gefüllte Pokale", (H II/1).   SATB, fl 2ob 2hn basso.
AutoMS score: D-SWl, Mus. 5127.   ★
*JWS-1va. Tantum ergo, in C, (J I/2).   SATB, 2ob 2cl 2hn 2bn 2tp vc+db timp.
AutoMS score (c.1810): D-SWl, Mus. 5131b.   *An arrangement of his own work originally with orchestral accompaniment (Mus. 5131a).*   ★
JWS-1d. Parthia in Dis (Eb), 6 mvts.   2cl 2hn bn.   MS parts: D-DO, Mus.Ms.1830.   *This is, in fact, by F.A. Rosetti (K. II 22), FAR-21; "Sperger" has been added in pencil.*
JWS-2d(-6d). 5 Parthien.   2ob 2hn bn.   MS parts: CZ-KRa.   *A ghost (Geisterwerk); MGG Citation = H-Bn set.*

SPILLER, Joseph *(1770)*
JKS-1. Partia in B[b]; 4 mvts.   2ob 2cl 2hn 2bn 2tp.   MS parts: D-LEt; D-Z.
JKS-2. Partia in Dis [Eb]; 5 mvts.   2cl 2hn 2bn tp(prin).
MS parts (by Augustin Erasmus Hübner, Langenbruck, 1801): CZ-Pu(dm), 59 R 3326.   ★

SPINDLER, Fritz *1817 - 1905, Germany*
FTS-1. Andantino.   2ob 2bn.
Pm (Music Publishers Holding Co.: New York, sd), ed. Lockhart, score & parts.   *Original provenance unknown.*

SPINO, Pasquale J. *1942, USA*
PAS-1. Statement.   2fl ob 4cl 4sax hn bn.
Pm (Standard: sl [USA], 1972).

*ŠPLICHAL (Splichal), Jan (Johann) *(1800)*
JVS-1. Andante[,] Marsche et [3] Feld Stücke [and 2 marches].
2cl(Bb vel C) cl(oblig, mvt 1 only) 2hn bn 2tp(clar) tp(prin) timp.
MS parts (by Augustin Erasmus Hübner, Schulfach, Anno 1816): CZ-Pu(dm), 59 R 3380.   ★
*JVS-2. Parthia in Dis [Eb]; 4 mvts.   2ob 2cl 2hn 2bn.   MS parts: CZ-Pnm, XX.F.114.   ★
JVS-1.1v. Quatour Stationes pro festo Corporis Christi.   CATB, fl 2cl 2hn bn 2tp(clar) tp(prin) timp.
MS pts: CZ-Pnm, XV.E.183, (missing fl; from Bohdaneč); CZ-Pu, 59 R 1601, (copy by Bergmann as "Nro 2.).   ★
JVS-1.2v. Quatour Stationes pro Festo Corporis Christi.   CATB, 2cl 2hn bn 2tp(clar) tp(prin) timp.
MS parts ("Z musikalú chrámn Páne Belohradského Ex Rebus [crossed out: Wen. Joh. Dobrovský] Val Zujíč"): CZ-Pu, 59 R 1534, (as "Nro 5").   *The flute part is not mentioned on the titlepage.*
JVS-2v. In Paradisum.   SATB, 3cl 2hn bn 2tp(clar) tp(prin) timp.
MS parts (by Johann Stephan, from Chroustovice): CZ-Pnm, XV.E.184.   ★
JVS-3v. Salve Regina, in Es [Eb].   CATB, 2cl 2hn bn.   MS pts: CZ-Pnm, XV.E.182, (from Mladá Boleslav, MS by Josef Dolensky); CZ-Pu, 59 R 1535, (copy by Joseph Bartmanny; for performance 1 Dec 1830, wind pts dated 30 Nov, voice pts dated 1 Dec.   Additional pts from 1844 simplify the cl pts, & add 2vl 2tp(11 bars) & organ).   ★

*SPOHR, Ludwig *5 April 1784, Braunschweig - 22 Oct 1859, Kassel*
*LXS-1. Notturno für Harmonie und Janitscharen-musik, in C, Op. 34; 6 mvts.
pic(fl, terz-fl) pic 2ob 2cl 2bn cbn+b-hn 2tp posthorn b-tb/tu b-dr+cym tri; (scoring varies for each mvt).
Pc (in Bureau de Musique von C.F. Peters: Leipzig, 1816), score (pn 1219) & parts (pn 1818): GB-Ob,
Mus 209.c.17, (score only); GB-DOTams, (photocopy, score only); D-SWl, (parts only). ★
Pc (Peters: Leipzig, 1853, reissued 1874), new edition, score & parts (pn 3598): GB-Lbl, (score) h.1099.c.(4),
(parts) h.1570.(4); I-Mc, Noseda V-47-a-b, (score & parts).
MS parts: D-DT, Mus-n 946, (fl-ottava 2ob 2cl 2hn 2bn 2tp tb b-hn timp); D-Rtt, Sm. 15, No. 64, (pre-1821,
purchased in Jan 1822 from Herrn Hauptmann von Vetter, Tischingen; missing pic II, cl I, and perc).
Pm (Alexander Broude: New York, 1966), score & parts.
Pm (Peer International Corp.: New York, sd), score & parts.
Pm (Mercury International Corp.: New York, sd), edited R.F. Goldman, score & parts.
Pm (T. Presser: Bryn Mawr, PA, sd), reprint of Mercury edition.

*SPONTINI, Gasparo (Luigi Pacifico) *14 Nov 1774, Maiolati, Italy - 24 Jan 1851, Maiolati*
GLS-1m. No 1º Ballo marziale, Evoluzioni Militar. 2fl 2ob 2cl(F) 2cl(C) 2bthn 4hn(F, C) 2bn cbn 2tp a-tb t-tb
b-tb b-hn perc("Janitscharen" - 2 staves: "triangelo, tamburro, Chinese), etc". MS score: I-Mc, Noseda R.19.36.★
GLS-2m. No 3º, Preludio ai Combattimenti, ed alla Vittoria sul Campo di Marte".
2fl 2ob 2cl(F) 2cl(C) 2bthn 4hn(C, G) 2bn cbn 2tp a-tb t-tb b-tb b-hn perc("Janitscharen" - 2 staves: "triangelo,
tamburro, Chinese, etc"). MS score: I-Mc, Noseda R.19.37. ★
GLS-3m. Grande Bacchanale. Instrumentation unknown.
Pc (sn: sl, sd), score: D-Bds, (?lost).
GLS-1mv. Borussia. TTBB, 2terz-fl(in 8) 2fl 2ob 2cl(C) 2bthn 4hn(C, F) 2bn cbn+b-hn(s) 2tp(C, at least 8
recommended) a-tb t-tb b-tb b-dr, tambour du soldat + tri, tambourino + cym, (2vl vla vc db timp ad lib, in
separate score).
MS: D-Bds, Hausbibl.M.M.283
Pc (Schelsinger: Berlin, pn S.1066, c.1830), score: CZ-Pnm, XXXIII.C.273; GB-Lbl, R.M.13.a.21.(1). ★
GLS-2mv. Grosser Sieges- und Festmarsch. Solo TTBB, TTBB chorus, 2fl terz-fl(8vo) terz-fl 2ob cl(F) 2cl(C)
2bthn 4hn(C, F) 2bn cbn 2tp 2t-tb b-tb b-hn(s) b-dr+cym tri, tambour du Soldat, tambourin, (2vl 2vla vc db timp
ad lib, in separate score).
Pc (Schlesinger: Berlin, pn S.1062, c.1830), score: A-Wgm; D-Bds; GB-Lbl, R.M.13.a.21.(2). ★
Pm (WINDS: Northridge, CA, pn W-160, c.1981), score & parts.
GLS-3mv. Preussischer Kriegsgesang (1840). Instrumentation unknown.
AutoMS score: D-Bds, Mus.Ms.Auto.G.Spontini.4.

*SPORCK, Georges *9 Mar 1870, Paris - 17 Jan 1943, Paris. Pupil of T Dubois and d'Indy.*
GOS-1. Paysages normandes; 6 mvts. 2fl 2ob 2cl 2hn 2bn.
Pc (Pfister frères: Paris, 1906), score & parts: F-Pn, Vm26 624.
Pm (A.J. Andraud: Cincinatti, now Southern Music Co.: San Antonio, Texas, sd), score & parts.

SPRONGL, Norbert *30 April 1892, Obermarkersdorf, Austria - 26 April 1983, Mödling, nr Vienna*
NRS-1. Octet, Op. 30. fl ob 2cl hn 2bn tp.
Pm (Döblinger: Wien, 1937), parts (copy in Döblinger archives).

*ŠRAMEK, Vladimír *10 March 1923, Košice*
VXK-1. Suita per accordeon; 5 mvts. Solo accordeon, 2cl bn tp.
Pm (SNKLHU: Prague, pn 2682, sd), score & parts.

SREBOTNJAK, Alojz (Aloyz) *27 June 1931, Postojna, Slovenia*
ALS-1a. Macedonian Dances [arranged]; 1974. 2ob 2cl 2bn perc.
Pm (G. Schirmer: New York, etc., pn BA 47550, 1978), score & parts.
ALS-1v. A Village Orpheus. Solo ST, SATB chorus, 2ob 2cl 2bn timp perc vla vc db.
Pm (G. Schirmer: New York, sd), hire score & parts.

*STAAB, Karspar (Caspar) *1717 - 1798, ?Frankfurt am Main*
KYS-1a. Mozart: Die Zauberflöte, VI Arien; (for the höchsten Namenstag of Archbishop Adalbert II).
2cl 2hn 2bn basso. MS parts: D-F, Mus.Hs.1179.

*STADLER, Josef de Wolfersgrün ("Giuseppe Stadler di Praga") *(1770)*
*JTS-1. 12 Tadeschi [sic] pour Musique d'Harmonie. 2cl 2hn 2bn.
MS parts: A-Wn, Mus.Hs.11,169; CZ-Pnm, XLII.B.5, (with dedication to Graf Philip Clam Gallas). ★
JTS-1m. Marche No. 17 pour la Musique et Harmonie et Turcaise ded. à son Alt. Ser. Msg. le Prince regnante
de Lobkowitz. pic 2ob 2cl 2hn 2bn 2tp, "clarino principale" b-dr s-dr(Tamborino) cym bells(Campunali=Jingling
Johnny?). MS parts: CZ-Pnm, Lobkovic X.H.a.86. ★
JTS-2m, 3m. Due Marcie; both in C. pic 2ob 2cl(C) 2hn 2bn tp(prin) b-dr s-dr.
Pc (Nel Magasino della Caes. Real, priv. Stamperia chymica: Vienna [sic], pn 108, 1804/1805), parts:
H-KE, K 2022/XI. ★

*STADLER, *Abbé* Maximilian *4 Aug 1748, Melk - 8 Sept 1833, Vienna*
*MXS-1v. Hoch du mein Oesterreich ein Jubellied zur Namensfeyer Seiner Majestät des Kaisers Franz I.
SATB, 2ob 2cl 2hn 2bn.
Pc (im Verlage der k.k. priv Chemie=Druckerey: Vienna, pn 2759, 1818), parts: A-Wgm, V 8650 (H 24435). ★

STADLMAIR, Hans *3 May 1929, Neuhofen, upper Austria*
HYS-1. Octet. 2ob 2cl 2hn 2bn. Pm (C.F. Peters: Leipzig, pn 8016, 1972), score & parts.

STAEMPFLI, Edward *1 Feb 1908, Bern*
EXS-1. Variations; 1950. 2fl 2ob 2cl 2hn 2bn 2tp tb. MS score: CH-Zma.
EXS-2. Sextet; 1979. 2cl 2hn 2bn. MS score: CH-Zma.

STALZER, Frank S. *25 April 1925, Kansas City*
FQS-1a. J.S. Bach, arrangement (G minor) of (?part of) "The Art of Fugue". 2ob 2ca 2bn.
Pm (International Double Reed Society: Indianola, Iowa), parts.

*STAMITZ, Carl (Karl) Philipp *7 May 1745, Mannheim - 9 Nov 1801, Jena*
The Stamitz sources are especially complicated with movements sometimes recombined into new groupings.
*CPS-1.1(-7.1). 7 Parties. 2fl 2ob 2cl 2hn 2bn.
MS parts: D-Bds, Hausbibl. 340; D-Dla, Mus.3528-P-1. ★
Pm (Mannheimer Musikverlag: Mannheim, pns E59-E61, sd), score & pts, ("Divertimento I - III", 7 mvts each).
Pm (Compusic: Amsterdam, pn 226, 1991), pts, (unidentified Parthia in E♭ for 2ob 2cl 2hn 2bn with 2fl ad lib).
CPS-1.2(-3.2). 3 Parthien/Oktetts. 2ob 2cl 2hn 2bn.
MS parts: D-Bds, (unverified); CZ-Pnm, (unverified); modern scores: D-KIZklöcker, (1.2 with a different Finale).
*CPS-8. Octet No. 1; in E♭ [not B♭. See: *The Wind Ensemble Source Book*], 3 mvts. 2ob 2cl 2hn 2bn.
MS score & parts: CZ-Pnm, (unverified); modern copy, D-KIZklöcker. ★
*CPS-9. Parthia in B♭; 5 mvts (mvts 2 - 5 = mvt 1 of CPS-11.1 and mvts 1, 3 & 4 of CPS-12.1). 2cl 2hn 2bn.
MS pts: (unverified: ?US-BETm); modern copy, D-KIZklöcker. *Mvt 1 may be by D.M. Michael.* ★
CPS-10.1(-13.1). 4 Divertissements; (all in E♭; 3, 4, 4, 4 mvts). 2cl 2hn 2bn.
MS parts (by Peter): US-BETm, Lititz Collegium Musicum 205 - 208. ★
*CPS-10.2(-13.2). No. I (-IIII [sic]) Parthia; (all in E♭, 3, 4, 4, 4, mvts). 2cl 2hn 2bn.
MS pts (by Bechler): US-BETm, Lititz Collegium Musicum 181 - 184. *Probably original in this scoring.* ★
*CPS-14. [12] Serenades, Oeuvre XXVIII [bn I: "Serenates Op: 28"]; each of 1 mvt. 2fl 2hn bn.
Pc (B. Hummel et Fils: Le Haye, Amsterdam, c.1785), parts: GB-Lbl, g.1065.d.(2), (with a printed slip giving the imprint of Longman & Broderip, London). ★
Pm (Sikorski: Hamburg, pn 562, 1961), ed. & arr. Walter Liebermann, parts, (Edition Sikorski No. 562).
*CPS-15. Divertimento in E♭ [from Six Quatuors, Op. 8, No. 2]. ob cl bn hn.
Pc (Seiber: Paris, c.1780), RISM [S 4487], parts: GB-Lbl, g.1065.b. ★
Pc (J.J. Hummel: Berlin, pn 352, c.1780), RISM [S 4488], parts: RF-Ssc.
Pm (In: Denkmäler der Tonkunst in Bayern, Bd. 15, 1915), score. Pm (Leuckart: München, 1937), score.
*CPS-1m. March. Comp[osed]. by Stamitz. 2ob 2bthn 2hn 2bn serp.
MS parts: GB-Lbl, RM.21.d.2. [= A-202.3/27(a)] *Probably an arrangement.* ★
CPS-1d (= Gyrowetz, ADG-2). Octet No. 2; in B♭, 3 mvts. 2ob 2cl 2hn 2bn.
MS parts: CZ-Pnm, XX.F.12, (as by Gyrowetz, with cbn); CZ-Bm, (as by Stamitz; unverified).
CPS-2d. (= XXI-1) Quartetto del Sigᵉ Ignoto; in F, 5 mvts. ob 2hn bn.
MS parts ("1802/Grdg."): D-Rtt, Inc.IIb/9. *"Stamitz" has been added in pencil on the titlepage.* ★

*STAMITZ (Stamic), Johann Wenzel (Ján Václav)
baptized 17 June 1717, Deutsch Brod (now Havíčkův Brod) - 27 March 1757, Mannheim
JLS-1. Adagio in F. 2cl 2hn. **JLS-2.** Adagio in F. 2cl hn bn.
Pc (In: VZR-1. V Roeser. *Essai d'Instruction à l'usage de ceux qui composent pour La Clarinette et le Cor.* Mercier: Paris, 1764; facsimile reprint: Minkoff: Geneva, 1972, pp. 21-22), scores of both works. ★
Pm (In: Albert R. Rice. *The Baroque Concerto.* Oxford University Press: London, 1992), pp. 129 - 132, score, JLS-1 only.

*STARCK, ( ) *Capellmeister*
XUS-1da. Dittersdorf: Hieronimus Knicker. 2ob 2cl 2hn 2bn. MS pts: D-DO, Mus.Ms.347. (= Went, JNW-14a)

*STARK, Wenzel *1670 - 1757*
WNS-1. A Quatro, E♭. 2cl 2hn. MS parts: A-KR, H 39/71. ★

*STARKE, Friedrich *1774, Elsterwerde, Saxony - 18 Dec 1835, Döbling, nr Vienna*
Here **JM** *stands for Starke's Journal militairische Musik in monatlichen Lieferungen. Whistling's annual lists first mention the journal in the 1819 Supplement 2 ("Wien Autor, Träg [sic: Traeg]", comprising Jahrgang 1 & 2, each of 12 Heften) but only begin to mention specific works with "Heft 61" in Supplement 4 (1821) - and even then, references are incomplete. Supplement 6 (1823) provides the important information, "(Zum Theil handschriftlich.)". However, a certain amount of caution is needed concerning the Journal since Whistling & Hofmeister's Ergänzungsband zum Handbuche of 1829 assigns opus numbers to works previously cited as "Heften". Other than FRS-30a, we have rarely found the journal title on any MSS that we have examined. Where a work is conjectured to be an earlier Heft of the Journal it is marked as* +**JM**.
Care must also be taken with MSS in CZ-Bm(au). It is now apparent that many are "pirated" copies, often with movements omitted, as, for example, in the case of FRS-10a.
FRS-1. Cahier I. contenant XII. Differentes Piéces [sic] en Musique Turque arrangé et Composée par Fr: Starke. Märtz [sic] 1807. 2pic("flautino") 2ob 3cl(C) 2hn 2bn 2tp(clar) b-dr s-dr.
MS parts: A-Ee, Mus.1161. *Nos. 3 - 12 appear to be original compositions.* ★
  1.1. M. Umlauf: Les Abencerrages und Tegris, overture. *(No. 1 in Starke's full arr.)*
  1.2. M. Umlauf: Les Abencerrages und Tegris, quintett. *(No. 4 in Starke's full arr.)*
  1.3. Marsch. 1.4. Danse Armée [sic]. 1.5. Starke: Marsch [&Trio]. 1.6. Poll[onoise] [& Trio].
  1.7. Quadril [& Trio]. 1.8. Allamant [sic] [& Trio]. 1.9. Menuetto [& Trio]. 1.10. Angl[aise] [& Trio].
  1.11. Rondo a la Turque [with Trio & Coda]. *Not Mozart's work of the same title.*
  1.12. La Schasse [sic] [& Trio].
FRS-2. 6 Variations sur l'Air "Wer hörte wohl jemals mich klagen" (in J. Weigl: *Die Schweizerfamilie*). 2ob pic-cl 2hn 2bn cbn 2tp. MS pts (July 1818): CZ-Bm(au), A.35.248. *The coda is marked "Pastorale Favorite le meme Opera [sic]".* ★
*FRS-3. Serenate; in E♭, 5 mvts. 2ob 2cl 2hn 2bn cbn. MS parts: A-Ee, Mus.1137. ★
FRS-4. [5] Variation über das Pas de deux auf dem Ballet "Die Tanzsucht". 2ob 2cl 2hn 2bn cbn.
MS parts: A-Ee, Mus.1160. *The Thema & Variations 1 - 5 are followed by a Nachspiel; the Coda (Allegro) is actually a 6th Variation.* ★

FRS-5. Thema mit [4] Variationen, Nachspiel und Coda. 2ob 2cl 2hn 2bn 2tp.
MS parts (**JM**, Heft 63, No. 3): CZ-Bm(au), A.35.251. ★
FRS-6. Die feindlichen Volksstämme (= M. Umlauf: Les Abencerrages), ein beliebtes Thema mit 4 Variationen
mit Nachspiel und Coda. 2ob 2cl 2hn 2bn 2tp. MS parts (1819, **JM**): CZ-Bm(au), A.35.252, No. 3. ★
FRS-7. Theme, 4 variations and coda on "Ich bin liederlich". 2ob 2cl(C) 2hn 2bn. MS pts: A-Ee, Mus.1136. ★
FRS-8. [2] Variations on Mozart's "O dolce Concento" (Die Zauberflöte: Das klinget so herrlich).
2ob 2cl 2hn 2bn. MS pts: CZ-Bm(au), A.40.170. *No. 2 of JFS- 2a.* ★
FRS-9. [4] Variations on Paisiello's "Nel cor più non mi sento" [La Molinara]. 2ob 2cl 2hn 2bn.
MS parts: CZ-Bm(au), A.40.170. *No. 3 of JFS- 2a.* ★
FRS-10.1. Tyroler Lied mit Veränderungen. ob/cl(C) ob/fl 2cl 2hn 2bn.
MS parts: A-Ee, Mus.1162. *The "Veränderungen" are changes rather than true variations; the title on the hn I
part gives, "2. Oboe oder Flute" rather than the alternatives listed on the wrapper.* ★
FRS-10.2. Tyroler Lied mit Verenderungen [sic] nebst einem Marsch. fl 2ob cl(Eb) 2cl(Bb) 2hn 2bn cbn.
MS parts: A-KR, H 41/95.
FRS-11. 6 Aline Walzer mit Coda. cl(Eb/F) 2cl(Eb) 2cl(Bb) 2hn bn(I) tp(Eb) basso.
MS parts: I-Mc, Noseda M.45.21. ★
FRS-12. National-Polonaise. 2ob 2cl 2hn 2bn cbn 2tp. MS parts (1819, **JM**): CZ-Bm(au), A.35.252, No. 2.
Probably an original piece by Starke. ★
FRS-1m. Marsch; in C. pic 2cl(F) 2cl(C) 3hn 2bn 2tp(prin, C, G) b-dr s-dr. MS pts: CZ-Pnm, XLII.F.149. ★
FRS-2m. Sechs Neue Original Maersche samt [sic] Trios der K.K. Oesterichschen Armée [sic] nach dem neuen,
bey derselben eingeführten geschwinden Tempo. 2ob cl(F) 2cl(C) 2hn 2bn cbn 2tp.
Pc (bey Joh. Cappi: Wien, pn 1282, 1812), parts: I-Fc, F.P. S.475, (uncut).
*FRS-3m. [6] Neue lebhafte militair Märsche…Nach dem neuen für die K. auch K.K. Oester. Armée [sic]
eingeführten geschwindern Tempo…Op. 14. 2ob 2cl(C) 2hn 2bn cbn 2tp.
Pc (Artaria und Comp.: Wien, pn 1830, 1812), parts: A-Wst, M 139006/c; GB-Ljag, (photocopy). ★
There are no divisi in the bn(II)+cbn part; the 2tp are divisi only in the 2nd march.
FRS-4m. 3 Märsche der oestreicher [sic] Truppen. pic 2cl 2hn 2bn tp(prin) posthorn.
MS parts (c.1820): CZ-Pnm, XLII.F.152. ★
   3.1m. Marsch, ¢. 3.2m. Jubelmarsch, ¢. 3.3m. Rüclmarsch aus Frankreich, ¢.
FRS-1a. Miscellanèes [sic] de la Musique . . . Anno 1817 - [1]819. 2ob 2cl 2hn 2bn cbn.
MS parts (+**JM**): CZ-Bm(au), A.35.253, Nos. 11 - 15.
   1.1a. Gyrowetz: Agnes Sorel, overture & 2 mvts. 1.2a. Zumsteeg: Tamira, polonaise.
   1.3a. Krommer: La Schasse [sic: "La Chasse", FVK-23, mvt 1 only, here in F].
FRS-2a. Production der berühmten Saengerin Madame Catalani bey Ihrer Durchrüse in Wien. 2ob 2c. 2hn 2bn.
MS parts (**JM**): CZ-Bm(au), A.40.170.
   2.1a. [unidentified] Sostenuto Larghetto, 2/4.
   2.2. (=FRS-8) Starke: Variations on Mozart's "O dolce contento".
   2.3. (=FRS-9) Starke: Variations on Paisiello's "Nel cor più mi sento". 2.4a.[unidentified] Russisch.
FRS-3.1a. Beethoven: Egmont, overture. pic 2fl 2ob cl(F) 2cl(Bb) cl(C) 4hn 2bn cbn 2tp b-tb tir.) s-dr.
AutoMS score: D-Bds, Mus.ms.auto.F.Starke 1.
FRS-3.2a. Beethoven: Egmont, overture. 2ob 2cl 2hn 2bn cbn.
Pc (Imprimerie Chimique: Vienna, pn 1905, 1812-13), parts: H-Bn, ZR 688.
MS parts: CZ-Pnm, Lobkovic X.G.f.57; D-Rtt, Sm. 14, No. 34, (as Anon, cb replaces cbn).
FRS-4a. Boieldieu: Le Petit Chaperon rouge, Röschens Aria & Chor der Holzbauer. 2ob 2cl 2hn 2bn cbn 2tp.
MS parts (**JM**, Heft 63, Nos. 1, 2): CZ-Bm(au), A.35.251.
FRS-5a. Carafa: Berenice in Siria, 1 mvt. 2ob 2cl 2hn 2bn cbn tp.
MS parts (**JM**, Heft 117, No. 5): CZ-Bm(au), A.36.892.
FRS-6a. Gallenberg: Joanna d'Arc, (1ter Theil) overture & 11 mvts. 2ob 2cl 2hn 2bn cbn 2tp.
MS parts (1825, **JM**, Heft 83): CZ-Bm(au), A.35.166. *Although some sources attribute the ballet to Vesque von
Püttingen (writing under the pseudonym "J. Hoven") the copy completion date of 1 Dec 1825 predates his opera
by 15 years; moreover, the wrapper clearly states "Ballet".*
FRS-7a. Generali: La Contessa di collo erboso, 1 mvt. 2ob 2cl 2hn 2bn cbn tp.
MS parts (**JM**, Heft 117, No. 12): CZ-Bm(au), A.36.892.
FRS-8a. Giuliani: Marsch. 2ob cl(F) 2cl 2hn 2bn 2tp.
MS parts (**JM**, Heft 63, No. 5): CZ-Bm(au), A.35.251. *The cl(F) only appears in this mvt.*
FRS-9a. Gyrowetz: Agnes Sorel, overture & 2 mvts. 2ob 2cl 2hn 2bn cbn. *See FRS-1.1a(-3a).*
FRS-10a. Gyrowetz: Der Augenartz, Abtheilung 1: overture & 8 mvts. Abth. 2: "Entre" [sic] & 7 mvts.
2ob 2cl 2hn 2bn cbn (2tp). *The 2tp are tacet in Abth. 1, Nos. 1 - 5 & 7, Abth. 2, Nos. 3, 5 & 6.*
Pc (bey Pietro Mechetti qᵐ Carlo: Wien, pn 78, 1812), RISM [G 5202], parts: CZ-Bm(au), A.18.863, (Abth. 1,
missing cbn); H-Bn, Z 43.671 (stamped "Industrie comtoir zu Pest", ?incomplete).
MS parts: CZ-Bm(au), A.35.167, ((1824, a compilation from the 2 Theils:Theil 1: overture & Nos. 1, 2, 7 & 8;
Theil 2: Nos. 1, 2 & 7); A-Wn, Mus.Hs.3795, Nos. 16 & 17, (= A-8.4a)
MS score (copy of the Mechetti edition, allegedly in the hand of J.S. Mayr): I-BGc, Mayr 597.
Modern MS score (ed. John Smit, Triebensee Ensemble, from CZ-Bm(au), A.35.167): GB-Ljag.
FRS-11a. Gyrowetz: Die Hochzeit der Thetis und Peleus, 6 mvts. 2ob 2cl 2hn 2bn cbn 2tp.
MS parts (1819, +**JM**): CZ-Bm(au), A.35.170.
FRS-12a. Gyrowetz: Die zwey Tanten, 1 Abt, 4 mvts. 2ob 2cl 2hn 2bn cbn 2tp.
MS parts (+**JM**): CZ-Bm(au), A.35.169.
FRS-13a. Gyrowetz & Persuis: Der Zauberschlaf. 2ob 2cl 2hn 2bn cbn 2tp.
MS parts (1819, +**JM**): CZ-Bm(au), (Abth 1, 5 mvts) A.35.205, (Abth 2, 8 mvts), A.35.204.
FRS-14a (attrib) Hummel: Die Eselshaut, overture & 6 mvts. pic 2ob 2cl 2hn 2bn (2tp) b-dr s-dr.
MS parts (**JM**, Heft 109): CZ-KRa, A3976/IV.B.142.
FRS-15a. Kalkbrenner: Rondo Villageoise, Op. 67. 2ob 2cl 2hn 2bn cbn 2tp.
MS parts (**JM**,"Zwey Rondeaux concertants, No. 1): CZ-Bm(au), A.36.667.

FRS-16a. Kauer: Die Brüder von Stauffenberg, overture & 6 mvts. 2ob 2cl 2hn 2bn cbn 2tp.
MS parts: CZ-Bm(au), A.36.880 (2ob 2cl 2hn 2tp) & A.35.249 (2bn cbn). *Bound with Triebensee's arrangement of Winter's Das Labyrinth.*
FRS-17a. Kinsky: Das ländlich Fest in Wäldchen bei Kis-Bér, overture & 8 mvts. 2ob 2cl 2hn 2bn cbn 2tp.
MS parts (**+JM**): CZ-Bm(au), A.35.172; D-Tl, Z 25, (No. 2, Ungaresi [Frissek], & No. 5, Verbunkos, only).
FRS-18a. Krommer: [Partita in E♭, FVK-23], La Schasse [sic "Chasse"]. 2ob 2cl 2hn 2bn cbn.
FRS-19a. Mayseder: Grand rondeau, Op. 21. 2ob 2cl 2hn 2bn cbn 2tp.
MS parts (**JM**, "Zwey Rondeaux Concertants" No. 2): CZ-Bm(au), A.36.667.
FRS-20a. Méhul: Joseph [und seiner Brüder], Abteilung 1: overture & 4 mvts, Abteilung 2: 3 mvts, Abteilung 3: 3 mvts. 2ob 2cl 2hn 2bn cbn 2tp. MS score (allegedly in the hand of J.S. Mayr): I-BGc, Mayr 616.
FRS-21a. Mercadante: Elisa e Claudio. 2ob 2cl 2hn 2bn cbn 2tp.
MS parts (**JM**, Hefts 128, 129, 1824): CZ-Bm(au), (Theil 1, overture & 7 mvts) A.35.186, (Theil 2, overture to Act II & Aria con Coro, "Se mi fai più lostradato") A.35.185.
FRS-22a. Meyerbeer: Il Crociato in Egitto, overture & 5 mvts. 2ob/fl 2cl 2hn 2bn 2tp b-tb.
MS parts (**JM**, Heft 138): CZ-Bm(au), A.35.190.
FRS-23a. Morlacchi: Tebaldo e Isolina, overture. 2ob 2cl(C) 2hn 2bn cbn 2tp.
MS parts (**JM**, Heft 130): CZ-Bm(au), A.35.191.
FRS-24a. Rossini: L'Inganno felice, 6 mvts. 2ob 2cl 2hn 2bn cbn.   MS parts: CZ-Bm(au), A.36.890.
FRS-25a. Rossini: Il Turco in Italia, Theil 1: overture & 11 mvts, Theil 2: mvts 1 - 3, 10, 11, (No. 1 is a Theme & 5 Variations). 2ob 2cl 2hn 2bn cbn tp.   MS parts (**JM**, Hefts 116, 117): CZ-Bm(au), A.36.892.
FRS-26a. Rossini: Sigismondo, recitative & aria. 2ob 2cl 2hn 2bn cbn tp.
MS parts (**JM**, Heft 117, No. 9): CZ-Bm(au), A.36.892.
FRS-27a. Rossini: Elisabetta, Regina de l'Inghilterra, Theil 1: overture & 9 mvts, Theil 2: 10 mvts.
2ob 2cl 2hn 2bn cbn 2tp. MS parts (**JM**, Hefts 134, 135): CZ-Bm(au), (Theil 1) A.35.214, (Theil 2) A.35.215.
*FRS-28.1a. Rossini: Otello, overture & 4 mvts. 2ob 2cl 2hn 2bn cbn 2tp.
MS parts ("31 Julii [1]819", **+JM**): CZ-Bm(au), A.35.218.
FRS-28.2a Rossini: Otello, Aria des Rodrigo. 2ob 2cl 2hn 2bn cbn 2tp.
MS parts (**JM**, Heft 63, No. 4): CZ-Bm(au), A.35.251.
FRS-28.3a. Rossini: Otello, 2 cavatinas. 2ob 2cl 2hn 2bn cbn tp.
MS parts (**JM**, Heft 117, Nos. 6 & 7): CZ-Bm(au), A.36.892.
FRS-29.1a. Rossini: La Gazza Ladra, Theil 1: overture & 11 mvts; Theil 2, 12 mvts. 2ob 2cl 2hn 2bn cbn 2tp.
MS parts (**JM**, Hefts 77 & 78): A-Wn, (?lost); CZ-Bm(au), A.36.889, (Theil 2); I-Fc, F.P. S.413, (complete).
FRS-29.2a Rossini: La Gazza Ladra, Schlusgesang & 1 mvt. 2ob 2cl 2hn 2bn cbn tp.
MS parts (**JM**, Heft 117, Nos. 3 & 8): CZ-Bm(au), A.36.892.
+FRS-30a. Rossini: Armida, (Abth 1) overture & 4 mvts: pic ob(I vel fl) ob (II vel cl in C) cl(F) 2cl(C) 2hn 2bn cbn 2tp(clar in C) 2tp(clar in D) b-tb b-dr s-dr; (Abth 2) 7 mvts: 2ob 2cl 2hn 2bn cbn 2tp.
MS parts (**JM**, Hefts 124, 125): CZ-Bm(au), (Abt 1) A.37.345, (Abt 2) A.35.208.
FRS-31a. Rossini: Ricciardo e Zoraide, Theil 1: sinfonia & 4 mvts, Theil 2: 4 mvts, Theil 3: 4 mvts.
2ob 2cl 2hn 2bn cbn. MS parts (**JM**, Hefts [?108, 109], 110): I-Fc, F.P. S.412.
FRS-32a. Rossini: La Donna del Lago, Abth 1: overture & 7 mvts, Abth 2: 6 mvts; Abth: 3: 7 mvts.
2ob 2cl 2hn 2bn cbn (2tp). MS parts (**JM**, Hefts 93 - 95): I-Fc, F.P. S.415, (without 2tp); CZ-Bm(au), A.36.874, (Abth 1: Nos. 1 - 4, 6, 7; Abth 2: No. 6; Abth 3: Nos. 2, 4, 6, 7). *The 2tp parts in CZ-Bm are ad lib.*
*FRS-33a. Rossini: Zelmira, overture & 6 mvts. 2ob 2cl 2hn 2bn cbn (2tp).
Pc (bey Artaria und Comp: Wien, pn 2685, c.1822), parts: A-Wst, M 13880/c; CZ-Pnm, XLI.B.122; GB-Ljag, (photocopy). *A tour de force for all instruments.*
FRS-34a. M. Umlauff: Les Abencerrages und Tegris oder Die feindlichen Volksstämme, overture & 13 mvts.
2ob 2cl 2hn 2bn cbn. MS parts: A-Ee, Mus.1163.   *See also supra: FRS-1.1, 1.2.*
FRS-35a. Weber: Oberon, Auswahlstücke, overture & 8 mvts. 2ob 2cl 2hn 2bn cbn (2tp).
MS parts (**+JM,**, 1828): CZ-Bm(au), A.35.244.
FRS-36a. J. Weigl: Nachtigall und Raabe, overture & 6 mvts. 2ob 2cl 2hn 2bn cbn 2tp.
MS score (allegedly in the hand of J.S. Mayr): I-BGc, Mayr 604.
MS parts (**+JM**): CZ-Bm(au), 35.246, (missing ob I).
FRS-37a. Zumsteeg: Tamira, 1 mvt. 2ob 2cl 2hn 2bn cbn. *See FRS-1.3a.*
FRS-38a. Rossini [sic; the attribution is incorrect; unidentified]: overture. 2ob 2cl 2hn 2bn cbn 2tp.
MS parts (1819, **JM**): CZ-Bm(au), A.35.252, No. 1.
FRS-1va Volkert: Der lustige Fritz, Romance Joyeuse mit Chor (Lied & Nachspiel).
TTBB, ob(v[el pic) 2ob cl(F) 2cl(C) 2hn 2bn cbn 2tp(clar) b-tb b-dr s-dr.
MS parts (**JM**, Heft 3): CZ-Bm(au), A.35.241, (probably a local copy).
FRS-1ad. P. Wranizky: Das Waldmädchen, as "Miscellans für 1816", sinfonia & 13 mvts. 2ob 2cl 2hn 2bn.
MS parts: CZ-KRa, A4168/IV.B.141. *We believe this arrangement to be by Went (JNW-72.1a), incorrectly labelled or with a misplaced wrapper.*

*STARZER, Joseph Franz *1726. Vienna - 22 April 1787, Vienna*
*JFS-1.1. Le Matin et Soir. 2ob 2cl 2hn 2bn.
Pc (Traeg: [Vienna], 1799-1804), No. 222, MS parts: A-Wgm, VIII 39992. ★
Pm (WINDS: Northridge, CA, pn W-67, c.1981), score & parts.
JFS-1.2. Le Matin et Le Soir. 2ob 2ca 2hn 2bn.
MS parts: CZ-K, symfonie 258.K.II, (with Starzer's printed program notes). *Probably a transcription by Went.*
*JFS-2. Musica di Camera Molto Particulare. 2chalumeaux/fl 3tp(C) 2tp(D)/hn timp.
MS parts: A-GÖ, MS.2901. ★
*JFS-1ad (= **A-538a**). Starzer: Les 3 Sultanes, 5 mvts. 2ob 2hn bn.
MS parts: CZ-Pnm, XLII.C.179; (modern MS copies: GB-Ljag, GB-DOTams).
*JFS-2ad (= **A-540a**). Starzer: Adéle de Ponthieu, 4 mvts. 2ob 2hn bn.   MS parts: CZ-Pnm, XLII.B.253.
*JFS-3ad (= **A-541a**). Starzer: Les Horaces et les Curiaces, 11 mvts 2ob 2hn bn. MS pts: CZ-Pnm, XLII.B.195.
*JFS-4ad (= **A-542a**). Starzer: Le Baal Angloise, 5 mvts. 2ob 2hn bn. MS parts: CZ-Pnm, XLII.B.161.

STEARNS, Peter Pindar *7 June 1931, New York*
PPS-1. Serenade; 1958. 3fl 3ob 3cl 3hn 2bn tu. Pm (American Composers Alliance: New York).
PPS-2. Octet. pic fl ob ca cl b-cl bn cbn. Pm (American Composers Alliance: New York).

*STEFFANI (Stefani), Jan (Jean), known as "*l'aîné*" *1746, Prague - 24 Feb 1829, Warsaw*
*JQS-1. Harmonie; in D, 4 mvts. 2ob 2cl 2hn 2bn.
MS parts: D-SWl, Mus. 5260. ★
Pm (Piper Publications: Barrhill by Girvan, pn P.P.PNC002, 1993), ed. David J. Rhodes, score & parts.
*JQS-2. Harmonie; in E♭, 5 mvts. 2cl 2hn bn.
MS parts: D-SWl, Mus. 5259. ★
Pm (Piper Publications: Barrhill by Girvan, pn P.P.PNC001, 1993), ed. David J. Rhodes, score & parts.
JQS-3. Parthia in E♭ [later wrapper: Serenata in E♭]; 4 mvts. 2ob 2cl 2hn (2)bn.
MS parts: CZ-Pnm, XXVII.B.117. *The original titlepage calls for "Fagotto", the wrapper for "Fagotti".* ★
Pm (Piper Publications: Barrhill by Girvan, pn P.P.PNC012, 1997), ed. David J. Rhodes, score & parts.
JQS-4(-9). Six Parties, Oeuvre Premier; (B♭, G minor, E♭, B♭, E♭, B♭; each of 4 mvts). 2cl 2hn 2bn.
Pc (J.J. Hummel: Berlin, 1786), parts: D-Bds, (?lost); RF-Ml, M3 Р-ИН/1506; RF-Ssc, 15. a. 56. 4. 246. ★
MS parts: CZ-OSr, 2136, (No. VI only, copy by Joseph Heber, as "Partitta").
Pm (Polskie Wydawnictwo Muzyczne: Kraków, 1993), ed. Jerzy Marowski, score, (Źródła do historii myzyki polskiej XXXIII), as "Sześć Partit".
JQS-10(-15). VI Partite da Stephani. 2ob 2cl 2hn 2bn.
Pc (Breitkopf: Leipzig, c.1785), ?MS pts: (untraced), advertized in catalog, *Supplement XVI, 1785, 1786, 1787.* ★

*STEINER, Franz *(?1780), Kapellmeister (? for the Löwenstein court, Wertheim am Main)*
FFS-1a. Reiser: 6 Walzer. cl(E♭) 2cl(B♭) 2hn 2bn cbn 2tp. (?Auto)MS parts: GB-Ljag(w), L.126.

STEINER, Johann Ludwig *(1770)*
QLS-1(-6). Six Quatuors, Oeuvre 20; (all in F). 2cl 2hn/tp timp(ad lib)
Pc (Johann André: Offenbach, pn 1575, 1802), RISM [S 5725], parts: D-Tu, (cl I, II only).

STENGEL, F. von
FVS-1. [Untitled work]. 2cl 2hn bn 2tp. MS parts: D-DS, (?lost in World War II).

*ŠTĚPÁN (Steffan, Stephani), Josef Antonín *bapt. 14 March 1726, Kopidlno, Bohemia-12 April 1797, Vienna*
Note: all works previously attributed to Štěpán are almost certainly by Jan Steffani (qv).

STEVENS, Richard John Samuel *27 March 1757, London - 23 Sept 1837, London*
RJS-1m, 2m. 2 Marches. Military band (instrumentation unknown). MS: GB-Cfm, (untraced).

*STEVENSON, *Sir* John Andrew *Nov 1761, Dublin - 14 Sept 1833, Meath.*
SAS-1m. Lord Donoughmore's First Grand March and Quick Step. 2cl/ob 2hn bn.
Pc (B. Cooke: Dublin, c.1795), RISM [S 6362], score: GB-Lbl, g.352.qq.(15). ★

STIEBER, Hans *1 March 1886, Naumberg, Saale - 18 Oct 1969, Halle, Saale*
HZS-1. Spielmusik, No. 3. fl 2ob 2cl hn 2bn. Pm (Hofmeister: Leipzig, etc., 1953), score & parts.

*ŠTIKA (Stika), Jan *(?1750)*
PJS-1t. Trauer Marsch des Fürsten v[on] S[ch]warzenberg; in C minor. fl 2cl 2hn 2bn tp.
MS parts (by Dominik Hübner, Langenbruck): CZ-Pu(dm), 59 R 3372. ★

STOCK, David (Frederick) *3 June 1939, Pittsburgh*
DFS-1. The 'Slibert Stomp. fl ob 2cl 2sax hn 3tp tb. Pm (American Composers Alliance: New York).

STOCKMEIER, Wolfgang *13 Dec 1931, Essen*
WOS-1. Credo. 2ob 2cl 4hn 2bn 2tp 3tb. Pm (Möseler Verlag: Wolfenbüttel), ?score.

*STONEHAM, (Arthur) Marshall *18 May 1940, Barrow-in-Furness, UK.*
Stoneham has also prepared performing versions of the complete wind music of Weber (e.g. the reconstruction of the Trauermusik, CMW-3v), Süssmayer & Dibdin and of works by Matthew Locke and Schetky.
AMS-1. Jenka. 2cl 2hn 2bn. AutoMS score & parts: GB-DOTams.
AMS-1a. Purcell (attrib): Prelude. ob 2cl 2hn 2bn. AutoMS score & parts: GB-DOTams.
AMS-1va. Willoughby Bertie (4th Earl of Abingdon) with accompaniments by F.J. Haydn: Catch ("Some kind Angel") & Glee ("Where shall a hapless lover find?"). 3 equal voices, cl 2hn bn. AutoMS parts: GB-DOTams.

STORARO, ( ) *(1800)*
ZCS-1. Marcia [& Trio]. (fl) 2cl 2hn tp(prin) tb vlne (bomb) timp organ(bc).
MS score: I-Vsmc, (with full organ part; the fl & bomb do not appear in the score). ★
ZCS-2. Marcia [& Trio]. 2cl 2hn tp(prin) tb basso timp organ. MS parts: I-Vsmc.

*STORL, Johann Georg Christian *1675 - 1719*
YJS-1m. Marsch [dedicated to *Herzog* Eberhard Ludwig von Württemberg]. 2ob 2hn bn.
MS: D-ROu, MS.1711.

STOSSEL, ( )
ZGS-1m. Militär-musik. Instrumentation unknown.
Pc (Schott: Mainz, post-1800), parts: D-MZsch.

STRÄNG, Kenneth *1959, Sweden*
KQS-1. Associations for winds, Op. 3; 1984. ob 3cl b-cl hn bn. MS score: The composer, c/o S-Sic.

STRAESSER, Joep *11 Mar 1934, Amsterdam*
JRS-1. Enclosures; 1970. 3fl 3ob 3cl 2hn 3bn 2tp 2tb tu perc. Pm (Donemus: Amsterdam, 1971), score.

STRAHAN, Derek *(1930), Australia*
DAS-1. Octet: Mutations II; 1964. 2ob 2ca 2cl 2bn. MS score: AUS-Smc.

STRANENSKY, ( ) *(1770)*
ZDS-1(-6). 6 Sinfonien; ("Parthien" on bn II part), (E♭, E♭, B♭, F, E♭, F), (c.1800).   2ob 2cl 2hn 2bn.
MS parts: D-W.
Pm (Das Erbe deutsche Musik, XIV, No. 7, 1941, repr 1961), No. 6 only, pp. 49 - 57, score. ★

STRANG, Gerald *13 Feb 1908, Claresholm, Canada - 2 Oct 1983, Lorna Linda, California*
GDS-1. Lost and Wandering.   2fl 2ca cl hn bn.   Pm (American Composers Alliance: New York).

STRAUB, Fritz *(1920)*
FWS-1a. Alte Tanzweisen (based on a piece by Carlo Farina, c.1600).   fl fl(pic) ob 2ca 2cl b-cl 2bn cbn(ad lib).
Pm (Ars Viva Verlag: Zürich; now B. Schott's Söhne: Mainz, 1954), score & parts.

*STRAUSS, Johann (Baptist) *the Younger* *25 Oct 1825, Vienna - 3 June 1899, Vienna*
SJS-1v. Graduale, "Tu qui regis totum orbem.   SATB, 2ob 2cl 2hn 2bn 3tb timp.
MS (1844): untraced but known to survive.

*STRAUSS, Richard Georg *11 June 1864, Munich - 8 Sept 1949, Garmisch-Partenkirchen*
*RGS-1. Serenade in E♭, Op. 7; 1881 - 1882.   2fl 2ob 2cl 4hn 2bn cbn/tu/db.
AutoMS score: A-Wue (Universal Edition archives).
Pc (J. Aibl: München, 1882), score: GB-Lbl, e.666.b.(12).
Pc (Jos. Aibl Verlag: Leipzig, c.1904), "In die 'Universal-Edition' aufgenommen", score: GB-Lbl, g.1138.r.(10).
Pm (Univeral Edition: Wien, London, sd), miniature score (pn Ph 246) & parts (pn 14326).
Pm (International Music Company: New York, pn 518, pre-1942), miniature score & parts.
*RGS-2. Suite in B♭, Op. 4; 1883/84.   2fl 2ob 2cl 4hn 2bn cbn/tu.
Pc (Adolphe Fürstner: Berlin, Paris, pn A.990P., 1911), score: GB-Lbl, h.3918.n.(1).
Pm (Leuckart: München, 1933, reprinted 1984), score & parts.
Pm (McGinnis & Marx: New York, sd).
Pm (Universal Edition: Wien, London, sd), miniature score (pn Ph 245).
*RGS-3. Erste Sonatine (Aus der Werkstatt eines Invaliden), AV 135, in F, 1943.
2fl 2ob cl(C) 2cl(B♭) bthn b-cl 4hn 2bn cbn.
AutoMS score: D-GSA; (photocopy held by Boosey & Hawkes, London).
Pm (Boosey & Hawkes: London, etc., pn 2606, 1964), score & miniature score (Hawkes Pocket Scores, No. 757),
parts on hire.
*RGS-4. Symphonie für Bläser (Zweite Sonatine; Fröhliche Werkstatte), AV 143, in E♭, 1944/45.
2fl 2ob cl(C) 2cl(B♭) bthn b-cl 4hn 2bn cbn.
AutoMS score: CH-Wr; (photocopy held by Boosey & Hawkes, London).
Pm (Hawkes & Son, now Boosey & Hawkes: London, etc., pn 2609, 1952), score & miniature score (Hawkes
Pocket Score, No. 677), parts on hire.
*RGS-1ed. Buhnenmusik zu Shakespeare's *Romeo und Julia*, 4 mvts, AV 86.
Pm (In: *Richard Strauss Jahrbuch* 1959 - 1960. pp. 42 - 50. Boosey & Hawkes: London, etc., 1960), score.
RGS-1evd. Vor dem Hochzeitsbette, Act 4, (mvt 3).   SSA, ob 2cl 2bn tri.
RGS-1ed. Trauermusik, Act 4, (mvt 4).   ob 2cl 2bn.

STRAVINSKY, Igor Theodorvich (Feodorovich) *17 June 1882, Orianenbaum - 6 April 1971, New York*
*ITS-1.1. Symphonies d'Instruments à vent à la mémoire de Claude Debussy; 1st version, 1920.
3fl a-fl(G) 2ob ca (??)cl bthn 4hn 2bn cbn 2tp(C) tp(A) 3tb tu.
AutoMS short score: CH-Bsacher (20 June 1920).
MS full score: CH-Bsacher (30 Nov 1920).
Pm (Boosey & Hawkes: London, 1972), score & hire parts.
*ITS-1.2. Symphonies of wind instruments, 1947 revision.   3fl 2ob ca 3cl 4hn 2bn cbn 3tp 3tb tu.
AutoMS score: US-Wc.
Pm (Edition russe de musique; Boosey & Hawkes: London, etc., 1952), score & min score (Hawkes Pocket
Scores, No. 672).
Pm (Boosey & Hawkes: London, 1972), score & hire parts.
*ITS-2. Concerto for piano and wind instruments, (1924, revised 1950).
Solo piano, 2fl 2ob ca 2cl 4hn 2bn (cbn) 4tp 3tb tu db timp.
Pc (Edition russe de musique: Berlin, 1936), score: GB-Lbl, i.105.g, (with MS corrections & revisions).
Pm (Boosey & Hawkes: London, 1960), miniature score (Hawkes Pocket Scores, No. 724).
*ITS-3. Concertino, 2nd version, 1952.   Violin, cello(oblig) fl(pic) ob ca cl 2bn 2tp 2tb.
Pm (William Hansen: Copenhagen, 1953), score (pn 3962a) & miniature score (pn 3962b).
*ITS-4. Octuor, 1922/23, revised 1952.   fl cl 2bn 2tp(C, A) t-tb b-tb.
Pc (Edition russe de musique: Berlin, 1924), score.
Pc (Berli: Moscow, 1924), score.
Pc (Boosey & Hawkes: London, 1948), miniature score, (Hawkes Pocket Scores, No. 630).
Pm (Edition Russe de Musique; Boosey & Hawkes: London, etc., pn B&H 17272, 1952), score.
ITS-5. Circus Polka, 1942.   fl(pic) 4cl 2sax 2hn 2crt 4tb 2bar 2tu organ perc.
Pm (B Schott's Söhne: Mainz, c.1950), score & hire parts.
ITS-6. Pesante (after No. 8 of *Les 5 doigts*, for piano duet).   2ob 2bn 3tp 3tb.
Pm (In: Robert Craft. *A Stravinsky Scrapbook.* London, 1983), pp. 103 - 106, score.
*ITS-1v. Mavra.   SMAT soli, 2fl(pic) 2ob ca pic-cl(E♭) 2cl 4hn 2bn 2tp(C) 2tp(A) 3tb tu, strings.
Pc (Edition russe de musique: Berlin, 1925), score.
Pm (Boosey & Hawkes: London, 1969), miniature score (Hawkes Pocket Scores, No. 843).
*ITS-2v. Symphony of Psalms, 1930, revised 1948.
Chorus, 4fl(pic) 4ob ca 4hn 3bn cbn 4tp tp(D) 3tb tu 3vc db 2pianos timp b-dr.
Pc (Edition russe de musique: Berlin, 1931, reprinted 1932), score.
Pm (Boosey & Hawkes: London, 1948), score & miniature score (Hawkes Pocket Scores, No. 637).
Pm (Muzyka: Moscow, etc., 1969), score.

*ITS-3v. Mass for Mixed Choir and Double Wind Quintet, 1948.   SATB, 2ob ca 2bn 2tp 3tb.
MS score: US-Wc.
Pm (Boosey & Hawkes: London, 1948), score & miniature score (Hawkes Pocket Scores, No. 655).
*ITS-4v. Canticum Sacrum ad honorem Sancti Marci nominis.
TB soli, chorus, fl 2ob ca 2bn cbn 3tp(C) b-tp 3tb cb-tb harp 4vla 3db organ.
Pm (Boosey & Hawkes: London, 1956), score & miniature score (Hawkes Pocket Scores, No. 691).
*ITS-5v. Threni: id est Lamentationes Jeremiae Prophetae.
SATTB & Basso profundo soli, SATB chorus, 2fl 2ob ca cl cl(bthn) b-cl sarrusophone 4hn flug 3tb tu timp
tam-tam piano celeste harp strings.
Pm (Boosey & Hawkes: London, 1958), score & miniature score (Hawkes Pocket Scores, No. 709).
ITS-6v. Variations on Bach's chorale "Vom Himmel hoch da komm' ich her".
Chorus, 2fl 2ob ca 4hn 2bn cbn 3tp 3tb vla db harp.
Pm (Boosey & Hawkes: London, 1956), score & miniature score (Hawkes Pocket Scores, No. 695).
ITS-7v. Cantata, 1952.   Solo ST, SSA chorus, 2fl ob ob/ca vc.
Pm (Boosey & Hawkes: London, pn HPS 666), miniature score.
*ITS-1a. Chant des Bataliers du Volga - Hymne à la nouvelle Russie, 1917.
pic fl 2ob 2cl 4hn 2bn cbn 3tp 3tb tu 2timp perc.
AutoMS score: GB-Lbl, Loan 75.47, (lent by J.W. Chester Ltd/Edition Wilhelm Hansen; 2 scores, one autograph
dated 8 April 1917, with piano reduction).
Pc (J. & W. Chester: London, 1920), score; reprinted 1923, (pn JWC 18).
Pm (J. & W. Chester: London, 1970), autograph edition, hire score & parts.
*ITS-2a. Sibelius: Canzonetta, Op. 62a, 1963.   cl b-cl 4hn db harp.
Pm (Breitkopf & Härtel: Leipzig, etc., pn PB3884, 1964), score.

*STRECK, Peter *(1800)*
PZS-1. 9 Pièces d'Harmonie.   fl 2cl 2hn bn.
Pc (Schott: Mainz; Falter: Munich, 1828), parts: D-MZsch.
PZS-1m. 12 Neue Märsche; (1833, für König Otto I von Grieschenland).
pic 2cl(Eb) 2cl(Bb) 4hn 2bn 3tp b-tb serp b-dr s-dr.   MS score: D-Mbs, Mus.Mss.3536.   ★
PZS-2m. 6 Militärische Alpen Märsche (dedicated to King Leopold I).   Large windband.   MS: B-Bc, W.13,411.
PZS-1a. Collection of 15 opera arrangements.   fl cl(D) 2cl(A) 2hn 2bn.   MS parts: D-Mbs, Mus.Mss.2570.
   1.1a. Hérold: Zampa, overture.   1.2a. Auber: Fra Diavolo, overture.
   1.3a. Boieldieu: La Dame blanche, overture.   1.4a, 1.5a. Weber: Oberon, overture & Chor.
   1.6a. Hérold: Zampa, potpourri.   1.7a. Lanner: Olymps-Walzer, Op. 67.
   1.8a. Lanner: Die Badner Ring'In Walzer, Op. 64.
   1.9a. Strauss the Elder: Mittelgegen den Schlaf Walzer, Op. 65.
   1.10a. Fahrbach the Elder: Beyfall mein schönster Lohn, Walzer.
   1.11a. Strauss the Elder: Der Pilger am Rhein Walzer, Op. 98.
   1.12a. Strauss the Elder: Ball-Racketen-Walzer, Op. 96.
   1.13a. Fahrbach the Elder: [unidentified] Galopp.   1.14a. Lanner: [unidentified] Galoppe.
   1.15a. Streck: Allemande.
PZS-2a. Collection of opera arrangments.   fl 2cl 2hn 2bn.   MS parts: D-Mbs, Mus.Mss.2569.
   2.1a. Spohr: Faust, Polonaise.   2.2a. Rossini: Semiramide, 1 mvt.
   2.3a. Chélard: Macbeth, Hexenterzett.   2.4. Weber: Oberon, overture & chorus.
   2.5a. Rossini: Guillaume Tell, overture.   2.6a. Lindpaintner: Janina, 1 long mvt.

*STREPPONI, Feliciano *1797, Milan - 13 Jan 1832, Trieste*
FES-1v. Dixit, Introduzione e Finale.   SATB, fl 2ob 2cl 2hn bn 2tp db perc.   MS: I-MZ, MS.87.
FES-2v. Gloria in Excelsis.   SATB, fl 2ob 2cl 2hn bn 2tp organ perc.   MS: I-MZ, MS.87.

STRNIŠTĚ, Jiří   *24 April 1914, Dašice*
IJS-1. Ottetto; 1975, 3 mvts.   2ob 2cl 2hn 2bn.
Pm (Panton: Prague, pn P 1789, 1978), score (Studijní Partitury 99).

*STROUHAL (Strauhal), Bernard, *Padre* *(1760), active pre-1800, Osek Monastery, Bohemia*
*BYS-1. N. 1 Parthia In C Le Galline Cioche [The Broody Hen"]; 5 mvts.   2ob 2hn 2bn.
MS parts: CZ-Pnm, XXXII.B.18.   ★
*BYS-2. Parthia in G, "Il Cuco", 4 mvts.   "Flauto traverso il cuco", 2ob 2hn 2bn.
MS parts: CZ-Pnm, XXXII.B.10. *The flute is only used in the last mvt.*   ★
*BYS-3. N. 3 Parthia In B[b] La Parussola [The Parosal]; 4 mvts.   2ob 2hn 2bn.
MS parts: CZ-Pnm, XXXII.B.22.   ★
*BYS-4. N. 4 Parthia in F La Zampagna [The Bagpipe"]; 4 mvts.   2ob 2hn 2bn.
MS parts: CZ-Pnm, XXXII.B.11.   ★
*BYS-5. N. 5 Parthia in B(b) La Quaglia [the Quail]; 4 mvts.   2ob 2hn 2bn.
MS parts: CZ-Pnm, XXXII.B.21.   ★
*BYS-6. N. 6 Parthia in C Il Echo Con Adieu; 4 mvts.   2ob 2hn 2bn.   MS parts: CZ-Pnm, XXXII.B.17.   ★
BYS-7. N. 1º Parthia In C; 5 mvts.   2ob 2hn bn.   MS parts: CZ-Pnm, XXXII.B.19.   ★
BYS-8. N. 2do Parthia In B[b]; 5 mvts.   2ob 2hn bn.   MS parts: CZ-Pnm, XXXII.B.23.   ★
BYS-9. N. 3º Parthia In G; 5 mvts.   2ob 2hn bn.   MS parts: CZ-Pnm, XXXII.B.9.   ★
BYS-10. N. 4to Parthia in F; 5 mvts.   2ob 2hn bn.   MS parts: CZ-Pnm, XXXII.B.12, (missing hn II).   ★
BYS-11. N. 5to Parthia In A; 5 mvts.   2ob 2hn bn.   MS parts: CZ-Pnm, XXXII.B.26.   ★
BYS-12. N. 6 Parthia In D; 5 mvts.   2ob 2hn bn.   MS parts: CZ-Pnm, XXXII.B.15.   ★
BYS-13. N. 1º Parthia In C; 5 mvts.   2ob 2hn bn.   MS parts: CZ-Pnm, XXXII.B.16.   ★
BYS-14. N. 2 Parthia in B[b]; 5 mvts.   2ob 2hn bn.   MS parts: CZ-Pnm, XXXII.B.21.   ★
BYS-15. N. 3 Parthia In F; 5 mvts.   2ob 2hn bn.   MS parts: CZ-Pnm, XXXII.B.13.   ★
BYS-16. N. 4 Parthia In D; 5 mvts.   2ob 2hn bn.   MS parts: CZ-Pnm, XXXII.B.23.   ★
BYS-17. N. 5 Parthia In A; 5 mvts.   2ob 2hn bn.   MS parts: CZ-Pnm, XXXII.B.24.   ★
BYS-18. N. 6 Parthia In B[b]; 5 mvts.   2ob 2hn bn.   MS parts: CZ-Pnm, XXXII.B.25.   ★

*STRUHAL, ( ) *(?active c.1800, zámek Svojšín, Moravia)*
QZS-1. Partia Turczia, 11 mvts.   2pic 2flautino 2ob 2cl 2hn bn tp(prin) timp
MS parts: CZ-Bm(sz), A.629, (timp part: "Nro IV. Struhalische Composition").   ★
QZS-1c. [Partia Turca], 28 mvts.   2pic 2flautino 2ob 2cl 2hn 2bn 2tp(prin) serp b-dr.
MS parts: CZ-Bm(sz), A.628, (missing flautino I).   ★
QZD-2c. Partia Turca, 9 mvts.   pic 2fl 2cl 2hn 2bn serp 2tp(clar) b-dr s-dr.   MS parts: CZ-Bm(sz), A.626.   ★
QZS-3d. Nro 7 [Partia Turca], 4 mvts.   pic 2fl 2cl 2hn 2bn 2tp s-dr.   MS parts: CZ-Bm(sz), A.627.   ★
QZS-4d. Partia Turzia [sic], 16 mvts.   cl(F) 2cl(C) 2hn 2bn 2tp b-dr s-dr.   MS parts: CZ-Bm(sz), A.630.   ★
QZS-1mc. Landwehr-Marsch.   pic 2flautino 2cl 2hn 2bn 2tp(prin) b-dr s-dr.   MS parts: CZ-Bm(sz), A.103.   ★

STRUTT, Clive
CLS-1. Fantasia; 1967.   2fl cl 2hn bn.   MS score: GB-Gsma, (available for purchase)
CLS-2. Partita; 1982.   fl ob cl b-cl hn bn.   MS score: GB-Gsma, (available for purchase).

*STÜCKEL, ( ) [?Ferdinand] *(1770)*
ZES-1a. J. Weigl: Richard Löwenherz.   2cl 2hn 2bn.   MS parts (by J.A. Buchal, 1803): PL-LA, RM 48.

STÜCKEL, Ferdinand
FDS-1. Partitta Turco; in C, 6 mvts.   pic 2fl 2cl(C) 2hn 2bn 2tp b-dr s-dr.   MS parts: H-KE, K 950.   ★
FDS-2. Partitta Turco; in C, 8 mvts.   pic 2fl 2cl(C) 2hn 2bn 2tp b-dr.   MS parts: H-KE, K 1134/IX.   ★

*STUMPF, Johann Christian *1763 - 1801*
JUS-1.1. Dous Pieses d'Harmonie [sic].   2fl 2ob 2cl 2hn 2bn cb(= cbn).   MS pts (1793): NL-DHgm, hk 19 C 1.   ★
JUS-1.2. Harmonie v[on] Stumpf arangiert v[on]. [Anton] Schneider.   fl 2ob 2cl(C & B♭) 2hn 2bn tp b-tb serp.
MS parts: D-Rtt, Sm. 16, Nos. 1 - 14, (only Nos. 1 & 2, 5 [= No. 6] and 13 [= No. 7] match; = AYS-94a).
JUS-2. 4 Allemandes.   2fl 2ob 2cl 2hn 2bn cbn.   MS parts: NL-DHgm, hk 19 C 2, (following JUS-1a).   ★
*JUS-3. Pièces d'harmonie, 1e Recueil; in E♭, 6 mvts.   2cl 2hn 2bn.
Pc (André: Offenbach am Main, pn 775, c.1796), parts: CZ-Pnm, XLI.B.134, (MS parts as "Parthia 2da", copy by Joseph Pražák).   ★
*JUS-4. Pièces d'harmonie, 2e Recueil; in B♭, 6 mvts.   2cl 2hn 2bn.
Pc (André: Offenbach am Main, pn 978, c.1796), parts: CZ-Pnm, XLI.B.135a, (missing titlepage).   ★
MS parts: CZ-Pnm, XLI.B.134, (by Joseph Pražák as "Parthia 1ma [sic]"); D-SWl, Mus. 5102, (missing mvts 4 & 5; the MS probably came from the Erdődy Harmonie, Pressburg, brought to Ludwigslust by Sperger).
Pm (Piper Publications: Barrhill By Girvan, pn P.P.PNC003, 1993), ed. David J. Rhodes, score & pts, (from the D-SWl MS copy, 4 mvts).
JUS-5. Pièces d'harmonie, 3e Recueil, 6 mvts.   2cl 2hn 2bn.
Pc (chez Johann André: Offenbach sur le Mein [sic], pn 979, c.1796), 1st ed., parts: CZ-Pnm, XLI.B.136.   ★
Pc (Johann André: Offenbach an Main, pn 3213, 1812/1813), 2nd ed., parts: D-Bhm.
JUS-6. Pièces d'Harmonie, Liv. 3 [without titlepage].   2fl 2hn 2bn serp b-dr s-dr cym.
Pc (Johann André: Offenbach am Main, pn 1836, c.1804), RISM [S 7078], parts: D-RH.
JUS-7. Pièces d'harmonie, Quartième Recueil.   2cl 2hn 2bn.
Pc (J. André: Offenbach am Main, pn 3214, 1812/1813), RISM [S 7077], parts: D-OF.
JUS-1a. Cimarosa: Il Matrimonio segreto, 2 Stücke ("aus der Heimlichen Ehe").   2fl 2ob 2cl 2hn 2bn cbn.
MS parts: NL-DHgm, hk 19 C 2, (followed by 4 Allemandes by Stumpf, JUS-2.).
JUS-2a. Devienne: Les Visitandines, 6 mvts.   2cl 2hn 2bn.
Pc (J.A. Böhme: Hambourg [sic], 1801), parts: D-Hs; H-KE, K 923/VIII; S-Skma.
JUS-3a. Martín y Soler: La Scuola dei maritati (as "La Capricciosa corretta"), overture & 5 mvts.   2cl 2hn 2bn.
Pc (Johann André: Offenbach am Main, pn 1359, 1799), Recueil 13, parts: A-KR; A-Wn; CH-Zz; D-Mbs, 4 Mus.pr 1359; H-Bn, Z 43,934; H-KE, K 1195 koll. 5; US-Wc; US-WS, (incomplete).   /
Pc (Imbault: Paris, c.1799), parts: D-AB.
JUS-4.1a, 4.2a. Mozart: Don Giovanni, Parthie 1ᵐ & 2ᵉ, each 7 mvts.   2fl 2ob 2cl 2hn 2bn tp basse.
MS parts: NL-DHgm, hk 19 C 3.
JUS-4.3a Mozart: Don Giovanni, 2 Pieces [sic], ["Deh vieni alla finestra"; "Non mi dir bell'idol mio"].
2fl 2ob 2cl 2hn 2bn tp basse.   MS parts: NL-DH, hk 19 C 2.
JUS-5a. Mozart: Così fan tutte, overture.   2fl 2ob 2cl 2hn 2bn tp basse.   MS parts: NL-DHgm, hk 18 A 4.
JUS-6.1a. Mozart: La Clemenza di Tito, overture & 11 mvts, liv. 1, 2.   2fl 2ob 2cl 2hn 2bn tp cb.
Pc (Chez Gombart et Comp: Augsbourg [sic], pn 369, 449, c.1798), RISM [M 5199], parts: D-AB, (liv. 1); D-HR, HR III 4 1/2 2° 389 (liv. 1); D-Mbs (liv. 1); D-NEhz (liv 1, 2); I-Fc, F.P. S.145. *Note: the copy of Liv. 1 cited in RISM in GB-Lbl is, in fact, Stumpf's arrangement for 2 violins, RISM [M 5225].*
MS pts: D-Rtt, Sm. 13, Nos. 1 - 11, (No. 12 has been copied and then crossed out in the fl I & II and ob I pts).
Pm (KGS), fiche (2370), of Gombart edition.
JUS-6.2a. Mozart: La Clemenza di Tito, overture & 11 mvts.   2ob 2cl 2hn 2bn.   MS pts: D-DO, Mus.Ms.1398.
JUS-7.1a(-7.3a). Mozart: Die Zauberflöte, 3 Recueils, each 6 mvts.   2cl 2hn 2bn.
Pc (chez Johann André: Offenbach sur le Mein [sic], pns 737, 751, 769, 1795), Recueils 1, 2, RISM [M 5053]; Recueil 3, RISM [M 5055]; parts: A-KR, (?rec.1-3); A-Sm, (rec. 2); CZ-Bm(no), A.16.669, A.16.670, (rec. 2 & 3: rec 3 with MS ob I & II parts transposed to replace or double the cl(B♭) parts): CZ-Pnm, XLII.B.135b, XLI.B.137, (rec. 2 & 3); D-AB, (rec. 3); D-OF, (rec.2); D-RH, (rec. 3, incomplete); S-Uu, utl.instr.mustr.142-144, Nos. 1-3, (missing hn II, 2bn); US-BETm, (rec. 1, 3), Philharmonic Society of Bethlehem PBS 1352.1, 1352.2.
MS parts (copy of the André edition): CZ-Pnm.
Pc (Johann André: Offenbach am Main, pn 2695, 3107, 2705; 1809, 1811, 1809), 3 Recueils, 2nd edition, RISM [M 5052, M 5054, M 5056], parts: D-B, (rec. 2, 3); D-F, (rec. 1); D-OF, (rec. 1, 3); GB-Ljag(w), (rec. 1, incomplete; rec. 3, complete).
Pc (Imbault: Paris, pns 623 - 625, c.1801), 3 Recueils, RISM [M 5063], parts: CH-Gpu, Ib.4853 (Recueil.1) Ib.4854 (Recueil 2); F-Pn, Vm27 4014 (1 - 3), (2 copies, complete).

JUS-7.4a, 7.5a. Mozart: Die Zauberflöte, 2 Livres, each 6 mvts.   2ob/fl 2cl 2hn 2bn.
Pc (Sieber pére: Paris, pns 1551, 1665, c.1804 - 1814), liv.1 (Suite 107), liv. 2, (Suite 122) RISM [M 5065, M 5066], parts: D-AB (liv. 1); GB-Ljag, (liv. 2).
JUS-8a. Mozart: String Quintet in E♭ (K.614), as "Grand serenade, tirée des oeuvres de Mozart".   2cl 2hn 2bn.
Pc (Gebrüder Meyn: Hamburg, pn 13, c.1799), RISM [M 6069], parts: D-DS; D-Dl; H-KE, 922/VIII.
JUS-9.1a, 9.2a. Paer: Camilla, 2 Recueils, each 6 mvts.   2cl 2hn 2bn.
Pc (Johann André: Offenbach am Main, pn 1366, 1367 (1st edition), c.1800), Recueils 14, 15, parts: H-KE, K 1195 koll. 6 & 7, (rec. 14 & 15).
Pc (Johann André: Offenbach am Main, pn 3119, (?3120), 1812), 2nd edition, parts: D-Mbs, (2 copies of rec. 14), 4 Mus.pr 14422, 44733.
JUS-10.1a, 10.2a. Paer: Il Morto vivo. 2 Recueils, each 6 mvts.   2cl 2hn 2bn.
Pc (Johann André: Offenbach am Main, pn 1578, 1579, 1801), Recueils 16, 17, parts: A-KR; A-Wn; D-Mbs, 4 Mus.pr 14442 (rec. 16); H-Bn, ZR 674, (rec. 17); H-KE, K 1195 koll. 8, (rec. 16); US-Wc.
JUS-11a. Paer: Poche ma buone (as "Der lustige Schuster").   2cl 2hn 2bn.
Pc (Johann André: Offenbach am Main, pn 1696, 1803), Recueil 18, parts: A-KR; A-Wn; D-Bhm, RA 3485, (?a reissue: the titlepage is formatted differently to the other Recueils & Stumpf's name is absent); D-SWl; US-Wc.
JUS-12a. Paisiello: L'Amor contrastato (as "La Molinara"), 6 mvts.   2cl 2hn 2bn.
Pc (Johann André: Offenbach am Main, pn 976, 1796), Recueil 7, RISM [P 126], parts: D-AB, (incomplete); D-OF; D-W; S-Uu, utl.instr.mustr.142- 144, No. 7, (missing hn II, 2bn); US-Wc.
Pc (Johann André: Offenbach am Main, pn 2698, 1809), 2nd edition, Recueil 7, RISM [P 127], parts: D-OF.
JUS-13a. Salieri: Il Talismano, 6 mvts.   2cl 2hn 2bn.
Pc (chez J. André: Offenbach sur le Mein [sic], pn 975, 1796), Recueil 6, parts: CZ-Pnm, XLI.B.133; S-Uu, utl.instr.mus.tr.142- 144, No. 6, (missing hn II, 2bn).
Pc (Johann André: Offenbach am Main, pn 3115, 1812), 2nd edition, Recueil 6, RISM [S 578], parts: A-KR; D-B, D.MS.197.131.an.3; H-KE, K 1195 koll 1, (incorrectly attributed as JUS-16.1a); US-Wc.
JUS-14a. Salieri: Tarare (as "Axur, Re d'Ormus"), 6 mvts.   2cl 2hn 2bn.
Pc (chez J. André: Offenbach sir le Mein [sic], pn 977, 1796), Recueil 8, RISM [S 459], parts: CZ-Pnm, XLI.B.138; D-AB; D-OF; D-W, (with MS bn parts).
Pc (Johann André: Offenbach am Main, pn 3120, 1812), 2nd edition, Recueil 8, RISM [S 460], parts: D-OF.
MS parts (copy of André edition): CZ-Pnm, XLI.B.138.
JUS-15.1a, 15.2a. J. Weigl: L'Amor marinaro, 2 Recueils, each 6 mvts.   2cl 2hn 2bn.
Pc (chez Jean André: Offenbach sur le Mein [sic], pn 2711, 2712, 1809), Recueils 19, 20, parts: A-KR; A-Wn rec. 19); GB-Ljag(w), (rec. 20); US-BETm, Philharmonic Society of Bethlehem 1352.3, 1352.4; US-Wc; US-WS.
MS parts (copy of André edition): CZ-Pnm, XLI.B.126.
JUS-16.1a(-16.4a). Winter: Das unterbrochene Opferfest, 4 Recueils, each 6 mvts.   2cl 2hn 2bn.
Pc (chez J. André: Offenbach °/M, pns (1st edition) 1139, 1140, 1204, 1205; 1798; (2nd edition) pns 3153, 3110, 3154, 3113, 1812), Recueils 9- 12, parts: A-KR; A-L (rec. 10); A-Wn; CZ-Pnm, XLI.B.139- 142, (rec. 9-12 in reverse order, all 1st ed.); D-B (rec. 11, 12); D-OF (rec. 10, 12, incomplete); GB-Ljag(w), (rec. 9 & 10, 2nd ed., both with the printed slip of the Frankfurt music seller, J. C. Gayl); D-SWl; H-Bn, ZR 698 (rec. 12); H-KE, K 1195 koll. 2-4, (rec. 10-12, all 1st ed.); S-Uu, utl.instr.mustr.142- 144, Nos. 9 - 12, (missing hn II, 2bn; rec. 9-12, all 1st ed.); US-Wc; US-WS.
MS parts: H-KE, K 0/108, (rec. 10).
JUS-16.5a. Winter: Das unterbrochene Opferfest, introductione & 7 mvts.   4cl 2hn 2bn.
Pc (Chez Vogt: Paris, sd), parts: CZ-Bm(au), 20.035.
JUS-16.6a(m). Marsches [sic] d'harmonie…Diexieme Recueil tiré de l'Opera [sic] Das unterbrochene Opferfest; 1 march. 2cl 2hn. MS pts: H-KE, K 0/108; H-Bn, (microfilm) FM 4/1988. *In fact, mvt 5 of JUS-16.2 only.*
JUS-17.1a, 17.2a. P. Wranizky: Oberon, 2 Recueils, each 6 mvts.   2cl 2hn 2bn.
Pc (Johann André: Offenbach am Main, pns 772, 774, 1795), Recueils 4 & 5, RISM [W 2039, W 2041], parts: A-KR; A-Wn; CH-Zz, AMG XIII 1086, (rec. 5); D-AB (rec. 4 & 5); D-OF, (rec. 5); D-HER (rec. 4); S-Uu, utl.instr.mustr.142- 144, Nos. 4 & 5, (rec. 4 & 5; missing hn II, bn I & II); US-Wc.
Pc (Johann André: Offenbach am Main, pns 3108, 3109, c.1811), 2nd edition, RISM [W 2040, W 2042], parts: D-B (rec. 4); D-OF (rec. 4 & 5).
JUS-17.3a(d). P. Wranizky: Oberon, overture & 12 mvts.   2cl 2hn 2bn.
MS parts: CZ-KRa, A4452/R.I.22, No. 6, (Havel's arrangement is credited "Auth: Stumpf"). *Possibly rescored or adapted - Stumpf's recueils do not include the Overture.*
JUS-1ca. Winter: Die Brüder als Nebenbuhler (I fratelli rivali), 3 mvts.   2fl 2ob 2cl 2hn 2bn tp basse.
MS parts: NL-DHgm, hk 19 C 1.

*STURMFEDER, Defours
DYS-1. Andante; in E♭.   2ob 2cl 2hn.
MS parts (from Hrádek nr Sušice): CZ-PLa, Hu 3178.   ★

*SUDA, Stanislav *22 March 1896, Plzeň - 13 Dec 1969, Plzeň*
See also: HORÁK, Josef, for a scoring of Suda's march, "Michálek".
SQS-1. Ballada; in D, 1906.   Solo violin, 2fl 2ob 2cl(A) 2hn 2bn harp.
MS score (by Jos. Reil, 18 June 1919): CZ-PLa, Hu 2356a. MS score: CZ-PLa, Hu 2356b.
MS score & parts (by Jos. Reil): CZ-PLa, Hu 2356c, (missing violin part).
SQS-2. Ecloga; in A. 1909.   Solo violin, 2fl 2ob 2cl(A) 2hn 2bn harp.
MS score: CZ-PLa, Hu 2374.
SQS-3. Elegie; in C. 1918.   Solo violin, 2fl 2ob 2cl(C) 2hn 2bn harp.
AutoMS score, MS scores & parts: CZ-PLa, Hu 2383a-ch.
SQS-4. Romance; in A. 1902.   Solo violin, 2fl 2ob 2cl(A) 2hn 2bn harp.
AutoMS score & MS score & parts (by Jos. Reil) & MS parts (by Jan Wurmser): CZ-PLa, Hu 2354.

SUDERBERG, Robert *28 Jan 1936, Spencer, Indiana*
RYS-1v. Choruses on themes of Yeats.   ST soli, Chorus, 2fl 2ob 3cl 2hn 2bn 2tp 2tb piano 2perc.
Pm (T. Presser: Bryn Mawr, PA, 1966), score.
RYS-2v. Second cantata.   T solo, 2fl cl 2hn 2tp piano vc db.
Pm (T. Presser: Bryn Mawr, PA, 1964), score.

*SÜSSMAYR (Süssmayer), Franz Xaver *1766, Schwanenstadt, Upper Austria - 16 Sept 1803, Vienna*
Performing editions of all of Süssmayr's wind works have been prepared by Marshall Stoneham (qv).
*FXS-1. [Untitled work] Nº 7; in F.   2bthn 2hn 2bn.
AutoMS score: GB-Lbl, Add.32181, ff. 242 - 242b.   MS: D-Bds (?lost, cited by Eitner).   ★
MS score & parts (modern): GB-DOTams.
FXS-1m. [March in C].   2ob 2cl 2hn 2bn tp.
AutoMS score: GB-Lbl, Add.32181, ff. 142 - 143.   MS score & parts (modern): GB-DOTams.   ★
Pm (WINDS: Northridge, CA, pn W-40, c.1981), photocopy of AutoMS & modern MS pts.
*FXS-2.1m. Contradanse [Marcia]; in Eb.   2ob 2cl 2hn 2bn.
AutoMS score (1793): GB-Lbl, Add.32181, f.131.   MS score & parts (modern): GB-DOTams.   ★
*FXS-2.2m. Marcia; Allegretto amoroso, in Eb.   2cl 2hn 2bn.
AutoMS score: GB-Lbl, Add.32181, f.133.   MS score & parts (modern): GB-DOTams.   ★
FXS-1.1e. Marsch aus der Cantatè: Der Retter in Gefahr.
2fl+pic 2ob(col fl) 2cl(C) 2hn 2bn 2tp(clar) b-dr+cym s-dr.   AutoMS score: H-Bn, Ms.mus.IV.43.   ★
FXS-1.2e. Recitatif und Aria aus der Cantat[a]: der Retter-Gefahr [sic].   2ob 2cl 2hn 2bn.
AutoMS score: GB-Lbl, Add. 32,181, ff. 27 - 35.   MS score (modern): GB-DOTams.   ★
FXS-1.1v. Frohnleichnams-Stationen in deutschen Texte.   CATB, 2fl 2ob 2cl 2hn 2bn cbn 2tp timp.
MS parts (from Langenbruck, now Dlouhý Most): CZ-Pu(dm), (2 copies), 59 R 3196/a, (1819, copy by Augustin
Erasmus Hübner; vocal pts with duplicate T & B pts) & 59 R 3196/b, (instrumental parts), 59 R 3197, (MS by
Dominik Hübner, Lehrer, c.1825-1850).   ★
FXS-1.2v. Pangelingua [sic] in C.   SATB, 2fl 2ob 2cl 2hn 2bn 2tp timp.
MS parts (1817): CZ-Bm(rj), A.13.058, (a note on the MS cites 4 performances between 15 Aug 1822 and 25
March 1831).   ★
*FXS-2v. Gesungen am [?Haimond]-Feyr Jubelfeyer, der Fraulein Anna Maria v Lang; "Sey uns dreymal hoch
willkommen".   SATB soli & chorus, 2ob 2cl(C) 2hn 2bn.
AutoMS score (1798): GB-Lbl, Add.32181, f.136.   MS score (modern): GB-DOTams.   ★
*FXS-1a. Kürzinger: Robert und Kalliste, quintetto.   2cl 2hn 2bn.
AutoMS score (1793): GB-Lbl, Add.32181, ff.156 - 160.   MS score & parts (modern): GB-DOTams.   ★

SULPIZI, Fernando *1936, Italy*
FNS-1. Punteggiatura, quattro pezzi, Op. 20.   fl 2cl hn bn.
Pm (Bérben: Anconia, Italy, pn 1659, c.1988), score & parts.

SULZER, Balduin *15 March 1932, Grossraming, Austria*
BAS-1. Octet; 1983.   2ob 2cl 2hn 2bn.
Pm (Astoria: Berlin. c.1983).

*SURINACH, Carlos *4 March 1915, Barcelona*
CZS-1. David and Bath-Sheba, ballet (A Place in the Sun).   2fl 2ob 2hn 2tp timp 2perc harp pf 2db.
Pm (Associated Music Publishers: New York, 1960), hire score & parts.

*SUTERMEISTER, Heinrich *12 Aug 1910, Feuerthalen, Canton Schaffhausen*
*HES-1. Modeste Mignon. D'après une valse d'Honoré de Balzac (or rather by D.F.E. Auber), 1973.
fl(pic) fl 2ob cl cl(Eb) 2hn bn bn(cbn).
Pm (B. Schott's Söhne: Mainz, 1974), score (pn 6500) & parts (pn 6500-10).

SUTTON, Wadham
WAS-1a. Mozart: Le Nozze di Figaro, Non più andrai.   2fl 3cl bn, *or* 2fl 4cl.
Pm (Mid Sussex Edition: Cleveleys, Blackpool, c.1985), score & parts.
WAS-2a. Mozart: Don Giovanni, "Il mio tesoro intanto".   2fl 3cl.
Pm (Mid Sussex Edition: Cleveleys, Blackpool, c.1985), score & parts.

*SVOBODA, Josef *(1800)*
FJS-1v. Missa quadragesimalis in Es [Eb].   SATB, 2cl 2hn 2vla organ
MS parts (by A.J. Hoke, Oberlehrer): CZ-Lla(je), No. 252 hud.   ★
FJS-2v. Missa quadragesimalis in Es [Eb].   SATB, 2cl 2hn 2vla organ.
MS parts (by A.J. Hoke, Oberlehrer): CZ-Lla(je), No. 253 hud.   ★

*SWEENEY, (John) William *5 Jan 1950, Glasgow*
WIS-1. Fantasias; 1986: 1. One night as I lay on my bed (English folk song); 2. By Hauchupside (Hugh
MacDiarmid).   2fl 2ob 2cl 4hn 2bn.   MS score: GB-Gsma, (available for purchase).

SYDEMAN, William T. *1928, USA*
WTS-1. Music.   2fl 2ob 2cl 2hn 2bn.
Pm (Seesaw Music Corp.: New York, sd).

*SYDOW, Samuel *c.1700 - 1754*
VYS-1. Concerto; in C, 4 mvts.   2ob taille 2bn.
MS parts: D-HRD, Fü 3741a, (55 - 58).   ★
Pm (Compusic: Amsterdam, pn 516, c.1994), score & parts.

*SYLVANI, ( ) VAN-, (Van-Sylvani), ( ) *(1770)*
XVS-1a. Harmonie . . . composée [sic] et Dediée [sic] à . . . Le Prince de Waldek, Op. 5; 8 mvts. 2cl 2hn 2bn.
Pc (Chanel: Lyon, c.1800), parts: CZ-Bm(au), A.28.038. ★
    1.1a. G.A. Walter: Allegro con brio.
    1.2a. G.A. Walter: Gratioso Siciliano
    1.3a. F.J. Haydn: Minuetto, (String Quartet, Hob. III/73iii.
    1.4a. G.A. Walter: Polacca Allegretto.
    1.5a. F.J. Haydn: Andantino con Variationi, (String Quartet, Hob. III/73ii).
    1.6a. Anon. [?Van Sylvani]: Allegretto.
    1.7a. Blasius: Waltz.
    1.8a. G.A. Walter: Potpourri, Allegretto.

*TAFFANEL, Claude Paul *16 Sept 1844, Bordeaux - 22 Nov 1908, Paris*
*CPT-1a. Saint-Saëns: Feuillet d'Album, Op. 81. fl ob 2cl 2hn 2bn.
Pc (Leduc: Paris, sd), score & parts: US-Wc, M859.S.
Pc (Durand: Paris, 1961), score (pn D.S.3893) & parts (pn 3894).

*TAG, Christian Gotthilf *2 April 1735, Beierfeld - 19 July 1811, Niederzwönitz bei Zwönitz*
CGT-1. Parthia a 2 Clarinetti in C; 3 mvts. 2fl 2ob 2cl(C) 2hn 3bn 2tp timp.
MS parts: D-LEm, Poel.Mus.Ms.326. ★
CGT-2. Choral Vorspiel zu Vom Himmel hoch. Coro 1: organ; Coro 2: ob 2cl 2hn 2bn.
MS parts: D-B, Mus.ms.21615.
CGT-1v. Cantata, "Schaffe in mir Gott ein neues Herz". CATB, 2ob 2hn organ.
MS: PL-GDj, Ms.Joh.422.
CGT-2v. Cantata, "Man singst mit Freuden". CATB, 2ob 2hn organ.
MS: PL-GDj, Ms.Joh.423.
CGT-3v. Gloria. SATB, winds.
MS score: D-Bds, Mus.Ms.21598.

*TANEYEV (Taneeff, Taneyef, Taniev, Taneev), Alexander Sergeivich (Sergei)
17 Jan 1850, St Petersburg - 7 Feb 1918, St Petersburg
AST-1. Andante. 2fl 2ob 2cl 2hn 2bn.
Pm (Muzgiz: Moscow, sd), edited B. Lamm, score & parts.
Pm (Leeds Music Corp.: New York, sd), score & parts (Musgis reprint).
Pm (McGinnis & Marx: New York, sd), score & parts.
Pm (Phylloscopus: Lancaster, UK, pn PP 20, c.1990), score & parts.

TANGAARD, Sven Erik *1942, Denmark*
SET-1. Forspil og 3 harmoniserede melodier; 1976. 2cl 2hn 2bn 2db 2perc. MS: DK-Kd.

*TANSMAN, Alexandre (Aleksander) *12 June 1897, Łódź - 15 Nov 1986, Paris*
AXT-1. Four Impressions (Prelude, Invention, Nocturne, Burlesque); 1945. 2fl 2ob 2cl 2bn.
Pm (Leeds Music Corp.: New York, etc., 1950), score & parts.

*TARCHI, Angelo (Angiolo) *1759/60 Naples - 19 Aug 1814, Paris*
Tarchi's 6 Sinfonien (I-Mc), often cited as "2ob 2hn" are actually for orchestra.
AYT-1ve. Ezio in Vicenza, cavatina, "A' voi, ò sponde amate". T, 2ob 2hn 2bn db timp.
MS parts (c.1793): D-Rtt, Tarchi 2. ★

TARDOS, Béla *1910 - 1966, Hungary*
BXT-1. Divertimento; 1935. 2ob 2cl 2hn 2bn.
MS score: H-Bmz.

*TAUSCH, Franz Wilhelm *26 Dec 1762, Heidelberg - 9 Feb 1817, Berlin*
*FWT-1. 6 Quatuors [sic; horns are ad lib], Op. 5; each of 1 mvt. 2bthn 2hn 2bn.
Pc (Werckmeister: Oranienburg, pn 72, 1805), parts: D-Bhm; I-Fc, F.P. S.475. ★
FWT-2. Serenata. 2cl 2hn 2bn.
MS parts: D-Bds, Hausbibl.No.341.
FWT-3. XIII Pièces en quatuors, Op. 22, Liv. 1 & 2. 2cl hn bn.
Pc (Adolph Martin Schlesinger: Berlin, pn 66, c.1808), parts: CH-E; GB-Ljag(w). ★
FWT-1m. Fünf Märsche und ein Choral für die Kaiserlich russische Garde.
fl cl(F) 2cl(C) 2hn 2bn 4tp(F, C) b-tb, (2pic cl(F) 2hn b-dr s-dr tri cym ad lib).
Pc (Schlessinger: Berlin, pn 138, 1810/11), parts: I-Fc, F.P. S.475, (uncut). ★
FWT-1a. Himmel: Fanchon, das Leiermädchen. fl ob 2cl 2hn 2bn vlne(ad lib).
Pc (Rudolphe Werckmeister: Berlin, pn 111, c.1804), RISM [H 5326], parts: D-AB; D-GOL.
MS parts: D-Rtt, Himmel 3/II, (Act II, 7 mvts, rescored for: 2fl 2cl 2hn 2bn cbn).
FWT-2a. Righini: Pièces d'Harmonie tirées de Minerve et Dédale, 8 mvts. 2cl 2hn 2bn.
Pc (Werckmeister: Oranienberg, pn 10, c.1801), RISM [R 1570], parts: CZ-Bm(au), A.35.207; S-Skma.

*TAUSINGER, Jan *1 Nov 1921, Piatra Neamt, Romania - 29 July 1980, Prague*
JAT-1. Prelude, sarabande & postlude. 3fl 2ob 2cl 4hn 3bn 3tp 3tb tu perc xyl harp pf.
Pm (Český hudební fond: Prague, 1967), hire score & parts.

*TAVERNER, John Kenneth *28 Jan 1944, London*
JOT-1. Credo. Solo T, SATB chorus, 3ob 3tp 2tb organ.
Pm (Chester Music: London, etc, 1960), hire score & parts.

*TAYLORSON, John Swainton *12 June 1923, County Durham, UK*
JST-1a. Bishop: The Comedy of Errors, "Lo! Here the Gentle Lark".   Solo S/cl & fl, 2ob 2cl 2hn 2bn cbn/db.
Pm (Castle Music: Sherrif Hutton, pn B7/123, 1992), score & parts.
JST-2a. Boyce: Symphony No. 4 in F.   fl 2ob 2cl 2hn 2bn cbn/db.
Pm (Castle Music: Sheriff Hutton, pn B8/102, 1992), score & parts.
JST-3a. Dvořák: Czech Suite, Op. 39, Romance.   2fl ob ca 2cl 2hn 2bn cbn/db.
Pm (Castle Music: Sherriff Hutton, pn D14/108, 1992), score & parts.
JST-4a. Dvořák: Slavonic Dance, Op. 46, No. 4.   fl 2ob 2cl 2hn 2bn cbn/db.
Pm (Castle Music: Sherriff Hutton, pn D10/120, 1992), score & parts
JST-5a. Fučik: Der Alte Brumbär, Op. 210.   Solo bn, fl 2ob 2cl 2hn 2bn cbn/db.
Pm (Castle Music: Sherriff Hutton, pn F2/118, 1992), score & parts.
JST-6a. Fučik: Florentine March, Op. 214.   fl(pic) 2ob 2cl 2hn 2bn cbn/db.
Pm (Castle Music: Sherriff Hutton, pn F1/118, 1992), score & parts.
JST-7a. Joplin: The Easy Winners.   fl 2ob 2cl 2hn 2bn cbn/db.
Pm (Castle Music: Sherriff Hutton, pn S3/115, 1992), score & parts.
JST-8a. Joplin: The Cascades.   fl 2ob 2cl 2hn 2bn cbn/db.
Pm (Castle Music: Sherriff Hutton, pn S4/114, 1992), score & parts.
JST-9a. Kéler Béla: Lustspiel Overture.   fl ob 2cl 2hn 2bn cbn/db.
Pm (Castle Music: Sherriff Hutton, pn K1/106, 1992), score & parts.
JST-10a. Lefébure-Wély: Sortie in B♭.   fl 2ob 2cl 2h 2bn cbn/db.
Pm (Castle Music: Sherriff Hutton, 1993), score & parts.
JST-11a. Mozart: Le Nozze di Figaro, 3 arias.   S, fl 2ob 2cl 2hn 2bn cbn/db.
Pm (Castle Music: Sherriff Hutton, pn M11/24/125, 1992), score & parts.
JST-12a. Mozart: Don Giovanni, "Là ci darem la mano".   fl 2ob 2cl 2hn 2bn cbn/db.
Pm (Castle Music: Sherriff Hutton, pn M14/104, 1992), score & parts.
JST-13a. Mozart: Don Giovanni, canzonetta.   ob ca 2cl 2hn 2bn cbn/db.
Pm (Castle Music: Sherriff Hutton, pn M15/109, 1992), score & parts.
JST-14.1a, 14.2a. Mozart: 2 Marches *(Die Zauberflöte & Idomeneo).* fl 2ob 2cl 2hn 2bn cbn/db.
Pm (Castle Music: Sherriff Hutton, pn M3/104, 1992), score & parts.
JST-15a. Mozart: Das Veilchen, (K.476).   fl 2ob 2cl 2hn 2bn cbn/db.
Pm (Castle Music: Sherriff Hutton, 1993), score & parts.
JST-16a. Mozart: Andante for flute, (K.315).   Solo fl, 2ob 2cl 2hn 2bn cbn/db.
Pm (Castle Music: Sherriff Hutton, 1993), score & parts.
JST-17a. Mozart: Adagio for Glass Harmonica, (K.356).   fl 2ob 2cl 2hn 2bn cbn/db.
Pm (Castle Music: Sherriff Hutton, pn 19/105, 1992), score & parts.
JST-18a. Rossini: Matilde di Shabran (Il Corradino), overture.   fl 2ob 2cl 2hn 2bn cbn/db.
Pm (Castle Music: Sherriff Hutton, pn R5/119, 1992), score & parts.
JST-19a. Rossini: Petite Messe Solennelle, O Salutaris.   S, fl 2ob 2cl 2hn 2bn cbn/db.
Pm (Castle Music: Sherriff Hutton, pn R6/1/124, 1992), score & parts.
JST-20a. Rossini: Petite Messe Solennelle, Domine Deus.   T, fl 2ob 2cl 2hn 2bn cbn/db.
Pm (Castle Music: Sherriff Hutton, 1993), score & parts.
JST-21a. F.P. Schubert: March in D.   fl 2ob 2cl 2hn 2bn cbn/db.
Pm (Castle Music: Sherriff Hutton, pn S10/110, 1992), score & parts.
JST-22a. J. Strauss the Younger: The Gypsy Baron, overture.   fl 2ob 2cl 2hn 2bn cbn/db.
Pm (Castle Music: Sherriff Hutton, pn S6/112, 1992), score & parts.
JST-23a. Josef Strauss: Frauenherz Polka, Op. 166.   fl 2ob 2cl 2hn 2bn cbn/db.
Pm (Castle Music: Sherriff Hutton, pn S7/128, 1992), score & parts.
JST-24a. Suppé: The Beautiful Galatea, overture.   fl 2ob 2cl 2hn 2bn cbn/db.
Pm (Castle Music: Sherriff Hutton, 1993), score & parts.
JST-25a. Vivaldi: [L'Estro armonico] Concerto Op. 3, No. 3.   Solo vl, fl 2ob 2cl 2hn 2bn cbn/db.
Pm (Castle Music: Sherriff Hutton, pn V4/113, 1992), score & parts.

*TCHAIKOVSKY (Chaikovsky), Peter (Pyotr) Il'yich *7 May 1840, Kamsko - 6 Nov 1893, St Petersburg*
PIT-1. Adagio in F, 1863/64.   2fl 2ob 2cl ca b-cl.
AutoMS score: RF-KL.
Pm (Gosudarstvennoe Istadel'stvo: Moscow, 1967), Tom. 58, pp. 26-28, score.
Pm (E.F. Kalmus: New York, etc., pn EK 601, 1974), miniature score.
PIT-1e. Yolante [Iolanthe; Yolande], Op. 69: Prelude.   3fl ob ca 2cl 4hn 2bn.
Pc (Jurgensen: Moscow, 1892), score.
Pm (Gosudarstvennoe Istadel'stvo: Moscow, 1953), Tom. 10, pp. 5-12, score.
PIT-1ad. Les Saisons, Op. 37a, No. 10, (Chant d'Automne).   ob 3cl 2bn.
Pm (Belwin Mills: Melville, NY, pn 9704, sd), parts, Kalmus Chamber Music Series, (original provenance unknown; possibly arranged Skinder).

*TCHEREPNIN (Cherepnin), Iwan (Ivan Alexandrovich) *5 Feb 1943, Paris*
IXT-1. Wheelwinds; 1960.   pic(fl) fl a-fl ob ob(ca) cl(E♭) cl(B♭) b-cl bn.
Pm (Ars Viva, *via* B Schott's Sohne: Mainz, 1971), score (pn AVV 112) and parts (pn AVV 113).

*TCHEREPNIN (Cherepnin), Nikolai Nikolaevich *15 May 1873, St Petersburg - 26 June 1945, Paris*
NNT-1. Sonatine, Op. 61.   pic fl ob ca cl hn 2bn 2tp tb timp xyl.
Pm (M. P. Balaieff/Russian State: Frankfurt, pn 3427, 1939, *reissued* 1967), study score.

*TEBAY, J. *(1770)*
JUT-1m. The Bath Volunteers March.   2cl 2hn 2bn.
Pc (T. & M. W. Cahusac: London, c.1800), RISM [T 378], score: GB-Lbl, h.1568.b.(22).   ★

*TELEMANN, Georg Philipp *14 March 1681, Magdeburg - 25 June 1767, Hamburg*
*GPT-1. Älster-Ouverture; in F, 9 mvts, (Hoffmann F/11).   2ob+2vl 4hn 2bn.
MS: D-DS, Mus.ms.1034/78, (without mvt 4); D-ROu, Mus.Saec. 3(VII=45/2, (19th century, for 2vl 4hn bn). ★
Pm (Musikverlag Hans Sikorski: Hamburg), ed. Winschermann, hire score & parts.
Pm (Ernst Eulenberg: London, etc., 1967), ed. Jürgen Braun, miniature score, (Edition Eulenburg, No. 1338).
Pm (Edition Eulenburg: Zürich, 1967), ed. Jürgen Braun, parts, (Praeclassica, No. 102).
Pm (WINDS: Northridge, CA, pn W-263, c.1981), score & parts.
*GPT-2. Overture; "La Joie"; in F, 6 mvts, (Hoffmann F/5; TWV 55:F5).   2ob/vl 2hn (2)bn.
MS: D-DS, Mus.ms.1034/29. ★
Pm (Möseler Verlag: Wolfenbüttel, sd), parts, (Corona, No. 118, No. 1).
Pm (WINDS: Northridge, CA, pn W-260, c.1981), score & parts.
*GPT-3. Ouverture, "La Chasse"; in F, 5 mvts, (Hoffmann F/9; TWV 55:F9).   2ob 2hn (2)bn; bc ad lib.
MS: D-DS, Mus.ms.1034/61. ★
Pm (Möseler Verlag: Wolfenbüttel, sd), ed. Hoffmann, parts, (Corona, No. 119).
Pm (WINDS: Northridge, CA, W-261, c.1981), score & parts.
*GPT-4. Ouverture; "La Fortuna"; in F, 4 mvts, (Hoffmann F/8; TWV 55:F8).   2ob 2hn (2)bn; bc ad lib.
MS: D-DS, Mus.ms.1034/58. ★
Pm (Möseler Verlag: Wolfenbüttel, sd), ed. Hoffmann, parts, (Corona, No. 118, No. 2).
Pm (WINDS: Northridge, CA, pn W-262, c.1981), score & parts.
*GPT-5. Ouverture [Concerto à 5, in D, 1733]; 6 mvts, (Hoffmann D/24; TWV 55:23).   2obdam 2hn bn.
MS: D-RH, Ms.728. ★
Pm (Leuckart: München, pn 105, 1937), ed. Johann P. Hinnenthal, parts.
Pm (Ernst Eulenberg: Zürich, pn GM987, 1983), score & pts, (2obdam replaced with parts for 2ob or 2cl in A).
*GPT-6. Ouverture [Suite à 5, in F]; 6 mvts, (Hoffmann F/18).   2obdam 2hn bn.
MS: D-RH, Ms.732. ★
Pm (Leuckart: München, pn 113, 1937), parts.
Pm (Joh. Philipp Hinnenthal (privately printed): Bielefeld, 1954), parts.
*GPT-7. Ouverture [Suitte, in F]; 8 mvts, (Hoffmann F/17; TWV 44:13).   2ob 2hn bn.
MS parts: D-ROu, Mus.Saec.XVII=45/17. ★
Pm (Leuckart: München, 1937), *unverified.*
*GPT-8. Ouverture [Suite à 5]; in F, (Hoffmann F/4), 5 mvts.   2vl/ob 2hn bn.
MS parts: D-DS, Mus.ms.1034/27. ★
Pm (Eulenburg: London, 1939), miniature score (Eulenburg Edition No. 889; as "Suite").
*GPT-9. Ouverture à 5; in F, 5 mvts, (Hoffmann F/15; TWV:44/12).   2ob 2hn bn.
MS parts: D-SWl, Mus. 5399/5. ★
Pm (Edition Corona: Berlin; *now* Möseler Verlag: Wolfenbüttel, sd), score & parts.
GPT-10. Concerto à 5; in D, (TWV 44/2). 4 mvts.   2obdam 2hn b+bc.
MS parts: D-MÜu; D-SWl, Mus. 5400/11, (MS by P.J. Fick). ★
*GPT-1m. Marche in F, 10 August 1716.   3ob 2hn bn 2tp.   AutoMS: D-F, Ms.Ff.Mus.1588. ★

*TEMPLETON, Alec Andrew *4 July 1909, Cardiff - 28 Mar 1963, Greenwich, Conn*
AQT-1. Passepied.   fl ob ca cl b-cl bn.
Pm (T. Presser: Bryn Mawr, pn 691, sd), score & parts.

TERMOS, Paul *1952, Netherlands*
PYT-1. Borstbeeld.   2fl 2ob 3cl 2hn 2bn 2tp db.
Pm (Donemus: Amsterdam, 1980), score.

TESTONI, Gianpaolo *1957, Italy*
GZT-1. Canzoni da Suonare, 3 mvts.   2fl(pic) 2ob 2cl(b-cl) 2hn 2bn.
Pm (G. Ricordi & Co.: Milano, pn 133381, 1982), score.

*THÄNN, ( ) *(1770)*
YXT-1. Partia in Dis [E♭]; 4 mvts.   2cl 2hn bn.
MS parts: (by Augustin Erasmus Hübner, Langenbruck, 1799): CZ-Pu(dm), 59 R 3336. ★

THÄRICHEN, Werner *12 March 1921, Kraków*
WXT-1. Divertimento, Op. 58.   2ob 2cl 2hn 2bn.
Pm (Bote & Bock: Berlin, 1979), hire score & parts.

*THAIM, ( ) (?possibly Thänn) *(1770)*
YYT-1. Parthia in Dis [E♭]; 4 mvts.   2cl 2hn bn.
MS parts (by Ignatius Hübner, Langenbruck): CZ-Pu(dm), 59 R 3344. ★

THELIN, Eje *9 June 1938 - 18 May 1990, Stockholm*
EJT-1. Circo della vita; 1986.   2fl 3ob(ca) 3cl 2hn 2bn db.   MS score: S-Sic.

*THENY, Jan (Joanne), Rev. D. Paroch Eccles. *10 March 1749, Jaroměř - 7 June 1828 Frenštat*
JQT-1v. Missa in Dis [E♭] Deutsch.   SAB, 2cl 2hn organ.   MS parts (1802): CZ-Bm(au), A.20.169. ★

THEUSS, Carl Theodor *(1800) - 1875, Weimar*
CTT-1. Serenade, Op. 21.   fl cl 2hn bn.
Pc (Gombart: Augsburg, sd), parts: D-Bds.
CTT-1a. Pourpourri [sic] milit[aire] des Chansons et Danses russes, Op. 41; 11 sections.
fl(E♭) cl(E♭) 2cl(Bb) 2hn 2bn tp 3tb b-dr+cym tri.
Pc (chez Frederic [sic] Hofmeister: Leipzig, pn 1102, 1813), parts: US-BETm, Philharmonic Society of Bethlehem
PSB Add 3. ★
Pm (Hofmeister: Leipzig, 1925), parts.

*THIEL, Ferdinand *(1800)*
FZT-1v. Graduale in A am Sonntage Quadregesima, "Angelus suis".   CATB, 2ob 2hn bn 2tp(clar) timp.
MS parts (c.1835): CZ-Bm(kb), A.36.458. ★

THIM, G.
GYT-1v. Lied Am St [word illegible] herfreitage Wenn nach dem St. Kreuzküssen des Kriesters [word illegible]
dem Altare, das hochwürdigste Gut ans der Sakristey auf den Altar getragen wird, - deutsche zu singen, anstatt
dem vexilla regis prodeunt etc. etc. "Des Königsfahre steigt empor, das Kreuzgeheimnis."
SSAATTBB, 2cl 2hn b-tb.   MS parts: CZ-Bm(lr), A.22.263, (missing A I, T I). ★

THOMAS, Eugen *30 Jan 1863, Surabaya, Java - Aug 1922, Schloss Orth, nr Gmunden*
EYT-1v. Der Spielmann, Op. 46; (words: M. Graf Stachwitz).   SATB soli & chorus, 2cl 3hn 2bn harp.
MS score: A-Wn, *unverified.*
Pc (Vocal piano score only:) (Deutsche Verlags AG: Leipzig, c.1905), "Ausgabe des "Wiener à capella Chor.
No. 11.": GB-Lbl, F.1267.cc.(9).

THOMMESSEN, Olav Anton *16 May 1946, Oslo*
OAT-1. The Phantom of Light; 1990.   2fl 2ob 2cl 2hn 2bn vc.   MS score: N-Oic.
OAT-1v. Gjensidig (Mutually).   2S, 2fl/pic 2cl perc.
Pm (Wilhelm Hansen: Copenhagen, 1973), hire score & parts.

*THOMPSON, Thomas *1777, Sunderland - post-1800*
TXT-1m. March . . . for the Use of the Sunderland Loyal Volunteer Corps.   2cl 2hn (2)bn tp.
Pc (Goulding, Phipps & D'Almaine: London, wm 1799), RISM [T 719], score: GB-Lbl, G.809.xx.(11);
GB-Lhumphries (modern MS copy). ★

*THOMSON, Virgil (Garnett) *25 Nov 1896, Kansas City - 30 Sept 1989, New York*
VGT-1. Barcarolle, 1940.   fl ob ca cl b-cl bn.
Pm (Mercury: New York, 1948), score.

*THOMU, M., *Signore* *(1760)*
MXT-1. Nro. 1 Türkische Stücke in F.   2fl cl(F) 2cl(C) 2hn 2bn cbn 2tp(clar) b-dr.
MS parts: A-KR, H 38/44. ★

*THURET, ( ) *(1740)*
XXT-1. Parthia ex B[♭]; 5 mvts.   2cl 2hn 2bn.   MS parts: CZ-NR, A.18.237/B.252. ★

TIRCUIT, Heuwell Andrew *18 Oct 1931, Plaque Mine, LA*
HXT-1. Concerto for Violin.   Solo violin, 2fl 2ob cl b-cl 2hn 2bn.
Pm (Associated Music Publishers: New York, s.d.), hire score & parts.

TIROBOSCHI, ( )
XYT-1v. Tantum ergo.   2cl(C) 2hn tp timp organ(con Strumenti).   MS parts: I-Vsmc, (missing voice parts). ★

*TISCHENKO, Boris (Ivanovich) *23 March 1939, Stalingrad (now Volgagrad)*
*BIT-1. Concerto for Cello No. 1, 1963.   Solo cello, 3ob 3cl 2hn 3bn 3tp 2tb tu 2timp org.
Pm (VAAP (Soviet Music): Moscow).

TISCHHAUSER, Franz *1921, Switzerland*
FRT-1. Beschallung der Stadt Kalau; 1989.   pic fl 2cl 2hn 2bn.   MS score: CH-Nf.

TISMÉ, Antoine *1932, France*
AOT-1. Arkham; [?the New England town which figures in H.P. Lovecraft's supernatural pulp fiction].
fl(pic) ob(ca) cl cl(b-cl) hn bn(cbn) tp tb 3perc piano vl vc.
Pm (Editions Française de Musique, now Billaudot: Paris, 1974), score & parts.

*TOCH, Ernst *7 Dec 1887, Vienna - 10 Oct 1964, Santa Monica, California*
EQT-1. Miniatur-Ouvertüre.   2fl ob cl b-cl bn 2tp tb perc.
Pm (Ars Viva *via* B. Schott's Söhne: Mainz, 1951), hire score & parts.
EQT-2. 5 Pieces: No. 4, Roundelay & No. 5, Cavalcade.   fl ob cl 2hn bn.
Pm (Mills Music: New York, 1963), score & parts.

*TOESCHI, Carlo Giuseppe *11 Nov 1731, Ludwigsburg - 12 April 1788, Munich*
CAT-1. La Chasse Royale.   2cl 2hn 2bn.   MS parts: F-Pa.

*TOJA, Giuseppe *(1800)*
*GXT-1. Serenata; in E♭, 4 mvts.   fl ob 2cl 2hn bn.
Pc (Presso Luigi Bertuzzi: Milano, pn 800, sd), parts: I-Mc, Da Camera A.137.1; GB-Ljag, (photocopy). ★
Pm (Ricordi: Milano, etc., pn 86045, sd), score & parts.

*TOMÁŠEK, Václav Jan Křtitel (Wenzel Johann Baptist) *17 April 1774, Skuteč - 3 April, 1850, Prague*
VJT-1m. Doppel-Marsch.   Instrumentation unknown.
MS: D-Bds, Mus.Ms.21945/20.
VJT-1t. Marcia funebre.   2ob 2cl 2hn 2bn cbn tp(clar).
AutoMS score: CZ-Pnm, III.E.107. ★
Pm (Compusic: Am Huizen, sd), score & parts.
VJT-1v. Korunovační mše [Coronation Mass], Op. 81.   CATB, fl ob 2cl(C) 2hn 2tp t-tb b-tb.
MS parts: CZ-Pnm, XLIII.E.5, (missing cl II; the instrumental introductions to the Benedictus & Agnus Dei are
missing in all parts). ★
VJT-2v. Karl is wieder da!   Voice (C/T), 2cl(A) 2hn 2bn.   AutoMS score: CZ-Pnm, III.E.112. ★

TOMASI, Henri *17 Aug 1901, Marseilles - 13 June 1971, Paris*
*HYT-1. La Moresco, Suite de Danses, 7 mvts.   2ob 2cl 2hn bn clavecin(piano à defaut) perc(3timballes 3tom-tom[grave, moyen, aigu] tam-tam gong, caisse claire).
Pm(Henry Lemoine: Paris, Brussels, 1965), miniature score.
HYT-2. Printemps; 1963.   fl fl(pic) ob cl sax hn bn.
Pm (Leduc: Paris, pn 23456, 1964), score & parts.

*TOMLINSON, Ernest *19 Sept 1924, Rawtenstall, Lancashire*
*EZT-1. Concertino.   pic fl ob ca 2cl 2hn 2bn.
Pm (Chandos: London, 1957), hire score & parts.   (MS score in GB-Lmic).

TOMMASINI, Domenico *(1820)*
DXT-1v. Ave Regina Celarum, 1851.   T solo, 2cl(C) 2hn bc (vlne/bn organ[bc-fig]).
MS score & parts: I-Vsmc, (the vlne/bn & organ(bc-fig) do not appear in the score).   ★
DXT-2vf. Tota pulcra. Fragment: ob I & II only.   MS parts: I-Vsmc.   ★

TÔN-THÂT, Tiêt *18 Oct 1933, Hue, Vietnam (resident in France)*
TTT-1. Vision.   Solo cello, 2fl 2ob 2cl hn 2bn tp tb piano 2perc.
Pm (Billaudot: Paris, 1966), score, (parts for hire).

TORRENGA, Benno *1942, Netherlands*
BYT-1. Serenade.   2fl 2ob 2cl 3hn 2bn vla 2vc db.
Pm (Donemus: Amsterdam, 1977), score.

TOST, František *1754/55 - 27 April 1829, Bratislava*
FXT-1(-6). Sei Parthia; E♭, 4 mvts; E♭, 4 mvts; E♭, 4 mvts; B♭, 4 mvts; B♭, 3 mvts; B♭, 3 mvts. 2cl 2hn 2bn.
MS parts (by Joseph Pražak): CZ-Pnm, XLI.B.174, (hn II missing the end of the last mvt of Parthia 6 after bar 58). *Following the 6 Parthien are a set of of 2 Arias & 2 Menuetti with Trios. We do not believe that these are by Tost and describe them under Anonymous Works.*   ★

TOTZAUER, Hans
HXT-1. Wallerstein: Bühnenmusik, (text: Schiller).   pic fl ob 2cl 2hn bn 6tp tb b-tu timp b-ft 6s-dr cym harp.
MS score & parts: A-Wn, BA 200.
HXT-2. Kriemhilds Rache: Bühnenmusik, (text: Max Mell).   fl ob 2hn 3tp 2tb tu timp b-dr s-dr tamb tri harp.
MS score & parts: A-Wn, BA 246.
HXT-3. Demetrius: Bühnenmusik, (text: Schiller).   fl ob 2hn 3tp tb tu timp glock harmonium.
AutoMS score & parts: A-Wn, BA 274.
HXT-4. Der Zweiköpfige Adler: Bühnenmusik, (text: Fritz Habreck, after Jean Cocteau).
fl ob cl 2hn 2tp tb b-dr.   AutoMS score & parts: A-Wn, BA 237.
HXT-5. Trio zu einem Marsch (Anon: Marsch für einer Geburtstag).   2cl 2hn 2tp 2tb perc.
MS score: A-Wn, BA 636.
HXT-6. Caesars Witwe: Bühnenmusik, (text Franz Theodor Gebor).   pic 2cl hn 2tp s-dr.
AutoMS score & parts: A-Wn, BA 298.

*TOUCHEMOULIN, Joseph *1727, Chalons sur Saône - 25 Oct 1801, Regensburg*
JXT-1. Divertimento per la Tavola; in E♭, 7 mvts.   2cl 4hn(Eb, B♭) 2bn 2tp 2vla vlne timp.
(?Auto)MS parts (c.1790): D-Rtt, Touchmoulin 13b.   ★
MS parts: D-Rtt, Touchmoulin 13a, (without timp).

TOWNSEND, Douglas *1921, USA*
DYT-1. Chamber Symphony.   fl ob cl 2hn bn tp tb tu.
Pm (Henmar Press, *via* C.F. Peters: New York, c.1987) score & parts, (copy in US-NYamc).

*TRAUTZL (FRANTZL), Jan Jakub Jacopo (pseud. Saputo) *22 Feb 1749, Židovice - 27 June 1834, Osek*
JYT-1. Parthia in b [B♭]; 3 mvts.   2cl 2hn 2bn.   AutoMS score: CZ-Pnm, XXXII.C.86(b).   ★
JYT-2. Allegro in E[♭] la fa.   2cl 2hn 2bn.   AutoMS score: CZ-Pnm, XXXII.C.86(c).   ★
JYT-3. Parthia in F; 5 mvts.   3bn vlne.
AutoMS pts: CZ-Pnm, XXXII.C.85, (with a slight defect in mvt 4 Menuetto & Trio of the violone part - which is also without the final Rondeau. The work is written out on earlier, spoiled MS sheets in several sizes).   ★
JYT-1a(f). [Fragment, possibly an arrangement of "Bei Männern" from Mozart's *Die Zauberflöte*, 37 bars, in G, 3/8, only partially laid out; the work has been crossed out in comtemporary crayon].   fl 2cl bn.
(Auto)MS score: CZ-Pnm, XXXIV.A.12, reverse of the first oblong sheet of JPF-3v.   ★
JYT-1v. Todtenklage (Cantata).   CATB, 2cl 2hn bn.
MS parts: CZ-Pnm, XXXII.D.176.   ★
JYT-2v. Cantata Funebris in Es [E♭] . . . [pro] defuncto Antonio Fleischer, auriga R.R.d.d. Mauritii, infurtunio costineto [sic] d'anno 1805 Sgtneto 30 Aprilis.   CATB, 2cl 2hn bn.   AutoMS score: CZ-Pnm, XXXIV.A.12.   ★
AutoMS parts: CZ-Pnm, XXXIV.A.11, (as "No. 17mo Cantata Funebris p[ro] defeto Antonio Fleischer[,] aurig[o] R:R:D:D: Ab[botis] Mauritio 1805").
FYT-3v. Cantate funebre due. P= V= P= [?]Gottroadí Trabac mercatore et defeto Prenobili O= Leuthenontio Feldkircher [added: d'anno 1806].   "Hier Mensch, hier [?]lerne, was du bist." CATB, 2cl(C) 2hn bn.
(?Auto)MS score: CZ-Pnm, XXXIV.A.13, (with a reduction for voice & piano - on the back of which (f.1b-2) is a very incomplete score for SATB, organ).   ★
JYT-4v. Cantata Funebris in E[♭].   CATB, 2cl 2hn bn.
(?Auto)MS score (1797): CZ-Pnm, XXXII.D.177. *An extensive work.*   ★

TREMAIN, Ronald *1923, New Zealand*
RXT-1. Mosiac; 1975.   pic 2fl 2ob 2cl 2bn.   MS score: NZ-Wmc.

*TRIEBENSEE (Trübensee), Josef *21 Nov 1772, Wittingau (now Třeboň) - 22 April 1846, Prague*
MISC: Miscellannées [sic] de Musique. 2ob 2cl 2hn 2bn, with cbn tp ad lib. **Note:** *A certain amount of confusion appears to have arisen during the distribution of Oeuvres 9 - 12 of Jahrgang I; we use the Austrian Imperial Harmonie (k.k. Hofharmonie) set (in A-Wn) as our reference, with information on the missing Oeuvres 4 - 6 of Jahrgang I taken from the set in the Florence Conservatorio (I-Fc). The ad lib tp (principale) & cbn parts are not as straightforward as they appear; in the lists below tacet tp parts & cbn parts which are identical to bn II are indicated by the use of an asterisk immediately following, e.g. cbn* tp* ad lib.*
  Pc (in MS:) (The Author: Feldsburg [?& Vienna - Stegmayr, as agent, advertized Jg. I, Oe. 1 & 2 in the Wiener Zeitung*), 1808 - 1814), parts, comprising 32 (or more) "Oeuvres" in three groups, styled "Jahrgangs". Sets of two Oeuvres were issued 3 times each year (See* The Wind Ensemble Sourcebook, *Chapter 1. Appendix 1 for details). Contrary to comments by earlier researchers, Triebensee only used the descriptive term "Lieferung" in his earlier* Harmonien Sammlung *of 1803/04 and in invoices for the Miscellanées.*
  MS parts: **A-Ee,** *Mus.1099, (Jg. I, Oe. 1), Mus.1098, (Jg. I, Oe. 2), Mus.1097, (Jg. I, Oe. 3), Mus.1096, (Jg. I, Oe. 4), Mus.1095, (Jg. I Oe. 5), Mus.1094, (Jg. I, Oe. 6), Mus.1093, (Jg. I, Oe. 7), Mus.1092, (Jg. I, Oe. 8), Mus.1172, (Jg. I, Oe. 9, as "Oeuvre 11"), Mus.1166 (Jg. I, Oe. 10 - Triebensee's arrangement of Nicolini's* Numa Pompilio *replaces the normal issue), Mus.1165, (Jg. I, Oe. 11, as "Oeuvre 9"), Mus.1173, (Jg. I, Oe. 12);* **A-Wgm,** *VIII 40733 (Jg. II, Oe. 5), VIII 47729 (Jg. II, Oe. 6);* **A-Wn,** *Mus.Hs.3739, (missing Jg. I, Oe. 4 - 6; otherwise complete);* **CZ-Bm(au),** *A.36.877, No. 1, (Jg. I, Oe. 2, No. 6, local copy without tp), A.36.878, (Jg. I, Oe. 4, Nos. 1, 5, 6, 8, 9, local copy), A.35.255, (Jg. I, Oe. 4, No. 7, local copy [20 Dec 1817] without tp), A.35.254, Nos. 1-4, (Jg. II, Oe. 1, Nos. 1, 7, 5, 3);* **CZ-KRa,** *A3978/IV.B.144 (Jg. I, Oe. 1, local copy missing 2ob cbn), A3930/IV.B.93, (Jg. I, Oe. 8, local copy with an additional tp II part by Havel for Nos. 6 & 10), A3877/IV.B.40, (Jg. I, Oe. 9, complete, local copy);* **CZ-Pnm,** *XX.F.19, (Jg. I, Oe. 1, Nos. 1, 2, 4 - 6, 9, 10, missing cbn & tp);* **CZ-Pnm,** *Lobkovic X.H.a.33 (Jg. I, Oe. 1), X.H.a.35 (Jg. I, Oe. 2), X.H.a.37 (Jg. I, Oe. 3), X.H.a.39 (Jg. I, Oe. 4), X.H.a.41 (Jg. I, Oe. 5), [missing Jg. I, Oe. 6], X.H.a.44 (Jg. I, Oe. 7), X.H.a.46 (Jg. I, Oe. 8), X.H.a.49 (Jg. I, Oe. 9, as "Oeuvre 12 "), X.H.a.50 (Jg. I, Oe. 10, missing hn I, as "Oeuvre 11"), X.H.a.51 (Jg. I, Oe. 11, missing tp, as "Oeuvre 9"), X.H.a.52 (Jg. I, Oe. 12, as "Oeuvre 10"), X.H.a.34 (Jg. II, Oe. 1), X.H.a.36 (Jg. II, Oe. 2), X.H.a.38 (Jg. I, Oe. 3), X.H.a.40 (Jg. II, Oe. 4), X.H.a.42 (Jg. II, Oe. 5), X.H.a.43 (Jg. II, Oe. 6), X.H.a.45 (Jg. II, Oe. 7), X.h.a.47 (Jg. II, Oe. 8), X.G.f.66 (Jg. II, Oe. 9), X.G.f.67 (Jg. II, Oe. 10);* **D-Mbs,** *Mus.Mss.2581 - 2584 (Jg. I, Oe. 5 - 8 only);* **D-NEhz,** *227, (Jg. I, Oe. 8; for 2ob 2cl 2hn 2bn cbn, with the extraordinary note, "Paris den 28 August 1810");* **I-Fc,** *F.P. S.448 (Jg. I, Oe. 1 -4), F.P. S.449 (Jg. I, Oe. 5 - 8), F.P. S.450 (Jg. I, Oe. 9 - 12; Oe. 10 & 11 possibly missing the ad lib trumpet part), F.P. S.451 (Jg. II, Oe. 1 - 4), F.P. S.452 (Jg. II, Oe. 5 - 8), F.P. S.453 (Jg. II, Oe. 9 - 12), F.P. S.453, (Jg. III, Oe. 1 - 4; the ad lib trumpet part of Oe. 1 may be inserted with Oe. 2), F.P. S.454 (Jg. III, Oe. 5 - 8).*
  The **CZ-Pnm** *Lobkovic collection also contains a compilation by F. Krechler (qv), "Miscellannées de Musique", X.H.a.53, drawn from the first five Oeuvres of Jahrgang I. The 28 movements are (Oeuvre / Number): 2/1, 2/2, 2/3, 2/5, 2/6, 2/7, 5/1, 5/2, 1/3, 1/4, 1/6, 1/7, 1/9, 2/9, 4/1, 4/3, 4/4, 4/6, 4/9, 4/10, 3/1, 3/5, 3/6, 3/7, 3/8, 3/9, 3/10. The first 7 mvts of CZ-Pnm, Lobkovic X.H.a.54 ("Miscellanees") are a compilation by Krechler of Jg II, Oe. 5, No. 4 & Jg. II, Oe. 6, Nos. 3, 7 - 11; the last 6 mvts are JZT-64a.*
  Hellyer & Whitwell attribute three anonymous collections in **A-Wn** *(Mus.Hs.3791 - 3793) to Triebensee. Mus.Hs.3791 is, in fact, drawn from arrangements by Sedlak (WXS-3a). Only the arrangements of Mozart in Mus.Hs.3792 can be attributed to Triebensee; the sets of variations added later to the volume may be by Triebensee and we list them below as JZT-1c - JZT-8c on p. 284. Mus.Hs.3793, entitled* Auszug Aus verschiedenen Ballets und Opern *and scored for 2ob 2cl 2hn 2bn cbn, is principally drawn from the Miscellanées: Nos. 2 - 9 from Jg. II, Oe. 7 (Nos. 2, 3, 6 - 8, 10 - 12; Nos. 10 - 14 from Jg. II, Oe. 8 (Nos. 1 - 4, 7), No. 15 from Jg. I, Oe. 7, No. 10; Nos. 18 - 22 from Jg. III, Oe. 6 (Nos. 1, 5, 6, 9 & 10). Only Nos. 1 (from Paer's* Il Morto vivo), *and Nos. 16 & 17 (from Gyrowetz's* Der Augenarzt) *are not found in Triebensee's collections. No. 1 has not been traced; however, Nos. 16 & 17 are drawn from Starke's arrangement (Mechetti: Vienna, pn 78, 1810), omitting the 2 ad lib trumpets.* **A-Wn** *Mus.Hs.3794 also poses problems: although the title bears the usual Triebensee misspelling (an additional "n" in "Miscellanées") this collection appears to have been produced by the Hoftheater-Musik-Verlag. Nos. 2 & 3 are drawn from P. Mašek's arrangement and Nos. 4 - 8 were arranged by Went. Nos. 1 & 9 date from after Went's death (as does the additional movement added after No. 9). However, there is no evidence to directly attribute these arrangements to Triebensee. It is possible that Krechler also compiled these collections through an involvement with the Hoftheater-Musik-Verlag (of which Prince Lobkowitz, his employer, was part-owner of the concession). Full listings for these collections can be found in the ARRANGEMENTS section under ANONYMOUS COLLECTIONS (A-6a - A-8a).*

*JZT-1. Partita; in E♭, 5 mvts.   2ob 2cl 2hn bn + (Echo) ob cl 2hn bn.
MS parts: A-Wgm, VIII 38669. ★
Pm (WINDS: Northridge, CA, pn W-28, c.1981), photocopy of original MS parts.
*JZT-2. Echostücke, 3 mvts.   ob cl hn bn + (offstage) ob cl hn bn; (cbn tp tacet).
Pc (MISC: Jg. II, Oe. 8, Nos. 8 - 10), MS parts. ★
Pm (WINDS: Northridge, CA, pn W-60, c.1981), photocopy of original parts.
JZT-3. Parthie in B♭, 4 mvts.   2ob 2cl 2hn 2bn cbn tp.
Pc (MISC: Jg. II, Oe. 4, Nos. 7 - 10), MS parts. ★
Pm (WINDS: Northridge, CA, pn W-83, c.1981), parts.
Pm (Compusic: Amsterdam, pn 228, 1988), score & parts.
JZT-4. Partitta, in B♭, 4 mvts.   2ob 2cl 2hn 2bn cbn.
Pc (in MS parts:) [The Author: Feldsberg, 1803], Harmonien Sammlung, Erster Jahrgang, Erster Lieferung:
A-Ee, Mus.1113; CZ-K, symfonie No.145.K.II; D-NEhz 228a. ★
*JZT-5. Partitta in E♭, 4 mvts.   2ob 2cl 2hn 2bn cbn.
Pc (in MS parts:) [The Author: Feldsberg, 1803], Harmonien Sammlung, Erster Jahrgang, Zweÿte Lieferung:
A-Ee, Mus.1114; A-Wgm, VIII 39986; CZ-Bm(au), A.35.240, (missing 2ob); CZ-K, symfonie No.146.K.II;
CZ-Pnm, (2 copies), Lobkovic X.H.a.32/1, 32/2; D-NEhz, 228c. ★
Pm (WINDS: Northridge, CA, pn W-85, c.1981), parts.
Pm (as an unidentified E♭ Parthia:) (Compusic: Amsterdam, pn 228, 1991), score & parts.

*JZT-6.1. Partitta in E♭, 4 mvts. 2ob 2cl 2hn 2bn cbn.
MS parts: A-Ee, Mus.1115, (the title does not mention a cbn part); CZ-Pnm, Lobkovic X.H.a.31, (as "Partita No.
2 in E♭"); D-NEhz, 228b, (mvts 2 & 3 reversed); I-Fc, (unverified); RF-SPc, (unverified). ★
JZT-6.2. Parthia in E♭; 4 mvts. 2cl 2hn 2bn. MS parts: PL-LA, RM 67, (?rescored by J.A. Buchal).
JZT-7. Concertino; in E♭, 5 mvts, (c.1798). Piano, 2ob 2cl 2hn 2bn.
MS parts: A-Wn, Mus.Hs.11077. ★
Pm (Northridge, CA, pn W-3, c.1981), modern MS score & photocopy of original MS parts.
Pm (Compusic: Amsterdam, pn 255, 1988), score & parts.
*JZT-8. Nro. 3 Parthia in B[♭]; 4 mvts. 2ob 2cl 2hn 2bn.
MS parts (by Johann Elssler, copyist at Esterháza): A-Wgm, VIII 39987. ★
Pm (WINDS: Northridge, CA, pn W-100, c.1981), photocopy of original MS parts.
*JZT-9. Partitta; in E♭, 4 mvts. 2ob 2cl 2hn 2bn (cbn). *A cbn is indicated in mvt 2 only in the bn II part but
is not mentioned on the title page.*
Pc (Traeg: Vienna, pre-1804), No. 223, MS parts: CZ-Bm(no), A.16.671; GB-BOlowe, (modern MS copy). ★
JZT-10. Partitta; in B♭, 4 mvts. 2ob 2cl 2hn 2bn.
Pc (Traeg: Vienna, pre-1804), No. 223, MS parts: CZ-Bm(no), A.16.672. ★
*JZT-11. Allegretto in B♭. 2ob 2cl 2hn 2bn, (cbn tp ad lib).
Pc (MISC: Jg. I, Oe. 12, No. 6), MS parts. ★
JZT-12. Andante Cantabile in F. 2ob 2cl 2hn 2bn, (cbn tp ad lib).
Pc (MISC: Jg. I, Oe. 12, No. 6), MS parts. ★
*JZT-13. Allegretto in E♭. 2ob 2cl 2hn 2bn, (cbn tp ad lib).
Pc (MISC: Jg. I, Oe. 12, No. 8), MS parts (A-Wn copy missing page 2 of Bn I). ★
JZT-14. Neuer Ländler in A♭. 2ob 2cl 2hn 2bn, (cbn tp ad lib).
Pc (MISC: Jg. I, Oe. 4, No. 7), MS parts. ★
JZT-15. Ländler in B♭. 2ob 2cl 2hn 2bn, (cbn tp ad lib).
Pc (MISC: Jg. I, Oe. 12, No. 4), MS parts. ★
JZT-16. Ländler. 2ob 2cl 2hn 2bn, (cbn tp ad lib).
Pc (MISC: Jg. III, Oe. 4, No. 10), MS parts. ★
JZT-17. Menuet & 2 Trios, E♭. 2ob 2cl 2hn 2bn, (cbn tp ad lib).
Pc (MISC: Jg. I, Oe. 12, No. 3), MS parts. ★
*JZT-18(-33). 16 pieces. 2ob 2cl 2hn 2bn, (cbn tp ad lib; tp in No. 14 only).
Pc (MISC: Jg. I, Oe. 9, Nos. 1 - 16), MS parts. *A 17th piece - a March with Trio - appears in the A-Wn copy
only; the composer was originally identified as Triebensee in the ob I part but this has been scraped off with
"Steibelt" overwritten in another hand (possibly that of the leader of the Imperial Harmonie).* ★
   18. Allo, in B♭, ¢, No. 1.   19. Menuetto & Trio, in B♭, 3/4, No. 2.   20. Presto, in B♭, 2/4, No. 3.
   21. And[an]tino, in E♭, 2/4, No. 4.   22. Allemande, in. B♭, 3/8, No. 5.
   23. Menuetto Cantabile & Trio, in E♭, 3/4, No. 6.   24. Presto, in B♭, 2/4, No. 7.
   25. Larghetto, in E♭, No. 8.   26. Allo assai, in B♭, 2/4, No. 9.
   27. Menuetto & Trio, in B♭, 3/4, No. 10.   28. Presto, in B♭, 2/4, No. 11.
   29. Andante, in E♭, ¢, No. 12.   30. Allemande & Trio & Coda, in B♭, 3/4, No. 13.
   31. Marcia Allo, in C, ¢, No. 14.   32. Allo, in B♭, 2/4, No. 15.   33. Menuetto & Trio, in E♭, 3/4, No. 16.
JZT-34. Ein neu componirtes Stük [sic], Andantino, in. 2ob 2cl 2hn 2bn, (cbn tp ad lib).
Pc (MISC: Jg. I, Oe. 6, Nos. 1 - 16), MS parts. ★
JZT-35. Ein neues Stük [sic], Allegro moderato, in. 2ob 2cl 2hn 2bn, (cbn tp ad lib).
Pc (MISC: Jg. I, Oe. 6, No. 6), MS parts. ★
JZT-36. Variations on a theme from T. Weigl's opera, *Ostrade.* 2ob 2cl 2hn 2bn (cbn, tp ad lib).
Pc (MISC: Jg. I, Oe. 4, No. 8), MS parts. ★
JZT-37. Andantino con variatione; 6/8. 2ob 2cl 2hn 2bn, (cbn tp ad lib).
Pc (MISC: Jg. I, Oe. 10, No. 9), MS parts. *This does not appear in CZ-Pnm Lobkovic X.H.a.50.* ★
*JZT-38. Variaz[ione].; on an original theme (Andantino, 2/4). 2ob 2cl 2hn 2bn (cbn tp ad lib).
Pc (MISC: Jg. I, Oe. 12, No. 2), MS parts. ★
Pm (WINDS: Northridge, CA, pn W-62, c.1981), photocopy of original parts.
*JZT-39. Variations on a theme by Gyrowetz *(Der Argonarzt:* "Mir leuchtet"). 2ob 2cl 2hn 2bn (cbn tp ad lib).
Pc (MISC: Jg. III, Oe. 4, No. 9), MS parts. ★
Pm (WINDS: Northridge, CA, pn W-64, c.1981), photocopy of original parts.
JXT-40. Variation on an (Andante) from Seyfried's opera (after Méhul), Euphrosine.
2ob 2cl 2hn 2bn (cbn tp ad lib). Pc (MISC: Jg. I, Oe. 6, No. 5), MS parts. ★
*JZT-41. Grand Quintuor; in G, 4 mvts. Piano, cl ca bthn bn.
Pc (Au Magasin de l'imprimerie chimique: Vienne, pn 666, c.1808), parts: A-Wgm, VIII 8541 (Q 18017). ★
A-Wgm, XI 10966 (Q 18019) is the same work scored for Piano, vl 2vla vc (pn 665).
JZT-42. No. I° Trio in F; 4 mvts. 2ob ca.
MS parts: CZ-K, No.34.K.23, No. 1, (the ob II pt also includes a part for "Grand Oboè" transposed to G). ★
Pm (Edition Kneuslin: Basle, 1979), ed. Antonín Myslík, parts, (Fur Kenner und Liebhaber No. 74).
JZT-43. Nro. IIdo. Trio in B[♭]; 4 mvts. 2ob ca.
MS parts: CZ-K, No.34.K.23, No. 2. ★
JZT-44. Nro. IIItio. Trio in C; 4 mvts. 2ob ca.
MS parts: CZ-K, No.34.K.23, No. 3. ★
JZT-45.1. Variazione in G. Thema di Haÿdn [sic]; [Hob. I/94ii, "Surprise Symphony", mvt 2]. 2ob ca.
MS parts: CZ-K, No.35.K.23. ★
Pm (Edition Robert Martin: Charney-Lès-Mâcon, pn R 2716 M, 1996), ed. Eric Baude-Delhommais, score & pts.
JZT-45.2. (N° 6) VI Variationi in C (Thema di Haydn). 2fl ca.
MS parts: A-Wgm, VIII 1288, No. 1.

For a further discussion of the following 8 works, see: The Wind Ensemble Sourcebook, *TRIEBENSEE.*
*JZT-1c (= A-6.38a). [5] Variazionen [sic]; on Mozart: Don Giovanni, minuet.   2ob 2cl 2hn 2bn.
MS parts: A-Wn, Mus.Hs.3792, No. 38.   ★
Pm (WINDS: Northridge, CA, pn W-32, c.1981), photocopy of original parts.
Pm (Nova Music: London, 1979), ed. James Brown, score & parts.
Pm (untraced), ed. William Martin, score & parts.
JZT-2c (= A-6.39a). Allegro con [5] Variaion [& Coda]; on Mozart: Don Giovanni, "Fin ch'han dal vino" (as
"Triebst der Champagner").   2ob 2cl 2hn 2bn.
MS parts: A-Wn, Mus.Hs.3792, No. 39.   ★
Pm (WINDS: Northridge, CA, pn W-69, c.1981), photocopy of original parts.
JZT-3c (= A-6.40a). [4] Variationen [& Coda] über einer [?original] Marsch.   2ob 2cl 2hn 2bn.
MS parts: A-Wn, Mus.Hs.3792, No. 40.   ★
Pm (WINDS: Northridge, CA, pn W-31, c.1981), photocopy of original parts.
*JZT-4c (= A-6.41a). [4] Variatione [& Coda] über das [?original] Zapfenstreich.   2ob 2cl 2hn 2bn.
MS parts: A-Wn, Mus.Hs.3792, No. 41.   ★
Pm (WINDS: Northridge, CA, pn W-71, c,1981), photocopy of original parts.
*JZT-5c (= A-6.43a). [6] Variátionen über das Volkslied [by Haydn]: Gott erhalte der [sic] Kaiser.
2ob 2cl 2hn 2bn cbn.
MS parts: A-Wn, Mus.Hs.3792, No. 43; CZ-Pnm, (A-120), Lobkovic X.G.f.75, (Anon).   ★
Pm (WINDS: Northridge, CA, pn W-29, c.1981), photocopy of original parts.
JZT-6c (=A-6.44a). [12] Variazione [über das Thema: O] du lieber Augustin.   2ob 2cl 2hn 2bn.
MS parts: A-Wn, Mus.Hs.3792, No. 44.   ★
Pm (WINDS: Northridge, CA, pn W-73, c.1981), photocopy of original parts.
*JZT-7c (= A-6.46a). Andante mit Variationen [Haydn: Symphony in E♭, Hob. I/103ii].   2ob 2cl 2hn 2bn cbn.
MS parts: A-Wn, Mus.Hs. 3792, No. 46. *This appears to be an arrangement rather than original variations.*   ★
Pm (WINDS: Northridge, CA, pn W-66, c.1981), photocopy of original parts.
JZT-8c (= A-6.45a). Menuetto mit 2 Trios.   2ob 2cl 2hn 2bn.   MS parts: A-Wn, Mus.Hs.3792, No. 45. *An
arrangement of the 3rd mvt of Haydn's Symphony in F, Hob. I/89iii.*   ★
***Marches.** Here WIN stand for: 6 Marches from the* Miscallannées de Musique.
Pm (WINDS: Northridge, CA, pn W-79, c.1981), photocopy of modern parts.
JZT-1m. Marsch von Triebensee, Volkshymn v[on]. Haydn' [Gott erhalte der Kaiser].
2ob 2cl 2hn 2bn (cbn tp ad lib).
Pc (MISC: Jg. II, Oe. 6, No. 11), MS parts.   ★
Pm (WIN: No. 1), photocopy of modern MS parts.
JZT-2m. Marsch.   2ob 2cl 2hn 2bn, (cbn tp ad lib).
Pc (MISC: Jg. II, Oe. 12, No. 11), MS parts.   ★
Pm (WIN: No. 2), photocopy of modern MS parts.
JZT-3m. Marsch; in E♭.   2ob 2cl 2hn 2bn, (cbn tp ad lib).
Pc (MISC: Jg. I, Oe. 11, No. 11), MS parts.   ★
Pm (WIN: No. 3), photocopy of modern MS parts.
JZT-4m. Marsch.   2ob 2cl 2hn 2bn, (cbn tp ad lib).
Pc (MISC: Jg III, Oe. 4, No. 8), MS parts.   ★
Pm (WIN: No. 4), photocopy of modern MS parts.
JZT-5m. Marche Douplée.   2ob 2cl 2hn 2bn, (cbn* tp ad lib).
Pc (MISC: Jg. I, Oe. 3, No. 5), MS parts.   ★
Pm (WIN: No. 5), photocopy of modern MS parts.
JZT-6m. Neuer Marsch, in E♭.   2ob 2cl 2hn 2bn, (cbn* tp ad lib).
Pc (MISC: Jg. I, Oe 3, No. 9), MS parts.   ★
Pm (WIN: No. 6), photocopy of modern MS parts.
JZT-7m. Neuer Marsch; in F.   2ob 2cl 2hn 2bn, (cbn tp ad lib).
Pc (MISC: Jg. I, Oe. 4, No. 3), MS parts.   ★
JZT-8m. Neuer Marsch, in C.   2ob 2cl 2hn 2bn, (cbn tp ad lib).
Pc (MISC: Jg. I, Oe. 4, No. 10), MS parts.   ★
JZT-9m. Original trio to a march from Gluck's *Armide.*   2ob 2cl 2hn 2bn, (cbn tp* ad lib). *(JZT-17a is an
arrangement of the march)*   Pc (MISC: Jg. I, Oe. 7, No. 5), MS parts.
*JZT-1.1tm. Trauer Marsch; (for the Funeral of Prince Alois Liechtenstein, 1805).
2ob 2cl 2hn 2bn (cbn tp ad lib).   Pc (MISC: Jg. I, Oe. 12, No. 5), MS parts.   ★
Pm (WINDS: Northridge, CA, pn W-39, c.1981), photocopy of original parts.
JZT-1.2tm. Trauer Marsch von Triebensee; welcher bei dem Leichenbegräbnis der Alois v[on] Li[e]chtenstein
zu Wranau in Mähren [now Vranov, Moravia] gespielt wurde.   2cl(C) 2cl(B♭) 2hn 2bn 2tp(clar).
MS parts (by Dominik Hübner, Langenbruck): CZ-Pu(dm), 59 R 3373.

Arrangements
*JZT-1a. (composer unidentified, ?compiler Anton Fischer): Figaro, overture & 5 mvts.
2ob 2cl 2hn 2bn (cbn tp ad lib).   Pc (MISC: Jg. I, Oe. 8, Nos. 5 - 10), MS parts.
JZT-2a. [J. Schuster, ?arr W. Müller]: Pas de deux, getanzt von Herr und Mad. Viganò.   2ob 2cl 2hn 2bn.
MS pts: A-Wn, (A-6.42a), Mus.Hs.3792. *See also: ARRANGEMENTS LIST, Müller, W.: Das neu Sonntagskind.*
JZT-3a. Beethoven: Piano Quintet, Op. 16, Andante.   2ob 2cl 2hn 2bn (cbn tp* ad lib).
Pc (MISC: Jg. I, Oe. 2, No. 2), MS parts.
JZT-4a. Belloli: Il trionfo di Vitellio Massimo, 3 mvts.   2ob 2cl 2hn 2bn (cbn tp ad lib).
Pc (MISC: Jg. I, Oe. 8, Nos. 2 - 4), MS parts.
JZT-5a. Boieldieu: Jean de Paris, (Act I, overture & 9 mvts; Act II, 7 mvts).   2ob 2cl 2hn 2bn (cbn tp ad lib).
Pc (MISC: (Act I) Jg. III, Oe. 3, Nos. 1 - 10; (Act II): Jg. III, Oe. 4, Nos. 1 - 7), MS parts.

JZT-6a. Bruni: Les Sabotiers, overture & 1 aria. 2ob 2cl 2hn 2bn (cbn tp ad lib).
Pc (MISC: Jg. I, Oe. 4, Nos. 1, 2), MS parts.
JZT-7a. Cherubini: Medée, sinfonia & 7 mvts. 2ob 2cl 2hn 2bn cbn/vlne. MS parts: I-Fc, F.P. S.392.
*__JZT-8.1a.__ Cherubini: La Prisonnière, overture & 8 mvts. 2ob 2cl 2hn 2bn cbn.
MS parts: A-Wn, Mus.Hs.3804, (8 mvts); CZ-K, opery No.52.K.I; I-Fc, F.P. S.359.
JZT-8.2a. Cherubini: La Prisonnière, duette (Allegretto). 2ob 2cl 2hn 2bn (cbn tp ad lib).
Pc (MISC: Jg. I, Oe. 4, No. 9), MS parts.
JZT-9a. Cherubini: Anacréon, "Grossen Tanz Aria". 2ob 2cl 2hn 2bn (cbn tp ad lib).
Pc (MISC: Jg. I, Oe. 1, No. 10), MS parts.
JZT-10a. J.B. Cramer: 4 Divertimentos, Op. 17, No. 3/i, Maestoso (as "Marcsh"). 2ob 2cl 2hn 2bn (cbn* tp ad lib).
Pc (MISC: Jg. I, Oe. 2, No. 4), MS parts.
JZT-11a. Della Maria: L'Oncle valet, duett. 2ob 2cl 2hn 2bn (cbn tp ad lib).
Pc (MISC: Jg. I, Oe. 6, No. 4), MS parts.
JZT-12a. Diabelli: Tambourin Solo der Mademoiselle Neumann. 2ob 2cl 2hn 2bn (cbn* tp ad lib).
Pc (MISC: Jg. I, Oe. 1, No. 4), MS parts.
JZT-13a. Duport (compiler): Zephir, overture & 11 mvts. 2ob 2cl 2hn 2bn (cbn tp ad lib).
Pc (MISC: Jg. III, Oe. 5, Nos. 1 - 12), MS parts.
JZT-14.1a. Duport (compiler = Steibelt, Persuis, et al.): Der blöde Ritter, overture & 11 mvts.
2ob 2cl 2hn 2bn (cbn tp ad lib). Pc (MISC: Jg. III, Oe. 6, Nos. 1 - 12), MS parts.
JZT-14.2a. (Duport (compiler = Steibelt, Persuis, et al.): Der blöde Ritter, 5 mvts. 2ob 2cl 2hn 2bn cbn.
MS parts: A-Wn, (A-8.5a), Mus.Hs.3793 (= Jg. III. Oe. 6, Nos. 1, 5, 6, 9 & 10).
JZT-15a. Esterházy von Galantha, *Prinzessin* Rosa: Ländler, in G. 2ob 2cl 2hn 2bn (cbn tp ad lib).
Pc (MISC: Jg. II, Oe. 12, No. 10), MS parts.
JZT-16a. Anton Fischer: Das Singspiel auf dem Dache, aria. 2ob 2cl 2hn 2bn (cbn tp ad lib).
Pc (MISC: Jg. I, Oe. 1, No. 9), MS parts.
JZT-17a. Gluck: Armide, Marsch (with an original Trio by Triebensee, JZT-9m).
2ob 2cl 2hn 2bn (cbn tp ad lib). Pc (MISC: Jg. I. Oe. 7, No. 5), MS parts.
JZT-18a. Gluck: Armide, Echo Arie der Wajaden, Act 2. 2ob 2cl 2hn 2bn (cbn tp* ad lib).
Pc (MISC: Jg. I. Oe. 7, No. 6), MS parts.
JZT-19a. Gluck: Iphigénie en Tauride, overture & 20 mvts. 2ob 2cl 2hn 2bn cbn.
MS parts: A-Ee, Mus.1138; A-Wn, (?lost); CZ-Pnm, Lobkovic X.H.a.66; I-Fc, D.V.509.
JZT-20a. Grétry: Zémire et Azor, Spiegel Terzett. 2ob 2cl 2hn 2bn (cbn* tp* ad lib).
Pc (MISC: Jg. I, Oe. 1, No. 8), MS parts.
JZT-21a. Gyrowetz: Federica ed Adolfo, (Act I, overture & 13 mvts; Act II, 7 mvts).
2ob 2cl 2hn 2bn (cbn tp ad lib).
Pc (MISC: (Act I) Jg. III, Oe. 1, Nos. 1 - 10 & Oe. 2, Nos. 1 - 4; (Act II) Jg. III, Oe. 2, Nos. 5 - 11), MS parts.
JZT-22a. Haydn: "Oxford" Symphony, (Hob. I/92). 2ob 2cl 2hn 2bn (cbn tp ad lib).
Pc (MISC: Jg. II, Oe. 11, Nos. 1 - 4), MS parts.
Pm (WINDS: Northridge, CA, pn W-97, c.1981), parts.
Pm (Emerson Edition: Ampleforth, sd), score & parts.
Pm (Compusic: Amsterdam, pn 210, 1991), score & parts.
JZT-23a. Haydn: Symphony in C, (Hob. I/97), Adagio, Menuetto & Presto. 2ob 2cl 2hn 2bn (cbn tp ad lib).
Pc (MISC: Jg. I, Oe. 3, Nos. 2 - 4), MS parts.
JZT-24a. Haydn: Symphony "The Miracle" (Hob. I/102), Presto. 2ob 2cl 2hn 2bn (cbn tp ad lib).
Pc (MISC: Jg. I, Oe. 2, No. 10), MS parts.
JZT-25a. Himmel: Fanchon, das Leiermädchen, overture & 9 mvts. 2ob 2cl 2hn 2bn (cbn tp ad lib).
Pc (MISC: Jg. I, Oe. 11, Nos. 1 - 10), MS parts.
JZT-26a. Hummel: Helena und Paris, Andante espressivo/Scherzando. 2ob 2cl 2hn 2bn (cbn tp ad lib).
Pc (MISC: Jg. I, Oe. 7, No. 8), MS parts.
JZT-27a. Isouard: Le Médecin turc (Der Türkische Artz), overture.
2ob 2cl 2hn 2bn (cbn tp ad lib). Pc (MISC: Jg. I, Oe. 3, No. 1), MS parts.
JZT-28a. Isouard: Cendrillon, overture & 16 mvts. 2ob 2cl 2hn 2bn (cbn tp ad lib).
Pc (MISC: Jg. II, Oe. 9, Nos. 1 - 11; Jg. II, Oe. 10, Nos. 1 - 6), MS parts.
JZT-29a. Kanne: Orpheus, duetto. 2ob 2cl 2hn 2bn (cbn tp* ad lib).
Pc (MISC: Jg. I, Oe. 7, No. 9), MS parts.
JZT-30a. Krommer: Symphony, Op. 12. 2ob 2cl 2hn 2bn (cbn tp ad lib).
Pc (MISC: Jg. I, Oe. 7, Nos. 1 - 4), MS parts. Modern MS score: GB-Ljag.
JZT-31a. Lesueur: Ossian, Marsch "Der Kaledonier". 2ob 2cl 2hn 2bn (cbn* tp ad lib).
Pc (MISC: Jg. I, Oe. 2, No. 9), MS parts.
JZT-32.1a. Maurer: Arlequin und Colombine auf der Alpes, pas de deux (Niederländen Bauern).
2ob 2cl 2hn 2bn (cbn tp ad lib). Pc (MISC: Jg. I, Oe. 1, No. 6), MS parts.
JZT-32.2a. Maurer: Arlequin und Colombine auf der Alpes, ballet music (1 mvt, Allo modto, 3/4).
2ob 2cl 2hn 2bn (cbn* tp* ad lib). Pc (MISC: Jg. I, Oe. 6, No. 3), MS pts.
JZT-33.1a. Mayr: Adelasia ed Aleramo, aria. 2ob 2cl 2hn 2bn (cbn tp ad lib).
Pc (MISC: Jg. I, Oe. 3, No. 7), MS parts.
JZT-33.2a. Mayr: Adelasia ed Aleramo, duetto. 2ob 2cl 2hn 2bn (cbn tp* ad lib).
Pc (MISC: Jg. I, Oe. 7, No. 7), MS parts.
JZT-34a. Méhul: Bion (as "Der Bauer"), overture. 2ob 2cl 2hn 2bn (cbn tp ad lib).
Pc (MISC: Jg. I, Oe. 8, No. 1), MS parts.
*__JZT-35a.__ Méhul: Le Trésor supposé, overture & 8 mvts. 2ob 2cl 2hn 2bn cbn.
MS parts: CZ-K, opery No.51.K.I; CZ-KRa, A3931/IV.B.94, (missing cbn); I-Fc, D.V.499, (missing cbn part).
JZT-36a. Méhul: L'Irato, aria. 2ob 2cl 2hn 2bn (cbn tp ad lib). Pc (MISC: Jg. I, Oe. 2, No. 7), MS parts.

JZT-37.1a. Möser: Die Berg-Schotten, contradanze (with 3 trios).   2ob 2cl 2hn 2bn (cbn tp ad lib).
Pc (MISC: Jg. I, Oe. 7, No. 10), MS parts.
JZT-37.2a. Möser: Die Berg-Schotten, quadrille (Allegro, contradanz, 2 trios & coda).   2ob 2cl 2hn 2bn cbn.
MS parts: A-Wn, (A-8.3a), Mus.Hs.3793.
JZT-38a. Mozart: Le Nozze di Figaro, duetto, "Sull' aria".   2ob 2cl 2hn 2bn (cbn tp ad lib).
Pc (MISC: Jg. I, Oe. 6, No. 2), MS parts.
*JZT-39.1a. Mozart: Don Giovanni, overture & 19 mvts.   2ob 2cl 2hn 2bn.
MS parts: A-Ee, Mus.1111; CZ-Bm(au), A.35.129, (local copy, mvts 2, 5-7, 9, 11, 12, 14-19); CZ-Pnm,
Lobkovic X.G.b.f.69; GB-Ljag(w), (local copy, as Anonymous); NL-DHgm, hk 19 B 20.
Pm (Musica rara: London, pn MR 1854, 1855, 1976), ed. H. Voxman, score & parts.
Pm (Emerson Edition: Ampleforth), score & parts.
JZT-39.2a. Mozart: Don Giovanni, duetto (Là ci darem).   2ob 2cl 2hn 2bn.
MS parts: A-Wn, Mus.Hs.3792.   (= A-6.11a)
JZT-40.1a. Mozart: La Clemenza di Tito, overture & 10 mvts.   2ob 2cl 2hn 2bn.
MS parts: I-Fc, F.P. S.358.
Pm (Musica rara: London, pn MR 1881, 1887, 1977), ed. H. Voxman, score & parts.
JZT-40.2a. Mozart: La Clemenza di Tito, terzetto & marcia.   2ob 2cl 2hn 2bn.
MS parts: A-Wn, Mus.Hs.3792.   (= A-6.6a, 6.17a)
JZT-41a. Mozart: "Linz" Symphony, (K.425), 2nd mvt.   2ob 2cl 2hn 2bn (cbn tp* ad lib).
Pc (MISC: Jg. I, Oe. 2, No. 8), MS parts.
JZT-42a. Mozart: Symphony in E♭, (K.543), 1st mvt.   2ob 2cl 2hn 2bn (cbn tp ad lib).
Pc (MISC: Jg. I, Oe. 1, No. 1), MS parts.
JZT-43a. W. Müller: Die Alte überall und nirgends, aria.   2ob 2cl 2hn 2bn (cbn tp ad lib).
Pc (MISC: Jg. I, Oe. 4, No. 4), MS parts.
JZT-44a Nicolini: Traiano in Dacia, overture & 19 (9 + 10) mvts.   2ob 2cl 2hn 2bn (cbn tp ad lib).
Pc (MISC: Jg. II, Oe. 5, Nos. 1-10; Jg. II, Oe. 6, Nos. 1-10), MS parts.
JZT-45a. Paer: I Fuorusciti, duettino.   2ob 2cl 2hn 2bn (cbn tp ad lib).
Pc (MISC: Jg. I, Oe. 6, No. 9), MS parts.
JZT-46a, Paer: Sargino, duet.   2ob 2cl 2hn 2bn.   MS parts: A-Wgm, VIII 43275, No. 5.
JZT-47.1a. Paer: Sofonisbe, overture.   2ob 2cl 2hn 2bn (cbn tp ad lib).
Pc (MISC: Jg. I, Oe. 2, No. 1), MS parts.
JZT-47.2a. Paer: Sofonisbe, duet.   2ob 2cl 2hn 2bn (cbn tp* ad lib)
Pc (MISC: Jg. I, Oe. 1, No. 5), MS parts.
JZT-47.3a. Paer: Sofonisbe, march.   2ob 2cl 2hn 2bn.   MS parts: A-Wgn, VIII 43275, No. 6.
JZT-48.1a. Paer: Numa Pompilio, sinfonia & (Act I) 9 mvts.   2ob 2cl 2hn 2bn (cbn tp ad lib).
MS parts: A-Ee, Mus.1165, (replaces Jg. I, Oe. 10 of the *Miscellannées*; sinfonia & Act I, Nos. 1 - 5, 7 - 9, 12,
15 of JZT-48.2a); CZ-Bm(au) A.40.163, (sinfonia, Nos. 2, 6 & 10; without cbn pt other than title listing).
JZT-48.2a. Paer: Numa Pompilio, (Act I) sinfonia & 15 mvts, (Act II) 8 mvts.   2ob 2cl 2hn 2bn (cbn).
Pc (Nel Magazino di Musica dei Teatri Imp-Reali: Vienna, c.1809), MS parts: A-Wn, Mus.Hs.3826;
CZ-KRa, A3946/IV.B.109; I-Fc, F.P. S.350. *The cbn pt only exists as part of title; actually for octet.*
JZT-49a. Pleyel: Piano Sonata; (actually "Air Ecossais", Adagio ma non troppo, from the Trio for Pf, vl, vc,
B.444/ii).   2ob 2cl 2hn 2bn (cbn tp* ad lib).
Pc (MISC: Jg. I, Oe. 1, No. 2), MS parts.
JZT-50a. Schulz: Die Jungfrau von Orleans, Harmonie-Begleitung zu dem sweiter Monolog.
2ob 2cl 2hn 2bn (cbn tp* ad lib).   Pc (MISC: Jg. I, Oe. 12, No. 9), MS parts.
JZT-51a. Seyfried: Zum goldenen Löwen, rondo.   2ob 2cl 2hn 2bn (cbn tp ad lib).
Pc (MISC: Jg. I, Oe. 6, No. 8), MS parts.
JZT-52.1a. Seyfried: Alamor der Mauer, marcia.   2ob 2cl 2hn 2bn (cbn* tp ad lib),
Pc (MISC: Jg. I, Oe. 1, No. 3), MS parts.
JZT-52.2a. Seyfried: Alamor der Mauer, marcia.   2cl 2hn bn.
MS parts: CZ-KRa, IV.B.144, (probably a local rescoring by V. Havel).
JZT-53a. Seyfried: Mitternacht, duet.   2ob 2cl 2hn 2bn (cbn tp* ad lib).
Pc (MISC: Jg. I, Oe. 2, No. 5), MS parts.
JZT-54a. Seyfried: Idas und Marpissa, duet.   2ob 2cl 2hn 2bn (cbn tp* ad lib).
Pc (MISC: Jg. I, Oe. 3, No. 6), MS parts.
JZT-55a. Spontini: La Vestale; (Act I) overture & 5 mvts, (Act II) 6 mvts, (Act III) 9 mvts.
2ob 2cl 2hn 2bn (cbn tp ad lib).   Pc (MISC: (Act I) Jg. II, Oe. 10, Nos. 7-12; (Act II) Jg. II, Oe. 11, Nos. 5-10;
(Act III) Jg. II, Oe. 12, Nos. 1-9), MS parts.
JZT-56a [=JZT-2d]. Steibelt: (Unidentified) March & Trio.   2ob 2cl 2hn 2bn (?cbn tp ad lib).
MS parts: A-Wn, *(as No. 17 of Jg. I, Oe. 9 of the* Miscellannées de Musique; *this only appears in the A-Wn
copy. Triebensee's name as composer has been scratched off and "Steibelt" added in another hand.*
JZT-57a. Süssmayr: Soliman der Zweite, overture & 7 mvts.   2ob 2cl 2hn 2bn (cbn tp ad lib).
Pc (MISC: Jg. I, Oe. 10, Nos. 1 - 8), MS parts.
JZT-58a. Taglioni: Divertissement, Pas de deux & marsch. *Possibly composed by Neumann.*
2ob 2cl 2hn 2bn (cbn tp ad lib).   Pc (MISC: Jg. I, Oe. 3, Nos. 9 & 10), MS parts.
JZT-59a. M. Umlauff: Der Quacksalber und die Zwerge, overture & 16 mvts.   2ob 2cl 2hn 2bn (cbn tp ad lib).
Pc (MISC: Jg. II, Oe. 3. Nos. 1-10; Jg. II, Oe. 4, Nos. 1-6), MS parts.
JZT-60.1a. M. Umlauff: Das eigensinnage Landmädchen, overture & 18 (11 + 7) mvts.
2ob 2cl 2hn 2bn (cbn tp ad lib).   Pc (MISC: Jg. II, Oe. 7, Nos. 1-12; Jg. II, Oe. 8, Nos. 1 - 7), MS parts.
JZT-60.2a. M. Umlauff: Das eigensinnage Landmädchen, (= Jg. II, Oe. 7, Nos. 2, 3, 7, 8, 10 - 12; Jg. II, Oe. 8,
Nos. 1 - 4, 7).   2ob 2cl 2hn 2bn cbn.   MS parts: A-Wn, (A-8.4a), Mus.Hs.3795, Nos. 2 - 14.

JZT-61a. Vogel: Démophon, overture. 2ob 2cl 2hn 2bn (cbn tp ad lib).
Pc (MISC: Jg. I, Oe. 12, No. 1), MS parts.
JZT-62a. Vogler: Castor e Polluce, 2 Theils. 2ob 2cl 2hn 2bn cbn.
MS parts: I-Fc, F.P. S.368. *Advertized in the* Allgemeinische Musikalische Zeitung, *Jan 1804.*
JZT-63a. (J. or T.) Weigl: Pas de deux [from an unidentified ballet choreographed by Taglioni] "mit den Masken von Weigl" & Allegretto moderato "Aus den demselben". 2ob 2cl 2hn 2bn (cbn tp ad lib).
Pc (MISC: Jg. I, Oe. 11, Nos. 9 & 10), MS parts. *The Allegretto moderato only appears in CZ-Pnm Lobkovic X.H.a.50 copy of the Miscellannées.*
JZT-64a. J. Weigl: Die isthmischen Spiele, 6 mvts. 2ob 2cl 2hn 2bn (cbn).
MS parts: CZ-Pnm (2 copies), Lobkovic X.H.a.54, Nos. 8 - 13, (with cbn); Lobkovic X.H.a.64, Nos. 11 - 16 of KRECHLER, FFK-17a, (without cbn). *Lobkovic X.H.a.54 is titled, "N° 72. Miscellanees [sic] de Musique... par Joseph Triebensee". The 6 mvts correspond to Nos. 3, 4, 6, 8, 5, 9 of the 2cl 2hn 2bn version (+WXS-65a) attributed to Sedlak, who is known to have made a number of reductions from Triebensee's arrangements. A complete octet/nonet version has not been traced. The second copy, in Krechler's "Auszuk [sic]...Vologesus.. [and] Istmischen Spielle ein Pallet von Giuseppe Weigel [sic]" is in keeping with Krechler's working as a compiler as well as an arranger. A complete copy of JZT-64a has not yet been traced.*
JZT-65.1a. J. Weigl: Kaiser Hadrian, overture & 9 mvts. 2ob 2cl 2hn 2bn (cbn tp ad lib).
Pc (MISC: Jg. I, Oe. 5, Nos. 1 - 10), MS parts.
JZT-65.2a. J. Weigl: Kaiser Hadrian, march. 2ob 2cl 2hn 2bn (cbn* tp ad lib).
Pc (MISC: Jg. I, Oe. 1, No. 7), MS parts.
JZT-66a. J. Weigl: Ostade, Arie mit obligater Harfe. 2ob 2cl 2hn 2bn (cbn tp ad lib).
Pc (MISC: Jg. I, Oe. 6, No. 7), MS parts.
JZT-67a. J. Weigl: Die Schweizerfamilie, (Act I) overture & 9 mvts; (Act II) overture & 9 mvts.
2ob 2cl 2hn 2bn (cbn tp ad lib). Pc (MISC: Jg. II, Oe. 1, Nos. 1-10; Jg. II, Oe. 2, Nos. 1-10), MS parts.
*****JZT-68a.** T. Weigl: Bacchus und Ariadne, overture & 12 mvts. 2ob 2cl 2hn 2bn cbn.
Pc (in MS parts:) [The Author: Feldsberg, 1803], *Harmonien Sammlung,* Erster Jahrgang Zweyte Lieferung": A-Ee, Mus.1084; A-Wn, Mus.Hs.3875, (as Anon.); CZ-Bm(au), A.36.877, (local copy: Nos. 2 - 6 = Nos. 3 - 6, & 10); CZ-K, balety No.179.K.II.
JZT-69.1a. Weiss: Amphion, Allegretto, ¢. 2ob 2cl 2hn 2bn (cbn tp* ad lib).
Pc (MISC: Jg. I, Oe. 2, No. 3), MS parts.
JZT-69.2a. Weiss: Amphion, Pas de deux. 2ob 2cl 2hn 2bn (cbn tp ad lib).
Pc (MISC: Jg. I, Oe. 2, No. 6), MS parts.
JZT-70a. Winter & Mederitsch: Babylons Pyramiden, overture & 12 mvts. 2ob 2cl 2hn 2bn.
Pc (Traeg: Vienna, 1798-1804), No. 204, MS pts: A-Ee, Mus.1083, (as Anon); A-Wgm(c), (lost); I-Fc, F.P. S.359.
*****JZT-71a.** Winter: Das Labyrinth, overture & 13 mvts. 2ob 2cl 2hn 2bn cbn.
Pc (in MS parts:) [The Author: Feldsberg, 1804], *Harmonien Sammlung,* Erster Jahrgang, Erste Lieferung: A-Ee, Mus.1085; A-Wn, Mus.Hs.3858, (13 mvts); CZ-Bm(au), A.36.880, (local copy, Nos. 1(overture), 2-4, 6, 8, 11, 13; parts (2ob 2cl 2hn with additional local parts for 2 trumpets), A.35.249, (parts = 2bn cbn); CZ-K, opery No.50.K.I; CZ-Pnm, Lobkovic X.H.a.10/2; D-NEhz, 83, (overture & 12 mvts); I-Fc, F.P. S.342. *The cbn is with bn II; however, there are no divisi & this work may really have been originally arranged as an octet.* MS score (allegedly in the hand of J.S. Mayr): I-BGc, Mayr 595.
JZT-72.1a. Winter: Tamerlan, overture & 19 mvts (9 + 10). 2ob 2cl 2hn 2bn (cbn tp ad lib).
Pc (MISC: Jg. III, Oe. 7, Nos. 1 - 10; Jg. III, Oe. 8, Nos. 1 - 10), MS parts.
JZT-72.2a. Winter: Tamerlan, Tanz Aria. 2ob 2cl 2hn 2bn (cbn tp ad lib).
Pc (MISC: Jg. I, Oe. 4, No. 6), MS parts.
JZT-73a. Winter: extra number (Polonaise "Ein Mädchen voll verlangen") for Dalayrac's opera *Les Deux Mots.*
Piano reductions were published by the Chemische Druckerei (Vienna, pn 713, c.1809; RISM [W 1602]) and Cappi (Vienna, pn 1603, sd; RISM [W 1603]). 2ob 2cl 2hn 2bn (cbn tp ad lib).
Pc (MISC: Jg. I, Oe. 4, No. 5), MS parts.
JZT-74a. Winter: Oboe Quartet, Presto. 2ob 2cl 2hn 2bn (cbn tp ad lib).
Pc (MISC: Jg. I, Oe. 12, No. 10), MS parts.
JZT-75a. Wölfl: Das Milchmädchen, overture. 2ob 2cl 2hn 2bn (cbn tp ad lib).
Pc (MISC: Jg. I, Oe. 6, No. 1), MS parts.
JZT-1d(-9d) = [A-34(-43)]. 9 Partiten. 2ca 2hn 2bn. MS parts: A-Wgm, VIII 8541, (?lost). *Cited as Anonymous in the original A-Wgm catalog; recent attributions to Triebensee are most unlikely. These works, for the Schwarzenberg Harmonie, may have been composed by Bonno or by Went.*
JZT-2d. Steibelt: (Unidentified) March & Trio. 2ob 2cl 2hn 2bn (?cbn tp ad lib).
MS parts: A-Wn, *(as No. 17 of Jg. I, Oe. 9 of the Miscellannées de Musique; this only appears in the A-Wn copy. Triebensee's name was originally present as composer but this has been scratched out and Steibelt's name overwritten in another hand. There is no question that Triebensee was the arranger (JZT-56a).*
JZT-1ad. Süssmayr: Der Spiegel in Arkadien, 19 mvts. 2ob 2cl 2hn 2bn.
MS parts: A-Wn, Mus.Hs.3854. *In fact, by Went. Statements that the ob I, bn I & II parts are in Triebensee's hand for 10 mvts are completely unfounded.*
JZT-2ad. J. Weigl: Der Tod der Hercules, 12 mvts. 2ob 2cl 2hn 2bn (bn III).
Pc (Nell' Magazino di Musicka [sic] dei Teatri imperiali: Vienna, c.1798), MS pts: A-Wn, Mus.Hs.3885. *"Fagoto 3to" appears in the bn II pt in No. 10, 8 bars divisi only. Modern attributions to Triebensee as arranger are unsubstantiated.*
JZT-3ad, 4ad. F.P. Schubert: Die Zauberharfe & Rosamunde. fl ob ob(ca) cl(tarogato) cl 2hn 2bn cb.
Original provenance unknown. Modern MS score & pts: D-KIZklöcker. *The scoring is uncharacteristic for Triebensee, suggesting an arranger from the German States (where such a configuration, with flute, was common). Triebensee is not known to have made any arrangements after his appointment as opera director in Prague in 1816.*

TRIMBLE, Lester Albert *1923, USA*
LAT-1. Double Concerto; 1964. 2 violins, fl ob 2cl hn 2bn tp tb. MS score: US-NYamc.

TRINKAUS, George J. *1878 - 1960, USA*
GJT-1a. Fibich: Nálady, dojni a upomínky. Series 1, Op. 41, Seš 4, No. 14, Poëm.
2cl 2hn bn tu *or* 2cl hn 2bn tu *or* 3cl hn bn tu.
Pm (Franklin Co: New York, sd).
GJT-2a. Franck: (Messe Solennelle), Op. 12, Panis Angeliscus. 2cl 2hn bn tu *or* 2cl hn 2bn tu *or* 3cl 2bn tu.
Pm (Franklin Co: New York, sd).

TROJAN, Pietro *(1810)*
PXT-1v. Tantum ergo, 1845. BB solo, (2cl(C)) 2hn (tb vlne) organ. MS score & pts: I-Vsmc, (the title states,"a
2. Bassi. Con Corni, ed Organo"; the 2cl tb & vlne pts do not appear in the score, and may be later additions). ★

*TROJAN, Václav *24 April 1907, Plzeň - 5 July 1983, Prague*
VXT-1. Čtyří karikaturi (s jednon navic), Four Caricatures (With One Added).
2fl 2ob 2cl 3hn 3bn 2tp tb timp perc piano.
Pm (Český hudební fond: Prague), hire score & parts.

*TROOP, A., (?pseudonym)
AZT-1m. 3 Scotch Quick-Steps des Regiments "Duke of Albany Highlanders". Military band, instrumentation
unknown. MS: D-Bds, Hausbibl.M.M.385.

*TROST, J.G.M. *Cited incorrectly in Eitner and Meyer as "Johann Kaspar"; not the J.G.M. Trost born c.1630.*
JGT-1. No. IV. Parthia; in C. 2 octavo-bn, 2 quarto-bn, 2hn 2bn.
MS parts (18 century): D-Z, Catalog. 738.
Pm (In: H. John Hedlund. *A Study of Some 18th century Woodwind Ensemble Music.* Ph.D. Dissertation,
University of Iowa, 1959), ed. Hedlund, score.

TSCHIRCH, Ernst (Leberecht) *3 July 1819, Lichtenun - 26 Dec 1854, Berlin*
ELT-1v. Rastlose Liebe. Male chorus, 2ob 2hn 2bn piano harp.
AutoMS score: D-Bds, Mus.Ms.Auto.E.Tschirch 22.

TUČAPSKÝ, Antonín *27 March 1928, Opotovice, nr Vyškov*
ANT-1v. La grande porte de la Thelemme; 1995. Chorus, 2ob ca 2bn. MS score & parts: F-TOep.

*TUČEK, J.F. *(1820) - active in Břetislav, nr Plzeň*
JFT-1.1(-1.3). 2. hé Pot-pouri - neb Michanice z Českých Národních písní.
cl(Eb) cl(B)b 2tp b-tp flug b-flug basso. MS parts (by J. Straka): CZ-PLa(ba), Hu 2823. ★
    1.1 Potpouri; 33 sections, commencing with "Těd já musín jít".
    1.2(a). F.J. Haydn: [Gott erhalte Franz den Kaiser], as Hymne. Bože zachovej nám Kráke.
    1.3. Hej Slované.

*TUČEK (Tuczek), Vincenc Tomaš Václav (Giovanni) *2 Feb 1773, Prague - 2 Nov 1820, Pest*
*VTT-1v. Pange lingua gloriosi In D## [D major]. CATB, 2fl 2ob/(cl(A) 2hn 2bn.
MS parts (by Johannis Kuczera, Vyšehrad): CZ-Pnm, XVII.A.126, (the cl pts are on the verso of the ob pts). ★
VTT-2v. Pange lingua. CATB, 2cl 2hn bn organ. MS: CZ-Pnm, L.C.151.

*TUCH, Heinrich Agatius Gottlob *1768, Gera - 1821, Dessau*
We have no locations for his Bläsermusik, Op. 22, *(Breitkopf & Härtel: Leipzig, 1808) for 2ob 2cl 2hn 2bn.*
HAT-1. Harmonia, Op. 35; 3 mvts. fl(Db) cl(Eb) 2cl(Bb) 2hn 2bn tp(Eb) b-tb serp b-dr cym.
Pc (Musik-Comptoir: Dessau-Leipzig, sd), RISM [T 1330], parts: A-Wmi, AR 760. ★
*HAT-2. Serenata in G, Op. 42; (dedicated to Fürst. Friedrich Leopold von Anhalt-Dessau). 2cl 2hn 2bn.
Pc (missing titlepage:) (Kollmann: Leipzig, pn 109, 1816), RISM [T 1332], parts: D-RUh.
*HAT-1t. Trauermarsch auf dem Heldentod des Herzogs von Braunschweig, im Jahr 1815. 10 winds.
MS parts: D-Bds.
HAT-1m(-3m). 3 Geschwindmärsche. Turkish music. MS parts: D-Bds.

*TÜRK (TUERK), Daniel Gottlob (Heinrich Anthon Gottlieb) *10 Aug 1756, Claussnitz - 26 Aug 1813, Halle*
DGT-1. Parthia, in Eb, 3 mvts. (?)2cl 2hn bn tp.
MS parts: US-BETm, Lititz Collegium Musicum 218, (here only the hn II & bn parts). ★
DGT-1.1m. March, in Eb, ¢. 2cl 2hn bn tp.
MS parts: US-BETm, Lititz Collegium Musicum 203, No. V. ★
DGT-1.2m. March, in Eb, ¢. 2cl 2hn bn tp.
MS parts: US-BETm, Lititz Collegium Musicum 203, No. X. ★
Pm (in Henry H. Hall, PhD dissertation: *The Moravian Wind Ensemble,* Vanderbilt Univiversity, 1967), score.

TÜTEL, ( )
YZT-1t. Trauermarsch; in B minor. fl(Eb) cl(Eb) 2cl(Bb) 2hn 2bn 2klappen-tp b-tb.
MS parts (by Johann Lapáček, from Veselí [?nad Lužnicí]): CZ-Pu, 59 r 90, (missing Eb cl). ★

TULL, Fisher Aubrey *24 Sept 1934, Waco, Texas*
FYT-1. Scherzino, Op. 27a. pic 3fl 3cl b-cl.
Pm (Boosey & Hawkes: New York, pn 2834, 1973), score & parts.

TURINSKY, František *(1780)*
FQT-1v. IV Stationes Theophoricae. "Die 22 May. 1807". CATB, 2cl 2hn 2bn cb.
MS parts (fromTrenčín church collection): SK-BRnm, Mus.XIII.245. ★

TUTINO, Marco *1954, Italy*
MYT-1. Gran Partita; 1982.   2fl 2ob 2cl 2hn 2bn.
Pm (Suvini-Zerboni: Milano, pn S.9042Z., c.1983), score & parts.

TUTSCH, ( )
ZXT-1t. Trauer Marsch; in C minor.   fl cl(E♭) cl(C) cl(B♭) 2hn 2bn 3tp(F, E♭, E♭) b-tb("obligat") bomb.
MS parts (by Johann Dráha): CZ-Pu, 59 r 86.   ★

TUULSE, Toomas *1946, Sweden*
TYT-1. Menuet; 1976.   2fl 2ob 2cl b-cl 2hn 2bn.   MS: S-Sic.

TYLŇÁK, Ivan *16 Jan 1910, Nižní Sinevir - 2 Jan 1969, Prague*
IYT-1. Divertimento; 1961.   fl 2cl hn.
Pm (Český hudební fond: Prague, 1961), hire score & parts.

TYRAY, ( )
XZT-1(-5). Parthia 1 [-5]; (all in B♭; Nos. 1 - 4: 3 mvts, No. 5: 4 mvts).   2ob 2cl 2hn 2bn.
MS parts (from the church collection at Půchov): SK-BRnm, Mus.XXV.9.   ★

UGOLETTI, Paolo *1956, Italy*
PAU-1. Gli orti epicuro; 1981.   2fl ob 2cl hn bn piano.
Pm (Suvini-Zerboni: Milano, pn S.9005Z., c.1982), score & parts.

UHL, Alfred *5 June 1909, Vienna - 8 June 1992, Vienna*
AXU-1. Eine vergnügliche Musik; 1944.   2ob 2cl 2hn 2bn.
Pm (Universal Edition: Wien, London, pn UE 11920, 1945, repr 1953), score & parts.
AXU-2. 3 Tänzstücke; 1986.   2ob 2cl 2hn bn.
Pm (Doblinger: Wien, pn 6593, 1987), score & parts.

ULBRECHT, Franz Joseph
FJU-1. 5 Sätze (Musica a Tavola nuovamente).   2cl 2hn bn (2tp ad lib).   MS parts: D-KA.

*UMLAUF, Ignaz *1746, Vienna - 8 June 1796, Meidling, nr Vienna*
IXU-1e. Musik von Bergleuten (in der Ferne); independent work in the Singspiel *Die Bergknappen*. 2ob 2hn 2bn.
Pm (In: Denkmäler der Tonkunst in Österreich. Artaria: Wien; Breitkopf & Härtel: Leipzig 1911), XVIII.1,
Bd. 36, pp. 100 - 101, ed. R Haas, score.   Photocopy: GB-Ljag.   ★

URBANI, Pietro (Peter) *1749, Milan - Dec 1816, Dublin.*
PXU-1m. Major Munro's March and Quick Step.   2cl 2hn 2bn.
Pc (Urbani & Liston: Edinburgh, c.1795), RISM [U 96], score: GB-Lbl, g.133.(61); GB-Ob.   ★

USHER, Julia *21 Sept 1945, Oxford*
JXU-1. Ra 1.   2fl 2ob 2cl 2bn.
Pm (Primavera: London, 1980), score.

USTVOLSKAYA, Galina Ivanova *17 June 1919, Petrograd*
GIU-1. Composition 3, "Benedictus qui venit"; 1974 - 1975.   2fl 2bn piano.
Pm (Sikorski: Hamburg, c.1977).

*VAČKÁŘ, Dalibor Cyril *19 Sept 1906, Korcula, (Dalmatia), formerly Yugoslavia*
DCV-1. Legenda o člověku (A Legend of Man).   2fl 2ob 2cl 2hn 2bn 3tp 2tb tu perc hpcd vibr.
Pm (Český hudební fond: Prague, 1966), score.

*VACTOR, Dan Van *1906, USA*
DVV-1, 2. 2 Double Quintets.   fl fl(pic) ob ob(ca) cl(A & B♭) cl(b-cl) 2hn bn bn(cbn).
Pm (Roger Rhodes Ltd.: New York, c.1975), score & parts.
DVV-3. Music for Woodwinds I.   fl fl(pic) ob ob(ca) cl cl(b-cl) 2hn bn bn(cbn).
Pm (Roger Rhodes Ltd.: New York, c.1975), score & parts.
DVV-4. Music for Woodwinds II.   fl fl(pic) ob ob(ca) cl cl(b-cl) 2hn bn bn(cbn).
Pm (Roger Rhodes Ltd.: New York, c.1975), score & parts.

*VÁLEK, Jiří *28 March 1923, Prague*
*JIV-1. 4th Symphony, "Dialogy s vnitřním hlasem" (Dialogues with Inner Voices, to words by Shakespeare).
M, BAR, winds, piano, perc.
Pm (Český hudební fond: Prague, 1965), hire score and parts.
JIV-2. Serenade [=Concertino?].   fl 2ob 2cl 2hn 2bn, piano.
Pm (Český hudební fond: Prague, 1963), hire score & parts.
JIV-1v. Sedm hudebních balek podle Ezopa (7 musical fables after Aesop; texts by František Branislav).
Low voice, piano *or* childrens' choir, child's games, fl 2cl bn pf.
Pm (Panton: Prague, 1972), score; recorded Panton.

*VALENTIN (Wallentin), ( ) *(1810), "Hautboistfeldwebel" (Brno)*
XXV-1a. Donizetti: Lucrezia Borgia, aria.   fl ob 4cl(C, B♭, C, C,) 2hn bn 2tp b-tb basso.
MS parts (1844): CZ-Bm(au), A.35.164.
XXV-2a. Lortzing: Czar und Zimmermann, overture.   2ob 2cl(A) 2hn 2bn cbn 2tp.
MS parts (1842): CZ-Bm(au), A.37.339.

VALERA, Roberto
RZV-1. Moviemento concertante.   Solo guitar, 3fl cl b-cl cb-cl hn 2bn cbn 2perc(incl vib).
Pm (C.F. Peters: New York).

VANDENBOGAERDE, Fernand *1946, France*
FEV-1. Masses/Fluides.   2cl 2hn 2bn 2tb tu 2perc 4vc(2 parts) db.
Pm (Mordant: ?Paris, c.1979).
FEV-2. Musique à dix.   fl(a-fl) ob(ca) cl(b-cl) 2hn bn 2tp 2tb.
Pm (Mordant: ?Paris, c.1981).

*VANDERHAGEN (Van-Der-Hagen), Armand Jean François Joseph *1753, Antwerp - July 1822, Paris*
We have no locations for surviving copies of his Suite d'harmonie militaire à dix parties Op. 14, 17, 20, 21, or his 2 Suites de pas redoublés.
*AJV-1. La Naissance du Roi de Rome, Symphonie Militaire, Dédié à l'Armée Française; C minor/major, 1 mvt.
2pic(F) 2cl(F) 2cl(C) 2hn 2bn 2tp 2tb 2serp b-dr+cym.
Pc (Chez Imbault: Paris, pn 961, 1811), parts: F-Pn, (2 copies), Vm25 75, Vm25 75A. ★
AJV-2. Pot-pourri pour huit instruments à vent.   2p-fl 2cl 2hn 2bn.
Pc (Imbault: Paris, pn 685, 1797), RISM [V 254], parts: F-Pn, (2 copies, including:) Vm27 4176. ★
AJV-1a. Troisième Suite d'airs de l'Opéra Buffa; 8 mvts.   2cl 2hn 2bn.
Pc (Chez Imbault: Paris, pn 915, c.1808), parts: F-Pn, Vm27 4177. *Suites 1 & 2 were arranged by G.F. Fuchs.*
  1.1a. Cimarosa: Il due Baroni, 4 mvts (duo & 3 arias).   Nos. 1 - 4.
  1.2a. Paisiello: La Modista raggiatrice, 2 mvts (arias).   Nos. 5 & 8.
  1.3a. Paer: Il Principe di Taranto, duo, "Per che mai sposina mia".   No. 6.
  1.4a. Cimarosa: I Nemici generosi, aria, "Fanciulla sventurata".   No. 7.
AJV-2.1a(-2.12a). (1ère - 12e) Suite des Amusements Militaires.   2cl 2hn 2bn.
Pc (M. de la Chevardière: Paris; Castaud: Lyon, c.1776), RISM [V 253; as published by Le Duc: V 252], pts:
F-BO, (Suite 1; as published by Le Duc); F-Pn, Vmg 14.854 (1 - 3), (Suites 2, 4 & 5; as published by Le Duc);
S-Uu, Utl.instr.mus.tr.145, 149 - 151, Takt 1 - 5, (Suites 1, 2, 4, 9 & 12; missing cl II, hn II; all 5 Nos. bear both the later signatures of Le Duc, the successor to De La Chevardière as of 1 Dec 1784, and overpasted printed slips with the imprint of Imbault dating from 1794 - 1799). *The contents of AJV-2.8a are taken from the Le Duc reissue, AJV-3.8a.*
  2.1/1a. Sacchini: La Colonie, "Si le ciel Est inexorable [sic]".   No. 1.
    2.1/2a - 4a. [unidentified]: "Elle reviens", "La colere sur la Face", "Tout succed ala tendresse [sic]".   Nos. 2-4.
    2.1/5a. Monsigny: La belle Arsène, 2 mvts.   Nos. 5 & 6.
  2.2/1a. Sacchini: La Colonie, 4 mvts.   2.2/2a. Grétry: La Rosière de Salency, 2 mvts.
  2.4/1a. F.A.D. Philidor: Les Femmes vengées, 4 mvts.   Nos. 1 - 4.
    2.4/2a. Sacchini: La Colonie, "N'est point une Folie" & overture.   Nos. 5 & 6.
  2.5/1a. Grétry: La Rosière de Salency, overture & 3 mvts.   Nos. 1, 2, 4 & 6.
    2.5/2a. Martini: Henri IV, "D'une folâtre adolescence".   No. 3.
    2.5/3a. Gossec: Les Pêcheurs, "Bernard est ma foi bon garçon".   No. 5.
  2.8/1a [= AJV-3.8a]. Monsigny: La belle Arsène, 4 mvts.   Nos. 1 - 4.
    2.8/2a. Sacchini: La Colonie, 2 mvts.   Nos. 5 & 6.
  2.9/1a. Rodolphe: L'Aveugle de Palmyre, 3 mvts.   Nos. 1 - 3.
    2.9/2a. Grétry: La Fausse Magie, "Qoi [sic] ce vieux coq".   No. 4.
    2.9/3a. Grétry: Les Mariages Samnites, "Dieu d'amour".   No. 5.
    2.9/4a. [unidentified mvt: "Quai je entendu [sic]"].   No. 6.
  2.12/1a. F.A.D. Philidor: Tom Jones, "D'un Cerf dix Cors". No. 1. (= RISM [P 1927]; all mvts attributed).
    2.12/2a. [2 unidentified mvts, "Aimable jenesse [sic]", "Dans le Brillante saisons", possibly from Lully's opera, *Psyché*].   Nos. 2 - 3.
    2.12/3a. [unidentified]: Polonaise [& Trio].
    2.12/4a. Audinot/Gossec: Le Tonellier, "Tu vois ton Serin dans sacage [sic]".   No. 5.
    2.12/5a. Audinot [probably falsely claimed]: Le Tonellier, "Pres fe moi Dans la boutique [sic]".   No. 6.
    2.12/6a. [unidentified mvt, "Pour qoi Craindreunamant" [sic: "Pourquoi craindre un'amant"].]   No. 7.
AJV-3.1a(-3.24a). Pièces d'harmonie Contenant des Ouvertures, Airs, et Ariettes d'Opera, et Opera comiques [sic]; Nos. [MS: 13 - 24 - and perhaps more; the continuation of AJV-2a].   2cl 2hn 2bn.
Pc (Le Duc: Paris, 1786/1787), RISM [V 250], parts: F-Pn, Vm27 4177, (Nos. 15 - 18, 21);
S-Uu, Utl.instr.mus.tr.145, 149 - 151, Takt 1 - 3, (Nos. 14, 24 & 8, respectively; missing cl II, hn II parts; a slip with the printed imprint of Imbault, dating from 1794 - 1799 is pasted over the original imprint); HR-Zha.
Le Duc purchased the firm of De La Chevardière and this periodical is, in fact, a continuation of AJV-2a; No. 8 is a reissue.
  3.8/1a. Monsigny: La belle Arsène, 4 mvts.   Nos. 1 - 4.
    3.8/2a. Sacchini: La Colonoie, 2 mvts.   Nos. 5 & 6.
  3.14/1a. Grétry: Panurge dans l'île des lanternes, overture & 7 mvts. [= RISM G 4286].
  3.15/1a. Dalayrac: L'Amant Statue, overture & 3 mvts.   Nos. 1 - 4.
    3.15/2a. Grétry: Panurge dans l'île des lanternes, 3 mvts.   Nos. 5 - 7.
    3.15/3a. Sacchini: Dardanus, "Lieux Funestes".   No. 8.
  3.16/1a. Sacchini: La [sic] Chimène, overture & 1 mvt ("Pardonnez").
    3.16/2a. Dezède: Blaise et Babet, duo ("Vous qui m'avois").
    3.16/3a. Grétry: Richard Coeur de Lion, 1 mvt (Allegretto, 2/4).
    3.16/4a. Grétry: L'Épreuve villageoise, ("Je vous revois").
    3.16/5a. Paisiello: Il Barbiere di Siviglia, "Saper bramante" (as "Je suis Lindor").
  3.17/1a. Dalayrac: L'Amant Statue, 4 mvts.
    3.17/2a. Sacchini: Dardanus, 2 airs de ballet.
  3.18/1 - 8. [?Vanderhagen]: 8 Marches.   3.18/9 - 14. [?Vanderhagen]: 6 Pas redoublés. ★
  3.21/1a. Dalayrac: La Dot, overture & 7 mvts.
  3.24/1a. Paisiello: Il Re Teodoro in Venezia, 7 mvts.

AJV-4a. Nº 21 Suitte D'Airs D'Harmonie [sic]; 8 mvts.   2cl 2hn 2bn.
Pc (Le Roy: Paris, pn 21, c.1784 - 1786), RISM [V 251], parts: S-Uu, Utl.instr.mus.tr.145, 149 - 151, Takt 13, (missing cl II, hn II parts; a printed slip with the imprint of Imbault is pasted over the original imprint).
    4.1a. Martini: Le Droit de Seigneur, 3 mvts.   4.2a. Sacchini: Chimène, air de ballet.
    4.3a. Grétry: L'Épreuve villageoise, 2 mvts.   4.4a. Piccinni: Didon, "Nous allons revoir".
    4.5a. Grétry: La Caravanne de Caire, menuetto grazioso.
AJV-5a. Nº [MS: 91] Suite d'Harmonie Tirées Des Opéras Buffon Qui ont Eté joués a Versailles; 11 mvts.
2cl 2hn 2bn.
Pc (Seiber père: Paris, pn 1164, c.1790), pts: S-Uu, Utl.instr.mus.tr. 145, 149 - 151, Takt 17 (missing cl II, hn II).
    5.1a. Dalayrac: Le Soirée orageuse, 5 mvts.   Nos. 1 - 4, 6.
    5.2a. Grétry: Raoul Barbe-Bleu, air de danse.   No. 5.
    5.4a. Beffroy de Reigny: Nicodème dans la lune, 2 mvts.   Nos. 7 & 11.
    5.5a. Pleyel: 6 Quartets dedicated to the Prince des Galles, No. 2, Andante poco Allegretto, (B.350ii).   No. 8.
    5.6a. Anon: Romance Amoroso, "Pauvre Jacques".   No. 9.
    5.7a. Méhul: Euphrosine, "Mes pastouraux".   No. 10.
AJV-6.1a. Berton: Le Grand Deuil, overture,   2fl(pic) 2cl(C) 2hn 2bn, (tp tb serp timp/t-dr/b-dr ad lib).
Pc (Chez Jᶜᵉ Pleyel: Paris, pn 1018, 1812), parts: F-Pn, Vm27 4175.
AJV-6.2a. Berton: Le Grand Deuil, airs.   2fl 2cl 2hn 2bn, (tp tb serp ad lib).
Pc (Pleyel: Paris, pn 1019, 1812), parts: F-Pn, Vm27 4174.
AJV-7a. Cimarosa: Le Astuzie femminili, [8] Airs.   2cl 2hn 2bn.
Pc (Chez Imbault: Paris, pn 913, c.1810), parts: F-Pn, Vm27 4171.
AJV-8a. Dalayrac: Le jeune Prude.   2fl 2cl 2hn 2bn, (tp tb serp ad lib).
Pc (Pleyel: Paris, 1806); ouverture, pn 657, RISM [D 330]; airs, pn 687, RISM [D 331]; parts: H-KE, (complete).
AJV-9a. Fioravanti: Le Cantatrici villane, [6] Airs.   2fl 2cl(C) 2hn 2bn.
Pc (Imbault: Paris, pn 943, 1811), RISM [V 256], parts: F-Pn, (2 copies), Vm27 4172; D-Rtt.
AJV-10a. Haydn: Morceaux choisis dans les oeuvres [Symphonies] du célèbre Haydn; Suite 1, 7 mvts [Hob.I/
95iv, 90ii, 90iv, 94ii, 95iii, 84ii, 97iii]; Suite 2, 6 mvts [89i, 103ii, 103ii, 97iv, 97ii, 99iv]. 2fl(pic) 2cl(C) 2hn 2bn.
Pc (Pleyel: Paris, pn 967, 968, 1817), 2 liv., parts: CH-Gpu, Ib.4855, 4856.
AJV-11a. Isouard: Michel-Ange, overture.   2fl 2cl 2hn 2bn (tp tb serp ad lib).
Pc (Magasin de musique Dirigé par MMʳˢ Chérubini [sic], Méhul, Kreutzer, Rode, N. Isouard et Boieldieu: Paris,
pn 75, 1803), parts: CZ-Bm(au), A.36.885.
MS parts: D-HER, Mus. N.1=2, (missing ad lib tb part).
AJV-12a. Isouard: Les Confidences.   2fl 2cl 2hn 2bn, (tp tb serp ad lib).
Pc (Magasin de musique Dirigé par MMʳˢ Chérubini [sic], Méhul, Kreutzer, Rode, N. Isouard et Boieldieu: Paris,
pn 203, 1803), parts: CZ-Bm(au), A.36.884, (missing tp tb serp parts).
AJV-13a. Isouard: Le Médecin Turc.   2fl 2cl 2hn 2bn, (tp tb serp ad lib).
Pc (Naigueli [Nägeli]: Zürich, pn 262, c.1803), ouverture, RISM [V 260], parts: H-KE, 977/VIII, (missing 2hn).
AJV-14a. F.C. Lefevbre: [9] Airs de Ballet de Venus et Adonis.   2cl 2hn 2bn.
Pc (Imbault: Paris, pn 909, c.1810), parts: CH-N; F-Pn, Vm27 4173.
AJV-15a. Lesueur: Paul et Virginie, (Suite No. 1).   2cl 2hn 2bn.
Pc (Sieber: Paris, pn 1197, c.1794), RISM [L 2146], parts: D-AB.
AJV-16a. Méhul: Une Folie, overture & 2 liv.   2fl 2cl 2hn 2bn tp.
Pc (Pleyel: Paris, 1803); ouverture, pn 518, RISM [M 2081]; Airs, 2 liv., pn 535, 536, RISM [M 2093]; parts:
D-AB, (overture); D-Rp, (complete).
AJV-17a. Méhul: Helena (Hélene), airs.   2fl 2cl 2hn 2bn, (tp tb serp ad lib)
Pc (Pleyel: Paris, c.1803), parts: I-Fc, F.P. S.385.
AJV-18a. Mozart: Le Nozze di Figaro, Airs, Liv. 1, 8 mvts, Liv. 2, 8 mvts, Liv. 3, 9 mvts.   2fl 2cl 2hn 2bn.
Pc (Sieber [fils]: Paris, pn 411 - 413, 1808), RISM [V 259], parts: CH-Gpu, Ib.4858, 4859 (vols. 2 & 3).
AJV-19a. Mozart: Don Giovanni, overture.   2fl 2cl(C) 2hn 2bn, (2tp tb ad lib).
Pc (Pleyel: Paris, pn 956, 1817), RISM [V 257], parts: CH-Gpu, Ib.4857.
AJV-20a. Paer: 6 Valses.   2cl 2hn 2bn, (fl(F) cl(F) tp tb serp b-dr cym ad lib).
Pc (Imbault: Paris, pn 957, c.1811), parts: F-Pn, Vm27 3300.

*VANĚČEK (Vaníček, Waníček), František S. (?Z)   *(?1800), active 1821 - 1849, Břevnice, South Bohemia*
FSV-1t. N: 10 Marcia a conduct defunctorum [pencil addition: Miserere romanorum"]; in E♭.   cl(E♭) 2hn 2bn.
(?Auto)MS parts (["František] Waněček [sic] m.p. 20/1 [1]839"): CZ-PLa(br), Hu 1692. ★
FSV-1v. Stace na slavnost božího Téla [4 Stationes].   CATB, fl 2cl(A) 2hn bn tp(prin) basso timp.
AutoMS ("6/6 [1]849 Wčk"): CZ-PLa(br), Hu 727. ★
FSV-2v. Litani de Sanc. Joanne Nepom[uk], 1833.   SATB, 2cl(A) 2hn bn 2tp(clar) timp.
AutoMS parts: CZ-Pnm, XVII.A.107, (with a later part transposed for clarinet I in C). ★
FSV-1tv. Pohřební; in C minor, 2 texts by M. Hovorky ("Aj umlkla ústa" & "Anděl smrti, anděl míru").
CATB, 2cl 2hn basso/bn basso.   AutoMS parts ("Vaněček m.p. 23/9 1848"): CZ-PLa(br), Hu 906. ★
FSV-2tv. Funebria No. 12; in C, "Sila, jharost zachá", text by Joseph Ulrych.   CATB, 2cl 2hn bn.
(?Auto)MS parts: CZ-PLa(br), Hu 908b. ★
FSV-3tv. [Funeral song]; in E♭, "Ach matko my syrotci [sic]", text by Joseph Ulrych.   CZTB, 2hn 2bn.
(?Auto)MS parts: CZ-PLa(br), Hu 908c, (with the note, "N.7. corr. dupp"; missing hn I). ★
FVS-4tv. Pís[eň] pohř[ební]. 4. Při poh[řbu]. Staré ženy [for the funerals of old women]; in B♭, "Všemohoucí
Bůh, jenž žáda od mládeže", text by Ulrych.   CATB, 2hn 2bn.   (?Auto)MS parts: CZ-PLa(br), Hu 908d. ★
FSV-5tv. N. 12 Při pohřbu člověka náhle zemřelého [for the funeral of an old person who died suddenly]; in C,
"Ach! jak velkého Boha slovo strašné se na mě vyplnilo", text by Joseph Ulrych.   CATB, 2hn basso.
AutoMS parts ("11/4 1840 Waněček [sic] m.p."): CZ-PLa(br). ★
FSV-6tv. Pís[eň] pohř[ební]. 11; in C minor, "Děsí nás hrobové brány", text by Joeph Ulrych.   CATB, 2hn bn.
(?Auto)MS parts (5 Oct 1848): CZ-PLa(br), Hu 908f. ★

*VANĚČEK (Vaniček, Waníček), Ladislav *brother of František (qv); active 1820s, Kasejovice, South Bohemia*
LYV-1. Předehra; in E♭.   cl(E♭) cl(B♭) 2hn flug a-hn basso.
(?Auto)MS parts: CZ-Pla(ka), Hu 937b.   ★

VANĚŘOVSKÝ (Wanerżowský, Wanczorjsky), František   *? - 22 Dec 1834, Prague*
FXV-1. Parthia, in E♭, 4 mvts.   2cl 2hn 2bn.
MS parts: CZ-Pnm, XLII.F.36, No. 4.   ★
FXV-2. Parthia, in E♭, 6 mvts.   2cl 2hn 2bn.
MS parts: CZ-Pnm, XLII.F.36, No. 6.   ★
FXV-3. Variaciones in F; in fact, 3 mvts.   cl 2bthn bn.   MS parts: CZ-Pnm, XX.F.22.   ★
FXV-4. Quartetto in F, 6 mvts.   cl 3bthn.   MS parts: CZ-Pnm, XLII.E.314.   ★
FXV-1v. Litania de Sanc. Joanne Nepom[uk].; in D.   SATB, 2cl 2hn bn 2tp timp.
AutoMS parts, (Rožmitál, 1833): CZ-Pnm, XVIII.A.107.   ★
FXV-2v. Requiem.   CATB, 2cl 2hn 2bn.   MS parts (from Kynšperk nad Ohří): CZ-Pnm, XVIII.A.162.   ★
FXV-1a. Müller: Die Schwestern von Prag, aria (cl I: "Quartetto / Larghetto").   2cl 2hn 2bn.
MS parts: CZ-KRa, A3933/IV.B.96.
FXV-2a. Salieri: Palmira, "I Nume eterno".   cl 3bthn.   *(See supra:* FXV-4, mvt 6).

*VANHAL (Wanhal, Wanhall, Vaňhal), Jan Křtitel (Johann Baptist)
12 May 1739, Nové Nechanice (Neu Nechaniz) - 26 Aug 1813, Vienna
JKV-1. [Serenade in E♭], 4 mvts.   fl 2ob 2hn 2bn..
MS parts: CZ-Pnm, XXXII.A.390, (missing titlepage; we assume that the title & attribution are derived from the old Clam Gallas catalog).   ★
JKV-2, 3. 2 Parthias in Dis [E♭]; each 5 mvts.   2cl 2hn bn.   MS parts: CZ-Pnm, XLII.E.325.   ★
JKV-4. Divertimento in C; 3 mvts.   2ob 2hn bn.
MS parts: CZ-Pnm, XLII.E.246.   ★
Pm (Eulenburg: Züruch & London, pn E.E.10007, 1971), ed. Hans Steinbeck, score & parts.
JKV-5. Divertimento in C; 4 mvts.   2ob 2hn bn.   MS parts: CZ-Pnm, XLII.E.247.   ★
JKV-6. Divertimento in C; 4 mvts.   2ob 2hn bn.   MS parts: CZ-Pnm, XLII.E.248.   ★
*JKV-7. Parthia N: 1mo; in E♭, 3 mvts.   2cl 2hn 2bn.
Pc (Breitkopf: Leipzig, c.1771), MS parts: UR-Ku, 1216054; CZ-Pu, mf637, (microfilm of UR-Ku MS).   ★
*JKV-8. Parthia N: 2; in E♭, 3 mvts.   2cl 2hn bn.
Pc (Breitkopf: Leipzig, c.1771), MS parts: UR-Ku, 1216054; CZ-Pu, mf637, (microfilm of UR-Ku MS).   ★
*JKV-9. Parthia N: 5; in E♭, 3 mvts.   2cl 2hn bn.
Pc (Breitkopf: Leipzig, c.1771), MS parts: UR-Ku, 1216054; CZ-Pu, mf637, (microfilm of UR-Ku MS); D-Rtt, Sammelband 8, Nos. 35 - 37, (for 2ob 2hn bn).   ★
*JKV-10. Parthia N: 4; in E♭, 3 mvts.   2cl 2hn bn.
Pc (Breitkopf: Leipzig, c.1771), MS parts: UR-Ku, 1216054; CZ-Pu, mf637, (microfilm of UR-Ku MS).   ★
*JKV-11. Parthia N: 6; in E♭, 3 mvts.   2cl 2hn bn.
Pc (Breitkopf: Leipzig, c.1771), MS parts: UR-Ku, 1216054; CZ-Pu, mf637, (microfilm of UR-Ku MS).   ★
*JVK-12. Parthia; in B♭, 3 mvts.   2cl 2hn bn.
MS parts: CZ-Pnm, XLII.F.36, No. 5; GB-Ljag, (modern MS score & parts).   ★
JVK-13. Trio [sic], in D; 3 mvts.   2fl 2hn basso.   MS parts: CZ-Bm(sz), A.272, (with an additional fl II pt).   ★
JKV-14.1. Divertimento; in G, 3 mvts.   fl 2hn bn.   MS parts: CZ-Bm(sz), A.124.   ★
JKV-14.2. Divertimento in G, 3 mvts.   ob 2hn bn.   MS parts: CZ-Bm(sz), A.122.   ★
JKV-1m, 2m. [2] March in C.   2fl 2cl(C) 2hn 2bn serp 2tp(clar) b-dr.
Pc (In **A-82.1m** Acht Märsche für Türkische Musick [sic], 1 Heft, Nos. 4 & 5:) (Johann André: Offenbach am Main, pn 1822, 1803), parts: H-KE, K 731/VIII.   ★
MS score & parts (copy of the André edition): I-Fc, F.P. S.553.
JKV-2.1m. March.   2cl 2hn 2bn.   MS parts: D-F, Mus. Hs.1172, No. 1, (?local arrangement).   ★
*JKV-1v. Pange lingua, in C.   SATB, 2cl/vl 2hn bn/(organ +vlne).
Pc (apud Ignatium Sauer: Viennæ [sic], pn 165, sd), RISM [V 288], parts: A-H; A-LA; A-Wgm, I 11479; A-Wst, (2 copies, including:) M 2222/c; CZ-Bm; CZ-Pnm, XVIII.B.126; GB-Ljag, (photocopy).
*JKV-2.1v. IV Brevis et faciles hymni [C, F, C, F] (I. O sacrum convivium, II. Da pacem Domine, III. Adjuva nos Deus, IV. O Salutaris hostia in honorem Sanctissimi Altaris Sacramenta).
SATB, 2cl(C)/vl 2hn bn/(organ, vlne).
Pc (apud Ignatium Sauer: Viennæ [sic], pn 166, sd), RISM [V 289], parts: A-M; A-TU; A-Wgm, I 11480; CZ-Pnm, (2 copies, including:) XVII.B.45.   ★
MS parts: A-Wn, (2 copies), Mus.Hs.2799, (Vienna "apud Ignatius Sauer"), Fond 5 MÖDLING 327, (as "Hymnen für den Frohnleichnahmstag [sic]"; incomplete: the Tenor & organ pts only; tenor pt dated 8 May 1891).; CZ-KV, B.197, (with additional basso & organ pts).
JKV-2.2v. Antiphonien pro Festo Corporis Christi.   CATB, 2cl 2hn bn.
MS parts: A-Wn, Mus.Hs.21,802, (the text "Quae coeli" replaces "O Salutaris hosta" in No. 4).
JKV-2.3v. [4] Antiphon.   CATB, 2cl(C) 2hn bn, (plus cl I vel Canto, cl II vel Alto).
MS parts: A-Wn, Mus.Hs.27,494, (with later parts for Soprano & keyed trumpet; the cl II vel Alto part has a later addition in the top left corner, "Flügelhorn"; with duplicate C & A parts). *As with JKV-2.2v, "O Salutaris hostia" in No. 4 has been replaced by the text "Quae coeli [here as "Qua Celi [sic]" although the Tenore & Canto parts also include the original setting (the Tenore part titled "Pass Tenor in Ersinlung [sic]") . A later set of Responsorien ("Ex hoc nunc et usque in Seculum" & "Qui fecit coelum et terram" have been added to all 4 hymns in all the vocal parts.*
JKV-3v. Libera me Domine; in C minor.   T/C solo, 2ob 2bn 2tp organ (+bc).
MS parts: CZ-PLa(cd), Hu 406.   ★
JKV-1mc(-4mc) (= **QYW-1m**). 4 Marches.   2cl 2hn 2bn.   MS parts: D-F, Mus.Hs.1170, (as by "W.").   ★

*VARÈSE, Edgard *22 Dec 1883, Paris - 6 Nov 1965, New York*
*EXV-1. Hyperprism, 1923. fl cl 3hn 2tp 2tp 7perc.
Pc (J. Curwen & Sons: London, 1924), score: GB-Lbl, g.727.e.(7).
Pm (Franco Colombo; Ricordi: Milano, 1961), score.
*EXV-2. Intégrales, 1925. 2pic ob 2cl hn 2tp(C,D) 3tb 4perc(17 instruments).
Pc (J. Curwen & Sons: London, pn 90794, 1926), miniature score.
Pm (Ricordi: New York, 1950), miniature score.
Pm (Franco Colombo; Ricordi: Milano & New York, pn COL7, 1980), revised & edited Chou Wen-Chung, score.

*VAUGHAN WILLIAMS, Ralph *12 Oct 1872, Down Ampney, UK - 26 Aug 1958, London*
*RWV-1e. Symphony No. 8 in D minor, mvt 2: Scherzo alla marcia. pic 2fl 2ob 2cl 2hn 2bn cbn(ad lib) 2tp 3tb.
Pm (Oxford University Press: London, pn 138 (complete symphony), 1956), score & parts.

VEIT, Václav Jindřich *(1810)*
VJV-1tv. Todtenaria. Lied in Es [E♭]. Bei der Leiche eines Vaters oder einer Mutter; "Lernt Kinden".
CATB, terz-fl cl 2hn bn. MS parts (by Josef Jentsch): CZ-LIa(je), No. 270 hud. ★

VELDEN, Renier van der *1910, Belgium*
RVV-1. Nocturne; 1985. fl ob ca 3cl 2hn bn cbn. MS score: B-Bcdm.

*VENTURINI, Francesco *c.1675, probably Brussels - 18 April 1745, Hanover*
*FYV-1(-3). Overture [Suites] à 6, Nos. 3 - 5; G minor, 5 mvts; E minor, 6 mvts; A minor, 4 mvts.
2ob hautcontre[obdam] taille 2bn.
MS (June 25, July 6, July 10, 1723): D-B, Mus.Ms.22305/2, ("No. 3"); 22305/6, ("No. 4"); 22305/4, ("No. 5"). ★
Pm (Ouverture in E minor only:) (Compusic: Amsterdam, pn 517, c.1994), score & parts.

*VERN, Auguste *(1780)*
*AXV-1. Nocturne in F; 4 mvts. fl 2cl(C) 2hn 2bn, (2ob cbn/serp tp tb ad lib).
MS parts ("Von Herrn Hauptmann v[on]. Vetter in anfang Janner [January] 1822 von Dischingen [sic] erhalten"):
D-Rtt, Sm.15, No. 62. ★
Pm (Phylloscopus Publications: Lancaster, Lancs, 1990), ed. C. & F. Nex, score & parts (cl pts in B♭).

*VERRALL, John Weedon *17 June 1908, Britt, Iowa*
JWV-1. Septet. fl ob 2cl hn 2bn.
Pm (Galaxy Music Corp: New York, 1966; reissued Highgate Press: New York, 1967), score & parts.
JWV-2. Serenata. 3cl a-cl bn.
Pm (Universal Edition: Vienna).

*VERSCHOOR, Onno *1965, Netherlands*
OXV-1. Oktet. 4ob 3bn cbn.
Pm (Compusic: Amsterdam, pn 518, c.1994), score & parts.

*VESELÝ (Wessely), R.P. Tadeáš (Tadeäs) *(1810)*
RTV-1v. Píseň Vánočni [Christmas song]. CAB, fl 2cl(C) 2tp(clar), tuba pastoralis, timp organ.
MS parts (from Rychov nad Kněžnou): CZ-Pnm, XVIII.F.14, (with a second organ part "organo senza
instrumenti", & with later duplicate parts: C, 2S, 3A 2B). *Two versions are present, the first with brass
accompaniment only, the second adding the fl & 2cl.* ★
RTV-1.1tv. Pjseň pokřebný [funeral song]. CATB, fl 2cl 2hn 2bn.
MS parts (by Jos. Neumann, Lukavice, 1845): CZ-Pnm, XVIII.F.12, (with later parts for cl(E♭ & tp). ★
RTV-1.2tv. Pjseň pokřebný. CATB, fl 2cl 2hn basso. MS pts (from Sadská): CZ-Pnm, XVIII.F.12, (with a
later set of parts, many of which have different instruments on the recto & verso: Flauto/Bass,
Clarinetto/Tromba[crossed out], Alto[viola]/Clarinetto 3, flug(B♭)/flug(E♭), Corno 1mo, Corno 2do, Tromba 1mo).

*VESQUE VON PÜTTINGEN, Johann Evangelist *(pseudonym: J Hoven)*
23 July 1803, Opole, Poland - 30 Oct 1883, Vienna
JEV-1v. Graduale, Nr 1: Felix es. SATB, 2ob/cl(C) 2bn.
MS score & parts (1852): A-Wn, HK 1192, (with 5 sets of vocal parts). ★

VIBERT, Mathieu *1920, Switzerland*
MXB-1. Intrada; 1979. 2fl 2ob ca 2cl 4hn 2bn 2tp tb. In MS: CH-Nf will assist in contacting the composer.

VICTORINI, Victorino Nepomuceno, de Lumenstein, Eccl. *(1740)*
VNV-1v. Hymnus Dulcior Saccaro. Jesu dulcil Memoria. CA, 2fl 2vla organ.
MS parts (c.1765): CZ-BR, sign. 395. ★

*VIGNALI, Gabriele
GXV-1a. Un Libro Solo Canzone Della B[eati]. V[irgine]. di S^n Lucca. 2fl 2cl(C) 2hn bn vc.
MS parts: I-Bl, S.G.-H 104. *An instrumental version, probably by the composer, of GXV-3v.*
GXV-1v. Alle Piaghe [i.e., Piaghe adorate]. TTB, 2ob 2cl(C) 2hn bn. AutoMS score: I-Bl, KK 301. ★
GXV-2v. Cantata - In occasione d'un Pranz data de Sua Emea Il Sig^r Card[ina]le Giovannetti alli Sig Sig^r
Missinoarj [sic]; "Al mirati in mezzo assiso". Solo & tutti TTB, 2ob 2cl(C) 2hn bn..
AutoMS score: I-Bl, KK 300. ★
*GXV-3v. Canzone Della B[eata] V[irgine] di S. Luc[c]a; "O bella mia speranza". TTB, 2ob 2cl(C) 2hn bn.
AutoMS score: I-Bl, KK 300. ★

VINTER, Gilbert *1909, ?Lincoln - 10 Oct 1969, Cornwall*
GYV-1. Dance of the Marionettes; 1956. fl fl(pic) ob(ca) 2cl bn.
Pm (Hawkes & Son, now Boosey & Hawkes: London, pn B&H 19134, 1963), score & parts.

*VITÁSEK (Witasek, Wittisek), Jan (Matyáš Nepomuk August) *22 Feb 1770, Hořín, - 7 Dec 1839, Prague*
*JMV-1. Quintet; in E♭, 7 mvts. 2cl 2hn bn. MS parts (by Havel, 9 June 1813): CZ-KRa, A4483/R.I.53. ★
JMV-1m, 2m. 2 Aufzüge Märsche. Winds & perc. MS: D-Bds, Mus.Ms.23209.
*JMV-1mv. Marsch mit Gesang, und als Kriegslied mit demselben Text, der Landwehrein den k:k: Oesterreichischen Sta[a]ten gewidmet. "Wzhuru Českj! podme smĕle, na hrdeho nepřitele."
Voice, 2pic 2cl(C) 2hn 2bn serp 2tp(clar) b-dr s-dr.
Pc (Im Verlage der Polt'schen Musikalienhandlung: Prag [Prague], sd), parts: CZ-Pnm, XX.F.1. ★
The march is in two sections: Marcia Vivace, 2/4, & Allegro, 2/4; the text is the same for each section. The parts are printed two to a large folio sheet (on one side only) and were intended to be cut into oblong quarto; the CZ-Pnm copy is uncut. The title page bears the note, "Anmerkung: das übrigen bei der militairischen Musick gebrächlichen Instrumente, richten sich nach den Hauptschlägen der grossen Trom[m]el". JMV-1m & 2m may be the same work without the voice part.
JMV-1v. Cantate. CATB, fl 2cl(C) 2hn 2bn 2tp(clar) tp(prin) timp.
MS parts (29 August 1839): CZ-Pu, 59 R 935. ★
JMV-2v. Pjseň Swatodussnj pro Zpĕw. CATB, 2cl 2hn 2bn 2tp cb timp organ.
MS parts: CZ-Pnm, XVII.B.77. ★
JMV-3.1v. Pjseň na weliký pátek při nessenj welebné swátosti Oltářny do Božjho hrobu.
CATB, 2cl 2hn 2bn 2tp.   MS parts: CZ-Pnm, (2 copies), XVIII.C.27, (by Ignaz Kulka, Česka Třeboň). ★
JMV-3.2v. Pjseň na weliký pátek. CATB, 2cl 2hn 2bn 2tp.   MS parts: CZ-Pnm, XXX.C.10. ★
JMV-4. Graduale in G ["Timete Deum omnes"]. CCATB, fl 2cl(A) 2hn bn.
MS parts (from Žleby nr Čáslav): CZ-Pnm, XVII.B.140. ★
JMV-5.1v. Graduale [Ave Maria] in B♭. CATB, 2cl 2hn 2bn.
MS parts: CZ-Bm(rj), A.13.121, (copied 1829, performed 15 August 1829, 24 March 1830, 8 December 1831); CZ-Pnm, (9 copies), XVII.B.82, (by Petter, Česká Třebová; František Křepelka, Plzeň; Wenc. Heidelberg, Příbram; [Anon], Střebsko; Wenzel Wawra [Vavra], Kostelec nad Labem, 1839; Kautzky, Žleby; O. Horník, 1900), III.C.195 (without provenance), XXIX.D.182 (without provenance). *A further, late, copy, for SATB, 2cl 2cl 2hn bn organ is at CZ-Pnm, III.B.69.* ★
JMV-5.2v. Ave Maria; in B♭. SATB, 2cl 2hn 2bn organ.
MS parts: CZ-Pnm, XLVII.E.14, No. 2, (missing organ).
JMV-5.3v. Graduale [in] B[♭]; "Ave Maria" with Czech text. CATB, fl 2cl 2hn keyed-tp b-tb.
MS parts (by Václav Kalenda): CZ-Pu, 59-R-1659, (Hummel's name has been incorrectly entered & crossed out; although the titlepage states "Possaunen [sic]", there is only one b-tb part, marked "Possaune [sic]").
JMV-5.4v. Zdrawas Maria in B[♭]. CATB, 2cl 2hn bn.
MS parts: CZ-BR, (2 copies), sign. 434, (MS by Antonín Horetsky and others, c.1820), sign. 512, (MS by Bedřich Porth, učitel, 14 Feb 1869); CZ-Pnm, (3 copies), XII.F.84 (copy by Ján Michalička, Kunvald, 1817, as "Zdrawas Marya a Otče náš"), III.E.150 (Latin text), XVI.E.164, (Latin text, copy by W. Bullirž).
JMV-6v. Terzetto. CTB, 2cl 2hn 2bn.
MS parts (by F. Krzepelka, Plzeň): CZ-Pnm, XVII.B.78.
JMV-7v. Ave Maria. SATTBB, 2cl 2hn 2bn. MS: A-TU, Ms. 401, (performed 1842/43).
JMV-8v. Salve Regina in B[♭]. CATB, 2cl 2hn bn. MS parts ("Hyan m.p. 1827"): CZ-Pla(bl), Hu 36. ★
JMV-9v. Ecce Sacerdos magnus. CATB, 2cl 2hn bn. MS parts: CZ-BR, (MS by Horetzky, 1818); CZ-Pnm, XXXVIII.F.511/c; CZ-SO, sign. 698, (MS by Jan Schlesinger, with the text, "Gegrusset seyst du Maria"). ★
JMV-1tv. Grablied; "Leutes Aechzen hohles banges Strönen", (Text by Ant. Kinzl, "bischöfl. Bezirks Vicar S.D. Aufseher Consistorialrath und Pfarrer zu Dlaschkowitz [sic]"). CATB, 2fl cl(E♭) 2cl(B♭) 2hn 2tp flug b-tb.
MS parts (by Jos. Patzelt): CZ-Lla(je), No. 190 hud. ★

*VITSKA (Witschka, Witska, Witzka), Carl (Karl) Bonaventura *1768 - 1848*
CBV-1v. [10] Lateinische Lÿtanei zum Gebrauche in der Bittwoche und monatlichen Prozession, Op. 53.
SATB, 2cl(C) 2hn tb/bn.
Pc (August Böhm: Augsburg, pn 1975, c.1820), parts: CZ-Pnm, XLIII.F.10. ★
AutoMS score (No. 1, Kyrie only): A-KR, H 134/52, 53, (scored for SATB, 2cl 2hn 2tb).
KBW-2v. Graduale "Beatam me dicent"; in E. CATB choir, 4hn 2bn. AutoMS score: A-KR, H 134/12. ★
KBW-3v. Graduale "Exaltabo Domine"; in C. CATB choir, 4hn 2bn. MS score: A-KR, H 134/11. ★

VIVALDI, Antonio *1678 - 1741*
ANV-1. Concerto; in F, RV 97 (Pincherle S.286; Fanna XII, 32; Rinaldi Op. 25, No. 1); 4 mvts.
Viola d'amore, 2ob 2hn bn bc.
AutoMS score: I-Tn, Foà vol. 29, ff. 272 - 292. ★
Pm (Ricordi: Milan), ed. Malpiero.

*VLAD, Roman *29 Dec 1919, Cernowitz (now Cernăuţi), Romania*
RYV-1. Serenata, 1959. fl 2ob 2cl 2hn 2bn 2va celeste.
Pm (Suvini-Zerboni: Milano, pn S.5654Z., 1963), score & parts.

*VLIJMEN, Jan Van *11 Oct 1935, Rotterdam*
JVV-1. Per diciasette; 1968. 3fl 3ob 2cl t-sax 4hn 4bn.
Pm (Donemus: Amsterdam, 1971), score.
JVV-2. Serenata 1; 1964-67. 2fl 2ob 2cl 2hn 2bn 2tb perc.
Pm (Donemus: Amsterdam, c.1971), score.

VOBROVSKÝ (Wobrovski), František *(?1760 - 1770)*
FAV-1. Parthia Pastorella; in C, 4 mvts. 2ob 2hn bn.
MS parts (pre-1800): CZ-Bm(au), A.20.925, (missing bn). ★

*VÖLKEL, Franz
FQV-1v. Pangelingua [sic]. CATB, 2cl 2hn 2bn tp(prin) timp organ(full part with bc-fig).
MS parts (by Fügerl): A-Wn, Mus.Hs.635, (with a later duplicate Canto part). ★
FQV-1.1tv. Trauer Lied ex Es [Eb], "Nun da ist die feyerliche Stunde". SATB, 2cl 2hn bn.
MS parts: A-GE, I 320. ★
FQV-1.2tv. Trauer Lied ex E(b), Für Erwachsene, "Wenn da ist die feyerliche Stunde"
MS parts: A-GE, I 329. *The music is the same as FQV-1.1tv.*

VOERT, Georg ter *1951, Germany*
GTV-1. Choral con Chorus. 4ob 2ca 4bn 2cbn.
Pm (self-published: sl, sd).

*VOGEL, Kajetan (Cajetan) *Pater (1750) Konojedy, nr Litoměřice - 27 Aug 1794, Prague*
KXV-1. Parthia in Dis [Eb] - Authore Vogel; 5 mvts. 2cl 2hn bn.
MS parts (by Dominik Hübner, Langenbruck): CZ-Pu(dm), 59 R 3337; (with an additional violin II part, in fact a transcribed clarinet II part). *The wind parts all bear the headtitle, "Parthia von Pleyel"; the vl II part bears the headtitle, "Sonata von Vogel". We believe that this work is, in fact, by Kajetan Vogel.* ★
KXV-1v. Litaniae Laurentanae ex B[b]. CATB, 3vl 2cl 2hn organ(bc).
MS parts (by Jan Augustin Fibiger, c.1815): CZ-BA, 142 (47-396).
KXV-1a. Kozeluch: Parthia in F, (2fl 2cl 2hn 2bn) as "Cassazion [sic],…angeschafft für braunschweigische Musikgesellschaft 1796 durch aldefeld". fl 2cl 2hn 2bn 2vla. MS: D-W, Ms.Vogel 141.
*KXV-2a. Mozart: Le Nozze di Figaro, sinfonia, (Act I) 8 mvts, (Act II) 5 mvts (including a 9-section Finale), (Act III) 8 mvts, (Act IV) 5 mvts (including a 6-section Finale). 2ob 2cl 2hn 2bn *or* 2cl 2hn 2bn.
Pc (Balzer: Vienna, 1787), parts: CZ-Pnm, XX.F.20, (missing Acts I/II: ob I, hn I & I; Acts III/IV: all but cl II).
*KXV-3a. Mozart: Don Giovanni, overture, (Act I) 7 mvts, (Act II) 10 mvts. 2cl 2hn 2bn.
MS parts: CZ-Pnm, XLII.E.365, (as by "P[ater]. Vogel").
*KXV-4a. Mozart: Così fan tutte, Act II, 12 mvts. 2ob 2cl 2hn 2bn. MS parts: CZ-Pnm, XX.F.21, (as Anon).

*VOGLER, Georg Joseph, *Abbé 15 June 1749, Pleichach, nr Würzburg - 6 May 1814, Darmstadt*
GJV-1v. Hessische Vater unser; "Vater unser beten wir!". SATB, 2fl 2ob 2cl 2hn 2bn cbn a-tb t-tb b-tb.
MS score & parts: D-DS, Mus.ms.1151 & 1151/a, (the flutes and oboes play in unison throughout; with an additional Corni Bassi part and duplicate vocal parts: S(11) A(9) T(8) B(10, 2bn(2); a note has been added in another hand, "Hessische Vater unser auf / den nahmlichen Melodie wie das Bairische [sic: Bayerische] / Vater Unser welches sich im Polymelos / von Abbé Vogler. Nro 3. befindet."). ★
GJV-2v. Auf unserm besten König. SATB, 2ob 2cl 2hn 2bn. AutoMS Score: D-Mbs, Mus.Mss.1710. ★
GJV-3v. Dixit Dominus. SATB, 2fl 2hn 2tp timp. AutoMS score: D-Bds, Mus.ms.auto.G.F.Vogler 2.
GJV-4.1v. Veni Sancte Spiritus; in Bb. SATB, 2ob/cl 2hn 2bn organ.
MS parts: D-HR, (2 copies), HR III 4 1/2 2° 567 (with cl parts on the reverse of the ob parts, c.1790), HR III 1/2 2° 248 (without alternate cl parts, c.1800). ★
Pm (KGS), fiche (2619, 2077).
GJV-4.2v. Veni Sancte Spiritus; in Bb. CATB, 2cl 2hn 2bn organ. MS parts (1799): D-Tl, B 110.
Note: the score, published by André: Offenbach, pn 3705, 1817, (RISM AI / V 2375) in a setting for CATB, 2cl 4hn 2bn 2vl is possibly a later rescoring by Vogler. ★

*VOGNER, František (Franz) *teacher in Litomyšl, active c.1881*
Vogner's funeral songs appear in Roman Nejedlý's 12 Pohřebních Písní. Pc (Ant. Kindl: Brno, 1881), parts.
FNV-1tv (= RZN-1.4tv). Uložme k spánku. S/T,A/T,B, 2cl 2hn basso
FNV-2tv (= RZN-1.6tv). Kynul Pán (Mládenci neb panně) [for funerals of youths or virgins].
S/T,A/T,B, 2cl 2hn basso.
FNV-3tv (= RZN-1.7tv). Slze bolné (U hrobu) [for performance at the grave]. SAB, 2cl 2hn basso.

*VOGT, Gustave *18 March 1781, Strasbourg - 3 June 1870, Paris*
*GUV-1. Sérénade [or rather, a potpourri] Dédiée à S.A.R. Le Duc de Berry Et arrangée à l'occasion du Mariage de S.A.R. 2fl 2cl 2hn 2tp.
Pc (Chez J. Frey: Paris, c.1816), parts: F-Pn, Vm27 4288, (2 copies). ★
GUV-2. Prière [Album Leaf for Alfred de Bezuchesne; complete composition]. 3ob.
AutoMS score (25 Oct 1838): F-Pn, W. 24,54, pp. 107 - 108. ★
GUV-3. Adagio religioso, Trio. 2ob ca, *or* 2cl a-sax.
Pc (Richault & Cie: Paris, pn R. 19488, 1893), parts: F-Pn, Vm7 12.011. ★
GUV-1a. Spontini: Fernand Cortez, Serenades en Harmonie, [MS: 1, 2] Livraison [continuous works].
2fl 2ob(2ca)/2cl(ripieno) 2cl(C) 2bthn 2hn 2bn 2tp tb serp timp b-dr+cym tri.
Pc (Mlles. Erard: Paris, pn 869 [both livraisons], 1819), CH-Gpu, Ib.4860, 4861.
MS parts: D-Rtt, Sammelbend 13, Nr. 38, (Suite 1 only).

VOGT, Hans *14 May 1911, Danzig (now Gdansk) - 19 May 1992*
HYV-1. Concertino. Piano, fl ob 2cl 2hn 2bn tp perc.
Pm (Bärenreiter: Kassel).

*VOJÁČEK (Wojáček, Wolacek), Hynek (Ignác František) *4 Dec 1825, Zlín - 9 Nov 1916, St Petersburg*
HXV-1. An die Zukunft!; (Intro & 5 Waltzes), 1843. cl(D) 2cl(A) 2hn 2bn cbn 2tp tb.
AutoMS parts: CZ-Bm(au), A.20.286. ★
HXV-2, 3. Ein Jux, Jux-walzer & Schon wieder ein Jux!, [Walzer], 1845. 2ob 2cl 2hn bn cbn 2tp tb.
MS parts: CZ-Bm(au), A.20.283. ★
HXV-4. Uvítání vesny; 2 mvts. fl ob 2cl 2hn 2bn cbn 2tp tb. MS parts: CZ-Bm(au), A.20.277. ★
HXV-5. Kuhreigen, Nocturne pastorale. fl 2ob cl(Eb) 2cl 2hn bn cbn 4tp(C, D) tb.
MS parts (1843): CZ-Bm(au), A.20.930, No. 2. (missing ob I, tp(D) I). ★

HXV-1a. Bellini: I Puritani, duetto. 2ob 2cl 2hn 2bn 2tp tb bassi. MS parts (1844): CZ-Bm(au), A.20.284.
HXV-2a. Diabelli: (unidentified) overture. fl ob 2cl 2hn bn cbn 2tp tb(2). MS pts (1844): CZ-Bm(au), A.20.282.
HXV-3a. Donizetti: L'Elixir d'Amore, potpourri. fl 2ob 2cl 2hn bn cbn 2tp tb. MS pts: CZ-Bm(au), A.20.292.
HXV-4a. Donizetti: La Fille du régiment, 3 mvts. fl 2ob 2cl 2hn 2bn cbn small-drum.
MS parts (1844): CZ-Bm(au), A.20.293.
HXV-5a. Meyerbeer: Les Huguenots, cavatina. fl 2ob 2cl 2hn bn cbn 4tp(C, D) tb.
MS parts (1843): CZ-Bm(au), A.20.930, (missing ob I, tp(D) I).
HXV-6a. Mozart: Così fan tutte, 1 mvt. 2ob 2cl 2hn 2bn cbn 2tp. MS pts: CZ-Bm(au), A.20.281, (missing cbn).
HXV-7a. Titl: Der Zauberschleier, 2tes Potpourri. fl 2ob 2cl(A) 2hn bn cbn 2tp tb.
MS parts (Jan 1844): CZ-Bm(au), A.20.929, (missing ob II, cl II, tp I).
HXV-8a. Titl: Der Totentanz, Ouverture aus dem Ballet. Incomplete, here only: 2ob 2cl.
MS parts (March 1844): CZ-Bm(au), A.20.928.
HXV-9.1a, 9.2a. [Reissiger: Danses Brillantes, Op. 26, No. 5, here attributed to C.M. Weber as "Das
Herzenload"] & Lortzing: Zar und Zimmermann, Aarie [sic], "Sanft spielt ich". fl(E♭) 2cl 2bn 2tp basso.
MS parts (1844): CZ-Bm, A.20.291.

*VOLÁNEK (Wollanek), Antonín (Anton) Josef Alois *1761 - 1817*
AAV-1(-4). [4] Trios; I: in C, 4 mvts; II: in F, 4 mvts; III: in F, 4 mvts; IV: in F, 5 mvts. 3bthn.
MS parts: PL-LA, RM 53 - 56. ★
AAV-1v. Pange lingua; in D. CATB, 2cl(A) 2hn 2bn 2tp(clar) timp organ.
MS parts (by Ferschmann): CZ-BR, sign. 439. ★
AAV-1a. Dittersdorf: Hieronimus Knicker, 13 mvts. 2cl 2hn bn. MS parts: CZ-Pnm, XLII.E.359.

*VOLÁNEK (Vollanek), Ignace
IXV-1. Nro VI M[arcia]: Turca[,] Contra Tanze [sic] et Marché [sic] ex F.
pic 2fl/flautino 2cl 2hn bn tp(prin) "virbel et Bom[ba]" (= t-dr b-dr). MS parts: CZ-Pnm, XXXII.E.64. ★

*VOLANS, Kevin *26 July 1949, Pietemaritzburg, South Africa*
*KYV-1. Concerto for Piano and Wind Instruments; 1995.
Solo piano, 3fl[fl II(pic)] 3ob 3cl(+E cl♭) 4hn 2bn cbn 2tp 3tb tu 3db 2perc.
Pm (Chester Music: London, 1996), hire score & parts.
KYV-2. Leaping Dance; 1984, transcribed 1995. fl ob(ca) 2cl 2bthn 2hn 2bn.
Pm (Chester Music: London, 1995), hire score & parts.

*VOLCKE, F. *(1790)*
XYV-1m. Musique militaire, Cahier 1; 6 mvts. fl(E♭) 2cl(E♭) 4cl(B♭) 2hn 2bn 2tp 2b-tb serp b-dr s-dr.
Pc (chez B. Schott fils: Mayence, pn 1538, 1822/23), parts: D-MZsch. ★
XYV-2m. [5 pieces, probably from one of the Schott Cahiers other than No. 1].
fl(E♭) 2cl(E♭) 4cl(B♭) 2hn 2bn 2tp 2tb serp b-dr s-dr.
MS parts: D-DT, Mus-n 2049, Nos. 1- 5, (Nos. 6 & 7 are by Küffner). ★

*VOLEDY, ( ) *(?1740)*
XZV-1. Parthia Ex F, 4 mvts. 2ob 2hn bn. MS parts: CZ-Pnm, XXXII.A.593. ★

*VOLKERT (Folgert), František Jan *4 Feb 1767, Friedlant (Frýdlant) - 12 March 1831, Králová*
FZV-1. Pastorella in B[♭] 2cl hn 2bn, tuba pastoralis. MS parts: CZ-KRa, A4171/IV.B.149. ★
*FZV-2. Echo und Rusische Arie. 2cl 2hn 2bn.
MS parts (by Havel): CZ-KRa, A3981/IV.B.151. ★
FZV-3. [6] Variationen [& Coda] in Dis [E♭]. 2cl 2hn 2bn.
MS parts: CZ-KRa, A3980/IV.B.148. ★
FZV-4. [7] Variationen [on a song from Haibel's *Tiroler Vastel].* 2cl 2hn 2bn.
MS parts: CZ-KRa, A4172/IV.B.150. ★
FZV-1v. Statio pro festo Corporis Christi. SATB, 2cl(C) 2hn 2bn.
MS parts: CZ-Pu, 59 R 1689. (with duplicate copies of vocal parts: 2S, 4A, 1T, 1B). ★

VOMÁČKA, Boleslav *28 June 1887, Mlada Boleslav - 1 March 1965, Prague*
BXV-1. Nonett, Op. 64. fl 2ob 2cl 2hn 2bn.
Pm (Český hudební fond: Prague, 1957), score & parts.

VOORN, Joop *16 Oct 1932, The Hague*
JXV-1. Symphony; 1981. 2fl 2ob 2cl 4hn 2bn db.
Pm (Donemus: Amsterdam, c.1982), score & parts.
JXV-2. Sucevita Chorals; 1974. 2ob 2cl b-cl bn.
Pm (Donemus: Amsterdam, 1975), score & parts.

*VOORTMAN, Roland *22 July 1953, Amsterdam*
RXV-1. Reminiscentie II. 2fl 2ob 2cl 2hn 2bn.
Pm (Donemus: Amsterdam, 1977), score & parts.
RXV-1v. Faustus (after Marlowe). M, chorus, 2fl(pic) 2ob(ca) 2cl(b-cl) 2hn 2bn(cbn).
Pm (Donemus: Amsterdam, 1982), score & parts.
RXV-2v. Abend. Contralto, 2fl ob ca cl b-cl 2hn 2bn.
Pm (Donemus: Amsterdam, 1982), score & parts.

*VOSTŘÁK, Zbyněk *10 June 1920, Prague - 4 Aug 1985, Strakonice*
ZBV-1. Krystalizace (Crystallisation), Op. 28; 1962. fl ob ca cl 2hn bn cbn 2tp 2tb.
MS score: (untraced; Český hudební fond: Prague?).

VRANKEN, Jaap *16 April 1897, Utrecht - 20 April 1956, The Hague*
JYV-1. Konzertierende Musik. Solo cello, 2fl 2ob 2cl 2hn bn tp tb.
Pm (Donemus: Amsterdam, 1938), score.

VRATNÝ (Wratni), J. *(?1780/1790)*
JQV-1a. March von Messano (possibly based on B.A. Weber's *Die Braut von Messina*). 2cl 2hn 2bn tp.
MS parts: D-DS, Mus.ms.1223/15. ★

*VRBA (Werba, Wrba), ( ) *(1770)*
YXV-1. Parthia in B[♭]; 4 mvts. 2cl 2hn bn.
MS parts (by Domink Hübner, Langenbruck): CZ-Pu, 59 R 3357, No. 1. ★
YXV-2(-10). [9 sets of] Pièces d'Harmonie; (B♭, 5 mvts; E♭, 4 mvts; E♭, 4 mvts; E♭, 6 mvts; B♭, 4 mvts; E♭, 4 mvts; E♭, 5 mvts; E♭, 4 mvts; E♭, 4 mvts). 2cl 2hn 2bn, (Sets 5 - 7: 2cl 2hn bn).
MS parts: RF-Ssc, Ф 891 собр юосуповъix N45, pp. 1 - 75, (Set 1 missing all but cl I). ★
YXV-11(-15). [5 sets of] Pièces d'Harmonie; (all E♭; 5, 4, 5, 4, 4 mvts). 2cl 2hn bn(Sets 1 & 4)/2bn(2, 3, 5).
MS parts: RF-Ssc, Ф 891 собр юосуповъix N46, pp. 2 - 40. *Set 2 headtitle, "Del S. Nicolai".* ★
QXW-1v. Messe in C. CATB, 2cl 2hn bn organ. MS parts: CZ-KV, B.275.

*VYCPÁLEK, Ladislav *23 Feb 1882, Prague - 9 Jan 1969, Prague*
LXV-1v. Tuláci ("Vagabonds", "Ramblers"), Op. 10, 1914. TTBB chorus, fl ob ca 2cl 2bn.
Pm (Artia: Prague), score & parts.

W., ( ), *1st of this pseudonym* **(? Vanhal)**
QYW-1m. 4 Marsch [sic]; (B♭, C, C, C; all tempi: ¢). 2cl 2hn 2bn. MS parts: D-F, Mus.Hs.1170. ★

W., ( ), *2nd of this pseudonym*
BZW-1a. Lindpaintner: Abrahams Opfer, overture. terz-fl cl(E♭) 3cl(B♭) 2hn 2bn 2tp serp+b-tb b-dr+s-dr.
MS score (post-1817): D-Tl, Z 87. *The wrapper bears the crossed-out title, "Ouverture v: Schmidt", & may indicate that Georg Schmitt was the arranger.*

WAGENAAR, Johan *1 Nov 1862, Utrecht - 17 June 1951, The Hague*
AJW-1. Kanon [double canon at the fourth). 2ob 2ca.
Pm (Karthause-Schmülling Verlag: Kamen, pn K 0079, sd), score & parts.

WAGENER, Heinrich *1930, Germany*
HER-1. Paraphrase über das liturgische Pater noster, Op. 13. 2ob cl bn organ.
Pm (Deutscher Tonkünstlerverband e.V.: München, 1978).

*WAGENSEIL (Vagenseil), Georg Christian (Christoph) *29 Jan 1715, Vienna - 1 March 1777, Vienna*
*GCW-1.1. Suite des Pièces in Es [E♭]; 4 mvts. 2cl 2hn 2bn fortepiano. MS parts: D-SWl, Mus. 5603. ★
*GCW-1.2. Divertimento in F; 4 mvts. 2ob 2ca 2hn 2bn.
MS parts: A-Wgm, VIII 8540 (Q 16423). ★
Pm (WINDS: Northridge, CA, pn W-1, c.1981), photocopy of original parts.
*GCW-2.1. Suite des Pièces, in E♭, 8 mvts. 2cl 2hn 2bn fortepiano.
MS parts: D-SWl, Mus. 5602; CZ-Pnm, XL.F.281, (4 mvts). ★
*GCW-2.2. Divertimento in F; 7 mvts. 2ob 2ca 2hn 2bn.
MS parts: A-Wgm, VIII 8540 (Q 16423), (mvts 5 - 7 are, in fact, mvts 1 - 3 of GCW-5). ★
Pm (WINDS: Northridge, CA, pn W-76, c.1981), parts.
*GCW-3.1. Suite des Pièces in B[♭]; 4 mvts. 2cl 2hn 2bn fortepiano. MS parts: D-SWl, Mus. 5606. ★
*GCW-3.2. Parthia in C; 6 mvts. 2ob 2ca 2hn 2bn.
MS parts: A-Wgm, VIII 8540 (Q 16423), (omits mvt 3; with 3 additional mvts). ★
Pm (Eulenburg: London, pn GM 884, 1978), ed. Kurt Janetzky, parts, (with an alternative of flutes for oboes).
Pm (WINDS: Northridge, CA, pn W-78, c.1981), parts.
GCW-4. Suite des Pièces in B[♭]; 4 mvts. 2cl 2hn 2bn fortepiano. MS parts: D-SWl, Mus. 5604. ★
GCW-5. Suite des Pièces in B[♭]; 7 mvts. 2cl 2hn 2bn fortepiano. MS pts: D-SWl, Mus. 5605. *cf. GCW-2.2.* ★

WAGMANN, ( ) *active 1st quarter of the 19th cetury, ?Wertheim am Main*
XAW-1. [Parthia in F, 6 mvts]. 2cl 2hn 2bn. MS parts: GB-Ljag(w), (old No. 375). ★

*WAGNER, ( ) *(?oboist/composer Jacob Karl Wagner, 22 Feb 1772, Darmstadt - 25 Nov 1822, Darmstadt)*
ZXW-1m. Militärmusik in F. Instrumentation unknown.
Pc (Schott: Mainz, sd), liv. 1, parts: D-MZsch.

*WAGNER, (Wilhelm) Richard *22 May 1813, Leipzig - 13 Feb 1883, Venice*
RW: Richard Wagners Werke. (Breitkopf & Härtel: Leipzig, Berlin, 1912 - 1923), ed. Michael Balling.
SW: Sämtliche Werke in Verbindung mit der Bayerischen Akademie der Schönen Künste, München. (B. Schott's Söhne: Mainz, 1970, etc.), ed. Carl Dahlhaus.
*WRW-1m. Huldigungs-Marsch, (RWV 97).
2p-fl 4fl 23cl b-cl 8hn 2bn 12tp 3flug 3a-hn 2t-hn 2bar-hn 6tb 6b-tb timp b-dr s-dr cym tri.
Pc (Bei B. Schott's Söhnen: Mainz, pn 24979, 1871, reissued c.1890), score: D-Bds, Mus.10779; D-MSsch. ★
Pc (E. Eulenberg: Leipzig, 1910), score, (kleine Orchester-Partitur-Ausgabe. Verschiedene Werke. No. 813).
*WRW-1t. Trauersinfonie zur feierlichen Beisetzung der Asche Carl Maria von Weber's . . . nach Melodien der Euryanthe arrangirt; (RWV 73). 5fl 7ob 20cl 14hn 10bn 6tp 9tb 4b-tb 6dr(muffled).
AutoMS score: D-Bds, Mus.Ms.Auto.R.Wagner 3. ★
Pm (SW, Bd. 18, II), score.

*WAILLY, Louis Auguste Paul Warnier de *16 May 1855, Amiens - 18 June 1933, Badoux*
LDW-1. Octet, Op. 22. fl ob 2cl hn 2bn tp.
Pc (Salabert: Paris).
Pc (Rouart Lerolle & Cie.: Paris, 1905), score & parts, (mvt 2 only): F-Pn.

*WALCH, Johann Heinrich *1776 - 2 Oct 1855, Gotha*
Here **PhilSoc** *stands for the Philharmonic Society of Bethlehem collection (which must be specified in all requests to US-BETm). We have no locations for:* 3 Marches *(fl 2ob 2cl 2bn tp serp, Breitkopf & Härtel, 1809).*
JHW-1. Pièces d'Harmonie, Liv. 1; 12 mvts. pic(Eb) cl(Eb) 3cl(Bb) 4hn(Eb, Bb) 2bn 2tp a-tb t-tb b-tb serp b-dr(+cym) s-dr; *or* pic cl(Eb) 2cl(Bb) 2hn(Eb) 2bn tp b-tb/serp.
Pc (C.F. Peters: Leipzig, pn 1455, 1818), parts: US-BETm, PhilSoc PSB Add 4. ★
MS parts: D-Rtt, Sm. 14, Nos. 13 - 24. *The titlepage is incorrectly copied from Liv. 2 (see infra).*
JHW-2. Pièces d'Harmonie, Liv. 2; 7 mvts. pic(Eb) cl(Eb) 3cl(Bb) 4hn(Eb, Ab) 2bn 2tp sig-hn a-tb t-tb b-tb serp b-dr s-dr; *or* pic cl(Eb) 2cl(Bb) 2hn(Eb) 2bn tp b-tb/serp.
Pc (C.F. Peters: Leipzig, pn 1488, 1818), pts: US-BETm, (2 copies), PhilSoc PSB L-2. *The sig-hn & 2hn(Ab) are tacet in the long (unnumbered) opening piece which includes a theme & 12 variations. One copy bears the printed slip, "Zu haben in August Cranz Musikhandlung in der grossen Reichenstrasse in Hamburg."* ★
MS parts: D-Rtt, Sm. 14, Nos. 7 - 12, (Nos. 1 - 6; omits unnumbered theme & variations).
JHW-3. Pièces d'Harmonie, Liv. 3; 12 mvts. terz-fl(F, fl in Eb, No. 8 in C) cl(Eb) 2cl(Bb) 2hn bn(I) bn(II)+serp 2tp/(2tp, Nos. 4, 6, 9; + signal-horn, Nos. 6 & 8) b-tb b-dr+cym.
Pc (C.F. Peters: Leipzig, pn 1610, 1820), parts: D-DT, Mus-n 2055. ★
*JHW-4. Pièces d'Harmonie, Liv. 4; 12 mvts. pic(Eb) cl(Eb) 3cl(Bb) 2hn 2bn serp 2tp sig-hn a-tb t-tb b-tb b-dr(+cym) s-dr tri.
Pc (C.F. Peters: Leipzig, pn 1672, 1820), parts: D-Rtt, Walch 2, (with MS parts for 2ob, essentially ripieno); US-BETm, PhilSoc PSB L-3. *The signal horn part is marked "Cor de Signale e Triangolo"; with Nos. 2, 4 - 6, 8 - 11 tacet; No. 12 is a triangle part only. One copy bears the printed slip, "Zu haben in August Cranz Musikhandlung in der grossen Reichenstrasse in Hamburg."* ★
JHW-5. Pièces d'Harmonie, Liv. 5; 12 mvts.
flautino(Eb) cl(Eb) 3cl(Bb) 2hn 2bn tp signal-hn(Ab, Nos. 3 & 4 only) a-tb t-tb b-tb serp b-dr s-dr.
Pc (C.F. Peters: Leipzig, pn 1751, 1825), parts: D-Rtt, Walch 1, (with MS parts for 2ob, essentially ripieno); GB-Ljag(w), (missing perc pts); US-BETm, (2 copies), PhilSoc PSB L-4. ★
*JHW-6. Pièces d'Harmonie, Liv. 6; 12 mvts.
fl(Eb) cl(Eb) 3cl(Bb) 2hn 2bn 2tp signal-horn(Nos. 2 - 4 & 11 only) a-tb t-tb b-tb serp b-dr s-dr t-dr.
Pc (C.F. Peters: Leipzig, pn 1814, 1826), pts: US-BETm, (2 copies), PhilSoc PSB L-5. *The terz-fl is used in Nos. 1 - 3 & 11; the Klappenhorn (signal horn) part bears the note, "Jn [sic] Ermanglung eines Klappenhorns, werden die in der 1ten Clarinetto angemerkten kleinen Noten gespielt." The tambour petit is replaced by tambour militaire in Nos. 2 & 9; in No. 3 both are used.* ★
JHW-7. Pièces d'Harmonie, Liv. 7, 12 mvts. flautino(Eb) cl(Eb) 3cl(Bb) 2hn 2bn 2tp a-tb t-tb b-tb serp b-dr s-dr.
Pc (C.F. Peters: Leipzig, pn 1852, 1826), parts: US-BETm, (2 copies), PhilSoc PSB L-6. ★
JHW-8. Pièces d'Harmonie, Liv. 8; 12 mvts. fl(Eb) cl(Eb) 3cl(Bb) 2hn 2bn 2tp a-tb t-tb b-tb serp b-dr-cym.
Pc (C.F. Peters: Leipzig, pn 1902, 1827), parts: GB-Ljag(w), (missing perc pts; with a MS signal-horn part transposed for tp in Eb). ★
JHW-9. Pièces d'Harmonie, Liv. 9; 12 mvts. fl(Eb)/terz-fl cl(Eb) 3cl(Bb) 2hn 2bn 2tp a-tb t-tb b-tb serp b-dr s-dr.
Pc (C.F. Peters: Leipzig, pn 1938, 1827), parts: US-BETm, PhilSoc PSB Add 4. ★
JHW-10. Pièces d'Harmonie, Liv. 10; 12 mvts.
fl(Eb)/terz-fl cl(Eb) 3cl(Bb) 2hn 2bn 2tp a-tb t-tb b-tb serp b-d s-dr.
Pc (C.F. Peters: Leipzig, pn 1987, 1827), parts: US-BETm, PhilSoc PSB Add 5. ★
JHW-11. Pièces d'Harmonie, Liv. 11; 12 mvts.
fl(Eb)/terz-fl cl(Eb) 3cl(Bb) 2hn 2bn 2tp a-tb t-tb b-tb serp b-dr(+cym) s-dr.
Pc (C.F. Peters: Leipzig, pn 1995, 1827/1828), parts: US-BETm, PhilSoc PSB L-8. *The terz-fl is used in Nos. 1, 2, 5, 6, 8 - 12; although cymbals are not specified, the second strain of the b-dr part for No. 1 bears the note, "ohne Becken".* ★
MS parts: D-DT, Mus-n 2062, (with added b-hn part; missing s-dr).
JHW-12. Douze Pièces d'Harmonie, Liv. 12; 12 mvts.
pic cl(Eb) 3cl(Bb) 2hn 2bn 2tp a-tb t-tb b-tb serp b-dr(+cym) s-dr.
Pc (Chez les fils de B. Schott: Pairs; chez les mêmes: Mayence; chez A. Schott: Anners, pn 2969, 18), parts: D-MZsch; F-Pn, Vm27 4311; US-BETm, PhilSoc PSB L-9. ★
JHW-13. Potpourri sur les Thêmes de Hummel et Weber et 4 Pièces d'Harmonie pour Musique militaire, Liv 13.
terz-fl/fl(Eb, No. 4) cl(Eb) 3cl(Bb) 2hn 2bn 2tp a-tb t-tb b-tb serp b-dr(+cym) s-dr.
Pc (C.F. Peters: Leipzig, pn 2045, 1828), parts: US-BETm, (2 copies), PhilSoc PSB L-10. ★
JHW-14. Pièces d'Harmonie, Liv. 14; 12 mvts.
terz-fl(= F, fl in Eb, No. 8 in C) ob(ad lib) cl(Eb) 3cl(Bb) 2hn bn(I) bn(II)+serp 2tp a-tb t-tb b-tb b-dr s-dr.
Pc (C.F. Peters: Leipzig, pn 2049, 1828), parts: D-DT, Mus-n 2072. ★
JHW-15. Potpourri, Liv 15.
Trumpet obligée, terz-fl/fl(Eb, No. 4) cl(Eb) 3cl(Bb) 2hn 2bn 2tp a-tb t-tb b-tb serp b-dr(+cym) s-dr.
Pc (C.F. Peters: Leipzig, pn 2091, c.1829), parts: GB-Ljag(w); US-BETm, PhilSoc PSB Add 6. ★
JHW-16. Variations sur un Air de Leonore [Paer] et 4 Pièces d'Harmonie pour Musique militaire, Liv. 16.
terz-fl cl(Eb) 3cl(Bb) 2hn 2bn 2tp a-tb t-tb b-tb serp b-dr s-dr.
Pc (C.F. Peters: Leipzig, pn 2122, c.1830), pts: GB-Ljag(w), (with a MS Contra Basso pt, identical to bn II). ★
JHW-17. Pièces d'Harmonie, Liv. 17; 12 mvts.
terz-fl ob(ad lib) cl(Eb) 3cl(Bb) 2hn bn(I) bn(II)+serp 2tp a-tb t-tb b-tb b-dr s-dr.
Pc (C.F. Peters: Leipzig, pn 2174, 1830), pts: D-DT, Mus-n 2072, (missing 3tb; with an extra MS hn II pt). ★
JHW-18. Pièces d'Harmonie, Liv. 18; 12 mvts. fl cl(Eb) 3cl(Bb) 4hn(Eb, Bb) 2bn 2tp a-tb t-tb b-tb b-dr(+cym) s-dr; *or* pic cl(Eb) 2cl(Bb) 2hn(Eb) 2bn tp b-tb/serp.
Pc (C.F. Peters: Leipzig, pn 2258, 1832), parts: D-DT, Mus-n 2066; US-BETm, PhilSoc PSB L-12. ★
JHW-19. Potpourri sur les Thêmes de l'Opéra: le Conte Ory de Rossini et 4 Pièces d'Harmonie pour Musique militaire, Liv 19. terz-fl cl(Eb) 3cl(Bb) 2hn 2bn 2tp a-tb t-tb b-tb serp b-dr s-dr.
Pc (C.F. Peters: Leipzig, pn 2362, 1833), parts: US-BETm, PhilSoc PSB L-13. ★
JHW-20. Pièces d'Harmonie, Liv. 20; 12 mvts.
terz-fl/fl(Eb)/fl(pic - No. 3) cl(Eb) 3cl(Bb) 2hn 2bn 2tp(and/or 2posthorns) a-tb t-tb b-tb serp b-dr s-dr.
Pc (C.F. Peters: Leipzig, pn 2446, 1833), parts: US-BETm, PhilSoc PSB L-14. *The tp pt is also marked "Corno di Posto in As (Ab)" & the cl I pt for No. 6 includes cues for this instrument.* ★

JHW-21. Pièces d'Harmonie, Liv. 21; 12 mvts.
fl(Eb)/terz-fl cl(Eb) 3cl(Bb) 2hn 2bn 2tp a-tb t-tb b-tb serp b-dr s-dr. Pc (C.F. Peters: Leipzig, pn 2501, 1834), parts: US-BETm, (3 copies), PhilSoc PSB Add 7. ★
JHW-22. Pièces d'Harmonie, Liv. 22; 12 mvts.
terz-fl ob(ad lib) cl(Eb) 3cl(Bb) 2hn bn(I) bn(II)+serp 2tp a-tb t-tb b-tb b-dr s-dr.
Pc (C.F. Peters: Leipzig, pn 2562, 1834), parts: D-DT, Mus-n 2072. ★
JHW-23. Pièces d'Harmonie, Liv. 23; 12 mvts.
terz-fl/fl(Eb)/fl(No. 7) ob(ad lib) cl(Eb) 3cl(Bb) 2hn 2bn 2tp a-tb t-tb b-tb serp b-dr(+cym) s-dr t-dr tri.
Pc (C.F. Peters: Leipzig, pn 2637, 1837), parts: US-BETm, PhilSoc PSB L-15. *No. 3, "Geschw[ind]. Marsch mit Militair Trommeln", includes a triangle solo and parts for tambour picolo & "Militair Trommeln" (which bear the instruction in the last strain, "auf den Stock").* ★
JHW-24. Pièces d'Harmonie, Liv. 24; 12 mvts.
terz-fl/fl(Eb) ob(ad lib) cl(Eb) 3cl(Bb) 2hn 2bn 2tp a-tb t-tb b-tb serp b-dr(+cym) s-dr.
Pc (C.F. Peters: Leipzig, pn 2664, c.1838), parts: US-BETm, PhilSoc PSB L-16. ★
JHW-25. Pièces d'Harmonie, Liv. 25, 12 mvts
fl ob(ad lib) cl(Eb) 3cl(Bb) 2hn 2bn 2tp a-tb t-tb b-tb serp b-dr s-dr.
Pc (C.F. Peters: Leipzig, pn 2697, 1839), parts: US-BETm, PhilSoc PSB Add 8. ★
JHW-26. Pièces d'Harmonie, Liv. 26; 12 mvts.
terz-fl ob(ad lib) cl(Eb) 3cl(Bb) 2hn bn(I) bn(II)+serp 2tp a-tb t-tb b-tb b-dr s-dr.
Pc (C.F. Peters: Leipzig, pn 2741, 1840), parts: D-DT, Mus-n 2072. ★
JHW-27. Pièces d'Harmonie, Liv. 27; 12 mvts.
terz-fl(fl No. 8) ob(ad lib) cl(Eb) 3cl(Bb) 2hn bn(I) bn(II)+serp 2tp a-tb t-tb b-tb b-dr s-dr.
Pc (C.F. Peters: Leipzig, pn 2755, 1841), parts: D-DT, Mus-n 2073. ★
JHW-28. Pieces of Harmony [sic], Liv. 28; 12 mvts.
terz-fl(pic) cl(Eb) 3cl(Bb) 2hn bn(I) bn(II)+serp 3tp a-tb t-tb b-tb b-dr s-dr t-tb+tri(Nos. 3 & 6 only).
Pc (C.F. Peters: Leipzig, pn 2782, 1841), parts: D-DT, Mus-n 2074. ★
JHW-29. Pièces d'Harmonie, Liv. 29; 12 mvts.
fl(ad lib) ob(ad lib) cl(Eb) 3cl(Bb) 2hn 2bn 2tp 2cap(ad lib) a-tb t-tb b-tb serp b-dr(+cym) s-dr.
Pc (Wessel & Stapleton: London, pn W&S. No. 5260, c.1845), parts: GB-Lbl, h.1555.(3). ★
*JHW-30. Potpourri [MS: 15; sic].   terz-fl cl(Eb) 3cl(Bb) 2hn 2tp b-tb serp b-dr.
Pc (C.F. Peters: Leipzig, pn 1509, 1819), parts: US-BETm, (3 copies), PhilSoc PSB L-1, (2 copies), PhilSoc PSB L-11. *The plate number of this work lies outside the main sequence, between Liv. 2 & 3.* ★
JHW-31. [5] Variations über des Thema Wenn ich in der Frühe aufstehe.   fl(Eb) 2ob(ad lib) cl(Eb) 4cl(Bb) 2hn 2bn tp b-tb serp b-dr s-dr. MS parts: D-DT, Mus-n 2079, (3tb listed in the title but no divisi in pt). ★
JHW-32. [23 pieces, probably drawn from Walch's *Pièces d'Harmonie.*]
fl(Eb) cl(Eb) 3cl(Bb) 2hn bn bn+serp 2tp a-tb t-tb b-tb b-dr. MS parts: D-DT, Mus-n 2052. ★
*JHW-1tm. Trauer Marsch. *An arrangement of Walch, and sometimes falsely attributed to Beethoven as K-H 13.*
2ob 2cl 2hn cbn.
Pc (Chemische Druckerei/Steiner: Vienna, pn 2563, 1816), parts: D-ESpriv; US-NRwhitwell, 183.
JHW-1a. Romberg: (unidentified) Simphonie.   fl ob 3cl 2hn 2bn 2tp b-hn db.   MS parts: D-RUI, RH.R25.
JHW-2a. Rossini: Mosè in Egitto, Geschwind-Marsch.   fl 3cl 2hn 2bn tp b-tb serp. MS pts: D-DT, Mus-n 1898.

WALDEK, Karl *(1840) - 25 March 1905, Linz*
KXW-1v. Christmas offertorium: Laetentur coeli, 1874.   SATB, fl 2cl 2hn 2bn.
AutoMS score: A-LIm, Automss. 1/4.

WALDENMAIER, August Peter *14 Oct 1915, Dachau*
APW-1a. Max Kunz: Bayernhymne.   2fl 2ob 2cl 2bn.
Pm (Vieweg: Berlin; now Leuckart: München, sd).

WALKER, James *1929, Stratford-on-Avon, UK*
JXW-1. Scherzo "Encore for winds".   2fl 2ob 2cl 2hn 2bn 2tp.
Pm (G. Schirmer: New York, London, 1975), score & parts.

WALLENREITER, Lorenz Josef
LJW-1v. Pange lingua, in Eb.   SATB (unison or pts), (ad lib organ; *or* 2hn 2tp(chromatic) tb + ad lib 2cl timp).
Pc (Anton Böhm: Augsburg, pn 3283, sd), parts: CZ-Pnm, XLIII.C.74, (here with trumpet parts: Hoch C & chromatic in Eb).

*WALTER, ( ) *(1800) Premier Basson au Grand Théâtre de Marseille*
*VYW-1.1, 1.2. Grand Walze du Dey d'Alger [sic] suivie de Celle de ses Favorites [2ᵉ Valse des favorites du Dey d'Alger].   1.1: pic(Db) cl(Eb) 3cl(Bb) 2hn tp bugle/cl(Bb) tb oph/tb serp b-dr; 1.2: pic(Db) cl(Eb) 2cl(Bb) 2hn tp tb serp b-dr.
Pc (Richault: Paris, pn 2752.R., 1830), parts: CH-Gpu, Ib.4921f; GB-Ljag, (photocopy).   ★

*WALTER, David *21 May 1959, Paris*
DYW-1a. J.S. Bach: Magnificat, extrait.   2ob obdam ca.   AutoMS score & parts: F-ANTwalter; F-TOep.
DYW-2a. J.S. Bach: Jesu meine Freunde.   2ob obdam ca.   AutoMS score & parts: F-ANTwalter; F-TOep.
DYW-3a. Brahms: Variations.   fl ob 2cl 2hn 2bn db.   AutoMS score & parts: F-ANTwalter; F-TOep.
DYW-4a. Haydn: Trio ("London").   2ob ca.   AutoMS score & parts: F-ANTwalter; F-TOep.
DYW-5a. Roost: Rikudim.   3fl 3ob 3cl 3hn 3bn.   AutoMS score & parts: F-ANTwalter; F-TOep.

WALTER, G. (?Johann/Giovanni) Ignaz *31 Aug 1755, Radoviče - 22 Feb 1822, Regensburg. We note also G. Walter, who was a violinist in Paris, 1790-1800, or I. Walter, a singer at Metz and a pupil of Starzer.*
IXW-1. Parthia a 6 voce; in Bb, 14 mvts.   2cl 2hn 2bn.   MS parts: D-F, Mus.Hs.1555. ★
IXW-2. Parthia in Dis [Eb].   2cl 2hn bn.   MS parts: A-KR, H 37/26. ★

*WANEK, Friedrich Karl *11 Nov 1929, Lugoj (Banat), Romania - 13 April 1991, Mainz*
FKW-1. 4 Grotesken. fl fl(pic) 2ob cl(B♭) cl(B♭, cl in E♭) 2hn 2bn tp perc(2templeblocks wood blocks, 3cym, hi-hat, tam-tam, 3tomtoms, b-dr, s-dr).
Pm (B. Schott's Söhne: Mainz, 1976), score (pn ED 6667) & parts (pn ED 6668).
FKW-2. Per fiati: concert suite. 2fl 2ob 2cl 2hn 2bn.
Pm (B. Schott's Söhne: Mainz, c.1980), score & parts.
FKW-1a. Français: L'Heure du Berger: musique du brasserie. fl ob 2cl hn 2bn tb piano.
Pm (B. Schott's Söhne: Mainz, 1972), score (pn ED 6271) & parts (pn ED 6272).
FKW-2a. Ligeti: 6 Miniatures, (1953-75). fl fl(pic) ob ob(ca) cl(B♭) cl(B♭, cl in E♭) 2hn 2bn.
Pm (B. Schott's Söhne: Mainz, c.1980), hire score & parts.
FKW-3a. Mahler: Fünf frühe Lieder, (1989). S solo, fl fl(pic) ob ob(ca) 2cl 2hn 2bn.
Pm (B. Schott's Sohne: Mainz), hire score & parts.
*FKW-4a. Orff: Carmina Burana, 5 mvts. fl fl(pic) ob ob(ca) 2cl 2hn bn cbn(bn).
Pm (B. Schott's Söhne: Mainz, 1981), score (pn ED 6950) & parts (pn ED 6951).
FKW-5a. Orff: Der Mond, Drei Tänze und Schluss-Szene. fl fl(pic) 2ob 2cl 2hn bn bn(cbn) tp. (Schott's catalog states, "für 12 Bläser" but names only 11 instruments - a trombone may also be needed.)
Pm (B. Schott's Sohne: Mainz), hire score & parts.
FKW-6a. Orff: Die Kluge, "Als die treue ward geboren" (Szene der drei Strolche).
fl fl(pic) 2ob 2cl 2hn cbn tp tb.
Pm (B. Schott's Sohne: Mainz), hire score & parts.

WANG, An-Ming
ANW-1. Promenade. 2fl 2ob 2cl 2hn 2bn tp 2tb. MS score: US-NYamc.

WANGEMANN, F.L. *(1790)*
XXW-1. Pièces d'Harmonie, Op. 3. fl 2ob bthn 2hn bn.
Pc (B. Schott's Söhne: Mainz, 1822), parts: D-MZsch.
XXW-2. Pièces d'Harmonie, in F, 3 mvts. fl ob/cl bthn hn bn.
MS parts (1822), D-Rtt, Wangemann 1. *Possibly an arrangement of XXW-1.* ★

*WARMERDAM, Desiree van *1959, Netherlands*
DEW-1. Xystus. 2ob obdam 2hn cbn.
Pm (Compusic: Amsterdam, pn 519, c.1994), score & parts.

WARREN, afterwards WARREN-DAVIS, Betsy Frost *(1950), Boston*
BFW-1. Octet for winds. 2ob 2cl 2hn 2bn.
Pm (Wiscasset Music Publishing Co.: Boston, 1984), score.

WARREN, Raymond Henry *7 Nov 1928, UK*
RHW-1. Music for Harlequin; 1964. 2fl 2ob 2cl 2hn 2bn 2tp 2tb tu perc.
Pm (Novello: London, 1966), score & hire parts.

WASHBURN, Robert Brooks *1928, USA*
RGW-1. Concertino. fl ob cl 2hn bn 2tp tb tu.
Pm (Oxford University Press: London, 1971), score & hire parts.

WATERS, Charles Frederick *1895, Epsom - 26 March 1975, London*
CFW-1. Solemn Minuet. fl ob 2cl 2bn.
Pm (Hinrichsen Edition: London, 1964), score & parts.

*WATLEN, John *(1770)*
JVW-1m (attributed). Newcastle Troop, Exordium. 2terz-fl 2cl 2hn bn.
Pc (In: *A Collection of Celebrated Marches & Quick Steps for the Piano Forte, Flute, Violin, &c. Composed by The Right Honble. Countess of Balcarras, Mrs. Major Tyler, [George] Muschett, Watlen &c.* Printed and Sold by J. Watlen: Edinburgh, c.1797), score: GB-Lbl, g.1780.q.(12). ★

WATSON, Walter C. (Robert) *13 Oct 1933, Canton, Ohio*
WCW-1. Divertimento. fl ob 2cl 2hn bn.
Pm (Witmark: New York, sd).

*WAWRA, Wenzel (Wenceslaus, Václav) *b. 1767, Niemeyez, Bohemia*
WQW-1m. Marsch für gantze türkische Musick [sic], in F.
pic 2ob 2cl 2hn 2bn 2tp(clar) b-tb b-dr s-dr cym tri tamb. MS parts: A-KR, H 37/1. ★
WQW-1v. Lied, "Der deutsche Jüngling", ("Ich bin ein deutscher Jüngling").
SA, pic 2fl pic-cl 2hn 2bn 2tp(clar) b-tb b-dr. MS parts: A-KR, I 16/31. ★
WQW-2v. Trauer amt and den Gedächtnistagen verstorbener stud render.
SATB choir, fl 2cl 2hn 2bn 2tp(clar) b-tb vlne timp organ.
(?Auto)MS score, MS parts & MS piano reduction: A-KR, E 4/14. *The MS score bears the note, "Requiem vor dem Evangelium, Offertorium, S, nach der Wandlung, A, Libe 'Bis unsers Bruders [sic] Trauerbahre' [,] Nach der Einsegnung."* ★

*WEAIT, Christopher Robert Irving *27 March 1939, Surrey, UK*
CIW-1a. 2 Canadian Folksongs. 2ob 2cl 2hn 2bn (cbn ad lib).
Pm (Compusic: Amsterdam, pn 260B, 1991), parts.
CIW-2a. A Nineteenth Century Scrapbook; 1971. 2ob 2cl 2hn 2bn. MS score: US-Wc.
CIW-1ma(-4ma). 4 Marches of the American Revolution. pic/fl/ob ob/ca/cl fl/bn bn/b-cl.
Pm (McGinnis & Marx: New York, 1973), score & parts.

WEBB, Peter
PTW-1. Sextet. 2cl 2hn 2bn. MS score: AUS-Smc.

*WEBB, William *(1780), Master of the Band of the Royal Victis Light Dragoons*
*WYW-1m. The Loyal Isle of Wight Volunteers Slow March.   4cl 2hn 2bn tp.
Pc (Preston: London, c.1810), score: GB-En, Glen 347-16.   ★
WYW-2m. A Set of Grand Military Divertimentos, Consisting of Slow & Quick Marches[,] And a Favorite Troop . . . No. 1; 12 mvts.   pic(G) 2fl 2cl(C; I divisi No. 12, II with some divisis) 2hn 2bn tp bugle serp/tb.
Pc (G.E. Black: Philadelphia, c.1828), parts: US-NYp, *MV-Amer.   ★
WYW-3m. A Second Set of Grand Military Divertimentos.   Military band (scoring possibly as WYW-2m).
Pc (G.E. Black: Philadelphia, c.1828), parts: US-Wc, Scala Collection.

*WEBER, Bernhard Anselm *18 April 1766, Mannheim - 22 March 1821, Berlin*
BAW-1m. Marsch.   Instrumentation unknown.
AutoMS score: D-Bds, Mus.ms.auto.B.A.Weber 8.
BAW-1e. Musig [sic] auf dem Theater zum Trauerspiel Klÿtemnestra.   4hn 2bn 3tb.
MS parts: A-Wn, Mus.Hs.2065.   ★
   1.1. Act I, Scene 2: 4hn 2bn 3tb.   1.2. Act II, Scene 7: 4hn.   1.3. Act II, Scene 8: 4hn.
   1.4. Act II, Scene 8, 4hn 2bn 3tb, (a reprise of 1.1, with a additional 2-bar conclusion).
BAW-2e. Die Jungfrau von Orleans.   Scoring varies.
MS score & parts: D-Sl, H.B.XVII. 654.   ★
Pc (Patern: Wien, c.1812), piano reduction by Anton Wranizky of the *Harmonie Monolog:* I-Fc, D.IX.24.
   2.1e. Vierter Aufzug 1ter Auftritt, "hinter den Coulishen, zu den Monolog der Johanna".
      Female voice, 2cl 2hn 2bn ("Auf dem Theater").   *A substantial piece; other versions and/or*
      arrangements can be found in the Arrangements List.
   2.2e. Vierter Aufzug 3tio Auftritt; 33 bars (then orchestra).   2fl 2cl(C) 2hn 2bn 2tp timp.
BAW-3e. Deodato.   Scoring varies.   MS score: D-Sl, H.B.XVII. 652 a.b.c.   ★
   3.1e. Act II, No. 5. Chor & Marsch; the final section, 14 bars.   TT, 2cl 2hn 2bn.
   3.2e. Act II, No. 6. Aus dem Theater.   TB, 2cl 2hn 2bn.
   3.3e. Act III, No. 17. Auf dem Theater [1st & 2nd Wächter]; 6 bars.   2cl 2hn 2bn 2tp 3tb.
   3.4e. Act III, No. 17. Four bars for 2cl 2hn 2bn 2tp 3tb.   *In the D-Sl score, this has been crossed out and 8*
      bars - possibly composed by Lindpaintner - for 2bthn 2hn 2bn has been substituted.
   3.5e. Act IV, No. 21, last section.   Voice, harp 2fl 2hn.
   The Act II, No. 8, Pas de deux is largely scored for ob(I) 2hn, with occasional strings.
BAW-1v. Sie Walken hin.   S solo, 2fl 2hn 2bn.   AutoMS score: D-Bds, mus.ms.auto.B.A.Weber 15.

*WEBER, Carl Maria Friedrich Ernst von *18 Nov 1786, Eutin, nr Lübeck - 5 June 1826, London*
Almost all works cited here with a Jähns number (e.g. J.303) are to be found as manuscript material (some autograph; sometimes incomplete), documents, printed editions, etc., in the F.W. Jähns collection "Weberiana" in D-B (formerly in D-Bds). We do not list this source separately where we give a number from Jähns's thematic catalog, Carl Maria von Weber in seinem Werken: chronologisch-thematisch Verzeichniss seiner sämmtlichen Compositionem *(Berlin 1871; repr 1967). Some rare works for winds are given (in piano reduction) in Leopold Hirschberg,* Reliquienschrein des Meisters Carl Maria von Weber, *Berlin: Morawe & Schieffelt Verlag, 1926 (a copy is at GB-Lbl, H.690.t)*
*CMW-1. March in C, for the Royal Society of Musicians; 1826, (J.303).   fl 2ob 2cl 2hn 2bn 2tp tb.
MS score (fair copy with Weber's signature, *not* by Fürstenau; Jähns collection): D-B, Web.IV B XIV, 1278.
Pc (au Bureau de Musique von C.F. Peters: Leipzig, c.1827), parts.
Pm (Deutscher Verlag für Musik: Leipzig, pn DVfM 8523, 1975), ed. Georg Meerwein, score & parts.
Pm (Musica rara: London, pn 1863, 1976), score & parts, (reissue of the preceding).
*CMW-2. Waltz "Maienblümlein"; (J.149).   fl 2cl 2hn 2bn tp.
MS score: D-B (Jähns collection).   MS score & parts (modern): GB-DOTams.
Pm (Eulenburg: London, pn GM 942, 1980), score & parts.
*CMW-3. Beim kindlichen Strahl des erwachenden Phobus; (J.153).   fl cl 2hn 2bn.
MS score: D-B (Jähns collection).   MS score & parts (modern): GB-DOTams.
*CMW-4. Ihr kleinen Vögelein, (J.150).   fl 2cl 2hn 2bn.
MS score: D-B (Jähns collection).   MS score & parts (modern): GB-DOTams.
*CMW-5. Lebewohl, mein süsses Leben, (J.151).   fl 2cl 2hn 2bn.
MS score: D-B (Jähns collection).   MS score & parts (modern): GB-DOTams.
*CMW-6. Die verliebte Schäferin, (J.152).   fl 2cl 2hn 2bn.
MS score: D-B (Jähns collection).   MS score & parts (modern): GB-DOTams.
*CMW-7. Adagio & Rondo; E♭, B♭.   2cl 2hn 2bn.
AutoMS score (1808): D-B, Mus.ms.auto.F.299.   MS score: F-Pn: Ms.408.   ★
Pm (Musica rara: London, pn M.R.1229, 1970), ed. Georgina Dobrée, score & parts.
Pm (B. Schott's Söhne: Mainz, pn 6446, 1973), ed. Wolfgang Sandner, score & parts.
*CMW-1e. Abu Hassan, (J.106), finale: march.   2ob 2hn.
Pm (Verlag der Seiboldschen Buchdruckerei Werner Dohany: Offenbach am Main, 1925; reprinted: Gregg International Publishers: Farnborough, 1968), score.
*CMW-2e. Der Freischütz, (J.277).
Pm (Gregg International Publishers: Farnborough, 1969), facsimile of the score pub. by Schlesinger: Berlin, 1848.
Pm (Ernst Eulenburg: London, 1976), ed. from the autograph by Hermann Albert, score (Édition Eulenburg, No.915).
Pm (Dover Publications: New York, 1977), facsimile of the edition published by C.F. Peters: Leipzig, 1871).
*CMW-3e. Preciosa (J.279), overture ("Gypsy March" section: 2fl 2ob 2cl 2hn 2bn) & No. 7 ("Zigeunermusik auf dem Theater", also known as "Frölicher Musik": 2pic 2hn 2bn s-dr cym tri tamb).
Pc/Pm (Schlesinger'sche Buch- und Musikhandlung: Berlin, c.1840, 1850, 1878, c.1890), (present copyright holder: Robert Lienau: Berlin), score: GB-Ob, Mus.22c.316.   ★
*CMW-4e. Euryanthe (J.291), Nos. 9 & 23.
Pm (Gregg International Publishers: Farnborough, 1969), facsimile of Schlesinger: Berlin, 1866), score.
   4.1e. No. 9, Finale Act I.   fl 2ob 2cl 2hn 2bn.
   4.2e. No. 23, Wedding March.   2pic 2ob 2cl 2hn 2bn 2tp 3tb timp (auf dem Bühne).

*CMW-5e. Oberon (J.306). (Nos. 6 & 9A also use winds auf dem Theater).
Pm (Gregg International Publishers: Farnborough, 1969), facsimile of (Schlesinger: Berlin, 1874), score.
    5.1e. No. 3. Vision, "O, why are thou sleeping".   2cl hn 2bn guitar
    5.2e. No. 9. March.   2fl 2cl 2hn 2bn tri tamb.   5.3e. No. 14. Melodram, Andante con moto.   2fl 2cl hn.
*CMW-6te. Musik zu Turandot, (J.75), Marcia funebre.   2fl 2ob 2cl 2hn 2bn 2tp(unison) b-tb timp b-dr s-dr tri.
Pm (Eulenburg: Zürich, pn 10120, 1975), score.
*CMW-7e. Musik zu Heinrich IV, König von Frankreich, (J.237).
MS score: D-B (Jähns collection).   *(7.6e = the Rondo of CMW-7)*
    7.1e. No. 1. "Vive Henri quatre".   2pic 2ob 2cl 2hn 2bn 2tp dr.   7.2e. No. 2. Tanz.   pic 2ob 2cl 2hn 2bn.
    7.3e. No.3 auf dem Theater. 2fl 2cl 2hn.   7.4e. No. 4. 2fl 2cl.   7.5e. No. 5.   2fl 2cl
    7.6e. No. 6. Act IV, Scene 2. 2cl 2hn 2bn.   Nos. 7 (& 8). Marcia. 2pic 2ob 2cl 2hn 2bn 2tp timp.
*CMW-8e. Musik zu Lieb' um Liebe, (J.246).   MS score: D-B (Jähns collection).
    8.1e. No. 2. Chor der Landleute. SATB, 2cl 2hn.   8.3e. No. 3.   Ländlicher Marsch. unspecified "Bläser".
    8.4e. No. 4. Melodram. 2ob 2cl 2hn 2bn 2tp.
*CMW-1v. Chor, "Heil dir, Sappho!", (J.240).   SSB, 2fl 2ob 2cl 2hn 2bn 2tp 2tb timp.   MS score: D-Dl.
*CMW-2v. Agnus Dei, (J.273).   SSA, 2fl 2cl 4hn 2bn *(Jähns catalog wrongly gives 2hn).*
MS score: D-B, (Jähns collection).   MS score & parts: GB-DOTstoneham, (modern copy).
*CMW-3tv. Trauermusik, "Hörst du der Klage" (J.116).   BAR solo, SATB chorus, fl 2cl 2hn 2bn 2tp b-tb timp.
MS sketches: D-B, (Jähns collection); GB-DOTams, (modern copy).
Pm (1986 reconstruction by M.T.A. Goddard and A.M. Stoneham), score & parts: GB-DOTams.
*CMW-4.1tv. Grablied, "Leis wandeln mir, wie Geisterhauch", (J.37).
CTTB, 2ob 2cl 2hn 2bn tb.   AutoMS score: (lost).
Pc (Schlesinger: Berlin, c.1840), score (with added piano accompaniment): D-B; GB-Lbl, F.665.b.; GB-DOTams.
*CMW-4.2tv. (Grablied, version 2) "Zerrissen hat des Todes Hand".   SATB, fl 2cl 2hn 2bn 3tb.
*CMW-5v. Kriegs-Eid, "Wir stehn vor Gott", (J.139).   Unison male chorus, 3hn bn 2tp b-tb.
Auto(?)MS score: D-B, (Jähns collection); GB-DOTams (modern copy).
*CMW-6v. Du hoher Rautenzweig, (J.251).   SATB, 2fl 2cl 2bn.
MS score: D-B (Jähns collection; incomplete).
MS score & parts (completed A.M. Stoneham): GB-DOTams.
*CMW-1d. Larghetto [& Allegro] on Mozart's *La Clemenza di Tito.* fl ob 3cl(C) bthn 2hn 2bn tp tb db.
MS score (in the hand of *Erbprinz* Carl Friedrich von Löwenstein) & MS parts: GB-Ljag(w).   ★
Pm (Musica rara: London, c.1981), ?project abandoned.
*CMW-2d. 5 Waltzes [No. 6 in the published set is an arrangement of a waltz from Weber's opera, *Oberon*].
Nos. 1 - 5: pic(D) cl(F) 3cl(C) 2hn 2bn b-tb; No. 6: terz-fl 2cl(E♭) 2cl(B♭) 2hn 2bn b-tb.
MS parts: GB-Ljag(w), (No. 6 is a later addition to the parts in the hand of F. Wieser).   ★
Pm (Musica rara: London, pn MR 2065, 1981), ed. Hermann Dechant, score & parts (with. ad lib cbn/db).
*CMW-3d. Tema con variazioni [the theme seems to be original].   fl(F) 2cl(E♭) 2cl(B♭) 2hn 2bn tp tb db.
MS score & parts: GB-L-jag(w).
Pm (Musica rara: London, pn 2073, 1984), ed. Robert Holeman, score & parts.
*CMW-4d. Concertino for Oboe; in F minor/major.   Solo oboe, fl 2cl(C) 2cl(B♭) 2hn 2bn b-tb cb.
MS score (in the hand of Friedrich Witt = FZW-7a): D-BABhüber.   MS parts: GB-Ljag(w).   ★
Pm (Musica rara: London, pn 1969A/B, 1980/81), ed. Hermann Dechant, score & parts, also piano reduction.
Pm (Nova Music: London, pn NM 137, 1980), oboe with piano reduction.
Pm (Kunzelmann: pn 10161, 1981), ed. Dieter Klöcker, score & parts.
Pm (WINDS: Northridge, CA, pn W-396, c. 1981), faint photocopy score (?copy of original) & modern MS pts.
*CMW-5d. Andante in C aus Titus [= Mozart: La Clemenza di Tito, Duetto, "Ah perdona al primo affetto"; in
fact, in B♭.].   2cl(E♭) 2cl(Bb) 2hn 2bn cb.
MS score (in the hand of Friedrich Witt = FZW-10.1a) & MS pts.   *See WITT, FZW-10a for a full discussion.*
MS parts: GB-Ljag(w), 414, No. 1.   ★
Pm (Musica rara: London, c.1981), as "Andante in C [sic]", project abandoned.   *Note: the introduction to the*
Musica rara edtion incorrectly identifies the scoring as: cl(F) 3cl(C) 2hn 2bn tp b-tb.
*CMW-6d. Harmonie in B[♭] (J.Anh.II/3l).   Instrumentation unknown.
MS score: D-Sl (among anonymous MS scores; Jähns suggests one of these items may be by Weber) Nos. 88,
92, 94, 107, 121, 126, 128, 145/3, 145/9. *Apparently lost in the Hoftheater fire in 1902; we believe that these*
works were, in fact, the 10 Harmonien by Johann David Schwegler.

*WEBER, Friedrich Dionys (Bedřich Diviš) *9 Oct 1766, Velichov, Bohemia - 25 Dec 1842, Prague*
FDW-1m. 6 Märsche.   pic fl 2ob 2hn 2bn cbn tp.
Pc (Breitkopf & Härtel: Leipzig, sd), parts: D-DS, (? lost in World War II); I-Fc, F.P. S.682, (for pic 2ob 2cl
2hn 2bn; Note: the catalog states that there are 11 parts).

*WEBER, (Jacob) Gottfried *1 March 1779, Freinsheim, nr Mannheim - 21 Sept 1839, Kreuznach*
JGW-1m. Triumphmarsch, Op. 20.   Large military band.
Pc (Schott: Mainz, pre-1820), parts: D-MZsch.
JGW-1v. Requiem den Manen der Sieger bei Leipzig und belle-alliance geweiht, Op. 21.
Male chorus, vla(s) basse 2hn organ/(or 2cl 2bn), (cbn 2tp tb ad lib).
Pc (André: Offenbach am Main, pn 3591, 1816), organ/piano score only, with German & Latin text:
CZ-Bm(au), A.20.227.   ★

*WEBER, S. J. *(1770)*
SJW-1a. Cherubini: Démophon, overture.   2fl 2ob 4cl 2hn 2bn 2tp tb serp perc.   MS parts: D-AB, S 74.
SJW-2a. Cherubini: Les deux Journées, 5 mvts.   2fl 2ob 2cl 2hn 2bn 2tp(clar) vlne+serp.
MS parts: D-AB, S.23, (?missing clarinets).

*WEBER, Wilhelm *(1780); Weber styles himself "Schullehrer" (schoolteacher) on the MSS.*
WXW-1tv. Leichenlied; in A♭, "Nichts auf Erden dauert immer". TTBB, 2cl 2hn bn.
AutoMS parts (1870): A-Wn, Mus.Hs.21692. ★
WXW-2tv. Leichenlied; in A♭, "Rosen auf den Weg gestreut". TTBB, 2cl 2hn basso.
AutoMS parts (1877): A-Wn, Mus.Hs.21693. ★

WEEKS, John *18 July 1934, Bath*
JBW-1. Octet, Op. 41; 1978. 2ob 2cl 2hn 2bn. MS score: GB-Gsma, (available for purchase).

*WEIDEMANN, Charles Frederick *d. 1782, London.*
CRW-1m. The Old Buff's March. 2ob/vl 2hn bn.
Pc (Benjamin Rhames: Dublin, c.1760), RISM [W 539], score: GB-Lbl, H.1601.a.(112); GB-Ljag, (modern score). ★

*WEIGERT (Weigart), Franz (Francesco) *(1740)*
FXW-1(-7). 7 Partittas; (D, B[♭], A, A, G, E♯ [E], D, C; all 5 mvts). 2ob 2hn bn.
MS parts: CZ-KRa, A3982-3989/IV.B.152 - IV.B.159. ★

*WEIGH, John *(1770), Master of the Band of the Royal Cheshire Militia.*
JPW-1m. Two marches . . . for the use of the Royal Cheshire Militia. [Slow & Quick Marches.] 2cl 2hn 2bn.
Pc (Printed for the Author by William Wright: Newcastle, c.1796), RISM [W 543], score: GB-Lbl, g.271.s.(14); GB-Ob, Mus.61.c.55(16). ★

*WEIGL, Joseph *28 March 1766, Eisenstadt - 3 Feb 1846, Vienna*
Kurtz reports a Marsch for 2ob 2cl 2hn 2bn in D-HR; this cannot be traced and may be a ghost.
*JYW-1. Parthia; in B♭, 6 mvts. 2ob 2cl 2hn 2bn. MS parts: A-Ee, Mus.1174. ★
JYW-2. Partia in B♭. 2ob 2cl 2hn 2bn. MS parts: D-Bds, Mus.Ms.22940.
JYW-1e. Pumpernickels Hochzeitstag, Harmoniestücke. Instrumentation unknown, probably 2ob 2cl 2hn 2bn.
Pc (N. Simrock: Bonn, c.1811), piano reduction only, in vocal score: GB-Lbl, E.96.b; GB-Ljag, (modern MS).
JYW-1a. Méhul: Joseph, overture & 6 mvts. 2ob 2cl 2hn 2bn (2tp) [b-tb].
MS parts: CZ-Bm(au), A.37.341, (the b-tb pt is not listed on the titlepage and is probably a later addition).
JYW-1v. Grosse Messe in Es [E♭]. Solo voice, SATB chorus, 2ob 2cl 2hn 2bn 2tp 2tb timp.
MS parts: A-Wn, A 304, Fond Nr.24 St-Peter-Wien.
JYW-1d. Harmonie in C; 2ob 2cl 2hn 2bn basso. MS parts: D-HR, HR III 4 1/2 2° 358. *This is, in fact, Went's arrangement of T. Weigl's ballet, Die Vermählung im Keller, (JNW-68.1a).*
JYW-1ad. J. Weigl: Das Waissenhaus, overture & 4 mvts. 2ob 2cl 2hn 2bn cbn.
MS parts: CZ-KRa, A3994/IV.B.164.

*WEIKERT, ( ) (? Franz WEIGERT) *(1770)*
UZW-1. Parthia in Dis [E♭]; 3 mvts. 2cl 2hn bn.
MS parts (by Dominik Hübner, Langenbruck): CZ-Pu(dm), 59 R 3341. ★
UZW-2. Ländler [& Trio] in Dis [E♭]. 2cl 2hn bn.
MS parts (by Dominik Hübner, Langenbruck): CZ-Pu(dm), 59 R 3342. ★

*WEILL, Kurt *2 March 1900, Dessau, Germany - 3 April 1950, New York*
Details of the complex copyrights, performance rights and hire facilities for Kurt Weill's works lie outside the scope of this volume. The places to start for hire of parts and performance rights are: [UK & Ireland] (as Agent): Alfred A. Kalmus Ltd., 2 Fareham St, London, W1V 2BN; [USA & BREV (former and present members of the British Commonwealth)]: European American Music Corporation., P.O. Box 850, Valley Forge, PA 19482, USA, herein abbreviated: (EAMC); [Other territories]: Universal Edition AG., Postfach 3, A-1015 Vienna.
*KYW-1. Kleine Dreigroschenoper Suite. 2fl(pic) 2cl a-sax t-sax(s-sax) 2bn 2tp tu banjo gtr/harp piano accordion/bandoneon timp perc. Pc (Universal: Wien, Leipzig, pn UE 9712 NJ, 1929), score: GB-Lbl, i.119.
*KYW-2. Concerto for Violin, Op. 12. Solo Violin, 2fl(pic) ob 2cl 2hn 2bn tp perc tinp 4db.
Pm (Universal Edition: Wien, pn UE 8339, 1965), study score.
*KYW-3. Gustav III. 2pic 2cl 2hn 2tp tb perc vl harmonium(piano) glock.
MS reconstructed by David Drew as Bastille Music, 6 mvts. Unpublished: EAMC, for all territories.
*KYW-4. Konjunktur, (surviving fragments arranged by David Drew in 1970 (final form, 1975) as *Öl [Oil] Music).* fl(pic) cl(a-sax, b-cl) 2tp tb vl piano timp perc. MS (fragments): US-NYweill.
Unpublished: EAMC, for USA, UK & BREV; Universal Edition AG. for all other territories.
*KYW-1v. Das Berliner Requiem. T & Bar soli, male chorus (or 2 male voices), 2cl 2a-sax(t-sax) 2hn 2bn 2tp 2tb tu(ad lib) banjo(guitar) piano(organ/harmonium), timp perc.
Pm (Universal Edition: Wien, pn UE 9789, 1977), ed. David Drew, score.
*KYW-2v. Ballade: Vom Tod im Wald, Op. 23. B solo, 2cl 2hn bn(cbn) 2tp t-tb b-tb. MS score: US-Wc.
Unpublished: EAMC for USAm UK & BREV; Universal Edition for all other territories.
*KYW-1e. Der Protagonist, Op. 15. *Stage band:* 2fl(pic) 2cl 2bn 2tp. Scene: M,T,BAR,B, 2fl 2cl 2bn 2tp.
Pm (Universal Edition: Wien, 1926), score. Scene: (hire pts), EAMC for US, UK, BREV; Universal all others.
*KYW-2.1e. Aufstieg und Fall der Stadt Mahagonny. *(Onstage)* 2pic 2cl s-sax a-sax t-sax 2hn 2bn 2tp 2tb tu perc piano zither/xylophone banjo bandoneon 3vl; *(Pit)* 2fl(pic) ob cl s-sax a-sax(bar-sax) t-sax 2hn bn bn(cbn) 3tp 2tb tu timp perc piano(harmonium ad lib) banjo b-gtr bandoneon, 6vl 3vla 2vc 2db.
MS Score: US-Wc. Pm (Universal Edition: Wien, 1929, revised 1931), score.
*KYW-2.2e. Die kleine Mahagonny (Mahagonny Songspiel).
TTBB and 2 Soubrettes (SS), 2vl, cl cl(b-cl) a-sax 2tp tb piano tinp perc.
Pm (Universal Edition: Wien, etc., 1963), score. New edition: (Universal: Wien, pn SF 10019, 1981), study score
*KYW-3e. Happy End. a-sax(fl, pic, cl) t-sax(cl, b-sax) tp tb banjo(Hawaiian slide guitar/mandolin) b-gtr bandoneon/accordion piano(harmonium) perc(tp II).
Pm (Universal Edition: Wien, etc., 1929), score.
Pm (European American Publishing Corp.: Valley Forge, PA, 1972), English adatation: Michael Feingold, (hire).
*KYW-4e. Die Dreigroschenoper. a-sax(fl, cl, bar-sax) t-sax(s-sax, b-cl, bn) tp(I)/tp(C), tb/db, banjo(guitar, vc, Hawaiian slide guitar, mandolin, bandoneon), harmonium(celeste, piano), timp/perc(tp II).
Pm (Universal Edition AG.: Wien, 1972), miniature score (Philharmonia, No. 400).

*WEILLAND, ( ) *(1770)*
*XZW-1. Harmonie; in E♭, 3 mvts.   2ob 2cl 2hn 2bn.
Pc (Pleyel: Paris, 1797), parts: D-DS, (?lost in World War II).
Pc (Printed by Broderip & Wilkinson: London, 1799), pts: GB-Lbl, h.125.(20); GB-Ob. Mus.Instr. I.231(5).   ★
MS parts: NL-DHgm; GB-Ljag (modern score & parts).
Pm (Phylloscopus: Lancaster, UK, pn PP39, 1990), score & parts.

WEINBERGER, Josef *(1780)*
JCW-1. Serenade concertante; in C, 5 mvts.   fl 2cl(C) 2hn 2vla vlne.   MS parts (1803): A-Sca, Hs.396.   ★

*WEINER, Lazar S. *27 Oct 1897, Cherkassy, nr Kiev - 10 Jan 1932, New York*
LSW-1v. Amos; 1970.   T & BAR soli, chorus, fl 2ob cl 2hn bn tp tb tu organ piano.
Pm (Bourne Co.: New York, c.1971), score.

WEINHORST, Richard W. *1920*
RWW-1. 6 Intradas, 1984.   3fl ob 2cl bn 3tp tb.
Pm (American Composers Alliance: New York, c.1984).

*WEINLICH, Johann *(1810)*
JMW-1a. J. Strauss, the Elder: Astraea Tänze, Op. 156.   fl ob 2cl 2hn 2bn cbn 2tp tb.
AutoMS score & MS parts, (1845): CZ-Bm(au), A.37.349.

*WEINMANN, Alexander (editor)
AXW-1ma. Historische Regimentsmärsche. Reconstructions from Ignaz Amon's 1794 set of marches "der Kays:
Konig: Armee für das Clavier oder Fortepiano".   fl 2ob 2cl 2hn 2bn cbn 2tp.
Pm (Doblinger: Wien, München, 1981), Diletto Musicale 196, piano score & parts (pn 06 610).
    1.1ma. F.J. Haydn (attributed): Marsche von den K K Infanterie Reg: Coloredo.
    1.2ma. Anon. Marsche von dem K. K. Infant: Reg: Teutschmeister [sic].
    1.3ma. Anon. Marsch von Anton Eszterházy.
    1.4ma. Anon. Marsch von dem K. K. Infant: Reg: Reisky.
    1.5ma. Major [Ignace] von Beecke. Marche pour le Clavecin faite à la Gloire des Armées de Prussiens et
        Hessoix à leur Entrée à Francfort.
    1.6ma. Marche von dem K. K. Infant: Reg: Lacsy.
    1.7ma. Anon. Marche von dem K. K. Infant: Reg: Preisz.
    1.8ma. Anon. Marsche des K. K. Infant: Reg: Huff.
    1.9ma. Anon. Margräfl Baden Durlachischer Truppenmarsch.

*WEIS, ( ) *(1770)*
UXW-1. Divertimento in Dis [E♭]; 4 mvts.   2vl 2cl 2hn bn.
MS parts (by Augustin Erasmus Hübner, Langenbruck, 1803): CZ-Pu(dm), 59 R 3400.   ★

*WEISGOTT, ( ) *(1770)*
UYW-1. Parthia in Dis [E♭]; 5 mvts.   2cl 2hn bn.
MS parts (by Augustin Erasmus Hübner, Langenbruck): CZ-Pu(dm), 59 R 3329.   ★

WEIS-OSTBORN, Rudolf von *8 Nov 1876, Graz - 18 Dec 1962, Graz*
ROW-1. Epilogue, Op. 17.   2hn 2bn.
Pm (Ries & Erler: Berlin, 1900), score & parts.

WEISS, ( ) *(?1810)*
QXW-1m. Acht Marsche [with Trios]; D, A, D, A, A, A, E, D.   Scoring varies.
(?Auto)MS score: A-Wn, Mus.Hs.2291.   *The score calls for "Tromboni" but there is only one part.*   ★
    1.1m. pic 2cl(D) 2cl(D) 4hn(D, G) 2bn cbn 2tp(D) tp(prin, D) tp(G) tp(A) tb(s)+serp[pts in octaves] b-dr s-dr.
    1.2m. pic cl(D) 2cl/(C) 4hn(A, D) 2bn cbn 4tp(A alto, 2D, E) tb(s)+serp[pts in octaves] b-dr s-dr.
    1.3m. pic cl(G) 3cl(D) 4hn(D, G) 2bn cbn+serp 4tp(2D, A, G) tb(s) b-dr s-dr.
    1.4m. pic cl(G) cl(D) 2cl(C) 4hn(D, A) 2bn cbn+serp 5tp(2D, A, E, [tief]-D) tb(s) b-dr s-dr.
    1.5m. pic cl(G) 2cl(D) 4hn(A, D) 2bn cbn+serp 4tp(2d, A alto, A basso) tb(s) b-dr s-dr.
    1.6m. pic cl(G) 3cl(D) 4hn(A,D) 2bn cbn+serp 3tp(2D, A) tb(s) b-dr s-dr.
    1.7m. pic cl(G) 3cl(D) 4hn(E, A) 2bn cbn+serp 3tp(D, E, A) tb(s) b-dr s-dr.
    1.8m. pic cl(G) 3cl(D) 4hn(D, G) 2bn cbn+serp 3tp(2D, A) tb(s) b-dr s-dr.

WEISS, Wenzel
WZW-1m. Marsch und Echo.   2ob 2cl 2hn 2bn.   MS: D-Bds, Hausbibl.M.M.145.

WELIN, Karl-Erik *31 May 1934, Genarp - 30 May 1992, Mallorca*
KEW-1. Viriditas per Omnibus; 1988.   2fl 2ob 3cl 2hn 2bn db.   MS score: S-Sic.

WELLER, Friedrich *c.1790, Dessau - 30 May 1870, Zerbst*
*FYW-1m(-4m). Acht Märsche für die Infanterie, Nos. 1 - 4, (Nos. 5 - 8 are by A.H. Neithardt).
pic 2ob cl(F) 3cl(C) 2bthn 4hn 3bn cbn+serp 4tp 3tb tri b-dr t-dr.
Pc (Eingenthum des Componisten: Berlin: c.1835), pp. 1 - 58, scores: D-Bds, (?lost); GB-Lbl, e.43.   ★
    1.1m. Marsch, in D.   1.2m. Marsch, in F.   1.3m. Ein musikalische Spass.
    1.4m. Marsch, in C, scored as the others except that the only percussion is the "Tambour militaire".
*FYW-1a. Weber: Oberon, overture & 3 Lieferungen, 19 mvts.   Scoring varies, total forces: fl fl(pic) 2ob 2cl(F,
E♭) 4cl(C & B♭) 2bthn 4hn(C) 2hn(G) 3bn cbn+serp 2tp(C) 2a-tb b-tb b-dr+cym s-dr t-dr tri.
Pc (Schlesinger: Berlin, pn 1384, 1833), score & parts: A-Wgm, VIII 44025, (overture, parts); D-DT, Mus-n 243,
(score, missing pp. 193/194 & all after p. 488); GB-Lbl, R.P.S.Pr.434, (parts, complete).
Pm (Overture, for 2ob 2cl 2hn 2bn cbn, 2tp ad lib) (Compusic: Amsterdam, pn 229, 1988), score & pts.

WELPMANN, Birgit
BRW-1a. Mozart: Sonata for Piano Duo, K.448.   2ob 2cl 2hn 2bn.
Pm (Karthause-Schmülling Internationale Musikverlage: Kamen, c.1993), score (pn 0047b) & parts (pn 0047a).

*WENT (Vent, Wendt, Wend, Wenth, Wennt, Venti), Johann (Jean) Nepomuk (Carlo) *1745 - 1801*
Versions of works by Rosetti, Starzer and Wagenseil scored for the Scharzenberg Harmonie (2ob 2ca 2hn 2bn)
may be transcriptions by Went. Went may also have prepared the anonymous arrangements of Starzer's works.
Works attributed to Went on strong evidence are indicated by +.
JNW-1.1. Parthia in Dis [E♭]; 5 mvts.   2ob 2cl 2hn 2bn.
MS parts (some pages reputedly by Johann Elssler, Haydn's copyist): A-Wgm, VIII 39988. ★
Pm (WINDS: Northridge, CA, pn W-34, c.1981), photocopy of original A-Wgm parts.
Pm (Compusic: Amsterdam, pn 257, 1988), score & parts.
JNW-1.2. Parthia No. 51; in E♭, 5 mvts.   2fl 2cl 2hn 2bn.
MS parts: RF-Ssc, Ф 891 собр юосуповьix N43, pp. 36 - 55.
Pm (Český hudební fond: Prague, 1961), ed. František Laštůvska, hire score No. 08667.
JNW-2. Parthia No. 17; in B♭, 4 mvts.   2fl 2cl 2hn 2bn.
MS parts: RF-Ssc, Ф 891 собр юосуповьix N43, pp. 2 - 17.
Pm (Český hudební fond: Prague, pn 3348, 1974), ed. František Laštůrka & Zdenčk Sesták, Musica antiqua
boemica, score & parts; also on hire, No. 5474.
JNW-3. Parthia in Dis [E♭] №1; 4 mvts.   2ob 2cl 2hn 2bn.
MS parts: H-Bn, Ms.Mus.IV 1521, (as by "Venti"). ★
JNW-4. Parthia No. 3, in B[♭]; 4 mvts.   2ob 2cl 2hn(B♭ alto) 2bn.
MS parts: H-Bn, Ms.Mus.IV 1484, (as by "Venti"). ★
JNW-5. Nro. 1mo Parthia In C; 4 mvts.   2ob 2cl 2hn 2bn.   MS parts: A-Ee, Mus.1166. ★
JNW-6.1. Nro. 2do Parthia In B[♭]; 6 mvts.   2ob 2cl 2hn 2bn.   MS parts: A-Ee, Mus.1167, (with local rescoring
in pencil in the final Rondo. Allo. modto.). ★
JNW-6.2. Parthia In B[♭]; mvts 1, 3, 4 & 6 of JNW-8.1.   2ob 2ca 2hn 2bn
MS parts: CZ-K, symphonie No.242.K.II.
JNW-7. Nro. 3tio Parthia In E♭; 6 mvts.   2ob 2cl 2hn 2bn.   MS parts: A-Ee, Mus.1168. ★
JNW-8. Nro. 4 Parthia in E♭; 6 mvts.   2ob 2cl 2hn 2bn.   MS parts: A-Ee, Mus.1169. ★
JNW-9.1. Nro. 5 Parthia in Dis [E♭]; 5 mvts.   2ob 2cl 2hn 2bn.   MS parts: A-Ee, Mus.1170. ★
JNW-9.2. Parthia in F; 5 mvts.   2ob 2ca 2hn 2bn.   MS parts: A-Wgm, VIII 8539. ★
JNW-10. N: 6 Parthia in Dis [E♭]; 5 mvts.   2ob 2cl 2hn 2bn.   MS parts: A-Ee, Mus.1171; D-RUl, RH. W55,
(as "N№ 6. Parthia in Es [E♭]"). ★
JNW-11. Parthia in F; 5 mvts.   2ob 2ca 2hn 2bn.   MS parts: CZ-K, symfonie No.229.K.II. ★
JNW-12. Parthia in C; 3 mvts.   2ob 2ca 2hn 2bn.   MS parts: CZ-K, symfonie No.230.K.II. ★
JNW-13. Parthia in F; 4 mvts.   2ob 2ca 2hn 2bn.   MS parts: CZ-K, symfonie No.241.K.II. ★
JNW-14. Parthia in C; 8 mvts.   2ob 2ca 2hn 2bn.   MS parts: CZ-K, symfonie No.245.K.II. ★
JNW-15. Parthia in B[♭]; 5 mvts.   2ob 2ca 2hn 2bn.   MS parts: CZ-K, symfonie No.246.K.II. ★
JNW-16. Parthia in F; 5 mvts.   2ob 2ca 2hn 2bn.   MS parts: CZ-K, symfonie No.247.K.II. ★
JNW-17. Parthia in F; 5 mvts.   2ob 2ca 2hn 2bn.   MS parts: CZ-K, symfonie No.248.K.II. ★
JNW-18. Parthia in C; 4 mvts.   2ob 2ca 2hn 2bn.   MS parts: CZ-K, symfonie No.249.K.II. ★
JNW-19. Parthia in F; 4 mvts.   2ob 2ca 2hn 2bn.   MS parts: CZ-K, symfonie No.251.K.II. ★
JNW-20. Parthia in F; 4 mvts.   2ob 2ca 2hn 2bn.   MS pts: CZ-K, symfonie No.252.K.II; CZ-Pnm, XLII.E.339,
(as an anonymous "Parthia ala Camera Ex Dis" for 2ca 2hn bn).   *In the CZ-Pnm (Clam Gallas) version an
additional Minuetto & Trio has been added at a later date; we do not believe that this mvt is by Went and treat
it as a separate anonymous work.* ★
JNW-21. Parthia in F; 4 mvts.   2ob 2ca 2hn 2bn.   MS parts: CZ-K, symfonie No.253.K.II. ★
JNW-22. Parthia in C Allelua; 4 mvts.   2ob 2ca 2hn 2bn.   MS parts: CZ-K, symfonie No.355.K.I. ★
JNW-23. Parthia in G; 5 mvts.   2ob 2ca 2hn 2bn.   MS parts: CZ-K, symfonie No.254.K.II. ★
JNW-24. Parthia in F; 4 mvts.   2ob 2ca 2hn 2bn.   MS parts: A-Wgm, VIII 8539. ★
JNW-25(-30). 6 Parthias [C, D# (=E♭), B♭, B♭, C minor, C minor].   2ob 2ca 2hn 2bn.
MS parts: A-Wgm, VIII 8539, (missing since 1989).
JNW-31. 18 Piéces [sic].   2ob 2ca 2hn 2bn.   MS parts: CZ-K, symfonie No.250.K.II. ★
JNW-32.1. 17 Piéces [sic].   2ob 2ca 2hn 2bn.   MS parts: CZ-K, symfonie No.255.K.II.   *"17" has been added
in pencil; the horn parts include two additional mvts.* ★
*JNW-32.2. Pièces en harmonie; Suite 1: Nos. 1 - 11; Suite 2, Nos. 12 - 23.   4cl 2hn bn.
Pc (Jean Henri Naderman: Paris, pn 133, 134, c.1792); 1e Suite, RISM [V 791]; 2e Suite, RISM [V 792], parts:
D-Tu, (suite 1 only); F-Pn, (2 complete copies), Vm7 6961, Vm27 4382 (1 - 2).   *Nos. 1 - 15 correspond to Nos.
1 - 15 of JNW-32.1; Nos. 22 & 23 may correspond to JNW-32.1, Nos. 16 (in horn pts only) & 17, respectively.
Nos. 16 - 21 do not match any of the other mvts in the sets of Piéces [sic] in CZ-K (JNW-31 - JNW-33).* ★
JNW-33. 12 Piéces [sic].   2ob 2ca 2hn 2bn.   MS parts: CZ-K, symfonie No.256.K.II. ★
JNW-34. Parthia IIda; in E♭, 4 mvts.   2cl 2hn 2bn.   MS parts: CZ-KRa, A4457/R.I.27 a-f, No. 2. ★
JNW-35. Parthia in B♭; 4 mvts.   2cl 2hn 2bn.
MS parts: H-KE, 0/128, (bequest from Johann Gallyus, Advokat in Zagreb, 1802); CZ-KRa, A4457/R.I.27 a-f,
No. 7, (as Anon, "Parthia Nro. 7mo"). ★
JNW-36. Parthia Nro. VIII; in E♭, 4 mvts.   2cl 2hn 2bn.
MS parts: CZ-KRa, A4457/R.I.27 a-f, No. 8, (as Anon). ★
JNW-37. Parthia Nro. IX; in E♭, 4 mvts.   2cl 2hn 2bn.
MS parts: CZ-KRa, A4457/R.I.27 a-f, No. 9, (as Anon). ★
JNW-38. Parthia Nro X; in B♭, 4 mvts.   2cl 2hn 2bn.
MS parts: CZ-KRa, A4457/R.I.27 a-f, No. 10, (as Anon). ★
*JNW-39. Parthia Nro. 11; in E♭, 4 mvts.   2cl 2hn 2bn.   MS parts: CZ-KRa, A4457/R.I.27 a-f, No. 11. ★
*JNW-40. Parthia Nro. 12; in E♭, 5 mvts.   2cl 2hn 2bn.   MS parts: CZ-KRa, A4457/R.I.27 a-f, No. 12. ★
JNW-41. Parthia In C; 4 mvts.   2ca 2hn 2bn.   MS parts: A-Wgm, VIII 8539, (missing hn I). ★
*JNW-42. Parthia in E♭; 4 mvts.   2ca 2hn bn.   MS parts: CZ-K, symfonie No.232.K.II.; CZ-Pnm, XLII.E.317,
(as "N: I Parthia a la Cammara (sic), in D."). ★

*JNW-43. Parthia in E♭; 4 mvts. 2ca 2hn bn. MS pts: CZ-K, symfonie No.234.K.II.; CZ-Pnm, XLII.E.316. ★
*JNW-44. Parthia ala Camera ex Dis [E♭]; 4 mvts. 2ca 2hn bn. MS parts: CZ-K, symfonie No.235.K.II. ★
*JNW-45. Parthia in E♭; 4 mvts. 2ca 2hn bn. MS parts: CZ-K, symfonie No.236.K.II.
*JNW-46. Parthia in Dis [E♭]; 5 mvts. 2ca 2hn bn. MS parts: CZ-Pnm, XLII.E.318. ★
JNW-47. N: 6 Parthia in Dis [E♭]; 6 mvts. 2ob 2hn bn. MS parts: CZ-Pnm, XLII.E.33. ★
JNW-48. Parthia alla Camera; in F, 4 mvts. 2ob 2hn bn. MS parts: CZ-Pnm, XLII.E.103. ★
JNW-49. Parthia in Dis [E♭]; 4 mvts. 2ob 2hn bn. MS parts: CZ-Pnm, XLII.E.315. ★
JNW-50(-52). [3 sets of] Pièces d'harmonie; (B♭, 3 mvts; B♭, 4 mvts; B♭, 4 mvts). 2fl 2cl 2hn 2bn.
MS parts: RF-Ssc, Ф 891 собр юосуповвіх N44, pp. 75 - 88, 89 - 102, 103 - 118. ★
JNW-1s. Divertimento in F No. IIItio a 3. 2ob ca. MS parts: CZ-K, No.36.III.K.23. ★
JNW-2s. Divertimento in C, No. VIto a 3. 2ob ca. MS parts: CZ-K, No.36.VI.K.23. ★
JNW-3s. Petite Sérénade Concertée [sic]; in F, 6 mvts. 2ob ca.
MS parts: CZ-K, No.23.K.23. ★
Pm (Edition Kneusslin: Basle, 1972), ed. Antonín Myslík, parts, (Für Kenner und Liebhaber No. 44).
JNW-4s. Trio Concerté [sic]. 2ob ca. MS parts: CZ-K, No.24.K.23. ★
JNW-5s. Trio in C: No. 1mo. 2ob ca. MS parts: CZ-K, No.36.I.K.23. ★
JNW-6s. Trio in B(♭) Nro. IIdo. 2ob ca. MS parts: CZ-K, No.36.II.K.23. ★
JNW-7s. Trio in C, Nro. IVto. 2ob ca. MS parts: CZ-K, No.36.IV.K.23. ★
JNW-8s. Trio in B(♭), No. Ca. 2ob ca. MS parts: CZ-K, No.36.I.K.23. ★
JNW-9.1s. [8] Variazioni in C: Thema di Giuseppe Haydn [Symphony in D, "L'Impériale", Hob.I/53/ii].
Acomodata [sic] di Went. 2ob ca. MS parts: CZ-K, No.35.K.23, No. 2. *The original Andante is not a theme*
& variations; it is possible that "Acomodata" here means composed by Went as well. ★
JNW-9.2s. [8] Variazioni in C: Thema di Giuseppe Haydn (Symphony in D, "L'Impériale", Hob.I/53/ii).
Acomodata [sic] di Went. 2fl ca. MS parts: A-Wgm, VIII 1228, No. 2.
JNW-10.1s. Variazioni in C: Del La Opera di Molinara [by Paisiello: "Nel cor più non mi sento"]. 2ob ca.
MS parts: CZ-K, No.35.K.23, No. 4. ★
Pm (Edition Kneusslin: Basle, 1972), ed. Antonín Myslík, parts, (Für Kenner und Liebhaber No. 64).
JNW-10.2s. Variazioni in C: Del La Opera di Molinara. 2fl ca. MS parts: A-Wgm, VIII 1228, No. 4.
JNW-11s [unidentified] Parthia; in E♭. 2ob 2cl 2hn 2bn. MS parts: D-Bds, Mus.Ms.23010/15.

JNW-1a. [Oktett], 7 mvts. 2ob 2cl 2hn 2bn. MS pts (1814): CZ-Bm(au), A.35.133, (No. 7 is by Mozart).
This is undoubtedly a compilation from a number of Went's works; all 7 mvts are Andante. Nos. 5 - 7 call for
clarinet I in Es [E♭] rather than in B♭, indicating that this is a local rescoring.
JNW-2.1a. Pies [sic] Di Diversi Balli; 13 mvts. 2ob 2ca 2hn 2bn. MS parts: A-Wgm, VIII 41158.
   2.1/1a. Dutillieu: Des Machte der schöne Geschichtes, sinfonia & 7 mvts. Nos. [0], 1 - 8.
   2.1/2a. Grétry: L'Amant jaloux, 2 mvts. Nos. 9 & 10.
   2.1/3a. Anon: Die Fogelsteler [sic], 1 mvt. No. 11.
   2.1/4a. Anon: Capiten Kok [sic], 1 mvt. No. 12.
JNW-2.2a. Dutillieu: Die Macht des schönen Geschlechts, sinfonia & 13 mvts. 2ob 2ca 2hn 2bn.
MS parts: CZ-K, balety No.174.K.II. *Nos. 11 & 12 correspond to the two sections of JNW-2.1/11a.*
JNW-3a. Diversi Opern Arien, (5 unidentified mvts). 2cl 2hn 2bn. MS parts: CZ-Pnm, XLI.B.115.
JNW-4a. Franzosische Stücke aus Opern, 21 mvts. 2ob 2ca 2hn 2bn.
MS parts: CZ-K, opery No.8.K.I, (there is no bn II part for No. 20). *On internal evidence we believe that Went*
was the arranger. Most mvts cannot be identified; only the following bear any information: No. 11, "de Midas",
No. 16, "Del Sig. Rubrecht" (probably the singer rather than composer), No. 20, "Aria von Rossen Mädchen".
JNW-5a. Vari Pezzi degli Balli, 9 mvts. 2cl 2hn 2bn. MS parts: CZ-Pnm, XLII.E.319.
+JNW-6a. Asplmayr: La Lavandara di Cittere, 8 mvts. 2ob 2ca 2hn (2)bn.
MS parts: (A-24a), CZ-K, No.175.K.II; CZ-Pnm, XLII.C.256. *On the titlepage of the CZ-Pnm copy (Clam*
Gallas collection), the "o" in "Fagotto" has been scratched out & the word altered to "Fagotti"; however, there
are no divisi passages.
+JNW-7a. Asplmayr: Agamemnon vengé, 8 mvts. 2ob 2ca 2hn 2bn.
MS parts: CZ-K, balety No.152/a.K.II.
+JNW-8a. Asplmayr: La Sposa Persiana, 20 mvts. 2ob 2ca 2hn 2bn.
MS parts (Fagotti part dated 1775): CZ-K, balety No.1.K.II.
+JNW-9a. Asplmayr: Il contra tempo, overture & 24 mvts. 2ob 2ca 2hn 2bn.
MS parts: CZ-K, balety No.2.K.II.
+JNW-10a. Asplmayr: A quelque chose malheur et bon, sinfonia & 9 mvts. 2ob 2ca 2hn 2bn.
MS parts: CZ-K, balety No.143.K.II.
JNW-11.1a. Cimarosa: Il Matrimonio segreto, introduzione (= overture) & 10 mvts. 2ob 2cl 2hn 2bn.
Pc (Traeg: Vienna, pre-1799), MS parts: A-Ee, Mus.1151; A-Wn, Mus.Hs.3807; I-Fc, F.P. S.346.
JNW-11.2a. Cimarosa: Il Matrimonio segreto, introduzione (= overture) & 10 mvts. 2ob 2ca 2hn 2bn.
MS parts: CZ-K, opery No.24.K.I.
JNW-11.3a. Cimarosa: Il Matrimonio segreto, overture & 10 mvts. 2cl 2hn 2bn.
MS parts: CZ-KRA, (2 copies; both incorrectly identify Mozart as the composer), A3935/IV.B.98, (copy by
Havel, 18 Dec 1813), A4454/R.I.24, No. 1; CZ-Pnm, XLI.A.92 (cl I & II, bn I) & XLI.D.321 (hn I & II, bn II).
JNW-12a. Cimarosa: Gli Orazi e Curiazi, sinfonia & 9 mvts. 2ob 2cl 2hn 2bn.
Pc (K.K. Hoftheater Musik Verlag: Wien, c.1796), MS parts: A-Ee, Mus.1082; CZ-KRa, A4010/IV.B.183;
I-Fc, F.P. S.330.
JNW-13.1a. Dittersdorf: Der Doktor und Apotheker. 2ob 2cl 2hn 2bn.
MS parts: D-DO, Mus.Ms.349, (Parts I & II; copy by Rosinack); NL-Ura/mZ, Z1175/M.A.Zcm.17, (sinfonia &
7 mvts; No. 9 is, in fact, the Marcia & "Amanti costanti seguaci d'amor" from Mozart's *Le Nozze di Figaro*, Act
III = mvt 13 in the A-Ee copy of JNW-28.1a).
JNW-13.2a. Dittersdorf: Der Doktor und Apotheker, 6 mvts. 2ob 2ca 2hn 2bn.
MS parts: CZ-K, opery No.17.K.I.
JNW-14a. Dittersdorf: Hieronymus Knicker, overture & 15 mvts. 2ob 2cl 2hn 2bn. MS parts: D-DO,
Mus.Ms.347, (arranger incorrectly given as "Capellmeister Starck" - or "Wast"); NL-DHgm, hk 19 C 3.

JNW-15.1a. Dutillieu: Die Macht des schönen Geschlechts, Pas de Deux del Signore Wulgani [sic] è Signora Muzarelli. 2ob ca. MS parts: CZ-K, No.35.K.23, No. 6.
JNW-15.2a. Dutillieu: Die Macht des schönen Geschlechts, Pas de Deux del Signore Vulgani è Signora Muzarelli. 2fl ca. MS parts: A-Wgm, VIII 1228, No. 6.
+JNW-16a. Gerl & Schack: Der dumme Gärtner aus dem Gebirge, 16 mvts. 2ob 2ca 2hn 2bn.
MS parts: CZ-K, opery No.15.K.I. *Probably a transcription of Heidenreich's octet arrangement, JYH-1a.*
+JNW-17.1a. Gluck: Le Rencontre imprévue. 2ob 2cl 2hn 2bn.
MS parts: F.P. S.325, CZ-Pnm, Lobkovic X.H.a57, Nos. 1 - 4 (= Krechler, FFK-1.1/1-3ad, "A ma maîtresse j'avais promis", "Mahomet, notre grand prophète", "Un ruisselet bien clair").
*+JNW-17.2/1-5a. Gluck: Le Rencontre imprévue, 5 mvts. 2ob 2ca 2hn 2bn; (1 ca in No. 31; 1 bn in No. 35)
MS parts: CZ-K, opery No.31.K.I and No.32.K.I, (2 arias, "aus Die Pilger nach Mecca": "J'ai perdu mon étalage" & "Vous ressemblez à la rose naissante"); CZ-K, No.33.K.I, ("das kleine Wasser" i.e., "Un ruisselet bien clair"); CZ-K, No.34.K.I, ("Mochomet, notre grand prophète"); CZ-K, No.35.K.I, (aria, "A ma maîtresse J'avais promis").
In both case where one instrument appears (No.32.K.I & No.35.K.I), the wrapper lists it in the singular; the parts are marked, "Corno Inglese Io" & "Fagotto 1mo", respectively. Both appear to be complete and we believe that this is just an indication of which player was to play the part..
*+JNW-18a. Gluck: Alceste (Italian version only), aria, "Non vi turbate". 2ob 2ca 2hn 2bn.
MS parts: CZ-K, No.36.K.I.
+JNW-19a. Grétry: L'Amant jaloux (as "Die ersterwichtig [sic] Liebhaber"), 6 mvts. 2ob 2ca 2hn 2bn.
MS parts: CZ-K, opery No.6.K.I. *Previous attributions of this work to Storace are unfounded.*
JNW-20.1a. Guglielmi: La Pastorella nobile, sinfonia & 9 mvts. 2ob 2cl 2hn 2bn.
Pc (Traeg: Vienna, pre-1799), MS parts: A-Ee, Mus.1109; A-Wgm(c), (?lost); I-Fc, F.P. S.331.
JNW-20.2a. Guglielmi: La Pastorella nobile, sinfonia & 9 mvts. 2ob 2ca 2hn 2bn.
MS parts: CZ-K, opery No.11.K.I.
JNW-21.1a. Guglielmi: La Bella Pescatrice, sinfonia & 11 mvts. 2ob 2cl 2hn 2bn.
Pc (Traeg: Vienna, pre-1799), MS parts: A-Ee, Mus.1102; A-Wgm(c), (?lost); I-Fc, F.P. S.336.
JNW-21.2a. Guglielmi: La Bella Pescatrice, sinfonia & 10 mvts. 2ob 2ca 2hn 2bn.
MS parts: CZ-K, opery No.10.K.I.
JNW-22.1a. Haydn: Symphony in G, "Surprise", (Hob. I/94ii), 2nd mvt, Andante. 2ob 2cl 2hn 2bn.
MS parts: I-Fc, (unverified). (= HAYDN, F.J., FJH-12d).
JNW-22.2a. Haydn: Symphony in G, "Surprise", (Hob. I/94ii), 2nd mvt, Andante. 2ob 2ca 2hn 2bn.
MS parts: CZ-K, symfonie No.121.K.II.
JNW-23a. Hoffmeister: Rosalinde, oder Die Macht der Feen, overture & 13 mvts. fl 2ob 2hn 2bn.
MS parts: H-Bn, Ms.Mus.IV.304, (as by "Carlo Went").
*JNW-24.1a. Kozeluch: La ritrovata Figlia d'Ottone II, overture & 16 mvts. 2ob 2cl 2hn 2bn.
Pc (Traeg: Vienna, c.1794-1798), MS parts: A-Ee, Mus.1156; A-KR, RH-K 74, (with minimal cbn pt); A-Wn, Mus.Hs.3866; CZ-Bm(no), A.16.644, (as Anon); D-DO, Mus.Ms.158; D-Rtt, Winter 5, (incorrectly titled, "Ballet / Das Waldmädchen oder die wiedergefundene Tochter / von Peter von Winter"; as a further confusion, the ob I part attributes this ballet to Haydn. The 1820 Gardemusik catalog notes, "Im Monat Juny 1820 bei H. Schaeffauer in Stuttgart . . . gekauft"); D-RUl, RH-K 74, (overture & 15 mvts, with minimal cbn pt).
JNW-24.2a. Kozeluch: La ritrovata Figlia d'Ottone II, overture & 16 mvts. 2ob 2ca 2hn 2bn.
MS parts: CZ-K, balety No.180.K.II, (as Anon). *Went also prepared a string quartet arrangement, CZ-K balety No.145.K.24, overture & 33 mvts (numbered [0], 1 - 3, 3½, 4 - 19, 19½, 20, 20½, 21 - 30).*
JNW-24.3a. Kozeluch: La ritrovata figlia d'Ottone II, overture & 16 mvts. 2cl 2hn 2bn.
MS parts: CZ-KRa, A4452/R.I.22, No. 7; CZ-Pnm, XLI.B.284, (overture & 13 mvts: Nos. 6 & 7, 11 & 12, 15 & 16 are combined; the last pair precede the usual final mvt, No. 17 Allegretto. 6/8 with minor & major sections).
JNW-25.1a. Martín y Soler: Una cosa rara, sinfonia & 17 mvts. 2ob 2cl 2hn 2bn.
Pc (Traeg,: Vienna, pre-1799), MS pts: A-Ee, Mus.1149; D-DO, Mus.Ms.1294, (as Anon; ?lost); I-Fc, F.P. S.323; D-Dl, Mus. 3946/F13; NL-DHgm, hk 19 C 1, (as arranged - & probably altered - by Rosinack, 7 mvts).
JNW-25.2a. Martín y Soler: Una cosa rara, sinfonia & 15 mvts. 2ob 2ca 2hn 2bn.
MS parts: CZ-K, opery No.22.K.I.
JNW-25.3a. Martín y Soler: Una cosa rara. 2ob 2bthn 2hn 2bn serp.
MS parts: GB-Lbl, R.M.21.d.3, (A-203, *VXM-1da:* Nos. 1 - 3 = JNW-25.2a, Nos. 11 [also found split at A-204.34(a) & 35(a)], 8 & 15 [also found at A-204.36(a)]; *VXM-2da:* Nos. 1 - 3 = JNW-25.2a, Nos. 12, 9 & 7; *VXM-3ad:* Nos. 1 - 4 = JNW-25.2a, Nos. 2, 3 & 16 (split). [also found at A-204.49(a)]; *VXM-4da:* Nos. 1 - 3 = JNW-25.2a, Nos. 5, 14 & 10).
JNW-26.1a. Martín y Soler: L'Arbore di Diana, overture & 24 mvts. 2ob 2cl 2hn 2bn.
Pc (Traeg: [Vienna], pre-1799), MS parts: A-Ee, Mus.1150; A-Wn, Mus.Hs.3816; CZ-Pnm, XLII.D.86; D-DO, Mus.Ms.1282; I-Fc, F.P. S.323.
JNW-26.2a. Martín y Soler: L'Arbore di Diana, overture & 24 mvts. 2ob 2ca 2hn 2bn.
MS parts: CZ-K, opery No.22.K.I.
*JNW-27.1a. Mozart: Die Entführung aus dem Serail, overture & 7 mvts. 2ob 2cl 2hn 2bn.
Pc (Traeg: [Vienna], pre-1799), MS parts: I-Fc, F.P. S.370.
Pm (Musica rara: London, pn 1826, 1975), ed. H. Voxman, score & parts.
*JNW-27.2a. Mozart: Die Entführung aus dem Serail, overture & 7 mvts. 2ob 2ca 2hn 2bn.
MS parts (1783): CZ-K, opery No.38.K.I.
Pm (Bärenreiter: Kassel, pn BA 3897, 1958), ed. Franz Giegling, score & parts.
*JNW-28.1a. Mozart: Le Nozze di Figaro, sinfonia & 14 mvts. 2ob 2cl 2hn 2bn.
MS parts: A-Ee, Mus.1152; D-Bds, König. Hausbibl. No. 345; D-DO, Mus.Ms.1394/1, (copy by Rosinack); I-Fc, F.P. S.329; NL-Z, Z1175/M.A.Zcm.17, (the Marcia & "Amanti costanti seguaci d'amor" from Act III included as No. 9 of Went's arrangement of Dittersdorf's opera, Der Doktor und Apotheker, JNW-8.1a).
Pm (Musica rara: London, pn 1825a/b, 1975), 2 vols., ed. R. Block & H. Voxman, (based on the I-Fc copy), score & parts.
Pm (WINDS: Northridge, CA, pn W-128, c.1980), based on D-Bds parts.

*JNW-28.2a. Mozart: Le Nozze di Figaro, sinfonia & 14 mvts. 2ob 2ca 2hn 2bn.
MS parts: CZ-K, opery No.39.K.I..
JNW-28.3a. Mozart: Le Nozze di Figaro. 2ob 2bthn 2hn 2bn.
MS parts: D-Bds, Mus.ms.15140/4.
JNW-29.1a. Mozart: Don Giovanni, overture & 10 mvts. 2ob 2cl 2hn 2bn.
MS parts: A-Ee, Mus.1110.
*JNW-29.2a. Mozart: Don Giovanni, sinfonia & 11 mvts. 2ob 2ca 2hn 2bn.
MS parts (1788): CZ-K, opery No.37.K.I, (Act I, mvts 2 - 8; Act II, mvts 9 - 12).
*JNW-30.1a. Mozart: Così fan tutte, overture & (?13) mvts. 2ob 2cl 2hn 2bn.
Pc (Traeg: [Vienna], pre-1799), MS parts: I-Fc, F.P. S.317.
Pm (Musica rara: London, pn 1876, 1877, 1976), 2 vols., score & parts, (overture & 13 mvts).
JNW-30.2a. Mozart: Così fan tutte, overture & 17 mvts. 2ob 2ca 2hn 2bn. MS parts: CZ-K, opery No.41.K.I.
*JNW-31.1a. Mozart: Die Zauberflöte, overture & 18 mvts. 2ob 2cl 2hn 2bn.
MS parts: A-Ee, Mus.1112, (omits Nos. 18 & 19); D-Rtt, W.A. Mozart 27/IV; D-W, Cod.Guelf.169
Mus.Handschr., (13 mvts, missing ob I, cl I & II, bn I; "Augeschaft [sic] für d[ie] M[usikalische] G[esellschaft
in Braunschweig], 1797 durch Aldefeld" - for another work for this society, *See* Vogel, KXV-1a).
JNW-31.2a. Mozart: Die Zauberflöte, overture & 14 mvts. 2ob 2ca 2hn 2bn. MS pts: CZ-K, opery No.41.K.I.
JNW-32a. W. Müller: Kaspar der Fagottist, sinfonia & 14 mvts. 2ob 2cl 2hn 2bn.
Pc (Traeg: [Vienna], pre-1799), No. 94, MS parts: A-Ee, Mus.1101; D-DO, Mus.Ms.1409; I-Fc, F.P. S.405, (with
cbn part); NL-DHgm, hk 19 B 19.
JNW-33a. W. Müller: Das neu Sonntagskind, 13 mvts (without overture). 2ob 2cl 2hn 2bn.
Pc (Traeg: [Vienna], pre-1799), MS parts: A-Ee, Mus.1158. *The arrangement does not include JNW-73a.*
JNW-34.1a. Naumann: Cora och Alonzo. 2ob 2cl 2hn 2bn. MS parts: I-Fc, F.P. S.354.
+JNW-34.2a. Naumann: Cora [och Alonzo], 19 mvts. 2ob 2ca 2hn 2bn.
MS parts: CZ-K, opery No.5.K.I, (incorrectly cites Méhul as the composer).
JNW-35.1a. Paer: Camilla, overture & 10 mvts. 2ob 2cl 2hn 2bn.
MS parts: A-Wn, Mus.Hs.3792, Nos. 18 - 23, (A-6.18a(-23a), sinfonia & 5 mvts); CZ-Bm(au), A.35.202, (6 mvts
following Krommer's Op. 73, local copy; No. 7 is a Duetto from Paer's *Sargines* = No. 7 of Sedlak's
arrangement); CZ-Bm(no), A.16.656; CZ-Pnm, (2 copies), XX.F.18, XLI.B.146.
MS score (as Anon, allegedly in the hand of J.S. Mayr): I-BGc, Mayr 566.
JNW-35.2a. Paer: Camilla, overture & 10 mvts. 2ob 2cl 2hn 2bn cbn.
Pc (Nel Magazzino [sic] di Musica dei teatri Reali: Vienna, post-1799), MS parts: A-Ee, Mus.1088;
A-Wn, Mus.Hs.3824; I-Fc, F.P. S.410; I-MOe, Mus.D.302, (without imprint). *The cbn part may be a later
addition - possibly by Triebensee.*
JNW-35.3a. Paer: Camilla, overture & 10 mvts. 2cl 2hn 2bn.
MS parts: CZ-Pnm, XLI.B.146, (local copy, with a set of horn & bn parts professionally copied in Vienna);
PL-LA, RM ?? (shelfmark omitted from catalog, Reference No. 2310; untraced). Although CZ-KRa,
A4452/R.I.22, No. 1 bears the note "Acom. Havel" it is essentially JNW-35.3a with some mvts transposed.
JNW-36.1a. Paisiello: La Frascatana. 2ob 2cl 2hn 2bn. *See also JNW-2ac.*
Pc (Traeg: [Vienna], pre-1799), No. 84, MS parts: A-Wgm(c), (?lost); D-DO, Mus.Ms.1544, (attributed to
Rosinack); I-Fc, F.P. S.327.
JNW-36.2a. Paisiello: La Frascatana, 9 mvts. 2ob 2ca 2hn 2bn. MS parts: CZ-K, opery No.25.K.I.
JNW-37.1a. Paisiello: Gli Astrologi immaginari (Die eingebildenten Philosophen), 10 mvts. 2ob 2cl 2hn 2bn.
MS parts: A-Wn, Mus.Hs.1961. *The 4th mvt does not appear in any known version of the opera. See also*
JNW-4.1ac & JNW-4.2ac.
JNW-37.2a. Paisiello: Gli Astrologi immaginari (Die eingenbildeten Philosophen), 10 mvts. 2ob 2ca 2hn 2bn.
MS parts: CZ-K, opery No.13.K.I. *See also JNW-4.1ac & JNW-4.2ac.*
JNW-38.1a. Paisiello: Il Matrimonio inaspettato (as "La Contadina di spirito"). 2ob 2cl 2hn 2bn.
Pc (Traeg: [Vienna], pre-1799), No. 98, MS parts: I-Fc, F.P. S.327.
JNW-38.2a. Paisiello: Il Matrimonio inaspettato (as "La Contadina di spirito"), 8 mvts. 2ob 2ca 2hn 2bn.
MS parts: CZ-K, opery No.28.K.I.
JNW-39.1a. Paisiello: La Finta amante, 7 mvts. 2ob 2cl 2hn 2bn. MS pts: I-Fc, F.P. S.353. *See also JNW-5ac.*
JNW-39.2a. Paisiello: La Finta amante, 7 mvts. 2ob 2ca 2hn 2bn. MS parts: CZ-K, opery No.21.K.I.
*JNW-40.1a. Paisiello: Il Barbiere di Siviglia, 10 mvts. 2ob 2cl 2hn 2bn.
MS parts: A-Ee, Mus.1100, (the MS incorrectly cites Salieri as the composer); A-Wgm(c), (?lost);
H-Bn, Ms.Mus.IV.305, (omits No. 7, Larghetto, 2/4, where the 2ob are tacet); I-Fc, F.P. S.324.
JNW-40.2a. Paisiello: Il Barbiere di Siviglia, overture & 9 mvts. 2ob 2ca 2hn 2bn.
MS parts: CZ-K, opery No.29.K.I.
JNW-40.3a. Paisiello: Il Barbiere di Siviglia, overture & 8 mvts (omits CZ-K, No. 9). 2ob 2bthn 2hn 2bn serp.
MS parts: GB-Lbl, R.M.21.d.2, Nos. 70 - 76, (= A-202.4/1-7).
JNW-41.1a. Paisiello: Il Re Teodoro in Venezia, introdutione & 13 mvts. 2ob 2cl 2hn 2bn.
Pc (Traeg: [Vienna], pre-1799), No. 83, MS parts: A-Ee, Mus.1148; A-K, H.42111; D-DO, Mus.Ms.1544, (copy
attributed to Rosinack); I-Fc, F.P. S.324.
JNW-41.2a. Paisiello: Il Re Teodoro in Venezia, introductione & 13 mvts. 2ob 2ca 2hn 2bn.
MS parts: CZ-K, opery No.30.K.I.
JNW-41.3a. Paisiello: Il Re Teodoro in Venezia, introductione & 13 mvts. 2fl 2ca 2hn 2bn.
MS parts: RF-Ssc, Ф 891 собр юосуповвьіх N19, pp. 156 - 210.
*JNW-42.1a. Paisiello: L'Amor contrastato ("La Molinara"), overture & 11 mvts. 2ob 2cl 2hn 2bn.
Pc (Traeg: [Vienna], pre-1799), No. 81, MS parts: A-Ee, Mus.1103; A-Wgm(c), (?lost); I-Fc, F.P. S.331. *Based
on Variant 8, performed at the Burgtheater, Vienna, 13 Nov 1790.*
*JNW-42.2a. Paisiello: L'Amor contrastato, ("La Molinara"), overture & 11 mvts. 2ob 2ca 2hn 2bn.
MS parts: CZ-K, opery No.27.K.I.

*JNW-42.3a. Paisiello: L'Amor contrastato ("La Molinara"), sinfonia & 11 mvts. 2cl 2hn 2bn.
Pc (Traeg: [Vienna], pre-1799), No. 39, MS parts: CZ-Pnm, XLI.B.161.
Pc (N. Simrock: Bonn, pn 559, 1807/1808), RISM [P 21], parts: CH-N, 5R.1576; D-Bhm; D-HR, HR III 4 1/2 2° 388 u. 4° 629; S-Skma, F6 A-R.
Pm (KGS), fiche (2369), of N. Simrock edition..
+JNW-42.4a. Paisiello: L'Amor contrastato ("La Molinara"), overture & 11 mvts. 2fl 2cl 2hn 2bn.
MS parts: RF-Ssc, Ф 891 собр юосуповъ ix N18, pp. 146 - 192.
JNW-43.1a. Paisiello: Nina, 7 mvts. 2ob 2ca 2hn 2bn. MS parts: CZ-K, opery No.25.K.I, (missing ob I).
JNW-43.2a. Paisiello: Nina. 2ob 2cl 2hn 2bn. MS parts: A-Wgm(c), (?lost).
JNW-44a. Pleyel: Symphony in F, (B.136), 4 mvts. 2ob 2ca 2hn 2bn.
MS parts (as "Parthia in F"): A-Wgm, VIII 8539.
JNW-45a. Pleyel: Symphony in A, (B.137), 3 mvts (omits mvt 3, Menuetto & Trio). 2ob 2ca 2hn 2bn.
MS parts (as "Parthia in C . . . accomodata di Went"): A-Wgm, VIII 8539.
JNW-46.1a. Righini: L'Incontro inaspettato, overture & 11 mvts. 2ob 2cl 2hn 2bn.
Pc (Traeg: [Vienna], pre-1799), No. 87, MS pts: A-Wn, Sm.3832, (12 mvts); I-Fc, F.P. S.325.
JNW-46.2a. Righini: L'Incontro inaspettato, overture & 12 mvts. 2ob 2ca 2hn 2bn.
MS parts: CZ-K, opery No.9.K.I.
JNW-47.1a. Salieri: Il Talismano, sinfonia & 15 mvts. 2ob 2cl 2hn 2bn.
Pc (Traeg: [Vienna], pre-1799), No114b, MS parts: A-Ee, Mus.1108; A-Wgm(c), (?lost); I-Fc, F.P. S.329.
JNW-47.2a. Salieri: Il Talismano, sinfonia & 15 mvts. 2ob 2ca 2hn 2bn. MS parts: CZ-K, opery No.44.K.I.
JNW-48a. Salieri: La Dama pastorella ("La Cifra"), sinfonia & 14 mvts. 2ob 2cl 2hn 2bn.
Pc (Traeg: [Vienna], pre-1799), No. 111, MS pts: A-Ee, Mus.1104; A-Wn, Mus.Hs.3846; I-Fc, F.P. S.346. *At the end of all parts in the A-Wn copy are 2 additional mvts, "Non ti par che mi guardassero" & "Chi mi sà dir cose quello" intended for insertion between mvts 8/9 & 11/12; is is possible that these insertions are in Went's hand.*
*JNW-49.1a. Salieri: Il Ricco d'un giorno, 7 mvts. 2ob 2cl(C) 2hn 2bn.
MS parts: A-Wn, Mus.Hs.3848. *Note: although the wrapper lists "2. Corni Basseti [sic]", these parts are not present; the 2cl(C) parts are in a different hand on slightly smaller paper, possibly prepared after Went's death. The missing basset horn parts may have been prepared for a special performance including itinerant players such as the Stadler brothers or Anton David, Valentin Springer and K. Franz Dworschack, cf. ANONYMOUS WORKS, England - Royal Music.*
JNW-49.2a. Salieri: Il Ricco d'un giorno, 7 mvts. 2ob 2ca 2hn 2bn. MS parts: CZ-K, opery No.45.K.I.
JNW-50.1a. Salieri: La Grotto di Trofonio, sinfonia & 14 mvts. 2ob 2cl 2hn 2bn.
Pc (Traeg: [Vienna], pre-1799), No. 112, MS parts: A-Ee, Mus.1107; A-Wgm(c), (?lost); I-Fc, F.P. S.323.
JNW-50.2a. Salieri: La Grotto di Trofonio, sinfonia & 12 mvts. 2ob 2ca 2hn 2bn.
MS parts: CZ-K, opery No.45.K.I.
JNW-51.1a. Salieri: Tarare (Axur, Re d'Ormus), introduzione & 17 short mvts. 2ob 2cl 2hn 2bn.
Pc (Traeg: [Vienna], pre-1799), MS pts: A-Ee, Mus.1153; A-Wn, Mus.Hs.3847, (as Anon); CZ-Pnm, XLI.B.116, (mvt 7 omitted); D-Rtt, Salieri 3, (as Anon, introduzione & 16 mvts -?mvt 7 omitted); I-Fc, F.P. S.329.
JNW-51.2a. Salieri: Tarare ("Axur, Rè d'Ormus), introduzione & 16 short mvts. 2ob 2ca 2hn 2bn.
MS parts: CZ-K, opery No.43.K.I.
JNW-52a. Salieri: Palmira, Regina di Persia, sinfonia & 22 mvts. 2ob 2cl 2hn 2bn.
Pc (k.k. Hoftheater Verlag: Vienna, 1796), MS pts: A-Ee, Mus.1144, (sinfonia & 16 mvts); A-Wn, Mus.Hs.3847; CZ-Bm(no), A.16.668, (sinfonia & 16 mvts; local copy, 1802); CZ-Pnm, XLI.B.171. (sinfonia & 16 mvts); D-DO, Mus.Ms.1709; I-Fc, F.P. S.326. *Also listed by Traeg as octet No. 220 in his 1804 Nachtrag.*
JNW-53.1a. Sarti: I Contratempi. 2ob 2cl 2hn 2bn.
Pc (Traeg: [Vienna], pre-1799), No. 88, MS parts: A-Wgm(c), (?lost); I-Fc, F.P. S.328.
JNW-53.2a. Sarti: I Contratempi, 10 mvts. 2ob 2ca 2hn 2bn. MS parts: CZ-K, opery No.20.K.I.
JNW-54.1a. Sarti: Giulio Sabino, 3 mvts. 2ob 2ca 2hn 2bn. MS parts: CZ-K, opery No.18.K.I.
+JNW-54.2a. Sarti: Giulio Sabino. 2ob 2cl 2hn 2bn.
MS parts: A-Wgm(c), (?lost); I-Fc, F.P. S.373, (Anon; with a later cbn part).
*JNW-55.1a. Sarti: Fra due Litiganti, 9 mvts. 2ob 2cl 2hn 2bn.
Pc (Traeg: [Vienna], pre-1799), No. 89, MS parts: A-Wn, Mus.Hs.3849; I-Fc, F.P. S.324.
JNW-55.2a. Sarti: Fra due Litiganti, 8 mvts. 2ob 2ca 2hn 2bn. MS parts: CZ-K, opery No.19.K.I.
+JNW-56a. Sarti: [unidentified] Terzetto. 2ob 2ca 2hn (2)bn.
MS parts: A-Wgm, VIII 8579, ("Fagotti" has been altered to "Fagotto" on the titlepage, there is only one part.).
The headtitle in some parts gives the work as "Aria Andantino"; not the same work as JNW-21ac.
JNW-57a. Stabinger: La Fête Flamande, sinfonia & 15 mvts. 2ob 2hn bn. MS parts: CZ-Pnm, XLII.B.162.
+JNW-58a. Starzer: La bianca e la rossa, 11 mvts. 2ob 2ca 2hn 2bn. MS parts: CZ-K, No.7.K.II.
JNW-59.1a. Storace: Gli Sposi malcontenti, 10 mvts. 2ob 2cl 2hn 2bn.
Pc (Traeg: [Vienna], pre-1799), No. 136, MS parts: H-Bn, Ms.Mus.IV.1,607; I-Fc, F.P. S.333.
JNW-59.2a. Storace: Gli Sposi malcontenti, 10 mvts. 2ob 2ca 2hn 2bn.
MS parts: CZ-K, opery No.4.K.I.
JNW-60.1a. J. Weigl: Il pazzo per forza. 2ob 2cl 2hn 2bn. MS parts: I-Fc, F.P. S.370.
JNW-60.2a. J. Weigl: Il pazzo per forza, overture & 14 mvts. 2ob 2ca 2hn 2bn.
MS parts: CZ-K, opery No.48.K.I.
JNW-61.1a. J. Weigl: La Principessa d'Amalfi, overture & 12 mvts. 2ob 2cl 2hn 2bn.
MS parts: A-Ee, Mus.1159, (omits No. 7); A-Wn, Mus.Hs.3855; I-Fc, F.P. S.349.
JNW-61.2a. J. Weigl: La Principessa d'Amalfi, overture & 11 mvts. 2ob 2ca 2hn 2bn.
MS parts: CZ-K, opery No.49.K.I. (same mvts as the A-Ee version supra).
JNW-62.1a. J. Weigl: Das Sinnbild des menschlichen Lebens, overture & 15 mvts. 2ob 2cl 2hn 2bn.
Pc (Traeg: [Vienna], pre-1799), No. 127, MS parts: A-Ee, Mus.1142; CZ-KRa, A4173/IV.B.167, No. 1, (copy by Havel, 26 July 1803). *Also published in MS by the k:k: Hoftheater-Musik-Verlag.*

JNW-62.2a. J. Weigl: Das Sinnbild des menschlichen Lebens, overture & 15 mvts.   2ob 2ca 2hn 2bn.
MS parts: CZ-K, balety No. 177.K.II.
JNW-62.3. J. Weigl: Das Sinnbild des menschlichen Lebens, overture & 15 mvts.   2cl 2hn 2bn.
MS parts: CZ-KRa, A4173/IV.B.167a, (copy by Havel, 26 July 1803); CZ-Pnm, XLI.B.125, (copy by Joseph Pražák; omits No. 3).
*JNW-63.1a. J. Weigl: Die Reue des Pigmalion, overture & 11 mvts.   2ob 2cl 2hn 2bn.
Pc (Traeg: [Vienna], pre-1799), No. 191, MS parts: A-Ee, Mus.1155; A-Wgm, VIII 39999; A-Wn, Mus.Hs.3872, (2 copies, the second incorporating the red crayon alterations on the first, Traeg, copy); D-DO, Mus.Ms.2014.
*JNW-63.2a. J. Weigl: Die Reue des Pygmalion, overture & 11 mvts.   2ob 2ca 2hn 2bn.
MS parts: CZ-K, opery No.47.K.I.
JNW-64a. J. Weigl: Giulietta e Pierotto, 12 mvts.   2ob 2ca 2hn 2bn.   MS parts: CZ-K, opery No.46.K.I.
JNW-65.1a. J. Weigl: Richard Löwenherz, overture & 14 mvts.   2ob 2cl 2hn 2bn.
Pc (Traeg: [Vienna], pre-1799), No. 125, MS parts: A-Ee, Mus.1154; CZ-Pnm, XLI.B.127.
Pc (Zu finden in einem K.K. Hof Theatral Musick [sic] Verlag: Wien, post-1796), MS rts: D-DO, Mus.Ms.2015; A-Wn, Mus.Hs.3792, No. 16, (marcia, No. 4; without MS imprint).
JNW-65.2a. J. Weigl: Richard Löwenherz, overture & 14 mvts.   2ob 2ca 2hn 2bn.
MS parts: CZ-K, balety No.176.K.II.
JNW-66.1a. J. Weigl: Der Raub der Helena, overture & 9 mvts.   2ob 2cl 2hn 2bn.
Pc (k.k. Hoftheater Verlag: Wien, 1796), MS parts: A-Ee, Mus.1143; D-DO, Mus.Ms.159.
JNW-66.2a. J. Weigl: Der Raub der Helena, overtrure & 9 mvts.   2ob 2ca 2hn 2bn.
MS parts: CZ-K, balety No.178.K.II.
+JNW-67a. J. Weigl: Alonzo e Cora, 10 mvts.   2ob 2cl 2hn 2bn.
Pc (Aus der K.K. Hoftheater Musik Verlag: Wien, c.1796), MS parts: A-Ee, Mus.1145.
+JNW-68.1a. T. Weigl: Die Vermählung im Keller, sinfonia & 11 mvts.   2ob 2cl 2hn 2bn.
Pc (Vienna: c.1796 - 1799), MS parts, No. 192: CZ-Bm(au), A.21.000 (2ob cl I, 2hn bn I) & CZ-Bm(au), A.35.259, (cl II, bn II), *local copy, 1817;* D-HR, HR III 4 1/2 2° 358, (as "Harmonie in C" with an additional basso part and a 13th mvt, the *Sinfonia Pastorale* from G. Bierey's opera, *Das Blumenmädchen;* this mvt may not be arranged by Went).
Pm (KGS), fiche (2309, 2310), of D-HR MS.
+JNW-68.2a. T. Weigl: Die Vermählung im Keller, sinfonia & 7 mvts.   2ob 2ca 2hn 2bn.
MS parts: CZ-K, balety No.78.K.II.
JNW-69a. T. Weigl: Die Hüldigung, overture & 11 mvts.   2ob 2cl 2hn 2bn.   MS parts: A-Wn, Mus.Hs.3876.
JNW-70a. T. Weigl: Das Gespenst im Traume, sinfonia & 12 mvts.   2ob 2cl 2hn 2bn.
MS parts: CZ-Pnm, Lobkovic X.G.f.60, (attributed to the choreographer, Clerico).
JNW-71a. Winter: Das unterbrochene Opferfest, overture & 10 mvts.   2ob 2cl 2hn 2bn.
MS parts: A-Ee, Mus.1087; A-Wn, Mus.Hs.3794, (A-7.3a; overture & 4 mvts); CZ-Bm(au), A.34.255, (A-4.1a; overture only).
Pc (In dem K.K. Hoftheater Musick [sic] Verlag: Wien, sd), MS parts: A-Wn, Mus.Hs.3859, (although the parts include one for "Fagotti Bassi" i.e., bn II + cbn, there are no divisi anywhere in the part); I-Fc, F.P. S.338.
+JNW-72.1a. P. Wranizky: Das Waldmädchen, overture & 13 mvts.   2ob 2cl 2hn 2bn.
MS parts: A-Wn, Mus.Hs.3871; A-Wn, Mus.Hs.3792, Nos. 32 & 33, (Nos. 11 & 12, Polonaise & La Russe, A-6.32a(-6.33a); CZ-Bm(no), A.16.676; CZ-KRa, A4168/IV.B.141, (as "Miscellans für 1816 del Sig. Starke" = STARKE, FRS-1ad); CZ-Pnm, XVIII.A.277, (modern MS copy by Robert Čech of the CZ-Bm(no) copy); D-DO, Mus.Ms.160; D-HR, HR III 4 1/2 2° 350, (as "Parthia. von Beecke"; probably only acquired by Beecke).
+JNW-72.2a. P. Wranizky: Das Waldmädchen, overture & 9 mvts.   2ob 2ca 2hn 2bn.   MS parts: H-KE, K 969.
+JNW-72.3a. P. Wranizky: Das Waldmädchen, overture & 11 mvts.   2cl 2hn 2bn.
MS parts: CZ-Pnm, (2 copies): XLI.A.90, (omits No. 8 of JNW-72.1a). XLI.D.322, (omits No. 8 of JNW-72.1a); CZ-KRa, A4454/R.I.24, No. 4, (Polonese & Masur only).
JNW-73.1a. J. Schuster [?arr. W. Müller]: Nro Vto Pas de Deux in C: del Signore é Signora Viganò.   2ob ca.
MS pts: CZ-K, No.35.V.K.23, No. 5.   *See also: ARRANGEMENTS LIST, MÜLLER, W.: Das neu Sonntagskind.*
JNW-73.2a. J. Schuster [?arr. W. Müller]: Nro Vto Pas de Deux in C: del Signore é Signora Viganò.   2fl ca.
MS parts: A-Wgm, VIII 1228, No. 5.
Unverified Attributions
JNW-1c. Parthia in Hes [B♭]; 5 mvts.   2ob 2ca 2hn 2bn.   MS parts: CZ-K, symfonie No.228.K.II.   ★
*JNW-1ac. Mozart: Serenade in C minor, K.388 (384a); 4 mvts.   2ob 2ca 2hn 2bn.
MS parts ("für die Kapelle Sr durchl[aucht] des Fürst Schwarzenberg"): A-Wgm, VIII 8570b.
MS score (by A. Unterreiter): D-B, Mus.ms.15339.   Modern MS score & parts: F-TOes; GB-Ljag.
JNW-2ac. Paisiello: La Frascatana, overture & 11 mvts.   2fl 2cl 2hn 2bn.
MS parts: RF-Ssc, Ф 891 собр юосуповьiх N17, pp. 1 - 61.
JNW-3ac. Paisiello: Le due Contesse.   2ob 2cl 2hn 2bn.   MS parts: I-Fc, F.P. S.328.
JNW-4.1ac. Paisiello: Gli Astrologi ammaginari, 2 Theils.   2ob 2cl 2hn 2bn cbn.   MS parts: I-Fc, F.P. S.371.
JNW-4.2ac. Paisiello: Gli Alstrologi immaginari (as "Due filosofi"), overture & 10 mvts.   2fl 2cl 2hn 2bn.
MS parts: RF-Ssc, Ф 891 собр юосуповьiх N16, pp. 140 - 177, (cl I part incomplete).
JNW-5ac. Paisiello: La finta Amante, overture & 9 mvts.   2fl 2cl 2hn 2bn.
MS parts: RF-Ssc, Ф 891 собр юосуповьiх N18, pp. 23 - 61.
JNW-6.1ac. Paisiello: La Serva Padrona, 2 Acts.   2ob 2cl 2hn 2bn.   MS parts: I-Fc, F.P. S.408.
JNW-6.2ac. Paisiello: La Serva Padrona, overture & 10 mvts.   2fl 2cl 2hn 2bn.
MS parts: RF-Ssc, Ф 891 собр юосуповьiх N17, pp. 62 - 109.
JNW-7ac. Paisiello: Il Barbiere di Siviglia, overture & 10 mvts.   2fl 2cl 2hn 2bn.
MS parts: RF-Ssc, Ф 891 собр юосуповьiх N19, pp. 1 - 153.
JNW-8ac. Paisiello: Le Gare generose.   2ob 2cl 2hn 2bn.
Pc (Traeg: [Vienna], pre-1799), No. 168, MS parts (A-254): A-Wgm(c), (?lost); I-Fc, F.P.S.331.
JNW-9ac. Paisiello: La Modista raggiatrice, overture & 7 mvts with "Credi...la mia ferita" from Paisiello's opera *Elfrida* and 2 unidentified mvts (JNW-9.2ac).   2fl 2cl 2hn 2bn.   MS pts: RF-Ssc, Ф 891 собр юосуповьiх N17.

JNW-10ac. Palma: La Pietra simpatica, sinfonia & 7 (+ 1) mvts.   2ob 2cl 2hn 2bn.
Pm (K.K. Hoftheater-Musik-Verlag: Wien, 1796), MS parts: A-Wn, Mus.Hs. 3830; I-Fc, F.P. S.326.
Statements that the A-Wn copy is partly in Went's hand & partly in Sedlak's are unfounded. The final mvt
(Quintetto, "Ecco l'amato aggetto") may be in Went's hand; this was originally intended for insertion after No. 6
(numbered "6½") but was later re-numbered "9" in red crayon. No. 2 has also been extended with the Duetto
"Mile volte mio tesoro" inserted after the initial Moderato; the hand is the same as that of the final Quintetto.
JNW-11ac. Salieri: La Fiera di Venezia, sinfonia & 15 mvts.   2ob 2cl 2hn 2bn. MS parts: A-Ee, Mus.1106.
JNW-12ac. Salieri: Der Rauchfangkehrer.   2ob 2cl 2hn 2bn.
Pc (Traeg: [Vienna], pre-1799), No. 113a, MS pts: I-Fc, F.P. S.328; CZ-Pnm, Lobkovic X.H.a.57, Nos. 8 & 9
(= KRECHLER, FFK-1.6/1-2ad).
JNW-13ac. Salieri: Falstaff.   2ob 2cl 2hn 2bn. MS parts: D-DO, (?lost); I-Fc, F.P. S.340.
JNW-14ac. Schenk: Die Weinlese, rondo.   2ob 2cl 2hn 2bn. MS parts: A-Wn, Mus.Hs.3850.
***JNW-15ac** (= **Triebensee, JZT-1ad**). Süssmayr: Der Spiegel von Arkadien, sinfonia & 18 mvts.
2ob 2cl 2hn 2bn. MS parts: A-Wn, Mus.Hs.3854. *Statements that this copy is partly in Went's hand &*
completed by Triebensee are completely unfounded; the parts are in several hands, none of which can be
identified as either Went or Triebensee. The arrangement is, however, almost certainly by Went.
Pc (Traeg: [Vienna], pre-1799), No, 92 (as Anon), MS parts: D-DO, Mus.Ms.1876; I-Fc, F.P. S.326.
JNW-16ac. J. Weigl: Das Petermännchen, Parts 1 - 4.   2ob 2cl 2hn 2bn.
MS parts: I-Fc, F.P. S.332, (as Anon).
JNW-17ac. J. Weigl: Die Verbrennung und Zestörung der Stadt Troja, overture & 9 mvts.   2ob 2cl 2hn 2bn.
MS parts: CZ-KRa, A3992/IV.B.162; D-DO, Mus.Ms.2016.
JNW-18ac. J. Weigl: I solitari, 2 mvts.   2ob 2cl 2hn 2bn. MS parts: A-Wn, Mus.Hs.3856.
JNW-19ac. J. Weigl: Alcina, overture & 16 mvts.   2ob 2cl 2hn 2bn.
MS parts: A-Ee, Mus.1086, (omits Nos. 15 & 17); A-Wn, Mus.Hs.3874; CZ-Bm(no), A.16.628, (omits No. 15).
Pc (Aus den K: K: Hof Theater Musik Verlag: Wien, c.1813), MS parts: D-Rtt, Weigl 4.
JNW-20ac. J. Weigl: Alceste, overture & 14 mvts.   2ob 2cl 2hn 2bn [cbn].
MS parts: A-Wn, Mus.Hs.3873; A-Wn, Mus.Hs.3792, No. 31, (duetto); CZ-Bm(no), A.16.674, (a cbn is listed
on the titlepage but no part - or divisi in the bn II pt - are present, so this is really an octet. This was a standard
publisher's ploy to insure sales to 9- or 8-part Harmonies; if available, the cbn was expected to double the bn II).
Pc (Aus den K: K: Hof Theater Musik Verlag: Wien, post-1813), MS parts: D-Rtt, Weigl 4.
JNW-21ac. P. Wranizky: (unidentified - ?Ballet) Terzetto [sic], overture & 6 mvts.   2ob 2cl 2hn 2bn.
MS parts: A-Ee, Mus.1077; A-Wn, Mus.Hs.3792, Nos. 34 & 35.
Pc (Aus den K.K Hoftheater Musik Verlag: Wien, c.1813): MS parts: D-Rtt, Weigl 4.
JNW-22ac. (= KRECHLER, FFK-1ad). Miselln [sic; pencil on bn I part].   2ob 2cl 2hn 2bn.
MS parts: CZ-Pnm, Lobkovic X.H.a.57. *These selections are almost certainly drawn from Went's arrangements.*
   22.1/1-3ad. Gluck: La Rencontre imprévue [Der Pilgrim aus Mekka], 3 mvts ("A ma maîtresse j'avais promis",
   "Mahomet, notre grand prophète", "Un ruisselet bien clair" [variant]. Nos. 1 - 3. (= JNW-17.1a)
   22.2ac. Gluck: Iphigénie aus Tauride, "Unis des la plus tendre enfance". No. 4.
   22.3/1-3ac. Gluck: Orfeo, 3 mvts. No. 5.   22.4ad. Gluck: Alceste, "Non vi turbate". No. 6.
   22.5/1-2ac. I. Umlauf: Das Irrlicht, 2 mvts. No. 7 (Andante) & 10 (Andante moderato).
   22.6/1-2ac. Salieri: Der Rauchfangkehrer, 2 mvts. Nos. 8 & 9. (= JNW-12ac)
   22.7ac. [unidentified] Andante, 2/4. No. 11.

WENUSCH, Stanislaus *(1810)*
Many of Wenusch's works bear lists of performance dates and the names of the deceased; we list dates only, in
italics, at the end of entries.
***SXW-1tv.** [Leichen-Arie]; "Hier stehen wir deinem Graben". SATB, fl 2cl(C) 2hn bn cbn.
AutoMS parts: A-Wn, Mus.Hs.21,771. ★
SXW-2tv. Non plus ultra. Trauer=Arie für das Fest Allerheiligen Nachmittag im Gottesacker.
CATB, fl 2cl 2hn bn bomb. MS parts: A-Wn, Mus.Hs.21,773, (with duplicate Canto part). ★
SXW-3tv. Bey einen King. Leichen Arie in Es [E♭]; "Lebt wohl o theure Eltern". CATB, fl 2cl 2hn bn.
AutoMS parts: A-Wn, Mus.Hs.21,764. *(27 April 1869; 24 Oct 1871; 20 Feb 1872, 12 March 1874.)* ★
SXW-4tv. Leichen-Arie; "Frommer Pilger dieser Erden". CATB, 2cl 2hn 2bn, (with later pts for 2cl(E♭) ad lib).
AutoMS parts: A-Wn, Mus.Hs.21,772. *(17 October 1839; 12 Sept 1858 (two funerals); 25 Nov 1861; 24 Dec*
1870; 4 Feb, 14 June 1884; 5 Dec 1887; 6 Jan 1889; 6 May 1896.) ★
SXW-5tv. Leichen=Arie in Es [E♭]. für 4 Singstimmen und Harmonie. Für kleine und erwachsene Kinder [small
and older children]; "Nun wohl an". CATB, 2cl 2hn tp(prin). AutoMS parts: A-Wn, Mus.Hs.21,766. ★
SXW-6tv. Leichen Arie in Es [E♭]; "Was sind doch der Menschen Jahre".
CATB, 2cl 2hn bn, (with a later bomb part).
AutoMS parts: A-Wn, Mus.Hs.21,770. *(Jan 1848; Jan 1870; 15 April, 19 Nov 1871.)* ★
SXW-7tv. Leichen Arie; "Selig, wer mit Ruhe dorthin blicket". CATB, 2cl 2hn bn; (with later parts for fl, cbn).
AutoMS parts: A-Wn, Mus.Hs.21,768. *(27 Sept 1839; 17 April 1841; 5 Feb 1842; 2 June 1843; 19 March, 24*
March 1846; 2 Dec 1847; 4 Jan, 1848; 12 Sept 1858; 18 May 1859; 4 Feb 1869; 24 Dec [no date]). ★
SXW-8tv. Leichen Arie in Es [E♭]; "Nun ist die Pilgerschaft vollbracht". CATB, 2cl 2hn bn.
AutoMS parts: A-Wn, Mus.Hs.21,765, (with a later duplicate bn part to repalce the water-damaged part probably
affected by rain during a graveside performance). ★
SXW-9tv. Leichen Arie in C; "Er ist nicht mehr, um dessen Sarg wir stehen". CATB, 2cl(C) 2hn bn; (with later
parts for fl cbn bomb). AutoMS parts: A-Wn, Mus.Hs.21,759. *(23 Sept 1868, 29 March 1871; 19 Jan 1872;*
8 Jan 1892.) ★
SXW-10tv. Leichen Arie in Es [E♭]; "Ach! wie bitter ist das Schieden". CATB, 2cl 2hn bn.
AutoMS parts: A-Wn, Mus.Hs.21,760. *(19 sept 1868; 27 Jan, 5 May, 26 Oct 1868; 18 April 1871.)* ★
SXW-11tv. Für eine u[nd] auch 2 grosse Leichen, dannauch für 2 Kinder. Leichen=Arie in Es [E♭] "Geliebte
Freunde stellet ein die Klagen". CATB, 2cl 2hn bn. AutoMS pts: A-Wn, Mus.Hs.21,761, (missing 2hn bn). ★

SXW-12tv. Leichen Arie in Es [E♭]; "Lebet wohl geliebte Kinder". CATB, 2cl 2hn bn.
AutoMS parts: A-Wn, Mus.Hs.21,763. ★
SXW-13tv. Leichen=Arie in Es [E♭]; für 4 Singstimmen und Harmonie. Bei einen kleine Kinde; "Schmücket
mich mit Blumen". CATB, 2cl 2hn bn. AutoMS parts: A-Wn, Mus.Hs.21,767. *(Jan 1869.)* ★
SXW-1a. VIII Stücke aus Opern und Balletts für Sechs oder Siebenstimmige Harmonie.
cl(E♭) 2cl(B♭) 2hn bn tp(prin). MS parts: A-Wn, Mus.Hs.21,790.
    1.1a. Anon: Andante, 2/4 / Scherzando modto, 3/4 / adagio, 3/4 / tempo Imo.
    1.2a. Rossini: Ciro in Babilonia, Allegretto, 2/4.
    1.3a. P. Wranizky: Das Waldmädchen, Allegro 6/8 / [no tempo marking], 3/8 / tempo 1mo, 6/8.
    1.4a. Rossini: Tancredi, Andte 2/4 / Allegro 2/4.
    1.5a. [C. or R.] Kreutzer: Adagio, 3/8.
    1.6a. J. Weigl: Der Tod der Hercules, Andte, ¢.
    1.7a. Anon: Die Seeräuber in Algir, Schlaven Tanz (Eccosaises, 2/4 & Trio). (pre-dates Bellini's *I Pirata*).
    1.8a. J. Weigl: Richard Löwenherz, Tempo di Marcia, Andante, 2/4.
*SXW-1avc. J. Weigl: IV Antiphonien. CATB, fl(ad lib) 2cl 2hn bn(I ad lib) bn(II oblig) kl-tp bomb.
MS parts: A-Wn, Mus.Hs.21,694. *The MS title page bears Wenusch's name beneath the title. We also believe
the arrangement is by Wenusch because of the unusual scoring, which matches his other vocal works with winds.
Another MS version for CATB with orchestra (A-Wn, Mus.Hs.22,625) does not mention Wenusch's name.*

*WERNER (Vernera), ( ) *(1800)*
QZW-1v. Salve Regina in B[♭]. Solo T(vel C), solo cl, solo vl, 2hn+2vla organ(bc).
MS parts (by Johann Josef Wagner, c.1825): CZ-NYc, DÚ 140. ★

*WERNER, F.W. *(1800), associated with the Löwenstein Kapelle*
FWW-1. Balletino; in B♭. pic(Eb) 2cl(E♭) 2cl(B♭) 4hn(E♭, B♭ basso) 2bn 2tp(B♭ basso) b-tb cb.
AutoMS score & MS parts: GB-Ljag(w). ★
FWW-1a. Bellini: Norma, Duett. terz-fl 2cl(E♭) 2cl(Bb) 4hn(E♭, B♭) 2bn 2tp b-tb cb.
AutoMS score & MS parts: GB-Ljag(w).
FWW-2a. A. Müller: Frühlingslied. terz-fl 2cl(E♭) cl(B♭) 3hn(2E♭, B♭) 2bn tp b-tb b.
AutoMS score & MS parts: GB-Ljag(w).
FWW-3a. [C.M. von Weber] Pieçen [sic] (quasi Potpourri) aus Euryanthe.
terz-fl 2cl(E♭) 2cl(B♭) 2hn 2bn tp b-tb cb. AutoMS score & MS parts: GB-Ljag(w), 6/371, No. 16.

*WERNER, Sven Eric 21 Feb *1937, Copenhagen*
SEW-1. Combinations; (1967-69). fl fl(pic) 2ob 2cl 2hn 2bn 2tp 2tb 3perc.
Pm (Wilhelm Hansen: Copenhagen, 1969), (hire) score & parts.
*SEW-2. Catch. 2ob 2cl 2hn 2bn.
Pm (Samfundet: Copenhagen, 1997).

WERNER, Vladimír 24 July *1937, Brno*
VXW-1. Divertimento. 2fl 2ob 2cl 2hn bn.
Pm (Český hudební fond: Prague), hire score & parts.

*WERTH, Francis *(1780), Master of the Royal South Gloucester Band*
FQW-1. The Celebrated Dutch Minuet - as Performed at Brighton, before His Royal Highness the Prince of
Wales, By the Royal South Gloces. [sic: Gloucester] Band. pic(solo) 2cl 2hn bn 2tp serp.
Pc (Longman & Co.: London, wm 1807), RISM [W 894], score: GB-Lbl, g.272.r.(41); I-Nc. ★
FQW-2. The Nightingale, a favorite Military Rondo, as Performed at Brighton, before His Royal Highness the
Prince of Wales, By the Royal South Glocester [sic] Band. pic(solo) 2cl 2hn bn 2tp serp.
Pc (Longman & Co: London, c.1807), score: GB-DOTstoneham; GB-Lbl, (3 copies), g.272.z.(31); g.1374.s.(1),
g.1780.q.(4); GB-Lhumphries (modern MS copy). ★

*WERTTIG, Joseph
JXW-1. 12 Pièces. 2ob 2cl 2bn tp. (?Auto)MS score: D-Bds, Hausbibl.M.M.342.
JQW-1m. 24 Märsche. 2pic 2fl 2ob 2cl 2hn 2bn serp 2tp tp(primo). MS parts: D-Bds, Hausbibl.M.M.147.
JXW-2m. 6 Märsche. 2ob 2cl 2bn tp. (?Auto)MS score: D-Bds, Hausbibl.M.M.146.

*WESLEY, Samuel 24 Feb *1766, Bristol - 11 Oct 1837, London.*
*SYW-1m. March in D. 2ob 2hn 2bn serp.
AutoMS score ("June 24th Finish'd 1777"): GB-Lbl, Add. 35,007, ff. 237 - 238. Modern MS: GB-Lbbc. ★
Pm (Facsimile in: *Hinrichsen's Musical Year Book* Vol. VII. Plates 6 - 8. Hinrichsen Edition: London, 1952).

WESSMANN, Harri *1949, Finland*
HAV-1. Capriccio. 2ob 2cl 2hn 2bn cbn. MS score: FIN-Hmt.

WESSNITZER, Ferdinand *(?1800), active in Cheb, formerly Eger, c.1830s/1840s)*
FEW-1v. Salve [Regina], Op. 33. CATB, fl cl(E♭) 2cl(B♭) 2hn bn 2tp(clar in E♭) bomb.
MS parts: CZ-PLa, Hu 1425, (missing C & fl parts). ★

*WESTERGAARD, Svend 8 Oct *1922, Copenhagen - 22 June 1988, Hillerød*
SZW-1. Transformazioni Sinfonische, Op. 32, 1976. Piano solo, 2fl(pic) 2ob 2cl 4hn 2bn 3tp 3tb tu timp perc.
Pm (Wilhelm Hansen: Copenhagen, 1976), score & (hire) parts.
SZW-2. Varianti Sinfonische, Op. 31, 1972. pic 2fl ob ob(ca) cl cl(b-cl) 4hn 2bn 3tp 3tb tu 3perc.
Pm (Wilhelm Hansen: Copenhagen, 1972), hire score & parts.
SZW-3. Music to Antigone; 1960. 2fl cl 2hn bn 3tp 2perc harp. MS score: DK-Kd.

WESTPHAL, August Wilhelm Franz 7 March *1789, Mecklenburg-Schwerin - 22 April 1883,
Mecklenburg-Schwerin*
AQW-1. Waltzer en Rondo; in C. 2fl 2cl(C) 2hn 2bn tp. AutoMS score: D-SWl, Mus. 5694/1. ★

*WETTICH, F. *(1770)*
FUW-1a. Cherubini: Le deux Journées. fl 2ob 2cl 2hn 2bn quart-bn. MS parts: D-RUl. RH-C-26.

*WHETTAM, Graham *7 Sept 1927, Swindon, UK*
GYW-1. Symphonietta. 2fl 2ob 2cl 2hn 2bn.
Pm (De Wolfe: London), score.
GYW-2. Concerto for Ten Wind; 1979. 2fl ob ca 2cl 2hn 2bn.
Pm (Meriden Music: Ingatestone, Essex, UK, 1979), parts.
GYW-3. Fantasy for Ten Wind; (1960, revised 1979). 2fl ob ca 2cl 2hn 2bn.
Pm (Meriden Music: Ingatestone, Essex, UK, 1979), parts.

WHITE, Edward
EYW-1. Romance in Blue. 2fl ob 2cl 2hn bn.
Pm (Boosey & Hawkes: London, etc).

*WIDDER, Johann Baptist *1797 - 1863*
*YYW-1a. 76 Stücke für Harmoniemusik. Nos. 1 - 56: 2fl 2cl 2hn 2bn; Nos. 57 - 76: fl ob 2cl 2hn 2bn.
MS scores: D-Mbs, Mus.Mss.2603.
    1.1a. Anon: Allegro Vivace, No. 39. 1.2a. Anon: Allegro Maestoso, Tempo di Marchia [sic], No. 43.
    1.3a. Anon: Allegro Moderato, No. 44. 1.4a. Anon: Allegro Moderato, No. 45.
    1.5a. Anon: Allegro Moderato, No. 55. 1.6a. Anon: Allegretto, No. 70. 1.7a. Anon: Andantino, No. 72.
    1.8a. Anon: Intrada. Andante, No. 73. 1.9a. Anon: Jagd, No. 74.
    1.10a. Anon: Allegretto, No. 75. 1.11a. Anon: Allegro, No. 76.
    1.12a. Anon: Allegro Moderato con [5] variazioni, No. 71.
    1.13a. Anon: Bertrands Abschied, Allegro Moderato, No. 41.
    1.14a. Auber: La Neige, 3 mvts, Nos. 11 - 13.
    1.15a. Auber: Le Maçon, 1 mvt, No. 38.
    1.16a. Auber: La Muette de Portici, 3 mvts, Nos. 23, 25, 26.
    1.17a. Auber: Fra Diavolo, 2 mvts, Nos. 26 & 28.
    1.18a. C. Cannabich: Palmer und Amalia, 2 mvts, Nos. 67, 68.
    1.19a. Chélard: Macbeth, 1 mvt, No. 18.
    1.20a. Chélard: Mitternacht, Ländler, No. 2.
    1.21a. Gyrowetz: Die schweizer Milchmädchen [Nathalie], 1 mvt, No. 50.
    1.22a. Hérold: Zampa, 1 mvt, No. 37.
    1.23a. Küffner: [unidentified] Polacca Moderato, No. 15.
    1.24a. Lindpaintner: Janina, 5 mvts, Nos. 14, 35, 47 - 49.
    1.25a. Lindpaintner: Alcibiades, 1 mvt, No. 27.
    1.26a. Meyerbeer: Emma di Resburgo, Polacca, No. 9.
    1.27a. Meyerbeer: Robert le Diable, Allegro Moderato, Tempo di Marchia [sic], No. 36.
    1.28a. Mozart: Don Giovanni, 3 mvts ("Risposate, verzoso ragazze!" [Act I Finale], "Vedrai carino", "Finch'
        han dal vino"), Nos. 57, 59, 60.
    1.29a. Mozart: Così fan tutte, overture, No. 58.
    1.30a. Paer: Camilla, 1 mvt, No. 63.
    YYW-1. Poissl: Alma Lied, with 3 variations (by Widder), No. 1.
    1.31a. Rossini: Tancredi, 1 mvt, No. 3.
    1.32a. Rossini: L'Italiana in Algeri, 1 mvt, No. 4.
    1.33a. Rossini: Il Barbiere di Siviglia, 1 mvt, No. 32.
    1.34a. Rossini: Ricciardo e Zoraide, 1 mvt, No. 5.
    1.35a. Rossini: La Donna del lago, 1 mvt, No. 8.
    1.36a. Rossini: Mathilda di Shabran [as "Mathilde"], 1 mvt, No. 16.
    1.37a. Rossini: Zelmira, Marche, No. 10.
    1.38a. Rossini: Semiramide, 4 mvts, Nos. 31, 52, 53, 65.
    1.39a. Rossini: Guillaume Tell, 4 mvts, Nos. 20 - 22, 26.
    1.40a. Salieri: Tarare [as "Axur"], 1 mvt, No. 61.
    1.41a. Salieri: Die Hussiten von Naumberg, Marche, No. 69.
    1.42a. Strauss the Elder: [unidentifed] Walzer, No. 62.
    1.43a. C.T. Toeschi: Ländler, No. 7.
    1.44a. C.M. von Weber: Preciosa, 4 mvts, Nos. 29, 40, 54, 64.
    1.45a. C.M. von Weber: Der Freischütz, 1 mvt, No. 30.
    1.46a. C.M. von Weber: Euryanthe, 1 mvt, No. 33.
    1.47a. C.M. von Weber: Oberon, 3 mvts, Nos. 17, 19, 34.
    1.48a. C.M. von Weber: Leyer und Schwert, Op. 42, No. 2, "Lützows wilde Jagd", No. 42.
    YYW-2. Widder: Dreher [revolution dance], Allegretto, No. 6.
    1.49a. Winter: Der Bettelstudent [Der Donnerwetter], 1 mvt, No. 66.
YYW-2a. Halévy: La Juive, Act I finale, ("Während des fierlichen Kirchenzuges").
pic fl 2cl(Eb) 3cl(Bb) 4hn(F, F, C, Bb alto) 2bn 3tp 3tb serp "bombartoni" b-dr s-dr tri.
MS score: I-Mc, Noseda M.34.12.
YYW-3a. I. Lachner: Lorelei, Gebet et Aria. 2fl cl(Ab) 2cl(Eb) 3cl(Bb) 4hn 2bn+baryton 3tp 3tb b-dr s-dr.
MS score (post-1846): GB-Ljag(w).
YYW-4a. Marschner: Der Templer und die Jüdin, Introduction mit Arie und Chor, Lied (des Narren),
Schlachtlied, Lied mit Chor. terz-fl(pic in Nos. 2 & 3) 2cl(Eb) 2cl(Bb) 2hn 2bn tp(chromatic) b-tb cb.
MS score & MS parts: GB-Ljag(w), (4 separate scores).
YYW-5a. Meyerbeer: Robert le Diable, Arie, Romance, Finale des 1<u>ten</u> Ackts [sic] (spiel Chor).
terz-fl 2cl(Eb) 2cl(Bb) 2hn 2bn tp(chromatic) b-tb cb. MS scores & MS parts: GB-Ljag(w), (3 separate scores).
YYW-6a. Rossini: Guillaume Tell, Overture, Introduction, Ballet, Ballet & Chor.
terz-fl 2cl(Eb) 2cl(Bb) 2hn 2bn tp(chromatic) b-tb cb. MS score & MS parts: GB-Ljag(w), (4 separate scores).

*WIDLAR, T.J. *(1970)*
*TJW-1a. Mozart: String Quintet in G minor, K.516.   2ob 2cl 2hn 2bn.
MS score & parts (1st performance: 19 June 1995, Bertranka, Prague): CZ-Pvent.
TJW-2a. Mozart: String Quintet in D, K. 593.   2ob 2cl 2hn 2bn.   MS score & pts (perf. as TJW-1a): CZ-Pvent.
TJW-3a. Mozart: String Quintet in E♭, K.614.   2ob 2cl 2hn 2bn.   MS score & pts (perf. as TJW-1a): CZ-Pvent.

*WIDMER, Ernst   *25 April 1927, Aarau, Switzerland (resident in Brasil)*
EXW-1. Notturno, Op. 79; 1973.   2fl 2ob 2cl 2hn 2bn.   MS score: CH-Zma.
EXW-2. Morfose II, Op. 92; 1974.   2ob 2hn bn.   MS score: CH-Zma.

*WIDOR, Charles Marie   *21 Feb 1844, Lyons - 12 March 1937, Paris*
CHW-1. Salvum fac populum tuum.   2fl ob cl 2hn bn 2tp 2tb perc timp.
Pm (Heugel & Cie.: Paris), score.   *Another edition in F-Pn is scored for 3tp 3tb tambour organ.*

*WIELAND, ( )   *Kapellmeister (1770)*
Works listed here are found in Sammelbänden 13, 14 & 15 in D-Rtt. The Regensburg Gardemusik Katalog includes a note that Sm. 15 was purchased from "Kapellmeister Weiland" in 1821; no other provenance in given. The Walch works at the beginning of the volume were published in 1818. Sm. 13 & 14 are also on the same paper type (watermark Rtt 164), not otherwise found at D-Rtt and we are confident that these volumes are also from the same source. However, it should be noted that Sm. 15, No. 62 (and probably Nos. 63 & 64) were added at a slightly later date on blank sheets at the ends of the volumes, having been acquired (?copied or purchased) "Von Herrn Hauptmann v[on]. Vetter in anfang Janner 1822 von Dischingen [sic]". A certain consistency of scoring indicative of a single Harmonie with a configuration often found in the German states emerges for the works listed below. Kapellmeister Wieland is probably not be the same as the "Weilland" whose Harmonie was published in Paris by Pleyel in 1797 and in London by Broderip and Wilkinson in London in 1799. All attributions listed in this entry must be treated with caution.
KZW-1d. Allemande.   fl ob cl(F) 2cl(C) hn hn(posthorn) 2bn tp cb.   MS parts: D-Rtt, Sm. 13, No. 51.   ★
KZW-2d(-6d). Allemande, Polonaise, Allemande & 2 Walzer.   fl 2ob 2cl 2hn 2bn tp(tacet No. 4) b-tb.
MS parts: D-Rtt, Sm. 15, Nos. 1 - 5.   ★
KZW-7d. Potpourri; in E♭.   fl(F) 2ob 2cl 3hn 2bn (2)b.   MS parts: D-Rtt, Sm. 15, No. 8.   ★
KZW-8d. Allemande; in C.   fl 2ob 2cl 2hn 2bn b.   MS parts: D-Rtt, Sm. 15, No. 9.   ★
KZW-9d. Polonaise; in C.   pic 2ob 2cl 2hn 2bn tp(C) tp(prin) posthorn serp/vlne.
MS parts: D-Rtt, Sm. 15, No. 14.   ★
KZW-10d. Polonaise; in F.   fl 2ob 2cl 2hn 2bn 2tp serp/vlne.   MS parts: D-Rtt, Sm. 15, No. 15.   ★
KZW-11d. Allemande; in F.   pic 2ob 2cl 2hn 2bn 2tp serp/vlne.   MS parts: D-Rtt, Sm. 15, No. 17.   ★
KZW-12d. Allegretto; in G.   fl 2ob 2cl 2hn 2bn b-tb+vlne.   MS parts: D-Rtt, Sm. 15, No. 20.   ★
KZW-13d. Andante mod[erato, B♭, ₵ / Andte con Var., ₵ / Allegretto, 6/8.   MS pts: D-Rtt, Sm. 15, No. 21. ★
KZW-14d. Allegretto; in B♭.   fl(D) 2ob 3cl 2hn 2bn b-tb serp/vlne.   MS parts: D-Rtt, Sm. 15, No. 22.   ★
KZW-15d. Poloneise [sic]; in C.   pic 2ob 2cl 2hn 2bn 2tp b-tb+serp timp.   MS pts: D-Rtt, Sm. 15, No. 23. ★
KZW-16d. Andante / Chasse Presto; in G.   pic 2ob 2cl 4hn 2bn serp/vlne.   MS pts: D-Rtt, Sm. 15, No. 24. ★
KZW-17d. Allegro / Andante Sostenuto.   fl(F) 2ob 2cl 3hn 2bn 2tp serp/vlne.   MS pts: D-Rtt, Sm. 15, No. 25. ★
KZW-18d. Allemande ["Walzer" in cl I pt]; in D.   fl(D) 2ob 2cl 2hn 2bn 2posthorn serp/vlne.
MS parts: D-Rtt, Sm. 15, No. 33.   ★
KZW-19d. Andantino.   fl 2ob 2cl 2hn 2bn serp/vlne.   MS parts: D-Rtt, Sm. 15, No. 35.   ★
KZW-20d. Allemande.   fl 2ob 2cl 2hn 2bn serp/vlne.   MS parts: D-Rtt, Sm. 15, No. 36.   ★
KZW-21d. Allemande.   fl 2cl 2hn 2bn serp/vlne.   MS parts: D-Rtt, Sm. 15, No. 37.   ★
KZW-22d. All[egr]o Brillant.   fl 2ob 2cl 2hn 2bn 2tp serp/vlne.   MS parts: D-Rtt, Sm. 15, No. 38.   ★
KZW-23d. Andantino con Var[iazioni].   fl 2ob 3cl 2hn 2bn 2tp b-tb.   MS parts: D-Rtt, Sm. 15, No. 38.   ★
KZW-1md. Pas redoublé; in C.   fl(pic) 2ob 2cl 2hn 2bn.
MS parts: D-Rtt, Sm. 15, No. 12.   ★
KZW-1ad. Anon: Andante [= God Save the King].   2cl(C) 2hn 2bn cb.   MS parts: D-Rtt, Sm. 13, No. 52.
KZW-2ad. Suite Harmonie Italienne, 8 mvts.   fl/ob ob/fl 2cl 2hn 2bn serp/b-tb.
MS parts: D-Rtt, Sm. 13, Nos. 39 - 46.
  2.1ad.   (unidentified) Cavatina Chante [sic] par Mme Catalani.
  2.2ad.   (unidentified) Conzoneta [sic] Siciliana.
  2.3ad.   Cimarosa: Gli Orazi e i Curiazi, "Quelle pupille tenere".
  2.4ad.   Rossini: Semiramide, (unidentified No.) Chante [sic] par Mme Catalani.
  2.5ad.   Mayr: Che Originali, Polacca Chante [sic] par Melle. Neri.
  2.6ad.   Cimarosa: Gli Orazi: "Frener vorrei le lagrime" Chanté par Md: Catalani.
  2.7ad.   Pucitta: "Mio ben per te questo anima".   Ch[anté]: par Catalani.
  2.8ad.   Anon: (unidentified) Tempo di Marcia.
KZW-3ad. Boieldieu: Jean de Paris, overture & 15 mvts.   2fl 2cl 2hn 2bn.
MS parts: D-Rtt, Sm. 13, Nos. 12 - 27, (mvt titles in German; includes Lorenz Schneider's "Vergiss mein nicht").
KZW-4ad. Himmel (misattributed to Beethoven, K.-H. Anh 14, No. 2): Schmerzenwalzer.   fl(F) 2ob 3cl 2hn 2bn b-tb serp.   MS parts: D-Rtt, Sm. 15, No. 26, (as "Allemand in F [minor] v[on]. Bethofen [sic]").
KZW-5ad. Hummel: Die gute Nachricht, overture, Op. 61.   fl 2ob 2cl 2hn 2bn serp/vlne.
MS parts: D-Rtt, Sm. 15, No. 10.
KZW-6ad. R. Kreutzer: Lodoiska, overture.   pic 2ob 2cl 2hn 2bn 2tp serp/vlne.
MS parts: D-Rtt, Sm. 15, No. 11.
KZW-7ad. Méhul: Le jeune Henri, overture (as "Jagd Symphonie").   fl(pic) 2ob 2cl 4hn 2bn serp/vlne timp.   MS parts: D-Rtt, Sm. 15, No. 6.
KZW-8ad. Paer: Achille, overture.   fl 2ob 2cl 2hn 2bn 2tp serp/vlne/b-tb.
MS parts (pre-1821): D-Rtt, Sm. 15, Nos. 16.

KZW-9ad. Rossini: Torvaldo e Dorliska, cavatina, "Tutto è vano".   fl(D & F) 2ob 2cl 2hn 2bn 2tp serp/vlne.
MS parts (pre-1821): D-Rtt, Sm. 15, No. 13.
KZW-10ad. Rossini: Otello, overture.   fl(D) 2ob 2cl 2hn 2bn 2tp serp/vlne.
MS parts (pre-1821): D-Rtt, Sm. 15, No. 18.
KZW-11ad. Rossini: La Gazza ladra, overture.   fl 2ob 2cl 2hn 2bn 2tp serp/vlne.
MS parts (pre-1821): D-Rtt, Sm. 15, No. 7.
KZW-12ad. Schaffner, Polonaise, in F.   fl(F) cl(F) 2cl(C) 2hn 2bn tp b-tb (serp) b-dr.
MS parts (pre-1821): D-Rtt, Sm. 14, No. 91.
KZW-13ad. Spontini: La Vestale, overture & 13 mvts.   2fl(overture only) 2ob cl(E♭) 2cl(B♭) 2hn 2bn cbn 2tp.
MS parts (pre-1821): D-Rtt, Sm. 14, Nos. 35 - 48. *Possibly a rescoring of the Chemische Druckerei Journal für neunstimmige Harmonie edition.*
KZW-14.1ad. Spontini: Fernand Cortez, overture & 6 mvts.   Incomplete: overture only: fl 4cl(C) cbn 2tp b-tb;
Nos. 50 - 55: cbn only.   MS parts (pre-1821): D-Rtt, Sm. 14, Nos. 49 - 55.
KZW-14.2ad. Spontini: Fernand Cortez, overture.   fl 2ob 2cl 2hn 2bn 2tp serp/vlne.
MS parts (pre-1821): D-Rtt, Sm. 15, No. 34.
KZW-15ad. Spontini: Lalla Rookh, march & 4 mvts.   fl 2ob 2cl 2hn 2bn 2tp b-tb serp.
MS parts (1820/21): D-Rtt, Sm. 15, Nos. 28 - 32.
KZW-1mad. (C. or R.) Kreutzer: Marsch, in D.   fl(F) 2ob 2cl 2hn 2bn 2tp b-tb serp.
MS parts (pre-1821): D-Rtt, Sm. 15, No. 27.
KZW-2mad. Neukomm (?rescored): Marsch, in C.   2fl 2ob/(cl ripieno) cl(E♭) 2cl(C) 2hn 2bn serp 2tp tb timp
tri cym.   MS parts (pre-1821): D-Rtt, Sm. 14, Nos. 71. *The cl(E♭) part bears Goepfert's name in pencil.*
KZW-3mad. Neukomm (?rescored): Marsch, in E♭.   2fl 2ob/(cl ripieno) cl(E♭) 2cl(C) 2hn 2bn serp 2tp tb timp
tri cym.   MS parts (pre-1821): D-Rtt, Sm. 14, Nos. 72.
KZW-4mad, 5mad. Neukomm (?rescored): 2 Marcia in C: Prinz Carl von Mecklenburg & Prinz Friedrich.
2pic 2ob 2cl(C) 2hn 2bn 2tp b-tb (serp).   MS parts (pre-1821): D-Rtt, Sm. 14, Nos. 92, 93.

WIELAND, Philipp   *(?1690)*
PQW-1. Ouverture [Suite] a 4; in A minor/C major, 7 mvts.   2ob/vl taille/vla b.   MS parts: S-Uu, IMHS 61:5.
*The number of instruments in the title has been altered from "4" to "6"; the violin parts duplicate the oboe parts
and this is reflected in the title, "Violon / Con Hautbois".* ★

*WIEPRECHT, Wilhelm Friedrich   *10 Aug 1802, Aschersleben - 4 Aug 1872, Berlin*
*WFW-1. Die Schlacht bei Leipzig.   Three wind orchestras.
MS score: D-Bds, Mus.Ms.23104 (?missing Orchestra I).
WFW-2. Notturno, Op. 8.   Instrumentation unknown.   MS score: D-Bds, Mus.Ms.23104/1.
WFW-1m. Postillion Marsch & Grand-Pas Redouble.   Instrumentation unknown.
AutoMS score: D-Bds, Mus.Ms.auto.W.F.Wieprecht 4.
WFW-2m. Marsch "Vorwarts" (22 June 1862).   Instrumentation unknown.
AutoMS score: D-Bds, Mus.Ms.auto.W.F.Wieprecht 2.
WFW-1v. Die Königskugel, "War einst ein alter König".   Unison male chorus, ob 2cl hn bn 2tp 2tb tu perc.
AutoMS score: D-Bds, Mus.Ms.auto.W.F.Wieprecht 3.

WIERNIK, Adam   *4 Jan 1916, Sweden*
AEW-1. Variations; 1994.   2fl 2ob 2cl 2hn 2bn.   MS score: S-Sic.

*WIESER, J.   *(1800), associated with the Löwensstein Kapelle, Wertheim*
FAW-1. Errinnerung [sic] an der Liedertafel, Poutpouri [sic].   terz-fl(pic) cl(E♭) cl(B♭) 2hn 2bn tp b-tb cb tri.
AutoMS score & MS parts: GB-jag(w). ★
FAW-2. Sylvester=Abend Walzer; in E♭.   terz-fl(pic) cl(E♭) cl(B♭) 2hn 2bn tp b-tb cb.
AutoMS score & MS parts: GB-Ljag(w). ★
FAW-3. Wolfsbrunner Galopp.   pic(D♭) cl(E♭) 3cl(B♭) 3hn 2bn tp tb cb.
AutoMS score & MS parts: GB-Ljag(w), 10/258, No. 5.3. ★
FAW-1m. Bavaria Marsch; in B♭.   terz-fl cl(E♭) 2cl(B♭) 2hn 2bn tp b-tb cb timp.
AutoMS score & MS parts: GB-Ljag(w). ★
FAW-1a. [Potpourri/Suite].   terz-fl cl(E♭) 2cl(B♭) 2hn 2bn tp b-tb cb.   AutoMS score & MS pts: GB-Ljag(w).
1.1a. Anon: Laendler, in B♭.   1.2a. Marschner: Trinklied, Den Stoepsolweg!.   1.3a. Anon: Speisezettel Gallop.
1.4a. Anon: And[ante]; 3/4.   1.5a. Anon: Des Deutschen Vaterland.   1.6a. Anon: Marsch Tempo.
1.7a. Zöllner: Leb wohl mein Liebchen.   1.8a. Anon: Marsch Tempo.   1.9a. [God Save the King].
1.10a. Anon: Allegro assai.
FAW-2a. Anon: Larghetto.   fl(F) cl(Eb) 2cl(B♭) 2hn 2bn tp b-tb cb timp.
MS parts: GB-Ljag(w), 7/258, No. 14, (missing hn II, bn II).
FAW-3a. Anon: Polka & Trio.   pic(Eb) cl(Eb) 3cl(B♭) 2hnn 2bn tp b-tb cb.
MS parts: GB-Ljag(w), 7/258, No. 7, (missing hn II, bn II).
FAW-4a. Anon: Schottischer & Trio.   pic(E♭) cl(Eb) 3cl(B♭) 2hn 2bn tp b-tb cb.
MS parts: GB-Ljag(w), 7/258, No. 8, (missing hn II, bn II).
FAW-5a. Anon: [4] Steurer [sic] Ländler.   fl(E♭) cl(Eb) 3cl(B♭) 2hnn 2bn tp b-tb cb.
MS parts: GB-Ljag(w), 7/258, No. 2, (missing hn II, bn II).
FAW-6a. Auber: Les Diamants de la couronne, [potpourri].   fl(pic) cl(E♭) 2cl(B♭) 2hn 2bn tp b-tb cb.
AutoMS score & MS parts: GB-Ljag(w).
FAW-7a. Auber: Le Duc d'Olonne, overture.   pic cl(E♭) 2cl(B♭) 2hn 2bn tp b-tb cb.
AutoMS score & MS parts: GB-Ljag(w).
FAW-8a. Beethoven: Adelaide, Op. 46.   terz-fl cl(E♭) 2cl(B♭) 2hn 2bn tp b-tb cb timp.
AutoMS score & MS parts: GB-Ljag(w).
FAW-9a. Bellini: I Puritani, Poutpouri [sic] N<u>r°</u> 4.   terz-fl(pic) cl(E♭) 2cl(B♭) 2hn 2bn tp b-tb cb.
AutoMS score & MS parts: GB-Ljag(w).

FAW-10a. Bendl: Humors-Organe Walzer.   pic(Db) cl(Eb) 3cl(Bb) 3hn 2bn tp tb cb.
AutoMS score & MS parts: GB-Ljag(w) 10/258, No. 5.6.
FAW-11a. Donizetti: Belisario, potpourri.   terz-fl cl(Eb) 2cl(Bb) 2hn 2bn tp b-tb cb.
MS parts: GB-Ljag(w).
FAW-12a. Donizetti: La Fille du régiment, poutpouri [sic] N° 1.
terz-fl cl(Eb) 2cl(Bb) 2hn 2bn tp b-tb cb timp b-dr.   AutoMS score & MS parts: GB-Ljag(w).
FAW-13a. Eschborn: Walzer.   pic(Eb) cl(Eb) 2cl(Bb) 2hnn 2bn tp b-tb cb timp.
MS parts: GB-Ljag(w), 7/258, No. 10, (missing hn II, bn II).
FAW-14a. Fischer: Lied, "Du mein lieber Engel Du!".   terz-fl cl(Eb) 2cl(Bb) 2hn 2bn tp b-tb cb timp.
AutoMS score & MS parts: GB-Ljag(w).
FAW-15a. Flotow: Alessandro Stradella, potpourri.   terz-fl cl(Eb) 2cl(Bb) 2hn 2bn tp b-tb cb.
MS parts: GB-Ljag(w).
FAW-16a. Fostlinger: Stey'rer Laendler.   pic(Eb) cl(Eb) 2cl(Bb) 2hn 2bn tp b-tb cb.
AutoMS score & MS parts: GB-Ljag(w).
FAW-17a. G. Hammer: Münchner Polka.   pic(Db) cl(Eb) 3cl(Bb) 2hn 2bn tp b-tb cb.
AutoMS score & MS parts: GB-Ljag(w).
FAW-18a. G. Hammer: Rheinländer-Polka.   pic(Eb) cl(Eb) 3cl(Bb) 2hn 2bn tp cb.
AutoMS score & MS parts: GB-Ljag(w).
FAW-19a. Labitzky: Die Elfen-Walzer, Op. 86.   terz-fl cl(Eb) 2cl(Bb) 2hn 2bn tp b-tb cb timp.
AutoMS score (c.1842) & MS parts: GB-Ljag(w).
FAW-20a. Labitzky: Walzer: Andenken an das Anith Koffsche Palais.
pic(terz-fl) cl(Eb) 2cl(Bb) 3hn(2Bb, F) 2bn tp b-tb cb.   AutoMS score & MS parts: GB-Ljag(w).
FAW-21a. Labitzky: Schottischer; in Bb.   pic cl(Eb) 2cl(Bb) 3hn(2Eb, Bb alto) 2bn tp b-tb cb.
AutoMS score & MS parts: GB-Ljag(w).
FAW-22a. Lanner: Tourbillon-Galopp, Op. 142a.   pic(Db) cl(Eb) 3cl(Bb) 3hn 2bn tp b-tb cb.
AutoMS score & MS parts: GB-Ljag(w).
FAW-23a. Lortzing: Zar und Zimmermann, Galopp.   pic(Db) cl(Eb) 3cl(Bb) 3hn 2bn tp b-tb cb.
AutoMS score & MS parts: GB-Ljag(w).
FAW-24a. Max[imilian], *Herzog:* Gesellschaft Potista [sic,?Schottische].   pic(Db) cl(Eb) 3cl(Bb) 2hn 2bn tp cb.
AutoMS score & MS parts: GB-Ljag(w).
FAW-25a. Max[imilian], *Herzog:* Hinneberger Schottische.   pic(Eb) cl(Eb) 3cl(Bb) 2hnn 2bn tp b-tb cb.
MS parts: GB-Ljag(w), 7/260, No. 6.
FAW-26a. Verdi: Nabucodonosor, Andante.   fl(F) cl(Eb) 2cl(Bb) 2hn 2bn tp b-tb cb timp.
AutoMS score & MS parts: GB-Ljag(w).

WIESLANDER, Ingvar *1917 - 1963, Sweden*
IYW-1. Missologi: Liten svit; 4 mvts, 1962.   2cl 2bn; *also piano reduction.*   MS score: S-Sic.

WIGGINS, Bram *1921, UK*
BXW-1a. Rameau: [Nouvelles suites . . . de clavecin, 1741], La Poule.   fl ob 2cl bn.
Pm (Fentone: Corby, pn F345, c.1990), score & parts.

WIGGINS, Christopher
CYW-1. Three Czech Dances.   fl/ob 2cl tp tb.
Pm (Ricordi: Chesham, pn LD 785, c.1988), score & parts.
CYW-2. Three French Dances.   fl/ob 2cl tp tb.
Pm (Ricordi: Chesham, pn LD 786, c.1988), score & parts.

*WILBY, Philip *1949, Pontefract, UK*
*PXW-1. And I move around the Cross: Concerto for Winds.   fl fl(pic) ob ca 2cl 2hn 2bn.
Pm (Chester Music: London, etc., 1985), (hire) score & parts; (copy in GB-Lmic).
See also: MOZART, WAM-6f, completed by Wilby.

*WILDER, Alec (Alexander Lafayette Chew) *16 Feb 1907, Rochester, NY - 24 Sept 1980, Gainesville, Florida*
AZW-1. Entertainment No. 7.   pic 2fl 2ob 3cl 4hn 2bn 4tp 3tb 2euph tu perc.
Pm (Margun Music: Newton Center, MA, pn 534SC, c.1975), score.
AZW-2. Serenade for Winds.   2fl 2ob 2cl 2hn 2bn cbn/tu.
Pm (Margun Music: Newton Center, MA, pn AW 544, 1979), score & parts.
AZW-3. Walking Home in the Spring.   fl ob ca 2cl b-cl bn.   *(See also AZW-4.4).*
Pm (McGinnis & Marx: New York, c.1939).
Pm (Margun Music: Newton Center, MA, pn AW 567, sd), score & parts (for fl/cl ob/ca cl b-cl bn hprd db dr).
AZW-4.1(-4.4). 1. She'll be seven in May; 2. A debutante's diary; 3. Such a tender night; 4. Walking home in Spring *(cf. AZW-3).*   fl ob ca/sax 2cl b-cl bn cbn piano perc.
Pm (Kendor: New York, sd).
AZW-5. Neurotic Goldfish; 1939.   ob 2cl b-cl bn db drum hpcd.
Pm (Margun Music: Newton Center, MA, sd), score & parts.
*AZW-1v. 5 Vocalises; c.1971.   Soprano, fl 2ob 2cl b-cl 3hn bn 3tp 3tb tu perc.
Pm (Margun Music: Newton Center, MA, pn AW 576, sd), hire score & parts.
AZW-2v. Childrens Plea for Peace; 1968.   Narrator, SSAA chorus, 2fl ob 3cl b-cl 1/2bn db hpcd dr.
Pm (Margun Music: Newton Center, MA, pn AW 541SS, sd), study score.

WILENSKI, Osias *1933*
OXW-1. Concertino.   2ob 2cl 2hn 2bn.
Pm (Barry Editorial: Buenos Aires, post-1955).

WILLIAMS, Graham *1940, UK*
GXW-1. Windsongs; 1988.   2ob 2cl 2hn 2bn.   MS parts: GB-BFlowes.

*WILLIAMSON, Thomas George *(1770)*
*TGW-1m. Six Grand Troops with Six Quick Steps, & Six Marches. Piano score only. [Each set bears a headtitle with an individual price and the notice: *"NB. This set of Six Troops are so arranged that Masters may easily form the parts for their Full Bands."* Occasional cues for flutes, clarinets & horns appear throughout.]
Pc (Printed for the Author, and Sold by Wm Napier: London, c.1800), RISM [W 1189], piano score: D-SWl;
GB-Lbl, g.137.(29). ★
    1.1m. H.M. 61st Regiment.   1.2m. H.M. 81st Regiment.   1.3m. Bengal Artillery.
    1.4m. 1st Regiment of Bengal European Infantry.   1.5m. 2d Regiment of Bengal European Infantry.
    1.6m. H.M. 91st Highland Regiment.

*WILLY, Jean (Johannes) *(1730)*
JZW-1. Barthia [sic], in D, 5 mvts.   2ob 2hn 2bn.   MS parts: CZ-KRa, A4004/IV.B.170. ★
JZW-2. Barthia, in G, 5 mvts.   2ob 2hn 2bn.   MS parts (1766): CZ-KRa, A3998/IV.B.171. ★
JZW-3. Barthia, in G, 5 mvts.   2ob 2hn 2bn.   MS parts: CZ-KRa, A3999/IV.B.172. ★
JZW-4. Barthia Pastorella, in G, 5 mvts.   2ob 2hn 2bn.   MS parts: CZ-KRa, A4000/IV.B.173a. ★
JZW-5. Barthia, in C, 5 mvts.   2ob 2hn 2bn.   MS parts: CZ-KRa, A4000/IV.B.173b. ★
JZW-6. Parthia a la Parade; in C, 4 mvts.   2ob 2hn 2bn.   MS parts (1766): CZ-KRa, A4001/IV.B.174. ★
JZW-7. Divertimento p: Variatio:, in C, 4 mvts.   2hn 2bn/(vla bn).   MS parts: CZ-KRa, A4002/IV.B.175. ★

WILSON, James Walter *1922, Ireland*
JUW-1. Nighttown; 1982.   cl b-cl 2 sax 2bn 2tp 2tb 2perc harm+gtr.   MS score: EIRE-Dcmc.
JUW-2. Duet for Ten; 1986.   2fl 2ob 2cl 2hn 2bn.   MS score: EIRE-Dcmc.

WILSON, Mortimer *6 Aug 1876, Charlton, Iowa - 27 Jan 1932, New York*
MYW-1. Pipes and Reeds.   2fl ob 2cl bn.
Pm (Albert J. Andraud: Cincinnati, now Southern Music Co.: San Antonio, Texas, sd).

WIMBERGER, Gerhard *30 Aug 1923, Vienna*
GZW-1. Stories.   3fl 2ob ca 2cl b-cl 4hn 2bn cbn 3tp 3tb tu piano db perc.
Pc (B Schott's Söhne: Mainz, pn 7194, 1962), score & parts.
GZW-2. Short Stories. Für elf Bläser, 1975.   2fl 2ob 2cl 2hn 2bn tp.
Pm (Bärenreiter, Kassel, etc., pn BA 6710, 1975), score.

WIND, Blasius *(pseud)*   *See: MENTNER, Karl.*

*WINEBERGER, Paul Anton *7 Oct 1758, Mergentheim am Tauber - 8 Feb 1821, Hamburg*
PAW-1. Parthia; in G, 1788, 4 mvts.   2fl 2ob 2cl 4hn 2bn vlne.
AutoMS score & MS parts: D-HR, HR III 4 1/2 2° 338.   ★
Pm (KGS), score (fiche 2269) & parts (fiche 2270, 2271).
PAW-2. Parthia; in D, 4 mvts.   2fl 2ob 2cl(A) 3hn 2bn vlne.
AutoMS score ("nel Mese di Settembre [1]785"): D-HR, HR III 4 1/2 4° 95.   ★   Pm (KGS), fiche (463).
*PAW-3. Partitta; in D, 6 mvts.   2fl 2ob 2cl 3hn 2bn vlne.
MS parts (1788): D-HR, HR III 4 1/2 2° 342.   ★   Pm (KGS), fiche (2279, 2280).
PAW-4. Parthia; in D, 4 mvts.   2fl 2ob 2cl(A) 3hn 2bn vlne.
AutoMS score (1788) & MS parts: D-HR, HR III 4 1/2 2° 349.   ★
Pm (KGS), score (fiche 2298) & parts (fiche 2299, 2300).
*PAW-5. Parthia; in C, 4 mvts.   2fl 2ob 2cl(C) 2hn 2bn tp vlne.
AutoMS score ("nel Mese di febraio 1789") & MS parts: D-HR, HR III 4 1/2 2° 340.   ★
Pm (KGS), score (fiche 2274) & parts (fiche 2275, 2276).
*PAW-6. Parthia en Chasse; in G, 4 mvts.   2fl ob 2cl(A) 4hn 2bn vlne.
AutoMS score (1786) & MS parts: D-HR, HR III 4 1/2 2° 348.   ★
Pm (KGS), score (fiche 2294, 2295) & parts (fiche 2296, 2297).
PAW-7. Parthia in F; 4 mvts.   2fl ob 2cl(A) 4hn(D, A) 2bn vlne.
MS parts (1786): D-HR, HR III 4 1/2 2° 346.   Pm (KGS), fiche (2291, 2292).
*PAW-8. Parthia; in D, 4 mvts.   2fl ob 2cl 4hn 2bn vlne.   AutoMS score (1786): D-SWl, Mus. 5715/1.   ★
*PAW-9. Parthia in G; 1785, 4 mvts.   2fl 2ob 2cl(A) 3hn 2bn vlne.
(?Auto)MS scores: D-Mbs, Mus.Mss.6411; D-SWl, Mus. 6411.   ★
MS parts (1785): D-HR, HR III 4 1/2 4° 92, (vlne with bn II, with a few divisi).   Pm (KGS), fiche (458, 459).
*PAW-10. Serenata; in D, 10 mvts.   2fl 2ob 2cl(A) 3hn 2bn (?2tp).
MS parts (1788): D-HR, HR III 4 1/2 2° 339, (?missing tp parts).   ★   Pm (KGS), fiche (2272, 2273).
PAW-11. Parthia in D; 4 mvts.   2fl 2ob 2cl(A) 2hn 2bn vlne.
AutoMS score (c.1785): D-HR, HR III 4 1/2 4° 89.   Pm (KGS), score, fiche (452, 453).   ★
*PAW-12. Parthia; in F, 4 mvts.   2fl 2ob 2cl(C) 2hn 2bn vlne.
MS parts (1793): D-HR, HR III 4 1/2 2° 343, (with a later cl II pt in B♭).   Pm (KGS), fiche (2281, 2282).   ★
*PAW-13. Partitta in F; 4 mvts.   2fl 2ob 2cl 2hn 2bn vlne.
AutoMS score (1794) & MS parts: D-HR, HR III 4 1/2 2° 345.   ★
Pm (KGS), score (fiche 2287) & parts (fiche 2288, 2289).
PAW-14. Parthia; in D, 4 mvts.   2fl 2ob 2cl(A) 3hn bn vlne.
AutoMS score & MS parts (c.1784): D-HR, HR III 4 1/2 4° 90.   ★
Pm (KGS), score (fiche 454) & parts (fiche 455, 56).
*PAW-15. Parthia; in F, 1786, 4 mvts.   2fl ob 2cl 3hn 2bn vlne.
AutoMS score & MS parts: D-HR, HR III 4 1/2 2° 337.   ★
Pm (KGS), score (fiche 2267) & parts (fiche 2268).
PAW-16. Parthia; in G, 1793, 4 mvts.   2fl 2ob cl(A) 2hn 2bn vlne.
MS parts: D-HR, HR III 4 1/2 2° 347.   ★Pm (KGS), fiche (2293).
PAW-17. Parthia in F; 4 mvts.   2fl 2ob cl 2hn 2bn vlne.
AutoMS score (1787): D-HR, HR III 4 1/2 2° 336.   Pm (KGS), fiche (2265, 2266).   ★

PAW-18. Parthia; in G, 1786, 4 mvts.   2fl ob 2cl(A) 2hn 2bn vlne.
MS parts: D-HR, HR III 4 1/2 2° 341.   ★Pm (KGS), fiche (2277, 2278).
PAW-19. Parthia; in F, 4 mvts.   2ob 2cl 3hn bn.
AutoMS score (1783): D-HR, HR III 4 1/2 2° 335.   Pm (KGS), fiche (2264).   ★
PAW-20. No: 1ᵐᵒ/ Nº: 27 / Parthia; in E♭, 4 mvts.   ob 2cl 2hn bn.
MS parts (c.1785): D-HR, HR III 4 1/2 4° 93.   Pm (KGS), fiche (460).   ★
***PAW-21.** Parthia; in E♭, 12 mvts.   2cl 2hn bn.
AutoMS parts (1782): D-HR, HR III 4 1/2 4° 91.   Pm (KGS), fiche (457).   ★

WINKLER, David *11 Oct 1948, Chicago*
DXW-1. Concerto.   pic fl cl b-cl bn cbn tp tb piano perc.
Pm (American Composers Alliance: New York).

***WINKLER, Johann (Jan)** *18 Nov 1794, Vsetín - 4 Jan 1874, Návsí u Jablunkova*
JOW-1. [untitled Parthia in F], 14 mvts.   2cl(C) 2hn bn.   MS parts: A-Wn, Mus.Hs.3028, No. 1.   ★
JOW-2. [untitled Parthia] Ex F; 19 mvts.   2cl 2hn 2bn.   MS parts: A-Wn, Mus.Hs.3028, No. 2.   ★
JOW-1tv, 2tv. 8 Trauer Arien, No. 4 ("Himmelunheilbare Wunden") in Dis [E♭], SATB, 2cl 2hn; No. 7 ("Wie Gras das an Morgenblühet"), in Dis [E♭], SATB, 2cl 2hn 2bn.
MS: A-Wn, Mus.Hs.3065, (Nos. 2, 3, 6 for SATB only; Nos. 1, 5, 8 for SATB, 2hn). *There are three other Trauer Arien for SATB + 2hn in A-Wn (Mus.Hs.2787, 2789, 2790), and one for SATB + 3tb (ad lib) at A-Wn, Mus.Hs.2792.*   ★

***WINKLER, Martin**
MXW-1a. II Parthie. 11 Ländler [without trios, all in C].   cl(F/E♭) cl(C) 2hn tp(C) tp(F/E♭) basso.
MS parts: A-Wn, Mus.Hs.23,971, (pencil inscriptions on the parts indicate cl(F) & tp(E♭) alternatives in E♭).   ★

***WINTER, Peter von** *baptized 28 Aug 1754, Mannheim - 17 Oct 1825, Munich*
PVW-1. A 2nd Set of Four Military Marches & Divertimentos For a Compleat [sic] Band Composed Expressely for M[ichael]. Kelly.   Nos. 1, 2 & 4: fl 2cl(C) 2hn 2bn basso tp; No. 3: terz-fl 2cl(C) 2hn 2bn basso.
Pc (Michael Kelly: London, wm1802, publication = c.1804), parts: GB-Lbl, R.M.17.f.9.(3).   ★
PVW-2. No. 1 Harmonie; in E♭, 4 mvts.   2ob 2cl 2hn 2bn cbn.
MS score: D-LEm, 1 an Becker III.11.67, S.1 - 20, (the original title, "Parthia" has been scraped off).   ★
***PVW-3.** Partita; in B♭, 3 mvts.   2ob 2cl 2hn 2bn.
Pc (Bureau des Arts et d'Industrie: Vienne, pn 442, 1804), RISM [W 1658], parts: A-Wgm, VIII 5221; CZ-Bm(au), A.20.257; CZ-Pk; D-Bds; D-HEms; D-RUl; H-KE, K 1129/IX.   ★
Pc (Breitkopf & Härtel: Leipzig, 1805), advertized in *AMZ*, Jan 1805, (probably only as Bureau des Arts agent).
Pm (WINDS: Northridge, PA, pn W-49, c.1980), photocopy of original parts.
PVW-4. Parthia. in E♭; 3 mvts.   2ob 2cl 2hn 2bn.   MS parts: D-DO, Mus.Ms.1597, No. 2.   ★
***PVW-5.** Parthia in Dis [E♭]; 4 mvts.   2cl 2hn 2bn.
Pc (Traeg: [Vienna], pre-1804), No. 210, MS parts: CZ-Pnm, XLI.B.129, (with an additional Echo mvt, Adagio, 2/4); PL-LA, RM 30, ("Eisenstadt den 11 Maj 1803").   ★
MS score: D-LEm, 1 an Becker III.11.67, S. 21 - 36, (as "No. 4 Harmonie")
***PVW-1v.** Veni Sancte Spiritus.   SATB, 2fl 2cl 2hn 2bn.
Partly AutoMS score: D-Mbs, Mus.Mss.2663. *The vocal lines are in faircopy; the wind parts have been added by the composer. A faircopy vocal score, SATB + organ(bc) follows the full score.*   ★
***PVW-2v.** Hymne: O könnt ich dich.   SATB, 2fl 2cl 2hn 2bn.
Partly AutoMS score: D-Mbs, Mus.Mss.2667. *The vocal lines are in fair copy and the majority of the wind parts are filled in by the composer.*   ★
***PVW-3v.** Chorale: Nun danket alle Gott.   SATB, (2)fl 2ob 2hn bn.
MS score: D-Mbs, Mus.Mss.2668. *Although the flute part calls for "Flauti", the part is in unison throughout.*   ★
***PVW-1tv.** [9] Responsiori pro defunctis.   Scoring varies.
MS score: A-Wn, HK 1966; D-Mh, Bl 116r, (1.1tv, as "Responsoria Nro 2, in Vigiliis Defunctorum", with additional timp & organ parts).   ★
    1.1tv. Responsorium I, Nocturno I; "Credo quod redemptor meus vivit". SATB, 2fl 2hn 2bn 2vc organ(bc-fig).
    1.2tv. Responsorium II; "Qui lazarum resuscitate". SATB, 2fl 2ob 2cl 4hn 2bn 2vc timp organ(bc-fig).
    1.3tv. Responsorium III; "Domine quando venereis judicare terram". SATB, 2fl 2cl 2hn 2bn 2vc organ(bc-fig).
    1.4tv. Responsorium IV, Nocturno II; "Momento mei Deus". SATB, 2cl 2hn 2bn 2vc organ(bc-fig).
    1.5tv. Responsorium VI; Recit: "Heu mei o Domini" & "Miserere mei dum veneris".
        SATB, 2fl 2cl 2hn 2bn 2vc organ(bc-fig).
    1.6tv. Responsorium VI; "Ne recorderis peccata mea Domine". SATB, 2fl 2cl 2hn 2bn 2vc organ(bc-fig).
    1.7tv. Responsorium VII, Nocturno III; "Pecantem me quotidie". SATB, 2fl·2cl 2hn 2bn 2vc organ(bc-fig).
    1.8tv. Responsorium VIII; "Domine, sedundum actum meum". SATB, 2bn 2vc basso.
    1.9tv. Responsorium IX; "Libera me Domine". SATB, 2fl 2ob 2cl 4hn 2bn 2vc organ(bc-fig).

WINTER, Tomas *1 March 1954, Sweden*
TZW-1. r - Aries [sic], Op. 151; 1991.   fl(pic) 2ob 2tp 2tb tu timp 2perc piano.   MS score: S-Sic.

WISKOTSHILL, ( )
YZW-1(-6). 6 Partie; (all in E♭).   2ob 2cl 2hn 2bn.
MS parts: D-Dl.

WISTER, Owen *1860 - 1938, USA*
OYW-1. Andante.   2fl 2ob 2cl hn 3bn harp.   MS score: US-Wc.

WITT, Christian Friedrich *(1660) - 1716*
CSW-1. Ouverture; in C.   3ob bn.
MS parts ("Sv Hof"): S-SK, 231:27.

*WITT, Friedrich *8 Nov 1770, Nieder Hallenstetten, Württemberg - 3 Jan 1836, Würzburg*
*FZW-1. Parthia in F; 4 mvts.   2fl 2ob 2cl 2hn 2bn vlne.
AutoMS score (1 March 1790) & MS parts: D-HR, HR III 4 1/2 2° 604.   ★
Pm (KGS), score (fiche 2719) & parts (fiche 2720, 2721).
FZW-2. Parthia in F; 4 mvts.   2fl 2ob 2cl 2hn 2bn vlne.
AutoMS score (2 Feb 1791) & MS parts: D-HR, HR III 4 1/2 2° 605.   ★
Pm (KGS), score, (fiche 2722, 2723), parts (fiche 2723, 2724).
*FZW-3. Parthia; in E♭, 1790, 4 mvts.   fl 2ob 2cl 2hn 2bn vlne.
MS parts: D-HR, HR III 4 1/2 2° 603.   ★
Pm (KGS), (fiche 2717, 2718).
*FZW-4. [7] Pièces d'harmonie.   cl(E♭) 2cl(B♭) 2hn 2bn tp b-tb serp.
Pc (chez les fils de B. Schott: Mayence, Paris; chez A. Schott: Anvers, pn 2583, 1826/1827), parts: D-MZsch; GB-Ljag(w). *The headtitle states, "Pieçes [sic] d'harmonie"; Küffner and Erbprinz Carl Friedrich von Löwenstein also use of this unusual misspelling.* Modern MS score (ed. Jon A. Gillaspie): GB-Ljag.   ★
FZW-4.1. [7] Pièces d'harmonie.   Additional timpani part specially composed for the Löwenstein Harmonie, Wertheim.   AutoMS part: GB-Ljag(w).
*FZW-5. Parthia; in E♭, 1792, 4 mvts.   fl ob 2cl 2hn 2bn vlne.
MS parts: D-HR, HR III 4 1/2 2° 602.   Pm (KGS), (fiche 2716).   ★
FZW-6. Duetto; in F.   2 solo basset horns, terz-fl 2cl(C) 2cl(B♭) 2hn 2bn basso.   AutoMS score: GB-Ljag(w).   ★
FZW-7 [= **Weber, CMW-4d**]. Concertino for Oboe; in F minor/major.
Solo oboe, fl 2cl(C) 2cl(B♭) 2hn 2bn tp b-tb cb.
AutoMS score: D-BABhüber.   MS parts: GB-Ljag(w).   ★
Pm (Musica rara: London, pn 1969A/B, 1980/81), ed. Hermann Dechant, score & parts, also piano reduction.
Pm (Nova Music: London, pn NM 137, 1980), oboe with piano reduction.
Pm (Kunzelmann: pn 10161, 1981), ed. Dieter Klöcker, score & parts.
Pm (WINDS: Northridge, CA, pn W-396, c. 1981), faint photocopy score (?copy of original) & modern MS pts.
FZW-8. Concertante per il Clarinetto ed Corno; 3 mvts.   Solo cl & hn, terz-fl 2cl(E♭) 2cl(B♭) 2hn 2bn tp b-tb cb.
AutoMS score: D-BABhuber, (missing most of 2nd mvt).   MS pts: GB-Ljag(w), 8/258, No. 4, (complete).   ★
FZW-9. Scena der il Corno di Bassetto; in F.   Solo basset horn, terz-fl 2cl(C) cl(B♭) 2hn 2bn tp b-tb cb.
AutoMS score ("Ottobre 1828"): D-BABhuber.   ★
FZW-10. [5] Variazioni Concertanti; in F.   2 solo horns, fl(F) 2cl(E♭) 2cl(B♭) 2bn tp b-tb cb.
AutoMS score: D-BABhuber.   MS parts: GB-Ljag(w), 8/264, No. 69.   ★
FZW-11. Walzer für das Klappenhorn.   Solo Klappenhorn, pic 2cl(C) 2cl(B♭) 2hn 2bn b-tb cb.
AutoMS score: GB-Ljag(w).   ★
FZW-12. [6] Walzer [with Trios; E♭, E♭, A♭, E♭, F, B♭].   terz-fl 2cl(E♭) 2cl(B♭) 2hn 2bn tp cb.
AutoMS score: GB-Ljag(w), (No. 5, in 2/4, is probably a Hopswalzer; another Walzer, scored for 2cl(E♭) 2cl(B♭) 2hn 2bn tp cb, has been cancelled on f.3b).   ★
FZW-13. [Parthia in E♭]; 3 mvts.   terz-fl 2cl(E♭) 2cl(B♭) 2hn 2bn tp cb.   AutoMS score: D-BABhuber.   ★
FZW-14. [Concertino]; in C, 1 continuous mvt in 2 sections.   terz-fl 2cl(E♭) 2cl(B♭) 2hn 2bn tp tb cb.
AutoMS score: D-BABhuber.   ★
FZW-15. Parthia Grande d'armonia [sic]; in E♭, 6 mvts.   2cl(E♭) 2cl(B♭) 2hn 2bn tp tb cb.
AutoMS score: GB-Ljag(w), 434.   ★
FZW-16. [Walzer & Trio in E♭].   2cl(E♭) 2cl(B♭) 2hn 2bn tp cb.   AutoMS score: GB-Ljag(w).   ★
FZW-17. [Single mvt, Allegretto, 3/4].   cl(E♭) 2cl(B♭) 2hn 2bn b-tb cb.   AutoMS score: GB-Ljag(w).   ★
FZW-18. Concertante; in F, 4 mvts.   2cl 2hn 2bn.   AutoMS score: GB-Ljag(w).   ★
FZW-19. [in pencil: "Quintett 1"]; in F, 2 mvts.   2cl 2hn bn.
AutoMS score: D-BABhuber, (formerly D-WEMl No. 440).   ★
FZW-20. [in pencil: "Quintett 2"]; in F, 2 mvts.   2cl 2hn bn.
AutoMS score: D-BABhuber, (formerly D-WEMl No. 441).   ★
FZW-21. Armonia dolorosa [in pencil: "Quintett 3"]; in B♭, 2 mvts.   2cl 2hn bn.
AutoMS score: D-BABhuber, (formerly D-WEMl No. 336).   ★
FZW-1s. Additional timpani part for Küffner's *Musique turque, 3 recueil*, JYK-14.   AutoMS part: GB-Ljag.
FZW-1t. Trauermarsch; in C minor.   4cl 2hn 2bn cb timp.   AutoMS score: D-BABhuber.   ★
FZW-1a. Auber: Le Maçon, overture & 13 mvts.   fl(F, terz-, pic in F) ob 2cl(E♭) 2cl(B♭) 2hn 2bn tp b-tb cb.
AutoMS score & MS parts: GB-Ljag(w), 2/261, No. 2.
FZW-2a. Auber: Le Philtre, overture & 12 mvts.   fl(pic) ob 2cl(E♭) 2cl(B♭) 2hn 2bn tp b-tb cb.
AutoMS score (1833) & MS parts: GB-Ljag(w)., 10/258, No. 4
FZW-3a. Boieldieu: Jean de Paris, overture.   terz-fl 2cl(C) 2cl(B♭) 2hn 2bn tp b-tb cb.
AutoMS score (1831; incomplete) & MS parts (complete): GB-Ljag(w).
FZW-4a. Boieldieu: La Dame blanche, overture & 14 mvts.   fl(F, terz-) 2cl(E♭) 2cl(B♭) 2hn 2bn tp b-tb cb.
AutoMS score & MS parts: GB-Ljag(w), 2/261, No. 1, (parts missing b-tb).
FZW-5a. Cherubini: Les deux Journées, overture & 5 mvts.   fl(terz-fl) cl(F) cl(C) 2cl(B♭) 2hn 2bn tp b-tb cb.
AutoMS score & MS parts: GB-Ljag(w), 1/263, No. 3.
FZW-6a. Mayseder: Variations.   Clarinet Principale in B♭, cl(E♭) 2cl(B♭) 2hn 2bn tp basso.
AutoMS score & MS parts: GB-Ljag(w).
FZW-7a. Meyerbeer: Robert le Diable, overture & 2 mvts.   fl(pic, terz-fl) ob 2cl(C) 2cl(B♭) 2hn 2bn tp b-tb cb.
AutoMS score (1833): GB-Ljag(w).
FZW-8a. Mozart: Le Nozze di Figaro, overture & 6 mvts.   fl(F, terz-) 2cl(E♭) 2cl(B♭) 2hn 2bn tp b-tbcb.
AutoMS score & MS parts: GB-Ljag(w).
FZW-9.1a. Mozart: Don Giovanni, overture & 19 mvts.   fl(F, terz-, D) 2cl(E♭, C) 2cl(B♭) 2hn 2bn tp b-tb cb.
AutoMS score & MS parts: GB-Ljag(w).
FZW-9.2a. Mozart: Don Giovanni, overture.   2cl(E♭) 2cl(B♭) 2hn 2bn cb.
AutoMS score: GB-Ljag(w), 346/11.
FZW-9.3a. Mozart: Don Giovanni, 8 mvts.   2cl 2hn 2bn.   AutoMS score (Nos. 1 - 5) & MS parts: Gb-Ljag(w).

FZW-10a. Mozart: La Clemenza di Tito, Andante aus Titus, ("Ah perdona al primo affetto"). *This is the "Andante in C [sic, in B♭]" often incorrectly attributed to Weber, CMW-5d.*; the MS includes 6 dances. 2cl(E♭) 2cl(B♭) 2hn 2bn cb.
AutoMS score: GB-Ljag(w), 346, No. 6.   MS parts: GB-Ljag(w), 414, No. 1. *The MS parts include an Allemande & Trio and a Walz [sic] in the original copyist's hand; these works were later renumbered as 3 & 5, respectively, and a further 3 dances were added. The Clarino part also includes 2 Adagios, the second a fragment only, unrelated to the other works in the set. The scoring varies for each number and it is impossible to determine whether Witt was the composer of FZW-10.3a (-10.6a), although this seems likely.*
    10.1a. Mozart: La Clemenza did Tito, Andante; arranged Witt.   2cl(E♭) 2cl(B♭) 2hn 2bn b-tb+cb
    10.2/1a. Witt: Allemande [& Trio]; B♭.   pic(E♭) 2cl(E♭) 2cl(B♭) 2hn 2bn tp b-tb+cb. Renumbered as "No. 3".
    10.2/2a. Witt: Allemande [& Trio] in B♭.   2pic(E♭) 2cl(E♭) 2cl(B♭) 2hn(E♭)+2hn(B♭) 2bn cb.
        AutoMS score: GB-L-jag(w).   ★
    10.3a. [?Witt:] Walz [sic]; B♭.   2cl(B♭) 2hn b-tb+cb. Renumbered as "No. 5".
    10.4a. [?Witt:] "No. 2 Walzer"; B♭.   terz-fl 2cl(E♭) 2cl(B♭) 2hn 2bn tp b-tb+cb.
    10.5a. [?Witt:] "No. 5. Walzer" [& Trio]; E♭.   terz-fl 2cl(E♭) 2cl(B♭) 2hn bn tp+tp(rip - in bn II pt) b-tb+cb.
    10.6a. [?Witt:] "No. 6. Deutsche"; E♭.   terz-fl 2cl(E♭) 2cl(B♭) 2hn 2bn b-tb+cb.
FZW-11a. Mozart: Die Zauberflöte, overture.   terz-fl 2cl(E♭) 2cl(B♭) 2hn 2bn tp b-tb cb.
AutoMS score & MS parts: GB-Ljag(w), 327.
FZW-12a. Paisiello: L'Olimpiade, recit & duet: Ne' giorni tuoi felici.   2fl 2ob 2cl 2hn 2bn vlne.
MS score & parts: D-HR, HR III 4 1/2 2° 421.   Pm (KGS), score (fiche 2423) & parts (fiche 2424).
FZW-13a. Righini: Armida, overture & 6 mvts.   cl(E♭) 2cl(B♭) 2hn 2bn tp b-tb cb.
AutoMS score & MS parts (1824): GB-Ljag(w).
FAW-14.1a. Spohr: Jessonda, overture & 8 mvts.   Scoring varies.
MS score with AutoMS alterations and a new cl(II E♭; No 8: 2cl in E♭) part: GB-Ljag(w).   cf. *FZW-15.2a.*
    [0]. Overture.   terz-fl fl(C) 2ob cl(E♭) 3cl(B♭) 4hn 2bn tp 2a-tb b-tb serp timp.
    1. Duett, Lass für ihn, den ich geliebet. №. 15.   terz-fl cl(E♭) 3cl(B♭) 2hn 2bn serp.
    2. Rondo, Dass mich Glück mit Rosen Kröne. №. 16.   (as No. 15.1/1).
    3. Aria, Der Kriegeslust ergeben. №. 12.   pic(fl) cl(E♭) 3cl(B♭) 2hn 2bn tp serp.
    4. Introduzion und Chor der Portugiesen. №. 10.   terz-fl cl(E♭) 3cl(B♭) 2hn 2bn 2tp serp.
    5. Waffentanz. 2ᵗᵉʳ Act. №. 10.   terz-fl cl(E♭) 3cl(B♭) 2hn 2bn serp.
    6. Terzett, Auf! und lasst die Fahnen fliegen, III. Akt, №. 25.   2terz-fl cl(E♭) 3cl(B♭) 2hn 2bn 2tp serp.
    7. Chor der Portugiesen, Heurlich ist es. 2ᵗᵉʳ Act. №. 10.   terz-fl ob 3cl(B♭) 2hn 2bn serp.
    8. Duett, Schönes Mädchen wirst mich hassen. №. 18.   terz-fl ob/fl 3cl(B♭) 2hn 2bn 2tp serp.
FZW-14.2a. Spohr: Jessonda, overture & 8 mvts.   fl(E♭) cl(E♭) cl(E♭/C) 2cl(B♭) 2hn 2bn tp tb cb.
AutoMS score (overture) & MS parts: GB-Ljag(w), 2/258, No. 2. *Rescored for Wertheim; cf. FZW-1ac.*
FZW-15.1a. C.M. Weber: Der Freischütz, overture & 14 mvts.   terz-fl(pic) 2cl(E♭) 2cl(B♭) 2hn 2bn tp b-tb cb.
AutoMS score & MS parts: GB-Ljag(w), (with additional pts: cl in C, in Witt's hand; tp & timp in another hand).
FZW-15.2a. C.M. Weber: Der Freischütz, Jäger Chor.   cl(F) 2cl(B♭) 2hn 2bn b-tb cb.
AutoMS score: GB-Ljag(w), 346, ("Clar in F" has been altered to "in E♭" but the part remains unchanged; beneath the two systems, Witt has added a second clarinet in E♭).
FZW-16a. Weber: Oberon, (arranged F. Weller, FYW-1.2a).   2cl(E♭) 2cl(B♭) 2hn 2bn tp tb cb.
AutoMS tp part & MS parts: GB-Ljag(w), (176). *A rescoring for the Wertheim Harmonie.*
FZW-17a. [Set of dances, composed & arranged by Witt].   Scoring varies.
AutoMS score (Nos. 1, 2, 7 & 8) & MS pts: GB-Ljag(w), 341, (Nos. 11 & 12 are later additions in another hand).
    17.1a. H. Stokmar: Oberwittbacher Fantasie [Walzer & Trio].   2cl(E♭) 2cl(B♭) 2hn 2bn tp b-tb.
    17.2a. H. Stokmar: Favorit Tanz.   2cl(E♭) 2cl(B♭) 2hn 2bn tp b-tb.
    17.3ac. Anon: Walzer.   2cl(E♭) 2cl(B♭) 2hn 2bn b-tb.
    17.4ac. Anon: Walzer & Trio.   2cl(E♭) 2cl(B♭) 2hn 2bn tp b-tb.
    17.5a. Witt: Oberwittbacher Walzer, non tanto.   pic(E♭) 2cl(E♭) 2cl(B♭) 2hn 2bn tp b-tb.
    17.6ac. Anon: Walzer.   fl(E♭) 2cl(E♭) 2cl(B♭) 2hn 2bn b-tb.
    17.7ac. [Schubert: Original-Tänze, No. 2, Sehnsuchtswalzer] as Beethoven: Walzer & Trio [K.-H. Anh. 14]. fl(E♭) 2cl(E♭) 2cl(B♭) 2hn 2bn tp b-tb.
    17.8ac. Witt: Walzer & Trio; in E♭.   terz-fl 2cl(E♭) 2cl(B♭) 2hn 2bn tp b-tb.
    17.9ac. Anon: Walzer & Trio.   terz-fl 2cl(E♭) 2cl(B♭) 2hn 2bn tp b-tb.
    17.10ac. Anon: Walzer.   terz-fl 2cl(E♭) 2cl(B♭) 2hn 2bn tp b-tb.
    17.11ac. Gumlich: Walzer.   terz-fl cl(E♭) 2hn bn b-tb.
    17.12ac. Anon: Ecossaise.   terz-fl cl(E♭) cl(B♭) 2hn 2bn b-tb.
FZW-1va. Witt: Requiem.   CATB, terz-fl 2cl(E♭) 2cl(B♭) 2hn 2bn tp b-tb cb timp.
AutoMS score (fragments): D-BABhuber.   MS parts (complete): GB-Ljag(w).   ★
FZW-1vac. [?Witt]: Mass in E♭.   CATB, fl(F) 2cl(E♭) 2cl(B♭) 2hn 2bn tp b-tb cb timp. MS pts: GB-Ljag(w). ★
FZW-1c [= **Hummel JNH-3d**]. Sextett für Bläser F-Dur; 4 mvts.   2cl 2hn bn bn/b-tb.
MS parts: D-BABhuber, (formerly D-WEMI, No. 417). *"Witt Sextett" has been added in pencil.*   ★
Modern MS score & parts: D-FIZklöcker, (recorded as "Hummel" with db).
FZW-1ac. Rossini: Le Siège de Corinthe, Aria.   fl(E♭) 2cl(E♭) 2cl(B♭) 2hn 2bn tp tb cb.
MS score & parts: GB-Ljag(w), 10/258, (No. 9 of the arrangement of Spohr's *Jessonda*, FZW-14.1a).
FZW-1f. [Single mvt in C; Adagio, C (27 bars) / 3/4, (21 bars) / Var I, (17 bars).
fl 2cl(C) 2cl(B♭) 2hn 2bn tp tb cb.   AutoMS score: GB-Ljag(w).   ★
FWZ-2f. [Single mvt in E♭; Adagio, 3/4 (21 bars) / Allo, C, (68 bars).]   2cl 2hn bn.
AutoMS score (1821): GB-Ljag(w).   ★
FZW-1caf. [?Witt]: Concertanto per Gli due oboe [sic]; in F.   2ob solo, 2cl(C) 2cl(B♭) 2hn 2bn tp b-tb cb.
AutoMS score & MS parts: D-BABhuber, (omits solo oboes in both score & parts; probably a transcription).   ★
CAL-2caf. [?Witt]: Concerto; in E♭, 2 mvts.   Corno Principale, terz-fl 2cl(E♭) 2cl(B♭) 2hn 2bn tp b-tb cb.
MS parts: GB-Ljag(w), 9/258, No. 4, (missing solo hn & one sheet of cl II in B♭).   ★

*WITTEK, Adolf *(1820), active in Břetislava nr Plzeň*
ADW-1. České Potpourri od: Pieníka pro Harmonii.   cl(Eb) cl(Bb) 2hn 2tp flug 2bassi.
MS parts (c.1850): CZ-PLa(ba), Hu 3822. ★

WITTENBERG, ( ) *active 2nd half of the 18th century, ?St Petersburg*
XIW-1. Pièces d'Harmonie.   2cl 2hn 1/2bn.
MS parts: RF-Ssc, Ф 891 собp юосуповьiх N46, pp. 76 - 129. ★

*WITTLINGER, H. *(1800)*
HYW-1v. Advent=Lied; "Ihr Himmel, taut aus euer'n Höhen".   CCB, 2cl 2hn 2bn.
MS parts (by the Schullehrer, Loritz, 5 Sept 1837): D-Tl, B 520.

*WITWAR, ( ) *(1740)*
YXW-1(-3). 3 Parthien; (Eb, 3 mvts; Eb, 3 mvts; Eb, 4 mvts).   2cl 2hn 2bn.
MS parts: CZ-NR, A.18.236/B.251. ★

*WOELFING, ( ) *(1810)*
ZZW-1a. Lanner: Regatta Galopp, Op. 134.   fl 2ob 2cl 2hn 2bn tb db.
MS parts: D-NEhz, 133, No. 26.
ZZW-2a. Lanner: Victoria Walzer, Op. 138.   fl 2ob 2cl 2hn 2bn tb db timp.
MS parts: D-NEhz, 133, No. 24.
ZZW-3a. Lanner: Die Osmanen Walzer, Op. 144.   fl 2ob 2cl 2hn 2bn tb db timp.
MS parts: D-NEhz, 133, No. 28.
ZZW-4a. Pixis: (unidentified) overture.   fl 2ob 2cl 3hn 2bn tp tb db timp.
MS score (in the hand of W E Scholz, beginning of score: "Schl[a]w[entzit]z d. 3ten Sept: [18]40", end of score
"d. 7ten Sept") & (MS missing cl I). D-NEhz, 58, No. 2. (parts missing cl I).
ZZW-5a. Strauss the Elder: Wiener-Gemüths-Walzer, Op. 116.   fl 2ob 2cl 3hn 2bn tp tb db timp.
MS parts (by W. E. Scholz, c.1841 - 1843): D-NEhz, 107, No. 1

*WOELFL (WÖLFL), Joseph *24 Dec 1773, Salzburg - 21 May 1812, London*
JSW-1(-6). VI Sonatas a 6. Oeuv. III; No. I in C, 3 mvts; No. II in G, 3 mvts; No. III in F, 2 mvts; No. IV in
G, 2 mvts; No. V in D, 2 mvts; No. VI in Bb, 2 mvts.   2ob 2hn 2bn.   AutoMS score: A-Sca, Hs. 688. ★
*JSW-7. Sei Sonate; here only: Nro I Sonata; in D, 5 mvts.   2ob 2hn 2bn.
AutoMS score: A-Sca, Hs.690. ★
Pm (Comes Verlag: Bad Reichenhall, 1992), ed. Gerhard Walterskirchen, score & parts.

WOESTYNE (Woestijne), David (van der) *18 Feb 1915, Llanidloes, Belgium*
DVW-1. Sérénades; 1946.   2cl b-cl 2hn 2bn cbn tp tb db piano.   MS: B-Bcdm.

WOHLMUTH, Andreas Michael *1809 - 1884*
AMW-1v. Offertorium in G.   CATB, 2fl 2ob 2cl 2hn bn vlne.   MS parts: CZ-Pnm, XXXII.E.98 (2).

*WOLF, Cyrill *9 March 1825, Müglitz - 21 Oct 1915, Vienna*
CXW-1v. Tantum ergo, "Comp. 29 Sept, [1]848".   SATB, 2cl 2hn 2bn *(there is an alternative version with*
organ instead of winds).   MS: A-Wn, Mus.Hs.22,748.

*WOLF (Wolff), Franz Xaver *(1760) Clarinettist, Royal Prussian Hohelohe Regt, 1797.*
FRW-1, 2. Deux Sérénades, Op. 1; both in Eb, 4 mvts.   2cl 2hn 2bn.
Pc (Johann André: Offenbach am Main, pn 836, 1795), RISM [W 1824], parts: D-W, (missing bn II part). ★
FRW-3. Parthia ex Es [Eb]; 4 mvts.   MS parts (1806): CZ-Bm(rj), A.13.125. ★

*WOLF, Hugo *13 March 1860, Windischgraz, Styria - 22 Feb 1903, Vienna*
HXW-1v. Gedichte von Eduard Mörike: No. 23, "Auf ein altes Bild" (revised orchestral version, 1889).
S solo, 2ob 2cl 2bn.
AutoMS: A-Wn, Mus.Hs.9. ★
Pc (C.F. Peters: Leipzig, 1904), score & parts (hire).
Pm (Belwin Inc.: New York, pn A4631, reprint of Peters edition, sd), score & parts.
Pm: (Musikwissenschaftlicher Verlag: Wien, 1983), Sämtlicher Werk Bd. 9, Lieder mit Orchesterbegleitung II,
ed. H. Jancik, pp. 86ff), score.

*WOLLE, Peter *1792 - 1871 (USA)*
PEW-1m. Madison's March; in Eb, ¢.   fl 2cl 2hn bn tp.
MS parts: US-BETm, Lititz Collegium Musicum 200.3. ★
Pm (in: Henry H. Hall, *The Moravian Music Ensemble*, PhD dissertation, Vanderbilt Univ, 1967), score.

WOOD, Kevin Joseph *1947, USA*
KJW-1. Kuretes Dance.   ob 2cl bn.
Pm (Highgate Press: New York, 1992).

WOOD, Ralph Walter *31 May 1902 - 28 March 1987, UK*
RLW-1. Sequenza; 1967.   2fl 2ob 2cl 2hn 2bn.   MS score: GB-Lmic.

*WOOLFENDEN, Guy Anthony *12 July 1937, Ipswich, UK*
Much of Woolfenden's music for winds is in MS, including incidental music for all Shakespeare plays and others.
Enquiries should be directed to: Ariel Music, Malvern House, Sibford Ferris, Banbury, Oxon, OX15 5RG, UK.
GAW-1. Suite française; 1991 commission.   2fl 2ob 2cl 2bn.
Pm (Ariel Music: Sibford Ferris, 1991), score & parts.
GAW-2. Prelude, In Memoriam and Finale.   fl ob cl b-cl hn bn.
Pm (Ariel Music: Sibford Ferris, c.1991), score & parts.
GAW-3. All's Well That Ends Well; incidental music, 1988.   2ob 2hn 2bn perc.   In MS *via* Ariel Music.

*WOOLRICH, John *3 Jan 1954, Cirencester, UK*
*JRW-1. Vaucanson's Machine. fl(a-fl) ob ca 2cl(E♭) 2hn 2bn.
Pm (Faber Music: London, 1988), hire score & parts.
JRW-2. The Way Out Discovered.   2ob 2cl 2bthn 4hn 2bn cbn.
Pm (Faber Music: London, 1997). *Commissioned for the Brighton Festival, 1st performance 10 May 1997.*
JRW-3. Quick Steps.   2ob cl(E♭) cl(B♭) 2hn 2bn.
Pm (Faber Music: London, 1990), study score, (parts for hire only).

*WORGAN, James (John), *the Younger* *(1770), London*
JJW-1m. A March . . . for the Loyal Essex Regiment of Fencible Infantry.
(2)fl(doubling obs) 2ob 2cl 2hn 2bn 2tp(doubling hns) serp timp.
Pc   (Broderip   &   Wilkinson: London,   c.1799),   RISM   [W   1877],   score: GB-Lbl,   g.133.(67);
GB-Ob, Mus.Instr.I.234(27). ★
JJW-2m. A celebrated French March Revived and Set for a Band with Variations for the Piano-forte.
2ob 2cl 2hn 2bn; piano.
Pc (Printed for the Author by Broderip and Wilkinson: London, 1802), RISM [W 1875], score:
GB-Lbl, g.139.(54); GB-Ob, Mus.Instr.I.234(25). ★

*WRANIZKY (Vranický, Wraniczky, Wranitzky), Anton (Antonín) *1761 - 1820*
MVH: Pochody pro dechové nástroje. Edited Antonín Myslík. (Editio Supraphon: Prague, 1970), Musica viva
*historica 26. **HMU**: Lovocké pochody pro dechové nástroje. (Hudebný matice Umélecké besedy: Prague, pn*
1060, 1948), miniature score, (Sbírka Kapesních Partitur Svazek 38).
*AYW-1. Grosser Quadrille Musik zum Karossal [sic]; 18 mvts. pic 2ob 2cl 2hn 2bn cbn 2tp 2tp(prin) b-dr cym.
(?Auto)MS parts: CZ-Pnm, Lobkovic X.H.a.68/1. ★
*AYW-2. IIda Harmonie zum Karossel.   2ob 2cl 2hn 2bn cbn tp.
(?Auto)MS parts: CZ-Pnm, Lobkovic X.H.a.68/1. ★
*AYW-3. Musique de grand Carouss., 15 mvts.   2ob 2cl 2hn 2bn (tp).
MS parts: H-KE, K 1182. ★
AYW-4. Nro Vto. Trio in C, 4 mvts.   2ob ca.
MS parts: CZ-K, No.34.K.23. ★
AYW-5. Parthia; in F.   2ob 2hn 2bn.   MS: CZ-Pnm, (unverified).
*AYW-1.1(-1.6)m. VI Kleinen Märsche; B♭, E♭, C, D, B♭, D minor.   2ob 2cl 2hn 2bn cbn tp.
MS parts: CZ-Pnm, Lobkovic X.h.b.9. ★
Pm (MVH), pp. 16 - 27, score & parts.
*AYW-2.1(-2.3)m. 3 Märsche /: auf französisch Art :/ [sic]; C, F, C.   2ob 2cl(C) 2hn 2bn cbn tp.
MS parts: CZ-Pnm, Lobkovic X.h.b.8. ★
Pm (MVH), pp. 13 - 15, score & parts.
*AYW-3.1, 3.2m. Jäger-Marasch: No. 9 (auf französische Arth) Marsch in 6/8 Takt; in D; Jägermarsch mit Solo
der Prinzipaltrompete; C.   2ob 2cl(1: A; 2: C) 2hn 2bn cbn tp(solo).
AutoMS parts: CZ-Pnm, Lobkovic X.h.b.7. ★
Pm (HMU), Nos. 5, 6, score.   Pm (MVH), pp. 9 - 12, score & parts.
*AYW-4.1(-4.4m). Vier Jägermarsche; B♭, F, B♭, B♭.   Nos. 1 & 4: 2cl 2hn 2bn; Nos. 2 & 3: 2ob 2hn 2bn.
AutoMS parts: CZ-Pnm, Lobkovic X.h.b.6. ★
MS parts of Nos. 1 & 3, for 2ob 2hn 2bn): CZ-Pnm, Lobkovic X.H.b.10.
Pm (HMU), Nos. 1 - 4, score.   Pm (MVH), pp. 1 - 8, score & parts.
AYW-1a. Cartellieri: 1 mvt. *See* AYW-1, mvt. 17.
AYW-2a. Salieri: Tarare ("La Tarare").   *See* AYW-1, mvt 4.
AYW-3.1a, 3.2a. J Weigl: Die isthmischen Spiel, 2 mvts. *See* AYW-1, mvts 5, 15.
AYW-1v. Gelegenheits-Lied und Chor. Bei Gelegenheit des 4ten Sept: [1]803 als Geburtstag Sr: Durchl. der
Fürsten.   CATB, 2ob 2cl 2hn 2bn 2tp timp.   MS parts: CZ-Pnm, Lobkovic X.B.f.25. ★
AYW-1mv. Saazer Kreis 1tes Bataillon. Volkslied . . . in Form eines Marscher; "Brüder auf! uns jedem Stande".
TTB, 2ob 2cl 2hn 2bn cbn tp.   MS parts ("Eisenberg in 7ber [Sept] 1808"): CZ-Pnm, Lobkovic X.I.b.101. ★

*WRANIZKY (Vranický, Wraniczky, Wranitzky), Paul (Pavel)
30 Dec 1756, Nová Říše - 26 Sept 1808, Vienna
*PYW-1. La Chasse, Op. 44; in D, 1 mvt.   Solo piano, 2fl 2ob 2cl 2hn 2bn timp b-dr.
Pc (Johann André: Offenbach am Main, pn 2425, 1807/1808), RISM [W 2081], parts: A-Wgm; D-Bds. ★
Pm (Castle Music: Sherriff Hutton, York, pn V3/117, 1992), ed. J.S. Taylorson, score & parts.
*PYW-2. Parthia in F; 4 mvts (often attributed to Haydn; see FJH-11d).   2ob 2cl 2hn 2bn.
MS parts: D-DO, Mus.Ms.2062 (with an extra final March).
For other locations, with a Haydn attribution, See: Haydn, **FJH-11d**.
Pm (International Music Co.: New York, 1951), miniature score (pn 999) & parts (pn 998).
Pm (Compusic: Amsterdam, pn 258, 1988), score & parts.

WRIGHT, Maurice Willis *1949, USA*
MWR-1. Chamber Symphony; c.1985.   2fl 2ob 2cl 2hn 2bn db.   MS score: US-NYamc.

*WRIGHT, Thomas *18 Sept 1763, Stockton-on-Tees - 24 Nov 1829, Barnard Castle*
TYW-1m. Two Marches [Slow & Quick] for the Volunteer Corps of Newcastle upon Tyne.   2cl 2hn bn.
Pc (Printed for G. Goulding: London, c.1795), score: GB-En, Glen 347-37/2. ★
TYW-2m. Two Marches . . . for the Use of The East York Militia.
(Quick March:) 2cl 2hn 2bn; (Slow March:) 2cl 2hn bn.
Pc (G. Goulding: London, c.1800), RISM [W 2176], score: GB-Lbl, g.133.(23). ★
TYW-3m. March . . . for the Use of the First Battalion of West York Militia.   2cl 2hn bn.
Pc (G. Goulding: London, c.1800), RISM [W 2177], score: GB-Lbl, g.133.(24), GB-Lhumphries (modern MS
score & parts). ★

*WUORINEN, Charles *9 June 1932, New York*
CAW-1. Concertino. Solo double bass, fl fl(pic) 2ob 3cl cl(in Bb)(cl in Eb) b-cl cb-cl 4hn bn bn(cbn), (optional strings, 2vl vla vc).
Pm (C.F. Peters: New York, 1984), hire score & parts.
CAW-2. Chamber Doncerto. Solo tuba; 4fl ob ca 4hn 2bn 1perc(12 drums).
Pm (C.F. Peters: New York, 1970), hire score & parts.
CAW-3. Composition. Solo violin, 2ob 2b-cl 2hn 2tb db piano perc.
Pm (C.F. Peters: New York, 1965), hire score & parts.

WYK, Carl Albert van *1942, South Africa*
CVW-1. Sextet; 1974. fl ob cl 2hn bn. MS score: SA-Jsamro.

*WYVILL (Wivill), Zerubbabel *1762, Maidenhead - 14 May 1837, Hounslow*
ZYW-1m. The Berkshire March in 8 Parts Composed for the Berkshire Militia at the Desire of the Right Honble. The Earl of Radnor.   2fl 2ob 2cl 2hn 2bn.
Pc (Printed and Sold for the Author by Messrs. Longman and Broderip: London, 1793), RISM [VV 2208], score: GB-Lbl, g.133.(64); GB-Ob, Mus.Instr.I.233(27); GB-DOTams, (modern score & pts); GB-Ljag (modern score), GB-Lhumphries (modern score & parts).   ★

XENAKIS (Xenakes), Iannis (Giannes, Yannis) *29 May 1922, Braila, Romania*
IXX-1. Akrata; 1964 - 1965.   pic ob s-cl(Eb) b-cl(Bb) cb-cl/bn 2hn bn 2cbn 3tp 2tb tu.
Pm (Boosey & Hawkes: London, etc., 1968), facsimile of AutoMS score.
Recorded on EMI CO 631001; Nonesuch H 71201; Angel S 36656; CBS 34-61226.
IXX-2. ST/10-1,080262; 1956 - 1962.   cl b-cl 2hn 2cbn 3tp 2tb tu.
Pm (Boosey & Hawkes: London, etc., 1967), score.
Recorded on EMI CO 631001; Angel S 36656; Columbia SCXG 55.
IXX-3. Oresteia, Suite.   fl ob 2cl hn bn 2tp tb tu vc perc.
Pm (Boosey & Hawkes: London, etc.), score.
IXX-1v. Oresteia; 1965 - 1966.   Chorus, fl ob 2cl hn bn 2tp tb tu vc perc.
Pm (Boosey & Hawkes: London, etc.), score. *Recorded on Erato STU 70656.*

YAVELOW, Christopher Johnson *15 June 1950, Cambridge, Mass*
CJY-1. Monday Morning Fantasy. 2fl ob ca 2cl hn tb; (ca, tb may be substituted by sax, bn).
Pm (American Composers Alliance: NY).

*YOST, Michel *(also used pseudonym:* **J. Michel)** *1754, Paris - 5 July 1786, Paris*
MXY-1. Suite (c.1780).   ob 2cl 2hn bn. MS parts: D-RH, MS.436.

YOUNG, Derek *12 July 1929, UK*
DXY-1. Serenade for flugelhorn.   Solo flug, 2fl ob cl b-cl 2hn bn.
MS: (location unknown: ?possibly on hire from Lynwood Music, West Hagby[?]).

YUN, Isang *17 Sept 1917, Tongyong*
IXY-1. Harmonia; 1974.   2fl 2ob 2cl 4hn 3bn harp glock 3cym 3gongs 2tomtoms, 3temple blocks; (ad lib: pic ca cl(III)/b-cl).
Pm (Bote & Bock: Berlin, 1975), score, (parts for hire).
IXY-2. Bläseroktett.   2ob 2cl 2hn 2bn (db ad lib).
Pm (Bote & Bock: Berlin, 1994), hire score & parts.

*ZACH, G[eorg] *(1740)*
*GYZ-1. Parthia Ex D, il 20 Ap: [1]771; 4 mvts.   2ob 2hn 2bn.
MS parts: CZ-Pnm, XXXII.A.96.   ★

*ZAIDEL-RUDOLPH, Jeanne *9 July 1948, Pretoria*
*JXZ-1. Kaleidescope.   fl ob 2cl 3hn bn tp 2tb tu perc.   MS score: SA-Jsamro.

*ZALUZAN (Valuzau), Johann *(1790)*
JYZ-1a. Harmonie Quodlibet aus dem Zauberspiel der Diamont des Geisterkönigs, [by Josef Dreschler, 1824].
2ob 2cl 2hn 2bn tp.   MS parts: CZ-KRa, A4007/IV.B.179.
JYZ-2a. Polonois für die Harmonie.   (instrumentation unknown).
MS parts: CZ-KRa, A4027/IV.B.200, (?lost, missing since 27 July 1981).

*ZÁMEČNÍK, Evžen *5 Feb 1939, Frýdek-Místek*
EXZ-1. Concerto Grosso for small wind ensemble & symphony orchestra.
Pm (Český hudební fond: Prague, 1984), hire score & parts.

ZANGL, Josef Gregor *12 March 1821, Steinach - 6 March 1897, Brixen*
JGZ-1v. Harmonie-Messe in Es [Eb], Op. 21. SATB, cl(Eb) 2cl(Bb) 2hn 2tp 2flug t-tb euph bomb timp organ(3).
Pc (Josef Anton Möst: Innsbruck, pn J.A.M.2, c.1850-1875), pts: CZ-Pnm, XLIII.E.4, (missing cl in Eb).   ★
JGZ-2v. Tantum ergo, Graduale und Offertorium, Op. 22; (all in Bb).
SATB, cl(Eb) 2cl(Bb) 2hn 2tp 2flug t-tb euph bomb timp organ.
Pc (sn: sl, [?Möst: Innsbruck], c.1850-75), pts: CZ-Pnm, XLIII.B.180, (printed vocal pts, MS instrumental pts).   ★
JGZ-3v. Fest-Messe in B[b]. [&] Es. [Eb], Op. 90.
SATB, 2cl 2hn 2tp 2flug t-tb b-tb timp organ/Directionsstimmen(4 copies).
Pc (Johann Gross S.A.Reiss: Innsbruck, pn 33, c.1890s), parts: CZ-Pnm, XLIII.D.23.   ★

ZANOLINI, Bruno *22 Aug 1945, Milan*
BXZ-1. Poursuite; 1 continuous mvt.   Piano, fl 2ob cl(Bb) 2hn 2bn. *Note: the cl & 2hn are written in C.*
Pm (Suvini Zerboni: Milano, pn S.9035Z., 1981), facsimile AutoMS score, (in "New Notation").

ZANONI, Ernesto
ERZ-1. Piccolo Concerto.   fl 2ob 2cl 2hn 2bn.
Pm (Edipan Edizione Musicale: Roma, sd).

*ZAPF, Johann Nepomuk   *2 or 21 Feb 1760, Mondsee, Upper Austria - post-1820*
JNZ-1. Parthia: in B[♭]; 4 mvts.   2ob 2cl 2hn 2bn.
MS parts: A-Wgm, VIII 8914.   ★

ZAPLETAL, ( )
ZXZ-1. Quartetto Nr. 6; in B♭, 4 mvts.   3cl bn.   MS parts: H-Bb, 1784.   ★

*ZASCHE (Czasche), Anton (Antonÿ)   *(1770)*
AZZ-1. Parthia in F; 3 mvts.   2fl(D) cl(F) 2cl(C) 2hn 2bn tp(prin) serp glock.
MS parts (by Dominik Hübner, Langenbruck): CZ-Pu(dm), 59 R 3320.   ★
AZZ-2. Parthia in Dis [E♭]; 4 mvts.   2fl 2cl 2hn 2bn.
MS parts (by Dominik Hübner, Langenbruck, 1800): CZ-Pu(dm), 59 R 3317, (missing bn II).   ★
AZZ-3. Parthia in Dis [E♭]; 4 mvts.   2fl 2cl 2hn 2bn.
MS parts (by Dominik Hübner, Langenbruck, 1800): CZ-Pu(dm), 59 R 3318, No. 1.   ★
AZZ-4. Parthia in Dis [E♭]; 4 mvts.   2fl 2cl 2hn 2bn.
MS parts (by Dominik Hübner, Langenbruck, 1800): CZ-Pu(dm), 59 R 3318, No. 2.   ★
AZZ-1a. V.V. Mašek: Parthia in Dis [E♭]; 3 mvts, (= VVM-8).
fl cl(F well [sic: vel] ob) 2cl(B♭) 2hn 2bn tp(prin).
MS parts (by Anton Zasche, Langenbruck, c.1800): CZ-Pu(dm), 59 R 3319.
AZZ-2a. Pleyel: Quartetto; (B.354/i, 354/ii), 1st 2 mvts only.   2fl(D) 2ob 2cl 2hn 2bn.
(?Auto)MS parts (Langenbruck, c.1800): CZ-Pu(dm), 59 R 3321.

ZDINKA, ( )
YYZ-1v. Missa.   Here only: 2cl 2hn.   MS parts: CZ-Bm(bh), A.9251.

*ZECH, Markus *1727 - 1770*
MXZ-1v. Lauda Syon Salvatorem; 7 mvts.   CCAATTBB, 2fl 2ob 2hn 2tp vc organ(bc-fig) timp.
MS parts: CH-E, Th. 277,16 (Ms.3154).   ★
MXZ-2v. Lauda Sion.   CATB, 2fl 2ob 2hn 2tp vc organ(bc-fig).
MS parts: CH-E, Th. 277,8 (Ms.3146).   ★
MXZ-3v. Lauda Syon.   CATB, 2fl 2ob 2hn 2tp vc organ(bc-fig).
MS parts: CH-E, Th. 280,15 (Ms.3226).   ★
MXZ-4v. Te Deum.   CATB, 2ob/vl 2hn 2tp vc organ.
MS parts: CH-E, Th. 297,4.   ★

*ZEHM, Friedrich *22 Jan 1923, Neusalz am Oder, Silesia*
*FXZ-1. Konzerstück: Schwierigkeiten und Unfälle mit einem Choral: Sonatine für einen Dirigenten und 10
Bläser, 1974.   2fl 2ob 2cl 2hn 2bn; *(the players also double on the following instruments: fl I, alarm whistle;*
fl II, piccolo & ratchet; ob I, siren whistle; ob II, click frog; cl I, cl(E♭) & bird-pipe; cl II, hooter; hn I, cuckoo;
hn II, rattle; bn I - no doubling; bn II, cbn; the conductor also plays triangle, slapstick & toy trumpet.)
Pm (B. Schott's Söhne: Mainz, etc., 1976), score (pn ED 6655) and hire parts.
FXZ-2. Musica pastorale für 6 Holzbläser.   2fl ob ca 2bn.
Pm (N. Simrock: Hamburg, London, 1966), parts.

*ZELINKA, Jan Evangelista *13 Jan 1893, Prague - 30 June 1969, Prague*
JEZ-1. Kratochvilné skladby; 1943.   2cl 2hn 2tp 2tb tu.
Pm (Český hudební fond: Prague), hire score & parts.

*ZELLNER, Leopold Alexander *23 Sept 1823, Zagreb - 24 Nov 1894, Vienna*
LAZ-1 (= LVB-5). Completion of Beethoven's Quintet in E♭, WoO 62.   ob 3hn bn.
Pm (B. Schott's Söhne: Mainz; Schott & Co.: London, 1954), score & parts.

ZETTLER, Richard *1 Nov 1921, Leutkirch/Allgäu*
RXZ-1. Allgäuer Skizzen.   cl/flug cl/flug/tp cl/tp/a-sax hn/a-sax hn/t-hn/t-sax bn/tb/bar/tu.
Pm (Möseler Verlag: Wolfenbüttel, pn 42121, sd), score & parts.

ZIELER, ( ) *active at Kremsmünster, early 19th century*
ZYZ-1m. Marsch in F.   2ob 2cl 2hn 2bn cbn tp(clar) b-dr.
MS parts: A-KR, H 59/238.   ★
ZYZ-2m. Marsch in F [Sturm Marsch].   Incomplete: here only: pic 2fl 2cl.
MS parts: A-KR, H36/36.   ★

*ZIFRA, Antonio *(1790)*
AXZ-1. Suonata No. 9, 1855, 1 long mvt, Allo. moderato.   fl 2cl 2hn bn 2tp tb vlne timp organ.
MS parts: I-Vsmc.   ★
AXZ-2. Marcia No. 2 in Cesolfaut, 1824.   2cl 2hn vlne timp organ(bc-fig & full pt).
MS parts: I-Vsmc, (the date has been added in another hand).   ★
AXZ-3. [No] IV Marcia in Fa (F), 1835, (Maestoso/Presto).   (2vl vla db+tb) 2cl(D) 2hn bn tp basso timp
organ(bc-fig).   MS parts: I-Vsmc, (the string parts of a later date; the note "e Trombon" has been added in a
later hand to the Contrabasso part. The dates on parts have been altered from 1824 to 1835).   ★
AXZ-1t. Marcia funebre.   (2cl(C)) 2hn 2tp 2tb organ.
MS score & parts: I-Vsmc, (missing cl I; the clarinets do not appear in the score).   ★
AXZ-1f. Suonata, in D, 1 long mvt, Allegro.   2cl(C) 2hn organ.   MS parts: I-Vsmc, (fragment only).   ★
AXF-2f. Marcia, in D.   Here 2ob/cl(C) only.   MS parts: I-Vsmc.   ★

*ZIHA, ( ) *(1730)*
XXZ-1. № 1 Partitta in C; 3 mvts.   2ob 2hn bn.   MS parts: CZ-Pnm, XLII.E.185. ★
XXZ-2. № 2 Partitta in C; 3 mvts.   2ob 2hn bn.   MS parts: CZ-Pnm, XLII.E.186. ★
XXZ-3. № 3 Partitta in D; 3 mvts.   2ob 2hn bn.   MS parts: CZ-Pnm, XLII.E.187. ★
XXZ-4. № 4 Partitta in D; 3 mvts.   2ob 2hn bn.   MS parts: CZ-Pnm, XLII.E.188. ★
XXZ-5. № 5 Partitta in F; 3 mvts.   2ob 2hn bn.   MS parts: CZ-Pnm, XLII.E.189. ★

ZILLIG, Winfried *1 April 1905, Würzburg - 17 Dec 1963, Hamburg*
WXZ-1. Konzert für Violoncello und Blasorchester, (revised 1952).
Solo cello, fl fl/pic ob ob/ca 2cl b-cl 4hn bn bn/cbn 2tp 2tb tu.
Pm (Bärenreiter: Kassel, Basel, 1960), score, (Taschenpartitur, No. 107).

*ZILLMANN, Eduard *1834 - post-1909*
EYD-1a. Anon: XII Walzer Arrangirt.   fl cl(E♭) 6cl(B♭) 2hn 2bn tp tb serp.
MS parts: D-DT, Mus-n 2103.

ZIMMER, L.
LXZ-1. Yankee Cakewalk.   2fl ob 2cl b-cl 2a-sax t-sax bar-sax/b-cl bn.
Pm (European American Music Corp.: Valley Forge, PA, sd), score & parts.

*ZIMMERMANN, Anton *1741, Pressburg (now Bratislava) - 16 Oct 1781, Pressburg*
AYZ-1. Parthia; in G, 3 mvts.   2ob 2hn bn.
MS parts: CZ-Bm(au), A.20.374. ★
AYZ-2. Parthia in C; 3 mvts.   2ob 2hn bn.
MS parts: CZ-Bm(au), A.20.375. ★
AYZ-3. Parthia in E♭; 5 mvts.   2talia 2hn bn.
MS parts: CZ-Bm(au), A.20.376. ★
AYZ-4. Parthia in C; 4 mvts.   2cl/ob bn 2tb.
MS parts: CZ-Bm(au), A.20.941, (incomplete, here only ob II, bn, tb I & II). ★
AYZ-5. Partia.   7 winds.
MS score & parts: D-B, (unverified).
AYZ-6. Partia.   2cl 2hn 2bn.
MS score & parts: A-Wgm, VIII 8571, (unverified).
AYZ-1v. Offertorium de Paschale de Martyre et de Sancto vel Santa, ("Veni, triumphos agito").
SATB, 2ob 2hn 2bn violone organ.   MS parts (c.1780): CZ-Bm(au), A.20.373. ★

*ZIMMERMANN, Bernd Alois *20 March 1918, Bliesheim, Cologne - 10 Aug 1970, Grosskönigsdorf*
*BAZ-1. Musique pour les soupers du Roi Ubu.   Ballet noir en sept parties et une entrée, 1966.
(*Orchestra & combo of:*) pic 3fl 3ob ca 3cl b-cl t-sax 4hn 3bn 3tp 3tb tu timp perc celeste guitar mandolin
electric-bass harp organ piano 4db.
Pm (Bärenreiter: Kassel, Basel, 1976), facsimile AutoMS score.
BAZ-2. Rheinische Kirmestänze; 1950, revised 1962.   fl fl/pic 2ob 2cl 2hn bn bn/cbn ct/tp tb db-tu/b-tu.
Pm (B. Schott's Söhne: Mainz, 1973), score (pn CON 176) & parts (pn CON 176-10).
BAZ-3. Söbensprung: ein norddeutsches Volkstanzpotpourri; 1950.   fl fl/pic 2ob 2cl 2hn 2bn 2tp 2tb tu 2perc.
Pm (B. Schott's Söhne: Mainz), hire score & parts.

*ZINEK, ( ) *Baron*
XBZ-1mv. Marsch Mit einem Kriegslied für Oestreichs [sic] Landwehr.   Voice(s), pic 2ob 2cl(C) 2hn 2bn cbn
tp b-dr s-dr tri.   MS parts: CZ-Pnm, XX.F.104, (the march & trio only; there is no cbn pt but it may have read
off the bn II pt). *See also KRECHLER, FFK-4.3a & 4.4a, for an arrangement,* ★

ZINGARELLI, Niccolò Antonio *4 April 1752, Naples - 5 May 1837 Torre del Greco, nr Naples*
NAZ-1. Sestetto; in B♭, 1 mvt (untitled 3/4 / Allo, C).   2fl 2cl 2bn.
(?Auto)MS score ("per ego di Francesco Vito"): I-Mc, Noseda R.23.8. ★
NAZ-1m. Marcie No. 10; (C, C, C, F, F, E♭, B[♭], D, C, C).   2ob 2hn 2bn 2tp timp.
MS score: CZ-Pnm, XLII.B.278. ★
NAZ-2m. Langsam Marsch.   pic quart-fl 2ob cl(F) 2cl(C) 4hn 2bn cbn+serp 2tp 3tb b-dr t-dr s-dr cym.
Pc (In: **A-74m**, Heft 6, No. 33), score. *Possibly an arrangement.*

ZÍTEK, ( ) *(?1770)*
XYZ-1v. Pange lingua in C.   CAB, 2fl 2cl 2hn 2tp(clar) tp(prin) timp organ.
MS parts (by Ambler, pre-1825): CZ-Pnm, XLIII.C.19, (missing cl I hn II, tp(clar) II). ★

ZOBL, ( )
XZZ-1. Parthia in Dis [E♭]; 3 mvts.   2cl 2hn 2bn.
MS parts: D-F, Mus.Hs.1557. ★

ZOEDLER (Zoëdler), ( ) *(1750)*
YXZ-1. Parthia in F; 4 mvts.   2ca 2hn bn.
MS parts: CZ-Pnm, XLII.C.156. ★

*ZONCADA, Giovanni *(1760), Horn player, London, 1790s.*
GXZ-1. Partita in E♭; 4 mvts.   Solo oboe, 2cl 2hn/2hn(muted) 2bn.
MS parts: I-Gc, SS.B.1.10.(H.8). ★
Pm (WINDS: Northridge, CA, pn W-47, c.1980), photocopy of original parts.
GXZ-2(-4). 3 Trios; (all in E♭, 3 mvts).   cl 2hn.
MS parts: NL-Z, Z1297. ★

*ZOPFF, Hermann *1 June 1826, Glogau, Silesia - 12 July 1883, Leipzig*
HXZ-1. Serenade, Op. 35.   2fl ob 2cl 2hn bn.
Untraced. *The only known score & pts were owned by the late John Parr, of Leeds; his ensemble played the work at least once. We would appreciate any further information.*

ZORZI, ( ) de, *di Udine (?1800)*
ZDZ-1v. Tantum ergo.   TTB(solo+rip), (2cl) 2hn (bn+vlne tp tb timp) organ.
MS score & parts: I-Vsmc, (instruments in parentheses do not appear in the score). ★

*ZULEHNER, Georg Carl *20 July 1770, Mainz - 27 Dec 1841, Munich*
Zulehner's arrangement of Mozart's Eine kleine Freimaurercantate *(K.623) has not been located; it is possible that earlier secondary sources have mistakenly identified the work cited here as Mozart's work.*
*GCZ-1v. Feier Gesang am Geburtsfeste des Hochw: Durchl: General=Grossmeisters Prinzen Carl von Hessen Gesungen in der g∴ u∴ v∴ ▭ [i.e. Masonic Lodge] zu den vereinigten Freunden im Or∴ von Mainz den 28ᵗᵉⁿ December 1817.   TTB, ob 2cl 2hn 2bn, *or* piano.
Pc (in der Grosherzogl: Hessischen Hofmuikhandlung von B. Schott: Mainz, pn 1085, 1818), score & piano accompaniment: D-MZsch, (2 copies). ★

*ZWECKSTETTER, Christoph *1772 - 1836*
CXZ-1v. Salve Regina.   CCA, fl 2cl 2hn bn.
AutoMS parts (c.1810): D-WS, MS. 721. ★

ZWING, M. (?Joseph Michael) *(1770)*
MJZ-1. Trois Grandes Pièces d'Harmonie Militaires, Oeuvre XI.
pic(D) cl(E♭) 2cl(B♭) 2hn 2bn 2tp tb serp b-dr s-dr.
Pc (G. Kreitner: Worms, pn 193, c.1800), RISM [Z 631], parts: D-HR, HR III 4 1/2 2° 385, (with MS parts for: fl(A), cl(E♭), and ob II/cl in C). ★
Pm (KGS), parts, fiche (2366).
MJZ-2. Six Pièces d'Harmonie, Oeuvre 2.   fl 2cl(C) 2hn(ad lib) bn vla(?ca).
Pc (G. Kreitner: Worms, pn 50, c.1800), RISM [Z 630], parts: D-HR, HR III 4 1/2 2° 384. ★
Pc (B. Schott: Mainz, c.1800), parts: D-Bhm.
Pm (KGS), fiche (2365)., of Kreitner edition

*ZWINGMANN, Johann Nicolaus (John N.) *28 Dec 1764, Stotternheim - post-16 Sept 1807, London*
*JOZ-1a. Steibelt: La belle Laitière, airs & march.   2fl 2cl 2hn 2bn tp buglehorn serp.
Pc (Robert Birchall: London, c.1805), RISM [S 4763], parts: D-BFb.

ANONYMOUS WORKS

Austria: Anonymous Instrumental Works

A-1. [2] Aufzüge in D . . . Pastoralla [sic]. 2fl 2cl 2hn bn tp(prin) timp.
MS pts ("pro me Johann Handl"): A-Wn, Mus.Hs.349, (missing 2fl, with a duplicate cl I pt in C). ★
An additional sheet is included, entitled "Aufzüge auf 4 Trompeten d.i.[sic]/ 2 Prinzipal et Clarin", probably in D; the two sets of parts are both on the same sheet. The Trio is marked "Trio Harmonie/ Clarinette et Corni" but no parts for these instruments survive. ★
A-2. [3] Aufzüge; all in D. 2tp(clar, D) 2tp(prin, D) timp; with later parts for 2cl(D) 2hn(D) bn.
MS pts ("pro me Johann Handl"): A-Wn, Mus.Hs.350. *The later wind parts are direct transcriptions - with the bassoon playing only the tonic & fifth below of the original timpani part.* ★
A-3. Harmonie-Stücke, 14 mvts. 2cl 2hn 2bn tp.
MS parts (by Mathias Zimma): A-Wn, Mus.Hs.37,399. ★
A-4. 21 Harmonie Stücke [in fact, 5 Parthien/Suites]. 2ca 2bthn 2hn bn, *later altered to:* 2/4cl(C) 2hn bn.
MS parts: A-Sca, Hs.1619. *The parts have been written into already bound small oblong volumes and the title slips have been pasted on after the scoring alteration; the calligraphy changes after No. 5. The clarinet parts were originally marked, "Cornu Passetto [sic] Primo/Secondo". The ca and bthn parts are not the same, although there are often long sections where the parts are unison. There are two bassoon parts: the original for use with the transposing instruments and a later part (with some variants) for use with the C clarinets.* ★
A-5. Intrade in C, zum Anfang u. Schluss Zum Gloria, Credo, Sanctus, und Ite missa est.
cl(C) 2hn tp 2flug basso. MS pts: A-Wn, Mus.Hs.409, (missing 2hn basso). ★
A-6. Dilectus [Offertorius]; in A. 2ob 2hn. MS pts: A-Wn, Fonds 5 MÖDLING 302. ★
A-7. Parthia in Dis [Eb], 4 mvts. 2cl 2hn 2bn. MS pts (by Johann Anton Handl): A-Wn, Mus.Hs.353, No 1. ★
A-8. Parthia, in Eb, 4 mvts. 2cl 2hn (2)bn.
MS parts (by Johann Anton Handl): A-Wn, Mus.Hs.353, No. 2, (with a later bassoon part transposed to F for use with C clarinets). ★
A-9. [Parthia in D; title in A-Wn catalog: "Suite in D"], 4 mvts. 2ob 2hn.
MS parts: A-Wn, Mus.Hs.3038, (ob pts missing mvts 3 & 4). ★
A-10. Nro. 3[,] Six Variatione; in Bb c.1805. Solo cl, 2ob cl 2hn 2bn.
MS parts: A-Wgm, VIII 2531. ★
Pm (WINDS: Northridge, CA, W-35), photocopy of original MS parts.
A-1m. 2 Märsche; Ab, Eb. 2ob 2cl 2hn 2bn cbn 2tp b-tb. MS parts (by Perschl): A-Wn, Mus.Hs.3787. ★
A-2m. Marsh [sic; in] C; with 2 Trios. 2terz-fl 2ob 2cl(C) 2hn 2bn tp(prin) "pagallo"[drum].
MS pts ("Anno 1796 / und 10te Martz"): A-Wgm, VIII 38672. *The 2 Trios are scored for 2ob 2cl 2hn 2bn only; on the verso of the sheets is an added "Trio 2do in Facanatasa [sic]", scored for 2terz-fl 2ob 2cl 2hn 2bn.* ★
A-3m. Märsche. 2ob 2hn 2bn 2vla. MS parts (1767): A-GO, MS.2970.
A-1ma. Sechs Märsch auf achstimmige Harmonie von verschiedenen Meistern. Zweiter Abteilung.
2ob 2cl 2hn 2bn.
Pc (kk Hof=Theater=Musik=Verlag, Wien, c.1801), MS parts: CZ-Pnm, XLII.B.320. ★
    1.1ma (-1.3ma): J. Weigl: Cleopatras Tod.   1.4ma: J. Weigl: Clothilde, Prinzessin von Salerno.
    1.5ma: Paer: Il Principe di Taranto.   1.6ma: J. Weigl: Rolla [Rollas Tod oder Die Spanier in Peru].
A-2ma. 2 Märsche für die Türkische Musick. cl(D) 2cl(C) 2hn 2bn tp(posthorn, No. 1 Trio) tp(II) serp b-dr s-dr.
Pc (Im Verlage der k:k: pr: chemy Druckery: Wien, pn 2295, 1814/1815), parts: E-Mam, K. 846.(12). ★
    2.1ma. [Starke] Alexander Marsch nach Starke. 2.2ma. [Persuis]: Blöde Ritter Marsch, (bn I, tp I with divisi).
A-3ma. Alexanders Favorit Marsch für die ganze türkische Musik Vom Regimento Colleredo.
pic(F) 2fl(Bb) cl(F) 2cl(C) 2hn(F) 2bn cbn 2tp(clar C) b-dr s-dr. MS parts (?from Vienna): GB-Ljag(w), 124. ★

Austria: Anonymous Vocal Works

A-1v. Gesang zur Messe [Deutsche Messe]. CATB, 2ob/cl 2hn bn organ.
MS parts (by Georg Schwiger): A-Wn, Fonds 5 MÖDLING 967, (missing hn I). ★
A-2v. Libera in Es [Eb]. (3)S(2)ATB, 2cl 2hn bn organ.
MS pts (by Josef Fügerl & Franz Gilg): A-Wn, Mus.Hs.670, (with later duplicate vocal parts: 2C, A, with a later Directionstimme/Orgel pt. One of the later Canto pts bears the note, "zu Allerheiligen /: Allerseelen :/ / Erue Domine animas eorum."). *On the final verso of the Directionstimme are performance dates: 9 Sept [19]00, 1 Nov [19]03.* ★
A-3v. Lied aus Aller=Seelentag [sic; All Souls's Day]. CATB, 2cl 2hn basso.
MS score & pts (by G. Zellner, Oberlehrer, dated 29/10 & 30/10 1867: A-Wn, Mus.Hs.31,214,(the score calls for "Canto" and "basso" but the parts are for Soprano & b-tb; with a duplicate S part). *Possibly by Zellner.* ★
A-4v. Deutsche Messe in D. [SATB], fl 2/3cl 2hn 1/2bn bombard organ. *This scoring comes from the MS title page; the parts comprise fl 2cl(C) cl(D) a-cl(A) 2hn bn cbn+bn(II) with later parts for 2flug.*
MS parts (by Stanislaus Wenusch): A-Wn, Mus.Hs.21,451, (missing choral parts). ★
A-5v. (?J Handl, JXH-1vd) Pange lingua a 4 Vocibus; in C. CATB, 2cl(D) 2hn bn organ(bc-fig).
MS parts (by Johann Handl): A-Wn, Mus.Hs.657, (with duplicate CAB, & 2 Organo pts - one in C and the other in D for use with clarinets in C; "Fagotto" is listed on the titlepage and probably read off the organ pt). ★
A-6v. 4 Responsorien am Frohnleichnamstage. 2cl(C) 2hn 2bn basso.
MS parts: A-Wn, Fonds 4 BADEN 589, (missing the vocal parts; the basso part bears the later note, "Fagotto"; the bn II pt is, in fact, a copy of the earlier basso part). ★
A-7v. Tantum [ergo in D]. CATB, fl 2tp(clar) b-tb vlne timp organ(bc-fig).
MS parts (by Coll): A-Wn, Fonds 4 BADEN 503, (with a duplicate C pt). ★
A-8v. Tantum ergo und Messe in Es [Eb]; 11 mvts. SATB, fl(F) 2ob 4cl 2hn 2bn cbn 2tp(clar) b-tb cb organ.
MS parts; A-Wn, Mus.Hs.2690. *The 4cl comprise pairs of solo and ripieno parts.* ★

Austria: Anonymous Funeral Music - Instrumental *See also infra: A-12tv.*
A-1t. Todten Marsch; in D minor. cl(F) 3cl(C) 2hn 2bn tp(prin in G) 2tp(prin in D).
MS pts (by Johann Handl): A-Wn, Mus.Hs.345, (there is 1 bar divisi in the 2tp(D) part; the tp(G) pt is missing 5 bars in the second strain; on the reverse of the bn I pt is the bn II pt transposed to C minor, marked "Fagotto"). ★
A-2t. Marcia Funebre; in G minor. 2ob 2cl 2hn 2bn cbn. MS parts: A-Wn, Mus.Hs.652. ★
A-3t. [Funeral March in G♭ minor]. 2cl 2hn 2bn.
MS parts: A-Wn, Mus.Hs.652. *On the reverse of the parts of A-3t.* ★
A-4t, 5t. [2] Trauermarsch; in C minor. 2cl 2hn bn.
MS parts (by Johann Handl): A-Wn, Mus.Hs.346, (with an additional - and probably later - cl in E♭ part). ★
A-6t. Marcia def[unctorum].; in D minor. 2ob 2cl(C) 2hn(D) 2bn 2tp(D); [tp(E♭), flug(B♭) b-flug(B♭) b-tb(G♭)].
MS score & parts: A-Wn, Mus.Hs.351, (with a duplicate cl II part). *The instruments above in square brackets are later additions; the wrapper - also a later addition - bears the title. "Marcia def. für große Besetzung".* ★

Austria: Anonymous Funeral Music - Vocal
A-1tv. Begräbnisgesang, "Trauert ihr englischen Chöre". CATB, 2cl(C) 2hn bn.
MS parts: A-Wn, Mus.Hs.9118. ★
A-2tv. Die Gottesacker. CATB, 2cl 2hn bn.
MS parts (by Leeder): A-Wn, Mus.Hs.34,760, (missing the instrumental parts). ★
A-3tv. Grablied [Todtenlied]; in E♭, "In den Frühling meine Jahre". CATB, 2cl(E♭) 2tp(clar).
MS parts: A-Wn, Fonds 4 BADEN 542, (with duplicate C & A pts; the b-tb pt is from a different work). ★
A-4tv. Requiem in F. CAT, 2cl 2hn vlne.
MS pts: A-Wn, Fonds 38 Langau bei Geras 60, (?missing B vocal pt). *Included with this work are 3 Soprano pts, 2 Alto parts and the organ part (Libera & Agnus only) of a Requiem by Karl Kempter.* ★
A-5tv. Todten=Aria; "Wir ruhen zu dir o grosser Gott!". CATB, 2cl 2hn.
MS parts (by Johann Handl): A-Wn, Mus.Hs.371. ★
A-6tv. Todten Aria in F; "Nun so seys ich bin geschieden". CATB, 2cl 2hn.
MS parts (by Johann Handl): A-Wn, Mus.Hs.378. ★
A-7tv. Todten Aria ex Dis [E♭]; "Was litt ich hier für Qualen". CATB, 2cl 2hn.
MS parts (by Johann Handl): A-Wn, Mus.Hs.369. ★
A-8tv. Todtenlied in Dis [E♭]; "Langsam Stunden". CATB, 2cl 2hn.
MS parts (by Johann Handl): A-Wn, Mus.Hs.375. ★
A-9tv. [Todtenlied] "Entflohen seiner morschen Hülle". CATB, 2cl(E♭) 2hn bn.
MS parts: A-Wn, Mus.Hs.27,479, (with a duplicate Canto part). ★
A-10tv. [Todtenlied] "Nun da ist die fayerliche Stunde". CATB, 2cl 2hn bn.
MS parts: A-Wn, Mus.Hs.27,478, (with duplicate vocal parts: 2C, A). ★
A-11tv. Trauergesang in Es [Eb]; "Selig der in Gottesfrinden!". CATB, 2cl 2hn.
MS parts (by Johann Handl): A-Wn, Mus.Hs.374. *The accompaniment is described as "Harmonia".* ★
A-12tv. [Collection of funeral music]. CATB, 2cl 2hn 2tp b-tb. MS parts: A-Wn, Mus.Hs.27,476; (with additional CATB parts for 2 other Begräbnissgesänge). ★
 12.1tv. Hier, Mensch! hier. CATB, 2cl 2hn b-tb. 12.2tv. Steh still, o Mensch. CATB, 2cl 2hn b-tb.
 12.3t(v). Miserere. 2cl 2hn 2tp b-tb. 12.4t(v). Trauer [Marsch]. 2cl 2hn 2tp b-tb.

Austria: Geras, Niederösterreich, Stift Geras
A-13tv. Grablied No. 10, "Im himmel ist Friede". CATB, 2cl 2hn bn tb. MS parts: A-GE, I 223. ★
A-14tv. Trauer-Lied ex Es [E♭], "Hier Mensch, hier lerne was du bist". CATB, 2cl 2hn bn.
MS parts: A-GE, I 232. ★
A-15tv. Trauer-Lied ex Es [E♭], "Nun woldan ach weh, ach Soll!". CATB, 2cl 2hn bn. MS pts: A-GE, I 240. ★
A-16tv. Todtenlied in Dis [E♭], "Hier lieg ich ohne Leben". CATB, 2cl 2hn. MS parts: A-GE, I 234. ★
A-17tv. Todtenlied in Dis [E♭] a 4tuor [sic]. Bey einer erwachsenen Person, "Christen! was zu suir ihn seht".
SATB, 2cl 2hn. MS parts: A-GE, I 235. ★
A-18tv. Todten Aria vor der Bahre zu singen. CCTB, 2cl 2hn.
MS parts (by Johann Anton Steiner): A-GE, I 123. ★
A-19tv. Todtenlied in Dis. CATB, 2cl 2hn bn. MS parts (by Franz Gahst): A-GE, I 128. ★
A-20tv. Todten Aria ex F, "Nun so segs ich bin geschieden". CATB, 2ob 2hn. MS parts: A-GE, I 192. ★
A-21tv. Aria pro de Functis [sic] in Dis. CATB, 2cl 2hn. MS parts: A-GE, I 131. ★
A-22tv. Aria pro definctis [sic] in B(♭). CATB, 2cl 2hn. MS parts: A-GE, I 139. ★

Austria: Kremsmünster, Benediktiner-Stift
A-11. Parthia Turcia in C. pic 2fl 2ob 2cl 2hn 2bn 2tp(clar) b-dr s-dr. MS parts: A-KR, H 37/28. ★
A-12. Marsch, Walzer[,] Menuetto. pic fl 2cl 2hn bn 3tp serp b-dr "tambur" glock. MS pts: A-KR, H40/78. ★
A-13. Variations; in B♭. 2cl 2hn 2bn. MS parts: A-KR, G 37/12. ★
A-14. Adagio; in F. fl ob cl 2hn bn. MS parts: A-KR, G 27/18b. ★
A-4m. Zapfenstreich; in D. pic 2cl(F) 2cl(C) 2hn 2bn 2tp serp cym glock. MS parts: A-KR, H 40/77. ★

Austria: Salzburg, Collegium Mariano Rupertinum
A-15. [Bound Collection of Pieces, some with identified composers and/or arrangers], 53 Nos. Scoring varies.
MS parts (c.1844/45): A-Sca, Hs.266, (the pic pts for Nos. 13 - 15 were pasted in and are now defective).
 15.1(m). No. 1. Mozartsmarsch [& Trio]. 2cl(E♭) 2cl(B♭) 2hn 2bn 2tp. ★
 15.2(m). No. 2. Neujahrsmarsch [& Trio]. 2cl(E♭) 2cl(B♭) 2hn 2bn 2tp. ★
 15.3(ma). No. 3. Alpenhornmarsch [& Trio]. 2cl(E♭) 2cl(B♭) 2hn 2bn 2tp. [cf. HANDL, JXH-1mad.] ★
 15.4(a). No. 4. Bellini: Norma, duetto. 2cl(B♭) 2hn bn 2tp.
 15.5(a), 15.6(a). Nos. 5, 6. Adolf Müller: Die Ballnacht, cavatina, arie. 2cl(B♭) 2hn bn 2tp flug(No. 6).
 15.7(a). No. 7. C. Kreutzer: Der Verschwender, introduction. 2cl(E♭) 2cl(B♭) 2hn 2bn 2tp.
 15.8(a). No. 8. [Anon]: Heimkehrmarsch. 2cl(E♭) 2cl(B♭) 2hn 2bn 2tp.
   No. 9. Totel: Trauermarsch [& Trio].
 15.9(a). No. 10. Bellini: Norma, Andante, C. cl(E♭) 2cl(B♭) 2hn 2bn 2tp.

15.10(a). No. 11. Bellini: La Sonnambula, Andante. fl 2cl(Bb) 2hn 2bn 2tp flug.
15.11(a). No. 12. Strauss (the Elder): Loreley-Klaenge Waltzer, Op. 154. 2cl(Eb) 2cl(Bb) 2hn 2bn 2tp flug.
15.12(m) (-15.15m). Nos. 13 - 15. 3 Märsche [all ¢, with Trios]. pic cl(Eb) 2cl(Bb) 2hn 2bn 2tp. ★
15.16(m), 15.17(m). Nos. 16, 17. 2 Märsche [¢, with Trios]. 2cl(Eb) 2cl(Bb) 2hn 2bn 2tp.
15.18(m) -15.35(m). Nos. 18 - 35. 18 Märsche [all ¢, with Trios]. fl(Db) cl(Eb) 2cl(Bb) 2hn 2bn 2tp.
15.36(m). Nos. 36. 15 Marsch [¢, with Trio]. fl(Db) cl(Eb) 2cl(Bb) 2hn 2bn tp posthorn.
        No. 37. Brechschloegl: National Stey'er. cl(Eb) 2cl(Bb) 2hn 2bn tp flug.
15.37(a). No. 38. L. Ricci: Chiara di Montalbano in Francia, cavatina.
15.38(a). No. 39. C.M. von Weber: Preciosa, Potpourri. fl(F) cl(Eb) 2cl(Bb) 2hn 2bn 2tp.
        No. 40. Hödl: Friedrichslust. No. 41. Heinrich: Harmonie Piece.
15.39(a). No. 42. Balfe: Les Quatre Fils de Aymon, cavatina. fl(D) 2cl(Bb) 2hn 2bn tp flug.
        No. 43. Hödl: Marsch v[on]. Marian Eleven. No. 44. Hödl: Marsch. No. 45. Kracher: Marsch.
        No. 46. Hödl: Trauermarsch und Grabgesang.
15.40(a). No. 47. Mozart: Così fan tutte, duetto. fl(Eb) cl(Eb) 2cl(Bb) 2hn 2bn 2tp.
        No. 48. Hödl: Quodlibet.
15.41. No. 49. Ferdinands=Polka [with Trio & Coda]. 2cl(Eb) 2cl(Bb) 2hn 2bn 2tp.
15.42(a). No. 50. Strauss (the Elder): [Quadrille . . . aus der Oper: Die vier Haimonskinder, i.e., Balfe:
        Les Quatre fils d'Aymon, Op. 169], as "Haimons=Quadrille". cl(Eb) 2cl(Bb) 2hn bn 2tp basso.
        No. 51. Hödl: Der Abschied, Marsch.
15.43(ma). No. 52. Auber [?arr. Hoedl]: Carlo Broschi, Marsch [& Trio]. 2cl(Eb) 2cl(Bb) 2hn bn tp flug.
        No. 53. Purebl: Marsch 1 - 4 (= JSP-1m).

Austro-Bohemia: Anonymous Instrumental Works
A-16. Parthia in Dis [Eb]; 4 mvts. 2cl 2hn bn. MS parts (by Wenceslas Kärby): CZ-Pnm, XIII.A.214. ★

Austro-Bohemia: Vocal Works (See also infra: Austro-Moravia, Brno)
A-9v. Missa Česka, (c.1830). CATB, 2cl 2hn bn organ. MS: CZ-MH, Hu.32.
A-10v. Pange lingua in D# [i.e. D major; with Tantum ergo, Genitori Genitoque & Sit et benedictus].
CA, 2ob 2hn bn(vel Organo). MS parts: CZ-Pnm, L.C.173. ★
A-11v. Te Deum Laudamus. Deutsche. CATB, 2fl 2ob 2hn bn tp(prin) timp organ.
MS parts (by Jos: Scholz; from Broumov monastery): CZ-Pnm, XXXVIII.B.268. ★

Austro-Bohemia: Bakov nad Jizerou (district)
A.17. Parthia in C; 3 mvts. 2fl 2cl 2hn 2bn 2tp(clar).
MS parts (by Jan Augustin Fibiger, c.1840): CZ-BA, 188 (45-599).
A-18. Messallan. (misspelling of "Miscellan"), 15 mvts. (fl) 2ob 2cl 2hn 2bn tp(prin).
MS parts (by Jan Augustin Fibiger, c.1825): CZ-BA, 193 (78-632). *Possibly a set of arrangements. The flute
part is unimportant.* ★
A-12v. Cantus Festivus ex D. C solo, CATB chorus, 2fl 2ob 2cl(A) 2hn 2bn cbn 2tp(clar) timp.
MS parts (c.1840): CZ-BA, 68 (22-164), (with a later Czech text, c.1870). ★
A-13v. Chválozpěz k svatému Janu Nepomuckému ex C. CATB, 2cl 2hn bn 2tp(clar) tp(prin) timp.
MS parts (c.1840): CZ-BA, 97 (109-251). ★
A-14v. Quadretto in F: O Salutaris hostia. CATB, 2cl 2hn bn.
MS parts (by Jan Augustin Fibiger, c.1825): CZ-BA, 62 (1-143). ★
A-15v. Pangelingua ex D. CATB, 2fl 2cl(A) 2hn bn klappen-tp timp.
MS parts (by Jan Augustin Fibiger, c.1840): CZ-BA, 160 (41-512). ★
A-16v. Pangelingua ex D dur. CATB, 2fl 2cl 2hn bn.
MS parts (by Jan Augustin Fibiger, c.1835): CZ-BA, 158 (38-509). ★
A-17v. Píseň postní k umučení Pána Ježíše Krista. CAB, 2fl/cl(C) 2hn(con sordini) fondamento.
MS parts (by Jan Augustin Fibiger, c.1845): CZ-BA, 177 (19-573). ★
A-18v. Pjseň in F k Panně Marii. CA, 2fl 2cl(C) 2hn organ+bn.
MS parts (by Jan Augustin Fibiger, c.1820): CZ-BA, 172 (13-568). ★
A-19v. Salve Regina in Dis [Eb]. CA, 2cl 2hn bn. MS pts (by Jan A. Fibiger, c.1820): CZ-BA 147 (78-427). ★
A-20v. Pjseň, která se při udělowánj swátosti Biřmowánj zpjwá, "Pleseyte nebesa".
Voice, 2fl 2cl 2hn bn tp(prin) timp org. MS parts (by Jan Augustin Fibiger, 1825): CZ-BA, 328 (F 2-39),
(voice with organ part; text by Vincenc Eduard Milde, Bishop of Litoměřice). ★
A-23tv. Cantus Funeralis: "Všickni lidé světě umíráme". CAB, 2cl 2hn bn.
MS parts (by Jan Augustin Fibiger, c.1850): CZ-BA, 327 (F 2-38). ★
A-24tv. Motetto Funebralis Credo quod Redemptor meus vivit. CATB, 2hn bn.
MS vocal score & instrumental parts (by Jan Augustin Fibiger, c.1810): CZ-BA, 81 (59-201). ★
A-25tv. Pohřební písně pro za malé dítky. CATB, 2fl 2cl 2hn bn.
MS parts (by Jan Augustin Fibiger, c.1845): CZ-BA, 326 (F 2-37). ★
        25.1tv. "V nevynosti andělské". 25.2tv. "Ach, jak jsem tak krátký čas byl daný na ten".
        25.3tv. "Vále falešný světe, já se již".
A-26tv. Pohřební píseň na ženskou osobo. (Nad manželkou), "Co to za novino"). CATB, 2cl 2hn bn.
MS parts (by Jan Augustin Fibiger, c.1840): CZ-BA, 325 (F 2-36). ★

Austro-Bohemia: Blovice (Blowitz), Church Band
A-21v. [9 religious songs]. Scoring varies. MS pts (? by Hyan, c.1840): CZ-PLa(bl), Hu 144, (missing vocal
parts; with duplicate pts for 2fl 2cl 2hn). *A final piece, "Píseň postní", is scored for CATB, organ(bc) only.* ★
        21.1v. Ó srdce kamené [sic]; 2fl 2cl(A & Bb) 2hn 2tp(clar) flug(A) tb.
        21.2v. Podte sem hříšnícky [sic]. 2fl 2cl 2hn 2tp(clar) flug. 21.3v. [Název neuveden]. 2fl 2cl(A) 2hn.
        21.4v. [Název neuveden]. 2fl 2cl(A) 2hn. 21.5v. Matka pláče etc. 2fl 2cl(Bb) 2hn flug tb.
        21.6v. Matka pláče a t.d. [sic]. 2fl 2cl(Bb) 2hn flug. 21.7v. Pohled ó hříšný člověče. 2fl 2cl 2hn.
        21.8v. Proč Mariá, proč si tak naříkáš. 2fl 2cl(A) 2hn flug tb.
        21.9v. Když v myšlení, usmrcení etc. 2fl 2cl(Bb) 2hn flug tb.

A-22v. Čtyry české písně a syce [4 Czech religious songs].   2fl 2cl(A, Bb) 2hn bn.
MS parts (by Hyan, c.1840): CZ-Pla(bl), Hu 134, (missing No 3; the title is taken from the titlepage). ★
  22.1v. Ku mši sv.: Bože Otče lid trůj verný etc.   22.2v. Na své tváře padamé etc.
  22.3v. k Requiem: Beže, jenž svou moudrostí.   22.4v. k Panně Maryi: O Maryá spomeň na mně.
A-23v. Píseň adventní.   S nebe posel vychází.   fl 2cl 2hn organ.
MS parts (by Hyan, c.1840): CZ-PLa(bl), Hu 1889. ★
A-24v. Dvě [or rather, 4] písně k Pánu Ježíši.   fl 2cl 2hn b-tb organ.
MS parts (by Hyan): CZ-Pla(bl), Hu 1885, (missing vocal parts). ★
  24.1v. Pochválen buď Pán Ježíš etc.   24.2v. Kde jsi můj Ježíši etc.
  27.3v. Ježíši náš nejmilejší etc.   24.4v. Kde jsi kde jsi lásko etc. [sic].
A-25v. [2 church songs].   2fl 2cl 2hn flug(C) organ.   MS parts (by Hyan, c.1840): CZ-PLa(bl), Hu 1892. ★
  25.1v. Píseň k Panně Marií [sic]. Kohobys ty matko milá!
  25.2v. Píseň k jmenoviném duchovního pastýře.   Milí spolužáci! Zase nastal v tomto etc.
A-26v. [3 short church songs].   2fl 2cl 2hn flug(C) b-tb; (No. 2: fl I only).
MS parts (by Hyan): CZ-PLa(bl), Hu 1886, (missing vocal parts). ★
  26.1v. Píseň při svěcení křížové - dle nápěvu již jsem dost pracoval.
  26.2v. Z nebe posel vychází.   26.3v. Při zpívané mši svaté.   Osrdce Kamené [sic] rozpomeň se.
A-27v. [3 short church songs].   Scoring varies.   MS pts (by Hyan): CZ-PLa(bl), Hu 1877, (missing vocal pts). ★
  27.1v. Tvůrce mocný nebes, země!   2fl 2cl 2hn bn.
  27.2v. Skroušeností srdce svého.   fl 2cl 2hn bn.
  27.3v. Vřelou láskou osloněný etc. [sic]. ke dni 29. ledna [January].   2cl 2hn bn b-tb.
A-28v. [4 short church songs].   2fl 2cl 2hn b-tb(No. 1 only).
MS parts: CZ-PLa(br), Hu 1872, (missing vocal pts). ★
  28.1v. Ó Maryá [sic] moje žádost.   28.2v. Zdrávas buď nebes královna.   28.3v & 28.4v. [Without title].
A-29v. [Religious song]; "Plesej srdce radostí".   fl 2cl 2hn b-tb.
MS parts (? by Hyan): CZ-PLa(bl), Hu 134a, (missing vocal parts). ★
A-30v. Tisíckrát pozdravujeme Tebe. Chválozpěv Panně Maryi [A thousand welcomes to you. Praises to Lady
Mary].   fl 2cl(C) 2hn bn 2tp(clar) b-tb organ.   MS parts: CZ-PLa(bl), Hu 1884, (missing vocal parts). ★
A-27tv. Píseň za mrtvé neb [song for the dead or] Requiem. No. 3.   2fl 2cl 2hn bn.
MS parts: CZ-PLa(bl), Hu 1875, (missing vocal parts). ★

Austro-Bohemia: Březnice (Bresnitz), Church (?& zámek) Band, (František Vaněčka bequest)
A-7t. 7. Aufzüge in C oder D . . . gewidmet von Jos. Scala [Skála] in Prag 1838.   pic fl 2cl(Bb, C) 2hn bn(I)
bn(II)+b-tb keyed-tp 2tp(clar) tp(Prin) timp; (with another set of parts transposed to D, including 2cl in D & A).
MS parts: CZ-BR, (2 copies), sign. 450, (complete), sign. 242, (No. 1 only, without klappen-trumpet; MS by
František Vaněček: "Kuru březnického chrámu P. na budancj památku od P. Josefa Skaly dne 12. Dubna [April]
1838. Vaněček mpria."   *A note on the bn(II)/b-tb pt suggests bthn or vla as alternatives if neither instrument
is present; a note on the b-dr part states that this was written for a large Turkish drum and should only be used
outdoors for funerals rather than in the church).* ★
A-19. Divertimento; in C, 5 mvts.   2fl bn.   MS parts (by Joseph Vaněček): CZ-PLa(br), Hu 719. ★
A-20. Divertimento; in C, 4 mvts.   2fl bn.   MS parts (by Joseph Vaněček): CZ-PLa(br), Hu 720. ★
A-21. [March, in C].   2fl 2cl 2hn bn tp(prin) timp.   MS parts: CZ-BR, sign. 541. ★
A-22. Marsch; in C.   2cl(C) 2hn bn tp(prin).   MS parts: CZ-BR, sign. 542. ★
A-23. [Parthia in C], 4 mvts.   Here only: ob II, cl I & II, hn I & II.   MS parts: CZ-Pl(br), Hu 1638. ★
A-24. Příchod třech kralů [Arrival of the 3 Kings]; in C, 3 mvts.   2cl(C) 2hn tp(prin).
MS parts: CZ-BR, sign. 539, (with Czech text added to tp part). ★
A-31v. Graduale [in] E dur; "Chval věrně".   CATB, 2cl(A) 2hn vlne organ(bc).
MS parts: CZ-PLa(br), Hu 929. ★
A-32v. Graduale; ("Chval věrně duše má"), in E.   CATB, 2cl(A) 2hn bn.
MS parts (by František Vaněček): CZ-PLa(br), Hu 1727.   *Followed by a Benediktu, "Chlebe pokrme duší", for
CATB only.* ★
A-33v. Hymnus de B:V: Maria; "Ave Maris stella", in D.   CATB, 2ob 2hn 2bn.
MS parts (by Fux/Fuchs): CZ-BR, sign. 394, (with a duplicate Canto part). ★
A-34v. Meší zpěv; in D; Czech text.   CATB, 2cl(A) 2hn con Fondamento et Fagotto.
MS parts ("Konec [finished] dne 3. August 1822 Franz Vaněček [sic] m.p."): CZ-PLa, Hu 1172. ★
A-35v. Pangelingua [sic] in C.   CATB, 2cl 2hn bn tp(prin) timp.
MS parts (by František Vaněček, 14 April 1821): CZ-PLa(br), Hu 604, (missing bn timp parts). ★
A-36v. Pange lingua ex D.   CATB, 2cl 2hn organ(bc).
MS parts by "Wenceslai Car. Kutschera", later addition: "Vaněček m.p."): CZ-PLa(br), Hu 1095, (with 2 sets
of clarinet parts, in C & Bb). ★
A-37v. Rorate. Quatuor vocibus; in Bb.   CATB, 2cl 2hn basso(vel fagotto) organ.
MS parts ("Red. Vaněček, 27/11 1847"): CZ-PLa(br), Hu 1096.   *Possibly a reduction.* ★
A-38v. Rorate; in Bb.   CATB, 2cl 2hn tp(prin).   MS parts: CZ-BR, sign. 537. ★
A-39v. [Salve] Regina; in D.   Here only: cl(II) 2hn bn 2tp(clar) timp.
MS parts (? by František Vaněček): CZ-PLa(br), Hu 1032, (missing voice parts & cl I). ★
A-40v. IV Stationes in Solennitatem Corporis Christi.   CATB, 2cl(D) 2cl(A) 2hn bn 2tp(clar) b-tb.
MS parts (by Joseph Spaula): CZ-BR, sign. 442. ★
A-41v. Stationes; in Eb.   CATB, 2cl 2hn bn.   MS parts: CZ-BR, sign. 538. ★
A-42v. Zpěw při Stacech ne Boží Tělo dne 10. dubna [April] 1823.
CAB, 2cl(D) 2cl(Bb) 2cl(A) 2hn bn tp(prin) timp.   MS parts (by František Vaněček): CZ-BR, sign. 433. ★
A-1va. Duetto Pastorale in F; "Zdawna žadany Krystus Syn Boži w Vetlemě na Seně".   CC, 2fl 2cl organ.
MS parts: CZ-BR, sign. 381, (a transcription of sign. 382, CC, 2fl 2vl organ). ★

Austro-Bohemia: Česká Třebová (Böhmische-Trübau), Church & Town Band
A-25. [3 Dances: 1. Sincoppen Galopp, 2: Postilion Polka, 3: La ciera Pola (franz:); possibly arrangements].
cl(Eb) 2cl(Bb) 2hn 2tp flug b-hn b-dr s-dr.   MS parts: CZ-TRB, H 87, (missing hn I).   ★
A-4m. [2 Marches].   terz-fl cl(Eb) cl(Bb) 2hn 2tp flug tb.   MS parts: CZ-TRB, H 120.   ★
A-8t. [2] Marcia Funebre für Orschester [sic]; in A minor & C minor.   fl(Eb) cl(Eb) 2cl(C/Bb) 2hn 2tp
flug(Bb hoch) flug(C tief) tb.   MS parts (by M. Březyna): CZ-TRB, H 72.   ★
A-9t. II Trauermärsche in Es [Eb].   cl(Eb) 2cl(Bb) 2hn 4tp(2Eb, Bb, C) tb.   MS parts: CZ-TRB, H 278.   ★
A-10t. Trauermarsch; in C minor.   cl(Eb) 2cl(Bb) 2hn 2tp(clar) flug tb.
MS parts (by Ignác Kulka): CZ-TRB, H 71.   ★
A-11t. 2 Todtenmaersche.   cl(G) 2hn 5tp(3D, G, A) flug(A) b-tb.   MS pts: CZ-TRB, H 280.   ★
A-12t. 2 Kurze Todtenmarsche [sic] für 6stimmige Harmonie.   cl(Eb) 2cl(Bb) 2hn tp(prin).
MS parts (by Ignác Kulka): CZ-TRB, H 279.   ★
A-43v. Cantilena pro Sepeliendis parvulos baptizatos; "Wssecko co se na Swět",   CATB, 2cl 2hn.
MS parts: CZ-TRB, H 437.   ★
A-44v. Cantilena pro Sepeliendis Parvulos baptizatos; "Cokoliw w Swětě gest wssechno marno".
CATB, 2cl 2hn 2bn.   MS pts: CZ-TRB, H 447, (with a pt for 2bn transposed to D for use with C clarinets).   ★
A-45.1v, 45.2v. [2] Cantilena pro Sepeliendis parvulos baptizatos; "Schlummer sanft du theurer süsser Liebling",
"Was ist doch der Menschen Leben".   CATB, 2cl 2hn.   MS parts: CZ-TRB, H 450.   ★
A-46v. Pjseň česká ke Mši swaté [Mass in C].   CATB, 2cl(C) 2hn bn organ.
MS parts (by Ignác Kulka): CZ-TRB, H 18, (missing vocal pts; these can be derived from the organ part).   ★
A-47v. Salve [Regina] et Animas [fidelium] in D.   CATB, 2cl(D) 2hn 2tp tb.
MS parts (by Ignác Kulka): CZ-TRB, H 281.   ★
A-28tv. Gesang bei dem Begräbnisse eines Seelforgens o[der]. Lehrers; "Gott! ein Lehrer deiner Herde".
CATB, 2cl 2hn 2bn 2tp.   MS parts (by Winzenz Matzke): CZ-TRB, H 453.   ★
A-29tv. Pohřebnj pjseň, Zhasla giž swjce.   CATB, 2cl 2hn 2tp tb.   MS parts: CZ-TRB, H 274.   ★
A-30tv. Cantilena pro defunctis adultis, Marnost nad Marnostj.   CATB, 2cl 2bthn 2hn bn(I).
MS parts: CZ-TRB, H 446, (possibly missing bn II).   ★
A-31tv. Pjseň pohřebnj u hrobu [at the grave]; "Wssecko ljbě odpočjwá".   B solo, 2cl 2hn 2bn.
MS parts (by Jos. J. Benesch): CZ-TRB, H 449.   ★
A-32tv. Cantilena pro defunctis adultis; "Ade se wssichnj posastawte".   CATB, 2cl 2hn 2bn.
MS parts: CZ-TRB, H 457.   ★
A-33tv. Trauergesang Bei einer Leiche erwachsener Person; "O! betrübte Sterbenszeiten".   B solo, 2cl 2hn tp tb.
MS parts (by Ignác Kulka): CZ-TRB, H 451.   ★
A-34tv. Leichenlied (bey Kleinen und Erwachsenen); "Der Todt ist eine Sündenstrafe".   CATB, 2cl 2hn bn.
MS parts (by Ignác Kulka): CZ-TRB, H 282.   ★
A-35tv. Pjseň Pohřebnj; "Pliň [sic] o dusse do wěčnosti mezy kůry".   CATB, 2cl 2hn bn.
MS parts (by A. Beran): CZ-TRB, H 444, (missing 2cl 2hn).   ★
A-36tv. [2] Leichenlieder; "Mach doch auf von deinem Schlummer" & "Ruhe sanft".   CATB, 2cl 2hn bn.
MS parts (by Ignác Kulka): CZ-TRB, H 448.   ★
A-37tv. Leichengesang bey Kindern; "O wie kurz war dein Leben".   CATB, 2cl 2hn bn.
MS parts (by Ignác Kulka): CZ-TRB, H 459.   ★
A-38tv. Cantilena pro defunctis adultis; "O Člowěče mysly předce".   CATB, 2bthn 2hn bn.
MS parts: CZ-TRB, H 456.   ★
A-39tv. Pjseň pohřebnj při mládency [youths]; "Spěssně hyne swěta sláva".   CATB, 2cl 2hn.
MS parts: CZ-TRB, H 455.   ★
A-40tv. Todtenlied in Es [Eb] bey einer ledigen Person; "O wie bald vergeht das Leben".   CATB, 2cl 2hn.
MS parts: CZ-TRB, H 452.   ★
A-41tv. Cantus funebris. Hinweg ihr Eitelkeiten.   CATB, 2cl 2hn.   MS parts: CZ-TRB, H 454.   ★
A-42tv. Pohřební píseň; "Unlkněte pozorugte".   CAB, 2cl 2hn.   MS parts: CZ-TRB, H 462.   ★

Austro-Bohemia: Český Krumlov (Krumau), Joannes Schimeczek family collection
A-26. Polka.   pic 2fl 2cl(D) 3cl(A) 2hn 3tp tb basso.   MS pts: CZ-K, Rodina Simečkova Sign. 0621/1.   ★
A-27. 4 mvts (1. Píseň [song], 2. Adagio, 3. Pochod poutnický [pilgrim's march], 4. Pochod [march]).
cl(Eb) 2cl(Bb) 3tp 2flug b-tu.   MS parts (c.1850): CZ-K, Rodina Simečkova Sign. 0624.   ★
A-28. Parthia Turtia [sic], in C, 5 mvts.   2fl 3cl(C) 2hn bn 2tp(clar).
MS parts (c.1820): CZ-K, Rodina Simečkova Sign. 0622.   ★
A-29. Parthia, in C, 5 mvts.   fl 3cl(C) 2hn bn 2tp(clar).
MS parts (c.1820): CZ-K, Rodina Simečkova Sign. 0623.   ★
A-13t. Trauer Marsch.   cl(Ab) cl(Eb) 2cl(Bb) 2hn 4tp táp 2flug 2b-flug b-tr basso.
MS parts (c.1850): CZ-K, Rodina Simečkova Sign. 0621/4.   ★
A-5m. Abschieds Marsch.   cl(Eb) cl(Bb) 2hn(Eb, Bb) 2tp flug.
MS parts: CZ-K, Rodina Simečkova Sign. 0621/3.   ★

Austro-Bohemia: Český Krumlov (Krumau), Třeboň, Prague, Vienna, Schwarzenberg Harmonie
A-30. Alle Mande [sic] ex C.   2cl 2hn bn.   MS parts: CZ-K, symfonie Nr 239.K.II.
A-31. Menuetto in C.   2ob 2hn basso.   MS parts: CZ-K, symfonie Nr 237.K.II, (missing ob II& hn I).
A-32. Minueto [sic] [pencil "in C (Hes)"].   2ob 2hn bn.   MS pts: CZ-K, symfonie Nr 259.K.II, (parts titled
"Minovetto Magiestoso [sic]"; the horns are tacet in the C minor Trio. At the bottom of the bn part the Minueto
alone is written out in Bb ("Hes"), possibly for use with Bb clarinets substituting for oboes).
A-33. (?Bonno or Went) Parthia in Eb, 4 mvts.   2ca 2hn bn.
MS parts: CZ-K, symfonie Nr 231.K.II; CZ-Pnm, XLII.B.307 (as: "Parthia ala Camera").   ★
A-34(-A-43). 10 Parthias.   No. 1: 2ob 2taille 2hn 2bn; Nos. 2 - 10: 2 taille 2hn 2bn.
MS parts: A-Wgm, VIII 8541, (?lost - not available as of 1 June 1996).

Austro-Bohemia: Cheb (Eger), district
A-48v. Lied für 4 Stimmen mit der Begleitung 1; ("Meine veil durchleben Zahre sind").
CATB, 2fl(F) fl(D) cl(E♭) 2cl(B♭) 2hn bn+b-tb 2tp.
MS parts (by Georg Käss[e], 1850-75): CZ-CH, S-40-195-3829, (with duplicate pts: 2cl(B♭) 2hn 2tp).   ⋆
A-49v. Pangelingua in Es [E♭].   CATB, organ+bn, (ad lib: cl(E♭) cl(B♭) 2hn 2tp(clar) timp).
MS parts (by F.J. Grimm, c.1800) CZ-CH, S-40-1-7.   ⋆

Austro-Bohemia: Dlouhý Most (Langenruck), Musikantengesellschaft
The substantial number of works in this collection were copied out by three members of the Hübner family (in chronological order:) Ignaz, Augustin Erasmus (styling himself either "Schulgehilf" [school assistant] or "beym [sic] Schulfach", and Dominik. Many of the approximately 80 works are by local composers; the majority of these anonymous works may be as well. CZ-Pu, 59 R 3371 comprises a MS compilation of 48/49 Stücke for 3 horns dating from 1808.
A-44. Parthia alla Turcia ex D; 4 mvts.   2fl(vel pic) 2cl(C) 2hn bn tp(prin, D) b-dr.
MS parts (by Augustin Erasmus Hübner, 1804): CZ-Pu(dm), 59 R 3363.   ⋆
A-45. Parthia ala Turcia in D; 4 mvts.   2fl 2cl(C) 2hn bn tp(prin, D) b-dr.
MS parts (by Augustin Erasmus Hübner, 1804): CZ-Pu(dm), 59 R 3364.
A-46. [5] Deutsche in C ala Turcia; without Trios.   pic 2cl(Bb) 2hn bn tp(prin, C) "bombass".
MS parts (by Augustin Erasmus Hübner, 1809): CZ-Pu(dm), 59 R 3365.
A-47. Divertimento in Dis [E♭]; 4 mvts.   2ob 2cl 2hn 2bn.
MS parts (by Dominik Hübner): CZ-Pu(dm), 59 R 3315.   ⋆
A-48. [Thema & 7] Variations in B[♭].   Solo clarinet, 2cl 2hn bn.
MS parts (by Augustin Erasmus Hübner, 1802): CZ-Pu(dm), 59 R 3368.   ⋆
A-49, A-50. Parthia in Dis [E♭] due; both 4 mvts.   2cl 2hn bn.
MS parts (by Augustin Erasmus Hübner, 1814): CZ-Pu(dm), 59 R 3358.   ⋆
A-51. Parthia in Dis [E♭]; 4 mvts.   2cl 2hn bn.
MS parts (by Augustin Erasmus Hübner, 1806, old No. 25): CZ-Pu(dm), 59 R 3359.   ⋆
A-52. Parthia in Dis [E♭]; 4 mvts.   2cl 2hn bn.
MS parts (by Augustin Erasmus Hübner, 1806, old No. 26): CZ-Pu(dm), 59 R 3359.   ⋆
A-53. Parthia in Dis [E♭]; 4 mvts.   2cl 2hn bn.
MS parts (by Augustin Erasmus Hübner, 1806, old No. 27): CZ-Pu(dm), 59 R 3359.   ⋆
A-54. Parthia in Dis [E♭] - Author Ignoto; 6 mvts.   2cl 2hn bn.
MS parts (by Augustin Erasmus Hübner, 1801, old No. 20): CZ-Pu(dm), 59 R 3359.   ⋆
A-55. Der treue Deutsche für das kleine Orchester; 6 mvts.   Incomplete: here only 2cl 2hn.
MS parts (by Dominik Hübner, cl I pt dated, 17. August 1812): CZ-Pu(dm), 59 R 3367, (parts imcomplete: cl II missing mvts 5 & 6, hn I missing mvt 6, hn II missing mvts 3 - 6).   ⋆
A-56(f). 3 fragments: 56.1 Polonese, 56.2 Nachtrag zur Polonese in F, mit Horn Aufgang, 56.3 Andante. Nos. 1 & 2 lined out without music or instrumentation; No 3: fl 2cl 2hn tp(prin).   MS pts: CZ-Pu(dm), 59-R3370.
A-6m. [2] Marsch; [without Trios], in D.   2pic 2cl(C) 2hn 3bn 2tp(clar) tp(prin) timp.
MS parts (by Augustin Erasmus Hübner, 1822): CZ-Pu(dm), 59 R 3384, No. III, (bn I & II parts are found on the reverse of the pic parts).   ⋆
A-7m. Aufzugs-Marsch für die Musikantengesellschaft; in C.   2fl 2cl(C) 2cl(B♭) 2hn 2bn tp(clar) timp.
MS pts (by Dominik Hübner): CZ-Pu(dm), 59 R 3387, (a school exercise is written on the back of the pts).   ⋆
A-8m. [Collection of 19 Aufzüge & Intradas].   pic 2fl 2cl 2hn bn 2tp(clar) tp(prin) timp.
MS parts (by Dominik Hübner): CZ-Pu(dm), 59 R 3399.   ⋆
A-9m. [4] Aufzüge in D.   2pic cl(C) 2hn 3bn 2tp(prin) timp.
MS parts (by Augustin Erasmus Hübner, 1822): CZ-Pu(dm), 59 R 3384, No. I.   ⋆
A-10m. [Intrade [sic] & [33] Marchia [sic] in D oder Dis [E♭] ohne Flauto.   2fl 2cl 2hn bn 2tp(clar) tp(prin) timp.   MS parts: CZ-Pu(dm), 59 R 3382. *The 2tp(clar) play only in March No. 32.*   ⋆
A-11m. [4] Marcia in F; with Trios.   2fl cl(F) 2cl(B♭) 2hn bn tp(prin).
MS parts (by Dominik Hübner): CZ-Pu(dm), 59 R 3376.   ⋆
A-12m. [2] Marcia in F; No 1: Aufzugs Marsche; Marcia Nro 2 [with Trio].   pic cl(F) cl(B♭) 2hn 2bn 2tp(prin).
MS parts (by Dominik Hübner): CZ-Pu(dm), 59 R 3377.   ⋆
A-13m. [10] Marchia [sic]; and other mvts.   2cl(C) 2cl(B♭) 2hn 2bn tp(prin in C, solo).
MS parts (?by Dominik Hübner): CZ-Pu(dm), 59 R 3323. *Nos. 1 - 3, 5 - 9 are all quick marches (tempo: ¢); No. 4 bears the title, "Brüner [Brno] Schützen Marsch" and No. 10 is a Contradance with Trio.*   ⋆
A-14m. [4] Marcia ex F [with Trios].   2fl cl(F) cl(B♭) 2hn bn tp(prin).
MS parts (by Dominik Hübner): CZ-Pu(dm), 59 R 3379.   ⋆
A-15m. [12] Aufzüge in Dis [E♭] oder F et [8 in] D oder C Nro II.   2cl(B vel C) 2hn bn tp(prin) timp.
MS parts (by Augustin Erasmus Hübner, 1805): CZ-Pu(dm), 59 R 3385.   ⋆
A-16m. [3] Marcia in Dis [E♭].   2cl 2hn 2bn tp(prin).
MS parts (by Dominik Hübner): CZ-Pu(dm), 59 R 3378. ⋆
A-17m. [26] Marchia [sic] in B[♭].   2cl 2hn bn.
MS parts (by Augustin Erasmus Hübner): CZ-Pu(dm), 59 R 3381.   ⋆
A-18m. [14] Aufzüge, Finale, Marchia [sic].   2cl 2hn bn.
MS parts (by Augustin Erasmus Hübner): CZ-Pu(dm), 59 R 3381.
A-19m. [14 Marches].   2cl 2hn bn.   MS parts (by Augustin Erasmus Hübner, 1808): CZ-Pu(dm), 59 R 3383, No. I. *Only 3 marches bear titles: No. 1, Marsch der französischen Jägen zu Fus; Nos. 5 & 6 are rescorings of Nos. 1 & 5 of Krommer's Op. 31 set (FVK-1m): Marsch du Regiment Archiduce Carles [sic] & Marsch du Regiment Prinz Auersberg [sic].*   ⋆

Austro-Bohemia: Hluboká nad Vltavou (Frauenberg), Church Band
A-50v. Píseň ke mši svaté; "Przdwihněm wrhůru myslí svých".   CCATB, 2cl(D) 2cl(A) 2hn bn.
MS parts: CZ-K, Sign. O171/1.

Austro-Bohemia: Jestřebí, Church Band
A-51v. Animus Fidelium; in F. CATB, 2cl 2hn bn. MS pts: CZ-LIa(je), No. 203 hud., (missing instruments). ★
A-52v. Der Gottesacker, ein Lied am Allerseelentage; "Wie sie so sanft ruhn". CATB, 2terz-fl 2cl 2hn bn 2tp.
MS parts (by Wolleschensky): CZ-LIa(je), No. 274 hud., (missing the bn pt; with an extra tp(prin) in B♭). ★
A-53v. Johanneslied; in C, "Grosses Beispiel edler Jugend". CAB, 2fl 2cl(C) 2hn bn 2tp(clar).
MS parts: CZ-LIa(je), No. 293 hud. ★
A-54v. [Píseň k svátky sv. Jana Nepomuckého]; "Ein Beispiel der Beständigkeit". CATB, 2fl 2cl(A) 2hn.
MS parts: CZ-LIa(je), No. 294 hud., (with duplicate Canto part). ★
A-55v. Salve in Es [E♭]. CATB, 2cl 2hn bn. MS pts (by A.J. Hoke, Oberlehrer): CZ-LIa(je), No. 199 hud. ★
A-56v. [Vater unser, in E♭]. CATB, fl 2cl 2hn 2tp(clar) b-tb.
MS parts: CZ-LIa(je), No. 206 hud., (with duplicate Canto part). ★
A-43tv. Grablied in Es [E♭]; "Nimm das letzte Lebewohl". CATB, terz-fl 2cl 2hn 2bn 2tp(con sordini) b-tb.
MS parts (by Ant. Joh. Hoke, 1842): CZ-LIa(je), No. 278 hud., (missing cl I, tp II, b-tb) ★
A-44tv. Grablied; "Todesgesang und Schmerzenstöne". CATB, 2fl 2cl 2hn 2bn 2tp.
MS parts (by Wenzel Zeisel): CZ-LIa(je), No. 214 hud., (with duplicate vocal, 2cl, 2tp pts & a later b-tb pt). ★
A-45.1tv. Grablied [in E♭] ["]Sollen nun die grünen Jahre[",] bei einer erwachsenen ledigen Person.
CATB, terz-fl 2cl 2hn 2tp bn+b-tb. MS parts (by N. Roesler, 6 Aug 1848): CZ-LIa(je), No. 189 hud., (the title
calls for bombardon to double the bassoon rather than the b-tb specified on the part). ★
A-45.2tv. Grablied in F [or rather E♭], Sollen nun die grünen Jahre etc. CATB, terz-fl 2cl 2hn 2tp b-tb.
MS parts: CZ-LIa(je), No. 189 hud., (missing terz-fl; the 2tp were later replaced by 2flug). ★
A-46tv. Grablied in Es [in E♭] "Die Stund ist uns verbogen". CATB, terz-fl 2cl 2hn b-tb.
MS parts (by A.J. Hoke, Oberlehrer): CZ-LIa(je), No. 245 hud, (with duplicate parts: 2S, A, T, 2B, cl II). ★
A-47tv. Grablied bei der Leiche eines Kindes; "O weinet nicht!". CATB, 2cl 2hn bn.
MS parts (by Josef Köhler): CZ-LIa(je), No. 261 hud. ★

Austro-Bohemia: Kasejovice (Kassejowitz), Church Band
A-14t. [Funeral march], in C minor. cl(E♭) 2cl(B♭) 2hn 2bn 2tp basso.
MS parts (by Ladislav Vaněček, učitel): CZ-Pl(ka), Hu 1643. ★
A-15.1t, 15.2t. [2 settings of a] Trauer Marsch. 2ob cl 2hn bn(I).
MS parts (by Ladislav Vaněček, 1837): CZ-Pl(ka), Hu 1644a, (?missing bn II). *In No. II, the clarinet and
oboe I parts are exchanged, with some other alterations.* ★
A-16t. [2 Trauer] Marche. Here only: cl I(E♭) bn.
MS parts (?by Ladislav Vaněček; "9/10 [1]837 Skadly"): CZ-Pl(ka), Hu 1644b & Hu 1644c. ★

Austro-Bohemia: Ledce, Church Band
A-57v. [4] Stationen pro Festo Corporis Christi. CATB, fl 2cl(C) 2hn bn 2tp timp.
MS parts: CZ-PLa, Hu 110, (with later parts for fl II, 2b-flug(B♭) 2b-tb and transposed parts for 2cl(A) &
2b-flug(A); 2 sets of duplicate vocal parts are present - as are duplicate parts for fl I, b-tb I). ★

Austro-Bohemia: Osek (Ossegg), Cistercian Monastery
A-57. Nro III [Parthia in C]; 5 mvts. pic 2fl 2cl(C) 2hn bn 2tp(clar) glock b-dr s-dr.
MS parts: CZ-Pnm, XXXII.C.314. ★
A-58v. Duetto; in C, "Tag der Plonne, Tag der Jubels". TB soli, 2solo ob, 2fl 2ob 2hn 2bn 2tp(clar) timp.
MS parts: CZ-Pnm, XXXIV.A.33. ★

Austro-Bohemia: Opočno (Opotschno), Castle Collection
A-93. Carroussel Musik aufgeführt an dem Glorreichen Nahmens Feste Ihrer Kais: Kön: Majestäat Maria
Lodovka in dem k:k: Schloss Garten zu Laxenburg arrangirt für die Türkische Musik.
pic 2fl cl(F) 2cl(C) 2hn 2bn cbn tp(C) tp(princ) b-dr small-dr.
Pc (Im Verlage der k: k: pr: chemischen Druckery: Wien, pn 1620, c.1810/11), parts: CZ-Pnm, XLII.F.772.
    93.1(a) Marsch la Familie Suisse (J. Weigl: Die Schweizerfamilie) zum Iten Einzug.
    93.2   Marsche de L: v: Beethoven zum Iten Abzug. (= LVB-2m)
    93.3   [Anon] La Chasse, wo Sr Majestät der Kaiser der Kronprintz Erzhersog Karl u: Anton ritten.
    93.4   [Anon] Ecoaise [sic] & Trio.   93.5 [Anon] Allemande & Trio.
    93.6   [Anon] Allemande & Trio.   93.7 [Anon] Marsch zum IIten Einzug, (without trio).
    93.8   [Anon] Allemande & Trio.   93.9 [Anon] Ecossaise & Trio.
    93.10   [Anon] Polonaise & Trio.   93.11 [Anon] Allemande Saxone & Trio.
    93.12   Marcia. Abzug des Carrousels. Del Sig. Beethoven. (= LVB-3m)

Austro-Bohemia: Panenský Týnec, Strachotů family
A-48tv. Pohřební píseň Marnost nad marností. CATB, 2cl 2hn bn. MS parts: CZ-Pu, 59 R 3616. ★

Austro-Bohemia: Plzeň (Pilsen), Městky (town) Archív, regional - but unknown - provenance
A-58. Arietta; in G. 2ob 2hn bn. Followed by a *"Chorus Recit. ["outrpností. Vidíti máte znepovážlivosti
[sic] & Aria. All[egr]o"* including voices & string parts. MS parts: CZ-PLa, Hu 1714, (?possibly from the
Dominican Monastery at Cheb, formerly Eger). ★
A-59. All[egr]o moderato; in E♭. 2cl 2hn bn. MS parts: CZ-Pl(br), Hu 1639. ★

Collections directly associated with Prague are listed alphabetically by collection or Harmonie.

Austro-Bohemia: Prague, Bertramka, Mozart Society *(In virtually all cases, original provenance is unknown.)*
A-60, 61. 2 Adagia [sic], D, D. cl(D) 2cl(C) 2hn bn 3tp(2D, A) tp(prin, D) b-hn.
MS parts: CZ-Pnm, XL.F.155. ★
A-62. Auszüge. pic 2fl 2cl(A)+2cl(A ad lib) 2hn 2bn 2tp(clar) 2tp(prin) timp.
MS parts (by Joseph Přibík): CZ-Pnm, XL.F.238, (missing bn I, tp(clar) I, tp(prin) II; although the title lists
"Picoli Due [sic]", the part bears the headtitle "Picolo [sic]"). ★
A-63. Auszüge, in C. fl 2cl 2hn bn 2tp(clar) tp(prin) timp. MS parts (by Joseph Přibík): CZ-Pnm, XL.F.352. ★

A-64. Chval Sione Spasitele in F.   cl(E♭) 2cl(B♭) 2hn 2tp 2flug(B♭) basso(2).
MS parts (c1850 - 1875): CZ-Pnm, XL.F.55. ★
A-65. Divertimento in F, 5 mvts.   2cl 2hn 2bn posthorn.   MS parts: CZ-Pnm, XL.E.340. ★
A-66, 67. 2 Quartetti; (E♭, 3 mvts; B♭, 2mvts).   ob 2cl bn.   MS score: CZ-Pnm, XL.E.338. ★
A-17t. Marcia funebre, in C minor.   fl 2cl 2hn 2bn 2tp(clar) b-tb.   MS score (c.1850): CZ-Pnm, XL.F.133. ★
A-59v. Domine audisti me; in C.   T, vla(oblig), 2cl 2hn.   MS parts: CZ-Pnm, XL.F.108. ★
A-60v. Ecce panis, in C.   CATB, 2fl 2cl(C) 2cl(Bb) 2hn bn tp(prin) timp.   MS parts: CZ-Pnm, XL.F.85. ★
A-61v. [Mše in C / Mass in C].   CATB, fl cl(C) cl(Bb) 2hn 2tp(clar) timp organ.
MS parts (c.1850): CZ-Pnm, XL.F.72, (?missing hn II, bn, tp I). ★
A-62v. Pange lingua; in D.   CAB, 2fl 2cl(A) 2hn bn+vlne timp.
MS parts: CZ-Pnm, XL.F.38, (with duplicate A & B parts). ★
A-63v. Pange lingua Ex C.   CATB, 2cl 2hn 2bn timp.   MS parts: CZ-Pnm, (2 copies), XL.E.277, (MS by Josef
Jakoubek), XL.E.278, (MS by Joseph Přibík; as "Pange lingua in C"; without timp pt). ★
A-64v. Stationes Quator.   CATB, 2fl 2cl 2hn bn 2tp(clar) 2tp(prin) timp.
MS parts (by Joseph Přibík): CZ-Pnm, XL.E.269, (missing all instruments except bn & timp). ★

Austro-Bohemia: Prague, zámek Veltrusy & zámek Káčina, Chotek Harmonie
A-68. 2 Arias & 2 Menuetti with Trios.   2cl 2hn bn.   MS parts: CZ-Pnm, XLI.B.174, (missing hn II; the 2 Arias
are in the bn I part & the 2 Menuetti in the bn II part).   *These works are written out in the empty spaces of*
Tost's Sei Parthien; we do not believe tha they are by Tost.   The cl I part for Aria 1 bears the note "aus Spigl
[sic] von [section of paper missing, ?] . . . eacun"; to our knowledge this piece does not match any number in
Süssmayr's opera, Der Spiegel in Arcadien. ★
A-20m. Marcia, in C.   2cl 2hn 2bn.   MS parts: CZ-Pnm, XLI.B.166.

Austro-Bohemia: Prague & Frýdlant (Friedland), Clam Gallas Harmonie
There is also in this collection a Parthia ala Camera in E♭, for 2 taille 2hn bn (MS pts: CZ-Pnm XLII.B.307,
perhaps by Bonno or Went) noted above as **A-21** *in the Schwarzenberg archives.*
A-69. Cassation; in E♭, 3 mvts.   fl 2ob 2taliae 2hn 2bn.   MS parts: CZ-Pnm, XLII.B.188, (missing 2taliae). ★
A-70. Contre Danse [sic; in fact, 4 mvts of which 1 & 4 bear this title - mvt 3, in 2/4 is also probably a
contratanz].   2ob 2hn bn.   MS parts: CZ-Pnm, XLII.B.160. ★
A-71. [untitled Divertimento, Cassation, or Parthia turca in D], 6 mvts.   2ob 2cl 2hn 2bn 2tp(clar) timp cym.
MS parts: CZ-Pnm, XLII.A.332.   *The 2bn are unison for much of the piece.* ★
A-72. Es [E♭]. Divertissement militaire . . . de differends [sic] Auteurs [not named]; 4 mvts.   2ob 2cl 2hn 2bn.
MS parts: CZ-Pnm, XLII.B.46. ★
A-73. Divertimento [ob II: "Postpuri [sic]"]; in C, 1 mvt in 7 sections.   2ob 2hn bn.
MS parts: CZ-Pnm, XLII.B.146. ★
A-74. [3] Ecosse; in F, C & F.   2ob 2cl 2hn 2bn.   MS parts: CZ-Pnm, XLII.C.401. ★
A-75. [untitled Parthia in C], 4 mvts.   2ob 2hn bn.   MS parts: CZ-Pnm, XLII.A.74. ★
A-76. Parthia Ex G; 4 mvts.   2ob 2hn bn.   MS pstts: CZ-Pnm, XLII.A.349, (missing ob I). ★
A-77. Parthia Pastoraly; in G, 4 mvts.   2ob 2hn 2bn.   MS parts: CZ-Pnm, XLII.C.219.   *Title in the ob I psrt.*
The bn pt is divisi only in the Andante & the Trio of the Menuetto.   Recorded on Supraphon 1111 2616 G. ★
A-78. Parthia in D; 5 mvts.   2ob 2hn bn.   MS parts: CZ-Pnm, XLII.B.110. ★
A-79. Parthia in C; 4 mvts.   2ob 2hn bn.   MS parts: CZ-Pnm, XLII.C.4. ★
A-80. [4] Parti [sic]; in B♭, each 1 mvt.   2tallÿ [sic] 2hn 2bn.   MS parts: CZ-Pnm, XLII.B.251. ★
A-81. [3] Ungarisch; all in C.   3bthn.   MS parts: CZ-Pnm, XLII.E.167, (missing bthn I). ★
A-82. [14 mvts - perhaps a ballet arrangement; titled mvts are: No. 1 Marcia; No. 2 Contradanz; No. 5 Marcia;
No. 6 Allegretto; No. 13 Quadrille alla Ungara; No. 14 Cosaka).   2 pic 2cl(C) 2cl(B♭) (2)bn.
MS parts: CZ-Pnm, XLII.A.334, (missing bn II). ★
A-83. [untitled work], 17 mvts.   cl 3bthn.   MS parts: CZ-Pnm, XLII.C.290. ★
A-21m. Pas redoubl. [sic] in C alla Turc.   2ob/(cl ripieno) 2cl(C) 2hn 2bn 2tp s-dr.
MS parts: CZ-Pnm, XLII.A.74. ★
A-22m. 2 Marcia la Turce [sic], D, D.   2ob 2cl 2hn bn.   MS pts: CZ-Pnm, XLII.E.38. ★

Austro-Bohemia: Prague & Budenický, Kinsky Harmonie
A-84. [untitled - ?March in F].   2ob 2cl 2hn 2bn cbn tp(princ).   MS parts: CZ-Pnm, XX.F.28. ★
A-85. Variazione, in F.   2ob 2cl 2hn 2bn.   MS parts: CZ-Pnm, XX.F.16.   *Theme, 4 Var, Coda.* ★

Austro-Bohemia: Prague & Raudnice nad Labem (Raudnitz), Lobkowitz (Lobkovic) Harmonie
A-86. Partie für Türkische Musik, 6 mvts.   pic 2fl(G) 2cl(F) 2cl(C) 2hn 2bn cbn 2tp b-dr s-dr.
MS parts: CZ-Pnm, Lobkovic X.H.a.74. ★
A-87. 8 Stücke für Türkische Musik.   pic(C) fl(G) 2cl(F) 2cl(C) 2hn 2bn serp 2tp s-dr b-dr (as "Tampouro Picolo
et Grande [sic]").   MS parts: CZ-Pnm, Lobkovic X.H.a.75. ★
A-88. [7] Variationen über das österreichs Volkshymne [Haydn's "Gott erhalte Franz den Kaiser"].
Clarinetto princpale(A), 2ob cl(A) 2hn 2bn cbn.   MS parts: CZ-Pnm, Lobkovic X.G.f.75. ★
A-89. [4] Märsche und [16] Carossel-Stücke.   2ob 2hn 2bn.   MS pts: CZ-Pnm, Lobkovic X.H.b.15. ★
A-90. Karossel Musik, 10 mvts.   2cl 2hn 2bn.   MS parts: CZ-Pnm, Lobkovic X.H.a.89. ★
A-91. Die so genanten Sächsischen Deutschen.   cl(F) cl(C) 2hn 2bn cbn.
MS parts: CZ-Pnm, Lobkovic X.H.b.24. ★
A-92. Die allgemein beliebten Sächsischen Deutschen.   cl(F) cl(C) 2hn 2bn cbn.
MS parts: CZ-Pnm, Lobkovic X.H.b.25. ★
A-23m. Marsch.   pic 2cl(D) cl(A) 2hn 3tp 2flug b-flug a-tb t-tb b-tb.
MS parts (1846): CZ-Pnm, Lobkovic X.H.b.73/1.
A-24m. Marsch, in F.   pic 2cl(C) 2hn 2bn tp(F; tacet in march, solo in trio).
MS parts: CZ-Pnm, Lobkovic, X.H.b.17. ★
A-18t. Todten Marsch.   2ob 2cl 2hn 2bn tp.   MS pts: CZ-Pnm, Lobkovic X.H.b.16. ★

Austro-Bohemia: Prague & Liblice, Pachta Harmonie
Prior to consolidation in CZ-Pnm, the collection was arranged in alphabetical order through Pichl; any works by composers with surnames beyond this point are assumed to be lost. Although a few of the anonymous (early) works listed below may be from this lost body of works, the majority bear consecutive numbers, indicative of a single composer (see e.g. Lorenz). Associated with this collection are 12 "Ariette per gli Corni [inserted later: o Clarinetti] di Cazzia [sic]", XXII.E.61/1-12; & 4 "Ariette per gli Clarinetti", XXII.E.61/13-16. Following these duets are two "Divertimento à Trée" [sic], both 12 mvts, for 2hn bn (XXII.E.61/17-18) and 6 Parthias for 2cl bn (XXII.E.61/19-24). Additional Parthias by Alexius for this configuration can also be found in CZ-Pnm.
A-94. Nro 1 Parthia in Dis (E♭), 5 mvts. 2ca/a-cl 2hn bn. MS pts: CZ-Pnm, XXII.E.61/26, ("o Clarinetti" has been added at a later date; the parts, however, are for alto clarinet in C). ★
A-95. N° 2 Partita a 5; in F, 4 mvts. 2tallis/a-cl 2hn bn. MS parts: CZ-Pnm, XXII.E.61/27, ("o Clarinetti" has been added at a later date; the cl parts are for a-cl). ★
A-96. Parthia Nro 1mo; in E♭, 5 mvts. 2cl 2hn bn. MS parts: CZ-Pnm, XXII.E.61/28. ★
A-97. Parthia Nro 2; in B♭, 4 mvts. 2cl 2hn bn. MS parts: CZ-Pnm, XXII.E.61/29. ★
A-98. Parthia Ex C Nro 3; 4 mvts. 2ob/cl 2hn 2bn. MS parts: CZ-Pnm, XXII.E.61/30. ★
A-99. Parthia in F Nro 4; 4 mvts. 2cl 2hn bn. MS parts: CZ-Pnm, XXII.E. 61/31. ★
A-100. Paradi Parthia ex D# [D major], Nro 2; 4 mvts. 2ob 2hn bn. MS parts: CZ-Pnm, XXII.E.61/32. ★
A-101. Parthia in D# [D major], Nro 3; 4 mvts. 2ob 2hn bn. MS parts: CZ-Pnm, XXII.E.61/33. ★
A-102. Partitta Nro 4; in C, 4 mvts. 2ob 2hn (2)bn. MS parts: CZ-Pnm, XXII.E.61/34, (although the title states "Fagotto", there is a divisi in the Trio of the Menuet). ★
A-103. Nro 6 Partitta, in F, 7 mvts. 2ob 2hn bn. MS parts: CZ-Pnm, XXII.E.61/35, (the 5th mvt, Poloneso, has been crossed out in all parts, but still remains legible). ★
A-104, 105. Nro 6, Nro 7, 2 Partitte; both in F, 7 mvts, 6 mvts. 2ob 2hn bn.
MS parts: CZ-Pnm, XXII.E.61/36, (?originally a single work: the mvts are numbered consecutively throughout; "Parthia 2d" has been added in a later hand after mvt 7). ★
A-106. Nro 8 Parthia; in D, 5 mvts. 2ob 2hn 2bn. MS parts: CZ-Pnm, XXII.E.61/37. ★
A-107. Parade Parthie in D# [D major] Nro 9; 4 mvts. 2ob 2hn bn(obl). MS parts: CZ-Pnm, XXII.E.61/38. ★
A-108. Parthia in C Nro 10; 4 mvts. 2ob 2hn bn(obl). MS parts: CZ-Pnm, XXII.E.61/39. ★
A-109. Parthia in C Nro 11; 4 mvts. 2ob 2hn bn(obl). MS parts: CZ-Pnm, XXII.E.61/40. ★
A-110. Parthie in C Nro 12; 4 mvts. 2ob 2hn bn(obl). MS parts: CZ-Pnm, XXII.E.61/41. ★
A-111. Parthia Ex G# [G major] Nro 13; 5 mvts. 2ob 2hn 2bn. MS parts: CZ-Pnm, XXII.E.61/42. ★
A-112. N° 14 Sonatini [sic]; in C, 5 mvts. 2ob 2hn 2bn. MS parts: CZ-Pnm, XXII.E.61/43. ★
A-113. Divertimento Ex G# [G major] Nro 15; 5 mvts. 2ob 2hn bn. MS parts: CZ-Pnm, XXII.E.61/44. ★
A-114. Parta [sic] Ex D## [D major] Nro 16; 5mvts. 2ob 2hn bn. MS parts: CZ-Pnm, XXII.E.61/45. ★
A-115. [wrapper missing: ? Parthia in D] Nro 17; 6 mvts. 2ob 2hn 2bn.
MS parts: CZ-Pnm, XXII.E.61/46 (missing bn I). ★
A-116. Parthia Ex G Nro 18; 4 mvts. 2ob 2hn 2bn. MS parts: CZ-Pnm, XXII.E.61/47. ★
A-117. Parthia Ex D Nro 19; 4 mvts. 2ob 2hn 2bn. MS parts: CZ-Pnm, XXII.E.61/48. ★
A-118. Divertimento Ex C Nro 20; 6 mvts. 2ob 2hn 2bn. MS parts: CZ-Pnm, XXII.E.61/49. ★
A-119. N° 21 Parthia ex D# [D major]; 4 mvts. 2ob 2hn bn. MS parts: CZ-Pnm, XXII.E.61/50. ★
A-120. Partia Ex G# [G major] Nro 22; 6 mvts. 2ob 2hn 2bn. MS parts: CZ-Pnm, XXII.E.61/51. ★
A-121. Parthia; in A, 5 mvts. 2ob 2hn 2bn. MS parts: CZ-Pnm, XXII.E.61/52. ★
A-122. N° 24 Parthia Ex Dis [E♭]; 4 mvts. 2ob 2hn 2bn. MS parts: CZ-Pnm, XXII.E.61/53. ★
A-123. Parthia in E♭. 2ob 2hn 2bn. MS pts: CZ-Pnm, XXII.E.61/54. *?A ghost (Geisterwerk): not located by us.*
A-25m. Marsch de l'Artillerie Tambourette. 2ob 2hn bn. MS parts: CZ-Pnm, XXII.E.61/25. ★

Austro-Bohemia: Prague, Strahov, Praemonstratensian Monastery, Funeral Music
A-19t. Todenmarsch [sic]; in C minor. 2fl 2ob 2cl 2hn 2bn 2tp(muted) b-tb timp(muted).
MS parts: CZ-Pnm, (2 copies), XLVI.F.63 (MS by Tomáš Macek), XLVI.F.68 (as "Toden=Marsch [sic]"; the b-tb part is marked "1 Basson C Basso"). ★
A-20t. Todten Marsch. 2ob 2cl 2hn bn 3tp tb. MS parts: CZ-Pnm, XLVI.F.17. ★
A-65v. Animas Fidelium; in D. CATB, 2fl 2ob 2hn bn 2tp(clar, muted).
MS parts (1782 or 1787): CZ-Pnm, XLVI.F.44. ★
A-48tv. Cantus funeralis pro Majoribus;"Du der du liebest hier auf Erden", C minor. CATB, 2cl 2hn bn.
MS parts (by Tomáš Macek): CZ-Pnm, XLVI.F.19. ★
A-49tv. Cantus funeralis pro Parvulis; "Finite parvules", E♭. CATB(+bn), 2cl 2hn.
MS parts: CZ-Pnm, XLVI.F.66. ★
A-50tv. Lied beym Grabe. "Alles schläft dem Todesschlummer". SATB, 2fl 2cl 2hn bn, (with later parts for 2tp & tb(doubles bn) & alterations to the forst 2 & last 6 bars). MS parts: CZ-Pnm, XLVI.F.45. ★
A-51tv. Todesfeyer bey Beerdigung einer erwachsiner Person nach dem lateinischen Dies irae [sic].
SATB, 2fl 2ob 2cl 2hn bn tb. MS parts: CZ-Pnm, CLVI.F.64, (with duplicate S & A parts). ★

Austro-Bohemia, Stráž pod Ralskem, Church/Castle Band
A-2va. [3] Lieder für Harmonimusik [sic]. 2cl 2hn 4tp(F, 3E♭) 2flug t-crt 2tb.
MS parts (by Josef Mitscherling, 5/11 1876): CZ-LIa(st). No. 133 hud.
2.1va. Dreschler: Das Gebet der Mutter für ihr Kind. 2.2va. Asberger: Das Kohlrösel.
2..3va. Gounod: [Chanson de Printemps] Frühlingslied.
A-80v. Lied bein einer Kreuzeinweihung [Cross installation/dedication], in F. CATB, 2cl(C) 2hn 2tp b-tb organ.
MS parts: CZ-LIa(st), No. 142 hud. ★
A-81v. Das deutsche Vexilla regis am Charfreitage. CATB, 2cl(A) 4hn(E, D) bn b-tb organ
MS parts: CZ-LIa(st), No. 141 hud. ★
A-82tv. Wenn von Schrecken etc. CATB, 2cl 2hn bn 2tp(clar) b-tb. MS parts: CZ-LIa(st), No. 106 hud. ★
A-83tv. In des Grabes Kühle. CATB, 2cl 2hn bn 2tp(clar) b-tb.
MS parts (by Peter Handschke): CZ-LIa(st), No. 107 hud, (missing instrumental parts). ★
A-84.1tv, 84.2tv. [2 funeral songs]. CATB, 2cl 2hn bn. MS parts: CZ-LIa(st), No. 151 hud. ★
84.1tv. Weinet nicht. 84.2tv. Die Blum tragen wir zu Grabe.
A-85tv. Begräbnisslied: "Da liegt er nun, in seiner Toderschlummer. CATB, 2cl 2hn bn.
MS parts (by Peter Handschke): CZ-Lia(st), No. 109 hud, (missing the instrumental parts). ★

Austro-Bohemia: Svojšín, Castle Colletion
A-124. Parthia in C; 3 mvts.   2cl(C) 2hn 2bn.   MS parts (by Ignaz Schödl): CZ-Pnm, XLII.F.150, (cf. A-30.1m). ★
A-125. Parthia, in C; 3 mvts.   terz-fl 2cl(C) 2hn bn.   MS parts: CZ-Pnm, XLII.F.36, No. 8.   ★
A-126. Parthia; in E♭, 4 mvts.   2cl 2hn 2bn.   MS parts: CZ-Pnm, XLII.F.36, No. 13.   ★
A-26m. Marcia.   2pic 2quart-pic 2cl 2hn tp b-dr s-dr.
MS parts: CZ-Pnm, XLII.F.198, (incomplete).
A-27m. Marsch.   pic cl(F) 2cl(C) 3hn 2bnb tp(prin, C) tp(prin, G) b-dr s-dr.
MS parts: CZ-Pnm, XLII.F.149.
A-28m. Marsch & Ecouse [sic].   terz-pic(vel fl) 2cl(C) 2hn 2bn tp(prin).
MS parts: CZ-Pnm, XLII.F.128.   *Possibly composed by Ascherl.*
A-29m. [Collection of pieces: 8 Marches, 2 Hopswalzer, 2 Langaus (3/8), 1 Russischer Hops[walzer]; No 7: "Marcia das Herrn [?]Jaester"].   2pic quart-pic 2cl(C) 2hn tp b-dr s-dr.
MS parts: CZ-Pnm, XLII.F.198, (missing bn part(s); defective cl I & II, b-dr, s-dr parts).
A-30.1m(-30.4m). Marsch, Walzer, Marsch, [Persuis] Alexander Marsch.   MS parts: CZ-Pnm, XLII.F.150, (following A-124; 2fl 2cl(C) 2hn); XLII.F.151, (Alexander Marsch only: cl(I) bn b-dr s-dr). ★

Austro-Bohemia: Úterý, Church Band
A-127. Divertimento in Dis [E♭]; 3 mvts.   Solo cl bn, 2hn 2vla basso.
MS parts: CZ-Pnm, XXXVIII.F.220, (with a later bassoon part c.1825 combining the concertant part with the basso part). ★
A-21t. Todten=Marsch in C.   2fl 2cl(C) 2hn bn cbn tp klappen-tp bomb.
MS parts: CZ-Pnm, XXXVIII.F.601, (with duplicate clarinet parts). ★
A-66v. Kaum gab der Herr; in E♭.   SATB, fl 2cl 2hn bn tp.   MS parts: CZ-Pnm, XXXVIII.F.607. ★
A-67v. Sbor ku cti sv. Jana Nepomuckého, in C.   SATB, 2fl 2hn organ.   MS pts: CZ-Pnm, XXXVIII.F.599. ★
A-68v. Predigt= u. Segenslied; both in D.   STB, 2fl 2cl 2hn vlne organ.   MS pts: CZ-Pnm, XXXVIII.F.512. ★
A-69v. Zu Weihnachten. Lied Zwischen den drey Lectionen von der 1. Strophe bis zur 4ten, 4. - 9., 9. - zu Ende. SATB, 2fl 2cl 2hn vlne organ.   MS parts (1825): CZ-Pnm, XXXVIII.F.499. ★
A-70.1v, 70.2v. [2] Advent Offertorium in C.   SATB, 2fl 2hn organ.
MS parts: CZ-Pnm, XXXVIII.F.472, (missing T). ★
A-71v. Offertorium In B[♭]; "Eja chori".   SATB, 2cl, 2vl(doubling cl) 2hn bn+organ.
MS parts (1795): CZ-Pnm, XXXVIII.F.416. ★
A-72v. Offertorium in F; "Eripe me".   SATB, 2fl 2hn organ organ-bc.   MS parts: CZ-Pnm, XXXVIII.F.293. ★
A-73v. Johannes=Lied sammt Begleitung; in C.   SATB, 2fl 2cl 2hn basso.   MS pts: CZ-Pnm, XXXVIII.F.292. ★
A-74v. Deutsche Messe; in F.   SATB, fl 2cl(C) 2hn organ.   MS parts: CZ-Pnm, XXXVIII.F.214. ★
A-75v. Deutscher Gesang.   SATB, 2fl 2cl(A/B♭) 2cl/vl 2hn 2bn 2tp vla vlne timp organ.
MS parts (1825): CZ-Pnm, XXXVIII.F.206, (possibly by Franz Bühler). ★
A-76v. Deutscher Gesang für ein hohes Amt [sic].   SATB, fl cl 2hn vlne organ.
MS parts: CZ-Pnm, XXXVIII.F.201. ★
A-77v. Deutscher Messgesang.   SATB, fl cl(C) 2hn vlne organ.
MS parts (19 March 1838): CZ-Pnm, XXXVIII.F.189. ★
A-78v. Gesang unter einem Hohamte.   SATB, 2fl 2hn organ.   MS parts: CZ-Pnm, XXXVIII.F.188. ★
A-79v. Gesang unter dem heil. Messopfer.   SATB, 2fl 2hn vlne organ.   MS pts: CZ-Pnm, XXXVIII.F.186. ★
A-52tv. Smuteční sbor [Funeral chorus]; in E♭.   SATB, 2fl 2cl 2hn bn tp.   MS pts: CZ-Pnm, XXXVIII.F.609. ★
A-53tv. Smuteční sbor; in E♭.   SATB, fl 2l 2hn bn tp.   MS parts: CZ-Pnm, XXXVIII.F.605. ★
A-54tv. Smuteční sbor; "Traurig klagen", in B♭.   SATB, 2cl 2hn bn.   MS parts: CZ-Pnm, XXXVIII.F.604. ★
A-55tv. Smuteční píseň; in E♭.   SATB, 2fl 2cl 2hn cbn tp.
MS parts (c1845): CZ-Pnm, XXXVIII.F.603, (with duplicate S & A parts). ★
A-56tv. Grablied für Grosse; "Wenn an des Kindes Leichenzuge".   SAB, 2cl 2hn bn 2tp.
MS parts: CZ-Pnm, XXXVIII.F.603, (missing all instruments except bn; with duplicate S, A & B parts). ★
A-57tv. Smuteční sbor, in E♭.   SATB, 2terz-fl 2cl 2hn 2bn tp.
MS parts: CZ-Pnm, XXXVIII.F.597, (with a duplicate S part). ★
A-58tv. Aus unserm Kreise gehet sie, in E♭.   CATB, 2fl 2cl 2hn bn tp.
MS parts: CZ-Pnm, XXXVIII.F.596, (with duplicate C, A & B parts). ★
A-59tv. Leichgesang für Erwachsene, "Schon schlug die Stunde mir [sic]", E♭.   CATB, 2fl 2cl 2hn cbn tp bomb.
MS parts (c.1845): CZ-Pnm, XXXVIII.F.595, (with duplicate C & T parts). ★
A-60tv. Endlich hörte Gott mein Flehen, in E♭.   SATB, 2fl 2cl 2hn bn tp bomb.
MS parts: CZ-Pnm, XXXVIII.F.594, (with duplicate 2cl, S, A & B parts). ★
A-61tv. Leichgesang für eine vereheligte Person. "Gottes Wille ist geschehen", in E♭.
MS parts: CZ-Pnm, XXXVIII.F.593. ★
A-62tv. Der grosse Gott, der alles schuf, in C.   SATB, 2cl 2hn bn.
MS parts: CZ-Pnm, XXXVIII.F.592, (with duplicate S & T parts). ★
A-63.1tv, 63.2tv. Grablieder in B[♭] u. Dis [E♭].   "Nach so manchen schweren Lieden" & "Dir o Vater der Natur".   SATB, fl 2cl 2hn bn.   MS parts (2 Dec 1817): CZ-Pnm, XXXVIII.F.591, (with duplicate S part). ★
A-64tv. Seht, nun ruhet diese Leiche, in E♭.   SATB, 2hn.
MS parts: CZ-Pnm, XXXVIII.F.590, (with duplicate S & A parts). ★
A-65tv. Leichgesang für Verehelichtgewesene. "Friede!".   SATB, 2cl 2hn 2tp tp(princ).
MS parts: CZ-Pnm, XXXVIII.F.589. ★
A-66tv. Smuteční sbor; "So welkt das Blüchen hin", in E♭.   SATB, fl 2cl 2hn bn 2tp.
MS parts: CZ-Pnm, XXXVIII.F.586. ★
A-67tv. Leichgesang. Schwermutsvoll und dumpfig hallt Geläute. Am Beerdigungstage der Überresste von Jungfer Julie Wurda den 7. März 1837, in E♭.   SATB, 2fl 2cl 2hn bn cbn tp.
MS parts: CZ-Pnm, XXXVIII.F.585, (with duplicate S & A parts). ★

A-68tv. Smuteční sbor; "Auferstehn, ja Auferstehn", in D. SATB, 2fl 2cl 2hn bn.
MS pts: CZ-Pnm, XXXVIII.F.584, (with duplicate S pt). ★
A-69tv. Gott will, wir sollen heilig seyn. SATB, 2fl 2cl(C) 2hn organ. MS parts: CZ-Pnm, XXXVIII.F.583. ★
A-70tv. Grabeslied. Wenn an des Vaters Aschenkruge, in E♭. SATB, 2fl 2cl 2hn 2bn 2tp b-tb timp.
MS parts (by Jos. Teuchner, c1845): CZ-Pnm, XXXVIII.F.582. ★
A-71tv. Smuteční sbor, in B♭. SATB, 2terz-fl 2cl 2hn 2bn. MS pts: CZ-Pnm, XXXVIII.F.581, (missing B). ★
A-72tv. Leichengesang für Verehelighte "Dir Gott, Vater der Natur", in E♭. SATB, 2fl 2cl 2hn basso tp
bomb(doubles basso). MS parts: CZ-Pnm, XXXVIII.F.580, (with duplicate S & A parts). ★
A-73tv. Smuteční píseň, "Nun hab ich ausgelitten", in E♭. SAB, 2cl 2hn bn tp bomb.
MS parts: CZ-Pnm, XXXVIII.F.576, (?missing T; with duplicate S part). ★
A-74tv. Leichgesang "Nach einer Prüfung kurzer Tage", in E♭. SATB, 2fl 2cl 2hn 2tp bomb.
MSS parts: CZ-Pnm, XXXVIII.F.575, (with a duplicate S part). ★
A-75tv. Smuteční píseň; "Lasst ach lasst die Kinde", in E♭. SATB, 2cl 2hn tp bomb.
MS parts: CZ-Pnm, XXXVIII.F.574. ★
A-76tv. Die sterbende Mutter, in E♭. SATB, 2fl 2cl 2hn 2bn. MS parts: CZ-Pnm, XXXVIII.F.573.
A-77tv. Begräbnislied Für ein Kind, "Jung, und doch der Leiden müde", in E♭. SATB, 2cl 2hn bn 2tp bomb.
MS parts: CZ-Pnm, XXXVIII.F.572. ★
A-78tv. Begräbnislied in Dis (E♭) für eine grosse Person, "So muss ich dann von hinnen scheiden", in E♭.
SATB, 2cl 2hn bn. MS parts: CZ-Pnm, XXXVIII.F.571. ★
A-79tv. Leichengesang, "Ruh' und Freunde ist gefunden." Für erwachsene Ledige, in E♭.
S(2)A(2)TB(2), terz-fl 2cl 2hn bn cbn tp(E♭) tp(princ). MS parts: CZ-Pnm, XXXVIII.F.570. ★
A-80tv. Leichengesang in Es (E♭), "Das Leiden der Erblasten ist vorüber durch den Tod".
S(2)A(2)T(2)B(2), 2fl 2cl 2hn bn 2tp. MS parts: CZ-Pnm, XXXVIII.F.569. ★
A-81tv. Leichgesang fü ein kleines Kind. "Abgeblühet ist ein Leben". SATB, fl 2cl(2) 2hn bn tp bomb.
MS parts: CZ-Pnm, XXXVIII.F.567. ★

Austro-Bohemia, Vejprnice, Town band (MSS by Jan Lašek, učitel, 1846 - 1867)
A-128. Není tu není, co by mě těšilo. Polka in B[♭]. cl(E♭) cl(B♭) 2hn 2tp.
MS parts: ("napsaná dne 17. ledne [January] 1864 v Manetíně [sic]): CZ-PLa(ve), Hu 2211. ★
A-129. [4 marches, all E♭], Nos. 42 - 46. cl(E♭, No 4: F) cl(B♭) 3keyed-tp 2basso(No. 4: bomb+basso II).
MS parts (1852): CZ-PLa(ve), Hu 2199, (No. 1 is dated 10 May 1852; the others bear only the year date). ★
A-31m. Abschied Marš No. 38; A♭. cl(E♭) cl(B♭) 2hn 4tp flug b-tb bomb. MS pts: CZ-PLa(ve), Hu 2196. ★
A-32m. Defiler [sic] Marsch in As [A♭]. terz-fl/cl(E♭) cl(E♭) cl(B♭) 2hn 3tp flug basso.
MS parts: CZ-PLa(ve), Hu 2801. ★
A-33m. Gruss von Wien-Marsch; in C. terz-fl/cl(E♭) cl(E♭) cl(B♭) 2hn 3tp flug b-flug a-hn basso.
MS parts: CZ-PLa(ve), Hu 2203. ★
A-34m. 2 Marše Mailand [&] Oster pro Zbor [sic, Sbor], No. 30, 31. cl(F) cl(B♭) 2hn 4tp flug b-tb bomb.
MS parts (by Jan Lašek): CZ-PLa(ve), Hu 2197. ★
A-35m. N. 50 Marš; in E♭. cl(E♭) cl(B♭) 2hn 3tp(2E♭, B♭) basso.
MS parts (by Jan Lašek, 16 září [Sept] 1853): CZ-PLa(ve), Hu 2000. ★
A-86tv. Píseň při pohřbu nevyňátka [sic] malého; "Pod do ráje neviňátko, křtem svatým.
CATB, 2cl 2hn 2bn org. MS parts (1867): CZ-PLa(ve), Hu 2237. ★

Austro-Bohemia, Velenice (Wellnitz), S. Trinitatis, Church Band
A-82v. Erstanden ist der heilige Christ. Am Ostersamstage bei der Prozession um die Kirche Abends nach der
Auferstehung und am heiligen Ostertage vor dem Hochamte. SAT, 2fl 2cl(C) 2hn bn+b-tb 2klappen-tp tp(prin).
MS parts: CZ-Lla(vl), No. 2375, (with duplicate S & A parts & 2 later klappen-trompett parts transposed). *The
MS bears the comment, "Wenn auch die Oster sonntage die Prozession un die Kirche geführt wird, so intonirt
der Priester zuerst Pange lingua und als dann beginnt der Zug und die erste Strophe des Pange lingua wird
ausgesungen, als dann Abend dieses Lied mit Musik produzirt.* ★
A-83v. Lied beim heiligen Grabe am Charfreitage. Ach! so ist denn Jesus todt. CATB, 2fl 2cl 2hn 2bn a-tb
t-tb b-tb. MS parts: CZ-Lla(vl), No. 2377, (with duplicate CAB parts). ★
A-84v. Lied zum heil: Johann v. Nepomuk; "Freunde schallt von allen Enden. CCAATB, 2fl 2cl(C) 2cl(A) 2hn
2tp b-tb. MS parts: CZ-Lla(vl), No. 2345 hud, (the 2cl in C parts may have been prepared later). ★
A-85v. Roratelied: Maria, sei gegrüsset, du lichter Morgenstern! CCAÄTTBB, 2fl 2cl(C) 2hn 2klappen-tp.
MS parts: CZ-Lla(vl), No. 2111 hud, No. 2b, (No. 2a is a setting of the same text for CATB). ★
A-86v. Stationen zum heiligen Corporis Christi Feste. CATB, 2fl 2ob 2cl(A) 2hn 2bn (cbn) 2tp(clar) (b-tb) timp.
MS parts: CZ-Lla(vl), No. 2113 hud, (the cbn & b-tb are not listed on the titlepage). *With the dates of 14
performances between 1854 and 1880.* ★
A-87v. Vexilla regis. CATB, 2cl 2hn bn. MS parts (c.1840): CZ-Lla(vl), No. 2105 hud. ★
A-87tv. 2 Grablieder. Scoring varies. MS parts: CZ-Lla(vl), No. 2455 hud. ★
    87.1tv. Jedes Wesen, das hier lebet. CATB, fl(F) 2cl 2hn 2tp b-tb.
    87.2tv. Hier bestehen keine Freuden. CATB, 2cl 2hn b-tb.
A-88.1tv. 2 Grablieder in As [A♭]. CATB, 2fl(F) cl(E♭) 2cl(B♭) 2hn 2bn 2tp(clar) b-tp b-tb.
MS parts: CZ-Lla(vl), No. 2448 hud. ★
    88.1/1tv. Trocknet eures Jammers Thränen. 88.1/2tv. Ruhe frei von aller Plage.
A-88.2tv. 2 Grablieder. Scoring varies. MS parts: CZ-Lla(vl), No. 2474 hud. ★
    88.2/1tv. Trocknet eures Jammers Thränen. CATB, 2fl(F) cl(E♭) 2cl(B♭) 2hn 2tp s-flug b-flug b-tb.
    88.2/2tv. Ruhe frei von aller Plage. CATB, 2fl(F) 2cl 2hn 2tp b-tb.
A-89tv. Grablied in Es [E♭], Ins stille Land [wer leitet uns hinüber?]. CATB, fl(F) 2cl 2hn 2bn 3tp bomb.
MS parts: CZ-Lla(vl), No. 2445 hud. ★
A-90tv. Grablied. Hier Mensch lerne. CATB, fl(E♭) 2cl 2hn 2tp(clar) s-flug b-flug b-tb.
MS parts: CZ-Lla(vl), No. 2468 hud. ★

A-91tv. Grablied in Es [E♭] "Die treue Gattin ist geschieden". CATB, terz-fl 2cl 2hn 2tp bomb.
MS parts: CZ-LIa(vl), No. 2495 hud. ★
A-92tv. 2 Grablieder. CATB, 2cl 2hn 2tp b-flug bomb. MS parts: CZ-LIa(vl), No. 2469 hud. ★
92.1tv. Im Leichentuche schläft sichs gut. 92.2tv. Im Grabe ist Ruh!
A-93tv. 2 Grablieder bei Kindern. CATB, 2fl cl(E♭) 2cl(B♭) 2hn bn 2tp. MS pts: CZ-LIa(vl), No. 2401 hud. ★
93.1tv. Ich schlafe sanft und sicher. 9.2tv. So sinken Blumen, die am Morgen blühen.
A-94tv. 2 Grablieder bei Kindern. CATB, 2fl 2cl 2hn 2bn 2tp(clar). MS pts: CZ-LIa(vl), No. 2411 hud. ★
94.1tv. Tief erschüttert stehn wir da. 94.2tv. Freunde denkt an meine Bahre.
A-95tv. 2 Begräbnisslieder bei Kindern. CATB, 2fl 2cl 2hn bn 2tp(clar). MS pts: CZ-LIa(vl), No. 2412 hud. ★
95.1tv. Schmücket mich mit Blumenkränzen. 95.2tv. Mein kurzes Wanderleben.
A-96tv. 2 Grablieder bei Kindern. CATB, 2terz-fl 2cl 2hn bn 2tp(clar). MS pts: CZ-LIa(vl), No. 2420 hud. ★
96.1tv. In des Lebens erster Blüthe. 96.2tv. So geh' nun hin dem Grabe zu.
A-97tv. 2 Grablieder bei Kindern. CATB, 2fl 2cl 2hn bn+b-tb 2tp(clar). MS pts: CZ-LIa(vl), No. 2417 hud. ★
97.1tv. So sankt du denn ins frühe Grab. 97.2tv. Eltern preiset Gottes Güte.
A-98tv. 2 Grablieder bei der Leiche eines Kindes. . CATB, fl 2cl 2hn bn 2tp b-tb. MS pts: CZ-LIa(vl),
No. 2418, (the notes have not been written out in the tp II pt). 98.1tv. Nimm dieses Kind des Lebensende.
98.2tv. Bei Kindern von mittlern und kleinen Jahren. "Bringt zur letzten Todtengabe". ★
A-99tv. 2 Grablieder bei Kindern. CATB, fl(F) 2cl 2hn bn 2tp(clar). MS parts: CZ-LIa(vl), No. 2433 hud. ★
99.1tv. Trocknet Eltern eure zähren. 99.2tv. Schlummre sanft du lieber Knabe!
A-100tv. 2 Grablieder bei Kindern. CATB, 2fl 2cl 2hn bn. MS parts: CZ-LIa(vl), No. 2413 hud. ★
100.1tv. Mein kurzes Wanderleben [another setting]. 100.2tv. Gib endlich fromme Christenschaar.
A-101tv. 2 Grablieder in Es [E♭] bei Kindern. CATB, 2cl 2hn 2tp b-tb. MS pts: CZ-LIa(vl), No. 2423 hud. ★
101.1tv. Traurig klagen ängstlich tönen. 101.2tv. Was ist der Mensch? ein Blümchen.
A-102tv. 2 Grab-Arien bei Kindern. Scoring varies. MS parts: CZ-LIa(vl), No. 2435 hud. ★
102.1tv. Kleiner Engel sich herab. CATB, 2cl 2hn 2tp b-tb.
102.2tv. So wellkt das Blümchen hin. CATB, 2cl 2hn.
A-103tv. 2 Grablieder bei Kindern. CATB, terz-fl 2cl 2hn b-tb. MS parts: CZ-LIa(vl), No. 2419 hud. ★
103.1tv. So wellkt das Blümchen hin [another setting to A-102.2tv]. 103.2tv. Ach wie unbeständig sind.
A-104tv. 2 Grablieder bei Kindern. CATB, 2cl 2hn bn. MS parts: CZ-LIa(vl), No. 2397. hud. ★
104.1tv. Ich sterbe früh, woll mir ich sterbe. 104.2tv. Früh beschloss der Tod dein Ziel hienieder.
A-105tv. 2 Grablieder bei Kindern. CATB, 2cl 2hn. MS parts: CZ-LIa(vl), No. 2415 hud. ★
105.1tv. Die Vorsicht Gottes waltet gleicht. 105.2tv. Aus des grabes Dunkelheit.
A-106tv. 2 Leichen-Arien bei Kindern. CATB, 2cl 2hn bn. MS parts: CZ-LIa(vl), No. 2421 hud. ★
106.1tv. Wenn kleinen Himmelserben. 106.2tv. So geh' nun dem Grabe zu.
A-107tv. 2 Grablieder bei Kindern. CATB, 2cl 2hn bn. MS parts: CZ-LIa(vl), No. 2434 hud. ★
107.1tv. Der Herr nach seinem weisen Rath. 107.2tv. Geliebte! nehmet hin den Dank.
A-108tv. 2 Grablieder bei Kindern. CATB, 2cl 2hn bn. MS parts: CZ-LIa(vl), No. 2436 hud. ★
108.1tv. Von der Todesnacht bedecket. 108.2tv. Ich bin noch ein Kind.
A-109tv. 2 Grablieder bei Kindern. CATB, 2cl 2hn. MS parts: CZ-LIa(vl), No. 2395 hud. ★
109.1tv. Kaum gab der Herr, der Welten schuf. 109.2tv. Soll dem nun der Unschuld Jugend.
A-110tv. 2 Grablieder bei Kindern; No. 2, "Die kalte Todeshand schont keines Alters nicht". CATB, 2cl 2hn.
MS parts: CZ-LIa(vl), No. 2403 hud., No. 2, (No.1, "Lebt wohl ihr Eltern" is for CATB, 2hn only). ★
A-111tv. 2 Grablieder bei Kindern; No. 2, So sey [sic] denn Gott zuück gegeben. CATB, 2cl 2hn.
MS pts: CZ-LIa(vl), No. 2404, No. 2, (No. 1, "Nimm dies Kind in deine Hände, Jesus" is scored for CATB). ★
A-112tv. 2 Grablieder bei jungen Personen und erwachsenen Kindern. CATB, 2fl(D) 2cl 2hn bn 2klappen-tp.
MS parts: CZ-LIa(vl), No. 2430 hud. ★
112.1tv. In dem Frühling meiner Jahre. 112.2tv. Geliebte! nehmet den Dank [another setting to A-207.2tv].
A-113tv. 2 Grablieder. Bei der Leiche einer jungen Person; No. 1, "Die Stund ist uns verborgen". CATB, fl(F) 2cl
2hn bn+b-tb 2tp. MS pts: CZ-LIa(vl), No. 2427 hud, (No. 2 is a setting for CATB, 2hn of the same piece). ★
A-114tv. 2 Trauergesänge: bei jungen Personen. CATB, 2cl 2hn 2tp b-tb. MS pts: CZ-LIa(vl), No. 2413 hud. ★
114.1tv. In dem Frühling meiner Jahre [another setting]. 114.2tv. Nun ist der Lebensstab.
A-115tv. 2 Grablider bei Erwachsenen jungen Personen. Scoring varies. MS parts: CZ-LIa(vl), No. 2426 hud ★
115.1tv. Schlummre sanft. CATB, terz-fl 2cl 2hn bn 3tp.
115.2tv. Am Grabe stehen wir. CATB, 2cl 2hn b-tb.
A-116tv. 2 Grablieder für Jünglinge. Scoring varies. MS parts: CZ-LIa(vl), No. 2437 hud. ★
116.1tv. Auch Rosen welken und verschwinden. CATB, fl(F vel cl in E♭) 2cl 2hn bn tp(clar) tp(prin).
116.2tv. Schlaf sanft und still im kühlen Grab! CATB, fl(F) 2cl 2hn bn tp(clar) tp(prin).
A-117tv. 2 Grablieder bei jungen unverheurathetan [sic, unmarried] Personen. CATB, 2fl(ad lib) 2cl 2hn
b-tb+bn 2klappen-tp. MS parts: CZ-LIa(vl), No. 2431 hud, (the ad lib flutes are not listed on the titlepage). ★
117.1tv. Erdentöchter, Erdentöchter. 117.2tv. Ach, es fliessen Trauerthränen.
A-118tv. 2 Beerdigungslieder für erwachsene Personen. Scoring varies. MS pts: CZ-LIa(vl), No. 2503 hud. ★
118.1tv. Ich scheide nun von euch Geliebte. CATB, 2fl(F) cl(E♭) 2cl(B♭) 2hn 4tp 2flug 2bomb.
118.1tv. Meine Reis ist nun vollendet. CATB, 2cl 2hn b-tb.
A-119tv. 2 Grablieder für Erwachsene. Scoring varies. MS parts: CZ-LIa(vl), No. 2440 hud. ★
119.1tv. Wie angstvoll war der Todesgang. CATB, 2terz-fl 2cl 2hn 2bn 2tp(clar) tp(II)+a-tb tp(I)+t-tb b-tb.
119.2tv. Das ziel von meinen Tagen. CATB, cl(E♭) 2cl(B♭) 2hn 2tp b-tb.
A-120tv. 2 Grablieder, No. 1 in As [A♭], No. 2 in Es [E♭]. Bei erwachsenen Personen. Scoring varies.
MS parts: CZ-LIa(vl), No. 2447 hud. ★
120.1tv. Schon so frühe musst du sterben. CATB, fl cl(E♭) 2cl(B♭) 2hn 2to flug bomb "Basso Grande".
120.2tv. Frühe schlug die ernste Schiedestunde. CATB, fl 2cl 2hn 4tp 2flug bomb+b-tb.
A-121tv. Zwei Grablieder für Erwachsene. Scoring varies. MS parts: CZ-LIa(vl), No. 2460 hud. ★
121.1tv. Tragt mich fort zu meinem Grabe. CATB, 2terz-fl 2cl 2hn bn 2tp(clar - missing notes).
121.2tv. Freunde! Die Todtenglocke ruft. CATB, 2terz-fl 2cl 2hn 2bn 2tp(clar).

A-122tv. 2 Grablieder bei Erwachsenen.   Scoring varies.   MS parts: CZ-LIa(vl), No. 2463 hud.   ★
  122tv. Nach so manchen schweren Leiden.   CATB, 2cl 2hn b-tb.
  122tv. Nimm das letzte Lebewohl.   CATB, 2terz-fl 2cl 2hn 2tp(clar) b-tb.   (Another scoring is at A-127.2tv)
A-123tv. 2 Grablieder bei Erwachsenen.   Scoring varies.   MS parts: CZ-LIa(vl), No. 2491 hud.   ★
  123.1tv. Erdentöchter, Erdensöhne.   CATB, fl 2cl 2hn b-tb.   [cf. A-117.1tv].
  123.2tv. Sei mir gegrüsst, du Ziel der Sorgen.   CAB, 2cl 2hn 2tp flug bomb.
A-124tv. Zwei Grablieder für Erwachsene.   Scoring varies.   MS parts: CZ-LIa(vl), No. 2501 hud.   ★
  125.1tv. Alles schlät den Todesschlummer.   CATB, 2terz-fl 2ob 2cl 2hn 2bn 2tp(clar) a-tb t-tb b-tb.
  125.2tv. Stiller Kirchhof, Trost der Müden [another setting].   CATB, fl 2cl 2hn 2bn 2tp a-tb t-tb b-tb.
A-125tv. 2 Grablieder bei Erwachsenen.   Scoring varies.   MS parts: CZ-LIa(vl), No. 2504 hud.   ★
  126.1tv. Alle Seelen ruhn in Frieden.   CATB, fl(E♭) cl(E♭) 2cl(B♭) 2hn 2tp 2flug 2tb bomb.
  126.2tv. Du nahst uns nicht vergebens.   CATB, terz-fl 2cl 2hn 2bn 2tp 2flug b-tb.
A-126tv. Zwei Grablieder für Erwachsene.   CATB, terz-fl 2cl 2hn bn 2tp(clar) a-tb t-tb b-tb.
  MS parts: CZ-LIa(vl), No. 2477 hud.   ★
  127.1tv. Selig, welche christlich sterben.   127.2tv. Mild und sanft sehn wir den Frommen.
A-127tv. 2 Grablieder bei Erwachenen, No. 1: Rings umher von Nacht umflossen.   CATB, 2fl(F) 2ob 2cl 2hn
  2bn cbn 2tp(clar) a-tb t-tb b-tb.   MS pts: CZ-LIa(vl), No. 2465 hud, (No. 2 is another version of A-122.2tv).   ★
A-128tv. 2 Grablieder für Erwachsene.   CATB, terz-fl 2cl 2hn 2bn b-tb.
  MS parts: CZ-LIa(vl), No. 2471 hud, (with 2 additional horn pts marked "ohne andere Begleitung").   ★
  128.1tv. Herr! Herr! was sind wir gegen dich wir Staub.   128.2tv. Nun bringet wir den Leib zur Ruh.
A-129tv. 2 Grablieder für Erwachsene, No. 1: Hier Mensch, hier lerne was du bist.   CAB, fl(F) 2cl 2hn b-tb.
  MS parts: CZ-LIa(vl), No. 2452 hud, (the 2nd Grablieder is set for CATB, 2hn only).   ★
A-130tv. 2 Grablieder bei Erwachsenen.   CATB, fl(F) 2cl 2hn bn b-tb.   MS pts: CZ-LIa(vl), No. 2476 hud.   ★
  130.1tv. Bei der Leiche eines Vaters oder Mutter. "Selig, welche christlich sterben" [another setting].
  130.2tv. Gieb endlich fromme Christenschaar [another setting].
A-131tv. 2 Grablieder bei Erwachsenen.   CATB, 2cl 2hn bn.   MS parts: CZ-LIa(vl), No. 2467 hud.   ★
  131.1tv. Alle müssen wir verwesen.   131.2tv. Stiller Kirchhof! Trost der Müder [another setting].
A-132tv. 2 Grablieder bei Erwachsenen.   CATB, 2cl 2hn bn.   MS parts: CZ-LIa(vl), No. 2479 hud.   ★
  132.1tv. Weinend und in vollem Jammer. (missing bn).   132.2tv. Werde munter meine Seele.
A-133tv. 2 Grab-Arien bei erwachsenen Personen.   CATB, 2cl 2hn bn.   MS pts: CZ-LIa(vl), No. 2480 hud.   ★
  133.1tv. Wenn einst mein Geist empor sich schwingt.   133.2tv. Schlummert süss ihr Jüngstgestorbnen alle.
A-134tv. 2 Grablieder bei Erwachsenen; No. 2: Begrabt den Leib in seine Grust.   CATB, 2cl 2hn bn.
  MS parts: CZ-LIa(vl), No. 2494 hud., (No. 1 is Gellert's "Ruhe frei von aller Klage", JXG-1.1/3)   ★
A-135tv. 2 Grablieder bei Erwachsenen.   CATB, 2cl 2hn bn.   MS parts: CZ-LIa(vl), No. 2505 hud.   ★
  135.1tv. Sey [sic] mir gegrüsst du Ziel der Sorgen.   135.2tv. Du nahst uns nicht vergebens.
A-136tv. 2 Grablieder bei einer erwachsenen Person, No. 1: Wohl dir, du bist entbunden.   CAB, 2cl 2hn b-tb.
  MS parts: CZ-LIa(vl), No. 2459 hud, (No. 2 is Josef Gellert's "Ach er ist von uns geschieden").   ★
A-137tv. 2 Grablieder bei Erwachsene.   CATB, 2cl 2hn b-tb.   MS parts: CZ-LIa(vl), No. 2461 hud.   ★
  137.1tv. Hier hört der Kampf des Christen auf.   137.2tv. Hier liegt der Mensch, die kleine Welt.
A-138tv. 2 Grablieder für Erwachsene.   CATB, 2cl 2hn b-tb.   MS parts: CZ-LIa(vl), No. 2473 hud.   ★
  138.1tv. Zum Grabe ich nun reise zu meinem.   138.2tv. So gib denn, fromme Christenschaar!
A-139tv. Grablied für Erwachsene; No. 1: "Hier sind wir an der Stätte".   CATB, 2cl 2hn b-tb.
  MS parts: CZ-LIa(vl), No. 2493 hud, (No. 2 is another scoring of A-134.2tv).   ★
A-140tv. 2 Grablieder bei Erwachsenen.   CATB, 2cl 2hn bomb.   MS parts: CZ-LIa(vl), No. 2490 hud.   ★
  140.1tv. In wehmuthsvoller Stiller.   140.2tv. Mein Gott ich bin genug gereist.
A-141tv. 2 Grablieder bei Erwachsene, No. 1: "Ach der Stunde voller Schmerzen".   CATB, 2cl 2hn.
  MS parts: CZ-LIa(vl), No. 2462 hud, (No. 2 is set for CATB only).   ★
A-142tv. 2 Grablieder bei Erwachsenen.   CATB, 2cl 2hn.   MS pts: CZ-LIa(vl), No. 2492 hud, (missing 2hn).   ★
  142.1tv. Der treue Gatte ist geschieden.   142.2tv. Ach es fliessen trauerthränen auf ein unerwartet Grab.
A-143tv. 2 Grablieder bei einer verstorb. Mutter, Vater, Freunde.
  CATB, 2cl 2hn bn.   MS parts: CZ-LIa(vl), No. 2489 hud.   ★
  143.1tv. Meiner Jahre Lauf hab ich vollstreckt.   143.2tv. Trocknet eures Jammers Thränen [another setting].
A-144tv. 2 Grablieder für Aeltern, Geschwister, Freunde.   Scoring varies.   MS pts: CZ-LIa(vl), No. 2443 hud.   ★
  144.1tv. Weinend, weinend, weinend.   CATB, 2fl cl(E♭) 3cl(B♭) 2hn 3tp tp(in E♭ allein) b-flug b-tb.
  144.2tv. O Mensch bedenk du bist.   CATB, 2cl 2hn b-tb.
A-145.1tv. 2 Grablieder bei Grossen.   CATB, 2fl 2cl 2hn b-tb.   MS parts: CZ-LIa(vl), No. 2442 hud.   ★
  145.1/1tv. Gott hat gewollt und meine Seele.   145.1/2tv. Wenn beklagt mit dumpfen Tönen.
A-145.2tv. Grablied für Erwachsene; No. 2: "Wenn beklagt mit dumpfen Tönen".   CATB, 2cl 2hn bn.
  MS parts: CZ-LIa(vl), No. 2493 hud., No. 2, (with 2 additional horn pts marked "ohne Clarinetten").   ★
A-146tv. 2 Grablieder bei Grossen.   CATB, 2cl 2hn.   MS parts: CZ-LIa(vl), No. 2466 hud.   ★
  146.1tv. So ruhe denn in deines Gottes.   146.2tv. Bei verunglückten Personen: "Auf allen unsern Wegen".
A-147tv. 2 Grablieder bei Grossen.   Scoring varies.   MS parts: CZ-LIa(vl), No. 2500 hud.   ★
  147.1tv. Ruhe sanft, endlich hast du überwunden.   CATB, fl(F) cl(E♭) 2cl(B♭) 2hn 2bn 2tp b-tb.
  147.2tv. Fliesst nur ihr Thränen fliesset.   CATB, fl(F) 2cl 2hn 2bn 2tp(clar) b-tb.

Austro-Bohemia, Veselí (? nad Lužnicí), Church band

A-130. Nro 2 Parthia in Dis [E♭] Cassatio; 7 mvts.   2cl 2hn 2bn.
  MS parts (by Josef Thomáš Lapáček [Lapaczek], 1823): CZ-Pu, 59 r 83.   ★
A-131. Nro 3 Parthia ex Dis; 4 mvts.   2cl 2hn bn.
  MS parts (by Josef Thomáš Lapáček [Lapaczek], 1823): CZ-Pu, 59 r 84.   ★
A-132. Parthia in Dis [E♭]; 4 mvts.   2cl 2hn bn.   MS parts ("Rerum Anton Pachta"): CZ-Pu, 59 r 85.   ★
A-22.1t, 22.2t. 2 Trauermärsche; both in C minor.   fl(E♭) 2cl 2hn 2bn 2klappen-tp(E♭) tp(E♭).
  MS parts (by Josef Thomáš Lapáček [Lapaczek]): CZ-Pu, 59 r 87, (No. 2 missing klappen-tp II & tp).   ★
A-23t. Trauermarsch; in C minor.   fl(E♭) 2cl 2hn 2bn 2tp b-tb.
  MS parts (by Josef Thomáš Lapáček [Lapaczek]): CZ-Pu, 59 r 88, (with a later flug(B♭) part).   ★

Austro-Bohemia, Zákupy, Church Band
A-148tv. Guter Vater [schlaf in Frieden]. CATB, 2cl 2hn 2tp flug b-tb. MS parts: CZ-LIa(za), No. 2662 hud.,
(with duplicate vocal parts: 3C, 2A, 2B). ★
A-149tv. [20 pohřebních písní - funeral songs - Nos. 10 - 20]. CATB, 2cl 2hn 2tp t-hn b-tb.
Pc (s.n.: s.l., s.d) parts: CZ-LIa(za), No. 2666 hud., (Nos. 1 - 9 are scored for CATB only). ★
    149.1tv. No. 10. Schonungslos und ohn' Erbarmen.   149.2tv. No. 11. Ruh' sanft, schlaf wohl!
    149.3tv. No. 12. Lebet wohl, o all' ihr Leben.   149.4tv. No. 13. Siehst des Thaues Perle du entschweben.
    149.5tv. No. 14. Es ist nicht mehr!   149.6tv. No. 15. Heisse Thränen träufeln heut hernieder.
    149.7tv. No. 16. Lebet wohl, ihr meine Lieben.   149.8tv. No. 17. Ach so früh schon musst du scheiden.
    149.9tv. No. 18. Unerbittlich ist der Todes Bote.   149.10tv. No. 19. Nimm dies Kind in deine Hände, Jesus.
    149.11tv. No. 20. So wie im Herbst des Sturmes Wüthen.

Austro-Hungary: Keszthely, Festhetics Harmonie/Helikon Conservatory
A-199. [5] Polonessens [sic]; with Trios. 2ob 2cl 2hn 2bn. MS parts: H-KE, K 951. ★
A-200. Harmonie; in E♭, 3 mvts. 2ob 2cl 2hn 2bn. MS parts: H-KE, K 956. ★

Austro-Moravia, Brno (Brünn)
A-36m. Abschied-Marsch für 10 Stimmige Harmonie. 2cl(D) 2hn bn 4tp(G, 3D) basso timp.
MS parts (c.1825 - 1850): CZ-Bu, St.Mus.2-622.422.

Austro-Moravia: Brno (Brünn), Augustinian Monastery Harmonie
A-133. Allegro in G. Large wind band. MS parts: CZ-Bm(au), Inv.43.095/A.31.137.
A-134. 3 Adagio [sic] und ein Poloness mit F clarinetto, (c.1817). 2ob (?)cl(F) 2cl 2hn 2bn.
MS parts: CZ-Bm(au), A.35.264, (?missing cl in F). ★
A-135. Baccanalia, c.1820. 2ob cl(C) cl(D) 2hn 2bn 2tp.
MS parts: CZ-Bm(au), A.36.849. *Possibly a ballet arrangement by P.A. Osswald.* ★
A-136. [8] Deutsche, c.1830. 2ob 2cl(C) 2hn cbn 2tp(F, D). MS parts: CZ-Bm(au), A.35.261. ★
A-137. [6] Deutsche. pic 3cl(C) cl(F) 4hn(C, F) 2bn 2tp b-tb db b-dr, tambour picc.
MS parts: CZ-Bm(au), A.35.260. ★
A-138. [10] Deutsche à Harmonie. pic 2cl(C) cl(D) 2hn 2bn cbn 2tp. MS parts: CZ-Bm(au), A.35.262. ★
A-139. Schlitasch Deutsche. 2ob 2cl(A, D) 2hn 2bn cbn 2tp. MS parts: CZ-Bm(au), A.36.893, No. 4. ★
A-140. Divertimento, 1827. Solo Klappen-trompett, 2ob 2cl 2hn 2bn cbn tp.
MS parts: CZ-Bm(au), A.37.322. *This may be Starke's untraced* Zweites Concertino für die Klappen-Trompette
mit Harmoniebegleitung, *c.1825, from the* Journal für militarische Musik, *Heft 120.* ★
A-141. 5 Ecossa a Harmonie. pic 2ob 2cl(C) cl(D) 2hn 2bn cbn 2tp posthorn.
MS parts (pre-1830): CZ-Bm(au), A.35.263. ★
A-142. Eccossaise et Walzer. pic cl(F) 2cl 2hn 2bn cbn 2tp. MS parts: CZ-Bm(au), A.37.323. ★
A-143. [2] Hongroises, 1817. 2ob cl(F) 3cl 2hn 2bn 2tp. MS parts: CZ-Bm(au), A.35.265. ★
A-144. [8] Ländler in Es [E♭]. 2cl cl(E♭) 2hn 2bn cbn 2tp. MS parts (c.1830): CZ-Bm(au), A.37.324. ★
A-145. 4 Ländler mit Trio. pic cl(F) 2cl(C) 2hn 2bn cbn 2tp. MS parts (c.1820): CZ-Bm(au), A.18.773. ★
A-146. [3 Marches & 1 Andante]. 2cl 2hn 2bn. MS parts: CZ-Bm(au), A.35.926. ★
A-147. Parthia in A, 5 mvts. 2cl(A) bn. MS parts: CZ-Bm(au), A.20.484. ★
A-148. [untitled Parthia in A♭], 4 mvts. 2ob 2cl 2hn 2bn. MS parts: CZ-Bm(au), A.36.852. ★
A-149. Nro 46 Parthia in Dis [E♭]; 4 mvts. 2cl 2hn bn.
MS parts (by P: Wosanlo, c.1800): CZ-Bsa, fond Staré Brno E4/1092. ★
A-150. Polonaise. pic cl(F) 3cl(C) 4hn(C, F) 2bn 5tp(C, C, F, F, B♭) tb db b-dr s-dr.
MS parts: CZ-Bm(au), A.36.854, (21 parts). ★
A-151. Pot Pourri, Nro 2. pic fl cl(F) 2cl(C) 2hn(C, F) 2bn 3tp b-tb b-dr s-dr.
MS parts: CZ-Bm(au), A.35.268. ★
A-152, 153. Quadrille Conversation; 5 mvts [and] Vorspiel Quadrille, 4 mvts, with 2 Mazurs.
cl(G) 2cl(D) 2hn bn cbn 2tp. MS parts: CZ-Bm(au), A.40.150. *The cl(D) leads throughout.* ★
A-154. Wachtel-Polka. fl ob 2cl(D) 2hn 2bn cbn 2tp. MS parts: CZ-Bm(au), A.35.269. ★
A-155. [5] Walzer a Harmonie. cl(F) 2cl 2hn 2bn cbn 2tp. MS parts: CZ-Bm(au), A.35.270. ★
A-156. 4 Walzer a Harmonie. cl(F) 2cl(C) 2hn 2bn cbn 2tp. MS parts (1817): CZ-Bm(au), A.35.271. ★
A-157. Introduzione [& 3 Walzer/Deutsche with Trios]. pic cl(F) 3cl(C) 4hn(C, G) 2bn cbn 4tp(2C, 2F) b-dr.
MS score & parts: CZ-Bm(au), A.36.855, (the parts end before the Trio to No. 2). ★
A-158. Walzer. 2ob cl(E♭) 2cl(B♭) 2hn 2bn. MS parts: CZ-Bm(au), A.37.329. ★
A-159. [6] Favorit-Walzer. pic cl(F) 2cl(C) 2hn 2bn cbn 2tp. MS parts (c.1818): CZ-Bm(au), A.37.328. ★
A-88v. Stationes Corporis Christi…quas procuravit Dominus Joannes Casparus Grosmuk Civis et Consul
(?)Vekro Brunensis descripsit et choro Parochiae hujus donavit Dominus Josephus Grosmuk tunc Regens Chori
in (?)balveis Carolianis in Bohemia Anno Domini 1794. SATB, 2fl 2cl 2hn 2bn 2tp(clarini) timp organ.
MS parts: CZ-Bm(au), A.20.505. ★

Austro-Moravia: Bystřice pod Hostýnem, Church Band
A-89v. Hymnus Pro Natalitia Christi Redemptor, "Jesu Redemptor omnium". CATB, 2cl 2hn bn organ.
MS parts (by Wendelin Lerch): CZ-Bm(bh), A.9274, (vocal parts only) & A.9272, (instrument parts, with
additional parts for: fl tp(prin)). ★
A-90v. Missa in C, Böhmischen Text. CATB, 2fl 2cl 2hn organ(oblig) basso.
MS parts (by Reg: W[endelin]: Lerch, 1863): CS-Bm(bh), A.9277, (missing A, basso). ★
A-91v. Mše. SATB, fl 2cl 2hn 2tp timp. MS parts: CZ-Bm(bh), A.9280. ★
A-92v. Pangelingua [sic] in D. CC, 2cl 2hn bn. MS parts: CZ-Bm(bh), A.9203. ★
A-93v. Pangelingua [sic] für Blech[bläser]. CATB, fl 2cl 2hn 2flug b-flug 5tb timp.
MS parts: CZ-Bm(bh), A.9297. ★
A-94v. Pastoral Graduale in C, "Jesu Redemptor omnium". CATBB, fl 2cl(C) 2hn 2flug bomb org.
MS parts (by W. Lerch, 23 XII [1]847): CZ-Bm(bh), A.9268. ★

Austro-Moravia: Čehovice (Čehowitz) u Prostějova (Prossnitz), Church Band
A-24t. 4 Smuteční pochody; (F minor, Ab, F minor, Ab). fl (solo)cl(Eb) 3cl(Bb) 2hn 4tp 2flug euph helikon b-tb b-dr s-dr. MS parts: CZ-Bm(cp), A.11.299. ★
A-25t. Trauer Marsch [Ab] für eine 10 stimmige Harmonie. 2cl 2hn 2tp flug b-flug basso.
MS parts ("Vttaslaw den 26/5 [1]867"): CZ-Bm(bh), A.11.302. ★
A-95v. Pastoral Pangelingua in Es (Eb). CATB, 2fl 2cl 2hn 2tp 4flug bomb.
MS parts (by Wyvlečka): CZ-Bm(cp), A.11.593, (here for CATB & organ only). ★
A-150tv. Píseň pohřební nad dospělyším dítětem: "Pohledte přatelé rozmalí". CATB, 2cl 2hn basso.
MS parts (by Karel Chlup): CZ-Bm(cp), A.11.598. ★
A-151tv. Píseň pohřební nad ditken: "Rodičove milí, proč pláčete. CATB, 2cl 2hn basso.
MS parts (by Karel Chlup): CZ-Bm(cp), A.11.597,)with duplicate CA parts). ★
A-152tv. 2 pohřební sbory ("Stalo se ře smrt ukrutná", "Hle tu příklad směnlivosti").
CATB, 2cl 2hn 2tp flug t-hn tb basso. MS vocal score & pts (by František Chlup): CZ-Bm(cp), A.11.603. *The same music is used for both settings.* ★
A-153tv. Smuteční sbor. "Vmavá rakev jest tvé luřko". CATB, 2cl 2hn t-hn flug(Bb) tb basso.
MS parts: CZ-Bm(cp), A.11.300. ★
A-154tv. Smuteční sbory. CATB/TTBB, 2cl hn 2tp crt 2flug tb basso.
MS vocal score & full parts: CZ-Bm(cp), A.301. *No. 1 bears the note, "Velmi zdlouha" (very long, extended); No. 3, "Vážuě s eitem"; No 4, "Zdlouka" (long, extended).* ★
154.1tv. U domu [at home] (Kuěre) "Pruchlotemné zvonů znění"
154.2tv. U hrobu [at the grave] (Kuěre) "Kráčí dělmík po sve práci".
154.3tv. U domu (učitele) Délmík kráčí po své práci". 154.4tv. U hrobu, "V libém dřímej spánku".

Austro-Moravia: České Křídlovice, Church Band
A-155tv. Todtenlied, "Eine Hand voll Erde". CATB, 2cl 2hn bonb. MS pts: A.43.566, (missing instruments). ★
A-156tv. Todten-Lied, "Zum Grabe geht die Reise". CATB, 2cl hn(II).
MS parts: CZ-Bm(ck), A.43.570, (probably missing hn(I) & bomb). ★

Austro-Moravia: Hranice (Mährische-Weisskirchen), Church Band.
A-157tv. Gesang bey dem Heilgen Mess-opfer. CATB, 2fl 2tp 2organ.
Pc (Bey Triedrich Eurich, k.k. priv. accademischen Kunst-Musik und Buchhandlung: Linz, sd), parts: CZ-Bm(hr), A.5901, (MS copy by Edmund Joannes Svaczek). ★

Austro-Moravia: Júr u Bratislavy, Svatý Júr, Church/Town Band
A-160. Pièces d'Harmonie, 8 mvts. 2cl 2hn 2bn.
MS score (c.1800): CZ-Bm(jb), A.52.111, (missing Nos. 2 - 6). ★
A-158tv. Cantio funebris, "In ictu oculi clanduntur". CAB, 2fl 2hn basso.
MS parts: CZ-Bm(jb), A.52.103, (missing C, B, fl I, hn I).

Austro-Moravia: Kamenice u Jihlavy, Church/Castle band
A-37m. [2] Marsch, Nur flott. cl(I, Eb) cl(II, Bb) 3tp flug b-flug basso. MS pts: CZ-Bm(kj), A.40.029. ★
A-96v. Nyní zde jest. CATB, 2cl 2hn flug basso. MS pts (c.1860): CZ-Bm(kj), A.40.030. ★
A-97v. Miserere mej Deus. C, 2cl 2hn tp. MS pts (c.1835): MS parts: CZ-Bm(kj), A.40.023. ★
A-98v. Cantilena, "Člověk z ženy narozený žije jenou". here: CATB, cl I & II, tp II & III.
MS parts ("Joseph Ulreich mpria den 11/3 1835"): CZ-Bm(kj), A.40.012, (missing tp I, ? and basso). ★

Austro-Moravia: Karlovice u Bruntálu (Freudenthal), Aloys Englisch[e] collection
CZ-Bm(kh), A.36.601 is a Todten-Arie ("Steh still o Mensch", c.1830) for CATB, 2cl.
A-26t. II Todten-Marsch mit gänzlich Orchester. cl(Eb) 2cl(Bb) 2hn basso.
MS parts (c.1840): CZ-Bm(kb), A.36.574. ★
A-159tv. Grab-Gesang, "Nun bringen wir dem Leib zur Ruh". Solo TB, terz-fl cl(Eb) 2cl(Bb) 2hn bn b-tb.
MS parts: CZ-Bm(kb), A.36.603. ★
A-160tv. Funeral chorus in Eb, "Alles schläft den Todesschlummer". CATB, 2cl 2hn bn tp(clar) 2tp(prin).
MS parts: CZ-Bm(kb), A.36.586, No. 2. ★
A-161tv. Todten-Lied, "O betrübte Lebenszeiten". B solo, fl 2cl 2hn bn tp. MS pts: CZ-Bm(kb), A.36.584. ★
A-162.1tv(-162.10tv). [10] Pohřební sbory. CATB, 2cl 2hn bn 2tp. MS pts (c.1835): CZ-Bm(kb), A.36.579. ★
162.1tv. "Hochst betrübt mit schweren Herzen". 162.2tv. "Herr ist deine kühle Ruhestätte".
162.3tv. "Ruhe Vater in der Gruft". 162.4tv. "Im Himmel ist Frieden, in Grabe ist Ruh".
162.5tv. "Senkt die Bahre still hier nieder". 162.6tv. "Lerne hier o! eitle Jungend".
162.7tv. "Wie der Baum entleert von Laube". 162.8tv. "Gute Nacht deine Wahlfart ist vollbrecht".
162.9tv. "Bald wirel nun die Stunde schlagen". 162.10tv. "Eine Hand voll Erde".
A-163.1tv(-163.3tv). 2 tříhlasé pohřební sbory. CAB, 2cl 2hn bn(vel tb). MS parts (c.1840): CZ-Bm(kb), A.36.600. *A-163.3tv is written on the verso of the instrumental parts and is probably of a later date.* ★
163.1tv. "O Traurigkeit, O Herzenslied". 163.2tv. "Hartes Herz lass dich erweichen". 163.3tv. "Seht heute an"
A-164.1tv(-164.23tv). [23] Todten-Marsch für Erwachsene. CATB, 2cl 2hn bn.
MS parts (c.1830): CZ-Bm(kb), A.36.578. ★
164.1tv. "Im Grabe ist Ruh". 164.2tv. "Der Herz der Ernte winket". 164.3tv. "Vollendet is dein Pilgerlauf".
164.4tv. "Alles alles ist auf Erden". 164.5tv. "Wir alle müussen, dieser alt und jung".
164.6tv. "Was frag ich nach der Welt". 164.7tv. "Hinweg ihr Eitelkeiten".
164.8tv. "Mein schmerzenvollen Leben". 164.9tv. "Hier senken wir".
164.10tv. "Geweichter Ort wo Saat von Gott". 164.11tv. "Welt mein Abschied ist gemacht".
164.12tv. "Deiner Pilgerlauf lasst du vollendet". 164.13tv. "Lasst dem Tode seiner Raub".
164.14tv. "Lebet wohl! Dieses Erdenlebens Stunden". 164.15.tv. "Meiner Jahre Lauf hab ich vollstrecket".
164.16tv. "Es sinkt der Leib ins kühle Grab". 164.17tv. "Kirchhof heil'ge Stätte, wenn ich dich betrete".
164.18tv. "Auferstehn ist des Christen". 164.19tv. "Ruhig ist des Todesschlummer".
164.20tv. "Nun ists geschehn mich trifft . . ." 164.21tv. "Nun sind sie hin die harten Stunden".
164.22tv. "Seelig die im Herrn verschieden". 164.23tv. "In den frühling meiner Jarhr . . . Herr!"

A-165.1tv(-165.16tv). [7] Todten-Arien für Kinder. CATB, 2cl 2hn bn.
MS parts: CZ-Bm(kb), A.36.580, Oddíl. a. ★
    165.1tv. "Schlummre senft du theurer süsser Liebling". 165.2tv. "Was was ist doch der Menschen Leben".
    165.3tv. "Du bist nicht mehr, du kleinen theures Wessen". 165.4tv. "Wenn kleine Himmelserben".
    165.5tv. "Du hast dein Ziel errungen". 165.6tv. "Schmerzenstöne hallen".
    165.7tv. "Weint Alern, weint denn eure Zähren".
A-166.1tv(-166.9tv). [9] Todten-Arien für Kinder. CATB, 2cl 2hn bn.
MS parts: CZ-Bm(kb), A.36.580, Oddíl. b. ★
    166.1tv. "Wie kurz ist doch die Lebensbahn". 166.2tv. "Du junge Christin lomm und schau".
    166.3tv. "Nimm diess Kind des lebensende". 166.4tv. "Die Rosen welken und verschwinden".
    166.5tv. "Von meinen Altern dich mich lieben". 166.6tv. "Ich sah kaum das Licht der Welt".
    166.7tv. "So wie nach Sturmes Wüthen". 166.8tv. "Sind denn die Todten zu beweinen".
    166.9tv. "Ruhe sanft endlich hast du überweinden".
A-167.1tv(-167.10tv). [10] Pohřební sbory pro smíšený volální čtyřlas. CATB, 2cl 2hn tb.
MS parts (c.1830): CZ-Bm(kb), A.36.574. ★
    167.1tv. "Aus der Tiefe rufe ich: Herr zu dir erhöre". 165.2tv. "Hier lieg ich im Sarge hier lieg ich im Grab".
    167.3tv. "Ich muss die Welt verlassen". 167.4tv. "Wir stehn beim Sarg und hoffen doch".
    167.5tv. "Schlummre sanft im kühlen Satten". 167.6tv. "Bethend lag ich auf den . . ."
    167.7tv. "Gedenk o Mensch, du bist von Staube". 167.8tv. "Wer ist der Mensch, der sagen darf".
    167.9tv. "Es ist vollbracht Was Gott beschlossen über mich".
    167.10tv. "Schlaf geliebte Schwester ein, schlaf im Grabe . . ."
A-168.1tv(-168.11tv). [11 funeral choruses]. here only: CATB, cl(I) 2hn.
MS parts: CZ-Bm(kb), A.36.581, (probably missing cl II, bn). ★
    168.1tv. " Schlafe wohl in kühler Erde". 168.2tv. "Aus der düstern Staubeswelt".
    168.3tv. "Ganz stille schleicht der kalte Tod". 168.4tv. "Aus sammelt Alle, Klein und Gross".
    168.5tv. "Immer näher kommt das Grab". 168.6tv. "Wiedersehn! Wort des Trostes!"
    168.7tv. "Freunde, denkt an meine Bahre". 168.8tv. "Dein Augenpaar von Gott erhellt".
    168.9tv. "Hier Mensch, hier lerne, was du bist". 168.10tv. "Holdes Kind! das schmerzlich wir beweinen".
    168.11tv. "Gefühlvoll. Salve Regina. "Sei Mutter der Bermherzigkeit".
A-169.1tv, 169.2tv. [2] Cantus Funebralis pro Parvulus. CATB, 2ob 2hn [bn].
MS parts (c.1835): CZ-Bm(kb), A.36.594. *A bn or other bass instrument may have read off the Bass voice pt.* ★
    169.1tv. "Nur fort mit mir zum Grabe fort". 169.2tv. "Ihr Ältern gute Nacht".
A-170.1tv, 170.2tv. [2] Cantus Funebralis in Dis (E♭). CATB, 2cl 2hn [bn].
MS parts (c.1830): CZ-Bm(kb), A.36.602. *A bn or other bass instrument may have read off the Bass voice pt.* ★
    170.1tv. "Mit meinen Wanderstabe". 170.2tv. "Was frag ich nach der Welt".

Austro-Moravia: Kojetín (Kojetein), Church Band
A-161. 5 Aufzüge in D oder C für ganz Harmonie. 2cl 2hn 2kl-tp 2tp(prin) tp(A) timp.
MS parts (by Anton Steinmacher, 10 March 1844): CZ-Bm(ko), A.11.671. ★
A-99v. Cur mundis militat. C, 2cl 2hn bn organ.
MS parts (c.1835): CZ-Bm(ko), A.11.818, (with performance dates between 1835 & 1846). ★
A-100v. Písen na weliky Pátek [Good Friday], CA, 2cl 2hn bn. MS parts (by Anton Steinmacher, 17 April 1835): CZ-Bm(ko), A.11.703, (with performance dates between 1835 & 1852). ★

Austro-Moravia: Kroměříž (Kremsier), Harmonie(n) of the Archbishops of Olmütz (Olomouc)
A-162. Adagio [& And[an]te Cantabile] et Variatione. 2fl 2cl 2hn 2bn. MS parts: CZ-KRa, A4489/R.I.59. ★
A-163. Divertimento in D, in one long mvt. Solo flute, solo klappen-trumpet, 2cl(A) 2hn 2bn.
MS parts (c.1824): CZ-KRa, A4020/IV.B.194. ★
A-164. Divertimento in E♭, 4 long mvts. 2cl bthn bn. MS parts: CZ-KRa, A4021/IV.B.195. ★
A-165(-A-184). 20 Parthien; (1: E♭, 5 mvts; 2: E♭, 6 mvts; 3: E♭, 4 mvts; 5: E♭, 6 mvts; 6: E♭, 6 mvts; 7: E♭, 5 mvts; 8: E♭, 5 mvts; 9: B♭, 6 mvts; 10: B♭, 4 mvts; 11: B♭, 5 mvts; 12: E♭, 6 mvts; 13: E♭, 6 mvts; 14: B♭, 6 mvts; 15: E♭, 3 mvts; 16: A, 7 mvts; 17: D, 9 mvts; 18: C, 7 mvts; 19: E♭, 7 mvts; 20: C, 5 mvts. Nos. 1 - 15 & 19: 2cl 2hn bn; Nos. 15 - 18 & 20, 2cl bn 2vla.
MS parts (1770s/1780s): CZ-KRa, A4023/IV.B.197, (the "Violetta" parts are written in the horn parts). *Neumann and Hantke are the likely composers for these works.* ★
A-185. Parthia Ex F; 4 mvts. 2ob 2hn 2bn. MS parts: CZ-KRa, A4031/IV.B.204. ★
A-186. [?Schuester:] Parthia ex C, 5 mvts. 2ob 2hn 2bn. MS parts: CZ-KRa, A4033/IV.B.206. ★
A-187. Parthia Ex C; 5 mvts. 2ob 2hn 2bn. MS parts: CZ-KRa, A.4034/IV.B.207. ★
A-188. [Parthia in C], 11 mvts. 2ob 2hn bn. MS parts: CZ-KRa, A.4035/IV.B.208. ★
A-189. [Parthia in A], 5 mvts. 2cl 2hn bn. MS parts: CZ-KRa, A.4036/IV.B.209. ★
A-190. [Parthia] Nro VI; in E♭, 4 mvts. 2cl 2hn 2bn. MS parts (by Havel, c.1805): A4455/R.I.21, No. 6. ★
A-191. Serenata [in pencil: 10]; in E♭, 2/3 mvts. MS parts (by Havel, c.1805): A4455/R.I.21, No. [10]. ★
A-192. [Parthia, pencil: 12]; in E♭, 4 mvts. MS parts (by Havel, c.1805): A4455/R.I.21, No. [12]. ★
A-193. [pencil: 13] Parthie; in E♭, 4 mvts. MS parts (by Havel, c.1805): A4455/R.I.21, No. [13]. ★
A-194. [pencil: 14] Parthie; in E♭, 4 mvts. MS parts (by Havel, c.1805): A4455/R.I.21, No. [14]. ★
A-195. Poloness /:Den so sehr geliebten Redout=paree:/, Poloness [with 3 Trios], Quadrille in C, Contra[tanz] in C, Polaca [sic], No. 2 [Polacca]. 2cl 2hn 2bn. MS score: CZ-KRa, A4037/IV.B.210. ★
A-196. [6] Waltzer, Baaden 1816. 2cl 2hn 2bn. MS parts: CZ-KRa, A4191/R.I.63. ★
A-101v. Hymnus pro Solemni (Iste confessor). SATB, 2ob 2cl 2hn 2bn 2tp. MS: CZ-KRa. ★

Austro-Moravia: Lomnice u Rýmařova, Church Band
A-102v. [4 Stationes] Für Frohleichnamsfest, Auf dem Wege von der Kirche bis zum ersten Oltar. CATB, 2hn 2bn bn. MS parts: CZ-Bm(lr), A.22.250, No. 1. *At the end of the Canto part is the date, "22/5 1878" - probably a performance date rather that of composition.* ★
A-103v. IV Stationes. SATB, cl I, 2hn 2flug basso. MS parts: CZ-Bm(lr): A.22.250, No. 2. ★

A-171tv. [7 funeral choruses]. CATB, fl 2cl 2hn bn. MS parts: CZ-Bm(lr), A.22.261.
  171.1tv. "Mutig mutig! Bald errungen est". 171.2tv."Ich weiss an wen ich glaube".
  171.3tv. "Wiederseh[e]n! Im Abenscheine flüsterts". 171.4tv. "Wie ein frühlingsmorgen schön frei".
  171.5tv. "Schlummare sanft Straub dem der Erde Schoss". 171.6tv. "Oede dumgt und schaurig ist das".
  171.7tv. "Wer versteht Gott! dienen Rat?"
A-172tv. Trauer Lied in Es [E♭], "Hier senken wir die schöne Gottessaat [sic]". B solo, SAT chorus, Harmonie.
MS parts: CZ-Bm(lr), A.22.242. *Pössel, ( ) may be either the composer or copyist.*

Austro-Moravia: Lukov - Horní Břečkov, Church Bands
A-104v. Animus [fidelium] in Es [E♭]. CATB, 2cl 2hn bn. MS parts (c.1850): CZ-Bm(lb), A.46.845. ★

Austro-Moravia: Nové Město na Moravě (Neustadl), Church Band *(See also: Johann Róhlík)*
A-105v. Echo Misa, in C. SS, 2cl 2hn bn tp(prin) timp.
MS parts (2 August 1821, copy by Kudrna): CZ-Bm(nm), A.551. ★

Austro-Moravia: Nová Říše (Neureisch), Monastery Kapelle & Harmonie
A-197. Parthia in Dis [E♭]; 6 mvts. 2cl 2hn bn. MS parts: CZ-NR, A.18.238. ★
A-106v. Pange lingua ex Dis [E♭] pro Festo S.S. Corporis Christi. SSATB, 2cl 2hn bn.
MS parts: CZ-NR, A.17.989. ★

Austro-Moravia: Ostrava, Český roshlas (Czech Radio) *In most cases, original provenance is unknown)*
A-107v. Missa in D. 2fl 2cl(vel oboe) 2hn 2bn 2tp(clar) tp(prin) 2vla timp.
MS parts: CZ-OScr, 2135, (missing vocal parts). ★
A-108v. [4 Stationes]. CATB, 2fl 2ob 2cl 2hn 2bn. MS parts: CZ-OScr, 2142. ★
A-173.1tv, 173.2tv. [2 Trauergesänge], "Sieh o Mensch", in A♭, & "Senkt ihm dem Todten", in E♭.
2cl 2hn flug b-flug b-tb. MS parts: CZ-OScr, 2144a, 2144b, (missing vocal parts). ★

Austro-Moravia: Ostrava (Ostrau), Church Band
A-109v. O Salutaris hostia. CATB, 2ob 2cl/fl 2hn bn. MS parts ("Ex Musicalibus Thomae Cžaban mp"):
CZ-Bm(os), A.48.455, (missing CA, 2cl/fl 2hn). *Tomáš Cžaban may possbily be the composer.*
A-110v. Salve Regina. 3 voices (?ATB), 2cl 2hn bn. MS score ("Gewidmet dem Herrn Valentin Bažan,
Recori=Chori in Mähr: Ostrau. A.D. 1830"): CZ-Bm(os), A.48.455. ★
A-111v. Salve Regina / Libera [me]. ATB, 2cl 2hn. MS parts (c.1840, by Valentin Bažan, Chor Rector
through at least 1859): CZ-Bm(os), A.48.472. *Composition by Rettig?* ★
A-174tv. [40] Begräbniss-Lieder pro Choro Morovo-Ostraviae, Zum Officium. AB, cl(E♭) cl(B♭) hn(II) bn(II).
MS parts (c.1820): CZ-Bm(os), A.48.478, (missing parts; texts primarily in Czech). ★

Austro-Moravia: Rajhrad (Gross Raigern), Benedictine Harmonie
A-198.1, 198.2. Duo [sic] Menueti com Trios. 2cl 2hn bthn bn.
MS parts ("Ex Rebus Ignatii Beck"): CZ-Bm(rj), A.14.436, (missing cl I). ★
A-199. Oktet; in E♭, 4 mvts. 2ob 2cl 2hn 2bn. MS parts: CZ-Bm(rj), A.14.435. ★
A-112v. Gelobt sey Jesus Christus! Gesang ohne oder mit Begleitung auf acterley Art. Auwerdbar: zu jeder Leis,
für Stadt und Land in und auser der Kirche. SATB, 2fl 2ob 4cl 2hn 4bn basso 4tp 2tb timp organ.
Pc (In Sauer's K.K. priv. Kunstverlag: Wien, pn S.S.179, c.1805), score: CZ-Bm(rj), A.14.428;
CZ-NR, A.18.133, (parts, for SATB, 2fl 2ob 4cl 2bn 2bn(basso) 2cbn 4tp 2tb timp harp hpcd/organ). ★
A-113v. Pangelingua [sic] ex Dis [E♭]. SAB, 2fl 2hn 2bn 2vla basso.
MS parts (1 Nov 1822): CZ-Bm(rj), A.13.246. ★
A-114v. Píseň, "Cur mundus milita". SATB, 2cl 2hn bn tb(doubles bn). MS parts: CZ-Bm(rj), A.14.460. ★
A-115v. Píseň ke Mssi Swalé we čsursek. SATB, 2cl 2hn organ.
MS parts (17 Nov 1831): CZ-Bm(rj), A.14.459. ★
A-175tv. Píseň pokřební; "Na den kněwu, na den žalosli". SATB, 2cl 2hn bn. MS pts: CZ-Bm(rj), A.14.455. ★
A-176tv. Píseň pokřební; "Již jest mně došli má léka". SATB, 2cl 2hn bn. MS pts: CZ-Bm(rj), A.14.457. ★
A-177tv. Píseň pokřební; "Nyní wiussawaná cesta". SATB, 2cl 2hn bn. MS parts: CZ-Bm)rj), A.14.474. ★

Austro-Moravia: Rešov, Church Band
A-116v. Pangelingua [sic] & Vexila regis. CATB, 2cl 2hn db/bn. MS parts (c.1850-75, "V. Moritz Hilscher /
Organist mpria"): CZ-Bm(re), A.42.710. ★

Austro-Moravia: Rozstání, Church Band
A-200. Märsche Frohnleichn[amsfest]. fl 3cl 2hn tp(clar) 2tp(prin) 3flug timp.
MS parts: CZ-Bm(ro), A.23.405, (missing hn II). ★
A-27t. Sbírka smutečných pochodů [collection of mourning marches]. 2cl 2tp 2flug basso.
MS parts (25 May 1870): CZ-Bm(ro), 27.213. *One march only.* ★
A-28t. Hudba byslivechá a Sbor poděkování. 2cl 2tp 2flug basso.
MS parts (26 July 1874): CZ-Bm(ro), A.27.245, (missing cl II, tp I, flug II). ★
A-117v. Brautlied ("Singt mit fröhlichen Gemüthe, Brätigan mit seiner Braut") vor und nach der Frauung
("Befehlt dem höchsten euer Leben). CAB, fl 2cl 2hn 2tp basso.
MS pts (by Leopold Kunerth): CZ-Bm(ro), A.23.398, (missing fl). *The fl probably doubled the S (vocal) pt.* ★
A-118v. [4 Stationes] pro Festo ad Prozessionen SS. Corporis Christi. CATB, fl 3cl 2hn tp(clar) tp(prin) flug
basso timp. MS parts (? by Leopold Kunerth): CZ-Bm(ro), A.23.403, (missing hn II). ★
A-119v. Stationes I - IV. CATB, 2cl 2hn 2tp t-hn basso. MS parts: CZ-Bm(ro), A.23.404. ★

Austro-Moravia: Trěbíč (Trebitsch), Church Band
No specific Harmonie works appear in this collection, but we note an Echo Missa in C *(MS parts: CZ-Bm(tr),
A.7568)* for CCAB, 2vl 2cl 2hn 2tp(clar) tp(prin) timp organ, with an Echo of CC, 2cl 2hn bn tp(prin) timp.

Austro-Slovakia: Kežmarok, Church Band
A-120v. Missa in C. TTBB, 2ob 2cl 2hn 2bn 2tp(clar) cb timp. MS parts: SK-BRnm, IX.438. ★
A-121v. Missa in E♭, 1807. TTBB, 2fl 2cl 4hn 2bn cb. MS parts: SK-BRnm, IX.180. ★

Austro-Slovakia: Trenčín (Trentschin), Church Band
A-122v. Sequentia ("Stabat Mater"). SATB, 2ob 2cl 2hn 2bn 2vla. MS parts: SK-BRnm, XIII.172. ★

France: Anonymous Works

Where applicable, works carry the reference numbers (such as P.2329) assigned by Constant Pierre in Musique des Fêtes et Cérémonies de la Révolution Français. Imprimerial Nationale: Paris, 1899.

A-39m. Marche, pour harmonie (F) (1er orchestre, No. 1); P.2329.
p-fl 2ob cl(F) 2cl(C) 2hn 2bn tp tb serp timp cym b-dr.
MS parts: F-Pn, (old shelfmark: Musique d'harmonie, paquet 50; untraced). ★
A-40m. Marche, pour harmonie (Bb) (1er orchestre, No. 2); P.2330.
p-fl 2ob cl(F) 2cl(C) 2hn 2bn tp tb serp timp cym b-dr.
MS parts: F-Pn, (old shelfmark: Musique d'harmonie, paquet 50; untraced). ★
A-41m. Marche, pour harmonie (Bb) (2e orchestre, No. 1), P.2331.
p-fl 2ob cl(F) 2cl(C) 2hn 2bn tp tb serp timp b-dr cym.
MS parts: F-Pn, (old shelfmark: Musique d'harmonie, paquet 50; untraced). ★
A-42m. Marche, pour harmonie (Eb) (2e orchestre, No. 2), P.2332.
p-fl 2ob cl(F) 2cl(C) 2hn 2bn tp tb serp timp b-dr cym.
MS parts: F-Pn, (old shelfmark: Musique d'harmonie, paquet 50; untraced). ★
A-43m. Marche religieuse, pour harmonie militaire (F); P.2281. (Harmonie pour les cérémonies lugubres, No. 6).
4cl 2hn 2bn. MS parts: F-Pn, (old shelfmark: Musique d'harmonie, paquet 30a; untraced). ★
A-44m. Marche religieuse, pour harmonie militaire; P.2282. (Harmonie pour les cérémonies lugubres, No. 2).
4cl 2hn 2bn. MS parts: F-Pn, (old shelfmark: Musique d'harmonie, paquet 30a; untraced). ★
A-45m. Recueil de Marches a 8 parties. 2vl 2ob 2hn 2bn. ★
Pc (chez Jolivet: Paris, sd), parts: CZ-Pnm, XLII.A.346. ★
   45.1m(a). Monsigny: Ouverture du Déserteur.   45.2m(a). Grétry: Marche du Huron.
   45.3m(a). Grétry: Marche Des janissaires dans les deux Avares.   45.4m. Anon: Marche Des Gardes Suisses.
   45.5m. Anon: Marche Des Gardes Françaises.   45.6m. Anon: Marche Des Mousquetaires.
A-46m(a). Recueil des Marches a 6 Parties. 2vl 2hn 2bn.
Pc (chez Jolivet: Paris, sd), parts: CZ-Pnm, XLII.A.346. ★
   46.1m(a). [Rameau: Castor et Pollux]: Marche de Castor.   46.2m(a). [Mondonville]: Marche de Thesée.
   46.3m(a). [Campra]: Marche de Tancrède.   46.4m(a). [Montclair]: Marche de Jepthé.
   46.5m(a). [Gervais]: Marche d'Hypermernestre.   46.6m(a). [Dauvergne]: Marche d'Hercule Mourant.
A-47m - A-54m are a fascinating set of marches, each part printed on stiff card (c.4½" x 4"; 115mm x 100mm), described as "detachées et mises dans une form portative". This is one of (if not the) earliest printed set specifically intended for bands either marching or on parade. Separate title cards are included with each March
A-47m. 1re Marche (celle des Gardes Françoises), à cinq parties, in C. 2cl 2hn bn
Pc (Mle Castagnery: Paris, sd, c.1755), RISM [AN 1658], pts: D-SWl, Mus. 571, (missing cl II). ★
A-48m. 2me Marche (celle des Gardes Suisses), à cinq parties, in C. 2cl(C) 2hn bn.
Pc (Mle Castagnery: Paris, sd, c.1755), RISM [AN 1658], parts: D-SWl, Mus. 571. ★
A-49m. 3me Marche (celle du [Grétry's opera] Huron), à cinq parties, in C. 2cl(C) 2hn bn.
Pc (Mle Castagnery: Paris, sd, c.1755), RISM [AN 1658[, parts: D-SWl, Mus. 571, (missing cl I). ★
A-50m. 4eme Marche (la 1re des Gardes Françoises), à cinq parties, in C. 2cl(C) 2hn bn.
Pc (Mle Castagnery: Paris, sd, c.1755), RISM [AN 1658[, parts: D-SWl, Mus. 571, (missing hn II). ★
A-51m. 5me Marche (la nouvelle des Gardes Françoises), à cinq parties, in C. 2cl(C) 2hn bn.
Pc (Mle Castagnery: Paris, sd, c.1755), RISM [AN 1658], parts: D-SWl, Mus. 571. ★
A-52m. 6eme Marche (celle des Mousquetaires), Six parties, in D. 2cl 2hn 2bn.
Pc (Mlle Castagnery: Paris, sd), RISM [AN 1659], parts: D-SWl, Mus. 571. ★
A-53m. [7me] Marche, à cinq parties, in Eb. 2cl 2hn bn.
Pc (Mle Castagnery: Paris, sd, c.1755), RISM [AN 1658], parts: D-SWl, Mus. 571, (missing title card). ★
A-54m. 8eme Marche (Allemande), à cinq parties, in Eb. 2cl 2hn bn.
Pc (Mle Castagnery: Paris, sd, c.1755), RISM [AN 1658], parts: D-SWl, Mus. 571. *The hn II has been mis-titled "Basson" & vice versa.* ★
A-4ma. Offrande à la Liberté, Arrangée en pot-pouri [sic] pour Musique Militaire; (on the songs: "Veillons au salut de l'Empire"; "La Marseillaise"; "La Carmagnole" and "Ah! ça ira"), (P.2275).
2fl 2cl(C oblig)+2cl(C ripieno) 2hn 2bn tp b-dr+cym.
Pc (Imbault: Paris, pn 391, c.1793/1794), RISM [G 3111], parts: F-Pn, Vm7 7113. ★
A-1mv. Hymne à la Liberté. Musique de ★★★; P.72. Solo voice, 2cl(C) 2hn bn.
Pc (Rec des époques: Paris, c.1799), liv. 1, No. 7, pp. 17 - 18, score: F-Pn, H2. 15,7. *Attributed to Catel by Whitwell; we have not been able to find any confirmation for this attribution.* ★
A-2mv. Le Rappel des Patriotes. Musique de ★★★. Solo voice, 2cl(C) 2hn (2)bn.
Pc (Rec des époques: Paris, c.1799), liv. 1, No. 34, pp. 95 - 96, score: F-Pn, H2. 15,34. ★

Great Britain: Anonymous Works

A-201. Quintetto; in F, 3 mvts. 2cl 2hn bn.
Pc (Longman and Broderip: London, [In: The Clarinet Instructor] c.1780), pp. 28 - 33, score: GB-Lbl, b.160.i.; GB-Ljag (modern score); US-BE; US-Wc. ★
A-55m. A New Set of Military Pieces....Composed in India...for His Majesty's 33rd Regt. [1st West Riding].
2fl cl(Eb) 3cl(Bb) 2hn bn tp serp("Serbando").
Pc (Thomas Key: London, c.1815), score: D-SWl, Mus. 570. ★
   55.1m. Lord Wellington's March.   55.2m. Colonel Gore's March.
   55.3m. Chundah's Song, Hindostan [sic] Air.   55.4m. Colonel Gore's favorite, Quick Step.
   55.5m. Tilby's Waltz.   55.6m. Monte Video [sic].
A-56m. Three Grand Marches, and Three Quick Steps...By an Eminent Master.
pic(Eb) cl(Eb) 2cl(Bb) 2hn (2)bn serp tb cym.
Pc (Wm Napier: London, c.1800), parts: GB-Lbl, R.M.15.g.11; GB-Lkc. ★

A-57m. Royal Westminster Regt. of Militia March. 2ob(& cl) 2hn (2)bn (2)tp serp drum.
Pc (Longman & Broderip: London, c.1790), score: GB-Lbl, g.352.ii.(19). ★
A-58m. Her Royal Highness The Princess Charlotte of Wales's Troop . . . for Her Highness's Regiment of Foot [Loyal MacLeod Fencibles]. 2fl(G) 2cl(B♭) 2hn 2bn tp serp.
Pc (Broderip & Wilkinson: London, wm1800), score: GB-Lbl, g.1780.nn.(17). ★
A-59m. Lord Lewisham's March as Performed by the Staffordshire Militia. 2vl 2ob 2hn 2tp basso timp.
Pc (J. Blundell: London, c.1780), score: GB-Lbl, g.271.t.(13). ★
A-60m. The Arch Duke Charles of Austria's March.   March: 4cl 2hn 2bn; Quick March: 3cl 2hn 2bn.
Pc (Longman & Broderip: London, c.1797), score: GB-Lbl, g.133.(72); GB-Ob. ★
A-61m. The Egyptian March. 2cl 2hn (2)bn tp.
Pc (T. & W.M. Cahusac: London, c.1801), score: GB-Lbl, h.1568.b.(13); GB-DOTams. ★
A-62m. The Grand Neopolitan March. 2cl 2hn (2)bn tp.
Pc (T. & W.M. Cahusac: London, c.1800), score: GB-Lbl, h.1568.b.(12). ★
A-63m. Twenty four Italian Pieces. 2fl 2cl/ob/vl 2hn bn/vc.
Pc (Longman, Lukey & Co.: London, c.1770), pts: GB-Lbl, b.78.a, (flute parts only); GB-CDp (incomplete). ★
A-64m. A Second Collection of XXIV Favourite Marches in 7 Parts As They Are Perform'd by His Majesty's Foot and Horse Guards. 2cl 2vl/fl/ob 2hn bn.
Pc (C. & S. Thompson: London, 1775), parts; GB-Lbl, a.226. ★
A-65m. Eighteen Marches in seven parts . . . by an Eminent Master. 2vl 2ob 2hn basso.
Pc (T. Cahusac & Sons: London), RISM [AN 1710], parts: US-R. ★
A-66m. 24 Military Pieces. Published for the use of his Majesty's Camps. 2cl/ob 2hn 2bn.
Pc (Longman & Broderip: London, sd), parts: D-SWl, Mus. 578. ★
  66.1m. The 20th Reg[i]ment March, ¢. 66.2m. Andante, 3/4.
  66.3m. Marche de Guard de Swiss De La France. 66.4m. Allegro, 2/4.   66.5m. March, 2/4.
  66.6m. March, 3/4. 66.7m. March, 2/4. 66.8m. Mineut [sic, without Trio], 3/4. 66.9m. Andante, 2/4.
  66.10m. Allegro, C. 66.11m. Allemande, 3/8. 66.12m. March, ¢. 66.13m. Polonoise [without Trio], 3/4.
  65.14m. March. 65.15m. Presto, 3/8. 65.16m. Minuetto [without Trio], 3/4. 65.17m. Allemande, 2/4.
  65.18m. The Hunters March. 65.19m. Boure [sic], 2/4. 65.20m. March d'Allarme.
  66.21m. Minuet [without Trio], 3/4. 66.22m. March.
  66.23m.The Royal Cheshire Militia March, ¢. 66.24m. Minuet [without Trio], 3/4.
A-67m. To be continued Monthly. Military Concertos . . . by Different Masters; 8 Nos. comprising 13 works. 2ob/2fl/2cl/2vl 2hn (2)bn.
Pc (Printed & Sold by J. Bremner, Sold also by R. Bremner: London, c.1770), parts: D-SWl, Mus. 344; GB-Lbl, (unconfirmed).
Nos. 1 - 4 are listed in Supplement 6, Part IV, , 1771, of the Breitkopf (Leipzig) catalog as "Concerti Militari da diversi Maestri, *intagl. in Londra / a 2 Oboi o Flauti, 2 Corni, 2 Clarini [sic] & 2 Fagotti";* the complete set is listed in Supplement of 1775; Breitkopf acted as German agent for Bremner. *Some confusion exists surrounding this set. The clarinet parts are, in fact, merely the oboe parts transposed for B♭ clarinet. After the 2nd issue, there is only a single "Fagotto" part, supplied in 2 copies. Issues 3 - 5, 7 & 8 comprise two Concerti; the issues were consecutively paginated. Although it has so far been impossible to identify the composers, we believe that these works are Parthien drawn from various European sources.* ★
  67.1m. Concerto I, in E♭, 5 mvts.
  67.2m. Concerto II, in e♭, 6 mvts. *The bassoons are divisi only in the 3rd mvt.*
  67.3m, 67.4m. Concerto III, in E♭, 3 mvts; Concerto IV, in E♭, 3 mvts.
  67.5m, 67.6m. Concerto V, in E♭, 3 mvts; Concerto VI, in E♭, 3 mvts.
  67.7m, 67.8m. Concerto VII, in E♭, 3 mvts; Concerto VIII, in E♭, 3 mvts.
  67.9m. Concerto IX, in E♭, 3 mvts.
  67.10m, 67.11m. Concerto X, in E♭, 3 mvts; Concerto XI, in E♭, 3 mvts.
  67.12m, 67.13m. Concerto XII, in E♭, 3 mvts; Concerto XIII, in E♭, 3 mvts.
A-68m. Marce e Minue; (11 marches, Nos. 1 - 8 followed by a minuet or balletto; an additional march, in a different hand, probably scored for 2 oboes, appears on f.25). 2ob 2hn basso.
MS score (?c.1740s): GB-Lbl, R.M.24.k.14. ★
A-69m. XXIV favourite Marches in five parts as they are performed by His Majesty's Foot and Horse Guards. 2vl/fl/ob 2hn basso.
Pc (Printed for C. & S. Thompson: London, c. 1765), pts: GB-Lbl, b.78.b, (the 1st & 2nd vl/fl/ob parts only). ★
A-70m. The Slow and Quick March of the Mid-Lothian Artillery. 2cl 2hn bn.
Pc (sn: sl, c.1800), score: GB-En, Glen 347-37/1. ★
A-71m. Lord Ancram's, or Janizaries March, Perform'd in the Two Misers [pastiche written by K. O'Mara] & by the 2d Regt. of Guards. 2cl (2vl *doubling cl, key signature as for B♭ cl*) 2hn basso.
Pc (Str[aight]: & Skill[ern]: London, c.1775), score: GB-Lbl (2 copies), h.1568.u.(12); Mad.Soc.21.(31). ★
A-72m. The Clarinet Instructor by which Playing on that Instrument is rendered easy to anyone unacquainted with Music . . . , by a Capital Performer on the above Instrument. To which is added several Duos for two Clarinets and a Quintetto for Horns, Clarinets and a Bassoon. *The Quintetto is also cited separately as A-151.* 2cl 2hn bn.
Pc (Longman & Broderip: London, c. 1780), score: GB-Lbl, b.160.i; GB-Ljag, (modern MS); US-BE; US-Wc. ★
A-73m. Collection of 47 marches, mostly for specific regiments, in piano score.
Nos. 1, 5, 6, 11, 12, 43, 46 & 47 are by J C. Bach; Nos. 2, 4, 7, 8, 9, 30 & 45 by C. F. Abel "for H.R.H. the Prince of Wales"; No. 3 is by Weideman[n].   MS piano score, (?mid-1780s): GB-Lbl, R.M.24.k.15.
A-3mv. Ye Sons of England take your Arms, A British Allons Enfans [sic] de la Patrie. Performed by the Band of His Royal Highness the Duke of York. 2cl 2hn 2bn.
Pc (Printed for & Sold by J. Dale: London, 1797/1798), score: GB-Lbl, G.376.(46); GB-Ob. ★

Great Britain: London, Royal Music Collection, Music for Harmonie with Basset Horns

The following 3 collections almost certainly date from the 1789 & 1791 visits to London by the itinerent basset horn players Anton David, Valentin Springer and K. Franz Dworschack. David (b. 1730) may have been ill for much of their visits. It is likely that these are the works performed by the wind band supplied by the Duke of York to Vauxhall Gardens - which may have drawn players from the band of the Coldstream Guards ("The Duke of York's Band"). Evidence suggests that C.F. Eley (qv) was cheifly responsible for preparing the music. The principal arrangements (Martín y Soler and Paisiello) appear to be adapted from Went's arrangements and were probably brought to London by the basset hornists.

A-202. [5 sets of original works and arrangements]. 2ob/terz-fl(Nos. 16 - 26, 28 - 47) 2bthn 2hn 2bn serp. MS pts: GB-Lbl, R.M.21.d.2, (missing bn II+serp after 203.3/17; 203.44 has been cut from all parts and tipped-in immediately before the *Divertimento* by Rosetti, FAR-6.1, in A-203; this also affect Nos. 44, 47 & 48).

202.1(a). Divertimento . . . Storace, Pleyel, Attwood.
    202.1/1(a). Storace] In the siege of Belgrade[,] Loud let the song of triumph. Maestoso, C.
    202.1/2(a). [Pleyel: B.111ii, IJP-12.5] Adagio, 2/4 / Allegretto, 2/4.
    202.1/3(a). [Storace] In the siege of Belgrade. Storace. Seize him I say. Allo Spirituoso, 6/8.
    202.1/4(a). Attwood. Mod[e]r[ato], 2/4.
202.2. [Divertimento - Set 2]. *Missing horn parts.*
    202.2/1. March, ¢.   202.2/2. Quick March, 2/4.
    202.2/3(a). [Pleyel: B.349/ii, iii, IJP-13.1, 13.2] Andante, 2/4 / Presto, 2/4.   202.2/4. Allemende [!], 2/4.
202.3. [Set 3, Collection of works].
    202.3/1(a). No. 1. [Pleyel: B.321/ii, IJP-13.3] Moderato, 2/4 [Theme , 2 Variations, Theme].
    202.3/2(a). No. 2. [Pleyel: B.322/i, B.deest, IJP-13.4] Andante Grazioso, 3/8 [f] / Swabisch, 3/8.
    202.3/3. No. 3. Mod[erato], ¢.   202.3/4. No. 4. Siciliano, 6/8.
    202.3/5(a). No. 5. Queen of Summer, 3/4 [2hn tacet].   202.3/6. No. 6. Engl[ese], 2/4.
    202.3/7(a). No. 7. Choral/O Ewigheit du Donner wort, C [bars - 7 :// 4].
    202.3/8(a). No. 8. Choral/Nun ruhen alle Wälder, ¢ [12 bars].
    202.3/9(a). No. 9. Pleyel. Andante con Vars (B.319ii, IJP-13.5). [Theme + 2 Variations].
    202.3/10(a).No. 10. Believe my Sighs my Tears my Dear. Comp by St[ephen]. Paxton. Glee Affectuoso, 3/4.
    202.3/11. No. 11. Allem[ande]: [& Trio] 3/4.   202.3/12. No. 12. Aria, 2/4.
    202.3/13(a). No. 13. Moder[ato]: di Rolle, ¢.   202.3/14. No. 14. Cottilion, [& Trio] 2/4.
    202.3/15. No. 15. Affectuoso, 3/4.   202.3/16(a). No. 16. Hook: Upon my Word I did.
    202.3/17(a). No. 17. [Grétry: Le Huron] March Des Hurons, ¢.
    202.3/18(a). No. 18. [M. Arne: Love in a Village] Affectuoso. Dans votre Lit [my Fanny].
    202.3/19. No. 19. Engl[ese]:, 2/4 [no Trio].   202.3/20(a). No. 20. [William Leeves] The Pigeon.
    202.3/21(a). No. 21. [Hook] Lowland Willy. Presto, 6/8.
    202.3/22. No. 22. Aria, C.   202.3/23. No. 23. Scherzando, 2/4.
    202.3/24(a). No. 24. [Storace] Gavotte. Jeunes Coeurs soyez fidelles. In the Opera La cameriera Astuta.
    202.3/25. No. 25. Cottilion, 2/4.   202.3/26(a). No. 26. [M. Arne] Song in the Heiress. 2/4.
    202.3/27(a). No. 27. Stamitz. March. Comp by Stamitz, ¢.   202.3/28. No. 28. Min[uet]: [& Trio], 3/4.
    202.3/29. No. 29. Allegro, 2/4.   202.3/30. No. 30. Adagio, 3/4.   202.3/31. No. 31. Min[uet]: [& Trio], 3/4.
    202.3/32. No. 32. Cottilion, [& Trio], 2/4.   202.3/33. No. 33. Marcia Moderato, ¢.
    202.3/34. No. 34. Min[uet]: [& Trio], 3/4.   202.3/35. No. 35. Cottilion [& Trio], 2/4.
    202.3/36. No. 36. Adagio, 3/4.   202.3/37. No. 37. March, 2/4.   202.3/38. No. 38. Min[uet]: [& Trio], 3/4.
    202.3/39. No. 39. Engl[ese]: [no Trio], 2/4.   202.3/40. No. 40. Andantino, 2/4.
    202.3/41. No. 41. Min[uet]: [& Trio], 3/4.   202.3/42. No. 42. Cott[ilion]: [& Trio], 2/4.
    202.3/43. No. 43. Min[uet]: [& Trio], 3/4.   202.3/44. No. 44. Pol[onaise]: [& Trio], 3/4.
    202.3/45. No. 45. Cott[ilion]: [& Trio], 2/4.   202.3/46. No. 46. March, ¢.
    202.3/47. No. 47. Min[uet]: [& Trio], 3/4.   202.3/48. No. 48. Min[uet]: [& Trio], 3/4.
    202.3/49. No. 49. Allegretto, 2/4.
Nos. 50, 51, 53, 54 & 56 are drawn from Stephen Paxton's A Collection of Glees, Catches, etc. Op. 5. *1782.*
    202.3/50(a). No. 50. [W. Paxton: Glee] Breathe soft ye Winds.
    202.3/51(a). No. 51. [S. Paxton: Glee] Cupid come without delay.   202.3/52. No. 52. Allegretto, 2/4.
    202.3/53(a). No. 53. Wm. Paxton. Glee. Grant me ye powers.
    202.3/54(a). No. 54. S. Paxton. [Glee] How sweet! How fresh!   202.3/55. No. 55. Andante affectuoso.
    202.3/56(a). No. 56. [W. Paxton: Glee] Soft God of Sleep.   202.3/57. No. 57. Allem[ande]: [& Trio].
Nos. 58 - 63 are probably drawn from a published set of dances.
    202.3/58. No. 58. Le Balon. Presto, C [sic, 2/4].   202.3/59. No. 59. Les Caprices des Hommes. Presto, 6/8.
    202.3/60. No. 60. Les Desirs des Dames. Presto, 6/8.   202.3/61. No. 61. The Brunette. Andante, C.
    202.3/62. No. 62. La Chateau. Presto, 6/8.   202.3/63. No. 63. La Fableau Partant. Cottilion [& Trio], 2/4.
    202.3/64. No. 64. Andante, 3/4.   202.3/65. No. 65. March, 2/4.   202.3/66. No. 66. March, 2/4.
    202.3/67. No. 67. March, 2/4.   202.3/68. No. 68. March, 2/4.   202.3/69. No. 69. March, C.
Nos. 70-76 are based on Went's arrangement for the Schwarzenberg Harmonie (2ob 2ca 2hn 2bn), JNW-40.2a.
[Paisiello] Opera, Il Barbiere di Siviglia. Del Sig. J. Baesello [!].
    202.4/1. No. 70. [Overture] / [I/1. Introduzion: Ecco l'ova s'avvicina] / [I/2. Scena. Dismo alla noja il bando].
    202.4/2. No. 71. [I/3. Aria. Scorsi già molti paesi].   202.4/3. No. 72. [I/3. Duet. Lode al ciel].
    202.4/4. No. 73. [I/6. Canzone. Saper bramante].
    202.4/5. No. 74. [I/10. Terzet: Ah! Rosina!]. *Segue* [I/10a. Ah! chi sa questo suo foglio] Andante, C.
    202.4/6. No. 75. [III/1. Duet: Oh! che umor!] Moderato, 3/4.
    202.4/7. No. 76. [IV/6. Finale. Cara, sei tu il mio bene / (Quand l'amour a la jeunesse)].
    202.5/1. No. 77. Rondo Allegro, 2/4.   202.5/2. No. 78. Andante ma Allegretto, 2/4.
    202.5/3. No. 79. Andante, 3/4 Sempre sotto voce (2hn tacet).   202.5/4. No. 80. Allem: [& Trio], 3/4.
    202.5/5. No. 81. Allem: [& Trio], 3/4.   202.5/6. No. 82. Allem: [& Trio], 3/4.

A-203. [7 Divertimentos].   2ob 2bthn 2hn 2bn serp.   MS parts: GB-Lbl, R.M.21.d.3. *The "No. 44 Polacca"*
parts cut from A-202 are tipped-in immediately before the Divertimento by Rosetti.
  203.1. [Divertimento 1], 15 mvts. 2fl/2ob(Nos. 2 & 12) 2bthn 2hn bn bn+serp.
    203.1/1. No. 1. His Royal Highness's March. March, ¢.   203.1/2. No. 2. Cantabile, 3/4.
    203.1/3(a). No. 3. de Cythere [sic; Gluck: Cythére assiégée]. Aria, "Sans lenteur", 3/4.
    203.1/4(a). No. 4. Roeser. Andante Grazioso, 6/8.   203.1/5. No. 5. Engl[ese]: 2/4 [& Trio]
    203.1/6(a). No. 6. [Handel]: Marcia in Giulio Cesare, C.   203.1/7. No. 7. Polonoise, 3/4 [& Trio].
    203.1/8. No. 8. Grazioso, 2/4.   203.1/9. No. 9. Engl[ese], 2/4 [no Trio].
    203.1/10(a). No. 10. [Handel]: March In Floridante, C.   203.1/11. No. 11. Air. Tempo di Min[uet]: 3/4.
    203.1/12. No. 12. Allegretto, 2/4.   [fl I: Allegretto ma non troppo; fl II: Dolce Sempre).
    203.1/13. No. 13. Cosaca, 2/4.   203.1/14(a). No. 14. [Storace]. Gavotte. Jeunes Cœurs soyez fidelles.
        In the Opera La Cameriera Astuta.   203.1/15. No. 15. Cotillion, 2/4 [& Trio].
  The 4 following Divertimentos are almost certainly based on Went's arrangement (2ob 2ca 2hn 2bn) for the
  Schwarzenberg Harmonie. Martín y Soler's opera, Una cosa rara, was first performed in London in 1789.
  The titlepages are similar: "N⁰ 2/ Divertimento / for / 2 Basset Horns / 2 Oboes / 2 French Horns in B♭ /
  2 Bassoons / & / Serpent / Comp. by Sig. Martini / [incipit]".
  VXM-1da. [Martín y Soler: Una cosa rara] N⁰ 2 [ob I: N⁰ 5] Divertimento. 2ob 2bthn 2hn 2bn serp.
    1.1da. (Act II, No. 17) Andantino, C / Allegretto, 6/8.
    1.2da. (Act I, No. 12.3, "Canone") Largo, 3/4 Sempre pianissimo / Allegretto, C
    1.3da. (Act I, No. 28) Andante Sostenuto, 6/8.   1.4da. [?Eley]: Cotillion, 2/4.
  VXM-2da. [Martín y Soler: Una cosa rara] N⁰ 3 Divertimento. 2ob 2bthn 2hn 2bn serp.
    2.1da. (Act II, No. 10) Larghetto, C / All⁰ mod: C.   2.2da. (Act I, No. 13, Aria) Andante Sostenuto, 6/8.
    2.3da. (Act I, No. 10) Allegro, 3/8.   2.4da. [?Eley: Cotillion] All⁰· molto, 2/4 [short & facile].
  VXM-3da. [Martín y Soler: Una cosa rara] N⁰ 4 Divertimento. 2ob 2bthn 2hn 2bn serp.
    3.1da. (Act I, No. 2, Terzetto) Allegro, 3/4 / Larghetto, C / All²·, 3/4.
    3.2da. (Act I, No. 4, Aria & Jägenchor) Andante poco Moto, 3/4 / Allegretto, 6/8.
    3.3da. (Act II, Finale, No. 30.3) Allegro, 6/8.
    3.4da. (Act II, Finale, No. 30.1) Allegretto, 6/8 / Andante 3/4 / Allegretto, 3/8
  VXM-4da. [Martín y Soler: Una cosa rara] N⁰ 6 Divertimento. 2ob 2bthn 2hn 2bn serp.
    4.1da. (Act I, No. 6, Duetto) All⁰, C.   4.2da. (Act II, No. 24, [Recit &] Duetto) Andante, 3/4.
    4.3da. (Act I, Finale, No. 15, Allegro Giusto) Allegro, 6/8.   4.4da. [?Eley]: Cotillion, 2/4 [& Trio]
  203.2. [?Divertimento], 4 mvts.   2ob 2bthn 2hn 2bn Serpani. ["Serpano" crossed out on Fagotto 2ᵈᵒ].
    203.2/1. March, 2/4.   203.2/2. Andante piu [sic] Allegretto, 6/8.
    203.2/3. Andante, 3/4 / Allegro, 3/4.   203.2/4. Allo, 2/4.
The tipped-in MSS parts from A-202: 45 Cottilion *follow A-203.2/3.*
  FAR-6.1. [Rosetti, Franz Anton]: Divertimento. Rosetty [sic]; 3 mvts.   2ob 2bthn 2hn 2vla vlne.
    Adagio, C / Allegro, 3/4 - Min[uet], 3/4 [& Trio] - Rondo, 2/4 [& Minore & Majore & Coda].
A-204. [Collection of 65 works]. 2ob/fl 2bthn 2hn 2bn serp. (Nos. 1, 5 - 12, 29 - 32, 48, 56 - 59: 2fl; No. 2:
  2ob *or* fl).   MS parts (1791): GB-Lbl, R.M.21.c.34-40. *In original soft bindings; a made-up set with many*
  works pasted in or copied from A-202 & A-203.
  204.1. March Bold, C.   204.2. Minuetto, 3/4 [& Trio].
  204.3(a). Glee. Andantino, 2/4. Sigh no more Ladies. [R.J.S.] Stevens.   204.4. Engl[ese], 2/4 [no Trio]
  204.5(t). March Fonebre [sic]. Adagio, C [= Eley. FCE-1.8].
  204.6(a). [Pleyel: B.112/iv & B.404/iii]. Adagio, 2/4 / Allegretto, 6/8.   (= Eley, FCE-3.1 & A-202.1/2).
  204.7. Menuetto Andantino, 3/4 [& Trio]. (= Eley. FCE-1.11).   204.8. Angloise, 2/4 [no Trio].
  204.9. March, ¢ [& Trio].   204.10. Andante, ¢.   204.11. Andante, 2/4.   204.12. Swab[isch]: 3/4.
  204.13. Andantino, C.   204.14. Min[uet]: 3/4 [& Trio + Coda].   204.15. Andantino, 3/8 Sotto voce.
  [204.15/1(a). [Under the pasted sheet: Martini. unidentified, probably a mvt from *Una cosa rara*]
  204.16. Polonoise [sic], 3/4 [& Trio].   204.17(a). Moderato, ¢, Di Rolla. (=A-202.3/13).
  204.18. Mod[e]r[ato]., 2/4 [pasted in].
  204.19. Affectuoso, 3/4.   204.20(a). [S. Paxton: Glee] Believe my Sighs my Tears my Dear. (= A-202.3/10).
  204.21. Engl[ese]: 2/4.   204.22. Marsch [sic], ¢.   204.23. Adagio, 6/8 / All²·, 2/4.
  204.24. Min[uet]:, 3/4 [& Trio].   204.25. Engl[ese], 2/4 [& Trio].
  204.26(a). March, ¢. [= Mozart: Le Nozze di Figaro, Non più andrai].   204.27. Andante, 2/4 [pasted in].
  204.28(a). Andantino un poco Sostenuto,6/8 ⇒ Allegretto, 2/4 [the Allegretto is sections 2 [major], 3 [minor]
        & 4 [major] of Mozart: K.331/iii, "Rondo alla turca"].
  204.29. March, C.   204.30. Andantino, 2/4 [pasted in].   204.31. Moder[ato], 2/4.
  204.32. All² modr:, 6/8.   204.33. Engl[ese], 2/4 [no Trio].
  204.34. Marcia [overpasted on 204.34/1 "Divertimento"] ⇒ 204.35(a). Allegretto, 6/8. (204.34/1 & 204.35 =
        Martín y Soler, VXM-1da, mvt 1).
  204.36(a). [Martín y Soler] In the Opera una Cosarara [sic] di Vinzens Martini. (= VXM-1da, mvt 3).
  204.37. Rondo, 2/4.   204.38. March, ¢ [pasted in].   204.39. Allegretto, 6/8 [& Trio].
  204.40. Adagio Sostenuto, 6/8.   204.41. Engl[ese], 2/4 [& Trio] [pasted in].   204.42. March, C.
  204.43. Andante poco Allegretto, 6/8.   204.44. Andante poco Allegretto, C.   204.45. Andante con moto, 3/4.
  204.46. Engl[ese], 2/4.   204.47. Engl[ese], 2/4 [& Trio].   204.48. March, C.
  204.49(a). Divertimento Allegro, 6/8 (= Martín y Soler. VXM-3da, mvt iii).
  204.50. Allegro non troppo, 2/4 / Andante, ¢, mezza voce.   204.51. Engl[ese], 2/4 [no Trio].
  204.52(a). Coro, ¢ [original number "4" crossed out; "Coro Rotorni o mai nel nostro &.c."].
  204.53. Swab[isch]: 6/8.
  204.54(a). Will great Lords and Ladies drest upon gay days come and visit you &c. Storace. [originally
        numbered "6" & crossed out] "Dialogue in the Haunted Tower".   Allegretto, 3/8.
  204.55. Cottilion, 2/4 [originally numbered "7" and crossed out].   204.56. March, [C / ¢]
  204.57. Polonoise, 3/4 [& Trio].   204.58. March, ¢.
  204.59. Adagio, 3/4 [pasted in] ⇒ Allegretto, 2/4.   204.60. Allegretto, 2/4.   204.61. Adagio, 2/4.
  204.62(a). [W. Paxton: Glee] Breathe soft ye Winds (= A-202.3/50).   204.63. Allegretto, 2/4 [G minor/majore].
  204.64(a). di Russa [sic] moderato, ¢.   204.65(a). Andantino by F. Herschel, 2/4, a mezzo voce [pasted in].

Germany: Unnamed Bands
A-205. Unidentified work.   2cl 2hn bn.   MS pts: D-Bds, Mus.Ms.anon.952.
A-206.1. General Bertrands Abschied.   2cl(C) 2hn bn.   MS score: F-Pn, D. 17240. (2.); (with a separate 4°
sheet of the song lyrics, "Les adieux de Bertand", in French, beginning, "Adieu, français, adieu franc chére").   ★
A-206.2. [3 variations & Coda on] Abschied das General Bertrand.   terz-fl 2cl 2hn 2bn.
MS score: F-Pn, D. 17240. (1).   ★
A-207. Concerto (? spurious Albinoni).   2obdam 2hn bn.   MS pts: D-BFb, Rheda MS.876.
A-208. Concerto; in B♭, 7 mvts.   3ob 2bn tp.
MS parts ("Wohl aus der Stuttgarter Erbprinzen-Slg."): D-ROu, Mus.Saec.XVII=51/30.   ★
A-209. Allegretto con Variazioni.   2fl 2cl 2hn bn.   MS pts: D-Dl, 2/P/2.
A-210. Tanz Musik; (12 Allemandes with Trios).   2cl(C) 2hn vlne.
MS parts ("Ad me Petrum Hueber"): D-Mbs, Mus.Ms.7615.   *Possibly by Holler.*   ★
A-211. Andante in C.   (?terz-)fl 2ob 2cl 2hn 2bn serp.   MS parts: D-Z, XLIX.156.
A-212. [15] Pièces d'Harmonie pour Musique turque par divers Compositeurs.   2fl 2cl(C) 2hn 2bn 2tp(clar) serp
b-dr cym tamburino.   (Nos. 1 - 3, 6 12 & 13 are arrangements of mvts by Pleyel: B.111/ii, 334/iii, 111/v,
319/ii, 433/ii & 395/ii, 128/iii, respectively.)
Pc (chez Jean André: Offenbach ª/M, pn 1836, 1803), parts: H-KE, K 1052/IX.   ★
MS parts: D-Tl, Gg 454, Nos. 35 - 49, (= A-248; missing 2fl 2cl 2hn 2tp).
A-74m. Sammlung von Maerschen für vollständige türkische Musik, zum bestimmten Gebrauch der Königlich
Preussischen Armée [sic]. [Heft 11, Nos. 67-72: Sammlung von Maerschen, auf allerhöchsten Befehl Sr. Majestät,
des Königs, zum bestimmten Gebrauche der Königl. Preuss. Infanterie.   Für vollständige türkische Musik.]
pic quart-fl 2ob cl(F) 2cl(C) 4hn 2bn cb+serp)/2b-hn 2tp 3tb b-dr cym, "Tamb: du Soldat", "Tamburen".
Pc (bei Adolph Martin Schlesinger: Berlin, c.1815 - 1825), 13 Heft, score: A-Wgm, (Hefts 1 - 10); D-Bds;
GB-Lbl, g.847.a, (Heft 3).
MS parts (Heft 12, No. 82; Heft 13, Nos. 86, 89, 90, for: pic 2ob cl(F) 2cl(C) 4hn 2bn 3tp tp(F, No. 1 only) 3tb
serp): D-DT, Mus-n 1870, (as "4 Königl. Preuss. Armee=Geschw. Märsche No. 82, 88 [sic], 89, 90".   *Although
all are attributed to A. Neithardt, only Heft 12, No. 86 is, in fact, an arrangement by this composer).*
Heft 1. 13 Geschwindmärsche (Quick marches)
　　1a. Dessauer Marsch.   2 - 6. von Satzenhofer.   7 - 9. von Boieldieu.
　　10. von Stackelberg.   11. aus dem Ballet: les Amours de Vénus.   12. von Cavos.
Heft 2. 12 langsame Märsche (Slow marches)
　　1-3. von Dörffeld.   4. aus dem Ballet: les Amours de Vénus.   5, 6. von Dörffeld.
　　7. des ersten Garde-Bataillons.   8. von Vogel.   9. des Herzogs von Braunschweig.
　　10 des Prinz August.   11, 12. von G. A. Schneider.
Heft 3. 12 Geschwindmärsche
　　13. bei der Kaiserlich Russischen Armee von Cavos, arrangirt von Dörffeld.
　　14. Sibirische Grenadier Regiment.   15. von Dörffeld.
　　16. aus dem Ballet: les Amours de Vénus, arrang[ed]: Cavos.   17. [aus Les] Deux Journées [Cherubini].
　　18. von Cavos, Arrang: von Dörffeld.   19. König von Preussen Grenadier No 2 von Dörffeld.
　　20, 21, 22. von Dörffeld.   23. Fangoriskische Grenadier Regiment.   24. von Nicolo [i.e. N. Isouard].
Heft 4. 12 Geschwindmärsche
　　25. des Königs von Preussen, [arranged] von Cavos.   26, 27. von Dörffeld.
　　28. Pariser Einzugsmarsch 1815.   29. von Boieldieu.   30. von Devienne.   31. von Steibelt.
　　32. der Reserve-Artillerie.   33. von Dörffeld.   34. von Paer.   35. von Dörffeld.   36. aus Spontini's Vestalin.
Heft 5. 12 langsame Märsche
　　13. von Koslowsky.   14. von Titoff.   15, 16. der Jasmaulaschen Garde.
　　17. aus Mozart's [La Clemenza di] Titus.   18. des Archangel-Gorodizkischen Regiments.   19, 20. von Cavos.
　　21. des Königs Friedrich II.   22, 23. à la Turque.   24. alter russischer Marsch von [W.F.] Gluck.
Heft 6. 12 langsame Märsche
　　25, 26, 27. des Prinzen von Coburg.   28. von Dörffeld.   29, 30, 31. aus Mozart's [Die] Zauberflöte.
　　32. von Dörffeld.   33. von Zingarelli.   34. von Spontini's Vestalin.
　　35. aus Mozart's [Le Nozze di] Figaro.   36. von Dörffeld.
Heft 7. 12 langsame Märsche
　　37. des Wjatkaschen Regiments.   38. Pariser Marsch, 1815.   39. von Gloger, 1815.
　　40. aus Spontini's [Fernand] Cortez.   41. des Polokischen Regiments.
　　42. des Regiments Erbach Eger, 1815.   43. Triumphmarsch aus Spontini's Vestalin.
　　44. aus [Gallenberg's] Alfred.   45. aus Spontini's Lalla Rakh [sic].   46, 47, 48. aus Calto und Colama.
Heft 8. 12 Geschwindmärsche
　　37. von Beethoven. (= LVB-2m)   38. Pariser Einzugsmarsch, 1814.   39. aus Spontini's Vestalin.
　　40. aus Spontini's [Fernand] Cortez.   41. Wiener Marsch.   42. des Collaredo.   43, 44. aus Flora und Zephire.
　　45. Polnischer Marsch.   46. aus Spontini's [Fernand] Cortez.   47. aus den vier Freiern.   48. la Castiglione.
Heft 9. 12 Geschwindmärsche
　　49, 50. des Grossfürsten Nicolaus.   51, 52. der Hannoverischen Grenadiers.
　　53. aus Schweden.   54. aus Spontini's Vestalin.   55, 56. aus Neapel.
　　57, 58. aus Rossini's Moses.   59. der Volhynischen Jäger.   60. von Seelicke.
Heft 10. 3 langsame Märsche
　　49, 50. von Naue.   51. von C. Eckard.
Heft 11. 6 Geschwindmärsche (& Sammlung von Märschen)
　　61. aus Spontini's Alcidor.   62. der Regiments Semenowsky.   63. Pratermarsch.
　　64. des Regiments Ismailowsky.   65. aus dem Ballet: la Festa di Terpsichore.
　　66. von Naue.   67. Marche du Ballet: "Malle Cadella" arranged Neithardt.
　　68. Marsche (Warschau), arranged Hasse.   69. Marsche de Posen.
　　70. Marsche de "Alcidor" de Spontini, arranged Neithardt.   71. Marsche des Grenadiers hongrois.

Heft 12. 12 Geschwind-Märsche
72. Marsche tirée de "La Dame blanche" de Boieldieu.
73. Marche raportée de S.A.R le Prince héréditaire de l'Italie.
74. Marche de "La Muette de Portici" d'Auber, arranged F Schick.
75. Marsche napolitaine, rapportée de l'Italie par S.A.R le Prince héréditaire.
76. Marsche Cavalleggiero della Guardia, rapportée de l'Italie par S.A.R le Prince héréditaire.
77. Marsche dal 3 Regimento Svizzero, rapportée de l'Italie par S.A.R le Prince héréditaire.
78, 79. Marsche de S.A.R le Prince Frederic de Prusse.   80. Marsche de C. Merz.
81. Marsche de "Le Siège de Corinte" de Rossini, des Grenadiers du Grand-Duc de Bade.
82. Marsche des Chansonniers des Alpes arranged N [sic] Neithardt.
83. Pasta-Marsche, arranged A. Neithardt.   84. Marsche rapportée du Hague, arranged A. Neithardt.
Heft 13. (10) Geschwind-Märsche
85. Marsche de la Garde russe, arranged Engelhardt.
86. Marsche de la Garde russe, Bat. de Sapeurs, arranged Engelhardt.
87, 88. Marsche de Weller.   89. Schweizermarsch.   90. Marsch aus den Kreuzrittern, von Meyerbeer.
91. Marsch des k.k. Regiments, Herzog Wellington.   92. Marsch des k.k. Regiments, Prinz Wasa.
93. Marsch aus Petersburg, arranged Engelhardt.   94. Marsch nach Steyerischen Alpenliedern, von Neithardt.
A-75m. Die Königlich Preussische Ordonance (200 marches, c.1766 - 1771).
MS parts: D-DS, (2 copies), Mus.Ms.1222, Mus.Ms.1225, (many of the marches are incomplete or in only 2 pts).
A-76m. 100 Marches (melodies only).   MS: D-Bds, Mus.Ms.anon.38214.
A-77m. Uniformirung und Organisation des Bürger-Militärs in dem Königreiche Baiern 1807; Partitur von Sechs Märschen für das gesammte Bürgermilitär des Königreichs Baiern. (Also includes "Ordananz für die Trompeter der bürgl: Cavatlerie [sic] des Königreichs Baiern" and "Ordananz Auf Trommel und Pfeiffen für die bürgl. Infanterie, Schützen und Artillerie des Königreichs Baiern".)
2flautino(Eb)/fl(F) 2cl(Eb) 2cl(Bb) 2hn 2bn 2tp b-dr+cym+"etc."
Pc (sn, sl [?Munich], 1807), scores: GB-Lbl, Hirsch III.544. *Nos. 1 - 3 are given as "88 Schritt in der Minute" but No. 3 is "Auf jedes ¼ Schritt in der Minute 88 Schritt"; Nos. 4 - 6 are "100 in der Minute."* ★
77.1m. Marsch.   77.2m. Marsch.   77.3m. Marcia Funebre.   (2fl replace pic, b-dr tacet, s-dr "vertimmt").
77.4m. Marche Allegretto.   77.5m. Marche Allegretto.   77.6m. Schützen March, (solo tp fanfare in trio).
A-78.1m. Journal de Musique militaire, 1e Moitié.   2ob 2cl 2hn 2bn tp.
Pc (Rudolf Werkmeister: Oranienburg, 1804), parts: CZ-KRa, (MS copy), A4178/IV.B.193; CZ-Pnm, Lobkovic X.H.a.59.
78.1/1m(a). Fleury: Ouverture; in F.   78.1/2m. Schmeling: Marche [& Trio].   78.1/3m(a). Haack: Walse.
78.1/4m. Von Sydow: Pas redoublé.   78.1/5m. Himmel: Pas de Manoeuvre.
A-78.2m. Journal de Musique militaire, 2do Moitié.   2pic 2quart-fl 2cl(C) 2hn 2bn 2tp serp b-dr+cym.
Pc (Rudolf Werkmeister: Oranienburg, 1804), parts: CZ-KRa, (MS copy), A4178/IV.B.193; CZ-Pnm, Lobkovic X.H.a.73, (missing 2hn).
78.2/1m(a). R. Kreutzer: Lodoiska, overture.   78.2/2m. B.A. Weber: Marsch, in C.
78.2/3m. Leroy: Pas de manoeuvre.   78.2/4m(a). Haydn: Walse [= Symphony Hob. I/101iii, Menuetto].
A-79m. Marsche der Kais. Russ. Cavalie-Garde.   fl 2ob cl(F) 2cl(Bb) 2bthn 4hn 2bn serp 3tp 3tb perc.
MS: D-Bds, Mus.ms.anon.38007.
A-80m. Marsch.   fl 4cl 3hn 3bn 4tp 3tb.   MS: D-Bds, Mus.ms.anon.1237.
A-81m. Marsch, (c.1830).   2fl 2cl 6hn 2tp bass timp.   MS: D-Bds, Ms.282.
A-82.1m. Acht Märsche für Türkische Musick [sic], 1 Heft.   2fl 2cl 2hn 2bn 2tp serp b-dr.
Pc (bei Johann André: Offenbach am Main, pn 1822, 1803), parts: H-KE, 731/VIII. *Works are also cataloged at individual composers.*
MS score & parts: I-Fc, F.P. S.553.   MS parts: D-Tl, Gg 454, Nos. 27 - 34, (missing 2fl 2cl 2hn).
82.1/1. Kozeluch: March in C, (as by "Kozeliuch").   82.1/2. Raffael: March in C.
82.1/3. Raffael: March in C.   82.1/4. Vanhal: March in C.·   82.1/5. Vanhal: March in C.
82.1/6. Beethoven: March in C.   [= LVB-8m, Grenadiers Marsch, WoO 29].
82.1/7. Krommer: March in C.   82.1/8. Lipavsky: March in C.
A-82.2m. Acht Maersch [sic] für Türkische Musik von versciedenen Komponisten, 2tes Heft.
2fl 2cl 2hn 2bn 2tp serp b-dr cym "Tamburino".
Pc (bei Johann André: Offenbach am Main, pn 1816, 1803), parts: CZ-KRa, A4019/IV.B.192; H-KE, 731/2. ★
MS pts: D-Tl, Gg 454, Nos. 50-57, (omits No. 7; missing 2fl 2cl 2hn 2tp). *Some pts are misnumbered: 1-6, 5, 6; composers are not identified. No. 1 is the Anonymous "Marche de Buonaparte à son entrée en Mantoue [sic]" also published by Meyn: Hamburg, sd, (H-KE, 2179); No. 7 is "Alles fühlt" from Mozart's Die Zauberflöte.*
A-82.3m. Sieben Märsche für Türckische Musick [sic], 3. Heft.   2fl 2cl(C) 2hn 2bn 2tp(clar) serp tamburino.
Pc (bei Johann André: Offenbach, pn 1840, 1803), parts: H-KE, K 731/3, (possibly missing hn II & tp II).   ★
A-83m. 6 Quick Märsche.   2ob 2cl 2hn bn tp.   MS: D-Bds, Mus.Ms.anon.1217.
A-84m. 12 Russische Märsche f[ü]r Harmonie Musik.   2ob 2cl 2hn 3bn.
MS: D-Bds, Mus.Ms.anon.38026 & 38027.
A-85m. Journal de Musique militaire.   2cl 2hn 2bn, (2pic/fife 2cl(ripieno) 2tp serp cym tri(s) s-dr tamb ad lib).
Pc (Chez J. Reinhard Storck: Strasbourg, April, 1784), parts: D-SWl, Mus. 3014, (No. 1 only).
85.1m(a). Mozart: Die Entführung aus dem Serail, overture.
85.2m(a). M[ons]. *** [sic]: Lise pénitente.
85.3m(a). Grétry: Colinette à la cour, air, (Moderato, 2/4).
85.4m(a). Monsigny: Félix, trio (Allegro, ¢).
85.5m. Müller, ( ): Marche.   85.6m. Müller, ( ): Allemande.
A-86m. 6 Neue Märsche.   ob 2cl tp.   MS: D-Bds, Mus.Ms.anon.1232.

Germany: Anonymous Vocal Works
A-123v. Cantata, "Auf den Abzug des Herrn".   SSAATB, 2fl 2cl 2hn 2bn tb.   MS parts: D-AG, 63.
A-124v. Cantata, "Singet dem Herrn ein neues Lied".   SATB, 2fl ob hn bn tp timp clavier organ.
MS parts: D-GOL, Nr. 26.

Germany: Anonymous Funeral Music
A-29t. Den Mänen des gefallenen Volkes von Unterwalden nied dem Walde am 9ten Herbstmonat 1798.
2fl 2cl 2hn(muted) 2bn.
Pc: (sn: sl, 1799), parts: CH-EN.
A-178tv. Still und Heilig (für) Fraulein Josepha von Menz, königl. Landrichters.   SATB fl 2cl 2hn tb.
MS: D-Ws, Ms. 779.
A-30t. Musik zur Toden-Feyer du Frau Herzogin Amelia; (20 April 1807).   fl 2ob 2cl 2hn 2bn cbn 2tb.
MS: D-WRl, Hofmarschllamt 3820.

Germany: Bad Buchau (Swabia), Harmonie
Note: A-299 & A-300, sold to the Thurn und Taxis regimental band at Schloss Taxis, Neresheim (qv), by Rath
und Oberförster Haeckel in 1821 probably came from this Harmonie.
A-230. 2 Polonaise; both in Ab [& 2 Valses].   pic(Db) cl(Eb) 2cl(Bb) 2hn 2bn tp serp+tb b-dr.
MS parts: D-Tl, Z 28. *The Valses (Nos. 3 & 4) have been added to the parts.* ★
A-231. [3 Polonaisen; all in D].   cl(D) 2cl(A) 2hn 2bn.   MS parts: D-Tl, Z 29. ★
A-232. Pottpouri [sic]; in Eb.   cl(Eb) 3cl(Bb) 2hn 2bn tp serp.   MS score: D-Tl,Z 43. ★
A-88m. Parademarsch; in C.   pic(Eb) 2cl(Eb) 3cl(Bb) 4hn 2bn 2tp (2)tb serp b-dr s-dr.
MS score: D-Tl, Z 27. ★
A-31t. Marche funèbre; in C minor.   pic(Db) cl(Eb) 2cl(Bb) 2hn 2bn tp tb+serp batterie(caisse & cimballe).
MS score: D-Tl, Z 136, No. 12, ff. 47 - 48b. ★

Germany: Bad Schussenried (Swabia)
A-233. [Oktett in Bb].   Solo clarinet, 2cl 2hn 2vl b.   MS parts: D-Tl, BB 3, (missing cl II). ★

Germany: Brackenheim, (Swabia), Church Band
A-125v. Palmer, "Macht hoch das Thor".   SATB, flautino, fl 2cl(C) 2cl(Bb) 3hn(2F, Eb) 4tp(Eb, F) b-tb vlne.
MS parts: D-Tl, EE 24, (with duplicate vocal parts: 4S, 7A, T, B).

Germany: Burgsteinfurt, Fürst Eugen zu Bentheim-Bentheim Harmonie
A-234. Zwölf Veränderungen [variations] über den beliebten Franzbrunner Deutschen.
terz-fl 2cl 2hn 2bn cbn timp.   MS parts: D-BFb, K-at 90 hoch b, (with duplicate bn pts).

Germany: Darmstadt, Fürst Ludewig IX zu Hesse-Darmstadt Harmonie (pre-1790)
D-DS collections, Mus.ms.1223 (Nos. 30 & 31) & Mus.ms.1224 also includes many piano versions of Marches.
The collection of 200 marches (c.1766 - 1771) Die Königlich Preussische Ordonance, A-75m is listed supra.
A-235. [2 mvts: Allegro, C minor - Presto & trio, C minor].   2ob 2bn tp.   MS pts: D-DS, Mus.ms.1223/9. ★
A-236. Aria; in G.   ob vl/ob 2hn basso.   MS parts: D-DS, Mus.ms.1224, S.21 - 29. ★
A-237. Polonoise; in Eb.   2ob bn tp.   MS parts: D-DS, Mus.ms.1224, S.269 - 275. ★
A-89m. Marsch; in C.   pic-fife 2fife 2cl(F) 2cl(C) 2hn bn 2tp.   MS parts: D-DS, Mus.ms.1223/25. ★
A-90m. La March Nº 2.   2pic 2cl 2hn 2bn 2tp b-dr s-dr.   MS score: D-DS, Mus.ms.1224, S.369a-c. ★
A-91m. La March Nº 3.   2cl+2flautini 2hn (2)bn 2tp.   MS score: D-DS, Mus.ms.1224, S.369e-g. *Although*
the score calls for "Fagotti" the parts are in unison throughout. ★
A-92m, 93m. Zwey Märsche [in a later hand: 1. Wilhelmus v[on]. Nassau[,] 2. Al is on Prinsje nog zoo Kleyn].
2ob 2cl(C) 2hn 2bn 2tp.   MS parts: D-DS, (2 copies), Mus.ms.1223/8a, b, (both in C), Mus.ms.1223/12, (as "II
Pieces 1ᵐᵉ Wilhelmus: 2ᵐᵉ Al is one &c. Arrangées"; here in C, G). ★
A-94m, 95m. Marche de Regiment General Leut. v. Bornstädt [&] Marche de Regiment General Major v. Köniz;
in Bb & Eb.   2ob 2cl 2hn 2bn 2tp(in the first march only).   MS parts: D-DS, Mus.ms.1223/20. *A note has*
been added in another hand, "Berliner Revue May 1786"; the oboe I part includes an alternative part transposed
up an octave for use when clarinets are not available; in the original, the oboe I lies beneath the oboe II part.
Another copy of the first march can be found in D-SWl (A-140m). ★
A-96m. Marsch; in Bb.   2ob 2cl 2hn 2bn 2tp.   MS parts: D-DS, Mus.ms.1223/11. ★
A-97m. Marsch Julius Caesar Pour tout la Musique turque Du Régiment d'alsace [sic]; in Eb.
2fl 2cl 2hn bn 2tp serp.   MS parts: D-DS, Mus.ms.1223/6, (with a duplicate cl I part). ★
A-98m. Marche a. 9 Parth:; in C.   2ob 2cl(C) 2hn 2bn tp(prin).   MS parts: D-DS, Mus.ms.1223/29. ★
A-99m. Marche von Regiment Landgraf[,] 1790.   2ob 2cl(C) 2hn 2bn 2tp.
MS scores (3 copies; one in C, two in Eb): D-DS, Mus.ms.1224, S.358 - 361. ★
A-100m. Marche von Leib-Regiment[,] 1790.   2ob 2cl(C) 2hn 2bn 2tp.   MS scores (three, all in C): D-DS,
Mus.ms.1224, S.362 - 365. *Mus.ms.365c-f is a contemporary piano reduction.* ★
A-101m. La Marche Nº 1.   2cl 2hn 2tp 2bassi.   MS score: D-DS, Mus.ms.1224, S.366 - 399. ★
A-102.1m, 102.2m. Marsch: 2. Regiment: K:. Exclenz [sic] v[on]. Moellendorff; (in fact, 2 settings of the same
march in Eb & C).   2ob 2cl 2hn bn tp.   MS parts: D-DS, Mus.ms.1223/22. ★
A-103m. 6 Märsche.   ob 2cl(C) 2hn bn 2tp(No 2 only).   MS parts: D-DS, Mus.ms.1223/19. *The titles are*
added in a later hand. Two additional Marches, added at a later date, are listed at A-104m. ★
   103.1m (= PVA-2.1m). Prinzess Amalie v Prussen. 94.2m. Der alte Dessauer.
   103.3m. Bataillonsmarsch v. Ludewig IX, comp[onirt]. 1.1.1764.
   103.4m. Aus "Julius Caesar" für das Reg. d'Alsace. (cf. A-97m)
   103.5m. Bataillonsmarsch, comp[onirt]. 1759 von Hesse.
   103.6m. Marsch, comp[onirt]. v[on]. Ludewig IX für sein französ[ische]. Regiment Royal Hesse Darmstadt.
A-104.1m, 104.2m. [2 additional Marches, numbered 7 & 8, added to A-103m].   2cl bn 2tp.
MS parts: D-DS, Mus.ms.1223/19, (the numbering is reversed in the cl II, hn I & II and tp I & II parts). ★
A-105.1m, 105.2m. [2] Märsche der Regiment von Ansalt Dessau vulgo der alte Dessauer und des Fürst
Moritzinsen Regiments. [In a later hand: Diese Märsche erhielt Ich von dem Hautboisten ersteren Regiments,
modo Thadden]. *[Headtitle:]* M[arsch] des R[egiment] v[on]. Thadden ehemals Anhalt Dessau. M[arsch]. des
R[egiment]. v[on]. Fürst Moriz [sic].   2ob 2cl 2bn 2tp.   MS parts: D-DS, Mus.Ms.1223/13. ★

A-106m. Marsch [added in a later hand: des k.k. Infanterie=Regiments von Ligne]; in D minor. 2cl 2hn 2tp b.
MS parts: D-DS, Mus.ms.1223/5. ★
A-107m. Marche von der Armee des Bouonapartes [sic]. 2cl 2hn 2bn tp.
MS parts: D-DS, Mus.ms.1223/16. ★
A-107m. Marche [in a later hand: "von dem Altenstein"]; in C. 2cl(C) 2hn 2bn tp.
MS parts: D-DS, Mus.ms.1223/28. *Although the titlepage states "Due Fagotti"/ the bassoon part, marked "Fagotto" is in unison throughout.* ★
A-109m. March; in E♭. 2cl 2hn 2tp basso. MS pts: D-DS, Mus.ms.1223/3. ★
A-110m. March; in E♭. 2ob 2cl 2hn 2tp basso. MS pts: D-DS, Mus.ms.1223/4. *The added oboe parts are generally ripieno in nature.*
A-111m. L'ordonnance pour la musique de la Legion Corse, 1772. 2cl(C) 2hn 2bn tambour.
MS score: D-DS, Mus.Ms.1186. ★
   111.1m. Le Thema. De La Retrait. 111.2m. Le Comencement [sic] De La Retrait; (the same as 111.1m).
   111.3m. un autre. 111.4m. un autre. 111.5m. un autre. 111.6m. Assemblé. 111.7m. un autre.
   111.8m. un autre assemblé. 111.9m. Marche des Drapeaux. 111.10m. un autre Marche des Drapeaux.
   111.11m. Autre Marche Trappo [sic]. 111.12m. Un autre Marche des trapeaux [sic]; (the same as 111.11m
    with an additional 8-bar second section). 111.13m. March au champ. 111.14m. Autre Marche au champ.
   111.15m. March Pas doubleé [sic]. 111.16m. autre Marche Pas doubleé [sic].
   111.17m. autre Marche doubleé [sic]. 111.18m. La Messe. 111.19m. autre Messe. 111.20. autre Messe.
A-112m(a). Les Aires ordinaires de la Musique de la legion corse 1772; Nos. 1 - 9 and 1 - 11. 2cl 2hn 2bn.
MS parts (c.1765): D-DS, Mus.ms.1187, (in the second set, the bn II part is missing & the cl I part is misbound).
   112.1m(a). N° 1. Grétry: [Le] Huron, Si jamias je prens un époux. 112.2m. N° 2. Allegro, 3/8.
   112.3m(a). N° 3. [Philidor: Le Sorcier]: Nous Etions dans Cette Etage encore [sic].
   112.4m(a). N° 4. Anon: Ah quel amour est jolie. 112.5m(a). N° 5. Anon: Ne fait il pas la Mineses.
   112.6m(a). N° 6. Monsigny: Le Deserteur, Javois egaré mon fuseau.
   112.7m. N° 7. La chasse. 113.8m(a). N° 8. [Monsigny: Rose et Colas]: Pauvre Colas.
   112.9m(a). N° 9. [Monsigny: Le Roy et le Fermier] Un fin chaseur.
   112.10m(a). N° 1. Monsigny: Le Deserteur, Marche. 112.11m(a). N° 2. Grétry: Lucille, Marche.
   112.12m(a). N° 3. Grétry: Les deux avares, Marche. 112.13m. N° 4. Lenterrement des Officiers Corsses [sic].
   112.14m(a). N° 5. Grétry: Huron, Marche. 112.15m. Marche des Turques. 112.16m. Marche général.
   112.17m. N° 8. Marche pour les Corses [added: favorite]. 112.18m(a). N° 9. Anon: On dit q'ua quinze ans.
   112.19m. Marche Des Dragons de Corsse. 112.20m. Marche de Corsses d'Infanterie.
A-113m. Marsch [in a later hand: Der Rheinströhmer, des das Regiment modo (1800). Kalksten zu Machtebrug, als Distinction wie Anhalt, nun Raunart [sic], den Sessauer hat v. Trompeter Huth zu Halle mir gegeben]; in E♭. ob 2cl 2bn tp. MS parts: D-DS, Mus.ms.1223/14. ★
A-114m. Geschwind Marsch. 2fife 2cl 2hn tp. MS parts: D-DS, Mus.ms.1223/27. ★
A-115m. [20 Marches, cited in RISM A/II as "20 Stücke"]. 2ob 2hn basso tp.
MS parts: D-DS, Mus.ms.1188a-f. ★
A-116m. Marsche; in F. 2ob 2bn 2tp. MS parts: D-DS, Mus.ms.1223/18. ★
A-117m. Marche. du quinzième Regiment d'Angleterre; in C. 2cl(C)/ob 2hn bn 2tp.
MS parts: D-DS, Mus.ms.1223/26. *Presumably the Royal Northumberland Fusiliers, whose official marches at that time were "Rule Britannia" and "The British Grenadiers". A piano reduction can be found at Mus.ms1224, S.141 - 143.* ★
A-118m. Marche; in F. 2ob 2bn tp. MS parts: D-DS, Mus.ms.1223/18. ★
A-119m. [March in B♭]. 2ob bn 2tp. MS parts: D-DS, Mus.ms.1223/30. ★
A-120m. Marsch; in F. 2ob 2hn basso. MS parts: D-DS, Mus.ms.1224, S.31 - 40. ★
A-121m. Marche; in G. 2ob 2hn basso. MS parts: D-DS, Mus.ms.1224, S.43 - 51. ★
A-122m. [4 Marches]. 2ob tp basso. MS parts: D-DS, Mus.ms.1224, S.91, 93, 105. ★
   122.1m. No. 1. March. Grenadier Guarde [sic]. 122.2m. No. 2. March. Fürtz [sic] de Hollstein.
   122.3m. No. 3. March Anhalt Zerbtz [sic]. 122.4m. No. 4. March General v[on]. Lewal.
A-123m. Marche de Regiment Graff-Brühl [sic]. 2ob 2hn bn.
MS parts: D-DS, Mus.ms.1224, S.97 - 103, 107. ★
A-124m. [3 Marches; all in D]. 2ob 2hn bn. MS parts: D-DS, Mus.ms.1224, S.119 - 138. ★
A-125m. [3 Marches; all in D]. 2ob 2hn bn. MS parts: D-DS, Mus.ms.1224, S.341 - 349. ★
A-126.1m. Marche du Regiment le Prince de Bervern. 2ob tp basso.
MS parts: D-DS, Mus.ms.1224, S. 141, 143. ★
A-126.2m. Marsch Printz von Bervern [sic]. 2ob bn tp. MS parts: D-DS, Mus.ms.1224, S.231 - 237, No. 3. ★
A-127m. March le Princ d[e] Bevern. 2ob tp basso. MS pts: D-DS, Mus.ms.1224, S.261. *A different march.* ★
A-128m. Marsh De la Primier Guarde de Roÿ [sic]. 2ob tp basso.
MS parts: D-DS, Mus.ms.1224, S. 221 - 227. ★
A-129m. [3 Marches]. 2ob bn tp. MS parts: D-DS, Mus.ms.1224, S.231 - 237. ★
   129.1m. [Friedrich II of Prussia: Mollen Marsch, 1741]. March Royal.
   129.2m. March Erb Printz von Darmstadt [sic].
   129.3m. Marsch Printz von Bervern [sic]. *(= A-126.2m).*
A-130m. March du Regiment Anhald Zerbst [sic]. 2ob tp basso.
MS parts: D-DS, Mus.ms.1224, S. 262. *Not the same as A-122.3m.* ★
A-131m. [Grenadier] March de alt Erb Württemb[erg] [sic]. 2ob bn tp.
MS parts: D-DS, Mus.ms.1224, S.319 - 323. ★
A-132m. Deux Marches; in C. 2ob bn tp. MS parts: D-DS, Mus.ms.1224, S.390 - 393. ★

Germany: Detmold, Lippe Harmonie
A-133m Geschwindmarsch. fl cl(E♭) 2cl(B♭) 2hn 2bn 2tp tb b-hn b-dr.
MS parts: D-DT, Mus-n 2089, No. 2.

Germany: Donauwörth (Swabia), Musiksammlung des Cassianeums
A-126v, 127v. Pange lingua in D u[nd]. Marienlied in C.   CAB, fl 2cl 2hn tp flug a-hn bomb vlne.
MS short score & parts: D-Tl, DWc 399.

Germany: Frankfurt am Main, Fürstbischöfliche (Fulda) Hofkapelle
A-238. Cassatio; in E♭, 17 mvts.   2fl 2cl 2hn 2bn.
MS parts: D-F, Mus.Hs.1564, (missing fl I; fl II missing all after mvt 7).   ★
A-239. N° I Divertissement in Dis [E♭] Per la Capella Principale das Bern, in der Schweitz; 6 mvts.
2cl 2hn bn.   MS parts: D-F, Mus.Hs.1560.   ★
A-240. N° 5 Divertissement in dis [E♭] Per la Capella Principale das Bern, in der Schweitz; 7 mvts.
2cl 2hn 2bn.   MS parts: D-F, Mus.Hs.1561, (bn I missing all after mvt 2; missing bn II).   ★
A-241. N° 7 Divertissement in B[♭] Per la Capella Principale das Bern, in der Schweitz; 6 mvts.   2cl 2hn 2bn.
MS parts: D-F, Mus.Hs.1562.   ★
A-242. Partia in F; 27 mvts.   2cl 2hn bn.   MS parts: D-F, Mus.Hs.1171, (incomplete: missing mvts 1 - 13).   ★
A-134m. [3] Marsch; (No. 5 Marsch; in C minor; No. 6 Geschwind Marsch; in E♭; No. 7 Marcia; in E♭).
pic cl(E♭) 2cl(B♭) 2hn 2bn 2tp(clar) b-tb serp.
MS parts: D-F, Mus.Hs.1173, (missing tp I).   *Originally part of a larger collection.*   ★
A-135m. 6 Marches.   2cl 2hn(3hn in Nos. 5 & 6) bn(2bn in Nos. 3 & 4).
MS parts: D-F, Mus.Hs.1172.   *Nos. 5 & 6 are later additions.*   ★
   135.1m. Vanhal: March; in B♭.   135.2m. Teyber: March; in E♭.   135.3m. Anon: Marsch in E♭.
   135.3m. Anon: Marsch Ponaparth [sic]; in F.   135.5m. Anon: Marsch; in C.   135.6m. Anon: Marsch; in E♭.

Germany: Füssen, Pfarrkiche St Mang, Church Band
A-243. [17 mvts].   pic 2cl(E♭) 2cl(B♭) 2hn bn 2tp.   MS parts (c.1830): D-FÜS, 220.   ★
   243.1. March; in F.   243.2. Adagio; in E♭.   243.3. Re Duple [sic]; in E♭.   243.4. Variacione [sic]; in E♭.
   243.5. Allegretto; in E♭.   243.6. Allomande [sic]; in E♭.   243.7. March; in A♭.   243.8. Angloise; in E♭.
   243.9. Allom [sic: Allemande]; in E♭.   243.10. March; in E♭.   243.11. Variatione; in E♭.
   243.12. Alloma [sic: Allemande]; in A♭.   243.13(a). Aus dem [unterbrochene] Opferfest [by P. von Winter].
   243.14. Angloise; in E♭.   243.15. Allma [sic: Allemande]; in A♭.   243.16. Andante; in E♭.
   243.17. Allma [sic: Allemande]; in E♭.
A-244. Graduale; in B♭.   fl 2cl 2hn 2tp(clar).   MS parts: D-FÜS 167, (missing tp I - ? and other parts).   ★
A-136.1m, 136.2m. Polka oder Parademarsch [E♭] & Parademarsch [B♭].   cl(E♭) 2cl(B♭) b-cl(B♭, No. 2 only).
MS parts: D-FÜS, 179, (? complete).   ★

Germany: Gutenzell, Swabia, Pfarramt (parich church) Band
A-245. 70 Stücke.   2ob 4cl 2hn 2bn 2tp serp timp.   MS pts: D-Tl, Gg 35, (unverified).
A-246. 12 Harmonie Stücke.   pic(D♭) 2fl cl(F) 2cl(C) 2hn 2bn tp(clar) tp(prin) b-dr s-dr.
MS parts ("Ad Chorum Bonac[ellensem] 1827 / Constitit 17."): D-Tl, Gg 99a.   ★
A-247. Harmonie; 4 mvts.   2terz-fl 2cl 2hn bn 2tp(clar).   MS parts: D-Tl, Gg 93.   ★
A-248. Harmonien; 79 mvts.   Incomplete, here only: 2cl(E♭, Nos. 58 - 74 only) 2bn serp timp b-dr tamb.
MS parts: D-Tl, Gg 454, (missing 2fl 2cl(B♭) & 2hns).   *The hand changes after No. 26 & again after No. 57;
Nos. 76-79 in the bn pts are the printed parts for Bühler's IV Hymni, FOB-4v. Nos. 27-34 are Acht Märsche
für Türkische Musick [sic], 1 Heft. (André: Offenbach am Main, pn 1822, [1803]), (A-81.1m). Nos. 35-49 are
Pièces d'Harmonie pour Musique turque par divers Compositeurs. (André: Offenbach S/M, pn 1836, [1803]).
Nos. 50-57 are Nos. 1-6 & 8 of Acht Maersch für Türkische Musik von verschiedenen Komponisten, 2tes Heft.
(André: Offenbach am Main, pn 1816, [1803]), (A-82.2m). Nos. 58-63 are J. Seiff's Militaer Musik. Bestimmt
fuer die National Garden dritter Klasse des Königreichs Baiern, 1tes Heft. (Falter und Sohn: Munich, [c.1802]).
Nos. 65-71 are by Joseph Küffner, probably from one of his Musique turque series (after Recueil No. 2).*   ★
A-249, 250. [2] Harmonien; I: in E♭, 7 mvts; II: in E♭, 6 mvts.   2cl 2hn bn.
MS parts ("Ad Chorum Bonac[ellensem] 1825. Const[itit]. 24x"): D-Tl, Gg 99.   ★
A-251. Geist der Wahrheit.   2cl 2hn.   MS parts: D-Tl, Gg 71.   ★
A-32t. No. IX Harmonien zur Trauer Musik; in C minor, 9 mvts.   2terz-fl(tacet Nos. 6 - 9) 2cl 2hn bn tp.
MS parts ("Ad Chorum Bonac[ellensem]"): D-Tl, Gg 98.   ★
A-128v. Deutscher Messgeseng; "VomStaub o Gott".   CCB, organ, *or* CCB, 2vl 2hn vlne organ.
MS parts ("Von Habsthal / Author unbekant / Text aus dem Konst[anzer]. Ges[ang] Buch"; "Script. ad Chorum
Bonacellensem 1831"): D-Tl, Gg 31.   ★
A-129v. Das Oelberglied, Kom[m]t, und seht, o Sünder!   CATB, (2cl(C) 2hn vlne ad lib).
MS parts ("Scripsimus 1837. ad Chorum Bonacellensem"): D-Tl, Gg 46, (missing A & B vocal parts).   ★
A-130v. Choral Vesper auf das hohe Frohnleichnamsfest über den Text des Konst[anzer]. Gesangbuch.
CAB, 2cl/fl 2hn basso organ.   MS parts ("Ad Chorum Bona[cellensem] 1827"): D-Tl, Gg 63.   ★
A-131v. [5] Gesänge zur Frohnleichnams-Prozession.   CAB, 2cl(E♭) 2cl(B♭) 2hn 2tp(clar) organ+basso.
MS parts ("Composer unbekan[n]t. von Wiesensteig"): D-Tl, Gg 64.   ★
A-132v. Harmonie-Chor; "Horch! wie die Schar dem Hirten signt".   CAB, 2fl 2cl 2hn b-hn vlne.
MS parts: D-Tl, Gg 86.   ★
A-179tv. Pour la Procession Funèbre [sic].   CATB, 2cl 2hn bn+hn(III)+b-tb (2)bn/hn(IV)+b-tb.
MS parts ("Ad chorum B[on]ac[ellem] 1826"): D-Tl, Gg 435; (2vl as alternative for 2cl in Nos. 10 & 11).   ★
Vocals are tacet in Nos. 2, 3, 8 & 11; instruments are tacet in Nos. 1, 4, 5 & 12.
   No. 1. Das Dies Ira [sic].   No. 2. Kozlowski: Marche pour la Procession Funèbre.
   No. 3. Kozlowski: Marche [funèbre].   No. 4. [incomplete vocal work without winds].
   No. 5. Benedictus.   **179.1tv.** No. 6. Am Grabe. Mit oder ohne bebleitung; "Hier, Mensch, Hier lerner.
   No. 7. Zum Graben.   **176.2t(v).** No. 8. Trauermarsch v[on] Norgen aus v[on] [sic] Jannerjungfrau.
   179.3tv. No. 9. Benedictus Contrapunct.   No. 10. Fr. Schneider: Agnus Dei.
   179.4tv(a). No. 11. [? Neefer]: Ad turbate; vocals tacet.   No. 12. Treukent nur ab Jai]ers [sic].

Germany: Herdringen, Schloss Herdringen Biblioteca Fürstenburgiana
A-252. Concerto; in B♭. 4ob bn. MS parts: D-HRD, Fü 3606a.
A-253. Concerto à 5; in F. 3ob 2bn. MS parts: D-HRD, Fü 3701a.
A-254. Concerto; in C, 5 mvts. 4ob 2bn. MS parts: D-HRD, Fü 3702a. ★
A-255. Concerto; in B♭. 3ob bn. MS parts: D-HRD, Fü 3704a.
A-256. Concerto; in C, 3 mvts. 3ob 2bn tp. MS parts: D-HRD, Fü 3715a. ★
Fü 3741a is a remarkable collection of 52 compositions of which the following specify instrumentation.
A-257. Ouverture; in C minor, 8 mvts. 3ob taille bn tp. MS parts: D-HRD, Fü 3741a, Nr. 1, (1 - 12). ★
A-258. Concerto; in D, 5 mvts. 3ob 2bn tp. MS pts: D-HRD, Fü 3741a, (23 - 28).
A-259. Concerto; in B♭. 4ob 2bn. MS parts: D-HRD, Fü 3741a, Nr. 6, (46 - 48).
A-260. Concerto; in F, 4 mvts. 2fl 2ob 2hn 2bn. MS parts: D-HRD, Fü 3741a, Nr. 7, (49 - 54). ★
A-261. Concerto; in C minor, 6 mvts. 3ob taille bn tp. MS parts: D-HRD, Fü 3741a, Nr. 9, (59 - 65). ★
A-262. Concerto in D. 4ob 2bn tp. MS parts: D-HRD, Fü 3741a, (74 - 80).
A-263. Concerto; in C. 3ob taille 2bn. MS parts: D-HRD, Fü 3741a, (122 - 126).
A-264. Simphonia; in B♭. 3ob 2bn tp. MS parts: D-HRD, Fü 3741a, (134 - 139).
A-265. Ouverture; in F, 8 mvts. 2fl 3ob 2hn bn. MS parts: D-HRD, Fü 3741a, Nr. 23, (140 - 149). ★
A-266. Ouverture; in F, 4 mvts. 3ob 2hn 2bn. MS parts: D-HRD, Fü 3741a, Nr. 24, (152 - 156). ★
A-267. Intrade; in B♭, 5 mvts. 4ob 2hn bn, cor de poste. MS parts: D-HRD, Fü 3741a, Nr. 25, (158 - 162). ★
A-268. Concerto; in F, 4 mvts. 3ob 2hnn 2bn. MS parts: D-HRD, Fü 3741a, (167 - 171). ★
A-269. Concerto; in A minor, 3 mvts. 4ob 2bn. MS parts: D-HRD, Fü 3741a, Nr. 28, (172 - 174).
A-270. Concerto; in C, 3 mvts. 4ob 2bn. MS parts: D-HRD, Fü 3741a, Nr. 29, (175 - 177).
A-271. Ouverture; in E♭, 5 mvts. 3ob taille bn tp. MS parts: D-HRD, Fü 3741a, Nr. 31, (186 - 192). ★
A-272. Ouverture; in E♭. 3ob bn tp. MS parts: D-HRD, Fü 3741a, (237 - 246).
A-273. [6] Arien. 4ob 2bn. MS parts: D-HRD, Fü 3741a, 255 - 260.
A-274. Concerto; in C minor, 4 mvts. 3ob taille 2bn tp. MS parts: D-HRD, Fü 3741a, Nr. 38, (261 - 266). ★
A-275. Concerto; in D. 2ob bn tp. MS parts: D-HRD, Fü 3741a, (292 - 306).
A-276. Concerto; in F, 3 mvts. 4ob 2bn. MS parts: D-HRD, Fü 3741a, (307 - 309).
A-277. Concerto; in C, 3 mvts. 4ob 2bn. MS parts: D=HRD, Fü 3741a, (315 - 318).
A-278. [2] Arien & Duett. 4ob 2bn. MS parts. D-HRD, Fü 3741a, (326 - 329).
A-279. Sinfonia; in F, 3 mvts. 2ob 2bn. MS parts: D-HRD, Fü 3741a, (330 - 332).

Germany: Herrenberg, Swabia, Church Band
A-133v. Parce Domine. ATB, 3hn bn. MS parts: D-Tl, Hh 1, (vocal pts without text).

Germany: Ludwigslust, Mecklenburg-Schwerin Court Harmonie (now in D-SWl)
A-301(-304). [Collection: Marsch, Andante maestoso, Allegretto, Quadrille.] 2fl 2ob 2cl 2hn 2bn tp.
MS parts: D-SWl, Mus. 568/1-4. ★
A-305. Allemande in F. ob 2cl 2hn 2bn tp. MS parts: D-SWl, Mus. 592. ★
A-306. 6 Angloises. 2cl 2hn 2bn tp.
MS parts (by Roschlaub, jun., oboist & copyist in the Hofkapelle, Ludwigslust): D-SWl, Mus. 561. ★
A-307. Concerto; in D. 2ob 2bn tp. MS parts: D-SWl, Mus. 327. ★
A-308. Marcia con Minuetto. 2cl 3hn 2bn. MS parts: D-SWl, Mus. 572. ★
A-309. Menuet & Gavotte, in C. 2ob 2hn 2bn tp. MS parts: D-SWl, Mus. 552. ★
A-310. Partia; in F, 3 mvts. 2cl(C) 2hn bn bn/basso. MS parts: D-SWl, Mus. 556. ★
A-311. Parthie in D; 4 mvts. 2ob 2hn bn tp.
MS parts: D-SWl, Mus. 557, (missing bn). ★
A-312. [6] Variations über O du lieber Augustine. 2pic 2cl(C) 2hn 2bn.
MS parts: D-SWl, Mus. 613. ★
A-313. Walzer; in E♭. ob(I) 2cl 2bn tp(prin). MS parts: D-SWl, Mus. 600/1. ★
A-314. Echo=Walzer; in C. fl ob 2cl(C) 2hn 2bn. MS parts ("Dessau, 1810"): D-SWl, Mus. 600/4. ★
A-139m. Friedenmarsch. fl 2ob 2cl 2hn 2bn 2tp(clar) timp b-dr cym tamb(B♭) tri(Bb) [sic].
MS parts: D-SWl, Mus. 575a. ★
A-140m. Marche du Régiment de Bornstädt [sic]. 2ob 2cl 2hn 2bn 2tp. MS parts: D-SWl, Mus. 575b. ★
A-141m. Marcha della Truppa Municipale. 2fl 2hn bn 2tp tb. MS score: D-SWl, Mus. 575c. ★
A-142m. 6 Märsche. 2ob 2hn 2bn tp. MS parts: D-SWl, Mus. 546, (missing bn I). ★
A-143m. 4 Märsche. 2ob 2hn bn tp. MS parts: D-SWl, Mus. 575b. ★
A-144m. Marsch, in E♭. 2ob 2hn bn tp. MS parts: D-SWl, Mus. 566. ★
A-145m. 5 Märsche. 2ob 2cl 2hn.
MS parts: D-SWl, Mus. 548/3, (?missing bn). *Only two marches are titled: No. 1, "March von Leib Regiment"*
& No. 4, "March. in der Areadne [sic, Ariadne]" ★
A-146m. 24 Märsche. 2ob 2hn bn. MS parts: D-SWl, Mus. 548/6. ★
A-147m. Marsch "Du Roy de Prusse". 2ob tp basso. MS: D-SWl, Mus. 569. ★

Germany: Munich (München), Harmonie of Ludwig I of Bavaria
A-137m. Marsch; in E♭. 2fl(E♭) 2cl(E♭) 2cl(B♭) 2cl(B♭, ripieno) 2hn 2bn 2tp b-tb serp b-dr s-dr.
MS parts: D-Mbs, Mus.Ms.2816. ★
A-138m. 5 Märsche. 2ob 2cl(Bb & D) 2hn (2)bn 2tp. MS parts: D-Mbs, Mus.Ms.3668. *Although the*
titlepage lists "Fagotti" the pt is unison throughout; the 2tp are tacet in No 5. With a later piano reduction. ★
  138.1m. March. Erbprinz v. Braunschweig. 138.2m. Zapfenstreich [& Trio].
  138.3m. March [& Trio]. Prinz Anton; (the 2cl are in D). 138.4m. Abtrupp [sic].
  138.5m. March. Leib Grenadiers Garde. d' Saxonie [sic].
Pc (No. 3 only. In: J.A. Kappey. *Military Music*. London: Boosey & Co., 1894), pp. 76 - 77, score.
Pm (No. 3 only. In: Swanzy), pp. 33 - 34, score.

Germany: Ochsenhausen, Kloster & Pfarramt Band
A-134v. [4 Stationes]. CATB, fl 3cl 2hn 2tp t-tb (2)b-tb.
MS parts: D-Tl, B 149, Nr. 2, (at the head of the 1st Lied is the note, "Wird sogleich nach dem Segen gesungen"). ★
A-135v. Lied beim Empfang des Bischofs; "O, der jubelnden Gemeine". CATB, 2cl 2hn 2bn (b-tb) organ.
MS parts: D-Tl, B 150, Nr. 1,2, (with duplicate parts: 3S, A, 2T, B; alternative parts for 2cl 2hn bn organ transposed to A are also present. The later b-tb part bears the title, "Harmonie Begleitung zu dem Lied, beim Empfange des Bischofs für den Firmungs=Akt"). ★
A-136v. Gesang bei der Ankunft des Bischofs; "Kommt, eilt in frohem Jubelton", in F. CATB, 2fl 2hn b-tb.
MS parts: D-Tl, B 150, Nr. 1,3, (with duplicate A, T & B parts). ★
A-137v. Vierstimmiger Gesang bei der Abreise des Bischofs nach dem vorgenommenen heil'[igen].
Firmungs=Akte; "Erschwing' dich, dankge stimmtes Herz". CATB, 2fl 2hn b-tb.
MS parts: D-Tl, B 150, Nr. 1, 4, (with duplicate CATB pts).
A-180tv. Grab lied: Süss u[nd] ruhig ist der Schlummer. Lied auch am Carfreitag bei der Abendandacht gesungen. CATB, fl 2cl 2hn bn basso. MS parts: D-Tl, B 144, Nr. 5,5.

Germany: Regensburg, Thurn und Taxis Harmonie, & Schloß Taxis, Neresheim, Württemberg
A-280. [Parthia in E♭], 11 mvts. 2cl 4hn(E♭, B♭) 2bn 2vla vlne. MS parts (c.1790): D-Rtt, Inc.IVa/16/I. ★
A-281. [?Parthia in E♭], 9 stimmig [sic] 51; 14 mvts. 2cl 2hn 2bn 2vla vlne.
MS parts (c.1790): D-Rtt, Inc.IVa/8, (missing bn I). *A note above No. 4 in the viola I part states "Favorite Von Rudolph und Wack".* ★
A-282. [? von Schacht] Larghetto [& Romance: Andante]; in C. cl(C) 2hn 2bn vlne.
MS score (c.1780): D-Rtt, Inc.IVa/24. ★
A-283. Parthia IIIio, in E♭, 5 mvts. 2cl 2hn bn. MS parts (1773): D-Rtt, Inc.IVa/31/I, Nos. 11 - 15. *A note beside the 3rd mvt states, "Mons: le Baron d'Horben", probably a title rather than the composer.* ★
A-284. Parthia IX; in E♭, 8 mvts. 2cl 2hn 2bn. MS pts (1773): D-Rtt, Inc.IVa/31/I, Nos. 41 - 48. *A note beside the 4th mvt states, "Mlle de Sternbach"; the name probably indicates a title rather than a composer.* ★
A-285. Parthia X; in E♭, 6 mvts. 2cl 2hn bn. MS parts (1773): D-Rtt, Inc.IVa/31/I, Nos. 49 - 54. ★
A-286. Parthia XI; in E♭, 6 mvts. 2cl 2hn bn. MS parts (1773): D-Rtt, Inc.IVa/31/I, Nos. 55 - 60. ★
A-287. A[nn]o 1773. in Januario. Parthia XII. 2cl 2hn bn. MS parts: D-Rtt, Inc.IVa/31/I, Nos. 61 - 65. ★
A-288. Parthia XIII; in E♭, 6 mvts. 2cl 2hn bn. MS parts (1773): D-Rtt, Inc.IVa/31/I, Nos. 66 - 71. ★
A-289. Parthia XIV; in E♭, 11 mvts. 2cl 2hn bn. MS parts (1773): D-Rtt, Inc.IVa/31/I, Nos. 72 - 82. *A pencil note in the hn I part beside the 8th mvt states, "Baron de Schacht"; this probably indicates that this mvt is arranged from Schacht's works rather than composed by him for Harmonie.* ★
A-290. Parthia XVII: E♭, 9 mvts. 2cl 2hn bn. MS parts (1773): D-Rtt, Inc.IVa/31/I, Nos. 96 - 103. *A note in the cl I parts beside the 3rd mvt states, "Cet No. 98. vient de Wallerstein par Mr Barone de Lasberg"; this probably indicates that the is an arrangement, possibly of a vocal work.* ★
A-291. [Parthia in G], Nº 3; 7 mvts. 2a-cl(G) 2vla b. MS parts (c.1780): D-Rtt, Inc.IVa/7/VI. ★
A-292. Six Anglaises. 2cl 2hn 2bn 2vla b. MS parts: D-Rtt, IVb/3. ★
A-293. [Divertimento; 6 Walzer, Ecos: Walzer, Adagio/Allegretto]. 4cl(C) 2hn bn. MS pts: D-Rtt, Inc. VIb/8.★
The 2 pieces below, (c.1802 - 05), may be drawn from J.S. Mayr & J. Wiegl's opera, Ginevra di Scotia.
A-294. Andantino. fl 2ob 2cl 2hn 2bn 2vla vlne. MS parts: D-Rtt, Sm. 32, No. 4. ★
A-295. Andante. fl 2/3ob 2cl 2hn 2bn 2/3vla vc vlne. MS parts: D-Rtt, Sm. 32, No. 5. *The oboe I part has a different part added as "No. 6"; on the last verso of the viola I part is another scoring for 2 violas with different parts; a crossed out "Oboe de Cour" [sic] part precedes the viola II part.* ★
A-296. [224 mvts]. (?Incomplete), here only: bthn hn(II) bn vla. MS parts: D-Rtt, IVa/22. *The bound pts includes arrs from Winter's* Das unterbrochene Opferfest *and Mozart's* Le Nozze di Figaro & Die Zauberflöte. ★
A-138v. Recitative [In così lieto giorno] und Cavatina [Con dolce riposo il cielo pietoso] der Euterpe.
S, ob 2hn bn, "Fagotto Basso" (= bn II), harp. MS score: D-Rtt, Inc.VI/6, (with a loose sheet for the singer with another text, "Rez.: Son pronta o Germane; Cavatina: Del tenero amor mio"). ★

Germany: Neresheim, Schloß Taxis, Württemberg, Thurn & Taxis Regimental Band, (now in D-Rtt)
A-297. Echo mit darauf folgenden 6 Laendler und Coda. 2fl 4cl(C) 4hn 2bn 2posthorn serp(vel tb).
MS score (Echo only) & MS parts (c.1820): D-Rtt, Inc.IVb/9. *The Gardemusik Catalog of 1821 notes that this work was purchased from Kapellmeister Richter in Stuttgart. The main instrumentation comprises 2fl 2cl(C) 2hn 2bn posthorn serp(vel tb), with an Echo of 2cl(C) 2hn posthorn.* ★
A-298. [?A. Schneider] Carousel [Music for the Riding School]; 9 mvts.
pic(D, E♭, F) cl(F) 2cl(C) 4hn 2bn cbn 4tp(clar, D) tp(prin) posthorn b-tb serp b-dr s-dr+t-dr, 2vl vlne.
MS parts ("Zu haben bey H. W. Sondermann in Regensburg", 1831): D-Rtt, Inc.IVa/29, (missing cl I in F, & all strings). ★
The Katalog der Gardemusik (1821) states that the 2 following works (A-299 & A-300) were acquired from Herrn "Rath und Oberförster Haeckel in [Bad] Buchau".
A-299. [35 Stücke]. 2cl(E♭) 2cl(B♭) 2hn bn. MS parts (c.1810): D-Rtt, Inc.IVa/28, (the bn pt ends after No. 26; 3 works have been added in the B♭ cl I pt only). ★
A-300. [87 Stücke]. 2cl 2hn bn. MS parts (c.1810): D-Rtt, Inc.IVa/27. ★

Germany: Wertheim-am-Main, Löwenstein Harmonie
A-301. Andante; in B♭. 2hn bn. MS parts: GB-Ljag(w). ★
A-302. [3 dances: Walzer, Polonaise, Dreher]. fl(F) 2cl(B♭) 2hn bn(I) bn(II)/b-tb tp(patent).
MS parts: GB-Ljag(w). ★
A-303. Marcia; in E♭. 2hn 2bn.
MS parts: GB-Ljag(w), (bn pts incomplete; with various fragments of other pieces added at a later date). ★
A-304. [Set of 13 movements & dances]. 2hn 1/2bn basso. MS parts: GB-Ljag(w).
A-305. [Set of 24 mvts & dances]. Incomplete: here only hn(I) bn(II). MS parts: GB-Ljag(w).

Italy: Anonymous Instrumental & Vocal Works
A-148.1m. Ordinance Del Reg[imen]to Della R[ea]le Guarda Swizzera [sic], [for the Band of the King of Sicily].
Melodies only except No. 9: 2ob 2hn bn. MS score: I-Mc, Noseda V.50.19. *All of the pieces are in two
sections except No. 9 which is in three.* ★
  148.1/1m. No. 1. La Generale, 3/8, f.1b.
  148.1/2m. No. 2. Drappò De Granatierei, 2/4, f.1b
  148.1/3m. No. 3. Samblé [assemblea], 2/4, f.1b.
  148.1/4m. No. 4. Retrette [ritirata], 3/8, f.1b.
  148.1/5m. No. 5. Marcia De Granatieri, Largo 2/4, f.2.
  148.1/6m. No. 6. Chiamata [call to arms], 3/8, f.2.
  148.1/7m. No. 7. Drappò De Mugchettieri [Moschettiere], 2/4, f.2.
  148.1/8m. No. 8. Marcia De Fucilieri, 2/4, f.2.
  148.1/9m. No. 9. Marcia Di Musica, Eb, ff.2b - 3.
A-148.2m. Originale Tocchi di Guerra O sia Ordinance Che devono sapere suonare tutte le Bande Di S.R.M.
Il Re delle Due Sicilie. pic quart-fl 2cl(Bb) 4hn(Eb) 2bn 2tp(keyed, Eb) tp(keyed, Ab) tp(Bb) tp(C) 3tb basso
b-dr s-dr. MS score: I-Mc, Noseda V.50.6. *This is a later rescoring of A-106.1m.* ▲
  148.2/1m. No. 1. L'Asseblera [sic], ¢, , ff.1b - 2, (= 106.1m/3).
  148.2/2m. No. 2. Il Drappò, ho [sic] sia La Bandiera, 2/4, ff. 2b -3, (= 148.1/2m).
  148.2/3m. No. 3. La Marcia di Fucilieri, ¢, ff.3b - 4, (= 148.1/8m).
  148.2/4m. No. 4. La Marcia di Granatiera, ¢, ff.4b - 5, (= 148.1/5m).
  148.2/5m. No. 5. La Vitorota [sic], ¢, ff.5b - 6, (no match).
  148.2/6m. No. 6. La Chiamata, 2/4, ff.6b - 7, (= 148.1/6m).
  148.2/7m. No. 7. La Massa, 3/8, ff.7b - 8, (= 148.1/4m).
  148.2/8m. No. 8. La Fascina, ho Sia il Vancia [sic], 2/4, ff.8b - 9, (= 148.1/7m).
  148.2/9m. No. 9. La Generale, 3/8, ff.9b - 10, (= 148.1/1m).
  148.2/10m. No. 10. Il Bando, 2/4, ff.10b - 11, (= 148.1/9m).
A-149m. Marciata E [5] Passi Padoppiati. pic("Decimino") cl(F, "Clarinetto Quartino") 2hn bn 2tp b-tb b-dr.
MS parts (c.1800): GB-Ljag, (possibly missing "Decimino Secondo"). ★
A-139v. Dio te salve Maria. TTB, 2pic(Db) 2hn 2cl(C) 2hn 2tp b. MS score: GB-Lhumphries. ★

Italy: Brescia, Archivo Capitolare del Duomo, Anonymous Vocal Works
A-140v. Beatus vir; in A minor. B solo, BB chorus, fl 2cl 2hn 2tp b-tb bombardino timp.
MS short score & MS parts: I-BRd, palch. 6-7/VII, (missing cl II).
A-141v. Confitebor tibi Domine; in F. TTB, fl 2cl 2hn 3tp b-tb cb organ.
MSS parts: I-BRd, palch. 6-7/XVII, (with a duplicate T(I) part).
A-142v. Dixit Dominus; in C. TTBB, 2cl 2hn 3tp tb bombardino vlne organ.
MS vocal score & instrumental parts: I-BRd, palch. 6-7/XVI, (missing cl I).

Italy: Venice, Pia Casa di Ricovero, Anonymous Vocal Works
A-143v. Gloria. TTB, 2ob 2hn bn organ. MS pts: I-Vcr, Busta II, N.25.
A-144v. Qui tollis. TTB, 2ob 2hn bn organ. MS pts: I-Vcr, Busta III, N.37.
A-145v. Tantum ergo. BAR solo, 2cl 2hn bn organ. MS pts: I-Vcr, Busta X, N.161.

Italy: Venice, Santa Maria Consolazione detta "della Fava", Anonymous Vocal Works
Duplicate vocal parts are indicated by a number in parentheses following the
A-146v. Beatus vir. TTB(solo+rip), 2ob 2hn 2tp timp.
MS parts: I-Vsmc, (missing T(II) di Ripieno, ?& organ). ★
A-147v. Criste a 3 Voci. TTB, fl 2cl 2hn basso/bn organ(full part). MS parts: I-Vsmc. ★
A-148v. Compieta. TTB(solo+rip), 2cl 2hn (vlne) organ(bc-fig).
MS parts: I-Vsmc, (the vlne part does not appear in the score. The organ part in score is a mixture of bc-fig
& written part; there is an additional full part). *Partly anonymous: the Qui habitat is by Fedeli; this segues to
the Ecce nunc benedicite Dominum by Fedeli; the Canticum Simonij [sic], 2 Nunc dimittis etc. a 3 Voci" are
by Deola & bear the date 1852.* ★
A-149v. Introito per la Funzion delle Relique nell'ultima Dom[ini]ca d'Agosto. TTB, 2ob 2hn vlne.
MS parts: I-Vsmc, (probably complete, with the vlne also serving as the organ(bc-fig) part). ★
  1. Sapientiam sanctorum, 2. Exultate justi in Domino, 3. Gloria. "Sicut erat in principo".
A-150v. Introito IIa. Domenica di Quaverima, "Reminiscere miseratiorum tuarum Domine".
T(3)T(3)T(3), 2cl 2hn vlne organ(bc-fig).
MS parts: I-Vsmc, (with an additional violone part, "senza Stromenti"). ★
A-151v. Salve Regina. T solo, 2ob 2hn organ. MS pts: I-Vsmc, (missing organ). ★
A-152v(f). Beati omnes. Here only: T II, cl(I & II) hn(I) bn. MS pts: I-Vsmc. ★
A-153v(f). Credo in Bb. TTB, 2cl 2hn bn timp organ.
MS score: I-Vsmc, (missing the opening section(s), complete from the Qui tollis onward).
A-154v(f). Credo. T(2)T(2)B(3), 2cl 2hn bn tp vlne timp organ.
MS score: I-Vsmc, (missing the first 79 bars; complete from the Qui sedes onward; with duplicate vocal parts).
A-155v(f). Credo. T(2)T(2)B(3), fl 2cl 2hn bn 2tp vlne timp organ.
MS score: I-Vsmc, (missing the opening: begins "... suscipe"; complete from the Qui sedes onward).
A-156v(f). Gloria. T(2)T(2)B(3), fl 2cl 2hn tp timp organ.
MS score: I-Vsmc, (missing part of the first section; with duplicate vocal parts).
A-157v(f). Gloria. TTB, 2cl 2hn tp basso organ(bc-fig).
MS score: I-Vsmc, (missiing the first 8 bars of the instrumental introduction).
A-158v(f). Mass in C. 2cl 2hn bn/basso organ. MS score: I-Vsmc, (missing vocal parts).
A-159v(f). Salve Regina. Here only: cl(I), hn(I&II). MS parts: I-Vsmc, (missing vocal parts, cl II, organ).

Netherlands: Zeist, Moravian Congregation
There are also many compositions for trombone choir in this collection.
A-315.1(-315.5). 5 compositions. 2fl ob cl(Eb) 2cl(Bb) 2hn 2bn 2tp.
MS parts: NL-Z, Z1133, Nos. 1 - 3, 5, 11, 12, (the cl in Eb pt is in another hand but is probably contemporary).
Identified compositions can be found at Mankell, Rauscher & Ries. In addition, there are three short pieces included in the horn I part & 7 in the horn II part. ★
    316.1. Allegro, Eb, 2/4.   316.2. Allegro, Eb, 6/8.   316.3. March (& Trio), in Eb, ¢.
    316.4(a). God Save the King.   316.5. Marsch, Eb, ¢. *Also appears as "Marche Française", scored for cl(Eb) 2cl(Bb) 2hn 2bn, at NL-Z, Z1137, No. 1, (missing the horn II part).*
    316.6. Marsch der polnischen Lensenträger (& Trio), in Eb, 2/4.
A-150.1m, 150.2m. 2 Marches, C, Eb. Incomplete, here only: cl(II) hn(I & II) bn(II) tp.
Pc (sn: sl, pn 489, sd), parts: NL-Z, Z1155.

Switzerland: Einsiedeln, Kloster Einsiedeln, Benedictiner Stift
A-316. [43] Kleine Stücke. fl cl 2hn 2bn. MS parts: CH-E, Th.51,40.
A-317. [8] Kleine Stücke. 2cl 2hn bn. MS parts: CH-E, Th.62,6.
A-318. [11 Stücke für Bläser]. 2fl 2hn bn.
Pc (sn: sl, sd), RISM [AN 3094], parts: CH-E, (bassoon pt in MS).
A-319. [3 Sätze, No 2 in F, No 3 in Bb; ? part of A-309]. Instrumentation unknown.
Pc (sn: sl, pn 170, sd), RISM [AN 3095], parts: CH-E (pp. 6 - 8, 10 - 13 only of the bassoonn part).
A-320. Adagio. fl 2ob 2cl 3hn 2bn 2tb piano. MS parts: CH-E, Th.60,12.
A-321. [35] Allemands. 2cl 2hn bn. MS parts: CH-E, Th.62,9.
A-322. Intrada Nr. 2, "per la Festa di Pentacoste" 1796). 2cl 2hn 3tp timp 2organs (?bns read from organ bass line). MS parts: CH-E, Th.60,22.
A-323. Intrada Nr. 1, "per la Festa di Pasqua", 1787. ob/cl 2hn 4tp timp 2organs (?bns read from organ bass line). MS parts: CH-E, Th.60,23.
A-324. Intrada, "Pastorale Nr. 1, per il S. Natale". 2cl bn 4hn 4tp timp 2organs.
MS parts: CH-E, Th.60,24.
A-325. Intrada, "Pastorale. Andantino "per il Santo Natale". 2cl 4hn 2tp timp 2 organs (?bns read from organ bass lines). MS parts: CH-E, Th.60,27a.
A-326. Intrada. Winds divided into two choruses; Chorus 1: 2cl 2hn bn 3tp; Chorus 2: 2fl 2hn tp timp.
MS parts: CH-E, Th.60,30.
A-327(-362). [36] Quintet, 1797. 2cl 2hn bn. MS parts: CH-E, Th.86,4.

Switzerland: Other works
A-363. [22] Kurze Stücke. fl 2cl 2hn tp.
MS parts: CH-Fcu, Ebaz IV-39, (?missing bn pts).

Ukraine: Tulchin (Tulczyn), Harmonie of Spohie (Zofia) Potocka
A-151m, 152m. [2] Marche; in Bb. 2fl 2cl 2hn 2bn.
MS parts: PL-LA, RM 81 / 1 - 5 / 11 & 12, (missing fl I, hn I, bn II).

United States of America: Bethlehem & Lititz, Pennsylvania: Moravian Brethren
A-153m. March, No. 13 [Kurek's Military Music]. pic cl(Eb) 3cl(Bb) 2hn 2valve-tp 2t-tb 2oph basso b-dr s-dr.
Pc (Published by C.H. Keith: Boston, 1843), parts: US-BETm, Philharmonic Society of Bethlehem PSB L-18. ★
A-154m. Winchester's Quick Step. Kurek's Military Music No. 14.
pic cl(Eb) 4cl(Bb) 2hn 2crt(Eb, Bb) 3t-tb 2oph basso b-dr s-dr.
Pc (Published by C.H. Keith: Boston, pn 116, 1843), parts: US-BETm, (2 copies), Philharmonic Society of Bethlehem PSB L-17. ★
A-155.1m(-155.7m). XII Marches. 2cl 2hn bn tp.
MS parts: US-BETm, Lititz Collegium Musicum 203. *Works without A-155.xm numbers can be found in the Main Works List under the relevant composer. We believe that both works by Rolle are arrangements of marches from his religious musical dramas.* ★
    155.1m(a).   I. Aus Wallenstein [? Wallensteins Lager], Eb, ¢.
                II. Di Bechler, ¢.
    155.2m.   III. Marsch der Leibgard zu Dresden, Eb, ¢.
    155.3m(a).   IV. Aus Turza [sic: Thirza und ihre Söhne] von Rolle, Eb, ¢.
                V. Di Türk, ¢.
    155.4m(a).   VI. Di Rolle, ¢.
                VII. Di Bechler, ¢.
    155.5m.   VIII. Bonoparte's [sic] March, Eb,¢.
    155.6m.   IX. Bonoparte's [sic] March, called the Mantuane, Eb, ¢.
                X. Di Türk, ¢.
                XI. Di Gebhard, ¢.
    155.7m.   XII. Washington's March, Eb, ¢.

ARRANGEMENTS

ANONYMOUS COLLECTIONS

A-1a. 88 Stücke (?original mvts & opera arrs). Nos. 1 - 48: 2cl 4hn 2bn 2tp 2vla cb; Nos. 49 - 81: 2cl 2hn 2bn.
MS parts: D-Rtt, Inc. IVa/21/II. *Nos. 1 - 48 may include original works. Nos. 49 - 81, a later addition, are scored for 2cl 2hn 2bn and may be arrangments drawn from Valentin Roeser's many published works, now lost.*
    A-1.29a. Vachon: Marche Lento.   A-1.37a (-41a, 44a). Schacht (after Grétry): La Rosière de Salenci, 6 mvts.
    A-1.42a, 43a, Monsigny: Le Déserteur, 2 mvts.   A-1.45a. Schacht: Rosamund, 1 mvt.
    A-1.49a. Anon: Hamlet (probably *Hamlet, Prinz von Dännemark*, Hamburg, c.1786), 1 mvt.
    A-1.55a, 57a. Grétry: Les deux Avares (as Die beiden Geizigen), march, vaudeville
    A-1.56a. Anon: Henriette, 1 mvt.   A-1.58a. [unidentified], 1 mvt "Sans l'amour".
    A-1.74a, 76a, 77a, 78a. Grétry: Zémire et Azor, "Veillons mes Soeurs", "Ah! quel torment", "Rassure mon
    père", Rose chérie", "Amour, Amour, quand ta rigueur".
    A-1.79a, 81a. Philidor: Tom Jones, "Amour, Amour", "Oui, toute ma vie".
    A-1.82a. [unidentified], "Dalbert, Sie wanckt dahin".
A-2a. 89 Stücke.   2cl 2hn 2bn.   MS parts: D-BAR.   *Composers are identified for the following mvts: No. 1, Distler; No. 6, Laussenmayer; No. 12, Collier; No. 18, Rosetti; No. 39, Wineberger; No. 73, [?Valentin] Roeser; Nos. 77 & 78, Vanhal; No. 79, [?Johann Samuel] Schröter; No. 80, Davaux; No. 81, Cramer.*
A-3a. Ouvertur und [11] Arien aus verschiedenen Opern.   2ob 2cl 2hn 2bn.
MS score (allegedly in the hand of J.S. Mayr): I-BGc, Mayr 596, (2 mvts are numbered "9").
    3.1a. Kauer: Ritter Willibald, overture. [unnumbered].
    3.2a. Winter: Das unterbrochene Opferfest, 5 mvts. Nos. 1 - 5.   (= WENT, JNW-71a)
    3.3a. Haydn: Die Schöpfung, Holch Gottin in zum seihe. No. 6.   (= DRUSCHETZKY, GYD-13a)
    3.4a. Paer: Camilla, terzetto. No. 7.   (= WENT, JNW-35.1a)
    3.5a (- 3.7a). [4 unidentified mvts]: No. 8, Moderato, 2/4; No. 9, Variazione, moderato, 2/4;
        No. 9 [sic] Maestoso, ¢; No. 10 [sic], Maestoso, 2/4, *Attacca* Rondo, 2/4.
A-4a. Miscellanées de la Musique arrangées . . . Brünn am 20 December [1]817.   2ob 2cl 2hn 2bn cbn.
MS parts: CZ-Bm, A.35.255, (without a separate cbn part).
    4.1a. Winter: Das unterbrochene Opferfest, overture.   (= WENT, JNW-71a)
    4.2a, 4.3a. Dalayrac: Sargines, 2 mvts.   4.4a. Kauer: Das Donauweibchen, 1 mvt.
    4.5a. Triebensee: Neuer Ländler in A♭. *In fact No. 7 of Triebensee's Miscellannées, Jg I, Oe 4, (JZT-16).*
A-5a. Sammlung; 11 mvts.   2cl 2hn 2bn.   MS parts: CZ-Pnm, XLI.B.124.
    5.1a. Rossini: Ciro in Babilonia, overture.
    5.2a - 5.11a. [10 unidentified mvts - not from *Ciro in Babilonia.*]

The following three collections are from the Nationalbibliothek, Vienna. Hellyer & Whitwell attribute these arrangements to Triebensee; Weinmann attributes A-6a to Druschetzky. We cannot accept these unverified suggestions. The majority of the arrangements appear to be drawn from anonymous arrangements issued in MS by the kk Hoftheater-Musik-Verlag - which may have been responsible for this compilation.
A-6a. Aus den besten Opera und Ballet. 2ob 2cl 2hn 2bn cbn. MS pts: A-Wn, Mus.Hs.3792. *Nos. 6.1a-6.5a call for "Fagotto 3zia Col Fagotto 2do"; divisi in the bn II part (for cbn) occur in Nos 6.20a, 6.22a-6.24a, 6.31a & 6.32a, 6.37a (without any mention of cbn on the bn II pt); Nos 6.45 & 6.46 specify a cbn (with a separate pt). For a further discussion of these collections, See: TRIEBENSEE, p. 278.*

A-6.1a, 6.2a.	Mayr: La Lodoiska, ouverture, aria.	(= H-M-V; ANON, A-289a)
A-6.3a.	Zingarelli: Pirro, Re d'Egitto, rondo.	(= H-M-V; ANON A-628a)
A-6.4a.	Mayr: La Lodoiska, polonoise.	(= H-M-V; ANON A-289a)
A-6.5a.	Zingarelli: Pirro, Re d'Egitto, rondo.	(= H-M-V; ANON A-628a)
A-6.6a.	Mozart: La Clemenza di Tito, Atto 2do Terzetto.	(= TRIEBENSEE, JZT-40a)
A-6.7a, 6.8a.	Salieri: Cesare in Farmacusa, terzetto, finale.	(= H-M-V; ANON A-491a)
A-6.9a, 6.10a.	Paer: L'Intrigo amoroso (as *Die wankelmüthige Frau*), duetto, aria.	(= H-M-V; ANON A-392a)
A-6.11a.	Mozart: Don Giovanni, duetto ("Là ci darem").	(= TRIEBENSEE, JZT-39.2a)
A-6.12a.	Paer: L'Intrigo amoroso (as *Die wankelmüthige Frau*), polonaise.	(= H-M-V; ANON A-392a)
A-6.13a, 6.14a.	Cimarosa: Gli Orazi e Curiazi (attrib. to Mayr), sinfonia & largo.	(= WENT; JNW-12a)
A-6.15a.	Zingarelli: Giulietta e Romeo, aria "Idola del mio cor".	(= ANON A-632a)
A-6.16a.	J. Weigl: Richard Löwenherz, marcia.	(= WENT, JNW-65.1a)
A-6.17a.	Mozart: La Clemenza di Tito, marcia.	(= TRIEBENSEE, JZT-40, Nos. 4 & 9)
A-6.18a(-23a).	Paer: Camilla, sinfonia & 5 arias.	(= WENT, JNW-35.1a)
A-6.24a.	Mayr: Lodoiska, marcia.	(= H-M-V; ANON A-289a)
A-6.25a(-29a).	J. Weigl: Alcina, overture & 4 nos.. (No. 29: "Andante Casantini Solo").	(= WENT, JNW-19ac)
A-6.30a.	J. Weigl: Rolla's Tod, marcia.	
A-6.32a, 33a.	P. Wranitzky & J. Kinsky: Das Waldmädchen, polonoise, La Russe.	(= WENT, JNW-72.1a)
A-6.34a, 6.35a.	Anon [here attributed to Pavel Wranitzky]: Terzetto, 2 mvts.	(= WENT, JNW-21ac)
A-6.36a, 37a.	J. Weigl: L'Amor marinaro, ouverture & polonoise.	(= ANON A-583a)

The following works were added at a later date in another hand and may be by Triebensee (JZT-1c - JZT-8c).

A-6.38a.	Variazionen über das Menuet aus Mozart's Don Juan [Don Giovanni].
A-6.39a.	Variazionen über ein Thema /: Triebst der Champagner:/ aus d°. [Mozart: Don Giovanni, "Finch' han dal vino"].
A-6.40a.	Variazionen über einer [?original] Marsch.
A-6.41a.	Variationen über das [? original] Zapfenstreich.
A-6.42a.	[J. Schuster, ?arr W. Müller: *Das neu Sonntagskind*]: Pas de deux getanzt von Hrn. und Mad. Viganò
A-6.43a.	Variationen über das Volkslied [by Haydn]: Gott erhalte der Kaiser [sic].
A-6.44a.	Variationen über das Thema: O du lieber Augustine.
A-6.45a.	Menuetto mit 2 Trios.
A-6.46a.	Andante mit Variationen. [= Haydn: Symphony in E♭ (Hob. I/103ii), "Drumroll"].

A-7a. № 54. Miscellannées [sic] de Musique; 9 (+1) mvts.   2ob 2cl 2hn 2bn cbn.
MS parts: A-Wn, Mus.Hs.3793. *Probably drawn from issues and reissues by the Hoftheater-Musik-Verlag, Wien.*
  A.7.1a. No. 1. Berton: Aline, Reine de Golconde, allegro [march in D, ¢]. (= ANON, A-56.1a, No. 4)
  A.7.2a. Nos. 2, 3. Cherubini: Les deux Journées (as *Der Tage der Gefahr*). (= P. MAŠEK, PLM-1.1a)
  A.7.3a. Nos. 4 - 8. Winter: Das unterbrochene Opferfest, overture & 4 mvts. (= WENT, JNW-71a)
  A.7.4a. No. 9. Federici: Zaira, aria con coro.
  A.7.5a. No. 10. [unidentified mvt: Andante Sostenuto 3/4 / Rondo Andante, C]. *Added later in another hand.*
A-8a. № 65. Auszug / Aus verschiedene Ballets und Opern [red pencil: No. 4]. 2ob 2cl 2hn 2bn cbn.
MS parts (post-1812): A-Wn, Mus.Hs.3794. *It is possible that KRECHLER (qv) was the compiler.*
  8.1a. No. 1. Paer: Il Morto vivo, Allegro vivace.
  8.2a. Nos. 2-14. M. Umlauf: Das eigensinnige Landmädchen, overture, 12 mvts. (TRIEBENSEE, JZT-60.2a)
  8.3a. No. 15. Moser: Quadrille aus Die Berg-Schotten. (TRIEBENSEE, JZT-37.2a)
  8.4a. Nos. 16, 17. Gyrowetz: Der Augenarzt, cavatina & sextetto.   (STARKE, FRS-10a)
  8.5a. Nos. 18 - 22. Duport: Der blöde Ritter, overture & 4 mvts.   (TRIEBENSEE, JZT-14,2a)
A-9a. Verschiedene Stücke aus Ballets und Opern. 3bthn. MS pts: CZ-Pnm, XLII.A.67. *Possibly by Volánek.*
  9.1a. Anon: Romanze poco Adagio.   10.2a. Anon: Menuetto Allegretto.
  9.3a. A.J.A. Volánek: Marsch v. Wolanek.
  9.4a. Anon: Andante del Opera Amore e Psiche [sic].   *The 3 following mvts may also be from this opera.*
  9.5a. Anon: Allegretto. 9.6a. Anon: Allegretto. 9.7a. Anon: Polonese.
  9.8a. Adagio v[on] Mozart.   9.9a. Anon: Langsam und Sanft. 9.10a. Anon: Adagio.
  9.11a. Anon: Selige Tage. 9.12a. Anon: Hebe sich in sanfte ruhe! 9.13a. Anon: Lebe wohl.
  9.14a. Anon: [-], 3/4. 9.15a. Mozart: La Clemenza di Tito. Allegro. 9.16a. Anon: Caros Marsh [sic].
  9.17a. Vogler: [Castor e Polluce] Cast. Pollux. 9.18a. Salieri: [Tarare] Axur, Re d'Ormus, Adagio.
  9.19a. Anon: Menuetto. 9.20a. Anon: Marcia de Buonap[arte]. 9.21a. Anon: Variationen.
  9.22a. Anon: Andante. 9.23a. Anon: Ländlerisch. 9.24a. P. Wranizky: Das Waldmädchen, Polonese.
A-10a. Collection of 61 dances (Hopwalzer, Walzer, Galopps, Marsch, Cottillon, Polonaisen) in the hands of
Georg Schmitt & W.E. Scholz. Only No. 32 (Kühn: Der alte Feldherr, Walzer) identifies Schmitt as the arranger,
and we list this work at GYS-37a; other arrangments in this volume are probably also by Schmitt. We list here
only the titled movements.) fl 2ob 3cl(cl III in Nos. 25 - 31 only) 2hn 2bn b-tb b.
MS parts (in the hands of Georg Schmitt & W.E. Scholz): D-NEhz, 134.
  10.25a. Anon: Skreyneckis Marsch.   10.26a. Anon: Polonaise zu Ehren Mysockis.
  10.29a. Meyerbeer: Robert le Diable, Galopp.
  10.30a. Anon: Marsch der Sensenträger beim Auszug aus Warschau.
  10.31a. Anon: Marsch der J. [i.e. I] National Guard in Warschau.
  10.32a. Kühn: Der alte Feldherr, Walzer.   (= Schmitt. GYS-37a)
  10.42a. C.M. Weber: Oberon, Walzer.   10.44a. C.M. Weber: Oberon, Walzer.
  10.45a. Paganini: [Violin Concerto in B minor, Op. 7, Rondo, "La Campanella"], Walzer.
  10.46a. C.M. Weber: Oberon, Walzer. 10.47a. Auber: [La Muette de Portici], Walzer Stummen v[on]. Pa. [sic].

Here we give details of anonymous arrangements found in the collection of the Löwenstein Kapelle, Wetheim-am-
Main. The scores, all in the same unidentifed hand, clearly originte with some other Harmonie - being on paper
not usually asociated with Wertheim with instrumentation other than that used by the Löwnestein Harmonie.
Versions of these works - and others where scores are not present - found in the bound parts are listed at A-20a.
A-11a. Bellini: La Straniera, Aria. fl(F) cl(E♭) 2cl(B♭) 2hn bn tp(patent, A♭) b-tb serp.
AutoMS score: GB-Ljag(w), 338.   MS parts: GB-Ljag(w), 371.38. (cb replaces serp).
A-12a. Küffner: XVIIIme Potpourri sur les motifs de l'opéra La Muette de Portici [by Auber], Op. 222.
fl(F) cl(E♭) 2cl(B♭) 2hn bn 2tp b-tb serp.   AutoMS score: GB-Ljag(w), 337.
A-13.1a(-13.4a). [Collection of 4 arrangements].   fl(F, pic F) cl(E♭) 2cl(B♭) 2hn bn tp(patent) tp b-tb serp.
AutoMS score: GB-Ljag(w), 355.1.   MS parts: GB-Ljag(w), 371.31, 371.32, 372/3.15, 3.16 (omits patent tp).
  13.1a. Bellini: [La Straniera], Potpourrÿ [sic] aus der Unbekante. pp. 1-16.
  13.2a. Lobe: Die Fürstin von Granada, Jagd-Chor. pp. 17-21.
  13.3a. Lanner: Olymp's Walzer, Op. 67. pp. 21-27.
  13.4a. Strauss *the Elder:* Fortuna Galopp, Op. 69. pp. 28-32.
A-14.1a, 14.2a. [Collection of 2 arrangements].   fl(pic E♭) ob cl(E♭) 2cl(B♭) 2hn bn 2tp b-tb serp.
AutoMS score: GB-Ljag(w), 371.40, 372/3.2.
  14.1a. Bellini: La Straniera, duetto.   pp. 1-7.   14.2a. Küffner: Vierzehn Tänze, Op. 252, Galopp. p. 8.
A-15.1a(-15.4a). [Collection of 4 arrangements.] pic(E♭, fl F) cl(E♭) 2cl(B♭) 2hn bn 2tp tb serp b-dr s-dr.
AutoMS score: GB-Ljag(w).   MS parts: GB-Ljag(w), 372/3.3 - 3.6.
  15.1a. Auber: Fra Diavolo, Walzer. pp. 1-3.   15.2a. Auber: Fra Diavolo, Galopp. pp. 4-5.
  15.3a. Hérold: Zampa, Walzer. pp. 5-8.   15.4a. Hérold: Zampa, Galopp. pp. 9-10.
A-16.1a, 16.2a. [Collection of 2 arrangements]. pic(E♭, fl F) cl(E♭) 2cl(B♭) 2hn bn 2tp tb serp b-dr t-dr.
AutoMS score: GB-Ljag(w).   MS parts: GB-Ljag(w), 3.7, 3.8
  16.1a. Meyerbeer: Robert le Diable, Walzer. pp. [1]-4.   16.2a. Marschner: Der Vampyr, Walzer. pp. [5-8].
A-17.1a(-17.3a). [Collection of 4 arrangements, missing No. 1.] fl(E♭) ob cl(E♭) 2cl(B♭) 2hn bn 2tp b-tb serp.
AutoMS score: GB-Ljag(w), 355.4.   MS pts: GB-Ljag(w), 372/3.10 - 3.12. (No. 1 is probably A.20.9a.)
  17.1a. Hérold: Zampa, Walzer. No. 2. pp. 5-7.   17.2a. Auber: Gustave III, Galopp. No. 3. pp. 8-9.
  17.3a. Hérold: Le Pré aux Clercs, Galopp. No. 4. pp. 10-11.
A-18.1a, 18.2a. [Collection of 2 arrangements, numbered 5 & 6.] fl(F) ob cl(E♭) 2cl(B♭) 2hn bn 2tp b-tb serp.
AutoMS score: GB-Ljag(w), 355.3.   MS parts: GB-Ljag(w), 371.39, 372/3.13.
  18.1a. Bellini: La Straniera, Introduzion. pp. 1-11.
  18.2a. Lanner: Die Badner Ring'In Walzer, Op. 64. pp. 12-16.
A-19.1a(-19.4a). [Collection of 6 arrangements.] fl(F) 2cl(E♭) 2cl(B♭) 2hn 2bn tp b-tb cb.
AutoMS parts: GB-Ljag(w), 111.
  19.1a. Strauss *the Elder:* Die Nachwandler Walzer, Op. 87.   19.2a. Auber: Le Domino noir, Galopp.
  19.3a. Strauss *the Elder:* Elisabethan-Walzer, Op. 71.
  19.4a. Strauss *the Elder:* Erinnerung an Deutschland, Walzer, Op. 87.
  19.5a. Strauss *the Elder:* Kettenbrüche-Galopp, Op. 21b. 19.6a. Strauss *the Elder* [spurious]: Eisenbahn Galopp.

A-20.1a(-A.20.16a). [Collection of 16 arrangements.] pic(E♭, fl F) cl(E♭) 2cl(B♭) 2hn 2bn 2tp(1 - 8)/tp(9 - 16) b-tb cb b-dr(Nos. 3 - 6).   MS parts: GB-Ljag(w), 372/3
   20.1a. Auber: Fra Diavolo, Walzer.   20.2a. Anon: Galopp.   20.3a. Auber: Fra Diavolo, Walzer.
   20.4a. Auber: Fra Diavolo, Galopp.   20.5a. Hérold: Zampa, Walzer.   20.6a. Hérold: Zampa, Galopp.
   20.7a. Meyerbeer: Robert le Diable, Walzer.   20.8a. Marschner: Der Vampyr, Walzer.
   20.9a. Marschner: Der Vampyr, Walzer.   20.10a. Hérold: Zampa, Walzer.
   20.11a. Auber: Gustave III, Galopp.   20.12a. Hérold: Le Pré aux Clercs, Galopp.
   20.13a. Strauss *the Elder:* Badner Ring'In Walzer.   20.14a. Küffner: Vierzehn Tänze, Op. 252, Galopp.
   20.15a. Lanner: Olymp's Walzer, Op. 67.   20.16a. Strauss *the Elder:* Fortuna Galopp, Op. 69.

Here we give details of anonymous and/or unidentified arrangements in the bound collection from the Tulchin (Ukraine) Harmonie (signed by Sophie Potacka) now held in Łańcut, Poland (PL-LA). Identified items can be found at: Bianchi, Boieldieu, Cherubini, Della Maria, Gassmann, Haydn, Kozlowski, Martín y Soler, Méhul, Mozart, Paisiello, Piccini, Pleyel, Salieri & Sarti, two anonymous marches are at A-151m, A-152m. It is possible that virtually all of these items were arranged by F.L. Michel (q.v.).
A-21a. Collection of anonymous arrangements.   2fl 2cl 2hn 2bn.
MS parts: PL-LA, RM 81/1-5/1-178, (missing cl I, hn I, bn II).
A-21.1a(-8a). Nos. 2-9. 8 short mvts, (Andante, Andante, Allegro, Allegro moderato, Andante affectuoso [sic], Andante non molto, Andante, Andantino).   *These movements follow a work by Kozlowski [JOK-1] for which the cl I part bears the heading "Stucke [sic] in B[♭]", but we cannot confirm they are also by Koslowski.*
A-21.9a. No. 10. Kantata, (Allegro maestoso, C minor; Andante, B♭; Poloneso & Trio, E♭).
A-21.10a. No. 13. Kantata, (Allegro assai, E♭; Andantino moderato, B♭; Polonosso & Trio, E♭).
A-21.11a. Nos. 14-30. Unidentified opera, overture & 16 mvts.
A-21.12a. No. 32. Single mvt, Andante.
A-21.13a. Nos. 33-40. Unidentified opera, overture and 7 mvts.
A-21.14a. No. 41. Single mvt, Allegro moderato in C.
A-21.15a. No. 42. Suita: Polonoises, E♭; Maldaviena, B♭; Quadrilla en militaire, E♭; Allemande, E♭.
A-21.16a. No. 43. Allegretto/Allegro.   A-11.17a. No. 44. Duetto, in B♭, Andante.
A-21.18a. No. 45. Rondo, in B♭. A-11.19a. No. 46. Single mvt, in B♭, Allegro con Spirito / Andante, in B♭.
The next group, Nos. 47 - 66 (A-11.20a - A-11.39a), may be from a single unidentifed opera.
A-21.20a. No. 47. Overtura, E♭, Allegro con brio.   A-11.21a. No. 48. Rondo, E♭, Allegro non moderato.
A-21.22a. No. 49. Allegro.   A-21.23a. No. 50. Vesalaja golova, Allegro.   A-21.24a. No. 51. Ach skučno mni.
A-21.25a. No. 52. Vo luzjach.   A-21.26a. No. 53. Andante.   A-21.27a. No. 54. Single mvt.
A-21.28a. No. 55. Andante, (fl II tacet).   A-21.29a. No. 56. Andante non molto.
A-21.30a. No. 57. Andantino.   A-21.31a. No. 58. Andante molto.   A-21.32a. No. 59. Andante grazioso.
A-21.33a. No. 60. Single mvt.   A-21.34a. No. 61. Rondo, B♭, Andante.
A-21.35a. No. 62. Romance, F minor, Adagio.   A-21.36a. No. 63. Adagio, in B♭.   A-21.37a. No. 64. Adagio.
A-21.38a. No. 65. Andante.   A-21.39a. No. 66. Single mvt.
A-21.40a. No. 67. Unidentified Overtura, [F minor] / Largo, [F major] / Allegro.
The next group, Nos. 76 - 86 (A-21.41a - A-21.51a), may be from a single unidentifed opera.
A-21.41a. No. 76. [?overture], Allegro Maestoso / Allo. assai / Più stretto.
A-21.42a. No. 77. La Chasse, E♭.
A-21.43a. No. 78. Allegro with 2 trios (trios marked "Allegretto [sic] Da capo").
A-21.44a. No. 79. Single mvt.   A-21.45a. No. 80. Andante; in C.   A-21.46a. No. 81. Allegretto.
A-21.47a. No. 82. Andante.   A-21.48a. No. 83. Allegretto.   A-21.49a. No. 84. Polonesse, B♭.
A-21.50a. No. 85. Menuetto [& Trio], B♭.   A-21.51a. No. 86. Polonese, B♭.
Nos. 88 - 92 may comprise items from Salieri's opera, La Fieri in Venezia.
A-21.52a. No. 88. Allegro.   A-21.53a. No. 89. Ballo [Ballet] vivace.
A-21.54a. No. 90. Vivace / Allegro.   A-21.55a. No. 91. Aria Calmica [B♭] / Ballo Calmuca [E♭].
A-21.56a. No. 92. Zingara Russa, E♭, Allegretto.
Nos. 123 - 125 may comprise iems from Gassmann's opera, L'Opera seria.
A-21.57a. No. 123. Largo / Andante sostenuto / All°.   A-21.58a. No. 124. Andantino Sostenuto.
A-21.59a. No. 125. Andante Sostenuto.   A-21.60a. No. 142. Polonesse, B♭.
A-21.61a. No. 143. Polonesse, B♭.   A-21.62a. No. 144. Menuetto [& Trio], B♭.
Nos. 146 - 148 may comprise items from Paisiello's opera, Didone abbandonata.
A-21.63a. No. 146. Andante.   A-21.64a. No. 147. Romance Andante, G minor.
A-21.65a. No. 148. Polonesse, B♭.
Nos. 150 - 154 may comprise items from Bianchi's opera, La Villanella rapita.
A-21.66a. No. 150. Che chiedi amor da me.   A-21.67a. No. 151. L'amorosa farfaletta.
A-21.68a. No. 152. Andante / Allegretto.   A-21.69a. No. 153. Allegro / Andante / Allegro.
A-21.70a. No. 154. Largo con Umil Riverenza / Poco Allo; *volte* Subito[:] Allo / Allegro assai.
Nos. 156 - 158 may comprise items from the same unidentified opera by Sarti as No. 155, "Rondo . Idolo amato".
A-21.71a. No. 156. Rondo, B♭, Allegro.   A-21.72a. No. 157. Duetto, B♭, Andantino.
A-21.73a. No. 158. Polonoises, E♭.   A-21.74a. No. 162. Andante (with Minore section).
A-21.75a. No. 163. Ariette, C minor.   A-21.76a. No. 164. Čto tak' nevessel' moj.
A-21.77a. No. 165. Single mvt.   A-21.78a. No. 167. Polonoises, B♭.
A-21.79a. No. fl I: "Adagio", cl I: "Andante".   A-21.80a. No. 169. Largo.
A-21.81a. No. 170. Ach gdě ukrytsja!, Allegro furioso.   A-21.82a. No. 171. Polon[oises]: E♭.
A-21.80a. No. 172. (unidentified; ?opera) Sinfonia in B[♭], 1 movement, Allegro.
A-21.83a. No. 173. Polonesso, in G.   A-21.84a. No. 174. Polonesso, in C.
A-21.85a. Unnumbered. The fl II pt only is marked "XXXXX op. 33", with "Potpourri allegro" in another hand.

ANONYMOUS (UNIDENTIFIED) SINGLE ARRANGEMENTS

Alle due grandi cascate d'acqua *(?ballet) Possibly composed or arranged by Giuseppe Magnelli (qv).*
    ANON **A-22a** (?2ob 2cl 2hn 2bn cbn).   MS parts (9): I-Fc, F.P. S.385.
Alpensänger Walzer
    ANON **A-23.1a** cl(E♭) 2hn 2bn 2tp.   MS parts: CZ-Bm(au), A.36.666, No 1.
L'Amour Turc (?opera, c.1787, Paris) Predates Cimarosa's opera, Les Amants turcs (I Traci amanti) *by 6 years.*
    OZI **EXO-1.22/3a** duo & air.   2cl 2hn 2bn.
Le bon Goût. (6) Valses alla [sic] Strauss *Apparently a local work from the Augustinian Monastery at Brno,*
composed in the style of Johann Strauss the Elder.
    ANON **A-24a** 2ob 2cl(D) 2hn bn cbn+serp 2tp.   MS parts: CZ-Bm(au), A.35.232, (missing ob I & II, cl I).
La Botte di Diogene *(?ballet) Possibly composed or arranged by Giuseppe Magnelli (qv).*
    ANON **A-25a** 5 MSS (?2cl 2hn 2bn).   MS parts: I-Fc, F.P. S.385.
Capitän Kok (ballet, ?c.1792, ?Vienna)
    WENT **JNW-2.1/4a** 1 mvt; WENT **JNW-2.2** No. 13 (= JNW-2.1/11a).   2ob 2ca 2hn 2bn.
Der Corsar aus Liebe (opera) Not the alternative title for J. Weigl's opera, L'amor marinaro; *we suggest that*
this may be the opera by Theodor von Schacht.
    SCHNEIDER, A. **AYS-8.1a** overture & 21 mvs.   fl 2ob 2cl 2hn 2bn 2vla (2)cb.
    SCHNEIDER, A. **AYS-8.2a** 1 mvt.   fl 2ob 4cl 2hn 2bn tp b-tb serp.
Couplet (?ballet, c.1770-74, Vienna) This title appears in two arranged Partitas by Asplmayr, and may refer
either to a work title or the common French generic movement titles. We believe that the composer is either
Asplmayr or Starzer. Although no contemporary ballet with this title is known, a slightly later Viennese ballet
choreographed by Armand bears the title, Glocken-Couplet. *(MS in A-Wn, Mus.Hs. 21,062).*
    ASPLMAYR **FDA-1a/FDA-46; FDA-4a/FDA-53**   2ob 2hn bn.
Figaro (ballet, choreographed Duport, 1808, Vienna) Not based on Mozart's opera, and probably unrelated
to either Dittersdorf's opera of 1789 or Peter von Winter's Munich ballet, Figaros Hochzeit, *of 1796.*
    PUREBL **JSP-1a** 3 Pièces.   2fl 3cl 2hn 2bn 2tp perc.
    PUREBL **JSP-2a** Rundtanz aus dem Ballet Figaro.   2ob 2cl 2hn 2bn.
    TRIEBENSEE **JZT-1a** overture & 5 mvts.   2ob 2cl 2hn 2bn (cbn tp ad lib).
Himnen. an die Nacht (?Lied)
    SCHNEIDER, A. **AYS-4a** fl 2ob 2cl+2cl(rip) 2hn 2bn tp b-tb serp.
Kaiser Alex (?ballet or Posse, Vienna, c.1800 - 1810) Havel, an unreliable source, attributes this to Josef Weigl;
it is possible that Havel was incorrectly citing Weigl's opera, Kaiser Hadrian.
    HAVEL **VXH-51a** Favorit Tänze. IV Poloness und Zwey Quadril [sic] *and* **VXH-53.1a** duett.   2cl 2hn 2bn.
Der kleine Hans (?opera)
    KIRCHHOFF **WZK-20a** "Nein ich will nicht länger leiden".   fl 2ob 2cl 2hn 2bn tp tb db.
Grösser Marsch aus der Trauerspiel König Lear *Only two sets of King Lear music are known from this*
period: one by the publisher Johann André the Elder, the other attributed to Haydn, also cited as perhaps by
Blumenthal (G6 App. K). Blumenthal is credited as composer in the Chemische Druckerei/Steiner printed parts.
    BLUMENTHAL **JVB-1a** 2ob 2cl 2bn 2bn tp.
Larighetto (?opera, ?c,1810s, ?Vienna) Possibly an original work by Josef Dobihal.
    DOBIHAL **JUD-1a** overture & 11 mvts.   2ob 2cl 2hn 2bn cbn.
Ludovisko (ballet, ?c.1800, ?Vienna) Not the versions of the opera, Lodoiska by Cherubini, Mayr, R. Kreutzer.
    ANON **A-26a** overture & 14 mvts.   MS parts: CZ-KRa, A4454/R.I.24, No. 6.
Das beliebte Lied "Mensch, Mensch Mensch", hat [?an] zu Brautweimarch [soc]
    ANON **A-27a** 2ob 2cl 2hn 2bn cbn 2tp.   MS parts: CZ-Bm(au), A.36.853.
Messano *(?opera, perhaps B.A. Weber's* Die Braut von Messina / La Sposa di Messina*)*
    VRATNÝ **JQV-1a** Marsch, in E♭.   2cl 2hn 2bn tp.
Monumento d'Alzinger (Alxinger) *(?ballet, sd, Florence) Possibly composed or arranged by G. Magnelli.*
    ANON **A-28a** (?2cl 2hn 2bn).   MS parts (5): I-Fc, F.P. S.385.
Un Nuit d'été (opera comique, ?c.1799, Paris)
    FUCHS, G.F. **GFF-1.5a** 1 mvt.   2fl 2cl(C) 2hn 2bn.
La Partenza, e il Ritorno Felice, doppo La Temposta Sofferta, etc. (Ballet, 1770s)
    ANON **A-29a** 10 mvts.   2ob 2hn bn.   MS parts: CZ-Pnm, XLII.C.327, (missing hn II).   *This is an*
        arrangement from the MS score at CZ-Pnm, XLII.C.328 (for 2vl vla basso 2fl 2ob 2hn bn); the horn pts of the
        arrangement differ only slightly from the full version & the missing horn part could easily be reconstructed.
Les Ruses d'amour (opera, c.1782, Paris) Too early for Chardinay's Le Pourvoir de la Nature, ou Le Suite de
la ruse d'amour *(comic opera, 1786, Paris)*
    ROESER **VAR-1.45/9-11** 3 mvts.   2cl 2hn 2bn.
Die Strickleiter *(Pastiche including Gyrowetz, J. Weigl, Boieldieu, J.N. Hummel, 1814, Vienna) Possibly based*
on P. Gaveaux's comic opera, L'Échelle de soie, *22 Aug 1808, Paris)*
    ANON **A-30a** 2ob 2cl 2hn 2bn cbn.   MS pts: I-Fc, F.P. S.387, (with Hummel (qv):* Die gute Nachricht).
Terzetto [in fact, overture & 6 mvts] Published without composer's name in a piano reduction as plate number
"op.127" by the k.k. Hoftheater-Musik Verlag, Vienna. This work is sometimes attributed either to Sacchini or
Sarti; however the Inhalt of A-Wn, Mus.Hs.3792 cites P. Wranizky as the composer.
    WENT **JNW-16.1ac** overture & 6 mvts.   2ob 2cl 2hn 2bn;   **JNW-16.2ac** overture & 6 mvts.   2ob 2ca 2hn 2bn.
Die Vogelsteler (Fogelsteller) (ballet, ?c.1792, ?Vienna)
    WENT **JNW-2.1/3a** 1 mvt;   **JNW-2.2a** Nos. 11 & 12 [= JNW-2.1/11a, sections 1 & 2].   2ob 2ca 2hn 2bn.
Unidentified operas See also: A-1a - A-11a.
    ANON **A-31a** overture & 4 mvts.   pic 2cl(F) 2cl(C) serp b-dr.   MS pts: CZ-Bm, A.35.266(au), (?missing pts).
    ANON **A-32a** "Ouverture, etc."   2ob 2cl 2hn 2bn cbn tp.   MS parts: CZ-Pnm, Lobkovic X.H.a.67.
Unidentified ballets
Ballo divertissiment [sic].   ANON **A-33a** 12 mvts.   3bthn.   MS parts: CZ-Pnm, XLII.E.233.
Pas de deux, getanzt von Herr und Mad. Viganò (by Joseph Schuster; See W. Müller Das neu Sonntagskind)
    TRIEBENSEE **JZT-2a** 2ob 2cl 2hn 2bn.   (= A-6.42a)
    WENT **JNW-73.1a** 2ob ca;   **JNW-73.2a** 2fl ca.

ARRANGEMENTS - MAIN SEQUENCE

ADAM, Adolphe Charles (1803 - 1856)
Le Chalet (comic opera, 25 Sept 1834, Paris)
  ANON **A-34a** overture. pic 2ob cl(Eb) cl(solo Bb) 3cl(Bb) 4hn 2bn 2tp 2tb serp b-dr t-dr.
    MS parts: D-DT, Mus-n 269.
Le Postillon de Lonjumeau (comic opera, 30 Oct 1836, Paris)
  ANON **A-35a** introduction. fl 2ob cl(Eb) cl(Bb solo) 3cl(Bb) 4hn 2bn 2tp tp("ventyli") kl-hn 3tb serp b-dr s-dr.
    MS parts: D-DT, Mus-n 271.
  BERR **FXB-1a** 2 Suites, each of 5 mvts. fl cl(Eb) cl(solo, Bb) 3cl(Bb) 4hn 2tp 2cap(Suite 2 only) 3tb
    serp/oph cb(obl. Suite 1, ad lib Suite 2).
  KIRCHHOFF **WZK-21a** 3 arias. fl 2ob 2cl 2hn 2bn tp tb db.
Le brasseur de Preston (comic opera, 31 Oct 1838, Paris)
  ANON **A-36a** aria. 2fl 2ob 2cl(Eb) cl(solo Bb) 4cl(Bb) bthn 4hn 2bn 5tp 3tb bomb b-dr t-dr.
    MS parts: D-DT, Mus-n 278.
  ANON **A-37a.** Galopp, Bb. fl 2ob 2cl 3hn 2bn tb basso. MS parts: D-NEhz, 133, No 21.
  LOUIS **FCL-1a** overture. fl cl(Eb) cl(solo Bb) 4cl(Bb) 4hn(Eb, Bb) 2bn 2cap 2tp 3tb oph/serp
    cb(ad lib) b-dr+cym s-dr.
Régine, ou Les deux nuits (comic opera, 17 Jan 1839, Paris).
  ANON **A-38a** Conversations-stücke (Masur, Marsch, Galopp, Walzer, Schottische).
    terz-fl cl(Eb) 2cl(Bb) 2hn bn 2tp b-tb. MS parts: CZ-Bm(au), A.36.659.
  ANON **A-39a** Unterhaltungs-stücke aus Adams Regine und Donizetti's Maria di Rudenza, (Marsch, Galopp,
    Schottische). terz-fl cl(Eb) 2cl(Bb) 2hn bn 2tp tb. MS parts: CZ-Bm(au), A.36.660.
Le Roi d'Ivetôt [d'Yvetôt] (comic opera, 13 Oct 1842, Paris)
  SCHOLZ **WES-21a** overture. fl 2ob 2cl 2hn 2bn tp tb db timp.

AIBLINGER, Johann Kaspar (1779 - 1867)
Demetrio (?ballet, untraced; possibly Rossini's opera, *Demetrio e Polibio*, misattributed)
  LEGRAND **WYL-1a** 1 mvt. fl ob 2cl 2hn 2bn.

ALBÉNIZ, Isaac (1860 - 1909)
España, Six album leaves, Op. 165, No. 2, Tango (piano, pub. 1889, London)
  CAMPBELL **AQC-1a** fl 2ob 2cl 2hn 2bn.

ALDAY, Paul (active c.1790s, France)
All꞉ Finale, in F
  LEROY **PQL-1.9/3** 2p-fl(F) 2ob 2cl(III & IV, C) 2hn 2bn tp serp.
Ouverture, in F
  LEROY **PQL-1.9/1a** 2p-fl(F) 2ob 2cl(III & IV, C) 2hn 2bn tp serp.
Rondeau, in F
  LEROY **PQL-1.6/3a**

ALESSANDRI, Felice (1742 - 1798)
Il Vecchio geloso (opera, autumn 1781, Milan)
  ANON **A-40a** 2ob 2cl 2hn 2bn. MS parts: I-Fc, F.P S.341, unverified, (the old shelfmark, D.V.496, converts
    to the shelfmark we have given. W. Müller's Singspiel *Der Alte überall und nirgends* is also at this shelfmark
    and there is a possibility that the earlier catalog entry may have misidentified this opera.)

ANDREOZZI, Gaetano (1775 - 1826)
Armide - pasticcio by Sarti & Joseph Mazzinghi, "Ah! quest' anima non speri" (interpolated) (?1790s, London)
  COURTIN **HZC-1.1a** 2ob/fl(ad lib) 2cl 2hn 2bn.

ARNE, Michael (1740/1741 - 1786)
The Heiress (comic opera, 21 May 1759, London)
  ANON **A-202.3/26(a)** Favorite Song. 2terz-fl 2bthn 2hn 2bn serp.
Love in a Village (comic opera, 1763, revived c.1775 & 1779; pub. a single song, c.1789, London)
  ANON **A-202.3/18(a)** "Dans votre lit, dear Fanny". 2terz-fl 2bthn 2hn 2bn serp.
Cymon (opera, 2 Jan 1767, revived 17 Jan 1778, London)
  ELEY **CFE-1ma** quick march. 2cl 2hn 2bn tp.

ARNE, Thomas Augustine (1710 - 1778)
Alfred (masque, Cliffden, 1 Aug 1740; 10 March 1744, Dublin; 20 March 1745, London; new version: 1793)
  SCHNEIDER, A. **AYS-14a** "Rule Britannia", (as "When Britann"). fl 2ob 2cl 2hn 2bn tp b-tb 2vla cb.

ARNOLD, Samuel (1740 - 1802)
The Surrender of Calais (opera, 30 July 1792, London)
  ELEY **CFE-2.7m(a)** duet, "From night to morn I take my glass". 2ob/cl 2cl 2hn 2bn tp.

ASBERGER, ( )
Das Kohlrösel (Lied)
  ANON **A-2.2va** 2cl 2hn 4tp(F, 3Eb) 2flug t-crt 2tb.   (*See* p. 331, Austro-Bohemia, Stráž pod Ralskem)

ASPLMAYR, Franz (1728 - 1786)   *See also supra: (UNIDENTIFIED) SINGLE ARRANGEMENTS* - Couplet.
Die kleine Weinlese (ballet, 1767, Vienna)
  ASPLMAYR **FDA-2ad** 8 mvts. 2ob 2hn bn.
La lavandara di Citere (ballet, 1771, Vienna)
  WENT **+JNW-6a** 8 mvts. 2ob 2ca 2hn (2)bn.

Agamemnon Vengé (ballet, 1771, revised 1772, Vienna)
  ASPLMAYR **FDA-53/FDA-4a** 1 mvt.   2ob 2hn bn.
  WENT **+JNW-7a** 8 mvts.   2ob 2ca 2hn 2bn.
Gli episodi (ballet, c.1772, Vienna)
  ASPLMAYR **FDA-46/FDA-1a** 2 mvts.   2ob 2hn bn.
  ASPLMAYR **FDA-47/FDA-2a** 1 mvt.   2ob 2hn bn.
  ASPLMAYR **FDA-58a/FDA-7a** 1 mvt.   2ob 2hn bn.
Alexandre et Campaspe de Larisse (ballet, 1773, Vienna)
  ASPLMAYR **FDA-1ad** 8 mvts.   2ob 2hn bn.
  ASPLMAYR **FDA-52/FDA-3a** 1 mvt.   2ob 2hn bn.
  ASPLMAYR **FDA-58/FDA-7a** 1 mvt.   2ob 2hn bn.
Acis et Galathée (ballet, 1773, Vienna)
  ASPLMAYR **FDA-55/FDA-6a** 1 mvt.   2ob 2hn bn.
  ASPLMAYR **FDA-58/FDA-7a** 1 mvt.   2ob 2hn bn.
La Sposa Persiana (ballet, pre-1775)
  WENT **+JNW-8a** 20 mvts.   2ob 2ca 2hn 2bn.
Il Contra Tempo o sia Il oportuno ritarno (ballet, pre-1775)
  WENT **+JNW-9a** overture & 24 mvts.   2ob 2ca 2hn 2bn.
A quelque chose malheur et bon (ballet, pre-1775)
  WENT **+JNW-10a** sinfonia & 9 mvts.

ATTWOOD, Thomas (1765 - 1838)
Divertimento . . . Storace, Pleyel, Attwood (c.1789, London)
  A-202.1/4(a) Moderato.   2ob 2bthn 2hn 2bn serp.

AUBER, Daniel François Esprit (1782 - 1871)
La Neige, ou Le Nouvel Éginard (Der Schnee) (comic opera, 8 Oct 1823, Paris)
  ANON **A-41a** 3 mvts.   fl(D, F) 2cl(C) 2hn 2bn.   MS parts: GB-Ljag(w), 5/262, Nos. 2, 3 & 16.
  LEGRAND **WYL-2a** 2 mvts.   fl ob 2cl 2hn 2bn.
  SCHMITT, G. **GYS-6a** 1 Bd.   fl 2ob 2cl 2hn 2bn tp 2tb db (timp).
  SCHNEIDER, A. **AYS-15a** overture & 15 mvts.   fl 2ob 2cl 2hn 2bn tp b-tb 2vla cb.
  WIDDER **YYW-1.14a** 3 mvts.   2fl 2cl 2hn 2bn.
Le Concert à la cour, ou La Débutante (Der Concerto am Hofe) (comic opera, 24 July 1824, Paris)
  KÜFFNER **JYK-4a** Potpourri, Op. 182.   fl 2cl 2hn 2bn.
  SCHMITT, G. **GYS-7.1a** fl 2ob 2cl 2hn 2bn tb(solo) 2tb db.
  SCHMITT, G. **GYS-7.2a** 1 mvt.   fl 2ob 2cl 2hn 2bn tp tb db.
Léocadie (comic opera, 4 Nov 1824, Paris)
  KIRCHHOFF **WZK-22a** 2 mvts.   fl 2ob 2cl 2hn 2bn tp tb basso.
Le Maçon (Der Maurer; Maurer und Schlosser) (comic opera, 3 May 1825, Paris)
  ANON **A-42a** overture.   cl(Eb) 2cl(Bb) 2hn cbn 2tp flug b-flug bomb.   MS parts: CZ-OScr, 2147.
  SCHMITT, G. **GYS-8a** 1 Bd.   fl 2ob 2cl 2hn 2bn 2tb db.
  SCHOLL **NYS-1ac** Marsch.   2ob 2cl 2hn 2bn cbn (2tp).
  WIDDER **YYW-1.15a** 1 mvt.   2fl 2cl 2hn 2bn.
  WITT **FZW-1a** overture & 13 mvts.   fl(F, terz-fl, pic in F) ob 2cl(Eb) 2cl(Bb) 2hn 2bn tp b-tb cb.
Fiorella (comic opera, 28 Nov 1826, Paris)
  KÜFFNER **JYK-5a** Ouverture & Airs, Op. 208.   fl 2cl 2hn 2bn.
La Muette de Portici (Die Stumme von Portici) (opera, 29 Feb 1828, Paris)
  ANON **A-10.47a** 1 mvt.   fl 2ob 2cl 2hn 2bn b-tb b.
  ANON **A-43a** overture.   2ob cl(F) 2cl(C) 2hn 2bn cbn 3tp tb.   MS pts: CZ-Bm(au), A.36.856, (missing ob II).
  ANON **A-44a** 1 mvt.   fl(F) 2cl(C) 2hn 2bn.   MS parts: GB-Ljag(w), 5/262, No. 21.
  BERR **FXB-2a** overture.   pic cl(Eb) 2cl(Bb) 2hn 2bn, (fl cl(III) tp 2tb serp ad lib).
  HASSE **YYH-1ma** Geschwindmarsch.   Instrumentation unknown.
  KAISER **KAK-1a** Schlummer-Arie.   cl(Eb) cl(solo Bb) 2cl(Bb) 4hn 2bn 2t-hn b.
  KÜFFNER **JYK-6a** potpourri.   fl(F) cl(Eb) 2cl(Bb) 2hn bn 2tp b-tb serp.
  KÜFFNER **JYK-7a** "La Guarache".   p-fl(Eb) 2cl(Eb) 3cl(Bb) 4hn 2hn 3tp(2Eb, 1Bb alto) 2tb serp b-dr t-dr.
  KÜFFNER **JYK-8a** Boléro, Op. 219.   Military band.
  LEGRAND **WYL-3a** 3 mvts.   fl ob 2cl 2hn 2bn (bn III ad lib).
  LÖWENSTEIN **CAL-14a** overture & 5 mvts.   fl(pic D) 2cl(Eb) 2cl(Bb) 2hn 2bn tp b-tb cb timp b-dr t-dr tri cym bell; (ad lib: hn III).
  MARPURG **WYM-4a** overture.   cl(Eb) 3cl(Bb) 2hn 2bn tp 3tb b-hn b-dr.
  SCHICK **FKS-1a** march.   pic quart-fl 2ob cl(F) 2cl(C) 4hn 2bn cbn+serp/2b-hn 2tp 3tb b-dr t-dr tamb cym.
  SCHMITT, G. **GYS-9a** 4 Bds.   pic fl 2ob 2cl 2hn 2bn 2tp b-tb db.
  SEDLAK **WYS-4a** Teil 1: overture & 11 mvts; Teil 2: 12 mvts; Teil 3: 13 mvts.   2ob 2cl 2hn 2bn cbn (2tp).
  SEIFF **JYS-1a** 2cl 2hn 2bn.
  WIDDER **YYW-1.16a** 3 mvts.   2fl 2cl 2hn 2bn.
La Fiancée (Die Verlobte) (comic opera, 10 Jan 1829, Paris)
  BERR **FXB-3a** overture.   pic cl(Eb) 2cl(Bb) 2hn bn(I) serp, (cl III & IV, bn II, tp 3tb db ad lib).
  SCHMITT, G. **GYS-10a** 2 Bds.   fl 2ob 2cl 2hn 2bn tp tb(solo) tb db.
Fra Diavolo, ou L'Hôtellerie de Terracine (comic opera, 28 Jan 1830, Paris)
  ANON **A-45a** romance.   fl 2ob cl(Eb) cl(solo Bb) 4hn 2bn 2tp a-hn 3tb b-hn/bomb.
    MS parts: D-DT, Mus-n 1660, No. 2.
  ANON **A-46a** overture.   2ob cl(F) 2cl(C) 2hn 2bn cbn 2tp b-tb s-dr.   MS parts (1831): CZ-Bm(au), A.35.148.

ANON **A-20.1, 20.3a, A-15.1a, 15.2a** 2 Walzer & 2 Galopps. pic(E♭, fl E♭) cl(E♭) 2cl(B♭) 2hn bn 2tp b-tb cb.
BERR **FXB-4a** overture. fl cl(E♭) solo+2cl(B♭) 2hn bn(I) serp 2tp, (ad lib: cl III, IV, bn(II) 2tb db b-dr tri).
KÜFFNER **JYK-9a** overture. pic fl cl(E♭) 3cl(B♭) 4hn 2bn 3tp 2/3tb b-hn("Russe") timp tri b-dr s-dr.
LANGE **GFL-1a** overture. 2cl bn.
MARPURG **WYM-2.3a** Lied. pic 2ob 2cl(E♭) 4cl(B♭) 5hn 2bn 2tp a-tb t-tb b-tb b-hn b-dr s-dr.
MARPURG **WYM-3.1a** overture. pic 2ob 2cl(E♭) 4cl(B♭) 2hn 2bn 2tp a-tb t-tb b-tb b-hn b-dr t-dr.
SCHMITT, G. **GYS-11a** overture & 3 Teils. fl 2ob 3cl 2hn 2bn tp tb(obl) 3tb db.
STRECK **PVS-1.2a** overture. fl cl(D) 2cl(A) 2hn 2bn.
WIDDER **YYW-1.17a** 2 mvts. 2fl 2cl 2hn 2bn.
Le Philtre (Der Liebestrank) (comic opera, 15 June 1831, Paris)
BERR **FXB-5a** overture. fl(E♭) cl(E♭) solo+2cl(B♭) 2hn bn serp; (ad lib: 2cl(B♭) bn(II) tp 3tb cb b-dr tri).
WITT **FZW-2a** overture & 12 mvts. fl(pic) ob 2cl(E♭) 2cl(B♭) 2hn 2bn tp b-tb cb.
Le Serment, ou Les faux monnayeurs (comic opera, 1 Oct 1832, Paris)
BERR **FXB-6a** pic cl(E♭) 2cl(B♭) 2hn bn serp, (cl III & IV, bn II, bugle 2tp 3tb b-dr s-dr ad lib).
Gustave III, ou Le Bal masqué (opera, 27 Feb 1833, Paris)
ANON **A-17.2a, 20.11a** Galopp. terz-fl cl(Eb) 2cl(Bb) 2hn bn 2tp b-tb serp.
GODFREY **CXG-1a** pic cl(E♭) 3cl(B♭) 2hn 2bn serp; (ad lib: cl(B♭) 2tp a-tb t-tb b-tb drums cym tri).
LEGRAND **WYL-4a** 1 mvt. fl ob 2cl 2hn 2bn (bn III ad lib).
POISSL **JNP-1.4a** "Au près de vous, Madame". fl ob 2cl 2hn 2bn.
Lestocq, ou L'Intrigue et l'amour (comic opera, 24 May 1834, Paris)
BERR **FXB-7a** overture. pic cl(E♭) 4cl(B♭) 4hn(E♭, Bb) 2bn 2cap 2tp 3tb serp+oph db b-dr cym.
KIRCHHOFF **WZK-23a** 2 mvts. fl 2ob 2cl 2hn 2bn tp tb db.
Le Cheval de bronze (comic opera, 21 March 1835, Paris)
BERR **FXB-8a** overture. pic cl(Eb) solo+2cl(Bb) 2hn bn(I) serp, (ad lib: cl III, IV; hn III, IV; 2tp 2tb b-tb db).
KIRCHHOFF **WZK-24a** 2 mvts. fl 2ob 2cl 2hn 2bn tp tb db.
Actéon (comic opera, 23 Jan 1836, Paris)
MOHR **JPM-1a** overture. pic(fl) cl(D) (solo)cl 4cl(A) 2hn bn cbn 2tp a-tb t-tb b-tb quint-oph oph+serp
b-dr+cym.
L'Ambassadrice (comic opera, 21 Dec 1836, Paris)
ANON **A-47a** romance. fl 2ob 2cl(E♭) cl(solo B♭) 3cl(B♭) 4hn 2bn 2tp a-hn 3tb b-hn/bomb.
MS parts: D-DT, Mus-n 1660.
Le Domino noir (comic opera, 2 Dec 1837, Paris)
ANON **A-19.2a** Galopp, (incorrectly attributed to Strauss *the Elder*). fl 2cl(E♭) 2cl(B♭) 2hn 2bn tp b-tb cb.
BERR **FXB-9a** overture. pic cl(E♭) (solo)cl(Bb) 4cl(Bb) 2hn 2bn 2tp(á piston) 2tp 3tb (solo)oph oph b-dr.
Zanetta, ou Jouer avec le feu (comic opera, 18 May 1840, Paris)
MOHR **JPM-2.1a** overture. pic cl(E♭) cl(B♭, solo) 4cl(B♭) 4hn(2B♭ basso obligés, 2F[ripieno]) bn(I)
bn(II)+cb/serp 2tp 2cap bugle 2a-tb b-tb a-oph oph(C) oph(B♭) b-dr tri.
MOHR **JPM-2.2a** airs, 5 mvts. fl cl(E♭) cl(B♭, solo) 4cl(B♭) 4hn bn(I) bn(II)+cb 2tp 2cap bugle 3tb oph.
Les Diamants de la couronne (Die Kromdiamanten) (comic opera, 6 March 1841, Paris)
SCHOLZ **WES-23.1a** ensemble. fl 2ob 2cl 2hn 2bn tp tb db.
SCHOLZ **WES-23.2a** duo & finale. fl 2ob 2cl 2hn 2bn tp tb db timp.
WIESER **FAW-6a** potpourri. fl(pic) cl(E♭) 2cl(B♭) 2hn 2bn tp b-tb cb.
Le Lac de fées (comic opera, 1 April 1842, Paris)
ANON **A-48a** pic terz-fl 2ob cl(E♭) 3cl(B♭) 4hn 2bn 3tp kl-hn 3tb bomb/b-hn b-dr t-dr.
MS parts: D-DT, Mus-n 280.
SCHOLZ **WES-22a** chor & duett. fl 2ob 2cl 3hn 2bn tp tb db timp.
Le Duc d'Olonne (Die Schwur, oder die Falshmünzer; Der Herzog von Olonne) (comic opera, 4 Feb 1842, Paris)
SCHOLL **NYS-2ac** 3 mvts (Ballade, Aria, Pas redoublé). 2ob 2cl 2hn 2bn cbn 2tp.
WIESER **FAW-7a** overture. pic cl(E♭) 2cl(B♭) 2hn 2bn tp b-tb cb.
Carlo Broschi, ou le Part du Diable (Des Teufels Antheil) (comic opera, 16 Jan 1843, Paris)
ANON [? Hoedl] **A-15.43(ma)** Marsch. 2cl(E♭) 2cl(B♭) 2hn bn tp flug.
SCHOLZ **WES-24.1a** overture. fl 2ob 2cl 2hn 2bn tp tb db timp.
SCHOLZ **WES-24.2a** aria. fl 2ob 2cl 2hn 2bn tb db.
Le Sirène (Die Syrene) (comic opera, 26 March 1844, Paris)
KIEL **AYK-1a** overture. 2fl 2ob cl(E♭) 4cl(B♭) 4hn 2bn 3tp a-hn 3tb b b-dr s-dr cym tri.
SCHOLZ **WES-25a** overture. fl 2ob 2cl 3hn 2bn 2tp tb db timp.
La Parisienne (Chant national, pub. c.1830, Paris)
KÜFFNER **JYK-2a** Military band.
Untraced arrangements: La Bergére Chatelaine (1820), Emma (1821), Léocadie (1824) et du Maçon (1825) arr.
Melchior (Pleyel: Paris, pn 1971, post-1825), Fiorello (overture & airs, arr. Henri Brod; Pleyel: Paris, pn 2447,
1830), Le Philtre (1831), Le Serment (1832), all published in Paris.

AUGUSTIN, ( )
12 Walzer (?piano, sl, pre-1825)
SCHNEIDER, A. **AYS-16a** fl 2ob 2cl 2hn 2bn tp b-tb 2vla cb.

BACH, Johann (John) Christian (1735 - 1782)
Lucio Silla (opera, 4 Nov 1776, Mannheim)
PICK **HXP-1a** overture. 2fl 2ob 3cl 2hn 2bn 2tp 2tb serp.

BACH, Johann Sebastian (1685 - 1750)
Englishe Suiten, No. 2: Sarabande in A minor (S.807) (cembalo, c.1725)
KENNAWAY **LXK-1a** 2fl ob 3cl bn.
3 Sarabandes
EMERSON **GZE-2a** 2fl ob 3cl bn.

BALFE, Michael William (1808 - 1870)
Falstaff (Italian comic opera, 19 July 1838, London)
 ANON **A-49a** 4 mvts. cl 3bthn. MS parts: CZ-Pnm, XLII.A.367.
The Bohemian Girl (The Gipsy; Die Zigeunerin) (opera, 12 Nov 1843, London)
 SCHOLZ **WES-26a** duet. fl 2ob 2cl 2hn 2bn tp tb db.
Les Quatre fils d'Aymon (Die vier Haimonskinder) (comic opera, 15 July 1844, Paris)
See also STRAUSS, Johann, *the Elder:* Quadrille . . . aus der Oper: Die vier Haimonskinder, Op. 169
 ANON **A-15.39(a)** cavatina. fl(D) 2cl(Bb) 2hn 2bn tp flug.
 SCHOLZ **WES-27a** aria. fl 2ob 2cl 2hn 2bn tp tb db.

BARNBY, *Sir* Joseph (1838 - 1896)
Sweet and Low (Part-song, ATTB or SATB, pub. 1868, London)
 ELGAR **EWE-6a** 2fl cl hn bn.

BEAUPLAN, Amadée de *(pseud. i.e. Amadée Rousseau)* (active 1820 - 1840)
Belle et Sensible (romance, c.1825, Paris)
 SCHNEIDER, A. **AYS-17a** fl 2ob 2cl 2hn 2bn tp b-tb 2vla cb.

BEECKE, *Notger* Ignaz Franz von (1773 - 1803)
Nina (Singspiel, Aschaffenburg, 1790)
 BEECKE **IVB-1ad** Parthia in C, overture & 6 mvts. 2fl 2ob 2cl 2hn 2bn cb.

BEETHOVEN, Ludwig van (1770 - 1827)
Fidelio (Lenore) (opera, 23 May 1814 (final version), Vienna)
 ANON **A-50a** overture. fl cl(Eb) cl(solo Bb) 3cl(Bb) 4hn 2bn 2tp 3tb serp b-dr t-dr.
  MS parts: D-DT, Mus-n 313.
 KIRCHHOFF **WZK-25a** overture & 1 Bd. fl 2ob 2cl 2hn 2bn 2tp tb db timp.
 SCHMITT, G. **GYS-12a** 2fl 2ob 2cl 2hn 2bn tp tb db.
 SCHOLZ **WES-28a** 3 mvts. fl 2ob 2cl 2/3hn 2bn tp b-tb db timp.
 SEDLAK **WXS-5a** overture & 10 mvts. 2ob 2cl 2hn 2bn cbn.
Lenore Overture No. 1 (orchestra, 1806-1807, performed 7 Feb 1828, Vienna; score published 1838)
 SCHOLZ **WES-29a** fl 2ob 2cl 2hn 2bn tp tb db timp.
Lenore Overture No. 2 (orchestra, 1804-1805, performed 20 Nov 1805, Vienna)
 SCHOLZ **WES-30a** fl 2ob 2cl 2hn 2bn tp tb db timp.
Das Geschöpfe des Prometheus (ballet, 28 March 1801, Vienna)
 SCHOLZ **WES-31a** overture. fl 2ob 2cl 2hn 2bn tp tb db timp.
Piano Sonata, Op. 10, No. 2 (pub. 1798, Vienna)
 SCHOENFELD **WCS-1.1a** Finale (Presto). fl ob 2cl 2bn.
 SCHOENFELD **WCS-1.2a** Finale (Presto). fl ob 2cl hn bn.
Sonata for Violin & Piano in A, Op. 12, No. 2 (published 1799, Vienna)
 SCHOLZ **WES-32a** Allego (mvt 3). fl 2ob 2cl 2hn 2bn tb db.
Piano Sonata ("Pathetique"), Op. 13 (published 1799)
 ANON **A-51a** 2ob 2cl 2hn 2bn cbn.
  Pc (Chemische Druckerei: Vienna, pn 1488, 1810), parts: NL-DHgm, hk 19 C 4.
   MS parts: CZ-Bm(au), A.37.330, (missing cbn; ob II marked "ad lib").
  Pm (performing edition prepared by Alexander Weinmann, broadcast ORF, Vienna, pre-1986, attributed
   without source to Druschetzky), MS score & parts: A-Worf.
  Pm (Compusic: Amsterdam, pn 202, 1991, attributed as "probably Druschetzky"), score & parts.
 DRUSCHETZKY **GYD-2ad** 2ob 2cl 2hn 2bn cbn. *(Entry as A-41a above)*.
 GEROLD **JWG-1a** terz-fl ob cl(Eb) 2cl(Bb) 2hn bn 2tp (2)crt a-crt tb euph tambours.
Quintet (pf, winds), Op. 16 (first performed 1797)
 TRIEBENSEE **JZT-3a** Andante, mvt 2 only. 2ob 2cl 2hn 2bn (cbn ad lib).
Septet, Op. 20 (published 1802)
 ANON **A-52a** (c.1810). terz-fl 2cl 2hn 2bn. MS parts (c.1800): D-Rtt, Beethoven 1, (as "Parthia in Es par
  Luis von [sic]] Beethoven").
 BEETHOVEN **LVB-1a(d)** (?fl,Eb) (?cl,Eb) 2cl(Bb) 3hns 2bn 2b-?.
 CRUSELL **BXC-1a** terz-fl cl(Eb) 2cl(Bb) 2hn 2bn b-tb serp.
 CZERNY **CYC-1a** 2cl 2hn 2bn.
 DRUSCHETZKY **GYD-8a** 2ob 2cl 2hn 2bn cbn.
 SCHMITT, G. **GYS-13a** 2fl 2ob 2cl 2hn 2bn tb db.
Symphony No. 1 in C, Op. 21 (perf c.1800, pub 1801)
 HÜTSCHENREIYTER the Elder **WOH-1a** 2fl 2cl 2hn 2bn tp.
 SCHMITT, G. **GYS-14a** 2fl 2ob 2cl 2hn 2bn tb db.
Violin Sonata in A minor, Op. 23 (pub. 1801, Vienna)
 ELGAR **EWE-7a** 2fl cl hn bn.
Piano Sonata in Ab, Op. 26 (published 1802, Vienna)
 RICHTER **QYR-1a** mvt 3 as "Todten Marsch". 2ob 2cl(Eb) 3cl(Bb) 2bthn 6hn 2bn 4tp a-tb t-tb b-tb serp.
 SCHOLZ **WES-33a** Andante con Variazioni (mvt 1). fl 2ob 2cl 2hn 2bn tb db.
Adelaide, Op. 46 (Lied, voice & piano, 1794 - 1795, pub. 1797, Vienna)
 KIRCHHOFF **WZK-26a** fl 2ob 2cl 2hn 2bn tb db.
 WIESER **FAW-8a** terz-fl cl(Eb) 2cl(Bb) 2hn 2bn tp b-tb cb timp.
Sechs Lieder (gedichte von Chr. Fr. Gellert), Op. 48 (pub. 1803, Vienna)
 KAISER, **KAK-2a** No. 4, Hymnus, "Die Ehre Gottes". fl cl(Eb) 2cl(Bb) 2hn 2tp 2t-hn tb b-dr s-dr.
Trois grand Marches, Op. 45 (piano, 4-hands, c.1803 London, 1804, Vienna)
 SCHNEIDER, A. **AYS-19a.** No 1 in D. fl 2ob 4cl 2hn 2bn tp b-tb serp.
Symphony No. 3 (Eroica) in Eb, Op. 55 (orchestra, 1803; performed 7 April 1805, Vienna)
 SCHOLZ **WES-34a** Scherzo. fl 2ob 2cl 3hn 2bn tb db.

Coriolan, Op. 62 (play - overture only, 1807, Vienna)
  SCHOLZ **WES-35a** overture. fl 2ob 4cl 2hn 2bn tb db timp.
Ah, perfido, Op. 65 (scena & aria, solo voice & orchestra, Vienna, 1795-96; published 1805)
  SCHOLZ **WES-36a** fl 2ob 2cl 2hn 2bn tp tb db timp.
Symphony No. 5 in C minor, Op. 67 (orchestra, 22 Dec 1808, published 1809, Vienna)
  SCHOLZ **WES-37a** mvts 1 & 2. fl 2ob 2cl 2hn 2bn tp tb db timp.
Egmont, Op. 84, Overture (Trauerspiel, 1810)
  ANON **A-53a** fl 2ob 2cl(E♭) cl(solo B♭) 3cl(B♭) 4hn 2bn 2tp 3tb b-dr s-dr. MS parts: D-DT, Mus-n 311.
  KIRCHHOFF **WZK-27a** fl 2ob 3cl 2hn 2bn tp tb db.
  SCHNEIDER, A. **AYS-17a** overture. fl 2ob 2cl 2hn 2bn tp b-tb 2vla cb.
  STARKE **FYS-3.1a** pic 2fl 2ob cl(F) 2cl(B♭) cl(C) 4hn cbn 2tp b-tb timp s-dr.
  STARKE **FYS-3.2a** 2ob 2cl 2hn 2bn cbn.
Wellingtons Sieg, oder die Schlacht bei Vittoria, Op. 91 (première 8 Dec 1813, Vienna)
  ANON (arrangement sometimes - probably wrongly - attributed to Beethoven) **A-54a** Abth. 1, Schlacht:
    pic(G) pic(F) fl(I, C) 2ob(ad lib) cl(E♭) 2cl(B♭) 2cl(C) 2hn 2bn cbn 4tp(2C, D, E♭) b-tb serp sym; Abth. 2,
    Sieges-Sinfonie: fl(II, C) replaces pic(F), 2cl(C) replace 2cl(B♭).
    Pc (Steiner: Wien, pn 2368, 1816), *Journal für Harmonie und türkische Musik*, Heft 1, parts:
    A-Wn, MS.14550; D-SWl, Mus. 1143; GB-Lbl, Hirsch IV.345.
    Pm (WINDS: Northridge, CA, pn W-158, 1981), score & parts.
Symphony No. 7 in A, Op. 92. (performed 8 Dec 1813, published 1816, Vienna)
  ANON **A-55a** fl 2ob 2cl 2hn 2bn tp tb db. MS pts: D-NEhz, 54, No. 7, (mvts 2 - 4 only, rescoring of A-46a).
  ANON **A-56a** here, in G. 2ob 2cl 2hn 2bn cbn.
    Pc (bei S. A. Steiner und Comp.: Wien, pn 2563, 1816), parts: B-BNbh; D-ESpriv.
    MS score (?c.1840): D-NEhz, 54, No. 7.
    Pm (WINDS: Northridge, CA, pn W-185, c.1981), parts.
    Pm (Compusic: Amsterdam, 1988), score (pn 231A) and parts (pn 231B).
    Pm (Doblinger: Wien, 1994), critical edition by Bastiaan Blomhert, score & parts.
  SEDLAK **WXS-1ad** 2ob 2cl 2hn 2bn cbn. (= A-46a, more likely to be by Druschetzky)
Overture Namensfeier, Op. 115 (orchestra, 25 Dec 1815, Vienna)
  SCHOLZ **WES-38a** fl 2ob 2cl 2hn 2bn tp tb db timp.
König Stephan, Op. 177 (play, 10 Feb 1812, Vienna)
  SCHOLZ **WES-39a** overture & 3 mvts. fl 2ob 2cl 2hn 2bn tp tb db timp.
Zapfenstreich No. 1 (Yorck' sche Marsch, Marsch des Fürst Joseph von Lobkowitzischen Bataillons), WoO 18
  KRECHLER **FFK-4.2a** 2ob 2lc 2hn 2bn cbn.
Andante favori in F, WoO 57 (piano, published 1805, Vienna)
  SCHOLZ **WES-40a** fl 2ob 2cl 2hn 2bn tb db.
Für Elise, WoO 59 (piano, 1808 or 1810, published posthumously, Vienna)
  HANMER **RCH-3.1(a)** fl fl/ob 2cl bn/b-cl.
5 Stücke für die Flötenuhr, K.-H.33.
  HESS **WZH-1a** No 1 (Adagio) only. fl 2ob 2cl 2hn 2bn.
Spurious Works
  Le Désir, Waltz [Sehnsuchtswalzer], K.-H.Anh.14, No. 1. See: SCHUBERT, F.P. Original-Tänze, Op. 9, No. 2.
  Schmerzenwalzer, K.-H.Anh.14, No. 2. See: HIMMEL, F H.
  Trauer Marsch, K.-H. Anh 13. See: WALCH, Johann Heinrich.
Untraced arrangements: Symphony No. 5 in C minor, Op. 67 (1809, 9-part version); Symphony No. 7 in A, Op.
92 (Chemische Druckerei: Vienna, late 1816, 6-part version); Symphony No. 8 in F, Op. 93 (Chemische
Druckerei, advertized in the *Wiener Zeitung* of 24 Dec 1817, in 6- and 9-part versions, pn 2572 and 2573).

BEFFROY DE REIGNY, Louis Abel ("Cousin Jacques") (1757 - 1811)
Nicodème dans la lune ou La Révolution pacifique (folie, 7 Nov 1790, Paris)
  VANDERHAGEN **AJV-5.4a** 2 mvts. 2cl 2hn 2bn.
Le Club des bonnes-gens (folie, 24 Sept 1791 Paris; collaboration with Gaveaux).
  DEVIENNE **FZD-1a** ouverture & 6 morceaux. 2pic/(2ob doubling ad lib) 2cl 2hn 2bn serp 2tr b-dr cym tri.

BELLINI Vincenzo (1801 - 1835)
Bianca e Gernando (arr. as: Bianca e Fernando, 3 April 1828, Genoa) (opera, 20 May 1826, Naples)
  ANON **A-57a** Aria, 1844. Solo tp, fl ob cl(B♭) 2cl(E♭) 2hn bn tp basso(2).
    MS parts: CZ-Bm(au). A.35.161, (here incorrectly attributed to Donizetti).
  CARULLI **BYC-1a** "All'udir del padre afflitto". 2fl 3cl 2hn 2bn 2tp.
Il Pirata (Die Seeräuber aus Algeri) (opera, 27 Oct 1827, Milan)
  SEDLAK **WXS-6a** Theil 1: overture & 11 mvts, Theil 2: 12 mvts. 2ob 2cl 2hn 2bn cbn (2tp).
La Straniera (Die Unbekante) (opera, 14 Feb 1829, Milan)
  ANON **A-11a** aria. fl(F) cl(E♭) 2cl(B♭) 2hn bn tp(patent in A♭) b-tb serp.
  ANON **A-13.1a** potpouri. fl(F) cl(E♭) 2cl(B♭) 2hn bn 2tp b-tb serp.
  ANON **A-14.1a** duetto. fl(F) cl(E♭) 2cl(B♭) 2hn bn 2tp b-tb serp.
  ANON **A-18.1a** introduzion[e]. fl(F) ob cl(E♭) 2cl(B♭) 2hn bn 2tp b-tb serp.
  MARPURG **WYM-1.2a(-1.4a)** 3 mvts. pic 2ob cl(E♭) 3cl(B♭) 2hn 2bn 2tp a-tb t-tb b-tb serp b-dr s-dr.
  SCHOLZ **NYS-3ac** introduzione & 10 mvts. 2ob 2cl 2hn 2bn cbn 2tp [b-tb].
I Capuleti ed i Montecchi (opera, 11 March 1830, Venice)
  ANON **A-58a** Cavatina, "È serba a quesdto acciaro", 1832. 2ob cl(E♭) 2c1(B♭) 2hn 2bn cbn 2tp tb.
    MS parts: CZ-Bm(au), A.36.857.
  ANON **A-59a** fl 2ob 2cl 2hn 2bn tp tb db. MS score & parts: D-NEhz, 54, No. 2, (parts missing tp).
  ANON **A-60a** duetto. 2ob 2cl 2hn 2bn cbn 2tp. MS parts: CZ-Bm(au), A.37.325.
  KIRCHHOFF **WZK-28a** overture & 2 Bds. fl 2ob 2cl 2hn 2bn tb db.
  SCHOLL **NYS-4ac** Theil 1: 2 mvts, Theil 2: 4 mvts. 2ob 2cl 2hn 2bn cbn (2tp, Theil 2 only).

La Sonnambula (opera, 6 March 1831, Milan)
  ANON **A-15.10(a)** 1 mvt.   fl 2cl(B♭) 2hn 2bn 2tp flug.
  KIRCHHOFF **WZK-29a** introduzion, arie & duetto.   fl 2ob 2cl 2hn 2bn tb db.
  LEGRAND **WYL-5a** 3 mvts.   fl ob 2cl 2hn 2bn (bn III ad lib).
  SCHOLL **NYS-5ac** 5 mvts.   2ob 2cl 2hn 2bn cbn 2tp [b-tb].
  SCHOLZ **WES-41a** quintett & finale.   fl 2ob 2cl 3hn 2bn tp tb db timp.
Norma (opera, 26 Dec 1831, Milan)
  ANON **A-61a** introduction & cavatine.   2fl 2ob cl(E♭) 3cl(B♭) 4hn 2bn 3tp a-hn kenthorn 3tb bomb b-hn
    b-dr t-dr.   MS parts: D-DT, Mus-n 343.
  ANON **A-62a** sinfonia.   2ob cl(F) 2cl(C) cl(C obl) 2cl(E♭) 2hn 2bn cbn 2tp b-tb.
    MS parts: CZ-Bm(au), A.35.150, (the cl obbligato doubles cl I in C; the cbn pt as titled "contrabasso").
  ANON **A-15.4(a)** duetto.   2cl 2hn bn 2tp.
  ANON **A-15.9(a)** 1 mvt.   cl(E♭) 2cl(B♭) 2hn 2bn 2tp.
  ANON **A-63a** aria e finale.   Here only cl(Eb) cl(C).   MS pts: CZ-Bm(au), A.35.150, (missing all other pts).
  LEGRAND **WYL-6a** 1 mvt.   fl ob 2cl 2hn 2bn.
  MARPURG **WYM-1.5a** overture.   pic 2ob cl(E♭) 3cl(B♭) 2hn 2bn 2tp a-tb t-tb b-tb serp b-dr s-dr.
  MOSELL **EQM-1a** 15 parts.
  SCHOLL **NYS-6ac** 4 mvts.   2ob 2cl 2hn 2bn cbn 2tp [b-tb].
  SCHOLZ **WES-42.1a** overture & 10 mvts.   fl 2ob 2cl 3hn 2bn tp tb db timp.
  SCHOLZ **WES-42.2a** finale Act II.   fl 2ob 2cl 2hn 2bn tp tb db timp.
  WERNER, F. **FWW-1a** duett.   terz-fl 2cl(E♭) 2cl(Bb) 4hn(E♭, B♭) 2bn 2tp b-tb cb.
Beatrice di Tenda (opera, 16 March 1833, Venice)
  SCHOLL **NYS-7ac** Terzetto.   2ob 2cl 2hn 2bn cbn 2tp [b-tb].
I Puritani di Scozia (opera, 24 Jan 1835, Paris)
  KIRCHHOFF **WZK-30.1a** "Diess war mein Leid, o Himmel".   fl 2ob 2cl 2hn 2bn tb db.
  KIRCHHOFF **WZK-30.2a** duetto, ("Den Rival").   fl 2ob 2cl 3hn 2bn tp tb db.
  SCHOLL **NYS-8ac** [2] duetti e aria.   2ob 2cl 2hn 2bn cbn 2tp [b-tb].
  SCHOLZ **WES-43a** 6 mvts.   fl 2ob 2cl 3hn 2bn tp tb db timp.
  VOJÁČEK **HXV-1a** duetto.   2ob 2cl 2hn 2bn 2tp tb bassi.
  WIESER **FAW-9a** poutpouri [sic] No. 4.   terz-fl(pic) cl(E♭) 2cl(B♭) 2hn 2bn tp b-tb cb.
Unidentified Works
  LEGRAND **WYL-7a** cavatine.   fl ob 2cl 2hn 2bn (bn III ad lib).

BELLMAN, Carl Michael (1740 - 1795)
  LUNDÉN **LYL-1a** unidentified mvts as: Blåsen nu alla: Bellmansvit.   2fl ob 2cl b-cl 2hn bn b.

BELLOLI Luigi (1770 - 1817)
I trionfo di Vitellio Massimo e la distruzzione di Pompejano (ballet, Milan 1803; Vienna 1808)
  TRIEBENSEE **JZT-4a** 3 mvts.   2ob 2cl 2hn 2bn (cbn tp ad lib).

BENDA, Georg (1709 - 1786)
Medea (melodrama, 1 May 1775, Leipzig; 26 March 1777, Berlin)
  ANON **A-64a** March.   fl ob 3cl 2hn 2bn tb.   MS parts: D-Rtt, G.Benda 2/IV.

BENDL, Conrad
Humors-Organe Walzer
  WIESER **FAW-10a** pic(D♭) cl(E♭) 2cl(B♭) 2hn 2bn t- b-tb cb.

BENEDICT, Julius (1804 - 1885)
The Gipsy's Warning (Das Zigeunerin Warnung) (opera, 19 April 1838, London)
  KÜFFNER **JYK-10a** Musique militaire.
  SCHOLZ **WES-44.1a** overture.   fl 2ob 2cl 2hn 2bn tp tb/bn db timp.
  SCHOLZ **WES-44.2a** arietta.   fl 2ob 2cl 2hn 2bn tb db timp.

BERBIGUIER, Antoine (Benoit) Tranquille (1782 - 1838)
Marche des volontaires Royaux (c.1814 - 1816, Paris)
  GAMBARO **VXG-4.5(a)** pic(D♭) cl(E♭) 2cl(B♭) 2hn (2)bn tp tb serp b-dr+cym.

BERLIOZ, Louis Hector (1803 - 1869)
Les Nuits d'été, Op. 7 (songs to texts by Gautier, composed 1834 - 1841)
  BAKER **LQB-1a** fl fl(pic) ob(ca) ca cl cl(b-cl) 2hn 2bn.
3 pièces pour harmonium (1845)
  GILLASPIE **JAG-1a** fl ob 2cl 2hn 2bn.

BERNARDINI, Marcello (known as "Marcello di Capua") (1752, Capua - post 1800)
Don Simoncino, ossia Furberia e Puntiglio (opera, 18 Sept 1798, Venice)
  FUCHS **GFF-2.4a** air, "Per amar Abbiamo il core".   2fl 2cl(C) 2hn 2bn.

BERNER, ( )
Grabgesang ("Horch wem hallt der Glocken dumpfer Klang"), in C minor.
  ANON **A-3va** TTBB, 2cl 2hn bn tb db.   MS score: D-NEhz, 163, No. 2.

BERNER, Louis
Myrthenblätter-Walzer ("Arr. nach d. Klavier")
  ANON **A-65a** winds.   MS score & parts: D-DT, Mus-n 1566.

BERTIE, Willoughby, *4th Earl of Abingdon* (1740 - 1799)
Twelve country dances and three capriccios...with three Minuets, (RISM [A 156]) (2fl 2hn 2vl b, c.1798, London)
  GILLASPIE **JAG-2a** 3 Minuets.   fl ob 2cl 2hn 2bn.
Catch, "Some kind Angel" & Glee "Where shall a hapless lover find" (with accompaniments by F.J. Haydn)
(3 equal voices, piano)
  STONEHAM **AMS-1va** 3 equal voices, cl 2hn bn.

BERTON, Henri Montan (1767 - 1844)
Montano et Stéphanie (comic opera, 15 April 1799, Paris)
    FUCHS **GFF-7a** 7 mvts.   2fl(ad lib) 2cl(C) 2hn 2bn.
Le grand Deuil (comic opera, 21 Jan 1801, Paris)
    VANDERHAGEN **AJV-6.1a** overture.   2fl(pic) 2cl(C) 2hn 2bn, (tp tb serp timp/t-dr/b-dr ad lib).
    VANDERHAGEN **AJV-6.2a** airs.   2fl 2cl 2hn 2bn, (tp tb serp ad lib).
Aline, Reine de Golconde (comic opera, 3 Sept 1803, Paris)
*The three nonet arrangements listed below show some divergence in mvts; we believe, however, that they share
a common (Viennese) source.*
    ANON **A-66.1a** overture & 13 mvts.   2ob 2cl 2hn 2bn cbn.   MS pts: CZ-KRa, A3839/IV.B.3, (pre-1811; with a
    note on the cover, "Revidi[rt]:"); A-Wn, Mus.Hs.3794, No. 1, (=A.7.1a; Marsch in C, ¢, No. 4 of CZ-KRa).
    ANON **A-66.2a** 2ob 2cl 2hn 2bn cbn.   overture & 9 mvts.   MS parts: I-Fc, F.P. S.345.
    ANON **A-66.3a** 2ob 2cl 2hn 2bn cbn.   overture & 8 mvts.   MS pts: I-Fc, F.P. S.381, (attributed to Gyrowetz).
    COURTIN **HZC-2.1a** overture, **HZC-2.2a** 11 airs.   4cl 2hn 2bn serp/cb, *or* 2cl 2hn 2bn.
    KROMMER **FVK-2.8ma** Marsch.   2ob 2cl 2hn 2bn cbn.
    SEDLAK **+WXS-7a** overture & 9 mvts.   2cl 2hn 2bn.
Untraced arrangements: Françoise de Foix (opera, 1809), Féodor (opera, 1816).

BERTONI, Fernando Gasparo (1725 - 1813)
Gloria, in Csolfaut (Venice)
    MARULLI **AXM-1av** Solo TTB, 2cl 2hn bn 2tp timp organ(bc-fig).

BIANCHI, Francesco (1752 - 1810)
La Villanella rapita (opera pasticcio, 1783, Venice) *See also MOZART, infra, for additional mvts for this opera.*
    ANON **A-67a** 2fl 2cl 2hn 2bn.   MS parts: RF-Ssc, Ф 891 собр юосуповыiх N18, pp. 62 - 110.
    FUCHS, G.F. **GFF-2.5a** duo, "Vanne in preda".   2fl 2cl(C) 2hn 2bn.
    GEBAUER, M.J. **MJG-2a** Suite.   2ob 2cl 2hn 2bn serp/db(ad lib).

BIBER, Heinrich Ignaz Franz von (1644 - 1704)
La Battalia (vl solo, strings, bc, 1673)
    BAUDE-DELHOMMAIS **EDB-1a** 3ob 2ca 2bn b.

BIEREY, Gottlob Benedikt (1772 - 1840)
Das Blumenmädchen oder besser Die Rosenkönigen (comic opera, 14 Feb 1801, Breslau; 1802, Leipzig)
    ANON **A-68a** Sinfonia Pastorale.   2ob 2cl 2hn 2bn basso.
    MS parts(c.1803): D-HR, HR III 4 1/2 2° 358, (mvt 13 of the arr of T. Weigl's *Die Vermählung im Keller*).
    Pm (KGS), fiche (2309, 2310).
Der Gemsenjäger (opera, 19 Jan 1811, Breslau; 18 Feb 1812, Vienna)
    ANON **A-69a** 2 Theils.   2ob 2cl 2hn 2bn cbn.   MS parts: I-Fc, F.P. S.375.
Die Pantoffeln (comic opera, 6 July 1811, Vienna)
    ANON **A-70a** 2ob 2cl 2hn 2bn cbn.   MS parts: I-Fc, F.P. S.375.
Die Herberge bei Parma (romantic opera, 27 Oct 1812, Vienna)
    ANON **A-61a** 2 Parts.   2ob 2cl 2hn 2bn cbn.
    Pc [T. Weigl: Wien, c.1813], MS parts: I-Fc, F.P. S.361.

BIRNBAUM, C.
[5] Brünner Redout Deutsche für das Jahr 1830 (?piano, 1830, Brno)
    ANON **A-23.4a** cl(D) 2hn 2bn 2tp.   MS parts: CZ-Bm(au), A.36.666, No 3.

BISHOP, *Sir* Henry Rowley (1786 - 1855)
The Comedy of Errors (comedy/opera, 11 Dec 1819, London)
    TAYLORSON **JST-1a** "Lo, Here the Gentle Lark".   Solo S *or* cl, fl 2ob 2cl 2hn 2bn cbn.

BIZET, (Alexandre César Léopold) Georges (1838 - 1875)
Carmen (opera, 3 March 1875, Paris)
    SHEEN **GHS-1a** Suite, 6 mvts.   fl ob ob(ca) 2cl 2hn 2bn cbn.
Jeux d'enfants (Piano, four hands, published 1872 Paris; orchestration published 1882, Paris)
    SHEEN **GHS-2a** fl(pic) 2ob 2cl 2hn 2bn.

BLANGINI, Giuseppe Maria Felice (1781 - 1841)
Nepthali ou Les Ammonites [oder der Macht des Glaubens] (opera, 15 April 1806, Paris)
    ANON **A-72a** 2 Abtheilungen.   2ob 2cl 2hn 2bn cbn.
    Pc (Thade [sic] Weigl: Wien, c.1807), MS parts: I-Fc, F.P. S.369.

BLASIUS, Frédéric Matthieu (1758 - 1829)
Unidentified works
    FUCHS **GFF-8a** Suite 110 (instrumentation unknown). *(Possibly the melodrama,* Don Pèdre et Zulika, *1802)*
Waltz
    SYLVANI **XSV-1.7a** 2cl 2hn 2bn.

BLAUVELS, ( )
Ouverture in Eb
    MEIER **GWM-1a** fl cl(Eb) cl(Bb obl) 3cl(Bb) 2hn 2bn tp 3tb serp b-dr.

BLUM, Karl (1786 - 1844)
Das Rosenhütchen (grosse Zauberoper, 28 June 1819, Vienna)
    ANON **A-73a** 2ob 2cl 2hn 2bn cbn.   MS parts: I-Fc, F.P. S.383.

BLUMENTHAL, Josef (Jacques) von (1782 - 1850)
König Lear (Trauerspiel, c.1810, Vienna)   (=JVB-1a)
  SCHNEIDER, A. **AYS-20a** Grosse Marsch. fl(D) 2ob 4cl(C) 2hn 2bn tp b-tb serp.

BOCCHERINI, Luigi
Ballet Espagnol (G.526) (orchestra, 1773)
  BACH, J.C. **JCB-1.2/iv** as last mvt Rondeau. 2cl 2hn 2bn.
Trio Sonata in D, No. 4 (G.146) Menuet militaire (hpcd/pf vl vc, pub. 1781, Paris - possibly spurious)
  ANON **A-74a** 2cl 2hn 2bn. MS parts (by John Liverins): US-BETm, Lititz Collegium Musicum 200.1.

BOCCHORONI, Raymond (appears to be neither Boccherini nor Pokorny)
(unidentified) Overture
  ANON **A-75.1a** 2ob 2cl 2hn 2bn 2tp. MS parts (1839), CZ-Bm(au), A.36.850, No. 1.

BOCHSA, Charles, père (c.1760 - 1821)
Marche Funèbre
  LEROY **PQL-1.4/3(a)** 2fl(F) 2cl(F) 2cl(C) 2hn 2bn tp serp b-dr
Valzer [sic]
  LEROY **PQL-1.9/5(a)** 2p-fl(F) 2cl(F) 2cl(C) 2hn 2bn tp serp.

BOCHSA Robert Nicolas Charles, fils (1789 - 1856)
Le Roi et la Ligue ou La ville assiégée (comic opera, 22 Aug 1815, Paris)
  BERR **FXB-1ac** overture. p-fl(A) (2)fl 2cl(F) 2cl(C) 2hn 2bn tp b-tb cb.
Ouverture, in F
  LEROY **PQL-1.4/1(a)** 2fl(F) 2ob 2cl(III & IV, C) 2hn 2bn tp serp b-dr.
Rondeau, in F
  LEROY **PQL-1.4/2(a)** 2fl(F) 2ob 2cl(III & IV, C) 2hn 2bn tp serp b-dr.

BOEHM, Theobald (1794 - 1881)
Grand Polonaise Op. 16 (fl & piano, c.1833)
  BENNETT **WXB-1a** solo fl, 2ob 2cl 2hn 2bn.

BÖHR, Josef
Rondo, Fresco Hungaria (?c.1805)
  DRUSCHETZKY **GYD-9a** 2ob cl bthn 2hn 2bn cbn.

BOIELDIEU, François Adrien (1775 - 1834)
See also Cherubini, *Le Prisonnière* (collaboration with Boieldieu).
Le Calife de Bagdad (comic opera, 16 Sept 1800, Paris)
  GEBAUER, E.F. (attributed) **EFG-1a** overture. pic 2cl 2hn 2bn.
Ma Tante Aurore ou Le roman impromptu (comic opera, 13 Jan 1803, Paris)
  KOSLOWSKY **JOK-1a** overture. 2fl 2cl 2hn 2bn, (incomplete).
Rien de trop (Nur mit Maass, oder die Neuvermeichlten) (comic opera, 6 Jan 1810, St Petersburg)
  ANON **A-76a** 2ob 2cl 2hn 2bn cbn 2tp. MS parts: I-Fc, F.P. S.360.
Le Nouveau Seigneur du village (Der neue Gutsherr) (comic opera, 1811, Paris) *Possibly adapted for Vienna by M. Umlauf.*
  ANON **A-77a** (?2ob 2cl 2hn 2bn cbn 2tp). MS parts (9): I-Fc, F.P. S.371, (here attributed to M. Umlauf).
Jean de Paris (Johann von Paris) (comic opera, 4 April 1812, Paris)
  ANON **A-78a** overture & 4 mvts. 2flautino cl(F) 3cl(C)+cl(I rip, C) 2hn s-dr.
    MS parts: CZ-Bm(au), A.35.154, (missing some parts, including 2bn).
  ANON **A-79a** overture. fl(I, D) fl(II, d or cl III in C) 2cl(C & Bb) 2hn bn 2tp b-tb/cb.
    MS parts (1824): D-Tl, Gg 306, No. 1, (missing cl II).
  ANON **A-80a** overture & 13 mvts. 2ob 2cl 2hn 2bn cbn tp. MS parts: A-Wn, Mus.Hs.3802.
  ANON **A-81.1a** overture & 9 mvts. 2ob 2cl 2hn 2bn cbn.
    Pc (Chemische Druckerei/Steiner: Wien, pn 2014 - 2015, 1813), **J9**, No. VI, parts: H-Bn, Z 37,642.
    MS parts: CZ-Bm(au), A.35.253, Nos. 1 - 10, (with later local parts for 2tp).
  ANON **A-81.2a** overture & 9 mvts. 2cl 2hn 2bn.
    Pc (Chemische Druckerei/Steiner: Wien, pn 2014 - 2015, 1813), **J6**, No. VI, parts: CZ-KRa, A4009/IV.B.182.
    MS parts (copy of J6 by Havel, made in Olomouc, 3 May 1813): CZ-KRa, A3840/IV.B.4.
  KRECHLER **FFK-17.1a** overture & 10 mvts. 2ob 2cl 2hn 2bn cbn 2tp.
  KRECHLER **FFK-17.2a** overture & 9 mvts. 2ob 2cl 2hn 2bn cbn.
  LÖWENSTEIN **CAL-15a** overture. 2cl 2hn bn tp.
  POESSINGER **FAP-1a** 2ob 2cl 2hn 2bn cbn.
  RUMMEL **CFR-2a** overture. fl(C) cl(I prin, C)/ob cl(II, C) 2cl(Bb) 2hn 2bn serp, (ad lib: fl(Eb) cl(III Bb) 2tp 2b-tb serp b-dr).
  SCHMITT, G. **GYS-15.1a** overture. 2fl 2ob 2cl 2hn 2bn tb db timp.
  SCHMITT, G. **GYS-15.2a** fl 2ob 2cl 2hn 2bn tp tb db.
  SCHNEIDER, A. **AYS-21a** overture & 13 mvts. fl 2ob 2cl 2hn 2bn tp b-tb 2vla cb.
  SEDLAK **WXS-8a** overture & 9 mvts. 2ob 2cl 2hn 2bn.
  TRIEBENSEE **JZT-5a** Act I, overture & 9 mvts; Act II, 7 mvts. 2ob 2cl 2hn 2bn (cbn tp ad lib).
  WIELAND **KZW-3ad** overture & 15 mvts. 2fl 2cl 2hn 2bn. *?Copy of an unknown French publication.*
  WITT **FZW-3a** overture. terz-fl 2cl(C) 2cl(Bb) 2hn 2bn tp b-tb cb.
Le Fête du village voisin (comic opera, 5 March 1816, Paris)
  SCHMITT, G. **GYS-16a** overture. 2fl 2ob 2cl 2hn 2bn tb db.

Le Petit Chaperon rouge (Das Rothkäppchen) (comic opera, 30 June 1818, Paris)
  RICHTER **QYR-3.4a(-3.7a)** overture & 3 mvts. fl(G)(2fl, F) cl(F, D) 3cl(C, B♭) 2hn 2bn serp/cbn 2tp b-tb.
  SCHMITT, G. **GYS-1.8a** (?) Walzer. 2fl 2ob 2cl 2hn 2bn tp (?t-)tb db.
  SCHMITT, G. **GYS-17.1a** 2fl 2ob 2cl 2hn 2bn (2)tp tb db timp.
  SCHNEIDER, A. **AYS-22a** overture. fl 2ob 2cl 2hn 2bn tp b-tb 2vla cb.
  STARKE **FRS-4a** Röschens Aria & Chor des Holzbauer. 2ob 2cl 2h 2bn cbn 2tp.
La Dame blanche (Die weisse Frau) (comic opera, 10 Dec 1825, Paris).
  BOCHSA, R.N.C. **RNB-1ac** cavatine. cl(E♭) cl(B♭ premier) 2cl(Bb) 2hn 2bn 2tp b-tb.
  BOUFFIL **JJB-1a** overture & 4 suites (14 mvts). fl(pic) 2cl 2hn 2bn, (ad lib: 2cl tp b-tb serp).
  ENGLEMANN **CZE-1a** 3 mvts. fl(E♭) cl(E♭) cl(solo B♭) 3cl(B♭) 2hn 2bn 2tp 3tb serp b-dr.
  FISCHER **CYF-3a** potpourri, Op. 7. (TTBB ad lib), terz-fl(fl in F, pic in D) cl(F) 4cl(C) 2hn 2bn 2tp a-tb t-tb b-tb serp b-dr s-dr.
  OSSWALD **PAO-3a** overture & 11 mvts. 2ob 2cl 2h 2bn cbn 2tp.
  SCHMITT, G. **GYS-18.1a** 2 Bds. fl 2ob 2cl 2hn 2bn tp tb db (timp).
  SCHMITT, G. **GYS-18.2a** 1 mvt. fl 2ob 2cl 2hn 2bn tp tb db.
  SCHOLZ **WES-45a** finale Act I. fl 2ob cl 2hn 2bn tp b-tb db timp.
  STRECK **PZS-1.3a** overture. fl cl(D) 2cl(A) 2hn 2bn.
  WITT **FZW-4a** overture & 14 mvts. fl(F, terz-) 2cl(E♭) 2cl(B♭) 2hn 2bn tp b-tb cb.
Les Deux Nuits (comic opera, 20 May 1829, Paris).
  ANON **A-82a** overture. fl 2ob cl(E♭) 2cl(C) 3cl(B♭) 4hn 2bn 2tp 3tb serp b-dr s-dr.
  MS parts: D-DT, Mus-n 367.
  BERR **FXB-10a** overture. pic cl(E♭) 2cl(B♭) 2hn 2bn serp, (cl III & IV, tp 2tb db ad lib).
  SEIFF **JYS-1a** 2cl 2hn 2bn.

BOLZONI, Giovanni (1841 - 1919)
Minuetto
  CONN **JPC-1a** fl ob 2cl a-cl b-cl bn.

BORGHI, Luigi (active 1774 - post-1790)
Litanies de la Vierge à 4 voix (Paris, sd)
  ANON **A-4va** TTB, 2cl 2hn tp timp organ(bc-fig).
  MS score & parts: I-Vsmc, (one piece only, as "Litanie della B.V. a 3 voci").

BOYCE, William (c.1710 - 1779)
Eight Symphonies in Eight Parts, Opera Seconda: No 4 in F (c.1750, London)
  TAYLORSON **JST-2a** fl 2ob 2cl 2hn 2bn cbn/db.

BRAHMS, Johannes (1833 - 1897)
Hungarian Dances, WoO (composed 1858 - 1869, Vienna; Books 1 & 2 pub. 1869, Books 3 & 4 pub. 1880)
  CLEMENTS **PYC-1a** (Nos. 3, 7). 2ob 2cl 2hn 2bn cbn/db.
  SHEEN **GHS-3a** (Nos. 3, 5, 11, 16). fl fl(pic) 2ob b-cl 4hn 2bn cbn.
Sextet, Op. 18 (2vl 2vla vc, published 1862)
  POPKIN **MZP-1a** 2fl 2ob 2cl 2hn 2bn.
Variations on a Theme by Schumann, Op. 23 (1861, pub. 1863, 1st performance 12 Jan 1864, Vienna)
  CONNOLLY **JZC-1a** fl 2ob 2cl 2hn 2bn.
Variations and Fugue on a theme by Handel for piano, Op. 24 (1862)
  SHEEN **GHS-4a** 2fl fl(pic) 2ob 2cl b-cl 3hn 2bn.
Intermezzo, Op. 117, No. 1 (piano, pub. 1892, Berlin)
  SKIRROW **ARS-1a** fl 2ob 2cl 2hn 2bn.

BRESCIANI, Pietro (1806 - 1872)
L'Arbore di Diana (ballet, spring 1827, Padua)
  SCHOLL **NYS-1.1a** overture. 2ob 2cl 2hn 2bn cbn 2tp.

BRUBECK, Dave (David W.) (b. 1920)
Three to get ready; Blue shadows in the street; Blue Rondo à la Turk (piano with jazz ensemble)
  LOWES **IYL-1a** 2cl 2hn 2bn.

BRUNI Antonio Bartolommeo (1751 - 1821)
Spinette et Marini, ou La leçon conjugale (comic opera, 21 June 1790, Paris)
  FUCHS **GFF-9a** overture. 4cl 2hn 2bn tp.
Taberne, ou Le pêcheur suédois (comic opera, 2 Dec 1795, Paris)
  GEBAUER, M.J. **MJG-3a** (fl pic ad lib) 2cl 2hn 2bn.
Les Sabotiers (Die Holzschuhmacher) (comic opera, 23 June 1796, Paris)
  TRIEBENSEE **JZT-6a** overture & 1 aria. 2ob 2cl 2hn 2bn (cbn tp ad lib).
La Rencontre en voyage (comic opera, 28 April 1798, Paris)
  FUCHS, G.F. **GFF-1.4a** 1 mvt. 2fl 2cl(C) 2hn 2bn.
  FUCHS, G.F. **GFF-10a** overture. 2fl 2cl(C) 2hn 2bn, (tp tb serp ad lib).

BURGMEIN, J. (*pseud.*, i.e. Giulio di Tito **RICORDI**) (1840 - 1912)
Sette Pezzi Caratteristici, No. 5, Il Racconto della Nonna, Preghiera, "O mamma cara" (c.1915)
  MUGNONE **LEM-1a** 2fl ob ca hn bn harp.
Impressions de route, No. 2, Dans la montagne (c.1915)
  MUGNONE **LEM-2a** 2ob 2cl 2hn 2bn cbn.
Mon carnot de jeunesse, "Dors, dors, mon enfant" (c.1915)
  MUGNONE **LEM-3a** fl ca 2cl hn bn harp.

BYRD, William (1543 - 1623)
Variations on the Tune "Walsingham" (virginal)
HODGES **MUH-1a** 2fl 2ob 2cl 2hn 2bn.
The Earl of Oxford's March (virginal)
JOUARD **PXJ-1a** 2fl 2ob 2cl 2hn 2bn 3tp tb tu.

CALLCOTT, John Wall (1766 - 1821)
Epitaph in the church yard of the parish of Brading, "Forgive Blest Shade" (SSB Glee, pre-1795, London)
ELGAR **EWE-8a** 2fl cl hn bn.
Glee (introduced in Samuel Arnold's opera, *The Battle of Hexham*, 11 Aug 1789, London)
ELEY **CFE-2.3m(a).** 2ob/cl 2hn 2bn tp.

CAMPRA, André (1660 - 1744)
Tancrède (opera, 7 Nov 1702, Paris; pub. 1737, Paris)
ANON **A-46.3m(a)** Marche. 2vl 2hn 2bn.

CANNABICH, Carl August (1771 - 1806)
Palmer und Amalia (opera, Aug 1803, Munich)
LEGRAND **WYL-8a** 3 mvts. fl ob 2cl 2hn 2bn, (fl III ad lib in mvt 3).
WIDDER **YYW-1.18a** 2 mvts. fl ob 2cl 2hn 2bn.
Grand Simphonie in C, Op. 8 (sd, Munich)
SCHNEIDER, A. **AYS-23a** mvt 1 only. fl(Eb) 2ob 2cl+2cl(rip) 2hn 2bn tp b-tb serp.

CARAFA di Colobrano, Michele (E. F. V. A. P.), *Prince* (1787 - 1872)
Die Millerin (?opera, unidentified)
ANON **A-83a** 1 mvt. fl(F) 2cl(C) 2hn 2bn. MS parts: GB-Ljag(w), 5/262, No. 23.
Gabriella di Vergy (opera, 3 July 1816, Naples)
SEDLAK **WXS-9a** overture & 10 mvts. 2ob 2cl 2hn 2bn cbn 2tp.
Berenice in Siria (opera/azione tragica, 29 July 1818, Naples)
STARKE **FRS-5a** 1 mvt. 2ob 2cl 2hn 2bn cbn 2tp.
Masaniello (drame lyrique, 27 Dec 1827, Paris)
BERR **FXB-11a** overture. pic cl(Eb) 2cl(Bb) 2hn bn(I) serp, (ad lib: cl III & IV, tp 2/3tb serp).
La Solitaire (Der Klausner) (comic opera, 22 Aug 1822, Paris)
ANON **A-84a** overture & 4 mvts. 2ob 2cl 2hn 2bn cbn 2tp.
MS parts: CZ-Bm(au), A.35.856, (here incorrectly attributed to Auber).
BERR **FXB-12a** overture. fl cl(Eb) 2cl(C) 2hn 2bn; (ad lib: cl III in C, tp (2)tb serp ripieno).
La Violette (opera, 7 Oct 1828, Paris)
NEUMANN, H. **HYN-1a** aria. terz-fl ob cl(Eb) 3cl(Bb) 4hn 2bn 2tp a-tb t-tb b-tb serp b-dr t-dr tri.
NEUMANN, H. **HYN-2a** 2 arias. terz-fl 2ob cl(Eb) 3cl(Bb) 4hn 2bn 2tp a-tb t-tb b-tb serp b-dr t-dr.
"Tema de Carraffa [sic]*"* (unidentified)
FISCHER **CYF-2a** Potpourri. fl(Eb) cl(Eb) 4cl(Bb) 4hn 2bn 2tp tp(clar)/posthorn a-tb t-tb b-tb serp b-dr s-dr.
Untraced arrangement: La Solitaire (opera, 1822, Paris).

CARMICHAEL, Hoagland "Hoagy" Howard (1899 - 1981)
Stardust (popular song, pub. 1929, New York)
KLICKMANN **QZK-1a** fl ob 2cl hn bn.

CARTELLIERI, Casimir Antonio (1772 - 1807)
WRANIZKY, A. **AYW-1a** 1 mvt. pic 2ob 2cl 2hn 2bn cbn 2tp(princ) b-dm cym.

CATEL Charles Simon (1773 - 1830)
Sémiramis (Sémiramide; Les Africains) (tragédie lyrique, 4 May 1802, Paris)
ANON **A-85a** 4 Theils. (?2ob 2cl 2hn 2bn cbn). MS parts (9): I-Fc, F.P. S.391.
ANON **A-86a** overture & 12 mvts. 2ob 2cl 2hn 2bn cbn.
MS parts: H-KE, 1175/IX, (without cbn); I-Fc, F.P. S.347
CATEL **CSC-1.1a, 1.2a** 2 Suites, each 5 mvts. 2fl 2cl(C) 2hn 2bn.
CATEL **CSC-1.3a** Air des Africains. 2cl 2hn 2bn; (ad lib: pic 2ob 2tp tb timp b-dr cym).
SCHMITT, G. **GYS-19a** air, Les Africains [sic]. 2pic 2ob cl(Eb) 2cl(Bb) 4hn 2bn 2tp serp timp.
SCHOLZ **WES-46a** overture. fl 2ob 2cl 3hn 2bn tb timp.
SCHNEIDER, A. **AYS-24a** overture & 1 mvt. fl 2ob 2cl 2hn 2bn tp b-tb 2vla b.
Les Aubergistes de qualité (Die vornehmen Wirthe) (comic opera, 11 June 1812, Paris) *Note: a 3-Act Parodie,*
Die vornehmen Wirtinnen, *by Franz de Paula Roser von Reiter was produced in Vienna on 6 April 1813.*
ANON **A-87a** Abtheilung 1 & 2. 2ob 2cl 2hn 2bn cbn.
Pc (Im Verlage Thade [sic] Weigl: Wien, c.1813), MS parts: I-Fc, F.P. S.363.
Untraced arrangements: Wallace (opera 1817), Zirphile et Fleur de Myrte (opéra féerie, 1818), L'Officier enlevé (opera 1819), all published in Paris.

CAVOS, Catterino (1775 - 1840)
See also: ANONYMOUS WORKS, A-74m.
Marsch (duple) bei der Kaiserlich Russischen Armee (band, c.1820, St Petersburg)
SCHNEIDER, A. **AYS-3ma** (rescoring of Dörffeld's arr). terz-fl 2ob 2cl+2cl(rip) 2hn 2bn tp b-tb serp.

CHABRIER Emanuel (1841 - 1894)
Huit pièces pittoresques (piano, 1880)
FRANÇAIX **JEF-1a** 2fl 2ob 2cl 2hn 2bn.
Cortège burlesque, Oeuvre posthume (piano duet, pub. 1921)
FRANÇAIX **JEF-2a** pic fl ob ca cl b-cl 2hn bn cbn.

CHAMPEIN, Stanislas (1753 - 1830)
La Mélomanie (comic opera, 23 Jan 1781, Versailles)
  BEINET **XJB-3.2/2a** 9 mvts.   2cl 2hn 2bn.
  GEBAUER, M.J. **MJG-4a** 2ob 2cl 2hn 2bn serp/db(ad lib).
  OZI **EXO-1.6/1a** overture.   2cl(C) 2hn 2bn.

CHAPELLE, Pierre David Augustin (1756 - 1821)
L'Heureux Dépit (comic opera, 16 Nov 1786, Paris)
  OZI **EXO-1.19/3a** "Toujours de tes rigeurs".   2cl(C) 2hn 2bn.

CHARDINAY, Louis Armand (1755/56/58 - 1793)
Le Pourvoir de la Nature, ou Le Suite de la ruse d'amour (comic opera, 1786, Paris)
  OZI **EXO-1.19/4a** "O moment délicieux".   2cl(C) 2hn 2bn.

CHARLES, ( ), *fils*
Marche, in F
  LEROY **PQL-1.1/1(a)** 2p-fl(F) 2cl(F) 2cl(C) 2hn 2bn tp serp b-dr.

CHÉLARD, Hippolyte André Jean Baptiste (1789 - 1861)
Macbeth (opera, 29 June 1827, Paris; revised version: 25 Aug 1828, Munich).
  ANON **A-88a** overture.   pic 2ob cl(E♭) 3cl(B♭) 2hn 2bn 2tp 3tb serp b-dr t-dr.   MS pts: D-DT, Mus-n 381.
  LEGRAND **WYL-9a** 1 mvt.   fl ob 2cl 2hn 2bn.
  SEIFF **JYS-1a** 2cl 2hn 2bn.
  STRECK **PZS-2.3a** Hexenterzett.   fl 2cl 2hn 2bn.
  WIDDER **YYW-1.19a** 1 mvt.   2fl 2cl 2hn 2bn.
Mitternacht (opera, 19 June 1831, Munich)
  ANON **A-89a** 1 mvt.   fl(D) 2cl(C) 2hn 2bn.   MS parts: GB-Ljag(w), 5/262, No. 25.
  LEGRAND **WYL-10a** 1 mvt (Ländler).   fl ob 2cl 2hn 2bn.
  WIDDER **YYW-1.20a** Ländler.   2fl 2cl 2hn 2bn.

CHERUBINI, Luigi (1760 - 1842)
Idalida (opera, 13 Feb 1784, Florence)
  ANON **A-90a** 2fl 2cl 2hn 2bn.   MS parts: RF-Ssc, Ф 891 собр юосуповьiх N16, pp. 96 - 139.
Giulio Sabino (opera, 1785, London)
  KRECHLER **FFK-11.1a** overture.   2ob 2cl 2hn 2bn cbn.
Démophon [Demophoon] (opera, 12 Dec 1788, Paris)
  WEBER, S.J. **SJW-1a** 2fl 2ob 4cl 2hn 2bn 2tp tb serp perc.
Lodoïska (opera/heroic comedy, 18 July 1791, Paris; March 1802,Vienna, with additions, 1805)
  ANON **A-91a** overture.   4cl 2hn 2bn tp.   MS parts: D-Dl, Mus. 401/F510, (formerly: D-Zl, Sigl. Exner).
  ANON **A-92a** overture & 14 mvts.   2ob 2cl 2hn 2bn+db(rip).   MS parts: I-Fc, F.P. S.392.
  ANON **A-93a** overture & 5 mvts, (not the same as A-83a).   2ob 2cl 2hn 2bn cbn.
    Pc ([Ignaz Sauer]: Wien, post-1805), MS parts: CZ-Pnm, XX.F.27; H-KE, K 2056.
  NEUMANN, H. **HYN-3a** overture.   fl fl(F) 2ob 2hn+(2hn ad lib) 2bn 2tp t-hn a-tb t-tb b-tb serp b/vc b-dr s-dr.
  SCHMITT, G. **GYS-20a** overture.   2pic 2ob cl(E♭) 2cl(B♭) 4hn 2bn 2tp serp timp.
  SEDLAK **WXS-10a** overture & 10 mvts.   2cl 2hn 2bn.
Élisa, ou Le Voyage au glaciers du Mont St-Bernard (Elisa von Bernhardsberg; Bernhardsberg) (opera, 13 Dec 1794, Paris; Vienna 1802)
  ANON **A-94a** overture & 13 mvts.   2ob 2cl 2hn 2bn cbn/vlne.   MS pts: I-Fc, F.P. S.373, as ("Bernhards Berg").
  ANON **A-95a** (? 2ob 2cl 2hn 2bn).   MS parts (8): I-Fc, F.P. S.392, (as "Elisa").
  ANON **A-96a** overture & 5 mvts.   2cl 2hn 2bn.   MS parts (5 Mar 1804): CZ-KRa, A4453/R.I.23, No. 5.
  KRECHLER **FFK-11.2a** 3 mvts.   2ob 2cl 2hn 2bn cbn.
Médée (Medea) (opera, 13 March 1797, Paris; 1802 Vienna)
  ANON **A-97a** (? 2ob 2cl 2hn 2bn).   MS parts (8): I-Fc, F.P. S.789.
  KRECHLER **FFK-18a** introduzione & 7 mvts.   2ob 2cl 2hn 2bn cbn.
  SCHOLZ **WES-47a** overture.   fl 2ob 2cl 2hn 2bn tp b-tb db timp.
  SEDLAK **WXS-11a** overture & 9 mvts.   2cl 2hn 2bn.   *Probably a reduction of Triebensee's arrangement.*
  TRIEBENSEE **JZT-7a** sinfonia & 9 mvts.   2ob 2cl 2hn 2bn cbn/vlne.
L'Hôtellerie Portugaise (L'Osteria Portughese; Die portugisische Gasthaus) (comic opera, 25 July 1798, Paris)
  ANON **A-98a** 8 mvts (without overture).   2ob 2cl 2hn 2bn cbn.
    Pc (In der Kunst und Musikhandlung des Thadé Weigl: Vienna, 1799), MS parts: I-Fc, F.P. S.338.
La Prisonnière (Die Gefangene) (pastiche, with Boieldieu, 12 Sept 1799, Paris)   *Cherubini contributed the overture & 4 numbers.*
  TRIEBENSEE **JZT-8.1a** overture & 8 mvts.   2ob 2cl 2hn 2bn cbn.
  TRIEBENSEE **JZT-8.2a** duett (Allegretto).   2ob 2cl 2hn 2bn (cbn tp ad lib).
Les deux Journées ou Le porteur d'eau (Die Tage der Gefahr, Il due giornati; Der Wasserträger; Graf Armand;) (opera, 16 Jan 1800, Paris; 1802 Vienna)
  ANON **A-74.3/5m(a)** march.   pic quart-fl 2ob cl(F) 2cl(C) 4hn 2bn cbn+serp/2b-hn 2tp 3tb b-dr t-dr tamb cym.
  ANON **A-99a** overture.   fl 2ob cl(E♭) 3cl(B♭) 4hn 2bn 2tp 3tb b-hn b-dr t-dr.   MS pts: D-DT, Mus-n 392.
  ANON **A-100a** overture.   fl 2ob cl(E♭) 4cl(B♭) 2hn 2bn 2tp 3tb serp b-dr.   MS parts: D-DT, Mus-n 394.
  ANON **A-101a** romance.   fl 2ob 2cl(C) 2hn 2bn tb db.   MS parts: D-NEhz, 233.
  ANON **A-102a** overture & 9 mvts.   2cl 2hn 2bn.   MS pts: CZ-KRa, A4456/R.I.26, No. 6.
  GOEPFERT **CAG-1a** 6 mvts.   fl 2cl 2hn bn tp serp.
  JAVAULT **AYJ-1.1a** overture, **AYJ-1.2a** Suite 1, 5 mvts.   fl ob 3cl 2hn 2bn tp tb serp.
  KRECHLER **FFK-8.4a, 8.5a** Marche & Choeur et marche.   2ob 2cl 2hn 2bn cbn tp.
  LEGRAND **WYL-11a** 1 mvt.   fl ob 2cl 2hn 2bn.
  MAŠEK, P. **PLM-1.1a, 1.2a** overture & 9 mvts.   2ob 2cl 2hn 2bn (cbn).

[Les deux Journées]
  SCHMITT, G. **GYS-17.2a** 2fl 2ob 2cl 2hn 2bn tp(2) tb db timp.
  SCHMITT, G. **GYS-21.1a** overture.   2pic 2ob cl(Eb) 2cl(Bb) 4hn 2bn 2tp serp timp.
  SCHMITT, G. **GYS-21.2a** overture.   2pic 2ob 2cl(Eb) 4cl(Bb) 3hn 2bn 2tp tb serp timp.
  SCHMITT, G. **GYS-21.3a** 3 Acts.   2fl 2ob 2cl 2hn 2bn tp tb db timp.
  SCHMITT, G. **GYS-21.4a** romance.   fl 2ob 2cl(C) 2hn 2bn tb db.
  SEYFRIED **IXS-1.5(a)** Marsch.   2ob 2cl 2hn cbn.
  WEBER, S.J **SJW-2a** 5 mvts.   2fl 2ob 2cl 2hn 2bn 2tp (clar) vlne+serp.
  WETTICH **FUW-1a** fl 2ob 2cl 2hn 2bn quart-bn.
  WITT **FZW-5a** overture & 5 mvts.   fl(terz-fl) cl(F) cl(C) 2cl(Bb) 2hn 2bn tp b-tb cb.
Anacéron ou L'amour fugitif (opéra-ballet, 4 Oct 1803, Paris)
  ANON **A-103a** overture & 9 mvts.   2ob 2cl 2hn 2bn cbn.   MS parts: I-Fc, F.P. S.343.
  TRIEBENSEE **JZT-9a** "Grossen Tanz Aria".   2ob 2cl 2hn 2bn (cbn tp ad lib).
Faniska (opera, 25 Feb 1806, Vienna)
  ANON **A-104a** overture & 10 mvts.   2cl 2hn 2bn.   MS parts: CZ-KRa, A3844/IV.B.8.
  SEDLAK **WXS-12a** overture & 11 mvts.   2ob 2cl 2hn 2bn cbn.
Messe No. 2 in D minor (c.1816, Paris)
  SEYFRIED **IXS-1av** Offertorium in D.   Solo SATB, 2fl 2ob 2cl 2hn 2bn 2tp timp, *or* 2ob 2tp 3tb timp.
Offertorium in F (Ave Maria) (Solo Soprano, solo clarinet, orchestra)
  LÖWENSTEIN **CAL-1va** S solo, cl solo/fl, 2cl(II, III, in C) 2hn bn(I = vla pt) vla.
Polonoise, in D (unidentified. Note: this piece also appears in Fuchs, GFF-3.1a atributed to Martín y Soler (in
La Capricciosa corretta) & in the D-Rtt score of Guglielmi's La Lanterne di Diogene, 1793)
  SCHNEIDER, A. **AYS-25a** fl 2ob 4cl 2hn 2bn tp b-tb serp.
Untraced arrangements: La Punition (opera 1799).

CHOPIN, Frédéric François (Fryderyk Franciszek) (1810 - 1849)
Valse brillante, Op. 18 (piano, 1831, pub. 1834)
  SCHOLZ **WES-48a** fl 2ob 2cl 3hn 2bn b-tb db.
Variations sur un air populaire Allemand ("Der Schweizerbub"), WoO, 1826 et Trois Ecossaises, Op. 72/3
  FRANÇAIX **JEF-3a** fl fl(pic) 2ob 2cl 2hn 2bn.

CIMAROSA, Domenico (1749 - 1801)
Giannina e Bernadone (comic opera, autumn 1781, Venice)
  FUCHS, G.F. **GFF-2.2a** duo, "Giannina amabile".   2fl 2cl(C) 2hn 2bn.
Il due Baroni di Rocca Azzurra (comic opera, Feb 1783, Rome)
  VANERHAGEN **AJV-1.1a** duo & 3 arias.   2cl 2hn 2bn
L'Impressario in Angustie (opera/farsa, 7 Feb 1786, Naples)
  ANON **A-105a** 2fl 2cl 2hn 2bn.   MS parts: RF-Ssc, Ф 891 собр юосуповьix N17, pp. 164 - 215.
  FUCHS, G.F. **GFF-2.1a** duo, "Che l'alma mia discacci" & air, "Chi dice mal d'amore".   2fl 2cl(C) 2hn 2bn.
  FUCHS, G.F. **GFF-11a** 2cl 2hn 2bn.
Il Matrimonio segreto (Die heimlichen Ehe) (comic opera, 7 Feb 1792, Vienna)
  ANON **A-106a** airs et ouverture. 4 suites, 24 mvts.   p-fl 2cl+(2cl ripieno) 2hn 2bn serp tp, *or* p-fl 2cl 2hn 2bn.
    Pc (Frères Gaveaux: Paris, c.1793), RISM [C 2313], pts: D-AB; NL-At, Zz-Cim-2, (Suite 1, overture & 5 mvts).
  ANON **A-107a** "Pria che spunti in ciel l'Aurora".   7 winds.   MS parts: I-Fc, F.P. S.353.
  ANON **A-108a** 2cl 2bn/vlne 2vla.   MS parts: I-Ria, Mus.648.
  FUCHS, G.F. **GFF-12.1a** ouverture; **GFF-12.2a** 8 morceaux choisis.   2fl 2cl(C) 2hn 2bn.
  FUCHS, G.F. **GFF-32** No. 6, "E vero che in casa".   2fl 2cl(C) 2hn 2bn.
  GUBICH **WZG-1a** 2ob 2cl 2hn 2bn.   *Possibly only the local copyist of Went's arrangement, JNW-11.1a.*
  KRECHELER **FFK-1.5ac** aria, Tempo Pollacco [sic].   2ob 2cl 2hn 2bn cbn tp.
  STUMPF **JUS-1a** 2 Stücke.   2fl 2ob 2cl 2hn 2bn cbn.
  WENT **JNW-11.1a** introduzione (overture) & 10 mvts.   2ob 2cl 2hn 2bn.
  WENT **JNW-11.2a** introduzione (overture) & 10 mvts.   2ob 2ca 2hn 2bn.
  WENT **JNW-11.3a** overture & 10 mvts.   2cl 2hn 2bn.
Amor rende sagace (comic opera, related to *Le Astuzie femminili*, 1 April 1793, Vienna)
  ANON **A-109a** symphonia [sic], introduzione & 8 mvts.   2ob 2cl 2hn 2bn.   MS parts: A-Ee, Mus.1105.
Le Astuzie femminili (comic opera, 26 Aug 1794, Naples)
  VANDERHAGEN **AJV-7a** Airs, 8 mvts.   2cl 2hn 2bn.
I Nemici generosi (comic opera, 26 Dec 1795, Rome)
  VANDERHAGEN **AJV-1.4a** aria, "Fanciulla sventurata".   2cl 2hn 2bn
Gli Orazi ed i Curiazi (opera/tragica per musica, 26 Dec 1796, Venice; 30 June 1797, Vienna)
  ANON **A-110a** Sinfonia, Act I: introduzione & 9 mvts.   2ob 2cl 2hn 2bn.
    Pc (sn: sl [K.K. Hoftheater Musik Verlag: Wien], c.1796), MS pts: CZ-Pnm, XX.F.54. *Not the Went version.*
  HAVEL **VXH-1a** Parthe [sic] I: overture & 8 mvts. Parthe [sic] IIdo: 9 mvts.   2cl 2hn 2bn.
  MÜNCHS **CNM-2/2/7(a)** overture.   p-fl(Db) cl(Eb) cl(Bb solo) 3cl(Bb) 2hn 2bn 2tp(hn) 2tb serp cb(ad lib).
  WENT **JNW-12a** sinfonia & 9 mvts.   2ob 2cl 2hn 2bn.
  WIELAND **KZW-2.3ad** "Quelle pupille tenore".   2fl 2ob 2cl 2hn 2bn serp/b-tb.
  WIELAND **KZW-2.6ad** "Frenar vorrei le lagrime".   2fl 2ob 2cl 2hn 2bn serp/b-tb.
Il Matrimonio per raggio (opera, revival of *L'Appresivo raggirato*, 1803, Padua)
  VANDERHAGEN **AJV-1.2a** No. 5 "Io son capriciosetta" & No. 8, "Vedete una ragazza".   2cl 2hn 2bn
Armonio composta d'alcuni motivi i più conosciuti dell' insigne Cimarosa (Bologna, 1826)
  AVONI **PYA-1a** 2fl 2ob 2cl 2hn 2bn 2tp b-tb.
Marche, in F
  LEROY **PQL-1.10/5a** 2p-fl(F) 2cl(F) 2cl(C) 2hn (2)bn tp serp timp.
Untraced (full) arrangements: I Nemici generosi (opera, 1795, Rome); Il Matrimonio per Raggio (opera, revival
of L'Apprensivo raggirato, 1803, Padua).

COCCIA, Carlo (1782 - 1873)
La Poeta fortunato ossia Tutto il male non vien dal mantello (opera, spring 1808, Florence)
 LEGRAND **WYL-14a** 1 mvt. fl ob 2cl 2hn 2bn.
Evvelina (opera seria, 26 Dec 1814, Milan)
 LEGRAND **WYL-13a** & **WYL-53.1a** overture. fl ob 2cl 2hn 2bn.
La Clothilde ossia La foresta di Hermannstadt (opera seria, 8 June 1815, Venice)
 LEGRAND **WYL-12a** 1 mvt. fl ob 2cl 2hn 2bn.

CORNELIUS, Peter (1824 - 1874)
6 Weihnachtslieder, Op. 8 (6 Christmas Songs) (voice & piano, 1856)
 EMERSON **GZE-1.5a** No. 1, "Der Tannenbaum" ("Der Christbaum"). 2fl ob 3cl hn bn.

COVALOVSKY, ( )
6 Deutsche (piano, 1820s)
 ANON **A-625.3a** 2ob cl(A) cl(C) 2hn 2bn cbn 2tp. MS parts (c.1827): CZ-Bm(au), A.36.893, No. 3.

CRAMER; Johann Baptist (1771 - 1858)
4 Divertimentos, Op. 17, No. 3, in D (piano, tamb & tri ad lib, pub: c.1798, London)
 TRIEBENSEE **JZT-10a** mvt 1, Maestoso (as "Marsch"). 2ob 2cl 2hn 2bn (tp ad lib).

CRUSELL, Bernhard Henrik (1775 - 1838)
Concertante for solo clarinet, horn & bassoon, with orchestra, Op. 3
 LÖWENSTEIN **CAL-16a** Solo cl, hn, bn, terz-fl 2cl(Eb) 2cl(Bb) 2hn (2)bn 2tp(clar) b-tb+cb.

D., Madame
Airs composés pour le clavecin ou piano-forte
 ANON **A-111a** 2cl 2hn 2bn.
  Pc (sn: sl, sd), RISM [IN 55], parts: F-Pn.

DALAYRAC (D'Alayrac; D-DO: "Tallirak"), Nicolas (1753 - 1809)
L'Amant Statue (comic opera, 2 Nov 1785, Fontainebleau; 6 Dec 1785, Paris)
 BEINET **XJB-3.1/1a** overture & 6 mvts. 2cl 2hn 2bn.
 OZI **EXO-1.17/2a** 6 mvts. 2cl(C) 2hn 2bn.
 VANDERHAGEN **AJV-3.15/1a** overture & 3 mvts; **AJV-3.17/1a** 4 mvts. 2cl 2hn 2bn.
La Dot (comic opera, 3 Nov 1785, Fontainebleau; 21 Nov 1785, Paris)
 OZI **EXO-1.18/2a** romance, "Vous que je viens de cueiller pour elle". 2cl(C) 2hn 2bn.
 VANDERHAGEN **AJV-3.21a** overture & 7 mvts.
Nina, ou La Folle par amour (comic opera, 15 May 1786, Paris) *See also:* PERSUIS, revival as a ballet, 1813.
 ANON (?Ehrenfried) **A-112a** 2ob 2cl 2hn 2bn. MS parts: D-DO, Mus.Ms.2017, (as by "Tallirak").
 EHRENFRIED **FHE-1a** 2 Parthias, (No. 1, 6 mvts; No. 2, 5 mvts). 2ob 2cl 2hn (2)basso.
 OZI **EXO-1.19/1a** overture & 4 mvts. 2cl(C) 2hn 2bn.
Azémia, ou Le nouveau Robinson [ou Les Sauvages] (Die Wilden; La Selvaggia) (opera, 17 Oct 1786, Fontainbleau)
 ANON **A-113a** overture. 2ob 2cl 2hn 2bn cbn. MS parts: D-RUl, RH-D1.
 ANON **A-114a** 2ob 2cl 2hn 2bn. MS score: S-St, (without shelfmark).
 FUCHS, G.F. **GFF-13a** 4cl 2hn 2bn serp/db; *or* 2cl 2hn 2bn.
 RIEGER **GYR-2a** overture & 6 mvts. 2cl 2hn 2bn.
Renaud d'Ast (opera, 19 July 1787, Paris)
 OZI **EXO-1.24/a** air; **EXO-1.26/2a** 4 mvts. 2cl(C) 2hn 2bn.
Sargines, ou L'élève de l'amour (oder der Triumph der Treue; Sargino) (comic opera, 14 May 1788, Paris)
 ANON **A-4.2a**, 4.3a 2 mvts. 2ob 2cl 2h 2bn cbn.
 GEBAUER, M.J. **MJG-5a** 8 mvts. 4cl 2hn 2bn.
Les Deux Petits Savoyards (Die beiden Savoyarden) (comic opera, 14 Jan 1789, Paris)
 ANON **A-115a** "Une petite Filette" & "Escoute d'Jeanette". fl ob 2cl 2hn.
  MS parts: NL-Z, Z1134, Nos 10 & 11, (possibly missing (2)bn).
 FUCHS, G.F. **GFF-4a** pot-pourri. 4cl 2hn 2bn.
 GEBAUER, M.J. **MJG-6a** 2ob 2cl 2hn 2bn serp/db(ad lib).
 PICK **HXP-2.10(a)** 5 mvts. 2fl(Bb, C, terz-fl) 4cl 2hn 2bn tp bugle-hn serp/b-tb b-dr.
 SEDLAK **WXS-13.1a** overture & 8 mvts. 2ob 2cl 2hn 2bn cbn.
 SEDLAK **WXS-13.2a** overture & 8 mvts. 2cl 2hn 2bn.
Le Soirée orageuse (comic opera, 29 May 1790, Paris)
 ANON **A-116a** 2fl 2cl 2hn 2bn. MS parts: RF-Ssc, Ф 891 собр юосуповъ i x N18, pp. 1 - 22.
 OZI **EXO-1.30/1a** overture & 2 mvts. 2cl 2hn 2bn.
 VANDERHAGEN **AJV-5.1a** 5 mvts. 2cl 2hn 2bn.
Camille, ou Le souterrain (comic opera, 19 March 1791, Paris)
 FUCHS, G.F. (attributed) **GFF-14a** overture. 4cl 2hn 2bn tp serp, *or* 2cl 2hn 2bn.
Gulnare, ou l'Esclave persanne (opera, 30 Dec 1798, Paris)
 FUCHS, G.F. (attributed) **GFF-15.1a** overture. 2pic(C) 2cl(C) 2hn 2bn tp.
 FUCHS, G.F. **GFF-15.2a** 6 airs. 2fl 2cl(C) 2hn 2bn; (the flute parts are essentially ripieno).
Adolphe et Clara, ou Les deux prisonniers (opera, 10 Feb 1799, Paris)
 KLEITZ **FZK-1a** 2ob/pic(ad lib) 2cl 2hn 2bn.
 SCHMITT, G. **GYS-22a** overture. 2fl 2ob 4cl 2hn 2bn serp 2tp.
Une Matinée [journée] de Catinat, ou Le Tableau (opera, 1 Oct 1800, Paris)
 ANON **A-117a** 2ob 2cl 2hn 2bn cbn. MS parts: I-Fc, F.P. S.376.
 FUCHS, G.F. **GFF-1.3a**. 2 mvts. 2fl 2cl(C) 2hn 2bn.

Maison à vendre (comic opera, 23 Oct 1800, Paris)
  BLASIUS **MFB-1a** overture & 5 airs. pic 2cl 2hn 2bn tp b-tb.
  SCHMITT, G. **GYS-23a** "O ciel! qu'ai-je lu?" 3fl 3ob 4cl 2hn 2bn serp tb.
Léhéman, ou La Tour de Neustadt (comic opera, 12 Dec 1801, Paris)
  GEBAUER, E.F. **EFG-2a** overture. Instrumentation unknown.
  LEGRAND **WYL-15a** 3 mvts. fl ob 2cl 2hn 2bn, (fl III ad lib).
La Boucle de cheveux (Die Haarlocke) (opera, 30 Oct 1802, Paris)
  GEBAUER, E.F. **EFG-3.1a** overture. Instrumentation unknown.
  GEBAUER, E.F. **EFG-3.2a** airs et duo. Instrumentation unknown.
Le jeune Prude, ou Les Femmes entre elles (opera, 14 Jan 1804, Paris)
  VANDERHAGEN **AJV-8a** ouverture & airs. 2fl 2cl 2hn 2bn, (tp tb serp ad lib).
Une Heure de Mariage (comic opera, 20 March 1804, Paris)
  ANON **A-118.1a,** overture; **118.2a** airs. 2fl 2cl 2hn 2bn.
  Pc (Pleyel: Paris, 1806), parts: (untraced; Pleyel 1806 catalog). *Not in F-Pn as sometimes stated.*
Gulistan, ou Le Hulla de Samarcande (comic opera, 30 Sept 1805, Paris)
  ANON **A-119a** overture & 11 mvts. 2fl 2ob 2cl 2hn 2bn cbn 2tp. MS parts: CZ-KRa, A3837/IV.B.1, (the
    wrapper bears of notes of 5 performances between 7 Oct 1816 & 15 Oct 1818). *The flute parts are for the*
    overture and Nos, 2 - 4 only.
  ANON **A-120a** 2ob 2cl 2hn 2bn. MS parts: I-Fc, F.P. S.344.
Deux Mots, ou Une Nuit dans la forêt (Die Nacht im Walde) (opera, 9 June 1806, Paris)
  SCHMITT, G. **GYS-24.1a** overture. 2fl 2ob 2cl 2hn 2bn 2tp tb db.
  SCHMITT, G. **GYS-24.2a** polonaise & pas redoublé. 2pic terz-fl 2ob cl(F) 2cl(B♭) 4hn 2bn cbn 2tp b-dr s-dr.
  SEIFF **JYS-1a** 2cl 2hn 2bn.
La Poète et le musicien (Der Dichter und Tonsetzer) (comic opera, 30 May 1811, Paris)
  ANON **A-121a** Marsch. pic cl(F) 3cl(C) 4hn(F, C) 2bn 4tp(F, C) b-dr. MS parts: CZ-Bm(au), A.35.157.
  ANON **A-122a** Marsch. 2ob cl(F) 2cl 2hn 2bn cbn 2tp. MS parts: CZ-Bm(au), A.35.267, (missing 2ob).
  SEDLAK **WXS-14a** overture & 10 mvts. 2ob 2cl 2hn 2bn cbn (2tp).
Untraced arrangement: L'Antichambre (later "Picaros et Diégo", opera 1802), overture & airs published by
Pleyel: Paris, pn 568, 1806.

DANZI Franz (1763 - 1826)
Lanassa (play with incidental music, 29 Dec 1782, Mannheim)
  ANON **A-123a** 2ob 2cl 2hn 2bn cbn. MS parts: I-Fc, F.P. S.382.
Freudenfest (cantata, 1804)
  SARTORIUS **GCS-1a** chorus. 2cl 2hn 2bn cbn.
Unidentified Works
  LEGRAND **WYL-16a** 1 mvt (Allegretto, 3/8, in G). fl ob 2cl 2hn 2bn, (fl III ad lib).

DAUVERGNE, Antoine (1713 - 1797)
Hercule Mourant (tragédie-lyrique, 3 April 1761, Paris)
  ANON **A-46.6m(a)** Marche. 2vl 2hn 2bn.

DAVAUX, Jean-Baptiste (1742 - 1822)   *See supra:* ANON **A-2a.**

DAVID, Félicien-Césaar (1810 - 1876)
Le Désert (L'Oasis; Der Karavane aus der Wüste) (ode-symphonique, 8 Dec 1844, Paris)
  SCHOLZ **WES-49a** Zug. fl 2ob 2cl 2hn 2bn tp tb db timp.

DEBUSSY, Claude Achille (1862 - 1918)
Petite Suite (piano, four hands, 1886 - 1889, pub. 1889, Paris)
  BRAKKEE **STB-1.1a** 2ob 2cl 2hn 2bn.
  BRAKKEE **STB-1.2a** 2ob 2ca 2hn 2bn.
Marche des anciens comtes de Ross (Marche écossaise sur un thême populaire) (piano four hands, 1891, Paris;
orchestration published c.1910, Paris)
  SHEEN **GHS-5a** fl fl(pic) ob ca 2cl b-cl 2hn 2bn cbn.
Coin des Enfants (piano suite, 1908)
  BUSHELL **GCB-1a** Golliwog's Cakewalk. 2fl 2ob 2cl b-cl/vc 2hn 2bn cbn/db.
  SHEEN **GHS-6a** 3 pieces. fl(pic) ob ca cl b-cl 2hn bn cbn.
Six Épigraphes antiques (piano four hands, 1915, Paris)
  SHEEN **GHS-7a** 2fl fl(pic) ob ca 2cl b-cl 2hn 2bn cbn.

DEDROI (?Dederoi), ( )
Marsch, in G
  SCHNEIDER, A. **AYS-3ma** fl 2ob 2cl+2cl(rip) 2hn 2bn tp b-tb serp.

DELLA MARIA, Pierre Antoine Dominique (1769 - 1800)
Le Prisonnière ou La resemblance (Die Ähnlichkeit) (opera, 29 Jan 1798, Paris)
  ANON **A-124a** 2ob 2cl 2hn 2bn cbn. MS parts: I-Fc, F.P. S.363.
L'Opéra Comique (Das Singspiel) (comic opera, 10 July 1798, Paris)
  GEBAUER, M.J. **MJG-7a** overture. fl 2cl(C) 2hn 2bn tp tb serp.
  JOERG **NXJ-2a** 2cl 2hn 2bn (cbn ad lib).
L'Oncle valet (comic opera, 8 Dec 1798, Paris)
  TRIEBENSEE **JZT-11a** duett. 2ob 2cl 2hn 2bn (cbn tp ad lib).
Untraced arrangement: Le vieux Château (opera, 1798).

DEMUT, ( )
Der Vampyr (opera, ?c.1830; *Note:* this is not the overture either for Lindpaintner's or Marschner's opera)
ANON **A-125a** overture.   fl cl(Eb) cl(solo Bb) 3cl(Bb) 3hn 2bn 2tp 3tb serp b-dr s-dr.
   MS parts: D-DT, Mus-n 679.

DESHAYES, Prosper Didier   (c.1760 - 1815)
Le faux serment, ou La matronne de Gonesse (opera, 31 Dec 1785, Paris)
OZI **EXO-1.20/1a** overture & 8 mvts.   2cl(C) 2hn 2bn.
Untraced arrangement: Zelia (opera, 1791, Paris).

DEVIENNE François   (1759 - 1803)
Les Visitandines (Die Herrhuterinnen) (opera, 7 July 1792, Paris)
FUCHS **GFF-16.1a** overture.   4cl 2hn 2bn tp serp; *or* 2cl 2hn 2bn.
FUCHS **GFF-16.2a** airs.   4cl 2hn 2bn; *or* 2cl 2hn 2bn.
STUMPF **JUS-2a** 6 mvts.   2cl 2hn 2bn.
Geschwindmarsch (unidentified)
ANON **A-74.4/6m** pic quart-fl 2ob cl(F) 2cl(C) 4hn 2bn cbn+serp/2b-hn 2tp 3tb b-dr t-dr tamb cym.
Untraced arrangement: Le valet de deux maitres (opera, 1799, Paris).

DEZÉDE, Nicolas   (1740/?1745 - 1792)
Blaise et Babet (comic opera,   4 April 1783, Versailles; 30 June 1783, Paris)
ANON **A-126a** (? 2ob 2cl 2hn 2bn).   MS parts (8): I-Fc F.P. S.335.
VANDERHAGEN **AJV-3.16/2a** duo, "Vous qui m'avois".   2cl 2hn 2bn.
Untraced arrangement: La Fête de la Cinquantaine (opera, 1796, Paris).

DIABELLI, Anton   (1781 - 1858)
Tambourin Solo der Mademoiselle Neumann, für das Pianoforte von Ant. Diabelli (ballet, original untraced)
TRIEBENSEE **JZT-12a** 2ob 2cl 2hn 2bn (tp ad lib).
Overture (original unidentified - possibly one of Diabelli's piano reductions mistaken for an original work)
VOJÁČEK **HXV-2a** fl ob 2cl 2hn bn cbn 2tp tb(2).

DIBDIN, Charles   (1745 - 1814)
[Unidentified piece]
BROOKS **JRB-1.1ma** 2cl 2hn bn.

DISTLER, Johann Georg   (1760 - 1799)   *See supra* ANON **A-2a.**

DITTERS VON DITTERSDORF, Carl   (1739 - 1799)
La Contadina fidele (opera, 20 Feb 1776, Johannisberg)
DRUSCHETZKY **GYD-34** last mvt (Aria).   2ob 2ca 2hn basso.
[Der] Doktor und [der] Apotheker (Singspiel, 11 July 1786, Vienna)
ANON **A-127a** 2ob 2cl 2hn 2bn.   MS parts: I-Fc, F.P. S.369.
ANON **A-128a** quintetto.   fl ob 2cl 2hn.   MS parts: NL-Z, Z1134, No. 12, (possibly missing some parts).
ROSINACK **FJR-1ad** (= WENT, JNW-13.1a).
WENT **JNW-13.1a** sinfonia & 7 mvts.   2ob 2cl 2hn 2bn.
WENT **JNW-13.2a** 6 mvts.   2ob 2ca 2hn 2bn.
Betrüg durch Aberglauben, oder Die Schatzgräber (Die Schatzgräber) (Singspiel, 30 Oct 1786, Vienna)
ANON **A-129a** 2ob 2cl 2hn 2bn.
   Pc (Traeg: [Vienna], pre-1799), No. 95, MS parts: I-Fc, F.P. S.333.
Hironimus Knicker (Singspiel, 7 July 1789, Vienna)
STARCK **XUS-1ad** 2ob 2cl 2hn 2bn. (= WENT JNW-14a)
VOLÁNEK **AYV-1a** 13 mvts.   2cl 2hn bn.
WENT **JNW-14a** overture & 15 mvts.   2ob 2cl 2hn 2bn.
Das rote Käppchen [Rotkäppchen] (operetta, 1788, Vienna)
SCHNEIDER, A. **AYS-26a** "Hab ich in den jungen Jahren".   fl 2ob 2cl 2hn 2bn tp b-tb 2vla vlne.

DONIZETTI, Gaetano   (1797 - 1848)
L'Esule di Roma, ossia Il proscritto (opera, 1 Jan 1828, Naples)
EGGAR **FXE-1a** cavatina.   t-fl cl(Eb) cl(Bb) 2hn 2bn, (keyed bugle, Eb, ad lib).
Anna Bolena (opera, 26 Dec 1830, Milan)
ANON **A-130a** Aria.   2ob 2cl 2hn 2bn cbn 2tp.   MS parts: CZ-Bm(au), A.35.160.
KIRCHHOFF **WZK-31a** 2 Bds.   fl 2ob 2cl 3hn 2bn (2)tp(clar) tb db timp.
L'Elisir d'amore (Die Liebestrank) (comic opera, 12 May 1832, Milan)
BELLOLI **ASB-1a** quinteto.   2fl 2ob cl(Eb) cl(Bb obbligato) 3cl(Bb) 4hn 2bn 6tp 2tb serp fagottone.
GILLASPIE **JAG-3a** overture.   2fl 2ob 2cl 2hn 2bn cbn/db.
GILLASPIE **JAG-4a** complete opera accompaniment.   2fl 2ob 2cl 2hn 2bn cbn/db.
SCHOLL **NYS-9ac** 4 mvts.   2ob 2cl 2hn 2bn cbn 2tp [b-tb].
SCHOLZ **WES-50a** overture & 8 mvts.   fl 2ob 2cl 3hn 2bn tp tb db timp.
VOJÁČEK **HXV-3a** potpourri.   fl 2ob 2cl 2hn bn cbn 2tp tb.
La Sancia di Castiglia (opera, 6 Nov 1832, Naples)
BASSI **LYB-1a** cavatina, "Se talor più nol rammento".   2cl hn bn tp tb.
Parisina (opera seria, 7 March 1833, Florence)
BERR **FXB-2ma** as "Pas Redoublé, No. 5".   fl cl(Eb) 2cl(Bb) 2hn 2bn 2tp 2tb oph b-dr s-dr.
Torquato Tasso (opera seria, 9 Sept 1833, Rome)
SCHOLL **NYS-10ac** 6 mvts.   2ob 2cl 2hn 2bn cbn 2tp [b-tb].

Lucrezia Borgia (opera, 26 Dec 1833, Milan)
ANON **A-131a** introduction.   fl 2ob cl(E♭) 3cl(B♭) 4hn 2bn 2tp tp(B♭ basso) kl-hn 3tb bomb b-dr s-dr.
ANON **A-132a** 3 mvts.   pic fl 2ob 2cl(E♭) cl(solo B♭) 3cl(B♭) 4hn 2bn cbn 4tp tp(ventilo) 3tb b-hn/serp b-dr
    t-dr tri.   MS parts: D-DT, Mus-n 414.
ANON **A-133a** finale.   pic fl 2ob cl(E♭) 3cl(B♭) 4hn 2bn 3tp a-hn 3tb b-hn timp b-dr.
    MS parts: D-DT, Mus-n 417.
ANON **A-134a** Chor & Trinklied.   fl 2ob cl(E♭) 3cl(B♭) 4hn 2bn 3tp kl-hn 3tb bomb b-dr s-dr.
    MS parts: D-DT, Mus-n 1597.
SCHOLZ **WES-51a** overture & 1 mvt.   fl 2ob 2cl 2hn 2bn tp tb db timp.
VALENTIN **XXV-1a** aria.   fl ob 4cl(C, B♭, C, C) 2hn bn 2tp b-tb basso.
Marino Faliero (opera, 12 March 1835, Paris)
HAUSSER **SJH-1a** aria.   (Solo) flug, fl(E♭) 2ob cl(A♭) cl(E♭) 2cl(B♭) 2hn 2bn cbn 2tp b-tb.
SCHOLL **NYS-11ac** 3 mvts.   2ob 2cl 2hn 2bn 2tp b-tb.
SCHOLZ **WES-52.1a** aria.   fl 2ob 2cl 3hn 2bn tb db timp.
SCHOLZ **WES-52.2a** aria.   fl 2ob 2cl 2hn 2bn tp tb db timp.
Lucia di Lammermoor (opera, 26 Sept 1835, Naples)
ANON **A-135a** Amusement.   pic fl 2ob cl(E♭) cl(solo B♭) 3cl(B♭) 4hn 2bn 3tp kl-hn a-hn 3tb b-hn/bomb
    b-dr t-dr.   MS parts: D-DT, Mus-n 1598.
SCHOLL **NYS-12ac** duetto e aria [& cavatina].   2ob 2cl 2hn 2bn cbn 2tp [b-tb].
SCHOLZ **WES-53.1a** 4 mvts.   fl 2ob 2cl 2hn 2bn tp tb db timp.
SCHOLZ **WES-53.2a** duet.   fl 2ob 2cl 2hn 2bn tp tb db timp.
SCHOLZ **WES-53.3a** 5 mvts.   fl 2ob 2cl 3hn 2bn 2tp tb db timp.
Belisario (opera, 4 Feb 1836, Venice)
ANON **A-136a** introduction & cavatina.   fl 2cl(E♭) 3cl(B♭) 4hn 2bn 2tp kl-hn/cap 3tb b-hn b-dr s-dr.
    MS parts: D-DT, Mus-n 1596.
ANON **A-137a** introduction, aria et choro.   fl 2ob cl(E♭) cl(solo B♭) 3cl(B♭) 2hn 2bn 4tp 3tb serp b-dr t-dr.
    MS parts: D-DT, Mus-n 411.
ANON **A-138a** Chor & Finale.   fl 2ob 2cl(E♭) 3cl(B♭) 4hn 2bn 2tp kl-hn/crt 3tb bomb/b-hn b-dr s-dr.
    MS parts: D-DT, Mus-n 412.
ANON **A-139a** cavatina.   fl ob 2cl(C) 2hn 2bn cbn 2tp; *or* 2ob 2cl(B♭) 2hn bn cbn+b-tb 2tp.
    MS pts: CZ-Bm(au), A.36.865.   *The alternate scoring appears in a pencil score on the inside of the wrapper.*
SCHOLZ **WES-54a** overture & 1 Bd.   fl 2ob 2cl 2hn 2bn tp tb db timp.
WIESER **FAW-11a** potpourri.   terz-fl cl(E♭) 2cl(B♭) 2hn 2bn tp b-tb cb.
Maria di Rudenz (opera, 30 Jan 1838, Venice)
ANON **A-140a** Marsch, schottische, galopp, walzer.   terz-fl cl(E♭) 2cl(B♭) 2hn bn 2tp basso.
    MS parts: CZ-Bm(au), A.35.162.
La Fille du régiment (Das regiments Tochter) (comic opera, 11 Feb 1840, Paris)
ANON **A-141a** Amusement.   pic fl 2ob cl(E♭) cl(solo B♭) 3cl(B♭) 4hn 2bn 3tp kl-hn 3tb bomb b-dr s-dr.
    MS parts: D-DT, Mus-n 1599.
ANON **A-142a** overture.   pic fl 2ob cl(E♭) cl(solo B♭) 3cl(B♭) 4hn 2bn 3tp kl-hn a-hn 3tb b-hn bomb b-dr
    t-dr s-dr.   MS parts: D-DT, Mus-n 419.
ANON **A-143a** Walzer, polonaise, schottische.   fl cl(E♭) 2cl(B♭) 2hn tb basso.
    MS parts (1843): CZ-Bm(au), A.37.327, (?missing bn(s) part).
MATYÁŠ, M. **MIM-1a** marziale, arie & rataplan.   fl 2cl(C & A) 2hn cbn 2tp flug b-flug tb tambure.
POISSL **JNP-1.7a(-1.10a)** 4 mvts.   fl ob 2cl 2hn 2bn.
SCHOLZ **WES-55.1a** overture.   fl 2ob 2cl 2hn 2bn tp tb db timp.
SCHOLZ **WES-55.2a** introduzione.   fl 2ob 2cl 3hn 2bn tb db timp.
SCHOLZ **WES-55.3a** duett.   fl 2ob 2cl 2hn 2bn tp tb db.
SCHOLZ **WES-55.4a** 3 mvts.   fl 2ob 2cl 2hn 2bn tp tb db timp.
SCHOLZ **WES-55.5a** aria.   fl 2ob 2cl 2hn 2bn tp tb db timp.
VOJÁČEK **HXV-4a** 3 mvts.   fl 2ob 2cl 2hn 2bn 2tp s-dr.
WIESER **FAW-12a** poutpouri [sic] No. 1.   terz-fl cl(E♭) 2cl(B♭) 2hn 2bn tp b-tb cb timp b-dr.
Linda di Chamounix (opera, 26 Dec 1841, Milan)
ANON **A-144a** duetto.   fl cl(I, D) cl(I, III, A) 2hn bn(I) cbn b-tb.
    MS parts (30/5 [May] [1]844): CZ-Bm(au), A.35.163, (possibly missing parts).
SCHOLZ **WES-56a** overture & 2 mvts.   fl 2ob 2cl 2hn 2bn tp tb db timp.
Don Pasquale (comic opera, 4 Jan 1843, Paris)
SCHOLZ **WES-57a** overture & 2 mvts.   fl 2ob 2cl 2hn 2bn 2tp s-dr.
Ispirazioni Viennesi. No 1. "La Zingara" [La Gitana] (voice & piano, pub. 1842, Milan & London)
NIPEL **FYN-1a** marcia.   pic cl(G) cl(D) cl(A) 2cl(C) 4hn 2bn 4tp flug 2tb b-tp b-tb 2bassi b-dr.

DOWLAND, John (1563 - 1626)
The First Booke of Songes or Ayres (pub. 1597, London)
ELGAR **EWE-9a** "Awake, Sweet Love" (as "Awake, Sweet Rose").   2fl cl hn bn.

DRESCHLER, Josef (1782 - 1852)
Der Diamont des Geisterkönigs (Feenmärchen, 17 Feb 1824, Vienna)
ZALUZAN **JYZ-1a** Harmonie Quodlibet.   2ob 2cl 2hn 2bn tp.
Das Gebet der Mutter für ihr Kind (Lied)
ANON **A-2.1va** 2cl 2hn 4tp(F, 3E♭) 2flug t-crt 2tb.   (*See* p. 331, Austro-Bohemia, Stráž pod Ralskem)
Nelsons Leichenfeier, Op. 5, ein Trauermarsch (piano, c.1805)
DRUSCHETZKY **GYD-10a** 2ob 2cl 2hn 2bn.   (as "Marcia Mor[te] di Nelson").

DROBISCH, Cark Ludwig (1803 - 1854)
Deutsche Messe "Ich komme vor dein Angesicht" (CATB, organ; published by Falter in Munich)
ANON **A-6va** 7 mvts. CATB, fl 2cl 2hn vlne. MS parts: D-FÜS, 18, (without vocal parts).

DUNI, Egidio Romualdo (c.1708 - 1775)
Ninette à la cour (pastiche, 1755, Parma; 1755, Paris; Duni's involvement is now the subject of debate)
ROESER **VAR-1.45/3(-8), 1.45/12** 7 mvts. 2cl 2hn 2bn.

DUPORT (Dupolt), Louis (b.1781)
We list here ballets choreographed by Duport where the composer, arranger or compiler has not been identified.
Figaro, ou La précaution inutile (ballet, *not* based on Mozart, c.1808, Vienna)
PUREBL **JSP-1a** 3 Pièces. 2fl 3cl 2hn 2bn 2tp perc.
PUREBL **JSP-2a** Rundtanz aus dem Ballet Figaro. 2ob 2cl 2hn 2bn.
TRIEBENSEE **JZT-2a** overture & 5 mvts. 2ob 2cl 2hn 2bn (cbn tp ad lib).
Zephir, oder die wiederkehrende Frühling (Zéphyr, ou le retour du printemps) (ballet, c.1814, many versions in different locations).
ANON **A-145.1a** overture & 9 mvts. 2ob 2cl 2hn 2bn cbn(ad lib).
    Pc (Im Verlage der k:k: priv chemischen Druckerey: Vienna, pn 2241, 2242, 1814), **J9**, No VII, RISM Supp [D 3853 III, 8], pts: CZ-Bm(au), A.18.709; CZ-KRa, A3858/IV.B.22, (MS copy); D-Rtt, Duport (Druck) 1.
ANON **A-145.2a** overture & 9 mvts. 2cl 2hn 2bn cbn(ad lib).
    Pc (Im Verlage der k:k: priv chemische Druckerey: Vienna, pn 2241, 2242, 1814), **J6**, No. VII, parts: CZ-Pnm, XLI.B.169; CZ-KRa, A3858a/IV.B.22, (MS copy by Havel).
TRIEBENSEE **JZT-13a** overture & 11 mvts. 2ob 2cl 2hn 2bn (cbn tp ad lib).
Der blöde Ritter (ballet, 1814, Vienna; overture from Steibelt's *La belle Laitière;* includes a march by Persuis)
SEDLAK **WXS-15.1a** overture & 9 mvts. 2ob 2cl 2hn 2bn cbn.
SEDLAK **WXS-15.2a** overture & 9 mvts. 2cl 2hn 2bn (cbn).
TRIEBENSEE **JZT-14.1a** overture & 11 mvts. 2ob 2cl 2hn 2bn (cbn tp ad lib).
TRIEBENSEE **JZT-14.2a** 5 mvts. 2ob 2cl 2hn 2bn cbn.
[Unidentified Ballet]
LEGRAND **WYL-17a** 1 mvt. fl ob 2cl 2hn 2bn.

DUSSEK, Jan Ladislav (1760 - 1798)
Rondo Allegretto, 6/8 (piano)
RUMMEL **CFR-1a** 2ob/fl 2cl 2hn 2bn cbn.

DUTILLIEU, Pierre (1754 - 1798)
Die Macht des schönen Geschlechtes (ballet, 25 June 1792, Vienna)
WENT **JNW-2.1a** sinfonia & 7 mvts; **JNW-2.2a** Nos. 1 - 8. 2ob 2ca 2hn 2bn.
WENT **JNW-15.1a** Pas de Deux del signore Vulgani è Signora Muzarelli. 2fl ca.
WENT **JNW-15.2a** Pas de Deux del signore Vulgani è Signora Muzarelli. 2ob ca.

DVOŘÁK, Antonín Leopold (1841 - 1904)
Suite in D ("Czech Suite") Op. 39 (orchestra, 1879)
SHEEN **GHS-8a** 2fl ob ob(ca) 2cl 2hn 2bn.
TAYLORSON **JST-3a** Romance. 2fl ob ca 2cl 2hn 2bn cbn/db.
Slavonic Dances (piano duet, Op. 46, 1878; Op. 72 1886; also orchestrated by the composer)
CLEMENTS **PYC-2a** Op. 46, Nos. 8 & 15; Op. 72, Nos. 1 & 7. 2ob 2cl 2hn 2bn cbn.
EMERSON **GZE-3a** Op. 46, No. 2. fl 2ob 2cl 2hn bn cbn(ad lib).
TAYLORSON **JST-4a** Op. 46, No. 4. fl 2ob 2cl 2h 2bn cbn/db.
Bagatelles (Maličkosti), Op. 47 (2vl vc harmonium/piano; 1878)
SHEEN **GHS-9a** 2ob 2cl 2bthn/cl 2hn 2bn cbn.

EGK, Werner (pseudonym of Werner Mayer) (1901 - 1983)
Die Zaubergeige (opera, 1935, Frankfurt am Main)
EGK **WXE-1a** overture. fl fl(pic) ob ob(ca) 2cl 2hn 2bn tp db.

ELGAR, *Sir* Edward William (1857 - 1924)
Salut d'amour, Op. 12 (orchestra, arrangement of a piano piece, 1889)
BARRÈRE **GOB-1a** fl + wind ensemble. *(recorded; location not known).*

EMMERT, Adam Josef (1765 - 1812)
Don Sylvio von Rosalva (opera, 1801, Ansbach, Schloss; pub. 1801, Salzburg)
EMMERT **AJE-1a** overture & 20 mvts. 2ob 2cl 2hn 2bn, (ad lib tp & turkish perc in Nos. 1 & 21).

ENDRES, ( ) *(probably August, who published* 6 Walzer. *Reitmayer: Regensburg, 1827)*
9 Walzer & 1 Allegretto
SCHNEIDER, A. **AYS-27a** fl 2ob 4cl 2hn 2bn tp(hn III) b-tb cb.

ERHARD, ( )
Der geistlichen Rath (?opera; orchestra MS parts, c.1823, at: D-Rtt, Erhard 1, Nos. 1 - 6)
SCHNEIDER, A. **AYS-28a** 6 Walzer. fl(in D, terz-fl) 2ob 4cl 2hn 2bn tp b-tb serp.

ESCH, Louis von (active 1786 - 1820)
7 Military Divertimentos (piano, sd)
JOUVE **JOJ-1ma** 2fl 2cl(F) 2cl(B♭) 2hn 2bn tp serp "big Drum Cimb &c".

ESCHBORN, Josef (?1800 - 1881)
Der Bastard oder Der Stiergefecht (grosse Oper, 31 Aug 1835, Aachen; Feb 1837, Cologne)
    ANON **A-146.1a** overture, introduzione & 1 mvt.   terz-fl 2cl(E♭) 2cl(B♭) 2hn 2bn tp b-tb cb timp.
      MS parts: GB-Ljag(w), 6/371, Nos. 29, 27, 28.
    ANON **A-146.2a** introduzione (variant).   terz-fl 2cl(E♭) 2cl(B♭) 2hn 2bn 2tp b-tb cb.
      MS parts: GB-Ljag(w), 6/371, No. 20, (with an additional chromatic tp part at No. 30).
Walzer
    WIESER **FAW-13a** pic(E♭) cl(Eb) 2cl(B♭) 2hn 2bn tp b-tb cb timp.

ESTERHÀZY VON GALANTHA, Rosa, *Prinzessin*
Ländler (piano, pre-1815)
    TRIEBENSEE **JZT-15a** 2ob 2cl 2hn2bn (cbn tp ad lib).
Walzer in G (piano, sd)
    SCHNEIDER, A. **AYS-29a** fl 2ob 2cl 2hn 2bn tp b-tb 2vla cb.

EUGEN FRIEDRICH PAUL LUDWIG, *Herzog von Württemberg* (1788 - 1857)
Der Geisterbraut (grand romantic opera, 22 Feb 1842, Breslau)
    SCHOLZ **WES-58a** quartett ("O reich dem Freunde").   fl 2ob 2cl 2hn 2bn tb db timp.
Scene aus Lenore ("Bald wird die Rache siegen")
    SCHOLZ **WES-59a** fl 2ob 2cl 2hn 2bn tp tb db timp.
Ballet Musik
    ANON **A-147a** 16 mvts.   fl(I) 2ob 3cl 2hn 2bn tp tb db.   MS parts: D-NEhz, 138, (?missing fl II).
Ouverture in C minor (possibly for *Der Wald von Hohenelbe*, romantic opera, April 1825, Karlsruhe)
    SCHMITT, G. **GYS-25a** 2fl 2ob 3cl 2hn 2bn tp tb db.

EULENSTEIN, Anton Heinrich, *Signore von* (1772 - 1821)
Vetter Damian (Singspiel, 16 May 1812, Vienna)
    ANON **A-148a** 2ob 2cl 2hn 2bn cbn.   MS parts: I-Fc, F.P. S.368.

EYBLER, Johann Leopold, *Edler* von (1765 - 1846)
Die Hirten an [bei] der Krippe zu Bethlehem (cantata, 1794, Vienna)
    ANON **A-149a** 2ob 2cl 2hn 2bn cbn.   MS parts: I-Fc, F.P. S.378.
7 Variations on "A Schüsserl und a Reinel" (piano, Vienna)
    HAVEL **VXH-2a** 2cl 2hn 2bn.

FAHRBACH, Josef, *the Elder* (1804 - 1883)
Erinnerung an Baden (6 Walzer & Coda, c.1840)
    ANON **A-150a** fl 2cl(C) 2hn 2bn 2tp.   MS parts: CZ-Bm(au), A.35.165.
Döblers Zauber Waltz (piano, sd)
    SCHOLZ **WES-60a** fl 2ob 2cl 2hn 2bn tp tb db timp.
Dumbronoc Polka (piano, sd)
    SCHOLZ **WES-61a** fl 2ob 2cl 2hn 2bn tp tb db timp.

FAHRBACH, Philipp *the Elder* (1815 - 1885)
Beyfall mein schönster Lohn, Walzer
    STRECK **PZS-1.10a** fl cl(D) 2cl(A) 2hn 2bn.
Galopp (unidentified)
    STRECK **PZS-1.13a** fl cl(D) 2cl(A) 2hn 2bn.

FARINELLI, Giuseppe (1769 - 1836)
Theresa e Claudio (farce, 9 Sept 1801, Venice)   *See also infra: MEYER.*
    ANON **A-151a** overture & 11 mvts.   2ob 2cl 2hn 2bn cbn.   MS parts: I-Fc, F.P. S.374.
La Locandiera (opera, 2 Jan 1803, Rome)
    LEGRAND **WYL-20a** 1 mvt (misattributed to Generali).   fl ob 2cl 2hn 2bn.

FAURÉ, Gabriel Urbain (1845 - 1924)
1er Nocturne pour piano, Op. 33, No. 1 (1883)
    GROVLEZ **GAG-1a** fl 2ob 2cl 2hn bn.
Dolly (Suite), Op. 56 (piano four-hands, No. 1, 1894, Nos. 2 -5, 1796, No. 6, 1897, Paris)
    CAMPBELL **AQC-2a** 4 pieces.   fl 2ob 2cl 2hn 2bn.

FEDERICI, Francesco (active c.1800, Italy)
Zaira ossia Il trionfo della religione (opera, March 1802, Reggio d'Emilia)
    ANON **A-7.4a** aria con coro.   2ob 2cl 2hn 2bn cbn.

FIBICH, Zdeněk (1850 - 1900)
Nálady, dojni a upomínky. Series 1, Op. 41 (piano, c.1910)
    TRINKAUS **GJT-1a** Seš [Book] 4, No 14: Poëm.   2cl 2hn bn tu; *or* 2cl hn 2bn tu; *or* 3cl hn bn tu.

FIORAVANTI, Valentino (1764 - 1837)
La Cantarici villane (comic opera, Jan 1799, Naples; 1799, Paris)
    SCHMITT, G. **GYS-26.1a** overture.   fl 2ob 2cl 2hn 2bn tp tb db.
    SCHMITT, G. **GYS-26.2a** overture & Act I (9 mvts).   2pic 2ob 3cl 4hn 2bn serp 2tp timp.
    SCHMITT, G. **GYS-26.3a** Act II, 6 mvts.   2fl 2ob 2cl 2hn 2bn 2tp.
    VANDERHAGEN **AJV-9a** 6 airs.   2fl 2cl 2hn 2bn.

La Capricciosa pentita (La Capricciosa ravveduta; Die gebesserte Eigensinnige) (comic opera, 2 Oct 1802, Milan; as *La Capricciosa ravveduta*; 26 June 1805, Vienna)
SEDLAK **WXS-16.1a** overture & 11 mvts. 2ob 2cl 2hn 2bn cbn.
SEDLAK **WXS-16.2a** overture & 11 mvts. 2cl 2hn 2bn.
Les Comédiens ambulans (I Virtuosi anbulanti) (comic opera, 26 Sept 1807, Paris)
GEBAUER, M.J. **MJG-1.2/3a, 1.2/4a** 2 mvts. fl(F) cl(F) 2cl(C) 2hn 2bn serp, *or* fl(F)2cl(C) 2hn 2bn serp.
[unidentified]
ANON **A-152a** Teatro dei Fiorentino. Aria. Ah si resta onor mi sgrida. Winds. MS pts (6): I-Fc, F.P. S.353.
SCHMITT, G. **GYS-3a(-5a)** unverified attribution: one of these may be an Overture by Fioravanti.

FISCHER, ( )
Du, mein lieber Engel Du! (Lied, 1830s)
WIESER **FAW-14a** terz-fl cl(Eb) 2cl(Bb) 2hn 2bn tp b-tb cb timp.

FISCHER, Anton (1777 - 1808)
For Fischer's adaptation of Raoul de Blaubart *with German text (1804, Vienna), See infra: GRÉTRY.*
Svetards Zaubergürtel (Zauberthal) (Komische Zauberoper, 3 July 1805, Vienna)
ANON **A-153a** (? 2ob 2cl 2hn 2bn cbn). MS parts (9): I-Fc, F.P. S.379.
KROMMER **FVK-2.3ma** Marsch. 2ob 2cl 2hn 2bn cbn.
Das Singspiel auf der Dache (Singspiel/opera, 5 Feb 1807, Vienna)
TRIEBENSEE **JZT-16a** aria. 2ob 2cl 2hn 2bn (cbn tp ad lib).

FLEURY, Charles (*1er Cor du Grand Théâtre de Lyon*) (active c.1800)
Chasse, in F
LEROY **PQL-1.12/4(a)** 2p-fl(F) 2ob 2cl(III & IV, C) 2hn 2bn tp serp timp.
Ouverture, in F
ANON **A-78.1/1m(a)** 2ob 2cl 2hn 2bn tp.
LEROY **PQL-1.2/1(a)** 2p-fl(F) 2ob 2cl(III & IV, C) 2hn 2bn tp serp b-dr.
Ouverture, in F
LEROY **PQL-1.5/1(a)** 2fl(F) 2ob 2cl(III & IV, C) 2hn 2bn tp serp b-dr.
Ouverture, in D minor/F major
LEROY **PQL-1.10/1(a)** 2p-fl(F) 2ob 2cl(III & IV, C) 2hn 2bn tp serp timp.
Pas Redoublé, in F
LEROY **PQL-1.10/6(a)** 2p-fl(F) 2cl(F) 2cl(C) 2hn (2)bn tp serp timp.
Polonaise, in F
LEROY **PQL-1.10/4(a)** 2p-fl(F) 2ob 2cl(III & IV, C) 2hn 2bn tp serp timp.

FLOTOW, Friedrich Ferdinand Adolf von (1812 - 1883)
Alessandro Stradella (opera, 30 Dec 1844, Hamburg)
ANON **A-154a** pic fl 2ob cl(Eb) cl(solo Bb) 3cl(Bb) 4hn 2bn 3tp a-hn kenthorn 3tb b-hn/bomb b-dr t-dr. MS parts: D-DT, Mus-n 450.
ANON **A-155a** Amusement. pic fl 2ob cl(Eb) cl(solo Bb) 3cl(Bb) 4hn 2bn 3tp kenthorn a-hn 3tb b-hn bomb b-dr t-dr. MS parts: D-DT, Mus-n 1622.
ANON **A-156a** Divertissement. pic fl 2ob cl(Eb) cl(solo Bb) 3cl(Bb) 4hn 2bn 3tp kenthorn/tp(Eb) a-hn 3tb b-hn/bomb t-dr. MS parts: D-DT, Mus-n 448/449.
SCHOLZ **WES-62.1a** 4 mvts. fl 2ob 2cl 2hn 2bn tp tb db timp.
SCHOLZ **WES-62.2a** finale Act II. fl 2ob 2cl 2hn 2bn tp tb db timp.
WIESER **FAW-15a** potpourri. terz-fl cl(Eb) 2cl(Bb) 2hn 2bn tp b-tb cb.
Martha (Der Markt zu Richmond) (opera, 25 Nov 1847, Vienna)
SCHOLZ **WES-63a** overture & finale Act I. fl 2ob 2cl 3hn 2bn tp tb db.
Die Grossfürstin (Sophie Katharina) (opera, 19 Nov 1850, Berlin)
ANON **A-157a** overture. 2fl 2ob cl(Eb) cl(solo Bb) 3cl(Bb) 4hn 2bn 3tp t-hn 3tb bomb b-hn vc/b timp b-dr. MS parts: D-DT, Mus-n 447, (the title also states "Nach dem Clavierauszug").
Indra (Indra das Schlangenmädchen) (opera, 18 Dec 1852, Vienna)
ANON **A-158a** Amusement. pic fl 2ob cl(Eb) cl(solo Bb) 3cl(Bb) 4hn 2bn 3tp t-hn 3tb b-hn bomb vc/b timp b-dr+tri+castanets s-dr. MS parts: D-DT, Mus-n 1621.
ANON **A-159a** Divertissement. pic fl 2ob cl(Eb) cl(solo Bb) 3cl(Bb) 4hn 2bn 3tp 3tb bomb b-hn vc/b timp-dr. MS parts: D-DT, Mus-n 445.
ANON **A-160a** overture. pic fl 2ob cl(Eb) cl(solo Bb) 3cl(Bb) 4hn 2bn 3tp t-hn 3tb b-hn/bomb vc/b timp b-dr. MS parts: D-DT, Mus-n 446.

FOIGNET, Jacques *dit* Charles Gabriel (1750 - 1823)
Le Mont Alphèa (opera, Dec 1792, Paris)
FUCHS, G.F. **GFF-17a** overture. 4cl(C) 2hn 2bn tp.

FOSTLINGER, ( )
Stey'rer Ländler
WIESER **FAW-16a** pic(Eb) cl(Eb) 2cl(Bb) 2hn 2bn tp b-tb cb.

FOURNIER, (?Alphonse)
Rondeau, in F
LEROY **PQL-1.9/6(a)** 2p-fl(F) 2cl(F) 2cl(C) 2hn 2bn tp serp.

FRANÇAIX, Jean (b. 1912)
L'Heure du Berger: musique de brasserie (fl ob cl hn bn piano, 1947)
WANEK **FKW-1a** fl ob 2cl hn 2bn tb piano.
Concerto pour Contrebasse (1974)
BLOMHERT **BQB-1a** Solo db, fl fl(pic) ob ob(ca) cl cl(b-cl) 2hn 2bn.

FRANCK, César Auguste Jean Guillaume Hubert (1822 - 1890)
Messe à 3 voix (solonnelle), Op. 12 (STB, vc db organ harp, 1860, performed 2 April 1861, pub. 1872, Paris)
  TRINKAUS **GJT-2a** Panis Angelicus. 2cl 2hn bn tu; *or* 2cl hn 2bn tu; *or* 2cl hn bn tu.

FRÄNZL (Fränzel), Ferdinand (1770 - 1833)
Carlo Fioras oder Die Stumme in der Sierra Morena (historisches Oper, 16 Oct 1810, Munich)
  MARPURG **WYM-2.1a** overture. pic 2ob 2cl(Eb) 4cl(Bb) 5hn 2bn 2tp a-tb t-tb b-tb b-hn b-dr s-dr.
[unidentifed] Allegro 6/8 (as "N. 1mo Serenatta [sic]")
  HAVEL **VXH-3a** 2cl 2hn 2bn.

FRIEDRICH, *Prince zu Hohenlohe-Öhringen* (1812 - 1892)
Polka in F (piano, sd)
  SCHOLZ **WES-64a** fl 2ob 2cl 2hn 2bn tp tb db
Walzer in C (piano, sd)
  KIRCHHOFF **WZK-32a** fl 2ob 2cl 2hn 2bn tb db.

FUCHS, Georg Friedrich (1752 - 1821)
6 Pièces (originals unidentified).
  GEBAUER, M.J. **MJG-1.3a** fl(F) cl(F) 2cl(C) 2hn 2bn tp serp/b-tb b-dr cym tri; *or* fl(F) 2cl(C) 2hn 2bn serp.

FUČIK, Julius (1872 - 1916)
Der Alte Brumbär, Op. 210 (1908)
  TAYLORSON **JST-5a** Solo bn, fl 2ob 2cl 2hn 2bn cbn/db.
Florentiner Marsch, Op. 214 (1908)
  TAYLORSON **JST-6a** fl(pic) 2ob 2cl 2hn 2bn cbn/db.

FUSS, Johann Nepomuk (1777 - 1819)
Isaak [Abraham] (melodrama, 12 Aug 1812, Vienna)
  ANON **A-161a** 2ob 2cl 2hn 2bn cbn.
    Pc (sn: sl [= T. Weigl: Vienna], c.1812), MS parts: I-Fc, F.P. S.362.
Judith (Die Belagerung von Bethulien) (Biblical opera, 20 April 1814, Vienna)
  ANON **A-162a** 2ob 2cl 2hn 2bn cbn. MS parts: I-Fc, F.P. S.378.

GABRIELI, Andrea (c.1510 - 1586)
Aria della Battaglia "per sonar d'Instrumenti da Fiato - a 8"
  GHEDINI **GFG-1a** fl fl(pic) 2ob ca 3cl b-cl 4hn 3bn 3tp 3tb b-tu.

GALLENBERG, Wenzel Robert, *Count* von (1783 - 1839)
Amleto (ballet, carnival 1815, Milan)
  GAMBARO **VXG-1a** overture.   fl 2cl 2hn bn bn+cb, (ad lib: cl(Eb ripieno) tp tb serp timp b-dr+cym).
Alfred der Grosse (ballet, 24 April 1820, Vienna)
  ANON **A-74.7/8m(a)** march. pic quart-fl 2ob cl(F) 2cl(C) 4hn 2bn cbn+serp/2b-hn 2tp 3tb b-dr t-dr tamb cym.
  ANON **A-163a** Marsch. 2cl 2hn 2bn tp(princ). MS parts: CZ-Bm(au), A.35.257, (?missing cbn).
  PAYER **JYP-1ma** Triumph-Marsch. pic(D) 4cl(D) cl(G) 4hn 2bn bn 7tp tb b-tb b-dr s-dr.
  SCHNEIDER, A. **AYS-30a** Grosser Marsch. fl 2ob 4cl 2hn 2bn tp b-tb cb.
  SEDLAK **WXS-17.1a** Theil 1: overture & 12 mvts, Theil 2: 12 mvts. 2ob 2cl 2hn 2bn cbn (2tp).
  SEDLAK **+WXS-17.2a** Marsch. 2ob 2cl 2hn 2bn cbn 2tp.
Jeanne d'Arc (Johanna d'Arc) (ballet, 7 May 1821, Vienna)
  STARKE **FRS-6a** (Ester Theil) overture & 11 mvts. 2ob 2cl 2hn 2bn cbn 2tp.
Die Psyche (Gallenberg was part-composer & co-compiler with Romani) (ballet, 29 May 1824, Vienna)
  ANON **A-164a** Theil 2, 12 mvts. 2ob 2cl 2hn 2bn cbn 2tp. MS parts: CZ-Bm(au), A.36.665.
Ottavio Pinelli (Ottavio Pisani) (ballet, 8 Nov 1827, Vienna)
  SEDLAK **WXS-18a** Theil 1: overture & 11 mvts, Theil 2: 13 mvts. 2ob 2cl 2hn 2bn cbn (2tp).

GALUPPI, Baldassare (1706 - 1785)
Il Filosofo di campagna (opera, autumn 1754, Venice)
  ANON **A-165a** 3 Parte. 2ob 2cl 2hn 2bn cbn. MS parts: I-Fc, F.P. S.394.

GARDEL (?Maximilien Léopold Philippe Joseph "l'aîné") (1741 - 1787)
  OZI **EXO-1.22/2aa** Gavotte, (possibly from *Le pied de boeuf*, ballet, 1787, Paris). 2cl 2hn 2bn.

GARNIE (?GARNIER, François Joseph) (1755 - 1825)
Polonaise, in D minor
  SCHNEIDER, A. **AYS-31a** fl 2ob 4cl 2hn 2bn tp b-tb serp.

GARRETT, George Mursell (1834 - 1897)
May Carol (Part-song, pub. 1870, London)
  ELGAR **EWE-10a** 2fl cl hn bn.

GASSMANN, Florian Leopold (1729 - 1774)
L'Opera seria (comic opera, 1769, Vienna)
  ANON **A-166a** overture. 2fl 2cl 2hn 2bn. MS parts: PL-LA, RM 81/1-5/122, (missing fl I, hn I, bn II).

GAVEAUX, Pierre (1761 - 1825)
See also supra: BEFFROY DE REIGNY, (collaborator, *Le Club de bonnes [sic] gens*).
L'Amour filial (opera, 7 March 1792, Paris)
  DEVIENNE **FZD-2a** overture & 6 morceaux. 2p-fl/ob 2cl 2hn 2bn 2tp serp b-dr cym tri.
Le Petit Matelot (opera, 7 Jan 1796, Paris)
  DEVIENNE **FZD-3a** 6 mvts. 2p-fl/ob 2cl 2hn 2bn, (ad lib: tp(s) serp b-dr cym tri).

Sophie et Moncars, ou L'intrigue portuguaise (opera, 30 Sept 1797, Paris)
  DEVIENNE **FZD-1ac** overture. 2p-fl/ob 2cl 2hn 2bn 2tp serp b-dr cym tri.
Le Diable couleur le rose, ou Le bonhomme misère (opera, 13 Sept 1803, Paris)
  GEBAUER, M.J. **MJG-8.1a** overture. 11 parts.
  GEBAUER, M.J. **MJG-8.2a** airs. 8 parts.
Monsieur Deschalumeaux (Monsieur des Chalumeaux) (opera bouffe, 17 Feb 1806, Paris)
  SCHMITT, G. **GYS-27a** overture. fl 2ob 2cl 2hn bn 2tp tb serp perc.
L'Échelle de soie (Die Strickleiter) (comic opera, 22 Aug 1808, Paris; c.1814 Vienna, possibly adapted Gyrowetz)
  ANON **A-30a** 2ob 2cl 2hn 2bn cbn.
    MS parts: I-Fc, F.P. S.387, (with Hummel (qv): *Die gute Nachricht). See also: p. 356.*
Untraced arrangements: Le traité nul (opera, 1797, Paris), Le diable en vacances (opera, 1807, Paris).

GENAST, Franz Eduard (1707 - 1866)
Der treue Herz (Lied)
  ANON **A-167a** fl 2ob 2cl(Eb) 3cl(Bb) 2hn 2bn 2cap/tp(obl) 3tb.
    MS parts: D-DT, Mus-n 1664.

GENERALI, Pietro (1782 - 1832)
Adelina (Luigina; Luisina) (farsa, 15 Sept 1810, Venice)
  ANON **A-168a** 2 Theils. 2ob 2cl 2hn 2bn 2tp.
    MS parts: CZ-Bm(au), A.20.947, (5 mvts; missing cbn 2tp); I-Fc, F.P. S.372, (2 Theils).
  LEGRAND **WYL-18a** overture & 1 mvt. fl ob 2cl 2hn 2bn.
La Contessa di collo erboso (opera buffa, Carnevale 1815, Genoa)
  LEGRAND **WYL-19a** 1 mvt. fl ob 2cl 2hn 2bn.
  STARKE **FRS-7a** 1 mvt. 2ob 2cl 2hn 2bn cbn 2tp.
L'Impostore (Il Marcotondo) (opera buffa, 21 May 1815, Milan)
  ANON **A-169a** duetto. 2ob 2cl 2hn 2bn 2tp.
    MS parts: CZ-Bm(au), A.18.817, (with incorrect contemporary identification as "Marc Antonio").
I Baccanti (Baccanali) di Roma (opera seria, 14 Jan 1816, Venice)
  SCHOLL **NYS-1.2a** 3 mvts. 2ob 2cl 2hn 2bn cbn 2tp.
La Locandiera (opera, untraced: probably a misattribution of Farinelli's opera)
  LEGRAND **WYL-20a** 1 mvt. fl ob 2cl 2hn 2bn.

GERL, Thaddäus (1764 - 1827)
Der dumme Gärtner aus dem Gebirge oder die zween Anton (opera, 12 July 1789, Vienna; with Benedikt Schack)
  HEIDENREICH **JYH-1a** 16 mvts. 2ob 2cl 2hn 2bn.
  WENT **+JNW-16a** 16 mvts. 2ob 2ca 2hn 2bn. *Probably a transcription of Heidenreich's arrangement.*
Der Stein der Weisen (Die Zauberinsel) (opera, 11 Sept 1790, Vienna; with Henneberg & Schack; includes music by Mozart)
  ANON **A-170a** 2 Theils. 2ob 2cl 2hn 2bn cbn.
    MS parts: I-Fc, F.P. S.372, (here attributed to Schikaneder, the librettist, as composer).

GERSHWIN, (Jacob) George (1898 - 1937)
Porgy and Bess (opera, 10 Oct 1935, New York)
  SKIRROW **ARS-2a** suite. 2ob 2cl 2hn 2bn.

GERVAIS, Charles-Henri (1671 - 1744)
Hypermernestre (tragédie en musique, possibly a collaboration with the Duc d'Orléans, 3 Nov 1716; revived 1728, 1746, 1765; performed as a ballet by Noverre, Stuttgart, 17 Feb 1758)
  ANON **A-46.5m(a)** Marche. 2vl 2hn 2bn.

GIANELLA, Luigi (1778 - 1817)
Untraced arrangement: Acis et Galathée, (ballet, 1805).

GIORNOVICHI, Giovanni Mane (1740-1804)
Allemande
  BEINET **XJB-3.1/7a** 2cl 2hn 2bn.

GIROUST (Giroult, Giroux), François (1738 - 1799)
  OZI **EXO-1.30/2a** Petit chœur. 2cl 2hn 2bn.

GIULIANI, Mario (1781 - 1828)
Marcia (probably for guitar)
  STARKE **FRS-8a** 2ob cl(F) 2cl(C) 2hn 2bn cbn 2tp.
Untraced arrangement: Der treue Tod (?Lied).

GLÄSER, Johann Franz (1798 - 1861)
Der Adlers Horst (opera, 29 Dec 1832, Berlin)
  SCHOLZ **WES-65a** terzett, "Die Flaschen zur Harnd". fl 2ob 2cl 3hn 2bn tp tb db timp.
Der Rattenfänger von Hameln (opera, 15 Oct 1837, Berlin)
  ANON **A-171a** Lied-Chor. 2fl 2ob 2cl(Eb) cl(solo Bb) 4cl(Bb) bthn 4hn 2bn 5tp tp("ventyli") 3tb bomb b-dr s-dr. MS parts: D-DT, Mus-n 278.

GLEISSNER, Franz Johann (1761 - 1818)
6 Missa brevis, Op. 2 (pub. Augsburg, 1789)
  ROSINACK **FJR-1va** *Missa brevis in C.* SATB. 2ob 2cl 2hn 2bn organ.

GLUCK (Gluk, Klik, Kluk, Rouck), Christoph Willibald (1714 - 1787)
Cythére assiégée (opera, summer, 1759, Schwetzingen nr Mannheim; revived 1 Aug 1775, Paris)
    ANON **A-203.1/3(a)** "Sans lenteur". 2ob 2bthn 2hn 2bn serp.
Don Juan, ou Le Festin de Pierre (pantomime ballet, 17 Oct 1761, Vienna)
    ANON **A-172a** sinfonia & 8 mvts & coda. 2ob 2hn bn.
    MS parts: CZ-Pnm, XLII.B.291, (the coda is not in the ballet).
Orfeo ed Euridice (Orpheé et Eurydice) (opera, 8 Oct 1762, Vienna; 1764, Paris)
    KRECHLER **FFK-1.3ad** 3 mvts. 2ob 2cl 2hn 2bn. (= Went, JNW-22.3ac)
La Rencontre imprévue (Les Pêlerins de la Mecque; Die Pilger von Mekka; Mochomet) (opera, 4 Jan 1764,
Schönbrunn Palace, Vienna)   *See also: MOZART, W.A., Variations on "Unser dummer Pöbel meint".*
    KRECHLER **FFK-1.1ad** 3 mvts, "A ma maîtresse j'avais promis", "Mahomet, notre grand prophète", "Un
    ruisselet bien clair" [variant]. 2ob 2cl 2hn 2bn.*Transcriptions of Went's arrangements.* (= Went, JNW-22.1ac)
    SEYFRIED **IXS-1.4/3(a)** "Unser dummer Pöbel meint". 2ob 2cl 2hn 2bn cbn.
    WENT **+JNW-17.1a** 2ob 2cl 2hn 2bn.
    WENT **+JNW-17.2/1-5a** 5 mvts.   2ob 2ca 2hn 2bn; (1 ca in JNW-17.2/2a, 1 bn in JNW-17.2/5a).
Alceste (Italian version) (opera, 26 Dec 1766, Vienna)
    KRECHLER **FFK-1.4ad** aria, "Non vi turbate". 2ob 2cl 2hn 2bn. *A transcription of WENT, +JNW-18a.*
    WENT **+JNW-18a** aria, "Non vi turbate". 2ob 2ca 2hn 2bn. (cf. Went, JNW-22.2ac)
Paride ed Elena (opera, 3 Nov 1770, Vienna)
    ASPLMAYR **FDA-5a/FDA-54** 1 mvt. 2ob 2hn bn.
Armide (opera, 23 Sept 1777, Paris)
    ANON **A-173a** 2ob 2cl 2hn 2bn cbn. MS parts: I-Fc, F.P. S.354.
    BACH, J.C. **JCB-3/ii** Act II ballet, as "Andante". 2cl 2hn (2)bn.
    BONASEGLA **B-2a** Gesang, "Reçois de notre amour". terz-fl ob 2cl 2hn bn tp(clar) cb.
    TRIEBENSEE **JZT-17a, 18a** March (with an original trio = JZT-9m). 2ob 2cl 2hn 2bn (cbn tp ad lib).
    TRIEBENSEE **JZT-18a** Echo Aria der Wajaden, Act 2. 2ob 2cl 2hn 2bn (cbn ad lib).
Iphigénie en Tauride (opera, 18 May 1779, Paris; 23 Oct 1781, Vienna)
    KRECHLER **FFK-1.2ad** "Unis de la plus tendre enfance", [variant]. 2ob 2cl 2hn 2bn.
    TRIEBENSEE **JZT-19a** overture & 20 mvts. 2ob 2cl 2hn 2bn cbn.
Russischer Marsch (unidentified)
    ANON **A-74.5/12m(a)** pic quart-fl 2ob cl(F) 2cl(C) 4hn 2bn cbn+serp/2b-hn 2tp 3tb b-dr t-dr tamb cym.
Untraced arrangement: Iphigénie en Aulide (opera, 1774, Paris)

GOSSEC, François Joseph (1734 - 1829)
Midas (pastiche, with contributions by Gossec, sd, Paris)
    ROESER **VAR-1.45/1** 2 mvts. 2cl 2hn 2bn.
Le Tonellier (adaptation of earlier opera by Audinot with additional pieces by Gossec, 16 March 1765, Paris)
    VANDERHAGEN **AJV-2.12/3a, 2.12/4a** 2 mvts. 2cl 2hn 2bn.
Les Pêcheurs (comic opera, 27 June 1765, Paris)
    VANDERHAGEN **AJV-2.5/3a** "Bernard est ma foi bon garçon". 2cl 2hn 2bn.
Le Triomphe de la République, ou Le Camp de Grand-Pré (opera-divertimento, 27 Jan 1793, Paris)
Gossec's revolutionary works, Chant de la Liberté & the Ronde nationale are based on numbers in this opera.)
    FUCHS **GFF-18.1a** overture. 4cl(C) 2hn 2bn tp.
    FUCHS **GFF-18.2a** 7 airs. 4cl(B♭ 2hn 2bn.
Te Deum
    SARTORIUS **GCS-21a** Chöre. 2cl 2hn 2bn cbn.
Citoyens dont Rome antique. Chant patriotique pour l'inauguration des bustes de Marat et de Lepelletier,
(= Chant en Honneur des Martyrs de la Liberté, P.979) (1793, Paris)
    ANON **A-7va** Solo voice, 2cl 2hn (2)bn.
    Pc (Rec des époques: Paris, c.1799), liv. 1, No. 13, score: F-Pn, H2. 15,13.
Motetto, O salutaris hostia
    ANON **A-8va** ATB, 2ob 2hn 2bn 2vla. MS parts (c.1780): D-Rtt, Gossec 15.
Symphony in E♭ Op. 12, No. 5 (c.1770)
    GILLASPIE **JAG-5a** fl 2ob 2cl 2hn 2bn cbn.

GOUNOD, Charles François (1818 - 1893)
Faust (Margarethe) (opera, 19 March 1859, Paris)
    ANON **A-174a** Adagio molto. fl 2ob cl(E♭) cl(B♭) 3hn 2bn 3tp t-hn 3tb vc/b timp b-dr+tri+cym s-dr.
    MS parts: D-DT, Mus-n 481, (missing ob I, bn I, & possibly 2cl).
Chanson du Printemps (chanson, voice & piano, 1860, Paris)
    ANON **A-2.3va** 2cl 2hn 4tp(F, 3E♭) 2flug t-crt 2tb. (*See* p. 331, Austro-Bohemia, Stráž pod Ralskem)
Marche funèbre d'une Marionette (piano, 1872, London; orchestrated 1879)
    HILL **PYH-1a.** 2fl 2ob 2cl 2hn 2bn.

GRANADOS, Enrique (1867 - 1930)
Goyescos: Quejas, ó La Maja y el ruiseñor (piano solo, published 1930)
    ELLIOT **WSE-1a** (as "Lament of the Maja and the Nightingale"). 2ob 2cl 2hn 2bn.

GRAUN, Carl Heinrich (1703/1704 - 1759)
Auferstehen (Grabgesang, "Auferstehn, ja auferstehn wirst du") (in *Geistliche Oden in Melodien,* 1758, Berlin)
    ANON **A-9.1va.** TTBB, 2cl 2bn. MS score: D-NEhz, 163, No 7, (incomplete).
    ANON **A-9.2va.** TTBB, 2hn 2bn. MS score: D-Nehz, 133, No 5.

GRÉTRY, André Ernest Modeste (1741 - 1813)
Le Huron (opera, 20 Aug 1768, Paris)
   ANON **A-45.2m(a)** Marche. 2vl 2ob 2hn 2bn.
   ANON **A-112.1m(a), 112.14m(a)** "Si jamais je prens un époux" & march.. 2cl 2hn 2bn
   ANON **A-202.3/17(a)** 1 mvt. 2terz-fl 2bthn 2hn 2bn serp.
Lucile (opera, 5 Jan 1769, Paris)
   ANON **A-112.11m(a)** march. 2cl 2hn 2bn.
   ROESER **VAR-2a** 2 ariettes. 2cl 2hn 2bn.
Silvain (Sylvain) (opera, 19 Feb 1770, Paris)
   ROESER **VAR-2a** 5 ariettes.
Les deux Avares (Die beiden Geizigen) (opera, Fontainebleau, 27 Oct 1770; 6 Dec 1770, Paris)
   ANON **A-45.3m(a)** Marche des janissaires. 2vl 2ob 2hn 2bn.
   ANON **A-112.14m(a)** march. 2cl 2hn 2bn.
   ANON **A-1.55a, 1.57a** 2 mvts. 2cl 2hn 2bn.
   SCHNEIDER, A. **AYS-32a** Marsch. fl 2ob 4cl 2hn 2bn tp b-tb serp.
Zémire et Azor (opera, 9 Nov 1771, Fontainebleau, 16 Dec 1771, Paris)
   ANON **A-1.74a, 1.76a, 1.77a, 1.78a** 4 mvts. 2cl 2hn 2bn.
   ANON **A-175a** Larghetto. 2fl 2ob 2cl 2hn 2bn. MS pts: CZ-Pnm, XLII.B.293, (here misattributed to Gluck).
   ANON **A-176a** 2ob 2cl 2hn 2bn.
     Pc (Traeg: [Vienna], pre-1799), No. 102, MS parts: I-Fc, F.P. S.335.
   ANON **A-177a** 3 (?possibly 7 mvts). fl ob 2cl 2hn. MS parts: NL-Z, Z1134, Nos. 1 - 7, (possibly missing
     some parts. No. 1, "Du moment qu'on aime", No. 2 "Ah quel tourment d'être sensible" & No. 4, "Ah! laissez
     moi" are identified; the other 4 mvts are unidentified).
   ANON **A-178a** "Suita", 6 mvts. 2cl 2hn 2bn. MS parts: CZ-Pnm, XLI.B.110.
   ANON **A-179a** Terzetto, Act III, scene 6, "Ah laissez-moi la plener". SSB, 2cl 2hn 2bn.
   MS parts: D-WRtl, Mus.II.c:5. *Although the lead pts are marked "Clarini" this undoubtedly means clarinets.*
   ANON **A-180a** Scène du père et des soeurs. 2fl 2cl 2hn 2bn.
     Pc (sn: sl [?Paris], sd), RISM [G 4543], parts: F-Pn, D. 16130, (missing titlepage; although a MS sheet bears
     the title and the note, "arrangée pour 6 instr. à vent", there are definitely 8 parts).
   DRUSCHETZKY **GYD-165.16(a)** Spiegel Aria. 2cl 2hn 2bn.
   SCHNEIDER, A. **AYS-33a** overture & 23 mvts. fl 2ob 2cl+2cl(rip) 2hn 2bn tp b-tb serp.
   TRIEBENSEE **JZT-20a** Spiegel Terzett (Andante). 2ob 2cl 2hn 2bn.
La Rosière de Salency (opera, 28 Feb 1774, Paris)
   BEINET **XJB-3.1/5a** "Quand le Rossignol". 2cl 2hn 2bn.
   VANDERHAGEN **AJV-2.2/2a** 2 mvts; **AJV-2.5/1a** overture & 3 mvts. 2cl 2hn 2bn.
Le Fausse Magie (opera, 1 Feb 1775, Paris)
   VANDERHAGEN **AJV-2.9/2a** "Qoi [sic] ce vieux coq". 2cl 2hn 2bn.
Les Mariages Samnites (opera, 12 Dec 1776, Paris)
   VANDERHAGEN **AJV-2.9/3a** "Dieu d'amour". 2cl 2hn 2bn.
L'Amant jaloux (Les fausses appearances; Die eifersüchtige [ersterwichtig] Liebhaber) (opera, 20 Nov 1778, Paris)
   WENT **JNW-2.1/2a** 2 mvts; **JNW-2.2** Nos. 9 & 10. 2ob 2ca 2hn 2bn.
   WENT **+JNW-19a** 6 mvts. 2ob 2ca 2hn 2bn.
Colinette à la cour, ou Le Double épreuve (opera, 1 Jan 1782, Paris)
   ANON **A-85.3m(a)** air. 2cl 2hn 2bn, (2pic/fife, 2cl(rip) 2tp cym tri(s) s-dr tamb ad lib).
   OZI **EXO-1.6/3a** 4 mvts. 2cl(C) 2hn 2bn.
Le Caravanne de Caire (opera, 30 Oct 1783, Fontainebleau; 12 Dec 1783, Paris)
   VANDERHAGEN **AJV-4.5a** menuetto grazioso. 2cl 2hn 2bn.
L'Épreuve villageoise (opera, 24 June 1784, Paris; revision of *Théodore et Paulin*, Fontainebleasu, 5 March 1784)
   VANDERHAGEN **AJV-3.16/4a** "Je vous revois". 2cl 2hn 2bn.
   VANDERHAGEN **AJV-4.3a** 2 mvts. 2cl 2hn 2bn.
Richard Coeur-de-Lion (Richard Löwenherz) (opera, 2 Oct 1784, Paris)
See also: SEYFRIED and J. WEIGL for ballets based on this opera.
   BEINET **XJB-1.3a** 6 mvts. 2cl 2hn 2bn.
   BEINET **XJB-3.1/4a** "Ô Richard, ô mon Roi". 2cl 2hn 2bn.
   BEINET **XJB-3.3/5a** 3 mvts.
   EHRENFRIED **FHE-2a** 3 Parthias, (No 1, 6 mvts; No 2, 6 mvts; No 3, 5 mvts). Nos 1, 3: 2ob 2cl 2hn
     (2)basso; No. 2: 2ob 2cl 2hn bn (2)basso.
   FUCHS **GFF-4a** pot-pourri. 4cl 2hn 2bn.
   HABERT **MQH-1a** 8 mvts. 2ob/fl+ob 2cl 2hn 2bn.
   KROMMER **FVK-2.4ma** Marsch. 2ob 2cl 2hn 2bn cbn.
   OZI **EXO-18.1a** overture & 5 mvts. 2cl(C) 2hn 2bn.
   VANDERHAGEN **AJV-3.16/3a** 1 mvt. 2cl 2hn 2bn.
Panurge dans l'ile des lanternes (opera, 25 Jan 1785, Paris)
   ANON **A-181a** 2fl 2cl 2hn 2bn. MS parts: RF-Ssc, Ф 891 собр юосуповьіх N19, pp. 54 - 90.
   BEINET **XJB-3.2/1a** overture & 3 mvts. 2cl 2hn 2bn.
   BEINET **XJB-3.1/3a** Marche. 2cl 2hn 2bn.
   VANDERHAGEN **AJV-3.14/1a** overture & 7 mvts; **AJV-3.15/2a** 2 mvts. 2cl 2hn 2bn.
Le rival Confident (opera, 26 July 1788, Paris)
   ANON **A-182a** overture. 2cl 2hn 2bn
     Pc (Imbault: Paris, pn 89, c.1789), RISM [G 4399], parts: S-Uu, (missing cl II, hn II).

Raoul Barbe-Bleue (Raoul der Blaubart; Blaubarth) (opera, 2 March 1789, Paris)
(Few works raise as many problems in identification. Anton Fischer (qv) freely arranged Grétry's opera to a German text (1804), but it is unlikely that Fischer prepared the Harmonie arrangements. We list all versions here - except the later pastiche based on Rossini's operas.
  ANON **A-183a** overture & 9 mvts. 2ob 2cl 2hn 2bn cbn. MS parts: I-Fc, F.P. S.347, (as "Fischer").
  ANON **A-184a** overture & 11 mvts. 2ob 2cl 2hn 2bn. MS parts: H-KE, 697/VIII, (as "Grétry und Fischer").
  EHRENFRIED **FHE-2a** Parthia No. 1, 6 mvts; No. 2, 6 mvts; No. 3, 5 mvts. 2ob 2cl 2hn bn(No. 3) (2)basso.
  KRECHLER **FFK-10.1a** overture & 2 mvts. 2ob 2cl 2hn 2bn cbn.
  SCHNEIDER, A. **AYS-34a** overture & 11 mvts. fl(Eb) 2ob 2cl 2hn 2bn tp(hn III) b-tb vlne.
  SEDLAK **WXS-19a** overture & 13 mvts. 2cl 2hn 2bn.
  SEYFRIED **IXS-1.1(a)** Marsch. 2ob 2cl 2hn 2bn cbn.
  VANDERHAGEN **AJV-5.2a** air de danse. 2cl 2hn 2bn.
Pierre le Grand (opera, 13 Jan 1790, Paris)
  ANON **A-185a** cavatina. 2ob 2cl 2hn 2bn cbn 2tp. MS parts: CZ-Bm(au), A.35.219.
  ANON **A-186a** cavatina. fl 3cl 2hn 2bn tp serp. MS parts: CZ-BA, 189/59-613.
  OZI **EXO-1.32/1a** overture. 2cl 2hn 2bn.
Untraced arrangement: La Caravane du Caire (opera, 1783, Paris).

GRIEG, Edvard Hagerup (1843 - 1907)
Poetiske Tonebilleder, Op. 3 (piano, pub. c.1870, Copenhagen)
  RALSTON **AFR-1.1a** No 5. fl ob 2cl bn/b-cl.
Humoresker, Op. 6 (piano, pub. c.1867, Berlin)
  RALSTON **AFR-1.3a** No 3. fl ob 2cl bn/b-cl.
Lyrischer Stücke - Selections
  ELLIOT **WSE-2a** 4 Nos. 2ob 2cl 2hn 2bn.
Lyrischer Stücke (Lyriske Smaastykker, Lyric Pieces), Op. 12 (piano, 1867, Copenhagen)
  RALSTON **AFR-1.2a, 1.4a - 1.7a** Nos. 5, 2, 1, 4, fl ob 2cl bn/b-cl.

GRISAR, Albert (1808 - 1869)
Sarah (opera, 26 April 1836, Paris)
  BERR **FXB-13a** overture. fl(Eb) cl(Eb) 4cl(Bb) 4hn 2bn 2cap 3tb (2)serp.

GUGLIELMI, Pierro Alessandro, *the Elder* (1728 - 1804)
La Pastorella nobile (opera, 19 April 1788, Naples; 25 May 1790, Vienna)
  ANON **A-187a** overture. 2cl 2hn 2bn.
    Pc (Imbault: Paris, c.1789), RISM [G 4942], parts: D-MÜu. MS parts: D-BFb, G-ug 41.
  WENT **JNW-20.1a** sinfonia & 9 mvts. 2ob 2cl 2hn 2bn.
  WENT **JNW-20.2a** sinfonia & 9 mvts. 2ob 2ca 2hn 2bn.
La Bella Pescatrice (opera, spring 1789, Naples; 26 April 1791, Vienna)
  ANON **A-188a** 5 mvts. 2ob 2cl 2hn 2bn [?cbn] 2tp. MS parts: CZ-Bm(no), A.18.855.
  WENT **JNW-21.1a** sinfonia & 11 mvts. 2ob 2cl 2hn 2bn.
  WENT **JNW-21.2a** sinfonia & 10 mvts. 2ob 2ca 2hn 2bn.
Due nozze ed un solo marito (opera, autumn 1800, Florence)
  ANON **A-189a** 2ob 2cl 2hn 2bn cbn. MS parts: I-Fc, F.P. S.393.

GUNGGERL, ( ) *Despite the similarity in spelling, we believe this is too early to be a work by Joseph Gung'l (qv).*
6 Walzer
  SCHNEIDER, A. **AYS-35a** fl 2ob 2cl 2hn 2bn tp b-tb 2vla cb.

GUNG'L, Joseph (1810 - 1889)
Sirenen-Galopp, Op. 20 (piano, c.1843)
  ANON **A-190a** fl 2ob cl(Eb) cl(solo Bb) 3cl(Bb) 4hn 2bn a-hn 3tb b-hn/bomb.
    MS parts: D-DT, Mus-n 1770, No. 2.
Venus-Reigen Walzer, Op. 63 (piano, c.1845)
  SCHOLZ **WES-66a** fl 2ob 2cl 2hn 2bn tp tb db timp.
Illustrirte-Polka, Op. 65 (piano, c.1845)
  SCHOLZ **WES-67a** fl 2ob 2cl 2hn 2bn tp tb db timp.
Ideal und Leben-Walzer, Op. 67 (piano, c.1845)
  SCHOLZ **WES-68a** fl 2ob 2cl 2hn 2bn tp tb db timp.
Träume auf dem Ocean Walzer, Op. 80 (piano, c.1847)
  SCHOLZ **WES-69a** fl 2ob 2cl 2hn 2bn tp tb db timp.
Klänge von Delaware Walzer, Op. 89 (piano, c 1848)
  SCHOLZ **WES-70a** fl 2ob 2cl 2hn 2bn tp tb db timp.
Columbinen-Galopp (piano, sd)
  SCHOLZ **WES-71a** fl 2ob 2cl 2hn 2bn tp tb db timp.
Der fröhliche Ulahne [sic], Mazurka (piano, sd)
  ANON **A-191a** pic fl 2ob cl(Eb) 3cl(Bb) 4hn 2bn 5tp t-hn 3tb b-hn/bomb b-dr t-dr s-dr.
    MS parts: D-DT, Mus-n 2035.
Gambrinus Polka (piano, sd)
  SCHOLZ **WES-72a** fl 2ob 2cl 2hn 2bn tp tb db timp.
Gazellen-Polka (piano, sd)
  SCHOLZ **WES-73a** fl 2ob 2cl 2hn2bn tp tb db timp.
Grazien-Polka (piano, sd)
  SCHOLZ **WES-74a** fl 2ob 2cl 2hn 2bn tp tb db timp.
Schlesische Lieder Walzer (piano, sd)
  SCHOLZ **WES-75a** fl 2ob 2cl 2hn 2bn tp tb db timp.

Vagabonden Polka (piano, sd)
ANON (? SCHOLZ) **A-180a** fl 2ob 2cl 2hn 2bn tp tb db.   MS score: D-NEhz, 114d.
SCHOLZ **WES-76a** fl 2ob 2cl 2hn 2bn tp tb db timp.
Vielliebschen Polka (piano, sd)
SCHOLZ **WES-77a** fl 2ob 2cl 2hn 2bn tp tb db timp.
Wiedershen Walzer (piano, sd)
SCHOLZ **WES-78a** fl 2ob 2cl 2hn 2bn tp tb db timp.

GYROWETZ (Jírovic), Adalbert Mathias (Vojtĕch Matyáš) (1763 - 1850)
Selico (Selico und Berissa) (Singspiel, 15 Oct 1804, Vienna)
KRECHLER **FFK-13.1a** overture & 2 mvts.   2ob 2cl 2hn 2bn.
Atlanta e Hypomenes (ballet divertissement, 30 Nov 1805, Vienna)
ANON **A-192a** overture & 12 mvts.   2ob 2cl 2hn 2bn.   MS parts: CZ-Pnm, XXVII.B.230.
Agnes Sorel (opera, 4 Dec 1806, Vienna)
ANON **A-193a** IItes Stueck [sic] zur Musikaliensammlung des Muzeums gehörig.
2fl 2ob 2cl 2hn 2bn 2bn 2tp(clar) s-dr.   MS parts (1806): A-KR, H 38/37.
SEDLAK **WXS-20.1a** overture & 12 mvts.   2ob 2cl 2hn 2bn cbn.   *See also* **WXS-3.1a** overture, Nos. 5 & 8.
SEDLAK **WXS-20.2a** overture & 12 mvts.   2cl 2hn 2bn.
STARKE **FRS-9a** (= **FRS-1.1a**) overture & 2 mvts.   2ob 2cl 2hn 2bn cbn.
Marina die Königin der Amazonen (melodrama, 27 May 1806, Vienna)
ANON **A-194a** overture & 11 mvts.   2ob 2cl 2hn 2bn (cbn).   MS parts: I-Fc, F.P. S.348.   *There is a single divisi bar in the bn II pt, suggesting a cbn; it is not listed on the titlepage.*
Emericke (Emerika) (comic opera, 11 Dec 1807, Vienna)
KRECHLER **FFK-4.6a** and **7.3a** arie & duetto.   2ob 2cl 2hn 2bn cbn, (2ob tacet in arie).
Der Samtrock (Singspiel, 24 Nov 1809, Vienna)
ANON **A-195a** 2ob 2cl 2hn 2bn cbn.   MS parts: I-Fc, F.P. S.395.
Der betrogene Betrüger (operette, 17 Feb 1810, Vienna)
ANON **A-196a.** 2ob 2cl 2hn 2bn cbn.   MS parts: I-Fc, F.P. S.395.
Wilhelm Tell (with J. Weigl) (incidental music/ballet 30 May 1810, Vienna)
ANON **A-197a** 2ob 2cl 2hn 2bn cbn.
Pc (sn: sl [= T. Weigl: Wien], c.1810), MS parts: I-Fc, F.P. S.360.
LÖWENSTEIN **CAL-3.1a** Hirtenlied.   fl 2cl 2hn 2bn.
Das zugemauerte Fenster (Singspiel, 18 Dec 1810, Vienna)
ANON **A-198a** 2ob 2l 2hn 2bn cbn.   MS parts: I-Fc, F.P. S.395.
Der Augenarzt (opera, 1 Oct 1811,Vienna)
Note, too, Triebensee's Variations on "Mir leuchet die Hoffnung", JZT-39.
ANON **A-199a** overture & 5 mvts.   2ob 2cl 2hn 2bn.   MS parts: CZ-KRa, A3867a/IV.B.31.
FENDT **AXF-3.2ad** overture, Act I: 8 mvts, Act II Entreact [sic] & 7 mvts.   2cl(E♭) 3cl(C & B♭) 2hn 2bn 2tp b-tb.   *Possibly adapted from Starke's arrangement, FRS-10a.*
SCHMITT, G. **GYS-28a** 1 mvt & 4 Walzer.   2fl 2ob cl(F) 2cl(B♭) 2bthn 4hn 2bn 2tp tb+db b-dr.
STARKE **FRS-10a** Abth. 1: overture & 8 mvts, Abth. 2: Entr'act & 7 mvts.   2ob 2cl 2hn 2bn cbn (2tp).
Frederica ed Adolfo (opera seria, 6 April 1812, Vienna)
TRIEBENSEE **JZT-21a** Act I: overture & 13; Act II: 7 mvts.   2ob 2cl 2hn 2bn (cbn tp ad lib).
Der Abschied (?= Der Abschied des Kriegers von seinen Mädchen, ländl. Duett von Castelli.) (Lied, c.25 July 1813, Vienna: k.k. Hofttheater-Musik-Verlag, pn Op. 172)
ANON **A-200a** 2ob 2cl 2hn 2bn cbn.   MS parts: I-Fc, F.P. S.396.
Robert oder die Prüfung (Singspiel, 15 July 1815, Vienna)
ANON **A-210a** 2ob 2cl 2hn 2bn cbn.   MS parts: I-Fc, F.P. S.396.
Die Pagen des Herzogs von Vendôme (ballet based on the 5 Aug 1808 comic opera, 16 Oct 1815, Vienna)
SEDLAK **WXS-2.1a** introduzione & 7 mvts.   2ob 2cl 2hn 2bn cbn (2tp).
Die Hochzeit der Thetis und des Peleus (with Persuis; ballet, 3 May 1816, Vienna)
SEDLAK **WXS-21.1a** overture & 11 mvts.   2ob 2cl 2hn 2bn cbn.
SEDLAK **WXS-21.2a** 5 mvts.   2ob 2cl 2hn 2bn cbn (2tp).
STARKE **FRS-11a** 6 mvts.   2ob 2cl 2hn 2bn cbn 2tp.
Helene (opera, 16 Feb 1816, Vienna)
ANON **A-202a** 2 Theils.   2ob 2cl 2hn 2bn cbn.   MS parts: I-Fc, F.P. S.370.
Die beiden Eremiten (opera, 1816, Vienna)
ANON **A-203a** 2ob 2cl 2hn 2bn.   MS parts: A-Wgm(c), (?lost).
Die zwei Tanten, oder Ehemals und Heute (ballet, 29 July 1816, Vienna)
STARKE **FRS-12a** 1 Abth, 4 mvts.   2ob 2cl 2hn 2bn cbn 2tp.
Der Zauberschlaft (with Persuis; ballet, 16 Jan 1818, Vienna)
SEDLAK **WXS-22a** overture & 13 mvts.   2ob 2cl 2hn 2bn cbn (2tp).
STARKE **FRS-13a** overture & 12 mvts, in 2 Abth.   2ob 2cl 2hn 2bn cbn 2tp.
Das Schweizer Milchmädchen (Nathalie) (ballet, 9 Oct 1821, Vienna)
WIDDER **YYW-1.21a** 1 mvt.   2fl 2cl 2hn 2bn.
Quodlibet (unidentified)
ANON **A-204a** 2ob 2cl 2hn 2bn cbn.   MS parts: I-Fc, F.P. S.396, 397.
Aria Russe ("Schöne Minka") (probably from *Sammlung russischer Volkslieder*, Ivan Pratsch: St Petersburg, 1790)
HAVEL **VXH-4a** 2cl 2hn 2bn
Dubious & Spurious Works
Aline (opera, sd)   *The MS cited below states "Oper . . . von Adalbert Gyrowetz". However, the Ouverture is, in fact, that of Berton's opera and many of the movements also appear to match.*
ANON **A-66.2a** overture & 7 mvts.   2ob 2cl 2hn 2bn cbn.   MS parts: I-Fc, F.P. S.381.

HAACK, ( )
March
 ANON **A-78.1/3m(a)** 2ob 2cl 2hn 2bn tp.

HÄNSEL (HAENSEL), Peter (1770 - 1831)
Rondo Allegretto à la ungaria [B♭]
 DRUSCHETZKY **GYD-11a** 2ob talia cl bthn 2hn 2bn.

HAIBL (HAIBEL), (Johann Petrus) Jakob (Jacob) (1762 - 1826)
Der Tiroller Wastel (opera, 14 May 1796, Vienna)
 HAVEL **VXH-12ac** 7 mvts. (misattributed to Wenzel Müller). 2cl 2hn 2bn.
Rochus Pumpernickel (dramatic quodlibet 13 Dec 1809, Vienna; a collaboration with Seyfried). *The music was drawn from the works of 16 composers, including Haydn & Mozart; Haibl's actual contribution is not known.*
 ANON **A-205a** 2ob 2cl 2hn 2bn cbn. MS pts: I-Fc, F.P. S.421, (under "Stegmayer", the librettist).
 LÖWENSTEIN **CAL-3.2a** overture & duetto. fl 2cl 2hn 2bn.
 SCHMETS **QYS-1a.** overture & polonese. 2ob 2cl 2hn 2bn cbn.

HALÉVY, Jacques François Fromental Élie (1799 - 1862)
La Dilettante d'Avignon (comic opera, 7 Nov 1829, Paris)
 BERR **FXB-14a** overture. fl solo+2cl 2cl 2hn bn(I) tp serp; (ad lib: cl III & IV, hn III & IV, bn II, tb b-dr).
La Juive (Die Jüdin) (opera, 23 Feb 1835, Paris)
 ANON **A-206a** introduction & Act I finale. fl 2ob 2cl(E♭) cl(solo B♭) 3cl(B♭) 4hn 2bn 2tp a-hn 3tb b-hn/bomb timp b-dr t-dr. MS parts: D-DT, Mus-n 1660, No. 1.
 ANON **A-207a** Act III finale. pic fl 2ob 2cl(E♭) cl(solo B♭) 3cl(B♭) 4hn 2bn 3tp kl-hn a-hn 3tb b-hn/bomb b-dr t-dr. MS parts: D-DT, Mus-n 1661.
 SCHOLZ **WES-79.1a** 4 mvts. fl 2ob 2cl 3hn 2bn tp tb timp.
 SCHOLZ **WES-79.2a** 4 mvts. fl 2ob 2cl 2hn 2bn tp tb db timp.
 WIDDER **YYW-2a** finale Act I. pic fl 2cl(E♭) 3cl(B♭) 4hn 2bn 3tp 3tb bombartoni b-dr s-dr tri.
L'Eclair (Der Blitz) (opera, 30 Dec 1835, Paris)
 ANON **A-208a** overture. fl(F) fl(E♭) 2ob cl(E♭) cl(solo B♭) 3cl(B♭) 4hn 2bn 4tp kenthorn t-hn 3tb b(=b-hn/bomb) vc/b b-dr s-dr. MS parts: D-DT, Mus-n 492.
 ANON **A-209a** Amusement [with Meyerbeer's *Les Huguenots*]. fl ob cl(E♭) cl(solo B♭) 3cl(B♭) 2hn 2bn 2tp 3tb b-hn b-dr s-dr. MS parts: D-DT, Mus-n 1860.
Le Guitarero (Der Guitarrespieler) (comic opera, 21 Jan 1841, Paris)
 ANON **A-210a** duett. fl 2ob cl(E♭) cl(solo B♭) 3cl(B♭) 2hn 2bn 2tp 3tb bomb b-dr s-dr. MS parts: D-DT, Mus-n 1659, No. 1.
 SCHOLZ **WES-80.1a** 3 mvts. fl 2ob 2cl 2hn 2bn tp tb db timp.
 SCHOLZ **WES-80.2a** ensemble & chor. fl 2ob 2cl 2hn 2bn tp tb db timp.
Le Reine de Chypre (Die Königin von Cypern) (opera, 22 Dec 1841, Paris)
 ANON **A-211a** overture. pic 2ob 2cl(E♭) cl(solo B♭) 3cl(B♭) 4hn 2bn 4tp kl-hn t-hn 3tb b-hn/bomb b-dr s-dr. MS parts: D-DT, Mus-n 1662, No. 1.
Les Mousquetaires de la Reine (Die Musquetiere der Königin) (comic opera, 2 Feb 1847, Paris)
 SCHOLZ **WES-81a** aria & ensemble. fl 2ob 2cl 2hn 2bn tp tb db timp.
Le Val d'Andorre (Thale von Andorra) (comic opera, 11 Nov 1848, Paris)
 SCHOLZ **WES-82a** overture & 3 mvts. fl 2ob 2cl 2hn 2bn tp tb db timp.

HAMMER, G.
Münchner Polka
 WIESER **FAW-17a** pic(D♭) cl(E♭) 3cl(Bb) 2hn 2bn tp b-tb cb.
Rheinländer-Polka
 WIESER **FAW-18a** pic(E♭) cl(E♭) 3cl(B♭) 2hn 2bn tp cb.

HANDEL (Händel, Haendel), George Frederick (Georg Friedrich) (1685 - 1759)
Floridante (opera, 1 Nov 1721, London)
 ANON **A-203.1/10(a)** march. 2ob 2bthn 2hn 2bn serp.
Giulio Cesare (opera, 20 Feb 1724, London)
 ANON **A-203.1/6(a)** march. 2ob 2bthn 2hn 2bn serp.
Judas Maccabeus (oratorio, 1 April 1747, London)
 ANON **A-212a** overture. 2cl 2hn 2bn. MS parts: CZ-Pnm, XLI.B.98, No. 3.
Solomon (oratorio, 17 March 1749, London)
 CAMPBELL **AWC-3a** sinfonia, "Arrival of the Queen of Sheba". 2ob 2cl 2hn 2bn.
Musick for the Royal Fireworks (7 Oct 1748, London)
 CAMPBELL **AQC-4a** 2ob 2cl 2hn 2bn.
Untraced arrangement: Saul (oratorio, 1739) for 6 or 7 winds (Sieber: Paris).

HANISCH, Franz (1749 - post-1789)
Polonaise, in B♭
 SCHNEIDER, A. **AYS-36a** fl 2ob 4cl 2hn 2bn tp b-tb serp.
Polacca, in B♭
 SCHNEIDER, A. **AYS-37a** fl 2ob 4cl 2hn 2bn tp b-tb serp.

HASSE, Johann Adolf (1699 - 1783)
Sant' Elena al Calvario (oratorio, 1746, Dresden, revived 1753; revived 1772, Vienna)
 ANON **A-213a** Parts 1 & 2. 2ob 2cl 2h 2bn cbn. MS parts: I-Fc, F.P. S.398 & 399.

HASSLER, ( )
[Single movement in F minor/major; And[an]te poco Largo / And[an]tino]
 DRUSCHETZKY **GYD-12a** 2ob cl bthn 2hn 2bn cbn.

HAYDN, Franz Joseph (1732 - 1809)
Die Schöpfung (The Creation; Le Création) Hob. XXI/2 (oratorio, 19 March 1798, Vienna)
  ANON **A-214a** 2 Suites, each 5 mvts. 2fl 2cl(C, principale) 2cl(C, ripieno) 2hn 2bn 2tp (2)tb serp.
    Pc (Pleyel: Paris, pn 414, 415, 1802), 2 suites, RISM [H 4112], parts: CH-Gpu, Ib.4866, 4867;
    CH-Zz, AMG. III 1091/1092 a-o, (Suite 2 missing fl I). *The trombone part is divisi in Suite 2, No. 2.*
  ANON **A-215a** Einleitung & 9/10 mvts. 2cl 2hn 2bn.
    MS parts: CZ-KRa, A3872/IV.B.35. *An additional mvt has been added on the cover of all parts.*
  DRUSCHETZKY **GXD-13a** Einleitung & 15 mvts. 2ob 2cl 2hn 2bn (cbn ad lib).
  SCHNEIDER, A. **AYS-38a** fl 2ob 2cl 2hn 2bn tp b-tb 2vla cb.
Die Jahreszeiten (The Seasons), Hob. XXI: 31 (oratorio, 24 April (private performance) & 30 Nov 1801, Vienna)
  DRUSCHETZKY **GYD-14a** overture & 13 mvts. 2ob 2cl 2hn 2bn.
  KRECHLER **FFK-5.4a, 5.6a, 5.7a** 3 mvts. 2ob 2cl 2hn 2bn (cbn tp ad lib).
  SCHNEIDER, A. **AYS-39a** Erste Abtheilung (Frühling - Sommer - Herbst - Winter), overture & 15 mvts.
    fl(pic) 2ob 2cl 2hn 2bn tp(hn III) b-tb 2vla cb.
  SCHOLZ **WES-83a** 2 Theils. fl 2ob 2cl 2hn 2bn 2tp(clar) tb db timp.
Orlando Paladino (Der Ritter Roland) (dramma eroicomico, 6 Dec 1782, Eszterháza)
  ROSINACK **FJR-1a** 2ob 2cl 2hn 2bn.
Gott erhalte Franz den Kaiser (Hob. XXVI/43) (song, 1797)
  DRUSCHETZKY **GYD-1.1va** SATB. 2ob 2cl 2hn 2bn.
  DRUSCHETZKY **GYD-1.2va** TTBB, ob cl hn bn.
  KROMMER **FVK-1ma** pic(Eb) cl(Ab) 4cl(Eb) 5hn 5tp 2tp(klappen) 2tb b-tb basse b-dr s-dr.
  SEYFRIED **IXS-1.4/24(a)** 2ob 2cl 2hn 2bn cbn + 2ob 2cl 2hn 2bn cbn.
  TRIEBENSEE **JZT-1m** as a march, Trio by Triebensee. 2ob 2cl 2hn 2bn (cbn tp ad lib).
Symphony in Bb, Hob. I/51 (c.1772 - 1774)
  GEBAUER, MJ. **MJG-9a** mvts 1 & 4 in C, 2 in F; omits 3. pic cl(F) 2cl(C) 2hn 2bn tp b-tb serp b-dr.
Symphony in D, ("L'Impériale"), Hob. I/53
  BEINET **XJB-3.1/2a** Andante, mvt 2. 2cl 2hn 2bn.
  GAMBARO **VXG-4.1(a)** mvts 2 & 3 only. pic(Db) cl(Eb) 2cl(Bb) 2hn (2)bn to tb serp b-dr+cym.
Symphony in Eb, "Schoolmaster", Hob. I/55 (1774)
  MICHEL **FLM-1a** 2fl 2cl 2hn 2bn.
Symphony in C, "La Roxolane", Hob. I/63 (c.1777 - 1780)
  FUCHS **GFF-37a** mvt 2, (in Steibelt's *Cinquième Potpourri).* 2cl 2hn 2bn.
  KLOB **STK-1a** mvt 2 only. 2cl 2hn bn 2vla vlne.
  SCHNEIDER, A. **AYS-40a** (Here with the title "Lieblings"). fl 2ob 2cl(C & Bb) 2hn 2bn tp b-tb 2vla cb.
Symphony in F, Hob. I/67 (1779)
  SCHNEIDER, A. **AYS-41a** (here in D). fl 2ob 2cl(C & Bb) 2hn 2bn tp b-tb 2vla cb.
Symphony in D. Hob. I/70 (1779)
  MICHEL **FLM-2a** 2fl 2cl 2hn 2bn.
Symphony in D, "La Chasse", Hob. I/73 (1780/1781).
  GEBAUER, F.R. **FRG-1a** mvts 1, 4 only. 2fl 2cl(C) 2hn 2bn tp(ad lib), *or* 2cl 2hn 2bn.
  LEROY **PQL-1.7/2a** mvt. 2 only. 2p-fl(F) 2cl(C) 2hn 2bn tp serp.
  MICHEL **FLM-3a** 2fl 2cl 2hn 2bn.
Symphony in D, Hob. I/75 (c.1780)
  MICHEL **FLM-4a** 2fl 2cl 2hn 2bn.
  SCHACHT **TVS-21** Menuetto & Trio. 2ca 2vla(con sordini).
Symphony in Eb, Hob. I/76 (c.1782)
  MICHEL **FLM-5a** 2fl 2cl 2hn 2bn.
Symphony in F, Hob. I/79 (c.1784)
  KLOB **STK-1a** mvts 2 & 3 only. 2cl 2hn bn 2vla vlne.
Symphony in G, Hob. I/81 (c.1784)
  KLOB **STK-1a** mvt 2 only. 2cl 2hn bn 2vla vlne.
Symphony in C, "L'Ours", Hob. I/82 (1786)
  ERNST **FRE-1a.** 2cl 2hn 2bn.
Symphony in Eb, Hob. I/84 (1786)
  VANDERHAGEN **AJV-10a** mvt 2 only, (Suite 1, No. 6). 2fl 2cl(C) 2hn 2bn.
Symphony in Bb, "La Reine", Hob. I/85 (1785/1786)
  BOCHSA, C. **CZB-1a** 2fl 2cl 2hn 2bn tp tb serp.
  KLOB **STK-1a** mvt 2 only. 2cl 2hn bn 2vla vlne.
Symphony in D, Hob. I/86 (1786)
  OZI **EXO-1.24/1a** mvt 1 only. 2cl(C) 2hn 2bn.
Symphony in F, Hob. I/89 (1787)
  KRECHLER **FFK-1.7ac** Menuetto, mvt 3 only. 2ob 2cl 2hn 2bn cbn tp.
  TRIEBENSEE **JZT-8ac** Menuetto mit 2 Trios. 2ob 2cl 2hn 2bn.
  VANDERHAGEN **AJV-11a** mvt 1 only, (Suite 2. No.1). 2fl(pic) 2cl(C) 2hn 2bn.
Symphony in C, Hob. I/90 (1788)
  KLOB **STK-1a** mvt 3 only. 2cl 2hn bn 2vla vlne.
  VANDERHAGEN **AJV-10a** mvts 2 & 4, (Suite 1, Nos. 2 & 3). 2fl 2cl(C) 2hn 2bn.
Symphony in Eb Hob. I/91 (1788)
  BOCHSA, C. **CZB-2a** 2fl 2cl 2hn 2bn tp tb serp.
  GAMBARO **VXG-.2.3/2a** Trio of Menuet only. 2fl 2cl 2hn 2bn, (ad lib: tp tb serp; all tacet in Trio).
  KLOB **STK-1a** mvts 2 & 3 only. 2cl 2hn bn 2vla vlne.

Symphony in G, "Oxford", Hob. I/92 (1789) *In F*
  LEROY **PQL-1.10/2a** mvt 2 only.   fl(F) 2ob 2cl(III & IV, C) 2hn 2bn serp.
  TRIEBENSEE **JZT-22a** 2ob 2cl 2hn 2bn (cbn tp ad lib).
Symphony in D, Hob. I/93 (1791)
  SCHNEIDER, A. **AYS-42a** fl 2ob 4cl 2hn 2bn tp b-tb cb.
Symphony in G, "Surprise" ("Mit dem Paukenschlag"), Hob. I/94 (1791, London)
  HAMMERL, P.C. **PCH-1.2(a)** Andante.   2ob 2cl 2hn 3bn tp serp.
  KLOB **STK-1a** mvts 2 & 3 only.   2cl 2hn bn 2vla vlne.
  LEROY **PQL-1.8/2a** mvt 2 only.   fl 2ob 2cl(III & IV, C) 2hn 2bn serp.
  SCHNEIDER, A. **AYS-43a** fl 2ob 4cl 2hn 2bn tp b-tb serp.
  VANDERHAGEN **AJV-10a** mvt 2 only.   2fl 2cl(C) 2hn 2bn.
  WENT **JNW-22.1a** Andante (mvt 2) only.   2ob 2cl 2hn 2bn.
  WENT **JNW-22.2a** Andante (mvt 2) only.   2ob 2ca 2hn 2bn.
Symphony in C minor, Hob. I/95 (1791)
  VANDERHAGEN **AJV-10a** mvts 3 & 4 only, (Suite 1, Nos. 5 & 1).   2fl 2cl(C) 2hn 2bn.
Symphony in C, Hob. I/97 (1792)
  KLOB **STK-1a** mvts 2 & 3 only.   2cl 2hn bn 2vla vlne.
  TRIEBENSEE **JZT-23a** mvts 2-4.   2ob 2cl 2hn 2bn (cbn tp ad lib).
  VANDERHAGEN **AJV-10a** mvts 2-4, (Suite 2, No. 5, Suite 1, No. 7, Suite 2, No. 4).   2fl 2cl(C) 2hn 2bn.
Symphony in E♭, Hob. I/99 (1793)
  ANON **A-216a** Adagio.   fl 2ob cl(E♭) cl(solo B♭) 3cl(B♭) 2hn 2bn 2tp 3tb serp b-dr t-dr.
    MS parts: D-DT, Mus-n 1893, No. 1.
  SCHNEIDER, A. **AYS-44a** fl 2ob 4cl 2hn 2bn tp b-tb cb.
  VANDERHAGEN **AJV-10a** mvt 4 only, (Suite 2, No. 6).   2fl 2cl(C) 2hn 2bn.
Symphony in G, "Military", Hob. I/100 (1794)
  HAYDN, F.J. **FJH-1m(a)** 2nd mvt: March in C.   fl 2ob 2cl(C) 2hn 2bn 2tp(C) tb serp s-dr.
  LEROY **PQL-1.12/2a** mvt 2 only.   2fl 2ob 2cl(III & IV, C) 2hn 2bn tp serp.
  LEROY **PQL-1.12/3a** mvt 3 only.   2p-fl(F) 2ob 2cl(III & IV, C) 2hn 2bn tp serp.
Symphony in D major/minor, "Clock", Hob. I/101 (1794)
  ANON **A-78.2/4m(a)** Menuetto & Trio.   2pic 2quart-fl 2cl(C) 2hn 2bn 2tp serp b-dr+cym.
  LEROY **PQL-1.6/2a** mvt 2 only.   2fl(F) 2ob 2cl(III & IV, C) 2hn 2bn tp serp b-dr.
  LEROY **PQL-1.2/5** mvt 3 only, (here attributed to Leroy).   2p-fl(F) 2cl(F) 2cl(C) 2hn 2bn tp serp b-dr.
  SCHNEIDER, A. **AYS-45a** fl 2ob 4cl 2hn 2bn tp b-tb cb.
Symphony in B♭, "Miracle", Hob. I/102 (1794)
  BOCHSA, C. **CZB-3a** 2fl 2cl 2hn 2bn tp tb serp.   *(The slow movement is replaced by that of Hob. I/104.)*
  KRECHLER **FFK-2.9a, FFK-9.6a** Menuetto, mvt 3 only.   2ob 2cl 2hn 2bn (cbn tp ad lib).
  TRIEBENSEE **JZT-24a** mvt 4 only.   2ob 2cl 2hn 2bn (cbn tp ad lib).
Symphony in E♭, "Drumroll" ("Mit dem Paukenwirbel"), Hob. I/103 (1795)
  ANON **A-217a** fl 2ob 2cl 2hn 2bn tp(prin).
    MS score (in the same hand as those in I-BGc allegedly by J.S. Mayr): I-Bl, TT 66.
  KRECHLER **FFK-2.10a, FFK-9.7a** 4th mvt only.   2ob 2cl 2hn 2bn (cbn tp ad lib).
  SCHNEIDER, A. **AYS-46a** fl 2ob 4cl 2hn 2bn tp b-tb cb.
  TRIEBENSEE **JZT-7ac** mvt 2, Andante.   2ob 2cl 2hn 2bn cbn.
  VANDERHAGEN **AJV-10a** mvts 2 & 3 only, (Suite 2, Nos. 2 & 3).   2fl 2cl(C) 2hn 2bn.
Symphony in D major/minor, "London", Hob. I/104 (1795)
  See also supra: Hob I/102, (= 2nd mvt, arranged Bochsa, CZB-3a).
  LEROY **PQL-1.9/2a** mvt 2 only.   2fl(F) 2ob 2cl(III & IV, C) 2hn 2bn serp.
  SCHNEIDER, A. **AYS-47a** fl 2ob 4cl 2hn 2bn tp b-tb cb.
Concerto for 2 Lire Organizzate, Hob. VIIh/5 (c.1786)
  KRECHLER **FFK-1.6ac** mvt 2, Andante, only.   2ob 2cl 2hn 2bn cbn tp.
String Quartet in B♭, Op. 44, No. 1 (King of Prussia set, No. 1, Hob. III/44ii) (1785)
  GAMBARO **VXG-2.2a** mvt 2, Adagio.   2cl 2hn 2bn.
String Quartet in G, Op. 54, No. 1 (Hob. III/58) (pub. 1789)
  GAMBARO **VXG-2.3/1a** Menuetto, (Trio. *See:* Symphony Hob. I/91).   2cl 2hn 2bn, (tp tb serp ad lib).
String Quartet in F minor & major, Op. 55, No. 2 (Hob. III/61) (pub. 1789)
  BLASIUS **MFB-2.2(a)** mvt 2, Adagio ma non troppo.   2cl 2hn 2bn.
String Quartet in F, Op. 74/2 (Hob. III/73) (1793)
  SYLVANI **XSV-1.3a, 1.5a** mvts 3 & 2, respectively.   2cl 2hn 2bn.
String Quartet in B♭ (Count Erdödy set, Op. 78, No. 4, Hob. III/78i) (1797)
  GAMBARO **VXG-2.1a** mvt 1, Allegro con spirito.   2cl 2hn 2bn, (ad lib: tp tb serp).
Piano Trio in A (Hob. XV/18) (piano, violin & cello, pre-1794)
  GAMBARO **VXG-2.4/1a** Andante, mvt 2.   2cl 2hn 2bn.
Piano Sonata in Eb (Hob. XVI/38ii) (1777 - 1779)
  LEROY **PQL-1.6/1a** mvt 2 only, (as "Ouverture").   2fl(F) 2cl(F) 2cl(C) 2hn 2bn tp serp b-dr.
Credo in B♭
  MAYR **JSM-1va** SATTB, 2cl 2hn tp tb vc vlne timp organ.
Die Beredsamkeit (Hob. XXVc, 4) (4-part song, 1796 - 1801)
  SONNENLEITER **LUS-1va** SATB, 2ob 2cl 2hn 2bn.
Der Greis (Hob. XXVc, 5) (4-part song, 1796 - 1801)
  ANON **A-8va** SATB, 2ob 2cl 2hn 2bn.   MS score & parts: A-Wgm.
Aus dem Danklied zu Gott (Hob. XXVc, 8) (4-part song, 1796 - 1801)
  SONNENLEITER **LUS-2va** SATB, 2ob 2cl 2hn 2bn.
Abendlied zu Gott, von Gellert (Hob. XXVc, 9) (4-part song, 1796 - 1801)
  ANON **A-10va** 2ob+fl 2cl(A) 3hn(E) 2bn tp tb.   MS score: D-DO, Mus.Ms.642; GB-Lgillaspie, (photocopy).

Chorlied: "Seele dein Heiland ist frei", (Hob. XXVc, B2) (4-part song)
ANON **A-11va** as "Zur Auferstehung Christi". SATB, fl 2cl 2hn 2bn.
MS parts: D-DO, Mus.Ms.738; GB-Lgillaspie, (photocopy).
Daphnens einziger Fehler &An die Frauen (Hob. XXVb, 2 & 4) (3-part songs, 1796 - 1801)
ANON **A-12va** 3 voices, bthn 2bn.
MS parts ("Walther Schulz, Stuttgart"): A-Wgm, (unverified, Hoboken citation).
Unidentified works
HAMMERL, C.A. **CAH-1** Partita; the 2nd mvt "da Haydn". ob 2cl 2hn bn.
Doubtful and Spurious Works
See: HOFFSTETTER, String Quartet in C, Trio, (formerly Hob. III/14).
Ochsen Menuet (Hob. IX/27, dubious)
KRECHLER **FFK-6.3a** 2ob 2cl 2hn 2bn cbn tp.
LÖWENSTEIN **CAL-1.2a** 2cl(C) 2hn bn b-tb/bn.
Polonaise in F
GAMBARO **VXG-2.4/2a** 2fl 2cl 2hn 2bn, (ad lib: tp tb serp).
Walzer [& Trio]
GEBAUER, MJ. **MJG-1.2/5a** fl(F) cl(F) 2cl(C) 2hn 2bn tp serp/b-tb b-dr cym tri; *or* fl(F) 2cl(C) 2hn 2bn serp.

HÉROLD, Louis Joseph Ferdinand (1791 - 1833)
La Clochette, ou le Diable page (Die Zauberglöcken) (opéra-féerie, 18 Oct 1817, Paris)
ANON **A-218a** overture & 8 mvts. (? 2ob 2cl 2hn 2bn cbn). MS parts (9): I-Fc, F.P. S.388.
Almédon ou le Monde renversé (later as: Marie) (opera, 12 Aug 1826, Paris)
BERR **FXB-15a** overture (as *Marie*). (Here only: pic cl(Eb) cl(Bb, IV) 2hn bn(I); (ad lib: tp (2)tb serp).
SCHMITT, G. **GYS-29a** 2 Bds. fl 2ob 3cl 2hn 2bn tp tb db.
Le Dernier Jour de Missolonghi (incidental music, 10 April 1828, Paris)
BERR **FXB-16a** overture. fl(Eb) cl(Bb solo) 2cl(Bb) 2hn bn (2)serp; (ad lib: 2cl(Bb) tp 2tb cb b-dr+cym tri).
Zampa, ou La Fiancée de marbre, (Zampa, oder die Marmorbraut) (opera, 2 March 1831, Paris)
ANON **A-219a** overture. 2ob cl(F) 2 cl(C) 2hn 2bn cbn. MS parts: CZ-Bm(au), A.35.297.
ANON **A-220a** potpourÿ [sic]. 2cl(Eb) 3cl(Bb) 2hn 2bn 2tp b-tb cb b-dr. MS pts: GB-Ljag(w), 10/258, No. 2.
ANON **A-15.3a, 15.4a (20.5a, 20.6a** Walzer & Galopp. fl(F) cl(Eb) 2cl(Bb) 2hn bn tp b-tb serp b-dr s-dr.
ANON **A-17.1a (20.10a)** Walzer. terz-fl cl(Eb) 2cl(Bb) 2hn bn 2tp b-tb serp.
BERR **FXB-17a** overture. fl cl(solo Bb) 2cl(Bb) 2hn bn(I) serp; (ad lib: 2cl(Bb) hn(III) bn(II) bugle tp 3tb db).
KIRCHHOFF **WZK-33.1a** 3 mvts. fl 2ob 2cl 2hn 2bn tp tb db.
KIRCHHOFF **WZK-33.2a** Zampa-Galopp. fl 2ob 2cl 2hn 2bn tp tb db.
KOLB, A. **AXK-1a** overture. pic(Eb) cl(Eb) 2cl(Bb) 2hn bn 2tp b-tb+cb serp b-dr s-dr.
SCHMITT, G. **GYS-30a** overture & 1 Bd. fl 2ob 3cl 3hn 2bn 2tp tb db timp.
SEDLAK (attrib) **+WXS-23a** Teil 1: overture & 8 mvts, Teil 2: 6 mvts. 2ob 2cl 2hn 2bn cbn 2tp.
STRECK **PZS-1.1a, 1.6a** overture & potpourri. fl cl(D) 2cl(A) 2hn 2bn.
WIDDER **YYW-1.22a** 1 mvt. 2fl 2cl 2hn 2bn.
Le Médecine sans Médecin (comic opera, 15 Oct 1832, Paris)
BERR **FXB-18a** overture. fl(Eb) cl(Eb) solo+2cl(Bb) 2hn bn serp; (ad lib: 2cl(Bb) tp bugle 3tb cb).
Le Pré aux Clercs (Zweikampf oder Schreiber Wiese bei Paris) (opera, 15 Dec 1832, Paris)
ANON **A-17.3a (20.12a)** Galopp. pic(Eb) cl(Eb) 2cl(Bb) 2hn bn 2tp b-tb serp.
BERR **FXB-19a** overture. fl(Eb) cl(Eb) solo+2cl(Bb) 2hn bn serp; (ad lib: 2cl(Bb) bn(II) tp bugle 3tb b-dr).
SCHOLL **NYS-13ac** 3 mvts. 2ob 2cl 2hn 2bn cbn 2tp.
[unidentified Overture - possibly a misattribution since it does not match any known Méhul overture]
SCHOLZ **WES-84a** fl 2ob 2cl 2hn 2bn 2tp tb timp tri.

HERZOG, August
Stradella-Polka (piano, based on Flotow's opera, post-1844)
ANON **A-221a** pic fl 2ob cl(Eb) 3cl(Bb) 4hn 2bn 5tp a-hn 3tb b-hn/bomb b-dr t-dr. MS pts: D-DT, Mus-n205

HIMMEL, Friedrich Heinrich (1765 - 1814)
Fanchon das Leyermädchen (Liederspiel, 16 May 1804, Berlin)
ANON **A-222a** 2ob 2cl 2hn 2bn cbn.
Pc (sn: sl [= T. Weigl: Vienna], c.1810), MS parts: I-Fc, F.P. S.336.
DÜRING **JCD-1a** overture & 12 mvts. 2fl 2ob 2cl 2hn 2bn tp cb.
FENDT **AXF-3.5ad** introduzione & 7 mvts. pic 2cl(Eb/ob 2cl(Bb) 2hn 2bn b-tb.
LÖWENSTEIN **CAL-17a** overture & 48 mvts. fl(F, D, pic F, D) 2cl(C)/2cl(Eb) 2cl(Bb) 2hn 2bn tp b-tb cb.
SARTORIUS **GCS-2a** 7 mvts. 2cl 2hn 2bn cbn.
TAUSCH **FWT-1a** fl ob 2cl 2hn 2bn (cbn/db ad lib).
TRIEBENSEE **JZT-25a** overture & 9 mvts. 2ob 2cl 2hn 2bn (cbn tp ad lib).
Der Kobold (comic opera, 19 May 1813, Vienna; 23 March 1814, Berlin)
ANON **A-223a** 2 Theils. 2ob 2cl 2hn 2bn. Ms parts: I-Fc, F.P. S.376.
Schmerzenwalzer (piano, misattributed to Beethoven as K.-H. Anh 14, No. 2, c.1808 - 1811)
WIELAND **KZS-4ad** fl(F) 2ob 3cl 2hn 2bn b-tb serp.
Alexis und Ida, Op. 43 (Schäferroman in 46 Liedern, voice & piano, 1814, Leipzig)
ANON **A-224a** No. 40, Die Sendung ("An Alexis"). fl 2ob 3cl 2hn 2bn b-hn/tb.
MS parts: D-DT,Mus-n 1884, (missing ob I, bn I, 2tp).
KIRCHHOFF **WZK-34a** No. 40, Die Sendung ("An Alexis". fl 2ob 2cl 2hn 2bn tp tb db (?timp).
Pas de Manoeuvre
ANON **A-78.1/5m(a)** 2ob 2cl 2hn 2bn tp.
[unidentified movement in Anton Schneider's Divertissement, in F, AYS-1.]
SCHNEIDER, A. **AYS-48a** fl 2ob cl hn bn.

HITZIGMANN ( )
6 Walzer
 SCHNEIDER, A. **AYS-49a** fl 2ob 2cl 2hn 2bn tp b-tb 2vla cb.

HOFFMANN, Leopold (c.1730 - 1793)
Salve Regina (CA, 2vl vla organ)
 ANON **A-13va** Salve Regina, in B♭. CATB, 2cl 2hn 2bn.
 MS parts (1840): CZ-Bm(kb), A.46.850, (with duplicate vocal parts: 3S, 3A, 2T; the T & B parts are later
 copies dated 1880).

HOFFMEISTER, Franz Anton (1754 - 1812)
Der Königssohn aus Ithaka (Telemach, der Königssohn aus Ithaka) (opera, 27 June 1795, Vienna)
 SARTORIUS **GCS-3a** 9 mvts. 2cl 2hn 2bn cbn.
Rosalinde, oder die Macht der Feen (opera, 23 April 1796, Vienna)
 WENT **JNW-23a** overture & 13 mvts. fl 2ob 2hn 2bn.
Arie et Echo
 HAVEL **VXH-15.3ac, VXH-16.2ac** 2cl 2hn 2bn. (At VXH-16.2 the Echo is attributed to Pleyel)
Untraced arrangements: Der Königsohn aus Ithaka (2ob 2cl 2hn 2bn & 2cl 2hn 2bn versions), possibly arranged
 by the composer (pub: Hoffmeister: Vienna; advertized in *Wiener Zeitung,* 5 Sept 1795).

HOFFSTETTER, Roman (1742 - 1815)
String Quartet in C (formerly misattributed to F.J. Haydn, "Op. 3, No 3", Hob. III/14).
 GEBAUER, MJ. **MJG-1.1/8a** Minuetto & Trio as "Walzer", (in 3/8 rather than 3/4).
 fl(F) cl(F) 2cl(C) 2hn 2bn tp serp/b-tb b-dr cym tri, *or* fl(F) 2cl(C) 2hn 2bn serp.

HOOK, James (1746 - 1827)
*12 Songs (Listen to the Voice of Love; Lucy Gray of Allendale; Tarry awhile with me, My Love; Sweet Kathlane
[sic] McCree; The Match Box; The Celedonian [sic] Laddy; The Linnet; She lives in the Valley below; The
Cottager's Daughter; The Turtle Dove Coos round my Cot; I never lov'd any, Dear Mary, but you; A Soldier
for Me)* (various dates, Parry's arrangements pub. c.1803, London)
 PARRY, J. **JBP-1am** 2fl 2cl 2hn bn bn/serp.
Lowland Willy (A Favorite Song sung by Mrs. Wrighten at Vaux-Hall Gardens (song, pub. c.1785, London)
 ANON **A-202.3/21(a)** 2terz-fl 2bthn 2hn 2bn serp.
Upon my Word I did (A Favorite scotch song sung by Miss Pool at Vauxhall) (song, pub. 1787, London)
 ANON **A-202.3/16(a)** 2terz-fl 2bthn 2hn 2bn serp.

HORZALKA, Johann Friedrich (1798 - 1860)
6 Bassionierte [sic] Walzer [& 5 Allemandes]
 SCHNEIDER, A. **AYS-50a** fl(D, terz-fl, pic) 2ob 2cl 2hn 2bn tp(hn III) b-tb 2vla cb.

HRADECKÝ, Friedric (1776 - 1820)
(6) Variationen ut Coda (piano)
 HAVEL **VXH-5a** 2cl 2hn 2bn.

HUGO, *Prinz zu Hohenlohe-Öhringen (Fürst from 1849)* (1816 - 1897)
Prince Hugo regularly use the pseudonym "Siebeneicher", Seven Oaks.
Bathy Massurka [sic] (piano, c.1840)
 SCHOLZ **WES-85a** fl 2ob 2cl 2hn 2bn tb db.
Furuska Polka (piano, c.1843)
 SCHOLZ **WES-86a** fl 2ob 2cl 2hn 2bn 2tp tb db timp.
Masurek (piano, c.1845)
 SCHOLZ **WES-87a** fl 2ob 2cl 2hn 2bn tp tb db timp.
Melancholie-Polka, in C minor (piano, c.1845)
 SCHOLZ **WES-88a** fl 2ob 2cl 2hn 2bn 2tp tb db timp.
Polka, in F (piano, c.1845)
 SCHOLZ **WES-89a** fl 2ob 2cl 2hn 2bn tp tb db timp.
Setimatäts Polka (piano, c.1843)
 SCHOLZ **WES-90a** fl 2ob 2cl 3hn 2bn 2tp tb db.
Sylvester Polka (piano, c.1843)
 SCHOLZ **WES-91a** fl 2ob 2cl 2hn 2bn tb db.
Attributed Works
3 mvts interpolated in Eugen, Herzog von Württemberg's opera, Der Geisterbraut (1843)
 SCHOLZ **WES-92a** Marsch, fl 2ob 2cl 2hn 2bn 2tp tb db.
Anna Polka (piano, c.1840)
 SCHOLZ **WES-93a** fl 2ob 2cl 2hn 2bn 2tp tb db.
Electricitäts-Polka, c.1843)
 SCHOLZ **WES-94a** fl 2ob 2cl 2hn 2bn 2tp tb db timp.
Mitternachts-Polka (piano, c.1843)
 SCHOLZ **WES-95a** fl 2ob 2cl 2hn 2bn 2tp tb db.
Polka (piano, c.1843)
 SCHOLZ **WES-96a** fl 2ob 2cl 2hn 2bn 2tp tb db timp.
Die Ungetauften, Mazurka (piano, c.1843)
 SCHOLZ **WES-97a** fl 2ob 2cl 2hn 2bn tp tb db.

HUMMEL, Johann Nepomuk (1778 - 1837)
Helene und Paris, Op. 26 (ballet, 29 July 1807, Vienna)
    SEDLAK **WXS-24a** overture & 13 mvts.   2ob 2cl 2hn 2bn cbn.
    TRIEBENSEE **JZT-26a** 1 mvt (Andante espressivo/Scherzando).   2ob 2cl 2hn 2bn (cbn tp ad lib).
Der Zauberkampf (Harlequin in der Heimat) (pantomime, 24 May 1812, Vienna)
    ANON **A-225a** 2 Theils.   2ob 2cl 2hn 2bn cbn.
      Pc (sn: sl [= T. Weigl: Vienna], 1812), MS parts: I-Fc, F.P. S.360.
Die Eselshaut, oder Die blaue Insel (Prinzessin Eselshaut) (opera, 10 March 1814).
    SEDLAK **WXS-25a** overture & 6 mvts.   2ob 2cl 2hn 2bn cbn.
    STARKE (attrib) **FRS-14a** overture & 6 mvts.   pic 2ob 2cl 2hn 2bn (2tp) b-dr s-dr.
Die gute Nachricht, Op. 61 (Singspiel pastiche, 11 April 1814, Vienna; music by Hummel: overture & 3 mvts,
Beethoven, Gyrowetz, Kanne, Mozart, J. Weigl)
    ANON **A-226a** overture & 6 mvts.   2ob 2cl 2hn 2bn cbn.
      MS parts: I-Fc, F.P. S.401.
    ANON **A-227a** 2ob 2cl 2hn 2bn cbn.
      MS parts: I-Fc, F.P. S.387, (also includes mvts from *Die Strickleiter*).
    WIELAND **KZW-5ad** overture.   fl 2ob 2cl 2hn 2bn 2tp serp/(vlne + tb).
Die Rückfahrt des Kaisers, Op. 69 (opera, 13 June 1814, Vienna)
    SCHNEIDER, A. **AYS-51a** overture.   fl 2ob 2cl 2hn 2bn tp b-tb 2vla cb.
Sappho von Mytilene (Die Rache der Venus) (ballet, 10 Aug 1812, Vienna)
    SEDLAK **WXS-26a** overture.   2ob 2cl 2hn 2bn cbn 2tp.
Variations on a Theme from Vogler's Castor e Polluce, *Op. 6* (piano & orchestra, c.1795, Vienna)
    ANON **A-228a** fl 2ob 2cl 2hn 2bn tb.   MS parts: D-NEhz, 203, (bn I part imcomplete).
12 Menuetten und Trios. Zur Eröffnung des Apollo Saales in Wien, Op. 27 (orchestra, 1807, Vienna; pub for pf)
    ANON **A-229a** 2ob 2cl 2hn 2bn.   MS parts: I-Fc, F.P. S.481, No. 1., (as "Apollo-Taenze Nº 1")
Tänze componirt für den Apollo Saal [12 Minuets & Trios], Op. 28 (orchestra, 1808, Vienna; pub for piano)
    ANON **A-230a** 2ob 2cl 2hn 2bn.   MS parts: I-Fc, F.P. S.481, No. 2, (as "Apolo-Taenze [sic] Nº 2") .
Apollo-Saal-Tänze [6 Allemandes, 6 Deutsche], Op. 31 (orchestra, 1809, Vienna; pub for piano)
    ANON **A-231.1a, 231.2a** 2ob 2cl 2hn 2bn.   MS parts, I-Fc, F.P. S.481, (as "Nº 3. Sechs Menuetten [sic] samt
      Trios" and "Nº 4. Sechs Deutsche samt Trios").
[conjectured] Apollo-Saal-Tänze [6 Allemandes, 6 Deutsche], Op. 39 (orchestra, 1811, Vienna; pub for piano)
    ANON **A-232.1a, 232.2a** 2ob 2cl 2hn 2bn.   MS parts: I-Fc, F.P. S.481, (as "Nº 6 Sechs Menuetten samt Trios"
      and "Nº 7 [?4] Deutsche samt vielen Trios und Coda. Der Ausbruch des Vesuv[iu]s".)
[conjectured] 12 Deutsche Tänze, Op. 44 (orchestra, c.1811, Vienna; pub for piano)
    ANON **A-233a** 2ob 2cl 2hn 2bn.   I-Fc, F.P. S.481, (as "Apollo-Taenze [sic] Nº 5 Zwolf Deutsche samt Trios
      und Coda"). *We have not been able to examine this work; another possibility is the set of Redout-Deutsche,
      Op. 29 (1808).*
Apollo-Saal-Tänze [Intrada. Marcia, 6 Allemandes, 6 Deutsche], Op. 45 (orchestra, 1812, Vienna; pub for pf)
    ANON **A-234.1a, 234.2a** 2ob 2cl 2hn 2bn.   I-Fc, F.P. S.481, (as "Nº 8 Introductions=Marsch. Sechs Menuetten
      samt Trios" and "Nº 9 Sechs Deutsche samt Trios").
Notturno, Op. 99 (piano 4 hands, 1822, pub. 1824, Leipzig)
    ROSE, J.D. **JDR-1a** fl 4cl 2hn 2bn tp tb.
Cello Sonata, Op. 104 (cello & piano, 1824, pub. 1826, London)
    ANON **A-235a** 2nd mvt (Romance).   fl 2ob 2cl 2hn 2bn tp tb db.
      MS score & parts: D-NEhz, 54, No 4, (parts missing).
[unidentified] Cantata (This may be either *Lob der Freundschaft*, 1807, or *Euterpens Abschied*, 1812)
    ANON **A-236a** (? 2ob 2cl 2hn 2bn cbn).   MS parts (9): I-Fc. F.P. S.401.
unidentified "Marscha" [sic]
    ANON **A-237a** fl 2ob 3cl 2hn 2bn b-hn/tb.   MS parts: D-DT.Mus-n 1884, (missing ob I, bn I, 2tp).

HUMPERDINCK, Engelbert (1854 - 1921)
Das Mirakel (Der Wunder, The Miracle) (pantomime, 23 Dec 1911, London)
    EMERSON **GZE-1.2a** prelude.   2fl ob 3cl hn bn.

ISOUARD (often known as "Nicolo"), Nicolò (1775 - 1818)
Michel-Ange (opera, 11 Dec 1802, Paris)
    ANON **A-238a** overture.   2ob 2cl 2hn 2bn cbn 2tp.   MS parts (c.1825): CZ-Bm(au), A.37.344.
    KRECHLER **FFK-19.1a** overture & 4 mvts.   2ob 2cl 2hn 2bn (cbn tp ad lib).
    SCHNEIDER, A. **AYS-52a** overture & 7 mvts.   fl 2ob 2cl 2hn 2bn cb.
    VANDERHAGEN **AJV-11a** overture.   2fl 2cl 2hn 2bn, (ad lib: tp serp).
Les Confidences (opera, 31 March 1803, Paris)
    VANDERHAGEN **AJV-12a** 2fl 2cl 2hn 2bn, (ad lib: tp tb serp).
Le Médecin Turc (Der türkische Arzt) (opera, 15 Nov 1803, Paris)
    SCHMITT, G. **GYS-31a** overture.   3fl 2ob 4cl 4hn 2bn 2tp serp.
    TRIEBENSEE **JZT-27a** overture.   2ob 2cl 2hn 2bn (cbn tp ad lib).
    VANDERHAGEN **AJV-13a** overture.   2fl 2cl 2hn 2bn, (ad lib: tp tb serp).
Un Jour à Paris (Ein Tag in Paris) (opera, 24 May 1808, Paris)
    ANON **A-239a** 3 Acts.   2ob 2cl 2hn 2bn cbn.
      Pc (Im Verlage des Thadé Weigl: Wien, sd, c.1809), MS parts: I-Fc, F.P. S.367.

Cendrillon (Aschenbrödel) (opera, 22 Feb 1810, Paris; 2 April 1811, Vienna)
ANON **A-240a** Romance, Almerlied, (2) Ländler. 2ob 2cl 2hn 2bn cbn 2tp. MS pts: CZ-Bm(au), A.36.851.
ANON **A-241.1a** overture & 12 mvts. 2ob 2cl 2hn 2bn cbn.
   Pc (Im Verlage der k:k: priv. chemischen Druckery: Vienna, pn 1701, 1702, 1811), **J9**, No. IV, Abtheil 1 & 2,
      parts: CZ-Bm(au), (MS parts) (Abth. 1, copy dated 29 Jan 1840) A.36.848, (Abth. 2) A.35.168; CZ-Pnm,
      Lobkovic X.G.f.68, (complete; there are also MS parts prepared by Krechler at X.G.f.64: overture, and
      X.G.f.65: overture with Nos. 8 & 12); H-Bn, Z 25,516, (Abth. 1 only); US-Wc, M959.I.
ANON **A-241.2a** overture & 12 mvts. 2cl 2hn 2bn.
   Pc (Im Verlage der k.k. pr. chemische Druckerey: Wien, pn 1703, 1704, 1811), **J6**, No. IV, Abtheil 1 & 2, pts:
      CZ-KRa, A3894/IV.B.57, (Abth. 1, overture & 4 mvts, MS by Havel, 1813/14); H-Bn, Z 25,515 (complete).
ANON **A-242a** overture & 11 mvts. 2ob 2cl 2hn 2bn cbn.
   Pc (T. Weigl: Wien, c.1810), MS parts: A-Ee, Mus.1124; I-Fc, F.P. S.356. *(A-Ee Doc. A.M. 4089 is*
   Weigl's bill of Sept. 4 1811, Prince Nikolas Esterházy's payment authorization for 100 gulden &
   Kapellmeister Johann Fuchs's receipt.
ANON **A-243a** overture & 7 mvts. 2ob 2cl 2hn 2bn cbn. MS pts: D-Rtt, Sm. 13, Nos. 26 - 33. *Probably*
   based on the T. Weigl: Vienna edition rather than that of the Chemische Druckerei.
GEBAUER, F.R. **FRG-2a** Suite 1: 6 mvts, Suite 2: 6 mvts. fl 2cl 2hn 2bn (serp/cb ad lib).
SCHNEIDER, A. **AYS-53a** overture & 16 mvts. fl(pic) 2ob 2cl 2hn 2bn tp b-tb 2vla vlne.
TRIEBENSEE **JZT-28a** overture & 16 mvts. 2ob 2cl 2hn 2bn (cbn tp ad lib).
Le Billet de loterie (Die Lotterieloos) (opera, 14 Sept 1811, Paris)
ANON **A-244a** 2 Theils. 2ob 2cl 2hn 2bn cbn tp.
   Pc (sn: sl [= T. Weigl: Vienna], c.1812), MS parts: I-Fc, F.P. S.357.
KRECHLER **FFK-22.2a** 5 mvts. 2ob 2cl 2hn 2bn (cbn tp ad lib).
Le Magicien sans magie (Die natürliche Zaubery) (comic opera, 4 Nov 1811, Paris)
ANON **A-245a** 2 Theils. 2ob 2cl 2hn 2bn cbn.
   Pc (sn: sl [= T. Weigl: Vienna], c.1812), MS parts: I-Fc, F.P. S.403.
Alamon, Prince de Catane (Le Prince de Catane; Monson Fürst von Cataneo) (opera, 4 March 1813, Paris)
ANON **A-246a** 2ob 2cl 2hn 2bn cbn. MS parts: I-Fc, F.P. S.403.
Joconde (opera, 28 Feb 1814, Paris)
· ANON **A-247a** overture. fl cl(Eb) 3cl(Bb) 2hn 2bn tp tb serp b-dr t-dr. MS parts: D-DT, Mus-n 549.
SEDLAK **WXS-1.1a.** overture & 9 mvts. 2ob 2cl 2hn 2bn cbn.
SEDLAK **WXS-27a** overture & 11 mvts. 2ob 2cl 2hn 2bn cbn (2tp).
Jeannot et Colin (opera, 17 Oct 1814, Paris)
ANON **A-248a** 4 Theils. 2ob 2cl 2hn 2bn cbn. Ms parts: I-Fc, F.P. S.403.
Geschwindmarsch (unidentified)
ANON **A-74.3/12m(a)** pic quart-fl 2ob cl(F) 2cl(C) 4hn 2bn cbn+serp/2b-hn 2tp 3tb b-dr t-dr tamb cym.
Untraced arrangements: L'Impromptu de Campagne (opera, 1797); Léonce (opera, 1805), L'Intrigue aux Fenêtres
(opera, 1805), Lully et Quinault (opera, 1812); Aladin (opera, 1822). In virtually all cases, these are arrangements
said to have been published in Paris.

JADIN, Louis Emmanuel (1768 - 1853)
Chasse, in F
LEROY **PQL-1.7/3(a)** 2fl(F) 2ob 2cl(III & IV, C) 2hn (2)bn tp serp timp.
Ouverture, in F
LEROY **PQL-1.3/1(a)** 2p-fl(F) 2cl(F) 2cl(C) 2hn 2bn tp serp b-dr.
Ouverture, in F
LEROY **PQL-1.7/1(a)** 2fl(F) 2ob 2cl(III & IV, C) 2hn 2bn tp serp timp
Rondeau, in F
LEROY **PQL-1.5/2(a)** 2fl(F) 2cl(F) 2cl(C) 2hn 2bn tp serp b-dr.

JANÁČEK, Leoš (1854 - 1928)
Valašské tance (Lašské tance; Lachian Dances) (orchestra, 1890, Brno)
SHEEN **GHS-10a** 2fl 2ob 2cl 2hn 2bn (cbn ad lib).

JESCHKO, L.
Grillchen Polka (piano)
ANON **A-249a** pic 2ob cl(Eb) cl(solo Bb) 3cl(Bb) 4hn 2bn 3tp t-hn 3tb b-hn/bomb timp b-dr s-dr.
   MS parts: D-DT, Mus-n 1525, No. 2, (the title states, "Nach dem Clavier[auszug]").

JOPLIN, Scott (1868 - 1917)
Great Crush Collision March (piano, 1896, Temple, Texas)
GILLASPIE **JAG-13a** 2ob/fl+ob 2cl 2hn 2bn cbn.
Maple Leaf Rag (piano, 1899, Sedalia, Missouri)
GILLASPIE **JAG-14a** 2ob/fl+ob 2cl 2hn 2bn cbn.
The Easy Winners (piano, 1901, St Louis, Missouri)
TAYLORSON **JST-7a** fl 2ob 2cl 2hn 2bn cbn/db.
A Breeze from Alabama, March and Two-Step (piano, 1902, St Louis, Missouri)
GILLASPIE **JAG-20a** 2ob 2ca 2hn 2bn db/cbn.
Cleopha, March and Two Step (piano, 1902, St Louis, Missouri)
GILLASPIE **JAG-6a** fl ob 2cl 2hn 2bn cbn.
The Entertainer, A Ragtime Two Step (piano, 1902, St Louis, Missouri)
CAWKWELL **RXC-1a.** No 1. 2ob 2cl 2hn 2bn cbn.
GILLASPIE **JAG-7a** fl ob 2cl 2hn 2bn cbn.
GILLASPIE **JAG-22a** 2ob 2ca 2hn 2bn db/cbn.

The Cascades, a Rag (piano, 1904, St Louis, Missouri).
GILLASPIE **JAG-11a** fl ob 2cl 2hn 2bn cbn.
TAYLORSON **JST-8a** fl 2ob 2cl 2hn 2bn cbn/db.
The Chrysanthemum - An Afro-Intermezzo (piano, 1904, St Louis, Missouri)
SCHMIDT, W.J. **WJS-1a** pic fl ob 2cl b-cl a-sax t-sax 2bn.
Bethena, a Concert Waltz (piano, 1905, St Louis, Missouri)
GILLASPIE **JAG-8a** fl ob 2cl 2hn 2bn cbn.
Eugenia (piano, 1905, Chicago).
GILLASPIE **JAG-15a** 2ob/fl+ob 2cl 2hn 2bn cbn.
The Ragtime Dance (piano, 1906, St Louis, Missouri & New York)
CAWKWELL **RXC-1a** No 2. 2ob 2cl 2hn 2bn cbn.
GILLASPIE **JAG-16a** fl ob 2cl 2hn 2bn cbn.
The Pine Apple Rag (piano, 1908, New York)
GILLASPIE **JAG-18a** 2ob/fl+ob 2cl 2hn 2bn cbn.
Euphonic Sounds, A Syncopated Novelty (piano, 1909, New York)
GILLASPIE **JAG-9a** fl ob 2cl 2hn 2bn cbn.
Pleasant Moments, Ragtime Waltz (piano, 1909, New York)
GILLASPIE **JAG-21a** 2ob 2ca 2hn 2bn db(ad lib).
Solace, A Mexican Serenade (piano, 1909, New York)
GILLASPIE **JAG-12a** fl ob 2cl 2hn 2bn cbn.
Stoptime Rag (piano, 1910, New York)
GILLASPIE **JAG-10a** fl ob 2cl 2hn 2bn cbn.
Scott Joplin's New Rag (piano, 1912, New York)
GILLASPIE **JAG-17a** 2ob/fl+ob 2cl 2hn 2bn cbn.
Magnetic Rag (piano, 1914, New York)
GILLASPIE **JAG-19a** 2ob/fl+ob 2cl 2hn 2bn cbn.

JOUVE, Joseph
The Austrian Retreat (piano or band, c.1800, London)
HALE **SYH-1.5m(a)** fl 2cl 2hn bn serp.
The Downfall of Paris (piano, c.1800, London)
HALE **SYH-1.11m(a)** 2fl 2cl 2hn bn serp.

KALKBRENNER, Friedrich Wilhelm Michael (1785 - 1849)
Rondo Villageoise, Op. 67 (piano, 1823)
STARKE **FRS-15a** 2ob 2cl 2hn 2bn cbn 2tp.
(unidentified movement, Allegro, 4/4 (piano)
RUMMEL **CFR-1a** 2ob/fl 2cl 2hn 2bn cbn.
(unidentified) Introduction et Polonaise d'après des Thémes de Kalkbrenner & Kalliwoda, Op. 13 (piano)
FISCHER **CYF-4a** fl(F) 2ob cl(Eb) 3cl(Bb) 4hn 2/3bn 2tp a-tb t-tb b-tb serp b-dr t-dr; (ad lib: fl in C).

KALLIWODA, Johann Wenzel (1801 - 1866)
Ouverture No. 1 in D minor, Op. 38 (orchestra, 1839, Leipzig)
SCHOLZ **WES-98a** fl 2ob 2cl 2hn 2bn tb db.
Messe
RINSLER **ZZR-1v** SATB, winds.
(unidentified) Introduction et Polonaise d'après des Thémes de Kalkbrenner & Kalliwoda, Op. 13 (piano)
FISCHER **CYF-4a** fl(F) 2ob cl(Eb) 3cl(Bb) 4hn 2/3bn 2tp a-tb t-tb b-tb serp b-dr t-dr; (ad lib: fl in C).

KANNE, Friedrich August (1778 - 1833)
Orpheus (opera, 10 Nov 1807, Vienna)
KRECHLER **FFK-6.10a, 12.4a** Marche. 2ob 2cl 2hn 2bn cbn tp.
TRIEBENSEE **JZT-29a** duetto. 2ob 2cl 2hn 2bn (cbn ad lib).
Miranda oder Das Schwert der Rache (heroische Oper, 14 Sept 1811, Vienna)
ANON **A-250a** 2ob 2cl 2hn 2bn cbn. MS parts: I-Fc, F.P. S.380.
KRECHLER **FFK-6.7a, FFK-7.5a** marche. 2ob 2cl 2hn 2bn cbn tp.

KAUER, Ferdinand (1751 - 1831)
Die Serenade (Singspiel, 4 June 1792, Vienna)
ANON **A-251a** 2ob 2cl 2hn 2bn cbn. MS parts: I-Fc, F.P. S.366.
Ritter Willibald oder Das goldene Garfäss (Singspiel, 13 June 1793, Vienna)
ANON **A-3.1a** overture. 2ob 2cl 2hn 2bn.
Das Donauweibchen (opera, Teil 1: 11 Jan 1798, Teil 2: 13 Feb 1798, Vienna)
ANON **A-4.4a** 1 mvt. 2ob 2cl 2hn 2bn cbn.
ANON **A-252a** 6 mvts. 2cl 2hn 2bn. MS parts: CZ-Kra, A4454/R.T.24, No 3.
ANON **A-253a** aria. 2cl 2hn 2bn. MS parts: CZ-KRa, A3878/IV.B.41. (3rd mvt added to Hoffmeister's Sextetto FAH-29).
SARTORIUS **GCS-4a** 7 mvts. 2cl 2hn 2bn cbn.
SCHMITT, G. **GYS-32a** overture. 2fl 2ob 2cl 2hn 2bn 2tp serp.
SCHNEIDER, A. **AYS-54a** 2 romances. (Theil 2, "Ich thron auf Silber wellen"; Theil 1, "In meinen Schloss ists gar fein"). fl 2ob 4cl 2hn 2bn tp b-tb serp.
Die Brüder von Stauffenberg (Volksmärchen, 5 Sept 1818, Vienna)
STARKE **FRS-16a** overture & 6 mvts. 2ob 2cl 2hn 2bn cbn 2tp.

KÉLER BÉLA, (*pseudonym* i.e., Adalbert Paul von Kéler) (1820 - 1882)
Lustspiel Overture, Op. 73 (orchestra, c.1863 - 1870, Wiesbaden)
  TAYLORSON **JST-9a** fl ob 2cl 2hn 2bn cbn/db.

KINSKY (Kinky), Josef (active 1790 - post-1815)
Das ländlich Fest im Wäldchen bei Kis-Ber (ballet divertimento, 19 Nov 1815, Vienna)
  SEDLAK **WXS-3.2a** 5 mvts. 2ob 2cl 2hn 2bn cbn.
  STARKE **FRS-17a** overture & 8 mvts. 2ob 2cl 2hn 2bn cbn 2tp.
Die kleine Dieben (ballet, 21 Nov 1815, Vienna).
  SEDLAK **WXS-1.3a** overture & 7 mvts. 2ob 2cl 2hn 2bn cbn.

KIRNBERGER, Johann Philipp (1721 - 1783)
Miserere (Introduzione, 14 mvts & Canon)
  DRUSCHETZKY **GYD-2va** SATB, 2cl 2hn 2bn organ.

KLIEGL, H.A.
Jägerlust Galopp
  ANON **A-254.1a** fl 2ob 2cl 3hn 2bn b+tb.   MS score: D-NEhz, 114b.
  ANON **A-254.2a** fl 2ob 2cl 2hn 2bn tb db.   MS parts: D-NEhz, 133, No. 27.

KLOSS, Carl (1792 - 1853)
"Da unten ist Friede" Militair-Musik
  KAISER **KAK-3a** cl(E♭) 2cl(B♭) 4hn 2tp t-hn bar tu.

KOCH, Erland von
En sommarlåt (A summer tune)
  MORBERG **GOM-1a** 2fl 2ob 2cl 2hn 2bn.

KÖHLER, Ernst
Fest Ouverture, in E♭ (organ, c.1840)
  SCHOLZ **WES-99a** fl 2ob 2cl 2hn 2bn tp tb db timp.

KORNLEIN, ( )
Kegeltanz (pre-1847)
  PIRNSLER **XYP-1a** fl ob 2cl 2hn bn tp tb.

KOTZWARA (Koczwara), Franz (František) (? - 1791)
The Battle of Prague (piano with vl vc & ad lib drum, pre-1789, London)
  HOLYOKE **SAH-1ma** 2cl(C) 2hn basso.

KOZELUCH (Koželuh), Leopold (1752 - 1818)
La ritrovata figlia di Ottone II (Die wiedergessundene Tochter Kaiser Otto des II) (ballo eroico, 24 Feb 1794, Vienna).
  HAVEL **VXH-6a** overture & 9 mvts. 2cl 2hn bn.
  HAVEL **VXH-1ad** overture & 16 mvts. 2cl 2hn 2bn. *Essentially WENT, JNW-24.3a with transpositions.*
  SARTORIUS **GCS-5a** Theil II: 9 mvts. 2cl 2hn 2bn cbn.
  WENT **JNW-24.1a** overture & 16 mvts. 2ob 2cl 2hn 2bn; (some MSS with later cbn pt).
  WENT **JNW-24.2a** overture & 16 mvts. 2ob 2ca 2hn 2bn.
  WENT **JNW-24.3a** overture & 13 mvts. 2cl 2hn 2bn.
Parthia in F (as "Cassazion") (2fl 2cl 2hn 2bn).
  VOGEL **KXV-1a** fl 2cl 2hn 2bn 2vla.

KRAUS, Joseph Martin (1756 - 1792)
Amphitryon (1784, Paris)
  GRENSER **JFG-1a** Intermedes. 2ob 3cl 2hn 2bn.

KREUTZER, [Conradin or Rodolphe]
Marche, in D
  WIELAND **KZW-1mad** fl(F) 2ob 2cl 2hn 2bn 2tp b-tb serp.
Adagio, 3/8
  WENUSCH **SXW-1.5a** cl(E♭) 2cl(B♭) 2hn bn tp(prin).

KREUTZER, Conradin (1780 - 1849)
Feodora (Fedora) (opera, 8 March 1812, Munich; 23 Feb 1818, Vienna)
  SCHMITT, G. **GYS-33.1a** overture & 6 mvts. 2fl 2ob 2cl 2hn 2bn tp tb db.
  SCHMITT, G. **GYS-33.2a** quartetto ("So sieget denn"). 2fl 2ob 2cl 2hn 2bn tp tb db.
Conradin von Schwaben (opera, 30 March 1812, Stuttgart; 1822, Vienna; composed 1805)
  ANON **A-255a** 2ob 2cl 2hn 2bn cbn. MS parts: I-Fc, F.P. S.402.
Die Alpenhütte (opera, 1 March 1815, Stuttgart)
  LÖWENSTEIN **CAL-18a** overture & 13 mvts. fl(D♭) 2cl(C, E♭) 2cl(B♭) 2hn 2bn tp b-tb cb.
  SCHMITT, G. **GYS-34a** overture & 6 mvts. 2fl 2ob 2cl 2hn 2bn tp tb db.
Das Nachtlager in Granada (opera, 14 Jan 1834, Vienna)
  ANON **A-256a** romance (Lied). fl 2ob cl(E♭) 3cl(B♭) 4hn 2bn 2tp tp(ventile) kl-hn 3tb serp b-dr s-dr.
    MS parts: D-DT, Mus-n 1696.
  KIRCHHOFF **WZK-35a** "Das mir alles". fl 2ob 2cl 2hn 2bn tp tb db.
  LEGRAND **WYL-21a** 2 mvts (Jagd Chor, Bolero). fl ob 2cl 2hn 2bn (bn III ad lib).
  SCHOLZ **WES-100.1a** overture. fl 2ob 2cl 2hn 2bn tp tb db timp.
  SCHOLZ **WES-100.2a** romance. fl 2ob 2cl 2hn tb db.
  SCHOLZ **WES-100.3a** quintett. fl 2ob 2cl 2hn 2bn tb db.
Der Verschwender oder Millionär und Bettler (opera, 20 Feb 1834, Vienna)
  ANON **A-15.7(a)** introduction. 2cl(E♭) 2cl(B♭) 2hn 2bn 2tp.

Der Apollosaal (operette, sd, Vienna)
ANON **A-257a** 2ob 2cl 2hn 2bn cbn.   MS parts: I-Fc, F.P. S.402.
Der deutshe Rhein (Männerchor, c.1830)
LÖWENSTEIN **CAL-19a** pic(F) cl(E♭) 2cl(B♭) 3hn 2bn tp b-tb+cb, (ad lib: tp II).
À la Chasse, col Echo
SCHNEIDER, A. **AYS-55a** fl 2ob 2cl+2cl(rip) 2hn 2bn b-tb.
Funf Frühlings Lieder von Uhland, Op. 33 (voice & piano, c.1820)
SCHNEIDER, A. **AYS-56a** fl 2ob 2cl+2cl(rip) 3hn 2bn b-tb serp.
Neun Wander Lieder von Uhland, Op. 34 (voice & piano, c.1820)
SCHNEIDER, A. **AYS-57a** fl 2ob 2cl+2cl(rip) 3hn 2bn b-tb serp.

KREUTZER, Rodolphe (1766 - 1831)
Paul et Virginie (opera, 15 Jan 1791, Paris)
FUCHS, G.F. **GFF-19a** overture. 4cl 2hn 2bn tp serp, *or* 2cl 2hn 2bn.
OZI **EXO-1.32/1a** 3 mvts. 2cl 2hn 2bn.
SCHMITT, G. **GYS-35.1a** overture. fl 2ob 4cl 4hn 2bn 2tp 2tb serp.
SCHMITT, G. **GYS-35.2a** untitled mvt. 3fl 2ob 4cl 2hn 2bn cbn 2tp tb perc.
SCHMITT, G. **GYS-35.3a** Chor des Nègres. 2fl 2ob 4cl 2hn 2bn cbn.
SCHMITT, G. **GYS-35.4a** finale. fl 2ob 4cl 4nn 2bn 2tp 2tb serp.
Lodoïska (opera, 1 Aug 1791, Paris)
ANON **A-78.2/1m(a)** overture. 2pic 2quart-fl 2cl(C) 2hn 2bn 2tp serp b-dr+cym.
HALE **SYH-1.10m(a)** march. 2fl 2cl 2hn bn serp.
KRECHLER **FFK-15a** overture & 2 mvts. 2ob 2cl 2hn 2bn cbn tp.
KRECHLER **FFK-16a** 2ob 2cl 2hn 2bn.
LÖWENSTEIN **CAL-20a** overture. 2cl(C) 2hn 2bn b-tb.
WIELAND **KZW-6ad** overture. pic 2ob 2cl 2hn 2bn 2tp serp/vlne.
Le Journée de Marathon (grand opera, 1793, Paris)
KREUTZER, R. **RZK-1ma** overture. 2p-fl 2cl(C) 2hn 2bn tp b-tb serp timp.
Antonius und Cleopatra (ballet, 1808, Vienna)
SEDLAK **WXS-3.4a** 2 mvts. 2ob 2cl 2hn 2bn cbn. 1 mvt & marcia.

KREUZENACHER, ( )
Favorit-Polka, in F (piano, c.1845)
SCHOLZ **WES-101a** fl 2ob 2cl 2hn 2bn tp tb db timp.

KROMMER (Kramář), Franz (František) (1759 - 1831)
Symphony (Op. 12) (1803, Vienna)
SCHMITT, G. **GYS-36a** 2fl 2ob 2cl 2hn 2bn tb db.
TRIEBENSEE **JZT-30a** 2ob 2cl 2hn 2bn (cbn tp ad lib).
Concerto for 2 clarinets, Op. 35
CRUSELL **BXC-2a** 2 solo cl, 2fl 2cl(Eb) 3cl(Bb) 4hn 2bn serp 2tp 3tb perc.
Unidentified 4 movement work as "Parthia, E♭" (The 1804 *Erster Nachtrag* of Johann Traeg und Sohn, Vienna, lists on p. 28 a "Parthia a la Turque [sic]" by Krommer as No. 235 of the section, "Harmonie pour plusieurs Instrumens". It is possible that this untraced work served as the basis for Reznicek's arrangement.)
REZNICEK **XZR-1a** pic(E♭) cl(A♭) 4cl(E♭) cl(B♭) 4hn 3bn 2kl-tp 5tp(2E♭, A♭, B♭, G) contrabassi b-dr s-dr.
Parthia in B♭, Op. 45, No. 1 (2ob 2cl 2hn 2bn cbn; tp ad lib, pub, 1803, Vienna = FVK-1)
HAVEL **VXH-7a** (as "Parthia 3tia", 1808). 2cl 2hn 2bn tp(ad lib).
Parthia in E♭, Op. 45, No. 2 (2ob 2cl 2hn 2bn cbn; tp ad lib, pub. 1803, Vienna = FVK-2)
HAVEL **VXH-8a** (as "Nro 3 [Parthia]"). 2cl 2hn 2bn.
Parthia in B♭, Op. 45, No. 3 (2ob 2cl 2hn 2bn cbn; tp ad lib, pub. 1803, Vienna = FVK-3)
HAVEL **VXH-9a** (as "Nro. 2 Parthia in B[♭]", 1808). 2cl 2hn 2bn tp(ad lib).
Harmonie in F, Op. 57 (2ob 2cl 2hn 2bn cbn, pub. 1807, Vienna = FVK-4)
HAVEL **VXH-10a** (as "Nro. 1mo Parthia in F", 1808). 2cl 2hn 2bn tp(ad lib).
Harmonie in B♭ Op. 67 (2ob 2cl 2hn 2bn cbn, pub. 1807/1808, Vienna = FVK-5)
HAVEL **VXH-11a** (as "Parthia V in B[♭]"). 2cl 2hn 2bn tp(ad lib).
Harmonie in E♭, Op. 69 (2ob 2cl 2hn 2bn cbn, pub. 1808, Vienna = FVK-6)
HAVEL **VXH-12a** (as "Parthia IVta", 1808). 2cl 2hn 2bn tp(ad lib).
Parthia in E♭ (2ob 2cl 2hn 2bn, FVK-14.1)
ROSINACK **FJR-3as** 2ob cl bn.
Partita in E♭ (2ob 2cl 2hn 2bn, FVK-16)
HAVEL **VXH-13a** (as "Nro 6 Parthia in dis", c.1808), 2 mvts. 2cl 2hn 2bn.
Partita in E♭ (2ob 2cl 2hn 2bn, FVK-17)
HAVEL **VXH-14a** (as "Partita Nro 1mo in dis", 1808). 2cl 2hn 2bn.
Parthia in E♭ (2ob 2cl 2hn 2bn, FVK-18.1)
ROSINACK **FJR-1as** 2ob cl bn.
Harmonie in Es [E♭] (2ob 2cl 2hn 2bn, FVK-19.1)
ROSINACK **FJR-5as** 2ob cl bn.
Partita in B♭ (2ob 2cl 2hn 2bn, FVK-20)
ROSINACK **FJR-2as** 2ob cl bn.
Parthia in B♭ (2ob 2cl 2hn 2bn, FVK-21.1)
HAVEL **VXH-15a** (as "Nro 2do Parthia in B", 1808). 2cl 2hn 2bn.
Parthia in E♭, "La Chasse" (2ob 2cl 2hn 2bn, FVK-23)
ROSINACK **FJR-6as** 2ob cl bn.
STARKE **FRS-18a** (= **FRS-1.3a**) mvt 1 only, here in F. 2ob 2cl 2hn 2bn cbn.
[4] Variatione & Finalle [sic]
HAVEL **VXH-15.1ac, 15.2ac** 2cl 2hn 2bn. (= KROMMER, FVK-12.1d, FVK-12.2d)
[unidentified work - ?String Quartet]
ROSINACK **FJR-4as** 2ob cl bn.

KRUMPHOLZ (as "Krämplpelz"), ( ) (?Wenzel, 1750 - 1817)
6 Walzer
SCHNEIDER, A. **AYS-58a** fl 2ob 2cl 2hn 2bn tp b-tb 2vla cb.

KUBÍČEK (Kubitschek), Adalbert (c.1776 - 1838)
4 Deutsche (piano, c.1830, Brno)
ANON **A-23.2a** cl(D) 2hn 2bn 2tp. MS parts: CZ-Bm(au), A.36.666, No. 2.
5 Deutsche (piano, c.1830, Brno)
ANON **A-23.3a** cl(D) 2hn 2bn 2tp. MS parts: CZ-Bm(au), A.36.666, No. 3.
2 Deutsche (piano, c.1830, Brno)
ANON **A-258.1a, 258.2a** incomplete: hn I, bn I, tp I & II only.
  MS parts (1831): CZ-Bm(au), A.35.235, Nos. 1 & 2. *(See also* STRAUSS, Johann, *the Elder)*
Untraced. Československý Hudební Slovník (Starní Vydavatelství: Praha, 1963) cites an arrangement of a set of piano variations on a theme from Rossini's *Tancredi* in CZ-Bm(rj); we have not been able to trace this work.

KÜCKEN, Friedrich Wilhelm (1810 - 1882)
Der Prätendent (comic opera, 19 Nov 1847, Hamburg)
ANON **A-259a** overture. pic 2ob cl(Eb) 3cl(Bb) 4hn 2bn 3tp kl-hn t-hn 3tb vc/b b-dr s-dr.
  MS parts: D-DT, Mus-n 593, (the title states, "aus dem Clavier=Auszug arrang:").
SCHOLZ **WES-102a** overture & 3 Bands. fl 2ob 2cl 2hn 2bn tp tb db timp.

KÜFFNER, Joseph (Josef) (1776 - 1856)
Der Kornett (Cornet) (operette, 12 May 1831, Würzburg)
MARPURG **WYM-1.1(a)** 1 mvt. pic 2ob cl(Eb) 3cl(Bb) 2hn 2bn 2tp a-tb t-tb b-tb serp b-dr t-dr.
Vierzehn Tänze für Orchester, Op. 252
ANON **A-14.2a, 20.14a** No. 5, Galope. fl(pic Eb) ob cl(Eb) 2cl(Bb) 2hn bn 2tp b-tb serp.
Polacca Moderato
WIDDER **YYW-1.23a** 2fl 2cl 2hn 2bn.
Walzer & Trio
LÖWENSTEIN **CAL-8.54(a)** terz-fl 2cl(Eb) 2cl(Bb) 2hn 2bn tp b-tb cb.

KÜHN, Josef Karl (1803 - ?)
Der alte Feldherr (Liederspiel, ?1830s) *Not listed in any source; we note a Liederspiel of this title by Karl von Holtei (1798 - 1880), performed 11 Dec 1825, Berlin.*
SCHMITT, G. **GYS-37a** (= **A-10.32a**) Walzer. fl 2ob 3cl 2hn 2bn tb db.

KÜHNER, Wilhelm (1812 - ?)
Errinerungs-Galopp (piano, c.1845)
SCHOLZ **WES-103a** fl 2ob 2cl 2hn 2bn tp tb db timp.
Europa-Walzer (piano, c.1845)
SCHOLZ **WES-104a** fl 2ob 2cl 3hn 2bn tb db timp.
Hugo Galopp (piano, c.1843)
SCHOLZ **WES-105a** fl 2ob 2cl 3hn 2bn tb db timp.
Potpourri über Tema's aus Auber's des Teufels Antheil [= Le Part du diable] (piano, c.1844)
ANON **A-260a** fl 2ob 2cl 2hn 2bn tb db. MS score: D-NEhz, 207, No 1.
Der Rheinländer, Walzer (piano, sd)
ANON **A-261a** fl 2ob 2cl 2hn 2bn tb db. MS score: D-NEhz, 207, No 2.
Tyrolienne, Op. 68, No. 3 (piano, sd)
ANON **A-262a** fl 2ob 2cl 2hn 2bn tb db. MS score: D-NEhz, 207, No 3.

KÜRZINGER, Paul Ignaz (c.1755 - post-1820)
Robert und Kallisto, oder Der Triumph der Treue (Singspiel, 15 Oct 1780, Regensburg; revived 1794, Vienna)
SÜSSMAYR **FXS-1a** 1 mvt, quintetto. 2cl 2hn 2bn

KUHLAU, Daniel Friedrich Rudolph (1786 - 1832)
Trylleharpen (Die Zauberharfe) (opera, 30 Jan 1817, Copenhagen)
SCHNEIDER, A. **AYS-59a** overture. fl 2ob 4cl(C) 3hn 2bn tp b-tb cb.
Elisa (Elise) (opera, 17 April 1820, Copenhagen)
SCHNEIDER, A. **AYS-60a** overture. fl 2ob 2cl(A)+2cl(rip, C) 2hn 2bn tp b-tb serp.

KUNZ, Max
Bayernhymne
WALDEMAIER **APW-1a** 2fl 2ob 2cl 2bn.

KUNZE, G.
Schottischer Walzer (Nachtviolen-Sternschnuppen)
ANON **A-263a** pic 2ob cl(Eb) 3cl(Bb) 4hn 2bn 2tp kl-hn t-hn 3tb b-hn b-dr s-dr. MS pts: D-DT, Mus-n 593.

KUNZEN, Friedrich Ludwig Aemilius (1761 - 1817)
Das Fest der Winter [Winzer], oder Die Weinlese (Das Winzerfest) (Singspiel, 3 May 1793, Frankfurt am Main)
LÖWENSTEIN **CAL-21a** overture. 2cl 2hn bn b-tb.
LÖWENSTEIN **CAL-3.3ac** aria. fl(D) 4cl(C) 2hn 2bn.
SIMONI (SIMONY) **ZYS-1a** 22 mvts. 2fl 2hn basso.

LAADE, Friedrich (1820 - ?)
Künstler-Grüsse Walzer (piano, c.1848)
SCHOLZ **WES-106a** fl 2ob 2cl 2hn 2bn tp tb db timp.

LABITZKY, Joseph (1802 - 1881)
Sophien-Walzer, Op. 51 (piano, c.1841)
   ANON **A-264.1a** fl 2ob 2cl 3hn 2bn tb. MS score: D-NEhz, 114a.
   ANON **A-264.2a** fl 2ob 2cl 2hn 2bn tb db. MS score: D-NEhz, 133, No 30.
Charlotten Polka (piano, c.1843)
   SCHOLZ **WES-107a** fl 2ob 2cl 2hn 2bn tp tb db timp.
Mephisto-Galopp, Op. 84 (piano, 1843)
   ANON **A-265a** fl 2ob cl(E♭) cl(solo B♭) 3cl(B♭) 4hn 2bn a-hn 3tb b-hn/bomb.
   MS parts: D-DT, Mus-n 1770, No. 1.
Die Elfen-Walzer, Op. 86 (piano, 1842, Prague)
   WIESER **FAW-19a** terz-fl cl(E♭) 2cl(B♭) 2hn 2bn tp b-tb cb timp.
Druskeniky-Mazurka, Op. 101 (piano, 1843)
   SCHOLZ **WES-108a** fl 2ob 2cl 2hn 2bn tp tb db timp.
Kinder-Freuden Polka, Op. 115 (piano, c.1844)
   SCHOLZ **WES-109a** fl 2ob 2cl 2hn 2bn tp tb db timp.
Seelen-Spiegel Walzer, Op. 126 (piano, c.1845)
   SCHOLZ **WES-110a** fl 2ob 2cl 2hn 2bn tp tb db timp.
Esterházy Walzer, Op. 129 (piano, 1846)
   SCHOLZ **WES-111a** fl 2ob 2cl 2hn 2bn tp tb db timp.
Carlsbader-Sprudel Galop, Op. 131 (piano, 1846)
   SCHOLZ **WES-112a** fl 2ob 2cl 2hn 2bn tp tb db timp.
Seraphinen Quadrille, Op. 135 (piano, 1846)
   SCHOLZ **WES-113a** fl 2ob 2cl 2hn 2bn tp tb db timp.
Chinesen-Galopp, Op. 137 (piano, 1846)
   ANON **A-266a** pic fl 2ob cl(E♭) cl(solo B♭) 3cl(B♭) 4hn 2bn 4tp kenthorn t-hn 2tb oph vc/b b-dr s-dr.
   MS parts: D-DT, Mus-n 2044, No. 2.
Sträusschen am Wege Walzer, Op. 143 (piano, 1847)
   SCHOLZ **WES-114a** fl 2ob 2cl 2hn 2bn tp tb db timp.
Verlobungs-Polka-Mazurka (Les Fiancailles), Op. 251 (piano, c.1861)
   ANON **A-267a** pic fl 2ob cl(E♭) cl(solo B♭) 3cl(B♭) 4hn 2bn 3tp t-hn 3tb b-hn bomb b-dr+cym s-dr.
   MS parts: D-DT, Mus-n 1995, No. 2.
Liverpool-Walzer (piano, 1846)
   SCHOLZ **WES-115a** fl 2ob 2cl 2hn 2bn tp tb db timp.
Liebes-Grüsse Walzer, (piano, 1847)
   SCHOLZ **WES-116a** fl 2ob 2cl 2hn 2bn tp tb db timp.
Mödlinger-Polka (piano, c.1847)
   SCHOLZ **WES-117a** fl 2ob 2cl 2hn 2bn tp tb db timp.
Andenken an das Anith Koffsche Palais (piano)
   WIESER **FAW-20a** pic(terz-fl) cl(E♭) 2cl(B♭) 3hn(2B♭, F) 2bn tp b-tb cb.
Wien-Prager Eisenbahn-Polka (piano)
   ANON **A-268a** pic 2ob cl(E♭) cl(solo B♭) 3cl(B♭) 4hn 2bn 3tp kenthorn a-hn 2tb b-hn/bomb vc/b b-dr t-dr.
   MS parts: D-DT, Mus-n 1899, No. 2b.
Unidentified Works
Gall[op] in E♭
   ANON **A-269a** fl 2ob cl(E♭) 3cl(B♭) 4hn 2bn 2tp kl-hn 3tb b-hn b-dr s-dr. MS pts: D-DT, Mus-n 2034, No. 2.
Galoppe
   STRECK **PZS-1.14a** fl cl(D) 2cl(A) 2hn 2bn.
Polka, in G (piano, c.1849)
   SCHOLZ **WES-118a** fl 2ob 2cl 2hn 2bn tp tb db timp.
Polka, in E♭ (piano, c.1849)
   SCHOLZ **WES-119a** fl 2ob 2cl 2hn 2bn tp tb db timp.
Polonaise, in A♭
   MARPURG **WYM-3.2a** pic 2ob 2cl(E♭) 4cl(B♭) 2hn 2bn 2tp 3tb b-hn b-dr s-dr.
Schottischer, in B♭
   WIESER **FAW-21a** pic(E♭) cl(E♭) 2cl(B♭) 3hn(2E♭, B♭ alto) 2bn tp b-tb cb.
Walzer, in F minor
   MARPURG **WYM-3.3a** pic 2ob 2cl(E♭) 4cl(B♭) 2hn 2bn 2tp 3tb b-hn b-dr s-dr.

LA BORDE (Delaborde, Laborde), Jean Benjamin de (1734 - 1794)
La Cinquantaine (opera pastorale, 13 Aug 1771, Paris)
   FUCHS, G.F. **GFF-20a** overture. 2cl 2hn 2bn.

LACHNER, Franz Paul (1803 - 1890)
Katherina (Catherino) Cornaro, Königin von Cypern (opera, 3 Dec 1841, Munich)
   ANON **A-270a** finale. 2fl 2ob cl(E♭) cl(solo B♭) 3cl(B♭) 4hn 2bn 3tp kenthorn a-hn 3tb b-hn bomb b-dr t-dr.
   MS parts: D-DT, Mus-n 620.
   ANON **A-271a** Chor. Terzett & Finale Act III. 2fl 2ob cl(E♭) cl(solo B♭) 3cl(B♭) 4hn(+hn ad lib) 2bn
   3tp+tp/kenthorn t-hn 3tb b-hn bomb vc/b b-dr t-dr. MS parts: D-DT, Mus-n 619.
   SCHOLZ **WES-120.1a** finale. fl 2ob 2cl 2hn 2bn tp tb db timp.
   SCHOLZ **WES-120.2a** aria & Act II finale. fl 2ob 2cl 2hn 2bn tp tb db timp.
Nachts in der Cajüte (Lieder)
   ANON **A-272a** No. 2, "Das Meer hat seine Perlen". Solo horn, fl 2ob cl(solo B♭) 3cl(B♭) 3hn 2bn 2tp 3tb (2)b.
   MS parts: D-DT, Mus-n 1838, No. 2.

LACHNER, Ignaz (1807 - 1895)
Lorelei (Loreley) (opera, 6 Sept 1846, Munich)
 WIDDER **YŸW-3a** Gebet et Aria.   2fl cl(A♭) 2cl(E♭) 3cl(B♭) 4hn 2bn+baryton 3tp 3tb b-dr s-dr.

LAFONT, Charles Philippe (1781 - 1839)
Polonoise, C minor
 SCHNEIDER, A. **AYS-61a** fl 2ob 4cl 2hn 2bn tp b-tb cb.

LANNER, Joseph Franz Carl (1801 - 1843)
Vermählungs Walzer, Op. 15 (advertized in *Wiener Zeitung,* 21 Jan 1828, Vienna)
 KIRCHHOFF **WZK-36a** fl 2ob 2cl 2hn 2bn tp tb db.   (Based on the piano arr by A. Hollenstein)
Amoretten Walzer, Op. 53 (26 July 1831, Vienna)
 ANON **A-273a** cl(G) cl(D) 2hn bn cbn+serp 2tp.   MS parts: CZ-Bm(au), A.35.233b.
Die Badner Ring'In Walzer, Op. 64 (15 Aug 1832, Vienna)
 ANON **A-18.2a, 20.13a** pic(E♭) ob cl(Eb) 2cl(B♭) 2hn bn 2tp b-tb serp.
 STRECK **PZS-1.8a** fl cl(D) 2cl(A) 2hn 2bn.
Olymp's Walzer, Op. 67 (28 Nov 1832, Vienna)
 ANON **A-13.3a, 20.15a** fl(F) cl(Eb) 2cl(B♭) 2hn bn tp(patent) tp b-tb serp.
 STRECK **PZS-1.7a** fl 3cl 2hn 2bn.
Tadolini-Galoppe, ohne Op. (21 Oct 1835, Vienna)
 ANON **A-274a** fl ob 2cl 3hn 2bn tp tb db.   MS score: D-NEhz, 212, No. 2.
Die Werber, Walzer, Op. 103 (Nov 1835, Pest; 24 Nov 1835, Vienna)
 ANON **A-275a** fl 2ob 2cl hn 2bn tb db.   MS parts: D-NEhz, 113, No. 7.
Hymens Feierklänge Walzer, Op. 115 (11 Jan 1837, Vienna)
 ANON **A-276.1a** fl ob 2cl 3hn 2bn tb+db.   MS score: D-NEhz, 212.
 ANON **A-276.2a** fl 2ob 2cl 2hn 2bn tb db timp.   MS parts: D-NEhz, 113, No. 25.
Amors Flügel Walzer, Op. 120 (Nov 1837, Graz)
 ANON **A-277.1a** fl 2ob 2cl 3hn 2bn tb+db.   MS score: D-NEhz, 114c.
 ANON **A-277.2a** fl 2ob 2cl 2hn 2bn tb db.   MS parts: D-NEhz, 113, No. 23.
Die Aelpler, Walzer, Op. 124 (Nov 1837, Graz)
 SCHOLZ **WES-121a** fl 2ob 2cl 2hn 2bn tp tb db.
Die Kösenden Walzer, Op. 128 (12 Feb 1838, Vienna)
 OLBRICH **FXO-1a** fl 2ob 2cl 2hn 2bn b-tb db.
Kroenungs-Walzer, Op. 133 (24 April 1838, Vienna)
 ANON **A-278a** fl 2ob 2cl 2hn 2bn tb db timp.   MS parts: D-NEhz, 113, No. 29.
Regata-Galoppe, Op. 134 (advertized in *Wiener Zeitung,* 6 Nov 1838, Vienna)
 WOELFING **ZZW-1a** fl 2ob 2cl 2hn 2bn tb db timp.
Roccoco-Walzer, Op. 136 (15 Jan 1839, Vienna)
 ANON **A-279.1a** 2ob 2cl(C) 2hn bn 2tp b-tb.   MS parts: CZ-Bm(au), A.37.337, No. 1.
Victoria-Walzer, Op. 138 (9 Feb 1839, Vienna)
 WOELFING **ZZW-2a** fl 2ob 2cl 2hn 2bn tb db timp.
Tourbillon-Galopp, Op. 142a (advertized in *Wiener Zeitung,* 24 Aug 1839, Vienna)
 WIESER **FAW-22a** pic(D♭) cl(E♭) 3cl(B♭) 3hn 2bn tp b-tb cb.
Marien-Walzer, Op.143 (20 May 1839, Vienna)
 ANON **A-280a** 2ob 2cl(A) 2hn 2bn cbn 2tp b-tb.   MS parts: CZ-Bm(au), A.37.335, (lacks ob I).
Die Osmanen, Walzer, Op. 146 (8 July 1839, Vienna)
 WOELFING **ZZW-3a** fl 2ob 2cl 2hn 2bn tb db timp.
Hoffnungs-Strahlen Walzer, Op. 158 (1840, Vienna)
 POKORNY, G.J. **GJP-1a** ob cl(D) cl(G) 2hn 2bn cbn 2tp.
Abendsterne Walzer, Op. 180 (7 June 1841, Vienna)
 SCHOLZ **WES-122a** fl 2ob 2cl 2hn 2bn tp tb db timp.
Nixen-Tänze, Walzer, Op. 198 (11 July 1842, Vienna)
 ANON **A-281a** fl cl(D) cl(A) 2hn bn basso 2tp tb.   MS parts: CZ-Bm(au), A.37.336.
s' Hoamweh, Original Steyrer Ländler, Op. 202 (4 March 1842, Vienna)
 ANON **A-282a** fl 2ob 2cl 2hn 2bn tb db.   MS score: D-NEhz, 207, No. 4.

LASSER, Johann Baptist (1751 - 1805)
Der Kapellmeister oder Ist's nicht die eine, so ist's die andere (comic opera, ?1789 Graz, 2 July 1790, Vienna)
 KROMMER **FVK-2.6ma** Marsch.   2ob 2cl 2hn 2bn cbn.

LEEVES, William (1748 - 1828)
The Pigeon (song, pub. 1784, London)
 ANON **A-202.2/20(a)** 2terz-fl 2bthn 2hn 2bn serp.

LEFÉBURE-WÉLY, Louis James Alfred (1817 - 1869)
Sortie in B♭ (organ)
 TAYLORSON **JST-10a** fl 2ob 2cl 2h 2bn cbn/db.

LEFEVBRE François Charlemagne (1775 - 1839)
Vénus et Adonis (ballet, 1 Sept, Versailles; 4 Oct 1808, Paris)
 VANDERHAGEN **AJV-14a** 9 mvts.   2cl 2hn 2bn.

LEIDERSDORF, Franz
Fest Overture bei Gelegenheit der Feyerlichen Krönung Ihrer Majestät Caroline, Kaiserin von Österreich, zur Königen von Ungarn (1837).
 KOLBE **OXK-1a** 2ob 2cl 2hn 2bn.

LEMOYNE, Jean Baptiste (1751 - 1796)
Les Prétendus (comédie lyrique, 2 June 1789, Paris)
    ANON **A-283a** 2fl 2cl 2hn 2bn. MS parts: RF-Ssc, Ф 891 собр юосуповьiх N18, pp. 111 - 145.
    ANON **A-284a** overture. 2cl 2hn 2bn.
    Pc (Imbault: Paris, pn H.105, c.1790), pts: S-Uu, Utl.inst.mus.tr.145, 148-150, Takt 24, (missing cl II, hn II).

LEONTIEFF, N.
Polonaise
    SCHNEIDER, L. **LXS-1a** fl 2ob 2hn 2bn serp.

LEROY, Pierre (active c.1800 - 1810, Lyon)
Pas de manoeuvre
    ANON **A-78.2/3m(a)** 2pic 2quart-fl 2cl(C) 2hn 2bn 2tp serp b-dr+cym.
Rondo, Allegretto non troppo, 2/4 (Note: this piece does not appear in Leroy's *Journal*, PQL-1)
    BLASIUS **MFB-2.5(a)** 2cl 2hn 2bn.

LESUEUR, Jean François (1760 - 1837)
La Caverne (drame lyrique, 6 June 1793, Paris)
    FUCHS, G.F. **GFF-21a** overture. 4cl 2hn 2bn tp.
Paul et Virginie, ou Le triomphe de la vertu (drame lyrique, 13 Jan 1794, Paris)
    FUCHS, G.F. **GFF-22a** overture. 4cl(C) 2hn 2bn tp.
    VANDERHAGEN **AJV-15a** Suite No. 1. 2cl 2hn 2bn.
Ossian, ou Les Bardes (opera, 10 July 1804, Paris)
    FUCHS, G.F. (attributed) **GFF-23.1a** ouverture. 2cl 2hn 2bn.
    FUCHS, G.F. **GFF-23.2a** Morceaux choisis, 2 Suites: 6 mvts, 8 mvts. 2cl 2hn 2bn.
    PERSUIS **LLP-1a** Songe d'Ossian, nocturne. fl 2cl 2hn 2bn (serp/db ad lib).
    SCHMITT, G. **GYS-38a** duo. 2fl 2ob 2cl 2hn 2bn.
    TRIEBENSEE **JZT-31a** Marsch "Der Kaledonier". 2ob 2cl 2hn 2bn (tp ad lib).
Marche séraphique (Taceat terra) du couronnement [of Napoleon] exécuté à Rhiems (orchestra, Rhiems, 1802)
    LOUIS **FCL-2a(m)** fl(E♭) cl(E♭) 2cl(B♭) 2hn 2bn tp b-tb serp b-dr.
Marche du Sacre de Sa Majesté L'Empereur. Esécutée Le jour de la bataille d'Austerlitz (1805)
    COURTIN **HZC-1ma** pic(D♭) cl(E♭) 2cl(B♭) 2hn 2bn 2cap 2tp 3tb b-dr s-dr.

LICKL, Karl Georg (1801 - 1877)
Bravour Galopp (piano, c.1840)
    SCHOLZ **WES-123a** fl 2ob 2cl 2hn 2bn tp tb db.

LIECHTENSTEIN (Lichtenstein), Karl August, *Freiherr* von (1767 - 1845)
Der steinerne Braut (Zauber-Oper, 25 Aug 1799, Dresden)
    RIEGER **GYR-1.2a** 1 mvt. 2cl 2hn 2bn.

LIEDER, ( )
Ruda-Klänge Masurka (piano, c.1845)
    SCHOLZ **WES-124a** fl 2ob 2cl 2hn 2bn tp tb db.

LIGETI, György (b. 1923)
Sechs Bagatellen (Miniatures) für Bläserquintet (1953).
    WANEK **FKW-2a** fl fl(pic) ob ob(ca) cl(B♭) cl(B♭ & cl E♭) 2hn 2bn.

LINDPAINTNER, Peter Joseph von (1791 - 1856).
Die Pflegekinder (operette, 1812 *or* 19 Nov 1814, Munich)
    ANON **A-285a** overture. cl(E♭) 4cl(B♭) 2hn 2bn 2tp b-hn. MS parts: D-DT, Mus-n 779.
Moses' Errettung (melodrama, 13 June 1813, Stuttgart; 1815 Munich)
    SCHMITT, G. **GYS-39a** overture. fl 2ob 2cl 2hn 2bn tp tb db.
Kunstsinn und Liebe (opera, May 1816, Munich)
    ANON **A-286a** overture. pic 2ob cl(E♭) 3cl(B♭) 2hn 2bn 2tp 3tb serp b-dr. MS parts: D-DT, Mus-n 937.
Abrahams Opfer (oratorio, 14 June 1817, Brno; 1819, Munich)
    W., *2nd of this pseudonym* **BZW-1a** overture. terz-fl cl(E♭) 2cl(B♭) 2hn 2bn 2tp serp+b-tb b-dr s-dr.
    ANON **A-287a** overture. cl(E♭) 3cl(B♭) 2hn 2bn 2tp b-hn. MS parts: D-DT, Mus-n 1838, No. 2.
Aglae (ou L'élève d'amour; Aglaia oder die Zögling [sic] der Liebe) (anacreontic ballet, 1826, Stuttgart)
    ANON **A-288a** Jagdgefolge aus dem Ballet. fl(F) 2cl(C) 2hn 2bn. MS parts: GB-Ljag(w), 5/262, No. 4.
    SCHMITT, G. **GYS-40a** 1 Bd. fl 2ob 2cl 2hn 2bn tp tb(solo) a-tb t-tb db.
Janina (Danina oder Joko, der brasilianische Affe) (ballet, 12 March 1826, Stuttgart)
    ANON **A-289a** 9 mvts. fl 2ob 2cl 2hn 2bn 2tp serp. MS score: D-Tl, Z 88.
    ANON **A-290a** 3 mvts. fl(D, F) 2cl(C) 2hn 2bn. MS parts: GB-Ljag(w), 5/262, Nos. 5, 12 & 18.
    SCHMITT, G. **GYS-41.1a** overture. fl 2ob 2cl 2hn 2bn tb(obl).
    SCHMITT, G. **GYS-41.2a** 2 mvts. fl 2ob 2cl 2hn 2bn 2tp b-tb db.
    SCHMITT, G. **GYS-41.3a** 1 Bd. fl 2ob 2cl 2hn bn 2tp 2tb db.
    STRECK **PZS-2.6a** 1 long mvt. fl 2cl 2hn 2bn.
    WIDDER **YYW-1.24a** 5 mvts. 2fl 2cl 2hn 2bn.
Zeila oder der kleine schottische Tambour (ballet, 1827, Stuttgart)
    SCHMITT, G. **GYS-42a** 2 Bds. fl 2ob 2cl 2hn 2bn tp 2a-tb b-tb db.
Der Vampyr (romantische Oper, 21 Sept 1828, Stuttgart)　　*See also:* Sieff **JYS-2a**.
    ANON **A-291a** overture & 1 mvt. 2ob 2cl(A) cl(G) 2hn 2bn cbn 2tp. MS parts: CZ-Bm(au), A.35.183.
Faust (Teil 1, Tragödie, 2 March 1829, Stuttgart)
    SCHOLZ **WES-125a** overture. fl 2ob 2cl 2hn 2bn tb db timp.

Quintette Concertante in B♭ (fl ob cl hn bn & orchestra, 1821, Stuttgart)
　　SCHNEIDER, A. **AYS-62a** fl 2ob 2cl 3hn 2bn b-tb 2vla cb.
Concertino for 2 horns & orchestra, Op. 60.
　　LÖWENSTEIN **CAL-22a** 2 solo horns, fl(pic) 2cl(A) 2bn tp b-tb cb.
Alcibiades (ballet, sd, sl; untraced)
　　WIDDER **YYW-1.25a** 1 mvt.　2fl 2cl 2hn 2bn.
(unidentified) Romance et Ballet
　　KIRCHHOFF **WZK-37a** fl 2ob 2cl 2hn 2bn tb db.
(unidentified) Arie Einlage
　　KIRCHHOFF **WZK-38a** fl 2ob 2cl 2hn 2bn tb db.
Untraced arrangement: Janina (Danina) oder Joko, der brasilianische Affe (ballet, 1826, Stuttgart); E Holmes
1828, *Rambles among the Musicians of Germany* p. 234 mentions the Overture to *Der Berg König* [sic] (opera,
1825, Stuttgart) arranged by Niedhárdt.

LISZT, Franz (Ferenc) (1811 - 1886)
Domine salvum fac regem (T solo, TTBB chorus, orchestra, 1853, Weimar)
　　RAFF **JJR-1a** T solo, TTBB chorus, 2ob 2cl 4hn 2bn 2tp 3tb tu db.

LITOLFF, Henry Charles (1818 - 1891)
Die Braut von Kynast (grand romantic opera, 3 Oct 1847, Braunschweig)
　　SCHOLZ **WES-126a** overture.　2ob 2cl 2hn 2bn tp tb vla vc db timp.

LIVERATI, Giovanni (1772 - 1846)
David oder Goliaths Tod (biblical opera, 8 April 1813, Vienna)
　　SEDLAK **WXS-28.1a** overture & 6 mvts.　2ob 2cl 2hn 2bn cbn.
　　SEDLAK **WXS-28.2a** overture & 6 mvts.　2cl 2hn 2bn.

LIVORKA (Liborka), ( ).
Walzer (c.1818)
　　HÖNIG **XZH-1a** 2ob 2cl 2hn 2bn cbn 2tp.

LOBE, Johann Christian (1797 - 1881)
Die Fürstin von Granada oder Der Zauberblick (grosses Zauberoper, 28 Spet 1833, Weimar)
　　ANON **A-13.2a** Jagd-Chor.　fl(F) cl(E♭) 2cl(B♭) 2hn bn 2tp b-tb serp.

LORTZING, Gustav Albert (1801 - 1851)
Undine (opera, 21 April 1845, Magdeburg)
　　KÉLER **BXK-1a** scena.　pic fl ob cl(A♭) cl(E♭) 3cl(B♭) 4hn 2bn 5tp tp(B♭ basso) cap 2flug b-flug 3tb euph
　　cb tambour.
Zar [originally "Czaar"] und Zimmermann, oder die zwei Peter (comic opera, 22 Dec 1837, Leipzig)
　　VALLENTIN **XXV-2a** overture.　2ob 2cl(A) 2hn 2bn cbn 2tp.
　　VOJÁČEK **HXV-9.2a** Aria, "Sanft spielt ich".　fl(E♭) 2cl 2hn 2bn 2tp basso.
　　WIESER **FAW-23a** Galopp.　pic(D♭) cl(E♭) 3cl(B♭) 3hn　2bn tp b-tb cb.
Der Waffenschmied (comic opera, 30 May 1846, Vienna)
　　SCHOLZ **WES-127.1a** overture.　fl 2ob 2cl 2hn 2bn tp tb vla db timp.
　　SCHOLZ **WES-127.2a** 3 mvts.　fl 2ob 2cl 2hn 2bn tp tb db timp.

LUMBYE, Hans Christian (1810 - 1874)
Mein Lebewohl an Berlin, Walzer (piano)
　　ANON **A-292a** fl 2ob cl(solo B♭) 3cl(B♭) 4hn 2bn 2tp 3tb (2)b.　MS parts: D-DT, Mus-n 1838, No. 1.
Fest-Galopp (piano, c.1845)
　　SCHOLZ **WES-128a** fl 2ob 2cl 2hn 2bn tp tb db timp.
Der Günstlings-Walzer (piano, c.1845)
　　SCHOLZ **WES-129a** fl 2ob 2cl 2hn 2bn tp tb db timp.

LUOPICCINI, ( ) (active at Březnice, Bohemia, 1765)
Vexilla Regis, in F (Březnice, 1765)
　　FUX **ZYF-1va** CATB, 2cl 2hn 2bn.

LYADOV, (Liadov, Liadow) Anatoly Konstantinovich (1885 - 1914)
8 Russian Folk Songs, Op. 58 (orchestra)
　　BROWN **WJB-1a** fl fl(pic) ob ob(ca) 2cl 2hn 2bn, (b-cl ad lib).

MAHLER, Gustav (1860 - 1911)
Fünf frühe Lieder
　　WANEK **FKW-3a.** Solo Soprano, fl fl(pic) ob ob(ca) 2cl 2hn 2bn.

MANFROCE, Nicoló Antonio (1791 - 1813)
No. 16 Duetto, "Quel presaggio fortunato" (possibly from his opera, Alzira, 10 Sept 1810, Rome)
　　ANON **A-293a** fl quart-fl 3cl 2hn tp tb 2serp.　MS parts: I-Mc, Noseda L.21.8.

MANNSFELDT, Edgar
An Madonna consolatrice (Lied)
　　ANON **A-294a** pic 2ob 2cl(E♭) cl(solo B♭) 3cl(B♭) 4hn 2bn 4tp kl-hn t-hn 3tb b-hn/bomb b-dr s-dr.
　　MS parts: D-DT, Mus-n 1662, No. 2.

MARIE, Gabriel, *sometimes given as:* **GABRIEL-MARIE, ( )** (1852 - 1928)
Deux Pièces, No. 2, La Cinquantaine (vc & pf, 1884, Paris; rescored 1886 for vc + string quintet)
  ANON **A-295a** fl ob 2cl 2hn bn.
    Pm (Boosey & Hawkes: London, sd).

MARSCHNER, Heinrich August (1795 - 1861)
Der Vampyr (opera, 29 March 1828, Leipzig)   *See also:* Sieff **JYS-2a.**
  ANON **A-16.a, 20.8a, 20.9a** 2 Walzer. fl(F) cl(Eb) 2cl(Bb) 2hn bn 2tp b-tb serp b-dr t-dr.
  SCHMITT, G. **GYS-43a** 2 Bds. fl 2ob 2cl 2hn 2bn 2tp a-tb t-tb b-tb db.
  SCHOLZ **WES-130a** 5 mvts. fl 2ob 2cl 2hn 2bn tp tb db timp.
Der Templer und die Jüdin (opera, 22 Dec 1829, Leipzig)
  ANON **A-296a** Marcia. (?3)fl ob cl(Eb) 2cl(Bb) 2hn 2bn tp tb serp b-dr cym, "Tambour militaire".
    MS parts: CZ-Bm(au), A.19.378, (?missing fl I & II). *Possibly based on No. 10 of Barth's arrangment.*
  BARTH **WLB-1a** 10 mvts. 2fl(terz-fl, pic) 2ob 4cl 2hn 2bn 2tp 3tb, (ad lib: serp b-dr+cym s-dr).
  KIRCHHOFF **WZK-39a** 3 Bds. fl 2ob 3cl 2hn 2bn tp tb db.
  LEGRAND **WYL-22a** 1 mvt (Tempo March). fl ob 2cl 2hn 2bn (bn III ad lib).
  SCHMITT, G. **GYS-44a** overture & 3 mvts in Act I. fl 2ob 3cl 2hn 2bn tp tb db.
  WIDDER **YYW-4a** 4 mvts. terz-fl(pic in Nos. 2 & 3) 2cl(Eb) 2cl(Bb) 2hn 2bn tp(chromatic) b-tb cb.
Hans Heiling (Opera und Vorspiel, 25 May 1833, Berlin)
  KIRCHHOFF **WZK-40a** arie & Act I finale ("Wehe mire wohin"). fl 2ob 2cl 2hn 2bn tp tb db.
Der Bäbu (comic opera, 19 Feb 1838, Hannover)
  SCHOLZ **WES-131a** 5 mvts. fl 2ob 2cl 2hn tp tb db timp.
Trinklied, "Den Stoepsolweg!"
  WIESER **FAW-1.2a** terz-fl cl(Eb) 2cl(Bb) 2hn 2bn tp b-tb cb.

MARTINI, Giovanni, *il Tedesco, (pseudonym* **i.e Johann Paul Aegidius Schwarzendorf)** (1741 - 1816)
Henri IV ou La Bataille d'Ivry (opera, 14 Nov 1774, Paris)
  ANON **A-297a** overture. fl 2ob 3cl(C) 2hn 2tp tb cb timp. MS parts: GB-:jag(w), 116, (a local rescoring
    of the orchestral arrangement by H. Hofmann, "Lieut. 6B. 60th Foot / Surinam August the 6th 1801".)
  VANDERHAGEN **AJV-2.5/2a** "D'une folâtre adolescence". 2cl 2hn 2bn.
Le Droit de Seigneur (opera, 17 Dec 1783, Versailles; 29 Dec 1783, Paris
  VANDERHAGEN **AJV-4.1a** 3 mvts. 2cl 2hn 2bn.
Untraced arrangement: Henri IV, full arrangement.

MARTÍN Y SOLER, Vincente (1754 - 1806)
Andromeda (Andromaca) (opera, 26 Dec 1780, Turin)
  ANON **A-298a** recitative and duet, "Lascia bel idol mio". SS, 2ob 2cl 2hn 2bn.
    MS score (c.1785): DK-Sa, R 128.
Una cosa rara, ossia Bellezza ed onestà (Lilla) (comic opera, 17 Nov 1786, Vienna)
See also infra: VIOTTI, *(Polacca inserted in the Paris version).*
  ANON **A-299a** overture & 13 mvts. 2fl 2cl 2hn 2bn.
    MS parts: PL-LA, RM 81/1-5/93-106, (missing fl I, hn I, bn II; in the fl II pt between Nos. 104 & 105, an
    additional mvt, Allegro Maestoso, C, 112 bars, has been crossed out). *Not based on the Went arrangement.*
  MOZART **WAM-2.1a** Act II, Finale. (1 section arranged in *Don Giovanni*). 2ob 2cl 2hn 2bn vlne.
  OZI **EXO-1.32/6a** aria. 2cl 2hn 2bn.
  ROSINACK **FJR-2ad** (= WENT, JNW-25.1a).
  SARTORIUS **GCS-6a** 9 mvts. 2cl 2hn 2bn cbn.
  WENT **JNW-25.1a** sinfonia & 17 mvts. 2ob 2cl 2hn 2bn.
  WENT **JNW-25.2a** sinfonia & 15 mvts. 2ob 2ca 2hn 2bn.
  WENT **JNW-25.3a** [= A-203a; VXM-1ad(-4ad)]. 2ob 2bthn 2hn 2bn serp.
L'Arbore di Diana (opera, 1 Oct 1787, Vienna)
Note: "*Occhietto furbetto*" *was also introduced into Bianchi's* La Villanella rapita *and Sarti's* Fra due Litiganti.
  ANON **A-300a** 2fl 2cl 2hn 2bn. MS parts: RF-Ssc, Ф 891 собр юосуповьіх N19, pp. 36 - 55.
  ANON **A-301.1a** 7 mvts, (also includes 2 pieces from Salieri's *Axur Re d'Ormus*). 2cl 2hn 2bn.
    MS parts: CZ-Pnm, XLII.D.86, Nos. 1 - 7.
  COURTIN **FJC-1.5a** "Occhietto furbetto". (2ob/fl ad lib) 2cl 2hn 2bn.
  HAVEL **VXH-16.1a** overture & 25 mvts. 2cl 2hn 2bn. *Possibly a reduction of WENT, JNW-26.1a.*
  HAVEL **VXH-16.2a** overture & 9 mvts. 2cl 2hn bn.
  SARTORIUS **GCS-7a** introduzione & 9 mvts. 2ob 2cl 2hn 2bn 2tp.
  WENT **JNW-26.1a** overture & 24 mvts. 2ob 2cl 2hn 2bn.
  WENT **JNW-26.2a** overture & 24 mvts. 2ob 2ca 2hn 2bn.
La Scuola dei maritati (La Capricciosa corretta; Die gebesserte Eigensinnige) (opera, 27 Jan 1791, London).
  FUCHS, G.F. **GFF-3.1a** polacca, "La Donna hà bello il core". 2fl 2cl(C) 2hn 2bn.
  SARTORIUS **GCS-8a** 6 mvts. 2cl 2hn 2bn cbn.
  STUMPF **JUS-3a** Recueil 13, overture & 5 mvts. 2cl 2hn 2bn.

MAŠEK (Maschek, Mashek), Václav Vincenc (Wenzel Vincent) (1755 - 1831)
Parthia in Dis [Eb] (VVM-8) (fl ob cl bthn 2hn 2bn (cbn tp ad lib)
  ZASCHE **AZZ-1a** fl cl(F vel ob) 2cl(Bb) 2hn 2bn tp(prin).
[7] Variationi in G (piano)
  HAVEL **VXH-17a** (here in F). 2cl 2hn 2bn
[7] Variationi in B[b] (piano)
  HAVEL **VXH-18a** 2cl 2hn 2bn.
[5] Variationi in B[b] (piano)
  HAVEL **VXH-19a** 2cl 2hn 2bn.

MATHILDE, *Fürstin von Schwarzberg-Sondershausen*
Lied von Prutz, "Um Mitternacht (voice & piano, c.1841)
   KIRCHHOFF **WZK-41a** fl ob(I) 2cl 2hn 2bn tp tb db.
2 Lieder, (Eb, F)
   ANON **A-302a** fl 2ob 2cl 3hn 2bn tb db timp.   MS parts: D-NEhz, 185, Nos. 4 & 5.
Lied
   ANON **A-303a** fl 2ob 2cl 2hn 2bn tb db.   MS score: D-NEhz, 241.

MAURER, Ludwig (Louis) Wilhelm   (1789 - 1878)
Arlequin et Colombine auf der Alpes (ballet, pre-1808, Vienna)
   HAVEL **VXH-20a** Niederländen Bauern, Pas de Deux. 2cl 2hn 2bn, tuba pastoralis. *Based on Triebensee's arr.*
   TRIEBENSEE **JZT-32.1a** Pas de deux (Niederländen Bauern).   2ob 2cl 2hn 2bn (cbn tp ad lib).
   TRIEBENSEE **JZT-32.2a** ballet music, 1 mvt.   2ob 2cl 2hn 2bn.

MAXIMILIAN, *Herzog*
Gesellschaft Potista [sic]
   WIESER **FAW-24a** pic(Db) cl(Eb) 3cl(Bb) 2hn 2bn tp cb.
Hinneberger Schottische
   WIESER **FAW-25a** pic(Eb) cl(Eb) 3cl(Bb) 2hnn 2bn tp b-tb cb.

MAYR (Mair, Mayer) Johann Simon (Giovanni Simone)   (1763 - 1845)
La Lodoiska (opera, 26 Jan 1796, Venice; 31 May 1798, Vienna; revivied 26 Dec 1799, Milan)
   ANON **A-304a** overture & 13 mvts.   2ob 2cl 2hn 2bn cbn(a few divisi bars in some mvts).
      Pc (Das Magazin de Musique des Théâtres national [sic]: Vienna, pn Op: 48, c.1800), parts:
      A-Wgm(c), (?lost); D-Rtt, Mayr 2/I; I-Fc, F.P. S.350.
      MS score (attributed to Cherubini, allegedly in the hand of J.S. Mayr, although it is highly unlikely that he
      would not recognize his own opera): I-BGc, Mayr 515, (without cbn).
      MS parts: A-Ee, Mus. 1091, (without cbn pt; 11 mvts - Nos. 6 & 7 and 9 & 10 are combined as single mvts);
      A-Wn, Mus.Hs.3792, Nos. 6.1a, 6.2a, 6.4a, 6.24a (= overture & Nos. 3, 13 & 6/7; incorrectly attributed
      to Zingarelli; with a later cbn pt).
   HAVEL **VXH-21a** overture & 13 mvts.   2cl 2hn 2bn.
   KRECHLER **FFK-12.2a** overture & 2 mvts.   2ob 2cl 2hn 2bn cbn tp.
   KRECHLER **FFK-13.2a** overture & 3 mvts.   2ob 2cl 2hn 2bn.
L'Intrigo della lettra (opera, 30 Nov 1797, Venice)
   KRECHLER **FFK-6.1a** overture.   2ob 2cl 2hn 2bn cbn tp.
Il Segreto (I Solitari) (opera, 24 Sept 1797, Venice)
   RATTI **LXR-1a** scene.   fl 2cl 2hn bn serp.
Che originali! (Il fanatico/pazzo per la musica) (opera, 18 Oct 1798, Venice; 1803, Vienna)
   WIELAND **KZW-2.5a** Polacca chanté par Melle. Neri.   fl/ob ob/fl 2cl 2hn 2bn serp/b-tb.
Il Carretto del venditor d'aceto (opera farce, 28 June 1800, Venice)
   RICHTER **QYR-2a** 2ob 2cl 2hn 2bn cbn.
Ginevra di Scozia (Vienna production with J. Weigl) (dramma serio comico per musica, 21 March 1801, Trieste)
   ANON **A-305.1a** "Vieni! colà t'attendo" (& possibly 2 other mvts).   fl 2ob 2cl 2hn 2bn 2vla vc+vlne.
      MS parts (c.1820): D-Rtt, Sm. 32, No. 3, (?4 & 5).
   ANON **A-306a** Parte 1: introduzione & 5 mvts; Parte 2: 6 mvts.   2ob 2cl 2hn 2bn cbn.
      MS parts: A-Ee, Mus. 1080, 1081 (the Partes have been reversed); I-Fc, (2 copies), F.P. S.339, F.P. S.404
   ANON **A-307a** (Part I) introduzione & 5 mvts, (Part II) 6 mvts.   2cl 2hn 2bn.
      MS parts: CZ-KRa, A4456/R.I.26 a-f, Nos. 3 & 4; CZ-Pnm, XLI.A.87, (missing cl I, 1805).
   ANON (?Buchnal = JWB-1ad) **A-308a** 2cl 2hn 2bn.   MS parts: PL-LA, RM 35.
   BUCHAL **JWB-1a** 2cl 2hn bn.
   ERCOLANI **GQE-1a** 2 marches.   Instrumentation unknown.
   KRECHLER **FFK-7.2a** cavatina.   2ob 2cl 2hn 2bn cbn tp.
   KRECHLER **FFK-1.3ac** marcia & duetto.   2ob 2cl 2hn 2bn cbn tp.
Alonso e Cora (dramma per musica, 26 Dec 1803, Milan; revived as *Cora,* 1815)
   KRECHLER **FFK-20a** overture & 7 mvts.   2ob 2cl 2hn 2bn cbn.
   SEDLAK **WXS-29a** sinfonia & 7 mvts.   2cl 2hn 2bn.
Ercole in Lidia (heroic opera, 29 Jan 1803, Vienna)
   ANON **A-309a** 2ob 2cl 2hn 2bn.   MS parts: I-Fc, F.P. S.337.
   KRECHLER **FFk-10.3a** overture & 1 mvt.   2ob 2cl 2hn 2bn cbn.
   SEDLAK **+WXS-30a** overture & 14 mvts.   2cl 2hn 2bn.
Adelasia ed Aleramo (melodramma serio, 25 Dec 1807, Milan)
   HEIDENREICH **JYH-2a** overture & 4 mvts.   2ob 2cl 2hn 2bn [cbn].
   KRECHLER **FFK-2.3a, 2.6a** quartetto ("Madre tu sei se l'amo") & duetto ("Che al bene al mio tesoro").
      2ob 2cl 2hn 2bn (cbn tp ad lib).
   TRIEBENSEE **JZT-33.1a** aria.   2ob 2cl 2hn 2bn (cbn tp ad lib).
   TRIEBENSEE **JZT-33.2a** duetto.   2ob 2cl 2hn 2bn (cbn ad lib).

MAYSEDER, Joseph   (1789 - 1863)
Grand Rondeau, Op. 21 (piano)
   STARKE **FRS-19a** 2ob 2cl 2hn 2bn cbn 2tp.
Variations (violin & piano)
   WITT **FZW-6a** clarinet principale in Bb, cl(Eb) 2cl(Bb) 2hn 2bn tp basso.

MEDERITSCH, Johann Georg Anton (*pseudonym* = Gallus)   (1752 - 1835)
Babylons Pyramiden (Act I; Act II by P. von Winter) (opera, 25 Oct 1797, Vienna). *See infra: WINTER.*

MÉHUL, Étienne Nicolas (1763 - 1817)
Euphrosine, ou Le tyran corrigé (opera, 4 Sept 1790; revived (3 acts) 1795, Paris; 14 Aug 1806, Vienna, with additional numbers composed by Seyfried)
 FUCHS, G.F. **GFF-24a** Suite, 7 mvts.   4cl(C) 2hn 2bn serp/cb; *or* 2cl 2hn 2bn.
 OZI **EXO-1.29/2a** quatuor & duo; **EXO-1.30/3a** 3 mvts.   2cl 2hn 2bn.
 VANDERHAGEN **AJV-5.7a** "Mes pastouraux".   2cl 2hn 2bn.
Le jeune Henri (Le Chasse du jeune Henri) (opera, 1 May 1797, Paris)
 ANON **A-310a** overture.   2fl 2ob 4cl 4hn(D, A) 2bn vc b timp.   MS parts (c.1800): D-Rtt, Méhul 12, (with duplicate 2hn in D parts & 3 basso parts).
 ANON **A-311a** overture.   2fl 2cl 2hn 2bn.   MS parts: PL-LA, RM 81/1-5/173, (missing fl I, hn I, bn II).
 JADIN, H. **HXJ-1a** overture.   2fl 2cl(C) 4hn 2bn tb serp.
 SCHMITT, G. **GYS-45a** overture.   fl 2ob 3cl 2hn 2bn tp tb db timp.
 WIELAND **KZW-7ad** overture.   fl(pic) 2ob 2cl 4hn 2bn serp/vlne timp.
Adrien (opera, 4 June 1799, Paris)
 ANON **A-312a** overture.   2p-fl 2cl 2hn 2bn.
 Pc (Pleyel: Paris, pn 387, 1802), RISM [M 1758], parts: D-Rp.
Ariodant (opera, 11 Oct 1799, Paris)
 FUCHS, G.F. **GFF-25a** morceaux choisis.   2fl 2cl 2hn 2bn.
Bion (Der Bauern; Der Bauer) (opera, 27 Dec 1800, Paris)
 TRIEBENSEE **JZT-34a** overture.   2ob 2cl 2hn 2bn (cbn tp ad lib).
L'Irato ou L'Emporté (Die Temperamente) (opera, 17 Feb 1801, Paris)
 OZI **EXO-2a** overture and 6 airs.   2cl(C & B♭) 2hn 2bn.
 TRIEBENSEE **JZT-36a** aria.   2ob 2cl 2hn 2bn (cbn tp ad lib).
Une Folie (Die beiden Füchse) (opera, 5 April 1802, Paris)
 ANON **A-313a** 2ob 2cl 2hn 2bn cbn.   MS parts: GB-Ljag(w), (overture & 7 mvts; with tp pt for the overture only); I-Fc, F.P. S.344.   MS score (allegedly in the hand of J.S. Mayr): I-BGc, Mayr 565.
 HAVEL **VXH-53.4a** 2 mvts, (incorrectly attributed to Josef Weigl).   2cl 2hn bn.
 LÖWENSTEIN **CAL-23a** overture & 9 mvts.   2cl 2hn 2bn.
 SEDLAK **WXS-31a** overture & 7 mvts.   2cl 2hn 2bn.
 VANDERHAGEN **AJV-16a** overture & 2 livres.   2fl 2cl 2hn 2bn tp.
Le Trésor supposé (Die Schatzgräber) (opera, 29 July 1802, Paris)
 KRECHLER **FFK-11.3a** 1 mvt.   2ob 2cl 2hn 2bn cbn.
 TRIEBENSEE **JZT-35a** overture & 8 mvts.   2ob 2cl 2hn 2bn cbn.
Helena (Hélène) (opera, 1 March 1803, Paris)
 ANON **A-314a** overture & 6 mvts.   2ob 2cl(C) 2hn 2bn.   MS parts: CZ-KRa, A3929/IV.B.92.
 KRECHLER **FFK-3.2a** overture.   2ob 2cl 2hn 2bn (cbn tp ad lib).
 VANDERHAGEN **AJV-17a** airs.   2fl 2cl 2hn 2bn, (ad lib: tp tb serp).
Les Deux Aveugles de Tolède (opera, 28 Jan 1806, Paris)
 SCHNEIDER, A. **AYS-63a** overture.   fl 2ob 2cl 2hn 2bn tp b-tb 2vla cb.
Joseph en Egypte (Joseph und seiner Brüder; J. in Ägypten; Jacob und seiner Söhne) (opera, 17 Feb 1807, Paris)
Note: The Schluss-Chor, "O gütiger Gott" in the Vienna production was composed by Ignaz von Seyfried.
 ANON **A-315a** romanze. "Ich war Jungling noch an Jahren".   fl 2ob 3cl 2hn 2bn b-hn/tb.
 MS parts: D-DT, Mus-n 1884, (missing ob I, bn I).
 ANON **A-316a** overture & 9 mvts.   2ob 2cl 2hn 2bn cbn. MS pts: I-Fc, F.P. S.356. *Not Sedlak, Starke or Weigl.*
 FENDT **AXF-3.3ad** 2 romanzes.   pic 2cl(E♭) 3cl(C & B♭) 2hn 2bn.
 KAISER **KAK-4a** overture.   fl cl(E♭) 2cl(B♭) 2hn 2tp t-hn tb tu b-dr s-dr.
 KÜFFNER **JYK-6.1/4(a)** romance.   fl 2cl hn bn.
 LEGRAND **WYL-23a** 1 mvt.   fl ob 2cl 2hn 2bn.
 SCHMITT, G. **GYS-46.1a** overture.   2fl 2ob 2cl 2hn 2bn tp tb db.
 SCHMITT, G. **GYS-46.2a** 6 mvts.   2fl 2ob 2cl 2hn 2bn (tp) tb db.
 SCHNEIDER, A. **AYS-64a** overture & 13 mvts.   fl(pic) 2ob 2cl 2hn 2bn tp(hn III) b-tb(tp II) 2vla cb.
 SEDLAK **WXS-32a** overture & 7 mvts; **WXS-1.2a**, overture & 5 mvts.   2ob 2cl 2hn 2bn cbn.
 STARKE **FRS-20a** (Abth 1: overture & 4 mvts, Abth. 2: 3 mvts, Abth. 3: 3 mvts.   2ob 2cl 2hn 2bn cbn 2tp.
 WEIGL, J. **JYW-1a** overture & 6 mvts.   2ob 2cl 2hn 2bn (2tp) b-tb.
Untraced arrangements: Stratonice (opera, 1792); Bion (opera, 1800); Les Deux Aveugles de Tolède (opera, 1806); La Journée aux Aventures (opera, 1816). All of these arrangements were published in Paris.

MENDELSSOHN BARTHOLDY, Jacob Ludwig Felix (1809 - 1847)
Ein Sommernachtstraum (A Midsummer Night's Dream) (play with incidental music, 14 Oct 1842, Potsdam)
 ANON **A-317a** Fest-Marsch.   fl 2ob 2cl(E♭) 2cl(C) 3cl(B♭) 4hn 2bn 4tp a-hn 3tb b-hn/bomb b-dr+cym s-dr tri.
 MS parts: D-DT, Mus-n 1946, No. 2.
 NESVADBA **XYN-1a** overture.   2fl(E♭) 2ob 2cl(E♭) 4cl(B♭) 4hn 2bn 2tp 2cap flug a-hn 3t-hn 3tb euph 2tu b-dr s-dr.
 SCHOLZ **WES-132a** Marsch.   fl 2ob 2cl 2hn 2bn tp tb db timp.
Sechs Lieder ohne Worte, Op. 19 (piano, pub. 1830)
 SCHOLZ **WES-133a** Nos. 1, 3 & 6.   fl 2ob 2cl 2hn 2bn tb db.
Overture: Die Hebriden (Fingals Höhle, Fingal's Cave), Op. 26 (16 Dec 1830; revised & published 1832)
 SCHOLZ **WES-134a** fl 2ob 2cl 3hn 2bn tp tb db.
Overture: Meeresstille und glückliche Fahrt, Op. 27 (18 April 1828, Berlin; pub. 1833)
 SCHOLZ **WES-135a** fl 2ob 2cl 3hn 2bn tp tb db timp.
Der schönen Melusine, Op. 32 (Overture zum Märchen, 14 Nov 1833; 1st performance, 7 April 1834, London)
 SCHOLZ **WES-136a** fl 2ob 2cl 3hn 2bn tp tb db timp.
6 Lieder, Op. 47 (voice & piano, pub. c.1840, Leipzig)
 KAISER **KAK-4a** No. 4, Volkslied ("Es ist bestimmt in Gottes Rath").   cl(E♭) 2cl(B♭) 2hn 2tp t-hn bar tu.

6 Kinderstücke, Op. 72 (6 Children's Pieces, 6 Christmas Pieces) (pub. 1847, Leipzig)
    EMERSON **GZE-1.1a** No. 1.   2fl ob 3cl hn bn.
Konzertstücke in F minor, Op. 113 (cl bthn piano, pub. 1869)
    SHEEN **GHS-11a** solo cl & bthn, fl 2ob 2hn 2bn.
Konzertstücke in D minor, Op. 114 (cl bthn piano, pub. 1869)
    SHEEN **GHS-12a** solo cl & bthn, fl 2ob 2hn 2bn.
Untraced arrangements: Unknown work arranged for 8 winds by C. H. Meyer (Breitkopf & Härtel: Leipzig);
F. L. Schubert (Breitkopf & Härtel; score & 8-part Harmoniemusik for *A Midsummer Night's Dream,* cited p. 38
of the Mendelssohn Thematic catalogue).

MERCADANTE, (Giuseppe) Saverio (Raffaele) (1795 - 1870)
Elisa e Claudio (melodramma semiserio, 30 Oct 1821, Milan)
    BERR **FXB-3.1/1(a)** overture.   fl(E♭) cl(E♭) cl(B♭ solo) 4cl(B♭) 2hn 2bn tp 3tb (2)serp cb.
    SEDLAK **WXS-33a** Theil 1: overture & 11 mvts; Theil 2: 6 mvts.   2ob 2cl 2hn 2bn cbn (2tp).
    STARKE **FRS-21a** Theil 1: overture & 7 mvts; Theil 2: overture & 1 long mvt.   2ob 2cl(C) 2hn 2bn cbn 2tp.
Andronico (melodramma tragico, 26 Dec 1821, Venice)
    CARULLI **BYC-2a** duetto, "Vanne se alberghi in petto".   fl 2cl hn bn.
    SCHOLL **NYS-14ac** duetto.   2ob 2cl 2hn 2bn cbn 2tp [b-tb].
Il Posto abbandanato (melodramma seriserio, 21 Sept 1822, Milan)
    ANON **A-318a** Harmoniestücke.   2ob 2cl 2hn 2bn cbn 2tp.   MS pts: CZ-Bm(au), A.35.189, (missing ob II).
    ANON **A-319a** Duetto, "Prendi rola al Capitano".   2ob 2cl 2hn 2bn cbn 2tp.
        MS parts (21 July 1824): CZ-Bm(au), A.19.412.
Amleto (melodramma lyrico, 26 Dec 1822, Milan)
    ANON **A-75.2a** aria.   2ob 2cl 2hn 2bn 2tp.   MS parts (1839): CZ-Bm(au), A.36.850, No 2.
Caritea, regina di Spagna (Donna Caritea) (melodramma serio, 21 Feb 1826, Venice)
    ANON **A-320a** overture, coro & aria.   2ob cl(I princ) cl(II) 2hn 2bn cbn 2tp.   MS pts: CZ-Bm(au), A.35.184.
I Briganti (melodramma, 22 March 1836, Paris)
    BERR **FXB-3ma** as "Pas Redoublé (No. 6)".   fl cl(E♭) 2cl(B♭) 2hn 2bn 2tp 2tb oph b-dr s-dr.
Il Bravo (opera, 9 March 1839, Milan)
    SCHOLZ **WES-137a** terzett & finale.   fl 2ob 2cl 3hn 2bn 2tp tb db timp.

MEYER, ( )
Theresa et Claudio (opera) *We have not been able to examine this work, but we believe it to be Farinelli's farce*
Terese e Claudio *(9 Sept 1801, Vienna), rearranged by Richter from one of C.H. Mayer's* Journals *(qv).*
    RICHTER **QYR-1ad** 2ob 2cl 2hn 2bn.   *See also supra: FARINELLI.*

MEYERBEER, Giacomo (1791 - 1864)
Emma di Ressburgo (melodramma eroica, 26 June 1819, Venice)
    LEGRAND **WYL-24a** 2 mvts.   fl ob 2cl 2hn 2bn.
    LEGRAND **WYL-52.4a, 52.5a** 2 mvts (as WYL-24a).   fl 2cl 2hn 2bn.
    WIDDER **YYW-1.26a** polacca.   2fl 2cl 2hn 2bn.
Margherita d'Anjou (melodramma semiserio, 14 Nov 1820, Milan)
    BERR **FXB-20a** overture. fl(pic) cl(E♭) solo+2cl(B♭) 2hn bn serp; (ad lib: cl(E♭) 2cl(B♭) bn(II) 2tb cb b-dr tri).
Il Crociato in Egitto (Die Kreuzfahrer in Ägypten) (melodramma eroico, 7 March 1824, Venice; revised 1826, Paris)
    ANON **A-74.13/6m(a)** march.   pic quart-fl 2ob cl(F) 2cl(C) 4hn 2bn cbn+serp/2b-hn 2tp 3tb b-dr t-dr tamb cym.
    SCHMITT, G. **GYS-47a** overture.   fl 2ob 2cl 2hn 2bn 2tb b-tb db.
    STARKE **FRS-22a** overture & 5 mvts, 1824.   2ob/fl 2cl 2hn 2bn 2tp b-tb.
Robert le Diable (grand opera, 21 Nov 1831, Paris)
    ANON **A-321a** Act V.   2fl 2ob cl(E♭) cl(solo B♭) 3cl(B♭) 4hn 2bn 3tp kenthorn/tp 3tb b-hn bomb vc/b
        b-dr(ad lib) t-dr.   MS parts: D-DT, Mus-n 722.
    ANON **A-322a** Robert Walzer sammt Marsche, 5 waltzes & march.   cl(E♭) 2cl(B♭) 2hn 2bn cbn 2tp b-tb.
        MS parts (1834): CZ-Bm(au), A.37.340, (missing tp II).
    ANON (G. Schmitt or W.E. Scholz) **A-323a** Walzer.   fl 2ob 2cl 2hn 2bn tb db.   MS pts: D-NEhz, 134, No. 29.
    ANON **A-16.1a, 20.7a** Walzer.   pic(E♭) cl(E♭) 2cl(B♭) 2hn bn 2tp tb serp b-dr t-dr.
    ANON **A-324a** 2tes Finale.   fl(F) 2cl(C) 2hn 2bn.   MS parts: GB-Ljag(w), 5/262, No. 10.
    ANON **A-10.29a** Galopp.   fl 2ob 3cl 2hn 2bn b-tb b.
    KIRCHHOFF **WZK-42a** overture & 5 acts.   fl 2ob 2cl 2hn 2bn (2)tp tb db timp.
    WIDDER **YYW-1.27a** 1 mvt (Allegro Moderato, Tempo di Marchia [sic]).   2fl 2cl 2hn 2bn.
    WIDDER **YYW-5a** 3 mvts.   terz-fl cl(E♭) 2cl(B♭) 2hn 2bn tp(chromatic) b-tb cb.
    WITT **FZW-7a** overture & 2 mvts.   fl(pic, terz-fl) ob 2cl(C) 2cl(B♭) 2hn 2bn tp b-tb cb.
Les Huguenots (Die Huguenotten) (grand opera, 29 Feb 1836, Paris)
    ANON **A-325a** Ouverture, Introduktion & Orgie.   pic terz-fl 2ob cl(E♭) cl(solo B♭) 3cl(B♭) 4hn 2bn 3tp
        kl-hn 2tb b-hn/bomb vc/b timp b-dr t-dr.   MS parts: D-DT, Mus-n 715.
    ANON **A-326a** Grand Duo.   2fl 2ob cl(E♭) cl(solo B♭) 3cl(B♭) 4hn 2bn 3tp kl-hn a-hn 3tb b-hn/bomb b timp
        b-dr s-dr.   MS parts: D-DT, Mus-n 717.
    ANON **A-327a** Chor und Gesang der 3 Mönche.   fl 2ob 2cl(E♭) 3cl(B♭) 4hn 2bn 3tp kenthorn 3tb b-hn/bomb
        vc/b timp b-dr t-dr.   MS parts: D-DT, Mus-n 1861.
    ANON **A-328a** Amusement [with Halévy's *L'Eclair*].   fl ob cl(E♭) cl(solo B♭) 3cl(B♭) 2hn 2bn 2tp 3tb b-hn
        b-dr s-dr.   MS parts: D-DT, Mus-n 1860.
    ANON **A-329a** Aria.   2ob 2cl 2hn bn basso(cbn) 2tp.   MS parts: CZ-Bm(au), A.40.157, (missing cbn, tp II).
    SCHOLL **NYS-15ac** 6 mvts.   2ob 2cl 2hn 2bn cbn 2tp [b-tb].
    SCHOLZ **WES-138.1a** overture & 2 Bds.   fl 2ob 2cl 3hn 2bn tp tb db timp.
    SCHOLZ **WES-138.2a** romance & chor.   fl 2ob 2cl 3hn 2bn tb db.
    VOJÁČEK **HXJ-5a** cavatina.   fl 2ob 2cl 2hn bn cbn 4tp(C, D) tb.

Die Gibellinen in Pisa (opera: all music drawn from *Les Huguenots,* c.1840)
ANON **A-330a** Scene du Bandeau. fl ob 2cl 2hn 2bn cbn (2tp) tb.
MS score: CZ-Bm(au), A.40.155.
ANON **A-331a** cavatine. Solo tp, terz-fl 2ob 2cl 2hn 2bn cbn.
MS parts (1842): CZ-Bm(au), A.40.156.
Ein Feldlager in Schlesien (Vielka) (Singspiel, 7 Dec 1844, Berlin Court; revised 18 Feb 1847, Vienna, as *Vielka)*
SCHOLZ **WES-139a** overture. fl 2ob 2cl 2hn 2bn tp tb db timp.
Struensee (Trauerspiel, 19 Nov 1846, Berlin)
SCHOLZ **WES-140.1a** overture. fl 2ob 2cl 2hn 2bn tp b-tb db timp.
SCHOLZ **WES-140.2a** 2 mvts. fl 2ob 2cl 2hn 2bn tp tb db timp.
Le Prophète (grand opera, 16 April 1849, Paris)
ANON **A-332a** Kornungsmarsch. pic 2fl 2ob cl(E♭) cl(solo B♭) 3cl(B♭) 2hn 2bn 4tp t-hn 3tb b-hn bomb vc
cb timp b-dr. MS parts: D-DT, Mus-n 721.
SCHOLZ **WES-141a** overture & 2 Bds. fl 2ob 2cl 2hn 2bn tp tb db timp.
Dinorah oder die Wallfahrt nach Ploërmel (Le Pardon de Ploërmel (opera, 4 April 1859, Paris)
ANON **A-333a** 1 mvt. 2fl 2ob cl(E♭) 3cl(B♭) 4hn 2bn 3tp t-hn 3tb b-hn bomb vc/b timp b-dr.
MS parts: D-DT, Mus-n 695.
Unidentified collections
LEGRAND **WYL-52** fl 2cl 2hn 2bn.

MINGOZZI, Giuseppe
"Se m'abbandonai mio delce amore" (Aria, original opera untraced)
ANON **A-334a** 7 winds. I-Fc, F.P. S.353.

MÖSER, ( ) (? Karl 1774 - 1851)
Die Berg-Schotten Quadrille (Berlin, post-1800)
TRIEBENSEE **JZT-37.1a** Contradance with 3 trios. 2ob 2cl 2hn 2bn (cbn tp ad lib).
TRIEBENSEE (attrib) **JZT-37.2a** Allegro, contradanz, 3 trios, coda. 2ob 2cl 2hn 2bn cbn.

MONDONVILLE, Jean-Joseph Cassanéa de (1711 - 1772)
Thésée (tragédie, 17 Nov 1765, Paris)
ANON **A-46.2m(a)** Marche. 2vl 2hn 2bn.

MONIUSZKO, Stanislav (1819 - 1872)
Untraced arrangement: Halka (opera 1854): Canzone (arr. ANON, for the unique combination of ob 2cl 2bn tp);
Pc (Oertel, Hamburg, sd).

MONSIGNY, Pierre (1729 - 1817)
Le Roy et le Fermier (comic opera, 22 Nov 1762, Paris)
ANON **A-112.9m(a)** "Un fin chasseur". 2cl 2hn 2bn.
Rose et Colas (comic opera, 8 March 1764, Paris)
ANON **A-112.8m(a)** "Pauvre Colas". 2cl 2hn 2bn.
Le Déserteur (drame, 6 March 1769, Paris)
ANON **A-335a** overture & 18 mvts. 2ob 2cl 2hn 2bn.
MS score & MS parts: D-Rtt, Monsigny 3/II.
ANON **A-112.6m(a)** "J'avois egaré mon fuseau. 2cl 2hn 2bn.
ANON **A-45.1m(a)** overture. 2vl 2hn 2bn.
ANON **A-1.42a, 1.43a** 2 mvts. 2cl 2hn 2bn.
EHRENFRIED **FHE-3a** 6 mvts. 2cl 2hn bn vlne.
La belle Arsène (opera, 16 Nov 1773, Fontainebleau; 14 Aug 1775, Paris)
VANDERHAGEN **AJV-2.1/5a** 2 mvts; **AJV-2.8/1a** 4 mvts. 2cl 2hn 2bn.
Félix ou L'enfant trouvé (comédie, 24 Nov 1777, Paris)
ANON **A-85.4m(a)** trio. 2cl 2hn 2bn, (2pic/fife, 2cl(rip) 2tp cym tri(s) s-dr tamb ad lib).
ANON **A-336a** "Ne vous repentes pas mon père". fl ob 2cl 2hn.
MS parts: NL-Z, Z1134, No. 8, (possibly missing some parts).
BEINET **XJB-3.1/6a** trio. 2cl 2hn 2bn

MONTCLAIR, Michel Pignolet (Pinolet) de (1667 - 1737)
Jepthé (tragédie, 28 Feb 1732, Paris)
ANON **A-46.4m(a)** Marche. 2vl 2hn 2bn.

MORLACCI, Francesco (1784 - 1841)
Tebaldo e Isolina (opera, 1820, Dresden; 4 Feb 1822, Venice)
STARKE **FRS-23a** overture. 2ob 2cl(C) 2hn 2bn cbn 2tp.

MORLEY, Thomas (c.1557 - 1602)
The First Booke of Balletts (1595, London)
ELGAR **EWE-13a** "Now is the Month of Maying", 5-part madrigal. 2fl cl hn bn.

MOSEL, Ignaz Franz von (1772 - 1844)
Der Feuerprobe (Singspiel, 28 April 1811, Vienna)
KRECHLER **FFK-8.2a, FFK-9.3a** 1 mvt. 2ob 2cl 2hn 2bn cbn.
Salem (opera, 5 March 1813, Vienna)
ROSER **FPR-1a** 3 Theils. 2ob 2cl 2hn 2bn cbn.

MOZART, Wolfang Amadeus (1756 - 1791)
See also: Schmitt, G. **GYS-3a(-5a)**.
Idomeneo (opera, 29 Jan 1781, Munich; March 1786, Vienna)
  ANON **A-337a** 2ob 2cl 2hn 2bn.   MS parts: I-Fc, F.P. S.337.
  KRAUS **JMK-1a** march. 2ob 2cl 2hn 2bn.
  LÖWENSTEIN **CAL-24a** overture & 14 mvts.   fl(F) 2cl(E♭) 2cl(B♭) 2hn 2bn tp b-tb cb.
  SCHMITT, G. **GYS-48.1a** overture. 4fl 2ob 4cl 2hn 2bn 2tp tb serp.
  SCHMITT, G. **GYS-48.2a** finale. 3fl 2ob 4cl 2hn 2bn 2tp tb serp.
  SCHOLZ **WES-142a** quartett, "Andrò ramingo". fl 2ob 2cl 2hn 2bn tb db.
  SHEEN **GHS-13a** overture. 2ob 2cl 2hn 2bn.
  TAYLORSON **JST-14.2a** march. fl 2ob 2cl 2hn 2bn cbn/db.
Die Entführung aus dem Serail (Singspiel, 16 July 1782, Vienna)
  ANON **A-338a** Arie, "Marten aller Arten". fl(E♭) cl(E♭) cl(solo B♭) 4cl(B♭) 2hn 2bn cbn 2tp 3tb b-dr t-dr.
    MS parts: D-DT, Mus-n 737.
  ANON **A-85.1m(a)** overture. 2cl 2hn 2bn, (ad lib: 2pic/fife, 2cl(rip) 2tp cym tri(s) s-dr tamb).
  ANON **A-339.3a** 3 mvts. 4cl 2hn bn. MS parts: D-Rtt, Mozart 17/I, Nr. 7 - 9.
  KIRCHHOFF **WZK-43a** overture & Act I (5 mvts). fl(pic) 2ob 2cl 2hn 2bn tb db.
  LÖWENSTEIN **CAL-13.1a** "Hiel soll ich dich dem sehen" & overture. 2cl(C) 2hn bn tb.
  MOZART **WAM-3a** overture & 16 mvts.   2ob 2cl 2hn 2bn.
  ROSINACK **FJR-3ad** (= MOZART, WAM-3a).
  SCHNEIDER, A. **AYS-66a** overture & 21 mvts. fl(pic) 2ob 2cl 3hn 2bn tp(hn III) b-tb 2vla cb.
  WENT **JNW-27.1a** overture & 7 mvts. 2ob 2cl 2hn 2bn.
  WENT **JNW-27.2a** overture & 7 mvts. 2ob 2ca 2hn 2bn.
Die Schauspieldirektor (Singspiel, 7 Feb 1786, Vienna - Schönbrunn Palace Orangery)
  ANON **A-339.2a** ?overture. 4cl 2hn bn. MS parts: D-Rtt, Mozart 17/I, Nr. 6.
  SHEEN **GHS-14a** overture. 2ob 2cl 2hn 2bn.
Le Nozze di Figaro (comic opera, 1 May 1786, Vienna)
  ANON **A-74.6/11m(a)** march. pic quart-fl 2ob cl(F) 2cl(C) 4hn 2bn cbn+serp/2b-hn 2tp 3tb b-dr t-dr tamb cym.
  ANON **A-340a** Act II finale. fl 2ob cl(E♭) 5cl(B♭) 2hn 2bn tb serp. MS parts: D-DT, Mus-n 743.
  ANON **A-341a** 2ob 2bthn 2hn 2bn. MS pts: D-Bds, Mus.Mss.15150/4. *(Probably adapted from Went, JNW-28.2a)*
  ANON **A-204.26(a)** march ("Non più andrai"). 2ob 2bthn 2hn 2bn serp. *Possibly arranged by C.F. Eley.*
  ANON **A-342a** 3 Märsche aus Figaro. 2ob 2hn 2bn 2tp. MS parts: D-Bds, Hausbibl. Nr.115.
  ANON **A-343a** march, (Act III Finale, "Ecco la marcia"). 2ob 2cl(C) 2hn 2bn cbn tp.
    MS parts: CZ-Pnm, Lobkovic X.H.a.84.
  ANON (In: Pätzig) **GDP-1.6m** Figaro Marsch. 2ob 2cl bn tp.
  ANON **A-344a** Winds & timp. MS parts: CH-E, Th.54,41 (Ms. 1928).
  ANON **A-296(a)** (?incomplete), here only for: bthn hn(II) bn vla.
  ELEY **CFE-1m** "Non più andrai", (as "The Duke of York's New March"). 2ob 2cl 2hn 2bn, *or* piano.
  GILLASPIE **JAG-23a** full opera accompaniment. 2fl 2ob 2cl 2hn 2bn cbn/db.
  GILLASPIE **JAG-24a** full opera accompaniment. fl ob cl hn bn hpcd.
  GILLASPIE **JAG-25a** "In quel'anni, in cui val poco". Solo horn, 2ob 2cl 2hn 2bn.
  HAEFFNER **CJH-2a** 4 mvts, Nos. 3, 20, 2 & 9. 2ob 2cl 2hn 2bn.
  HALE **SYH-1m(a)** "Non più andrai" (as "The Duke of York's New March"). 2fl 2cl 2hn bn serp.
  HAMMERL **PCH-1a** overture. 2fl 2cl(C) 2hn 2bn tp serp/cbn.
  KRECHLER **FFK-5.2a** "Non più andrai". 2ob 2cl 2hn 2bn (cbn tp ad lib).
  LEGRAND **WYL-25a** 3 mvts. 2ob 2cl 2hn 2bn, (fl III ad lib in mvt 3).
  MOZART **WAM-2.3a** "Non più andrai" in *Don Giovanni*. 2ob 2cl 2hn 2bn vlne.
  NOVOTNÝ **AYN-1a** overture. 2ob 2cl(C) 2hn 2bn cbn 2tp.
  ROSINACK **FJR-4ad** (= WENT, JNW-28.1a).
  SARTORIUS **GCS-9a** overture & 5 mvts. 2cl 2hn 2bn cbn.
  SCHACHT **TVS-1.6a, 1.7a** duettino, ("Cinque, dieci, venti") & overture. 2cl 2hn 2bn 2vla cb.
  SCHMITT, G. **GYS-49.1a** overture & Act II finale. 2fl 2ob 2cl 2hn 2bn tp tb(2) db timp.
  SCHMITT, G. **GYS-49.2a** 1 mvt. 2fl 2ob 2cl 2hn 2bn tp tb db.
  SCHNEIDER, A. **AYS-66a** overture & 23 mvts. fl 2ob 2cl 2hn 2bn tp(hn III) b-tb 2vla cb.
  SCHOLZ **WES-143a** terzett ("Cosa sento"). fl 2ob 2cl 2hn 2bn tb db.
  SEYFRIED **IXS-1.4/21(a)** "Non più andrai". 2ob 2cl 2hn 2bn.
  SUTTON **WAS-1a** "Non più andrai". 2fl 3cl bn, *or* 2fl 4cl.
  TAYLORSON **JST-11a** 3 arias. S, fl 2ob 2cl 2hn 2bn cbn/db.
  TRIEBENSEE **JZT-38a** duetto, "Sull' aria". 2ob 2cl 2hn 2bn (cbn tp ad lib).
  VANDERHAGEN **AJV-18a** 25 numbers, in 3 livres. 2fl 2cl 2hn 2bn.
  VOGEL **KXV-2a** sinfonia & 26 mvts. 2ob 2cl 2hn 2bn; *or* 2cl 2hn 2bn.
  WENT **JNW-28.1a** sinfonia & 14 mvts. 2ob 2cl 2hn 2bn.
  WENT **JNW-28.2a** sinfonia & 14 mvts. 2ob 2ca 2hn 2bn.
  WENT **JNW-28.3a** 2ob 2bthn 2hn 2bn.
  WITT **FZW-8a** overture & 6 mvts. fl(F, terz-) 2cl(E♭) 2cl(B♭) 2hn 2bn tp b-tb cb.
Don Giovanni (Don Juan) (opera, 29 Oct 1787, Prague; 7 May 1788, Vienna)
  ANON **A-345a** overture. fl 2ob cl(E♭) 4cl(B♭) 2hn 2bn 2tp 3tb serp b-dr. MS parts: D-DT, Mus-741.
  ANON **A-346a** aria & duet. fl 2ob cl(E♭) cl(solo B♭) 3cl(B♭) 2hn 2bn 2tp 3tb bomb b-dr s-dr.
    MS parts: D-DT, Mus-n 1659, Nos. 2 & 3.
  ANON **A-347a** "Dalla sua pace". Solo althorn, fl 2ob cl(E♭) 3cl(B♭) 2hn 2bn 3tb bomb.
    MS parts: D-DT, Mus-n 1659.
  ANON **A-348a** "Il mio tesoro in tanto". fl 2ob cl(E♭) cl(solo B♭) 3cl(B♭) 4hn 2bn tp(B♭ solo) 2tp(E♭) 3tb
    b-hn b-dr t-dr.   MS score (23 Dec 1845): D-DT, Mus-n 9078.

ANON **A-349a** Finch'han dal vino (as "Gran Marcia"). flautino quartino 2cl(C) 4hn 2bn 4tp tb serp b-dr t-dr.
  MS score: I-MOe, Mus.F.794.
ANON **A-350a** aria. 2ob 2cl 2hn bn cbn 2tp tb. MS parts (1845): CZ-Bm(au), A.36.866.
ANON **A-351a** recitative & aria. 2ob 2cl 2hn 2bn cbn 2tp.
  MS parts (1845): CZ-Bm(au), A.40.159, (missing cl II).
ANON **A-352a** 7 mvts. 2ob 2cl 2hn 2bn. (= HEIDENREICH, JYH-2ad)
  MS parts: D-DO, Mus.Ms.1388.
  Pm (Schott: London, Mainz, 1957), score (pn 6621) & parts (pn 6622), (without attribution).
ANON **A-353a** 15 mvts. 2cl 2hn 2bn.
  MS parts: CZ-KRa, A3934/IV.B.97, (as "Don Juan"). *The wrapper identifies this local copy as part of the*
  Journal für Sechstimmige Harmonie *(Chemische Druckerei: Vienna); the phrasing of the title & the format*
  tend to support this identification, although the publisher's lists do not include this particular item.
ANON **A-354a** overture & 19 mvts. 2cl 2hn 2bn. MS parts: CZ-Pnm, XLI.B.150. *Probably a reduction*
  of Triebensee's arrangement, JZT-39.1a
ANON **A-355a** 2fl bn/vc.
  Pc (B. Schott's Söhne: Mainz, pn 1269, c.1820), RISM [M 4633], parts: A-Wn; D-MZsch.
EHRENFRIED **FHE-4a** 2ob 2cl 2hn 2bn vlne/cb.
FUCHS **GFF-26a** 7 mvts. (2fl ad lib) 2cl 2hn 2bn.
KIRCHHOFF **WZK-44.1a** overture. fl 2ob 2cl 2hn 2bn tp tb db timp.
KIRCHHOFF **WZK-44.2a** introduzione. fl 2ob 2cl 2hn 2bn tp tb db.
KIRCHHOFF **WZK-44.3a** finale Act I. fl 2ob 2cl 2hn 2bn tp tb db timp.
KIRCHHOFF **WZK-44.4a** sextett ("Sola, sola in bujo loco"). fl 2ob 2cl 2hn 2bn tp tb db timp.
KIRCHHOFF **WZK-44.5a** finale Act II. fl 2ob 2cl 2hn 2bn tp tb db timp.
LÖWENSTEIN **CAL-25a** overture. 2cl(C) 2hn bn b-tb.
LÖWENSTEIN **CAL-3.7ac** "Madamina". fl(D) 2cl(C) 2cl(A) 2hn 2bn.
LÖWENSTEIN **CAL-3.8ac** "Finch' han dal vino". 2cl(Eb) 2cl(Bb) 2hn 2bn.
MERKLEIN **ZXM-1a** overture & 19 mvts. 2cl 2hn 2bn. *The same as XLI.B.150, except for cuts.*
NOVOTNÝ **AYN-2a** aria. 2ob 2cl 3hn 2bn cbn tp.
OSSWALD **PAO-2a** overture. 2ob 2cl(C) 2hn 2bn cbn 2tp.
RICHTER **QYR-1a** finale Act I, in 3 parts. fl cl(F) 3cl(C) 2hn 2bn 2tp b-tb serp/cbn.
SARTORIUS **GCS-10a** 6 mvts. 2cl 2hn 2bn cbn.
SCHACHT **TVS-1.3a, 1.5a** finale Act I & "Là ci darem la mano". 2cl 2hn 2bn 2vla db.
SCHMITT, G. **GYS-50.1a** 2 Bds. fl 2ob 2cl 3hn bn 2tp 2tb db.
SCHMITT, G. **GYS-50.2a** 2 Bds. 2fl 2ob 3cl 2hn 2bn tp 2tb db.
SCHNEIDER, A. **AYS-67a** overture & 35 mvts. fl 2ob 2cl+2cl(rip) 2hn 2bn tp b-tb serp.
SCHOLZ **WES-144a** 2 arias ("In quali eccessi", "Batti, batti"). fl 2ob 2cl 3hn 2bn tp tb db timp.
STUMPF **JUS-4.1a, 4.2a** Parthie 1: 7 mvts, Parthie 2: 7 mvts. 2fl 2ob 2cl 2hn 2bn tp basse.
STUMPF **JUS-4.3a** "Deh vieni alla fenestra" & "Non mi di bell'idol mio". 2fl 2ob 2cl 2hn 2bn tp basse.
SUTTON **WAS-2a** "Il mio tesoro intanto". 2fl 3cl.
TAYLORSON **JST-12a** "Là ci darem la mano". fl 2ob 2cl 2hn 2bn cbn/db.
TAYLORSON **JST-13a** canzonetta. ob ca 2cl 2hn 2bn cbn/db.
TRIEBENSEE **JZT-39.1a** overture & 19 mvts. 2ob 2cl 2hn 2bn.
TRIEBENSEE (attributed - A-6.11a) **JZT-39.2a** Duetto, ("Là ci darem la mano"). 2ob 2cl 2hn 2bn.
VANDERHAGEN **AJV-19a** overture. 2fl 2cl(C) 2hn 2bn, (2tp tb ad lib).
VOGEL **KXV-3a** overture, Act I: 7 mvts, Act II: 10 mvts. 2cl 2hn 2bn.
WENT **JNW-29.1a** overture & 10 mvts. 2ob 2cl 2hn 2bn.
WENT **JNW-29.2a** sinfonia & 11 mvts. 2ob 2ca 2hn 2bn.
WIDDER **YYW-1.28a** 3 mvts. fl ob 2cl 2hn 2bn.
WITT **FZW-9.1a** overture & 19 mvts. fl(F, terz-, D) 2cl(Eb, C) 2cl(Bb) 2hn 2bn tp b-tb cb.
WITT **FZW-9.2a** overture. 2cl(Eb) 2cl(Bb) 2hn 2bn basso.
WITT **FZW-9.3a** 8 mvts. 2cl 2hn bn.
Così fan tutte (opera buffa, 26 Jan 1790, Vienna)
ANON **A-356a** overture. 2ob 2cl 2hn 2bn cbn 2tp. MS parts: CZ-Bm(au), A.20.281.
ANON **A-15.40(a)** duetto. fl(Eb) cl(Eb) 2cl(Bb) 2hn 2bn 2tp. MS parts: A-Sca, Hs.266, No. 47.
ANON **A-339.1a** 5 mvts. 4cl 2hn bn. MS parts: D-Rtt, Mozart 17/I.
ANON **A-357a** overture & 21 mvts. 2cl 2hn 2bn. MS parts: CZ-KRa, A4456/R.I.26, No. 5.
BAKER **LQB-1va** "E amore un ladroncello" (Act 4). S or cl solo. 2fl 2ob 2cl 2hn 2bn.
FENDT **AXF-2.2ad** overture & 28 mvts. 2fl 2cl(C & Bb) 2cl(C) 2hn 2bn cb/cbn.
GEBAUER, MJ. **MJG-10a** overture & 6 mvts. (No. 108, 1e liv). 2fl/ob 2cl 2hn 2bn.
GEBAUER, MJ. **MJG-11a** 7 mvts. No.13. Suite 115, 8me liv. 2fl/ob 2cl 2hn 2bn.
GEBAUER, MJ. **MJG-12a** No.23. Suite 116, 9e liv. 2fl/ob 2cl 2hn 2bn.
LEGRAND **WYL-26a** overture. fl ob 2cl 2hn 2bn, (fl III [sic] ad lib).
LEGRAND **WYL-54a** 8 mvts. fl ob 2cl 2hn 2bn.
SARTORIUS **GCS-11a** overture & 11 mvts. 2cl 2hn 2bn cbn.
SCHACHT **TVS-2.13a** "Il core vi dono". 2cl 2hn 2bn 2vla vlne.
SCHNEIDER, A. **AYS-68a** overture. fl 2ob 2cl+2cl(rip) 2hn 2bn tp b-tb serp.
STUMPF **JUS-5a** overture. 2fl 2ob 2cl 2hn 2bn tp basse.
VOGEL **KXV-4a** Act II, 12 mvts. 2ob 2cl 2hn 2bn.
VOJÁČEK **HXV-6a** 1 mvt. 2ob 2cl 2hn 2bn cbn 2tp.
WENT **JNW-30.1a** overture & (?13) mvts. 2ob 2cl 2hn 2bn.
WENT **JNW-30.2a** overture & 17 mvts. 2ob 2ca 2hn 2bn.
WIDDER **YYW-1.29a** overture. fl ob 2cl 2hn 2bn.

La Clemenza di Tito (Kaiser Titus der Grossmüthige) (opera seria, 6 Sept 1791, Prague; 8 Sept 1798, Vienna)
ANON **A-74.5/5m(a)** march. pic quart-fl 2ob cl(F) 2cl(C) 4hn 2bn cbn+serp/2b-hn 2tp 3tb b-dr t-dr tamb cym.
ANON **A-358a** 12-part Harmonie. MS parts: D-DO, (?lost). *This was probably Stumpf, JUS-6.1a.*
ANON (attributed Mozart) **A-259a** overture. pic(Db) cl(Eb) 2cl(Bb) 2hn 2/3bn(divisi in bn I) tp serp b-dr.
   Pc (J.J. Hummel: Berlin, Amsterdam, pn 1151, 1799), RISM [M 5219], parts: D-Tl, Z 92; NL-Z, Z1235.
ANON **A-360a** aria, "Non più di fiori". fl(D) 2cl(C) cl(Bb) 2hn 2bn tp b-tb cb. MS pts: GB-Ljag(w), 400/2.
ANON **A-361a** overture & 2 mvts. 2cl 2hn 2bn. MS parts: CZ-Pnm, XLI.B.158; PL-LA, RM 14, (omits
   mvt 2, Aria). *The mvts arranged correspond to those arranged for nonet by Krechler, FFK-21a.*
ANON **A-362a** 10 mvts, (without overture). 2cl 2hn 2bn. MS parts: CZ-Pnm, XLI.B.156, (parts initialed
   "G.M[?erklein].", more clarinet driven than CZ-Pnm, XLI.B.158).
ANON **A-363a** overture & 7 mvts. 2cl 2hn 2bn. MS parts: CZ-KRa, A4454/R.I.24, No. 7.
ANON **A-364a** overture & "Parto, parto". 2cl 2hn 2bn. MS parts (by Pražák): CZ-Pnm, XLI.B.157.
ANON **A-9.15a** 1 mvt. 3bthn.
AIBLINGER **JCA-1va** Act II, Scene 6, recitative. T, 2fl 2ob 2cl 2hn 2bn 2tp.
COURTIN **HZC-1.4a** "Ah perdo". 2ob/fl(ad lib) 2cl 2hn 2bn.
FISCHER **ZZF-1a** "Parto, parto". fl cl(Bb obl) cl(Bb solo) 3cl(Bb) 2hn 2bn cbn/serp 2tp b-tb.
FUCHS **GFF-27.1a** overture (I Suite). 2ob 2hn 2bn.
FUCHS **GFF-27.2a** 6 mvts, (2 Suite). 2fl 2cl 2hn 2bn.
FUCHS **GFF-27.3a** 5 mvts, (3 Suite). 2cl 2hn 2bn.
HAMMERL **PCH-2a** overture. 2fl 2cl(C) 2hn 2bn tp serp.
KRECHLER **FFK-12.1a** overture & 2 mvts. 2ob 2cl 2hn 2bn cbn tp.
KRECHLER **FFK-10.2a** overture & 2 mvts. 2ob 2cl 2hn 2bn.
KRECHLER **FFK-21a** overture & 12 mvts. 2ob 2cl 2hn 2bn (cbn - listed but no divisi).
KROMMER **FVK-2.5ma** Marsch. 2ob 2cl 2hn 2bn cbn.
LEGRAND **WYL-27a** overture. fl ob 2cl 2hn 2bn, (fl III ad lib).
LÖWENSTEIN **CAL-26.1a** overture. 2fl 2cl(C) 2cl(B) 2hn 2bn tp(clar) b-tb cb timp.
LÖWENSTEIN **CAL-26.2a** 26 mvts. fl(F, Eb, C) 1/2cl(Eb, C, Bb) 2cl(C, Bb) 2hn 2bn tp b-tb timp.
LÖWENSTEIN **CAL-26.3a** overture & 26 mvts. fl(C, D, F) 2cl(Eb, C) 2cl(Bb, C) 2hn 2bn tp b-tb cb timp.
RIEGER **GYR-3a** overture & 5 mvts. 2cl 2hn 2bn.
SARTORIUS **GCS-12a** 6 mvts. 2cl 2hn 2bn.
SCHMITT, G. **GYS-51.1a** overture. 2pic 2ob cl(Eb) 2cl(Bb) 4hn 2bn 2tp serp timp.
SCHMITT, G. **GYS-51.2a** 1 Bd. 2fl 2ob 2cl 2hn 2bn tp tb cb.
SCHNEIDER, A. **AYS-69a** overture & 26 mvts. fl 2ob 2cl 2hn 2bn tp b-tb 2vla b.
SEYFRIED **IXS-1.4/1(a)** overture. 2ob 2cl 2hn 2bn cbn.
SEYFRIED **IXS-1va** Coro, "Che del ciel". CATB, orchestra *or* 2cl 2hn 2bn.
SHEEN **GHS-15a** overture. 2ob 2cl 2hn 2bn.
STUMPF **JUS-6.1a** overture & 11 mvts (in 2 liv.). 2fl 2ob 2cl(C) 2hn 2bn tp basse.
STUMPF **JUS-6.2a** 2ob 2cl 2hn 2bn.
TRIEBENSEE **JZT-40a** overture & (Act 1) 10 mvts. 2ob 2cl 2hn 2bn (cbn).
TRIEBENSEE **JZT-40.2a** terzetto & marcia. 2ob 2cl 2hn 2bn. (= A.6a, 6.17a)
WEBER, C.M. **CMW-5d** Andante aus Titus. (= WITT, FZW-10a)
WITT **FZW-10a** Andante aus Titus, ("Ah perdona al primo affetto". 2cl(Eb) 2cl(Bb) 2hn 2bn cb.
Die Zauberflöte (La Flûte enchantée; Les Mystères d'Isis) (Singspiel, 30 Sept 1791, Vienna)
ANON **A-74.6/5(-7)m(a)** 3 langsame Märsche. pic quart-fl 2ob cl(F) 2cl(C) 4hn 2bn cbn+serp/2b-hn 2tp 3tb
   b-dr t-dr tamb cym.
ANON **A-365a** overture. fl 2ob cl(Eb) 4cl(Bb) 2hn 2bn 2tp 3tb serp b-dr. MS parts: D-DT, Mus-741.
ANON **A-366a** "Bei Männern" & Marcia (No. 9). fl 2ob 3cl 2hn 2bn b-hn/tb. MS parts: D-DT, Mus-n 1884,
   Nos. 6 & 7, (missing ob I, bn II).
ANON **A-82.2/7m(a)** "Alles fühlt der Liebe Freuden". 2fl 2cl 2hn 2bn 2tp serp b-dr cym tamburino.
ANON **A-367a** overture & 14 mvts. 2fl 2cl 2hn 2bn.
   MS pts: PL-LA, RM 81/1-5/107 - 121, (missing fl I, hn I, bn II); RF-Ssc,Ф 891 собр юосуповыix N19,
   pp. 36 - 55. *Possibly arranged by F. Michel.*
ANON **A-368a** 12 mvts (without overture). 2ob 2cl 2hn 2bn (vlne).
   MS parts: D-Rtt, Mozart 27/V. *Does not match any other arrangement for this configuration.*
ANON **A-369a** Douze airs choisis. 2ob 2cl 2hn 2bn. *Does not match any other arr. for this configuration.*
   Pc (Pleyel: Paris, pn 82, c.1806), RISM [M 5067], parts: A-Wn; CH-Gpu, Ib.4864 (two sets);
   CZ-Pnm, XLII.A.3, (missing ob I, cl I (Nos. 1 & 2), hn I); GB-Ljag, (photocopy).
ANON **A-370a** overture & 7 (Act I, Nos. 1 - 7) mvts. 2ob 2cl 2hn 2bn.
   MS pts (local copy): CZ-KRa, A3936/IV.B.99. *Does not match any other arrangement for this configuration.*
ANON **A-371a** overture. 2cl 2hn 2bn. MS parts: CZ-Bm(no), A.15.816. *Possibly arranged by Rieger.*
ANON **A-372a** overture & 16 mvts. 2cl 2hn 2bn. MS parts: CZ-KRa, A4456/R.I.26 a-f, No. 1.
ANON **A-373a** "Pamina", (in fact "Bei Männern"). 2cl 2hn 2bn. MS parts: CZ-NR, A.18.233, No. 1.
ANON **A-374a** overture & 27 mvts. 2cl 2hn 2bn. MS parts: PL-LA, RM 13.
ANON **A-375a** 2cl 2hn 2bn. MS parts: D-Bds, Mus.Ms.15153/30.
ANON **A-376a** Divertimento, 5 mvts. 2cl 2hn bn.
   MS parts (by Augustin Erasmus Hübner, Langenbruck, 1801): CZ-Pu, 59 R 3355.
ANON **A-377.1a** Act 1: 7 mvts, Act 2: 6 mvts. 3bthn. MS parts (post-1791): CZ-Pnm, XLII.C.159, ("Arien
   aus den Opern Zauberflöte und Zauberzitter [W. Müller]").
ANON **A-296(a)** (?incomplete), here only: bthn hn(II) 2bn vla.
BLOMHERT **BQB-2a** complete opera acompaniment. fl(pic) ob ob(ca) 2cl 2hn 2bn db glock.

DRUSCHETZKY **GYD-15.1a** 18 mvts.   2cl 2hn 2bn.   *Authentic: not the Stumpf arr. misattributed.*
DRUSCHETZKY **GYD-15.2a** Priester Marsch.   2cl 2hn 2bn.
FELDMAYR **GJF-1a** as "Parthia in F", 9 or 11 mvts.   2ob 2hn bn vla.
HAERING **JQH-2.18(a)** "Bei Mannern".   2pic 2cl 2hn 2bn tp timp.
HAGNER **MEH-1a** overture.   2cl 2hn 2bn.
HEIDENREICH **JYH-3a** sinfonia & 17 mvts.   2ob 2cl 2hn 2bn.
HIEBSCH **JNH-1a** Parthia (JNH-4, mvts partly from Die Zauberflöte).   fl 2ob cl 3hn 2bn vlne.
KIRCHHOFF **WZK-45.1a** introduzione.   fl 2ob 2cl 2hn 2bn tb db.
KIRCHHOFF **WZK-45.2a** "Dies Bildnis ist bezaubrend schön".   fl 2ob 2cl 2hn 2bn tb db.
KIRCHHOFF **WZK-45.3a** finale Act I.   fl 2ob 2cl 2hn 2bn tp tb db timp.
KIRCHHOFF **WZK-45.4a** Act II, Priester Marsch.   fl 2ob 2cl 2hn 2bn tp tb db timp.
KIRCHHOFF **WZK-45.5a** Act II, Aire-Chor-Terzett.   fl 2ob 2cl 2hn 2bn tp tb db timp.
KIRCHHOFF **WZK-45.6a** finale Act II.   fl 2ob 2cl 2hn 2bn tp tb db timp.
KRECHLER **FFK-6.9a** arie [sic], "Der Hölle Rache".   2ob 2cl 2hn 2bn cbn tp.
KRECHLER **FFK-12.3a** 5 mvts.   2ob 2cl 2hn 2bn tp.
KINSKY **HXK-2a** overture.   2pic 2cl(E♭) 2cl(B♭) 4hn 2bn cbn serp 3tp b-tb b-dr s-dr cym.
LÖWENSTEIN **CAL-27a** overture.   2cl 2hn bn tp(clar) b-tb/bn(II).
OSSWALD **AZO-2a** Theil 1, overture & 6 mvts; Theil 2, 6 mvts.   2ob 2cl 2hn 2bn cbn (2tp).
RINCK **JCR-2a** Arie.   Solo B, fl 2cl 2hn 2bn cbn.
ROSINACK **FJR-2a** March of the Priests (Act 2, No. 9).   2ob 2cl 2hn 2bn.
ROSINACK **FJR-5ad** (= HEIDENREICH. JYH-3a)
SARTORIUS **GCS-13.1a** 7 mvts.   pic-fife 2fife 2ob 2cl(C) 2hn 2bn 2tp serp b-dr s-dr cym+"Halber Mond".
SARTORIUS **GCS-13.2a** 12 mvts.   2cl 2hn 2bn cbn.
SCHMITT, G. **GYS-52.1a** overture.   2fl 2ob 4cl 2hn 2bn tp tb db.
SCHMITT, G. **GYS-52.2a** overture & 4 mvts.   4cl 2hn 2bn.
SCHNEIDER, A. **AYS-85a** overture & 21 mvts.   fl(pic) 2ob 4cl 2hn 2bn tp(hn III) b-tb cb.
SEYFRIED **IXS-1.4/5(a)** "Dies Bildnis ist bezaubernd schön".   2ob 2cl 2hn 2bn cbn.
SEYFRIED **IXS-1.4/14(a)** "In dienen heilgen Hallen".   2cl hn(solo) 2bn.
SEYFRIED **IXS-1.4/23(a)** "Zum Ziele".   2cl 2hn 2bn cbn.
SHEEN **GHS-16a** "Alles fühlt der Liebe Freuden".   pic ob 2cl 2hn 2bn.
STAAB **KYS-1a** 6 mvts.   2cl 2hn 2bn basso.
STUMPF **JUS-7.1a(-7.3a)** Recueils 1 - 3, each 6 mvts.   2cl 2hn 2bn.
STUMPF **JUS-7.5a, 7.6a** 2 livs. (Suite 107, 6 mvts; Suite, 122, 6 mvts).   2ob/fl 2cl 2hn 2bn.
TAYLORSON **JST-14.1a** march.   fl 2ob 2cl 2hn 2bn cbn/db.
WENT **JNW-31.1a** overture & 18 mvts.   2ob 2cl 2hn 2bn.
WENT **JNW-31.2a** overture & 14 mvts.   2ob 2ca 2hn 2bn.
WITT **FZW-11a** overture.   terz-fl 2cl(E♭) 2cl(B♭) 2hn 2bn tp b-tb cb.
Additional numbers for F. Bianchi's opera La Villanella rapita *(28 Nov 1785, Vienna) (See also: Sinfonia, K.318)*
MICHEL **FLM-6.2a** terzetto, "Mandina amabile", K.480.   2fl 2cl 2hn 2bn.
SCHNEIDER, A. **AYS-72a** quartetto, "Dite almeno", K.479, & terzetto, "Mandina amabile", K.480.
fl 2ob 4cl 3hn 2bn b-tb cb.
(unidentified) Scene, aus Einer Italienische Oper
SCHNEIDER, A. **AYS-73a** fl 2ob 2cl 2hn 2bn tp b-tb 2vla cb.
Alma Dei (Offertorium de B. V. Maria, K 277) (1777)
SCHUBERT, F.L. **FLS-1va** Voices, fl 2ob 2hn bn 2tp timp.
Lieder, K.530, 529, Anh 246 (Anh C.8.06), 596, 392 (340a), 518
GOEPFERT **CAG-2a** 2ob/fl 2cl 2hn bn+serp/2bn (tp ad lib).
Lieder, K.391 (340b), 468, 531, 597, 433 (416c)
GOEPFERT **CAG-3a** 2ob/fl 2cl 2hn bn+serp/2bn tp(ad lib).
Lieder, K.523, 476, 524, 264, 307 (284d), 539
GOEPFERT **CAG-4.1a** ob 2cl(C) 2hn 2bn tp.
Lieder, K.523, 476, 524, 441, 307 (284d), 539
GOEPFERT **CAG-4.2a** fl 2cl 2hn 2bn tp.
Das Veilchen, K.476 (Lied, 1785, Vienna)
TAYLORSON **JST-15a** fl 2ob 2cl 2hn 2bn cbn/db.
Symphony in D, "Paris", K.297 (300a) (1778, Paris)
GOEPFERT **CAG-5a** 2ob/fl 2cl(C) 2hn 2bn/bn+serp tp.
Sinfonia in G (Symphony No. 32), K.318, known as the overture to Zaide *(unfinished opera, 1779, Salzburg);
often used as an Overture to Bianchi's* La Villanella rapita.
MICHEL, F. **FLM-6.1a** (as overtue to Bianchi's opera).   2fl 2cl 2hn 2bn.
SCHNEIDER, A. **AYS-71a** (as overture to Bianchi's opera).   fl 2ob 4cl 3hn 2bn tp(with hn III) b-tb cb.
Symphony in C, "Linz", K.425. (1783, Linz)
ANON **A-378a** 2terz-fl 2cl 2hn 2bn.   MS parts: D-Rtt, Mozart 17/II, (missing terz-fl I; the Gardemusik
Katalog of 1821 states that this work was acquired "von Regierungsrath von Peter Regensburg").
TRIEBENSEE **JZT-41a** Andante, mvt 2 only.   2ob 2cl 2hn 2bn (cbn ad lib).
Symphony in E♭, K.543 (1788, Vienna)
TRIEBENSEE **JZT-42a** mvt 1 only.   2ob 2cl 2hn 2bn (cbn tp ad lib).
Symphony in G minor, K 550 (1788, Vienna)
SCHOLZ **WES-145a** fl 2ob 2cl 3hn 2bn tb db.

Gran Partita, K.361 (1782-3, Vienna)
Arrangements for 2ob 2cl 2hn 2bn cbn:
  ANON **A-379a** MS parts: CZ-Pnm, XX.F.55, (7 mvts).
  GOEPFERT **CAG-6a** *with opening Largo & an extra Trio to the 2nd Menuet,* (c.1813).
Arrangements for 2ob 2cl 2hn 2bn (Traeg MS, pre-1799). Parthia II (mvts 5,4,6), Parthia IV (mvts 1,2,3,7).
  ANON **A-380a** MS score and/or parts: CZ-Pu, M.1/31 (complete); D-DO, Mus.Ms.1359, (Parthia II);
    D-F, Mus.Hs.221, 222, (parts, complete).
  Pm (WINDS: Northridge, CA, pn W-42, W-44, c.1981), photocopy of CZ-Pu score & modern pts: GB-Lwpl.
  ANON **A-381a** K.Anh.182, often - wrongly - attributed to Mozart. *Missing the opening Largo of mvt 1.*
    Pc (Breitkopf & Härtel: Leipzig, pn 61, 1801), Nos. 1 & 3 of "Trois Pièces d'harmonie", pts: A-Sm; A-Wgm
    (2 copies); A-Wn; CZ-Bm(au), A.19.490; D-Dmb; D-ZI, (missing horns & bassoons); GB-DOTams; I-Fc.
    MS parts: CH-E, Th.91,18, Nos. 1 & 3, (the cl pts are at Th.982.18)
    Pm (Peters: New York, pn 6306, 1971), ed. A. Einstein, No. 1 of A-367a only, miniature score.
  ANON **A-382a** MS score (by O. Jähns): D-B, Mus.Ms.15351, Nr.1. *Probably of A-365a.*
  GEBAUER, M.J. **MJG-13a** Suite 109, liv. 2, (mvts 1, 2, 3 & 7). 2fl/ob 2cl 2hn 2bn. *With opening Largo.*
  HEIDENREICH **JYH-1ad** mvts 1 - 3, 7. 2ob 2cl 2hn 2bn. *With opening Largo.*
  KLEITZ, F. & FALTZANN **XFK-2.1a** Liv. 1, (mvts 1, 2, 3 & 7). 2ob/fl+ob 2cl 2hn 2bn. *Essentially A-365a.*
Other arrangements of Mozart
Andante for Flute, K.315 (flute + orchestra, 1778, Mannheim)
  TAYLORSON **JST-16** Solo flute, 2ob 2cl 2hn 2bn cbn/db.
Eine kleine Nachtmusik, K.525 (string orchestra, 1787, Vienna)
  SMET **RDS-1a** 2ob 2cl 2bn.
  SHEEN **GHS-17a** 2ob 2cl 2hn 2bn.
Serenade in C minor, K.388 (WAM-4) (2ob 2cl 2hn 2bn, 1783, Vienna)
  HALE **SYH-1.13m(a)** Quick March, loosely based on the finale. 2fl 2cl 2hn bn serp.
  WENT **JNW-1ac** as "Parthia, In E♭ [sic]". 2ob 2ca 2hn 2bn.
Horn Quintet in E♭, K. 407 (K.6 386c) (hn vl 2vla vc, 1782, Vienna)
  ANON (falsely attributed to Mozart) **A-383a** 2cl 2hn 2bn.
    Pc (In: *Pièces d'Harmonie par W.A. Mozart):* (Breitkopf & Härtel: Leipzig, pn 285, c.1805), Liv. 4, RISM
    [M 6079], parts: A-Wgm (3 copies); A-Wn; CH-Zz, Z.Mus.109.a-e; CZ-Bm(rj), A.12.792, (as "Parthia ex
    E♭"); CZ-Bm(au), A.19.490, (MS parts); D-Mmb; GB-DOTams, (photocopy and modern MS score).
    Includes the Menuetto & Trio of K.563.
    Pm (Compusic: Amsterdam, pn 272, c.1994), score & parts.
  HEIDENREICH **JYH-4a** (includes the 2nd Minuet & Trio from K.375). 2ob 2cl 2hn 2bn.
String Quintet in D minor, K.516 (2vl 2vla vc, 1787, Vienna)
  WIDLAR **TJW-1a** 2ob 2cl 2hn 2bn.
String Quintet in D, K.593 (2vl 2vla vc, 1790, Vienna)
  WIDLAR **TJW-2a** 2ob 2cl 2hn 2bn.
String Quintet in E♭, K.614 (2vl 2vl a vc, 1791, Vienna)
  HEIDENREICH **JYH-5a** 2ob 2cl 2hn 2bn.
  ROSINACK **FJR-6ad** (= HEIDENREICH, JYH-5a). Minuet & Trio only.
  STUMPF **JUS-7a** 2cl 2hn 2bn.
  WIDLAR **TJW-3a** 2ob 2cl 2hn 2bn.
String Quartet (Haydn Set, No. 3) in E♭, K.428 (1783, Vienna)
  HERMSTEDT **EJH-1.1a** terz-fl 2ob 2cl 2hn 2bn 2tp(prin) b-tb b-hn.
String Quartet (King of Prussia Set No. 1), in D, K.575 (1789, Vienna)
  HERMSTEDT **EJH-2a** Allegro (1st mvt) only. fl 2ob 3cl 2hn 2bn 2tp b-tb(C, G) b-hn timp.
Divertimento in E♭, K.563 (vl vla vc, Vienna, 1788)
  ANON **A-384a** Menuet & Trio. 2cl 2hn 2bn.
    Pc (An extra mvt in A-369a:) (Breitkopf & Härtel: Leipzig, pn 285, c.1805), Liv.7, Nr.7, parts: *See above.*
    MS score (contemporary copy): D-B, Mus.Ms.15351.
Sonata in D (2 pianos), K.448 (1781)
  WELPMANN **BRW-1a** 2ob 2cl 2hn 2bn.
Sonata in F (pf duet), K.497 (1786)
  RUDOLPH, *Archduke* **JRR-1a** 2ob 2cl 2hn 2bn.
Variations on "Ah, vous dirai-je, Maman", K.265 (K6 300e) (piano, 1778, Paris)
  DRUSCHETZKY **GYD-1.2a** 2cl 2hn 2bn.
Variations on "Lison dormait" from Dezéde's opera, Julie (piano, 1778, Paris)
  GOEPFERT **CAG-4.1/4a** ob 2cl(C) 2hn 2bn tp.
Sonata in A, K.331/iii - Rondo à la turque (1778)
  ANON **A-203.28(a)** sections 2 - 4. 2ob 2bthn 2hn 2bn serp.
  GOEPFERT **CAG-7a** pic 2ob/fl 2cl, (ad lib: 2hn bn tp(clar) serp b-dr).
Variations on "Unser dummer Pöbel meint" from Gluck's La Rencontre imprévue, *K.455* (piano, 1782, Vienna)
  DRUSCHETZKY **GYD-1.5a** 2cl 2hn 2bn.
Adagio in C, for Glass Harmonica, K.356 (1791, Vienna)
  TAYLORSON **JST-17a** fl 2ob 2cl 2hn 2bn cbn/db.
Adagio & Allegro for a mechanical organ, K.594 (1790)
  BLOMHERT **BQB-3a** 2ob 2cl 2hn 2bn.
  PARRY-JONES **GWP-1a** 2ob 2cl 2hn 2bn cbn.

Fantasy in F minor for a mechanical organ, K.608 (1791)
  BLOMHERT **BQB-4a** 2ob 2cl 2hn 2bn.
  PARRY-JONES **GWP-2a** fl 2ob 2cl 2hn 2bn cbn.
  PILLNEY **KHP-1a** fl 2ob 2cl 2hn 2bn.
Andante in F for a mechanical organ, K.616 (1791)
  BLOMHERT **BQB-5a** 2ob 2cl 2hn 2bn.
Vl Marches pour harmonie, K.408/1 (383e), 335/1 (320a), 408/3 (383f), 335/2 (320a), 621/4, 366/8.
  GOEPFERT **CAG-8a** 2ob/fl 2cl(C) 2hn 2bn tp(clar) serp b-dr.
Sinfonia Concertante for winds, K.297b (attributed to Mozart)
  EGK **WXE-2a** 2ob 2cl 2hn 2bn db.
Dem höchsten Regierer sich Jubelsang (unidentified)
  RINCK **JCR-3va** SATB, fl 2cl 2hn 2bn cbn.
[Parthia in B♭] No. 7 (largely based on Mozart themes)
  SCHACHT **TVS-2a** 13 mvts. 2cl 2hn 2bn 2vla vlne.
Spurious Works
Divertimento in E♭, K.Anh.226/K3. 196e/K.C.17.01; WAM-3d (2ob 2cl 2hn 2bn, *or* 2cl/ob 2hn 2bn)
  HAVEL **VXH-22a** 5 mvts. 2cl 2hn 2bn.
Untraced arrangements: Anon, "Parthia in C minore" (K.388) for 2cl 2hn 2bn, advertized as No. 197 in Traeg's
Vienna Nachtrag for 1804; Fleischmann: "Mozart Opern" (André: Offenbach), 2ob 2cl 2hn 2bn; Hermstedt: "3
Quartets" (Peters: Leipzig), Nos. 2 & 3; Goepfert: *Die Zauberflöte.* Holmes (p. 234 of *A Ramble among the
Musicians of Germany,* 1828) mentions arrangments by Neidhardt of *Die Zauberflöte* and the *Fantasia K.475.*

MÜLLER, Adolf (1801 - 1886)
Die Ballnacht oder Die Faschingdienstag (Posse, 6 Feb 1836, Vienna)
  ANON **A-15.5(a), A-15.6(a)** cavatina & arie. 2cl 2hn bn 2tp flug(15.6(a) only).
Tivoli (farce, 31 Dec 1830, Vienna)
  ANON **A-385a** overture, 1835. 2ob cl(F) 2cl(C) 2hn 2bn cbn 2tp tb. MS parts: CZ-Bm(au), A.35.194.
Zu ebner Erde und im ersten Stock (Posse, 24 Sept 1835, Vienna; 1839, Stuttgart)
  LEGRAND **WYL-28a** 1 mvt. fl ob 2cl 2hn 2bn (bn III ad lib).
Frühlingslied
  WERNER, F. **FWW-2a** terz-fl 2cl(E♭) cl(B♭) 3hn(2E♭, B♭) 2bn tp b-tb b.

MÜLLER, Ivan (1786 - 1854)
Unidentified Duetto e Terzetto
  MOSELL **EGM-2a** fl 2cl bn.

MÜLLER, Wenzel (1767 - 1835)
Das Sonnenfest der Braminen (heroic-comic Singspiel, 9 Sept 1790, Vienna)
  ANON **A-386a** 1 mvt (Larghetto). 2cl 2hn 2bn. MS parts: CZ-Pnm, XLII.F.36, inserted between Nos 7 & 8.
  DRUSCHETZKY **GYD-7.1a** sinfonia & 10 mvts. 2cl 2hn 2bn.
  DRUSCHETZKY **GYD-165.17(a)** 2 mvts (= GYD-7.1a, Nos. 6 & 11). 2cl 2hn 2bn
  HEIDENREICH **JYH-6a** 2ob 2cl 2hn 2bn.
Kaspar der Fagottist, oder die Zauberzither (Der Faggotist) (Singspiel, 8 June 1791, Vienna)
  ANON **A-387a** finale 1mo. 2fl 2cl 2hn 2bn. MS parts: CZ-KRa, A3932/IV.B.95, (the flute parts are on
    different paper in a different hand and may be additional parts added by Havel).
  ANON **A-388a** sinfonia & 7 mvts. 2cl 2hn 2bn.
    Pc (Traeg: [Vienna], pre-1799), No. 40, MS pts: CZ-Pnm, XLI.B.172. *Possibly from Druschetzky, GYD-7.6a.*
  ANON **A-377.2a** 7 mvts. 3bthn. MS pts: CZ-Pnm, XLII.C.159, ("Arien aus den Opern Zauberflöte [Mozart]
    und Zauberzitter").
  ANON (?Nudera) **A-389a** 5 mvts. 3bthn. MS parts: CZ-Pnm, XXVII.C.52.
  DRUSCHETZKY **GYD-7.6a** sinfonia & 14 mvts. 2cl 2hn 2bn.
  DRUSCHETZKY **GYD-165.22(a)** 1 mvt (= GYD-7.6, No. 39). 2cl 2hn 2bn.
  SARTORIUS **GCS-14a** 8 mvts. 2cl 2hn 2bn.
  SCHMITT, G. **GYS-53a** cavatina. 2fl 2ob 2cl 2hn 2bn tb serp.
  WENT **JNW-32a** sinfonia & 14 mvts. 2ob 2cl 2hn 2bn (cbn).
Das neu Sonntagskind (Singspiel, 10 Oct 1793, Vienna) *Note: the "Tempo a Polonese" appearing as the last mvt
of Heidenreich's arrs is an adaptation by Müller of Joseph Schuster's aria, "La Polonese. Le Donne han tanti
inganni". A piano red (CZ-Bm, A.27.114) cites the ballet with the Viganòs' Pas de deux as* Diana et Endimione.
  ANON **A-390a** sinfonia & 10 mvts. 2cl 2hn 2bn.
    MS parts (?local copy): CZ-KRa, A3937/IV.B.100. *Does not match the Went or Heidenreich arrangements.*
  ANON **A-391.1a** 22 mvts. 3bthn. MS parts (post-1794): CZ-Pnm, XLII.C.231, ("Arien aus den Opera
    Spiegel von Arkadien [Süssmayr] un[d] Sonntagskind").
  DRUSCHETZKY **GYD-7.3a** sinfonia & 2 mvts. 2cl 2hn 2bn.
  HEIDENREICH **JYH-7.1a** sinfonia & 12 mvts. 2ob 2cl 2hn 2bn.
  HEIDENREICH **JYH-7.2a** sinfonia & 10 mvts. 2cl 2hn 2bn.
  ROSINACK **FJR-7ad** 2cl 2hn 2bn. *Probably the Heidenreich arrangement.*
  SCHMITT, G. **GYS-54.1a** overture. 2pic 2ob cl(E♭) 2cl(B♭) 4hn 2bn 2tp serp timp.
  SCHMITT, G. **GYS-54.2a** 3 mvts. 2fl 2ob 4cl 4hn 2bn 2tp serp perc.
  SCHMITT, G. **GYS-54.3a** duett ("Wenn lieserl nur wollt"). 2fl 2ob 2cl 2hn 2bn serp.
  SCHMITT, G. **GYS-19.3a** 2fl 2ob 2cl 2hn 2bn serp.
  TRIEBENSEE **JZT-2a** (= **A-6.42a**) (Tempo a Polonese, as "Pas de deux getanzt…Viganò"). 2ob 2cl 2hn 2bn
  WENT **JNW-33a** 13 mvts (without overture). 2ob 2cl 2hn 2bn.
  WENT **JNW-73.1a** 2ob ca; **JNW-73.2a** 2fl ca. (Tempo a Polonese, as "Pas de deux getanzt von…Viganò").
Die [zwei] Schwestern von Prag (Singspiel, 11 March 1794, Vienna)
  DRUSCHETZKY **GYD-7.2a** sinfonia & 2 mvts. 2cl 2hn 2bn.
  HEIDENREICH **JYH-8a** sinfonia & 13 mvts. 2ob 2cl 2hn 2bn.
  VANĚRZOVSKÝ **ZYW-1a** Aria in F, (cl I: "Quartetto / Larghetto"). 2cl 2hn 2bn.

Der Alte überall und nirgends (play with songs, Teil 1: 10 June 1795, Teil 2: 10 Dec 1795, Vienna)
  HEIDENREICH **JYH-9a** sinfonia & 10 mvts.   2ob 2cl 2hn 2bn.
  TRIEBENSEE **JZT-43a** aria.   2ob 2cl 2hn 2bn (cbn tp ad lib).
Das Schlagenfest in Sangora [in Braminen] (opera, 15 Dec 1796, Vienna)
  RIEGEL **JZR-1a** quartetto, "Was nüken Trepter".   2cl 2hn 2bn.
  SCHNEIDER, A. **AYS-74a** overture & 5 mvts.   fl 2ob 2cl 2hn 2bn tp(hn III) b-tb 2vla cb.
Die zwölf schlafenden Jungfrauen (play with songs, Teil 1: 12 Oct 1797, Teil 2: 24 July 1798, Teil 3: 27 May 1800, Vienna)
  HEIDENREICH **JYH-10a** sinfonia & 11 mvts.   2ob 2cl 2hn 2bn.
Der lustige Beilager (Singspiel, 14 Feb 1797, Vienna; re-staged 1825)
  CIBULKÁ **MAC-1a** 2 mvts.   2cl 2hn 2bn.
Die Teufelsmühle am Wienerberge (Singspiel/Legend with songs, 12 Nov 1799, Vienna)
  HAVEL **VXH-23a** overture & 20 mvts.   2cl 2hn 2bn.
  HAVEL **VXH-53.4a** 5 mvts, (misattributed to Josef Weigl).   2cl 2hn bn.
  SCHMITT, G. **GYS-55a** overture & 9 mvts.   2fl 2ob 2cl 2bthn 2hn 2bn 2tp vlne/serp.
Der Schusterfeierabend (Singspiel, 23 July 1801, Vienna)
  ANON **A-392a** 2 Theils.   2ob 2cl 2hn 2bn cbn.   MS parts: I-Fc, F.P. S.368.
Der österreichische (ungarische) Grenadier (Singspiel, 8 Sept 1813, Vienna)
  SCHNEIDER, A. **AYS-75a** overture.   fl 2ob 4cl 2hn 2bn tp b-tb serp.
Hamlet (opera, sd, pre-1824, ?Vienna)
  SCHNEIDER, A. **AYS-76a** overture & 13 mvts.   fl 2ob 2cl 2hn 2bn tp b-tb 2vla cb.

MUSARD, Philippe (1793 - 1859)
Suite de Valses sur Les Deux Aveugles, de J. Offenbach (orchestra, 1855, Paris; *Note:* the published version states, "Arrangée pour le Piano par Desgranges")
  ANON **A-393a** pic fl 2ob cl(A) cl(C) 4hn 2bn 2tp 3tb bomb timp b-dr+tri.   MS parts: D-DT, Mus-n 1872.

MUSSINI, Natale Nicola (1765 - 1837)
Overture (unidentified, possibly *Les Caprices du poëte*, Berlin, 1803, or *Das befreite Bethulien*, Berlin, 1806)
  HAMMERL **PCH-1.1(a)** 2ob 2cl 2hn 3bn tp serp.

MUSSORGSKY (Musorgsky), Modest Petrovich (1839 - 1881)
Pictures at an Exhibition (Kartinki s vistavki) (piano, 1874, St Petersburg)
  MAGANINI **QEM-1a** Ballet of the Chicks in their Shells.   fl ob 2cl bn 2tp.

NASOLINI Sebastiano (1768 - c.1806)
La Morte di Semiramide (opera, Carnevale 1792, Florence)
  ANON **A-394a** 4 parts.   (? 2ob 2cl 2hn 2bn cbn).   MS parts (36): I-Fc, F.P. S.406.
Le Feste d'Iside (Il Sesostri) (opera, 1794, Florence; new setting 2 Oct 1798, Trieste; with additions, 1799, Vienna)
  HEIDENREICH **JYH-11a** 2ob 2cl 2hn 2bn.
La Pietra simpatica (opera, untraced: this is almost certainly a misattribution of Palma's opera)
  ANON **A-395a** 2 Acts.   (? 2ob 2cl 2hn 2bn cbn).   MS parts (18): I-Fc, F.P. S.424.

NAUMANN, Johann Gottlieb (1741 - 1801)
Elisa (opera seria, 21 April 1781, Dresden)
  ANON **A-396a** Marsch, E minor.   2fl 2ob 4cl 2bthn 4hn 2bn cbn 2tp a-tb t-tb b-tb b-dr s-dr cym tri.
  MS parts: D-B, Mus.ms.15969/17.
Cora och Alonzo (Alonzo und Cora; Cora und Alonzo) (opera seria, 30 Sept 1782, Stockholm)
  DRUSCHETZKY **GYD-7.5a** 8 mvts.   2cl 2hn 2bn.
  WENT **JNW-34.1a** 2ob 2cl 2hn 2bn.
  WENT **JNW-34.2a** 19 mvts.   2ob 2ca 2hn 2bn.
Protesilao (with J. Reichardt) (opera seria with choruses & ballet, 26 Jan 1789, Berlin; revived Feb 1793, Berlin)
  SCHMITT, G. **GYS-56a** overture.   2fl 2ob 2cl 2bthn 2hn 2bn 2tp db.
La Dama Soldato [Was tut die Liebe nicht] (opera, 7 March 1791, Dresden)
  ANON **A-397a** 6 Märsche.   2ob 2cl 2hn 2bn cbn 2tp.   MS parts: D-Bds, Hausbibl. M.M.172.
  ANON (?Nudera) **A-398a** Marcia.   3bthn.   MS parts: CZ-Pnm, XXVII.C.53, No. 4.
  NAUMANN **JGN-1.5m** Marsch, in B♭.   2ob 2cl 2bn basso(?serp).
  NAUMANN **JGN-1mad** Retiret, in C.   2ob 2cl(C) 2hn 2bn 2tp serp.

NEEFE, Christian Gottlob (1748 - 1798)
Der Friedhof
  KAISER **KAK-5a** cl(E♭) 2cl(B♭) 2hn 2tp t-hn bar tu.

NEUBAUER, Franz Christian (1750 - 1795)
Quatuor Stationes (FCN-1v)
  KNECHT **ZZK-1va** with different texts.   CATB, (ad lib: organ *and/or* 3cl(C) 2hn b-tb vlne).
Quatuor Stationes (FCN-3.2v)
  KNECHT **ZZK-2va** CATB, 3cl 2hn basso.

NEUKOMM, Sigismund, *Ritter* von (1778 - 1858)
2 Märsche, in C, E♭
  GOEPFERT **CAG-1ad** 2fl 2ob/cl cl(E♭) 2cl(B♭) 2hn 2bn 2tp tb serp timp tri cym. (= WIELAND, KZW-2ad, 3ad)
  WIELAND **KZW-2mad, 3mad** 2fl 2ob/cl(rip) 2cl(C) 2hn 2bn 2tp tb serp timp tri cym.
2 Marcia in C: Prinz Carl von Mecklenburg & Prinz Friedrich
  WIELAND **KZW-4mad, 5mad** 2pic 2ob 2cl(C) 2hn 2bn 2tp b-tb (serp).
2 Marcia in E♭: Prinz Albert & Prinz Heinrich
  SCHNEIDER, A. **AYS-5ma, 6ma** 2pic 2ob(non obligat) 3cl 2hn 2bn tp b-tb serp.

NICOLAI, Otto (1810 - 1849)
Gildippe e Odoardo (Odoardo e Gildippe) (melodramma, 26 Dec 1840, Genoa)
  SCHOLZ **WES-146a** cavatine ("Ach ewig füllt die Seele"). fl 2ob 2cl 2hn tp tb db.
Il Proscritto (Die Heimkehr des Verbannten) (opera, 13 March 1841, Milan; in German: 3 Feb 1846, Vienna)
  SCHOLZ **WES-147a** Introduzion. fl 2ob 2cl 2hn 2bn tp tb db timp.
Die lustige Weiber von Windsor (comic opera, 9 March 1849, Berlin)
  ANON **A-399a** overture. 2fl 2ob cl(Eb) cl(solo Bb) 3cl(Bb) 4hn 2bn 3tp t-hn 3tb b-hn bomb timp b-dr.
    MS parts: D-DT, Mus-n 774.

NICOLINI (Niccolini), Giuseppe (1762 - 1842)
Rondo, "Gia un dolce raggio" [? actually J.S. Mayr's additional polacca for Andreozzi's *La Principessa Filosofa*]
  COURTIN **HZC-1.6a** (2fl/ob ad lib) 2cl 2hn 2bn.
Traiano in Dacia (Trajan in Dacia) (opera, 3 Feb 1807, Rome)
  ANON **A-400a** overture & 12 long mvts, (Act I, Nos. 2 - 7; Act II, Nos. 8 - 13). 2ob 2cl 2hn 2bn cbn.
    Pc (sn: sl [= T. Weigl: Vienna], 1810), MS parts: CZ-KRa, A4014/IV.B.187. *Advertized in the* Wiener
      Zeitung, *Nr. 74, 3 October 1810.*
  KRECHLER **FFK-1.4ac** duetto. 2ob 2cl 2hn 2bn cbn tp.
  SEDLAK **WXS-34a** Theil 1: overture & 9 mvts. 2ob 2cl 2hn 2bn cbn (2tp).
  TRIEBENSEE **JZT-44a** overture & 19 mvts (Act 1: 9, Act 2: 10). 2ob 2cl 2hn 2bn (cbn tp ad lib).
Coriolano ossia L'assedio di Roma (opera, 26 Dec 1808, Milan)
  ANON **A-401a** overture & 5 mvts. 2ob 2cl 2hn 2bn cbn. MS parts: CZ-Bm(au), A.35.195.
Quinto Fabio Rutiliano (opera, 24 April 1811, Vienna)
  ANON **A-402a** march. 2ob 2cl(C) 2hn 2bn cbn tp. MS parts: CZ-Pnm, Lobkovic X.H.a.85.
  ANON **A-403a** overture. 2pic 2fl 2cl(A) 4hn 2bn 2tp timp b-dr.
    MS parts: CZ-KRa, A.4017/IV.B.190, (at the end of the cl I part only is the instruction, "Siegue [sic] Subito
      in C:", indicating that this may have been drawn of a larger arrangement).
  ANON **A-404a** overture & 10 mvts. 2ob 2cl 2hn 2bn cbn. MS parts: CZ-KRa, A4013/IV.B.186.
  LEGRAND **WYL-30a** 2 mvts. fl ob 2cl 2hn 2bn.
  LEGRAND **WYL-52.1a** 1 mvt (as WYL-30.1a). fl 2cl 2hn 2bn.
  PUREBL **JSP-4a** Marsch. pic 2fl cl(F) 2cl(C) 2hn 2bn cbn tp(prin) b-dr s-dr.
Carlo Magno (opera, Feb 1813, Piacenza)
  LEGRAND **WYL-53.2a** 2 mvts. fl ob 2cl 2hn 2bn.
Balduino duca di Spoleto (opera, 15 April 1816, Venice)
  LEGRAND **WYL-29a** 2 mvts. fl ob 2cl 2hn 2bn.
  LEGRAND **WYL-52.3a** 1 mvt (as WYL-29.1a). fl 2cl 2hn 2bn.
Unidentified collections
  LEGRAND **WYL-52a** fl 2cl 2hn 2bn.

NIEDERMEYER, (Abraham) Louis (1802 - 1861)
La Ronde du Sabbat! (Ballade, c.1830, Paris)
  BERR **FXB-29.3a** p-fl(Eb) cl(Eb) 3cl(Bb) 2hn 2bn tp 3tb serp b-dr t-dr; (ad lib: hn III, bugle).

NIELSEN, Carl August (1865 - 1931)
6 Humoresques-Bagatelles, Op. 11 (piano, 1897)
  MANN **TXM-1a** fl 2cl bn.

OFFENBACH, Jacques (1819 - 1880)
Polka Dance (possibly the *Polka burlesque,* orchestra, c.1840, Vienna)
  SCHOLZ **WES-148a** fl 2ob 2cl 3hn 2bn tb db.
Les deux Aveugles (operette, 5 July 1855, Paris) *See* MUSARD.

OLBRICH, ( )
Polon[e]se (?piano, c.1843, Neuenstein)
  SCHOLZ **WES-149a** fl 2ob 2cl 3hn 2bn tb db timp.

ORFF, Carl (1895 - 1982)
Carmina Burana (scenic cantata, 1937, Frankfurt oder Main)
  WANEK **FKW-4a** 5 mvts. fl fl(a-fl) ob ob(ca) 2cl 2hn bn bn(cbn).
Der Mond (kleines Welttheater, 1939, Munich)
  WANEK **FKW-5a** 3 dances & closing scene. fl(pic) fl 2ob 2cl 2hn bn bn(cbn) tp.
Die Kluge: Als die treue Ward geborn (Scene of the three vagabonds) (Frankfurt, 1943)
  WANEK **FKW-6a** fl(pic) fl 2ob 2cl 2hn bn cbn tp tb.

ORLANDI (ORLANDO), Ferdinando (1773 - 1848)
Il Podestà di Chioggia (opera, 12 March 1801, Milan)
  SCHMITT, N **NXS-1.3a, 1.6a** "Degl' angelletti al canto" & "Cheta cheta qui masscondo". 4cl 2hn 2bn.
La Dama Soldata (opera, 20 Sept 1808, Milan)
  ANON **A-405a** 2 Acts. 2ob 2cl 2hn 2bn cbn. MS parts: I-Fc, F.P. S.377.
  LEGRAND **WYL-31a** 1 mvt. fl ob 2cl 2hn 2bn.

OSSWALD, Paul Anton (1790; active 1815 - 1830s)
L'Uomo Négro (Der schwarz Mann) (Zauber-Oper, 1820s, Brno)
  OSSWALD **PAO-6a** overture & 20 mvts in 3 Theils. 2ob 2cl(C) 2hn 2bn cbn 2tp.

OTTANI, Bernardino (1736 - 1827)
L'Amore industrioso (L'Industrie amorose) (opera, 1769, Dresden)
  ANON **A-406a** 2fl 2cl 2hn 2bn. MS parts: RF-Ssc, Ф 891 собр юосуповъix N16, pp. 1 - 52.

PACINI, Giovanni (1796 - 1867)
See also: LEGRAND **WYL-53.3a**.
Il Barone di Dolsheim (Baron Dolsheim) (opera, 25 Sept 1818, Milan)
  ANON **A-407a** 2ob 2cl 2hn 2bn cbn. MS parts: I-Fc, F.P. S.389, ("Harmonie oder Husarenstreiche").
La Vestale (Die Vestalin) (opera seria, 6 Feb 1823, Milan)
  ANON **A-408a** introduzione & duetto. 2ob 2cl 2hn 2bn cbn 2tp. MS parts: CA-Bm(au), A.40.162.
Alessandro nell'Indie (Alexander von Indien) (opera seria, 29 Sept 1824, Naples)
  ANON **A-409a** 2 mvts. 2ob cl(F) 2cl(B♭) 2hn 2bn cbn 2tp b-tb.
    MS parts (c.1830): CZ-Bm(au), A.35.201, (?arranger identified by illegible cipher).
  SCHOLL **NYS-1.3a** cavatina. 2ob 2cl 2hn 2bn cbn 2tp.
L'Ultimo giorno di Pompei (opera seria, 19 Nov 1825, Naples)
  SCHMITT, G. **GYS-57a** 2 Bds. fl 2ob 2cl 3hn 2bn tp tb db.
  SEDLAK **WXS-35a** Theil 1: 8 mvts; Theil 2: 6 mvts. 2ob 2cl 2hn 2bn cbn (2tp).
Amazilla (opera seria, 6 July 1825; revived (2 acts) 1827, Vienna)
  SCHOLL **NYS-16ac** overture & 4 mvts. 2ob 2cl 2hn 2bn cbn 2tp.

PAER (Pär, Baer), Ferdinando (1771 - 1839)
L'Intrigo Amoroso (Die wankelmüthige Frau) (opera, 4 Dec 1795, Venice; 26 April 1798, Vienna)
  ANON **A-410a** sinfonia & 11 mvts. 2ob 2cl 2hn 2bn (cbn).
    Pc (Nel Magazine di Musica dei Teatri Imp. Reali: Vienna [sic], c.1796), MS parts: A-Ee, Mus.1090;
    A-Wn, Mus.Hs.3825, (cbn with bn II, no divisi), *and* Mus.Hs.3792, (A-6.9a, 6.10a, 6.12a); I-Fc, F.P. S.340.
  ANON **A-411a** overture & 10 mvts. 2cl 2hn 2bn. MS parts: CZ-KRa, A4454/R.I.24, No. 2.
  ANON **A-412a** (No. 11: Thema, 5 Vars *attaca* Allegro, 2/4). 2cl 2hn 2bn. MS pts: CZ-KRa, A4480/R.I.50.
  HAVEL **VXH-24** overture & 11 mvts. 2cl 2hn bn.
Il Principe di Taranto (dramma giocoso, 11 Feb 1797, Parma)
  ANON **A-413a** sinfonia & 9 mvts. 2ob 2cl 2hn 2bn cbn.
    Pc (In dem k.k. Hof-Theat[er]-Mus[ik]: Verlag: Wien, sd), MS parts: A-Wn, Mus.Hs.3827;
    D-DO, Mus.Ms.1508; I-Fc, F.P. S.410.
  VANDERHAGEN **AJV-1.3a** duo, "Per che mai sposina mia". 2cl 2hn 2bn.
Griselda, ou La virtù al cimento (dramma semiserio, Jan 1798, Parma)
  AHL **CXA-1a** recueils 1 & 2, each 6 mvts. 2cl 2hn bn.
  AVONI **PYA-2a** "Vederlo sol bramo". 2fl 2ob 2cl 2hn 2bn 2tp b-tb.
  FUCHS, G.F. (attributed) **GFF-28.1a** overture. 2cl 2hn 2bn
  FUCHS, G.F. **GFF-28.2a** 9 mvts. 2cl 2hn bn.
Camilla, ossia Il sotteraneo (La Camilla) (drama semiserio, 28 Feb 1799, Vienna)
  ANON **A-414.1a** overture & 4 mvts. fl 2ob 2cl 2hn 2bn 2vla vc+vlne. MS pts: D-Rtt, Sm. 33, Nos. 1 - 5.
  HAVEL **VXH-25a** overture & 3 mvts. 2cl 2hn bn.
  HAVEL **VXH-2ad** overture & 10 mvts. 2cl 2hn 2bn. *Essentially WENT, JNW-35.3a, with transpositions.*
  KRECHLER **FFK-7.8a** duetto. 2ob 2cl 2hn 2bn cbn (?2)tp.
  LEGRAND **WYL-33a** 2 mvts. fl ob 2cl 2hn 2bn, (fl III ad lib).
  SCHMITT, G. **GYS-58.1a** overture & 2 mvts. 2fl 2ob 4cl 2hn 2bn 2tp tb serp.
  SCHMITT, G. **GYS-58.2a** Act I, Nos. 4 & 5. 2fl 2ob 4cl 2hn 2bn 2tp tb serp.
  SCHMITT, G. **GYS-58.3a** Act I, Nos. 6 & 7. 2fl 2ob 2cl(C) 2cl(B♭) 2hn 2bn 2tp tb serp.
  SCHMITT, G. **GYS-58.4a** Act II, Nos. 8 & 9. 2fl 2ob 2cl 2hn 2bn tb serp.
  SCHMITT, G. **GYS-58.5a** Act II, No. 10, duett. 2fl 2ob 2cl 2hn 2bn tb serp.
  SCHOLZ **WES-150a** introduzione. fl 2ob 2cl 3hn 2bn tp tb db timp.
  STUMPF **JUS-9.1a, 9.2a** Recueils 14 & 15, each 6 mvts. 2cl 2hn 2bn.
  WENT **JNW-35.1a** overture & 10 mvts. 2ob 2cl 2hn 2bn.
  WENT **JNW-35.2a** overture & 10 mvts. 2ob 2cl 2hn 2bn cbn.
  WENT **JNW-35.3a** overture & 10 mvts. 2cl 2hn 2bn.
  WIDDER **YYW-1.30a** 1 mvt. fl ob 2cl 2hn 2bn.
Il Morto vivo (opera buffa, 12 July 1799, Vienna)
  ANON **A-8.1a** 1 mvt, Allegro vivace. 2ob 2cl 2hn 2bn cbn.
  STUMPF **JUS-10.1a, 10.2a** Recueils 16 & 17, each 6 mvts. 2cl 2hn 2bn.
La Testa riscaldata (farsa, 20 Jan 1800, Venice)
  KRECHLER **FFK-2.1a, 2.2a, 2.4a** overture (also **FFK-4.1a**) & 2 arias ("La donna com amore" & "Calma mio
    bene"). 2ob 2cl 2hn 2bn (cbn tp ad lib).
Ginevra degli Almieri (La Peste di Firenze) (opera tragicomica, 2 Sept 1800, Vienna)
  KRECHLER **FFK-2.5a** overture. 2ob 2cl 2hn (cbn tp ad lib).
  KRECHLER **FFK-9.1a** overture. 2ob 2cl 2hn 2bn cbn.
Poche ma buone, ossia Le Donna cambiate (Der lustige Schuster) (opera buffa, 18 Nov 1800, Vienna)
  KRECHLER **FFK-2.8a, FFK-9.5a** overture. 2ob 2cl 2hn 2bn (cbn tp ad lib).
  SCHMITT, G. **GYS-59a** overture. 2pic 2ob cl(E♭) 2cl(B♭) 2hn 2bn 2tp serp timp.
  STUMPF **JUS-11a** Recueil 18, 6 mvts. 2cl 2hn 2bn.
Achille (melodramma eroico, 6 June 1801, Vienna)
  ANON **A-415a** Marsch. pic 2ob 2cl 2hn 2bn 2tp serp perc. MS parts: D-Bds, Hausbibl., (?lost).
  ANON **A-416a** 2 pochody [marches]. 2ob 2cl 2hn 3bn cbn tp. MS parts: CZ-TRB, H 438.
  BUCHAL **JWB-2a** 2cl 2hn 2bn.
  FUCHS, G.F. **GFF-29a** overture. 2cl(C) 2hn 2bn; (ad lib: 2fl tp b-tb b-dr).
  HAVEL **VXH-26a** overture & 16 mvts. 2cl 2hn bn. *Essentially a rescoring of SEDLAK, WXS-36.2a.*
  SCHMITT, G. **GYS-60.1a** overture. 2fl 2ob 4cl 2hn 2bn 2tp tb serp.
  SCHMITT, G. **GYS-60.2a** terzetto ("Dunque andiam"). 2fl 2ob 2cl 2hn 2bn tp tb db.
  SCHNEIDER, A. **AYS-77a** Trauer Marsch, C minor. fl 2ob 2cl 2hn 2bn tp b-tb 2vla cb.
  SEDLAK **WXS-36.1a** overture & 14 mvts. 2ob 2cl 2hn 2bn cbn.
  SEDLAK **WXS-36.2a** overture & 14 mvts. 2cl 2hn 2bn.
  WIELAND **KZW-8ad** overture. fl(D) 2ob 2cl 2hn 2bn b-tb+vlne.

Il Fuorusciti di Firenze (Der Triumpf der Treue) (opera semiseria, 27 Nov 1802, Dresden)
KRECHLER **FFK-1.1ac** overture. 2ob 2cl 2hn 2bn cbn tp.
TRIEBENSEE **JZT-45a** duettino. 2ob 2cl 2hn 2bn (cbn tp ad lib).
Sargino, o L'allievo dell' amore (Sargines) (dramma eroicomico, 26 May 1803, Dresden)
ANON **A-417a** overture. fl 2ob 2cl(Eb) 3cl(Bb) 4hn 2bn 2tp 3tb serp b-dr t-dr.
    MS parts: D-DT, Mus-n 1877, No. 1.
ANON **A-418a** Marsch. pic 2ob 2cl 2hn 2bn 2tp perc. MS parts: D-Bds, Hausbibl. Thouret Nr. 121.
ANON **A-419a** duett, "Voi non vedeste mai". 2cl 2hn 2bn. MS parts: CZ-KRa, A3963a/IV.B.127.
LÖWENSTEIN **CAL-1ac** overture. 2cl(Bb) 2hn 2bn tp.
SCHMITT, G. **GYS-61.1a** 1 Bd. 2fl 2ob 3cl 2hn 2bn tp tb db.
SCHMITT, G. **GYS-61.2a** Larghetto. 2fl 2ob 2cl 2hn 2bn tp tb db.
SEDLAK **WXS-37.1a** overture & 12 mvts. 2ob 2cl 2hn 2bn cbn.
SEDLAK **WXS-37.2a** overture & 8 mvts. 2ob 2cl 2hn 2bn.
SEDLAK **WXS-37.3a** overture & 12 mvts. 2cl 2hn 2bn.
TRIEBENSEE **JZT-46a** duet. 2ob 2cl 2hn 2bn.
Léonora, ossia L'amore coniugale (dramma semiserio, 3 Oct 1804, Dresden)
BARTH **WLB-2a** introduzione & 7 mvts. fl 2cl 2hn 2bn.
Una in bene ed una in male (opera, Dec 1804, Rome)
FUCHS, G.F. **GFF-30.1a** overture. 2fl(ad lib) 2cl(C) 2hn 2bn.
FUCHS, G.F. **GFF-30.2a** 8 airs. 2fl(ad lib) 2cl(C) 2hn 2bn.
Sofonisba (dramma serio, 19 May 1805, Bologna)
TRIEBENSEE **JZT-47.1a** overture. 2ob 2cl 2hn 2bn (cbn tp ad lib).
TRIEBENSEE **JZT-47.2a** duet. 2ob 2cl 2hn 2bn (cbn ad lib).
TRIEBENSEE **JZT-47.3a** march. 2ob 2cl 2hn 2bn.
Numa Pompilio (dramma serio, March 1809, Paris)
ANON **A-420a** overture. 2fl 2cl(C) 2hn 2bn (b-tb ad lib).
    Pc (Imbault: Paris, pn O.H.H.196, 1809), parts: F-Pn, Vm27 3296.
KRECHLER **FFK-5.5a, 5.3a, 5.9a, 5.10a** overture, 1 mvt (2/4), ballo, 1 mvt (Allegro maestoso).
    2ob 2cl 2hn 2bn (cbn tp ad lib; tp tacet in 5.3a & 5.9a).
SCHMITT, G. **GYS-62a** overture. 2fl 2ob 2cl 2hn 2bn tp tb db.
TRIEBENSEE **JST-48.1a** sinfonia & (Act I) 9 mvts. 2ob 2cl 2hn 2bn (cbn tp ad lib).
TRIEBENSEE **JZT-48.2a** Act I: sinfonia & 15 mvts, Act II: 8 mvts. 2ob 2cl 2hn 2bn.
Agnese di Fitz-Henry (dramma semiserio, Oct 1809, Ponte d'Altara near Parma)
GAMBARO **VXG-3a** Suites 1 & 2, each 4 mvts. fl 2cl 2hn 2bn; (ad lib: 2cl tp tb serp).
La Passione di Gesù Cristo (oratorio, 1810, Parma)
DRUSCHETZKY **GYD-16a** 2ob 2cl 2hn 2bn.
Der Kapellmeister von Venedig (Der Scheinbetrügt) (quodlibet, 1813, Schwerin & Berlin; 29 March 1821, Paris)
SCHNEIDER, A. **AYS-78a** overture. fl 2ob 2cl 2hn 2bn tp b-tb 2vla cb.
Cantata per la festività del S. Natale (sd, Florence)
DRUSCHETZKY **GYD-17a** 2ob 2cl 2hn 2bn.
Six Valses
VANDERHAGEN **AJV-20a** 2cl 2hn 2bn; (ad lib: fl(F) cl(F) tp tb serp b-dr cym).
Polonaise in Bb (unidentified)
KRECHLER **FFK-2.7a** 2ob 2cl 2hn 2bn (cbn tp ad lib).
KRECHLER **FFK-16.2a** 2ob 2cl 2hn 2bn.
Composite Arrangements
ANON **A-421a** 6 pièces d'harmonie. 2cl 2hn 2bn.
    Pc (André: Offenbach a/Main, sd), parts: I-Nc, 48.2.25. *Probably one of the Stumpf livraisons.*
Unidentified Works
ANON **A-422a** duetto, (c.1829). 2ob 2cl 2hn 2bn 2tp. MS parts: CZ-Bm(au), A.20.880.
ANON **A-74.4/10m(a)** march. pic quart-fl cl(F) 2cl(C) 4hn 2bn cbn+serp/2b-hn 2tp 3tb b-dr t-dr tamb cym.
Die wanterten Komedianten (comic opera, sd, Vienna) *Not listed in any opera lexicon; a MS orchestral score in D-S identifies the work as freely adapted by Matthias Stegmayr.*
ANON **A-423a** overture & 9 mvts. 2ob 2cl 2hn 2bn. MS parts (by Havel): CZ-KRa, A3944/IV.B.107.
Pirro (opera, ?c.1812) *Not listed in any opera lexicon; however, Breitkopf & Härtel (Leipzig) published a piano reduction of the overture in 1812, (pn 1644).*
ANON **A-424a** overture. 2fl 2cl(C) 2hn 2bn tb.
    Pc (Chez Imbault: Paris, pn O.H.199, 1805-14), parts: F-Pn, Vm27 3299.
La Contessa (untraced: probably a misattribution; it has been impossible to match with works with similar titles)
ANON **A-425a** 1 mvt. fl(D) 2cl(C) 2hn 2bn. MS parts: GB-Ljag(w), 5/262, No. 17.
Untraced arrangement: La Maître de Chapelle (opera, 1821, Paris).

PÄRT, Arvos (b. 1935)
Fratres (fl ob cl hn bn 2vl vla vc db claves tomtom, 1977)
BRINER **BEB-1a** 2ob 2cl 2hn 2bn claves tomtom.

PAGANINI, Ercole (c.1770 - 1825)
Olimpia (opera seria, 15 Sept 1804, Florence)
ANON **A-426a** 2ob 2cl 2hn 2bn cbn. MS parts: I-Fc, F.P. S.377.

PAGANINI, Nicolò (1782 - 1840)
24 Cappricci, Op. 1, No. 24 (A minor) (unaccompanied violin, pub. 1820)
BLANK **AZB-1a** 2fl 2ob 2cl 2hn.
Violin Concerto No. 2, in B minor, Op. 7, Rondo ("La Clochette") (c.1824; pub. 1851, Paris & Mainz)
ANON **A-10.45a** fl 2ob 2cl 2hn 2bn b-tb b.
BERR **FXB-29.2a** p-fl(Eb) cl(Eb) 3cl(Bb) 2hn 2bn tp 3tb serp b-dr t-dr; (ad lib: hn III, bugle).

PAISIELLO, Giovanni (1740 - 1816)
La Frascatana (Das Mädchen von Frascati) (opera, autumn 1774, Naples)
  ANON **A-427a** overture.   2cl 2hn 2bn.   MS parts: F-Pa, MS.6784.
  ROSINACK **FJR-8ad** (= WENT, JNW-36.1a; as composed by "G. Pizzini").
  SARTORIUS **GCS-15a** overture & 7 mvts.   2cl 2hn 2bn cbn.
  WENT **JNW-36.1a** 2ob 2cl 2hn 2bn.
  WENT **JNW-36.2a** 9 mvts.   2ob 2ca 2hn 2bn.
  WENT **JNW-2ac** overture & 11 mvts.   2fl 2cl 2hn 2bn.
Le Due Contesse (intermezzo, 3 Jan 1776, St Petersburg)
  BEINET **XJB-3.3/1a** overture.   2cl 2hn 2bn.
  WENT **JNW-3ac.** 2ob 2cl 2hn 2bn.
Dal Finto il vero (opera, spring 1776, Naples)
  SCHMITT, N. **NYS-1.1a, 1.2a** "Reste in pace" & "Se constante, se fidele".   4cl 2hn 2bn.
La Nitteti (opera seria, 28 Jan 1777, St Petersburg)
  ANON **A-428a** 2fl 2cl 2hn 2bn.   MS parts: PL-LA, RM 81/1-5/126, (missing fl I, hn I, bn II).
Gli Astrologi immaginari (I filosofi immaginari; Die eingebildeten Philosophen; Le Philosophe immaginaire)
(opera buffa, 14 Feb 1779, St Petersburg)
  ANON **A-429a** 5 mvts.   Instrumentation unknown.   MS parts: D-Bds, Hausbibl. 347.
  WENT **JNW-36.1a** 10 mvts.   2ob 2cl 2hn 2bn.
  WENT **JNW-36.2a** 10 mvts.   2ob 2ca 2hn 2bn.
  WENT **JNW-4.1ac** 2 Theils.   2ob 2cl 2hn 2bn cbn.
  WENT **JNW-4.2ac** overture & 10 mvts.   2fl 2cl 2hn 2bn.
Il Matrimonio inaspettato (La Contadina di spirito, Il Marchese Tulipano, La Finte Contessa) (opera, 1 Nov
[21 Oct old date] 1779, St Petersburg)
  WENT **JNW-38.1a** 2ob 2cl 2hn 2bn.
  WENT **JNW-38.2a** 8 mvts.   2ob 2ca 2hn 2bn.
La Finta Amante (opera, 15 June 1780, Mogilev, Poland)
  WENT **JNW-39.1a** 7 mvts.   2ob 2cl 2hn 2bn.
  WENT **JNW-39.2a** 7 mvts.   2ob 2ca 2hn 2bn.
  WENT **JNW-5ac** overture & 9 mvts.   2fl 2cl 2hn 2bn.
La Serva Padrona (intermezzo, 10 Sept 1781, St Petersburg)
  FETTER & ERCOLANI **FFF-1a** Parte Primo.   2ob 2cl 2hn 2bn.
  WENT **JNW-6.1ac** 2 Acts.   2ob 2cl 2hn 2bn.
  WENT **JNW-6.2ac.** overture & 10 mvts.   2fl 2cl 2hn 2bn.
Il Barbiere di Siviglia (opera buffa, 26 Sept 1782, St Petersburg; 13 Aug 1783, Vienna; 1784, Paris)
  VANDERHAGEN **AJV-3.16/5a** "Saper bramante" (as "Je suis Lindor").   2cl 2hn 2bn.
  WENT **JNW-40.1a** 2ob 2cl 2hn 2bn.
  WENT **JNW-40.2a** overture & 9 mvts.   2ob 2ca 2hn 2bn.
  WENT **JNW-40.3a** overture & 8 mvts (omits 40.2a, No. 9).   2ob 2bthn 2hn 2bn serp.
  WENT **JNW-7ac** overture & 10 mvts.   2fl 2cl 2hn 2bn.
La Passione di Gesù Cristo (oratorio, March 1783, St Petersburg)
  ANON **A-430a** 2ob 2cl 2hn 2bn.   MS parts: I-Fc, F.P. S.352, (old shelfmark, D.V.507).
Il Re Teodoro in Venezia (dramma eroicomico, 23 Aug 1784, Vienna; in French: 28 Oct 1786, Fontainebleau)
  ANON **A-431a** Marsch.   2fl 2ob 2hn bn.   MS parts: CZ-KRa, A3940/IV.B.103.
  ANON **A-432a** Suite d'harmonie.   4cl 2hn 2bn.
  Pc (Sieber: Paris, sd), RISM [P 518], parts: D-AB, (missing one cl part).
  BEINET **XJB-1.1a** overture & 3 mvts.   2ob 2cl 2hn 2bn.
  BEINET **XJB-3.3/3a** 2 mvts, "L'orgue il vous enflamme" & "Sort cruel".   2cl 2hn 2bn.
  GUERINGE **ZXG-1a** overture & 21 mvts.   2cl 2hn 2bn.
  KRECHLER **FFK-7.9a** Marche.   2ob 2cl 2hn 2bn cbn tp.
  KREITH **CXK-1a** quintet (in fact, 8 mvts).   2fldam 2hn bn.
  OZI **EXO-1.21/1a** overture & 4 mvts.   2cl 2hn 2bn
  ROSINACK **FJR-9ad** (= WENT, JNW-41.1a).
  VANDERHAGEN **AJV-3.24/1a** 7 mvts.   2cl 2hn 2bn.
  WENT **JNW-41.1a** introductione & 13 mvts.   2ob 2cl 2hn 2bn.
  WENT **JNW-41.2a** introductione & 13 mvts.   2ob 2ca 2hn 2bn.
  WENT **+JNW-41.3a** introductione & 13 mvts.   2fl 2cl 2hn 2bn.
La Gare generosa (opera, Carnevale 1786, Naples)
  WENT **JNW-8ac** 2ob 2cl 2hn 2bn.
L'Olimpiade (dramma per musica, 30 Jan 1786, Naples)
  WITT **FZW-12a** "Ne` giorni tuoi felici".   2fl 2ob 2cl 2hn 2bn vlne.
L'Amore vendicato (cantata/favola boschiereccia, 4 Oct 1786, Naples)
  ANON **A-433a** Rondo, "Oh Perduta il bel sembiante".   6 parts.   MS parts: I-Fc, F.P. S.353.
La Modista raggiatrice (opera, autumn 1787, Naples)
  VANDERHAGEN **AJV-1.2a** 2 arias.   2cl 2hn 2bn.
  WENT **JNW-9ac.** overture & 7 mvts (+ "Credi...la mia ferita" from Paisiello's opera *Elfrida* & 2 unidentified
    mvts, = 10 mvts).   2fl 2cl 2hn 2bn.
L'Amor contrasto (La Molinara; Die [schöne] Müllerin) (opera, 1788, Naples; 13 Nov 1790, Vienna)
  ANON **A-434a** Instrumentation unknown.   MS parts: D-DS, (?lost in World War II; probably by Sartorius).
  SEYFRIED **IXS-1.4/6(a)** 1 mvt.   2ob 2hn 2bn.
  STUMPF **JCS-12a** Recueil 7, 6 mvts.   2cl 2hn 2bn.
  WENT **JNW-42.1a** overture & 11 mvts.   2ob 2cl 2hn 2bn.
  WENT **JNW-42.2a** overture & 11 mvts.   2ob 2ca 2hn 2bn.
  WENT **JNW-42.3a** overture & 11 mvts.   2cl 2hn bn.
  WENT **JNW-42.4a** overture & 11 mvts.   2fl 2cl 2hn 2bn.

Nina, ossia La Pazza per amore (commedia in prosa e versi, 25 June 1789, with continuous music, 1790, Naples)
    FETTER & ERCOLANI **FFF-2a** 2 Parts. 2ob 2cl 2hn 2bn. Ms parts: I-Fc, F.P. S.408.
    FUCHS, G.F. **GFF-38a** Steibelt: Cinquième pot-pourry, 1 mvt. 4cl 2hn 2bn.
    GIANELLA **LXG-1a** overture & 11 mvts. fl 2ob 2hn 2bn.
    OZI **EXO-1.32/4a** duetto. 2cl 2hn 2bn.
    WENT **JNW-43.1a** 7 mvts. 2ob 2ca 2hn 2bn.
    WENT **JNW-43.2a** 2ob 2cl 2hn 2bn.
I Zingari in fiera (Les Bohémiens en foire) (opera, 21 Nov 1789, Naples)
    FUCHS, G.F. **GFF-31a** Nos. 1 - 5, (No. 6 is from Cimarosa: Il Matrimonio segreto). 2fl 2cl(C) 2hn 2bn.
Elfrida (tragedia per musica, 4 Nov 1792, Naples)   *See also supra:* La Modista raggiratrice.
    ANON **A-435a** 2pic 2cl 2hn 2bn b-dr s-dr. MS parts: I-Rvat, 19(Vat.Mus.148).
    ANON **A-436a** aria, "Regnate tradito" & duetto "Credi...la mia ferita". 2ob 2cl 2hn 2bn cbn.
    MS parts: I-Fc, F.P. S.353.
Il Giochi d'Agrigento (opera, 16 May 1792, Venice)
    ANON **A-437a** sinfonia & 11 mvts. 7 parts. MS parts: I-Fc, F.P. S.409.
Didone abbandonata (La Didone) (opera seria, 4 Nov 1794, Naples)
    ANON **A-438a** duetto. 2fl 2cl 2hn 2bn. MS parts: PL-LA, RM 81/1-5/145, (missing fl I, hn I, bn II).
    ANON **A-439a** 6 mvts. 2ob 2cl 2hn 2bn. MS parts: I-Fc, F.P. S.409.
Andromaca (dramma per musica, 4 Nov 1797, Naples)
    ANON **A-440a** duetto. 8 parts. MS parts: I-Fc, F.P. S.353.
L'Inganno felice (comic opera, winter 1798, Naples)
    FUCHS, G.F. **GFF-3.2a** quatuor ("Infedeli dov' è l'affetto") & duo ("Via dite cosa avete". 2fl 2cl(C) 2hn 2bn.
Proserpine (opera seria/tragédie lyrique, 28 March 1803, Paris)
    FUCHS **GFF-32.1a** overture. 2cl 2hn 2bn; (pic & serp ad lib).
    FUCHS **GFF-32.2a** Suite 1: 7 mvts, Suite 2: 8 mvts. 2cl 2hn 2bn.
Sinfonia in tre tempi, D major
    MOZART *See:* **WAM-1a** 1 mvt in K.166 (WAM-3). 2ob 2ca 2cl 2hn 2bn.
2 Marches & 2 Pas redoublés
    GEBAUER, MJ. **MJG-1.1/1a, 1.1/3a, 1.1/5a, 1.1/7a** fl(F) cl(F) 2cl(C) 2hn 2bn tp serp/b-tb b-dr cym tri; *or*
    fl(F) 2cl(C) 2hn 2bn serp.
Catch (unidentified; ?spurious)
    ELEY **CFE-3.7m(a)** 2ob/cl 2cl(C) 2hn 2bn tp.

PALMA (de Palma), Silvestro (1754 - 1834)
La Pietra simpatica (opera, autumn 1795, Naples)
    FUCHS **GFF-2.3a** Polaca [sic], "Sento che son vicino". 2fl 2cl(C) 2hn 2bn.
    SEDLAK **WXS-2ad** 2ob 2cl 2hn 2bn. (= WENT, JNW-10ac)
    WENT **JNW-10ac** sinfonia & 7 (+ 1) mvts. 2ob 2cl 2hn 2bn.

PANSERON, Auguste Mathieu (1796 - 1859)
Petit blanc! (Chanson créole, 1826, Paris)
    BERR **FXB-29.4a** p-fl(E♭) cl(E♭) 3cl(B♭) 2hn 2bn tp 3tb serp b-dr t-dr; (ad lib: hn III, bugle).
Le petit Porteur d'eau (Chansonette, 1828, Paris)
    BERR **FXB-29.4a** p-fl(E♭) cl(E♭) 3cl(B♭) 2hn 2bn tp 3tb serp b-dr t-dr; (ad lib: hn III, bugle).

PAVESI, Stefano (1779 - 1850)
Ser Marcantonio (opera, 26 Sept 1810, Milan)
    LEGRAND **WYL-34a** 2 mvts. fl ob 2cl 2hn 2bn.
    SEDLAK **WXS-38a** overture & 12 mvts. 2ob 2cl 2hn 2bn cbn (2tp).
La Celanira (opera seria, 27 May 1815, Venice)
    LEGRAND **WYL-33a** 2 mvts. fl ob 2cl 2hn 2bn.
    LEGRAND **WYL-52.2a, 52.6a** 2 mvts (as WYL-33a). fl 2cl 2hn 2bn.
L'Opera o Divertimento (opera, original unidentified, possibly *Un avvertimento ai gelosi*, autumn 1803, Venice)
    ANON **A-441a** overture & 9 mvts. 2ob 2cl 2hn 2bn cbn. MS parts: I-Fc, F.P. S.374.

PAXTON, Stephen (1735 - 1787)
A Collection of Glees, Catches, etc., Op. 5 (pub. 1782, London)
    ANON **A-202.3/10(a)** *and* **A-204.20(a)** Glee, (TTB), "Believe my Sighs, my Tears, my Dear".
    2ob 2bthn 2bn serp.
    ANON **A-202.3/51(a)** Glee, (ATTB), "Cupid come without delay. 2ob 2bthn 2hn 2bn serp.
    ANON **A-202.3/54(a)** Glee, (ATTB), "How sweet! How fresh!". 2ob 2bthn 2hn 2bn serp.

PAXTON, William (1737 - 1781; brother of Stephen)
A Collection of Glees, Catches, etc., Op. 5 (pub. 1782, London)
    ANON **A-204.62(a)** Glee, (TTB), "Breathe soft ye Winds". 2fl 2bthn 2hn 2bn serp.
    ANON **A-202.3/50(a)** Glee, (TTB), "Breathe soft ye Winds". 2ob 2bthn 2hn 2bn serp.
    ANON **A-202.3/53(a)** Glee, (ATB), "Grant me ye Powers". 2ob 2bthn 2hn 2bn serp.
    ANON **A-202.3/56(a)** Glee, (ATB), "Soft god of Sleep". 2ob 2bthn 2hn 2bn serp.

PEASLEA, Richard C.
Nightsongs
    DOTAŠ **CZD-1a** Solo flug/tp, 2fl ob ca 3cl 2hn 2bn piano db 2perc.

PERGLER, L.
Polka
    KUTTICH **FWK-1a** fl 2ob 2cl 2hn 2bn cbn 2tp tb.

PERSUIS, Louis Luc Loiseau de (1769 - 1819)   *For co-composed works, See: Gyrowetz; Spontini.*
Estelle (comic opera, 1794, Paris)
  FUCHS, G.F. **GFF-33a** overture.   4cl 2hn 2bn tp.
Nina, ou La folle per amour (oder die Wahnsinnige aus Liebe) (ballet after Dalayrac's opera, 23 Nov 1813, Paris)
  ANON **A-442a** 8 mvts.   2ob 2cl 2hn 2bn.   MS parts: CZ-KRa, A3947/IV.B.110, A3948/IV.B.111.
  SEDLAK **WXS-2.2a** 4 mvts.   2ob 2cl 2hn 2bn cbn.
  SEDLAK **WXS-39a** introdutione & 11 mvts.   2ob 2cl 2hn 2bn cbn.
Alexander Marsch (1816; often falsely attributed to Beethoven, K.-H. Anh 11)   *This march was also arranged*
by F. Starke, and also included in the pastiche ballet, Der blöde Ritter, *choreographed by DUPORT (qv).*
  ANON **A-4ma** pic fl cl(F) 2cl(C) 4hn(D, F) 2bn cbn 3tp(D, D, F) b-dr s-dr.
    MS parts: CZ-Bm(au), A.35.256, (?missing cl I).
  ANON **A-5ma** cl(D) 3cl(C) 2hn 2bn cbn 2tp serp b-dr s-dr.   MS parts (?from Vienna): GB-Ljag(w), 176/129,
    (as "Alexanders Favorit=Marsch für die ganze türkische Musik Vom Regiment Kaiser Alexander").
  ANON **A-2.2ma** Märsche, "blöde Ritter".   cl(D) cl(C) 2hn 2bn 2tp serp b-dr s-dr.
Vive le Roi, Vive la France, Marche de M.M. Les Gardes du corps Musique (post-1814, Paris)
  GAMBARO **VXG-4a** fl(F) cl(F) 2cl(B♭) 2hn (2)bn tp tb serp(B)♭ b-dr.

PHILIDOR, François André Danican (1726 - 1795)
Le Sorcier (comic opera, 2 Jan 1764, Paris)
  ANON **A-112.3m(a)** "Nous étions dans cet âge".   2cl 2hn 2bn.
Tom Jones (opera, 27 Feb 1765, Paris)
  ANON **A-1.79a, 1.81a** 2 mvt, "Amour, Amour" and "Oui, toute ma vie".   2cl 2hn 2bn.
  VANDERHAGEN **AJV-2.12/1a** "D'un Cerf dix Cors".   2cl 2hn 2bn.
Ernelinde, Princesse de Norvège (tragédie, 24 Nov 1767, Paris)
  ROESER **VAR-3a** 2cl 2hn 2bn.
Les Femmes vengées (opera, 20 March 1775, Paris)
  VANDERHAGEN **AJV-2.4/1a** 4 mvts.   2cl 2hn 2bn.
Thémistocle (opera, 18 Oct 1785, Fontainebleau; 23 May 1786, Paris)
  OZI **EXO-1.19/2a.** 1 mvt.   2cl(C) 2hn 2bn.
La belle Esclave (comic opera, 6 Nov 1787, Paris)
  OZI **EXO-1.26/1a** overture (2 parts) & 1 mvt.   2cl(C) 2hn 2bn.

PICCINNI, Nicolo (1728 - 1800)
Didon (tragédie lyrique, 16 Oct 1783, Fontainebleau)
  ANON **A-443a** (Traeg, 1799).   2ob 2cl 2hn 2bn.   MS parts: I-Fc, F.P. S.325.
  ANON **A-444a** "Ah! prends pitié de ma foiblesse".   fl ob 2cl 2hn.   MS parts: NL-Z, Z1134, No. 9, (possibly
    missing some parts).
  SARTORIUS **GCS-16a** 8 mvts.   2cl 2hn 2bn cbn.
  VANDERHAGEN **AJV-4.4a** "Nous allons revoir".   2cl 2hn 2bn.
Pénélope (opera, 2 Nov 1785, Fontainebleau; 6 Dec 1785, Paris)
  OZI **EXO-1.17/1a** overture & air de danse.   2cl 2hn 2bn.
Unidentified excerpt: "Lasciarmi respirar".
  ANON **A-445a** 2fl 2cl 2hn 2bn.   MS parts: PL-LA, RM 81/1-5/137, (missing fl I, hn I, bn II).
Pas redoublé
  GAMBARO **VXG-4.6(a)** pic(d♭) cl(E♭) 2cl(B♭) 2hn (2)bn tp tb serp b-dr+cym.

PINSUTI, Ciro Ercole, *Cavaliero* (1829 - 1888)
Tell me, Flora (glee for SATB, pub. 1867, London)
  ELGAR **EWE-14a** 2fl cl hn bn.

PIXIS, Johann Baptist (1788 - 1874)
Overture (unidentified, possibly the *Overture in F*, for orchestra)
  WOELFING **ZZW-4a** fl 2ob 2cl 3hn 2bn tb db timp.

PLEYEL, Ignaz Joseph (Ignace Jan) (1757 - 1831)
Virtually all of Pleyel's "Harmoniemusik" is found in other versions. We list here works by known arrangers
(or postumous arrangements). Works by Pleyel or attributed to him are listed in the Main Works List.
Symphony (B. deest)
  ANON **A-446a** fl ob/(cl IV) cl(E♭) 3/4cl(B♭) 2hn 2bn 2tp tb serp b-dr.   MS parts: D-DT, Mus-n 790.
Symphony in F (B.136) (Strasbourg, 1786)
  WENT **JNW-44a** 4 mvts.   2ob 2ca 2hn 2bn.
Symphony in A (B.137) (Strasbourg, 1788)
  WENT **JNW-45a** 3 mvts (omits Menuetto & Trio, mvt 3).   2ob 2ca 2hn 2bn.
Quintetto No. 4, in E♭, (B.283) (2vl 2vla vc, 1788)
  MICHEL **FLM-7a** 2fl 2cl 2hn 2bn.
6 Quartets, Oeuvre 1, (B.301 - 306) (string quartet, 1782 - 1783)
  ELEY **CFE-3.3m(a)** No. 2, mvts 3 & 4, (B.302iii, iv - actually one continuous mvt).   2cl 2hn bn.
  MICHEL **FLM-8a** No. 4, (B.304).   2fl 2cl 2hn 2bn.
6 Quartets, "Oeuv. 2" (B.307 - 312) (string quartets, 1784, Vienna)
  HAVEL **VXH-27** No. 2, (B.308), complete.   2cl 2hn 2bn.
  HAVEL **VXH-28** No. 4, (B.310), complete.   2cl 2hn 2bn.
  OZI **1.18/3a** No. 2, Finale Allegro (B.308iii).   2cl 2hn 2bn.

6 Quartets, Op. 6, (B.319 - 324) (string quartet, 1786)
  ÉLEY **CFE-3.5m(a)** No. 4, mvt 3, Meneutto & Trio, (B.322iii, iiia). 2cl 2hn bn.
  HAVEL **VXH-29a** No. 1, (B.319/i), Moderato, (as "Serenatta [sic] 2da"). 2cl 2hn 2bn.
  HAVEL **VXH-30a** No. 3, (B.321), complete, (as "Parthie 7"). 2cl 2hn 2bn.
  HAVEL **VXH-31a** No. 4, (B.322), complete, (as "Parthie 9"). 2cl 2hn 2bn.
  HAVEL **VXH-32a** No. 5, (B.323), complete, (as "Parthie 15"). 2cl 2hn 2bn
  HAVEL **VXH-33a** No. 6, (B.324). complete, (as "Parthie 10"). 2cl 2hn 2bn.
  MICHEL **FLM-9a** No. 3, (B.321); **FQM-10a** No. 4, (B.322). 2fl 2cl 2hn 2bn.
6 Quartets, (B.325 - 330) (string quartet, 1786)
  HAVEL **VXH-34a** No. 1, (B.325), mvts 1 & 4 only, (as "Nro 15"). 2cl 2hn 2bn.
12 Quartets, dedicated to the King of Prussia, (B.331 - 342) (string quartet, 17)
  ÉLEY **CFE-2.5m(a)** No. 1, mvt 2, (B.331ii), followed by B.350/ii. 2cl 2hn bn.
  HAVEL **VXH-34a** No. 4, (B.334), complete, (as "Parthie 16"). 2cl 2hn 2bn.
  KROMMER **FVK-1a.** No. 8, mvt 2, Variazione, (B.338ii). 2ob ca.
3 Quartets, (B.343 - 345) (string quartet, 1788)
  HAVEL **VXH-35a** No. 1, (B.343), complete, (as "Parthae 12"). 2cl 2hn 2bn.
6 Quartets, dedicated to the Prince des Galles, (B.346 - 351) (string quartet, 1791)
  ÉLEY **CFE-2.5m(a)** No. 4, (B.350ii, joined onto B.331/ii). 2cl 2hn bn.
  HAVEL **VXH-37a** No. 1, (B.347), complete, (as "Parthia 19"). 2cl 2hn 2bn.
  VANDERHAGEN **AJV-5.5a** No. 2, Andante poco Allegretto, (B.350/ii). 2cl 2hn 2bn.
6 Quartets, dedicated to the King of Naples, (B.353 - 358) (string quartet, 1791)
  HAVEL **VXH-38a** (B.358), mvts 1 & 2. 2cl 2hn 2bn.
  ZASCHE **AZZ-2a** No. 2 (B.351), mvts 1 & 2 only. 2fl(D) 2ob 2cl 2hn 2bn.
6 Quartets (B.381 - 386) (fl vl vla vc, 1780) *Note: B.384 = B.2909/2910, IJP-16, Trois Harmonies, No. 3.*
  HAVEL **VXH-39a** Nro VIta Partita, 3 mvts (B.384/i, B.386/ii, B.384/iii). 2cl 2hn 2bn.
  MICHEL **FLM-15a** B.384, complete. 2fl 2cl 2hn 2bn.
Trio for piano, violin & cello, (B.444)
  TRIEBENSEE **JZT-49a** 2nd mvt, "Air Ecossais". 2ob 2cl 2hn 2bn (cbn ad lib).
3 Sonatas (Sonatinas VII - IX), B.580 - 582 (piano & violon, c.1800, Paris)
  HAMMERL, P.C. **PCH-3.1a** No. 1, (B.580), 2nd mvt, Andante. 2ob 2cl 2hn 2bn tp serp.
Echo Nᵒ 2 in F, (B. deest)
  HAVEL **VXH-16.2ac** 2cl 2hn 2bn. (Attributed to Hoffmeister at Havel, VXH-15.3ac)
Composite Works
  MICHEL **FLM-7a** B.321i, B.134iv, iva, B.321ii. 2fl 2cl 2hn 2bn.
  MICHEL **FLM-8a** B.111v, ?B.433i, B.111ii, B.322iii (all variants). 2fl cl 2hn 2bn.
  MICHEL **FLM-9a** B.312ii; B.331ii; B.349ii; B.349iii.
  MICHEL **FLM-10a** B.331ii (variant?); B.303ii; B.303iii; B.304iii. 2fl 2cl 2hn 2bn.
  MICHEL **FLM-11a** B.386i; B.338ii; B.386ii; B.334iii. 2fl 2cl 2hn 2bn.
  MICHEL **FLM-12a** B.111i; B.382ii; B.382iii; ?variant of B.381iii. 2fl 2cl 2hn 2bn.
  MICHEL **FLM-13a** B.304i; B.355ii; B.354ii variant; B.353iii. 2fl 2cl 2hn 2bn.
  MICHEL **FLM-14a** B.322i; B.322iii, iiia; B.319/ii; B.323iii. 2fl 2cl 2hn 2bn.
  MICHEL **FLM-16a** B.216i; B.359iii; B.258iii, iiia; B.216v. 2fl 2cl 2hn 2bn.
  MICHEL **FLM-17a** B.346i; B.346ii; B.382ii; B.382iii; B.284iv.
Pièces d'Harmonie (B.2038 / 2040: 338/ii; 350/ii; 339/iv, iva; 346/iii; 342/iv; 349/ii; 347/iii; X41)
  BISCH **YXB-1a** 2cl 2hn 2bn

POULENC, Francis (1899 - 1963)
 FRANÇAIX **JEF-4a** Musique pour faire plaisir [composite work]. 2fl ob ob(ca) cl cl(b-cl) 2hn bn bn(cbn).
L'histoire de Babar (melodrama, reciter & piano, 1940 - 1945)
  BLOMHERT **BQB-6a** Speaker, fl fl(pic) ob ob(ca) cl cl(b-cl) 2hn bn(cbn) tp tu.

PROCH, Heinrich (1809 - 1878)
Das Alpenhorn, 18 Werk (Lied for solo voice, piano & horn or cello, c.1835, Vienna)
  ANON **A-447a** fl 2ob cl(Eb) cl(solo Bb) 3cl(Bb) 4hn 2bn a-hn 3tb b-hn/bomb.
    MS parts: D-DT, Mus-n 1770, No. 3.
  ANON **A-448a** Variationen. fl 2ob cl(Eb) cl(solo Bb) 3cl(Bb) 4hn 2bn 3tp a-hn 3tb bomb b-dr s-dr.
    MS parts: D-DT, Mus-n 1888.

PROCHASKA, ( )
Theresien-Polka (?piano, c.1843)
  SCHOLZ **WES-151a** fl 2ob 2cl 2hn 2bn tp tb db.

PUCITTA, Vincenzo (1778 - 1861)
Mio ben per te quest' anima (aria)
  WIELAND **KZW-2.7ad** fl/ob ob/fl 2cl 2hn 2bn cb.

PURCELL, Henry (1659 - 1695)
Prelude (attributed)
  STONEHAM **AMS-1a** ob 2cl 2hn 2bn.

QUILTER, Roger (1877 - 1953)
4 Child Songs, Op. 5 (voice & piano, 1914)
  CAMPBELL **AQC-5a** 2ob 2cl 2hn 2bn.

RAMEAU, Jean-Philippe (1683 - 1764)
Castor e Pollux (opera, 24 Oct 1737, revived 8/11 Nov 1754 & 24 Jan 1764 (with minor revisions), Paris)
  ANON **A-46.1m(a)** Marche. 2vl 2hn 2bn
Nouvelles suites . . . de clavecin (1741, Paris)
  WIGGINS, B. **BXW-1a** La Poule. fl ob 2cl bn.

RAVEL, (Joseph) Maurice (1875 - 1937)
Pavane pour une infante défunte (piano, later orchestrated, 1899, Paris)
BAKER **LQB-2a** 2fl ob ob(ca) 2cl 2hn 2bn.

RAYMOND, (?Georges-Marie) (1769 - 1839)
Wintergarten-Polka (?piano, c.1835)
SCHOLZ **WES-152a** fl 2ob 2cl 2hn 2bn tp tb db timp.

REDERN, Friedrich Wilhelm, *Graf* von (1802 - 1883)
Geschwind Marsch Konig Pr[eussischer] Armeem[arsch] No. 155
ANON **A-449a** pic fl 2ob cl(E♭) cl(solo B♭) 3cl(B♭) 4hn 2bn 3tp t-hn 3tb bomb/b-hn vc/cb b-dr s-dr.
MS parts: D-DT, Mus-n 1891, No. 1.

REEVE, William (1757 - 1827)
Oscar & Malvina (with William Shield, pantomime ballet, 20 Oct 1791)
ELEY **CFE-2.2m(a) & 2.7m(a)** 2 mvts. 2ob/2cl 2hn 2bn tp.

REISER, ( )
6 Walzer
STEINER **FFS-1a** cl(E♭) 2cl(B♭) 2hn 2bn 2tp.

REISSIGER, Carl Gottlieb (1798 - 1859)
Yelva, die Waise aus Russland (melodrama, 21 Oct 1828, Dresden)
KIRCHHOFF **WZK-46a** overture. fl 2ob 3cl 2hn 2bn tp tb db.
Die Felsenmühle zu Estalières (opera, 10 April 1831, Dresden)
ANON **A-450a** overture. 2ob 2cl 2hn 2bn cbn 2tp tb. MS parts: CZ-Bm(au), A.36.886.
KIRCHHOFF **WZK-47a** 8 mvts. fl 2ob 2cl 2hn 2bn tp tb db.
Adele de Foix (opera, 26 Nov 1841, Dresden)
SCHOLZ **WES-153a** terzett. fl 2ob 2cl 2hn 2bn tp tb db timp.
Danses Brillantes, Op. 26, No. 5 (often known as the "Dernière Pensée de C.M. von Weber" or as the song "Das Herzenload") (1822, pub 1824).
BERR **FXB-21a** Military band.
VOJÁČEK **HXV-9.1a** as "Das Herzenload". fl(E♭) 2cl 2bn 2tp basso.

RESCH, Johann (1830 - 1889)
Eisenbahn-Polka (piano)
ANON **A-451a** pic fl 2ob cl(E♭) 3cl(B♭) 4hn 2bn 5tp a-hn 3tb b-hn/bomb b-dr t-dr s-dr.
MS parts: D-DT, Mus-n 2035, No. 1.
Oesterreische [sic] Zapfenstreich-Polka (piano)
ANON **A-452a** pic fl 2ob cl(E♭) 3cl(B♭) 4hn 2bn 5tp a-hn 3tb b-hn/bomb b-dr t-dr s-dr.
MS score: D-DT, Mus-n 1899. MS parts: D-DT, Mus-n 2035, No. 2a.

RICCI, Luigi (1805 - 1859)
Il nuovo Figaro (opera, 15 Feb 1832, Parma)
SCHOLL **NYS-17ac** overture. 2ob 2cl 2hn 2bn cbn 2tp b-tb.
Chiara di Montalbano in Francia (opera, 15 Aug 1835, Milan)
ANON **A-15.37(a)** cavatina. cl(E♭) 2cl(B♭) 2hn 2bn tp flug.
Il Desertore per amore (opera, 16 Dec 1836, Naples)
SCHOLL **NYS-18ac** cavatina & scene e cavatina. 2ob 2cl 2hn 2bn cbn 2tp [b-tb].

RIEGEL (Rigel), Henri-Jean (1772 - 1852)
Untraced arrangement: Les deux Meuniers (opera, 1799/1800, Cairo; overture).

RIEGER, Gottfried (1764 - 1839)
Allegretto, in F
DRUSCHETZKY **GYD-18a** 2ob 2cl 2hn 2bn.

RIES, Ferdinand (1784 - 1838)
Grande Ouverture e Marche triomphale pour la Fête Musicale de Cologne, Op. 172. (orchestra, 1832)
KÜFFNER **JYK-11a** Instrumentation unknown (military band).

RIGHINI, Vincenzo (1756 - 1812)
Armida (opera, 23 Feb 1782, Vienna; revived 21 Feb 1797, Berlin)
EHRENFRIED **FHE-5a** overture & 17 mvts. 2ob 2cl 2hn 2bn vlne/db.
SCHNEIDER, A. **AYS-79a** overture. fl 2ob 4cl 2hn 2bn tp b-tb serp.
WITT **FZW-13a** overture & 6 mvts. cl(E♭) 2cl(B♭) 2hn 2bn tp b-tb cb.
L'Incontro inaspettato (opera, 27 April 1785, Vienna; revived 1795, Berlin)
DRUSCHETZKY **GYD-7.4a** sinfonia & "Sposa Sonia". 2cl 2hn 2bn.
DRUSCHETZKY **GYD-165.18(a)** "Sposa Sonia". 2cl 2hn 2bn.
WENT **JNW-46.1a** overture & 11/12 mvts. 2ob 2cl 2hn 2bn.
WENT **JNW-46.2a** overture & 12 mvts. 2ob 2ca 2hn 2bn.
Il Natal d'Apollo (cantata, 1789, Vienna; performed as an opera, 1794, Berlin)
ANON **A-453a** Parte 1 & 2. 9 winds (?2ob 2cl 2hn 2bn cbn). MS parts: I-Fc, F.P. S.411.
Enea nel Lazio (opera, 7 Jan 1793, Berlin)
ANON **A-454a** Parte 1 & 2. 9 winds (? 2ob 2cl 2hn 2bn cbn). MS parts: I-Fc, F.P. S.411.
SCHMITT, G. **GYS-63a** terzetto. 2fl 2ob 2cl 2bthn 2hn 2bn 2tp db.

Tigrane, Re d'Armenia (opera, 20 Jan 1800, Berlin)
    SCHOLZ **WES-154a** overture. fl 2ob 2cl 3hn 2bn tp tb db timp.
Minerve et Dédale (ballet, 23 April 1802, Berlin)
    TAUSCH **FWT-2a** 8 mvts. 2cl 2hn 2bn.
La Gerusalemme liberata (Armida al campo di Franchi) (opera, 17 Jan 1803, Berlin).
    ANON **A-14va** 2 choruses. Instrumentation unknown. MS: D-SWl, (old Catalog: Righini 6).
    SCHMITT, G. **GYS-64a** quartetto ("Fallisce in orni impressa"). 2fl 2ob 2cl 2hn 2bn (tp) tb db.

RIOTTE, Philipp Jacob (1776 - 1856)
Wanda, Königin der Sarmaten (romantic tragedy, 16 March 1812, Vienna)
    ANON **A-455a** 2 Theils. 2ob 2cl 2hn 2bn cbn tp.
    Pc (sn: sl [= T. Weigl: Vienna], c.1812), MS parts: I-Fc, F.P. S.357.

RODE, Pierre Jacques Joseph (1774 - 1830).
Air varié in G, Op. 10 (violin, c.1807) *Adapted by Madame Angelina Catalani for the singing lesson in the Vienna production of Rossini's opera,* Il Barbiere di Siviglia.
    SEDLAK **WXS-40a** 2ob 2cl 2hn 2bn cbn (2tp).

RODOLPH Rodolph), Jean-Joseph (Johann Joseph) (1730 - 1812)
L'Aveugle de Palmire (Palmyre) (comédie-pastoral mêlée d'ariettes, 5 March 1767, Paris)
    VANDERHAGEN **AJV-2.9/1a** 3 mvts. 2cl 2hn 2bn.

ROESER, Valentin (?1735 - ?1782) *See also supra:* ANON **A-2a.**
    ANON **A-203.1/4(a)** (= **ROESER, VZR-3a**) Andante grazioso. 2ob 2bthn 2hn 2bn serp.

ROHM, Karl
Erinnerung an Pyrmont, Walzer (piano)
    ANON **A-456a** fl 2ob 1cl(E♭) cl(solo B♭) 3cl(B♭) 2hn 2bn 2tp 3tb serp b-dr t-dr. MS pts: D-DT, Mus-n 1893.
6 dances (piano)
    ANON **A-457a** fl 2ob cl(E♭) cl(solo B♭) 3cl(B♭) 4hn 2bn 2tp kl-hn 3tb b-hn b-dr s-dr.
    MS parts: D-DT, Mus-n 2034.

ROLLE, Johann Heinrich (1718 - 1785)
Thirza und ihre Söhne (musikalische Drama, 1781, Leipzig)
    ANON **A-155.4m(a)** March in E♭. 2cl 2hn bn tp.
Unidentified Marches
    ANON **A-202.3/13(a)** *and* **A-204.17(a)** March; in B♭, ₵. 2ob 2bthn 2hn 2bn serp.
    ANON **A-155.6m(a)** March in E♭, ₵. 2cl 2hn bn tp.

ROMANI, Pietro, (composer & compiler) (1791 - 1877) *See also: Gallenberg:* Der Psyche.
Die Fee und der Ritter (ballet, 1824, Vienna). *The composers include Aiblinger, Dobihal, Mercadante, Pacini, Payer, Pensel, Rossini & Romani, (and possibly Gyrowetz).*
    SEDLAK **WXS-41a** Theil 1: overture & 11 mvts; Theil 2: 12 mvts. 2ob 2cl 2hn 2bn cbn (2tp).

ROMBERG, Andreas Jakob (1767 - 1821)
Simphonie (unidentified)
    WALCH **JHW-1a** fl ob 3cl 2hn 2bn 2tp db.

RONALD *(actually RUSSELL), Sir* Landon (1873 - 1938)
Summertime (song cycle, voice & piano, 1901, London)
    ANON **A-458a** "O lovely Night!". Solo voice, 2fl 2ob 2cl 2hn 2bn 2tp 3tb timp.
    Pm (Edwin Ashdown: London, etc, sd), hire score & parts.

ROSER von REITER, Franz de Paula (1779 - 1830)
Das Lebendige Weinfass (Grosses Quodlibet in drei Acten; 21 Jan 1812, Vienna; includes music by Beethoven, Giuliani, Haydn, Hoffmeister, Queen Hortense, Mozart, W. Müller, Pechatschek, I. Unlauf, J. Weigl, Woelfl, Anonymous & Traditional)
    ANON **A-459a** 2 acts. Instrumentation unknown, (includes pic and tp).
    Pc (Verlage [T.] Weigl: Wienn [sic], c.1812), MS parts (23): I-Fc, F.P. S.363, (? Acts 2 & 3 only).
    ANON **A-460a** (?2ob 2cl 2hn 2bn cbn 2tp). MS parts (9): I-Fc, F.P. S.379.
Johann von Wieselburg (parodie, 3 acts, 28 Nov 1812, Vienna)
    KÜFFNER **JYK-12a** potpourri. 2fl 2cl(E♭) 3cl(B♭) 4hn 2bn 2tp 2sig-hn 2tb serp b-dr s-dr.

ROSETTI (Rössler), Francesco Antonio (Franz Anton) (1750 - 1792). *See supra:* ANON **A-2a.**

ROSSINI, Gioachino Antonio (1792 - 1868)
L'Inganno felice (opera, 8 Jan 1812, Venice)
    LEGRAND **WYL-37a** 1 mvt. fl ob 2cl 2hn 2bn.
    LEGRAND **WYL-55a** 2 airs. Nos. 4 & 5 (with *La gazza ladra)*. fl 2cl 2hn 2bn.
    STARKE **FRS-24a** 6 mvts. 2ob 2cl 2hn 2bn cbn.
Ciro in Babilonia (Cyrus in Babylon, La caduta di Baldassare) (opera, 14 March 1812, Ferrara)
    ANON **A-3.1a** overture. 2cl 2hn 2bn. MS parts: CZ-Pnm, XLI B.124.
    SEDLAK **WXS-42a** Theil I: overture & 11 mvts, Theil 2: Act II overture & 11 mvts. 2ob 2cl 2hn 2bn cbn (2tp).
    WENUSCH **SXW-1.2a** 1 mvt. cl(E♭) 2cl(B♭) 2hn bn tp(prin).
La Scala di seta (opera, 9 May 1812, Venice)
    ANON **A-461a** overture & 2 mvts. 2ob 2cl 2hn 2bn cbn 2tp tb. MS parts (1833): CZ-Bm(au), A.35.221.
    GILLASPIE **JAG-26a** overture. fl(pic) 2ob 2cl 2hn 2bn cbn.

Demetrio e Polibio (opera, 18 May 1812, Rome)   *See also supra: AIBLINGER.*
  LEGRAND **WYL-35a** 1 mvt. fl ob 2cl 2hn 2bn.
La Pietra di Paragone (opera, 26 Sept 1812, Milan)
  LEGRAND **WYL-36a** 5 mvts. fl ob 2cl 2hn 2bn.
Tancredi (opera, 6 Feb 1813, Venice)
  ANON **A-462a** introduction. terz-fl cl(Eb) 3cl(Bb) 2hn 2bn 2tp b-tb serp b-dr. MS parts: D-DT, Mus-n 869.
  ANON **A-463a** "Die soll mit treuster Zärtlichkeit". fl cl(Eb) 3cl(Bb) 2hn bn bn/serp 2tp b-tb b-dr.
    MS parts: D-DT, Mus-n 870.
  ANON **A-464a** coro e cavatina Amenaide. 2fl ob 2cl(C) 2hn bn(II) 2tp 2tb.
    MS parts: I-OS, Mus.Musiche 4185, (probably missing bn I).
  ANON **A-465a** sinfonia & 12 mvts. 2ob 2cl 2hn 2bn tp. MS parts: CZ-KRa, A4016/IV.B.189.
  ANON **A-466a** overture. fl(F) 2cl 2hn basso. MS parts (1826): D-Tl, Gg 305.
  BERR **FXB-22** overture. (instrumentation unknown; possibly as Berr's arr. of *La Siège de Corinthe* infra).
  FLACHS **KXF-1a** overture. fl ob 2cl 2hn 2bn.
  KÜFFNER **JYK-15a** potpouri, 5 mvts. pic 2cl(Eb) 2cl(Bb) 2hn 2bn 2tp posthorn 2tb serp b-dr t-dr.
  LEGRAND **WYL-38a** overture & 6 mvts. fl ob 2cl 2hn 2bn.
  LEGRAND **WYL-56a** overture & 5 mvts. fl ob 2cl 2hn 2bn.
  RUMMEL **CFR-2a** overture. pic(D) cl(Eb) cl(Bb prin) 3cl(Bb) 2hn 2bn 2tp 2tb 2serp b-dr.
  SCHMITT, G. **GYS-65a** 1 Bd. 2fl 2ob 2cl 2hn 2bn tp 2tb db.
  SEDLAK **WXS-43.1a** overture & 11 mvts. 2ob 2cl 2hn 2bn cbn (2tp).
  SEDLAK **WXS-43.2a** 5 mvts (Nos. 6 - 11 of *L'Italiana in Algeri*, WXS-44a). 2ob 2cl 2hn 2bn cbn (2tp).
  WENUSCH **SXW-1.4a** 1 mvt. cl(Eb) 2cl(Bb) 2hn bn tp(prin).
  WIDDER **YYW-1.31a** 1 mvt. 2fl 2cl 2hn 2bn.
  WIELAND **KZW-14ad** overture & 9 mvts. 2fl 2ob 2cl 2hn 2bn.
L'Italiana in Algeri (opera buffa, 22 May 1813, Venice)
  ANON **A-467a** polonaise. 2fl(D)/fl+cl(III, C) 2cl 2hn bn 2tp b-tb/cb.
    MS parts (1824): D-Tl, Gg 306, No. 3, (missing cl II).
  ANON **A-468a** overture. 2cl 2hn 2bn tp. MS parts: CZ-Pnm, XLI.B.121.
  ANON **A-469a** sinfonia & 15 mvts. 2ob 2cl 2hn 2bn. MS pts: I-OS, Mus.Musiche 4078. *Not Sedlak, WXS-44a.*
  FLACHS **KXF-2a** overture. fl ob 2cl 2hn 2bn.
  GAMBARO **VXG-5a** overture. fl 2cl(Bb) 2hn 2bn; (ad lib: cl(Eb) 2cl(Bb) 2tp b-tb serp b-dr.
  LEGRAND **WYL-39a** overture & 6 mvts. fl ob 2cl 2hn 2bn.
  LEGRAND **WYL-57a** overture & 5 mvts. fl ob 2cl 2hn 2bn.
  LÖWENSTEIN **CAL-2ac** overture. cl(C) 3cl(C) 2hn 2bn tp b-tb timp.
  SCHNEIDER, A. **AYS-80a** overture & 6 mvts. fl 2ob 2cl 2hn 2bn tp b-tb 2vla cb.
  SEDLAK **WXS-44a** overture & 11 mvts [sic: Nos. 6 - 11 are from *Tancredi*, (qv)]. 2ob 2cl 2hn 2bn cbn (2tp).
  WIDDER **YYW-1.32a** 1 mvt. 2fl 2cl 2hn 2bn.
Il Turco in Italia (opera buffa, 14 Aug 1814, Milan)
  BERR **FXB-23a** oveture. (instrumentation unknown; possibly as Berr's arr. of *La Siège de Corinthe* infra).
  SCHMITT, G. **GYS-66a** 1 Bd. 2fl 2ob 2cl 2hn 2bn tp tb db.
  SCHNEIDER, A. **AYS-81a** overture & 14 mvts. fl 2ob 2cl 2hn 2bn tp b-tb 2vla cb.
  STARKE **FRS-25a** Theil 1: overture & 11 mvts, Theil 2: Nos. 1 - 3, 10, 11. 2ob 2cl 2hn 2bn cbn 2tp.
Sigismondo (opera, 26 Dec 1814, Venice)
  STARKE **FRS-26a** recitative & aria. 2ob 2cl 2hn 2bn cbn 2tp.
Elisabetta, Regina d'Inghilterra (opera, 8 Oct 1815, Naples) (For the relationship between the overture *and that*
of Il Barbiere di Siviglia, *see Norman del Mar:* Orchestral Variations. *London: Eulenburg, 1981.)*
  ANON **A-470a** overture. pic 2fl 3cl(C) cl(D) 4hn(D, G) 2bn cbn 6tp(3D, 2A, F) b-tb b-dr cym s-dr.
    MS parts (1824): CZ-Bm(au), A.35.213.
  C., J. **XJC-1a** Chor (Marziale). pic fl 2ob 2cl(A) 2hn 2bn tp b-dr s-dr.
  LEGRAND **WYL-40a** 1 mvt. fl ob 2cl 2hn 2bn.
  SCHNEIDER, A. **AYS-82.1a** overture. fl 2ob 2cl(A) 2cl(C) 2hn 2bn tp b-tb serp.
  SCHNEIDER, A. **AYS-82.2a** overture & 11 mvts. fl(pic) ob 2cl 2hn 2bn tp(hn III) b-tb 2vla cb.
  SEDLAK **WXS-45a** 26th/27th Werk, Theil 1: overture & 11 mvts; Theil 2: 12 mvts. 2ob 2cl 2hn 2bn cbn (2tp).
  STARKE **FRS-27a** Theil 1: overture & 9 mvts, Theil 2: 10 mvts. 2ob 2cl 2hn 2bn cbn 2tp.
Torvaldo e Dorliska (opera, 26 Dec 1815, Rome)
  ANON **A-471a** 3 Theils. 2ob 2cl 2hn 2bn cbn. MS parts: I-Fc, F.P. S.389.
  WIELAND **KZW-9ad** cavatina, "Tutto è vano". fl(D & F) 2ob 2cl 2hn 2bn 2tp serp/vlne.
Il Barbiere di Siviglia (Almaviva) (opera, 5 Feb 1816, Rome; 28 Sept 1819, Vienna)
  ANON **A-472a** overture & 8 mvts. 2ob 2cl 2hn 2bn. MS parts: CZ-Bm(au), A.36.888. (Not Sedlak's arr.)
  ANON **A-473a** 2 mvts. fl 2cl 2hn 2bn. MS parts: A-FK, IV 30.
  ANON **A-474a** cavatina. Instrumentation unknown. MS score: A-Wn, Mus.Hs.20,620, (stamped: "Anton
    Sitter Musik Director vormals Capelle Fahrbach").
  ANON **A-475a** 3 mvts. fl(D) 2cl(C) 2hn 2bn. MS parts: GB-Ljag(w), 5/262, Nos. 6, 9 & 20.
  FUCHS **GFF-34.1a** overture. pic cl(F) 2cl(Bb) 2hn 2bn b-tb serp.
  FUCHS **GFF-34.2a** Suite 1: Nos. 1 - 6, Suite 2: Nos. 7 - 13. 2fl cl(F) 2cl(Bb) 2hn 2bn b-tb serp.
  GAMBARO **VXG-6a** overture & 4 suites (4, 4, 5, 5 mvts). fl cl(Eb, overture) 2cl(Bb) 2hn 2bn; (ad lib:
    cl(III & IV Bb) tp[2tp in Suites 2 - 4] tb serp).
  HNOJIL **JAH-1.1a** 10 mvts (without overture). 2ob 2cl 2hn 2bn cbn 2tp.
  HNOJIL **JAH-1.2a** Alla marcia. 2ob 2cl 2hn 2bn cbn.
  LEGRAND **WYL-41a** 11 mvts. fl ob 2cl 2hn 2bn.

LEGRAND **WYL-53.3a** 1 mvt (as by Pacini). fl ob 2cl 2hn 2bn.
OSSWALD **AZO-4a** overture. 2ob 2cl 2hn 2bn cbn 2tp tb.
SCHMITT, G. **GYS-67a** 1 Bd. 2fl 2ob 2cl 2hn 2bn tp tb db.
SCHNEIDER, A. **AYS-83.1a** overture. fl 2ob 2cl 2hn 2bn tp b-tb 2vla cb.
SCHNEIDER, A. **AYS-83.2a** 15 mvts (without overture). fl 2ob 2cl 2hn 2bn tp b-tb 2vla cb.
SEDLAK **WXS-46.1a** 22/30 Werk, Theil 1: overture & 11 mvts, Theil 2: 12 mvts. 2ob 2cl 2hn 2bn cbn (2tp).
SEDLAK **WXS-46.2a** overture & 11 mvts. 2cl 2hn 2bn.
WIDDER **YYW-1.33a** 1 mvt. 2fl 2cl 2hn 2bn.
Otello, ossia il Moro [L'Africano] di Venezia (opera, 4 Dec 1816, Naples)
ANON **A-476a** romance. 2ob 2cl 2hn 2bn cbn 2tp. MS parts: CZ-Bm(au), A.36.875.
GAMBARO **VXG-7a** overture. fl(Eb) 2cl(Bb) 2hn 2bn; (ad lib: cl(Eb) 2cl(Bb ripieno) tp 3tb timp b-dr).
GILLASPIE **JAG-27a(v)** "Sommeil à me priére". Soprano, fl ob 2cl 2hn 2bn cbn.
KIRCHHOFF **WZK-48a** arie. fl 2ob 2cl 2hn 2bn tb db.
KÜFFNER **JYK-3a** Pièces d'Harmonie. fl 2cl 2hn 2bn.
KÜFFNER **JYK-14.1m** Potpourri. 1/2pic(Eb, F, fl in F) 2cl(Eb) 3cl(Bb) 2hn 2bn 2tp 2tb serp b-dr t-dr.
KÜFFNER **JYK-14.2m** Potpourri militaire. pic 2cl(Eb) 3cl(Bb) 2hn 2bn 2tp(clar) 2tp(prin) 2tb serp b-dr t-dr.
LEGRAND **WYL-42a** overture & 1 mvt. fl ob 2cl 2hn 2bn.
SCHMITT, G. **GYS-68a** 1 Bd. 2fl 2ob 2cl 2hn 2bn tp tb db.
SCHNEIDER, A. **AYS-84a** 12 mvts. fl 2ob 2cl 2hn 2bn 2vla cb.
SCHOLZ **WES-155.1a** finale Act III. fl 2ob 2cl 3hn 2bn tp tb db timp.
SCHOLZ **WES-155.2a** finale Act III. fl 2ob 2cl 3hn 2bn tp tb db timp.
SEDLAK **WXS-47a** Theil 1: overture & 11 mvts; Theil 2, overture & 9 mvts. 2ob 2cl 2hn 2bn cbn (2tp).
STARKE **FRS-28.1a** overture & 4 mvts. 2ob 2cl 2hn 2bn cbn 2tp.
STARKE **FRS-28.2a** Aria des Rodrigo. 2ob 2cl 2hn 2bn 2tp.
WIELAND **KZW-10ad** overture. fl(D) 2ob 2cl 2hn 2bn 2tp serp/vlne.
La Cenerentola ossia La Bontà in trionfo (opera buffa, 25 Jan 1817, Rome)
ANON **A-477a** 2 mvts. fl(D) 2cl(C) 2hn 2bn. MS parts: GB-Ljag(w), 5/262, No. 8.
BERR **FXB-24a** Airs. (instrumentation unknown; possibly as Berr's arr. of *La Siège de Corinthe* infra).
LEGRAND **WYL-44a** 5 mvts. fl ob 2cl 2hn 2bn.
SCHMITT, G. **GYS-69a** overture & Act I. 2fl 2ob 2cl 2hn 2bn tp tb db timp.
SCHOLZ **WES-156a** 5 mvts. fl 2ob 2cl 2hn 2bn tp tb db timp.
SEDLAK **WXS-48a** Theil 1: overture & 7 mvts; Theil 2, 8 mvts; Theil 3: 8 mvts. 2ob 2cl 2hn 2bn cbn (2tp).
La Gazza ladra (Die diebische Elster, La Pie voleuse) (opera buffa, 31 May 1817, Milan)
ANON **A-478a** ariette. 2fl(Eb) 2cl(Eb) 2cl(Bb) 4hn 2bn 2tp 2tb serp. MS parts: D-Tl, Z.117.
ANON **A-479a** overture. 2ob cl(Eb) 4cl(Bb) 2hn 2bn 2tp b-hn. MS pts: D-DT, Mus-n 779, (missing ob I).
ANON **A-480a** aria "Was ich oft im Traume sah". fl 2ob 3cl 2hn 2bn b-hn/tb.
  MS parts: D-DT, Mus-n 1884, No. 4, (missing ob I, bn I).
ANON **A-481a** 1 mvt. fl(F) 2cl(C) 2hn 2bn. MS parts: GB-Ljag(w), 5/262, No. 8.
CALEGARI **GFC-1a** sinfonia. Instrumentation unknown: "Grande Armonia".
GAMBARO **VXG-8a** overture. fl cl(Eb) 2cl(Bb) 2hn 2bn; (ad lib: tp tb serp timp).
LEGRAND **WYL-43a** overture & 8 mvts. fl ob 2cl 2hn 2bn.
LEGRAND **WYL-55a** overture & 2 airs (Nos. 1 - 3, with *L'inganno felice).* fl 2cl 2hn 2bn.
SCHMITT, G. **GYS-70a** 2 acts. pic 2fl 2ob 2cl 2hn 2bn tp tb db.
STARKE **FRS-29.1a** Theil 1: overture & 11 mvts; Theil 2: 12 mvts. 2ob 2cl 2hn 2bn cbn 2tp.
STARKE **FRS-29.2a** Schlusgesang & 1 mvt. 2ob 2cl 2hn 2bn cbn tp.
WIELAND **KZW-11ad** overture. fl 2ob 2cl 2hn 2bn 2tp serp/vlne.
Armida (opera, 9 Nov 1817, Naples)
ANON **A-482a** overture & 11 mvts. 2ob 2cl 2hn 2bn cbn. MS parts: I-Fc, F.P. S.417.
SCHMITT, G. **GYS-71a** 1 Bd. 2fl 2ob 2cl 2hn 2bn tp tb db (timp).
STARKE **FRS-30a** Abth. 1: overture & 4 mvts, pic 2ob/fl cl(F) 2cl(C) 2hn 2bn cbn 2tp(C) 2tp(D) b-tb b-dr s-dr;
  Abth 2: 7 mvts, 2ob 2cl 2hn 2bn cbn 2tp.
Mosè in Egitto (Moses oder Der Auszug aus Ägypter; Moïse) (opera, 5 March 1818, Naples)
ANON **A-74.9/9m(a), 10m(a)** 2 marches. pic quart-fl 2ob cl(F) 2cl(C) 4hn 2bn cbn+serp/2b-hn 2tp 3tb b-dr
  t-dr tamb cym.
ANON **A-483a, 484a** 2 mvts & 3 mvts. fl 4cl(Bb) 2hn 2bn 2tp b-tb serp. MS parts: D-DT, Mus-n 864, 865.
ANON **A-485a** Allegro. 2fl 2cl 2hn bn 2tp tb/cb. MS parts: D-Tl, Gg. 306, No. 2, (missing cl II).
ANON **A-486a** Allegro, C. 2fl(D)/fl+cl(III, C) 2cl 2hn bn 2tp b-tb/cb.
  MS parts (1824): D-Tl, Gg 306, No. 2, (missing cl II).
GAMBARO **VXG-9a** overture. 12 parts [? fl cl(Eb) 2cl(Bb) 2hn 2tp tb serp b-dr].
KÜFFNER **JYK-13a** potpourri. fl 2cl 2hn 2bn.
LEGRAND **WYL-45a** 2 mvts. fl ob 2cl 2hn 2bn.
LEGRAND **WYL-53.4a** 1 mvt. fl ob 2cl 2hn 2bn.
SCHMITT, G. **GYS-72a** 5 mvts. Incomplete; here only: fl 2ob cl 2hn tp tb db timp.
SCHOLZ **WES-157.1a** 4 mvts. fl 2ob 2cl 2hn 2bn tp tb db timp.
SCHOLZ **WES-157.2a** invocazione & duett. fl 2ob 2cl 2hn 2bn tp tb db timp.
SEDLAK **WXS-49.1a** Theil 1: introduzione & 11 mvts, Theil 2: 12 mvts. 2ob 2cl 2hn 2bn cbn (2tp).
SEDLAK **WXS-49.2a** duetto. 2ob 2cl 2hn 2bn cbn 2tp.
SEDLAK **WXS-49.3a** Preghiera. 2ob 2cl 2hn 2bn 2tp.
WALCH **JHW-2a** Geschwind-Marsch. fl 3cl 2hn 2bn tp b-tb serp.

Ricciardo e Zoraide (opera, 8 Dec 1818, Naples)
 ANON **A-487a** Gran Terzetto. pic fl 2ob cl(F) 3cl(C) 4hn 2bn fagottone 2tp b-dr b-dr s-dr.
  MS parts: I-OS, Mus.Musiche B 865.
 ANON **A-488a** Marziale. fl(F) 2cl(C) 2hn 2bn. MS parts: GB-Ljag(w), 5/262, No. 24.
 GAMBARO **VXG-10a** overture. fl 2cl 2hn 2bn, (ad lib: cl(E♭) tp tb serp timp).
 LEGRAND **WYL-46a** 4 mvts. fl ob 2cl 2hn 2bn.
 SCHMITT, G. **GYS-73a** 1 Bd. 2fl 2ob 2cl 2hn 2bn tp tb db.
 SEDLAK **WXS-50a** Theil 1, overture & 10 mvts; Theil 2, 14 mvts. 2ob 2cl 2hn 2bn cbn (2tp).
 STARKE **FRS-31a** Theil 1: sinfonia & 4 mvts, Theil 2: 4 mvts; Theil 3: 4 mvts. 2ob 2cl 2hn 2bn cbn.
 WIDDER **YYW-1.34a** 1 mvt. 2fl 2cl 2hn 2bn.
Eduardo e Cristina (pasticcio, 24 April 1819, Venice)
 ANON **A-489a** overture & 8 mvts. 2ob 2cl 2hn 2bn cbn. MS parts: I-Fc, F.P. S.414.
La Donna del Lago (Das Fräulein vom See) (opera, 24 Oct 1819, Naples)
 ANON **A-490a** 1 mvt. fl(D) 2cl(C) 2hn 2bn. MS parts: GB-Ljag(w), 5/262, No. 13.
 STARKE **FRS-32a** Abth 1: overture & 6 mvts; Abth 2: 6 mvts; Abth 3: 7 mvts. 2ob 2cl 2hn 2bn cbn (2tp).
 WIDDER **YYW-1.35a** 1 mvt. 2fl 2cl 2hn 2bn.
Bianca e Falliero, ovvero Il consiglio dei tre (opera, 26 Dec 1819, Milan)
 SKÁCEL **ZZS-1a** quartetto. 2ob 2cl 2hn 2bn cbn 2tp.
Matilda di Shabran, ossia Bellezza e cuor di ferro (Il Corradino) (opera, 24 Feb 1821, Rome)
 ANON **A-491a** 1 mvt. fl(F) 2cl(C) 2hn 2bn. MS parts: GB-Ljag(w), 5/262, No. 1.
 BERR **FXB-25a** overture. (instrumentation unknown; possibly as Berr's arr. of *La Siège de Corinthe* infra).
 KÜFFNER **JYK-13a** potpourri. fl 2cl 2hn 2bn.
 SEDLAK **WXS-51a** 46 - 48 Werk; Theil 1: overture & 11 mvts, Theil 2: 12 mvts, Theil 3: 12 mvts.
  2ob 2cl 2hn 2bn cbn (2tp).
 TAYLORSON **JST-18a** fl 2ob 2cl 2hn 2bn cbn/db.
 WIDDER **YYW-1.36a** 1 mvt. 2fl 2cl 2hn 2bn.
Zelmira (opera, 10 Feb 1822, Naples; 13 April 1822, Vienna)
 SEDLAK **WXS-52.1a** 39/40 Werk; Theil 1, overture & 11 mvts; Theil 2, 13 mvts. 2ob 2cl 2hn 2bn cbn (2tp).
 SEDLAK **WXS-52.2a** 39/40 Werk; [Theil 1] overture & 13 mvts, [Theil 2] 1st finale & 9 mvts. 2cl 2hn 2bn.
 STARKE **FRS-33a** 6 long bravura mvts. 2ob 2cl 2hn 2bn cbn (2tp).
 WIDDER **YYW-1.37a** 1 mvt. 2fl 2cl 2hn 2bn.
Semiramide (Sémiramis, Semiramis) (opera, 3 Feb 1823, Venice)
 GAMBARO **VXG-11a** overture, here as inserted in *Ivanhoé.* 15 parts.
 HEUSCHKEL **JEH-1a** 5 mvts. fl 2cl 2hn 2bn.
 HEUSCHKEL **JEH-2a** Nos 1 - 3. fl 2cl 2hn 2bn.
 KIRCHHOFF **WZK-49a** overture & 1 Bd. fl 2ob 2cl 2hn bn(I)/tb bn(II).
 MÜNCHS **CNM-2.2/2(a)** Pas redoublé. p-fl(D♭) cl(E♭) cl(B♭ solo) cl(I B♭) 2cl(II B♭) 2hn 2bn tp(crt)
  2tp(hn B♭ alto) 2tb serp+oph b-dr+cym t-dr.
 SEDLAK **WXS-53a** 52/53 Werk; Theil 1: overture & 11 mvts, Theil 2: 13 mvts. 2ob 2cl 2hn 2bn cbn (2tp).
 STRECK **PZS-2.2a** 1 mvt. fl 2cl 2hn 2bn.
 WIDDER **YYW-1.38a** 4 mvts. No. 1: 2fl 2cl 2hn 2bn; Nos. 2 - 4: fl ob 2cl 2hn 2bn.
La Siège de Corinthe (revision of Maometto II) (opera, 9 Oct 1826, Paris)
 ANON **A-74.12/9m(a)** march. pic quart-fl 2ob cl(F) 2cl(C) 4hn 2bn cbn+serp/2b-hn 2tp 3tb b-dr t-dr tamb cym.
 ANON **A-492a** introduction & Act I finale. pic fl 2ob cl(E♭) cl(solo B♭) 3cl(B♭) 4hn 2bn 3tp tp/kl-hn a-hn
  3tb serp b-hn bomb timp b-dr t-dr. MS parts: D-DT, Mus-n 857, (some parts may be later additions).
 BERR **FXB-26a** overture. fl(E♭) cl(E♭) 2cl(B♭) 2hn 2bn; (ad lib: 2cl(B♭) tp 3tb/b-tb serp cb).
 SCHMITT, G. **GYS-74a** 2 Bds. fl 2ob 2cl 2hn 2bn tp tb 2tb db.
 SEDLAK **WXS-54a** Theil 1, overture & 13 mvts; Theil 2, 6 mvts. 2ob 2cl 2hn 2bn cbn (2tp).
Le Comte Ory [music from Il viaggio a Reims, *1825]* (comic opera, 20 Aug 1828, Paris).
 SCHOLZ **WES-158a** Act II finale, 2 sections. fl 2ob 2cl 2hn 2bn tp tb db timp.
 SEDLAK **+WXS-55a** Theil 1: 5 mvts, Theil 2: 7 mvts. 2ob 2cl 2hn 2bn cbn 2tp.
 SEIFF **JYS-1a** 2cl 2hn 2bn.
 SEIFF **JYS-2a** 2cl 2hn 2bn.
 SIRLETTI **LQS-1a** terzetto. fl ob 2cl(A) 2hn bn.
 SIRLETTI **LQS-2a** coro e preghiera. fl ob 2cl 2hn bn.
Guillaume Tell (Wilhelm Tell) (opera, 3 Aug 1829, Paris).
 ANON **A-493a** Chor & Ballet-Musik. fl 2ob cl(E♭) 2cl(B♭) 4hn 2bn 2tp 2tb b-hn b-dr t-dr tri.
  MS parts: D-DT, Mus-n 872(a).
 ANON **A-494a** 2 mvts. 2fl 4cl 2hn 2bn 2tp 3tb(No. 2 + basso). MS score: I-OS, Mus.Musiche B 807.
 ANON **A-495a** 1 mvt. fl(D) 2cl(C) 2hn 2bn. MS parts: GB-Ljag(w), 5/262, No. 15.
 BERR **FXB-27a** overture. (instrumentation unknown; possibly as Berr's arr. of *La Siège de Corinthe* supra).
 SCHMITT, G. **GYS-75a** overture & 3 mvts. fl 2ob 2cl 2hn 2bn tp tb db.
 SCHOLZ **WES-159.1a** overture, introduzione & 1 aria. fl 2ob 2cl 3hn 2bn tb db timp.
 SCHOLZ **WES-159.2a** 2 Bds. fl 2ob 2cl 2hn 2bn tp tb db timp.
 SEDLAK **+WXS-56a** Theil 1: overture & 7 mvts, Theil 2: 8 mvts. 2ob 2cl 2hn 2bn cbn (2tp) b-tb).
 SEIFF **JYS-2a** 2cl 2hn 2bn.
 STRECK **PZS-2.5a** overture. fl 2cl 2hn 2bn.
 WIDDER **YYW-1.39a** 4 mvts. 2fl 2cl 2hn 2bn.
 WIDDER **YYW-6a** overture & 3 mvts. terz-fl 2cl(E♭) 2cl(B♭) 2hn 2bn tp(chromatic) b-tb cb.
Petite Messe Solennelle (1st version: voices, 2pf & harm, 1863; 2nd, with orchestra: 1867; pub. 1869, Paris)
 TAYLORSON **JST-19a** O Salutaris. S, fl 2ob 2cl 2hn 2bn cbn/db.
 TAYLORSON **JST-20a** Domine Deus. T, fl 2ob 2cl 2hn 2bn cbn/db.

Stabat Mater (second version: 1841, Paris)
ANON **A-496a** Cujus animam. pic 2ob cl(Eb) cl(solo Bb) 3cl(Bb) 4hn 2bn 3tp kenthorn a-hn 3tb b-hn/bomb
vc/b b-dr s-dr. MS parts: D-DT, Mus-n 1899, No. 1.
ANON **A-497a** Quartet. fl 2ob cl(Eb) cl(solo Bb) 3cl(Bb) 4hn 2bn 4tp a-hn 3tb b-hn/bomb.
MS parts: D-DT, Mus-n 868.
Pastiches
Blaubart (ballet, post-1814, Vienna)
SEDLAK **WXS-57a** overture & 11 mvts. 2ob 2cl 2hn 2bn cbn (2tp).
Pietro il Grand (opera, ?Vienna - cavatina possibly interpolated in Vaccai's opera, 17 Jan 1824, Parma)
ANON **A-498a** cavatina. 2ob 2cl 2hn 2bn cbn 2tp. MS parts: CZ-Bm(au), 35.219.
ANON **A-499a** cavatina. terz-fl(vel cl in Eb) 2cl 2hn tp serp.
MS parts (by Augustin Fibiger, 1843): CZ-BA, 189 (59-613).
Die Fee und der Ritter (ballet, Vienna) *See:* ROMANI, Pietro, (compiler).
Ivanhoé (opera, adapted Pacini with Rossini's participation, 12 Sept 1826, Paris) *See supra:* ROSSINI: *Semiramide*
Composite works
MOSELL **EGM-2a** VII Quartetti. fl 2cl bn.
KÜFFNER **JYK-16a** VII Potpurri, Op. 126 (d'opéras de Rossini), 6 mvts.
2pic 2cl(Eb) 3cl(Bb) 4hn 2bn 2tp 2signal-hn b-tb serp b-dr t-dr.
MÜNCHS **CNM-2.2/3(a)** Pas redoublé Sur des motifs de Rossini.
p-fl(Db) cl(Eb) 2cl(Bb solo) 2cl(Bb) 2hn 2bn tp 2tp(hn Bb alto) 2tb serp+oph b-dr+cym t-dr.
Unidentified works
Marche
BERR **FXB-29.1a** p-fl(Eb) cl(Eb) 3cl(Bb) 2hn 2bn tp 3tb serp b-dr t-dr; (ad lib: hn III, bugle).
Marziale
ANON **A-500a** 2cl 2hn (bn vlne tp) organ. MS score & parts: I-Vsmc.
Duett
SCHOLZ **WES-160a** fl 2ob 2cl 2hn 2bn tb db.
Quartetto in Bb
SCHNEIDER, A. **AYS-86a** fl 2ob 2cl 2hn 2bn tp b-tb 2vla cb.
Untraced arrangements: Torvaldo e Dorliska (opera, 1815, arr. Fuchs); for an arrangement of an untraced
(spurious) opera, *see:* Legrand, **WYL-1a**, Evelina, overture [by Coccia].

ROUGET DE LISLE, Claude Joseph (1760 - 1836)
La Marseillaise (Chant de guerre pour l'armée du Rhine) (song, 25 April 1792, Strassbourg)
ANON **A-501a** La Marseillaise Marsche ("Ludwig und Louise auf dem Theater"). 2ob 2cl(A) 2hn 2bn tp.
MS score: A-Wn, Mus.Hs.2092, (the 2bn have only 1 bar divisi).
Pm (WINDS: Northridge, CA, pn W-37, c.1981), photocopy of contemporary score & modern parts.
GOSSEC **FJG-1.1amv** ATB chorus, 2p-fl 2cl 2hn 2bn 2tp serp timp. *(Note also a reconstruction, scored as
the original, by John Humphries (GB-Lhumphries).*
GOSSEC **FJG-1.2am** 2fl 2cl 2hn 2bn 2tb timp.
OZI **EXO-1.32/7a** 2cl 2hn 2bn.

RUMMEL, Christian Franz Ludwig Friedrich Alexander (1787 - 1849)
5 Walzer
SCHNEIDER, A. **AYS-87a** fl(Eb) 2ob 2cl(Eb, Bb) 2cl(Bb) 2hn 2bn tp(posthorn) b-tb cb.
2 Valses
GAMBARO **VXG-4.1(a), 4.2(a)** pic(Db) cl(Eb) 2cl(Bb) 2hn (2)bn tp tb serp b-dr+cym.
Andante with 4 Variations
GAMBARO **VXG-5.1(a)** pic(Db) cl(F) 2cl(C) 2hn 2bn tp tb serp b-dr.
Valse
GAMBARO **VXG-5.2(a)** pic(Db) cl(F) 2cl(C) 2hn 2bn tp tb serp b-dr.

RYBA, Jakub Šimon Jan (1768 - 1815)
Octo Ariae et Duetto
[?RYBA] **JSR-1va, 2va** Aria I ("Offero tibi cor meum") & Aria II ("O Deus ego amo te").
S solo, 2cl(No I: Bb; No II: A) 2hn vla organ+basso.
MS parts (MS by Schreyer, 1817; Chrám sv. Mikuláše collection): CZ-CH, S-40-5-102.

SACCHINI, Antonio Maria Gasparo (1730 - 1786)
La Colonie (comic opera, 16 Aug 1775, Paris; revision of *L'Isola d'amore*, Jan 1766, Rome)
VANDERHAGEN **AJV-2.1/1a** 1 mvt; **AJV-2.2/1a** 4 mvts; **AJV-2.4/2a** 1 mvt & overture; **AJV-2.8/2a**
(= AJV-3.8/2a), 2 mvts. 2cl 2hn 2bn.
Renaud (opera, 25 Feb 1783, Paris)
OZI **EXO-1.6/2a** 2 airs. 2cl(C) 2hn 2bn.
Chimème (lyric tragedy, 18 Nov 1783, Fontainebleau; 9 Feb 1784, Paris)
VANDERHAGEN **AJV-3.16/1a** overture & 1 mvt ("Pardonnez"). 2cl 2hn 2bn.
VANDERHAGEN **AJV-4.2a** air de ballet. 2cl 2hn 2bn.
Dardanus (tragédie lyrique, 18 Sept 1784, Versailles; 30 Nov 1784, Paris)
VANDERHAGEN **AJV-3.15/3a** "Lieux Funestes"; **AJV-3.17/2** 2 airs de ballet. 2cl 2hn 2bn.
Oedipe á Colonne (opera, 4 Jan 1786, Versailles; 1 Feb 1787 Paris)
ANON **A-502a** ballet. fl(F) 2ob cl(F) cl(solo Bb) 2cl(Bb) bthn 2hn 2bn tp 3tb serp timp b-dr.
MS parts: D-DT, Mus-n 880.
ANON **A-503a** airs. 2cl 2hn 2bn.
Pc (Schott: Mainz, sd), Suite 1 & 2, parts: D-MZsch. *Probably the Ernst arrangement.*
ERNST **FRE-2a** Suite 1: 8 mvts, Suite 2: 8 mvts. 2cl 2hn 2bn
OZI **EXO-1.24/3a** dui [sic], gavotte & air. 2cl(C) 2hn 2bn.

SAINT-SAËNS, Charles Camille (1835 - 1921)
Feuillets d'album, Op. 81 (piano duet, c.1889)
  TAFFANEL **CPT-1a** fl ob 2cl 2hn 2bn.

SALIERI, Antonio (1750 - 1825)
La Fiera in Venezia (opera, 29 Jan 1772, Vienna)
  ANON **A-504a** overture. 2fl 2cl 2hn 2bn.
    MS parts: PL-LA, RM 81/1-5/87, (missing fl I, hn I, bn II; Nos. 88 - 92 may also be from this opera);
    RF-Ssc, Ф 891 собр юосуповъ ix N16, pp. 53 - 95.
  ASPLMAYR **FDA-4a/FDA-53** Menuet. 2ob 2hn bn.
  WENT **JNW-11ac** sinfonia & 15 mvts. 2ob 2cl 2hn 2bn
Il Talismano (opera, 1779, Milan; rescored: 20 Sept 1788, Vienna) *All arrangements use the later version.*
  STUMPF **JUS-13a** Recueil 6, 6 mvts. 2cl 2hn 2bn.
  WENT **JNW-47.1a** sinfonia & 15 mvts. 2ob 2cl 2hn 2bn.
  WENT **JNW-47.2a** sinfonia & 15 mvts. 2ob 2ca 2hn 2bn.
La Dama pastorella (revived as La Cifra*)* (opera, 27 Dec 1779, Rome; 11 Dec 1789, Vienna).
  WENT **JNW-48a** sinfonia & 14 mvts. 2ob 2cl 2hn 2bn.
Der Rauchfangkehrer (Singspiel, 30 April 1781, Vienna)
  WENT **JNW-12ac** 2ob 2cl 2hn 2bn
Il Ricco d'un giorno (opera, 6 Dec 1784, Vienna)
  WENT **JNW-49.1a** 7 mvts. 2ob 2ca 2hn 2bn.
  WENT **JNW-49.2a** 7 mvts. 2ob 2bthn 2hn 2bn.
La Grotto di Trofonio (opera, 12 Oct 1785, Vienna)
  ANON (?von Schacht) **A-505a** 2fl 2ob 2cl 2hn 2bn 2vla vlne. MS parts: D-Rtt, Salieri 10/V.
  ANON **A-414.2a.** overture & 4 mvts. fl 2ob 2cl 2hn 2bn 2vla vc vlne.
    MS parts (pre-1820: D-Rtt, Sm. 33, Nos. 6 - 10.
  ANON **A-506a.** Terzett, "Mie care figliuole". fl 2ob 2cl 2hn 2bn 2vla vlne.
    MS parts (pre-1820): D-Rtt, Sm. 32, No. 1.
  ANON **A-507a** sinfonia, Act I: 9 mvts, Act II: 8 mvts. 2cl 2hn 2bn.
    MS parts: CZ-Pnm, XLII.A.103, (missing 2cl 2bn for the sinfonia & Act I; Act II is complete).
  WENT **JNW-50.1a** sinfonia & 14 mvts. 2ob 2cl 2hn 2bn.
  WENT **JNW-50.2a** sinfonia & 12 mvts. 2ob 2ca 2hn 2bn.
Axur, Re d'Ormus (originally: Tarare; all arrs use the later title) (opera, 8 June 1787, Paris; 8 Jan 1788, Vienna)
  ANON **A-301.2a** 2 mvts (also includes 7 mvts from Martín y Soler's *L'Arbore di Diana*). 2cl 2hn 2bn.
    MS parts: CZ-Pnm, XLII.D.86, Nos. 8 & 9.
  ANON **A-9.18a** 1 mvt. 3bthn.
  BEINET **XJB-1.3a** 2 mvts. 2ob 2cl 2hn 2bn.
  BEINET **XJB-3.3/2** 5 mvts. 2cl 2hn 2bn.
  ERNST **FRE-3a** Pièces d'harmonie, Suite 1: 13 mvts, Suite 2: 12 mvts. 2cl 2hn 2bn.
  OZI **EXO-1.24/2a** 3 mvts. 2cl(C) 2hn 2bn.
  PICK **HXP-2.8(a)** introduzione & 5 mvts. 2fl(B♭, C, terz-fl) 4cl 2hn 2bn tp bugle-hn serp/b-tb b-dr.
  STUMPF **JUS-14a** Recueil 8, 6 mvts. 2cl 2hn 2bn.
  WENT **JNW-51.1a** introduzione & 17 short mvts. 2ob 2cl 2hn 2bn.
  WENT **JNW-51.2a** introduzione & 16 short mvts. 2ob 2ca 2hn 2bn.
  WIDDER **YYW-1.40a** 1 mvt. fl ob 2cl 2hn 2bn.
  WRANIZKY, A. **AYW-2a** 1 mvt. pic 2ob 2cl 2hn 2bn cbn 4tp b-dr cym.
Palmira, Regina di Persia (opera, 15 Oct 1795, Vienna)
  ANON. **A-508a** 10 mvts. 2cl 2hn 2bn
    Pc (sn: sl, sd), RISM [S 558], parts: CZ-KRa, (missing titlepage), unverified.
  ANON **A-509a** quartetto. cl 3bthn. MS parts: CZ-Pnm, XLII.A.112.
  HANDL **JXH-1a** Stuck in Dis [E♭]. 2cl 2hn bn tp(prin).
  SCHMITT, G. **GYS-76a** overture. 2pic 2ob cl(E♭) 2cl(B♭) 4hn 2bn 2tp serp timp.
  SEYFRIED **IXS-1.4/19(a)** 1 mvt. 2bn + 2bn.
  VANĚROVSKÝ **FXV-2a** "I Nume eterno". cl 3bthn.
  WENT **JNW-52a** sinfonia & 22 mvts. 2ob 2cl 2hn 2bn.
Falstaff ossia Il tre burle (König von England) (opera, 8 Jan 1799, Vienna)
  WENT **JNW-13ac** 2ob 2cl 2hn 2bn,
Cesare in Farmacusa (opera, 2 June 1800, Vienna)
  ANON **A-510a** overture & 9 mvts. 2ob 2cl 2hn 2bn cbn.
    Pc (Aus den K: K: Hof Theater Musik Verlag: Wien, post-1813), MS pts: D-Rtt, Weigl 4; I-Fc, F.P. S.340,
    (with MS imprint in Italian, "Nel magazzino [sic] di Musica dei Teatri Imperiali"); A-Wn, Sm.3792, Nos.
    6 & 7, (terzetto, finale; = A-6.7a, 6.8a).
Die Hussiten vor Naumburg (Schauspiel by Kotzebue, 2 March 1803, Vienna)
  WIDDER **YYW-1.41a** marche. fl ob 2cl 2hn 2bn.

SARTI, Giuseppe (1729 - 1802). See: Courtin, **HYC-1a.**
I Contratempi (opera, Nov 1778, Venice)
  WENT **JNW-53.1a** 2ob 2cl 2hn 2bn.
  WENT **JNW-53.2a** 10 mvts. 2ob 2ca 2hn 2bn.
Giulio Sabino (opera, Jan 1781, Venice).
  ANON **A-511a** 2ob 2cl 2hn 2bn cbn 2tp. MS parts: CZ-Bm(au), A.35.227, (overture & 5 mvts);
    A-Wgm(w), (lost). *Pohl's transfer list states "9 stimmige Harm" but lists the 2tp, suggesting that this may
    be an arr. by Sedlak "mit Begleitung 2 Trompetten"; however, if complete, the CZ-Bm format suggests Starke.*
  WENT **JNW-54.1a** 3 mvts. 2ob 2ca 2hn 2bn.
  WENT **JNW-54.2a** 2ob 2cl 2hn 2bn.

Fra due Litiganti, il terzo gode (Les Noces de Dorine; Le Nozze di Dorina) (opera, 14 Sept 1782, Milan)
 ANON **A-512a** 11 mvts.   2cl 2hn bn.   MS parts: CZ-Pnm, XLI.D.89.   *Possibly a reduction of WENT,*
  JNW-55.1a (with the two sections of Nos. 6 & 8 split into two mvts)
 FUCHS, G.F. **GFF-3.3a** polacca.   2fl 2cl(C) 2hn 2bn.
 FUCHS, G.F. **GFF-38a** Steibelt: Cinquième pot-pourry, 1 mvt.   4cl 2hn 2bn.
 MOZART **WAM-2.2a** "Com' un agnelo", in *Don Giovanni*.   2ob 2cl 2hn 2bn.
 WENT **JNW-55.1a** 9 mvts.   2ob 2cl 2hn 2bn.
 WENT **JNW-55.2a** 8 mvts.   2ob 2ca 2hn 2bn.
Unidentified excerpts
 ANON **A-513a** Rondo: "Idolo amato".   2fl 2cl 2hn 2bn.
  MS parts: PL-LA, RM 81/1-5/155, (missing fl I, hn I, bn II).
 WENT **+JNW-56a** terzetto.   2ob 2ca 2hn (2)bn.   *Not the same work as JNW-21ac (P. Wranizky: Terzetto).*

SATIE, Erik Alfred Leslie (1866 - 1925)
4 Pieces
 SOETEMAN **IZS-1a** ob ob(ca) cl(Eb) 2cl b-cl 4hn 2bn cbn/db.

SATZENHOVEN (Satzenhöfer), Friedrich (dates unknown; active 1798 - 1821, Vienna)
Der Körbchenflechter an der Zauberquelle (Zaubrer-Oper, 19 June 1805, Vienna)
 HEIDENREICH **JYH-12a** introduzione & 15 mvts.   2ob 2cl 2hn 2bn cbn.

SCARLATTI, Domenico (1685 - 1757)
Sonatas, K.446 (keyboard)
 EMERSON **GZE-1.3a** Siciliano, in F.   2fl ob 3cl hn bn.
Two Scarlatti Pieces: Pastorale (L.413) & Capriccio (L.375) (keyboard)
 SHOSTAKOVICH **DDS-1a** pic 2fl 2ob 2cl 2hn 2bn 2tp tb timp.
Allegro in Sib [Bb] della Suite VIIIa per clavicembalo (unidentified)
 SETACCIOLI **GIS-1a** fl 2ob 2cl hn 2bn.

SCHACHT, Theodor von (1748 - 1823)
Rosamund (Rosamunde) (ballet, 7 Nov 1778, Regensburg)
 ANON **A-1.45a** 1 mvt.   2cl 2hn 2bn.
La Rosière de Salency (ballet after the opera by Grétry, 1778, Regensburg)
 ANON **A-1.37a(-4a), 1.44a** 6 mvts.   2cl 4hn 2bn 2tp 2vla vlne.

SCHAFFNER, Nicolas Anton (Albert?) (born c.1790
Ouverture du Chasse
 GAMBARO **VXG-12a** fl 2cl 2hn 2bn, (ad lib: 2cl 2tp tb serp).
Polonaise, in F
 WIELAND **KZW-12ad** fl(F) cl(F) 2cl(C) 2hn 2bn tp b-tb (serp) b-dr.
Rondo, in Bb
 GAMBARO **VXG-4.4(a)** pic(Db) cl(Eb) 2cl(Bb) 2hn (2)bn tp tb serp b-dr+cym.
Marche, in Bb
 GAMBARO **VXG-5.3(a)** pic(Db) cl(F) 2cl(C) 2hn (2)bn tp tb serp b-dr.

SCHENK (Schenck), Johann (1753 - 1836)
Die Weinlese [Weinlesse] (Singspiel, 12 Oct 1785, Vienna)
 WENT **JNW-14ac** rondo.   2ob 2cl 2hn 2bn.
Der Dorfbarbier (Singspiel, 30 Oct 1796, Vienna)
 RIEGER **GYR-1.4a** Alla Pollaca.   2cl 2hn 2bn.
 SCHNEIDER, A. **AYS-88.1a** overture.   fl 2ob 2cl 2hn 2bn tp b-tb 2vla cb.
 SCHNEIDER, A. **AYS-88.2a** polonoise, in Bb.   fl 2ob 4cl 2hn 2bn tp b-tb serp.

SCHIEDEMAYR, Johann Baptist (1779 - 1840)
Deutsche Nro. 2 (Introduction & 4 Deutsche)
 OSSWALD **PAO-5a** incomplete: here only ob I & II, cl(C).

SCHMELLING, ( )
Marche (& Trio)
 ANON **A-78.1/3m(a)** 2ob 2cl 2hn 2bn tp.

SCHMID, Joseph, *of Vienna* (piano virtuoso, active 1820s)
Polonoise, in D minor
 SCHNEIDER, A. **AYS-89a** fl 2ob 4cl 2hn 2bn tp b-tb serp.

SCHMITT, ( )
Ouverture in Bb ("Ouverture di Lipsia"), Op. 36a (orchestra, Leipzig, pre-1826)
 SCHNEIDER, A. **AYS-90a** fl 2ob 2cl 2hn 2bn tp b-tb 2vla cb.

SCHÖRTZEL, ( )
Balli Tedeschi (3 sets)
 ROSINACK **FJR-7as(-9as)** 2ob cl bn.

SCHROETER (Schröter), Johann Samuel (c.1752 - 1788)   *See supra:* ANON **A-2a.**

SCHUBERT, Franz Peter (1797 - 1828)
Die Zauberharfe, D.644 (melodrama, 19 Aug 1820, Vienna)
  TRIEBENSEE **JZT03ad** (Scoring uncertain; with *Rosamunde* includes:) fl ob ob(ca) cl(tarogato) cl 2hn 2bn cb.
Rosamunde, Fürstin von Zypern, D.767 (opera, incidental music to romantic play, 20 Dec 1823, Vienna)
  TRIEBENSEE **JZT-4ad** (Scoring uncertain: with *Die Zauberharfe:*) fl ob ob(ca) cl(tarogato) cl 2hn 2bn cb.
Fierabras, D.796 (opera, 29 March 1828, Leipzig; composed 1823)
  SCHOLZ **WES-161a** overture.   fl 2ob 2cl 2hn 2bn tp tb db timp.
Mass No. 2 in G, D.167 (SATB, strings, organ, 1815, Vienna)
  DERENZIS **RZD-1va** SATB soli, SATB chorus, 2fl 2cl a-cl b-cl.
Salve Regina, in F, D.386 (chorus & orchestra, 1816, Vienna)
  SCHUBERT, F.L. **FLS-2va** SATB chorus, 2ob 2hn 2bn 2tp 3tb organ(ad lib).
Ellens zweiter Gesang, Op. 52, No. 2, D.838 (voice & piano, pub. 1826, Vienna)
  BRAHMS **JHB-1va** Solo &, SSA chorus, 4hn 2bn.
  NEX **CYN-1a** rescoring of the Brahms arrangement.   2ob 2cl 4hn 2bn.
Ellens dritter Gesang ("Ave Maria"), Op. 52, No. 6, D.839 (voice & piano, pub. 1826, Vienna)
  ANON **A-514a** fl ob ca cl(E♭) 3cl(B♭) 2hn 2bn 2tp t-hn 3tb b-hn bomb.   MS parts: D-DT, Mus-n 1622.
Schwanengegang, D.957 (voice & piano, pub. 1829, Vienna)
  ANON **A-515a** No. 4, Ständchen.   2ob fl ob ca 3cl 4hn 2bn 2tp a-hn 3tb b-hn/bomb.   MS parts: D-DT, Mus-n 868.
Original-Tänze, Op. 9, No. 2 (commonly misattributed to Beethoven as "Le Désir Waltz", K.-H.Anh.14, No. 1)
  BERR **FXB-28a** fl(E♭) cl(E♭) 2cl(C) 2hn 2bn; (ad lib: cl III in C, tp (2)tb, serp ripieno).
  KÜFFNER **JYK-5.1(a)** fl(F) 2cl 2hn 2bn.
  WITT **FZW-17.7ac** fl(E♭) 2cl(E♭) 2cl(B♭) 2hn 2bn tp b-tb.
Trois Marches Militaires, Op. 51, D.733 (piano duet, pub. 1826, Vienna)
  FRANÇAIX **JEF-5a** fl fl(pic) 2ob 2cl 2hn bn bn(cbn).
  TAYLORSON **JST-21a** March in D.   fl 2ob 2cl 2hn 2bn cbn/db.
16 Deutsche (German Dances), Op. 33, D.783 (Jan 1823 - July 1824; pub. 1825, Vienna)
  BERKES **KYB-1a** Nos. 6 & 7, (as "German Dances").   2ob 2cl 2hn 2bn.
  SHEEN **GHS-18a** fl(pic) ob ca cl b-cl 2hn bn cbn.
20 Waltzes, D.146 (piano, Nos. 1, 3 - 11, 1815, Nos. 2, 12 - 20, 1823; pub. 1830 as "Op. 127", Vienna)
  BERKES **KYB-2a** Nos. 12 & 20.   2ob 2cl 2h 2bn.

SCHUBRY, ( )
  BERR **FXB-4ma** as "Pas Redoublé No. 3".   fl cl(E♭) 2cl(B♭) 2hn 2bn tp 3tb oph b-dr s-dr.

SCHULZ, Johann Philipp Christian (1773 - 1827)
Die Jungfrau von Orleans (play with music, c.1801, Leipzig)
  SCHULZ **JCS-1.1a** Harmonie zum Monolog.   fl 2cl 2hn bn.
  TRIEBENSEE **JZT-50a** Harmonie zum Monolog.   2ob 2cl 2hn 2bn (cbn ad lib).   *A rescoring of JCS-1.1a.*
Schulz's VIII pièces dharmonies de diverses Comédies favorites (JCS-1a) includes the following works which
we believe to be arrangements of original works for (untraced) plays in Leipzig: fl cl(C & B♭) 2hn bn.
  JCS-1.2a. Menikov und Natalie, 1 mvt. No. 2.   JCS-1.3a. Aus dem Soldaten, 2 mvts. Nos. 3 & 7.
  JCS-1.4a. Die Kreuzfahrer, 2 mvts. Nos. 4 & 5.   JCS-1.5a. Aus dem Schreibepult, 1 mvt. No. 8.

SCHUMANN, Robert Alexander (1810 - 1856)
Introduction, Allegro & Finale (Conzertstück), Op. 92 (14 Feb 1850, Leipzig)
  SKIRROW **ARS-3a** fl ob 2cl 2hn 2bn cbn(ad lib).

SCHWARZ, Ch(ristian)
Huit Allemandes avec Introduction, Trios et Coda (piano, c.1820)
  ANON **A-625.2a** Intro[duction] & 6 Deutsche.   2ob cl(A) cl(D) 2hn 2bn cbn 2tp.
  MS parts (c.1827): CZ-Bm(au), A.36.893, No. 3.

SEYFRIED, Ignaz, *Ritter* von (1776 - 1841)
Cyrus in Persia (grosse heröische Oper, 22 Nov 1803)
  KROMMER **FVK-2.7ma** Marsch.   2ob 2cl 2hn 2bn cbn.
Zum goldenen Löwen (opera, 12 Nov 1806, Vienna)
  TRIEBENSEE **JZT-51a** rondo.   2ob 2cl 2hn 2bn (cbn tp ad lib).
Alamor der Mauer (opera, 1 Jan 1807, Vienna)
  ANON **A-516a** Act I - IV (? 3 Teils).   (? 2ob 2cl 2hn 2bn cbn).
  MS parts (27): I-Fc, F.P. S.390, (here incorrectly attributed to Bruni).
  TRIEBENSEE **JZT-52.1a** march.   2ob 2cl 2hn 2bn (tp ad lib).
  TRIEBENSEE **JZT-52.2a** march.   2cl 2hn bn.   *Probably a local rescoring by Václav Havel.*
Mitternacht (opera, 22 April 1807, Vienna)
  TRIEBENSEE **JZT-53a** duet.   2ob 2cl 2hn 2bn (cbn ad lib).
Idas und Marpissa (opera, 10 Oct 1807, Vienna)
  TRIEBENSEE **JZT-54a** duet.   2ob 2cl 2hn 2bn (cbn ad lib).
Rochus Pumpernickel (quodlibet, 13 Dec 1809, Vienna; compiled & arranged by Seyfried & Haibel)
  ANON **A-517a** 2ob 2cl 2hn 2bn cbn.   MS parts: I-Fc, F.P. S.421, (cataloged under "Stegmayer").
  SCHMETS **QYS-1a** "Overture a [i.e., and] Polonese".   2ob 2cl 2hn 2bn cbn.
Die Familie Pumpernickel [Rochus Pumpernickel, Teil 2] (quodlibet, 13 Feb 1810, Vienna)
  ANON **A-518a** overture & 2 acts.   2ob 2cl 2hn 2bn cbn.   MS parts: I-Fc, F.P. S.421.
Saul, König von Israel (biblical opera/melodrama, 7 April 1810, Vienna)
  ANON (sometimes attributed to Seyfried IXS-1ad) **A-519.1a** overture & 14 mvts.   2ob 2cl 2hn 2bn cbn.
    Pc (Im Verlage der k: k: priv: chemischen Druckerey: Wien, pn 1486, 1487, 1810), **J9**, No. II, parts:
    A-Wst, M.24772/c; CZ-KRa, A3842/IV.B.6, (MS parts; overture, Nos 3, 4, 9 & 12; missing cbn; here
    attributed to "Cherubiny [sic]"); GB-Ljag, (photocopy); H-Bn, Z 22,012; I-Fc, F.P. S.355, (? MS parts).
  ANON **A-519.2a** overture & 14 mvts.   2cl 2hn 2bn.
    Pc (Im Verlage der k: k: priv: chemischen Druckerey: Wien, pn 1486, 1810), **J6**, No. II, parts:
    CZ-Bm(au), A.35.228.
  SCHNEIDER, A. **AYS-91a** overture & 9 mvts.   fl 2ob 4cl 2hn 2bn tp b-tb serp.

Richard Löwenherz (ballet after Grétry's opera *Richard, Coeur-de-Lion*, 1810 Vienna)
 SEDLAK **+WXS-58a** overture & 12 mvts, in 2 Abtheilungen. 2ob 2cl 2hn 2bn cbn.
Friedrich von Minsky oder Das Familiengericht (melodrama, 5 Jan 1811, Vienna)
 ANON **A-520a** 2ob 2cl 2hn 2bn cbn. Ms parts: I-Fc, F.P. S.358.
Pumpernickels Hochzeitstag [Rochus Pumpernickel, Teil 3] (quodlibet, 9 Sept 1811, Vienna)
 ANON **A-521a** 3 parts. 2ob 2cl 2hn 2bn cbn. MS parts: I-Fc, F.P. S.422.
Die Cisterne (melodrama, 17 Dec 1811, Vienna)
 ANON **A-522a** overture & 4 acts. 2ob 2cl 2hn 2bn cbn tp. MS parts (40): I-Fc, F.P. S.365.
Faust (dramatic legende, 13 March 1816, Vienna)
 SCHOLZ **WES-162a** overture. fl 2ob 2cl 2hn 2bn 2tp tb db timp.
Salmonnäa und ihre Söhne oder Die Makkabäer (Biblical drama, 21 Nov 1818, Vienna)
 ANON **A-523a** (?2ob 2cl 2hn 2bn cbn). MS parts (9): I-Fc, F.P. S.420.
Requiem in A♭ Con Libera (IXS-2v) (SATB, 2bthn 2bn 2tp 3tb organ timp)
 MAYR, J.S. **JSM-2va** Libera. STBB, 2fl 2ob 2cl 2hn bn 2tp 2tb timp.

SHIELD, William (1748 - 1829)
See also: REEVE. *Oscar & Malvina.*
The Woodman (comic opera, 26 Dec 1791, London)
 ELEY **CFE-3.2m(a)** finale. 2ob/cl 2cl 2hn 2bn tp.

SIBELIUS, Jean (Johan Julias Christian) (1865 - 1957)
Canzonetta, Op. 62a (adaptation by the composer from *Kuolema, Op. 44;* strings, pub. 1911)
 STRAVINSKY **ITS-2a** cl b-cl 4hn cb harp.

SIXT, J.
6 Allemandes ROSINACK **FJR-3a** 2ob 2cl 2hn 2bn.
12 Waltzes ROSINACK **FJR-4a** 2ob 2cl 2hn 2bn.

SOLIÉ (Solier, Soulier), Jean Pierre (1755 - 1812)
Jean et Geneviève (opéra comique, 7 Dec 1792, Paris)
 FUCHS, G.F. **GFF-35.1a** [3] Airs . . . mèlés de [4] petits Airs Patriotiques. 4cl 2hn 2bn.
 FUCHS, G.F. **GFF-35.2a** Airs. 2fl 2cl 2hn 2bn.
Le Jockei (Le Jockey) (opéra comique, 6 Jan 1796, Paris)
 SIMONET **FMS-1a** overture. 2fl 2cl 2hn 2bn.
 SIMONET **FMS-2a** suite. 2fl 2cl 2hn 2bn.
Le Chapitre second (Das zweite Capitel; Das zweyte Kapitel) (opera, 17 June 1799, Paris)
 FUCHS, G.F. **GFF-36.1a** overture. 2fl 2cl 2hn 2bn.
 FUCHS, G.F. **GFF-36.2a** airs. 2fl 2cl(C) 2hn 2bn.
 HAVEL **VXH-12ac** overture & 13 mvts. 2cl 2hn 2bn.
Mademoiselle (Madame) de Guise (opera, 17 March 1808, Paris)
 GEBAUER, M.J. **MJG-1.4a** overture & 5 mvts. fl(F) cl(F) 2cl(C) 2hn 2bn tp serp/b-tb b-dr cym tri; *or*
  fl(F) 2cl(C) 2hn 2bn serp.

SOUSA, John Philip (1854 - 1932)
Washington Post, March (military band, 15 June 1889, Washington, DC).
 GODDARD **MXG-2a** 2cl 2hn 2bn.

SOWINSKI, Albert
Marche Héroïque des Parisiens (dédiée au Général Lafayette) (?piano, c.1793, Paris)
 BERR **FB-1ma** pic(D♭) cl(E♭) cl(B♭ solo) 4cl(B♭) 2hn 2bn tp 3tb serp b-dr t-dr.

SPINTLER, Chr[istian]
Soldatenlust, Defilermarsch
 ANON **A-524a** pic fl 2ob cl(E♭) cl(solo B♭) 3cl(B♭) 4hn 2bn 3tp t-hn 3tb bomb/b-hn vc/b b-dr s-dr.
  MS parts: D-DT, Mus-n 1891, No. 2.

SPOFFORTH, Reginald (1770 - 1827)
Six Glees, No. 6, Hail Smiling Morn (ATTB Glee, pub. c.1820, London)
 ELGAR **EWE-16a** 2fl cl hn bn.

SPOHR, Louis (1784 - 1859)
Alruna die Eulenkönigin (opera, ?1808, Weimar)
 SCHOLZ **WES-164a** overture. fl 2ob 2cl 2hn 2bn tp tb db timp.
Faust (opera, 1 Sept 1816, Prague; March 1818, Frankfurt am Main; 7 July 1818, Vienna)
 ANON **A-525a** overture. pic 2ob cl(E♭) cl(C) 2cl(B♭) 2hn 2bn 2tp 3tb serp b-dr. MS pts: D-DT, Mus-n 937.
 ANON **A-526a** overture & 9 mvts. 2ob 2cl 2hn 2bn cbn. MS pts: CZ-KRa, A3974/IV.B.138; I-Fc, F.P. S.380.
 KIRCHHOFF **WZK-50a** aria ("Der Hölle selbst"). fl 2ob 2cl 3hn 2bn tb db.
 SCHNEIDER, A. **AYS-92a** overture. fl 2ob 2cl(C) 2hn 2bn tp b-tb 2vla cb.
 SCHOLZ **WES-164.1a** overture. fl 2ob 2cl 2hn 2bn tp tb db timp.
 SCHOLZ **WES-164.2a** scene & chor. fl 2ob 2cl 3hn 2bn tp tb db timp.
 SCHOLZ **WES-164.3a** introduction. fl 2ob 2cl 3hn 2bn tb db timp.
 SCHOLZ **WES-164.4a** aria with chorus. fl 2ob 2cl 2hn 2bn tp tb db timp.
 SCHOLZ **WES-164.5a** sextet & aria. 2ob 2cl 2hn 2bn tp tb db timp.
 STRECK **PZS-2.1a** polonaise. fl 2cl 2hn 2bn.
Zemire und Azor (opera, 4 April 1819, Frankfurt am Main)
 ANON **A-527a** overture & 5 mvts. 2ob 2cl 2hn 2bn cbn. MS parts: I-Fc, F.P. S.388.
 KIRCHHOFF **WZK-51a** romance ("An die Rose"). fl 2ob 2cl 2hn 2bn tb db.

Jessonda (opera, 28 July 1823, Kassel)
  BARTH **WLB-3.1a** overture. fl(pic E♭) terz-fl(pic E♭) 2ob cl(E♭) 3cl(B♭) 4hn 2bn tp a-tb t-tb b-tb serp timp.
  BARTH **WLB-3.2a** 8 mvts. fl(pic E♭) terz-fl(pic E♭) 2ob cl(E♭) 3cl(B♭) 2hn 2bn (2)tp serp.
  MARPURG **WYM-1.2(a)** 1 mvt. pic 2ob cl(E♭) 3cl(B♭) 2hn 2bn 2tp a-tb t-tb b-tb serp b-dr t-dr.
  MINAŘIK **YXM-1a** aria & duett. 2ob 2cl 2hn 2bn cbn 2tp.
  SCHMITT, G. **GYS-77a** introduzione & 4 mvts. fl 2ob 2cl 2hn 2bn tp 2tb db.
  SCHNEIDER, A. **AYS-93a** overture. fl(C, E♭, pic in E♭) 2ob 2cl(A & B♭) 2hn 2bn tp b-tb 2vla cb.
  SCHOLZ **WES-165.1a** overture. fl 2ob 2cl 3hn 2bn tp tb db timp.
  SCHOLZ **WES-165.2a** introductione. fl 2ob 2cl 2hn 2bn tb db.
  SCHOLZ **WES-165.3a** duet ("Schönes Mädchen"). fl 2ob 2cl 2hn 2bn tb db.
  WITT **FAW-14.1a** overture & 8 mvts. (Scoring varies; total forces:) terz-fl(pic) fl(C, terz-) 2ob cl(E♭)
  3cl(B♭) 4hn/2hn 2bn tp 2a-tb b-tb serp timp.
  WITT **FZW-14.2a** overture & 8 mvts. fl(E♭) 2cl(E♭) 2cl(B♭) 2hn 2bn tp b-tb cb.
Der Berggeist, WoO 54 (opera, 24 March 1825, Kassel)
  ANON **A-528a** overture. fl cl(solo) 3cl 2hn 2bn 2tp 3tb serp.   MS parts: D-DT, Mus-n 924.
Der Alchymist (Der Alchimisten) (opera, 28 July 1830, Kassel)
  KIRCHHOFF **WZK-52a** 2 mvts. fl 2ob 2cl 2hn 2bn tp tb db.
Des Heilands letzte Stunden, WoO 62 (oratorio, Kassel, 1835; Norwich, 19 Sept 1839)
  SCHOLZ **WES-166a** aria ("Ewig fliesset meine Zähren"). fl 2ob 2cl 2hn 2bn tb db.
[unidentified movement]
  SCHMITT, G. **GYS-78a** 2fl 2ob 2cl 2hn 2bn tp tb db.

SPONTINI, Gasparo Luigi Pacificus, *Conte de S. Andrea* (1774 - 1851)
Milton (comic opera, 27 Nov 1804, Paris)
  KRECHLER **FFK-8.3a** Schluss Chor. 2ob 2cl 2hn 2bn cbn tp.
  KRECHLER **FFK-9.4a** Schluss Chor. 2ob 2cl 2hn 2bn cbn.
La Vestale (Die Vestellen) (opera, 25 Dec 1807, Paris; 12 Nov 1810, Vienna)
  ANON **A-74.4/12m(a), A-74.6/10m(a), A-74.8/3m(a), A-74.9/6m(a)** 4 Märsche.
  pic quart-fl 2ob cl(F) 2cl(C) 4hn 2bn cbn+serp/2b-hn 2tp 3tb b-dr t-dr tamb cym.
  ANON **A-74.7/7m(a)** Triumphmarsch. (scoring as above)
  ANON **A-515a** overture. fl 2ob cl(E♭) 4cl(B♭) 2hn(+2hn ad lib) 2bn 2tp 3tb serp b-dr s-dr.
  MS parts: D-DT, Mus-n 963.
  ANON **A-520a** overture. pic fl ob cl(F) 2cl(C) 3hn 2bn 2tp tb serp. MS parts: D-Tl, Z 125.
  ANON **A-530a** Marcia. 2fl 2ob 2cl 2hn 2bn 2tp tb. MS parts: D-Dl.
  ANON **A-531a** 2 mvts. 2ob 2cl 2hn 2bn cbn 2tp. MS parts: CZ-Bm(au), A.40.162.
  ANON **A-532a** overture & 7 mvts. 2ob 2cl 2hn 2bn cbn tp.
  Pc (T. Weigl: Vienna, 1811), MS parts: A-Ee, Mus.1123; I-Fc, F.P. S.356.
  ANON **A-533.1a** overture & 13 mvts. 2ob 2cl 2hn 2bn cbn.
  Pc (In Verlage der k: k: priv: chemischen Druckerey: Wien, pn 1641, 1811), **J9**, No. III, pts: H-Bn, Z 22,011.
  ANON **A-533.2a** overture & 13 mvts. 2cl 2hn 2bn.
  Pc (Im Verlage der k: k: priv: chemischen Druckerey: Wien, pn 1640, 1641, 1811), **J6**, No. III, parts:
  CZ-KRa, A4015/IV.B.188; CZ-Pnm, XLI.B.103, (missing pages 7/8 & 11/12 of the cl I pt).
  ANON **A-534a** overture & 6 mvts. 2ob 2cl 2hn 2bn. MS parts: CZ-KRa, A3975/IV.B.139.
  GEBAUER, E.F. **EFG-4a** overture. 2fl 2ob 2cl 2hn 2bn tp tb serp.
  KRECHLER **FFK-25a** overture & 7 mvts. 2ob 2cl 2hn 2bn cbn.
  LEZGUS **DHL-1** Theil 3, No. 8, March. 2cl 2hn bn.
  SCHMITT, G. **GYS-79.1a** overture & 7 mvts. 2fl 2ob cl(E♭ obl) 2cl(B♭) 2bthn 4hn 2bn cbn 2tp tb b-dr
  s-dr tri.
  SCHMITT, G. **GYS-79.2a** overture & 1 Bd. fl 2ob 2cl 2hn 2bn tp 2tb db timp.
  SCHOLZ **WES-165.1a** 3 mvts. fl 2ob 2cl 2hn 2bn tp tb db timp.
  SCHOLZ **WES-165.2a** ensemble & finale. fl 2ob 2cl 2hn 2bn tp tb db timp.
  TRIEBENSEE **JZT-55a** overture, Act I: 5 mvts, Act 2: 6 mvts, Act III: 9 mvts. 2ob 2cl 2hn 2bn (cbn tp ad lib).
  WIELAND **KZW-13ad** overture & 13 mvts. 2fl 2ob cl(E♭) 2cl(B♭) 2hn 2bn cbn 2tp.
Fernand Cortez, ou La Conquète du Mexique (opera, 28 Nov 1809, Paris)
  ANON **A-74.8/4m(a), 10m(a)** 2 Märsche. pic quart-fl 2ob cl(F) 2cl(C) 4hn 2bn cbn+serp/2b-hn 2tp 3tb b-dr
  t-dr tamb cym.
  ANON **A-535a** overture. pic 2ob cl(E♭) 3cl(B♭) 4hn 2bn 2tp 3tb serp b-dr t-dr. MS pts: D-DT, Mus-n 959.
  ANON **A-536.1a** overture & 14 mvts. 2ob 2cl 2hn 2bn cbn.
  Pc (In Verlage der k: k: priv: chemischen Druckerey: Wien, pn 1944, 1810), **J9**, No. V, pts: H-Bn, Z 22,012;
  CZ-KRa, A4167/IV.B.142, (MS parts, 14 mvts without overture); I-Fc, F.P. S.357, (?MS parts).
  ANON **A-536.2a** overture & 14 mvts. 2cl 2hn 2bn.
  Pc (Im Verlage der k: k: priv: chemischen Druckerey: Wien, pn 1944, 1945, 1810), **J6**, No. V, parts: CZ-KRa,
  A4009/IV.B.181, (missing cl II, hn II & wrapper); CZ-Pnm, XLI.B.104. MS pts (1825): D-Tl, Gg 353.
  GEBAUER, E.F. **EFG-5a** overture. 2pic 2fl 2ob 2cl(F) 2cl(C) 2hn 3bn 2tp timp b-dr tri tambour.
  KRECHLER **FFK-22a** overture & 14 mvts. 2ob 2cl 2hn 2bn cbn (tp), (later parts: pic b-dr t-dr cym tri).
  KRECHLER **FFK-4.5a** Marché [sic] espagnol. 2ob 2cl 2hn 2bn cbn.
  KRECHLER **FFK-7.1a** choeur (Tempo di Marcia). 2ob 2cl 2hn 2bn cbn tp.
  SCHMITT, G. **GYS-80a** overture & 1 Bd. fl 2ob 2cl 2hn 2bn tp 2tb db timp.
  SCHOLZ **WES-168a** overture & 1 Band. fl 2ob 2cl 3hn 2bn tp tb db timp.
  VOGT **GUV-1a** Liv. 1, 2. fl fl(pic) 2ob/cl(C ripieno) 3cl(C) 2ca bthn 2hn 2bn 2tp tb serp timp b-dr cym tri.
  WIELAND **KZW-14.1ad** overture & 6 mvts. *Incomplete:* (overture), 2fl 4cl(C) 2hn cbn; (6 mvts) cbn only.
  WIELAND **KZW-14.2ad** overture. fl 2ob 2cl 2hn 2bn 2tp serp/vlne.

Les Dieux rivaux (opera, 21 June 1816, Paris; collaboration with Berton, R. Kreutzer & Persuis)
  GEBAUER, E.F. **EFG-6a** Instrumentation unknown.
Olympie (Olympia) (opera, 22 Dec 1819, Paris)
  SCHNEIDER, A. **AYS-94a** overture. fl 2ob 2cl(C) 2hn 2bn tp b-tb 2vla cb.
  SCHOLZ **WES-169a** overture. fl 2ob 2cl 2hn 2bn tp tb db timp.
Lalla Rookh (Lalla Rakh) (tableaux vivants, 27 Jan 1821, Berlin, Royal Palace)
  ANON **A-74.11/m(a)** march. pic quart-fl 2ob cl(F) 2cl(C) 4hn 2bn cbn+serp/2b-hn 2tp 3tb b-dr t-dr tamb cym.
  WIELAND **KZW-15ad** march & 4 mvts. fl 2ob 2cl 2hn 2bn 2tp b-tb serp.
Alcidor (opera, 23 May 1825, Berlin)
  NEITHARDT **AHN-1a** march. pic quart-fl 2ob cl(F) 2cl(C) 4hn 2bn cbn+serp/2b-hn 2tp 3tb b-dr t-dr tamb cym.
Sieges- und Festmarsch in C (voice & winds)
  SCHOLZ **WES-170a** fl 2ob 2cl 2hn 2bn tp tb vc db timp.
Untraced arrangements: Milton (opera, 1804, Paris); Julie (opera, 1805, Paris).

STABINGER, Mattia (active c.1765 - 1780)
La Fête Flamande (ballet, c.1769; CZ-K full score dated October 1769)
  WENT **JNW-57a** sinfonia & 15 mvts. 2ob 2hn bn.

STARKE, Friedrich (1774 - 1835)
Alexander-Marsch
  A-2.1ma. Alexander Marsch nach Starke. cl(D) 2cl(C) 2hn 2bn tp(posthorn in Trio) tp(II) serp b-dr s-d.

STARZER, Josef (c.1726 - 1787)
Anonymous arrangements in the Clam Gallas collection (CZ-Pnm, XLII) may be very early arrangements by Went.
Diana ed Endimione (ballet, Vienna, 1770)
  ANON **A-537a** Allegro, 6/8. 2ob 2hn bn. MS parts: CZ-K, symfonie No.238.K.II, (missing hn II; incorrectly
    identified as "Parthia in C Nro 12", this is, in fact, No. 12 in the full ballet at CZ-K, balety 149.K.II).
  ASPLMAYR **FDA-4a/FDA-53** Minuet & Trio; Andante cantabile. 2ob 2hn bn.
Les cinques Soltanes (ballet, 1771, Vienna)
  ANON (?Starzer, JFS-1ad) **A-538a** 5 mvts. 2ob 2hn bn. MS pts: CZ-Pnm, XLII.C.179, (as "Les 3 Sultanes").
Adèle de Ponthieu (Adelheid von Ponthieu, Adelheit von Ranthau) (ballet, 1773, Vienna)
  ANON **A-539a** 14 mvts. fl 2cl 2hn 2bn. MS parts: CZ-Pnm, XLII.A.226.
  ANON (?Starzer, JFS-2ad) **A-540a** 4 mvts. 2ob 2hn bn. MS parts: CZ-Pnm, XLII.B.253.
  ASPLMAYR **FDA-1a/FDA-46** Adagio. 2ob 2hn bn.
Les Horaces et les Curiaces (ballet, 1774, Vienna)
  ANON (?Starzer, JFS-3ad) **A-541a** 11 mvts. 2ob 2hn bn. MS parts: CZ-Pnm, XLIL B.195.
Le Baal Angloise (ballet, sd, Vienna)
  ANON (?Starzer, JFS-4ad) **A-542a** 5 mvts. 2ob 2hn bn. MS parts: CZ-Pnm, XLII.B.161.
La Bianca e la Rossa (ballet, sd, Vienna)
  WENT **+JNW-58a** 11 mvts. 2ob 2ca 2hn 2bn.

STASNY, Ludwig (1823 - 1883)
Papageno-Polka (piano)
  ANON **A-543a** pic 2ob cl(E♭) cl(solo B♭) 3cl(B♭) 4hn 2bn 3tp t-hn 3tb b-hn/bomb timp b-dr s-dr.
    MS parts: D-DT, Mus-n 1525, No. 1, (the title states, "Nach dem Clavier[auszug]").

STEIBELT, Daniel (1765 - 1823)
La belle Laitière, ou Blanche, Reine de Castille (ballet, 26 Jan 1805, London)
See also supra DUPORT: *Der blöde Ritter.*
  ZWINGMANN **JOZ-1a** 2fl 2cl 2hn 2bn tp bugle-horn serp.
Britannia, Allegorical Overture, Op. 41. (Combat Naval; (piano, 1797)
  GOEPFERT **CAG-9a** 2ob 2cl 2hn 2bn; (ad lib: tp b-tbn serp).
La Battaille d'Austerlitz (piano, 1806)
  FUCHS **GFF-37a** 2cl(C) 2hn 2bn; (ad lib: pic tp tb timp b-dr).
Cinquième potpourri (pf c.1793) *Includes 1 mvt from Paisiello's Nina, an Andante from Haydn's "La Roxolane"
Symphony (Hob. 1/63ii) & 1 mvt from Sarti's Fra due Litiganti (as "Les Noces de Dorine")*
  FUCHS **GFF-38a** 4cl 2hn 2bn.
La Journée d'Ulm, fantasie pour le piano forte (1805)
  FUCHS **GFF-39a** 2cl 2hn 2bn; (ad lib: fl tp tb b-dr).
March & Trio (original piano version unidentified) *Falsely attributed to Triebensee as composer (JZT-2d).*
  TRIEBENSEE **JZT-56a** 2ob 2cl 2hn 2bn (cbn tp ad lib). *Unquestionably arranged by Triebensee.*
Geschwindmarsch (unidentified)
  ANON **A-74.4/7m(a)** pic quart-fl 2ob cl(F) 2cl(C) 4hn 2bn cbn+serp/2b-hn 2tp 3tb b-dr t-dr tamb cym.

STEIBELT, Daniel, PERSUIS, Louis Luc Loiseau de, et al.
Der blöde Ritter (ballet, c.1810,Vienna). *Duport, the choreographer is usually cited as the compiler of this work.
The overture is Steibelt's overture to* La Belle laitière; *Persuis' "Alexander Marsch" is also used. All entries
are listed supra at* DUPORT.

STEINECKER, ( )
4 Polonaises (piano duet, Vienna, 1808)
  SCHNEIDER, A. **AYS-95a** fl 2ob 4cl 2hn 2bn tp(hn III) b-tb cb.
Walzer, in D (piano duet, 1810-1813, Vienna)
  SCHNEIDER, A. **AYS-96a** fl 2ob 2cl(A)+2cl(rip, C) 2hn 2bn tp b-tb serp.

STERKEL, Johann Franz Xaver (1750 - 1817)
Farnace, Op. 18 (opera, 12 Jan 1782, Naples)
 SCHMITT, G. **GYS-81a** overture.   2fl 2ob 2cl 2hn 2bn tb db.

STOKMAR, H.
Oberwittbacher Fantasie [Walzer & Trio] and *Favorit Tanz*
 WITT **FZW-17.1a, 17.2a** 2cl(E♭) 2cl(B♭) 2hn 2bn tp b-tb.

STORACE, Stephen (1763 - 1796)
Gli Sposi malcontenti (opera, 1 June 1785, Vienna)
 WENT **JNW-59.1a** 10 mvts.   2ob 2cl 2hn 2bn.
 WENT **JNW-59.2a** 10 mvts.   2ob 2ca 2hn 2bn.
La Cameriera astuta (opera, 4 March 1788, London)
 ANON **A-202.3/24(a)** "Jeunes Cœurs soyez fidelles".   2terz-fl 2bthn 2hn 2bn serp.
 ANON **A-203.1/14(a)** "Jeunes Cœurs soyez fidelles".   2ob 2bthn 2hn 2bn serp.
The Haunted Tower (comic opera, 24 Nov 1789, London)
 ANON **A-204.54(a)** "Will great Lords and Ladies drest upon gay days".   2ob 2bthn 2hn 2bn serp.
The Siege of Belgrade (opera, 1 Jan 1791, London)
 ANON **A-202.1(a)** "Divertimento . . . Storace, Pleyel, Attwood", mvts 1 & 3, "Loud let the song of triumph"
  & "Seize him I say".   2ob 2bthn 2hn 2bn serp.
Andante (unidentified)
 ELEY **CFE-3.6m(a)** 2ob/cl 2cl 2hn 2bn tp.

STRAUSS Johann, *the Elder (vater)* (1804 - 1849)
Note: Anonymous arrangements from D-NEhz are most likely by W.E. Scholz.
Carolinen und Kettenbrüche-Galopp, Op. 21a/b (*Wiener Zeitung* advertizements, 16 Nov 1827, 25 Jan 1828, respectively, Vienna)
% ANON **A-258.4a** incomplete: hn I, bn I, tp I & II only.   MS parts: CZ-Bm(au), A.35.325, No. 4.
Benefice-Walzer, Op. 33 (12 Feb 1830, Vienna)
% ANON **A-258.3a** incomplete: hn I, bn I, tp I & II only.   MS parts: CZ-Bm(au), A.35.235, No. 3.
Tivoli-Rutsch-Walzer (Wiener-Tivoli-Rutschwalzer), Op. 39 (9 Oct 1830, Vienna)
 ANON **A-544a** cl(G) cl(D) 2hn 2bn cbn 2tp serp.   MS parts: CZ-Bm(au), A.35.239.
Das Leben ein Tanz, oder Der Tanz ein Leben, Walzer, Op. 49 (23 Nov 1836, Vienna)
 ANON **A-545a** cl(G) 2cl(D) 2hn bn 2tp tb.   MS parts: CZ-Bm(au), A.35.236.
Alexandra Walzer, Op. 56 (10 July 1832, Vienna)
 ANON **A-546a** pic 2ob cl(E♭) 3cl(B♭) 2hn 2bn 2tp 3tb serp b-dr s-dr.   MS pts: D-DT, Mus-n 1935, No. 2.
Der Frohsinn, mein Ziel. Walzer, Op. 63 (16 May 1833, Vienna)
 ANON **A-547a** cl(E♭) 2cl(B♭) 2hn 2bn cbn 2tp b-tb.   MS parts: CZ-Bm(au), A.35.233a.
Mittel gegen der Schlaf, Walzer, Op. 65 (28 Aug 1833, Vienna)
 ANON **A-548a** cl(I, E♭) cl(II & III, B♭) 2hn bn cbn 2tp b-tb.   MS parts: CZ-Bm(au), A.35.237.
 STRECK **PZS-1.9a** fl cl(D) 2cl(A) 2hn 2bn.
Emlék Pestre, Erinnerung an Pest, Walzer, Op. 66 (7/13Nov 1834, Pest)
 HLADKÝ **XXH-1a** 3cl(B♭) 2hn bn cbn 2tp b-tb.   MS parts: CZ-Bm(au), A.37.350.
Gabrielen-Walzer, Op. 68 (20 Jan 1834, Vienna)
 ANON **A-549a** fl 2ob cl(E♭) 3cl(B♭) 2hn 2bn 2tp 3tb serp b-dr s-dr.   MS parts: D-DT, Mus-n 1935, No. 1.
Fortuna Galopp, Op. 69 (9 Jan 1834, Vienna)
 ANON **A-13.4a, 20.16a** pic(E♭) cl(E♭) 2cl(B♭) 2hn bn 2tp b-tb serp.
Pfenning-Walzer, Op. 70 (5 March 1834, Vienna)
 ANON **A-550a** fl 2ob 2cl 2hn 2bn b-tb basso.   MS parts: D-NEhz, 133, No. 6.
Elisabethan-Walzer, Op. 71 (26 June 1834, Vienna)
 ANON **A-551a** pic 2ob cl(E♭) 3cl(B♭) 2hn 2bn 2tp 3tb serp b-dr s-dr.   MS parts: D-DT, Mus-n 1935.
 ANON **A-19.3a** fl(F) 2cl(E♭) 2cl(B♭) 2hn 2bn tp b-tb cb.
Venetianer-Galopp, Op. 74 (21 July 1834, Vienna)
 DASSEL **JBD-1.1a** fl 2ob cl(E♭) 3cl(B♭) 2hn 2bn 2tp 3tb serp b-dr t-dr.
 KIRCHHOFF **WZK-53a** fl 2ob 2cl 2hn 2bn tb db.
Grazien-Tänze, Walzer, Op. 81 (7 July 1835, Vienna)
 ANON **A-552a** pic 2ob 3cl 2hn 2tp 3tb serp b-dr.   MS parts: D-DT, Mus-n 1945, No. 1.
 ANON **A-553a** fl 2ob 2cl 2hn 2bn b-tb basso.   MS parts: D-NEhz, 133, No. 5.
Heimat-Klänge, Walzer, Op. 84 (1836, Vienna)
 SCHOLZ **WES-171a** fl 2ob 2cl 3hn 2bn tb db.
Reise-Galopp, Op. 85 (*Wiener Zeitung* advertizement, 15 Feb 1836, Vienna)
 DASSEL **JBD-1.2a** fl 2ob cl(E♭) 3cl(B♭) 2hn 2bn 2tp 3tb serp b-dr t-dr.
Ballnacht-Galopp, Op. 86 (*Wiener Zeitung* advertizement, 15 Feb 1836, Vienna)
 ANON **A-554a** pic 2ob 3cl 2hn 2bn 2tp 3tb serp b-dr.   MS parts: D-DT, Mus-n 1945, No. 2.
Erinnerung an Deutschland Walzer, Op. 87 (10 Feb 1836, Vienna)
 ANON **A-13.4a** fl(F) 2cl(E♭) 2cl(B♭) 2hn 2bn tp b-tb cb.
Die Nachtwandler Walzer, Op. 88 (23 June 1836, Vienna)
 ANON **A-555a** fl 2ob 2cl 2hn 2bn b-tb basso.   MS score (incomplete) & MS parts: D-NEhz, 133, No. 10.
 ANON **A-19.1a** fl(F) 2cl(E♭) 2cl(B♭) 2hn 2bn tp b-tb cb.
Jugendfeuer Gallopp, Op. 90 (22 Aug 1836, Vienna)
 ANON **A-556a** fl 2ob 2cl(E♭) 3cl(B♭) 4hn 2bn 3tp kenthorn 3tb b-hn/bomb vc/b b-dr t-dr.
  MS parts: D-DT, Mus-n 1861.
 ANON **A-557a** fl 2ob 2cl 2hn 2bn b-tb basso.   MS parts: D-NEhz, 133, No 8.

Hugenotten-Galopp nach . . . der Oper Meyerbeers, Op. 93 (Weiner Zeitung advertizement, 7 Feb 1837, Vienna)
  ANON **A-558a** fl 2ob 2cl(E♭) 3cl(B♭) 4hn 2bn 2tp 3tb serp b-dr t-dr. MS parts: D-DT, Mus-n 1887, No. 2.
Künstler-Ball-Tänze, Op. 94 (17 Jan 1837, Vienna)
  SCHOLZ **WES-172a** fl 2ob 2cl 2hn 2bn tp tb db timp.
Brüssler Spitzen, Walzer, Op. 95 (31 Nov 1837, Vienna)
  SCHOLZ **WES-173a** fl 2ob 2cl 2hn 2bn tp tb db timp.
Ball-Raketen, Walzer, Op. 96 (26 Feb 1837, Vienna)
  STRECK **PZS-1.12a** fl cl(D) 2cl(A) 2hn 2bn.
Pilger am Rhein, Walzer, Op. 98 (19 Dec 1836, Bonn; 10 July 1837, Vienna)
  STRECK **PZS-1.11a** fl cl(D) 2cl(A) 2hn 2bn.
Die Berggeister, Walzer, Op. 113 (5 Aug 1839, Vienna)
  ANON **A-559a** 2ob(2) 2cl(C) 2hn 2bn cbn b-tb. MS parts: CZ-Bm(au), A.35.231, (?missing 2tp).
Rosenblätter, Walzer, Op. 115 (25 June 1839, Vienna)
  SCHOLZ **WES-174a** fl 2ob 2cl 3hn 2bn tb db.
Wiener-Gemüths-Walzer, Op. 116 (25 Nov 1839, Vienna)
  WOELFING **ZZW-5a** fl 2ob 2cl 3hn 2bn tp db timp.
Gibellinnen-Galopp, Op. 117 (11 Jan 1840, Vienna)
  ANON **A-279.2a** 2ob 2cl(C) 2hn 2bn cbn 2tp tb. MS parts: CZ-Bm(au), A.37.337, No. 2.
Beliebte Annen-Polka, Op. 137 (2 Aug 1842, Vienna)
  SCHOLZ **WES-175a** fl 2ob 2cl 2hn 2bn tp tb db.
Mode-Quadrille, Op. 138 (17 Jan 1842, Vienna)
  ANON **A-560a** pic ob cl(E♭) cl(C) cl(B♭) 2hn 2bn basso(cbn) 2tp. MS parts (1843): CZ-Bm(au), A.35.238.
Haute Volée-Quadrille, Op. 142 (31 May 1842, Vienna)
  ANON **A-561a** fl 2ob 2cl(E♭) 3cl(B♭) 4hn 2bn 4tp a-hn 3tb b-hn/bomb b-dr+cym t-dr+tri.
  MS parts: D-DT, Mus-n 1946, No. 1.
  ANON **A-562a** ob cl(A, II) 2cl(C) 2hn bn cbn 2tp tb vl II. MS pts (1843): CZ-Bm(au), A.35.234, (?complete).
  SCHOLZ **WES-176a** fl 2ob 2cl 2hn 2bn tp tb db.
Loreley-Rhein-Klänge, Waltzer, Op. 154 (19 Aug 1844, Vienna)
  ANON **A-15.11(a).** 2cl(E♭) 2cl(B♭) 2hn 2bn 2tp flug.
Walhalla-Toaste, Walzer, Op. 147 (15 Feb 1843, Vienna)
  SCHOLZ **WES-177a** fl 2ob 2cl 2hn 2bn tp tb db timp.
Astrea Tänze, (Asträa Tänzen Walzer), Op. 156 (17 Jan 1844, Vienna)
  WEINLICH **YXW-1a** fl ob 2cl 2hn 2bn cbn 2tp tb.
Wilkommen-Rufe, Walzer, Op. 168 (20 May 1844, Vienna)
  SCHOLZ **WES-178a** fl 2ob 2cl 2hn 2bn tp tb db timp.
Quadrille über beliebte Motive aus der Oper [by Balfe]: Die vier Hamoniskinder, Op. 169 (19 Jan 1845, Vienna)
  ANON **A-15.42(a)** cl(E♭) 2cl(B♭) 2hn bn 2tp basso.
Maskenlieder, Walzer, Op. 170 (24 Nov 1844, Vienna)
  SCHOLZ **WES-179a** fl 2ob 2cl 2hn 2bn tp tb db timp.
Eunomien-Tänze, Op. 171 (Wiener Zeitung advertizement, 19 May 1845, Vienna)
  SCHOLZ **WES-180a** fl 2ob 2cl 2hn 2bn tp tb db timp.
Flora-Quadrille, Op. 177 (Wiener Zeitung advertizement, 8 Oct 1845, Vienna)
  SCHOLZ **WES-181a** fl 2ob 2cl 2hn 2bn tp tb db timp.
Sommernachts-Träume, Walzer, Op. 180 (17 June 1845, Vienna)
  SCHOLZ **WES-182a** fl 2ob 2cl 2hn 2bn tp tb db timp.
Amoretten-Quadrille, Op. 183 (25 July 1845, Vienna)
  SCHOLZ **WES-183a** fl 2ob 2cl 2hn 2bn tp tb db timp.
Bouquets, Walzer, Op. 197 (24 July 1846, Vienna)
  SCHOLZ **WES-184a** fl 2ob 2cl 2hn 2bn tp tb db timp.
Themis-Klänge, Walzer, Op. 201 (13 Jan 1847, Vienna)
  SCHOLZ **WES-185a** fl 2ob 2cl 2hn 2bn tp tb db timp.
Eisele- und Beisele-Sprünge, Polka, Op. 202 (14 Feb 1847, Vienna)
  SCHOLZ **WES-186a** fl 2ob 2cl 2hn 2bn tp tb db timp.
Herz-Töne, Walzer, Op. 203 (29 Jan 1847, Vienna)
  SCHOLZ **WES-187a** fl 2ob 2cl 2hn 2bn tp tb db timp.
Helenen-Walzer, Op. 204 (1 Oct 1846, Vienna)
  SCHOLZ **WES-188a** fl 2ob 2cl 2hn 2bn tp tb db timp.
Triumph-Quadrille, Op. 205 (18 Oct 1846, Vienna)
  SCHOLZ **WES-189a** fl 2ob 2cl 2hn 2bn tp tb db timp.
Najaden-Quadrille, Op. 206 (2 Feb 1847, Vienna)
  SCHOLZ **WES-190a** fl 2ob 2cl 2hn 2bn tp tb db timp.
Schwedische Lieder, Walzer, Op. 207 (9 Feb 1847, Vienna)
  SCHOLZ **WES-191a** fl 2ob 2cl 2hn 2bn tp tb db timp.
Marien-Walzer, Op. 212 (20 July 1847, Vienna)
  SCHOLZ **WES-192a** fl 2ob 2cl 2hn 2bn tp tb db timp.
Martha Quadrille, Op. 215 (18 Dec 1847, Vienna)
  SCHOLZ **WES-193a** fl 2ob 2cl 2hn 2bn tp tb db timp.
Sorgenbrecher, Walzer, Op. 230 (22 Feb 1848, Vienna)
  SCHOLZ **WES-194a** fl 2ob 2cl 2hn 2bn tp tb db timp.
Louisen-Quadrille, Op. 234 (Wiener Zeitung advertizement, 1 Feb 1849, Vienna)
  SCHOLZ **WES-195a** fl 2ob 2cl 2hn 2bn tp tb db timp.

Unidentified, Dubious & Spurious Attributions
Walzer
  LEGRAND **WYL-47a** fl ob 2cl 2hn 2bn.
Walzer
  WIDDER **YYW-1.42a** 2fl 2cl 2hn 2bn.
Eisenbahn-Galopp (Not by Strauss)
  ANON **A-20.6a** fl(F) 2cl(E♭) 2cl(B♭) 2hn 2bn tp b-tb cb.
Domino Galopp. See: AUBER. Le Domino noir
Untraced arrangements: Krapfen-Walden-Walzer, Op.12 (1828), Haslinger: Vienna, 6- and 9-part Harmonie.

STRAUSS, Johann, *the Younger* (1825 - 1899)
Die Fledermaus (operetta, 5 April 1874, Vienna)
  BLOMHERT **BQB-7a** fl(pic) fl 2ob 2cl 2hn 2bn db/cbn.
Die Zigeunerbaron [The Gypsy Baron] (operetta, 24 Oct 1885, Vienna)
  TAYLORSON **JST-22a** overture. fl 2ob 2cl 2hn 2bn cbn/db.
Kaiser Franz-Josef I Rettungs-Jubel-Marsch No. 1, Op. 126 (6 March 1853, Vienna)
  ANON **A-563a** pic fl 2ob cl(E♭) cl(solo B♭) 3cl(B♭) 4hn 2bn 3tp t-hn 3tb b-hn/bomb vc/b b-dr+tri s-dr.
    MS pts: D-DT, Mus-n 1984, No. 1.
Reise-Abenteuer Walzer, Op. 227 (23 or 11 July 1859, Vienna)
  ANON **A-564a** pic fl 2ob cl(E♭) cl(solo B♭) 3cl(B♭) 4hn 2bn 3tp t-hn 3tb b-hn bomb vc/b timp b-dr s-dr.
    MS pts: D-DT, Mus-n 2000.
Niko-Polka, Op. 228 (18 Dec 1859, Vienna)
  ANON **A-565a** pic fl 2ob cl(E♭) cl(solo B♭) 3cl(B♭) 4hn 2bn 3tp t-hn 3tb b-hn bomb b-dr+cym s-dr.
    MS parts: D-DT, Mus-n 1995, No. 1.
Kammerball-Polka, Op. 230 (11 Jan 1860, Vienna)
  SARO **HNS-1a** fl 2ob cl(E♭) cl(solo B♭) 3cl(B♭) 4hn 2bn 3tp t-hn 3tb b-hn bomb b-dr s-dr.
Luzifer-Polka (Lucifer-Polka), Op. 266 (22 Feb 1862, Vienna)
  ANON **A-566a** pic 2ob cl(E♭) cl(solo B♭) 3cl(B♭) 4hn 2bn 3tp t-hn 3tb b-hn/bomb vc/b b-dr s-dr.
    MS parts: D-DT, Mus-n 1903, No. 2.
Geschichten aus dem Wienerwald (Tales from the Vienna Woods), Walzer, Op. 325 (9 June 1868, Vienna)
  GILLASPIE **JAG-28a** fl 2ob 2cl 2bthn 4hn 2bn db/cbn.

STRAUSS, Josef (1827 - 1870)
Schwert und Leier Walzer, Op. 71 (16 Aug 1859, Vienna)
  ANON **A-567a** pic fl 2ob cl(E♭) cl(solo B♭) 3cl(B♭) 4hn 2bn 3tp t-hn 3tb b-hn bomb vc/b timp b-dr s-dr.
    MS parts: D-DT, Mus-n 2022.
Frauenherz, Polka-Mazurka, Op. 166 (6 Sept 1864, Vienna)
  TAYLORSON **JST-23a** fl 2ob 2cl 2hn 2bn cbn/db.

STRAVINSKY, Igor Feodorovich (1882 - 1971)
Four Norwegian Moods (orchestra, 1942, pub. 1944, New York)
  BRINER **BEB-2a** 2ob 2cl 2hn 2bn.

STUMPF, Johann Christian ([1740] - 1801)
Harmonie (JUS-1.1, 14 mvts)
  SCHNEIDER, A. **AYS-97a** overture & 13 mvts. (rescored for:) 2ob 4cl 2hn 2bn 2tp b-tb serp.
4 unidentified movements
  FENDT **AXF-2.6ad** pic 2cl(C & B♭) 2cl(C) 2hn 2bn cb/cbn.

SUDA, Stanislav (1896 - 1969) (qv)
  HORÁK **RJH-1am.** "Michálek" pochod [march]. pic fl cl(E♭) 3cl(B♭) 4hn 2flug t-hn bar-hn 2basso b-dr s-dr.

SÜSSMAYR, Franz Xaver (1766 - 1803)
Der Spiegel in [von] Arkadien (Singspiel, 14 Nov 1794, Vienna)
  ANON **A-568a** 3 mvts. 3bthn. MS parts: CZ-Pnm, XXVII.C.53.
  ANON **A-391.2a** 8 mvts. 3bthn. MS parts (post-1794): CZ-Pnm, XLII.C.231, ("Arien aus den Opera Spiegel
    von Arkadien un[d] [Die neu] Sonntagskind [W. Müller]").
  DRUSCHETZKY **GYD-165.21(a)** 2 mvts. 2cl 2hn 2bn.
  DRUSCHETZKY **GYD-19a** Länderlische. 2cl 2hn 2bn
  SARTORIUS **GCS-17a** overture & 8 mvts. 2cl(C) 2hn 2bn cbn.
  SCHMIDT, G. **GYS-82a** duetto. 2fl 2ob 2cl 2hn 2bn serp.
  WENT **JNW-15ac** (= TRIEBENSEE **JZT-1ad**) sinfonia & 18 mvts. 2ob 2cl 2hn 2bn.
Der Retter in Gefahr (patriotic cantata, 1796, Vienna)
  ANON **A-569a** recitativo & aria. 2ob 2cl 2hn 2bn.
    MS parts: A-Wn, Mus.Hs.3853. (= SEDLAK WXS-3ad)
Soliman der Zweite (Solymander) (opera, 5 Oct 1799, Vienna)
  TRIEBENSEE **JZT-57a** overture & 7 mvts. 2ob 2cl 2hn 2bn (cbn tp ad lib).

SULLIVAN, *Sir* Arthur Seymour (1842 - 1900)
The Yeomen of the Guard (opera, 3 Oct 1888, London)
  GILLASPIE **JAG-29a** overture. 2fl ob 2cl 2hn 2bn cbn/vc/db.
  GILLASPIE **JAG-30a** complete opera accompaniment. 2fl ob 2cl 2hn 2bn cbn/vc/db.

SUPPÉ, Franz von (1819 - 1895)
Dichter und Bauer (Poet and Peasant) (play, 24 Aug 1846, Vienna).
  GILLASPIE **JAG-31a** overture.   2fl 2ob 2cl 2hn 2bn cbn/vc/db.
Die schöne Galathea (operetta, 9 Sept 1865, Vienna)
  TAYLORSON **JST-24a** overture.   fl 2ob 2cl 2hn 2bn cbn/db.
Selection of mvts
  GILLASPIE **JAG-32a** A von Suppé Potpourri.   2ob 2cl 2hn 2bn cbn.

SYDOW, ( ) Von
Pas redoublé
  ANON **A-78.1/4m(a)** 2ob 2cl 2hn 2bn tp.

TAGLIONI, Maria *(it is likely that Taglioni was only the dancer associated with the work below.)*
Divertissement (ballet, original unidentified)
  TRIEBENSEE **JZT-58a** Pas de deux & Marsch.   2ob 2cl 2hn 2bn (cbn tp ad lib).

TARCHI, Angelo (1760 - 1814)
Le Trente et Quarante (comic opera, 19 May 1798, Paris)
  FUCHS, G.F. **GFF-1.1a** 3 mvts.   2fl 2cl(C) 2hn 2bn.
Le Cabriolet jaune (comic opera, 6 Nov 1798, Paris)
  FUCHS, G.F. **GFF-1.2a** 1 mvt.   2fl 2cl(C) 2hn 2bn.

TAUSCH, Franz Wilhelm (1762 - 1817)
Rondo aus einer [unidentified - ?clarinet] Concerto
  FISCHER **ZZF-2a** fl cl(E♭) 3cl(B♭) 2hn 2bn 2tp 3tb serp b-dr s-dr.

TCHAIKOVSKY (Chaikovsky), Peter (Pytor) Il'yich (1840 - 1893)
Deux morceaux pour piano, Op. 10 (1871, pub. 1876, St Petersburg; arranged by the composer for vl & pf, 1877)
  SKIRROW **ARS-4a** No. 2, Humoresque.   2ob 2cl 2hn 2bn.
Serenate (Serenata), Op. 48 (strings, 1880, pub. 1881, 1st performance 30 Oct 1881, St Petersburg)
  SERAFINO **NQS-1a** Elegia.   fl ob 2cl 2hn bn tp.
16 Chansons pour la Jeunesse (Children's Songs), Op. 54 (voice & piano, pub. 1883, St Petersburg)
  EMERSON, **GZE-1.3a** No. 5, Légende (as "Legend, Christ in His Garden").   2fl ob 3cl hn bn.

TEMPLETON, Alex Andrew (1909 - 1963)
Merry Christmas
  JOUARD **PXJ-2a** 2fl 2ob 2cl 2hn 2bn.

THOMAS, Charles Louis Ambroise (1811 - 1896)
Le Panier fleuri (Der Blumenkorb) (comic opera, 6 May 1839, Paris)
  SCHOLZ **WES-196a** overture.   fl 2ob 2cl 3hn 2bn 2tp tb db timp.

TITL, Anton Emil (1809 - 1882)
Die Zauberschleier oder Maler, Fee und Wirtin (Zauberspiel, 11 Feb 1842, Vienna)
  VOJÁČEK **HXV-7a** 2tes potpourri.   fl ob cl 2hn bn cbn 2tp tb.
Der Totentanz (Zauberspiel, 8 Nov 1843, Vienna)
  VOJÁČEK **HXV-8a** ouverture aus dem Ballet.   Incomplete: 2ob 2cl only.

TOESCHI, Karl Theodor (1731 - 1788)
Ländler (?piano, sd)
  WIDDER **YYW-1.43a** 2fl 2cl 2hn 2bn.

TOST, František (Johann) (1754/55 - 1829)
Der Lügner (Singspiel, 1795, Bratislava)
  HAVEL **HXV-40a** Cadentz, 6 Ländler (No. 1 = "Wenn ich in der Früh aufsteh") & Coda.   2cl 2hn 2bn.

TRENTO, Vittorio (1761 - 1833)
Unidentified Polacca, "Sento che sono vicino"
  SCHMITT, N. **NYS-1.5a** 4cl 2hn 2bn.

TRIEBENSEE, Josef (1772 - 1846)
Miscellannees [sic] de Musique, Jg. I, Oe. 1 (2ob 2cl 2hn 2bn, cbn tp ad lib)
  HAVEL **VXH-41a** rescored for: 2cl 2hn 2bn tp.
Echo N⁰ 1 in F
  HAVEL **VXH-16.1ac** 2cl 2hn 2bn.

TRIETTO, ( ) (? Domenico TRITTO) (1776 - 1851)
  OZI **EXO-1.32/2a** duetto (possibly from *La Virgine del Sol).*   2cl 2hn 2bn.

TUČEK (Tuczec, Tuczeck), František Vinzenz (Franz Vincent) Ferrarius (1773 - post-1821)
Lanassa oder Die Eroberung von Malabar (opera, 13 Dec 1805, Pest)
  ANON **A-570a** (? 2ob 2cl 2hn 2bn).   MS parts: I-Fc, F.P. S.380.

UMLAUF, Ignaz (1746 - 1796)
Das Irrlicht [Der Irrwisch; Endlich fand er sie] (opera, 17 Jan 1782, Vienna)
  KRECHLER **FFK-10.9, 10.12a** 2 mvts.   2ob 2cl 2hn 2bn.
Untraced arrangement: Die schöne Schusterin (opera, 1779, Vienna) for 3bthn 2hn (Traeg catalog 1799).

UMLAUF, Michael (1781 - 1842)
Der Tiroler Jahrmarkt (with T. Weigl & P. Wranizky; ballet divertissement, 26 Feb 1805, Vienna)
  ANON **A-571a** sinfonia & 9 mvts. 2ob 2cl 2hn 2bn cbn.
  Pc (Johann Cappi: Vienna, c.1805), MS parts: GB-Ljag, (the MS attributes the ballet to M. Umlauf).
  ANON **A-572a** 2 mvts & coda. 2cl 2hn 2bn. MS parts: CZ-KRa, A3997/IV.B.166.
Paul et Rosette oder Der Winzer (ballet pantomime, 5 March 1806, Vienna)
  SEDLAK +**WXS-59a** overture & 11 mvts. 2ob 2cl 2hn 2bn cbn.
Die Spiele des Paris auf dem Berg Ida (ballet divertissement, 11 July 1806, Vienna)
  SEDLAK **WXS-60a** overture & 9 mvts. 2ob 2cl 2hn 2bn cbn.
Les Abenceragen und Zegris oder Die feindlichen Volksstände (Singspiel/ballet, 24 Nov 1806, Vienna)
  STARKE **FRS-35a** overture & 13 mvts. 2ob 2cl 2hn 2bn cbn.
Die Hochzeit des Gamacho, oder Don Quixote (ballet, 7 March 1807, Vienna)
  SEDLAK **WXS-3.3a.** 2 mvts. 2ob 2cl 2hn 2bn cbn.
Der Quacksalber und die Zwerge (Ⅱ Ciralatano) (ballet, 25 Feb 1810, Vienna)
  TRIEBENSEE **JZT-59a** overture & 16 mvts. 2ob 2cl 2hn 2bn (cbn tp ad lib).
Das eigensinnige Landmädchen (Das eigensinnige Bäuerin) (ballet, 9 April 1810, Vienna)
  HAVEL **VXH-42a** overture & 9 mvts. 2cl 2hn 2bn.
  TRIEBENSEE **JZT-60.1a** overture & 18 mvts. 2ob 2cl 2hn 2bn (cbn tp ad lib).
  TRIEBENSEE (= A-8.2a) **JZT-60.2a** overture & 12 mvts. 2ob 2cl 2hn 2bn cbn.
Aeneas in Karthago (Aeneas in Carthago) (ballet, 5 Oct 1811, Vienna)
  KRECHLER **FFK-8.4a, 15.2a** 4 mvts. 2ob 2cl 2hn 2bn cbn tp.
  SEDLAK +**WXS-61a** 2 mvts. 2ob 2cl 2hn 2bn cbn.
Der Grenadier (Die Medaille) (operette, 8 July 1812, Vienna)
  ANON **A-573a** 2ob 2cl 2hn 2bn cbn. MS parts: I-Fc, F.P. S.368.

VACHON, Pierre (1731 - 1802)
Marche Lento
  A-1.29a 2cl 4hn 2bn 2tp 2vla cb.

VANHAL (Wanhal), Jan Křtitel (1739 - 1813)   *See supra* ANON **A-2a.**

VERDI, Guiseppe (Fortunino Francesco) (1813 - 1901)
Oberto di San Bonifazio (Bonifacio) (opera, 17 Nov 1839, Milan)
  SCHOLZ **WES-197a** cavatine & finale. fl 2ob 2cl 2hn 2bn tp tb db timp.
Nabucodonosor (Nabucco) (opera, 9 March 1842)
  ANON **A-574a** pic fl 2ob cl(Eb) cl(solo Bb) 3cl(Bb) 4hn 2bn 4tp kenthorn t-hn 2tb oph vc/b b-dr s-dr.
    MS parts: D-DT, Mus-n 2044, No. 1.
  ANON **A-575a** cavatina. fl 2ob 2cl(C) cl(D) cl(A) 2hn bn 4tp(F, C) b-tb t-bomb.
    MS parts (c.1844): CZ-Pnm, XL.F.118.
  MATYÁŠ, M. **MIM-2a** "Sperate, o figli". cl(G) 2cl(C oblig) 2hn bn 3tp flug(C) 2bomb.
  WIESER **FAW-26a** Andante. fl(F) cl(Eb) 2cl(Bb) 2hn 2bn tp b-tb cb timp.
I Lombardi alla prima crociata (opera, 12 Feb 1842, Milan)
  SCHOLZ **WES-198.1a** 6 mvts. fl 2ob 2cl 2hn 2bn tp tb db timp.
  SCHOLZ **WES-198.2a** 4 mvts. fl 2ob 2cl 2hn 2bn tp tb db timp.
Ernani (opera, 9 March 1844, Venice)
  ANON **A-576a** cavatine. pic 2ob cl(Eb) cl(solo Bb) 3cl(Bb) 4hn 2bn 4tp kenthorn 3tb bassi b-dr s-dr.
    MS parts: D-DT, Mus-n 976.
  ANON **A-577a** Potpourri. pic fl 2ob cl(Eb) cl(solo Bb) 3cl(Bb) 4hn 2bn 4tp t-hn 3tb bassi b-hn/bomb vc/b.
    MS parts: D-DT, Mus-n 2042, (possibly missing perc: timp b-dr, *See infra: Il Trovatore)*
  SCHOLZ **WES-199.1a** overture & 2 Bds. fl 2ob 2cl 2hn 2bn tp tb db timp.
  SCHOLZ **WES-199.2a** overture & 2 Bds. 2ob 2cl 2hn 2bn tp tb db timp.
Alzira (opera, 12 Aug 1845, Naples)
  MATYÁŠ, M. **MIM-3a** cavatina. cl(C) obbligato, fl cl(D) cl(II C) 2hn bn 3tp 2flug bomb.
Macbeth (1st version) (opera, 14 March 1847, Florence)
  SCHOLZ **WES-200a** overture & 2 Bds. fl 2ob 2cl 2hn 2bn tp tb db timp.
Rigoletto (opera, 11 March 1851, Venice)
  ANON **A-578a** Potpourri. pic 2ob cl(Eb) cl(solo Bb) 3cl(Bb) 4hn 2bn 4tp kenthorn 3tb bassi timp b-dr.
    MS parts: D-DT, Mus-n 2045.
Il Trovatore (opera, 19 Jan 1853, Rome)
  ANON **A-579a** Potpourri. fl 2ob 2cl 2hn 2bn tp tb serp.
    MS parts: D-DT, Mus-n 976.
  GILLASPIE **JAG-33a** Tango Paraphrase on the Miserere Scene. 2ob 2cl 2hn 2bn cbn.
Les Vêpres siciliennes (opera, 13 June 1855, Paris)
  BILLEMA **CBB-1a** "Polka-Mazurka". pic fl 2ob 2cl 4hn 2bn 2tp 3tb bomb timp b-dr+tri.
Aroldo (= Stiffelio, revised) (opera, 16 Aug 1857, Rimini)
  ANON **A-580a** sinfonia. fl(Db) cl(Eb) 2cl(Bb) 2hn 2tp 2flug b-flug tb euph basso. MS pts: CZ-TRB, H 192.
La Forza del Destino (opera, 10 Nov 1862, St Petersburg)
  GODDARD **MXG-1a** overture. fl 2ob 2cl 2hn 2bn.
Aida (opera, 24 Dec 1871, Cairo)
  FAHRBACH **JBF-1a** Due Fantasie, Op. 86. fl cl(Eb) cl(Bb) 2hn bombardino/bn tp flug bombardone.

VIGUERIE, Bernard (c.1761 - 1819)
La Bataille de Marengo (piano, violin & bass, c.1806, Paris)
  ANON **A-581a** 2cl 2hn (2)bn tp(clar). MS parts: US-BETm, Lititz Collegium Musicum 200.2.

VIOTTI, Giovanni Battista (1755 - 1824)
Simphonie (not otherwise known as a work by Viotti)
GEBAUER, MJ. **MJG-1.2/1a** Maestoso / Allegro. fl(F) cl(F) 2cl(C) 2hn 2bn tp serp/b-tb b-dr cym tri; *or* fl(F) 2cl(C) 2hn 2bn serp.
Polacca (inserted in the Paris version of Martín y Soler's Una cosa rara).
OZI **EXO-1.32/5a** 2cl 2hn 2bn.

VIVALDI, Antonio (1678 - 1741)
L'Estro armonico, [12 concerti] Op. 3 (c.1710, Venice)
TAYLORSON **JST-25a** Concerto No. 3. Solo violin, fl 2ob 2cl 2hn 2bn cbn/db.

VIVIANI, (? Luigi Maria; ? - 1856)
La Morte de Virginia (ballet, ?Vienna)
SCHOLL **NYS-2a** sinfonia, (Act I) 5 mvts, (Act II) 4 mvts. 2ob 2cl 2hn 2bn (cbn 2tp).

VOGEL, Johann Christoph (1756 - 1788)
Le Toison d'or (opera, 29 Aug 1786, Versailles; 3 Sept 1786, Paris)
BEINET **XJB-3.3/4a** Marche. 2cl 2hn 2bn.
OZI **EXO-1.22/1a** overture & 4 mvts. 2cl 2hn 2bn.
Démophon (opera, performed posthumously 15 Sept 1789, Paris)
ANON **A-582a** overture. 2ob 2cl 2hn 2bn tp serp, *or* 2cl 2hn 2bn.
   Pc (au Bureau de Musique de Hoffmeister et Kühnel: Leipsic [sic], pn 408, 1805), parts: CZ-Pnm, Lobkovic X.H.a.4.
   Pc reprint (Ambrosius Kühnel: Leipzig, pn 408, post-1806), RISM [V 2275], parts: D-AB; H-KE, 683/VIII.
   Pc reprint (C.F. Peters: Leipzig, pn 408, post-1813), RISM [V 2276], parts: D-NEhz.
ERNST **FAE-3a** Suite No. 87, 10 mvts. 2cl 2hn 2bn; (ad lib: tp serp b-dr cym).
FUCHS **GFF-40a** overture. 4cl 2hn 2bn, *or* 2cl 2hn 2bn.
OZI **EXO-1.29/1a** overture & 4 mvts. 2cl 2hn 2bn.
TRIEBENSEE **JZT-61a** overture. 2ob 2cl 2hn 2bn (cbn tp ad lib).
Marsch langsam (unidentified)
ANON **A-74.2/8m(a)** pic quart-fl 2ob cl(F) 2cl(C) 4hn 2bn cbn+serp/2b-hn 2tp 3tb b-dr t-dr tamb cym.

VOGLER, Georg Joseph (1749 - 1814)
Castor e Polluce (Castor und Pollux) (opera, 12 Jan 1787, Munich; revised 1790, 1806)
ANON **A-9.17a** 1 mvt. 3bthn.
TRIEBENSEE **JZT-62a** 2 Theils. 2ob 2cl 2hn 2bn cbn.
Samori (opera, 17 May 1804, Vienna)
KRECHLER **FFK-23a** overture & 23 mvts. 2ob 2cl 2hn 2bn (cbn tp ad lib).
Sinfonia, in C ("The Scala", "Bayerische National-Sinfonie") (orchestra, pub. 1799, Offenbach am Main)
SCHNEIDER, A. **AYS-98a** fl 2ob 2cl 2hn 2bn tp b-tb 2vla cb.
Hymnus (Pfingsten u[nd]. Reformationsfest)
SILCHER **FIS-1va** TTBB. 2cl 2hn 2bn basso.

VOLKERT, Franz (1767-1845)
Der lustige Fritz (Zauberspiel Quodlibet, 17 June 1818, Vienna)
STARKE **FRS-1va** Romance Joyeuse mit Chor. TTBB, ob(vel pic) 2ob cl(F) 2cl(C) 2hn 2bn cbn 2tp b-tb b-dr s-dr.

W., ( )
Ouverture in C minor
SCHMITT, G. **GYS-83a** 2fl 2ob 3cl 2hn 2bn tp tb db.

WAGNER, Jakob Karl (1772 - 1822)
Untraced arrangement: Liebe und Freundschaft (cantata), arranged Sartorius - the one known MS copy (D-DS) appears to have been lost during World War II.

WAGNER, Richard (1813 - 1883)
Tannhäuser (opera, 19 Oct 1845, Dresden)
ANON **A-583a** Scenen, Act II. 2fl 2ob cl(E♭) cl(solo B♭) 3cl(B♭) 4hn 2bn 3tp t-hn 3tb bom b b-hn timp b-dr.
   MS parts: D-DT, Mus-n 1000.

WALCH, Johann Heinrich (c.1775 - 1855)
Trauermarsch (often attributed to Beethoven, K.-H. Anh. 13)
ANON **A-584a** terz-fl cl(E♭) 2cl(B♭) 2hn 2bn cbn 2keyed-tp 3tb s-dr(damped), (ad lib: cl III in B♭, tb II & III).
   MS parts (in the same hand as many of the later b-tb parts in Perschl's arrangements): A-Wn, Mus.Hs.5793, (tb I & II pts marked "entbehrlich", dispensible; *headtitle*: "Trauer-Marsch / von L: v: Beethoven").

WALTER, Georg Anton (violinist, active c.1790 - 1800, Paris)
Allegro con brio, Gratioso Siciliano, Polacca, Potpourri Allegretto
SYLVANI **XSV-1.1a, 1.2a, 1.4a, 1.8a** 4 mvts. 2cl 2hn 2bn.
Ouverture, in F
LEROY **PQL-1.8/1(a)** 2p-fl(F) 2ob 2cl(III & IV, C) 2hn 2bn tp serp.
Ouverture, in F minor/major
LEROY **PQL-1.11/1(a)** 2fl(F) 2ob 2cl(III & IV, C) 2hn 2bn 2tp serp timp.
Marche, in F
LEROY **PQL-1.11/5(a)** 2p-fl(F) 2cl(F) 2cl(C) 2hn (2)bn 2tp serp timp.
Polonaise, in F
LEROY **PQL-1.8/3(a)** 2p-fl(F) 2ob 2cl(III & IV, C) 2hn 2bn tp serp.
Rondeau, in F
LEROY **PQL-1.11/4(a)** 2p-fl(F) 2ob 2cl(III & IV, C) 2hn 2bn 2tp serp timp.

WALTER (?Ignaz, 1759 - 1822)
Marsch, in D
	SCHNEIDER, A. **AYS-7ma** fl 2ob 4cl 2hn 2bn tp b-tb serp.

WALTON, *Sir* William Turner (1902 - 1983)
Façade (reciter, fl(pic) cl(b-cl) sax tp vc perc, 1921-1922, later arranged as a ballet; final revision 1942, London)
	SKIRROW **ARS-5a** 7 mvts. fl 2ob 2cl 2hn 2bn.

WARLOCK, Peter *(pseudonym.* i.e. Philip Haseltine) (1894 - 1930)
Capriol Suite (string orchestra *or* piano duet, 1926, London; arranged for orchestra, 1928, London)
	CAMPBELL **AQC-6a** 2ob 2cl 2hn 2bn.
Milkmaids (song with piano accompaniment, 1923, London)
	ANON **A-585a** Solo voice, 2fl ob 2cl 2hn bn 2tp 2tb timp perc celeste harp.
		Pm (E. Ashdown: London, post-1924), hire score & parts.

WEBER, Bernhard Anselm (1766 - 1821)
Jolanta, Königin von Jerusalem (Trauerspiel, 26 Aug 1797, Berlin)
	SCHMITT, G. **GYS-84a** 3 mvts. 2cl 2hn bn.
Die Weihe der Kraft (Martin Luther) (Schauspiel, 11 June 1806, Berlin)
	ANON **A-586.1a** Ausgewaehlte Stücke, 10 mvts. 2ob 2cl 2hn 2bn (cbn).
		MS parts: H-KE, 2054, (without cbn pt); I-Fc, F.P. S.362. *Mvt 10 is, in fact, the Krönungs-Marsch from
		B.A. Weber's Schauspiel* Die Jungfrau von Orleans. *The MS attributes the Choral (mvt 1, "Ein feste Burg
		ist unser Gott", taken from the Ouverture) to Martin Luther, Koburg, 1530.*
Der Ganz nach dem Eisenhammer (spoken melodrama, c.1810, Berlin)
	SCHOLZ **WES-201a** 1 mvt. fl 2ob 2cl 2hn 2bn tb db timp.
Die Jungfrau von Orleans (Tragödie/Schauspiel, 29 Nov 1801, Berlin)
	ANON **A-586.2a** Krönungs-Marsch. 2ob 2cl 2h 2bn cbn. *Mvt 10 of A-576.1a supra.*
	ANON **A-587a** Harmonie monolog. 2cl 2hn 2bn cb. MS pts: D-AB, S.52. *Possibly Schulz rather than Weber.*
Marche, in C
	ANON **A-78.1/5m(a)** 2pic 2quart-fl 2cl(C) 2hn 2bn 2tp serp b-dr+cym.

WEBER, Carl Maria Friedrich Ernst von (1786 - 1826)
For the spurious work, "Weber's Last Waltz", "Das Herzenload", etc., See: REISSIGER.
See also: BISCHOFF, EIB-1.
Peter Schmoll und seine Nachbarn (opera, ?March, 1803, Augsburg; some sources give: Salzburg, June 1802)
	ELLIOT **WSE-3a** overture. 2ob 2cl 2hn 2bn.
Turandot (Musik zu Turandot) (play with music, 1809, Stuttgart)
	ELLIOT **WSE-4a** march. 2ob 2cl 2hn 2bn.
Silvana (Sylvana) (romantic comic opera, 16 Sept 1810, Frankfurt am Main)
	LÖWENSTEIN **CAL-28a** overture & 19 mvts. terz-fl(fl in F, pic in F) 2cl(Eb) 2cl(Bb) 2hn 2bn tp b-tb cb.
Abu Hassan (Singspiel, 4 June 1811, Munich, Residenz)
	SCHNEIDER, A. **AYS-99a** overture. fl 2ob 2cl 2hn 2bn tp b-tb 2vla cb.
Overture: Der Beherrscher der Geister, Op. 27 (1811, Munich)
	SCHNEIDER, A. **AYS-100a** fl 2ob 2cl 2hn 2bn tp b-tb 2vla cb.
	SCHOLZ **WES-202.1a** fl 2ob 2cl 3hn 2bn tp tb db timp.
	SCHOLZ **WES-202.2a** fl 2ob 2cl 2hn 2bn tp tb db timp.
Preciosa (music for Wolff's drama, 14 March 1821, Berlin)
	ANON **A-588a** overture. terz-fl 2ob cl(Eb) 3cl(Bb) 4hn 2bn 3tp kenthorn a-hn 3tb b-hn/bomb vc/b b-dr t-dr tri.
		MS parts: D-DT, Mus-n 1018.
	ANON **A-589a** Lied. fl 2ob 3cl(Bb) 2hn 2bn b-hn/b-tb. MS parts: D-DT, Mus-n 1010, (missing ob I, bn I).
	ANON **A-15.38(a)** potpourri. fl(F) cl(Eb) 2cl(Bb) 2hn 2bn 2tp.
	KÜFFNER **JYK-3a** Pièces d'Harmonie. fl 2cl 2hn 2bn.
	LÖWENSTEIN **CAL-29a** overture & 10 mvts. fl(F, Eb; pic in F & Eb) 2cl(Eb) 2cl(Bb) 2hn 2bn tp b-tb+cb.
	SCHMITT, G. **GYS-1.40a** Walzer. 2fl 2ob 2cl 2hn 2bn 1/2tp (?t-)tb db.
	SCHMITT, G. **GYS-85.1a** 1 mvt. fl 2ob 2cl 2hn 2bn tp tb db.
	SCHMITT, G. **GYS-85.2a** 1 Bd. 2fl 2ob 2cl 2hn 2bn tp 2tb db.
	SCHMITT, G. **GYS-85.3a** Zigeuner Marsch. fl 2ob 2cl 2hn 2bn 2tp b-tb db.
	SCHNEIDER, A. **AYS-101a** overture & 8 mvts. fl(drum) 2ob 2cl 2hn 2bn tp(hn III, tri) b-tb 2vla cb.
	WIDDER **YYW-1.44a** 4 mvts. Nos 1 & 2: 2fl 2cl 2hn 2bn; Nos 3 & 4: fl ob 2cl 2hn 2bn.
Der Freischütz (Robin des Bois) (opera, 13 June 1821, Berlin)
	ANON **A-590a** overture. terz-fl 2ob cl(Eb) cl(solo Bb) cl(C) 3cl(Bb) 4hn 2bn 2tp(+2tp ad lib) t-hn 3tb serp
		b-dr t-dr. MS parts: D-DT, Mus-n 1010.
	FLACHS **KXF-3a** overture & 8 mvts. fl 2ob 2cl 2hn 2bn db. *(Not 2fl, as stated by Jähns)*
	HAGMANN **LQH-1ac** Podpouri [sic]. 2cl 2hn bn tp.
	KIRCHHOFF **WZK-54a** scene & aria. fl 2ob 2cl 2hn 2bn tb db.
	KÜFFNER **JYK-17a** VIII Pot-pourri. 2fl 2cl(Eb) 3cl(Bb) 2hn 2bn 3tp 2signal-hn 2tb serp b-dr t-dr.
	KÜFFNER **JYK-18.1a** IX Pot Pourri. 2fl(F, Eb) 2cl(Eb) 3cl(Bb) 2hn 2bn 2tp 2signal-hn(a clefs) 2tb b-dr t-dr.
	KÜFFNER **JYK-18.2a** Neufième pot pourri sur Robin des Bois, Op. 134. 2fl 2cl(Eb) 3cl(Bb) 4hn 2bn 2(+1)tp
		2tb serp t-dr. [the extra tp = corno à signal à clefs en Sib].
	KÜFFNER **JYK-19a** 5 Stücke. fl cl bthn 2hn bn.
	LÖWENSTEIN **CAL-4.4ac** 1 mvt. 2cl(C) 2cl(A) 2hn 2bn cb+bn.
	RINCK **JCR-4va** "Leise, leise, fromme Weise". STB, fl 2cl 2hn 2bn cbn.
	SCHMITT, G. **GYS-1.32a** Walzer. 2fl 2ob 2cl 2hn 2bn 2tp (?t-)tb db.

[Der Freischütz]
SCHMITT, G. **GYS-86.1a** 1 Bd. 2fl 2ob 2cl 3hn 2bn tp tb db (timp).
SCHMITT, G. **GYS-86.2a** Jägerchor. 2fl 2ob 2cl 4hn 2bn tb db.
SCHMITT, G. **GYS-86.3a** 2 mvts. fl 2ob 2cl 2hn 2bn tp tb db.
SCHNEIDER, A. **AYS-102.1a** overture & 16 mvts.
   fl 2ob 4cl(hn IV replaces cl II in overture) 2hn 2bn 2tp(hn III) b-tb serp.
SCHNEIDER, A. **AYS-102.2a** overture & 16 mvts. fl 2ob 4cl 2hn(2tp) 2bn b-tb cb.
SCHNEIDER, A. **AYS-102.3a** overture. fl(pic) 2ob 2cl+2cl(rip) 2hn 2bn tp b-tb serp.
SCHNEIDER, A. **AYS-102.4a** Marsch. fl ob 2cl+2cl(rip) 2hn 2bn tp b-tb serp.
SEDLAK **WXS-62a** 35/36 Werk. Theil 1: overture & 11 mvts, Theil 2: 9 mvts. 2ob 2cl 2hn 2bn cbn (2tp).
WIDDER **YYW-1.45a** 1 mvt. 2fl 2cl 2hn 2bn.
WITT **FZW-15.1a** overture & 14 mvts. terz-fl(terz-pic) 2cl(E♭) 2cl(B♭) 2hn 2bn tp b-tb cb.
WITT **FZW-15.2a** Jäger Chor. cl(F) 2cl(B♭) 2hn 2bn tp b-tb.
Euryanthe (Euryanthe, ou La Forêt de Senard) (opera, 25 Oct 1823, Vienna)
ANON (?Küffner) **A-591a** fl 2cl 2hn 2bn.
   Pc: (Schott: Mainz, c.1824), parts: D-MZsch.
C., J. **XJC-2a** Jaegerchor. 2ob 2cl 2hn 2bn.
HEUSCHKEL **JEH-2a** Nos 4 - 7. fl 2cl 2hn 2bn.
HEUSCHKEL **JEH-3a** 6 mvts. fl 2cl 2hn 2bn.
KIRCHHOFF **WZK-55.1a** overture. fl 2ob 2cl 3hn 2bn tp tb db timp.
KIRCHHOFF **WZK-55.2a** romance ("Unter blühenden Mandelbäumen"). fl 2ob 2cl 2hn 2bn tb db.
KIRCHHOFF **WZK-55.3a** Jägerchor. fl 2ob 2cl 2hn 2bn tb db.
KÜFFNER **JYK-20a** Pot-Pourri. fl(F, pic E♭) 2cl(E♭) 3cl(B♭, all divisi) 4hn 2bn 4tp 2tb serp b-dr t-dr.
SCHMITT, G. **GYS-87a** Jägerchor. 2fl 2ob 2cl 5hn(B♭, 4E♭) bn tb db.
SCHNEIDER, A. **AYS-103.1a** overture, 8 mvts & finale. fl 2ob 2cl 2hn 2bn tp(hn III) b-tb 2vla cb.
SCHNEIDER, A. **AYS-103.2a** Jägerchor. fl 2ob 2cl 5hn 2bn tp b-tb 2vla cb.
SCHOLZ **WES-203.1a** finale Act I. fl 2ob 2cl 3hn 2bn tp tb db timp.
SCHOLZ **WES-203.2a** scene & aria ("Wo berg ich mich"). fl 2ob 2cl 3hn 2bn tp tb db timp.
SCHOLZ **WES-203.3a** cavatina ("Glocklein im Thale"). fl 2ob 2cl 2hn 2bn tb db timp.
SCHOLZ **WES-203.4a** aria ("Wehen mir Lüfte"). fl 2ob 2cl 2hn 2bn tb db timp.
SCHOLZ **WES-203.5a** scene & cavatine. fl 2ob 2cl 2hn 2bn tp tb db timp.
SCHOLZ **WES-203.6a** Act I introduzion ("Dem Frieden Heil"). fl 2ob 2cl 2hn 2bn tp tb db timp.
SEDLAK **+WXS-63a** overture & 16 mvts. 2ob 2cl 2hn 2bn cbn 2tp.
WERNER, F. **FWW-3a** potpourri. terz-fl 2cl(E♭) 2cl(B♭) 2hn 2bn tp b-tb cb.
WIDDER **YYW-1.46a** 1 mvt. 2fl 2cl 2hn 2bn.
Oberon, or The Elf King's Oath (opera, 1826, 12 April London)
ANON **A-592a** overture. pic(E♭) 2ob cl(E♭) cl(solo B♭) 3cl(B♭) 4hn 2bn 3tp kenthorn a-hn 3tb b-hn/bomb vc/b b-dr t-dr. MS parts: D-DT, Mus-n 1014.
ANON **A-593a** overture. 2fl 2ob cl(E♭) 2cl(C) 4cl(B♭) 4hn 2bn 2tp 3tb serp b-dr t-dr tri.
   MS parts: D-DT, Mus-n 1015.
ANON **A-594a** overture & 10 mvts. 2cl(E♭) 2cl(B♭) 2hn 2bn tp b-tb cb. MS parts: GB-Ljag(w), 176.
ANON **A-10.42a** Walzer. fl 2ob 2cl 2hn 2bn b-tb b.
ANON **A-10.46a** Walzer. fl 2ob 2cl 2hn 2bn b-tb b.
KIRCHHOFF **WZK-56a** ariette. fl 2ob 2cl 2hn 2bn tb db.
LÖWENSTEIN **CAL-6.46(a), 6.53(a)** Walzer. terz-fl 2cl(E♭) 2cl(B♭) 2hn 2bn tp b-tb cb.
SCHMITT, G. **GYS-88.1a** 3 Bds. fl 2ob 2cl 2hn 2bn 2tp tb 3tb db timp.
SCHMITT, G. **GYS-88.2a** overture. fl 2ob 2cl 2hn tp 2tb db.
SCHNEIDER, A. **AYS-104a** overture. fl 2ob 2cl 2hn 2bn tp b-tb 2vla cb.
SCHOLZ **WES-204a** overture. fl 2ob 2cl 2hn 2bn tb db timp.
STARKE **FRS-36a** Auswahlstücke, overture & 8 mvts. 2ob 2cl 2h 2bn cbn (2tp).
STRECK **PZS-1.4a, 1.5a** overture & chorus. fl cl(D) 2cl(A) 2hn 2bn.
WELLER **FYW-1.1a** overture & 19 mvts. *Scoring varies:* 2fl 2ob 2cl(F) 3cl(C) 2bthn 4hn cbn serp tp 3tb perc.
WELLER **FYW-1.2a** overture & 17 mvts. 2ob 2cl 2hn 2bn cbn+tb, (ad lib: fl 2tp).
WIDDER **YYW-1.47a** 3 mvts. 2fl 2cl 2hn 2bn.
WITT **FZW-16a** overture & 17 mvts. 2cl(E♭) 2cl(B♭) 2hn 2bn tp b-tb. *A rescoring of WELLER, FYW-1.2a.*
Grosse Symphonie No. 1, in C (comp. 1807; published 1812, Offenbach am Main)
SCHNEIDER, A. **AYS-105a** fl 2ob 2cl(C) 2hn 2bn tp b-tb(tp III) 2vla cb.
Jubel-Overture (Ouverture Jubilate) (1818, Berlin; published 1819)
KIRCHHOFF **WZK-57a** fl 2ob 2cl 2hn 2bn tp tb db timp.
MARPURG **WYM-2.2a** pic 2ob 2cl(E♭) 4cl(B♭) 5hn 2bn 2tp a-tb t-tb b-tb b-hn b-dr s-dr.
RUMMEL **CFR-1a** 2ob/fl 2cl 2hn 2bn bn.
Piano Sonata No. 2 in A♭, Op. 39 (published 1816, Berlin)
SCHOLZ **WES-205a** capriccioso. fl 2ob 2cl 2hn 2bn tb db.
Leyer und Schwert, Op. 42, No. 2, "Lützow's wilde Jagd", J.169 (partsong, 1814; published 1816, Berlin)
LEGRAND **WYL-48a** fl ob 2cl 2hn 2bn.
LEZGUS **DHL-1** Theil 3, No. 9. 2cl 2hn bn.
SCHNEIDER, A. **AYS-106a** fl 2ob 3cl 4hn 2bn b-tb cb.
WIDDER **YYW-1.48a** 2fl 2cl 2hn 2bn.
Aufforderung zum Tanze, Rondo brillant, Op. 65 (piano, published 1821, Berlin)
KÜFFNER **JYK-5.3(a)** fl(F) 2cl 2hn 2bn.
SCHOLZ **WES-206a** fl 2ob 2cl 2hn 2bn tp tb db timp.
Volkslied, "Mein Schatzerl is hübsch", J.234 (voice & piano, 1818)
LÖWENSTEIN **CAL-7.2c(a)** fl(F) 2cl(E♭) 2cl(B♭) 2hn 2bn b-tb.
5 Weber Movements
CAMPBELL **AQC-7a** 2ob 2cl 2hn 2bn.

WEBER, Jacob Gottfried (1779 - 1839)
Triumph Marsch, Op. 20, in F
  SCHNEIDER, A. **AYS-107a** pic(fl) 2ob 2cl(F) 2cl(C) 2hn 2bn tp b-tb cb.

WEIGL, [Joseph or Thaddeus]
Pas de deux (from an unidentified ballet, choreographed by Taglioni "mit den Masken von Weigl" & Allegretto moderato. (sd, Vienna). These works may have been composed as additional mvts for the ballet in Süssmayr's opera, Solimann der II.
  TRIEBENSEE **JZT-63a** Pas de deux "Mit dem Masken von Weigl" & 1 mvt. 2ob 2cl 2hn 2bn (cbn tp ad lib).

WEIGL, Joseph (1766 - 1846)
Il pazzo per forza (opera, 14 Nov 1788, Vienna).
  WENT **JNW-60.1a** 2ob 2cl 2hn 2bn.
  WENT **JNW-60.2a** overture & 14 mvts. 2ob 2ca 2hn 2bn.
Venere e Adonis (Venus und Adonis) (cantata, 1792, Vienna, Esterházy Palace)
  ANON **A-595a** 2 Theils. 2ob 2cl 2hn 2bn. MS parts: I-Fc, F.P. S.423.
La Principessa [Contessa] d'Amalfi (opera, 12 Jan 1794, Vienna)
  WENT **JNW-61.1a** overture & 12 mvts. 2ob 2cl 2hn 2bn.
  WENT **JNW-61.2a** overture & 11 mvts. 2ob 2ca 2hn 2bn.
Das Petermännchen (Schauspiel mit Gesänge; Teil 1: 8 April 1794; Teil 2: 20 May 1794; Vienna)
  WENT **JNW-16ac** Parts 1 - 4. 2ob 2cl 2hn 2bn.
Das Sinnbild des menschlichen Lebens (ballet-divertissement, 10 May 1794, Vienna)
  HAVEL **VXH-43a** overture & 6 mvts. 2cl 2hn bn. *Essentially a reduction of Went's sextet arrangement.*
  WENT **JNW-62.1a** overture & 15 mvts. 2ob 2cl 2hn 2bn.
  WENT **JNW-62.2a** overture & 15 mvts. 2ob 2ca 2hn 2bn.
  WENT **JNW-62.3a** overture & 15 mvts. 2cl 2hn 2bn.
Die Reue des Pygmalion (ballet, 1 Aug 1794, Vienna)
  HAVEL **VXH-53.3a** 1 mvt. 2cl 2hn bn.
  SEDLAK **+WXS-64a** overture & 8 mvts. 2cl 2hn 2bn.
  WENT **JNW-63.1a** overture & 11 mvts. 2ob 2cl 2hn 2bn.
  WENT **JNW-63.2a** overture & 11 mvts. 2ob 2ca 2hn 2bn.
Giulietta e Pierotto (opera, 16 Oct 1794, Vienna)
  WENT **JNW-64a** 12 mvts. 2ob 2ca 2hn 2bn.
Richard Löwenherz (Riccardo Cor di Leone) (ballet, 2 Feb 1795, Vienna)
  ANON **A-596a** overture & 14 mvts. 2cl 2hn 2bn.
    Pc (Traeg: [Vienna], pre-1799), No. 71, MS parts: CZ-Pnm, XLI.B.127.
  ANON **A-597a** marcia. 2cl 2hn 2bn. MS parts: CZ-KRa, A4454/R.I.24, No. 6, mvt 17.
  HAVEL **VXH-44** overture & 16 mvts. 2cl 2hn 2bn.
  KRECHLER **FFK-5.1a** Marche. 2ob 2cl 2hn 2bn (cbn tp ad lib).
  STÜCKEL **ZES-1a** overture & 13 mvts. 2cl 2hn 2bn.
  WENUSCH **SXW-1.8a** 1 mvt, Tempo di Marcia. cl(E♭) 2cl(B♭) 2hn bn tp(prin).
  WENT **JNW-65.1a** overture & 14 mvts. 2ob 2cl 2hn 2bn.
  WENT **JNW-65.2a** overture & 14 mvts. 2ob 2ca 2hn 2bn.
Der Raub der Helena (ballet, 16 May 1795, Vienna)
  WENT **JNW-66.1a** overture & 9 mvts. 2ob 2cl 2hn 2bn.
  WENT **JNW-66.2a** overture & 9 mvts. 2ob 2ca 2hn 2bn.
Die Verbrennung und Zerstörung der Stadt Troja (Il Incendio di Troja; Trojas Brand) (ballet, 2 Jan 1796, Vienna)
  WENT **JNW-17ac** overture & 9 mvts. 2ob 2cl 2hn 2bn.
Alonzo e Cora (ballet, 30 March 1796, Vienna)
  WENT **JNW-67a** 10 mvts. 2ob 2cl 2hn 2bn.
I solitari (opera seria, 15 March 1797, Vienna)
  WENT **JNW-18ac** duetto & terzeto [sic]. 2ob 2cl 2hn 2bn. MS parts: A-Wn, Mus.Hs.3856.
L'Amor marinaro (Der Korsar [Corsar] aus Liebe) (opera, 15 Oct 1797, Vienna)
  ANON **A-598a** 2ob 2cl 2hn 2bn. MS parts: CZ-Pnm, XLII.B.54; I-Fc, F.P. S.330; A-Wn, Mus.Hs.3792,
    (overture & polonaise = A-6.36a, 6.37a);.
  ANON **A-599a** overture & 12 mvts. 2cl 2hn 2bn.
    MS parts: CZ-KRa, A3941/IV.B.104, (attributed to Paisiello); CZ-Pnm, XLI.B.126, (missing cl I & II).
  ANON **A-600a** terzetto. 2cl 2hn 2bn. MS pts: CZ-KRa, A4454/R.I.24, No. 6, mvt 16.
  LEGRAND **WYL-58a** 1 mvt. fl ob 2cl 2hn 2bn.
  SEYFRIED **IXS-1.4/6(a)** 1 mvt. 2ob 2cl 2hn 2bn cbn.
  STUMPF **JUS-15.1a, 15.2a** Recueils 19 & 20, each 6 mvts. 2cl 2hn 2bn.
Alcina (ballet, 25 Jan 1798, Vienna)
  ANON **A-601a** overture & 16 mvts. 2cl 2hn 2bn. MS parts: CZ-Pnm, XLI.B.168, (as "Suita", omits No. 15);
    CZ-KRa, A4454/R.I.24, No. 5, (overture & 19 mvts; Nos. 3 & 12 split into 2 numbers; includes No. 15);
    PL-LA, RM 45, (overture & 16 mvts; parts signed by Buchal, "Wien 22 - 23 April . . . 803 [sic]").
    Probably a reduction of the Went octet arrangement, JNW-19ac. Although it is possible that Went prepared this version, other arrangers such as Sedlak must also be considered.
  BUCHAL **JWB-3a** Stücke aus Allcina [sic]. 2cl 2hn bn. ("Łańcut den 23 Jully . . . 804 [sic]").
  HAVEL **VXH-53.2a** 1 mvt. 2cl 2hn bn.
  WENT **JNW-19ac** overture & 16 mvts. 2ob 2cl 2hn 2bn.
Das Dorf im Gebirge (Gebürge) (Schauspiel mit Gesänge, 17 April 1798, Vienna)
  SCHMITT, G. **GYS-89a** overture. 2fl 2ob 2cl 2hn 2bn db.

Die Spanier in Peru, oder Rolla (Rolla[']s Tod) (ballet, 13 March 1799, Vienna)
  ANON **A-6.30a** Marsch. 2ob 2cl 2hn 2bn. MS parts: A-Wn, Mus.Hs.3792.
  ANON **A-602a** overture & 10 mvts. 2cl 2hn 2bn. MS parts: CZ-KRa, A4454/R.I.24, No. 8.
Clothilde, Prinzessin von Salerno (Anton Capucci: Hefts 1, 2, 4 ,5, Weigl: Heft 3; ballet, 1799, Vienna)
  ANON **A-603a** overture & 13 mvts. 2ob 2cl 2hn 2bn cbn.
    Pc (Traeg: [Vienna], 1799-1804), No. 225 *(Erster Nachtrag)*, MS parts: A-Ee, Mus.1135; D-Tl, Z 129.
  ANON **A-604a** overture & 13 mvts. 2cl 2hn 2bn. MS parts: CZ-KRa, A3996/IV.B.165b, (in the same hand
    as A-590a, Vienna scribal copy).
  HAVEL **VXH-45a** overture & 3 mvts, (with 3 original mvts, VXH-2). 2cl 2hn bn.
Alceste (ballet, 6 Aug 1800, Vienna)
  ANON **A-605a** overture & 14 mvts. 2cl 2hn 2bn. MS parts: CZ-KRa, A3990/IV.B.160, (in the same
    hand as A-589, Vienna scribal copy).
  WENT **JNW-20ac** overture & 14 mvts. 2ob 2cl 2hn 2bn [cbn].
Cleopatras Tod (ballet, choreographed by Clerico, 1800, Vienna)
  ANON **A-1.1ma** 3 Märsche. 2ob 2cl 2hn 2bn.
  ANON **A-606a** 13 mvts. 2ob 2cl 2hn 2bn cbn. MS parts: CZ-KRa, A3846/IV.B.10, (attributed to Clerico).
Die Athenienische Tänzerin (ballet, 16 March 1802, Vienna)
  ANON **A-607a** sinfonia & 9 mvts. 2cl 2hn 2bn. MS parts (1804): CZ-Pnm, XLl.B.285.
  ANON **A-608a** overture & 7 mvts. 2cl 2hn 2bn. MS parts: CZ-KRa, A4456/R.I.26 a-f, No 7.
  KULAK **JQK-1ad** overture & 9 mvts. 2cl 2hn 2bn. *Probably A-593a with minor alterations.*
  MAŠEK, P. **PLM-2a** 10 mvts. 2ob 2cl 2hn 2bn cbn.
Die Spanier auf der Insel Christina (I spagnoli nell'isola Cristina) (ballet, 31 Aug 1802, Vienna)
  ANON **A-609a** Instrumentation unknown. MS: D-DS. *Unverified; cited in* The New Grove, *Vol. 20, p.298;
    probably by Sartorius and lost in World War II).*
  ANON **A-610a** overture & 10 mvts. 2cl 2hn 2bn. MS parts ("Finis 1803. P:W:"): PL-LA, RM 46.
Die isthmischen Spiele (ballet, 13 July 1803, Vienna)
  KRECHLER **FFK-14.2a(d)** 6 mvts. 2ob 2cl 2hn 2bn cbn. (= TRIEBENSEE, JZT-64a)
  KROMMER **FVK-2.11ma** Marsch. 2ob 2cl 2hn 2bn cbn.
  SEDLAK +**WXS-65a** overture & 8 mvts. 2cl 2hn 2bn.
  TRIEBENSEE **JZT-64a** 6 mvts. 2ob 2cl 2hn 2bn (cbn).
  WRANIZKY, A. **AYW-3.1a, 3.2a** 2 mvts. pic 2ob 2cl 2hn 2bn cbn 4tp b-drum cym.
Die Uniform (L'uniforme) (opera, German version: 15 Feb 1805, Vienna; French version: 1803, Schönbrunn)
  SEDLAK **WXS-66a** overture & 11 mvts. 2ob 2cl 2hn 2bn.
Vesta's Feuer (heroic opera, 10 Aug 1805, Vienna)
  ANON **A-611a** overture & 9 mvts. 2ob 2cl 2hn 2bn. MS parts: I-Fc, F.P. S.348.
  SCHMITT, G. **GYS-90a** overture. 2fl 2ob 4cl 2hn 2bn tp tb timp.
Kaiser Hadrian (opera, 21 May 1807, Vienna)
  ANON **A-612a** overture & 4 mvts. 2ob 2cl 2hn 2bn cbn 2tp. MS parts: CZ-Bm(au), A.35.245.
  ANON **A-613a** marsch. 2ob 2cl 2hn 2bn.
    Pc (Chemische Druckerei: Wien, pn 670, c.1803), pts: CZ-Pnm, Lobkovic X.H.b.3.
  KRECHLER **FFK-6.5a, 7.6a** duetto. 2ob 2cl 2hn 2bn cbn (?2)tp.
  KRECHLER **FFK-8.7a** duetto. 2ob 2cl 2hn 2bn cbn tp.
  TRIEBENSEE **JZT-65.1a** overture & 9 mvts. 2ob 2cl 2hn 2bn (cbn tp ad lib).
  TRIEBENSEE **JZT-65.2a** Marsch. 2ob 2cl 2hn 2bn (tp ad lib).
Ostade oder Adrian von Ostade (opera, 3 Oct 1807, Vienna)
  ANON **A-614a** introduzione & 5 mvts. 2ob 2cl 2hn 2bn. MS parts: I-Fc, F.P. S.355.
  TRIEBENSEE **JZT-66a** Aria mit obligater Harfe. 2ob 2cl 2hn 2bn (cbn tp ad lib)
Das Waisenhaus (Singspiel, 4 Oct 1808, Vienna)
  ANON **A-615a** overture & 9 mvts. 2ob 2cl 2hn 2bn cbn.
    MS parts: CZ-Pnm, (2 copies), Lobkovic X.H.a.8/1, X.H.a.8/2; I-Fc, F.P. S.336, (without cbn),
    CZ-KRa, A3994/IV.B.164. (local copy; overture & Nos. 2, 3, 7 & 10).
  ANON **A-616a** Marsch. 2ob 2cl 2hn 2bn cbn.
    Pc (Chemische Druckerei: Wien, pn 1114, 1810), parts: CZ-Pnm, Lobkovic X.H.b.4.
  KRECHLER **FFK-15.1a** overture & 5/6 mvts. 2ob 2cl 2hn 2bn cbn tp.
  LEGRAND **WYL-49a** 1 mvt. fl ob 2cl 2hn 2bn.
  LÖWENSTEIN **CAL-3.4a** overture. fl cl 2hn 2bn.
Die Schweizerfamilie (Singspiel, 14 March 1809, Vienna)
  ANON **A-93.1(a)** Marsch (Carousel Musik). pic 2fl cl(F) 2cl(C) 2hn 2bn cbn tp(princ) tp(C) b-dr s-dr.
  ANON **A-617a** overture. fl cl(Eb) 2cl(Bb) 2hn 2bn 2tp tb b-hn b-dr. MS pts: D-DT, Mus-n 2083, No. 1.
  ANON **A-618a** Liv. I, overture & 4 mvts; Liv. II, 8 mvts. 2ob 2cl 2hn 2bn cbn(ad lib).
    Pc (Chez Thadé Weigl: Vienna, pn 1114, 1115, 1810), parts: A-Ee, Mus.1121, 1122; CZ-Pnm, Lobkovic
    X.H.a.7, (with ob I & II, bn I, bn II+cbn MS parts for the overture, Nos. 5 & 4, transposed (with some
    alterations) to allow all mvts to be played on clarinets in C; the 1st 14 bars of the overture in cl II have been
    overpasted with MS alterations which elaborate the accompaniment, and an altered cl II part to No. 4 has
    been added loose in MS; the 2hn parts for these mvts remain the same with the keys altered in crayon);
    D-DT, Mus-n 1313.
  ANON **A-619.1a** overture & 12 mvts. 2ob 2cl 2hn 2bn cbn.
    Pc (Im Verlage der k: k: priv: chemischen Druckerey: Wien, pn 1449, 1810), **J9**, No. I, parts:
    CZ-Bm(au), A.20.232; H-Bn, Z 25.514; I-Fc, F.P. S.364, (?MS parts); CZ-Bm(au), A.35.247. (MS parts,
    1829; Nos. 2, 4, 6, 11, 13).
  ANON **A-619.2a** overture & 12 mvts. 2cl 2hn 2bn.
    Pc (Im Verlage der k: k: priv: chemischen Druckerey: Wien, pn 1448, 1449, 1810), **J6**, No. I, pts: CZ-Pnm,
    XLI.B.165, (with MS bn I & II parts for Nos. 1-3, 5, 6 & 13 transposed so that the 2cl can read their parts
    as Bb cls); CZ-KRa, A4175/IV.B.168 (MS pts, copy by Havel); CZ-Pnm, XLII.B.36, (MS pts, Nos. 2-4, 6).
  AHL **CXA-2a** Recueils 3 & 4, each 7 mvts. 2cl 2hn bn.

[Die Schweizerfamilie]
   BARTH **WLB-4a** overture & 3 mvts.   fl 2cl 2hn 2bn.
   FENDT **AXF-3.4ad** overture & 12 mvts.   pic 4cl(B♭ & C) 2hn 2bn 2tp.
   KÜFFNER **JYK-6.1/1(a), 6.1/2(a)** 2 mvts.   fl 2cl hn bn.
   LEGRAND **WYL-50a** 2 mvts.   fl ob 2cl 2hn 2bn.
   LÖWENSTEIN **CAL-3.4a** overture.   fl 2cl 2hn 2bn.
   POESSINGER **FAP-1a** Parts 1 & 2.   2ob 2cl 2hn 2bn cbn.
   SCHMITT, G. **GYS-91.1a** overture.   2pic 2ob cl(E♭) 2cl(B♭) 4hn 2bn 2tp serp timp.
   SCHMITT, G. **GYS-91.2a** overture & 6 mvts.   2fl 2ob 2cl 2hn 2bn tb db.
   SCHNEIDER, A. **AYS-108a** overture & 18 mvts.   fl 2ob 2cl 2hn 2bn tp(hn III) b-tb 2vla cb.
   TRIEBENSEE **JZT-67a** Act I: overture & 9 mvts, Act II: overture & 9 mvts.   2ob 2cl 2hn 2bn (cbn tp ad lib).
Franziska [Francesca] von Foix (heroic-comic opera, 7 Feb 1812, Vienna)
   ANON **A-620a** 2 Theils.   2ob 2cl 2hn 2bn cbn.
      Pc (sn: sl [= T. Weigl: Vienna], c.1812), MS parts: I-Fc, F.P. S.358.
Die Nachtigall und der Raabe (opera, 20 April 1818, Vienna)
   SCHMITT, G. **GYS-92a** 1 Bd.   2fl 2ob 2cl 2hn 2bn tp tb db.
   STARKE **FRS-37a** overture & 6 mvts.   2ob 2cl 2hn 2bn cbn 2tp.
IV Antiphonen [for Corpus Christi] (Vienna, post-1820)
   WENUSCH **SXW-1vac** CATB, fl(ad lib) 2cl 2hn bn(I ad lib) bn II(oblig) kl-tp bomb.
Composite Works
   ANON **A-621a** Rolla, oder Die Spanier in Peru (ballet) with 3 unidentified operas.   2ob 2cl 2hn 2bn.
      MS parts: A-Wgm(c), (?lost).
   BUCHAL **JWB-4a** Stücke aus Richard Löwenherz und Insel Christina.   2cl 2hn bn.

WEIGL, Thaddeus (Thaddäus) (1776 - 1844)
Die Vermählung im Keller (comic ballet, 2 Aug 1796, Vienna)
   WENT **+JNW-68.1a** sinfonia & 11 mvts.   2ob 2cl 2hn 2bn.
   WENT **+JNW-68.2a** sinfonia & 7 mvts.   2ob 2ca 2hn 2bn.
Die Hüldigung (ballet divertissement, 15 June 1796, Vienna)
   WENT **JNW-69a** overture & 11 mvts.   2ob 2cl 2hn 2bn.
Der Tod der Hercules (ballet, 4 Oct 1798, Vienna)
   ANON **A-622a** overture & 11 mvts.   2ob 2cl 2hn 2bn (cbn).
      Pc (Nell' Magazino di Musicka [sic] dei Teatri imperiali: Vienna [sic], c.1798), MS pts: A-Wn, Mus.Hs.3885.
      "Fagoto 3to" appears in the bn II part in No. 10, 8 bars divisi only.
   ANON **A-623a** overture & 11 mvts.   2cl 2hn 2bn.   MS parts: CZ-KRa, A4453/R.I.23, No. 7.
   TRIEBENSEE **JZT-2d** overture & 11 mvts.   2ob 2cl 2hn 2bn.   (= A-609a; modern attribution unsubstantiated)
   WENUSCH **WXS-1.6a** 1 mvt.   cl(E♭) 2cl(B♭) 2hn bn tp(prin).
Das Gespenst im Traume (ballet, 20 Nov 1798, Vienna)
   WENT **JNW-70a** sinfonia & 12 mvts.   2ob 2cl 2hn 2bn.
Bacchus und Ariadne (ballet, 13 Dec 1803, Vienna)
   HAVEL **VXH-46a** overture & 12 mvts.   2cl 2hn 2bn.   *Probably a reduction of the Triebensee arrangement.*
   KRECHLER **FFK-14a** 2ob 2cl 2hn 2bn cbn.
   KROMMER **FVK-2.12ma** Marsch.   2ob 2cl 2hn 2bn cbn.
   TRIEBENSEE **JZT-68a** overture & 12 mvts.   2ob 2cl 2hn 2bn cbn.
Der Tiroler Jahrmarkt (with P. Wranizky & M. Umlauf; ballet divertissement, 26 Feb 1805, Vienna)
   ANON **A-571a** sinfonia & 9 mvts.   2ob 2cl 2hn 2bn cbn.
      Pc (bei Johann Cappi: Wien, c.1805), MS parts: GB-Ljag(w), (the MS attributes the ballet to M. Umlauf).
   ANON **A-624a** 2 mvts & coda.   2cl 2hn 2bn.   MS parts: CZ-KRa, A3997/IV.B.166.

WEINER, Léo (1885 - 1960)
Two Hungarian Dances
   BERKES **KYB-3a** 2ob 2cl 2hn 2bn.

WEISS, Franz   See: COLLECTIONS, ANON. **A-3a.**
Amphion, oder Der Zögling der Musen (ballet, 20 Sept 1806, Vienna)
   TRIEBENSEE **JZT-69.1a** Allegretto.   2ob 2cl 2hn 2bn (cbn ad lib).
   TRIEBENSEE **JZT-69.2a** Pas de deux.   2ob 2cl 2hn 2bn (cbn tp ad lib).

WESTERHOLD, ( ) *Graf*
11 Walzer
   SCHNEIDER, A. **AYS-109a** fl(C, D, E♭) 2ob 2cl 2hn 2bn tp b-tb 2vla cb.

WHITLOCK, Percy William (1903 - 1946)
Five short pieces for organ, No. 2: Folk Tune
   EMERSON **GZE-4a** 2fl ob 3cl hn bn.

WILDE, Joseph
Tänze des Brassilianischen Ballfests welche bei dem von Sr Excellenz dem Hochgebornen Herrn Marquis von Marialva ausserordentlichen Rothsehafter Sr Majestäat des Königs von Portugall, gegeben grossen Hof=Feste in k:k: Ausgarten zu Wien mit 80 Personen aufgeführt wurden. - Polonaise, Walzes avec Coda et une Quadrille executees a [sic] l'occasion de la Féte [sic] de cour dormée pour son Excellence M' l'embassadour du Roi de Portugall, dans le jardin imp. rou. dit Augarten a Vienne. composees et dedies a [sic] son Excellence Mr le Marquis Marialva. Grand Euyer de SR M: Tré fidéle et son Ambassadeur Extraordinaire et Plenipotentiare par Joseph Wilde Chef d'Orchestre a [sic] la Salle Imp. et Roiale de Redout. Diese Tänze sind auch bei dem — von dem Central=Verein zur unterstützing der Hothliedenden veranstatteten Ball mit einem gleich starken Orchester Personale gegeben werden. 8te Lieferung der Tänze Einzig rechtmässige Original Ausgabe. Wien bei S:A: Steiner und Comp: (orchestra, 8 Waltzes & Coda, Quadrille, Polonaise)
   HAVEL **VXH-47a** 2cl(C) 2hn 2bn.

WILHELM, Joseph
4 Deutsche (piano, post-1820)
ANON **A-625.1a** 2ob cl(A) 2cl(D) 2hn 2bn cbn 2tp.   MS parts (c.1827): CZ-Bm(au), A.36.893, No. 1.

WINEBERGER, Paul Anton (1758 - 1821)   *See supra:* ANON **A-2a.**

WINTER, Ernst
Elisabeth-Marsch
ANON **A-626a** pic fl 2ob cl(E♭) cl(solo B♭) 3cl(B♭) 4hn 2bn 3tp t-hn 3tb b-hn/bomb vc/b b-dr+tri s-dr
MS parts: D-DT, Mus-n 1984, No. 2.

WINTER, Peter von (1754 - 1825)
Der Liebe Heinrichs IV und der Gabriele (Henri IV) (ballet, 1779, Munich)
ROSINACK **FJR-5a** overture & 17 mvts.   2ob 2cl 2hn 2bn.
Helena und Paris (Paris und Helena (opera, 5 Feb 1782, Munich)
SARTORIUS **GCS-18a** 6 mvts.   2cl 2hn 2bn cbn.
Der Bettelstudent (Der Donnerwetter) (opera, 2 Feb 1785, Munich)
LEGRAND **WYL-51a** 1 mvt.   fl ob 2cl 2hn 2bn.
WIDDER **YYW-1.49a** 1 mvt.   fl ob 2cl 2hn 2bn.
I Fratelli rivali (Die Brüder als Nebenbuhler) (dramma giocoso, Nov 1793, Venice)
STUMPF **JUS-1ca** 3 mvts.   2fl 2ob 2cl 2hn 2bn tp basse.
Belisa (opera, 5 Feb 1794 Venice; 30 Jan 1798, Vienna, as "Elise (Gräfin) von Hildburg")
ANON **A-627a** overture & 11 mvts.   2ob 2cl 2hn 2bn cbn.   MS parts: I-Fc, F.P. S.343, unverified.
SARTORIUS **GCS-19a** 6 mvts.   2cl 2hn 2bn cbn.
Das unterbrochene Opferfest (Le Sacrifice interrompu) (opera, 14 June 1796, Vienna)
ANON **A-628a** Nouvelles Suites d'harmonie. Suite 111.   Instrumentation unknown (?2fl 2cl 2hn 2bn).
Pc (Seiber: Paris, pn 1566, 1802), RISM [W 1590], parts: D-AB.
ANON **A-629a** 1 mvt.   fl(D) 2cl(C) 2hn 2bn.   MS parts: GB-Ljag(w), 5/262, No. 22.
ANON **A-296(a)** (?incomplete); here only for: bthn hn 2bn vla.
BUCHAL **JWB-5a** Stücke aus Montalban und Opferfest.   2cl 2hn bn.
CZERNY **CYC-2a** overture & 10 mvts.   2cl 2hn 2bn. *Possibly a reduction of WENT, JNW-71a.*
HAMMERL **PCH-1.3(a)** 1 mvt, Allegretto.   2ob 2cl 2hn 3bn tp serp.
HAVEL **VXH-48a** overture & 4 mvts.   2cl 2hn 2bn. *Possibly related to Czerny's arrangement.*
HAVEL **VXH-15.6ac** arie.   2cl 2hn 2bn. *Possibly related to Czerny's arrangement.*
KROMMER **FVK-2.11ma** Marsch.   2ob 2cl 2hn 2bn cbn.
RIEGER **GYR-4a** overture & 7 mvts.
SARTORIUS **GCS-20a** Bd 1: 9 mvts, Bd. 2: 6 mvts.   2cl 2hn 2bn cbn.
SCHMITT, G. **GYS-93a** duetto.   2fl 2ob 2cl 2hn 2bn tp b-tb db.
SCHNEIDER, A. **AYS-110a** overture & 22 mvts.   fl 2ob 4cl 2hn 2bn tp(hn III) b-tb cb.
STUMPF **JCS-16.1a(-16.4a)** Recueils 9 - 12, each 6 mvts.   2cl 2hn 2bn.
STUMPF **JCS-16.6a** introductione & 4 mvts.   4cl 2hn 2bn.
STUMPF **JUS-16.7a(m).** Marsches d'harmonie [sic] . . . Dixième Recueil tiré de l'Opera [sic] Das
unterbrochene Opferfest; 1 march (= mvt 5 of Recueil 10).   2cl 2hn 2bn.
WENT **JNW-71a** overture & 10 mvts.   2ob 2cl 2hn 2bn [cbn].
Babylons Pyramiden (opera, 25 Oct 1797, Vienna; Act I by J.G.A. Mederitsch)
TRIEBENSEE **JZT-70a** overture & 12 mvts.   2ob 2cl 2hn 2bn.
Das Labyrinth [Labirint], oder der Kampf mit den Elementen (opera, 12 June 1798, Vienna)
SCHNEIDER, A. **AYS-111a** overture.   fl 2ob 2cl 2hn 2bn tp b-tb 2vla cb.
SEDLAK **WXS-67a** overture & 13 mvts.   2cl 2hn 2bn.
TRIEBENSEE **JZT-71a** overture & 13 mvts.   2ob 2cl 2hn 2bn (cbn - listed with bn II but no divisi).
Marie von Montalban (opera, 28 Jan 1800, Munich)
ANON **A-630a** [Theil 1:] overture & 5 mvts, [Theil 2:] 6 mvts.   2ob 2cl 2hn 2bn (cbn).
Pc (In der Kunst und Musikhandlung der Thade Weigl: Wien, 1800), MS parts: CZ-Bm(no), A.16.675,
(local copy); I-Fc, F.P. S.338, (there are no divisi in the bn II/cbn part).
MS score (allegedly in the hand of J.S. Mayr): I-BGc, Mayr 609, (Theil 1 only, for 2ob 2cl 2hn 2bn).
ANON **A-631a** [MS: 1ᵉʳ] Suitte d'harmonie; overture.   2fl 2cl(C) 2hn 2bn tp.
Pc (H. Naderman: Paris, pn 1233, c.1800 - 1802), RISM [W 1374], parts: CH-Gpu; Ib. 4862, (with the printed
slip of Marcillac dit Le Jeune: Geneva; au dépôt de musique: Lausanne; the stamp signature of "Vve
Naderman" indicates that the CH-Gpu copy was sold after Nadermann's death, 4 Feb 1799).
BUCHAL **JWB-5a** Stücke aus Montalban und Opferfest.   2cl 2hn bn.
SEDLAK **WXS-68a** overture & 11 mvts.   2cl 2hn 2bn.
Tamerlan (opera, 14 Sept 1802, Paris)
ANON **A-632a** overture.   cl(E♭) 2cl(B♭) 2hn 2bn 2tp flug b-flug bomb.   MS parts: CZ-OScr, 2148.
ANON **A-633a** Deuxième Suite d'Harmonie Extraite des Opéras; overture & 10 mvts.   2fl 2cl 2hn 2bn.
Pc (Nadermann: Paris; Geneva: Marcillac, c.1803), RISM [W 1466], parts: CH-Gpu, Ib.4863, (with the printed
imprint slip of Marcillac dit Le Jeune: Geneva; au dépôt de musique: Lausanne).
ANON **A-634a** 2ob 2cl 2hn 2bn.   MS parts (20 [sic]): I-Fc, F.P. S.361. *Possibly TRIEBENSEE, JZT-72.1a.*
SCHOLZ **WES-207a** overture.   fl 2ob 2cl 3hn 2bn tp tb db timp.
TRIEBENSEE **JZT-72.1a** overture & 19 (9 + 10) mvts.   2ob 2cl 2hn 2bn (cbn tp ad lib).
TRIEBENSEE **JZT-72.2a** Tanz Aria.   2ob 2cl 2hn 2bn (cbn tp ad lib).
Vologesus oder Der Triumph der Treue (ballet, 17 Dec 1804, Vienna)
KRECHLER **FFK-24a** overture & 9 mvts.   2ob 2cl 2hn 2bn cbn.
KRECHLER **FFK-14.1a** overture & 9 mvts.   2ob 2cl 2hn 2bn.
KROMMER **FVK-2.12a** Marsch.   2ob 2cl 2hn 2bn cbn.

Additional polonaise ("Ein Mädchen voll verlangen") for Dalyrac's opera, Deux Mots (Vienna, c.1809)
  TRIEBENSEE **JZT-73a** 2ob 2cl 2hn 2bn (cbn tp ad lib).
Oboe Quartet Possibly based on Cinq pièces concertantes...[Das unterbröchene Opferfest]...arrangées en
  quatuors pour haut-bois, violon, alto et violoncelle. *(André: Offenbach am Main, pn 2104, 1805); RISM*
  [W 1589].
  TRIEBENSEE **JZT-74a** Presto. 2ob 2cl 2hn 2bn (cbn tp ad lib).
Composite works
  ANON **A-635a** Suite d'harmonie Tirée des Ouvrages de Winter; 8 mvts. 2fl 2cl(C) 2hn 2bn serp/cb.
    Pc (A l'Imprimerie du Conservatoire de Musique: Paris, c.1797 - 1805), parts: F-Pn, Vm7 6963.
  BUCHAL **JWB-5a** Stücke aus Montalban und Opferfest. 2cl 2hn bn.
Unidentified arrangements
"Serenate. Opera di Winter"
  ANON **A-636a** (?2ob 2cl 2hn 2bn). MS parts (8): I-Fc, F.P. S.372.
"Andante. Thema di Winter"
  HAMMERL **PCH-1.7(a)** 2ob 2cl 2hn 3bn tp serp.

WITT, Friedrich (1770 - 1836)
Requiem, in Eb (?CATB, orchestra)
  WITT **FZW-1va** CATB, terz-fl 2cl(Eb) 2cl(Bb) 2hn 2bn tp b-tb cb timp.
Pollaca [sic] in C (unidentified)
  HAMMERL, P.C. **PCH-3.2a** 2ob 2cl(C) 2hn 2bn tp serp.

WOELFL (Wölfl), Joseph (1773 - 1812)
Das schöne Milchmädchen oder Der Guckkasten (comic opera, 5 Jan 1797, Vienna)
  TRIEBENSEE **JZT-75a** overture. 2ob 2cl 2hn 2bn (cbn tp ad lib).

WOLFRAM, Joseph Maria (1789 - 1839)
Der Bergmönch (opera, 14 March 1830, Dresden)
  MARPURG **WYM-1.1a** overture. pic 2ob cl(Eb) 3cl(Bb) 2hn 2bn 2tp 3tb serp b-dr s-dr.
Schloss Candra (heroic romantic opera, 7 Dec 1832, Dresden)
  ANON (?Kuttich - FWK-1ad) **A-637a** overture. 2ob 2cl 2hn 2bn cbn 2tp
    MS parts (copy by Kuttich, c.1835): CZ-Bm(au), A.40.169, (missing cl I, hn II).

WRANIZKY (Vranicky, Wraniztky), Paul (Pavel) (1756 - 1802)
Oberon, König der Elfen (romantic opera, 7 Nov 1789, Vienna)
  ANON **A-638.1a** 2ob 2cl 2hn 2bn cbn. MS parts: I-Fc, F.P. S.364.
  ANON **A-638.2a** 2ob 2cl 2hn 2bn. MS parts: D-DO, Mus.Ms.2067, (attributed to Rosinack, FJR-10ad).
  HAVEL **VXH-49a** overture & 13 mvts. 2cl 2hn 2bn.
  HAVEL **VXH-15.4ac** arie (opera attributed to Stumpf). 2cl 2hn 2bn.
  ROSINACK **FJR-10ad** 2ob 2cl 2hn 2bn.
  STUMPF **JUS-17.1a, 17.2a** Recueils 4 & 5, each 6 mvts. 2cl 2hn 2bn.
  STUMPF **JUS-17.3a(d)** overture & 12 mvts. 2cl 2hn 2bn.
Das Waldmädchen (La Selvaggia; Die Wilden) (with Joseph Kinsky; ballet, 23 Sept 1796, Vienna)
Note: the popular movement "La Russe" is, in fact, by Giornovichi.
  ANON **A-639a** Duetto aus Salvaggia [sic]. 2ob 2cl 2hn 2bn 2tp b-tb.
    MS parts: CZ-Bm(au), A.36.891, (missing 2hn cbn 2tp b-tb; cataloged at Rossini: *Il Barbiere di Siviglia*).
  ANON **A-9.24a** polonese. 3bthn.
  BEECKE **IVB-2ad** Parthia, overture & 12 mvts. 2ob 2cl 2hn 2bn. (= WENT, JNW-72.1a)
  STARKE **FRS-1ad** overture & 12 mvts. 2ob 2cl 2hn 2bn. (= WENT, JNW-72.1a)
  WENT **JNW-72.1a** overture & 12 mvts. 2ob 2cl 2hn 2bn.
  WENT **JNW-72.2a** overture & 9 mvts. 2ob 2ca 2bn.
  WENT **JNW-72.3a** overture & 11 mvts. 2cl 2hn 2bn.
  WENUSCH **SXW-1.3a** 1 mvt. cl(Eb) 2cl(Bb) 2hn bn tp(prin).
Das Urtheil des Paris (ballet, 13 July 1801, Vienna)
  HAVEL **VXH-14ac** overture & 12 mvts. 2cl 2hn 2bn. MS parts: CZ-KRa, A44453/R.I.23, No. 6.
Der Tiroler Jahrmarkt (with M. Umlauf & T. Weigl; ballet divertissement, 26 Feb 1805, Vienna)
  ANON **A-556a** sinfonia & 9 mvts. 2ob 2cl 2hn 2bn cbn.
    Pc (Johann Cappi: Wien, c.1805), MS parts: GB-Ljag, (the MS attributes the ballet to M. Umlauf).
  ANON **A-640a** 2 mvts & coda. 2cl 2hn 2bn. MS parts: CZ-KRa, A3997/IV.B.166.
Terzetto (?ballet, untraced)
  WENT **A-21ac** overture & 6 mvts. 2ob 2cl 2hn 2bn.

WUNDERLICH, ( )
6 Walzer
  SCHNEIDER, A. **AYS-112a** fl(C, D, Eb) 2ob 2cl 2hn 2bn tp b-tb 2vla cb.

ZABEL, Carl (1822 - 1883)
Front-Marsch
  ANON **A-641a** pic fl 2ob cl(Eb) cl(solo Bb) 3cl(Bb) 4hn 2bn 3tp t-hn 3tb b-hn/bomb vc/b b-dr s-dr.
    MS parts: D-DT, Mus-n 2089.

ZERGANSY, ( )
6 Walzer
  SCHNEIDER, A. **AYS-113a** fl 2ob 2cl 2hn 2bn tp b-tb 2vla cb.

ZIMMAROTSKY, ( )
5 Walzer
SCHNEIDER, A. **AYS-114a** fl 2ob 2cl 2hn 2bn tp b-tb 2vla cb.

ZINEK, ( ) *Baron*
Romance & Marche, für Oestreichs [sic] Landswehr
KRECHLER **FFK-4.3a, 4.4a** 2ob 2cl 2hn 2bn cbn.

ZINGARELLI, Nicolo Antonio (1752 - 1837)
Pirro, Re d'Epiro (opera, 26 Dec 1791, Milan; 9 May 1798, Vienna)
ANON **A-642a** 4 mvts. 2ob 2cl 2hn 2bn.
Pc: (In den Kais: König Hoftheater Musick Verlag: Wien, c.1798), MS parts: A-Ee, Mus.1079;
CZ-KRa, A4008/IV.B.180; I-Fc, F.P. S.339; A-Wn, Mus.Hs.3792, (2 rondos; with cbn; = A-6.3a, 6.5a).
Quinto Fabio (opera, autumn 1794, Livorno)
ANON **A-643a** 4fl 2ob 2cl 4hn 2bn 2tp tb perc. MS parts: CZ-KRa, IV.B.19.
La Gerusalemme distrutta (Das Zerstorte Jerusalem) (opera, March 1794, Florence)
ANON **A-644a** 2ob 2cl 2hn 2bn cbn (2tp). MS parts: I-Fc, F.P. S.364.
Giulietta e Romeo (opera, 30 Jan 1796, Milan; 28 April 1804, Vienna)
ANON **A-645a** overture & 8 mvts. 2ob 2cl 2hn 2bn cbn. MS parts: A-Ee, Mus.1089; CZ-Bm(au), A.20.942,
(8 mvts). *Probably the same as the following entry, with a (?later) added cbn part.*
ANON **A-646a** overture & 8 mvts. 2ob 2cl 2hn 2bn. MS parts: CZ-Pnm, XLII.C.118; D-DO, Mus.Ms.2082;
I-Fc, F.P. S.3130; A-Wn, Mus.Hs.3792, No. 15, (A-6.15a).
COURTIN **HZC-1.3a** rondo, "Ombra adorata aspetta". (2ob/fl ad lib) 2cl 2hn 2bn.
HAVEL **VXH-50.1a** overture & 6 mvts. 2cl 2hn 2bn.
HAVEL **VXH-50.2a** overture. 2cl 2hn 2bn.
SEDLAK **WXS-69a** overture & 8 mvts. 2cl 2hn 2bn.
6 Walzer (unidentified; attributed to "Zinggarnelly")
SCHNEIDER, A. **AYS-115a** fl 2ob 2cl 2hn 2bn tp b-tb 2vla cb.
Marsch langsam (unidentified)
ANON **A-74.6/9m(a)** pic quart-fl 2ob cl(F) 2cl(C) 4hn 2bn cbn+serp/2b-hn 2tp 3tb b-dr t-dr tamb cym.

ZUMSTEEG, Johann Randolph (1760 - 1802)
Tamira (duodrama, 13 June 1788, Stuttgart)
STARKE **FRS-38a** (= **FRS-1.2a**) polonaise. 2ob 2cl 2hn 2bn cbn.

ZWERGER, ( )
Walzer
SCHNEIDER, A. **AYS-116a** fl 2ob 2cl 2hn 2bn tp b-tb 2vla cb.

APPENDIX: ALTERNATIVE OPERA AND BALLET TITLES

To assist the user, we list here the most common alternative opera and ballet titles used in Harmoniemusik arrangements. Initial articles are ignored.

Abraham → FUSS: Isaak
Adelheid von Ponthieu → STARZER: Adèle de Pontheiu
Les Africains → CATEL: Sémiramis
Die Ähnlichkeit → DELLA MARIA: Le Prisonnière
Alonzo und Cora → NAUMANN: Cora och Alonzo
Aschenbrödel → ISOUARD: Cendrillon

Der Bauern [Der Bauer] → MÉHUL: Bion
Die beiden Füchse → MÉHUL: Une Folie
Die beiden Geizigen → GRÉTRY: Les deux Avares
Die beiden Savoyarden → DALAYRAC: Les Deux Petites Savoyards
Die Belagerung von Bethulien → FUSS: Judith
Bernhardsberg → CHERUBINI: Élisa
Bianca e Fernando → BELLINI: Bianca e Gernando
Blaubarth → GRÉTRY: Raoul Barbe-Bleu
Der Blitz → HALÉVY: L'Eclair
Les Bohémiens en foire → PAISIELLO: I Zingari in fiera
Die Brüder als Nebenbuhler → WINTER: I Fratelli rivali

La Capricciosa corretta → MARTÍN Y SOLER: La Scuola dei maritati
La Capricciosa ravveduta → FIORAVANTI: La Capricciosa pentita
La Chasse de jeune Henri → MÉHUL: Le jeune Henri
La Cifra → SALIERI: La Dama pastorella
Combat Naval → STEIBELT: Britannia
Der Concert am Hof → AUBER: La Concert à la Cour
La Contadina di spirito → PAISIELLO: Il Matrimonio inaspettato
Il Corradino → ROSSINI: Matilda di Shabran
The Creation (Le Création) → HAYDN: Die Schöpfung

Danina → LINDPAINTNER: Janina
Der Dichter und Tonsetzer → DALAYRAC: La Poète et le musicien
Die diebische Elster → ROSSINI: La Gazza ladra
Don Quixote → UNLAUF, M.: Die Hochzeit des Gamacho
La Donna cambiate → PAER: Poche ma buone
Donna Caritea → Meyerbeer: Caritea, regina di Spagna
Der Donnerwetter → WINTER: Der Bettelstudent
Due filosifi → PAISIELLO: Gli Astrologi immaginari
Il due giornati → CHERUBINI: Les deux Journées

Die eifersüchtige [ersterwichtig] Liebhaber → GRÉTRY: L'Amant jaloux
Die eingebildeten Philosophen → PAISIELLO: Gli Astrologi immaginari

Der Fagottist → MÜLLER, W.: Kaspar der Fagottist
Le Festin de Pierre → GLUCK: Don Juan
I filosofi immaginari → PAISIELLO: Gli Astrologi immaginari
La Finte Contessa → PAISIELLO: Il Matrimonio inaspettato
La Forêt de Senard → WEBER, C.M.: Euryanthe
Das Fräulein vom See → ROSSINI: La Donna del Lago
Furberia e Puntiglio → BERNARDINI: Don Simoncino

Die gebesserte Eigensinnige → FIORAVANTI: La Capricciosa pentita
Die gebesserte Eigensinnige → MARTÍN Y SOLER: La Scuola dei maritati
Die Gefangene → CHERUBINI (with Boieldieu): La Prisonnière
Graf Armand → CHERUBINI: Les deux Journées
Der Guitarrespieler → HALÉVY: Le Guitarero
The Gypsy → BALFE: The Bohemian Girl

Die Haarlocke → DALAYRAC: La Boucle de cheveux
Die Heimkehr des Verbannten → NICOLAI: Il Proscritto
Die heimlichen Ehe → CIMAROSA: Il Matrimonio segreto
Die Holzschuhmacher → BRUNI: Les Sabotiers

L'Industrie amorose → OTTANI: L'Amore industrioso

Jacob und seiner Söhne → MÉHUL: Joseph en Egypte
Johann von Paris → BOIELDIEU: Jean de Paris
Joko → LINDPAINTNER: Janina
Die Jüdin → HALÉVY: La Juive

Kaiser Titus der Grossmüthige → MOZART: La Clemenza di Tito
Der Kampf mit den Elementen → WINTER: Das Labyrinth
Der Klausner → CARAFA: La Solitaire
Die Königin von Cypern → HALÉVY: La Reine de Chypre
Der Korsar aus Liebe → WEIGL, J.: L'Amor marinaro
Die Kreuzfahrer in Ägypten → MEYERBEER: Il Crociato in Egitto
Die Krondiamanten → AUBER: Les Diamants de la couronne

Der Liebertrank → AUBER: Le Philtre
Die Liebestrank → DONIZETTI: L'Elisir d'amore
Die Lotterieloos → ISOUARD: Le Billet de loterie
Die lustige Schuster → PAER: Poche ma buone

Machomet → GLUCK: La Rencontre imprévu
Marc Antonio → GENERALI: L'Impostore
Il Marchese Tulipano → PAISIELLO: Il Matrimonio inaspettato
Marie → HÉROLD: Almédon
Der Maurer → AUBER: Le Maçon
Maurer und Schlosser → AUBER: Le Maçon
Die Medaille → UMLAUF, M.: Der Gernadier
La Molinaro → PAISIELLO: L'Amor contrasto
Monson Fürst von Cataneo → ISOUARD: Alamon
Die Müllerin → PAISIELLO: L'Amor contrasto
Die Musquetiere der Königen → HALÉVY: Las Mousquetaires de la Reine
Les Mystères d'Isis → MOZART: Die Zauberflöte

Die Nacht im Walde → DALAYRAC: Deux Mots
Nathalie → GYROWETZ: Das Schweizer Milchmädchen
Die natürliche Zaubery → ISOUARD: Le Magicien sans magie
Der neue Gutsherr → BOIELDIEU: Le Nouveau Seigneur du village
Les Noces de Dorine → SARTI: Fra due Litiganti
Le Nozze di Dorina → SARTI: Fra due Litiganti
Nur mit Maas → BOIELDIEU: Rien de trop

Odoardo e Gildippe → NICOLAI: Gildippe e Odoardo
L'Osteria Portughese → CHERUBINI: L'Hôtellerie Portugaise

Le Pardon de Ploërmel → MEYERBEER: Dinorah
Les Pelerins de la Mecque → GLUCK: La Rencontre imprévu
Die Pilger von Mekka → GLUCK: La Rencontre imprévu
Die portugisische Gasthaus → CHERUBINI: L'Hôtellerie Portugaise
Le Prince de Catane → ISOUARD: Alamon
Die Prufung → GYROWETZ: Robert

Das regiments Tochter → DONIZETTI: La Fille du régiment
Richard Löwenherz → GRÉTRY: Richard Coeur-de-Lion
Der Ritter Roland → HAYDN: Orlando Paladino
Robin des Bois → WEBER, C.M.: Der Freischütz
Das Rothkäppchen → BOIELDIEU: Le Petit Chaperon rouge

Le Sacrifice interrompu → WINTER: Das unterbrochene Opferfest
Die Schatzgräber → DITTERSDORF: Betrüg durch Aberglauben
Die Schatzgräber → MÉHUL: Le Trésor supposé
Der Scheinbetrügt → PAER: Der Kapellmeister von Venedig
Der Schnee → AUBER: La Neige
Die schöne Müllerin → PAISIELLO: L'Amor contrasto

Der schwarz Mann → OSSWALD: L'Uomo Negro
Die Schwur → AUBER: Le Duc d'Olonne
The Seasons → HAYDN: Die Jahreszeiten
Die Seeräuber aus Algeri → BELLINI: I Pirata
La Selvaggia → DALAYRAC: Azémia
La Selvaggia → WRANIZKY, P.: Das Waldmädchen
Il Sesostri → NASOLINI: Le Feste d'Iside
Das Singspiel → DELLA MARIA: L'Opéra Comique
I Solitari → MAYR: Il Segreto
Die Strickleiter → GAVEAUX: L'Échelle de soie
Die Stumme von Portici → AUBER: La Muette de Portici
Die Syrene → AUBER: Le Sirène

Ein Tag in Paris → ISOUARD: Un Jour à Paris
Die Tage der Gefahr → CHERUBINI: Les deux Journées
Tarare → SALIERI: Axur, Re d'Ormus
Telemach → HOFFMEISTER: Der Königssohn aus Ithaka
Die Temperamente → MÉHUL: L'Irato
Terzetto → WRANIZKY, P.
Der Teufels Antheil → AUBER: Carlo Broschi
Thale von Andorra → HALÉVY: Le Val d'Andorre
Les Trois Sultanes → STARZER: Les cinques Soltanes
Trojas Brand → WEIGL, J.: Die Verbrennung und Zerstörund der Stadt Troja
Der türkische Arzt → ISOUARD: Le Médecin Turc

Die ungarische Grenadier → MÜLLER, W.: Der österreichische Grenadier

Die Verlobte → AUBER: La Fiancée
Vielka → MEYERBEER: Eil Feldlage in Schlesien
Die vier Haimonskinder → BALFE: Les Quatre fils d'Aymon
I Virtuosi ambulanti → FIORAVANTI: Les Comédiens ambulans
Die vornehmen Wirthe → CATEL: Les Aubergistes de qualité

Die wankelmüthige Frau → PAER: L'Intrigo Amoroso
Was tut die Liebe nicht → NAUMANN: La Dama Soldato
Der Wasserträger → CHERUBINI: Les deux Journées
Die weisse Frau → BOIELDIEU: La Dame blanche
Die wiedergessundene Tochter Kaiser Otto des II → KOZELOCH: La ritrovata figlia di Ottone II
Die Wilden → DALAYRAC: Azémia
Die Wilden → WRANIZKY, P.: Das Waldmädchen
Das Winzerfest → KUNZEN: Das Fest der Winter

Der Zauberblick → LOBE: Die Fürstin von Granada
Die Zauberglöcken → HÉROLD: La Clochette
Die Zauberharfe → KUHLAU: Trylleharpen
Die Zauberzitter → Kaspar der Fagottist
Das Zerstorte Jerusalem → ZINGARELLI: La Gerusalem distrutta
Die Ziguenerin → BALFE: The Bohemian Girl
Das Ziguererin Warnung → BENEDICT: The Gypsy's Warning
Die Zween Anton → GERL: Der dumme Gärtner
Zweikampf → HÉROLD: Le Pré aux Clercs
Das zweite Capitel (Das zweyte Kapitel) → SOLIÉ: Le Chapitre second

About the Authors

JON A. GILLASPIE is a freelance musicologist and music cataloger as well as a composer, arranger, record producer, and experienced bassoonist and keyboard player. Born in Potsdam, New York, he studied social anthropology before emigrating to England in 1973. His extensive travels researching into primary sources of wind harmony now total more than three years in the field, and his own extensive collection includes the former wind harmony of the Löwenstein Kapelle. He has composed and arranged widely for wind ensemble, including works for the London Wind Soloists, the Ensemble Philidor, and the Dorchester Wind Players.

MARSHALL STONEHAM is Massey Professor of Physics, University College London, a Fellow of the Royal Society, and Chief Scientist of AEA Technology. He has written extensively not only on the physical sciences, but on music as well. He has taken the opportunity to visit libraries in many countries when on travels associated with his scientific work. He is an experienced horn player and the founder and organizer of the Dorchester Wind Players, which, over the past twenty years, has played many works of the genre documented in this catalog.

DAVID LINDSEY CLARK is a former music librarian to Oxfordshire County Libraries, Oxford, England. He has been involved in the revision of the music catalogs of a number of libraries, including the Bodleian of Oxford University. Now retired, he continues his bibliographical work exploring the repertoire of music about which he has written for many years.

ISBN 0-313-25394-3

90000>

EAN

9 780313 253942

HARDCOVER BAR CODE